[redacted]

ANNUAL REGISTER OF GRANT SUPPORT™

A DIRECTORY OF FUNDING SOURCES

[redacted]

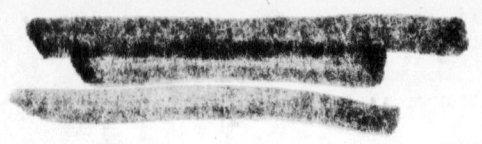

Annual Register of Grant Support™
50th Edition

ANNUAL REGISTER OF GRANT SUPPORT™

A DIRECTORY OF FUNDING SOURCES

50th EDITION | 2017

Published by

Information Today, Inc.
143 Old Marlton Pike
Medford, NJ 08055-8750
Phone: (609) 654-6266
Fax: (609) 654-4309
E-mail (Orders): **custserv@infotoday.com**
Web site: http://www.infotoday.com

ISSN 0066-4049
ISBN 978-1-57387-523-3
Library of Congress Catalog Card Number: 69-18307

Information Today, Inc.
143 Old Marlton Pike
Medford, NJ 08055-8750
Phone: 800-300-9868 (Customer Service)
800-409-4929 (Editorial)
Fax: 609-654-6098
E-mail (orders): custserv@infotoday.com
Web Site: www.infotoday.com

Printed and bound in the United States of America

US $349.50
ISBN 978-1-57387-523-3
34950>
9 781573 875233

Contents

Continued

Preface

Now in its 50th edition, the *Annual Register of Grant Support™: A Directory of Funding Sources* has achieved a deserved reputation as an authoritative standard reference source on financial support. Known and relied upon by academic scholars and researchers, *Grant Support* also responds to the needs of those in the fields of business, civic improvement, and social welfare. Recognized for its value to the individual, *Grant Support* assists hospitals, arts organizations, community service groups, medical research facilities, and other institutional applicants as well.

The 2017 edition includes details of 2,598 grantmaking organizations including government agencies, public and private foundations, corporations, community trusts, unions, educational and professional associations, and special interest organizations. These organizations support a total of 4,026 grant programs and cover a broad spectrum of interests from academic and scientific research, project development, travel and exchange programs, and publication support to equipment and construction grants, in-service training, and competitive awards and prizes in a variety of fields. Please see the "Key to entry information" and associated definitions on pages xxvi and xxvii. This feature illustrates a sample listing with all the data elements defined.

Grant Support attempts to be as comprehensive as possible by including the following forms of financial aid: programs that offer non-repayable financial assistance directly to the grantee or indirectly through payment to the sponsoring institution; programs that accept applicants from the United States or Canada or directly benefit the United States or Canada; study grants and fellowships aimed principally though not exclusively at the graduate or postgraduate levels; grants for construction, facilities, or project costs for education, medical research, health care, civic improvement, etc.; and programs donating consulting services in lieu of a direct monetary grant.

Funding sources are given the opportunity annually to update entry data. Staff research continues to within weeks of *Grant Support*'s publication date to assure information is as current and complete as possible and to identify new funding sources for inclusion. Essential programs for which no updated information has been returned are included, either as they appeared in the last edition, revised where possible, or compiled entirely through secondary research.

Support programs are divided into eleven major areas, further subdivided into more specific subject fields. Each entry contained in *Grant Support* has been placed in the section that reflects its principal interest. If program interests equally emphasize diverse fields, such as communications and business and economics, one full entry and an abbreviated cross-reference will appear in the relevant sections. Similarly, a program for minority political scientists will appear in either "Special Populations" or "Political Science," with a cross-reference in the appropriate section. However, organizations with broad support purposes or interests in three or more well-defined areas are listed in the "Multiple Special Purpose" section.

Four helpful indexes conclude the volume: Subject, Organization and Program, Geographic, and Personnel. Please note: *References in each index point to the entry number visible in the listing—not to a page number.*

In the Subject Index, each grant has been indexed in terms of the specific areas to which it may be applied (e.g., Cartography, Mathematics), the type of grant (e.g., Medical Research, Theology), and the individuals or organizations eligible for support, if limitations are specified (e.g., Religious Institutions, Women). The Organization and Program Index lists grant programs in upper/lower case and funding organizations in all upper case. Programs are also listed following the organizations that sponsor them. The Geographic Index groups grantmaking organizations according to the state or country in which they are located. In the Personnel Index, officers of the organizations, trustees, directors, and awards committee members are listed with their program entry number.

While consulting the Subject Index, should the reader wish to know in which chapter a particular entry appears, he or she may consult the Entry Listing by Chapter Index, a one-page outline that precedes the Subject Index.

The editorial staff of *Annual Register of Grant Support* strives continually to provide the professional community with the most current and comprehensive information on existing forms of financial aid from as wide a variety of sources as possible. The staff urges the users of this edition to inform us of any corrections or additions to existing entries and of funding sources not included, and cordially invites suggestions for improvement of future editions.

In closing, we would like to mark the retirement of associate editor Daniel Bazikian. Dan has been a dedicated editor and researcher on *Grant Support* for fifteen years. We are grateful for his conscientious service and wish him the best in his well-deserved retirement.

Introduction

In the United States today, the support of human services through grants, awards, fellowships, and private gifts is a multibillion-dollar enterprise. Private foundations, corporations, individuals, charitable organizations, and agencies gave an estimated $373.25 billion to charity in 2015, an increase of 4.1 percent compared with the revised estimate of $358.83 billion given in 2014, according to the Giving USA Foundation.

Of the total $373.25 billion given in 2015, $265.01 billion came from individuals and accounts for 71 percent of all estimated giving. Grants from foundations, excluding those affiliated with business enterprises, totalled $59.72 billion, an increase of 10.7 percent. Gifts received through bequests increased an estimated 19.4 percent to $33.59 billion; corporations contributed $18.66 billion, an increase of 5.0 percent.

When total charitable giving is analyzed by recipient fields, religion received the largest share of 2015 dollars—$119.44 billion—followed by education ($55.99 billion); human services ($44.79 billion); foundations ($41.06 billion); health ($29.86 billion); public-society benefit ($26.13 billion); arts, culture, and humanities ($18.66 billion); international affairs ($14.93 billion); and environment and animals ($11.2 billion).

The 2,598 entries listed in this edition of *Annual Register of Grant Support*™ represent billions of dollars in financial assistance to potential grant seekers.

Part of the success in using the *Annual Register of Grant Support*™ will depend on an understanding of the various types of grantmaking entities, how they differ in their objectives and grantmaking procedures, what they look for in the grant applicant, and how they are approached. It is hoped that the following descriptions of grant-supporting organizations will increase the usability of Grant Support to the potential grant seeker.

PRIVATE FOUNDATIONS

Probably no area of philanthropy is so misunderstood and misused as that of private foundations. According to studies, as many as 80 percent of all applications to private foundations are incorrect, inappropriate or misdirected. While at least part of the blame for this error must be attributed to the private foundations themselves, grant seekers often compound the error by tending to lump all private foundations together as if they shared a common purpose.

Not only do private foundations differ greatly from public funding sources, but there is a wide diversity among private foundations themselves. What may be an appropriate application to The Ford Foundation, for example, may be totally inappropriate to the San Francisco Foundation.

There are more than 75,000 grantmaking foundations in the United States. The reason that an approximate figure must be used is that the federal government defines private foundations more by exclusion than by anything else. If an organization cannot qualify as a charitable, religious, educational, scientific, or governmental organization, it may be classified as a private foundation even if it has never made a grant nor intends to make one. Potential grant seekers should be aware that the mere use of the word "foundation" in the title of an organization is not evidence that the organization will make grants.

Until the tax reform act of 1976, private foundations bore a 4 percent excise tax on net investment income (Section 4940 of the Tax Reform Act of 1969), and annual giving requirements were based on the greater of "adjusted net income" or a *variable* percentage of the market value of investment assets—in effect discouraging the foundations from building their assets.

After 1976, the variable percentage was eliminated, and giving requirements were set at 5 percent of market value of assets or of net income. The Economic Recovery Tax Act of 1981 (ERTA) further amended the requirements to a flat 5 percent of market value of assets. In addition, the excise tax on net investment income was reduced to 2 percent in 1978, which further encouraged growth by private foundations.

Several provisions of the Tax Reform Act of 1969 still regulate the activities of foundations. For instance, foundations face restrictions on self-dealing and are limited in the ownership of businesses. One provision of particular interest to the potential grant seeker is a requirement that every private foundation with assets of $5,000 or more (virtually all of them) must submit an annual report that is available for public inspection. These annual reports, printed on special Internal Revenue Service form 990-PF (Private Foundation), include the names and addresses of all principal officers of the foundation, the total assets and investments of the foundation and, most important, a complete listing of every grant made during the year of record. Readers of *Grant Support* may wish to review selected 990-PFs of those foundations included in this edition in order to supplement information on current grants.

These 990-PF forms may be obtained directly from the private foundations themselves, or they may be found in over 200 Foundation Center Network member libraries located throughout the country, and are available for

public use. (A list of these libraries may be obtained by contacting the Foundation Center, 79 Fifth Avenue, New York, NY 10003-3076, or via their web site at www.foundationcenter.org).

A substantial number of private foundations publish their own annual reports, over and above the 990-PF requirement mentioned earlier. Copies of these annual reports may be obtained by writing the foundation directly.

TYPES OF FOUNDATIONS

There are certain aspects common to all private foundations in the United States. However, foundations can be broken down into five types, which will assist the grant seeker in understanding their current objectives and grant distribution patterns.

1. National Foundations

Most of the foundations listed in Grant Support are national foundations, meaning that they are not limited to any geographic area in their grant support. National foundations are usually quite large, with assets of $25 million or more. They include all the better-known foundations, such as The Ford Foundation, the Lilly Endowment, Inc., The Rockefeller Foundation, and the Carnegie Corporation of New York. Because national foundations may make grants anywhere in the country, it is important to remember that these foundations are usually more attracted to programs and proposals with national, or at least regional, implications. Most of the national foundations are staffed with professional grantmakers, publish their own annual reports, and often have well-defined philanthropic goals.

While national foundations are large enough to fund projects of almost any size—and have been known to make grants of a million dollars or more—it should be remembered that competition for these national foundation grants is extremely fierce. The Ford Foundation, for example, will receive as many as 30,000 proposals every year and will fund only about 2,000.

2. Special-Interest Foundations

Many foundations listed in this edition of Grant Support devote their entire grant efforts to programs within a single field of interest. These special-interest foundations, just as the national foundations, often make grants without any geographic limitations so long as the projects relate to the specific areas. Special-interest foundations range from the massive Robert Wood Johnson Foundation (health) to the Joseph P. Kennedy Foundation (mental retardation) to those supporting research on a single disease.

Some of the larger special-interest foundations employ staff whose purpose is not only to review grants but to stay abreast of information being gathered about that special field of interest. Grant seekers, then, should consider special-interest foundations as a potential source of information about a given subject as well as a potential source of funds.

3. Corporate Foundations

During the 1950s, many major corporations created private foundations to serve as the corporate philanthropic arm, although the Tax Reform Act of 1969 greatly slowed the increase in their number. The ExxonMobil Corporaton, Inc. is an example. Readers should be alerted to the fact that while many foundations carry names of large corporations, they are not corporate foundations. The Ford Foundation, for example, is not a corporate foundation; it was created by the Ford family.

Most corporate foundations, while "independent," are very much creatures of the corporations that founded them and fund them. Corporate foundations will, therefore, often be more receptive to proposals that are in line with their corporate interest. Historically, corporate foundations more often have made grants in the fields of education, federated giving (United Way, etc.), minority enterprises, and local social services that demonstrate a benefit to the company employees as well as the community at large.

Most corporate foundations will have relatively small assets in comparison with the amount of grants. This is because once the money has moved from the corporation to the corporate foundation, it can never go back to the corporation. Usually corporations will keep only enough funds in the corporate foundation to sustain the foundation's grant efforts without harming the corporate financial position.

4. Family Foundations

By far, the largest number of private foundations are family foundations. They range in assets from hundreds of millions of dollars, such as those of the several Rockefeller Foundations, to a few thousand dollars.

The grant support pattern of family foundations is very often a personal matter. Often the family foundation will be controlled entirely by family members, and even when these family members have died, the family foundation will often continue to reflect their wishes. Unlike special-interest foundations, family foundations seldom have set fields of interest. Grants more probably will reflect areas of current family interest rather than any recognizable pattern of traditional philanthropy.

Most family foundations are small, and few will have staff or guidelines for submitting proposals. A vast majority of family foundations limit their grants to the city or locality in which the family resides and accumulated its wealth. Unlike national foundations, family foundations are best approached as if they were individual donors, not private foundations.

Because most family foundations are relatively small

and have such a limited geographic giving pattern, few are included in *Grant Support*. These foundations should be explored, however, for modest gifts of a local nature. While the average gift of small family foundations is less than $5,000, the sheer volume of family foundations makes them an important factor in grant support.

5. Community Foundations

In a strictly legal sense, community foundations are not really foundations at all but rather public charities. Community foundations maintain this favored tax status by collecting money from the public and directing grants within the community for which they are named. Because community foundations are not private foundations, they have no minimum giving requirements and pay no excise taxes on their net investment income. This is partly responsible for their rapid growth during the past decade, for hundreds of foundations (including some with assets in the many millions of dollars) have given all their money to community foundations.

A number of the larger community foundations, such as The Cleveland Foundation and The New York Community Trust, are listed in *Grant Support*. It is easy to distinguish a community foundation, for it will always be named for the community it serves. The San Francisco Foundation serves San Francisco, The Chicago Community Trust serves Chicago, and so forth. Readers of *Grant Support* should bear in mind that community foundations cannot, by law, make grants outside the geographic regions they serve. The San Francisco Foundation, for example, would not fund a project in Texas, regardless of the merit of the proposal.

For more information about the existence of a community foundation in a given city, readers may wish to consult the local trust bank in that city. (Information can also be obtained by writing the Council on Foundations, Inc., 2121 Crystal Drive, Suite 700, Arlington, VA 22202 or via their web site at www.cof.org.)

CORPORATE GIVING

Although the practice of corporations making grants and gifts to charity is now largely accepted, it was not until 1935 that the Internal Revenue Service allowed a charitable deduction for corporate gifts. In 1982, changes in the tax law enhanced the value of donations of company products, and increased the deduction of corporate contributions from 5 to 10 percent of net income.

Yet while this modest federal government incentive has spurred corporate philanthropy, approximately only one-third of all corporations in the United States make corporate gifts.

Corporations made the largest percentage of their donations to education over the last several years, with health and human services receiving the second largest amounts. Cultural and arts groups, civic and community activities, and various other recipients received the balance of corporate dollars.

Most corporations do not have professional grant reviewers but will often have grant guidelines, specific philanthropic objectives, or well-defined procedures for grant applicants.

An important consideration when approaching corporations is to introduce a benefit, either directly to the company or indirectly through its employees, that grant support can make. A proposal for support of an alcoholism program may be received more readily if the corporation feels alcoholism is a problem among its employees.

Many corporations are willing to provide volunteer service and specific expert assistance as well as money. Corporations also make in-kind contributions, such as free printing, equipment, etc., and will sometimes match gifts made by individual employees.

FEDERATED GIVING

Grant Support lists many grant opportunities from funding sources which, though neither foundations nor corporations, provide many millions of dollars of grant support every year. These funding sources can best be described as federated giving organizations, in that a number of small organizations combine their funding efforts for maximum effect.

The largest and best known federated agency is, of course, United Way. Most United Ways, however, do not make grants so much as they support existing agencies.

There are a number of other federated agencies that do make grants. The Catholic Campaign for Human Development, which is the federated arm of the Catholic Church in America, provides some $14 million in grant support annually. Other federated agencies include the United Negro College Fund (UNCF), the United Jewish Appeal, and the American Association of University Women.

PUBLIC MONEY

Government funding is as complex and confusing as it is big, and the special terms and language of government grants make the subject seem more confusing than it really is. An understanding of the various types of grants and some of the most often used terms may help readers break through the perplexing language of government grants.

Types of Grants

The federal government makes grants in many forms, some of which allow the independent grant seeker an

opportunity to be funded, and some which do not. Below are some of the most common types of government grants.

Block Grants: Sometimes called "bloc" grants, these are made from the federal government directly to states or local units of government, such as counties and municipalities. The grant most often comes to the state in a "block," and the state may spend the money as it wishes as long as the funds are being used to fulfill the basic purposes for which they were authorized. Many of the more recent federal grants under what is called "new federalism" have been block grants such as the Housing and Community Development Act money, the Comprehensive Employment and Training Act money, and funds to support programs for older Americans. Under the rules of most block grants, the state must submit an annual "state plan" to the federal government explaining how and where the funds are to be used. This state plan is public information, and potential grant seekers may wish to review it for programs under which they wish to seek grant support. One important aspect of block grants is that while the money is federal, the authority to spend it is local, and the recipients of block grant funds are allowed great flexibility in how they use the money.

Capitation Grants: Stemming from a concept of providing funds per capita of service, capitation grants are awarded based on the actual number of people served, rather than on the task to be performed. For example, an organization may be providing housing for runaway youths. This organization's annual budget is $100,000, and last year it provided housing for 1,000 youths. A capitation grant would provide $100 for each youth housed during the coming year ($100,000 divided by 1,000 youths). Capitation grants are most often used for training grants where payment is based on enrollment, rather than training outcome.

Categorical Grants: Simply stated, funds under a certain "category" must be expended within a certain field of interest, such as mental health, services for the handicapped, or maternity and child care. Although the number of categorical grants provided by the federal government has decreased in the past few years because of an increase in block grants, there are still more than 850 federal grant programs active within the federal government.

Construction Grants: Unless specifically stated, most federal grants will not provide funds for capital purposes, requiring instead that the grantee rent or lease the appropriate facility. Special construction grants, especially in the fields of health and mental health, have been made in the past for construction, renovation, and expansion. Many more important construction grant programs have been severely cut in the past few years, however, and it appears that the federal government is less enamored with this type of grant than in the past.

Demonstration Grants: Among the most common types of grants made in the human services field, demonstration grants, as opposed to basic research grants, are made to agencies in order to illustrate the effectiveness of a certain procedure or methodology, while at the same time providing a direct benefit to a group of clients. Unlike research grants, there is usually a large amount of evidence that the methodology to be demonstrated should prove effective before the grant is awarded. Often, demonstration grants are the second step of research grants, attempting to show that the success of a research grant may have greater applicability or a wider target population than originally envisioned.

Formula Grants: Not so much a type of grant as a method of determining the amount of funds to be made available, formula grants are based most often on the population, income, taxation, and special need of a given area.

The formula for grants will be written into the legislation or regulation that established the fund. The capitation grant mentioned earlier is one type of formula.

Matching Grants: Often confused with formula grants in that there is usually a "formula" for establishing the matching grant requirement, a matching grant means that the agency or individual who is receiving the grant guarantees to provide a certain portion of the total grant funds from sources other than the government. This "match" may be as small as 1 percent to as much as 50 percent with organizations such as the National Endowment for the Arts and National Endowment for the Humanities. Often there is a "sliding match" requirement, which means that the agency receiving the grant will provide a greater share of the total costs in the second and subsequent years of the award. Matching requirements may be for a "hard" or "soft" match. A "hard" match means that actual dollar matches must be secured, whereas a "soft" match allowed for such donated services as volunteer time and goods or equipment to be counted in lieu of "hard" dollars.

Project Grants: The grants allow the granting agency, usually a department or agency of the federal government, to determine funding based solely on the merits of the project of an individual or organization, rather than by formula requirements mentioned earlier. This is one of the most flexible types of grants in that the granting agency may have complete control in selecting the project, the grant recipient, and the amount of the award.

Research Grants: As opposed to demonstration grants and project grants, research grants are provided to test theories and hypotheses, develop or interpret new information, or revise accepted theories without the requirement that some benefit be immediately passed on to the clients. In fact the term "client" is often replaced with the term "subject" in research grants. There are two types, basic and applied. Basic research, which enjoyed great favor in the 1960s, has found funding harder to obtain lately, while applied research funds have continued to grow, especially in environmental programs.

Staffing Grants: As the phrase implies, these grants are provided for support of salaries of professional and technical staff members, plus in-service training in many cases. Most staffing grants come with a sliding match requirement.

Training Grants: These are awarded to organizations, corporations, or individuals to support the costs of training existing staff, students, or potential staff in the techniques or procedures needed to develop skills in a particular field, such as nursing, paramedical training and legal aid.

Seeking Governmental Sources

In addition to the *Annual Register of Grant Support*™, there are several places potential grant seekers can look for information about federal grants.

Catalog of Federal Domestic Assistance

The most important index for identifying federal resources is the *Catalog of Federal Domestic Assistance* (CFDA). Available online at www.cfda.gov, the catalog gives you access to a database of all Federal programs available to State and local governments (including the District of Columbia); federally recognized Indian tribal governments; Territories (and possessions) of the United States; domestic public, quasi-public, and private profit and nonprofit organizations and institutions; specialized groups; and individuals.

Available from the web site as a PDF download, the first section contains the indexes. An Agency Index Summary describes the functions and activities of the respective agencies responsible for administering the programs. The Agency Program Index lists, in numerical order, all programs, titles, the agency responsible, and the kind of assistance being offered—financial, nonfinancial, or combined. The Functional Index Summary lists categories of support, while a Subject Index provides a listing of programs by various topics. The second section provides the Program Descriptions, including detailed information for each program. Also included in the CFDA is a deadlines index and several informational appendices. After you find the program you want, contact the office that administers the program and find out how to apply.

Federal Register

Another valuable source is the *Federal Register*, available at www.federalregister.gov. Published by the Office of the Federal Register, National Archives and Records Administration (NARA), the Federal Register is the official daily publication for rules, proposed rules, and notices of Federal agencies and organizations. It includes such items as presidential orders, advisory meetings, program announcements, requests for applications and deadline dates.

Grants.gov

Grants.gov is a central storehouse for information on over 1,000 grant programs and provides access to approximately $500 billion in annual awards. The Department of Health and Human Services is the Grants.gov program's managing partner, and allows access to 26 federal grant-making agencies through the grants.gov web site.

Clearinghouses

Begun in the 1960s on a limited basis, a coordinated grant support process known as clearinghouse review was once required on hundreds of government grants.

As part of this review process, an applicant submits a brief description of the project or activity for which federal support is sought. Some clearinghouses have developed special forms for this "notification of intent," while others ask for a simple program description, along with the name and location of the applicant agency. Clearinghouses then notify the government agencies and elected officials of local governments that might be interested in the project, in order for the departments and agencies to comment.

If the clearinghouse does not identify any problems or possible conflicts, the applicant may complete and submit the proposal to the funding agency unless the clearinghouse specifies that it wants to review the completed proposal.

If there are concerns or unresolved issues, the clearinghouse may arrange a meeting between the applicant and the various departments that have expressed the concern. After any issues have been addressed, the applicant may wish to rewrite the proposal, continue discussions with the departments that are expressing concern, or submit the proposal to the funding source with the comments of the clearinghouse attached.

Program planning and proposal writing

Introductory version

By Norton J. Kiritz and Jerry Mundel

Proposals written for private foundations and those written for government grants (Federal, State, County or City) usually differ in their final form. Foundations often require a brief letter as an initial approach. A full proposal may follow in many situations. Government funding sources almost always require completion of a number of forms along with a detailed proposal narrative. Therefore, proposals to private and government grantmakers look quite different.

The package to a foundation or corporation will usually contain these elements:

1. **The cover letter**
2. **The proposal**
3. **Additional materials.**

1. The cover letter is signed by the Chairperson of the Board of a nonprofit agency, or the top authority in a governmental agency. It briefly describes the program, and tells the grantmaker how important the grant would be to the community served by the applicant agency. It shows strong support of the Board of Directors, which is essential in gaining foundation grants.

2. The body of the proposal may be as modest as one page (in the case of a foundation that limits requests to a page) or voluminous. It may be in letter form or a more formal presentation. In either case, following the instructions in Program Planning & Proposal Writing (PP&PW) will help to assure that the necessary items are included and are presented in a logical manner. Remember one thing: PP&PW can help you structure your thinking and even plan your project or program. It can serve as your proposal format where the funding source has not provided one as often the case with foundation proposals. But it should not be substituted for any format required by a foundation. If they ask you to follow a set format, do it!

3. Additional materials should be limited to those required by the funding source supplemented by only the most important addenda. Reviewers don't grade proposals by the pound, so save your postage.

The proposal package to a government funding source usually contains these elements:

1. **Letter of transmittal**
2. **The proposal**
3. **Additional materials.**

1. **The letter of transmittal** is a brief statement (2-3 paragraphs) signed by the highest level person within your organization. It briefly describes the request, the amount asked for, and may indicate the significance and importance of the proposed project. It should reflect the Board's support and approval of the request as reflected in the signature of the Board Chairperson (possibly as a dual signature along with the Executive Director/Chief Executive Officer).

2. The proposal going to a government funding source will generally be more lengthy than one going to a private foundation. It will often be 10-20 pages long, and the funding source guidelines will contain the sequence to be followed in writing the narrative portion.

It is a good idea to read the information describing how your proposal will be evaluated. Quite often, government agency guidelines describe exactly how each section of your proposal will be weighed. This tells you what the reviewers look for and helps you to organize your thoughts. If you are told to limit your proposal to 10 single-spaced pages, don't include one or two more thinking that it won't be viewed in a negative light. Follow the guidelines meticulously, because the reviewers will. Proposals can be deemed inappropriate simply because you failed to follow specific instructions.

Proposals going to government funders may also contain unique forms such as fact sheet forms where the entire project, names of key staff, budget, numbers of people impacted by the

---

project, etc. are indicated; assurance forms (addressing issues such as human subjects at risk); equal opportunity policy statements, facility access to the handicapped; and a number of other such forms. It is important to understand which items must be submitted along with your proposal and how they are to be completed, so read the instructions carefully.

3. Additional materials will generally include those items suggested by the funding source. This usually consists of job descriptions, resumes, letters of support or commitment, your IRS tax exemption designation, an annual report, financial statement, and related documents. This section (or Appendix) can be extensive when a funding source requests a great deal of information. There are instances in which the funding source will request copies of certain agency policies and procedures, copies of negotiated indirect cost rates, etc.

Generally, this will happen only once, and for refunding packages to the same public agency, you will probably not need to resubmit the same documents.

We suggest the following as a basic format for planning all of your proposals. Thinking through the various sections should enable you to create virtually all that either a private or government funding source will ask of you. It will also enable you to develop a logical approach to planning and proposal writing.

This is our proposed format:

PROPOSAL SUMMARY

I. INTRODUCTION
II. PROBLEM STATEMENT
III. PROGRAM GOALS AND OBJECTIVES
IV. METHODS
V. EVALUATION
VI. FUTURE FUNDING
VII. BUDGET
VIII. APPENDIX

PROPOSAL SUMMARY

The summary is a very important part of a proposal, not just something you jot down as an afterthought. There may be a box for a summary on the first page of a federal grant application form. It may also be called a proposal abstract. In writing to a foundation, the summary should be the first paragraph of a letter-type proposal, or the first section of a more formal proposal. The summary is probably the first thing that a funding source will read. It should be clear, concise and specific. It should describe who you are, the scope of your project, and the cost. The summary may be all that some in the review process will see, so make it good.

I. INTRODUCTION

In this part of the proposal you introduce your organization as an applicant for funds. More often than not proposals are funded on the reputation of the applicant organization or its key personnel, rather than on the basis of the program's content alone. The Introduction is the section in which you build your credibility, and make the case that your organization should be supported.

Credibility

What gives an organization credibility in the eyes of a funding source? First of all, it depends on the funding source. A traditional, conservative funding source might be more responsive to persons of prominence on your Board of Directors, how long you have been in existence and how many other funding sources have been supporting you. An avant garde funding source might be more interested in a Board of community persons rather than of prominent citizens and in organizations that are new rather than established.

Potential funding sources should be selected because of their possible interest in your type of organization as well as the kind of program you offer. You can use the Introduction to reinforce the connection you see between your interests and those of the funding source.

What are some of the things you can say about your organization in an introductory section?

- How you got started, your purpose and goals
- How long you have been around, how you've grown, and the breadth of your financial support
- Unique aspects of your agency (the fact that you were the first organization of its kind in the nation, etc.)
- Some of your most significant accomplishments as an organization or, if you are a new organization, some of the significant accomplishments of your Board or staff in their previous roles
- Your success with related projects
- The support you have received from other organizations and individuals (accompanied by a few letters of endorsement which can be attached in the Appendix)

We strongly suggest that you start a credibility file which you can use as a basis for the Introduction in your future proposals. In this file you can keep copies of newspaper articles about your organizations, letters of support you receive from other agencies and from your clients. Include statements made by key figures in your field or in the political arena that endorse your kind of program even if they do not mention your agency. For example, by including a presidential commission's statement that the type of program which you are proposing has

the most potential of solving the problems with which you deal, you can borrow credibility from those who made the statement (if they have any).

Remember, in terms of getting funded, the credibility you establish in your Introduction may be more important than the rest of your proposal. Build it! But here, as in all of your proposal, be as brief and specific as you can. Avoid jargon and keep it simple.

II. PROBLEM STATEMENT OR ASSESSMENT OF NEED

In the Introduction you have told who you are. From the Introduction we should know your areas of interest—the field in which you are working. Now you will zero in on the specific problem or problems that you want to solve through your proposed program. If the Introduction is the most important part of your proposal in getting funded, the Problem Statement is most important in planning a good program.

The Problem Statement or Needs Assessment describes the situation that caused you to prepare this proposal. It should refer to situation(s) that are outside of your organization (i.e. situations in the life of your clients or community). It does not refer to need internal to your organization, unless you are asking someone to fund an activity to improve your own effectiveness. In particular, the Problem Statement does not describe your lack of money as the problem. Everyone understands that you are asking for money in your solicitation. That is a given. But what external situation will be dealt with if you are awarded the grant? That is what you should describe, and document, in the Problem Statement.

Problem Statements deal with such issues as the homeless, offenders returning to prison with regularity, children who are far behind in their reading skills, youths dropping out of school, and the myriad other problems in contemporary society. Needs Statements are often used when dealing with a less tangible subject. They are especially useful in programs that are artistic, spiritual, or otherwise value-oriented. These are certainly no less important as subjects, but they do not lend themselves as directly to the problem-solving model of PP&PW. You would ordinarily deal with them as Needs and Satisfaction of Needs instead of Problems and Objectives.

You should not assume that "everyone knows this problem is valid." That may be true, but it doesn't give a fund source assurance about your expertise if you fail to demonstrate your knowledge of the problem. Use some appropriate statistics. Augment them with quotes from authorities, especially those in your own community. And make sure that you make the case for the problem in your area of service, not just on a national level. Charts and graphs will probably turn off the reader. If you use excessive statistics, save them for an Appendix, but pull out the key figures for your Problem Statement. And know what the statistics say.

In the Problem Statement, you need to do the following:

- Make a logical connection between your organization's background and the problems and the needs with which you propose to work.
- Clearly define the problem(s) with which you intend to work. Make sure that what you want to do is workable—that it can be done within a reasonable time, by your agency and with a reasonable amount of money.
- Support the existence of the problem by evidence. Statistics, as mentioned above, are but one type of support. You may also use statements from groups in your community concerned about the problem, from prospective clients, and from other organizations working in your community and from professionals in the field.
- Be realistic—don't try and solve all the problems in the world in the next six months.

Note: Many grant applicants fail to understand the difference between problems or needs and methods of solving problems or satisfying needs. For example, an agency working with the elderly in an urban area said that what the community needed were vans to get the elderly to various agencies. They determined that this need existed because not enough seniors were able to get to the social security office, health services, and related human service programs. What they had done was to immediately jump to a method by which the seniors would now be able to readily receive services. The problem with that logic is that the transportation suggested is a method and there are other methods as well. For example, what about the possibility of working with the agencies to decentralize services? Alternatively, volunteer advocates could work with seniors, acting on their behalf with some of these service providers. Ultimately, buying vans might be the best method, but it is clearly a method and not a problem or client need. Be very cautious about this. If you find yourself using lack of statements in the problem section, you are probably saying lack of method. This starts you on a circular reasoning track that will ruin the planning process.

III. PROGRAM GOALS AND OBJECTIVES

A well-prepared proposal has continuity—a logical flow from one section to another. Your Introduction can establish the context for your Problem Statement. Similarly, the Problem Statement will prepare the funding source for your logical Goals and Objectives.

Goals are broad statements such as: Develop additional resources to provide AIDS information to bilingual populations; Reduce underemployment rates among adults; Increase the availability of resources to address the problem of adolescent pregnancies; Create an environment in which folk art is fully

appreciated; or Enhance self-images of senior adults. These types of statements cannot be measured as they are stated. They offer the reader an understanding of the general thrust of a program. They are not the same as objectives.

Objectives are specific, measurable outcomes of your program. Objectives are your promised improvements in the situation you described in the Problem Statement. When you think of Objectives this way, it should be clear in most proposals what your Objective should look like. For example, if the problem was that certain children in your school read at least three grade levels below the norm for their age, then an objective would be that a certain number of those children would read significantly better when you had classmates who had also been reading poorly, but who did not have the benefit of your intervention. These outcome Objectives should state who is to change, what behaviors are to change, in what direction the changes will occur, how much change will occur, and by what time the change will occur.

Another example of a measurable objective would be:

"Within 30 days of completion of the JTPA Classroom Training Program, 75% of the 80 participating welfare recipients will have secured unsubsidized employment at a minimum of $5.25 per hour, and will maintain those positions for a minimum of 90 days."

The Importance of Distinguishing Between Methods and Objectives

Many, if not most, proposals state that the purpose of the program is to establish a program or provide a service. This is consistent with most thinking in the nonprofit sector, which sees the nonprofit organization as a "service provider." This results in Objectives that read like this:

"The objective of this project is to provide counseling and guidance services to delinquent youth between the ages of 8 and 14 in the blank community."

The difficulty with this kind of objective is that it says nothing about outcome. It says nothing about the change in a situation that was described in the Problem. That is, unless the Problem Statement (perish the thought) said that the problem was a "lack of counseling." Presumably the Problem Statement said something about youth being arrested, going to jail, dropping out of school, or whatever.

Objectives should be specific, estimating the amount of benefit to be expected from a program. Some applicants, trying to be as specific as they can, pick a number out of the air. For example, an agency might say that their objective was to decrease unemployment among adults in the XYZ community by 10% within a certain time period. The question you need to ask is: where did that figure come from? Usually it is made up because it sounds good. It sounds like a real achievement. But it should be made of something more substantial than that. Perhaps no program has ever achieved that high a percentage. Perhaps similar programs have resulted in a range of achievement of from 2-6% decrease in unemployment. In that case, 5% would be very good and 6% would be as good as has ever been done. Ten percent is just plain unrealistic. And it leads one to expect that you don't really know the field very well. Just remember that Objectives should be realistic and attainable. Decide whether the 10% figure is attainable. If not, then it is a poor objective because you cannot achieve it.

If you are having difficulty in defining your Objectives, try projecting your agency a year or two into the future. What differences would you hope to see between then and now? What changes would have occurred? These changed dimensions may be the Objectives of your program.

A Note About Process Objectives

You may be used to seeing Objectives that read like this:

"The objective of this training program is to offer classes in automotive repair three times each week, for a period of 36 weeks, to a group of 40 unemployed individuals,"

or

"The objective of this program is to provide twice-weekly counseling sessions, for a period of 18 weeks, to no less than 50 parents who have been reported to Child and Protective Services for child abuse."

These are Process Objectives, and belong in the Methods section of your proposal. They tell what you will do, and do not address the outcome or benefit of what you will do. It is critically important to distinguish between these process Objectives and true outcome Objectives. If you do not do so, you will end up knowing only what has occurred during your program, and will not have dealt with the changes attributed to your program. Remember, you have proposed your program in order to make some change in the world, not to add one more service to a world already overcrowded with services and service providers.

Process Objectives may be very useful, but they should only appear in the Methods section of your proposal, so they are not confused with the results of your proposed program.

IV. METHODS

You now have told the reviewer who you are, the problems you intend to work with, and your Objectives (which promise a solution to or reduction of the problems). Now you are going to describe the Methods you will use to accomplish your Objectives.

The Methods component of your proposal should describe, in some detail, the activities that will take place in order to achieve the desired results. It is the part of the proposal where the reader should be able to gain a picture in his/her mind of exactly how things work, what your facility looks like, how staff are deployed, how clients are dealt with, what the exhibits look like, how the community center recruits and assigns volunteers, or how the questionnaires will be administered and results interpreted.

There are two basic issues to be dealt with in the Methodology section. What combination of activities and strategy have you selected to employ to bring about the desired results? And why have you selected this particular approach, of all the possible approaches you could have employed?

Justifying your approach requires that you know a good deal about other programs of a similar nature. Who is working on the problem in your community or elsewhere? What Methods have been tried in the past and are being tried now and with what results? In other words, you need to substantiate your choice of Methods.

The consideration of alternatives is an important aspect of describing your methodology. Showing that you are familiar enough with your field to be aware of different program models and showing your reasons for selecting the model you have gives a funding source a feeling of security and adds greatly to your credibility. Obviously then, building credibility only starts in your Introduction, and can be enhanced as you demonstrate that you are knowledgeable throughout your proposal.

Your methodology section should describe who is doing what to whom, and why it is being done that way. Your approach should appear realistic to the reviewer, and not suggest that so much will be performed by so few that the program appears unworkable. A realistic and justified program will be impressive. An unrealistic program will not win you points for good intentions.

V. EVALUATION

Evaluation of your program can serve two purposes. Your program can be evaluated in order to determine how effective it is in reaching its stated Objectives. This concept of Evaluation is aimed at measuring results of your program (outcome Evaluation).

Evaluation can also be used as a tool to provide information necessary to make appropriate changes and adjustments in your program as it proceeds. This concept is focused on the way your program has been conducted (process Evaluation).

Measurable Objectives set the stage for effective outcome Evaluation. If you have difficulty in determining what criteria to use in evaluating your program, better take another look at your Objectives. They probably aren't very specific.

Subjective and Objective Evaluations

Many Evaluation plans are subjective in nature. Subjective Evaluations tell you how people feel about a program, but seldom deal with the concrete results of a program. For example, the Evaluation of an educational program that surveyed students, parents, teachers and administrators of the program would be eliciting attitudes about the program. It would not speak to the tangible improvement in performance attributed to the program.

Subjectivity also allows the introduction of our own biases into an Evaluation. This could easily happen if you evaluate your own programs, especially if you feel that continued funding depends on producing what looks like good results.

One way of obtaining a more objective Evaluation, and sometimes a more professionally prepared Evaluation, is to look to an outside organization to conduct an Evaluation for you. Sometimes it is possible to get an outside organization to develop an Evaluation design that can be submitted to a funding source as part of your proposal. This not only can suggest a more objective Evaluation, but can also add to the credibility of your proposal, since you have added the credibility of the evaluating institution.

It is essential to build an Evaluation plan into your proposal and be prepared to implement your Evaluation at the same time that you start your program. If you want to determine change along some dimension, then you have got to show where your clients have come from. It is very difficult to start an Evaluation at or near the conclusion of the program, for at that time you may not know the characteristics of your clients at the time of their entry into the program.

VI. FUTURE AND OTHER NECESSARY FUNDING

No grantmaker wants to adopt you. Funding sources want to know how you will continue your program when their grant runs out. If you are requesting funds to start a new program, or to expand an existing program, then how will you maintain it after the grant funds have been spent?

A promise to continue looking for alternative sources of support is not sufficient. You should present a plan that will assure the funding source, to the greatest extent possible, that you will be able to maintain this new program after the grant has been completed. Indeed, if you are having difficulty keeping your current operations supported, you will probably have more difficulty in maintaining a level of operation which includes additional programs. The funding source may be doing you no favor by supporting a new project and putting you in the position of having to raise even more money next year than you do now.

At this point in your planning you may realize that there is little likelihood of any other sources of support one or two years hence. This ought to bring you to a decision-making point whether you should even try to implement a new program at this time in your agency's history.

What would constitute a satisfying response in this proposal component? Could you get a local institution or governmental agency to agree to continue to support your program, should it demonstrate the desired results? Can you get such a commitment in writing? Can you generate funds through the project itself—such as fees from services that will build up over a year or two, subscriptions to publications, etc.? Are there third parties available to provide reimburse-

ment for services? Are you expanding your non-grant fundraising activities? The best plan for Future Funding is the plan that does not require continued grant support.

Other Necessary Funding

Other necessary funding refers to what are sometimes called "non-recurring grants." That is, one-time only requests. This could be a request for a vehicle to transport your clientele, or the purchase of a piece of medical equipment for your hospital. While these are not program grants, the funds you request are not all you will need either to utilize the vehicle, or to operate the medical device. For the vehicle to be used, you must cover the costs of a driver, insurance, gas and maintenance. Similarly, the medical equipment must be operated by trained personnel. The funding source will want to know if you are aware of what you need beyond the purchase requested in your grant, and have the funds needed to cover these costs. They surely will not want to fund a bus that will sit in your garage for a year.

VII. BUDGET

Funding source requirements for Budgets vary, with foundations requiring less extensive Budgets than government funding sources. The following Budget design should satisfy most funding sources that allow you to design your own Budget and, with minor changes that the sources will tell you about, can be adapted to fit most government agency requirements. This recommended Budget contains three sections: The first is Personnel, the second is Non-Personnel, and the third is Indirect Costs.

When planning your Budget, it is wise to look closely at your Goals and Objectives to determine the level of activity in the program, and at your Methods section to review the specific plan you have proposed. For example, a Volunteer Senior Peer Counseling program would, one hopes, be less costly to operate than a Senior Peer Counseling program involving paid staff. Budgets should be built from the ground up—that is, based on your Goals and Objectives and the methodology you have proposed. In the context of your program you can begin to itemize such things as the staffing called for, the facilities needed, the equipment required, the supplies necessary, travel costs to be paid, and the range of costs for which your agency must be reimbursed, i.e., time of the CEO, bonding of employees, fundraising, use of space, payroll services, in-service training offered, etc.

It is important to go through this exercise in developing a Budget. Without it, there is a risk of developing unrealistic or impractical requests, where program and Budget are unrelated.

This is how we suggest you structure your Budget:

I. PERSONNEL

A. Salaries & Wages

In this section you can list all full- and part-time staff in the proposed program. We suggest a format which includes the following information:

# of persons per title	Title	Full monthly salary	% of time employed in grant	# of months during grant period	Amount requested	Amount donated or volunteered	Total

How does this look on a completed line item of a Budget? If you are employing a Project Coordinator at a salary of $2,000 per month, working full time (100%) for the entire grant period (12 months) and are asking the funding source to provide the full amount of this salary, then it looks like this:

	Req.	Donated	Total
Proj Coord @ $2,000/ea. 100% x 12 months	$24,000	-0-	$24,000

You can list all of your staff in the same way. If any of your staff are being paid out of another source of funds (for example, a staff person assigned to your project by a County agency), then you total up their salary and put it in the donated column (also referred to as in-kind, local share, or applicant share). Like this:

	Req.	Donated	Total
Soc Workers @ $1500 ea. 50% x 12 months	-0-	$18,000	$18,000

This means that you will have two half-time Social Workers on your staff for the full year and their salaries are being paid by somebody other than the funding source. You take their full salary in the Budget ($1,500/mo.) and halve it ($750) as they are only working 50% time; multiply the $750 by 12 months they will be working (giving you $9,000) and multiply it by 2 (the number of people employed in this capacity). This gives you a total of $18,000 of donated Social Worker services in this project.

What does the $2,000 per month figure for the salary of the Project Coordinator represent? It may represent the actual salary paid the Project Coordinator, but not necessarily. If this is a new project, and if your organization has a typical five-step salary schedule for job classifications, the monthly salary range for the Project Coordinator may look like this:

Step A	Step B	Step C	Step D	Step E
$1,500	$1,750	$2,000	$2,250	$2,500

If you have developed a salary schedule like this for each position, then you should request the mid-point ($2,000) unless you know in advance who will fill that position. In that case, list the actual salary anticipated. If not, the mid-point of the salary schedule allows you to hire someone currently making $1,300/mo., who would welcome the increase even in Step A. You have the flexibility to hire at any point along the range with the assumption that all staff salaries will average out toward the

middle of the salary range. (This works if there are a number of positions in your project, not just one or two.)

How do you determine what the salary range of a Project Coordinator ought to be? The federal government prefers that salaries be comparable to the prevailing practice in similar agencies in your community. To justify the salaries you build into your Budget you should obtain information from other local agencies regarding the salaries of persons with job descriptions, qualifications, and responsibilities similar to those of the jobs in your agency. You might go to the local city and/or county government, the school district, or United Way. By comparing the jobs at your agency with the jobs at other local agencies, you plan a salary for each position, and you keep the comparability data on hand, should you be asked by the funding source to justify your staff salaries.

Another final item to be included in your Budget for most public agency applications is the matching support being contributed by your organization, or the donated services. They can either be personnel contributed by you (the applicant organization), or by a third party (another participating agency, a corporation giving you a loaned executive, students, etc.). In many cases this will involve the use of volunteers. You should place a value on the service being performed by that volunteer, e.g. plumber, attorney, carpenter, receptionist, etc. That value is based upon the function being performed by the volunteer, not the professional background or education of the volunteer. A physician volunteering time at a community center where he/she helps out in painting the facility is shown at the hourly wage paid painters, not physicians.

Governmental grantmakers sometimes require financial participation on the part of an applicant, i.e., 10% or 25% match. You may be able to make this contribution in "cash" or in-kind. For example, if you are going to pay the salary of a staff member, that is cash. If you are using volunteers, or receive an executive on loan from a local corporation, that is "in-kind."

If you promise volunteers in your program, you are required to deliver the required volunteer services, just as if the funding source was actually paying their salary. You will be asked to document the work they perform and to keep records of their time. Records may be audited in the case of a government grant. Always be able to document 5-10% more than the required percentage match just in the event that you are audited and some of your volunteer time is disallowed.

Why is it important to develop a match (applicant share) and show the total costs of a project when some of the money or services are not being provided by the funding source? There are several reasons. First the government funding source wants to know that there is a commitment on the part of your agency—a commitment beyond just conducting a program. It helps for them to know there is some likelihood that you have resources with which to continue the program after the funding has ceased. It also provides some clarity as to the exact cost in delivering a service. If the program were to be replicated elsewhere, and donated services are not available, it tells the funding source what the total cost would be. Finally, when you have local resources (volunteers, cash, staff, equipment, etc.), it reduces the amount of money required of the grantor, thereby allowing additional projects to be funded in other locations.

B. Fringe Benefits

In this section you list the fringe benefits your employees will be receiving, and the dollar cost of these benefits. Some fringe benefits are mandatory, but they vary from state to state, so you will have to determine what they are for your agency in your state. Mandatory fringe benefits may include State Disability Insurance, State Unemployment, FICA, etc. They are usually based on percentages of salaries. For example, if FICA is currently 7.51% of the first $45,000 of each person's salary, an entry for FICA on your Budget might look like this:

	Req.	Donated	Total
FICA @ 7.51% of $90,000	$6,759	-0-	$6,759

$90,000 would be the total of all your salaries, up to $45,000 for any one person.

Some fringe benefits are calculated on a flat amount per month per staff member, and not on a percentage, e.g., health insurance. For example:

	Req.	Donated	Total
Health insurance @ $100/mo. per staff member x 4 staff @ 12 months	$4,800	-0-	$4,800

As with your salary schedule, your fringe benefits should be comparable to the benefits offered in similar agencies in your community.

While you will need to calculate fringe benefits for your own information, in some grant applications you simply indicate the fringe benefit total as a percentage of salary.

C. Consultant and Contract Services

This is the third and final part of the Personnel section of your Budget. In this section you include paid and unpaid consultants (i.e., volunteers). You can differentiate between which items go here and which go in Salaries and Wages on the basis of the manner in which the individual or business normally operates. If a bookkeeping firm generally operates on a fee-for-service basis and is volunteering their service to your organization, that would fit best under Consultant and Contract Services. Essentially, be logical and if a Fed yells at you, change it. (Foundation persons never yell.) Entries might look like these:

	Req.	Donated	Total
Bookkeeping Services @ $200/mo. x 12 mos.	-0-	$2,400	$2,400

Contracted Fundraising Svc. @ $400/day x 10 days	$4,000	-0-	$4,000
Trainer @ $250/day x 8 days	$2,000	-0-	$2,000

II. NON-PERSONNEL

A. Space Costs

In this section, you list all of the facilities you will be using, both those on which you pay rent and those which are being donated for your use. Rent you pay, or the valuation of donated facilities, should be comparable to prevailing rents in the geographic area in which you are located. In addition to the actual rent, you should also include the cost of utilities, maintenance services and renovations, if they are absolutely essential to your program, insurance on the facility, telephones (number of instruments needed, installment costs, and monthly cost of instruments), and out-of-town facilities needed. Include these items in line item fashion like this:

	Req.	Donated	Total
Office Space of 900 sq. feet $1.25/foot/mo. x 12 mos.	$13,500	-0-	$13,500
Facility insurance	-0-	$600	$600

B. Rental, Lease or Purchase of Equipment

Here you list all the equipment, donated or to be purchased, that will be used in the proposed program. This includes office equipment, desks, duplicating machines, word processors, etc. Let discretion be your guide in this section. Try to obtain as much donated equipment as you can. It not only lowers the funding source cost, but it shows the funding source that other people are involved in trying to make the program happen. Be careful to read guidelines closely when working with government grant applications—especially as to their definition of equipment and restrictions which apply. For example, equipment is often defined as something costing more than $500 per unit and/or having a lifetime of greater than one year. Additionally, there may be prohibitions against purchasing equipment, and you may be encouraged to lease rather than purchase.

C. Supplies

This generally means "desk top" supplies such as paper clips, pens, paper, stationery, etc. A reasonable figure to use is $125 per year for each of your staff. If you have any unusual needs for supplies—perhaps you are running an art education program, a sheltered workshop, or some classroom activity requiring a good deal of educational materials—then have a separate line item for such supplies. This component can also include publications, subscriptions, and postage.

D. Travel

All transportation related expenses are included here. Don't put in any big lump sums which will require interpretation or raise a question by the funding source. Include all staff travel, per diem rates approved by your agency and/or the state or federal agency you are applying to, ground transportation, taxi, reimbursement to staff for use of their automobiles, consultant travel costs, use of agency vans or automobiles (if this has not been included under equipment), etc. Examples include the following:

	Req.	Donated	Total
Four round trip air fares LA-NY for workshop on Creative Accounting @ $550/each	$2,000	-0-	$2,000
Reimbursement for staff travel @ .20/mile x average of 400 miles/mo. x 12 mos.	$960	-0-	$960
Per Diem (NY) @ $150/day x 8 days for 4 staff at Creative Accounting Workshop	$1,200	-0-	$1,200

Be sure that you use per diem (hotel and meals) rates which are consistent for the location. Attending a workshop in Weed, California will be considerably less expensive than New York City.

E. Other Costs

This is generally a catch-all category which includes items not reasonable to include elsewhere. For example:

1. Bonding of employees
2. Tuition for classes
3. Professional Association dues
4. Printing (unless you placed this under Consultant and Contract Services)

III. INDIRECT COSTS

The third component of your Budget is called Indirect Costs. The federal government defines indirect costs as those costs of an institution which are not readily identifiable with a particular project or activity, but nevertheless are necessary to the general operation of the institution and the conduct of the activities it performs. The cost of operating and maintaining buildings and equipment, depreciation, administrative salaries, general telephone expenses, general travel and supplies expenses are types of expenses usually considered as indirect costs. While it is possible for all such costs to be charged directly—that is, to the line items listed above—this is often impractical, and you may group them into a common pool. The federal government indicates that "an Indirect Cost Rate is simply a device for determining fairly and expeditiously ... that proportion of an institution's general expenses each of its projects or activities should bear." An organization or institution can negotiate an Indirect Cost Rate (generally a percentage of Salaries and Wages or Total Direct Costs) with any federal agency from whom it has received funds. This is an important issue since many larger institutions find that

SAMPLE BUDGET

	Req.	Donated	Total	
I. PERSONNEL				
A. Salaries and Wages				
Project Coordinator @$2,000/month @ 100% x 12 months	24,000	-0-	24,000	
2 Social Workers @$1,500/month each @50% time x 12 months	-0-	18,000	18,000	
20 Volunteer Recreational Aides @50 hours each/year x 7.00/hour		-0-	7,000	7,000
B. Fringe Benefits				
20% of $42,000	4,800	3,600	8,400	
C. Consultant and Contract Services				
Bookkeeping Services @$200/month x 12 months	-0-	2,400	2,400	
Fundraising Services @$400/day x 10 days	4,000	-0-	4,000	
Trainer @$250/day x 8 days	2,000	-0-	2,000	
Annual Audit	2,000	2,000	4,000	
II. NON-PERSONNEL				
A. Space				
900 square feet @$1.25/square foot/month x 12 months		13,500	-0-	13,500
Telephones @$200/month x 12 months	2,400	-0-	2,400	
Utilities @$300/month x 12 months	-0-	3,600	3,600	
Facility Insurance @$600/year	600	-0-	600	
B. Rental, Lease, Purchase of Equipment				
Word Processor/printer	2,000	-0-	2,000	
12-passenger van @$400/month x 10 months		4,000	-0-	4,000
3 desk/chair sets @$250/each	750	-0-	750	
C. Supplies				
Desk top supplies @$125/year/staff x 3	375	-0-	375	
Educational materials @$50/month x 12 months	600	-0-	600	
D. Travel				
4 roundtrip airfares LA-NY @$500/each	2,200	-0-	2,200	
Reimbursement for staff auto travel @$.20/mile x average of 400 miles/month x 12 months	960	-0-	960	
8 days per diem (NY) @$1.50/day		1,200	-0-	1,200
E. Other Costs				
Conference Tuition (Creative Accounting) @$200/each x 4 staff		800	-0-	800
Board Liability Insurance	600	-0-	600	
III. INDIRECT COSTS				
15.3% of TADC (Total Allowable Direct Costs) as per att. negot. rate with Dept. of Labor, 1998	10,860	-0-	10,860	
TOTAL PROJECT COST:	**77,645**	**36,600**	**114,245**	

every new project undertaken costs the institution money unless it is reimbursed for the indirect cost associated with operating the institution.

For further clarification of Indirect Cost Rates, contact the Federal Office's Regional Comptroller or your Program Officer for Contract Officer to find out exactly how to go about negotiating Indirect Cost Rates. Once you have such a rate, there may still be instances in which the funding source refuses to pay indirect cost rates or places a cap (a maximum) on the percentage of total direct costs they will pay. Nevertheless, this is an area which should be explored and understood.

VIII. APPENDIX

Addenda to a foundation or corporate proposal should be limited. It is an imposition to suggest that a reviewer plod through many pages of additional material that you decided were important enough to include with your proposal. In the case of a government grant, however, the Appendix may be longer than the body of the proposal. It contains material which needs to be submitted to the funding source, but should not detract from the continuity and flow of the proposal by being included in the narrative. The rationale for any decision about what to include in the body of a proposal should be based on your answering the question, "Do I really want the funding source to read/scan the census runs, flow chart, or job descriptions while reading the proposal?" If the answer is "Yes" then definitely include the item at that juncture. If the answer is "No" then include the item in the Appendix and refer the reader to it.

Funding sources will usually stipulate the attachments they want you to include with your grant application. This will involve a variety of documents, many of which will be required routinely by other funding sources. It is a good idea for Development Officers, Program Planners, Grantwriters, or related personnel to maintain a file of materials which can be included in a proposal package. Such items ought to be accessible to you at all times.

Items which are routinely requested by many funding sources include the following:

1. An Audited Financial Statement

Funding sources generally require an audited financial statement. Many smaller organizations do not routinely have an audit conducted, or cannot afford an audit, and an "unaudited" financial statement is often developed by the agency's accountant or bookkeeper. it is important that the applicants know whether the funding source will accept an unaudited financial statement. A telephone call to the program officer, foundation staff member, or related contact person at the offices of the funding source will provide you with the answer.

2. I.R.S. Documentation Letter

This letter from the I.R.S. indicates that your organization is exempt from federal corporate income taxes. It contains important information regarding the basis for your exemption and the requirements associated with maintaining it. In some cases, individual states may also grant such exemptions, and copies of both letters may be appropriate for submission.

3. Indication of Nonprofit Corporation Status

A copy of the receipt of nonprofit corporation status by the state in which your organization was incorporated may be required by funding sources. In most instances, the favorable determination of tax exemption (above) will be sufficient in that it lists the name of the incorporated nonprofit organization.

4. Roster of Board of Directors

A document more and more requested by funding sources is a roster of board members by affiliation. Of concern is more than simply the names of your board members, but who they represent. By this is meant their job function: minister, doctor, banker, social worker, building contractor, etc. In the cases of retired individuals, indicate their former job or profession.

In situations where organizations have board members who are welfare recipients, housewives, unemployed persons, students, etc., select an area of interest or specialty for such individuals, and indicate that after their name. Don't just list a name without any affiliation.

5. Table of Organization

Another item which may be useful is a table of organization. This table should include the proposed staffing pattern for the project for which funds are being requested, and should also include the larger agency/department/section to whom the new project personnel report. With large organizations, it is not critical that each position be indicated, but units or departments should be shown. In many instances it is more important that the funding source understand how the major "functions" of the organization are carried out, and how boards, committees and staff interrelate. The only problem with these tables is that they often present such a confusing picture that one wonders how the organization could ever work.

6. Organizational Budget

Some funding sources will require submission of an organizational Budget for the current or forthcoming program year. This organizational Budget differs from the Budget for the project itself, previously discussed. This allows the reviewer to put the grant request in a larger context.

7. Summary Chart of Key Events

Most public grant applications will require that you submit some form of timeline for major milestones or activities. This can be done in a variety of formats—Gantt charts, PERT charts, flow charts, etc., and can be done by month, quarterly, or by time elapsed from the initiation of the project. Whatever format you use, it should be clear and easily understood by the funding source.

Other documents are often needed for inclusion as an attachment to a proposal:

8. Negotiated Indirect Cost Rate

A copy of your agency's negotiated indirect cost rate should be included in the Appendix when you are citing a "percentage" amount for indirect costs. This is required when submitting public agency applications where such costs are being charged.

Private foundations may also pay indirect cost rates, but be sure to review foundation guidelines closely in that some place a limit on the percentage they will pay. In some cases this percentage is only ten percent (10%) of total direct costs—considerably less than the negotiated percentage with the federal agency.

9. Letters of Support or Endorsement

Letters from elected officials, other organizations and individuals will need to be submitted as required by a funding source or on the basis of your organization's decision that such indicators of support would be a good idea.

In general, such letters should be addressed to your organization (Executive Director, Board Chairman, etc.) and sent to you for submission along with the proposal. Letters should not be sent under separate cover to the funding source because they may not get there in time or may not be filed appropriately with your proposal. More significantly, many funding sources simply will not accept documents submitted separately.

To aid in the process of securing letters of support, many grantwriters and development officers have developed a procedure designed to aid those individuals and organizations from whom you want such letters. Many elected officials and agency executives are continually asked for such letters of support, but it speeds up the process if they can see an example of the type of letter desired.

It is a good idea to draft letters of support and share them with potential signees. This will ensure that you do not receive a glowing endorsement for your program "to provide a shelter for homeless immigrant families" when you are actually seeking support for "establishing a source of food and shelter for migrating birds." Telephone discussions which summarize project ideas often do not get heard exactly as you think you've transmitted them.

If you plan to include "motherhood letters" along with your proposal, i.e., "As a mother in Centerville with six children, I have nothing but praise for the Headstart program and urge you to continue funding it," try to keep such endorsements to a minimum—no more than two such letters per proposal!

10. Resumes

Whenever possible, resumes/curriculum vitae of key staff should be updated periodically so that you are not submitting the exact resume which was placed in the agency's file ten years ago when the person was hired.

Also, it helps the ease of reading if different resumes are written in the same format, so when updating resumes you might consider developing a similar format for each. With the exclusion of academic and medical personnel, they need be no longer than 2-3 pages.

11. Job Descriptions

While in some instances it is important to create a capsule resume for inclusion in the body of the proposal, in most cases the description of positions ought to be an Appendix item.

Key to entry information

(1) **XYZ FOUNDATION** (2) **[101]**

(3) One Central Commerce Building
Main and Division Streets
Anytown, IL 60009

(4) (312) 555-5555
Fax: (312) 555-1234
E-Mail: abcd@xyzfdn.edu
Web Site: www.xyzfdn.edu

(5) FOUNDED: 1990

(6) AREAS OF INTEREST:
Education, medical research, the environment, youth groups, law and social welfare.

(7) CONSULTING OR VOLUNTEER SERVICES:
Technical assistance to community groups, particularly to those providing cultural activities.

(8) NAME OF PROGRAM
•. John Doe Project Grants Fund

(9) TYPE:
Project/Program grants. Support for a variety of activities in the areas of education, medical research, desert research, atmospheric, earth, and oceanographic sciences, youth organizations, libraries, conservation projects, water pollution studies, fish and game management, preservation, parks and recreation, environmental studies, law, judicial education, crime delinquency, law enforcement, relief and social agencies, museums and historical projects, health, hospitals, and community improvement organizations. Awards are not available for endowment, contingency or reserve purposes.

(10) YEAR PROGRAM STARTED: 1950

(11) PURPOSE:
To support endeavors for the benefit of mankind.

(12) LEGAL BASIS:
Private foundation; tax-exempt under statute 501(c)(3) of the Internal Revenue Code.

(13) ELIGIBILITY:
U.S. tax-exempt nonprofit organizations with appropriate interests are eligible to apply. Grants are not made, however, to organizations which distribute them to beneficiaries of their own selection. Priority is given to projects which are not normally financed by public tax funds.

(14) GEOG. RESTRICTIONS: United States.

(15) FINANCIAL DATA:
Grants vary in amount depending upon the needs and nature of the request.

(16) *Amount of support per award:* $1,000 to $500,000.

(17) *Total amount of support:* $6,005,000 for the year ended May 31, 2016.

(18) *Matching fund requirements:* Grants exceeding $25,000 must be matched by an amount not less than one-third the total amount of the grant.

(19) CO-OP FUNDING PROGRAMS: The Foundation prefers joint funding whenever possible.

(20) NO. MOST RECENT APPLICANTS: 512

(21) NO. AWARDS: 92 for the year ended May 31, 2016.

(22) REPRESENTATIVE AWARDS:
$75,000 to Anytown Hospital, toward facilities and equipment for its new Community Health Center; $25,000 to State University, for development of an interdisciplinary studies program; $15,000 to City Youth Center, toward purchase of equipment for its model reading laboratory program for youths.

(23) APPLICATION INFO.:
No official application forms are issued. Interested applicants should submit an informal proposal which briefly includes:
(1) amount requested and an explanation of the necessity or purpose therefore;
(2) aid sought and amounts received from other foundations and sources (include names) during the preceding three years;
(3) aid presently being sought from other sources (or whether such solicitation is contemplated) and, if so, from whom;
(4) copy of tax-exempt letter from the U.S. Treasury and Section 509 classification determination;
(5) latest audited balance sheet and detailed income account and;
(6) signature and approval of the overall head of the applicant institution or organization. Seven copies of application proposals and covering letters should be submitted. Letters of support from appropriate authorities and/or organizations are also encouraged.

(24) *Duration:* Varies according to length of project. Grants may be renewed if continued support can be shown to be beneficial and vital to project success.

(25) *Deadline:* Formal proposals and supporting documents must be received two months prior to board meetings, held in June and December.

(26) PUBLICATIONS:
Annual report; application guidelines.

(27) IRS I.D.: 00-1234567

(28) BOARD OF TRUSTEES:
John Doe III, Chairman
Margaret Lee, Vice Chairman
Samuel Smith, Treasurer
Robert Johnson, Secretary
Arthur Boyle
Anthony Cates
Phillip Sevoy

(29) OFFICERS:
Phyllis Hartley, Executive Director
David Lisle, President
Susan Banks, Vice President
John Quincy Smith, Project Grants Coordinator

(30) ADDRESS INQUIRIES TO:
John Quincy Smith, Project Grants Coordinator
P.O. Box 777
Neartown, IL 60008

(31) * PLEASE NOTE:
If an applicant is unclear as to the Foundation's current fields of interest, an inquiry directed to it describing the applicant's project may save the trouble or expense of preparing and submitting a formal application.

(1) Grantmaking organization.
(2) Entry number, reference corresponding to numbers used in all the indexes.
(3) Address.
(4) Telephone numbers, E-mail, and Web Site addresses when available.
(5) Date organization was founded.
(6) Major fields of organizational interest.
(7) Fields in which the organization donates consulting, volunteer, or similar services, and the nature of the service.
(8) Name(s) of grant program(s).
(9) Nature of support available under the program(s), e.g., fellowships, project grants, research grants, technical assistance, etc.
(10) Date program was established.
(11) Objective of the grant program and/or sponsoring institution.
(12) Organization's legal status or type (e.g., IRS ruling, state statute, corporate giving program, etc.); legal authority for expenditure of government funds, etc.
(13) Qualifications required of the applicant individual or project and/or sponsoring institution.
(14) Restrictions or preferences as to geographic location of the applicant individual or project and/or sponsoring institution.
(15) Fiscal nature of the grant, including expenses to which it may be applied, restrictions on its use and noncash benefits.
(16) Fixed sum, average amount, or range of funds offered for each award.
(17) Total funding available for the program or, when indicated, for all programs of a grantmaking organization, and the year in question.
(18) Cost-sharing stipulations.
(19) Nature of participation with other donors for project support.
(20) Total applicants, for the most recent year statistics are available.
(21) Total recipients, and the year in question.
(22) Representative awards made under the program for the most recent year, including the amount, recipient, and project title or purpose of the award.
(23) Application requirements and procedures, or references for further information.
(24) Period for which support is provided; renewal possibilities.
(25) Closing date(s) for application submission; award announcement date(s).
(26) Publications that are available from the organization, e.g., annual report, application guidelines, program announcements, etc.
(27) Internal Revenue Service tax identification number, if applicable.
(28) Names and titles of principal personnel, e.g., Trustees, Directors, Awards Committee members, etc.
(29) Names and titles of organization and/or program officers.
(30) Source of further information and/or recipient of applications.
(31) Unusual specifications or conditions concerning the program.

An asterisk (*) following an organization name indicates no or incomplete data was received from the source to update or compile the entry. The program listing is then reprinted from the last edition of *Grant Support*, revised where possible, or compiled entirely through staff research.

New listings in 2017 edition

The following is a list of foundations that are offering new grant programs. Bulleted items (•) reflect new program names for the foundation listed.

EDUCATION

Scholar aid programs (all disciplines)

Congressional Hispanic Caucus Institute, Washington, DC
- (•) Scholar Intern Programs

Davidson Institute, Reno, NV
- (•) Davidson Fellows

The Kosciuszko Foundation, Inc., New York, NY
- (•) Wisconsin Study in Poland WSIP

HUMANITIES

Arts (multiple disciplines)

New Mexico Arts, Santa Fe, NM

Utah Division of Arts & Museums, Salt Lake City, UT
- (•) Artist in Residence
- (•) Arts Education Projects
- (•) Arts Organization Capacity Building
- (•) Arts Project A&B
- (•) Folk Arts Scholarships
- (•) Local Arts Agencies
- (•) Museum: Tiers One and Two
- (•) Sustainability: Tiers One and Two

History

Cushwa Center for the Study of American Catholicism, Notre Dame, IN
- (•) Peter R. D'Agostino Research Travel Grant
- (•) Theodore M. Hesburgh Research Travel Grant

History Colorado State Historical Fund, Denver, CO

Omohundro Institute of Early American History and Culture, Williamsburg, VA
- (•) Georgian Papers Programme Fellowships
- (•) Jamestown Rediscovery Omohundro Institute JR OI Short Term Visiting Fellowship

Franklin D. Roosevelt Library and Museum, Hyde Park, NY
- (•) Roosevelt Institute Research Grants

LIFE SCIENCES

Life sciences (general)

The Wiley Foundation, Hoboken, NJ
- (•) Wiley Prize in Biomedical Sciences

Medicine (multiple disciplines)

National Institutes of Health, Bethesda, MD
- (•) Small Research Grant Program Parent R03

Internal medicine

The Leukemia & Lymphoma Society, Rye Brook, NY
- (•) Screen to Lead Program SLP

Neurology

Parkinson's Disease Foundation, Inc., New York, NY
- (•) Stanley Fahn Junior Faculty Award

Obstetrics and gynecology

The Lalor Foundation, Inc., Boston, MA
- (•) Anna Lalor Burdick Program

Psychiatry, psychology, mental health

American Academy of Child and Adolescent Psychiatry, Washington, DC
- (•) Educational Outreach Program

(•) Paramjit T. Joshi, M.D., International Scholars Award
(•) Junior Investigator Award
(•) Life Members Mentorship Grant for Medical Students
(•) Pilot Awards
(•) Ulku Ulgur, M.D., International Scholar Award

American Psychological Association, Washington, DC
(•) MFP Services for Transition Age Youth

SOCIAL SCIENCES

Communications

National Association of Science Writers, Inc., Berkeley, CA
(•) NASW Idea Grants

SPECIAL POPULATIONS

African-American

National Black MBA Association, Atlanta, GA
(•) NBMBAA Undergraduate Scholarship Program

Native American

Bureau of Indian Affairs, Lakewood, CO
(•) Tribal Energy Development Capacity TEDC Grant
(•) Energy and Mineral Development Program EMDP Grant

Bureau of Indian Affairs, Washington, DC
(•) Native American Business Development Institute NABDI

Special populations

Caring for Military Families: The Elizabeth Dole Foundation, Washington, DC
(•) Innovation Grants Program

The Joseph P. Kennedy, Jr. Foundation, Washington, DC
(•) Public Policy Fellowship

TECHNOLOGY AND INDUSTRY

Home economics and nutrition

Canadian Foundation for Dietetic Research (CFDR), Toronto, ON, Canada
(•) Research Grants in Dietetics

URBAN AND REGIONAL AFFAIRS

Community development and services

The Harry and Jeanette Weinberg Foundation, Inc., Owings Mills, MD
(•) Basic Human Needs and Health
(•) Disabilities
(•) Education
(•) General Community Support
(•) Older Adults
(•) Veterans
(•) Workforce Development

MULTIPLE SPECIAL PURPOSE

Multiple special purpose

ABBOTT FUND [1]

100 Abbott Park Road, D379/AP6D
Abbott Park, IL 60064-3500
(847) 937-7075
Fax: (847) 935-5051
Web Site: www.abbottfund.org

FOUNDED: 1951

AREAS OF INTEREST:
Health and welfare, education, culture and arts, civic and public policy.

NAME(S) OF PROGRAMS:
- **General Grant Program**

TYPE:
General operating grants; Project/program grants. Primary interest in the fields of higher education and human health and welfare. In addition, support of appropriate programs in culture, the arts and civic activities will continue to be a portion of Abbott's program.

YEAR PROGRAM STARTED: 1951

PURPOSE:
To provide support through cash grants to U.S.-based recipients whose areas of interest are consistent with Abbott's basic philanthropic policies and objectives.

LEGAL BASIS:
Corporate nonprofit giving program.

ELIGIBILITY:
Grants will be made only to associations and organizations and not directly to individuals. Grantees must be able to provide evidence of nonprofit, tax-exempt status and must complete the eligibility test to ensure that the organization or program falls within the funding criteria.

Preference is given to requests for one-time contributions and for programmatic and operating purposes. However, grants extending over a defined period of years or directed towards the support of specific building or other capital projects will be considered on an exception basis.

Priority will be given to organizations serving communities in which Abbott has significant operations or employee populations, to organizations whose activities are directed towards the support of professions which provide, directly or indirectly, health care or other services related to Abbott's primary areas of operation.

Grants will not be made to individuals, purely social organizations, political parties or candidates, religious organizations, advertising journals, booklets, symposiums or conferences, social events, for ticket purchases, memberships, business-related purposes or for-profit entities.

FINANCIAL DATA:
Grants vary in amount, depending upon the needs and nature of the request.

APPLICATION INFO:
Online application only.

Duration: One year. Possible multiyear.

Deadline: Applications may be submitted at any time. Most proposals are reviewed within 12 weeks after receipt.

ADDRESS INQUIRIES TO:
Grant Program
(See address above.)

THE ABELL FOUNDATION, INC. [2]

111 South Calvert Street
Suite 2300
Baltimore, MD 21202-6174
(410) 547-1300
Fax: (410) 539-6579
E-mail: abell@abell.org
Web Site: www.abell.org

FOUNDED: 1953

AREAS OF INTEREST:
Arts and culture, community development, education, conservation and environment, health and human services, workforce development, criminal justice and addictions.

TYPE:
Capital grants; Challenge/matching grants; Demonstration grants; Development grants; General operating grants; Matching gifts; Project/program grants; Seed money grants.

YEAR PROGRAM STARTED: 1953

PURPOSE:
To improve the quality of life in the area around Baltimore, MD.

LEGAL BASIS:
Private foundation.

ELIGIBILITY:
Individuals are not eligible for grants. Qualifying organizations must have IRS 509(a) and 501(c)(3) not-for-profit status. Religious organizations are eligible.

GEOG. RESTRICTIONS: Maryland.

FINANCIAL DATA:
Amount of support per award: $500 to $500,000; average: $43,644.

Total amount of support: Approximately $10,256,348 for the year 2013.

NO. MOST RECENT APPLICANTS: 504.

NO. AWARDS: 154 for the year 2014.

REPRESENTATIVE AWARDS:
$20,000 to Banner Neighborhoods Community Corporation, Baltimore, MD, for continued support of the Home Maintenance Program providing minor but necessary repair services for elderly low-income homeowners in southeast Baltimore to enable them to stay in their homes; $75,000 to Druid Heights Community Development, Baltimore, MD, toward the purchase of a six-unit apartment building to provide supportive housing and services to clients in the Maryland Re-entry program; $120,000 to The Urban Alliance Foundation, Inc., Baltimore, MD, to provide two-year funding for staffing costs of the Urban Alliance Baltimore Program, a pilot youth employment program for students at Northwestern High School.

APPLICATION INFO:
Foundation application form must be completed and submitted. Applicant organizations must provide IRS 501(c)(3) and 509(a) documentation, the most recently audited financial statement, operating budget, projected budget for each year funding is requested, a list of the board of directors as well as pertinent information regarding the program. Application needs to be preceded by a two-page letter of inquiry.

Duration: Primarily one-year grants; few multiyear awards.

Deadline: Grants will be awarded six times a year; January 1, March 1, May 1, August 1, September 1 and November 1.

PUBLICATIONS:
Annual Report; *Abell Report*, newsletter; periodic research reports.

IRS I.D.: 52-6036106

OFFICER:
Robert C. Embry, Jr., President
Lynn Heller, Vice President

ADDRESS INQUIRIES TO:
Lynn Heller, Vice President
(See address above.)

THE ABNEY FOUNDATION [3]

100 Vine Street
Anderson, SC 29621
(864) 964-9201
Fax: (864) 964-9209
E-mail: info@abneyfoundation.org
Web Site: www.abneyfoundation.org

FOUNDED: 1957

AREAS OF INTEREST:
Religious, charitable, scientific, literary or educational, including encouragement of art and music.

TYPE:
Capital grants; Development grants; Endowments; Project/program grants; Research grants.

YEAR PROGRAM STARTED: 1957

PURPOSE:
To make grants for innovative and creative projects and to programs which are responsive to changing community needs in the areas of education, health, social service and cultural affairs.

LEGAL BASIS:
Tax-exempt, private foundation.

ELIGIBILITY:
Applicants must be tax-exempt organizations. No grants to individuals.

GEOG. RESTRICTIONS: South Carolina.

FINANCIAL DATA:
Amount of support per award: $1,000 to $250,000.

Total amount of support: $1,920,000 for the year 2014.

NO. MOST RECENT APPLICANTS: 100.

NO. AWARDS: 35.

APPLICATION INFO:
Applicants may submit a Letter of Intent briefly describing the project before submitting a proposal in order to find out if their ideas are potentially fundable by the Foundation.

Duration: No grants on a continuing basis.

Deadline: November 15.

PUBLICATIONS:
Application guidelines.

IRS I.D.: 57-6019445

STAFF:
David C. King, Executive Director

TRUSTEES AND OFFICERS:
John R. Fulp, Jr., Chairman
David C. King, Vice Chairman
Johnnye K. Palmer, Treasurer and Secretary
Lebrena Fulp Campbell
Carl T. Edwards
John R. Fulp, III
Edd Sheriff

ADDRESS INQUIRIES TO:
David C. King, Executive Director
(See address above.)

ACADIA UNIVERSITY [4]

18 University Avenue
Wolfville NS B4P 2R6 Canada
(902) 585-1498
Fax: (902) 585-1096
E-mail: theresa.starratt@acadiau.ca
Web Site: www.acadiau.ca

AREAS OF INTEREST:
English, political science, sociology, biology, chemistry, computer science, geology, psychology, education, recreation management, mathematics, statistics and applied geomatics, and social and political thought.

NAME(S) OF PROGRAMS:
- **Acadia Graduate Scholarships/Acadia Graduate Teaching Assistantships**

TYPE:
Awards/prizes.

PURPOSE:
To financially support graduate students.

ELIGIBILITY:
Open to registered full-time graduate students at Acadia University. Candidates must possess a 3.0/4.0 grade point average in each of the last two years of undergraduate study in their major.

FINANCIAL DATA:
Amount of support per award: Up to $9,000 for first-year students and a maximum of $8,000 for second-year students.

APPLICATION INFO:
Consult the University for guidelines.

Duration: One or two years.

Deadline: February.

ADDRESS INQUIRIES TO:
Theresa Starratt, Graduate Studies Officer
(See address above.)

*SPECIAL STIPULATIONS:
Acadia Graduate Teaching Assistantship recipients should expect to undertake certain duties during the academic year (up to maximum of 12 hours per week and to a maximum of 144 hours per semester) as a condition of tenure. Specific duties will be established by agreement at the beginning of each academic year. An Acadia Graduate Scholarship does not require students to do any work.

THE ACHELIS FOUNDATION [5]

767 Third Avenue, 4th Floor
New York, NY 10017-2023
(212) 644-0322
Fax: (212) 759-6510
E-mail: main@achelis-bodman-fnds.org
Web Site: www.achelis-bodman-fnds.org

FOUNDED: 1940

AREAS OF INTEREST:
Primarily arts and culture, education, employment, health, public policy and youth and families.

TYPE:
Challenge/matching grants; Conferences/seminars; Development grants; General operating grants; Internships; Matching gifts; Project/program grants; Research grants; Scholarships; Technical assistance; Training grants. Over 90% of the Foundation's grants fall into its six program categories.

PURPOSE:
To impact the greater New York City region and enhance the quality of life for its people, especially the disadvantaged; to advance human dignity, inspire personal achievement and foster self-reliance.

LEGAL BASIS:
Private foundation under Section 501(c)(3) of the Internal Revenue Code.

ELIGIBILITY:
Nonprofit organizations based in New York City and northern New Jersey that are tax-exempt under Section 501(c)(3) of the Internal Revenue Code and fall within the program areas of the Foundation are welcome to submit an inquiry or proposal letter.

The Foundation generally does not make grants to nonprofit organizations outside of New York, annual appeals, dinner functions and fund-raising events, endowments and capital campaigns, loans and deficit financing, direct grants to individuals (such as scholarships and financial aid), individual day-care and after-school programs, housing, international projects, films and travel, projects for the elderly, small art, dance, music and theater groups, independent or public K-12 schools (except charter schools), national health and mental health organizations, and government agencies and nonprofit programs and services significantly funded or substantially reimbursed by government.

GEOG. RESTRICTIONS: Northern New Jersey and New York, New York.

FINANCIAL DATA:
Amount of support per award: $5,000 to $125,000 for the year 2013.

Total amount of support: $1,990,000 for the year 2014.

APPLICATION INFO:
It is recommended that an organization's initial contact with the Foundation include only the following items:
(1) an inquiry or proposal letter briefly summarizing the history of the project, need, research, objectives, time period, key staff, project budget, and evaluation plan emphasizing measurable outcomes and specific program results;
(2) latest annual report;
(3) current and complete audited financial statements and;
(4) copy of the organization's IRS 501(c)(3) tax-exemption letter.

Duration: One year.

OFFICERS:
John N. Irwin, III, Chairman
Russell P. Pennoyer, President
Peter Frelinghuysen, Vice President
Mary S. Phipps, Vice President
Tatiana Pouschine, Vice President
Horace I. Crary, Jr., Treasurer
John B. Krieger, Executive Director, Secretary and Assistant Treasurer

BOARD OF TRUSTEES:
Horace I. Crary, Jr.
Walter J.P. Curley, Jr.
Peter Frelinghuysen
John N. Irwin, III
Leslie Lenkowsky
Russell P. Pennoyer
Mary S. Phipps
Tatiana Pouschine
Magdalena Zavalia de Miguens

ADDRESS INQUIRIES TO:
John B. Krieger, Executive Director
(See address above.)

AETNA FOUNDATION, INC. [6]

151 Farmington Avenue
Hartford, CT 06156-3180
(860) 273-6382
Fax: (860) 273-7764
E-mail: aetnafoundation@aetna.com
Web Site: www.aetna-foundation.org

FOUNDED: 1972

AREAS OF INTEREST:
Obesity, racial and ethnic health care equity, and integrated health care.

NAME(S) OF PROGRAMS:
- **National Grants**
- **Regional Grants**

TYPE:
Matching gifts; Project/program grants; Research grants.

YEAR PROGRAM STARTED: 1972

PURPOSE:
To promote wellness, health and access to high-quality health care for everyone, while supporting the communities Aetna serves.

LEGAL BASIS:
Corporate giving program.

ELIGIBILITY:
Nonprofit organizations with evidence of IRS 501(c)(3) designation of de facto tax-exempt status may apply for a grant. Complete details available on the Foundation web site.

APPLICATION INFO:
Guidelines available on the Foundation web site.

Duration: Varies.

Deadline: Varies.

PUBLICATIONS:
Aetna Annual Giving Report.

IRS I.D.: 23-7241940

STAFF:
Garth N. Graham, M.D., M.P.H., President
Gillian R. Barclay, D.D.S., Dr.P.H., Vice President
Sharon C. Dalton, MBA, Vice President
Sharon R. Ions, Program Officer
Kristyn L. Neal, Program Officer
Alyse B. Sabina, M.P.H., Program Officer
Saima R. Siddiqi, Program Associate
Cheryl A. Tourigny, Program Associate
Melenie O. Magnotta, Grants Manager

BOARD OF DIRECTORS:
Mark T. Bertolini
Donna Checkett
Shawn Guertin
Nancy Ham
Steven B. Kelmar
Mark LaBorde
Andy Napoli
Harold Paz, M.D., M.S.

ADDRESS INQUIRIES TO:
See e-mail address above.

THE AHMANSON FOUNDATION [7]

9215 Wilshire Boulevard
Beverly Hills, CA 90210
(310) 278-0770
E-mail: info@theahmansonfoundation.org
Web Site: www.theahmansonfoundation.org

FOUNDED: 1952

AREAS OF INTEREST:
Arts and humanities, education, human services, medicine and health.

TYPE:
Capital grants; Endowments; Matching gifts; Project/program grants; Scholarships.

PURPOSE:
To support programs that improve the quality of life in Los Angeles County.

LEGAL BASIS:
Private family foundation.

ELIGIBILITY:
Grants are made to organizations that have tax-exempt status under Section 501(c)(3) of the Internal Revenue Code. No grants are made to individuals. Nonsectarian religious programs may apply.

GEOG. RESTRICTIONS: Los Angeles County, California.

FINANCIAL DATA:
Amount of support per award: Varies.

NO. AWARDS: Approximately 400 to 500.

APPLICATION INFO:
Send letter of inquiry to the Grants Administrator.

Duration: Varies.

ADDRESS INQUIRIES TO:
Grants Administrator
(See address above.)

ALABAMA POWER FOUNDATION [8]

600 North 18th Street
Birmingham, AL 35291
(205) 257-2508
Web Site: powerofgood.com

FOUNDED: 1989

AREAS OF INTEREST:
Education, arts and culture, civic and community, health and human services, and environment.

NAME(S) OF PROGRAMS:

- **Educational Grant Program**
- **Foundation Grants**
- **Gateway Grant**
- **Good Roots Grant**
- **Students to Stewards Program**

TYPE:
Capital grants; Challenge/matching grants; Endowments; General operating grants; Project/program grants; Scholarships; Seed money grants.

PURPOSE:
To improve the quality of life of Alabamians and to strengthen the communities in which they live.

LEGAL BASIS:
Corporate foundation.

ELIGIBILITY:
Applicant must be a 501(c)(3) tax-exempt, nonprofit Alabama organization. No grants to individuals, religious or political groups.

GEOG. RESTRICTIONS: Alabama.

FINANCIAL DATA:
Amount of support per award: Foundation Grants: Varies; Gateway: Up to $2,000; Good Roots: Up to $1,000; Students to Stewards: Up to $7,500.

Total amount of support: Approximately $8,000,000 annually.

NO. AWARDS: Good Roots: 38 for the year 2014.

APPLICATION INFO:
All grant applications are received online. Applicants will be asked for specific information about their organization. On the last page, applicants will be prompted to attach the following:
(1) actual grant request with cover letter outlining goals, objectives and specific needs addressed, including an implementation plan and timeline with an outline for any activities planned in the near future and achievements thus far (no more than four pages);
(2) project budget with an evaluation plan with specific criteria for judging the effectiveness;
(3) a copy of the program's most recent audited financial statement;
(4) a copy of the program's current operating budget and;
(5) a copy of the program's Section 501(c)(3) IRS determination letter.

Attachments must be in MS Word, MS Excel or Adobe Acrobat file formats to be accepted.

Duration: One-time funding.

Deadline: Foundation Grant requests over $50,000: February, June, August and November. Requests under $50,000 are reviewed on an ongoing basis; Gateway: Late June; Good Roots: Applications are accepted February 1 to April 1; Students to Stewards: Applications are accepted May through June 30.

PUBLICATIONS:
Annual report; information and guidelines.

ADDRESS INQUIRIES TO:
President
(See address above.)

ALCOA FOUNDATION [9]

201 Isabella Street
Pittsburgh, PA 15212-5858
(412) 553-4545
Fax: (412) 553-4532
Web Site: www.alcoa.com

FOUNDED: 1952

AREAS OF INTEREST:
Environment, education and community enhancement.

TYPE:
Project/program grants. In the area of education, the Foundation supports STEM education and workforce training initiatives to help build the advanced technology workforce.

In the area of environment, the Foundation supports programs that drive measurable and systematic improvements in environmental sustainability through innovative solutions that incorporate the next generation of products, practices and systems.

In the area of community enhancement, the Foundation supports local initiatives that address unique community needs.

YEAR PROGRAM STARTED: 1964

PURPOSE:
To strengthen the communities where employees live and in which the company does business.

LEGAL BASIS:
Nonprofit foundation.

ELIGIBILITY:
Organizations and programs must meet the following basic requirements in order to be considered for funding:
(1) must serve communities where Alcoa has operating plants or offices;
(2) organizations must be classified as not-for-profit public charities and tax-exempt under Section 501(c)(3) of the U.S. Internal Revenue Code. Public educational institutions and government entities, while not classified as 501(c)(3) public charities, may be eligible for grant funds provided that funds are used for charitable purposes;
(3) non-U.S. organizations must either agree to receive a grant under an Expenditure Responsibility Agreement or operate as the equivalent to a U.S. 501(c)(3) public charity;
(4) program must fall within Alcoa Foundation guidelines and;
(5) request must be a minimum of $15,000.

FINANCIAL DATA:
Amount of support per award: Varies.

Total amount of support: Varies.

APPLICATION INFO:
Applications are accepted on an invitation-only basis.

Duration: Varies.

Deadline: Generally July 31.

GEORGE I. ALDEN TRUST [10]

c/o Fletcher Tilton P.C.
370 Main Street, 11th Floor
Worcester, MA 01608
(508) 459-8005
Fax: (508) 459-8305
E-mail: trustees@aldentrust.org
Web Site: www.aldentrust.org

FOUNDED: 1912

AREAS OF INTEREST:
Higher education.

TYPE:
Capital grants; Challenge/matching grants. Capital projects related to teaching and learning technology, in general, and to the sciences, in particular; some support for need-based scholarship endowment and faculty development.

YEAR PROGRAM STARTED: 1912

LEGAL BASIS:
Probate Trust.

ELIGIBILITY:
Principal focus is on independent colleges and universities with full-time traditional undergraduate enrollments of at least 1,000 students and with a total undergraduate and graduate student population (full-time equivalents) of under 5,000. Also, educationally related entities in the Worcester (MA) area and at YMCAs in Massachusetts.

GEOG. RESTRICTIONS: New Jersey, New York, Pennsylvania and the six New England states.

FINANCIAL DATA:
Total amount of support: $9,500,000 for the year 2014.

Matching fund requirements: Usually 1:2 or 1:3 (Alden Trust:matching dollars), with 18-month challenge period. The Trust only pays when the challenge is met in full. The Trust makes no interim or partial payments.

APPLICATION INFO:
Guidelines for colleges and universities are available on the web site.

Deadline: Completed proposals received for March, June, September and December meetings must be received by the 15th of the month prior to the meeting.

IRS I.D.: 04-6023784

ADDRESS INQUIRIES TO:
Warner S. Fletcher, Chairperson
(See address above.)

ALLEGHENY FOUNDATION [11]

One Oxford Centre
301 Grant Street, Suite 3900
Pittsburgh, PA 15219-6401
(412) 392-2900
Web Site: www.scaife.com

AREAS OF INTEREST:
Education, civic development and historic preservation.

TYPE:
General operating grants.

ELIGIBILITY:
Applicant must be a 501(c)(3) nonprofit organization.

GEOG. RESTRICTIONS: Western Pennsylvania.

FINANCIAL DATA:
Amount of support per award: Varies.

Total amount of support: $3,738,500 in grants paid for the year 2014.

APPLICATION INFO:
Contact Foundation for guidelines.

Duration: Typically one year.

Deadline: The Foundation normally considers grants at an Annual Meeting held in November. However, grant requests may be submitted at any time.

ADDRESS INQUIRIES TO:
Matthew A. Groll, Chairman
(See address above.)

THE PAUL G. ALLEN FAMILY FOUNDATION [12]

505 Fifth Avenue South, Suite 900
Seattle, WA 98104
(206) 342-2030
Fax: (206) 342-3030
E-mail: info@pgafamilyfoundation.org
Web Site: www.pgafamilyfoundation.org

FOUNDED: 1988

NAME(S) OF PROGRAMS:
- **Arts and Culture**
- **Asset Building**
- **Basic Needs**
- **Education**
- **Libraries**
- **Science and Technology**

TYPE:
Awards/prizes; Capital grants; Challenge/matching grants; Conferences/seminars; Matching gifts; Project/program grants; Research grants.

PURPOSE:
To create meaningful change in communities by partnering with exceptional organizations and leaders who are bold enough to reinvent the world.

LEGAL BASIS:
Private family foundation.

ELIGIBILITY:
Applicants must be organizations organized and operated exclusively for charitable purposes in the Pacific Northwest area, tax-exempt under 501(c)(3) of the IRS code, and not be a private foundation as defined in Section 509(a).

GEOG. RESTRICTIONS: Alaska, Idaho, Montana, Oregon and Washington.

FINANCIAL DATA:
Amount of support per award: Varies.

Total amount of support: Varies.

Matching fund requirements: Varies by grant.

NO. MOST RECENT APPLICANTS: 125 for the year 2012.

NO. AWARDS: 120.

REPRESENTATIVE AWARDS:
$100,000 to Adelante Mujeres for the expansion of a microenterprise assistance program; $100,000 to Bellingham Food Bank for the addition of fresh produce and essential items to its food distribution program in the northern Puget Sound region; $10,000 to Bunnell Street Gallery for its 2013 Visual Arts Exhibition program; $150,000 to Pierce County Library Foundation to build an interactive platform on its web site; $600,000 to Seattle Public Schools to improve graduation rates.

APPLICATION INFO:
The Foundation encourages applicants to contact it via its web site if their projects are aligned with Foundation's programs.

Duration: One year. Some multiyear.

Deadline: Varies.

PUBLICATIONS:
Grants List, online.

IRS I.D.: 94-3082532

STAFF:
Susan Coliton, Vice President
Dave Ferrero, Senior Program Officer
Jim McDonald, Senior Program Officer
Kathy Richmond, Senior Program Officer
Lisa Arnold, Manager, Grants and Library Program
Val Bush, Grants Specialist

ADDRESS INQUIRIES TO:
Lisa Arnold, Grants Manager
(See address above.)

AMERICAN PHILOSOPHICAL SOCIETY [13]

104 South Fifth Street
Philadelphia, PA 19106-3387
(215) 440-3429
E-mail: lmusumeci@amphilsoc.org
Web Site: www.amphilsoc.org

FOUNDED: 1743

AREAS OF INTEREST:
Scholarly research.

NAME(S) OF PROGRAMS:
- **Franklin Research Grants**

TYPE:
Grants-in-aid; Research grants. Postdoctoral grants toward the cost of scholarly research in all areas of knowledge except those in which support by government or corporate enterprise is more appropriate. Scholarly research covers most kinds of scholarly inquiry by individuals. It does not include journalistic or other writing for general readership; the preparation of textbooks, casebooks, anthologies, or other materials for classroom use by students; or the work of creative and performing artists.

The Society does not have fellowships or scholarships for study, nor does it give grants for travel to conferences.

YEAR PROGRAM STARTED: 1933

PURPOSE:
To support scholarly research by individual scholars.

LEGAL BASIS:
Nonprofit learned society.

ELIGIBILITY:
Applications may be made by residents of the U.S., by American citizens resident abroad and by foreign nationals. American citizens and foreign nationals employed by an American institution may apply for support to carry out work anywhere in the world. Foreign nationals not employed by an American institution may apply for funding to work in the U.S. Applicants expecting to use materials or conduct interviews in a foreign language must possess the necessary competence in the language or languages involved. Grants are never made for predoctoral study or research.

It is the Society's long-standing practice to encourage research by younger and less well-established scholars.

FINANCIAL DATA:
Grants are made payable to the applicant.

The Society offers no funds for conference support, fellowships and scholarships, maintenance work already done, or costs of publication.

Amount of support per award: Funding is offered up to a maximum of $6,000.

Total amount of support: $463,000 for the year 2013-14.

CO-OP FUNDING PROGRAMS: If an applicant receives an award for the same project from another granting insititution, the Society will consider limiting its award to costs that are not covered by the other grant.

NO. AWARDS: 85 for the year 2013-14.

APPLICATION INFO:
Applications are submitted through the Society's online application portal.

Duration: One year.

Deadline: October 1 and December 1.

ADDRESS INQUIRIES TO:
Linda Musumeci
Director of Grants and Fellowships
(See address above.)

AMERICAN PHILOSOPHICAL SOCIETY [14]

The Lewis and Clark Fund
104 South Fifth Street
Philadelphia, PA 19106-3387
(215) 440-3429
E-mail: lmusumeci@amphilsoc.org
Web Site: www.amphilsoc.org

FOUNDED: 1743

AREAS OF INTEREST:
Scholarly research.

NAME(S) OF PROGRAMS:
- **The Lewis and Clark Fund for Exploration and Field Research**

TYPE:
Research grants. The Lewis and Clark Fund for Exploration and Field Research (initially supported by the Stanford Ascherman/Baruch Blumberg Fund for Basic Science,

established by a benefaction from the late Stanford Ascherman, M.D., of San Francisco) encourages exploratory field studies for the collection of specimens and data and to provide the imaginative stimulus that accompanies direct observation. Applications are invited from disciplines with a large dependence on field studies, such as archeology, anthropology, biology, ecology, geography, geology, linguistics, paleontology and population genetics, but grants will not be restricted to these fields.

YEAR PROGRAM STARTED: 2005

PURPOSE:
To support scholarly research by individual scholars.

LEGAL BASIS:
Nonprofit learned society.

ELIGIBILITY:
Grants will be available to doctoral students. Postdoctoral fellows, Master's degree candidates, and undergraduates are not eligible. Applicants who have received Lewis and Clark Fund grants may reapply after an interval of two years.

The competition is open to U.S. residents wishing to carry out research anywhere in the world. Foreign applicants must either be based at a U.S. institution or plan to carry out their work in the U.S.

Funding is contingent on successful applicants demonstrating that required permits and permissions have been secured.

FINANCIAL DATA:
Amount of support per award: Up to $5,000.

Total amount of support: $104,400 for the year 2013.

NO. MOST RECENT APPLICANTS: 444 for the year 2013.

NO. AWARDS: 29 for the year 2014.

APPLICATION INFO:
The applicant should ask his or her academic advisor to write one of the two letters of recommendation, specifying the student's qualifications to carry out the proposed work and the educational content of the trip. Budgets should be limited to travel and related expenses, including personal field equipment.

When appropriate, the applicant should provide assurances that safety measures will be taken for potentially hazardous projects. When necessary, the applicant and his or her supervisor should discuss the field training that will be provided and the provisions for experienced supervision.

Duration: Preferably one year.

Deadline: February 1, with notification in May, for work in June and beyond.

ADDRESS INQUIRIES TO:
Linda Musumeci
Director of Grants and Fellowships
(See address above.)

AMERICAN SCHLAFHORST FOUNDATION [15]

P.O. Box 242610
Charlotte, NC 28224
(704) 554-0800
Fax: (704) 556-1643

AREAS OF INTEREST:
Arts, children, education, health care, sciences, senior citizens and social services.

TYPE:
Capital grants; Endowments; General operating grants; Research grants; Scholarships; Seed money grants.

PURPOSE:
To improve the quality of life in the community.

LEGAL BASIS:
Corporate foundation.

ELIGIBILITY:
Grants are made to organizations that have tax-exempt status under Section 501(c)(3) of the Internal Revenue Code. No grants are made to individuals.

GEOG. RESTRICTIONS: Greater Charlotte, North Carolina.

FINANCIAL DATA:
Amount of support per award: Varies.

Total amount of support: Varies.

APPLICATION INFO:
Applicants should submit a Letter of Inquiry to the Foundation at the address above.

Duration: Varies.

Deadline: October.

ADDRESS INQUIRIES TO:
Dan Loftis, Grant Administrator
(See address above.)

AMGEN FOUNDATION, INC. [16]

One Amgen Center Drive, M.S. 28-1-B
Thousand Oaks, CA 91320
(805) 447-4056
Fax: (805) 376-1258
E-mail: amgenfoundation@amgen.com
Web Site: www.amgen.com/citizenship/foundation.html

FOUNDED: 1991

AREAS OF INTEREST:
Science education, human services and community life including arts and culture, social services and environment.

TYPE:
Challenge/matching grants; General operating grants; Grants-in-aid; Matching gifts; Project/program grants. The Foundation funds national-level science education programs.

YEAR PROGRAM STARTED: 1991

PURPOSE:
To advance excellence in science education to inspire the next generation of innovators; to invest in strengthening communities where Amgen staff members live and work.

LEGAL BASIS:
Company-sponsored foundation.

ELIGIBILITY:
The Foundation will consider grant requests from nonprofit organizations that are recognized by the IRS as tax-exempt public charities under Sections 501(c)(3) and 509(a)(1), (2) or (3) of the Internal Revenue Code, located in the U.S. and Puerto Rico. In addition, the Foundation will consider requests for funding from governmental organizations located in the U.S. where the purpose of the grant is to support a charitable, educational, scientific or literary purpose. Thus, eligible grantees may include public elementary and secondary schools, as well as public colleges and universities, public libraries and public hospitals. Successful requests will fall within both the current eligibility guidelines and funding priority areas established by the Foundation. The Foundation has established a grantmaking partnership with United Way Worldwide (UWW) to manage donations to organizations chartered in Europe.

GEOG. RESTRICTIONS: California, Colorado, Massachusetts, Puerto Rico, Rhode Island, Washington, and parts of Europe.

FINANCIAL DATA:
Amount of support per award: Varies.

Total amount of support: Varies.

NO. AWARDS: 140 for the year 2012.

APPLICATION INFO:
Letter of intent must first be submitted online.

Duration: Typically one year. Possible multiyear funding.

THE ANNENBERG FOUNDATION [17]

2000 Avenue of the Stars
Suite 1000 S
Los Angeles, CA 90067
(310) 209-4560
Fax: (310) 209-1631
E-mail: requests@annenberg.org
Web Site: www.annenbergfoundation.org

FOUNDED: 1989

AREAS OF INTEREST:
Arts, culture and humanities; animal welfare; civic and community; environment; education; human health and wellness; military veterans.

TYPE:
General operating grants; Grants-in-aid; Project/program grants; Technical assistance.

PURPOSE:
To provide funding and support to nonprofit organizations in the U.S. and globally; to advance the public well-being through improved communication; to encourage the development of effective ways to share ideas and knowledge.

ELIGIBILITY:
The Foundation seeks to fund organizations that have a deep level of community involvement, are led by effective leaders and tackle challenging and timely problems. The Foundation values the following organizational attributes: visionary leadership, impact, sustainability, innovation, organizational strength, network of partnerships, plus the population being served (hence the acronym VISION).

Only organizations that have 501(c)(3) not-for-profit status are eligible.

GEOG. RESTRICTIONS: Greater Los Angeles, California area (five-county region including Los Angeles, Orange, Riverside, San Bernardino and Ventura.

FINANCIAL DATA:
Total assets of $1.6 billion for year ended June 30, 2014.

Amount of support per award: Typically, $10,000 to $100,000. Average grant: $75,000.

Total amount of support: $70,030,812 for year ended June 30, 2013.

APPLICATION INFO:
Application guidelines are available on the Foundation web site.

Duration: One year. Grants are renewable, but applicant must reapply.

APPLIED MATERIALS, INC. [18]

3050 Bowers Avenue
Mail Stop 0106
Santa Clara, CA 95052-3299
(408) 727-5555
Fax: (408) 986-7115
E-mail: community_affairs@amat.com
Web Site: www.appliedmaterials.com

FOUNDED: 1967

AREAS OF INTEREST:
Arts and culture, community development, education and the environment.

NAME(S) OF PROGRAMS:

- **Applied Materials Corporate Philanthropy Program**

TYPE:
Project/program grants.

YEAR PROGRAM STARTED: 1990

PURPOSE:
To support the arts and culture, education, community development and the environment.

LEGAL BASIS:
Corporate giving program.

ELIGIBILITY:
Organizations classified as 501(c)(3) by the IRS can apply. Preference is given to areas of company operation. Individuals and religious organizations are ineligible.

FINANCIAL DATA:
Amount of support per award: Varies.

Total amount of support: Varies.

APPLICATION INFO:
Application procedures are available online.

Duration: One year. May be renewed for up to two additional years based on results.

PUBLICATIONS:
Annual report; community report; guidelines.

ADDRESS INQUIRIES TO:
See e-mail address above.

*SPECIAL STIPULATIONS:
Progress is requested to be shared in writing with the Corporate Contribution Committee at least once a year.

APS CORPORATE GIVING PROGRAM [19]

Arizona Public Service Company
400 North 5th Street, 10th Floor
Phoenix, AZ 85004
(602) 250-2702
Fax: (602) 250-2113
E-mail: corporategiving@aps.com
Web Site: www.aps.com/corporategiving

FOUNDED: 1888

AREAS OF INTEREST:
Education, most specifically STEM engineering; community vitality; community and economic development in APS service territories.

TYPE:
Challenge/matching grants; Development grants; Project/program grants. Primary focus is on program support.

YEAR PROGRAM STARTED: 1981

PURPOSE:
To enhance the quality of life in Arizona.

LEGAL BASIS:
Corporate giving program.

ELIGIBILITY:
Applicants must be 501(c)(3) nonprofit organizations for a minimum of three years. Preference is given to organizations within the APS service territory, although there are exceptions. No funds for individuals, individual scholarships, religious, political, fraternal, legislative or lobbying efforts, travel or hotel expenses. The program will not fund any organization that discriminates.

GEOG. RESTRICTIONS: Arizona.

FINANCIAL DATA:
Amount of support per award: $2,500 to $250,000.

Total amount of support: Over $9,900,000 for the year 2015.

NO. AWARDS: Varies.

APPLICATION INFO:
Applications must be submitted online and will require the following documentation:
(1) 501(c)(3) IRS letter of determination;
(2) current list of board members;
(3) list of sponsorship levels (if applicable);
(4) line-item budget;
(5) list of other funders and dollar amounts and;
(6) grant evaluation form (if applicable).

Duration: One year. Renewable by reapplication.

Deadline: APS Foundation: March 1 and September 1. Corporate Funding is on a rolling basis.

PUBLICATIONS:
Community Investment Report.

IRS I.D.: 95-3735903

THE ARCA FOUNDATION [20]

1308 19th Street, N.W.
Washington, DC 20036
(202) 822-9193
E-mail: proposals@arcafoundation.org
Web Site: www.arcafoundation.org

FOUNDED: 1952

AREAS OF INTEREST:
Wall Street reform, financial regulation, corporate accountability, and advocating for a U.S. foreign policy approach that increases peace and security.

TYPE:
General operating grants; Project/program grants.

YEAR PROGRAM STARTED: 1952

PURPOSE:
To provide funding for nonprofit organizations working on ways to engage citizens in social change, promote democracy, and reform unjust practices in public policy.

LEGAL BASIS:
Private foundation.

ELIGIBILITY:
Nonprofit organizations.

GEOG. RESTRICTIONS: United States.

FINANCIAL DATA:
Amount of support per award: $50,000.

Total amount of support: Approximately $2,500,000 annually.

NO. MOST RECENT APPLICANTS: 500.

NO. AWARDS: Approximately 60 to 70 annually.

APPLICATION INFO:
Applications must be submitted online. Applications submitted by any other method will not be considered.

The Foundation highly recommends the applicant review the instructions on using the system and online application system FAQs before beginning the application process. The Proposal FAQs outlines the information to be included in the narrative of the proposal, as well as the list of documents that the organization should be prepared to submit/upload electronically. Documents include the organization's IRS 501(c)(3) letter and Arca's Lobbying Expenditure Form. As always, the Foundation only considers full proposals and does not accept letters of inquiry.

Duration: One year, or the program period.

Deadline: February 1 or August 1 by 5 P.M., or first business day following if the first falls on a weekend.

STAFF:
Anna Lefer Kuhn, Executive Director
Becca Freedman, Grants Officer

BOARD OF DIRECTORS AND OFFICERS:
Nancy R. Bagley, President
Nicole Bagley, Vice President
Mary E. King, Secretary
Rev. Joseph Elderidge
Omaha Kassa
Mike Lux
Janet Shenk
Margery Tabankin

ASSISI FOUNDATION OF MEMPHIS INC. [21]

515 Erin Drive
Memphis, TN 38117
(901) 684-1564
Fax: (901) 684-1997
Web Site: www.assisifoundation.org

AREAS OF INTEREST:
Education, health and human services, social justice, ethics and literacy.

TYPE:
Challenge/matching grants; Endowments; General operating grants; Matching gifts; Project/program grants; Research grants; Technical assistance.

YEAR PROGRAM STARTED: 1994

PURPOSE:
To support health, lifelong learning, social justice, and community enrichment.

ELIGIBILITY:
Grants are made to organizations that already have tax-exempt status under Section 501(c)(3) of the Internal Revenue Code.

GEOG. RESTRICTIONS: Memphis area and Shelby County, Tennessee.

FINANCIAL DATA:
Amount of support per award: Varies.

Total amount of support: Varies.

APPLICATION INFO:
Grant application process and required forms are available to download from the Foundation's web site.

Duration: Varies.

ADDRESS INQUIRIES TO:
Dr. Jan Young, Executive Director
(See address above.)

ATHWIN FOUNDATION [22]

5200 Wilson Road
Suite 307
Edina, MN 55424
(612) 616-0256
E-mail: jstormcod1@aol.com
Web Site: www.catchcod.com

FOUNDED: 1956

AREAS OF INTEREST:
Arts and humanities, education, human services, environmental enhancement and organizational capacity building.

TYPE:
Capital grants; General operating grants; Project/program grants.

YEAR PROGRAM STARTED: 1956

PURPOSE:
To provide funds for charitable, scientific, literary or educational purposes.

LEGAL BASIS:
Tax-exempt private foundation.

ELIGIBILITY:
Only tax-exempt organizations may apply. No grants are awarded to individuals.

GEOG. RESTRICTIONS: Primarily greater Minnesota.

FINANCIAL DATA:
Amount of support per award: Varies.

NO. MOST RECENT APPLICANTS: 250.

NO. AWARDS: Varies.

REPRESENTATIVE AWARDS:
$1,000 to American Indian OIC for program support; $25,000 to the American Red Cross-Minneapolis Chapter for a capital campaign; $100,000 to Blake School for a two-year capital campaign.

APPLICATION INFO:
The Foundation will initiate communication with those organizations it selects for potential funding. All organizations receiving notification will complete the application process and submit material by the date identified by the Foundation.

Duration: Varies.

PUBLICATIONS:
Annual report.

IRS I.D.: 41-6021773

TRUSTEES:
Bruce W. Bean
Glen Bean
Mary F. Bean
Eleanor Nolan

ADDRESS INQUIRIES TO:
Jim Storm, Administrator
(See address above.)

ATKINSON FOUNDATION [23]

c/o Pacific Foundation Services
1600 Bush Street, Suite 300
San Francisco, CA 94019
(650) 357-1101
(415) 561-6540
Web Site: www.atkinsonfdn.org
www.pfs-llc.net

FOUNDED: 1939

AREAS OF INTEREST:
Social services and education in San Mateo County, CA, as well as American private volunteer organizations providing technical assistance and development in Mexico and Central America.

TYPE:
Development grants; General operating grants; Project/program grants; Seed money grants.

YEAR PROGRAM STARTED: 1939

PURPOSE:
To foster the efforts of individuals and families to become socially, economically and physically self-sufficient, and to increase their economic and social welfare.

LEGAL BASIS:
Private foundation.

ELIGIBILITY:
Applicants must be organizations with Internal Revenue Code 501(c)(3) status.

No loans or grants to individuals or for doctoral study or research. The Foundation does not sponsor nor contribute to one-time events or nationwide appeals from organizations and does not fund publications, films or conferences.

GEOG. RESTRICTIONS: San Mateo County, California, Mexico and Central America.

FINANCIAL DATA:
Amount of support per award: $1,000 to $30,000. Average $8,000.

Total amount of support: $601,503 for the year 2014.

NO. MOST RECENT APPLICANTS: 173 for the year 2014.

NO. AWARDS: 95 for the year 2014.

REPRESENTATIVE AWARDS:
$10,000 to Boys & Girls Club of the Coastside for general program support; $15,000 to Second Harvest Food Bank for mobile pantry program; $9,000 to San Mateo Union High School District for workability program; $10,000 to Adelante Foundation microcredit programs, Honduras.

APPLICATION INFO:
Application information is available on the Foundation web site.

Duration: Usually one year.

Deadline: February 1, May 1, August 1 and November 1.

IRS I.D.: 94-6075613

OFFICERS AND DIRECTORS:
Linda L. Lanier, President
Elizabeth H. Curtis, Vice President, Administration
James R. Avedisian, Vice President, Finance
William Crandall, Assistant Treasurer
Jean S. Atkinson, Secretary
Olivia O. Aranda, Director
Susan R. Atkinson, Director
Robert H. Griffin, Director
John E. Herrell, Director
Stephen A. Way, Director
Elizabeth Woodward, Director

ATRAN FOUNDATION, INC. [24]

155 North Dean Street, Suite 3-B
Englewood, NJ 07631
(201) 569-9677
Fax: (201) 569-2290
E-mail: foundatran@gmail.com

FOUNDED: 1948

AREAS OF INTEREST:
Civic, medical, charitable and educational organizations aligned with the Foundation's principles.

TYPE:
General operating grants; Project/program grants.

YEAR PROGRAM STARTED: 1948

PURPOSE:
To support worthy civic, medical, charitable, or educational organizations that align with the founding philanthropic principles of the Foundation.

LEGAL BASIS:
Tax-exempt under Section 501(c)(3) of the Internal Revenue Code.

ELIGIBILITY:
Grants are made only to 501(c)(3) tax-exempt organizations. No grants to individuals.

GEOG. RESTRICTIONS: United States.

FINANCIAL DATA:
Amount of support per award: Varies.

Total amount of support: Varies.

NO. MOST RECENT APPLICANTS: 50.

NO. AWARDS: Approximately 35 per year.

APPLICATION INFO:
No formal application form is required. Application guidelines may be requested from the Foundation.

Duration: One year.

Deadline: September 30.

PUBLICATIONS:
Guideline for application procedure.

IRS I.D.: 13-5566548

OFFICERS:
Diane Fischer, President
Robert Kaplan, Vice President
Samuel Norich, Treasurer
Alison Fischer, Secretary

ADDRESS INQUIRIES TO:
Judah Fischer, Executive Director
(See address above.)

MARY REYNOLDS BABCOCK FOUNDATION [25]

2920 Reynolda Road
Winston-Salem, NC 27106
(336) 748-9222
Fax: (336) 777-0095
E-mail: info@mrbf.org
Web Site: www.mrbf.org

FOUNDED: 1953

AREAS OF INTEREST:
Racism and poverty in the southeastern U.S.

NAME(S) OF PROGRAMS:

- **Moving People and Places Out of Poverty**

TYPE:
Challenge/matching grants; Development grants; General operating grants; Travel grants. Program-related investments.

YEAR PROGRAM STARTED: 2005

PURPOSE:
To help to move people and places out of poverty.

LEGAL BASIS:
Private foundation.

ELIGIBILITY:
Applicants must be nonprofit tax-exempt organizations with appropriate interests, located or working in the Southeast.

GEOG. RESTRICTIONS: Southeastern United States.

FINANCIAL DATA:
Amount of support per award: Varies.
Total amount of support: Approximately $7,000,000.
Matching fund requirements: Varies.

NO. MOST RECENT APPLICANTS: 382 for the year 2014.

NO. AWARDS: Varies.

APPLICATION INFO:
Applications must be submitted electronically.
Duration: One to three years depending on the grant.
Deadline: Applications are accepted on a rolling basis.

PUBLICATIONS:
Application form.

IRS I.D.: 56-0690140

BOARD OF DIRECTORS:
Dee Davis, President
Mary Mountcastle, Vice President
Laura Mountcastle, Treasurer
Ivan Kohar Parra, Secretary
Bruce Babcock
LaVeeda Battle
Chad Berry
Jerry Gonzalez
Derrick Johnson
Barbara Millhouse
James Mitchell
Katharine B. Mountcastle
Katherine R. Mountcastle
Ken Mountcastle
Kevin Trapani

ADDRESS INQUIRIES TO:
Program Officers
(See address above.)

BADER PHILANTHROPIES, INC. [26]

233 North Water Street, 4th Floor
Milwaukee, WI 53202
(414) 224-6464
Fax: (414) 224-1441
E-mail: info@bader.org
Web Site: www.bader.org

FOUNDED: 1991

AREAS OF INTEREST:
Alzheimer's disease and dementia, workforce development, children and youth, Jewish education, program-related investments, and youth development.

TYPE:
Capital grants; Challenge/matching grants; Conferences/seminars; General operating grants; Matching gifts; Project/program grants; Technical assistance; Training grants.

YEAR PROGRAM STARTED: 1991

PURPOSE:
To fund innovative projects and programs in four primary areas including Alzheimer's disease and dementia, workforce development, children and youth, and Jewish education.

LEGAL BASIS:
Family foundation.

ELIGIBILITY:
U.S. organizations must be tax-exempt under Section 501(c)(3) of the IRS or governmental entities. Grants will only be approved for foreign entities which meet specific charitable status requirements.

GEOG. RESTRICTIONS: Milwaukee, Wisconsin.

FINANCIAL DATA:
Amount of support per award: $500 to $180,000. Median is $10,000.
Total amount of support: $10,852,468 for the year 2013-14.

CO-OP FUNDING PROGRAMS: Milwaukee Area Workforce Funding Alliance.

NO. MOST RECENT APPLICANTS: 565 for the year 2013-14.

NO. AWARDS: 262 grants awarded for the year 2013-14.

REPRESENTATIVE AWARDS:
$5,000 to Alverno College; $80,000 to EMDA - Alzheimer's Association of Israel; $40,000 to SHARP Literacy, Inc.

APPLICATION INFO:
Application information is available on the Foundation web site.
Duration: Varies. Renewal possible.
Deadline: Applications are accepted at any time.

IRS I.D.: 39-1710914

BOARD OF DIRECTORS:
Jere D. McGaffey, Chairman and Treasurer
Daniel J. Bader, President
David M. Bader, Vice President
Deirdre Britt, Secretary
Linda C. Bader
Margaret Foster
Adina Shapiro
Frances Wolff

ADDRESS INQUIRIES TO:
Daniel J. Bader, President
(See address above.)

R.C. BAKER FOUNDATION [27]

330 Encinitas Boulevard
Suite 101
Encinitas, CA 92024-8705
(760) 632-8322

FOUNDED: 1952

AREAS OF INTEREST:
Education, health, cultural, scientific research, social services for youth and elderly, and crime prevention.

TYPE:
Capital grants; Fellowships; General operating grants; Project/program grants; Scholarships; Technical assistance; Training grants; Work-study programs.

LEGAL BASIS:
Private foundation.

ELIGIBILITY:
Applicant organizations must have IRS tax-exempt status. No grants are made to individuals, endowments or loans. No grants to capital programs of tax-supported institutions.

GEOG. RESTRICTIONS: United States.

FINANCIAL DATA:
Amount of support per award: Varies.
Total amount of support: $1,564,600.

APPLICATION INFO:
Applications should include a description of the proposed project and goals, a recently audited financial statement, amount requested, and a list of other sources of support. In addition, the applicant should include its IRS statement of tax-exempt status. The Foundation does not grant personal interviews.
Duration: Typically, one-time grants.
Deadline: May 1 and October 1.

IRS I.D.: 95-1742283

BOARD OF TRUSTEES:
Frank L. Scott, Chairman
James Benedict
Dennis Cronin
F. Lawrence Scott, Jr.

ADDRESS INQUIRIES TO:
F. Lawrence Scott, Jr., Board of Trustees
(See address above.)

BALL BROTHERS FOUNDATION [28]

222 South Mulberry
Muncie, IN 47305
(765) 741-5500
Fax: (765) 741-5518
E-mail: info@ballfdn.org
Web Site: www.ballfdn.org

FOUNDED: 1926

AREAS OF INTEREST:
Education, arts, culture and humanities, human services, public/society benefit, health and environment.

TYPE:
Challenge/matching grants; General operating grants; Project/program grants; Seed money grants; Technical assistance; Training grants.

YEAR PROGRAM STARTED: 1926

PURPOSE:
To promote recreational, educational or charitable purposes within the state of Indiana.

LEGAL BASIS:
Private foundation.

ELIGIBILITY:
Indiana not-for-profit organizations or institutions are eligible to apply. No grants to individuals.

GEOG. RESTRICTIONS: Indiana.

FINANCIAL DATA:
Amount of support per award: $1,000 to $1,000,000.
Total amount of support: $6,889,927 for the year 2015.

NO. MOST RECENT APPLICANTS: 251 for the year 2015.

NO. AWARDS: 124 for the year 2015.

REPRESENTATIVE AWARDS:
$30,000 to Conner Prairie Museum; $100,000 to Greater Muncie, Indiana Habitat for Humanity; $30,000 to Inside Out, CDC; $40,000 to Music for All; $188,000 to Project Leadership.

APPLICATION INFO:
Application must include a description of the project, project staff and budget, IRS determination letter, objective of the proposal, plan of development, expected results and method of evaluation.
Duration: One year.
Deadline: February 15 and July 15.

PUBLICATIONS:
Guidelines; annual report.

IRS I.D.: 35-0882856

OFFICERS:
James A. Fisher, Chairman
Frank B. Petty, Vice Chairman

Tammy Phillips, Treasurer
Terry L. Walker, Secretary

DIRECTORS:
Charles Ball
William Bracken
Stephanie Duckmann
Jud Fisher
Douglas J. Foy
Nancy B. Keilty
Terri Matchett
Stacy McHenry
Judy Oetinger
Scott E. Shockley

ADDRESS INQUIRIES TO:
Donna Munchel, Grant Process Manager
(See address above.)

GEORGE AND FRANCES BALL FOUNDATION [29]

222 South Mulberry
Muncie, IN 47305
(765) 741-5500
Fax: (765) 741-5518
E-mail: kris@ballassociates.org

FOUNDED: 1937

AREAS OF INTEREST:
Education, arts and culture, civic community projects, health and human services, environment and conservation.

TYPE:
Challenge/matching grants; Endowments; General operating grants; Matching gifts; Project/program grants.

LEGAL BASIS:
Family foundation.

ELIGIBILITY:
Applicants must be 501(c)(3) organizations or institutes.

GEOG. RESTRICTIONS: East central Indiana, primarily Delaware County.

FINANCIAL DATA:
Amount of support per award: $25,000 median.

Total amount of support: $4,863,000 for the year ended December 31, 2015.

Matching fund requirements: Usually 1:1.

NO. MOST RECENT APPLICANTS: 46.

NO. AWARDS: 46 for the year 2015.

APPLICATION INFO:
General grant request guidelines provided upon request.

Deadline: Applications accepted year-round.

OFFICERS AND DIRECTORS:
Stefan S. Anderson, Chairman
Jon H. Moll, Vice Chairman
Thomas C. Bracken, President
Tamara S. Phillips, Treasurer
Carol E. Seals, Assistant Treasurer
Joan H. McKee, Secretary
Norman E. Beck
Ronald K. Fauquher
Mike Galliher
Robert M. Smitson
Joseph F. Wiese, III

ADDRESS INQUIRIES TO:
Kris Gross, Executive Assistant
(See address above.)

BALTIMORE COMMUNITY FOUNDATION [30]

2 East Read Street, 9th Floor
Baltimore, MD 21202
(410) 332-4171
Fax: (410) 837-4701
E-mail: info@bcf.org
Web Site: www.bcf.org

FOUNDED: 1972

AREAS OF INTEREST:
Education and neighborhoods.

TYPE:
Scholarships. Neighborhood grants. Education grants.

YEAR PROGRAM STARTED: 1972

PURPOSE:
To work for a healthy productive Baltimore region and to provide a flexible effective way for charitable individuals, corporations and foundations to invest in those efforts.

LEGAL BASIS:
Community foundation.

ELIGIBILITY:
The Foundation welcomes grant applications from organizations in the Greater Baltimore region that are tax-exempt under Section 501(c)(3) of the Internal Revenue Code.

The Foundation will be most likely to fund programs that:
(1) address underlying causes of specific problems and seek long-term systemic solutions;
(2) are preventive rather than remedial;
(3) reach a broad segment of the community;
(4) increase individual access and opportunity;
(5) attract financial or volunteer resources or involve collaboration;
(6) build the capacity of grantee organizations and;
(7) strengthen the private, nonprofit sector.

The Foundation does not make grants for annual fund campaigns, operating support except for start-up, religious or sectarian purposes, capital campaigns, or individuals (including scholarships and fellowships).

GEOG. RESTRICTIONS: Baltimore city and Baltimore County, Maryland.

FINANCIAL DATA:
Amount of support per award: Varies.

Total amount of support: Approximately $20,409,748 in grants and scholarships for the year 2014.

REPRESENTATIVE AWARDS:
$15,000 to create a support network for charter schools; $20,000 to increase affordable housing opportunities; $10,000 for consulting services to a growing arts organization.

APPLICATION INFO:
Contact the Foundation for guidelines and application form.

Duration: Typically one year; multiyear grants are dependent upon funds available and is at the discretion of the board committee.

Deadline: Letters of inquiry are welcomed throughout the year. Proposal deadlines vary by grant program.

PUBLICATIONS:
The BCF Edge, newsletter; annual report.

OFFICERS:
Ray Bank, Chairman
Thomas E. Wilcox, President
Josh E. Fidler, Treasurer
Marsha Y. Reeves, Secretary

STAFF:
Thomas E. Wilcox, President and Chief Executive Officer
Amy Seto, Executive Vice President and Chief Operations Officer
Danista Hunte, Vice President, Community Investments
Ralph Serpe, Vice President, Development

ADDRESS INQUIRIES TO:
Danista Hunte
Vice President, Community Investments
(See address above.)

C.R. BARD FOUNDATION [31]

730 Central Avenue
Murray Hill, NJ 07974
(908) 277-8182
Fax: (908) 277-8098
E-mail: linda.hrevnack@crbard.com
Web Site: www.crbard.com

FOUNDED: 1988

AREAS OF INTEREST:
Health care, community, employee activities and education.

TYPE:
Matching gifts; Project/program grants; Scholarships.

YEAR PROGRAM STARTED: 1988

PURPOSE:
To assist nonprofit organizations which improve the quality of life for local communities in areas where Bard has a facility or substantial employee population.

LEGAL BASIS:
Corporate foundation.

ELIGIBILITY:
The Foundation does not contribute to private foundations, individuals, political parties, fraternal groups, religious groups, veterans' organizations or sectarian groups. Organizations receiving major support from the United Way or similar programs are also not eligible. For matching gifts, the individual must be a member of the board of directors or an active U.S. employee of C.R. Bard, Inc., or any of its domestic operating divisions or subsidiaries at the time of the contribution. Nonprofit organizations eligible for matching gifts must be recognized as tax-exempt by the IRS under Section 501(c)(3) of the Internal Revenue Code and must be open to, or operated for the benefit of, the general public.

FINANCIAL DATA:
Amount of support per award: $1,000 to $25,000.

Total amount of support: Varies.

Matching fund requirements: Bard will match employee gifts of $25 to $15,000 per employee per calendar year and $25 to $5,000 per director per calendar year.

NO. AWARDS: Varies.

APPLICATION INFO:
Requests for funding must be submitted through the Foundation's web site and include the following:
(1) name, address, history, objectives and description of the organization;
(2) the purpose for which the grant is requested and the amount requested;
(3) a copy of the organization's IRS

document indicating 501(c)(3) status;
(4) a copy of the organization's operating budget and its most recent audited financial statement and;
(5) a list of the organization's Board of Directors and/or trustees.

Duration: One to five years.

Deadline: Quarterly.

PUBLICATIONS:
Guidelines.

ADDRESS INQUIRIES TO:
Linda Hrevnack
Manager, Community Affairs and Contributions
(See address above.)

BARRA FOUNDATION [32]

200 West Lancaster Avenue
Suite 202
Wayne, PA 19087-4046
(610) 964-7601
Fax: (610) 964-0155
E-mail: info@barrafoundation.org
Web Site: www.barrafoundation.org

FOUNDED: 1963

AREAS OF INTEREST:
Arts and culture, human services, education and health.

TYPE:
Demonstration grants; Project/program grants; Seed money grants.

LEGAL BASIS:
Private foundation.

ELIGIBILITY:
501(c)(3) nonprofit organizations only.

GEOG. RESTRICTIONS: Philadelphia, Pennsylvania metropolitan area.

FINANCIAL DATA:
Amount of support per award: $2,000 to $100,000.

Total amount of support: Approximately $3,005,000.

APPLICATION INFO:
Applications are accepted online only.

Duration: Varies.

Deadline: Applications accepted on a continuous basis.

PUBLICATIONS:
Policy statement.

STAFF:
Kristina L. Wahl, President

ADDRESS INQUIRIES TO:
Kristina L. Wahl, President
(See address above.)

*SPECIAL STIPULATIONS:
No grants for environmental programs, exhibitions, publications or religious organizations.

BATTLE CREEK COMMUNITY FOUNDATION [33]

34 West Jackson Street
One Riverwalk Center
Battle Creek, MI 49017-3505
(269) 962-2181
Fax: (269) 962-2182
E-mail: bccf@bccfoundation.org
Web Site: www.bccfoundation.org

FOUNDED: 1974

AREAS OF INTEREST:
Education, health, and liveable communities.

TYPE:
Challenge/matching grants; Conferences/seminars; Demonstration grants; Development grants; Endowments; Exchange programs; Internships; Matching gifts; Project/program grants; Research grants; Scholarships; Technical assistance; Training grants; Travel grants. Emerging needs grants.

YEAR PROGRAM STARTED: 1974

PURPOSE:
To promote philanthropic giving and the use of endowment funds; to serve as a leader in coordinating local resources to meet the current and future needs of the Battle Creek community.

LEGAL BASIS:
Community foundation.

ELIGIBILITY:
Applicants must be nonprofit organizations whose programs will benefit residents or students of the greater Battle Creek community.

No grants for general operating support, endowments, annual fund-raising programs, or projects outside of the Battle Creek area which do not benefit the local community.

General operating support is only given for arts and culture initiatives.

GEOG. RESTRICTIONS: Battle Creek, Michigan area.

FINANCIAL DATA:
Amount of support per award: Average: $10,000 to $15,000.

Total amount of support: $8,500,000.

NO. MOST RECENT APPLICANTS: 1,824.

NO. AWARDS: 1,234.

APPLICATION INFO:
Prospective grant applicants must attend a grantseeker orientation and should contact Foundation staff to gather information on upcoming orientations, dates/times, etc.

Duration: One year.

Deadline: Varies by program.

PUBLICATIONS:
Guidelines; annual report.

ADDRESS INQUIRIES TO:
Annette Chapman, Vice President of Grantmaking and Scholarships
(See address above.)

THE BAXTER INTERNATIONAL FOUNDATION [34]

One Baxter Parkway
Deerfield, IL 60015
(847) 948-4605
Fax: (847) 948-2887
E-mail: fdninfo@baxter.com
Web Site: www.baxter.com

FOUNDED: 1981

AREAS OF INTEREST:
Health care and its enhancement.

TYPE:
Matching gifts; Project/program grants. The Foundation supports health care awards programs, including the Foster G. McGaw Prize, a $100,000 grant awarded annually to a U.S. hospital that has distinguished itself in community service and the William Graham Health Services Research Award, a $50,000 award made annually to an individual who has made significant contributions to the improved delivery of medical care through innovative health-services research.

YEAR PROGRAM STARTED: 1982

PURPOSE:
To increase access to health care services for the disadvantaged; to improve the quality and cost-effectiveness of health care.

LEGAL BASIS:
Corporate foundation.

ELIGIBILITY:
Grants are made to nonprofit 501(c)(3) organizations with new or expanded programs or direct health care services proposals consistent with the Foundation's priorities. In evaluating a grant application, the Foundation looks for eligibility under Foundation guidelines, including geographies where Baxter employees work and live, evidence that the project is a response to a valid need and is superior to other competing projects, and evidence of the agency's capacity to accomplish its goals.

In general, the Foundation does not make grants to capital and endowment campaigns, hospitals, disease-specific organizations, educational institutions, individuals, organizations with a limited constituency such as fraternal, veterans' or religious organizations, organizations soliciting contributions for advertising space, tickets to dinners and fund-raising events and promotional materials.

FINANCIAL DATA:
Amount of support per award: Varies.

Total amount of support: Varies.

REPRESENTATIVE AWARDS:
$50,000 to Health and Medicine Policy Research Group; $87,027 to Irish Hospice Foundation; $98,175 to The Trevor Project, Inc.

APPLICATION INFO:
All grants must utilize the Foundation's online application process. Requirements of the application include:
(1) organization's full legal name, complete mailing address, phone number, fax number, contact person's name and e-mail address;
(2) if applicable, a description of the organization's relationship with the local Baxter facility;
(3) a brief but complete description of the organization, its purpose, history, governance, programs and achievements;
(4) a statement describing the specific purpose of the grant requested, including how the project meets the priorities of the Foundation;
(5) a statement of the amount of money requested in U.S. dollars and over what period of time;
(6) a plan for how the program or services will be sustained after the conclusion of funding;
(7) a plan for measuring results and reporting periodic progress, as well as for a final evaluation;
(8) financial information, including the organization's current operating full budget and the budget for the proposed project;
(9) a list of sources of income and amounts, including support from corporate donors, foundations, the United Way and the government - committed and approaching - for both the organization and the proposed project;

(10) audited financial statements for the most recent fiscal year and the two previous years (total of three);
(11) a copy of the organization's certificate of tax exemption for the IRS as a 501(c)(3) or equivalent organization. For organizations outside the U.S., a copy of the charitable certificate and exemption from taxes from the local or national government;
(12) a list of officers and board members, with their home addresses and their affiliations and;
(13) a list of the names and home addresses of the five highest paid employees.

Duration: Typically one to two years.

Deadline: Submissions accepted December 1 to January 11, May 1 to June 11 and September 1 to October 11.

ADDRESS INQUIRIES TO:
See e-mail address above.

ADELAIDE BREED BAYRD FOUNDATION [35]

350 Main Street
Suite 13
Malden, MA 02148
(781) 324-0322
Fax: (781) 397-0531
E-mail: kezer@kezer.com

FOUNDED: 1927

AREAS OF INTEREST:
Community services, education and cultural projects, health-related projects and youth-related projects.

TYPE:
Capital grants; Project/program grants; Seed money grants.

PURPOSE:
To support organizations whose activities are centered in the Malden, MA, area, and to support organizations elsewhere, whose activities give substantial benefit to the citizens of Malden.

LEGAL BASIS:
Private foundation.

ELIGIBILITY:
Grants are made to nonprofit, 501(c)(3) organizations in the Foundation's areas of interest. Requests from individuals, endowment funds, performing arts (excepting educational projects and programs) and research will generally be excluded.

In general, the Foundation favors grants toward project services over operational expenditures.

GEOG. RESTRICTIONS: Boston area, with emphasis on Malden and vicinity.

FINANCIAL DATA:
Amount of support per award: Varies.

Total amount of support: Average $700,000 annually.

REPRESENTATIVE AWARDS:
$33,000 to ABBF New Scholarships; $5,000 to Agassiz Village; $10,000 to American Red Cross; $3,000 to Boston Ballet.

APPLICATION INFO:
No particular form of request is required. A letter stating the need, the purpose of the organization and other salient matters will suffice. Copies of summaries of current budget or recent financial statements may be helpful. Organizations should be prepared to furnish a copy of IRS tax form 501(c)(3) or another tax-exempt certificate.

Duration: Typically one year.

Deadline: Second Tuesday in February.

PUBLICATIONS:
Annual report.

IRS I.D.: 04-6051258

ADDRESS INQUIRIES TO:
C. Henry Kezer, President
(See address above.)

BEMIS COMPANY FOUNDATION [36]

One Neenah Center
P.O. Box 669
Neenah, WI 54957
Fax: (920) 527-7600
E-mail: kwetzel@bemis.com
Web Site: www.bemis.com

FOUNDED: 1959

AREAS OF INTEREST:
Education, social welfare and health, cultural and civic needs.

NAME(S) OF PROGRAMS:

- **Bemis Scholarship Program**
- **Educational Gift Matching**
- **FoodShare Program**
- **Nonprofit Gift Matching Program**
- **United Way Program**

TYPE:
Capital grants; Challenge/matching grants; General operating grants; Matching gifts; Project/program grants. Grants to tax-exempt organizations in the communities in which the Bemis Company operates. Scholarships, matching educational and matching nonprofit gifts are for employees only.

The Bemis Scholarship Program provides financial aid to sons and daughters of employees of the company and its subsidiaries. The Program is open to the sons and daughters under age 25 who wish to attend community colleges, four-year colleges, universities or vocational schools.

The Educational Gift Matching program gives employees an opportunity to have their personal contributions to eligible secondary schools, vocational/technical schools, colleges and universities double-matched by the Bemis Company.

Through the Bemis FoodShare Program, employees have the opportunity to have their contributions to local food banks and food shelves matched by the company.

In the United Way program, Bemis contributes to the United Way in communities where the company has facilities.

YEAR PROGRAM STARTED: 1959

PURPOSE:
To match available funds with those public needs where the interests of the company and its employees are inseparable.

LEGAL BASIS:
Corporate foundation.

ELIGIBILITY:
Grants are made to tax-exempt, U.S.-based organizations only. Priorities in grants will be given to those organizations and/or programs that will contribute the most to advancing the quality of life for all peoples in the communities in which the Bemis Company operates. Emphasis will be on those programs that encourage the development of our human resources, education programs and, in a lesser degree, civic and art institutions that encourage participation by the general public. Special consideration will be given to those programs in which the company's employees actively participate or are directly benefited.

The Foundation will not make grants to individuals or to organizations for religious purposes or for political purposes, either for lobbying efforts or campaigns. The Foundation prefers not to make grants for educational capital funds programs, endowment purposes or to support trips or tours. Grants will not exceed 5% of the total requirements of any organization or specific campaign goal.

GEOG. RESTRICTIONS: United States.

FINANCIAL DATA:
Amount of support per award: Varies.

Total amount of support: Approximately $3,250,000 per year.

Matching fund requirements: Educational Gift Matching: The Plan provides that the employee's contribution to an eligible educational institution will be double-matched.

APPLICATION INFO:
Complete application information may be obtained online. Grant proposals need not follow a specific format, but all proposals should include:
(1) name of the organization and amount requested;
(2) brief description of the objectives for which the grant is sought;
(3) details as to how the objectives are to be attained;
(4) budget, including information about existing and other possible sources of income;
(5) officers and board members and;
(6) statement that the organization has tax-exempt status under Section 501(c)(3) of the Internal Revenue Code and that contributions to it are tax-deductible.
It is preferred that all initial inquiries be by e-mail and not by telephone or personal visits.

Duration: Varies.

Deadline: March, June and December.

PUBLICATIONS:
Application guidelines.

IRS I.D.: 41-6038616

ADDRESS INQUIRIES TO:
See e-mail address above.

*SPECIAL STIPULATIONS:
All initial inquiries should be made by e-mail.

H.N. AND FRANCES C. BERGER FOUNDATION [37]

P.O. Box 13390
Palm Desert, CA 92255
(760) 341-5293
Fax: (760) 341-3518
Web Site: www.hnberger.org

FOUNDED: 1961

AREAS OF INTEREST:
Arts, culture, children, education, environment, health, human services and youth.

TYPE:
Project/program grants.

PURPOSE:
To provide people with the opportunity to improve their own situations.

LEGAL BASIS:
Private family foundation.

ELIGIBILITY:
Grants are made to organizations that have tax-exempt status under Section 501(c)(3) of the Internal Revenue Code. No grants are made to individuals. Nonsectarian religious programs may apply.

GEOG. RESTRICTIONS: United States, primarily southern California.

FINANCIAL DATA:
Amount of support per award: Grants vary in amount, depending upon the needs and nature of the request.

Total amount of support: Varies.

APPLICATION INFO:
Submit a one- to two-page request for consideration. This should include a concise statement of intent as well as a brief history of the organization and its activities.

Duration: Typically one year.

ADDRESS INQUIRIES TO:
Christopher McGuire
Vice President of Programs
(See address above.)

THE GRACE AND FRANKLIN BERNSEN FOUNDATION [38]

15 West 6th Street, Suite 1308
Tulsa, OK 74119-5407
(918) 584-4711
Fax: (918) 584-4713
E-mail: info@bernsen.org
Web Site: www.bernsen.org

FOUNDED: 1968

AREAS OF INTEREST:
Arts, civic, education, medical, religious, United Way, and children.

TYPE:
Capital grants; Challenge/matching grants; Project/program grants.

YEAR PROGRAM STARTED: 1968

PURPOSE:
To provide grants in support of religious, charitable, scientific, literary or educational purposes, or for the prevention of cruelty to children.

LEGAL BASIS:
Private family foundation.

ELIGIBILITY:
The Foundation gives priority to applications from nonprofit organizations with clearly defined benefits, such as those for building and capital funding purposes, and other special program needs. Education programs, including those in the arts, higher education, human services and community programs, religious causes and youth programs are eligible for support.

Grants may require matching funds to be raised by the recipient.

No grants are made to elementary or secondary education institutions unless they involve programs for at-risk, handicapped or learning-disabled children. No grants are made to individuals, or for the benefit of specific individuals.

GEOG. RESTRICTIONS: Tulsa, Oklahoma area.

FINANCIAL DATA:
Amount of support per award: Average: $5,000.

Total amount of support: $1,300,000.

Matching fund requirements: Typically one half.

NO. MOST RECENT APPLICANTS: 135.

NO. AWARDS: 50 to 75.

APPLICATION INFO:
Applications should be submitted in writing by the chief executive officer of the applicant organization. They must include a brief description of the organization, an explanation of its importance, a clear statement of its goals, financial need including the other sources of funds and copies of a tax-exemption letter from the IRS.

Additional information required with summary letter:
(1) list of current officers and Board of Trustees;
(2) most recent audited financial statement or last year's IRS Form 990;
(3) current year-to-date financial statements and budget;
(4) project budget (if applicable) and plans to support the project after the grant period and;
(5) a one-page abstract e-mailed to apps@bensen.org in advance of submitting the full request.

If additional information is required, the organization making application will be notified by the Foundation.

Applicants should review Foundation guidelines at the website above and contact staff by phone or e-mail with any questions.

Deadline: Grant applications must be received before noon on the first day of any given month in order to be considered for the next trustee meeting.

IRS I.D.: 23-7009414

TRUSTEES:
Melissa Easterainy
Barbara Pray
Donald E. Pray
W. Bland Williamson

ADDRESS INQUIRIES TO:
David M. Zemel, Director
(See address above.)

BERRIEN COMMUNITY FOUNDATION [39]

2900 South State Street
Suite 2 East
St. Joseph, MI 49085
(269) 983-3486
Fax: (269) 983-4939
E-mail: bcf@berriencommunity.org
Web Site: www.berriencommunity.org

FOUNDED: 1952

AREAS OF INTEREST:
Building spirit of community/arts and culture, nurturing our children, encouraging youth leadership and development.

TYPE:
Development grants; General operating grants; Project/program grants; Scholarships; Seed money grants; Technical assistance.

PURPOSE:
To promote philanthropy, build a spirit of community and enhance the quality of life in Berrien County, MI.

ELIGIBILITY:
501(c)(3) or equivalent.

GEOG. RESTRICTIONS: Berrien County, Michigan.

FINANCIAL DATA:
Amount of support per award: Varies.

Total amount of support: More than $4,800,000 for the year 2014.

APPLICATION INFO:
Contact the Foundation.

Duration: Typically one year.

ADDRESS INQUIRIES TO:
Lisa Cripps-Downey, President
(See address above.)

BERWIND CORPORATION [40]

3000 Centre Square West
1500 Market Street
Philadelphia, PA 19102
(215) 575-2350
Fax: (215) 575-2314
E-mail: mlarue@berwind.com
Web Site: www.berwind.com

FOUNDED: 1886

AREAS OF INTEREST:
Education and community development.

TYPE:
Matching gifts.

LEGAL BASIS:
Nonprofit 501(c)(3) philanthropic organization.

ELIGIBILITY:
Applicants must be 501(c)(3) organizations within Berwind operating areas.

GEOG. RESTRICTIONS: Primarily Philadelphia area, Pennsylvania.

FINANCIAL DATA:
Amount of support per award: Varies.

Matching fund requirements: Dollar-for-dollar up to $10,000 for employee grants only.

APPLICATION INFO:
Contact the Corporation.

Duration: One year.

Deadline: Varies.

ADDRESS INQUIRIES TO:
Mary A. LaRue, Matching Gift Officer
(See address above.)

BING FUND [41]

9700 West Pico Boulevard
Los Angeles, CA 90035
(310) 277-5711
Fax: (310) 277-6368

FOUNDED: 1920

AREAS OF INTEREST:
Museums, higher education, performing arts, population control, and hospitals.

TYPE:
Project/program grants.

PURPOSE:
To fund a variety of worthwhile projects in the community.

LEGAL BASIS:
501(c)(3) tax-exempt organizations.

ELIGIBILITY:
Must be a tax-exempt organization under Section 501(c)(3) of the Internal Revenue Code. Funding is at the discretion of the Directors.

GEOG. RESTRICTIONS: Southern California.

FINANCIAL DATA:
Amount of support per award: Varies.
Total amount of support: Varies.

NO. MOST RECENT APPLICANTS: 100.

NO. AWARDS: Varies.

APPLICATION INFO:
Contact the Fund for details.
Duration: Varies. Renewal possible.
Deadline: Varies.

ADDRESS INQUIRIES TO:
Sue Porto, Office Manager
(See address above.)

THE WILLIAM BINGHAM FOUNDATION [42]

1111 Superior Avenue, Suite 700
Cleveland, OH 44114-2540
(216) 363-6482
E-mail: info@wbinghamfoundation.org
Web Site: www.wbinghamfoundation.org

FOUNDED: 1955

AREAS OF INTEREST:
Education, science, health and human services, and the arts.

TYPE:
Capital grants; Challenge/matching grants; Endowments; General operating grants; Project/program grants.

YEAR PROGRAM STARTED: 1955

PURPOSE:
To provide funding to nonprofit organizations that sponsor programs in the areas of education, science, health and human services, and the arts; to strengthen civil society and its institutions.

LEGAL BASIS:
Private family foundation.

ELIGIBILITY:
Grants are made only to public charities. Grants are not made to individuals or to organizations located outside of the U.S.

GEOG. RESTRICTIONS: United States.

FINANCIAL DATA:
Amount of support per award: $50,000 average.
Total amount of support: $791,000 for the year 2014.

NO. MOST RECENT APPLICANTS: 600.

NO. AWARDS: 20.

REPRESENTATIVE AWARDS:
$60,000 to Denison University, Granville, OH, for two-year Sustainability Fellows Program; $50,000 to Environmental Learning Center, Inc., Vero Beach, FL, for general operating support; $250,000 to Hawken School, Gates Mills, OH, for renovation of Stirn Hall.

APPLICATION INFO:
The majority of grantmaking is by invitation only.
Duration: Generally one year.

ADDRESS INQUIRIES TO:
Laura H. Gilbertson, Chief Administrator
(See address above.)

THE BLUESCOPE FOUNDATION NORTH AMERICA [43]

1540 Genessee Street
Kansas City, MO 64102
(816) 968-3208
Fax: (816) 627-8993
E-mail: jcharmon@butlermfg.com
Web Site: www.butlermfg.com

FOUNDED: 1952

AREAS OF INTEREST:
United charities, scholarship program, aid to education, community needs, youth and civic cultural activities, hospitals and health, and minorities.

TYPE:
Capital grants; General operating grants; Matching gifts; Project/program grants; Scholarships. Scholarship program available to children of Company employees only. Matching gift program for employee contributions to eligible educational or cultural institutions.

In the area of community needs, support is given to organizations which serve broadly the communities in which the Company has employees and significant capital investment. Programs falling within this category include United Way organizations in Company plant cities, minority assistance limited to nonprofit agencies that help provide jobs or job training for the disadvantaged, foster the movement of minorities into the mainstream of economic life and enable minorities to improve their level of educational attainment, and neighborhood and nonresidential building programs utilizing the company's products.

In the area of education, grants are made to colleges and universities which supply significant numbers of employees to the Company and/or which provide opportunities for continuing education to employees, help disadvantaged students who demonstrate ability and desire to prepare for and remain in colleges and universities, have programs which have the objective of providing education to residents of Company plant locations and provide educational opportunities which advance minorities, women and individuals with disabilities.

In the area of culture, the Foundation considers programs which help broaden the cultural experience of the residents of local communities through the support of visual and performing arts organizations, demonstrate concern for excellence and innovation in the arts, and bring cultural opportunity to the economically disadvantaged.

In the area of public affairs, the Foundation helps promote strong relationships between the public and private sectors to assist in the solution to urban problems, reinforce the efforts of groups formed to gather and disseminate information that is in the general public interest, encourage community volunteerism, and promote economic education and the merits of the free enterprise system.

YEAR PROGRAM STARTED: 1952

PURPOSE:
To provide sustained financial assistance to worthy charitable, educational, health and welfare programs in the U.S.; to enhance the quality of life in those communities where employees of BlueScope Steel reside.

LEGAL BASIS:
A nonprofit, benevolent and charitable corporation under the laws of the State of Missouri. A 501(c)(3) private foundation under IRS code.

ELIGIBILITY:
Grants are made only to nonprofit organizations located in areas where the company has facilities. Organizations must have a clear statement of purpose in the public interest, a program consistent with the organization's stated purpose, evidence of interagency cooperation to avoid duplication of services, an active and responsive governing body of volunteers holding regular meetings, evidence of professional program management and reasonable fund-raising expenses, maintenance of ethical publicity and promotion of the program that excludes exaggerated or misleading claims, and fund solicitation policies which prohibit the payment of commission or other compensation based on total funds raised or undue pressures.

Grants are not normally made to individuals, political organizations, religious organizations for sectarian purposes, pre-school, primary and secondary educational institutions, fraternal or veteran's organizations, organizations receiving United Way support for operating expenses, national health organizations, including local or regional chapters, hospitals (except those providing unique services, burn centers or children's services), tours, conferences, seminars, workshops, testimonial dinners, tables, tickets, advertisements, walk-a-thons, endowment funds, and other foundations of any type providing grants to not-for-profits or programs beyond the Foundation's stated geographic areas of interest.

GEOG. RESTRICTIONS: Rainsville, Alabama; Pine Bluff, Arkansas; Turlock and Visalia, California; Kansas City and St. Joseph, Missouri; Greensboro and Laurinburg, North Carolina; Annville, Pennsylvania; Jackson and Memphis, Tennessee; San Marcos, Texas; and Evansville, Wisconsin.

FINANCIAL DATA:
Amount of support per award: $1,000 to $10,000.
Total amount of support: $300,000 annually.
Matching fund requirements: The minimum single gift the Foundation will match per eligible donor is $25. The maximum single gift or total of annual gifts to be matched per eligible donor for full-time employees is $2,000 per calendar year.

NO. MOST RECENT APPLICANTS: 100.

NO. AWARDS: 90 for fiscal year 2012, excluding matching gifts.

REPRESENTATIVE AWARDS:
$7,500 to Harvesters, Kansas City, MO; $1,500 to River City Dance Theatre, San Marcos, TX; $4,000 to Genesis School, Kansas City, MO.

APPLICATION INFO:
Initial contact should be made by phone, e-mail or letter addressed to the Foundation Administrator or, in non-Kansas City locations, to the plant or division manager describing the need, purpose and general activities of the requesting charitable organization. The letter will be reviewed by

the plant or division manager to assure compliance with the policies established by the Foundation Trustees with a recommendation and forwarded to the Foundation Administrator.

Applicants must provide evidence of compliance with eligibility requirements, plus an annual report describing program activities and supporting services including financial statements, detailed annual budget and copy of IRS not-for-profit determination.

Duration: One year.

Deadline: Announcements are made after quarterly Trustee meetings.

PUBLICATIONS:
Annual report; contributions policy; application guidelines.

IRS I.D.: 44-0663648

ADDRESS INQUIRIES TO:
Jill Harmon, Foundation Director
(See address above.)

THE BODMAN FOUNDATION [44]

767 Third Avenue, 4th Floor
New York, NY 10017-2023
(212) 644-0322
Fax: (212) 759-6510
E-mail: main@achelis-bodman-fnds.org
Web Site: www.achelis-bodman-fnds.org

FOUNDED: 1945

AREAS OF INTEREST:
Primarily arts and culture, education, employment, health, public policy and youth and families.

TYPE:
Challenge/matching grants; Conferences/seminars; Development grants; General operating grants; Internships; Matching gifts; Project/program grants; Research grants; Scholarships; Technical assistance; Training grants. Over 90% of the Foundation's grants fall into its six program areas.

PURPOSE:
To impact the greater New York City region and enhance the quality of life for its people, especially the disadvantaged; to advance human dignity, inspire personal achievement and foster self-reliance.

LEGAL BASIS:
Private foundation under Section 501(c)(3) of the Internal Revenue Code.

ELIGIBILITY:
Nonprofit organizations based in New York City and northern New Jersey that are tax-exempt under Section 501(c)(3) of the Internal Revenue Code and fall within the program areas of the Foundation are welcome to submit an inquiry or proposal letter.

The Foundation generally does not make grants to nonprofit organizations outside of New York and New Jersey; annual appeals, dinner functions and fund-raising events; endowments and capital campaigns; loans and deficit financing; direct grants to individuals (such as scholarships and financial aid); individual day-care and after-school programs; housing; international projects; films and travel; projects for the elderly; small art, dance, music and theater groups; independent or public K-12 schools (except charter schools); national health and mental health organizations and; government agencies and nonprofit programs and services significantly funded or substantially reimbursed by government.

GEOG. RESTRICTIONS: Primarily New York City, but also northern New Jersey.

FINANCIAL DATA:
Amount of support per award: $1,000 to $200,000 for the year 2014.

Total amount of support: $2,061,000 for the year 2014.

APPLICATION INFO:
It is recommended that an organization's initial contact with the Foundation include only the following items:
(1) an inquiry or proposal letter briefly summarizing the history of the project, need, research, objectives, time period, key staff, project budget, and evaluation plan emphasizing measurable outcomes and specific program results;
(2) latest annual report;
(3) current and complete audited financial statements and;
(4) copy of the organization's IRS 501(c)(3) tax-exemption letter.

Duration: One year. Renewal does not generally follow the year of a grant.

OFFICERS:
John N. Irwin, III, Chairman
Russell P. Pennoyer, President
Peter Frelinghuysen, Vice President
Mary S. Phipps, Vice President
Horace I. Crary, Jr., Treasurer
John B. Krieger, Executive Director, Secretary and Assistant Treasurer

BOARD OF TRUSTEES:
Horace I. Crary, Jr.
Walter J.P. Curley, Jr.
Peter Frelinghuysen
John N. Irwin, III
Leslie Lenkowsky
Russell P. Pennoyer
Mary S. Phipps
Tatiana Pouschine
Magdalena Zavalia de Miguens

ADDRESS INQUIRIES TO:
John B. Krieger, Executive Director
(See address above.)

THE BOOTH-BRICKER FUND [45]

826 Union Street
Suite 300
New Orleans, LA 70112
(504) 581-2430
Fax: (504) 566-4785
E-mail: hriley@boo-ker.com

FOUNDED: 1966

AREAS OF INTEREST:
The Fund focuses exclusively on taking advantage of the historic opportunity to reform public education in New Orleans.

TYPE:
Capital grants; Development grants; Project/program grants.

PURPOSE:
To promote, develop and foster religious, charitable, scientific, literary and educational nonprofit organizations.

ELIGIBILITY:
The Fund generally does not provide sustaining (operations and maintenance) funding. Requests are welcomed for capital needs, special projects and other one-time requirements. No grants are made to individuals or supporting organizations (i.e., a Section 501(c)(3) organization with further designation under Section 509(a)(3)).

GEOG. RESTRICTIONS: Louisiana, with priority given to the New Orleans area.

FINANCIAL DATA:
Market value of assets as of December 31, 2015: $43,645,474.

Amount of support per award: Varies.

Total amount of support: Charitable distributions of $2,072,960 for the year 2015. Since its inception, the Fund has made charitable contributions exceeding $40,000,000.

NO. AWARDS: 70 for the year 2015.

APPLICATION INFO:
Applications, which should be made by letter, are considered by the board of trustees at its quarterly meetings. There are no forms or deadlines. Requests should include complete information about the applicant organization, including its history, purpose, finances, current operations, governing board and tax status. A detailed explanation of the proposed use of the funds must be provided. Videotapes or DVDs should not be submitted.

Duration: Varies.

BOARD OF TRUSTEES:
Charles B. Mayer
Gray S. Parker
Mary Kay Parker
Nathaniel P. Phillips, Jr.
H. Hunter White, Jr.

OFFICERS:
Gray S. Parker, Chairman
Ingrid C. Laffont, Treasurer
Heather A. Riley, Secretary

ADDRESS INQUIRIES TO:
Gray S. Parker, Chairman
(See address above.)

JAMES GRAHAM BROWN FOUNDATION, INC. [46]

4350 Brownsboro Road
Suite 200
Louisville, KY 40207
(502) 896-2440
Fax: (502) 896-1774
E-mail: grants@jgbf.org
Web Site: www.jgbf.org

FOUNDED: 1943

AREAS OF INTEREST:
Education, economic development, cultural and human services.

TYPE:
Capital grants; Project/program grants.

YEAR PROGRAM STARTED: 1943

PURPOSE:
To foster the well-being, quality of life and image of Louisville and Kentucky.

LEGAL BASIS:
Private foundation.

ELIGIBILITY:
Only Kentucky organizations that have a tax-exempt designation under Section 501(c)(3) of the IRS Code can apply.

GEOG. RESTRICTIONS: Kentucky, with emphasis on Louisville.

FINANCIAL DATA:
Amount of support per award: $25,000 and up.

NO. AWARDS: 70.

REPRESENTATIVE AWARDS:
$500,000 to Asbury University for support of a Virtual Teaching School; $400,000 to Boys and Girls Clubs of Kentuckiana for support of three new clubs to serve at-risk youth; $1,000,000 to Filson Historical Society for capital campaign to expand the Old Louisville Campus; $750,000 to Habitat for Humanity of Metro Louisville for the Portland Initiative; $100,000 to Kentuckiana Works Foundation for SummerWorks 2012 Summer Jobs program.

APPLICATION INFO:
Contact the Foundation for details.

Duration: One year.

PUBLICATIONS:
Annual report.

ADDRESS INQUIRIES TO:
Mason Rummel, President
(See address above.)

THE JOE W. AND DOROTHY DORSETT BROWN FOUNDATION [47]

320 Hammond Highway, Suite 500
Metairie, LA 70005
(504) 834-3433
Fax: (504) 834-3441
E-mail: bethbuscher@thebrownfoundation.org
Web Site: www.thebrownfoundation.org

FOUNDED: 1959

AREAS OF INTEREST:
Health and science, community benefit, human services, education, conservation, and environment.

TYPE:
General operating grants; Project/program grants; Research grants; Training grants.

PURPOSE:
To alleviate human suffering.

ELIGIBILITY:
Applicants must be nonprofit 501(c)(3). The Foundation favors requests for funds where funds are generally unavailable from most other sources. Within the five focus areas, the focus is primarily on relieving human suffering; secondary interest includes cultural, spiritual, educational or scientific initiatives. No grants are made to individuals.

GEOG. RESTRICTIONS: Louisiana and Mississippi. Preference is given to the greater New Orleans area and Mississippi gulf coast.

FINANCIAL DATA:
Amount of support per award: Varies.

Total amount of support: Varies.

APPLICATION INFO:
Contact the Foundation.

Duration: One year. Must reapply.

Deadline: August 30.

THE MARGARET E. BURNHAM CHARITABLE TRUST [48]

c/o H.M. Payson & Co.
P.O. Box 31
Portland, ME 04112-0031
(207) 772-3761
Fax: (207) 871-7508
E-mail: jbe@hmpayson.com
Web Site: www.megrants.org/burnham.html

AREAS OF INTEREST:
Community/social services, medical, educational, arts and culture, and environment.

TYPE:
Grants-in-aid; Project/program grants. Annual grant dedicated to responding to the needs of the Maine communities served.

PURPOSE:
To benefit nonprofit organizations located or operating in the state of Maine.

ELIGIBILITY:
Organizations must be 501(c)(3) and must operate in and serve the state of Maine. Individuals, private foundations under Section 509, and religious organizations are not eligible.

GEOG. RESTRICTIONS: Maine.

FINANCIAL DATA:
Amount of support per award: $1,000 to $20,000.

Total amount of support: Varies.

APPLICATION INFO:
A completed application consists of the following:
(1) certification, application, project description, and budget pages;
(2) copy of the organization's most recent 501(c)(3) IRS ruling;
(3) copy of the organization's most recent financial statement or tax return and;
(4) list of the organization's officers and directors.

Duration: One year.

Deadline: October 1.

ADDRESS INQUIRIES TO:
Thomas M. Pierce, Trustee
(See address above.)

EDYTH BUSH CHARITABLE FOUNDATION, INC. [49]

199 East Welbourne Avenue, Suite 100
Winter Park, FL 32789
(407) 647-4322
(888) 647-4322
Fax: (407) 647-7716
E-mail: jdixon@edythbush.org
Web Site: www.edythbush.org

FOUNDED: 1973

AREAS OF INTEREST:
Children, youth and families, education, health care, limited interest in the arts, improvement of nonprofit organizations, and human services.

TYPE:
Capital grants; Challenge/matching grants; Demonstration grants; Development grants; Matching gifts; Project/program grants; Technical assistance; Training grants.

PURPOSE:
To provide nonprofit programs and grantmaking designed to help people help themselves.

LEGAL BASIS:
Private foundation.

ELIGIBILITY:
The Foundation welcomes grant applications from nonprofit organizations that have secured their 501(c)(3) and 509(a) IRS rulings. The Foundation has elected to focus its resources within Lake, Orange, Osceola and Seminole counties, FL. The Foundation will not fund organizations that are chiefly tax-supported, nor does it fund individual scholarships, individual research (even if through an exempt or otherwise qualified educational organization), alcoholism or drug abuse programs or facilities, routine operating expenses, the pay-off of deficits or pre-existing debt, foreign organizations or foreign expenditures, travel projects or fellowships, chiefly church, sacramental, denominational or interdenominational purposes (except those outreach programs for elderly, indigents, needy, youth or homeless, regardless of belief, race, color, creed, or sex), endowment funds, advocacy organizations, cultural or arts organizations or organizations that have receipts or revenues from memberships and/or contributions of less than $25,000.

GEOG. RESTRICTIONS: Lake, Orange, Osceola and Seminole counties, Florida.

FINANCIAL DATA:
Amount of support per award: Typically $5,000 to $50,000. Maximum grant has been $1,000,000 spread over five years. Large grants are typically spread over two or three years.

Total amount of support: Varies.

Matching fund requirements: Must be new or increased cash contributions or pledges.

APPLICATION INFO:
Detailed information is available on the web site.

Duration: One year.

Deadline: Applications are accepted year-round.

PUBLICATIONS:
Guidelines; brochure.

IRS I.D.: 23-7318041

OFFICERS:
David A. Odahowski, President and Chief Executive Officer
Mary Ellen Hutcheson, CPA, Vice President and Treasurer
Matthew W. Certo, Corporate Secretary

BOARD OF DIRECTORS:
Gerald F. Hilbrich, Chairman
Herbert F. Holm, Vice Chairman
Matthew W. Certo
Elizabeth Dvorak
Deborah C. German, M.D.
Harvey Massey
David A. Odahowski

ADDRESS INQUIRIES TO:
Jaime Dixon, Grants Manager
(See address above.)

CABOT FAMILY CHARITABLE TRUST [50]

70 Federal Street
Boston, MA 02110
(617) 226-7505
Fax: (617) 451-1733
E-mail: kmchugh@cabotwellington.com
Web Site: www.cabotfamilytrust.org

FOUNDED: 1942

AREAS OF INTEREST:
Arts and culture, education and youth development, environment and conservation, health and human services, and for the public benefit.

TYPE:
Capital grants; General operating grants; Project/program grants. Capital campaigns.

YEAR PROGRAM STARTED: 1942

PURPOSE:
To provide funding for nonprofit organizations working in the arts, environment, youth development, education, health and human services.

LEGAL BASIS:
Charitable trust.

ELIGIBILITY:
The Trust supports only nonprofit organizations holding active 501(c)(3) status under the IRS code. The Trust does not make contributions to individuals, political organizations, religious institutions, advertising, sponsorship or fraternal organizations.

Applicants must meet the following criteria:
(1) extend important services to individuals and groups not served adequately through other programs and institutions;
(2) manage change by assessing community needs and developing programs to meet emerging needs;
(3) promote productive cooperation and full use of resources by nonprofit organizations and community groups and;
(4) test new approaches to problems or adapt solutions that have been successful elsewhere.

GEOG. RESTRICTIONS: Boston and other contiguous communities.

FINANCIAL DATA:
Assets of $44,000,000.

Amount of support per award: $5,000 to $50,000 per year.

Total amount of support: $1,800,000.

NO. MOST RECENT APPLICANTS: 380 for the year 2014.

NO. AWARDS: Approximately 80.

REPRESENTATIVE AWARDS:
$25,000 to Reach Out and Read for an early reading program for infants in the Neonatal Intensive Care Unit at Boston Medical Center; $40,000 to Urban Farming Institute to train inner city residents interested in careers in agriculture and farming; $100,000 (over two years) to Artists for Humanity for expansion of facilities serving teen entrepreneurs in the arts and design.

APPLICATION INFO:
Applicants should submit a concept paper of three pages plus cover sheet and budget. Application form is available on the web site.

Duration: Usually, one year; multiyear considered.

Deadline: February 1 and September 1.

PUBLICATIONS:
Annual report.

IRS I.D.: 04-6035446

TRUSTEES:
Frank Bradley
John G.L. Cabot
Laura C. Carrigan
Mary Schneider Enriquez
Greenfield Sluder
Hendrika Sluder

EXECUTIVE DIRECTOR:
Katherine S. McHugh

ADDRESS INQUIRIES TO:
Katherine S. McHugh, Executive Director
(See address above.)

THE MORRIS AND GWENDOLYN CAFRITZ FOUNDATION [51]

1825 K Street, N.W.
Suite 1400
Washington, DC 20006
(202) 223-3100
Fax: (202) 296-7567
E-mail: info@cafritzfoundation.org
Web Site: www.cafritzfoundation.org

FOUNDED: 1948

AREAS OF INTEREST:
Community services, arts and humanities, education, health and the environment.

TYPE:
Challenge/matching grants; General operating grants; Project/program grants; Scholarships; Technical assistance.

YEAR PROGRAM STARTED: 1948

PURPOSE:
To build a stronger community for residents of the Washington, DC area through support of programs in arts and humanities, community services, education, health and the environment.

LEGAL BASIS:
Private foundation.

ELIGIBILITY:
Grants are made only to charitable, educational and cultural institutions exempt from taxation under the Internal Revenue Code. IRS-registered, tax-exempt, 501(c)(3) organizations with a public charity status of 509(a)(1) or 509(a)(2) only. The general policy is to concentrate grants to organizations, operating within the greater Washington metropolitan area, with projects of direct assistance to the District of Columbia and its environs. Grants are not made for capital purposes, endowments or to individuals.

GEOG. RESTRICTIONS: Montgomery and Prince George's counties in Maryland; Arlington and Fairfax counties, and the cities of Alexandria and Falls Church in Virginia; and Washington, DC.

FINANCIAL DATA:
Amount of support per award: Varies.

Total amount of support: $17,392,760 for the fiscal year ended April 30, 2015.

NO. MOST RECENT APPLICANTS: 700.

NO. AWARDS: 424 for the year 2015.

REPRESENTATIVE AWARDS:
$50,000 to Round House Theatre, Bethesda, MD, for general support; $30,000 to Alexandria Seaport Foundation, Alexandria, VA, for general support for the apprenticeship program; $55,000 to Education Pioneers, Washington, DC, for the DC Metro Area Fellowship and Alumni Programs; $30,000 to Natural Resources Defense Council, New York, NY, for the Anacostia Cleanup Initiative; $25,000 to DC Greens, Washington, DC, for general support.

APPLICATION INFO:
To be considered for funding, an organization must submit a complete proposal, not a Letter of Inquiry (LOI). LOIs are not required. Organizations may submit a proposal for only one deadline within a 12-month period. The Foundation requires that all organizations use the Washington Grantmakers' Common Grant Application.

Duration: One year.

Deadline: November 1, March 1 and July 1.

PUBLICATIONS:
Annual report; application guidelines.

OFFICERS:
Calvin Cafritz, President and Chief Executive Officer
John E. Chapoton, Vice Chairman
Ed McGeogh, Vice President, Asset Management
Rohan Rodrigo, Vice President, Finance

STAFF:
Rose Ann Cleveland, Executive Director
Mardell Moffett, Associate Director
Mary Mulcahy, Senior Program Officer
Tobi Printz-Platnick, Senior Program Officer
Kara Blankner, Program Officer
Debbi Lindenberg, Program Officer
Jessica Plocher, Program Officer
Jacqueline Prior, Program Officer
Miyesha Perry, Manager, Grants and Administration
Armaine Decastro, Grants and Communications Assistant
Messay Derebe, Program Assistant

DIRECTORS:
Calvin Cafritz, Chairman of the Board
Michael F. Brewer
Jane Lipton Cafritz
John E. Chapoton
LaSalle D. Leffall, Jr., M.D., F.A.C.S.
Patricia McGuire
Robert Peck
Earl A. Powell, III
Alice M. Rivlin, Ph.D.

ADVISORY BOARD:
Anthony W. Cafritz
Elliot S. Cafritz
Carolyn J. Deaver
The Hon. Constance A. Morella
Elizabeth M. Peltekian

ADDRESS INQUIRIES TO:
Rose Ann Cleveland, Executive Director
(See address above.)

THE CALERES CARES CHARITABLE TRUST [52]

8300 Maryland Avenue
St. Louis, MO 63105
(314) 854-4000
Web Site: caleres.com/community

FOUNDED: 1951

AREAS OF INTEREST:
Family, healthy living/wellness, arts and culture, local community, and footwear industry.

TYPE:
Project/program grants.

YEAR PROGRAM STARTED: 1951

PURPOSE:
To help develop stronger families by providing opportunities for enrichment; to encourage individuals to live better lives through health and wellness efforts; to provide occasions for families and individuals to step feet-first into the arts and cultural opportunities in the community.

LEGAL BASIS:
Corporate contributions program.

ELIGIBILITY:
The Caleres Trust encourages tax-exempt, nonprofit organizations who meet the Trust's funding priorities to apply. Organization must be located in St. Louis, MO, or in communities around the world where the company operates.

The Trust supports charitable organizations which are either strategically aligned with the Trust's mission, vision and values, focused on advancing the footwear industry or benefit the overall St. Louis community in growing and attracting new businesses and residents.

Grants are not made to individuals. In general, the Trust does not support galas, walks, golf outings, trivia nights, etc.

FINANCIAL DATA:
To date, Caleres has donated more than $20,000,000 to 501(c)(3) organizations.

APPLICATION INFO:
Guidelines and application forms are available on the Company web site.

Applicants will be asked to supply information about their organization, key leadership, details about their request, the impact they expect the grant to have on their organization or community, and how they will measure success. The application requires the following attachments:
(1) current year's operating budget;
(2) list of board members and;
(3) program or project budget (if applicable).
Attachments can be in Microsoft Word, Excel or Adobe PDF format. Compressed ZIP files must not be included.

Deadline: Grant proposals: March 31, June 30, September 30 and December 31.

*PLEASE NOTE:
The Caleres Cares Charitable Trust was formerly known as the Brown Shoe Company, Inc. Charitable Trust.

CAMPBELL SOUP FOUNDATION [53]

One Campbell Place
Camden, NJ 08103-1799
(856) 342-6423
E-mail: wendy_milanese@campbellsoup.com
Web Site: www.campbellsoupcompany.com

FOUNDED: 1953

AREAS OF INTEREST:
Nourishing the lives of the people of Camden, particularly the children; organizations that focus on community well-being, youth empowerment and economic sustainability programming which support the development of a healthy community; particular emphasis on Camden, NJ.

NAME(S) OF PROGRAMS:
- **Dollars for Doers Fund**
- **Matching Gift Program**
- **United Way Match Program**

TYPE:
Matching gifts. Dollars for Doers Program provides financial support to nonprofit organizations where Campbell employees volunteer in Campbell communities.

Matching Gift Program supports employee's gifts to higher education and to six pre-selected nonprofit organizations whose mission closely meets the Foundation's CSR goals.

The Campbell Soup Foundation also supports 15 separate United Way campaigns hosted at Campbell and Pepperidge Farm operating facilities throughout the U.S.

YEAR PROGRAM STARTED: 1954

PURPOSE:
To provide financial support to local champions that inspire positive change in communities throughout the U.S. where Campbell Soup Company employees live and work.

LEGAL BASIS:
Tax-exempt private foundation.

ELIGIBILITY:
Grants are made to tax-exempt organizations providing service consistent with Foundation's goals. Grants are not directed at supporting individuals.

GEOG. RESTRICTIONS: United States.

FINANCIAL DATA:
Amount of support per award: Varies.

Total amount of support: Approximately $1,600,000 each fiscal year.

APPLICATION INFO:
Online grant submission. Foundation guidelines are available online.

Duration: Usually one-time grants.

Deadline: Two funding cycles per year, one in the fall and one in the spring, typically four months in length. Fall cycle runs September through December and Spring cycle runs January through April.

OFFICERS:
Kim Fortunato, President
Ashok Madhavan, Treasurer
Andrew Kupchik, Secretary
Bill O'Shea, Controller
Wendy Milanese, Program Manager

TRUSTEES:
Gary Biscoll
Mark Cacciatore
Kim Fortunato
E.J. Henry
Richard Landers
Helen Le Du
Karen Lewis
Harry Miller
Anthony Sanzio
Dave Stangis

ADDRESS INQUIRIES TO:
Wendy Milanese, Program Manager
(See address above.)

CAMPBELL SOUP FOUNDATION [54]

One Campbell Place
Camden, NJ 08103-1799
(856) 342-6423
E-mail: wendy_milanese@campbellsoup.com
Web Site: www.campbellsoupcompany.com

FOUNDED: 1953

AREAS OF INTEREST:
Nourishing the lives of the people of Camden, particularly the children; organizations that focus on community well-being, youth empowerment and economic sustainability programming which support the development of a healthy community, with particular emphasis on Camden, NJ.

NAME(S) OF PROGRAMS:
- **Healthy Impact Awards**

TYPE:
Awards/prizes. Recognizes and rewards partnership among nonprofit organizations and other key stakeholders in advancing real change in building healthy communities where Campbell has operations in the U.S.

PURPOSE:
To provide financial support to local champions that inspire positive change in communities throughout the U.S. where Campbell Soup Company employees live and work.

LEGAL BASIS:
Tax-exempt private foundation.

ELIGIBILITY:
Programs that apply should focus their work in one or more of these key areas: access to healthy food, nutrition education and increased physical activity in order to advance improvement in the health of the community's young people. Partnership among several key stakeholders is required of awardees.

GEOG. RESTRICTIONS: United States.

FINANCIAL DATA:
Amount of support per award: $7,500 and $12,500.

Total amount of support: $40,000 annually.

NO. AWARDS: 4; 2 per award, twice annually.

APPLICATION INFO:
Guidelines are available online.

OFFICERS:
Kim Fortunato, President
Ashok Madhavan, Treasurer
Andrew Kupchik, Secretary
Bill O'Shea, Controller
Wendy Milanese, Program Manager

TRUSTEES:
Gary Biscoll
Mark Cacciatore
Kim Fortunato
E.J. Henry
Richard Landers
Helen Le Du
Karen Lewis
Harry Miller
Anthony Sanzio
Dave Stangis

ADDRESS INQUIRIES TO:
Wendy Milanese, Program Manager
(See address above.)

THE CANNON FOUNDATION, INC. [55]

52 Spring Street, N.W.
Concord, NC 28025
(704) 786-8216
Fax: (704) 782-2812
E-mail: vskahen@cannonfoundation.org
info@cannonfoundation.org
Web Site: www.cannonfoundation.org

FOUNDED: 1943

AREAS OF INTEREST:
Primarily health care, higher education and human services. Limited grants to arts, historical preservation and environment.

TYPE:
Capital grants.

YEAR PROGRAM STARTED: 1943

LEGAL BASIS:
Private foundation.

ELIGIBILITY:
Applicant must be 501(c)(3) nonprofit organization. No grants to individuals.

GEOG. RESTRICTIONS: North Carolina.

FINANCIAL DATA:
Amount of support per award: $5,000 to $200,000.

Total amount of support: Approximately $8,650,508 for fiscal year ended September 30, 2014.

NO. MOST RECENT APPLICANTS: 168 for the year 2014.

NO. AWARDS: 119 for the year 2014.

APPLICATION INFO:
Applications are requested through the web site. Links to the online application are sent to the applying organization's chief executive officer/executive director, not to grant writers or consultants.

Duration: One year.

Deadline: January 5, April 5, July 5 and October 5. Notification within two months of deadlines.

STAFF:
Venetia Skahen, Executive Director

ADDRESS INQUIRIES TO:
Venetia Skahen, Executive Director
(See address above.)

CARNEGIE CORPORATION OF NEW YORK [56]

437 Madison Avenue
New York, NY 10022
(212) 371-3200
Fax: (212) 754-4073
E-mail: grantsinfo@carnegie.org
Web Site: www.carnegie.org

FOUNDED: 1911

AREAS OF INTEREST:
Education, democracy, international peace and security, and higher education and research in Africa.

TYPE:
Conferences/seminars; Development grants; Project/program grants; Research grants; Seed money grants.

YEAR PROGRAM STARTED: 1911

PURPOSE:
To promote the advancement and diffusion of knowledge and understanding.

LEGAL BASIS:
Private foundation.

ELIGIBILITY:
Grants are made primarily to academic institutions and national or regional organizations.

FINANCIAL DATA:
Amount of support per award: Average $450,000.

Total amount of support: Approximately $120,000,000 for the year 2014.

NO. AWARDS: Varies.

APPLICATION INFO:
Only Letters of Inquiry submitted via the Corporation's online system will be considered.

Duration: Varies.

PUBLICATIONS:
Program guidelines; pamphlet; meeting and occasional papers; *Carnegie Reporter*, magazine; annual report.

IRS I.D.: 13-1628151

ADDRESS INQUIRIES TO:
See e-mail address above.

AMON G. CARTER FOUNDATION [57]

201 Main Street, Suite 1945
Fort Worth, TX 76102
(817) 332-2783
Fax: (817) 332-2787
E-mail: terry@agcf.org
Web Site: www.agcf.org

FOUNDED: 1945

AREAS OF INTEREST:
The arts, health and medical services, youth and elderly, and human and social services.

TYPE:
Capital grants; Challenge/matching grants; Development grants; Matching gifts; Project/program grants; Seed money grants.

PURPOSE:
To support arts, education, health and medical services, programs benefiting youth and elderly, and civic and community endeavors that enhance quality of life.

LEGAL BASIS:
Private foundation.

ELIGIBILITY:
Applicants must be 501(c)(3) organizations. Board focus on Fort Worth and Tarrant County, TX.

No loans. No grants to individuals.

GEOG. RESTRICTIONS: Texas.

FINANCIAL DATA:
Amount of support per award: $1,000 to $500,000.

Total amount of support: Varies.

NO. MOST RECENT APPLICANTS: 400 for the year 2014.

NO. AWARDS: 200 for the year 2014.

REPRESENTATIVE AWARDS:
$7,557,570 to Amon Carter Museum; $2,500,000 to Texas Christian University.

APPLICATION INFO:
Send brief letter request supplemented with project budget and/or other pertinent information in support of request.

Duration: Three years maximum. Renewal rare.

PUBLICATIONS:
Grant policy and guideline statement.

OFFICERS:
Robert W. Brown, M.D., Vice President
W. Patrick Harris, Executive Vice President-Investments
John H. Robinson, Executive Vice President, Grant Administration
Kathy King, Controller

BOARD OF DIRECTORS:
Robert W. Brown, M.D.
Kate L. Johnson
Mark L. Johnson
Sheila B. Johnson

ADDRESS INQUIRIES TO:
John H. Robinson
Executive Vice President
Grant Administration
(See address above.)

HAROLD K.L. CASTLE FOUNDATION [58]

1197 Auloa Road
Kailua, HI 96734-4606
(808) 263-7073
Fax: (808) 261-6918
E-mail: amatsukado@castlefoundation.org
Web Site: www.castlefoundation.org

FOUNDED: 1962

AREAS OF INTEREST:
Hawaii's public education redesign and enhancement, Hawaii's nearshore marine resource conservation, strengthening the communities of Windward Oahu, and other areas of focus when the Foundation sees a special opportunity to make a difference with limited resources.

TYPE:
Capital grants; Project/program grants; Seed money grants.

PURPOSE:
To benefit the people of Hawaii.

LEGAL BASIS:
Family foundation.

ELIGIBILITY:
Nonprofit organizations serving the state of Hawaii with Internal Revenue Code Sections 501(c)(3) and 509(a) public charity status and public schools in Hawaii.

GEOG. RESTRICTIONS: Hawaii.

CO-OP FUNDING PROGRAMS: Hawaii Community Stabilization Initiative.

NO. MOST RECENT APPLICANTS: 116.

NO. AWARDS: 48.

REPRESENTATIVE AWARDS:
$922,815.33 to University of Hawaii Foundation; $475,000 to Teach for America; $95,000 to Hawaii Conservation Alliance Foundation; $750,000 to Bishop Museum.

APPLICATION INFO:
Prospective grant applicants must submit an Online Inquiry Form, which is the first step in requesting funds from the Foundation. The Foundation will contact applicants within one month to request more information, invite the submission of a full proposal, or to inform applicant that the Foundation will be unable to consider a full proposal due to limited resources and/or a mismatch with Foundation priorities.

Duration: Program grants: Up to five years.

Deadline: Applications accepted on a rolling basis. Capital support requests due each year by October 1.

PUBLICATIONS:
Application guidelines; annual report.

IRS I.D.: 99-6005445

STAFF:
Terrence R. George, President and Chief Executive Officer
Carlton K.C. Au, Vice President, Chief Financial Officer and Treasurer
Eric Co, Senior Program Officer for Marine Conservation
Alex Harris, Senior Program Officer for Education
Ann Matsukado, Controller

BOARD OF DIRECTORS:
H. Mitchell D'Olier, Chairman of the Board
Dr. Claire L. Asam
Dr. Kittredge A. Baldwin
Debbie Berger
Corbett A.K. Kalama
James C. McIntosh
Eric K. Yeaman

ADDRESS INQUIRIES TO:
Ann Matsukado, Grants Manager
(See address above.)

CENTRAL MAINE POWER COMPANY [59]

83 Edison Drive
Augusta, ME 04336
(800) 565-0121 ext. 2967
(207) 629-1067
Fax: (207) 623-5908
Web Site: www.cmpco.com

AREAS OF INTEREST:
Education, civic, science, technology education and economic development.

NAME(S) OF PROGRAMS:
- **Central Maine Power Company Corporate Contributions Program**

TYPE:
Capital grants; Challenge/matching grants; Demonstration grants; General operating grants; Project/program grants; Research grants.

LEGAL BASIS:
Corporation giving program.

ELIGIBILITY:
Applicants must be nonprofit organizations, limited to the area serviced by Central Maine Power.

GEOG. RESTRICTIONS: Maine.

FINANCIAL DATA:
Amount of support per award: $100 to $1,000.

NO. MOST RECENT APPLICANTS: 500.

NO. AWARDS: 100.

APPLICATION INFO:
Applicants should send a proposal letter.

Duration: Typically one year. Some multiyear funding.

Deadline: Applications accepted throughout the year. Grants announced monthly.

STAFF:
John H. Carroll, Manager of Public Affairs

ADDRESS INQUIRIES TO:
Public Affairs Department
(See address above.)

*SPECIAL STIPULATIONS:
Only available to schools and nonprofits within company's service territory in Maine.

CENTRAL VALLEY COMMUNITY FOUNDATION [60]

5260 North Palm Avenue
Suite 122
Fresno, CA 93704
(559) 226-5600
Fax: (559) 230-2078
E-mail: info@centralvalleycf.org
Web Site: fresnoregfoundation.org

FOUNDED: 1966

AREAS OF INTEREST:
Primarily arts and culture, health and human services, and youth services, environment, high impact with a lesser emphasis on parks and music.

NAME(S) OF PROGRAMS:
- **Arts and Culture**
- **Environment**
- **High Impact**
- **Regional Sustainability**
- **Teen Pregnancy Prevention Initiative**
- **Youth Grants**

TYPE:
General operating grants; Project/program grants.

PURPOSE:
To improve the quality of life for the people of the Central San Joaquin Valley.

LEGAL BASIS:
Community foundation.

ELIGIBILITY:
To apply, an organization should be a 501(c)(3) nonprofit, government agency, community group with fiscal agent, public agency, or educational institution.

The Foundation does not consider requests for previously incurred expenses, fund-raising by one agency on behalf of another, endowments, individuals, or institutions limiting their services to persons of a single religious sect or denomination.

GEOG. RESTRICTIONS: Central San Joaquin Valley, California; primarily the counties of Fresno, Kings, Madera, Mariposa, Merced, and Tulare.

FINANCIAL DATA:
Amount of support per award: Varies.

Total amount of support: Varies.

APPLICATION INFO:
There is an online application process; the beginning step is to complete the organization card.

Duration: One year. Renewal possible. High Impact grants: Multiyear. Teen Pregnancy Prevention Initiative: Two-year grants.

Deadline: Varies.

STAFF:
Hugh J. Ralston, President and Chief Executive Officer
Sandra Flores, Senior Program Officer

ADDRESS INQUIRIES TO:
Sandra Flores, Senior Program Officer
(See address above.)

THE CHAMPLIN FOUNDATIONS [61]

2000 Chapel View Boulevard, Suite 350
Cranston, RI 02920
(401) 944-9200
Fax: (401) 944-9299
Web Site: champlinfoundations.org

FOUNDED: 1932

AREAS OF INTEREST:
Conservation, environment, education, health, cultural programs, youth, social service, historic preservation and libraries.

TYPE:
Capital grants; Challenge/matching grants; Scholarships. Direct grants for capital needs including the purchase of equipment, real estate, renovations, construction and reduction of mortgage indebtedness.

Other grants are made only in certain circumstances.

Challenge grants are made at the Foundations' discretion.

Scholarships are only to Brown University for graduates of Rhode Island public high schools.

YEAR PROGRAM STARTED: 1932

PURPOSE:
To make grants to qualified charitable organizations to promote the general well-being of humanity, with preference to Rhode Island.

LEGAL BASIS:
Tax-exempt private foundation.

ELIGIBILITY:
Tax-exempt organizations, preferably in Rhode Island, may apply. No grants are awarded to individuals. Scholarships are limited to Rhode Island public high school graduates accepted at Brown University.

GEOG. RESTRICTIONS: Rhode Island.

FINANCIAL DATA:
Amount of support per award: Average: $25,000 to $65,000.

Total amount of support: $18,533,450 for the year 2015.

NO. MOST RECENT APPLICANTS: Approximately 400.

NO. AWARDS: 200 for the year 2015.

REPRESENTATIVE AWARDS:
Health Care: $250,000 to Blackstone Valley Community Health Care; Education: $535,000 to Brown University; Libraries: $257,795 to Ocean State Libraries; Youth/Fitness: $117,500 to Girl Scouts of Southeastern New England; Open Space/Parks/Environment: $600,000 to Rhode Island Zoological Society; Social Services: $750,000 to Ronald McDonald House of Providence.

APPLICATION INFO:
Applicants must submit a brief letter concisely describing the project and its intended purpose, status of any fund-raising effort and other sources of funds available. Copies of IRS 501(c)(3) tax-exemption and 509(a) letters must be furnished. Audited financial statements may be required on request.

Duration: No grants are awarded on a continuing basis. Applicants may apply annually.

Deadline: April 30. Grants awarded in November; checks issued in December. Invited public schools: June 30.

PUBLICATIONS:
Annual report; guidelines; Report on Open Space and Recreation Grants.

IRS I.D.: 51-0165988

EXECUTIVE COMMITTEE:
John Gorham, Chairman
Keith H. Lang, Executive Director
Timothy N. Gorham, Associate Director

ADDRESS INQUIRIES TO:
Keith H. Lang, Executive Director
(See address above.)

*SPECIAL STIPULATIONS:
Preference is given to Rhode Island tax-exempt organizations.

All initial inquiries must be made by mail.

BEN B. CHENEY FOUNDATION [62]

3110 Ruston Way, Suite A
Tacoma, WA 98402
(253) 572-2442
E-mail: info@benbcheneyfoundation.org
Web Site: www.benbcheneyfoundation.org

AREAS OF INTEREST:
Charity, civic affairs, culture, education, the elderly, health, social services and youth.

TYPE:
Capital grants; Project/program grants; Seed money grants.

PURPOSE:
To improve the quality of life in communities where the Cheney Lumber Company operated.

LEGAL BASIS:
Foundation.

ELIGIBILITY:
Applicants must be 501(c)(3) tax-exempt organizations.

GEOG. RESTRICTIONS: Tacoma and Pierce County, Washington; Medford and Jackson County, Oregon and the seven northernmost counties in California.

FINANCIAL DATA:
Amount of support per award: $1,000 to $15,000 for small grants; $16,000 to $125,000 for regular grants.

Total amount of support: Varies.

NO. MOST RECENT APPLICANTS: 300.

NO. AWARDS: 110.

APPLICATION INFO:
Begin with a query letter; projects of interest will be contacted for a follow-up interview.

Duration: Typically one to two years. No renewals.

ADDRESS INQUIRIES TO:
Brad Cheney, Executive Director
(See address above.)

CHICAGO TRIBUNE FOUNDATION [63]

Community Giving, 2nd Floor
435 North Michigan Avenue
Chicago, IL 60611-4041
(312) 222-3928
Fax: (312) 222-3882
E-mail: jwoelffer@chicagotribune.com
Web Site: www.chicagotribunecommunitygiving.com

FOUNDED: 1958

AREAS OF INTEREST:
Civic, culture, employee matching gifts and journalism.

TYPE:
General operating grants; Internships; Matching gifts; Project/program grants. Sponsorships. Civic: Grants in this program area primarily support initiatives that focus on providing educational opportunities for low-income youth from the Chicago area. Grant requests in the civic program area will be considered by invitation only.

Culture: Grants support arts organizations within the Chicago metropolitan area that provide access to the arts through educational programs for low-income youth in grades K-12. Grant support priority is given to arts organizations with an operating budget of less than $2,000,000. (The definition of cultural organizations is organizations whose entire mission is the arts or arts education.)

Journalism: The Foundation strives for journalistic excellence by building a broad and diverse pool of journalists to serve readers in Chicago and encouraging youths to have a voice. It seeks to focus its resources on local programs that will help train journalists who might otherwise not enter the field, and help them thrive in newsrooms. The Foundation provides support in five categories: (1) internships; (2) training and education programs; (3) hands-on journalism production or media literacy programs offered by local nonprofit organizations that reach low-income youth and diverse students in metropolitan Chicago; (4) local reading services of media news and information and; (5) programs that provide opportunities for youth or diverse journalists to attend journalism conferences held in Chicago.

PURPOSE:
To improve the future of the Chicago metropolitan area by helping underserved youth succeed and be safe; to provide resources, partnerships and a voice to help strengthen at-risk youths and families in its diverse community; to support educational civic programs for at-risk families, access to the arts for low-income youths, and diversity and youth voices in journalism.

LEGAL BASIS:
Corporate private foundation.

ELIGIBILITY:
All grant requests must fall within the described geographic and program areas in order to be considered for either general support or program support. The Foundation does not fund individual, capital or international grants. The grant requests must be received by the required dates described in the program area.

GEOG. RESTRICTIONS: City of Chicago, Illinois and the Chicago metropolitan area.

FINANCIAL DATA:
Amount of support per award: $2,500 to $7,500.

Total amount of support: $155,900 for the year 2014.

Matching fund requirements: The Foundation matches Chicago Tribune employee donations to most U.S. nonprofit organizations on a 2:1 basis; the match is $1,000 per employee on the calendar year.

CO-OP FUNDING PROGRAMS: Chicago Tribune Company bears the administrative costs of Chicago Tribune Foundation. Donations from Chicago Tribune's pretax profits or assets of the Foundation fund Chicago Tribune Foundation.

REPRESENTATIVE AWARDS:
Civic: $5,000 to Chicago Youth Centers, Chicago, IL, to develop college-to-career readiness programs; Culture: Near South Planning Board for a creative writing program including children's authors visiting classrooms; Journalism: Community Renewal Society, Chicago, IL, to support journalism internships focusing on issues of race or poverty.

APPLICATION INFO:
The Foundation advises the applying organization to initially send a one-page e-mail of inquiry that briefly includes organization's mission, geographic area and population served, program summary, organization budget and program budget. Include contact name, phone number and e-mail. To submit this letter of inquiry, please contact Jan Ellen Woelffer, Chicago Tribune, at the above address, phone number, fax number or e-mail. Foundation funds are limited.

The Foundation accepts, but does not require, the Chicago Area Grant Application Form. Use the information requested on the Chicago Area Grant Application Form as a guide for the proposal. Provide the information requested on the Form in a two-page narrative. The following attachments must be included with the proposal:
(1) a one-sided, one-page list of one's board of directors and their business affiliation and title;
(2) a copy of the most recent IRS tax-exempt status form;
(3) audited financial statements or Form 990 from the most recent fiscal year;
(4) organization budget for year in which funding is sought;
(5) sources of support listing which funds have been committed and;
(6) annual report or other literature on the organization's programmatic, financial and strategic accomplishments.

PUBLICATIONS:
Corporate contributions guidelines; annual report.

IRS I.D.: 36-3689171

STAFF:
Jan Ellen Woelffer, Grant and Charitable Programs Specialist

BOARD OF DIRECTORS AND OFFICERS:
Tony Hunter, Chairman
Joseph Schiltz, President
Joetta Fields-Taylor, Secretary
Maggie Wartik
Joyce Winnecke

ADDRESS INQUIRIES TO:
Jan Ellen Woelffer, Grant and Charitable Programs Specialist
(See address above.)

*SPECIAL STIPULATIONS:
If an organization previously received a grant from the Foundation, an updated report on that year's grant must be received before another grant request can be submitted. The report can be a two-page summary of accomplishments and challenges including the financial summary about the program supported by the grant.

If an organization has received grant support from the Foundation for three consecutive years, the organization is not eligible for funding in the fourth year. The organization can re-apply after taking a year away from funding.

THE CHRISTENSEN FUND [64]

487 Bryant Street
Second Floor
San Francisco, CA 94107
(415) 644-1630
Fax: (415) 644-1601
E-mail: info@christensenfund.org
Web Site: www.christensenfund.org

FOUNDED: 1957

AREAS OF INTEREST:
Supporting organizations working on biological and cultural diversity.

NAME(S) OF PROGRAMS:
- **African Rift Valley**
- **Central Asia**
- **Global**
- **Melanesia**
- **Northern Australia**
- **Northwest Mexico**
- **San Francisco-Bay Area**
- **Southwest U.S.**

TYPE:
General operating grants; Project/program grants; Research grants.

YEAR PROGRAM STARTED: 2004

PURPOSE:
To buttress the efforts of people and institutions who believe in a biodiverse world infused with artistic expression and who work to secure ways of life and landscapes that are beautiful, bountiful and resilient.

LEGAL BASIS:
Private, independent foundation.

ELIGIBILITY:
Must have nonprofit 501(c)(3) status or similar not-for-profit organization based either in the U.S. or another country.

GEOG. RESTRICTIONS: Southwest United States, northwest Mexico, Central Asia, Northern Australia, Melanesia, and the Africa Rift Valley (Southwest Ethiopia/Northern Kenya).

FINANCIAL DATA:
Amount of support per award: $50,000 to $100,000.

Total amount of support: $13,400,000 for the year 2014.

NO. MOST RECENT APPLICANTS: 250.

NO. AWARDS: 170 on average.

APPLICATION INFO:
Information may be obtained from the Fund's web site.

Duration: Typically one to two years.

Deadline: Varies.

ADDRESS INQUIRIES TO:
See e-mail address above.

EDNA MCCONNELL CLARK FOUNDATION [65]

415 Madison Avenue, 10th Floor
New York, NY 10017
(212) 551-9100
Fax: (212) 421-9325
E-mail: info@emcf.org
Web Site: www.emcf.org

FOUNDED: 1970

AREAS OF INTEREST:
Youth development.

NAME(S) OF PROGRAMS:
- **Youth Development Fund**

TYPE:
General operating grants. Business planning grants. Focus areas for the Youth Development Fund are academic achievement, preparation for workforce, and avoidance of risky behavior.

PURPOSE:
To support efforts by high-performing nonprofit organizations to increase their capacity to serve more kids (ages 9 to 24) with proven programs during the nonschool hours.

LEGAL BASIS:
Private foundation.

GEOG. RESTRICTIONS: United States.

FINANCIAL DATA:
Amount of support per award: Varies.

CO-OP FUNDING PROGRAMS: When Foundation interests are shared with other organizations.

APPLICATION INFO:
Organizations need to complete survey online.

Duration: Varies.

Deadline: No official deadlines. Board meets four times a year, plus standing committee meetings.

PUBLICATIONS:
Annual report.

IRS I.D.: 23-7047034

OFFICERS:
Nancy Roob, President
Ralph Stefano, Vice President, Chief Financial and Administrative Officer
Woodrow McCutchen, Managing Director

TRUSTEES:
H. Lawrence Clark, Chairman
James McConnell Clark, Jr.
W. Don Cornwell
Alice F. Emerson
Simon Hemus
Kevin W. Kennedy
Janice C. Kreamer
Nancy Roob
Joyce Shields

ADDRESS INQUIRIES TO:
Albert Chung
Director of Communications
(See address above.)

*PLEASE NOTE:
The Foundation does not accept unsolicited proposals.

THE CLIFFS FOUNDATION [66]

200 Public Square
Suite 3300
Cleveland, OH 44114-2589
(216) 694-5700
Fax: (216) 694-4880
Web Site: www.cliffsnaturalresources.com

FOUNDED: 1962

AREAS OF INTEREST:
Education and community building.

TYPE:
Capital grants; General operating grants.

PURPOSE:
To enhance the quality of life of the Company's employees and communities in which the Company operates.

ELIGIBILITY:
501(c)(3) organizations, as defined by the IRS, may apply. Request must address Cliffs Foundation funding priorities, including geographical and cause areas of interest. Organizations and their proposed programs must address specific community needs.

GEOG. RESTRICTIONS: Upper Peninsula of Michigan; northeastern Minnesota and Cleveland, Ohio.

FINANCIAL DATA:
Amount of support per award: $250 minimum.

APPLICATION INFO:
All requests for support must be in writing.

Duration: One year.

Deadline: Applications accepted throughout the year.

PUBLICATIONS:
Guidelines.

ADDRESS INQUIRIES TO:
Anna Ediger, Manager of Government Relations
(See address above.)

COASTAL BEND COMMUNITY FOUNDATION [67]

615 North Upper Broadway
Suite 1950
Corpus Christi, TX 78401
(361) 882-9745
Fax: (361) 882-2865
E-mail: kwesson@cbcfoundation.org
Web Site: www.cbcfoundation.org

FOUNDED: 1981

AREAS OF INTEREST:
Arts, children and youth, community development, crime prevention, elderly, environment, health, social welfare, education and human services.

TYPE:
Project/program grants; Research grants; Scholarships; Seed money grants; Training grants.

YEAR PROGRAM STARTED: 1981

PURPOSE:
To improve the quality of life in the Coastal Bend area.

LEGAL BASIS:
Community foundation.

ELIGIBILITY:
Grants are made to organizations that have tax-exempt status under Section 501(c)(3) of the Internal Revenue Code. No grants are made to individuals.

GEOG. RESTRICTIONS: Aransas, Bee, Jim Wells, Kleberg, Nueces, Refugio and San Patricio counties, Texas.

FINANCIAL DATA:
Amount of support per award: Varies.

Total amount of support: $6,658,935 for the year 2014.

Matching fund requirements: Determined on individual basis.

CO-OP FUNDING PROGRAMS: Coastal Bend Day of Giving.

NO. MOST RECENT APPLICANTS: 155.

NO. AWARDS: 131 (includes many partial grants).

APPLICATION INFO:
Applications accepted online between May 1 and June 15. Organizations should submit application with requested documentation by the application deadline. Applications that do not conform to the required format will not be considered.

Duration: Grants must be completed by the following September 30.

Deadline: Posted online.

PUBLICATIONS:
Annual report.

IRS I.D.: 74-2190039

ADDRESS INQUIRIES TO:
Karen W. Selim
President and Chief Executive Officer
(See address above.)

THE COCKRELL FOUNDATION [68]

1000 Main Street
Suite 3250
Houston, TX 77002
(713) 209-7500
Fax: (713) 209-7599
E-mail: foundation@cockrell.com
Web Site: www.cockrell.com

FOUNDED: 1957

AREAS OF INTEREST:
Education, arts, health care, youth activities and medical research.

TYPE:
Capital grants; Challenge/matching grants; Endowments; Fellowships; Professorships; Project/program grants; Scholarships. Endowments, fellowships, professorships and scholarships at University of Texas, Cockrell School of Engineering.

YEAR PROGRAM STARTED: 1966

PURPOSE:
To provide financial support for charitable organizations in the Houston area in support of education, health, civic, religious and social services.

LEGAL BASIS:
Private foundation.

ELIGIBILITY:
Endowments, fellowships, professorships and scholarships to the University of Texas Cockrell School of Engineering only.

In general, the Foundation gives support for annual and capital campaigns, building funds, endowment funds, general purposes, matching funds, and special projects. Grants are made only to nonprofit, tax-exempt organizations. To be eligible, an organization must have a determination letter from the IRS indicating that it is an organization described in Section 501(c)(3) of the Internal Revenue Code and is not a private foundation within the meaning of Section 509(a) of the Code.

GEOG. RESTRICTIONS: Primarily Houston, Texas.

FINANCIAL DATA:
Amount of support per award: Varies.

Total amount of support: $8,035,354 in grants for the year 2015.

NO. MOST RECENT APPLICANTS: 200.

NO. AWARDS: 54 grants for the year 2015.

APPLICATION INFO:
The Foundation supplies no application form. Applicants should submit a written description, no longer than five pages, of how the grant money will be used, covering the following items:
(1) description of the need or problem;
(2) a simple statement of what is hoped to be accomplished;
(3) a budget for the project, giving the total cost, the amount raised to date toward the project or program, the sources from which it has come, including private, religious organizations and/or government sources, and, in particular, the amount contributed by the individuals on the Board of Directors;
(4) plans for raising any uncovered balance;
(5) an explanation of why it is necessary to seek outside support;
(6) the current status of the project - where it stands now and how long it will take to complete;
(7) the specific sum being requested of the Foundation;
(8) plans for putting continuing projects on a self-sustaining basis and an estimate of when this will occur;
(9) name and address of tax-exempt organization which will be the recipient if a donation is made and a copy of the exemption letter from the U.S. Treasury Department;
(10) copy of the organization's current annual budget;
(11) copy of the organization's latest IRS-990;
(12) copy of the organization's latest audited financials;
(13) a list of the members of the Board of Directors;
(14) a list of the officers of the organization and;
(15) an Executive Summary Sheet.

Duration: One year.

IRS I.D.: 74-6076993

OFFICERS AND DIRECTORS:
Ernest H. Cockrell, President and Director
M. Nancy Williams, Executive Vice President
Milton T. Graves, Vice President and Director
David A. Cockrell, Director
Ernest D. Cockrell, Director
Janet S. Cockrell, Director
Carol Cockrell Curran, Director
Richard B. Curran, Director
J. Webb Jennings, III, Director
Laura Jennings Turner, Director

ADDRESS INQUIRIES TO:
M. Nancy Williams
Executive Vice President
(See address above.)

THE OGDEN CODMAN TRUST [69]

c/o Rackemann, Sawyer & Brewster
160 Federal Street, 15th Floor
Boston, MA 02110-1700
(617) 951-1108
Fax: (617) 542-7437
E-mail: smonahan@rackemann.com
Web Site: www.codmantrust.org

FOUNDED: 1968

AREAS OF INTEREST:
Environment, conservation, historic preservation, cultural, health and social services in the town of Lincoln, MA.

TYPE:
Project/program grants. Support for special programs.

YEAR PROGRAM STARTED: 1972

PURPOSE:
To improve the quality of life in Lincoln.

LEGAL BASIS:
Private independent foundation.

ELIGIBILITY:
Organizations must be IRS 501(c)(3) tax-exempt.

GEOG. RESTRICTIONS: Lincoln, Massachusetts.

FINANCIAL DATA:
Amount of support per award: $2,000 to $50,000.

Total amount of support: $177,000 for the year 2015.

Matching fund requirements: Case-by-case basis.

NO. MOST RECENT APPLICANTS: 12 for the year 2015.

NO. AWARDS: 10 for the year 2015.

REPRESENTATIVE AWARDS:
Town of Lincoln; Codman Community Farm; Lincoln School Foundation.

APPLICATION INFO:
Contact Grants Coordinator prior to submitting an application.

Duration: Varies.

Deadline: Applications are reviewed on a rolling basis.

PUBLICATIONS:
Application guidelines.

TRUSTEES:
Susan T. Monahan
Maura E. Murphy, Esq.
Michael F. O'Connell, Esq.

ADDRESS INQUIRIES TO:
Susan T. Monahan
Grants Coordinator and Trustee
(See e-mail address above.)

THE GEORGE W. CODRINGTON CHARITABLE FOUNDATION [70]

3900 Key Center
127 Public Square
Cleveland, OH 44114-1291
(216) 566-5699
Fax: (216) 566-5800
E-mail: craig.martahus@thompsonhine.com

FOUNDED: 1955

AREAS OF INTEREST:
Humanitarian projects.

TYPE:
Capital grants; Challenge/matching grants; Endowments; General operating grants; Matching gifts. Annual grants to public charitable or educational projects.

YEAR PROGRAM STARTED: 1955

PURPOSE:
To assist, encourage and promote the well-being of mankind, regardless of race, color or creed.

LEGAL BASIS:
Private foundation.

ELIGIBILITY:
The Foundation's supportive services are limited to public charitable or educational projects. No grants are made to individuals.

GEOG. RESTRICTIONS: Cuyahoga County, Ohio and immediately adjacent areas.

FINANCIAL DATA:
Amount of support per award: $1,000 to $200,000.

Total amount of support: Varies.

NO. MOST RECENT APPLICANTS: 130.

NO. AWARDS: 70.

REPRESENTATIVE AWARDS:
$5,000 to Business Volunteers Unlimited; $15,000 to Friends of Breakthrough Schools; $2,000 to Junior Achievement; $7,000 to Near West Theater; $30,000 to United Way of Greater Cleveland.

APPLICATION INFO:
Applications should be directed to the Supervisory Board of the Foundation. The application should state fully but briefly the amount requested, the need for the grant, the area served by the applicant, a brief history of the applicant's organization, description of the applicant's contributions to the area and listing of the applicant's officers and trustees. Original plus three copies should be submitted. Must also include IRS letter as evidence of Section 501(c)(3) status.

Deadline: Pending applications are considered at meetings of the Supervisory Board held in April, June, September and December.

IRS I.D.: 34-6507457

TRUSTEES:
Robyn Minter Smyers

SUPERVISORY BOARD:
Craig R. Martahus, Esq., Chairman
William R. Seelbach, Vice Chairman
Raymond T. Sawyer, Esq., Secretary

ADDRESS INQUIRIES TO:
Craig R. Martahus, Esq.
Chairman, Supervisory Board
(See address above.)

THE COLEMAN FOUNDATION, INC. [71]

651 West Washington Boulevard
Suite 306
Chicago, IL 60661-2134
(312) 902-7120
Fax: (312) 902-7124
E-mail: info@colemanfoundation.org
Web Site: www.colemanfoundation.org

FOUNDED: 1951

AREAS OF INTEREST:
Entrepreneurship education, cancer care, and developmental disability services.

TYPE:
Capital grants; Challenge/matching grants; Conferences/seminars; Project/program grants. The major areas of grantmaking include:
(1) education, with a strong emphasis on entrepreneurship education (national in scope, with focus in Chicago);
(2) cancer care and treatment in the Chicago metropolitan area and;
(3) services for the disabled in the Chicago metropolitan area, with a strong emphasis on developmental disabilities.

ELIGIBILITY:
Grants are only made to IRS-certified tax-exempt nonprofit organizations, 501(c)(3) or 509(a)(1) and that are not supporting foundations. Funding is prohibited to individuals, for-profit businesses, advertising books and tickets. General solicitations and annual appeals will not be considered.

Only programs within the Foundation's region of focus will be considered.

GEOG. RESTRICTIONS: Primarily metropolitan Chicago and other select parts of the Midwest.

FINANCIAL DATA:
Amount of support per award: Varies.
Total amount of support: Varies.

NO. AWARDS: Approximately 100.

APPLICATION INFO:
A two-page letter of inquiry should be sent by the applicant which includes the following:
(1) brief description of the organization;
(2) synopsis of the program to be proposed;
(3) clear statement of program/grant objectives and how they will be evaluated;
(4) estimate of the size grant to be proposed or range of proposed funding;
(5) statement of how the program/project will be sustained following the grant period and;
(6) contact name and information, including e-mail address of the project manager, for further communication.

Brochures, video tapes, CDs and other attachments should not be sent with the letter of inquiry. Any such attachments will not be considered at this stage of review.

Duration: Typically one year.

Deadline: Letters of Inquiry are accepted on a continuing basis.

ADDRESS INQUIRIES TO:
Michael Hennessy
President and Chief Executive Officer
(See address above.)

THE COLLINS FOUNDATION [72]

1618 S.W. First Avenue
Suite 505
Portland, OR 97201
(503) 227-7171
Fax: (503) 295-3794
E-mail: information@collinsfoundation.org
Web Site: www.collinsfoundation.org

FOUNDED: 1947

AREAS OF INTEREST:
Quality of life issues. Projects that will have an immediate and long-term impact on life in the community.

TYPE:
Challenge/matching grants; Project/program grants. Grants made to agencies exclusively in the state of Oregon to improve, enrich and give greater expression to its religious, educational, cultural and scientific endeavors. Also, to assist in improving the quality of life in the state.

YEAR PROGRAM STARTED: 1947

PURPOSE:
To help fund programs or projects that will make life better in the community.

LEGAL BASIS:
Private, nonprofit foundation.

ELIGIBILITY:
The Foundation is organized in the state of Oregon for projects within the state. All applicant agencies must be tax-exempt, as established by the Treasury Department of the United States. No support is given to individuals.

GEOG. RESTRICTIONS: Oregon.

FINANCIAL DATA:
Amount of support per award: Varies.
Total amount of support: $10,406,000 for the year 2014.
Matching fund requirements: The Foundation looks favorably on grants which must be matched.

NO. AWARDS: 264 for the year 2014.

APPLICATION INFO:
Application information is available online.
Duration: Varies.
Deadline: Not specified. Awards are announced periodically throughout the year.

OFFICERS:
Truman W. Collins, Jr., President
Cynthia G. Addams, Executive Vice President
Timothy R. Bishop, Treasurer

BOARD OF TRUSTEES:
Ralph Bolliger
Truman W. Collins, Jr.
Jerry E. Hudson
Alayna Luria
Cherida Collins Smith
Lee Diane Collins Vest

ADDRESS INQUIRIES TO:
Cynthia G. Addams, Executive Vice President
(See address above.)

COMMUNITIES FOUNDATION OF TEXAS, INC. [73]

Grants Department
5500 Caruth Haven Lane
Dallas, TX 75225
(214) 750-4222
Fax: (214) 750-4210
E-mail: donorservices@cftexas.org
Web Site: www.cftexas.org

AREAS OF INTEREST:
Arts, community improvement, disaster relief, education, health, housing, religion, scientific research, social services and youth.

NAME(S) OF PROGRAMS:
- **Community Impact Grants**
- **Donor-Advised Grants**
- **Educate Texas**
- **Entrepreneurs for North Texas**

TYPE:
Project/program grants.

YEAR PROGRAM STARTED: 1953

LEGAL BASIS:
Public charity.

ELIGIBILITY:
Organizations with IRS 501(c)(3) tax-exempt designation.

GEOG. RESTRICTIONS: Primarily Dallas, Denton, Colin, Rockwell and Tarrant counties in Texas.

FINANCIAL DATA:
Amount of support per award: Varies.
Total amount of support: Varies.

APPLICATION INFO:
Requests must be submitted using the Foundation Letter of Inquiry checklist and form, which can be downloaded from the web site above.
Duration: Varies.
Deadline: Letter of Intent: April 1.

ADDRESS INQUIRIES TO:
Grants Processing
(See address above.)

THE COMMUNITY FOUNDATION [74]

7501 Boulders View Drive, Suite 110
Richmond, VA 23225
(804) 330-7400
Fax: (804) 330-5992
E-mail: info@tcfrichmond.org
Web Site: www.tcfrichmond.org

FOUNDED: 1968

AREAS OF INTEREST:
Basic human needs for children and families, child and youth development, community and economic development, community enrichment and promoting philanthropy/strengthening nonprofit capacity.

NAME(S) OF PROGRAMS:
- **Strengthening Families - Strengthening Communities**

TYPE:
Awards/prizes; Capital grants; Challenge/matching grants; Conferences/seminars; Development grants; General operating grants; Project/program grants; Research grants; Scholarships; Seed money grants; Technical assistance; Training grants. Community grants programs.

YEAR PROGRAM STARTED: 1995

PURPOSE:
To give financial assistance to worthwhile charitable organizations serving people in the community.

LEGAL BASIS:
Community foundation.

ELIGIBILITY:
Proposals will be accepted from charitable organizations which serve the city of Richmond, outlying counties or the Tri-Cities.

GEOG. RESTRICTIONS: Richmond, Virginia metropolitan area and the Tri-Cities, Colonial Heights, Goochland, Hopewell and Petersburg.

FINANCIAL DATA:
Amount of support per award: Average $30,000.

Total amount of support: $50,000,000 for the year 2013.

NO. AWARDS: 1,000 organizations and 240 individuals for the year 2013.

APPLICATION INFO:
Instructions for submitting preliminary proposals are available on the Foundation's web site.

Duration: Usually one year. Renewal possible.

Deadline: May 5 and November 5. Announcement in September and March.

PUBLICATIONS:
Annual report; policy and guidelines for grant requests.

IRS I.D.: 23-7009135

OFFICERS:
Thomas N. Chewning, Chairperson
Thomas S. Gayner, Vice Chairperson
Sherrie Branch, President and Chief Executive Officer
Robert C. Sledd, Treasurer
Dee Ann Remo, Secretary

ADDRESS INQUIRIES TO:
Susan H. Hallett or
Elaine Summerfield
Vice President, Programs
(See address above.)

COMMUNITY FOUNDATION FOR SOUTHEAST MICHIGAN [75]

333 West Fort Street
Suite 2010
Detroit, MI 48226
(313) 961-6675
Fax: (313) 961-2886
E-mail: cfsem@cfsem.org
Web Site: www.cfsem.org

FOUNDED: 1984

AREAS OF INTEREST:
Environment, health, arts and culture, economic development, human services and civic affairs.

TYPE:
Development grants; Project/program grants; Seed money grants.

LEGAL BASIS:
Public Foundation.

ELIGIBILITY:
No grants for buildings, equipment, religious programs, fund-raising, individuals, conferences or annual meetings.

GEOG. RESTRICTIONS: The seven counties of southeast Michigan: Livingston, Macomb, Monroe, Oakland, St. Clair, Washtenaw and Wayne.

FINANCIAL DATA:
Amount of support per award: Varies.

NO. AWARDS: 3,000 grants were awarded for the year 2013.

APPLICATION INFO:
Telephone Foundation to discuss proposal before submitting application.

Duration: One year.

Deadline: Generally quarterly: March, June, September and December.

PUBLICATIONS:
Annual report; newsletters.

STAFF:
Mariam C. Noland, President
Karen L. Leppanen, Vice President, Finance and Administration
Robin D. Ferriby, Vice President, Philanthropic Services
Katie G. Brisson, Vice President, Programs

OFFICERS OF THE TRUSTEES:
James B. Nicholson, Chairman
Joseph L. Hudson, Jr., Founding Chairperson
Penny B. Blumenstein, Vice Chairman
W. Frank Fountain, Vice Chairman
David M. Hempstead, Vice Chairman
Michael T. Monahan, Treasurer
Mary M. Weiser, Secretary
Vivian Day Stroh, Program and Distribution Committee Chair

ADDRESS INQUIRIES TO:
Mariam C. Noland, President
(See address above.)

COMMUNITY FOUNDATION OF EASTERN CONNECTICUT

68 Federal Street
New London, CT 06320
(860) 442-3572
(877) 442-3572
Fax: (860) 442-0584
E-mail: jennob@cfect.org
Web Site: www.cfect.org

TYPE:
General operating grants; Project/program grants; Scholarships.

See entry 1199 for full listing.

COMMUNITY FOUNDATION OF GREATER MEMPHIS [76]

1900 Union Avenue
Memphis, TN 38104
(901) 728-4600
Fax: (901) 722-0010
E-mail: aharper@cfgm.org
Web Site: www.cfgm.org

FOUNDED: 1969

AREAS OF INTEREST:
Grants administered for charitable purposes in metropolitan Memphis.

NAME(S) OF PROGRAMS:
- **Nonprofit Capacity Building Grants**
- **Scholarship Funds**

TYPE:
Challenge/matching grants; Project/program grants; Scholarships; Technical assistance.

YEAR PROGRAM STARTED: 1974

PURPOSE:
To provide support for the benefit of the geographic area that the Foundation serves; to strengthen the community through philanthropy.

LEGAL BASIS:
Community foundation.

ELIGIBILITY:
Applicants must be charitable and nonprofit under IRS regulations, holding a 501(c)(3) tax-exempt status. Applicants must be located in the geographic area that the Foundation serves.

GEOG. RESTRICTIONS: Metropolitan Memphis, Tennessee.

FINANCIAL DATA:
Amount of support per award: Varies.
Total amount of support: Varies.
Matching fund requirements: Stipulated with some grant awards.

NO. MOST RECENT APPLICANTS: Varies.

APPLICATION INFO:
Grant guidelines and application forms are available online.

Duration: One year. Some grants are awarded on a multiyear basis.

Deadline: Varies.

PUBLICATIONS:
Newsletters; annual report.

IRS I.D.: 58-1723645

ADDRESS INQUIRIES TO:
Ashley Harper
Director of Grants and Initiatives
(See address above.)

THE COMMUNITY FOUNDATION OF MOUNT VERNON & KNOX COUNTY [77]

One South Main Street
Mount Vernon, OH 43050
(740) 392-3270
Fax: (740) 399-5296
E-mail: sbarone@mvkcfoundation.org
Web Site: www.mvkcfoundation.org

FOUNDED: 1944

AREAS OF INTEREST:
New projects in educational, charitable and civic fields.

TYPE:
Capital grants; Challenge/matching grants; Matching gifts; Project/program grants; Scholarships; Seed money grants.

YEAR PROGRAM STARTED: 1944

PURPOSE:
To improve the quality of life for the people of Mount Vernon and Knox County, OH.

LEGAL BASIS:
Nonprofit, community foundation.

ELIGIBILITY:
Grants from unrestricted funds generally limited to projects in Knox County, OH.

GEOG. RESTRICTIONS: Knox County, Ohio.

FINANCIAL DATA:
Amount of support per award: Varies.
Total amount of support: $2,500,000 annually.

APPLICATION INFO:
Application forms are available online. Personal presentations only at invitation of Distribution Committee.

PUBLICATIONS:
Annual report.

IRS I.D.: 23-7002871

BOARD OF DIRECTORS:
Karen Buchwald Wright, Chairman
Terry L. Divelbiss, Vice Chairman
Kurt E. Schisler, Treasurer
Kim Rose, Secretary
Jeffrey L. Boucher
R. Leroy Bumpus
Sean Decatur, Ph.D.
Marc Hawk
Richard K. Mavis
Dr. Amy Murnen
Susan Sukys

ADDRESS INQUIRIES TO:
Sam Barone, Executive Director
(See address above.)

COMMUNITY FOUNDATION OF THE EASTERN SHORE

1324 Belmont Avenue, Suite 401
Salisbury, MD 21804
(410) 742-9911
Fax: (410) 742-6638
E-mail: hmahler@cfes.org
Web Site: www.cfes.org

TYPE:
Awards/prizes; Challenge/matching grants; Demonstration grants; Project/program grants; Scholarships; Seed money grants; Technical assistance; Training grants.

See entry 1212 for full listing.

THE COMMUNITY FOUNDATION OF THE HOLLAND/ZEELAND AREA [78]

85 East Eighth Street
Suite 110
Holland, MI 49423
(616) 396-6590
Fax: (616) 396-3573
E-mail: info@cfhz.org
Web Site: www.cfhz.org

FOUNDED: 1951

AREAS OF INTEREST:
Education, arts and culture, recreation, community and economic development, the needs of youth and the elderly, health and human services, environment and housing.

TYPE:
Research grants; Scholarships; Technical assistance.

YEAR PROGRAM STARTED: 1951

PURPOSE:
To create lasting positive change; to work to build a permanent community endowment that supports high-impact charitable projects; to help donors achieve their charitable goals; to lead and partner in community-level initiatives.

LEGAL BASIS:
Corporation and public charity, 501(c)(3).

ELIGIBILITY:
Grants are made to organizations that have tax-exempt status under Section 501(c)(3) of the Internal Revenue Code or governmental agencies. No grants are made to individuals. Nonsectarian religious programs may apply.

GEOG. RESTRICTIONS: Holland and Zeeland, Michigan area only.

FINANCIAL DATA:
Amount of support per award: $500 to $75,000.

Total amount of support: Varies.

NO. MOST RECENT APPLICANTS: 770.

NO. AWARDS: 285.

APPLICATION INFO:
Grant applicants must contact the Foundation to discuss a proposal prior to submitting an application.

Scholarship applications must be completed on the Foundation web site.

Duration: One year.

Deadline: Varies.

PUBLICATIONS:
Annual report; application guidelines.

IRS I.D.: 38-6095283

STAFF:
Elizabeth Kidd, Vice President of Community Impact
Stacy Timmerman, Director of Scholarship

ADDRESS INQUIRIES TO:
Vice President of Community Impact
(See address above.)

THE COMMUNITY FOUNDATION OF WESTERN NORTH CAROLINA [79]

4 Vanderbilt Park Drive
Suite 300
Asheville, NC 28803
(828) 254-4960
Fax: (828) 251-2258
E-mail: info@cfwnc.org
Web Site: www.cfwnc.org

FOUNDED: 1978

AREAS OF INTEREST:
Food and farming, people in need, early childhood development, and natural and cultural resources.

TYPE:
Project/program grants; Scholarships.

YEAR PROGRAM STARTED: 1978

PURPOSE:
To inspire philanthropy and mobilize resources to enrich lives and communities in western North Carolina.

ELIGIBILITY:
Grants are awarded to tax-exempt organizations. Eligibility varies by program.

GEOG. RESTRICTIONS: Western North Carolina.

FINANCIAL DATA:
Total amount of support: Approximately $15,000,000 in grants and scholarships for the fiscal year 2015.

NO. AWARDS: Varies.

APPLICATION INFO:
Application information is available on the web site.

Duration: Varies.

PUBLICATIONS:
Quarterly newsletter; annual report.

IRS I.D.: 56-1223384

ADDRESS INQUIRIES TO:
Diane Crisp, Grants Manager
(See address above.)

COMPTON FOUNDATION, INC. [80]

101 Montgomery Street, Suite 850
San Francisco, CA 94104
(415) 391-9001
E-mail: info@comptonfoundation.org
Web Site: www.comptonfoundation.org

FOUNDED: 1946

AREAS OF INTEREST:
Climate change, peace and national security, and reproductive rights and justice.

TYPE:
Project/program grants.

PURPOSE:
To ignite change; to support transformative leadership and courageous storytelling, inspiring action toward a peaceful, just, sustainable future.

ELIGIBILITY:
501(c)(3) nonprofit organizations in the U.S. that are working domestically may apply.

The Foundation does not support organizations that work solely in one city or state.

FINANCIAL DATA:
Amount of support per award: Varies.

Total amount of support: $5,200,000 for the year 2015.

NO. AWARDS: 172 for the year 2015.

APPLICATION INFO:
Proposals are by invitation only. Unsolicited proposals are not accepted. The Foundation does, however, have an open inquiry process available online.

Duration: One year. Grants are renewable.

PUBLICATIONS:
Grant Highlights (available on web site).

STAFF:
Ellen Friedman, Executive Director
Deborah K. Daughtry, Director of Operations
Jennifer L. Sokolove, Program Director
Jennifer Turnage, Manager of Grants and Accounting
Johanna Marie Pederson Hanson, Program Associate
Nicole Lopez-Hagen, Foundation Assistant

BOARD OF DIRECTORS:
Vanessa Compton, President
Rebecca DiDomenico, Vice President
Emilie Cortes, Treasurer
W. Danforth Compton, Secretary
Betty L. Farrell
Jakada Imani
Stephen Perry
Steven M. Riskin

ADDRESS INQUIRIES TO:
Deborah K. Daughtry, Director of Operations
(See address above.)

THE CONNELLY FOUNDATION [81]

One Tower Bridge
100 Front Street, Suite 1450
West Conshohocken, PA 19428
(610) 834-3222
Fax: (610) 834-0866
E-mail: eawilcox@connellyfdn.org
Web Site: www.connellyfdn.org

FOUNDED: 1955

AREAS OF INTEREST:
Educational, civic and cultural institutions, health with emphasis on human services. A significant portion of funding is directed toward organizations affiliated with the Catholic Church.

TYPE:
Capital grants; General operating grants; Project/program grants.

PURPOSE:
To enhance the quality of life in the Delaware Valley.

LEGAL BASIS:
Private foundation.

ELIGIBILITY:
No grants to individuals, political or national organizations or other foundations, nor does the Foundation respond to annual appeals or general letters of solicitation. Foundation guidelines restrict funding any organization more than once during a 12-month period. Applicants who have received previous grants from the Foundation should submit final reports under separate cover.

GEOG. RESTRICTIONS: Camden, New Jersey; Bucks, Chester, Delaware and Montgomery counties and city of Philadelphia, Pennsylvania.

FINANCIAL DATA:
Amount of support per award: $5,000 to $50,000.

Total amount of support: $10,898,166 for the year 2015.

NO. AWARDS: 639 for the year 2015.

APPLICATION INFO:
Foundation requires grantees to use the Philanthropy Network Greater Philadelphia Common Grant Application Form, available on the Foundation web site.

Duration: One year.

Deadline: Written proposals are accepted and reviewed by the Foundation throughout the year. With the exception of Foundation initiatives, there are no deadlines. Applicants receive a response within approximately three months.

PUBLICATIONS:
Application guidelines.

OFFICERS:
Josephine C. Mandeville, President
Emily C. Riley, Executive Vice President
Lewis W. Bluemle, Senior Vice President
Victoria K. Flaville, Senior Vice President and Chief Operating Officer
Thomas A. Riley, Vice President for Strategy
Amy M. Snyder, Chief Financial Officer

ADDRESS INQUIRIES TO:
E. Ann Wilcox
Associate Vice President, Administration
(See address above.)

*PLEASE NOTE:
Visits to the Foundation office or contacts with its staff initiated by applicants during the proposal review process are discouraged.

CONSUMERS ENERGY FOUNDATION [82]

One Energy Plaza, Room EP8-210
Jackson, MI 49201-2276
(517) 788-0432
(877) 501-4952
Fax: (517) 788-2281
E-mail: foundation@consumersenergy.com
Web Site: www.consumersenergy.com/foundation

FOUNDED: 1989

AREAS OF INTEREST:
Social welfare, education, culture and arts, community and civic affairs, and environment.

CONSULTING OR VOLUNTEER SERVICES:
Employee volunteer program.

NAME(S) OF PROGRAMS:
- **Caring for Community**
- **Volunteer Investment Program**

TYPE:
Capital grants; Challenge/matching grants; General operating grants; Matching gifts; Project/program grants; Scholarships; Seed money grants; Technical assistance. Volunteer grants.

YEAR PROGRAM STARTED: 1990

PURPOSE:
To support the charitable interest of Consumers Energy.

LEGAL BASIS:
Corporate program.

ELIGIBILITY:
501(c)(3) tax-exempt status, nonprofit organizations are eligible for support. The Foundation will not fund individuals, political, religious, labor or veteran's organizations.

Requests will be considered from organizations elsewhere for programs or projects that significantly benefit the state of Michigan.

GEOG. RESTRICTIONS: Michigan.

FINANCIAL DATA:
Amount of support per award: $1,000 to $200,000.

Total amount of support: $3,300,000 for the year 2015.

Matching fund requirements: Foundation will match employee and retiree contributions to Michigan higher education, food banks, homeless shelters and community foundations. Minimum $25 and maximum $1,000 per year per employee and retiree. Retirees eligible for 50% match.

NO. MOST RECENT APPLICANTS: 1,800.

NO. AWARDS: 920 for the year 2013.

REPRESENTATIVE AWARDS:
$250,000 to Detroit Zoological Society; $100,000 to Food Bank of Eastern Michigan; $50,000 to Great Start Collaborative of Traverse Bay; $75,000 to Impression 5 Science Center; $150,000 to Michigan State University, College of Engineering.

APPLICATION INFO:
Cover letter and completed grant application required by mail only.

Duration: Varies. Renewal unlikely.

PUBLICATIONS:
Guidelines brochure.

DIRECTORS:
J.G. Russell, Chairman
David G. Mengebier, President
Carolyn A. Bloodworth, Secretary and Treasurer
John M. Butler
Daniel J. Malone
Patricia K. Poppe
Catherine M. Reynolds
Garrick J. Rochow
T.J. Webb

ADDRESS INQUIRIES TO:
Carolyn A. Bloodworth
Secretary and Treasurer
(See address above.)

V.V. COOKE FOUNDATION [83]

220 Mount Mercy Drive
Suite 2
Pewee Valley, KY 40056
(502) 241-0303
E-mail: carl.vvcooke@att.net

FOUNDED: 1947

AREAS OF INTEREST:
Civic affairs, education, religion and humanitarianism.

TYPE:
Capital grants; Endowments; General operating grants; Scholarships; Seed money grants.

LEGAL BASIS:
Private foundation.

ELIGIBILITY:
Grants are made to organizations that have tax-exempt status under Section 501(c)(3) and are not described in Section 509(a)(3) of the Internal Revenue Code. Grants are made for religious, educational, humanitarian and civic purposes. No grants are made to individuals.

GEOG. RESTRICTIONS: Metropolitan Louisville, Kentucky and the Commonwealth of Kentucky.

FINANCIAL DATA:
Amount of support per award: $250 to $25,000.

Total amount of support: $171,000 for the year ended August 31, 2013.

NO. MOST RECENT APPLICANTS: 54.

NO. AWARDS: 75.

REPRESENTATIVE AWARDS:
$2,000 to Alice Lloyd College; $10,000 to Cardiovascular Innovation Institute.

APPLICATION INFO:
Applications should be in letter form. Applicants must:
(1) outline the organization's goals and purposes, and the intended use and amount of the grant requested;
(2) list other organizations that serve the needs addressed by this application and what distinguishes this organization and;
(3) identify the percentage of the organization's budget that is used for fund-raising and for administrative expenses.

Eight copies of the application are required.

Deadline: Applications are considered in mid-February, May, August and November.

PUBLICATIONS:
Application guidelines.

IRS I.D.: 61-6033714

STAFF:
Carl M. Thomas, Executive Director

ADDRESS INQUIRIES TO:
Carl M. Thomas, Executive Director
(See address above.)

COOPER FOUNDATION [84]

1248 O Street, No. 870
Lincoln, NE 68508-1493
(402) 476-7571
Fax: (402) 476-2356
E-mail: info@cooperfoundation.org
Web Site: www.cooperfoundation.org

FOUNDED: 1934

AREAS OF INTEREST:
Education, human services, arts and humanities, and the environment.

TYPE:
Challenge/matching grants; Demonstration grants.

PURPOSE:
To support the operations and core programs of strong, well-managed and effective nonprofit organizations located in and working in Lancaster County, NE.

LEGAL BASIS:
Private foundation.

ELIGIBILITY:
Most grants are made to organizations located in and impacting residents of Lancaster County, NE.

The Foundation does not fund individuals, businesses, health organizations or issues, churches, religious organizations or issues, travel, memberships, endowments, non-501(c)(3) organizations, 509(a)(3) supporting organizations, fiscal agents, or private foundations.

GEOG. RESTRICTIONS: Nebraska.

FINANCIAL DATA:
Amount of support per award: $1,000 to $15,000; Average: $5,000.

Total amount of support: $556,362 for the year 2013.

NO. MOST RECENT APPLICANTS: 60.

NO. AWARDS: 60.

APPLICATION INFO:
The Foundation accepts formal applications only from organizations that have already communicated with them and have been asked to complete an application form. The initial communication may be in person, by phone, by mail or by facsimile. The Foundation staff is available for consultation at any stage in the process.

Reapplication cannot be made sooner than 12 months after grant approval or decline, or the final payment date, whichever is later. Organizations submitting a collaborative grant may apply on their own, but not during the same grant application cycle.

Duration: One year. Must reapply annually.

Deadline: January 15, April 1, August 1 and October 1.

ADDRESS INQUIRIES TO:
Victoria Kovar, Program Officer
(See address above.)

THE MARY S. AND DAVID C. CORBIN FOUNDATION [85]

Akron Centre Plaza
50 South Main Street, Suite 703
Akron, OH 44308-1830
(330) 762-6427
Fax: (330) 762-6428
E-mail: corbin@nls.net
Web Site: fdnweb.org/corbin

AREAS OF INTEREST:
Arts, culture, environment, health, housing, human services, education, youth and medical research.

TYPE:
Project grants.

PURPOSE:
To benefit charities in the Akron and Summit County, OH areas and national charities that have a presence in the Akron and Summit County areas of Ohio.

ELIGIBILITY:
Organizations classified as 501(c)(3) by the IRS and non-private foundations can apply. The Foundation gives primary consideration to the City of Akron and Summit County, OH charitable organizations and/or local chapters of national charities located in the Akron, Summit County area of Ohio.

The Foundation does not fund individuals, annual fund-raising campaigns, ongoing requests for general operating support, operating deficits, or organizations which in turn make grants to others. The Foundation generally does not fund religious organizations.

GEOG. RESTRICTIONS: City of Akron and Summit County, Ohio.

FINANCIAL DATA:
Amount of support per award: $250 to $500,000.

APPLICATION INFO:
Contact the Foundation for application procedures. The Foundation application can also be downloaded from the web site. Organizations should send a brief letter on their letterhead and should submit one original and one copy of all application materials. Letter should include:
(1) a brief description of the organization and;
(2) a description of the proposed project, proposed accomplishments, duration, the total cost of the project and the specific amount requested from the Foundation.

Duration: One year.

Deadline: March 1 and September 1, for consideration in May and November respectively.

ADDRESS INQUIRIES TO:
Erika J. May, Grants Administrator
(See address above.)

*SPECIAL STIPULATIONS:
Only written applications will be considered. Both telephone and personal interviews are discouraged unless requested by the Foundation.

MARION STEDMAN COVINGTON FOUNDATION [86]

P.O. Box 29304
Greensboro, NC 27429-9304
(336) 282-0480
E-mail: info@mscovingtonfoundation.org
Web Site: www.mscovingtonfoundation.org

AREAS OF INTEREST:
Historic preservation.

TYPE:
Capital grants; Challenge/matching grants; Conferences/seminars; General operating grants; Project/program grants; Research grants; Seed money grants.

YEAR PROGRAM STARTED: 1986

PURPOSE:
To provide grants to nonprofit organizations operating in the area of historic preservation.

ELIGIBILITY:
Grants are made to federally tax-exempt, nonprofit organizations.

GEOG. RESTRICTIONS: Primarily North Carolina.

FINANCIAL DATA:
Amount of support per award: $10,000 average.

Total amount of support: Approximately $300,000.

NO. AWARDS: Varies.

APPLICATION INFO:
Application procedures are available on the web site.

Duration: Varies.

Deadline: August 1 and March 1. Announcements in mid-October and mid-May.

PUBLICATIONS:
Annual report; guidelines.

IRS I.D.: 56-6286555

ADDRESS INQUIRIES TO:
Alexa S. Aycock, Executive Director
(See address above.)

*PLEASE NOTE:
Challenge grants may be requested or the Foundation may designate a grant as such. In either event, there will be a specified time period in which the matching funds are to be raised.

S.H. COWELL FOUNDATION [87]

595 Market Street, Suite 950
San Francisco, CA 94105
(415) 397-0285
Fax: (415) 986-6786
Web Site: shcowell.org

FOUNDED: 1955

AREAS OF INTEREST:
Family resource centers, public education, youth development, and improving the quality of life of low-income children and families in neighborhoods that meet the Foundation's place-based criteria.

TYPE:
Capital grants; Challenge/matching grants; Project/program grants; Technical assistance; Training grants. Community building. Operating support.

YEAR PROGRAM STARTED: 1955

PURPOSE:
To improve the quality of life of children living in poverty in northern California by making grants that support and strengthen their families and the neighborhoods where they live.

LEGAL BASIS:
Independent nonprofit foundation.

ELIGIBILITY:
Organization must be tax-exempt and must submit evidence that a grant would qualify under the Tax Reform Act of 1969. Grants are restricted to organizations, projects and programs in northern California, except by invitation of the Foundation.

As a matter of policy, the Foundation typically does not make grants to hospitals for construction or research, sectarian religious groups, individuals for scholarships or financial aid.

GEOG. RESTRICTIONS: Northern and central California.

FINANCIAL DATA:
Amount of support per award: $1,000 to over $500,000.

APPLICATION INFO:
The application process is rigorous, and prospective grantees should expect to work with Cowell staff before, during, and after a formal proposal is submitted. There are five

steps to the process:
(1) make sure that your project meets Foundation funding criteria;
(2) call the Foundation;
(3) if asked to do so, submit a letter of inquiry;
(4) if asked to do so, submit a full proposal. Please do not send a formal proposal unless a program officer requests one. If you are asked to submit a proposal, staff will give you a list of required information and;
(5) plan on at least one site visit.

Duration: Varies.

Deadline: The Directors meet regularly and review only those proposals recommended by staff.

OFFICERS AND BOARD OF DIRECTORS:
Ann Alpers, President
Lisa Backus
Charles E. Ellwein
Charles A. Higueras
Dr. Mikiko Huang
Scott Mosher
Lydia Tan
Kim Thompson

ADDRESS INQUIRIES TO:
Lise Maisano
Vice President, Grant Programs
(See address above.)

*SPECIAL STIPULATIONS:
No grants to individuals, for media projects, conferences, seminars, to sectarian organizations, hospitals or public/governmental agencies.

HENRY P. AND SUSAN C. CROWELL TRUST [88]

102 North Cascade Avenue
Suite 300
Colorado Springs, CO 80903
(719) 645-8119
Fax: (719) 418-2695
E-mail: info@crowelltrust.org
Web Site: www.crowelltrust.org

FOUNDED: 1927

AREAS OF INTEREST:
Evangelical foreign missions.

TYPE:
General operating grants; Project/program grants.

YEAR PROGRAM STARTED: 1927

PURPOSE:
To aid evangelical Christianity by support to organizations having for their purposes its teaching, advancement and active extension at home and abroad.

LEGAL BASIS:
Private foundation.

ELIGIBILITY:
No grants to churches, individuals or for endowment funds or research. No loans.

GEOG. RESTRICTIONS: United States.

FINANCIAL DATA:
Amount of support per award: Average $35,000.

Total amount of support: $3,500,000.

NO. MOST RECENT APPLICANTS: 375.

NO. AWARDS: 100.

APPLICATION INFO:
Applicants must ensure the project fits the guidelines of the Trust by completing the online Self-Screening Aid to determine eligibility and begin the application process. If the organization and project fit the minimum requirements, applicants should proceed to the online grant management system. No proposals will be accepted in hard copy or through e-mail.

Duration: One year. May resubmit annually.

Deadline: Proposals should be submitted by February 28 for spring and July 31 for fall consideration. Proposals received after the deadline may be held over for the following grant cycle.

PUBLICATIONS:
Application guidelines.

IRS I.D.: 36-6038028

STAFF:
Candace Sparks, Chief Executive Officer

ADDRESS INQUIRIES TO:
Angela Hunter
Assistant to the Executive Director
(See address above.)

THE CULLEN FOUNDATION [89]

601 Jefferson, 40th Floor
Houston, TX 77002
(713) 651-8837
Fax: (713) 651-2374
E-mail: gina@cullenfdn.org
Web Site: www.cullenfdn.org

FOUNDED: 1947

AREAS OF INTEREST:
Arts, education, medicine, science, handicapped and public service.

TYPE:
Capital grants; Challenge/matching grants; Development grants; Endowments; Fellowships; General operating grants; Professorships; Project/program grants; Research grants; Scholarships.

PURPOSE:
To provide charitable, educational and medical grants for hospitals, medical research, higher education and music and the performing arts; to provide aid to the handicapped and community funds.

LEGAL BASIS:
Tax-exempt, private foundation.

ELIGIBILITY:
Grants are limited to the state of Texas by indenture. No grants are made to individuals or businesses.

GEOG. RESTRICTIONS: Texas, primarily Houston.

FINANCIAL DATA:
Amount of support per award: $10,000 to $5,000,000.

NO. MOST RECENT APPLICANTS: 117.

NO. AWARDS: 31 new grants.

APPLICATION INFO:
Applications are accepted online only through the link on the Foundation web site.

Duration: No grants are awarded on a continuing basis.

IRS I.D.: 76-0647361

OFFICERS:
Isaac Arnold, Jr., President
Wilhemina E. Robertson, Vice President, Assistant Treasurer and Secretary
Meredith T. Cullen, Vice President, Assistant Secretary and Assistant Treasurer
Alan M. Stewart, Treasurer

DIRECTORS:
Alan M. Stewart, Executive Director
Isaac Arnold, Jr.
Bert L. Campbell
William H. Drushel, Jr.
Wilhemina E. Robertson

ADDRESS INQUIRIES TO:
Gina McEvily, Grant Administrator
(See address above.)

*SPECIAL STIPULATIONS:
Grants are made to qualified charities in the state of Texas, primarily in the Houston area. No grants to individuals or businesses.

THE NATHAN CUMMINGS FOUNDATION, INC. [90]

475 10th Avenue, 14th Floor
New York, NY 10018
(212) 787-7300
Fax: (212) 787-7377
E-mail: contact@nathancummings.org
Web Site: www.nathancummings.org

FOUNDED: 1949

AREAS OF INTEREST:
Inequality and climate change.

NAME(S) OF PROGRAMS:
- **Arts and Culture**
- **Constituency Building**
- **Disruptive Ideas**
- **Religious Traditions and Contemplative Practice**

TYPE:
General operating grants; Project/program grants.

YEAR PROGRAM STARTED: 1989

PURPOSE:
To promote democratic values and social justice, including fairness, diversity and community; to build a socially and economically just society that values and protects the ecological balance for future generations; to promote humane health care; to foster arts and culture that enrich communities.

LEGAL BASIS:
Private foundation.

ELIGIBILITY:
Applying organizations must be recognized as 501(c)(3) tax-exempt public charities, as defined by the IRS. Projects that are not recognized as tax-exempt public charities must have a fiscal sponsor.

GEOG. RESTRICTIONS: United States.

FINANCIAL DATA:
Amount of support per award: Varies.

APPLICATION INFO:
Letter of Inquiry is required for funding consideration. The application process is very competitive; only those organizations whose projects fit most closely with the Foundation's programmatic goals will be invited to submit a Foundation Application Form.

Duration: Varies.

Deadline: Prior to Board of Trustees meetings held in April and November.

IRS I.D.: 23-7093201

STAFF:
Sharon Alpert, President and Chief Executive Officer
Loren Harris, Vice President of Programs
Ethan O. Richards, Director of Information Technology and Communications

Laura Shaffer Campos, Director of Shareholder Activities
Janet Disla, Grants Manager

ADDRESS INQUIRIES TO:
Sharon Alpert
President and Chief Executive Officer
(See address above.)

THE CUMMINS FOUNDATION [91]

500 Jackson Street, MC 60113
Columbus, IN 47201
(812) 377-3114
Fax: (812) 377-7897
E-mail: cummins.foundation@cummins.com
Web Site: www.cummins.com

FOUNDED: 1954

AREAS OF INTEREST:
Focus on environment, education and social justice.

TYPE:
Development grants. Incubator grants. Matching grants.

YEAR PROGRAM STARTED: 1954

PURPOSE:
To improve the quality of life in communities where Cummins has manufacturing operations and subsidiaries; to promote the Foundation's philanthropic objectives through grants in priority areas as well as projects of special interest in Columbus and subsidiary communities.

LEGAL BASIS:
Corporate foundation.

ELIGIBILITY:
Grantees must be tax-exempt organizations or institutions located in areas where Cummins has a presence. Organizations must have proof of past Cummins employee engagement.

No grants are made to individuals or for denominational religious organizations. No scholarships are granted.

FINANCIAL DATA:
Amount of support per award: Varies.
Total amount of support: Varies.

APPLICATION INFO:
The Foundation requires initial contact via e-mail.

PUBLICATIONS:
Sustainability report.

DIRECTORS:
N. Thomas Linebarger, Chairman
Robert J. Bernhard
Franklin Chang-Diaz
Bruno V. Di Leo
Stephen B. Dobbs
Robert K. Herdman
Alexis M. Herman
Thomas J. Lynch
William I. Miller
Georgia R. Nelson

ADDRESS INQUIRIES TO:
See e-mail address above.

DANIELS FUND [92]

101 Monroe Street
Denver, CO 80206-4467
(303) 393-7220
Fax: (720) 941-4110
E-mail: info@danielsfund.org
grantsinfo@danielsfund.org
Web Site: www.danielsfund.org

FOUNDED: 2000

AREAS OF INTEREST:
Daniels Fund Grants Program: Aging, alcoholism and substance abuse, amateur sports, disabilities, early childhood education, K-12 education reform, ethics and integrity in education, homeless and disadvantaged, youth development.

NAME(S) OF PROGRAMS:
- **Daniels Fund Grants Program**
- **Daniels Fund Scholarship Program**

TYPE:
Capital grants; General operating grants; Project/program grants; Scholarships. Daniels Fund Grants Program supports highly effective nonprofit organizations in Colorado, New Mexico, Utah and Wyoming.

Daniels Fund Scholarship Program consists of the Daniels Scholarship Program and the Daniels Boundless Opportunity Scholarship Program. The Daniels Scholarship Program provides a comprehensive, four-year annually-renewable college scholarship for graduating high school seniors who demonstrate exceptional character, leadership, and a commitment to serving their communities, and applies toward the expense of attaining a Bachelor's degree at any nonprofit, accredited college or university in the U.S. The Daniels Boundless Opportunity Scholarship Program provides college scholarships for non-traditional students of all ages, awarded by select colleges and universities using funds provided by the Daniels Fund.

PURPOSE:
To help excellent nonprofits achieve a high level of effectiveness and impact.

ELIGIBILITY:
Daniels Grants Program: Applying organizations must have 501(c)(3) not-for-profit status.

Daniels Scholarship Program: High school seniors seeking to obtain a Bachelor's degree. Applicants must meet the core values of character, leadership and service, and demonstrate financial need.

Boundless Opportunity Scholarship: Applicants must demonstrate financial need and be:
(1) an adult entering or returning to college;
(2) a GED recipient;
(3) a former foster care youth;
(4) a former juvenile justice youth;
(5) returning military;
(6) an individual pursuing EMT/paramedic training or;
(7) an individual pursuing Early Childhood Education (ECE) certification.

GEOG. RESTRICTIONS: Colorado, New Mexico, Utah and Wyoming.

FINANCIAL DATA:
Total assets of $1,307,235,276 for the year ended December 31, 2015.
Amount of support per award: Varies.
Total amount of support: $62,800,000 in grants and scholarships for the year ended December 31, 2015.

NO. AWARDS: Daniels Fund Grants Program and Daniels Boundless Opportunity Scholarship: Varies. Daniels Scholarship Program: Approximately 230.

APPLICATION INFO:
Online application process. Daniels Scholarship Program application process opens in September.

Duration: Grants: Typically one year. Must reapply. Daniels Scholarship Program: Four years. Daniels Boundless Opportunity Scholarship: Varies.

Deadline: Daniels Scholarship Program: November 30.

MARGARET A. DARRIN FOUNDATION, INC. [93]

120 Columbia Turnpike
Florham Park, NJ 07932
(973) 822-2995

FOUNDED: 1987

AREAS OF INTEREST:
Arts, humanities, civic affairs, education, health, social services and women's issues.

TYPE:
General operating grants.

YEAR PROGRAM STARTED: 1987

ELIGIBILITY:
No restrictions or limitations on funding. Grants made to nonprofit 501(c)(3) organizations only.

GEOG. RESTRICTIONS: Northeastern United States.

FINANCIAL DATA:
Amount of support per award: Maximum approximately $500 to $5,000.

REPRESENTATIVE AWARDS:
$41,000 to Hague Adirondacks Historical Museum; $10,000 to Williston Northampton School, Easthampton, MA; $1,000 to Hutchinson Island Fire Department.

APPLICATION INFO:
Applications should take the form of a brief letter describing the charity, its background and the purpose of the contribution.

Applicant will be notified only if approved.

Duration: One year. Must reapply for additional funding.

Deadline: October 31.

IRS I.D.: 22-6426771

STAFF:
Michael Hanifin, President

ADDRESS INQUIRIES TO:
Charitable Contributions
(See address above.)

THE ARTHUR VINING DAVIS FOUNDATIONS [94]

225 Water Street
Suite 1510
Jacksonville, FL 32202
(904) 359-0670
Fax: (904) 359-0675
E-mail: office@avdf.org
Web Site: www.avdf.org

FOUNDED: 1952

AREAS OF INTEREST:
Private higher education, health care (caring attitudes), graduate theological education (seminaries fully accredited by the Association of Theological Schools), public television (major educational series for viewing nationally on PBS), secondary education (professional development programs that strengthen teachers and

teaching in grades nine-12), and programs that promote and strengthen caring attitudes in health care.

TYPE:
Project/program grants.

LEGAL BASIS:
Privately endowed foundation established by the will of Arthur Vining Davis.

ELIGIBILITY:
Grants are limited to institutions in the U.S. and its territories. Activities and functions not supported include assistance to individuals (except as participants in an organized institutional scholarship program), voter registration drives and voter education, efforts to influence elections or legislation, expenditures for noncharitable purposes and projects incurring obligations extending over many years. Support is not granted to institutions primarily supported by government funds except medical institutions and secondary education programs.

GEOG. RESTRICTIONS: United States.

FINANCIAL DATA:
Amount of support per award: $150,000 to $400,000, depending on program area.

Total amount of support: Approximately $9,600,000 for the year 2014.

CO-OP FUNDING PROGRAMS: As a policy, the Foundations' support increased cooperation among foundations and expanded communication with the public. The staff has taken an active part in national and regional efforts in this direction.

APPLICATION INFO:
Application information is available online.

Duration: Re-grants in higher education and religion generally are not considered until at least four years after a previous grant.

Deadline: Varies by program.

PUBLICATIONS:
Guideline brochure; annual report.

OFFICERS:
Dr. Nancy J. Cable, President
Cheryl Tupper, Vice President for Programs
Doreen Flippin, Chief Operations Officer

TRUSTEES:
J.H. Dow Davis, Chairman
Caleb N. Davis
Dr. Christopher V. Davis
Haley T. Davis
Tamara Davis
Serena Davis Hall
Alicia Davis Jaworski
Dorothy Davis Kee
Dr. William Given Kee

ADDRESS INQUIRIES TO:
Dr. Nancy J. Cable, President
(See address above.)

JOHN DEERE FOUNDATION [95]

One John Deere Place
Moline, IL 61265
(309) 748-7950
Fax: (309) 748-7953
E-mail: corpcitizenship@johndeere.com
Web Site: www.deere.com

FOUNDED: 1948

AREAS OF INTEREST:
Higher education, community development, and solutions for world hunger.

TYPE:
Project/program grants.

PURPOSE:
To support programs and activities that responsibly seek to build a better future for everyone.

LEGAL BASIS:
Corporate foundation.

ELIGIBILITY:
The Foundation only considers grant requests from tax-exempt, nonprofit organizations located in the U.S. or its possessions. No grants to individuals.

GEOG. RESTRICTIONS: United States and its territories.

FINANCIAL DATA:
Amount of support per award: Varies.

Total amount of support: Approximately $15,000,000 annually.

APPLICATION INFO:
Application is available online.

Duration: One to two years, with review.

OFFICERS:
Mara Downing, President
Nate Clark, Vice President

ADDRESS INQUIRIES TO:
Corporate Citizenship
(See address above.)

DELAWARE COUNTY FOUNDATION

3954 North Hampton Drive
Powell, OH 43065
(614) 764-2332
Fax: (614) 764-2333
E-mail: foundation@delawarecf.org
Web Site: www.delawarecf.org

TYPE:
Scholarships.

See entry 1226 for full listing.

DELUXE CORPORATION FOUNDATION [96]

3680 Victoria Street North
Shoreview, MN 55126-2966
(651) 787-5124
(651) 483-7842
Fax: (651) 481-4371
E-mail: pam.bridger@deluxe.com
Web Site: www.deluxe.com/foundation

FOUNDED: 1952

AREAS OF INTEREST:
K-12 economic education programs, tutoring programs, employment programs, small business coaching and arts.

TYPE:
Capital grants; General operating grants; Project/program grants. Volunteer match on behalf of employee volunteerism at 501(c)(3) nonprofit.

LEGAL BASIS:
Corporate foundation.

ELIGIBILITY:
The Foundation will generally not make grants to organizations that are not exempt under Sections 501(c)(3) or 509(a)(1), (2) or (3), individuals, colleges and universities, religious organizations, organizations designed primarily for lobbying, seminars, conferences, workshops or fund-raisers, endowments, research projects, tours and travel expenses, health, start-up organizations, athletic events or sponsorships.

It is not a common practice of the Foundation to consider requests for multiyear commitments.

GEOG. RESTRICTIONS: United States and Canada.

FINANCIAL DATA:
Amount of support per award: $5,000 to $10,000 average.

Total amount of support: Varies.

Matching fund requirements: Qualifying organizations for matching funds: Accredited educational institutions; public television and radio; professional arts; historical societies; museums.

CO-OP FUNDING PROGRAMS: United Way.

NO. AWARDS: 144.

REPRESENTATIVE AWARDS:
WBDC, Chicago, IL; Junior Achievement of South Florida, Coconut Creek, FL; Genesys Works, San Francisco, CA; Women's Employment Network, Kansas City, MO; Make A Difference WI, Milwaukee, WI.

APPLICATION INFO:
Online grant inquiry and application process is available at deluxecares.com.

Duration: One year.

BOARD OF DIRECTORS:
Lee J. Schram, President
Jennifer A. Anderson, Director of Foundations and Community Affairs
Amanda K. Brinkman
Julie Loosbrock
Edward A. Merritt
Terry Peterson
J. Michael Schroeder

ADDRESS INQUIRIES TO:
Pamela G. Bridger, Grants Administrator
(See address above.)

GERALDINE R. DODGE FOUNDATION [97]

14 Maple Avenue, Suite 400
Morristown, NJ 07960
(973) 540-8442
Fax: (973) 540-1211
E-mail: info@grdodge.org
Web Site: www.grdodge.org

FOUNDED: 1974

AREAS OF INTEREST:
The arts, environment, education, and Morris County projects.

TYPE:
General operating grants; Project/program grants. Grants in four key areas:
(1) Art grants enhance the cultural richness of the community in which citizens reside and contribute to New Jersey's creative economy;
(2) Educational grants provide transformational experiential educational opportunities both inside and outside of the classroom for young people who have limited access to educational excellence;
(3) Environmental grants help to achieve ecosystem resilience and sustainable community solutions and;
(4) Media grants support traditional and innovative uses of media to educate and engage the public around issues of importance to New Jersey and its citizens, as well as efforts to uncover the abuses of power by the institutions in which citizens have placed their trust.

PURPOSE:
To support and encourage those educational, cultural, social and environmental values that contribute to making our society more humane and our world more livable.

LEGAL BASIS:
Private foundation.

ELIGIBILITY:
Applicants must be nonprofit, 501(c)(3) tax-exempt organizations located in or providing benefits to the residents of the state of New Jersey. No grants in areas of higher education, health and religion. No support for capital programs, endowments, equipment purchases, scholarships, indirect costs or deficit reduction. No direct awards to individuals nor grants to conduit organizations, nor is funding made for lobbying efforts.

GEOG. RESTRICTIONS: New Jersey.

APPLICATION INFO:
Unsolicited requests for scholarships and grants are not accepted. New applicants should submit a one-page letter of inquiry to determine if a project falls within the Foundation's guidelines. Letters of inquiry may be submitted throughout the year, but must be received at least two weeks prior to the corresponding submission deadline. Letters of inquiry must be submitted online or e-mailed, without attachments. Following staff review of initial inquiries, applicants will be notified whether or not to submit a full proposal.

Applicants invited to apply are then required to submit an electronic copy of their proposal.

Duration: Typically 12 months.

Deadline: Letter of Inquiry: February 15 and August 1; Application: March 1 and September 1. Notification early July and mid-December, respectively.

PUBLICATIONS:
Application guidelines; biannual report.

IRS I.D.: 23-7406010

STAFF:
Christopher J. Daggett, President and Chief Executive Officer

ADDRESS INQUIRIES TO:
RoseAnn DeBois, Grants Manager
Tel: (973) 695-1175
E-mail: rdebois@grdodge.org

*SPECIAL STIPULATIONS:
The Foundation does not accept fax proposals or proposals sent via express mail carriers.

DOMINION FOUNDATION [98]

701 East Cary Street
Richmond, VA 23219
(804) 771-3169
Fax: (804) 771-3910
E-mail: dominionfoundation@dom.com
Web Site: www.dom.com/foundation

FOUNDED: 1985

AREAS OF INTEREST:
Basic human needs, environmental protection, education and community vitality.

TYPE:
Capital grants; General operating grants; Matching gifts; Project/program grants.

PURPOSE:
To improve the physical, social and economic well-being of the communities served by Dominion companies.

ELIGIBILITY:
Applicants must be 501(c)(3) organizations. No grants to individuals, sectarian purposes, fraternal, political, advocacy or labor organizations, religious programs of churches, or operating funds of individual United Way agencies.

FINANCIAL DATA:
Amount of support per award: Generally $1,000 to $15,000.

Total amount of support: Approximately $20,000,000 annually.

Matching fund requirements: Must be employee or retiree of Dominion.

NO. AWARDS: Over 1,400.

APPLICATION INFO:
Individual program criteria can be found on the Foundation web site.

PUBLICATIONS:
Grant guidelines.

IRS I.D.: 47-2746460

EXECUTIVE DIRECTOR:
Katharine Bond

ADDRESS INQUIRIES TO:
Dominion Foundation
P.O. Box 26666
Richmond, VA 23261-2666
(See e-mail address above.)

*SPECIAL STIPULATIONS:
Organizations seeking support should direct their requests to the operating company in their area.

GAYLORD AND DOROTHY DONNELLEY FOUNDATION [99]

35 East Wacker Drive, Suite 2600
Chicago, IL 60601
(312) 977-2700
Fax: (312) 977-1686
E-mail: info@gddf.org
Web Site: www.gddf.org

FOUNDED: 1952

AREAS OF INTEREST:
Artistic vitality, land conservation and collections in Chicago or the Lowcountry of South Carolina.

TYPE:
Challenge/matching grants; Development grants; General operating grants; Matching gifts; Project/program grants; Technical assistance.

YEAR PROGRAM STARTED: 1952

PURPOSE:
To promote artistic vitality and land conservation.

LEGAL BASIS:
Tax-exempt, private foundation.

ELIGIBILITY:
Grants are made to tax-exempt, nonprofit 501(c)(3) organizations. Grants are not made to individuals, for community welfare, education, benefits, conferences, loans or pledges.

GEOG. RESTRICTIONS: Chicago region and South Carolina's Lowcountry.

FINANCIAL DATA:
Amount of support per award: Varies.

Total amount of support: Varies.

NO. MOST RECENT APPLICANTS: 270.

NO. AWARDS: 211.

APPLICATION INFO:
Proposals should be submitted in response to guidelines, if projects are applicable.

Duration: Typically one year.

Deadline: Varies.

OFFICERS AND DIRECTORS:
Laura Donnelley, Chairman
David Farren, Executive Director
Gerald W. Adelmann, Director
Julia Antonatos, Director
Timothy Brown, Director
Shawn M. Donnelley, Director
Vivian Donnelley, Director
Cheryl Mayberry McKissack, Director
Dr. John Rashford, Director
Alex Shuford, Director
Alaka Wali, Director
Trenyholm Walker, Director
Mimi Wheeler, Director
Tom Trinley, Director of Finance and Administration

ADDRESS INQUIRIES TO:
Program Director
(See address above.)

R.R. DONNELLEY [100]

4101 Winfield Road
Warrenville, IL 60555-3521
(630) 322-6946
Fax: (630) 322-6994
E-mail: communityrelations@rrd.com
Web Site: www.rrdonnelley.com

FOUNDED: 1864

AREAS OF INTEREST:
Youth, education, inclusion and diversity.

NAME(S) OF PROGRAMS:
- **Corporate Contributions Program**

TYPE:
Capital grants; Internships; Scholarships. Scholarships are for children of employees only. Geographical focus on communities with manufacturing operations.

YEAR PROGRAM STARTED: 1964

PURPOSE:
To exercise corporate social responsibility, with special emphasis on enhancing the Company's manufacturing communities.

LEGAL BASIS:
Corporate contributions program.

ELIGIBILITY:
Grants are made only to nonprofit organizations. No grants are made to individuals.

FINANCIAL DATA:
Amount of support per award: Varies.

Total amount of support: Varies.

APPLICATION INFO:
Grant requests should be made online. Requests should be in the form of a short proposal containing a description of the organization, its activities and its clients, a clear statement of what the organization wants from R.R. Donnelley and an explanation of what it plans to accomplish with such assistance. Attach a copy of the organization's IRS status letter, a list of board members and an audited financial statement. A limited amount of other supporting materials, such as an annual report, brochure or newsletter, is also welcome.

Duration: One year. Must reapply for additional funding.

Deadline: Proposals are accepted from January 1 to November 1 and referred to the next Contributions Committee meeting.

PUBLICATIONS:
Corporate Social Responsibility Report.

ADDRESS INQUIRIES TO:
Kamala L. Martinez
Community Relations Director
(See address above.)

THE DOUTY FOUNDATION [101]

P.O. Box 1437
Philadelphia, PA 19105
(215) 620-1869
E-mail: jennifer@doutyfoundation.org
Web Site: www.doutyfoundation.org

FOUNDED: 1968

AREAS OF INTEREST:
Economic and educational opportunities to disadvantaged people, especially children.

TYPE:
General operating grants; Project/program grants. Projects with social impact, innovative projects and general operations.

YEAR PROGRAM STARTED: 1969

PURPOSE:
To support programs that provide either educational opportunities for the disadvantaged or local innovative social services.

LEGAL BASIS:
Tax-exempt private foundation.

ELIGIBILITY:
Qualifying tax-exempt organizations are eligible. Grants are not made for capital expenditures, agency promotions, annual reports, renovations or to organizations with annual budgets of more than $1,000,000. Grants are not made to individuals or for religious or political purposes.

GEOG. RESTRICTIONS: Greater Philadelphia, Pennsylvania area with preference to Montgomery and Philadelphia counties.

FINANCIAL DATA:
Amount of support per award: Up to $7,500.

Total amount of support: $268,100 for the year 2015.

NO. AWARDS: 60 for the year 2015.

APPLICATION INFO:
Applications may be submitted online via the Foundation web site.

Duration: One year. Renewals are usually limited to six years.

Deadline: March 15 and September 15.

IRS I.D.: 46-3309525

TRUSTEES:
Judith L. Bardes
Carrolle Perry Devonish
Peter Gonzales, Esq.
Thomas B. Harvey, Esq.
Nancy J. Kirby
Elbert Sampson
Ludy Soderman

STAFF:
Jennifer Leith, Executive Director

ADDRESS INQUIRIES TO:
Jennifer Leith, Executive Director
(See address above.)

*SPECIAL STIPULATIONS:
Organizations that have been funded for a six-year period may not reapply until at least two years have passed.

DOW JONES FOUNDATION [102]

1211 Avenue of the Americas, 7th Floor
New York, NY 10036
(212) 416-3202
E-mail: brad.rolston@dowjones.com

FOUNDED: 1954

AREAS OF INTEREST:
Journalism, free press, literacy and education, arts and culture, and community.

TYPE:
General operating grants. Program support.

PURPOSE:
To support causes engaged in the promotion and protection of journalism and free press, as well as causes devoted specifically to literacy and education, arts and culture, or local communities.

LEGAL BASIS:
Corporate foundation.

ELIGIBILITY:
The Foundation does not currently make grants in medical and scientific research.

FINANCIAL DATA:
Amount of support per award: Varies.

APPLICATION INFO:
All requests for Foundation support must be submitted in writing. Each request must indicate IRS tax-exemption certificate number.

Deadline: Normally, requests received will be considered by the board of directors only at their annual meeting in June for distribution in the next fiscal year.

PUBLICATIONS:
Application guidelines.

IRS I.D.: 13-6070158

OFFICERS:
Bradley P. Rolston, Esq., Secretary and Director

ADDRESS INQUIRIES TO:
Bradley P. Rolston, Esq., Director
(See address above.)

JOSEPH DROWN FOUNDATION [103]

1999 Avenue of the Stars, Suite 2330
Los Angeles, CA 90067
(310) 277-4488
Fax: (310) 277-4573
E-mail: alyssa@jdrown.org
Web Site: www.jdrown.org

FOUNDED: 1953

AREAS OF INTEREST:
Education.

TYPE:
General operating grants; Project/program grants.

YEAR PROGRAM STARTED: 1953

PURPOSE:
To assist individuals in becoming successful, self-sustaining and contributing members of society.

ELIGIBILITY:
No funds to individuals, endowments, capital campaigns or building funds. The Foundation will not underwrite annual meeting or conferences. No funding for religious programs and special events.

In the area of medical research, the Foundation does not accept unsolicited requests.

GEOG. RESTRICTIONS: Los Angeles, California.

FINANCIAL DATA:
Amount of support per award: $5,000 to $50,000.

Total amount of support: Approximately $4,000,000 for the fiscal year ended March 31, 2016.

NO. MOST RECENT APPLICANTS: 1,200.

NO. AWARDS: 150.

APPLICATION INFO:
No special application form is required. Proposals should include a letter with information about both the organization as a whole and the project in particular, a 501(c)(3) tax determination letter from the IRS, a budget for both the organization as a whole and the project in particular, the most recent audited financial statements, a copy of the most recent Form 990 filed with the IRS and a list of the current board of directors. Any additional materials, such as an annual report, may be attached.

Duration: One year.

Deadline: January 15, April 15, July 15 and October 15 (postmark).

PUBLICATIONS:
Application guidelines.

OFFICERS AND STAFF:
Norman C. Obrow, Chairman
Wendy Wachtell, President
Ann T. Miller, Chief Financial Officer
Alyssa Ichelberger, Program Officer

ADDRESS INQUIRIES TO:
Alyssa Ichelberger, Program Officer
(See address above.)

*SPECIAL STIPULATIONS:
In the area of medical research, the Foundation does not accept unsolicited requests.

DORIS DUKE CHARITABLE FOUNDATION [104]

650 Fifth Avenue, 19th Floor
New York, NY 10019
(212) 974-7000
Fax: (212) 974-7590
Web Site: www.ddcf.org

FOUNDED: 1996

AREAS OF INTEREST:
Environment, performing arts, child abuse prevention and clinical research.

NAME(S) OF PROGRAMS:
- **Arts Program**
- **Child Well-being Program**
- **Environment Program**
- **Medical Research Program**

TYPE:
Grants-in-aid. The Arts Program supports performing artists with the creation and public performance of their work. The Program focuses its support on contemporary dance, jazz and theatre, and the organizations that nurture, present and produce them.

The Child Well-being Program promotes children's healthy development and protects them from abuse and neglect. The Program favors a public health approach and is especially interested in place-based,

whole-community approaches that seek to engage a range of participants from various disciplines to ensure that family well-being is supported by strong communities.

The Environment Program enables communities to protect and manage wildlife habitat and create efficient built environments. The Program's awareness of climate change as the greatest emerging threat to biodiversity - and the need to aggressively mitigate it without unnecessarily sacrificing wildlife habitat - shapes the Program's grantmaking priorities.

The Medical Research Program supports the prevention, treatment and cure of human disease. The goal of the Program is to strengthen and support clinical research to help advance the translation of basic biomedical discoveries into new treatments, preventions and cures for human diseases.

YEAR PROGRAM STARTED: 1997

PURPOSE:
To improve the quality of people's lives through grants supporting the performing arts, environmental conservation, medical research and the prevention of child abuse, and through the preservation of the cultural and environmental legacy of Doris Duke's properties.

LEGAL BASIS:
Nonprofit foundation.

ELIGIBILITY:
While all Foundation programs require that grantee organizations be publicly supported 501(c)(3) tax-exempt organizations based in the U.S., each program has a customized approach to its grantmaking strategy.

FINANCIAL DATA:
Amount of support per award: $315,000 average.

Total amount of support: Approximately $76,000,000.

APPLICATION INFO:
The majority of the Foundation's grants are awarded through competitive (request-for-proposal) processes or by invitation. Open competitions and funding opportunities for grants are listed on the Foundation's web site. Foundation staff also welcome letters of inquiry from qualifying organizations.

To submit a letter of inquiry, the Foundation requests that organizations visit its web site and submit letters of inquiry through the online form. To do so, applicant will need a nonprofit tax ID as well as the title of the proposed project, a brief description of the specific project for which funding is sought, the requested funding amount, a description of how the objectives of the proposed project relate to those of the Foundation, the organization's mission and strategies, and a primary contact for the organization. Staff will respond to the letters of inquiry within two months and will notify the writer if additional information is desired.

Duration: Short-term or multiyear grants are awarded.

TRUSTEES:
John E. Zuccotti, Chairperson
Anthony S. Fauci, Vice Chairperson
Harry B. Demopoulos
James F. Gill
Kathy Halbreich
Nannerl O. Keohane
Angela K. Mwanza
Peter A. Nadosy
William H. Schlesinger
Nicholas Scoppetta
Jide J. Zeitlan

STAFF:
Edward P. Henry, President

THE DUKE ENDOWMENT [105]

800 East Morehead Street
Charlotte, NC 28202
(704) 376-0291
Fax: (704) 376-9336
E-mail: cperkins@tde.org
Web Site: www.dukeendowment.org

FOUNDED: 1924

AREAS OF INTEREST:
Not-for-profit hospitals in North Carolina and South Carolina; children's welfare and adoption assistance institutions in North Carolina and South Carolina; rural United Methodist churches and retired ministers in North Carolina and four colleges: Duke, Furman and Johnson C. Smith universities and Davidson College.

TYPE:
Capital grants; General operating grants; Project/program grants.

YEAR PROGRAM STARTED: 1924

PURPOSE:
To carry out the terms of the Trust Indenture, as written by James B. Duke, by supporting four institutions in higher education, not-for-profit hospitals and children's homes in North Carolina and South Carolina, retired pastors of the United Methodist Church and programs and projects of rural United Methodist Churches in North Carolina.

LEGAL BASIS:
Charitable trust.

ELIGIBILITY:
North and South Carolina organizations and institutions with appropriate interests and activities are eligible.

GEOG. RESTRICTIONS: North Carolina and South Carolina.

FINANCIAL DATA:
Amount of support per award: Varies.

Total amount of support: $140,000,000 in total grants, including $96,940,111 in new grants for the year 2014.

Matching fund requirements: Varies with grant.

NO. MOST RECENT APPLICANTS: Varies.

NO. AWARDS: Varies.

REPRESENTATIVE AWARDS:
$35,000,000 multiyear grant to Johnson C. Smith University to support science programs, scholarships and capital improvements on campus; $11,250,000 multiyear grant to Health Science South Carolina to advance leading-edge programs; $2,000,000 to Furman University to enrich the University's fine arts program.

APPLICATION INFO:
Applicants must check the eligibility criteria before applying. Complete guidelines and application form are available on the web site.

Duration: Varies. All eligible beneficiaries may request continued and renewed support.

Deadline: Varies.

PUBLICATIONS:
Annual report; e-newsletter, occasional papers and reports on projects and programs.

IRS I.D.: 56-0529965

TRUSTEES AND OFFICERS:
Minor Mickel Shaw, Chairperson
Dennis M. Campbell, Ph.D., Vice Chairperson
Mary Duke Trent Jones, Vice Chairperson
Eugene W. Cochrane, Jr., President
Arthur E. Morehead, IV, Vice President/General Counsel
Mary L. Piepenbring, Vice President
Karen H. Rogers, Chief Financial Officer/Treasurer
Terri W. Honeycutt, Corporate Secretary
K. Todd Walker, Managing Director, Investments
William Barnet, III
John F.A.V. Cecil
Ravenel B. Curry, III
Harris E. DeLoach, Jr.
Constance F. Gray
Thomas S. Kenan, III
Charles C. Lucas, III
Wilhelmina M. Reuben-Cooke, J.D.
Russell M. Robinson, II
Jean G. Spaulding, M.D.
Kenneth D. Weeks, Jr., M.D.
Judy Woodruff

ADDRESS INQUIRIES TO:
Eugene W. Cochrane, Jr., President
(See address above.)

DUNSPAUGH DALTON FOUNDATION [106]

1501 Venera Avenue, Suite 312
Coral Gables, FL 33146
(305) 668-4192
Fax: (305) 668-4247
E-mail: ddf@dunspaughdalton.org
Web Site: dunspaughdalton.org

AREAS OF INTEREST:
Higher, secondary, and elementary education; social services; youth; health associations and hospitals; cultural programs; and civic affairs.

TYPE:
Capital grants; General operating grants; Project/program grants.

ELIGIBILITY:
Grants are made to organizations that have tax-exempt status under Section 501(c)(3) of the Internal Revenue Code. No grants are made to individuals.

GEOG. RESTRICTIONS: Monterey County, California; Miami-Dade County, Florida; Charlotte and Mecklenburg County, North Carolina.

FINANCIAL DATA:
Amount of support per award: $5,000 average.

APPLICATION INFO:
Applicant must submit:
(1) proposal summary (not to exceed one-half page) explaining why the grant is requested, what outcomes are hoped to be achieved and how funds will be spent;
(2) narrative including background, funding requirements and evaluation (not to exceed five pages);
(3) completed Grant Application Form and;
(4) the most recent financial statements used as the basis for filing IRS Form 990.

Submit all application documents to either office listed on the Grant Application Form.

Duration: One year. Can reapply.

OFFICERS:
Alexina H. Lane, President
Robert C. Bonner, III, Vice President/Treasurer
Leslie W. Buchanan, Vice President/Secretary

ADDRESS INQUIRIES TO:
Leslie W. Buchanan, Secretary or
Alexina Lane, President
(See address above.)

JESSIE BALL DUPONT FUND [107]

40 East Adams Street
Suite 300
Jacksonville, FL 32202-3302
(904) 353-0890
(800) 252-3452
Fax: (904) 353-3870
Web Site: www.dupontfund.org

FOUNDED: 1976

AREAS OF INTEREST:
Education, religion, health and human services, arts and culture, juvenile justice, environment, housing, community and economic development, historic preservation, nonprofit capacity building and financial asset building.

TYPE:
Challenge/matching grants; General operating grants; Project/program grants; Technical assistance. Organizational capacity building.

Geared to nonprofit, religious organizations and educational institutions.

YEAR PROGRAM STARTED: 1976

PURPOSE:
To expand access and create opportunity through investing in people, organizations and communities that were important to Jessie Ball duPont.

LEGAL BASIS:
Private foundation.

ELIGIBILITY:
The Fund makes grants only to a defined universe of organizations. An organization is eligible if it received a contribution from Mrs. duPont between January 1, 1960 and December 31, 1964. Proof of eligibility is determined by examining Mrs. duPont's personal or tax records or by the applicant presenting written, verifiable evidence of having received a contribution during the eligibility period.

GEOG. RESTRICTIONS: Primarily the South, especially Delaware, Florida, and Virginia.

FINANCIAL DATA:
Amount of support per award: Executive Director's Discretionary Fund: Average $10,000; Feasibility Grants: Up to $5,000; Independent Schools Initiative: $10,000 over three years; Technical Assistance Grants: Up to $4,000.

Total amount of support: $12,525,980 in grants awarded for the year 2014.

NO. MOST RECENT APPLICANTS: Varies.

NO. AWARDS: 290 for the year 2015.

APPLICATION INFO:
Duration: One to three years.

Deadline: Trustees meet quarterly in February, May, August and November to consider grant applications. Awards are announced immediately after the meetings.

PUBLICATIONS:
Annual report; policy briefings; *Notes from the Field.*

IRS I.D.: 59-6368632

TRUSTEES:
Rev. Eddie E. Jones, Jr., Chairperson and Clerical Trustee
Leroy Davis, Vice Chairperson
David Llewellyn, Representing Corporate Co-Trustee, Northern Trust
Mary Lynn Huntley
Thomas H. Jeavons
Martha T. Lanahan
Mary K. Phillips

STAFF:
Sherry P. Magill, Ph.D., President
Mark Constantine, Senior Vice President
Katie Ensign, Senior Program Officer
Barbara Roole, Senior Program Officer
Chris Crothers, Program Officer
Mark Walker, Knowledge Management and Technology Officer

ADDRESS INQUIRIES TO:
Sherry P. Magill, Ph.D., President
(See address above.)

*PLEASE NOTE:
Guidelines must be followed carefully when submitting proposal.

EASTERN BANK CHARITABLE FOUNDATION [108]

195 Market Street
Lynn, MA 01901
(781) 598-7595
Fax: (781) 596-4445
E-mail: l.kurzrok@easternbank.com
Web Site: www.easternbank.com

FOUNDED: 1994

AREAS OF INTEREST:
Human services, family and children, affordable housing, community health, civil liberties, sustainability, and workforce development.

NAME(S) OF PROGRAMS:
- **Community Grants**
- **Partnership Grants**
- **Targeted Grants**

TYPE:
Capital grants; Endowments; General operating grants; Project/program grants. Community grants; Partnership grants.

YEAR PROGRAM STARTED: 1994

PURPOSE:
To contribute, in a meaningful way, to the health and vitality of the various communities which are served by Eastern Bank, by providing financial support to selected nonprofit organizations operating within those communities; to support organizations providing services to the underserved and neediest members of our community; to ensure all our neighbors have equal access to food, shelter, education, employment, child care and other basic human needs.

LEGAL BASIS:
Corporate foundation.

ELIGIBILITY:
Applicants must be nonprofit 501(c)(3) organizations and be located in the market area served by Eastern Bank. The Foundation does not accept applications from organizations with 509(a)(3) designation or private foundations.

GEOG. RESTRICTIONS: Eastern Massachusetts and southern and coastal New Hampshire.

FINANCIAL DATA:
Amount of support per award: $50 to $50,000.

Total amount of support: $6,900,000 for the year 2015.

Matching fund requirements: Full-time employees, trustees and directors: Minimum $50, maximum $1,000 per year.

NO. MOST RECENT APPLICANTS: 3,000.

NO. AWARDS: 2,000.

APPLICATION INFO:
Applications are only accepted through the online application site.

Deadline: Ongoing for requests up to $10,000. Requests for Eastern Bank Partnership Grants ($10,000 to $50,000): August 1. Targeted grants ($10,000 to $50,000): March 1.

PUBLICATIONS:
Annual report, available online.

IRS I.D.: 22-3317340

ADDRESS INQUIRIES TO:
Laura Kurzrok, Executive Director
(See address above.)

EATON CHARITABLE FUND [109]

Eaton Center
1000 Eaton Boulevard
Cleveland, OH 44122
(440) 523-4502
E-mail: tarasgszmagala@eaton.com
Web Site: www.eaton.com

FOUNDED: 1953

AREAS OF INTEREST:
Education, arts and culture, children at-risk, community improvement and neighborhood development.

TYPE:
Capital grants; Challenge/matching grants; Matching gifts; Product donations; Project/program grants. The Corporation places a priority on contributing to those organizations in which Eaton employees are personally involved and which serve their needs. Contributions are made to health, human service, civic, arts and cultural organizations and educational institutions.

Support of capital campaigns at educational institutions is generally limited to programs of direct interest to Eaton, which prefers to invest in engineering, scientific, technological and business-related projects.

YEAR PROGRAM STARTED: 1953

PURPOSE:
To contribute to the betterment of life in communities where Eaton employees live and work; to support employee involvement and investment; to promote self-sufficiency; to sustain arts and cultural institutions; to enhance education.

LEGAL BASIS:
Corporate foundation.

ELIGIBILITY:
501(c)(3) organizations within the Corporation's areas of interest are eligible for support. Grants are not made to religious, fraternal or labor organizations; to individuals or individual endeavors; debt retirement; medical research; endowment funds;

fund-raising benefits, sponsorships or other events; or annual operating budgets of United Way agencies or hospitals.

Grants are only made in communities where Eaton has operations.

FINANCIAL DATA:
Cash grants are mainly from the Charitable Fund, but also from the company.

Amount of support per award: Typically, $1,000 to $100,000. Average: $5,000 to $15,000.

Total amount of support: Approximately $9,100,000 for the year 2015.

Matching fund requirements: The Corporation single-matches employee contributions to nationally accredited educational institutions and arts and cultural organizations approved by the Corporate Contributions Committee.

APPLICATION INFO:
Send requests to the nearest company facility. All requests for contributions must be in writing. Each should include a one-page cover letter (on organization letterhead), a one- to three-page description of organization's program, and an attached description of the organization's history and purpose, identification of other organizations (including corporations) involved in funding the program and gift amounts committed, names of Eaton employees and a description of their involvement (if applicable), copies of the most recently audited financial statements and the current budget, a roster of officers and directors or trustees of the organization and their affiliations, and official government documentation of the organization's 501(c)(3) tax-exempt IRS status (or its non-U.S. equivalent).

Grants are generally limited to one grant per organization in a given year. Previous grants are not considered as precedent for additional support. Proposals should not be submitted in binders or with videotapes, CD-ROMs and/or in other costly manners.

Duration: Grants are typically given for one year. Multiyear commitments are usually capital grants.

Deadline: Grant requests are accepted and reviewed throughout the year.

PUBLICATIONS:
Annual report; guidelines.

STAFF:
Lisa Durst, Manager, Community Affairs

CONTRIBUTIONS COMMITTEE:
Taras Szmagala, Jr., Chairman
Revathi Advaithi
Bill Blausey
Cynthia Brabander
Ken Semelsberger
Uday Yadav

ADDRESS INQUIRIES TO:
Taras Szmagala, Jr., Senior Vice President
Public and Community Affairs
(See address above.)

EDISON INTERNATIONAL [110]

2244 Walnut Grove Avenue
Quad 4A G.O. No. 1
Rosemead, CA 91770
(626) 302-5538
Fax: (626) 302-7985
E-mail: tami.bui@sce.com
Web Site: www.sce.com

FOUNDED: 1996

AREAS OF INTEREST:
Education (science, technology, engineering, arts and math), environment, public safety and emergency preparedness, and civic engagement.

CONSULTING OR VOLUNTEER SERVICES:
Volunteer Program, Energy in Action.

NAME(S) OF PROGRAMS:
- **Corporate Contributions Program**
- **Edison Scholars Program**
- **Employee Matching Gifts Program**

TYPE:
Challenge/matching grants; General operating grants; Matching gifts; Project/program grants; Scholarships. Matching gifts and employees for education only: private and public schools (K-University).

YEAR PROGRAM STARTED: 1986

PURPOSE:
To promote the economic prosperity and overall quality of life in the areas where its employees live and work by supporting numerous community initiatives and historically supporting a variety of effective educational, civic and charitable activities.

ELIGIBILITY:
Primary focus on Southern California and other areas where Edison International operates.

No grants to individuals, political organizations or candidates, veterans organizations, fraternal orders, labor groups, commercial profit-making enterprises, religious or sectarian organizations or any group whose activities are not in the best interests of Edison International, its employees, shareholders, customers or the communities it serves.

FINANCIAL DATA:
Amount of support per award: Community Grants: Up to $5,000 for non-established grantees; Edison Scholars: $40,000 over four years.

Matching fund requirements: Equal match to $2,000 for accredited public and private educational institutions; Up to $2000 for Energy Assistance Fund.

NO. MOST RECENT APPLICANTS: Edison Scholars: 30 annually; Grants: Varies.

NO. AWARDS: Varies.

REPRESENTATIVE AWARDS:
$1,500,000 to American Red Cross for public safety and awareness in southern California.

APPLICATION INFO:
Applications for Edison grants and sponsorships must be submitted online during Edison's funding cycles. Application links are active only during funding cycles.

Deadline: Funding cycles are during the months of March and June.

PUBLICATIONS:
Annual report; contributions policy; application guidelines.

OFFICERS:
Theodore Craver, Chairman

ADDRESS INQUIRIES TO:
Tami Bui
Principal Manager, Corporate Philanthropy
(See address above.)

EL POMAR FOUNDATION [111]

10 Lake Circle
Colorado Springs, CO 80906
(719) 633-7733
Fax: (719) 577-5702
E-mail: fellowship@elpomar.org
grants@elpomar.org
Web Site: www.elpomar.org

FOUNDED: 1937

AREAS OF INTEREST:
Health, education, welfare, arts and culture, humanities, civic and community, and leadership.

NAME(S) OF PROGRAMS:
- **Fellowship Program**
- **Grants Program**

TYPE:
Capital grants; Challenge/matching grants; Fellowships; General operating grants; Matching gifts; Project/program grants; Scholarships; Technical assistance. The Fellowship Program brings highly qualified college graduates with diverse backgrounds and interests to the Foundation. This program focuses on professional development and prepares Fellows for positions of leadership in Colorado and the nation.

Grants Program is to support construction, development and acquisition of buildings and equipment and other projects in education, health, humanities, resources, environment and welfare in the state of Colorado.

PURPOSE:
To support general-purpose grantmaking, civic collaboration, projects of major community importance and initiatives that provide various kinds of assistance to nonprofit organizations; to provide leadership development opportunities for a range of individuals, from those just out of college to those responsible for the state's most important nonprofits; to help those least able to help themselves.

LEGAL BASIS:
Private nonprofit charitable foundation.

ELIGIBILITY:
Priority consideration will be provided to capital projects that have received local community and other support. The Foundation does not accept grant applications for grant support to:
(1) other foundations or nonprofits that distribute money to recipients of its own selection;
(2) endowments;
(3) organizations that practice discrimination of any kind;
(4) organizations that do not have fiscal responsibility for the proposed project;
(5) organizations that do not have an active 501(c)(3) nonprofit IRS determination letter;
(6) camps, camp programs, or other seasonal activities;
(7) religious organizations for support of religious programs;
(8) cover deficits or debt elimination;
(9) cover travel, conferences, conventions, group meetings, or seminars;
(10) influence legislation or support candidates for political office;
(11) produce videos or other media projects;
(12) fund research projects or studies and;
(13) primary or secondary schools (K-12).
The Foundation will consider, on a limited basis, capital requests from nonpublicly funded secondary schools.

Capital grant requests exceeding $100,000, unless initiated by the Foundation, will not be considered.

GEOG. RESTRICTIONS: Colorado.

FINANCIAL DATA:

Amount of support per award: Fellowship Program: $30,000; Grants Program: $2,500 to $50,000.

Total amount of support: $25,000,000 in grants approved for the year 2016.

NO. AWARDS: 700 grants approved for the year 2016.

APPLICATION INFO:

The Trustees have established no set form for grant applications. A proposal should include a concise statement of the project according to the requirements. Fellowship and grant guidelines are available on the Foundation web site.

Duration: Fellowship Program: Two years; Grant Program: Typically one year.

PUBLICATIONS:

Annual report; application guidelines.

IRS I.D.: 84-6002373

OFFICERS:

William J. Hybl, Chairman and Chief Executive Officer
R. Thayer Tutt, Jr., President and Chief Investment Officer
Elaine Martinez, Chief Financial Officer
Kyle H. Hybl, Chief Operating Officer and General Counsel

TRUSTEES:

Judy Bell
Michael Gould
Nechie Hall
Robert J. Hilbert
Kyle H. Hybl
William J. Hybl
Charles H. Jacoby, Jr.
Jen Livsey
David J. Palenchar
Brenda Smith
R. Thayer Tutt, Jr.
William R. Ward

ADDRESS INQUIRIES TO:

William J. Hybl
Chairman and Chief Executive Officer
(See address above.)

RUTH H. AND WARREN A. ELLSWORTH FOUNDATION [112]

c/o Fletcher Tilton
370 Main Street, 11th Floor
Worcester, MA 01608
(508) 459-8000
(508) 459-8042
Fax: (508) 459-8342
E-mail: stilton@fletchertilton.com

AREAS OF INTEREST:

Culture, education, health and human services.

TYPE:

Project/program grants.

PURPOSE:

To support organizations that are providing solutions to or preventing problems within the immediate community.

ELIGIBILITY:

Grants are made to organizations that have tax-exempt status under Section 501(c)(3) of the Internal Revenue Code. No grants are made to individuals. Nonsectarian religious programs may apply.

The Foundation does not usually fund grants for general operating expense.

GEOG. RESTRICTIONS: Worcester, Massachusetts and surrounding area.

FINANCIAL DATA:

Amount of support per award: $5,000 to $25,000.

Total amount of support: Varies.

APPLICATION INFO:

Submit a proposal in a letter form and a grant application summary.

Duration: Varies.

Deadline: June 1.

ADDRESS INQUIRIES TO:

Sumner B. Tilton, Jr., Trustee
(See address above.)

EMD MILLIPORE [113]

290 Concord Road
Billerica, MA 01821-7037
(781) 533-6000
Web Site: www.emdmillipore.com

FOUNDED: 1985

AREAS OF INTEREST:

Science, education (K-12), sustainability, and health care.

TYPE:

Capital grants; Challenge/matching grants; Matching gifts; Project/program grants; Research grants; Scholarships.

YEAR PROGRAM STARTED: 1985

PURPOSE:

To serve the public interest in ways that are meaningful to the company and its employees.

ELIGIBILITY:

Organizations, excluding religious and political, classified as 501(c)(3) by the IRS can apply.

FINANCIAL DATA:

Since inception, over $20,000,000 has been distributed to deserving nonprofit programs on a local and national level.

Amount of support per award: $5,000 to $10,000.

Matching fund requirements: $25 minimum gift.

APPLICATION INFO:

Eligible programs may submit a copy of the 501(c)(3) certificate, tax identification number, and a letter of inquiry no more than two pages in length briefly describing the organization, the program for which funding is sought, and the amount of funding requested. Those organizations whose programs are of interest to Millipore will be invited to submit full proposals.

Millipore also accepts the Associated Grant Makers Common Proposal Form.

Duration: One year. Grants are renewable.

Deadline: Proposals are considered quarterly at Review Committee meetings.

ADDRESS INQUIRIES TO:

Johanna Jobin, Director of Corporate Responsibility
(See address above.)

EMERSON [114]

8000 West Florissant Avenue
St. Louis, MO 63136
(314) 553-2000
(314) 553-3621
Web Site: www.emerson.com

FOUNDED: 1944

AREAS OF INTEREST:

Education; youth, culture and the arts; health, welfare and civic needs.

TYPE:

Capital grants; Challenge/matching grants; Development grants; Endowments; General operating grants; Matching gifts; Project/program grants.

YEAR PROGRAM STARTED: 1950

PURPOSE:

To encourage sound, innovative programs that enrich human lives, promote volunteerism, provide services directly to those in need and increase the overall impact of contributed funds.

LEGAL BASIS:

Corporate contributions program.

ELIGIBILITY:

Grants are made to organizations having IRS 501(c)(3) tax-exempt status, located in areas where Emerson has facilities. The Trust does not contribute to organizations that practice discrimination by race, color, creed, sex, age or national origin, religious or politically partisan organizations, projects requiring funding directly to an organization located outside the U.S. or its territories, loans or investment funds, fraternal, veterans' or labor groups unless they furnish services benefiting the general public, aid to individuals, underwriting of deficits or post-event funding.

FINANCIAL DATA:

Amount of support per award: Varies.

Total amount of support: $35,763,000 for the year 2015.

Matching fund requirements: Dollar-for-dollar match of employee donations to institutions of higher learning (up to $10,000 annual maximum) and cultural arts organizations (up to $5,000 annually to any one organization, up to $10,000 maximum).

APPLICATION INFO:

Proposals should be submitted in writing and include the following information:
(1) brief description and history of the organization submitting the proposal;
(2) a clear statement of the purpose and objectives of the project or program (including expected results), the program budget, the amount requested, a statement of how the funds will be used and a timetable of project completion;
(3) statement of the relationship of the project's goals to the priorities of the Emerson Charitable Trust;
(4) annual report or audited financial statement of the requesting organization showing income and expenses, operational budget and which may include a copy of the most recent IRS 990 report;
(5) supporting factual information that may be useful as a basis of evaluation, such as a list of sources providing support to the organization;
(6) copy of the organization's IRS 501(c)(3) tax-exemption statement;
(7) listing of the organization's Board of Directors and a statement regarding staff who will manage the project and;

(8) statement of general plans for sustaining activities and post-grant evaluation of the project.
Applicants should expect a 30- to 60-day turnaround on all written proposals.
Duration: One year. Must reapply, unless multiyear funding at outset.

PUBLICATIONS:
Annual report; guidelines.

ADDRESS INQUIRIES TO:
Patrick J. Sly, Executive Vice President
(See address above.)

ERION FOUNDATION [115]

P.O. Box 732
Loveland, CO 80539
(970) 667-4549
Fax: (970) 663-6187
E-mail: contact@erionfoundation.org
Web Site: www.erionfoundation.org

FOUNDED: 1986

AREAS OF INTEREST:
Education, health, welfare, and culture.

TYPE:
Capital grants; Challenge/matching grants; Development grants.

YEAR PROGRAM STARTED: 1986

PURPOSE:
To support the Loveland, Colorado community.

LEGAL BASIS:
Private foundation.

ELIGIBILITY:
Eligible organizations must be IRS 501(c)(3) tax-exempt.

GEOG. RESTRICTIONS: Loveland, Colorado and the immediate surrounding area.

FINANCIAL DATA:
Amount of support per award: Varies.

APPLICATION INFO:
Applicants must submit via mail:
(1) completed application form;
(2) a copy of the organization's 501(c)(3) designation letter;
(3) page one of the organization's most recent IRS Form 990;
(4) a list of all members of the organization's board of directors and;
(5) the title of the person signing the application.
Duration: Varies.

ADDRESS INQUIRIES TO:
Doug Erion, President
(See address above.)

EVERSOURCE FOUNDATION [116]

One NSTAR Way
Westwood, MA 02090
(781) 441-3587
E-mail: responsibleenergy@eversource.com
Web Site: www.eversource.com

FOUNDED: 1981

AREAS OF INTEREST:
Health and well-being of youth and advancement and promotion of clean energy and related technologies.

TYPE:
Challenge/matching grants; Development grants; Matching gifts; Project/program grants; Research grants; Scholarships; Technical assistance. Grants to nonprofit charitable organizations in the Foundation's service territory.

YEAR PROGRAM STARTED: 1981

PURPOSE:
To make a positive difference in the lives of Eversource customers.

LEGAL BASIS:
Corporate foundation.

ELIGIBILITY:
Applicants must be institutions and organizations with a 501(c)(3) tax-exempt designation.

The Foundation does not support personal expenses related to events, conferences or travel, corporations that do not qualify as charitable organizations as defined by the IRS Code, projects benefiting limited groups (religious, fraternal or political), private foundations or endowments, requests aimed at reducing or eliminating a pre-existing debt, golf outings, organizations located outside the Foundation areas served and whose services do not benefit Eversource customers, and advertising. Generally speaking, grants are not provided to organizations that receive direct support from United Way or other federated funds, as these umbrella agencies are supported through Eversource direct giving and employee giving campaigns.

FINANCIAL DATA:
Amount of support per award: $1,000 to $100,000. $2,500 average.
Total amount of support: $1,000,000 to $1,500,000.
Matching fund requirements: The Foundation matches dollar-for-dollar employee gifts to approved educational or cultural organizations and homeless shelters. Minimum of $100 and maximum of $2,500 in any calendar year.

APPLICATION INFO:
Applications for support must be submitted through the online application form. Requests by e-mail or other means will not be considered.
Duration: Usually one year.
Deadline: November 15.

PUBLICATIONS:
Guidelines; matching grants program brochure.

EXELON CORPORATION [117]

Corporate Relations
10 South Dearborn Street
Chicago, IL 60603
(312) 394-4361
E-mail: steve.solomon@exeloncorp.com
Web Site: www.exeloncorp.com

FOUNDED: 1888

AREAS OF INTEREST:
Math and science, environmental education, arts and culture, neighborhood development, and environmental conservation.

NAME(S) OF PROGRAMS:
- **Corporate Giving Program**

TYPE:
General operating grants; Matching gifts; Project/program grants. Sponsorship for events.

PURPOSE:
To strengthen customer and community relations by promoting the advancement of math, science and energy education, contributing to charitable organizations that promote efficiency and renewable energy, promoting economic and community development, and contributing to organizations that promote diversity in the workplace and community.

LEGAL BASIS:
Corporate contributions program.

ELIGIBILITY:
Grants are made to institutions, organizations and agencies located in Exelon's service area (northern Illinois, central Maryland and southeastern Pennsylvania). The company does not purchase ads in benefit programs. No contributions are made to religious organizations for religious purposes, political organizations, or to individuals.

GEOG. RESTRICTIONS: Northern Illinois, central Maryland and southeastern Pennsylvania.

FINANCIAL DATA:
Total amount of support: $33,100,000 to nonprofit organizations for the year 2015.

NO. AWARDS: 3,000.

APPLICATION INFO:
Application must be submitted online.
Duration: One year.
Deadline: Applications are reviewed on an ongoing basis.

PUBLICATIONS:
Guidelines.

STAFF:
Christopher M. Crane, President and Chief Executive Officer of Exelon Corporation

ADDRESS INQUIRIES TO:
Steve Solomon
Vice President, Corporate Relations
(See address above.)

EXXON MOBIL CORPORATION [118]

5959 Las Colinas Boulevard
Irving, TX 75039
(972) 444-1106
Fax: (972) 444-1405
E-mail: citizenship@exxonmobil.com
Web Site: www.exxonmobil.com/community

FOUNDED: 1998

AREAS OF INTEREST:
Environment, public information and policy research, higher education and pre-college education, health, minority and women-oriented service organizations.

CONSULTING OR VOLUNTEER SERVICES:
The corporation encourages its employees and annuitants to volunteer at nonprofit agencies which serve their local communities with Volunteer Involvement Fund (VIF) grants of up to $500 each.

TYPE:
Capital grants; General operating grants; Matching gifts; Project/program grants.

YEAR PROGRAM STARTED: 1998

PURPOSE:
To provide funding to worthwhile organizations with interests that mirror those of the company.

LEGAL BASIS:
Corporate contributions program.

ELIGIBILITY:
Exxon Mobil makes grants to organizations which have tax-deductible status under Section 501(c)(3) of the Internal Revenue

Code. In general, Exxon Mobil contributes to organizations and activities which are national or international in scope or significance and to local agencies only in geographic areas where there is a significant concentration of Exxon Mobil employees or facilities.

Exxon Mobil does not provide funds to be used for religious or political purposes or to individuals. Generally excluded from the grants program are contributions to endowments, organizations formed to combat a single disease and operating support to agencies funded by United Way. Exxon Mobil does not seek, and rarely funds, unsolicited applications and project proposals.

GEOG. RESTRICTIONS: Baldwin and Mobile counties, Alabama; Anchorage, Fairbanks, Juneau and North Slope, Alaska; Santa Barbara County and Torrance, California; District of Columbia; Joliet and vicinity, Illinois; Kingman and Stevens County, Kansas; Baton Rouge, Chalmette, Louisiana; Billings, Montana; Clinton and Paulsboro, New Jersey; Lea County, New Mexico; Akron, Ohio; Texas County, Oklahoma; Baytown, Beaumont, Dallas/Fort Worth, Houston and vicinity, Midland/Odessa and Tyler/Longview, Texas; San Juan County, Utah; northern Virginia; Lincoln, Sublette and Sweetwater counties, Wyoming.

FINANCIAL DATA:
Amount of support per award: Varies.

APPLICATION INFO:
Exxon Mobil does not seek, and rarely funds, unsolicited applications and project proposals.

PUBLICATIONS:
Annual report.

ADDRESS INQUIRIES TO:
Kevin Murphy
Manager, Corporate Citizenship
(See address above.)

FAIRFIELD COUNTY'S COMMUNITY FOUNDATION [119]

383 Main Avenue
Norwalk, CT 06851
(203) 750-3200
Fax: (203) 750-3232
E-mail: info@fccfoundation.org
Web Site: www.fccfoundation.org

FOUNDED: 1992

AREAS OF INTEREST:
Community development, housing, education, youth development, health and human services, and arts and culture.

NAME(S) OF PROGRAMS:
- **Competitive Grantmaking Program**

TYPE:
General operating grants; Project/program grants. Capacity building grants. Scholarships are for high school students pursuing college or postsecondary training.

YEAR PROGRAM STARTED: 1992

PURPOSE:
To promote philanthropy as a means to create change in Fairfield County, CT, focusing on innovative and collaborative solutions to critical issues impacting the community.

ELIGIBILITY:
Grants are made to organizations that have tax-exempt status under Section 501(c)(3) of the Internal Revenue Code. No grants are made to individuals.

Competitive grants are awarded to nonprofit organizations benefitting residents of Fairfield County, CT.

Discretionary grants are only made to organizations serving Fairfield County, CT.

Donor-advised grants can be awarded to nonprofits throughout the U.S. and also abroad.

FINANCIAL DATA:
Assets over $179,700,000 for the year ended June 30, 2014.

Amount of support per award: Grants vary in amount, depending upon the needs and nature of the request.

Total amount of support: $12,000,000 in grants for fiscal year 2014.

NO. AWARDS: 119 competitive grants awarded for fiscal year 2014.

APPLICATION INFO:
Application information is available on the web site.

Duration: One year. Renewal possible.

STAFF:
Juanita T. James, President and Chief Executive Officer

ADDRESS INQUIRIES TO:
Sharon Jones, Program Assistant
E-mail: sjones@fccfoundation.org
(See address above.)

FARGO-MOORHEAD AREA FOUNDATION [120]

409 7th Street South
Fargo, ND 58103
(701) 234-0756
Fax: (701) 234-9724
E-mail: lexi@areafoundation.org
Web Site: www.areafoundation.org

FOUNDED: 1960

AREAS OF INTEREST:
Basic human needs, education, community building, arts, culture and creativity.

TYPE:
Project/program grants; Scholarships.

PURPOSE:
To encourage philanthropy; to develop a permanent endowment to assess and respond to emerging and changing community needs; to provide a permanent charitable trust to donors with varied interests and giving capacities.

ELIGIBILITY:
Must be 501(c)(3) nonprofit organization.

GEOG. RESTRICTIONS: Cass and Clay counties, Minnesota and North Dakota.

FINANCIAL DATA:
Amount of support per award: Varies per award.

Total amount of support: Approximately $2,300,000 annually.

NO. AWARDS: Varies.

APPLICATION INFO:
Organizations applying for funds are required to use the Foundation Grant Proposal Forms available online.

Duration: One year.

ADDRESS INQUIRIES TO:
Lexi Oestreich, Program Officer
(See address above.)

FIELD FOUNDATION OF ILLINOIS [121]

200 South Wacker Drive, Suite 3860
Chicago, IL 60606
(312) 831-0910
Fax: (312) 831-0961
E-mail: apennick@fieldfoundation.org
Web Site: www.fieldfoundation.org

FOUNDED: 1960

AREAS OF INTEREST:
Health, community welfare, primary and secondary education, cultural activities, conservation/environmental, and urban and community affairs.

TYPE:
Capital grants; Challenge/matching grants; General operating grants; Matching gifts; Project/program grants; Research grants; Technical assistance; Training grants. Support is available for general and capital support and special programs.

Requests from major cultural institutions for capital gifts is restricted to repairs/maintenance or replacement.

Urban affairs grants are made for programs that strengthen, unify and build urban communities' metropolitan areas or neighborhoods.

Through its grants program in primary and secondary education, the Foundation is interested in supporting individual public schools or clusters of schools in three areas:
(1) curriculum development;
(2) teaching quality and;
(3) parental involvement.

YEAR PROGRAM STARTED: 1960

PURPOSE:
To provide support for community, civic and cultural organizations in the Chicago area, enabling both new and established programs to test innovations, to expand proven strengths or to address specific, time-limited operational needs.

LEGAL BASIS:
Private foundation.

ELIGIBILITY:
Support is limited to programs primarily serving Chicago residents. Grants are made to nonprofit institutions. Grants are not made directly to individuals.

GEOG. RESTRICTIONS: Chicago, Illinois.

FINANCIAL DATA:
Amount of support per award:
Programs/projects: $10,000 to $25,000. Grants to individual schools do not exceed $20,000 a year.

Total amount of support: Approximately $3,000,000 annually.

Matching fund requirements: Only Board of Directors and staff can submit matching gift applications.

NO. MOST RECENT APPLICANTS: 282.

NO. AWARDS: 121.

APPLICATION INFO:
In order to facilitate staff review, prospective grantees must complete the Self-Certification Checklist.

Duration: One year. Project/program and capital funding: Possible renewals up to three years.

PUBLICATIONS:
Biennial reports; information brochure (including application guidelines).

IRS I.D.: 36-6059408

OFFICERS:
Lyle Logan, Chairman
Aurie A. Pennick, Executive Director and Treasurer
Sarah M. Linsley, Secretary and General Counsel

BOARD OF DIRECTORS:
Judith S. Block
Gloria Castillo
Marshall Field, V
Rita A. Fry
Stephanie Field Harris
Kym Hubbard
Philip Wayne Hummer
Jamie Field Kane
F. Oliver Nicklin
George A. Ranney, Jr.

ADDRESS INQUIRIES TO:
Operations/Grants Manager
(See address above.)

FIRMAN FUND [122]

1422 Euclid Avenue
Hanna Building, Suite 1150
Cleveland, OH 44115
(216) 303-8060
Fax: (216) 862-2737

AREAS OF INTEREST:
Medicine, education, culture, youth, welfare, conservation and community funds.

TYPE:
Capital grants; Endowments; General operating grants; Project/program grants; Research grants.

LEGAL BASIS:
Tax-exempt, private foundation.

ELIGIBILITY:
No grants are awarded to individuals. No unsolicited requests accepted.

GEOG. RESTRICTIONS: Denver, Colorado; Thomasville, Georgia and Cleveland, Ohio.

FINANCIAL DATA:
Amount of support per award: $1,000 to $250,000.

Total amount of support: Approximately $400,000 for the year 2015.

NO. AWARDS: Approximately 25.

APPLICATION INFO:
First Contact: Letter or Proposal.

Duration: Grants awarded are not to be considered on a continuing basis. Yearly renewal on request.

Deadline: Six weeks prior to the board meetings (April and November).

TRUSTEES:
Royal Firman, III, President
Stephanie Firman
Cynthia F. Webster

*PLEASE NOTE:
The Fund does not accept unsolicited requests for funds.

FIRST COMMUNITY FOUNDATION PARTNERSHIP OF PENNSYLVANIA [123]

330 Pine Street, Suite 400
Williamsport, PA 17701
(570) 321-1500
(866) 901-2372
Fax: (570) 321-6434
E-mail: FCFP@fcfpartnership.org
Web Site: www.fcfpartnership.org

FOUNDED: 1916

AREAS OF INTEREST:
Arts and culture, education, recreation and environment, health, human services, economic and community development.

CONSULTING OR VOLUNTEER SERVICES:
Estate planning seminars, grant applicant training.

NAME(S) OF PROGRAMS:
- **Ralph and Josephine Smith Fund for Northumberland County**
- **Margaret E. Waldron Memorial Fund**
- **Williamsport Lycoming Community Fund**

TYPE:
Project/program grants; Scholarships.

PURPOSE:
To improve the quality of life in Williamsport and Lycoming County, PA.

LEGAL BASIS:
Community foundation.

ELIGIBILITY:
Central and northcentral Pennsylvania qualified 501(c)(3) organizations only.

GEOG. RESTRICTIONS: Bradford, Clinton, Columbia, Lycoming, Montour, Northumberland, Potter, Snyder, Sullivan, Tioga and Union counties, Pennsylvania.

FINANCIAL DATA:
Amount of support per award: Varies.

Total amount of support: $3,398,224 for the year ended December 31, 2015.

CO-OP FUNDING PROGRAMS: Scholarships in combination with donor-advised funds.

APPLICATION INFO:
Application information is available on the web site. Application must include a copy of the IRS tax determination letter.

Duration: Typically one year.

Deadline: Varies.

PUBLICATIONS:
Annual report; grants and loans policy; *Insights in Estate and Financial Planning*; other tax and estate planning brochures.

IRS I.D.: 24-6013117

ADDRESS INQUIRIES TO:
Betty Gilmour
Director of Grantmaking
E-mail: bettyg@fcfpartnership.org

FIRSTENERGY FOUNDATION [124]

76 South Main Street
Akron, OH 44308-1890
(330) 384-5022
Web Site: www.firstenergycorp.com/community/firstenergy_foundation.html

FOUNDED: 1961

AREAS OF INTEREST:
Principally education, the arts, community improvements, professional development and literacy, and overall health of the community.

TYPE:
Capital grants; General operating grants; Matching gifts; Project/program grants.

PURPOSE:
To improve the vitality of our communities and support key safety initiatives; to promote local and regional economic development and revitalization efforts; to support FirstEnergy employees' community leadership and volunteer interests; to advance an educated workforce by supporting professional development and literacy, and science, technology, engineering and mathematics education initiatives.

LEGAL BASIS:
Corporate foundation.

ELIGIBILITY:
The Foundation supports nonprofit, tax-exempt organizations within the FirstEnergy operating companies' service area including Ohio Edison, The Illuminating Company and Toledo Edison in Ohio; Met-Ed, Penelec, Penn Power and West Penn Power in Pennsylvania; Jersey Central Power and Light in New Jersey; Mon Power and Potomac Edison in West Virginia and Maryland; and where FirstEnergy Solutions Corp., FirstEnergy Generation and FirstEnergy Nuclear Operations conduct business.

Generally, no grants are made to individuals or for political organizations, endowment funds, deficit financing, research, scholarships or fellowships. No loans.

FINANCIAL DATA:
Amount of support per award: Grants vary in amount, depending upon the needs and nature of the request.

Matching fund requirements: Employees only.

NO. AWARDS: Varies.

APPLICATION INFO:
The Foundation does not accept unsolicited grant applications. Applicants are encouraged to discuss grant inquiries with the local management of FirstEnergy companies and the staff of FirstEnergy's Community Involvement Department.

ADDRESS INQUIRIES TO:
Dee Lowery, President
(See address above.)

*SPECIAL STIPULATIONS:
Unsolicited grant applications are not accepted.

A.J. FLETCHER FOUNDATION [125]

909 Glenwood Avenue
Raleigh, NC 27605
(919) 322-2580
Fax: (919) 322-2581
E-mail: natalie@ajf.org
contact@ajf.org
Web Site: ajf.org

AREAS OF INTEREST:
Artistic endeavors, education, elderly, infirm and indigent, media and communication, public recreation, and religious faith.

TYPE:
General operating grants; Project/program grants.

PURPOSE:
To support nonprofit organizations in their endeavors to improve the quality of life in North Carolina.

ELIGIBILITY:
Eligible organizations must be IRS 501(c)(3) tax-exempt.

GEOG. RESTRICTIONS: North Carolina.

FINANCIAL DATA:
Amount of support per award: Varies.
Total amount of support: Varies.

APPLICATION INFO:
Applications for funding are by request only.
Duration: One-time to multiyear funding.

ADDRESS INQUIRIES TO:
Natalie Fogg, Director of Operations and Grants Administration
(See address above.)

THE FLINN FOUNDATION [126]

1802 North Central Avenue
Phoenix, AZ 85004
(602) 744-6800
Fax: (602) 744-6815
E-mail: info@flinn.org
Web Site: www.flinn.org

FOUNDED: 1965

AREAS OF INTEREST:
Biosciences, education, arts and culture, and civic leadership in Arizona.

NAME(S) OF PROGRAMS:
- **Arizona Center for Civic Leadership**
- **Flinn Scholars Program**

TYPE:
Demonstration grants; Fellowships; Project/program grants; Scholarships; Seed money grants. The arts and culture grants program assists Arizona's large arts and culture organizations in generating capital through creative programming and fiscal planning.

The Foundation's biosciences grant projects aim to strengthen Arizona's biosciences infrastructure and thereby improve the state's capacity to compete nationally and internationally in the biosciences economy.

The Arizona Center for Civic Leadership seeks to strengthen civic leadership in Arizona.

The Flinn Scholars Program annually awards top Arizona high school graduates full scholarship support.

YEAR PROGRAM STARTED: 1981

PURPOSE:
To improve the quality of life in Arizona to benefit future generations through support of the biosciences, arts and culture, the Flinn Scholars and civic leadership.

LEGAL BASIS:
Tax-exempt private foundation.

ELIGIBILITY:
Grant applicants must be tax-exempt, nonprofit organizations which have qualified for exemption under Section 501(c)(3) of the IRS code and, generally, are not those classified as private foundations.

Grants are made only for charitable purposes that support organizations and activities in Arizona. The Foundation generally does not make grants to support individuals, building and equipment projects, endowment or annual fund-raising campaigns or to meet ongoing operating costs or deficits.

GEOG. RESTRICTIONS: Arizona.

FINANCIAL DATA:
Foundation assets of approximately $220,000,000.
Amount of support per award: Varies.
Total amount of support: Varies.

CO-OP FUNDING PROGRAMS: The Flinn-Brown Civic Leadership Academy, a component of the Arizona Center for Civic Leadership, is co-funded by the Thomas R. Brown Foundations.

NO. AWARDS: Flinn Scholars: Approximately 20 annually.

REPRESENTATIVE AWARDS:
$504,000 to Arizona State University for Flinn Scholarship awards; $1,500,000 to Translational Genomics Research Institute for support of three genomic-based research projects in collaboration with Arizona institutions; $100,000 to Mesa Arts Center to choose and expand programming that connects to the Center's audiences and donors under age 40.

APPLICATION INFO:
No unsolicited applications accepted. There is no standard application form, except for those proposals submitted in response to a Foundation-initiated program.
Duration: Varies.

PUBLICATIONS:
Annual report; special reports; electronic newsletters.

ADMINISTRATIVE STAFF:
Jack B. Jewett, President and Chief Executive Officer
Bradley W. Halvorsen, Executive Vice President
William A. Read, Ph.D., Senior Vice President, Research and Special Programs
Stacy L. Tucker, Vice President and Chief Financial Officer
Nancy Welch, Vice President, Arizona Center for Civic Leadership
Matt Ellsworth, Vice President, Communications

*SPECIAL STIPULATIONS:
No unsolicited applications accepted.

THE FORD FOUNDATION [127]

320 East 43rd Street
New York, NY 10017
(212) 573-5000
Fax: (212) 351-3677
E-mail: office-secretary@fordfoundation.org
Web Site: www.fordfoundation.org

FOUNDED: 1936

NAME(S) OF PROGRAMS:
- **Civic Engagement and Government Program**
- **Equitable Development Program**
- **Free Expression and Creativity Program**
- **Gender, Racial and Ethnic Justice Program**
- **Inclusive Economies Program**
- **Internet Freedom Program**
- **Youth Opportunity and Learning Program**

TYPE:
Conferences/seminars; Endowments; Fellowships; General operating grants; Matching gifts; Project/program grants; Research grants; Seed money grants; Technical assistance. General purposes, publications, program-related investments, special projects, individual grants.

Civic Engagement and Government Program deals with the issues of expanding participation, engaging government and equitable resources.

Equitable Development Program deals with the issues of just cities and regions and natural resources and climate change.

Free Expression and Creativity Program deals with the issues of social justice storytelling and 21st century arts infrastructure.

Gender, Racial and Ethnic Justice Program deals with the issues of freedom and dignity and rights of women and girls.

Inclusive Economies Program deals with the issues of quality work, economic security and impact investing.

Internet Freedom Program deals with the issues of digital rights and access and tecnology for the public interest.

Youth Opportunity and Learning Program deals with the issues of pathways for youth success and next generation leadership.

PURPOSE:
To reduce poverty and injustice and to promote democratic values, free expression and human achievement.

LEGAL BASIS:
Private foundation.

ELIGIBILITY:
Qualified institutions, individuals and communities with appropriate interests are eligible to apply. Most of the Foundation's grant funds are given to organizations. Although the Foundation also makes grants to individuals, such grants are few in number relative to demand. These are limited to research, training and other activities related to the Foundation's program interests and subject to certain limitations and procedural requirements under the U.S. Internal Revenue Code.

The Foundation does not award undergraduate scholarships or make grants for purely personal or local needs. Support for graduate fellowships is generally funneled through grants to universities and other organizations, which are responsible for the selection of recipients. Support is not normally given for routine operating costs of institutions or for religious activities. Except in rare cases, funding is not available for the construction or maintenance of buildings.

FINANCIAL DATA:
Amount of support per award: Grants vary in amount, depending upon the needs and nature of the request. Average grant to organizations: $230,000.
Total amount of support: $609,127,646 total grants, program-related investments and Foundation-administered projects for fiscal year ended December 31, 2015.

NO. MOST RECENT APPLICANTS: Approximately 40,000 grant proposals annually.

NO. AWARDS: 1,565 grants for the year 2015.

APPLICATION INFO:
Prospective applicants should, as a first step, submit a brief letter of inquiry in order to determine whether the Foundation's present interests and funds permit consideration as a proposal.

There is no application form. Proposals should set forth objectives, the proposed program for pursuing objectives, qualifications of persons engaged in the

work, a detailed budget, present means of support and status of applications to other funding sources and legal and tax status.

Duration: Varies.

Deadline: Applications are considered throughout the year.

PUBLICATIONS:
Annual report; program policy statement including application guidelines; *Ford Foundation Report*, issued quarterly.

IRS I.D.: 13-1684331

OFFICERS:
Darren Walker, President
John W. Bernstein, Vice President, Treasurer and Chief Operating Officer
Kenneth T. Monteiro, Vice President, Secretary and General Counsel
Eric W. Doppstadt, Vice President and Chief Investment Officer
Martin Abregu, Vice President, Democracy, Rights and Justice
Xavier de Souza Briggs, Vice President, Economic Opportunity and Markets
Hilary Pennington, Vice President, Education, Creativity and Free Expression
Alfred Ironside, Vice President, Global Communications
Samantha Gilbert, Vice President, Talent and Human Resources

BOARD OF TRUSTEES:
Kofi Appenteng, Chairperson of the Board
Tim Berners-Lee
Ursula Burns
Francisco G. Cigarroa
Martin Eakes
Amy C. Falls
Irene Hirano Inouye
J. Clifford Hudson
Lourdes Lopez
Thurgood Marshall, Jr.
Paula Moreno
N.R. Narayana Murthy
Peter A. Nadosy
Cecile Richards
Darren Walker

ADDRESS INQUIRIES TO:
Office of the Secretary
(See address above.)

FORD MOTOR COMPANY FUND AND COMMUNITY SERVICES [128]

One American Road
Dearborn, MI 48126-2798
(888) 313-0102
E-mail: fordfund@ford.com
Web Site: corporate.ford.com/company/community.html

FOUNDED: 1949

AREAS OF INTEREST:
Education, community development and auto-related safety.

NAME(S) OF PROGRAMS:
- **Community Grants Program**

TYPE:
Capital grants; Project/program grants; Scholarships. Support largely for education, including basic research grants, community funds and urban affairs, and civic and cultural programs.

PURPOSE:
To support initiatives and institutions that enhance and/or improve opportunities for those who live in communities where Ford Motor Company operates.

LEGAL BASIS:
Corporate foundation.

ELIGIBILITY:
No grants are made directly to individuals. Not-for-profit organizations with 501(c)(3) tax-exempt status may apply.

GEOG. RESTRICTIONS: United States.

FINANCIAL DATA:
Amount of support per award: Varies.

Total amount of support: Varies.

APPLICATION INFO:
Application form is available online. Paper applications are not accepted.

Duration: Varies.

Deadline: Requests for support are accepted and reviewed throughout the year.

ADDRESS INQUIRIES TO:
Jim Vella, President
(See address above.)

FREEMAN FOUNDATION [129]

c/o The Rockefeller Trust Company, N.A.
10 Rockefeller Plaza, Third Floor
New York, NY 10020
(212) 549-5270
Fax: (212) 549-5519

FOUNDED: 1993

AREAS OF INTEREST:
Asian studies, environmental conservation and preservation, and Hawaii and Vermont programs.

TYPE:
Challenge/matching grants; Exchange programs; Fellowships; General operating grants; Professorships; Project/program grants; Research grants; Scholarships; Seed money grants; Technical assistance; Training grants; Travel grants; Visiting scholars.

PURPOSE:
To support a range of charitable organizations; to strengthen the bonds of friendship between the U.S. and the countries of East Asia; to preserve and protect the forests, lands and natural resources of the U.S. for future generations; to contribute to and enhance the development of a vibrant, international free enterprise system.

ELIGIBILITY:
Eligible organizations must be IRS 501(c)(3) tax-exempt.

GEOG. RESTRICTIONS: Hawaii, Vermont and Asia.

FINANCIAL DATA:
Foundation grants since inception now total over $800,000,000.

Amount of support per award: Generally, $5,000 to $750,000.

Total amount of support: $15,000,000 in total grants for 2017.

APPLICATION INFO:
Letters of Inquiry: Applicants should submit a letter describing the program and financial needs.

A grant proposal should:
(1) include a cover letter for the grant request;
(2) provide a brief history of one's organization, its mission and leadership;
(3) provide financial information for the most recent fiscal year as well as financials for the next fiscal year, if available, and;
(4) provide a list of current funding sources, including amounts.

Six sets of the proposal should be mailed. Two of the six sets should include the organization's IRS Form 990, the IRS 501(c)(3) determination letter and the most recent audit. The length of the proposal, including cover letter and project budget sheet, should not exceed six pages.

Mail proposals to Mr. Graeme Freeman; President; The Freeman Foundation; 1601 East-West Road; Honolulu, HI 96848-1601.

Duration: Varies by the program. Renewal possible.

Deadline: Applications must be received at least one month prior to Trustees' meetings, which occur three times yearly.

PUBLICATIONS:
Annual report.

IRS I.D.: 13-2965090

TRUSTEES AND OFFICERS:
Graeme Freeman, President
David Stack, Trustee
George Tsandikos, Trustee

ADDRESS INQUIRIES TO:
The Rockefeller Trust Company
George S. Tsandikos, Managing Director
(See address above.)

FREEPORT-MCMORAN COPPER & GOLD FOUNDATION [130]

333 North Central Avenue
Phoenix, AZ 85004
(602) 366-8018
(602) 366-8100
Fax: (602) 366-7368
E-mail: foundation@fmi.com
communitydevelopment@fmi.com
Web Site: www.fcx.com
www.freeportinmycommunity.com

FOUNDED: 1953

AREAS OF INTEREST:
Community safety, health and wellness, environment, cultural preservation and the arts, economic development, and education and training.

NAME(S) OF PROGRAMS:
- **Matching Gifts Program**
- **Social Investment Program**

TYPE:
Matching gifts; Project/program grants.

YEAR PROGRAM STARTED: 1932

PURPOSE:
To serve as a catalyst of positive change in the communities where the company has major facilities and update the quality of life.

LEGAL BASIS:
Corporate foundation.

ELIGIBILITY:
Nonprofit programs and organizations aligned with the core values of the company. Must be located in communities where the company has a presence.

GEOG. RESTRICTIONS: United States.

FINANCIAL DATA:
Amount of support per award: Varies.

Matching fund requirements: Minimum $25. First $500 is matched 2:1; above $500 is matched dollar-for-dollar.

APPLICATION INFO:
Guidelines and application are available on the Foundation web site.

Duration: One year. Renewable.

Deadline: Proposals are accepted throughout the year. Social Investment Program: August 30 for grant award the following year.

OFFICERS:
Tracy Bame, Director of Social Responsibility and Community Development

ADDRESS INQUIRIES TO:
Contributions Administrator
(See address above.)

FREY FOUNDATION [131]

40 Pearl Street, N.W.
Suite 1100
Grand Rapids, MI 49503-3028
(616) 451-0303
Fax: (616) 451-8481
E-mail: contact@freyfdn.org
Web Site: www.freyfdn.org

FOUNDED: 1974

AREAS OF INTEREST:
Children and their families, environment, community arts, civic progress, and philanthropy.

NAME(S) OF PROGRAMS:
- **Building Community**
- **Enhancing the Lives of Children and Their Families**
- **Nurturing Community Arts**
- **Protecting the Environment**

TYPE:
Capital grants; Demonstration grants; Project/program grants; Seed money grants; Technical assistance. Grants are available for special one-time only or time-limited purposes, such as "start-up" or program expansion, demonstration projects, planning or other forms of technical assistance, evaluation, advocacy, and applied research. Capital is available in some program areas.

YEAR PROGRAM STARTED: 1974

PURPOSE:
To promote healthy development of children and their families, particularly infants and children under the age of six and their parents, with special attention to traditionally disadvantaged populations; to protect, preserve and improve the ecological health of natural resources; to stimulate vitality, effectiveness and growth of community-based arts; to encourage civic action to improve the livability of cities and communities; to improve the effectiveness of organized philanthropy and stimulate its growth.

LEGAL BASIS:
Private family foundation.

ELIGIBILITY:
Applicants must be public institutions and 501(c)(3) nonprofit organizations. No grants to individuals, endowment funds, debt retirement, general operating expenses, scholarships, travel, to cover routine, current or emergency expenses and/or sectarian charitable activities.

GEOG. RESTRICTIONS: Charlevoix, Emmet or Kent counties and lower western Michigan.

FINANCIAL DATA:
Amount of support per award: Varies upon nature of request.

Total amount of support: Over $5,000,000 for the year 2017.

NO. AWARDS: Approximately 85 per year.

APPLICATION INFO:
Applicants must submit a brief inquiry using the online system.

Duration: One year.

Deadline: February 15, May 15, August 15 and November 15.

PUBLICATIONS:
Annual report; *Taking Care of Civic Business*; *Charting the Course; Today's Winners, Tomorrow's Losers.*

STAFF:
Steve Wilson, President
Randy A. VanAntwerp, Director of Financial Operations
Lynne J. Ferrell, Program Officer
Jill M. May, Program Officer
Teresa J. Crawford, Grants Manager

BOARD OF TRUSTEES:
David G. Frey, Chairman
John M. Frey, Vice Chairman
Edward J. Frey, Jr., Secretary, Treasurer and Trustee

ADDRESS INQUIRIES TO:
Steve Wilson, President
(See address above.)

THE FROST FOUNDATION, LTD. [132]

511 Armijo Street, Suite A
Santa Fe, NM 87501
(505) 986-0208
Fax: (505) 986-0430
E-mail: frost0729@aol.com
info@frostfound.org
Web Site: www.frostfound.org

FOUNDED: 1959

AREAS OF INTEREST:
Social service and humanitarian needs, the environment and education.

CONSULTING OR VOLUNTEER SERVICES:
Professional services of staff are offered for special projects.

TYPE:
Challenge/matching grants; Project/program grants; Research grants; Seed money grants.

YEAR PROGRAM STARTED: 1959

PURPOSE:
To seek and assist innovative projects that will have positive impact beyond the boundaries of a single state.

LEGAL BASIS:
Tax-exempt private foundation.

ELIGIBILITY:
The Foundation encourages self-reliance, creativity and ingenuity on the part of prospective recipients.

Its efforts are directed primarily to support exemplary organizations and programs which can generate positive change beyond traditional boundaries, to encourage creativity which recognizes emerging needs, and to assist innovation which addresses current urgent problems.

Within these parameters, it provides initial impetus to exemplary organizations and programs, to operating funds, to pioneering organizations and programs which other institutions might similarly use, and to programs which have potential for wider service or educational exposure than an individual community.

The Foundation encourages collaborations, mergers and the formation of alliances among agencies within the community to reduce duplication of effort and to promote a maximum effective use of funds. The Foundation also considers requests for operating. It is prepared to review applications of human service needs, environmental and education programs in New Mexico and Louisiana from organizations which have an IRS 501(c)(3) determination.

GEOG. RESTRICTIONS: Louisiana and New Mexico.

FINANCIAL DATA:
Amount of support per award: $15,000 average.

Total amount of support: Approximately $2,000,000 annually.

NO. MOST RECENT APPLICANTS: Approximately 500.

NO. AWARDS: Approximately 65.

APPLICATION INFO:
A brief description of the institution/organization, including its mission, must be submitted along with evidence of tax-exempt status, the amount requested, a statement of the specific need(s) to be met by the project, a budget projection with the time frame expected and the qualifications of the staff members selected to serve the project. Faxed summaries are not accepted.

Duration: Typically one year. On rare occasions, because of special circumstances, grants will be renewed.

Deadline: December 1 for March Board meeting and June 1 for September Board meeting.

PUBLICATIONS:
Annual report; application guidelines.

OFFICERS:
Mary Amelia Whited-Howell, President
Philip B. Howell, Executive Vice-President
Taylor F. Moore, Secretary/Treasurer

BOARD OF DIRECTORS:
Ann Rogers Gerber
Philip B. Howell
Taylor F. Moore
Mary Amelia Whited-Howell

EXECUTIVE COMMITTEE:
Philip B. Howell
Mary Amelia Whited-Howell

ADDRESS INQUIRIES TO:
Mary Amelia Whited-Howell, President
(See address above.)

LLOYD A. FRY FOUNDATION [133]

120 South LaSalle Street
Suite 1950
Chicago, IL 60603
(312) 580-0310
Fax: (312) 580-0980
E-mail: usong@fryfoundation.org
Web Site: www.fryfoundation.org

FOUNDED: 1983

AREAS OF INTEREST:
Education, arts and culture education, access to health care, and employment, with special emphasis on support of inner-city projects.

TYPE:
Project/program grants.

LEGAL BASIS:
Private foundation.

ELIGIBILITY:
501(c)(3).

GEOG. RESTRICTIONS: Inner-city Chicago, Illinois.

FINANCIAL DATA:
Amount of support per award: $15,000 to $50,000 average.

Total amount of support: $7,000,755 in total grants and awards for fiscal year 2015.

APPLICATION INFO:
Application guidelines are available at the Foundation web site.

Duration: One year.

Deadline: Arts Learning: June 1, September 1 and March 1. Education: June 1, December 1 and March 1. Employment: June 1, September 1 and December 1. Health: September 1, December 1 and March 1.

PUBLICATIONS:
Annual report.

IRS I.D.: 36-6108775

STAFF:
Unmi Song, President
Diane Sotiros, C.P.A., Controller
Soo Na, Senior Program Officer, Health
Nicole Woodard-Iliev, Program Officer, Education
Jennifer Miller Rehfeldt, Program Officer, Employment
Jessica Leggin, Program Assistant
Jennifer Moss, Program Assistant

ADDRESS INQUIRIES TO:
Ms. Unmi Song, President
E-mail: applications@fryfoundation.org
(See address above.)

GANNETT FOUNDATION [134]

7950 Jones Branch Drive
McLean, VA 22107-0150
(703) 854-6047
(703) 854-6000
Fax: (703) 854-2167
E-mail: gannettfoundation@gannett.com
Web Site: www.gannettfoundation.org

FOUNDED: 1991

AREAS OF INTEREST:
Education and neighborhood improvement, economic development, youth development, community problem-solving, assistance to disadvantaged people, environmental conservation and cultural enrichment.

TYPE:
General operating grants; Matching gifts; Project/program grants.

PURPOSE:
To improve the education, health and advancement of the people who live in Gannett communities.

LEGAL BASIS:
Corporate foundation.

ELIGIBILITY:
Local organizations determined by the IRS to be tax-exempt under 501(c)(3) in communities where the Gannett Company, Inc. owns a daily newspaper or broadcast station.

FINANCIAL DATA:
Amount of support per award: Average $1,000 to $5,000.

Total amount of support: $4,500,000 in grants for the year 2015.

Matching fund requirements: Gifts for programs or initiatives where the primary purpose is the promotion of religious doctrine or tenets are excluded.

NO. AWARDS: 1,200.

APPLICATION INFO:
Application form and guidelines are available online.

Duration: One year. Renewal possible.

ADDRESS INQUIRIES TO:
Meg Kennedy, Program Administrator
(See address above.)

GATX CORPORATION [135]

222 West Adams Street
Chicago, IL 60606
(312) 621-6200
Fax: (312) 621-6648
E-mail: community@gatx.com
contactgatx@gatx.com
Web Site: www.gatx.com

FOUNDED: 1898

AREAS OF INTEREST:
Education, family and environment, cultural, health care, and social service issues.

NAME(S) OF PROGRAMS:

- **Dollars-for-Doers**
- **Employee Matching Gifts**

TYPE:
Challenge/matching grants; Development grants; General operating grants; Grants-in-aid; Internships; Matching gifts; Project/program grants; Seed money grants; Technical assistance. United Way support, employee matching gift program for 501(c)(3) organizations, education, family issues, and environment.

YEAR PROGRAM STARTED: 1953

PURPOSE:
To improve communities by proactively supporting significant issues relevant to the economic viability of the Corporation's local communities through initiatives that are consistent with the Corporation's business interests.

LEGAL BASIS:
Corporate contributions program.

ELIGIBILITY:
Applicants must be nonprofit tax-exempt organizations with a 501(c)(3) tax-exempt status. The Corporation will not fund individuals, political or religious organizations, foundations, capital campaigns or endowment funds.

GEOG. RESTRICTIONS: Chicago neighborhoods of Englewood, Grand Boulevard and Humboldt Park.

FINANCIAL DATA:
Matching fund requirements: $50 minimum and $2,000 maximum per employee and calendar year.

NO. MOST RECENT APPLICANTS: 295.

NO. AWARDS: 75.

REPRESENTATIVE AWARDS:
Education: $20,000 to Chicago Communities in Schools; $53,000 to Waterford Institute; Families: $14,600 to the Robert Crown Center for Health Education; Environment: $25,000 to Wildlife Habitat Council.

APPLICATION INFO:
All applicants must use the Chicago Area Grant Application. A complete application includes the following materials:
(1) Chicago Area Grant Application (CAGA);
(2) application narrative as described in the CAGA;
(3) itemized budget for the project;
(4) itemized organizational budget for the current fiscal year;
(5) audited financial statement for the most recently completed fiscal year;
(6) brief biographies of key organizational staff, including job description and professional qualifications;
(7) list of institutional funding for the current fiscal year, including amounts;
(8) a list of members of the board of directors, including affiliations;
(9) annual report for the most recently completed fiscal year, if available, and;
(10) IRS tax determination letter indicating the applicant's status as a 501(c)(3) nonprofit organization or equivalent.

Duration: One year. Renewals are possible after formal request has been received.

Deadline: January 15, April 15, July 15 and October 15. Announcement approximately three weeks after committee meeting.

PUBLICATIONS:
Application guidelines; grant application form.

THE CARL GELLERT AND CELIA BERTA GELLERT FOUNDATION [136]

2171 Junipero Serra Boulevard, Suite 310
Daly City, CA 94014
(650) 985-2080
Fax: (650) 985-2084
E-mail: info@gellertfoundation.org
Web Site: www.gellertfoundation.org

FOUNDED: 1958

AREAS OF INTEREST:
Religious, charitable, scientific, literary or educational purposes.

TYPE:
Capital grants; Development grants; Endowments; General operating grants; Project/program grants; Scholarships; Technical assistance.

YEAR PROGRAM STARTED: 1958

LEGAL BASIS:
Private foundation.

ELIGIBILITY:
Grants are available for nonprofit tax-exempt organizations which are not private foundations, that have and can prove 501(c)(3) and 509(a)170(b) status. No grants to individuals.

GEOG. RESTRICTIONS: Alameda, Contra Costa, Marin, Napa, San Francisco, San Mateo, Santa Clara, Solano and Sonoma, the nine counties of the Greater San Francisco Bay area, California.

FINANCIAL DATA:
Amount of support per award: Varies.

APPLICATION INFO:
Application information can be found at the Foundation's web site. Application must be submitted online.

Deadline: August 15, annually or following Monday if 15th falls on a weekend.

IRS I.D.: 94-6062858

DIRECTORS:
Carol Conroy
Andrew A. Cresci
Jack Fitzpatrick
Kevin Flynn
Robert J. Grassilli, Jr.

Michael J. King
J. Malcolm Visbal
Christine Whelan

ADDRESS INQUIRIES TO:
Jack Fitzpatrick, Executive Director
(See address above.)

THE FRED GELLERT FAMILY FOUNDATION [137]

1038 Redwood Highway
Building B, Suite 2
Mill Valley, CA 94941
(415) 381-7570
Fax: (415) 381-8526
E-mail: FGFamilyFoundation@gmail.com
Web Site: www.FGFamilyFoundation.com

FOUNDED: 1958

AREAS OF INTEREST:
Long-term sustainability planning: Environmental, advanced and specialized education, local community support through social service organizations, and reproductive health.

TYPE:
Challenge/matching grants; Endowments; Fellowships; General operating grants; Matching gifts; Professorships; Project/program grants; Research grants; Seed money grants.

YEAR PROGRAM STARTED: 1958

PURPOSE:
To advance positive forces for social change to ensure quality of life for future generations.

LEGAL BASIS:
Private family foundation.

ELIGIBILITY:
Applicants must be 501(c)(3) organizations. No grants to individuals or for purchasing development rights or land. No unsolicited grant proposals are accepted.

FINANCIAL DATA:
Amount of support per award: $500 to $40,000; Average: $5,000.

Total amount of support: $235,677 for the year 2015.

Matching fund requirements: Provide information on challenge grant.

NO. MOST RECENT APPLICANTS: Approximately 100 for the year 2014.

NO. AWARDS: Approximately 45 for the year 2015.

REPRESENTATIVE AWARDS:
$10,000 to Marin General Hospital; $5,000 to Aim High; $25,000 to Green Science Policy Institute; $1,500 to NatureBridge.

APPLICATION INFO:
The Foundation does not accept unsolicited inquiries.

Duration: Typically one year.

IRS I.D.: 94-6062859

STAFF:
Serena Lim
Patty O'Day
Heather Wyatt

*PLEASE NOTE:
Grant monies released April to October.

GENERAL SERVICE FOUNDATION [138]

557 North Mill Street
Suite 201
Aspen, CO 81611
(970) 920-6834
Fax: (970) 920-4578
E-mail: info@generalservice.org
Web Site: www.generalservice.org

FOUNDED: 1946

AREAS OF INTEREST:
Human rights and economic justice, reproductive justice, and Colorado.

NAME(S) OF PROGRAMS:
- **Colorado Program**
- **Human Rights and Economic Justice**
- **Reproductive Justice**

TYPE:
Challenge/matching grants; Demonstration grants; Development grants; General operating grants; Project/program grants; Seed money grants; Technical assistance; Travel grants. The goal of the Human Rights and Economic Justice program is to advance and strengthen human rights, democratic reform, and economic justice in Mexico.

The goal of the Reproductive Justice program is to ensure that women and girls in the U.S. have the power and resources to make healthy decisions about their bodies, sexuality and reproduction.

The goal of the Foundation's grantmaking program in Colorado is to build the capacity of key base-building organizations committed to justice and equity in the state and to facilitate collaboration among its grantees and also between its grantees and other sectors (including media, research, leadership, policy and issue-advocacy groups) to create a powerful, permanent infrastructure capable of affecting statewide policy change over the long term.

YEAR PROGRAM STARTED: 1946

PURPOSE:
To address some of the world's basic long-term problems; to bring about a more just and sustainable world; to nurture and learn from strategic partnerships, embracing risk and possibility; to align every aspect of Foundation's organization with its deeply held values which include a commitment to leadership, integrity, diversity, experimentation, accountability, justice and excellence.

LEGAL BASIS:
Private foundation, tax-exempt under IRS statute 501(c)(3).

ELIGIBILITY:
Organizations must be tax-exempt under U.S. law.

In general, the Foundation does not contribute to annual campaigns, nor to capital campaigns, to individuals or for relief.

Because the Foundation's areas of concern are broad, the Board has determined guidelines within each area. All applicants are urged only to submit applications falling within the Foundation's Contribution Policy and Guidelines.

GEOG. RESTRICTIONS: Mexico and the United States.

FINANCIAL DATA:
Amount of support per award: $2,000 to $50,000.

NO. MOST RECENT APPLICANTS: Approximately 165.

NO. AWARDS: 66.

APPLICATION INFO:
The Foundation requests that applications for contributions be in line with the approved guidelines and be submitted online.

Duration: One to two years.

Deadline: February 1 and September 1 for letters of inquiry.

IRS I.D.: 36-6018535

OFFICERS:
Robin Snidow, Board Chairperson
Zoe L. Foxley, Vice Chairperson
Griff Foxley, Treasurer
Marcie J. Musser, Secretary
William M. Repplinger, Assistant Treasurer
Sara Samuels, Assistant Secretary

DIRECTORS:
Eliot Estrin
Jesse Estrin
Mary Lloyd Estrin
Robert L. Estrin
Griff Foxley
Zoe L. Foxley
Sarita Gupta
Peter Halby
Will Halby
Silvia Henriquez
Cleo Hill
Marcie J. Musser
Robert W. Musser
Robby Rodriguez
Robin Snidow

THE GEORGE FOUNDATION [139]

215 Morton Street
Richmond, TX 77469
(281) 342-6109
Fax: (281) 341-7635
E-mail: grants@thegeorgefoundation.org
Web Site: www.thegeorgefoundation.org

FOUNDED: 1945

AREAS OF INTEREST:
Basic human needs, community enhancement, education and health.

TYPE:
General operating grants; Project/program grants; Scholarships. Preventative programs for children and families.

YEAR PROGRAM STARTED: 1947

PURPOSE:
To address critical community needs, enhance the quality of life and provide opportunities for Fort Bend County residents.

ELIGIBILITY:
An organization must:
(1) be tax-exempt under Section 501(c)(3) and further classified as a public charity under Section 509(a) of the Internal Revenue Code, or be tax-exempt under Section 170(c) of the Internal Revenue Code;
(2) provide programs or services that benefit Fort Bend County residents;
(3) meet the Foundation's funding issue areas;
(4) demonstrate the proposed activities are in response to a documented community need and;
(5) be in compliance with the Foundation on all previous grants.

No grants to individuals.

GEOG. RESTRICTIONS: Fort Bend County area, Texas.

FINANCIAL DATA:
Amount of support per award: Varies.
Total amount of support: $12,000,000.

APPLICATION INFO:
Guidelines and application are available at the web site.

Duration: One year. Reapplication must be made for additional funding.

Deadline: Letters of Inquiry are received and reviewed throughout the year. Application deadlines are January 15, April 15, July 15 and October 15.

TRUSTEES:
William Jameson
Pat McDonald
Thomas McNutt
John Null
Don Wenzel

ADDRESS INQUIRIES TO:
Quynh-Anh McMahan
(See address and e-mail above.)

GEORGIA-PACIFIC FOUNDATION [140]

133 Peachtree Street, N.E.
32nd Floor
Atlanta, GA 30303
(404) 652-4182
Fax: (404) 749-2754
Web Site: www.gp.com/company/community/foundation

FOUNDED: 1958

AREAS OF INTEREST:
Education, environment, entrepreneurship, community enrichment and employee involvement.

TYPE:
Project/program grants; Scholarships.

PURPOSE:
To fund and support community-based programs, volunteer service projects, disaster relief and other initiatives that improve the quality of life in communities where Georgia-Pacific employees live and work.

LEGAL BASIS:
Corporate foundation.

ELIGIBILITY:
Organizations must have 501(c)(3) tax-exemption status from the IRS.

The Foundation does not support organizations that discriminate on the basis of race, color, creed, national origin or gender; private organizations; "bail-out" funds given to provide emergency assistance to organizations for general operating purposes; individuals, other than through scholarship and community service programs; political causes, candidates and legislative lobbying or advocacy efforts of any type; churches or religious denominations, religious or theological schools; general operating support for United Way member agencies; operating support for colleges and universities; fund-raising events such as raffles, telethons, walk-a-thons and auctions; and for trips and tours.

FINANCIAL DATA:
Amount of support per award: Minimum $1,000.

APPLICATION INFO:
Prospective applicants must first complete the Eligibility Quiz. If their program meets the initial criteria for funding, the applicant will be invited to submit a full proposal.

Only one copy of the proposal is required. Proposals must be sent via mail. E-mails or faxes will not be accepted.

Deadline: Charitable contribution requests are reviewed on a rolling cycle. Within 60 days of receipt of the request with the appropriate documentation, the Foundation will respond with written notification as to whether the grant is accepted.

GHEENS FOUNDATION [141]

401 West Main Street
Suite 705
Louisville, KY 40202
(502) 584-4650
Fax: (502) 584-4652
E-mail: barry@gheensfoundation.org
Web Site: gheensfoundation.org

FOUNDED: 1957

AREAS OF INTEREST:
Culture, education and health.

TYPE:
Capital grants; Challenge/matching grants; Development grants; General operating grants; Project/program grants; Research grants; Scholarships; Technical assistance.

YEAR PROGRAM STARTED: 1957

PURPOSE:
To support programs that meet the needs of society and improve the quality of life in the community.

LEGAL BASIS:
501(c)(3), private foundation.

ELIGIBILITY:
Grants are made to organizations that have tax-exempt status under Section 501(c)(3) of the Internal Revenue Code. No grants are made to individuals.

GEOG. RESTRICTIONS: Louisville, Kentucky; Lafourche and Terrebone parishes in Louisiana.

FINANCIAL DATA:
Amount of support per award: Varies depending on the nature of the request.
Total amount of support: Varies.

NO. MOST RECENT APPLICANTS: 250.

NO. AWARDS: 122 for the year 2015.

APPLICATION INFO:
Application is available on the Foundation web site.

Duration: One year. May reapply.

Deadline: Prior to meetings in March, June, September and December.

ADDRESS INQUIRIES TO:
Barry G. Allen, Executive Director
(See address above.)

HERMAN GOLDMAN FOUNDATION [142]

44 Wall Street
Suite 1212
New York, NY 10005
(212) 461-2132
Fax: (212) 461-2223
E-mail: rbaron@hermangoldman.com

FOUNDED: 1942

AREAS OF INTEREST:
Arts, health, social justice and education.

TYPE:
General operating grants; Grants-in-aid; Project/program grants.

YEAR PROGRAM STARTED: 1943

PURPOSE:
To benefit those in need.

LEGAL BASIS:
Private foundation.

ELIGIBILITY:
Grants for individuals are not considered. It is not possible to respond to emergency requests, nor to financial needs of crash programs because of the time the Foundation requires to study grant proposals. Applicants must be tax-exempt organizations.

GEOG. RESTRICTIONS: Primarily, New York City metropolitan area.

FINANCIAL DATA:
Amount of support per award: $1,000 to $50,000.
Total amount of support: Varies.

APPLICATION INFO:
Applicants should submit one copy only of a written proposal and/or can use the New York-New Jersey area Common Grant Application Form. No letter of inquiry required. Applicants must provide IRS tax-exempt documentation.

Duration: One year.

Deadline: Applications accepted throughout the year.

PUBLICATIONS:
Annual report.

ADDRESS INQUIRIES TO:
Richard K. Baron, Executive Director
(See address above.)

THE GOODYEAR TIRE & RUBBER COMPANY [143]

200 Innovation Way
Akron, OH 44316-0001
(330) 796-2244
Web Site: www.goodyear.com
corporate.goodyear.com/en-US/about.htmlabout_community.html

FOUNDED: 1898

AREAS OF INTEREST:
Safety, health and human services, culture and the arts, education, civic and community improvement.

TYPE:
Project/program grants.

PURPOSE:
To promote healthy, high-functioning communities in locations where Company major plants and offices reside; to be a socially aware and responsive global citizen wherever the Company operates or does business.

LEGAL BASIS:
Corporate contributions program.

ELIGIBILITY:
Grants are made to nonprofit, tax-exempt organizations in communities where Goodyear plants and headquarters offices are located. No grants are made to individuals.

Requests are required to meet guidelines of strategic giving based on safety by focusing on safety programs plus at least one

additional category noted below and/or provide volunteer opportunities for Company associates which are appropriately aligned with Company strategy:
(1) Civic and Community and Other: Grant awards will depend on local needs and customs in the communities in which the Company operates;
(2) Culture and the Arts: Requests from organizations and institutions serving plant communities and selected national arts organizations will be considered provided they comply with the connection to safety;
(3) Education: Requests for support from colleges, universities, and other educational institutions serving the areas in which Company plants and principal offices are located must demonstrate a connection with safety and/or must be a source of subsidized educational opportunities for Company associates and their families; a limited number of private and public universities of national or regional significance whose programs are of special interest or those that provide a continuing source of associates to the Company may also receive priority and;
(4) Health and Human Services: Highest priority is given to United Way campaigns in communities where Company plants and principal offices are located; organizations receiving United Way support may not be eligible for additional funding.

A limited number of traditional grants will be honored at the Company's discretion.

FINANCIAL DATA:

Amount of support per award: Varies.

Total amount of support: Varies.

APPLICATION INFO:

Applicants should visit the web site for complete application information. Application may be made online. The following documents and information are required:
(1) the purpose, amount and community need that will be met by the request;
(2) the program's potential connection to safety for priority consideration;
(3) the geographical area and audience served by the applicant's organization and the request;
(4) a board of trustees list;
(5) a copy of the organization's 501(c)(3) IRS Letter of Determination proving tax-exempt status or equivalent;
(6) the most recent organizational financial statement and income-and-expense budget;
(7) a list of other current and projected sources of funding for the program;
(8) a breakdown, by percentage, of how grant funds are utilized by the organization (i.e., administration, services, research, etc.) and;
(9) the nature of Goodyear goods and services utilized by the organization.

Organizations in the greater Akron, OH area should send requests to the address listed above. Those located in U.S. communities where Goodyear has plants and major facilities should contact the local plant manager's office for mailing instructions.

PUBLICATIONS:

Overview.

ADDRESS INQUIRIES TO:

Community Affairs
(See address above.)

*PLEASE NOTE:

The Company does not accept grant requests by telephone. E-mail requests accepted per guidelines on web site.

W. R. GRACE FOUNDATION, INC. [144]

7500 Grace Drive
Columbia, MD 21044
(410) 531-4000
Fax: (410) 531-4233
E-mail: shirley.hewitt@grace.com
Web Site: www.grace.com

FOUNDED: 1961

AREAS OF INTEREST:

Higher education, civic, youth development, cultural programs, community funds, health and human services, and science, technology, engineering and mathematics education (STEM).

TYPE:

Challenge/matching grants; Matching gifts; Project/program grants.

YEAR PROGRAM STARTED: 1961

PURPOSE:

To provide primary support for education, particularly programs emphasizing math, sciences and chemistry.

LEGAL BASIS:

Company-sponsored foundation.

ELIGIBILITY:

Nonprofit, tax-exempt organizations with a 501(c)(3) tax-exempt status are eligible for support. The Foundation will not support individuals, political or religious organizations.

Grants to organizations in communities where W. R. Grace & Co. has significant employee population.

GEOG. RESTRICTIONS: United States and Canada.

FINANCIAL DATA:

Amount of support per award: Grants vary in amount based on the needs and nature of the request; Average: $1,000.

Total amount of support: Approximately $761,000 for the year 2013.

NO. AWARDS: Approximately 200 each year.

APPLICATION INFO:

Applications accepted online only. Complete details available at the web site.

Duration: Usually one year. Multiyear commitments possible.

Deadline: November 30.

DIRECTORS:

Mark A. Shelnitz, Chairman

ADDRESS INQUIRIES TO:

Shirley Hewitt, Deputy Executive Director
(See address above.)

GRAHAM HOLDINGS COMPANY [145]

1300 North 17th Street
Suite 1700
Arlington, VA 22209
(703) 345-6450
E-mail: pinkie.mayfield@ghco.com
Web Site: www.ghco.com

FOUNDED: 1947

AREAS OF INTEREST:

Civic and community, health and human services, education and cultural programs.

TYPE:

General operating grants. Employee Matching Gifts Program.

PURPOSE:

To support communities where Graham Holdings Company operates.

ELIGIBILITY:

Applicants must be nonprofit 501(c)(3) organizations.

GEOG. RESTRICTIONS: Metropolitan Washington, DC area.

FINANCIAL DATA:

Amount of support per award: Average $500 to $2,500.

Total amount of support: Varies.

Matching fund requirements: $25 minimum, $2,000 per year/per employee maximum. 1:1 or 1:2 for schools or where employee is an active volunteer.

REPRESENTATIVE AWARDS:

The Phillips Collection; Martha's Table; Capital Area Food Bank; Inner City-Inner Child; Northern Virginia Family Services.

APPLICATION INFO:

Send a short letter describing proposed program and budget.

Duration: One year. Renewal possible.

Deadline: Proposals are accepted on an ongoing basis.

ADDRESS INQUIRIES TO:

Pinkie Mayfield
Vice President-Corporate Affairs
Special Assistant to the Chairman
(See address above.)

PHILIP L. GRAHAM FUND [146]

c/o Graham Holdings Company
1300 North 17th Street, Suite 1700
Arlington, VA 22209
(703) 345-6515
E-mail: plgfund@ghco.com
Web Site: www.plgrahamfund.org

FOUNDED: 1963

AREAS OF INTEREST:

Primarily health and human services, education, arts and humanities, and community endeavors in the Washington, DC metropolitan area.

TYPE:

Capital grants; Project/program grants. Technology enhancement. Other infrastructure investments.

YEAR PROGRAM STARTED: 1963

PURPOSE:

To use resources for the betterment of the Washington, DC metropolitan area.

LEGAL BASIS:

General interest foundation.

ELIGIBILITY:

Applicants must be 501(c)(3) organizations located in the Washington, DC metropolitan area.

No grants to individuals, for religious or political purposes, research, conferences, travel, fund-raising, event sponsorships, hospitals or publications.

GEOG. RESTRICTIONS: Primarily Washington, DC metropolitan area.

FINANCIAL DATA:

Amount of support per award: $25,000 to $150,000. Average grant approximately $40,000.

NO. AWARDS: 86 for the year 2015.

APPLICATION INFO:
Organizations interested in applying for funding must first submit a letter of inquiry (LOI) through the online application system prior to one of the three deadlines each year.

Duration: Varies.

Deadline: Early April, August and December.

IRS I.D.: 52-6051781

TRUSTEES:

ADDRESS INQUIRIES TO:
Eileen Daly, President
(See address above.)

*PLEASE NOTE:
Proposals accepted only through the Fund web site.

GRAND RAPIDS COMMUNITY FOUNDATION [147]

185 Oakes Street, S.W.
Grand Rapids, MI 49503
(616) 454-1751
Fax: (616) 454-6455
E-mail: grfound@grfoundation.org
Web Site: www.grfoundation.org

FOUNDED: 1922

AREAS OF INTEREST:
Education, environment, engagement, health, neighborhoods and prosperity.

NAME(S) OF PROGRAMS:

- **Access Camps**

TYPE:
Capital grants; Challenge/matching grants; Demonstration grants; Development grants; Project/program grants; Scholarships; Technical assistance.

YEAR PROGRAM STARTED: 1922

PURPOSE:
To build and manage our community's permanent endowment and lead the community to strengthen the lives of its people.

LEGAL BASIS:
Nonprofit organization established by resolution and declaration of trust. Incorporated in 1989.

ELIGIBILITY:
Applicant must have a current 501(c)(3) nonprofit designation from the IRS or be a governmental organization located in Kent County and serve local residents. No grants to individuals except through the scholarship program.

GEOG. RESTRICTIONS: Grand Rapids, Michigan and surrounding communities.

FINANCIAL DATA:
Amount of support per award: General grants vary by fund; typically $2,000 to $250,000.

Total amount of support: $9,800,000 in grants authorized for fiscal year ended June 30, 2015.

NO. MOST RECENT APPLICANTS: 1,743 for the year 2013-14.

NO. AWARDS: 1,686 for the year 2013-14.

REPRESENTATIVE AWARDS:
Kent School Services Network to continue the work of a school-based program that will coordinate and deliver health and human services to students and their families.

APPLICATION INFO:
For the general fund, applicants fill out an online pre-application on the Foundation's web site. After committee review, applicants may be asked to submit a Full Proposal, with final grant disposition determined by the Board of Trustees.

Duration: Generally, one-time grants. Foundation will, under certain circumstances, award multiyear grants.

Deadline: Varies by Fund. No deadline for the General Fund; pre-applications are reviewed every two weeks.

PUBLICATIONS:
Annual report; quarterly newsletter.

IRS I.D.: 38-2877959

OFFICERS:
Paul M. Keep, Chairperson
Diana R. Sieger, President
Marilyn Zack, Vice President of Development
Lynne Black, Vice President of Finance and Administration
Roberta F. King, Vice President of Public Relations and Marketing

ADDRESS INQUIRIES TO:
Shavon Doyle-Holton, Grants Management Assistant
(See address above.)

JOHN SIMON GUGGENHEIM MEMORIAL FOUNDATION [148]

90 Park Avenue
New York, NY 10016
(212) 687-4470
Fax: (212) 697-3248
E-mail: fellowships@gf.org
Web Site: www.gf.org

FOUNDED: 1925

AREAS OF INTEREST:
Sciences, social sciences, humanities and the creative arts.

NAME(S) OF PROGRAMS:

- **Guggenheim Fellowships**

TYPE:
Fellowships.

YEAR PROGRAM STARTED: 1925

PURPOSE:
To further the development of scholars and artists by assisting them to engage in research in any field of knowledge and creation in any of the arts.

LEGAL BASIS:
Private foundation.

ELIGIBILITY:
The Fellowships are awarded to men and women who have already demonstrated exceptional capacity for productive scholarship or exceptional creative ability in the arts.

Fellowships are awarded through two annual competitions: one open to citizens and permanent residents of the U.S. and Canada, and the other open to citizens and permanent residents of Latin America and the Caribbean. The Fellowships will be awarded by the Trustees upon nominations made by a Committee of Selection.

FINANCIAL DATA:
The amounts of the grants will be adjusted to the needs of the Fellows, considering their other resources and the purpose and scope of their plans, in accord with the Foundation's annual fellowship budget.

Amount of support per award: Varies.

Total amount of support: Approximately $8,100,000 annually.

NO. AWARDS: Approximately 180 annually.

APPLICATION INFO:
Online application is available at the Foundation web site.

Duration: Appointments must be from six to 12 months. Fellows of the Foundation, until further notice from the Board of Trustees, may no longer seek renewed assistance.

Deadline: Applications must be submitted on or before September 18 for U.S. and Canadian competition. Fellowships to be announced the following April for U.S. competition. Latin American competition: December 1, with fellowship awards to be announced the following June.

PUBLICATIONS:
Annual report; announcement of Fellowship competition and recipients; application guidelines.

IRS I.D.: 13-5673173

OFFICERS:
Edward Hirsch, President
Andre Bernard, Vice President and Secretary

TRUSTEES:

ADDRESS INQUIRIES TO:
Keith Lewis, Program Officer
Fellowships Program
(See address above.)

THE GEORGE GUND FOUNDATION [149]

1845 Guildhall Building
45 Prospect Avenue West
Cleveland, OH 44115
(216) 241-3114
Fax: (216) 241-6560
E-mail: info@gundfdn.org
Web Site: www.gundfoundation.org

FOUNDED: 1952

AREAS OF INTEREST:
Education, economic development and community revitalization, human services, arts and environment.

TYPE:
General operating grants; Project/program grants.

YEAR PROGRAM STARTED: 1952

PURPOSE:
To enhance the quality of life, particularly for those living in the greater Cleveland area; to solve community problems; to improve living conditions, particularly for the poor and

underprivileged; to provide opportunities for all people to live constructive lives in a peaceful world.

LEGAL BASIS:
Private foundation.

ELIGIBILITY:
Grants are made only to nonprofit, tax-exempt educational and philanthropic organizations. No awards are made to individuals. Grants for operating budget support will be considered only if the need is for limited duration and will accomplish some important purpose which will strengthen the future position of the institution. Preference will be given to pilot projects, innovative programs and research which hold promise of significant benefits of broad applicability.

GEOG. RESTRICTIONS: Primarily greater Cleveland and Cuyahoga County, Ohio.

FINANCIAL DATA:
Amount of support per award: Varies.

Total amount of support: $7,083,637 for the year 2016.

NO. AWARDS: 58 grants for the year 2016.

APPLICATION INFO:
Foundation requires that all applications for grants be submitted online at the Foundation's web site. Application materials to be uploaded with application include:
(1) organizational background;
(2) project description;
(3) project budget;
(4) organizational budget;
(5) list of current trustees;
(6) most recent audited financial statements and;
(7) climate change statement.

Duration: One year.

Deadline: March 15, July 15 and November 15, for board meetings to be held in July, November and February, respectively.

PUBLICATIONS:
Annual report; Guidelines for Grant Applicants (on Foundation web site).

TRUSTEES:
Geoffrey Gund, President and Treasurer
Ann L. Gund, Vice President
Catherine Gund, Secretary
George Gund, IV
Lara Gund
Zachary Gund
Randell McShepard
Robyn Minter Smyers
Anna Traggio

ADMINISTRATIVE STAFF:
David T. Abbott, Executive Director
Robert B. Jaquay, Associate Director and Senior Program Officer for Economic Development and Community Revitalization
Jennifer Coleman, Senior Program Officer, Arts
Ann K. Mullin, Senior Program Officer, Education
John Mitterholzer, Senior Program Officer, Environment
Marcia Egbert, Senior Program Officer, Human Services

ADDRESS INQUIRIES TO:
David T. Abbott, Executive Director or
Cynthia Gasparro
Grants and Office Administrator
(See address above.)

HALL FAMILY FOUNDATION [150]

P.O. Box 419580
Mail Drop 323
Kansas City, MO 64141-6580
(816) 274-8516
Fax: (816) 274-8547
Web Site: www.hallfamilyfoundation.org

FOUNDED: 1943

AREAS OF INTEREST:
Early and K-12th-grade education, higher education, children, youth and families, community development, the arts, and support of community-wide efforts that seek to provide long-term solutions to high-priority local issues.

TYPE:
Capital grants; Project/program grants; Technical assistance; Training grants.

YEAR PROGRAM STARTED: 1943

PURPOSE:
To promote the health, welfare and happiness of school-age children; to promote the advancement and diffusion of knowledge; to fund activities for the improvement of public health; to advance social welfare.

ELIGIBILITY:
Applying nonprofit organizations must be 501(c)(3) and must have been in operation for at least five years. No grants are made to individuals. Grants are made to a religious organization only if its program is of a nonsectarian nature.

GEOG. RESTRICTIONS: Usually, organizations in the greater Kansas City, Missouri area.

FINANCIAL DATA:
Total assets of approximately $822,800,000 for the year 2015.

Amount of support per award: Varies.

Total amount of support: Approximately $41,700,000 for the year 2015.

APPLICATION INFO:
Prospective grant recipients should first submit a brief letter of inquiry. Those applicants whose request appears to fall within the Foundation's areas of interest and to meet its guidelines will be asked to submit a full proposal.

Duration: Two to five years, depending on the type of project.

ADDRESS INQUIRIES TO:
William A. Hall, President
(See address above.)

HANCOCK COUNTY COMMUNITY FOUNDATION

312 East Main Street
Greenfield, IN 46140
(317) 462-8870
Fax: (317) 467-3330
E-mail: mgibble@giveHCgrowHC.org
Web Site: givehcgrowhc.org

TYPE:
Project/program grants; Scholarships.

See entry 1268 for full listing.

HARDEN FOUNDATION [151]

1636 Ercia Street
Salinas, CA 93906
(831) 442-3005
Fax: (831) 443-1429
E-mail: joe@hardenfoundation.org
Web Site: www.hardenfoundation.org

FOUNDED: 1963

AREAS OF INTEREST:
Children, youth and family, senior citizens, animal welfare and the environment, agriculture, education, arts and culture, and health.

TYPE:
Capital grants; General operating grants; Project/program grants.

YEAR PROGRAM STARTED: 1963

PURPOSE:
To fund groups working in the Foundation's areas of interest.

LEGAL BASIS:
Private foundation.

ELIGIBILITY:
The Foundation does not fund schools, churches or religious activities, or individuals for endowments or fund-raising. Eligible organizations must be of a 501(c)(3), not-for-profit character.

GEOG. RESTRICTIONS: Monterey County, California.

FINANCIAL DATA:
Amount of support per award: Typically $5,000 to $100,000.

Total amount of support: $2,236,967.50 in grants awarded for the year 2013.

APPLICATION INFO:
Guidelines and application forms are available online.

Duration: Operating grants for start-up programs: Generally up to two years.

Deadline: March 1 and September 1.

ADDRESS INQUIRIES TO:
Joseph C. Grainger, Executive Director
(See address above.)

THE JOHN A. HARTFORD FOUNDATION, INC. [152]

55 East 59th Street, 16th Floor
New York, NY 10022
(212) 832-7788
Fax: (212) 593-4913
E-mail: mail@jhartfound.org
Web Site: www.jhartfound.org

FOUNDED: 1929

AREAS OF INTEREST:
Aging and health.

NAME(S) OF PROGRAMS:
- **Aging and Health Program**

TYPE:
Demonstration grants; Matching gifts; Project/program grants; Research grants; Technical assistance.

YEAR PROGRAM STARTED: 1983

PURPOSE:
To improve the care of older adults.

LEGAL BASIS:
Private foundation.

ELIGIBILITY:
Grantee organizations must be located in the U.S. and must have 501(c)(3) IRS tax-exempt designation.

The Foundation's prior grantmaking related to enhancing geriatric research and training, and integrating and improving health-related services to the elderly. Currently, the Foundation makes grants that will put geriatrics expertise to work in all health care settings by:

(1) advancing practice change and innovation;
(2) supporting team-based care through interdisciplinary education of all health care providers;
(3) supporting policies and regulations that promote better care and;
(4) developing and disseminating new, evidence-based models that deliver better, more cost-effective health care.

The Foundation awards both single and multiple-year grants. No support for general purposes, endowment funds or capital budgets.

GEOG. RESTRICTIONS: United States.

FINANCIAL DATA:
Amount of support per award: $600 to more than $2,600,000.

Total amount of support: $21,009,452 for the year 2015.

NO. MOST RECENT APPLICANTS: 102 for the year 2015.

NO. AWARDS: 45 for the year 2015.

APPLICATION INFO:
All proposals are by invitation only from one of the Foundation's program officers, the program director, or the president.

Duration: One to three years.

PUBLICATIONS:
Annual report.

TRUSTEES:
Margaret L. Wolff, Chairperson
Christopher T.H. Pell, Co-Vice Chairperson
Barbara Paul Robinson, Co-Vice Chairperson
John H. Allen
Charles A. Dana
Charles M. Farkas
Lile R. Gibbons
John R. Mach, Jr., M.D.
Audrey A. McNiff
Elizabeth A. Palmer
Earl A. Samson, III

STAFF:
Terry Fulmer, Ph.D., RN, President
Eva Cheng, Chief Financial Officer and Treasurer
Amy J. Berman, RN, Senior Program Officer
Marcus R. Escobedo, M.P.A., Senior Program Officer
Nora OBrien-Suric, Ph.D., Senior Program Officer
Rani E. Snyder, M.P.A., Program Director
Wally B. Patawaran, M.P.H., Program Officer
Ann E. Raffel, Information Technology Officer
Francisco J. Doll, M.P.A., Grants Manager and Corporate Secretary
Rutuma M. Gandhi, Accounting Manager
Melida Galvez, Junior Accountant
Julianne N. McLean, Program Secretary

ADDRESS INQUIRIES TO:
Francisco J. Doll, Grants Manager
(See address above.)

H.J. HEINZ COMPANY FOUNDATION [153]

One PPG Place, Suite 3100
Pittsburgh, PA 15222
(412) 456-5773
Web Site: www.heinz.com/sustainability/communities/heinz-foundation.aspx

FOUNDED: 1951

AREAS OF INTEREST:
Nutrition, diversity and fostering healthy communities.

CONSULTING OR VOLUNTEER SERVICES:
Employee volunteer program.

TYPE:
Matching gifts; Project/program grants.

YEAR PROGRAM STARTED: 1951

PURPOSE:
To fulfill corporate responsibility through philanthropic giving in communities with Heinz operating companies and in cities where Heinz holds a major corporate presence.

LEGAL BASIS:
Corporate foundation.

ELIGIBILITY:
All organizations seeking funding must be tax-exempt under 501(c)(3) of the Internal Revenue Code.

The Foundation does not make grants for loans or assistance to individuals, general scholarships, fellowships, travel grants, political campaigns either local or national and/or sectarian religious purposes.

FINANCIAL DATA:
Amount of support per award: Varies.

Total amount of support: Varies.

Matching fund requirements: The Foundation will match gifts in amounts of no less than $25 and no more than $5,000 for employees. A personal gift must be made to an eligible organization in the form of cash or securities and must be paid, not merely pledged. The market value of the securities will be the closing price on the day the gift was made or if there was no sale on that day, the most recently published closing price preceding the date of the gift.

The Foundation will not match payments made for services, tuition, membership dues, subscriptions, preferential seating or any type of payment not made as a direct contribution. In addition, the Foundation will not match any payment to the extent that the match would satisfy a pledge which the individual has made.

REPRESENTATIVE AWARDS:
Extra Mile Education Foundation; Make-A-Wish Foundation of Western Pennsylvania.

APPLICATION INFO:
A written project summary may be sent including the goals of the applying organization, the specific purpose for which funds are requested, how the objective will be accomplished, to whom and where the program will be offered and whether the project is a single project or one that requires additional phases. A letter of intent is recommended to approach the H.J. Heinz Company Foundation.

Duration: Mostly one year. Renewal requests are considered.

TRUSTEES:
Tammy B. Aupperle, Chairperson
Ted Bobby
Kristen Clark
Beth Eckenrode
Michael Mullen
Michael Okoroafer

ADDRESS INQUIRIES TO:
Jenece Upton, Manager
(See address above.)

HENDERSON FOUNDATION [

P.O. Box 420
Sudbury, MA 01776-0420
(978) 443-4646
Fax: (978) 443-9510
E-mail: robertahenderson@comcast.net

FOUNDED: 1947

AREAS OF INTEREST:
Charitable, educational, religious, health, political, environmental, and community outreach.

TYPE:
General operating grants.

PURPOSE:
To continue support to general operations of those organizations now supported.

LEGAL BASIS:
Nonprofit foundation.

ELIGIBILITY:
Funding limited to public charities with a nonprofit 501(c)(3) tax-exempt status. The Foundation does not support activities for which the IRS requires grantor's responsibility and reports.

GEOG. RESTRICTIONS: United States.

FINANCIAL DATA:
Amount of support per award: Minimum $500.

Total amount of support: Varies.

NO. MOST RECENT APPLICANTS: 150.

NO. AWARDS: 100.

APPLICATION INFO:
Send letter of inquiry with documentation of nonprofit 501(c)(3) tax-exempt status.

Duration: Varies.

Deadline: December 31.

TRUSTEES:
Barclay G. Henderson
Roberta Henderson
Mrs. Joseph C. Petrone

ADDRESS INQUIRIES TO:
Roberta Henderson, Trustee
(See address above.)

B. KEITH & NORMA F. HEUERMANN FOUNDATION [155]

Whitney, Newman, Mersch and Otto
1228 L Street
Aurora, NE 68818
(402) 694-3161

FOUNDED: 1994

AREAS OF INTEREST:
Children, the aged, the developmentally challenged, disabled, physically impaired, youth education and agriculturally related activities.

TYPE:
Capital grants; Matching gifts; Project/program grants; Research grants; Technical assistance.

YEAR PROGRAM STARTED: 1994

PURPOSE:
To support programs that meet the needs of society and improve the quality of life preferably in communities in rural Nebraska.

LEGAL BASIS:
Private foundation.

ganizations that have
er Section 501(c)(3) of
Code. No grants are
The Foundation does not
plicants.

GEOG. RESTRICTIONS: Rural areas in Nebraska.

FINANCIAL DATA:
Amount of support per award: $1,000 to $25,000.

Total amount of support: Varies.

APPLICATION INFO:
The Foundation does not have an application form. The Grant Proposal should identify a special need or project to which funds will be applied including the objectives to be attained, people or groups who will benefit, work plans or timetables for achieving the stated objectives, and any other means of support. A copy of the 501(c)(3) letter from the IRS should accompany the application. Provide the grant applicant's federal ID number.

Grant Proposal should be limited to two pages. Supporting documents such as project budget, other resources, names of supporters, and background information about the organization may be attached to the proposal. Stapled proposals are favored over bound ones. Brevity is appreciated.

Applicants must submit five original copies of the proposal.

Duration: Proposal may be for a project which extends over several years; however, the Foundation may review and make grants only on an annual basis.

Deadline: Proposals may be submitted at any time. The Directors convene at least three times per year at meetings to be scheduled in its discretion to review requests for grants.

PUBLICATIONS:
Guidelines.

IRS I.D.: 47-0748466

ADDRESS INQUIRIES TO:
Timothy J. Otto
(See address above.)

THE WILLIAM AND FLORA HEWLETT FOUNDATION [156]

2121 Sand Hill Road
Menlo Park, CA 94025
(650) 234-4500
Fax: (650) 234-4501
E-mail: communications@hewlett.org
Web Site: www.hewlett.org

FOUNDED: 1966

AREAS OF INTEREST:
Education, the environment, performing arts, philanthropy, and global development and population.

NAME(S) OF PROGRAMS:
- **Education**
- **Environment**
- **Global Development and Population**
- **Performing Arts**
- **Philanthropy**

TYPE:
Capital grants; Challenge/matching grants; Conferences/seminars; Development grants; Endowments; General operating grants; Project/program grants; Research grants; Seed money grants; Technical assistance; Training grants; Travel grants.

YEAR PROGRAM STARTED: 1966

PURPOSE:
To help people build measurably better lives.

LEGAL BASIS:
Private foundation.

ELIGIBILITY:
The Foundation does not fund individuals and generally does not fund scholarships, building construction, or unincorporated associations or groups.

Requirements vary by area of interest and are available on the Foundation web site.

FINANCIAL DATA:
Total assets of $9 billion as of December 31, 2015.

Amount of support per award: $555,396 average for the year 2015.

Total amount of support: $400,398,000 in grants awarded for the year ended December 31, 2015.

Matching fund requirements: Foundation matches eligible employees' contributions to qualifying organizations.

NO. AWARDS: 726 for the year 2015.

APPLICATION INFO:
Information may be obtained at the Foundation web site.

Duration: Generally, one to three years.

Deadline: Varies according to program.

PUBLICATIONS:
Annual report; application guidelines.

BOARD OF DIRECTORS:
Stephen C. Neal, Chairman
Larry Kramer, President
Mariano-Florentino Cuellar
Alecia A. DeCoudreaux
Harvey V. Fineberg
Eric Gimon
Ben V. Hewlett
Walter B. Hewlett
Patricia A. House
Koh Boon Hwee
Mary H. Jaffe
Richard C. Levin
Rakesh Rajani

ADDRESS INQUIRIES TO:
Vidya Krishnamurthy
Director of Communications
(See address above.)

CORINA HIGGINSON TRUST [157]

2001 Bryan Point Road
Accokeek, MD 20607
(301) 292-5665
Fax: (301) 292-1070
E-mail: info@corinahigginsontrust.org
Web Site: corinahigginsontrust.wordpress.com

AREAS OF INTEREST:
Education and human services.

TYPE:
General operating grants.

PURPOSE:
To improve the quality of life in the mid-Atlantic region.

ELIGIBILITY:
Eligible organizations must be IRS 501(c)(3) tax-exempt. An organization cannot be awarded more than one grant per year.

GEOG. RESTRICTIONS: Maryland, Virginia and Washington, DC.

FINANCIAL DATA:
Amount of support per award: Typically $5,000.

NO. MOST RECENT APPLICANTS: 20.

APPLICATION INFO:
Applicants must include a copy of the tax-exempt determination letter with the application.

Duration: One year.

Deadline: Spring and fall for Letters of Inquiry. Full proposals by invitation only.

ADDRESS INQUIRIES TO:
Laura Ford, Program Officer
(See address above.)

HILLSDALE FUND, INC. [158]

701 Green Valley Road, Suite 300
Greensboro, NC 27408
(336) 574-8696

FOUNDED: 1963

TYPE:
Project/program grants.

LEGAL BASIS:
Family foundation.

ELIGIBILITY:
Must have 501(c)(3) status of Internal Revenue Code to be eligible. Grants will not be made available for indirect costs or overhead as opposed to direct funding, routine, recurring operating expenses, conferences and seminars, travel and study, or individuals for any purpose.

FINANCIAL DATA:
Amount of support per award: Varies.

Total amount of support: $1,300,000 for the year 2015.

APPLICATION INFO:
Applicants should contact the Foundation for guidelines and application form.

Duration: Varies.

Deadline: Varies. Contact Fund for specific deadlines.

ADDRESS INQUIRIES TO:
Mary Scott, Executive Director
P.O. Box 20124
Greensboro, NC 27420

THE HITACHI FOUNDATION [159]

1215 17th Street, N.W.
Washington, DC 20036
(202) 457-0588
Fax: (202) 296-1098
E-mail: info@hitachifoundation.org
Web Site: www.hitachifoundation.org

FOUNDED: 1985

AREAS OF INTEREST:
Entrepreneurship and workforce development.

NAME(S) OF PROGRAMS:
- **Entrepreneurship @ Work: SOURCE**
- **Good Companies @ Work Program**

TYPE:
Project/program grants. Entrepreneurship @ Work: SOURCE links entrepreneurs and investors focused on social challenges that affect low-wealth Americans.

Good Companies @ Work program is designed to achieve integration between business actions and societal well-being.

YEAR PROGRAM STARTED: 1985

PURPOSE:
To improve the ability of individuals, institutions and communities to participate in a global society, one which manifests itself in every aspect of our lives, including environmental, economic, cultural and social.

LEGAL BASIS:
Private foundation.

ELIGIBILITY:
Grant applicants must be nonprofit 501(c)(3) organizations.

GEOG. RESTRICTIONS: United States.

FINANCIAL DATA:
Amount of support per award: Varies.
Total amount of support: Varies.

APPLICATION INFO:
Guidelines and application are available on the Foundation web site.
Duration: Varies.
Deadline: Varies.

STAFF:
Mark G. Popovich, Senior Program Officer
Katrinka Hall, Manager of Executive Operations

OFFICERS AND BOARD OF DIRECTORS:
Patrick Gross, Chairman
Barbara Dyer, President and Chief Executive Officer
Jason Baron
Sherry Salway Black
Albert Fuller
David Langstaff
Bruce MacLaury, Ph.D.
Jennifer Pryce
Kelly Ryan

ADDRESS INQUIRIES TO:
See e-mail address above.

HOBLITZELLE FOUNDATION [160]

5556 Caruth Haven Lane, Suite 200
Dallas, TX 75225
(214) 373-0462
Fax: (214) 750-7412
E-mail: pharris@hoblitzelle.org
Web Site: www.hoblitzelle.org

FOUNDED: 1942

AREAS OF INTEREST:
Education, cultural affairs, social welfare and health.

TYPE:
Capital grants; Challenge/matching grants; Matching gifts. Project grants.

YEAR PROGRAM STARTED: 1942

LEGAL BASIS:
Private foundation.

ELIGIBILITY:
Educational institutions, hospitals, community agencies, youth and other welfare programs and organizations with appropriate interests are eligible.

GEOG. RESTRICTIONS: Texas, primarily Dallas.

FINANCIAL DATA:
Amount of support per award: $25,000 to $500,000.
Total amount of support: Approximately $6,500,000 annually.

NO. MOST RECENT APPLICANTS: 600.

NO. AWARDS: 70.

REPRESENTATIVE AWARDS:
University of Texas Southwestern Medical Center; Carter Bloodcare World Affairs Council of Greater Dallas.

APPLICATION INFO:
Applications for grants should be made in writing to the Foundation. Formal oral presentations to the Board are not allowed.
Duration: One year and multiyear.
Deadline: April 15 for May meeting, August 15 for September meeting and December 15 for January meeting. If holiday or weekend, next business day.

PUBLICATIONS:
Annual report; application guidelines.

IRS I.D.: 75-6003984

OFFICERS:
William T. Solomon, Chairman
Caren H. Prothro, Vice Chairman
Paul W. Harris, President
Jere W. Thompson, Jr., Treasurer
Kathy Stone, Corporation Secretary

DIRECTORS:
Raphael M. Anchia
John Dayton
Lydia Novakov
Daniel K. Podolosky, M.D.
Karen L. Shuford
Jere W. Thompson, Jr.

ADDRESS INQUIRIES TO:
Paul W. Harris, President and Chief Executive Officer
(See address above.)

HOUSTON ENDOWMENT INC. [161]

600 Travis, Suite 6400
Houston, TX 77002-3000
(713) 238-8100
Fax: (713) 238-8102
E-mail: info@houstonendowment.org
Web Site: www.houstonendowment.org

FOUNDED: 1937

AREAS OF INTEREST:
Arts, education, environment, health and human services.

TYPE:
Capital grants; General operating grants; Project/program grants. Program support. Building completion.

LEGAL BASIS:
Private foundation.

ELIGIBILITY:
Organizations exempt under Section 501(c)(3). No grants are made directly to individuals. All scholarship funds are disbursed through recipient institutions. No grants made outside the U.S.

GEOG. RESTRICTIONS: Harris County and contiguous counties (Brazoria, Chambers, Fort Bend, Galveston, Liberty, Montgomery and Waller).

FINANCIAL DATA:
Amount of support per award: Varies.

APPLICATION INFO:
Application must be made online. Written applications will not be considered. Scholarships are never awarded directly on the basis of personal inquiry but are administered by colleges and universities.
Duration: One year to multiyear.

PUBLICATIONS:
Annual report.

MABEL Y. HUGHES CHARITABLE TRUST [162]

Wells Fargo Bank
MAC No. C7300-493
1740 Broadway
Denver, CO 80274
(720) 947-6766
Fax: (720) 947-6804
E-mail: kathy.cordova@wellsfargo.com
Web Site: www.wellsfargo.com/privatefoundationgrants/hughes

FOUNDED: 1969

AREAS OF INTEREST:
Arts, animals, environment, humanities, religion, health, education, culture and human services in the state of Colorado, with emphasis on Denver metropolitan area.

TYPE:
General operating grants; Project/program grants.

PURPOSE:
To provide funding to nonprofit and educational institutions that address vital community needs especially, but not limited to, human services.

LEGAL BASIS:
Private tax-exempt foundation.

ELIGIBILITY:
501(c)(3) tax-exempt organizations in Colorado only may apply. No grants are awarded to individuals.

GEOG. RESTRICTIONS: Colorado.

FINANCIAL DATA:
Amount of support per award: $5,000 to $25,000.
Total amount of support: Approximately $500,000 per year.

NO. MOST RECENT APPLICANTS: Approximately 300.

NO. AWARDS: 50.

APPLICATION INFO:
Submit a brief letter describing project, why needed, population to be served, brief line-item budget, information about organization seeking funds and its accomplishments to date, starting and ending dates, plans for postgrant funding and project evaluation, and a copy of latest 501(c)(3) exemption.
Duration: No grants awarded on a continuing basis.
Deadline: March 1, July 1 and November 1.

TRUSTEES:
W.R. Alexander

ADDRESS INQUIRIES TO:
Kathy Cordova
(See e-mail address above.)

THE HYDE AND WATSON FOUNDATION [163]

31-F Mountain Boulevard
Warren, NJ 07059-5617
(908) 753-3700
Fax: (908) 753-0004
E-mail: info@hydeandwatson.org
Web Site: www.hydeandwatson.org

FOUNDED: 1983

AREAS OF INTEREST:
Broad fields include education, social services, arts, health, religion and humanities.

TYPE:
Capital grants; Challenge/matching grants. The Foundation supports capital projects such as hard costs related to purchase and relocation of facilities and/or building improvements, purchase of capital equipment, and other one-time capital needs.

LEGAL BASIS:
Private.

ELIGIBILITY:
Grants are made to nonprofit organizations that have received 501(c)(3) and 509(a)(1) or 509(a)(2) status from the IRS. In general, the Foundation does not accept applications for endowment, operating support, benefit fund-raisers, annual fund appeals, or from fiscal agents.

GEOG. RESTRICTIONS: Primarily the five boroughs of New York City, and Essex, Morris and Union counties in New Jersey.

FINANCIAL DATA:
Amount of support per award: Average grant: $10,000.

Total amount of support: $4,989,650 for the year ended December 31, 2015.

NO. MOST RECENT APPLICANTS: 749 for the year 2015.

NO. AWARDS: 470 for the year 2015.

APPLICATION INFO:
Applicants must submit the following:
(1) a completed Grant Application Form; document is available at the Foundation web site;
(2) a brief narrative (no longer than three pages), signed by an authorized official, summarizing the background of the organization and constituency served, the purpose of the appeal, project total and amount requested, anticipated time frame for the project and how the equipment/capital improvement will benefit the organization;
(3) a project budget with line items, including amount raised and balance needed;
(4) an operating budget for the current fiscal year;
(5) a list of corporate and foundation supporters for the most recent fiscal year;
(6) a list of the board of directors/trustees and their business affiliations;
(7) a copy of the most recent audited financial report is strongly preferred; if not available, the most recent Form 990 will be accepted; if neither are available, call the Foundation to discuss;
(8) a copy of the organization's annual report (if available);
(9) a copy of the organization's most recent 501(c)(3) and 509(a) IRS ruling letter(s) and;
(10) written confirmation by an authorized official of one's organization that this organization is currently in compliance with all mandatory federal and state tax and filing regulations.

If one's organization is a former grantee, in accordance with current guidelines, the Foundation will not consider any future proposals from one's organization until a report is provided for any previous grants received from the Foundation. The "Grant Report Form" is available on the Foundation web site.

Appeals or inquiries submitted by e-mail will not be considered.

Duration: Typically one year.

Deadline: Applications are accepted between November 15 and February 15 for consideration at the Spring meeting, and between June 15 and September 15 for the Fall meeting. Please note that there is an ongoing review of proposals; therefore, it is strongly suggested that applicants do not wait until the deadline to submit proposals. Late appeals will likely be deferred for consideration at subsequent meetings to allow sufficient time for evaluation.

PUBLICATIONS:
Program policy statement and grant application guidelines.

IRS I.D.: 22-2425725

OFFICERS:
Hunter W. Corbin, Chairman
William V. Engel, President
Brunilda Moriarty, Executive Vice President
Thomas W. Berry, Treasurer
Hans Dekker, Secretary
John W. Holman, III, Assistant Treasurer
Maureen T. McCutcheon, Assistant Treasurer
Sarah A. Kalra, Assistant Secretary
Allison J. Pena, Assistant Secretary

DIRECTORS:
Deborah J. Barker
Thomas W. Berry
Hunter W. Corbin
Hans Dekker
William V. Engel
John W. Holman, Jr.
John W. Holman, III
Thomas H. MacCowatt
Robert W. Parsons, Jr.
Anita V. Spivey
Andrew J. Thompson
Kate B. Wood

ADDRESS INQUIRIES TO:
William V. Engel, President
(See address above.)

*PLEASE NOTE:
Appeals or inquiries submitted by e-mail will not be considered.

IDAHO COMMUNITY FOUNDATION [164]

210 West State Street
Boise, ID 83702
(208) 342-3535
Fax: (208) 342-3577
E-mail: info@idcomfdn.org
Web Site: www.idcomfdn.org

FOUNDED: 1988

AREAS OF INTEREST:
Arts, civic affairs, community, conservation, culture, education, environment, health and human services.

NAME(S) OF PROGRAMS:
- **IFFT Fund Grants**
- **Northern, Eastern and Southwestern Region Competitive Grants**
- **Perc H. Shelton and Gladys A. Pospisil Shelton Foundation Advised Fund Grants**

TYPE:
Capital grants; General operating grants; Scholarships.

YEAR PROGRAM STARTED: 1988

PURPOSE:
To enrich the quality of life throughout Idaho.

LEGAL BASIS:
Community foundation; 501(c)(3) public charity.

ELIGIBILITY:
Grants are made to organizations that are nonprofit. Nonsectarian religious programs and government entities may apply. No grants are made to individuals.

GEOG. RESTRICTIONS: Idaho.

FINANCIAL DATA:
Amount of support per award: Competitive grants to $5,000. Others unlimited.

Total amount of support: Varies.

NO. MOST RECENT APPLICANTS: 311 through competitive programs for the year 2013.

NO. AWARDS: 154 in competitive programs for the year 2013.

APPLICATION INFO:
Form can be downloaded from the Foundation web site.

Duration: Varies.

Deadline: Varies per grant or scholarship.

IRS I.D.: 82-0425063

ADMINISTRATION:
Karen Belowith, Chief Financial Officer
Elly Davis, Director of Donor Services

ADDRESS INQUIRIES TO:
Elly Davis, Director of Donor Services
(See address above.)

INDEPENDENCE FOUNDATION [165]

Offices at the Bellevue
200 South Broad Street, Suite 1101
Philadelphia, PA 19102
(215) 985-4009
Fax: (215) 985-3989
E-mail: ssherman@independencefoundation.org
Web Site: www.independencefoundation.org

FOUNDED: 1932

AREAS OF INTEREST:
Community-based care, health promotion, family planning and comprehensive health care services where issues of quality, access and cost are taken into consideration; culture, arts and legal aid and assistance to the disadvantaged; visual and performing arts.

NAME(S) OF PROGRAMS:
- **Individual Artists Fellowship/Performing and Visual Arts**
- **New Theater Works Initiative**
- **Public Interest Law Fellowships**

TYPE:
Challenge/matching grants; Fellowships; General operating grants; Project/program grants.

YEAR PROGRAM STARTED: 1993

PURPOSE:
To encourage and support health services; to have a valuable impact on the quality of health care services; to strengthen nursing education's focus on community-based care in both Philadelphia and surrounding Pennsylvania counties.

LEGAL BASIS:
Private foundation.

ELIGIBILITY:
No grants to individuals.

GEOG. RESTRICTIONS: Philadelphia and four surrounding counties of Bucks, Chester, Delaware and Montgomery.

FINANCIAL DATA:
Unaudited net assets of $73,000,000 for the year ended December 31, 2014.

Amount of support per award: Average: $3,000 to $10,000; Multiyear: Up to $50,000.

Total amount of support: $3,500,000 in unaudited grants for the year ended December 31, 2014.

Matching fund requirements: Match of contributions by individual new donors or increase in contributions by current individual donors (nongovernmental/nonfoundation funds).

NO. AWARDS: 128.

REPRESENTATIVE AWARDS:
Culture and the Arts: $5,000 to Headlong Dance Theater, Philadelphia, PA, for general operating support; Health and Human Services: $10,000 to Overbrook School for the Blind, Philadelphia, PA, for project support; Public Interest Law: $10,000 to Homeless Advocacy Project, Philadelphia, PA, for general operating support.

APPLICATION INFO:
Each year the Foundation sends out a limited number of Requests for Proposals (RFP) in each of the funding initiatives. Organizations not previously funded by the Foundation are encouraged to send a two-page Letter of Inquiry including organizational background information, amount being requested, and a description of the program/services for which the funds will be used.

Duration: Varies.

Deadline: Letters of Inquiry are accepted January 1 to January 31. Deadlines vary.

PUBLICATIONS:
Annual report; application guidelines.

IRS I.D.: 23-1352110

DIRECTORS AND OFFICERS:
Hon. Phyllis W. Beck, Chairperson
Susan E. Sherman, President and Chief Executive Officer
Andre Dennis, Esq., Vice President
Pedro A. Ramos, Esq., Director
Barton Silverman, Director
Andrea Mengel, Secretary

ADDRESS INQUIRIES TO:
Susan E. Sherman
President and Chief Executive Officer
(See address above.)

ANN JACKSON FAMILY FOUNDATION [166]

P.O. Box 5580
Santa Barbara, CA 93150-5580
(805) 455-0505
Fax: (805) 969-0315
Web Site: www.annjacksonfamilyfoundation.org

FOUNDED: 1978

AREAS OF INTEREST:
Community infrastructure, art, human services and health.

TYPE:
Capital grants; General operating grants.

PURPOSE:
To enhance the community.

LEGAL BASIS:
Private foundation.

ELIGIBILITY:
Grants are made to organizations that have tax-exempt status under Section 501(c)(3) of the Internal Revenue Code. No grants are made to individuals.

GEOG. RESTRICTIONS: Primarily Santa Barbara County, California.

FINANCIAL DATA:
Amount of support per award: Typically $1,000 to $10,000 for general operating grants.

Total amount of support: Varies.

NO. AWARDS: Over 100 annually.

APPLICATION INFO:
The Foundation encourages applicants to use the Common Grant Application form, a link to which is available on the web site.

Duration: One year, with occasional multiyear. Renewal by reapplication.

ADDRESS INQUIRIES TO:
Palmer G. Jackson, Sr., President
(See address above.)

THE JACKSON FOUNDATION [167]

c/o U.S. Bank, NA
P.O. Box 3168
Portland, OR 97208
(503) 464-4920
E-mail: march.voyles@usbank.com
Web Site: www.thejacksonfoundation.com

FOUNDED: 1960

AREAS OF INTEREST:
Arts/performing arts, economic development, substance abuse, human services, minorities, housing, disabilities, humanities, education, environment, health, children/youth, aged and women.

TYPE:
Capital grants; Challenge/matching grants; Development grants; General operating grants; Matching gifts; Project/program grants; Research grants.

YEAR PROGRAM STARTED: 1963

PURPOSE:
To support new programs that will enhance and expand the well-being of individuals, with a focus on children in the Portland metropolitan area, by granting funds for the purpose of health and education.

LEGAL BASIS:
Private foundation.

ELIGIBILITY:
Grants are made to 501(c)(3) organizations.

GEOG. RESTRICTIONS: Oregon.

FINANCIAL DATA:
Amount of support per award: $1,000 to $50,000; average $3,370.

NO. MOST RECENT APPLICANTS: 250.

NO. AWARDS: 125.

APPLICATION INFO:
Guidelines and application forms are available online.

Duration: One year.

Deadline: March 31, June 30, September 30 and December 31.

ADDRESS INQUIRIES TO:
Trustees, Jackson Foundation
(See address or e-mail above.)

HENRY M. JACKSON FOUNDATION [168]

1501 Fourth Avenue
Suite 1580
Seattle, WA 98101
(206) 682-8565
Fax: (206) 682-8961
E-mail: foundation@hmjackson.org
Web Site: www.hmjackson.org

FOUNDED: 1983

AREAS OF INTEREST:
International affairs, public service, environment/natural resources and human rights.

NAME(S) OF PROGRAMS:
- **Environmental and Natural Resources Management Program**
- **Human Rights Program**
- **International Affairs Education Program**
- **Public Service Program**

TYPE:
Challenge/matching grants; Conferences/seminars; Internships; Professorships; Project/program grants; Seed money grants.

YEAR PROGRAM STARTED: 1983

PURPOSE:
To advance education and public understanding of critical public policy issues in the four priority areas above.

LEGAL BASIS:
Publicly supported foundation.

ELIGIBILITY:
Grants are made to private, nonprofit, tax-exempt organizations under 501(c)(3) and public, tax-exempt entities under 170(c). No grants are made to individuals.

No grants for capital or general operating expenses.

FINANCIAL DATA:
Amount of support per award: $1,000 to $50,000.

Total amount of support: Average: $250,000 per year.

NO. AWARDS: 10 to 15 per year.

REPRESENTATIVE AWARDS:
$71,000 to support guest faculty on topics of current foreign policy concerns for senior-level courses at the University of Washington's Jackson School of International Studies; $15,000 to support the publication and dissemination of a report on urban sprawl's toll on open space and farmland; $10,000 to create two new exhibits representing gulag life during different epochs of Soviet history on the site of a former prison labor camp; $34,536 for a program that places young adults on city boards and commissions.

APPLICATION INFO:
Proposals should include:
(1) a cover letter summarizing the project and amount requested;
(2) a detailed budget, implementation strategy, identification of board and/or those responsible for the project and plans for evaluation and;
(3) IRS tax-exempt status determination letter.

Duration: Varies.

Deadline: December 1, March 1, June 1 and September 1, for awards announced in March, June, September and December, respectively.

PUBLICATIONS:
Application guidelines; annual report; newsletter.

IRS I.D.: 52-1313011

OFFICERS:
Helen H. Jackson, Chairman
John Hempelmann, President
Craig Gannett, Vice President
Linda Mason Wilgis, Vice President
David Rostov, Treasurer
Anna Marie Laurence, Secretary
Joel C. Merkel, General Counsel

ADDRESS INQUIRIES TO:
Lara Iglitzin, Executive Director
(See address above.)

JACKSONVILLE JAGUARS FOUNDATION [169]

One EverBank Field Drive
Jacksonville, FL 32202
(904) 633-5437
Fax: (904) 633-5683
Web Site: www.jaguars.com/foundation-community/index.html

FOUNDED: 1993

AREAS OF INTEREST:
Social welfare for disadvantaged youths.

TYPE:
General operating grants; Project/program grants. Limited capital grants that target economically and socially "at-risk" youths in northeast Florida.

YEAR PROGRAM STARTED: 1994

PURPOSE:
To support programs benefiting economically and socially disadvantaged youth, families and other NFL and team charitable initiatives.

LEGAL BASIS:
Corporation foundation.

ELIGIBILITY:
Organizations in northeast Florida that work for disadvantaged youths on a nonsectarian basis. Must have 501(c)(3) IRS documentation.

No grants to individuals, schools or single-disease organizations.

GEOG. RESTRICTIONS: Baker, Clay, Duval, Nassau, and Saint Johns counties, Florida.

FINANCIAL DATA:
Amount of support per award: Varies.
Total amount of support: Over $2,000,000 for the year 2015.

CO-OP FUNDING PROGRAMS: Youth Anti-Obesity Grants with Baptist Health; Teen Pregnancy Prevention Grants with Blue Cross Blue Shield of Florida.

NO. MOST RECENT APPLICANTS: 42.

NO. AWARDS: 37.

APPLICATION INFO:
Submit a one-page summary that includes the specific goals, objectives, proposed activities and results expected to the Foundation.
Duration: One year. Renewal by reapplication.
Deadline: July and February.

ADDRESS INQUIRIES TO:
Peter Racine, President
(See address above.)

JOHNSON & JOHNSON FAMILY OF COMPANIES [170]

One Johnson & Johnson Plaza
New Brunswick, NJ 08933
(732) 524-0400
Fax: (732) 524-3300
Web Site: www.jnj.com

FOUNDED: 1953

AREAS OF INTEREST:
Health care and education.

TYPE:
Matching gifts; Project/program grants; Research grants. International programs, product donation, cash grants. Emphasis on health care, with a special interest in maternal and child health care issues. The Company administers major programs in partnership with selected nonprofit organizations. Grants largely extended through these programs on a Request for Proposal basis.

The Corporation conducts extensive product giving program but only through established partnerships with selected nonprofit organizations. No unsolicited requests accepted.

The Corporation also conducts large matching gifts program in areas of higher education, hospitals, disease-specific organizations, cultural organizations and prevention and treatment of substance abuse.

PURPOSE:
To make life-changing, long-term differences in human health by targeting the world's major health-related issues through community-based partnerships.

ELIGIBILITY:
Grants are made to organizations with 501(c)(3) status. Grants are not made for endowments, appeals for unrestricted funds, tours, fund-raising galas and sporting events, political, fraternal or athletic groups, sectarian or religious organizations, capital expenditures, individuals or loans. Priority is given to activities and needs in locations where the company has a presence in the U.S. and Puerto Rico.

FINANCIAL DATA:
Amount of support per award: Grant amounts vary.
Total amount of support: Varies.

NO. AWARDS: More than 600 grants.

APPLICATION INFO:
No unsolicited requests are accepted.

PUBLICATIONS:
Corporate Contributions report; application guidelines, policy statement.

STAFF:
Shaun Mickus, Director, Corporate Citizenship and Community Relations
Michael J. Bzdak, Director, Corporate Contributions
Alice Lin Fabiano, Director, Corporate Contributions
William Lin, Ph.D., Director, Corporate Contributions
Joy Marini, Director, Corporate Contributions
Conrad Person, Director, Corporate Contributions
Bonnie J. Petrauskas, Director, Corporate Contributions
Katsura Tsuno, Director, Corporate Contributions
Frank Welvaert, Director, Corporate Social Responsibility

ADDRESS INQUIRIES TO:
William Lin, Ph.D., Director
Corporate Contributions
(See address above.)

JOHNSON CONTROLS FOUNDATION [171]

5757 North Green Bay Avenue
Milwaukee, WI 53209-4408
(414) 524-2296
Web Site: www.johnsoncontrols.com

FOUNDED: 1952

AREAS OF INTEREST:
Higher education, health and social services, civic activities, culture and arts.

TYPE:
Matching gifts; Project/program grants. The Foundation matches the personal gifts of employees, retirees and directors to accredited colleges and universities, community arts and cultural organizations and to United Way in the aggregate from its U.S. company units.

PURPOSE:
To be operated for charitable purposes which include the distribution and application of financial support to soundly managed and operated organizations or causes which are fundamentally philanthropic.

LEGAL BASIS:
Corporate foundation.

ELIGIBILITY:
Contributions are limited to organizations which are exempt from taxation under the Internal Revenue Code. Applicant must meet one or more of the Foundation's funding priorities and benefit communities where Johnson Controls, Inc. has operations and employees work and live. Special consideration is given to those requests which impact the Milwaukee community.

No gifts will be made to any municipal, state, federal agency or department or to any organization established to influence legislation. No distribution will be made to a private individual. No gifts will be made to sectarian institutions or programs whose services are limited to members of any one religious group or whose funds are used primarily for the propagation of a religion. Grants are not usually given to public or private pre-schools, elementary or secondary institutions, but are limited to colleges and universities.

GEOG. RESTRICTIONS: United States.

FINANCIAL DATA:
Amount of support per award: Varies.
Total amount of support: Grants of more than $7,000,000 annually.
Matching fund requirements: $50 to $5,000 on a 1:1 basis per individual, per organization, per year to culture and arts as well as education nonprofit organizations.

NO. AWARDS: Up to 40.

REPRESENTATIVE AWARDS:
$50,000 to Discovery World Museum; $75,000 to Milwaukee Symphony Orchestra; $50,000 to Milwaukee Performing Arts; $125,000 to the University of Wisconsin, Milwaukee.

APPLICATION INFO:
Proposals, preferably in concise letter form, should include statement regarding tax-exempt status, description of the structure, governing board, purpose, history and programs of the organization, summary of the need for support and how it will be used, geographic areas served by the organization, budget information about the

organization and statement regarding other sources of income from corporations and foundations, community support and involvement. Must include 501(c)(3) letter.

Duration: Most grants are one-time only.

Deadline: Proposals are accepted and reviewed throughout the year.

ADDRESS INQUIRIES TO:
Johnson Controls Foundation
P.O. Box 591
Milwaukee, WI 53201-0591

MAGIC JOHNSON FOUNDATION, INC. [172]

9100 Wilshire Boulevard
Suite 700, East Tower
Beverly Hills, CA 90212
(310) 246-4400
Fax: (310) 786-8796
Web Site: www.magicjohnson.org

FOUNDED: 1991

AREAS OF INTEREST:
Youth; HIV/AIDS education, prevention and care.

NAME(S) OF PROGRAMS:
- **Magic Johnson Foundation HIV/AIDS Grant**
- **Taylor Michaels Scholarship**

TYPE:
Project/program grants; Scholarships; Technical assistance.

PURPOSE:
To support organizations and programs specializing in HIV/AIDS education, prevention and care, and in the areas of education, social needs and health issues of young people.

LEGAL BASIS:
National public charity.

ELIGIBILITY:
Organizations classified as 501(c)(3) by the IRS can apply. Funding will not be considered for projects by individuals and families. Advertising or sponsorship for other funding events are not eligible to receive funds. Research grants, conferences, travel, videos and capital acquisitions are also excluded.

GEOG. RESTRICTIONS: Northern and southern California; Washington, DC; Atlanta, Georgia; Chicago, Illinois; Baltimore, Maryland; New York, New York; Cleveland, Ohio; Houston, Texas.

FINANCIAL DATA:
Amount of support per award: Grants: $5,000 to $25,000; Scholarships: $2,000 to $5,000 per year.

Total amount of support: Varies.

NO. AWARDS: 30 to 35 new scholarships annually.

APPLICATION INFO:
By invitation only, but do accept letters of intent on an ongoing basis. Applicants should request in writing (maximum two pages) to be placed on the Magic Johnson Foundation's database. Requests must contain the name of the organization, address, telephone and fax numbers, e-mail address, contact person, a brief explanation of specific funding needs and a history of services provided.

Duration: Grants: One year. Scholarships: Up to five years.

Deadline: Letters of Intent accepted on an ongoing basis.

PUBLICATIONS:
Annual report; grant guidelines.

ADDRESS INQUIRIES TO:
Shane Jenkins, Vice President of HIV and Social Programs
(See address above.)

DAISY MARQUIS JONES FOUNDATION [173]

1600 South Avenue
Suite 250
Rochester, NY 14620-3921
(585) 461-4950
Fax: (585) 461-9752
E-mail: mail@dmjf.org
Web Site: www.dmjf.org

FOUNDED: 1968

AREAS OF INTEREST:
Disadvantaged children and families, access to health care, assistance to senior citizens and economic security for families.

TYPE:
Capital grants; Challenge/matching grants; Development grants; General operating grants; Matching gifts; Project/program grants.

YEAR PROGRAM STARTED: 1968

PURPOSE:
To improve the well-being of residents of Monroe and Yates counties, NY, particularly within the city of Rochester; to meet the needs of the disadvantaged, focusing on prevention; to develop children and families to their maximum potential.

LEGAL BASIS:
Not-for-profit, private foundation.

ELIGIBILITY:
Applicants must be nonprofit, tax-exempt organizations in Monroe and Yates counties, NY. The Foundation does not consider requests for aid for basic research, private schools, the arts, or religious purposes. The Foundation does not make grants to individuals.

GEOG. RESTRICTIONS: Monroe and Yates counties, New York.

FINANCIAL DATA:
Amount of support per award: Varies.

Total amount of support: $2,577,200 in grants committed in 2015.

Matching fund requirements: Stipulated with specific programs.

NO. AWARDS: 86 grants in 2013.

REPRESENTATIVE AWARDS:
$125,000 to Center for Youth Services to support the Alternative to Out-of-School Suspension Program and New Beginnings School; $50,000 to Greater Rochester Summer Learning Association for PreK-3rd grade reading skills; $45,000 to Seneca Park Zoo Society to support the Butterfly Beltway Program; $50,000 to Lifespan of Greater Rochester to support senior citizens; $25,000 to Neighborworks Rochester to support the neighborhood reviltalization program.

APPLICATION INFO:
Applicant must complete the inquiry form that is available on the Foundation web site. The Foundation will reply by e-mail.

Duration: Typically one year.

PUBLICATIONS:
Annual report.

TRUSTEES AND OFFICERS:
Donald W. Whitney, President
Roger L. Gardner

ADDRESS INQUIRIES TO:
Donald W. Whitney, President
(See address above.)

THE JOYCE FOUNDATION [174]

321 North Clark Street
Suite 1500
Chicago, IL 60654
(312) 782-2464
Fax: (312) 595-1350
E-mail: info@joycefdn.org
Web Site: www.joycefdn.org

FOUNDED: 1948

AREAS OF INTEREST:
Education, employment, environment, gun violence prevention, democracy, and culture.

TYPE:
Awards/prizes; Challenge/matching grants; Demonstration grants; Development grants; General operating grants; Research grants; Technical assistance.

YEAR PROGRAM STARTED: 1948

PURPOSE:
To support efforts to protect the natural environment of the Great Lakes; to reduce poverty and violence in the region; to ensure that its people have access to good schools, decent jobs, and a diverse and thriving culture; to reform the system of financing elections campaigns to ensure that public policies truly reflect public rather than private interests.

LEGAL BASIS:
Private foundation.

ELIGIBILITY:
Applicants must be tax-exempt, charitable organizations that are based or have a program in the Midwest, which the Foundation defines as including Illinois, Indiana, Michigan, Minnesota, Ohio and Wisconsin. A limited number of environment grants are made to organizations in Canada. The Foundation generally does not support capital proposals, endowment campaigns, religious activities, commercial ventures, direct service programs or scholarships.

GEOG. RESTRICTIONS: Midwest, including Illinois, Indiana, Michigan, Minnesota, Ohio and Wisconsin.

FINANCIAL DATA:
Amount of support per award: Up to $1,000,000 over three years; average grant: $250,000.

Total amount of support: $34,312,903 in grants awarded in the year 2013.

NO. MOST RECENT APPLICANTS: 713.

NO. AWARDS: 280.

REPRESENTATIVE AWARDS:
$1,000,000 to the Illinois Community College Board, Springfield, IL, to test new programs and policies aimed at increasing the number of adult basic and developmental education students who transition to postsecondary occupational education and ultimately to better jobs in Illinois; $350,000 to William J. Brennan, Jr. Center for Justice, New York, NY, to support its campaign finance and judicial reform initiatives,

particularly in the Midwest; $50,000 to the Cuyahoga Community College Foundation, Cleveland, OH, to support a multiyear collaborative that includes a long-term residency and commissioning of a new work by African-American jazz artist and composer, Cecilia Smith.

APPLICATION INFO:
Guidelines on how to apply and other details are available on the web site.

Duration: The majority of awards are for one year, although multiyear grants are also considered. Renewal of funding is primarily based on grantee's fulfillment of terms and goals of the previous grant and the program's continued advancement of Foundation priorities.

Deadline: Early April for July; August 10 for December; December 1 for the following April.

PUBLICATIONS:
Program and Grant Proposal Guidelines (online); newsletters; annual report.

IRS I.D.: 36-6079185

STAFF:
Ellen S. Alberding, President
Deborah Gillespie, Vice President of Finance and Administration, Secretary and Treasurer
Beth Swanson, Vice President of Strategy and Programs
Bill Strong, Director of Communications
Jane R. Patterson, Chief Investment Officer
Whitney Smith, Senior Program Director, Employment
Angelique Power, Program Director, Culture
Edmund Miller, Program Director, Environment
Nina Vinik, Program Director, Gun Violence Prevention
Elizabeth Cisar, Senior Program Officer, Environment
Jason Quiara, Program Officer, Education
Matthew M. Muench, Program Officer, Employment
Jessyca Dudley, Program Officer, Gun Violence Prevention
Pablo Merchan, Senior Accountant
Veronica Salter, Manager of Grants and Technology Specialist
Kerry M. Goese, Controller

BOARD OF DIRECTORS:
Roger R. Fross, Chairman
Charles U. Daly, Vice Chairman
Ellen S. Alberding
Jose B. Alvarez
John T. Anderson
Michael F. Brewer
Anthony S. Earl
Carlton L. Guthrie
Daniel P. Kearney
Tracey L. Meares
Margot M. Rogers
Paula Wolff

ADDRESS INQUIRIES TO:
E-mail: applications@joycefdn.org

ALICE AND JULIUS KANTOR CHARITABLE TRUST [175]

809 North Bedford Drive
Beverly Hills, CA 90210
(310) 360-7541

FOUNDED: 1977

AREAS OF INTEREST:
Medical research, arts and cultural programs, education and human services.

TYPE:
Development grants; Project/program grants; Research grants.

YEAR PROGRAM STARTED: 1977

PURPOSE:
To find cures for diseases and aid mankind.

LEGAL BASIS:
Trust.

ELIGIBILITY:
Grants are made to organizations that have tax-exempt status under Section 501(c)(3) of the Internal Revenue Code. No grants are made to individuals, religious organizations or political organizations.

FINANCIAL DATA:
Amount of support per award: Varies.

Total amount of support: Varies.

APPLICATION INFO:
Applicants must submit a brief letter outlining the purpose of the grant, as well as a letter certifying the organization's 501(c)(3) status under the Internal Revenue Code.

Duration: Varies.

ADDRESS INQUIRIES TO:
Arnold Seidel, Trustee
(See address above.)

THE J.M. KAPLAN FUND, INC. [176]

71 West 23rd Street
9th Floor
New York, NY 10010
(212) 767-0630
Fax: (212) 767-0639
E-mail: acarabine@jmkfund.org
Web Site: www.jmkfund.org

FOUNDED: 1945

AREAS OF INTEREST:
Marine conservation, cultural heritage/historic preservation and immigration.

NAME(S) OF PROGRAMS:
- **Discretionary Grants**
- **Environment Program Grant**
- **Furthermore Grant**
- **Historic Preservation Grant**
- **The J.M.K. Innovation Prize**
- **Migrations Grant**

TYPE:
General operating grants; Project/program grants.

YEAR PROGRAM STARTED: 1945

PURPOSE:
To champion inventive giving that supports transformative social, environmental and cultural causes.

LEGAL BASIS:
Family foundation.

ELIGIBILITY:
No grants are made to individuals. Unsolicited requests are not accepted.

FINANCIAL DATA:
Amount of support per award: $30,000 to $200,000 for program grants; $2,500 to $50,000 for discretionary grants.

Total amount of support: $8,000,000 for the year 2015.

NO. MOST RECENT APPLICANTS: Over 750.

APPLICATION INFO:
Application is by invitation only.

Duration: 12 to 24 months.

TRUSTEES:
Peter Davidson, Chairman
Betsy Davidson
Bradford Davidson
Joan K. Davidson
J. Matthew Davidson
Caio Fonseca
Elizabeth K. Fonseca
Isabel Fonseca
Quina Fonseca
Mary E. Kaplan

STAFF:
Amy L. Freitag, Executive Director
William P. Falahee, Controller
Angela D. Carabine, Grants Manager
Charles Moore, Program Director, Environment
Ann Birckmayer, Program Associate, Furthermore Grants in Publishing

ADDRESS INQUIRIES TO:
Angela D. Carabine, Grants Manager
(See address above.)

KATE SPADE & COMPANY FOUNDATION [177]

2 Park Avenue, 12th Floor
New York, NY 10016
(212) 626-5704
E-mail: foundation@katespade.com
Web Site: www.katespadeandcompany.com

FOUNDED: 1981

AREAS OF INTEREST:
Women's programs only, specifically economic empowerment.

TYPE:
Challenge/matching grants; General operating grants; Matching gifts; Project/program grants; Seed money grants; Technical assistance.

YEAR PROGRAM STARTED: 1981

PURPOSE:
To support multidimensional programs that transition women from underserved communities into successful individuals that inspire the people around them.

LEGAL BASIS:
Corporate foundation.

ELIGIBILITY:
Organizations classified as 501(c)(3) by the IRS can apply. Individuals and religious, political and fraternal organizations are ineligible.

GEOG. RESTRICTIONS: Hudson County, New Jersey and New York, New York.

FINANCIAL DATA:
Amount of support per award: $15,000 to $120,000.

Total amount of support: Approximately $1,200,000 annually.

Matching fund requirements: 1:1; $25 minimum and $10,000 annual total per employee; includes arts, education, health, human services and the environment.

REPRESENTATIVE AWARDS:
$50,000 to WomenRising, Jersey City, NJ; $95,000 to Per Scholas, Women in Tech Training, Bronx, NY.

APPLICATION INFO:
Guidelines and application form are available online.

Duration: One year. Grants are renewable.

Deadline: Applications are accepted throughout the year.

PUBLICATIONS:
Application guidelines.

IRS I.D.: 13-3060673

ADDRESS INQUIRIES TO:
Valerie Biberaj, Director
(See address above.)

MAY GORDON LATHAM KELLENBERGER HISTORICAL FOUNDATION [178]

529 South Front Street
New Bern, NC 28562
(252) 639-3500
Fax: (252) 514-4876

FOUNDED: 1978

AREAS OF INTEREST:
Historic preservation in the city of New Bern and Craven County, NC.

TYPE:
Project/program grants.

YEAR PROGRAM STARTED: 1978

PURPOSE:
To aid in the preservation of significant structures in New Bern as well as to assist in historical research and study pertaining to the city of New Bern and Craven County, NC.

LEGAL BASIS:
Special-interest foundation.

ELIGIBILITY:
Applicants must be organizations, agencies and institutions which are tax-exempt under the provisions of the U.S. Internal Revenue Code.

GEOG. RESTRICTIONS: Craven County and New Bern, North Carolina.

APPLICATION INFO:
Contact Foundation for application form and guidelines.

Duration: One year. Can be renewed for one additional year.

Deadline: June 10 and December 10. Announcement on August 1 and February 1.

PUBLICATIONS:
Application guidelines.

OFFICERS:
Millie Barbee, Chairperson
William C. Cannon, Secretary and Treasurer
Nelson McDaniel, Project Review Committee Chairperson

ADDRESS INQUIRIES TO:
Laurie Bowles, Administrative Support
(See address above.)

W.K. KELLOGG FOUNDATION [179]

One Michigan Avenue East
Battle Creek, MI 49017-4012
(269) 968-1611
Fax: (269) 968-0413
E-mail: proposalsprocessing@wkkf.org
Web Site: www.wkkf.org

FOUNDED: 1930

AREAS OF INTEREST:
Family economic security; education and learning; food, health and well-being; community and civic engagement (WKKF Community Leadership Network); and racial equity.

TYPE:
Challenge/matching grants; Development grants; Endowments; Fellowships; General operating grants; Matching gifts; Project/program grants; Seed money grants. Grants for pilot projects to improve human well-being are made in the U.S., Mexico, Haiti, northeastern Brazil, Southern Africa, and with sovereign tribes.

The Foundation encourages grant seekers to review the latest information on its web site regarding its focus areas of educated kids, healthy kids, secure families, racial equity, and civic engagement before beginning the application process. This will assist in determining if/how grant seeker's idea might be a fit with the Foundation's current programming framework.

YEAR PROGRAM STARTED: 1930

PURPOSE:
To support children, families and communities as they strengthen and create conditions that propel vulnerable children to achieve success as individuals and as contributors to the larger community and society.

LEGAL BASIS:
Independent private foundation.

ELIGIBILITY:
To be eligible for support, applying organization or institution, as well as the purpose of the proposed project, must qualify under the regulations of the U.S. IRS. Grantees must have the financial potential to sustain the project on a continuing basis after Foundation funding is ended. The Foundation is not able to provide funding directly to individuals.

GEOG. RESTRICTIONS: Haiti, Mexico and United States, with priority in Michigan, Mississippi, New Mexico and New Orleans, Louisiana.

FINANCIAL DATA:
Total assets of $8,447,155,607 for the year ended August 31, 2015.

Amount of support per award: Varies.

Total amount of support: New commitments of $267,822,524 and total grant expenditures of $301,711,594 for the year ended August 31, 2015.

NO. MOST RECENT APPLICANTS: 2,304 for fiscal year 2015.

NO. AWARDS: 658 for fiscal year 2015.

REPRESENTATIVE AWARDS:
$1,900,000 to Food Corps; $600,000 to Accion, The U.S. Network.

APPLICATION INFO:
The preferred method for grant submissions is the Foundation's online application. The Foundation will give prompt consideration to all preproposal submissions. The initial review may take up to three months to complete. If the proposed project falls within the Foundation's priorities and available resources, applicants may be asked to develop a more detailed proposal.

Duration: Varies.

Deadline: The Foundation accepts proposals on an ongoing basis, and staff members review them as they are received.

PUBLICATIONS:
Annual report.

BOARD OF TRUSTEES:
Ramón Murguía, Chairman
Celeste Clark
Roderick Gillum
Fred Keller
Cathann Kress
Hanmin Liu
Cynthia Milligan
Richard Tsoumas

EXECUTIVE STAFF:
La June Montgomery Tabron, President and Chief Executive Officer
Hong Linh Nguyen, Chief Operating Officer
Aranthan (A.J.) Jones, II, Chief Policy and Communications Officer
Barbara Ferrer, Chief Strategy Officer
Joel Wittenburg, Vice President and Chief Investment Officer
Donald Williamson, Vice President for Finance and Treasurer
Ross Comstock, Vice President for Information Systems and Technology
Cindy Smith, Vice President for Integrated Services
Gail Christopher, Vice President for Policy and Senior Advisor
Joseph Scantlebury, Vice President for Program Strategy
Carla Thompson, Vice President for Program Strategy
Alandra Washington, Vice President for Quality and Organizational Effectiveness
Dianna Langenburg, Vice President for Talent and Human Resources
Kathryn Krecke, General Counsel and Corporate Secretary

ADDRESS INQUIRIES TO:
See e-mail address above.

HARRIS AND ELIZA KEMPNER FUND [180]

2201 Market Street, Suite 1250
Galveston, TX 77550-1529
(409) 762-1603
Fax: (409) 762-5435
E-mail: information@kempnerfund.org
Web Site: www.kempnerfund.org

FOUNDED: 1946

AREAS OF INTEREST:
Arts, historic preservation, community development, education, environment, and health and human services.

NAME(S) OF PROGRAMS:
- **Matching Gifts Program**
- **Primary Grant Program**
- **Program Related Investments**

TYPE:
Capital grants; Challenge/matching grants; Conferences/seminars; Demonstration grants; Endowments; Fellowships; General operating grants; Matching gifts; Professorships; Project/program grants; Scholarships; Seed money grants. Primary Grant Program provides grants to qualifying organizations in the greater Galveston, TX area in the arts and historic preservation, community development, education, environment, and health and human services.

Program Related Investments are recommended by Fund trustees for Galveston projects.

YEAR PROGRAM STARTED: 1946

PURPOSE:
To support a wide range of innovative as well as traditional programs for the enhancement of the local community.

LEGAL BASIS:
Independent private foundation.

ELIGIBILITY:
Primary Grant Program: Preferred applicants are programs/projects that benefit the greater

Galveston, TX community. Seed money, operating funds, small capital needs and special projects, and partnering with other funding sources are supported. Proposals will not be considered for fund-raising benefits, direct-mail solicitations, grants to individuals, or grants to non-U.S.-based organizations.

Matching Gifts Program: Restricted to Kempner family members and trustees of the Kempner Fund.

GEOG. RESTRICTIONS: Galveston, Texas.

FINANCIAL DATA:

Amount of support per award: Grants: $1,000 to $75,000 for the year ended December 31, 2015.

Total amount of support: $1,798,000 in grants and $273,000 in matching gifts for the year ended December 31, 2015.

Matching fund requirements: Restricted to descendants of Harris and Eliza Kempner.

NO. MOST RECENT APPLICANTS: 80 for the year 2014.

NO. AWARDS: 71 for the year 2015.

REPRESENTATIVE AWARDS:

$50,000 to the Grand 1894 Opera House; $40,000 to the Galveston ISD Educational Foundation; $4,000 to the Galveston Symphony; $40,000 to the City of Galveston, Planning Department; $60,000 to the Family Service Center.

APPLICATION INFO:

Applicants should submit a brief cover letter, signed by the Executive Director and Board Chairman, stating the need and amount being requested. Complete guidelines and forms are available at the web site.

The following project/program information also needs to be submitted:
(1) name and telephone number of contact person;
(2) description;
(3) timeline;
(4) budget (income and expenses);
(5) list of sources and amounts being solicited and/or received or pledged;
(6) future funding plans (for new and continuing programs) and;
(7) plans for evaluating program's progress and/or results.

The following organization information should be attached:
(1) statement of purpose and brief history;
(2) names of present officers and board members;
(3) operating budget (revenue and expenses) for year for which funds are sought;
(4) financial statements (year-to-date), audit, and/or Tax Form 990 for most recent fiscal year;
(5) copy of post-1969 IRS determination letter to document tax-exempt status and;
(6) statement on organization letterhead that there has been no change in IRS status since issuance of ruling letter.

Duration: Varies.

Deadline: Health or Human Services: March 15. Arts, Community Development, Environment, Historic Preservation or Education: October 15.

IRS I.D.: 74-6042458

STAFF:
Anne Brasier, Executive Director

DIRECTORS:
Barbara W. Sasser, Honorary Director
Lyda Ann Thomas, Honorary Director
Lisa Allen, Director
Carroll Goldstone, Director
Hetta T. Kempner, Director
Victoria Marchand, Director
Andrew Mytelka, Director
Carol Roberts, Director
Brooke Thompson, Director

OFFICERS AND TRUSTEES:
Robert K. Lynch, President
Daniel Thorne, Vice President
Randall Kempner, Treasurer
Armin Cantini, Secretary

*SPECIAL STIPULATIONS:

Funding is limited to Galveston, TX area only.

JOHN F. KENNEDY PRESIDENTIAL LIBRARY [181]

Columbia Point
Boston, MA 02125-3313
(617) 514-1653
Fax: (617) 514-1625
E-mail: kennedy.library@nara.gov
Web Site: www.jfklibrary.org

FOUNDED: 1964

AREAS OF INTEREST:

History, government, archival administration and library science, journalism, communications and other related disciplines.

NAME(S) OF PROGRAMS:

- **Kennedy Library Archival Internships**

TYPE:

Internships. Awarded to undergraduate and graduate students majoring in history, government, archival administration, library science, journalism, communications and related disciplines for on-site work with the archives staff at the Kennedy Library.

YEAR PROGRAM STARTED: 1970

LEGAL BASIS:

Private foundation in cooperation with a U.S. government agency.

FINANCIAL DATA:

Amount of support per award: Monthly stipend of $560 for part-time interns (16 hours per week); $1,120 for full-time interns (32 hours per week); $1,400 for full-time summer interns (40 hours per week).

APPLICATION INFO:

Candidate must complete application form, submit a copy of current college transcript, and a letter of reference.

Duration: Varies.

THE KERR FOUNDATION, INC. [182]

12501 North May Avenue
Oklahoma City, OK 73120
(405) 749-7991
Fax: (405) 749-2877
Web Site: www.thekerrfoundation.org

FOUNDED: 1963

AREAS OF INTEREST:

Education, cultural activities, and health and human services.

TYPE:

Capital grants; General operating grants; Project/program grants.

YEAR PROGRAM STARTED: 1986

PURPOSE:

To support programs of interest to the Foundation in the areas of health, education, youth services and cultural activities.

LEGAL BASIS:

Private, charitable foundation.

ELIGIBILITY:

Application is limited to nonprofit, 501(c)(3) tax-exempt organizations. No grants to individuals.

GEOG. RESTRICTIONS: Arkansas, Colorado, Kansas, Missouri, New Mexico, Oklahoma, Texas, and Washington, D.C.

FINANCIAL DATA:

Grant-seeking organizations must first raise a specified amount in actual new dollars donations or up-to-three-year pledges. The grant will be paid upon successful raising of the funds or pledges, which must occur within one year or a mutually agreed-upon time limit.

Amount of support per award: $5,000 to $50,000.

CO-OP FUNDING PROGRAMS: All Oklahoma foundations.

NO. MOST RECENT APPLICANTS: 150.

NO. AWARDS: 50.

APPLICATION INFO:

Forms and guidelines are available online.

Duration: Most grants awarded on a one-time basis.

OFFICERS AND TRUSTEES:
Mrs. Robert S. Kerr, Jr., President and Chairperson
Steven Kerr, Treasurer
Laura Kerr Ogle, Secretary
Cody T. Kerr

ADDRESS INQUIRIES TO:
Mrs. Robert S. Kerr, Jr.
President and Chairman of the Board
(See address above.)

GRAYCE B. KERR FUND, INC. [183]

117 Bay Street
Easton, MD 21601
(410) 822-6652
Fax: (410) 822-4546
E-mail: office@gbkf.org
Web Site: www.gbkf.org

FOUNDED: 1986

AREAS OF INTEREST:

Education, cultural programs, and public policy research, with major emphasis on education.

TYPE:

Project/program grants. Grants to nonprofit organizations. Grants are not limited to any one specific area of interest or geographical location. Currently, the Fund's principal areas of interest include nurturing educational achievement and excellence, fostering life skills critical to self-sufficiency, and encouraging cultural growth. The Fund supports research and other activities directed toward improving the information base available to the public.

YEAR PROGRAM STARTED: 1986

PURPOSE:

To provide financial support to worthy nonprofit organizations that enhance the quality of life, significantly impact and sustain long-term change and growth in organizations and institutions.

LEGAL BASIS:
Private, charitable foundation.

ELIGIBILITY:
Applicants must be nonprofit, 501(c)(3) tax-exempt organizations. No grants to individuals.

GEOG. RESTRICTIONS: United States.

FINANCIAL DATA:
Grant minimums and maximums are not designated. Preference may be given, in some years, to large grants where a genuine impact may be accomplished.

Amount of support per award: Varies.

Total amount of support: Varies.

APPLICATION INFO:
The Foundation self-selects grantees based on the interests of the family and Trustees.

Duration: Usually one year.

PUBLICATIONS:
Annual report; application.

IRS I.D.: 73-1256124

BOARD OF TRUSTEES:
Marcy Kerr Yuknat, Chairperson
John R. Valliant, President and Trustee
David A. Yuknat, Secretary and Treasurer

ADDRESS INQUIRIES TO:
John R. Valliant, President
(See address above.)

KIMBERLY-CLARK FOUNDATION, INC. [184]

P.O. Box 619100
Dallas, TX 75261-9100
(972) 281-1477
E-mail: kcfoundation@kcc.com
Web Site: www.kimberly-clark.com

FOUNDED: 1952

AREAS OF INTEREST:
Social welfare, medicine and health.

TYPE:
Project/program grants.

YEAR PROGRAM STARTED: 1952

PURPOSE:
To support organizations that strengthen today's families.

LEGAL BASIS:
Corporate foundation.

ELIGIBILITY:
Grants are made to tax-exempt, charitable, 501(c)(3) nonprofit organizations in communities where Kimberly-Clark has operations. There are a limited number of contributions to national organizations.

FINANCIAL DATA:
Amount of support per award: Varies.

Total amount of support: $700,000 in grants for the year 2015.

REPRESENTATIVE AWARDS:
$1,300,000 to Boys and Girls Clubs of America; $20,000 to Susan G. Komen Foundation; $50,000 to Catalyst for Women; $200,000 to American Red Cross.

APPLICATION INFO:
Written requests must be sent to the Foundation. Please call before sending requests.

Duration: One to five years.

PUBLICATIONS:
Annual report.

OFFICERS:
Tony Palmer, President
Mark A. Buthman, Vice President
Jenny Lewis, Vice President
Nancy Loewe, Treasurer
John Wesley, Secretary

DIRECTORS:
Mark A. Buthman
Thomas J. Falk
Tony Palmer

ADDRESS INQUIRIES TO:
Jenny Lewis, Vice President
(See address above.)

STEPHEN AND TABITHA KING FOUNDATION [185]

P.O. Box 855
Bangor, ME 04402
(207) 990-2910
Fax: (207) 990-2975
E-mail: info@stkfoundation.org
Web Site: www.stkfoundation.org

FOUNDED: 1986

AREAS OF INTEREST:
Arts, children/youth, health, education, libraries, recovery, women's issues, human rights and literacy.

TYPE:
Awards/prizes; Capital grants; Challenge/matching grants; Demonstration grants; Development grants; Endowments; General operating grants; Matching gifts; Project/program grants; Seed money grants; Training grants.

PURPOSE:
To improve the quality of life in Maine.

LEGAL BASIS:
Private family foundation.

ELIGIBILITY:
Organizations classified as 501(c)(3) by the IRS and located in Maine can apply. Grants are only awarded to nonprofit organizations operating in the state of Maine. Individuals and religious organizations are ineligible.

GEOG. RESTRICTIONS: Maine.

FINANCIAL DATA:
Amount of support per award: Grants: $500 to $50,000.

Total amount of support: Varies, dependent on investment revenue.

Matching fund requirements: Must be met through grassroots local community funding.

NO. MOST RECENT APPLICANTS: 1,000.

NO. AWARDS: Approximately 250.

APPLICATION INFO:
Applications are submitted online.

Duration: Foundation prefers one-time grants. Multiyear commitments occasionally.

Deadline: June 30 and December 31. Decisions on grants may take as long as eight weeks.

IRS I.D.: 13-3364647

STAFF:
Stephanie Leonard, Administrator

ADDRESS INQUIRIES TO:
Stephanie Leonard, Administrator
(See address above.)

F.M. KIRBY FOUNDATION, INC. [186]

17 DeHart Street
Morristown, NJ 07963
(973) 538-4800
Fax: (973) 538-4801
Web Site: www.fmkirbyfoundation.org

FOUNDED: 1931

AREAS OF INTEREST:
General charitable support.

TYPE:
Capital grants; Challenge/matching grants; Endowments; Fellowships; General operating grants; Professorships; Project/program grants; Research grants; Scholarships. Grants usually are reflective of personal interest by one or more members of the Kirby family who are, or have been, active in the affairs of the Foundation.

YEAR PROGRAM STARTED: 1931

LEGAL BASIS:
Private foundation.

ELIGIBILITY:
Organizations must be tax-exempt under applicable provisions of the IRS code and not private foundations. No grants are made to individuals. No grants are made to public foundations which would, as a result thereof, become private foundations. No grants for fund-raising activities such as benefits, charitable dinners, sports or theater events, etc. No loans are made.

GEOG. RESTRICTIONS: Morris County, New Jersey; Hillsborough, North Carolina area and Wilkes-Barre, Pennsylvania area.

FINANCIAL DATA:
Amount of support per award: Varies.

Total amount of support: $18,600,000 for the year 2016.

Matching fund requirements: Determined on a case-by-case basis.

NO. MOST RECENT APPLICANTS: Approximately 500 for the year 2014.

NO. AWARDS: 265 for the year 2014.

APPLICATION INFO:
The preferred method of initial contact is a full proposal with a cover letter. The Foundation provides no formal application forms and sets down no specific guidelines. Proposals should include:
(1) a report on the use of previous grants if applicable;
(2) a description of the organization, its purpose and the project, if any;
(3) an indication of the budget for which financial support is requested;
(4) roster of directors and principal officers;
(5) copy of the current audited financial statement;
(6) copy of the valid IRS tax determination letter and;
(7) copy of current annual budget.

Duration: One year. Renewal possible.

Deadline: October 31. Solicitations received after deadline will be held over to following year.

PUBLICATIONS:
Application guidelines.

IRS I.D.: 51-6017929

STAFF:
Thomas J. Bianchini, Financial Advisor

DIRECTORS AND OFFICERS:
S. Dillard Kirby, President and Director

Jefferson W. Kirby, Vice President and Director
William H. Byrnes, Vice President-Grants
Frank N. Barra, Treasurer and Secretary
Alice K. Horton, Director
Ward K. Horton, Director
F.M. Kirby, Director
Walker D. Kirby, Director
Laura H. Virkler, Director
JoAnn F. Tiefau, Program Officer

ADDRESS INQUIRIES TO:
William H. Byrnes, Vice President-Grants
(See address above.)

KITSAP COMMUNITY FOUNDATION

9657 Levin Road, N.W.
Suite 260
Silverdale, WA 98383
(360) 698-3622
Fax: (360) 698-6043
E-mail: kcf@kitsapfoundation.org
Web Site: www.kitsapfoundation.org

TYPE:
General operating grants; Project/program grants; Scholarships.

See entry 1282 for full listing.

ROBERT J. KLEBERG, JR. AND HELEN C. KLEBERG FOUNDATION [187]

700 North St. Mary's Street
Suite 1200
San Antonio, TX 78205
(210) 271-3691 ext. 39
Fax: (210) 299-1541
E-mail: margretb@alexventures.com
Web Site: www.klebergfoundation.org

FOUNDED: 1950

AREAS OF INTEREST:
Basic science and clinical research; community and health services based primarily in south Texas; education; arts and humanities; and wildlife, and veterinary and animal sciences.

TYPE:
Project/program grants; Research grants.

PURPOSE:
To provide financial support for research projects or actual programs in the area of biomedical research, education, health and welfare.

LEGAL BASIS:
Private foundation.

ELIGIBILITY:
Applicants must be IRS 501(c)(3) organizations or public universities under Section 170(c) of the Internal Revenue Code. No grants to individuals. No grants for endowments, deficit financing, community organizations outside of Texas, indirect costs or overhead for research projects.

GEOG. RESTRICTIONS: United States.

FINANCIAL DATA:
The Foundation has awarded nearly $262,000,000 since its founding.

Amount of support per award: Varies.

Total amount of support: Approximately $12,000,000 annually.

APPLICATION INFO:
Detailed information is available on the web site.

Duration: Project support can be up to five years.

Deadline: April 15 for consideration in June; October 15 for consideration in December. Should the deadline fall on a weekend, it will be extended to the following Monday. Should the deadline fall on a weekend and the following Monday is a holiday, it will be extended to the following Tuesday. Late proposals will not be accepted.

PUBLICATIONS:
Guidelines.

ADDRESS INQUIRIES TO:
Margret Bamford, Grant Coordinator
(See address above.)

JOSIAH W. AND BESSIE H. KLINE FOUNDATION, INC. [188]

515 South 29th Street
Harrisburg, PA 17104
(717) 561-4373
Fax: (717) 561-0826
E-mail: info@kline-foundation.org
Web Site: www.kline-foundation.org

FOUNDED: 1952

AREAS OF INTEREST:
Medical, academic, benevolent, community and cultural.

NAME(S) OF PROGRAMS:

- **Kline Foundation Grants**

TYPE:
Project/program grants; Research grants.

YEAR PROGRAM STARTED: 1952

PURPOSE:
To aid blind or incapacitated persons or crippled children in need of financial assistance; to make grants to Pennsylvania colleges and universities, to hospitals and institutions for crippled children or to any other benevolent or charitable institution; to make grants for scientific or medical research to be performed by scientific persons or by colleges, universities or research institutions.

LEGAL BASIS:
Community foundation.

ELIGIBILITY:
The Foundation does not make loans and does not make grants to individuals and generally does not make grants for normal operational phases of established programs or to national organizations or religious programs.

Normally grants are not made to state-affiliated schools, colleges, or universities.

GEOG. RESTRICTIONS: South central Pennsylvania, with emphasis on Cumberland and Dauphin counties.

FINANCIAL DATA:
Amount of support per award: $500 to $250,000.

Total amount of support: Varies.

APPLICATION INFO:
Application information is available on the web site. To be considered for Foundation aid, a copy of the Foundation's completed application form must be submitted and the following information must be fully stated:
(1) a description of the need and purpose, the qualifications of the requesting organization and the location as to where and how the support will be used;
(2) a budget for the project and any support that will be received from other sources;
(3) the amount of the request from the Foundation and the dates the funds are needed and;
(4) a copy of a letter from the IRS showing that the organization is exempt from federal income tax under Section 501(c)(3) of the Internal Revenue Code and that the organization is not a private foundation under Section 509(a).

Application may be submitted online.

Deadline: April and October. Some grants are awarded in June, while others are generally awarded after December 1 of each year.

PUBLICATIONS:
Annual report; application guidelines; application.

ADDRESS INQUIRIES TO:
John A. Obrock, C.P.A.
(See address above.)

*SPECIAL STIPULATIONS:
One grant per year per organization.

JOHN S. AND JAMES L. KNIGHT FOUNDATION [189]

200 South Biscayne Boulevard
Suite 3300
Miami, FL 33131-2349
(305) 908-2600
Fax: (305) 908-2698
E-mail: grants@knightfoundation.org
Web Site: www.knightfoundation.org

FOUNDED: 1950

AREAS OF INTEREST:
Journalism and engaged and informed communities.

NAME(S) OF PROGRAMS:

- **Arts Program**
- **Communities Program**
- **Journalism Program**
- **National Program**

TYPE:
Capital grants; Challenge/matching grants; Development grants; Endowments; Matching gifts; Project/program grants; Seed money grants; Technical assistance. The Foundation promotes excellence in journalism worldwide and invests in the vitality of 26 U.S. communities.

The Foundation focuses on three areas:
(1) Innovating Media and Journalism: The Foundation aims to help sustain democracy by leading journalism to its best possible future in the 21st century;
(2) Engaging Communities: To sustain healthy communities in a democracy, the Foundation's community engagement initiatives aim to give all residents a strong sense of belonging and caring, timely access to relevant information, the ability to understand that information, and the motivation to take sustainable action on the issues that matter most to them and;
(3) Fostering the Arts: Through its national arts program, the Foundation seeks to weave the arts into the fabric of the Knight resident communities to engage and inspire their residents; the Foundation believes that the arts are a catalyst for public dialogue, and that shared cultural experiences contribute to a sense of place and communal identity.

YEAR PROGRAM STARTED: 1950

PURPOSE:
To sustain democracy in the digital age by fostering informed and engaged communities;

to back transformational ideas at the intersection of media, journalism, community engagement and the arts; to advance media innovation with a wide range of initiatives; to support projects, including in the arts, that increase community engagement through the use of technology and other innovative approaches.

LEGAL BASIS:
Private non-operating foundation.

ELIGIBILITY:
A segment of the Foundation's activities focuses on 26 communities where the Knight brothers owned newspapers, with donor-advised programs in 18 and program director-led programs in the eight "resident Knight communities."

An applicant organization must have received a letter of determination from the IRS granting it 501(c)(3) tax-exempt status and stating that it is not a private foundation according to the definition in Section 509(a) of the Internal Revenue Code.

The Knight News Challenge permits for-profit entities and individuals to apply from anywhere in the world.

The Knight Community Information Challenge accepts applications from community and place-based foundations in the U.S. and its territories, as well as Mexico and Canada.

The Knight Arts Challenge accepts applications from South Florida, Detroit (MI), and Greater Philadelphia individuals, for-profit and nonprofit organizations.

FINANCIAL DATA:
Amount of support per award: Varies.
Total amount of support: $151,161,532 for the year 2015.

NO. AWARDS: 599 grants for the year 2015.

APPLICATION INFO:
Applicants must submit an online letter of inquiry. If the inquiry is determined to fall into Knight Foundation funding priorities, applicants are asked to submit a full proposal.
Duration: Varies per project; usually from one to five years.

PUBLICATIONS:
Evaluation and Assessment publications; Reporter Analysis evaluation articles; KnightBlog posts.

IRS I.D.: 65-0464177

STAFF:
Terese Coudreaut, Vice President and Chief Administrative Officer
Juan Martinez, Vice President and Chief Financial Officer
Victoria Rogers, Vice President/Arts
Andrew Sherry, Vice President of Communications
Jorge Martinez, Vice President of Information Technology
Michael Maness, Vice President/Journalism Program
Mayur Patel, Vice President/Strategy and Assessment

TRUSTEES AND OFFICERS:
John Palfrey, Chairman
Alberto Ibarguen, President and Chief Executive Officer
Stephanie Bell-Rose
Francisco L. Borges
William H. Considine
Marjorie Knight Crane
James N. Crutchfield
Chris Hughes
Joichi Ito
Susan D. Kronick
Rolfe Neill
Anna Spangler Nelson
Mariam C. Noland
Beverly Knight Olson
Earl W. Powell
Ray Rodriguez
E. Roe Stamps, IV
Paul E. Steiger

ADDRESS INQUIRIES TO:
Grants Administrator
(See address above.)

MARION I. AND HENRY J. KNOTT FOUNDATION, INC. [190]

3904 Hickory Avenue
Baltimore, MD 21211
(410) 235-7068
Fax: (410) 889-2577
E-mail: choffman@knottfoundation.org
Web Site: www.knottfoundation.org

FOUNDED: 1977

AREAS OF INTEREST:
Education (private and Catholic schools only), health care, human and social services, arts and humanities.

TYPE:
Capital grants; Challenge/matching grants; Development grants; General operating grants; Matching gifts; Project/program grants; Technical assistance; Training grants.

YEAR PROGRAM STARTED: 1977

PURPOSE:
To further Roman Catholic activities and other charitable, cultural, educational, health care and human service activities within the meaning of Section 501(c)(3) of the Internal Revenue Code.

LEGAL BASIS:
Private family foundation.

ELIGIBILITY:
Applicants must be nonprofit, charitable organizations with evidence of tax-exemption ruling under Section 501(c)(3) of the Internal Revenue Code. No grants pertaining to scholarships, individuals, annual giving, pro-choice causes, public education or institutions, or politically oriented activities.

The Foundation does not favor multiyear requests.

GEOG. RESTRICTIONS: All counties in the state of Maryland excluding the entire Eastern Shore, Calvert, Cecil, Charles, Montgomery, Prince George's, and St. Mary's counties.

FINANCIAL DATA:
Amount of support per award: $10,000 to $100,000. Average $40,000.
Total amount of support: $2,312,979 for the year 2015.
Matching fund requirements: Specific to grantee. Usually matched within a six-month period.

NO. MOST RECENT APPLICANTS: 210.

NO. AWARDS: 52.

REPRESENTATIVE AWARDS:
$85,175 to St. Francis Parish; $46,243 to Parks & People Foundation; $70,000 to St. Philip Neri School; $25,000 to Art with a Heart; $40,000 to Dyslexia Tutoring.

APPLICATION INFO:
Required documentation includes proof of 501(c)(3) status, brief narrative of objective of proposal, history of requesting agency, list of trustees and officers, administrating personnel with resume, budget for project, most recent audited report and list of foundations and corporations that have supported previous requests and are being solicited for this request. Must call Executive Director before submitting a proposal.
Duration: Usually one year.
Deadline: Letters of Inquiry and Financials: February, June and October. Full Proposal: March 24, July 21 and November 24, respectively.

IRS I.D.: 52-1517876

TRUSTEES AND OFFICERS:
Patrick Rodgers, President
Daniel Gallagher
David Gallagher
Lindsay R. Gallagher
Marty Voelkel Hanssen
E.B. Harris
Kelly L. Harris
Thomas Harris
Carlisle Hashim
Erin Knott
Marion I. Knott
Martin G. Knott, Jr.
Martin G. Knott, Sr.
Owen M. Knott
Teresa A. Knott
Brian McDonald
Meghan McDonald
Peter McGill
David L. Porter
Joanna O. Porter
Laurel Porter
Margie Riehl
Michael Riehl
Brooke Rodgers
Michael Rodgers
Geralynn D. Smyth
John Smyth
Peggy Smyth
Jan Steendam
Emmett Voelkel

ADDRESS INQUIRIES TO:
Kelly Medinger, Executive Director
(See address above.)

KORET FOUNDATION [191]

611 Front Street
San Francisco, CA 94111-1963
(415) 882-7740
Fax: (415) 882-7775
E-mail: koret@koretfoundation.org
Web Site: www.koretfoundation.org

FOUNDED: 1979

AREAS OF INTEREST:
Arts, community service and volunteerism, Jewish community services, education and employment for youth, elderly, hunger and homelessness.

TYPE:
Capital grants; General operating grants; Project/program grants; Seed money grants.

YEAR PROGRAM STARTED: 1979

PURPOSE:
To address societal challenges and strengthen Bay Area life; to invest in strategic, local solutions that help to inspire a multiplier effect, encouraging collaborative funding and developing model initiatives.

LEGAL BASIS:
Private foundation.

ELIGIBILITY:
Grant applicants must be 501(c)(3) organizations. Private foundations are not eligible to apply.

Although the majority of funding is granted to six of nine bay area counties, the Foundation will consider national and Israeli projects.

GEOG. RESTRICTIONS: Alameda, Contra Costa, Marin, San Francisco, San Mateo and Santa Clara counties, California.

FINANCIAL DATA:
Amount of support per award: Grants vary in amount, depending upon the needs and nature of the request.

Total amount of support: $35,551,100 for the year 2014.

APPLICATION INFO:
The Foundation considers grant requests by invitation only.

Duration: Varies.

PUBLICATIONS:
Annual report; application guidelines.

IRS I.D.: 94-1624987

OFFICERS:
Jeffrey A. Farber, Chief Executive Officer

ADDRESS INQUIRIES TO:
Marina Lum, Grants Manager
(See address above.)

THE KRESGE FOUNDATION [192]

3215 West Big Beaver Road
Troy, MI 48084
(248) 643-9630
Fax: (248) 643-0588
E-mail: info@kresge.org
Web Site: www.kresge.org

FOUNDED: 1924

AREAS OF INTEREST:
Arts and culture, Detroit/community development, education, environment, and health and human services.

TYPE:
General operating grants; Project/program grants. Program-related investments.

YEAR PROGRAM STARTED: 1924

PURPOSE:
To expand opportunity for low-income people so they can gain the tools and support needed to lead self-determined lives and join the economic mainstream.

LEGAL BASIS:
Independent private foundation.

ELIGIBILITY:
Tax-exempt charitable organizations operating in the fields of higher education (including community colleges), health care and long-term care, human services, science and the environment, arts and humanities and public affairs. Governmental agencies are also eligible to apply. Full accreditation is required for higher education and hospital applicants and preferred in all other fields that offer it. Evidence of initial funding for the requested project is considered essential.

The following projects are eligible:
(1) construction of facilities;
(2) renovation of facilities;
(3) purchase of major equipment or an integrated system at a cost of at least $300,000; equipment costs may include computer software expenses, if applicable and;
(4) purchase of real estate.

Religious organizations, elementary and secondary schools, private foundations and individuals are not eligible to apply. However, accredited seminaries are eligible to apply. Also, agencies operated by religious organizations that serve secular needs may be eligible if the programs have financial and governing autonomy separate from the parent organization. They must also have space formally dedicated to their programs.

Some elementary and secondary schools may be eligible in the Foundation's Human Services category, if they predominantly serve individuals with physical and/or developmental disabilities.

FINANCIAL DATA:
Amount of support per award: Varies.

Total amount of support: $120,000,000 to $150,000,000 annually.

NO. AWARDS: 150 for the year 2015.

REPRESENTATIVE AWARDS:
$100,000,000 in 2014 to the Foundation for Detroit's Future, a fund created to soften the impact of the city's bankruptcy on pensioners and to safeguard cultural assets at the Detroit Institute of Arts.

APPLICATION INFO:
Grant and social investment opportunities are announced online. Only electronic application is accepted.

Duration: Varies.

PUBLICATIONS:
Annual report.

ADDRESS INQUIRIES TO:
Grants Inquiry Coordinator
(See address above.)

ALBERT AND BESSIE MAE KRONKOSKY CHARITABLE FOUNDATION [193]

112 East Pecan, Suite 830
San Antonio, TX 78205
(210) 475-9000
Fax: (210) 354-2204
E-mail: kronfndn@kronkosky.org
Web Site: www.kronkosky.org

FOUNDED: 1991

AREAS OF INTEREST:
Elderly, youth, child abuse and neglect, persons with disabilities, culture and the arts, museums, libraries, prevention of cruelty to animals, health, parks, zoos and wildlife sanctuaries.

TYPE:
Capital grants; Challenge/matching grants; Endowments; General operating grants; Matching gifts; Project/program grants; Research grants; Seed money grants; Technical assistance; Training grants; Research contracts.

YEAR PROGRAM STARTED: 1999

PURPOSE:
To produce profound good that is tangible and measurable in Bandera, Bexar, Comal, and Kendall counties in Texas by implementing the Kronkoskys' charitable purposes.

LEGAL BASIS:
Private foundation.

ELIGIBILITY:
Corporate organizations that are exempt under Section 501(c)(3) of the Internal Revenue Code. The Foundation will not make grants to individuals or for-profit organizations. In addition, the Foundation has a geographic limitation that requires that grant funds be used in the specific counties listed below.

GEOG. RESTRICTIONS: Bandera, Bexar, Comal and Kendall counties, Texas.

FINANCIAL DATA:
Amount of support per award: $2,080 to $1,000,000 for the year 2015. Average grant: $75,000.

Total amount of support: $17,066,566 for the year 2015.

NO. MOST RECENT APPLICANTS: 213 for the year 2015.

NO. AWARDS: 169 grants for the year 2015.

APPLICATION INFO:
Send a Letter of Inquiry to the address above. If the Letter of Inquiry meets requirements, it will be reviewed by Foundation's staff within 10 days of receipt. If the proposal is accepted, an application package as well as a timeline for submission of the grant proposal will be forwarded. If proposal is not accepted, notification in writing will be sent. Please note geographic requirement.

Duration: Usually one year.

Deadline: Letters of Inquiry will be accepted throughout the year and reviewed on a rolling basis.

PUBLICATIONS:
Program guidelines; annual report (online only).

IRS I.D.: 74-6385152

ADDRESS INQUIRIES TO:
Tullos Wells, Managing Director
(See address above.)

THE JEAN AND E. FLOYD KVAMME FOUNDATION

P.O. Box 2494
Saratoga, CA 95070
(408) 395-2829
Fax: (408) 354-0804

TYPE:
Capital grants; Development grants; General operating grants; Project/program grants. Medical grants are given primarily in the areas of Alzheimers, leukemia, arthritis, and spondylitis; however, grants for research in other areas are considered.

See entry 1515 for full listing.

LAIDLAW FOUNDATION [194]

365 Bloor Street East
Suite 2000
Toronto ON M4W 3L4 Canada
(416) 964-3614 ext. 307
Fax: (416) 975-1428
E-mail: bkeles@laidlawfdn.org
Web Site: laidlawfdn.org

FOUNDED: 1949

AREAS OF INTEREST:
Youth engagement, youth social infrastructure and policy development.

NAME(S) OF PROGRAMS:

- **Youth-led Community Change (YLCC)**

TYPE:
Project/program grants.

YEAR PROGRAM STARTED: 1949

PURPOSE:
To invest in innovative ideas, convene interested parties, share learning and advocate for change in support of young people becoming healthy, creative and fully engaged citizens.

LEGAL BASIS:
Private family foundation.

ELIGIBILITY:
The Foundation will fund youth-led initiatives. Applicants must be young people 14 to 25 years of age.

GEOG. RESTRICTIONS: Ontario, Canada.

FINANCIAL DATA:
Amount of support per award: Project Grants: Up to $25,000.

Total amount of support: Approximately $650,000.

APPLICATION INFO:
Applicants must submit:
(1) Grant Application Cover Sheet;
(2) three- to five-page proposal;
(3) work plan;
(4) budget;
(5) contact information for other community groups, agencies or individuals that will play a role in the proposal, if applicable;
(6) partnership agreement between main applicant and administrative partner and/or letter from administrative partner, if applicable;
(7) list of board of directors or governing committee members, if applicable;
(8) current operating budget for the group/organization, if applicable;
(9) most recent audited financial statements, if applicable and;
(10) most recent final report if applicant has been previously funded from Laidlaw.

Submit 12 hard copies and one electronic copy (by e-mail). Confirmation will be sent by e-mail when proposal is received.

Duration: Typically one year.

Deadline: Varies.

ADDRESS INQUIRIES TO:
Betul Keles
Program Manager, Youth Organizing
(See address and e-mail above.)

LAMB FOUNDATION [195]

P.O. Box 1705
Lake Oswego, OR 97035
(503) 635-8010
Fax: (503) 635-6544
E-mail: lambfdn@lambfoundation.org
Web Site: www.lambfoundation.org

FOUNDED: 1971

AREAS OF INTEREST:
Social services for youth and children, arts, and environment.

TYPE:
Challenge/matching grants; General operating grants; Project/program grants.

LEGAL BASIS:
Private foundation.

ELIGIBILITY:
Applicants must be nonprofit 501(c)(3) public charity organizations.

GEOG. RESTRICTIONS: Pacific Northwest.

FINANCIAL DATA:
Amount of support per award: Typical grants: $5,000 to $15,000.

Total amount of support: Approximately $250,000.

NO. MOST RECENT APPLICANTS: 17 for the year 2015.

NO. AWARDS: 41.

REPRESENTATIVE AWARDS:
$15,000 to p:ear for an arts and culture program; $15,000 to The Freshwater Trust for the Scalable Tools for Freshwater Restoration Project; $15,000 to Mountain Star Family Relief Nursery for the expansion of services in Prineville, OR.

APPLICATION INFO:
The Foundation does not accept unsolicited applications. Upon invitation, application information will be sent to the prospective applicant.

Duration: One year.

Deadline: Included in application materials sent to invited applicants.

PUBLICATIONS:
Brochure.

IRS I.D.: 23-7120564

STAFF:
Debra Iguchi, Administrator

ADDRESS INQUIRIES TO:
Debra Iguchi, Administrator
(See address above.)

*PLEASE NOTE:
Prospective applicants are encouraged to contact the office or web site periodically for changes.

LAND O'LAKES FOUNDATION [196]

4001 Lexington Avenue North
Arden Hills, MN 55126
(651) 375-2470
E-mail: landolakesfoundation@landolakes.com
Web Site: www.foundation.landolakes.com

FOUNDED: 1997

AREAS OF INTEREST:
Hunger, education and community.

CONSULTING OR VOLUNTEER SERVICES:
Group projects.

NAME(S) OF PROGRAMS:

- **California Regions Grant Program**
- **Community Grants Program**
- **Dollars for Doers Program**
- **Matching Gifts to Education Program**
- **Member Co-op Match Program**
- **Mid-Atlantic Grant Program**

TYPE:
Capital grants; Endowments; General operating grants; Matching gifts; Project/program grants. Major support is in the form of cash contributions, supplemented with food and product donations to Feeding America National Food Bank Network only.

California Regions Grant Program funds community projects in three areas of California: Orland, Tulare/Kings/Bakersfield and Ontario, initiated by Land O'Lakes dairy member-leaders.

Community Grants Program provides support through cash grants to nonprofit organizations that are working to improve communities where Land O'Lakes has a significant concentration of members or employees. Foundation's primary focus area is hunger and hunger-related issues.

Dollars for Doers Program recognizes employee and retiree volunteerism with financial contributions to 501(c)(3) nonprofit organizations based on volunteer hours.

Matching Gifts to Education Program matches gifts by full- and part-time employees, Board of Directors members and Leadership Council members to grades K-12, postsecondary education, and public radio and public television stations.

Member Co-op Match Program matches dollar-for-dollar the cash donations of member cooperatives, thus doubling the funds available for hometown projects.

Mid-Atlantic Grant Program funds community projects in Maryland, New York, Pennsylvania and Virginia, initiated by Land O'Lakes dairy member-leaders.

YEAR PROGRAM STARTED: 1981

PURPOSE:
To demonstrate a commitment to improving and enhancing the quality of life in communities where Land O'Lakes has facilities, plants, members and employees; to invest and participate in community programs that strengthen and preserve the quality of rural life; to encourage and support employee volunteerism.

LEGAL BASIS:
Corporate foundation.

ELIGIBILITY:
Contributions are generally restricted to organizations which have been granted 501(c)(3) tax-exempt status and are working to improve communities where Land O'Lakes has a significant concentration of members or employees. Contributions are focused in the western, north central and eastern states. Of our donations, 85% will be made in rural areas and 15% in urban areas within those states.

Funds generally will not be used for lobbying, political and religious organizations, veteran, fraternal and labor organizations, fund-raising events, benefits or advertising, national groups, individuals, scholarships, private colleges and universities, disease/medical research or treatment or racing/sports sponsorships.

Matching Gift recipient organizations must be located in the U.S. and be tax-exempt under Section 501(c)(3) of the Internal Revenue Code. Eligible institutions include the following:
(1) elementary and secondary schools that are fully accredited by the Department of Education;
(2) public or private colleges, universities, junior colleges, technical/vocational institutes, community colleges and graduate professional schools with appropriate regional or professional accreditation, or tax-exempt alumni funds, foundations or associations that collect funds exclusively for the direct benefit of an eligible institution and;
(3) public radio and television stations that meet the criteria established by the Corporation for Public Broadcasting.

Organizations are eligible for only one grant per calendar year.

FINANCIAL DATA:
Amount of support per award: Varies.

Total amount of support: Approximately $7,600,000 for the year 2015.

Matching fund requirements: Cash only.

CO-OP FUNDING PROGRAMS: Through the Member Co-op Match Program, Land O'Lakes member cooperatives may request that the Foundation match their donations to local nonprofits, within the parameters of the program.

REPRESENTATIVE AWARDS:
Feeding America National Food Bank Network.

APPLICATION INFO:
Duration: Varies.

PUBLICATIONS:
Contributions program guidelines.

IRS I.D.: 41-1864977

ADDRESS INQUIRIES TO:
Executive Director
Land O'Lakes Foundation
P.O. Box 64150
St. Paul, MN 55164-0150

LAND O'LAKES FOUNDATION [197]

4001 Lexington Avenue North
Arden Hills, MN 55126
(651) 375-2470
E-mail: landolakesfoundation@landolakes.com
Web Site: www.foundation.landolakes.com

AREAS OF INTEREST:
Dairy science or dairy manufacturing/marketing.

NAME(S) OF PROGRAMS:
- **John Brandt Memorial Scholarship Fund**

TYPE:
Scholarships. John Brandt Memorial Scholarship Program is a $25,000 scholarship available to graduate students pursuing dairy-related degrees. One or two scholarships are awarded annually to deserving candidates who have demonstrated exceptional commitment and aptitude toward their field of study.

PURPOSE:
To encourage graduate study in dairy science or dairy marketing/manufacturing.

LEGAL BASIS:
Corporate foundation.

ELIGIBILITY:
Applicants must be pursuing a program of study leading to a Master's or Doctorate degree in dairy cattle nutrition, genetics, physiology or management, or the manufacturing, processing or marketing of milk and dairy products at one of the four following institutions: University of Minnesota, University of Wisconsin, Iowa State University and South Dakota State University. Such factors as personal recommendations, scholastic record, planned program of study and research and future plans for working in the dairy industry or closely related fields shall be considered in making the award.

FINANCIAL DATA:
Amount of support per award: $25,000.

Total amount of support: Up to $75,000, depending on need and endowment market performance.

NO. AWARDS: Up to 3 annually.

APPLICATION INFO:
The Foundation sends out Requests for Proposals (RFPs) to the qualifying schools to begin the application process. Those with recommendations should send an application form including personal history, transcripts of scholastic record, and a plan of study and research to be followed in pursuit of an advanced degree. Applications should be sent to the Executive Director, Land O'Lakes Foundation, P.O. Box 64150, St. Paul, MN 55164-0150.

Duration: One academic year. No renewals.

ADDRESS INQUIRIES TO:
Executive Director
Land O'Lakes Foundation
P.O. Box 64150
St. Paul, MN 55164-0150

*SPECIAL STIPULATIONS:
Scholarships for graduate-level studies.

HERBERT AND GERTRUDE LATKIN CHARITABLE FOUNDATION [198]

P.O. Box 2340
Santa Barbara, CA 93120-2340
(805) 899-8471

FOUNDED: 1991

AREAS OF INTEREST:
Animal cruelty, child abuse, emergency medical services, health and welfare to elderly and needy people, scholarships to deserving college students.

TYPE:
Project/program grants; Scholarships.

YEAR PROGRAM STARTED: 1991

PURPOSE:
To promote the health and welfare of the elderly; to prevent cruelty to animals; to provide emergency medical service for persons suffering as a result of calamity or disaster; to prevent child abuse; to provide assistance to the needy; to provide scholarships to college students.

LEGAL BASIS:
Private family foundation.

ELIGIBILITY:
Grants are made to organizations that have tax-exempt status under Section 501(c)(3) of the Internal Revenue Code. No grants are made to individuals or religious organizations.

GEOG. RESTRICTIONS: Santa Barbara County, California.

FINANCIAL DATA:
Amount of support per award: Varies.

Total amount of support: $213,500 for the year 2014.

NO. MOST RECENT APPLICANTS: 65.

NO. AWARDS: 57.

APPLICATION INFO:
Send a letter of inquiry outlining the organization's goal and purposes, the intended use and amount of the grant requested and 501(c)(3) letter.

Duration: One year. Renewal possible.

Deadline: April 1 and October 1.

IRS I.D.: 77-6070540

ADDRESS INQUIRIES TO:
Stephanie Eubanks, Trust Officer
(See address above.)

THE BLANCHE AND IRVING LAURIE FOUNDATION [199]

P.O. Box 53
Roseland, NJ 07068-5788
(973) 993-1743
Fax: (973) 993-3146

AREAS OF INTEREST:
Arts, children, needs of the elderly, education, medical care and needs of the Jewish community.

TYPE:
Capital grants; Project/program grants.

LEGAL BASIS:
Private foundation.

ELIGIBILITY:
Funds given for specific projects only. No funds for general organization endowments, nor to meet general operating expenses or budget deficits.

GEOG. RESTRICTIONS: Social service programs: New Jersey.

FINANCIAL DATA:
Amount of support per award: $25,000 to $50,000.

APPLICATION INFO:
Submit seven copies of proposal including statement of program objectives, project budget, plans for publicizing the project, background information about the organization and copy of IRS tax-exemption letter.

Duration: Varies.

Deadline: Proposals accepted year-round.

PUBLICATIONS:
Informational brochure.

BOARD OF TRUSTEES:
Laura Barron
Gene R. Korf, Esq.
Scott Korf
Richard A. Patt
Harvey Rich
Robert M. Zagoren

ADDRESS INQUIRIES TO:
Gene R. Korf, Esq., Executive Director
(See address above.)

LIBRA FOUNDATION [200]

Three Canal Plaza, Suite 500
Portland, ME 04101
(207) 879-6280
Fax: (207) 879-6281
E-mail: kathi@librafoundation.org
Web Site: www.librafoundation.org

FOUNDED: 1989

AREAS OF INTEREST:
Arts, culture and humanities, education, environment, health, human services, public/society benefit and religion.

TYPE:
Grants-in-aid; Project/program grants.

YEAR PROGRAM STARTED: 1989

PURPOSE:
To strive for innovative ways to enrich Maine, empower communities, and enhance the quality of life of all Maine citizens.

ELIGIBILITY:
Charitable nonprofit organizations whose activities, operations, or purposes take place only within the state of Maine. Religious organizations are eligible. Organizations must supply a copy of tax-exempt 501(c)(3) letter. Grants are not made to individuals.

GEOG. RESTRICTIONS: Maine.

FINANCIAL DATA:

Amount of support per award: Up to $25,000.

Total amount of support: Approximately $4,656,000 for the year 2015.

NO. MOST RECENT APPLICANTS: 305.

NO. AWARDS: 60.

APPLICATION INFO:

Applicants are asked to complete a two-paged application in accordance with the Foundation's guidelines, both of which may be obtained from the Foundation web site.

Duration: One-time grant. May reapply after expiration of one year.

Deadline: February 15, May 15, August 15 and November 15.

ADDRESS INQUIRIES TO:
Jennifer A. Cook, Financial Assistant
(See address above.)

LILLY ENDOWMENT INC. [201]

2801 North Meridian Street
Indianapolis, IN 46208
(317) 924-5471
Fax: (317) 926-4431
E-mail: cebulaj@lei.org
Web Site: www.lillyendowment.org

FOUNDED: 1937

AREAS OF INTEREST:
Religion, education and community development.

TYPE:

Awards/prizes; Challenge/matching grants; Conferences/seminars; Development grants; Fellowships; General operating grants; Matching gifts; Project/program grants; Research grants. In the area of religion, support for programs that enrich the religious lives of American Christians, mainly by supporting efforts to call, support and educate a new generation of talented pastors and to strengthen current pastors in their capacities for excellence in ministry; support for programs that seek to help congregations be healthy communities of faith; support for theological seminaries and other educational and religious institutions that share these aims; support for projects which strengthen the contributions that religious ideas, practices, values and institutions make to the common good.

In the area of education, support for initiatives and programs that improve education in Indiana, with special emphasis on higher education and on programs designed to increase the number of Indiana residents with Bachelor's degrees; support for a number of invitational grant programs, many of which are aimed at Indiana's colleges' and universities' abilities to increase the state's educational attainment level; support on an invitational basis for minority higher education.

In the area of youth, support for direct-service organizations in central Indiana; support for building capacity of intermediary organizations throughout the state; support for professional development for the staff and volunteer leadership of these organizations.

In the area of leadership education, support for projects that nurture good stewardship among the trustees and executives of charitable organizations; support for scholarship on the characteristics of able trusteeship and good governance of nonprofit organizations.

In the area of fund-raising and philanthropy, support for programs (nationally and in Indiana) to increase the charitable giving among Americans; support for efforts to create a body of reliable knowledge about giving and fund-raising; support for scholarly pursuit of the subject.

In the areas of community development, support is available for programs that involve Indianapolis initiatives in the arts, culture and preservation, human services and community development and revitalization. Indiana initiatives include Indiana United Ways and community foundations. Economic public-policy general support grants are offered on an invitational basis to a limited number of organizations that promote free market and democratic principles.

YEAR PROGRAM STARTED: 1937

PURPOSE:
To support the causes of religion, education and community development.

LEGAL BASIS:
Private foundation.

ELIGIBILITY:
Applicants must be 501(c)(3) tax-exempt public organizations and institutions with appropriate interests in targeted areas. Grantmaking prohibitions generally include loans or cash to individuals, health care projects, mass media projects, endowments, libraries outside Indianapolis, and general operating support/capital campaigns for organizations outside of Indiana.

GEOG. RESTRICTIONS: Community development and education in Indiana.

FINANCIAL DATA:

Grants vary in amount depending on the needs and nature of the request.

Amount of support per award: Varies.

Total amount of support: $439,968,365 in grants paid for the year 2015.

Matching fund requirements: Varies.

NO. MOST RECENT APPLICANTS: 446 proposals for the year 2015.

NO. AWARDS: 766 approved grants for the year 2015.

APPLICATION INFO:

Except for specialized programs, no official application forms are required. Guidelines for applicants are found on the web site. The usual first step is a two-page letter outlining the project and budget and a description of the applicant organization, including a statement of federal tax-exempt status.

Duration: One to three years; typically, one year.

Deadline: Applications accepted on an ongoing basis.

PUBLICATIONS:
Application guidelines; annual report.

IRS I.D.: 35-0868122

OFFICERS:
N. Clay Robbins, Chairman, President and Chief Executive Officer
Diane M. Stenson, Vice President and Treasurer
Wallace R. (Ace) Yakey, Jr., Vice President, Community Development
Sara B. Cobb, Vice President, Education
E.G. White, Vice President, Finance
Christopher L. Coble, Vice President, Religion
David D. Biber, Secretary and Director, Youth Programs

DIRECTORS:
Daniel P. Carmichael
Craig R. Dykstra
William G. Enright
Charles E. Golden
Jennett M. Hill
Eli Lilly, II
Mary K. Lisher
N. Clay Robbins
David N. Shane

ADDRESS INQUIRIES TO:
Program Office
(See address above.)

*SPECIAL STIPULATIONS:
Awards are made to 501(c)(3) groups only.

LINCOLN FINANCIAL FOUNDATION [202]

1300 South Clinton Street
Fort Wayne, IN 46802
(260) 455-3868
Fax: (260) 455-4004
E-mail: deb.washler@lfg.com
Web Site: www.lincolnfinancial.com

FOUNDED: 1962

AREAS OF INTEREST:
Arts, youth education, human services and workforce/economic development.

CONSULTING OR VOLUNTEER SERVICES:
Volunteer Involvement Program for employees of Lincoln Financial Group.

TYPE:
Matching gifts; Project/program grants.

YEAR PROGRAM STARTED: 1962

PURPOSE:
To enhance the quality of life and help individuals face their futures with confidence in communities where employees work.

LEGAL BASIS:
Corporate Foundation.

ELIGIBILITY:

Applicants must be 501(c)(3) organizations.

No grants to individuals, for endowments, for sponsorship of sporting events or for the purchase of tickets.

GEOG. RESTRICTIONS: Hartford, Connecticut; Fort Wayne, Indiana; Omaha, Nebraska; Concord, New Hampshire; Greensboro, North Carolina; Philadelphia, Pennsylvania.

FINANCIAL DATA:

Amount of support per award: Varies.

Total amount of support: Up to 2% of the corporation's pre-tax earnings annually.

Matching fund requirements: Qualified 501(c)(3).

NO. MOST RECENT APPLICANTS: 420.

NO. AWARDS: 340.

APPLICATION INFO:

Online application form required. Some attachments requested.

Duration: Quarterly.

Deadline: Varies.

PUBLICATIONS:
Guidelines.

IRS I.D.: 35-6042099

ADDRESS INQUIRIES TO:
Program Officer
(See address above.)

THE LOATS FOUNDATION, INC. [203]

35 East Church Street
Frederick, MD 21701
(301) 663-6361
Fax: (301) 663-7747

FOUNDED: 1979

AREAS OF INTEREST:
Scholarship for Frederick County residents only and charitable organizations of Frederick County, MD.

TYPE:
Scholarships.

YEAR PROGRAM STARTED: 1979

PURPOSE:
To help residents of Frederick County, MD go on to higher education by providing financial aid.

LEGAL BASIS:
Nonprofit foundation.

ELIGIBILITY:
Applicant must be a resident of Frederick County, MD. Scholarships are distributed by colleges on a need basis.

GEOG. RESTRICTIONS: Frederick County, Maryland.

FINANCIAL DATA:
Amount of support per award: $3,000 cap.

Total amount of support: Varies.

APPLICATION INFO:
Applications for scholarships are available at all Maryland colleges and universities.

Duration: One year. Renewable on need basis.

ADDRESS INQUIRIES TO:
Helen Hahn, Secretary
(See address above.)

THE LUBRIZOL FOUNDATION [204]

29400 Lakeland Boulevard, Mail Drop 054B
Wickliffe, OH 44092-2298
(440) 347-1797
Fax: (440) 347-1858
E-mail: karen.lerchbacher@lubrizol.com
Web Site: www.lubrizol.com

FOUNDED: 1952

AREAS OF INTEREST:
Education, health and human services, civic, cultural, environmental and youth activities.

NAME(S) OF PROGRAMS:
- **Community Connection Employee Volunteer Gift Program**
- **Matching Gift Program**

TYPE:
Capital grants; Fellowships; General operating grants; Matching gifts; Project/program grants; Scholarships. The Foundation has scholarship programs at 38 selected colleges and universities. It also matches gifts of Lubrizol employees to most charitable organizations on a dollar-for-dollar basis.

In the area of education, support is given for scholarships, fellowships and awards in selected fields of study through selected colleges and universities, with major emphasis on the study of chemistry and chemical and mechanical engineering, capital and operating grants to colleges, universities, schools, educational programs and combined educational funds.

In the area of health and human services, support is provided for combined funds, direct grants to health and human service activities.

In the area of civic and cultural, support is provided for public television stations, performing arts organizations, schools of fine arts and museums.

In the area of youth activities, support is given to programs that contribute to character-building, such as those which promote good citizenship, self-reliance, an understanding of free enterprise and an appreciation of nature and the environment.

In the environmental area, support is given to parks, nature centers, conservancies and local environmental education efforts.

YEAR PROGRAM STARTED: 1952

PURPOSE:
To support educational, youth, health, human services, civic and cultural and environmental activities of a tax-exempt, charitable nature.

LEGAL BASIS:
Private, tax-exempt foundation.

ELIGIBILITY:
Grants are made to U.S. nonprofit, educational or other charitable tax-exempt organizations. Grants are not generally made to endowments, religious or political purposes or individuals.

GEOG. RESTRICTIONS: Primarily Greater Cleveland, Ohio and Houston, Texas.

FINANCIAL DATA:
Amount of support per award: Grants vary in amount, depending upon the needs and nature of the request.

Total amount of support: $4,539,563, including matching gifts, for the year 2015.

Matching fund requirements: 1:1 match; $100 minimum; $5,000 maximum, and five gifts maximum.

NO. MOST RECENT APPLICANTS: 100.

NO. AWARDS: 55 discretionary grants; 199 total awards including operating, capital and discretionary.

REPRESENTATIVE AWARDS:
$110,200 to the United Way of Lake County, Inc. for general operating support; $84,800 to the United Way of the Texas Gulf Coast for general operating support; $183,300 to the United Way Services of Cleveland for general operating support.

APPLICATION INFO:
Grant proposals should include the following:
(1) a cover letter that summarizes the purpose of the request signed by the executive officer of the organization;
(2) a narrative of specific information related to the subject of the request;
(3) current audited financial statements and a specific project budget, if applicable and;
(4) documentation of the organization's Federal tax-exempt status.

Additional descriptive literature (annual report, brochures, etc.) that accurately characterizes the overall activities of the organization is appreciated. Upon review, further information may be requested including an interview or site visit.

Applicants will receive written notification of the decision on their proposal. An organization whose request has been declined should not submit another proposal for at least 12 months after such notification.

Duration: One year, with possible renewal. Some grants are ongoing.

PUBLICATIONS:
Annual report.

IRS I.D.: 34-6500595

OFFICERS:
J.L. Hambrick, Chairman
J. Mark Sutherland, President
B.A. Valentine, Treasurer
K.A. Lerchbacher, Secretary

TRUSTEES:
R.T. Graf
J.L. Hambrick
K.L. Jethrow
K.A. Lerchbacher
J. Mark Sutherland
B.A. Valentine

ADDRESS INQUIRIES TO:
Karen A. Lerchbacher
Grants Manager
(See address above.)

THE HENRY LUCE FOUNDATION, INC. [205]

51 Madison Avenue, 30th Floor
New York, NY 10010
(212) 489-7700
Fax: (212) 581-9541
E-mail: hlf1@hluce.org
Web Site: www.hluce.org

FOUNDED: 1936

AREAS OF INTEREST:
Interdisciplinary exploration of higher education, increased understanding between Asia and the U.S., the study of religion and theology, scholarship in American art, opportunities for women in science and engineering, and environmental and public policy programs.

NAME(S) OF PROGRAMS:
- **American Art Program**
- **Clare Boothe Luce Program**
- **Luce Foundation Theology Program**
- **Henry Luce III Fellows in Theology Program**
- **Luce Scholars Program**

TYPE:
Fellowships; Project/program grants; Scholarships. American Art Program focuses on the American fine and decorative arts and is committed to scholarship and the overall enhancement of this field. The program is national in scope and provides support for all periods and genres of American art history.

The Clare Boothe Luce Program promotes the advancement of American women through higher education in the sciences, engineering and mathematics.

The Luce Foundation's Theology program encourages the development of leadership for religious communities through theological education, and fosters scholarship that links the academy to churches and the wider public. The program provides funding for seminary education, leadership, ecumenical and interreligious programs, and religion and the arts.

The Henry Luce III Fellows in Theology program, administered by the Association of Theological Schools, supports innovative research and publication by full-time seminary faculty.

The Luce Scholars Program provides stipends and internships for young Americans to live and work in Asia each year.

PURPOSE:
To promote interdisciplinary exploration of higher education, increased understanding between Asia and the U.S., the study of religion and theology, scholarship in American art, opportunities for women in science and engineering, and environmental and public policy programs.

ELIGIBILITY:
The Foundation does not support health care or medical projects and does not fund development assistance work overseas. It does not normally assist journalism, media and film projects or the performing arts. The Foundation does not offer funding for individuals.

FINANCIAL DATA:
Amount of support per award: Varies.

Total amount of support: Varies.

APPLICATION INFO:
No special forms are required, although separate guidelines and deadlines exist for specific programs. In most cases, an initial letter of inquiry, to determine whether a project falls within the Foundation's guidelines, can be addressed to the appropriate program director or officer.

Duration: Varies.

ADDRESS INQUIRIES TO:
Appropriate Program Director or see e-mail address above.

LYNDHURST FOUNDATION [206]

517 East Fifth Street
Chattanooga, TN 37403-1826
(423) 756-0767
Fax: (423) 756-0770
E-mail: bclark@lyndhurstfoundation.org
Web Site: www.lyndhurstfoundation.org

FOUNDED: 1938

AREAS OF INTEREST:
Education, conservation, arts, culture, economy, urban design and development, neighborhood revitalization and physical health.

Enhancing the quality of Chattanooga's public gathering places in downtown and along the riverfront, plus its public schools, its diverse arts and cultural organizations and its natural environment. Beyond the city's boundaries, the Foundation wants to be involved in projects that protect and enhance the natural environment of the southern Appalachian region.

TYPE:
Challenge/matching grants; Conferences/seminars; Demonstration grants; Development grants; Endowments; General operating grants; Matching gifts; Project/program grants; Seed money grants; Technical assistance. The Foundation intends to focus upon continued development of the Tennessee Riverpark, redevelopment of the Southside as a live-and-work urban neighborhood, facilitation of historic preservation, stimulation of downtown housing development, strengthening of the city's arts and cultural life, protection and enhancement of the community's natural environment, the reform of the community's public schools, the continued development of improved housing opportunities for people of modest means and innovations in social service programs that provide genuine progress against social problems and genuine enhancement of community strengths in Chattanooga.

YEAR PROGRAM STARTED: 1978

PURPOSE:
To identify and invest in initiatives, institutions, people and programs that contribute to the long-term livability and resilience of the greater Chattanooga, TN region.

LEGAL BASIS:
Private foundation.

ELIGIBILITY:
Applicants must be 501(c)(3) organizations in the southeastern U.S.

Grants are distributed primarily at the initiative of the Foundation through the cultivation of strategic partnerships with nonprofit organizations which have the demonstrated capacity and leadership to engender positive and measurable outcomes within the Foundation's declared areas of interest.

Unsolicited proposals will not be eligible for consideration.

GEOG. RESTRICTIONS: The greater Chattanooga, Tennessee region.

FINANCIAL DATA:
Amount of support per award: Approximately $96,000 average grant for the year 2014.

Total amount of support: Grants of $4,807,438 for the year 2014.

NO. AWARDS: Varies.

REPRESENTATIVE AWARDS:
$10,000 to Cumberland Trail Conference for the construction of a foot bridge; $100,000 to Public Education Foundation in support of an education data analyst for the Hamilton County Department of Education; $55,000 to Chattanooga Neighborhood Enterprise for technical assistance and neighborhood revitalization activities.

APPLICATION INFO:
Potential partners will be invited to submit grant proposals that:
(1) describe the program of work to be undertaken;
(2) indicate the desired level of funding;
(3) list the results that should be achieved and;
(4) define the means by which the project outcomes will be evaluated.

The narrative section of the proposal should be limited to three pages and include the following attachments:
(1) a description of the sponsoring organization;
(2) a list of the board of directors and staff;
(3) a copy of the organization's annual budget (both income and expenditures);
(4) an estimated project budget with line items and;
(5) a copy of the organization's tax-exempt ruling from the IRS.

Duration: One year. Renewal possible for up to three years.

Deadline: Proposals are due six weeks in advance of the Foundation's quarterly board meeting dates, which typically occur in February, May, August and November. Program staff will be available to work with applicants to ensure that materials are delivered on a timely basis and in the required format.

PUBLICATIONS:
Annual report.

OFFICERS:
Robert C. Taylor, Jr., Chairman of the Board
Benic M. Clark, III, President/Treasurer
Katherine N. Currin, Secretary

TRUSTEES:
Stephen A. Culp
Katherine N. Currin
Kathleen S. Hunt, M.D.
James O. Kennedy
Alison G. Lebovitz
James J. McGinness
Robert K. Mills
Robert C. Taylor, Jr.
Margaret W. Townsend

STAFF:
Benic M. Clark, III, President/Treasurer
Macon C. Toledano, Associate Director
Margaret Stakely, Controller
Kathleen Nolte, Program Officer

ADDRESS INQUIRIES TO:
Catherine C. Cox
(See phone number above.)

M & M AREA COMMUNITY FOUNDATION

1110 10th Avenue, Suite L-1
Menominee, MI 49858
(906) 864-3599
Fax: (906) 864-3657
E-mail: info@mmcommunityfoundation.org
Web Site: www.mmcommunityfoundation.org

TYPE:
Project/program grants; Scholarships.

See entry 1289 for full listing.

THE J.E. AND L.E. MABEE FOUNDATION, INC. [207]

401 South Boston Avenue
Suite 3001
Tulsa, OK 74103-4017
(918) 584-4286
Fax: (918) 585-5540
Web Site: www.mabeefoundation.com

FOUNDED: 1948

AREAS OF INTEREST:
Education, scientific and medical research, religion and charities.

TYPE:
Challenge/matching grants.

PURPOSE:
To assist religious, charitable and educational organizations.

LEGAL BASIS:
Nonprofit foundation.

ELIGIBILITY:
Grants are awarded to nonprofit, tax-exempt, non-tax-supported, established institutions which combine sound character and stability with progressiveness and purpose. The Foundation does not generally favor deficit financing and debt retirement, operating or program funds, annual fund-raising campaigns, endowments, government-owned or -operated institutions, educational

institutions below the college level, furnishings or equipment (except major medical equipment) or grants to churches.

Grants are made toward building and facility construction, renovation projects and the purchase of major medical equipment.

GEOG. RESTRICTIONS: Arkansas, Kansas, Missouri, New Mexico, Oklahoma and Texas.

FINANCIAL DATA:
Amount of support per award: $25,000 to $1,000,000.

Total amount of support: $35,000,000 to $45,000,000.

NO. MOST RECENT APPLICANTS: 190.

NO. AWARDS: 100.

APPLICATION INFO:
There is no application form. Proposals must contain the following items:
(1) the legal name and address of the organization;
(2) name, title, address and telephone number of the primary contact person;
(3) brief description of the organization;
(4) description of the project, with goals and objectives;
(5) description of the population expected to benefit from the project;
(6) detailed budget for the project;
(7) a list of funding sources including those received and any pending or pledged;
(8) the cut-off date for a challenge grant;
(9) a time schedule for start of construction;
(10) indicate how the project will be sustained after the grant expires;
(11) verification of IRS tax-exempt status under Section 501(c)(3) and not a private foundation under Section 509(a);
(12) the organization's most recent audited financial statement and interim financial statement for the current fiscal period or current IRS 990 and;
(13) a list of officers with titles and names of the governing body with primary professional affiliations.

Duration: Varies.

Deadline: March 1, June 1, September 1 and December 1.

PUBLICATIONS:
Program announcement; proposal guidelines.

ADDRESS INQUIRIES TO:
Ray Tullius, Vice Chairman
(See address above.)

JOHN D. AND CATHERINE T. MACARTHUR FOUNDATION [208]

140 South Dearborn Street
Chicago, IL 60603-5285
(312) 726-8000
E-mail: 4answers@macfound.org
Web Site: www.macfound.org

FOUNDED: 1978

NAME(S) OF PROGRAMS:
- **Big Bets**
- **Changing Work**
- **Enduring Commitments**
- **Impact Investments**

TYPE:
Fellowships; General operating grants; Project/program grants. The following specific programs are found under the above general program areas:

Big Bets: Climate Solutions; Criminal Justice; Nuclear Challenge Project.

Enduring Commitments: Chicago; Journalism & Media; MacArthur Award for Creative & Effective Institutions; MacArthur Fellows.

Changing Work: American Democracy; Cities; Community & Economic Development; Conservation & Sustainable Development; Digital Media & Learning; Girls' Secondary Education in Developing Countries; Housing; Human Rights; International Peace & Security; Juvenile Justice; Migration; Policy Research; Population & Reproductive Health.

YEAR PROGRAM STARTED: 1978

PURPOSE:
To build a more just, verdant and peaceful world.

LEGAL BASIS:
Private, independent foundation.

ELIGIBILITY:
The Foundation develops grantmaking strategies designed to meet very specific goals. Please consult the Foundation's web site regarding the grantmaking guidelines for each program.

The Foundation does not support political activities or attempts to influence action on specific legislation, and does not provide the following:
(1) scholarships/tuition assistance for undergraduate, graduate or postgraduate studies;
(2) annual fund-raising drives;
(3) institutional benefits;
(4) honorary functions or similar projects and;
(5) unsolicited grants to individuals (except for the MacArthur Fellows, which operates through a separate nominating process that is not open to public nominations).

GEOG. RESTRICTIONS: With a global reach, the Foundation supports organizations working in 50 countries. United States grantmaking impacts nearly every state in the nation. The Foundation is also very active in the headquarters city of Chicago, Illinois.

FINANCIAL DATA:
Amount of support per award: Varies.

Total amount of support: $231,400,000 in 2014.

NO. MOST RECENT APPLICANTS: 5,200.

NO. AWARDS: 560.

APPLICATION INFO:
Complete details are available on the Foundation web site.

Duration: One to five years. Renewals by reapplication.

PUBLICATIONS:
Annual report.

IRS I.D.: 23-7093598

ADDRESS INQUIRIES TO:
Web site:
macfound.fluxx.io/user_sessions/new

*PLEASE NOTE:
The Foundation awards the majority of its grants to organizations identified by its staff. Each year it also awards grants to individuals through the MacArthur Fellows program, which does not accept applications or nominations.

MARBROOK FOUNDATION [209]

730 Second Avenue South
Suite 1300
Minneapolis, MN 55402
(612) 752-1783
Fax: (612) 752-1780
E-mail: mbrooks@marbrookfoundation.org
Web Site: www.marbrookfoundation.org

FOUNDED: 1948

AREAS OF INTEREST:
The Foundation's primary interest is in initiatives or organizations that create equal opportunity for immigrants and refugees in the Twin Cities metro area.

TYPE:
Capital grants; Endowments; General operating grants; Project/program grants; Scholarships; Technical assistance. As the immigrant and refugee populations grow and become increasingly diverse, so does the potential for enrichment and transformation in our communities. The Foundation believes that addressing the opportunities and challenges that come with blending cultures, languages and beliefs will help to revitalize our communities and contribute to our well-being.

YEAR PROGRAM STARTED: 1948

PURPOSE:
To promote the values of the Brooks Family by making grants and focusing involvement in designated charitable areas and causes that reflect those values.

LEGAL BASIS:
Tax-exempt, private foundation.

ELIGIBILITY:
The Foundation will give priority to projects or organizations that address at least one of the following areas:
(1) initiatives working to create equal opportunity or to empower immigrants and refugees (e.g., affordable housing, job training, life skills);
(2) environmental conservation and access to green space for neighborhoods with a high concentration of immigrants and refugees;
(3) expanding access to healthy food for neighborhoods with a high concentration of immigrants and refugees;
(4) academic success for children of immigrants and refugees;
(5) English language instruction for immigrants and refugees;
(6) cultural preservation for new Americans;
(7) integrating a comprehensive approach (of body, mind and spirit) to the well-being of immigrants and refugees, with a special interest in programs honoring the inherent spiritual and cultural richness of immigrant communities and;
(8) arts organizations/projects that highlight cultural awareness or address social issues of immigrants and refugees.

The Foundation does not fund start-up organizations, programs for the elderly, domestic abuse programs, disease-related organizations, homeless shelters, food shelves, early-childhood education, legal services, conferences and events, programs serving the physically or mentally disabled, or individuals or organizations which attempt to influence legislation or to intervene in any political campaign.

GEOG. RESTRICTIONS: Minnesota, with emphasis on Minneapolis and St. Paul.

FINANCIAL DATA:
Amount of support per award: Grants vary in amount, depending upon the needs and nature of the request.

Total amount of support: $800,000 for the year 2015.

NO. AWARDS: 99 for the year 2014.

REPRESENTATIVE AWARDS:
$10,000 to the CSJ Ministry Collaborative for Learning in Style; $10,000 to the Sierra Club for the MN Environmental Justice Project; $15,000 to the Trust for Public Land for the Frogtown Park and Farm; $15,000 to the African Development Center for general operating support.

APPLICATION INFO:
Applications must be submitted online.

Deadline: March and September.

TRUSTEES:
Markell Kiefer, Chairperson
Edward A. Brooks
Katherine Brooks
Markell Brooks
Sarah Brooks
Bill King
John Larsen

EXECUTIVE DIRECTOR:
Minna K. Brooks

MARIN COMMUNITY FOUNDATION [210]

5 Hamilton Landing, Suite 200
Novato, CA 94949
(415) 464-2500
Fax: (415) 464-2555
E-mail: info@marincf.org
Web Site: www.marincf.org/grants-and-loans-grantmaking-approach-and-process

FOUNDED: 1986

AREAS OF INTEREST:
Education, economic opportunity, health and environment.

TYPE:
Awards/prizes; Capital grants; Challenge/matching grants; Conferences/seminars; General operating grants; Project/program grants; Scholarships; Technical assistance.

YEAR PROGRAM STARTED: 1987

PURPOSE:
To encourage and apply philanthropic contributions to help improve the human condition, embrace diversity, promote a humane and democratic society, and enhance the community's quality of life, now and for future generations.

LEGAL BASIS:
Community foundation.

ELIGIBILITY:
Proposals must be consistent with the Foundation's program goals and must meet two additional requirements. First, the applicant must be a public or nonprofit organization and, second, the proposed project must be conducted in and/or benefit the residents of Marin County, CA. Projects with a regional or multi-county benefit may be funded only in proportion to the extent that they benefit the Marin County community.

Ineligible activities include for-profit purposes, basic research, the start-up of new nonprofit organizations that will unnecessarily duplicate existing programs or services or undertake services that can be more effectively provided by other organizations and grants to individuals. Other limitations specific to each program area are outlined in the funding guidelines. No grants are made to individuals.

Buck Trust grants are limited to Marin County.

GEOG. RESTRICTIONS: Grants from the Buck Trust are restricted to Marin County, California.The Foundation's donor-advised funds support efforts locally and in communities around the world.

FINANCIAL DATA:
The Foundation manages more than $1.6 billion in total assets.

Amount of support per award: $50,000 to $150,000.

Total amount of support: Over $60,000,000 in grants annually.

NO. AWARDS: 345.

APPLICATION INFO:
The following procedures apply:
(1) The Foundation issues a Request for Proposals (RFP);
(2) If interested, a representative from a nonprofit organization can register on the Foundation's online Grant Center;
(3) The nonprofit representative can then submit an online Letter of Intent (LOI) for the RFP and;
(4) Following the Foundation's review of the LOIs, selected applicants are invited to submit a full proposal through the Grant Center.
Consult the web site address above for further details.

Duration: Varies. Renewal possible.

Deadline: Applications are accepted according to a schedule posted on the Foundation's web site.

PUBLICATIONS:
General information brochure.

IRS I.D.: 94-3007979

OFFICERS:
Thomas Peters, Ph.D., President and Chief Executive Officer
Sid Hartman, Chief Financial and Operating Officer

BOARD OF TRUSTEES:
Cleveland Justis, Chairperson
Marilee Eckert
Miguel Gavaldón
Andrew Giacomini
Peter Hamilton
Robert J. Reynolds
Fu Schroeder
Steven Schroeder, M.D.
Julia Sze

MARRIOTT INTERNATIONAL, INC. [211]

10400 Fernwood Road
Bethesda, MD 20817
E-mail: community.engagement@marriott.com
Web Site: marriott.versaic.com

FOUNDED: 1927

AREAS OF INTEREST:
Shelter and food, environment, readiness for hotel careers, vitality of children, and embracing diversity and people with disabilities.

TYPE:
Project/program grants. Support to national and global nonprofits that address help, support readiness for jobs, diversity and inclusion, poverty alleviation, and the environment.

LEGAL BASIS:
Corporate contributions program.

ELIGIBILITY:
Grants are made to tax-exempt 501(c)(3) organizations which fulfill important community needs.

FINANCIAL DATA:
Amount of support per award: Varies.

Total amount of support: Varies.

APPLICATION INFO:
The Corporation only accepts requests online via its web site.

Duration: Varies.

Deadline: Before end of October.

PUBLICATIONS:
Application guidelines.

ROBERT R. MCCORMICK FOUNDATION [212]

205 North Michigan Avenue
Suite 4300
Chicago, IL 60601-5927
(312) 445-5000
Fax: (312) 445-5001
E-mail: info@mccormickfoundation.org
Web Site: www.mccormickfoundation.org

FOUNDED: 1955

AREAS OF INTEREST:
Community strengthening, democracy, youth media, early childhood education, and veterans affairs.

NAME(S) OF PROGRAMS:

- **Communities Program**
- **Democracy Program**
- **Education Program**
- **Veterans Program**

TYPE:
General operating grants; Project/program grants.

YEAR PROGRAM STARTED: 1955

PURPOSE:
To foster communities of educated, informed and engaged citizens.

FINANCIAL DATA:
Total amount of support: $48,722,343 in total grants approved for the year ended December 31, 2014.

NO. AWARDS: 598 total grants approved for the year ended December 31, 2014.

PUBLICATIONS:
Annual report; program brochures; conference reports.

J.M. MCDONALD FOUNDATION, INC. [213]

P.O. Box 3219
Evergreen, CO 80437-3219
(303) 674-9300
Fax: (303) 674-9216
E-mail: info@jmmcdonaldfoundation.org
Web Site: jmmcdonaldfoundation.org

FOUNDED: 1952

AREAS OF INTEREST:
Education, humanities, health, and a variety of social and human services.

TYPE:
Capital grants; Development grants; Project/program grants.

YEAR PROGRAM STARTED: 1952

LEGAL BASIS:
Private foundation.

ELIGIBILITY:
Nonprofit organizations with appropriate interests are eligible for support. Applicants must be located in the U.S. and have IRS-509A and 501(c)(3) letter. No grants are made to individuals, for projects to influence legislation or elections, or solely for conferences, seminars, workshops, travel or exhibits.

GEOG. RESTRICTIONS: Primarily upstate New York.

FINANCIAL DATA:
Amount of support per award: Grants vary in amount, depending upon the needs and nature of the request.

APPLICATION INFO:
Application for funding through online granting process is available at the Foundation web site.

Duration: One year.

Deadline: April 15 and September 15, with responses in May and October, respectively.

PUBLICATIONS:
Application guidelines.

OFFICERS AND TRUSTEES:
Donald R. McJunkin, President
Nancy J. Palmer, Vice President
Janet E. Stanton, Vice President
Pamela Criswell, Treasurer
Dana Amundson, Secretary
Scott Palmer

JAMES S. MCDONNELL FOUNDATION [214]

1034 South Brentwood Boulevard
Suite 1850
St. Louis, MO 63117
(314) 721-1532
E-mail: info@jsmf.org
Web Site: www.jsmf.org

FOUNDED: 1950

AREAS OF INTEREST:
Mathematical and complex systems approaches for brain cancer, studying complex systems, understanding human cognition, and cognitive rehabilitation.

NAME(S) OF PROGRAMS:
- **Collaborative Activity Awards**
- **Postdoctoral Fellowship Awards in Studying Complex Systems**
- **Scholar Awards**

TYPE:
Fellowships; Research grants. Collaborative Activity Awards are to initiate interdisciplinary discussions on problems or issues, to help launch interdisciplinary research networks, or to fund communities of researchers dedicated to developing new methods, tools and applications of basic research.

Postdoctoral Fellowship Awards are intended to provide students in the final stages of completing a Ph.D. degree more leeway in identifying and securing postdoctoral training opportunities in complex systems research.

Scholar Awards provide funding in the area of Understanding Human Cognition.

YEAR PROGRAM STARTED: 2000

PURPOSE:
To encourage investigators to engage difficult problems; to support ideas and approaches departing from conventional wisdom; to fund novel or interdisciplinary proposals.

LEGAL BASIS:
Private foundation.

FINANCIAL DATA:
Amount of support per award: Collaborative Activity Awards: Varies; Postdoctoral Fellowship: $200,000; Scholar Awards: Up to $600,000, depending on award.

NO. MOST RECENT APPLICANTS: 160 for the year 2015.

NO. AWARDS: 28.

APPLICATION INFO:
Guidelines and all program applications are available on the Foundation's web site.

Duration: Varies.

Deadline: Postdoctoral Fellowship and Scholars Award: Varies. There are no deadlines for Collaborative Activity Awards.

Letters of inquiry are accepted year-round for collaborative fund seekers.

IRS I.D.: 54-2074788

OFFICERS:
Dr. Susan Fitzpatrick, President

BOARD OF DIRECTORS:
Jeanne M. Champer
Holly M. James
Alicia S. McDonnell
James S. McDonnell, III
Jeffrey M. McDonnell
John F. McDonnell
Marcella M. Stevens

ADDRESS INQUIRIES TO:
See e-mail address above.

MCGREGOR FUND [215]

333 West Fort Street, Suite 2090
Detroit, MI 48226-3134
(313) 963-3495
Fax: (313) 963-3512
E-mail: info@mcgregorfund.org
Web Site: www.mcgregorfund.org

FOUNDED: 1925

AREAS OF INTEREST:
Human services, education, health, the arts and public benefit in metropolitan Detroit.

TYPE:
General operating grants; Project/program grants. Limited capital grants; program and operational support. The Fund also supports aid to private liberal arts colleges and universities in Michigan.

YEAR PROGRAM STARTED: 1925

PURPOSE:
To relieve misfortunes and promote the well-being of mankind.

LEGAL BASIS:
Tax-exempt private foundation.

ELIGIBILITY:
Tax-exempt, Internal Revenue Code 501(c)(3) organizations in the Detroit metropolitan area.

The Fund does not provide loan funds, make direct grants to students for scholarships, make grants for travel, conferences, seminars or workshops, or make grants to individuals.

GEOG. RESTRICTIONS: Metropolitan Detroit, Michigan.

FINANCIAL DATA:
Amount of support per award: $25,000 to $50,000.

Total amount of support: Varies.

NO. AWARDS: 45 for the year 2014.

REPRESENTATIVE AWARDS:
$250,000 to Coalition on Temporary Shelter to support homeless shelters; $200,000 to Forgotten Harvest to support the campaign to acquire and retrofit a new facility for food rescue operations.

APPLICATION INFO:
Guidelines are available on the Fund web site.

Duration: No grants are made on a continuing basis.

Deadline: Submit applications three months prior to Board meeting dates in March, June, September and December.

PUBLICATIONS:
Annual report; guidelines; application procedures.

IRS I.D.: 38-0808800

OFFICERS:
Reuben A. Munday, Chairman
Denise J. Lewis, Vice Chairman

BOARD OF TRUSTEES:
Kate Levin Markel, President and Secretary
Gerard M. Anderson
Cynthia N. Ford
Denise J. Lewis
Leslie Murphy
Richard L. Rogers
Susan Schooley, M.D.
William W. Shelden, Jr.

ADDRESS INQUIRIES TO:
See e-mail address above.

THE MCLEAN CONTRIBUTIONSHIP [216]

Sugartown Square Offices, Suite 30
230 Sugartown Road
Wayne, PA 19087
(610) 989-8090
Web Site: fdnweb.org/mclean

FOUNDED: 1951

AREAS OF INTEREST:
Education, environment, health and hospitals, care of the elderly and youth development.

TYPE:
Capital grants; Endowments. The Contributionship makes a relatively limited number of grants for projects of long-term benefit. Its trustees focus on capital projects: bricks and mortar and endowment; they may make grants in ways to encourage the successful funding of projects.

PURPOSE:
To support understanding and preserving the environment; to encourage compassionate and cost-effective health care; to improve the quality of life through education and through support of the communities' cultural assets usually in the form of capital projects.

LEGAL BASIS:
Private foundation.

ELIGIBILITY:
Organizations, including some religious, classified as 501(c)(3) by the IRS can apply. Individuals are ineligible.

The Contributionship favors projects that:
(1) stimulate a better understanding of the natural environment, and encourage the preservation of its important features;
(2) encourage more compassionate and cost-effective care for the ill and aging, in an atmosphere of dignity and self-respect and;
(3) promote education, or medical, scientific or (on occasion) cultural developments enhancing the quality of life.

In addition, the trustees from time to time support projects which:
(1) motivate promising young people to assess and develop their talents despite social and economic obstacles and;
(2) encourage those in newspaper and related fields to become more effective and responsible in helping people understand better how events in their communities and around the world affect them.

GEOG. RESTRICTIONS: Mainly in the Greater Philadelphia area.

FINANCIAL DATA:
Amount of support per award: $1,000 to $100,000.

Total amount of support: Approximately $2,301,784 for the year 2015.

NO. MOST RECENT APPLICANTS: 187 for the year 2014.

NO. AWARDS: 122 for the year 2015.

REPRESENTATIVE AWARDS:
$25,000 to Cradles to Crayons, Conshohocken, PA, for the Cradles to Crayons Growth Campaign: The Campaign to do More, specifically the construction costs of the new 40,000 square foot warehouse ($50,000 total multiyear grant, $25,000 remaining to be paid); $10,000 to North Light Community Center, Philadelphia, PA, for the design and installation of a wooden playground; $12,000 to Philadelphia Wooden Boat Factory, Philadelphia, PA, for the purchase of two rigid inflatable boats for the organization's on-water programming; $30,000 to South Of South Neighborhood Association Inc, for Carpenter Green, a multiyear effort to transform a vacant lot at 17th and Carpenter into a public park.

APPLICATION INFO:
The Contributionship accepts the common grant application form of the Philanthropy Network Greater Philadelphia. Application should include:
(1) a letter, which describes and justifies the project;
(2) a budget and timetable, strategy for securing funding and latest financial statement;
(3) interim operating statements or budgets for future periods if appropriate;
(4) evidence of tax-exempt status and;
(5) a list of officers and directors.

Application can be submitted online (preferred) or mailed to Sandra L. McLean, Executive Director, at the address above.

Duration: One to three years.

Deadline: Applications must be received six weeks prior to meeting date.

PUBLICATIONS:
Application guidelines.

IRS I.D.: 23-6396940

TRUSTEES:
Sandra L. McLean, Executive Director and Trustee
John F. Bales
Diana L. McLean
Wendy McLean
Carolyn M. Raymond
Susannah McLean, Advisory Trustee

ADDRESS INQUIRIES TO:
Sandra L. McLean
Executive Director and Trustee
(See address above.)

*PLEASE NOTE:
No grants to individuals.

THE JOSEPH AND MERCEDES MCMICKING FOUNDATION [217]

1004B O'Reilly Avenue
San Francisco, CA 94129
(415) 474-1784
Fax: (415) 474-1754
E-mail: miriam@mcmickingfoundation.org
Web Site: mcmickingfoundation.org

AREAS OF INTEREST:
Arts, computer science, education and science.

TYPE:
Project/program grants.

PURPOSE:
To improve the quality of life for San Francisco Bay Area residents through grants and scholarships for the education and welfare of children and their families.

ELIGIBILITY:
The Foundation makes grants only to organizations that are exempt from federal tax under Section 501(c)(3) of the Internal Revenue Code and are not classified as private foundations under Section 509(a) of the Code.

The Foundation does not provide support for grants to individuals or loans.

GEOG. RESTRICTIONS: San Francisco Bay Area, California.

FINANCIAL DATA:
Amount of support per award: Varies.

Total amount of support: $650,000 in total grants for the year 2015.

APPLICATION INFO:
Organizations seeking information should mail a letter and application to the Executive Director. The Foundation will not accept proposals sent by facsimile.

Complete guidelines and application form are available on the web site.

Duration: One year.

Deadline: Proposals are accepted throughout the year.

ADDRESS INQUIRIES TO:
Miriam deQuadros White, Executive Director
(See address or phone number above.)

THE MARGARET MCNAMARA EDUCATION GRANTS (MMEG) [218]

The World Bank Family Network
1818 H Street, N.W.
MSN J2-202
Washington, DC 20433
(202) 473-8751
E-mail: mmeg@worldbank.org
Web Site: www.mmeg.org

FOUNDED: 1981

AREAS OF INTEREST:
Agriculture, architecture and urban planning, civil engineering, education, forestry, journalism, nursing, nutrition, pediatrics, public administration, public health, social sciences, social work and others.

TYPE:
Scholarships. Education grants are awarded to women from developing and middle-income countries who, upon obtainment of their degree, intend to return to or remain in their countries or other developing countries, and work to improve the lives of women and/or children.

YEAR PROGRAM STARTED: 1981

PURPOSE:
To support the education of women from developing countries and underserved communities in the U.S. who are committed to improving the lives of women and children in their home countries.

LEGAL BASIS:
501(c)(3) public charity.

ELIGIBILITY:
Applicants must be nationals of developing countries, enrolled in U.S., Canadian, South African or Latin American universities, that are current clients of the World Bank. The U.S./Canada program is open to women enrolled in an accredited educational institution in the U.S. or Canada where the grant will be used. The South Africa program is for students enrolled at the Universities of Pretoria, Cape Town, Witwatersrand, Stellenbosch or Free State. The Latin American program is for students enrolled at the Universities of Austral, Argentina; Iberoamericana, Mexico; Catolica del Peru, Peru; Nacional de Columbia, Columbia; Rafael Landivar, Guatemala and FLACSO Facultad Latinoamericana de Ciencias Sociales. Women must be at least 25 years old, planning to return to their home country or another developing country within two years of program completion, and have demonstrated financial need.

GEOG. RESTRICTIONS: United States, Canada, South Africa and Latin America.

FINANCIAL DATA:
Amount of support per award: Average of $15,000 in U.S./Canada; $7,000 in South Africa and Latin America.

NO. AWARDS: 34 for the year 2015.

APPLICATION INFO:
Complete application information is available on the web site.

Duration: One year.

Deadline: Varies.

ADDRESS INQUIRIES TO:
MMMF Coordinator
(See address above.)

MEADOWS FOUNDATION, INC. [219]

Wilson Historic District
3003 Swiss Avenue
Dallas, TX 75204-6049
(214) 826-9431
(800) 826-9431
Fax: (214) 827-7042
E-mail: webgrants3003@mfi.org
Web Site: www.mfi.org

FOUNDED: 1948

AREAS OF INTEREST:
Arts and culture, civic and public affairs (including the natural environment), education, health (including mental health), and human services.

TYPE:
Awards/prizes; Capital grants; Challenge/matching grants; Demonstration grants; Development grants; Endowments; General operating grants; Matching gifts; Project/program grants; Research grants; Seed money grants; Technical assistance; Training grants; Loan forgiveness programs. Program-related investments. Support for organizations, agencies, programs and projects within the areas of the Foundation's interest. Areas of high interest: environment, mental health and public education.

YEAR PROGRAM STARTED: 1948

PURPOSE:
To assist people and institutions of Texas improve the quality and circumstances of life for themselves and future generations.

LEGAL BASIS:
Tax-exempt, private foundation.

ELIGIBILITY:
Applicants must be tax-exempt organizations, benefitting Texas. No grants are awarded to individuals. Generally, no contributions for church or seminary construction, annual fund-raising drives, out-of-state travel, or professional conferences/symposia.

GEOG. RESTRICTIONS: Texas.

FINANCIAL DATA:
Amount of support per award: $25,000 to $500,000.
Matching fund requirements: Stipulated with specific grants.

NO. MOST RECENT APPLICANTS: 700 to 800.

NO. AWARDS: More than 200.

APPLICATION INFO:
Application/proposal should include:
(1) a brief history of the organization, its current focus and recent accomplishments;
(2) a copy of the latest verification of tax-exempt status from the IRS;
(3) certified audits for the last three years, current operating budget and year-to-date financial statements;
(4) statement of need for the proposed project, to include population served, and how project will address need;
(5) a list of trustees or directors, corporate officers and key staff;
(6) the specific dollar amount requested and the date payment is needed;
(7) a list of all entities asked to give financial support and their responses;
(8) project line-item budget (include income and expenses);
(9) plans to evaluate the project (include measurable, time-specific goals) and;
(10) support for the project after the grant period.
Duration: Grants are seldom awarded on a continuing basis.
Deadline: Proposals are accepted throughout the year.

PUBLICATIONS:
Annual report; guidelines.

IRS I.D.: 75-6015322

STAFF:
Cynthia Cass, Grants Administrator
Charles Glover, Senior Program Officer
Michael K. McCoy, Senior Program Officer
Cindy M. Patrick, Senior Program Officer
Kathy Smith, Senior Program Officer
Celeste Arista, Senior Program Associate

OFFICERS AND DIRECTORS:
Robert A. Meadows, Chairman, Board of Trustees, Director and Vice President
Linda Perryman Evans, President and Chief Executive Officer, Trustee and Director
Paula Herring, Vice President and Treasurer
Tom Gale, Vice President and Chief Investment Officer
Bruce H. Esterline, Senior Vice President for Strategic Initiatives and Grants
Holli Leigh Broadfoot, Director
Daniel H. Chapman, Trustee and Director
Deborah Gill, Trustee and Director
Virginia Hanson, Director
P. Mike McCullough, Trustee and Director
Karen L. Meadows, Trustee and Director
Peter Miller, Director
William A. Nesbitt, Trustee and Director
Keith Rhodus, Director
Jason Ritzen, Director
Dudley Lee Rouse, Jr., Director
Joel T. Williams, III, Trustee and Director

ADDRESS INQUIRIES TO:
Bruce H. Esterline
Senior Vice President for
Strategic Initiatives and Grants
(See address above.)

MEDICAL LIBRARY ASSOCIATION [220]

65 East Wacker Place
Suite 1900
Chicago, IL 60601-7246
(312) 419-9094
Fax: (312) 419-8950
E-mail: awards@mlahq.org
Web Site: www.mlanet.org

FOUNDED: 1898

AREAS OF INTEREST:
Health sciences librarianship.

NAME(S) OF PROGRAMS:
- **MLA Continuing Education Grants**

TYPE:
Grants-in-aid. The Continuing Education Grants are designed to aid in the study of the theoretical, administrative and technical aspects of library and information science.

PURPOSE:
To provide professional health science librarians with the opportunity to continue their education.

ELIGIBILITY:
Candidates must be U.S. or Canadian citizens, or permanent residents who are mid-level librarians with a graduate degree in library science and a practicing health sciences librarian with at least two years of work experience at the professional level. Membership in MLA is required. In exceptional cases, consideration will be given to an outstanding candidate not meeting the above eligibility criteria.

FINANCIAL DATA:
Amount of support per award: $100 to $500.

NO. AWARDS: 1 to 2.

APPLICATION INFO:
Applicants must complete and submit an application form which is available online. Candidates should also identify a continuing education program.
Duration: One year.
Deadline: December 1.

STAFF:
Maria Lopez, Grants, Scholarships and Awards Coordinator

ADDRESS INQUIRIES TO:
Coordinator
Grants, Scholarships and Awards
(See address above.)

*PLEASE NOTE:
The award is not to support work towards a degree or certificate.

MEDTRONIC PHILANTHROPY [221]

710 Medtronic Parkway, LC110
Minneapolis, MN 55432-5604
(763) 505-2639
(800) 328-2518
Fax: (763) 505-2648
Web Site: www.medtronic.com/philanthropy

FOUNDED: 1979

AREAS OF INTEREST:
Health, education, arts, civic affairs, culture and human services.

NAME(S) OF PROGRAMS:
- **Community Education**
- **Community Health Grants**
- **HeartRescue**
- **Patient Link**
- **Strengthening Health Systems**

TYPE:
Challenge/matching grants; Fellowships; Matching gifts; Scholarships. Matching Gifts to Education involves employees.

YEAR PROGRAM STARTED: 1979

PURPOSE:
To benefit the socioeconomically disadvantaged of Medtronic communities in the areas of education, health, human services, and arts, civic affairs and culture.

LEGAL BASIS:
Corporate foundation.

ELIGIBILITY:
Grants are made to 501(c)(3) tax-exempt organizations, schools or government agencies for specific projects or programs. The Foundation does not support individuals, continuing medical education, religious groups for religious purposes, fund-raising and social events, general operating support, political or fraternal activities, reimbursable health treatment, or scientific research.

GEOG. RESTRICTIONS: Primarily Tempe/Greater Phoenix, Arizona; Goleta, Santa Ana, Santa Rosa and Sunnyvale, California; Louisville and Metro Denver, Colorado; Jacksonville, Florida; Warsaw, Indiana; Beverly and Danvers, Massachusetts; Twin Cities and seven-county metropolitan area, Minnesota; Memphis, Tennessee; Fort Worth and San Antonio, Texas; Redmond, Washington; and Humacao and Villalba, Puerto Rico.

FINANCIAL DATA:
Amount of support per award: Varies depending on need and nature of request.

APPLICATION INFO:
Applicants should review the General Foundation Guidelines to ensure eligibility. Each grant program has its own set of guidelines and deadlines. U.S organizations must apply via the online application process. In addition to the completion of the online application, the following documents are required:

(1) budget form;
(2) interim/final report on the organization's most recent Medtronic Foundation Grant (if funding has previously been received);
(3) list of officers and directors and their affiliations;
(4) IRS tax exemption letter;
(5) latest annual report (only required if available electronically) and;
(6) financial statement from most recently completed fiscal year (whether audited or not).

Organizations based outside the U.S. must first complete a Letter of Inquiry. Upon receiving the letter, a Foundation representative may recommend the organization submit a full application.

Duration: Varies.

Deadline: Grants are generally reviewed within 90 days.

IRS I.D.: 41-1306950

THE ANDREW W. MELLON FOUNDATION [222]

140 East 62nd Street
New York, NY 10065
(212) 838-8400
Fax: (212) 500-2302
E-mail: inquiries@mellon.org
Web Site: www.mellon.org

FOUNDED: 1969

AREAS OF INTEREST:
Higher education and scholarship in the humanities, scholarly communications, arts and cultural heritage, diversity, and international higher education and strategic projects.

TYPE:
Challenge/matching grants; Endowments; General operating grants; Project/program grants; Research grants. Grants on a selective basis to institutions in the Foundation's areas of interest.

PURPOSE:
To build, strengthen and sustain institutions and their core capacities, rather than be a source for narrowly defined projects.

LEGAL BASIS:
Not-for-profit corporation.

ELIGIBILITY:
Organizations and institutions with appropriate interests are eligible. The Foundation does not award fellowships or grants to individuals or make grants to primarily local organizations.

FINANCIAL DATA:
Amount of support per award: Varies.

APPLICATION INFO:
Applications are considered throughout the year and no special forms are required. Ordinarily a simple letter setting forth the need, the nature and the amount of the request and the justification for it, together with evidence of suitable classification by the IRS and any supplementary exhibits an applicant may wish to submit, will suffice to assure consideration. Unsolicited applications are rarely funded.

Duration: Varies.

PUBLICATIONS:
Annual report.

OFFICERS:
Earl Lewis, President
Mariet Westermann, Vice President
Michele S. Warman, Vice President, General Counsel and Secretary
John E. Hull, Financial Vice President and Chief Investment Officer

TRUSTEES:
Danielle S. Allen, Chairperson
Richard H. Brodhead
Katherine Farley
Kathryn A. Hall
Earl Lewis
Glenn D. Lowry
Jane L. Mendillo
Eric Mindich
L. Rafael Reif
Sarah E. Thomas

ADDRESS INQUIRIES TO:
Michele S. Warman
Vice President, General Counsel and Secretary
(See address above.)

*PLEASE NOTE:
The Foundation rarely funds unsolicited proposals.

MERCK FAMILY FUND [223]

P.O. Box 870245
Milton Village, MA 02187
(617) 696-3580
Fax: (617) 696-7262
E-mail: merck@merckff.org
Web Site: www.merckff.org

FOUNDED: 1954

AREAS OF INTEREST:
Protecting the natural environment, meeting human needs and addressing the root causes of problems faced by social and economically disadvantaged people.

TYPE:
General operating grants; Project/program grants; Seed money grants.

YEAR PROGRAM STARTED: 1993

PURPOSE:
To protect and restore vital eastern ecosystems and promote economic practices for a sustainable environment.

LEGAL BASIS:
Tax-exempt corporation.

GEOG. RESTRICTIONS: Northeastern and southeastern United States.

FINANCIAL DATA:
Amount of support per award: $10,000 to $50,000.

Total amount of support: $2,500,000 for the year 2015.

APPLICATION INFO:
New requests for support should be made through the online application system rather than with a full proposal or a request for a personal meeting. Applicants will be contacted if a full proposal is warranted. Unsolicited proposals will not be acknowledged.

Duration: Grants may be from one to two years. Progress reports must be received before continuation or renewal support will be considered.

Deadline: February 1 for spring; August 1 for fall.

PUBLICATIONS:
Annual report; grants list; guidelines.

IRS I.D.: 22-6063382

STAFF:
Jenny D. Russell, Executive Director
James Maguire, L
Management and
Ruth Goldman, Co

OFFICERS AND TRUSTE
Nathaniel Chamberl
Whitney Hatch, Vice
Wilhelm Merck, Trea
Patience Chamberlin,
Katie Chamberlin
Oona Coy
Eliza Hatch
Henry Hatch
Elliott Merck
George Whitridge

ADDRESS INQUIRIES TO:
Jenny D. Russell, Executive Director
(See address above.)

METLIFE FOUNDATION [224]

1095 Avenue of the Americas
New York, NY 10036
(212) 578-6272
Fax: (212) 578-0617
E-mail: metlifefoundation@metlife.com
Web Site: www.metlife.org

FOUNDED: 1976

AREAS OF INTEREST:
Financial empowerment and program-related investments.

CONSULTING OR VOLUNTEER SERVICES:
Employee volunteer programs.

TYPE:
Matching gifts; Project/program grants; Scholarships. Program-related investments. Grants are made in the areas of financial empowerment.

MetLife Foundation has a new global focus - financial inclusion - and it has committed $200,000,000 over a five-year period to this initiative. These grants are focused in the following three categories:
(1) Access and Knowledge: Grants to partners with the ability to reach large numbers of underserved households around the world and work with them to develop financial strategies and capabilities to improve lives;
(2) Access to Services: Partnering with experts in financial inclusion to deliver high-quality services like savings, microinsurance and credit to individuals in need and ensure they are prepared, incentivized and motivated to improve the lives of their families and communities and;
(3) Access to Insights: Sharing what the Foundation learns by gathering knowledge from its partners and the communities with which it works; the Foundation offers its insights to the financial inclusion community to help enhance the approach and advance the goals they share in common.

MetLife and the Foundation make below-market-rate investments with groups and projects working to improve communities across the country. Either directly or through relending with nonprofit intermediaries, social investments reach every major city in the nation and over 30 states. Loans support affordable housing developments with social services, organizations serving the homeless and mentally ill, health care services and community-based economic development.

YEAR PROGRAM STARTED: 1976

advance financial inclusion, helping to build a secure future for individuals and communities around the world.

LEGAL BASIS:
The Foundation is a tax-exempt organization under Section 501(c)(3) and is classified as a private foundation as defined by Section 509(a) of the Internal Revenue Code.

ELIGIBILITY:
Applicants must be 501(c)(3) tax-exempt organizations in the Foundation's areas of interest.

No grants are made to private foundations or religious, fraternal, political, athletic, or social organizations, organizations receiving support from United Way, hospitals, capital fund campaigns, local chapters of national organizations, disease-specific organizations, labor groups, organizations primarily engaged in patient care or direct treatment, drug treatment centers and community health clinics, elementary and secondary schools, courtesy advertising or festival participation or individuals. Generally, no support is given for endowment funds.

FINANCIAL DATA:
Total amount of support: $42,573,607 for the year 2015.

Matching fund requirements: Employee contributions to colleges and universities.

NO. AWARDS: Varies.

APPLICATION INFO:
The Foundation only accepts online grant proposals. Details available on the web site.

Duration: Generally one year. Two or three years occasionally.

Deadline: Requests and applications are reviewed throughout the year.

PUBLICATIONS:
Annual report of contributions; guidelines (available online).

BOARD OF DIRECTORS:

ADDRESS INQUIRIES TO:
A. Dennis White
President and Chief Executive Officer
(See address above.)

MEYER MEMORIAL TRUST [225]

425 N.W. 10th Avenue, Suite 400
Portland, OR 97209
(503) 228-5512
E-mail: mmt@mmt.org
Web Site: www.mmt.org

FOUNDED: 1978

AREAS OF INTEREST:
Education, environment, affordable housing and building community.

YEAR PROGRAM STARTED: 1982

PURPOSE:
To work with and invest in organizations, communities, ideas and efforts that contribute to a flourishing and equitable Oregon.

LEGAL BASIS:
Private, independent foundation.

ELIGIBILITY:
Applicants must:
(1) be an IRS-sanctioned tax-exempt organization;
(2) be requesting support for a program that operates in Oregon and;
(3) provide equal opportunity in leadership, staffing and service regardless of age, gender, race, ethnicity, sexual orientation, disability, national origin, political affiliation or religious belief.

GEOG. RESTRICTIONS: Oregon.

FINANCIAL DATA:
Amount of support per award: Varies.

APPLICATION INFO:
Organizations must register on the Trust's online system to complete and submit the application.

Duration: Varies.

TRUSTEES:

STAFF:
Doug Stamm, Chief Executive Officer
Rukaiyah Adams, Chief Investment Officer
Candy Solovjovs, Director of Programs

ADDRESS INQUIRIES TO:
Phoebe O'Leary
Director of Operations
(See address above.)

*SPECIAL STIPULATIONS:
No grants given to individuals or for businesses.

ROBERT R. MEYER FOUNDATION [226]

1900 5th Avenue North, Suite 2500
Birmingham, AL 35203
(205) 264-7881
Fax: (205) 326-7767
E-mail: marcie.braswell@regions.com

FOUNDED: 1942

AREAS OF INTEREST:
Arts, education, humanities, civic affairs, health and human services, and charitable work.

TYPE:
Assistantships; Challenge/matching grants; Conferences/seminars; Development grants; General operating grants; Matching gifts; Project/program grants; Research grants; Technical assistance; Training grants; Work-study programs.

YEAR PROGRAM STARTED: 1942

PURPOSE:
To help in community affairs.

LEGAL BASIS:
Private foundation.

ELIGIBILITY:
Grants restricted to organizations that benefit the Birmingham, AL area, or to Birmingham, AL nonprofit organizations. No grants to individuals or corporations.

GEOG. RESTRICTIONS: Birmingham, Alabama area.

FINANCIAL DATA:
Amount of support per award: $2,500 to $200,000; Average: $30,000.

Total amount of support: Approximately $2,000,000 for the year 2015.

NO. MOST RECENT APPLICANTS: Approximately 140 for the year 2013.

NO. AWARDS: Approximately 70.

APPLICATION INFO:
Call for grant guidelines and application.

Duration: One year.

Deadline: March 1 and September 1.

PUBLICATIONS:
Application form.

ADVISORY COMMITTEE:

ADDRESS INQUIRIES TO:
Marcie P. Braswell, Senior Vice President
(See address above.)

THE MIAMI FOUNDATION [227]

40 N.W. 3rd Street
Suite 305
Miami, FL 33128
(305) 371-2711
Fax: (305) 371-5342
E-mail: jbrown@miamifoundation.org
Web Site: www.miamifoundation.org

FOUNDED: 1967

AREAS OF INTEREST:
Education, health and human services, arts and culture, the environment, economic development and community.

NAME(S) OF PROGRAMS:
- **Community Grants Program**
- **GLBT Community Projects Fund**
- **Denise Moon Memorial Fund**

TYPE:
Project/program grants. Special initiative grants.

YEAR PROGRAM STARTED: 1967

PURPOSE:
To enhance the quality of life for all the residents of Greater Miami.

LEGAL BASIS:
Community foundation.

ELIGIBILITY:
Applicants must be 501(c)(3) organizations as well as some grassroots organizations.

No grants to individuals. No grants for memberships, fund-raising events or memorials.

GEOG. RESTRICTIONS: Miami-Dade County, Florida.

FINANCIAL DATA:
Amount of support per award: Varies.

Total amount of support: Varies.

NO. MOST RECENT APPLICANTS: 600.

NO. AWARDS: 130.

APPLICATION INFO:
Responsive grant applications must be made online. Application includes cover letter with the purpose of the grant and the amount requested as well as a narrative about the applicant organization and budget. Attachments should include IRS

determination letter, board list, and current fiscal year operating budget. Slight variations per grant program may apply.

Duration: Typically one year.

Deadline: Varies.

PUBLICATIONS:
Annual report; quarterly newsletter; grant guidelines; professional advisors guides.

STAFF:
Javier Alberto Soto, President and Chief Executive Officer
Charisse Grant, Senior Vice President for Programs
Stuart Kennedy, Director of Programs and Strategy
Jordan De Leon, Senior Programs Assistant
Jenna Brown, Programs Assistant

ADDRESS INQUIRIES TO:
Jenna Brown, Programs Assistant
(See address above.)

MICROSOFT CORPORATION [228]

One Microsoft Way
Redmond, WA 98052-6399
(425) 882-8080
(425) 706-8185
Fax: (425) 706-7329
Web Site: www.microsoft.com/citizenship

FOUNDED: 1983

AREAS OF INTEREST:
U.S. Program Areas: Expanding opportunities through technology access, strengthening nonprofits through technology, developing a diverse technology workforce and building community through corporate funding and through matching employees' individual giving.

International Program Areas: Improving the quality of life for people in countries and communities where Corporation employees live and do business.

NAME(S) OF PROGRAMS:
- **Disaster Response and Humanitarian Relief**
- **Employee Giving and Volunteer Programs**
- **Microsoft YouthSpark**
- **Nongovernmental Organization Capacity Building**
- **Software Donations**

TYPE:
Grants-in-aid; Matching gifts; Product donations; Scholarships; Technical assistance.

YEAR PROGRAM STARTED: 1983

PURPOSE:
To bring the benefits of information technology to underserved people and communities who do not have access to this technology; to support organizations in the communities in which Microsoft employees live and work; to support Microsoft employees taking an active role in their community through volunteer and matching gift programs.

LEGAL BASIS:
Corporate giving program.

ELIGIBILITY:
Grants are restricted to nonprofit organizations with tax-exempt 501(c)(3) status.

Microsoft does not make charitable grants to individuals; private foundations; political, labor, religious or fraternal organizations; amateur or professional sports groups, teams or events; conferences or symposia; hospitals or medical clinics; sponsorship of events, tables, exhibitions or performances; fund-raising events such as luncheons, dinners, walks, runs or sports tournaments; or programs serving people and communities outside the U.S. (exceptions may be made for pilot programs initiated by a Microsoft subsidiary in another country).

No monetary or in-kind donations to individuals.

FINANCIAL DATA:
Total amount of support: Approximately $922,000,000 in in-kind donations and $135,000,000 in cash donations for fiscal year 2015.

Matching fund requirements: Employee donations of money and time to eligible organizations are matched up to $15,000 per employee per year.

APPLICATION INFO:
All proposals should include:
(1) a copy of the organization's tax-exempt notification letter from the IRS;
(2) a description of the organization (including its mission, accomplishments, governance, area and population served);
(3) the operating budget for the current fiscal year including funding sources and;
(4) lists of current board members and key organizational staff.

Additional information may be requested by Microsoft. Proposal materials, including photographs, videos and special binders, cannot be returned.

Funding proposals are accepted through Microsoft subsidiary offices throughout the world. Locations can be found online.

Deadline: Proposals are reviewed February 15, May 15, and October 30. Award announcement approximately six weeks following deadline.

PUBLICATIONS:
Program brochure; annual report of giving.

ADDRESS INQUIRIES TO:
Community Affairs
(See address above.)

*SPECIAL STIPULATIONS:
Proposals submitted by e-mail, fax or phone will not be accepted.

MID-NEBRASKA COMMUNITY FOUNDATION, INC. [229]

121 North Dewey Street, Suite 112
North Platte, NE 69101
(308) 534-3315
Fax: (308) 534-6117
E-mail: mncf@hamilton.net
Web Site: www.midnebraskafoundation.org

FOUNDED: 1978

AREAS OF INTEREST:
Arts, education, civic development, environment, health and welfare.

TYPE:
Capital grants; Demonstration grants; Development grants; Endowments; Project/program grants; Scholarships.

PURPOSE:
To serve charitable people and nonprofit causes in North Platte and the surrounding area.

GEOG. RESTRICTIONS: Custer, Dawson, Frontier, Hayes, Keith, Lincoln, Logan, McPherson, and Perkins counties, Nebraska.

FINANCIAL DATA:
Amount of support per award: Varies.

Total amount of support: Average: $1,000,000 to $1,500,000.

APPLICATION INFO:
Application form required. Initial approach by letter or telephone.

Duration: Varies.

Deadline: April 15, July 15, October 15 and January 15.

IRS I.D.: 47-0604965

ADDRESS INQUIRIES TO:
Eric Seacrest, Executive Director
(See address above.)

ADAH K. MILLARD CHARITABLE TRUST [230]

Northern Trust Company
One Oakbrook Terrace, Suite 200
Oakbrook Terrace, IL 60181
(630) 932-6981
Fax: (630) 932-6968

FOUNDED: 1976

AREAS OF INTEREST:
Youth agencies, arts, cultural programs and hospitals.

TYPE:
Capital grants; Project/program grants. Project grants in areas of the Foundation's interest.

YEAR PROGRAM STARTED: 1976

PURPOSE:
To make grants to charitable agencies in Omaha and Douglas County, NE.

LEGAL BASIS:
Tax-exempt.

ELIGIBILITY:
Tax-exempt organizations in Omaha and Douglas County, NE. No grants are awarded to individuals.

GEOG. RESTRICTIONS: Douglas County and Omaha, Nebraska.

FINANCIAL DATA:
Amount of support per award: $1,000 to $35,000.

Matching fund requirements: Stipulated with specific programs.

NO. AWARDS: 35.

REPRESENTATIVE AWARDS:
Salvation Army; United Way; Nebraska Food Bank.

APPLICATION INFO:
A request should be made for guidelines to submit grant applications. Six copies of the application are required.

Duration: No grants are awarded on a continuing basis.

Deadline: March 20 and October 1. Announcements in May and November.

PUBLICATIONS:
Application guidelines.

IRS I.D.: 36-6629069

ADDRESS INQUIRIES TO:
Paul Pedersen, Senior Vice President
(See address above.)

THE MOODY FOUNDATION [231]

2302 Post Office Street, Suite 704
Galveston, TX 77550
(409) 797-1500
Fax: (409) 763-5564
E-mail: info@moodyf.org
Web Site: www.moodyf.org

FOUNDED: 1942

AREAS OF INTEREST:
Arts, education, medical research, community and economic development, environment and youth programs.

TYPE:
Capital grants; Challenge/matching grants; Endowments; Grants-in-aid; Project/program grants; Research grants; Scholarships. Capital campaigns; Equipment; Matching funds; Building/renovation; Program development and research.

YEAR PROGRAM STARTED: 1942

PURPOSE:
To assist in supporting activities that are directed toward improving the general well-being of the citizens of the state of Texas, especially Galveston.

LEGAL BASIS:
Private family foundation.

ELIGIBILITY:
Tax-exempt 501(c)(3) organizations in the state of Texas only are eligible to apply. The Foundation generally does not make grant awards for deficit financing, operational expenses of established organizations, or grants for any activities considered a taxable expenditure under the 1969 Tax Reform Act. No grants to individuals (except for one scholarship program). No loans.

GEOG. RESTRICTIONS: Texas.

FINANCIAL DATA:
Amount of support per award: Varies.
Total amount of support: Varies.

NO. AWARDS: 20 to 30.

REPRESENTATIVE AWARDS:
$30,000 to American Cancer Society Inc./Cattle Baron's Ball, Dallas, TX; $15,000 to Community Schools in Dallas; $5,000 to Garland Family Outreach, Inc., Garland, TX.

APPLICATION INFO:
Prospective candidates should consult the Foundation's web site for an online inquiry to ascertain if appropriate to request guidelines for making application.
Duration: Generally, grants are awarded for one year at a time.

PUBLICATIONS:
Annual report; application guidelines.

IRS I.D.: 74-1403105

STAFF:
Frances Anne Moody-Dahlberg, Executive Director
Garrik Addison, Chief Financial Officer
Allan Matthews, Grants Director
Bernice C. Torregrossa, Regional Grants Director for Central Texas and Grants Analyst
Jamie Williams, Regional Grants Director for North Texas and Human Resources
Samantha Seale, Scholarship Director
Gerald Smith, Program Officer

BOARD OF TRUSTEES:
Frances Anne Moody-Dahlberg, Chairperson
Elizabeth Moody
Ross R. Moody

FOUNDERS:
Libbie Shearn Moody
W.L. Moody, Jr.

ADDRESS INQUIRIES TO:
See e-mail address above.

THE CLARENCE E. MULFORD TRUST [232]

P.O. Box 290
Fryeburg, ME 04037
(207) 935-2061
Fax: (207) 935-3939

AREAS OF INTEREST:
Animals, education, literature, religion, science and youth.

TYPE:
Project/program grants.

PURPOSE:
To support charitable organizations that are working to improve the quality of life for Maine residents.

LEGAL BASIS:
Trust fund.

ELIGIBILITY:
Grants are made to organizations that have tax-exempt status under Section 501(c)(3) of the Internal Revenue Code. No grants are made to individuals. Religious organizations may apply.

GEOG. RESTRICTIONS: Fryeburg, Maine and adjoining towns.

FINANCIAL DATA:
Amount of support per award: $500 to $10,000.
Total amount of support: Approximately $500,000 for the year 2015.

APPLICATION INFO:
Organizations should submit IRS tax exemption letter under 501(c)(3) of the Internal Revenue Code.
Duration: One year. Renewal by reapplication.
Deadline: January 10 and July 10.

TRUSTEES:
David R. Hastings, III
Peter Hastings

ADDRESS INQUIRIES TO:
Peter Hastings, Trustee
(See address above.)

M.J. MURDOCK CHARITABLE TRUST [233]

703 Broadway, Suite 710
Vancouver, WA 98660
(360) 694-8415
Fax: (360) 694-1819
E-mail: stevem@murdock-trust.org
Web Site: www.murdock-trust.org

FOUNDED: 1975

AREAS OF INTEREST:
Education, science, health and human services, arts and culture.

TYPE:
Capital grants; Challenge/matching grants; Development grants; Project/program grants; Research grants. Equipment grants. In addition to a special interest in education and scientific research, the Trust partners with a wide variety of organizations that serve the arts, public affairs, health and medicine, human services, leadership development and persons with disabilities.

PURPOSE:
To enrich the quality of life in the Pacific Northwest by providing grants and enrichment programs to organizations seeking to strengthen the region's educational, spiritual and cultural base in creative and sustainable ways.

LEGAL BASIS:
Private foundation.

ELIGIBILITY:
Applications for grants are considered only from organizations which have been ruled to be tax-exempt under Section 501(c)(3) of the Internal Revenue Code and are not private foundations. Primary attention is given to applications for the support of projects and programs conducted by qualified institutions within five states of the Pacific Northwest, including Alaska, Idaho, Montana, Oregon and Washington. Priority is given to organizations and projects which are not primarily or normally financed by public tax funds.

Applications are not considered for loans, endowment, debt retirement, operational deficits, contributions to general fund drives or annual charitable appeals, continuation of programs previously financed from external sources or emergency funding.

GEOG. RESTRICTIONS: Pacific Northwest.

FINANCIAL DATA:
Amount of support per award: $100,000 to $200,000.
Total amount of support: Varies.

NO. MOST RECENT APPLICANTS: 303.

NO. AWARDS: 265 grants approved for the year 2013.

APPLICATION INFO:
Submit a letter of inquiry and request for guidelines to loi@murdock-trust.org.
Duration: One year to multiyear.
Deadline: Varies.

PUBLICATIONS:
Annual report; *Grants Proposal Guidelines*; proposal form.

TRUSTEES:
John W. Castles
Jeffrey T. Grubb
Lynwood W. Swanson

OFFICERS AND STAFF:
Steven G.W. Moore, Executive Director
Terry Stokesbary, Senior Program Director for Enrichment Programs
Dana L. Miller, Senior Program Director for Grant Programs
David Austin, Program Director
Lorin Dunlop, Program Director
John Franklin, Program Director
Jan Kennedy, Program Director
Moses Lee, Program Director
Jill Tatum, Program Director

ADDRESS INQUIRIES TO:
E-mail: info@murdock-trust.org

NATIONWIDE INSURANCE FOUNDATION [234]

One Nationwide Plaza
Mail Drop 1.2.16
Columbus, OH 43215-2220
(614) 249-4310
Fax: (866) 212-7960
E-mail: blicklk@nationwide.com
Web Site: www.nationwide.com/foundation

FOUNDED: 1959

AREAS OF INTEREST:
Health and welfare, education, culture and the arts, and civic and community affairs. Highest priorities are emergency and basic needs and crisis stabilization.

TYPE:
Capital grants; Challenge/matching grants; General operating grants; Matching gifts; Project/program grants.

YEAR PROGRAM STARTED: 1959

PURPOSE:
To provide financial support for qualified tax-exempt organizations whose programs address basic human needs.

LEGAL BASIS:
Corporate foundation.

ELIGIBILITY:
Qualified, tax-exempt organizations in Columbus, OH and locations with a large number of Nationwide associates are eligible.

GEOG. RESTRICTIONS: Primarily Scottsdale, Arizona; Des Moines, Iowa and Columbus, Ohio. Tiers One and Two funding considered in Sacramento, California; Denver, Colorado; Gainesville, Florida; Raleigh/Durham, North Carolina; Cleveland, Ohio; Harrisburg and metropolitan Philadelphia, Pennsylvania; Nashville, Tennessee; San Antonio, Texas; and Wausau, Wisconsin.

FINANCIAL DATA:
Amount of support per award: $5,000 to $7,000 average.

Matching fund requirements: Matching gifts to accredited colleges and universities.

APPLICATION INFO:
Guidelines and application form are available at the Foundation web site.

Duration: One year. Renewal possible.

Deadline: September 1. Announcement in mid-March.

PUBLICATIONS:
Contributions guidelines.

ADDRESS INQUIRIES TO:
Karen H. Blickley, Senior Director
(See address above.)

NEW ENGLAND BIOLABS FOUNDATION [235]

240 County Road
Ipswich, MA 01938
(978) 998-7990
E-mail: info@nebf.org
Web Site: www.nebf.org

FOUNDED: 1982

AREAS OF INTEREST:
Environmental issues: landscapes and seascapes, and the associated biocultural diversity, ecosystem services and foodways.

TYPE:
Grants-in-aid; Project/program grants; Seed money grants. The Foundation prefers to help organizations start their projects with the understanding that once they are established, funding from other sources will be sought.

YEAR PROGRAM STARTED: 1982

PURPOSE:
To support grassroots organizations working with the environment.

ELIGIBILITY:
The Foundation prefers to fund grassroots organizations and/or projects (i.e., those conceived, developed and managed by the community). Grassroots organizations, emerging support groups and charitable organizations may apply. Grants are not made to religious organizations.

FINANCIAL DATA:
Amount of support per award: Average $3,000 to $10,000.

Total amount of support: Approximately $400,000 annually.

NO. MOST RECENT APPLICANTS: 200.

NO. AWARDS: 70.

APPLICATION INFO:
Letters of Inquiry and Proposals should be submitted electronically to the e-mail address listed above.

Duration: Typically one year.

ADDRESS INQUIRIES TO:
Deborah Fraize, Assistant Director
(See address above.)

THE NEW YORK COMMUNITY TRUST [236]

909 Third Avenue, 22nd Floor
New York, NY 10022
(212) 686-0010
Fax: (212) 532-8528
Web Site: www.nycommunitytrust.org

FOUNDED: 1924

AREAS OF INTEREST:
Children, youth and families, community development and the environment, education, arts, human justice, health, people with special needs and special projects.

TYPE:
Project/program grants; Technical assistance. Since 1924, The New York Community Trust has built a permanent endowment to support the nonprofits that make New York City a vital and secure place in which to live and work. With thousands of charitable funds set up by individuals, families, and businesses, the Trust helps donors with their giving today and enables their generosity to continue after their lifetimes, supporting the causes they cared about and solving problems of the future.

Additionally, the Trust has an environmental program that makes grants to organizations working nationally and internationally.

Grants to improve the social work profession are made to groups nationwide.

YEAR PROGRAM STARTED: 1924

PURPOSE:
To support the nonprofits that make New York City a vital and secure place to live and work.

LEGAL BASIS:
Public nonprofit foundation.

ELIGIBILITY:
Priority is given to grant proposals from nonprofit organizations which deal with the problems of the New York metropolitan region. Preference is given to proposals that support specific programs or projects.

Grants are not made to support endowments or building fund campaigns, deficit financing or annual giving, religious purposes or financial assistance or to individual applicants.

GEOG. RESTRICTIONS: Primarily New York, New York.

FINANCIAL DATA:
Amount of support per award: $5,000 to $200,000.

Total amount of support: Competitive grants: Approximately $35,000,000 annually.

APPLICATION INFO:
Applicants should begin by going to the Grantee Application Hub on the Trust's web site; click on "How to Apply," where one can read the Trust's guidelines for grant applicants and start the application process by completing the Proposal Cover Sheet.

Duration: Usually one year.

Deadline: Grant applications are accepted throughout the year. Trust's Board reviews grants five times per year.

PUBLICATIONS:
Annual report; application and individual program guidelines; proposal cover sheet; newsletter.

OFFICERS:
Lorie A. Slutsky, President
Patricia Jenny, Vice President, Grants
Mercedes Leon, Vice President, Administration
Carolyn M. Weiss, C.P.A., Chief Financial Officer

DISTRIBUTION COMMITTEE:
Charlynn Goins, Chairman
Jamie Drake
Roger J. Maldonado
Anne Moore, M.D.
Raffiq Nathoo
Valerie Peltier
Judith O. Rubin
Lorie A. Slutsky
Barron Tenny
Ann Unterberg
Mary Kay Vyskocil
Jason H. Wright

THE NORCLIFFE FOUNDATION [237]

Wells Fargo Center
999 Third Avenue, Suite 1006
Seattle, WA 98104
(206) 682-4820
Fax: (206) 682-4821
E-mail: arline@thenorcliffefoundation.com
Web Site: www.thenorcliffefoundation.com

FOUNDED: 1952

AREAS OF INTEREST:
Health, education, social services, civic improvement, religion, historic preservation, culture and the arts, youth programs, and environment.

TYPE:
Capital grants; General operating grants; Project/program grants. Social service grants.

YEAR PROGRAM STARTED: 1952

PURPOSE:
To improve the lives of people.

LEGAL BASIS:
Private foundation.

ELIGIBILITY:
Eligible organizations must be of IRS 501(c)(3), not-for-profit status. Grants are not given to individuals.

GEOG. RESTRICTIONS: Puget Sound area of Washington state.

FINANCIAL DATA:
Amount of support per award: Varies.

Total amount of support: $20,868,537 for the year 2015.

NO. AWARDS: Over 279 for the year 2015.

APPLICATION INFO:
Application details can be found on the Foundation web site.

Duration: Varies by project. Grants are generally not renewable.

Deadline: Applications are accepted throughout the year.

ADDRESS INQUIRIES TO:
Arline Hefferline, Foundation Manager
(See address above.)

THE NORDSON CORPORATION FOUNDATION [238]

28601 Clemens Road
Westlake, OH 44145-1148
(440) 892-1580
Fax: (440) 414-5751
E-mail: crender@nordson.com
Web Site: www.nordson.com

FOUNDED: 1952

AREAS OF INTEREST:
Education, human welfare, civic, arts and culture.

CONSULTING OR VOLUNTEER SERVICES:
Corporate volunteer program.

NAME(S) OF PROGRAMS:

- **Time and Talent**

TYPE:
Capital grants; Challenge/matching grants; General operating grants; Matching gifts; Project/program grants; Technical assistance.

YEAR PROGRAM STARTED: 1988

PURPOSE:
To improve the quality of life in our communities by improving educational outcomes that enable individuals to become self-sufficient, active participants in the community.

LEGAL BASIS:
Corporate foundation.

ELIGIBILITY:
Grants are made to tax-exempt organizations, as defined in Section 501(c)(3) of the Internal Revenue Code. No grants to religious organizations.

GEOG. RESTRICTIONS: Mainly "North" San Diego County, California; northern Colorado; Emanuel and Gwinnett counties, Georgia; Mercer County, New Jersey; Youngstown and Lorain County, Ohio; New Castle, Pennsylvania; Providence, Rhode Island; Pulaski, Virginia; and Chippewa Falls, Wisconsin.

FINANCIAL DATA:
Amount of support per award: Varies.

Total amount of support: $8,000,000 for the year 2014.

Matching fund requirements: Foundation will match minimum contributions of $25 to a maximum of $10,000 for any calendar year.

NO. MOST RECENT APPLICANTS: 290 for the year 2014.

NO. AWARDS: 255 for the year 2014.

APPLICATION INFO:
Application forms are available online.

Duration: Typically one year.

Deadline: February 15, May 15, August 15 and November 15 for meetings held in January, April, July and October, respectively.

TRUSTEES:
Doug Bloomfield
Michael Hilton
John Keane
Greg Merk
Shelly Peet
Greg Thaxton

STAFF:
Kathy Ladiner, Grants Manager and Matching Gifts Coordinator
Jennifer Kuhn, Community Relations Liaison/New Jersey
Shannon Aiton, Community Relations Liaison/Rhode Island
Sara Vaz, Program Officer/California and Colorado
Cindy Baumgardner, Program Officer/Georgia and Virginia
Joan Szczepanik, Program Officer
Amonica Davis, Manager, Student Outreach

ADDRESS INQUIRIES TO:
Cecilia H. Render, Tel: (440) 892-1580
Kathy Ladiner, Tel: (440) 892-1580 (Matching Gifts)
Jennifer Kuhn, Tel: (609) 259-9222 (NJ)
Johanna Friedrich, Tel: (330) 726-4000 ext. 6321 (Youngstown, OH)
Marcus Kinkaid, Tel: (970) 226-8254 (Fort Collins, CO)
Cindy Baumgardner, Tel: (770) 497-3672 (GA and VA)
Wendy Crotteau, Tel: (715) 726-1201 ext. 184 (WI)
Shannon Aiton, Tel: (401) 431-7094 (RI)
Sara Vaz, Tel: (760) 930-7246 (CA and CO)
Joan Szczepanik, Tel: (440) 414-5440
Amonica Davis, Tel: (440) 414-5444

KENNETH T. AND EILEEN L. NORRIS FOUNDATION [239]

11 Golden Shore, Suite 450
Long Beach, CA 90802
(562) 435-8444
Fax: (562) 436-0584
E-mail: grants@norrisfoundation.org
Web Site: www.norrisfoundation.org

FOUNDED: 1963

AREAS OF INTEREST:
Funding categories include medicine, education and science, youth, community and culture.

TYPE:
Capital grants; Challenge/matching grants; Endowments; General operating grants; Project/program grants; Research grants.

YEAR PROGRAM STARTED: 1963

PURPOSE:
To support programs that advance better health and intellectual enlightenment through education, cultivation of the arts, individual responsibility, freedom and dignity.

LEGAL BASIS:
Family foundation.

ELIGIBILITY:
Applicants must be nonprofit, tax-exempt organizations. The Foundation does not support individuals and/or political or religious organizations.

GEOG. RESTRICTIONS: Southern California.

FINANCIAL DATA:
Amount of support per award: Grants vary in amount, depending upon the needs and nature of the request.

Total amount of support: Varies.

APPLICATION INFO:
Potential applicants should contact the Foundation for guidelines and application form.

Duration: Most grants are for one year.

Deadline: Education/Science and Medical: May 1 to June 30. Decision in October; Youth: February 15 to March 31. Decision in August; Community and Cultural: December 1 to January 31. Decision in May.

PUBLICATIONS:
Biannual report.

IRS I.D.: 95-6080374

TRUSTEES AND OFFICERS:
Lisa D. Hansen, Chairman
Ronald R. Barnes
James R. Martin
Bradley K. Norris
Harlyne J. Norris
Kimberley Presley
Walter J. Zanino

ADDRESS INQUIRIES TO:
Walter J. Zanino, Executive Director
(See address above.)

NORTH CAROLINA COMMUNITY FOUNDATION [240]

4601 Six Forks Road, Suite 524
Raleigh, NC 27609-5286
(919) 828-4387
(800) 201-9533
Fax: (919) 828-5495
E-mail: info@nccommunityfoundation.org
Web Site: www.nccommunityfoundation.org

FOUNDED: 1988

AREAS OF INTEREST:
Arts and conservation, education, health, historical and culture resources, preservation of environmental and social services.

TYPE:
General operating grants; Project/program grants; Scholarships.

YEAR PROGRAM STARTED: 1988

PURPOSE:
To inspire North Carolinians to make lasting and meaningful contributions to their communities.

LEGAL BASIS:
501(c)(3).

ELIGIBILITY:
Nonprofit, tax-exempt organizations. No grants are made to individuals.

GEOG. RESTRICTIONS: North Carolina.

FINANCIAL DATA:
Amount of support per award: Varies.

Total amount of support: Approximately $11,000,000 distributed in 2014, including $800,000 from application process.

APPLICATION INFO:
Details regarding eligibility criteria, program guidelines, and application process can be found on the Foundation web site.

ADDRESS INQUIRIES TO:
Grants and Scholarships
North Carolina Community Foundation
(See address above.)

THE NORTHWEST MINNESOTA FOUNDATION

201 Third Street, N.W.
Bemidji, MN 56601
(218) 759-2057
Fax: (218) 759-2328
E-mail: nwmf@nwmf.org
Web Site: www.nwmf.org

TYPE:
Challenge/matching grants; Demonstration grants; Project/program grants; Research grants; Scholarships; Seed money grants; Technical assistance.

See entry 1305 for full listing.

WILLIAM J. AND DOROTHY K. O'NEILL FOUNDATION [241]

7575 Northcliff Avenue, Suite 205
Cleveland, OH 44144
(216) 831-4134
Fax: (216) 378-0594
E-mail: info@oneill-foundation.org
Web Site: www.oneill-foundation.org

FOUNDED: 1987

AREAS OF INTEREST:
Capacity building - all program areas.

TYPE:
Matching gifts. Capacity building; Proactive grants; Gifts in recognition of service; Youth Philanthropy grants; Responsive grants; Special initiative grants; Rapid responsive grants. In the area of capacity building, the Foundation funds projects that create and implement strategic plans, governance and board development, leadership succession planning, planning and implementing technology systems, fund development, and communications and marketing strategies.

Matching gifts and gifts in recognition of service are directed by O'Neill Family members.

Youth Philanthropy grants are made by O'Neill Family youth.

YEAR PROGRAM STARTED: 1987

PURPOSE:
To fund programs that address root causes of family strength and family disintegration, capacity building for nonprofits and areas of interest to individual family members.

LEGAL BASIS:
Family foundation.

ELIGIBILITY:
Nonprofit organizations with IRS 501(c)(3) tax-exempt status are eligible for support. No grants to individuals or to organizations which operate wholly outside the U.S. No grants in response to annual appeal form letters.

In order to be eligible, you must have either received a grant from the Foundation already and/or be notified that you are eligible.

GEOG. RESTRICTIONS: Washington, DC; Bonita Springs, Greater Orlando and Naples, Florida; Big Island, Hawaii; Annapolis and Baltimore, Maryland; New York, New York; Cleveland, Columbus and Licking counties, Ohio; Houston, Texas; Dorset, Manchester, Pawlet and Rupert, Vermont; and Richmond, Virginia.

FINANCIAL DATA:
Amount of support per award: Average: $35,000.

Total amount of support: $3,628,947 for the year 2015.

NO. AWARDS: 123 Responsive Grants for the year 2015.

REPRESENTATIVE AWARDS:
$50,000 to Autism Speaks, New York, NY; $20,000 to Columbus Housing Partnership, Columbus, OH; $12,000 to Hope Alliance, Round Rock, TX; $28,000 to YWCA of Annapolis and Anne Arundel County, Arnold, MD.

APPLICATION INFO:
Complete details can be found on the Foundation web site. Letter of inquiry must be submitted online.

Duration: One year.

Deadline: Letters of Inquiry: February 22 and August 22.

PUBLICATIONS:
Annual report; application guidelines.

IRS I.D.: 34-1560893

OFFICERS:
Leah S. Gary, President and Chief Executive Officer
Robert W. Donahey, Treasurer
Sara O'Neill Sullivan, Secretary

TRUSTEES:
Kelly Sweeney McShane, Chairperson
Leah S. Gary, President and Chief Executive Officer
Shirley Cohen
Robert W. Donahey
Connie Bowen Korzenski
Timothy M. O'Neill
Sara O'Neill Sullivan

ADDRESS INQUIRIES TO:
Symone McClain, Vice President
(See address above.)

THE JOHN R. OISHEI FOUNDATION [242]

726 Exchange Street
Suite 510
Buffalo, NY 14210
(716) 856-9490
Fax: (716) 856-9493
E-mail: info@oishei.org
Web Site: www.oishei.org

FOUNDED: 1940

AREAS OF INTEREST:
Strengthening neighborhoods and building communities, self-sufficiency, education and employment, community health and medical research, expanding the impact of regional assets, and building organizational strength through operational improvements.

TYPE:
Capital grants; Challenge/matching grants; General operating grants; Project/program grants; Seed money grants; Technical assistance; Training grants. Education grants.

PURPOSE:
To be a catalyst for change; to enhance the economic vitality and the quality of life for the Buffalo Niagara region through grantmaking, leadership and network building.

LEGAL BASIS:
Private foundation.

ELIGIBILITY:
An organization seeking support must be determined by the Internal Revenue Code to be tax-exempt under Section 501(c)(3). Private foundations, a
509(a) of the Internal
be eligible for Found
Foundation support,
well managed, incluc
drawn from a cross
community. It must have a consistent record of sound fiscal management and a demonstrated track record of efficient operations and effective programming. The Foundation does not make grants to governmental institutions, agencies or projects. Organizations that rely heavily on government funding are eligible to apply, but must be able to demonstrate that a grant from the Foundation would supplement rather than supplant public funding.

GEOG. RESTRICTIONS: Erie and Niagara counties, New York.

FINANCIAL DATA:
Amount of support per award: $10,000 to $1,000,000.

Total amount of support: $8,642,248 for the year 2015.

NO. AWARDS: 133 for the year 2015.

REPRESENTATIVE AWARDS:
$150,000 to Buffalo State College Foundation; $200,000 to Buffalo Arts and Technology Center; $375,000 to Local Initiatives Support Corporation.

APPLICATION INFO:
Letters of Inquiry (LOIs) and applications for general funding requests must be submitted online.

Duration: One to four years.

Deadline: The Foundation accepts and processes applications throughout the year. Notification generally within three months.

PUBLICATIONS:
Catalyst for Change, annual report and guidelines.

OFFICERS:
James M. Wadsworth, Chairman
Ann M. McCarthy, Vice Chairman
Robert D. Gioia, President
Edward F. Walsh, Jr., Treasurer
Gayle L. Houck, Secretary
Jackie Reisdorf, Recording Secretary

DIRECTORS:
Robert M. Bennett
Florence M. Conti
William G. Gisel, Jr.
Luke T. Jacobs
Ann M. McCarthy
Yvonne Minor-Ragan, Ph.D.
Francisco M. Vasquez, Ph.D.
James M. Wadsworth
Edward F. Walsh, Jr.

ADDRESS INQUIRIES TO:
Robert D. Gioia, President
(See address above.)

OMAHA COMMUNITY FOUNDATION [243]

302 South 36th Street
Suite 100
Omaha, NE 68131
(402) 342-3458
Fax: (402) 342-3582
E-mail: tina@omahafoundation.org
Web Site: www.omahafoundation.org

FOUNDED: 1982

AREAS OF INTEREST:
General philanthropy.

CONSULTING OR VOLUNTEER SERVICES:
Nonprofit Capacity Building Initiative.

NAME(S) OF PROGRAMS:
- **African American Unity Fund**
- **Endowment Funds of Southwest Iowa**
- **Fund for Omaha**
- **Futuro Latino Fund**

TYPE:
Capital grants; Project/program grants; Scholarships. Donors can contribute through the Omaha Community Foundation to any nonprofit agency. The OCF also has four discretionary grant programs.

PURPOSE:
To facilitate charitable giving and serve as a vehicle for community improvement; to improve the quality of life in Greater Omaha by supporting needs not being met in the areas of civic, cultural, health, education and social service.

LEGAL BASIS:
Public foundation.

ELIGIBILITY:
Organizations applying for grants must be tax-exempt as defined by IRS 501(c)(3) status. Except under unusual circumstances, no grants for endowments, capital campaigns, deficit financing, annual fund drives or fund-raising activities. The grant request must have the approval of the governing board of the requesting organization.

GEOG. RESTRICTIONS: Greater Omaha area.

FINANCIAL DATA:
Amount of support per award: $5,000 to $15,000.

Total amount of support: Varies.

NO. AWARDS: Approximately 425.

APPLICATION INFO:
Contact the Foundation for details.

Duration: Varies.

Deadline: African American Unity Fund and Futuro Latino Fund: August 1; Endowment Funds: February 1; Fund for Omaha: March 1 and September 1.

PUBLICATIONS:
Newsletter.

IRS I.D.: 47-0645958

STAFF:
Tina McGaugh, Program Assistant

ADDRESS INQUIRIES TO:
Program Assistant
(See address above.)

ORANGE COUNTY COMMUNITY FOUNDATION [244]

4041 MacArthur Boulevard
Suite 510
Newport Beach, CA 92660-2503
(949) 553-4202
Fax: (949) 553-4211
E-mail: thanson@oc-cf.org
Web Site: www.oc-cf.org

FOUNDED: 1989

AREAS OF INTEREST:
Children and youth, family relationships, diverse communities, music education and performance, classical music and education, health, environment and education.

TYPE:
Endowments; General operating grants; Project/program grants; Scholarships. The Foundation offers several grant programs throughout the year in human services, education, health, arts and culture, veterans, citizenship, and the environment. Other special grant competitions also occur throughout the year.

YEAR PROGRAM STARTED: 1990

PURPOSE:
To encourage, support and facilitate philanthropy in Orange County.

LEGAL BASIS:
Community foundation.

ELIGIBILITY:
Applicant agencies must be tax-exempt, serve its residents, and operate without discrimination on the basis of race, religion, gender, sexual orientation, age, national origin or disability.

GEOG. RESTRICTIONS: Primarily Orange County, California.

FINANCIAL DATA:
Amount of support per award: Average grant: $5,000 to $25,000.

Total amount of support: $59,000,000 for fiscal year ending June 30, 2015.

CO-OP FUNDING PROGRAMS: Accelerate Change Together Anaheim; OC Veterans Initiative; I Heart OC Giving Day; OC Founders Roundtable.

APPLICATION INFO:
All applications and transcripts must be submitted through the online application system. Guidelines are available on the web site.

Duration: Generally one year for unrestricted grants. Renewal occasionally possible for scholarships.

Deadline: Varies.

PUBLICATIONS:
Annual report; newsletters; guidelines.

IRS I.D.: 33-0378778

ADDRESS INQUIRIES TO:
Todd Hanson, Vice President of Donor and Community Engagement
(See address above.)

THE BERNARD OSHER FOUNDATION [245]

One Ferry Building, Suite 255
San Francisco, CA 94111
(415) 861-5587
Fax: (415) 677-5868
E-mail: info@osherfoundation.org
Web Site: www.osherfoundation.org

FOUNDED: 1977

AREAS OF INTEREST:
Scholarship funding to selected colleges and universities, integrative medicine, lifelong learning for seasoned adults, arts and humanities.

TYPE:
Project/program grants; Scholarships. The Foundation provides scholarship funding nationally to selected colleges and universities and funds integrative medicine centers at Harvard University, Northwestern University, Vanderbilt University, the University of California at San Francisco, and the Karolinska Institute in Stockholm. It also supports a growing network of lifelong learning institutes for seasoned adults located at nearly 120 colleges and universities from Maine to Hawaii. Arts and humanities grants are made to nonprofit organizations principally in the Greater San Francisco Bay Area, specifically Alameda and San Francisco counties, as well as the state of Maine.

YEAR PROGRAM STARTED: 1977

PURPOSE:
To provide scholarship funding nationally to selected colleges and universities and to fund integrative medicine centers; to support a network of lifelong learning institutes for seasoned adults; to support the arts and humanities.

ELIGIBILITY:
Requests will be accepted only from organizations which are classified by the IRS as nonprofit and designated as IRS 501(c)(3). Organizations seeking funds should have experience which is relevant to the proposed project.

The Foundation is precluded by its policies from making direct grants to individuals.

FINANCIAL DATA:
Amount of support per award: Varies.

Total amount of support: Varies.

APPLICATION INFO:
A letter of inquiry is invited as the first step in communicating with the Foundation. Details can be found on the Foundation web site.

Duration: Generally one year.

STAFF:
Mary G.F. Bitterman, President
Thomas Moffett, Chief Financial Officer/Chief Investment Officer
David Blazevich, Senior Program Director
Eric Gillespie, Program Director
Jeanie Hirokane, Corporate Secretary and Program Director

BOARD OF DIRECTORS:
Barbro Osher, Chairman
Bernard Osher, Founder and Treasurer
Mary G.F. Bitterman, President
David Agger
Phyllis Cook
Robert Friend
John Gallo
Laura Lauder
John Pritzker

ADDRESS INQUIRIES TO:
Mary G.F. Bitterman, President
(See address above.)

*PLEASE NOTE:
The Foundation is not currently accepting new proposals, except in the areas of local arts and educational.

PACCAR FOUNDATION [246]

777 106th Avenue, N.E.
Bellevue, WA 98004
(425) 468-7400
Fax: (425) 468-8216
E-mail: ken.hastings@paccar.com
Web Site: www.paccar.com/foundation.asp

FOUNDED: 1951

AREAS OF INTEREST:
Education, science, arts and humanities.

TYPE:
Capital grants.

LEGAL BASIS:
Private foundation.

ELIGIBILITY:
No grants to individuals, political or lobbying groups, fraternal organizations or religious organizations for sectarian purposes.

GEOG. RESTRICTIONS: Columbus, Mississippi; Chillicothe, Ohio; Broken Arrow, Oklahoma; Denton, Texas; Bellevue, Kirkland, Renton, Seattle and Skagit, Washington.

FINANCIAL DATA:
Amount of support per award: $10,000 to $250,000.

Total amount of support: $5,000,000.

APPLICATION INFO:
Guidelines and application procedures are available on the Foundation web site.

Duration: One year. Must reapply for continued funding.

Deadline: Applications accepted throughout the year. Decisions made semiannually.

STAFF:
Ken Hastings, Vice President and General Manager

ADDRESS INQUIRIES TO:
Ken Hastings
Vice President and General Manager
(See address above.)

PACIFIC GAS AND ELECTRIC COMPANY [247]

77 Beale Street
San Francisco, CA 94105
(415) 973-1150
Fax: (415) 973-5411
E-mail: pmm2@pge.com
Web Site: www.pge.com/giving

AREAS OF INTEREST:
Education, economic and community vitality, and environment.

CONSULTING OR VOLUNTEER SERVICES:
Volunteer program.

TYPE:
Project/program grants; Scholarships. Signature programs.

YEAR PROGRAM STARTED: 2001

LEGAL BASIS:
Corporate contributions program.

ELIGIBILITY:
Applicants must have tax-deductible status from the IRS under Section 501(c)(3) or be a unit of government (including a public school). Contributions are not made to individuals, for tickets for contests, raffles or other prize-oriented activities, to religious organizations (unless for a program offered to the public on a nondiscriminatory basis and without regard to the recipient's religious affiliation), endowments, debt-reduction campaigns, films, or to political or partisan organizations or events.

The most successful grant applications are those that:
(1) address a demonstrated community need;
(2) link a nonprofit or government program to the Company's business goals and employee presence in the community and;
(3) can provide the grantee and the Company with recognition in the community.

GEOG. RESTRICTIONS: Northern and central California.

FINANCIAL DATA:
Amount of support per award: $1,000 to $25,000. Most grants are under $5,000.

Total amount of support: $25,000,000 for the year 2015.

Matching fund requirements: 1:1 basis: $25 to $2,500 per calendar year, per employee.

NO. MOST RECENT APPLICANTS: Over 2,500.

NO. AWARDS: 1,500 for the year 2015.

APPLICATION INFO:
Prior to applying for a grant, applicants should contact the local PG&E representative in their project area to discuss the grant proposal. All applicants must use the online grant application. PG&E will neither accept nor process grant proposals in any other format. Please submit only a fully completed application. Incomplete applications will not be considered.

Duration: Generally one year.

Deadline: Applications are preferred before September 30 of each year.

ADDRESS INQUIRIES TO:
Pat Mora, Executive Administrator
(See address above.)

PACIFIC LIFE FOUNDATION [248]

700 Newport Center Drive
Newport Beach, CA 92660-6397
(949) 219-3787
E-mail: plfoundation@pacificlife.com
Web Site: www.pacificlifefoundation.com

FOUNDED: 1984

NAME(S) OF PROGRAMS:
- **Arts and Culture**
- **Civic, Community, and Environment**
- **Education**
- **Health and Human Services**

TYPE:
Capital grants; General operating grants; Matching gifts; Project/program grants. Arts and Culture: Funds nonprofit agencies that provide the public with a broad spectrum of arts and cultural initiatives (e.g., workshops, performances) to help build the public's appreciation of and participation in dance, music, and theater.

Civic, Community, and Environment: Funding is directed to a wide range of programs that enhance communities through leadership development and environmental protection, as well as fund research to learn more about marine mammals.

Education: Funds nonprofit agencies committed to providing quality educational programs for youth and adults (e.g., mentoring, tutoring, literacy) to help them excel academically and in life.

Health and Human Services: Contributions are allocated to agencies that seek to improve the quality of life of those in need, including the working poor, the homeless, and individuals with physical or developmental disabilities.

PURPOSE:
To recognize and support employees' varied interests and community involvement and, through focus programs, to identify and respond to particular community needs so that, whenever possible, funds may be channeled to those areas in which the most good can be accomplished with the funds available.

LEGAL BASIS:
Corporate foundation and corporate contributions program.

ELIGIBILITY:
Grants are made to nonprofit, tax-exempt, 501(c)(3) organizations. The Foundation does not provide support for individuals, for political parties, candidates or partisan political organizations, for labor organizations, fraternal organizations, athletic clubs or social clubs, for K-12 schools, school districts, or school foundations (contact Foundation for exceptions), for sectarian or denominational religious organizations, except for programs which are broadly promoted, available to anyone, and free from religious orientation, for fund-raising events (e.g., membership drives, luncheons/dinners, tournaments and benefits), or for advertising sponsorships.

GEOG. RESTRICTIONS: The Greater Orange County, California area and other areas, such as Omaha, Nebraska.

FINANCIAL DATA:
Amount of support per award: General grants: $5,000 to $15,000 for a one-year period of funding; Capital grants: $20,000 to $100,000, paid out over multiple years; Matching Gift Program for Higher Education: Up to $2,000; Matching Gift Program to Nonprofits: Up to $500.

Total amount of support: Matching Gift Program: $247,623 for the year 2014. Pacific Life Charitable Contributions and Pacific Life Foundation Charitable Grants: $6,000,000 for the year 2014.

NO. AWARDS: Matching Gift Program for Higher Education: 73 colleges and universities for the year 2014.

APPLICATION INFO:
Grant guidelines and application form are available online.

Duration: Agencies may reapply annually for funding; however, grants are made to any one agency for no more than three consecutive years. Support may again be requested after a two-year interim period.

Deadline: Submissions accepted July 15 to August 15.

PUBLICATIONS:
Annual report.

OFFICERS:
James T. Morris, Chairman and Chief Executive Officer
Carol R. Sudbeck, Vice Chairman
Tennyson S. Oyler, President
Michele A. Townsend, Vice President
Edward R. Byrd, Chief Financial Officer
Joseph J. Tortorelli, General Counsel
Jane M. Guon, Secretary
Marryn D. Santucci, Assistant Secretary

BOARD OF DIRECTORS:
Thomas D. Billiard
David R. Finear
Lorene C. Gordon
Douglas P. Jackson
James T. Morris
John F. O'Donnell
Tennyson S. Oyler
Joshua D. Scott
Carol R. Sudbeck
Michele A. Townsend
Rebecca Warwar

ADDRESS INQUIRIES TO:
Tennyson S. Oyler, President
(See address above.)

THE DAVID AND LUCILE PACKARD FOUNDATION [249]

343 Second Street
Los Altos, CA 94022
(650) 948-7658
Fax: (650) 948-5793
E-mail: inquiries@packard.org
Web Site: www.packard.org

FOUNDED: 1964

AREAS OF INTEREST:
Arts; children and youth, families and communities, food and shelter; conservation and sciences; organizational effectiveness; philanthropy; and Pueblo, CO.

NAME(S) OF PROGRAMS:
- **Children, Families and Communities**
- **Conservation and Science**
- **Local Grantmaking Program**
- **Population and Reproductive Health**

TYPE:
Capital grants; Challenge/matching grants; Conferences/seminars; Demonstration grants; Development grants; Fellowships; General operating grants; Matching gifts; Project/program grants; Research grants; Scholarships; Seed money grants; Technical assistance. Grants are made to provide support in the local five-county area for organizational development, arts education and traditional performing arts, as well as for areas of wetlands preservation and restoration, marine fisheries protection and restoration.

Funds are also provided to support fellowships for 20 young professors in science and engineering.

In addition, the Foundation supports children's health programs through children, families, and communities programs, population and family planning services.

Support is given for research of the deep ocean in the Monterey, CA area and community grants in Pueblo County, CO.

YEAR PROGRAM STARTED: 1964

PURPOSE:
To support private, voluntary charities.

LEGAL BASIS:
Private foundation incorporated under California law.

ELIGIBILITY:
Applicants must be qualified tax-exempt charitable organizations. Most community-oriented grants are made to organizations that serve the people of Monterey, San Benito, San Mateo, Santa Clara and Santa Cruz counties. Requests for support of community and local activities outside of these geographical areas will rarely be considered. Grants are also made in Pueblo (CO) and for national and international programs in conservation, population, public policy and children's health. No proposals may be accepted that benefit individuals or that are for religious purposes.

FINANCIAL DATA:
Total amount of support: Approximately $296,000,000 in general program grant awards for the year 2014.

APPLICATION INFO:
Contact the Foundation for guidelines.

Duration: Grants are made for one year, with occasional multiyear grants.

PUBLICATIONS:
Annual report; guideline brochures.

OFFICERS:
Susan Packard Orr, Chairperson
Nancy Packard Burnett, Vice Chairperson
Julie E. Packard, Vice Chairperson
Carol S. Larson, President and Chief Executive Officer
Chris DeCardy, Vice President and Director of Programs
Craig Neyman, Vice President and Chief Financial Officer
John H. Moehling, Chief Investment Officer
Mary Anne Rodgers, Secretary and General Counsel

BOARD OF TRUSTEES:
Ned Barnholt
Jason K. Burnett
Nancy Packard Burnett
James Clark
Sierra Clark
Linda Griego
Michael J. Klag
Carol S. Larson
Jane Lubchenco
Linda A. Mason
David Orr
Susan Packard Orr
Julie E. Packard
Louise Stephens
Ward W. Woods

PARK BANK FOUNDATION, INC. [250]

330 East Kilbourn Avenue
Milwaukee, WI 53202
(414) 270-3209
Fax: (414) 223-3022
E-mail: susanb@parkbankonline.com

FOUNDED: 1980

AREAS OF INTEREST:
Arts and culture, community development, conservation, education, health, historic preservation and social services.

TYPE:
Capital grants; Development grants; General operating grants.

YEAR PROGRAM STARTED: 1980

PURPOSE:
To fund qualifying organizations in the Milwaukee Metropolitan area as well as surrounding communities.

ELIGIBILITY:
Must have 501(c)(3) status and be located in the Milwaukee area and surrounding communities. No grants are made to individuals. Nonsectarian religious programs may apply.

GEOG. RESTRICTIONS: Milwaukee, Wisconsin metropolitan area.

FINANCIAL DATA:
Amount of support per award: $50 to $6,000.

APPLICATION INFO:
Send a request on the organization's letterhead, a copy of the 501(c)(3) status, a current financial statement of the organization, and a current listing of the Board of Directors.

Duration: One year.

Deadline: Request needs to be received six weeks prior to the meeting dates to be held mid-April, mid-August and mid-December.

THE PARKER FOUNDATION [251]

2604-B El Camino Real
Suite 244
Carlsbad, CA 92008
(760) 720-0630
Fax: (760) 720-1239
E-mail: mail@theparkerfoundation.org
Web Site: www.theparkerfoundation.org

FOUNDED: 1971

AREAS OF INTEREST:
Adult and youth services, visual and performing arts, museums and zoos, education, medical purposes, environment and community activities.

TYPE:
Capital grants; Challenge/matching grants; Matching gifts; Project/program grants. Programs and capital funding.

YEAR PROGRAM STARTED: 1971

PURPOSE:
To improve all aspects of life of the people of San Diego County, CA.

LEGAL BASIS:
Tax-exempt, independent private foundation.

ELIGIBILITY:
Applicants must be organizations operating in San Diego County, CA, qualified under IRS 501(c)(3). No grants to individuals or for support of conferences or symposia. No support provided for any project to the extent that it becomes dependent on the Foundation for continued existence.

GEOG. RESTRICTIONS: San Diego County, California.

FINANCIAL DATA:
Amount of support per award: Varies.

Total amount of support: $1,792,622 in grants paid in fiscal year 2015.

NO. MOST RECENT APPLICANTS: 227 for the year 2015.

NO. AWARDS: 75 for the year 2015.

ADDRESS INQUIRIES TO:
Robbin C. Powell
Chief Administrative Officer
(See address above.)

*SPECIAL STIPULATIONS:
Limited by governing documents to San Diego County, CA.

PARKER HANNIFIN CORPORATION FOUNDATION [252]

6035 Parkland Boulevard
Cleveland, OH 44124
(216) 896-3000
Fax: (216) 896-4057
E-mail: parkerfoundation@parker.com
Web Site: www.parker.com

AREAS OF INTEREST:
Educational, health, welfare, youth and other charitable organizations.

TYPE:
Capital grants; Matching gifts; Project/program grants. Through the National Merit Scholarship for Parker employee children only. Matching gifts are for education.

LEGAL BASIS:
Corporate foundation.

ELIGIBILITY:
Grants are made to nonprofit organizations. Emphasis will be placed on organizations that benefit Parker employees and shareholders by improving services in communities with Parker operations and educational opportunities for current and potential employees.

Contributions will not be made to fraternal or labor organizations. Donations to religious organizations are limited to organizations serving the general public on a nondenominational basis, such as the Y's, Salvation Army, educational institutions, hospitals, etc.

GEOG. RESTRICTIONS: United States.

FINANCIAL DATA:
Amount of support per award: $20 to $600,000.

Total amount of support: $6,000,000 annually.

APPLICATION INFO:
Applicants should submit a proposal stating needs and what the grant will be used for, to the Parker division in their locality.

Duration: One-time award.

Deadline: June 30.

THE RALPH M. PARSONS FOUNDATION [253]

888 West 6th Street, 7th Floor
Los Angeles, CA 90017
(213) 362-7600
Fax: (213) 362-7601
Web Site: www.rmpf.org

FOUNDED: 1961

AREAS OF INTEREST:
Social impact, health, civic and cultural affairs, and higher education in Los Angeles County.

TYPE:
General operating grants; Project/program grants.

YEAR PROGRAM STARTED: 1978

LEGAL BASIS:
Not-for-profit corporation.

ELIGIBILITY:
Applicants must be 501(c)(3) organizations not classified under 509(a). Grants limited to organizations providing services in Los Angeles County.

No funding for mass mailings, fund-raisers, individuals, conferences, religious or political activities and/or dinners or endowments.

GEOG. RESTRICTIONS: Los Angeles County, California.

FINANCIAL DATA:
Amount of support per award: Varies.

Total amount of support: $19,000,000 for the year 2015.

NO. AWARDS: 250 for the year 2015.

REPRESENTATIVE AWARDS:
$25,000 to Bet Tzedek, Los Angeles, CA, to train, recruit and evaluate the work of pro bono attorneys.

APPLICATION INFO:
Submit preliminary letter outlining project and amount requested. Program staff will determine whether applicant is qualified and may request additional information.

Applicants are encouraged to visit the Foundation web site prior to submitting Letter of Inquiry.

Duration: One year.

PUBLICATIONS:
Annual report.

STAFF:
Wendy Garen, President and Chief Executive Officer
Astra Galang, Chief Financial Officer
Thomas Brewer, Senior Program Officer
Jennifer Price-Letscher, Senior Program Officer
Nicole Larsen, Grants Administrator

BOARD OF DIRECTORS:
Linda Griego
Paul Haaga
Elizabeth Lowe
Karen Hill Scott
Peter J. Taylor
James A. Thomas
Robert Tranquada, M.D.
Franklin Ulf
Gayle Wilson

ADDRESS INQUIRIES TO:
Wendy Garen
President and Chief Executive Officer
(See address above.)

AMELIA PEABODY CHARITABLE FUND [254]

185 Devonshire Street
Suite 600
Boston, MA 02110
(617) 451-6178
Web Site: apcfund.org

FOUNDED: 1984

AREAS OF INTEREST:
Social service and youth services in Massachusetts; environment, health and historic preservation.

TYPE:
Capital grants; Challenge/matching grants.

PURPOSE:
To support organizations that work to improve the quality of life in New England.

LEGAL BASIS:
Private foundation.

ELIGIBILITY:
Eligible organizations must be IRS 501(c)(3) tax-exempt and classified as a public charity under Section 509(a)(1) or 509(a)(2) of the Internal Revenue Code. No grants to individuals or religious organizations. No funding is provided for operating costs, start-ups or salaries, or education.

GEOG. RESTRICTIONS: New England states, primarily Massachusetts.

FINANCIAL DATA:
Amount of support per award: Varies per program.

Total amount of support: Approximately $8,000,000 annually.

NO. MOST RECENT APPLICANTS: Approximately 300.

NO. AWARDS: 100.

APPLICATION INFO:
All proposals are submitted online via the web site above.

Duration: Renewal possible after three years.

Deadline: February 1 and July 1.

PUBLICATIONS:
Guidelines.

IRS I.D.: 23-7364949

STAFF:
Bethany B. Kendall, Executive Director
Cheryl Gideon, Business and Grants Coordinator

ADDRESS INQUIRIES TO:
Cheryl Gideon
Business and Grants Coordinator
(See address above.)

PEACOCK FOUNDATION, INC. [255]

100 S.E. Second Street, Suite 2370
Miami, FL 33131-2145
(305) 373-1386
Fax: (305) 375-0660
Web Site: peacockfoundationinc.org

AREAS OF INTEREST:
Elderly, children, youth, art for educational purposes, environmental education, disabilities, health and hospitals, medical research and human services.

TYPE:
General operating grants; Project/program grants. Support is provided for projects/programs and limited operating funds.

ELIGIBILITY:
Organizations classified as 501(c)(3) by the IRS can apply. Individuals are ineligible.

GEOG. RESTRICTIONS: Broward, Miami-Dade and Monroe counties, Florida.

FINANCIAL DATA:
Amount of support per award: Average $25,000.

NO. AWARDS: 65.

APPLICATION INFO:
Applicants must initially submit letter of inquiry.

Duration: One year.

ADDRESS INQUIRIES TO:
Joelle Allen, Executive Director
(See address above.)

THE WILLIAM PENN FOUNDATION [256]

Two Logan Square, 11th Floor
100 North 18th Street
Philadelphia, PA 19103-2757
(215) 988-1830
Fax: (215) 988-1823
E-mail: grants@williampennfoundation.org
Web Site: www.williampennfoundation.org

FOUNDED: 1945

AREAS OF INTEREST:
Art, communities, culture, environment, children, youth and families.

NAME(S) OF PROGRAMS:

- **Creative Communities**
- **Great Learning**
- **Watershed Protection**

TYPE:
Capital grants; Challenge/matching grants; Demonstration grants; Development grants; General operating grants; Project/program grants; Research grants; Seed money grants; Technical assistance. Planning grants; Implementation grants.

In the areas of children, youth and families, grants are made to promote a better early care and education system, more effective and equitable education policies, networks of developmental opportunities for older youth, and improvements to the systems supporting families. The program focuses on critical transitions in the lives of children as they progress from birth, through early childhood, and into young adulthood.

In the area of environment and communities, grants are made to foster greater cross-sector collaborations that build on the assets of our region through revitalization of its urban core and protection and restoration of watersheds, with a focus on key waterways. Investments are intended to catalyze innovation and leadership in the region.

In the area of arts and culture, the Foundation provides various types of core operating support for arts groups and cultural institutions, enabling them to pursue their creative missions. Work is also funded that broadly advances the region's cultural sector. General operating grants are made only for arts funding.

YEAR PROGRAM STARTED: 1945

PURPOSE:
To improve the quality of life in the Greater Philadelphia area, particularly for its economically disadvantaged residents; to serve nonprofit organizations that help people improve their lives within a more just and caring society.

LEGAL BASIS:
Private foundation.

ELIGIBILITY:
Applicants must be organizations which are defined as tax-exempt under Section 501(c)(3) of the Internal Revenue Code and which are not private foundations. Grants may be made to religious institutions for nonsectarian purposes, to governments and national organizations in support of policy and advocacy projects.

The Foundation does not fund scholarships, fellowships, or grants to individuals; loans or investment programs; debt reduction; sectarian religious activities; housing capital projects; exempt organizations that pass funds to nonexempt groups; profit-making enterprises; nonpublic schools; programs for rehabilitation or research; programs to replace discontinued government support or national or international grants.

GEOG. RESTRICTIONS: Philadelphia area (Bucks, Chester, Delaware and Montgomery counties), Pennsylvania and Camden, New Jersey.

FINANCIAL DATA:
Amount of support per award: Varies.

Total amount of support: $110,000,000 in total grants for year ended December 31, 2015.

CO-OP FUNDING PROGRAMS: The Foundation regularly joins with other foundations and institutions to fund projects.

APPLICATION INFO:
All applicants must first submit a letter of inquiry. Guidelines are available on the Foundation web site.

PUBLICATIONS:
Annual report.

IRS I.D.: 23-1503488

BOARD OF DIRECTORS:
Janet Haas, M.D., Chairperson
Leonard C. Haas, Vice Chairperson
Frederick R. Haas, Secretary
Judith Freyer
Andrew Haas
Christina Haas
David Haas
Thomas W. Haas
Katherine Hanrahan
Don Kimelman
Dennis Maple
Howard Meyers

OFFICERS AND STAFF:
Laura Sparks, Executive Director
Olive Mosier, Director, Arts Funding
Barbara Scace, Director, Grants Management

ADDRESS INQUIRIES TO:
See e-mail address above.

PEPSICO FOUNDATION [257]

700 Anderson Hill Road
Purchase, NY 10577
(914) 253-2000
Fax: (914) 253-2070
Web Site: www.pepsico.com

FOUNDED: 1962

AREAS OF INTEREST:
Education, environment and health.

TYPE:
Capital grants.

PURPOSE:
To support programs that encourage healthy lifestyles, improve availability of affordable nutrition, expand access to clean water, enhance sustainable agriculture capability, enable job readiness, and empower women and girls.

LEGAL BASIS:
Nonprofit under 501(c)(3).

ELIGIBILITY:
Organizations seeking a grant must be registered and have an official tax-exemption under Section 501(c)(3) of the Internal Revenue Code, or the equivalent. The Foundation does not make grants to individuals, religious organizations or political causes.

FINANCIAL DATA:
Amount of support per award: Varies.

APPLICATION INFO:
Submit a brief Letter of Interest. Complete details are available on the Foundation web site.

ADDRESS INQUIRIES TO:
Grants Manager
(See address above.)

THE CARL AND LILY PFORZHEIMER FOUNDATION, INC. [258]

950 Third Avenue, 30th Floor
New York, NY 10022
(212) 223-6500
Fax: (212) 223-2222

FOUNDED: 1942

AREAS OF INTEREST:
Education, primarily early 19th century English literature.

TYPE:
Grants-in-aid; Project/program grants.

PURPOSE:
To provide resources for the in-depth study of 19th century English literature.

LEGAL BASIS:
Private foundation.

ELIGIBILITY:
Grants are awarded only to IRS 501(c)(3) tax-exempt organizations. No grants are made directly to individuals.

GEOG. RESTRICTIONS: Primarily United States.

FINANCIAL DATA:
Amount of support per award: Average: $25,000 to $50,000.

APPLICATION INFO:
Organizations may submit a proposal.

Duration: Varies.

ADDRESS INQUIRIES TO:
Carl H. Pforzheimer III, President
(See address above.)

THE ALBERT PICK, JR. FUND [259]

70 East Lake Street
Suite 1120
Chicago, IL 60601
(312) 236-1192
Fax: (312) 236-1209
E-mail: iris@albertpickjrfund.org
Web Site: www.albertpickjrfund.org

FOUNDED: 1947

AREAS OF INTEREST:
Civic and community, culture, education, health and human services.

TYPE:
Challenge/matching grants; Demonstration grants; Development grants; General operating grants; Project/program grants; Technical assistance.

YEAR PROGRAM STARTED: 1947

PURPOSE:
To offer a hand when help is needed.

LEGAL BASIS:
Private family foundation.

ELIGIBILITY:
Nonprofits with offices and budgeted programs operating within the city of Chicago.

GEOG. RESTRICTIONS: Chicago, Illinois.

FINANCIAL DATA:
Amount of support per award: Minimum $15,000.

NO. MOST RECENT APPLICANTS: 196.

NO. AWARDS: 53.

APPLICATION INFO:
Eligible nonprofits are requested to complete an application form, available from the Fund. Only those proposals which completely meet the requirements outlined in the guidelines will be reviewed. Complete details are available on the Fund's web site.

Duration: Generally, one year.

Deadline: January 21 for the Spring quarter, March 23 for the Summer quarter, June 15 for Fall quarter and September 14 for Winter quarter.

PUBLICATIONS:
Guidelines; grant application form.

IRS I.D.: 36-6071402

OFFICERS AND BOARD OF DIRECTORS:
Robert B. Lifton, President
Shelly A. Davis, Vice President
Howard A. Sulkin, Treasurer

Gwendolyn M. Rice, Secretary
James W. Mabie

ADDRESS INQUIRIES TO:
Iris Krieg, Executive Director
(See address above.)

THE HAROLD WHITWORTH PIERCE CHARITABLE TRUST [260]

c/o Nichols and Pratt
50 Congress Street
Boston, MA 02109
(617) 523-8368
Fax: (617) 523-8949
E-mail: piercetrust@nichols-pratt.com
Web Site: www.piercetrust.org

AREAS OF INTEREST:
Education, green and public spaces, capital projects and arts education.

TYPE:
Capital grants; Project/program grants.

PURPOSE:
To support projects that will bring long-range benefits to Boston's citizens.

ELIGIBILITY:
Eligible organizations must be IRS 501(c)(3) tax-exempt.

No grants are made for scholarships to individuals. In addition, no grants are made for fund-raising events, films, videos, travel, fund-raising training or advocacy.

GEOG. RESTRICTIONS: Boston, Massachusetts area.

FINANCIAL DATA:
Amount of support per award: $10,000 to $60,000.

Total amount of support: Average: $1,000,000.

NO. AWARDS: Varies.

REPRESENTATIVE AWARDS:
Education: $20,000 to Associated Day Care Services, Boston, MA, to train and mentor teachers of infants and toddlers in an intensive Literacy Curriculum specifically designed for infants and toddlers; Capital Projects: $50,000 to Ballet Theatre of Boston, Cambridge, MA, for a capital grant to help make possible the construction of a new home for the Ballet Theater within a church in Cambridge; Green and Public Spaces: $10,000 to Boston GreenSpace Alliance for a second installment of a two-year grant for operating support for the Alliance.

APPLICATION INFO:
The application process consists of three steps:
(1) a telephone call to the Trust's grant administrator to determine eligibility;
(2) a concept letter describing the applicant organization and its mission, etc., and;
(3) after review of concept letters by the trustees, full proposals will be invited from a limited number of applicants. The Trust will then decide which proposals to fund.

Duration: Typically one year.

Deadline: Concept letter due (postmarked) March 1 and September 30; Invited proposals: mid-April and early November.

PUBLICATIONS:
Application guidelines.

ADDRESS INQUIRIES TO:
Elizabeth D. Nichols, Program Director
(See address above.)

IRWIN ANDREW PORTER FOUNDATION [261]

7201 Ohms Lane
Suite 100
Edina, MN 55439
E-mail: iapfound@gmail.com
Web Site: www.iapfoundation.org

FOUNDED: 1996

AREAS OF INTEREST:
Arts, education, environment and social programs.

TYPE:
Challenge/matching grants; Grants-in-aid; Project/program grants.

PURPOSE:
To fund innovative projects that foster connections between individuals, communities, the environment and the world at large.

ELIGIBILITY:
The Foundation provides funding for a variety of interest areas. The quality, innovation, thoughtfulness and effectiveness of a project are of more importance than the specific interest area. However, its areas of interest are the arts, education, environment and social programs.

International projects should be applicable to, and repeatable in, other regions. The Foundation gives funding to nonprofit organizations with U.S. IRS tax-exempt status only. International organizations must have a fiscal agent incorporated in the U.S. with an appropriate U.S. IRS tax-exempt designation.

The Foundation does not provide financial support for:
(1) general operating expenses;
(2) capital projects;
(3) endowments;
(4) scholarships;
(5) fund-raising events or activities, social events, goodwill advertising or marketing;
(6) lobbying, political, fraternal, athletic, social or veterans organizations;
(7) religious programs;
(8) travel for individuals or groups;
(9) individuals or;
(10) ordinary school funding.

GEOG. RESTRICTIONS: Illinois, Iowa, Michigan, Minnesota, North Dakota, South Dakota and Wisconsin.

FINANCIAL DATA:
Amount of support per award: Grants: $500 to $30,000 annually.

Total amount of support: Approximately $135,000 annually.

APPLICATION INFO:
Organizations are selected for an invitation to apply from a group of secret nominators.

Duration: Generally, one year.

ADDRESS INQUIRIES TO:
Amy L. Hubbard, Chairman
(See address above.)

*PLEASE NOTE:
Foundation grantmaking is by invitation only; unsolicited proposals will not be considered.

PPG INDUSTRIES FOUNDATION [262]

One PPG Place
Pittsburgh, PA 15272
E-mail: foundation@ppg.com
Web Site: www.ppgcommunities.com

FOUNDED: 1951

AREAS OF INTEREST:
Education, human services, culture and the arts, civic and community affairs.

NAME(S) OF PROGRAMS:
- **Grant Incentives for Volunteerism by PPG Employees and Retirees (GIVE)**
- **Innovative Classroom Grant Program**
- **Matching Gifts Program**
- **National Merit Scholarships**
- **PPG CARE Fund**

TYPE:
Capital grants; General operating grants; Project/program grants; Scholarships. Grant Incentives for Volunteerism by PPG Employees and Retirees (GIVE) is a program to encourage PPG employee involvement in volunteerism. The GIVE Program recognizes personal involvement by active PPG employees and retirees who volunteer on their own time by providing grants to eligible institutions in the U.S.

Innovative Classroom Grant Program provides grants up to $1,000 that specifically support projects designed to spark student interest and achievement related to science, technology, engineering and mathematics (STEM). PPG employees in the U.S. have an opportunity to help their local schools apply for these grants.

Matching Gifts Program matches gifts of PPG employees and directors to qualified institutions.

National Merit Scholarships are awarded in three categories. The Employee-Child Scholarship Program is for sons and daughters of PPG Industries, Inc. employees. The Plant Community Scholarship Program offers a community scholarship program to major PPG facilities. The National Achievement Scholarship Program awards two scholarships per year to outstanding African-American students in this program.

YEAR PROGRAM STARTED: 1951

PURPOSE:
To enhance the quality of life in those communities within the U.S. where PPG Industries has a major presence; to develop human potential.

LEGAL BASIS:
Corporate, nonprofit foundation.

ELIGIBILITY:
Grants are made to tax-exempt organizations in the Foundation's areas of interest. Priority is given to applications from organizations dedicated to enhancing the welfare of communities in which PPG Industries is a resident. It gives consideration to those organizations whose activities either enhance individual opportunities or help to strengthen the nation's human services, educational, or economic systems on a regional or nationwide basis.

In general, the Foundation will not award grants to advertisement sponsorship for benefit purposes, endowments, individuals, organizations established to influence legislation or support political activities, organizations outside of the U.S. or its territories, projects which would directly benefit PPG Industries, Inc., religious groups

solely for religious purposes, special events and telephone solicitations or United Way agencies for operating support.

FINANCIAL DATA:
Amount of support per award: Varies.
Total amount of support: $5,700,000 in support paid for the year 2014.
Matching fund requirements: Contributions by PPG employees and members of the board of directors of the company are matched on a 1:1 basis by the Foundation; $25 minimum, $10,000 maximum per year per donor.

APPLICATION INFO:
Grant policies, guidelines and online application are available on the Foundation web site.
Duration: Varies.
Deadline: Requests for funding are accepted year-round.

STAFF:
Sue Sloan, Executive Director, PPG Industries Foundation

BOARD OF DIRECTORS:
Charles E. Bunch, Executive Chairman
Michael H. McGarry, President and Chief Executive Officer
Frank S. Sklarsky, Executive Vice President and Chief Financial Officer
Glenn E. Bost, Senior Vice President and General Counsel
J. Craig Jordan, Vice President, Human Resources

PRINCIPAL FINANCIAL GROUP FOUNDATION INC. [263]

711 High Street
Des Moines, IA 50392-0150
(515) 247-7227
Fax: (515) 246-5475; (866) 496-6547
E-mail: mcreynolds.mandi@principal.com
Web Site: www.principal.com/about-us/corporate-citizenship

FOUNDED: 1987

AREAS OF INTEREST:
Financial security, education and strong communities.

CONSULTING OR VOLUNTEER SERVICES:
The mission of the Principal Volunteer Network is to be the primary volunteer network for community service to educate and recruit employees, agents and retirees of the Principal Financial Group; thus enhancing the company's social responsibility goals and business objectives.

NAME(S) OF PROGRAMS:
- **Charitable Giving Program**

TYPE:
Capital grants; General operating grants; Project/program grants.

YEAR PROGRAM STARTED: 1987

LEGAL BASIS:
Corporate foundation.

ELIGIBILITY:
Applicants must be nonprofit IRS 501(c)(3) organizations located in communities with significant employee presence.

Grants are generally not made to athletes or athletic organizations, conference or seminar attendance, goodwill advertising, endowments or memorials, festival participation, fraternal organizations, hospital or health care facility capital fund drives, individuals, K-12 schools, libraries, partisan political organizations, private foundations, sectarian, religious or denominational organizations, social organizations, tax-supported organizations, or United Way organizations seeking funds for United Way-funded programs.

GEOG. RESTRICTIONS: Wilmington, Delaware; Cedar Falls, Greater Des Moines, Mason City and Waterloo, Iowa; Grand Island, Nebraska; Spokane, Washington; Appleton, Wisconsin.

FINANCIAL DATA:
Amount of support per award: Varies.
Total amount of support: Varies.

NO. MOST RECENT APPLICANTS: Over 900.

APPLICATION INFO:
Proposals should include:
(1) a grant application form;
(2) cover letter with amount requested, background and mission of organization, purpose of funding, desired outcome and how measured;
(3) evaluation of previous funding;
(4) budget;
(5) board list;
(6) IRS exemption letter of 501(c)(3) status;
(7) one audit 990 form and;
(8) annual report.
Deadline: March 15 for health and human services, June 15 for education, and October 15 for Strong Communities (civic, community and environment).

PUBLICATIONS:
Guidelines.

ADDRESS INQUIRIES TO:
Mandi McReynolds
Global Community Relations Manager
(See address above.)

PUBLIC WELFARE FOUNDATION, INC. [264]

1200 U Street, N.W.
Washington, DC 20009-4443
(202) 965-1800
Fax: (202) 265-8851
E-mail: info@publicwelfare.org
Web Site: www.publicwelfare.org

FOUNDED: 1947

AREAS OF INTEREST:
Workers' rights, criminal justice and juvenile justice.

NAME(S) OF PROGRAMS:
- **Criminal Justice**
- **Juvenile Justice**
- **Workers' Rights**

TYPE:
General operating grants; Project/program grants.

YEAR PROGRAM STARTED: 1947

PURPOSE:
To support efforts to ensure fundamental rights and opportunities for people in need; to look for carefully defined points where the Foundation's funds can make a difference in bringing about systemic changes that can improve the lives of countless people.

LEGAL BASIS:
Private foundation.

ELIGIBILITY:
Applicants' requests must adhere to the Foundation's funding guidelines.

GEOG. RESTRICTIONS: United States.

FINANCIAL DATA:
Amount of support per award: Varies.
Total amount of support: $21,400,000 allocated for fiscal year 2016.

NO. MOST RECENT APPLICANTS: 410 for fiscal year 2015.

NO. AWARDS: 165 approved grants for fiscal year 2015.

APPLICATION INFO:
Applicants should submit letters of inquiry using the online application system. This letter should contain facts and figures about the organization, describe its mission and explain the purpose of the request, including the Program under which a grant is being requested. Applicants will be invited by e-mail to submit full proposals. The Foundation cannot consider full proposals which have not been invited.
Duration: Usually one to two years. Renewal possible.

IRS I.D.: 54-0597601

BOARD OF DIRECTORS AND OFFICERS:
Lydia Micheaux Marshall, Chairperson
Phillipa Taylor, Secretary and Treasurer
Craig Aase
Stephanie Bell-Rose
Jackie Clegg
Colin Diver
David Dodson
Mary McClymont
Maria Otero
Shirley Sagawa
Cliff Sloan
Landis Zimmerman

ADDRESS INQUIRIES TO:
Grants Management
(See address above.)

THE QUAKER CHEMICAL FOUNDATION [265]

901 East Hector Street
Conshohocken, PA 19428-2380
(610) 832-4301
Fax: (610) 832-4496
E-mail: quakerfoundation@quakerchem.com
Web Site: www.quakerchem.com

FOUNDED: 1959

AREAS OF INTEREST:
Civic and community; cultural, health and welfare; and education.

NAME(S) OF PROGRAMS:
- **Grant Program**
- **Matching Gift Program**
- **Scholarship Program**

TYPE:
Matching gifts; Project/program grants; Scholarships. The Foundation matches employee gifts to qualified educational institutions, health and welfare organizations, civic and community, and arts or cultural institutions which are operated for the benefit of the general public.

YEAR PROGRAM STARTED: 1959

PURPOSE:
To help community projects where the company has domestic operations.

LEGAL BASIS:
Corporate foundation.

ELIGIBILITY:
Applicants must be IRS 501(c)(3) tax-exempt organizations. As a general rule, the Foundation does not support national organizations, limiting its interest to those organizations that are active in the areas in

which the Quaker Chemical Corporation has operations, generally located within a five-mile radius of company facilities and locations.

FINANCIAL DATA:
Amount of support per award: $1,000 to $5,000; average: $1,500.

Matching fund requirements: Minimum $25 and maximum $1,000 per employee, retiree, director or spouse thereof per fiscal year.

REPRESENTATIVE AWARDS:
Conshohocken Fellowship House; Delaware Valley Science Fairs.

APPLICATION INFO:
Application must include the following information:
(1) project description;
(2) budget;
(3) list of board of directors and officers and;
(4) organization's tax-exempt ruling under Section 501(c)(3) of the Internal Revenue Code.

Duration: One year.

Deadline: April 30.

PUBLICATIONS:
Grant application guidelines.

IRS I.D.: 23-6245803

TRUSTEES:
Palitha Abeywardena
Cindy Cemar
Jennifer Hill
Irene M. Kisleiko
Christian Scholund
Jan Waldauer

ADDRESS INQUIRIES TO:
Quaker Chemical Foundation Secretary
(See address above.)

THE NELL J. REDFIELD FOUNDATION [266]

P.O. Box 61
Reno, NV 89504
(775) 323-1373
Fax: (775) 323-4476
E-mail: redfieldfoundation@yahoo.com

FOUNDED: 1974

AREAS OF INTEREST:
Aged, disadvantaged children, education, religion, health care and the homeless poor.

TYPE:
Capital grants; Challenge/matching grants; Development grants; Matching gifts; Project/program grants. Grants for higher education. Medical and social welfare for disadvantaged children and seniors.

PURPOSE:
To promote education, health care and care for the homeless poor.

LEGAL BASIS:
Nonprofit foundation.

ELIGIBILITY:
Grants are made to organizations that have tax-exempt status under Section 501(c)(3) of the Internal Revenue Code. Nonsectarian religious programs may apply. No grants are made to individuals or private foundations.

Grants are restricted to organizations in northern Nevada.

GEOG. RESTRICTIONS: Northern Nevada.

FINANCIAL DATA:
Amount of support per award: Varies.

Total amount of support: Varies.

NO. MOST RECENT APPLICANTS: 125.

NO. AWARDS: 75.

APPLICATION INFO:
Initially, contact the fund with a two-page summary that includes the specific goals, objectives, proposed activities and results expected.

Duration: One year. Renewal possible.

Deadline: Quarterly during each calendar year.

ADDRESS INQUIRIES TO:
Gerald C. Smith, Director
(See address above.)

THE REEBOK FOUNDATION [267]

1895 J.W. Foster Boulevard
Canton, MA 02021
(781) 401-5000
Fax: (781) 401-4744
Web Site: www.adidas-group.com/en/brands/reebok

FOUNDED: 1986

AREAS OF INTEREST:
Programs for underserved youth in the greater Boston, MA area.

TYPE:
General operating grants; Matching gifts.

YEAR PROGRAM STARTED: 1986

PURPOSE:
To help children fulfill their potential.

LEGAL BASIS:
Corporate foundation.

ELIGIBILITY:
Grant applicants must be nonprofit organizations that provide equal access to funding and equal opportunity, and do not discriminate based on race, religion or sex. Grants are not made to individuals, political or fraternal organizations, or for advertising in program books or medical research.

GEOG. RESTRICTIONS: Greater Boston, Massachusetts area.

FINANCIAL DATA:
Amount of support per award: $500 to $10,000.

Matching fund requirements: Employees of Reebok International Ltd, its subsidiaries and divisions. Organizations must be IRS 501(c)(3). Employee contributions to qualified organizations are matched dollar-for-dollar, up to $1,500 maximum.

APPLICATION INFO:
An initial letter is requested to determine the interest and appropriateness of a full proposal.

Deadline: Applications accepted throughout the year.

PUBLICATIONS:
Guidelines.

IRS I.D.: 04-3073548

STAFF:
Alisha Collins, Manager

ADDRESS INQUIRIES TO:
Alisha Collins, Manager
(See address above.)

THE REGEN FOUNDATIO

225 West Wacker I
Suite 1500
Chicago, IL 60606
(312) 917-1833
Fax: (312) 917-1822
E-mail: regfound@a

FOUNDED: 1950

AREAS OF INTEREST:
Education, community services, medicine and health, urban affairs, arts and music.

TYPE:
Capital grants; Endowments. Most grants are made to organizations located in and directly serving the residents of Illinois, basically in the metropolitan Chicago area.

YEAR PROGRAM STARTED: 1950

PURPOSE:
To help improve life and the community in and around Chicago.

LEGAL BASIS:
Private foundation.

ELIGIBILITY:
Any charitable organization other than private foundations for exempt purposes. No grants are made to individuals or for the benefit of designated individuals.

GEOG. RESTRICTIONS: Chicago, Illinois.

FINANCIAL DATA:
Only a small number of applicants will receive funds due to the relatively limited amount available and the number of organizations funded on trustee initiative.

Amount of support per award: Varies.

Total amount of support: Varies.

NO. MOST RECENT APPLICANTS: 45 for the year 2013.

NO. AWARDS: 35.

APPLICATION INFO:
Contact the Foundation in writing for an application.

Duration: One year. Renewable.

Deadline: March 31 and September 30.

OFFICERS:
Susan Regenstein, Chairperson

EXECUTIVE DIRECTOR:
Patricia Wallies

ADDRESS INQUIRIES TO:
Susan Regenstein, Chairperson
(See address above.)

THE CHARLES H. REVSON FOUNDATION [269]

55 East 59th Street
23rd Floor
New York, NY 10022
(212) 935-3340
Fax: (212) 688-0633
E-mail: info@revsonfoundation.org
Web Site: www.revsonfoundation.org

FOUNDED: 1956

AREAS OF INTEREST:
Urban affairs, with emphasis on New York City, education, biomedical research policy and Jewish philanthropy and education.

TYPE:
Fellowships; Project/program grants; Research grants. The Foundation supports a

of ongoing fellowship programs in c policy, biomedical research and Jewish ucation.

YEAR PROGRAM STARTED: 1978

PURPOSE:
To make a commitment to spread knowledge and to improve human life.

LEGAL BASIS:
Private foundation.

ELIGIBILITY:
Grants are made to nonprofit, tax-exempt organizations. The Foundation does not make grants to individuals or for endowments, local health appeals, direct-service programs, building or construction funds, or routine budgetary support.

GEOG. RESTRICTIONS: New York, New York and Israel.

FINANCIAL DATA:
Amount of support per award: Varies.

APPLICATION INFO:
The Foundation welcomes letters of inquiry from prospective grantees. Letters should be no longer than two pages and include:
(1) Revson program area of proposed project;
(2) brief description of project and of sponsoring organization and;
(3) amount requested.

In response to a letter of inquiry, the Foundation may invite the submission of a complete proposal.

Proposals can be sent to loi@revsonfoundation.org. No proposals accepted by fax.

Duration: Varies.

IRS I.D.: 13-6126105

STAFF:
Julie Sandorf, President
Azade Ardali, Administrative Officer
Nessa Rapoport, Senior Program Officer
Maria Marcantonio, Program Officer
Katie Shragge, Grants Administrator
Karen Yu, Controller

BOARD OF DIRECTORS:
Reynold Levy, Chairman
Cheryl Cohen Effron, Treasurer
Gerald Rosenfeld, Secretary
Stacy Dick
Suzanne Gluck
Jeffrey Goldberg
Sharon Greenberger
Steven Hyman
Charles H. Revson, Jr.
Clifford Tabin

ADDRESS INQUIRIES TO:
See e-mail address above.

Z. SMITH REYNOLDS FOUNDATION, INC. [270]

102 West Third Street
Suite 1110
Winston-Salem, NC 27101-3940
(336) 725-7541 ext. 116
(800) 443-8319
Fax: (336) 725-6069
E-mail: patw@zsr.org
Web Site: www.zsr.org

FOUNDED: 1936

AREAS OF INTEREST:
Community economic development, environment, public education, social justice and equity, and strengthening democracy.

TYPE:
Challenge/matching grants; General operating grants; Project/program grants; Seed money grants. Sabbatical Program.

YEAR PROGRAM STARTED: 1936

PURPOSE:
To support charitable causes within the state of North Carolina.

LEGAL BASIS:
Private foundation.

ELIGIBILITY:
North Carolina public and nonprofit private institutions and organizations are eligible. No grants are made to individuals for any purpose.

GEOG. RESTRICTIONS: North Carolina.

FINANCIAL DATA:
Amount of support per award: $500 to $1,200,000.

Total amount of support: Approximately $17,589,177 for the year ended December 2014.

NO. MOST RECENT APPLICANTS: 399 for the year 2014.

NO. AWARDS: 166 for the year 2014.

APPLICATION INFO:
Application information can be downloaded from the web site.

Deadline: February 1 for the spring meeting and August 1 for the fall meeting.

PUBLICATIONS:
Annual report (online).

IRS I.D.: 58-6038145

OFFICERS:
Lloyd P. Tate, Jr., President
Jane S. Patterson, Vice President
W. Noah Reynolds, Treasurer
Terry Lockamy, Assistant Treasurer
Maurice O. Green, Secretary
Patricia B. Williamson, Assistant Secretary

TRUSTEES:
Nancy R. Bagley
Piper Neal Beveridge
Anita Brown-Graham
Daniel G. Clodfelter
Ilana Dubester
John O. McNairy
Katharine B. Mountcastle, Life Trustee
Mary Mountcastle
David L. Neal
Stephen L. Neal
Jane S. Patterson
W. Noah Reynolds
Virgil Smith
Lloyd P. Tate, Jr.

ADDRESS INQUIRIES TO:
Maurice O. Green, Secretary
(See address above.)

THE RHODE ISLAND FOUNDATION/RHODE ISLAND COMMUNITY FOUNDATION [271]

One Union Station
Providence, RI 02903-1746
(401) 274-4564
Fax: (401) 331-8085
Web Site: www.rifoundation.org

FOUNDED: 1916

TYPE:
Challenge/matching grants; Conferences/seminars; Demonstration grants; Development grants; Fellowships; General operating grants; Project/program grants; Research grants; Scholarships; Technical assistance; Travel grants; Loan forgiveness programs. Strategy grants; Small grants; Basic human needs grants; Regional grants.

YEAR PROGRAM STARTED: 1916

PURPOSE:
To improve the living conditions and well-being of the inhabitants of Rhode Island.

LEGAL BASIS:
Community foundation.

ELIGIBILITY:
Grants are not generally made directly to individuals. Programs must primarily benefit Rhode Island.

GEOG. RESTRICTIONS: Rhode Island.

FINANCIAL DATA:
Amount of support per award: Varies.

APPLICATION INFO:
Guidelines are available at the Foundation web site.

PUBLICATIONS:
Annual report; newsletter; guidelines; reports.

BOARD OF DIRECTORS:
Marie J. Langlois, Chairman
Michael K. Allio
Frederick K. Butler
Mary W.C. Daly
Ned Handy
Ann-Marie Harrington
Mary F. Lovejoy
Hon. Ronald K. Machtley
Cynthia Stewart Reed
Neil D. Steinberg
Howard G. Sutton
Hon. Ernst C. Torres

ADDRESS INQUIRIES TO:
Jennifer Pereira
Director of Grant Programs
(See address above.)

SID W. RICHARDSON FOUNDATION [272]

309 Main Street
Fort Worth, TX 76102
(817) 336-0494
Fax: (817) 332-2176
E-mail: sranelle@sidrichardson.org
Web Site: www.sidrichardson.org

FOUNDED: 1947

AREAS OF INTEREST:
Education, health, human service, and the arts.

TYPE:
Capital grants; Challenge/matching grants; Development grants; General operating grants; Matching gifts; Project/program grants; Research grants.

PURPOSE:
To support organizations that serve the people of Texas.

LEGAL BASIS:
Private foundation.

ELIGIBILITY:
All funds must be limited to the state of Texas for IRS 501(c)(3) tax-exempt institutions and organizations or 509(a) organizations (other than a private foundation under the latter code). An organization also may qualify if it falls within the terms of

Section 170(c)(1) and the contribution requested is to be used exclusively for public purposes. No grants are made to individuals.

GEOG. RESTRICTIONS: Texas.

FINANCIAL DATA:

Amount of support per award: $5,000 to $5,000,000.

Matching fund requirements: Varies.

NO. MOST RECENT APPLICANTS: Approximately 500 to 600.

NO. AWARDS: Approximately 120 to 145.

REPRESENTATIVE AWARDS:

Education: $150,000 to Communities in Schools, Fort Worth, Inc. for the program to place counselors in public schools across Tarrant County; Health: $75,000 to Child Study Center for diagnostic and treatment services for children with disabilities; Human Services: $110,000 to Catholic Charities Diocese of Fort Worth for the transportation program; Cultural: $50,000 to National Cowgirl Museum and Hall of Fame, Inc. for operational support.

APPLICATION INFO:

Initial contact should be by letter briefly explaining project or program. If the project is within areas of current activity, an application will be provided.

Duration: Typically one year.

Deadline: January 15.

PUBLICATIONS:

Annual report.

IRS I.D.: 75-6015828

BOARD OF DIRECTORS:

ADDRESS INQUIRIES TO:

Pete Geren, President
(See address above.)

ROCKEFELLER FAMILY FUND [273]

475 Riverside Drive
Suite 900
New York, NY 10115-0066
(212) 812-4252
Fax: (212) 812-4299
E-mail: ccaddle-steele@rffund.org
Web Site: www.rffund.org

FOUNDED: 1967

NAME(S) OF PROGRAMS:

- **Economic Justice for Women**
- **Environment**
- **Institutional Accountability and Individual Liberty**

TYPE:

Challenge/matching grants; General operating grants. Economic Justice for Women program seeks to improve the quality of life for working women and their families by advocating for equitable employment opportunities and updated employment standards.

Initiatives under the Environment program are designed to enact aggressive policies at the state and national levels to reduce carbon emissions, highlight the risks of coal-burning power plants and mountaintop removal coal-mining, and sound climate science, while exposing those who distort it.

The Institutional Accountability and Individual Liberty program encourages the active participation of citizens in government, seeks to make government and private institutions more accountable and responsive, and supports efforts to ensure that individuals' rights and liberties under the Constitution are protected.

YEAR PROGRAM STARTED: 1967

PURPOSE:

To make grants to nonprofit organizations in the areas of economic justice for women, the environment, and institutional accountability and individual liberty.

LEGAL BASIS:

A not-for-profit charitable corporation existing under the New York state not-for-profit corporation law.

ELIGIBILITY:

Tax-exempt organizations engaged in educational and charitable activities of national significance are eligible for support.

The Fund does not ordinarily consider projects that pertain to a single community, except in the rare instance where a project is unique, strategically placed to advance a national issue, or is likely to serve as a national model. Grants are rarely made to organizations which traditionally enjoy popular support, such as universities, museums, hospitals or endowed institutions.

The Family Fund does not make grants for academic or scholarly research or social or human service programs. Grants are also not made to support individuals, scholarships, international programs, domestic programs dealing with international issues, profit-making businesses, construction or restoration projects, or to reduce an organization's debt. Instead, support is offered for advocacy efforts that are action-oriented and likely to yield tangible public policy results.

GEOG. RESTRICTIONS: United States.

FINANCIAL DATA:

Total net assets of $94,751,000 as of December 31, 2013.

Amount of support per award: $25,000 to $75,000.

Total amount of support: Approximately $2,500,000 annually.

Matching fund requirements: Fund will match employee contributions.

REPRESENTATIVE AWARDS:

Citizen Participation and Government Accountability: $50,000 to the William J. Brennan Jr. Center for Justice, Inc., New York, NY, to support the Center's work to restore voting rights to citizens with criminal convictions; Economic Justice for Women: $50,000 to the National Partnership for Women & Families, Washington, DC, to support the Partnership's state and local paid sick days campaigns; Environment: $50,000 to CommunityWise Bellingham, Bellingham, WA, to support work on anti-coal issues; Institutional Responsiveness: $55,000 to MAPLight.org, Berkeley, CA, to continue publishing data on the connections between political contributions and votes.

APPLICATION INFO:

Applications are submitted online.

Duration: Grants are normally given for no more than two years at a time and are normally not given for more than three or four consecutive years.

Deadline: Letters of inquiry are accepted throughout the year.

PUBLICATIONS:

Annual report.

TRUSTEES:

ADDRESS INQUIRIES TO:

Carolyn Caddle-Steele, Grants Manager
(See address above.)

ROCKWELL FUND, INC. [274]

770 South Post Oak Lane
Suite 525
Houston, TX 77056
(713) 629-9022
Fax: (713) 629-7702
E-mail: grantsinfo@rockfund.org
Web Site: www.rockfund.org

FOUNDED: 1931

AREAS OF INTEREST:

Education, health, housing and workforce development.

NAME(S) OF PROGRAMS:

- **Operating Funds**
- **Program/Project Support**

TYPE:

Challenge/matching grants; Development grants; General operating grants; Matching gifts; Project/program grants; Seed money grants; Technical assistance. Capacity building grants.

YEAR PROGRAM STARTED: 1949

PURPOSE:

To improve the quality of life in the greater Houston area; to pursue change through cooperative philanthropy.

LEGAL BASIS:

Nonprofit organization.

ELIGIBILITY:

Eligible organizations must have IRS 501(c)(3) not-for-profit status. A church or political subdivision that is not required to obtain a Section 501(c)(3) designation in order to be a permitted donee of a private foundation is also eligible. Grants are not made to individuals. The Fund does not provide financial support to programs or organizations outside of its stated issue areas.

GEOG. RESTRICTIONS: Greater Houston, Texas area.

FINANCIAL DATA:

Amount of support per award: Varies.

Total amount of support: $3,175,080 in total grants in 2015.

APPLICATION INFO:

Applying organizations must have IRS Form 990 and Internal Revenue Code 501(c)(3) documentation. Consult the web site for application details. The Fund only accepts electronic submission of completed applications via e-mail. It does not accept applications sent via fax, mail or hand delivery.

Duration: One year. Renewable by reapplication.

Deadline: Varies.

IRS I.D.: 74-6040258

STAFF:
R. Terry Bell, President and Chief Executive Officer
Margaret E. McConn, C.P.A., Vice President, Chief Financial Officer and Chief Investment Officer
Don A. Titcombe, M.S.S.W., Program Officer
Judy A. Ahlgrim, Grants Administrator
G. Charmaine Glaze, MBA, Accountant

ADDRESS INQUIRIES TO:
Judy A. Ahlgrim, Grants Administrator
(See address above.)

ROLEX SA [275]

665 Fifth Avenue
New York, NY 10022-5385
(212) 758-7700
Fax: (212) 371-0371
Web Site: www.rolexawards.com

FOUNDED: 1976

AREAS OF INTEREST:
Science and medicine, technology, exploration, environment and cultural heritage.

NAME(S) OF PROGRAMS:
- **Rolex Awards for Enterprise Program**

TYPE:
Awards/prizes; Project/program grants; Seed money grants. Awards are given biennially.

YEAR PROGRAM STARTED: 1976

PURPOSE:
To encourage groundbreaking personal enterprise and initiative; to improve the quality of life and expand the knowledge of the world.

ELIGIBILITY:
Awards given for original and innovative projects in the areas of science and medicine, technology and innovation, exploration and discovery, the environment and cultural heritage. Given to an individual based on originality, feasibility and potential impact and exceptional spirit of enterprise.

FINANCIAL DATA:
Amount of support per award: Varies.

Total amount of support: Varies.

NO. MOST RECENT APPLICANTS: 1,500 to 2,500.

NO. AWARDS: 5.

APPLICATION INFO:
Complete application information is available on the web site.

Duration: One time per project.

Deadline: Varies.

PUBLICATIONS:
Applications; winners publication; journal.

ADDRESS INQUIRIES TO:
The Secretariat
P.O. Box 1311
1211 Geneva 26, Switzerland

S&P GLOBAL [276]

55 Water Street, 46th Floor
New York, NY 10041
(212) 438-1273
E-mail: louise.raymond@spglobal.com
Web Site: www.spglobal.com

AREAS OF INTEREST:
Corporate giving program: Financial essentials/economic empowerment, women entrepreneurs and STEM.

CONSULTING OR VOLUNTEER SERVICES:
Employee Volunteer Grant, Community Impact Month and Grants.

NAME(S) OF PROGRAMS:
- **Employee Giving Programs**

TYPE:
Matching gifts; Project/program grants. Employee Giving Programs including Matching Gift, Employee Volunteer Grants, Signature Volunteer Program (Community Impact Month), and Direct Grants that focus on women entrepreneurs and STEM.

PURPOSE:
To contribute to the vitality and well-being of the communities in which it is involved.

LEGAL BASIS:
Corporate giving program.

ELIGIBILITY:
Applicants must be organizations that qualify as public charities under the Internal Revenue Code 501(c)(3) or international equivalent. Preference given to areas containing an employee base.

FINANCIAL DATA:
Total amount of support: $3,700,000 for the year 2015.

APPLICATION INFO:
Contact the organization for guidelines.

Duration: One year unless multiyear pledge. Reapply each year.

PUBLICATIONS:
Corporate annual report and Corporate Responsibility report.

BOARD OF DIRECTORS:
Charles E. Haldeman, Jr., Chairman
Sir Winfried F.W. Bischoff
William D. Green
Rebecca Jacoby
Hilda Ochoa-Brillembourg
Douglas L. Peterson
Sir Michael Rake
Edward B. Rust, Jr.
Kurt L. Schmoke, Esq.
Richard E. Thornburgh

ADDRESS INQUIRIES TO:
Louise Raymond
Vice President, Corporate Responsibility
(See address above.)

ST. CROIX VALLEY FOUNDATION

516 Second Street, Suite 214
Hudson, WI 54016
(715) 386-9490
Fax: (715) 386-1250
E-mail: info@scvfoundation.org
Web Site: www.scvfoundation.org

TYPE:
Project/program grants; Scholarships. Environmental and humane grants.

See entry 1329 for full listing.

SALISBURY COMMUNITY FOUNDATION [277]

220 North Tryon
Charlotte, NC 28202
(704) 973-4559
Fax: (704) 973-4959
E-mail: cabinanti@fftc.org
Web Site: www.salisbury-cf.org

FOUNDED: 1944

AREAS OF INTEREST:
Arts and culture, public education K-12, higher education, environment and human services.

TYPE:
Project/program grants.

YEAR PROGRAM STARTED: 1944

PURPOSE:
To support charitable organizations in the Salisbury and Rowan County areas.

LEGAL BASIS:
Community foundation.

ELIGIBILITY:
Applicants must be 501(c)(3) organizations.

GEOG. RESTRICTIONS: Rowan County, North Carolina.

FINANCIAL DATA:
Amount of support per award: Varies.

APPLICATION INFO:
Application information is available on the web site.

Duration: One year.

Deadline: September 30, 2016.

PUBLICATIONS:
Annual report.

IRS I.D.: 56-0772117

BOARD OF TRUSTEES:
Edward P. Norvell, Chairperson
Kathleen S. Boyd, Vice Chairperson
Gwin C. Barr
Sarah Busby
Sara D. Cook
Diane L. Fisher
J. Steven Fisher
Dr. Michael M. Goodman
Shari M. Graham
Richard L. Huffman
William Pete Kennedy
Vergel L. Lattimore
Laura Lewis
Lynn P. Moody, Ed.D.
C. Cliff Ritchie
Charles D. Taylor, Jr.
Bill Wagoner
Leo Wallace, III

ADDRESS INQUIRIES TO:
Candice Abinanti, Board and Grant Specialist
(See address above.)

THE FAN FOX AND LESLIE R. SAMUELS FOUNDATION, INC. [278]

350 Fifth Avenue
Suite 4301
New York, NY 10118
(212) 239-3030
Fax: (212) 239-3039
E-mail: info@samuels.org
Web Site: www.samuels.org

FOUNDED: 1959

AREAS OF INTEREST:
Performing arts, health care, and quality of life for the elderly.

NAME(S) OF PROGRAMS:
- **Performing Arts**

TYPE:
Development grants; Project/program grants. General operating grants for performing artists only.

The majority of the Foundation's funding is for the performing arts. In the area of health care, the Foundation will consider funding direct health care and social service programs to improve quality of life for New York City elderly.

The Foundation realizes that it cannot support an organization indefinitely and expects the programs it funds to become self-supporting within a few years.

YEAR PROGRAM STARTED: 1959

PURPOSE:
To provide funding for the performing arts; to improve the health care and quality of life of the elderly in New York, NY.

LEGAL BASIS:
Private foundation.

ELIGIBILITY:
Grants are made to organizations that are tax-exempt under Section 501(c)(3) of the Internal Revenue Code. The Foundation does not give grants to individuals or for scholarships. General operating support is for performing arts only.

GEOG. RESTRICTIONS: New York City.

FINANCIAL DATA:
Amount of support per award: $2,000 to $300,000.

Total amount of support: Varies.

APPLICATION INFO:
A letter should briefly summarize the proposal and state the amount of the grant being requested. A copy of the organization's tax exemption letter issued by the IRS, most recent audited financial report, organization brochure (if available), Board of Directors list, project budget and current contributors list should be included.

Duration: Health Care: One to two years; Performing Arts: One year.

Deadline: December 1, March 1, June 1 and September 1.

IRS I.D.: 13-3124818

STAFF:
Alexandra Francis, Program Associate

OFFICERS AND DIRECTORS:
Robert Marx, President
Julio Urbina, Vice President
Joseph Mitchell, Managing Director

ADDRESS INQUIRIES TO:
Alexandra Francis, Program Associate
(See address above.)

THE SAN FRANCISCO FOUNDATION [279]

One Embarcadero Center
Suite 1400
San Francisco, CA 94111
(415) 733-8500
Fax: (415) 477-2783
E-mail: info@sff.org
Web Site: www.sff.org

FOUNDED: 1948

AREAS OF INTEREST:
Community health, education, arts and culture, community development, and the environment.

NAME(S) OF PROGRAMS:
- **Koshland Young Leader Awards**

TYPE:
Scholarships. The Koshland Young Leader Awards recognize the next generation of leadership in the local community. This scholarship program provides financial assistance to college-bound San Francisco public high school students from economically disadvantaged backgrounds.

PURPOSE:
To promote change in the areas of community health, education, arts and culture, community development, and the environment.

LEGAL BASIS:
Community foundation.

ELIGIBILITY:
Koshland Young Leaders are strongly motivated to achieve despite facing multiple challenges such as economic and family responsibilities.

GEOG. RESTRICTIONS: San Francisco, California.

FINANCIAL DATA:
Award to be used for education-related expenses such as academic test fees, computers, books and supplies for classes.

Amount of support per award: Two-year award of $7,000.

NO. AWARDS: Up to 10 each year.

APPLICATION INFO:
Contact the Foundation.

Duration: Two years.

SARKEYS FOUNDATION [280]

530 East Main Street
Norman, OK 73071
(405) 364-3703
Fax: (405) 364-8191
E-mail: sarkeys@sarkeys.org
Web Site: www.sarkeys.org

FOUNDED: 1962

AREAS OF INTEREST:
Education, health care and medical research, cultural and humanitarian programs of regional interest.

TYPE:
Capital grants; Challenge/matching grants; Development grants; Endowments; Matching gifts; Professorships; Project/program grants; Research grants; Technical assistance; Training grants.

YEAR PROGRAM STARTED: 1962

PURPOSE:
To improve the quality of life in Oklahoma.

LEGAL BASIS:
Private charitable foundation.

ELIGIBILITY:
Applicants must be 501(c)(3) organizations which are not private foundations under 509(a) of the Internal Revenue Code. Organization must be headquartered and operating within the state of Oklahoma.

GEOG. RESTRICTIONS: Oklahoma.

FINANCIAL DATA:
Amount of support per award: Varies.

Total amount of support: $3,460,547 in grants for fiscal year 2014-15.

NO. MOST RECENT APPLICANTS: 92.

NO. AWARDS: 55.

APPLICATION INFO:
The application form should be typed and all space limitations observed. The attachments should also be typed, unbound and printed on one side only. The Foundation does not accept faxed or e-mailed proposals. A new application form should be requested each year.

Duration: Varies.

Deadline: Letters of inquiry: December 1 and June 1.

PUBLICATIONS:
Application guidelines; annual report.

BOARD MEMBERS:
Teresa B. Adwan
Elizabeth Base
Dr. John Bell
Clay Christensen
Dan Little
Jim Loftis
Joseph W. Morris
Terry W. West

ADDRESS INQUIRIES TO:
Kim Henry, Executive Director
Susan Frantz, Senior Program Officer
Linda English Weeks, Senior Program Officer
or
Natalie Carns, Program Officer
(See address above.)

*SPECIAL STIPULATIONS:
The recipient must sign an agreement outlining the terms of the award and provide reports as requested. Outside independent audit required for organizations whose operating budget exceeds $500,000 per year.

DR. SCHOLL FOUNDATION [281]

1033 Skokie Boulevard
Suite 230
Northbrook, IL 60062-4109
(847) 559-7430
Web Site: www.drschollfoundation.com

FOUNDED: 1947

AREAS OF INTEREST:
Private education at all levels, including elementary and secondary schools, colleges and universities, and medical and nursing institutions; general charitable programs, including grants to hospitals and programs for children, developmentally disabled and senior citizens, civic, cultural, social services, health care, economic and religious activities.

TYPE:
Project/program grants.

YEAR PROGRAM STARTED: 1947

PURPOSE:
To help support worthwhile projects and activities.

LEGAL BASIS:
Private foundation.

ELIGIBILITY:
Organization must submit copy of tax-exemption letter from the IRS identifying that the applicant is a tax-exempt organization under Internal Revenue Code 501(c)(3), but is not a private foundation under 509(a) of the Internal Revenue Code. All grant requests should be in the form of a special project or program.

GEOG. RESTRICTIONS: United States.

FINANCIAL DATA:
Amount of support per award: Average $1,000 to $25,000.

Total amount of support: Varies.

NO. MOST RECENT APPLICANTS: 1,100.

NO. AWARDS: 330.

APPLICATION INFO:
A formal application form is required together with the tax-exemption letter, budget, financial statements and details about the organization, its officers, directors and specialized personnel.

Duration: Usually one year.

Deadline: March 1. Notification in November and distribution in December.

OFFICER:
Pamela Scholl, President

ADDRESS INQUIRIES TO:
Pamela Scholl, President
(See address above.)

CHARLES AND HELEN SCHWAB FOUNDATION [282]

201 Mission Street, Suite 1950
San Francisco, CA 94105
(415) 795-4920
Fax: (415) 795-4921
E-mail: info@schwabfoundation.org
Web Site: www.schwabfoundation.org
www.chsf.org

FOUNDED: 1987

AREAS OF INTEREST:
K-12 education reform, community needs, human services and health, and trustee grants.

NAME(S) OF PROGRAMS:
- **Foundation Initiative Grants**

TYPE:
General operating grants; Project/program grants; Technical assistance. Capacity building and human services programs.

YEAR PROGRAM STARTED: 2001

PURPOSE:
To improve education and student learning for children in the San Francisco Bay area, the state of California, and the nation more broadly.

LEGAL BASIS:
Private foundation.

ELIGIBILITY:
The Foundation supports organizations characterized by strong leadership, a compelling track record and future potential.

GEOG. RESTRICTIONS: San Francisco Bay area, California; national.

FINANCIAL DATA:
Amount of support per award: Varies.

Total amount of support: $19,918,712 in total grants for the year ended December 31, 2014.

APPLICATION INFO:
The Foundation does not accept unsolicited grant applications, grant proposals or letters of inquiry.

Duration: Varies.

PUBLICATIONS:
Foundation brochure; program reports.

IRS I.D.: 94-3188972

STAFF:
Kristi Kimball, Executive Director
Erin Gilbert, Program Officer and Administrative Director

BOARD OF DIRECTORS AND OFFICERS:
Helen O. Schwab, President
Charles R. Schwab, Chairman
Nancy Bechtle, Director
Katie Schwab Paige, Director
Matt Wilsey, Director

ADDRESS INQUIRIES TO:
Human Services Program
(See address above.)

THE ELLEN BROWNING SCRIPPS FOUNDATION [283]

6121 Terryhill Drive
La Jolla, CA 92037
(858) 212-3311
Fax: (858) 459-4809
E-mail: dougdawson46@yahoo.com

FOUNDED: 1935

AREAS OF INTEREST:
Health care, medical research, education, conservation, recreation, family, youth and child welfare agencies, wildlife and animals, libraries and literacy.

TYPE:
Project/program grants; Research grants; Scholarships; Technical assistance.

YEAR PROGRAM STARTED: 1935

PURPOSE:
To provide funding for a number of social causes including medical research, health care, the arts, conservation and programs to help children.

LEGAL BASIS:
Private foundation.

ELIGIBILITY:
Applicant must be a tax-exempt, 501(c)(3) organization within San Diego County, CA.

GEOG. RESTRICTIONS: San Diego County, California.

FINANCIAL DATA:
Amount of support per award: $5,000 to $125,000.

Total amount of support: $1,125,000.

NO. AWARDS: 54.

APPLICATION INFO:
Information is available from the Foundation.

Deadline: May 1.

ADDRESS INQUIRIES TO:
E. Douglas Dawson, Executive Director
(See address above.)

THE SEATTLE FOUNDATION [284]

1200 Fifth Avenue, Suite 1300
Seattle, WA 98101-3151
(206) 515-2131
Fax: (206) 622-7673
E-mail: c.erickson@seattlefoundation.org
Web Site: www.seattlefoundation.org

FOUNDED: 1946

AREAS OF INTEREST:
Arts and culture, education, basic needs, environment, economy, health and wellness, neighborhoods and communities.

NAME(S) OF PROGRAMS:
- **Community Grantmaking Program**

TYPE:
Capital grants; Development grants; General operating grants; Technical assistance. Equipment purchases; Facility renovation grants.

YEAR PROGRAM STARTED: 1946

PURPOSE:
To improve the quality of life in the Puget Sound area.

LEGAL BASIS:
Community foundation.

ELIGIBILITY:
Organizations must be IRS 501(c)(3) tax-exempt. No grants to individuals.

GEOG. RESTRICTIONS: King County, Washington.

FINANCIAL DATA:
Amount of support per award: Average $25,000.

APPLICATION INFO:
Application form and guidelines are available on the web site.

Duration: One-time grants.

PUBLICATIONS:
Annual report; *Healthy Communities Report.*

STAFF:
Ceil Erickson, Director, Community Programs

ADDRESS INQUIRIES TO:
Ceil Erickson
Director, Community Programs
(See address above.)

THE SEAVER INSTITUTE [285]

12400 Wilshire Boulevard
Suite 1240
Los Angeles, CA 90025
(310) 979-0298
Fax: (310) 979-0297
E-mail: vsd@theseaverinstitute.org

FOUNDED: 1955

AREAS OF INTEREST:
Arts and the sciences.

TYPE:
Project/program grants; Research grants; Seed money grants.

YEAR PROGRAM STARTED: 1955

PURPOSE:
To provide seed money to highly regarded organizations for particular projects which offer the potential for significant advancement in their fields.

LEGAL BASIS:
Tax-exempt private foundation.

ELIGIBILITY:
Applicant must be a legally tax-exempt organization. The Institute does not support endowments, scholarships, construction, ongoing projects or deficit grants.

GEOG. RESTRICTIONS: United States.

FINANCIAL DATA:
Amount of support per award: $75,000 to $400,000.

NO. MOST RECENT APPLICANTS: 30.

NO. AWARDS: 20.

REPRESENTATIVE AWARDS:
University of Hawaii for foundation reefs; National Geographic for Timur's Garrison at Lake Issyk Kul; Massachusetts Institute of Technology for music21: a toolkit for computer-aided musicology; Sustainable Conservation for ecosystem services.

APPLICATION INFO:
A written request is required. No formal guidelines.

Duration: One year. Renewal is possible.

Deadline: Early April and early October.

PUBLICATIONS:
Official guidelines letter; annual report.

BOARD OF TRUSTEES:

ADDRESS INQUIRIES TO:
Victoria Seaver Dean, President
(See address above.)

SIMMONS FAMILY FOUNDATION [286]

722 West Shepard Lane
Suite 103
Farmington, UT 84025
(801) 550-5026
Fax: (801) 323-9314
E-mail: elizabeth@simmonsfoundation.org
Web Site: www.simmonsfoundation.org

FOUNDED: 1986

AREAS OF INTEREST:
Religion, community enhancement, education, art and medicine.

TYPE:
Challenge/matching grants; Development grants; General operating grants; Matching gifts; Project/program grants; Research grants; Scholarships; Seed money grants.

PURPOSE:
To foster virtues of good citizenship through religious, medical, community, art and educational purposes.

LEGAL BASIS:
Private family foundation.

ELIGIBILITY:
Grants to nonprofit organizations that are tax-exempt under Section 501(c)(3) or Section 170(c) of the Internal Revenue Code. No grants to individuals.

GEOG. RESTRICTIONS: Utah.

FINANCIAL DATA:
Amount of support per award: Varies.

APPLICATION INFO:
E-mail a one-page letter of intent summarizing the organization and project to the address posted. Organizations will then be invited to submit a formal application. Additional information is available on the Foundation web site.

Deadline: August 15.

PUBLICATIONS:
Application guidelines.

IRS I.D.: 13-3420599

ADDRESS INQUIRIES TO:
Elizabeth W. Gerner
Executive Director
(See address above.)

J. MARION SIMS FOUNDATION, INC. [287]

800 North White Street
Lancaster, SC 29720
(803) 286-8772
Fax: (803) 286-8774
E-mail: sdevenny@jmsims.org
Web Site: www.jmsims.org

FOUNDED: 1995

AREAS OF INTEREST:
Education, community health and wellness, and adult literacy.

NAME(S) OF PROGRAMS:
- **Adult Literacy Partnership Grants**
- **Responsive Grants**
- **Teachers' Pet Grants**

TYPE:
Challenge/matching grants; General operating grants; Project/program grants; Seed money grants; Technical assistance.

YEAR PROGRAM STARTED: 1995

PURPOSE:
To provide community support.

LEGAL BASIS:
Private foundation.

ELIGIBILITY:
Organizations and agencies classified as 501(c)(3) by the IRS can apply. Individuals are ineligible.

GEOG. RESTRICTIONS: Fort Lawn, Great Falls and Lancaster County, South Carolina.

FINANCIAL DATA:
Amount of support per award: $67,686.

Total amount of support: $1,895,203 for fiscal year ended December 31, 2015.

NO. MOST RECENT APPLICANTS: 39 for fiscal year ended December 31, 2015.

NO. AWARDS: 28 for fiscal year ended December 31, 2015.

APPLICATION INFO:
Contact the Foundation for application guidelines.

Duration: Typically one year. Grants are renewable.

Deadline: April 15 and October 15. Preapplication meeting with program officer no less than 30 days prior to deadlines required.

PUBLICATIONS:
Annual report.

IRS I.D.: 57-0355295

STAFF:
Susan W. DeVenny, President
Holly C. Furr, Program Officer
Mary D. Henderson, Program Officer

ADDRESS INQUIRIES TO:
Susan W. DeVenny, President
(See address above.)

THE SIRAGUSA FOUNDATION [288]

One East Wacker Drive
Suite 2910
Chicago, IL 60601-1474
(312) 755-0064
Fax: (312) 755-0069
E-mail: info@siragusa.org
Web Site: www.siragusa.org

FOUNDED: 1950

AREAS OF INTEREST:
Arts learning, education and social services.

TYPE:
General operating grants; Project/program grants; Scholarships; Technical assistance. Project grants or unrestricted support.

YEAR PROGRAM STARTED: 1950

PURPOSE:
To help people help themselves with the ultimate goal of improving their quality of life.

LEGAL BASIS:
Tax-exempt private foundation, incorporated in Illinois.

ELIGIBILITY:
Tax-exempt organizations are eligible. No grants are made to individuals.

GEOG. RESTRICTIONS: Greater Chicago, Illinois area.

FINANCIAL DATA:
Amount of support per award: $5,000 to $20,000.

NO. AWARDS: 143 grants for the year 2016.

APPLICATION INFO:
Unsolicited letters of inquiry and proposals are not currently accepted.

Duration: Varies.

PUBLICATIONS:
Annual report; guidelines.

STAFF:
Irene S. Phelps, President and Chief Executive Officer

BOARD OF DIRECTORS:

ADDRESS INQUIRIES TO:
Sharmila Rao Thakkar
Executive Director
(See address above.)

THE SKILLMAN FOUNDATION [289]

100 Talon Centre Drive
Suite 100
Detroit, MI 48207
(313) 393-1185
Fax: (313) 393-1187
E-mail: grants@skillman.org
Web Site: www.skillman.org

FOUNDED: 1960

AREAS OF INTEREST:
Education, neighborhoods, community leadership, safety, social innovation and youth development.

NAME(S) OF PROGRAMS:
- **Good Neighborhood**
- **Good Opportunities**
- **Good Schools**

TYPE:
Matching gifts; Project/program grants. Good Neighborhood Program strives to guide young people to be safe, healthy, well-educated and prepared for adulthood when they are embedded in a strong system of supports and opportunities, when they

attend high-quality schools, when their neighborhoods have the capacities and resources to support youth and families, and when broader systems and policies create conditions under which youth can thrive. The program is targeted in six Detroit neighborhoods - Brightmoor, Chadsey Condon, Cody Rouge, Northend Central Woodward, Osborn, Southwest Detroit.

Good Opportunities Program is designed to support the Foundation's primary work and to invest in special opportunities that can accomplish significant results for children.

Good Schools Program aims to have children attend high-quality schools, to graduate from high school and to attend college so they can lead self-sufficient and prosperous lives. To accomplish this goal the Foundation focuses on four areas: creating a citywide schools infrastructure, ensuring high-quality early care and education opportunities, improving schools in target neighborhoods, and generating parent and public will for high-quality education.

YEAR PROGRAM STARTED: 1960

PURPOSE:
To improve the lives of children in metropolitan Detroit by improving their homes, schools and neighborhoods.

LEGAL BASIS:
Private foundation.

ELIGIBILITY:
Foundation grantseekers and grantees must:
(1) be a nonprofit 501(c)(3) tax-exempt organization and provide its tax identification (EIN) number or be a government or public agency (city, county, state, public school district);
(2) be a publicly supported charity as defined in Section 509(a) of the Internal Revenue Code;
(3) have total revenues of at least $100,000 for its preceding fiscal year and be able to provide a copy of a current financial audit conducted by an independent certified public accountant and;
(4) in policy and practice, offer opportunity and service to all, regardless of age, race, creed, gender, religion, disability, sexual orientation and ethnicity.

GEOG. RESTRICTIONS: Detroit, Michigan.

FINANCIAL DATA:
Amount of support per award: Generally $20,000 to $200,000.

Total amount of support: Annual grants budget of approximately $17,000,000.

REPRESENTATIVE AWARDS:
$85,000 to Arab Community Center for Economic and Social Services to support a project that mobilizes Arab-American and non-Arab organizers to engage residents and plan projects that create positive change in Chadsey Condon and Cody Rouge neighborhoods; $300,000 to Black Family Development, Inc., to support for community engagement in Osborn and Cody Rouge and to promote block club development and leadership training (the MAN Network collaboration will continue as a joint venture for community policing); $85,000 to Detroit Hispanic Development Corporation to support an afterschool program that promotes life skills and academic achievement through structured activities in the graphic arts for southwest Detroit youth, ages 11 to 18; $100,000 to First Children's Finance to continue the efforts to stabilize, improve and expand high-quality childcare businesses serving low- and moderate-income families in Detroit with a specific focus on the six Skillman neighborhoods; $90,000 to Michigan College Access Network to support the expansion of the National College Advising Corps in the Good Neighborhood Schools, a nationally recognized program that returns recent college graduates to their home communities as college advisors at neighborhood high schools.

APPLICATION INFO:
Consult the Foundation web site.

Duration: Generally one year.

Deadline: New grant inquiries should be submitted approximately two months in advance of Trustee meetings in March, June, September and December.

PUBLICATIONS:
Annual report; application guidelines.

IRS I.D.: 38-1675780

TRUSTEES:
Lizabeth Ardisana, Chairperson
Herman B. Gray, Vice Chairperson
Tonya Allen
Bill Emerson
Denise Ilitch
Mary L. Kramer
Amyre Makupson
Eddie R. Munson
Jerry Norcia
Mark Reuss

OFFICERS AND STAFF:
Tonya Allen, President and Chief Executive Officer
Maria Woodruff Jordan, Vice President, Operations and Chief Financial Officer
Kristen McDonald, Vice President, Program and Policy
Chris Uhl, Vice President, Social Innovation
William Hanson, Chief of Staff
Sarah Mather, Controller
Marie Colombo, Director of Evaluation and Learning
Danielle McLaughlin, Grants Manager
Robert Thornton, Senior Program Officer
Punita Dani Thurman, Senior Program Officer

ADDRESS INQUIRIES TO:
Danielle McLaughlin, Grants Manager
(See address above.)

ALFRED P. SLOAN FOUNDATION [290]

630 Fifth Avenue
Suite 2200
New York, NY 10111
(212) 649-1649
Fax: (212) 757-5117
E-mail: lin@sloan.org
Web Site: www.sloan.org

FOUNDED: 1934

AREAS OF INTEREST:
Research and related programs in science and technology, education in science, technology, management, economic growth, industrial competitiveness and selected national issues.

TYPE:
Fellowships; Project/program grants; Research grants. Grants for imaginative and constructive projects in the Foundation's areas of interest.

YEAR PROGRAM STARTED: 1934

PURPOSE:
To support imaginative and constructive approaches to problems of domestic needs and uses.

LEGAL BASIS:
Private foundation.

ELIGIBILITY:
Recognized tax-exempt educational and research institutions with appropriate interests are eligible to apply. The Foundation's activities do not extend to primary or secondary education, religion, the creative or performing arts, medical research, health care or to the humanities. Grants are not made for endowments, buildings or equipment and are very rarely made for general support or for activities outside the U.S.

GEOG. RESTRICTIONS: United States.

FINANCIAL DATA:
Amount of support per award: Varies.

Total amount of support: $78,000,000 in grants annually.

APPLICATION INFO:
A brief letter of inquiry, rather than a fully developed proposal, is an advisable first step for an applicant, conserving his or her time and allowing the Foundation to make a preliminary response as to the possibility of support.

Duration: One to three years. Extensions or renewals are possible.

PUBLICATIONS:
Annual report.

BOARD OF TRUSTEES:
Sandra O. Moose, Chairperson
Cynthia Barnhart
Bonnie Bassler
Francine Berman
Richard Bernstein
Kevin Burke
Mary Schmidt Campbell
Frederick Henderson
Freeman A. Hrabowski, III
Paul L. Joskow
Robert Litterman
James Poterba
Michael Purugganan
Marta Tienda

ADMINISTRATIVE OFFICERS AND STAFF:
Paul L. Joskow, President
Leisle Lin, Senior Vice President, Finance and Operations
Christopher T. Sia, Treasurer and Chief Technology Officer
Gayle Myerson, Fellowship Coordinator

A.O. SMITH FOUNDATION [291]

11270 West Park Place
Milwaukee, WI 53224-3690
(414) 359-4107
Fax: (414) 359-4180
Web Site: www.aosmith.com

FOUNDED: 1955

AREAS OF INTEREST:
Education, civic and cultural affairs, human services, health and hospital, and United Way.

TYPE:
Project/program grants. Employee Education Matching Gift to secondary, four-year colleges and universities, junior colleges, community colleges, graduate and professional schools, technical and specialized schools.

YEAR PROGRAM STARTED: 1955

PURPOSE:
To strengthen higher education throughout the country; to promote the civic, cultural and social welfare of communities; to advance medical research and improve local health services where A.O. Smith plants are located.

LEGAL BASIS:
Corporate foundation.

ELIGIBILITY:
Organization must be located where A.O. Smith has operating facilities. The Foundation does not make contributions to politically active organizations or any other organization whose chief purpose is to influence legislation.

FINANCIAL DATA:
Amount of support per award: $500 minimum.

Total amount of support: $1,800,000.

NO. AWARDS: Over 200 annually.

APPLICATION INFO:
No specific application form is required. Inquiries should be made on organization's letterhead and include the following information:
(1) the exact name and location of the organization;
(2) a description of the organization, including its objectives and purpose;
(3) verification of IRS 501(c)(3) tax-exempt status;
(4) the geographic area served by the organization;
(5) an explanation of the activity for which support is being requested;
(6) the amount of support being requested;
(7) a description of the benefits to be achieved and who will receive them;
(8) budget information about the organization, including other sources of income and;
(9) plans for reporting results.

Duration: Varies.

Deadline: October 31.

PUBLICATIONS:
Annual report.

ADDRESS INQUIRIES TO:
Roger S. Smith
Director of Community Affairs
(See address above.)

THE ETHEL SERGEANT CLARK SMITH MEMORIAL FUND [292]

Wells Fargo Bank, N.A.
123 South Broad Street
Philadelphia, PA 19109
(215) 670-4225
Fax: (215) 670-4190
E-mail: paralee.knight@wellsfargo.com
Web Site: www.wellsfargo.com/privatefoundationgrants/smith

FOUNDED: 1977

AREAS OF INTEREST:
Arts and culture, hospitals, education, libraries, social services, women's programs and people with disabilities in Delaware County, PA.

TYPE:
Capital grants; Challenge/matching grants; Development grants; Project/program grants. Grants and challenge grants to community interest organizations in southeastern Pennsylvania. Grants to hospitals, colleges and schools for program and capital projects. Grants for social services, arts/cultural events and centers.

YEAR PROGRAM STARTED: 1977

PURPOSE:
To promote the public welfare in Delaware County, PA.

LEGAL BASIS:
Private foundation.

ELIGIBILITY:
Candidates must be tax-exempt organizations not classified as private foundations or private operating foundations within the terms of the Tax Reform Act of 1969. Primary emphasis is on those serving community needs in Delaware County, the former home of Ethel Sergeant Clark Smith. Grants will be made for capital projects, operating expenses and special programs that are meaningful to the success of the individual endeavors of the organizations. As a general rule, requests for funds on a long-term basis or for deficit financing will not be considered.

GEOG. RESTRICTIONS: Southeastern Pennsylvania.

FINANCIAL DATA:
Amount of support per award: $5,000 to $25,000.

Total amount of support: Approximately $540,000 annually.

Matching fund requirements: Varies.

NO. MOST RECENT APPLICANTS: Approximately 200.

NO. AWARDS: Approximately 60 annually.

APPLICATION INFO:
Application process is online only.

Duration: Three consecutive years maximum.

Deadline: March 1 and September 1.

PUBLICATIONS:
Biennial report.

IRS I.D.: 23-6648857

ADVISORY COMMITTEE:
Diane R. Bricker
Jack Holefelder
Dr. Joseph E. Pappano, Jr.
Sen. Dominic Pileggi
Alice Strine, Esq.

ADDRESS INQUIRIES TO:
Paralee Knight, Grant Administrator
(See address above.)

THE W.W. SMITH CHARITABLE TRUST [293]

200 Four Falls Corporate Center
Suite 300
West Conshohocken, PA 19428
(610) 397-1844
Fax: (610) 397-1680
E-mail: mmontgomery@wwsmithcharitabletrust.org
Web Site: www.wwsmithcharitabletrust.org

FOUNDED: 1976

AREAS OF INTEREST:
Basic medical research protocols dealing with cancer, AIDS and heart disease, financial aid programs for qualified needy undergraduate students at accredited four-year universities and colleges, and programs providing shelter, food and clothing for children and needy families with children and the elderly.

NAME(S) OF PROGRAMS:
- **College Scholarships**
- **Food, Clothing and Shelter**
- **Maritime Education**
- **Medical Research**

TYPE:
Project/program grants; Research grants; Scholarships. By invitation only, these grants are offered to provide financial aid programs for qualified needy undergraduate students at accredited four-year universities and colleges and also provide shelter, food and clothing for children and needy families with children and the elderly.

YEAR PROGRAM STARTED: 1978

PURPOSE:
To enhance medical excellence; to enable children, families and the elderly to improve their lives; to assure students of a college education.

LEGAL BASIS:
Private foundation.

ELIGIBILITY:
Grants are limited to nonprofit organizations within the Delaware Valley area: Bucks, Chester, Delaware, Montgomery and Philadelphia (PA), as well as the city of Camden (NJ). Grants are made only to tax-exempt, 501(c)(3) organizations, not classified as private foundations or private operating foundations within the terms of the Tax Reform Act of 1969.

Grants will be made for programs or organizations with proven or prudently predictable records of performance; never directly to individuals. Renovation projects, special programs that deal with food, clothing and shelter for children and the elderly may be funded, but requests for general operating expenses, deficit financing and capital campaigns are not considered.

As a rule, under the Basic Needs Grants, the further away any request is from direct provision of literal food, clothing or shelter, the less likely funding may be granted.

The Trust budgets no funds to purchase charity tables, program advertisements, golf tournament sponsorships, organizational memberships or analogous fund-raising events.

GEOG. RESTRICTIONS: Bucks, Chester, Delaware, Montgomery and Philadelphia counties, Pennsylvania and Camden, New Jersey.

FINANCIAL DATA:
Amount of support per award: $6,000 to $300,000 for fiscal year 2013-14.

Total amount of support: $6,582,954 for fiscal year 2013-14.

NO. MOST RECENT APPLICANTS: 173 for fiscal year 2013-14.

NO. AWARDS: 124 for fiscal year 2013-14.

APPLICATION INFO:
Complete application information is available online. Proposals will be considered only for the following purposes:
(1) specific, basic medical research projects dealing with cancer, heart disease or AIDS;
(2) by invitation of the Trust only, accredited, four-year university and college financial aid programs for needy, worthy, full-time undergraduate students (no requests ever accepted directly from individual students) and;
(3) providing shelter, food or clothing for

children age 18 or under (including needy families with dependent children) or the elderly age 60 and above.

The trustees endeavor to keep abreast of the needs and conditions in the area served by the Trust and variations from these policies may be made at their discretion.

Duration: Scholarship and Food, Clothing and Shelter grants: One year; Medical Research grant: Typically one year.

Deadline: Cancer and AIDS Research: June 15; Food, Clothing, and Shelter: December 15 and June 15; Heart Research: September 15; Scholarships: May 1.

PUBLICATIONS:
Biennial report (includes application guidelines).

IRS I.D.: 23-6648841

TRUSTEES:
Mary L. Smith

ADMINISTRATORS:
Michelle Montgomery, Grant Administrator, Food, Clothing and Shelter/Scholarships
Louise A. Havens, Grant Administrator, Medical Research
Deborah J. McKenna, Advisor

ADDRESS INQUIRIES TO:
Michelle Montgomery, Grant Administrator
(See address above.)

*SPECIAL STIPULATIONS:
Grants only in the Philadelphia, PA area and surrounding five counties, plus the city of Camden, NJ.

THE JOHN BEN SNOW FOUNDATION, INC. [294]

50 Presidential Plaza
Suite 106
Syracuse, NY 13202
(315) 471-5256
Fax: (315) 471-5256
E-mail: johnbensnow@verizon.net
Web Site: www.johnbensnow.com

FOUNDED: 1948

AREAS OF INTEREST:
Arts and culture, community initiatives, education, environment, journalism, special grants, youth programs and historic preservation.

TYPE:
Capital grants; Challenge/matching grants; Development grants; Fellowships; Project/program grants; Scholarships; Seed money grants; Technical assistance.

YEAR PROGRAM STARTED: 1948

PURPOSE:
To grant funds for educational, cultural and humanitarian purposes.

LEGAL BASIS:
Corporation.

ELIGIBILITY:
Applicants must be IRS 501(c)(3) organizations primarily in central and northern New York state. Grants are made to qualified organizations for educational and humanitarian purposes.

The general policy of the Board of Directors gives preference to proposals seeking one-year funding of program-related grants, matching grants, startup grants and capital grants and to reject proposals from individuals, religious organizations, government agencies, or for endowments, contingency funding, or general operating support.

GEOG. RESTRICTIONS: Central and northern New York state.

FINANCIAL DATA:
Amount of support per award: Typically $5,000 to $15,000.

Total amount of support: $307,565 in total grants for the year ended December 31, 2011.

NO. MOST RECENT APPLICANTS: More than 60.

NO. AWARDS: 27.

REPRESENTATIVE AWARDS:
Arts and Culture: $2,500 to Syracuse Shakespeare Festival, Syracuse, NY, for Kids Doing Shakespeare Theatre Camp; Community Initiatives: $25,000 to Northern Oswego County Ambulance, Pulaski, NY, for facility expansion; Education: $20,000 to Clarkson University, Postdam, NY, for endowed scholarship fund; Historic Preservation: $5,000 to Half-Shire Historical Society, Richland, NY, for facility renovation; Literacy: $20,000 to ProLiteracy, Syracuse, NY, for LifeLinks on North Side.

APPLICATION INFO:
The Foundation is pro-active in seeking grant proposals from qualifying 501(c)(3) organizations. Additionally, the Foundation accepts unsolicited proposals from qualifying organizations.

Applicants should inquire about funding first. Foundation will then supply guidelines and a formal application to be filled out. The inquiry should include:
(1) the name and complete address of the organization;
(2) a brief summary of the project to be funded;
(3) the name and address of the person responsible for the use of funds and;
(4) a photocopy of the organization's IRS tax-exemption letter.

If the proposal meets the stated guidelines and priorities of the Foundation, a grant application will be forwarded. All grant applications must be submitted using the Foundation grant application form and must be received by April 1 of the year in which a grant is requested.

Duration: One year. Renewals depend on the project.

Deadline: Letter of inquiry: No later than January 1 of the year in which the grant is requested. Grant application: April 1. Final or progress report: March 1 of the year following grant.

PUBLICATIONS:
Guidelines; annual report.

STAFF:
Ann M. Scanlon, Program Officer

BOARD MEMBERS:
Jonathan L. Snow, President
David H. Snow, Vice President and Treasurer
Valerie A. MacFie, Secretary
Angus M. Burton
Marion Hancock Fish
Emelie M. Williams

ADDRESS INQUIRIES TO:
Jonathan L. Snow, President
(See address above.)

SOUTHWEST FLORIDA COMMUNITY FOUNDATION

8771 College Parkway
Building 2, Suite 201
Fort Myers, FL 33919
(239) 274-5900
Fax: (239) 274-5930
E-mail: info@floridacommunity.com
Web Site: www.floridacommunity.com

TYPE:
Capital grants; Challenge/matching grants; Demonstration grants; Project/program grants; Scholarships; Seed money grants; Technical assistance; Training grants.

See entry 1341 for full listing.

SOWERS CLUB OF NEBRASKA FOUNDATION [295]

1701 South 17th Street
Suite 1H
Lincoln, NE 68502
(402) 438-2244
Fax: (402) 438-2426
E-mail: sowersclub@windstream.net
Web Site: www.thesowersclub.com

FOUNDED: 1986

AREAS OF INTEREST:
Charity and education.

TYPE:
Project/program grants; Scholarships.

PURPOSE:
To offer assistance to organizations that serve and educate the community.

ELIGIBILITY:
Agency must have been in existence for a minimum of five years and must qualify as exempt under Section 501(c)(3) of the Internal Revenue Code. Grant requests will not be considered for individuals, promoting religious purposes or for political purposes.

GEOG. RESTRICTIONS: Lincoln, Nebraska and surrounding communities.

FINANCIAL DATA:
Total amount of support: $75,000 per year.

APPLICATION INFO:
Grant request must include eight copies of the following:
(1) Letter of Determination from the IRS regarding 501(c)(3) status and;
(2) annual report or current balance sheet outlining the organization's administrative costs. All information will be treated with strict confidentiality.

All blanks on the grant request form must be completed. Do not answer a question on the request form by reference to another question, document or party.

Deadline: February 15, June 15 and September 15.

BOARD OF DIRECTORS AND OFFICERS:
Stan Dinges, President
Michael Fiene, Vice President
Roger Zajicek, Treasurer
Dick Stephenson, Secretary
Ed Packard
Robby Robinson
John Trayer

ADDRESS INQUIRIES TO:
Dick Stephenson, Secretary
(See address above.)

SETH SPRAGUE EDUCATIONAL AND CHARITABLE FOUNDATION [296]

c/o US Trust
114 West 47th Street, 10th Floor
New York, NY 10036
(646) 855-1011
Fax: (646) 855-5463

AREAS OF INTEREST:
Hospitals, educational institutions and social agencies.

TYPE:
Project/program grants.

ELIGIBILITY:
The Foundation makes grants to hospitals, educational institutions, social agencies and other charitable organizations. No grants to individuals.

GEOG. RESTRICTIONS: San Diego, California; Maine; Boston area, Massachusetts; and New York City, New York.

FINANCIAL DATA:
Amount of support per award: $10,000 to $20,000.

Total amount of support: $1,000,000 for the year 2013.

NO. MOST RECENT APPLICANTS: 450.

NO. AWARDS: 100.

APPLICATION INFO:
Contact the Foundation for application information.

Duration: One year.

Deadline: April 1 and September 1. Award announcement in June and December.

ADDRESS INQUIRIES TO:
Christine O'Donnell, Senior Vice President
(See address above.)

THE STATE STREET FOUNDATION [297]

State Street Financial Center
One Lincoln Street
Boston, MA 02111-2900
(617) 664-8720
Fax: (617) 664-9577
E-mail: wyoung@statestreet.com
Web Site: www.statestreet.com

FOUNDED: 1804

AREAS OF INTEREST:
Providing economically disadvantaged citizens with the skills they need to be successful, with a focus on initiatives that seek to achieve systemic change and address core problems affecting local communities.

NAME(S) OF PROGRAMS:

- **Global Philanthropy Program**

TYPE:
Conferences/seminars; Development grants; General operating grants; Internships; Matching gifts; Project/program grants. Particular emphasis is on programs that help the disadvantaged in the Greater Boston inner-city neighborhoods and communities where State Street has a presence. The Foundation supports public/private partnerships that serve this need, build community capabilities and promote collaborations between community institutions to increase effectiveness.

YEAR PROGRAM STARTED: 1977

PURPOSE:
To channel funds back into the communities where State Street employees work and live.

LEGAL BASIS:
Corporate foundation.

ELIGIBILITY:
Grant applicants must be tax-exempt, 501(c)(3) organizations located in communities where State Street has a presence.

The Foundation does not make individual scholarship grants, nor does it fund research, having a preference for programs emphasizing direct delivery of services. It does not support organizations by purchasing advertisements, tables or tickets at dinners or other functions.

FINANCIAL DATA:
Amount of support per award: $20,000 to $50,000.

Total amount of support: Approximately $17,800,000.

APPLICATION INFO:
Grant Proposal Summary Form and instructions are available at the Foundation web site.

Duration: One year.

Deadline: April 1, August 1 and December 1. Notification of decision mid-July, mid-November and mid-March, respectively.

PUBLICATIONS:
Contributions guidelines.

ADDRESS INQUIRIES TO:
Wayne Young, Global Grants Manager
(See address above.)

JOHN STAUFFER CHARITABLE TRUST [298]

301 North Lake Avenue, Suite 1000
Pasadena, CA 91101-4108
(626) 793-9400
Fax: (626) 793-5900
E-mail: lsjaynes@lagerlof.com

FOUNDED: 1974

AREAS OF INTEREST:
Colleges, universities and hospitals within California.

TYPE:
Capital grants; Challenge/matching grants; Endowments; Fellowships; Matching gifts; Professorships; Project/program grants; Scholarships.

YEAR PROGRAM STARTED: 1974

PURPOSE:
To support universities and colleges located in the U.S. in acquiring land, erecting buildings and other facilities, obtaining equipment, instruments, books, furnishings, and providing scholarships, fellowships and professorships; to support hospitals located in the U.S. which are organized and operated for charitable purposes in acquiring land, erecting buildings and other facilities, and obtaining equipment, instruments and furnishings.

LEGAL BASIS:
Tax-exempt private foundation founded in 1974 as a Testamentary Trust under will of John Stauffer by Order of the Superior Court of the State of California in and for the County of Los Angeles.

ELIGIBILITY:
Each university, college or hospital that receives funds from the Trust must be, at the time of the receipt of the funds:
(1) an exempt organization under Section 501(c)(3) of the Internal Revenue Code;
(2) an organization described in Section 170(c) of the Internal Revenue Code (or the corresponding provisions of any subsequent federal tax law) and;
(3) an organization meeting the qualifications of Sections 13842 and 23701(d) of the Revenue and Taxation Code of the state of California (or the corresponding provisions of any subsequent California tax law).
The organization must not be a private foundation.

Because of the Trust's finite resources, its Trustees must focus their attention on a few fields of activity and on certain priorities. The Trustees will favor:
(1) projects or programs of private nonprofit universities, colleges and hospitals within southern California;
(2) grants for facilities, educational or medical equipment, scholarships, professorships and fellowships;
(3) projects and programs that link science and medicine in education, research and treatment;
(4) projects and programs that emphasize chemistry as an integral component of education or treatment;
(5) institutions and organizations that as a matter of policy and practice maintain balanced operating budgets and avoid deficit financing and;
(6) projects and programs supported by matching funds from other donors.

Contact the Trust for full details.

GEOG. RESTRICTIONS: California, with a focus on southern California.

FINANCIAL DATA:
Amount of support per award: $100,000 to $3,000,000.

Total amount of support: Varies.

NO. MOST RECENT APPLICANTS: Approximately 200.

REPRESENTATIVE AWARDS:
$3,000,000 to Huntington Hospital; $300,000 to Claremont McKenna College; $500,000 to Stanford University; $2,500,000 to California Institute of Technology.

APPLICATION INFO:
All applications must be presented to the Trustees in writing and in digital format, with proposals clear and concise. Each application should include:
(1) a brief summary that sets forth the exact amount requested, an explanation of the need for the subject of the grant, the objectives to be achieved and the manner in which John Stauffer's name will be memorialized;
(2) full financial information, including a detailed budget for the project to be assisted by the grant;
(3) a statement indicating whether a grant for the same or similar purpose is presently being sought from other foundations or other sources, and, if so, which ones;
(4) the application's being executed by an officer of the applicant institution;
(5) (preferably) accompanying letters of support from board members or authorities and/or organizations in the applicant's field and;
(6) where applicable, copies of the latest exemption determination letter from the IRS and the corresponding state tax authorities in the state in which the applicant is located; the IRS determination that the applicant is

not a private foundation; the latest audited balance sheet; and the latest audited statement of income and expenditures.

Duration: For large grants, up to two or more years.

PUBLICATIONS:
Application guidelines.

IRS I.D.: 23-7434707

ADDRESS INQUIRIES TO:
John Stauffer Charitable Trust
c/o Timothy J. Gosney, Esq.
(See address above.)

*SPECIAL STIPULATIONS:
Each grantee is required to make a report on the use of the funds granted by the Trustees, including a certification that the funds have been used for the purpose(s) for which the grant was made. In addition, grantees shall comply with all reporting requirements contained in conditions of the grant, which will be set forth in writing by the Trustees. The Trustees reserve the right to require a reasonable audit of the use of grant funds conducted by their representative at the Trust's expense.

STEELCASE FOUNDATION [299]

P.O. Box 1967 GH-4E
Grand Rapids, MI 49501-1967
(616) 246-4695
Fax: (616) 475-2200
E-mail: jridenou@steelcase.com
Web Site: www.steelcasefoundation.org

FOUNDED: 1951

AREAS OF INTEREST:
Human service, health, education, social welfare, the arts and culture, and the environment in the areas of Steelcase, Inc. manufacturing plants. Particular concern is given to people who are disadvantaged, disabled, and young or elderly in an attempt to improve the quality of their lives.

TYPE:
Capital grants; Challenge/matching grants; Demonstration grants; Development grants; General operating grants; Matching gifts; Project/program grants; Seed money grants. Special projects, startup, capital and capacity building.

The Steelcase Foundation believes quality, accessible public education is paramount to achieving its vision. The Foundation assists its philanthropic partners in generating education initiatives, in addition to work and cultural opportunities.

YEAR PROGRAM STARTED: 1951

PURPOSE:
To improve the quality of life in the communities where Steelcase employees live; to empower people to reach their full potential.

LEGAL BASIS:
Corporate foundation.

ELIGIBILITY:
The Foundation makes grants to IRS-certified nonprofit organizations in areas where Steelcase manufacturing plants are located.

GEOG. RESTRICTIONS: Athens, Alabama and primarily western Michigan.

FINANCIAL DATA:
Amount of support per award: $1,000 to $1,000,000.

Total amount of support: $5,340,000 for the year 2013.

NO. MOST RECENT APPLICANTS: 300.

NO. AWARDS: 60.

APPLICATION INFO:
To obtain a grant application, send a letter on organization's letterhead and signed by the Chief Executive Officer. Include the following items with the letter:
(1) description of organization or project;
(2) expected results of the project;
(3) amount of grant funds requested and;
(4) copy of IRS 501(c)(3) nonprofit certification.

If the proposal meets the Foundation criteria, a detailed application form will be sent to the organization.

Duration: Varies.

Deadline: Grant requests are reviewed quarterly.

PUBLICATIONS:
Annual report; application; guidelines.

IRS I.D.: 38-6050470

STAFF:
Phyllis A. Gebben, Coordinator of Donations

ADDRESS INQUIRIES TO:
Phyllis A. Gebben, Coordinator of Donations
(See address above.)

THE WILLIAM B. STOKELY, JR. FOUNDATION [300]

620 Campbell Station Road, Station West
Suite 27
Knoxville, TN 37934
(865) 966-4878
Fax: (865) 675-5095

FOUNDED: 1951

AREAS OF INTEREST:
College and university scholarship programs and cultural, educational, religious and health service organizations.

TYPE:
General operating grants; Matching gifts; Scholarships.

YEAR PROGRAM STARTED: 1951

PURPOSE:
To provide funds for colleges and universities for scholarships.

LEGAL BASIS:
Tax-exempt private foundation.

ELIGIBILITY:
The Foundation does not extend funds to individuals but rather to colleges and universities in the form of scholarships to disburse under the guidelines of their particular program. Also considered are the needs of cultural, educational, religious (Christian) and health service organizations in areas where the Stokely family has ties. Regional priority is given to the southeastern U.S. and eastern Tennessee.

Organizations requesting funds must be approved, listed nonprofit organizations with 501(c)(3) status. All proposals must be submitted in writing for review by the Board of Directors.

GEOG. RESTRICTIONS: Southeastern United States and Eastern Tennessee.

FINANCIAL DATA:
Amount of support per award: $25 to $100,000.

APPLICATION INFO:
All proposals must be submitted in writing for review by the Board of Directors.

Duration: Varies.

Deadline: Proposals are reviewed on an ongoing basis.

IRS I.D.: 35-6016402

ADDRESS INQUIRIES TO:
William B. Stokely, III, President
(See address above.)

ROY AND CHRISTINE STURGIS CHARITABLE AND EDUCATIONAL TRUST [301]

c/o Bank of America, N.A.
901 Main Street, 19th Floor
Dallas, TX 75202-3714
E-mail: tx.philanthropic@ustrust.com
Web Site: www.bankofamerica.com/philanthropic/foundation

FOUNDED: 1981

AREAS OF INTEREST:
Education, arts and culture, youth and social services, science and health.

TYPE:
Capital grants; Challenge/matching grants; Matching gifts; Project/program grants.

LEGAL BASIS:
Private foundation (charitable trust).

ELIGIBILITY:
Applicants must have a 501(c)(3) exempt status from federal income tax as determined by the IRS before applying for a grant.

Charitable organizations which receive a one-payment grant must skip a year before applying again. Charitable organizations which receive multiyear payments cannot apply again while receiving payments and must skip a year after the last payment is received.

Trustee will consider grant requests for supplements for capital improvements, special projects, medical research and equipment, grants to meet challenges, endowments, start-up funds (extraordinary review), limited general operating expenses and construction or renovation of facilities.

The Trustee may favorably consider proposals which are unique, necessary and of high priority for the charitable organizations and which do not duplicate other services which are available, proposals for which funding may not be readily available from

other sources and essential projects which are sufficiently described as worthwhile, important and of a substantive nature.

The Trustee will not consider providing support for political organizations, loans, scholarships for individuals, tuition for individuals or for seminars. No grants to individuals or for mass appeals for funding.

GEOG. RESTRICTIONS: Arkansas and Dallas area in Texas.

FINANCIAL DATA:
Amount of support per award: $5,000 to $200,000 for multiyear payments. Average: $23,500.

APPLICATION INFO:
Guidelines and application forms are available on the Trust web site.

Duration: One year; occasional multiyear.

Deadline: March 1. Notification on or before June 30.

PUBLICATIONS:
Guidelines.

IRS I.D.: 75-6331832

SUNTRUST FOUNDATION [302]

919 East Main Street
Richmond, VA 23219
(804) 782-7907
E-mail: jane.markins@suntrust.com

AREAS OF INTEREST:
Education, health and human services, culture and art, civic and community.

TYPE:
General operating grants; Matching gifts; Project/program grants. Employee matching gifts program is designed to encourage SunTrust employees to support educational institutions and cultural organizations.

PURPOSE:
To improve the quality of life in the communities in which SunTrust operates.

LEGAL BASIS:
Corporate giving program.

ELIGIBILITY:
Applicants must be 501(c)(3) organizations.

When considering a specific contribution request, the following are among the criteria that SunTrust applies:
(1) does the cause fall under one or more of the areas of interest of the Foundation?;
(2) does SunTrust have a business presence in the geographic area in which the contribution will have impact?;
(3) will the contribution support programs and activities for improvement of the quality of life in the community served? and;
(4) will the organization requesting financial support have good management and active involvement of community leaders?

No grants to individuals.

GEOG. RESTRICTIONS: Florida, Georgia, Maryland, North Carolina, South Carolina, Tennessee, Virginia and Washington, DC.

FINANCIAL DATA:
Amount of support per award: Varies.

Total amount of support: $12,000,000.

Matching fund requirements: SunTrust will match employee contributions to eligible educational institutions and arts/cultural enrichment programs.

APPLICATION INFO:
Well-organized, fully documented requests for aid will facilitate the review process. The proposal must be in writing with appropriate documentation. The documentation should include project and/or operating budgets and a full description of the area of need and the reasons for the request. The applicant should give special attention to the guidelines applied by the Foundation when considering a proposal.

Applications are reviewed and approved on a local basis.

Duration: Varies. Renewal possible.

Deadline: September 1 for the next year's budget.

PUBLICATIONS:
Guidelines.

ADDRESS INQUIRIES TO:
Regional Headquarters or
SunTrust Foundation
(See address above.)

SURDNA FOUNDATION INC. [303]

330 Madison Avenue, 30th Floor
New York, NY 10017-5001
(212) 557-0010 ext. 237
Fax: (212) 557-0003
E-mail: grants@surdna.org
Web Site: www.surdna.org

FOUNDED: 1917

AREAS OF INTEREST:
Sustainable environments, strong local economies, and thriving cultures.

NAME(S) OF PROGRAMS:
- **Strong Local Economy**
- **Sustainable Environments**
- **Thriving Cultures**

TYPE:
General operating grants; Project/program grants; Research grants; Technical assistance.

YEAR PROGRAM STARTED: 1917

PURPOSE:
To foster catalytic, entrepreneurial programs which offer viable solutions to difficult systemic problems.

ELIGIBILITY:
Grant applicants must be 501(c)(3) nonprofits located within the U.S.

No grants to individuals. No grants for capital support.

GEOG. RESTRICTIONS: United States.

FINANCIAL DATA:
Amount of support per award: Varies.

Total amount of support: Approximately $40,000,000 allocated for fiscal year 2015.

NO. MOST RECENT APPLICANTS: Approximately 1,300 per year.

NO. AWARDS: 253 for fiscal year 2014.

APPLICATION INFO:
Letters of Inquiry should be submitted on the Foundation web site. Application guidelines are available online.

Duration: One to three years. Grants are renewable.

Deadline: Letters of Inquiry are reviewed on a rolling basis.

PUBLICATIONS:
Annual report.

ADDRESS INQUIRIES TO:
See e-mail address above.

TAHOE TRUCKEE COMMUNITY FOUNDATION [304]

11071 Donner Pass Road
Truckee, CA 96161
(530) 587-1776 ext. 106
Fax: (530) 550-7985
E-mail: phyllis@ttcf.net
Web Site: www.ttcf.net

FOUNDED: 1998

AREAS OF INTEREST:
Education, environment, arts and culture, civic benefits, health, human services, youth development, recreation and animal welfare.

TYPE:
Block grants; Challenge/matching grants; Demonstration grants; General operating grants; Project/program grants; Scholarships. Capacity building.

YEAR PROGRAM STARTED: 1998

PURPOSE:
To enhance the quality of life in the Truckee Tahoe community.

ELIGIBILITY:
Grants are made to organizations that have tax-exempt status under Section 501(c)(3) of the Internal Revenue Code. No grants are made to individuals.

GEOG. RESTRICTIONS: Truckee and Tahoe region, California.

FINANCIAL DATA:
Amount of support per award: $5,000 to $10,000.

Total amount of support: $1,100,000 to $1,500,000.

NO. MOST RECENT APPLICANTS: 151.

NO. AWARDS: 42.

APPLICATION INFO:
Contact the Foundation for application procedures.

Duration: One year.

Deadline: Varies.

IRS I.D.: 68-0416404

ADMINISTRATIVE STAFF:
Phyllis McConn, Community Impact Officer

EXECUTIVE OFFICERS:
Stacy Caldwell, Chief Executive Officer

ADDRESS INQUIRIES TO:
Phyllis McConn, Community Impact Officer
(See address above.)

S. MARK TAPER FOUNDATION [305]

12011 San Vicente Boulevard, Suite 400
Los Angeles, CA 90049
(310) 476-5413
Fax: (310) 471-4993
E-mail: questions@smtfoundation.org
Web Site: www.smtfoundation.org

FOUNDED: 1989

AREAS OF INTEREST:
Including, but not limited to, environment, independent living for the disabled, children, hunger, AIDS, teenage pregnancy prevention, economic revitalization, the arts, public education and civic affairs.

TYPE:
Capital grants; Challenge/matching grants; Demonstration grants; Development grants; Endowments; General operating grants; Matching gifts; Project/program grants; Scholarships; Seed money grants; Technical assistance; Training grants. Specific project grants.

YEAR PROGRAM STARTED: 1989

PURPOSE:
To enhance the quality of people's lives.

LEGAL BASIS:
Independent foundation.

ELIGIBILITY:
No grants to individuals. Applicants must be certified tax-exempt under Section 501(c)(3) of the Internal Revenue Code.

Previously funded nonprofit organizations are not eligible for another grant until after three full cycles have elapsed following the grant cycle during which previous grant was made.

GEOG. RESTRICTIONS: Southern California, primarily Los Angeles County.

FINANCIAL DATA:
Amount of support per award: Small grants: up to $50,000; medium grants: $50,001 to $250,000; large grants: over $250,000.

Total amount of support: Varies.

NO. MOST RECENT APPLICANTS: 400.

NO. AWARDS: 80.

APPLICATION INFO:
Application form required. Make initial contact by way of Letter of Inquiry. Letter must include organization background information, purpose of project, amount requested and anticipated results. Documentation of 501(c)(3) status required. Letters of Inquiry submitted by e-mail or fax will not be accepted.

Duration: One year unless paid in installments.

Deadline: Letters of Inquiry are accepted December through February. Applications are mailed in April through June. Notification in September.

PUBLICATIONS:
Letter of Inquiry Guidelines.

OFFICERS:
Janice Taper Lazarof, President

ADDRESS INQUIRIES TO:
Adrienne Wittenberg, Grants Director
(See address above.)

JOHN TEMPLETON FOUNDATION [306]

300 Conshohocken State Road
Suite 500
West Conshohocken, PA 19428
(610) 941-2828
Fax: (610) 825-1730
Web Site: www.templeton.org

FOUNDED: 1987

AREAS OF INTEREST:
Higher education, science and religion, theology, medicine, philosophy, spirituality and health, character development and free enterprise education.

TYPE:
Awards/prizes; Challenge/matching grants; Project/program grants; Research grants. Awards are financial in nature.

PURPOSE:
To promote and support relationships and progress between science and religion.

LEGAL BASIS:
Private foundation.

ELIGIBILITY:
Organizations classified as 501(c)(3) by the IRS can apply.

FINANCIAL DATA:
Amount of support per award: Varies.

Total amount of support: Varies.

Matching fund requirements: Defined on an individual grant basis.

APPLICATION INFO:
Funding guidelines can be found at web site.

Duration: Varies.

PUBLICATIONS:
Brochures; newsletter; articles.

IRS I.D.: 62-1322826

TEXAS INSTRUMENTS FOUNDATION [307]

12500 TI Boulevard
Dallas, TX 75243
(972) 995-2011
Web Site: www.ti.com/giving

FOUNDED: 1964

AREAS OF INTEREST:
Education, arts and culture, and community investment.

TYPE:
Matching gifts; Project/program grants. Education grants.

YEAR PROGRAM STARTED: 1965

PURPOSE:
To better the communities in which Texas Instruments operates.

LEGAL BASIS:
Nonprofit foundation.

ELIGIBILITY:
Organization must be 501(c)(3) and tax-exempt. No grants to individuals, student scholarships, good will advertising or for contributions of Texas Instruments products.

GEOG. RESTRICTIONS: Texas.

FINANCIAL DATA:
Total amount of support: $11,600,000 for the year 2013.

Matching fund requirements: Up to $10,000 per person per category each year for education and arts and culture.

APPLICATION INFO:
All requests for funding should be submitted online.

Duration: Varies. Renewals possible.

PUBLICATIONS:
Guidelines.

IRS I.D.: 75-6038519

STAFF:
Andy Smith, Executive Director

TEXTRON CHARITABLE TRUST [308]

40 Westminster Street
Providence, RI 02903
(401) 421-2800
Fax: (401) 457-3598
Web Site: www.textron.com

FOUNDED: 1969

AREAS OF INTEREST:
Culture and the arts, education, job training, health care, minorities and women, United Way, environment/conservation and youth groups.

TYPE:
Project/program grants. Employee matching gift programs.

YEAR PROGRAM STARTED: 1969

PURPOSE:
To support organizations, institutions and programs that contribute significantly to the quality of life in the communities where Textron employees live and work.

LEGAL BASIS:
Corporate contributions program.

ELIGIBILITY:
Grants are made to nonprofit, tax-exempt organizations. The Trust cannot contribute to organizations which are not determined to be a tax-exempt public charity as defined by the Internal Revenue Code 501(c)(3), separate appeals for operating funds by local United Way agencies, however, capital fund campaigns approved by local United Ways can be considered for support, fund-raising appeals from, or matching program contributions to churches, seminaries or other directly related religious organizations, individuals, including political candidates, endowment funds, or requests that intend to reduce operating deficits.

GEOG. RESTRICTIONS: Rhode Island.

FINANCIAL DATA:
Amount of support per award: Employee Matching Gifts: $25 to $7,500 per employee annually.

Total amount of support: Varies.

NO. AWARDS: Varies.

APPLICATION INFO:
Applications will be accepted online only.

Duration: Generally one year. Multiyear commitments are kept to a minimum.

Deadline: March 1 and September 1.

PUBLICATIONS:
Policy statement; guidelines.

ADDRESS INQUIRIES TO:
Karen Warfield
Community Affairs Manager
(See address above.)

3M FOUNDATION, INC. [309]

Community Affairs
3M Center Building 225-01-S-23
St. Paul, MN 55144-1000
(651) 733-1721
(651) 733-0144
Fax: (651) 737-3061
E-mail: cfkleven@mmm.com
Web Site: www.3Mgives.com

FOUNDED: 1953

AREAS OF INTEREST:
Education, arts and culture, human services and environment.

TYPE:
Capital grants; General operating grants; Matching gifts; Product donations; Project/program grants. 3Mgives consists of gifts by the 3M Foundation, cash and product donations by 3M and employee/retiree volunteerism.

YEAR PROGRAM STARTED: 1953

PURPOSE:
To improve every life.

LEGAL BASIS:
Corporate contributions program.

ELIGIBILITY:
Grants are made in the program areas of interest to established, well-managed organizations which have an IRS 501(c)(3) nonprofit status, and which are located in and serving 3M communities. Essential qualities are programs with broad-based community support, a reputation for leadership and high-quality service delivery and measurable results.

The 3M Foundation will not fund organizations in non-3M communities, individuals, for-profit organizations, disease-related organizations, hospitals, (in general) individual K-12 schools, organizations with a limited constituency, such as religious, fraternal, social, veterans or military organizations, and scholarship funds or organizations.

Grants are not awarded for advocacy and lobbying efforts to influence legislation; conferences, seminars, workshops or publications of their proceedings; endowments; film/video production; fund-raising, testimonial, athletic and special events; purchase of equipment that has not been manufactured by 3M; and travel for individuals or groups.

3Mgives generally will not consider organizations or causes that do not impact 3M communities, lease, conferences, seminars, workshops, symposia, publication of proceedings and all aspects relating to conferences, fund-raising and testimonial events/dinners, grants to individual K-12 schools, including tickets, silent auctions, raffles, telethons, etc., not more than 10% of the organization's campaign goal or annual budget, whichever is smaller, programs or projects beyond three years.

FINANCIAL DATA:
Amount of support per award: Varies.

Total amount of support: $58,200,000 for the year 2013.

Matching fund requirements: Limited to 3M employees and retirees.

NO. MOST RECENT APPLICANTS: 10,000.

NO. AWARDS: Approximately 3,000.

APPLICATION INFO:
Applications are by invitation only.

Duration: Generally one year, and not more than three years.

Deadline: April and October.

PUBLICATIONS:
Annual report; contributions guidelines.

IRS I.D.: 41-6038262

BOARD:
I.F. Hardgrove, President
K.F. Price, Vice President
S.D. Krohn, Treasurer
C.F. Kleven, Secretary
D.M. Amsden, Assistant Secretary
I.K. Fong
J. Garcia Galiana
H.M. Gindre
A.M. Hanrahan
A.K. Khandpur
J.R. Lavers
R. Rao
J.B. Sweeney
I.G. Thulin
S.K. Tokach

JOHN H. AND H. NAOMI TOMFOHRDE FOUNDATION [310]

c/o Rackemann, Sawyer & Brewster
160 Federal Street, 15th Floor
Boston, MA 02110-1700
(617) 951-1108
Fax: (617) 542-7437
E-mail: smonahan@rackemann.com
Web Site: www.cybergrants.com/tomfohrde

FOUNDED: 1996

AREAS OF INTEREST:
Cultural, social and civic betterment, community health, higher education, scientific research within the New England area with a special focus on Greater Boston.

TYPE:
Capital grants; Conferences/seminars; Matching gifts; Product donations; Project/program grants; Seed money grants; Technical assistance. The Foundation's particular focus is on supporting the work of charitable institutions, organizations and agencies in the New England area and particularly in Greater Boston, which are dedicated to the cultural, social and civic betterment of the community and particularly which foster the advancement of higher education, the classic arts, scientific research in biomedicine and the improvement of community health.

PURPOSE:
To bring about the cultural, social and civic betterment of the community and particularly to foster the advancement of higher education, the classic arts, scientific research in biomedicine and the improvement of community health.

LEGAL BASIS:
Private, independent foundation.

ELIGIBILITY:
The Foundation supports nonprofit 501(c)(3) organizations only.

GEOG. RESTRICTIONS: New England, with a preference for Greater Boston.

FINANCIAL DATA:
Amount of support per award: $5,000 to $10,000.

Total amount of support: $190,750 for the year 2013.

Matching fund requirements: Determined on a case-by-case basis.

NO. MOST RECENT APPLICANTS: 100 for the year 2013.

NO. AWARDS: 24 for the year 2013.

REPRESENTATIVE AWARDS:
Boston Health Care for the Homeless; Boston History Center and Museum.

APPLICATION INFO:
Applicants are required to submit a Preliminary Application-Concept Cover Letter. Only applicants whose preliminary application has been approved will be invited to submit a full proposal.

Deadline: January, April and August for trustees meetings in February, June and October, respectively.

IRS I.D.: 04-3338742

TRUSTEES:
Albert M. Fortier, Jr., Esq.
William B. Tyler, Esq.

STAFF:
Susan T. Monahan, Grants Coordinator

ADDRESS INQUIRIES TO:
Susan T. Monahan, Grants Coordinator
(See e-mail address above.)

TOPFER FAMILY FOUNDATION [311]

3600 North Capital of Texas Highway
Building B, Suite 310
Austin, TX 78746
(512) 329-0009
(866) 897-0298
Fax: (512) 329-6462
E-mail: info@topferfoundation.org
Web Site: www.topferfoundation.org

FOUNDED: 2000

AREAS OF INTEREST:
Child abuse prevention and treatment, youth enrichment, job training and support services, children's health, and aging in place.

TYPE:
Capital grants; Challenge/matching grants.

PURPOSE:
To help people connect to the tools and resources needed to build self-sufficient and fulfilling lives; to address the needs of the communities in which the Topfer family resides.

ELIGIBILITY:
Organizations must be nonprofit, classified 501(c)(3). No grants to individuals.

GEOG. RESTRICTIONS: Greater Chicago, Illinois and greater Austin, Texas metropolitan areas. In Illinois, preference is given to Cook and DuPage counties.

FINANCIAL DATA:
Amount of support per award: $5,000 to $100,000.

Total amount of support: $2,800,000.

NO. MOST RECENT APPLICANTS: 150.

NO. AWARDS: 113.

APPLICATION INFO:
Application should be submitted online.

Duration: One year. Must reapply.

Deadline: Varies.

ADDRESS INQUIRIES TO:
Erica Gustafson, Program Officer
(See address above.)

*PLEASE NOTE:
Unsolicited requests are not accepted in the greater Chicago, IL area. Must be by invitation only.

TOTAL PETROCHEMICALS & REFINING USA FOUNDATION [312]

1201 Lousiana, Suite 1800
Houston, TX 77002
(713) 483-5000
Fax: (713) 483-5429
Web Site: www.totalpetrochemicalsrefiningusa.com
www.usa.total.com

FOUNDED: 1974

AREAS OF INTEREST:
Education.

TYPE:
Development grants; Matching gifts; Project/program grants.

LEGAL BASIS:
Corporate foundation.

ELIGIBILITY:
Grants are made to organizations which are tax-exempt under Section 501(c)(3) of the Internal Revenue Code. Grants may not be made to individuals nor are grants made to private foundations as defined in Section 509(a) of the Internal Revenue Code.

GEOG. RESTRICTIONS: Louisiana and Texas.

FINANCIAL DATA:
Amount of support per award: Varies.

Total amount of support: Varies.

Matching fund requirements: All gifts from Total Petrochemicals & Refining USA, Inc. full-time employees are matched to four-year educational institutions from which the donor received a degree. The minimum gift that will be matched is $25 and the maximum gift per person per calendar year is $5,000. The contribution must be a personal gift of the eligible donor and cannot include resources from other people or institutions.

NO. MOST RECENT APPLICANTS: Approximately 500.

NO. AWARDS: Varies.

APPLICATION INFO:
No form is prescribed for submitting grant applications; however, budgets and statements of financial condition will assist the Foundation in acting upon any request for funds. A categorized statement regarding the expected sources of funds, excluding individual contributors and specifically whether the organization is supported by the United Way, are also of interest. Prior to issuance of a grant, an organization will be requested to furnish documentation of its status under the Code and a statement regarding its present operation and sources of support.

Duration: Varies.

OFFICERS:
Philippe Doligez, Chief Executive Officer
Tricia Fuller, Secretary

ADDRESS INQUIRIES TO:
Tricia Fuller, Manager, Public Affairs
(See address above.)

THE HARRY A. AND MARGARET D. TOWSLEY FOUNDATION [313]

P.O. Box 349
Midland, MI 48640-0349
(989) 837-1100
Fax: (989) 837-3240
E-mail: chatland@towsleyfoundation.org

FOUNDED: 1959

AREAS OF INTEREST:
Education, cultural arts, health and community service.

TYPE:
Project/program grants.

YEAR PROGRAM STARTED: 1959

PURPOSE:
To assist religious, educational, charitable and scientific organizations with their programs; to prevent cruelty to children.

LEGAL BASIS:
Private foundation.

ELIGIBILITY:
The Foundation does not make direct grants to individuals, provide loan funds, fund travel or conferences, or make grants to students for scholarships, books or other media. Grants are not made to institutions which in policy or practice unfairly discriminate against age, race, color, creed or sex.

GEOG. RESTRICTIONS: Primarily Michigan.

FINANCIAL DATA:
Amount of support per award: $5,000 to $1,000,000.

Total amount of support: Varies.

APPLICATION INFO:
Organizations seeking aid should submit verification of tax-exempt and nonprofit status, amount of requested funds, explanation of need, and most recent financial statement along with operating budget and other funding sources.

Duration: Varies. Renewal possible.

PUBLICATIONS:
Brochure; annual report.

IRS I.D.: 38-6091798

OFFICERS:
Lynn T. White, President
Wendel Dunbar, Vice President
Judith D. Rumelhart, Vice President
Mary Ivers, Treasurer
Margaret E. Thompson, M.D., Secretary

TRUST FUNDS INCORPORATED [314]

1104 Corporate Way
Sacramento, CA 95831-3875
(916) 395-4472
Fax: (415) 434-2936

FOUNDED: 1934

AREAS OF INTEREST:
Elementary, secondary and graduate Catholic education, Catholic religious and social service organizations and programs, and religious arts.

TYPE:
General operating grants; Grants-in-aid.

YEAR PROGRAM STARTED: 1934

PURPOSE:
To support worthwhile projects and programs that share the interests of the Foundation.

LEGAL BASIS:
Private foundation.

ELIGIBILITY:
Grants are usually limited to the San Francisco Bay area. No grants to individuals. No grants for buildings or endowments, annual campaigns, or to organizations which draw substantial public support.

GEOG. RESTRICTIONS: San Francisco, California and surrounding area.

FINANCIAL DATA:
Amount of support per award: $1,000 to $15,000.

APPLICATION INFO:
Application forms provided for all grant proposals complying with guidelines. Write or call first.

PUBLICATIONS:
Applications and guidelines.

IRS I.D.: 94-6062952

DIRECTORS:
James T. Healy, President
Thomas F. Kubasak, Chief Financial Officer
John Strain, Secretary
Lisa Kelley, Director
Joan C. O'Rourke, Director

ADDRESS INQUIRIES TO:
James T. Healy, President
(See address above.)

TULL CHARITABLE FOUNDATION, INC. [315]

191 Peachtree Street, N.E.
Suite 3950
Atlanta, GA 30303
(404) 659-7079
Fax: (404) 659-1223
E-mail: carol@tullfoundation.org
Web Site: www.tullfoundation.org

FOUNDED: 1952

AREAS OF INTEREST:
Education, health and human services, youth development and the arts.

TYPE:
Capital grants.

YEAR PROGRAM STARTED: 1952

PURPOSE:
To respond to charitable and community needs in the Atlanta metropolitan area and in Georgia.

LEGAL BASIS:
Converted from Trust to Nonprofit Corporation of Georgia.

ELIGIBILITY:
Nonprofit 501(c)(3) organizations located within Georgia are eligible for support.

The Foundation does not make grants to individuals or churches and does not participate in the operation of a project other than that of providing start-up funds.

The Foundation's trustees prefer to make grants that will have a significant and lasting impact on an organization, as well as the community. Priority is given to grant requests that:
(1) are strategically important to an organization's growth and capacity;
(2) enable the organization to more effectively address important community needs and;
(3) are cost-effective.

Proposals that address education, health and human services, youth development, and the arts are given priority by Foundation trustees.

GEOG. RESTRICTIONS: Georgia.

FINANCIAL DATA:
Amount of support per award: Average $50,000.

Total amount of support: $2,100,000 for the year 2013.

APPLICATION INFO:
Prior to receiving a full proposal, the Foundation prefers a concise letter-of-intent providing a brief description of the applicant organization, the project for which funding is being requested, the total cost of the project and the amount being requested and a copy of the organization's 501(c)(3) certification. If the Foundation determines that further consideration is to be given to the proposed project, additional information will be requested.

Duration: Typically one year.

Deadline: December 1, March 1, June 1 and September 1.

PUBLICATIONS:
Guidelines; policies.

TRUSTEES AND OFFICERS:
Larry Prince, Chairman
Claire Arnold
Sylvia Looney Dick
Lillian Giornelli
Jack Guynn
B. Harvey Hill, Jr.
Warren Jobe
Clay Rolader
Napoleon Rutledge

ADDRESS INQUIRIES TO:
Barbara T. Cleveland, Executive Director or Carol Aiken, Assistant
(See address above.)

UNION PACIFIC FOUNDATION [316]

1400 Douglas, Stop 1560
Omaha, NE 68179
(402) 544-5600
Fax: (402) 501-0011
E-mail: upf@up.com
Web Site: www.up.com/found

FOUNDED: 1955

AREAS OF INTEREST:
Health and human services, community and civic, and fine arts in communities served by Union Pacific.

TYPE:
Capital grants; General operating grants; Project/program grants. Support generally for capital campaigns, building funds, equipment and materials, renovation and operating support.

YEAR PROGRAM STARTED: 1959

PURPOSE:
To improve the quality of life in the communities served by Union Pacific and where its employees live and work.

LEGAL BASIS:
Incorporated in Utah, May 13, 1955.

ELIGIBILITY:
Organization must be a public charity, 501(c)(3) tax-exempt and located in a community served by Union Pacific.

GEOG. RESTRICTIONS: Arizona, Arkansas, California, Colorado, Idaho, Illinois, Iowa, Kansas, Louisiana, Minnesota, Missouri, Montana, Nebraska, Nevada, New Mexico, Oklahoma, Oregon, Texas, Utah, Washington, Wisconsin and Wyoming.

FINANCIAL DATA:
Amount of support per award: Varies.

Total amount of support: $8,500,000 for fiscal year 2015.

NO. MOST RECENT APPLICANTS: 2,300.

NO. AWARDS: 913 for fiscal year 2015.

APPLICATION INFO:
Details may be obtained from the Foundation web site.

Duration: Most grants are awarded annually.

Deadline: August 15 for consideration for the following year's budget.

TRUSTEES:
E.L. Butler
Diane Duren
Lance Fritz
R.M. Knight, Jr.
S.D. Moore

*PLEASE NOTE:
Due to the Foundation undergoing a strategic plan, some of this information is subject to change.

THE UPS FOUNDATION [317]

55 Glenlake Parkway, N.E.
Atlanta, GA 30328
(404) 828-6374
Fax: (404) 828-7435
E-mail: community@ups.com
Web Site: www.community.ups.com

FOUNDED: 1951

AREAS OF INTEREST:
Economic and global literacy, environmental sustainability, nonprofit effectiveness, encouraging diversity and community safety, and volunteerism.

NAME(S) OF PROGRAMS:
- **James E. Casey Scholarship Program**
- **Neighbor to Neighbor**
- **George D. Smith Scholarship Program**

TYPE:
Project/program grants; Scholarships. James E. Casey Scholarship Program provides the opportunity for children of UPS employees to earn four-year scholarships at colleges and universities.

Neighbor to Neighbor program mobilizes UPS employees and their families to serve as volunteers in their communities.

George D. Smith Scholarship Program provides scholarships for children of full- and part-time UPS employees enrolled in a full-time study program of up to two years.

YEAR PROGRAM STARTED: 1951

PURPOSE:
To improve lives and strengthen the capacity of nonprofits through volunteerism, community grants and creative programs.

LEGAL BASIS:
Corporate foundation.

ELIGIBILITY:
Grant applicants must be any worthy philanthropic, nonprofit project or organization that is tax-exempt under 501(c)(3). The Foundation does not fund annual campaigns, building or endowment funds, deficit financing, emergency funds, individuals, land acquisition, loans, operating costs or capital expenses, publications, or religious organizations or theological functions.

FINANCIAL DATA:
Amount of support per award: Varies.

Total amount of support: Varies.

APPLICATION INFO:
The Foundation does not accept or respond to unsolicited grant proposals.

Duration: James E. Casey: Up to four years; Neighbor to Neighbor: Varies; George D. Smith: Up to two years.

Deadline: Varies.

ADDRESS INQUIRIES TO:
Eduardo Martinez, President
(See address above.)

USG FOUNDATION, INC. [318]

550 West Adams Street
Chicago, IL 60661
(312) 436-4021
(312) 436-4000
Fax: (312) 672-4021
E-mail: maclark@usg.com
Web Site: www.usg.com

FOUNDED: 1978

AREAS OF INTEREST:
Community, arts and culture, health and welfare, and education.

TYPE:
Project/program grants.

YEAR PROGRAM STARTED: 1978

PURPOSE:
To provide assistance to nonprofit organizations seeking solutions to educational, social or health problems or whose work contributes to cultural enrichment.

LEGAL BASIS:
Tax-exempt, corporate foundation.

ELIGIBILITY:
Applicants must be tax-exempt 501(c)(3) organizations. The Foundation supports the creation of economic opportunity through grants to organizations that provide affordable housing/shelter, encourage self-sufficiency and assist economic development.

The Foundation does not contribute to organizations without IRS tax-exempt 501(c)(3) status, sectarian organizations having an exclusively religious nature, individuals, political parties, offices or candidates, fraternal organizations, primary or secondary schools, organizations that cannot provide adequate accounting records, procedures or courtesy advertising.

GEOG. RESTRICTIONS: Primarily Chicago, Illinois.

FINANCIAL DATA:
Amount of support per award: Varies.

Total amount of support: Varies.

APPLICATION INFO:
Grant proposals should be submitted in writing to receive consideration. Application form is available on the Foundation web site.

Duration: One year. Renewal possible upon reapplication.

PUBLICATIONS:
Guidelines.

OFFICER:
Brian Cook, President

ADDRESS INQUIRIES TO:
Margaret Clark, Assistant Secretary
(See address above.)

VERIZON FOUNDATION [319]

One Verizon Way
Basking Ridge, NJ 07920
(866) 247-2687 (volunteers program)
Fax: (908) 630-2660
E-mail: cgsupport@cybergrants.com
Web Site: www.verizon.com/about/responsibility/verizon-foundation

FOUNDED: 2001

AREAS OF INTEREST:
Health care for children, women and seniors; STEM education for K-12 youth; and energy management.

TYPE:
Matching gifts; Project/program grants.

PURPOSE:
To address critical disparities among targeted segments in education, family, safety, health care and sustainability.

LEGAL BASIS:
Private, nonprofit organization.

ELIGIBILITY:
To be considered for an invitation, an organization must be classified as tax-exempt under Section 501(c)(3) of the Internal Revenue Code and further classified as a public charity under Section 509(a)(1)-(3).

Proposals will also be considered from elementary and secondary schools (public and private) that are registered with the National Center for Education Statistics (NCES), providing that the grant is not for the sponsorship of a field trip.

GEOG. RESTRICTIONS: United States.

FINANCIAL DATA:
Amount of support per award: Average $5,000 to $10,000.

Total amount of support: $6,468,984 in grants paid for the year 2013.

APPLICATION INFO:
Grants applications are by invitation only.

IRS I.D.: 13-3319048

THE WALLACE FOUNDATION [320]

5 Penn Plaza, 7th Floor
New York, NY 10001
(212) 251-9700
Fax: (212) 679-6990
E-mail: grantrequest@wallacefoundation.org
Web Site: www.wallacefoundation.org

FOUNDED: 1965

AREAS OF INTEREST:
Education leadership, arts education, building audiences for the arts, summer and expanded learning, and afterschool learning.

NAME(S) OF PROGRAMS:
- **After School System Building**
- **Building Audiences for Sustainability**
- **Principal Pipeline Initiative**
- **Principal Supervisor Initiative**
- **Summer Learning District Demonstration Project**
- **University Principal Preparation Initiative**

TYPE:
Conferences/seminars; Project/program grants; Research grants; Technical assistance; Research contracts.

YEAR PROGRAM STARTED: 2003

PURPOSE:
To foster improvements in learning and enrichment for disadvantaged children and the vitality of the arts for everyone; to catalyze broad impact by supporting the development, testing and sharing of new solutions and effective practices.

LEGAL BASIS:
Private foundation.

ELIGIBILITY:
Grant applicants must be 501(c)(3) tax-exempt organizations. No grants are made to individuals.

GEOG. RESTRICTIONS: United States.

FINANCIAL DATA:
Estimated assets of $1.463 billion as of December 31, 2015.

Amount of support per award: Varies depending on needs and nature of request.

Total amount of support: Approximately $55,200,000 in grants paid for calendar year 2015.

NO. MOST RECENT APPLICANTS: 240.

NO. AWARDS: 141.

APPLICATION INFO:
In most cases, the Foundation evaluates prospective grantees through the issuance of Requests for Proposals or other careful screening processes. Nevertheless, an organization may submit an inquiry by e-mail briefly describing the project, the organization, the estimated total for the project, and the portion requiring funding.

Duration: Varies.

Deadline: Varies.

PUBLICATIONS:
Annual report.

IRS I.D.: 13-6183757

OFFICERS AND BOARD OF DIRECTORS:
Kevin W. Kennedy, Chairman
Will Miller, President
Stacy J. Martin, Chief Financial Officer and Treasurer
Rob D. Nagel, Chief Investment Officer and Assistant Treasurer
Kenneth W. Austin, Corporate Secretary
Lawrence T. Babbio, Jr., Director
Candace K. Beinecke, Director
Augusta Souza Kappner, Director
Richard Kauffman, Director
Kent McGuire, Director
Ann S. Moore, Director
Joseph W. Polisi, Director
Debora L. Spar, Director
Amor H. Towles, Director
Mary Beth West, Director

ADDRESS INQUIRIES TO:
See e-mail address above.

*PLEASE NOTE:
Grants are rarely made to unsolicited projects, especially from local organizations.

THE WASIE FOUNDATION [321]

230 Manitoba Avenue South
Suite 110
Wayzata, MN 55391-1612
(952) 955-8500
Fax: (952) 955-8509
Web Site: www.wasie.org

FOUNDED: 1966

AREAS OF INTEREST:
Postsecondary educational scholarship programs for people of Polish ancestry in Minnesota; care, treatment and research regarding schizophrenia and arthritis; children's health; and organizations providing services and programs to people living with cancer.

NAME(S) OF PROGRAMS:
- **Arthritis Grants**
- **Cancer Grants**
- **Children's Medical Health Grants**
- **Schizophrenia Grants**
- **Scholarship Program**

TYPE:
Capital grants; Challenge/matching grants; Conferences/seminars; Development grants; General operating grants; Matching gifts; Project/program grants; Research grants. The grant program provides funding in four health areas, specifically: schizophrenia, arthritis, cancer, and children with medical problems.

YEAR PROGRAM STARTED: 1966

LEGAL BASIS:
Private foundation.

ELIGIBILITY:
Grants are made to 501(c)(3) nonprofit organizations.

GEOG. RESTRICTIONS: Minnesota and South Florida (Broward, Miami-Dade, and Palm Beach counties).

FINANCIAL DATA:
Amount of support per award: Varies.

Total amount of support: $1,562,642 in grants paid for the year 2014.

NO. AWARDS: 34 grants paid for the year 2014.

REPRESENTATIVE AWARDS:
$150,000 to Joe DiMaggio Children's Hospital Foundation; $25,000 to Franciscan End of Life Care; $10,000 to Vail Place; $10,000 to Epilepsy Foundation of Minnesota; $25,000 to Gilda's Club Twin Cities.

APPLICATION INFO:
The Foundation encourages organizations which believe they fall within their funding guidelines to initiate contact through a telephone call to one of the program staff who will gather information and assist with the proposal process.

Proposal submission is by invitation only.

Duration: One to three years. Renewal possible.

Deadline: Submissions are invited throughout the year.

STAFF:
Gregg D. Sjoquist, President and Chief Executive Officer
Dani Mathison, Chief Operating Officer
Jan Preble, Vice President of Programs

ADDRESS INQUIRIES TO:
Jan Preble
Vice President of Programs
(See address above.)

*PLEASE NOTE:
The Foundation is not inviting proposal submissions in 2016.

*SPECIAL STIPULATIONS:
Grant proposals are by invitation only. Inquiries open to any organization falling within funding areas and within demographic areas noted.

EDWIN S. WEBSTER FOUNDATION [322]

c/o GMA Foundations
77 Summer Street, Suite 800
Boston, MA 02110-1006
(617) 391-3087
Fax: (617) 426-7087
E-mail: mjenney@gmafoundations.com
Web Site: www.gmafoundations.com

FOUNDED: 1948

AREAS OF INTEREST:
Charitable purposes, with emphasis on hospitals, medical research and education, youth agencies, cultural activities and programs addressing the needs of minorities.

TYPE:
Capital grants; Challenge/matching grants; Endowments; General operating grants.

YEAR PROGRAM STARTED: 1982

PURPOSE:
To work towards a better society by giving grants to organizations trying to help people with serious needs not otherwise being addressed.

LEGAL BASIS:
Nonprofit foundation.

ELIGIBILITY:
No grants are given to individuals or organizations outside the U.S. The majority of contributions are made to organizations in the New England area. It is the policy of the Foundation to support charitable organizations that are well known to the Trustees, with emphasis on hospitals, medical research, education, youth agencies, cultural activities and programs addressing the needs of minorities. Grantees must have tax-exempt status.

GEOG. RESTRICTIONS: Primarily New England.

FINANCIAL DATA:
Amount of support per award: $5,000 to $25,000.

Total amount of support: Approximately $1,800,000.

APPLICATION INFO:
Proposals are submitted by using the online application form.

Duration: One year.

Deadline: For consideration at spring meeting, proposals should arrive by May 1. For consideration at the fall meeting, proposals should arrive by November 1.

PUBLICATIONS:
Guidelines.

TRUSTEES:
Henry U. Harris, III
Alexander Hiam
Suzanne Harte Sears

ADDRESS INQUIRIES TO:
Michelle Jenney, Administrator
(See address above.)

WEINGART FOUNDATION [323]

1055 West 7th Street
Suite 3200
Los Angeles, CA 90017-2305
(213) 688-7799
Fax: (213) 688-1515
E-mail: info@weingartfnd.org
Web Site: www.weingartfnd.org

FOUNDED: 1951

AREAS OF INTEREST:
Human services, health and education, with an emphasis on projects that benefit children and youth.

NAME(S) OF PROGRAMS:

- **Capacity Building**
- **Capital Support**
- **Core Support**
- **Program Support**
- **Small Grant Program**

TYPE:
Capital grants; General operating grants; Project/program grants. The Foundation makes grants to assist organizations that work in the areas of health, human services and education. The Foundation gives highest priority to activities that provide greater access to people who are economically disadvantaged and underserved. The Foundation has particular interest in applications that specifically address the needs of low-income children and youth, older adults and people affected by disabilities and homelessness. The Foundation also funds activities that benefit the general community and improve the quality of life for all individuals in southern California.

Core Support: Unrestricted funding that enables an organization to carry out its mission. It can be used to underwrite administrative infrastructure and/or to maintain core programs and essential staff.

Capacity Building: For new or enhanced activities aimed at strengthening an organization's programmatic and/or administrative capacity. Projects must evidence a credible plan for sustaining costs.

Capital Support: For specific projects with capital expenditures. Funding is available to support land, facility, equipment purchases, renovations or new construction.

Program Support: For new, expansion or enhancement program requests. Projects must evidence a viable fund-raising and sustainability plan.

Small Grant Program: For increasing access to funding and strengthening the capacity of small, community-based, and developing organizations, with priority given to organizations with operating budgets under $1,000,000. The Program also supports small capital projects for organizations of any size.

PURPOSE:
To assist credible agencies and institutions serving children and youth, the aged, the disabled, the homeless, the sick, the poor or otherwise disadvantaged and projects benefiting the general community.

ELIGIBILITY:
An organization that is certified as tax-exempt under Section 501(c)(3) of the U.S. Internal Revenue Code and is not a private foundation as defined in Section 509(a) of that Code is eligible for consideration. The Foundation does not fund Section 509(a)(3) Type III nonfunctionally integrated supporting organizations.

Grants are not made:
(1) to organizations that discriminate against certain groups or individuals in the delivery of programs and services on the basis of race, religion, national origin, gender, age, sexual orientation or disability;
(2) for propagandizing, influencing legislation and/or elections, promoting voter registration; for political candidates, political campaigns; for litigation;
(3) for social or political issues outside the U.S.;
(4) to individuals;
(5) to federated appeals or for the collection of funds for redistribution to other nonprofit groups;
(6) for conferences, workshops, temporary exhibits, travel, surveys, films or publishing activities;
(7) for endowment funds;
(8) for contingencies, deficits or debt reduction;
(9) for fund-raising dinners or events or;
(10) for research.

Grants generally are not approved for:
(1) national organizations that do not have local chapters operating in the geographic area of grant focus;
(2) projects or programs normally financed by government sources;
(3) refugee or religious programs, consumer interest or environmental advocacy or;
(4) feasibility studies.

GEOG. RESTRICTIONS: Southern California, with priority given to Los Angeles, Orange, Riverside, San Bernardino, Santa Barbara, and Ventura counties.

FINANCIAL DATA:
Assets of $798,922,695 for the year ended June 30, 2014.

Amount of support per award: $5,000 to $750,000.

Total amount of support: $32,081,941 in grants approved for the fiscal year ended June 30, 2014.

Matching fund requirements: Organization matches 1:1.

CO-OP FUNDING PROGRAMS: Nonprofit Sustainability Initiative, Home for Good.

NO. AWARDS: 643 for the fiscal year ended June 30, 2014.

APPLICATION INFO:
It is recommended that all applicants apply to the Regular Grant Program using the online LOI process. If submitting the request online is not an option, applicants may also submit a letter via regular mail. The letter, which should be limited to two pages, should include a brief description of the organization's mission and activities, a brief explanation of how the funds would be used, and the total amount of funding requested from the Foundation. If the request is for a specific project or activity (capital, capacity building, or program), the applicant should also include the total cost of the project for which funding is sought and the amount raised to date.

If it is determined from the Letter of Inquiry that the request meets the Foundation's priorities and interests, the applicant will be provided with the instructions and forms required to prepare and submit a formal application.

There is no Letter of Inquiry required for the Small Grant Program.

Duration: Mostly, one to two years. Core Support grants are generally made for a two-year period.

Deadline: The Foundation accepts applications throughout the year.

PUBLICATIONS:
Annual report, only available on web site.

IRS I.D.: 95-6054814

OFFICERS:
Fred J. Ali, President and Chief Executive Officer
Deborah M. Ives, Vice President and Treasurer
Belen Vargas, Vice President, Programs

BOARD OF DIRECTORS:
Monica C. Lozano, Chairman
Aileen Adams
Fred J. Ali
William C. Allen
Andrew E. Bogen
Steven D. Broidy
John W. Mack
Miriam Muscarolas
Steve L. Soboroff

ADDRESS INQUIRIES TO:
President and Chief Executive Officer
Weingart Foundation
(See address above.)

HERMAN O. WEST FOUNDATION [324]

530 Herman O. West Drive
Exton, PA 19341
(610) 594-2900
Web Site: www.westpharma.com

FOUNDED: 1972

AREAS OF INTEREST:
Funding of nonprofit organizations serving cultural, health and public service needs of the areas/communities where West Pharmaceutical Services maintains operations.

TYPE:
Capital grants; Challenge/matching grants; General operating grants; Matching gifts; Project/program grants; Scholarships.

YEAR PROGRAM STARTED: 1972

PURPOSE:
To fund nonprofit organizations, provide employee scholarship programs and employee matching gifts program.

LEGAL BASIS:
Corporate contributions program; private foundation.

ELIGIBILITY:
Grant applicants must be organizations with tax-exempt status, located in areas where the company maintains operations in the U.S.

Employees of West Pharmaceutical Services may participate in the Employee Matching Gifts Program and Matching Gifts to Non-Profit Organizations Program.

Scholarships are available to children of West Pharmaceutical Services employees.

GEOG. RESTRICTIONS: United States.

FINANCIAL DATA:
Amount of support per award: $500 to $150,000.

Total amount of support: Approximately $1,294,478 for the year 2015.

APPLICATION INFO:
Application includes description of service provided, financial statement, including sources of funding and how dispersed, list of future needs and services of program and documentation of tax-exempt status.

Duration: Varies. Renewal possible.

PUBLICATIONS:
Application guidelines.

OFFICERS AND TRUSTEES:
George R. Bennyhoff, Chairman
Annette Favorite, Trustee
Paula Johnson, M.D., Trustee

ADDRESS INQUIRIES TO:
Maureen B. Goebel, Administrator
Tel: (610) 594-2945
(See address above.)

WESTERN INTERSTATE COMMISSION FOR HIGHER EDUCATION [325]

3035 Center Green Drive
Suite 200
Boulder, CO 80301
(303) 541-0270
E-mail: info-sep@wiche.edu
Web Site: www.wiche.edu/psep

FOUNDED: 1953

AREAS OF INTEREST:
Allopathic medicine, dentistry, physical and occupational therapy, optometry, podiatry, osteopathic medicine, veterinary medicine, physician assistant and pharmacy.

NAME(S) OF PROGRAMS:
- **Professional Student Exchange Program (PSEP)**

TYPE:
Scholarships. Tuition assistance/loan for service.

YEAR PROGRAM STARTED: 1953

PURPOSE:
To provide affordable access to professional health care education.

ELIGIBILITY:
Must be a resident of a state listed below. Rules vary by state.

GEOG. RESTRICTIONS: Alaska, Arizona, Colorado, Hawaii, Montana, Nevada, New Mexico, North Dakota, Utah and Wyoming.

FINANCIAL DATA:
Amount of support per award: Varies.

Total amount of support: Varies.

NO. AWARDS: 657 for the year 2014-15.

APPLICATION INFO:
Applicants should contact their state certifying officers, listed on the web site above, for more information.

Duration: One year. Grants are renewable for course of study; subject to available funding.

Deadline: October 15 of the year prior to admission.

ADDRESS INQUIRIES TO:
Director of Student Exchange
(See address above.)

*PLEASE NOTE:
Grant is for residents of one western state making applications to participating schools in another western state.

E. L. WIEGAND FOUNDATION [326]

Wiegand Center
165 West Liberty Street, Suite 200
Reno, NV 89501
(775) 333-0310 ext. 112
Fax: (775) 333-0314

FOUNDED: 1982

AREAS OF INTEREST:
Education, medical research, civic and community affairs, arts and cultural affairs, and public affairs.

TYPE:
Capital grants; Project/program grants.

YEAR PROGRAM STARTED: 1982

PURPOSE:
To support charitable organizations and Roman Catholic charitable institutions.

LEGAL BASIS:
Private charitable trust.

ELIGIBILITY:
The Foundation will consider applications from institutions that are tax-exempt under Section 501(c)(3) of the IRS, and which are not private foundations as defined in Section 509.

The review process by the Foundation will consider institutions that:
(1) are exemplary in their field;
(2) have a history of high achievement and sound management;
(3) demonstrate a stable financial condition;
(4) have the potential to be self-supporting after the stage of initial funding by the Foundation;
(5) focus on strengthening traditional values essential to the preservation of a democratic society nurtured by free market principles (in the area of public affairs) and;
(6) are developing programs and projects that have a significant impact in the area for which the grant is requested.

GEOG. RESTRICTIONS: Arizona, Hawaii, Idaho, Montana, Nevada, Oregon, Utah, Washington, and New York City/Washington, DC (public policy).

FINANCIAL DATA:
Amount of support per award: $1,000 to $1,000,000.

Total amount of support: $5,361,252 for the year 2015.

NO. MOST RECENT APPLICANTS: 120 for the year 2015.

NO. AWARDS: 42 for the year 2015.

APPLICATION INFO:
A prospective applicant should describe the highlights of the proposal (including data regarding the organization, sources of funding, a brief description of the project or program, estimated budget and timeline) in a letter addressed to the Foundation. If, after staff consideration, it is determined that the program or project complies with the preliminary review, a prospective applicant shall receive an application for grant form which shall be assigned numerically to such applicant. The Foundation is only able to support a small percentage of the proposals it receives.

Deadline: Letters of Inquiry accepted throughout the year.

IRS I.D.: 94-2839372

ADDRESS INQUIRIES TO:
Kristen A. Avansino
President and Executive Director
Grants Program
(See address above.)

*PLEASE NOTE:
Written communications to the Foundation are preferred.

MATILDA R. WILSON FUND [327]

6th Floor at Ford Field
1901 St. Antoine Street
Detroit, MI 48226
(313) 259-7777
Fax: (313) 393-7579
E-mail: roosterveen@bodmanlaw.com

FOUNDED: 1944

AREAS OF INTEREST:
Arts, education, health and human services.

TYPE:
Capital grants; Project/program grants.

PURPOSE:
To primarily fund pre-selected organizations supported by Matilda R. Wilson during her lifetime.

ELIGIBILITY:
Applicants must be 501(c)(3) organizations. No grants to individuals.

GEOG. RESTRICTIONS: Primarily southeast Michigan.

FINANCIAL DATA:
Amount of support per award: $500 to $50,000.
Total amount of support: Varies.

NO. MOST RECENT APPLICANTS: 60.

NO. AWARDS: 35.

REPRESENTATIVE AWARDS:
$7,000,000 to Oakland University, Rochester, MI, for exterior restoration projects at Meadow Brook Hall.

APPLICATION INFO:
No application form. Applicants must submit tax-exempt documentation.
Duration: One year; some multiyear.
Deadline: January, April and August.

IRS I.D.: 38-6087665

STAFF:
Robin L. Oosterveen, Program Director

ADDRESS INQUIRIES TO:
Robin L. Oosterveen, Program Director
(See address above.)

*PLEASE NOTE:
Priority given to organizations that Mrs. Wilson supported during her lifetime, or with which the Fund has a long-standing commitment.

WOLFE ASSOCIATES, INC. [328]

34 South Third Street
Columbus, OH 43215
(614) 460-3782
Fax: (614) 469-6173
E-mail: rwolfe@10tv.com

FOUNDED: 1973

AREAS OF INTEREST:
Health and medicine, education, culture, community service and environment.

TYPE:
Project/program grants.

YEAR PROGRAM STARTED: 1973

LEGAL BASIS:
Private foundation.

ELIGIBILITY:
Grants are made to tax-exempt public foundations and charities.

GEOG. RESTRICTIONS: Primarily the central Ohio area.

FINANCIAL DATA:
Amount of support per award: Varies.
Total amount of support: Varies.

APPLICATION INFO:
Applicants should submit a cover letter with a brief summary of the proposal and amount requested.
Deadline: The Foundation accepts and reviews applications throughout the year.

ADDRESS INQUIRIES TO:
Rita J. Wolfe, Vice President
(See address above.)

THE ROBERT W. WOODRUFF FOUNDATION [329]

191 Peachtree Street, N.E.
Suite 3540
Atlanta, GA 30303
(404) 522-6755
Fax: (404) 522-7026
E-mail: fdns@woodruff.org
Web Site: www.woodruff.org

FOUNDED: 1937

AREAS OF INTEREST:
K-12th-grade and higher education; health care and health outreach; human services, particularly for children and youth; community development in metropolitan Atlanta; major Atlanta arts and cultural institutions; large-scale conservation projects; and Atlanta parks and greenspaces.

TYPE:
Capital grants; Project/program grants.

YEAR PROGRAM STARTED: 1937

PURPOSE:
To improve the quality of life in Georgia by investing in health, education, economic opportunity and the vitality of the community.

LEGAL BASIS:
Independent, private foundation with a broad charter to support charitable activities in the areas of health, education, environment, human services, arts and culture, and community development.

ELIGIBILITY:
Grants generally are limited to 501(c)(3) public charities located and operating in metropolitan Atlanta, GA, although grants are occasionally considered for significant institutions and initiatives in communities throughout Georgia. Grants are typically awarded for one-time capital or capacity needs of well-established charitable organizations with strong leadership, sustainable operations, a broad base of financial support, and proven program effectiveness.

Grants for ongoing operating support or endowments are avoided. No grants are made for individuals, loans, churches, conferences, startup organizations, debt relief, political activities, professional associations, festivals, performances, exhibits, fund-raising events or sponsorships.

GEOG. RESTRICTIONS: Georgia, with a focus on metropolitan Atlanta.

FINANCIAL DATA:
Amount of support per award: $25,000 to $80,000,000. Average award (2011-15): $3,000,000. Median award: (2011-15): $750,000.
Total amount of support: Varies.

NO. MOST RECENT APPLICANTS: 300.

NO. AWARDS: 21.

REPRESENTATIVE AWARDS:
$500,000 to Jewish Family & Career Services for $5,100,000 campaign to improve campus, including the addition of a building to provide a work program for the disabled; $1,250,000 to Trees Atlanta for $5,000,000 Branching Out campaign to increase tree plantings, expand educational offerings and strengthen conservation initiatives; $1,500,000 to Atlanta Police Foundation for $12,000,000 campaign to support a comprehensive public safety strategy to reduce crime.

APPLICATION INFO:
Application form not required. Proposal (one copy) should be made in letter form and should briefly describe the organization (its mission, history and programs) and the proposed project or initiative, including the challenge it addresses, project goals and/or expected outcomes. Proposals that are concise and to the point are preferred.

Applicant must include these attachments:
(1) itemized project budget, including other sources of support in-hand or anticipated;
(2) a list of executive staff and board members, including an address for the board chairperson;
(3) financial statements, including most recent audit report and;
(4) the current IRS determination letter.
Deadline: September 1 and February 1.

PUBLICATIONS:
Application guidelines.

OFFICERS:
P. Russell Hardin, President
Erik S. Johnson, Treasurer and Secretary

TRUSTEES:
James B. Williams, Chairman
E. Jenner Wood, III, Vice Chairman
Lawrence L. Gellerstedt, III
Thomas J. Lawley
Wilton D. Looney

ADDRESS INQUIRIES TO:
P. Russell Hardin, President
(See address above.)

WYMAN-GORDON FOUNDATION [330]

c/o Fletcher Tilton P.C.
370 Main Street, 12th Floor
Worcester, MA 01608
(508) 798-8621
(508) 459-8000
Fax: (508) 791-1201

FOUNDED: 1966

AREAS OF INTEREST:
Health and human services, education, civic and community affairs, culture and arts.

TYPE:
Grants-in-aid. The Foundation focuses its grantmaking in non-operating areas (i.e., capital campaigns, equipment).

YEAR PROGRAM STARTED: 1966

PURPOSE:
To operate exclusively for charitable, scientific and/or educational purposes.

ELIGIBILITY:
Applicants must be nonprofit organizations with a 501(c)(3) tax-exempt status.

GEOG. RESTRICTIONS: Primarily Worcester area, Massachusetts.

FINANCIAL DATA:
Amount of support per award: $100 to $150,000.

NO. MOST RECENT APPLICANTS: 200.

NO. AWARDS: 50.

REPRESENTATIVE AWARDS:
$150,000 to United Way of Central Massachusetts; $10,000 to Worcester Public Library; $3,000 to Mechanics Hall; $3,500 to Worcester Municipal Research Bureau.

APPLICATION INFO:
Application includes 501(c)(3) tax-exempt letter, statement of purpose and specifics regarding project or program to be funded.
Deadline: April 1, August 1 and December 1.

IRS I.D.: 04-6142600

OFFICERS AND TRUSTEES:
David P. Gruber, President
Wallace F. Whitney, Jr., Secretary and Treasurer
Warner S. Fletcher, Trustee

ADDRESS INQUIRIES TO:
Warner S. Fletcher, Trustee
(See address above.)

THE WYOMISSING FOUNDATION [331]

960 Old Mill Road
Wyomissing, PA 19610-2522
(610) 376-7494
Fax: (610) 372-7276
E-mail: pswavely@wyofound.org
Web Site: www.wyofound.org

FOUNDED: 1929

AREAS OF INTEREST:
Charitable purposes, primarily local giving, with emphasis on hospitals, higher education, youth agencies and community funds, conservation, music and economic development.

TYPE:
Capital grants; Challenge/matching grants; Development grants; Grants-in-aid; Project/program grants; Research grants; Seed money grants.

YEAR PROGRAM STARTED: 1929

LEGAL BASIS:
Private donor foundation.

ELIGIBILITY:
No grants to individuals. Applicants must be 501(c)(3) organizations.

GEOG. RESTRICTIONS: Primarily Berks County, Pennsylvania.

FINANCIAL DATA:
No fiscal restrictions.

Amount of support per award: $5,000 to $250,000.

Total amount of support: Varies.

APPLICATION INFO:
Guidelines available at the web site.

Duration: Primarily one year.

Deadline: Quarterly.

IRS I.D.: 23-1980570

OFFICERS AND BOARD OF DIRECTORS:
Glenn Moyer, Chairman
Alex Frazee, Vice Chairman
Karen A. Rightmire, President
Chris Pruitt, Treasurer

ADDRESS INQUIRIES TO:
Karen A. Rightmire, President
(See address above.)

XCEL ENERGY FOUNDATION [332]

414 Nicollet Mall
Minneapolis, MN 55401-1993
(800) 328-8226
E-mail: lauren.c.olson@xcelenergy.com
Web Site: www.xcelenergy.com

FOUNDED: 2001

AREAS OF INTEREST:
Environment, math and science education, job training and placement, and access to the arts.

TYPE:
Project/program grants. Employee/retiree matching gifts program. Project/program grants in the areas of STEM education, economic sustainability, arts and culture, and environmental stewardship.

YEAR PROGRAM STARTED: 2001

PURPOSE:
To help promote a desirable, healthy environment in those areas served by Xcel Energy.

ELIGIBILITY:
Applicants must be 501(c)(3) nonprofit organizations in the service area. Grants will not be made to individuals, political parties, national organizations, research programs or government agencies. Grants are made to religious organizations only if program sponsored has a direct benefit to the community and not the religious organization.

GEOG. RESTRICTIONS: Cities within Xcel Energy service areas.

FINANCIAL DATA:
Amount of support per award: $1,000 to $30,000.

Total amount of support: Varies.

Matching fund requirements: 501(c)(3) nonprofits. Employee and retiree matching gifts program: Minimum donation $50, maximum $500.

APPLICATION INFO:
The Foundation utilizes an online grant application system. Applications are accepted by invitation only.

Duration: Varies.

Deadline: Varies by location.

STAFF:
Jeanne Fox, Representative, Michigan and Wisconsin
Terry Price, Representative, New Mexico and Texas

ADDRESS INQUIRIES TO:
Lauren Olson, Grants Manager
(See address above.)

THE XEROX FOUNDATION [333]

45 Glover Avenue
Norwalk, CT 06856
(203) 849-2453
Fax: (203) 849-2479
E-mail: mark.conlin@xerox.com

FOUNDED: 1972

AREAS OF INTEREST:
Education and workforce preparedness, science and technology, employee and community affairs, cultural affairs, and national affairs.

TYPE:
Assistantships; Challenge/matching grants; Development grants; Fellowships; General operating grants; Grants-in-aid; Internships; Matching gifts; Professorships; Project/program grants; Research grants; Scholarships; Seed money grants; Technical assistance; Training grants.

YEAR PROGRAM STARTED: 1972

PURPOSE:
To assist a variety of social, civic, and cultural organizations that provide broad-based community programs and services in the cities where Xerox employees live and work; to support higher education to prepare qualified men and women for careers in business, government and education; to advance knowledge in science and technology; to enhance learning opportunities for minorities and disadvantaged; to foster debate on major national public policy issues; to support national leadership efforts around major social problems, education, employability and cultural affairs.

LEGAL BASIS:
Corporate foundation.

ELIGIBILITY:
Grants are made only to organizations that have been granted exemption from Federal Income Tax under Section 501(c)(3) and ruled to be publicly supported under Section 509(a) of the Internal Revenue Code. No grants for individuals; capital grants (except for special circumstances and approved by Board of Trustees); endowments or endowed chairs; political organizations or candidates; religious or sectarian groups; municipal, county, state, federal or quasi-government agencies.

GEOG. RESTRICTIONS: United States.

FINANCIAL DATA:
Amount of support per award: Grants vary in amount, depending upon the needs and nature of the request.

Total amount of support: $13,500,000 for the year 2014.

Matching fund requirements: Will match colleges/universities up to $1,000 per institution.

NO. MOST RECENT APPLICANTS: Approximately 600 for the year 2014.

APPLICATION INFO:
No specific application form is used. Applications must be submitted in letter form. The letter should contain:
(1) the legal name of the organization;
(2) the official contact person;
(3) its tax-exempt status;
(4) a brief description of its activities and programs;
(5) the purpose for which the grant is being requested;
(6) the benefits expected;
(7) the plans for evaluation;
(8) the projected budget and;
(9) the expected sources and amount of funds needed.

Any additional factual material related to the organization or request that may be deemed useful for evaluation, plus a copy of the latest annual financial statement if available, should also be included.

Duration: The Foundation usually does not make grants for continuing support without a follow-up request. Large grants may be approved for one year or on a multiyear basis.

Deadline: Grant reviews take place monthly.

OFFICERS:
Mark J. Conlin, President

ADDRESS INQUIRIES TO:
Mark J. Conlin, President
(See address above.)

HUMANITIES

Humanities (general)

AMERICAN ACADEMY IN ROME [334]

7 East 60th Street
New York, NY 10022-1001
(212) 751-7200
Fax: (212) 751-7220
E-mail: info@aarome.org
Web Site: www.aarome.org

FOUNDED: 1894

AREAS OF INTEREST:
Arts and humanities.

NAME(S) OF PROGRAMS:
- **Rome Prize Fellowships**

TYPE:
Awards/prizes; Fellowships; Residencies. Fellowships for independent work in architecture, landscape architecture, design, musical composition, visual arts, historic preservation/conservation, ancient studies, medieval studies, renaissance and early modern studies, and modern Italian studies. Supported projects must be conducted at American Academy in Rome facilities.

YEAR PROGRAM STARTED: 1894

PURPOSE:
To support emerging artists and scholars in the early or middle stages of their careers; to refine and expand their professional, artistic or scholarly aptitudes, drawing on their colleagues' erudition and experience, as well as on the inestimable resources of the Italian capital of Rome, Europe and the Mediterranean.

LEGAL BASIS:
Private, not-for-profit.

ELIGIBILITY:
Must be U.S. citizen at the time of application. Graduate students in the humanities may apply only for Predoctoral Fellowships. Previous winners of the Rome Prize are not eligible to reapply. Undergraduate students are not eligible for Rome Prize Fellowships.

U.S. citizens and foreign nationals who have lived in the U.S. for three years immediately preceding the application deadline may apply for the NEH Postdoctoral Fellowships.

FINANCIAL DATA:
Rome Prize includes stipend, meals, a bedroom with private bath, and a study or studio. Winners of six-month and 11-month fellowships receive stipends.

Amount of support per award: Fellowships provide stipends of $16,000 (six-month) and $28,000 (11-month).

Total amount of support: $2,700,000.

CO-OP FUNDING PROGRAMS: National Endowment for the Arts, National Endowment for the Humanities, Andrew W. Mellon Foundation, Samuel Kress Foundation and American Academy of Arts and Letters.

NO. MOST RECENT APPLICANTS: 902.

NO. AWARDS: 31.

APPLICATION INFO:
Application forms are available online.

Duration: Six-month and 11-month fellowships depending on field of application. Predoctoral awards in the humanities include 11-month and two-year fellowships.

Deadline: November 1.

STAFF:
Shawn Miller, Program Director

ADDRESS INQUIRIES TO:
Programs Department
(See address above.)

AMERICAN ANTIQUARIAN SOCIETY (AAS) [335]

185 Salisbury Street
Worcester, MA 01609-1634
(508) 755-5221
Fax: (508) 754-9069
E-mail: perickson@mwa.org
Web Site: www.americanantiquarian.org

FOUNDED: 1812

AREAS OF INTEREST:
American history and culture through 1876.

NAME(S) OF PROGRAMS:
- **AAS American Society for Eighteenth Century Studies Fellowship**
- **AAS National Endowment for the Humanities Fellowships**
- **AAS-Northeast Modern Language Association Fellowship**
- **American Historical Print Collectors Fellowship**
- **Stephen Botein Fellowships**
- **The "Drawn to Art" Fellowship**
- **Linda F. and Julian L. Lapides Fellowship**
- **Jay and Deborah Last Fellowship**
- **The Legacy Fellowship**
- **Barbara Packer Fellowship**
- **Kate B. and Hall J. Peterson Fellowships**
- **The Reese Fellowship**
- **Justin G. Schiller Fellowship**
- **Joyce A. Tracy Fellowship**

TYPE:
Conferences/seminars; Fellowships. Fellowships provide support for residence at the Society's library for research on any topic supported by the collections. All awards are for research and writing using the library's resources.

YEAR PROGRAM STARTED: 1972

PURPOSE:
To enable scholars to come to Worcester for an extended period to do research in the Society's collections.

LEGAL BASIS:
AAS was incorporated by the legislature of Massachusetts, October 24, 1812.

ELIGIBILITY:
Fellows are selected on the basis of the applicant's scholarly qualifications, the scholarly significance of the project, and the appropriateness of the proposed study to the Society's collections.

The National Endowment for the Humanities Fellowships are intended for scholars beyond the Doctorate, for which senior and midcareer scholars are encouraged to apply. Applicant must be a U.S. citizen.

Short-term fellowships are available for scholars holding Ph.D. and for doctoral candidates engaged in dissertation research.

FINANCIAL DATA:
Amount of support per award: Long-term fellowships carry stipends up to $4,200 per month. Short-term fellowships are $1,850 per month.

Total amount of support: Varies.

NO. MOST RECENT APPLICANTS: 170.

NO. AWARDS: Up to 40.

APPLICATION INFO:
Application information is available online.

Duration: One month for short-term fellowships. Four to 12 months for long-term fellowships.

Deadline: January 15. Announcement by March 30.

ADDRESS INQUIRIES TO:
Paul Erickson
Director of Academic Programs
(See address above.)

*SPECIAL STIPULATIONS:
Recipient must maintain regular and continuous residence at the Society during his or her period of tenure.

AMERICAN ANTIQUARIAN SOCIETY (AAS) [336]

185 Salisbury Street
Worcester, MA 01609-1634
(508) 755-5221
Fax: (508) 753-3311
E-mail: cmcrell@mwa.org
Web Site: www.americanantiquarian.org

AREAS OF INTEREST:
American history, literature and culture through 1876.

NAME(S) OF PROGRAMS:
- **AAS Fellowship for Creative and Performing Artists and Writers**

TYPE:
Fellowships. Visiting fellowship for historical research by creative and performing artists, writers, filmmakers and journalists.

YEAR PROGRAM STARTED: 1995

PURPOSE:
To multiply and improve ways in which an understanding of history is communicated to the American people.

ELIGIBILITY:
Creative and performing artists, writers, filmmakers, journalists, and others whose goals are to produce imaginative, non-formulaic works dealing with pre-20th century American history. Works are for the general public, rather than for academic or educational audiences.

FINANCIAL DATA:
Amount of support per award: Stipend of $1,150 to $1,350 for Fellows living on campus; $1,850 for Fellows residing off-campus.

Total amount of support: Varies.

NO. MOST RECENT APPLICANTS: 40.

NO. AWARDS: 5.

APPLICATION INFO:
A complete fellowship application consists of the following materials:
(1) cover sheet;
(2) current resume, including a list of any awards, scholarships or grants received;
(3) a statement of not more than five typed, double-spaced pages briefly summarizing the applicant's educational and professional background and goals, describing the research for the project including readings in primary and secondary sources, and indicating the nature of the research program proposed for the AAS fellowship;
(4) 10 copies of representative samples of previous works must be included for distribution to the selection committee.

Written works (play and video scripts; prose and poetry; works of nonfiction, etc.) cannot exceed 25 pages in length. Applicants are welcome to send two or three copies of full, completed works in addition to the 25-page sample. If submitting samples of films, videos, audio and music recordings, or reproductions (digital versions and/or photographs) of paintings, sculptures, prints and other art works, please send only three copies or sets with the completed application. Applicants are encouraged to include any relevant reviews of their work by professional critics. If the applicant wishes to have any of these samples returned, please enclose a self-addressed, stamped envelope and; (5) two letters of reference should be sent directly to AAS by individuals familiar with the applicant's career accomplishments and goals.

Duration: Four-week residency.

Deadline: October 5, with notification on or about December 5.

ADDRESS INQUIRIES TO:
James David Moran
Director of Outreach
(See address above.)

AMERICAN COUNCIL OF LEARNED SOCIETIES [337]

633 Third Avenue, 8th Floor
New York, NY 10017-6795
(212) 697-1505 ext. 136 or 138
E-mail: fellowships@acls.org
Web Site: www.acls.org

FOUNDED: 1919

AREAS OF INTEREST:
The humanities and related social sciences.

NAME(S) OF PROGRAMS:
- **ACLS Fellowship**

TYPE:
Fellowships. Postdoctoral fellowships to support research in the humanities or research projects with a predominantly humanities-related emphasis in the social sciences.

PURPOSE:
To provide opportunities for scholars to engage in humanities research.

LEGAL BASIS:
Nonprofit.

ELIGIBILITY:
U.S. citizens or permanent residents holding a Ph.D. degree conferred two years before application deadline or its equivalent (taken to mean scholarly maturity as demonstrated by professional experience and publications) may apply.

FINANCIAL DATA:
Amount of support per award: Fellowships are up to $70,000 for full professor (and career equivalent), up to $45,000 for associate professor (and career equivalent), and up to $35,000 for assistant professor (and career equivalent).

Total amount of support: Varies.

NO. MOST RECENT APPLICANTS: 1,050.

NO. AWARDS: 70.

APPLICATION INFO:
Applications must be submitted through the ACLS Online Fellowship Application system.

Duration: Fellows must devote six to 12 continuous months to full-time work on supported projects.

Deadline: September.

THE AMERICAN NUMISMATIC SOCIETY [338]

75 Varick Street, Floor 11
New York, NY 10013
(212) 571-4470 ext. 153
Fax: (212) 571-4479
E-mail: vanalfen@numismatics.org
Web Site: www.numismatics.org

FOUNDED: 1858

AREAS OF INTEREST:
Numismatics (coins and medals), history and archeology.

NAME(S) OF PROGRAMS:
- **The Eric P. Newman Graduate Summer Seminar**

TYPE:
Grants-in-aid. Grants for graduate students and junior faculty to attend the Society's summer seminar held at its museum in New York. The Graduate Seminar in Numismatics is an intensive program of study including lectures and conferences conducted by specialists in various fields, preparation and oral delivery of a research paper and actual contact with the coinage in the Society's collection. Curatorial staff and other experts from the U.S. and abroad will participate in the seminar.

YEAR PROGRAM STARTED: 1952

PURPOSE:
To familiarize students with numismatic methodology and scholarship; to provide a deeper understanding of the contributions made by numismatics to other fields of study.

ELIGIBILITY:
Applications are accepted from students of demonstrated competence who will have completed at least one year of graduate work in history, art history, classical studies, economics, economic history or other related fields. Applications are encouraged from junior faculty members with an advanced degree in one of these fields.

Applications are also accepted from outstanding students from foreign institutions who have completed at least one year of graduate work and are able to demonstrate fluency in English; however, no financial aid for them is offered.

FINANCIAL DATA:
Stipends are available to qualified applicants who are citizens or permanent residents of the U.S.

Amount of support per award: Stipends up to $4,000.

Total amount of support: Varies.

CO-OP FUNDING PROGRAMS: Support of attendance at the Seminar is made possible by a generous donation from Mr. and Mrs. Eric P. Newman.

NO. MOST RECENT APPLICANTS: 50.

NO. AWARDS: Up to 6.

APPLICATION INFO:
Applications must be supported by three letters of recommendation. Additional information and application forms will be provided upon request.

Duration: Seven to eight weeks, June through July.

Deadline: February 14.

OFFICERS:
Dr. Peter Van Alfen, Director

ADDRESS INQUIRIES TO:
Dr. Peter Van Alfen, Director
(See address above.)

AMERICAN PHILOSOPHICAL SOCIETY [339]

c/o American Philosophical Society Library
104 South Fifth Street
Philadelphia, PA 19106-3386
(215) 440-3443
Fax: (215) 440-3423
E-mail: libfellows@amphilsoc.org
Web Site: www.amphilsoc.org/grants/resident

FOUNDED: 1743

AREAS OF INTEREST:
Scholarly research.

NAME(S) OF PROGRAMS:
- **The Library Resident Research Fellowships**

TYPE:
Fellowships; Grants-in-aid; Research grants. Short-term residential fellowships for conducting research in the Library's collections.

YEAR PROGRAM STARTED: 1991

PURPOSE:
To encourage research by scholars in the Library's collections.

LEGAL BASIS:
Nonprofit learned society.

ELIGIBILITY:
Open to both U.S. citizens and foreign nationals who are holders of a Ph.D. or the equivalent, Ph.D. candidates who have passed their preliminary exams and degreed independent scholars. Applicants in any relevant field of scholarship may apply.

FINANCIAL DATA:
Amount of support per award: $3,000 per month.

NO. MOST RECENT APPLICANTS: 69.

NO. AWARDS: 27.

APPLICATION INFO:
Applications must be submitted online. Applicants will provide name, project title, affiliation, address, e-mail and telephone number. Project description must state the specific relevance of the American Philosophical Society's collections to the project and indicate expected results of the research (such as publications), a curriculum vitae or resume and two letters of reference (doctoral candidates must use their dissertation advisor). Referees will also provide letters online. Instructions are in application information.

Duration: One to three months, taken between June 1 and May 31.

Deadline: Beginning of March. Notification in early May.

PUBLICATIONS:
Program announcement; list of guides to the Society's collections.

ADDRESS INQUIRIES TO:
Earle Spamer
The Library Resident Research Fellowships
(See address above.)

*SPECIAL STIPULATIONS:
Fellows are expected to be in residence during the period of their award.

THE AMERICAN SCHOOL OF CLASSICAL STUDIES AT ATHENS
6-8 Charlton Street
Princeton, NJ 08540-5232
(609) 683-0800
Fax: (609) 924-0578
E-mail: ascsa@ascsa.org (for information)
application@ascsa.org (to apply)
Web Site: www.ascsa.edu.gr

TYPE:
Fellowships. Several Fellowships awarded by the School for the full academic year: the Samuel H. Kress Fellowship in art and architecture of antiquity; the Gorham Phillips Stevens Fellowship in the history of architecture; the Ione Mylonas Shear Fellowship in Mycenaean archaeology or Athenian architecture and/or archaeology; the Homer A. and Dorothy B. Thompson Fellowship in the study of pottery. Additionally, three Fellowships are unrestricted as to field: the Edward Capps, the Doreen Canaday Spitzer, and the Eugene Vanderpool Fellowships.

See entry 874 for full listing.

THE AMERICAN SCHOOL OF CLASSICAL STUDIES AT ATHENS
6-8 Charlton Street
Princeton, NJ 08540-5232
(609) 683-0800
Fax: (609) 924-0578
E-mail: ascsa@ascsa.org (for information)
application@ascsa.org (to apply)
Web Site: www.ascsa.edu.gr

TYPE:
Scholarships. Four-week program in intermediate-level Medieval Greek language and philology at the Gennadius Library, with site and museum trips. Seminar given every other year. Next seminar to be held in 2017.

See entry 877 for full listing.

THE AMERICAN SCHOOL OF CLASSICAL STUDIES AT ATHENS
6-8 Charlton Street
Princeton, NJ 08540-5232
(609) 683-0800
Fax: (609) 924-0578
E-mail: ascsa@ascsa.org (for information)
application@ascsa.org (to apply)
Web Site: www.ascsa.edu.gr

TYPE:
Fellowships. Fellowships for postdoctoral scholars and professionals in the humanities.

See entry 872 for full listing.

THE AMERICAN SCHOOL OF CLASSICAL STUDIES AT ATHENS
6-8 Charlton Street
Princeton, NJ 08540-5232
(609) 683-0800
Fax: (609) 924-0578
E-mail: ascsa@ascsa.org (for information)
application@ascsa.org (to apply)
Web Site: www.ascsa.edu.gr

TYPE:
Fellowships. The M. Alison Frantz Fellowship and The Jacob Hirsch Fellowship are part of the Student Associate Program, which is open to advanced graduate students in the same fields as the Regular Academic Program (classical studies and ancient Mediterranean studies and related fields such as history of art, anthropology, prehistory, studies in postclassical Greece, etc.), who plan to pursue independent research projects and who do not wish to commit to the full Regular Academic Program.

The Jacob Hirsch Fellowship is also open to students from Israel.

See entry 873 for full listing.

ARCHAEOLOGICAL INSTITUTE OF AMERICA [340]
656 Beacon Street, 6th Floor
Boston, MA 02215
(617) 358-4184
Fax: (617) 353-6550
E-mail: lsparks@aia.bu.edu
Web Site: www.archaeological.org

FOUNDED: 1879

AREAS OF INTEREST:
Archaeological research and publication.

NAME(S) OF PROGRAMS:
- **John R. Coleman Traveling Fellowship**
- **Olivia James Traveling Fellowship**

TYPE:
Fellowships. John R. Coleman Traveling Fellowship: Awarded to be used for travel and study in Italy, the western Mediterranean, or North Africa. Applicants must be engaged in dissertation research in a U.S. graduate program.

Olivia James Traveling Fellowship: Awarded, preferably, to individuals engaged in dissertation research or to recent recipients of the Ph.D. (within five years of the application deadline) for travel and study in Greece, the Aegean Islands, Cyprus, Sicily, Southern Italy, Asia Minor or Mesopotamia to conduct a project in (most suitably) classics, sculpture, architecture, archaeology or history.

YEAR PROGRAM STARTED: 1961

PURPOSE:
John R. Coleman Traveling Fellowship: To encourage the continued study of archaeological sites; to provide funding for travel and study in Italy, the western Mediterranean or North Africa.

Olivia James Traveling Fellowship: To encourage the continued study of archaeological sites; to provide fellowships for travel and study in Greece, the Aegean Islands, Cyprus, Sicily, Southern Italy, Asia Minor or Mesopotamia.

LEGAL BASIS:
Nonprofit, scientific and educational organization.

ELIGIBILITY:
John R. Coleman Traveling Fellowship: Applicants must be members of the AIA at the time of application. The recipient should remain a member until the end of the fellowship term and subsequent submission of an abstract and/or presentation at the AIA annual meeting. Applicants must be engaged in dissertation research in a U.S. graduate program.

Olivia James Traveling Fellowship: Applicants must be U.S. citizens. Preference is given to individuals engaged in dissertation research or to recent Ph.D. recipients (within five years of application deadline). Preference is also given to projects of at least a half-year's duration. The award is for travel and study in Greece, the Aegean Islands, Cyprus, Sicily, Southern Italy, Asia Minor or Mesopotamia and is not intended to support field excavation projects. Recipients may not hold other major fellowships during the requested tenure.

FINANCIAL DATA:
Amount of support per award: John R. Coleman Traveling Fellowship: $11,000. Olivia James Traveling Fellowship: $25,000.

Total amount of support: John R. Coleman Traveling Fellowship: $11,000. Olivia James Traveling Fellowship: $25,000.

NO. MOST RECENT APPLICANTS: John R. Coleman Traveling Fellowship: 12. Olivia James Traveling Fellowship: 11.

NO. AWARDS: John R. Coleman Traveling Fellowship: 1. Olivia James Traveling Fellowship: 1.

APPLICATION INFO:
John R. Coleman Traveling Fellowship: Official application materials are available August of each year on the Institute's web site. Graduate transcripts, two letters of reference and a summary statement of proposed project are required. Applications for the fellowship can be submitted electronically.

Olivia James Traveling Fellowship: Official application materials are available August of each year on the Institute's web site. Graduate transcript(s), two letters of reference, and a summary statement of proposed project are required. Applications for the fellowship can be submitted electronically.

Duration: John R. Coleman Traveling Fellowship: Single fellowship for work to be conducted between July 1 of the award year and the following June 30. Olivia James Traveling Fellowship: Single fellowship for work to be conducted between July 1 and the following June 30.

Deadline: John R. Coleman and Olivia James Traveling Fellowships: November 1. Announcement by February 1.

ADDRESS INQUIRIES TO:
Laurel Nilsen Sparks
Lecture and Fellowship Coordinator
(See address above.)

ARCHAEOLOGICAL INSTITUTE OF AMERICA [341]
656 Beacon Street, 6th Floor
Boston, MA 02215
(617) 358-4184
Fax: (617) 353-6550
E-mail: lsparks@aia.bu.edu
Web Site: www.archaeological.org

FOUNDED: 1879

AREAS OF INTEREST:
Archaeological research and publication.

NAME(S) OF PROGRAMS:
- **Harriet and Leon Pomerance Fellowship**

TYPE:
Fellowships. Awarded to support a person on an individual project of a scholarly nature relating to Aegean Bronze Age Archaeology.

Preference will be given to candidates whose project requires travel to the Mediterranean for the purpose stated above.

YEAR PROGRAM STARTED: 1972

PURPOSE:
To promote serious scholarly study of Aegean Bronze Age Archaeology.

LEGAL BASIS:
Nonprofit, scientific and educational organization.

ELIGIBILITY:
Applicants must be citizens or permanent residents of the U.S. or Canada, or be actively pursuing an advanced degree at a North American college or university. Previous Harriet Pomerance Fellows are not eligible. At the conclusion of the fellowship tenure, the recipient must submit a report on the use of the stipend to the president of the Institute.

FINANCIAL DATA:
Amount of support per award: $5,000.

Total amount of support: $5,000.

NO. MOST RECENT APPLICANTS: 6.

NO. AWARDS: 1.

APPLICATION INFO:
Official application materials are available online in August of each year. Graduate transcript(s), two letters of reference, and a summary statement of proposed project are required. Applications for the fellowship can be submitted electronically.

Duration: Work to be conducted between July 1 of the award year and the following June 30.

Deadline: November 1. Announcement by February 1.

ADDRESS INQUIRIES TO:
Laurel Nilsen Sparks
Lecture and Fellowship Coordinator
(See address above.)

ARCHAEOLOGICAL INSTITUTE OF AMERICA [342]

656 Beacon Street, 6th Floor
Boston, MA 02215
(617) 358-4184
Fax: (617) 353-6550
E-mail: fellowships@aia.bu.edu
Web Site: www.archaeological.org

FOUNDED: 1879

AREAS OF INTEREST:
Archaeological research and publication.

NAME(S) OF PROGRAMS:
- **Anna C. and Oliver C. Colburn Fellowship**

TYPE:
Fellowships. Awarded to an applicant every other year contingent upon his or her acceptance as an incoming Associate Member or Student Associate Member of the American School of Classical Studies at Athens, Greece.

YEAR PROGRAM STARTED: 1991

PURPOSE:
To support studies at the American School of Classical Studies at Athens, Greece.

LEGAL BASIS:
Nonprofit, scientific and educational organization.

ELIGIBILITY:
Applicants must be U.S. or Canadian citizens or permanent residents, or those who are actively pursuing an advanced degree at a North American college or university, who are at the predoctoral stage or who have recently received the Ph.D. degree (within five years of the date of application). They must apply concurrently to the American School for Senior Associate Membership or Student Associate Membership. Applicants may not be Members of the American School during the year of application.

The fellowship recipient is required to submit a report on the use of the stipend both to the President of the Archaeological Institute of America and to the Director of the American School of Classical Studies at Athens at the conclusion of the tenure of the fellowship.

FINANCIAL DATA:
Amount of support per award: $5,500.

Total amount of support: $11,000.

NO. MOST RECENT APPLICANTS: 5.

NO. AWARDS: 2.

APPLICATION INFO:
Official application materials are available on the web site. Graduate transcript(s), three letters of reference, and a summary statement of the proposed project are required. Candidates must apply concurrently to the American School for Senior Associate Membership or Student Associate Membership.

Duration: Work to be conducted between July 1 of the award year and the following June 30.

Deadline: January 15, 2018 and every other year thereafter.

ADDRESS INQUIRIES TO:
Laurel Nilsen Sparks
Lecture and Fellowship Coordinator
(See address above.)

*SPECIAL STIPULATIONS:
After the tenure of their fellowship, all fellows are expected to submit an abstract to the Program Committee within two years, in accordance with that committee's guidelines, in order to present a paper on their research at the Institute annual meeting.

ARCHAEOLOGICAL INSTITUTE OF AMERICA [343]

656 Beacon Street, 6th Floor
Boston, MA 02215
(617) 358-4184
Fax: (617) 353-6550
E-mail: fellowships@aia.bu.edu
Web Site: www.archaeological.org

FOUNDED: 1879

AREAS OF INTEREST:
Archaeological research and publication.

NAME(S) OF PROGRAMS:
- **Jane C. Waldbaum Archaeological Field School Scholarship**

TYPE:
Scholarships. Award to support participation in an archaeological excavation or survey project.

YEAR PROGRAM STARTED: 2006

ELIGIBILITY:
Open to junior and senior undergraduates or first-year graduate students. Applicants cannot previously have participated in archaeological excavation and must be at least a junior at the time of application. Applicants must be enrolled in a college or university in the U.S. or Canada, but do not have to be U.S. citizens or residents.

FINANCIAL DATA:
Amount of support per award: $1,000.

Total amount of support: Varies.

NO. MOST RECENT APPLICANTS: 80.

NO. AWARDS: 20.

APPLICATION INFO:
All applications must be submitted electronically through the AIA web site. Required materials include the application form, two letters of reference, official transcript(s) and a letter of acceptance from the field school. All application materials must be received by the deadline.

Duration: Minimum one-month stay at the field school. Nonrenewable.

Deadline: March 1.

ADDRESS INQUIRIES TO:
Laurel Nilsen Sparks
Lecture and Fellowship Coordinator
(See address above.)

THE AUSTRALIAN NATIONAL UNIVERSITY [344]

Humanities Research Centre, RSHA
A.D. Hope Building, No. 14
Union Court ANU Campus
Canberra, ACT 0200 Australia
(61) 2 612 54357
Fax: (61) 2 612 51380
E-mail: colette.gilmour@anu.edu.au
Web Site: hrc.anu.edu.au

FOUNDED: 1973

AREAS OF INTEREST:
European thought and culture, their influence overseas, any area of research in the humanities (broadly interpreted), and human rights.

NAME(S) OF PROGRAMS:
- **Visiting Fellowships**

TYPE:
Conferences/seminars; Fellowships. Visiting Fellowships are offered with a grant, without a grant or with a partial grant.

YEAR PROGRAM STARTED: 1973

PURPOSE:
To stimulate research in the humanities throughout Australia.

LEGAL BASIS:
Integral part of the Australian National University, Research School of Humanities.

ELIGIBILITY:
Applicants are usually established academics and must have a higher degree. Relevance of project proposed to research platforms, publications.

FINANCIAL DATA:
Visiting Fellowships provide accommodation for up to 60 days plus airfare.

Total amount of support: Up to $150,000 (AUD) annually.

NO. AWARDS: Approximately 12 to 18.

APPLICATION INFO:
Application form, curriculum vitae, publications and three reports from referees are required.

Duration: Up to 60 days.

Deadline: Late February. Award announcement around June.

PUBLICATIONS:
Annual report; descriptive brochure; journal; application guidelines; forms and HRC bulletin.

ADDRESS INQUIRIES TO:
Colette Gilmour, Administrator
(See address above.)

JOHN CARTER BROWN LIBRARY

Brown University
94 George Street
Providence, RI 02906
(401) 863-2725
Fax: (401) 863-3477
E-mail: jcb-fellowships@brown.edu
Web Site: www.jcbl.org

TYPE:
Fellowships. The John Carter Brown Library (JCB), an independently funded institution for advanced research at Brown University, contains one of the world's premier collections of primary materials related to the discovery, exploration, and settlement of the New World to 1825, including books, maps, newspapers and other printed objects.

The Library offers both Short-term and Long-term Fellowships.

See entry 570 for full listing.

CANADIAN FEDERATION FOR THE HUMANITIES AND SOCIAL SCIENCES

275 Bank Street, Suite 300
Ottawa ON K2P 2L6 Canada
(613) 238-6112 ext. 352
Fax: (613) 238-6114
E-mail: aspp-paes@ideas-idees.ca
Web Site: www.ideas-idees.ca

TYPE:
Grants-in-aid. Grants to support the publication of scholarly books in the social sciences and humanities.

See entry 1795 for full listing.

CANADIAN INSTITUTE IN GREECE/L'INSTITUT CANADIEN EN GRECE [345]

330 Albert Street
Waterloo ON N2L 3T8 Canada
(519) 886-4428
E-mail: gschaus@wlu.ca
Web Site: www.cig-icg.gr

FOUNDED: 1974

AREAS OF INTEREST:
Modern Greek, classical languages and literatures, history, archaeology, history of art and music.

NAME(S) OF PROGRAMS:
- **Elizabeth Alfoldi-Rosenbaum Fellowship**
- **Franz and Neda Leipen Fellowship**
- **Homer and Dorothy Thompson Fellowship**

TYPE:
Fellowships. Intended to support the graduate work of a person who needs to study in Greece.

YEAR PROGRAM STARTED: 1974

PURPOSE:
To promote the study of classical languages and literatures, history, archaeology, history of art and music in Greece.

LEGAL BASIS:
Incorporated in Canada and Greece.

ELIGIBILITY:
Open to Canadian citizens or landed immigrants.

FINANCIAL DATA:
Amount of support per award: $8,000 (CAN) plus housing at the Institute.

Total amount of support: Varies each year.

NO. MOST RECENT APPLICANTS: 2 to 3.

NO. AWARDS: 1.

APPLICATION INFO:
Applicants must write, enclosing a curriculum vitae and an outline of the proposed research. Applicants must also arrange for three referees to send letters to the Canadian address.

Duration: Nine months.

Deadline: March 1. All fellowships are not offered every year.

PUBLICATIONS:
CIG Bulletin, semi-annually.

STAFF:
David Rupp, Director
Jonathan Tomlinson, Assistant Director

ADDRESS INQUIRIES TO:
E-mail: cig-icg@cig-icg.gr

CENTER FOR HELLENIC STUDIES [346]

3100 Whitehaven Street, N.W.
Washington, DC 20008
(202) 745-4400
Fax: (202) 797-1540
E-mail: chs@chs.harvard.edu
fellowships@chs.harvard.edu
Web Site: www.chs.harvard.edu

FOUNDED: 1961

AREAS OF INTEREST:
Postdoctoral ancient Greek studies.

TYPE:
Fellowships; Residencies; Visiting scholars. The Center offers Residential Fellowships to scholars working on various aspects of ancient Greek civilization. Eligible fields of research include archaeology, art history, epigraphy, history, literary criticism, philology, philosophy, pedagogical applications and interdisciplinary research.

YEAR PROGRAM STARTED: 1961

PURPOSE:
To encourage research in Hellenic studies.

LEGAL BASIS:
A unit of Harvard University.

ELIGIBILITY:
Investigators holding a Ph.D. degree or equivalent are eligible to apply. Professional competence in ancient Greek, as evidenced by publication, is essential.

FINANCIAL DATA:
Residential fellowships provide a stipend (maximum $17,000) plus lodging. Travel and research assistance available ($1,000).

CO-OP FUNDING PROGRAMS: Joint Fellowships with German Archaeological Institute.

NO. MOST RECENT APPLICANTS: 79.

NO. AWARDS: CHS/DAI Joint Fellowships: 2; Residential Fellowships: 17 semester.

APPLICATION INFO:
Official application materials are available on the web site.

Duration: Support is available for a nine-month period beginning September 1 and ending May 31. Fellowships are available for an 18-week period in the spring or the fall.

Deadline: October.

PUBLICATIONS:
Application form and guidelines.

DIRECTORS:
Gregory Nagy

ADDRESS INQUIRIES TO:
Fellowships and Curricular Development
(See address above.)

CENTER FOR MEDIEVAL AND RENAISSANCE STUDIES [347]

University of California, Los Angeles
302 Royce Hall
Box 951485
Los Angeles, CA 90095-1485
(310) 825-1880
Fax: (310) 825-0655
E-mail: cmrs@humnet.ucla.edu
Web Site: www.cmrs.ucla.edu

FOUNDED: 1963

AREAS OF INTEREST:
All aspects related to the Medieval and Renaissance periods.

NAME(S) OF PROGRAMS:
- **Ahmanson Research Fellowships for the Study of Medieval and Renaissance Books and Manuscripts**
- **CMRS Travel Grants**
- **Research Assistantships in Medieval and Renaissance Studies**
- **The George T. and Margaret W. Romani Fellowship**
- **Lynn and Maude White Fellowship**

TYPE:
Assistantships; Awards/prizes; Conferences/seminars; Fellowships; Project/program grants; Research grants; Travel grants; Visiting scholars.

PURPOSE:
To promote interdisciplinary and cross-cultural studies of modern civilization in its formative period between the fourth and mid-17th centuries and to provide added research opportunities, facilities and assistance.

LEGAL BASIS:
Nonprofit university research organization.

ELIGIBILITY:
For the Ahmanson Research Fellowships, graduate students or scholars holding a Ph.D. (or the foreign equivalent) who are engaged in graduate-level, postdoctoral or independent research are invited to apply.

For the CMRS Travel Grants, applicant must be a UCLA graduate student attending conferences, symposia or meetings of professional organizations to present research papers on any topic in the field of Medieval and Renaissance Studies.

For Research Assistantships, the applicant must expect to be a registered graduate student at UCLA and must have the goal of obtaining a Ph.D. in the field of Medieval and Renaissance Studies.

For Romani Fellowship, students must be nominated by their academic departments, pursuing studies in an aspect of the Middle Ages or Renaissance under mentorship of an active CMRS faculty member.

For the Lynn and Maude White Fellowship, the applicant must be a graduate student advanced to candidacy for the Ph.D. at UCLA in a department associated with the Center for Medieval and Renaissance Studies.

FINANCIAL DATA:
Amount of support per award: Ahmanson Research Fellowships: A stipend of $2,500 per month for fellowships lasting up to three months; CMRS Travel Grants: Varies; Romani Fellowship: $20,000 per year; Lynn and Maude White Fellowship: $15,000.

CO-OP FUNDING PROGRAMS: Ahmanson Research Fellowships are offered through the generosity of the Ahmanson Foundation, the UCLA Center for Medieval and Renaissance Studies (CMRS) and the UCLA Library Special Collections (LSC).

NO. AWARDS: CMRS Travel Grants: Varies; Research Assistantships: 3; Romani Fellowship and Lynn and Maude White Fellowship: 1 every other year.

APPLICATION INFO:
For the Ahmanson Research Fellowships, the application should include a cover letter, a curriculum vitae, an outline of research and special collections to be used (two pages maximum), dates to be spent in residence, and two letters of recommendation from faculty or other scholars familiar with the research project. Application materials may be submitted by e-mail (PDF format preferred) to the e-mail address above or to the postal address above, Attention: Ahmanson Fellowships.

For CMRS Travel Grants, submit letter of request with conference or meeting name, date and place; title of paper or research project being presented; travel expense budget; and conference program.

For Research Assistantships, applicant must submit a curriculum vitae, transcripts, statement of purpose and three letters of recommendation.

For the Romani Fellowship, applicant must be nominated by department, pursuing study in Middle Ages or Renaissance topic, under CMRS faculty member mentorship in three categories: (1) graduate students newly admitted to UCLA; (2) continuing UCLA graduate students and; (3) graduate or postdoctoral students from other universities who have been invited to study at UCLA for a full academic year.

For the Lynn and Maude White Fellowship, applicant must submit a curriculum vitae, a research proposal, three current letters of recommendation and a letter from the student's dissertation director.

Duration: Ahmanson Research Fellowships: Up to three months. Research Assistantships: Nine months, October through June annually. Lynn and Maude White Fellowship: One year.

Deadline: Ahmanson Research Fellowships: Applications are due March 1 for fellowships to be taken within the 12-month period beginning July 1. Research Assistantships and Lynn and Maude White Fellowship: Early April with announcement in May.

PUBLICATIONS:
Viator, annual journal; *Comitatus*, graduate journal; *Cursor Mundi*, book series.

STAFF:
Massimo Ciavolella, Director
Karen E. Burgess, Assistant Director
Benay Furtivo, Administrative Analyst
Brett Landenberger, Programmer Analyst
Blair Sullivan, Publications Director
Sasha Wadman, Program Coordinator

ADDRESS INQUIRIES TO:
Karen E. Burgess, Assistant Director
(See address above.)

CENTER FOR 17TH AND 18TH CENTURY STUDIES [348]

University of California, Los Angeles
10745 Dickson Plaza, 310 Royce Hall
Los Angeles, CA 90095-1404
(310) 206-8552
Fax: (310) 206-8577
E-mail: c1718cs@humnet.ucla.edu
Web Site: www.1718.ucla.edu/research/

FOUNDED: 1985

AREAS OF INTEREST:
England between 1640 and 1830 (history, language and literature, religion and theology), Oscar Wilde and the 1890s, and modern fine printing.

NAME(S) OF PROGRAMS:
- **Clark Predoctoral Fellowships**

TYPE:
Fellowships. Offered for three consecutive months during the period July 1 through June 30 to registered University of California doctoral candidates whose dissertation project is on a specific subject relevant to the collections and interests of the Clark Library.

YEAR PROGRAM STARTED: 1990

PURPOSE:
To provide support for research in the humanities.

LEGAL BASIS:
University.

ELIGIBILITY:
Advanced, registered University of California doctoral candidates are eligible.

GEOG. RESTRICTIONS: California.

FINANCIAL DATA:
Amount of support per award: $2,500 per month for one to three months.

Total amount of support: $7,500.

APPLICATION INFO:
Applicants must submit:
(1) a curriculum vitae (maximum of two pages);
(2) a bibliography of scholarly works (published and unpublished) and;
(3) a statement of research plans (maximum 1,000 words, double-spaced).

In addition to the information provided on the application form, applicants must submit three scholarly references with required reference cover sheets.

Duration: Three months. Nonrenewable.

Deadline: February 1 of each year.

PUBLICATIONS:
Application guidelines; brochure on the Center and Library and its holdings; biennial newsletters; proceedings of conferences.

OFFICERS:
Candis Snoddy, Assistant Director

ADDRESS INQUIRIES TO:
Myrna Ortiz, Fellowship Coordinator
(See address above.)

CENTER FOR 17TH AND 18TH CENTURY STUDIES [349]

University of California, Los Angeles
10745 Dickson Plaza, 310 Royce Hall
Los Angeles, CA 90095-1404
(310) 206-8552
Fax: (310) 206-8577
E-mail: c1718cs@humnet.ucla.edu
Web Site: www.1718.ucla.edu/research/

FOUNDED: 1985

AREAS OF INTEREST:
England between 1640 and 1750 (history, language and literature, religion and theology), Oscar Wilde and the 1890s, and modern fine printing.

NAME(S) OF PROGRAMS:
- **ASECS/Clark Library Fellowships**

TYPE:
Fellowships. Postdoctoral fellowships for research in residence for a period of one month any time from July 1 through June 30 at the William Andrews Clark Memorial Library on a project in The Restoration or 18th century.

YEAR PROGRAM STARTED: 1985

PURPOSE:
To provide support for research in the humanities.

LEGAL BASIS:
University.

ELIGIBILITY:
Candidates must:
(1) have received the Doctorate prior to appointment;
(2) be members in good standing of the American Society for Eighteenth-Century Studies and;
(3) be working on a project in The Restoration or the eighteenth century.

FINANCIAL DATA:
Amount of support per award: $2,500 for one month.

APPLICATION INFO:
Application information may be obtained from the Center.

Duration: One month. Nonrenewable.

Deadline: February 1 of each year.

PUBLICATIONS:
Application guidelines; brochure on the Center and Library and its holdings; biennial newsletters; proceedings of conferences.

OFFICERS:
Candis Snoddy, Assistant Director

ADDRESS INQUIRIES TO:
Myrna Ortiz, Fellowship Coordinator
(See address above.)

CENTER FOR 17TH AND 18TH CENTURY STUDIES [350]

University of California, Los Angeles
10745 Dickson Plaza, 310 Royce Hall
Los Angeles, CA 90095-1404
(310) 206-8552
Fax: (310) 206-8577
E-mail: c1718cs@humnet.ucla.edu
Web Site: www.1718.ucla.edu/research/

FOUNDED: 1985

AREAS OF INTEREST:
England between 1640 and 1830 (history, language and literature, religion and theology), Oscar Wilde and the 1890s, and modern fine printing.

NAME(S) OF PROGRAMS:
- **Ahmanson and Getty Postdoctoral Fellowships**

TYPE:
Fellowships. With the support of the Ahmanson Foundation of Los Angeles and the J. Paul Getty Trust, the UCLA Center for 17th- and 18th-Century Studies and the William Andrews Clark Memorial Library have a theme-based fellowship program to encourage the participation of junior scholars in the Center's cross-disciplinary, comparative research projects. The major theme for a given year is announced the preceding fall.

Participating fellows will be expected to make a substantive contribution to program seminars.

YEAR PROGRAM STARTED: 1992

PURPOSE:
To provide support for research in the humanities.

LEGAL BASIS:
University.

ELIGIBILITY:
Candidates must have received their Ph.D. in the last six years prior to application and be engaged in research pertaining to the theme.

FINANCIAL DATA:
Amount of support per award: Stipend of $43,692 plus paid medical benefits for scholar and dependents for the academic year.

APPLICATION INFO:
Applicants must submit:
(1) a curriculum vitae (maximum of two pages);
(2) a bibliography of scholarly works (published and unpublished) and;
(3) a statement of research plans (maximum 1,000 words, double-spaced).

In addition to the information provided on the application form, applicants must submit three scholarly references with required reference cover sheets.

Duration: Three academic quarters. Nonrenewable.

Deadline: February 1 of each year preceding the award.

PUBLICATIONS:
Application guidelines; brochure on the Center and Library and its holdings; fellowships brochure; biennial newsletters; proceedings of conferences.

OFFICERS:
Candis Snoddy, Assistant Director

ADDRESS INQUIRIES TO:
Myrna Ortiz, Fellowship Coordinator
(See address above.)

CENTER FOR 17TH AND 18TH CENTURY STUDIES [351]

University of California, Los Angeles
405 Hilgard Avenue, 310 Royce Hall
Los Angeles, CA 90095-1404
(310) 206-8552
Fax: (310) 206-8577
E-mail: c1718cs@humnet.ucla.edu
Web Site: www.1718.ucla.edu/research/

FOUNDED: 1985

AREAS OF INTEREST:
England between 1640 and 1830 (history, language and literature, religion and theology), Oscar Wilde and the 1890s, and modern fine printing.

NAME(S) OF PROGRAMS:
- **Short-Term Research Fellowships**

TYPE:
Fellowships. Short-term (one to three months) postdoctoral fellowships for research in residence for any period of the year (July 1 through June 30) at the William Andrews Clark Memorial Library on specific subjects relevant to the collections and interests of the Library.

YEAR PROGRAM STARTED: 1985

PURPOSE:
To provide support for research in the humanities.

LEGAL BASIS:
University.

ELIGIBILITY:
Candidates must have received the Doctorate prior to appointment. Preference will be given to applicants outside the southern California area.

FINANCIAL DATA:
Amount of support per award: $2,500 per month.

Total amount of support: Varies.

NO. AWARDS: Varies.

APPLICATION INFO:
Application information may be obtained from the Center.

Duration: One to three months. Nonrenewable.

Deadline: February 1 of each year.

PUBLICATIONS:
Application guidelines; brochure on the Center and Library and its holdings; biennial newsletters; proceedings of conferences.

OFFICERS:
Candis Snoddy, Assistant Director

ADDRESS INQUIRIES TO:
Myrna Ortiz, Fellowship Coordinator
(See address above.)

CENTER FOR THE HUMANITIES [352]

Mellon Postdoctoral Fellowship Program
Wesleyan University
95 Pearl Street
Middletown, CT 06459-0069
(860) 685-3044
Fax: (860) 685-2171
E-mail: esavage@wesleyan.edu
Web Site: www.wesleyan.edu/humanities

FOUNDED: 1959

AREAS OF INTEREST:
The Center aims to explore fresh and vital aspects of the humanities, to realize an interdisciplinary response to human problems and to generate new possibilities for curricular reform. In fulfilling these aims, the Center must also examine the assumptions that underlie academic disciplines and humanistic theories. It must encourage research as well as the fundamental discourse of teachers and students.

NAME(S) OF PROGRAMS:
- **Andrew W. Mellon Postdoctoral Fellowship**

TYPE:
Fellowships. The aims of the Center are reflected in its constituency which includes scholars, artists, public figures and students. Fellows range in age and achievement from undergraduates to the most eminent humanists. Departments at Wesleyan University participating in the Center include Classics, Modern Languages and Literatures, English, the College of Letters, Philosophy, History, Religion, Anthropology, Psychology and the Fine Arts.

PURPOSE:
To promote advanced study and research in the humanities, arts and qualitative social sciences; to provide scholars who have lately completed their Ph.Ds. with free time to further their own work in a cross-disciplinary setting, and to associate them with a distinguished faculty.

LEGAL BASIS:
Grant from Andrew W. Mellon Foundation to Wesleyan University.

ELIGIBILITY:
Scholars who have received their Ph.D. degree after June 2011 in any field of inquiry in the humanities or humanistic social sciences - broadly conceived - are invited to apply.

Fellows will be expected to participate in the lectures, colloquia and discussion groups that are organized each semester around a specific theme chosen for its theoretical interest and its pertinence to crucial problems in related disciplines of the humanities, the qualitative social sciences or the arts. Additional duties of the fellows will be to teach one course and to give one public lecture.

Fellow must reside in Middletown, CT for tenure of fellowship.

FINANCIAL DATA:
Amount of support per award: $40,000.

CO-OP FUNDING PROGRAMS: Andrew W. Mellon Foundation.

NO. MOST RECENT APPLICANTS: 250.

NO. AWARDS: 1 to 2 each year.

APPLICATION INFO:
There is no official application form. Applications should include:
(1) a letter from the applicant, including a statement of current research interests and a brief proposal for a one-semester undergraduate course related to the Center for the Humanities theme;
(2) a full curriculum vitae;
(3) three letters of recommendation and;
(4) copies of published work, extracts from the dissertation, or drafts of work in progress (not to exceed 25 pages).

Duration: Two years.

PUBLICATIONS:
Brochure.

ADDRESS INQUIRIES TO:
Ethan Kleinberg, Director
(See address above.)

CORNELL UNIVERSITY [353]

Society for the Humanities
A.D. White House
27 East Avenue
Ithaca, NY 14853-1101
(607) 255-9274
(607) 255-4086
Fax: (607) 255-1422
E-mail: humctr-mailbox@cornell.edu
Web Site: www.arts.cornell.edu/sochum

FOUNDED: 1966

AREAS OF INTEREST:
Postdoctoral fellowships in the humanities.

NAME(S) OF PROGRAMS:
- **Mellon Postdoctoral Fellowships**

TYPE:
Fellowships. Postdoctoral teaching-research fellowships in the humanities, each awarded for a two-year period. While in residence at Cornell, postdoctoral fellows hold department affiliation and have limited teaching duties and the opportunity for scholarly work.

PURPOSE:
To encourage the academic growth of promising humanists with recent Ph.D. degrees.

LEGAL BASIS:
University.

ELIGIBILITY:
Applicants who will receive the Ph.D. degree by June 30 of the beginning program year are eligible to apply. Such applicants must include a letter of confirmation.

FINANCIAL DATA:
Fellows receive stipend while in residence.

Amount of support per award: $50,000 per year.

Total amount of support: Varies.

CO-OP FUNDING PROGRAMS: Funded by a grant from the Andrew W. Mellon Foundation.

NO. AWARDS: 2 for the year 2016.

APPLICATION INFO:
Application procedures are found on the web site.

If the applicant does not have a Ph.D. in hand at the time of application, a letter of confirmation must be received from applicant's committee chair or department stating that applicant will have the Ph.D. degree before the term of the fellowship begins on July 1 of the beginning program year. Faxed applications will not be accepted.

Duration: Two years.

ADDRESS INQUIRIES TO:
Emily Parsons, Program Administrator
Mellon Postdoctoral Fellowships
(See address above.)

CORNELL UNIVERSITY [354]

Society for the Humanities
A.D. White House
27 East Avenue
Ithaca, NY 14853-1101
(607) 255-9274
(607) 255-4086
Fax: (607) 255-1422
E-mail: humctr@cornell.edu
Web Site: www.arts.cornell.edu/sochum/society_fellowships.html

FOUNDED: 1966

AREAS OF INTEREST:
Humanities studies.

NAME(S) OF PROGRAMS:
- **Society for the Humanities Fellowships**

TYPE:
Fellowships. Yearly fellowships with a new focal theme each year. Fellows include scholars from other universities and members of the Cornell faculty released from regular duties.

The Focal Theme for 2017-18: Corruption.

PURPOSE:
To support research and encourage imaginative teaching in the humanities.

LEGAL BASIS:
University.

ELIGIBILITY:
Applicants must have received the Ph.D. degree before January 1 of the year of their application. They must have one or more years of teaching experience, which may include teaching as a graduate student. Fellows should be working on topics related to the year's theme. Their approach to the humanities should be broad enough to appeal to students and scholars in several humanistic disciplines.

FINANCIAL DATA:
Fellows receive a stipend and spend most of their time in research and writing but are encouraged to offer an informal seminar related to their research. Applicants living outside North America are eligible for an additional $2,000 to assist with travel costs.

Amount of support per award: $50,000.

Total amount of support: Varies.

NO. MOST RECENT APPLICANTS: 150.

NO. AWARDS: 6 to 8 each year.

APPLICATION INFO:
Candidates should inform the Society of their intention to apply. The following materials must be submitted through the application link on the Society's web site:
(1) a curriculum vitae and a copy of one scholarly paper (no more than 35 pages in length);
(2) a one-page abstract and a detailed statement of the research project the applicant would like to pursue during the term of the fellowship (1,000 to 3,000 words);
(3) a two-page proposal for a seminar related to the applicant's research and;
(4) two letters of recommendation from senior colleagues to whom candidates should send their research proposal and teaching proposal.

Referees should send their letters of recommendation directly to the Society before the closing date. Faxed applications will not be accepted.

Duration: One academic year.

Deadline: Application materials, including letters of recommendation, must be submitted on or before October 1 of the year prior to the beginning of the fellowship. Awards are announced by the end of December of that year of application.

PUBLICATIONS:
Brochure.

ADDRESS INQUIRIES TO:
Emily Parsons, Program Administrator
Society for the Humanities
(See address above.)

*SPECIAL STIPULATIONS:
Fellows spend their time in research and writing, participate in the weekly Fellows Seminar, and offer one seminar related to their research.

CULTURAL SERVICES OF THE FRENCH EMBASSY

972 Fifth Avenue
New York, NY 10075
(212) 439-1463
Fax: (212) 439-1455
E-mail: puf.scac@ambafrance-us.org
Web Site: face-foundation.org

TYPE:
Project/program grants; Research grants. Grants provided by this Fund support research and graduate education partnerships between French and American universities with emphasis placed on novel, innovative and interdisciplinary projects when relevant.

See entry 892 for full listing.

GLADYS KRIEBLE DELMAS FOUNDATION [355]

275 Madison Avenue, 33rd Floor
New York, NY 10016-1101
(212) 687-0011
Fax: (212) 687-1470
E-mail: info@delmas.org
Web Site: www.delmas.org

FOUNDED: 1976

AREAS OF INTEREST:
Humanities, research libraries, performing arts and research in the history and culture of Venice and the Veneto.

NAME(S) OF PROGRAMS:
- **Humanities Program**
- **Performing Arts Program**
- **Research Library Program**
- **Venetian Research Program**

TYPE:
Fellowships; General operating grants; Project/program grants; Research grants.

YEAR PROGRAM STARTED: 1977

PURPOSE:
To provide grants for research projects in Venice and the Veneto; to support performing arts organizations in New York and research libraries and humanities projects.

LEGAL BASIS:
Private foundation.

ELIGIBILITY:
For Venetian Research Program, applicants must be U.S. citizens or permanent residents at the predoctoral and postdoctoral levels. If graduate students, applicants must have fulfilled all doctoral requirements except for completion of the dissertation at the time of application.

GEOG. RESTRICTIONS: Performing Arts Grants to New York City only.

FINANCIAL DATA:
Amount of support per award: Up to $20,000.

NO. MOST RECENT APPLICANTS: 300.

NO. AWARDS: 150.

REPRESENTATIVE AWARDS:
$210,000 over three years to the New York Public Library for the Performing Arts; $25,000 to the American Philological Association for the Classical Atlas Project; $4,200 for "Theatrical Dance in 17th Century Venetian Opera;" $7,000 for "Pseudo-Dionysius and the Mathematical Culture of 16th Century Venice."

APPLICATION INFO:
Contact the Foundation.

Duration: Varies.

Deadline: Venetian Research Program: December 15.

DISTRICT OF COLUMBIA COMMISSION ON THE ARTS AND HUMANITIES

200 I Street, S.E.
Washington, DC 20003
(202) 724-5613
Fax: (202) 727-4135
TDD: (202) 727-3148
E-mail: steven.mazzola@dc.gov
Web Site: www.dcarts.dc.gov

TYPE:
Awards/prizes; Capital grants; Challenge/matching grants; Conferences/seminars; Exchange programs; Fellowships; General operating grants; Grants-in-aid; Project/program grants; Research grants; Residencies. Services provided to arts institutions and individual artists including inquiry services, technical assistance and funding.

See entry 434 for full listing.

DUMBARTON OAKS [356]

1703 32nd Street, N.W.
Washington, DC 20007
(202) 339-6401
(202) 339-6413
Fax: (202) 339-6416
E-mail: FellowshipPrograms@doaks.org
Web Site: www.doaks.org

FOUNDED: 1940

AREAS OF INTEREST:
Archaeology, gardens, history, history of art, philosophy, landscape, language, literature, religion and theology.

NAME(S) OF PROGRAMS:

- **Fellowships and Project Grants in Byzantine Studies, Pre-Columbian Studies and Garden and Landscape Studies**

TYPE:
Awards/prizes; Fellowships; Internships; Project/program grants; Residencies. Residential fellowships and project support in the area of Byzantine studies (including related aspects of late Roman, early Christian, western medieval, Slavic and Near Eastern studies), Pre-Columbian studies (of Mexico, Central America and Andean South America), and Garden and Landscape studies (including garden history, landscape architecture and related disciplines).

YEAR PROGRAM STARTED: 1941

PURPOSE:
To promote research in Byzantine studies, Pre-Columbian studies, and Garden and Landscape studies.

LEGAL BASIS:
Research institute affiliated with Harvard University.

ELIGIBILITY:
Fellowships are awarded on the basis of demonstrated scholarly ability and preparation of the candidate, including knowledge of the requisite languages, interest and value of the study or project and the project's relevance to the resources of Dumbarton Oaks.

Junior Fellowships are awarded to degree candidates who at the time of application have fulfilled all preliminary requirements for a Ph.D. or appropriate final degree and plan to work on a dissertation or final project at Dumbarton Oaks under the direction of a faculty member from their own university.

Fellowships are awarded to scholars who hold a Ph.D. or appropriate final degree or have established themselves in their field and wish to pursue their own research. Graduate students who expect to have a Ph.D. prior to taking up residence at Dumbarton Oaks may also apply.

Summer Fellowships are awarded to Byzantine, Pre-Columbian, or Garden and Landscape scholars on any level beyond the first year of graduate (post-Baccalaureate) study.

FINANCIAL DATA:
Fellowships and Junior Fellowships: Award includes stipend, housing (with the exception of residents from the greater Washington, DC metropolitan area), a research expense allowance, lunch on weekdays, and a health insurance contribution from Dumbarton Oaks. Travel expense reimbursement may be provided for Fellows and Junior Fellows if support cannot be obtained from other sources.

Summer Fellowships: Besides maintenance allowance, support includes housing in a Dumbarton Oaks apartment, lunch on weekdays, Dumbarton Oaks's health insurance contribution, and travel expense reimbursement if other travel support cannot be obtained. No housing allowances or dependents' allowances for families are available in the summer.

Amount of support per award: Support includes a stipend of approximately $21,000 for a Junior Fellow; $35,000 stipend for a Fellow for the full academic year.

A maintenance allowance of $250 per week for Summer Fellowships.

NO. MOST RECENT APPLICANTS: 250.

NO. AWARDS: 50 Fellowships (23 in Byzantine Studies, 16 in Garden and Landscape Studies and 11 in Pre-Columbian Studies); 8 Project Grants for the year 2015-16.

APPLICATION INFO:
Applications must be submitted electronically. A brochure is available upon request to the Director's office.

Duration: Fellowships are usually awarded for a full academic year (mid-September to mid-May); however, requests for a single term of support (mid-September to early January or mid-January to mid-May) are also considered. Summer Fellowships are awarded for periods of seven to nine weeks, beginning early June and ending early August.

Deadline: Varies. Contact Dumbarton Oaks for detailed information.

PUBLICATIONS:
Fellowship and Project award brochure; application guidelines.

OFFICERS:
Jan Ziolkowski, Director

ADDRESS INQUIRIES TO:
E-mail specific program:
Byzantine@doaks.org
Pre-Columbian@doaks.org or
Landscape@doaks.org

*SPECIAL STIPULATIONS:
Fellowships are tenable only for full-time resident work.

DUQUESNE UNIVERSITY, DEPARTMENT OF PHILOSOPHY [357]

600 Forbes Avenue
Pittsburgh, PA 15282
(412) 396-6500
Fax: (412) 396-5353
E-mail: polansky@duq.edu
Web Site: www.duq.edu/academics/schools/liberal-arts/graduate-school/programs/philosophy

FOUNDED: 1878

AREAS OF INTEREST:
The Ph.D. program in the Department of Philosophy at Duquesne University emphasizes continental philosophy, i.e., phenomenology and 20th century French and German philosophy, as well as the history of philosophy.

NAME(S) OF PROGRAMS:

- **Duquesne University Graduate Assistantship**

TYPE:
Assistantships; Conferences/seminars; Exchange programs. Philosophy assistantship.

PURPOSE:
To provide a stipend to enable students to obtain a Ph.D. in philosophy.

ELIGIBILITY:
Open to holders of a Bachelor's degree in philosophy, or its equivalent, who have a grade point average of at least 3.7 and an excellent graduate record examination score. Candidates should have knowledge of a second language.

FINANCIAL DATA:
Amount of support per award: Stipend of $17,000 plus all tuition for coursework.

NO. MOST RECENT APPLICANTS: 170.

NO. AWARDS: 17.

APPLICATION INFO:
Applicants must complete an application including a statement of intent and three letters of recommendation, Graduate Record Examination scores and application form and fee, plus test of English as a Foreign Language scores.

Duration: Four years.

Deadline: Ph.D. January 15; M.A. March 1.

ADDRESS INQUIRIES TO:
Ronald Polansky, Chairperson
(See address above.)

EARTHWATCH INSTITUTE

114 Western Avenue
Boston, MA 02134
(800) 776-0188
Fax: (978) 461-2332
E-mail: fellowshipawards@earthwatch.org
Web Site: www.earthwatch.org/education

TYPE:
Fellowships. Teachers in grades K-12 apply for seven- to 10-day Earthwatch expedition

fellowships that take place during the summer. Earthwatch selects over 50 teachers from all subject areas across the U.S. to assist scientists on expeditions by collecting data on climate change and sustainable resource management. Funding for these fellowships comes from a variety of donors, e.g., individuals, corporations, family foundations, community organizations and nonprofits. On their return from the field, these teachers must develop a lesson or action plan that ties their experience back to their classroom or community.

See entry 1765 for full listing.

THE FIELDSTONE FOUNDATION [358]

14 Corporate Plaza, Suite 100
Newport Beach, CA 92660
(949) 873-2717
Fax: (949) 515-8520
E-mail: janinem@fieldstonefoundation.org
Web Site: www.fieldstonefoundation.org

FOUNDED: 1983

AREAS OF INTEREST:
Educational, humanitarian, and Christian ministries and cultural arts.

CONSULTING OR VOLUNTEER SERVICES:
Nonprofit executive leadership training and peer coaching.

TYPE:
Challenge/matching grants; General operating grants; Project/program grants.

YEAR PROGRAM STARTED: 1983

PURPOSE:
To improve the quality of life for children and families.

ELIGIBILITY:
Eligible organizations must be IRS 501(c)(3) tax-exempt. The Foundation does not fund grants to individuals or churches. Funding by invitation only.

GEOG. RESTRICTIONS: Orange and San Diego counties, California.

FINANCIAL DATA:
Amount of support per award: Varies.
Total amount of support: Varies.

NO. AWARDS: 44.

APPLICATION INFO:
The application must include a copy of the IRS tax determination letter. Proposals by invitation only. Foundation staff will initiate all grant considerations.

Unsolicited requests will not be accepted.

Duration: One year.

STAFF:
Heather Cova
Robin Stropko

ADDRESS INQUIRIES TO:
Janine Mason, Executive Director
(See address above.)

*PLEASE NOTE:
Unsolicited requests will not be considered.

THE FOLGER INSTITUTE [359]

Folger Shakespeare Library
201 East Capitol Street, S.E.
Washington, DC 20003-1094
(202) 675-0333
Fax: (202) 544-4623
E-mail: institute@folger.edu
Web Site: www.folger.edu/institute

FOUNDED: 1970

AREAS OF INTEREST:
Early modern history, literature, political science, art and cultural studies.

NAME(S) OF PROGRAMS:
- **Early Modern Studies**

TYPE:
Conferences/seminars; Grants-in-aid; Internships; Travel grants. Fall and Spring seminars and workshops. Yearlong colloquia. Stipends for institutes. Grants for travel and lodging expenses, according to need, for workshops and seminars.

YEAR PROGRAM STARTED: 1986

PURPOSE:
To advance the teachings and study of the early modern period.

LEGAL BASIS:
Research center at an independent research library.

ELIGIBILITY:
Grants in support of program participation are available to affiliates of the member universities. The Folger Institute does not offer grants-in-aid support of scholars from outside of the consortium.

FINANCIAL DATA:
Amount of support per award: Long-term research fellowship: $50,000 stipend; Short-term research fellowship: $2,500 stipend per month.

APPLICATION INFO:
Application information and forms are available on the web site. Letters of recommendation should be sent to the e-mail address listed above.

Duration: Long-term research fellowship: Six to nine months; Short-term research fellowship: One to three months.

Deadline: Long-term research fellowships: November 1. Short-term fellowships: March 1.

OFFICERS:
Kathleen Lynch, Executive Director
Owen Williams, Assistant Director, Scholarly Programs
Carol Brobeck, Fellowships Administrator

ADDRESS INQUIRIES TO:
Elyse Martin, Program Assistant
(See address above.)

*PLEASE NOTE:
Scholars wishing to apply for long- or short-term fellowships should contact the e-mail address or phone number listed above.

THE GWATHMEY MEMORIAL TRUST [360]

Bank of America Center
VA2-300-12-92
1111 East Main Street
Richmond, VA 23219-3500
(804) 887-8773
E-mail: sarah.kay@ustrust.com
Web Site: www.bankofamerica.com/philanthropic

FOUNDED: 1982

AREAS OF INTEREST:
History, literature, art and architecture, and direct services.

TYPE:
Development grants; Project/program grants.

YEAR PROGRAM STARTED: 1982

ELIGIBILITY:
Grants are made to Virginia institutions and organizations which are tax-exempt 501(c)(3) organizations and operate for charitable, scientific, literary, or educational purposes. Preference is given to specific, well-defined projects and programs whose results can be evaluated.

Grants are not made to private foundations, national or community organizations, or to individuals.

GEOG. RESTRICTIONS: Virginia.

FINANCIAL DATA:
Amount of support per award: $5,000 to $50,000; Average: $15,000 to $20,000.
Total amount of support: Average $650,000 annually.

NO. AWARDS: 30 to 40.

APPLICATION INFO:
All applicants must submit a description of the organization, evidence of the organization's tax-exempt and private foundation status, financial statements, and names and affiliations of the organization's trustees, directors, advisors and principal staff. In addition, a concise description of the project including the needs and anticipated benefits to be met, detailed financial plan, brief biographical background of the person who will conduct or supervise the proposed program, plans for evaluation of the project's results, and covering letter from an official of the organization stating that the organization has formally approved the proposed program are required.

Duration: One year.

Deadline: March 1 and September 1.

PUBLICATIONS:
Guidelines for applicants.

ADDRESS INQUIRIES TO:
Sarah Kay, Vice President, Senior Philanthropic
Relationship Manager
(See address above.)

THE HASTINGS CENTER

21 Malcolm Gordon Road
Garrison, NY 10524
(845) 424-4040
Fax: (845) 424-4545
E-mail: visitors@thehastingscenter.org
Web Site: www.thehastingscenter.org

TYPE:
Residencies; Visiting scholars. Independent study.

See entry 2041 for full listing.

HAWAII STATE FOUNDATION ON CULTURE AND THE ARTS

250 South Hotel Street
Second Floor
Honolulu, HI 96813
(808) 586-0301
Fax: (808) 586-0308
TTY: (808) 586-0740
E-mail: jonathan.johnson@hawaii.gov
Web Site: hawaii.gov/sfca

TYPE:
Project/program grants.

See entry 443 for full listing.

THE GEORGE A. AND ELIZA GARDNER HOWARD FOUNDATION

346 Brook Street
Marston Hall, Room B-9
Providence, RI 02912
(401) 863-2640
Fax: (401) 863-6280
E-mail: howard_foundation@brown.edu
Web Site: www.brown.edu/Howard_Foundation

TYPE:
Fellowships. The Foundation awards a limited number of fellowships each year for independent projects in fields selected on a rotational basis.

See entry 1578 for full listing.

HENRY E. HUNTINGTON LIBRARY AND ART GALLERY [361]

1151 Oxford Road
San Marino, CA 91108
(626) 405-2194
Fax: (626) 449-5703
E-mail: cpowell@huntington.org
Web Site: www.huntington.org

FOUNDED: 1919

AREAS OF INTEREST:
British and American art history, history, literature and history of science.

NAME(S) OF PROGRAMS:
- **Research Awards at the Huntington Library and Art Gallery**

TYPE:
Fellowships; Research grants; Visiting scholars. Grants for studies in American or British literature, history, art history and history of science.

YEAR PROGRAM STARTED: 1927

PURPOSE:
To encourage significant scholarship in the areas of the Huntington collections.

LEGAL BASIS:
Private, nonprofit.

ELIGIBILITY:
Persons who have demonstrated unusual abilities as scholars are encouraged to apply. Consideration is given to the value of the candidate's project and the degree to which the Huntington Library will be used. Projects to be used for doctoral dissertations will be considered.

FINANCIAL DATA:
Amount of support per award: Short-term: $3,000 per month; Long-term: $50,000 for the academic year.

Total amount of support: Varies.

NO. MOST RECENT APPLICANTS: Short-term: 325; Long-term: 119.

NO. AWARDS: Short-term: 128; Long-term: 11.

APPLICATION INFO:
Contact the Library.

Duration: Short-term grants: One to five months. Long-term awards: Minimum of nine months.

Deadline: November 15 for commencement on July 1.

IRS I.D.: 95-1644589

OFFICERS:
Laura Trombley, President
Coreen Rodgers, Vice President, Financial Affairs
Randy Shulman, Vice President, Advancement
Laurie Sowd, Vice President, Operations
Susan Turner-Lowe, Vice President, Communications
Catherine Allgor, Director, Education
James Folsom, Director, Botanical Gardens
Steve Hindle, Director, Research
Kevin Salatino, Director, Art Collections
David Zeidberg, Director, Library

TRUSTEES:
Stewart R. Smith, Chairman
Andrew F. Barth
Anne F. Rothenberg
Loren R. Rothschild
Geneva H. Thornton

ADDRESS INQUIRIES TO:
Steve Hindle, Director of Research
(See address above.)

*SPECIAL STIPULATIONS:
Recipients of all fellowships are expected to be in continuous residence at the Huntington.

THE INSTITUTE FOR ADVANCED STUDIES IN THE HUMANITIES [362]

The University of Edinburgh
Hope Park Square
Edinburgh EH8 9NW Scotland
(44) 0131 650 4671
Fax: (44) 0131 651 1176
E-mail: iash@ed.ac.uk
Web Site: www.iash.ed.ac.uk/

FOUNDED: 1969

AREAS OF INTEREST:
Humanities and social science.

CONSULTING OR VOLUNTEER SERVICES:
Institute has connections with and is within easy reach of the National Library of Scotland, the National Archives of Scotland, the Royal Museum of Scotland and the Edinburgh University Library.

NAME(S) OF PROGRAMS:
- **Visiting Research Fellowships**

TYPE:
Fellowships. Visiting Research Fellowships with the use of a private office in the Institute with all the usual research facilities. Recipients of the Fellowships are expected to play a full part in the activities of the Institute.

YEAR PROGRAM STARTED: 1970

PURPOSE:
To further advanced studies in the humanities, broadly conceived.

LEGAL BASIS:
Institution of University of Edinburgh.

ELIGIBILITY:
Applicants should be scholars of established reputation or younger scholars holding a Doctorate or offering equivalent evidence of aptitude for advanced study.

The Election Committee will consider the academic record and the publications of all applicants, their capacity to disseminate their views effectively in public and the likelihood of completing the proposed research by task by the end of the fellowship or shortly afterwards. Students who have not completed their studies for a particular degree are not eligible.

No teaching is required of Fellows in the project, but each Fellow will be expected to make at least one public presentation of his or her research activities.

NO. MOST RECENT APPLICANTS: 21.

NO. AWARDS: Up to 20.

APPLICATION INFO:
Apply online through the Institute web site. The Election Committee will only consider applications accompanied by full documentation and supported by a minimum of two and a maximum of three references. It is the responsibility of each applicant to ensure that their referees submit their reports directly to Edinburgh. Candidates may like to submit a copy of an article or publication relevant to their application. The Institute will not return any documents to applicants.

Duration: Fellowships are tenable for two to six months. Nonrenewable.

Deadline: February 28, 2016. Notification by e-mail by end of April.

PUBLICATIONS:
Application guidelines.

OFFICERS:
Prof. Jo Shaw, Director

ADDRESS INQUIRIES TO:
Prof. Jo Shaw, Director
(See address above.)

*SPECIAL STIPULATIONS:
Fellows, as well as carrying out research, are required to live in or near Edinburgh and will be asked to give one seminar.

INSTITUTE FOR ADVANCED STUDY

One Einstein Drive
Princeton, NJ 08540
(609) 734-8250
Fax: (609) 951-4457
E-mail: donne@ias.edu
Web Site: www.sss.ias.edu

TYPE:
Fellowships; Residencies. Postdoctoral research fellowships at the School of Social Science.

See entry 1801 for full listing.

INSTITUTE FOR HUMANE STUDIES (IHS)

3434 Washington Boulevard, MS 1C5
Arlington, VA 22201
(703) 993-4880
Fax: (703) 993-4890
E-mail: funding@theihs.org
Web Site: www.theihs.org

TYPE:
Fellowships; Research grants. Humane Studies Fellowships cover the fields of the social sciences and humanities.

See entry 1940 for full listing.

MASS HUMANITIES [363]

66 Bridge Street
Northampton, MA 01060-2406
(413) 584-8440
Fax: (413) 584-8454
E-mail: info@masshumanities.org
Web Site: www.masshumanities.org

FOUNDED: 1974

AREAS OF INTEREST:
Humanities and areas of special concern in Massachusetts, historic societies and libraries.

NAME(S) OF PROGRAMS:
- **Project Grants**
- **Public Squared Challenge Grant**
- **Reading and Discussion Grants**
- **Research Inventory Grants**
- **Scholar in Residence Grants**

TYPE:
Project/program grants.

PURPOSE:
To identify and develop major initiatives in areas of special interest or concern.

LEGAL BASIS:
Private, nonprofit corporation.

ELIGIBILITY:
Applicants must be nonprofit organizations. The Foundation does not fund refreshments or indirect costs.

GEOG. RESTRICTIONS: Massachusetts.

FINANCIAL DATA:
Amount of support per award: Varies.

Matching fund requirements: Outright Funds must be matched equally by your organization through cost-sharing.

REPRESENTATIVE AWARDS:
"Shifting Gears: The Changing Meaning of Work in Massachusetts," for study of economic change; "Understanding the AIDS Challenge;" "Knowing Our Place: Humanistic Aspects of Environmental Issues;" "Seeing Through the Media: The Crisis of our Cultural Environment," for studying the impact of the media on American society.

APPLICATION INFO:
Applicants should submit the Foundation's web-based Letter of Inquiry form six weeks before final proposal deadline. Application is an online process.

Duration: Typically one year.

Deadline: Varies.

PUBLICATIONS:
Newsletter; application guidelines; brochure.

STAFF:
David Tebaldi, Executive Director
Pleun Bouricius, Director of Grants and Programs
John Sieracki, Director of Development and Communications
Anne Rogers, Systems Manager
Rose Sackey-Milligan, Program Officer
Melissa Wheaton, Grant Administrator

ADDRESS INQUIRIES TO:
Pleun Bouricius
Director of Grants and Programs
(See address above.)

ALLETTA MORRIS MCBEAN CHARITABLE TRUST [364]

1200 Central Boulevard
Suite B
Brentwood, CA 94513
(925) 516-6212
Fax: (925) 516-4496
E-mail: mcbeanproperties@att.net
Web Site: allettamcbeancharitabletrust.org

FOUNDED: 1986

AREAS OF INTEREST:
Historic and land preservation in and around Newport, RI.

TYPE:
Capital grants; Challenge/matching grants; Endowments; Project/program grants.

YEAR PROGRAM STARTED: 1986

PURPOSE:
To enhance the quality of life in and around Newport and Aquidneck Island, RI.

LEGAL BASIS:
Private charitable trust.

ELIGIBILITY:
Applicants must be tax-exempt organizations.

GEOG. RESTRICTIONS: Aquidneck Island, Rhode Island.

FINANCIAL DATA:
Amount of support per award: $25,000 to $100,000.

Total amount of support: $2,800,000 per year.

Matching fund requirements: Varies.

NO. MOST RECENT APPLICANTS: 20 to 25.

REPRESENTATIVE AWARDS:
$50,000 to Edward King House Senior Citizens Center for building renovations; $6,000 to Lucy's Hearth for kitchen renovation; $250,000 to Newport Performing Arts Center Task Group for acquisition and facade restoration of the opera house.

APPLICATION INFO:
Six formal proposals with budgets are preferred, as well as other sources of funding for project, tax-exempt status and other background material.

Deadline: February 28 and July 31.

IRS I.D.: 94-3019660

OFFICERS:
Donald C. Christ, Chairman
John J. Slocum, Jr., Secretary
Charlene C. Kleiner, Assistant Secretary
Dorienne Farzan
Walter G.D. Reed
Gladys V. Szapary

ADDRESS INQUIRIES TO:
Donald C. Christ, Chairman
Charlene C. Kleiner, Assistant Secretary
(See address above.)

MICHIGAN SOCIETY OF FELLOWS [365]

University of Michigan
0540 Rackham Building
915 East Washington Street
Ann Arbor, MI 48109-1070
(734) 763-1259
E-mail: society.of.fellows@umich.edu
Web Site: www.societyoffellows.umich.edu

FOUNDED: 1970

AREAS OF INTEREST:
All schools and colleges at the University of Michigan.

NAME(S) OF PROGRAMS:
- **Postdoctoral Fellowships in the Humanities and the Arts, Sciences and Professions**

TYPE:
Fellowships. Fellows are appointed as Assistant Professors in appropriate departments and as Postdoctoral Scholars in the Michigan Society of Fellows. They are expected to be in residence in Ann Arbor during the academic years of the fellowship, to teach for the equivalent of one academic year, to participate in the informal intellectual life of the Society, and to devote time to their independent research or artistic projects.

YEAR PROGRAM STARTED: 1970

PURPOSE:
To recognize and support academic and creative excellence in humanities and the arts, the social, physical, and life sciences, and the professions.

LEGAL BASIS:
Nonprofit, tax-exempt organization.

ELIGIBILITY:
Candidates should be near the beginning of their professional careers, but not more than three years beyond completion of their degrees. The Ph.D. degree or comparable professional or artistic degree, received prior to appointment, is required.

Applications from degree candidates and recipients of the Ph.D. from the University of Michigan will not be considered.

FINANCIAL DATA:
Amount of support per award: $55,000 annually plus health benefits for 2016-19 fellowships. $1,500 per year allowance toward travel and research expenses.

CO-OP FUNDING PROGRAMS: Mellon Foundation.

NO. MOST RECENT APPLICANTS: 961 for the year 2015.

NO. AWARDS: 6 each year.

APPLICATION INFO:
Applications will be reviewed by members of the Society of Fellows and by faculty in appropriate University of Michigan departments. Final selection of candidates will be made by the senior fellows of the Society.

Duration: Three years.

Deadline: September 28. Final selections made end of February.

PUBLICATIONS:
Application guidelines.

OFFICERS:
Donald S. Lopez, Jr., Chairperson of Society

*SPECIAL STIPULATIONS:
Fellows are expected to reside in Ann Arbor during the academic years of the fellowship.

NATIONAL ENDOWMENT FOR THE HUMANITIES [366]

The Constitution Center
400 7th Street, S.W.
Washington, DC 20001
(202) 606-8424
Fax: (202) 606-8240
E-mail: info@neh.gov
Web Site: www.neh.gov

FOUNDED: 1965

AREAS OF INTEREST:
Scholarship, research, education and public programs in the humanities. In the act that established the Endowment, the term humanities includes, but is not limited to, the study of history, philosophy, languages, linguistics, literature, archaeology, jurisprudence, the history, theory and criticism of the arts, ethics, comparative religion and those aspects of the social sciences that employ historical or philosophical approaches.

NAME(S) OF PROGRAMS:
- **Research Program**

TYPE:
Research grants. Grants provide support for collaborative research in the preparation for publication of editions, translations and other important works in the humanities and in the

conduct of large or complex interpretive studies including archaeology projects and the humanities studies of science and technology. Grants also support research opportunities offered through independent research centers and scholarly organizations and international research centers.

YEAR PROGRAM STARTED: 1967

PURPOSE:
To provide funding for research and the publication of that research. The work must be in a field of interest to the National Endowment.

LEGAL BASIS:
Federal agency, established by act of Congress: The National Foundation on the Arts and Humanities Act of 1965, Public Law 89-209, as amended.

ELIGIBILITY:
Applicants can be individuals, institutions of higher education, nonprofit professional associations, scholarly societies and other nonprofit organizations.

GEOG. RESTRICTIONS: United States.

FINANCIAL DATA:
Amount of support per award: Varies.
Total amount of support: Varies.

APPLICATION INFO:
Application can be downloaded from the web site.
Duration: Varies.
Deadline: Varies.

PUBLICATIONS:
Annual report; *Grant Programs*; *Humanities Magazine.*

IRS I.D.: 52-1098584

ADDRESS INQUIRIES TO:
Paula Wasley, Public Affairs Specialist
(See address above.)

NATIONAL ENDOWMENT FOR THE HUMANITIES [367]

The Constitution Center
400 7th Street, S.W.
Washington, DC 20001
(202) 606-8424
Fax: (202) 606-8240
E-mail: info@neh.gov
Web Site: www.neh.gov

FOUNDED: 1965

AREAS OF INTEREST:
Scholarship, research, education and public programs in the humanities. In the act that established the Endowment, the term humanities includes, but is not limited to, the study of history, philosophy, languages, linguistics, literature, archaeology, jurisprudence, the history, theory and criticism of the arts, ethics, comparative religion and those aspects of the social sciences that employ historical or philosophical approaches.

NAME(S) OF PROGRAMS:
- **Creating Humanities Communities**
- **Humanities Access Grants**
- **Next Generation Humanities PhD**

TYPE:
Capital grants; Challenge/matching grants; Professorships; Residencies; Visiting scholars. The Office of Challenge Grants offers grants that "challenge" local, state and national institutions to respond to opportunities that exist in this country's humanities ecosystem.

Creating Humanities Communities supports partnerships and collaborations between multiple institutions to seed grassroots humanities infrastructure in incentive states.

Humanities Access Grants funds capacity-building for humanities programs that benefit youth, communities of color and economically disadvantaged populations.

Next Generation Humanities PhD program assists universities and graduate programs in devising new models of doctoral education to transform the understanding of what it means to be a humanities scholar and to promote the integration of the humanities with the public sphere.

YEAR PROGRAM STARTED: 1977

PURPOSE:
To encourage long-range financial and program planning within humanities institutions and organizations; to provide means for humanities organizations and institutions to increase levels and kinds of continuing financial support; to sustain or develop high-quality work within the humanities; to join federal with nonfederal support so that those institutions in which teaching, learning and research of the humanities occur may achieve greater financial stability.

LEGAL BASIS:
Federal agency, established by act of Congress: The National Foundation on the Arts and Humanities Act of 1965, Public Law 89-209, as amended.

ELIGIBILITY:
Nonprofit postsecondary, educational, research or cultural institutions and organizations working within the humanities are eligible for support.

GEOG. RESTRICTIONS: United States.

FINANCIAL DATA:
Amount of support per award: Varies.
Total amount of support: Varies.

REPRESENTATIVE AWARDS:
$75,000 to Lenox Library Association, Lenox, MA, to support construction of a special collections research area, renovation of archival storage facilities, collection preservation, automation of acquisitions, circulation and endowment expansion; $150,000 to Saint Louis University, St. Louis, MO, to support an endowment for Saint Louis University's Center for Medieval and Renaissance Studies that will provide library materials, fellowships and a professorship in Byzantine and classical studies; $125,000 to Historical Society of Cheshire County, Keene, NH, to support renovation and expansion of a new site for a consolidated museum and archival center.

APPLICATION INFO:
Applications can be downloaded from the above web site.
Duration: Varies.
Deadline: Varies.

PUBLICATIONS:
Annual report; *Grant Programs*; *Humanities Magazine.*

IRS I.D.: 52-1098584

ADDRESS INQUIRIES TO:
Paula Wasley, Public Affairs Specialist
(See address above.)

NATIONAL ENDOWMENT FOR THE HUMANITIES [368]

The Constitution Center
400 7th Street, S.W.
Washington, DC 20001
(202) 606-8424
Fax: (202) 606-8240
E-mail: info@neh.gov
Web Site: www.neh.gov

FOUNDED: 1965

AREAS OF INTEREST:
Scholarship, research, education and public programs in the humanities.

NAME(S) OF PROGRAMS:
- **Fellowships**
- **Summer Stipends**

TYPE:
Awards/prizes; Fellowships. Grants provide support for scholars to undertake full-time independent research and writing in the humanities. Grants are available for a maximum of one year and a minimum of six weeks to two months of summer study.

Grants also provide support for historically Black college and university faculty to undertake one year of full-time study leading to a doctoral degree in the humanities with preference given to those individuals who are at the dissertation stage of their work.

YEAR PROGRAM STARTED: 1967

PURPOSE:
To encourage continued research and study in the humanities discipline.

LEGAL BASIS:
Federal agency, established by act of Congress: The National Foundation on the Arts and Humanities Act of 1965, Public Law 89-209, as amended.

GEOG. RESTRICTIONS: United States.

FINANCIAL DATA:
Amount of support per award: Varies.
Total amount of support: Varies.

APPLICATION INFO:
Application can be downloaded from the web site.
Duration: Up to one year.
Deadline: Fellowships: April 26; Summer Stipends: Late September.

PUBLICATIONS:
Annual report; *Grant Programs*; *Humanities Magazine.*

IRS I.D.: 52-1098584

ADDRESS INQUIRIES TO:
Paula Wasley, Public Affairs Specialist
(See address above.)

NATIONAL ENDOWMENT FOR THE HUMANITIES [369]

The Constitution Center
400 7th Street, S.W.
Washington, DC 20001
(202) 606-8424
Fax: (202) 606-8240
E-mail: info@neh.gov
Web Site: www.neh.gov

FOUNDED: 1965

AREAS OF INTEREST:
Scholarship, research, education and public programs in the humanities. In the act that established the Endowment, the term humanities includes, but is not limited to, the

study of history, philosophy, languages, linguistics, literature, archaeology, jurisprudence, the history, theory and criticism of the arts, ethics, comparative religion and those aspects of the social sciences that employ historical or philosophical approaches.

NAME(S) OF PROGRAMS:
- **Seminars and Institutes Program**

TYPE:
Conferences/seminars. Grants support summer seminars and national institutes in the humanities for college and school teachers. These faculty development activities are conducted at colleges and universities across the country. Lists of pending seminars and institutes are available from the program.

YEAR PROGRAM STARTED: 1983

PURPOSE:
To provide opportunities for teachers to study under the direction of a master teacher and distinguished scholar in an area of mutual interest at a college or university during the summer.

LEGAL BASIS:
Federal agency, established by act of Congress: The National Foundation on the Arts and Humanities Act of 1965, Public Law 89-209, as amended.

ELIGIBILITY:
Applicants can be individuals or institutions of higher learning.

GEOG. RESTRICTIONS: United States.

FINANCIAL DATA:
Amount of support per award: Varies.
Total amount of support: Varies.

APPLICATION INFO:
Complete application information can be found online. Participant application forms and instructions can be obtained from seminar directors at the host institutions. Those wishing to participate in seminars should submit their applications to the seminar director. Information about the program is publicized in the fall preceding the summer in question.

Duration: Seminars last four, five, or six weeks, depending on the choice of the director.

Deadline: Late February to early March.

PUBLICATIONS:
Annual report; *Grant Programs*; *Humanities Magazine*.

IRS I.D.: 52-1098584

ADDRESS INQUIRIES TO:
Paula Wasley, Public Affairs Specialist
(See address above.)

NATIONAL ENDOWMENT FOR THE HUMANITIES [370]

The Constitution Center
400 7th Street, S.W.
Washington, DC 20001
(202) 606-8424
Fax: (202) 606-8240
E-mail: info@neh.gov
Web Site: www.neh.gov

FOUNDED: 1965

AREAS OF INTEREST:
Scholarship, research, education and public programs in the humanities. In the act that established the Endowment, the term humanities includes, but is not limited to, the study of history, philosophy, languages, linguistics, literature, archaeology, jurisprudence, the history, theory and criticism of the arts, ethics, comparative religion and those aspects of the social sciences that employ historical or philosophical approaches.

NAME(S) OF PROGRAMS:
- **Preservation and Access**

TYPE:
Project/program grants. Support may be sought to preserve the intellectual content and aid bibliographic control of collections, to compile bibliographies, descriptive catalogs and guides to cultural holdings, to create dictionaries, encyclopedias, databases and other types of research tools and reference works and to stabilize material culture collections through the appropriate housing and storing of objects, improved environmental control and the installation of security, lighting and fire-prevention systems.

Applications may also be submitted for national and regional education and training projects, regional preservation field service programs and research and demonstration projects that are intended to enhance institutional practice and the use of technology for preservation and access.

YEAR PROGRAM STARTED: 1985

PURPOSE:
To advance study in the area indicated.

LEGAL BASIS:
Federal agency, established by act of Congress: The National Foundation on the Arts and Humanities Act of 1965, Public Law 89-209, as amended.

GEOG. RESTRICTIONS: United States.

FINANCIAL DATA:
Amount of support per award: Varies.
Total amount of support: Varies.

REPRESENTATIVE AWARDS:
$90,000 to Atlanta University Center, Atlanta, GA, to support a project to arrange and describe archival collections that document the African-American experience in the arts, religion, education, race relations and civil rights; $138,914 to Baltimore Museum of Industry, Baltimore, MD, to support the arrangement, description and preservation microfilming of the corporate records of the Canton Company of Baltimore, Maryland, dating from 1836 to 1981; $110,281 to Santa Barbara Museum of Natural History, Santa Barbara, CA, to support the computerization of the catalog and accession records of the museum's archaeological and ethnographic collections.

APPLICATION INFO:
Application can be downloaded from the web site.

Duration: Varies.

Deadline: Varies.

PUBLICATIONS:
Annual report; *Grant Programs*; *Humanities Magazine*.

IRS I.D.: 52-1098584

ADDRESS INQUIRIES TO:
Paula Wasley, Public Affairs Specialist
(See address above.)

NATIONAL ENDOWMENT FOR THE HUMANITIES

The Constitution Center
400 7th Street, S.W.
Washington, DC 20506
(202) 606-8269
Fax: (202) 606-8557
E-mail: publicpgms@neh.gov
Web Site: www.neh.gov

TYPE:
Project/program grants. Public Humanities Projects grants support projects that bring the ideas and insights of the humanities to life for general audiences. Projects must engage humanities scholarship to illuminate significant themes in disciplines such as history, literature, ethics and art, or to address challenging issues in contemporary life. NEH encourages projects that involve members of the public in collaboration with humanities scholars or that invite contributions from the community in the development and delivery of humanities programming. The grant program supports a variety of forms of audience engagement:
Community Conversations: This format supports one- to three-year-long series of community-wide public discussions in which diverse residents creatively address community challenges, guided by the perspectives of the humanities;
Exhibitions: This format supports permanent exhibitions that will be on view for at least three years, or traveling exhibitions that will be available to public audiences in at least two venues in the U.S. (including the originating location) and;
Historic Places: This format supports the interpretation of historic sites, houses, neighborhoods and regions, which might include living history presentations, guided tours, exhibitions and public programs.

See entry 1886 for full listing.

NATIONAL HUMANITIES CENTER [371]

7 T.W. Alexander Drive
Research Triangle Park, NC 27709
(919) 549-0661
Fax: (919) 990-8535
E-mail: nhc@nationalhumanitiescenter.org
Web Site: www.nationalhumanitiescenter.org

FOUNDED: 1976

AREAS OF INTEREST:
History, literature, philosophy, classics, political theory, law, religion, anthropology, art history, folklore and other humanistic fields.

NAME(S) OF PROGRAMS:
- **National Humanities Center Fellowships**

TYPE:
Fellowships; Visiting scholars. Awards for advanced study in the humanities in residence at the Center.

YEAR PROGRAM STARTED: 1978

PURPOSE:
To support advanced study in the humanities; to encourage the exchange of ideas among humanist scholars; to enhance the influence of the humanities in the U.S.

LEGAL BASIS:
Privately incorporated nonprofit institute for advanced study.

ELIGIBILITY:
Open to scholars in the humanities. As a rule, the Center does not consider applications from candidates who have not yet completed the Doctorate. Fellowships for younger scholars are not intended for an immediate postdoctoral year but are awarded to individuals who have begun their professional careers and are undertaking research significantly beyond their dissertations.

FINANCIAL DATA:
Fellows receive travel expenses to and from the Center for themselves and their families.

Amount of support per award: Individually determined based on need.

Total amount of support: Varies.

Matching fund requirements: Stipulated with specific grants.

CO-OP FUNDING PROGRAMS: Scholars who have financial support from university or other funding agencies are welcome to apply and receive from the Center the difference between that support and their normal academic salaries.

NO. AWARDS: 40.

APPLICATION INFO:
Applications accepted online only.

Duration: One academic year, September through May.

Deadline: October 15. Announcement in February.

PUBLICATIONS:
Annual report; application guidelines; semiannual newsletter.

IRS I.D.: 59-1735367

OFFICERS:
Patricia R. Morton, Chairman
William C. Jordan, Vice Chairman
Lawrence R. Ricciardi, Treasurer
Thomas Scherer, Secretary

STAFF:
Robert Newman, President and Director
Anthony E. Kaye, Vice President for Scholarly Programs

ADDRESS INQUIRIES TO:
Lois Whittington, Program Coordinator
Fellowship Program
(See address above.)

NEW YORK COUNCIL FOR THE HUMANITIES [372]

150 Broadway
Suite 1700
New York, NY 10038
(212) 233-1131
Fax: (212) 233-4607
E-mail: nych@nyhumanities.org
Web Site: www.nyhumanities.org

FOUNDED: 1975

AREAS OF INTEREST:
Humanities, public programs and education.

NAME(S) OF PROGRAMS:
- **Action Grants**
- **Community Conversations Program**
- **Reading and Discussion Program**
- **Speakers in the Humanities Program**
- **Vision Grants**

TYPE:
Challenge/matching grants; Project/program grants; Seed money grants. Action Grants help launch public programs that use the humanities to activate conversations within a community. Projects that encourage participants to reflect on their values, explore new ideas, and connect with others across New York state are encouraged. These grants require matching funds to demonstrate your community's investment in the project.

Community Conversations Program promotes thoughtful, engaged community dialogue, using a short text and a facilitator from the local community.

Reading and Discussion Programs are awarded to involve community members in ongoing discussions of books and ideas.

Speakers in the Humanities Program allows local organizations to present distinguished lectures by a select group of scholars and professionals to community audiences on various topics.

Vision Grants help groups brainstorm, connect, research, strategize, and design engaging public humanities programs. Innovation is welcomed, and projects that use the tools of the humanities (civic engagement, critical inquiry, debate, discussion, historical framing, etc.) to address contemporary issues are encouraged.

YEAR PROGRAM STARTED: 1975

PURPOSE:
To help all New Yorkers become thoughtful participants in our communities by promoting critical inquiry, cultural understanding, and civic engagement.

LEGAL BASIS:
State humanities council, nonprofit under Internal Revenue Code 501(c)(3).

ELIGIBILITY:
Tax-exempt, nonprofit 501(c)(3) organizations in New York state.

GEOG. RESTRICTIONS: New York state.

FINANCIAL DATA:
Amount of support per award: Action Grants: Typically $1,501 to $5,000; Vision Grants: Typically $200 to $1,500.

Total amount of support: $430,000.

Matching fund requirements: All Action Grants must be matched (at least dollar-for-dollar) with cash and/or in-kind contributions. Vision Grants do not require a match.

NO. MOST RECENT APPLICANTS: Action Grants: 134; Speakers in the Humanities Awards: 350; Vision Grants: 25.

NO. AWARDS: Action Grants: 76; Speakers in the Humanities Awards: 168; Vision Grants: 2.

APPLICATION INFO:
All applications are available online.

PUBLICATIONS:
Application guidelines.

IRS I.D.: 51-0152266

ADDRESS INQUIRIES TO:
Lauren Kushnick, Director of Grants
E-mail: grants@nyhumanities.org

Michael Washburn, Director of Programs
E-mail: programs@nyhumanities.org

*SPECIAL STIPULATIONS:
Grants available only to New York-based, tax-exempt organizations, but fiscal sponsorship is permitted.

THE NEWBERRY LIBRARY [373]

Office of Research and Academic Programs
60 West Walton Street
Chicago, IL 60610
(312) 255-3666
E-mail: research@newberry.org
Web Site: www.newberry.org/fellowships

FOUNDED: 1887

AREAS OF INTEREST:
The humanities of Western Europe, England and the Americas from the late Middle Ages to the early 20th century.

NAME(S) OF PROGRAMS:
- **Newberry Library Short-Term Fellowships**

TYPE:
Fellowships; Residencies. Fellowships of one to two months for advanced research, including doctoral dissertations, in history and the humanities. Fellowships provide access to the Newberry's collections for those who live and work beyond commuting distance from Chicago.

YEAR PROGRAM STARTED: 1942

PURPOSE:
To give scholars engaged in research in the fields listed above the opportunity to utilize the specialized collections of the Newberry Library.

LEGAL BASIS:
Private research library.

ELIGIBILITY:
Applicants must have the Ph.D. or terminal degree in their field, or have completed all requirements except the dissertation. Preference will be given to applicants from outside the greater Chicago area whose research particularly requires study at the Newberry. Applicants must live and work outside of the Chicago area.

FINANCIAL DATA:
Amount of support per award: $2,500 per month.

NO. MOST RECENT APPLICANTS: 170.

NO. AWARDS: 40 to 45.

APPLICATION INFO:
Applications must be submitted through the online webform.

Duration: One to two months.

Deadline: December 15.

STAFF:
D. Bradford Hunt, Vice President for Research and Academic Programs

ADDRESS INQUIRIES TO:
See e-mail address above.

THE NEWBERRY LIBRARY [374]

Office of Research and Academic Programs
60 West Walton Street
Chicago, IL 60610
(312) 255-3666
E-mail: research@newberry.org
Web Site: www.newberry.org/fellowships

FOUNDED: 1887

AREAS OF INTEREST:
Late Medieval and Renaissance studies.

NAME(S) OF PROGRAMS:
- **The Audrey Lumsden-Kouvel Fellowship**

TYPE:
Fellowships. The Audrey Lumsden-Kouvel Fellowship is for postdoctoral scholars conducting extended research in residence at

the Newberry Library in the areas of late medieval and early modern history and literature.

LEGAL BASIS:
Private research library.

ELIGIBILITY:
Preference will be given to projects focusing on Romance cultures, including work that draws on sources from the colonial Americas. Topics in Portuguese, Spanish and Latin American Studies are especially welcome, as are translation projects. Recent recipients of Ph.Ds. are encouraged to apply.

FINANCIAL DATA:
Amount of support per award: $4,200 per month.

NO. MOST RECENT APPLICANTS: 40.

NO. AWARDS: 1.

APPLICATION INFO:
Applications must be submitted through the online webform.

Duration: Four to six months.

Deadline: November 15.

STAFF:
D. Bradford Hunt, Vice President for Research and Academic Programs

ADDRESS INQUIRIES TO:
See e-mail address above.

THE NEWBERRY LIBRARY [375]

Office of Research and Academic Programs
60 West Walton Street
Chicago, IL 60610
(312) 255-3666
E-mail: research@newberry.org
Web Site: www.newberry.org/fellowships

FOUNDED: 1887

AREAS OF INTEREST:
The humanities of Western Europe, England and the Americas from the late Middle Ages to the early 20th century.

NAME(S) OF PROGRAMS:
- **National Endowment for the Humanities (NEH) Fellowships**

TYPE:
Fellowships; Residencies. Support for projects in any field appropriate to the Library's collections.

YEAR PROGRAM STARTED: 1975

PURPOSE:
To encourage the individual scholar's research and to deepen and enrich the opportunities for serious intellectual exchange.

LEGAL BASIS:
Private research library.

ELIGIBILITY:
Established scholars at the postdoctoral level or its equivalent may apply. Awards are open to U.S. citizens and foreign nationals who have been living in the U.S. for at least three years. Preference is given to applicants who have not held major fellowships for three years preceding the proposed period of residency.

Projects must be appropriate for research in the Newberry collection.

FINANCIAL DATA:
Applicants may combine grants with sabbaticals or other stipendiary support.

Amount of support per award: $4,200 per month.

NO. MOST RECENT APPLICANTS: 95.

NO. AWARDS: Approximately 4.

APPLICATION INFO:
Applications must be submitted through the online webform.

Duration: Four to 12 months.

Deadline: November 15.

STAFF:
D. Bradford Hunt, Vice President for Research and Academic Programs

ADDRESS INQUIRIES TO:
See e-mail address above.

THE NEWBERRY LIBRARY [376]

Office of Research and Academic Programs
60 West Walton Street
Chicago, IL 60610
(312) 255-3666
E-mail: research@newberry.org
Web Site: www.newberry.org/fellowships

FOUNDED: 1887

AREAS OF INTEREST:
The humanities of Western Europe, England and the Americas from the late Middle Ages to the early 20th century.

NAME(S) OF PROGRAMS:
- **Arthur and Lila Weinberg Fellowship for Independent Scholars and Researchers**

TYPE:
Fellowships; Residencies. Weinberg Fellowship is for scholars working outside traditional acedemic settings. The program seeks scholars, journalists, writers, filmmakers, visual and performing artists and other humanists. Preference is given to scholars working on historical issues related to social justice or reform.

LEGAL BASIS:
Private research library.

ELIGIBILITY:
Candidates are those working in a field appropriate to the Newberry collections. Preference is given to scholars working on historical issues related to social justice and reform. Applicants for this fellowship need not be from outside the Chicago area.

FINANCIAL DATA:
Amount of support per award: $2,500 total stipend.

NO. MOST RECENT APPLICANTS: 8.

NO. AWARDS: 1.

APPLICATION INFO:
Applications must be submitted through the online webform.

Duration: One to 12 months.

Deadline: December 15.

STAFF:
D. Bradford Hunt, Vice President for Research and Academic Programs

ADDRESS INQUIRIES TO:
See e-mail address above.

THE NEWBERRY LIBRARY

Office of Research and Academic Programs
60 West Walton Street
Chicago, IL 60610
(312) 255-3666
E-mail: research@newberry.org
Web Site: www.newberry.org/fellowships

TYPE:
Fellowships. For scholars wishing to use the Newberry's collections to study the period 1660 to 1815.

See entry 611 for full listing.

THE NEWBERRY LIBRARY [377]

Office of Research and Academic Programs
60 West Walton Street
Chicago, IL 60610
(312) 255-3666
E-mail: research@newberry.org
Web Site: www.newberry.org/fellowships

FOUNDED: 1887

AREAS OF INTEREST:
The humanities of Western Europe, England and the Americas from the late Middle Ages to the early 20th century.

NAME(S) OF PROGRAMS:
- **Lloyd Lewis Fellowship in American History**

TYPE:
Fellowships. The Lloyd Lewis Fellowship in American History is awarded to postdoctoral scholars pursuing projects in any area of American history appropriate to the Newberry's collections.

PURPOSE:
To further research in American history.

ELIGIBILITY:
Applicants must hold a Ph.D. at the time of application.

FINANCIAL DATA:
Applicants may combine these fellowship awards with sabbatical or other stipendiary support.

Amount of support per award: Monthly stipend of $4,200.

APPLICATION INFO:
Applications must be submitted through the online webform.

Duration: Four to 12 months.

Deadline: November 15.

ADDRESS INQUIRIES TO:
See e-mail address above.

*PLEASE NOTE:
The Newberry's long-term fellowship grants support individual research and promote serious intellectual exchange through active participation in the Newberry's scholarly activities, including fellows' seminars and a weekly colloquium.

THE NEWBERRY LIBRARY [378]

Office of Research and Academic Programs
60 West Walton Street
Chicago, IL 60610
(312) 255-3666
E-mail: research@newberry.org
Web Site: www.newberry.org/fellowships

FOUNDED: 1887

AREAS OF INTEREST:
The humanities of Western Europe, England and the Americas from the late Middle Ages to the early 20th century.

NAME(S) OF PROGRAMS:
- **Monticello College Foundation Fellowship for Women**

TYPE:
Fellowships. The Monticello College Foundation Fellowship for Women is

intended to help a postdoctoral woman scholar at an early stage (pre-tenure) of her academic career.

PURPOSE:
To provide assistance to postdoctoral woman scholars at an early stage of their academic careers.

ELIGIBILITY:
Applicants must hold a Ph.D. at the time of application. This award is intended for a postdoctoral woman scholar at an early stage (pre-tenure) of her academic career. Preference will be given to proposals particularly concerned with the study of women.

FINANCIAL DATA:
Applicants may combine these fellowship awards with sabbatical or other stipendiary support.

Amount of support per award: Monthly stipend of $4,200 per month.

APPLICATION INFO:
Applications must be submitted through the online webform.

Duration: Four to six months.

Deadline: November 15.

ADDRESS INQUIRIES TO:
See e-mail address above.

*PLEASE NOTE:
The Newberry's long-term fellowship grants support individual research and promote serious intellectual exchange through active participation in the Newberry's scholarly activities, including fellows' seminars and a weekly colloquium.

THE NEWBERRY LIBRARY [379]

Office of Research and Academic Programs
60 West Walton Street
Chicago, IL 60610
(312) 255-3666
E-mail: research@newberry.org
Web Site: www.newberry.org/fellowships

FOUNDED: 1887

AREAS OF INTEREST:
The humanities of Western Europe, England and the Americas from the late Middle Ages to the early 20th century.

NAME(S) OF PROGRAMS:
- **Newberry Consortium of American Indian and Indigenous Studies (NCAIS) Faculty Fellowship**

TYPE:
Fellowships.

PURPOSE:
To promote research in American Indian studies.

ELIGIBILITY:
This award is intended for faculty members at institutions participating in the Consortium. Preference is given to scholars at an early career stage.

FINANCIAL DATA:
Applicants may combine these fellowship awards with sabbatical or other stipendiary support.

Amount of support per award: Monthly stipend of $4,200.

APPLICATION INFO:
Awardees must indicate in their applications how many months they intend to be in residence at the Newberry. Applications must be submitted through the online webform.

Duration: Four to six months.

Deadline: November 15.

ADDRESS INQUIRIES TO:
See e-mail address above.

*PLEASE NOTE:
The Newberry's long-term fellowship grants support individual research and promote serious intellectual exchange through active participation in the Newberry's scholarly activities, including fellows' seminars and a weekly colloquium.

THE NEWBERRY LIBRARY [380]

Office of Research and Academic Programs
60 West Walton Street
Chicago, IL 60610
(312) 255-3666
E-mail: research@newberry.org
Web Site: www.newberry.org/fellowships

FOUNDED: 1887

AREAS OF INTEREST:
The humanities of Western Europe, England and the Americas from the late Middle Ages to the early 20th century.

NAME(S) OF PROGRAMS:
- **Sixteenth Century Society and Conference (SCSC) Fellowship**

TYPE:
Fellowships; Research grants; Residencies. Support for projects in any field appropriate to the Library's collection.

PURPOSE:
To support research in residence at The Newberry Library.

LEGAL BASIS:
Private research library.

ELIGIBILITY:
Applicants must have the Ph.D. or terminal degree in their field, or have completed all doctoral requirements except the dissertation. Preference will be given to those working in the early modern era, broadly defined (*circa* 1450 - *circa* 1660). Applicants must be members of the SCSC at the time of application and through the period of the fellowship.

Applicants must live and work outside the greater Chicago area.

FINANCIAL DATA:
Amount of support per award: $2,500 for one month in residence.

APPLICATION INFO:
Applications must be submitted through the online webform. Application form must be completed.

Duration: One-month residency.

Deadline: December 15.

EXECUTIVE STAFF:
D. Bradford Hunt, Vice President for Research and Academic Programs

ADDRESS INQUIRIES TO:
See e-mail address above.

THE NEWBERRY LIBRARY [381]

Office of Research and Academic Programs
60 West Walton Street
Chicago, IL 60610
(312) 255-3666
E-mail: research@newberry.org
Web Site: www.newberry.org/fellowships

FOUNDED: 1887

AREAS OF INTEREST:
The humanities of Western Europe, England and the Americas from the late Middle Ages to the early 20th century.

NAME(S) OF PROGRAMS:
- **Newberry Library - Jack Miller Center Fellowship**

TYPE:
Fellowships; Residencies. Support for projects in any field appropriate to the Library's collection.

PURPOSE:
To advance scholarship in those fields of study that will contribute to a deeper understanding of America's founding principles and history and wider traditions that influenced its development.

LEGAL BASIS:
Private research library.

ELIGIBILITY:
Applicants must have the Ph.D. or terminal degree in their field, or have completed all doctoral requirements except the dissertation. Preference will be given to applicants whose research particularly requires study at the Newberry.

Applicants must live and work outside the greater Chicago area.

FINANCIAL DATA:
Amount of support per award: $2,500 per month in residence.

APPLICATION INFO:
Applications may be submitted through the online webform. Applicants must request one or two months of support at the time of application.

Duration: One to two months.

Deadline: December 15.

EXECUTIVE STAFF:
D. Bradford Hunt, Vice President for Research and Academic Programs

ADDRESS INQUIRIES TO:
See e-mail address above.

THE NEWBERRY LIBRARY [382]

Office of Research and Academic Programs
60 West Walton Street
Chicago, IL 60610
(312) 255-3666
E-mail: research@newberry.org
Web Site: www.newberry.org/fellowships

FOUNDED: 1887

AREAS OF INTEREST:
The humanities of Western Europe, England and the Americas from the late Middle Ages to the early 20th century.

NAME(S) OF PROGRAMS:
- **Susan Kelly Power and Helen Hornbeck Tanner Fellowship**

TYPE:
Fellowships; Residencies. Support for projects in any field appropriate to the Library's collection.

PURPOSE:
To support Ph.D. candidates and postdoctoral scholars of American Indian heritage for one or two months of residential research in any field in the humanities using the Newberry collection.

LEGAL BASIS:
Private research library.

ELIGIBILITY:
Applicants must have the Ph.D. or terminal degree in their field, or have completed all doctoral requirements except the dissertation. Preference will be given to applicants whose research particularly requires study at the Newberry. Applicants must be U.S. citizens of American Indian heritage.

FINANCIAL DATA:
Amount of support per award: $2,500 per month in residence.

APPLICATION INFO:
Applications must be submitted through the online webform. Applicants must complete a supplementary application form, detailing American Indian heritage.

Duration: One to two months of residential research.

Deadline: December 15.

EXECUTIVE STAFF:
D. Bradford Hunt, Vice President for Research and Academic Programs

ADDRESS INQUIRIES TO:
See e-mail address above.

THE NEWBERRY LIBRARY [383]

Office of Research and Academic Programs
60 West Walton Street
Chicago, IL 60610
(312) 255-3666
E-mail: research@newberry.org
Web Site: www.newberry.org/fellowships

FOUNDED: 1887

AREAS OF INTEREST:
The humanities of Western Europe, England and the Americas from the late Middle Ages to the early 20th century.

NAME(S) OF PROGRAMS:
- **Society of Mayflower Descendants in the State of Illinois Fellowship**

TYPE:
Fellowships; Residencies. Support for projects in any field appropriate to the Library's collection.

PURPOSE:
To encourage research work, especially those working in early American history.

LEGAL BASIS:
Private research library.

ELIGIBILITY:
Applicants must have the Ph.D. or terminal degree in their field, or have completed all doctoral requirements except the dissertation. Preference will be given to applicants whose research particularly requires study at the Newberry, and whose research work is in early American history.

Applicants must live and work outside the greater Chicago area.

FINANCIAL DATA:
Amount of support per award: $2,500 for one month in residence.

APPLICATION INFO:
Applications must be submitted through the online webform.

Duration: One month.

Deadline: December 15.

EXECUTIVE STAFF:
D. Bradford Hunt, Vice President for Research and Academic Programs

ADDRESS INQUIRIES TO:
See e-mail address above.

THE NEWBERRY LIBRARY [384]

Office of Research and Academic Programs
60 West Walton Street
Chicago, IL 60610
(312) 255-3666
E-mail: research@newberry.org
Web Site: www.newberry.org/fellowships

FOUNDED: 1887

AREAS OF INTEREST:
The humanities of Western Europe, England and the Americas from the late Middle Ages to the early 20th century.

NAME(S) OF PROGRAMS:
- **Charles Montgomery Gray Fellowship**

TYPE:
Fellowships; Residencies. Support for projects in any field appropriate to the Library's collection.

PURPOSE:
To encourage the individual scholar's research and to deepen and enrich the opportunities for serious intellectual exchange.

LEGAL BASIS:
Private research library.

ELIGIBILITY:
Applicants must have the Ph.D. or terminal degree in their field, or have completed all doctoral requirements except the dissertation. Projects must be appropriate for research in residence, within the Newberry's collection. Preference will be given to applicants whose research particularly requires study at the Newberry. Preference may be given to those working in the early modern period or Renaissance, as well as English history, legal history or European history.

Applicants must live and work outside the greater Chicago area.

FINANCIAL DATA:
Amount of support per award: $2,500 per month of residency.

APPLICATION INFO:
Applications must be submitted through the online webform. Applicants may request one or two months of support at the time of application.

Duration: One to two months.

Deadline: December 15.

EXECUTIVE STAFF:
D. Bradford Hunt, Vice President for Research and Academic Programs

ADDRESS INQUIRIES TO:
See e-mail address above.

THE NEWBERRY LIBRARY [385]

Office of Research and Academic Programs
60 West Walton Street
Chicago, IL 60610
(312) 255-3666
E-mail: research@newberry.org
Web Site: www.newberry.org/fellowships

FOUNDED: 1887

AREAS OF INTEREST:
The humanities of Western Europe, England and the Americas from the late Middle Ages to the early 20th century.

NAME(S) OF PROGRAMS:
- **Newberry Library - American Society for Environmental History (ASEH) Fellowship**

TYPE:
Fellowships; Residencies. This fellowship supports one month's work in residence at the Newberry Library.

PURPOSE:
To offer support for qualified applicants working on a European art history project covering the period prior to 1830.

LEGAL BASIS:
Private research library.

ELIGIBILITY:
Applicants must have the Ph.D. or terminal degree in their field, or have completed all doctoral requirements except the dissertation.

Applicants must live and work outside the greater Chicago area and have a specific need for research in the Newberry collection. Applicants must be members of the ASEH at the time of the award.

FINANCIAL DATA:
Amount of support per award: $2,500 for one month in residence.

APPLICATION INFO:
Applications must be submitted through the online webform.

Duration: One month.

Deadline: December 15.

EXECUTIVE STAFF:
D. Bradford Hunt, Vice President for Research and Academic Programs

ADDRESS INQUIRIES TO:
See e-mail address above.

THE NEWBERRY LIBRARY [386]

Office of Research and Academic Programs
60 West Walton Street
Chicago, IL 60610
(312) 255-3666
E-mail: research@newberry.org
Web Site: www.newberry.org/fellowships

FOUNDED: 1887

AREAS OF INTEREST:
The humanities of Western Europe, England and the Americas from the late Middle Ages to the early 20th century.

NAME(S) OF PROGRAMS:
- **Andrew W. Mellon Foundation Fellowship**

TYPE:
Fellowships; Residencies. Support for projects in any field appropriate to the Library's collection.

PURPOSE:
To encourage the individual scholar's research and to deepen and enrich the opportunities for serious intellectual exchange.

LEGAL BASIS:
Private research library.

ELIGIBILITY:
Established scholars at the postdoctoral level may apply. An established scholar, as defined by the Awards Committee, is generally someone who has at least two published articles in refereed journals or the equivalent at the time of application. Projects must be appropriate for research in residence, within the Newberry's collection. There may be preference given for scholars who live and work outside of the Chicago area.

FINANCIAL DATA:
Amount of support per award: $4,200 per month of residency.

APPLICATION INFO:
Applications may be submitted through the online webform. Applicants must request at least four and no more than 12 months of support at the time of application.

Duration: Four to 12 months.

Deadline: November 15.

EXECUTIVE STAFF:
D. Bradford Hunt, Vice President for Research and Academic Programs

ADDRESS INQUIRIES TO:
See e-mail address above.

THE PHI BETA KAPPA SOCIETY

1606 New Hampshire Avenue, N.W.
Washington, DC 20009
(202) 745-3287
Fax: (202) 986-1601
E-mail: awards@pbk.org
Web Site: www.pbk.org

TYPE:
Fellowships. Grant to women scholars made in alternate years for advanced research dealing with Greek language, literature, history or archaeology (odd-numbered years) or with French language or literature (even-numbered years).

See entry 1071 for full listing.

THE ROYAL SOCIETY OF CANADA

Walter House
282 Somerset Street West
Ottawa ON K2P 0J6 Canada
(613) 998-9920
Fax: (613) 991-6996
E-mail: nominations@rsc-src.ca
Web Site: www.rsc-src.ca/en/fellows/medals-awards

TYPE:
Awards/prizes. The Konrad Adenauer Research Award is intended to promote academic collaboration between Canada and the Federal Republic of Germany.

The Bancroft Award is given for publication, instruction and research in the earth sciences that have conspicuously contributed to public understanding and appreciation of the subject.

The Pierre Chauveau Medal is awarded for a distinguished contribution to knowledge in the humanities.

The Flavelle Medal is awarded for an outstanding contribution to biological science during the preceding 10 years or for significant additions to a previous outstanding contribution to biological science.

The Ursula Franklin Award in Gender Studies is intended to recognize significant contributions by a Canadian scholar in the humanities and social sciences to furthering our understanding of issues concerning gender.

The Innis-Gérin Medal is presented for a distinguished and sustained contribution to the literature of the social sciences.

The McLaughlin Medal is awarded for important research of sustained excellence in any branch of the medical sciences.

The McNeil Medal for the Public Awareness of Science is awarded to a candidate who has demonstrated outstanding ability to promote and communicate science to students and the public (in the broadest sense of the latter term) within Canada.

The Willet G. Miller Medal is given for outstanding research in any branch of earth sciences.

The Lorne Pierce Medal is awarded for an achievement of special significance and conspicuous merit in imaginative or critical literature written in either English or French (critical literature dealing with Canadian subjects has priority over critical literature of equal merit that does not deal with Canadian subjects).

The Miroslaw Romanowski Medal is awarded for significant contributions to the resolution of scientific aspects of environmental problems or for important improvements to the quality of an ecosystem in all aspects - terrestrial, atmospheric and aqueous - brought about by scientific means.

The Rutherford Memorial Medals are awarded for outstanding research in any branch of physics and chemistry.

The John L. Synge Award is given to acknowledge outstanding research in any of the branches of the mathematical sciences.

The Henry Marshall Tory Medal is given for outstanding research in any branch of astronomy, chemistry, mathematics, physics or an allied science.

The J.B. Tyrrell Historical Medal is awarded for outstanding work in the history of Canada.

The Alice Wilson Award is given to three women of outstanding academic qualifications in the arts and humanities, social sciences or science who are entering a career in scholarship or research at the postdoctoral level.

See entry 1784 for full listing.

THE SCHOMBURG CENTER FOR RESEARCH IN BLACK CULTURE [387]

515 Malcolm X Boulevard
New York, NY 10037-1801
(212) 491-2228
E-mail: sir@nypl.org
Web Site: schomburgcenter.org/scholarsinresidenceprogram

FOUNDED: 1925

AREAS OF INTEREST:
African, African-American and Afro-Caribbean history and culture.

NAME(S) OF PROGRAMS:

- **Scholars-in-Residence**

TYPE:
Fellowships. Awarded to scholars and professionals whose research in the Black experience can benefit from extended access to the Center's collections. Seminars, colloquia, forums, symposia and conferences complement the residency program.

YEAR PROGRAM STARTED: 1983

PURPOSE:
To encourage research and writing in Black history and culture; to facilitate interaction among the participants, including fellows funded by other sources; to provide for widespread dissemination of findings through lectures, publications and the Schomburg Center Seminars.

ELIGIBILITY:
Applicants must be professionals and/or scholars in the humanities studying Black history and culture and fields related to the Schomburg Center's collections and program activities, including librarianship, archives and museum administration, special collections, photographs, audiovisual materials and publications. Studies in the social sciences, the arts, science and technology, psychology, education and religion are also eligible if they utilize a humanistic approach and contribute to humanistic knowledge. Creative writing projects (works of poetry and fiction) and projects that result in a performance are not eligible.

Persons seeking support for research leading to degrees are not eligible under this program. Candidates for advanced degrees must have received the degree or completed all requirements for it by the application deadline. Foreign nationals are ineligible unless they will have resided in the U.S. for three years immediately preceding the award date of the fellowship.

FINANCIAL DATA:
Amount of support per award: Stipend of $30,000 per six months.

CO-OP FUNDING PROGRAMS: Funded by the National Endowment for the Humanities, the Ford Foundation, the Samuel I. Newhouse Foundation, the Andrew W. Mellon Foundation, the Rockefeller Foundation, the Aaron Diamond Foundation, and the Irene Diamond Foundation.

NO. MOST RECENT APPLICANTS: 100.

NO. AWARDS: 6.

APPLICATION INFO:
Applications are accepted electronically only.

Duration: Six consecutive months.

Deadline: December 1.

PUBLICATIONS:
Program announcement.

STAFF:
Farah Griffin, Director

ADDRESS INQUIRIES TO:
Scholars-in-Residence Program
(See address or e-mail above.)

*PLEASE NOTE:
The Center will assist scholars in locating housing.

*SPECIAL STIPULATIONS:
Fellows may not be employed or hold other major fellowships or grants during period of residency.

SOCIAL SCIENCES AND HUMANITIES RESEARCH COUNCIL OF CANADA

350 Albert Street
Ottawa ON K1P 6G4 Canada
(613) 943-7777
Fax: (613) 943-1329
E-mail: fellowships@sshrc-crsh.gc.ca
Web Site: www.sshrc-crsh.gc.ca

TYPE:
Awards/prizes; Fellowships; Scholarships. Through its Doctoral Awards program, SSHRC offers two types of funding for doctoral students:

(1) SSHRC Doctoral Fellowships and;
(2) Joseph-Armand Bombardier (JAB) Canada Graduate Scholarships (CGS) program - Doctoral Scholarships.

See entry 1815 for full listing.

SOCIAL SCIENCES AND HUMANITIES RESEARCH COUNCIL OF CANADA

350 Albert Street
Ottawa ON K1P 6G4 Canada
(613) 943-7777
Fax: (613) 943-1329
E-mail: fellowships@sshrc-crsh.gc.ca
Web Site: www.sshrc-crsh.gc.ca

TYPE:
Fellowships. For Canadian citizens or permanent residents of Canada, to support postdoctoral research in the humanities and social sciences.

See entry 1816 for full listing.

SOCIAL SCIENCES AND HUMANITIES RESEARCH COUNCIL OF CANADA

350 Albert Street
Ottawa ON K1P 6G4 Canada
(613) 943-7777
Fax: (613) 943-1329
E-mail: vanier@cihr-irsc.gc.ca
fellowships@sshrc-crsh.gc.ca
Web Site: www.vanier.gc.ca
www.sshrc-crsh.gc.ca

TYPE:
Awards/prizes; Fellowships; Scholarships. For full-time doctoral students in the humanities and social sciences.

See entry 1817 for full listing.

SOCIAL SCIENCES AND HUMANITIES RESEARCH COUNCIL OF CANADA

350 Albert Street
Ottawa ON K1P 6G4 Canada
(613) 943-7777
Fax: (613) 943-1329
E-mail: fellowships@sshrc-crsh.gc.ca
Web Site: www.sshrc-crsh.gc.ca

TYPE:
Fellowships. For Canadian citizens, permanent residents of Canada and foreign citizens to support postdoctoral research in the humanities and social sciences.

See entry 1818 for full listing.

SOCIAL SCIENCES AND HUMANITIES RESEARCH COUNCIL OF CANADA

350 Albert Street
Ottawa ON K1P 6G4 Canada
(613) 943-7777
Fax: (613) 943-1329
E-mail: fellowships@sshrc-crsh.gc.ca
Web Site: www.sshrc-crsh.gc.ca

TYPE:
Awards/prizes; Fellowships; Scholarships.

See entry 1819 for full listing.

STANFORD HUMANITIES CENTER [388]

Stanford University
424 Santa Teresa Street
Stanford, CA 94305-4015
(650) 723-3052
Fax: (650) 723-1895
E-mail: shc-fellowships@stanford.edu
Web Site: shc.stanford.edu

FOUNDED: 1980

AREAS OF INTEREST:
History, literature, philosophy, classics, languages, social theory, political theory, law, religion, anthropology, art history, folklore and other areas of the humanities.

NAME(S) OF PROGRAMS:
- **External Faculty Fellowships**

TYPE:
Fellowships. Fellowships are awarded to support research projects in the humanities; creative arts projects are not eligible. The Humanities Center seeks candidates whose research is likely to contribute to intellectual exchange among a diverse group of scholars within the disciplines of the humanities.

YEAR PROGRAM STARTED: 1982

PURPOSE:
To promote the humanities and humanistic study at Stanford and nationally, primarily through a research fellowship program.

LEGAL BASIS:
Private, nonprofit research center at Stanford University.

ELIGIBILITY:
Postdoctoral level research in the humanities. Applicants must be at least three years beyond receipt of their Ph.D. at the start of their fellowship year.

FINANCIAL DATA:
Amount of support per award: $70,000, plus a moving and housing allowance of $30,000.

Matching fund requirements: Applicants are encouraged to seek supplementary financial support.

NO. MOST RECENT APPLICANTS: 350.

NO. AWARDS: 10.

APPLICATION INFO:
Online application is required and may be obtained directly from the Humanities Center web site.

Duration: Academic year. Normally September 15 to June 15. No renewals.

Deadline: October. Award announcement by late March.

ADVISORY BOARD:
Jayna Brown, Ethnic Studies, University of California, Riverside
Zephyr Frank, History, Stanford
Sally Haslanger, Linguistics and Philosophy, Massachusetts Institute of Technology
Margaret Imber, Classical and Medieval Studies, Bates College
Robert Katz, President's Office, Stanford
Steven Mavromihalis, Pacific Union International and Christie's Great Estates
Linda R. Meier, Former Trustee, Stanford
Peggy Phelan, Theater and Performance Studies, Stanford
Harsha Ram, Slavic Languages and Literatures, University of California, Berkeley
Mary Anne Rothberg Rowen, Provenance Productions
Donna Schweers, Community and Stanford Volunteer
Elaine Treharne, English, Stanford
Jun Uchida, History, Stanford
Ben Wang, East Asian Languages and Cultures, Stanford
Connie Wolf, Cantor Arts Center, Stanford

ADDRESS INQUIRIES TO:
See e-mail address above.

STIFTELSEN RIKSBANKENS JUBILEUMSFOND [389]

Kungstradgardsg. 18
SE-114 86 Stockholm Sweden
(46) 08-50 62 64 00
Fax: (46) 08-50 62 64 31
E-mail: rj@rj.se
Web Site: www.rj.se

FOUNDED: 1964

AREAS OF INTEREST:
Scientific research in humanities and social sciences.

NAME(S) OF PROGRAMS:
- **Europe and Global Challenges**
- **Flexit**
- **Pro Futura**
- **Research Grants**

TYPE:
Conferences/seminars; Research grants.

YEAR PROGRAM STARTED: 1965

PURPOSE:
To support and promote scientific research in humanities and social sciences.

LEGAL BASIS:
Independent, non-governmental foundation.

ELIGIBILITY:
Open to single researchers or research groups. The Foundation is interested in supporting multidisciplinary or interdisciplinary research projects in which researchers from different disciplines, faculties, localities or countries collaborate with Swedish scholars.

FINANCIAL DATA:
Amount of support per award: Average SEK 3,600,000.

Total amount of support: Approximately SEK 400,000,000.

CO-OP FUNDING PROGRAMS: Occasional co-financing for large projects.

NO. MOST RECENT APPLICANTS: Approximately 900.

NO. AWARDS: Approximately 80 larger projects.

APPLICATION INFO:
Applicants should first submit a short outline sketch and a publication list. If the preliminary proposal is accepted, applicants will be required to send a complete application.

Duration: Three years average for projects; six to eight years for programs.

Deadline: End of January.

PUBLICATIONS:
Annual report; program publications; yearbook.

STAFF:
Goran Blomquist, Managing Director
Bjorn Olsson, Finance Director
Dr. Jenny Bjorkman, Head of Communications
Hanna Kollerstrom, Public Relations Officer
Robert Hamren, Research Secretary, Economics, Law, and Political Science

Dr. Britta Lovgren, Research Secretary, Humanities
Dr. Maria Wikse, Research Secretary, Humanities
Dr. Torbjorn Eng, Research Secretary, Social Science
Dr. Fredrik Lundmark, Research Secretary, Social Science

ADDRESS INQUIRIES TO:
Dr. Jenny Bjorkman
Head of Communications
(See address above.)

SWANN FOUNDATION FOR CARICATURE AND CARTOON [390]

Prints and Photographs Division
Library of Congress
101 Independence Avenue, S.E.
Washington, DC 20540-4730
(202) 707-9115
Fax: (202) 707-6647
E-mail: swann@loc.gov
Web Site: www.loc.gov/rr/print/swann/swann-fellow.html

FOUNDED: 1967

AREAS OF INTEREST:
Caricature and cartoons.

NAME(S) OF PROGRAMS:
- **Swann Foundation Fellowship**

TYPE:
Conferences/seminars; Fellowships; Internships; Project/program grants; Visiting scholars. Small grants. Annual fellowship awarded to candidate for a Ph.D. or Master's degree.

YEAR PROGRAM STARTED: 1995

PURPOSE:
To support the documentation and understanding of caricature and cartoon as art.

LEGAL BASIS:
Nonprofit, federal agency.

ELIGIBILITY:
Fellowships are awarded to active Ph.D. candidates, M.A. candidates and those people who have received an advanced degree within the last three years.

GEOG. RESTRICTIONS: North America.

FINANCIAL DATA:
Amount of support per award: $5,000.
Total amount of support: Varies.

NO. MOST RECENT APPLICANTS: Approximately 20.

NO. AWARDS: Varies.

APPLICATION INFO:
Applicants should submit a project proposal and budget.
Duration: One academic year, generally fall through following late spring.
Deadline: February 15.

ADDRESS INQUIRIES TO:
Martha Kennedy
Curator, Popular and Applied Graphic Art
(See address above.)

*SPECIAL STIPULATIONS:
Must be a graduate student or a postgraduate within three years of receiving an M.A. or Ph.D. from a university in the U.S., Canada, or Mexico.

UCLA CHICANO STUDIES RESEARCH CENTER

193 Haines Hall
Box 951544
Los Angeles, CA 90095
(310) 825-2363
Fax: (310) 206-1784
E-mail: csrcinfo@chicano.ucla.edu
Web Site: www.chicano.ucla.edu
www.iac.ucla.edu/

TYPE:
Fellowships; Visiting scholars.

See entry 1049 for full listing.

UNIVERSITY OF PENNSYLVANIA, PENN HUMANITIES FORUM [391]

3260 South Street
Penn Museum
Philadelphia, PA 19104-6324
(215) 898-8220
Fax: (215) 746-5946
E-mail: phf@sas.upenn.edu
Web Site: www.phf.upenn.edu

FOUNDED: 1999

AREAS OF INTEREST:
Humanities.

NAME(S) OF PROGRAMS:
- **Andrew W. Mellon Postdoctoral Fellowships in the Humanities**

TYPE:
Fellowships. Fellows conduct research and teach one course.

YEAR PROGRAM STARTED: 1976

PURPOSE:
To support and encourage the intellectual development of untenured scholars in the humanities.

LEGAL BASIS:
Nonprofit, non-taxable university.

ELIGIBILITY:
Candidates must have research interests that relate to the forum's topic of study for the year of the fellowship. Preference is given to proposals that are interdisciplinary and to candidates who have not previously used the resources of the University of Pennsylvania and whose work would allow them to take advantage of the research strengths of the institution and to make a contribution to its intellectual life. Research proposals are invited in all areas of humanistic studies except educational curriculum-building and performing arts.

FINANCIAL DATA:
Fellowships include health insurance and a $3,000 research fund.
Amount of support per award: $53,000.

NO. AWARDS: 5.

APPLICATION INFO:
Applications are available, commencing in May, on the web site. Applicants are expected to submit the application, which includes a description of their proposed project, as well as recommendations.
Duration: One year in residence at University of Pennsylvania.
Deadline: October 15 of the year preceding the fellowship. Announcement in January of the fellowship year.

STAFF:
James F. English, Director
Jennifer Conway, Associate Director
Sara Varney, Program Manager

ADDRESS INQUIRIES TO:
Jennifer Conway, Associate Director
(See address above.)

VILLA I TATTI: THE HARVARD UNIVERSITY CENTER FOR ITALIAN RENAISSANCE STUDIES

Via di Vincigliata, 26
50135 Florence Italy
(39) 055 603251
(39) 055 608909
Fax: (39) 055 603383
E-mail: info@itatti.harvard.edu
Web Site: www.itatti.harvard.edu/fellowships

TYPE:
Fellowships. Stipendiary and nonstipendiary fellowships for the academic year July 1 through June 30 in residence in Florence for study on any aspect of the Italian Renaissance. There are also a limited number of short-term fellowships. Details are available online.

See entry 931 for full listing.

LEWIS WALPOLE LIBRARY [392]

Yale University
154 Main Street
Farmington, CT 06032
(860) 677-2140
Fax: (860) 677-6369
E-mail: walpole@yale.edu
Web Site: www.library.yale.edu/walpole

FOUNDED: 1979

AREAS OF INTEREST:
18th century studies (mainly British), the study of Horace Walpole and Strawberry Hill, 18th century British satirical prints.

NAME(S) OF PROGRAMS:
- **Visiting Research Fellowship Program**

TYPE:
Conferences/seminars; Fellowships; Travel grants. 18th century studies (mainly British), including history, literature, theatre, drama, art, architecture, politics, philosophy or social history.

YEAR PROGRAM STARTED: 1979

PURPOSE:
To fund study into any aspect of British 18th century studies in the Library's collection of 18th century British prints, paintings, books and manuscripts.

ELIGIBILITY:
Applicants should normally be pursuing an advanced degree or must be engaged in postdoctoral research or equivalent research. Study is at doctoral, postdoctoral, postgraduate and research levels.

FINANCIAL DATA:
Amount of support per award: Research Fellowship: Includes round-trip travel to the Library from the fellow's home location, a per diem for days in residence at the Library, and free accommodation in the fellows' quarters on the Lewis Walpole Library campus.

Travel Grant: Includes round-trip travel to the Library from the fellow's home location and free accommodation in the fellows' quarters on the Lewis Walpole Library campus but not the per diem.

Total amount of support: Varies.

CO-OP FUNDING PROGRAMS: ASECS Library fellowship; Lewis Walpole Library/Beinecke Rare Book & Manuscript Library joint eight-week fellowship.

NO. MOST RECENT APPLICANTS: 50.

NO. AWARDS: Up to 15.

APPLICATION INFO:
Applicants must submit a curriculum vitae, a brief outline of research proposal of up to three pages and two confidential letters of recommendation.

Duration: Four-week and eight-week Visiting Research Fellowship; two-week travel grants.

Deadline: Second Monday in January.

ADDRESS INQUIRIES TO:
Nicole L. Bouché
W.S. Lewis Librarian
and Executive Director
Lewis Walpole Library
Yale University
P.O. Box 1408
Farmington, CT 06034

WOODROW WILSON INTERNATIONAL CENTER FOR SCHOLARS [393]

One Woodrow Wilson Plaza
1300 Pennsylvania Avenue, N.W.
Washington, DC 20004-3027
(202) 691-4170
Fax: (202) 691-4001
E-mail: fellowships@wilsoncenter.org
Web Site: www.wilsoncenter.org

FOUNDED: 1968

AREAS OF INTEREST:
Social sciences, humanities and public policy.

NAME(S) OF PROGRAMS:
- **Fellowship Program at the Woodrow Wilson International Center for Scholars**

TYPE:
Fellowships; Research grants; Residencies; Scholarships; Visiting scholars. The Center seeks to commemorate, through its residential fellowship program of advanced research, both the scholarly depth and the public concerns of Woodrow Wilson. The Center welcomes outstanding project proposals in the social sciences and humanities on global issues - topics that intersect with questions of public policy or provide the historical framework to illume policy issues of contemporary importance. The Center especially welcomes projects likely to foster communication between the world of ideas and the world of public affairs.

Projects should have relevance to the world of public policy. Fellows should be prepared to interact with policymakers in Washington and with the Center's staff working on similar areas.

Fellowships are tenable in residence only at the Woodrow Wilson International Center for Scholars. The Center will not provide support for research to be carried out elsewhere. Fellows devote their full time to research and writing.

YEAR PROGRAM STARTED: 1970

LEGAL BASIS:
Government agency.

ELIGIBILITY:
The Center seeks individuals from throughout the world with superior projects representing diverse scholarly interests in the social sciences and humanities - topics that intersect with questions of public policy.

Academic participants are normally established scholars at the postdoctoral level but cannot be currently working on a Ph.D.

For nonacademic participants, namely those from careers in government, journalism, business, diplomacy and other professions, an equivalent degree of professional achievement is required.

Criteria for selection include scholarly capabilities, promise and achievements, the importance and originality of the proposed research, and the likelihood of the applicant being able to accomplish what he or she proposes.

Applicants should have a very good command of spoken English, since the Center is designed to encourage the exchange of ideas among its Fellows.

FINANCIAL DATA:
The Center tries to ensure that the stipend provided under the fellowship, together with fellow's other sources of funding (e.g., grants secured by applicant and sabbatical allowances), approximate a fellow's regular salary.

Amount of support per award: Varies.

Total amount of support: $1,400,000 for the year 2015.

NO. MOST RECENT APPLICANTS: 320.

NO. AWARDS: 15 to 20.

REPRESENTATIVE AWARDS:
"Technology and the Rise of the U.S. Global Security State: How Can History Inform Policy?;" " The Organizational Roots of Persistent Electoral Violence in Africa;" "Rule of Law and Open Governance Reforms in China: Implications for China, U.S.-China Relations and International Relations."

APPLICATION INFO:
Applicant must submit:
(1) the two-page, single-sided Fellowship Application Form (preferably typed);
(2) a list of publications that includes exact titles, names of publishers, dates of publication and status of forthcoming publications (not to exceed three pages);
(3) a Project Proposal (not to exceed five single-spaced typed pages, using 12-point type). The Center reserves the right to omit from review applications that are longer than the requested page length;
(4) a bibliography for the project that includes primary sources and relevant secondary sources (not to exceed three pages);
(5) the one-page Financial Information Form and;
(6) a curriculum vitae (not to exceed three pages). The Center will only accept the first three pages. Please list publications separately.

All application materials must be submitted in English. Applications submitted via fax will not be considered.

Duration: Fellowships of usually nine months are tenable September 1 of the fellowship year.

Deadline: October 1 for receipt of applications. Decisions announced by March of the following year.

PUBLICATIONS:
Annual report; application guidelines.

OFFICERS:
Jane Harman, Director, President and Chief Executive Officer

ADDRESS INQUIRIES TO:
Kim Conner, Fellowship Specialist
(See address above.)

WINTERTHUR MUSEUM, GARDEN & LIBRARY [394]

5105 Kennett Pike
Winterthur, DE 19735
(302) 888-4876
Fax: (302) 888-4870
E-mail: croeber@winterthur.org
Web Site: www.winterthur.org

FOUNDED: 1951

AREAS OF INTEREST:
American decorative arts, American art, American cultural and social history and horticulture.

NAME(S) OF PROGRAMS:
- **Dissertation Fellowships**
- **Winterthur Fellowships**

TYPE:
Fellowships. Long-term and short-term fellowships to be held in residence at Winterthur Museum.

The Dissertation Fellowships are for doctoral candidates. The award is a four- to eight-month fellowship.

Winterthur Fellowships consist of one- to three-month fellowships designed to promote research and study in topics of relevance to Winterthur's collections.

All fellowships are residential, requiring research and writing at Winterthur.

YEAR PROGRAM STARTED: 1977

PURPOSE:
To promote research in any humanistic field related to Winterthur's collections (museum, library, garden), work of an interdisciplinary nature and/or research with both objects and documents.

LEGAL BASIS:
Tax-exempt, public charitable organization.

ELIGIBILITY:
Applicants for a Dissertation Fellowship must have completed coursework, passed qualifying exams, fulfilled language requirements, and have an approved prospectus. The fellowship is open to students in departments of history, anthropology, folklore, art history, American studies, African-American history, historic preservation, and related fields.

Winterthur Fellowships are available to academic, museum and independent scholars and to support dissertation research.

FINANCIAL DATA:
Applicants may hold sabbaticals and grants from their own institutions, but may not simultaneously hold other major fellowships. Housing is available in a cottage on the museum grounds (full housekeeping facilities and furnished rooms).

Amount of support per award: Dissertation Fellowships: $7,000 per semester; Winterthur Fellowships: $1,750 per month.

Total amount of support: Varies.

REPRESENTATIVE AWARDS:
John Lardas Modern, Professor of Religious Studies, Franklin & Marshall College,

Lancaster, PA, "Haunted Modernity; or, the Metaphysics of Secularism in Antebellum America;" Julia A. Sienkewicz, University of Illinois, "Citizenship by Design: the Creation of Identity through Art, Architecture and Landscape in the Early Republic;" Sarah Carter, Harvard University, "A Basket, A Needle, A Penknife: Object Lessons in Nineteenth-Century American Material and Visual Culture;" Nicole Belolan, Ph.D. candidate, University of Delaware, Newark, DE, "Navigating the World: The Material Culture of Physical Mobility Impairment in the Early American North, 1700-1861."

APPLICATION INFO:
Application instructions and materials are available online at the Winterthur web site. Applicants for each fellowship should submit a three- to five-page statement of purpose, a curriculum vitae and two letters of recommendation. Supporting materials for dissertation research must include a letter from the dissertation advisor.

Duration: Dissertation Fellowships: Four to eight months; Winterthur Fellowships: One to three months.

Deadline: January 15. Announcement by April 30.

IRS I.D.: 51-0066038

ADDRESS INQUIRIES TO:
Research Fellowship Program
Academic Programs Department
(See address and e-mail above.)

CARTER G. WOODSON INSTITUTE FOR AFRICAN-AMERICAN AND AFRICAN STUDIES [395]

University of Virginia
McCormick Road, 108 Minor Hall
Charlottesville, VA 22903
(434) 924-3109
Fax: (434) 924-8820
E-mail: woodson@virginia.edu
Web Site: woodson.virginia.edu

FOUNDED: 1981

AREAS OF INTEREST:
Those disciplines of the humanities and social sciences which concern themselves with Afro-American and African Studies.

NAME(S) OF PROGRAMS:
- **African-American and African Studies Fellowships**

TYPE:
Fellowships. The Woodson Institute offers residential fellowships to predoctoral and postdoctoral scholars. These fellowships are designed to facilitate the completion of works in progress by providing scholars with unencumbered leave.

Afro-American and African Studies is considered to cover Africa, Africans and peoples of African descent in North, Central and South America and the Caribbean, past and present.

YEAR PROGRAM STARTED: 1981

PURPOSE:
To help researchers complete dissertations, books and other research projects focusing on the Black experience.

LEGAL BASIS:
University.

ELIGIBILITY:
Applicants for the predoctoral fellowships must have completed all requirements for the Ph.D. except the dissertation prior to August 1. Applicants for the postdoctoral fellowship must have been awarded their Ph.D. by the time of application or furnish proof that it will have been received prior to June 30. There are no restrictions as to citizenship or current residence. Employees of the University of Virginia may not apply.

Proposals will be judged on the basis of the significance of the proposed work, the applicant's qualifications, familiarity with existing relevant research literature, the research design of the project and the promise of completion within the award period. Preference will be given to projects whose field research is already substantially completed.

Fellowship recipients must be in residence at the University of Virginia for the duration of the award period and are expected to contribute to the intellectual life of the University. In pursuit of these goals, predoctoral fellows will become visiting graduate students attached to their respective disciplinary departments, and postdoctoral fellows will receive the status of visiting scholars in their respective fields.

FINANCIAL DATA:
Amount of support per award: Predoctoral Fellowship: $20,000 per year; Postdoctoral Fellowship: $45,000.

NO. MOST RECENT APPLICANTS: 149; 58 predoctoral and 91 postdoctoral.

NO. AWARDS: 5.

APPLICATION INFO:
Complete guidelines are available on the Institute web site.

Duration: Two years.

Deadline: December 1. Notification by mail early March.

PUBLICATIONS:
Program guidelines.

STAFF:
Deborah E. McDowell, Director

ADDRESS INQUIRIES TO:
Program Administrator
(See address above.)

*SPECIAL STIPULATIONS:
Fellows are required to present a formal paper to the University community at least once a year.

YALE CENTER FOR BRITISH ART [396]

1080 Chapel Street
New Haven, CT 06520
(203) 432-9805
Fax: (203) 432-4538
E-mail: ycba.research@yale.edu
Web Site: britishart.yale.edu/research/residential-scholar-awards

FOUNDED: 1977

AREAS OF INTEREST:
British art, history and literature.

NAME(S) OF PROGRAMS:
- **Visiting Scholar Awards**

TYPE:
Fellowships; Research grants; Residencies; Visiting scholars. Short-term resident fellowships for scholars of literature, history, the history of art or related fields.

YEAR PROGRAM STARTED: 1978

PURPOSE:
To allow scholars of literature, history, the history of art or related fields to study the Center's holdings of paintings, sculpture, drawings, prints and rare books and to make use of its research facilities (photograph archive and reference library).

LEGAL BASIS:
University-affiliated museum and research center.

ELIGIBILITY:
Open to scholars engaged in predoctoral and postdoctoral or equivalent research related to British art and to museum professionals whose responsibilities and research interests include British art.

FINANCIAL DATA:
Fellowships include the cost of travel to and from New Haven and also provide accommodation and a living allowance. Recipients will be required to be in residence in New Haven during the Fellowship period.

Amount of support per award: Varies.

CO-OP FUNDING PROGRAMS: One fellowship per annum is reserved for members of the American Society for Eighteenth-Century Studies; by arrangement with the Huntington Library and the Delaware Art Museum, scholars may apply for tandem awards.

NO. MOST RECENT APPLICANTS: Average 47 to 50.

NO. AWARDS: Approximately 20.

REPRESENTATIVE AWARDS:
Anya Matthews, Ph.D. candidate, Courtauld Institute of Art, "Picturing London's Post-Fire Livery Halls;" Helen McCormack, Lecturer, Forum for Critical Inquiry, Glasgow School of Art, "William Hunter and his Eighteenth-Century Cultural Worlds: The Anatomist and the Fine Arts;" Julia Sienkewicz, Assistant Professor of Art History, Duquesne University, "Epic Landscapes: Benjamin Henry Latrobe's Virginian Watercolors, 1795-1799."

APPLICATION INFO:
Application must be submitted online. Complete application information is available on the web site.

Duration: One to four months.

Deadline: January.

PUBLICATIONS:
Brochure.

STAFF:
Amy Meyers, Director
Martina Droth, Associate Director of Research
Lisa Ford, Assistant Director

ADDRESS INQUIRIES TO:
Lisa Ford, Assistant Director
P.O. Box 208280
New Haven, CT 06520
E-mail: lisa.ford@yale.edu

*SPECIAL STIPULATIONS:
Inquiries by e-mail only.

Architecture

AMERICAN ARCHITECTURAL FOUNDATION [397]

c/o AAF-RMHP
740 15th Street, N.W., Suite 225
Washington, DC 20005
(202) 787-1001
Fax: (202) 787-1002
E-mail: info@archfoundation.org
Web Site: www.archfoundation.org

FOUNDED: 1942

AREAS OF INTEREST:
Architecture, urban design and leadership development.

NAME(S) OF PROGRAMS:
- **The Richard Morris Hunt Prize**

TYPE:
Exchange programs; Fellowships; Research grants; Travel grants. Six-month professional study in France awarded in alternate years to midcareer American architects and urbanists pursuing careers with an emphasis on historic preservation topics.

YEAR PROGRAM STARTED: 1990

PURPOSE:
To study American and French architecture heritage.

ELIGIBILITY:
Open to architects and urban design professionals who have written and oral proficiency in French and are pursuing a career in historic preservation. In alternate years, open to French architects. Applicants must be U.S. or French citizens.

GEOG. RESTRICTIONS: United States and France.

FINANCIAL DATA:
Amount of support per award: $20,000.

CO-OP FUNDING PROGRAMS: Co-sponsored by the AAF and the French Heritage Society.

NO. MOST RECENT APPLICANTS: 9.

NO. AWARDS: 1.

APPLICATION INFO:
Applicants should submit a recent biography, three letters of recommendation, examples of professional work such as slides, sketches or photographs, a statement explaining how academic background and work experience relate to the Fellowship and how the Fellowship will benefit professionally. Applicants must demonstrate French language proficiency.

Duration: Six months.

Deadline: July 31.

PUBLICATIONS:
Program announcement.

STAFF:
Thom Minner, Program Director

ADDRESS INQUIRIES TO:
Thom Minner, Program Director
(See address above.)

THE AMERICAN INSTITUTE OF ARCHITECTS [398]

1735 New York Avenue, N.W.
Washington, DC 20006-5292
(202) 626-7539
Fax: (202) 626-7399
E-mail: rhayes@aia.org
infocentral@aia.org
Web Site: www.aia.org

FOUNDED: 1952

AREAS OF INTEREST:
Health care, facility planning, design and construction, facilities management, clinical engineering, and safety and security.

NAME(S) OF PROGRAMS:
- **AIA Arthur N. Tuttle, Jr. Graduate Fellowship in Health Facility Planning and Design**

TYPE:
Fellowships; Research grants. The American Institute of Architects and the American Hospital Association sponsor this program with additional support from the Steris Corporation, which offers one or more graduate fellowships.

YEAR PROGRAM STARTED: 1952

PURPOSE:
To increase the amount of research being done in the area of health care facility design and planning.

LEGAL BASIS:
Nonprofit organization.

ELIGIBILITY:
Open to graduate and postgraduate students enrolled at an accredited school of architecture. Applicants must be citizens of Canada, Mexico or the U.S.

FINANCIAL DATA:
Amount of support per award: Varies.

APPLICATION INFO:
Guidelines and application forms are available on the Institute web site.

Duration: One to two years depending on proposal.

Deadline: June.

PUBLICATIONS:
Guidelines.

ADDRESS INQUIRIES TO:
Richard L. Hayes, Ph.D., AIA
Director of Knowledge Resources
(See address above.)

THE AMERICAN INSTITUTE OF ARCHITECTS [399]

1735 New York Avenue, N.W.
Washington, DC 20006-5292
(202) 626-7529
Fax: (202) 626-7399
E-mail: scholarships@aia.org
Web Site: www.aia.org

FOUNDED: 1943

AREAS OF INTEREST:
Architecture.

NAME(S) OF PROGRAMS:
- **AIA/F Diversity Advancement Scholarship**

TYPE:
Scholarships. Awards to provide an opportunity for financially disadvantaged and/or minority groups to pursue a professional degree in architecture.

YEAR PROGRAM STARTED: 1973

PURPOSE:
To provide scholarships for those who would not otherwise have the opportunity to be enrolled in professional architecture studies.

ELIGIBILITY:
Applicants must be residents of the U.S. High school seniors, technical school/junior college students transferring to an NAAB school of architecture or college freshmen who are entering a program leading to a professional degree (Bachelor, Master's of Architecture or D.Arch.) are eligible to apply. Students who have completed the first year of a standard four-year curriculum are not eligible.

GEOG. RESTRICTIONS: United States.

FINANCIAL DATA:
Scholarship awards vary according to financial need. The amount of the award is determined based on the financial information and consultation with the Director of Financial Aid at the student's school.

Amount of support per award: $3,000 to $4,000.

Total amount of support: $20,000.

NO. MOST RECENT APPLICANTS: 120.

NO. AWARDS: Approximately 5.

APPLICATION INFO:
Candidates must submit:
(1) a letter of recommendation completed by an architect, an AIA component, a community design center representative, a guidance counselor or teacher, a director of a community, civic, or religious organization, or the dean, administrative head, or professor at an NAAB-accredited professional program;
(2) a completed application form;
(3) a copy of transcripts of all high school and college records, including SAT or ACT scores;
(4) a copy of a written acceptance from an NAAB-accredited professional program in architecture (can be provided at time of acceptance);
(5) a personal statement outlining interests, experience, and career plans related to architecture;
(6) a statement describing the applicant's disadvantaged circumstances;
(7) one freehand drawing on an 8 1/2 x 11-inch page depicting any subject; cannot be drafted or done using computer-aided design and;
(8) completed portion of the last page of the application by the high school guidance counselor or the administrative head at the NAAB-accredited professional program.

Duration: One academic year. Renewable up to five years.

Deadline: Postmarked by May 2.

OFFICERS:
Robert Ivey, Executive Vice President and Chief Executive Officer, American Institute of Architects

ADDRESS INQUIRIES TO:
Jamie Yeung, Manager
Professional Development and Resources
(See address above.)

THE AMERICAN SCHOOL OF CLASSICAL STUDIES AT ATHENS

6-8 Charlton Street
Princeton, NJ 08540-5232
(609) 683-0800
Fax: (609) 924-0578
E-mail: ascsa@ascsa.org (for information)
application@ascsa.org (to apply)
Web Site: www.ascsa.edu.gr

TYPE:
Fellowships.

See entry 419 for full listing.

AMERICAN SOCIETY OF INTERIOR DESIGNERS EDUCATIONAL FOUNDATION [400]

718 7th Street N.W., 4th Floor
Washington, DC 20001
(202) 546-3480
Fax: (202) 546-3240
E-mail: foundation@asid.org
Web Site: www.asidfoundation.org

FOUNDED: 1931

AREAS OF INTEREST:
Interior design (commercial and residential) and interior design-related industry.

NAME(S) OF PROGRAMS:
- **ASID Foundation Legacy Scholarship for Graduate Students**
- **ASID Foundation Legacy Scholarship for Undergraduates**
- **Irene Winifred Eno Grant**
- **Joel Polsky Academic Achievement Award**
- **Joel Polsky Prize**

TYPE:
Awards/prizes; Research grants; Scholarships. Irene Winifred Eno Grant provides financial assistance to individuals or groups engaged in the creation of an educational program(s) or an interior design research project dedicated to health, safety and welfare.

The Legacy Scholarship for Graduate Students is awarded on the basis of academic/creative accomplishment.

The Legacy Scholarship for Undergraduates is given to a creatively outstanding student as demonstrated through their portfolio.

The Polsky Academic Achievement Award is given annually to recognize an outstanding undergraduate or graduate student's interior design research or thesis project.

The Joel Polsky Prize recognizes outstanding academic contributions to the discipline of interior design through literature or visual communication.

PURPOSE:
To encourage excellence in the field of interior design.

LEGAL BASIS:
Nonprofit foundation.

ELIGIBILITY:
The Legacy Scholarship for Graduate Students is open to students who are enrolled in or have been accepted to a graduate-level interior design program at a degree-granting institution.

The Legacy Scholarship for Undergraduates is open to all students in their junior or senior year of undergraduate study and enrolled in at least a three-year program of interior design.

The Irene Winifred Eno Grant is open to students, educators, interior design practitioners, institutions or other interior design-related groups.

The Joel Polsky Academic Achievement Award judges interior design research or doctoral and Master's thesis projects.

The Joel Polsky Prize entrants should address the needs of the public, designers and students on such topics as educational research, behavioral science, business practice, design process, theory or other technical subjects. High school students and college freshmen are not eligible.

GEOG. RESTRICTIONS: United States.

FINANCIAL DATA:
Amount of support per award: Irene Winifred Eno Grant, Joel Polsky Academic Achievement Award and Joel Polsky Prize: $5,000; Legacy Scholarship for graduate and undergraduate students: $4,000.

APPLICATION INFO:
Complete details are available online.

Duration: One-time award.

PUBLICATIONS:
ASID ICON, magazine; application guidelines.

OFFICERS:
Valerie O'Keefe, Foundation Manager

ADDRESS INQUIRIES TO:
Valerie O'Keefe, Foundation Manager
(See address above.)

ARCHITECTURAL LEAGUE OF NEW YORK [401]

594 Broadway, Suite 607
New York, NY 10012
(212) 753-1722
Fax: (212) 486-9173
E-mail: info@archleague.org
Web Site: www.archleague.org

FOUNDED: 1881

AREAS OF INTEREST:
Architecture, architectural history and urban studies.

NAME(S) OF PROGRAMS:
- **Deborah J. Norden Fund**

TYPE:
Travel grants. The Deborah J. Norden Fund, established in 1995 in memory of architect and arts administrator Deborah Norden, awards travel/study grants to students and recent graduates in the field of architecture, architectural history, and urban studies.

YEAR PROGRAM STARTED: 1995

PURPOSE:
To support genuinely independent projects that require travel.

ELIGIBILITY:
Students or recent graduates in the fields of architecture, architectural history and urban studies may apply.

The intention of the fund is to support genuinely independent projects. Grant funds cannot be used for tuition or for participation in an organized program, such as a university's summer abroad program.

FINANCIAL DATA:
Amount of support per award: Up to $5,000.

Total amount of support: $5,000.

NO. MOST RECENT APPLICANTS: 110.

NO. AWARDS: 2.

APPLICATION INFO:
Applicants should submit a brief proposal in letter form, no more than three pages, which succinctly describes the objectives of the grant request and how it will assist the applicant's intellectual and creative development. The grant amount requested must be specified. The submission should also include a resume of not more than two pages, project schedule, and budget for travel and other project costs. Two letters of recommendation must be requested from individuals who are knowledgeable about the applicant's ability and project. The applicant's name and brief project title must appear on the first page of the proposal.

Deadline: Mid-April. Announcement in late May.

ADDRESS INQUIRIES TO:
Jessica Liss, Program Associate
(See address above.)

ARCHITECTURAL LEAGUE OF NEW YORK [402]

594 Broadway, Suite 607
New York, NY 10012
(212) 753-1722
Fax: (212) 486-9173
E-mail: info@archleague.org
Web Site: www.archleague.org

FOUNDED: 1881

AREAS OF INTEREST:
Young architects.

NAME(S) OF PROGRAMS:
- **The League Prize for Young Architects and Designers**

TYPE:
Awards/prizes; Conferences/seminars. A catalogue of winning work will be published by the Architectural League and Princeton Architectural Press. Winning work will be displayed.

YEAR PROGRAM STARTED: 1982

PURPOSE:
To recognize specific works of high quality and to encourage the exchange of ideas among young architects and designers who might otherwise not have a forum; to focus on the aesthetic, cultural, and social concerns of architecture and the allied arts; to help architects, artists, and the public enrich their understanding of the purposes and importance of the art of architecture.

ELIGIBILITY:
Entrants may submit work done independently. Entrants must be 10 years or less out of graduate or undergraduate school; students are not eligible for this competition. Work completed for fulfillment of course requirements at academic institutions is not eligible.

GEOG. RESTRICTIONS: United States, Canada and Mexico.

FINANCIAL DATA:
Amount of support per award: $2,000.

NO. MOST RECENT APPLICANTS: 100.

NO. AWARDS: 6 per year.

APPLICATION INFO:
A call for entries is issued each fall. A written statement (not to exceed 250 words) is requested, which defines and considers the work under the rubric of the competition theme. Significant weight is given to how an applicant's work addresses the theme. A single portfolio, which may include several projects, must be bound and no larger than 11x14 inches. The portfolio may not contain more than 30 double-sided pages. CDs, models, slides and transparencies will not be accepted.

Each submission must include an entry form and $25 entry fee. Insert form, intact, into an unsealed envelope attached to the inside back cover of the submission. To maintain

anonymity, no identification of the entrant may appear on any part of the submission, except on the entry form and return envelope.

Portfolios will be returned by mail only if a self-addressed envelope with postage is also enclosed. The Architectural League assumes no liability for original drawings. The League will take every precaution to return submissions intact, but can assume no responsibility for loss or damage. Portfolios may be discarded after six months if no return envelope is provided.

Deadline: Varies.

ADDRESS INQUIRIES TO:
Anne Rieselbach, Program Director
(See address above.)

THE COMMUNITY FOUNDATION OF LOUISVILLE, INC.

325 West Main Street, Suite 1110
Louisville, KY 40202
(502) 585-4649
Fax: (502) 587-7484
E-mail: giving@cflouisville.org
Web Site: www.cflouisville.org

TYPE:
Endowments; General operating grants; Scholarships.

See entry 428 for full listing.

ENTERPRISE COMMUNITY PARTNERS [403]

334 Boylston Street, Suite 400
Boston, MA 02116
(781) 235-2006
(781) 591-4702
Fax: (781) 235-4011
E-mail: rosefellowship@enterprisecommunity.org
Web Site: www.enterprisecommunity.org

AREAS OF INTEREST:
Architecture and community development.

NAME(S) OF PROGRAMS:
- **Enterprise Rose Architectural Fellowship**

TYPE:
Fellowships.

YEAR PROGRAM STARTED: 2000

PURPOSE:
To promote architectural and community design in low-income communities and to encourage architects to become lifelong leaders in public service and community development.

ELIGIBILITY:
Applicant must have an NAAB-accredited Professional Architecture Degree (B.Arch, M.Arch or D.Arch) and must be eligible to work in the U.S. for the entire fellowship period.

GEOG. RESTRICTIONS: United States.

FINANCIAL DATA:
Fellowship package includes the standard insurance and benefits package (provided by the host organization), two annual week-long fellowship retreats and professional development allowance and opportunities.

Amount of support per award: $52,000 annual stipend.

Matching fund requirements: Community-based organizations must match Rose Fellowship funds 2:1.

NO. MOST RECENT APPLICANTS: 150.

NO. AWARDS: Average of 5.

APPLICATION INFO:
Contact Enterprise Community Partners.

Duration: Three years.

Deadline: Midsummer.

ADDRESS INQUIRIES TO:
Christopher Scott, Director
Enterprise Rose Architectural Fellowship
(See address above.)

THE JAMES MARSTON FITCH CHARITABLE FOUNDATION [404]

c/o The Neighborhood Preservation Center
232 East 11th Street
New York, NY 10003
(212) 252-6809
Fax: (212) 471-9987
E-mail: cpena@fitchfoundation.org
Web Site: www.fitchfoundation.org

FOUNDED: 1989

AREAS OF INTEREST:
Architecture, engineering, environmental planning, and historic preservation.

NAME(S) OF PROGRAMS:
- **Richard L. Blinder Award**
- **Mid-Career Fellowship**

TYPE:
Research grants. Richard L. Blinder Award was created to promote studies that explore the architecture of cultural buildings which integrate historic preservation and new construction - past, present and future; presented biennially.

Mid-Career Fellowship: This grant is the primary mission and the signature grant of this Foundation. The grants are intended to support projects of innovative original research or creative design that advance the practice of historic preservation in the U.S.

PURPOSE:
To support professionals in the field of historic preservation by providing midcareer grants to those working in preservation, landscape architecture, urban design, environmental planning, decorative arts, and architectural design and history.

ELIGIBILITY:
Richard L. Blinder Award proposal must demonstrate that it fosters architectural preservation in the U.S. Applicant must be an architect holding a professional degree or a valid license to practice architecture with at least 10 years experience in architecture, historic preservation or related fields. Grants are awarded only to individuals, not organizations or university-sponsored research projects. Grants are not awarded for professional fees.

Mid-Career Fellowship is for college graduates with a postgraduate degree and at least 10 years of professional experience in historic preservation or related fields.

GEOG. RESTRICTIONS: United States.

FINANCIAL DATA:
Amount of support per award: Up to $15,000.

NO. AWARDS: Richard Blinder Award: 1 biennially; Mid-Career Grant: 1 to 2.

APPLICATION INFO:
Contact the Foundation for guidelines and application.

Duration: One year.

Deadline: October 15.

ADDRESS INQUIRIES TO:
See e-mail address above.

GRAHAM FOUNDATION FOR ADVANCED STUDIES IN THE FINE ARTS [405]

Madlener House
4 West Burton Place
Chicago, IL 60610
(312) 787-4071
E-mail: grantprograms@grahamfoundation.org
Web Site: www.grahamfoundation.org

FOUNDED: 1956

AREAS OF INTEREST:
Architecture and related spatial practices that engage a wide range of cultural, social, political, technological, environmental and aesthetic issues. The Foundation is interested in projects that investigate the contemporary condition, expand historical perspectives, or explore the future of architecture and the designed environment.

NAME(S) OF PROGRAMS:
- **Carter Manny Award**
- **Production and Presentation Grants**
- **Research and Development Grants**

TYPE:
Awards/prizes; Project/program grants; Research grants. Grants to organizations, individuals and public programs.

Carter Manny Award: To support research for academic dissertations by promising scholars who are presently candidates for a doctoral degree, and whose dissertations focus on areas traditionally supported by the Foundation. Students must be nominated by their department to apply for this Award.

Production and Presentation Grants: To assist individuals and organizations with the production-related expenses that are necessary to take a project from conceptualization to realization and public presentation. These projects may include, but are not limited to, publications, exhibitions, installations, conferences, films, new-media projects, and other public programs.

Research and Development Grants: To assist individuals with seed money for research-related expenses such as travel, documentation, materials, supplies and other development costs.

YEAR PROGRAM STARTED: 1956

PURPOSE:
To make project-based grants to individuals and organizations and to produce public programs to foster the development and exchange of diverse and challenging ideas about architecture and its role in the arts, culture and society.

LEGAL BASIS:
Private foundation.

ELIGIBILITY:
Individuals and institutions may apply. No grants for endowments, general operating expenses, capital projects, scholarship aid or for work in pursuit of an academic degree (except for the Carter Manny Award), debt or expenses incurred prior to the date of grant request.

APPLICATION INFO:
Application to the Foundation involves a two-stage process and is open submission.

Stage One/Inquiry Form: Eligible candidates interested in applying for a grant must first submit an Inquiry Form. The Inquiry Form is available on the Foundation web site with each grant cycle and must be submitted online.

Stage Two/Proposal Form: Applicants whose projects best match the Foundation's priorities and interests are invited to submit a Proposal Form and supplementary materials. Applicants not invited to submit a Proposal Form are sent a decline letter at this stage. An invitation to submit a Proposal Form does not guarantee eventual funding.

Award Decision: Funding recommendations are presented to the Board of Trustees for consideration. If a grant is awarded, applicant will be asked to sign a Grant Agreement that outlines the conditions of the award, such as annual reporting. Funding decisions at all stages of the review are based on the priority of the proposed project as related to the Foundation's mission and interests, the project's fulfillment of the Foundation's criteria for evaluation, and availability of Foundation funds.

Duration: Varies.

Deadline: February 25 for organizations; September 15 for individuals.

PUBLICATIONS:
Annual report; guidelines.

OFFICERS:
Sarah Herda, Director
Ellen Hartwell Alderman, Managing Director
Stephanie Whitlock, Program Officer
Carolyn T. Kelly, Grants Manager

ADDRESS INQUIRIES TO:
See e-mail address above.

THE LEF FOUNDATION [406]

P.O. Box 382066
Cambridge, MA 02238-2066
(617) 492-5333
Fax: (617) 868-5603
E-mail: sara@lef-foundation.org
gen@lef-foundation.org
Web Site: www.lef-foundation.org

FOUNDED: 1985

AREAS OF INTEREST:
Nonfiction film and video.

NAME(S) OF PROGRAMS:
- **Moving Image Fund**

TYPE:
The Foundation gives grants for preproduction, production and post production of nonfiction film and video.

PURPOSE:
To fund the work of independent documentary film and video artists in the region; to broaden recognition and support for the artist's work both locally and nationally.

ELIGIBILITY:
Grants are made to organizations that have tax-exempt status under Section 501(c)(3) of the Internal Revenue Code, as well as individuals with 501(c)(3) fiscal sponsors.

GEOG. RESTRICTIONS: New England.

FINANCIAL DATA:
Amount of support per award: $5,000 to $25,000.

Total amount of support: $200,000 annually.

NO. AWARDS: 400.

APPLICATION INFO:
Application form and guidelines are available on the Foundation web site.

Duration: Varies.

Deadline: Varies.

ADDRESS INQUIRIES TO:
Sara Archambault, Program Director or
Genevieve Carmel, Program Assistant
E-mail: gen@lef-foundation.org
(See address above.)

THE PAUL MELLON CENTRE FOR STUDIES IN BRITISH ART [407]

16 Bedford Square
London WC1B 3JA England
(44) 0 20 7580 0311
Fax: (44) 0 20 7636 6730
E-mail: grants@paul-mellon-centre.ac.uk
Web Site: www.paul-mellon-centre.ac.uk

FOUNDED: 1970

AREAS OF INTEREST:
British art and architectural history.

NAME(S) OF PROGRAMS:
- **Educational Programme Grants**
- **Junior Fellowships**
- **Paul Mellon Centre Rome Fellowship**
- **Postdoctoral Fellowships**
- **Research Support Grants**
- **Senior Fellowships**

TYPE:
Conferences/seminars; Fellowships; Project/program grants; Research grants. Educational Programme Grants for lectures, symposia, seminars or conferences on British art or architectural history.

The Junior Fellowship is to pursue ongoing doctoral research at an American or British university.

The Paul Mellon Centre Rome Fellowship offers fellowships to scholars working on Grand Tour subjects or in the field of Anglo-Italian cultural and artistic relations.

The Postdoctoral Fellowship works to transform doctoral research into publishable form such as a book, series of articles, or exhibition catalogues.

Research Support Grants are for expenses in pursuit of research.

The Senior Fellowship supports an established scholar in the field of British art and architectural history to complete a manuscript or book for immediate publication.

YEAR PROGRAM STARTED: 1998

PURPOSE:
To promote scholarship and publications.

LEGAL BASIS:
University-affiliated research center.

ELIGIBILITY:
Candidates for the Junior Fellowship may be of any nationality but must be enrolled in a graduate program at an American or other non-British university for study in the U.K. or at a non-American university for study in the U.S.

The Postdoctoral Fellowship is awarded within four years of an applicant's doctoral award. Applicants must have had their doctoral theses successfully examined.

Applicants for the Rome Fellowship should, preferably, be competent in spoken and written Italian.

FINANCIAL DATA:
Amount of support per award: Varies.

APPLICATION INFO:
Full details and application forms are available online.

Duration: Junior Fellowship: Three months. Postdoctoral Fellowship: Six months. Rome Fellowship: Three months. Senior Fellowship: Nine months.

Deadline: Fellowships and grants: January 31. Grants: September 15.

ADDRESS INQUIRIES TO:
Fellowships and Grants Manager
(See e-mail address above.)

NATIONAL SOCIETY DAUGHTERS OF THE AMERICAN REVOLUTION [408]

1776 D Street, N.W.
Washington, DC 20006-5303
(202) 879-3263
Fax: (202) 879-3348
E-mail: scholarships@dar.org
Web Site: www.dar.org

FOUNDED: 1895

AREAS OF INTEREST:
Historic preservation.

NAME(S) OF PROGRAMS:
- **J.E.R. Caldwell Centennial Scholarship**

TYPE:
Scholarships.

YEAR PROGRAM STARTED: 1985

PURPOSE:
To provide ways and means to aid students in attaining higher education.

LEGAL BASIS:
Incorporated historical society.

ELIGIBILITY:
Applicants must be enrolled in the junior or senior year of a fully accredited college or university in the U.S. and pursuing a degree in the field of historic preservation, may reside in any state, and must be a U.S. citizen. All applicants must be sponsored by a local DAR chapter.

GEOG. RESTRICTIONS: United States.

FINANCIAL DATA:
Amount of support per award: Varies.

APPLICATION INFO:
Application information is available online. All scholarship applicants are required to have a letter of sponsorship from a chapter. Individuals interested in obtaining a letter of sponsorship from a local chapter are encouraged to contact the DAR State Chairman.

Duration: One year.

Deadline: February 15.

PUBLICATIONS:
American Spirit, magazine.

ADDRESS INQUIRIES TO:
Office of the Reporter General
DAR Scholarship Committee
(See address above.)

ROTCH TRAVELLING SCHOLARSHIP IN ARCHITECTURE [409]

Boston Society of Architects
290 Congress Street, Suite 200
Boston, MA 02210
(617) 391-4000
Fax: (617) 951-0845
E-mail: sgarber@architects.org
Web Site: www.rotch.org

FOUNDED: 1883

AREAS OF INTEREST:
Architecture.

NAME(S) OF PROGRAMS:
- **Rotch Travelling Scholarship**
- **Rotch Travelling Studio**

TYPE:
Awards/prizes; Fellowships; Travel grants. Traveling Fellowships. Rotch Travelling Scholarship awards a minimum of six months of foreign travel and study in the field of architecture and allied subjects.

Rotch Travelling Studio allows faculty to take architecture students for a one-month travelling program.

YEAR PROGRAM STARTED: 1883

PURPOSE:
To provide young architects with the opportunity to gain experience with other cultures; to augment the architectural education of students of architecture at the highest level of scholarship within a studio format.

LEGAL BASIS:
Private trust.

ELIGIBILITY:
Rotch Travelling Scholarship: Candidates must be U.S. citizens who have obtained a professional degree (B.Arch./M.Arch.) from an accredited school in the last 10 years. Candidates must have one year full-time professional experience in a Massachusetts architecture firm as of January 1 of the competition year, or have obtained an accredited degree from an accredited Massachusetts school of architecture as of January 1 of the competition year.

Rotch Travelling Studio: Applicants are invited from faculty members in all NAAB-accredited schools of architecture in the U.S. for travel anywhere in the world during the following calendar year.

GEOG. RESTRICTIONS: United States.

FINANCIAL DATA:
Amount of support per award: Travelling Scholarship: Up to $38,500; Travelling Studio: Up to $20,000.

APPLICATION INFO:
Official application forms are available online.

Duration: Travelling Scholarship: Minimum six months. Travelling Studio: One month.

Deadline: Travelling Scholarship: January.

ADDRESS INQUIRIES TO:
Sara Garber, Program Manager
Boston Society of Architects
(See e-mail address above.)

*PLEASE NOTE:
Rotch Travelling Studio is not being offered in the fall of 2016.

*SPECIAL STIPULATIONS:
No Rotch scholar may hold simultaneously another travelling scholarship, nor may he or she be employed during the period of the scholarship without special permission.

ROYAL INSTITUTE OF BRITISH ARCHITECTS [410]

RIBA Research Trusts
Education Department
66 Portland Place
London W1B 1AD England
(44) 0 20 7307 3678
E-mail: education@riba.org
Web Site: www.architecture.com

FOUNDED: 1834

AREAS OF INTEREST:
Architecture, and the arts and sciences connected therewith, in the U.K.

NAME(S) OF PROGRAMS:
- **RIBA Research Trust Awards**

TYPE:
Awards/prizes; Research grants; Seed money grants; Travel grants. Merit-based award to support recent architecture graduates who are pursuing research in the field of architecture.

PURPOSE:
To support individuals who are pursuing research in the field of architecture, with the anticipation that award winners may, in subsequent years, undertake a career as skilled researchers in the architectural field or be practicing architects developing a research trajectory.

ELIGIBILITY:
Open to applicants interested in a wide range of subject matter relevant to the advancement of architecture, and connected arts and sciences, in the U.K.

The Institute Research Trust Award is for a closely defined piece of architectural research. The committee will support practice-led or academic research, but it will not support course fees and subsistence costs for Ph.D./M.Phil. or Master's programmes. Awards are given only to named individuals, not organisations.

Applicants based outside the U.K. are also eligible to apply; however, the research work must in the main be undertaken within the U.K.

The Institute may support recent graduates or individuals who are already further into their careers. The committee will particularly welcome applications from practice-led researchers as this is an area from which it has historically received very few applications.

GEOG. RESTRICTIONS: United Kingdom.

FINANCIAL DATA:
The value of an award will be determined by the estimated requirements of the project.

Amount of support per award: Maximum award not to exceed GBP 10,000.

CO-OP FUNDING PROGRAMS: A candidate may have funding from other sources.

APPLICATION INFO:
Application forms are available from the Institute. Only requests up to GBP 10,000 will be considered.

Duration: Up to two years.

Deadline: Varies.

OFFICER:
Alan Vallance, Interim Chief Executive

ADDRESS INQUIRIES TO:
RIBA Education Projects
E-mail: hayley.russell@riba.org

SIR JOHN SOANE MUSEUM FOUNDATION [411]

1040 First Avenue, Suite 311
New York, NY 10022
(212) 223-2012
Fax: (866) 841-1928
E-mail: info@soanefoundation.com
Web Site: www.soanefoundation.com

AREAS OF INTEREST:
Education of the public in architecture and the fine and decorative arts.

NAME(S) OF PROGRAMS:
- **Sir John Soane Museum Foundation Traveling Fellowship**

TYPE:
Fellowships. Designed to help graduate students and scholars pursue research projects related to the work of Sir John Soane's Museum and its collections.

PURPOSE:
To educate and inspire the general and professional public in architecture and the fine and decorative arts.

ELIGIBILITY:
Applicants must be enrolled in a graduate degree program in a field appropriate to the Foundation's purpose. Level of study is postgraduate.

FINANCIAL DATA:
Amount of support per award: $5,000 plus economy airfare.

NO. MOST RECENT APPLICANTS: 20.

NO. AWARDS: 2.

APPLICATION INFO:
Applicants must submit a formal proposal of not more than one page describing the goal, scope and purpose of the research project, in addition to three letters of recommendation.

Duration: One year.

Deadline: March 1.

ADDRESS INQUIRIES TO:
Chas Miller, Executive Director
(See address above.)

SOCIETY OF ARCHITECTURAL HISTORIANS [412]

1365 North Astor Street
Chicago, IL 60610-2144
(312) 573-1365
Fax: (312) 573-1141
E-mail: chiggins@sah.org
Web Site: www.sah.org

FOUNDED: 1940

AREAS OF INTEREST:
Architecture and its related arts.

NAME(S) OF PROGRAMS:
- **Sally Kress Tompkins Fellowship**

TYPE:
Fellowships; Internships; Travel grants. The Sally Kress Tompkins Fellowship, a joint program of the Society of Architectural Historians and the National Park Service's Historic American Buildings Survey, permits an architectural historian to work on a 12-week project during the summer. The Fellow will prepare a written history to become part of the permanent collection focusing on either a specific nationally significant building/site, or a broader architectural history topic. The Fellow will

be stationed in the field working in conjunction with a measured drawings team, or in the Washington, DC office. The Fellow will be selected by a jury of two SAH members and one HABS representative.

PURPOSE:
To advance the knowledge and understanding of architecture, design, landscape and urbanism worldwide.

LEGAL BASIS:
Nonprofit professional organization.

ELIGIBILITY:
Graduate students and member of SAH.

FINANCIAL DATA:
Amount of support per award: $500 to $9,200.

Total amount of support: $10,000.

CO-OP FUNDING PROGRAMS: National Park Service's Historic American Buildings Survey (HABS).

NO. MOST RECENT APPLICANTS: 5.

NO. AWARDS: 1.

APPLICATION INFO:
Details are available online, for members.

Duration: One year.

Deadline: October 1.

PUBLICATIONS:
Newsletter; *Journal of the Society of Architectural Historians.*

ADDRESS INQUIRIES TO:
Christopher Higgins, Programs Coordinator
(See address above.)

THE SOCIETY OF NAVAL ARCHITECTS AND MARINE ENGINEERS

99 Canal Center Plaza, Suite 310
Alexandria, VA 22314
(703) 997-6709
Fax: (703) 997-6702
E-mail: bgreer@sname.org
Web Site: www.sname.org

TYPE:
Scholarships. The Society annually awards both graduate and undergraduate scholarships to encourage study in naval architecture, marine engineering, ocean engineering or marine industry-related fields.

Graduate Scholarships are made for one year of study leading to a Master's in naval architecture, marine engineering, ocean engineering or in fields directly related to the marine industry.

Undergraduate Scholarships are administered by schools offering undergraduate programs on grants given to the schools.

See entry 2577 for full listing.

VIRGINIA POLYTECHNIC INSTITUTE AND STATE UNIVERSITY

MAOP Office
110 Femoyer Hall
Blacksburg, VA 24061
(540) 231-5023
Fax: (540) 231-2618
E-mail: maop@vt.edu
Web Site: www.maop.vt.edu

TYPE:
Assistantships; Fellowships; Internships; Scholarships. The program assists with graduate school financing in exchange for assistance to MAOP administration. Graduate students assist with programming implementation such as mentoring to undergraduate students.

See entry 1000 for full listing.

WASHINGTON UNIVERSITY [413]

School of Architecture
Campus Box 1079
One Brookings Drive
St. Louis, MO 63130-4899
(314) 935-6200
Fax: (314) 935-7656
E-mail: abowles@wustl.edu
Web Site: www.samfoxschool.wustl.edu/steedman

FOUNDED: 1925

AREAS OF INTEREST:
Architectural education.

NAME(S) OF PROGRAMS:
- **James Harrison Steedman Memorial Fellowship in Architecture**

TYPE:
Awards/prizes; Fellowships; Travel grants. An award made on the basis of a design competition that requires the recipient to travel and study abroad for nine months. Not to be used towards tuition.

YEAR PROGRAM STARTED: 1925

PURPOSE:
To assist well-qualified architectural graduates to benefit by travel and study of architecture in foreign countries.

ELIGIBILITY:
Open to graduates of an accredited school of architecture, regardless of age, for a period up to eight years after the receipt of their first professional degree. Candidates must have at least one year of practical experience in the office of a practicing architect. Citizens of all countries are eligible.

FINANCIAL DATA:
Amount of support per award: $50,000 stipend for nine months of travel abroad.

Total amount of support: $50,000.

NO. MOST RECENT APPLICANTS: 125.

NO. AWARDS: 1 awarded biennially.

APPLICATION INFO:
Registration forms are available online. Applications are available in late October every odd year and fellowships are awarded in the spring every even year.

Duration: Nine months.

PUBLICATIONS:
Application guidelines.

GOVERNING BOARD:
William Wischmeyer

ADDRESS INQUIRIES TO:
Amanda Bowles, Assistant to Dean
(See address above.)

Arts (multiple disciplines)

ACADEMY FOUNDATION OF THE ACADEMY OF MOTION PICTURE ARTS AND SCIENCES

1313 North Vine Street
Los Angeles, CA 90028
(310) 247-3000 ext. 1131
E-mail: sguthrie@oscars.org
Web Site: www.oscars.org

TYPE:
Awards/prizes.

See entry 529 for full listing.

ALABAMA STATE COUNCIL ON THE ARTS [414]

201 Monroe Street
Suite 110
Montgomery, AL 36104-3721
(334) 242-4076
Fax: (334) 240-3269
E-mail: staff@arts.alabama.gov
Web Site: www.arts.alabama.gov

FOUNDED: 1966

AREAS OF INTEREST:
Architecture, literature, fine arts, arts in education, museums and libraries, music, and creative and performing arts.

CONSULTING OR VOLUNTEER SERVICES:
Strengthens cultural activities already in existence, assists in formation of new cultural activities, works towards improving the quality of presentations by both professional and amateur organizations and offers assistance to culturally oriented groups.

NAME(S) OF PROGRAMS:
- **Art and Cultural Facilities**
- **Arts-in-Education**
- **Community Arts Development**
- **Folk Arts**
- **Literary Art**
- **Performing Arts**
- **Visual Arts and Crafts**

TYPE:
Awards/prizes; Challenge/matching grants; Conferences/seminars; Development grants; Fellowships; General operating grants; Internships; Project/program grants; Residencies; Technical assistance. Grants to various disciplines comprising technical and financial assistance to local organizations in sponsoring activities of quality and promise in the various arts disciplines of the visual and performing arts within communities throughout Alabama.

YEAR PROGRAM STARTED: 1967

PURPOSE:
To increase interest, participation and support in the arts by supplementing local initiatives and local funds in order to enable a greater number of quality activities to be seen or heard throughout the state.

LEGAL BASIS:
Alabama Law, Act No. 551, Regular Session 1967 and Act No. 1065, Regular Session, 1969.

ELIGIBILITY:
Applicants must be qualified organizations sponsoring arts events or programs for communities. Such groups include local arts councils, arts associations, museums, literary associations, colleges and universities, dance and theatre groups. Evidence of nonprofit status is required.

GEOG. RESTRICTIONS: Alabama.

FINANCIAL DATA:
Amount of support per award: $500 to $250,000 for the year 2016.
Total amount of support: $3,600,000 for the year ended September 30, 2016.
Matching fund requirements: Equal amounts from other sources with exception of Artists Fellowships.

APPLICATION INFO:
A special application form can be obtained and submitted by using the Council eGRANT system which is available on their web site.
Duration: One year. Renewal by reapplication.
Deadline: March 1, June 1 and September 1.

PUBLICATIONS:
Guide to Programs; *Alabama Arts*, magazine; *Touring & Presenting Guide*.

IRS I.D.: 63-6000619

EXECUTIVE COUNCIL:
Dora H. James, Chairman
Joel T. Daves, IV, Vice Chairman
Rachel B. Fowler, Secretary

ADDRESS INQUIRIES TO:
Albert B. Head, Executive Director
(See address above.)

ALASKA STATE COUNCIL ON THE ARTS [415]

161 Klevin Street
Suite 102
Anchorage, AK 99508-1508
(907) 269-6610
Fax: (907) 269-6601
E-mail: aksca.info@alaska.gov
Web Site: www.education.alaska.gov/aksca

FOUNDED: 1966

AREAS OF INTEREST:
Alaska arts and culture.

CONSULTING OR VOLUNTEER SERVICES:
Technical assistance for grantees.

TYPE:
General operating grants; Project/program grants; Residencies. Grants in 16 categories for organizations and individuals based in Alaska.

YEAR PROGRAM STARTED: 1966

PURPOSE:
To foster the development of the arts for all Alaskans through education, partnerships, grants and services.

LEGAL BASIS:
State agency.

GEOG. RESTRICTIONS: Alaska.

FINANCIAL DATA:
Amount of support per award: Varies according to program.
Matching fund requirements: All organizational grants require at least 1:1 match (cash).

APPLICATION INFO:
Specific guidelines and applications are available online.
Duration: One year.
Deadline: Varies according to program.

PUBLICATIONS:
Annual report; individual grant program guidelines.

STAFF:
Laura Forbes, Grants Administrator
Saunders McNeill, Grants Administrator
Andrea Noble-Pelant, Grants Administrator

ADDRESS INQUIRIES TO:
Executive Director
(See address above.)

THE ALLIANCE FOR YOUNG ARTISTS & WRITERS [416]

557 Broadway
New York, NY 10012
Fax: (212) 389-3939
E-mail: kat@artandwriting.org
Web Site: www.artandwriting.org

FOUNDED: 1923

AREAS OF INTEREST:
Art and writing.

NAME(S) OF PROGRAMS:
- **The Scholastic Art and Writing Awards**

TYPE:
Awards/prizes; Scholarships. The Alliance for Young Artists & Writers identifies teenagers with exceptional artistic and literary talent and brings their remarkable work to a national audience through The Scholastic Art and Writing Awards.

YEAR PROGRAM STARTED: 1923

PURPOSE:
To provide guidance and support for the next generation of artists and writers and reward outstanding achievement in the creative arts.

LEGAL BASIS:
501(c)(3) organization.

ELIGIBILITY:
Public, private, parochial, or home-school students (grades 7 to 12) in the U.S., Canada, or American schools abroad, regardless of citizenship, may submit work. Foreign exchange students who are temporarily residing in the U.S. may also participate.

FINANCIAL DATA:
Scholarship recipients are additionally eligible for school-specific, tuition scholarships at more than 50 colleges.
Amount of support per award: $500 to $10,000.
Total amount of support: More than $250,000 given annually through the Scholastic Awards program in awards and scholarships to top Awards recipients and their educators.

NO. AWARDS: Approximately 100.

APPLICATION INFO:
Contact the Alliance.
Duration: One year.
Deadline: Varies by geographic location, approximately December 15 to January 15.

IRS I.D.: 13-3780998

ADDRESS INQUIRIES TO:
Debra Samdperil
Assistant Executive Director, Programs
(See address above.)

AMERICA-ISRAEL CULTURAL FOUNDATION

1140 Broadway
Suite 304
New York, NY 10001
(212) 557-1600 ext. 801
Fax: (212) 557-1611
E-mail: admin@aicf.org
Web Site: www.aicf.org

TYPE:
Awards/prizes; Endowments; Fellowships; Project/program grants; Scholarships. For study in the arts of music, painting and sculpture, dance and drama, film and television, to be pursued either in Israel or in other countries.

See entry 934 for full listing.

THE AMERICAN CERAMIC SOCIETY [417]

600 North Cleveland Avenue, Suite 210
Westerville, OH 43082
(614) 794-5827
Fax: (614) 794-5817
E-mail: tfreshour@ceramics.org
Web Site: ceramics.org

FOUNDED: 1898

AREAS OF INTEREST:
Ceramic education and glass.

NAME(S) OF PROGRAMS:
- **Graduate Student Poster Contest**
- **Outstanding Educator Award**
- **Student Speaking Contest**
- **Undergraduate Student Poster Contest**

TYPE:
Awards/prizes.

PURPOSE:
To promote and encourage materials science and engineering studies in the discipline of glass and ceramics.

FINANCIAL DATA:
Amount of support per award: Varies.
Total amount of support: $2,000 for the year 2013.

APPLICATION INFO:
Contact the Society.
Duration: One-time awards.
Deadline: Graduate Student Poster Contest: March; Outstanding Educator Award: April; Student Speaking and Undergraduate Student Poster Contests: September.

ADDRESS INQUIRIES TO:
Tricia Freshour, Membership Services Manager
(See address and e-mail above.)

AMERICAN FIDELITY FOUNDATION [418]

2000 North Classen, Suite 7N
Oklahoma City, OK 73106
(405) 523-5008
Fax: (405) 523-5421
E-mail: joella.ramsey@americanfidelity.com
Web Site: americanfidelityfoundation.org

AREAS OF INTEREST:
Education, arts, culture, health and human services, and civic and economic development.

TYPE:
Endowments; General operating grants; Research grants. Employment Matching Gifts.

ELIGIBILITY:
Organizations with 501(c)(3) status.

FINANCIAL DATA:
Amount of support per award: Grants to a single charity are typically $500 to $5,000.
Total amount of support: Varies.

NO. AWARDS: 100.

APPLICATION INFO:
Organizations that wish to be considered for a grant are asked to submit a letter of interest. If the Foundation chooses to pursue the project or program described, a formal application will be sent for completion to the organization within two weeks.

ADDRESS INQUIRIES TO:
Jo Ella Ramsey, Administrator
(See address above.)

THE AMERICAN SCHOOL OF CLASSICAL STUDIES AT ATHENS [419]

6-8 Charlton Street
Princeton, NJ 08540-5232
(609) 683-0800
Fax: (609) 924-0578
E-mail: ascsa@ascsa.org (for information)
application@ascsa.org (to apply)
Web Site: www.ascsa.edu.gr

FOUNDED: 1881

AREAS OF INTEREST:
Financial support for individuals involved in research.

NAME(S) OF PROGRAMS:
- **CAORC Multi-Country Research Fellowships**

TYPE:
Fellowships.

PURPOSE:
To provide support for individuals whose research has regional significance and requires travel to multiple countries, at least one of which hosts an American overseas research center such as the American School.

ELIGIBILITY:
Fellowship is limited to U.S. citizens. Open to U.S. doctoral candidates who have completed all Ph.D. requirements except the dissertation and U.S. postdoctoral scholars at all levels with research requiring travel to several countries with an American overseas research center.

School programs are generally open to qualified students and scholars at colleges or universities in the U.S. or Canada; restrictions may apply for specific fellowships and programs. The American School of Classical Studies at Athens does not discriminate on the basis of race, age, sex, sexual orientation, color, religion, ethnic origin, or disability when considering admission to any form of membership.

FINANCIAL DATA:
School fees are to be paid out of the fellowship stipend by the recipient. Fellowship does not include travel costs, housing, board, and other living expenses.

Amount of support per award: Doctoral candidates/postdoctoral scholars: $12,000 for all centers.

CO-OP FUNDING PROGRAMS: Fellowships for Multi-Country Research are funded by the Bureau of Educational and Cultural Affairs of the U.S. Department of State through a grant to the Council of American Overseas Research Centers.

NO. MOST RECENT APPLICANTS: 8.

NO. AWARDS: 1.

APPLICATION INFO:
Application guidelines are available at CAORC's web site (www.caorc.org). Associate Member application to ASCSA.

Duration: Doctoral and postdoctoral scholars: Minimum of 90 days.

Deadline: January 15. Awards announced on April 15.

STAFF:
James C. Wright, Director

ADDRESS INQUIRIES TO:
E-mail: ascsa@ascsa.org

*SPECIAL STIPULATIONS:
Research and reporting must be completed by October 31, 2016. Recipients may not hold any other federally funded grant at the same time, such as a Fulbright or NEH Fellowship.

Membership application to the ASCSA must be made online on the web site at the same time one applies to any outside funding organization for work at the School.

A final report is due at the end of the award period, and the ASCSA expects that copies of all publications that result from research conducted as a Fellow of the ASCSA be contributed to the relevant library of the School.

ARIZONA COMMISSION ON THE ARTS [420]

417 West Roosevelt Street
Phoenix, AZ 85003
(602) 771-6502
Fax: (602) 256-0282
E-mail: info@azarts.gov
Web Site: www.azarts.gov

FOUNDED: 1967

AREAS OF INTEREST:
Performing arts, visual arts and literary arts.

TYPE:
Challenge/matching grants; Conferences/seminars; Development grants; General operating grants; Internships; Project/program grants; Research grants; Residencies; Technical assistance; Travel grants. Specialized library services to artists and arts organizations.

YEAR PROGRAM STARTED: 1967

PURPOSE:
To stimulate and encourage public interest in the arts. Dedicated to making quality arts opportunities available to its citizens, the Arts Commission takes a leadership role in broadening the support systems for the arts and demonstrating how the arts are integral to the vitality of our communities and citizens.

Commission goals are to increase opportunities for all residents of Arizona to experience the arts; assist individual artists and arts organizations in Arizona; stimulate support and visibility for the arts in Arizona; foster the preservation, promotion and availability of Arizona's diverse ethnic arts; make the arts fundamental to education.

LEGAL BASIS:
State agency.

GEOG. RESTRICTIONS: Arizona.

FINANCIAL DATA:
Amount of support per award: Varies.

Total amount of support: Varies.

APPLICATION INFO:
Call for application or access from web site.

Duration: Varies.

Deadline: Varies.

ASIAN CULTURAL COUNCIL [421]

6 West 48th Street, 12th Floor
New York, NY 10036-1802
(212) 843-0403
Fax: (212) 843-0343
E-mail: acc@accny.org
Web Site: www.asianculturalcouncil.org

FOUNDED: 1980

AREAS OF INTEREST:
Visual and performing arts of Asia.

TYPE:
Exchange programs; Fellowships; Project/program grants; Research grants; Residencies; Travel grants; Visiting scholars. Support of cultural exchange in the visual and performing arts between the U.S. and those countries of Asia extending from Afghanistan through Japan.

YEAR PROGRAM STARTED: 1980

PURPOSE:
To award fellowships to individuals and grants to organizations to support projects that foster exchange between Asia and the U.S.; to fund regional travel within Asia.

LEGAL BASIS:
Public foundation organized under Section 501(c)(3).

ELIGIBILITY:
Grants are open to citizens and permanent residents of the countries of Asia from Afghanistan eastward through Japan and Indonesia, and citizens and permanent residents of the U.S. Individuals pursuing projects in their home countries are not supported. Priority consideration is generally given to individuals who have not previously received funding support from the Council.

FINANCIAL DATA:
The Asian Cultural Council's grant programs are supported by endowment income and annual contributions from foundations, corporations, and individuals in the U.S. and Asia. Levels of grant activity are based on financial resources available.

Amount of support per award: Varies.

Total amount of support: Varies.

NO. MOST RECENT APPLICANTS: 500 for the year 2014.

NO. AWARDS: 100.

APPLICATION INFO:
Grant applicants must first submit the appropriate online Individual or Organization Inquiry form. Applications are available through the web site September 1 through October 31 of each calendar year for grants in the following year.

Duration: Three months to one year. Renewals are rare.

Deadline: Full application: November 1 (postmarked).

PUBLICATIONS:
Annual report.

IRS I.D.: 13-3018822

OFFICERS:
Wendy O'Neill, Chairman
Hans Michael Jebsen, Vice Chairman
Josie Cruz Natori, Vice Chairman
Jonathan Fanton, Treasurer
Hope Aldrich, Secretary

TRUSTEES:
Jane DeBevoise

John Foster
Curtis Greer
David Halpert
Douglas Tong Hsu
J. Christopher Kojima
Richard S. Lanier
Erh-fei Liu
Elizabeth J. McCormack
Ken Miller
Carol Rattray
David Rockefeller, Jr.
Lynne Rutkin
Marissa Fung Shaw
William G. Spears
Yuji Tsutsumi
Valerie Rockefeller Wayne

ADDRESS INQUIRIES TO:
E-mail: applications@accny.org

ASTRAEA LESBIAN FOUNDATION FOR JUSTICE

116 East 16th Street, 7th Floor
New York, NY 10003
(212) 529-8021
Fax: (212) 982-3321
Web Site: www.astraeafoundation.org

TYPE:
Awards/prizes.

See entry 957 for full listing.

THE WILLIAM G. BAKER, JR. MEMORIAL FUND [422]

2 East Read Street, Ninth Floor
Baltimore, MD 21202
(410) 332-4171
Fax: (410) 837-4701
E-mail: mwarlow@bcf.org
Web Site: www.bcf.org/baker

FOUNDED: 1964

AREAS OF INTEREST:
Arts and culture.

TYPE:
Awards/prizes; Challenge/matching grants; Development grants; General operating grants; Project/program grants.

YEAR PROGRAM STARTED: 1964

PURPOSE:
To strengthen Baltimore's arts and culture sector.

LEGAL BASIS:
Private, nonprofit foundation.

ELIGIBILITY:
Cultural organizations (or their fiscal agents) serving the Baltimore area that qualify as public charities under Section 501(c)(3) of the Internal Revenue Code.

The fund does not normally make grants to endowment campaigns, annual appeals, event sponsorships, services outside the greater Baltimore area, or art programs and projects that use the arts as a mechanism to achieve other ends such as community development, health, social justice, arts education or youth development objectives.

GEOG. RESTRICTIONS: Greater Baltimore area.

FINANCIAL DATA:
Amount of support per award: $1,500 to $50,000.

Total amount of support: $1,181,859 for the year 2015.

NO. MOST RECENT APPLICANTS: 41.

NO. AWARDS: 41 for the year 2015.

APPLICATION INFO:
Applicants must complete the online application and evaluation chart. Maryland Cultural Data Project data profile is required.

Duration: Varies.

IRS I.D.: 52-6057178

GOVERNING BOARD:
Connie E. Imboden, President
Gwen Davidson
Laura L. Gamble
Steven G. Ziger

ADDRESS INQUIRIES TO:
Melissa Warlow, Director
(See address above.)

BATON ROUGE AREA FOUNDATION [423]

402 North Fourth Street
Baton Rouge, LA 70802
(225) 387-6126
Fax: (225) 387-6153
E-mail: jcarpenter@braf.org
Web Site: www.braf.org

AREAS OF INTEREST:
Arts, cultural programs, education, community development, human services, environment, scholarships, medical and health.

TYPE:
Capital grants; Challenge/matching grants; Conferences/seminars; Demonstration grants; Development grants; Matching gifts; Project/program grants; Scholarships; Seed money grants; Technical assistance; Training grants; Visiting scholars.

PURPOSE:
To connect philanthropists with capable nonprofits to make sure the needs of the community are met; to invest in and manage pivotal projects that can change the community.

ELIGIBILITY:
Eligible organizations must be IRS 501(c)(3) tax-exempt.

GEOG. RESTRICTIONS: Baton Rouge area, Louisiana.

FINANCIAL DATA:
Amount of support per award: Varies.

Total amount of support: Varies.

APPLICATION INFO:
Application details are available online. All applications must include a copy of the IRS tax determination letter.

Duration: One year. Must reapply for additional funding.

ADDRESS INQUIRIES TO:
John K. Carpenter, Director of Donor Services
(See address above.)

CALIFORNIA ARTS COUNCIL [424]

1300 I Street, Suite 930
Sacramento, CA 95814
(916) 322-6555
(800) 201-6201
Fax: (916) 322-6575
E-mail: caitlin.fitzwater@arts.ca.gov
Web Site: www.arts.ca.gov

FOUNDED: 1976

AREAS OF INTEREST:
Operating and creative support to art organizations, artists, visual and performing arts programs in schools and after-school programs.

CONSULTING OR VOLUNTEER SERVICES:
Sponsor conferences and technical assistance to art organizations.

NAME(S) OF PROGRAMS:
- **Accessibility Grant**
- **Artists in Schools**
- **Creative California Communities**
- **Jump Starts**
- **Local Impact**
- **Professional Development and Consulting**
- **State-Local Partnership Program in the Arts**
- **Statewide Service Networks in the Arts**
- **Veterans Initiative in the Arts**

TYPE:
Challenge/matching grants; Project/program grants.

YEAR PROGRAM STARTED: 1976

PURPOSE:
To advance California in the arts and creativity.

LEGAL BASIS:
State arts agency, funded by state budget and other sources.

ELIGIBILITY:
To be eligible for funding, a California-based group or organization should be an incorporated nonprofit and have been in existence at least two years and be able to demonstrate fiscal and managerial responsibility. Grants are given to provide in-school and after-school arts educational activities, assistance for specific artistic services such as events, exhibitions and publications, to expand participation by segments of the public who have had limited access to cultural events, and to encourage and enhance communication among artists, organizations and the general public.

GEOG. RESTRICTIONS: California.

FINANCIAL DATA:
Amount of support per award: Varies according to program.

Total amount of support: Varies.

NO. MOST RECENT APPLICANTS: 300.

NO. AWARDS: Approximately 200.

APPLICATION INFO:
Contact the Council.

Duration: Six months to one year.

Deadline: Varies according to program.

PUBLICATIONS:
Guide to programs; applications; newsletters.

COUNCIL MEMBERS:
Donn K. Harris, Chairperson
Nashormeh Lindo, Vice Chairperson
Larry Baza
Phoebe Beasley
Christopher Coppola
Juan Devis
Kathleen Gallegos
Jaime Galli
Louise McGuinness
Steven H. Oliver
Rosalind Wyman

ADDRESS INQUIRIES TO:
Caitlin Fitzwater
Communications Director
(See address above.)

CANADA COUNCIL FOR THE ARTS [425]

150 Elgin Street
Ottawa ON K1P 5V8 Canada
(800) 263-5588 ext. 5060 (Canada only)
(613) 566-4414 ext. 4681
Fax: (613) 566-4390
TTY: (866) 585-5559
E-mail: info@canadacouncil.ca
Web Site: www.canadacouncil.ca

FOUNDED: 1957

AREAS OF INTEREST:
The arts in Canada (dance, music, inter-arts, theatre, visual arts, media arts, creative writing and publishing).

NAME(S) OF PROGRAMS:
- **Grants to Professional Canadian Artists and Arts Organizations**

TYPE:
Awards/prizes; Block grants; Development grants; Endowments; Fellowships; Formula grants; General operating grants; Project/program grants; Research grants; Residencies; Scholarships; Training grants; Travel grants; Visiting scholars. Several programs of support providing grants and services to professional Canadian artists and nonprofit arts organizations.

PURPOSE:
To provide grants and services to professional Canadian artists and arts organizations in dance, music, theatre, media arts (film video, audio, new media), inter-arts (including contemporary circus art), visual arts and creative writing to help them pursue professional development, independent artistic creation or production.

LEGAL BASIS:
Independent agency established by the Parliament of Canada in 1957.

ELIGIBILITY:
Individual professional artists must be Canadian citizens or permanent residents of Canada. They do not have to be living in Canada when they apply. The Canada Council defines a professional artist as someone who has specialized training in the field (not necessarily in academic institutions), who is recognized as such by her or his peers (artists working in the same artistic tradition) and who has a history of public presentation or publication.

Canadian arts organizations, such as theatre companies, art museums, public galleries, artist-run centres, dance companies, orchestras and film cooperatives, that are staffed by arts professionals who create artistic works or present them to the Canadian public, are also eligible, as are professional publishing houses.

Canadian arts organizations are assessed on the basis of criteria such as professionalism, artistic excellence, community support, stability and sound financial management.

GEOG. RESTRICTIONS: Canada.

FINANCIAL DATA:
Grants for Professional Artists contribute towards living expenses, cost of materials related to the project, professional development, or independent artistic creation or production. Funds may not be used for capital costs.

Amount of support per award: Grants for Professional Artists: $3,000 to $20,000 (CAN) in increments of $1,000 (CAN); Travel grants: $500 to $2,500 (CAN), depending on need.

Total amount of support: Varies.

NO. MOST RECENT APPLICANTS: 14,900.

NO. AWARDS: 5,800.

APPLICATION INFO:
Prospective applicants should specify their citizenship and their field of interest and indicate whether they are professional. Further information and brochures are available on request.

The Council does not accept applications that are sent by fax or e-mail.

PUBLICATIONS:
Program information sheets.

ADDRESS INQUIRIES TO:
Christian Mondor, Information Officer
(See address above.)

CINTAS FOUNDATION [426]

c/o MDC Museum of Art and Design
600 Biscayne Boulevard
Miami, FL 33132
(305) 237-7901
Fax: (305) 373-0056
E-mail: lescobar@mdc.edu
Web Site: www.cintasfoundation.org

FOUNDED: 1981

AREAS OF INTEREST:
Architecture, creative writing, music composition and the visual arts.

NAME(S) OF PROGRAMS:
- **Cintas Fellowships in the Arts**

TYPE:
Awards/prizes; Fellowships. Awarded to persons of Cuban citizenship or lineage residing outside Cuba for achievement of a creative nature in architecture, painting, sculpture, printmaking, music composition and literature.

PURPOSE:
To recognize outstanding creative work done by a person from Cuba or a person of Cuban descent.

LEGAL BASIS:
Private, not-for-profit agency.

ELIGIBILITY:
Applications are open to professionals in the creative arts, of Cuban citizenship or lineage, who can give evidence of their creative production by records of exhibitions, performances or (when appropriate) by published books or scores. Students wishing to pursue academic programs are not eligible for awards nor are performing artists as opposed to creative artists. Although there is no fixed age limit, the Fellowships are intended for young professionals in the arts who have completed their academic and technical training. The program focuses on one creative genre per grant cycle.

FINANCIAL DATA:
Amount of support per award: $10,000, paid in four equal quarterly stipends.

Total amount of support: Varies.

NO. MOST RECENT APPLICANTS: 150.

NO. AWARDS: 3 to 4 annually.

APPLICATION INFO:
Eligible candidates may request application forms and letter of reference forms from the Foundation. Applications should be in English and should be accompanied by supporting documentation of an appropriate nature, such as published books or music scores or photographs and color slides of paintings or sculpture.

Duration: 12 consecutive months beginning October 10.

Deadline: July 1.

ADDRESS INQUIRIES TO:
Laurie Escobar, Administrator
(See address and e-mail above.)

COLORADO CREATIVE INDUSTRIES [427]

1625 Broadway, Suite 2700
Denver, CO 80202
(303) 892-3802
Fax: (303) 892-3848
TDD: (303) 894-2664
E-mail: coloarts@state.co.us
Web Site: www.coloradocreativeindustries.org

FOUNDED: 1967

AREAS OF INTEREST:
Visual arts, literature, performing arts, folk arts and media arts, youth-at-risk and economic benefits.

NAME(S) OF PROGRAMS:
- **Career Advancement**
- **Colorado Creates**
- **Creative Districts**

TYPE:
Project/program grants.

PURPOSE:
To promote, support and expand the creative industries to drive Colorado's economy, grow jobs and enhance the quality of life.

LEGAL BASIS:
State government agency.

ELIGIBILITY:
Colorado artists, creative small business and nonprofit tax-exempt organizations and municipalities.

GEOG. RESTRICTIONS: Colorado.

FINANCIAL DATA:
Amount of support per award: Career Advancement: Up to $2,500; Colorado Creates: $4,000 to $10,000.

Total amount of support: Varies.

Matching fund requirements: Career Advancement: 1:1 cash match; Colorado Creates: Based on cash operating income. Creative Districts: 1:1 match.

NO. MOST RECENT APPLICANTS: 380.

NO. AWARDS: 300.

APPLICATION INFO:
Contact Colorado Creative Industries.

Duration: Colorado Creates: Two years on, one year off. Other programs: Generally one year.

PUBLICATIONS:
Annual report; guidelines; press releases; news clips; strategic plan.

OFFICERS:
John Hickenlooper, Governor
Robert Clasen, Chairperson
Margaret Hunt, Director

ADDRESS INQUIRIES TO:
Sheila Sears, Deputy Director
(See address above.)

THE COMMUNITY FOUNDATION OF LOUISVILLE, INC. [428]

325 West Main Street, Suite 1110
Louisville, KY 40202
(502) 585-4649
Fax: (502) 587-7484
E-mail: giving@cflouisville.org
Web Site: www.cflouisville.org

AREAS OF INTEREST:
Visual arts, crafts, theatre, historic preservation, environment, education, religion and humanities.

TYPE:
Endowments; General operating grants; Scholarships.

PURPOSE:
To enrich the quality of life for all citizens in the Louisville area and to serve as a catalyst for promoting philanthropy within the local community.

ELIGIBILITY:
Grants are made to organizations that have tax-exempt status under Section 501(c)(3) of the Internal Revenue Code.

GEOG. RESTRICTIONS: Louisville, Kentucky and surrounding communities.

FINANCIAL DATA:
Amount of support per award: Varies.
Total amount of support: Varies.

APPLICATION INFO:
Contact the Foundation.
Duration: One year.
Deadline: Details are available on the web site.

ADDRESS INQUIRIES TO:
For Scholarships:
Ebony O'Rea
E-mail: ebonyo@cflouisville.org

For Grants:
Program Officer
(See address above.)

CONGRESSIONAL BLACK CAUCUS FOUNDATION, INC.

1720 Massachusetts Avenue, N.W.
Washington, DC 20036
(202) 263-2800
Fax: (202) 263-0846
E-mail: scholarships@cbcfinc.org
Web Site: www.cbcfinc.org

TYPE:
Scholarships. CBC Spouses-Heineken USA Performing Arts Scholarship, developed in honor of the late Curtis Mayfield, is intended to ensure that students pursuing a career in the performing arts receive the financial assistance to achieve their goals.

CBC Spouses Visual Arts Scholarship was established for students who are pursuing a career in the visual arts.

See entry 1004 for full listing.

CONSEIL DES ARTS DE MONTREAL [429]

1210 East Sherbrooke Street
First Floor
Montreal QC H2L 2L9 Canada
(514) 280-3582
E-mail: nathalie.maille@ville.montreal.qc.ca
Web Site: www.artsmontreal.org

FOUNDED: 1956

AREAS OF INTEREST:
Visual arts, dance, theatre, music, literature, cinema, new artistic practices, video and electronic arts.

NAME(S) OF PROGRAMS:
- **Programme de tournees**
- **Programme General**

TYPE:
Awards/prizes; Development grants; Exchange programs; General operating grants; Project/program grants; Technical assistance. Grants to nonprofit professional organizations having their head offices in Montreal.

YEAR PROGRAM STARTED: 1956

PURPOSE:
To assist Montreal's artistic and cultural organizations.

LEGAL BASIS:
Regional organization.

ELIGIBILITY:
Professional, nonprofit organizations in Montreal.

GEOG. RESTRICTIONS: Montreal, Quebec.

FINANCIAL DATA:
Amount of support per award: Varies.
Total amount of support: $11,955,681 (CAN) for the year 2015.

NO. MOST RECENT APPLICANTS: 522.

NO. AWARDS: 425 for the year 2015.

APPLICATION INFO:
Contact the Conseil des Arts.
Duration: One fiscal year.
Deadline: Programme de tournees: September. Programme General: Varies by type of grant.

PUBLICATIONS:
Annual report.

STAFF:
Sylviane Martineau, Cultural Advisor, Dance
Rejane Bouge, Cultural Advisor, Literature, Cinema
Claire Metras, Cultural Advisor, Music
Christiane Bonneau, Cultural Advisor, New Artist Practices, Multidisciplinary, Circus Arts
Isabelle Boisclair, Cultural Advisor, Theatre
Marie-Michele Cron, Cultural Advisor, Visual Arts, Media Arts

ADDRESS INQUIRIES TO:
Cultural Advisor
(See address above.)

THE CORPORATION OF YADDO [430]

312 Union Avenue
Saratoga Springs, NY 12866
(518) 584-0746
Fax: (518) 584-1312
E-mail: chwait@yaddo.org
Web Site: www.yaddo.org

FOUNDED: 1900

AREAS OF INTEREST:
Literature, visual arts, music composition, filmmaking, choreography, performance art and other creative arts.

NAME(S) OF PROGRAMS:
- **Artist Residencies**

TYPE:
Residencies; Travel grants.

YEAR PROGRAM STARTED: 1926

PURPOSE:
To enable artists to work in a quiet, protected and supportive environment.

LEGAL BASIS:
A publicly supported charity.

ELIGIBILITY:
For creative artists working at a professional level in their field.

FINANCIAL DATA:
No cash grants. The award covers room, board and studio costs. A small fund exists to provide limited help towards the expenses of travel or renting equipment to invited guests of any discipline who otherwise might not be able to visit.

NO. MOST RECENT APPLICANTS: 1,542 for the year 2013.

NO. AWARDS: 186 for the year 2013.

APPLICATION INFO:
Applicants should apply to the Admissions Panel that best represents the project they wish to undertake should they be invited for a residency. Applicants may apply to only one admissions panel, in one genre, at a time. Applicants with concerns about choice of panel should contact the Program Director.

All application materials, including contact information, resume, work sample, and reference letters must be submitted electronically.

Duration: Up to two months.
Deadline: January 1 and August 1.

PUBLICATIONS:
Annual report; newsletter; case statement.

IRS I.D.: 14-1343055

OFFICERS:
A.M. Homes, Chairperson
Susan Unterberg, Chairperson
Peter Kayafas, Vice Chairperson
Elaina Richardson, President
Patricia Sopp, Vice President, Finance and Assistant Treasurer
Candace Weir, Treasurer
Gardner McFall, Corporate Secretary
Susan Brynteson, Recording Secretary

ADDRESS INQUIRIES TO:
Candace Wait, Program Director
The Corporation of Yaddo
P.O. Box 395
Saratoga Springs, NY 12886-0395

COSTUME SOCIETY OF AMERICA [431]

P.O. Box 852
Columbus, GA 31902-0852
(706) 615-2851
(800) 272-9447 (U.S.)
E-mail: national.office@costumesocietyamerica.com
Web Site: www.costumesocietyamerica.com

FOUNDED: 1973

AREAS OF INTEREST:
Costume, art history, research, textile and fashion design, museum studies and anthropology.

NAME(S) OF PROGRAMS:
- **Stella Blum Research Grant**
- **CSA Travel Research Grant**
- **Adele Filene Student Presenter Grant**

TYPE:
Awards/prizes; Conferences/seminars; Development grants; Fellowships; General operating grants; Project/program grants; Research grants; Scholarships; Travel grants. Stella Blum Research Grant is a merit award for a student researching a North American costume topic.

CSA Travel Research Grant aids in travel to collections to any library, archive, museum or site for research to further an ongoing project.

Adele Filene Student Presenter Grant assists the travel of a CSA student member to that year's CSA national symposium to present either a juried paper or poster.

YEAR PROGRAM STARTED: 1987

PURPOSE:
To advance the global understanding of all aspects of dress and appearance.

ELIGIBILITY:
Must be a Costume Society of America member for all awards.

CSA Travel Research Grant: Must be a CSA nonstudent member. Proof must be given that work on the project is already underway.

Adele Filene Student Presenter Grant: Must be currently enrolled as a student with a juried paper or poster accepted by the CSA symposium.

FINANCIAL DATA:
Amount of support per award: Stella Blum Research Grant: $2,000, plus up to $500 to present completed research at the National Symposium and one day presentation registration fee; CSA Travel Research Grant: $1,500; Adele Filene Student Presenter Grant: Up to $500, plus one day presentation registration fee.

Total amount of support: Varies.

NO. MOST RECENT APPLICANTS: 12.

NO. AWARDS: 3.

APPLICATION INFO:
Information is available, under "Resources/Grants, Awards and Honors," on the Society's web site.

Duration: One year.

Deadline: Grant deadlines are posted online.

ADDRESS INQUIRIES TO:
Executive Director
(See e-mail address above.)

DELAWARE DIVISION OF THE ARTS [432]

Carvel State Office Building
820 North French Street
Wilmington, DE 19801
(302) 577-8278
Fax: (302) 577-6561
E-mail: delarts@state.de.us
Web Site: www.artsdel.org

FOUNDED: 1969

AREAS OF INTEREST:
Performing arts, visual arts, literature and media.

CONSULTING OR VOLUNTEER SERVICES:
Technical assistance to community groups and arts organizations.

NAME(S) OF PROGRAMS:
- **Arts in Education**
- **Arts Organizations Grants**
- **Community Based Organizations Grants**
- **Gallery Program**
- **Individual Artist Fellowships**
- **Opportunity Grants**

TYPE:
Challenge/matching grants; Conferences/seminars; Fellowships; General operating grants; Project/program grants; Residencies; Technical assistance. Grants to Delaware nonprofit, tax-exempt organizations for projects in the arts. Fellowships program for individual creative artists who reside in Delaware.

YEAR PROGRAM STARTED: 1970

PURPOSE:
To nurture and support the arts to enhance the quality of life for all Delawareans.

LEGAL BASIS:
State agency.

ELIGIBILITY:
Applicants must be nonprofit, tax-exempt organizations in the state of Delaware. Fellowship applicants are individual creative artists who reside in Delaware.

GEOG. RESTRICTIONS: Delaware.

FINANCIAL DATA:
Amount of funds available is determined by state appropriation and funding from the National Endowment for the Arts.

Amount of support per award: Variable according to program.

Total amount of support: $3,100,000.

Matching fund requirements: Organization grants matching requirements vary according to program.

NO. MOST RECENT APPLICANTS: 253.

NO. AWARDS: 168.

APPLICATION INFO:
Application must be made on forms available on the web site.

Duration: Varies.

Deadline: March 1 for most grants. Announcement July 1 for most grants.

ADDRESS INQUIRIES TO:
Paul Weagraff, Director
(See address above.)

DEPARTMENT OF ECONOMIC AND COMMUNITY DEVELOPMENT/CONNECTICUT OFFICE OF THE ARTS [433]

One Constitution Plaza, 2nd Floor
Hartford, CT 06103
(860) 256-2753
(860) 256-2727
Fax: (860) 256-2811
E-mail: kristina.newmanscott@ct.gov
Web Site: www.cultureandtourism.org

FOUNDED: 1965

AREAS OF INTEREST:
Fine arts, literature, museums and libraries, music, creative and performing arts, theatre, dance, arts in education, community arts development programs, public art slide bank, art in public spaces, history, tourism and colleges/universities.

CONSULTING OR VOLUNTEER SERVICES:
Volunteer Lawyers for the Arts program.

TYPE:
Challenge/matching grants; Conferences/seminars; Endowments; Fellowships; General operating grants; Internships; Project/program grants; Technical assistance. Grants are available to Connecticut artists, arts institutions, arts organizations and nonprofit arts-sponsoring organizations for program support and technical assistance.

Project grants are available to non-arts organizations using arts or conducting arts programming, as well as schools, libraries and PTOs.

YEAR PROGRAM STARTED: 1965

PURPOSE:
To invest in the state's art-based cultural activities and infrastructure in ways that will advance the attractiveness and competitiveness of Connecticut cities, towns and villages as meaningful communities in which to live, work, learn and play.

LEGAL BASIS:
The State of Connecticut Enabling Legislation, Public Act No. 78-187 created the original Connecticut Commission on the Arts.

ELIGIBILITY:
Connecticut artists, art institutions, units of state or local government, art organizations and nonprofit arts-sponsoring associations whose principle residence is in Connecticut. Ineligible programs are those which take place out of state, student projects, fund-raising benefits, social activities, membership activities, scholarships, underwriting of past deficits or capital expenditures.

GEOG. RESTRICTIONS: Connecticut.

FINANCIAL DATA:
Amount of support per award: $1,000 to $35,000 for the year 2016.

Total amount of support: Approximately $2,000,000 for the year 2016.

CO-OP FUNDING PROGRAMS: Matching funds, Federal-state partnership and designated regional service organizations.

NO. MOST RECENT APPLICANTS: 300.

NO. AWARDS: 265 for the year 2016.

APPLICATION INFO:
A guidelines brochure may be requested from the Commission three to four months in advance to the project.

Duration: Varies.

Deadline: Varies.

PUBLICATIONS:
Copyright Law; *Non-Profit Incorporation-A Guide for Artists and Organizations*; *Contract Law for Artists and Organizations*; *Culture and Tourism Newsletter*; Bi-Monthly Bulletin; *Art in Public Spaces Program Guide*; *Hot Schools Transform Education*; *Economic Impact of the Nonprofit Arts Industry in Connecticut*; *Performing Artists*, online directories.

STAFF:
Kristina Newman-Scott, Director of Culture

ADDRESS INQUIRIES TO:
Rhonda Olisky, Special Projects Coordinator
(See address above.)

DISTRICT OF COLUMBIA COMMISSION ON THE ARTS AND HUMANITIES [434]

200 I Street, S.E.
Washington, DC 20003
(202) 724-5613
Fax: (202) 727-4135
TDD: (202) 727-3148
E-mail: steven.mazzola@dc.gov
Web Site: www.dcarts.dc.gov

FOUNDED: 1968

AREAS OF INTEREST:
The arts and humanities in the District of Columbia.

NAME(S) OF PROGRAMS:

- **Artist Fellowship Program**
- **Arts Education Program**
- **City Arts Projects**
- **Cultural Facilities Program**
- **East of the River Program**
- **Grants-in-Aid**
- **Mid Atlantic Performing Arts Presenters**
- **Public Art Building Communities**
- **Sister Cities International Arts Grant**
- **UPSTART Program**

TYPE:
Awards/prizes; Capital grants; Challenge/matching grants; Conferences/seminars; Exchange programs; Fellowships; General operating grants; Grants-in-aid; Project/program grants; Research grants; Residencies. Services provided to arts institutions and individual artists including inquiry services, technical assistance and funding.

YEAR PROGRAM STARTED: 1968

PURPOSE:
To administer funds to arts organizations, community organizations and individual artists to support arts endeavors within the District of Columbia.

LEGAL BASIS:
State arts agency authorized by executive order.

ELIGIBILITY:
Applicants must be residents of Washington, DC. Organizations must be located in Washington, DC and be nonprofit IRS 501(c)(3) arts organizations within the District of Columbia at least two years prior to application in some programs and one year in most others. Organizations are also required to participate in the DC Cultural Data Project.

Grant funds cannot be used for scholarships, reserve funds, or any food/receptions. Fiscal agents are strictly prohibited.

GEOG. RESTRICTIONS: Washington, DC.

FINANCIAL DATA:
Amount of support per award: $1,000 to $30,000. For capital funding projects and for organizations: Up to $200,000.

Total amount of support: Varies.

Matching fund requirements: Matching funds are required for organizations.

CO-OP FUNDING PROGRAMS: National Endowment for the Arts.

NO. MOST RECENT APPLICANTS: 750.

REPRESENTATIVE AWARDS:
$5,000 to Thomas Circle Singers for general operating support; $15,000 to Kennedy Center for project support for its Millenium Stage; $11,162 to Shakespeare Theatre Company for a security camera.

APPLICATION INFO:
Application information is available on the web site.

Duration: All expenses must be paid within the District's fiscal year of October 1 to September 30.

Deadline: Varies per grant cycle.

PUBLICATIONS:
Application guidelines.

ADDRESS INQUIRIES TO:
Steven Mazzola, Director of Grants
(See address above.)

EAST TENNESSEE FOUNDATION

520 West Summit Hill Drive
Suite 1101
Knoxville, TN 37902
(865) 524-1223
(877) 524-1223
Fax: (865) 637-6039
E-mail: etf@etf.org
Web Site: www.easttennesseefoundation.org

TYPE:
Project/program grants; Scholarships; Seed money grants; Technical assistance. The Foundation is comprised of 400 philanthropic funds and nine supporting organizations.

See entry 1099 for full listing.

THE FIELDSTONE FOUNDATION

14 Corporate Plaza, Suite 100
Newport Beach, CA 92660
(949) 873-2717
Fax: (949) 515-8520
E-mail: janinem@fieldstonefoundation.org
Web Site: www.fieldstonefoundation.org

TYPE:
Challenge/matching grants; General operating grants; Project/program grants.

See entry 358 for full listing.

FLORIDA DEPARTMENT OF STATE, DIVISION OF CULTURAL AFFAIRS [435]

500 South Bronough Street
Tallahassee, FL 32399-0250
(850) 245-6470
Fax: (850) 245-6497
E-mail: info@florida-arts.org
Web Site: www.florida-arts.org

FOUNDED: 1969

AREAS OF INTEREST:
The Division of Cultural Affairs administers the cultural grant programs of the Department of State and is responsible for planning and implementing arts programs statewide, providing technical assistance to artists and arts organizations, awarding, administering, monitoring and evaluating the grants program, disseminating arts-related information and encouraging cultural development in Florida.

CONSULTING OR VOLUNTEER SERVICES:
Facilitative services in all areas are available.

NAME(S) OF PROGRAMS:

- **Capitol Complex Exhibition Program**
- **Cultural Facilities Program**
- **Florida Cultural Endowment Program**
- **Florida Individual Artist Fellowship Program**
- **General Program Support Grants Program**
- **Specific Cultural Projects Grants Program**
- **State Touring Program**

TYPE:
Awards/prizes; Capital grants; Conferences/seminars; Endowments; Fellowships; Formula grants; General operating grants; Grants-in-aid; Project/program grants. Cultural facilities grants. State touring grants. Fellowships to individual artists residing in the state of Florida. Program provides a limited number of unmatched fellowships for creative artists in dance, folk arts, inter-disciplinary, literature, media arts, music, theatre and visual arts.

YEAR PROGRAM STARTED: 1969

PURPOSE:
To encourage the creation of projects that promote excellence in the arts and that strive to bring arts to a communitywide audience.

LEGAL BASIS:
State government agency.

ELIGIBILITY:
To apply for a grant, an organization must qualify as a political subdivision of a municipal, county or state government in Florida or be a not-for-profit, tax-exempt Florida corporation, meet specific budgetary and program requirements as outlined for the appropriate artistic disciplines, special programs and funding categories, match dollar-for-dollar, in most cases, the grant amount requested from the Division and meet all legal and financial requirements described in the *Guide to Cultural Programs*.

To apply for and retain a fellowship, an applicant must be a Florida citizen, at least 18 years old, and maintain Florida residency for the duration of the grant period. The applicant must not be a degree-seeking student at the time of application or at any time during the grant period. Applicant must not have received a Division fellowship during the past four years at the time of the application.

GEOG. RESTRICTIONS: Florida.

FINANCIAL DATA:
Cash grants are for program expenses rather than for capital improvements.

Amount of support per award: Varies depending upon grant program and specific eligibility.

Total amount of support: Varies by program.

Matching fund requirements: Fellowships: Unmatched. In most cases, grants are matched 1:1.

NO. MOST RECENT APPLICANTS: More than 1,400.

NO. AWARDS: More than 100 awards for fiscal year 2012-13.

APPLICATION INFO:
Program guidelines can be downloaded from the web site.

Duration: One year.

Deadline: June for General Program Support and Specific Cultural Projects grants. July for fellowships.

OFFICERS:
Sandy Shaughnessy, Director, Division of Cultural Affairs

STAFF:
Gaylen Phillips, Associate Director of Arts Resources and Services

ADDRESS INQUIRIES TO:
Tim Storhoff, Arts Consultant
(See address above.)

FONDATION DES ETATS-UNIS [436]

15, boulevard Jourdan
75014 Paris France
(33) 1 53 80 68 82
Fax: (33) 1 53 80 68 99
E-mail: culture@feusa.org
Web Site: www.feusa.org/harriet-hale-woolley-scholarship/

FOUNDED: 1929

AREAS OF INTEREST:
Grants for musicians, artists, and interns in psychiatry.

CONSULTING OR VOLUNTEER SERVICES:
Office of Cultural Affairs.

NAME(S) OF PROGRAMS:
- **Harriet Hale Woolley Scholarships**

TYPE:
Awards/prizes; Development grants; Scholarships. Bequeathed to the Fondation des Etats-Unis, Cite Internationale Universitaire de Paris in the early 1930s, the Harriet Hale Woolley Scholarship is awarded annually to a select number of exceptional American artists and musicians who plan to pursue their studies in Paris.

A scholarship is also available to French, Swiss and American medical postgraduates specializing in psychiatry with an internship in a Parisian hospital.

The scholarship is not intended for research in art history or musicology, nor for dance or theater.

YEAR PROGRAM STARTED: 1933

PURPOSE:
To promote artistic and cultural exchange between the U.S. and France.

LEGAL BASIS:
Fondation Reconnue d'Utilite Publique (FRUP).

ELIGIBILITY:
Requirements include:
(1) American citizenship;
(2) between 21 and 29 years of age;
(3) graduation with high academic standing from an American college, university, or professional school of recognized standing;
(4) evidence of accomplishment in the candidate's field of expertise;
(5) proposal of a unique and detailed artistic project related to one's field of study that requires a one-year residency in Paris and;
(6) good moral character, personality and adaptability, plus good physical health and emotional stability.

Scholarship recipient must reside at the Fondation des Etats-Unis for the academic year.

FINANCIAL DATA:
The Scholarship is designed to assist with living expenses while in Paris.

Amount of support per award: Stipend of EUR 10,000 (may vary subject to fund earnings), payable in four installments during the academic year (October 1 to June 30).

Total amount of support: A maximum amount of EUR 10,000.

NO. MOST RECENT APPLICANTS: 15 to 20.

NO. AWARDS: Up to 4 annually.

APPLICATION INFO:
Application should be made by e-mail. See web site for instructions.

Duration: One academic year.

Deadline: All application dossiers and their supporting materials must be received no later than January 31, for the following academic year.

OFFICER:
Dr. Anne Cremieux, Director
Dr. Sophie Vasset, Director
Noëmi Haire-Sievers, Cultural Attaché

ADDRESS INQUIRIES TO:
Harriet Hale Woolley Scholarship
(See address above.)

*SPECIAL STIPULATIONS:
As this project should include enrollment in a recognized institution, it is strongly suggested that the candidate establish a significant contact with a teacher or institution prior to arriving in France and to show evidence of this contact in his or her application dossier.

FORECAST PUBLIC ART [437]

2300 Myrtle Avenue
Suite 160
St. Paul, MN 55114
(651) 641-1128
Fax: (651) 641-1983
E-mail: grants@forecastpublicart.org
Web Site: www.forecastpublicart.org

FOUNDED: 1978

AREAS OF INTEREST:
Public art.

CONSULTING OR VOLUNTEER SERVICES:
Consulting for public artists and communities.

NAME(S) OF PROGRAMS:
- **Emerging Artist Project Grant**
- **Emerging Artist Research and Development Grant**
- **Mid-Career Professional Development Grant**
- **Mid-Career Project Grant**

TYPE:
Awards/prizes; Project/program grants; Research grants.

YEAR PROGRAM STARTED: 1988

PURPOSE:
To fund emerging and midcareer artists of all disciplines to develop and/or produce public art projects.

LEGAL BASIS:
Private nonprofit corporation.

ELIGIBILITY:
Open to emerging and midcareer artists of all disciplines. Applicant must be a Minnesota resident.

Mid-Career Project Grant applicants must be midcareer public artists.

GEOG. RESTRICTIONS: Minnesota.

FINANCIAL DATA:
Amount of support per award: Emerging Artist Project Grant: $8,000; Emerging Artist Research and Development Grant: $2,500; Mid-Career Professional Development Grant: $5,000; Mid-Career Project Grant: $50,000.

NO. MOST RECENT APPLICANTS: 50 to 100 per competition.

APPLICATION INFO:
Application information is available online.

Duration: Up to one year.

Deadline: Mid-Career Project Grant: July. Emerging Artist Project Grant, Emerging Artist Research and Development Grant, and Mid-Career Professional Development Grant: October.

PUBLICATIONS:
Public Art Review, a semiannual publication focusing on public art projects and issues.

IRS I.D.: 41-1361351

STAFF:
Jack Becker, Executive Director
Laura Ayers, Interim Associate Director
Kirstin Wiegmann, Consultant and Education and Community Engagement Program Director
Jessica Fiala, Artist Services Program Coordinator
Karen Olson, Executive Editor, *Public Art Review*

ADDRESS INQUIRIES TO:
Jessica Fiala
Artist Services Program Coordinator
(See address above.)

CARL M. FREEMAN FOUNDATION [438]

31556 Winterberry Parkway
Selbyville, DE 19975
(302) 436-3015
E-mail: info@freemanfoundation.org
Web Site: www.carlfreemanfoundation.org

FOUNDED: 1960

AREAS OF INTEREST:
Facilitating, supporting and promoting innovative community-based leadership and giving.

NAME(S) OF PROGRAMS:
- **FACES Grant**

TYPE:
Capital grants; Challenge/matching grants; General operating grants.

YEAR PROGRAM STARTED: 2000

PURPOSE:
To provide funding and capacity-building support to nonprofit organizations in the communities served by the Carl M. Freeman Companies.

ELIGIBILITY:
Must be IRS-recognized 501(c)(3) tax-exempt, nonprofit organizations or public agencies serving the residents of the Companies' funding areas.

GEOG. RESTRICTIONS: Sussex County, Delaware and Montgomery County, Maryland.

FINANCIAL DATA:
Amount of support per award: $2,500 or $5,000.

Total amount of support: $50,000 annually.

APPLICATION INFO:
Guidelines are available on the web site.

Duration: Six months; possible several-month renewal.

Deadline: Varies.

ADDRESS INQUIRIES TO:
Melissa Rizer, Grant Manager
(See address above.)

FREER GALLERY OF ART AND ARTHUR M. SACKLER GALLERY [439]

Smithsonian Institution, MRC 707
1050 Independence Avenue, S.W.
Washington, DC 20560
(202) 633-0401
Fax: (202) 633-0067
Web Site: www.asia.si.edu/research/fellowships.asp

FOUNDED: 1923

AREAS OF INTEREST:
Asian art, 19th and early 20th century American art.

CONSULTING OR VOLUNTEER SERVICES:
Docent tours for the public through Freer Gallery of Art and Arthur M. Sackler Gallery.

NAME(S) OF PROGRAMS:
- **The J.S. Lee Memorial Fellowship**
- **Smithsonian Institution Fellowship**
- **Anne van Biema Fellowship**

TYPE:
Awards/prizes; Fellowships; Internships; Project/program grants; Research grants; Technical assistance; Visiting scholars. The J.S. Lee Memorial Fellowship facilitates the international exchange of curatorial expertise and contributes to the professional development of Chinese art curators and academics.

Anne van Biema Fellowship is established to promote excellence in research and publication on the Japanese visual arts. One award is made each year to support a scholar at the postdoctoral level for a period of two to nine months.

YEAR PROGRAM STARTED: 1923

PURPOSE:
To advance scholarship of Asian art and 19th and early 20th century American art.

LEGAL BASIS:
U.S. government agency.

ELIGIBILITY:
Varies with each fellowship.

FINANCIAL DATA:
Amount of support per award: Senior and Postdoctoral: Up to $45,000 per year; Predoctoral: $30,000 per year; van Biema Fellowship: Maximum $35,000 stipend.

Total amount of support: Varies.

CO-OP FUNDING PROGRAMS: Smithsonian Office of Fellowships and Grants, University of Michigan.

APPLICATION INFO:
For Smithsonian Fellowship, write to Office of Fellowships and Internships in the Smithsonian. For the J.S. Lee Memorial Fellowship, visit the fellowship page at www.jsleefellowship.org. Van Biema Fellowship information is available on the web site.

Duration: Varies.

Deadline: Varies.

PUBLICATIONS:
Annual report.

OFFICERS:
Dr. Julian Raby, Director

THE DAVID GEFFEN FOUNDATION

12011 San Vicente Boulevard
Suite 606
Los Angeles, CA 90049
(310) 581-5955
Fax: (310) 581-5949
E-mail: ddishman@geffenco.com

TYPE:
General operating grants; Project/program grants.

See entry 1396 for full listing.

GEORGIA COUNCIL FOR THE ARTS [440]

75 Fifth Street, N.W.
Suite 1200
Atlanta, GA 30308
(404) 962-4827
E-mail: gaarts@gaarts.org
Web Site: gaarts.org

FOUNDED: 1968

AREAS OF INTEREST:
The arts.

CONSULTING OR VOLUNTEER SERVICES:
Extensive technical assistance to nonprofit arts organizations in all disciplines on matters of artistic, administrative or technical concern.

NAME(S) OF PROGRAMS:
- **Georgia Masterpieces**
- **Literary Events Grants**
- **Poet Laureate**
- **Poetry Out Loud**
- **State Art Collection**

TYPE:
Awards/prizes; Challenge/matching grants; Conferences/seminars; Demonstration grants; Development grants; Formula grants; General operating grants; Grants-in-aid; Internships; Matching gifts; Project/program grants; Research grants; Residencies; Seed money grants; Technical assistance; Training grants; Visiting scholars; Research contracts. Capacity building; Poetry competitions; Traditional arts apprenticeships; Partner grants. Technical assistance and grants in categories including, but not limited to, architecture/environmental arts, dance, education (arts-related), filmmaking, folk arts/heritage arts and crafts, historic preservation (arts-related), literary arts, multimedia, museums, music, photography, public radio, television, theatre and visual arts.

YEAR PROGRAM STARTED: 1968

PURPOSE:
To cultivate the growth of Georgia communities through the arts.

LEGAL BASIS:
Government agency.

ELIGIBILITY:
Grants are made to nonprofit, tax-exempt arts organizations or units of government which are incorporated in the state of Georgia.

GEOG. RESTRICTIONS: Georgia.

FINANCIAL DATA:
Amount of support per award: $1,500 to $25,000 for the year 2015.

Total amount of support: $830,000 for the year 2015.

Matching fund requirements: Varies.

NO. AWARDS: 77 for the year 2015.

APPLICATION INFO:
Grant applications are available online.

Duration: One year. Must reapply for additional funding.

PUBLICATIONS:
Application guidelines; quarterly newsletter.

ADDRESS INQUIRIES TO:
Tina Lilly, Grants Program Manager
(See address above.)

NANCY GRAVES FOUNDATION [441]

33-20 48th Avenue, 2nd Floor
Long Island City, NY 11101
(212) 560-0602
(718) 482-1100
E-mail: mail@nancygravesfoundation.org
Web Site: www.nancygravesfoundation.org

FOUNDED: 1996

AREAS OF INTEREST:
Visual arts.

NAME(S) OF PROGRAMS:
- **Grants for Visual Artists**

TYPE:
Grant for nominated visual artists for work in any medium other than their own.

YEAR PROGRAM STARTED: 2000

PURPOSE:
To give assistance to individual artists; to maintain an archive of the Founder's life and work and organize exhibitions of her art.

ELIGIBILITY:
Grantees must be residents of the U.S. who have been working as artists for at least five years beyond his or her schooling. Grants will not be awarded to students. Applications will be solicited from nominated visual artists who wish to have the opportunity to master a technique, medium or discipline that is different from the one in which he or she is primarily recognized.

GEOG. RESTRICTIONS: United States.

FINANCIAL DATA:
Amount of support per award: $5,000.

NO. AWARDS: 2 annually.

APPLICATION INFO:
Artist applicants must be nominated by Foundation nominators and will subsequently receive an application for consideration by a second panel of jurors.

STAFF:
Christina Hunter, Director

ADDRESS INQUIRIES TO:
Christina Hunter, Director
(See address above.)

HAMBIDGE [442]

P.O. Box 339
Rabun Gap, GA 30568
(706) 746-5718
Fax: (706) 746-9933
E-mail: center@hambidge.org
Web Site: www.hambidge.org

FOUNDED: 1934

AREAS OF INTEREST:
Artist residency program.

NAME(S) OF PROGRAMS:
- **Hambidge Residency Program Fellowships**

TYPE:
Fellowships; Residencies. The Hambidge Center awards residency fellowships to distinguished artists and scientists at its 600-acre creative sanctuary in the Blue Ridge Mountains. Fellowships apply to any field or discipline of creative work. They consist of the following:
(1) The Antinori Fellowship for Ceramic Artists awards a scholarship to a ceramic artist;
(2) The Bella Cucina (Art of Food) Fellowship awards a scholarship to a culinary artisan;
(3) The Elfster Fellowship awards a scholarship to a residency applicant in any discipline;
(4) The Neva Langley Fickling Fellowship for Piano awards a scholarship to a musician concentrating on work with the piano;
(5) The Friends of Hambidge Fellowship awards a scholarship to a residency applicant in any discipline;
(6) The Fulton County Arts & Culture Fellowship awards scholarships to three artists from Fulton County, GA;
(7) The Griffith Fellowship awards a scholarship to a residency applicant in any discipline;
(8) The Holland & Knight Fellowship awards a scholarship to a residency applicant in any discipline;
(9) The W.S. Hopkins Fellowship for Photography awards a scholarship to an applicant in the field of photography;
(10) The King & Spalding Fellowship awards a scholarship to a residency applicant in any discipline;
(11) The National Endowment for the Arts Fellowship awards scholarships to nine artists from across the U.S.;
(12) The Post Hope Fellowship awards a scholarship to a residency applicant in any discipline;
(13) The Joe Quattlebaum Fellowship awards a scholarship to a southern artist actively involved in sustainability, environmental consciousness or gardening and botany;
(14) The Rogers Fellowship for Textile Arts awards a scholarship to a textile or fiber artist;
(15) The Nellie Mae Rowe Fellowship, endowed by Judith Alexander, awards a scholarship to an African American artist of any discipline;
(16) The Ron Sanders Fellowship awards a scholarship to a residency applicant in any discipline;
(17) The Judith C. Simmons Fellowship for Visual Arts awards a scholarship to a visual artist and;
(18) The Lillian Thomas Fellowship awards a scholarship to a ceramic artist.

PURPOSE:
To provide applicants with an environment for creative work in the arts and sciences.

ELIGIBILITY:
Open to qualified applicants in all disciplines who can demonstrate seriousness, dedication and professionalism. International residents are welcome.

FINANCIAL DATA:
Each of the individuals in residence has private accommodations and studio space, and shares communal dinners prepared by an in-residence chef. Eight individuals are in residence at any given time.

Amount of support per award: Each artist receives a two-week residency with no fees, a $700 stipend, and the honor of a Distinguished Fellowship.

APPLICATION INFO:
Application information is available on the web site.

Duration: Two weeks.

Deadline: January 15, April 15 and September 15.

ADDRESS INQUIRIES TO:
Debra Sanders, Office Manager
(See address above.)

HAWAII STATE FOUNDATION ON CULTURE AND THE ARTS [443]

250 South Hotel Street
Second Floor
Honolulu, HI 96813
(808) 586-0301
Fax: (808) 586-0308
TTY: (808) 586-0740
E-mail: jonathan.johnson@hawaii.gov
Web Site: hawaii.gov/sfca

FOUNDED: 1965

AREAS OF INTEREST:
Arts education, community arts, heritage and preservation, presentation, and community arts.

NAME(S) OF PROGRAMS:
- **Biennium Grants Program**

TYPE:
Project/program grants.

YEAR PROGRAM STARTED: 1965

PURPOSE:
To stimulate, encourage and promote culture, the arts and humanities throughout the state of Hawaii.

LEGAL BASIS:
State arts agency.

ELIGIBILITY:
Hawaii Revised Statutes for organizations and individuals as defined in Section 9-11.

GEOG. RESTRICTIONS: Hawaii.

FINANCIAL DATA:
Limits on the amount of funding for any one project are established by the SFCA Board. Certain costs are not allowable for SFCA funding.

Amount of support per award: Varies.

Total amount of support: Over $500,000 for fiscal year 2016.

Matching fund requirements: 1:1 match required.

NO. MOST RECENT APPLICANTS: 110.

NO. AWARDS: 62 for the year 2016.

APPLICATION INFO:
Applicants must complete the required application forms and attachments.

Duration: Funds are awarded on a biennial basis. No funds are awarded on a continuing basis.

Deadline: Grant applications are received and reviewed during the State budgetary process.

PUBLICATIONS:
Annual Report; application guidelines.

ADDRESS INQUIRIES TO:
Jonathan Johnson, Executive Director
(See address above.)

HAYSTACK MOUNTAIN SCHOOL OF CRAFTS [444]

89 Haystack School Drive
Deer Isle, ME 04627
(207) 348-2306
Fax: (207) 348-2307
E-mail: haystack@haystack-mtn.org
Web Site: www.haystack-mtn.org

FOUNDED: 1950

AREAS OF INTEREST:
Craft education and exploration in ceramics, metals, wood, fibers, graphics, glass and blacksmithing.

NAME(S) OF PROGRAMS:
- **Conferences/Seminars**
- **Exhibitions**
- **Maine Programs**
- **Open Studio Residency**
- **Summer Conference**
- **Summer Workshops**

TYPE:
Conferences/seminars; Fellowships; Residencies; Scholarships; Visiting scholars; Work-study programs. Minority scholarships; Technical Assistant and Work Study Scholarships. Awards for study in diverse craft media and workshops in six studios including ceramics, metals, wood, fibers, graphics, glass and blacksmithing.

YEAR PROGRAM STARTED: 1950

PURPOSE:
To offer professional instruction and demonstration in crafts.

LEGAL BASIS:
Nonprofit educational organization.

ELIGIBILITY:
U.S. and foreign citizens who are capable of doing graduate-level work are eligible for technical assistant scholarships. Candidates must be at least 18 years of age.

FINANCIAL DATA:
Annual scholarships cover the cost of tuition, or tuition and room and board.

Amount of support per award: $1,400.

Total amount of support: $120,000.

NO. MOST RECENT APPLICANTS: 259.

NO. AWARDS: 101 (45 work-study students; 56 technical assistants).

APPLICATION INFO:
Guidelines and application form are available at the web site.

Duration: One- to two-week sessions.

Deadline: Scholarship applications: March 1; Regular applications: April 1.

PUBLICATIONS:
Catalog; newsletter; scholarly monographs; regional program brochures; eNewsletters.

IRS I.D.: 01-0243548

ADDRESS INQUIRIES TO:
Paul Sacaridiz, Director
Haystack Mountain School of Crafts
22 Church Street (November to April)
89 Haystack School Drive (May to October)
Deer Isle, ME 04627

THE MAXIMILIAN E. & MARION O. HOFFMAN FOUNDATION, INC.

970 Farmington Avenue, Suite 203
West Hartford, CT 06107
(860) 521-2949
Fax: (860) 561-5082

TYPE:
Project/program grants.

See entry 2196 for full listing.

HUTCHINSON COMMUNITY FOUNDATION [445]

One North Main Street
Suite 501
Hutchinson, KS 67501
(620) 663-5293
Fax: (620) 663-9277
E-mail: info@hutchcf.org
Web Site: www.hutchcf.org

FOUNDED: 1989

AREAS OF INTEREST:
Arts, civic improvements, education, health and human services.

TYPE:
Project/program grants; Seed money grants.

YEAR PROGRAM STARTED: 1989

PURPOSE:
To make Hutchinson area a better place to work and live.

LEGAL BASIS:
501(c)(3) public foundation.

ELIGIBILITY:
Organizations that support innovative projects located in Reno County, KS, and government units that work in the Foundation's objective.

GEOG. RESTRICTIONS: Reno County, Kansas.

FINANCIAL DATA:
Amount of support per award: Varies.

Total amount of support: Varies.

NO. MOST RECENT APPLICANTS: 50.

NO. AWARDS: 28.

APPLICATION INFO:
One copy of the applicant's current IRS determination letter Section 501(c)(3) or 509(a) is required. Contact the Foundation for application procedures.

Duration: One year. Reapplication possible.

Deadline: Early September. Contact Foundation for exact date.

PUBLICATIONS:
Annual report; application guidelines.

OFFICERS AND STAFF:
Aubrey A. Patterson, President and Executive Director
Kari Jackson Mailloux, Program Officer

ADDRESS INQUIRIES TO:
Aubrey A. Patterson
President and Executive Director
(See address above.)

IDAHO COMMISSION ON THE ARTS [446]

2410 Old Penitentiary Road
Boise, ID 83712
(208) 334-2119
(800) 278-3863 (Idaho residents only)
Fax: (208) 334-2488
E-mail: info@arts.idaho.gov
Web Site: www.arts.idaho.gov

FOUNDED: 1966

AREAS OF INTEREST:
All disciplines in the arts.

CONSULTING OR VOLUNTEER SERVICES:
Technical assistance in arts management.

NAME(S) OF PROGRAMS:

- **Arts Education Projects**
- **Directory of Teaching Artists**
- **Entry Track**
- **Fellowships**
- **Public Programs in the Arts**
- **Quick Funds**
- **Traditional Arts Apprenticeship Program**
- **Tumblewords**
- **Writer-in-Residence Program**

TYPE:
Conferences/seminars; Fellowships; General operating grants; Project/program grants; Residencies; Technical assistance. Fellowship/apprenticeship, touring/sponsorship, immediate assistance.

YEAR PROGRAM STARTED: 1966

PURPOSE:
To develop the artistic and cultural life of Idaho.

LEGAL BASIS:
State agency.

ELIGIBILITY:
Applicants must be nonprofit, tax-exempt organizations or artists living in Idaho.

GEOG. RESTRICTIONS: Idaho.

FINANCIAL DATA:
Fiscal restrictions, non-cash benefits.

Amount of support per award: Up to $25,000.

Total amount of support: $848,224 in grants and services for fiscal year 2015.

Matching fund requirements: 50:50, cash or in-kind.

NO. MOST RECENT APPLICANTS: 292 for fiscal year 2015.

NO. AWARDS: 194 for fiscal year 2015.

APPLICATION INFO:
Applications must be on the appropriate form and are available on the Commission web site. Do not use application forms from previous years. Review the checklist carefully because the panel will review the application as submitted. Answer the required narrative questions, paying close attention to the page limitations, and check to see that the application is complete, signed and dated. Incomplete applications are subject to return.

Duration: 12 months.

Deadline: Varies. Consult the Commission.

PUBLICATIONS:
Application guidelines.

IRS I.D.: 82-6000952

OFFICERS:
Kay Hardy, Chairperson
Stuart Weiser, Deputy Director
Michelle Coleman, Community Development Director
John McMahon, Director of Artist Services
Ruth Piispanen, Education Program Director
Steven Hatcher, Folk Arts Program Director
Jocelyn Robertson, Literature Director and Public Information Officer

ADDRESS INQUIRIES TO:
Jadee Carson
Grants Manager or
Stuart Weiser
Deputy Director
(See address or phone numbers above.)

ILLINOIS ARTS COUNCIL [447]

James R. Thompson Center
100 West Randolph, Suite 10-500
Chicago, IL 60601
(312) 814-6750
Fax: (312) 814-1471
E-mail: iac.info@illinois.gov
Web Site: www.arts.illinois.gov

FOUNDED: 1965

AREAS OF INTEREST:
The arts.

TYPE:
General operating grants; Project/program grants.

PURPOSE:
To make the arts more widely available to Illinois residents; to promote an environment that is beneficial to artistic activities; to aid the continuing development of the state's cultural resources.

ELIGIBILITY:
Applicants must be tax-exempt 501(c)(3) organizations registered as not-for-profit corporations in good standing with the Illinois Secretary of State, or units of government (i.e., school, school district, park district, library district), or institutions of higher education. Applicant organizations must have been in active service to the public for at least one year prior to the date of application.

Applicant organizations must be involved in the above-mentioned fields.

GEOG. RESTRICTIONS: Illinois.

FINANCIAL DATA:
Amount of support per award: Varies depending on needs and nature of the request.

APPLICATION INFO:
Guidelines available on the Council web site.

Duration: Up to one year.

OFFICERS:
Shirley R. Madigan, Chairperson
Rhoda A. Pierce, Vice Chairperson

INDIANA ARTS COMMISSION [448]

100 North Senate Avenue
Room N505
Indianapolis, IN 46204
(317) 232-1278
Fax: (317) 232-5595
TDD: (317) 233-3001
E-mail: GrantsAdmin@iac.in.gov
Web Site: www.in.gov/arts

FOUNDED: 1969

AREAS OF INTEREST:
The arts including crafts, dance, design, education, expansion arts, folk, literature,

media, multiarts, museums, music, presenters, statewide arts service organizations, theatre and visual and local arts agencies.

CONSULTING OR VOLUNTEER SERVICES:
Consultation on a limited basis to Indiana organizations and artists.

TYPE:
Block grants; Conferences/seminars; Development grants; General operating grants; Project/program grants; Technical assistance. Arts in education; Arts organizations and services; Capacity building; Individual artist projects. Most grants are awarded through a network of regional partners which serve all 92 counties.

YEAR PROGRAM STARTED: 1969

PURPOSE:
To act as public catalyst, partner and investor that serves the citizens of Indiana by funding, encouraging, promoting and expanding all the arts.

LEGAL BASIS:
State agency.

ELIGIBILITY:
Applicants must be private tax-exempt, not-for-profit arts organizations or public agencies or individual artists. Eligible organizations without tax-exempt status should submit a fiscal year budget. IAC does not fund capital improvements, purchase of permanent equipment, costs of receptions, foods or beverages or agents fees for programs contracted through commercial agencies.

Must have impact on the state of Indiana.

GEOG. RESTRICTIONS: Indiana.

FINANCIAL DATA:
Amount of support per award: Varies.

Total amount of support: $3,600,000.

Matching fund requirements: Matching funds may include in-kind as well as cash.

NO. MOST RECENT APPLICANTS: 573.

NO. AWARDS: 455.

APPLICATION INFO:
Applicants must complete an application, grant agreement and any reporting required by the program guidelines. Program guidelines are available from the Commission. Potential applicants should contact the agency before applying.

Duration: July 1 through June 30, fiscal year.

PUBLICATIONS:
Monthy newsletters; press releases; grant/program guidelines.

IRS I.D.: 35-6000158

COMMISSION MEMBERS:
Nancy Stewart, Chairperson
Kathy Ziliak Anderson, Vice Chairperson
Linda S. Levell, Secretary
Gilberto Cardenas
Libby Chiu
Ruth Ann Cowling
M. Susan Hardwick
Jeffrey Kirk, II
Jennifer Perry
Allen C. Platt, III
J. Allan Rent
Micah L. Smith
Sherry Stark
Yolanda Stemer
Trevor Yager

ADDRESS INQUIRIES TO:
Paige Sharp, Director of Programs or
Adrian Starnes, Grants Manager
(See address above.)

INTERNATIONAL DOCUMENTARY ASSOCIATION [449]

3470 Wilshire Boulevard
Suite 980
Los Angeles, CA 90010
(213) 232-1660
Fax: (213) 232-1669
E-mail: toni.b@documentary.org
Web Site: www.documentary.org

FOUNDED: 1982

AREAS OF INTEREST:
Documentary film.

NAME(S) OF PROGRAMS:
- **IDA Documentary Awards**
- **IDA/David L. Wolper Student Documentary Achievement Award**
- **Pare Lorentz Award**
- **Pare Lorentz Documentary Fund**
- **Los Angeles County Arts Commission Internships**

TYPE:
Awards/prizes; Internships. IDA Documentary Awards celebrate the best nonfiction films and programs of the year. Prize awarded in seven categories: feature, short, episodic series, curated series, short film series, limited series, and the David L. Wolper Student Documentary Award.

IDA/David L. Wolper Student Documentary Achievement Award recognizes exceptional achievement in nonfiction film and video production at the university level and brings greater public and industry awareness to the work of students in the documentary field.

The Pare Lorentz Award is awarded for films that reflect the spirit and tradition of Pare Lorentz's work. The film should demonstrate one or more of Lorentz's central concerns (the appropriate use of the natural environment, justice for all, and the illumination of pressing social problems) presented as a compelling story by skillful filmmaking.

Pare Lorentz Documentary Fund supports full-length documentary films that reflect the spirit and nature of Pare Lorentz's work, exhibiting objective research, artful storytelling, strong visual style, high production values, artistic writing and outstanding music composition, as well as skillful direction, camerawork and editing.

Los Angeles County Arts Commission Internships are offered to undergraduate students who currently reside or are enrolled in a college or university located in Los Angeles County, CA. Those interested should consult the Association web site for up-to-date details.

YEAR PROGRAM STARTED: 1984

PURPOSE:
To provide resources, create community, and defend rights and freedoms for documentary artists, activists, and journalists.

LEGAL BASIS:
501(c)(3).

ELIGIBILITY:
Varies by program or award.

FINANCIAL DATA:
Amount of support per award: IDA/David L. Wolper Student Documentary Achievement Award: $1,000 honorarium; Pare Lorentz Award: $2,500 honorarium. Pare Lorentz Documentary Fund: $15,000 to $25,000; Los Angeles County Arts Commission Internships: $400 per week (2015 Internships).

Total amount of support: Pare Lorentz Documentary Fund: $195,000 for the year 2017.

NO. AWARDS: IDA Documentary Awards: 14 including 2 for the IDA/David L. Wolper Student Documentary Achievement Award. Pare Lorentz Documentary Fund: Up to 12. Los Angeles County Arts Commission Internships: 1 to 2. Pare Lorentz Award: 2.

APPLICATION INFO:
Pare Lorentz Documentary Fund: Guidelines are available on the Association web site.

Duration: Los Angeles County Arts Commission Internships: 10 weeks in the summer (2015 Internships). Pare Lorentz Documentary Fund: One year.

Deadline: IDA Documentary Awards: July 11; Pare Lorentz Documentary Fund: July 31.

IRS I.D.: 95-3911227

EXECUTIVE DIRECTOR:
Simon Kilmurry

ADDRESS INQUIRIES TO:
Toni Bell
Filmmaker Services Coordinator
(See e-mail address above.)

IOWA ARTS COUNCIL [450]

600 East Locust Street
Des Moines, IA 50319-0290
(515) 281-4641
Fax: (515) 242-6498
E-mail: matthew.harris@iowa.gov
Web Site: www.iowaculture.gov/arts

FOUNDED: 1967

AREAS OF INTEREST:
All arts disciplines, primarily in Iowa.

CONSULTING OR VOLUNTEER SERVICES:
Technical assistance in a variety of disciplines and subject areas, including information.

NAME(S) OF PROGRAMS:
- **Arts Resources and Artists Programs**
- **Funding and Arts in Education Programs**
- **Technical Assistance and Community Development Programs**

TYPE:
Challenge/matching grants; Conferences/seminars; Development grants; General operating grants; Project/program grants; Residencies; Scholarships; Technical assistance; Training grants. Seminars, technical assistance and funding. Services provided to institutions and individuals statewide.

YEAR PROGRAM STARTED: 1967

PURPOSE:
To cultivate creativity, learning and participation of the arts in Iowa.

LEGAL BASIS:
State agency established under Chapter 304A, Code of Iowa.

ELIGIBILITY:
Applicants must be nonprofit, tax-exempt 501(c)(3) organizations incorporated and located in Iowa, schools or institutions of higher education located in Iowa, units of

local, county or federally recognized tribal government located in Iowa, or Iowa residents, age 18 or older.

GEOG. RESTRICTIONS: Iowa.

FINANCIAL DATA:
Amount of support per award: Varies.

Matching fund requirements: One-to-one cash or in-kind match for most grant programs.

REPRESENTATIVE AWARDS:
$9,500 to University of Iowa, Iowa City, for City of Literature documentary; $6,700 to Quad City Symphony Orchestra for Midori Residency; $9,500 to Civic Center of Greater Des Moines to support the Dance Series project.

APPLICATION INFO:
Refer to the Council web site.

Duration: 12 months or less.

Deadline: November 1 and May 1 annually.

PUBLICATIONS:
Online e-newsletter (bimonthly).

IRS I.D.: 42-6004812

STAFF:
Matthew Harris, Division Administrator
Veronica O'Hern, Grants Administrator

ADDRESS INQUIRIES TO:
Veronica O'Hern
Grants Administrator
(See address above.)

JEROME FOUNDATION, INC. [451]

400 Sibley Street, Suite 125
St. Paul, MN 55101
(651) 224-9431
(800) 995-3766 (MN and NYC only)
Fax: (651) 224-3439
E-mail: info@jeromefdn.org
Web Site: www.jeromefdn.org

FOUNDED: 1964

AREAS OF INTEREST:
Arts with a focus on film and video, literature, dance, music, theater and visual arts. Emphasis is on creation of new works by emerging artists.

TYPE:
Awards/prizes; Development grants; Fellowships; General operating grants; Project/program grants; Residencies; Seed money grants; Travel grants.

YEAR PROGRAM STARTED: 1964

PURPOSE:
To contribute to a dynamic and evolving culture by supporting the creation, development and production of new works by emerging artists.

LEGAL BASIS:
Tax-exempt, private foundation.

ELIGIBILITY:
Foundation grants are made primarily to not-for-profit arts organizations and to individual professional artists through specific programs. The Foundation accepts requests from new organizations. It also supports not-for-profit fiscal sponsors that apply on behalf of artists. The Foundation is flexible and will consider various funding mechanisms if they provide significant assistance to emerging artists.

The Foundation does not support capital (building and endowment) campaigns, nor does it offer travel grants other than the specific Travel and Study Grant Program it administers.

Foundation support is restricted to emerging artists who are legal residents of Minnesota and/or New York City, NY.

GEOG. RESTRICTIONS: Minnesota and the five boroughs of New York City, New York.

FINANCIAL DATA:
Amount of support per award: Average grant: $24,908.

Total amount of support: Average $3,100,000 annually.

NO. MOST RECENT APPLICANTS: 757.

NO. AWARDS: 144.

REPRESENTATIVE AWARDS:
$20,000 to Aaron Davis Hall, New York, NY, for fund for new works.

APPLICATION INFO:
Guidelines and application forms are available on the web site.

Duration: One to two years. Renewal possible.

PUBLICATIONS:
Annual report.

STAFF:
Ben Cameron, President
Robert Byrd, Program Director
Eleanor Savage, Senior Program Officer

DIRECTORS:
Philip Bither
Carlyle Brown
Linda Earle
Patricia Hampl
Barbara McLanahan
Gary Nan Tie
Calogero Salvo
Elizabeth Streb
Charles Zelle

ADDRESS INQUIRIES TO:
Ben Cameron, President
(See address above.)

*PLEASE NOTE:
Ongoing programs and initiatives will continue as the program is under review. New programs will not be considered in the 2016-17 fiscal year.

KENTUCKY ARTS COUNCIL [452]

500 Mero Street, 21st Floor
Frankfort, KY 40601-1987
(502) 564-3757 ext. 469
Fax: (502) 564-2839
E-mail: kyarts@ky.gov
Web Site: artscouncil.ky.gov

FOUNDED: 1966

AREAS OF INTEREST:
Arts development (visual arts, performing arts, literature and media), community development, arts-in-education and individual artists.

CONSULTING OR VOLUNTEER SERVICES:
Staff available for assistance in planning in above areas and in applying for grants.

NAME(S) OF PROGRAMS:

- **Arts Education Programs**
- **Arts Organizations**
- **Community Arts**
- **Individual Artists**

TYPE:
Awards/prizes; Fellowships; General operating grants; Project/program grants; Residencies; Technical assistance. Arts development and artist support.

YEAR PROGRAM STARTED: 1966

PURPOSE:
To help sponsoring organizations and artists reach and develop new audiences or strengthen themselves artistically or managerially; to act as the funding and program coordinating organization for the arts in Kentucky.

LEGAL BASIS:
State Arts Agency of the Commonwealth of Kentucky.

ELIGIBILITY:
Nonprofit organizations incorporated in the state of Kentucky or Kentucky artists. Most grant programs require IRS tax-exempt status.

GEOG. RESTRICTIONS: Kentucky.

FINANCIAL DATA:
Amount of support per award: $200 to $135,000.

Total amount of support: $2,000,000 annually.

Matching fund requirements: Varies by program.

CO-OP FUNDING PROGRAMS: Support for Kentucky arts partnership organizations through power2give.

NO. MOST RECENT APPLICANTS: 500.

NO. AWARDS: 175.

APPLICATION INFO:
Guidelines and applications are found on the Council web site.

Duration: One fiscal year, July 1 through June 30.

Deadline: Varies.

PUBLICATIONS:
Bimonthly newsletter; annual report.

IRS I.D.: 61-0600439

OFFICERS:
Lori Meadows, Executive Director

ADDRESS INQUIRIES TO:
Lori Meadows, Executive Director
(See address above.)

THE LEEWAY FOUNDATION

1315 Walnut Street
Suite 832
Philadelphia, PA 19107
(215) 545-4078
Fax: (215) 545-4021
E-mail: info@leeway.org
Web Site: www.leeway.org

TYPE:
Awards/prizes; Project/program grants. Art and Change Grants provide project-based grants to fund art for social change projects.

Leeway Transformation Award is an unrestricted award (not project-based) for women and trans people demonstrating a commitment to art for social change work.

See entry 1065 for full listing.

LEHIGH VALLEY COMMUNITY FOUNDATION [453]

840 West Hamilton Street
Suite 310
Allentown, PA 18101
(610) 351-5353
Fax: (610) 351-9353
E-mail: lvcfoundation@lvcfoundation.org
Web Site: www.lvcfoundation.org

FOUNDED: 1967

AREAS OF INTEREST:
Arts and culture, community development, education, environment, health care, history and heritage, human services and science.

TYPE:
Endowments; Scholarships.

YEAR PROGRAM STARTED: 1967

PURPOSE:
To promote philanthropy in order to improve the quality of life in the Foundation's region.

LEGAL BASIS:
Nonprofit, tax-exempt 501(c)(3) organization.

ELIGIBILITY:
Limited to nonprofit, tax-exempt organizations serving citizens within the geographic limits of its outreach.

GEOG. RESTRICTIONS: Lehigh and Northampton counties, Pennsylvania.

FINANCIAL DATA:
Amount of support per award: Average discretionary grant: $5,000.

Total amount of support: $3,000,000 for fiscal year 2014-15.

NO. AWARDS: Over 350 grants for fiscal year 2014-15.

APPLICATION INFO:
Application can be downloaded from the Foundation's web site. Financial sheet must be submitted with grant application.

Deadline: July 1. Notification December 15. Grants: Varies.

IRS I.D.: 23-1686634

STAFF:
Bernard Story, President and Chief Executive Officer

ADDRESS INQUIRIES TO:
Bernard Story
President and Chief Executive Officer
(See address above.)

THE JOHN J. LEIDY FOUNDATION

c/o Pierson & Pierson
305 West Chesapeake Avenue, Suite 308
Towson, MD 21204
(410) 821-3006
Fax: (410) 821-3007
E-mail: info@leidyfoundation.org
Web Site: www.leidyfoundation.org

TYPE:
General operating grants; Project/program grants.

See entry 1286 for full listing.

LOUISIANA DIVISION OF THE ARTS, DEPARTMENT OF CULTURE, RECREATION AND TOURISM [454]

1051 North Third Street, Room 420
Baton Rouge, LA 70802
(225) 342-8200
Fax: (225) 342-8173
E-mail: arts@crt.state.la.us
Web Site: www.crt.state.la.us/arts

FOUNDED: 1976

AREAS OF INTEREST:
Dance, design, folklife, literature, media, music, theater, visual arts and crafts, arts-in-education, and arts service organizations.

CONSULTING OR VOLUNTEER SERVICES:
Grants writing, program development, community development, and alternate funding sources.

NAME(S) OF PROGRAMS:
- **Decentralized Arts Funding Program**
- **Statewide Arts Grants Programs**

TYPE:
General operating grants; Technical assistance. Grants in a variety of programs are offered to arts organizations across the state.

General operating support grants are offered in three levels of operating support to nonprofit arts organizations.

YEAR PROGRAM STARTED: 1977

PURPOSE:
To support established and emerging arts organizations; to stimulate public participation in the arts.

LEGAL BASIS:
Government agency (the official state arts agency of Louisiana).

ELIGIBILITY:
Grants are available for nonprofit arts organizations. Organizations domiciled in Louisiana are eligible to apply for grants to support arts activities taking place in Louisiana.

Eligible applicants generally fall into one of the following categories: nonprofit 501(c)(3) organizations, public or private educational institutions, colleges or universities sponsoring arts activities intended for community participation (not academic, credit-producing, or curriculum-oriented projects), agencies of local, parish, or state government such as state or parish libraries, units of municipal government, parish police juries and agencies of state government.

GEOG. RESTRICTIONS: Louisiana.

FINANCIAL DATA:
Amount of support per award: Decentralized Arts Funding Program: $500 to $15,000; General Operating Support: $1,000 to $40,000; Local Arts Agencies: $1,000 to $123,600.

Matching fund requirements: Decentralized Arts Funding Program: No minimum match requirement; Stabilization and Local Arts Agencies: Dollar-for-dollar or as high as 3:1.

APPLICATION INFO:
Applications are available online.

Duration: One year.

Deadline: Statewide Arts Grants Program: First business day in March. Decentralized Arts Funding Program: Varies by region.

ADDRESS INQUIRIES TO:
Director of Organization and
Community Development
Tel: (225) 342-8175
E-mail: info@crt.state.la.us

THE MACDOWELL COLONY [455]

100 High Street
Peterborough, NH 03458
(603) 924-3886
(212) 535-9690
Fax: (603) 924-9142; (212) 737-3803
E-mail: info@macdowellcolony.org
admissions@macdowellcolony.org
Web Site: www.macdowellcolony.org

FOUNDED: 1907

AREAS OF INTEREST:
Writing, theatre, visual art, music composition, filmmaking, architecture and interdisciplinary art.

NAME(S) OF PROGRAMS:
- **Artist Residency Program**

TYPE:
Fellowships; Residencies; Travel grants. Residency fellowships awarded to emerging and established artists across a spectrum of disciplines - architecture, film, interdisciplinary practices, literature, music, visual art, and theatre - to support studio time and artistic exchange in an ideal environment for the creative process.

YEAR PROGRAM STARTED: 1907

PURPOSE:
To nurture the arts by offering creative individuals of the highest talent an inspiring environment in which they can produce enduring works of the imagination.

LEGAL BASIS:
Nonprofit corporation, certified by IRS as falling under Code Section 509(a)(2).

ELIGIBILITY:
Talent is the sole criterion for acceptance. Established artists as well as emerging artists of promising talent are encouraged to apply.

FINANCIAL DATA:
No residency fees. Fellowships cover costs of living accommodations, all meals, and use of an individual studio building. Travel reimbursement and stipends are available for artists who demonstrate need.

Amount of support per award: Stipends and travel grants up to $2,000.

Total amount of support: $3,500,000.

NO. MOST RECENT APPLICANTS: 1,931.

NO. AWARDS: Approximately 288 artists-in-residence.

APPLICATION INFO:
Application forms are available on the web site. There is a $30 application fee. Work samples must be submitted digitally with the application. Read guidelines before applying.

Duration: Residence periods are from two weeks to two months. No more than one application per 24-month period.

Deadline: January 15, April 15 and September 15.

PUBLICATIONS:
Application guidelines.

OFFICERS AND STAFF:
Michael Chabon, Chairman, Board of Directors

Susan Davenport Austin, President
Cheryl A. Young, Executive Director

ADDRESS INQUIRIES TO:
Courtney Bethel, Admissions Director
(See address above.)

MAINE ARTS COMMISSION [456]

193 State Street
25 State House Station
Augusta, ME 04333-0025
(207) 287-2724
(207) 287-2750
Fax: (207) 287-2725
TTY: (877) 887-3878
E-mail: kathy.shaw@maine.gov
Web Site: www.mainearts.com

FOUNDED: 1966

AREAS OF INTEREST:
Arts.

CONSULTING OR VOLUNTEER SERVICES:
Opportunities for artists and arts organization.

NAME(S) OF PROGRAMS:

- **Arts and Humanities Grants**
- **Arts Learning**
- **CCED Grant**
- **Creative Aging Grant**
- **Maine Artist Fellowship**
- **Jane Morrison Film Fund**
- **Organizational Development**
- **Partnership Grant**
- **Project Grant for Artists**
- **Project Grant for Organizations**
- **Traditional Arts Apprenticeship**
- **Traditional Arts Fellowship**

TYPE:
Awards/prizes; Conferences/seminars; Fellowships; General operating grants; Matching gifts; Project/program grants; Residencies; Technical assistance.

YEAR PROGRAM STARTED: 1966

PURPOSE:
To encourage and stimulate public interest and participation in the cultural heritage and cultural programs of our state; to expand the state's cultural resources; to encourage and assist freedom of artistic expression for the well-being of the arts; to meet the needs and aspirations of persons in all parts of the state.

LEGAL BASIS:
Government agency.

ELIGIBILITY:
Applicants must be nonprofit Maine arts organizations, individual artists, schools and/or certain units of city/state or tribal government.

GEOG. RESTRICTIONS: Maine.

FINANCIAL DATA:
Amount of support per award: Generally $1,500 to $75,000.

Total amount of support: $450,000 for the year 2015.

Matching fund requirements: 1:1, cash or in-kind for most grants. No matching requirement for grants to individual artists.

CO-OP FUNDING PROGRAMS: Maine Community Foundation; Maine Humanities Council.

NO. MOST RECENT APPLICANTS: 607.

NO. AWARDS: 132.

APPLICATION INFO:
Applicant may speak with a staff member about the project before submitting an application.

Application forms must be submitted electronically.

Duration: Varies from 30 days to a full fiscal year period.

Deadline: Varies for all programs.

IRS I.D.: 01-6000001

COMMISSION MEMBERS:
Charles Stanhope, Chairperson

ADDRESS INQUIRIES TO:
Kathy Ann Shaw
Senior Grants Director
(See address above.)

ROBERT MAPPLETHORPE FOUNDATION, INC. [457]

477 Madison Avenue, 15th Floor
New York, NY 10022-5835
(212) 755-3025
Fax: (212) 941-4764
E-mail: joree@mapplethorpe.org
Web Site: www.mapplethorpe.org

FOUNDED: 1988

AREAS OF INTEREST:
Photography as an art form; scientific study of AIDS and AIDS-related research in order to help find a cure.

NAME(S) OF PROGRAMS:

- **Photography Program**

TYPE:
Project/program grants. Funds medical research in the fight against AIDS and HIV infection and supports the promotion of photography as a fine art, embracing exhibitions, acquisitions, and publications.

YEAR PROGRAM STARTED: 1988

ELIGIBILITY:
The Foundation will not provide grants or scholarships to individual photographers. The Foundation will supply museums and other public institutions by assisting in the creation or expansion of photographic departments.

GEOG. RESTRICTIONS: United States.

FINANCIAL DATA:
Amount of support per award: Varies.

Total amount of support: Varies.

APPLICATION INFO:
There is no formal application form.

Duration: Varies.

Deadline: Proposals are accepted on a continuing basis.

ADDRESS INQUIRIES TO:
Joree Adilman, Foundation Manager
(See address above.)

MARYLAND STATE ARTS COUNCIL [458]

175 West Ostend Street
Suite E
Baltimore, MD 21230
(410) 767-6555
Fax: (410) 333-1062
TDD/TTY: (410) 333-4519
E-mail: msac@maryland.gov
Web Site: www.msac.org

FOUNDED: 1967

AREAS OF INTEREST:
Arts.

NAME(S) OF PROGRAMS:

- **Artists in Education**
- **Arts and Entertainment Districts Program**
- **Community Arts Development**
- **Grants for Organizations**
- **Individual Artist Awards**
- **Maryland Folklife Program**
- **Public Art Program**

TYPE:
Awards/prizes; Block grants; General operating grants; Project/program grants; Residencies; Technical assistance. Arts program, arts project grants. Individual artist awards. The Council awards grants to county arts councils in Maryland through its Community Arts Development program.

The Maryland Folklife program is dedicated to the identification, documentation and presentation of Maryland traditional artists to general audiences through public life and educational activities.

The Artists in Education program is designed to increase access to a range of artistic disciplines and to assist schools in integrating the arts into the curriculum. Projects vary in length from one-day visits to four-week residencies.

The Grants for Organizations Program provides support to those who produce or present the arts to the public.

YEAR PROGRAM STARTED: 1967

PURPOSE:
To make the arts more widely available to all Maryland residents, to strengthen the state's cultural institutions and to encourage the development of resident artistic activity throughout the state.

LEGAL BASIS:
Article 41 of the Annotated Code of Maryland as amended, Sections 387 to 395, inclusive.

ELIGIBILITY:
Applying organizations must be not-for-profit, tax-exempt and incorporated in the state of Maryland. Individuals must be 18 years of age or older and a Maryland resident.

Funding is not provided for acquisition of capital assets, capital improvements, depreciation, deficits, capital debt reduction and contributions to endowments.

GEOG. RESTRICTIONS: Maryland.

FINANCIAL DATA:
Amount of support per award: Varies.

Total amount of support: Varies.

APPLICATION INFO:
Guidelines and grant application forms may be acquired by writing to the Council office.

Duration: Up to one year. No grants are automatically renewable.

EXECUTIVE DIRECTOR:
Theresa Colvin

ADDRESS INQUIRIES TO:
Theresa Colvin, Executive Director
(See address above.)

THE METROPOLITAN MUSEUM OF ART [459]

1000 Fifth Avenue
New York, NY 10028-0198
(212) 650-2763
Fax: (212) 570-3972
E-mail: academic.programs@metmuseum.org
Web Site: www.metmuseum.org

FOUNDED: 1870

AREAS OF INTEREST:
Study or research in American visual and decorative arts.

NAME(S) OF PROGRAMS:

- **The Douglass Foundation Fellowship in American Art**

TYPE:
Fellowships. Fellowship is awarded in honor of John K. Howat. It is given to a promising young scholar for one year's study or research in the American Wing (in either the Department of American Paintings and Sculpture or the Department of American Decorative Arts) on an aspect of the Museum's collection.

PURPOSE:
To promote study and research in American visual and decorative arts.

ELIGIBILITY:
Applicants should have been enrolled for at least one year in an advanced degree program in the field of American art or culture.

FINANCIAL DATA:
Amount of support per award: $42,000, plus up to $6,000 for travel and miscellaneous expenses.

Total amount of support: Varies.

NO. AWARDS: 1.

APPLICATION INFO:
Current application may be obtained from the Museum's web site.

Duration: One year.

Deadline: First Friday in November. Announcements of awards will be made by late March.

STAFF:
Marcie Karp, Managing Museum Educator, Academic Programs, Education Department

ADDRESS INQUIRIES TO:
See e-mail address above.

MICHIGAN COUNCIL FOR ARTS AND CULTURAL AFFAIRS [460]

Michigan Economic Development Corporation
300 North Washington Square
Lansing, MI 48913
(888) 522-0103
E-mail: braceyj@michigan.org
Web Site: www.michiganbusiness.org/arts

FOUNDED: 1966

AREAS OF INTEREST:
Arts.

CONSULTING OR VOLUNTEER SERVICES:
Consulting services in the arts, management, development, consultations and workshops, conferences, communications, media development and artist services.

NAME(S) OF PROGRAMS:

- **Arts in Education Residency Program**
- **Capital Improvement Program**
- **Operational Support Grants**
- **Project Support Grants**

TYPE:
General operating grants; Project/program grants.

PURPOSE:
To develop and encourage programs and projects that make music, painting, literature, cinema, dance, sculpture, crafts, architecture and all the arts available to the people of Michigan, regardless of their age, location, background or economic status; to support activities of Michigan artists.

LEGAL BASIS:
State agency.

ELIGIBILITY:
Generally, grants will be awarded only for activities within the state of Michigan. For most programs, applicants should be Michigan-based nonprofit tax-exempt organizations residing in Michigan. The Council ordinarily does not finance an existing deficit, capital improvements, curriculum-oriented activities or permanent equipment.

GEOG. RESTRICTIONS: Michigan.

FINANCIAL DATA:
Amount of support per award: Varies.

Total amount of support: $2,079,391 for the year 2016.

Matching fund requirements: Varies with program.

CO-OP FUNDING PROGRAMS: Re-Granting and Partnership programs.

APPLICATION INFO:
Applicants are required to use the Council's online eGrant system.

Duration: One year, October 1 through September 30.

Deadline: Primary programs: June 1. All other programs: Varies.

PUBLICATIONS:
Program guidelines; factsheet.

IRS I.D.: 38-6000134

OFFICERS:
Andrew Buchholz, Chairman
John Bracey, Executive Director

ADDRESS INQUIRIES TO:
John Bracey, Executive Director
(See address above.)

MID-AMERICA ARTS ALLIANCE [461]

2018 Baltimore Avenue
Kansas City, MO 64108
(816) 421-1388
Fax: (816) 421-3918
E-mail: christine@maaa.org
Web Site: www.maaa.org

FOUNDED: 1972

AREAS OF INTEREST:
Performing and visual arts (traveling exhibits) throughout the U.S.

NAME(S) OF PROGRAMS:

- **Regional Touring Program**
- **Touring Exhibits through ExhibitsUSA**

TYPE:
Project/program grants; Technical assistance. Support and project/program grants for community arts projects and touring performing arts.

YEAR PROGRAM STARTED: 1973

PURPOSE:
To increase the access to high-quality arts programs and to sponsor competency.

LEGAL BASIS:
Missouri corporation, 501(c)(3).

ELIGIBILITY:
Nonprofit organizations presenting M-AAA touring programs in Arkansas, Kansas, Missouri, Nebraska, Oklahoma and Texas may apply. Visual arts exhibitors throughout the country may request traveling exhibits.

GEOG. RESTRICTIONS: Arkansas, Kansas, Missouri, Nebraska, Oklahoma and Texas.

FINANCIAL DATA:
Amount of support per award: $500 to $15,000.

Total amount of support: Varies.

Matching fund requirements: Most grants require a dollar-for-dollar match.

CO-OP FUNDING PROGRAMS: State arts agencies of Arkansas, Kansas, Missouri, Nebraska, Oklahoma, Texas, corporations and foundations, and the National Endowment for the Arts.

NO. MOST RECENT APPLICANTS: 129.

NO. AWARDS: 57.

APPLICATION INFO:
Application information is available on the web site.

PUBLICATIONS:
Annual report; exhibit catalogs.

IRS I.D.: 23-7303693

OFFICERS:
Mary Kennedy, Chief Executive Officer

ADDRESS INQUIRIES TO:
Linda Gramse, Executive Assistant
(See address above.)

MID ATLANTIC ARTS FOUNDATION [462]

201 North Charles Street
Suite 401
Baltimore, MD 21201
(410) 539-6656 ext. 104
Fax: (410) 837-5517
E-mail: maaf@midatlanticarts.org
Web Site: www.midatlanticarts.org

FOUNDED: 1979

AREAS OF INTEREST:
Regional arts activities crossing state lines in Delaware, District of Columbia, Maryland, New Jersey, New York, Pennsylvania, Virginia, West Virginia and the U.S. Virgin Islands; national and international funding through Southern Exposure and USArtists International.

NAME(S) OF PROGRAMS:

- **ArtsConnect**
- **French-American Jazz Exchange**
- **Jazz Touring Network**
- **Living Legacy Jazz Award**
- **Mid Atlantic Creative Fellowships**
- **Mid Atlantic Folk Arts Outreach Program**
- **Mid Atlantic Tours**
- **On Screen/In Person**
- **Southern Exposure**
- **Special Presenter Initiatives**
- **USArtists International**

TYPE:
Fellowships; Project/program grants; Residencies; Technical assistance.

YEAR PROGRAM STARTED: 1979

PURPOSE:
To promote the sharing of arts resources among the Foundation's partner states, regionally, nationally and internationally.

LEGAL BASIS:
Private, not-for-profit organization.

ELIGIBILITY:
Individuals and organizations must be based in the region for most programs. Other requirements vary according to the specific program.

ArtsConnect provides artist fee support to not-for-profit presenting networks comprised of at least three Mid Atlantic-based organizations.

French-American Jazz Exchange supports projects between French and American jazz artists.

Mid Atlantic Creative Fellowships places an artist from each member state in residence at selected organizations. A different artistic discipline is selected each year for foundation support.

Mid Atlantic Tours provide fee support for foundation-initiated performing arts tours.

On Screen/In Person provides fee subsidy to film series host sites.

Southern Exposure provides support to U.S. presenters for foundation-initiated tours of artists from Latin America.

USArtists International supports U.S. music, dance, and theatre artists at international festivals and performing arts markets.

GEOG. RESTRICTIONS: Delaware, District of Columbia, Maryland, New Jersey, New York, Ohio, Pennsylvania, Virginia, West Virginia and the U.S. Virgin Islands for all programs except Southern Exposure and USArtists International.

FINANCIAL DATA:
Amount of support per award: $1,000 to $25,000.

Matching fund requirements: Varies according to program.

NO. MOST RECENT APPLICANTS: More than 1,000.

NO. AWARDS: More than 500.

APPLICATION INFO:
Guidelines are available on the web site. The Foundation utilizes an electronic application process.

Duration: Varies.

Deadline: Varies.

PUBLICATIONS:
Guidelines; monthly e-mail newsletter; biennial report.

IRS I.D.: 52-1169382

STAFF:
Alan W. Cooper, Executive Director

THE MILLAY COLONY FOR THE ARTS, INC. [463]

454 East Hill Road
Austerlitz, NY 12017-0003
(518) 392-3103
Fax: (518) 392-4144 (call first)
E-mail: apply@millaycolony.org
Web Site: www.millaycolony.org

FOUNDED: 1973

AREAS OF INTEREST:
Writing, composing, music and visual arts.

TYPE:
Residencies. The Millay Colony offers a variety of residencies from the months of April through November for visual artists, writers and composers in order to immerse themselves in creative work. The Colony accommodates a multidisciplinary group of six to seven artists each month and offers special residencies to collaborating groups of artists. It also offers free arts education programs in local schools.

YEAR PROGRAM STARTED: 1973

PURPOSE:
To provide space, studio and time for writers and composers to immerse themselves in their work.

ELIGIBILITY:
Residents are selected after undergoing an application and juried process. Juries make selections anonymously.

FINANCIAL DATA:
No cash grant is made, nor is any residency fee required. Meals are provided.

NO. MOST RECENT APPLICANTS: 1,300 for the year 2015.

NO. AWARDS: 69 for the year 2015.

APPLICATION INFO:
Online application process is available. An application form may also be requested by sending a self-addressed, stamped envelope to the address above.

An application fee of $35 is required.

Duration: Residencies are for one month.

Deadline: October 1 for the following April through July. March 1 for the following August through November.

DIRECTORS:
Caroline Crumpacker, Executive Director

ADDRESS INQUIRIES TO:
Calliope Nicholas, Residency Director
(See address above.)

JOAN MITCHELL FOUNDATION [464]

545 West 25th Street, 15th Floor
New York, NY 10001
(212) 524-0100
Fax: (212) 524-0101
E-mail: info@joanmitchellfoundation.org
Web Site: www.joanmitchellfoundation.org

AREAS OF INTEREST:
Art: painting, sculpture and/or drawing.

NAME(S) OF PROGRAMS:
- **Emergency Grant Program**

TYPE:
Grants-in-aid. The Foundation provides emergency support to U.S.-based visual artists working in the mediums of painting, sculpture and/or drawing, who have suffered significant losses after natural or manmade disasters that have affected their community. Artists who have been negatively impacted due to catastrophic situations of this nature can apply to the Foundation for funding.

Information on the full range of Foundation programs can be found online.

PURPOSE:
To provide emergency support to visual artists in need.

GEOG. RESTRICTIONS: United States.

FINANCIAL DATA:
Amount of support per award: Up to $6,000.

Total amount of support: Varies yearly.

NO. AWARDS: Varies.

APPLICATION INFO:
Contact the Foundation.

ADDRESS INQUIRIES TO:
Grants Program Director
(See e-mail address above.)

THE MOODY FOUNDATION

2302 Post Office Street, Suite 704
Galveston, TX 77550
(409) 797-1500
Fax: (409) 763-5564
E-mail: info@moodyf.org
Web Site: www.moodyf.org

TYPE:
Capital grants; Challenge/matching grants; Endowments; Grants-in-aid; Project/program grants; Research grants; Scholarships. Capital campaigns; Equipment; Matching funds; Building/renovation; Program development and research.

See entry 231 for full listing.

MARIETTA MCNEILL MORGAN AND SAMUEL TATE MORGAN, JR. FOUNDATION

U.S. Trust, Philanthropic Solutions
1111 East Main Street, 12th Floor
Richmond, VA 23219
(804) 887-8773
Fax: (804) 887-8854
E-mail: va.grantmaking@ustrust.com
Web Site: www.bankofamerica.com/grantmaking

TYPE:
Capital grants. Grants for capital only. No grants to individuals, for endowment funds or operating funds.

See entry 1455 for full listing.

WILLIAM MORRIS SOCIETY IN THE U.S. [465]

P.O. Box 53263
Washington, DC 20009
E-mail: us@morrissociety.org
ecmill@ucdavis.edu
Web Site: www.morrissociety.org

FOUNDED: 1957

AREAS OF INTEREST:
The life and work of William Morris as a craftsman, designer and writer.

NAME(S) OF PROGRAMS:
- **Joseph R. Dunlap Memorial Fellowship**
- **William Morris Society Award**

TYPE:
Fellowships; Research grants; Scholarships; Travel grants; Visiting scholars; Research contracts. Supports scholarly, creative, and translation projects about William Morris and his designs, writings and other work.

YEAR PROGRAM STARTED: 1995

PURPOSE:
To support research projects that deal with any subject relating to William Morris.

LEGAL BASIS:
Society.

ELIGIBILITY:
Projects may deal with any subject - biographical, literary, historical, social, artistic, political, typographical - relating to Morris. They may be scholarly or creative, and may include translations or the preparation of educational materials. Applicants for all awards may be from any country. Applications are particularly encouraged from younger members of the Society and from those at the beginning of their careers. Recipients need not have an academic or institutional appointment and the Ph.D. is not required.

FINANCIAL DATA:
Amount of support per award: Up to $1,000.

APPLICATION INFO:
Applicants are asked to submit a resume and a two-page description of their projects, including a timeline and an indication of where the results might be published. At least one recommendation should be sent separately. Submissions will not be accepted via e-mail.

For translation submissions, send one copy of the translation (of the published version, if relevant), with a letter of reference from someone acquainted with both languages assessing the quality of the translation. Translations should have been completed within the past five years.

For teaching materials, no letters of recommendation are needed, but enclose a cover letter describing the ways in which the materials might be (or already have been) used in learning situations.

Duration: One year.

Deadline: December 15. Announcement by January 15.

PUBLICATIONS:
Announcement.

ADDRESS INQUIRIES TO:
Linda K. Hughes, Vice President
(See address above.)

NATIONAL ENDOWMENT FOR THE ARTS [466]

400 7th Street, S.W.
Washington, DC 20506
(202) 682-5400
(202) 682-5403
Fax: (202) 682-5609
E-mail: webmgr@arts.gov
Web Site: www.arts.gov/grants

FOUNDED: 1965

AREAS OF INTEREST:
National artistic accomplishments of the past, present and future.

NAME(S) OF PROGRAMS:

- **Art Works**
- **Challenge America**
- **Creative Writing Fellowships**
- **Our Town**
- **Partnership Agreements**
- **Research: Art Works**
- **Translation Projects**

TYPE:
Fellowships; Project/program grants. The National Endowment for the Arts has three grant categories: Grants for Organizations, Grants for Individuals and Partnership Agreements. Under Grants for Organizations, the Endowment funds projects only.

Art Works: An organization grant to support the creation of art that meets the highest standards of excellence, public engagement with diverse and excellent art, lifelong learning in the arts and the strengthening of communities through the arts.

Challenge America: An organization grant to support projects that extend the reach of the arts to underserved populations.

Creative Writing Fellowships: An individual grant offering fellowships in fiction, poetry and creative nonfiction which enable recipients to set aside time for writing, research, travel and general career advancement.

Our Town: An organization grant for creative placemaking projects that contribute to the livability of communities and place the arts at their core. The Our Town program offers support for projects in two areas: Arts Engagement, Cultural Planning, and Design Projects; and Projects that Build Knowledge About Creative Placemaking.

Partnership Agreements: Operates in conjunction with state arts agencies (SAAs) and regional arts organizations (RAOs).

Research: Art Works: An organization grant to support research that investigates the value and/or impact of the arts, either as individual components of the U.S. arts ecology or as they interact with each other and/or with other domains of American life.

Translation Projects: An individual grant that enables recipients to translate work from other languages into English.

YEAR PROGRAM STARTED: 1966

PURPOSE:
To support artists, art forms, art events, art education, and to conserve highly significant works of art.

LEGAL BASIS:
The National Foundation on the Arts and Humanities Act of 1965, Public Law 89-209, as amended.

ELIGIBILITY:
Contact the Endowment for details.

GEOG. RESTRICTIONS: United States, American Samoa, Guam, Puerto Rico or the United States Virgin Islands.

FINANCIAL DATA:
Amount of support per award: Art Works: Grants generally $10,000 to $100,000. Challenge America: Grants for $10,000. Creative Writing Fellowships: $25,000. Our Town: Grants $25,000 to $200,000. Research: Art Works: Grants $10,000 to $30,000. Translation Projects: $12,500 or $25,000.

Total amount of support: Varies.

Matching fund requirements: Art Works and Challenge America: A minimum cost share/match equal to the grant amount is required. Our Town and Research: Art Works are also matching grants.

APPLICATION INFO:
Contact Endowment or consult its web site.

ADDRESS INQUIRIES TO:
Nicki Jacobs, Grants Director
Tel: (202) 682-5546

NATIONAL FOUNDATION FOR ADVANCEMENT IN THE ARTS [467]

2100 Biscayne Boulevard
Miami, FL 33137
(305) 377-1140
(800) 970-2787
Fax: (305) 377-1149
E-mail: jclark@youngarts.org
Web Site: www.youngarts.org

FOUNDED: 1981

AREAS OF INTEREST:
To identify and nurture the most accomplished young artists in the visual, literary, design and performing arts and assist them at critical junctures in their educational and professional development.

CONSULTING OR VOLUNTEER SERVICES:
Offers the names of registrants and awardees of its YoungArts® program nationally to colleges, universities and performing arts institutions which subscribe to the Foundation's Scholarship List Service (SLS).

NAME(S) OF PROGRAMS:

- **National YoungArts Week**
- **YoungArts Los Angeles**
- **YoungArts Miami**
- **YoungArts New York**
- **YoungArts Outside the Box Series**
- **YoungArts Salon Series**

TYPE:
Awards/prizes; Conferences/seminars; Internships. Cash grants and scholarship opportunities to young artists.

YEAR PROGRAM STARTED: 1981

PURPOSE:
To recognize and support aspiring artists in their formative years and provide career entry opportunities.

LEGAL BASIS:
Private nonprofit, 501(c)(3), operating national foundation.

ELIGIBILITY:
YoungArts applicant must be 15 to 18 years old, or a high school student in grades 10 to 12. Participants must be U.S. citizens or permanent residents.

NFAA offers a conference for high school arts educators on preparing students for college auditions.

20 U.S. Presidential Scholars in the Arts are selected exclusively from YoungArts participants by the White House Commission on Presidential Scholars.

GEOG. RESTRICTIONS: United States.

FINANCIAL DATA:
Up to 150 national finalists attend YoungArts Week in Miami, all expenses paid.

Amount of support per award: YoungArts Gold Awards: $10,000 each; YoungArts Silver Awards: $5,000; YoungArts Award: Level I, $3,000; Level II, $1,500; Level III, $1,000; Honorable Mention, $250.

Total amount of support: Approximately $800,000 annually.

CO-OP FUNDING PROGRAMS: NFAA works in partnership with other arts organizations to offer workshops, internships and residencies to students in advanced stages of their arts training.

NO. MOST RECENT APPLICANTS: YoungArts: Approximately 11,000 per year.

NO. AWARDS: Approximately 800 total awards per year; approximately 450 cash awards per year.

APPLICATION INFO:
There is a $35 registration fee per category.

Deadline: YoungArts: Early registration May 16, regular registration through October 14. Audition/portfolio materials due late October.

IRS I.D.: 59-2141837

ADDRESS INQUIRIES TO:
John D. Clark
Vice President of Development
Tel: (305) 377-1140 ext. 1801
(See e-mail address above.)

NEBRASKA ARTS COUNCIL [468]

1004 Farnam Street, Lower Level
Omaha, NE 68102
(402) 595-2122
Fax: (402) 595-2334
E-mail: nac.grants@nebraska.gov
Web Site: www.nebraskaartscouncil.org

FOUNDED: 1965

AREAS OF INTEREST:
Architecture, visual arts, artists, art organizations, literature, museums and libraries, performing arts, aged, children and youth, community and rural development and services and education.

CONSULTING OR VOLUNTEER SERVICES:
Technical (staff) services for requesting organizations who desire assistance in arts programming efforts. Developmental aspects of assistance to arts organizations and/or individuals is predominant.

NAME(S) OF PROGRAMS:
- **Artists-in-Schools/Communities Grants**
- **Arts Learning Projects**
- **Arts Project Grants**
- **Basic Support Grants**
- **Individual Artist Fellowships**
- **Mini Grants**
- **Nebraska Touring Program**
- **School Bus for the Arts Grants**

TYPE:
Fellowships; General operating grants; Matching gifts; Project/program grants. Grants to encourage growth and activity in the arts for the citizens of the state of Nebraska.

YEAR PROGRAM STARTED: 1965

PURPOSE:
To stimulate and encourage, throughout the state, the study and presentation of the visual and performing arts and public interest and participation therein; to promote the arts, cultivate resources and support excellence in artistic endeavors for all Nebraskans.

LEGAL BASIS:
Government agency under state legislation. Agency also accepts federal funds (from the National Endowment for the Arts) and private funds for purposes of its intent.

ELIGIBILITY:
Nonprofit, incorporated status is required of applying organizations. Applicant organizations must have federal tax-exempt status or proof of application for that status at the time of application. Individuals not connected with nonprofit organizations are eligible only for Individual Artist Fellowships and must be Nebraska residents. The NAC does not provide funding for capital expenditures or existing deficits.

GEOG. RESTRICTIONS: Nebraska.

FINANCIAL DATA:
Amount of support per award: Basic Support Grants: Up to $50,000; All other grants: Up to $7,500.

Total amount of support: Approximately $1,200,000.

Matching fund requirements: Must be in cash.

CO-OP FUNDING PROGRAMS: Support is provided for organizations desiring programming in the Mid-America Arts Alliance (six-state consortium consisting of Arkansas, Kansas, Missouri, Nebraska, Oklahoma and Texas).

APPLICATION INFO:
Application form is available on the web site.

Duration: One year.

Deadline: March 1 and October 1.

PUBLICATIONS:
Guide to Programs and Services; Artist Directory.

STAFF:
Jane Ji, Grants Manager

ADDRESS INQUIRIES TO:
See e-mail address above.

*SPECIAL STIPULATIONS:
Please contact NAC prior to applying for the first time.

NEVADA ARTS COUNCIL [469]

716 North Carson Street
Suite A
Carson City, NV 89701
(775) 687-6680
Fax: (775) 687-6688
E-mail: sboskoff@nevadaculture.org
Web Site: nac.nevadaculture.org

FOUNDED: 1967

AREAS OF INTEREST:
Visual, literary, performing, design and folk arts, as well as community development.

CONSULTING OR VOLUNTEER SERVICES:
Consulting on arts management, resources in the arts, grants workshops, community arts and professional arts needs.

NAME(S) OF PROGRAMS:
- **Artist Services Program**
- **Arts Learning Program**
- **Community Arts Development**
- **Folklife Program**
- **Grants Program**

TYPE:
Awards/prizes; Challenge/matching grants; Conferences/seminars; Development grants; Fellowships; General operating grants; Project/program grants; Residencies; Technical assistance; Training grants; Work-study programs. Grants to Nevada nonprofit groups, individual artists, public institutions and for arts in education.

YEAR PROGRAM STARTED: 1967

PURPOSE:
To enrich the cultural life of the state through leadership that preserves, supports, strengthens and makes accessible excellence in the arts to all Nevadans.

LEGAL BASIS:
Government agency.

ELIGIBILITY:
Nevada nonprofit organizations with IRS tax-exempt status and individual artists with one-year minimum residency may apply for grants. Artists may also apply for artist residencies. Fellowships require residency.

GEOG. RESTRICTIONS: Nevada.

FINANCIAL DATA:
Amount of support per award: $250 to $10,000.

Matching fund requirements: Usually 1:1. Challenge grants 3:1.

APPLICATION INFO:
Applications are available on the web site.

Duration: Length of project can usually be no longer than one fiscal year, July 1 to June 30, except for challenge grants and quarterly grants.

IRS I.D.: 88-6000022

OFFICERS:
Julia Arger, Chairperson
Susan Boskoff, Executive Director
Linda Ficklin, Administrative Services Officer

ADDRESS INQUIRIES TO:
Susan Boskoff, Executive Director
(See address above.)

NEW ENGLAND FOUNDATION FOR THE ARTS [470]

145 Tremont Street
Seventh Floor
Boston, MA 02111-1254
(617) 951-0010
Fax: (617) 951-0016
E-mail: info@nefa.org
Web Site: www.nefa.org

FOUNDED: 1975

AREAS OF INTEREST:
Performing artists, ensembles, literary artists, composers, public art and Native American art.

NAME(S) OF PROGRAMS:
- **Center Stage**
- **Expeditions**
- **Fund for the Arts**
- **National Dance Project**
- **National Theater Pilot**
- **New England States Touring Program**
- **Presenter Travel Fund**

TYPE:
Awards/prizes; Development grants; Project/program grants; Travel grants. Production and touring grants.

PURPOSE:
To facilitate the movement of people, ideas and resources in the arts within New England and beyond; to make vital connections between artists and audiences; to build the strength, knowledge and leadership of the region's creative sector.

LEGAL BASIS:
Public/private partnership.

FINANCIAL DATA:
Amount of support per award: Varies by program.

Total amount of support: Varies.

NO. AWARDS: 450.

APPLICATION INFO:
Contact the Foundation.

Duration: Varies.

Deadline: Varies.

NEW HAMPSHIRE STATE COUNCIL ON THE ARTS [471]

19 Pillsbury Street
Concord, NH 03301
(603) 271-2789
Fax: (603) 271-3584
TTY/TDD: (800) 735-2964
E-mail: cassandra.mason@dcr.nh.gov
Web Site: www.nh.gov/nharts

FOUNDED: 1965

AREAS OF INTEREST:
The arts in New Hampshire.

CONSULTING OR VOLUNTEER SERVICES:
Artists as Entrepreneurs Workshops, Fall Arts in Education Partnership Conference and Grants Information Services Workshops.

NAME(S) OF PROGRAMS:
- **Apprenticeships**
- **Artist Entrepreneurial Workshops**
- **Artist in Residence**
- **Artist Services**
- **Arts in Education**
- **Arts in Health Project Grants**
- **Cultural Conservation**
- **General Project Grants**
- **Operating Grants**
- **Percent for Art**
- **Public Value Partnerships**
- **Traditional Arts Apprenticeship**
- **Youth Arts Project Grants**

TYPE:
Awards/prizes; Challenge/matching grants; Conferences/seminars; Fellowships; General operating grants; Project/program grants; Residencies; Technical assistance. Grant assistance to New Hampshire organizations and individual artists.

YEAR PROGRAM STARTED: 1965

PURPOSE:
To support and promote excellence, education and community investment in the arts for people in New Hampshire.

LEGAL BASIS:
Agency of the state of New Hampshire.

ELIGIBILITY:
Organizations must be incorporated in New Hampshire. Individual artists must reside in New Hampshire for at least one year.

GEOG. RESTRICTIONS: New Hampshire.

FINANCIAL DATA:
Amount of support per award: $250 to $26,000.

Total amount of support: $544,864 for fiscal year 2016.

Matching fund requirements: Varies.

NO. MOST RECENT APPLICANTS: 204 for fiscal year 2013.

NO. AWARDS: 148 funded for fiscal year 2013.

APPLICATION INFO:
A completed application form is required for all grants. Submissions must be made online. Support materials are required from all applicants; work sample required from individual artists. IRS tax-exempt 501(c)(3) letter is required from nonprofit organizations.

Duration: One to two years.

Deadline: Varies.

PUBLICATIONS:
E-News; *E-Opps.*

STAFF:
Ginnie Lupi, Director

ADDRESS INQUIRIES TO:
Cassandra Mason
Chief Grants Officer
(See address above.)

*SPECIAL STIPULATIONS:
Funding is restricted to New Hampshire artists, organizations, schools, libraries, branches of government and communities.

NEW JERSEY STATE COUNCIL ON THE ARTS [472]

225 West State Street, 4th Floor
Trenton, NJ 08608
(609) 292-6130
Fax: (609) 989-1440
Web Site: www.artscouncil.nj.gov
www.nj.gov/state/njsca/index.html

FOUNDED: 1966

AREAS OF INTEREST:
Dance, music, opera, musical theatre, theatre, visual arts, design arts, crafts, media arts, presenters, multi- and interdisciplinary, arts education, folk art, local arts, literary arts, stabilization and advancement.

NAME(S) OF PROGRAMS:
- **Artists-in-Education Residency Grant Program (AIE)**
- **Arts Project Support (APS)**
- **Folk Arts Apprenticeships**
- **General Operating Support (GOS)**
- **General Program Support (GPS)**

TYPE:
Fellowships; General operating grants; Internships; Project/program grants; Residencies; Technical assistance. Apprenticeships; local arts grants. Fellowships and matching grants to provide money to New Jersey artists and organizations. Local arts grants (for local arts) are available to designated county arts agencies only.

Artists-in-Education Residency Grant Program places practicing professional artists in long-term residencies (20-100 days) in schools across the state.

Arts Project Support: awarded annually to New Jersey-based, nonprofit organizations and agencies to help support single public arts events.

Folk Arts Apprenticeships: awarded to New Jersey residents to support an apprentice learning a traditional art form from a master in their shared community.

General Operating Support Grants: awarded every three years to New Jersey-based, nonprofit arts organizations to help underwrite the expense of their total operation including their expense of producing and presenting arts events.

General Program Support Grants: awarded every three years to other New Jersey-based, nonprofit organizations, agencies, institutions or units of local government to help underwrite the expense of presenting major, ongoing arts programs.

YEAR PROGRAM STARTED: 1966

PURPOSE:
To improve the quality of life of New Jersey, its people and communities by helping the arts to flourish.

LEGAL BASIS:
State governmental agency.

ELIGIBILITY:
The Council awards grants on a highly competitive basis, employing standardized criteria for eligibility and evaluation published in guidelines and convening panels of independent experts in the various fields of endeavor for objective feedback and recommendations. A New Jersey resident or a nonprofit organization incorporated in the State of New Jersey committed to professionalism in the arts may apply.

GEOG. RESTRICTIONS: New Jersey.

FINANCIAL DATA:
Amount of support per award: Varies.

Total amount of support: $15,000,000 for fiscal year 2013.

Matching fund requirements: Fellowships are non-matching. Matching grants to organizations must be on a basis of at least 1:1, 3:1 for operating and program support grants.

NO. MOST RECENT APPLICANTS: Approximately 400 fellowship applications and 300 organization/project applications for fiscal year 2013.

APPLICATION INFO:
Details available on the Council web site.

Duration: Annual.

STAFF:
Julie Ellen Prusinowski, Director of Programs and Services

ADDRESS INQUIRIES TO:
Julie Ellen Prusinowski, Director of Programs and Services
(See address above.)

NEW MEXICO ARTS [473]

Bataan Memorial Building
407 Galisteo Street, Suite 270
Santa Fe, NM 87501
(505) 827-6490
Fax: (505) 827-6043
E-mail: JeniceE.Gharib@state.nm.us
Web Site: www.nmarts.org

FOUNDED: 1966

AREAS OF INTEREST:
Arts.

TYPE:
General operating grants; Project/program grants. Funds are available for arts projects; arts in social service; traditional folk arts; arts learning; colleges, universities and government entities; major cultural organizations; local arts councils and service organizations; economic and entrepreneurial development; arts trails; and community arts development.

PURPOSE:
To promote the arts in New Mexico.

ELIGIBILITY:
Applicants must be a New Mexico organization, government or tribal entity. Organizations must have 501(c)(3) not-for-profit status, although they can use a fiscal agent. Religious organizations can apply for grants. No grants are made to individuals.

GEOG. RESTRICTIONS: New Mexico, with a preference for rural New Mexico.

FINANCIAL DATA:
Amount of support per award: Average: $3,000 to $9,000.

Matching fund requirements: 50% match is required; half of the match can be in-kind.

APPLICATION INFO:
Application is online and available each September and must include the organization's 501(c)(3) letter from the IRS. New applicants must submit an advance review application in October.

Duration: One year; applicants must reapply for renewal each year.

Deadline: Advance review in October; final review in December. Contact organization for exact dates.

ADDRESS INQUIRIES TO:
Jenice E. Gharib
Grants Program Manager
(See address or e-mail above.)

*SPECIAL STIPULATIONS:
Consult guidelines for eligible expenses and specific category eligibility requirements.

NEW YORK FOUNDATION FOR THE ARTS [474]

20 Jay Street, Suite 740
Brooklyn, NY 11201
(212) 366-6900
Fax: (212) 366-1778
E-mail: fellowships@nyfa.org
dterry@nyfa.org
Web Site: www.nyfa.org

FOUNDED: 1971

AREAS OF INTEREST:
The arts, with a primary focus on New York state.

NAME(S) OF PROGRAMS:

- **Artists' Fellowships**

TYPE:
Awards/prizes; Development grants; Fellowships; Grants-in-aid. Cash awards made to individual or pairs of originating artists living and working in the state of New York for use in career development. Funds are unrestricted.

YEAR PROGRAM STARTED: 1985

PURPOSE:
To provide the time and resources for the creative mind and the artistic spirit to think, work and prosper.

ELIGIBILITY:
Applicant must be 25 years of age or older and cannot be enrolled in a degree-granting program. Applicant must be a resident of New York state for the two years prior to the deadline.

GEOG. RESTRICTIONS: New York state.

FINANCIAL DATA:
Since its inception, the program has provided over $27,000,000 in unrestricted cash grants to artists in 15 disciplines at critical stages in their creative development.

Amount of support per award: $7,000 cash awards.

Total amount of support: $642,000 in 2015.

NO. AWARDS: 91 grants to 95 awardees with 4 collaborations in 2015.

APPLICATION INFO:
Contact the Foundation.

Deadline: January 28, 11:59 P.M.

STAFF:
Michael L. Royce, Executive Director

NEW YORK STATE COUNCIL ON THE ARTS [475]

300 Park Avenue South, 10th Floor
New York, NY 10010
(212) 459-8800
Fax: (212) 477-1471
E-mail: public.affairs@arts.ny.gov
Web Site: www.arts.ny.gov

FOUNDED: 1960

AREAS OF INTEREST:
Public support for the arts in New York state.

CONSULTING OR VOLUNTEER SERVICES:
Technical assistance is available for eligible nonprofit arts organizations.

TYPE:
Awards/prizes; Capital grants; Challenge/matching grants; Conferences/seminars; Development grants; General operating grants; Internships; Residencies; Technical assistance. Grants are awarded to eligible New York state nonprofit organizations through 16 discipline-based funding programs: Architecture and Design; Facilities; Arts Education; Dance; Electronic Media and Film; Folk Arts; Individual Artists; Literature; Museum; Music; Presenting; Regional Economic Development; Special Arts Services; State and Local Partnerships; Theater; and Visual Arts. In addition, NYSCA support reaches an additional 1,500 community-based organizations each year in the form of regrants, which are administered by a statewide network of Local Arts Councils through NYSCA's Decentralization program.

YEAR PROGRAM STARTED: 1960

PURPOSE:
To ensure that the role of the arts in New York's communities will continue to grow and play a more significant part in the welfare and education of New York's citizens.

LEGAL BASIS:
State agency.

ELIGIBILITY:
Grants are awarded to nonprofit organizations incorporated in New York state, Indian tribes, and units of local government. Individuals and unincorporated groups may only apply through an eligible nonprofit organization.

GEOG. RESTRICTIONS: New York state.

FINANCIAL DATA:
Amount of support per award: Varies by program.

Matching fund requirements: Varies by program.

NO. AWARDS: Over 2,400 annually.

APPLICATION INFO:
Applications and guidelines are available online. New applicants (except municipalities and Indian tribes) must submit proof of nonprofit status. Returning applicants who have applied in the past three years must certify that their nonprofit status remains valid.

Duration: One calendar year. Organizations may reapply each year.

PUBLICATIONS:
Program guidelines.

STAFF:
Dr. Barbaralee Diamonstein-Spielvogel, Vice Chairperson
Jackie Snyder, Interim Executive Director
Petra Maxwell, Deputy Executive Director of Agency Operations
Megan White, Deputy Executive Director of Programs

ADDRESS INQUIRIES TO:
Office of Public and Governmental Affairs
(See address above.)

NEW YORK STATE HISTORICAL ASSOCIATION [476]

5798 State Highway 80
Cooperstown, NY 13326
(607) 547-1418
Fax: (607) 547-1404
E-mail: publications@nysha.org
Web Site: www.nysha.org

FOUNDED: 1899

AREAS OF INTEREST:
New York state and culture.

NAME(S) OF PROGRAMS:

- **Henry Allen Moe Prize**

TYPE:
Awards/prizes. Prizes for published catalogues treating collections located or exhibited in New York state.

YEAR PROGRAM STARTED: 1983

PURPOSE:
To foster and recognize scholarship in art history and decorative arts studies in the form of published catalogues located or exhibited in New York state.

LEGAL BASIS:
Private.

ELIGIBILITY:
Entries should add new information to what is known about the subject and may completely document an exhibition. Only catalogues treating collections located or exhibited in New York state qualify.

FINANCIAL DATA:
Amount of support per award: $250 to $1,000.

NO. MOST RECENT APPLICANTS: 8 for the year 2015.

NO. AWARDS: 1 for the year 2015.

APPLICATION INFO:
Entries published in the previous two years only should be submitted in four copies accompanied by a letter of transmittal.

Deadline: On or before February 15 for awards in the current year.

PUBLICATIONS:
New York History; *Heritage Magazine*.

OFFICERS AND TRUSTEES:
Jeffrey H. Pressman, M.D., Chairman of the Board
Thomas O. Putnam, Vice Chairman
Kathleen Flanagan
Nellie Gipson
Shelley Graham
Doris Fischer Malesardi
Erna Morgan McReynolds
John B. Stetson
Ellen Tillapaugh
Richard C. Vanison
Craig S. Wilder, Ph.D.

ADDRESS INQUIRIES TO:
Cynthia G. Falk
Assistant Professor of Material Culture
(See address above.)

NORTH CAROLINA ARTS COUNCIL [477]

Department of Natural
and Cultural Resources
109 East Jones Street
Raleigh, NC 27601
(919) 807-6500
Fax: (919) 807-6532
E-mail: ncarts@ncdcr.gov
Web Site: www.ncarts.org

FOUNDED: 1964

AREAS OF INTEREST:
Arts development throughout North Carolina.

CONSULTING OR VOLUNTEER SERVICES:
Consulting services to arts organizations.

NAME(S) OF PROGRAMS:
- **Artist Fellowships**
- **Arts and Audiences**
- **Arts in Education Grants**
- **Grassroots Arts Program**
- **Regional Artist Project Grants**
- **State Arts Resources**
- **Statewide Service Organizations**

TYPE:
Challenge/matching grants; Development grants; Fellowships; General operating grants; Internships; Project/program grants; Residencies; Technical assistance. Per capita distribution of funds for arts development, general operating support, project grants, local government challenge grants, arts-in-education grants, new works grants, discipline-development grants, individual artist fellowships, fee subsidy for touring groups, consultant grants, scholarship grants and workshops.

Artist Fellowships: To support the creative development of North Carolina artists. In even years, fellowships are awarded to writers, songwriters, composers, playwrights and screenwriters. In odd years, fellowships are awarded in the areas of visual art, craft, film/video and choreography.

Arts and Audiences: To help arts organizations broaden, deepen and diversify participation in their arts programs.

Arts in Education Grants: For schools and nonprofit organizations to strengthen the use of the arts in pre-K-through-12 settings.

Grassroots Arts Program: Distributes funds for arts programming, primarily through local arts councils, to all 100 North Carolina counties using a per capita-based formula.

Regional Artist Project Grants: For regional consortia of local arts councils, which award project grants to artists in their regions.

State Arts Resources: For mature arts organizations that, over time, have consistently produced strong arts programs and demonstrated strong management and financial accountability.

Statewide Service Organizations: Support is provided to organizations that provide programs and services to the arts community on a statewide or regional basis.

YEAR PROGRAM STARTED: 1967

PURPOSE:
To enrich cultural life in North Carolina by nurturing and supporting excellence in the arts and by providing opportunities for every North Carolinian to experience the arts.

LEGAL BASIS:
Agency of the state of North Carolina.

ELIGIBILITY:
Except for fellowships to individual artists who are North Carolina residents, the Council awards grants only to North Carolina organizations which qualify as tax-exempt and nonprofit under Section 501(c)(3) of the Internal Revenue Code of 1954.

GEOG. RESTRICTIONS: North Carolina.

FINANCIAL DATA:
Amount of support per award: $20,000 average grant. Project and challenge grants generally do not exceed $10,000. General operating support as much as $95,000, per capita distribution as much as $217,000 per grant and artist fellowships as much as $10,000.

Total amount of support: Varies.

Matching fund requirements: 1:1 cash match, except for fellowships.

APPLICATION INFO:
Application form is available online.

Deadline: Organizational grant applications: March 1. Individuals: November 1.

STAFF:
Wayne Martin, Executive Director

ADDRESS INQUIRIES TO:
Joyce Spivey, Grants and Finance Officer
(See address above.)

NORTH DAKOTA COUNCIL ON THE ARTS [478]

1600 East Century Avenue
Suite 6
Bismarck, ND 58503
(701) 328-7590
Fax: (701) 328-7595
E-mail: comserv@nd.gov
Web Site: www.nd.gov/arts

FOUNDED: 1967

AREAS OF INTEREST:
Arts.

NAME(S) OF PROGRAMS:
- **Arts-in-Education/Artists in Residence**
- **Arts-in-Education/STE[A]M**
- **Arts-in-Education/Teacher Incentive**
- **Community Arts Access**
- **Individual Artists Fellowships**
- **Institutional Support**
- **Presenter Support**
- **Professional Development**
- **Special Projects**
- **Traditional Arts Apprenticeships**

TYPE:
Challenge/matching grants; Conferences/seminars; Exchange programs; Fellowships; General operating grants; Grants-in-aid; Project/program grants; Residencies; Technical assistance. Funding and technical assistance provided to institutions and organizations statewide for special projects and administration of special projects.

YEAR PROGRAM STARTED: 1967

PURPOSE:
To stimulate and encourage the study and presentation of and public participation in the performing and visual arts in North Dakota.

LEGAL BASIS:
North Dakota Legislative Assembly.

ELIGIBILITY:
Grants are awarded only to nonprofit organizations, schools, government subdivisions and individuals in North Dakota. Requirements vary according to program. Organizations which do not have 501(c)(3) status may be considered for funding on a case-by-case basis.

GEOG. RESTRICTIONS: North Dakota.

FINANCIAL DATA:
Amount of support per award: Varies by program.

Total amount of support: $961,824.65 for fiscal year 2015.

Matching fund requirements: Varies by grant.

CO-OP FUNDING PROGRAMS: Institutional Support and Arts-in-Education.

NO. MOST RECENT APPLICANTS: 283 for fiscal year 2015.

NO. AWARDS: 280 funded for fiscal year 2015.

APPLICATION INFO:
Contact the Council.

Duration: Up to one year.

Deadline: Varies.

PUBLICATIONS:
Newsletter; guidelines; brochures; eNewsletter; cultural guide.

OFFICER:
David Trottier, Chairperson

ADDRESS INQUIRIES TO:
Beth Klingenstein, Executive Director
(See address above.)

OHIO ARTS COUNCIL [479]

30 East Broad Street
33rd Floor
Columbus, OH 43215
(614) 728-4429
Fax: (614) 466-4494
TDD: (800) 750-0750
E-mail: dia.foley@oac.state.oh.us
Web Site: www.oac.state.oh.us

FOUNDED: 1965

AREAS OF INTEREST:
Arts.

CONSULTING OR VOLUNTEER SERVICES:
Staff assistance related to applications and program development.

NAME(S) OF PROGRAMS:
- **Artists with Disabilities Access**
- **Arts Access**
- **Arts Learning: Artist Express**
- **Arts Learning: Artist in Residence/Artists**
- **Arts Learning: Artist in Residence/Sponsors**
- **Arts Learning: Arts Partnership**
- **ArtsNEXT**
- **ArtSTART**
- **Big Yellow School Bus**
- **Building Cultural Diversity**
- **Individual Artist Grants and Services: Traditional Arts Apprenticeships**
- **Ohio Artists on Tour**
- **Ohio Heritage Fellowship Awards**
- **Sustainability**

TYPE:
Assistantships; Awards/prizes; Conferences/seminars; Fellowships; Formula grants; General operating grants; Internships; Matching gifts; Project/program grants; Residencies; Technical assistance. Special projects and general programming.

YEAR PROGRAM STARTED: 1965

PURPOSE:
To fund and support quality arts experiences to strengthen Ohio communities culturally, educationally and economically.

LEGAL BASIS:
State agency.

ELIGIBILITY:
All applicants for grants must meet the following legal requirements including intending your project to be nonprofit, having the fact that every tax-exempt organization must have an Employer Identification Number, every applicant having to be an Ohio resident or Ohio-based to receive direct grant support, producing projects of high aesthetic quality and artistic merit, providing at least one-half of the activity cost, preferably in dollars (in-kind services may be used as a part of the required match), submitting accurate budgets that are appropriate to the proposed project or creative work, demonstrating financial responsibility and methods to provide community access and involvement.

No person or persons shall, on the grounds of race, color, national origin, handicap, age, sex or religion, be excluded from participation in, be denied benefits of or be otherwise subjected to discrimination under any program, service or benefit advocated, authorized or provided by the state of Ohio.

GEOG. RESTRICTIONS: Ohio.

FINANCIAL DATA:
Amount of support per award: $200 to $400,000.

Total amount of support: $9,700,000 for fiscal year 2014.

Matching fund requirements: Generally, 1:1 cash match.

REPRESENTATIVE AWARDS:
Cleveland Orchestra, Cleveland, OH; Worthington Arts Council, Worthington, OH; Lima Symphony Orchestra, Lima, OH; Actor's Summer Theatre, Columbus, OH; Southern Ohio Museum, Portsmouth, OH.

APPLICATION INFO:
Applicants must use OAC's web-based application system to submit an application.

Duration: July 1 through June 30.

Deadline: Artists with Disabilities Access and Big Yellow School Bus: Application accepted anytime; Arts Access and ArtsNEXT: March 1; Arts Learning-Artist Express: Application due in six weeks prior to the date of the visit; Arts Learning-Artist in Residence/Artists: July 1; Arts Learning-Artist in Residence/Sponsors: February 1; Arts Learning: Arts Partnership: March 1; ArtSTART: April 1; Building Cultural Diversity: March 1, June 1, September 1 and December 1; Individual Artist Grants and Services: January 15 for Traditional Arts Apprenticeships and September 1 for Individual Excellence Awards; Ohio Artists on Tour: May 15; Ohio Heritage Fellowship Awards: January 15; Sustainability: February 1.

PUBLICATIONS:
Guidelines; *Arts Ohio*; *Ohio Festivals & Competitions Guide*; *Focusing the Light: The Arts and Practice of Planning*; *Appreciative Journey: A Guide to Developing International Cultural Exchange.*

IRS I.D.: 31-1334820

OFFICERS:
Donna S. Collins, Executive Director
Dan Katona, Deputy Director
Dia Foley, Grants Office Director

ADDRESS INQUIRIES TO:
Dan Katona, Deputy Director
(See address above.)

OKLAHOMA ARTS COUNCIL [480]

Jim Thorpe Building, Room 640
2101 North Lincoln Boulevard
Oklahoma City, OK 73105
(405) 521-2931
Fax: (405) 521-6418
E-mail: grants@arts.ok.gov
Web Site: www.arts.ok.gov

FOUNDED: 1965

AREAS OF INTEREST:
Arts.

NAME(S) OF PROGRAMS:
- **Capitol Art Travel Subsidies**
- **Major Grant Support**
- **Organizational Support**
- **Small Grant Support**
- **Small Grant Support for Schools**

TYPE:
Project/program grants; Technical assistance. State-appropriated funds and federal funds from the National Endowment for the Arts are disbursed to nonprofit, tax-exempt and nonreligious organizations for arts projects statewide.

YEAR PROGRAM STARTED: 1965

PURPOSE:
To further the arts in the state of Oklahoma.

LEGAL BASIS:
State agency.

ELIGIBILITY:
Nonprofit, tax-exempt and nonreligious Oklahoma organizations are eligible to apply. Funding is also provided for schools, universities, libraries as well as city, county and tribal governments.

GEOG. RESTRICTIONS: Oklahoma.

FINANCIAL DATA:
Amount of support per award: Varies.

APPLICATION INFO:
Contact the Council.

Duration: Projects receiving funding must be completed during the fiscal year.

Deadline: Capitol Art Travel Subsidies: 30 days before travel. Major Grant Support: February 18. Organizational Support: March 15. Small Grant Support and Small Grant Support for Schools: 60 days before program.

PUBLICATIONS:
Program Guidelines; general brochures.

OFFICERS:
Holbrook Lawson, Chairperson
Amber Sharples, Executive Director

ADDRESS INQUIRIES TO:
Maya Hering, Grants Director
(See address above.)

OREGON ARTS COMMISSION [481]

775 Summer Street, N.E.
Suite 200
Salem, OR 97301-1280
(503) 986-0082
Fax: (503) 986-0260
E-mail: oregon.artscomm@state.or.us
Web Site: www.oregonartscommission.org

FOUNDED: 1967

AREAS OF INTEREST:
Arts.

NAME(S) OF PROGRAMS:
- **Access Reimbursement Grants**
- **Art Acquisition Funding**
- **Arts Build Communities**
- **Arts Learning Grants**
- **Arts Services Grants**
- **Capacity Building Grants**
- **Career Opportunity Grants**
- **Individual Artists Fellowship Grants**
- **Operating Support Grants**
- **Oregon Media Arts Fellowship**
- **Small Operating Grants**

TYPE:
Awards/prizes; Conferences/seminars; Fellowships; General operating grants; Project/program grants; Technical assistance; Training grants; Travel grants. Services provided to arts institutions statewide.

YEAR PROGRAM STARTED: 1967

PURPOSE:
To enhance the quality of life for all Oregonians through the arts bystimulating creativity, leadership and economic vitality.

LEGAL BASIS:
Agency of the state of Oregon.

ELIGIBILITY:
Grants are available to nonprofit organizations and professional, nonstudent artists.

GEOG. RESTRICTIONS: Oregon.

FINANCIAL DATA:
Amount of support per award: Varies.

Matching fund requirements: Minimum 1:1.

NO. MOST RECENT APPLICANTS: Varies.

NO. AWARDS: Varies.

APPLICATION INFO:
Detailed information is available on the web site.

Duration: One year.

Deadline: Varies.

PUBLICATIONS:
Program guide; monographs of Arts Build Communities Program, Arts Learning Program and Percent for Art Program; guidelines for various grant programs; Creative Vitality Index Report.

IRS I.D.: 93-0563386

PENNSYLVANIA COUNCIL ON THE ARTS [482]

216 Finance Building
Commonwealth and North Streets
Harrisburg, PA 17120
(717) 787-6883
Fax: (717) 783-2539
E-mail: ra-arts@pa.gov
phorn@pa.gov
Web Site: www.arts.pa.gov

FOUNDED: 1966

AREAS OF INTEREST:
Arts.

NAME(S) OF PROGRAMS:
- **Arts Organization Grants**

TYPE:
General operating grants; Residencies. General support grants, specific support grants, and peer-to-peer consultation.

YEAR PROGRAM STARTED: 1966

PURPOSE:
To foster the excellence, diversity and vitality of the arts in Pennsylvania; to broaden the availability and appreciation of those arts throughout the state.

LEGAL BASIS:
State agency.

ELIGIBILITY:
Incorporated nonprofit organizations located in Pennsylvania and serving residents of the state may apply.

GEOG. RESTRICTIONS: Pennsylvania.

FINANCIAL DATA:
Funding comes from state-appropriated funds and federal grants.

Total amount of support: Varies.

Matching fund requirements: Usually a dollar-for-dollar match for organizations.

APPLICATION INFO:
Contact the Council.

Duration: One year.

Deadline: Varies.

PUBLICATIONS:
Guide to Fellowship Programs; Guide to Programs and Services; Guide to the Arts-in-Education Program.

ADMINISTRATIVE STAFF:
Seth Poppy, Grants Manager

DIRECTORS:
Philip Horn, Executive Director
Amy Gabriele, Deputy Director for Administration and Program Director for Music
Heather Doughty, Deputy Director for Communications
Charon Battles, Deputy Director for Programs and Program Director for Dance and Preserving Diverse Cultures
Caroline E. Savage, Program Director for Art Museums, Crafts, Folk and Traditional Arts
Jamie Dunlap, Program Director for Arts in Education
Matt Serio, Program Director for Entry Track, Partners in the Arts

ADDRESS INQUIRIES TO:
Program Director of Pertinent Arts Discipline
(See address above.)

PERPETUAL TRUSTEE COMPANY LTD [483]

GPO Box 4172
Sydney N.S.W. 2001 Australia
(61) 1800 501 227
Fax: (61) 02 8256 1471
E-mail: philanthropy@perpetual.com.au
Web Site: www.perpetual.com.au/philanthropy-awards.aspx

FOUNDED: 1961

AREAS OF INTEREST:
Portrait painting.

NAME(S) OF PROGRAMS:
- **Portia Geach Memorial Award**

TYPE:
Awards/prizes. Cash award for the best portrait painted from life of a man or woman distinguished in Art, Letters or the Sciences, by any female artist resident in Australia.

YEAR PROGRAM STARTED: 1965

PURPOSE:
To recognize the portrait painted from life of the highest artistic merit.

LEGAL BASIS:
Trustees of the Portia Geach Memorial Fund.

ELIGIBILITY:
Entrants must be female Australian residents who are either Australian-born, naturalized, or British-born. Entries must be the original work of the competitor. Works must have been executed entirely during the commenced year previously. Each entry must be a portrait painted from life of a man or woman distinguished in Art, Letters or the Sciences. Self-portraits are accepted. Works must be two-dimensional and must use the medium of paint.

Sculptures, photographic and video works are not eligible. There is no limit to the number of entries an artist can submit.

GEOG. RESTRICTIONS: Australia.

FINANCIAL DATA:
Amount of support per award: $30,000 (AUD) (2014 prize).

NO. AWARDS: 1.

APPLICATION INFO:
Application information will be available on the web site when the award cycle opens.

Duration: Annual award.

ADDRESS INQUIRIES TO:
Philanthropic Services
Portia Geach Memorial Award
(See e-mail address above.)

RAGDALE FOUNDATION [484]

1260 North Green Bay Road
Lake Forest, IL 60045
(847) 234-1063
E-mail: admissions@ragdale.org
Web Site: www.ragdale.org

FOUNDED: 1976

AREAS OF INTEREST:
Visual arts, poetry, fiction, nonfiction writing, music composition, performance art, play/screenwriting and interdisciplinary arts.

NAME(S) OF PROGRAMS:
- **Residencies at Ragdale Foundation**

TYPE:
Awards/prizes; Fellowships; Internships; Residencies. Low-cost subsidized residencies at Ragdale Foundation, an artist's community, providing a place to work undisturbed on creative projects. Some financial aid and fellowships are available upon acceptance.

YEAR PROGRAM STARTED: 1976

PURPOSE:
To provide a place for artists to work undisturbed on creative projects.

LEGAL BASIS:
Not-for-profit, tax-exempt foundation.

ELIGIBILITY:
Residents are chosen by selection committees composed of professionals in the arts. Writers, composers, visual artists and artists of other disciplines are accepted. Couples and collaborators are not accepted unless each qualifies independently.

FINANCIAL DATA:
Amount of support per award: Residencies with room and board provided. Standard fee is $630 for 18-day residencies and $875 for 25-day residencies.

Total amount of support: Varies.

NO. MOST RECENT APPLICANTS: 600.

NO. AWARDS: Approximately 200.

APPLICATION INFO:
Completed application must be submitted along with references, resume, work samples and project description. Application process is online through the Submittable portal. A $25 application fee is required. Financial aid application must be completed after acceptance.

Duration: 18 or 25 days.

Deadline: May 15.

PUBLICATIONS:
Application guidelines; two newsletters annually.

IRS I.D.: 36-2937927

OFFICER:
Sally McDonald, President

ADDRESS INQUIRIES TO:
Amy Sinclair
Grants and Admissions Manager
(See address above.)

RHODE ISLAND STATE COUNCIL ON THE ARTS [485]

One Capitol Hill, 3rd Floor
Providence, RI 02908
(401) 222-3880
(401) 222-3882
Fax: (401) 222-3018
E-mail: adrienne.adeyemi@arts.ri.gov
Web Site: www.arts.ri.gov

FOUNDED: 1967

AREAS OF INTEREST:
Arts.

NAME(S) OF PROGRAMS:
- **Arts Access Grant (AAG)**
- **Design Innovation Grants (DIG)**
- **Fellowships**
- **Folk Arts Apprenticeships and Fellowships**
- **Investments in Arts and Culture (IAC)**
- **Project Grants for Education (PGE and PGA)**
- **Project Grants for Individuals (PGI)**

TYPE:
Fellowships; General operating grants; Project/program grants. Organizational support includes general operating grants and project/program grants; funding for Rhode Island nonprofit organizations doing arts programming. Individual artist support includes Fellowships, Project Grants for Individuals, and Folk Arts Apprenticeships. Educational Support includes Project Grants in Education.

YEAR PROGRAM STARTED: 1967

PURPOSE:
To support and develop increased and substantial arts opportunities for Rhode Island.

LEGAL BASIS:
Agency of the state of Rhode Island.

ELIGIBILITY:
Varies with each grant category.

GEOG. RESTRICTIONS: Rhode Island.

FINANCIAL DATA:
Amount of support per award: Varies.

Total amount of support: $1,530,525 for fiscal year 2015.

Matching fund requirements: Matching funds required for all grants, except for individual artists.

CO-OP FUNDING PROGRAMS: State and local cooperative programs.

APPLICATION INFO:
Contact the specific Program Director.

Duration: Varies with program.

Deadline: April 1 and October 1.

IRS I.D.: 05-6000523

OFFICERS:
Randall Rosenbaum, Executive Director
Sherilyn Brown, Program Director, Arts in Education (Education Partnerships)
Elena Calderon-Patino, Program Director, Community Arts and Atrium Gallery
Adrienne Adeyemi, Program Director, Grants for Organizations
Cristina DiChiera, Program Director, Individual Artists
Elizabeth Keithline, Program Director, Public Art
Daniel L. Kahn, Program Assistant, Arts in Education (Grants)
Donna Fiske, Fiscal and Office Manager

ADDRESS INQUIRIES TO:
Adrienne Adeyemi, Program Director
Grants for Organizations
(See address or e-mail above.)
Tel: (401) 222-3882

Cristina DiChiera, Program Director
Individual Artists
(See address or e-mail above.)
Tel: (401) 222-3881

Elena Calderon-Patino, Program Director
Community Arts and Atrium Gallery
(See address or e-mail above.)
Tel: (401) 222-6996

Dan Kahn, Program Assistant
Arts in Education
(See address or e-mail above.)
Tel: (401) 222-1146

THE SAN FRANCISCO FOUNDATION [486]

One Embarcadero Center, Suite 1400
San Francisco, CA 94111
(415) 733-8500
Fax: (415) 477-2783
E-mail: artsinfo@sff.org
Web Site: www.sff.org

FOUNDED: 1948

AREAS OF INTEREST:
Fine arts.

NAME(S) OF PROGRAMS:
- **Edwin Anthony and Adelaide Boudreaux Cadogan Scholarships**
- **Jack K. and Gertrude Murphy Fellowships**

TYPE:
Fellowships; Scholarships.

YEAR PROGRAM STARTED: 1986

PURPOSE:
To assist San Francisco Bay Area students in pursuing graduate academic fine arts study at various Bay Area institutions.

LEGAL BASIS:
Community foundation.

ELIGIBILITY:
Applicants must be M.F.A. students currently pursuing a graduate degree in one of the following San Francisco Bay Area colleges and universities: Mills College, San Francisco State University, Stanford University, The California College of the Arts, The San Francisco Art Institute, and UC Berkeley. Students may self-nominate for the award.

Students must have completed at least one semester of graduate school by the time they apply, must be continuously enrolled in the same program and be in good academic standing.

GEOG. RESTRICTIONS: San Francisco Bay Area, California.

FINANCIAL DATA:
Amount of support per award: Awardees receive $6,000 for the Cadogan Award in tuition assistance and have their work displayed in a professionally curated exhibition at SOMArts Cultural Center. The Murphy Award is received by one student; the amount is determined based on the amount in the Murphy Fund.

Total amount of support: $6,000 for Cadogan; amount is determined based on the fund amount for the one recipient of the Murphy Award.

NO. MOST RECENT APPLICANTS: 100 for the year 2015.

NO. AWARDS: 24 for the year 2015.

APPLICATION INFO:
Contact the Foundation.

Deadline: May of each year.

ADDRESS INQUIRIES TO:
See e-mail address above.

THE SAN FRANCISCO FOUNDATION [487]

One Embarcadero Center
Suite 1400
San Francisco, CA 94111
(415) 733-8500
Fax: (415) 477-2783
E-mail: artsinfo@sff.org
Web Site: www.sff.org

FOUNDED: 1948

AREAS OF INTEREST:
Arts and artists.

NAME(S) OF PROGRAMS:
- **Art Awards**

TYPE:
Awards/prizes.

PURPOSE:
To foster individual artistic growth within the community.

LEGAL BASIS:
Community foundation.

ELIGIBILITY:
Poets, writers, sculptors, painters, filmmakers, media artists, photographers, printmakers and performing artists are eligible.

GEOG. RESTRICTIONS: Alameda, Contra Costa, Marin, San Francisco and San Mateo counties, California.

FINANCIAL DATA:
Amount of support per award: $2,000 to $10,000.

Total amount of support: Varies.

NO. AWARDS: Varies.

APPLICATION INFO:
Contact the Foundation.

Deadline: Varies.

ADDRESS INQUIRIES TO:
Art Awards Program
(See e-mail address above.)

*PLEASE NOTE:
Some art awards that are administered by the Foundation are by nomination only. They are not open application processes.

SILICON VALLEY CREATES [488]

38 West Santa Clara Street
San Jose, CA 95113
(408) 998-2787 ext. 204
Fax: (408) 971-9458
E-mail: audreys@svcreates.org
Web Site: www.svcreates.org

FOUNDED: 1982

AREAS OF INTEREST:
Arts organizations, individual artists and community arts.

NAME(S) OF PROGRAMS:
- **Artist Laureates**
- **Local Arts Grants**

TYPE:
Awards/prizes; Conferences/seminars; General operating grants; Technical assistance. Laureate awards.

Artist Laureate Awards provide awards to recognize the accomplishments of individual artists.

Local Arts Grants provide general operating support to arts organizations for activities that:
(1) promote artistic excellence while reflecting the dynamic diverse and innovative character of Santa Clara County;
(2) support the professional development of small and mid-sized arts organizations;
(3) recognize and encourage nonprofessional, volunteer involvement as an essential part of the county's cultural environment and;
(4) stimulate local support, particularly at the grassroots level.

LEGAL BASIS:
Private, nonprofit arts council.

GEOG. RESTRICTIONS: Santa Clara County, California.

FINANCIAL DATA:
Amount of support per award: Artist Laureates: $5,000.

Total amount of support: Approximately $420,000 for fiscal year 2015.

NO. AWARDS: Artist Laureates: 6.

PUBLICATIONS:
Annual report.

IRS I.D.: 94-2825213

ADDRESS INQUIRIES TO:
Audrey Struve, Program Manager
(See address above.)

SMITHSONIAN INSTITUTION

Office of Fellowships and Internships
470 L'Enfant Plaza, S.W., Suite 7102
MRC 902, P.O. Box 37012
Washington, DC 20013-7012
(202) 633-7070
Fax: (202) 633-7069
E-mail: siofi@si.edu
Web Site: www.smithsonianofi.com

TYPE:
Fellowships. Offered to qualified scholars for research to be conducted in residence at the Smithsonian in association with the staff, using collections and research facilities.

See entry 1787 for full listing.

SOUTH CAROLINA ARTS COMMISSION [489]

1026 Sumter Street, Suite 200
Columbia, SC 29201
(803) 734-8696
Fax: (803) 734-8526
E-mail: info@arts.sc.gov
Web Site: www.southcarolinaarts.com

FOUNDED: 1967

AREAS OF INTEREST:
Arts education, community arts development and artist development.

NAME(S) OF PROGRAMS:
- **Arts Education**
- **Community Organizations Grants/Programs**
- **Individual Artist Grants/Programs**

TYPE:
Awards/prizes; Fellowships; General operating grants; Project/program grants; Seed money grants; Technical assistance; Training grants; Travel grants.

ELIGIBILITY:
Individuals who apply must be citizens or residents of the U.S. Grants are awarded to South Carolina artists and organizations only.

FINANCIAL DATA:
Amount of support per award: Varies.

Total amount of support: Varies.

APPLICATION INFO:
Consult the Commission web site.

Deadline: Varies.

SOUTH DAKOTA ARTS COUNCIL [490]

711 East Wells Avenue
Pierre, SD 57501-3369
(605) 773-3301
Fax: (605) 773-5977
E-mail: sdac@state.sd.us
Web Site: www.artscouncil.sd.gov

FOUNDED: 1966

AREAS OF INTEREST:
Statewide arts programming in all arts disciplines.

NAME(S) OF PROGRAMS:
- **Artist Grants**
- **Artist-in-Schools & Communities**
- **Arts Organization Challenge Grants**
- **Professional Development**
- **Project Grants**
- **Technical Assistance**
- **Touring Arts**

TYPE:
Challenge/matching grants; Fellowships; General operating grants; Grants-in-aid; Project/program grants; Residencies; Seed money grants; Technical assistance; Travel grants. Artist grants; arts challenge grants/general operating support.

YEAR PROGRAM STARTED: 1968

PURPOSE:
To support development of the arts.

LEGAL BASIS:
State agency.

ELIGIBILITY:
Requirements vary with projects. Most grants are available to South Dakota residents only, with the exception of Touring Arts and Artist-in-Schools & Communities.

GEOG. RESTRICTIONS: South Dakota.

FINANCIAL DATA:
Amount of support per award: $100 to $45,000.

Total amount of support: $1,300,000 for fiscal year 2016.

Matching fund requirements: Required except for Artist Grants.

NO. AWARDS: 500.

APPLICATION INFO:
Applications are accepted through an online e-grant system.

Duration: Generally one fiscal year. Renewable.

Deadline: March 1 for Organizations and Artist Grants. September 1 for Touring Arts and Artist-in-Schools & Communities.

PUBLICATIONS:
Quarterly newsletter; strategic long-range plan; annual report.

STAFF:
Michael Pangburn, Director
Rebecca Cruse, Assistant Director
Paul Mehlhaff, Grants Officer
Heather Davidson, Program Coordinator

ADDRESS INQUIRIES TO:
Michael Pangburn, Director
(See address above.)

H. CHASE STONE TRUST [491]

c/o JPMorgan
370 17th Street, Suite 3200
Denver, CO 80202
(303) 607-7810
Fax: (303) 607-7761
E-mail: julie.golden@jpmorgan.com
Web Site: www.jpmorgan.com/onlinegrants

AREAS OF INTEREST:
Primarily performing, literary and fine arts.

TYPE:
Project/program grants.

PURPOSE:
To support, sustain and develop charitable organizations operating in the El Paso County community.

ELIGIBILITY:
Performing, literary and fine arts organizations serving the entire El Paso County community are eligible to apply. Must have 501(c)(3) not-for-profit status. No grants to individuals.

GEOG. RESTRICTIONS: El Paso County, Colorado.

FINANCIAL DATA:
Amount of support per award: $3,000 to $10,000.

APPLICATION INFO:
Application and guidelines are available online. Organization must provide current copy of IRS determination letter showing tax-exempt status under Section 501(c)(3) and public charity status under Section 509(a).

Duration: One year. No renewals.

Deadline: October 31, 2016.

ADDRESS INQUIRIES TO:
Julie Golden, Trust Advisor
(See address above.)

*SPECIAL STIPULATIONS:
JPMorgan will only accept applications submitted online.

THE FRANK M. TAIT FOUNDATION

40 North Main Street
Suite 1530
Dayton, OH 45423
(937) 222-2401
Fax: (937) 224-6015
E-mail: taitfoundation@gmail.com

TYPE:
Project/program grants. Focus on youth development, particularly early childhood development.

See entry 1126 for full listing.

TENNESSEE ARTS COMMISSION [492]

401 Charlotte Avenue
Nashville, TN 37243-0780
(615) 741-6395
Fax: (615) 741-8559
E-mail: diane.williams@tn.gov
Web Site: www.tn.gov/arts

FOUNDED: 1967

AREAS OF INTEREST:
All arts disciplines in Tennessee.

CONSULTING OR VOLUNTEER SERVICES:
Consultant, informational and developmental services are offered to arts groups, individual artists, museums and arts councils throughout the state.

NAME(S) OF PROGRAMS:
- **Division of Arts Programs**
- **Division of Communications, Information & Technology**

TYPE:
Conferences/seminars; Fellowships; General operating grants; Project/program grants; Residencies; Technical assistance; Training grants. Professional development. Matching grants. Arts Programs consist of grants to institutions, individuals, coordinating agencies and entities of government. Consultation information and development assistance to state arts constituency is also provided.

Grant Programs: Funds may not be used for capital improvements or for permanent equipment.

YEAR PROGRAM STARTED: 1967

PURPOSE:
To support and encourage the life and growth of the arts and craft in the state of Tennessee and preservation of the state's cultural heritage.

LEGAL BASIS:
Independent state agency.

ELIGIBILITY:
Grants categories are limited to residents, artists and organizations of Tennessee. Grants are made to individuals, nonprofit organizations and/or entities of government.

GEOG. RESTRICTIONS: Tennessee.

FINANCIAL DATA:
Amount of support per award: $200 to $100,000.

Matching fund requirements: Most grant awards require a 1:1 match.

NO. MOST RECENT APPLICANTS: 1,200.

NO. AWARDS: 1,000.

APPLICATION INFO:
Details are available on the web site.

Duration: One fiscal year, July to June.

Deadline: Varies.

PUBLICATIONS:
Weekly online newsletter.

COMMISSION MEMBERS:
Patsy White Camp, Chairperson
Stephanie B. Conner, Vice Chairperson
Ann C. Smith, Secretary
Steve Bailey
Lisa Bobango
Ritche Bowden
Donna Chase
Ed Gerace
Waymon L. Hickman, Sr.
Andrea Loughry
Chancellor Carol L. McCoy
Leo McGee
Jan Ramsey
Connie S. Weathers
Lee D. Yeiser

ADDRESS INQUIRIES TO:
Diane Williams, Director of Grants Management
(See address above.)

TEXAS COMMISSION ON THE ARTS [493]

E.O. Thompson Building
920 Colorado, 5th Floor
Austin, TX 78701
(512) 463-5535
(800) 252-9415 (Texas only)
Fax: (512) 475-2699
E-mail: laura@arts.texas.gov
Web Site: www.arts.texas.gov

FOUNDED: 1965

AREAS OF INTEREST:
Operational support and project support to nonprofit Texas arts organizations for ongoing programs and/or arts education, health and human services, economic development, public safety and criminal justice, and natural resources and agriculture; performance support for civic, cultural and other nonprofit organizations.

CONSULTING OR VOLUNTEER SERVICES:
Seminars, information services, technical assistance and funding. Services provided to institutions statewide.

NAME(S) OF PROGRAMS:
- **TCA Grant Programs**

TYPE:
Block grants; Challenge/matching grants; Conferences/seminars; Exchange programs; General operating grants; Project/program grants; Residencies; Technical assistance; Training grants; Travel grants; Visiting scholars. Organizational support, project support and touring support.

YEAR PROGRAM STARTED: 1965

PURPOSE:
To advance the state economically and culturally by investing in a creative Texas.

LEGAL BASIS:
Texas Government Code, Chapter 444, Section 021.

ELIGIBILITY:
Any 501(c)(3) organization, educational institution, or form of government may apply. Presenters and producers of performing arts whose programs are designed to stimulate artistic activity and to heighten awareness of and broaden public access to the arts in rural and underserved areas of the state are eligible to apply.

Award made according to project cost, program limits, ability to meet funding criteria and available funds.

GEOG. RESTRICTIONS: Texas.

FINANCIAL DATA:
Total amount of support: $8,000,000 for the year 2016.

Matching fund requirements: Funds provided by the state through the grants process must be matched by the applicant organization. Matching funds are generally expected to be in cash.

NO. MOST RECENT APPLICANTS: 1,500.

APPLICATION INFO:
Guidelines available online. All applications submitted electronically. Contact TCA staff to obtain user ID and password.

Duration: Up to one year.

Deadline: Varies.

PUBLICATIONS:
Guide to Programs and Services.

STAFF:
Dr. Gary Gibbs, Executive Director

COMMISSION MEMBERS:
Patricia A. Bryant, Chairperson
Dale W. Brock, Vice-Chairperson
David Garza, Treasurer
Rita E. Baca, Secretary
S. Shawn Stephens, Parliamentarian
Alphonse A. Dotson, At-Large
Linda Hatchel, At-Large
Mila Gibson
Liza Lewis
Ronald Sanders

ADDRESS INQUIRIES TO:
Laura Wiegand
Director of Programs and Technology
(See address above.)

TWO TEN FOOTWEAR FOUNDATION

1466 Main Street
Waltham, MA 02451
(800) 346-3210 ext. 1512
Fax: (781) 736-1555; (781) 736-1554
E-mail: contactus@applyists.com
Web Site: www.twoten.org

TYPE:
Scholarships. Intended for students who are interested in pursuing a career in footwear design.

See entry 1715 for full listing.

UNITARIAN UNIVERSALIST ASSOCIATION OF CONGREGATIONS [494]

UU Funding Program
P.O. Box 301149
Jamaica Plain, MA 02130
(617) 971-9600
Fax: (617) 971-0029
E-mail: uufunding@gmail.com
Web Site: uua.org/care/scholarships/stanfield

FOUNDED: 1986

AREAS OF INTEREST:
Limited to the fine arts of painting, drawing, enameling, printmaking, photography and sculpture.

NAME(S) OF PROGRAMS:
- **Stanfield and D'Orlando Art Scholarship**

TYPE:
Scholarships. Annual scholarship to be awarded to an applicant majoring in art, for further study in that major, at an accredited school.

YEAR PROGRAM STARTED: 1980

PURPOSE:
To aid a Unitarian Universalist student majoring in fine arts.

LEGAL BASIS:
Religious organization.

ELIGIBILITY:
Applicants must be members in good standing for at least one year before date of application or sponsored by a member of a Unitarian Universalist Congregation and must be enrolled in an accredited school. Eligible art fields include drawing, painting, sculpture, enameling, printmaking and photography.

GEOG. RESTRICTIONS: United States.

FINANCIAL DATA:
Payment is made directly to the recipient.

Amount of support per award: Average $1,000.

Total amount of support: Varies.

NO. MOST RECENT APPLICANTS: 19 for the year 2014.

NO. AWARDS: Varies.

APPLICATION INFO:
Applications should include a short essay on applicant, photos or slides of at least six works by applicant, a letter of recommendation, statement of tuition costs where applicant is enrolled and an application which has been signed.

Duration: One academic year. May reapply.

Deadline: February 15. Notification in May.

UNITED ARTS COUNCIL OF RALEIGH AND WAKE COUNTY, INC. [495]

410 Glenwood Avenue, Suite 170
Raleigh, NC 27603
(919) 839-1498 ext. 203
Fax: (919) 839-6002
E-mail: eoakley@unitedarts.org
Web Site: www.unitedarts.org

FOUNDED: 1990

AREAS OF INTEREST:
Arts, arts education, music education, theatre arts education, humanities-community development, and teacher-preparation education.

NAME(S) OF PROGRAMS:
- **Artists-in-Schools Grants Program**
- **Program Support Grants**
- **Regional Artist Grants**

TYPE:
Project/program grants; Seed money grants.

YEAR PROGRAM STARTED: 1989

PURPOSE:
To enhance and strengthen arts and arts education in Wake County, NC.

ELIGIBILITY:
Funds are available to Wake County (NC) grades K-12 schools, individual artists, arts organizations and municipalities with specific arts programming.

GEOG. RESTRICTIONS: Wake County, North Carolina.

FINANCIAL DATA:
Amount of support per award: $1,000 to $30,000.

Total amount of support: Varies.

Matching fund requirements: Required for some programs.

NO. MOST RECENT APPLICANTS: Over 200.

NO. AWARDS: Varies.

APPLICATION INFO:
Application information is available on the web site.

Duration: Varies by grant program annually.

Deadline: Varies by grant program annually.

PUBLICATIONS:
Guidelines.

IRS I.D.: 56-0770175

UNIVERSITY OF MINNESOTA

Room 113, Elmer L. Andersen Library
222 21st Avenue South
Minneapolis, MN 55455
(612) 624-4576
E-mail: asc-clrc@umn.edu
Web Site: lib.umn.edu/clrc

TYPE:
Travel grants. Award to travel to Kerlan Collection, University of Minnesota, plus per diem.

See entry 692 for full listing.

UNIVERSITY OF MINNESOTA [496]

Room 113, Elmer L. Andersen Library
222 21st Avenue South
Minneapolis, MN 55455
(612) 624-4576
E-mail: asc-clrc@umn.edu
Web Site: special.lib.umn.edu/clrc/

AREAS OF INTEREST:
Research and children's literature.

NAME(S) OF PROGRAMS:
- **Marilyn Hollinshead Fellowship**

TYPE:
Travel grants. Award to travel to Kerlan Collection, University of Minnesota, as well as per diem.

PURPOSE:
To fund children's literature research with manuscripts and/or original illustrations.

FINANCIAL DATA:
Award covers travel, food or lodging.

Amount of support per award: Up to $1,500.

Total amount of support: $1,500.

NO. AWARDS: 1.

APPLICATION INFO:
Electronic application acceptable by deadline.

Duration: Grants are awarded annually and are nonrenewable.

Deadline: January 30 of research year.

ADDRESS INQUIRIES TO:
Fellowship Committee
(See address above.)

THE UNIVERSITY OF TEXAS AT AUSTIN AND THE TEXAS INSTITUTE OF LETTERS [497]

The Graduate School
110 Inner Campus Drive, Main 101
Austin, TX 78705
(512) 232-3609
Fax: (512) 471-7620
E-mail: adameve@mail.utexas.edu
gbarton@austin.utexas.edu
Web Site: www.utexas.edu/ogs/Paisano

AREAS OF INTEREST:
Competitive writing fellowships.

NAME(S) OF PROGRAMS:
- **The Dobie Paisano Fellowship Program**

TYPE:
Project/program grants. Provides an opportunity for creative or nonfiction writers to live and write for an extended period in an environment that offers isolation and tranquility.

Ralph A. Johnston Memorial Fellowship is aimed at writers who have demonstrated some publishing and critical success.

Jesse H. Jones Writing Fellowship is aimed at, but not limited to, writers who are early in their careers.

Both fellowships provide and require free residence at the ranch.

YEAR PROGRAM STARTED: 1967

PURPOSE:
To stimulate creative writing by making it possible for a person to work without distractions in an environment that offers isolation and tranquility.

ELIGIBILITY:
Criteria for making the awards include quality of work, character of the proposed project, and suitability of the applicant for life at Paisano, the late J. Frank Dobie's ranch near Austin, TX.

At the time of application, the applicant must meet one of the following:
(1) be a native Texan;
(2) have lived in Texas at some time for at least three years or;
(3) have published significant work with a Texas subject.

FINANCIAL DATA:
Amount of support per award: Ralph A. Johnston Memorial Fellowship: $25,000 over four or five months; Jesse H. Jones Writing Fellowship: $18,000 over five-and-a-half months.

NO. MOST RECENT APPLICANTS: Ralph A. Johnston Memorial Fellowship: 22; Jesse H. Jones Writing Fellowship: 67.

NO. AWARDS: 1 each annually.

APPLICATION INFO:
Application process begins on November 1. Application fee of $20 for one fellowship or $30 for both fellowships is required. If applying for both fellowships, include the fee with the Johnston Memorial Fellowship application and check the appropriate box at the top of the Johnston application form. Application fees are nonrefundable.

Applicants must submit each application in triplicate and its accompanying materials in separate packets. Make checks or money orders payable to The University of Texas at Austin.

Both application forms can be downloaded and printed from the web site. To request a printed copy of either application, send a self-addressed, stamped envelope (2 ounces postage) to the address above.

Duration: Ralph A. Johnston Memorial Fellowship: Four or five months. Jesse H. Jones Writing Fellowship: Five-and-a-half months. Both nonrenewable.

Deadline: December 15.

ADDRESS INQUIRIES TO:
Michael Adams or
Gwen Barton
(See address above.)

*SPECIAL STIPULATIONS:
Applicant must demonstrate ability to live in a rustic secluded rural location. Fellows must reside at Paisano Ranch.

UTAH DIVISION OF ARTS & MUSEUMS [498]

617 East South Temple
Salt Lake City, UT 84102
(801) 236-7550
Fax: (801) 236-7556
E-mail: lalder@utah.gov
Web Site: artsandmuseums.utah.gov

FOUNDED: 1899

AREAS OF INTEREST:
Arts and museums funding in Utah.

NAME(S) OF PROGRAMS:
- **Artist-In-Residence**
- **Arts Education Projects**
- **Arts Organization Capacity Building**
- **Arts Project A/B**
- **Folk Arts Scholarships**
- **Local Arts Agencies**
- **Museum: Tiers 1 & 2**
- **Sustainability: Tiers 1 & 2**

TYPE:
Development grants; General operating grants; Matching gifts; Residencies; Scholarships.

PURPOSE:
To provide funding to art and museum organizations in Utah.

ELIGIBILITY:
Varies with the program. Organizations must have IRS 501(c)(3) not-for-profit status or be government entities. No grants to individuals or religious organizations.

GEOG. RESTRICTIONS: Utah.

FINANCIAL DATA:
Amount of support per award: $500 to $80,000.

APPLICATION INFO:
Procedure is done online. Applying organizations must have a Charitable Solicitation Permit.

Duration: One year; nonrenewable.

Deadline: Contact the organization.

ADDRESS INQUIRIES TO:
Laurel Cannon Alder
Grants Manager
(See address above.)

VCCA (VIRGINIA CENTER FOR THE CREATIVE ARTS) [499]

154 San Angelo Drive
Amherst, VA 24521
(434) 946-7236
Fax: (434) 946-7239
E-mail: vcca@vcca.com
Web Site: www.vcca.com

FOUNDED: 1971

TYPE:
Exchange programs; Fellowships; Residencies. VCCA is a creative space offering exchange programs, fellowships and residencies. It is open to writers, visual artists and composers. VCCA enables these artists,

both professional and upcoming, to concentrate on their work and take it to new heights.

YEAR PROGRAM STARTED: 1971

PURPOSE:
To provide visual artists, writers and composers with a creative space so they can pursue their projects with a minds-wide-open focus, free from the distractions and responsibilities of daily life.

LEGAL BASIS:
Nonprofit corporation.

ELIGIBILITY:
Achievement or outstanding promise within a field of art must be demonstrated.

FINANCIAL DATA:
All fellowships are for periods of residency. No cash awards are offered. Some fellowships do offer stipends.

Amount of support per award: Varies.

Total amount of support: Varies.

NO. AWARDS: Over 400.

APPLICATION INFO:
Application must include two references from professionals in applicant's field, samples of applicant's work and a curriculum vitae. Residencies available for three composers, nine visual artists and 13 writers at any time.

Duration: Two to eight weeks.

Deadline: January 15 for fellowships running from June to September. May 15 for fellowships running from October to January. September 15 for fellowships running from February to May.

PUBLICATIONS:
Application form; annual report; newsletters.

STAFF:
Sheila Gulley Pleasants, Artists Services Director

ADDRESS INQUIRIES TO:
Sheila Gulley Pleasants, Artists Services Director
(See address above.)

VERMONT ARTS COUNCIL [500]

136 State Street
Montpelier, VT 05633
(802) 828-3293
Fax: (802) 828-3363
E-mail: info@vermontartscouncil.org
Web Site: www.vermontartscouncil.org

FOUNDED: 1964

AREAS OF INTEREST:
Visual arts including painting, sculpture, drawing, printmaking, architectural and cultural facilities design, crafts, film and photography; performing arts in music, theatre and dance; literature.

CONSULTING OR VOLUNTEER SERVICES:
Staff members may counsel and assist individuals and organizations in the development of arts projects and activities.

NAME(S) OF PROGRAMS:

- **Artist Development Grants**
- **Artists in Schools**
- **Arts Partnership Grants**
- **Creation Grants**
- **Cultural Facilities Grants**
- **Cultural Routes Grants**
- **Project Grants**
- **Technical Assistance Grants**

TYPE:
Conferences/seminars; Development grants; Project/program grants; Seed money grants; Technical assistance; Training grants; Travel grants. Professional development grants. Cultural facilities improvements. Arts partnerships.

YEAR PROGRAM STARTED: 1966

PURPOSE:
To advance and preserve the arts at the center of Vermont communities.

LEGAL BASIS:
Official state arts agency and a nonprofit membership corporation.

ELIGIBILITY:
Applicants must be nonprofit organizations, agencies of town, county, state government and/or individual artists of demonstrated ability who are residents of Vermont for at least one year.

Funding is not available for:
(1) academic tuition;
(2) activities in which artists are not appropriately compensated;
(3) construction of new facilities, renovation of existing facilities, or other capital improvements (exceptions in cases that comply with Cultural Facilities Grants);
(4) deficits and debts incurred from past activities;
(5) events that present faculty members on the campus of their own institutions;
(6) events which are predominantly religious or sectarian;
(7) events whose sponsors are not in compliance with the requirements of the Americans with Disabilities Act of 1990 and Section 504 of the Rehabilitation Act of 1973;
(8) food and beverages;
(9) for-profit organizations;
(10) fund-raising events;
(11) international travel (airline tickets);
(12) lobbying expenses;
(13) private events to which the public is not invited and;
(14) purchase of permanent equipment (exceptions in cases that comply with Cultural Facilities Grants).

GEOG. RESTRICTIONS: Vermont.

FINANCIAL DATA:
Amount of support per award: Varies according to each program.

Total amount of support: $1,200,000 in grants and services and $579,000 in grants only for the average fiscal year.

Matching fund requirements: Generally 1:1.

CO-OP FUNDING PROGRAMS: Cultural Facilities Grants with the state of Vermont.

NO. MOST RECENT APPLICANTS: 250.

NO. AWARDS: 135.

APPLICATION INFO:
Interested applicants can view the *Arts Council Grant Guidelines* and application online. Individual artists are required to submit samples of work.

Duration: Typically one to three years.

Deadline: Varies.

PUBLICATIONS:
Grant guidelines; *Art Directory*; *ArtMail*.

IRS I.D.: 03-0218115

ADDRESS INQUIRIES TO:
Thaddeus Gibson, Executive Assistant
(See address above.)

VETERANS OF FOREIGN WARS AUXILIARY [501]

National Headquarters
406 West 34th Street, 10th Floor
Kansas City, MO 64111
(816) 561-8655
Fax: (816) 931-4753
E-mail: info@vfwauxiliary.org
Web Site: www.vfwauxiliary.org

AREAS OF INTEREST:
Creative art for patriotic American youth.

NAME(S) OF PROGRAMS:

- **Young American Creative Patriotic Art Awards**

TYPE:
Awards/prizes.

YEAR PROGRAM STARTED: 1947

PURPOSE:
To promote artistic creativity in patriotic American youth.

LEGAL BASIS:
Nonprofit.

ELIGIBILITY:
Students must be in grades 9 through 12 and must attend school in the same state as the sponsoring VFW Auxiliary. Home-schooled students are eligible; foreign exchange students are not. National winners of the past contests may not compete in future Young American Creative Patriotic Art Contests. Students must be no older than 18 years of age and U.S. citizens.

GEOG. RESTRICTIONS: United States.

FINANCIAL DATA:
Amount of support per award: National Scholarships: $10,000 for first place; $5,000 for second place; $2,500 for third place; $1,500 for fourth place; $500 for fifth through eighth place.

Total amount of support: $21,000.

NO. AWARDS: 8.

APPLICATION INFO:
Art must be on paper or canvas. Water color, pencil, pastel, charcoal, tempera, crayon, acrylic, pen-and-ink, or oil may be used. Digital art is not accepted.

Art work must not be framed. Canvas entries must be submitted on stretcher frames or canvas board. Other entries must be matted on white. Other color mats must not be used. In matting, heavy paper must be used to reinforce back. Mounted and floating mats may also be used. The art should be no smaller than 8" x 10" but no larger than 18" x 24", not including mat.

Applicant must be sure to complete entry form and to attach to back of entry.

Applicant must be sponsored by a VFW Auxiliary or a foreign-based VFW Auxiliary or Post.

If American flag is used in entry, it must conform to the Federal Flag Code as far as color, number of stars and stripes, and other pertinent rules of the Code.

Entry must have been done during the current school year and be submitted with teacher's signature. One entry only per student.

Deadline: Student: Participants must submit entries to a local VFW Auxiliary Scholarships Chairman by March 31. Department: VFW Auxiliary or District entries must be received by the Department

Scholarships Chairman by April 15. National: Department entries in the National Contest must be received at VFW Auxiliary VFW National Headquarters by May 5.

ADDRESS INQUIRIES TO:
Connie Wahlen
Administrator of Programs
(See address above.)

*SPECIAL STIPULATIONS:
Only the first place department winner (from each state and D.C.) is eligible for the national competition.

VIRGIN ISLANDS COUNCIL ON THE ARTS [502]

5070 Norre Gade, Suite 1
St. Thomas, VI 00802-6762
(340) 774-5984
Fax: (340) 774-6206
E-mail: tasidakelch@yahoo.com
Web Site: www.vicouncilonarts.org

FOUNDED: 1966

AREAS OF INTEREST:
Fine arts, language and literature, music, creative, visual and performing arts and crafts.

NAME(S) OF PROGRAMS:
- **Expanding Opportunities for Participation in the Arts**

TYPE:
Awards/prizes; Exchange programs; General operating grants; Project/program grants; Residencies; Technical assistance; Training grants; Travel grants. Professional development artist or art teacher grants. Grants and technical assistance to individual artists, arts organizations and arts institutions in the Virgin Islands.

YEAR PROGRAM STARTED: 1966

PURPOSE:
To encourage wider participation in the arts by means of individual creative development and the strengthening of cultural organizations.

LEGAL BASIS:
Government agency.

ELIGIBILITY:
Applicants must be residents of the Virgin Islands for at least two years. Grants are made to Virgin Island-based projects or applicants.

GEOG. RESTRICTIONS: Virgin Islands.

FINANCIAL DATA:
Amount of support per award: Up to approximately $10,000. Organizations can receive a maximum of $10,000 and individuals can receive a maximum of $5,000.

Total amount of support: Depends on government, local and federal funding.

Matching fund requirements: The amount varies depending on category of grant. Usually 1:1.

NO. MOST RECENT APPLICANTS: 183 grant requests for the year 2014-15.

NO. AWARDS: 159 grants awarded for the year 2014-15.

REPRESENTATIVE AWARDS:
$10,000 to Reichhold Center for the Performing Arts; $5,000 to the Farmers Association.

APPLICATION INFO:
Official application information is available on the Council's web site.

Duration: One year. Renewable on reapplication and reconsideration by the Board of Directors.

Deadline: January 31 and August 31.

STAFF:
Tasida Kelch, Acting Executive Director

ADDRESS INQUIRIES TO:
Tasida Kelch, Acting Executive Director
(See address above.)

VIRGINIA COMMISSION FOR THE ARTS [503]

1001 East Broad Street, Suite 330
Richmond, VA 23219
(804) 225-3132
Fax: (804) 225-4327
E-mail: margaret.vanderhye@arts.virginia.gov
Web Site: www.arts.virginia.gov

FOUNDED: 1968

AREAS OF INTEREST:
Arts activities including but not limited to performances, exhibitions, demonstrations, workshops, readings and other presentations or participatory experiences in the fields of crafts, dance, folk arts, literature, museum work, music, public media, theatre and visual arts, provided by artists or arts organizations located in the state of Virginia.

TYPE:
Fellowships; General operating grants; Project/program grants; Technical assistance. Touring grants. Residency, afterschool/arts programs, training programs for artists. Local government challenge grants. Arts and education grants. Cultural/arts tourism marketing program.

YEAR PROGRAM STARTED: 1968

PURPOSE:
To encourage participation and invest in the arts for all Virginians.

LEGAL BASIS:
State agency.

ELIGIBILITY:
Applicants must be nonprofit, tax-exempt organizations, schools or professional artists, government units.

GEOG. RESTRICTIONS: Virginia.

FINANCIAL DATA:
Amount of support per award: Varies.

Total amount of support: $3,360,000 for fiscal year 2014-15.

Matching fund requirements: Varies according to program.

NO. MOST RECENT APPLICANTS: Approximately 1,000 for fiscal year 2014-15.

NO. AWARDS: Approximately 740 for fiscal year 2014-15.

APPLICATION INFO:
Contact the Commission.

Duration: One year.

Deadline: March 1 and April 1 for most programs. Varies for other programs.

PUBLICATIONS:
Tour directory.

IRS I.D.: 54-0843105

STAFF:
Margaret Vanderhye, Executive Director

ADDRESS INQUIRIES TO:
Margaret Vanderhye, Executive Director
(See address above.)

VIRGINIA MUSEUM OF FINE ARTS [504]

Art and Education Division
200 North Boulevard
Richmond, VA 23220-4007
(804) 204-2685
Fax: (804) 204-2675
E-mail: Jenny.Harding@vmfa.museum
Web Site: www.vmfa.museum/fellowships

FOUNDED: 1940

AREAS OF INTEREST:
Education and careers in the visual arts.

NAME(S) OF PROGRAMS:
- **Professional Fellowship Program**
- **Student Fellowship Program**

TYPE:
Awards/prizes; Fellowships. Awards for undergraduate students, graduate students and professionals in the visual arts including painting, sculpture, crafts, photography, filmmaking, video, printmaking, mixed media, new/emerging media, and drawing. Art history is for graduate students only.

YEAR PROGRAM STARTED: 1940

PURPOSE:
To aid Virginians who seek financial aid for additional education or experience in the arts.

LEGAL BASIS:
State agency administering funds from an endowment and private foundations.

ELIGIBILITY:
All Applicants: Persons must be citizens or permanent residents of the U.S. and current legal residents of Virginia. A legal resident has a valid Virginia driver's license and/or pays income taxes in Virginia and/or is a registered Virginia voter. Applicants must be able to provide verification of residency upon request.

Student Applicants: Persons must be current legal residents of Virginia, and must have been legal residents for at least 12 consecutive months prior to the application deadline. Students paying in-state tuition to an accredited Virginia college, university or school of the arts qualify as legal residents of Virginia. Students must be enrolled full-time at an accredited college, university or school of the arts for the grant period of August 2017 to May 2018. Half-year fall semester Fellowship awards will be considered on a case-by-case basis for full-time students in the final year of a degree program who plan to graduate in December 2017.

Professional Applicants: Persons must be current legal residents of Virginia, and must have been legal residents for at least 24 consecutive months prior to the application deadline. Professional applicants must not be degree-seeking students at the time of the application deadline nor during the grant period of August 2017 to May 2018.

GEOG. RESTRICTIONS: Virginia.

FINANCIAL DATA:
Amount of support per award: Professional Fellowships: $8,000; Undergraduate Fellowships: $4,000; Graduate Fellowships: $6,000.

Total amount of support: $162,000 for the year 2016.

NO. MOST RECENT APPLICANTS: 750.

NO. AWARDS: 27.

APPLICATION INFO:
Contact the Museum or visit its web site.

Duration: August 2017 to May 2018. No renewals.

Deadline: November 4, 2016. Notification in February 2017.

STAFF:
Jenny Harding, Coordinator, Fellowship Program

ADDRESS INQUIRIES TO:
Fellowship Program
(See e-mail address above.)

*PLEASE NOTE:
Awards are made to applicants of highest artistic merit whose education and/or careers will benefit from financial assistance.

KURT WEILL FOUNDATION FOR MUSIC [505]

7 East 20th Street, 3rd Floor
New York, NY 10003-1106
(212) 505-5240
Fax: (212) 353-9663
E-mail: kwfinfo@kwf.org
Web Site: www.kwf.org

FOUNDED: 1962

AREAS OF INTEREST:
The study and performance of music by Kurt Weill and Marc Blitzstein.

TYPE:
Grants-in-aid; Project/program grants; Research grants. Broadcasts: Proposals are welcome from producers and not-for-profit broadcasters to support programs that feature Kurt Weill's or Marc Blitzstein's life and/or music.

College/University Performance: Grants to colleges and universities in support of general production expenses for performances of Kurt Weill's and Marc Blitzstein's stage works; grants are available to cover musical expenses in connection with performance of complete Weill and Blitzstein concert works.

Educational Outreach: Grants are awarded to performing and educational organizations which may request funding for educational activities (workshops, symposia, scholarly conferences, lectures in connection with performances, study days, secondary and college-level educational initiatives, etc.) focusing on Kurt Weill, Lotte Lenya and/or Marc Blitzstein, including payment of speakers' honoraria and travel expenses, preparation and printing of supporting materials, etc.

Professional Performance Grants: Funding may be requested by professional opera companies, theater companies, dance companies and concert groups in support of production expenses for performances of works by Kurt Weill or Marc Blitzstein.

Publication Assistance: Grants assist in expenses related to preparing manuscripts for publication in a recognized scholarly medium, including editing, indexing, design and reproduction fees. Not-for-profit publishing companies are encouraged to apply.

Research and Travel: Grants support research and travel expenses to locations of primary source material for applicants who are researching a topic related to Kurt Weill, Lotte Lenya and/or Marc Blitzstein.

Kurt Weill Dissertation Fellowship: Assists Ph.D. candidates in Weill-research activities.

Kurt Weill Mentors: Grants are awarded to aid in preparation of Weill or Blitzstein stage or concert performances, to present workshops or lectures or to participate in scholarly symposia; performing arts organizations and educational institutions may request support to engage performers, conductors, directors and scholars who have been designated "Weill Mentors" by the Kurt Weill Foundation.

PURPOSE:
To preserve and perpetuate the legacies of composer Kurt Weill (1900-1950) and actress-singer Lotte Lenya (1898-1981).

ELIGIBILITY:
Broadcasts: Proposals are welcome from producers and not-for-profit broadcasters to support programs that feature Kurt Weill's or Marc Blitzstein's life and/or music. A complete description of the project must be accompanied by a written commitment from the broadcaster.

College/University Performance: Stage Works - All works must be presented in their authorized versions and orchestrations. Performances of *Die sieben Todsonden* are fundable only in Weill's original orchestration and keys. Concert works - Grants are available to cover musical expenses in connection with performance of complete Weill and Blitzstein concert works. Compilation properties consisting solely of Weill's or Blitzstein's songs do not qualify for support.

Educational Outreach: Performing and educational organizations may request funding for educational activities (workshops, symposia, scholarly conferences, lectures in connection with performances, study days, secondary and college-level educational initiatives, etc.) focusing on Weill, Lenya and/or Blitzstein, including payment of speakers' honoraria and travel expenses, preparation and printing of supporting materials, etc.

Professional Performance: Funding may be requested by professional opera companies, theater companies, dance companies and concert groups. All works must be presented in their authorized versions and orchestrations. Applicants must furnish evidence (recordings, reviews) of the artistic merit of the organization's previous performances. Productions of *The Threepenny Opera* are not eligible for funding in the professional production and performance category, and performances of *Die sieben Todsunden* are fundable only in Weill's original orchestration and keys. Performances of *Kleine Dreigroschenmusik* alone are normally not eligible for funding, unless the piece is programmed as part of a group of Weill works. Compilation properties consisting solely of Weill's songs do not qualify for support.

Publication Assistance: Funds may be requested to assist in expenses related to preparing manuscripts for publication in a recognized scholarly medium, including editing, indexing, design and reproduction fees. Not-for-profit publishing companies are encouraged to apply. All proposals must have been subject to peer review. Normally conference proceedings are ineligible unless the essays have undergone significant revision and editing as components of a book.

Research and Travel: Applicants must be researching a topic related to Kurt Weill, Lotte Lenya and/or Marc Blitzstein.

Kurt Weill Dissertation Fellowship: Applicants must be writing their dissertation on a topic related to Kurt Weill.

Kurt Weill Mentors: To aid in preparation of Weill or Blitzstein stage or concert performances, to present workshops or lectures or to participate in scholarly symposia; performing arts organizations and educational institutions may request support to engage performers, conductors, directors and scholars who have been designated "Weill Mentors" by the Kurt Weill Foundation. Such requests may be considered even when the relevant performances would not otherwise be eligible for support under the Foundation's grant program. Applicants should contact the Foundation for further information.

FINANCIAL DATA:
Amount of support per award: Varies.

Total amount of support: Varies.

NO. MOST RECENT APPLICANTS: 19.

NO. AWARDS: 16.

APPLICATION INFO:
All applications must include the following:
(1) Application Cover Sheet and Performance Grant Fact Sheet, if applying for a performance grant, available at the Foundation web site;
(2) a detailed description of the project;
(3) information about the applicant, including relevant qualifications and past achievements; performance grant applicants should also include a DVD or audio recording of a past performance and;
(4) a detailed and itemized budget specifying entire project expenses and income, including ticket revenue and income anticipated from other funding sources and date of determination. Applicants must notify the Foundation if other grants are awarded.

In addition, specific items are requested for each category:
Broadcasts: a complete description of the project must be accompanied by a written commitment from the broadcaster;
College/University Performance: applicants must furnish evidence (recordings, reviews) of the artistic merit of the organization's previous performances;
Educational Outreach: applications must include detailed description of the educational activities and vitae for expert participants;
Professional Performance: applicants must furnish evidence (recordings, reviews) of the artistic merit of the organization's previous performances;
Publication Assistance: all proposals must have been subject to peer review; such reviews must be submitted in support of the application, along with a copy of the manuscript;
Research and Travel: grant applicants must submit a detailed outline of the proposed project, a writing sample, and at least one letter of recommendation;
Weill Dissertation Fellowship: applicants must include a copy of the dissertation proposal, at least one writing sample, and two letters of recommendation, one of which must be from the applicant's faculty advisor.

Deadline: November 1 for the following calendar year, academic year or cultural season. Applications for support of major professional productions/festivals/exhibitions, etc., will be evaluated on a case-by-case basis without application or performance deadlines. An additional application deadline of June 1 has been established, limited exclusively to College/University Performance grants for productions taking place in the fall semester of the current academic year.

ADDRESS INQUIRIES TO:
Brady Sansone, Director
(See address above.)

WEST VIRGINIA DIVISION OF CULTURE AND HISTORY [506]

The Culture Center
State Capitol Complex
1900 Kanawha Boulevard East
Charleston, WV 25305-0300
(304) 558-0220
(304) 558-0240
Fax: (304) 558-2779
E-mail: renee.margocee@wv.gov
Web Site: www.wvculture.org

FOUNDED: 1967

AREAS OF INTEREST:
Artists and arts organizations, including community development, touring, institutions, special projects and support for artists, cultural facilities purchase and rehabilitation.

CONSULTING OR VOLUNTEER SERVICES:
Consultation in a variety of fields is available.

TYPE:
Capital grants; Challenge/matching grants; General operating grants; Internships; Project/program grants; Residencies; Technical assistance; Training grants; Travel grants. Long-range planning. Individual artists grants.

YEAR PROGRAM STARTED: 1967

PURPOSE:
To provide financial and technical assistance to further the promotion, presentation and development of the arts throughout the state of West Virginia.

LEGAL BASIS:
Government agency.

ELIGIBILITY:
Nonprofit organizations and public agencies may apply. Nonprofits must have been based in West Virginia one year prior to application. Individual artists must be residents of West Virginia one year prior to application.

GEOG. RESTRICTIONS: West Virginia.

FINANCIAL DATA:
Generally, grants cover 50% of project cost.

Amount of support per award: $125 to $100,000.

Total amount of support: Approximately $2,600,000 for the year 2013.

Matching fund requirements: Dollar-for-dollar.

CO-OP FUNDING PROGRAMS: Ohio River Border Initiative (ORBI) with Ohio Arts Council.

NO. MOST RECENT APPLICANTS: 26.

NO. AWARDS: 12.

APPLICATION INFO:
Copies of application guidelines and application forms are available upon request to the Commission or can be found on the Division web site. Online applications are preferred.

Duration: One year. Must reapply for additional funding.

Deadline: Varies.

PUBLICATIONS:
Annual report; application guidelines; *ArtWorks*, newsletter.

OFFICERS:
Randall Reid-Smith, Division Commissioner
Karen Gresham, Deputy Commissioner

ADDRESS INQUIRIES TO:
Renée Margocee, Director of Arts
West Virginia Commission on the Arts
(See address above.)

WHITAKER FOUNDATION [507]

308 North 21st Street
Suite 400
St. Louis, MO 63103
(314) 241-4352
E-mail: info@thewhitakerfoundation.org
Web Site: www.thewhitakerfoundation.org

FOUNDED: 1975

AREAS OF INTEREST:
The arts, the use of and preservation of parks.

TYPE:
Project/program grants. Project/program grants are for urban parks and the arts.

PURPOSE:
To enrich lives through the arts; to encourage the preservation and use of parks.

LEGAL BASIS:
Private foundation.

ELIGIBILITY:
Organizations must be tax-exempt 501(c)(3). Project support is preferred. No support for social events.

The Foundation does not make grants to individuals.

GEOG. RESTRICTIONS: Metropolitan area of St. Louis, Missouri.

FINANCIAL DATA:
Amount of support per award: Varies.

Total amount of support: $704,575 for the year 2014.

NO. AWARDS: 18 for the year 2014.

APPLICATION INFO:
Application process begins with a Letter of Inquiry, which must be submitted online. Applicants, even those previously funded, must call the Foundation in advance to discuss their intent to apply.

Duration: Varies.

Deadline: Letters of Inquiry: August 1, November 1 and February 1; Invited Proposals: December 1, March 1 and September 1, respectively.

PUBLICATIONS:
Guidelines.

ADDRESS INQUIRIES TO:
Christy Gray, Executive Director
(See address above.)

WISCONSIN ARTS BOARD [508]

201 West Washington Avenue
2nd Floor
Madison, WI 53703
(608) 266-0190
Fax: (608) 267-0380
E-mail: artsboard@wisconsin.gov
Web Site: www.artsboard.wisconsin.gov

FOUNDED: 1973

AREAS OF INTEREST:
All arts disciplines in Wisconsin.

CONSULTING OR VOLUNTEER SERVICES:
Workshops and individual consultations.

NAME(S) OF PROGRAMS:

- **Creation and Presentation**
- **Creative Communities**
- **Folk Arts Apprenticeship Program**
- **Wisconsin Regranting Program**

TYPE:
Challenge/matching grants; Internships; Project/program grants; Technical assistance. Inquiry services, research and funding. Services provided to institutions and individuals statewide in Wisconsin.

Creative Communities Grants include Arts in Education, Local Arts and Folk Arts.

PURPOSE:
To provide support of arts projects and activities in the state of Wisconsin.

LEGAL BASIS:
Agency of the state of Wisconsin.

ELIGIBILITY:
Applicants must be organizations located in Wisconsin, operating for three years and have 501(c)(3) tax-exempt status.

GEOG. RESTRICTIONS: Wisconsin.

FINANCIAL DATA:
Amount of support per award: $1,500 to $20,000 depending on the program.

Total amount of support: $1,000,000 for fiscal year 2015.

Matching fund requirements: All grants must be matched.

NO. AWARDS: Varies.

APPLICATION INFO:
Application form is available online.

Duration: One year.

Deadline: Varies.

STAFF:
George Tzougros, Executive Director

ADDRESS INQUIRIES TO:
Karen Goeschko, Assistant Director
Programs and Services
(See address above.)

WOMEN IN FILM

6100 Wilshire Boulevard
Suite 710
Los Angeles, CA 90048
(323) 935-2211
Fax: (323) 935-2212
E-mail: mgreen@wif.org
Web Site: www.wif.org/programs/film-finishing-fund

TYPE:
Project/program grants. Awards for completion of films on subjects that meet the stated guidelines of WIF on an annual basis.

See entry 1079 for full listing.

WOMEN'S STUDIO WORKSHOP (WSW) [509]

722 Binnewater Lane
Rosendale, NY 12401
(845) 658-9133
Fax: (845) 658-9031
E-mail: info@wsworkshop.org
Web Site: www.wsworkshop.org

FOUNDED: 1974

AREAS OF INTEREST:
Book arts.

NAME(S) OF PROGRAMS:
- **Artists' Book Residency Grants**

TYPE:
Project/program grants; Residencies.

YEAR PROGRAM STARTED: 1979

PURPOSE:
To enable artists to produce a limited edition artists' book while in residence at the Women's Studio Workshop.

ELIGIBILITY:
Women artists working in printmaking or the book arts.

FINANCIAL DATA:
Amount of support per award: $350 per week artist stipend, up to $750 materials, up to $250 travel costs within the continental U.S., access to all studios, and housing.

NO. MOST RECENT APPLICANTS: 100.

NO. AWARDS: 3 to 5.

APPLICATION INFO:
Application must include:
(1) application form;
(2) 100-word description of the project (one copy), which should also include studios/media needed;
(3) a structural dummy to demonstrate how the book will appear; it does not have to be a complete representation of the finished piece; however, please include one to two spreads that are fully sketched out; the dummy should be actual size; (the Workshop anticipates that, if funded, applicant will refine her ideas before her residency);
(4) materials budget;
(5) resume;
(6) 10 images of recent work plus an image script, which should include title, media, dimensions and date and;
(7) self-addressed, stamped envelope or appropriate postage, if applicant wishes to have her application materials or dummy returned (please indicate if one wishes to have one's book dummy returned).

Duration: Six to eight weeks. Nonrenewable.

Deadline: November 15.

ADDRESS INQUIRIES TO:
Ann Kalmbach, Executive Director
(See address above.)

WOMEN'S STUDIO WORKSHOP (WSW) [510]

722 Binnewater Lane
Rosendale, NY 12401
(845) 658-9133
Fax: (845) 658-9031
E-mail: info@wsworkshop.org
Web Site: www.wsworkshop.org

FOUNDED: 1974

AREAS OF INTEREST:
Art-in-education.

NAME(S) OF PROGRAMS:
- **Art-in-Education Artists' Book Residency Grant**

TYPE:
Residencies. With National Endowment for the Arts (NEA) support, WSW awards two eight-week residencies to artists in the book arts. This is a residency grant.

PURPOSE:
To help grantees create new work while they simultaneously teach young people through the workshop's studio-based art-in-education program.

ELIGIBILITY:
Women artists working in printmaking or the book arts.

FINANCIAL DATA:
Amount of support per award: $350 per week stipend, $750 materials budget, housing, travel costs up to $250 within the continental U.S. and unlimited studio access.

APPLICATION INFO:
Application should include:
(1) application form;
(2) 100-word description of the project, which should include media or studio needed to produce the edition;
(3) a one-page description of applicant's relevant experience working with children;
(4) a structural dummy to demonstrate how the book will be bound or function when handled; it does not have to be a complete representation of the finished piece; however, please include one to two spreads that are fully sketched out; the dummy should be actual size (the Workshop anticipates that, if funded, applicant will refine her ideas before her residency);
(5) materials budget;
(6) a CD with 10 clearly marked images of recent work; an image list should also be provided and include title, media, dimensions and date; check the Workshop Faq Sheet on its web site for digital specifications and;
(7) application materials/book dummies will not be returned unless requested; a self-addressed, stamped envelope or appropriate postage should be included if applicant wishes to have her application materials or dummy returned.

Duration: Eight to 10 weeks.

Deadline: November 15.

ADDRESS INQUIRIES TO:
Ann Kalmbach, Executive Director
(See address above.)

*PLEASE NOTE:
Normally, residencies are September to October and March to April. Specific dates are determined by the academic calendar and vary annually.

WOMEN'S STUDIO WORKSHOP (WSW) [511]

722 Binnewater Lane
Rosendale, NY 12401
(845) 658-9133
Fax: (845) 658-9031
E-mail: info@wsworkshop.org
Web Site: www.wsworkshop.org/residencies/studio-residency-grant

FOUNDED: 1974

AREAS OF INTEREST:
Visual artists.

NAME(S) OF PROGRAMS:
- **Studio Residency Grant**

TYPE:
Residencies.

YEAR PROGRAM STARTED: 1999

PURPOSE:
To provide artists with time and resources to create a new body of work.

ELIGIBILITY:
Women printmakers, papermakers, book artists, ceramists, photographers or artist collaborators can apply.

FINANCIAL DATA:
Amount of support per award: $350 per week artist stipend, up to $500 for materials, up to $250 for travel within the continental U.S., plus housing and unlimited studio use.

NO. MOST RECENT APPLICANTS: 177 in 2014.

NO. AWARDS: 2.

APPLICATION INFO:
All applications must be submitted through the web site listed above. Application must include:
(1) a current resume;
(2) a description of the project (100 to 200 words), including the studio the applicant would prefer to work in;
(3) 10 images of recent work and;
(4) an image script, including title, medium, dimension and date of each image.

Duration: Six to eight weeks. Nonrenewable.

Deadline: February 1.

ADDRESS INQUIRIES TO:
Ann Kalmbach, Executive Director
(See address above.)

THE HELENE WURLITZER FOUNDATION OF NEW MEXICO [512]

218 Los Pandos Road
Taos, NM 87571
(575) 758-2413
Fax: (575) 758-2559
E-mail: hwf@taosnet.com
Web Site: www.wurlitzerfoundation.org

FOUNDED: 1954

AREAS OF INTEREST:
Creative, not interpretive, work in all media and allied fields.

TYPE:
Residencies. Residence grants for national and international artists involved in creative work, including writing, painting, sculpture and musical composition.

YEAR PROGRAM STARTED: 1954

PURPOSE:
To encourage and stimulate creative work in all media, including visual arts, literary arts and musical composition.

LEGAL BASIS:
Tax-exempt under Section 501(c)(3) and Section 4945(j)(3), (g)(3) and (g)(1).

ELIGIBILITY:
No restrictions are made on the basis of race, sex, age or religious or ethnic background or national origin.

FINANCIAL DATA:
No direct monetary grants are made. Residences are located in Taos, NM and are furnished with free utilities and rent.

Amount of support per award: Varies.

Total amount of support: Varies.

CO-OP FUNDING PROGRAMS: Robert Chesley Foundation.

NO. MOST RECENT APPLICANTS: 355.

NO. AWARDS: 33.

APPLICATION INFO:
Application must include five samples maximum (photographs or digital images) from visual artists (please list medium and dimensions), writing sample not to exceed 35 double-spaced pages or six poems from literary artists, or one CD/DVD from composers. Failure to comply with the guidelines will result in elimination from the review process. The Foundation will not retain samples of work and recommends a self-addressed, stamped envelope be included with samples if applicant wishes to have samples returned.

Applicant should also send self-addressed, stamped envelope if requesting application via mail.

Duration: Three-month residencies.

Deadline: January 18.

IRS I.D.: 85-0128634

OFFICERS AND BOARD OF DIRECTORS:
Rena Rosequist, President
Peggy Nelson, Vice President
Bill Ebie, Treasurer
Harold Hahn, Secretary
Nic Knight, Executive Director
Joseph Caldwell
Michael A. Knight
Tito Naranjo

ADDRESS INQUIRIES TO:
Nic Knight, Executive Director
(See address above.)

*SPECIAL STIPULATIONS:
Single occupancy only; no pets, no smoking, no outside employment while in residence.

WYOMING ARTS COUNCIL [513]

2301 Central Avenue
Barrett Building, 2nd Floor
Cheyenne, WY 82002
(307) 777-7742
Fax: (307) 777-5499
Web Site: wyoarts.state.wy.us

FOUNDED: 1967

AREAS OF INTEREST:
Arts within the state of Wyoming.

CONSULTING OR VOLUNTEER SERVICES:
Assistance for 501(c)(3) nonprofit and government organizations.

NAME(S) OF PROGRAMS:

- **Blanchan/Doubleday Fellowships**
- **Capital Support Grants**
- **Community Support Grants**
- **Folk Arts Apprenticeships**
- **Literary Arts Fellowships**
- **Performing Arts Fellowships**
- **Professional Development Grants**
- **Rural Arts Access Grants**
- **Visual Arts Fellowships**

TYPE:
Awards/prizes; Capital grants; Development grants; Fellowships; Formula grants; General operating grants; Project/program grants; Technical assistance. Blanchan/Doubleday Fellowships, Individual Artist Grants, Literary Arts Fellowships, Performing Arts Fellowships and Visual Arts Fellowships are for individual artists.

YEAR PROGRAM STARTED: 1967

PURPOSE:
To assist artistic programs of outstanding quality that serve the needs of Wyoming citizens, further public interest in the state's cultural heritage and resources and encourage artistic expression, essential for the well-being of the arts.

LEGAL BASIS:
Agency of the state of Wyoming.

ELIGIBILITY:
Grants are provided to 501(c)(3) nonprofit organizations, educational institutions and governmental entities within the state, including arts centers, museums, symphonies, schools, dance workshops, theatre and local arts councils. Professional Development Grants and the individual fellowships are provided in visual, literary and performing arts to Wyoming residents.

GEOG. RESTRICTIONS: Wyoming.

FINANCIAL DATA:
Amount of support per award: Varies.

Total amount of support: Varies.

Matching fund requirements: A one-to-one cash match is required on most grants.

NO. MOST RECENT APPLICANTS: More than 300.

NO. AWARDS: Over 300 grants are awarded each year.

APPLICATION INFO:
Apply online for most grant programs.

Duration: One fiscal year (July 1 to the following June 30).

Deadline: Varies.

PUBLICATIONS:
Newsletter.

STAFF:
Michael Lange, Executive Director
Karen Merklin, Grants Manager
Rachel Clifton, Public Art and Creative Sector Individuals Supervisor
Danee Hunzie, Community Development and Independent Music Specialist
Annie Hatch, Folklorist and Arts Specialist

ADDRESS INQUIRIES TO:
Karen Merklin, Grants Manager
(See address above.)

Performing arts

ACADEMY FOUNDATION OF THE ACADEMY OF MOTION PICTURE ARTS AND SCIENCES [514]

1313 North Vine Street
Los Angeles, CA 90028
(310) 247-3010
Fax: (310) 247-3794
E-mail: nicholl@oscars.org
Web Site: www.oscars.org/nicholl

FOUNDED: 1927

AREAS OF INTEREST:
Motion picture arts and sciences.

NAME(S) OF PROGRAMS:

- **The Academy Nicholl Fellowships in Screenwriting**

TYPE:
Awards/prizes; Fellowships. Awards provide a portion of living expenses for one year for promising new writers so that they may concentrate during that period on writing for the screen.

YEAR PROGRAM STARTED: 1985

PURPOSE:
To foster the development of the art of motion picture screenwriting.

LEGAL BASIS:
Nonpublic foundation.

ELIGIBILITY:
Applicants may not have earned more than $25,000 or any other consideration as a screenwriter for theatrical films or television or sold or optioned screen or television rights to any original story, treatment, outline screenplay or teleplay.

FINANCIAL DATA:
Amount of support per award: $35,000 each.

Total amount of support: $175,000 for the year 2015.

NO. MOST RECENT APPLICANTS: 7,442 for the year 2015.

NO. AWARDS: Up to 5 fellowships each year.

APPLICATION INFO:
Applicants must submit one copy of an original screenplay in PDF format, no shorter than 70 pages, and no longer than 160 pages in length, written in screenplay format standard to the U.S. motion picture industry. Submissions must have been written originally in English; translations will not be accepted. Submissions must be the original work of the applicant and may not be based, in whole or in part, on any other person's or persons' fictional or nonfictional material, published or unpublished, produced or unproduced. Sequels utilizing characters or storylines from produced motion pictures, television shows or published fiction are not eligible. Nor are adaptations eligible, unless the source material is solely the entrant's original work.

Applicants must also fill out an application form via an online account, completed in its entirety and pay a nonrefundable entry fee. This fee will be applied against judging and administrative costs. Applications and screenplays are accepted online only. Submitted materials will not be returned.

Duration: One year. Commencing around the first week of November.

Deadline: Uploaded by 11:59 P.M., May 2. Announcement in late October.

PUBLICATIONS:
Guidelines.

FELLOWSHIP COMMITTEE:
Robin Swicord, Chairperson
Buffy Shutt, Vice Chairperson
Stephanie Allain
John Bailey
Albert Berger
Julia Chasman
Tina Gordon Chism
Naomi Foner
Marcus Hu
Julie Lynn
Ron Mardigian
Eric Roth
Eva Marie Saint
Peter Samuelson
Kirsten Smith
Dana Stevens
Tyger Williams

ADDRESS INQUIRIES TO:
Academy Nicholl Fellowships
(See address above.)

*PLEASE NOTE:
Each fellowship is payable quarterly for one year. The first payment will be made at the

start of the fellowship year. The second, third, fourth and final payments will be made subject to satisfactory progress of the recipient's work, as judged by the Academy's Nicholl Fellowship Committee. The Academy reserves the right to grant no awards if, in the opinion of the Academy Nicholl Fellowship Committee, no application is of sufficient merit.

*SPECIAL STIPULATIONS:

Academy Nicholl Fellowships may not be held concurrently with other fellowships. During the fellowship year, Academy Nicholl Fellows are expected to complete an original screenplay approximately 90 to 120 pages in length.

AMERICAN DANCE FESTIVAL [515]

Box 90772
Durham, NC 27708-0772
(919) 684-6402
Fax: (919) 684-5459
E-mail: adf@americandancefestival.org
Web Site: www.americandancefestival.org

NAME(S) OF PROGRAMS:

- **Tuition Scholarships**

TYPE:

Scholarships.

PURPOSE:

To offer assistance to promising students.

ELIGIBILITY:

Open to promising students who have a high level of technical ability, creative potential and who have experience in either performing and/or choreography.

GEOG. RESTRICTIONS: Primarily United States.

FINANCIAL DATA:

Amount of support per award: Quarter to full tuition.

Total amount of support: Varies.

APPLICATION INFO:

Students must either submit their application before their audition date or be prepared to turn it in at the audition site. Students unable to attend an audition may submit a DVD containing two minutes of technique and a one-minute solo.

Duration: Six-and-a-half weeks.

Deadline: Details are available on the web site.

ADDRESS INQUIRIES TO:

Nicolle Wasserman Greenhood
Director of School Administration
(See address above.)

AMERICAN SOCIETY FOR THEATRE RESEARCH (ASTR) [516]

1000 Westgate Drive
Suite 252
Saint Paul, MN 55114
(847) 447-1701
Fax: (847) 447-1150
E-mail: fellowships@astr.org
Web Site: www.astr.org

FOUNDED: 1956

AREAS OF INTEREST:

Theatre studies (history, criticism, theory) and performance studies.

NAME(S) OF PROGRAMS:

- **The ASTR Collaborative Research Award**
- **Biennial Sally Banes Publication Prize**
- **Oscar G. Brockett Essay Prize**
- **Cambridge University Press Prize**
- **Chinoy Dissertation Research Fellowships**
- **Co-sponsored Events Awards**
- **Selma Jeanne Cohen Conference Presentation Award**
- **Distinguished Scholar Award**
- **Grants for Researchers with Heavy Teaching Loads**
- **Barnard Hewitt Award**
- **Errol Hill Award**
- **Gerald Kahan Scholar's Prize**
- **David Keller Travel Grants**
- **Thomas F. Marshall Graduate Student Awards**
- **Brooks McNamara Publishing Subvention**
- **Research Fellowships**
- **Targeted Research Areas Grants**

TYPE:

Awards/prizes; Conferences/seminars; Development grants; Exchange programs; Fellowships; Research grants; Scholarships; Seed money grants; Travel grants; Visiting scholars. The ASTR Collaborative Research Award aims to foster the exchange of research across different academic and community contexts within the U.S. or between U.S. scholars/artists and those abroad. It also aims to foster long-term relationships benefiting faculty who work in different types of institutional environments and to foster the exchange of research in subject areas underrepresented in U.S. theatre scholarship, pedagogy, and performance practice.

Biennial Sally Banes Publication Prize is presented in even-numbered years for the publication (book or essay) that best explores the intersections of theatre and dance/movement in the previous two calendar years.

Oscar G. Brockett Essay Prize is jointly awarded by the Society and the Oscar G. Brockett Center for Theatre History and Criticism at the University of Texas - Austin for the best essay published in English in a refereed scholarly journal or volume published by a scholarly press. The essay can relate to any subject in theatre research, broadly construed.

The Cambridge University Press Prize is given for a Society conference plenary paper written by a first-time plenary presenter.

Chinoy Dissertation Research Fellowships assist Ph.D. candidates with travel to national and international collections to conduct research connected with their dissertations.

Co-sponsored Events Awards assist with events that fulfill ASTR's purpose through collaboration with other organizations and institutions and increase the visibility of the work of both ASTR and the award recipient within a wider professional context.

Selma Jeanne Cohen Conference Presentation Award goes to a scholar to participate in a plenary or working session at the ASTR conference. The presentation must explore the intersections of theatre and dance/movement.

Distinguished Scholar Award is given each year to a scholar whose body of work has made a significant contribution to the field of theatre, dance, opera, and/or performance studies.

Grants for Researchers with Heavy Teaching Loads promote scholarly and practical exchange among theatre researchers by providing opportunities to faculty at institutions with heavy teaching loads and limited support for scholarship.

The Barnard Hewitt Award for Outstanding Research in Theatre History is awarded each year to the best book in "theatre history or cognate disciplines" published during the previous calendar year. The Department of Theatre at the University of Illinois, Urbana-Champaign, provides the monetary prize.

Errol Hill Award is given in recognition of outstanding scholarship in African American theatre, drama, and/or performance studies. The book or article must be published during the previous calendar year.

Gerald Kahan Scholar's Prize is awarded for the best essay written by a junior scholar and published in English in a refereed scholarly journal on any subject in theatre research, broadly construed.

David Keller Travel Grants encourage untenured scholars with terminal degrees to become active members of the Society by helping them to meet the expenses of attending the ASTR annual meeting in November.

Thomas F. Marshall Graduate Student Awards encourage active student membership in the Society by helping to meet the expenses of attending the ASTR annual meeting.

Brooks McNamara Publishing Subvention supports the costs of securing rights to reproduce illustrations for publication, costs of acquiring illustrations, and/or the costs of reproducing illustrations in conjunction with a book under contract for publication. (Electronic publications will also be considered.)

Research Fellowships underwrite some expenses associated with projects in the field of theatre and/or performance studies.

Targeted Research Areas Grants support specific projects in areas currently underrepresented. Such areas include, but are not limited to, pre-1900 research; Asian, African, Latin American, and Middle Eastern theatre, dance and performance. Translations of important theatre documents, including plays, are also considered.

YEAR PROGRAM STARTED: 1976

LEGAL BASIS:

Nonprofit learned society.

ELIGIBILITY:

The ASTR Collaborative Research Award: At least one participant from a host institution must be a current ASTR member.

Biennial Sally Banes Publication Prize: Any independent, tenured or untenured scholar; eligible books and articles must have been published in the previous two calendar years.

Oscar G. Brockett Essay Prize: Author must have been a member of ASTR for at least three years and be at least seven years beyond the Ph.D. Essays must have been published in the previous calendar year and may not have appeared elsewhere previously.

Cambridge University Press Prize: ASTR conference plenary paper written by a first-time plenary presenter.

Helen Krich Chinoy Dissertation Research Fellowships: Ph.D. candidates who have passed their qualifying exams within the last two years (or will have passed their qualifying exams by June of the current year) and have begun working on their dissertations. The project must be part of the dissertation research.

Co-sponsored Events Awards: Applications may come from individuals, institutions or a combination, to support events of regional, national or international significance in the form of conferences, colloquia, symposia, summits, etc. Events must foster scholarship on theatre and performance.

Selma Jeanne Cohen Conference Presentation Award: Tenured, untenured and contingent faculty, independent scholars and graduate students are eligible to apply.

Distinguished Scholar Award: Nominations are accepted from ASTR members and previous recipients of the award. In addition to contributions made to theatre, dance, opera and/or performance studies, involvement in ASTR is also a criterion of the award.

Grants for Researchers with Heavy Teaching Loads: Any full-time or contingent instructor at the college level, with a terminal degree and a heavy teaching load or the equivalent load based on heavy production and/or service obligations.

Barnard Hewitt Award: Eligible books must have been published in the previous calendar year. They must be written by a scholar or scholars residing in the Americas, or by a scholar or scholars located outside the Americas but writing on an American topic. Plays, edited collections and anthologies are not eligible for this prize.

Errol Hill Award: The book or article must have been published in the previous calendar year. Authors may nominate their own works; nominations from publishers and editors are also accepted.

Gerald Kahan Scholar's Prize: The author must be untenured and within seven years of the Doctorate, or must be enrolled in a doctoral program, at the time the essay is published.

David Keller Travel Grants: Any untenured scholars with terminal degrees, including independent scholars and tenure-track and adjunct faculty.

Thomas F. Marshall Graduate Student Awards: Any student majoring in theatre/performance studies in any academic department at any level of higher education.

Brooks McNamara Publishing Subvention: Any scholar holding a terminal degree and who has been a member of ASTR for at least three years. Applicant must hold a book contract to qualify. Preference is given to junior scholars.

Research Fellowships: Anyone who holds a terminal degree and has been a member of the Society for at least three years is eligible to apply.

Targeted Research Areas Grants: Any independent, tenured or untenured scholar who is currently a member of the Society and holds a terminal degree, or any graduate student who is applying in support of a project that is not directly related to her/his dissertation.

FINANCIAL DATA:
Total amount of support: Varies.

APPLICATION INFO:
Application information is available on the web site, under "Awards."

Duration: Varies.

Deadline: Varies.

ADDRESS INQUIRIES TO:
Director of Fellowships and Awards
(See address above.)

ARTS MIDWEST [517]

2908 Hennepin Avenue, Suite 200
Minneapolis, MN 55408-1954
(612) 341-0755
Fax: (612) 341-0902
E-mail: christy@artsmidwest.org
Web Site: www.artsmidwest.org

FOUNDED: 1985

AREAS OF INTEREST:
Performing arts booking conference and performing arts grants to presenting organizations.

NAME(S) OF PROGRAMS:
- **Arts Midwest Conference**
- **Arts Midwest Touring Fund**

TYPE:
Conferences/seminars. Performing arts grants.

YEAR PROGRAM STARTED: 1985

PURPOSE:
To connect people throughout the Midwest and the world to meaningful arts opportunities, sharing creativity, knowledge, and understanding across boundaries.

LEGAL BASIS:
Nonprofit.

ELIGIBILITY:
Nonprofit performing arts presenters within our nine-state region.

GEOG. RESTRICTIONS: Illinois, Indiana, Iowa, Michigan, Minnesota, North Dakota, Ohio, South Dakota and Wisconsin.

FINANCIAL DATA:
Amount of support per award: Up to 20% of the artist's contracted fee, $500 to $4,000.

Total amount of support: Varies.

NO. MOST RECENT APPLICANTS: 200.

APPLICATION INFO:
Application information is available online. Only one application may be submitted.

Duration: Varies.

Deadline: Varies.

THE BANFF CENTRE [518]

107 Tunnel Mountain Drive
Banff AB T1L 1H5 Canada
(403) 762-6180
Fax: (403) 762-6345
E-mail: arts_info@banffcentre.ca
Web Site: www.banffcentre.ca/programs

FOUNDED: 1933

AREAS OF INTEREST:
Performing arts, literary, visual and new media arts.

TYPE:
Conferences/seminars; Residencies; Scholarships. Practicum.

PURPOSE:
To provide financial assistance to deserving artists for a residency at The Banff Centre.

ELIGIBILITY:
Open to advanced students who have been accepted for a program at The Banff Centre.

FINANCIAL DATA:
Amount of support per award: Varies.

Total amount of support: Varies depending on program.

APPLICATION INFO:
Application information can be accessed online. Applicants must submit a completed application form, accompanied by requested documentation.

Duration: Varies.

Deadline: Varies per program.

ADDRESS INQUIRIES TO:
Office of the Registrar
The Banff Centre
(See address above.)

CHOPIN FOUNDATION OF THE U.S.

1440 79th Street Causeway, Suite 117
Miami, FL 33141
(305) 868-0624
Fax: (305) 865-5150
E-mail: info@chopin.org
Web Site: www.chopin.org

TYPE:
Scholarships. Scholarship program supporting young American pianists, 14 to 17 years of age.

See entry 747 for full listing.

COLONIAL PLAYERS, INC. THEATER-IN-THE-ROUND [519]

108 East Street
Annapolis, MD 21401
(410) 268-7373 (Box Office)
E-mail: info@thecolonialplayers.org
Web Site: thecolonialplayers.org

FOUNDED: 1949

AREAS OF INTEREST:
Theatre and the arts.

NAME(S) OF PROGRAMS:
- **Biennial Promising Playwright Award**

TYPE:
Awards/prizes. Monetary award and showcase for an outstanding script by an aspiring playwright.

YEAR PROGRAM STARTED: 1973

PURPOSE:
To foster the arts and to encourage aspiring playwrights and promising talent in every aspect of the theatre.

LEGAL BASIS:
501(c)(3) nonprofit.

ELIGIBILITY:
Competition is open to any aspiring playwright residing in any of the states descendant from the original 13 colonies (Connecticut, Delaware, Georgia, Maryland, Massachusetts, New Hampshire, New Jersey, New York, North Carolina, Pennsylvania, Rhode Island, South Carolina, Virginia, Washington, DC and West Virginia).

Only full-length plays, suitable for arena production, with up to two settings, and running not less than 90 minutes and not more than two hours, excluding intermission, will be considered. Cast sizes are limited to 10 actors or fewer. Musicals and adaptations in copyright will not be considered. In

addition, plays that have been previously produced professionally will not be considered.

Plays submitted must be free of royalty and copyright restrictions which would prevent Colonial Players from producing the play. Collaborations of two or more authors are acceptable. Musicals and adaptations in copyright will not be considered. The play must not have been professionally produced elsewhere at the time of submission. Nonprofessional productions, staged readings and/or workshop productions prior to submission are permitted. (Please list places and dates along with name, address, phone number of the playwright in a sealed envelope attached to the manuscript.) Only plays which receive Honorable Mention from previous Colonial Players' contests may be resubmitted for consideration.

GEOG. RESTRICTIONS: Connecticut, Delaware, Georgia, Maryland, Massachusetts, New Hampshire, New Jersey, New York, North Carolina, Pennsylvania, Rhode Island, South Carolina, Virginia, Washington, DC and West Virginia.

FINANCIAL DATA:
Amount of support per award: $1,000 and workshop reading of the play.

NO. MOST RECENT APPLICANTS: 200.

NO. AWARDS: 1.

APPLICATION INFO:
Scripts must be typewritten and firmly bound in a cover (no brads, no staples and no ring binders). The first sheet must include only the title of the play. The second sheet must contain a description of the setting(s), characters and the time of action. In a separate packet, author should submit the same first two pages bound with a one-page synopsis of the play and a 10-page sample from the play. The author's name, address and phone number may not appear anywhere on the manuscripts (no headers or footers) but must be attached to the manuscript in a sealed envelope. Scripts will be numbered for judging.

Duration: Colonial Players reserves the right to work with the Director in a workshop production of the play within two years after the award is announced. Subsequent productions of the play at other theaters must give credit to Colonial Players, Inc. for premiering the play.

Deadline: Manuscripts will be accepted only if they bear postmarks between September 1 and December 31. Those received before or after will not be considered. Final decision of the judges will be announced no later than June 30 of the following year.

IRS I.D.: 23-7074203

OFFICERS:
Darice Clewell, President

ADDRESS INQUIRIES TO:
Coordinator
The Colonial Players, Inc.
Promising Playwright Contest
(See address above.)

Manuscripts must be sent to
The Colonial Players, Inc.
Promising Playwright Contest
(See address above.)

*PLEASE NOTE:
The award-winning playwright will be invited to a weekend workshop devoted entirely to the winning play the summer after the contest winner is announced. The workshop will include intensive discussions with directors, designers and actors, and a rehearsed reading in front of an audience.

MARTHA GRAHAM SCHOOL OF CONTEMPORARY DANCE, INC. [520]

55 Bethune Street, 11th Floor
New York, NY 10014
(212) 838-5886
(212) 229-9200
Fax: (212) 838-0339
E-mail: info@marthagraham.org
jpatten@marthagraham.org
Web Site: marthagraham.org

FOUNDED: 1926

AREAS OF INTEREST:
Training professional dancers.

NAME(S) OF PROGRAMS:
- **Graham II Performing Group Scholarship**
- **Independent Program**
- **Professional Trainee Program**
- **Summer Intensive**
- **Teens Program**
- **Third Year Post Certificate Program**
- **Winter Intensive**

TYPE:
Conferences/seminars; General operating grants; Internships; Matching gifts; Project/program grants; Research grants; Residencies; Scholarships; Work-study programs. Awards for class tuition.

Scholarship students work at the school.

YEAR PROGRAM STARTED: 1966

PURPOSE:
To provide help to the most promising dance students who are studying at the Martha Graham School.

LEGAL BASIS:
Nonprofit private school.

ELIGIBILITY:
Proficiency in dancing with special proficiency in the Martha Graham Technique is required. On-site scholarship auditions.

FINANCIAL DATA:
Scholarships are full (minimum of eight classes a week) or partial (student pays approximately half tuition per quarter for a minimum of eight classes a week). Scholarships require regular attendance.

Amount of support per award: Full $5,000; Half $2,500. Both for a 10-month school year.

Total amount of support: Varies.

NO. MOST RECENT APPLICANTS: 210.

NO. AWARDS: 24.

APPLICATION INFO:
Applicants are students at the School at the time they apply. Award is by competition judged by the School faculty.

Duration: Normally awarded on a 12-month basis, on the basis of competition.

IRS I.D.: 13-1834089

STAFF:
LaRue Allen, Executive Director
Jennifer Patten, Director of Education and Training
Tami Alesson, Director of Student Affairs

BOARD OF TRUSTEES:
Kenneth Bloom, Chairman
Inger Witter, President
LaRue Allen
Amy Blumenthal
Audra D. Cohen
Janet Eilber
Beau Gage
Inga M. Golay
Jon Gralnick
John Hotta
John R. Keller
Jean-Paul Lafaye
Jayne Millard
Lorraine Oler
Judith Schlosser
Janis Bishop Tripodakis

ADDRESS INQUIRIES TO:
Jennifer Patten
Director of Education and Training
(See address above.)

JACOB'S PILLOW DANCE FESTIVAL, INC. [521]

358 George Carter Road
Becket, MA 01223
(413) 243-9919
Fax: (413) 243-4744
E-mail: info@jacobspillow.org
Web Site: www.jacobspillow.org

FOUNDED: 1932

AREAS OF INTEREST:
Nurturing and sustaining artistic creation, presentation, education and preservation as well as engaging and deepening public appreciation and support for dance.

NAME(S) OF PROGRAMS:
- **The Intern Program at Jacob's Pillow**
- **The School at Jacob's Pillow**

TYPE:
Assistantships; Awards/prizes; Exchange programs; Fellowships; Internships; Residencies; Scholarships; Training grants; Visiting scholars. The Intern Program at Jacob's Pillow has training in arts administration and technical theater production. The School at Jacob's Pillow has four intensive programs: Ballet, Cultural Traditions, Contemporary and Musical Theatre Dance, all including awards/prizes/scholarships.

There are creative development residencies available.

PURPOSE:
The Intern Program at Jacob's Pillow: To train aspiring young professionals and career-changers in arts administration and technical theater production during the Festival season and in arts administrations during the fall/winter/spring. The School at Jacob's Pillow: To provide professional development training to advanced dancers in summer dance programs.

ELIGIBILITY:
The Intern Program at Jacob's Pillow provides professional training experience in arts administration and technical theater production to aspiring young professionals and career-changers. The School at Jacob's Pillow is open to U.S. and foreign nationals who are 16 years of age or older and complete application requirements for the program(s) selected.

FINANCIAL DATA:
The School at Jacob's Pillow provides scholarships applicable toward tuition, room

and board. Festival performances are an integral part of The School and Intern programs.

Amount of support per award: The School at Jacob's Pillow: Varies.

Total amount of support: Varies.

NO. MOST RECENT APPLICANTS: Over 1,000 for both programs.

NO. AWARDS: 100 per year.

APPLICATION INFO:
Intern Program at Jacob's Pillow: Applicants must write a cover letter explaining why they wish to intern at Jacob's Pillow, what position(s) they are applying for and in what priority order, their qualifications and interests, and their goals and expectations for the internship. Complete application instructions are downloadable from the web site.

The School at Jacob's Pillow: All applicants must audition. Initially, applicants must submit a complete, legible program application, assembled and mailed as instructed on the Application Checklist. Enclosures vary by program. Complete application instructions are downloadable from the web site.

Duration: The Intern Program at Jacob's Pillow: Up to three months. The School at Jacob's Pillow: One to three weeks.

Deadline: Intern Program: February; School: March.

ADDRESS INQUIRIES TO:
See e-mail address above.

NATIONAL OPERA ASSOCIATION, INC.

2403 Russell Long Boulevard
Canyon, TX 79016
(806) 651-2843
Fax: (806) 651-2958
E-mail: rhansen@noa.org
Web Site: www.noa.org

TYPE:
Awards/prizes. Cash prizes awarded to Artist Division winners and Scholarship Division winners. Also scholarships to AIMS, awarded in both divisions. Productions of winning operas in Chamber Opera Competition will be scheduled for annual convention.

See entry 767 for full listing.

NEW DRAMATISTS [522]

424 West 44th Street
New York, NY 10036
(212) 757-6960
Fax: (646) 390-8705
E-mail: newdramatists@newdramatists.org
Web Site: www.newdramatists.org

FOUNDED: 1949

AREAS OF INTEREST:
Service organization for member playwrights. Work with member writers on new plays, providing them with workshops, readings and staged readings. Involves directors and dramaturges in workshops.

TYPE:
Awards/prizes; Internships; Residencies. Resident playwrights are selected by an admissions panel which consists of current resident playwrights, alumni playwrights, and other theatre professionals. The panel changes completely from year to year.

YEAR PROGRAM STARTED: 1949

PURPOSE:
To provide playwrights with the tools and freedom to make lasting contributions to the theatre.

LEGAL BASIS:
Not-for-profit corporation.

ELIGIBILITY:
Open to U.S. citizens.

GEOG. RESTRICTIONS: United States.

FINANCIAL DATA:
Internships include college credit, where available. Full-time interns work 40 hours per week with a stipend of $50 to cover transportation and lunch. Part-time interns work a minimum of 15 hours per week with a stipend of $25.

NO. MOST RECENT APPLICANTS: 350 for the year 2014.

NO. AWARDS: 5 to 8 residencies per year.

APPLICATION INFO:
Information is available online.

Deadline: Varies.

PUBLICATIONS:
Application guidelines; brochure.

OFFICERS:
Seth Gelblum, Chairman
Isobel Robins Konecky, President

NEW MUSIC USA

90 Broad Street, Suite 1902
New York, NY 10004
(212) 645-6949
Fax: (646) 490-0998
E-mail: info@newmusicusa.org
Web Site: www.newmusicusa.org

TYPE:
Awards/prizes; General operating grants; Project/program grants; Residencies.

See entry 770 for full listing.

PEN AMERICAN CENTER [523]

588 Broadway, Suite 303
New York, NY 10012-5246
(212) 334-1660
Fax: (212) 334-2181
E-mail: awards@pen.org
Web Site: www.pen.org

FOUNDED: 1922

AREAS OF INTEREST:
American theater.

NAME(S) OF PROGRAMS:
- **PEN/Laura Pels Foundation Awards for Drama**

TYPE:
Awards/prizes. Honors a Grand Master of American Theater, Playwright in Mid-Career, and Emerging Playwright.

PURPOSE:
To honor the accomplishments of American playwrights.

ELIGIBILITY:
Candidates for the award to a senior American playwright are proposed by the judges. Candidates for the award to an American playwright in midcareer must be playwrights writing in English who have had a professional production of at least two full-length works mounted in a theatre of at least 299 seats and contracted specifically for either limited or open runs. Candidates for Emerging Playwright must have had a professional production of at least one full-length work.

Nominated playwrights must be U.S. citizens or permanent residents.

FINANCIAL DATA:
Amount of support per award: Emerging Playwright: cash prize of $2,500; Master American Dramatist: a specially commissioned art object; Mid-Career American Playwright: cash prize of $7,500.

NO. AWARDS: 3 annually.

APPLICATION INFO:
Playwrights may not apply on their own behalf. They must be nominated by their peers - producers, agents, critics, or other playwrights who are expected to write a letter of support, describing in some detail the literary character of the candidate's work, accompanied by a list of the candidate's produced work. Do not send scripts.

Deadline: Summer of each year.

PERPETUAL TRUSTEE COMPANY LTD [524]

GPO Box 4172
Sydney N.S.W. 2001 Australia
(61) 1800 501 227
Fax: (61) 02 8256 1471
E-mail: philanthropy@perpetual.com.au
Web Site: www.perpetual.com.au/philanthropy-awards.aspx

FOUNDED: 1979

AREAS OF INTEREST:
Personal management and furtherance of education of classical musicians in the arts (i.e., music, visual arts, literature, performing arts, etc.).

NAME(S) OF PROGRAMS:
- **Lady Mollie Isabelle Askin Ballet Scholarship**
- **Sir Robert William Askin Operatic Scholarship**
- **Kathleen Mitchell Award**

TYPE:
Awards/prizes; Scholarships. The scholarships shall be used for study, maintenance and travel either in Australia or overseas.

The Lady Mollie Isabelle Askin Ballet Scholarship is awarded every two years for outstanding ability and promise in ballet.

The Sir Robert William Askin Operatic Scholarship is awarded every two years for outstanding ability and promise as a male operatic singer.

The Kathleen Mitchell Award is awarded to young Australian writers aged under 30 at the time their novel is published. Prize is awarded every two years.

The above scholarships and award are entirely separate and are from separate charitable bequests.

YEAR PROGRAM STARTED: 1996

PURPOSE:
Lady Mollie Isabelle Askin Ballet Scholarship and Sir Robert William Askin Operatic Scholarship: To augment a scholar's own resources affording him or her a cultural education by means of a travelling scholarship. Kathleen Mitchell Award: To advance the improvement of Australian literature; to improve the educational style of

young authors, and to provide them with additional amounts to improve their literary efforts.

LEGAL BASIS:
Trust.

ELIGIBILITY:
Lady Mollie Isabelle Askin Ballet Scholarship: Must be Australian citizen 17 to 29 years of age at the closing date of entries; Sir Robert William Askin Operatic Scholarship: Must be male Australian citizen 18 to 29 years of age; Kathleen Mitchell Award: Australian, British-born or naturalized Australian who has been a resident of Australia for the 12 months preceding close of entries date, and 29 years of age or less at the time of one's book's first publication.

FINANCIAL DATA:
Amount of support per award: Lady Mollie Isabelle Askin Ballet Scholarship, Sir Robert William Askin Operatic Scholarship and Kathleen Mitchell Award: $20,000 (AUD).

NO. AWARDS: Lady Mollie Isabelle Askin Ballet Scholarship and Sir Robert William Askin Operatic Scholarship: 3 each; Kathleen Mitchell Award: 1.

APPLICATION INFO:
Application information will be available on the web site when the award cycle opens.

Duration: Every two years.

PUBLICATIONS:
Application guidelines.

ADDRESS INQUIRIES TO:
Philanthropic Services
(See e-mail address above.)

PEW FELLOWSHIPS AT THE PEW CENTER FOR ARTS & HERITAGE

1608 Walnut Street, 18th Floor
Philadelphia, PA 19103
(267) 350-4920
Fax: (267) 350-4997
E-mail: mfranklin@pcah.us
Web Site: www.pcah.us/fellowships

TYPE:
Fellowships. Opportunities for contemporary artists in the Philadelphia five-county area to concentrate on the development and creation of art. Fellowships to support artists at critical junctures in any stage of their career development. Fellows will be expected to participate annually in at least three meetings with other fellowship recipients.

See entry 551 for full listing.

PRINCESS GRACE FOUNDATION-USA [525]

150 East 58th Street, 25th Floor
New York, NY 10155
(212) 317-1470
Fax: (212) 317-1473
E-mail: grants@pgfusa.org
Web Site: www.pgfusa.org

FOUNDED: 1982

AREAS OF INTEREST:
Theater, dance, choreography, film and playwriting.

NAME(S) OF PROGRAMS:
- **Princess Grace Awards**

TYPE:
Awards/prizes; Fellowships; Scholarships. Dedicated to identifying and assisting emerging artists in theater, dance and film through grants.

YEAR PROGRAM STARTED: 1984

PURPOSE:
To identify and assist emerging artists in the fields of dance, theater and film within the U.S.

LEGAL BASIS:
Not-for-profit, tax-exempt, publicly supported charity.

ELIGIBILITY:
Must be a U.S. citizen or permanent resident.

GEOG. RESTRICTIONS: United States.

FINANCIAL DATA:
Amount of support per award: Theater, Dance and Film Awards: $7,500 to $30,000 average; Playwrighting Award: $7,500; Choreography Awards: $10,000.

Total amount of support: More than $13,000,000 since inception.

NO. MOST RECENT APPLICANTS: Theater, dance, choreography and film: 50 to 60; Playwrighting: 250 to 300.

NO. AWARDS: Over 900 since inception.

APPLICATION INFO:
All applicants, except playwrights, must be nominated by a school department chair/dean or company artistic director. The nominating organization must be a registered 501(c)(3). Detailed information is available online.

Duration: September 1 to August 31.

Deadline: Must be postmarked by March 31 for theater and playwriting; April 30 for dance and choreography; June 1 for film.

PUBLICATIONS:
Fact sheet; mission statement; press releases; newsletter.

IRS I.D.: 23-2218331

OFFICERS:
Hon. John F. Lehman, Chairman
Robert O. Marx, Vice Chairman
Toby E. Boshak, Secretary and Treasurer
Amy B. Desmond, Assistant Treasurer

ADDRESS INQUIRIES TO:
Diana Kemppainen, Program Director
(See address above.)

FOREST ROBERTS THEATRE [526]

Northern Michigan University
1401 Presque Isle Avenue
Marquette, MI 49855-5364
(906) 227-2559
Fax: (906) 227-2567
E-mail: newplays@nmu.edu
Web Site: www.nmu.edu/theatre

FOUNDED: 1977

AREAS OF INTEREST:
Performing arts and playwriting.

NAME(S) OF PROGRAMS:
- **Mildred and Albert Panowski Playwriting Award**

TYPE:
Awards/prizes.

YEAR PROGRAM STARTED: 1977

PURPOSE:
To encourage and stimulate artistic growth among educational and professional playwrights; to provide students with the creative opportunity to produce an original work on the university stage.

LEGAL BASIS:
Tax-exempt, nonprofit.

FINANCIAL DATA:
The award will include a spring or summer workshop reading of the play and fully mounted production in the subsequent production season, and a trip to Marquette to act as Artist-in-Residence during the reading of the play and dress rehearsals leading to opening night of the show. Room and board will be provided. Conducting informal seminars and workshops will be a part of this residency. A professional dramaturge will respond to the script and work with the playwright and director.

Amount of support per award: $2,000.

NO. MOST RECENT APPLICANTS: 430.

NO. AWARDS: Generally 1 award in even-numbered years.

REPRESENTATIVE AWARDS:
Mark Rigney for "Bears;" David J. Swanson for "A Paper Tiger in the Rain."

APPLICATION INFO:
The contest has a different theme for each cycle. Applications are to be submitted online.

Duration: One year. Renewal possibilities on a biennial basis.

Deadline: Entries accepted in odd-numbered years only. Entries must be received on or before September 1 to be considered for the current theme. Winner will be announced within six months after the September 1 deadline.

PUBLICATIONS:
Brochure.

ADDRESS INQUIRIES TO:
Playwriting Coordinator
(See address above.)

THE SHUBERT FOUNDATION, INC. [527]

234 West 44th Street
New York, NY 10036
(212) 944-3777
Fax: (212) 944-3767
Web Site: www.shubertfoundation.org

FOUNDED: 1945

AREAS OF INTEREST:
Arts-related organizations, dance, education, human services and theatre.

TYPE:
General operating grants.

YEAR PROGRAM STARTED: 1945

PURPOSE:
To sustain and advance the live performing arts, in particular the American theatre and secondarily dance.

LEGAL BASIS:
Private foundation.

ELIGIBILITY:
The Foundation supports not-for-profit theatre and dance companies, as well as some arts-related organizations that assist in the development of the theatre. Applicants must be nonprofit organizations with Internal Revenue Code 501(c)(3) status. Organizations must submit audited financial statements. No grants to individuals.

GEOG. RESTRICTIONS: United States.

FINANCIAL DATA:
All grants cover general operating support only.

Amount of support per award: $10,000 to $275,000.

Total amount of support: $22,500,000 for the year 2013.

NO. MOST RECENT APPLICANTS: 500.

REPRESENTATIVE AWARDS:
$20,000 to Open Stage of Harrisburg, Harrisburg, PA; $145,000 to La Jolla Playhouse, La Jolla, CA; $210,000 to Manhattan Theatre Club.

APPLICATION INFO:
A comprehensive application form, including audited financial data, must be submitted to the Foundation in duplicate. Applications, guidelines and instructions can be downloaded from the web site August to December; however, applications cannot be requested or submitted via e-mail.

Duration: One year. Renewal only with reapplication.

Deadline: December 1 for theatre category; October 15 for dance and other categories. Announcement in May each year.

PUBLICATIONS:
Annual report with application guidelines.

OFFICERS:
Philip J. Smith, Chairman of the Board
Michael I. Sovern, President
Wyche Fowler, Jr.
Lee J. Seidler
Stuart Subotnick
Robert E. Wankel

ADDRESS INQUIRIES TO:
Vicki Reiss, Executive Director
(See address above.)

WAGNER COLLEGE [528]

Wagner College Theater
One Campus Road
Staten Island, NY 10301
(718) 390-3223
Fax: (718) 390-3323
E-mail: diane.catalano@wagner.edu
Web Site: www.wagner.edu/theatre/stanley-drama

FOUNDED: 1957

AREAS OF INTEREST:
Playwriting.

NAME(S) OF PROGRAMS:
- **Stanley Drama Award**

TYPE:
Awards/prizes; Project/program grants. Annual award for the best play or musical submitted to the competition.

YEAR PROGRAM STARTED: 1957

PURPOSE:
To call attention to and encourage new playwrights.

LEGAL BASIS:
University.

ELIGIBILITY:
The Award is offered for an original full-length play, musical or one-act play sequence that has not been professionally produced or received tradebook publication. Writers of musicals are urged to submit music on tape or CD.

The Stanley Award competition will consider only one submission (a single full-length play, musical or one-act sequence) per playwright. Plays entered previously in the competition may not be resubmitted. Former Stanley Award winners are not eligible to compete.

FINANCIAL DATA:
Amount of support per award: $2,000.

NO. MOST RECENT APPLICANTS: 100.

NO. AWARDS: 3 (1 winner, 2 finalists).

APPLICATION INFO:
Applications may be obtained by sending a self-addressed, stamped envelope to the address above or on the web site. All scripts must be accompanied by a completed application. A reading fee of $30 must accompany the manuscript.

Deadline: October 31. Announcement the following March.

PUBLICATIONS:
Application guidelines.

ADDRESS INQUIRIES TO:
Diane Catalano
Stanley Drama Award
(See address above.)

*SPECIAL STIPULATIONS:
Previous winners are ineligible.

THE LOREN L. ZACHARY SOCIETY FOR THE PERFORMING ARTS

2250 Gloaming Way
Beverly Hills, CA 90210-1717
(310) 276-2731
Fax: (310) 275-8245
E-mail: infoz@zacharysociety.org
Web Site: www.zacharysociety.org

TYPE:
Awards/prizes.

See entry 785 for full listing.

Fine arts

ACADEMY FOUNDATION OF THE ACADEMY OF MOTION PICTURE ARTS AND SCIENCES [529]

1313 North Vine Street
Los Angeles, CA 90028
(310) 247-3000 ext. 1131
E-mail: sguthrie@oscars.org
Web Site: www.oscars.org

AREAS OF INTEREST:
Filmmakers.

NAME(S) OF PROGRAMS:
- **Student Academy Awards Competition**

TYPE:
Awards/prizes.

PURPOSE:
To recognize outstanding achievements in student filmmaking; to support and encourage filmmakers with no previous professional experience who are enrolled in accredited colleges and universities.

ELIGIBILITY:
To be eligible, the filmmaker must be a full-time student at an accredited U.S. college, university, film school or art school. The film must have been made in a teacher-student relationship within the curricular structure of that institution. The film must be in one of the following categories: Alternative, Animated, Documentary and Narrative.

FINANCIAL DATA:
Amount of support per award: $5,000 Gold Award, $3,000 Silver Award, and $2,000 Bronze Award.

NO. MOST RECENT APPLICANTS: 500.

NO. AWARDS: Approximately 15.

APPLICATION INFO:
Regional juries have sole responsibility for the determination of final selections for submission to the Academy. Each regional jury may consider only films from schools within its own region.

Deadline: June 1.

ADDRESS INQUIRIES TO:
Shawn Guthrie
Student Academy Awards and Grants Manager
(See address above.)

AMERICAN ORIENTAL SOCIETY [530]

Hatcher Graduate Library, Room 110
University of Michigan
Ann Arbor, MI 48109-1205
(734) 764-7555
Fax: (734) 763-6743
E-mail: jrodgers@umich.edu
Web Site: www.umich.edu/~aos

FOUNDED: 1842

AREAS OF INTEREST:
Archaeology, fine arts, history, philosophy, language, literature, religion and theology.

NAME(S) OF PROGRAMS:
- **Louise Wallace Hackney Fellowship**

TYPE:
Fellowships. Fellowship for the study of Chinese art with special relation to painting.

YEAR PROGRAM STARTED: 1946

PURPOSE:
To encourage basic research in the languages and literatures of Asia.

LEGAL BASIS:
Nonprofit.

ELIGIBILITY:
Graduate students who have successfully completed at least three years of Chinese language study at a recognized university and have some knowledge or training in art. Students must have completed all requirements for the Ph.D. except research, travel and the written dissertation. Applicants should have the sponsorship of recognized scholars in the fields of Chinese language and culture.

U.S. citizenship is required.

GEOG. RESTRICTIONS: United States.

FINANCIAL DATA:
Amount of support per award: $8,000.

Total amount of support: $8,000 annually.

NO. MOST RECENT APPLICANTS: Approximately 3.

NO. AWARDS: 1 annually.

APPLICATION INFO:
Applicants should write to the secretary, at the address given above, outlining the proposed plan of study and accompany the

letter with a curriculum vitae, an academic record and no less than three letters of recommendation.

All materials must be submitted in duplicate or application will be considered incomplete.

Duration: Renewals of appointment are possible but not usually considered.

Deadline: Applications should be submitted no later than March 1. Announcement in May.

PUBLICATIONS:
Application guidelines.

DIRECTORS AND OFFICERS:
Jonathan Rodgers, Secretary and Treasurer
Stephanie W. Jamison, Editor

ADDRESS INQUIRIES TO:
Jonathan Rodgers, Secretary and Treasurer
(See address above.)

BRUCEBO FINE ART SCHOLARSHIP FOUNDATION [531]

Studio Arts, EV Building
Sir George William Campus
Concordia University
1455 De Maisonneuve Boulevard West
Montreal QC H3G 1M8 Canada
(514) 848-2424 (University)
Fax: (514) 909-5115 (mobile)
E-mail: brucebosubmission@gmail.com
jessica@jessicaauer.com
Web Site: www.bruceboscholarships.ca

FOUNDED: 1971

AREAS OF INTEREST:
Promotion of fine arts; Canada-Sweden relationships; artist residencies.

CONSULTING OR VOLUNTEER SERVICES:
Evaluation Committee members provide free services.

NAME(S) OF PROGRAMS:
- **W.B. Bruce European Fine Art Travel Scholarship**
- **Brucebo Fine Art Summer Residency Scholarship**

TYPE:
Development grants; Research grants; Residencies; Scholarships; Travel grants. Grant principally in the fields of fine arts, visual art and design. Grant is either for stay at the Brucebo Studio on the Island of Hanseatic Gotland, Sweden, in the Baltic Sea, for three months during the summer annually, or for undertaking a European Fine Art Travel-Study journey.

YEAR PROGRAM STARTED: 1971

PURPOSE:
To support talented Canadian fine arts graduated students and fine arts practitioners, B.F.A. or M.F.A. persons, in the emerging years of their respective careers.

LEGAL BASIS:
Private.

ELIGIBILITY:
Qualified emerging Canadian artists with appropriate project plans are eligible to apply. Must hold Canadian citizenship.

GEOG. RESTRICTIONS: Europe, with specific reference to the Nordic countries and Baltic Rim (coastal corridor).

FINANCIAL DATA:
Amount of support per award: SEK 30,000, the equivalent of approximately $5,000 (CAN).

Total amount of support: SEK 60,000.

NO. MOST RECENT APPLICANTS: 85.

NO. AWARDS: 2.

APPLICATION INFO:
Application form and guidelines can be found on the Foundation web site.

Duration: Three months.

Deadline: January 31.

PUBLICATIONS:
Research reports.

STAFF:
Jessica Auer, Chairperson, Brucebo Fine Art Evaluation Committee

ADDRESS INQUIRIES TO:
Jessica Auer, Chairperson
Brucebo Fine Art Evaluation Committee
Faculty of Studio Arts
Concordia University
E-mail: brucebosubmission@gmail.com
(See address above.)

*SPECIAL STIPULATIONS:
Canadian citizens only. Recipient submits a report on his or her activities engaged in after return to Canada.

THE CENTER FOR PHOTOGRAPHY AT WOODSTOCK [532]

59 Tinker Street
Woodstock, NY 12498
(845) 679-9957
Fax: (845) 679-6337
E-mail: info@cpw.org
Web Site: www.cpw.org

FOUNDED: 1977

AREAS OF INTEREST:
Photography.

NAME(S) OF PROGRAMS:
- **Art Administration Interns**
- **The Photographers' Fund**
- **Woodstock A-I-R**
- **Workshop Interns**

TYPE:
Project/program grants; Residencies; Work-study programs. Photography Workshops. Photographers' Fund awards fellowships to regional photographers of vision and talent, selected by portfolio review by a panel of noted national artists.

Woodstock A-I-R is a residency program for artists of color working in the photographic arts.

PURPOSE:
To support artists working in photography and related media and engaging their audiences through opportunities in which creation, discovery and learning are made possible.

LEGAL BASIS:
Not-for-profit arts and educational organization.

ELIGIBILITY:
Fellowship applicants must live and work in upstate New York.

FINANCIAL DATA:
Amount of support per award: Art Administration Interns and Woodstock A-I-R: Varies; Photographers' Fund: $2,500; Workshop Interns: $650 in-kind tuition.

CO-OP FUNDING PROGRAMS: The Center receives funds from the National Endowment for the Arts and the New York State Council on the Arts and has received grants from IBM and the New York Council for the Humanities, The Avery Foundation, Eastman Kodak, Canon, U.S.A. and Andy Warhol Foundation.

NO. AWARDS: Art Administration Interns: Up to 4 seasonally; Photographers' Fund: 1 fellowship; Woodstock A-I-R: 8; Workshop Interns: 4.

APPLICATION INFO:
Application information can be found on the web site.

IRS I.D.: 14-1592639

OFFICERS:
Hannah Frieser, Executive Director

ADDRESS INQUIRIES TO:
Hannah Frieser, Executive Director
(See address above.)

DALLAS MUSEUM OF ART [533]

1717 North Harwood
Dallas, TX 75201
(214) 922-1334
Fax: (214) 922-1354
E-mail: a2a@dma.org
Web Site: www.dma.org

FOUNDED: 1903

AREAS OF INTEREST:
Contemporary art.

NAME(S) OF PROGRAMS:
- **Clare Hart DeGolyer Memorial Fund**

TYPE:
Awards/prizes.

YEAR PROGRAM STARTED: 1980

PURPOSE:
To support younger, emerging visual artists who reside in the southwestern part of the U.S.

LEGAL BASIS:
Nonprofit, tax-exempt arts organization.

ELIGIBILITY:
Applicants must be between 15 and 25 years of age, have lived in the southwestern part of the U.S. for the past four years and currently reside there.

Grants are not available for college or art school tuition.

GEOG. RESTRICTIONS: Arizona, Colorado, New Mexico, Oklahoma and Texas.

FINANCIAL DATA:
Amount of support per award: Approximately $1,500.

NO. MOST RECENT APPLICANTS: 25.

NO. AWARDS: Varies.

APPLICATION INFO:
Applications can be downloaded online.

Deadline: Mid-January.

PUBLICATIONS:
Bimonthly *DMAgenda*; permanent collection and exhibition catalogues.

ADDRESS INQUIRIES TO:
Awards to Artists
(See address above.)

DALLAS MUSEUM OF ART [534]

1717 North Harwood
Dallas, TX 75201
(214) 922-1334
Fax: (214) 922-1354
E-mail: a2a@dma.org
Web Site: www.dma.org

FOUNDED: 1903

AREAS OF INTEREST:
Contemporary art.

NAME(S) OF PROGRAMS:
- **Arch and Anne Giles Kimbrough Fund**

TYPE:
Awards/prizes. Direct grants to artists.

YEAR PROGRAM STARTED: 1980

PURPOSE:
To support younger, emerging visual artists in Texas.

LEGAL BASIS:
Nonprofit, tax-exempt arts organization.

ELIGIBILITY:
Applicants must be under 30 years of age, have lived in Texas for the past three years and currently reside there.

Funds are not available for college or art school tuition.

GEOG. RESTRICTIONS: Texas.

FINANCIAL DATA:
Amount of support per award: Approximately $3,500.

NO. MOST RECENT APPLICANTS: 35.

NO. AWARDS: Varies.

APPLICATION INFO:
Applications can be downloaded online.

Deadline: Mid-January.

PUBLICATIONS:
Bimonthly *DMAgenda*; permanent collection and exhibition catalogues.

ADDRESS INQUIRIES TO:
Awards to Artists
(See address above.)

DALLAS MUSEUM OF ART [535]

1717 North Harwood
Dallas, TX 75201
(214) 922-1334
Fax: (214) 720-0862
E-mail: a2a@dma.org
Web Site: www.dma.org

FOUNDED: 1903

AREAS OF INTEREST:
Art. Collections include contemporary art, Pre-Columbian, Asian, African, American and European painting and sculpture, decorative arts and textiles.

NAME(S) OF PROGRAMS:
- **Otis and Velma Davis Dozier Travel Grant**

TYPE:
Awards/prizes; Travel grants.

YEAR PROGRAM STARTED: 1990

PURPOSE:
To recognize exceptional talent in professional artists who wish to expand their artistic horizons through domestic or foreign travel.

LEGAL BASIS:
Nonprofit, tax-exempt arts organization.

ELIGIBILITY:
Artists eligible for the grant must be practicing professionals, be 30 years of age or older, have lived in Texas for the past three years and be currently living in Texas. Financial need will be given consideration but will not be the determining factor in making the awards.

GEOG. RESTRICTIONS: Texas.

FINANCIAL DATA:
Amount of support per award: Varies.

Total amount of support: Approximately $6,000.

NO. MOST RECENT APPLICANTS: 40.

APPLICATION INFO:
Applications can be downloaded online.

Deadline: January 17.

PUBLICATIONS:
Bimonthly *DMAgenda*; permanent collection and exhibition catalogues.

ADDRESS INQUIRIES TO:
Awards to Artists
(See address above.)

FINE ARTS WORK CENTER IN PROVINCETOWN [536]

24 Pearl Street
Provincetown, MA 02657
(508) 487-9960
Fax: (508) 487-8873
E-mail: info@fawc.org
Web Site: www.fawc.org

FOUNDED: 1968

AREAS OF INTEREST:
Visual arts and creative writing.

NAME(S) OF PROGRAMS:
- **Visual Arts Fellowship**
- **Writing Fellowship**

TYPE:
Fellowships; Residencies.

YEAR PROGRAM STARTED: 1968

PURPOSE:
To offer opportunities to emerging artists and writers.

LEGAL BASIS:
Nonprofit corporation.

ELIGIBILITY:
Fellowships are offered to selected writers and visual artists. Applicants must be in the emerging phase of their careers and must demonstrate significant talent and commitment.

Applicants must be individuals (visual artists and creative writers) who have spent time working on their own and have created a considerable body of work which can be presented in the form of slides or manuscript.

FINANCIAL DATA:
In addition to the stipend, fellows are provided with an apartment and studio in Provincetown, MA, and have the support of a resident staff. Each residency includes private living and/or working studio in Provincetown, MA.

Amount of support per award: Stipend of $750 per month.

Total amount of support: $5,250.

NO. MOST RECENT APPLICANTS: 1,000.

NO. AWARDS: 20.

APPLICATION INFO:
Forms and application information may be requested from the Center by sending a self-addressed, stamped envelope. Applications can also be downloaded at the web site. Application fee is $45.

Duration: Seven months, October 1 to May 1.

Deadline: Writers: December 1. Visual Arts: February 1. Announcement by May 15.

PUBLICATIONS:
Shankpainter, online literary magazine.

OFFICERS OF THE TRUSTEES:
Hatty Walker Fitts, Co-Chairperson
Lynne Kortenhaus, Co-Chairperson
Ted Chapin, President
Barbara Kapp, Vice President

ADDRESS INQUIRIES TO:
Melenie Flynn, Grant Writer
(See address above.)

*SPECIAL STIPULATIONS:
Fellowships are reserved for emerging writers and visual artists.

J. PAUL GETTY TRUST, GETTY FOUNDATION [537]

1200 Getty Center Drive
Suite 800
Los Angeles, CA 90049-1685
(310) 440-7320
Fax: (310) 440-7703
E-mail: gettyfoundation@getty.edu
Web Site: www.getty.edu/foundation

FOUNDED: 1984

AREAS OF INTEREST:
Strengthening art history as a global discipline, promoting the interdisciplinary practice of conservation, increasing access to museums and archival collections, and developing current and future professionals and leaders.

TYPE:
Conferences/seminars; Fellowships; Internships; Matching gifts; Project/program grants; Research grants; Training grants.

YEAR PROGRAM STARTED: 1984

PURPOSE:
To advance the understanding and preservation of the visual arts locally and throughout the world.

ELIGIBILITY:
Requirements vary according to grant category. Individuals at the undergraduate and graduate level may be eligible to apply for internships. Eligibility for all other grant categories is limited to nonprofit organizations.

Generally, grants are not made for operating or endowment purposes, for construction or maintenance of buildings or for acquisition of works of art.

FINANCIAL DATA:
Amount of support per award: Varies.

Total amount of support: $9,411,147 for the year 2015.

NO. MOST RECENT APPLICANTS: Approximately 1,000.

NO. AWARDS: 258 for the year 2015.

REPRESENTATIVE AWARDS:
$247,000 to Trustees of Columbia University, New York, NY, for research seminars "Spanish Italy and the Iberian Americas;"

$50,000 to Duke University, Durham, NC, for the summer institute "Visualizing Venice: The Biennale and the City;" $42,000 to Library Foundation of Los Angeles, Los Angeles, CA, for research planning for "Visualizing Language;" $120,000 to Wellesley College, Wellesley, MA, for the preparation of a conservation management plan for Paul Rudolph's Jewett Arts Center; $44,000 to Los Angeles County Arts Commission, Los Angeles, CA, for educational programming related to the 2015 Arts Internship Program.

APPLICATION INFO:
Funding priorities and application information are available on the Foundation web site.

Duration: One to three years, depending upon the grant category.

Deadline: November 1. Internships: Varies.

PUBLICATIONS:
Annual report of J. Paul Getty Trust.

IRS I.D.: 95-1790021

OFFICERS:
Deborah Marrow, Director, The Getty Foundation
Rebecca Martin, Associate Director
Joan Weinstein, Deputy Director

ADDRESS INQUIRIES TO:
The Getty Foundation
(See address above.)

ADOLPH AND ESTHER GOTTLIEB FOUNDATION, INC. [538]

380 West Broadway
New York, NY 10012
(212) 226-0581
Fax: (212) 274-1476
E-mail: sross@gottliebfoundation.org
Web Site: www.gottliebfoundation.org

FOUNDED: 1976

AREAS OF INTEREST:
Visual artists.

NAME(S) OF PROGRAMS:

- **Emergency Assistance Program**
- **Individual Support Program**

TYPE:
Grants-in-aid. Emergency Assistance Program provides cash award to mature creative painters, sculptors and printmakers who are experiencing financial hardship resulting from a current or recent emergency.

Individual Support Program was designed to encourage those artists who have dedicated their lives to developing their art, regardless of their level of commercial success.

YEAR PROGRAM STARTED: 1984

PURPOSE:
To provide interim financial assistance to qualified artists during times of emergencies (such as fire, flood, medical or other unexpected, catastrophic events), or to provide financial assistance as an encouragement to artists who have dedicated their lives to developing their art.

LEGAL BASIS:
Nonprofit corporation.

ELIGIBILITY:
Emergency Assistance Program: Applicant must be able to demonstrate a minimum involvement of 10 years in a mature phase of his or her work as a creative painter, sculptor or printmaker and his or her need must result from current or recent emergency beyond the artist's usual circumstances (medical, fire, flood, etc.). This Program does not consider requests for dental work, chronic situations, capital improvements, or projects of any kind; nor can it consider situations resulting from general indebtedness or lack of employment.

Individual Support Program: Applicant will be able to demonstrate work in a mature phase of his or her art for at least 20 years. Eligibility is also determined by applicant's current financial need. The Foundation does not provide funding for organizations, projects of any type, educational institutions, students, graphic artists, or those working in crafts. The disciplines of photography, film, video or related forms are not eligible unless the work directly involves, or can be interpreted as, painting, printmaking or sculpture.

FINANCIAL DATA:
Amount of support per award: Emergency Assistance Program: Maximum $15,000; typical amount is $5,000. Individual Support Program: $25,000.

Total amount of support: $300,000 per program.

NO. AWARDS: Individual Support Grants: 12.

APPLICATION INFO:
Emergency Assistance Program: Application forms are available online.

Individual Support Program: Application forms are available by mail in early September. Only written requests for application forms will be honored.

Deadline: Emergency Assistance Program: Available throughout the year, as budget permits. Individual Support Program: December 15.

PUBLICATIONS:
Information brochure.

BOARD OF DIRECTORS:
Sanford Hirsch, Executive Director
Lynda Benglis
Charlotta Kotik
Robert Mangold
Gordon Marsh

ADDRESS INQUIRIES TO:
Sheila Ross, Grants Manager
(See address above.)

*SPECIAL STIPULATIONS:
The Emergency Assistance Program is to assist individuals in emergency situations only.

THE ELIZABETH GREENSHIELDS FOUNDATION [539]

1814 Sherbrooke Street West
Montreal QC H3H 1E4 Canada
(514) 937-9225
E-mail: info@greenshieldsfoundation.ca
Web Site: www.elizabethgreenshieldsfoundation.org

FOUNDED: 1955

AREAS OF INTEREST:
Painting, drawing, printmaking and sculpture.

NAME(S) OF PROGRAMS:

- **The Elizabeth Greenshields Foundation Grants**

TYPE:
Grants for artists.

YEAR PROGRAM STARTED: 1955

PURPOSE:
To provide financial assistance, by way of grants, to students and artists in the early or developmental stage of their career who work in a representational style of painting, drawing, sculpture or printmaking and demonstrate a commitment to making art a lifetime career.

LEGAL BASIS:
Charitable foundation.

ELIGIBILITY:
Candidates must be at least 18 years of age at the time of submitting their application, and must meet the following criteria:
(1) be in the early or developmental stage of their career;
(2) be enrolled or completed training in an established school of art or demonstrate, through past work and future plans, a commitment to making art a lifetime career and;
(3) work in a representational style of painting, drawing, sculpture or printmaking.

Previous recipients of a grant who have complied with the terms and conditions of a grant previously awarded to them by the Foundation may apply for a second or third grant one year after the award of their previous grant. Previous applicants who have not received a grant may reapply after two years.

The Foundation does not accept applications from commercial artists, graphic designers and illustrators, photographers, cartoonists, animation artists, video artists, filmmakers and digital artists, craft-makers or any artist whose work falls primarily into these categories. The Foundation does not provide funding for the pursuit of abstract or nonobjective art.

GEOG. RESTRICTIONS: The Foundation welcomes applicants from around the world.

FINANCIAL DATA:
Amount of support per award: First grants are in the amount of $15,000 (CAN) each. Subsequent grants are in the amount of $18,000 (CAN) each (maximum of three grants per artist). The Foundation reserves the right to award grants in other amounts and to disburse funds in whole or in part, as it deems advisable. Grants are made directly to the beneficiaries, not through other organizations.

Total amount of support: Maximum of three grants per artist.

APPLICATION INFO:
Applications may only be accessed through the Foundation's web site. The Foundation does not mail or provide application forms to applicants. Applications must be completed online, then printed, dated and signed by the applicant, and submitted by mail. Applicants may not submit applications by fax, e-mail, Internet or other electronic means. All information, supporting documentation and material required in the application form must be provided. Incomplete, unsigned or undated applications will not be considered. The documents required include:
(1) proof of identity: a copy of an official photograph attesting to the identity, date of birth and address of the applicant (driver's license, citizenship card, passport photo, student ID, etc.);
(2) proof of acceptance: if the applicant is applying for a grant to further his or her art

education or training, a letter or other proof of acceptance from the school, university or other institution where the applicant intends to study or train confirming his or her acceptance, by name, to the selected program of studies or training for the period or academic year(s) specified;
(3) exhibition and press materials: copies of invitations, reviews, announcements, press clippings or press releases and other written material relating to any exhibitions or shows of the applicant's work;
(4) portfolio: images of six representative original works (no more or less) produced by the applicant alone in the last two years, on a USB key or a PC-compatible CD; works submitted with an application for a second or a third grant must not have been submitted with a previous application(s); images must be submitted in the required format (see the "Format of Images" section in the Instructions that accompany the Application Form;
(5) artistic proposal: a detailed description (maximum 750 words) of the proposed work, project, course of study or training that the applicant intends to undertake with a grant from The Foundation, explaining its significance to the advancement of the applicant's artistic practice;
(6) artist statement: a brief artist statement (350 to 500 words) relating to the applicant's previous and current work;
(7) budget: a detailed budget for the proposed work, project, course of study or training described in the applicant's artistic proposal and;
(8) letter of reference: a signed letter of reference from a teacher or professor, an artist or a gallery, museum or exhibition curator who is known to the applicant and able to support his or her application.

Duration: Award winners may reapply for another grant one year after a grant was awarded. Applicants who were not awarded a grant may reapply two years from the last decision.

Deadline: The Foundation welcomes applications throughout the year. However, in order to allow for proper response time, it is strongly recommended that applicants file their applications at least six months prior to the date on which funds are required.

PUBLICATIONS:
Application guidelines.

ADDRESS INQUIRIES TO:
Applications Coordinator
(See address above.)

*PLEASE NOTE:
The Elizabeth Greenshields Foundation grant is one of the most prestigious grants available to emerging figurative artists, as well as one of the most substantial. It is one of the longest standing, with an illustrious history of recipients spanning more than half a century. It is also unique in its scope, in that it is available to students and artists around the world. To date, the Foundation has provided financial assistance to more than 1,600 students and artists in 40 countries.

SAMUEL H. KRESS FOUNDATION [540]

174 East 80th Street
New York, NY 10075
(212) 861-4993
E-mail: wyman.meers@kressfoundation.org
Web Site: www.kressfoundation.org

FOUNDED: 1929

AREAS OF INTEREST:
Art history, art conservation and art interpretation in museums.

NAME(S) OF PROGRAMS:
- **Conservation Fellowships**
- **Conservation Grant Program**
- **Digital Resources Grant Program**
- **History of Art Grant Program**
- **History of Art: Institutional Fellowships**
- **Interpretive Fellowships at Art Museums**

TYPE:
Fellowships; Research grants; Travel grants. Grants: Competitive grants only awarded to nonprofit institutions. The grant programs support scholarly projects that promote the appreciation, interpretation, preservation, study and teaching of European art from antiquity to the early 19th century.

Fellowships: Competitive fellowships are awarded to art historians and art conservators in the final stages of their preparation for professional careers, as well as to students of art history and related fields who are interested in art museum education and curating.

YEAR PROGRAM STARTED: 1963

PURPOSE:
To advance the history, conservation and enjoyment of European art, architecture and archaeology from antiquity to the pre-modern era.

LEGAL BASIS:
Private foundation.

ELIGIBILITY:
Contact the Foundation for specific eligibility and application requirements for each grant and fellowship program.

FINANCIAL DATA:
Amount of support per award: Varies.
Total amount of support: Varies.

NO. MOST RECENT APPLICANTS: Approximately 500 in fiscal year 2015.

APPLICATION INFO:
Application information and forms are available on the web site ("How to Apply").

Duration: Varies.

Deadline: Fellowships: Conservation Fellowships: January 22. Institutional Fellowships: November 30. Interpretive Fellowships: April 1.

Grants: Conservation and History of Art Grants: January 15, April 1 and October 1. Digital Resources Grants: April 1 and October 1.

PUBLICATIONS:
Annual Report.

IRS I.D.: 13-1624176

STAFF:
Wyman Meers, Program Administrator

OFFICERS AND TRUSTEES:
Frederick W. Beinecke, Chairman
David Rumsey, Vice Chairman
Max Marmor, President
Barbara A. Shailor

ADDRESS INQUIRIES TO:
Wyman Meers, Program Administrator
(See address above.)

*SPECIAL STIPULATIONS:
No applications accepted via fax or e-mail.

LIGHT WORK [541]

316 Waverly Avenue
Syracuse, NY 13210
(315) 443-1300
Fax: (315) 443-9516
E-mail: info@lightwork.org
Web Site: www.lightwork.org

FOUNDED: 1972

AREAS OF INTEREST:
Photography.

CONSULTING OR VOLUNTEER SERVICES:
All aspects of visual arts and programs for artists.

NAME(S) OF PROGRAMS:
- **Central New York Light Work Grant**
- **Light Work Artist-in-Residence Program**

TYPE:
Project/program grants; Residencies; Visiting scholars. Artist-in-Residence, exhibitions, publications, sponsored projects, lectures and regrants.

Central New York Light Work Grant supports photographers, critics and photo historians in central New York.

YEAR PROGRAM STARTED: 1973

PURPOSE:
To support artists in photography.

LEGAL BASIS:
Not-for-profit organization.

ELIGIBILITY:
Applicants must be working in photography or related visual arts including video, installation and electronic media. Students are ineligible to apply.

GEOG. RESTRICTIONS: Central New York Light Work Grant: Central New York.

FINANCIAL DATA:
Amount of support per award: $5,000.
Total amount of support: Varies.

CO-OP FUNDING PROGRAMS: Yes.

NO. MOST RECENT APPLICANTS: 500 to 600.

NO. AWARDS: 12 to 15.

APPLICATION INFO:
Applicants are encouraged to use the online application process.

Duration: One month.

Deadline: July 1.

STAFF:
Shane Lavalette, Director

ADDRESS INQUIRIES TO:
Shane Lavalette, Director
(See address above.)

*PLEASE NOTE:
Housing is provided for residencies.

THE ROBERTO LONGHI FOUNDATION FOR THE STUDY OF THE HISTORY OF ART [542]

Via Benedetto Fortini, 30
50125 Florence Italy
(39) 055 6580794
Fax: (39) 055 6580794
E-mail: longhi@fondazionelonghi.it
Web Site: www.fondazionelonghi.it

FOUNDED: 1971

AREAS OF INTEREST:
Italian painting from the 13th to the 18th centuries.

NAME(S) OF PROGRAMS:
- **Art History Fellowships in Florence**

TYPE:
Fellowships.

PURPOSE:
To promote and further the study of art history by keeping Roberto Longhi's cultural legacy and methods alive.

LEGAL BASIS:
Private foundation.

ELIGIBILITY:
Open to Italian citizens who possess a degree from an Italian university with a thesis in the history of art, and to non-Italian citizens who have fulfilled the preliminary requirements for a doctoral degree in the history of art at an accredited university or an institution of equal standing. Students who have reached their 32nd birthday before the application deadline are not eligible.

Designed for those who want to seriously dedicate themselves to research in the history of art. Fellowship holders may make use of the study materials available in the Institute. They must frequent the Institute and collaborate on a specific group research project selected by the Scientific Committee. In particular, successful candidates must give the assurance that they can dedicate their full time to the research for which the fellowship is assigned. They must live in Florence for the duration of the fellowship, except for travel required for their research. They may not exceed the periods of vacation fixed by the Institute. They are required to attend seminars, lectures and other activities arranged by the Institute. In addition, Fellows must submit a written report at the end of their stay in Florence, relating the findings of their individual research undertaken at the Longhi Foundation. The nonobservance of the above conditions will be considered sufficient grounds for the cancellation of a fellowship.

FINANCIAL DATA:
Amount of support per award: EUR 5,400 (paid in monthly installments over a period of nine months).

APPLICATION INFO:
Applications should be addressed to the Secretariat of the Foundation at the address above and should contain the candidate's biographical data (place and date of birth, domicile, citizenship), a transcript of the candidate's undergraduate and graduate records, a copy of the degree thesis (if available) and other original works, published or unpublished, a "curriculum studiorum," also indicating the knowledge of foreign languages spoken and written, letters of reference from at least two persons of academic standing who are acquainted with the candidate's work, the subject of the research that the candidate is interested in pursuing within the range of the history of art and two passport photographs.

Recipients of fellowships are asked to communicate within 15 days of notification their acceptance and willingness to comply with the conditions and rules as stated.

Duration: Nine months beginning in October.

Deadline: May 15.

PUBLICATIONS:
Proporzioni, art review.

OFFICERS:
Mina Gregori, Chairman and President

MARYLAND INSTITUTE COLLEGE OF ART [543]

Office of Graduate Admission
131 North Avenue
Baltimore, MD 21201
(410) 225-2256
Fax: (410) 225-5275
E-mail: graduate@mica.edu
Web Site: www.mica.edu

FOUNDED: 1823

AREAS OF INTEREST:
Fine arts, design and art education.

NAME(S) OF PROGRAMS:
- **Art Education (Low-residency/online MA)**
- **Business of Art and Design (MPS)**
- **Filmmaking (MFA)**
- **Hoffberger School of Painting (MFA)**
- **MA in Critical Studies**
- **MA Social Design**
- **Master of Arts in Teaching**
- **MBA/MA in Design Leadership**
- **MFA Community Arts**
- **MFA Curatorial Practice**
- **MFA Illustration Practice**
- **MFA in Graphic Design**
- **Mt. Royal School of Art (MFA)**
- **MPS in Art and Design**
- **MPS in Information Visualization**
- **Photographic and Electronic Media (MFA)**
- **Post-Baccalaureate Program in Fine Arts**
- **Post-Baccalaureate Program in Graphic Design**
- **Rinehart School of Sculpture (MFA)**
- **Studio Art (Low-residency MFA)**
- **UX Design (MPS)**

TYPE:
Awards/prizes; Challenge/matching grants; Conferences/seminars; Fellowships; Internships; Research grants; Residencies; Scholarships; Travel grants; Visiting scholars. Teaching internships. Post-Baccalaureate Program awards certificates in fine arts and graphic design.

YEAR PROGRAM STARTED: 1896

LEGAL BASIS:
Nonprofit institution.

ELIGIBILITY:
Bachelor's degree is required.

FINANCIAL DATA:
Amount of support per award: M.I.C.A. scholarship awards for students in all graduate programs based on merit, up to half of tuition.

Total amount of support: Varies.

NO. MOST RECENT APPLICANTS: 1,200.

NO. AWARDS: 215.

APPLICATION INFO:
Candidates apply for all programs online through mica.slideroom.com.

Duration: One to two years. Renewable upon application for the second year.

Deadline: January 15. Announcement April 1.

ADDRESS INQUIRIES TO:
Christopher Harring
Director of Graduate Admission
E-mail: charring@mica.edu or

Erin High
Graduate Admissions Counselor
E-mail: ehigh@mica.edu

THE PAUL MELLON CENTRE FOR STUDIES IN BRITISH ART

16 Bedford Square
London WC1B 3JA England
(44) 0 20 7580 0311
Fax: (44) 0 20 7636 6730
E-mail: grants@paul-mellon-centre.ac.uk
Web Site: www.paul-mellon-centre.ac.uk

TYPE:
Conferences/seminars; Fellowships; Project/program grants; Research grants. Educational Programme Grants for lectures, symposia, seminars or conferences on British art or architectural history.

The Junior Fellowship is to pursue ongoing doctoral research at an American or British university.

The Paul Mellon Centre Rome Fellowship offers fellowships to scholars working on Grand Tour subjects or in the field of Anglo-Italian cultural and artistic relations.

The Postdoctoral Fellowship works to transform doctoral research into publishable form such as a book, series of articles, or exhibition catalogues.

Research Support Grants are for expenses in pursuit of research.

The Senior Fellowship supports an established scholar in the field of British art and architectural history to complete a manuscript or book for immediate publication.

See entry 407 for full listing.

THE METROPOLITAN MUSEUM OF ART [544]

1000 Fifth Avenue
New York, NY 10028-0198
(212) 570-3710
Fax: (212) 570-3782
E-mail: mmainterns@metmuseum.org
Web Site: www.metmuseum.org

FOUNDED: 1870

AREAS OF INTEREST:
Internships in art museums.

TYPE:
Internships. Internships for graduate and undergraduate students.

YEAR PROGRAM STARTED: 1972

PURPOSE:
To provide pre-career training and experience for students and graduates in art museums.

ELIGIBILITY:
Many projects require strong preparation in the history of art. Applicants of diverse backgrounds and disciplines are encouraged to apply.

FINANCIAL DATA:
Amount of support per award: Varies by program.
Total amount of support: Varies.

NO. MOST RECENT APPLICANTS: 477.

NO. AWARDS: 42.

APPLICATION INFO:
Application information is available on the Museum's web site.
Duration: Up to 12 months.
Deadline: Varies.

ADDRESS INQUIRIES TO:
Internship Programs
(See address and e-mail above.)

THE METROPOLITAN MUSEUM OF ART [545]

1000 Fifth Avenue
New York, NY 10028-0198
(212) 650-2763
Fax: (212) 570-3972
E-mail: academic.programs@metmuseum.org
Web Site: www.metmuseum.org

FOUNDED: 1870

AREAS OF INTEREST:
Museum conservation work.

NAME(S) OF PROGRAMS:
- **The Sherman Fairchild Foundation Fellowships**

TYPE:
Fellowships. Fellowships are awarded annually and make possible study and training in the following Museum conservation departments: Paintings Conservation, Objects Conservation (including sculpture, metalwork, glass, ceramics, furniture and archaeological objects), Musical Instruments, Arms and Armor, Paper Conservation, Textile Conservation, The Costume Institute Conservation.

The Museum offers junior-level and senior-level fellowships in conservation and scientific research. Junior fellowships are intended for those who have recently completed graduate-level training. Senior fellowships are intended for well-established professionals with advanced training in the field and a proven publication record.

All fellowships must take place between September 1 and the following August 31.

PURPOSE:
To make possible study and training in conservation departments of the Museum.

ELIGIBILITY:
Qualified candidates from the U.S. and abroad who have already reached an advanced level of training or experience.

FINANCIAL DATA:
Amount of support per award: $42,000 plus up to $6,000 for travel and miscellaneous expenses for Junior Conservation Fellow; $52,000 plus up to $6,000 for travel and miscellaneous expenses for Senior Conservation Fellow.
Total amount of support: Varies.

NO. AWARDS: Varies.

APPLICATION INFO:
Application may be obtained from the Museum's web site.
Duration: Up to one year.
Deadline: First Friday in December. Announcements of awards will be made by late March.

STAFF:
Marcie Karp, Managing Museum Educator, Academic Programs, Education Department

ADDRESS INQUIRIES TO:
See e-mail address above.

THE METROPOLITAN MUSEUM OF ART [546]

1000 Fifth Avenue
New York, NY 10028-0198
(212) 650-2763
Fax: (212) 570-3972
E-mail: academic.programs@metmuseum.org
Web Site: www.metmuseum.org

NAME(S) OF PROGRAMS:
- **Andrew W. Mellon Fellowships**

TYPE:
Fellowships. Awarded to promising young scholars with commendable research projects related to the Metropolitan Museum's collections and to distinguished visiting scholars from the U.S. and abroad who can serve as teachers and advisors making their expertise available to catalogue and refine the collections. Fellows are expected to spend most of their tenure at the Metropolitan Museum.

YEAR PROGRAM STARTED: 1974

PURPOSE:
To promote research in the fine arts.

ELIGIBILITY:
Applicants should have received the Doctorate or have completed substantial work toward it.

FINANCIAL DATA:
Amount of support per award: $52,000 stipend for senior fellows for one year, $42,000 for predoctoral fellows, and up to an additional $6,000 for travel and miscellaneous expenses.

APPLICATION INFO:
Application may be obtained from the Museum's web site.
Duration: Normally, a fellow will be in residence at the Metropolitan for a maximum of one year. Fellowships for senior scholars are also available for as short a term as one month.
Deadline: Application and required letters of recommendation must be received by the first Friday in November. Announcement of awards will be made by late March.

STAFF:
Marcie Karp, Managing Museum Educator, Academic Programs, Education Department

ADDRESS INQUIRIES TO:
See e-mail address above.

THE METROPOLITAN MUSEUM OF ART [547]

1000 Fifth Avenue
New York, NY 10028-0198
(212) 650-2763
Fax: (212) 570-3972
E-mail: academic.programs@metmuseum.org
Web Site: www.metmuseum.org

AREAS OF INTEREST:
Scholarly research in the fine arts.

NAME(S) OF PROGRAMS:
- **Chester Dale Fellowships**

TYPE:
Fellowships. Awarded for independent scholarly study or research related to the fine arts of the Western world at the Metropolitan Museum.

PURPOSE:
To promote research in the fine arts.

ELIGIBILITY:
Individuals whose fields of study are related to the fine arts of the Western world and who are preferably American citizens under the age of 40.

FINANCIAL DATA:
Fellowships are awarded as available funds permit.
Amount of support per award: $52,000 stipend for senior fellows, $42,000 for predoctoral fellows, and up to an additional $6,000 for travel and miscellaneous expenses.

APPLICATION INFO:
Application may be obtained from the Museum's web site.
Duration: The grants typically cover periods from three months to one year.
Deadline: Application and required letters of recommendation must be received by the first Friday in November. Announcements of awards will be made by late March.

STAFF:
Marcie Karp, Managing Museum Educator, Academic Programs, Education Department

ADDRESS INQUIRIES TO:
See e-mail address above.

THE METROPOLITAN MUSEUM OF ART [548]

1000 Fifth Avenue
New York, NY 10028-0198
(212) 650-2763
Fax: (212) 570-3972
E-mail: academic.programs@metmuseum.org
Web Site: www.metmuseum.org

NAME(S) OF PROGRAMS:
- **J. Clawson Mills Scholarships**

TYPE:
Fellowships. Awarded to scholars interested in pursuing research projects at the Metropolitan Museum or abroad in any branch of the fine arts related to the Museum's collections.

PURPOSE:
To promote research in the fine arts.

ELIGIBILITY:
In general, these grants are reserved for mature scholars of demonstrated ability.

FINANCIAL DATA:
Scholarships are awarded as available funds permit.
Amount of support per award: $52,000 stipend for one year for senior fellows, $42,000 for predoctoral fellows, and up to an additional $6,000 for travel and miscellaneous expenses.

APPLICATION INFO:
Application may be obtained from the Museum's web site.
Duration: One year.
Deadline: Application and required letters of recommendation must be received by the first Friday in November. Announcement of awards will be made by March 4.

STAFF:
Marcie Karp, Managing Museum Educator, Academic Programs, Education Department

ADDRESS INQUIRIES TO:
See e-mail address above.

THE METROPOLITAN MUSEUM OF ART [549]

1000 Fifth Avenue
New York, NY 10028-0198
(212) 650-2763
Fax: (212) 570-3972
E-mail: academic.programs@metmuseum.org
Web Site: www.metmuseum.org

NAME(S) OF PROGRAMS:
- **The Bothmer Fellowship**

TYPE:
Fellowships. Awarded to an outstanding graduate student who has been admitted to the doctoral program of a university in the U.S., and who has submitted an outline of a thesis dealing with either Greek or Roman art.

YEAR PROGRAM STARTED: 1976

PURPOSE:
To promote research in the fine arts.

ELIGIBILITY:
An applicant must be an outstanding graduate student who has been admitted to the doctoral program of a university in the U.S. and who has submitted an outline of a thesis dealing with either Greek or Roman art. Preference will be given to the applicant who, in the opinion of the Grants Committee, would profit most from utilizing the resources of the Museum's Department of Greek and Roman Art: its collections, library, photographs and other archives with the guidance of its curatorial staff.

FINANCIAL DATA:
Amount of support per award: $42,000 for one year for predoctoral fellows with up to an additional $6,000 for travel and miscellaneous expenses.

APPLICATION INFO:
Application may be obtained from the Museum's web site.

Duration: One academic year.

Deadline: Application and required letters of recommendation must be received by the first Friday in November. Announcements of awards will be made by late March.

STAFF:
Marcie Karp, Managing Museum Educator, Academic Programs, Education Department

ADDRESS INQUIRIES TO:
See e-mail address above.

MUSEUM OF EARLY SOUTHERN DECORATIVE ARTS (MESDA) [550]

924 South Main Street
Winston-Salem, NC 27101-5335
(336) 721-7369
Fax: (336) 721-7367
E-mail: mesdamail@gmail.com
Web Site: www.mesda.org

FOUNDED: 1965

AREAS OF INTEREST:
Decorative arts of the South before 1860.

NAME(S) OF PROGRAMS:
- **Horton Fellowship**

TYPE:
Fellowships.

YEAR PROGRAM STARTED: 1976

PURPOSE:
To combine the study of history and objects in a museum context.

LEGAL BASIS:
Nonprofit.

ELIGIBILITY:
Graduate student status or present employment in museum-related professions required.

FINANCIAL DATA:
Covers partial tuition for three credit hours.

Amount of support per award: $150 to $500.

Total amount of support: $5,000 for the year 2015.

NO. MOST RECENT APPLICANTS: Approximately 15 per year.

NO. AWARDS: Up to 10 per year.

APPLICATION INFO:
Applicant must submit a completed application form and letters of recommendation.

Duration: Four weeks.

Deadline: March 11. Notification April 1.

IRS I.D.: 56-0587289

STAFF:
April Strader Bullin, Director of Museum Programs

ADDRESS INQUIRIES TO:
April Strader Bullin
Director of Museum Programs
(See address above.)

PEW FELLOWSHIPS AT THE PEW CENTER FOR ARTS & HERITAGE [551]

1608 Walnut Street, 18th Floor
Philadelphia, PA 19103
(267) 350-4920
Fax: (267) 350-4997
E-mail: mfranklin@pcah.us
Web Site: www.pcah.us/fellowships

FOUNDED: 1991

AREAS OF INTEREST:
Fellowships are awarded for various art forms, including Choreography, Craft Arts, Folk and Traditional Arts, Literature (Fiction, Literary Non-Fiction and Poetry), Media Arts, Music Composition, Painting, Performance Art, Playwriting, Works on Paper and Visual Arts 3-D.

TYPE:
Fellowships. Opportunities for contemporary artists in the Philadelphia five-county area to concentrate on the development and creation of art. Fellowships to support artists at critical junctures in any stage of their career development. Fellows will be expected to participate annually in at least three meetings with other fellowship recipients.

YEAR PROGRAM STARTED: 1991

PURPOSE:
To provide financial support directly to artists so that they will have the opportunity to dedicate themselves wholly to the development of their artwork; to provide such support at a critical juncture in an artist's career, when a concentration on artistic development and exploration is most likely to contribute to personal and professional growth.

ELIGIBILITY:
Artists are nominated and invited to apply for the fellowship. Candidates must be residents of Bucks, Chester, Delaware, Montgomery or Philadelphia counties, PA, for two years or longer. Matriculated students, full or part-time, or immediate family members of a panelist for the year applied or of Pew Fellowships staff are not eligible.

There is no restriction as to citizenship.

GEOG. RESTRICTIONS: Bucks, Chester, Delaware, Montgomery and Philadelphia counties, Pennsylvania.

FINANCIAL DATA:
Fellowship includes stipend. Funds may be used to support costs such as equipment, materials, assistants, training and travel. The specific use of grant funds will be up to the recipient artist.

Amount of support per award: $75,000.

Total amount of support: Up to $900,000 each year.

CO-OP FUNDING PROGRAMS: Program funded by the Pew Charitable Trusts.

NO. MOST RECENT APPLICANTS: Varies.

NO. AWARDS: Up to 12 each year.

APPLICATION INFO:
Application by nomination only.

The application procedure involves a panel review by artists and arts professionals. The first level of review is discipline-based; the second level of review is interdisciplinary; the final selection of candidates is based on the applicant's accomplishments or promise in his or her discipline, and the degree to which the fellowship will address a critical juncture in the artist's career and/or artistic development.

Duration: Up to two years.

STAFF:
Melissa Franklin, Director
Laura Paige Kyber, Program Associate

ADDRESS INQUIRIES TO:
Melissa Franklin, Director
(See e-mail address above.)

THE POLLOCK-KRASNER FOUNDATION, INC. [552]

863 Park Avenue
New York, NY 10075
(212) 517-5400
Fax: (212) 288-2836
E-mail: grants@pkf.org
Web Site: www.pkf.org

FOUNDED: 1985

AREAS OF INTEREST:
Visual arts.

TYPE:
Grants-in-aid. Grants to individual visual artists for personal and professional needs.

YEAR PROGRAM STARTED: 1985

PURPOSE:
To aid internationally working artists who have embarked on professional careers.

LEGAL BASIS:
Private foundation.

ELIGIBILITY:
Grants are made to painters, sculptors and artists who work on paper, including printmakers who have taken up art as a

professional career. The Foundation will not accept applications from commercial artists, photographers, video artists, filmmakers, craft-makers or any artist whose work primarily falls into these categories. It does not make grants to students nor fund academic study.

The Foundation does not make grants to pay for past debts, legal fees, the purchase of real estate, moves to other cities or to pay for the costs of installations, commissions or projects ordered by others. With very few exceptions, the Foundation will not fund travel expenses.

FINANCIAL DATA:

Amount of support per award: The size of the grant is determined by the individual circumstances of the artist.

Total amount of support: Varies.

APPLICATION INFO:

Artists are required to submit a cover letter, an application, and 10 images of current work. Applications are to be submitted online.

Duration: One year.

Deadline: Grants are awarded throughout the year.

PUBLICATIONS:

Biannual report; application guidelines.

OFFICERS:

Charles C. Bergman, Chairman of the Board and Chief Executive Officer
Samuel Sachs, II, President
Kerrie Buitrago, Executive Vice President

STAFF:

Caroline Black, Program Director
Beth Cochems, Grants Manager

ADDRESS INQUIRIES TO:

Charles C. Bergman, Chairman of the Board and Chief Executive Officer
(See address above.)

ROSWELL ARTIST-IN-RESIDENCE PROGRAM [553]

409 East College Boulevard
Roswell, NM 88201
(575) 622-6037
Fax: (575) 623-5603
E-mail: stephen@rair.org
Web Site: www.rair.org

FOUNDED: 1967

AREAS OF INTEREST:

Studio-based, fine-art residencies.

TYPE:

Residencies. Roswell Artist-in-Residence Program is for artists who work in drawing, painting, sculpture, photography, printmaking, video and other fine art media.

YEAR PROGRAM STARTED: 1967

PURPOSE:

To provide time for artists to focus on their work, without distractions or interruptions.

FINANCIAL DATA:

Amount of support per award: $800 per month, plus housing, studio and utilities and $100 per dependent.

Matching fund requirements: Artists cover phone service, food, art materials and transportation.

NO. MOST RECENT APPLICANTS: Approximately 200 average.

NO. AWARDS: 6 each year.

APPLICATION INFO:

Application information is available on the web site.

Duration: One year.

Deadline: Varies from year to year.

IRS I.D.: 33-0999247

STAFF:

Stephen Fleming, Director
Nancy Fleming, Programs and Publications and Co-Director

ADDRESS INQUIRIES TO:

Roswell Artist-in-Residence Program
P.O. Box One
Roswell, NM 88202

SAN DIEGO ART INSTITUTE [554]

1439 El Prado
House of Charm, Balboa Park
San Diego, CA 92101
(619) 236-0011
Fax: (619) 236-1974
E-mail: admin@sandiego-art.org
director@sandiego-art.org
Web Site: www.sandiego-art.org

FOUNDED: 1941

AREAS OF INTEREST:

Visual arts.

NAME(S) OF PROGRAMS:

- **Annual International Juried Award Exhibition**
- **Southern California Regional Juried Award**
- **Youth Art**

TYPE:

Awards/prizes; Conferences/seminars; Internships. Monthly juried exhibitions; monthly youth art exhibitions; awarded member solo shows; annual international juried award exhibition; annual city/county youth art award show; quarterly informational lecture series; biannual art tours; newsletter/journal.

YEAR PROGRAM STARTED: 1954

PURPOSE:

To advance the visual arts through exhibition, outreach and education.

LEGAL BASIS:

501(c)(3) nonprofit arts organization.

ELIGIBILITY:

For the International Juried Award, the exhibition is open to any artist (digital entry only). There are no residency restrictions. Art must be original.

For the Southern California Regional Juried Award, southern California residency is required.

FINANCIAL DATA:

Awards include monetary compensation.

Amount of support per award: For the International Juried Award Exhibition, one award of $2,000; two awards of $1,000; one award of $500; two awards of $150; three awards of $100. For Southern California Regional Juried Award Exhibition: one award of $1,000; two awards of $500.

Total amount of support: $7,100.

NO. AWARDS: 13.

APPLICATION INFO:

Work may be two- or three-dimensional. All media are welcome except crafts or functional art. For the Southern California Regional, one art work per artist. Entry fee required.

Duration: One-time awards.

PUBLICATIONS:

Journal; guidelines.

IRS I.D.: 95-1816068

ADDRESS INQUIRIES TO:

Ginger Shulick Porcella, Executive Director
(See address and e-mail above.)

*PLEASE NOTE:

All shows are juried by outside juror.

SCHOOL OF THE MUSEUM OF FINE ARTS, BOSTON [555]

230 The Fenway
Boston, MA 02115
(617) 369-3656
Fax: (617) 369-3856
Web Site: www.smfa.edu

FOUNDED: 1876

AREAS OF INTEREST:

Contemporary visual art.

NAME(S) OF PROGRAMS:

- **Traveling Fellowship Award**

TYPE:

Fellowships. Awarded for travel and study abroad.

YEAR PROGRAM STARTED: 1899

PURPOSE:

To further the professional development of the artist recipients.

LEGAL BASIS:

A part of the Museum of Fine Arts, a nonprofit Massachusetts corporation.

ELIGIBILITY:

Applicants must be alumni of the School of the Museum of Fine Arts.

FINANCIAL DATA:

Amount of support per award: Up to $10,000.

Total amount of support: Approximately $100,000 annually.

NO. MOST RECENT APPLICANTS: 190.

APPLICATION INFO:

Proposed plan of travel and study, including itinerary, must be submitted with a presentation of art work.

Duration: Varies according to proposal. Normally not more than one year. Nonrenewable.

Deadline: June. Announcement in September.

ADDRESS INQUIRIES TO:

Office of Exhibitions
(See address above.)

SKOWHEGAN SCHOOL OF PAINTING AND SCULPTURE [556]

136 West 22nd Street
New York, NY 10011
(212) 529-0505
Fax: (212) 473-1342
E-mail: mail@skowheganart.org
Web Site: www.skowheganart.org

FOUNDED: 1946

AREAS OF INTEREST:

All visual arts.

TYPE:

Scholarships; Travel grants.

YEAR PROGRAM STARTED: 1946

PURPOSE:
To bring together a gifted and diverse group of individuals who have demonstrated a commitment to art-making and inquiry to create the most stimulating environment possible for a concentrated period of artistic creation, interaction and growth.

LEGAL BASIS:
Not-for-profit educational institution.

ELIGIBILITY:
Based on need. Candidate must be at least 21 years old.

FINANCIAL DATA:
Scholarships cover room, board and tuition.

Amount of support per award: Varies.

NO. MOST RECENT APPLICANTS: 2,102.

NO. AWARDS: 65.

APPLICATION INFO:
Application information is available online.

Duration: Nine-week summer program, mid-June to mid-August.

Deadline: February 1 for all applications. Notification in mid-April.

ADDRESS INQUIRIES TO:
Sarah Workneh, Director
(See address above.)

W. EUGENE SMITH MEMORIAL FUND [557]

c/o International Center of Photography
1114 Avenue of the Americas
New York, NY 10036
(212) 857-0062
Fax: (212) 857-0091
E-mail: smithfund@icp.edu
Web Site: www.smithfund.org

FOUNDED: 1979

AREAS OF INTEREST:
Photography.

NAME(S) OF PROGRAMS:
- **W. Eugene Smith Grant in Humanistic Photography**

TYPE:
Project/program grants.

PURPOSE:
To support a photographer working on a project in the humanistic tradition of W. Eugene Smith, in order to pursue the work.

ELIGIBILITY:
Open to outstanding photographers of any nationality.

FINANCIAL DATA:
Amount of support per award: $30,000 and a possible additional $5,000 fellowship.

NO. MOST RECENT APPLICANTS: Approximately 200 annually.

NO. AWARDS: 1 annually.

APPLICATION INFO:
Initial application is online only. Applicants should include a written proposal, resume of educational and professional qualifications, and 20 to 40 images. Entry fee of $50 is required.

Duration: One year.

Deadline: May 31.

*SPECIAL STIPULATIONS:
Grant recipients agree to give to the W. Eugene Smith Memorial Fund, Inc., as an unrestricted gift, 12 digital images and 12 prints of work completed as part of the project proposed, within 18 months of the award and shall become part of the Legacy Collection.

SIR JOHN SOANE MUSEUM FOUNDATION

1040 First Avenue, Suite 311
New York, NY 10022
(212) 223-2012
Fax: (866) 841-1928
E-mail: info@soanefoundation.com
Web Site: www.soanefoundation.com

TYPE:
Fellowships. Designed to help graduate students and scholars pursue research projects related to the work of Sir John Soane's Museum and its collections.

See entry 411 for full listing.

THE JOHN F. AND ANNA LEE STACEY SCHOLARSHIP FUND [558]

c/o National Cowboy and Western Heritage Museum
1700 N.E. 63rd Street
Oklahoma City, OK 73111
(405) 478-2250
Fax: (405) 478-4714
E-mail: mleslie@nationalcowboymuseum.org
Web Site: www.nationalcowboymuseum.org

FOUNDED: 1955

AREAS OF INTEREST:
Drawing and painting in the conservative mode.

TYPE:
Awards/prizes. Cash awards to be used to further the development of young painters in the classical conservative tradition.

YEAR PROGRAM STARTED: 1975

PURPOSE:
To foster a high standard in the study of form, color, drawing, painting, design and technique, as these are expressed in modes showing patent affinity with the classical tradition of western culture.

LEGAL BASIS:
Nonprofit.

ELIGIBILITY:
Open to U.S. citizens between 18 and 35 years of age. Only those who are skilled and devoted to the painting or drawing of classical or conservative tradition of western culture should apply.

GEOG. RESTRICTIONS: United States.

FINANCIAL DATA:
Amount of support per award: $1,000 to $4,000.

Total amount of support: Varies.

NO. MOST RECENT APPLICANTS: More than 200.

NO. AWARDS: 3 to 5.

APPLICATION INFO:
Guidelines and application are posted online by November 1 for the following year. All applicants will be required to upload images to the Fund's FTP site. Not more than six images of their work (clearly labeled with name, title, dimensions, medium and date of execution of the work) in the following categories: painting from life, drawing from the figure (nude), composition, landscape and others. Application forms must accompany all submissions.

Duration: One year.

Deadline: Entries need to be uploaded by February 1 of each year.

PUBLICATIONS:
Guidelines.

STAFF:
Mike Leslie, Assistant Director

ADDRESS INQUIRIES TO:
See e-mail address above.

STUDIO ARTS CENTERS INTERNATIONAL (SACI) [559]

Palazzo dei Cartelloni
Via Sant' Antonino 11
50123 Florence Italy
(39) 055-289948
(212) 248-7225
Fax: (39) 055-2776408
E-mail: admissions@saci-florence.edu
Web Site: www.saci-florence.edu

FOUNDED: 1975

AREAS OF INTEREST:
Studio art, art history, art conservation, Italian language and culture.

NAME(S) OF PROGRAMS:
- **Fall/Spring/Summer Study Abroad**
- **MA in Art/History**
- **MFA in Communication Design**
- **MFA in Photography**
- **MFA in Studio Art (Painting or Drawing)**
- **Post Baccalaureate Certificate Programs**

TYPE:
Awards/prizes; Scholarships.
Fall/Spring/Summer Study Abroad: Undergraduate and graduate visiting students may attend for a term or more. SACI offers a wide variety of both traditional and cutting-edge studio art and design courses as well as classes in art history covering medieval and contemporary art. For conservation students, there is the unique opportunity to participate hands-on in the conservation of historic works in Florence. Studio Art courses include Fresco Painting, Serigraphy, Printmaking, Photography, Digital Multimedia, Video, Jewelry Making, Batik, Book Making, Sculpture, Ceramics, and many more.

MFA in Studio Art (Painting or Drawing)/MFA in Photography/MFA in Communication Design: SACI's MFAs are two-year programs in which students work in a creative environment of rigorous critical and technical inquiry utilizing the unique artistic and cultural resources of Florence to prepare for careers as artists and college instructors. Students pursue a curriculum integrating practical and critical skills that encourages individual innovation, creative collaboration, mentorships and instruction from SACI's outstanding faculty.

Post Baccalaureate Certificate Programs: SACI's Post Baccalaureate Certificate Programs are one-year programs of intensive graduate study in a selected major discipline within Conservation or Studio Art. The study program includes graduate seminars, reviews, field trips, lecture series and exhibitions.

YEAR PROGRAM STARTED: 1975

PURPOSE:
To study Studio Art, Art History or Conservation at a U.S.-accredited institution in Florence, Italy.

ELIGIBILITY:
Selection is based on academic/artistic merit as well as financial need.

FINANCIAL DATA:
Amount of support per award: $500 up to full tuition.

APPLICATION INFO:
Application information is available on the web site.

Duration: Semester.

Deadline: Fall: March 15. Spring: October 15. Summer: April 1.

ADDRESS INQUIRIES TO:
Studio Arts Centers International (SACI)
25 Broadway, Ninth Floor
New York, NY 10004-1058
(See e-mail address above.)

UNIVERSITY OF ILLINOIS AT URBANA-CHAMPAIGN [560]

College of Fine and Applied Arts
608 East Lorado Taft Drive, Suite 100
Champaign, IL 61820
(217) 333-1661
(217) 333-1660
Fax: (217) 244-8381
E-mail: faa@illinois.edu
Web Site: www.faa.illinois.edu/alumni-friends/kate-neal-kinley-memorial-fellowship

FOUNDED: 1931

AREAS OF INTEREST:
Art, architecture, dance, landscape architecture, music, theatre, and urban and regional planning.

NAME(S) OF PROGRAMS:
- **Kate Neal Kinley Memorial Fellowship**

TYPE:
Fellowships. Awarded for advanced study in the fine arts in the U.S. or abroad, in an approved educational institution, with an approved private teacher or in independent study.

Three major Fellowships will be awarded:
(1) one in any field of music;
(2) one in architectural design and history, art and design, theatre, dance, or instrumental or vocal music and;
(3) one in art, architecture, dance, landscape architecture, theatre, or urban and regional planning.

YEAR PROGRAM STARTED: 1931

PURPOSE:
To help defray expenses of advanced study of the fine and applied arts in America or abroad.

Provides a meaningful opportunity for students to enhance their professional status, aid their pursuit of an advanced degree, or finance a special project within the field.

ELIGIBILITY:
Open to graduates of the College of Fine and Applied Arts of the University of Illinois at Urbana-Champaign and to graduates of similar institutions of equal educational standing whose principal or major studies have been in the fields of art, architecture, dance, landscape architecture, music, theatre, and urban and regional planning.

Although there is no age limitation for applicants, other factors being equal, preference will be given to applicants who have not reached their 25th birthday.

Fellowships will be awarded upon the basis of unusual promise in the fine arts as attested by:
(1) high attainment in the applicant's major field of study as evidenced by academic marks and quality of work submitted or performed;
(2) high attainment in related cultural fields as evidenced by academic marks;
(3) the character, merit and suitability of the program proposed by the applicant and;
(4) excellence of personality, seriousness of purpose and good moral character.

FINANCIAL DATA:
The fellowships are to be used by the recipients toward defraying the expenses of advanced study in America or abroad.

Amount of support per award: Major fellowships: Up to $20,000 in any field of music, up to $20,000 in architectural design and history, art and design, theatre, dance, or instrumental or vocal music, and up to $9,000 in art, architecture, dance, landscape architecture, theatre, or urban and regional planning.

CO-OP FUNDING PROGRAMS: Funded partially by the John Robert Gregg Fund at Community Funds, Inc. and the New York Community Trust.

NO. AWARDS: 3 major fellowships, plus up to 3 additional fellowships of lesser amounts, depending upon committee recommendations.

APPLICATION INFO:
Application form and guidelines are available online.

Duration: Tenable for one academic year.

Deadline: December 1.

ADDRESS INQUIRIES TO:
Edward Feser, Dean
Kate Neal Kinley
Memorial Fellowship Committee
(See address and telephone number above.)

UNIVERSITY OF SOUTHERN CALIFORNIA ROSKI SCHOOL OF ART AND DESIGN [561]

851 Downey Way
HSH-101
Los Angeles, CA 90089-1058
(213) 740-9153
Fax: (213) 740-8938
E-mail: roski@usc.edu
Web Site: roski.usc.edu

FOUNDED: 1883

AREAS OF INTEREST:
Art.

NAME(S) OF PROGRAMS:
- **International Artist Fellowships**
- **M.F.A. Teaching Assistantships**
- **Post-M.F.A. Teaching Fellowship**

TYPE:
Assistantships; Travel grants. Tuition remission. International artist fellowships. Awards are for people pursuing M.F.A. degree, for experience in teaching art on a college level.

YEAR PROGRAM STARTED: 1960

PURPOSE:
To educate artists.

LEGAL BASIS:
Private university.

ELIGIBILITY:
Applicants must be accepted into the Roski School of Art and Design two-year M.F.A. program at University of Southern California.

All applicants to the program are considered for awards regardless of national origin.

FINANCIAL DATA:
Teaching Assistantship includes full tuition remission, generous monthly stipend and private studio. Post-M.F.A. Fellowship includes a stipend plus teaching two studio art courses. International Artist Fellowship supports an international student for two years, plus full tuition remission and travel stipend.

Amount of support per award: Teaching Assistantship: $53,000 per year; Summer Travel Fellowship: Up to $7,500; Post-M.F.A. Fellowship: $25,000.

Total amount of support: $400,000.

NO. MOST RECENT APPLICANTS: 391.

NO. AWARDS: International Artist Fellowship, Post-M.F.A. Teaching Fellowship and Travel grant: 1 per award; Teaching Assistantships: 7.

APPLICATION INFO:
Applications are available online.

Duration: One year. Assistantships are renewable.

Deadline: January 15.

ADDRESS INQUIRIES TO:
Penelope Jones
Assistant Dean for Student Affairs
(See address above.)

History

AGRICULTURAL HISTORY SOCIETY [562]

MSU History Department
P.O. Box H
Mississippi State, MS 39762
(662) 268-2247
E-mail: jgiesen@history.msstate.edu
Web Site: www.aghistorysociety.org

AREAS OF INTEREST:
Agricultural and rural history.

NAME(S) OF PROGRAMS:
- **Everett E. Edwards Awards in Agricultural History**
- **Gilbert C. Fite Dissertation Award**
- **Wayne D. Rasmussen Award**
- **Theodore Saloutos Book Award**
- **Henry A. Wallace Award**

TYPE:
Awards/prizes. The Everett E. Edwards Award is presented to the graduate student who submits the best manuscript on any aspect of agricultural history and rural studies during the current calendar year.

The Gilbert C. Fite Dissertation Award will be presented to the author of the best dissertation on any aspect of agricultural history completed during the current calendar year.

The Wayne D. Rasmussen Award is given to the author of the best article on agricultural history published by a journal other than *Agricultural History* during the current calendar year.

The Theodore Saloutos Book Award is presented to the author of a book on any aspect of agricultural history in the U.S. within the current year, broadly interpreted.

The Henry A. Wallace Award is presented to the author of a book on any aspect of agricultural history outside of the U.S. within the current year, broadly interpreted.

PURPOSE:
To promote research and publication in the field of agricultural and rural history.

FINANCIAL DATA:
Amount of support per award: Edwards Award: Honorarium of $200 and publication in *Agricultural History*; Fite Dissertation Award: Honorarium of $300 and a certificate; Rasmussen Award: Honorarium of $200 for the author and certificates for the author and publisher; Saloutos Book Award: $500 to the author.

APPLICATION INFO:
Contact the Society for details.

Deadline: December 31.

AMERICAN ANTIQUARIAN SOCIETY (AAS)

185 Salisbury Street
Worcester, MA 01609-1634
(508) 755-5221
Fax: (508) 753-3311
E-mail: cmcrell@mwa.org
Web Site: www.americanantiquarian.org

TYPE:
Fellowships. Visiting fellowship for historical research by creative and performing artists, writers, filmmakers and journalists.

See entry 336 for full listing.

AMERICAN ANTIQUARIAN SOCIETY (AAS)

185 Salisbury Street
Worcester, MA 01609-1634
(508) 755-5221
Fax: (508) 754-9069
E-mail: perickson@mwa.org
Web Site: www.americanantiquarian.org

TYPE:
Conferences/seminars; Fellowships. Fellowships provide support for residence at the Society's library for research on any topic supported by the collections. All awards are for research and writing using the library's resources.

See entry 335 for full listing.

AMERICAN CATHOLIC HISTORICAL ASSOCIATION [563]

Department of African & African-American Studies
Fordham University, Dealy Hall, Room 637
441 East Fordham Road
Bronx, NY 10458
(718) 817-3830
Fax: (718) 817-5690
E-mail: acha@fordham.edu
Web Site: www.achahistory.org

FOUNDED: 1919

AREAS OF INTEREST:
The history of Catholicism from antiquity to the present.

NAME(S) OF PROGRAMS:

- **The Howard R. Marraro Prize**

TYPE:
Awards/prizes. This Prize is given annually to the author of a book that is judged by a committee of experts to be the most distinguished work dealing with Italian history or Italo-American history or relations that has been published in a preceding 12-month period. It is named in memory of Howard A. Marraro (1879-1972), professor, Columbia University and the author of more than a dozen books on Italian literature, history and culture.

YEAR PROGRAM STARTED: 1973

PURPOSE:
To stimulate interest in the history of Catholicism among young scholars.

LEGAL BASIS:
An endowed fund owned by the Association.

ELIGIBILITY:
To be entered in the competition, a work must be of book length, in English, already published and must deal with Italian history or Italian-American history or relations. To be eligible for the prize, an author must be a citizen or resident of the U.S. or Canada. The work must have been published since June 1 of the previous year.

FINANCIAL DATA:
Amount of support per award: $750.

NO. AWARDS: 1 per annum.

APPLICATION INFO:
Three copies, if possible, of the work to be considered should be sent, together with a brief curriculum vitae and bibliography of the author, to the American Historical Association, 400 A Street, S.E., Washington, DC 20003.

Deadline: May 15.

ADDRESS INQUIRIES TO:
Prize Administrator
Tel:(202) 544-2422
E-mail: dschaffer@historians.org

AMERICAN CATHOLIC HISTORICAL ASSOCIATION

Fordham University, Dealy Hall, Room 637
441 East Fordham Road
Bronx, NY 10458
(718) 817-3830
Fax: (718) 817-5690
E-mail: acha@fordham.edu
Web Site: www.achahistory.org

TYPE:
Awards/prizes; Challenge/matching grants; Conferences/seminars; Travel grants. A prize awarded annually to the author whose article, dealing with the history of the Catholic Church, is the first of his or her professional career and is judged to be the best of those in that category accepted for publication in any given year by the editors of the *Catholic Historical Review*.

See entry 790 for full listing.

AMERICAN CATHOLIC HISTORICAL ASSOCIATION

Fordham University, Dealy Hall, Room 637
441 East Fordham Road
Bronx, NY 10458
(718) 817-3830
Fax: (718) 817-5690
E-mail: acha@fordham.edu
Web Site: www.achahistory.org

TYPE:
Awards/prizes. This Prize is given annually to the author of a book, published during a preceding 12-month period, which is judged by a committee of experts to have made the most original and distinguished contribution to knowledge of the history of the Catholic Church.

See entry 791 for full listing.

AMERICAN CATHOLIC HISTORICAL ASSOCIATION

Fordham University, Dealy Hall, Room 637
441 East Fordham Road
Bronx, NY 10458
(718) 817-3830
Fax: (718) 817-5690
E-mail: acha@fordham.edu
Web Site: www.achahistory.org

TYPE:
Awards/prizes; Challenge/matching grants; Conferences/seminars; Research grants; Travel grants. ACHA Graduate Student Summer Research Grant is awarded to an ACHA graduate student member who has completed all requirements for the Doctorate except the dissertation.

ACHA Junior Faculty Grant is awarded to an ACHA tenure-track scholar to assist in summer travel to conduct research.

John Tracy Ellis Dissertation Award memorializes the scholarship and teaching of Monsignor Ellis (1905-1992).

Graduate Student Travel Grant was created in 2010 by the Association from donations from former presidents.

See entry 788 for full listing.

AMERICAN CATHOLIC HISTORICAL ASSOCIATION

Fordham University, Dealy Hall, Room 637
441 East Fordham Road
Bronx, NY 10458
(718) 817-3830
Fax: (718) 817-5690
E-mail: acha@fordham.edu
Web Site: www.achahistory.org

TYPE:
Awards/prizes. The Msgr. Harry C. Koenig Award for Catholic Biography is offered every two years (in even-numbered years) and recognizes outstanding biographies of members of the Catholic Church who have lived in any age or country.

See entry 789 for full listing.

THE AMERICAN HISTORICAL ASSOCIATION [564]

400 A Street, S.E.
Washington, DC 20003
(202) 544-2422
Fax: (202) 544-8307
E-mail: awards@historians.org
Web Site: www.historians.org

FOUNDED: 1884

AREAS OF INTEREST:
Promotion of historical studies, the collection and preservation of historical manuscripts and the dissemination of historical research.

NAME(S) OF PROGRAMS:

- **The Herbert Baxter Adams Prize**
- **The George Louis Beer Prize**

- **The Jerry Bentley Prize**
- **The Albert J. Beveridge Award**
- **The Albert J. Beveridge Grant**
- **The Paul Birdsall Prize**
- **The James Henry Breasted Prize**
- **The Albert B. Corey Prize in Canadian-American Relations**
- **The John H. Dunning Prize in United States History**
- **The John K. Fairbank Prize in East Asian History**
- **The Herbert Feis Award**
- **The Morris D. Forkosch Prize**
- **The Leo Gershoy Award**
- **The Clarence H. Haring Prize**
- **J. Franklin Jameson Award**
- **The Friedrich Katz Prize**
- **The Joan Kelly Memorial Prize in Women's History**
- **Martin A. Klein Prize in African History**
- **Michael Kraus Research Grant**
- **The Waldo G. Leland Prize**
- **Littleton-Griswold Grant**
- **The Littleton-Griswold Prize in American Law and Society**
- **The J. Russell Major Prize**
- **The Helen and Howard R. Marraro Prize in Italian History**
- **The George L. Mosse Prize**
- **The John E. O'Connor Film Award**
- **The Premio Del Rey**
- **The James A. Rawley Prize in Atlantic History**
- **John F. Richards Prize in South Asian History**
- **The James Harvey Robinson Prize**
- **The Dorothy Rosenberg Prize**
- **Bernadotte E. Schmitt Grant**
- **The Wesley-Logan Prize**

TYPE:
Awards/prizes; Fellowships; Research grants. Prizes and awards for distinguished scholarly publications written in English on historical subjects as follows:

Herbert Baxter Adams Prize: Awarded annually for a distinguished book by an American author in the field of European history.

Beer Prize: Awarded annually for the best work on European international history by a U.S. citizen.

Bentley Prize: Awarded annually for the best book in the field of world history.

Beveridge Award: Awarded annually for the best book in English on the history of the U.S., Canada, or Latin America from 1492 to the present.

Beveridge Grant: Given for research pertaining to the Western Hemisphere.

Birdsall Prize: For the best work in European military and strategic history. Awarded biennially in even years.

Breasted Prize: Awarded annually for an outstanding book in English in any field of history prior to 1000 A.D.

Corey Prize: Awarded biennially in even years for a book on the history of Canadian-U.S. relations, or on the history of both countries.

Dunning Prize: For a book on any subject relating to American history. Awarded biennially in odd years.

Fairbank Prize: Awarded annually for an outstanding book on the history of China proper, Vietnam, Chinese Central Asia, Mongolia, Manchuria, Korea or Japan since the year 1800.

Feis Award: Awarded for distinguished contributions to public history.

Forkosch Prize: Awarded annually in recognition of the best book in English in the field of British, British Imperial or British Commonwealth History.

Gershoy Prize: Awarded annually for an outstanding work published in English on any aspect of the fields of 17th and 18th century western European history.

Haring Prize: For a Latin American who, in the opinion of the committee, has published the most outstanding book on Latin American history during the preceding five years. Awarded every five years.

J. Franklin Jameson Award: Given for outstanding achievement in the editing of historical sources.

Friedrich Katz Prize: Awarded annually for the best book in Latin American and Caribbean history.

Kelly Memorial Prize: Awarded annually for the best work in women's history and/or feminist theory.

Martin A. Klein Prize: Awarded in the study of African history.

Michael Kraus Research Grant: Awarded for the study of colonial American history.

Leland Prize: Offered every five years for the outstanding reference tool in the field of history, i.e., bibliographies, indexes, encyclopedias and other scholarly apparatus.

Littleton-Griswold Grant: Awarded in U.S. legal history and law and society, broadly defined.

Littleton-Griswold Prize: Awarded annually for the best book in any subject on the history of American law and society, broadly defined.

J. Russell Major Prize: Awarded annually for the best work in English on any aspect of French history.

Marraro Prize: Awarded annually for the best work on any epoch of Italian history or Italian-American relations.

George L. Mosse Prize: Awarded annually for an outstanding major work of extraordinary scholarly distinction, creativity, and originality in the intellectual and cultural history of Europe since the Renaissance.

John E. O'Connor Film Award: Awarded annually to recognize outstanding interpretations of history through the medium of film.

Premio del Rey: Awarded biennially, in even years, for the best book in English in the field of early Spanish history, 500 to 1516 A.D.

James A. Rawley Prize in Atlantic History: Awarded annually in recognition of outstanding historical writing that explores aspects of integration of Atlantic worlds before the 20th century.

John F. Richards Prize in South Asian History: Awarded annually for the most distinguished work of scholarship on South Asian history published in English.

Robinson Prize: Awarded biennially in even years for the teaching aid that has made the most outstanding contribution to the teaching of history in any field. Award encompasses textbooks, source materials, audio-visual and computer-assisted instruction programs/techniques.

Dorothy Rosenberg Prize: Book prize for the Jewish Diaspora Community.

Bernadette Schmitt Grant: Given for research of Europe, Asia and Africa.

Wesley-Logan Prize: Awarded annually for an outstanding book on African diaspora history.

PURPOSE:
To promote and honor good historical writing and scholarship.

LEGAL BASIS:
Nonprofit association.

ELIGIBILITY:
Applicant must be a member to apply for grants. Preference will be given to Ph.D. candidates and postgraduates.

FINANCIAL DATA:
Amount of support per award: Varies.

NO. AWARDS: 1 in each program on the yearly basis.

PUBLICATIONS:
Annual report; *American Historical Review*; *Perspectives in History*.

OFFICERS:
Vicki Ruiz, President
James R. Grossman, Executive Director
Robert A. Schneider, Editor, *American Historical Review*
Randy B. Norell, Controller

ADDRESS INQUIRIES TO:
Prize or Grant Administrator
(See e-mail address above.)

THE AMERICAN HISTORICAL ASSOCIATION [565]

400 A Street, S.E.
Washington, DC 20003
(202) 544-2422
Fax: (202) 544-8307
E-mail: awards@historians.org
Web Site: www.historians.org

FOUNDED: 1884

AREAS OF INTEREST:
Scholarly research.

NAME(S) OF PROGRAMS:
- **The J. Franklin Jameson Fellowship**

TYPE:
Fellowships. Award in American history offered annually by the Library of Congress and the American Historical Association.

YEAR PROGRAM STARTED: 1977

PURPOSE:
To support significant scholarly research in the collections of the Library of Congress by scholars at an early stage in their careers in history.

LEGAL BASIS:
Nonprofit association.

ELIGIBILITY:
At the time of application, applicants must hold the Ph.D. degree or equivalent, must have received this degree within the past seven years and must not have published or had accepted for publication a book-length historical work. The fellowship will not be awarded to complete a doctoral dissertation.

The applicant's project in American history must be one for which the general and special collections of the Library of Congress offer unique research support. Applicants should include a statement substantiating this relationship.

Before the conclusion of the fellowship, the Jameson fellow will summarize the results of his or her research at a professional gathering arranged by the American Historical Association and the Library of Congress. Jameson fellows are not required to complete their project during the tenure of the fellowship, nor need they necessarily have published the results as a discrete work.

The American Historical Association encourages nontenured faculty, public historians, independent scholars and two-year faculty to apply.

FINANCIAL DATA:
Amount of support per award: $5,000 stipend.

NO. MOST RECENT APPLICANTS: 5 to 10 annually.

NO. AWARDS: 1 annually.

APPLICATION INFO:
Letter of application should include a vitae, statement concerning the proposed project and its relationship to Library of Congress holdings, tentative schedule for tenure of the fellowship and three letters of recommendation by persons qualified to judge the project and the applicant's fitness to undertake it.

Duration: Two to three months.

Deadline: April 1. Award announced in June.

PUBLICATIONS:
Annual report.

OFFICERS:
Vicki Ruiz, President
James R. Grossman, Executive Director
Robert A. Schneider, Editor, *American Historical Review*
Randy B. Norell, Controller

ADDRESS INQUIRIES TO:
J. Franklin Jameson Fellowship
(See e-mail address above.)

THE AMERICAN HISTORICAL ASSOCIATION [566]

400 A Street, S.E.
Washington, DC 20003
(202) 544-2422
Fax: (202) 544-8307
E-mail: awards@historians.org
Web Site: www.historians.org

FOUNDED: 1884

AREAS OF INTEREST:
Scholarly research.

NAME(S) OF PROGRAMS:
- **Fellowship in Aerospace History**

TYPE:
Fellowships. The Association annually funds at least one fellow for a period of six to nine months, to undertake a proposed research project related to aerospace history. The Fellowship is supported by the National Aeronautics and Space Administration (NASA).

YEAR PROGRAM STARTED: 1986

PURPOSE:
To provide a fellow with an opportunity to engage in significant and sustained advanced research in all aspects of the history of aerospace from the earliest human interest in flight to the present, including cultural and intellectual history, economic history, history of law and public policy and the history of science, engineering and management.

LEGAL BASIS:
Nonprofit association.

ELIGIBILITY:
Applicants must possess a Doctorate degree in history or in a closely related field or be enrolled as a student, having completed all course work, in a doctoral degree-granting program.

The Fellowship term is for a period of at least six months, but not more than nine months, and should commence no later than November 15. The fellow will be expected to devote the term entirely to the proposed research project. Office space is not provided with the Fellowship, and residency is not required; however, fellows are encouraged to take advantage of the resources of the National Aeronautics and Space Administration, the National Academies of Science, the Library of Congress, the Smithsonian Air and Space Museum and other collections in the Washington, DC area.

FINANCIAL DATA:
Amount of support per award: $20,000 stipend for a six- to nine-month fellowship. The stipend is adjustable to the length of the fellowship term.

NO. AWARDS: 1 per year.

APPLICATION INFO:
Applicants must complete an application form, available online, and offer a specific and detailed research proposal that will be the basis of the fellow's research during the term. At the term's conclusion, the fellow will be expected to write a report and present a paper or public lecture on the Fellowship experience.

Duration: Six to nine months.

Deadline: April 1.

PUBLICATIONS:
Annual report.

OFFICERS:
Vicki Ruiz, President
James R. Grossman, Executive Director
Robert A. Schneider, Editor, *American Historical Review*
Randy B. Norell, Controller

ADDRESS INQUIRIES TO:
Fellowship in Aerospace History
(See address above.)

*SPECIAL STIPULATIONS:
Funds may not be used to support tuition or fees. A fellow may not hold other major fellowships or grants during the fellowship term, except sabbatical and supplemental grants from their own institutions and small grants from other sources for specific research expenses. Sources of anticipated support must be listed in the application form.

AMERICAN INSTITUTE OF THE HISTORY OF PHARMACY

University of Wisconsin School of Pharmacy
Rennebohm Hall
777 Highland Avenue
Madison, WI 53705-2222
(608) 262-5378
E-mail: gia@aihp.org
Web Site: www.aihp.org

TYPE:
Grants-in-aid; Research grants.

See entry 2458 for full listing.

THE AMERICAN NUMISMATIC SOCIETY [567]

75 Varick Street, Floor 11
New York, NY 10013-1917
(212) 571-4470
Fax: (212) 571-4479
E-mail: ans@numismatics.org
Web Site: www.numismatics.org

FOUNDED: 1858

AREAS OF INTEREST:
Numismatics, history and archaeology.

NAME(S) OF PROGRAMS:
- **Frances M. Schwartz Fellowship**

TYPE:
Fellowships.

YEAR PROGRAM STARTED: 1994

PURPOSE:
To support work and the study of numismatic and museum methodology at the Society.

ELIGIBILITY:
Applicants must have a B.A. or equivalent.

GEOG. RESTRICTIONS: United States.

FINANCIAL DATA:
Amount of support per award: The stipend will vary with the term of tenure (normally the academic year) but will not exceed $2,000.

NO. AWARDS: 1.

APPLICATION INFO:
Detailed guidelines are available from the Society.

Duration: Up to one year.

ADDRESS INQUIRIES TO:
Board Secretary
(See address above.)

THE AMERICAN NUMISMATIC SOCIETY [568]

75 Varick Street, 11th Floor
New York, NY 10013
(212) 571-4470 ext. 110
Fax: (212) 571-4479
E-mail: ans@numismatics.org
Web Site: www.numismatics.org

FOUNDED: 1858

AREAS OF INTEREST:
Numismatics (coins and medals), history and archaeology.

NAME(S) OF PROGRAMS:
- **The Donald Groves Fund**

TYPE:
Fellowships.

YEAR PROGRAM STARTED: 1958

PURPOSE:
To promote publication in the field of early American numismatics involving material dating no later than 1800.

LEGAL BASIS:
Nonprofit.

GEOG. RESTRICTIONS: United States.

FINANCIAL DATA:
Groves funding is available for travel and other expenses in association with research as well as for publication costs.

Amount of support per award: Varies.

Total amount of support: Varies.

APPLICATION INFO:
Applications should be addressed to the Secretary of the Society and should include an outline of the proposed research, the method of accomplishing the research, the funding requested and the specific uses to which funding will be put. Applications are reviewed periodically by a committee, which makes its recommendations to the Society's Board of Trustees.

Duration: Varies.

OFFICERS:
Dr. Ute Wartenberg Kagan, Executive Director

ADDRESS INQUIRIES TO:
Secretary of the Society
(See address above.)

BERKSHIRE CONFERENCE OF WOMEN HISTORIANS [569]

543 Bramhall Avenue
Jersey City, NJ 07304
(201) 521-9195
(201) 463-6749
E-mail: secretary@berksconference.org
Web Site: www.berksconference.org

FOUNDED: 1930

AREAS OF INTEREST:
Women's history.

TYPE:
Awards/prizes. One prize awarded annually for the best first book and one for the best article of historical scholarship published by a woman historian in any field of history during the preceding year.

YEAR PROGRAM STARTED: 1972

PURPOSE:
To promote historical scholarship by women.

ELIGIBILITY:
The book or article must have been published in the year preceding the award date.

FINANCIAL DATA:
Amount of support per award: $1,000 for each book prize; $500 for each article prize.

Total amount of support: $1,500.

NO. MOST RECENT APPLICANTS: 150.

NO. AWARDS: 1 award in each category per year.

APPLICATION INFO:
Detailed guidelines are available on the Conference web site.

Deadline: January 15. Notification in June.

ADDRESS INQUIRIES TO:
Barbara Balliet, Secretary
(See e-mail address above.)

JOHN CARTER BROWN LIBRARY [570]

Brown University
94 George Street
Providence, RI 02906
(401) 863-2725
Fax: (401) 863-3477
E-mail: jcb-fellowships@brown.edu
Web Site: www.jcbl.org

FOUNDED: 1846

AREAS OF INTEREST:
Historical studies pertaining to the Age of Exploration, Latin American history before 1830, North American history to approximately 1800, European impressions of America, New World travel, exploration and colonization. Also, Indian language, cartography, West Indies and Caribbean studies, maritime, slave trade, and the Jewish Experience in the colonial Americas, north and south.

NAME(S) OF PROGRAMS:

- **The John Carter Brown Library Research Fellowships**

TYPE:
Fellowships. The John Carter Brown Library (JCB), an independently funded institution for advanced research at Brown University, contains one of the world's premier collections of primary materials related to the discovery, exploration, and settlement of the New World to 1825, including books, maps, newspapers and other printed objects.

The Library offers both Short-term and Long-term Fellowships.

YEAR PROGRAM STARTED: 1981

PURPOSE:
To promote scholarly research at the library.

LEGAL BASIS:
Independently funded and administered library and research center.

ELIGIBILITY:
Fellowships and grants will be awarded on the basis of the applicant's scholarly qualifications, the merits of the project, and the appropriateness of the inquiry in relation to the holdings of the John Carter Brown Library.

Fellowships are open to scholars and writers working on all aspects of the Americas in the early modern period.

Short-term Fellowships are open to U.S. and foreign citizens who are engaged in predoctoral or postdoctoral, or independent research. Graduate students must have passed their preliminary or general examinations at the time of application.

Long-term Fellowships, some of which are funded by the National Endowment for the Humanities (NEH), for which an applicant must be an American citizen or have been resident in the U.S. for the three years preceding the application deadline. There are other long-term JCB Fellowships for which all nationalities are eligible. Graduate students are not eligible for Long-term Fellowships.

FINANCIAL DATA:
Amount of support per award: Short-term Fellowships: $2,100 per month; Long-term Fellowships: $4,200 per month.

Total amount of support: Varies.

NO. AWARDS: Approximately 40 for the year 2014-15.

APPLICATION INFO:
Application form is available online; only online applications will be accepted.

Duration: Short-term Fellowships: Two to four months; Long-term Fellowships: Five to 10 months.

Deadline: December 1. Announcements by April 15.

PUBLICATIONS:
Application guidelines.

STAFF:
Valerie Andrews, Fellowship Coordinator

ADDRESS INQUIRIES TO:
See e-mail address above.

*PLEASE NOTE:
Recipients of all Fellowships must relocate to Providence and be in continuous residence at the John Carter Brown Library for the entire term of the award. Rooms are available for rent at Fiering House, the JCB Fellows' residence, a beautifully restored 1869 house just four blocks from the Library. Those living within commuting distance of the Library (approximately 45 miles distant) are ordinarily not eligible for JCB Fellowships.

CANADIAN INSTITUTE OF UKRAINIAN STUDIES [571]

University of Alberta
430 Pembina Hall
Edmonton AB T6G 2H8 Canada
(780) 492-2972
Fax: (780) 492-4967
E-mail: cius@ualberta.ca
Web Site: www.cius.ca

FOUNDED: 1976

AREAS OF INTEREST:
Studies in history, literature, language, education, social sciences, library sciences and women's studies.

NAME(S) OF PROGRAMS:

- **The Helen Darcovich Memorial Doctoral Fellowship**
- **Neporany Doctoral Fellowship**
- **Research Grants**
- **Stasiuk Master's Research Fellowship**

TYPE:
Fellowships; Research grants; Scholarships.

PURPOSE:
Fellowships: To aid students to complete a thesis on a Ukrainian or Ukrainian and Canadian topic in education, history, law, humanities, social sciences, women's studies or library sciences. Research grants: To aid scholars with research-related costs.

FINANCIAL DATA:
Total amount of support: Over $100,000 for the year 2015.

NO. MOST RECENT APPLICANTS: Over 100.

NO. AWARDS: Helen Darcovich Memorial Doctoral Fellowship, Neporany Doctoral Fellowship and Stasiuk Master's Research Fellowship: 2 per fellowship; Research grants: 46.

APPLICATION INFO:
Applicants should contact the Institute.

Duration: Varies.

Deadline: March 1.

ADDRESS INQUIRIES TO:
Iryna Fedoriw, Administrator
(See address above.)

COLLEGE OF PHYSICIANS OF PHILADELPHIA [572]

Francis Clark Wood Institute for the History of Medicine
19 South 22nd Street
Philadelphia, PA 19103-3097
(215) 399-2305
Fax: (215) 575-3499
E-mail: blander@collegeofphysicians.org
Web Site: www.collegeofphysicians.org

FOUNDED: 1787

AREAS OF INTEREST:
The history of medicine.

NAME(S) OF PROGRAMS:
- **Wood Institute Travel Grants**

TYPE:
Travel grants; Visiting scholars. This program allows scholars to conduct short-term research in the College's Library and/or Mutter Museum.

YEAR PROGRAM STARTED: 1983

PURPOSE:
To encourage the study and appreciation of medicine in the broader historical and social context in response to current health care issues and public and professional interests.

LEGAL BASIS:
501(c)(3) not-for-profit educational institution.

ELIGIBILITY:
Applicants must reside more than 75 miles from Philadelphia to be eligible. Grants are available to scholars and bona fide researchers.

FINANCIAL DATA:
Amount of support per award: Up to $1,500.
Total amount of support: Up to $1,500.

NO. MOST RECENT APPLICANTS: 15.

NO. AWARDS: Varies.

APPLICATION INFO:
Applicants should submit:
(1) one-page statement of the research project and the applicability of the College's resources;
(2) curriculum vitae (not to exceed three pages in length);
(3) budget estimate of travel and lodging needs and;
(4) one letter of reference (to be sent directly from the source to the College).

Electronic applications are strongly encouraged.

Duration: One to four weeks.

ADDRESS INQUIRIES TO:
Beth Lander, Librarian
(See address above.)

COLUMBIA UNIVERSITY [573]

517 Butler Library
535 West 114th Street
New York, NY 10027
(212) 854-2247
Fax: (212) 854-4972
E-mail: annthornton@columbia.edu
Web Site: library.columbia.edu/about/awards/bancroft.html

FOUNDED: 1754

NAME(S) OF PROGRAMS:
- **Bancroft Prizes**

TYPE:
Awards/prizes. Prizes of equal rank to be awarded to the authors of distinguished works in either or both American History, including biography and diplomacy.

YEAR PROGRAM STARTED: 1948

PURPOSE:
To honor the authors of books of distinguished merit and distinction, upon the subject of American history in its broadest sense.

LEGAL BASIS:
University.

ELIGIBILITY:
Awards are made for books first published in the previous calendar year. The competition is open to all persons whether connected with Columbia University or not, and whether citizens of the U.S. or any other country.

The word "American" is interpreted to include all the Americas, North, Central and South; however, the award is confined to works originally written in English or of which there is a published translation in English. Volumes of papers, letters and speeches of famous Americans, unless edited by the author himself, are not eligible. Autobiography comes within the terms of the prize, but books reporting on recent personal experiences of Americans, within a limited area both in time and geography, are not considered eligible.

Previous winners are eligible for an award in a later year.

FINANCIAL DATA:
Amount of support per award: $10,000.
Total amount of support: $20,000 to $30,000 annually.

NO. MOST RECENT APPLICANTS: 225.

NO. AWARDS: 2 to 3.

APPLICATION INFO:
Works submitted in competition may be sent to the Bancroft Prize Committee at the address above. It is requested that four copies be furnished, three for jury members and one for the Libraries of Columbia University. A letter should accompany the books so that acknowledgement may be made.

Deadline: Works may be submitted after June 1 and before November 1. Page-proof copy may be submitted after November 1 provided the work will be published after that date and before December 31 of the year preceding the award.

ADDRESS INQUIRIES TO:
Bancroft Prize Committee
(See address above.)

THE COORDINATING COUNCIL FOR WOMEN IN HISTORY, INC.

6042 Blue Point Court
Clarksville, MD 21209
(805) 705-7097
E-mail: execdir@theccwh.org
Web Site: www.theccwh.org

TYPE:
Awards/prizes. The Catherine Prelinger Award is given to a scholar, with a Ph.D. or A.B.D., whose career has not followed a traditional academic path through secondary and higher education and whose work has contributed to women in the historical profession.

See entry 1057 for full listing.

THE COORDINATING COUNCIL FOR WOMEN IN HISTORY, INC. [574]

6042 Blue Point Court
Clarksville, MD 21209
(805) 705-7097
E-mail: execdir@theccwh.org
Web Site: www.theccwh.org

AREAS OF INTEREST:
Women's history.

NAME(S) OF PROGRAMS:
- **CCWH/Berkshire Conference of Women Historians Graduate Student Fellowship**
- **Nupur Chaudhuri First Article Prize**
- **Carol Gold Best Article Award**
- **Ida B. Wells Graduate Student Fellowship**

TYPE:
Awards/prizes; Fellowships.

PURPOSE:
To support the exploration of the diverse experiences and histories of all women; to educate men and women on the status of women in the historical profession; to promote research and interpretation in areas of women's history.

ELIGIBILITY:
CCWH/Berkshire Conference of Women Historians Graduate Student Fellowship: Applicant must be a woman graduate student completing a dissertation in a history department.

Nupur Chaudhuri First Article Prize: Applicant must be a CCWH member whose first article is published in a refereed journal.

Carol Gold Best Article Award: Applicant must have received the rank of Associate Professor at the time of publication and must be a current member of the CCWH.

Ida B. Wells Graduate Student Fellowship: Applicant must be an A.B.D. woman graduate student working on a historical dissertation, not necessarily in a history department. Applicants in interdisciplinary areas such as women's studies or ethnic studies are particularly welcome.

GEOG. RESTRICTIONS: United States.

FINANCIAL DATA:
Amount of support per award: CCWH/Berkshire Conference, Nupur Chaudhuri Prize and Wells Fellowships: $1,000; Carol Gold Best Article Award: $500.

APPLICATION INFO:
Applications are available on the Council web site.

Deadline: May 15.

ADDRESS INQUIRIES TO:
Sandra Trudgen Dawson, Executive Director
(See e-mail address above.)

CUSHWA CENTER FOR THE STUDY OF AMERICAN CATHOLICISM [575]

407 Geddes Hall
University of Notre Dame
Notre Dame, IN 46556
(574) 631-5441
Fax: (574) 631-8471
E-mail: cushwa@nd.edu
Web Site: www.cushwa.nd.edu

NAME(S) OF PROGRAMS:
- **Hibernian Research Award**

TYPE:
Research grants; Travel grants. The Hibernian Research Award is offered to further the scholarly study of Irish America by scholars of any academic discipline engaged in a research project studying the Irish experience in the U.S.

PURPOSE:
To promote the scholarly study of the Irish in the U.S.

ELIGIBILITY:
Awards are made to scholars in any academic discipline.

FINANCIAL DATA:
Amount of support per award: Maximum $2,000.

APPLICATION INFO:
Applicants must include the following:
(1) a current curriculum vitae;
(2) a brief 1,000-word description of the research project;
(3) a proposed budget and;
(4) letters of recommendation from two people familiar with the applicant's work. These letters of recommendation should be sent directly to the Cushwa Center.

Deadline: December 31. Applicants will be notified in March.

DIRECTORS:
Kathleen Sprows Cummings

ADDRESS INQUIRIES TO:
Kathleen Sprows Cummings, Director
(See address above.)

CUSHWA CENTER FOR THE STUDY OF AMERICAN CATHOLICISM [576]

407 Geddes Hall
University of Notre Dame
Notre Dame, IN 46556
(574) 631-5441
Fax: (574) 631-8471
E-mail: cushwa@nd.edu
Web Site: www.cushwa.nd.edu

FOUNDED: 1980

AREAS OF INTEREST:
Catholicism in the U.S.

NAME(S) OF PROGRAMS:
- **Research Travel Grants**

TYPE:
Travel grants. Research Travel Grants support projects that require substantial use of the collection of the library and/or the archives of the University of Notre Dame and help to defray travel and lodging costs.

YEAR PROGRAM STARTED: 1980

PURPOSE:
To make it possible for scholars to make use of the Notre Dame archives.

LEGAL BASIS:
University.

ELIGIBILITY:
Grants are made to scholars in any academic discipline.

FINANCIAL DATA:
Amount of support per award: Typically, Research Travel Grants are $1,000 or less, unless extenuating circumstances necessitate greater funding. Assistance at finding affordable accommodations is available.

Total amount of support: Varies.

APPLICATION INFO:
Applicant must include the following:
(1) one copy of the application form;
(2) current curriculum vitae;
(3) 1,000-word description of the project to be undertaken at the center and;
(4) proposed budget estimating lodging and research expenses.

Duration: Varies.

Deadline: December 31. Applicants will be notified in March.

STAFF:
Kathleen Sprows Cummings, Director

ADDRESS INQUIRIES TO:
Kathleen Sprows Cummings, Director
(See address above.)

CUSHWA CENTER FOR THE STUDY OF AMERICAN CATHOLICISM [577]

407 Geddes Hall
University of Notre Dame
Notre Dame, IN 46556
(574) 631-5441
Fax: (574) 631-8471
E-mail: cushwa@nd.edu
Web Site: www.cushwa.nd.edu

FOUNDED: 2012

AREAS OF INTEREST:
Catholicism in the U.S.

NAME(S) OF PROGRAMS:
- **Peter R. D'Agostino Research Travel Grant**

TYPE:
Travel grants. Offered in conjunction with Italian Studies at Notre Dame, the Peter R. D'Agostino Research Travel Grant supports research in Roman archives for a significant publication project on U.S. Catholic history.

YEAR PROGRAM STARTED: 2012

PURPOSE:
To facilitate the study of the American past from an international perspective.

LEGAL BASIS:
University.

FINANCIAL DATA:
Amount of support per award: $5,000 annually.

APPLICATION INFO:
Applicant must include the following:
(1) one copy of the application form;
(2) current curriculum vitae and;
(3) 1,000-word description of the project to be undertaken.

Deadline: December 31.

ADDRESS INQUIRIES TO:
Kathleen Sprows Cummings, Director
(See address above.)

CUSHWA CENTER FOR THE STUDY OF AMERICAN CATHOLICISM [578]

407 Geddes Hall
University of Notre Dame
Notre Dame, IN 46556
(574) 631-5441
Fax: (574) 631-8471
E-mail: cushwa@nd.edu
Web Site: www.cushwa.nd.edu

AREAS OF INTEREST:
Catholicism in the U.S.

NAME(S) OF PROGRAMS:
- **Theodore M. Hesburgh Research Travel Grant**

TYPE:
Travel grants.

YEAR PROGRAM STARTED: 2016

PURPOSE:
To support research and writing projects that make use of materials pertaining to Father Hesburgh.

LEGAL BASIS:
University.

FINANCIAL DATA:
Amount of support per award: Varies, depending on budget.

APPLICATION INFO:
Applicant must include the following:
(1) one copy of the application form;
(2) current curriculum vitae;
(3) 1,000-word description of the project to be undertaken and;
(4) two letters of recommendation.

Deadline: April 1 and October 1.

ADDRESS INQUIRIES TO:
Kathleen Sprows Cummings, Director
(See address above.)

SHELBY CULLOM DAVIS CENTER FOR HISTORICAL STUDIES [579]

Princeton University
129 Dickinson Hall
Princeton, NJ 08544-1017
(609) 258-4997
Fax: (609) 258-5326
E-mail: jhoule@princeton.edu
Web Site: www.princeton.edu/dav

FOUNDED: 1968

AREAS OF INTEREST:
Historical research.

TYPE:
Fellowships.

YEAR PROGRAM STARTED: 1969

LEGAL BASIS:
Center is part of a Charitable Educational Institution.

ELIGIBILITY:
Candidates must have a Ph.D. degree. Fellowships are awarded on the strength of the candidate's research projects, the relationship of those projects to the Center's theme, the candidate's previous scholarly work, and the candidate's ability to contribute to the intellectual life and intellectual exchange of the Center.

Princeton faculty members are not eligible.

Applicants who are non-U.S. nationals or who are members of traditionally underrepresented groups are encouraged to apply.

FINANCIAL DATA:
Fellowship includes salary plus research expenses.

Amount of support per award: Varies.

Total amount of support: Varies.

NO. AWARDS: 7 for the year 2015-16.

APPLICATION INFO:
Applicants must apply online and submit the following:
(1) cover letter;
(2) curriculum vitae;
(3) research proposal, preceded by a one paragraph abstract and;
(4) contact information for three references.

Duration: One semester or one academic year. Nonrenewable.

Deadline: December 1. Notification in early March.

EXECUTIVE COMMITTEE:
Philip Nord, Director

ADDRESS INQUIRIES TO:
Jennifer Goldman, Manager
(See address above.)

THE DIRKSEN CONGRESSIONAL CENTER

2815 Broadway
Pekin, IL 61554
(309) 347-7113
Fax: (309) 347-6432
E-mail: fmackaman@dirksencenter.org
Web Site: www.dirksencongressionalcenter.org

TYPE:
Research grants; Seed money grants; Travel grants. Financial awards to individuals conducting research about the U.S. Congress and its leaders.

See entry 1933 for full listing.

GERMAN HISTORICAL INSTITUTE [580]

1607 New Hampshire Avenue, N.W.
Washington, DC 20009-2562
(202) 387-3355
Fax: (202) 387-6437
E-mail: fellowships@ghi-dc.org
Web Site: www.ghi-dc.org

FOUNDED: 1987

AREAS OF INTEREST:
German and U.S. history, transatlantic studies and comparative studies in economic, social, cultural and political history.

NAME(S) OF PROGRAMS:
- **Doctoral and Postdoctoral Fellowships**

TYPE:
Fellowships. The Institute awards short-term fellowships to German and American doctoral students as well as postdoctoral scholars/Habilitanden in the fields of German history, the history of German-American relations, and the role of Germany and the U.S. in international relations.

YEAR PROGRAM STARTED: 1989

PURPOSE:
To support research programme for doctoral students and postdoctoral scholars in the fields of German history, the history of German-American relations, the role of Germany and the U.S. in international relations and the history of consumption and consumerism.

ELIGIBILITY:
Open to German and U.S. doctoral and postdoctoral students.

FINANCIAL DATA:
Amount of support per award: Monthly stipend for Europeans: EUR 1,700 for doctoral students and EUR 3,000 for postdoctoral scholars. Monthly stipend for Americans: $1,900 for doctoral students and $3,200 for postdoctoral scholars.

NO. MOST RECENT APPLICANTS: 150 annually.

NO. AWARDS: 40 to 50 annually.

APPLICATION INFO:
Applications should include cover letter, curriculum vitae, proof of academic degree (or transcripts), project description (3,000 words), research schedule for the fellowship period, and at least one letter of reference. Although applicants may write in either English or German, it is recommended that they use the language in which they are most proficient.

Duration: One to five months, but can be extended one month.

Deadline: April 1 and October 1 annually.

ADDRESS INQUIRIES TO:
Bryan Hart, Program Officer
(See address above.)

HAGLEY MUSEUM AND LIBRARY [581]

Center for the History of
Business, Technology and Society
298 Buck Road
Wilmington, DE 19807
(302) 658-2400 ext. 243
Fax: (302) 655-3188
E-mail: clockman@hagley.org
Web Site: www.hagley.org

FOUNDED: 1953

AREAS OF INTEREST:
American business, economic and labor history and the history of technology and science.

NAME(S) OF PROGRAMS:
- **Henry Belin du Pont Dissertation Fellowship in Business, Technology, and Society**
- **Henry Belin du Pont Research Grants**
- **Hagley Exploratory Research Grant**

TYPE:
Fellowships; Research grants; Travel grants; Visiting scholars. Grants to support short-term research in the imprint, manuscript, pictorial and artifact collections of the Hagley Museum and Library.

The Henry Belin du Pont Dissertation Fellowship in Business, Technology, and Society supports research and writing by candidates for doctoral degrees. Projects should demonstrate superior intellectual quality and make substantial use of Hagley's collections.

Henry Belin du Pont Research Grants support research in the collections of the museum and library.

Hagley Exploratory Research Grant supports a one-week visit by scholars who believe that their project will benefit from Hagley research collections, but need the opportunity to explore them on-site to determine if a Henry Belin du Pont research grant application is warranted.

YEAR PROGRAM STARTED: 1962

PURPOSE:
To encourage and support research in the collections.

LEGAL BASIS:
Nonprofit educational institution.

ELIGIBILITY:
Degree candidates and advanced scholars working in Hagley's areas of collecting and research interest are invited to apply. Applications should include research proposals specifying the collections or materials to be studied. Residential award, not a scholarship for college or graduate school.

Hagley Exploratory Research Grant: Priority will be given to junior scholars with innovative projects that seek to expand on existing scholarships.

FINANCIAL DATA:
Amount of support per award: Hagley Exploratory Research Grant: Stipend of $400; Henry Belin du Pont Dissertation Fellowship: Up to $6,500; Henry Belin du Pont Research Grants: $400 per week for recipients residing more than 50 miles from Hagley, and $200 per week for those within 50 miles.

Total amount of support: Approximately $50,000.

APPLICATION INFO:
Application forms and guidelines are available online.

Duration: Hagley Exploratory Research Grant: One week; Henry Belin du Pont Dissertation Fellowship: Up to four months; Henry Belin du Pont Research Grants: Up to eight weeks.

Deadline: Hagley Exploratory Research Grant and Henry Belin du Pont Research Grants: March 31, June 30 and October 31; Henry Belin du Pont Dissertation Fellowship in Business, Technology, and Society: November 15.

PUBLICATIONS:
Guides to Collection; application; guidelines.

STAFF:
David A. Cole, Executive Director
Roger Horowitz, Center Director
Carol Ressler Lockman, Center Manager

RESEARCH STAFF:
Lynn Catanese, Chief Curator of Library Collections
Max Moeller, Curator, Published Collections
Kevin Martin, Andrew W. Mellon Curator of Audiovisual Collections

ADDRESS INQUIRIES TO:
Carol Ressler Lockman, Center Manager
(See address above.)

THE HISTORIC NEW ORLEANS COLLECTION [582]

533 Royal Street
New Orleans, LA 70130
(504) 523-4662
Fax: (504) 293-8162
E-mail: wrc@hnoc.org
Web Site: www.hnoc.org

FOUNDED: 1966

AREAS OF INTEREST:
Louisiana history and support of research in the field.

NAME(S) OF PROGRAMS:
- **Kemper and Leila Williams Prize in Louisiana History**

TYPE:
Awards/prizes.

YEAR PROGRAM STARTED: 1975

PURPOSE:
To encourage excellence in the writing and publishing of Louisiana history.

LEGAL BASIS:
Nonprofit foundation.

ELIGIBILITY:
Published books are eligible, but only in the year of their publication or completion.

FINANCIAL DATA:
Amount of support per award: $1,500.
Total amount of support: $1,500.

NO. MOST RECENT APPLICANTS: 20.

NO. AWARDS: 1.

APPLICATION INFO:
Application forms are available on the web site. Four copies of each entry must be submitted.

Deadline: January 16 for works published the previous calendar year. Announcement in March.

PUBLICATIONS:
Application guidelines.

OFFICERS:
Mrs. William K. Christovich, Chairperson
Drew Jardine, President
John Kallenborn, Vice President
Hilton S. Bell
Bonnie Boyd
E. Alexandra Stafford
John E. Walker

STAFF:
Priscilla Lawrence, Executive Director

ADDRESS INQUIRIES TO:
John Lawrence, Chairman
Williams Prize Committee
(See address above.)

THE HISTORIC NEW ORLEANS COLLECTION [583]

533 Royal Street
New Orleans, LA 70130
(504) 523-4662
Fax: (504) 598-7108
E-mail: wrc@hnoc.org
Web Site: www.hnoc.org

FOUNDED: 1966

AREAS OF INTEREST:
Louisiana history and support of research in the field.

NAME(S) OF PROGRAMS:
- **The Dianne Woest Fellowship in the Arts and Humanities**

TYPE:
Fellowships.

YEAR PROGRAM STARTED: 2005

PURPOSE:
To encourage research using The Historic New Orleans Collection, as well as other research facilities in the greater New Orleans area.

ELIGIBILITY:
Open to doctoral candidates, academic and museum professionals and independent scholars. U.S. citizenship not required, but applicants should be fluent in English.

Fellows will be expected to:
(1) present a public lecture during their term of residence and;
(2) acknowledge The Collection in any published work drawing on fellowship research.

FINANCIAL DATA:
Amount of support per award: Approximately $4,000 stipend.

Total amount of support: Varies.

NO. MOST RECENT APPLICANTS: 60.

NO. AWARDS: 1 to 3.

APPLICATION INFO:
Information may be obtained by e-mailing Jason Wiese, Associate Director, at jasonw@hnoc.org.

Duration: One to three months.

Deadline: November 1. Announcement February 1. Research to begin on or after April 1.

ADDRESS INQUIRIES TO:
Jason Wiese, Associate Director
(See address above.)

*SPECIAL STIPULATIONS:
Fellows may select their period of residence, but all research must commence and conclude during the specified fiscal year April 1 to May 31.

HISTORY COLORADO STATE HISTORICAL FUND [584]

1200 Broadway
Denver, CO 80203
(303) 866-2825
Fax: (303) 866-2041
E-mail: shf@state.co.us
Web Site: www.historycolorado.org/oahp/state-historical-fund

FOUNDED: 1990

AREAS OF INTEREST:
Historic preservation.

TYPE:
Project/program grants. Grants for historic preservation projects.

The State Historical Fund was created by the 1990 constitutional amendment allowing limited gaming in the towns of Cripple Creek, Central City and Black Hawk. The amendment directs that a portion of the gaming tax revenues be used for historic preservation throughout the state.

YEAR PROGRAM STARTED: 1990

PURPOSE:
To promote historic preservation throughout the state of Colorado.

ELIGIBILITY:
Criteria vary for different types of grants. Funds are distributed through a competitive process, and all projects must demonstrate strong public benefit and community support. The Fund assists in a wide variety of preservation projects, including restoration and rehabilitation of historic buildings, architectural assessments, archaeological excavations, designation and interpretation of historic places, preservation planning studies, and education and training programs.

Organizations have to have 501(c)(3) not-for-profit status. Religious organizations may apply, but no grants are given to individuals.

Historic preservation projects in the state of Colorado only.

GEOG. RESTRICTIONS: Colorado.

FINANCIAL DATA:
Varies for different types of grants.

Amount of support per award: Mini-grants: Up to $35,000. Full grants: Up to approximately $200,000.

APPLICATION INFO:
Contact the History Colorado office and use the application on its web site. Colorado Substitute W9 Form for documentation required.

Duration: Varies; grantees can reapply for new projects.

Deadline: April 1 and October 1.

ADDRESS INQUIRIES TO:
Outreach Specialist
(See phone number above.)

HISTORY OF SCIENCE SOCIETY [585]

440 Geddes Hall
University of Notre Dame
Notre Dame, IN 46556
(574) 631-1194
Fax: (574) 631-1533
E-mail: info@hssonline.org
Web Site: www.hssonline.org

FOUNDED: 1924

AREAS OF INTEREST:
History of science and its cultural influences.

NAME(S) OF PROGRAMS:
- **Derek Price/Rod Webster Prize**

TYPE:
Awards/prizes. Prize for the best scholarly article published in *Isis* during the past three years.

YEAR PROGRAM STARTED: 1979

PURPOSE:
To acknowledge the best scholarly work to appear in *Isis*.

LEGAL BASIS:
Nonprofit 501(c)(3).

ELIGIBILITY:
Applicant must have published an article in *Isis*.

FINANCIAL DATA:
Amount of support per award: $1,000.

NO. AWARDS: 1 per year.

PUBLICATIONS:
Syllabus samplers, Topical Essays for Teachers, Non-Western Science.

ADDRESS INQUIRIES TO:
Robert J. Malone, Executive Director
(See address above.)

HISTORY OF SCIENCE SOCIETY [586]

440 Geddes Hall
University of Notre Dame
Notre Dame, IN 46556
(574) 631-1194
Fax: (574) 631-1533
E-mail: info@hssonline.org
Web Site: www.hssonline.org

FOUNDED: 1924

AREAS OF INTEREST:
History of science, women in science and science service.

NAME(S) OF PROGRAMS:
- **Watson Davis and Helen Miles Davis Prize**
- **Joseph H. Hazen Education Prize**
- **Suzanne J. Levinson Prize**
- **Pfizer Prize**
- **Nathan Reingold Prize**
- **Margaret W. Rossiter History of Women in Science Prize**

TYPE:
Awards/prizes. The Davis Prize honors books in the history of science directed to a wide public and was established through a long-term pledge from Miles and Audrey Davis.

The Joseph H. Hazen Education Prize recognizes excellence in teaching in the history of science.

The Levinson Prize is awarded in even-numbered years to an outstanding book in the life sciences and natural history.

The Pfizer Prize honors the best English-language work related to the history of science published in the preceding three years.

The Nathan Reingold Prize is given for an original essay in the history of science and its cultural influences. Essay must be no more than 8,000 words in length and thoroughly documented.

The Margaret W. Rossiter History of Women in Science Prize honors an outstanding book, or in even-numbered years an article, published in the preceding four years.

YEAR PROGRAM STARTED: 1955

PURPOSE:
To recognize and reward distinguished writing in the field of the history of science.

LEGAL BASIS:
Nonprofit.

ELIGIBILITY:
For the Davis Prize, books should be introductory in assuming no previous knowledge of the subject and be directed to audiences of beginning students and general readers. Books should introduce an entire field, a chronological period, a national tradition or the work of a noteworthy individual. Multi-authored or edited books are eligible, whereas unrevised reprints of previously published works are ineligible.

For the History of Women in Science Prize, books may take a biographical, institutional, theoretical or other approach. Include in the topic, "Women in Science," discussions of women's activities in science, analyses of past scientific practices that deal explicitly with gender and investigations regarding women as viewed by scientists. These may relate to medicine, technology and the social sciences as well as the natural sciences.

The Levinson Prize is open to all books in the life sciences and natural history published in the four years prior to the award year.

The Pfizer Prize is open to all books published in English. The quality of the work is the overriding criterion.

The Reingold Prize is open to graduate students at any International college. Essays dealing with medical subjects are not accepted, though papers dealing with the relations between medicine and the natural sciences are welcome.

FINANCIAL DATA:
Amount of support per award: Davis, Hazen, Levinson and Rossiter History of Women in Science Awards: $1,000; Pfizer Prize: $2,500; Reingold Prize: $500 award, $500 in travel expenses.

APPLICATION INFO:
Contact the Society for details.

Deadline: April 1.

PUBLICATIONS:
Newsletter.

OFFICERS:
Janet Browne, President
Bernard Lightman, Vice President
Adam Apt, Treasurer
Marsha Richmond, Secretary
H. Floris Cohen, Editor

ADDRESS INQUIRIES TO:
Robert J. Malone, Executive Director
(See address above.)

*PLEASE NOTE:
Society does not give grants, scholarships or fellowships.

HOOVER PRESIDENTIAL FOUNDATION

302 Parkside Drive
West Branch, IA 52358
(319) 643-5327
Fax: (319) 643-2391
E-mail: info@hooverassociation.org
Web Site: www.hooverassociation.org

TYPE:
Travel grants. Money is only available for travel to the Hoover Presidential Library in West Branch, IA. The program seeks to encourage scholarly use of the holdings of the Herbert Hoover Presidential Library. It is specifically intended to promote the study of subjects of interest and concern to Herbert Hoover, Lou Henry Hoover, their associates and other public figures as reflected in the Library's 150 manuscript collections.

See entry 1939 for full listing.

IEEE HISTORY CENTER [587]

Stevens Institute of Technology
Samuel C. Williams Library, Third Floor
One Castle Point on Hudson
Hoboken, NJ 07030
(732) 562-5468
Fax: (732) 562-6020
E-mail: ieee-history@ieee.org
Web Site: www.ieee.org/history_center

FOUNDED: 1884

AREAS OF INTEREST:
History of technology and sociology of technology.

NAME(S) OF PROGRAMS:
- **IEEE Fellowship in the History of Electrical and Computing Technology**
- **Internship in Electrical History**

TYPE:
Fellowships; Internships. Fellowship in the History of Electrical and Computing Technology: Award for one year of full-time doctoral or postdoctoral work in the history of electrical engineering and technology at a college or university of recognized standing.

Internship in Electrical History: Two-month internship for graduate research.

YEAR PROGRAM STARTED: 1980

ELIGIBILITY:
Fellowship in the History of Electrical and Computing Technology: Individuals doing graduate or postgraduate work in the history of electrical technology. Internship in Electrical History: Scholars at the beginning of their career studying the history of electrical technology and computing.

FINANCIAL DATA:
Total amount of support: Fellowship in the History of Electrical and Computing Technology: $17,000 annually; Internship in Electrical History: $3,500.

NO. MOST RECENT APPLICANTS: 12.

NO. AWARDS: 1 Fellowship and 1 Internship annually.

APPLICATION INFO:
Identification and description of a research project of value is an important part of the application procedure. Further information is available upon request to the Institute.

Duration: Fellowship in the History of Electrical and Computing Technology: One academic year; Internship in Electrical History: Two months.

Deadline: Fellowship in the History of Electrical and Computing Technology: February 1; Internship in Electrical History: March 1.

PUBLICATIONS:
Newsletter.

ADDRESS INQUIRIES TO:
Director, IEEE History Center
(See address above.)

IRISH AMERICAN CULTURAL INSTITUTE

P.O. Box 1716
Morristown, NJ 07962
(973) 605-1991
E-mail: info@iaci-usa.org
Web Site: www.iaci-usa.org

TYPE:
Awards/prizes; Exchange programs; Fellowships. Awards to artists, writers and organizations in Ireland for their efforts in Irish history, literature and art.

See entry 665 for full listing.

ISTITUTO ITALIANO PER GLI STUDI STORICI [588]

Via Benedetto Croce, 12
80134 Naples Italy
(39) 081 5517159
(39) 081 5512390
Fax: (39) 081 5514813
E-mail: info@iiss.it
Web Site: www.iiss.it

FOUNDED: 1947

AREAS OF INTEREST:
Postgraduate institute for the study of history, philosophy and literature.

NAME(S) OF PROGRAMS:
- **Federico II Scholarship**
- **Scholarships Istituto italiano per gli studi storici for Graduate Students and Young Postdocs, Italian and Foreign**

TYPE:
Awards/prizes; Conferences/seminars; Research grants; Scholarships. Awards for historical, literature and philosophical studies at the Istituto Italiano per gli Studi Storici in Naples.

Federico II Scholarship: Offered by the Universita di Napoli for graduates from Italian universities whose final thesis is in medieval studies.

YEAR PROGRAM STARTED: 1947

PURPOSE:
To promote historical, philosophical and literature studies.

LEGAL BASIS:
Private institution.

ELIGIBILITY:
These annual scholarships are offered to young graduates and those with a Doctorate, both Italian and non-Italian, in the disciplines of history, philosophy and literature. Applicants must have presented their final university dissertation before the final application date and must be less than 32 years of age.

Applications will not be accepted from candidates who:
(1) already received a scholarship from the

Istituto;
(2) will receive payment from another type of activity or;
(3) will be carrying out a research Doctorate or another scholarship (with financing).

FINANCIAL DATA:
The scholarship will be paid to the successful candidates in 12 monthly installments starting from November of the year of application.

Amount of support per award: Scholarships: EUR 9,700 for Campania Region; EUR 12,000 for students residing outside of Campania; Federico II Scholarship: EUR 10,300.

Total amount of support: EUR 260,000.

NO. MOST RECENT APPLICANTS: 171.

NO. AWARDS: 1 for Federico II; 15 Scholarships for Graduate Students and Young Postdocs, Italian and Foreign.

APPLICATION INFO:
Applications (including personal details, citizenship, residence, telephone numbers, e-mail address and a declaration of a clean police record) must be accompanied by the following documents:
(1) certificate of nationality (or photocopy of official identity card or passport);
(2) curriculum of studies, including languages spoken;
(3) degree certificate showing marks for individual exams, or Doctorate degree (for non-Italians, an equivalent degree certificate is required);
(4) copy of graduation or doctoral dissertation and of publications, both in hard copy and digital file;
(5) research project that the student intends to carry out at the Institute, including aims and objectives, timing, materials to be used and the research location;
(6) academic letters of reference and;
(7) list of other applications already made or to be made for similar scholarships and grants by November 1 of the year in which one is applying.

Applications which do not conform to the above requirements will not be considered.

Candidates who are shortlisted on the basis of their curriculum may be called for an interview by a Board of Examiners. Scholarships will be assigned by the Commission on evaluation of curriculum and interview results.

Duration: Twelve months (November to June for courses and July to October for research). The scholarship can be renewed for a second year.

Deadline: Application materials must be received no later than July 29. (Postal dates will not be accepted.)

PUBLICATIONS:
Annali Dell' Istituto Italiano Per Gli Studi Storici; series of monographs; series of historical, philosophical and literary texts.

DIRECTORS:
Prof. Natalino Irti, President
Dr. Marta Herling, Secretary-General
Dr. Elli Catello, Librarian
Dr. Stefano Palmieri, Editor of Publications
Piero Craveri
Giulio de Caprariis
Melina Decaro Bonella
Paola Franchomme
Giuseppe Galasso
Roberto Giordano
Maurizio Mattioli
Alberto Quadrio Curzio
Gennaro Sasso
Fulvio Tessitore

ADDRESS INQUIRIES TO:
Dr. Marta Herling, General Secretary
(See address above.)

*SPECIAL STIPULATIONS:
Fellows must carry out their research project and attend lessons until the end of the academic year.

From December to May, fellows must reside in Naples in order to follow the courses and seminars organized by the Institute. In the five months that follow, they can carry out their research at another institution, either in Italy or abroad. They must make a first report about their research activities by July 31 and a final one by October 31.

The Institute reserves the right to withdraw funding should fellows prove themselves to be seriously inadequate.

ITALIAN AMERICAN STUDIES ASSOCIATION [589]

P.O. Box 487
Millbrae, CA 94030
(408) 738-4564
Fax: (408) 864-5629
E-mail: quinnroseanne@deanza.edu
Web Site: www.italianamericanstudies.net

FOUNDED: 1966

AREAS OF INTEREST:
Encouragement of Italian-American studies, collection, preservation, study and popularization of materials that illuminate the Italian-American experience in the U.S. and Canada.

CONSULTING OR VOLUNTEER SERVICES:
Sponsors an annual national conference, resource depositories and maintains an information network.

NAME(S) OF PROGRAMS:
- **IASA Memorial Fellowship**

TYPE:
Fellowships.

YEAR PROGRAM STARTED: 1970

PURPOSE:
To promote understanding of the Italian experience in America.

LEGAL BASIS:
Nonprofit, tax-exempt organization.

FINANCIAL DATA:
Amount of support per award: $1,000.

Total amount of support: $1,000.

NO. AWARDS: 1.

APPLICATION INFO:
Contact the Association for details.

Duration: One year.

Deadline: September 29.

PUBLICATIONS:
Annual Proceedings.

OFFICERS:
George Guida, President

ADDRESS INQUIRIES TO:
Dr. Roseanne Giannini Quinn
(See address above.)

THE LYNDON BAINES JOHNSON FOUNDATION

2313 Red River Street
Austin, TX 78705-5702
(512) 232-2266
Fax: (512) 232-2285
E-mail: grants@lbjfoundation.org
Web Site: www.lbjfoundation.org

TYPE:
Fellowships; Research grants.

See entry 1943 for full listing.

KENTUCKY HISTORICAL SOCIETY [590]

100 West Broadway
Frankfort, KY 40601
(502) 564-1792
Fax: (502) 564-4701
E-mail: kent.whitworth@ky.gov
Web Site: history.ky.gov

FOUNDED: 1836

AREAS OF INTEREST:
Historical research and publishing.

NAME(S) OF PROGRAMS:
- **Scholarly Research Fellowship Program**

TYPE:
Fellowships; Research grants; Travel grants. Scholarly Research Fellowship Program encourages and promotes advanced research on all aspects of Kentucky-related local, regional, national and transnational history.

PURPOSE:
To assist - through these fellowships - researchers with travel and living expenses while using the Kentucky Historical Society research collections.

ELIGIBILITY:
These short-term fellowships are intended to support serious scholarly work. They enable individuals to pursue advanced study and research in the collections of the Kentucky Historical Society. Applications are welcome from independent scholars, as well as from college and university teachers, graduate students, scholars working in other related disciplines and public school teachers.

FINANCIAL DATA:
Amount of support per award: Typically $400 (for one week) to $1,600 (for four weeks).

NO. AWARDS: Typically 20 to 30 each year.

APPLICATION INFO:
Applications are available on the Kentucky Historical Society web site. All applications are peer-reviewed by a panel of leading historians.

Deadline: September 1 and March 1.

ADDRESS INQUIRIES TO:
Dr. Amanda Higgins
Coordinator, Research Fellowship Program
E-mail: amanda.higgins@ky.gov
Tel: (502) 564-1792 ext. 4440

LIBRARY COMPANY OF PHILADELPHIA [591]

1314 Locust Street
Philadelphia, PA 19107
(215) 546-3181
Fax: (215) 546-5167
E-mail: jgreen@librarycompany.org
Web Site: www.librarycompany.org

FOUNDED: 1731

AREAS OF INTEREST:
American studies.

NAME(S) OF PROGRAMS:
- **Albert M. Greenfield Foundation Dissertation Fellowships**
- **NEH Postdoctoral Fellowships**
- **Program in African-American History**
- **Program in Early American Economy and Society**
- **Research Fellowships in American History and Culture**

TYPE:
Fellowships. Albert M. Greenfield Foundation Dissertation Fellowship: Supports dissertation research in residence at the Library Company on any subject relevant to its collections.

Program in African-American History: Its Mellon Scholars Fellowship Program offers postdoctoral, dissertation and short-term fellowships to support scholarly work in African-American history from the 17th through the 19th centuries.

Program in Early American Economy and Society: Pre-1860 American economic and business history.

Research Fellowships in American History and Culture: 18th and 19th Century American social and cultural history.

YEAR PROGRAM STARTED: 1988

PURPOSE:
To promote early American historic studies.

ELIGIBILITY:
Both the short-term and long-term Fellowships support postdoctoral and dissertation research. Both also require that the project proposal demonstrate that the Library Company has a primary source central to the research topic. NEH fellows must be U.S. citizens or residents at least three years.

FINANCIAL DATA:
Amount of support per award: Long-term: $20,000 to $50,000; Short-term: $2,000.

Total amount of support: Approximately $170,000 annually.

CO-OP FUNDING PROGRAMS: The short-term fellowships are jointly sponsored with the Historical Society of Pennsylvania.

NO. MOST RECENT APPLICANTS: 200.

NO. AWARDS: Long-term: 15; Short-term: 32.

APPLICATION INFO:
For the short-term fellowships, applicants must complete the required electronic cover sheet and submit one portable document format (PDF) containing a resume and a two- to four-page description of the proposed research. One letter of recommendation should arrive under separate cover in PDF format as well. E-mail materials to fellowships@librarycompany.org.

Duration: Short-term: One month; Long-term: One semester.

Deadline: Program and Research Fellowships: March 1; Long-term Postdoctoral Fellowships: November 1.

ADDRESS INQUIRIES TO:
Jim Green, Fellowship Office
(See address above.)

JAMES MADISON MEMORIAL FELLOWSHIP FOUNDATION [592]

1613 Duke Street
Alexandria, VA 22314
(800) 525-6928
Fax: (319) 337-1204
E-mail: madison@scholarshipamerica.org
Web Site: www.jamesmadison.gov

FOUNDED: 1986

AREAS OF INTEREST:
The roots, principles, framing and development of the U.S. Constitution.

NAME(S) OF PROGRAMS:
- **James Madison Fellowship Program**

TYPE:
Fellowships. The Foundation awards fellowships to college seniors and college graduates without teaching experience (Junior Fellows) and to experienced secondary school teachers in grades seven-12 (Senior Fellows) who will normally enroll respectively in full- and part-time graduate study leading to one of the following Master's degrees: Master's degree in American history or political science, a degree of Master of Arts in Teaching in history or political science, or a related Master's degree in education that permits a concentration in American history, American government or social studies.

YEAR PROGRAM STARTED: 1992

PURPOSE:
To support the graduate study of the roots, principles, framing and development of the U.S. Constitution.

LEGAL BASIS:
Foundation.

ELIGIBILITY:
Each fellowship recipient must take at least 12 semester hours or their equivalent in topics directly related to the framing and history of the U.S. Constitution.

A James Madison Fellow must be a U.S. citizen or U.S. national, qualify for study toward one of the qualifying Master's degrees indicated and agree to teach full-time in a secondary school for no less than one year for each full academic year of study under a fellowship.

A Senior Fellow must be a full-time teacher of American history, American government, or social studies in grades seven through 12 during the previous year and be under contract or prospective contract to teach full-time as a secondary school teacher of the same subjects for the upcoming academic year.

A Junior Fellow must possess a Bachelor's degree or plan to receive a Bachelor's degree no later than August 31 of the year of application.

GEOG. RESTRICTIONS: United States and its territories.

FINANCIAL DATA:
Amount of support per award: Up to $24,000 for each award.

NO. MOST RECENT APPLICANTS: 400.

NO. AWARDS: 1 per state per year, as funding permits.

APPLICATION INFO:
Applicant must register online to complete the application process.

Duration: Up to five years for Senior Fellows. Up to two years for Junior Fellows.

Deadline: March 1, annually.

ADDRESS INQUIRIES TO:
James Madison Fellowship Program
One Scholarship Way
St. Peter, MN 56082

*SPECIAL STIPULATIONS:
No funding for Ph.D. programs.

JACOB RADER MARCUS CENTER OF THE AMERICAN JEWISH ARCHIVES

3101 Clifton Avenue
Cincinnati, OH 45220-2408
(513) 221-1875
Fax: (513) 221-7812
E-mail: kproffitt@huc.edu
Web Site: www.americanjewisharchives.org

TYPE:
Fellowships. The Marcus Center's Fellowship Program provides recipients with month-long fellowships for research and writing at The Jacob Rader Marcus Center of the American Jewish Archives. Fellowship stipends will be sufficient to cover transportation and living expenses while in residence. Applicants must be conducting serious research in some area relating to the history of North American Jewry.

See entry 804 for full listing.

THE MASSACHUSETTS HISTORICAL SOCIETY [593]

1154 Boylston Street
Boston, MA 02215-3695
(617) 536-1608
(617) 646-0557
Fax: (617) 859-0074
E-mail: education@masshist.org
programs@masshist.org
Web Site: www.masshist.org

FOUNDED: 1791

AREAS OF INTEREST:
Massachusetts, New England and U.S. history.

NAME(S) OF PROGRAMS:
- **Swensrud Teacher Fellowships at MHS**

TYPE:
Fellowships. Swensrud Teacher Fellowships are offered to public and/or parochial schoolteachers and library media specialists for on-site research at the Society.

YEAR PROGRAM STARTED: 2001

PURPOSE:
To support four weeks of research at the Society for a specific project.

ELIGIBILITY:
Applications are welcome from any K-12 teacher or library media specialist who has a serious interest in using the collections at the MHS to prepare primary-source-based curricula, supported by documents and visual aids, in the fields of American history, world history or English/language arts.

The fellowship process is competitive. Awards are made on the strength of:
(1) project design;
(2) the plan for using the Society collections;
(3) the creativity of the proposed classroom activities;
(4) usability in other classrooms and;
(5) recommendations.

Open to national and international applicants.

FINANCIAL DATA:
Amount of support per award: Stipend of $4,000.

NO. AWARDS: Minimum of 3.

APPLICATION INFO:
Application information is available on the web site.

Duration: Four weeks.

Deadline: February 28 (postmark).

ADDRESS INQUIRIES TO:
Kathleen Barker, Assistant Director of Education and Public Programs
Tel: (617) 646-0557
(See address above.)

THE MASSACHUSETTS HISTORICAL SOCIETY [594]

1154 Boylston Street
Boston, MA 02215
(617) 646-0512
Fax: (617) 859-0074
E-mail: research_programs@masshist.org
cwright@masshist.org
Web Site: www.masshist.org

FOUNDED: 1791

AREAS OF INTEREST:
Civil War history, Massachusetts, New England, and U.S. history.

NAME(S) OF PROGRAMS:
- **Suzanne and Caleb Loring Fellowship**

TYPE:
Fellowships; Research grants; Visiting scholars. Fellowship funds research on the Civil War, its origins, and consequences, for projects that use the resources at the Massachusetts Historical Society and the Boston Athenaeum. Research must be conducted for at least four weeks at each of the two participating institutions.

YEAR PROGRAM STARTED: 2008

PURPOSE:
To encourage projects that draw on the Civil War resources of the participating organizations.

ELIGIBILITY:
Open to independent scholars, advanced graduate students and holders of a Ph.D. or equivalent. Applicants must be U.S. citizens or already hold the J-1 visa or equivalent documents that will allow them to accept the stipend.

FINANCIAL DATA:
Amount of support per award: $4,000.

NO. AWARDS: 1.

APPLICATION INFO:
Applicants must submit the following materials online:
(1) cover letter;
(2) current curriculum vitae;
(3) project proposal, approximately 1,000 words in length, which includes a description of the project, a statement explaining the historiographical significance of the project, and an indication of the specific Massachusetts Historical Society and Boston Athenaeum collections the applicant wishes to consult and;
(4) for those not holding a Ph.D., a letter of recommendation from a faculty member familiar with the student's work and with the project being proposed.

Duration: Minimum of 20 days at each of the two institutions, for a total of 40 days.

Deadline: Applications must be submitted by 11:59 P.M. on February 15.

ADDRESS INQUIRIES TO:
The Massachusetts Historical Society
E-mail: fellowships@masshist.org
Tel: (617) 646-0568

THE MASSACHUSETTS HISTORICAL SOCIETY [595]

1154 Boylston Street
Boston, MA 02215
(617) 646-0512
Fax: (617) 859-0074
E-mail: research_programs@masshist.org
cwright@masshist.org
Web Site: www.masshist.org

FOUNDED: 1791

AREAS OF INTEREST:
Massachusetts, New England and U.S. history.

NAME(S) OF PROGRAMS:
- **Short-Term Research Fellowship**

TYPE:
Fellowships; Research grants; Visiting scholars. Research fellowship to use the Society's collection to complete a major project.

YEAR PROGRAM STARTED: 1983

PURPOSE:
To support at least 20 days of research at the Society for a specific project.

ELIGIBILITY:
Must be U.S. citizens or foreign nationals holding appropriate U.S. government status. Open to independent scholars, advanced graduate students, and holders of a Ph.D. or equivalent.

FINANCIAL DATA:
Amount of support per award: Stipend of $2,000.

NO. AWARDS: Approximately 20.

APPLICATION INFO:
Applicants must submit the following materials online:
(1) cover letter;
(2) current curriculum vitae;
(3) project proposal, approximately 1,000 words in length, which includes a description of the project, a statement explaining the historiographical significance of the project, and an indication of the specific MHS collections the applicant wishes to consult and;
(4) for applicants not holding a Ph.D., a letter of recommendation from a faculty member familiar with the student's work and with the project being proposed.

Duration: Minimum of 20 days.

Deadline: Applications must be submitted by 11:59 P.M. on March 1.

ADDRESS INQUIRIES TO:
The Massachusetts Historical Society
E-mail: fellowships@masshist.org
Tel: (617) 646-0568

THE MASSACHUSETTS HISTORICAL SOCIETY [596]

1154 Boylston Street
Boston, MA 02215
(617) 646-0512
Fax: (617) 859-0074
E-mail: research_programs@masshist.org
cwright@masshist.org
Web Site: www.masshist.org

FOUNDED: 1791

AREAS OF INTEREST:
Massachusetts, New England and U.S. history.

NAME(S) OF PROGRAMS:
- **Long-Term Research Fellowship**

TYPE:
Fellowships; Research grants; Visiting scholars. Research fellowship to use the Society's collection to complete a major project.

YEAR PROGRAM STARTED: 1983

PURPOSE:
To support four to 12 months of research at the Society for a specific project.

ELIGIBILITY:
Applicants must be U.S. citizens or foreign nationals who have lived in the U.S. for at least three years prior to the application deadline. Applicants must have completed their professional training. Fellowship is not available to graduate students. Awards committee will pay special attention both to the quality of proposed projects and to their relationship to the Society's collections. Preference will be given to candidates who have not held a long-term grant during the preceding three years.

FINANCIAL DATA:
There is an allowance for professional expenses.

Amount of support per award: $4,200 per month stipend with up to $500 per month housing allowance.

NO. AWARDS: Minimum of 2.

APPLICATION INFO:
Applicants must submit the following materials online:
(1) cover letter;
(2) current curriculum vitae;
(3) project proposal, approximately 1,000 words in length, which includes a description of the project, a statement explaining the historiographical significance of the project, and an indication of the specific MHS collections the applicant wishes to consult;
(4) Certification for Participants form and;
(5) two letters of recommendation.

Duration: Four to 12 months of continuous tenure.

ADDRESS INQUIRIES TO:
The Massachusetts Historical Society
E-mail: fellowships@masshist.org
Tel: (617) 646-0568

THE MASSACHUSETTS HISTORICAL SOCIETY [597]

1154 Boylston Street
Boston, MA 02215
(617) 646-0512
Fax: (617) 859-0074
E-mail: research_programs@masshist.org
cwright@masshist.org
Web Site: www.masshist.org

FOUNDED: 1791

AREAS OF INTEREST:
Massachusetts, New England and U.S. history.

NAME(S) OF PROGRAMS:
- **New England Regional Fellowship Consortium**

TYPE:
Fellowships; Research grants; Travel grants; Visiting scholars. Research fellowship to use the resources at a minimum of three different participating institutions.

YEAR PROGRAM STARTED: 1999

PURPOSE:
To encourage projects that draw on the resources of the participating organizations.

ELIGIBILITY:
Open to individuals with a serious need to use the collections and facilities of the participating organizations.

Fellows must work at each of at least three chosen organizations for at least two weeks.

FINANCIAL DATA:
Amount of support per award: Stipend of $5,000 for a minimum of eight weeks of research at participating institutions.

NO. AWARDS: Minimum of 15.

APPLICATION INFO:
Guidelines and fellowship applications are available on the New England Regional Fellowship Consortium (NERFC) web site. (The Massachusetts Historical Society web site provides a link to it.)

Duration: Minimum of eight weeks.

Deadline: February 1.

ADDRESS INQUIRIES TO:
Katheryn P. Viens, Research Coordinator
E-mail: fellowships@masshist.org
Tel: (617) 646-0568

THE MEDIEVAL ACADEMY OF AMERICA [598]

17 Dunster Street, Suite 202
Cambridge, MA 02138
(617) 491-1622
Fax: (617) 492-3303
E-mail: info@themedievalacademy.org
Web Site: www.medievalacademy.org/awards

FOUNDED: 1925

AREAS OF INTEREST:
Any aspect of medieval studies, 500 to 1500 A.D.

NAME(S) OF PROGRAMS:
- **Birgit Baldwin Fellowship**
- **John Nicholas Brown Prize**
- **Van Courtlandt Elliott Prize**
- **Medieval Academy Dissertation Grants**
- **Schallek Awards**
- **Schallek Fellowship**

TYPE:
Awards/prizes; Fellowships; Research grants. Cash prizes for publications of material on medieval topics.

Birgit Baldwin Fellowship supports a graduate student studying in a North American university researching and writing a significant dissertation for a Ph.D. on any subject in French medieval history. Research must be in archives and libraries of France.

The Brown Prize is awarded annually to a first book or monograph on a medieval topic.

The Elliott Prize is awarded annually for a first published article in the medieval field, judged by the selection committee to be of outstanding quality.

Medieval Academy Dissertation Grants support advanced graduate students who are writing Ph.D. dissertations on medieval topics.

Schallek Awards support graduate students conducting doctoral research in any relevant discipline dealing with late-Medieval Britain (*circa* 1350-1500).

Schallek Fellowship supports Ph.D. dissertation research in any relevant discipline dealing with late-Medieval Britain (*circa* 1350-1500).

YEAR PROGRAM STARTED: 1940

PURPOSE:
To promote publication on medieval topics.

LEGAL BASIS:
Nonprofit corporation.

GEOG. RESTRICTIONS: North America.

FINANCIAL DATA:
Medieval Academy Dissertation Grants and Schallek Awards: These programs help defray research expenses such as the cost of travel to research collections and the cost of photographs, photocopies, microfilms and other research materials. The cost of books or equipment (e.g., computers) is not included.

Amount of support per award: Birgit Baldwin Fellowship: $20,000; Brown Prize: $1,000; Elliott Prize: $500; Medieval Academy Dissertation Grants and Schallek Awards: $2,000; Schallek Fellowship: $30,000.

NO. MOST RECENT APPLICANTS: 30.

NO. AWARDS: Medieval Academy Dissertation Grants: 9. Schallek Awards: 5. Other programs: 1 each annually.

APPLICATION INFO:
All submissions must be made online.

Duration: Fellowships: One year. Baldwin Fellowship is renewable for a second year.

Deadline: Baldwin: November 15. Schallek Fellowships and Brown Prize: October 15. Announcement in April. Medieval Academy Dissertation Grants and Schallek Awards: February 15.

ADDRESS INQUIRIES TO:
Sheryl Mullane-Corvi
Assistant to the Executive Director
(See address above.)

MOUNT VERNON HOTEL MUSEUM & GARDEN [599]

421 East 61st Street
New York, NY 10065
(212) 838-6878
Fax: (212) 838-7390
E-mail: t.daly@mvhm.org
Web Site: www.mvhm.org

AREAS OF INTEREST:
American social history, material culture, historic preservation and museum education.

NAME(S) OF PROGRAMS:
- **William Randolph Hearst Foundation Fellowship**

TYPE:
Fellowships. Provides fellowships to graduate or undergraduate students who are interested in American social history, material culture, historic preservation and museum education.

YEAR PROGRAM STARTED: 1984

PURPOSE:
To promote the study of American history.

ELIGIBILITY:
Applicants must currently be enrolled in a college, university or graduate program.

FINANCIAL DATA:
Amount of support per award: $2,750.
Total amount of support: $5,500.

CO-OP FUNDING PROGRAMS: Fellowship is funded by the William Randolph Hearst Foundation.

NO. AWARDS: 2.

APPLICATION INFO:
Students must submit the completed application form, a short essay explaining the applicant's interest in the fellowship, resume and two letters of recommendation e-mailed directly from the individuals writing the recommendations. Applications are available on the web site.

Duration: Nine weeks in June and July.

Deadline: Approximately March.

ADDRESS INQUIRIES TO:
Terri Daly, Director
(See address above.)

NANTUCKET HISTORICAL ASSOCIATION [600]

P.O. Box 1016
Nantucket, MA 02554-1016
(508) 228-1655
E-mail: btyler@nha.org
Web Site: www.nha.org/library/verney.html

AREAS OF INTEREST:
History.

NAME(S) OF PROGRAMS:
- **E. Geoffrey and Elizabeth Thayer Verney Fellowship**

TYPE:
Fellowships; Residencies. The Verney Fellowship, which is a residency program to pursue historical research pertaining to Nantucket, MA, encourages research in the collections of the Nantucket Historical Association Research Library. The Association is the principal repository of Nantucket history, with extensive archives, collections of historic properties, and art and artifacts that broadly illustrate Nantucket's past.

YEAR PROGRAM STARTED: 1999

PURPOSE:
To enhance the public's knowledge and understanding of the heritage of Nantucket, MA.

ELIGIBILITY:
Open to graduate students, independent scholars and academics in any field to conduct research in the collections of the Association.

FINANCIAL DATA:
Amount of support per award: $300 per week stipend; housing will be provided. Travel is reimbursed up to $600.

NO. AWARDS: 1.

REPRESENTATIVE AWARDS:
Verney Fellows: (2013) Edward D. Melillo, "Out of the Blue: Nantucket and the Pacific World."

APPLICATION INFO:
Applicants must send a full description of the proposed project, a curriculum vitae, the names of three references, and an estimate of anticipated time and duration of stay. Send application packet to: Betsy Tyler, Obed Macy Research Chair and Editor of *Historic Nantucket*, Nantucket Historical Association, at the address above.

Duration: Up to three weeks.

Deadline: December 31.

ADDRESS INQUIRIES TO:
Betsy Tyler, Obed Macy Research Chair
(See address above.)

*PLEASE NOTE:
The Verney Fellow resides in the Thomas Macy House, a historic property owned by the Association, for up to a three-week period.

*SPECIAL STIPULATIONS:
NHA Visiting Research Scholars are expected to produce an article suitable for publication in *Historic Nantucket*, the NHA's biannual journal, and to deliver a public lecture on the subject of their research. Projects resulting in the publication of a book, article, conference paper, or other media, are looked upon favorably.

NATIONAL HISTORICAL PUBLICATIONS AND RECORDS COMMISSION [601]

National Archives and Records Administration
700 Pennsylvania Avenue, N.W., Room 114
Washington, DC 20408-0001
(202) 357-5010
Fax: (202) 357-5914
E-mail: nhprc@nara.gov
Web Site: www.archives.gov/nhprc

FOUNDED: 1934

AREAS OF INTEREST:
Archives and historical manuscripts relating to American history.

TYPE:
Project/program grants; Research grants; Technical assistance; Training grants. Grants to support the collection, preservation, digitization, arrangement, description, editing and publishing of documentary source material relating to the history of the U.S., the papers of American leaders and documents treating major subjects and events in American history.

YEAR PROGRAM STARTED: 1964

PURPOSE:
To promote the preservation and use of historical records important for an understanding and appreciation of the history of the U.S.

LEGAL BASIS:
44 U.S.C. 2501-2506.

ELIGIBILITY:
Tribal, state and local government agencies, nonprofit organizations and institutions.

GEOG. RESTRICTIONS: United States and its territories.

FINANCIAL DATA:
Amount of support per award: Average $70,000.

Total amount of support: $5,000,000 for fiscal year 2014.

Matching fund requirements: Generally, 1:1.

NO. MOST RECENT APPLICANTS: 240 for fiscal year 2014.

NO. AWARDS: 82 for fiscal year 2014.

REPRESENTATIVE AWARDS:
$148,000 to the Massachusetts Historical Society to edit *The Papers of John Adams*; $112,693 to Appalachian State University, Boone, NC to process and provide online access to primary research materials within the W.L. Eury Appalachian Collection.

APPLICATION INFO:
All applications must be submitted through Grants.gov.

Duration: Up to three years, depending on the individual project.

Deadline: Varies by program.

PUBLICATIONS:
Newsletter and special reports.

NATIONAL SOCIETY DAUGHTERS OF THE AMERICAN REVOLUTION [602]

1776 D Street, N.W.
Washington, DC 20006-5303
(202) 879-3263
Fax: (202) 879-3348
E-mail: scholarships@dar.org
Web Site: www.dar.org

FOUNDED: 1895

AREAS OF INTEREST:
American history.

NAME(S) OF PROGRAMS:

- **Dr. Aura-Lee A. and James Hobbs Pittenger American History Scholarship**

TYPE:
Scholarships. The American History Scholarship is awarded to graduating high school students in the upper one-fifth of the class or home schooled who will have a concentrated study of a minimum of 24 credit hours in American History and American Government.

PURPOSE:
To provide ways and means to help students to attain higher education; to perpetuate the memory and spirit of men and women who achieved American independence by acquisition and protection of historical spots and erection of monuments; to carry out injunction of Washington in his farewell address to American people; to maintain institutions of American Freedom; to aid liberty.

LEGAL BASIS:
Incorporated historical society.

ELIGIBILITY:
Scholarships are awarded without regard to race, religion, sex or national origin. All four-year, or more, scholarships must be for consecutive years and are renewable only upon review and approval of annual transcript. Candidates must be U.S. citizens and must attend an accredited college or university in the U.S. No affiliation or relationship to DAR is required for qualification, but candidate must be sponsored by a local DAR Chapter. Awards are judged on the basis of academic excellence, commitment to field of study, as required, and financial need.

GEOG. RESTRICTIONS: United States.

FINANCIAL DATA:
Amount of support per award: $2,000 per year for maximum of $8,000.

Total amount of support: Varies.

NO. AWARDS: Varies.

APPLICATION INFO:
Application information is available online. The application package must be completed. All transcripts, letters of recommendation and other required documents must be in a single package.

Included with the application packet is the list of DAR State Scholarship Chairmen. All scholarship applicants are required to have a letter of sponsorship from a chapter. Individuals interested in obtaining a letter of sponsorship from a local chapter are encouraged to contact the DAR State Chairman.

Duration: One academic year. Renewable for up to four years upon annual transcript review and approval.

Deadline: February 15.

PUBLICATIONS:
American Spirit, magazine.

ADDRESS INQUIRIES TO:
Office of the Reporter General
DAR Scholarship Committee
(See address above.)

NATIONAL TRUST FOR HISTORIC PRESERVATION [603]

2600 Virginia Avenue, N.W.
Suite 1100
Washington, DC 20037
(202) 588-6277
Fax: (202) 588-6223
E-mail: grants@savingplaces.org
Web Site: www.preservationnation.org/funding

FOUNDED: 1949

AREAS OF INTEREST:
To encourage public participation in the preservation of sites, buildings and objects significant in American history and culture.

NAME(S) OF PROGRAMS:

- **National Trust Preservation Funds (NTPF)**

TYPE:
Challenge/matching grants; Project/program grants; Seed money grants; Technical assistance; Training grants. Education program curricula. Project grants to support consultants with professional expertise in areas such as architecture, law, planning, economics, archeology and graphic design. Conferences that address subjects of particular importance to historic preservation also are funded. In addition, grants are made for curriculum development in preservation education directed at select audiences.

YEAR PROGRAM STARTED: 1979

PURPOSE:
To increase the flow of information and ideas in the field of preservation by helping stimulate public discussion, enabling local groups to gain the technical expertise needed for particular projects, introducing students to preservation concepts and crafts and encouraging participation by the private sector in preservation.

LEGAL BASIS:
Nonprofit corporation.

ELIGIBILITY:
Applicants must be nonprofit incorporated organizations or public agencies. Applicants are eligible for no more than three NTPF grants in any two-year period.

Activities eligible for National Trust Preservation Funds grants include hiring consultants to undertake preservation planning or design projects, obtaining professional advice to strengthen management capabilities, sponsoring preservation conferences, designing and implementing innovative preservation

education programs targeted to a specific audience and undertaking other planning activities that will lead to implementation of a specific preservation project.

Grants can be used for professional consultant services, preservation education programs and conferences and rehabilitation feasibility studies. Projects, programs and conferences are not funded retroactively.

Bricks-and-mortar construction projects and the funding of ongoing staff positions are not eligible activities. In addition, historic resource surveys to create inventories or to list resources on local, state or national registers are generally not eligible for funding.

GEOG. RESTRICTIONS: United States and its territories.

FINANCIAL DATA:

Amount of support per award: $2,500 to $5,000.

Total amount of support: $1,200,000 for fiscal year 2015.

Matching fund requirements: Each grantee must match the funds on at least a dollar-for-dollar basis using cash contributions.

NO. AWARDS: 196 grants for fiscal year 2015.

APPLICATION INFO:

Guidelines and application forms may be found on the web site. Applications must be completed and submitted online by the appropriate deadline. Incomplete applications will not be considered.

Duration: Usually a one-time award.

Deadline: Applicants should contact the National Trust Grants Office to obtain information regarding application deadlines.

IRS I.D.: 53-0210807

ADDRESS INQUIRIES TO:
Grants Coordinator
National Trust Preservation Funds
(See address above.)

NEW JERSEY HISTORIC TRUST [604]

101 South Broad Street
Trenton, NJ 08608-2401
(609) 984-0473
Fax: (609) 984-7590
E-mail: njht@dca.nj.gov
Web Site: www.njht.org

FOUNDED: 1967

AREAS OF INTEREST:
Historic preservation.

NAME(S) OF PROGRAMS:

- **Discover New Jersey History License Plate Fund for Heritage Tourism**

TYPE:

Challenge/matching grants; Conferences/seminars; Demonstration grants; Project/program grants; Technical assistance; Training grants. Planning Grants. Provides funding for the preservation of historic properties.

YEAR PROGRAM STARTED: 2013

PURPOSE:

To develop and promote visitor-ready sites as heritage tourism destinations.

ELIGIBILITY:

Applicants must be state, county or municipal governments or nonprofit organizations.

GEOG. RESTRICTIONS: New Jersey.

FINANCIAL DATA:

Amount of support per award: Discover New Jersey History License Plate Fund: Up to $5,000.

Total amount of support: Varies.

NO. MOST RECENT APPLICANTS: 12.

NO. AWARDS: 5.

REPRESENTATIVE AWARDS:

$3,000 to First Presbyterian Church of Elizabeth for development of Historic Burial Groups Visitor App.

APPLICATION INFO:

Duration: Varies.

PUBLICATIONS:

Annual report; program announcement; *Economic Impact of Historic Preservation in New Jersey* (1997), funding resources for history; *Economic and Fiscal Impacts of Heritage Tourism in New Jersey*; *Keeping the Past Present: The New Jersey Historic Trust, 1967-2013.*

IRS I.D.: 22-3113979

STAFF:
Dorothy Guzzo, Executive Director

NEW JERSEY HISTORIC TRUST [605]

101 South Broad Street
Trenton, NJ 08608-2401
(609) 984-0473
Fax: (609) 984-7590
E-mail: njht@dca.nj.gov
Web Site: www.njht.org

FOUNDED: 1967

AREAS OF INTEREST:
Capital preservation of historic properties.

NAME(S) OF PROGRAMS:

- **Emergency Loans**

TYPE:

Capital grants; Matching gifts; Project/program grants. Loans. Activities which qualify for funding include emergency repair or stabilization, planning or research necessary to preserve an endangered property, limited rehabilitation, restoration or improvement, acquisition of a historic property or the purchase of an option to acquire a historic property.

YEAR PROGRAM STARTED: 1990

PURPOSE:

To provide emergency funding for capital preservation projects of historic properties.

LEGAL BASIS:

Government-approved program. Statutory Citation: P.L. 1967, c. 124.

ELIGIBILITY:

Applicants must be nonprofit, tax-exempt organizations or agencies of county or municipal governments. All properties must be listed or eligible for listing in the State and National Registers of Historic Places. For all requests other than acquisition, applicants must demonstrate control of the property through a deed or a valid lease.

GEOG. RESTRICTIONS: New Jersey.

FINANCIAL DATA:

Awards are short-term low-interest loans.

Amount of support per award: $1,000 to $10,000.

Matching fund requirements: Matching funds for loans are encouraged but not required.

REPRESENTATIVE AWARDS:

$10,000 to Newark Museum for stabilization of skylight in historic Polhemus House.

APPLICATION INFO:

A nonrefundable application fee of $25 must be submitted with each application. Applicants must consult with Trust staff before making application for these funds.

Duration: Varies.

Deadline: Notification two months after submission of complete application.

PUBLICATIONS:
Program announcement.

IRS I.D.: 21-6000928

ADDRESS INQUIRIES TO:
Lauren Giannullo
(See address above.)

NEW JERSEY HISTORICAL COMMISSION [606]

New Jersey Department of State
225 West State Street, Fifth Floor
Trenton, NJ 08625-0305
(609) 292-6062
Fax: (609) 633-8168
E-mail: cristen.piatnochka@sos.nj.gov
Web Site: www.history.nj.gov

FOUNDED: 1969

AREAS OF INTEREST:
New Jersey history.

NAME(S) OF PROGRAMS:

- **General Operating Support Grants**

TYPE:

General operating grants. Provide general assistance to historical organizations, museums, historic sites, archives, libraries and similar organizations with collections or programming relating to the history of New Jersey.

YEAR PROGRAM STARTED: 2000

PURPOSE:

To provide operating support for New Jersey history organizations.

LEGAL BASIS:

Agency within the Department of State, State of New Jersey.

ELIGIBILITY:

To be eligible to apply for a General Operating Support Grant, an organization must:
(1) be a not-for-profit corporation or government (municipal or county) agency, commission or other organization;
(2) be based in New Jersey;
(3) be governed by a board responsible for the programs and policies of the organization;
(4) have a clearly stated mission of service to the promotion, preservation, research, interpretation or public presentation of New Jersey history and;
(5) have a two-year track record of providing programs and services to the public that fulfill that mission.

Eligible applicants include a wide variety of organizations, both public and private, that:
(1) have an annual budget of at least $100,000 and;
(2) document that 25% of its audience (both virtual and actual) comes from beyond a 20-mile radius from its headquarters location.

GEOG. RESTRICTIONS: New Jersey.

FINANCIAL DATA:
Amount of support per award: General Operating Support: Applicants may apply for grants of up to 33% of the nonstate operating income for either the current or next fiscal year.

Total amount of support: $2,294,506 for fiscal year 2016.

Matching fund requirements: Matching fund ratio of 3:1 (grantee: Commission).

NO. MOST RECENT APPLICANTS: 106 for fiscal year 2014.

NO. AWARDS: 84 for fiscal year 2016.

REPRESENTATIVE AWARDS:
$43,008 to Hoboken Historical Museum; $72,360 to Historic Cold Spring Village.

APPLICATION INFO:
The Commission offers assistance to applicants in the technical aspects of completing the application. Applicants may call the Grants Program Officer at (609) 943-3304 for information or check the web site.

Duration: Three-year funding cycle. Successful applicants will receive a grant for fiscal year 2017, and a commitment to support in fiscal years 2018 and 2019 if funds are available and all reporting obligations are met.

Deadline: Applicants must notify the Commission of their intent to apply for the grant by March 1. Full proposals must be received in the Commission office by April 1.

PUBLICATIONS:
Application guidelines.

ADMINISTRATION:
Cristen Piatnochka, Grants Program Officer

ADDRESS INQUIRIES TO:
Cristen Piatnochka
Grants Program Officer
P.O. Box 305
Trenton, NJ 08625-0305

*SPECIAL STIPULATIONS:
All funding is based on state appropriations.

NEW JERSEY HISTORICAL COMMISSION [607]

New Jersey Department of State
225 West State Street, Fifth Floor
Trenton, NJ 08625-0305
(609) 292-6062
Fax: (609) 633-8168
E-mail: sara.cureton@sos.nj.gov
Web Site: www.history.nj.gov

FOUNDED: 1969

AREAS OF INTEREST:
New Jersey history.

NAME(S) OF PROGRAMS:
- **Alfred E. Driscoll Dissertation Prize**
- **Mildred Barry Garvin Prize**
- **Richard P. McCormick Prize for Scholarly Publication**

TYPE:
Awards/prizes. The Driscoll Dissertation Prize is awarded in even years to the author of an outstanding doctoral dissertation on any topic on New Jersey history.

The Garvin Prize is awarded annually to a New Jersey teacher, guidance counselor or school librarian for outstanding teaching of Black American history or related activity at any grade, K-12.

The McCormick Prize is awarded in odd years for an outstanding scholarly work on any aspect of New Jersey history.

YEAR PROGRAM STARTED: 1981

PURPOSE:
To stimulate the study and public knowledge of the history of New Jersey.

LEGAL BASIS:
Agency within the Department of State, State of New Jersey.

ELIGIBILITY:
Driscoll Prize: Doctoral dissertations in New Jersey history are eligible.

Garvin Prize: Applicant must be a New Jersey teacher, guidance counselor or school librarian.

McCormick Prize: Scholarly books published in the preceding two years are eligible.

FINANCIAL DATA:
Amount of support per award: $1,500 for each prize.

NO. AWARDS: Garvin Prize: 1 per year. Driscoll and McCormick Prizes alternate; each year the Historical Commission may award either 1 Driscoll Prize or 1 McCormick Prize.

APPLICATION INFO:
Guidelines and application forms are available on the web site.

Duration: One-time award. Not renewable.

Deadline: Driscoll (2016) and McCormick (2017) Prizes: March; Garvin Prize: September/October.

PUBLICATIONS:
Annual report; application guidelines.

ADMINISTRATION:
Sara R. Cureton, Director, New Jersey Historical Commission

ADDRESS INQUIRIES TO:
For the Driscoll or Garvin Prize:
Niquole Primiani, Chief Programs Officer

For the McCormick Prize:
Sara Cureton, Director, Grants Program
(See address above.)

NEW JERSEY HISTORICAL COMMISSION [608]

New Jersey Department of State
225 West State Street, Fifth Floor
Trenton, NJ 08625-0305
(609) 292-6062
Fax: (609) 633-8168
E-mail: cristen.piatnochka@sos.nj.gov
Web Site: www.history.nj.gov

FOUNDED: 1967

AREAS OF INTEREST:
New Jersey history.

NAME(S) OF PROGRAMS:
- **Project Grants**

TYPE:
Project/program grants. Funding for expenses of specific projects relating to New Jersey history. Examples of successful projects include conservation of historical materials (manuscripts, books, costumes, historical visuals), editorial and publication projects, educational initiatives, exhibitions, media (films, radio, videotape, digital media), public programs, and research (including archaeological projects, fellowships, oral history, and national and New Jersey registers of historic places nominations).

YEAR PROGRAM STARTED: 1975

PURPOSE:
To engage diverse audiences in the active exploration, enjoyment, interpretation, understanding and preservation of New Jersey history.

LEGAL BASIS:
Agency within the New Jersey Department of State.

ELIGIBILITY:
Grants are available for both individuals and organizations. There are general standards of eligibility, as well as specific requirements for programs. Organizations must have an annual budget of at least $100,000 and must document that 25% of its audience (both virtual and actual) comes from beyond a 20-mile radius from its headquarters location.

FINANCIAL DATA:
Amount of support per award: Projects: $1 to $15,000.

Matching fund requirements: Organizations with annual operating budgets of at least $500,000 are expected to show a match equal to 50% of the grant request.

NO. AWARDS: 27 for fiscal year 2016.

REPRESENTATIVE AWARDS:
$10,620 to Monmouth County Historical Association; $8,915 to Atlantic City Public Library.

APPLICATION INFO:
Applicants must submit a Declaration of Intent online prior to submitting an application.

Deadline: Declaration of Intent: January 15. Application: February 15.

PUBLICATIONS:
Application guidelines.

ADMINISTRATION:
Cristen Piatnochka, Grants Program Officer

ADDRESS INQUIRIES TO:
Cristen Piatnochka, Grants Program Officer
P.O. Box 305
Trenton, NJ 08625-0305

NEW YORK LANDMARKS CONSERVANCY [609]

One Whitehall Street, 21st Floor
New York, NY 10004-2127
(212) 995-5260
Fax: (212) 995-5268
E-mail: nylandmarks@nylandmarks.org
Web Site: www.nylandmarks.org

FOUNDED: 1973

AREAS OF INTEREST:
Historic preservation and restoration of buildings.

NAME(S) OF PROGRAMS:
- **City Ventures Fund**
- **EZ (Empowerment Zone) Consulting Grants**
- **Historic Properties Fund**
- **Sacred Sites Program**
- **Technical Services Program**

TYPE:
Project/program grants.

PURPOSE:
To provide financial and technical services to nonprofit housing corporations, community development organizations, social service agencies, homesteading groups, and mutual housing associations.

LEGAL BASIS:
501(c)(3) not-for-profit.

ELIGIBILITY:
Eligible organizations must be IRS 501(c)(3) tax-exempt.

GEOG. RESTRICTIONS: New York.

FINANCIAL DATA:
Amount of support per award: Varies.
Total amount of support: Varies.

APPLICATION INFO:
Prospective applicants should first contact the Conservancy. Applications must include a copy of the IRS tax determination letter.
Duration: Varies.
Deadline: Varies.

IRS I.D.: 23-7181785

ADDRESS INQUIRIES TO:
See phone or e-mail address above.

NEW YORK STATE HISTORICAL ASSOCIATION [610]

5798 State Highway 80
Cooperstown, NY 13326
(607) 547-1416
Fax: (607) 547-1404
E-mail: c.miosek@nysha.org
Web Site: www.nysha.org

FOUNDED: 1899

AREAS OF INTEREST:
The history of New York state.

NAME(S) OF PROGRAMS:
- **The Dixon Ryan Fox Manuscript Prize of the New York State Historical Association**

TYPE:
Awards/prizes. Annual cash prize and publication assistance.

YEAR PROGRAM STARTED: 1973

PURPOSE:
To award the best unpublished, book-length monograph dealing with the history of New York state, as judged by an editorial committee.

LEGAL BASIS:
Private nonprofit association.

ELIGIBILITY:
Manuscripts may deal with any aspect of New York state history. Biographies of individuals whose careers illuminate aspects of the history of the state are also eligible, as are manuscripts dealing with such cultural matters as literature and the arts, provided that in such cases the methodology used is historical. Works of fiction are not eligible.

FINANCIAL DATA:
Amount of support per award: $3,000.
Total amount of support: $3,000.

NO. MOST RECENT APPLICANTS: 9 for the year 2015.

NO. AWARDS: 1 annually.

APPLICATION INFO:
Manuscripts must be typed, double-spaced, with at least one-inch margins. Please send two copies. Clear, readable photocopies or computer printouts are acceptable.
Duration: One-time award. Nonrenewable.
Deadline: March 1. Announcement by July 30 annually.

PUBLICATIONS:
Application guidelines.

OFFICERS AND TRUSTEES:

ADDRESS INQUIRIES TO:
Caitlin Miosek
Executive Coordinator to the President
(See address above.)

NEW YORK STATE HISTORICAL ASSOCIATION

5798 State Highway 80
Cooperstown, NY 13326
(607) 547-1418
Fax: (607) 547-1404
E-mail: publications@nysha.org
Web Site: www.nysha.org

TYPE:
Awards/prizes. Prizes for published catalogues treating collections located or exhibited in New York state.

See entry 476 for full listing.

THE NEWBERRY LIBRARY [611]

Office of Research and Academic Programs
60 West Walton Street
Chicago, IL 60610
(312) 255-3666
E-mail: research@newberry.org
Web Site: www.newberry.org/fellowships

FOUNDED: 1887

AREAS OF INTEREST:
The humanities of Western Europe, England and the Americas from the late Middle Ages to the early 20th century.

NAME(S) OF PROGRAMS:
- **American Society for Eighteenth-Century Studies (ASECS) Fellowships**

TYPE:
Fellowships. For scholars wishing to use the Newberry's collections to study the period 1660 to 1815.

PURPOSE:
To help provide access to Newberry resources for people who live beyond commuting distance.

LEGAL BASIS:
Private research library.

ELIGIBILITY:
Applicants must have received their Ph.D. or equivalent degree, or be a Ph.D. candidate at dissertation level.

Applicants must be members of the ASECS at the time of award.

Applicants must live outside the Chicago area.

FINANCIAL DATA:
Amount of support per award: $2,500 per month.

NO. MOST RECENT APPLICANTS: 15.

NO. AWARDS: 1 per year.

APPLICATION INFO:
Applications must be submitted through the online webform.
Duration: One month.
Deadline: December 15.

STAFF:
D. Bradford Hunt, Vice President for Research and Academic Programs

ADDRESS INQUIRIES TO:
See e-mail address above.

OMOHUNDRO INSTITUTE OF EARLY AMERICAN HISTORY AND CULTURE [612]

400 Landrum Drive, Ground Floor
Swem Library
Williamsburg, VA 23185
(757) 221-1116
Fax: (757) 221-1047
E-mail: nizimmerli@wm.edu
Web Site: oieahc.wm.edu/books/bookprize.html

FOUNDED: 1943

AREAS OF INTEREST:
Manuscripts about any area of early American studies.

NAME(S) OF PROGRAMS:
- **Jamestown Prize**

TYPE:
Awards/prizes. Prize to the author of the best book-length scholarly manuscript pertaining to the early American period. Subject of the manuscript must pertain to America circa 1450 to 1820 or to the related history of the British Isles, Europe, West Africa or the Caribbean. The award also guarantees publication by the Institute in association with the University of North Carolina Press.

YEAR PROGRAM STARTED: 1957

LEGAL BASIS:
Independent, nonprofit research institution.

ELIGIBILITY:
The competition is open only to authors who have not previously published a book. Previous and current holders of Institute postdoctoral fellowships are not eligible.

FINANCIAL DATA:
Amount of support per award: $3,000, plus publication.

NO. AWARDS: 1 every two years.

APPLICATION INFO:
Applicants must first send a letter of inquiry with a book prospectus and current curriculum vitae. Mail all materials to the Editor of Publications; OIEAHC; P.O. Box 8781; Williamsburg, VA 23187-8781. The Institute will then invite the authors of all promising proposals to send their complete work.
Deadline: Late April (odd-numbered years). Contact Institute for exact date.

STAFF:
Karin A. Wulf, Director

ADDRESS INQUIRIES TO:
Associate Editor of Publications
Jamestown Prize
(See e-mail address above.)

*SPECIAL STIPULATIONS:
Past and current holders of Institute postdoctoral fellowships are ineligible.

OMOHUNDRO INSTITUTE OF EARLY AMERICAN HISTORY AND CULTURE [613]

400 Landrum Drive, Ground Floor
Swem Library
Williamsburg, VA 23185
(757) 221-1110
Fax: (757) 221-1047
E-mail: oieahc@wm.edu
Web Site: oieahc.wm.edu/fellowship

FOUNDED: 1943

AREAS OF INTEREST:
Research leading to book publication on any area of early American studies.

NAME(S) OF PROGRAMS:
- **Omohundro Institute-NEH Postdoctoral Fellowship**

TYPE:
Fellowships. The Omohundro Institute of Early American History and Culture, located on the campus of The College of William and Mary, annually offers one postdoctoral fellowship to a promising young scholar in any area of early American studies whose dissertation shows potential for making a significant book-length contribution to scholarship.

Fellows have the opportunity of teaching at the College of William and Mary with a concurrent appointment as visiting assistant professor in the appropriate department.

YEAR PROGRAM STARTED: 1945

LEGAL BASIS:
Independent, nonprofit research institution.

ELIGIBILITY:
Fellows must have successfully defended their dissertation and completed all requirements for the Doctorate by the time they begin the fellowship and may not have previously published a book or have a book under contract. Applications are due the end of October for the term beginning the following July. Foreign nationals are eligible to apply.

FINANCIAL DATA:
Amount of support per award: $50,400 per year stipend.

CO-OP FUNDING PROGRAMS: The fellowships are supported by the Omohundro Institute and the National Endowment for the Humanities.

NO. MOST RECENT APPLICANTS: 27 for the 2015-17 fellowship.

NO. AWARDS: 1 annually.

APPLICATION INFO:
Applicants should apply via the Institute web site.

Duration: Two years.

Deadline: End of October for the term beginning the following July 1.

PUBLICATIONS:
William and Mary Quarterly, scholarly journal; *Uncommon Sense*, newsletter; books.

STAFF:
Karin A. Wulf, Director

ADDRESS INQUIRIES TO:
Karin A. Wulf, Director
(See e-mail address above.)

*SPECIAL STIPULATIONS:
The Institute holds first rights to publishing the resulting book manuscript.

OMOHUNDRO INSTITUTE OF EARLY AMERICAN HISTORY AND CULTURE [614]

400 Landrum Drive, Ground Floor
Swem Library
Williamsburg, VA 23185
(757) 221-1114
(757) 221-1110
Fax: (757) 221-1047
E-mail: oieahc@wm.edu
Web Site: oieahc.wm.edu/fellowship

FOUNDED: 1943

AREAS OF INTEREST:
Graduate student research related to Early American and transatlantic print culture.

NAME(S) OF PROGRAMS:
- **Lapidus-OI Fellowship**

TYPE:
Fellowships. The Lapidus-OI Fellowship is offered annually to support advanced graduate student research related to Early American and transatlantic print culture, including authorship, production, circulation and reception.

LEGAL BASIS:
Independent, nonprofit research institution.

FINANCIAL DATA:
Amount of support per award: $500.

CO-OP FUNDING PROGRAMS: Fellowships are made possible through the generous support of Sid Lapidus.

NO. AWARDS: Up to 8 annually.

APPLICATION INFO:
Duration: Application information is available on the web site.

Deadline: January 15. Fellowship recipients may expect to be notified of the award by early spring.

STAFF:
Karin A. Wulf, Director

ADDRESS INQUIRIES TO:
Fellowship Program
(See e-mail address above.)

*SPECIAL STIPULATIONS:
Fellowship recipients must provide a one-page report of their progress no more than 12 months after notification of their award.

OMOHUNDRO INSTITUTE OF EARLY AMERICAN HISTORY AND CULTURE [615]

400 Landrum Drive, Ground Floor
Swem Library
Williamsburg, VA 23185
(757) 221-1114
(757) 221-1110
Fax: (757) 221-1047
E-mail: oieahc@wm.edu
Web Site: oieahc.wm.edu/fellowship

FOUNDED: 1943

AREAS OF INTEREST:
Promoting the study of early American history and culture.

NAME(S) OF PROGRAMS:
- **Georgian Papers Programme Fellowships**
- **Jamestown Rediscovery-Omohundro Institute (JR-OI) Short-Term Visiting Fellowship**

TYPE:
Fellowships. Georgian Papers Programme Fellowships: With support from the Lapidus Initiative, the Omohundro Institute has entered into an international partnership that will provide opportunities for scholars to do research in the historically rich trove of Georgian materials housed at the Royal Archives in Windsor Castle's Round Tower. The Georgian Papers Programme is a five-year project that by 2020 will create an open online archive and library of approximately 350,000 digitized items from the Georgian monarchs.

Jamestown Rediscovery-Omohundro Institute (JR-OI) Short-Term Visiting Fellowship: Fellows in this program will make use of the College of William and Mary's Swem Library and collections at Historic Jamestowne as well as other resources in the Historic Triangle and Richmond region. This fellowship will also provide the opportunity to experience the Omohundro Institute's editorial expertise and intellectual community of early Americanists.

LEGAL BASIS:
Independent, nonprofit research institution.

ELIGIBILITY:
Georgian Papers Programme Fellowships: Open to scholars - from advanced graduate students to senior scholars; restricted to U.S. or U.K. citizens. Successful applicants will be required to undergo a security clearance before beginning work at Windsor Castle.

JR-OI Short-Term Visiting Fellowship: Open to scholars - from advanced graduate students to senior scholars. Scholars with strong interests in colonial history, historical archaeology, Atlantic history, Native American history, African American studies, early Jamestown, the Chesapeake, and material culture, 1500-1720, are encouraged to apply.

FINANCIAL DATA:
Amount of support per award: Georgian Papers Programme Fellowships: $2,500 stipend with up to $1,500 in additional support for travel. JR-OI Short-Term Visiting Fellowship: Stipend of $2,500 per month.

CO-OP FUNDING PROGRAMS: JR-OI Short-Term Visiting Fellowship: This program is offered in conjunction with the Jamestown Rediscovery Foundation.

NO. AWARDS: Georgian Papers Programme Fellowships: Up to 8 annually. JR-OI Short-Term Visiting Fellowship: Up to 4 annually.

APPLICATION INFO:
Georgian Papers Programme Fellowships: Applicants need to submit a letter of application (including a description of the proposed project and its potential match with the collections), a curriculum vitae and two letters of recommendation. The letter and curriculum vitae should be uploaded via the Institute web site (above). Recommenders should e-mail letters directly to the e-mail address listed above.

JR-OI Short-Term Visiting Fellowship: Applicants need to submit an electronic file with a brief project description (1,000 words maximum) and a curriculum vitae via the Institute web site. In addition, two letters of recommendation should be sent directly to the Institute via the e-mail address above.

Duration: Georgian Papers Programme Fellowships: One month. JR-OI Short-Term Visiting Fellowship: One to two months.

Deadline: Georgian Papers Programme Fellowships: Varies each year. Contact Institute for up-to-date information. JR-OI Short-Term Visiting Fellowship: April 15 and October 15.

ADDRESS INQUIRIES TO:
Omohundro Institute of Early American History and Culture
(See e-mail address above.)

PHI ALPHA THETA HISTORY HONOR SOCIETY [616]

University of South Florida
4202 East Fowler Avenue, SOC107
Tampa, FL 33620-8100
(800) 394-8195
(813) 974-8212
Fax: (813) 974-8215
E-mail: info@phialphatheta.org
Web Site: www.phialphatheta.org

FOUNDED: 1921

AREAS OF INTEREST:
History.

NAME(S) OF PROGRAMS:
- **Member's Best First Book Award**
- **Member's Best Subsequent Book Award**

TYPE:
Awards/prizes. Awards for the best books published by members of Phi Alpha Theta, one for his or her first book, one for subsequent books (second, third, etc.), published in the field of history.

PURPOSE:
To encourage the publication of distinctive books in history.

LEGAL BASIS:
Nonprofit, 501(c)(3).

ELIGIBILITY:
Books to be judged must be published from August 1 of the previous year to June 30 of the following (award) year to be eligible for that year's award. Awards restricted to society members.

FINANCIAL DATA:
Amount of support per award: $1,000 each.

Total amount of support: $2,000.

NO. AWARDS: 2 for the year 2013.

APPLICATION INFO:
Six copies of each book and a completed application must be forwarded to the Society's Book Award Committee at the address above.

Deadline: July 1 of the award year.

OFFICERS:
Dr. Graydon A. Tunstall, Jr., Executive Director

ADDRESS INQUIRIES TO:
Dr. Graydon A. Tunstall, Jr.
Executive Director
(See address above.)

PHI ALPHA THETA HISTORY HONOR SOCIETY [617]

University of South Florida
4202 East Fowler Avenue, SOC107
Tampa, FL 33620-8100
(800) 394-8195
(813) 974-8212
Fax: (813) 974-8215
E-mail: info@phialphatheta.org
Web Site: www.phialphatheta.org

FOUNDED: 1921

AREAS OF INTEREST:
History.

NAME(S) OF PROGRAMS:
- **Thomas S. Morgan Memorial Scholarship**
- **William E. Parrish Scholarship**
- **Phi Alpha Theta Scholarship**
- **John Pine Memorial Award**
- **Graydon A. Tunstall Undergraduate Student Scholarship**
- **A.F. Zimmerman Scholarship**

TYPE:
Awards/prizes; Scholarships. The Thomas S. Morgan, William E. Parrish and A.F. Zimmerman Scholarships are given to student members entering graduate school for the first time for work leading to a Master's degree in history.

The Phi Alpha Theta Scholarship, the John Pine Memorial Award and two additional awards are given to graduate student members for work leading to a Ph.D. in history.

The Graydon A. Tunstall Undergraduate Student Scholarship is given to exceptional junior-year students majoring in Modern European History (1815 to present).

PURPOSE:
To promote the study of history at the graduate level.

LEGAL BASIS:
Nonprofit, 501(c)(3).

ELIGIBILITY:
Applicants must be initiated members of the Phi Alpha Theta History Honor Society. Applicant must not be enrolled in an online degree program.

For the Morgan, Parrish and Zimmerman Scholarships, members must be entering graduate school for the first time in the fall of the award year and must be pursuing a Master's degree in History. Students currently enrolled in a graduate program are not eligible to apply.

For the Phi Alpha Theta Scholarship and the John Pine Memorial Award, graduate students must be pursuing a Ph.D. in History and must have passed general examinations by February 15 of the award year and be ready to start dissertations.

For the Graydon A. Tunstall Undergraduate Student Scholarship, students must be entering the fall semester of their senior year and majoring in Modern European History (1815 to the present).

FINANCIAL DATA:
Amount of support per award: Morgan and Parrish Scholarships, Phi Alpha Theta Scholarship, Pine Memorial and Graydon A. Tunstall Scholarship: $1,000 each; Zimmerman Award: $1,250. In some years, there may be two additional awards of $850 each for Doctoral Scholarships.

Total amount of support: Varies.

NO. AWARDS: Master's degree: 3; Ph.D. in history: 4; Undergraduate: 1.

APPLICATION INFO:
Consult the Society web site.

Duration: One year.

Deadline: Applications must be received on or before March 1.

OFFICERS:
Dr. Graydon A. Tunstall, Jr., Executive Director

ADDRESS INQUIRIES TO:
Dr. Graydon A. Tunstall, Jr.
Executive Director
(See address above.)

*SPECIAL STIPULATIONS:
Applicants must be members of Phi Alpha Theta.

PHI ALPHA THETA HISTORY HONOR SOCIETY [618]

University of South Florida
4202 East Fowler Avenue, SOC107
Tampa, FL 33620-8100
(800) 394-8195
(813) 974-8212
Fax: (813) 974-8215
E-mail: info@phialphatheta.org
Web Site: www.phialphatheta.org

FOUNDED: 1921

AREAS OF INTEREST:
History.

NAME(S) OF PROGRAMS:
- **The Nels Andrew Cleven Founder's Paper Prize Awards**
- **Dr. George P. Hammond Paper Prize**
- **Dr. Lynn W. Turner Paper Prize**

TYPE:
Awards/prizes. The George P. Hammond Prize award is for the best paper by a graduate student member of the Society.

The Dr. Lynn W. Turner Prize is awarded for the best paper by an undergraduate student member of the Society.

The four Founder's Paper Prizes are awarded to two graduate and two undergraduate student members of the Society.

PURPOSE:
To promote historical research.

LEGAL BASIS:
501(c)(3).

ELIGIBILITY:
All students must be initiated members. All manuscripts must carry a letter of recommendation from either the faculty advisor or the chair of the department of history. Papers should not exceed 25 typewritten double-spaced pages in length.

FINANCIAL DATA:
Amount of support per award: Founder's Awards: $400; Hammond Prize and Turner Award: $500 each.

NO. AWARDS: 6.

APPLICATION INFO:
Essay should combine original historical research on significant subjects, based on source material and manuscripts if possible, with good English composition and superior style. Papers should not exceed 25 typewritten double-spaced pages in length, excluding bibliography. Entries received that do not comply with these guidelines will be disqualified.

Title page of the paper must include the applicant's name, mailing address, phone number and e-mail address, as well as the college/university, graduate or undergraduate status and year at which he or she joined Phi Alpha Theta.

Entrants must submit five copies of each manuscript and a letter of recommendation from either the Faculty Advisor or History Department Chair indicating the applicant's

chapter affiliation and whether the individual is a graduate or an undergraduate student.
Send to:
Dr. Clayton Drees
Department of History
Virginia Wesleyan College
1584 Wesleyan Drive
Norfolk, VA 23502-5599
E-mail: cdrees@vwc.edu.

Deadline: July 1.

OFFICERS:
Dr. Graydon A. Tunstall, Jr., Executive Director

ADDRESS INQUIRIES TO:
Dr. Graydon A. Tunstall, Jr.
Executive Director
(See address above.)

PONTIFICAL INSTITUTE OF MEDIAEVAL STUDIES [619]

59 Queen's Park Crescent East
Toronto ON M5S 2C4 Canada
(416) 926-7142
Fax: (416) 926-7292
E-mail: allan.smith@utoronto.ca
Web Site: www.pims.ca

FOUNDED: 1929

AREAS OF INTEREST:
Medieval studies.

NAME(S) OF PROGRAMS:
- **Mellon Postdoctoral Fellowships**

TYPE:
Fellowships.

YEAR PROGRAM STARTED: 1998

PURPOSE:
To develop a candidate's personal research in the context of the Institute's mission.

ELIGIBILITY:
Open to scholars engaged in medieval studies. Level of study is postdoctoral.

FINANCIAL DATA:
Amount of support per award: $40,000 (CAN).

Total amount of support: Approximately $160,000 (CAN).

NO. MOST RECENT APPLICANTS: 58 for the year 2014.

NO. AWARDS: Up to 4.

APPLICATION INFO:
Application must include official confirmation that the Ph.D. has been examined and that its award has been approved by the appropriate authority.

Duration: One year.

Deadline: February 1.

ROCK ISLAND ARSENAL MUSEUM [620]

Rock Island Arsenal Historical Society
R. Maguire Scholarship Committee
One Rock Island Arsenal
Rock Island, IL 61299-5000
(309) 782-5021
Fax: (309) 782-3598
E-mail: rimahoch@aol.com
Web Site: www.arsenalhistoricalsociety.com

AREAS OF INTEREST:
Postgraduate, Master's or Doctorate studies in history and museum study.

NAME(S) OF PROGRAMS:
- **Richard C. Maguire Scholarship**

TYPE:
Scholarships.

PURPOSE:
To provide financial support to a student working for a Master's or Doctorate degree in the fields of history, archaeology or museum study.

ELIGIBILITY:
Applicants must be U.S. citizens. Grants will be awarded on an objective and nondiscriminatory basis without regard to age, sex, race, religion or affiliation. Level of study is postdoctoral and postgraduate.

GEOG. RESTRICTIONS: United States.

FINANCIAL DATA:
Amount of support per award: $1,000.

APPLICATION INFO:
Write to the Museum for an application form. Applicant must enclose a self-addressed, stamped envelope.

Duration: One year.

Deadline: May 2.

ADDRESS INQUIRIES TO:
Dick Hochstetler
(See e-mail address above.)

ROCKEFELLER ARCHIVE CENTER [621]

15 Dayton Avenue
Sleepy Hollow, NY 10591
(914) 366-6309
Fax: (914) 361-6017
E-mail: archive@rockarch.org
Web Site: www.rockarch.org

FOUNDED: 1974

AREAS OF INTEREST:
Preservation of and research in the records of The Rockefeller University, the Rockefeller Foundation, the Rockefeller Brothers Fund, the Rockefeller family, the Ford Foundation, the Commonwealth Fund, the Social Science Research Council, the Asian Cultural Council, and other foundations, cultural organizations, research institutions and associated organizations and individuals which include major concentrations in philanthropy, education, history of medicine, science, public health, the arts, agriculture, social sciences, urban affairs and public policy.

CONSULTING OR VOLUNTEER SERVICES:
Reports on holdings and their relevance to research topics and provides assistance to visiting scholars.

NAME(S) OF PROGRAMS:
- **Grants-in-Aid for Research at the Rockefeller Archive Center**

TYPE:
Grants-in-aid. Grants-in-Aid to individual scholars to defray costs of travel and accommodation expenses while doing research at the Rockefeller Archive Center in the Center's collections.

YEAR PROGRAM STARTED: 1977

PURPOSE:
To foster, promote and support research by serious scholars in the collections located at the Rockefeller Archive Center, which includes the records of the Rockefeller Family and their far-reaching philanthropic endeavors, such as the Rockefeller University, Rockefeller Foundation, and Rockefeller Brothers Fund.

LEGAL BASIS:
Nonprofit and educational.

ELIGIBILITY:
Grants will be made on a competitive basis to applicants from any discipline, usually graduate students or postdoctoral scholars, who are engaged in research that requires use of the collections at the Center.

FINANCIAL DATA:
Grants are for receipted, approved expenses. Expenses are reimbursed after the completion of the research visit.

Amount of support per award: Up to $4,000.

Total amount of support: $140,000 for the year 2016.

NO. MOST RECENT APPLICANTS: 73 for the year 2016.

NO. AWARDS: 51 for the year 2016.

APPLICATION INFO:
Two letters supporting the Grant-in-Aid application are required.

Duration: Applications for second- and third-year support will be considered, but preference is given to new applicants.

Deadline: November 1. Announcement of awards at the beginning of March.

PUBLICATIONS:
Research Reports OnLine from the Rockefeller Archive Center; guides to manuscripts and photograph collections; surveys of holdings on specific subjects.

OFFICERS AND STAFF:
Jack Meyers, President
James A. Smith, Vice President and Director of Research and Education

ADDRESS INQUIRIES TO:
Norine Hochman, Executive Assistant
(See address above.)

FRANKLIN D. ROOSEVELT LIBRARY AND MUSEUM [622]

4079 Albany Post Road
Hyde Park, NY 12538
(845) 486-7770
E-mail: grants.fdr@nara.gov
Web Site: fdrlibrary.org/research-grants

FOUNDED: 1941

AREAS OF INTEREST:
Archives, museum, education and public programs relating to the life and times of Franklin and Eleanor Roosevelt.

NAME(S) OF PROGRAMS:
- **Roosevelt Institute Research Grants**

TYPE:
Grants-in-aid; Research grants. The Roosevelt Institute - the Library's nonprofit partner - supports a program of small grants-in-aid, in support of research on the "Roosevelt years" or clearly related subjects.

PURPOSE:
To foster research and education on the life and times of Franklin and Eleanor Roosevelt.

ELIGIBILITY:
The grants program is particularly designed to encourage younger scholars to expand the knowledge and understanding of the Roosevelt period. The Roosevelt Institute Grants Committee makes its decision on whether or not to provide a grant based on the merits of each research topic and its potential contribution to scholarship.

FINANCIAL DATA:
Funds are awarded for the sole purpose of helping to defray living, travel and related expenses incurred while conducting research at the Roosevelt Library.

Amount of support per award: Up to $2,500.

NO. AWARDS: Determined based on the merit of the applications.

APPLICATION INFO:
Application instructions are found on the Library web site. Applicants are required to submit to the grants administrator an original grant application and one copy detailing the nature and scope of their research project, the names and institutions of three references and a budget outlining the amount needed for travel, lodging and any other research expenses. Each application is evaluated by the Library's archival staff to ascertain that there is material at the Library appropriate for the research topic, approximately how long such research might be expected to take, and per diem.

Duration: Use of the grants is to occur within a year of the grant announcement letter.

Deadline: November 15. Grants are awarded at the beginning of each year.

ADDRESS INQUIRIES TO:
See e-mail address above.

*SPECIAL STIPULATIONS:
Letters are sent to all applicants informing them of the Roosevelt Institute Grants Committee's decision on whether or not to grant funding. Grantees are informed that the use of their grants is to occur within a year of their letter. Grantees will receive their award when they arrive for research at the Library.

SANTA BARBARA MISSION ARCHIVE-LIBRARY [623]

2201 Laguna Street
Santa Barbara, CA 93105
(805) 682-4713 ext. 152
E-mail: director@sbmal.org
Web Site: www.sbmal.org

FOUNDED: 1786

AREAS OF INTEREST:
Preservation, cataloging and public history.

NAME(S) OF PROGRAMS:
- **Geiger Memorial Internship**

TYPE:
Internships; Residencies.

YEAR PROGRAM STARTED: 1978

PURPOSE:
To support an opportunity to gain experience working in an archive.

ELIGIBILITY:
Consideration will be given to graduate and undergraduate students furthering their studies or a career in public history, art history, library and information technology, archive management or museum studies.

FINANCIAL DATA:
Amount of support per award: $2,500 stipend.

NO. AWARDS: 1 annually.

APPLICATION INFO:
Application information is available online.

Duration: Eight weeks during the summer.

Deadline: April 29. Announcement June 1.

ADDRESS INQUIRIES TO:
Chair of the Award Committee or
Dr. Monica Orozco, Director
(See address and e-mail above.)

SMITHSONIAN NATIONAL AIR AND SPACE MUSEUM

601 Independence Avenue, S.W.
Room P700, MRC 305
Washington, DC 20560
(202) 633-2542
Fax: (202) 633-8928
E-mail: banksscottm@si.edu
Web Site: airandspace.si.edu/research/internships/

TYPE:
Internships. Full-time interns work 40 hours per week from approximately the first week in June until the second week in August.

See entry 2544 for full listing.

SOCIETY FOR FRENCH HISTORICAL STUDIES [624]

Department of History
University of Vermont
133 South Prospect Street
Burlington, VT 05405-0164
E-mail: steven.zdatny@uvm.edu
Web Site: www.societyforfrenchhistoricalstudies.net

FOUNDED: 1955

AREAS OF INTEREST:
French history.

NAME(S) OF PROGRAMS:
- **The Gilbert Chinard Prize**
- **Natalie Zemon Davis Graduate Student Award**
- **Marjorie M. and Lancelot L. Farrar Memorial Awards**
- **The William Koren, Jr. Prize**
- **The David H. Pinkney Prize**
- **Research Travel Award**
- **John B. and Theta H. Wolf Travel Fellowship**

TYPE:
Awards/prizes. The Chinard Prize is for a recent book on historical relations between France and the Americas.

Davis Graduate Student Award is given for the best paper presented by a graduate student at the Society's annual meeting.

Farrar Award is for dissertation research.

The Koren Prize is for a recent journal article written on French history.

The Pinkney Prize is for a recent book written on French history.

Research Travel Award is for recent recipients of doctorates (awarded jointly with Western Society for French History).

Wolf Travel Fellowship is for research travel pertaining to a dissertation.

YEAR PROGRAM STARTED: 1955

PURPOSE:
To further the study of French history in the U.S. and Canada.

ELIGIBILITY:
Gilbert Chinard Prize: Historical studies of any area or period are acceptable.

Marjorie M. and Lancelot L. Farrar Awards: Must be a doctoral student in French history at a North American university.

William Koren, Jr. Prize: Must be a North American scholar who published an article on any era of French History in an American, European or Canadian journal.

David Pinkney Prize: Must be a citizen of the U.S. or Canada or an author with a full-time appointment at a U.S. or Canadian college or university. Books on any aspect and period of French history will be considered.

Research Travel Award: Granted to an outstanding American or Canadian scholar who has received the Doctorate in History in the five-year period prior to the award.

John B. and Theta H. Wolf Travel Fellowship: Must be a doctoral student at a university in the U.S. or Canada.

FINANCIAL DATA:
Amount of support per award: Chinard and Koren Prize: $1,000; Davis Graduate Student Award: $500; Farrar Awards: $2,500 each; Pinkney Prize: $1,500; Research Travel Award and Wolf Travel Fellowship: $2,000.

NO. AWARDS: Chinard Prize, Davis Graduate Student Award, Koren Prize, Pinkney Prize, Research Travel Award and Wolf Travel Fellowship: 1; Farrar Awards: 2.

APPLICATION INFO:
Application information is available on the web site.

Deadline: Chinard Prize and Pinkney Prize: December 31; Davis Graduate Student Award: May 15; Farrar Memorial Awards, Research Travel Award and Wolf Travel Fellowship: January 31.

ADDRESS INQUIRIES TO:
Dr. Steven Zdatny, Executive Director
(See address above.)

THE SOCIETY OF AMERICAN HISTORIANS [625]

Columbia University
Graduate School of Journalism
2950 Broadway
New York, NY 10027
(212) 854-6495
E-mail: amhistsociety@columbia.edu
Web Site: www.sah.columbia.edu

FOUNDED: 1939

AREAS OF INTEREST:
American history and biography.

NAME(S) OF PROGRAMS:
- **James Fenimore Cooper Prize**
- **Allan Nevins Dissertation Prize**
- **Francis Parkman Prize**

TYPE:
Awards/prizes. James Fenimore Cooper Prize: Biennial award in odd-numbered years for a book of historical fiction on an American subject that makes a significant contribution to historical understanding, portrays authentically the people and events of the historical past, and displays skills in narrative construction and prose style published within the previous two calendar years.

Allan Nevins Dissertation Prize: Annual award for the best written doctoral dissertation on an American subject completed in the previous year.

Francis Parkman Prize: Annual award for the best nonfiction book in American history published the previous calendar year that is distinguished for its literary merit.

YEAR PROGRAM STARTED: 1960

PURPOSE:
To encourage literary distinction in the writing of history and biography.

LEGAL BASIS:
Nonprofit.

ELIGIBILITY:
Allan Nevins Dissertation Prize: Eligible dissertation must have been defended or the Ph.D. received in the previous calendar year; dissertations must be nominated and submitted by the student's program chair or dissertation sponsor.

FINANCIAL DATA:
Amount of support per award: $2,000 per prize.

NO. AWARDS: James Fenimore Cooper Prize: 1 biennially in odd-numbered years; Allan Nevins Dissertation and Francis Parkman Prizes: 1 each biennially.

APPLICATION INFO:
Application information and guidelines are available online.

Deadline: James Fenimore Cooper Prize: December 1, 2016. Allan Nevins Dissertation Prize: December 31 annually. Francis Parkman Prize: December 1 annually.

OFFICERS:
Jill Lepore, President
Tony Horwitz, Vice President
Andie Tucher, Executive Secretary

ADDRESS INQUIRIES TO:
See e-mail address above.

THE SONS OF THE REPUBLIC OF TEXAS [626]

SRT Office
1717 Eighth Street
Bay City, TX 77414
(979) 245-6644
Fax: (979) 244-3819
E-mail: aa-srt@son-rep-texas.net
Web Site: www.srttexas.org

FOUNDED: 1893

AREAS OF INTEREST:
Republic of Texas (1836-1846).

NAME(S) OF PROGRAMS:
- **Summerfield G. Roberts Award**

TYPE:
Awards/prizes. Cash award to the author of a work of creative writing on the Republic of Texas.

PURPOSE:
To encourage literary effort and research about historical events and personalities during the days of the Republic of Texas (1836-1846), and to stimulate interest in this period.

LEGAL BASIS:
Nonprofit organization.

ELIGIBILITY:
The competition is open to all writers everywhere; they need not reside in Texas nor must the publishers be in Texas. Manuscripts may be either fiction or nonfiction, poems, essays, plays, short stories, novels, or biographies.

FINANCIAL DATA:
Amount of support per award: $2,500.

Total amount of support: $2,500 annually.

NO. AWARDS: 1 annually.

APPLICATION INFO:
Manuscripts must be written or published during the calendar year for which the award is given. No entry may be submitted more than one time. There is no word limit on the material submitted for the award. The title page must have the contestant's full name, address and phone number. Five copies of each entry must be mailed to the General Office of The Sons of the Republic of Texas at the address above. No copies will be returned.

Duration: One-time award.

Deadline: Postmarked no later than January 15 of the year following the qualifying year of the award.

ADDRESS INQUIRIES TO:
Janet Knox, Administrative Assistant
The Sons of the Republic of Texas
(See address above.)

THE SONS OF THE REPUBLIC OF TEXAS [627]

SRT Office
1717 Eighth Street
Bay City, TX 77414
(979) 245-6644
Fax: (979) 244-3819
E-mail: aa-srt@son-rep-texas.net
Web Site: www.srttexas.org

FOUNDED: 1893

AREAS OF INTEREST:
Spanish colonial period of Texas history.

NAME(S) OF PROGRAMS:
- **Presidio La Bahia Award**

TYPE:
Awards/prizes. Presidio La Bahia Award is intended to promote suitable preservation of relics, appropriate dissemination of data, and research into Texas heritage, with particular emphasis on the Spanish colonial period.

PURPOSE:
To encourage literary effort and research about historical events and personalities during the days of the Spanish colonial period of Texas history, and to stimulate interest in this period.

ELIGIBILITY:
Open to all persons interested in the Spanish colonial influence on Texas culture.

Research writings have proved in the past to be the most successful type of entry. However, careful consideration will be given to other literary forms, as well as to art, architecture, and archaeological discovery.

FINANCIAL DATA:
Amount of support per award: First place: a minimum of $1,200 for the best published book. At its discretion, the organization may award a second-place book prize. There is a separate category with a prize for the best published paper, article published in a periodical, or project of a nonliterary nature.

Total amount of support: A total of $2,000 is available annually for winning participants in the competition at the discretion of the judges.

NO. AWARDS: 3 for the year 2015.

APPLICATION INFO:
Applicants must submit four copies of published writings to the office. Galley proofs are not acceptable.

Deadline: Entries are accepted from June 1 to September 30.

ADDRESS INQUIRIES TO:
Janet Knox, Administrative Assistant
The Sons of the Republic of Texas
(See address above.)

THE SUMMERLEE FOUNDATION

5556 Caruth Haven Lane
Dallas, TX 75225
(214) 363-9000
Fax: (214) 363-1941
E-mail: info@summerlee.org
Web Site: www.summerlee.org

TYPE:
Project/program grants; Research grants; Technical assistance.

See entry 1347 for full listing.

HARRY S. TRUMAN LIBRARY INSTITUTE

500 West U.S. Highway 24
Independence, MO 64050
(816) 268-8248
Fax: (816) 268-8299
E-mail: sullivan.hstli@gmail.com
Web Site: www.trumanlibraryinstitute.org

TYPE:
Awards/prizes; Fellowships; Grants-in-aid; Research grants; Travel grants. The Dissertation Year Fellowships are given to encourage historical scholarship of the public career of Harry S. Truman or the Truman era. Support is given annually to one or two graduate students who have completed the dissertation research and are in the writing stage. Preference will be given to projects based on extensive research at the Truman Library. Successful applicants will be expected to deposit one copy of their completed dissertation, or any publication resulting therefrom, with the Truman Library.

Research Grants are intended to enable graduate students as well as postdoctoral scholars to come to the Library for one to three weeks to use its archival facilities.

The Scholar's Award is given every other year, even-numbered years only, to a scholar engaged in a study of either the public career of Harry S. Truman or some aspect of the history of the Truman administration or of the U.S. during that administration. The scholar's work must be based on extensive research at the Truman Library and must be designed to result in the publication of a book-length manuscript. One copy of such book (and/or any other publication resulting from work done under this award) shall be deposited by the author with the Harry S. Truman Library.

The Harry S. Truman Book Award is given in even years for the best book dealing with some aspect of history of the U.S. between April 12, 1945 and January 20, 1953 or with the public career of Harry S. Truman.

See entry 1955 for full listing.

U.S. ARMY CENTER OF MILITARY HISTORY [628]

Dissertation Fellowship Committee
Collins Hall, Building 35
102 Fourth Avenue, Fort Lesley J. McNair
Washington, DC 20319-5060
(202) 685-2252
Fax: (202) 685-2077
E-mail: cmhonline@us.army.mil
usarmy.mcnair.cmh.mbx.answers@mail.mil
Web Site: www.army.mil/cmh-pg

FOUNDED: 1942

AREAS OF INTEREST:
History of warfare on land, with special emphasis on the history of the U.S. Army.

NAME(S) OF PROGRAMS:
- **Dissertation Year Fellowships**

TYPE:
The Center offers two Dissertation Fellowships each year and sometimes awards a third fellowship to exceptional dissertations on museum-related topics. The Center will consider dissertations on the history of land warfare; preference is given to topics on the history of the U.S. Army.

YEAR PROGRAM STARTED: 1970

PURPOSE:
To encourage scholarship in military history.

LEGAL BASIS:
Government agency.

ELIGIBILITY:
Applicants must be civilian citizens or nationals of the U.S. that have demonstrated ability and special aptitude for advanced training and study in military history, be enrolled in a recognized graduate school and have successfully completed by September of the year of the award all requirements for the Ph.D. except the dissertation.

FINANCIAL DATA:
Amount of support per award: Stipend of $10,000.

Total amount of support: Up to $30,000.

NO. MOST RECENT APPLICANTS: 26 for the year 2013.

NO. AWARDS: Up to 3 annually.

REPRESENTATIVE AWARDS:
"A Crisis of Faith: Chaplains, Vietnam and Religion in the American Military;" "Conflict and Change during the U.S. Occupation of Cuba, 1898-1902;" "Creature Comforts: The Exchange and Consumption of Sugar, Tobacco, and Other Everyday Stimulants during the Great War."

APPLICATION INFO:
Applicants must submit by mail or fax the following materials:
(1) completed, typed application form;
(2) proposed research plan and reasons for interest in this topic (not to exceed 10 double-spaced, typed pages);
(3) letter from dissertation director confirming dissertation proposal has been accepted by the committee;
(4) letters of recommendation;
(5) a writing sample of approximately 25 double-spaced, typed pages (e.g., seminar paper, published scholarly article, excerpt from M.A. thesis or Ph.D. dissertation) and;
(6) transcripts from all undergraduate and graduate schools attended.

Duration: One year.

Deadline: January 15. Announcement April 1.

ADDRESS INQUIRIES TO:
Dr. Thomas Boghardt
CMH Dissertation Fellowship Committee
(See address above.)

U.S. ARMY MILITARY HISTORY INSTITUTE [629]

U.S. Army Heritage and Education Center
950 Soldiers Drive
Carlisle, PA 17013-5021
(717) 245-4240 (office)
Fax: (717) 245-4370
E-mail: thomas.l.hendrix10.civ@mail.mil
Web Site: www.carlisle.army.mil/ahec/ridgway.cfm

FOUNDED: 1967

AREAS OF INTEREST:
Military history with emphasis on the U.S. Army.

NAME(S) OF PROGRAMS:
- **General and Mrs. Matthew B. Ridgway Research Grant**

TYPE:
Research grants; Travel grants. Research and travel fellowships to cover expenses incurred while conducting individual research in USAMHI holdings. These grants may not be used to cover costs for travel to and research at other institutions.

YEAR PROGRAM STARTED: 1977

PURPOSE:
To stimulate utilization of holdings of the Institute in preparation of scholarly, mature publications in military history (theses, dissertations or books).

LEGAL BASIS:
U.S. Department of the Army.

ELIGIBILITY:
Applicants must be scholars at the undergraduate, graduate, postgraduate, or instructor/professor level; or be other professional scholars or authors; or have comparable qualifications based on experience who are pursuing research topics on significant subjects in the field of military history which are well represented in USAMHI holdings.

Government historians researching for official projects are not eligible.

FINANCIAL DATA:
Amount of support per award: Up to $2,500.

Total amount of support: Varies.

NO. MOST RECENT APPLICANTS: 18 for the year 2014.

NO. AWARDS: 8 for the year 2014.

APPLICATION INFO:
Applications can be downloaded online.

Duration: Until December 31 of the following year.

Deadline: Postmarked by December 31, to be considered when review panel meets in January.

ADDRESS INQUIRIES TO:
Ridgway Research Grants
(See address above.)

*SPECIAL STIPULATIONS:
Must do research in U.S. Army Military History Institute holdings.

U.S. MARINE CORPS [630]

Marine Corps History Division
3078 Upshur Avenue
Quantico, VA 22134
(703) 432-5058
Fax: (703) 432-5054
E-mail: paul.j.weber1@usmc.mil
Web Site: www.history.usmc.mil

FOUNDED: 1919

AREAS OF INTEREST:
U.S. military and naval history and history-based studies in the social and behavioral sciences with a direct relationship to the USMC.

NAME(S) OF PROGRAMS:
- **Marine Corps Historical Program Research Grants**

TYPE:
Awards/prizes; Internships; Research grants. Grants in areas of tangible benefit to the Marine Corps to support research that will add materially to the sum of knowledge regarding the Marine Corps and will not duplicate official projects.

YEAR PROGRAM STARTED: 1975

PURPOSE:
To promote the scholarly study of the USMC from 1775 to the present.

LEGAL BASIS:
Funds provided by the Marine Corps Heritage Foundation, a nonprofit, educational organization.

ELIGIBILITY:
Graduate students, postdoctoral scholars and others with demonstrated professional competence to pursue research projects.

FINANCIAL DATA:
Grants ordinarily will be paid in two installments. Half on the initiation of the approved project and half on its successful conclusion. There are no restrictions on how the recipients apply these funds.

Amount of support per award: $400 to $3,000.

NO. MOST RECENT APPLICANTS: 14 for the year 2015.

NO. AWARDS: 11 for the year 2015.

APPLICATION INFO:
A letter should be submitted prior to formal application if the applicant feels that the project involved is within the scope of the program as outlined in the brochure describing the program. This letter should describe concisely the project and its intended purpose and will serve to initiate a request for formal application if deemed appropriate.

Duration: Varies.

Deadline: Applications accepted throughout the year. Decisions on applicants are announced as soon as possible.

PUBLICATIONS:
Brochure describing program.

OFFICER:
Paul J. Weber, Deputy Director

ADDRESS INQUIRIES TO:
Paul J. Weber, Deputy Director
Marine Corps History Division
(See address above.)

U.S. MARINE CORPS [631]

Marine Corps History Division
3078 Upshur Avenue
Quantico, VA 22134
(703) 432-5058
Fax: (703) 432-5054
E-mail: paul.j.weber1@usmc.mil
Web Site: www.history.usmc.mil

FOUNDED: 1919

AREAS OF INTEREST:
U.S. military and naval history and history-based studies in the social and behavioral sciences with a direct relationship to the history of the USMC.

NAME(S) OF PROGRAMS:
- **Dissertation Fellowships in Marine Corps History**

TYPE:
Awards/prizes; Fellowships; Internships. Awarded to a qualified graduate student working on a doctoral dissertation pertinent to U.S. Marine Corps history. Topics in U.S. military and naval history and history-based topics in the social and behavioral sciences with a direct relationship to the history of the U.S. Marine Corps will be considered.

YEAR PROGRAM STARTED: 1975

PURPOSE:
To promote the scholarly study of the USMC from 1775 to the present.

LEGAL BASIS:
Funds provided by the Marine Corps Heritage Foundation, a nonprofit, educational organization.

ELIGIBILITY:
Applicants must be enrolled in a recognized graduate school, have completed all requirements for the Ph.D. degree except the dissertation and have a university-approved dissertation topic pertinent to U.S. Marine Corps history.

FINANCIAL DATA:
Stipend will be provided directly to the recipient in two equal payments. The first upon acceptance of the award and the second at the completion of the program.

Amount of support per award: $10,000.

Total amount of support: Varies.

NO. MOST RECENT APPLICANTS: 6 for the year 2014.

NO. AWARDS: 1 for the year 2015.

APPLICATION INFO:
Applications may be obtained from the chairman of the history department of the applicant's institution or from the Coordinator, Grants and Fellowships, at the address above.

Duration: One year. No renewals.

Deadline: May 1.

PUBLICATIONS:
Brochure.

OFFICER:
Paul J. Weber, Deputy Director

ADDRESS INQUIRIES TO:
Paul J. Weber, Deputy Director
Marine Corps History Division
(See address above.)

U.S. MARINE CORPS [632]

Marine Corps History Division
3078 Upshur Avenue
Quantico, VA 22134
(703) 432-5058
Fax: (703) 432-5054
E-mail: paul.j.weber1@usmc.mil
Web Site: www.history.usmc.mil

FOUNDED: 1919

AREAS OF INTEREST:
U.S. military and naval history and history-based studies in the social and behavioral sciences with a direct relationship to the history of the USMC.

NAME(S) OF PROGRAMS:
- **Master's Thesis Fellowships in Marine Corps History**

TYPE:
Awards/prizes; Fellowships. Awarded to qualified graduate students with university-approved thesis topics pertinent to U.S. Marine Corps history. Topics may be in U.S. military and naval history or in history-based studies in the social and behavioral sciences, with a direct relationship to the history of the U.S. Marine Corps.

YEAR PROGRAM STARTED: 1986

PURPOSE:
To promote the scholarly study of all aspects of Marine Corps activities from 1775 to the present.

LEGAL BASIS:
Funds provided by the Marine Corps Heritage Foundation, a nonprofit, educational organization.

ELIGIBILITY:
Applicants must be actively enrolled in an accredited Master's degree program requiring a Master's thesis and have a university-approved topic pertinent to U.S. Marine Corps history. Applicants must be U.S. citizens or nationals and must not have held or accepted an equivalent fellowship from any other Department of Defense agency.

FINANCIAL DATA:
Stipend will be provided directly to the recipient in two equal payments. The first upon acceptance of the award and the second upon completion.

Amount of support per award: $3,000.

Total amount of support: Varies.

NO. MOST RECENT APPLICANTS: 2 for the year 2015.

NO. AWARDS: 1 for the year 2015.

APPLICATION INFO:
Applications may be obtained from the chairman of the history department of the applicant's institution or from the Coordinator, Grants and Fellowships, at the address above.

Duration: One year. No renewal; however, thesis fellows are eligible to apply for the Marine Corps Historical Program's doctoral dissertation fellowship when qualified.

Deadline: May 1.

PUBLICATIONS:
Brochure.

OFFICER:
Paul J. Weber, Deputy Director

ADDRESS INQUIRIES TO:
Paul J. Weber, Deputy Director
Marine Corps History Division
(See address above.)

UNITED STATES HOLOCAUST MEMORIAL MUSEUM - JACK, JOSEPH AND MORTON MANDEL CENTER FOR ADVANCED HOLOCAUST STUDIES [633]

100 Raoul Wallenberg Place, S.W.
Washington, DC 20024-2126
(202) 314-7829
Fax: (202) 479-9726
E-mail: vscholars@ushmm.org
Web Site: www.ushmm.org/research/competitive-academic-programs/fellowship-competition

FOUNDED: 1993

AREAS OF INTEREST:
Holocaust and genocide studies.

NAME(S) OF PROGRAMS:
- **Visiting Scholar Program**

TYPE:
Exchange programs; Fellowships. The Jack, Joseph and Morton Mandel Center for Advanced Holocaust Studies is an integral part of the United States Holocaust Memorial Museum, which serves as America's national institution for Holocaust education and remembrance. The Mandel Center awards fellowships to support significant research and writing about the Holocaust. Awards are granted on a competitive basis. The Mandel Center welcomes proposals from scholars in all relevant academic disciplines, including history, political science, literature, Jewish studies, philosophy, religion, psychology, comparative genocide studies, law and others.

Visiting Scholar Program participants at the Mandel Center have access to more than 100 million pages of Holocaust-related archival documentation; the Museum's extensive library; oral history, film, photo, art, artifacts and memoir collections; and Holocaust survivor database.

YEAR PROGRAM STARTED: 1994

PURPOSE:
To support scholarship and publication in the field of Holocaust studies; to promote the growth of Holocaust studies at universities; to seek to foster strong relationships between American and international scholars; to organize programs to ensure the ongoing training of future generations of scholars specializing in the Holocaust.

ELIGIBILITY:
Fellowships are awarded to candidates working on their dissertations (ABD), postdoctoral researchers, and senior scholars. Immediate postdoctorals and faculty between appointments will also be considered.

FINANCIAL DATA:
Amount of support per award: Up to $3,500 monthly.

Total amount of support: Varies.

NO. MOST RECENT APPLICANTS: 146.

NO. AWARDS: Approximately 30.

APPLICATION INFO:
Application information is available at the web site address above.

Duration: Three to eight months. Must be a minimum of three consecutive months.

Deadline: Typically, November of each year.

PUBLICATIONS:
Program announcement.

ADDRESS INQUIRIES TO:
Jo-Ellyn Decker, Program Manager
(See address above.)

THE UNIVERSITY OF DELAWARE-HAGLEY GRADUATE PROGRAM [634]

Department of History, John Munroe Hall
University of Delaware
Newark, DE 19716
(302) 831-8226
Fax: (302) 831-1538
E-mail: dianec@udel.edu
Web Site: www.udel.edu/hagley
www.history.udel.edu

FOUNDED: 1954

AREAS OF INTEREST:
Technology, business, consumption, and work in industrial and post-industrial societies.

TYPE:
Assistantships; Fellowships. The University of Delaware, in association with the Hagley Museum, sponsors a premier graduate resident program for the study of technology, business, consumption, and work in industrial and post-industrial societies leading to a Master of Arts or Ph.D. in History. Students have access to faculty with international reputations in American, European and non-Western history, and benefit from strong interdisciplinary ties to museum studies and material culture programs, as well as the Hagley Museum and Library.

YEAR PROGRAM STARTED: 1954

PURPOSE:
To prepare students planning careers as college teachers and as professionals in museums and historical agencies.

LEGAL BASIS:
Not-for-profit organization classified by IRS as 501(c)(3) organization.

ELIGIBILITY:
All Hagley Scholars are required to complete 30 credits (ten classes). Some of these classes must be selected to fulfill History Department requirements. Hagley Scholars also must take two "Hagley courses" which reflect student and faculty interests. These are offered every semester. Ph.D. students take a written comprehensive examination and write a dissertation. A thesis is optional for M.A. students.

FINANCIAL DATA:
All Hagley Scholars receive a stipend and tuition remission. M.A. students are supported for two years. Ph.D. students receive five years of funding. In exchange, Scholars work as teaching assistants during half the semesters in which they are funded. Hagley Scholars also receive an allowance of $600 a year for travel and research expenses. The Program and the History Department also have additional funds which can be used to support internships and Ph.D. research.

Amount of support per award: M.A. students receive $18,000, plus tuition; Ph.D. students receive $19,500, plus tuition.

APPLICATION INFO:
Interested applicants should complete the online application for the UD History Graduate Program. Applicant should clearly indicate on the top of the personal statement that he or she wishes to be considered for the Hagley Program.

Duration: Nine-month fellowships/assistantships may be renewed once for those seeking a terminal Master's degree and up to four times for those seeking a Ph.D.

Deadline: January 5.

ADDRESS INQUIRIES TO:
Diane Clark, Academic Support Coordinator
(See address above.)

*SPECIAL STIPULATIONS:
This is a resident graduate program.

UNIVERSITY OF DELAWARE, DEPARTMENT OF HISTORY [635]

46 West Delaware Avenue
Newark, DE 19716
(302) 831-8226
Fax: (302) 831-1538
E-mail: dianec@udel.edu
Web Site: www.udel.edu
www.history.udel.edu

AREAS OF INTEREST:
Professional training in historical studies.

NAME(S) OF PROGRAMS:
- **E. Lyman Stewart Fellowship**

TYPE:
Fellowships. Residential program in history.

PURPOSE:
To provide a program of graduate study leading to an M.A. or Ph.D. degree for students who plan careers as museum professionals, historical agency administrators or seek careers in college teaching and public history.

ELIGIBILITY:
Open to nationals of any country.

FINANCIAL DATA:
Amount of support per award: M.A. students receive $18,000, plus tuition; Ph.D. students recieve $19,500, plus tuition.

Total amount of support: Varies.

NO. AWARDS: Varies.

APPLICATION INFO:
Applications must be submitted online using the University of Delaware application form and include transcripts, Graduate Record Examination scores, TOEFL scores (where applicable), plus three letters of recommendation and a writing sample.

Duration: Two to five years.

Deadline: January 5.

ADDRESS INQUIRIES TO:
Diane Clark, Academic Support Coordinator
(See address above.)

WISCONSIN HISTORICAL SOCIETY PRESS [636]

816 State Street
Madison, WI 53706-1482
(608) 264-6582
Fax: (608) 264-6486
E-mail: whspress@wisconsinhistory.org
Web Site: www.wisconsinhistory.org/whspress

FOUNDED: 1846

AREAS OF INTEREST:
Wisconsin history and culture.

NAME(S) OF PROGRAMS:
- **D.C. Everest Fellowship**
- **Amy Louise Hunter Fellowship**
- **Alice E. Smith Fellowship**

TYPE:
Fellowships; Research grants. Fellowships awarded for research and writing for publication in book form by the Society press on Wisconsin history topics.

YEAR PROGRAM STARTED: 2000

PURPOSE:
To promote research and writing on Wisconsin history topics.

LEGAL BASIS:
Agency of the state of Wisconsin.

ELIGIBILITY:
Fellowships are awarded to individuals. Organizations are not eligible to apply.

FINANCIAL DATA:
Amount of support per award: $1,000 to $2,000.

NO. AWARDS: 1 per award.

APPLICATION INFO:
Application form available online.

Duration: One-time award.

PUBLICATIONS:
Program announcement.

ADDRESS INQUIRIES TO:
See e-mail address above.

YIVO INSTITUTE FOR JEWISH RESEARCH [637]

15 West 16th Street, 3rd Floor
New York, NY 10011-6301
(917) 606-8290
Fax: (212) 292-1892
E-mail: jyoung@yivo.cjh.org
Web Site: www.yivo.org

FOUNDED: 1925

AREAS OF INTEREST:
Yiddish, East European and American Jewish history and culture.

NAME(S) OF PROGRAMS:
- **Fellowship in American Jewish Studies**

TYPE:
Fellowships. Fellowship in American Jewish Studies is dedicated to doctoral or postdoctoral research in American Jewish history, with special consideration given to scholars working on some aspect of the Jewish labor movement. This Fellowship is for research at the YIVO Library and Archives.

YEAR PROGRAM STARTED: 1990

PURPOSE:
To further research of American Jewish history, based on resources from the YIVO Library and Archives.

LEGAL BASIS:
Tax-exempt 501(c)(3) organization.

ELIGIBILITY:
Applicants must be working in American Jewish history with special consideration toward the Jewish Labor Movement. The research must be conducted at YIVO in New York City.

FINANCIAL DATA:
Amount of support per award: Stipend of $5,500.

Total amount of support: $5,500.

NO. AWARDS: 1.

APPLICATION INFO:
Application materials should be sent by regular mail, fax or e-mail to:
Chairperson, Fellowship Committee
YIVO Institute for Jewish Research.

Applicants should include the following materials:
(1) curriculum vitae, including all contact information and detailing education,

publications, other scholarly activity (papers presented, etc.), teaching and other relevant work experience, knowledge of relevant languages, honors, awards and fellowships, etc.;
(2) research proposal of no more than four pages, including aims for research during the period of fellowship; whether the proposed work is part of a larger project, such as a dissertation, book, etc.; how the resources of YIVO will contribute to the work and;
(3) two letters of support, which discuss the importance of the applicant's work for the relevant field, as well as the applicant's ability to carry out the proposed work.

Applicants may apply for only one fellowship.

Deadline: January 15, 2016.

PUBLICATIONS:
YIVO-bleter; *Yedies fun YIVO*.

BOARD OF DIRECTORS:
Ruth Levine, Chairman
Jonathan Mishkin, Chairman
Rosina Abramson
Jack Bendheim
Martin Flumenbaum
Sherry Gordon
Fanya Gottesfeld Heller
Solomon Krystal
Dr. Chava Lapin
Jacob Morowitz
Bernard Nussbaum
Doris Payson
Martin Peretz
Irena Pletka
Dr. Arnold Richards
Joseph S. Steinberg
Jodi Sweed
Michael Trock

ADDRESS INQUIRIES TO:
Jennifer Young, Director of Education
Max Weinreich Center for
Advanced Jewish Studies
(See address above.)

*PLEASE NOTE:
Each fellowship requires up to three months' research stay and at least one public lecture by the holder.

YIVO INSTITUTE FOR JEWISH RESEARCH [638]

15 West 16th Street, 3rd Floor
New York, NY 10011-6301
(917) 606-8290
Fax: (212) 292-1892
E-mail: jyoung@yivo.cjh.org
Web Site: www.yivo.org

FOUNDED: 1925

AREAS OF INTEREST:
Yiddish, East European and American Jewish history and culture.

NAME(S) OF PROGRAMS:
- **Fellowship in East European Jewish Literature and Arts**

TYPE:
Fellowships. Fellowship in East European Jewish Literature and Arts is designed to assist an undergraduate, graduate or postgraduate researcher in Eastern European Jewish music, art and theater or Yiddish literature. The stipend is intended to defray expenses connected with research in YIVO's music, art and theater collections and library.

YEAR PROGRAM STARTED: 1994

PURPOSE:
To further research in Yiddish Studies, based on resources from the YIVO Library and Archives.

LEGAL BASIS:
Tax-exempt 501(c)(3) organization.

FINANCIAL DATA:
Amount of support per award: Stipend of $6,500.

NO. AWARDS: 1.

APPLICATION INFO:
Application materials should be sent by regular mail, fax or e-mail to:
Chairperson, Fellowship Committee
YIVO Institute for Jewish Research.

Applicants should include the following materials:
(1) curriculum vitae, including all contact information and detailing education; publications; other scholarly activity (papers presented, etc.); teaching and other relevant work experience; knowledge of relevant languages; honors, awards and fellowships, etc.;
(2) research proposal of no more than four pages, including aims for research during the period of fellowship; whether the proposed work is part of a larger project, such as a dissertation, book, etc.; how the resources of YIVO will contribute to the work and;
(3) two letters of support, which discuss the importance of the applicant's work for the relevant field, as well as the applicant's ability to carry out the proposed work.

Applicants may apply for one fellowship only.

Deadline: January 15.

PUBLICATIONS:
Yedies fun YIVO; *YIVO-bleter*.

BOARD OF DIRECTORS:
Ruth Levine, Chairman
Jonathan Mishkin, Chairman
Rosina Abramson
Jack Bendheim
Martin Flumenbaum
Sherry Gordon
Fanya Gottesfeld Heller
Solomon Krystal
Dr. Chava Lapin
Jacob Morowitz
Bernard Nussbaum
Doris Payson
Martin Peretz
Irena Pletka
Dr. Arnold Richards
Joseph S. Steinberg
Jodi Sweed
Michael Trock

ADDRESS INQUIRIES TO:
Jennifer Young, Director of Education
Max Weinreich Center for
Advanced Jewish Studies
(See address above.)

*PLEASE NOTE:
Each fellowship requires up to three months' research stay and at least one public lecture by the holder.

YIVO INSTITUTE FOR JEWISH RESEARCH [639]

15 West 16th Street, 3rd Floor
New York, NY 10011-6301
(212) 246-6080
Fax: (212) 292-1892
E-mail: eportnoy@yivo.cjh.org
Web Site: www.yivo.org

FOUNDED: 1925

AREAS OF INTEREST:
Eastern European Jewish studies.

NAME(S) OF PROGRAMS:
- **Fellowship in Baltic Jewish Studies**
- **Fellowship in Polish Jewish Studies**

TYPE:
Fellowships. Fellowship in Baltic Jewish Studies supports original doctoral or postdoctoral research in the field of Lithuanian Jewish history at the YIVO Library and Archives or travel for Ph.D. dissertation research in archives and libraries of the Baltic states.

Fellowship in Polish Jewish Studies supports doctoral or postdoctoral research on Polish-Jewish history in the modern period, particularly Jewish-Polish relations, including the Holocaust period, and Jewish contributions to Polish literature and culture. This Fellowship is for research at the YIVO Library and Archives.

PURPOSE:
To advance Eastern European Jewish studies.

FINANCIAL DATA:
Amount of support per award: Fellowship in Baltic Jewish Studies: $5,000. Fellowship in Polish Jewish Studies: $4,000.

APPLICATION INFO:
Applications should include a curriculum vitae, a research proposal (four-page maximum), and two letters of support.

Duration: Varies.

Deadline: January 1.

ADDRESS INQUIRIES TO:
Dr. Eddy Portnoy
Max Weinreich Center Academic Advisor
and Research Associate
(See address above.)

*PLEASE NOTE:
Fellows are usually expected to spend four to six weeks in residence and are required to give one public lecture.

*SPECIAL STIPULATIONS:
Applicants may apply for one fellowship only.

YIVO INSTITUTE FOR JEWISH RESEARCH [640]

15 West 16th Street, 3rd Floor
New York, NY 10011-6301
(212) 246-6080
Fax: (212) 292-1892
E-mail: eportnoy@yivo.cjh.org
Web Site: www.yivo.org

FOUNDED: 1925

AREAS OF INTEREST:
Eastern European Jewish studies.

NAME(S) OF PROGRAMS:
- **The Dina Abramowicz Emerging Scholar Fellowship**
- **The Workmen's Circle/Dr. Emanuel Patt Visiting Professorship**

TYPE:
Fellowships; Visiting scholars. The Dina Abramowicz Emerging Scholar Fellowship is intended for postdoctoral research on a topic in Eastern European Jewish studies. The work should lead to a significant scholarly publication and may encompass the revision of a doctoral dissertation. The Fellowship carries a stipend for the holder to conduct research at the YIVO Library and Archives.

The Workmen's Circle/Dr. Emanuel Patt Visiting Professorship in Eastern European Jewish Studies, established by the Van Cortlandt Workmen's Circle Community House, is designed to support postdoctoral research at the YIVO Library and Archives.

PURPOSE:
To advance Eastern European Jewish studies.

FINANCIAL DATA:
Amount of support per award: Abramowicz Fellowships: $3,000; Workmen's Circle: $5,000.

APPLICATION INFO:
Applications should include a cover letter indicating one choice of fellowship, a curriculum vitae, a research proposal (four-page maximum), and two letters of support.

Duration: Varies.

Deadline: January 1.

ADDRESS INQUIRIES TO:
Dr. Eddy Portnoy
Max Weinreich Center Academic Advisor and Research Associate
(See address above.)

*PLEASE NOTE:
Fellows are usually expected to spend four to six weeks in residence and are required to give one public lecture.

*SPECIAL STIPULATIONS:
Applicants may apply for one fellowship only.

Languages

THE AMERICAN CLASSICAL LEAGUE [641]

860 N.W. Washington Boulevard
Suite A
Hamilton, OH 45013
(513) 529-7741
Fax: (513) 529-7742
E-mail: info@aclclassics.org
Web Site: www.aclclassics.org

FOUNDED: 1919

AREAS OF INTEREST:
Latin and Classical Studies of ancient Rome and Greece.

CONSULTING OR VOLUNTEER SERVICES:
Placement service for teachers of Latin.

NAME(S) OF PROGRAMS:
- **McKinlay Scholarship**

TYPE:
Grants-in-aid; Scholarships.

YEAR PROGRAM STARTED: 1975

PURPOSE:
To assist high school teachers of Latin to further their educational background.

LEGAL BASIS:
Nonprofit.

ELIGIBILITY:
Applicant must be a member of American Classical League for the preceding three years and current year and teaching high school Latin courses.

GEOG. RESTRICTIONS: United States.

FINANCIAL DATA:
Amount of support per award: Varies.

Total amount of support: Varies.

NO. MOST RECENT APPLICANTS: 15.

NO. AWARDS: 14.

APPLICATION INFO:
The application form and guidelines are available on the League web site.

Duration: One-time award.

Deadline: January 15. Award announcement March 15.

ADDRESS INQUIRIES TO:
Sherwin Little, Administrative Secretary
(See address above.)

AMERICAN INSTITUTE OF INDIAN STUDIES [642]

1130 East 59th Street
Chicago, IL 60637
(773) 702-8638
Fax: (773) 702-6636
E-mail: aiis@uchicago.edu
Web Site: www.indiastudies.org

FOUNDED: 1961

AREAS OF INTEREST:
Indian studies.

NAME(S) OF PROGRAMS:
- **Advanced Language Program in India**

TYPE:
Fellowships. Awards for graduate studies in India in an Indian language.

YEAR PROGRAM STARTED: 1969

PURPOSE:
To provide advanced language training in India.

LEGAL BASIS:
Cooperative, nonprofit organization of 47 American colleges and universities.

ELIGIBILITY:
Open to graduate students in U.S. colleges and universities who have had a minimum of two years or 240 class hours of classroom instruction in Bengali, Hindi or Tamil and intend to pursue teaching degrees. Applicants for other Indian languages may be considered, but they should contact the AIIS for further information and advice. Applicants must be U.S. citizens.

FINANCIAL DATA:
Grants will be awarded on a competitive basis and will include round-trip airfare to India and a maintenance allowance sufficient to cover living expenses. No funding will be provided for dependents.

APPLICATION INFO:
Application forms are available from the address above. All applications must include a $25 processing fee.

Duration: Nine months.

Deadline: January 31.

OFFICERS:
Frederick Asher, President
Elise Auerbach, Administrator

ADDRESS INQUIRIES TO:
Fellowship Coordinator
(See address above.)

AMERICAN RESEARCH INSTITUTE IN TURKEY, INC.

c/o The University of Pennsylvania Museum
3260 South Street
Philadelphia, PA 19104-6324
(215) 898-3474
Fax: (215) 898-0657
E-mail: leinwand@sas.upenn.edu
Web Site: ccat.sas.upenn.edu/ARIT

TYPE:
Fellowships. Bogazici University Summer Language Program: For summer study in Turkey. Also offer travel, stipend and tuition grants. This intensive program offers the equivalent of one full academic year of study in advanced Turkish language at the college level.

See entry 869 for full listing.

AXE-HOUGHTON FOUNDATION [643]

c/o Foundation Source
55 Walls Drive, 3rd Floor
Fairfield, CT 06824
(800) 839-1754
Fax: (800) 421-6579
Web Site: www.foundationcenter.org/grantmaker/axehoughton

FOUNDED: 1965

AREAS OF INTEREST:
Improvement of English speech and its uses in the areas of public affairs, education, theatre, poetry and debate. A portion of available funds may be devoted to speech remediation.

TYPE:
Project/program grants.

YEAR PROGRAM STARTED: 1965

PURPOSE:
To foster and encourage an appreciation of the English language, with emphasis on the spoken language.

LEGAL BASIS:
Tax-exempt eleemosynary foundation.

ELIGIBILITY:
Applicant institutions must have tax-exempt status. No grants to individuals or for operating budgets, general purposes, continuing support, annual campaigns, emergency funds, deficit financing, capital funds, endowment funds, loans, matching gifts, scholarships, fellowships or publications.

Grants are rarely made to organizations outside of the New York City metropolitan area.

GEOG. RESTRICTIONS: Primarily New York City.

FINANCIAL DATA:
Amount of support per award: $2,000 to $6,000; Average: $4,000.

APPLICATION INFO:
Applications are only accepted by organizations who have been invited to apply.

Duration: One year. Renewals generally of no more than three years.

Deadline: Submit invited proposals between June 1 and September 1. Award announcements are made in late December.

PUBLICATIONS:
Program policy statement; application guidelines.

OFFICERS AND TRUSTEES:
Jeffrey Steinman, President

Robert B. von Mehren, Vice President
Bruce D. Haims, Treasurer
Suzanne Schwartz Davidson, Secretary

ADDRESS INQUIRIES TO:
John Johnson
(See address above.)

*PLEASE NOTE:
Communications by mail only.

THE JAPAN FOUNDATION, NEW YORK

1700 Broadway
15th Floor
New York, NY 10019
(212) 489-0299
Fax: (212) 489-0409
E-mail: info@jfny.org
Web Site: www.jfny.org
www.cgp.org

TYPE:
Conferences/seminars; Fellowships; Professorships; Project/program grants; Research grants; Travel grants.

See entry 837 for full listing.

KOBE COLLEGE CORPORATION-JAPAN EDUCATION EXCHANGE

540 West Frontage Road, Suite 3335
Northfield, IL 60093
(847) 386-7661
Fax: (847) 386-7662
E-mail: kccjee@comcast.net
Web Site: www.kccjee.org

TYPE:
Awards/prizes. The KCC-JEE High School Essay Contest includes a one-month trip to Japan. It incorporates intensive language study, college credit and a home stay with a Japanese family.

See entry 905 for full listing.

LUSO-AMERICAN EDUCATION FOUNDATION [644]

7080 Donlon Way
Suite 200
Dublin, CA 94568
(925) 828-3883
Fax: (925) 828-4554
E-mail: education@luso-american.org
Web Site: www.luso-american.org/laef.php

FOUNDED: 1963

AREAS OF INTEREST:
Perpetuation of the Portuguese language and culture in the U.S., Portuguese education and the teaching of Portuguese in California schools and universities.

CONSULTING OR VOLUNTEER SERVICES:
Provides advisory and reference services, assists teachers and school districts in setting up Portuguese language and literature courses, choosing texts, etc., makes referrals to other sources of information, permits on-site use of collection and holds annual Conference on Portuguese-American Education for educators, administrators and community persons. Services are free and available to people across the U.S.

NAME(S) OF PROGRAMS:
- **Educational Grant Program**

TYPE:
Grants-in-aid; Research grants; Scholarships. The Foundation provides a variety of grant and scholarship programs: research grants, Portuguese language-program grants, study-abroad (in Portugal) grants; educator (of Portuguese language and/or culture) grants, and scholarships for undergraduate and graduate students.

YEAR PROGRAM STARTED: 1970

PURPOSE:
To lead initiatives for the advances of the Portuguese culture and language; to support qualified students in accessing higher education; and to foster life-long learning programs.

LEGAL BASIS:
Tax-exempt corporation.

ELIGIBILITY:
Varies with the program.

FINANCIAL DATA:
Amount of support per award: Grants vary in amount, depending on the applicant's need and Foundation funds allocated.

Total amount of support: Varies.

APPLICATION INFO:
Call and request application form.

Deadline: For most programs, all materials pertinent to an application must be postmarked by February 15. For the Luso-American Fraternal Federation 20-30s and Adult College Scholarships: All materials pertinent to this application must be postmarked by April 1.

PUBLICATIONS:
The Luso-American, annual; *Portuguese Presence in California*; *Literatura de Expressao Portuguesa Nos Estados Unidos*; bibliographies; annual report.

ADDRESS INQUIRIES TO:
Sara Rodrigues
Administrative Director
(See address above.)

LUSO-AMERICAN EDUCATION FOUNDATION [645]

7080 Donlon Way
Suite 200
Dublin, CA 94568
(925) 828-3883
Fax: (925) 828-4554
E-mail: education@luso-american.org
Web Site: www.luso-american.org/laef.php

FOUNDED: 1963

AREAS OF INTEREST:
Perpetuation of the Portuguese language and culture in the U.S.

NAME(S) OF PROGRAMS:
- **Luso-American Education**

TYPE:
Scholarships.

LEGAL BASIS:
Tax-exempt corporation.

ELIGIBILITY:
For the General Youth Scholarship, the applicant must currently be a high school graduating senior, enrolled to begin classes at a community or four-year college/university, and an official U.S. resident. He or she must also meet one of the following requirements:
(1) being of Portuguese descent, with a minimum grade point average of 3.5;
(2) currently taking Portuguese classes at high school level, with a minimum grade point average of 3.0 or;
(3) having attended the Luso-American Education Foundation Cultural Youth Summer Camp for a minimum of two years, with a minimum grade point average of 3.0.

FINANCIAL DATA:
Amount of support per award: Varies in amount, depending on applicant's need and Foundation funds allocated.

NO. MOST RECENT APPLICANTS: 112.

APPLICATION INFO:
The following materials must be submitted:
(1) a complete application by printing (in pen) or typing all information requested;
(2) an official transcript of all completed high school work and SAT/ACT scores (if applicable); these must be issued and certified by a school official, along with a completed Student Counselor Report (found on web site);
(3) a letter of recommendation submitted directly from two individuals who can attest to applicant's character and/or financial needs; each letter of recommendation must be submitted with a Letter of Recommendation Cover Sheet (found on web site) and;
(4) a recent wallet-size photo of applicant (no photocopies).

Duration: Nonrenewable.

Deadline: All materials pertinent to this application must be postmarked by February 15. Announcement prior to June 1.

PUBLICATIONS:
Program announcement.

ADDRESS INQUIRIES TO:
Sara Rodrigues
Administrative Director
(See address above.)

MODERN LANGUAGE ASSOCIATION OF AMERICA [646]

85 Broad Street, Suite 500
New York, NY 10004-2434
(646) 576-5000
(646) 576-5141
Fax: (646) 458-0030
E-mail: awards@mla.org
Web Site: www.mla.org

FOUNDED: 1883

AREAS OF INTEREST:
Literary studies, languages and education.

NAME(S) OF PROGRAMS:
- **Morton N. Cohen Award for a Distinguished Edition of Letters**
- **Kenneth W. Mildenberger Prize**
- **Modern Language Association Prize for a Scholarly Edition**
- **Modern Language Association Prize for Independent Scholars**
- **Mina P. Shaughnessy Prize**

TYPE:
Awards/prizes.

PURPOSE:
To recognize outstanding scholarly work.

LEGAL BASIS:
Membership association.

ELIGIBILITY:
Authors are not required to be members of the Association.

The Morton N. Cohen Award is presented biennially in odd-numbered years for important collections of letters published in either of the two preceding years. A multivolume edition is eligible if at least one volume was published during that period. Editors can apply regardless of the fields they and the authors of the letters represent. The winning collection will be one that provides a clear, accurate and readable text, necessary background information, and succinct and eloquent introductory material and annotations. The collection should be in itself a work of literature.

The Kenneth W. Mildenberger Prize is presented biennially in odd-numbered years for an outstanding publication in the field of teaching foreign languages and literatures.

The Modern Language Association Prize for a Scholarly Edition will be given biennially in odd-numbered years to a book published in either of the two preceding years without regard to the field or language either of the editor or of the text presented in the edition. To qualify for the award, an edition should be based on an examination of all available relevant textual sources; the source texts and the edited text's deviations from them should be fully described; the edition should employ editorial principles appropriate to the materials edited, and those principles should be clearly articulated in the volume; the text should be accompanied by appropriate textual and other historical contextual information; the edition should exhibit the highest standards of accuracy in the presentation of its text and apparatus; and the text and apparatus should be presented as accessibly and elegantly as possible.

The Modern Language Association Prize for Independent Scholars is awarded biennially in even-numbered years for a distinguished scholarly book published in the field of English or another modern language or literature. Authors enrolled in a program leading to an academic degree and authors holding a tenured, tenure-accruing or tenure-track position in a postsecondary institution at the time of publication of the book are not eligible. Tenure is understood to include any comparable provision for job security in a postsecondary educational institution.

The Mina P. Shaughnessy Prize is presented biennially in even-numbered years for an outstanding scholarly book in the fields of language, culture, literacy and literature that has a strong application to the teaching of English.

FINANCIAL DATA:

Amount of support per award: Varies.

Total amount of support: Varies.

APPLICATION INFO:

Application form is required for submissions to the Prize for Independent Scholars. To enter book into competition for other prizes, no special form or procedure is needed. Shipments of books should be preceded or accompanied by letters identifying the works.

Duration: One-time award.

Deadline: May 1.

ADDRESS INQUIRIES TO:

Annie M. Reiser, Coordinator of Book Prizes (See address above.)

MODERN LANGUAGE ASSOCIATION OF AMERICA [647]

85 Broad Street, Suite 500
New York, NY 10004-2434
(646) 576-5000
(646) 576-5141
Fax: (646) 458-0030
E-mail: awards@mla.org
Web Site: www.mla.org

FOUNDED: 1883

AREAS OF INTEREST:

Literary studies, languages and education.

NAME(S) OF PROGRAMS:

- **Matei Calinescu Prize**
- **Katherine Singer Kovacs Prize**
- **Fenia and Yaakov Leviant Memorial Prize in Yiddish Studies**
- **James Russell Lowell Prize**
- **Howard R. Marraro Prize**
- **MLA Prize for a Bibliography, Archive, or Digital Project**
- **MLA Prize for a First Book**
- **MLA Prize in United States Latina and Latino and Chicana and Chicano Literary and Cultural Studies**
- **Lois Roth Award for a Translation of a Literary Work**
- **Aldo and Jeanne Scaglione Prize for a Translation of a Literary Work**
- **Aldo and Jeanne Scaglione Prize for a Translation of a Scholarly Study of Literature**
- **Aldo and Jeanne Scaglione Prize for Comparative Literary Studies**
- **Aldo and Jeanne Scaglione Prize for French and Francophone Studies**
- **Aldo and Jeanne Scaglione Prize for Italian Studies**
- **Aldo and Jeanne Scaglione Prize for Studies in Slavic Languages and Literatures**
- **Aldo and Jeanne Scaglione Prize for Studies in Germanic Languages and Literatures**
- **Aldo and Jeanne Scaglione Publication Award for a Manuscript in Italian Literary Studies**
- **William Sanders Scarborough Prize**

TYPE:

Awards/prizes. To recognize outstanding scholarly works in the fields of English, French, Italian, Germanic languages and Slavic languages, Yiddish literature and culture, Black American literature and culture, Latino/Latina and Chicana/Chicano literature and culture. Germanic languages include Danish, Dutch, German, Icelandic, Norwegian, Swedish and Yiddish.

The Fenia and Yaakov Leviant Memorial Prize in Yiddish Studies, the Howard R. Marraro Prize, the MLA Prize for a Bibliography, Archive, or Digital Project, the Aldo and Jeanne Scaglione Prize for a Translation of a Literary Work and the Aldo and Jeanne Scaglione Prize for Studies in Germanic Languages and Literatures are offered biennially in even-numbered years. The MLA Prize in United States Latina and Latino and Chicana and Chicano Literary and Cultural Studies, the Lois Roth Award for a Translation of a Literary Work, the Aldo and Jeanne Scaglione Prize for a Translation of a Scholarly Study of Literature, the Aldo and Jeanne Scaglione Prize for Italian Studies, and the Aldo and Jeanne Scaglione Prize for Studies in Slavic Languages and Literatures are offered biennially in odd-numbered years. All others are awarded annually.

PURPOSE:

To recognize outstanding scholarly work.

LEGAL BASIS:

Membership association.

ELIGIBILITY:

For all awards, works of literary history, literary criticism, philology or literary theory are eligible. Except for translation prizes, books that are primarily translations are ineligible. For French, Germanic, Italian, Lowell, First Book and Marraro Prizes, books must be written by a current member of the Association.

FINANCIAL DATA:

Amount of support per award: Varies.

APPLICATION INFO:

To enter books into competition for prizes, no special form or procedure is needed. Four to six copies of each work are required, depending upon the prize. Shipments of books should be preceded or accompanied by letters identifying the works and where necessary, confirming the author's membership in the MLA.

Duration: One-time awards.

Deadline: James Russell Lowell Prize and Prize for a First Book: March 1. Matei Calinescu Prize, Lois Roth Award and Scaglione Prize for a Translation of a Literary Work: April 1. Scaglione Publication Award for a Manuscript in Italian Literary Studies: June 1. All other awards: May 1.

ADDRESS INQUIRIES TO:

Annie M. Reiser, Coordinator of Book Prizes (See address above.)

NATIONAL SCIENCE FOUNDATION [648]

Linguistics Program
Division of Behavioral and Cognitive Sciences
4201 Wilson Boulevard, Suite 995
Arlington, VA 22230
(703) 292-8046
Fax: (703) 292-9068
E-mail: jmaling@nsf.gov
Web Site: www.nsf.gov

FOUNDED: 1950

NAME(S) OF PROGRAMS:

- **Doctoral Dissertation Research Improvement Grants (DDRIG)**
- **Documenting Endangered Languages (DEL)**
- **Linguistics Program**

TYPE:

Research grants. Conferences/workshops. Awards provide support for research into the syntactic, morphological, semantic, phonological and phonetic properties of individual languages and of language in general. Research into the acquisition of language, the psychological processes in the production and perception of language, the biological foundations of language, the social influences on and effects of language and dialect variation, and the formal and mathematical properties of language models are also supported.

YEAR PROGRAM STARTED: 1975

PURPOSE:

To support scientific research and education to strengthen research potential in language sciences.

LEGAL BASIS:

National Science Foundation Act of 1950.

ELIGIBILITY:
Applicants may be U.S. colleges and universities on behalf of their staff members, nonprofit, nonacademic research institutions, such as independent museums, observatories, research laboratories, stock centers and similar organizations, private profit organizations and, under special circumstances, unaffiliated U.S. scientists.

FINANCIAL DATA:
Support may cover salaries, research assistantships, staff benefits if a direct cost, permanent equipment, travel, publication costs, computer costs and certain other direct and indirect costs.

Amount of support per award: Averages $350,000 over three-year grant period; Doctoral Dissertation Research Improvement Grants: Not more than $12,000 in indirect costs.

Total amount of support: Approximately $6,000,000 for fiscal year 2014; $3,100,000 for DEL.

CO-OP FUNDING PROGRAMS: DEL in partnership with the National Endowment for the Humanities.

NO. MOST RECENT APPLICANTS: Approximately 250 for the year 2014; 80 for DEL.

APPLICATION INFO:
Proposal should include information about the institution, principal investigator and business administrator, title and description of proposed research, desired effective date of grant, duration of support, facilities, personnel, biographical sketches, current support and pending applications and budget.

Duration: Research grants may be for periods of up to five years. Most grants are for three years, except dissertation awards which are typically for 12 to 24 months.

Deadline: Linguistics Program: Target dates are July 15 for Fall review and January 15 for Spring review. Proposals received too late for one round of review will be reviewed in the following round with a corresponding delay in the availability of funding. Documenting Endangered Languages Program: September 15 annually.

PUBLICATIONS:
NSF grant proposal guide.

STAFF:
Joan Maling, Program Director

ADDRESS INQUIRIES TO:
Joan Maling, Program Director
(See address above.)

PEN AMERICAN CENTER [649]

588 Broadway, Suite 303
New York, NY 10012-5246
(212) 334-1660
Fax: (212) 334-2181
E-mail: awards@pen.org
Web Site: www.pen.org

FOUNDED: 1922

AREAS OF INTEREST:
Intellectual cooperation among men and women of letters in all countries in the interests of literature, the exchange of ideas, freedom of expression and goodwill.

NAME(S) OF PROGRAMS:
- **PEN Translation Prize**

TYPE:
Awards/prizes. Translation prize awarded for a distinguished translation into English from any language published in the U.S. in 2016.

YEAR PROGRAM STARTED: 1962

PURPOSE:
To promote the art of translation; to pay tribute to the profession.

LEGAL BASIS:
Nonprofit organization affiliated with International PEN.

ELIGIBILITY:
Although all eligible books must have been published in the U.S. in 2016, translators may be of any nationality; U.S. residency or citizenship is not required. There are no restrictions on the subject matter of translated works, although eligible titles should be of a literary character; technical, scientific, or bibliographical translations will not be considered. Translators and authors may not submit their own work. Submissions will only be accepted from publishers and literary agents.

FINANCIAL DATA:
Amount of support per award: $3,000.

Total amount of support: $3,000 annually.

NO. MOST RECENT APPLICANTS: 130.

NO. AWARDS: 1 each year.

REPRESENTATIVE AWARDS:
Tiina Nunnally, translator of *Kristin Lavransdottir*, by Sigrid Undset.

APPLICATION INFO:
Online application form can be found on the Center web site. One copy of a book-length literary translation published during the calendar year under consideration may be submitted by publishers or literary agents. Self-published books are not eligible. Early submissions are strongly recommended.

Duration: One year.

Deadline: Summer.

BOARD OF TRUSTEES:
Andrew Solomon, President

ADDRESS INQUIRIES TO:
PEN Literary Awards
(See address above.)

THE PHI BETA KAPPA SOCIETY

1606 New Hampshire Avenue, N.W.
Washington, DC 20009
(202) 745-3287
Fax: (202) 986-1601
E-mail: awards@pbk.org
Web Site: www.pbk.org

TYPE:
Fellowships. Fellowship for at least six months of study in France. One award given annually.

See entry 916 for full listing.

SOUTH ATLANTIC MODERN LANGUAGE ASSOCIATION [650]

Georgia State University
Department of English
25 Park Place N.E., Suite 2425
Atlanta, GA 30303
(404) 413-5816
E-mail: samla@gsu.edu
Web Site: samla.memberclicks.net

FOUNDED: 1928

AREAS OF INTEREST:
All humanities.

NAME(S) OF PROGRAMS:
- **Graduate Student Creative Writing Award**
- **Graduate Student Essay Prize**
- **Harper Fund Award**
- **SAMLA Studies Award**
- **SAR Prize**

TYPE:
Assistantships; Awards/prizes; Conferences/seminars; Internships; Professorships; Travel grants. SAMLA Studies Award is for the best scholarly book written by a SAMLA member. Presses and individual members may nominate their recent publications in the year prior to the year of the convention.

YEAR PROGRAM STARTED: 1934

PURPOSE:
To encourage and honor distinguished scholarship in the modern languages and literatures.

LEGAL BASIS:
Nonprofit organization.

ELIGIBILITY:
Open to SAMLA members.

GEOG. RESTRICTIONS: Alabama, District of Columbia, Florida, Georgia, Kentucky, Maryland, North Carolina, South Carolina, Tennessee, Virginia, and West Virginia.

FINANCIAL DATA:
Amount of support per award: Graduate Student Creative Writing Award and Graduate Student Essay Prize: $250 per award; Harper Fund Award: Up to $500; SAMLA Studies Award: $1,000; SAR Prize: $500.

Total amount of support: Varies.

NO. MOST RECENT APPLICANTS: SAMLA Studies Award: 8; SAR Prizes: 25.

NO. AWARDS: SAMLA Studies Award, SAR Prizes and Graduate Student Essay Prize: 4. Harper Fund Award: Varies.

APPLICATION INFO:
SAMLA Studies Award: Applicants must be SAMLA members who have had a scholarly book published in the preceding year. No bibliographies or editions. Must be written in English. Presses and individuals may nominate their recent publications.

Duration: One-time award. Nonrenewable.

Deadline: May 1.

PUBLICATIONS:
South Atlantic Review, quarterly journal; *SAMLA News*, newsletter.

IRS I.D.: 62-0800246

OFFICERS:
Ruth Sanchez Imizcoz, President
Scott Yarbrough, First Vice President
Rafael Ocasio, Second Vice President

EXECUTIVE COMMITTEE:
Silvia Giovanardi Byer
Chris Cairney
Christina Russell McDonald
Tara Powell
Susan Canty Quinlan
Sabine Smith

ADDRESS INQUIRIES TO:
Paul Donnelly, Associate Director
(See address above.)

U.S. DEPARTMENT OF EDUCATION [651]

International and Foreign Language Education (IFLE)
Advanced Training and Research Division
1990 K Street, N.W., Suite 6087
Washington, DC 20006-8521
(202) 502-7634
(202) 502-7700
Fax: (202) 502-7860
E-mail: ifle@ed.gov
Web Site: www.ed.gov/ope/iegps

AREAS OF INTEREST:
Foreign language and area studies.

NAME(S) OF PROGRAMS:
- **Foreign Language and Area Studies Fellowships**

TYPE:
Fellowships. The Foreign Language and Area Studies Fellowships program provides allocations of academic year and summer fellowships to institutions of higher education or consortia of institutions of higher education to assist meritorious undergraduate students and graduate students undergoing training in modern foreign languages and related international or area studies.

YEAR PROGRAM STARTED: 1959

LEGAL BASIS:
Section 602, Title VI of the Higher Education Act of 1965, as amended.

ELIGIBILITY:
FLAS grants are awarded to institutions for a four-year project period. Institutions conduct competitions to select eligible undergraduate and graduate students to receive fellowships.

Funds may be used overseas with prior approval from IFLE.

GEOG. RESTRICTIONS: United States.

FINANCIAL DATA:
Each fellowship includes an institutional payment and a subsistence allowance.

Amount of support per award: The estimated institutional payment for 2015-16 academic year fellowship is $18,000 for a graduate student and $10,000 for an undergraduate student. The estimated institutional payment for summer 2016 fellowship is $5,000 for graduate and undergraduate students.

The estimated subsistence allowance for academic year 2015-16 fellowship is $15,000 for a graduate student and $5,000 for an undergraduate student. The subsistence allowance for summer 2016 fellowship is $2,500 for graduate and undergraduate students.

APPLICATION INFO:
An electronic application form is available at the web site.

Duration: Institutions: Four years. Individuals: Academic year or summer.

ADDRESS INQUIRIES TO:
Carolyn Collins, Program Officer
(See address above.)

*PLEASE NOTE:
The next competition will take place in 2018.

U.S. DEPARTMENT OF EDUCATION [652]

International and Foreign Language Education (IFLE)
International Studies Division
Room 6084, 6th Floor
1990 K Street, N.W.
Washington, DC 20006-8521
(202) 502-7589
(202) 502-7700 (main office)
Fax: (202) 502-7860
E-mail: ddra@ed.gov
Web Site: www.ed.gov/programs/iegpsddrap/index.html

AREAS OF INTEREST:
Foreign languages.

NAME(S) OF PROGRAMS:
- **Fulbright-Hays Doctoral Dissertation Research Abroad**

TYPE:
Fellowships. Fellowships to support doctoral dissertation research abroad in modern foreign languages and related area studies. For the purpose of these programs, area studies is defined as a program of comprehensive study of the aspects of a society or societies, including the study of their geography, history, culture, economy, politics, international relations and languages. The program is designed to develop research knowledge and capability in world areas not widely included in American curricula. Awards will not be available for projects focusing on Western Europe.

YEAR PROGRAM STARTED: 1964

PURPOSE:
To enable graduate students who plan to teach in the U.S. to undertake doctoral dissertation research in the field of modern foreign languages and area studies; to assist with the development of language and area studies specialists.

LEGAL BASIS:
The Mutual Educational and Cultural Exchange Act of 1961, Public Law 87-256, as amended (commonly known as the Fulbright-Hays Act), Section 102(b)(6).

ELIGIBILITY:
A student is eligible to receive a fellowship if he or she:
(1) is a citizen or national of the U.S. or is a permanent resident of the U.S.;
(2) is a graduate student in good standing at an institution of higher education who, when the fellowship begins, is admitted to candidacy in a doctoral program in modern foreign languages and area studies at that institution;
(3) is planning a teaching career in the U.S. upon graduation and;
(4) possesses adequate skills in the language(s) necessary to carry out the dissertation project.

FINANCIAL DATA:
Travel expenses, including excess baggage to and from the residence of the fellow to the host country of research. Maintenance allowance based on the cost of living in country(ies) of research for the fellow and his or her dependent(s). Project allowance for research-related expenses such as books, affiliation fees, local travel and other incidental expenses. Health and accident insurance premiums. $100 administrative fee to applicant institution.

Amount of support per award: $33,000 average for the year 2014.

Total amount of support: $3,000,000 for the year 2014.

NO. MOST RECENT APPLICANTS: 380.

NO. AWARDS: 84.

REPRESENTATIVE AWARDS:
$19,303 for "Testing AIDS Treatment Efficacy by a Northern Thai Community;" $28,565 for "Rethinking Community Through Suburban Nepal;" $22,364 for "Culture, Nationalism and Ethnicity in Twentieth Century Lesotho."

APPLICATION INFO:
Official application materials are available from college and university graduate schools concerned with the fellowship program. Prospective applicants must apply electronically through their institutions. The completed materials are then forwarded electronically by the institution to the U.S. Education Department's Application Control Center (ACC) in accordance with instructions published in the *Federal Register*.

Duration: Fellowships provide support for a minimum period of six months and a maximum period of 12 months.

ADDRESS INQUIRIES TO:
Dr. Pamela Maimer
E-mail: pamela.maimer@ed.gov

U.S. DEPARTMENT OF EDUCATION [653]

Higher Education Programs
International and Foreign Language Education (IFLE)
National Resource Centers Program
1990 K Street, N.W., Room 6087
Mail Stop K-OPE-6-6078
Washington, DC 20006
(202) 502-7634
(202) 502-7700
Fax: (202) 502-7860
E-mail: IFLE@ed.gov
Web Site: www.ed.gov/ope/iegps

AREAS OF INTEREST:
Foreign language and area studies.

NAME(S) OF PROGRAMS:
- **National Resource Centers (NRC) Program**

TYPE:
Project/program grants; Training grants. The NRC Program provides grants to institutions of higher education and consortia of institutions to establish, strengthen and operate comprehensive and undergraduate centers that will be national resources for:
(1) teaching of any modern foreign language;
(2) instruction in fields needed to provide full understanding of areas, regions or countries in which the modern foreign language is commonly used;
(3) research and training in international studies and the international and foreign language aspects of professional and other fields of study and;
(4) instruction and research on issues in world affairs that concern one or more countries.

LEGAL BASIS:
Authorized under Section 602, Title VI of the Higher Education Act, as amended.

FINANCIAL DATA:
Amount of support per award: $115,000 to $285,000 per year.

NO. AWARDS: 100 to 110 institutional grants; 100 new awards in fiscal year 2014.

APPLICATION INFO:
Duration: Four years.

ADDRESS INQUIRIES TO:
Cheryl E. Gibbs, Director
Advanced Training and Research Division
(See address above.)

*PLEASE NOTE:
The NRC Program competes every four years. The next competition will be in fiscal year 2018. This is not a cost-share or matching grant program.

U.S. DEPARTMENT OF EDUCATION [654]

Higher Education Programs
International and Foreign Language Education (IFLE)
Language Resource Centers Program
1990 K Street, N.W., 6th Floor
Mail Stop K-OPE-6-6078
Washington, DC 20006
(202) 502-7589
Fax: (202) 502-7860
E-mail: stephanie.mckissic@ed.gov
Web Site: www.ed.gov/ope/iegps

AREAS OF INTEREST:
Foreign language education.

NAME(S) OF PROGRAMS:
- **Language Resource Centers Program**

TYPE:
General operating grants. Language Resource Centers Program provides grants for establishing, strengthening and operating centers that serve as resources for improving the nation's capacity for teaching and learning foreign languages through teacher training, research, materials development and dissemination projects.

PURPOSE:
To provide grants to institutions of higher education to establish, strengthen and operate resource centers that serve to improve the nation's capacity to teach and learn foreign languages.

ELIGIBILITY:
Applicant organizations must be institutions of higher education.

FINANCIAL DATA:
Amount of support per award: Average new award for fiscal year 2014: $171,673.

Total amount of support: $2,762,068 appropriated for fiscal year 2014.

NO. AWARDS: 16 new awards for fiscal year 2014.

APPLICATION INFO:
Duration: Four years.

ADDRESS INQUIRIES TO:
Dr. Stephanie McKissic
Program Officer
Language Resource Centers Program
(See address above.)

*PLEASE NOTE:
The next competition will be in fiscal year 2018.

U.S. DEPARTMENT OF EDUCATION

International and Foreign Language Education
1990 K Street, N.W., 6th Floor
Mail Stop K-OPE-6-6078
Washington, DC 20006-8521
(202) 502-7626
(202) 502-7700
Fax: (202) 502-7860
E-mail: tanyelle.richardson@ed.gov
Web Site: www2.ed.gov/programs/iegpsgpa/index.html

TYPE:
Exchange programs; Project/program grants; Seed money grants; Training grants; Travel grants. Also, study grants and grants for foreign language and area study programs of educational development for projects to be undertaken abroad. Grants are awarded to higher education institutions, nonprofit educational organizations, state department of education and consortium of such institutions, departments, organizations and institutions which, in turn, enable professors, college and elementary and secondary school teachers and advanced students to attend seminars abroad and to travel and study in foreign countries in order to strengthen the institution's programs in foreign languages, area studies and world affairs.

See entry 924 for full listing.

U.S. DEPARTMENT OF EDUCATION

Office of Postsecondary Education
International and Foreign Language Education
1990 K Street, N.W., 6th Floor
Washington, DC 20006-8521
(202) 502-7589
(202) 502-7700
Fax: (202) 502-7860
E-mail: stephanie.mckissic@ed.gov
Web Site: www2.ed.gov/programs/iegpsfra/index.html

TYPE:
Fellowships; Research grants. This program funds fellowships through institutions of higher education (IHEs) to faculty members who propose to conduct research abroad in modern foreign languages and area studies to improve their skill in language and their knowledge of the culture of the people of these countries.

See entry 925 for full listing.

U.S. DEPARTMENT OF EDUCATION

International and Foreign Language Education Office
1990 K Street, N.W., Sixth Floor
Washington, DC 20006-8521
(202) 502-7626
Fax: (202) 502-7860
E-mail: tanyelle.richardson@ed.gov
Web Site: www.ed.gov/ope/iegps

TYPE:
Project/program grants; Seed money grants. Grants to plan, develop, and carry out a program to strengthen and improve undergraduate instruction in international studies and foreign languages. Projects primarily focus on curriculum and faculty development. Institutions of higher education and public and private nonprofit agencies and organizations may apply for funds to develop projects which have the potential for making an especially significant contribution to the improvement of undergraduate instruction in international and foreign language studies in the U.S.

See entry 1589 for full listing.

YIVO INSTITUTE FOR JEWISH RESEARCH

15 West 16th Street, 3rd Floor
New York, NY 10011-6301
(917) 606-8290
Fax: (212) 292-1892
E-mail: jyoung@yivo.cjh.org
Web Site: www.yivo.org

TYPE:
Fellowships. Fellowship in East European Jewish Literature and Arts is designed to assist an undergraduate, graduate or postgraduate researcher in Eastern European Jewish music, art and theater or Yiddish literature. The stipend is intended to defray expenses connected with research in YIVO's music, art and theater collections and library.

See entry 638 for full listing.

Literature

THE AMERICAN-SCANDINAVIAN FOUNDATION [655]

58 Park Avenue
New York, NY 10016
(212) 879-9779
(212) 847-9728
Fax: (212) 249-3444
E-mail: grants@amscan.org
Web Site: www.amscan.org

FOUNDED: 1910

AREAS OF INTEREST:
Translations of poetry, fiction, drama or literary prose by a Scandinavian author born after 1800.

NAME(S) OF PROGRAMS:
- **American-Scandinavian Foundation Translation Competition**

TYPE:
Awards/prizes. Prize for translation of fiction (50 double-spaced manuscript pages) or poetry (25 double-spaced manuscript pages).

YEAR PROGRAM STARTED: 1980

PURPOSE:
To encourage English translation of contemporary Scandinavian literature.

LEGAL BASIS:
Nonprofit educational institution qualifying under statutes 501(c)(3), 509(a)(1) and 170(c)(2) of the IRS code.

ELIGIBILITY:
Entry must be work by one author, though not necessarily from a single work. It should be conceived as part of a book manuscript. A table of contents for the proposed book should also be included.

FINANCIAL DATA:
Amount of support per award: First prize: $2,500; Second Prize: $2,000.

Total amount of support: $4,500.

NO. MOST RECENT APPLICANTS: 20.

NO. AWARDS: 2.

APPLICATION INFO:
Request rules for Translation Prize Competition. Applicants should submit one copy of work in original language and one copy of translation, including title page and table of contents. Name, address and phone number of translator and title and author of the manuscript with the original language specified should be on a separate page. Translator must include written permission from author or author's agent for translation to be entered in competition and published in *Scandinavian Review*. Manuscripts accompanied by self-addressed, stamped envelope will be returned.

Duration: One-time award.

Deadline: June 1. Awards announced by November 1.

PUBLICATIONS:
Competition rules.

OFFICER:
Edward P. Gallagher, President

ADDRESS INQUIRIES TO:
Translation Prize Committee
(See address above.)

AMERICAN SOCIETY OF COMPOSERS, AUTHORS AND PUBLISHERS (ASCAP) [656]

1900 Broadway, 7th Floor
New York, NY 10023
(212) 621-6588
Fax: (212) 595-3276
E-mail: jsteinblatt@ascap.com
Web Site: www.ascap.com

FOUNDED: 1914

AREAS OF INTEREST:
Writing on the subject of music.

NAME(S) OF PROGRAMS:

- **ASCAP Deems Taylor/Virgil Thomson Awards**

TYPE:
Awards/prizes. The ASCAP Deems Taylor/Virgil Thomson Awards program recognizes books and articles on the subject of music selected for their excellence.

YEAR PROGRAM STARTED: 1967

PURPOSE:
To encourage, recognize and reward excellence in a field that is vital to the health and growth of America's musical heritage.

LEGAL BASIS:
Membership association.

ELIGIBILITY:
Any books or articles published anywhere in the U.S. (the 50 states and Puerto Rico) in English during the calendar year preceding the award will be eligible. The subject matter may be biographical or critical, reportorial or historical - almost any form of nonfiction prose about music and/or its creators - not an instructional textbook, how-to guide, or a work of fiction.

Paperbacks that were originally published in hardcover are not eligible.

GEOG. RESTRICTIONS: United States.

FINANCIAL DATA:
Amount of support per award: Several categories of cash prizes, from $200 to $500.

Total amount of support: Varies.

NO. AWARDS: 15 for the year 2014.

APPLICATION INFO:
Application may be made online. The following information is required:
(1) title of the book or article;
(2) copyright date of book or date of publication for the article;
(3) name, street address, e-mail address and daytime phone number of all authors of the book or article and;
(4) contact name, address and daytime phone number of the publisher or publication in which the article appeared.

Four copies of each entry are required. Submissions will not be returned. For articles and books, submissions are limited to one entry per author. When submitting one or more articles, be sure that a copy of every article is put into each of four letter-sized file folders. Label each folder with one's full name only. (This is for the competition judges who will review the entries.)

Submissions should be addressed to ASCAP Deems Taylor/Virgil Thomson Awards; American Society of Composers, Authors and Publishers at the address listed above.

Duration: Annual award.

Deadline: May 31.

ADDRESS INQUIRIES TO:
Julie Lapore
ASCAP-Deems Taylor/Virgil Thomson Awards
(See address above.)

THE ASSOCIATION OF WRITERS & WRITING PROGRAMS [657]

Mail Stop 1E3, 4400 University Drive
George Mason University
Fairfax, VA 22030
(703) 993-4301
Fax: (703) 993-4302
E-mail: supriya@awpwriter.org
Web Site: www.awpwriter.org

FOUNDED: 1967

AREAS OF INTEREST:
Creative writing; four genres: short fiction, poetry, creative nonfiction and the novel.

CONSULTING OR VOLUNTEER SERVICES:
The office provides information on curricula for courses or programs in creative writing and members of the Board of Directors occasionally visit campuses in order to consult with departments wishing to establish or improve creative writing programs. The office also sponsors the INTRO Journals Project, an annual competition of fiction, nonfiction and poetry by students of creative writing; runs job placement service for members interested in obtaining teaching and writing-oriented positions.

NAME(S) OF PROGRAMS:

- **AWP Award Series in Creative Nonfiction**
- **AWP Award Series in the Novel**
- **Donald Hall Prize in Poetry**
- **Grace Paley Prize in Short Fiction**

TYPE:
Awards/prizes. Annual open competitions for book-length manuscripts: a collection of short stories, a collection of poems, or a work of creative nonfiction of more than 60,000 words. The award in each case is the publication of the winning manuscript by a university press and a cash honorarium from AWP in addition to royalties from the publisher.

YEAR PROGRAM STARTED: 1974

PURPOSE:
To support American writers and creative writing programs in U.S. colleges and universities; to encourage the publication and distribution of good fiction, poetry and other creative writing; to improve the quality of literary education primarily at the college level, as well as at the public school level; to disseminate information useful to writers and students of writing.

LEGAL BASIS:
Nonprofit, tax-exempt corporation.

ELIGIBILITY:
Original works written in English are eligible.

Only book-length manuscripts are eligible (poetry: 48 pages minimum; short story collection and creative nonfiction: 150 to 300 manuscript pages; novel: at least 60,000 words).

The AWP Award Series is open to all authors writing original works in English. No mixed-genre manuscripts can be accepted. Criticism and scholarly monographs are not acceptable for creative nonfiction, which the Award Series defines as factual and literary writing that has the narrative, dramatic, meditative and lyrical elements of novels, plays, poetry, and memoirs.

To avoid conflict of interest and to avoid the appearance of a conflict of interest, former students of a judge (former students who studied with a judge in an academic degree-conferring program or its equivalent) are ineligible to enter the competition in the genre for which their former teacher is serving as judge.

FINANCIAL DATA:
Negotiations regarding book royalties are left to the author and publisher, but AWP has established minimum standards.

Amount of support per award: AWP Prize for Creative Nonfiction and AWP Prize for the Novel: $2,500 each; Donald Hall Prize in Poetry and Grace Paley Prize in Short Fiction: $5,500 each.

Total amount of support: $16,000.

CO-OP FUNDING PROGRAMS: Donald Hall Prize in Poetry and Grace Paley Prize for Short Fiction are made possible by the generous support of amazon.com.

NO. MOST RECENT APPLICANTS: Nonfiction: 223; Novel: 293; Poetry: 780; Short Fiction: 332.

NO. AWARDS: 1 winner per genre; 2 finalists per genre.

APPLICATION INFO:
For the Award Series, submissions are only accepted via Submittable (online submissions manager).

Manuscripts must be uploaded between January 1 and February 28. If the author's name appears anywhere except the cover page, the manuscript will be disqualified. Do not attach acknowledgement of previous publications or a biographical note. No manuscripts will be returned. There is a $30 entry/reading fee for nonmembers, $20 for AWP members. Please read guidelines on Association's web site before uploading one's manuscript through Submittable.

Deadline: Manuscripts are accepted only with postmark between January 1 and February 28.

PUBLICATIONS:
Guidelines; *The Writer's Chronicle*, six times per year.

IRS I.D.: 05-0314999

EXECUTIVE DIRECTOR:
D.W. Fenza

ADDRESS INQUIRIES TO:
Supriya Bhatnagar
Director of Publications
(See address above.)

*PLEASE NOTE:
Reading period from February 1 to September 30 each year.

BREAD LOAF WRITERS' CONFERENCE [658]

Middlebury College
204 College Street
Middlebury, VT 05753
(802) 443-5286
Fax: (802) 443-2087
E-mail: blwc@middlebury.edu
Web Site: www.middlebury.edu/bread-loaf-conferences/bl_writers

FOUNDED: 1926

AREAS OF INTEREST:
Poetry, fiction and nonfiction.

NAME(S) OF PROGRAMS:
- **Fellowship and Scholarship Program for Writers**

TYPE:
Fellowships; Scholarships; Work-study programs. Fellowships and scholarships pay all or part of conference fees.

YEAR PROGRAM STARTED: 1926

PURPOSE:
To encourage writers at the beginning of their careers.

LEGAL BASIS:
Nonprofit.

ELIGIBILITY:
Fellowship candidates must have had one or two original books published. Privately printed books are not considered.

Candidates for tuition scholarships must have had their work published in recognized literary periodicals, but will not have published in book form.

Working scholarships as waiters and waitresses are available for people who have not had their work published but who show promise as writers.

People under 18 are not eligible.

FINANCIAL DATA:
Fellowships pay all conference fees, tuition, room and board. Tuition scholarships pay full tuition but not room and board. Working scholarships pay part of tuition and room and board; recipients earn the remainder.

Amount of support per award: Varies.

Total amount of support: Varies.

NO. MOST RECENT APPLICANTS: 1,600.

NO. AWARDS: 60.

APPLICATION INFO:
Information is available online.

Duration: Usually one-time award.

Deadline: March 1. Announcement in May.

DIRECTORS:
Michael Collier, Director
Jennifer Grotz, Assistant Director

ADDRESS INQUIRIES TO:
Jason Lamb, Coordinator
(See address above.)

THE WITTER BYNNER FOUNDATION FOR POETRY, INC. [659]

P.O. Box 10169
Santa Fe, NM 87504-0169
(505) 913-0082
E-mail: witterb123@gmail.com
Web Site: bynnerfoundation.org

FOUNDED: 1972

AREAS OF INTEREST:
Poetry, with special interest in developing the poetry audience, the process of poetry translation, uses of poetry (including but not limited to dramatic, educational, therapeutic, etc.) and the support of individual poets through existing institutional programs.

TYPE:
Project/program grants; Residencies; Scholarships.

YEAR PROGRAM STARTED: 1972

PURPOSE:
To develop the poetic art through grant support to nonprofit organizations and individuals represented by such organizations.

LEGAL BASIS:
Exempt, private foundation.

ELIGIBILITY:
Only applications from nonprofit tax-exempt organizations will be accepted. No grants to individuals. Publication projects, endowment funds, capital improvements, continued support and operating expenses are not generally funded.

GEOG. RESTRICTIONS: United States.

FINANCIAL DATA:
Amount of support per award: $1,000 to $10,000.

Total amount of support: $62,500 for the year 2015-16.

NO. MOST RECENT APPLICANTS: 115 letters of intent for the year 2015-16.

NO. AWARDS: 13 grant programs for the year 2015-16.

REPRESENTATIVE AWARDS:
Library of Congress/Fellowships in Poetry; Santa Fe Girls School/Poetry Workshops; Santa Fe Arts Commission/Poetry Works; Teatro Paraguas; New Mexico Culture Net; Santa Fe Playhouse; Forest Woods Media Productions.

APPLICATION INFO:
Upon request, the Foundation's guidelines, an annual report, and a list of the most recent grants will be provided. Applicants must submit a letter of intent prior to application.

Duration: One-year grants only. May be renewed at the discretion of the Board of Directors.

Deadline: February 15 annually. Announcement in May. Letters of intent accepted from August 1 to December 31 annually.

PUBLICATIONS:
Annual report; application guidelines.

IRS I.D.: 23-7169999

BOARD OF DIRECTORS:
Dr. Douglas Schwartz, Chairman
Robert Kurth, Vice President
Fletcher Catron, Secretary/Treasurer
Dr. Mark McDaniel

ADMINISTRATIVE STAFF:
Steven D. Schwartz, Executive Director
Nanci Caldwell, Business Manager

ADDRESS INQUIRIES TO:
Steven D. Schwartz, Executive Director
(See address above.)

*SPECIAL STIPULATIONS:
The Foundation is interested particularly in using its limited funds as a means to help attract additional monies from other sources to advance the art of poetry. Applications to support the development of seed-money proposals in each of the above areas, therefore, are especially encouraged. While the Foundation has traditionally been supportive of the four areas listed above, it may consider the support of other creative and innovative projects in poetry.

CANADA COUNCIL FOR THE ARTS [660]

150 Elgin Street
Ottawa ON K1P 5V8 Canada
(613) 566-4414 ext. 4681
(800) 263-5588 ext. 5060 (Canada and U.S. only)
Fax: (613) 566-4390
TTY: (866) 585-5559 (hearing-impaired)
E-mail: info@canadacouncil.ca
Web Site: www.canadacouncil.ca/writing-and-publishing

FOUNDED: 1957

AREAS OF INTEREST:
The arts in Canada (dance, media arts, music, theatre, creative writing and publishing, inter-arts and visual arts).

NAME(S) OF PROGRAMS:
- **Writing and Publishing Section Grants**

TYPE:
Development grants; General operating grants; Grants-in-aid; Project/program grants; Residencies; Travel grants. Council grants support the following types of activities:
(1) Grants for Individual Professional Writers: These grants can help one create new work or travel to events important to one's career. Support is also available for storytellers and spoken word artists.
(2) Operating Funding: These grants offer operating support to book and periodical publishers and nonprofit arts service organizations.
(3) Project Funding: Project grants are available to nonprofit arts organizations, magazine and book publishers, artists' collectives or groups to cover some of the costs of specific, time-limited activities.

PURPOSE:
To provide support for the creation, translation, publication and promotion of Canadian literature.

LEGAL BASIS:
Independent agency established by the Parliament of Canada in 1957.

ELIGIBILITY:
Council grants cannot be used to start a business or to buy capital items, such as computers, musical instruments, film and video equipment, or printing presses.

GEOG. RESTRICTIONS: Canada.

FINANCIAL DATA:
Amount of support per award: Varies depending on project.
Total amount of support: Varies.

APPLICATION INFO:
The Council does not send or accept applications by fax or e-mail.
Deadline: Varies.

PUBLICATIONS:
Program information sheets.

ADDRESS INQUIRIES TO:
Christian Mondor, Information Officer
(See address above.)

CARNEGIE FUND FOR AUTHORS [661]

P.O. Box 409
Lenox Hill Post Office
New York, NY 10021

FOUNDED: 1942

AREAS OF INTEREST:
Literary interests.

TYPE:
Grants-in-aid.

YEAR PROGRAM STARTED: 1942

PURPOSE:
To award grants to authors whose need has come about because of illness or other emergency.

ELIGIBILITY:
Applicants must be authors who have had at least one book of reasonable length published by a mainstream publisher. Applicants cannot use any publication they paid to have published.

Grants are made to individuals who must be U.S. citizens or residents. Applicants must live in the U.S.

FINANCIAL DATA:
Amount of support per award: No fixed sum; based on need.

APPLICATION INFO:
Applicants must request an application form and submit to the address above with all supporting documentation.
Duration: Lump-sum grant. Must reapply.
Deadline: Grants are voted on and distributed year-round.

IRS I.D.: 13-6084244

CHILDREN'S LITERATURE ASSOCIATION [662]

1301 West 22nd Street
Suite 202
Oak Brook, IL 60523
(630) 571-4520
Fax: (708) 876-5598
E-mail: info@childlitassn.org
Web Site: www.childlitassn.org

FOUNDED: 1973

AREAS OF INTEREST:
All aspects of children's literature scholarship, research and criticism.

NAME(S) OF PROGRAMS:
- **ChLA Diversity Research Grant**

TYPE:
Project/program grants; Research grants. ChLA Diversity Research Grant is a grant to support research related to children's and young adult cultural artifacts (including media, culture and texts) about populations that have been traditionally underrepresented or marginalized culturally and/or historically. Applications for this grant are to be considered annually and will be awarded as warranted.

YEAR PROGRAM STARTED: 2013

PURPOSE:
To promote scholarship and criticism in children's literature.

LEGAL BASIS:
International; tax-exempt 501(c)(3), nonprofit scholarly organization.

ELIGIBILITY:
Applications will be evaluated based upon the quality of the proposal and the potential of the project to enhance or advance Children's Literature studies. Funds may be used for - but are not restricted to - research-related expenses such as travel to special collections, subvention funds, or purchasing materials and supplies. The awards may not be used for obtaining advanced degrees, for researching or writing a thesis or dissertation, for textbook writing or for pedagogical projects. Winners must be members of the Children's Literature Association before they receive any funds. Winners must acknowledge ChLA in any publication or other presentation resulting from the grant.

Members of the ChLA Diversity Committee are not eligible to apply. Recipients of a Diversity Research Grant are not eligible to reapply until the third year from the date of the first award. (In the event the ChLA Board institutes another time interval - whether longer or shorter - the vote of the Board shall supersede the three-year interval rule.)

In a given year, if there are no proposals for the Diversity Research Grant that the Diversity and/or Grants Committee deems of sufficient quality to support ChLA's aims, no grants will be given; conversely, if there are multiple Diversity Research Grant proposals of high quality, it is possible that multiple grants will be made, in which case the award may be less than the proposed budget.

FINANCIAL DATA:
Amount of support per award: $500 to $1,000, depending upon the winning proposal's projected budgetary considerations.

APPLICATION INFO:
Proposals should take the form of a single Word document and include the following information:
(1) cover page including name, telephone number, mailing address and e-mail address, as well as academic institution and status/rank (student, professor, librarian, etc.) or institution applicant is affiliated with (library, publisher, etc.), if any;
(2) a detailed description of the research proposal (not to exceed three single-spaced pages), indicating the nature and significance of the project, where it will be carried out, rough budget and the expected date of completion and;
(3) a vitae that includes a bibliography of major publications and scholarly achievements (degrees, honors, etc.).
E-mail the completed proposal as an attachment to: ChLA Association Manager at the e-mail address above. Subject line should read: "ChLA Diversity Research Grant Application." A confirmation e-mail will be sent to acknowledge receipt of proposal.

The following general guidelines apply:
(1) e-mail the proposal as an attachment dated within the application period (January 1 to February 1 annually); incomplete or late applications will not be considered; applications and supporting materials should be written in, or translated into, English; if applicant is applying for both a Diversity Research Grant and a general ChLA Research Grant, applicant must state this in the application;
(2) The ChLA Diversity Committee will screen all proposals and select the awardee(s);
(3) The ChLA Diversity Committee is encouraged to communicate openly with the Grants Committee since some submissions could be appropriate for both submission processes and;
(4) winners are urged to attend the annual conference if at all possible to receive the award.
Deadline: Only applications that are complete and received as of midnight on February 1 will be considered. Winners will be notified in April, and the awards will be announced at the ChLA annual conference.

IRS I.D.: 38-2005828

ADDRESS INQUIRIES TO:
ChLA Grants Committee
(See address above.)

*SPECIAL STIPULATIONS:
Grant recipients are required to submit a progress report of the project to the chair of the Diversity Committee by April/May of the year following the award and a summary report of the completed project to the chair of the Diversity Committee by April/May of the second year, prior to the presentation of the ideas at the conference.

Each grant will be awarded with the expectation that the undertaking will lead to publication and make a significant contribution to the field of children's literature scholarship or criticism. Within two years of receiving the grant, the recipient will be asked to submit a paper proposal based upon the project for presentation at a ChLA annual conference.

CHILDREN'S LITERATURE ASSOCIATION [663]

1301 West 22nd Street
Suite 202
Oak Brook, IL 60523
(630) 571-4520
Fax: (708) 876-5598
E-mail: info@childlitassn.org
Web Site: www.childlitassn.org

FOUNDED: 1973

AREAS OF INTEREST:
All aspects of children's literature scholarship, research and criticism.

NAME(S) OF PROGRAMS:
- **ChLA Beiter Graduate Student Research Grants**
- **ChLA Faculty Research Grants**

TYPE:
Conferences/seminars; Grants-in-aid; Project/program grants; Research grants. ChLA Beiter Graduate Student Research Grants are awarded for proposals of original scholarship with the expectation that the undertaking will lead to publication or a conference presentation and contribute to the field of children's literature criticism.

ChLA Faculty Research Grants are awarded for proposals dealing with criticism or original scholarship with the expectation that the undertaking will lead to publication and make a significant contribution to the field of children's literature in the area of scholarship or criticism. Proposals that deal with critical or original work in the areas of fantasy or science fiction for children or adolescents will be awarded the Margaret P. Esmonde Memorial Scholarship.

YEAR PROGRAM STARTED: 1978

PURPOSE:
To promote scholarship and criticism in children's literature.

LEGAL BASIS:
International; tax-exempt 501(c)(3), nonprofit scholarly organization.

ELIGIBILITY:
ChLA Beiter Research Grants for Graduate Students: Grant funds are not intended as income to assist in the completion of a graduate degree, but as support for research that may be related to the dissertation or Master's thesis. The grant may be used to purchase supplies and materials (e.g., books, videos, equipment), as research support (photocopying, etc.), or to underwrite travel to special collections or libraries. Winners must either be members of the Children's Literature Association or join the Association before they receive any funds. Students of ChLA Executive Board members or Scholarship Committee members are not eligible to apply.

ChLA Faculty Research Grants: Applications will be evaluated based upon the quality of the proposal and the potential of the project to enhance or advance children's literature studies. Funds may be used for (but are not restricted to) research-related expenses such as travel to special collections or purchasing materials and supplies. The awards may not be used for obtaining advanced degrees, for researching or writing a thesis or dissertation, for textbook writing, or for pedagogical projects. Winners must either be members of the Children's Literature Association or join the Association before they receive any funds. Members of the Executive Board of ChLA and of the Scholarship Committee are not eligible to apply.

FINANCIAL DATA:
ChLA Faculty Research Grants may be used for such expenses as transportation, living expenses or materials and supplies, but not for obtaining advanced degrees.

Amount of support per award: $500 to $1,500.

Total amount of support: Up to $10,000 annually for both grants.

NO. AWARDS: Varies.

APPLICATION INFO:
E-mail proposals as an attachment dated within the application period of January 1 to February 1. Incomplete or late applications will not be considered. Subject line should read: ChLA Faculty Research Grant Application or ChLA Beiter Graduate Research Grant Application. Applications should include name, mailing address, phone, e-mail address, academic institution, academic status or institution applicant is affiliated with (library, publisher, etc.), a detailed description of the research proposal, a vitae that includes a bibliography of major publications and scholarly achievements (for Beiter Grants, just a curriculum vitae), and two letters of reference (for Beiter Grant applicants only). One letter must be from applicant's dissertation or thesis advisor. For more information, write to the address listed above.
For a printed copy of guidelines, please send a self-addressed, stamped envelope.

Duration: Varies. Usually a one-time award to run the length of the project or course of study.

Deadline: February 1. Announcement at the annual conference.

PUBLICATIONS:
Application guidelines.

IRS I.D.: 38-2005828

ADDRESS INQUIRIES TO:
ChLA Grants Committee
(See address above.)

*SPECIAL STIPULATIONS:
Winners should acknowledge ChLA in any publication resulting from the award.

GREAT LAKES COLLEGES ASSOCIATION NEW WRITERS AWARDS [664]

535 West William Street
Suite 301
Ann Arbor, MI 48103
(734) 661-2350
Fax: (734) 661-2349
E-mail: wegner@glca.org
Web Site: www.glca.org

FOUNDED: 1962

AREAS OF INTEREST:
Education.

NAME(S) OF PROGRAMS:
- **New Writers Awards**

TYPE:
Awards/prizes. Winners invited to tour up to 13 Great Lakes Colleges. Honorarium and expenses included. Awards are made for yearly, first published best book of fiction, best book of poetry and best book of creative nonfiction. Judges of the awards are faculty members of literature and creative writing at member colleges.

YEAR PROGRAM STARTED: 1970

PURPOSE:
To promote new writers, literature and colleges.

LEGAL BASIS:
Association of independent, liberal arts colleges in Michigan, Indiana, Ohio and Pennsylvania.

ELIGIBILITY:
The book must be the first published volume in fiction, poetry, or creative nonfiction by the author. Only publishers may submit, on behalf of the author, one book in each category, four copies.

Entries submitted must be written in English and published in the U.S. or Canada.

GEOG. RESTRICTIONS: United States and Canada.

FINANCIAL DATA:
The award also covers the costs of a writer's travel when visiting GLCA member colleges.

Amount of support per award: At least $500 per college visited.

NO. MOST RECENT APPLICANTS: 133.

NO. AWARDS: 1 each for creative nonfiction, fiction and poetry.

APPLICATION INFO:
Applicants should send for rules and enclose self-addressed, stamped envelope or visit the GLCA web site to download submission packet.

Deadline: July 25.

ADDRESS INQUIRIES TO:
New Writers Awards
(See address above.)

IRISH AMERICAN CULTURAL INSTITUTE [665]

P.O. Box 1716
Morristown, NJ 07962
(973) 605-1991
E-mail: info@iaci-usa.org
Web Site: www.iaci-usa.org

FOUNDED: 1962

AREAS OF INTEREST:
Promotion of better understanding of Ireland through publications and educational programs such as the Institute's IRISH WAY Program for high school students and its Irish Perceptions Series which brings Irish lecturers and performers to the U.S. to tour.

NAME(S) OF PROGRAMS:
- **IACI Awards**

TYPE:
Awards/prizes; Exchange programs; Fellowships. Awards to artists, writers and organizations in Ireland for their efforts in Irish history, literature and art.

YEAR PROGRAM STARTED: 1966

PURPOSE:
To stimulate, develop and disseminate information pertinent to the Irish culture.

LEGAL BASIS:
Public foundation under IRS code 501(c)(3).

ELIGIBILITY:
Open to residents of Ireland only.

REPRESENTATIVE AWARDS:
$5,000 to painter Basil Blackshaw; $5,000 to author Michael Davitt; $5,000 to poet Patrick Galvin.

APPLICATION INFO:
Projects are generally initiated by the Institute with pertinent announcements distributed when necessary. However, brief descriptive statements of appropriate proposed projects are welcomed. Such requests should outline the objectives to be accomplished, the proposed means of accomplishment and the type and amount of assistance desired.

Duration: One-time awards.

Deadline: December 31.

PUBLICATIONS:
Eire-Ireland, magazine.

OFFICERS:
Peter Halas, Chairman
Brian Stack, Vice Chairman
Barbara Lyons, Treasurer
Edward F. Ginty, Secretary

ITALIAN AMERICAN STUDIES ASSOCIATION

P.O. Box 487
Millbrae, CA 94030
(408) 738-4564
Fax: (408) 864-5629
E-mail: quinnroseanne@deanza.edu
Web Site: www.italianamericanstudies.net

TYPE:
Fellowships.

See entry 589 for full listing.

JEWISH BOOK COUNCIL [666]

520 Eighth Avenue, 4th Floor
New York, NY 10018-4393
(212) 201-2920
Fax: (212) 532-4952
E-mail: jbc@jewishbooks.org
Web Site: www.jewishbookcouncil.org

FOUNDED: 1943

AREAS OF INTEREST:
Jewish literature.

NAME(S) OF PROGRAMS:

- **National Jewish Book Award-American Jewish Studies**
- **National Jewish Book Award-Anthologies and Collections**
- **National Jewish Book Award-Biography, Autobiography and Memoir**
- **National Jewish Book Award-Children's Literature**
- **National Jewish Book Award-Contemporary Jewish Life and Practice**
- **National Jewish Book Award-Debut Fiction**
- **National Jewish Book Award-Education and Jewish Identity**
- **National Jewish Book Award-Fiction**
- **National Jewish Book Award-History**
- **National Jewish Book Award-Holocaust**
- **National Jewish Book Award-Modern Jewish Thought and Experience**
- **National Jewish Book Award-Poetry**
- **National Jewish Book Award-Scholarship**
- **National Jewish Book Award-Sephardic Culture**
- **National Jewish Book Award-Visual Arts**
- **National Jewish Book Award-Women's Studies**
- **National Jewish Book Award-Writing Based on Archival Material**
- **National Jewish Book Award-Young Adult Literature**

TYPE:
Awards/prizes. National Jewish Book Awards:
(1) Award to the author of a nonfiction book about the Jewish experience in North America;
(2) Award to the author of a book of essays, biographies, short stories, or other collected works by more than one author;
(3) Award to the author of a biography, autobiography, personal memoir or family history. The subject need not be a Jewish person or family, but must have significant relevance to the Jewish experience;
(4) Award to the author of a book on a Jewish theme that is intended for children;
(5) Award to the author of a nonfiction book about current tools and resources of Jewish living within the greater Ashkenazic and Sephardic communities. These include, but are not limited to, cookbooks, holiday how-to books and life-cycle books;
(6) Award to the author of a debut novel or short-story collection with Jewish content;
(7) Award to the author of a nonfiction work that focuses on theory, history and/or practice of Jewish education. Textbooks are not eligible;
(8) Award to the author of a novel or short-story collection with Jewish content;
(9) Award to the author of a nonfiction work about the Jewish historical experience. Books focusing primarily on the Holocaust do not belong in this category;
(10) Award to the author of a nonfiction book concerning the Holocaust including autobiographies, memoirs and academic studies;
(11) Award to the author of a nonfiction work addressing Sephardic and/or Ashkenazic Jewish thought and experience;
(12) Award to the author of a book of verse consisting primarily of poems of Jewish concern;
(13) Award to the author of a nonfiction selection that makes an original contribution to Jewish learning. This includes, but is not limited to, works on Bible, Rabbinics and Jewish Law;
(14) Award to the author of a book that explores the traditions and practices unique to Sephardic Jews;
(15) Award to the author of a work of one or more visual artists (painters, weavers, sculptors, photographers, etc.) which includes illustrations and images of Jewish content as a dominant component;
(16) Award to the author of a nonfiction book about women's role in the Jewish experience;
(17) Award to the author of a book of modern historical writing published in English based on archival material including footnotes and bibliography and;
(18) Award to the author of a book on a Jewish theme that is intended for young adults.

YEAR PROGRAM STARTED: 1949

PURPOSE:
To promote greater awareness of works of Jewish literature and scholarship.

LEGAL BASIS:
Not-for-profit organization.

ELIGIBILITY:
Books published during the current calendar year will be eligible, except anthologies of previously published material or collections of writings by various authors or reprints and revised editions, unless otherwise specified. No manuscripts are accepted.

Books must be published in the English language unless otherwise specified. This includes books translated into English from any other language.

FINANCIAL DATA:
Amount of support per award: Varies.

Total amount of support: Varies.

NO. MOST RECENT APPLICANTS: 400.

NO. AWARDS: 18 to 20 each year. Some awards are biennial.

APPLICATION INFO:
Guidelines and submission forms are available online in June.

Duration: One year.

Deadline: Submissions accepted early summer to late September.

PUBLICATIONS:
Application guidelines.

EXECUTIVE DIRECTOR:
Naomi Firestone-Teeter

ADDRESS INQUIRIES TO:
Naomi Firestone-Teeter
Executive Director
(See address above.)

JEWISH BOOK COUNCIL [667]

520 Eighth Avenue, 4th Floor
New York, NY 10018
(212) 201-2920
Fax: (212) 532-4952
E-mail: samirohrprize@jewishbooks.org
Web Site: www.jewishbookcouncil.org

AREAS OF INTEREST:
Jewish literature.

NAME(S) OF PROGRAMS:

- **Sami Rohr Prize for Jewish Literature**

TYPE:
Awards/prizes. In celebration of Sami Rohr's 80th birthday, his children and grandchildren instituted the Sami Rohr Prize for Jewish Literature to honor his lifelong love of Jewish writing. The annual award recognizes the unique role of contemporary writers in the transmission and examination of Jewish values, and is intended to encourage and promote outstanding writing of Jewish interest.

In conjunction with this award, the Rohr family has established the Sami Rohr Jewish Literary Institute, a forum devoted to the continuity of Jewish Literature. The Prize and Institute are coordinated and administered under the exclusive auspices of the Jewish Book Council. Winners will be selected by an independent panel of judges.

YEAR PROGRAM STARTED: 2006

PURPOSE:
To reward an emerging writer of Jewish literature whose work has demonstrated a fresh vision and evidence of future potential.

ELIGIBILITY:
Recipients must have written a book of exceptional literary merit that stimulates an interest in themes of Jewish concern. Fiction and nonfiction books will be considered in alternate years. Books published during the current calendar year and previous publishing year are eligible. Books must be published in the English language unless otherwise specified. This includes books translated into English from any other language.

FINANCIAL DATA:
Amount of support per award: $100,000.

NO. AWARDS: 1.

APPLICATION INFO:
An author may not submit directly to the Prize, but may submit their title for review in the Jewish Book Council publication *Jewish Book World* or in National Jewish Book Awards so that the Rohr committee can be made aware of their title.

STAFF:
Carolyn Starman Hessel, Director

ADDRESS INQUIRIES TO:
Carolyn Starman Hessel, Director
Sami Rohr Prize for Jewish Literature
(See address above.)

ROBERT F. KENNEDY HUMAN RIGHTS [668]

1300 19th Street, N.W.
Suite 750
Washington, DC 20036
(202) 463-7575
Fax: (202) 463-6606
E-mail: info@rfkhumanrights.org
Web Site: www.rfkhumanrights.org

FOUNDED: 1968

NAME(S) OF PROGRAMS:
- **RFK Book Award**
- **RFK Journalism Awards**

TYPE:
Awards/prizes. The RFK Book Award recognizes authors whose works of moral insight and imagination uphold a vision of political inclusion, compassion and justice.

The RFK Journalism Awards celebrate excellence in journalism in 13 categories, from investigative journalism to satirical cartoons and documentary film.

YEAR PROGRAM STARTED: 1980

PURPOSE:
To carry forward the mission of Robert F. Kennedy.

LEGAL BASIS:
Tax-exempt public charity.

ELIGIBILITY:
Fiction and nonfiction books published in the U.S. in the previous calendar year are eligible.

FINANCIAL DATA:
Amount of support per award: Book Award: $2,500 Grand Prize; Journalism Awards: $1,000 to individual or news organization and $500 to college and high school winners.

Total amount of support: Varies.

NO. MOST RECENT APPLICANTS: 75.

NO. AWARDS: Varies.

APPLICATION INFO:
Entries may be made by either individual authors or publishers. There is a handling fee of $75 per entry. Books must be submitted in quadruplicate with an entry form clipped inside the front cover of each book.

Duration: One-time award.

Deadline: Varies.

PUBLICATIONS:
Rules for entry.

ADDRESS INQUIRIES TO:
Jae Regala
E-mail: Regala@rfkhumanrights.org

KNIGHTS OF COLUMBUS VATICAN FILM LIBRARY AT ST. LOUIS UNIVERSITY [669]

Pius XII Memorial Library
St. Louis University
3650 Lindell Boulevard
St. Louis, MO 63108-3302
(314) 977-3090
Fax: (314) 977-3108
E-mail: vfl@slu.edu
Web Site: lib.slu.edu/special-collections/research/fellowship

AREAS OF INTEREST:
Classical languages and literature, palaeography, scriptural and patristic studies, history, philosophy and sciences in the Middle Ages and the Renaissance, early Romance literature, history of music, manuscript illumination, mathematics and technology, theology, liturgy, Roman and canon law or political theory.

NAME(S) OF PROGRAMS:
- **Vatican Film Library Mellon Fellowship**

TYPE:
Fellowships; Travel grants. Stipendiary fellowship which includes cost of air travel within the continental U.S.

YEAR PROGRAM STARTED: 1976

PURPOSE:
To assist scholars wishing to conduct research in the manuscript collections in the Vatican Film Library at St. Louis University.

ELIGIBILITY:
Applicants must be at the postdoctoral level or be a graduate student formally admitted to Ph.D. candidacy and working on their dissertation. U.S. citizens and foreign nationals are eligible.

FINANCIAL DATA:
Fellowship provides the cost of air travel within the continental U.S.

Amount of support per award: $2,250 per month living allowance.

Total amount of support: Varies. Maximum allowance of $4,500 plus air travel.

NO. AWARDS: Varies.

APPLICATION INFO:
Applicants must write a brief project description and notify of the manuscripts to be consulted (for availability), including dates of proposed study, a curriculum vitae, as well as a select bibliography on titles related to project. Proposals should not exceed more than two to three pages. Doctoral applicants must include a letter of recommendation from their advisor.

Duration: Two to eight weeks. Fellows can reapply the following year.

Deadline: March 1 for June to August. June 1 for September to December. October 1 for January to May.

STAFF:
Gregory A. Pass, Ph.D., Assistant Dean for Special Collections and Director, Vatican Film Library

ADDRESS INQUIRIES TO:
See e-mail address above.

STEPHEN LEACOCK ASSOCIATION [670]

149 Peter Street North
Orillia ON L3V 4Z4 Canada
(705) 835-3218 (Judith Rapson)
E-mail: judith.rapson@gmail.com
Web Site: www.leacock.ca

FOUNDED: 1946

AREAS OF INTEREST:
Writing of humour by Canadians.

NAME(S) OF PROGRAMS:
- **Stephen Leacock Memorial Medal for Humour**

TYPE:
Awards/prizes. Stephen Leacock Memorial Medal for Humour is presented for a book of humour published in the current calendar year and written by a Canadian. A cash prize from the TD Bank Financial Group accompanies this award.

YEAR PROGRAM STARTED: 1947

PURPOSE:
To promote the writing of Canadian humour.

LEGAL BASIS:
Nonprofit charitable organization.

ELIGIBILITY:
Author must be a Canadian citizen or landed immigrant. Books to be published in year current to year award given. Content to be humour. E-books are eligible if they have been published in book form.

FINANCIAL DATA:
Amount of support per award: Awardee receives a sterling silver medal plus a $15,000 (CAN) cash prize; four finalists receive $1,500 (CAN) each.

CO-OP FUNDING PROGRAMS: The T.D. Financial Group of Canada provides the major sponsorship for the prize money.

NO. AWARDS: 1.

APPLICATION INFO:
There is an entry fee of $200 per entry to be sent by check in Canadian funds. Send 10 copies of each title plus author biography and 8 x 10-inch photo to Stephen Leacock Associates. Photographs may be sent electronically. Work must be published in previous calendar year. Not more than two authors. All authors must be Canadian citizens or landed immigrants. Books are nonreturnable. Entries should be sent to: Stephen Leacock Association; Attention: Mrs. Bette Walker; at the address above.

Deadline: December 31, 2015. (No submissions until August 31 of that year.) Long list announced on or about April 25, 2016, published on the web site and in the media. Short list of three published on May 6, 2016 on the web site and in the media. Winner announced on June 11, 2016. Presentation of cash prize and medal in June during Gala dinner weekend.

PUBLICATIONS:
Newspacket.

BOARD OF DIRECTORS:
Michael Hill, President
Judith Rapson, Chairman, Award Committee
Bette Walker, Secretary

ADDRESS INQUIRIES TO:
Judith Rapson
Chairman, Award Committee
P.O. Box 854
Orillia, ON Canada L3V 6K8
(See phone and e-mail address above.)

*SPECIAL STIPULATIONS:
Authors must agree to be present for the Gala dinner weekend, June 10-12, 2016.

WILLIAM MORRIS SOCIETY IN THE U.S.

P.O. Box 53263
Washington, DC 20009
E-mail: us@morrissociety.org
ecmill@ucdavis.edu
Web Site: www.morrissociety.org

TYPE:
Fellowships; Research grants; Scholarships; Travel grants; Visiting scholars; Research contracts. Supports scholarly, creative, and translation projects about William Morris and his designs, writings and other work.

See entry 465 for full listing.

NATIONAL FEDERATION OF STATE POETRY SOCIETIES, INC. [671]

P.O. Box 1352
Los Lunas, NM 87031
E-mail: sonneteer@earthlink.net
Web Site: www.nfsps.com

AREAS OF INTEREST:
Poetry.

NAME(S) OF PROGRAMS:

- **NFSPS College Undergraduate Poetry (CUP) Competition**

TYPE:
Awards/prizes. The College Undergraduate Poetry Competition consists of two awards: The Edna Meudt Memorial Award and the Florence Kahn Memorial Award.

YEAR PROGRAM STARTED: 1989

PURPOSE:
To encourage the study and writing of poetry.

ELIGIBILITY:
All undergraduate levels of study at an accredited U.S. university or college are eligible (freshman through senior).

GEOG. RESTRICTIONS: United States.

FINANCIAL DATA:
Amount of support per award: Each awardee receives $500 plus 75 copies of published manuscript and an additional $300 stipend for travel to the NFSPS Convention to give a reading.

NO. MOST RECENT APPLICANTS: 35.

NO. AWARDS: 2.

APPLICATION INFO:
Applicant must submit a manuscript of 10 original poems. Consult web site for complete application information. Submissions may be made online via submittable.com.

Deadline: Applications are accepted December 1 to January 31. One anonymous, highly qualified judge will evaluate, judge and select scholarship winners on or before April 1.

ADDRESS INQUIRIES TO:
Shirley Blackwell, Chairperson
College/University Level Poetry Awards
(See address above.)

THE NATIONAL POETRY SERIES [672]

57 Mountain Avenue
Princeton, NJ 08540
(609) 430-0999
Fax: (609) 430-9933
E-mail: npspoetry@gmail.com
Web Site: www.nationalpoetryseries.org

FOUNDED: 1978

AREAS OF INTEREST:
Poetry.

NAME(S) OF PROGRAMS:

- **National Poetry Series Open Competition**

TYPE:
Awards/prizes.

YEAR PROGRAM STARTED: 1978

PURPOSE:
To publish five books of poetry each year through sponsorship of a contest and arrangement for publication through two trade publishing houses, two small presses and one university press.

LEGAL BASIS:
Nonprofit, private.

ELIGIBILITY:
The National Poetry Series seeks book-length manuscripts of poetry written by American residents or American citizens living abroad. All manuscripts must be previously unpublished, although some or all of the individual poems may have appeared in periodicals. Translations, chapbooks, small groups of poems and books previously self-published are not eligible. Manuscript length is not limited; however, a length of 48 to 64 pages is suggested.

GEOG. RESTRICTIONS: United States.

FINANCIAL DATA:
Arrangements are between author and publisher.

Amount of support per award: $10,000 and book publication.

Total amount of support: $50,000.

NO. MOST RECENT APPLICANTS: 1,850.

NO. AWARDS: 5.

APPLICATION INFO:
Manuscripts are submitted online via the web site. Each manuscript must be accompanied by an entrance fee of $30.

Manuscripts must include two cover pages:
(1) title of manuscript, author's name, address and telephone number (this should be the only page with author's identification) and;
(2) title of manuscript only.

Manuscripts must be typed on standard white paper, on one side of the page only, paginated (include a table of contents), and bound only by a clip as more permanent bindings are very difficult to handle. Do not include acknowledgments, explanatory statements, resumes, autobiographical statements, photographs, illustrations or artwork. These will not be considered.

Manuscripts cannot be returned.

Please include a self-addressed, stamped postcard if you would like confirmation of receipt of the manuscript. Include a self-addressed, stamped envelope if you would like to be notified of the NPS winners (announced in August).

Duration: One-time award.

Deadline: February 23 (postmark).

PUBLICATIONS:
Guidelines.

STAFF:
Daniel Halpern, Director
Stephanie Stio, Coordinator

ADDRESS INQUIRIES TO:
Coordinator, National Poetry Series
(See address above.)

PEN AMERICAN CENTER [673]

588 Broadway, Suite 303
New York, NY 10012-5246
(212) 334-1660 ext. 4813
Fax: (212) 334-2181
E-mail: awards@pen.org
Web Site: www.pen.org

FOUNDED: 1922

AREAS OF INTEREST:
Promoting the professional development of talented fiction writers.

NAME(S) OF PROGRAMS:

- **PEN/Robert W. Bingham Prize**

TYPE:
Awards/prizes. The PEN/Robert W. Bingham Prize is awarded annually and honors an exceptionally talented fiction writer whose debut work - a first novel or collection of short stories published in the prior year - represents distinguished literary achievement and suggests great promise.

YEAR PROGRAM STARTED: 1990

PURPOSE:
To promote the professional careers of exceptionally talented fiction writers.

LEGAL BASIS:
Nonprofit organization affiliated with International PEN.

ELIGIBILITY:
Candidate's first (and only the first) novel or first collection of short fiction must have been published by a U.S. trade publisher between January 1 and December 31 of the prior year. Candidates must be U.S. residents. American citizenship is not required. There are no restrictions on the candidate's age or on the style of his or her work. Self-published books are not eligible. Authors may not submit their own work. Submissions will only be accepted from publishers and literary agents.

FINANCIAL DATA:
Amount of support per award: Stipend of $25,000.

NO. AWARDS: 1.

APPLICATION INFO:
Submissions will only be accepted from publishers and literary agents. Submitter is expected to mail one copy of book to mailing address provided.

Deadline: Summer of each year.

ADDRESS INQUIRIES TO:
Arielle Anema
Literary Awards Coordinator
(See e-mail address above.)

PEN AMERICAN CENTER [674]

588 Broadway, Suite 303
New York, NY 10012-5246
(212) 334-1660
Fax: (212) 334-2181
E-mail: awards@pen.org
Web Site: www.pen.org

FOUNDED: 1922

AREAS OF INTEREST:
Fiction, literary nonfiction, biography/memoir and poetry.

NAME(S) OF PROGRAMS:

- **PEN Open Book Award**

TYPE:
Awards/prizes. Invites submissions of book-length writings by authors of color, published during the calendar year.

PURPOSE:
To encourage racial and ethnic diversity within the literary and publishing communities.

ELIGIBILITY:
Open to authors of color who have not received wide media coverage. U.S. residency or citizenship is not required. Works of fiction, literary nonfiction, biography/memoir and other works of literary character are

strongly preferred. Authors may not submit their own work. Submissions will only be accepted from publishers or literary agents.

FINANCIAL DATA:
Amount of support per award: $5,000.

NO. MOST RECENT APPLICANTS: 90.

NO. AWARDS: 1.

APPLICATION INFO:
Online application form can be found on the Center web site. Publishers and agents may submit one copy of a book-length writing by an author of color published during the calendar year under consideration, with an official letter of recommendation.
Self-published books are not eligible. Early submissions are strongly recommended.
Deadline: Summer of each year.

ADDRESS INQUIRIES TO:
See e-mail address above.

PEN AMERICAN CENTER [675]

588 Broadway, Suite 303
New York, NY 10012-5246
(212) 334-1660 ext. 4813
Fax: (212) 334-2181
E-mail: awards@pen.org
Web Site: www.pen.org

FOUNDED: 1922

AREAS OF INTEREST:
Poetry.

NAME(S) OF PROGRAMS:
- **PEN/Joyce Osterweil Award for Poetry**

TYPE:
Awards/prizes. Recognizes the high literary character of the published work to date of a new and emerging American poet of any age and the promise of further literary achievement.

PURPOSE:
To recognize the achievements of new and emerging American poets.

ELIGIBILITY:
Poets nominated for the Award have to be selected by a PEN member.

FINANCIAL DATA:
Amount of support per award: $5,000 awarded in odd-numbered years.

NO. AWARDS: 1.

APPLICATION INFO:
Letters of nomination are accepted from PEN members only.
Deadline: Summer of even-numbered years.

ADDRESS INQUIRIES TO:
See e-mail address above.

PEN AMERICAN CENTER [676]

588 Broadway, Suite 303
New York, NY 10012-5246
(212) 334-1660 ext. 4813
Fax: (212) 334-2181
E-mail: awards@pen.org
Web Site: www.pen.org

FOUNDED: 1922

AREAS OF INTEREST:
Children's/young adult fiction.

NAME(S) OF PROGRAMS:
- **PEN/Phyllis Naylor Working Writer Fellowship**

TYPE:
Awards/prizes. The Fellowship is offered annually to an author of children's or young adult fiction.

PURPOSE:
To recognize the fact that many writers' work is of high literary caliber but has not yet attracted a broad readership.

ELIGIBILITY:
A candidate is a writer of children's or young adult fiction demonstrating financial need. Candidate must have published at least one novel for children or young adults which have been warmly received by literary critics, but have not generated sufficient income to support the author. The writer's books must be published by a U.S. publisher.

FINANCIAL DATA:
Amount of support per award: $5,000.

NO. AWARDS: 1.

APPLICATION INFO:
Writers may nominate themselves or a fellow writer. This Fellowship will be judged blindly - the administrators will be aware of the nominee's names, but the judges will not. The application process is entirely online. Hard copy materials will no longer be accepted. The online application will require the following materials:
(1) a letter describing in some detail how they meet the criteria for the Fellowship, including a list of their published novel(s) for children or young adults;
(2) copies of at least three reviews of their novel(s) from professional publications;
(3) a letter of recommendation from an editor or fellow writer;
(4) one copy of the outline of the current novel in progress;
(5) one copy of 50 to 75 pages of the text. Picture books are not eligible. The writers' name should not appear anywhere on the manuscript, in order to ensure anonymity for the judging process and;
(6) on a separate piece of paper, a brief description of the candidate's recent earnings and a statement about why monetary support will make a particular difference in the applicant's writing life at this time. If the candidate is married or living with a domestic partner, please include a brief description of total family income and expense.
Deadline: Summer.

ADDRESS INQUIRIES TO:
See e-mail address above.

PEN AMERICAN CENTER [677]

588 Broadway, Suite 303
New York, NY 10012-5246
(212) 334-1660 ext. 4813
Fax: (212) 334-2181
E-mail: awards@pen.org
Web Site: www.pen.org

FOUNDED: 1922

AREAS OF INTEREST:
Poetry in translation.

NAME(S) OF PROGRAMS:
- **PEN Award for Poetry in Translation**

TYPE:
Awards/prizes. The award recognizes book-length translations of poetry from any language into English published during the current calendar year and is judged by a single translator of poetry appointed by the PEN Translation Committee. The award was made possible originally by a bequest from the late translator and PEN member Rae Dalven, and has received current support from The Kaplen Foundation. It is conferred every spring in New York.

YEAR PROGRAM STARTED: 1963

PURPOSE:
To recognize book-length translations of poetry from any language into English published during the current calendar year.

ELIGIBILITY:
Although all eligible books must have been published in the U.S., translators may be of any nationality; U.S. residency or citizenship is not required.

Self-published books or books with more than two translators are not eligible. Translators and authors may not submit their own work. Submissions will only be accepted from publishers and literary agents.

FINANCIAL DATA:
Amount of support per award: $3,000.

NO. AWARDS: 1.

APPLICATION INFO:
One copy of book-length translations of poetry published during the calendar year under consideration may be submitted by publishers, agents, or the translators themselves. Early submissions are strongly recommended.
Deadline: Summer.

ADDRESS INQUIRIES TO:
See e-mail address above.

PEN AMERICAN CENTER [678]

588 Broadway, Suite 303
New York, NY 10012-5246
(212) 334-1660 ext. 4813
Fax: (212) 334-2181
E-mail: awards@pen.org
Web Site: www.pen.org

FOUNDED: 1922

AREAS OF INTEREST:
Poetry.

NAME(S) OF PROGRAMS:
- **PEN/Voelcker Award for Poetry**

TYPE:
Awards/prizes. The Award, established by a bequest from Hunce Voelcker, will be presented to an American poet whose distinguished and growing body of work to date represents a notable and accomplished presence in American literature, for whom the promise seen in earlier work has been fulfilled, and who has matured with each successive volume of poetry.

PURPOSE:
To honor an American poet whose distinguished and growing body of work to date represents a notable and accomplished presence in American literature.

ELIGIBILITY:
Candidates must be American residents and can be nominated only by members of PEN. It is understood that all nominations made for the Award supplement internal nominations made by the panel of judges. There are no restrictions whatsoever to the age of the poet or to the style of his or her work.

FINANCIAL DATA:
Amount of support per award: $5,000 awarded in even-numbered years.

NO. AWARDS: 1.

APPLICATION INFO:
All letters of nomination (one to two pages is expected) should describe the scope and literary caliber of the candidate's work, and summarize the candidate's publications. Most importantly, nominations should articulate the degree of accomplishment the nominated poet has attained, and the esteem in which the candidate's work is held within the American literary community. Letters of nomination must be submitted through PEN's online nomination portal.

Deadline: Offered in even-numbered years. Application cycle begins in the summer of the preceding odd-numbered year.

ADDRESS INQUIRIES TO:
See e-mail address above.

PEN AMERICAN CENTER [679]

588 Broadway, Suite 303
New York, NY 10012-5258
(212) 334-1660 ext. 103/117
Fax: (212) 334-2181
E-mail: prisonwriting@pen.org
Web Site: www.pen.org

FOUNDED: 1922

AREAS OF INTEREST:
Writing of literature and poetry.

NAME(S) OF PROGRAMS:
- **PEN Prison Writing Program**

TYPE:
Awards/prizes.

YEAR PROGRAM STARTED: 1971

PURPOSE:
To help incarcerated writers develop their writing talents and to promote writing as a means of rehabilitation.

LEGAL BASIS:
Tax-exempt, nonprofit organization.

ELIGIBILITY:
U.S. federal, state or county prisoners in the year before the deadline may apply. Only unpublished manuscripts will be considered, except those that have appeared in a prison publication.

GEOG. RESTRICTIONS: United States.

FINANCIAL DATA:
In addition to prize money, all winners are awarded the opportunity to correspond with a writing mentor.

Amount of support per award: Five first prizes at $200 each, five second prizes at $100 each, five third prizes at $50 each, five Fielding Dawson prizes at $50 each, and fifteen honorable mentions at $25 each. Prizes are given for each of five categories: Poetry, Fiction, Essay, Memoir and Drama.

Total amount of support: $2,375 annually.

NO. MOST RECENT APPLICANTS: 1,500.

NO. AWARDS: 35 annually.

APPLICATION INFO:
Manuscripts must be typewritten (double-spaced) or clearly printed on standard letter-size paper. Also accept alternative submissions. Authors must not submit more than one entry in each category except in poetry. Name, inmate number and address must appear on each submission.

Duration: One-time award.

Deadline: September 1. Winners announced in Spring.

PUBLICATIONS:
PEN Handbook for Writers in Prison (lists resources available to inmates and journals interested in prison writing).

STAFF:
Jackson Taylor, Prison Writing Program Director
Tim Small, Prison Writing Mentorship Program Coordinator

ADDRESS INQUIRIES TO:
Director
PEN Writing Award for Prisoners
(See address above.)

PEN AMERICAN CENTER [680]

588 Broadway, Suite 303
New York, NY 10012-5246
(212) 334-1660 ext. 4813
Fax: (212) 334-2181
E-mail: info@pen.org
Web Site: www.pen.org/writersfund

FOUNDED: 1922

AREAS OF INTEREST:
Literature, free expression and international literary fellowship.

NAME(S) OF PROGRAMS:
- **PEN Writers' Fund**

TYPE:
Grants-in-aid. Emergency fund for professional (published or produced) writers in acute, emergency financial crisis.

YEAR PROGRAM STARTED: 1958

PURPOSE:
To assist professional literary writers in times of short-term financial emergency and also to assist writers and editors with AIDS or HIV; to advance literature, defend free expression and foster international literary fellowship.

LEGAL BASIS:
Nonprofit organization affiliated with International PEN.

ELIGIBILITY:
The fund aims to assist professional (published or produced) writers facing unexpected financial and medical emergencies, and those who are HIV-positive. The fund does not exist for research purposes, for completing projects or to support publications or organizations. Must be a U.S. resident. Self-published writers are not eligible.

GEOG. RESTRICTIONS: United States.

FINANCIAL DATA:
Amount of support per award: Up to $2,000.

APPLICATION INFO:
Applicants should submit a completed application form, published writing samples, documentation of financial emergency and professional resume. Applications are accepted year-round and are reviewed every three months by the Writers' Fund Committee.

Application can be found at the above web site address.

Deadline: Mid-March, mid-June, mid-September and mid-December.

PUBLICATIONS:
Application; guidelines.

STAFF:
Arielle Anema, Writers' Fund Coordinator

ADDRESS INQUIRIES TO:
Arielle Anema, Writers' Fund Coordinator
(See address above.)

*SPECIAL STIPULATIONS:
Repeat grants to any one individual will not be given within a three-year period since last grant.

PEN NEW ENGLAND [681]

Massachusetts Institute of Technology
14N-221A
77 Massachusetts Avenue
Cambridge, MA 02139
(617) 324-1729
E-mail: pen-newengland@mit.edu
Web Site: www.pen-ne.org

FOUNDED: 1975

AREAS OF INTEREST:
Authors.

NAME(S) OF PROGRAMS:
- **PEN New England Awards**

TYPE:
Awards/prizes. Three prizes will be awarded annually for best book of fiction, nonfiction and poetry by New England authors or books with a New England topic or setting.

YEAR PROGRAM STARTED: 1975

PURPOSE:
To recognize literary excellence and honor works of fiction, nonfiction and poetry by New England authors.

LEGAL BASIS:
Nonprofit organization affiliated with International PEN.

ELIGIBILITY:
Books of fiction, nonfiction and poetry by New England authors or with a New England topic or setting.

FINANCIAL DATA:
Amount of support per award: $1,000 in each category.

Total amount of support: $3,000.

NO. MOST RECENT APPLICANTS: Approximately 500.

NO. AWARDS: 3; 1 for fiction, 1 for nonfiction and 1 for poetry.

APPLICATION INFO:
Full guidelines available on web site. Submit three copies of eligible books and an entry fee of $50 per title to the PEN New England Award, at the address above.

Deadline: December 1, 2016. Awards ceremony in April 2017 held at the John F. Kennedy Library, Boston.

ADDRESS INQUIRIES TO:
See e-mail address above.

*SPECIAL STIPULATIONS:
Self-published books, electronic submissions or e-books are not eligible for consideration.

PEN NEW ENGLAND [682]

Massachusetts Institute of Technology
14N-221A
77 Massachusetts Avenue
Cambridge, MA 02139
(617) 324-1729
E-mail: pen-newengland@mit.edu
Web Site: www.pen-ne.org

NAME(S) OF PROGRAMS:
- **PEN/Hemingway Award for Debut Fiction**

TYPE:
Awards/prizes. Awarded annually for the first published book-length work of fiction by an American writer.

YEAR PROGRAM STARTED: 1976

PURPOSE:
PEN New England: To celebrate literature and free expression. PEN/Hemingway Award: To recognize literary excellence and to honor debut fiction.

LEGAL BASIS:
Nonprofit organization affiliated with International PEN.

ELIGIBILITY:
First published book-length work of fiction (a novel or book of short stories) by an American citizen or resident, published in the U.S. in 2016, may be submitted by publishers, agents or the authors themselves. Authors are not disqualified by the previous publication of nonfiction, poetry, drama or books for children.

GEOG. RESTRICTIONS: United States.

FINANCIAL DATA:
Amount of support per award: $25,000.
Total amount of support: $25,000.

NO. MOST RECENT APPLICANTS: 450.

NO. AWARDS: 1 winner, 2 finalists, and 2 honorable mentions.

APPLICATION INFO:
Full guidelines are available on the web site. Submit four copies of eligible books and an entry fee of $50 per title to the PEN Hemingway Award, at the address above.

Duration: One-time award.

Deadline: December 1, 2016. Awards ceremony in April 2017 held at the John F. Kennedy Library, Boston.

ADDRESS INQUIRIES TO:
See e-mail address above.

*SPECIAL STIPULATIONS:
Self-published books, electronic submissions or e-books are not eligible for consideration.

PEN/FAULKNER FOUNDATION [683]

PEN/Faulkner Foundation
201 East Capitol Street, S.E.
Washington, DC 20003
(202) 898-9063
Fax: (202) 544-4623
E-mail: esnyder@penfaulkner.org
Web Site: www.penfaulkner.org

FOUNDED: 1980

AREAS OF INTEREST:
Fiction.

NAME(S) OF PROGRAMS:
- **PEN/Faulkner Award for Fiction**

TYPE:
Awards/prizes. Cash awards for a published winning author and four nominees.

YEAR PROGRAM STARTED: 1981

PURPOSE:
To honor literary excellence.

LEGAL BASIS:
Nonprofit 501(c)(3) organization.

ELIGIBILITY:
Candidates must be living American citizens. Books must be published within the calendar year of the award. No self-published books.

GEOG. RESTRICTIONS: United States.

FINANCIAL DATA:
Amount of support per award: $15,000 for the winner. $5,000 to each of four finalists.
Total amount of support: $35,000.

NO. MOST RECENT APPLICANTS: 350.

NO. AWARDS: 5.

APPLICATION INFO:
Candidates should submit four copies of their book.

Deadline: Submissions must be postmarked by October 31. Announcement by mid-March.

IRS I.D.: 52-1431622

OFFICERS:
Susan Richards Shreve, Chairperson

ADDRESS INQUIRIES TO:
Executive Director
(See address above.)

*PLEASE NOTE:
This is not a grant program, but a prize for published work.

PERPETUAL TRUSTEE COMPANY LTD [684]

GPO Box 4172
Sydney N.S.W. 2001 Australia
(61) 1800 501 227
Fax: (61) 02 8256 1471
E-mail: philanthropy@perpetual.com.au
Web Site: www.milesfranklin.com.au/newhome

FOUNDED: 1954

AREAS OF INTEREST:
The advancement, improvement and betterment of Australian literature.

NAME(S) OF PROGRAMS:
- **Miles Franklin Literary Award**

TYPE:
Awards/prizes. Annual cash award for a published book on Australian life.

YEAR PROGRAM STARTED: 1957

PURPOSE:
To improve the educational style of authors; to help and give incentive to authors and to provide them with additional monetary support to enable them to improve their literary efforts.

LEGAL BASIS:
Trustees of estate of the late Miles Franklin.

ELIGIBILITY:
All works must be in English. No special requirements as regards nationality, age, etc. The book must be published in the year of entry of the award and be of the highest literary merit and must present Australian life in any of its phases. More than one entry may be submitted by each author. Novels or plays written by two or more authors in collaboration are eligible.

Biographies, collections of short stories, children's books and poetry are not eligible. Judges will not consider any text that has only had Internet publication.

FINANCIAL DATA:
Amount of support per award: $60,000 (AUD) (2015 prize).

NO. AWARDS: 1 per year.

APPLICATION INFO:
Application information is available on the web site when the award cycle opens. Publishers are required to submit the novels on the authors' behalf.

Duration: Annual.

PUBLICATIONS:
Application guidelines.

ADDRESS INQUIRIES TO:
Scholarship and Awards
Miles Franklin Literary Award
(See e-mail address above.)

THE PHI BETA KAPPA SOCIETY [685]

1606 New Hampshire Avenue, N.W.
Washington, DC 20009
(202) 745-3287
Fax: (202) 986-1601
E-mail: awards@pbk.org
Web Site: www.pbk.org

FOUNDED: 1776

NAME(S) OF PROGRAMS:
- **Ralph Waldo Emerson Award**
- **Christian Gauss Award**
- **Phi Beta Kappa Award in Science**

TYPE:
Awards/prizes. Three book awards given annually to outstanding scholarly books that have been published in the U.S. in the fields of the humanities, the social sciences, the natural sciences and mathematics.

The Ralph Waldo Emerson Book Award is offered annually for scholarly studies that contribute significantly to interpretations of the intellectual and cultural condition of humanity. This award may recognize work in the fields of history, philosophy and religion; these fields are conceived in sufficiently broad terms to permit the inclusion of appropriate work in related fields such as anthropology and the social sciences. Biographies of public figures may be eligible if their critical emphasis is primarily on the intellectual and cultural condition of humanity.

The Christian Gauss Award is offered for books in the field of literary scholarship or criticism. The prize honors the late Christian Gauss, the distinguished Princeton University scholar, teacher, and dean, who also served as president of the Phi Beta Kappa Society. To be eligible, a literary biography must have a predominantly critical emphasis.

Phi Beta Kappa Book Award in Science is offered for outstanding contributions by scientists to the literature of science. The Award's intent is to encourage literate and scholarly interpretations of the physical and biological sciences and mathematics; monographs and compendiums are not eligible. To be eligible, biographies of scientists must have a substantial critical emphasis on their scientific research.

YEAR PROGRAM STARTED: 1950

PURPOSE:
To recognize outstanding printed work in several fields including the social sciences, humanities, natural science and math.

LEGAL BASIS:
National scholarly honorary society.

ELIGIBILITY:
Awards are given for works published in the U.S. during the previous calendar year. Entries must be original publications. Translations and works previously published as a whole are not eligible. Books that contain chapters or sections previously published as articles in periodicals will be considered only if they have very clear, unifying themes and are not random

collections. Books that consist entirely of previously published articles are unlikely to qualify.

Entries ordinarily will be the work of a single writer. Exceptions may be made for books written by small teams of scholars working in close collaboration. Books that are collections of chapters by several different authors are not eligible. Entries should not be highly technical in character, nor should they treat subjects of narrowly limited interest. Monographs and reports on research as such are not eligible. In all cases, the subject and style of the entries should be accessible to the general, literate reader.

Authors must be citizens or residents of the U.S. Entries must have been published originally in the U.S. A book may not be entered for more than one of the awards. All entries must be submitted by the publisher. Publishers may submit no more than one entry for each award.

GEOG. RESTRICTIONS: United States.

FINANCIAL DATA:
Amount of support per award: $10,000 to the winning author.

Total amount of support: $30,000 annually.

NO. MOST RECENT APPLICANTS: 80 for each program for the year 2013.

NO. AWARDS: 1 award in each category each year.

APPLICATION INFO:
Inquiries and entries should be addressed to the appropriate award committee at the address above. Entries must be submitted by the publisher.

Duration: No renewal.

Deadline: February 15.

PUBLICATIONS:
Application guidelines.

OFFICERS:
Catherine White Berheide, President
John Churchill, Secretary

ADDRESS INQUIRIES TO:
Laura Hartnett
Program and Event Specialist
(See address above.)

PITT POETRY SERIES [686]

University of Pittsburgh Press
7500 Thomas Boulevard
Pittsburgh, PA 15260
(412) 383-2456
Fax: (412) 383-2466
E-mail: info@upress.pitt.edu
Web Site: www.upress.pitt.edu

FOUNDED: 1967

AREAS OF INTEREST:
Contemporary American poetry.

NAME(S) OF PROGRAMS:
- **Agnes Lynch Starrett Poetry Prize**

TYPE:
Awards/prizes. Cash prize, plus publication in the Pitt Poetry Series.

YEAR PROGRAM STARTED: 1980

LEGAL BASIS:
University.

ELIGIBILITY:
Starrett Prize awarded annually for a manuscript in English by a writer who has not previously published a full-length book of poetry.

FINANCIAL DATA:
Amount of support per award: $5,000, plus book publication.

Total amount of support: $5,000.

NO. MOST RECENT APPLICANTS: Approximately 350 to 400 per year.

NO. AWARDS: 1 each year.

REPRESENTATIVE AWARDS:
Michael McGriff, *Dismantling the Hills*.

APPLICATION INFO:
Send one copy of manuscript on good quality white paper, with no fewer than 48 and no more than 100 typescript pages. Clean, legible photocopies are acceptable. Name, address, phone number, and e-mail address should be on the title page. Also include curriculum vitae. A $25 reading fee per manuscript is required.

Deadline: Between March 1 and April 30 only. Announcement in the fall.

PUBLICATIONS:
Competition rules.

OFFICERS:
Ed Ochester, Editor, Pitt Poetry Series

ADDRESS INQUIRIES TO:
See e-mail address above.

*SPECIAL STIPULATIONS:
Competition for the Starrett Prize is severe. Casual submissions are not encouraged. Publisher cannot provide critiques of manuscripts.

Manuscripts will not be returned.

THE PLAYWRIGHTS' CENTER [687]

2301 Franklin Avenue East
Minneapolis, MN 55406
(612) 332-7481
Fax: (612) 332-6037
E-mail: info@pwcenter.org
Web Site: www.pwcenter.org

FOUNDED: 1971

AREAS OF INTEREST:
Playwriting.

CONSULTING OR VOLUNTEER SERVICES:
Advice on career development, jobs and production for playwrights.

NAME(S) OF PROGRAMS:
- **Affiliated Writer Program**
- **Core Apprentice Program**
- **Core Writer Program**
- **Jerome Fellowships**
- **Many Voices Fellowships**
- **McKnight Advancement Fellowship**
- **McKnight National Residency and Commission**
- **McKnight Theater Artist Fellowships**
- **New Plays on Campus**

TYPE:
Awards/prizes; Conferences/seminars; Fellowships; Internships; Project/program grants. Core Apprentice Program provides student playwrights with such benefits as a year of mentorship with a professional playwright and a full workshop of a new play at the Playwrights' Center.

Core Writer Program confers additional membership benefits to committed professional playwrights.

Jerome Fellowships provide grants to emerging playwrights, who receive access to Center's developmental services.

Many Voices Fellowships are awarded to playwrights of color.

McKnight Advancement Fellowship provides grants to midcareer Minnesota playwrights.

McKnight National Residency and Commission aids in the creation and development of new works from nationally recognized playwrights not residing in Minnesota.

McKnight Theater Artist Fellowships are awarded to Minnesota theater artists (other than playwrights).

YEAR PROGRAM STARTED: 1971

PURPOSE:
To assist playwrights.

LEGAL BASIS:
Tax-exempt and nonprofit.

ELIGIBILITY:
Core Writer Program is open to professional playwrights in the U.S.

Jerome Fellowships are open to emerging playwrights in the U.S. (citizens or permanent residents).

Many Voices Fellowships are available to national and local writers of color.

McKnight Advancement Fellowships and McKnight Theater Artist Fellowships are open to Minnesota writers only.

McKnight National Residency and Commission is for playwrights residing outside of Minnesota.

Additional criteria vary for each program.

FINANCIAL DATA:
Amount of support per award: Varies.

Total amount of support: Over $250,000.

NO. MOST RECENT APPLICANTS: 200 for fellowships. 500 for all programs.

NO. AWARDS: For the year 2014-15: Core Apprentices: 5; Core Writer: Varies; Jerome Fellowships: 4; Many Voices Fellowships: 2; Many Voices Mentorship: 2; McKnight Advancement Fellowships: 2; McKnight National Residency and Commission: 1; McKnight Theater Artist Fellowships: 3.

APPLICATION INFO:
Application information is available on the web site.

Duration: Core Writer: Three years; All other fellowships: One year.

Deadline: Varies.

PUBLICATIONS:
Annual report; newsletter.

IRS I.D.: 41-6170139

STAFF:
Jeremy Cohen, Producing Artistic Director
Hayley Finn, Associate Artistic Director
Amanda Robbins-Butcher, Artistic Administrator
Christina Ham, Many Voices Program Coordinator

ADDRESS INQUIRIES TO:
Julia Brown, Office Manager
(See address above.)

*SPECIAL STIPULATIONS:
Playwright must be in residence in Minnesota for one year for Jerome Fellowship. Recipients of McKnight Advancement Fellowships, McKnight Theater Artist

Fellowships, and Many Voices Fellowships must maintain residence in Minnesota during program year.

SOCIETY OF CHILDREN'S BOOK WRITERS AND ILLUSTRATORS [688]

4727 Wilshire Boulevard, Suite 301
Los Angeles, CA 90010
(323) 782-1010
Fax: (323) 782-1892
E-mail: scbwi@scbwi.org
Web Site: www.scbwi.org

FOUNDED: 1968

AREAS OF INTEREST:
Writers, editors and illustrators of children's books.

NAME(S) OF PROGRAMS:
- **Don Freeman Memorial Grant-in-Aid**
- **Work-In-Progress Grants**

TYPE:
Grants-in-aid; Project/program grants. The Freeman Memorial Grant-In-Aid has been established to enable picture-book artists to further their understanding, training and work in any aspect of the picture-book genre.

Work-In-Progress Grants have been established to assist children's book writers to complete a specific project. Grants are given in four categories: General Work-in-Progress Grant; Grant for a Contemporary Novel for Young People; Nonfiction Research Grant; and Grant for a work whose author has never had a book published.

YEAR PROGRAM STARTED: 1974

PURPOSE:
To encourage continuing excellence in the creation of children's literature and to provide assistance and support to those working in the children's book field.

LEGAL BASIS:
Corporation.

ELIGIBILITY:
Both grants are available to full and associate members of the Society of Children's Book Writers. The SCBW Grant Committee reserves the right to withhold the grants for any given year.

FINANCIAL DATA:
Amount of support per award: Freeman Memorial Grant-In-Aid: $2,000, plus a runner-up grant of $500; Work-In-Progress Grants: $2,000 in each category, plus runner-up grants of $500 in each category.

NO. MOST RECENT APPLICANTS: 285.

NO. AWARDS: 1 Freeman Memorial Grant-In-Aid and 4 Work-In-Progress Grants are awarded each year. Runner-up grants are made in each category.

APPLICATION INFO:
Applications may be obtained by sending a self-addressed, stamped envelope to the address above beginning October 1 of each year. Instructions for mailing the completed applications and written materials will be sent with the application.

Applicants for the Freeman Memorial Grant-In-Aid must enclose either (a) a rough picture-book dummy, the picture-book text in manuscript form and two finished illustrations (one color and one black-and-white); or (b) 10 finished illustrations that would make a suitable portfolio presentation expressly intended for picture books. Specifications will be sent with the application.

Applicants for the Work-In-Progress Grants must enclose three clearly reproduced copies of a synopsis of the work for which the grant will be used and a two- to 10-page writing sample from that work.

Duration: One-time grant.

Deadline: Freeman Memorial Grant-In-Aid: applications accepted between February 1 and May 1. Announcement on June 15. Work-In-Progress Grants: applications accepted between February 1 and May 1. Announcement the following September.

PUBLICATIONS:
Grants brochure.

OFFICERS:
Stephen Mooser, President
Lin Oliver, Executive Director

ADDRESS INQUIRIES TO:
For the Freeman Memorial Grant-In-Aid:
SCBW Don Freeman Grant-In-Aid
(See address above.)

For the Work-In-Progress Grants:
SCBW Grant Committee
(See address above.)

SYRACUSE UNIVERSITY [689]

English Graduate Office
420 Hall of Languages
Syracuse, NY 13244-1170
(315) 443-9480
Fax: (315) 443-3660
E-mail: tazollo@syr.edu
Web Site: english.syr.edu

FOUNDED: 1861

AREAS OF INTEREST:
Creative writing in poetry and fiction.

NAME(S) OF PROGRAMS:
- **Graduate Program in Creative Writing**

TYPE:
Assistantships; Awards/prizes; Fellowships; Scholarships; Travel grants. Fellowships and teaching assistantships in creative writing.

YEAR PROGRAM STARTED: 1963

PURPOSE:
To assist talented writers to pursue graduate degrees at Syracuse University.

ELIGIBILITY:
Applicant must have a B.A., B.F.A. or B.S. degree.

FINANCIAL DATA:
Fellowships and assistantships include remission of tuition costs for graduate study.

Amount of support per award: University Fellowships: $19,196; Cornelia Carhart Award: $18,367(fiction only); Mead Fellowship: $18,367 (poetry only); Teaching Assistantships: $14,826; Creative Writing Scholarships: $14,535 (fiction and poetry).

Total amount of support: Varies.

APPLICATION INFO:
An applicant must submit a writing sample (poetry or fiction), statement of purpose, teaching statement, official transcripts, and letters of recommendation.

Duration: Three years.

Deadline: December 15 for writing sample and complete application.

ADDRESS INQUIRIES TO:
Terri Zollo
Graduate English Office Coordinator
(See e-mail address above.)

TOWSON UNIVERSITY [690]

College of Liberal Arts
8000 York Road
Towson, MD 21252
(410) 704-2128
Fax: (410) 704-6392
E-mail: cla@towson.edu
Web Site: www.towson.edu/cla

FOUNDED: 1866

NAME(S) OF PROGRAMS:
- **Towson University Prize for Literature**

TYPE:
Awards/prizes. Awarded to Maryland writer of a single book or book-length manuscript of fiction, poetry, drama or imaginative nonfiction.

YEAR PROGRAM STARTED: 1980

PURPOSE:
To honor a published work of fiction, poetry or imaginative nonfiction by a Maryland resident.

LEGAL BASIS:
Special endowment.

ELIGIBILITY:
Applicant must be a Maryland resident for at least three years at the time of the award. Prize is awarded on the basis of literary and aesthetic excellence. Book must have been published in the three years prior to the award.

The winning author must be willing to be present at the awards ceremony and to grant to Towson State University the right to quote from the winning work in any publicity related to the prize.

GEOG. RESTRICTIONS: Maryland.

FINANCIAL DATA:
Amount of support per award: Generally $1,000.

Total amount of support: $1,000.

NO. MOST RECENT APPLICANTS: 14.

NO. AWARDS: 1 annually.

APPLICATION INFO:
Any individual, institution, group or publisher may nominate one or more works for the prize. Submit three copies of the work by certified mail, bound if published or typewritten if manuscript. If manuscript, proof of acceptance by a publisher and proposed date of publication must be provided. A completed nomination form must accompany entry.

Duration: One-time award.

Deadline: June 15 each year. Announcement in early Spring.

ADDRESS INQUIRIES TO:
Dean, College of Liberal Arts, LA 2213
Towson University
(See address above.)

THE UNIVERSITY OF IOWA [691]

Iowa Writers' Workshop
102 Dey House
507 North Clinton Street
Iowa City, IA 52242-1000
(319) 335-0416
Fax: (319) 335-0420
E-mail: kelly-a-smith@uiowa.edu
Web Site: writersworkshop.uiowa.edu

AREAS OF INTEREST:
Short story collection.

NAME(S) OF PROGRAMS:
- **The Iowa Short Fiction Award**
- **The John Simmons Short Fiction Award**

TYPE:
Awards/prizes. Publication of short story collection/manuscript.

YEAR PROGRAM STARTED: 1969

PURPOSE:
To encourage writing of short stories.

ELIGIBILITY:
Any writer who has not previously published a volume of prose fiction is eligible. Revised manuscripts which have been previously entered may be resubmitted. Writers who have published a volume of poetry are eligible.

The manuscript must be a collection of short stories of at least 150 word-processed, double-spaced pages. Stories previously published in periodicals are eligible.

CO-OP FUNDING PROGRAMS: The awards are provided with cooperation of the Iowa Writers' Workshop and the University of Iowa Press.

NO. MOST RECENT APPLICANTS: 400.

NO. AWARDS: 1 of each annually.

APPLICATION INFO:
No application forms are necessary. Manuscripts should be mailed to: Iowa Short Fiction Award, Iowa Writers' Workshop, at the address listed above. Do not send the only copy of the manuscript. Xeroxed copies are encouraged. Stamped, self-addressed packaging may be included for return of the manuscript, but is not required.

Deadline: Entries should be postmarked between August 1 and September 30. Announcement of the winners will be made early in the following year.

STAFF:
Lan Samantha Chang, Director

ADDRESS INQUIRIES TO:
Connie Brothers, Program Associate
(See address above.)

UNIVERSITY OF MINNESOTA [692]

Room 113, Elmer L. Andersen Library
222 21st Avenue South
Minneapolis, MN 55455
(612) 624-4576
E-mail: asc-clrc@umn.edu
Web Site: lib.umn.edu/clrc

AREAS OF INTEREST:
Children's book artist development.

NAME(S) OF PROGRAMS:
- **The Ezra Jack Keats/Kerlan Memorial Fellowship**

TYPE:
Travel grants. Award to travel to Kerlan Collection, University of Minnesota, plus per diem.

PURPOSE:
To fund the artist development of a talented writer and/or illustrator of children's books.

ELIGIBILITY:
Grants are awarded to individuals based on need. Special consideration will be given to those who would find it difficult to finance a visit to the Kerlan Collection. Candidates do not have to be U.S. citizens or residents.

FINANCIAL DATA:
Recipient will receive transportation cost and a per diem allotment.

Amount of support per award: Up to $1,500.

Total amount of support: Up to $1,500.

NO. AWARDS: 1.

APPLICATION INFO:
Electronic application acceptable by deadline.

Duration: Grants are awarded annually and are nonrenewable.

Deadline: January 30 (postmark).

ADDRESS INQUIRIES TO:
Ezra Jack Keats/Kerlan Collection
Memorial Fellowship Committee
(See address above.)

UNIVERSITY OF NEW MEXICO [693]

MSC03 2170
One University of New Mexico
Albuquerque, NM 87131-0001
(505) 277-5572
E-mail: taosconf@unm.edu
Web Site: taosconf.unm.edu

FOUNDED: 1999

AREAS OF INTEREST:
Fiction, nonfiction and poetry workshops.

NAME(S) OF PROGRAMS:
- **Taos Summer Writers' Conference**

TYPE:
Assistantships; Awards/prizes; Conferences/seminars; Fellowships; Scholarships. The Taos Summer Writers' Conference has a number of scholarships to provide support for talented writers.

The D.H. Lawrence Fellowship is intended for emerging writers with one book in print. It provides tuition remission and the cost of lodging.

The Taos Resident Writer Award provides tuition remission for one workshop to a resident of the Taos area.

The Hispanic Writer Award is open to any New Mexican resident of Hispanic, Latino, or Spanish heritage. The award provides tuition remission for one workshop and the cost of lodging.

The Leo Love Merit Scholarships are available to any potential conference participant. It pays tuition for a weeklong workshop or partial tuition for a master class. Recipient is responsible for her or his transportation and/or lodging costs.

The Native Writer Award is open to any Native American writer who is a resident of New Mexico. It provides tuition remission for one workshop and the cost of lodging.

YEAR PROGRAM STARTED: 1999

PURPOSE:
To help up-and-coming writers hone their skills by continuing to take courses to advance their writing career.

LEGAL BASIS:
University.

ELIGIBILITY:
Qualified individuals involved in the fields listed above are eligible to apply.

FINANCIAL DATA:
Recipients receive tuition remission, lodging, and breakfast and lunch. Lodging costs are excluded from the Leo Love Merit Scholarships.

Amount of support per award: Up to $700.

Total amount of support: Varies.

NO. MOST RECENT APPLICANTS: 50.

NO. AWARDS: 6 annually.

APPLICATION INFO:
Application information is available on the web site.

Duration: Conference: Six to eight days.

IRS I.D.: 85-6000642

STAFF:
Sharon Oard Warner, Founding Director
Eva Lipton-Ormand, Assistant Director

ADDRESS INQUIRIES TO:
Eva Lipton-Ormand, Assistant Director
Taos Summer Writers' Conference
(See address above.)

THE UNIVERSITY OF SOUTHERN MISSISSIPPI [694]

118 College Drive
Box 5148
Hattiesburg, MS 39406
(601) 266-4349
Fax: (601) 266-6269
E-mail: ellen.ruffin@usm.edu
Web Site: www.lib.usm.edu/degrummond

FOUNDED: 1966

AREAS OF INTEREST:
American and British children's literature.

NAME(S) OF PROGRAMS:
- **Ezra Jack Keats/Janina Domanska Children's Literature Research Fellowship**

TYPE:
Fellowships; Research grants.

PURPOSE:
To support research in children's literature.

FINANCIAL DATA:
Amount of support per award: Varies.

Total amount of support: Varies.

NO. MOST RECENT APPLICANTS: Average 5 to 7.

NO. AWARDS: 1 for the year 2014.

APPLICATION INFO:
Application information is available on the web site.

Duration: One year. Grants not renewable.

Deadline: November. Announcement in mid-December.

ADDRESS INQUIRIES TO:
Ellen H. Ruffin, Curator
de Grummond Children's Literature Collection
(See address above.)

UNIVERSITY OF VIRGINIA PRESS [695]

P.O. Box 400318
Charlottesville, VA 22904-4318
(434) 924-3361
Fax: (434) 982-2655
E-mail: arh2h@virginia.edu
Web Site: www.upress.virginia.edu

FOUNDED: 1963

AREAS OF INTEREST:
18th century studies.

NAME(S) OF PROGRAMS:

- **Walker Cowen Memorial Prize**

TYPE:
Awards/prizes.

YEAR PROGRAM STARTED: 1989

LEGAL BASIS:
University.

ELIGIBILITY:
Author of work in 18th century studies (i.e., the "long" 18th century, from the 1690s to 1815) in history (including the history of science), literature, philosophy or the arts. The work may cover Europe, the Americas, or the Atlantic world.

New manuscripts: Any unpublished, book-length (60,000 to 150,000 words) manuscript in English. The author may be of any nationality. Only manuscripts that are not under review (i.e., not being considered for publication at another press) elsewhere will be considered.

Translation candidates: Books published within the last three years in a European language may be submitted.

Contact the Press for complete details.

FINANCIAL DATA:
Amount of support per award: $5,000, plus publication by The University of Virginia Press.

NO. MOST RECENT APPLICANTS: 10.

NO. AWARDS: 1 annually.

APPLICATION INFO:
Include three copies of applicant's curriculum vitae and a description (one to two typescript pages) of the manuscript's content, scope and intended readership. New manuscripts: Submit two identical copies of the manuscript simultaneously. Translation candidates: Submit one copy of the work in the original language together with copies of any published reviews.

Submissions should be mailed to the address given above, or, if mailing by courier, to the following:
Cowen Award Judges
c/o The University of Virginia Press
210 Sprigg Lane
Charlottesville, VA 22904-4318.

Deadline: November 1 (postmark). Award announcement in the following March.

ADDRESS INQUIRIES TO:
Angie Hogan, Assistant Editor
(See address above.)

THE WORD WORKS, INC. [696]

P.O. Box 42164
Washington, DC 20015
(301) 581-9439
E-mail: editor@wordworksbooks.org
Web Site: www.wordworksbooks.org

FOUNDED: 1974

AREAS OF INTEREST:
Poetry and literature.

NAME(S) OF PROGRAMS:

- **The Washington Prize**

TYPE:
Awards/prizes.

YEAR PROGRAM STARTED: 1981

PURPOSE:
To encourage and promote contemporary American poetry.

LEGAL BASIS:
Nonprofit corporation.

ELIGIBILITY:
The Washington Prize is awarded for a volume of original poetry in English by a living American or Canadian writer.

GEOG. RESTRICTIONS: Canada and United States.

FINANCIAL DATA:
Amount of support per award: $1,500 plus book publication.

NO. AWARDS: 1 each year.

APPLICATION INFO:
Application may be submitted online. There is an entry fee of $25 (U.S.) drawn on a U.S. bank only, payable to The Word Works.

Applications mailed through the postal service should be addressed to: The Word Works Washington Prize, Adirondack Community College, 640 Bay Road, Queensbury, NY 12804.

Deadline: January 15 to March 15. Decision by August.

IRS I.D.: 52-1042022

BOARD OF DIRECTORS:
Karren L. Alenier, Chairperson of the Board
Nancy White, President
J.H. Beall
Todd Ibrahim
Rebecca Kutzer-Rice

ADDRESS INQUIRIES TO:
Nancy White, Executive Director
The Word Works Washington Prize
Adirondack Community College
640 Bay Road
Queensbury, NY 12804

*PLEASE NOTE:
The Washington Prize is for support of poets. It is not an academic scholarship for higher education.

THE WORD WORKS, INC. [697]

P.O. Box 42164
Washington, DC 20015
(301) 581-9439
E-mail: editor@wordworksdc.com
Web Site: www.wordworksbooks.org

FOUNDED: 1974

AREAS OF INTEREST:
Poetry.

NAME(S) OF PROGRAMS:

- **Tenth Gate Prize**

TYPE:
Awards/prizes. Award is given to a living poet with at least two full-length collections of poetry published by literary presses.

PURPOSE:
To encourage and promote contemporary American poetry.

ELIGIBILITY:
Submitted work must be a volume of original poetry written in English. Applicant must have had at least two full-length collections of poetry published by literary presses.

FINANCIAL DATA:
Amount of support per award: $1,000 plus book publication.

APPLICATION INFO:
Application may be made online. There is an entry fee of $25 (U.S.). Detailed information can be found on the web site.

Deadline: June 1 to July 15. Decision by November 15.

ADDRESS INQUIRIES TO:
Leslie McGrath, Series Editor
The Tenth Gate, English Department
Central Connecticut State University
1615 Stanley Street
New Britain, CT 06050
(See e-mail address above.)

*PLEASE NOTE:
Include a self-addressed, stamped envelope with all regular mail inquiries.

Museums and libraries

ALABAMA LIBRARY ASSOCIATION SCHOLARSHIP LOAN FUND, INC. [698]

Alabama Library Association
6030 Monticello Drive
Montgomery, AL 36117
(334) 414-0113
E-mail: allanet.org@gmail.com
Web Site: www.allanet.org

FOUNDED: 1904

AREAS OF INTEREST:
Library science.

NAME(S) OF PROGRAMS:

- **Scholarships in Library Science**

TYPE:
Scholarships. Scholarships for graduate study in library science/library media.

YEAR PROGRAM STARTED: 1945

PURPOSE:
To provide professional training for librarians and prospective librarians.

LEGAL BASIS:
Nonprofit corporation.

ELIGIBILITY:
Residents of Alabama who have been accepted by an accredited institution offering a graduate course in library science are eligible to apply.

GEOG. RESTRICTIONS: Alabama.

FINANCIAL DATA:
Amount of support per award: ALLA Centennial Memorial Scholarship and ALLA Memorial Scholarship: Up to $1,000 per award.

Total amount of support: Up to $2,000.

NO. AWARDS: 2.

APPLICATION INFO:
Application forms are available online or from the Association Administrator. Three references are required and proof of admission to school.

Duration: One academic year.

Deadline: June 1.

PUBLICATIONS:
Brochure; application guidelines.

OFFICERS:
Dena Luce, President

ADDRESS INQUIRIES TO:
See e-mail address above.

AMERICAN ASSOCIATION OF LAW LIBRARIES [699]

105 West Adams Street
Suite 3300
Chicago, IL 60603
(312) 939-4764
Fax: (312) 431-1097
E-mail: membership@aall.org
Web Site: www.aallnet.org

FOUNDED: 1906

AREAS OF INTEREST:
Librarianship, law librarianship and law.

NAME(S) OF PROGRAMS:
- **Library Degree for Law School Graduates**
- **Library Degree for Non-Law School Graduates**
- **Library School Graduates Attending Law School**
- **Library School Graduates Seeking a Non-Law Degree**

TYPE:
Scholarships. For study of law or librarianship, with support intended for prospective law librarians.

YEAR PROGRAM STARTED: 1966

PURPOSE:
To assist qualified persons who are interested in becoming professional law librarians.

LEGAL BASIS:
Not-for-profit corporation.

ELIGIBILITY:
Preference is given to AALL members, but scholarships are not restricted to members. Evidence of financial need must be submitted.

GEOG. RESTRICTIONS: United States.

FINANCIAL DATA:
Amount of support per award: $1,000 to $3,000. Amounts vary according to available funds and may be limited at the discretion of the Scholarships Committee.

Total amount of support: Varies.

NO. MOST RECENT APPLICANTS: 30.

NO. AWARDS: Varies.

APPLICATION INFO:
Application information is available on the web site.

Duration: Varies by scholarship.

Deadline: April 1.

ADDRESS INQUIRIES TO:
Hannah Phelps Proctor
Membership Services Coordinator
(See address above.)

AMERICAN ASSOCIATION OF LAW LIBRARIES [700]

105 West Adams Street
Suite 3300
Chicago, IL 60603
(312) 939-4764
Fax: (312) 431-1097
E-mail: membership@aall.org
Web Site: www.aallnet.org

FOUNDED: 1906

AREAS OF INTEREST:
Librarianship, law librarianship and minorities.

NAME(S) OF PROGRAMS:
- **George A. Strait Minority Stipend Scholarship Endowment**

TYPE:
Scholarships. Stipend for graduate study leading to a degree at an accredited school of library or information science or an accredited law school. Preference will be given to individuals with previous service to, or interest in, law librarianship.

YEAR PROGRAM STARTED: 1966

PURPOSE:
To assist qualified persons who are interested in becoming professional law librarians.

LEGAL BASIS:
Not-for-profit corporation.

ELIGIBILITY:
Application is limited to minority group members defined by current guidelines of the U.S. government. Applicant must be a degree candidate in an ALA-accredited library school or ABA-accredited law school and intend to have a career in law librarianship.

GEOG. RESTRICTIONS: United States.

FINANCIAL DATA:
Amount of support per award: Up to $2,500.

Total amount of support: Varies.

NO. MOST RECENT APPLICANTS: 17.

NO. AWARDS: Varies.

APPLICATION INFO:
Application packet must include:
(1) an official transcript or unofficial copy of transcript from the school where applicant completed most recent degree;
(2) a letter from the Admissions Officer of the library school, stating the program for which the applicant has been accepted and the date the courses begin, or, if applicant has already begun pursuing the degree, a transcript showing they are a degree candidate in good standing, or, if the applicant is attending law school, a transcript showing they are a degree candidate in good standing;
(3) two letters of recommendation from persons who have knowledge of the applicant's abilities and who can evaluate and comment upon law library employment experience;
(4) a personal statement discussing the applicant's interest in law librarianship, reason for applying for this scholarship, career goals as a law librarian, and statement of financial need and;
(5) a resume.

Duration: One year.

Deadline: April 1.

ADDRESS INQUIRIES TO:
Hannah Phelps Proctor
Membership Services Coordinator
(See address above.)

AMERICAN ASSOCIATION OF SCHOOL LIBRARIANS [701]

50 East Huron Street
Chicago, IL 60611
(800) 545-2433 ext. 4382
Fax: (312) 280-5276
E-mail: aasl@ala.org
Web Site: www.ala.org/aasl

FOUNDED: 1951

AREAS OF INTEREST:
Libraries and librarianship.

NAME(S) OF PROGRAMS:
- **AASL Collaborative School Library Award**
- **AASL Frances Henne Award**
- **AASL Innovative Reading Grant**
- **AASL National School Library Program of the Year Award**
- **ABC-CLIO Leadership Grant**

TYPE:
Awards/prizes; Development grants; Project/program grants.

PURPOSE:
To honor distinguished service and foster professional growth in the school library profession.

ELIGIBILITY:
Frances Henne Award: The applicant must be a full-time student preparing to be a school librarian at the preschool, elementary or secondary level.

Applicants for awards/grants must be members of the American Association of School Librarians.

FINANCIAL DATA:
Amount of support per award: $1,000 to $10,000.

Total amount of support: Varies.

NO. MOST RECENT APPLICANTS: 50.

NO. AWARDS: Varies.

APPLICATION INFO:
Application form and information are available from the Association.

Deadline: AASL National School Library Program of the Year Award: January 1; AASL Collaborative School Library Award, AASL Frances Henne Award, and ABC-CLIO Leadership Grant: February 1.

EXECUTIVE DIRECTOR:
Sylvia Norton

ADDRESS INQUIRIES TO:
See e-mail address above.

AMERICAN ASSOCIATION OF SCHOOL LIBRARIANS [702]

50 East Huron Street
Chicago, IL 60611
(800) 545-2433 ext. 4382
Fax: (312) 280-5276
E-mail: aasl@ala.org
Web Site: www.ala.org/aasl

FOUNDED: 1951

AREAS OF INTEREST:
Libraries.

NAME(S) OF PROGRAMS:
- **Distinguished Service Award**

TYPE:
Awards/prizes. Baker and Taylor provides funding for this award.

YEAR PROGRAM STARTED: 1978

PURPOSE:
To honor distinguished service and foster professional growth in the school library field.

ELIGIBILITY:
Nominator must be a member of AASL.

FINANCIAL DATA:
Amount of support per award: $3,000 and a citation.

Total amount of support: $3,000.

NO. AWARDS: 1.

APPLICATION INFO:
Application form and information are available from the Association.

Deadline: February 1.

ADDRESS INQUIRIES TO:
See e-mail address above.

AMERICAN LIBRARY ASSOCIATION (ALA) [703]

50 East Huron Street
Chicago, IL 60611-2795
(312) 280-3247
(800) 545-2433 ext. 3247
Fax: (312) 280-5014
E-mail: awards@ala.org
Web Site: www.ala.org

FOUNDED: 1876

AREAS OF INTEREST:
Librarianship.

NAME(S) OF PROGRAMS:
- **ALA Awards**

TYPE:
Awards/prizes; Conferences/seminars; Development grants; Fellowships; Research grants; Scholarships; Seed money grants; Travel grants. Cash and noncash awards for achievement/distinguished service, authors/illustrators/publishers, exhibits, funding, intellectual freedom, literacy, professional development, public relations, publications/articles and special services, as well as scholarships, fellowships and research grants sponsored by ALA and its units.

PURPOSE:
To honor distinguished service and foster professional growth.

FINANCIAL DATA:
Amount of support per award: Awards: $250 to $10,000; Research Grants and Fellowships: $500 to $10,000.

Total amount of support: Varies.

CO-OP FUNDING PROGRAMS: Some grants are sponsored by Baker and Taylor, H.W. Wilson Company and Voice of Youth Advocates.

NO. AWARDS: More than 150 annually.

REPRESENTATIVE AWARDS:
Academic or Research Librarian of the Year Award for outstanding contribution to academic and research librarianship and library development, $3,000 (donated by Baker & Taylor); The H.W. Wilson Library Staff Development Grant to library organization for a program to further its goals and objectives, $3,500 (donated by The H.W. Wilson Company); Frances Henne Research Grant to provide seed money to an individual, institution or group for a project to encourage research on library service to young adults, $500 minimum (donated by Voice of Youth Advocates); David H. Clift Scholarship to worthy U.S. or Canadian citizen to begin an M.L.S. degree in an ALA-accredited program, $3,000 (donated by scholarship endowment interest, individual contributions).

APPLICATION INFO:
Application information is available on the web site.

Duration: Varies.

Deadline: December 1.

ADDRESS INQUIRIES TO:
Cheryl Malden, Program Officer
(See address above.)

ASSOCIATION FOR LIBRARY AND INFORMATION SCIENCE EDUCATION [704]

2150 North 107th Street, Suite 205
Seattle, WA 98133
(206) 209-5267
Fax: (206) 367-8777
E-mail: office@alise.org
Web Site: www.alise.org

FOUNDED: 1915

AREAS OF INTEREST:
Library and information science education.

NAME(S) OF PROGRAMS:
- **ALISE Research Awards**

TYPE:
Awards/prizes; Research grants. Award for an outstanding research proposal in the field of librarianship and information science.

YEAR PROGRAM STARTED: 1976

PURPOSE:
To provide support for research which will help to promote excellence in education for librarianship and information science.

LEGAL BASIS:
Nonprofit 501(c)(3) corporation.

ELIGIBILITY:
Determined on the basis of the project's appropriateness to the goals of the ALISE, evidence of an established methodology and a viable research design, likelihood of completion in 12 to 18 months and on the qualifications of the researcher, who should be an ALISE member. Evidence that other funds are not available for the project should be presented.

The award cannot be used to support a doctoral dissertation. At least one applicant in a group submitting a proposal must be a personal member of the Association as of the deadline date. Staff training, general operating or overhead expenses, and other indirect costs are not funded.

Recipients of the award must present a progress report at the ALISE Annual Conference, submit written quarterly reports to the Executive Director of ALISE, who will pay the grant in periodic installments as the research progresses, submit the results of the funded study to the Association's Journal of Education for Library and Information Science (JELIS) for possible publication prior to submission to other publications, that is, the Journal will have first option on publication, acknowledge the support of ALISE in any publicity or presentation based on the funded study and inform the Executive Director if they receive research funding in addition to that provided by ALISE.

FINANCIAL DATA:
Staff training, general operating or overhead expenses, and other indirect costss are not funded.

Amount of support per award: Up to $5,000.

Total amount of support: $5,000 annually.

NO. AWARDS: 1.

REPRESENTATIVE AWARDS:
Laurie Bonnici, University of Alabama for "Non-Verbal Communication in Information Behavior: Ischemic Stroke and Partial Facial Paralysis."

APPLICATION INFO:
Proposals should be succinct and precise. No more than 20 double-spaced, typed pages. If necessary, supporting information may be included in an appendix. Proposals must include the following information to be considered in the competition:
(1) abstract of the project in no greater than 200 words;
(2) problem statement and literature review including justification and need for the research;
(3) project objectives;
(4) project description;
(5) research design, methodology and analysis techniques;
(6) detailed budget (including institutional or departmental contributions, if any);
(7) expected benefits and impact from the research and;
(8) vita(e) of project investigator(s).

Duration: One year.

Deadline: October 1.

PUBLICATIONS:
Application guidelines.

IRS I.D.: 51-0193882

STAFF:
Andrew Estep, Executive Director

BOARD OF DIRECTORS AND OFFICERS:
Samantha Hastings, President
Denise Adkins, Secretary/Treasurer
Carol Tilly, Director for External Relations
Laurie Bonnici, Director for Membership Services
Leanne Bowler, Director for Special Interest Groups

ADDRESS INQUIRIES TO:
ALISE Awards
(See address above.)

*SPECIAL STIPULATIONS:
The Research Grant award cannot be used to support a doctoral dissertation.

ASSOCIATION FOR LIBRARY AND INFORMATION SCIENCE EDUCATION [705]

2150 North 107th Street, Suite 205
Seattle, WA 98133
(206) 209-5267
Fax: (206) 367-8777
E-mail: office@alise.org
Web Site: www.alise.org

FOUNDED: 1915

AREAS OF INTEREST:
Library and information science education.

NAME(S) OF PROGRAMS:
- **ALISE/ProQuest Methodology Paper Competition**
- **The Eugene Garfield/ALISE Doctoral Dissertation Competition**
- **Bohdan S. Wynar Research Paper Competition**

TYPE:
Awards/prizes. Awards for an outstanding unpublished research paper, methodology paper and for each of two outstanding doctoral dissertations, respectively.

YEAR PROGRAM STARTED: 1977

PURPOSE:
To encourage research in the field of library and information science education and related areas.

LEGAL BASIS:
Nonprofit 501(c)(3) corporation.

ELIGIBILITY:
ALISE/ProQuest Methodology Paper Competition is open to all types of methodology. Papers must be limited to description and discussion of a research method or a technique associated with a particular research method. Papers must explain the particular method/technique, including methodological implications for library and information science. Examples to illustrate its value can come from LIS-related published studies, proposed studies, and works in progress. Papers that stress findings are not eligible.

The Eugene Garfield/ALISE Doctoral Dissertation Competition is open to doctoral students who have recently graduated in any field of study, or who will have completed their dissertations by the deadline. Dissertations must deal with substantive issues related to library and information science, but applicants may be from within or outside LIS programs.

Bohdan S. Wynar Research Paper Competition is open to research papers concerning any aspect of library and information science. This competition is not limited to research regarding LIS education. Any research methodology is acceptable.

FINANCIAL DATA:
Amount of support per award: ALISE/ProQuest Methodology Paper and The Eugene Garfield/ALISE Doctoral Dissertation Competitions: $500 each.

NO. AWARDS: ALISE/ProQuest Methodology Paper Competition: 1; The Eugene Garfield/ALISE Doctoral Dissertation and Bohdan S. Wynar Research Paper Competitions: Up to 2 each.

APPLICATION INFO:
Application information is available on the web site.

Deadline: ALISE/ProQuest Methodology Paper and Bohdan S. Wynar Research Paper Competitions: September; The Eugene Garfield/ALISE Doctoral Dissertation Competition: June 30.

IRS I.D.: 51-0193882

STAFF:
Andrew Estep, Executive Director

BOARD OF DIRECTORS AND OFFICERS:
Samantha Hastings, President
Denise Adkins, Secretary/Treasurer
Carol Tilly, Director for External Relations
Laurie Bonnici, Director for Membership Services
Leanne Bowler, Director for Special Interest Groups

ADDRESS INQUIRIES TO:
ALISE Awards
(See address above.)

BETA PHI MU [706]

Drexel University
College of Computing and Informatics
3141 Chestnut Street
Philadelphia, PA 19104
(215) 895-2492
Fax: (215) 895-2494
E-mail: betaphimu@drexel.edu
Web Site: www.beta-phi-mu.org

FOUNDED: 1948

AREAS OF INTEREST:
Library and information studies.

NAME(S) OF PROGRAMS:
- **Eugene Garfield Doctoral Dissertation Fellowship**
- **Harold Lancour Scholarship for Foreign Study**
- **Sarah Rebecca Reed Scholarship**
- **Frank B. Sessa Scholarship for Continuing Education of a Beta Phi Mu Member**
- **Blanche E. Woolls Scholarship for School Library Media Service**

TYPE:
Fellowships; Scholarships. Eugene Garfield Doctoral Dissertation Fellowship is funded through the generosity of Eugene Garfield, and provides fellowships for up to six students per year. They are awarded to foster high-quality research in the field and to expedite the movement of new Doctorates into teaching positions.

The Harold Lancour Scholarship is given for foreign study.

The Sarah Rebecca Reed Scholarship is given to a beginning student at the Master's level accepted in an American Library Association-accredited program.

The Frank B. Sessa Scholarship is given for Continuing Education for a Beta Phi Mu member.

The Blanche Woolls Scholarship is given to a beginning student at the Master's level accepted in an American Library Association-Accredited Program majoring in School Media Services.

PURPOSE:
To assist qualified persons who are interested in completing a course of advanced study in library and information studies.

LEGAL BASIS:
Nonprofit organization.

FINANCIAL DATA:
Amount of support per award: Garfield Doctoral Dissertation Fellowship: $3,000; Lancour Scholarship: $1,750; Reed and Woolls Scholarships: $2,250 each; Sessa Scholarship: $1,500.

Total amount of support: Up to $28,000.

NO. MOST RECENT APPLICANTS: 142.

NO. AWARDS: 10.

APPLICATION INFO:
Forms are available on the Society's web site.

Duration: One-time award. Nonrenewable.

Deadline: March 15.

PUBLICATIONS:
The Pipeline, online newsletter.

STAFF:
Alison M. Lewis, Ph.D., Executive Director
Isabel Gray, Program Director

ADDRESS INQUIRIES TO:
Isabel Gray, Program Director
(See address above.)

GLADYS BROOKS FOUNDATION

1055 Franklin Avenue
Suite 208
Garden City, NY 11530-2903
(516) 746-6103
Web Site: www.gladysbrooksfoundation.org

TYPE:
Capital grants; Challenge/matching grants; Demonstration grants; Development grants; Endowments; Matching gifts; Project/program grants; Scholarships. Grants to private, not-for-profit publicly supported libraries, educational institutions, hospitals and clinics in the eastern U.S.

See entry 1163 for full listing.

CALIFORNIA LIBRARY ASSOCIATION [707]

248 East Foothill Boulevard
Suite 101
Monrovia, CA 91016
(626) 239-1776
Fax: (626) 239-1776
E-mail: info@cla-net.org
Web Site: www.cla-net.org

FOUNDED: 1896

AREAS OF INTEREST:
Librarianship.

NAME(S) OF PROGRAMS:
- **Begun Scholarship**
- **CLA Scholarship for Minority Students in Memory of Edna Yelland**
- **Reference Service Press Fellowship**

TYPE:
Fellowships; Scholarships. Support for minority library school students. Support for graduate students in reference/information service librarianship.

YEAR PROGRAM STARTED: 1973

PURPOSE:
To help support the educational goals of minority students in the library service field.

LEGAL BASIS:
Nonprofit.

ELIGIBILITY:
Applicant must be accepted by a graduate library school in California, accredited by the American Library Association, be of ethnic origin and show financial need. California residents and U.S. citizens or permanent U.S. residents may apply. For fellowships, applicants must be preparing for a career in reference or information service librarianship. Students pursuing an M.L.S. on a part-time or full-time basis are equally eligible.

GEOG. RESTRICTIONS: California.

FINANCIAL DATA:
Amount of support per award: Generally $2,500 per Edna Yelland Scholarship; $3,000 for Begun Scholarship; $3,000 for fellowship.

Total amount of support: $10,500 for scholarships; $3,000 for fellowship.

NO. MOST RECENT APPLICANTS: 25.

NO. AWARDS: 4 scholarships and 1 fellowship each year.

APPLICATION INFO:
Application information can be found on the Association's web site.

Duration: One-time award.

Deadline: Mid-March.

CAMBRIDGE UNIVERSITY LIBRARY [708]

West Road
Cambridge CB3 9DR England
(44) 0 1223 333000
Fax: (44) 0 1223 333160
E-mail: library@lib.cam.ac.uk
Web Site: www.lib.cam.ac.uk

FOUNDED: 1400

AREAS OF INTEREST:
Bibliographic research.

NAME(S) OF PROGRAMS:
- **The Munby Fellowship in Bibliography**

TYPE:
Fellowships. Graduate fellowships for bibliographical research based on the collections of Cambridge libraries.

YEAR PROGRAM STARTED: 1977

LEGAL BASIS:
University.

ELIGIBILITY:
Open to university graduates in any discipline, with preference given to graduates of postdoctoral or equivalent level, of any nationality or age. Research must be bibliographical.

FINANCIAL DATA:
Amount of support per award: GBP 33,574 for the year 2016-17.

NO. MOST RECENT APPLICANTS: 50.

NO. AWARDS: 1.

APPLICATION INFO:
Applicants must send a completed cover sheet (available from the Library), curriculum vitae and statement of proposed research.

Duration: 10 months, October 1 to July 31.

Deadline: October 31. Election made in early January.

PUBLICATIONS:
Application guidelines.

ADDRESS INQUIRIES TO:
Head of Special Collections
(See address above.)

CATHOLIC LIBRARY ASSOCIATION [709]

8550 United Plaza Boulevard
Suite 1001
Baton Rouge, LA 70809
(225) 408-4417
E-mail: cla2@cathla.org
Web Site: www.cathla.org

FOUNDED: 1921

AREAS OF INTEREST:
Promotion of Catholic principles by the improvement of library resources and services.

NAME(S) OF PROGRAMS:
- **Junior Library Guild-Sister Sally Daly Grant**

TYPE:
Conferences/seminars.

YEAR PROGRAM STARTED: 2007

PURPOSE:
To allow a member to attend their first CLA Convention.

ELIGIBILITY:
Applicant must be attending the CLA Convention for the first time.

FINANCIAL DATA:
Amount of support per award: Up to $1,500.

Total amount of support: Up to $1,500.

NO. AWARDS: 1 annually.

APPLICATION INFO:
Application information is available on the web site.

Duration: One-time award.

ADDRESS INQUIRIES TO:
CLA Office
(See address above.)

CONNECTICUT LIBRARY ASSOCIATION [710]

234 Court Street
Middletown, CT 06457
(860) 346-2444
Fax: (860) 344-9199
E-mail: cla@ctlibrarians.org
Web Site: www.ctlibraryassociation.org

NAME(S) OF PROGRAMS:
- **Proficiency Enhancement Grants (PEG)**

TYPE:
Grants-in-aid. Grants for personnel at all levels of library work.

YEAR PROGRAM STARTED: 1976

PURPOSE:
To support the educational goals of library science students in Connecticut.

LEGAL BASIS:
Nonprofit organization.

ELIGIBILITY:
Grants are made to CLA members only.

GEOG. RESTRICTIONS: Connecticut.

FINANCIAL DATA:
Amount of support per award: Up to $400.

Total amount of support: Up to $2,500 annually.

NO. AWARDS: Up to 4 or 5 grants per year.

APPLICATION INFO:
Apply to the Chairperson, Program for Educational Grants, at the address above.

Duration: One year. Not renewable.

Deadline: September 1, November 1, January 2 and July 1.

ADDRESS INQUIRIES TO:
Peter F. Ciparelli, PEG Chairman
Killingly Public Library
25 Westcott Road
Danielson, CT 06239-2928
E-mail: pciparelli@biblio.org
Tel: (860) 779-5383

*PLEASE NOTE:
Only for continuing education, workshops and seminars. Any other applications will be considered at the discretion of the committee.

COOPERSTOWN GRADUATE PROGRAM [711]

SUNY College at Oneonta
Cooperstown Graduate Program in Museum Studies
5838 State Route 80
Cooperstown, NY 13326-2502
(607) 547-2586
Fax: (607) 547-8926
E-mail: rosemary.craig@oneonta.edu
gretchen.sorin@oneonta.edu
Web Site: www.oneonta.edu/academics/cgp

FOUNDED: 1964

AREAS OF INTEREST:
History museum studies and science museum studies.

TYPE:
Assistantships; Fellowships; Scholarships. Awards for museum studies for Cooperstown Graduate Program students only.

YEAR PROGRAM STARTED: 1964

PURPOSE:
To provide professionally trained individuals for the museum field.

ELIGIBILITY:
Applicants must have a strong academic record, an interest in public service, excellent writing skills and a demonstrated commitment to the field through museum work in either staff or volunteer capacity.

FINANCIAL DATA:
Amount of support per award: $4,000 to $12,000 per year.

Total amount of support: $175,000.

CO-OP FUNDING PROGRAMS: Co-sponsored with SUNY College at Oneonta.

NO. MOST RECENT APPLICANTS: 70 to 80.

NO. AWARDS: Approximately 20 awards for students.

APPLICATION INFO:
Applications and further information may be obtained from the web site. Applications are to be submitted online.

Duration: Tenable in Cooperstown, NY, for 24 months.

Deadline: July 1 for fellowship application.

PUBLICATIONS:
Viewbook.

ADDRESS INQUIRIES TO:
Rosemary Craig
Assistant to Program Director
P.O. Box 4
Cooperstown, NY 13326-0004

FOUNDATION OF THE AMERICAN INSTITUTE FOR CONSERVATION OF HISTORIC AND ARTISTIC WORKS (FAIC) [712]

1156 15th Street, N.W., Suite 320
Washington, DC 20005
(202) 452-9545
Fax: (202) 452-9328
E-mail: cap@conservation-us.org
Web Site: www.conservation-us.org

FOUNDED: 1973

AREAS OF INTEREST:
Conservation assessment of museum collections.

CONSULTING OR VOLUNTEER SERVICES:
Professional consulting services.

NAME(S) OF PROGRAMS:
- **Collections Assessment for Preservation (CAP)**

TYPE:
Technical assistance. Provides funds for an independent, professional conservation assessment of a museum's collections and building environment. The assessor's resulting report will identify conservation priorities to assist the museum in developing a long-term plan for collections care and management.

YEAR PROGRAM STARTED: 1990

PURPOSE:
To make collections care and conservation a fundamental priority of museums and historical societies.

LEGAL BASIS:
Private and nonprofit.

ELIGIBILITY:
Institutions including museums, zoos, aquariums, botanical gardens and arboreta are eligible for assistance. CAP will also support the on-site participation of an architectural assessor. Zoos and aquariums that do not have an assessment of the animals' physical conditions and habitats can use the program for a general assessment of those collections.

GEOG. RESTRICTIONS: United States.

FINANCIAL DATA:
Amount of support per award: $5,040 to $10,080, depending on institution and collections.

Total amount of support: Varies.

NO. MOST RECENT APPLICANTS: 140.

NO. AWARDS: 78.

APPLICATION INFO:
Notification of the release of CAP application online will be publicized on the FAIC web site by November 1.

Duration: One year.

Deadline: February 1.

PUBLICATIONS:
Sample CAP application with guidelines; CAP brochure.

STAFF:
Tiffani Emig, Coordinator, Collections Assessment for Preservation

ADDRESS INQUIRIES TO:
Collections Assessment for Preservation
(See address above.)

GEORGIA LIBRARY ASSOCIATION [713]

P.O. Box 793
Rex, GA 30273
(678) 466-4325
Fax: (678) 466-4349
E-mail: gordonbaker@clayton.edu
Web Site: gla.georgialibraries.org/scholarship.htm

FOUNDED: 1897

AREAS OF INTEREST:
Library professional development.

NAME(S) OF PROGRAMS:
- **Beard Scholarship**
- **Hubbard Scholarship**

TYPE:
Scholarships. Awards for graduate study of library science.

PURPOSE:
To recruit excellent librarians for Georgia.

LEGAL BASIS:
Professional association.

ELIGIBILITY:
Applicants must be accepted for admission to a Master's program at an ALA-accredited library school and must indicate intention to complete the Master's program within three years. Recipient must work in a library in Georgia for at least one year after graduation from ALA-accredited library school. Beard Scholarship is for candidates who demonstrate leadership potential.

GEOG. RESTRICTIONS: Georgia.

FINANCIAL DATA:
Amount of support per award: Beard Scholarship: $1,000; Hubbard Scholarship: $3,000.

Total amount of support: $4,000 annually.

NO. AWARDS: 1 each annually.

APPLICATION INFO:
Applicant must submit to the Chair the following:
(1) one official application form (applicant may be considered for both scholarships via one form and other accompanying documentation; do not submit duplicate materials);
(2) proof of admission to an American Library Association-accredited Master's program/library school, i.e., a letter from the dean of the school/program certifying acceptance (photocopy is acceptable);
(3) three letters of reference sent directly from the reference to the Committee Chair and;
(4) official transcripts of all academic work sent directly to the Chair from each college or university attended.

Duration: Beard Scholarship: Up to two semesters; Hubbard Scholarship: Up to four semesters. Both are nonrenewable.

Deadline: Beard and Hubbard Scholarships: May 21.

ADDRESS INQUIRIES TO:
Linh Uong
GLA Scholarship Committee
c/o Northeast Georgia Regional Library
P.O. Box 2020
Clarkesville, GA 30523

*SPECIAL STIPULATIONS:
The scholarship winners must agree to work in Georgia for one year following receipt of the Master's degree or agree to pay back a prorated amount of the award plus interest. Repayment must be made within two years.

HARTFORD PUBLIC LIBRARY [714]

500 Main Street
Hartford, CT 06103-3075
(860) 695-6300
Fax: (860) 722-6900
E-mail: billings@hplct.org
Web Site: www.hplct.org

FOUNDED: 1774

NAME(S) OF PROGRAMS:
- **The Caroline M. Hewins Scholarship**

TYPE:
Scholarships. Awarded to candidates for M.L.S. who will work with children.

YEAR PROGRAM STARTED: 1926

PURPOSE:
To assist in graduate Library Science study, leading to a career in library service with children.

ELIGIBILITY:
Students who plan to specialize in library work with children, who have received or are about to receive a four-year undergraduate degree and who have been admitted to or are attending an ALA-accredited library school are eligible. Preference is given to applicants who plan to pursue a career in public library service.

FINANCIAL DATA:
Amount of support per award: Up to $4,000.

Total amount of support: Up to $4,000 annually.

NO. AWARDS: 1 annually.

APPLICATION INFO:
The application form can be downloaded from the web site or obtained by writing to the Library, at the above address.

Deadline: Completed applications must be submitted by May 1.

ADDRESS INQUIRIES TO:
Mary Billings
Chief Public Services Officer
(See address above.)

INDIANA LIBRARY FEDERATION [715]

941 East 86th Street
Suite 260
Indianapolis, IN 46240
(317) 257-2040
Fax: (317) 257-1389
E-mail: askus@ilfonline.org
Web Site: www.ilfonline.org

FOUNDED: 1891

AREAS OF INTEREST:
Librarian education and training.

NAME(S) OF PROGRAMS:
- **The Esther Schlundt Fund**
- **The Sue Marsh Weller Fund**

TYPE:
Scholarships. Awards for graduate study of library science at ALA-accredited schools.

PURPOSE:
To aid students in financial need who have strong undergraduate records and who show unusual ability in the library field either public or academic.

LEGAL BASIS:
Professional association.

ELIGIBILITY:
Applicants must be legal residents of Indiana who intend to work in an Indiana library for at least one year after completing library education and must be enrolled in an ALA-accredited graduate program of library science.

GEOG. RESTRICTIONS: Indiana.

FINANCIAL DATA:
Amount of support per award: Up to $2,500.

Total amount of support: Varies.

APPLICATION INFO:
Application must be made in writing. Further information may be requested from the Federation.

Deadline: June 30.

ADDRESS INQUIRIES TO:
Lucinda Nord, Executive Director
(See address above.)

INSTITUTE OF MUSEUM AND LIBRARY SERVICES [716]

955 L'Enfant Plaza, S.W.
Suite 4000
Washington, DC 20024
(202) 653-4657
Fax: (202) 653-4600
TTY: (202) 606-8636
E-mail: imlsinfo@imls.gov
Web Site: www.imls.gov

FOUNDED: 1996

AREAS OF INTEREST:
Museums in all disciplines including art, history, science, as well as aquariums and zoological parks, botanical gardens, arboretums, planetariums, nature centers, natural history and children's museums.

NAME(S) OF PROGRAMS:
- **Museum Assessment Program**
- **Museum Grants for African American History and Culture**
- **Museums for America**
- **National Leadership Grants for Museums**
- **National Medal for Museum and Library Service**
- **Native American/Native Hawaiian Museum Services Program**
- **Sparks! Ignition Grants for Museums**

TYPE:
Awards/prizes; Challenge/matching grants; Conferences/seminars; Demonstration grants; Development grants; Fellowships; Formula grants; Internships; Project/program grants; Research grants; Scholarships; Seed money grants; Technical assistance; Training grants; Research contracts. Museum Assessment Program (MAP) grants help strengthen museum operations, plan for the future and meet national standards through self-study and a site visit from a peer reviewer.

Museum Grants for African American History and Culture strengthen African American museums by improving care of collections, developing professional management or providing internships and fellowship opportunities.

Museums for America grants support activities that strengthen museums as active resources for lifelong learning, vital components of livable communities and good stewards of the nation's collections.

National Leadership Grants for Museums support projects that address challenges or needs of the museum field, have broad impact and demonstrate innovation and collaboration.

National Medal for Museum and Library Service is the nation's highest honor for libraries and museums and is awarded by IMLS to outstanding institutions that make exceptional contributions to their communities.

Native American/Native Hawaiian Museum Services Program grants enhance museum services to sustain heritage, culture and knowledge.

Sparks! Ignition Grants for Museums provide an opportunity to expand and test the boundaries of museum services and practices.

YEAR PROGRAM STARTED: 1977

PURPOSE:
To foster leadership, innovation and lifetime learning by supporting museums and libraries.

LEGAL BASIS:
Federal independent agency within the Executive Branch.

ELIGIBILITY:
All types of museums, large and small, are eligible for funding. An eligible museum must be a public or private nonprofit institution that exists on a permanent basis for educational or aesthetic purposes.

Funds cannot be used for construction, renovation of facilities, endowment or acquisition of objects. Contact IMLS for program-specific eligibility.

GEOG. RESTRICTIONS: United States, American Samoa, Guam, the Marshall Islands, Micronesia, Northern Mariana Islands, Palau, Puerto Rico or the Virgin Islands.

FINANCIAL DATA:
Amount of support per award: Varies.
Total amount of support: Varies.

CO-OP FUNDING PROGRAMS: The Museum Assessment Program is funded by the Institute of Museum and Library Services and administered by the American Alliance for Museums.

NO. MOST RECENT APPLICANTS: Varies.

NO. AWARDS: Varies.

APPLICATION INFO:
Grant program guidelines and application instructions are available at IMLS web site.
Deadline: Varies.

PUBLICATIONS:
Annual report.

INSTITUTE OF MUSEUM AND LIBRARY SERVICES [717]

955 L'Enfant Plaza, S.W.
Suite 4000
Washington, DC 20024
(202) 653-4657
Fax: (202) 653-4600
E-mail: imlsinfo@imls.gov
Web Site: www.imls.gov

FOUNDED: 1996

AREAS OF INTEREST:
Libraries, including public libraries, school libraries, state libraries, college and university libraries, digital libraries, research libraries and archives that are not an integral part of an institution of higher education and that make publicly available library services and materials, and private or special libraries deemed eligible to participate by the state in which the library is located. Organizations, including graduate schools of library and information science, library consortia and library associations. There are special funding categories for state library administrative agencies, tribal libraries and organizations providing library services to Native Hawaiians.

NAME(S) OF PROGRAMS:
- **Laura Bush 21st Century Librarian Program**
- **Grants to State Library Administrative Agencies**
- **National Leadership Grants for Libraries**
- **Native American Library Services: Basic Grants and Enhancement Grants**
- **Native Hawaiian Library Services Grant**
- **Sparks! Ignition Grants for Libraries**

TYPE:
Project/program grants. Laura Bush 21st Century Librarian Program: Grants support professional development, graduate education and continuing education to help libraries and archives develop human capital capacity.

Grants to State Library Administrative Agencies: This is the largest grant program run by IMLS. It provides funds to State Library Administrative Agencies (SLAAs) using a population-based formula.

National Leadership Grants for Libraries: This program supports projects that address challenges faced by the library and archive fields and that have the potential to advance practice in those fields.

Native American Library Services: Basic Grants and Enhancement Grants: Provide funds for core library operations, technical assistance, and innovative project grants for libraries serving Native Americans and Alaska Native villages.

A Native Hawaiian Library Services Grant is awarded annually to organizations providing library services to Native Hawaiians.

Sparks! Ignition Grants for Libraries provide an opportunity to expand and test the boundaries of library and archive services and practices.

PURPOSE:
To foster leadership, innovation and lifetime learning by supporting museums and libraries.

LEGAL BASIS:
Federal independent agency within the Executive Branch.

ELIGIBILITY:
Restricted funding categories exist for state library administrative agencies and for library services to Native Americans and Native Hawaiians.

Funds cannot be used for construction, renovation of facilities, endowment or acquisition of objects. Contact IMLS for program-specific eligibility.

GEOG. RESTRICTIONS: United States and territories.

FINANCIAL DATA:
Amount of support per award: Varies.
Total amount of support: Varies.

NO. MOST RECENT APPLICANTS: Varies.

NO. AWARDS: Varies.

APPLICATION INFO:
Application information is available online.
Duration: Varies per award.
Deadline: Varies.

MEDICAL LIBRARY ASSOCIATION [718]

65 East Wacker Place
Suite 1900
Chicago, IL 60601-7246
(312) 419-9094
Fax: (312) 419-8950
E-mail: awards@mlahq.org
Web Site: www.mlanet.org

FOUNDED: 1898

AREAS OF INTEREST:
Health sciences librarianship.

NAME(S) OF PROGRAMS:
- **MLA Scholarship**
- **Thomson Reuters/MLA Doctoral Fellowship**

TYPE:
Fellowships; Scholarships. Awarded for study and doctoral work in health sciences librarianship.

Thomson Reuters/MLA Doctoral Fellowship is awarded biennially (in even-numbered years). It was established by the Institute for Scientific Information (ISI) and is administered by the MLA.

YEAR PROGRAM STARTED: 1986

PURPOSE:
To support and encourage individuals who are qualified to make a contribution to librarianship.

LEGAL BASIS:
Nonprofit.

ELIGIBILITY:
Citizens or permanent residents of the U.S. or Canada are eligible to apply.

Applicants for the MLA Scholarship must be entering an ALA-accredited graduate library school Master's program or, at the time of the granting of the scholarship (February), have completed no more than one-half of the academic requirements of the graduate program. An applicant who is a past recipient of the MLA Scholarship or the MLA Scholarship for Minority Students is ineligible.

For the Thomson Reuters/MLA Doctoral Fellowship, applicants must be members of MLA and graduates of an ALA-accredited library school or have equivalent graduate credentials in related information science disciplines (i.e., computer science, biomedical informatics). They must also have been accepted to candidacy in a Ph.D. program in health sciences librarianship with an emphasis on biomedical and health-related information science. A past recipient of the MLA Doctoral Fellowship is ineligible.

GEOG. RESTRICTIONS: United States and Canada.

FINANCIAL DATA:
Amount of support per award: MLA Scholarship: Up to $5,000; Thomson Reuters/MLA Doctoral Fellowship: $2,000.

NO. AWARDS: MLA Scholarships: 1 each per year; Thomson Reuters/MLA Doctoral Fellowship: 1 every two years.

APPLICATION INFO:
For the MLA Scholarship, applicant must submit an application form, essay, and all related documents plus a single copy of transcripts, two letters of reference and a copy of applicant's library school catalog or web page, which states the number of credits needed for one's degree.

For the Thomson Reuters/MLA Doctoral Fellowship, applicant must submit the following:
(1) application form and pertinent documentation;
(2) signed statement of terms and conditions;
(3) two letters of reference, submitted by the reference directly to MLA, Professional Development Department;
(4) transcripts of graduate work or proof of enrollment in the graduate program and a list of courses completed and;
(5) name, title, address, phone and e-mail of doctoral advisor.

Application and all supporting documents must be received by the deadline to be valid.

Duration: One year.

Deadline: December 1.

STAFF:
Maria Lopez, Grants, Scholarships and Awards Coordinator

ADDRESS INQUIRIES TO:
Coordinator
Grants, Scholarships and Awards
(See address above.)

MEDICAL LIBRARY ASSOCIATION [719]

65 East Wacker Place
Suite 1900
Chicago, IL 60601-7246
(312) 419-9094
Fax: (312) 419-8950
E-mail: awards@mlahq.org
Web Site: www.mlanet.org

FOUNDED: 1898

AREAS OF INTEREST:
Health sciences librarianship.

NAME(S) OF PROGRAMS:
- **Estelle Brodman Award for the Academic Medical Librarian of the Year**
- **Lois Ann Colaianni Award for Excellence and Achievement in Hospital Librarianship**
- **Louise Darling Medal for Distinguished Achievement in Collection Development in the Health Sciences**
- **Janet Doe Lectureship**
- **Ida and George Eliot Prize**
- **Erich Meyerhoff Prize**
- **Marcia C. Noyes Award**
- **Rittenhouse Award**
- **Thomson Reuters/Frank Bradway Rogers Information Advancement Award**

TYPE:
Awards/prizes; Visiting scholars. Awards to honor service to libraries and librarianship.

The Lois Ann Colaianni Award for Excellence and Achievement in Hospital Librarianship is given to an MLA-member who has made significant contributions to the profession in the area of hospital librarianship.

The Estelle Brodman Award for the Academic Medical Librarian of the Year recognizes an academic medical librarian at the midcareer level who demonstrates significant achievement or the potential for leadership and continuing excellence.

The Louise Darling Medal for Distinguished Achievement in Collection Development in the Health Sciences is given annually for outstanding collection development in the health sciences.

The Janet Doe Lectureship chooses an individual to present the lecture at the MLA's annual meeting. Recipients are chosen for their unique perspective on the history or philosophy of medical librarianship.

The Ida and George Eliot Prize is presented annually for a work published in the preceding calendar year that has been judged most effective in furthering medical librarianship.

The Erich Meyerhoff Prize is awarded annually for the best unpublished essay on the history of medicine and allied health sciences written by a health sciences librarian.

The Marcia C. Noyes Award is the highest professional distinction of the MLA. It recognizes a career that has resulted in lasting and outstanding contributions to medical librarianship.

The Rittenhouse Award recognizes an outstanding unpublished paper written by a library student or intern on health sciences librarianship or medical informatics.

The Thomson Reuters/Frank Bradway Rogers Information Advancement Award is presented annually to recognize the application of technology to the delivery of health sciences information to the science of information, or to the facilitation of the delivery of health sciences information.

Fellows and Honorary Members are selected for outstanding lifetime contributions to the advancement of the purposes of the MLA and are ordinarily chosen from members at or near the close of an active professional career. Honorary members are nonmembers who have made outstanding contributions to the advancement of the purposes of the Association.

PURPOSE:
To honor those who have rendered distinguished service to libraries and medical librarianship.

LEGAL BASIS:
Nonprofit organization.

ELIGIBILITY:
Applicants must be health science librarians. Essays submitted must be on the history of medicine or the allied sciences and must be unpublished.

Membership in MLA is required.

FINANCIAL DATA:
Amount of support per award: Colaianni Award for Excellence and Achievement in Hospital Librarianship, Rittenhouse Award and Rogers Award: $500 each; Janet Doe Lectureship: $250; Eliot Prize: $200; Meyerhoff Prize: $500.

CO-OP FUNDING PROGRAMS: The Rittenhouse Award established and sponsored by the Rittenhouse Book Distributors, Philadelphia, PA. The Erich Meyerhoff Prize is given by the MLA History of the Health Sciences Section.

NO. AWARDS: 1 per award each year.

APPLICATION INFO:
Nominations forms and guidelines are available on the web site.

Deadline: November 1.

PUBLICATIONS:
Honors and awards program announcement.

STAFF:
Maria Lopez, Grants, Scholarships and Awards Coordinator

ADDRESS INQUIRIES TO:
Coordinator
Grants, Scholarships and Awards
(See address above.)

MEDICAL LIBRARY ASSOCIATION

65 East Wacker Place
Suite 1900
Chicago, IL 60601-7246
(312) 419-9094
Fax: (312) 419-8950
E-mail: awards@mlahq.org
Web Site: www.mlanet.org

TYPE:
Fellowships; Travel grants; Work-study programs. Work-study program for medical librarians from countries other than the U.S. or Canada for a time period of at least two weeks.

See entry 941 for full listing.

MEDICAL LIBRARY ASSOCIATION

65 East Wacker Place
Suite 1900
Chicago, IL 60601-7246
(312) 419-9094
Fax: (312) 419-8950
E-mail: awards@mlahq.org
Web Site: www.mlanet.org

TYPE:
Awards/prizes; Scholarships. Awarded for study in health sciences librarianship.

See entry 977 for full listing.

THE METROPOLITAN MUSEUM OF ART [720]

1000 Fifth Avenue
New York, NY 10028-0198
(212) 650-2763
Fax: (212) 570-3972
E-mail: academic.programs@metmuseum.org
Web Site: www.metmuseum.org

NAME(S) OF PROGRAMS:
- **Theodore Rousseau Fellowships**

TYPE:
Fellowships. Awarded for the training of students whose goal is to enter museums as curators of painting, by enabling them to undertake related study in Europe, made possible by a bequest from the late Curator-in-Chief of the Metropolitan Museum of Art.

PURPOSE:
To develop the skills of connoisseurship by supporting firsthand examination of paintings in major European collections, rather than by supporting library research for the completion of degree requirements.

ELIGIBILITY:
Applicants should have been enrolled for at least one year in an advanced degree program in the field of art history.

FINANCIAL DATA:
Amount of support per award: Stipends vary in amount. For one year: $42,000 for predoctoral fellows, and up to an additional $6,000 for travel and miscellaneous expenses.

APPLICATION INFO:
Current application information may be obtained from the Museum's web site.

Duration: Three to 12 months.

Deadline: Application and required letters of recommendation must be received by the first Friday in November. Announcement of awards will be made by late March.

STAFF:
Marcie Karp, Managing Museum Educator, Academic Programs, Education Department

ADDRESS INQUIRIES TO:
See e-mail address above.

THE METROPOLITAN MUSEUM OF ART [721]

1000 Fifth Avenue
New York, NY 10028-0198
(212) 650-2763
Fax: (212) 570-3972
E-mail: academic.programs@metmuseum.org
Web Site: www.metmuseum.org

NAME(S) OF PROGRAMS:
- **Andrew W. Mellon Conservation Fellowship**

TYPE:
Fellowships. The Fellowship is awarded for training in one or more of the following Departments of the Metropolitan Museum: Arms and Armor, Asian Art Conservation, The Costume Institute, Musical Instruments, Objects Conservation (including sculpture, metalwork, glass, ceramics, furniture and archaeological objects), Paintings Conservation, Paper Conservation, Photograph Conservation, Scientific Research, or Textile Conservation, and made possible by the Andrew W. Mellon Foundation.

All fellowship recipients will be expected to spend the fellowship in residence in the department with which they are affiliated.

The Museum offers junior-level and senior-level fellowships in conservation and scientific research. Junior fellowships are intended for those who have recently completed graduate-level training. Senior fellowships are intended for well-established professionals with advanced training in the field and a proven publication record.

All fellowships must take place between September 1 and the following August 31.

ELIGIBILITY:
Applicants should have reached an advanced level of experience or training.

FINANCIAL DATA:
Amount of support per award: Stipend: $42,000 per year for junior-level conservators and researchers, $52,000 for senior-level, plus $6,000 for travel and miscellaneous expenses.

APPLICATION INFO:
Current application may be obtained from the Museum's web site.

Duration: Usually one year in duration. Shorter-term fellowships for senior scholars are also available.

Deadline: Application and required letters of recommendation must be received by the first Friday in December. Announcements of awards will be made by late March.

STAFF:
Marcie Karp, Managing Museum Educator, Academic Programs, Education Department

ADDRESS INQUIRIES TO:
See e-mail address above.

*SPECIAL STIPULATIONS:
All fellowship recipients will be expected to spend the fellowship in residence in the department with which they are affiliated.

MINNESOTA DEPARTMENT OF EDUCATION [722]

State Library Services
1500 Highway 36 West
Roseville, MN 55113
(651) 582-8791
Fax: (651) 582-8752
E-mail: mde.lst@state.mn.us
Web Site: education.state.mn.us/MDE/StuSuc/Lib/StateLibServ/index.html

FOUNDED: 1899

AREAS OF INTEREST:
Supporting innovation in library services, cooperation among all types of libraries, public library accessibility, library technology and resource sharing.

CONSULTING OR VOLUNTEER SERVICES:
Consultant assistance provided on a range of library issues.

NAME(S) OF PROGRAMS:
- **Library Accessibility and Improvement Grants**
- **Library Services and Technology Act Competitive Grants**
- **Multi-Type Library Cooperation Aid**
- **Regional Library Telecommunications Aid**
- **Regional Public Libraries Systems Support**

TYPE:
Capital grants; Development grants; Formula grants; General operating grants; Project/program grants; Seed money grants; Technical assistance; Training grants. Matching capital grants for library accessibility and improvement. Competitive grants that address activities and priorities in the Minnesota Five-Year Plan.

YEAR PROGRAM STARTED: 1957

PURPOSE:
To extend and improve library and information services for the people of Minnesota through public libraries and cooperation among all types of libraries.

LEGAL BASIS:
Government agency.

ELIGIBILITY:
Specific requirements vary by program, and include local public libraries, Minnesota county and regional public library systems, and multicounty, multitype library systems meeting minimum support requirements, academic libraries and school library media centers are eligible to apply. Contact the Department for details.

GEOG. RESTRICTIONS: Minnesota.

FINANCIAL DATA:
Amount of support per award: Varies by grant program.

Total amount of support: Varies by year.

Matching fund requirements: Varies by program.

NO. MOST RECENT APPLICANTS: Varies by grant program.

NO. AWARDS: Varies by grant program.

APPLICATION INFO:
Applications available online.

Duration: Varies by grant program.

Deadline: Varies by grant program.

ADDRESS INQUIRIES TO:
Jennifer R. Nelson, Director and State Librarian
(See address above.)

NATIONAL HOME LIBRARY FOUNDATION [723]

3804 Williams Lane, Lower Level
Chevy Chase, MD 20815
(301) 986-4854
Fax: (301) 986-4855
E-mail: natlhomelibrary@yahoo.com
Web Site: www.homelibraryfoundation.org

FOUNDED: 1932

AREAS OF INTEREST:
Literacy.

TYPE:
Project/program grants. Grants in support of libraries, books and publications.

PURPOSE:
To assist in the distribution of books and other literacy-related resources to libraries

and community groups with limited access to sources of specific areas of information; to assist in support, promotion and development of programs with the goal of combating illiteracy and/or encouraging an interest in reading and the literacy arts among all ages; to encourage development of programs relating primarily to literary or cultural topics that utilize various means of communications.

ELIGIBILITY:
Applicants must be tax-exempt groups with appropriate interests and activities.

GEOG. RESTRICTIONS: United States, with preference to Maryland, Virginia and Washington, DC, areas.

FINANCIAL DATA:
Amount of support per award: $500 to $5,000.

REPRESENTATIVE AWARDS:
$1,000 to the city of Coffman Cove, AK, to fund fledgling community library; $2,000 to Calvin Coolidge High, DC, to purchase contemporary books for school library; $5,000 to Washington Jesuit Academy, DC, to fund books for the tuition-free middle school for disadvantaged minority students.

APPLICATION INFO:
Application takes the form of a proposal stating the nature of the project and its sponsors, along with a budget and financial statement.

Duration: Grants are usually awarded for one year.

Deadline: Applications may be submitted at any time and are reviewed at thrice-annual board meetings.

IRS I.D.: 52-6051013

OFFICERS:
Lynda J. Robb, President
Ervin S. Duggan, Secretary and Treasurer

TRUSTEES:
Sue Bell
Vandna Wendy Bhagat
Ervin S. Duggan
Michael R. Gardner
Lynda J. Robb
Ricardo Urbino
Kathleen M. Vance

ADDRESS INQUIRIES TO:
Joan Sahlgren, Executive Director
(See address above.)

NEW HAMPSHIRE LIBRARY ASSOCIATION [724]

c/o NH State Library
20 Park Street
Concord, NH 03301-6314
(603) 673-2288
E-mail: sleonardi@amherstlibrary.org
Web Site: www.nhlibrarians.org

FOUNDED: 1889

AREAS OF INTEREST:
Library and information science education.

NAME(S) OF PROGRAMS:
- **Rosalie Norris Scholarship**
- **F. Mabel Winchell Loan Fund**

TYPE:
Scholarships. The Norris Scholarship is awarded to New Hampshire residents or individuals working in a New Hampshire library for graduate library study. The Winchell Loan Fund provides for interest-free loans to New Hampshire residents or individuals working in a New Hampshire library to attend graduate library schools.

YEAR PROGRAM STARTED: 1949

PURPOSE:
To promote good library service from all types of libraries to all people of the state.

LEGAL BASIS:
Nonprofit.

ELIGIBILITY:
An applicant must be a member of the New Hampshire Library Association and have been accepted into the appropriate program. Applicant must live in New Hampshire or be employed by a New Hampshire library and must be enrolled in an ALA- accredited program.

GEOG. RESTRICTIONS: New Hampshire.

FINANCIAL DATA:
Amount of support per award: Scholarship grant provides a maximum of $1,000. Loan provides $1,500 (interest-free) to be repaid in five years.

Total amount of support: Varies.

NO. MOST RECENT APPLICANTS: 8 for scholarships and 3 for loans in 2015.

NO. AWARDS: 4 Norris Scholarships and 1 F. Mabel Winchell Loan for the year 2015.

APPLICATION INFO:
Applications are approved by the New Hampshire Library Association Scholarship Committee. Mail applications to: Sarah Leonardi, Scholarship Chairperson, New Hampshire Library Association, c/o Amherst Town Library, 14 Main Street, Amherst, NH 03031.

Duration: One year.

Deadline: April 1 and September 1.

ADDRESS INQUIRIES TO:
Sarah Leonardi, Scholarship Chairperson
(See address above.)

NEW JERSEY LIBRARY ASSOCIATION [725]

P.O. Box 1534
Trenton, NJ 08607
(609) 394-8032
Fax: (609) 394-8164
E-mail: njla_office@njla.org
Web Site: www.njla.org

FOUNDED: 1890

AREAS OF INTEREST:
Education, training of members and recruitment into the profession.

NAME(S) OF PROGRAMS:
- **Scholarships**

TYPE:
Scholarships. Offered to residents of New Jersey for study leading to a degree in library science at a graduate library school with an ALA-accredited degree program.

YEAR PROGRAM STARTED: 1926

PURPOSE:
To give financial support for tuition to worthy candidates, of New Jersey residency, desiring to work toward a graduate degree in library service as a profession.

LEGAL BASIS:
Nonprofit status.

ELIGIBILITY:
Applicants for scholarships must:
(1) be residents of New Jersey at the time of application or have worked in any New Jersey library for at least 12 months on a full-time or part-time basis;
(2) show substantial financial need and;
(3) present worthy scholarship, as shown by official transcript, a written essay describing what the applicant can contribute to librarianship, and two recommendations by people in the field of librarianship if possible.

FINANCIAL DATA:
Scholarships are awarded in the spring for the following school year for full- or part-time study. Funds must be used for tuition only and are sent directly to the college. Any unused monies are refunded to the treasurer of the New Jersey Library Association.

Amount of support per award: Varies depending on funding.

Total amount of support: $8,000 for the year 2014-15.

NO. AWARDS: 4 for the year 2014-15.

APPLICATION INFO:
Applications and guidelines are available on the Association web site.

Duration: One year.

Deadline: March 11.

ADDRESS INQUIRIES TO:
See e-mail address above.

NEW MEXICO LIBRARY ASSOCIATION [726]

P.O. Box 26074
Albuquerque, NM 87125
(505) 400-7309
E-mail: contact@nmla.org
Web Site: nmla.org

FOUNDED: 1923

AREAS OF INTEREST:
Promoting libraries and librarianship in New Mexico.

NAME(S) OF PROGRAMS:
- **College Scholarship Fund**
- **Continuing Education Grants**
- **Marion Dorroh Memorial Scholarship**

TYPE:
Scholarships. The scholarships support study in an accredited library school program. The continuing grants support attending workshops, conferences and educational activities of practicing New Mexico librarians.

YEAR PROGRAM STARTED: 1953

PURPOSE:
To support and promote libraries and the development of library personnel.

LEGAL BASIS:
Nonprofit corporation.

ELIGIBILITY:
College Scholarship Fund: Application is intended for New Mexico library workers who are pursuing an undergraduate program culminating in a degree in Library Technology or school library certification. It can also be used for graduate study toward a teacher-librarian endorsement.

Marion Dorroh Memorial Scholarship: Applicant must be accepted or currently enrolled in an ALA-accredited college or university as a full- or part-time student for an advanced degree in Library and Information Science.

The Continuing Education Grants support is based upon financial need. The Grants are intended for New Mexico library workers to promote professional development. They may be used to attend workshops, conferences and related activities.

GEOG. RESTRICTIONS: New Mexico.

FINANCIAL DATA:

Amount of support per award: College Scholarship: $1,000; Marion Dorroh Memorial Scholarship: $1,500; Continuing Education Grants: Up to $200.

APPLICATION INFO:

Application forms are available on the Association web site.

Duration: One year.

Deadline: College Scholarship and Marion Dorroh Memorial Scholarship: May 1. Continuing Education Grants: Applications are accepted on a rolling basis.

IRS I.D.: 23-7024820

ADDRESS INQUIRIES TO:

Kevin Comerford, Chairperson
NMLA Education Committee
(See address above.)

NORTH CAROLINA LIBRARY ASSOCIATION [727]

c/o Scholarships Committee
1841 Capital Boulevard
Raleigh, NC 27604
(919) 839-6252
Fax: (888) 977-3143
E-mail: nclaonline@gmail.com
Web Site: www.nclaonline.org

FOUNDED: 1904

AREAS OF INTEREST:

The promotion of libraries and library service in North Carolina.

NAME(S) OF PROGRAMS:

- **The Appalachian Scholarship**
- **The McLendon Scholarship**
- **The North Carolina Library Association Memorial Scholarship**
- **The Query-Long Scholarship**

TYPE:

Scholarships. Scholarships and loans to promote the education of qualified librarians.

PURPOSE:

To promote library science education.

LEGAL BASIS:

Professional association.

ELIGIBILITY:

Applicants must have been a legal resident of North Carolina for two years, have a genuine interest in professional library work, demonstrate need of financial assistance, hold an undergraduate degree and be accepted by a library school. (Persons whose library school applications are pending may apply for the scholarships.)

GEOG. RESTRICTIONS: North Carolina.

FINANCIAL DATA:

Amount of support per award: Appalachian, North Carolina Library Association Memorial and Query-Long Scholarships: $1,000 each; McLendon Scholarship: $400.

Total amount of support: Varies.

APPLICATION INFO:

Application forms and instructions can be found on the Association web site.

Duration: One year.

Deadline: May 30. Notification in the summer. Awarded biennially in Conference years.

ADDRESS INQUIRIES TO:

Libby Stone
Chairperson for Scholarships
North Carolina Library Association
(See address above.)

ROCK ISLAND ARSENAL MUSEUM

Rock Island Arsenal Historical Society
R. Maguire Scholarship Committee
One Rock Island Arsenal
Rock Island, IL 61299-5000
(309) 782-5021
Fax: (309) 782-3598
E-mail: rimahoch@aol.com
Web Site: www.arsenalhistoricalsociety.com

TYPE:

Scholarships.

See entry 620 for full listing.

STATE LIBRARY AND ARCHIVES OF FLORIDA [728]

R.A. Gray Building
500 South Bronough Street
Tallahassee, FL 32399-0250
(850) 245-6620
Fax: (850) 245-6643
E-mail: marian.deeney@dos.myflorida.com
Web Site: info.florida.gov/services-for-libraries/grants/lsta/

FOUNDED: 1925

AREAS OF INTEREST:

Public libraries, public elementary school or secondary school libraries, academic libraries, research libraries, private libraries, or library consortium.

CONSULTING OR VOLUNTEER SERVICES:

Consultant advice to public and institution libraries and libraries for the blind and handicapped.

NAME(S) OF PROGRAMS:

- **Library Services and Technology Act**

TYPE:

Project/program grants. Project grants congruent with the state long-range plan.

YEAR PROGRAM STARTED: 1997

PURPOSE:

To stimulate excellence and promote access to learning and information resources in all types of libraries for individuals of all ages; to promote library services that provide all users access to information through state, regional, national, and international electronic networks; to provide linkages among and between libraries; to promote targeted library services to people of diverse geographic, cultural, and socioeconomic backgrounds, to individuals with disabilities and to people with limited functional literacy or information skills.

LEGAL BASIS:

Based on U.S. Library Services and Technology Act (P.L. 104-208, as amended) and Florida Statutes 257.12, 257.191 and 257.192.

ELIGIBILITY:

Applicants must be Florida libraries that provide free library service or institution libraries that are operated or substantially supported by the state.

GEOG. RESTRICTIONS: Florida.

FINANCIAL DATA:

Amount of support per award: Varies.

Total amount of support: $8,048,596 for fiscal year 2015; $8,259,897 for fiscal year 2016.

Matching fund requirements: Matching funds must equal at least one-third of the grant request or award.

NO. MOST RECENT APPLICANTS: 33.

NO. AWARDS: 30.

APPLICATION INFO:

Application must be submitted online. Applicants should supply project proposal.

Duration: One year. Must reapply for each year.

Deadline: Varies.

PUBLICATIONS:

Grant guidelines.

IRS I.D.: 59-3466865

ADDRESS INQUIRIES TO:

David Beach, Library Program Specialist
(See address above.)

TEXAS LIBRARY ASSOCIATION [729]

3355 Bee Cave Road, Suite 401
Austin, TX 78746-6763
(512) 328-1518
(800) 580-2852
Fax: (512) 328-8852
E-mail: tla@txla.org
Web Site: www.txla.org

FOUNDED: 1902

AREAS OF INTEREST:

Library and information science.

NAME(S) OF PROGRAMS:

- **Walter H. Escue Memorial Scholarship**
- **Vivian Greenfield Education Award**
- **Ray C. Janeway Scholarship**
- **TLA Summer School Scholarship**
- **Van Dusen-Tobin-Kaiser Scholarship**

TYPE:

Scholarships. Awards for graduate study leading to a Master's degree in library science.

YEAR PROGRAM STARTED: 1998

PURPOSE:

To help support the educational goals of students who want to get an advanced degree in library science.

LEGAL BASIS:

Professional association.

ELIGIBILITY:

Applicants must be members of TLA.

Walter Escue Scholars must be Texas residents concentrating studies in technical services, systems administration or library automation, attained at least a "B" average during the last two years of a Baccalaureate degree program and have been accepted as a graduate student to a Texas ALA-accredited library education program.

Vivian Greenfield Award applicants must reside in Texas and write a goals statement outlining a desired educational endeavor revolving around youth services.

Janeway Scholarship applicants must be Texas residents, attained at least a "B" average during the last two years of a

Baccalaureate program and have been accepted as a graduate student at a Texas ALA-accredited library education program.

TLA Summer School Scholar must be a Texas resident, attained at least a "B" average during the last two years of a Baccalaureate degree program, and must be registered for MLS degree courses during a summer session at a Texas ALA-accredited library education program. (The scholarship applies only to the summer session.)

Van Dusen-Tobin-Kaiser Scholars must be Texas residents and must be pursuing graduate studies leading to a career as an elementary school or children's librarian, attained at least a "B" average during the last two years of a Baccalaureate degree program, and accepted as a graduate student at a Texas ALA-accredited library education program.

Contact the Association for complete details.

GEOG. RESTRICTIONS: Texas.

FINANCIAL DATA:

Amount of support per award: Escue Scholarship: $1,000; Greenfield Award: $1,500; Janeway Scholarship: $2,000, awarded annually; TLA Summer School Scholarship: $500; Van Dusen-Tobin-Kaiser Scholarship: $1,000, awarded biennially in even-numbered years.

Total amount of support: Varies.

NO. AWARDS: Varies.

APPLICATION INFO:

Application must be submitted online.

Duration: One year.

Deadline: Completed applications must be submitted no later than January 31.

IRS I.D.: 74-6014110

ADDRESS INQUIRIES TO:

Glenda Genchur, Director of Administration
(See address above.)

*SPECIAL STIPULATIONS:

Scholarships and grants are to be awarded to Texas residents only and only to applicants attending an institution of higher learning in Texas with an accredited School of Library Science.

UKRAINIAN RESEARCH INSTITUTE, HARVARD UNIVERSITY [730]

34 Kirkland Street
Cambridge, MA 02138
(617) 495-4053
Fax: (617) 495-8097
E-mail: huri@fas.harvard.edu
Web Site: www.huri.harvard.edu

FOUNDED: 1980

AREAS OF INTEREST:

Ukrainian studies.

NAME(S) OF PROGRAMS:

- **Eugene and Daymel Shklar/USF Research Fellowships in Ukrainian Studies**

TYPE:

Fellowships.

YEAR PROGRAM STARTED: 1980

PURPOSE:

To promote scholarship in history, literature, philology and other disciplines relating to the Ukraine.

LEGAL BASIS:

Nonprofit organization.

ELIGIBILITY:

Individuals who hold a Doctorate in Ukrainian history, literature, philology or culture and other fields in the humanities and social sciences and have demonstrated scholarship in Ukrainian studies are eligible to apply.

FINANCIAL DATA:

In addition to the stipend, the award provides for the cost of direct round-trip travel to Harvard University and, during the fellow's stay, supplemental funding to attend one established conference connected with Ukrainian studies.

Amount of support per award: $3,300 per month.

Total amount of support: Average: $13,200.

APPLICATION INFO:

Application information is available on the web site.

Duration: Three to eight months; average: four months.

ADDRESS INQUIRIES TO:

The HURI Fellowships in Ukrainian Studies
c/o Tamara H. Nary, Programs Administrator
Ukrainian Research Institute
Harvard University
(See address above.)

UNITED STATES HOLOCAUST MEMORIAL MUSEUM - JACK, JOSEPH AND MORTON MANDEL CENTER FOR ADVANCED HOLOCAUST STUDIES

100 Raoul Wallenberg Place, S.W.
Washington, DC 20024-2126
(202) 314-7829
Fax: (202) 479-9726
E-mail: vscholars@ushmm.org
Web Site: www.ushmm.org/research/competitive-academic-programs/fellowship-competition

TYPE:

Exchange programs; Fellowships. The Jack, Joseph and Morton Mandel Center for Advanced Holocaust Studies is an integral part of the United States Holocaust Memorial Museum, which serves as America's national institution for Holocaust education and remembrance. The Mandel Center awards fellowships to support significant research and writing about the Holocaust. Awards are granted on a competitive basis. The Mandel Center welcomes proposals from scholars in all relevant academic disciplines, including history, political science, literature, Jewish studies, philosophy, religion, psychology, comparative genocide studies, law and others.

Visiting Scholar Program participants at the Mandel Center have access to more than 100 million pages of Holocaust-related archival documentation; the Museum's extensive library; oral history, film, photo, art, artifacts and memoir collections; and Holocaust survivor database.

See entry 633 for full listing.

UNIVERSITY OF ARIZONA SCHOOL OF INFORMATION [731]

University of Arizona
1515 East First Street, Room 3
Tucson, AZ 85719
(520) 621-3565
Fax: (520) 621-3279
E-mail: sirls@email.arizona.edu
Web Site: si.arizona.edu

FOUNDED: 1963

AREAS OF INTEREST:

Promoting new knowledge and practice in the library and information professions with research, education, and public service through degree programs at the Master's, doctoral, and certificate levels.

TYPE:

Assistantships; Internships; Scholarships. Graduate assistantships; Research assistantships; Undergraduate internships and scholarships. Awarded to qualified students to attend the School of Information.

YEAR PROGRAM STARTED: 1963

PURPOSE:

To engage in research and education around all aspects of information science without regard for disciplinary boundary.

LEGAL BASIS:

Nonprofit, tax-exempt.

ELIGIBILITY:

Any student receiving financial aid must be accepted into the SI degree program. Awards are made to students who meet the criteria set by the School. (This includes students participating in the program online.) The School requires that the student be enrolled for the required number of hours for the semester of award. Assistance is awarded on a semester basis.

A new financial aid form must be completed each semester that a student wishes to be considered for aid. To be considered for financial assistance, an applicant must meet the deadlines posted. Criteria for financial aid are: stellar academic performance, financial status, and other qualifications as defined by specific scholarships.

FINANCIAL DATA:

Amount of support per award: Varies by program.

Total amount of support: Varies.

APPLICATION INFO:

Applicant must complete the Financial Assistance Application section of Library Science Application for Admission.

Duration: One or two semesters.

Deadline: March 1.

ADDRESS INQUIRIES TO:

See e-mail address above.

THE UNIVERSITY OF DELAWARE-HAGLEY GRADUATE PROGRAM

Department of History, John Munroe Hall
University of Delaware
Newark, DE 19716
(302) 831-8226
Fax: (302) 831-1538
E-mail: dianec@udel.edu
Web Site: www.udel.edu/hagley
www.history.udel.edu

TYPE:
Assistantships; Fellowships. The University of Delaware, in association with the Hagley Museum, sponsors a premier graduate resident program for the study of technology, business, consumption, and work in industrial and post-industrial societies leading to a Master of Arts or Ph.D. in History. Students have access to faculty with international reputations in American, European and non-Western history, and benefit from strong interdisciplinary ties to museum studies and material culture programs, as well as the Hagley Museum and Library.

See entry 634 for full listing.

THE UNIVERSITY OF SOUTHERN MISSISSIPPI [732]

118 College Drive
Box 5148
Hattiesburg, MS 39406
(601) 266-4349
Fax: (601) 266-6269
E-mail: ellen.ruffin@usm.edu
Web Site: www.lib.usm.edu/degrummond/research/fellowships.html

NAME(S) OF PROGRAMS:
- **H.A. and Margret Rey Research Fellowship**

TYPE:
Fellowships. Rey Fellowship is awarded to hire translators (French, German, Portuguese or Russian) for the purpose of translating the H.A. and Margret Rey documents into English to further facilitate use in research, as needed. Funds may also be used for the preservation and conservation of the Rey documents or to provide funding for an individual conducting research on the life and work of the Reys.

ELIGIBILITY:
Rey Translation Fellowship: Applicant must demonstrate through formal education or other experience expertise in translating material. Funding is also provided for an individual conducting research on the life and work of the Reys.

FINANCIAL DATA:
Amount of support per award: Varies.

NO. AWARDS: Rey Translation Fellowship: 1 to 2 awards as needed.

APPLICATION INFO:
Application information is available on the web site.

Duration: Rey Translation Fellowship: One year. Nonrenewable.

Deadline: Contact the University.

ADDRESS INQUIRIES TO:
Ellen H. Ruffin, Curator, de Grummond Children's Literature Collection
The University of Southern Mississippi
(See address above.)

UNIVERSITY OF TORONTO [733]

Faculty of Information
140 St. George Street, Room 211
Toronto ON M5S 3G6 Canada
(416) 978-3234
Fax: (416) 978-5762
E-mail: inquire.ischool@utoronto.ca
Web Site: www.ischool.utoronto.ca

FOUNDED: 1928

AREAS OF INTEREST:
Education.

NAME(S) OF PROGRAMS:
- **Patricia Fleming Visiting Fellowship in Bibliography and Book History**

TYPE:
Fellowships. Fellowship is awarded biennially in even-numbered years.

YEAR PROGRAM STARTED: 1928

PURPOSE:
To encourage outstanding scholars to conduct research in the field of bibliographical studies or book history.

LEGAL BASIS:
University.

GEOG. RESTRICTIONS: Canada.

FINANCIAL DATA:
Amount of support per award: $2,000 (CAN).

NO. MOST RECENT APPLICANTS: 7.

NO. AWARDS: 1.

APPLICATION INFO:
Applicants should submit a resume, two letters of recommendation, and a one- to two-page research proposal describing the project.

Duration: One month.

Deadline: February/March.

ADDRESS INQUIRIES TO:
Adriana Rossini, Registrar and Director of Student Services
Faculty of Information
(See address above.)

UTAH DIVISION OF ARTS & MUSEUMS

617 East South Temple
Salt Lake City, UT 84102
(801) 236-7550
Fax: (801) 236-7556
E-mail: lalder@utah.gov
Web Site: artsandmuseums.utah.gov

TYPE:
Development grants; General operating grants; Matching gifts; Residencies; Scholarships.

See entry 498 for full listing.

Music

ACCADEMIA MUSICALE CHIGIANA [734]

Via di Città, 89
53100 Siena Italy
(39) 0577 22091
Fax: (39) 0577 288124
E-mail: accademia.chigiana@chigiana.it
Web Site: www.chigiana.it

FOUNDED: 1932

AREAS OF INTEREST:
Music.

NAME(S) OF PROGRAMS:
- **Scholarships for Summer Music Courses**

TYPE:
Awards/prizes; Scholarships. Merit scholarships to those who are registered as active students at the Academy, which offers various summer music master courses in orchestral conducting, composition, voice and various instruments.

In addition, there are other scholarships financed by public institutions or private donors and are awarded at the discretion of the Accademia Chigiana Direction.

YEAR PROGRAM STARTED: 1932

PURPOSE:
To allow young musicians from all over the world to perfect themselves in the principal instruments, studying with many world famous musicians.

ELIGIBILITY:
Applicants can be students of any nationality. Active students must hold an Italian music diploma or an equivalent foreign certificate (exception made for the courses of guitar and singing) and must pass an entrance examination. Age limits are as follows: Conducting, 30 years for the session dedicated to the classical orchestral repertoire; 40 years for the session dedicated to the modern symphonic repertoire; Voice, 32 years (sopranos and tenors), 34 years (mezzo sopranos, baritones and basses); Instruments, 30 years; Chamber Music, average of 30 years. The Italian government also finances scholarships for attendance of summer master classes at the Accademia Chigiana.

Scholarships offered by the Accademia Musicale Chigiana are awarded on the basis of the results of the entrance examination and student merit.

No scholarship will be granted to students already benefiting from financial help from other institutions or to those who do not take the entrance examination on the established date.

FINANCIAL DATA:
Amount of support per award: Scholarships consist of reimbursement of tuition fees (after detraction of the added value tax) plus a daily grant of EUR 35 gross.

Total amount of support: EUR 60,000 (with funds of the Academy) plus EUR 30,000 (by public institutions or private donors).

APPLICATION INFO:
Detailed information and application forms are available from the address above. For details of requirements and application formalities about scholarships awarded by the Italian government, candidates should write directly to the Italian Culture Institute or to the Italian Embassy in their own country.

Deadline: May 31 for the Orchestral Conducting Course; May 31 for Composition Course; June 10 for all other courses.

PUBLICATIONS:
Courses booklet (information and application form).

OFFICERS:
Marcello Clarich, President
Angelo Armiento, Managing Director
Nicola Sani, Artistic Director

ADDRESS INQUIRIES TO:
Fondazione Accademia Musicale Chigiana
(See address above.)

AMERICAN ACADEMY OF ARTS AND LETTERS [735]

633 West 155th Street
New York, NY 10032-7599
(212) 368-5900
Fax: (212) 491-4615
E-mail: academy@artsandletters.org
Web Site: www.artsandletters.org

FOUNDED: 1898

NAME(S) OF PROGRAMS:
- **The Richard Rodgers Awards**

TYPE:
Awards/prizes. Completed musical scripts are accepted by the Academy for this annual competition. The award subsidizes staged readings, studio productions or productions in New York City by a not-for-profit theater group of a musical play by composers and writers who are not already established in this field.

YEAR PROGRAM STARTED: 1978

PURPOSE:
To further the art of the musical theater in the U.S.

LEGAL BASIS:
Nonprofit Internal Revenue Code 501(c)(3).

ELIGIBILITY:
Open only to U.S. citizens or permanent residents of any age. While students may enter the competition, it is primarily intended for work at a professional level.

GEOG. RESTRICTIONS: United States.

FINANCIAL DATA:
Award money is given to the not-for-profit theater for production expenses.

Amount of support per award: Varies.

NO. MOST RECENT APPLICANTS: 133.

NO. AWARDS: 1 to 4.

APPLICATION INFO:
Application form can be downloaded from the Academy web site. The name(s) of the author(s) must be blocked out on each of the items submitted, with the exception of the application form. Write only the title of the work on the script, plot summary and CD. Entries must include the following items:
(1) script with lyrics, preferably with no binders or metal clips. Do not send score, videos or visuals;
(2) half-page synopsis of the action and a list of characters;
(3) CD which must contain at least 45 minutes of music, including a minimum of eight songs, recorded in chronological order. Orchestrations are not necessary; piano and vocals are sufficient. Songs must be in sequence on the CD and each song clearly keyed into the script. Please include a separate track sheet of recorded songs with page numbers indicating where they appear in the script, and specify the total number of minutes recorded. Audio tapes will not be accepted and;
(4) application form signed by all collaborators in a sealed envelope with the title of the work on the outside. Applicants submitting work which has already been produced must give full information concerning these productions, including programs. A work is not eligible if one of the collaborators is deceased.

If the submitted work (or a portion thereof) is an adaptation of material which is not in the public domain, candidates must submit licenses, permissions, or authorizations necessary to permit the work to be produced in conformity with applicable copyright laws. The music must be original.

Materials will be returned if a self-addressed, stamped mailer is enclosed. Addresses must be valid for at least six months. The Academy will take all due care of materials, but it cannot be held responsible for their safe return.

Deadline: November 1. Notification by March.

PUBLICATIONS:
Application guidelines.

STAFF:
Virginia Dajani, Executive Director
Jane Bolster, Coordinator, Richard Rodgers Awards

ADDRESS INQUIRIES TO:
The Richard Rodgers Awards
(See address above.)

*SPECIAL STIPULATIONS:
Musical submitted may not be entered again, even if revised.

AMERICAN ACCORDION MUSICOLOGICAL SOCIETY [736]

322 Haddon Avenue
Westmont, NJ 08108
(856) 854-6628
E-mail: accordion.1@verizon.net
Web Site: www.aamsaccordionfestival.com

FOUNDED: 1968

AREAS OF INTEREST:
Research and symposiums on accordion history in the U.S.

CONSULTING OR VOLUNTEER SERVICES:
Library services, books and music on the accordion, and records, CDs and DVDs for rental.

NAME(S) OF PROGRAMS:
- **Annual Symposium and Festival**

TYPE:
Awards/prizes; Work-study programs. The Annual Symposium and Festival is held on a weekend in March.

YEAR PROGRAM STARTED: 1970

PURPOSE:
To help and stimulate young composers to write for the accordion.

LEGAL BASIS:
Nonprofit professional association.

ELIGIBILITY:
Composer must be acquainted with the various types of accordions.

FINANCIAL DATA:
Amount of support per award: $600.

NO. AWARDS: 1.

APPLICATION INFO:
Applicants should write for entry forms or send an e-mail to the address above.

Deadline: Contact the Society.

PUBLICATIONS:
Annual news bulletin on classical/folk accordion; annual booklet of accordion information.

ADDRESS INQUIRIES TO:
Joanna Darrow, Director
(See address above.)

THE AMERICAN BANDMASTERS ASSOCIATION [737]

Westlake High School
4100 Westbank Drive
Austin, TX 78746
(512) 732-9280 ext. 33820
E-mail: ktaylor@eanesisd.net
colburnmj@gmail.com
Web Site: www.americanbandmasters.org

FOUNDED: 1929

AREAS OF INTEREST:
Concert band and band music.

NAME(S) OF PROGRAMS:
- **Sousa/Ostwald Award**

TYPE:
Awards/prizes. Prize sponsored by the American Bandmasters Association and Sousa Foundation, involving cash award and performance of the winning band or wind ensemble composition. One award is presented in odd years for grades 1-4; one award is presented in even years for grades 5-6.

YEAR PROGRAM STARTED: 1955

PURPOSE:
To enrich the spectrum of concert band activity.

ELIGIBILITY:
Details are available on the Association web site.

FINANCIAL DATA:
Amount of support per award: $5,000.

Total amount of support: $5,000.

NO. MOST RECENT APPLICANTS: 91.

NO. AWARDS: 1.

APPLICATION INFO:
Send scores (PDFs only) and recordings (mp3 of live performances only) and direct all inquiries to the Chairman of the Contest Committee at the e-mail address above.

Deadline: October 1.

PUBLICATIONS:
Journal of Band Research.

IRS I.D.: 36-6112860

OFFICERS:
Terry Austin, President
Dr. Timothy Rhea, President-Elect
Gary E. Smith, Vice President
Thomas V. Fraschillo, Secretary-Treasurer
David Waybright, Chairperson, Nominating Committee

BOARD OF DIRECTORS:
Dennis Zeisler, Chairman
Jay Gephart
Col. Lowell Graham
William Johnson
Linda Moorhouse
Bruce Moss
Ray Toler

ADDRESS INQUIRIES TO:
Kerry Taylor, Co-Chairperson
ABA/Ostwald Committee (Grades 1-4)
Michael Colburn, Co-Chairperson
ABA/Ostwald Committee (Grades 5-6)
(See e-mail addresses above.)

*SPECIAL STIPULATIONS:
All inquiries and correspondence must be in the form of an e-mail.

AMERICAN CONSERVATORY OF MUSIC [738]

252 Wildwood Road
Hammond, IN 46324
(219) 931-6000
Fax: (219) 931-6089
E-mail: registrar@americanconservatory.edu
Web Site: www.americanconservatory.edu

FOUNDED: 1886

AREAS OF INTEREST:
Music performance, conducting, composition, theory and music technology.

NAME(S) OF PROGRAMS:
- **Leo Heim Presidential Scholarships**

TYPE:
Scholarships.

YEAR PROGRAM STARTED: 1984

PURPOSE:
To provide excellent musical instruction for talented students at all levels of ability.

LEGAL BASIS:
Not-for-profit corporation since 1941; partnership, multiple partners.

ELIGIBILITY:
Applicants must be students with strong musical background.

FINANCIAL DATA:
Award to be applied solely towards tuition at the Conservatory.

Amount of support per award: Varies based on merit and need.

Total amount of support: Varies.

APPLICATION INFO:
Applicants should submit a standard application form and audition.

Duration: One year.

IRS I.D.: 84-1454666

ADDRESS INQUIRIES TO:
Admissions
(See address above.)

AMERICAN MATTHAY ASSOCIATION FOR PIANO [739]

405 East Hermosa Circle
Tempe, AZ 85282
(480) 829-0228
Fax: (480) 829-0228 (notice required)
E-mail: mcpiano2@aol.com
Web Site: www.matthay.org

FOUNDED: 1925

AREAS OF INTEREST:
Piano performance and teaching.

NAME(S) OF PROGRAMS:
- **Clara Wells Scholarships for Piano Study**

TYPE:
Conferences/seminars; Scholarships; Work-study programs. Prize funds for study of piano with member of the Association, emphasizing the performance and teaching principles of Tobias Matthay. The Clara Wells Scholarships are awarded biennially.

The next Clara Wells Auditions will be held in June 2016 at the Festival of the American Matthay Association for Piano. Contact the Association for the specific date and time.

YEAR PROGRAM STARTED: 1970

PURPOSE:
To foster the teaching principles of Tobias Matthay.

LEGAL BASIS:
Nonprofit organization.

ELIGIBILITY:
Entrants must submit CD recordings for the preliminary phases. Finals require live performance.

FINANCIAL DATA:
Funds must be used to study piano with a member of the Association.

Amount of support per award: First prize: $2,000. Second Prize: $1,500.

Total amount of support: Varies.

NO. MOST RECENT APPLICANTS: 6 to 10 per year.

NO. AWARDS: 2.

APPLICATION INFO:
Contact the Association.

Deadline: April 2016.

PUBLICATIONS:
The Matthay News.

ADDRESS INQUIRIES TO:
Dr. Mary Pendleton Hoffer
Competition Chairperson
(See address and e-mail above.)

AMERICAN MUSICOLOGICAL SOCIETY [740]

Bowdoin College
6010 College Station
Brunswick, ME 04011-8451
(207) 798-4243
(877) 679-7648
Fax: (207) 798-4254
E-mail: ams@ams-net.org
Web Site: www.ams-net.org

FOUNDED: 1934

AREAS OF INTEREST:
Scholastic work in musicology published in any country, any language.

NAME(S) OF PROGRAMS:
- **The Philip Brett Award**
- **The Alfred Einstein Award**
- **Noah Greenberg Award**
- **Thomas Hampson Award**
- **The Otto Kinkeldey Award**
- **Lewis Lockwood Award**
- **Music in American Culture Award**
- **Claude V. Palisca Award**
- **Paul A. Pisk Prize**
- **H. Colin Slim Award**
- **Ruth A. Solie Award**
- **Robert M. Stevenson Award**

TYPE:
Awards/prizes. The Philip Brett Award honors exceptional musicological work in the field of gay, lesbian, bisexual, transgender/transsexual studies completed during the previous two academic years (ending June 30), in any country and in any language. By "work" is meant a published article, book, edition, annotated translation, a paper read at a conference, teaching materials (course descriptions and syllabi), and other scholarly work accepted by the award committee that best exemplifies the highest qualities of originality, interpretation, theory and communication in this field of study.

The Alfred Einstein Award honors a musicological article of exceptional merit, published during the previous year in any language and in any country, by a scholar in the early stages of his or her career.

The Noah Greenberg Award is intended as a grant-in-aid to stimulate active cooperation between scholars and performers by recognizing and fostering outstanding contributions to historical performing practices. Both scholars and performers may apply, since the Award may subsidize the publication costs of articles, monographs, or editions, as well as public performance, recordings, or other projects.

The Thomas Hampson Award is dedicated to fostering editions and scholarship on classic song in all its contexts as well as new and innovative technologies for promoting and understanding classic song via interactive media and the Internet.

The Otto Kinkeldey Award will honor each year a musicological book of exceptional merit published during the previous year in any language and in any country by a scholar who is past the early stages of his or her career.

The Lewis Lockwood Award honors each year a musicological book of exceptional merit published during the previous year in any language and in any country by a scholar in the early stages of his or her career who is a member of the AMS or a citizen or permanent resident of Canada or the U.S.

The Music in American Culture Award honors each year a book of exceptional merit that both illuminates some important aspect of the music of the U.S. and places that music in a rich cultural context. Books published in the previous year in any language and in any country are eligible. The author must be a citizen or permanent resident of the U.S. or Canada.

The Claude V. Palisca Award honors each year a scholarly edition or translation in the field of musicology published during the previous year in any language and in any country by a scholar who is a member of the AMS or a citizen or permanent resident of Canada or the U.S., deemed by a committee of scholars to best exemplify the highest qualities of originality, interpretation, logic and clarity of thought, and communication.

The Paul A. Pisk Prize is awarded annually to a graduate music student for a scholarly paper to be presented at the Annual Meeting of the Society.

The H. Colin Slim Award honors each year a musicological article of exceptional merit, published during the previous year in any language and in any country by a scholar who is past the early stages of his or her career and who is a member of the AMS or a citizen or permanent resident of Canada or the U.S.

The Ruth A. Solie Award honors each year a collection of musicological essays of exceptional merit published during the preceding calendar year in any language and in any country and edited by a scholar or scholars who are members of the AMS or citizens or permanent residents of Canada or the U.S.

The Robert M. Stevenson Award recognizes outstanding scholarship in Iberian music. The prize will be awarded annually to a book, monograph, edition, or journal article by a member of the AMS. The publication must be written in English and must have been published during the preceding three calendar years.

Winners of all awards receive a monetary prize, conferred at the Annual Business Meeting and Awards Presentation of the Society by the chair of the committee.

YEAR PROGRAM STARTED: 1967

LEGAL BASIS:
Private.

GEOG. RESTRICTIONS: United States and Canada.

FINANCIAL DATA:
Amount of support per award: Varies.

Total amount of support: Maximum $1,000 (U.S.).

APPLICATION INFO:
Application information is available on the web site.

Deadline: Philip Brett Award: July 1. Noah Greenburg Award: August 15. Paul A. Pisk Prize: October 1. All others: May 1.

IRS I.D.: 23-1577392

AMERICAN MUSICOLOGICAL SOCIETY [741]

Bowdoin College
6010 College Station
Brunswick, ME 04011-8451
(207) 798-4243
(877) 679-7648
Fax: (207) 798-4254
E-mail: ams@ams-net.org
Web Site: www.ams-net.org

FOUNDED: 1934

AREAS OF INTEREST:
Research in the various fields of music as a branch of learning and scholarship.

NAME(S) OF PROGRAMS:
- **Howard Mayer Brown Fellowship**
- **Alvin H. Johnson AMS 50 Dissertation Fellowships**

TYPE:
Fellowships; Grants-in-aid. The Publications Committee of the American Musicological Society makes available funds to help individuals with expenses involved in the publication of works of musical scholarship, including books, articles and works in nonprint media.

The Howard Mayer Brown Fellowship is intended to increase the presence of minority scholars and teachers in musicology. The fellowship supports one year of graduate work for a member of a group historically underrepresented in the discipline.

The Alvin H. Johnson AMS Dissertation Fellowships are intended for full-time study. It is expected that the recipient's dissertation be completed within the fellowship year.

YEAR PROGRAM STARTED: 1989

PURPOSE:
To support the advancement of research in various fields of music.

LEGAL BASIS:
Nonprofit organization.

ELIGIBILITY:
For the AMS Fellowship, applicants must be registered for a doctorate at a North American university and have completed all formal degree requirements except the dissertation.

The Howard Mayer Brown Fellowship will be awarded to a student who has completed at least one year of graduate work, and who intends to complete a Ph.D. in the field. Applications are encouraged from African-Americans, Native Americans, Latinos, Asian-Americans and, in Canada, visible minorities. There are no restrictions as to age or sex.

FINANCIAL DATA:
Amount of support per award: AMS 50 Fellowship: $21,000 stipend; Brown Fellowship: $20,000.

Total amount of support: Varies.

APPLICATION INFO:
Applications must be submitted electronically.

Duration: One year. No individual can receive a subvention more than once in a three-year period.

Deadline: December 15.

IRS I.D.: 23-1577392

AMERICAN SOCIETY OF COMPOSERS, AUTHORS AND PUBLISHERS (ASCAP)

1900 Broadway, 7th Floor
New York, NY 10023
(212) 621-6588
Fax: (212) 595-3276
E-mail: jsteinblatt@ascap.com
Web Site: www.ascap.com

TYPE:
Awards/prizes. The ASCAP Deems Taylor/Virgil Thomson Awards program recognizes books and articles on the subject of music selected for their excellence.

See entry 656 for full listing.

ARD INTERNATIONAL MUSIC COMPETITION [742]

Internationaler Musikwettbewerb der ARD
Bayerischer Rundfunk
Rundfunkplatz 1
D-80335 Munich Germany
(49) 89 5900 42471
Fax: (49) 89 5900 3573
E-mail: ard.musikwettbewerb@br.de
Web Site: www.ard-musikwettbewerb.de

FOUNDED: 1952

AREAS OF INTEREST:
International music competition.

NAME(S) OF PROGRAMS:
- **Music Competition**

TYPE:
Awards/prizes. Cash prizes; Competition for music.

Intended for a selection of young musicians who are interested in following an international career. The standards are, therefore, high and the prizes are awarded only for outstanding performances. Program categories differ each year. For 2017: piano, violin, oboe and guitar.

YEAR PROGRAM STARTED: 1952

PURPOSE:
To create gifted musicians and international soloists.

ELIGIBILITY:
Instrumentalists should be born between 1988 and 2000.

FINANCIAL DATA:
Amount of support per award: Soloists: First prize, EUR 10,000; Second prize, EUR 7,500; Third prize, EUR 5,000. Wind Quintet: First prize, EUR 25,000; Second prize, EUR 20,000; Third prize, EUR 15,000. Piano Duo: First prize, EUR 12,000; Second prize, EUR 9,000; Third prize, EUR 6,000. String Quartet (2016): First prize, EUR 24,000; Second prize, EUR 18,000; Third prize, EUR 12,000. Piano Trio (2018): First Prize, EUR 18,000; Second prize, EUR 13,500; Third prize, EUR 9,000.

Total amount of support: EUR 90,000 for the year 2017.

CO-OP FUNDING PROGRAMS: Theodor - Rogler - Foundation, Alice - Rosner - Foundation, and others.

NO. MOST RECENT APPLICANTS: Approximately 400 each year.

NO. AWARDS: 12.

APPLICATION INFO:
A valid statement of type and duration of study should accompany the entry form. Students must have permission from their current teacher to participate. A list of the applicant's complete repertoire is required. Upon arrival in Munich, each competitor should present a birth certificate or a valid passport at the Competition Office.

Preselections with CD are obligatory for all categories.

PUBLICATIONS:
Annual prospectus with application guidelines and programs.

OFFICERS:
Oswald Beaujean, Artistic Director
Elisabeth Kozik, Administrative Director

ADDRESS INQUIRIES TO:
Competition Office
(See address above.)

THE ASCAP FOUNDATION [743]

1900 Broadway, 7th Floor
New York, NY 10023
(212) 621-6588
Fax: (212) 595-3276
E-mail: concertmusic@ascap.com
Web Site: www.ascapfoundation.org

FOUNDED: 1975

AREAS OF INTEREST:
Music, music composition and music education.

NAME(S) OF PROGRAMS:
- **The ASCAP Foundation Morton Gould Young Composer Awards**

TYPE:
Awards/prizes.

YEAR PROGRAM STARTED: 1978

PURPOSE:
To encourage talented young American composers.

LEGAL BASIS:
Publicly supported foundation, 501(c)(3) organization.

ELIGIBILITY:
Individuals must have not reached their 30th birthday as of January 1 of the year of application and must be U.S. citizens, permanent residents or enrolled students with student visas.

Previous recipients are eligible to reapply for the award.

GEOG. RESTRICTIONS: United States.

FINANCIAL DATA:
Amount of support per award: $500 to $3,500, at discretion of judges.
Total amount of support: $25,000.

NO. MOST RECENT APPLICANTS: Approximately 700.

NO. AWARDS: 15 or more.

APPLICATION INFO:
A completed application form must be submitted along with one reproduction of an original manuscript or score, a listing of music studies and compositions to date, and biographical information.
Deadline: February 1.

PUBLICATIONS:
Annual report; contributions policy; application guidelines.

BOARD OF DIRECTORS:
Paul Williams, President
Irwin Z. Robinson, Vice President
Dean Kay, Treasurer
Ginny Mancini, Secretary
Marilyn Bergman
Charles Bernstein
Bruce Broughton
Tita Cahn
Alf Clausen
Dan Foliart
Arthur Hamilton
Wayland Holyfield
James M. Kendrick
Robert Kimball
Ed London
Johnny Mandel
James McBride
Marcus Miller
Jay R. Morgenstern
Stephen Schwartz
Alex Shapiro
Valerie Simpson
Charles Strouse
Doug Wood

ADMINISTRATION:
Colleen McDonough, Executive Director
Julie Lapore, Program Manager

ADDRESS INQUIRIES TO:
Cia Toscanini, Vice President
Concert Music ASCAP
(See address above.)

BRANDON UNIVERSITY [744]

School of Music
270 18th Street
Brandon MB R7A 6A9 Canada
(204) 727-7388
Fax: (204) 728-6839
E-mail: music@brandonu.ca
Web Site: www.brandonu.ca/music

AREAS OF INTEREST:
Music education, performance and literature (piano, collaborative piano, strings, composition, clarinet, trumpet, conducting and jazz).

TYPE:
Assistantships; Scholarships.

YEAR PROGRAM STARTED: 1980

PURPOSE:
To afford graduate students the opportunity to gain professional experience while studying and to provide monetary assistance.

ELIGIBILITY:
Open to candidates with a Bachelor's degree in music or music education with a minimum grade point average of 3.0 during the final year.

FINANCIAL DATA:
Amount of support per award: Up to $5,000 per year.
Total amount of support: $20,000 per year.

NO. MOST RECENT APPLICANTS: 15.

NO. AWARDS: 11.

APPLICATION INFO:
Applications available both online and from the Graduate Music Office.
Duration: Two years.
Deadline: May 1.

ADDRESS INQUIRIES TO:
Megumi Masaki, Chairperson
Graduate Music Department
(See address above.)

CHAMBER MUSIC AMERICA [745]

12 West 32nd Street, 7th Floor
New York, NY 10001
(212) 242-2022 ext. 102
Fax: (212) 967-9747
E-mail: sdadian@chamber-music.org
Web Site: www.chamber-music.org

FOUNDED: 1977

AREAS OF INTEREST:
The promotion of public interest in and appreciation of chamber music and the promotion of cooperation among and advancement of professional American chamber music ensembles and presenters.

CONSULTING OR VOLUNTEER SERVICES:
Technical assistance provided in such areas as fund-raising, marketing and residency design and implementation.

NAME(S) OF PROGRAMS:
- **Residency Partnership Program**

TYPE:
Project/program grants. Direct grants for ensembles and concert presenters.

YEAR PROGRAM STARTED: 1978

PURPOSE:
To stimulate the establishment of chamber music residencies.

LEGAL BASIS:
Nonprofit arts service organization.

ELIGIBILITY:
Candidates must be an ensemble member or a presenter in good standing of CMA and have experience in workshops or other residency-related activities.

GEOG. RESTRICTIONS: United States.

FINANCIAL DATA:
Amount of support per award: $2,500 to $12,000.
Total amount of support: Varies.
Matching fund requirements: CMA funds up to 75% of the requested amount.

NO. MOST RECENT APPLICANTS: 38.

NO. AWARDS: 8.

APPLICATION INFO:
Telephone consultations and workshops held by teleconference with CMA staff are available for organizations with questions about the application process.
Duration: Three days to one year.
Deadline: Fall 2016.

PUBLICATIONS:
Chamber Music, magazine; newsletter; application guidelines.

ADDRESS INQUIRIES TO:
Susan Dadian, Program Director
CMA Classical/Contemporary
(See address above.)

*SPECIAL STIPULATIONS:
Residencies must take place within the U.S.

CHAMBER MUSIC AMERICA [746]

12 West 32nd Street, 7th Floor
New York, NY 10001
(212) 242-2022 ext. 102
Fax: (212) 967-9747
E-mail: sdadian@chamber-music.org
Web Site: www.chamber-music.org

FOUNDED: 1977

AREAS OF INTEREST:
The promotion of public interest in and appreciation of chamber music and the promotion of cooperation among and advancement of professional American chamber music ensembles and presenters.

NAME(S) OF PROGRAMS:
- **Chamber Music America Classical Commissioning Program**

TYPE:
Project/program grants. Classical Commissioning provides support to U.S. member ensembles and presenters for commissions of new chamber works. Grants are made for commissioning fees, copying costs and ensemble rehearsal honoraria.

YEAR PROGRAM STARTED: 1983

PURPOSE:
To stimulate the composition of new works for chamber ensembles.

LEGAL BASIS:
Nonprofit arts service organization.

ELIGIBILITY:
Ensembles and presenters must be organizational members of Chamber Music America. Compositions must be written for small ensembles (two to 10 musicians) performing one to a part, and may represent a diverse musical spectrum, including contemporary art music, world music, and works that include electronics.

GEOG. RESTRICTIONS: United States.

FINANCIAL DATA:
Amount of support per award: Up to $20,000 for composer fee, copying allotment of $1,000 and subsidy of $1,000 per musician.
Total amount of support: Varies.

NO. MOST RECENT APPLICANTS: 132.

NO. AWARDS: 10 to 12.

APPLICATION INFO:
Guidelines may be obtained in the fall from the address above.
Duration: Applicants may reapply after one cycle.
Deadline: March 31, 2017.

PUBLICATIONS:
Guidelines and applications.

ADDRESS INQUIRIES TO:
Susan Dadian, Program Director
CMA Classical/Contemporary
(See address above.)

CHOPIN FOUNDATION OF THE U.S. [747]

1440 79th Street Causeway, Suite 117
Miami, FL 33141
(305) 868-0624
Fax: (305) 865-5150
E-mail: info@chopin.org
Web Site: www.chopin.org

FOUNDED: 1977

AREAS OF INTEREST:
Chopin and the promotion of classical music in the community by the support of young American pianists.

NAME(S) OF PROGRAMS:
- **Scholarship Program for Young Pianists**

TYPE:
Scholarships. Scholarship program supporting young American pianists, 14 to 17 years of age.

YEAR PROGRAM STARTED: 1997

PURPOSE:
To support talented young American musicians in their struggle for career recognition; to make classical music available to the community.

ELIGIBILITY:
Open to any qualified American pianists (citizens or legal residents) not younger than 14 and not older than 17 years of age on the application deadline, whose field of study is music and whose major is piano. If applicant is older than 17 years of age, he or she may only be accepted if currently in this scholarship program.

GEOG. RESTRICTIONS: United States.

FINANCIAL DATA:
Amount of support per award: $1,000.

Total amount of support: $10,000 for the year 2014.

NO. MOST RECENT APPLICANTS: 17 for the year 2015.

NO. AWARDS: 10 for the year 2015.

APPLICATION INFO:
Submit application along with the following documents:
(1) statement of career goals;
(2) minimum of two references from piano teachers or performers;
(3) video recording of 20 to 30 minutes of Chopin's works. Each piece must be an unedited performance on the DVD media. Recording must be clearly labeled, including applicant's name, address and works performed and;
(4) $25 registration fee.

Duration: One year. Renewable up to four years as long as the recipient continues to study piano, maintains satisfactory progress, and each year submits an audiocassette, CD or DVD recording of unedited performances of Chopin's works for evaluation as per renewal information.

Deadline: April 15.

IRS I.D.: 59-1778404

ADDRESS INQUIRIES TO:
Jadwiga Gewert, Executive Director
(See address above.)

*SPECIAL STIPULATIONS:
Registration fee of $25 must be included with application.

CINCINNATI WORLD PIANO COMPETITION [748]

Music Hall
1241 Elm Street
Cincinnati, OH 45202
(513) 744-3501
Fax: (513) 744-3504
E-mail: wpc@cincinnatiwpc.org
Web Site: www.cincinnatiwpc.org

FOUNDED: 1956

AREAS OF INTEREST:
Musical education and identification of piano talent worldwide.

CONSULTING OR VOLUNTEER SERVICES:
Development of piano artistry and education directed by well renowned artists.

NAME(S) OF PROGRAMS:
- **Cincinnati World Piano Competition**

TYPE:
Awards/prizes; Challenge/matching grants; Demonstration grants; Endowments; Internships; Matching gifts; Scholarships. Annual awards.

YEAR PROGRAM STARTED: 1956

PURPOSE:
To develop talent of young piano prodigies and artists.

LEGAL BASIS:
Nonprofit association.

FINANCIAL DATA:
Amount of support per award: Gold: $20,000 cash prize, solo performance with the Cincinnati Symphony Orchestra, and recital in New York, NY. Silver: $15,000 cash prize. Bronze: $10,000 cash prize. Also $1,000 to each semifinalist not advancing to the final round.

NO. MOST RECENT APPLICANTS: 38 for the 2014 competition.

NO. AWARDS: 6.

APPLICATION INFO:
Applications available upon request.

Duration: One-time awards.

Deadline: February 22.

IRS I.D.: 31-0711247

BOARD OF DIRECTORS:
Jack Rouse, Chairman
Jennifer McFarland Barrett, Vice-Chairman
Gary Smith, Treasurer
Jerome Eichert, Finance Officer and Secretary
Sam Ross, Branding Officer
Mary Jo Barnett, Volunteer Coordinator
Mrs. Jackie Lett Brown
Trish Bryan
Brad Cerra
Suzanne Costandi
Brent Ludwick
Pamela E. McDonald
Danute Miskinis
Robert Plageman
Kirk Polking
Ernest L. Robinson
Bryce Yoder

ADDRESS INQUIRIES TO:
Jack Rouse, Chairman
(See address above.)

CIVIC ORCHESTRA OF CHICAGO [749]

220 South Michigan Avenue
Chicago, IL 60604
(312) 294-3420
Fax: (312) 294-3329
E-mail: civic@cso.org
Web Site: www.cso.org/civic

FOUNDED: 1919

AREAS OF INTEREST:
Training young musicians for professional work in the orchestral field at the highest level with an emphasis on artistic excellence, community engagement and advocacy.

NAME(S) OF PROGRAMS:
- **Civic Orchestra Lesson Scholarship Stipends**

TYPE:
Fellowships; Scholarships. Stipends to help defray cost of private study with Chicago Symphony members and additional music training-related costs. Scholarship funds may be used for full-time two-year graduate-level study at a local academic institution.

YEAR PROGRAM STARTED: 1919

PURPOSE:
To promote the development of aesthetic sensitivity and playing technique through personal instruction with skilled pedagogues.

LEGAL BASIS:
The Civic Orchestra is a training orchestra under the auspices of the Chicago Symphony Orchestra, which is incorporated as a nonprofit, tax-exempt organization.

ELIGIBILITY:
Scholarships are available to all Civic Orchestra members.

FINANCIAL DATA:
Amount of support per award: $7,100 average for 30-week season.

Total amount of support: Varies.

NO. MOST RECENT APPLICANTS: 604.

NO. AWARDS: 90 each season.

APPLICATION INFO:
Application forms can be filled out when auditioning for the Civic Orchestra. Membership application forms are available from the Civic Orchestra office. Auditions are held in February and March.

Duration: 30 weeks, September to May or June. Renewal possible for up to two years.

Deadline: Mid-January.

OFFICERS:
Jay L. Henderson, Chairperson
Jeff Alexander, President, Chicago Symphony Orchestra

ADDRESS INQUIRIES TO:
Yoo-Jin Hong, Director
Civic Orchestra and Training Programs
(See address above.)

CLEVELAND INSTITUTE OF MUSIC [750]

11021 East Boulevard
Cleveland, OH 44106
(216) 795-3160
Fax: (216) 791-3063
E-mail: laura.orazi@cim.edu
Web Site: www.cim.edu

FOUNDED: 1920

NAME(S) OF PROGRAMS:
- **Cleveland Institute of Music Scholarships**

TYPE:
Scholarships.

PURPOSE:
To provide talented students with a professional, world-class education in the art of music.

ELIGIBILITY:
Candidates must be enrolled in the Bachelor or Master's program.

FINANCIAL DATA:
Amount of support per award: Varies.

NO. MOST RECENT APPLICANTS: Varies.

APPLICATION INFO:
Students must apply online.

Deadline: Returning students: March 1. New students: February 15.

ADDRESS INQUIRIES TO:
Lynn Johnson, Director of Admissions
(See address above.)

COLUMBIA UNIVERSITY

709 Pulitzer Hall
2950 Broadway
New York, NY 10027
(212) 854-3841
Fax: (212) 854-3342
E-mail: pulitzer@pulitzer.org
Web Site: www.pulitzer.org

TYPE:
Awards/prizes; Fellowships. Awards in journalism, books and music.

Pulitzer Prizes in Journalism are awarded based on material appearing in a text-based U.S. newspaper or news site that publishes at least once a week during the year. Awards given for:
(1) meritorious public service by a newspaper through the use of its journalistic resources which may include editorials, cartoons, photographs, graphics and online material;
(2) local reporting of breaking news;
(3) investigative reporting by an individual or team, presented as a single article or series;
(4) explanatory journalism that illuminates a significant or complex subject, demonstrating mastery of the subject, lucid writing and clear presentation;
(5) local reporting;
(6) reporting on national affairs;
(7) reporting on international affairs, including United Nations correspondence;
(8) feature writing giving prime consideration to high literary quality and originality;
(9) commentary;
(10) criticism;
(11) editorial writing;
(12) cartoon or portfolio of cartoons;
(13) breaking news photography in black and white or color, which may consist of a photograph or photographs, a sequence or an album and;
(14) feature photography in black and white or color with the same stipulations as above.

Prizes in Letters are restricted to works first published in the U.S. during the year in book form and available for purchase by the general public. Awards given for:
(1) fiction by an American author, preferably dealing with American life;
(2) a play by an American author, preferably original in its source and dealing with American life, produced in the U.S. January 1 to December 31;
(3) appropriately documented book on the history of the U.S.;
(4) appropriately documented biography or autobiography by an American author;
(5) volume of original verse by an American author and;
(6) appropriately documented book of nonfiction by an American author that is not eligible for consideration in any other category.

A prize in music is given for distinguished musical composition by an American that has had its first performance in the U.S. during the year.

Four fellowships enable outstanding graduates to travel, report and study abroad. One fellowship is given to an outstanding graduate who wishes to specialize in drama, music, literary, film or television criticism.

See entry 1864 for full listing.

AARON COPLAND FUND FOR MUSIC, INC. [751]

254 West 31st Street, 15th Floor
New York, NY 10001
(212) 461-6956
Fax: (212) 810-4567
E-mail: info@coplandfund.org
Web Site: www.coplandfund.org

FOUNDED: 1992

AREAS OF INTEREST:
Music.

NAME(S) OF PROGRAMS:
- **Performance Program**
- **Recording Program**
- **Supplemental Program**

TYPE:
General operating grants; Project/program grants. Performance Program: Provides support to performing organizations whose artistic excellence encourages and improves public knowledge and appreciation of serious contemporary American music. Organizations whose principal function is to support a specific performing ensemble should apply to this program.

Recording Program: Documents and provides wider exposure for the music of contemporary American composers, develops audiences for contemporary American music through record distribution and other retail markets, and supports the release and dissemination of recordings of previously unreleased contemporary American music and the reissuance of recordings that are no longer available.

Supplemental Program: Provides support to nonprofit organizations that have a history of substantial commitment to contemporary American music but whose needs are not addressed by the Fund's programs of support for performing organizations and recording projects, such as presenters and music service organizations.

YEAR PROGRAM STARTED: 1992

PURPOSE:
To encourage and improve public knowledge and appreciation of contemporary American music.

LEGAL BASIS:
Foundation.

ELIGIBILITY:
For the Performance Program, applicants must be nonprofit professional performing ensembles with a history of substantial commitment to contemporary American music and with plans to continue that commitment. Ensembles must have been in existence for at least two years at the time of application. Festivals are only eligible to apply for their professional core ensembles. Individuals, student ensembles, presenters without a core ensemble are not eligible. Grants will not be made for the purpose of commissions to composers.

For the Recording Program, applicants must be nonprofit performance ensembles, presenting institutions or nonprofit or commercial recording companies. Any applicant who, as of the deadline date, has one or more Recording Program grants that have been paid but that have not been released within two years after receiving funds will not be eligible to apply for a Recording Program grant. Grants will not be made for the purpose of commissions to composers.

Supplemental Program: Applications may be submitted by nonprofit organizations that have a history of substantial commitment to contemporary American music but whose needs are not addressed by the Fund's programs of support for performing organizations and recording projects. Organizations must have been in existence for at least two years at the time of application.

FINANCIAL DATA:
Grants for recordings of orchestral works may cover up to 50% of the total project costs, including musicians' recording fees, production, marketing and distribution.

Amount of support per award: $1,000 to $20,000 for Performance Program and Supplemental Program; Up to $20,000 for the Recording Program.

Total amount of support: $1,500,000.

NO. MOST RECENT APPLICANTS: Approximately 550.

NO. AWARDS: 139 Ensemble and Recording grants for the year 2014.

APPLICATION INFO:
Fund guidelines and application procedures are available to prospective applicants on the Fund's web site.

Duration: Varies depending on needs and nature of the request.

ADDRESS INQUIRIES TO:
Grants Manager
E-mail: grantsmanager@coplandfund.org
(See address above.)

THE CURTIS INSTITUTE OF MUSIC [752]

1726 Locust Street
Philadelphia, PA 19103
(215) 717-3117
Fax: (215) 893-7900
E-mail: admissions@curtis.edu
Web Site: www.curtis.edu

FOUNDED: 1924

AREAS OF INTEREST:
Musical performance.

NAME(S) OF PROGRAMS:
- **Bachelor of Music Degree Program**
- **Diploma Program**
- **Master of Music in Opera**

TYPE:
Scholarships. The training of young performing musicians, admitted by competitive audition for a tuition-free musical education.

YEAR PROGRAM STARTED: 1924

PURPOSE:
To train exceptionally gifted young musicians for careers as performing artists on the highest professional level.

LEGAL BASIS:
The school is operated under a Charter granted by the Commonwealth of Pennsylvania and is also included in the list of "Colleges and Universities in Pennsylvania approved by the State Council of Education for the Granting of Degrees."
The U.S. Government has duly approved the Curtis Institute of Music as an institution of learning for the attendance of nonimmigrant students, under the Immigration and Nationality Act.

ELIGIBILITY:
All are eligible for the competitive audition, regardless of race, origin or geographic distribution.

For Bachelor of Music Degree Program and Diploma Program, eligibility requirements consist of a competitive audition, high school diploma or GED, SAT Scores, English achievement scores and TOEFL for foreign students.

For Master of Music Degree Programs, eligibility requirements consist of a competitive audition and previous Bachelor's degree.

FINANCIAL DATA:
All students are on a scholarship basis exclusively and pay no tuition fees.

Amount of support per award: Varies depending upon award program.

Total amount of support: Varies.

APPLICATION INFO:
An application form with requested information completed in detail and transcript of high school, college and other academic records should be submitted to the Admissions Officer.

Duration: One-time award.

Deadline: December 12, 2016.

PUBLICATIONS:
The Curtis Institute of Music Catalogue (includes application form).

IRS I.D.: 23-1585611

ADDRESS INQUIRIES TO:
Christopher Hodges, Director of Admissions
(See address above.)

EASTMAN SCHOOL OF MUSIC OF THE UNIVERSITY OF ROCHESTER [753]

26 Gibbs Street
Rochester, NY 14604
(585) 274-1560
Fax: (585) 274-1088
E-mail: gdean@esm.rochester.edu
Web Site: www.esm.rochester.edu

AREAS OF INTEREST:
Music.

NAME(S) OF PROGRAMS:
- **Eastman School of Music Graduate Awards**

TYPE:
Assistantships; Fellowships; Scholarships; Visiting scholars.

PURPOSE:
To support the School's academic programs.

ELIGIBILITY:
Open to nationals of all countries. Candidates should have the qualifications necessary for admission to the Eastman School of Music. Non-U.S. citizens are usually offered service scholarships in ensemble work at graduate level.

FINANCIAL DATA:
Amount of support per award: Up to $21,000 in stipend and $41,720 in tuition scholarship per year.

Total amount of support: Approximately $6,500,000 annually.

NO. AWARDS: 300.

APPLICATION INFO:
Applicants must complete an application form. In addition, awards require an interview in Rochester or at one of the regional auditions.

Duration: One academic year. Renewable.

Deadline: December 1.

ADDRESS INQUIRIES TO:
Admissions Office
Eastman School of Music
(See address above.)

AVERY FISHER ARTIST PROGRAM [754]

c/o M.L. Falcone
155 West 68th Street, Suite 1114
New York, NY 10023
(212) 580-4302
Fax: (212) 787-9638
Web Site: www.averyfisherartistprogram.org

FOUNDED: 1974

AREAS OF INTEREST:
Music, specifically classical instrumentalists.

NAME(S) OF PROGRAMS:
- **The Avery Fisher Career Grants**
- **The Avery Fisher Prize**

TYPE:
Awards/prizes; Grants-in-aid. Awards for excellence and help in launching major careers.

YEAR PROGRAM STARTED: 1974

PURPOSE:
To recognize outstanding classical instrumentalists and chamber ensembles.

LEGAL BASIS:
Not-for-profit, tax-exempt.

ELIGIBILITY:
Instrumentalists who are U.S. citizens or permanent residents may be nominated.

FINANCIAL DATA:
Amount of support per award: Avery Fisher Career Grants: $25,000 each; Avery Fisher Prize: $75,000.

NO. AWARDS: Up to 5 Career Grants per year. Avery Fisher Prize considered every year, but not necessarily awarded.

APPLICATION INFO:
Individual artists may not apply directly. Nominations are made by the Recommendation Board, which comprises nationally known instrumentalists, conductors, music educators and presenters. Final selections are made by the Executive Committee. The Program is administered by the Lincoln Center for the Performing Arts, Inc.

Deadline: Varies.

EXECUTIVE COMMITTEE:
Emanuel Ax
Jed Bernstein
David Finckel
Henry Fogel
Anthony Fogg
Pamela Frank
Ara Guzelimian
Wu Han
Yo-Yo Ma
Jane S. Moss
Joseph W. Polisi
Chad Smith
Matias Tarnopolsky
Matthew VanBesien

ADDRESS INQUIRIES TO:
Joseph W. Polisi, Chairman
(See address above.)

FROMM MUSIC FOUNDATION AT HARVARD [755]

Department of Music
3 Oxford Street
Harvard University
Cambridge, MA 02138
(617) 495-2791
Fax: (617) 496-8081
E-mail: moncrief@fas.harvard.edu
Web Site: frommfoundation.fas.harvard.edu

FOUNDED: 1972

AREAS OF INTEREST:
Commissioning and performance of contemporary music.

TYPE:
Commission and grant-in-aid.

YEAR PROGRAM STARTED: 1952

PURPOSE:
To bring contemporary music closer to the public by providing support to composers and performers.

LEGAL BASIS:
Private foundation.

ELIGIBILITY:
Composers must be citizens or residents of the U.S. For these purposes, "residents" shall be deemed to include only lawful permanent residents, temporary residents, asylees, refugees and nonimmigrants who have lawfully been admitted to the U.S. for a term of one year or more.

FINANCIAL DATA:
Amount of support per award: $12,000.

NO. MOST RECENT APPLICANTS: 200.

NO. AWARDS: 12.

APPLICATION INFO:
Applicants must contact the Foundation for an application.

Deadline: June 1 for consideration in following fall. Commissions will be awarded in December.

PUBLICATIONS:
Application guidelines.

STAFF:
Jean Moncrieff, Administrator

DIRECTORS:
Suzannah Clark, Chairperson
Marilyn Nonken
Chen Yi

ADDRESS INQUIRIES TO:
Jean Moncrieff, Administrator
(See address above.)

*SPECIAL STIPULATIONS:
For those who have previously received a Fromm Commission, there is a 15-year waiting period before you can apply again. The Fromm Commission cannot be applied to projects that have been awarded other commissions.

THE GRAMMY FOUNDATION [756]

3030 Olympic Boulevard
Santa Monica, CA 90404
(310) 392-3777
Fax: (310) 392-2188
E-mail: grants@grammy.com
Web Site: www.grammy.org/grammy-foundation/grants

FOUNDED: 1989

AREAS OF INTEREST:
Music research, archiving and preserving and the medical and occupational well-being of music professionals.

TYPE:
Challenge/matching grants; Project/program grants; Research grants. The GRAMMY Foundation Grant Program funds the following areas:
(1) Scientific Research Projects - Grants to organizations and individuals to support efforts that advance the research and/or broad reaching implementations of original scientific research projects related to the impact of music on the human condition, such as the links between music study and early childhood development, the effects of music therapy and the medical and occupational well-being of music professionals.
(2) Archiving and Preservation Projects - Grants to organizations and individuals to support efforts that advance the archiving and preservation of the music and recorded sound heritage of the Americas. The Archiving and Preservation area has two funding categories: (a) Preservation Implementation and (b) Planning, Assessment and/or Consultation.

YEAR PROGRAM STARTED: 1989

PURPOSE:
To cultivate the understanding, appreciation and advancement of the contribution of recorded music to American culture.

ELIGIBILITY:
Priority is given to music projects of national significance that achieve a broad reach and whose final results are accessible to the general public.

The GRAMMY Foundation, Inc., will not fund:
(1) chapters, trustees, officers or staff;
(2) organizations that discriminate on the basis of race, sex, religion, national origin, disability or age;
(3) recording projects, demo tapes or live performances designed to promote the career of an individual or group;
(4) faculty and staff salaries unrelated to the project;
(5) performance events;
(6) purchase or repairs of music instruments or equipment;
(7) competitions and related expenses;
(8) work toward academic degrees;
(9) regular ongoing business activities of corporate clients;
(10) organizations or individuals for more than three consecutive years;
(11) organizations not based in the U.S. or;
(12) documentaries, endowments and web sites.

FINANCIAL DATA:
Amount of support per award: $5,000 to $20,000.

NO. MOST RECENT APPLICANTS: Varies.

NO. AWARDS: 14 for the year 2015.

APPLICATION INFO:
Letters of inquiry are only accepted online. Guidelines are available on the Foundation web site. Applicants must use current grant application only and should also include:
(1) evidence of organization's nonprofit status and copy of IRS tax determination letter;
(2) general description, history and accomplishments of the organization;
(3) current resume for individual applicants and organization's key personnel;
(4) two letters of support for the project and;
(5) an itemized budget.

Late or incomplete applications will not be reviewed.

Duration: Six to 24 months.

Deadline: October 1. Invitation to submit full proposal sent in November. Notification by March 15.

*SPECIAL STIPULATIONS:
Projects must be completed and a final report submitted within 12 to 24 months of project start date. A full set of the completed project is due to The GRAMMY Foundation within 90 days of the project completion date. Grantees must formally credit The GRAMMY Foundation in all published materials and announcements.

GUITAR FOUNDATION OF AMERICA [757]

P.O. Box 2900
Palos Verdes Peninsula, CA 90274
(877) 570-1651
E-mail: info@guitarfoundation.org
Web Site: www.guitarfoundation.org

FOUNDED: 1973

AREAS OF INTEREST:
Classical guitar.

NAME(S) OF PROGRAMS:
- **International Concert Artists Competition**
- **International Youth Competition**
- **Regional Events**

TYPE:
Awards/prizes; Conferences/seminars. International Youth Competition awarded in two divisions: Division I for ages 15 to 18 years old and Division II for ages 14 years old and under.

PURPOSE:
To support the serious study of the guitar in its historic and performance aspects; to promote the guitar as an ensemble instrument; to encourage composition and arrangements of ensemble music involving the guitar; to preserve and make available literature on the guitar.

LEGAL BASIS:
501(c)(3).

ELIGIBILITY:
Open to competitors worldwide.

FINANCIAL DATA:
Amount of support per award: Varies.
Total amount of support: Varies.

NO. AWARDS: 3 annually.

IRS I.D.: 51-0147668

ADDRESS INQUIRIES TO:
E-mail: emarkham@guitarfoundation.org

THE KOSCIUSZKO FOUNDATION, INC. [758]

15 East 65th Street
New York, NY 10065
(212) 734-2130
Fax: (212) 628-4552
E-mail: info@thekf.org
Web Site: www.thekf.org/programs/competitions/chopin/

FOUNDED: 1925

AREAS OF INTEREST:
Polish culture in the U.S., friendship and understanding between the U.S. and Poland through educational and cultural programs.

NAME(S) OF PROGRAMS:
- **Chopin Piano Competition**

TYPE:
Awards/prizes; Scholarships.

YEAR PROGRAM STARTED: 1949

PURPOSE:
To encourage gifted young pianists to further their studies and perform the works of Chopin, Szymanowski and other Polish composers.

LEGAL BASIS:
501(c)(3) not-for-profit organization.

ELIGIBILITY:
The competition is open to citizens and permanent residents of the U.S., Polish citizens, and to international full-time students with valid student visas. Applicants must be between the ages of 16 and 26. It is expected that applicants will have demonstrated exceptional talent and artistic achievement. Contestants may apply to compete in the preliminaries in New York. Each contestant should have a program of at least 60 minutes and is expected to perform complete works from memory.

GEOG. RESTRICTIONS: United States.

FINANCIAL DATA:
Amount of support per award: $5,000 first prize; $2,500 second prize; $1,500 third prize.

Total amount of support: $9,000.

APPLICATION INFO:
Official application materials are available upon request to the Foundation. Send business-size, self-addressed, stamped envelope. These materials are also available on the web site.

PUBLICATIONS:
KF newsletter; annual report.

IRS I.D.: 13-1628179

STAFF:
John S. Micgiel, President and Executive Director

ADDRESS INQUIRIES TO:
Chopin Piano Competition
(See address above.)

THE LEEDS INTERNATIONAL PIANO COMPETITION [759]

The Piano Competition Office
The University of Leeds
Woodhouse Lane
Leeds LS2 9JT England
(44) 0 113 244 6586
Fax: (44) 0 113 234 6106
E-mail: info@leedspiano.com
Web Site: www.leedspiano.com

FOUNDED: 1961

AREAS OF INTEREST:
Piano.

NAME(S) OF PROGRAMS:
- **Leeds International Piano Competition**

TYPE:
Awards/prizes. Prizes in piano awarded every third year.

YEAR PROGRAM STARTED: 1963

PURPOSE:
To provide a competition for professional pianists.

LEGAL BASIS:
Charity.

ELIGIBILITY:
The Competition is open to professional pianists of all nationalities up to 30 years of age.

FINANCIAL DATA:
Amount of support per award: GBP 1,500 to GBP 20,000.

Total amount of support: Prize money in excess of GBP 70,000.

APPLICATION INFO:
Application may be made online. Application information and forms are available from the Administrator at the address above. The official application form must be completed in English.

Deadline: The application form, with enclosures, must arrive no later than February 1 of the year of the competition.

ADDRESS INQUIRIES TO:
Administrator
(See address above.)

THE LESCHETIZKY ASSOCIATION, INC. [760]

880 West 181st Street
Apartment 3H
New York, NY 10033
(212) 781-5377
E-mail: alison.thomas@verizon.net
marafw@gmail.com
Web Site: www.leschetizky.org

FOUNDED: 1942

AREAS OF INTEREST:
Organization founded by Theodor Leschetizky's pupils to honor the memory of a great and beloved master and to perpetuate his principles in piano playing, teaching and composing.

CONSULTING OR VOLUNTEER SERVICES:
Offers teaching and consulting services in piano playing and piano education.

NAME(S) OF PROGRAMS:
- **Concerto Competition "Theodor Leschetizky"**

TYPE:
Awards/prizes. Competition for a debut recital in New York and cash awards.

PURPOSE:
To perpetuate Theodor Leschetizky's principles in playing and teaching.

LEGAL BASIS:
Tax-exempt organization under the IRS code 501(c)(3).

ELIGIBILITY:
Open to pianists ages 13 to 17.

FINANCIAL DATA:
Amount of support per award: $300 to $1,000.

Total amount of support: $10,000.

NO. MOST RECENT APPLICANTS: 20.

NO. AWARDS: 3.

APPLICATION INFO:
Information is available online. Entry materials may be mailed to Mara Waldman at the address below.

Deadline: March 1, 2017 postmarked. Biennial competition in odd-numbered years.

PUBLICATIONS:
Annual bulletin.

OFFICERS:
Mara Waldman, Chairperson
Dr. Alison Thomas, President

ADDRESS INQUIRIES TO:
Mara Waldman, Chairperson
884 West End Avenue, Suite 105
New York, NY 10025-3517
Tel: (212) 222-2733

LONG-THIBAUD-CRESPIN COMPETITION [761]

32, avenue Matignon
75008 Paris France
(33) 1 42 66 66 80
Fax: (33) 1 42 66 06 43
E-mail: contact@long-thibaud-crespin.org
Web Site: www.long-thibaud-crespin.org

FOUNDED: 1943

AREAS OF INTEREST:
Music.

TYPE:
Awards/prizes. International competition for piano, violin and voice. The competition varies yearly: The Crespin Singing Competition (2017); The Thibaud Violin Competition (2018); The Long Piano Competition (2019).

ELIGIBILITY:
Candidate maximum age of 30 years on January 1 of the year of the contest.

FINANCIAL DATA:
Amount of support per award: First Grand Prize: EUR 25,000. There are other prizes also in each competition.

NO. MOST RECENT APPLICANTS: 57.

NO. AWARDS: Varies with the competition.

APPLICATION INFO:
Information about the various competitions can be found on the web site.

Duration: One week.

Deadline: Varies.

PUBLICATIONS:
Brochures.

OFFICERS:
Jean-Philippe Schweitzer, President

ADDRESS INQUIRIES TO:
Delegate General
Long-Thibaud-Crespin Competition
(See address above.)

E. NAKAMICHI FOUNDATION [762]

5013 Maytime Lane
Culver City, CA 90230
(714) 771-9677
Fax: (866) 879-2140
E-mail: yas@enfoundation.com
Web Site: www.enfoundation.com

FOUNDED: 1985

AREAS OF INTEREST:
Music.

TYPE:
Project/program grants. Performance of music by classical and romantic period composers.

YEAR PROGRAM STARTED: 1986

PURPOSE:
To support appreciation of music by classical and romantic period composers.

LEGAL BASIS:
Private foundation.

ELIGIBILITY:
Eligible organizations must be 501(c)(3) tax-exempt. Individuals and religious organizations are ineligible.

GEOG. RESTRICTIONS: Japan and United States.

FINANCIAL DATA:
Amount of support per award: $3,000 to $20,000.

Total amount of support: Generally $350,000 to $400,000 per year.

NO. MOST RECENT APPLICANTS: 100.

NO. AWARDS: 35.

APPLICATION INFO:
Contact the Foundation for application procedures.

Duration: Single/multiple performances.

Deadline: March 15 and October 15.

IRS I.D.: 95-3870341

ADDRESS INQUIRIES TO:
Yas Yamazaki, President and Executive Director
(See address above.)

*PLEASE NOTE:
The Foundation is only accepting grant applications from those organizations that were successfully awarded a grant in the years 2000 through 2007.

NATIONAL ASSOCIATION OF COMPOSERS, USA (NACUSA) [763]

P.O. Box 49256
Barrington Station
Los Angeles, CA 90049
(541) 765-2406
E-mail: gsteinke9@gmail.com
nacusa@music-usa.org
Web Site: www.music-usa.org/nacusa

FOUNDED: 1932

AREAS OF INTEREST:
The performance, publication, broadcasting and archiving of new American concert hall music.

NAME(S) OF PROGRAMS:
- **Young Composers' Competition**

TYPE:
Awards/prizes; Conferences/seminars. Cash awards and guaranteed performances.

YEAR PROGRAM STARTED: 1978

PURPOSE:
To recognize and encourage young talent.

LEGAL BASIS:
501(c)(3) nonprofit organization.

ELIGIBILITY:
Open to all NACUSA members between the ages of 18 and 30. Compositions submitted should not exceed 15 minutes in length. Compositions should not require more than five players; an additional person for tape playback will not be counted as a performer. Compositions submitted must not have been previously published nor won any other musical competition. Instrumentation will be specified on a yearly basis.

GEOG. RESTRICTIONS: United States.

FINANCIAL DATA:
Amount of support per award: First prize: $400 and a guaranteed performance at a Los Angeles NACUSA concert; Second prize: $100 and a guaranteed performance at a NACUSA concert.

CO-OP FUNDING PROGRAMS: Contest is supported, in part, by grants from ASCAP and BMI.

NO. MOST RECENT APPLICANTS: 63.

NO. AWARDS: Varies.

APPLICATION INFO:
Complete information and electronic application submission is available on the Association web site. One copy of the score is to be submitted. Recordings of the entire composition are highly desirable, but not mandatory. Return postage must accompany each score if the composer wishes to maintain possession of the music. Scores will be judged, in part, on clear and legible music copying. Composers may submit up to two compositions. Scores should be submitted anonymously with an envelope attached containing the name of the work, the name of the composer and the composer's address and phone number.

Deadline: October 31.

PUBLICATIONS:
Composer/USA, newsletter.

IRS I.D.: 51-0166704

ADDRESS INQUIRIES TO:
Dr. Greg A. Steinke, President
(See address above.)

NATIONAL FEDERATION OF MUSIC CLUBS [764]

1646 West Smith Valley Road
Greenwood, IN 46142
(317) 882-4003
Fax: (317) 882-4019
E-mail: info@nfmc-music.org
Web Site: www.nfmc-music.org

FOUNDED: 1898

AREAS OF INTEREST:
Vocal and instrumental music, dance and composition.

NAME(S) OF PROGRAMS:
- **NFMC Competitions and Awards**

TYPE:
Awards/prizes. Competitions. Awards for students and adults who show proficiency in the fields of voice, instrumental performance, dance, composition, etc. The Federation provides a wide range of awards.

PURPOSE:
To support performance and promotion of American music.

LEGAL BASIS:
Nonprofit.

ELIGIBILITY:
Competitions cover a wide range of age groups from age 10 through adult. In general, applicants must be native-born or naturalized American citizens and must be members or become members of the National Federation of Music Clubs either by individual or group affiliation before applications are accepted.

GEOG. RESTRICTIONS: United States.

FINANCIAL DATA:
Amount of support per award: $50 to $15,000.

APPLICATION INFO:
Except in a few instances, applicants must become members of the NFMC on or before application either through individual or group affiliation before applications are considered. Application forms and information may be obtained from the NFMC at the address above. Enclose a self-addressed, stamped envelope. All requests for information must include $2 for material, postage and handling.

Duration: One-time award.

PUBLICATIONS:
Competitions and awards chart; *Junior Keynotes Magazine*; *Music Club Magazine*.

OFFICERS:
Michael Edwards, President
Barbara Hildebrand, Treasurer
Jeanne Hryniewicki, Recording Secretary

STAFF:
Jennifer Griffin, Administrative Manager

ADDRESS INQUIRIES TO:
Jennifer Griffin, Administrative Manager
(See address above.)

NATIONAL FEDERATION OF MUSIC CLUBS [765]

1646 West Smith Valley Road
Greenwood, IN 46142
(317) 882-4003
Fax: (317) 882-4019
E-mail: info@nfmc-music.org
Web Site: www.nfmc-music.org

FOUNDED: 1898

AREAS OF INTEREST:
Vocal and instrumental music and composition.

NAME(S) OF PROGRAMS:
- **Award Program for Summer Music Festivals and Music Centers**

TYPE:
Awards/prizes. Prizes for the performance and promotion of American music at summer music festivals.

PURPOSE:
To support performance and promotion of American music.

LEGAL BASIS:
Nonprofit.

ELIGIBILITY:
Program open to summer music festivals, centers and camps in the U.S. and its territories. In general, applicants must be native-born or naturalized American citizens and must be members or become members of the National Federation of Music Clubs either by individual or group affiliation before applications are accepted.

GEOG. RESTRICTIONS: United States.

FINANCIAL DATA:
Amount of support per award: Average $175 to $3,000.

NO. AWARDS: Over 39.

OFFICERS:
Michael Edwards, President
Barbara Hildebrand, Treasurer
Jeanne Hryniewicki, Recording Secretary

STAFF:
Jennifer Griffin, Administrative Manager

ADDRESS INQUIRIES TO:
Jennifer Griffin, Administrative Manager
(See address above.)

NATIONAL FEDERATION OF MUSIC CLUBS [766]

1646 West Smith Valley Road
Greenwood, IN 46142
(317) 882-4003
Fax: (317) 882-4019
E-mail: info@nfmc-music.org
Web Site: www.nfmc-music.org

FOUNDED: 1898

AREAS OF INTEREST:
Dedicated to finding and fostering young musical talent.

NAME(S) OF PROGRAMS:
- **Dorothy Dann Bullock Music Therapy Award**

TYPE:
Grants-in-aid. Financial assistance.

PURPOSE:
To support performance and promotion of American music.

LEGAL BASIS:
Nonprofit.

ELIGIBILITY:
Offered to Music Therapy Majors (college sophomores, juniors or seniors) in accredited schools offering Music Therapy degrees approved by American Music Therapy Association. Applicants must be native-born or naturalized American citizens and must be members or become members of NFMC either by individual or group affiliation before applications are accepted.

GEOG. RESTRICTIONS: United States.

FINANCIAL DATA:
Amount of support per award: $1,350.

Total amount of support: $1,350 annually.

NO. AWARDS: 1 annually.

APPLICATION INFO:
Application information is available on the web site.

Deadline: March 1.

OFFICERS:
Michael Edwards, President
Barbara Hildebrand, Treasurer
Jeanne Hryniewicki, Recording Secretary

STAFF:
Jennifer Griffin, Administrative Manager

ADDRESS INQUIRIES TO:
Bullock Music Therapy Award
(See address above.)

NATIONAL OPERA ASSOCIATION, INC. [767]

2403 Russell Long Boulevard
Canyon, TX 79016
(806) 651-2843
Fax: (806) 651-2958
E-mail: rhansen@noa.org
Web Site: www.noa.org

FOUNDED: 1955

AREAS OF INTEREST:
Opera production, opera composition, promotion of operatic talent and opera education.

CONSULTING OR VOLUNTEER SERVICES:
Distinguished members available for consultation and workshops.

NAME(S) OF PROGRAMS:

- **Carolyn Bailey and Dominick Argento Vocal Competition**
- **Biennial Dissertation Competition**
- **Chamber Opera Competition**
- **Collegiate Opera Scenes Competition**
- **Opera Production Competition**
- **Scholarly Paper Competition**

TYPE:
Awards/prizes. Cash prizes awarded to Artist Division winners and Scholarship Division winners. Also scholarships to AIMS, awarded in both divisions. Productions of winning operas in Chamber Opera Competition will be scheduled for annual convention.

YEAR PROGRAM STARTED: 1977

PURPOSE:
To assist young opera singers in furthering their training for an operatic career and to honor the best of the new chamber operas and the outstanding opera productions by universities and colleges.

LEGAL BASIS:
Nonprofit organization.

ELIGIBILITY:
All applicants must submit an entrance fee depending on category and membership status.

FINANCIAL DATA:
Amount of support per award: $500 to $2,000 for singing competitors.

Total amount of support: $10,000.

NO. MOST RECENT APPLICANTS: 150 for vocal competition, 25 for opera production competition and over 100 for chamber opera competition.

NO. AWARDS: Approximately 10.

APPLICATION INFO:
Application information is available on the web site.

Duration: Nonrenewable.

Deadline: Varies by contest.

PUBLICATIONS:
Opera Journal; NOA Newsletter.

ADDRESS INQUIRIES TO:
Robert Hansen, Executive Director
(See address above.)

NATIONAL ORCHESTRAL INSTITUTE [768]

3800 Clarice Smith Performing Arts Center
University of Maryland School of Music
College Park, MD 20742
(301) 405-2317
Fax: (301) 405-5977
E-mail: noi@umd.edu
Web Site: www.noi.umd.edu

FOUNDED: 1988

AREAS OF INTEREST:
Orchestral music.

TYPE:
Residencies; Scholarships; Training grants; Visiting scholars. Advanced orchestral training program offering talented musicians on the threshold of their professional careers a four-week opportunity to study and perform under internationally renowned conductors and principal musicians from leading American orchestras.

YEAR PROGRAM STARTED: 1988

PURPOSE:
To prepare musicians for professional orchestral careers.

LEGAL BASIS:
University.

ELIGIBILITY:
Applicants must be between the ages of 18 and 28 with appropriate orchestral music skill.

FINANCIAL DATA:
Support includes tuition at the Institute.

Amount of support per award: Over $4,000.

Total amount of support: Varies.

NO. MOST RECENT APPLICANTS: 750 for the year 2013.

NO. AWARDS: Over 80 annually.

APPLICATION INFO:
Applicants should submit an application, resume and one letter of recommendation. They should also audition at one of the audition centers in cities across the U.S. between January and March.

Duration: June 1 to June 30.

Deadline: Varies by audition location.

PUBLICATIONS:
Program announcement.

ADDRESS INQUIRIES TO:
Richard Scerbo, General Manager
(See address above.)

THE WALTER W. NAUMBURG FOUNDATION, INC. [769]

120 Claremont Avenue
New York, NY 10027
(212) 362-9877
(917) 493-4040
E-mail: naumburgfoundation@gmail.com
Web Site: www.naumburg.org

FOUNDED: 1925

AREAS OF INTEREST:
Sponsorship of international competitions for violin, cello, piano, voice, chamber music and composition.

TYPE:
Awards/prizes.

ELIGIBILITY:
Requirements differ with various categories of violin, cello, piano, voice, chamber music and composition. This competition is open to musicians and composers of every nationality.

The competitors may not be under 17 years of age or more than 31 years of age, and may not have had a birthday before 1985 for the 2016 Violin and Cello Competitions. Voice applicants may not be under 20 years of age or more than 35 years of age.

Chamber Music Award for string quartets, piano trios and ensembles including at least three members and not more than eight without a conductor. Chamber Music Group requirements include:
(1) in residence in North America;
(2) confirmation of a concert career from three years or more (must include original printed programs, or copies of) and;
(3) average age of ensemble members must not exceed 34 as of 2016 Competition.

FINANCIAL DATA:
Solo Competition: First prize award includes two fully subsidized New York Recitals - Debut in Weill Hall, Carnegie Hall, recital and orchestral performances, in addition to a cash award. Chamber Music Award: Recital with commission work.

Amount of support per award: Solo Competition: $15,000 first prize, $10,000 second prize and $5,000 third prize.

APPLICATION INFO:
Application forms and a CD of no less than 30 minutes of satisfactory audible quality must be received at the Naumburg office by the deadline. Application forms may be obtained online.

Duration: One-time award.

Deadline: Contact the Foundation for exact date.

BOARD OF DIRECTORS AND OFFICERS:
David Geber, President
Nicholas Mann, President
Marshal Gibson, Treasurer
Lucy Rowan Mann, Assistant Treasurer
John Corigliano
Bonnie Hampton
Joel Krosnick
Claude Mann
Judith Naumburg
Charles Neidich
Anton Nel
Ursula Oppens
Robert Sherman
Benita Valente

ADDRESS INQUIRIES TO:
Lucy Rowan Mann, Executive Director
(See address above.)

*PLEASE NOTE:
The solo competition disciplines rotate from year to year.

NEW MUSIC USA [770]

90 Broad Street, Suite 1902
New York, NY 10004
(212) 645-6949
Fax: (646) 490-0998
E-mail: info@newmusicusa.org
Web Site: www.newmusicusa.org

FOUNDED: 2011

AREAS OF INTEREST:
Living composers and contemporary music of all kinds.

NAME(S) OF PROGRAMS:

- **Music Alive**
- **NYC New Music Impact Fund**
- **Project Grants**

TYPE:
Awards/prizes; General operating grants; Project/program grants; Residencies.

PURPOSE:
To increase opportunities for composers by fostering the creation, performances, dissemination, and appreciation for their music; to fund the creation of new work; to

support direct contact between composers and audiences; to create education programs that deepen the understanding of composers and their work; to establish innovative private- and public-sector partnerships that create new opportunities.

LEGAL BASIS:
Nonprofit corporation.

GEOG. RESTRICTIONS: United States.

FINANCIAL DATA:
Amount of support per award: Varies. Project Grants: $250 to $15,000.

Total amount of support: $990,327 in grants to the field for fiscal year 2015 (unaudited).

APPLICATION INFO:
Refer to the web site.

Duration: Varies.

Deadline: Varies.

IRS I.D.: 13-0432981

BOARD OF DIRECTORS:
Frederick Peters, Chairperson
Joseph Walker, Treasurer
Kristin Lancino, Secretary
Ed Harsh, President and Chief Executive Officer

ADDRESS INQUIRIES TO:
Scott Winship
Director of Grantmaking Programs
(See address above.)

ORCHESTRE SYMPHONIQUE DE MONTREAL (OSM) [771]

1600, rue Saint-Urbain
Montreal QC H2X 0S1 Canada
(514) 840-7400 ext. 7415
Fax: (514) 842-0728
E-mail: concours@osm.ca
Web Site: www.osm.ca/competition

FOUNDED: 1937

AREAS OF INTEREST:
Music.

NAME(S) OF PROGRAMS:
- **OSM Manulife Competition**

TYPE:
Awards/prizes; Scholarships. Grand prize includes money prize, a performance with the Orchestre symphonique de Montreal, concert opportunities with various organizations throughout Canada, scholarships at Canada's leading summer academies and a professional recording in one of Radio-Canada's studios. 2015 competition for piano and percussion.

YEAR PROGRAM STARTED: 1937

PURPOSE:
To encourage young Canadian musicians.

LEGAL BASIS:
Symphony orchestra.

ELIGIBILITY:
Open to Canadian citizens or landed immigrants in the following categories: Piano and Strings, up to 25 years of age; Woodwinds and Brass, 16 to 25 years of age (except tuba, 16 to 30 years of age); Percussion, 16 to 30 years of age; Voice, 22 to 30 years of age.

Each year is for a different category.

FINANCIAL DATA:
Amount of support per award: One grand prize: $15,000 (CAN); two first prizes: $10,000 (CAN). Three second prizes: $5,000 (CAN). Three third prizes: $2,500 (CAN). Three prizes for the best interpretation of a Canadian work: $2,500 (CAN). The Paul Merkelo Scholarship: $2,500 (CAN).

Total amount of support: More than $100,000 (CAN) in prizes, scholarships and concert opportunities.

NO. MOST RECENT APPLICANTS: 85 to 95.

NO. AWARDS: Approximately 15 annually.

APPLICATION INFO:
Include application form, registration fee, proof of age and of Canadian citizenship and curriculum vitae. Applicants must contact OSM Competition to acquire full details of application process.

Deadline: May 1, 2017.

ADDRESS INQUIRIES TO:
Concours OSM Standard Life Competition
(See address above.)

*PLEASE NOTE:
Musical program approved by the jury members of the competition.

PERCUSSIVE ARTS SOCIETY [772]

110 West Washington Street
Suite A
Indianapolis, IN 46204
(317) 974-4488
Fax: (317) 974-4499
E-mail: percarts@pas.org
Web Site: www.pas.org

FOUNDED: 1961

AREAS OF INTEREST:
Percussive arts, including music education, performance and literature related to percussion instruments.

CONSULTING OR VOLUNTEER SERVICES:
Consulting committees on acoustics, education curricula, literature, etc.

NAME(S) OF PROGRAMS:
- **Internship Program**
- **PASIC International Scholarship**
- **PASIC Scholarships**
- **PAS/Armand Zildjian Percussion Scholarship**
- **PAS/Remo, Inc. Fred Hoey Memorial Scholarship**
- **PAS/Sabian, Ltd. Larrie Londin Memorial Scholarship**
- **PAS/Yamaha Terry Gibbs Vibraphone Scholarship**
- **Percussion Composition Contest**
- **Zildjian Family Opportunity Fund**

TYPE:
Awards/prizes; Internships; Project/program grants; Scholarships.

YEAR PROGRAM STARTED: 1961

PURPOSE:
To promote percussion education, research, performance and appreciation.

LEGAL BASIS:
Not-for-profit corporation.

ELIGIBILITY:
Applicants must be members of the Society.

Internships are open to enrolled music business major students in an accredited university program.

FINANCIAL DATA:
Amount of support per award: Varies.

Total amount of support: Varies; approximately $25,000 to $30,000 per year.

NO. AWARDS: 12.

APPLICATION INFO:
Application may be submitted online. Consult Society web site.

Duration: Education scholarships and grants: One year.

Deadline: Varies.

PUBLICATIONS:
Percussive Notes, magazine; *Percussion News*, newsletter.

IRS I.D.: 73-1385751

STAFF:
Jeff Hartsough, Executive Director

ADDRESS INQUIRIES TO:
Jeff Hartsough, Executive Director
(See address above.)

THE PITTSBURGH NEW MUSIC ENSEMBLE, INC. [773]

P.O. Box 111581
Pittsburgh, PA 15238
(512) 785-6255
E-mail: kevinpnme@gmail.com
Web Site: www.pnme.org

FOUNDED: 1975

AREAS OF INTEREST:
New music.

NAME(S) OF PROGRAMS:
- **Harvey Gaul Music Composition Contest**

TYPE:
Awards/prizes.

YEAR PROGRAM STARTED: 1975

PURPOSE:
To promote new music and support composers.

LEGAL BASIS:
Nonprofit corporation.

ELIGIBILITY:
Contestants must be U.S. citizens.

FINANCIAL DATA:
Amount of support per award: $6,000 commission.

NO. AWARDS: 1.

APPLICATION INFO:
An entry form is required. An entry fee of $20 must accompany each composition. Contestants should send a score and CD of a representative instrumental work, along with a current biography and contact information. No MIDI realizations.

PUBLICATIONS:
Application guidelines.

IRS I.D.: 25-1364030

OFFICERS:
Kevin Noe, Executive Artistic Director

ADDRESS INQUIRIES TO:
Kevin Noe, Executive Artistic Director
(See address above.)

*PLEASE NOTE:
Contest is on an as needed basis, not every year.
The Ensemble does not award scholarships.

PRESSER FOUNDATION [774]

1501 Cherry Street
Philadelphia, PA 19102
(267) 519-5350
Fax: (267) 519-5349
E-mail: trodgers@presserfoundation.org
Web Site: www.presserfoundation.org

FOUNDED: 1916

AREAS OF INTEREST:
Music education and music philanthropy.

NAME(S) OF PROGRAMS:
- **Advancement of Music**
- **Assistance to Worthy Music Teachers**
- **Capital Support**
- **The Presser Foundation Graduate Music Award**
- **The Presser Foundation Undergraduate Scholar Award**
- **Special Projects**

TYPE:
Awards/prizes; General operating grants; Project/program grants.

YEAR PROGRAM STARTED: 1916

PURPOSE:
To provide financial awards to promising undergraduate and graduate students at qualified higher education institutions; to provide grants for the construction and renovation of suitable buildings for musical instruction and performance; to administer emergency aid to worthy music teachers in distress; to provide support to innovative projects and collaborations between music organizations; to provide operating support to worthy music organizations in the Greater Philadelphia area.

LEGAL BASIS:
Private foundation.

GEOG. RESTRICTIONS: United States.

APPLICATION INFO:
Application form can be downloaded from the Foundation web site.

ADDRESS INQUIRIES TO:
Teresa Araco Rodgers, Executive Director
(See address above.)

THE QUEEN ELISABETH INTERNATIONAL MUSIC COMPETITION OF BELGIUM [775]

20, rue aux Laines
B-1000 Brussels Belgium
(32) 2 213 40 50
Fax: (32) 2 514 32 97
E-mail: info@qeimc.be
Web Site: www.qeimc.be
www.cmireb.be/en

FOUNDED: 1951

AREAS OF INTEREST:
Voice, violin, piano and cello.

TYPE:
Awards/prizes.

PURPOSE:
To support young artists and thus help to establish their reputations with both professionals and the public through an international competition for music interpretation.

LEGAL BASIS:
Nonprofit organization.

ELIGIBILITY:
Programs alternate each year. The competition is reserved for violin in 2015, piano in 2016, cello in 2017, and voice in 2018.

The competition is open to musicians of all nationalities. The minimum age for applicants is 18. Maximum age is 30 for piano, violin, cello and singers. Instrumental competitors play both assigned works and pieces of their own selection. The competition is divided into selection rounds and final round.

FINANCIAL DATA:
Amount of support per award: Varies.

NO. MOST RECENT APPLICANTS: 214 singers for the year 2014.

NO. AWARDS: 12 for the year 2014.

APPLICATION INFO:
Applications for registration should be downloaded online and accompanied by the following:
(1) a copy of birth certificate;
(2) proof of nationality;
(3) one photograph in the form of a TIFF file (minimum 300 dpi) for the programme;
(4) curriculum vitae;
(5) documentation providing proof of his or her skill (for example, higher diplomas, repertoire list with works performed in public, prizes and diplomas received from other competitions, press reviews, etc.) and;
(6) a DVD recording (image and sound) with appropriate music programme.

Deadline: January 10 of the year of the competition.

PUBLICATIONS:
Competition announcement and rules; brochures.

OFFICERS:
Baron Jan Huyghebaert, Chairman
Michel-Etienne Van Neste, Secretary General

ADDRESS INQUIRIES TO:
The Secretariat of the Competition
(See address above.)

SAN FRANCISCO CONSERVATORY OF MUSIC [776]

50 Oak Street
San Francisco, CA 94102
(415) 503-6214
Fax: (415) 503-6299
E-mail: dhoward@sfcm.edu
Web Site: www.sfcm.edu

FOUNDED: 1917

AREAS OF INTEREST:
Music.

NAME(S) OF PROGRAMS:
- **Performance Scholarships in Music for Students in Bachelor and Master of Music Programs**

TYPE:
Assistantships; Scholarships; Work-study programs. Awards for the study of music at the Conservatory.

YEAR PROGRAM STARTED: 1917

PURPOSE:
To enable talented, needy students to attend the Conservatory.

LEGAL BASIS:
Conservatory of Music.

ELIGIBILITY:
U.S. and foreign citizens may apply. Candidates must have had considerable experience in musical performance and must attend the Conservatory on a full-time basis.

FINANCIAL DATA:
Scholarships are to be applied toward tuition at the Conservatory.

Amount of support per award: $1,000 and up.

Total amount of support: $7,491,204 for the academic year 2014-15.

NO. MOST RECENT APPLICANTS: 950.

NO. AWARDS: 406 for the academic year 2014-15.

APPLICATION INFO:
Applicants must submit the San Francisco Conservatory of Music Application and either the Free Application for Federal Student Aid or International Student Certification of Finances. CSS/Financial Aid Profile is required for all international students and domestic students under the age of 26.

Duration: Tenable for one year and may be renewed.

Deadline: February 15.

OFFICER:
Doris Howard, Director of Financial Aid

ADDRESS INQUIRIES TO:
Financial Aid
E-mail: finaid@sfcm.edu
(See address above.)

SAN FRANCISCO OPERA CENTER [777]

War Memorial Opera House
301 Van Ness Avenue
San Francisco, CA 94102-4509
(415) 565-3245
Fax: (415) 551-6305
E-mail: sfoperacenter@sfopera.com
Web Site: www.sfopera.com/about-us/opera-center/

FOUNDED: 1954

AREAS OF INTEREST:
Young professional singers, pianists/accompanists and stage directors interested in a sequence of opera performance and career development opportunities.

CONSULTING OR VOLUNTEER SERVICES:
Board of Directors of Merola Opera Program and a full staff of conductors, coaches, stage directors and instructors in singing, acting, movement, stage combat, auditioning, career development and other activities.

NAME(S) OF PROGRAMS:
- **Adler Fellowships**
- **Merola Opera Program**

TYPE:
Fellowships; Internships; Technical assistance. Auditions by application are held in the fall of each year for the following summer's Merola Opera Program in various cities throughout the U.S. Participants will also be considered for Adler Fellowships (singers/pianists).

YEAR PROGRAM STARTED: 1954

PURPOSE:
To provide professional opera training and performance opportunities for talented young opera professionals.

LEGAL BASIS:
Nonprofit.

ELIGIBILITY:
Merola Opera Program: Open to all singers, pianists/accompanists and stage directors. All voice types are eligible, between the ages of 20 and 34.

FINANCIAL DATA:
Merola Opera Program participants receive shared housing accommodations, weekly

allowance and round-trip airfare from place of residence to San Francisco. Adler Fellowships are for a salaried 12-month contract.

Total amount of support: Varies.

APPLICATION INFO:
Application form is required. Details available on the web site.

Duration: Adler Fellowships: 12-month contract. Merola Opera Program: June to August.

Deadline: Merola Opera Program: Fall of each year.

PUBLICATIONS:
Application guidelines.

OFFICERS:
Sheri Greenawald, Director

ADDRESS INQUIRIES TO:
Jo Ann McStravick, Artists' Services and Auditions Administrator
(See address above.)

SIGMA ALPHA IOTA PHILANTHROPIES, INC. [778]

One Tunnel Road
Asheville, NC 28805-1229
(828) 251-0606
Fax: (828) 251-0644
E-mail: nh@sai-national.org
sarabande88@yahoo.com
Web Site: www.sai-national.org

FOUNDED: 1903

AREAS OF INTEREST:
Music, new compositions.

CONSULTING OR VOLUNTEER SERVICES:
Local volunteers in music.

NAME(S) OF PROGRAMS:
- **Inter-American Music Awards**

TYPE:
Awards/prizes. Music composition contest. The 2018 prize will go to a piano composition.

YEAR PROGRAM STARTED: 1948

PURPOSE:
To give to the fraternity, and to the public, compositions of high musical merit; to bring distinction to winning composers; to offer royalties and other benefits coincident with publication of winning music.

LEGAL BASIS:
Nonprofit corporation.

ELIGIBILITY:
Requirements change each triennium; however, applicants must be residents of North, Central or South America.

GEOG. RESTRICTIONS: North, Central and South America.

FINANCIAL DATA:
Amount of support per award: $2,500 prize, plus winning composition published by a major music publisher.

NO. MOST RECENT APPLICANTS: 15.

NO. AWARDS: 1.

APPLICATION INFO:
Application information is available on the web site.

Duration: One-time award.

Deadline: September 1, 2017.

PUBLICATIONS:
Brochure.

STAFF:
Ruth Sieber Johnson, SAI Executive Director

ADDRESS INQUIRIES TO:
SAI Philanthropies, Inc.
(See address above.)

SYMPHONY OF THE MOUNTAINS [779]

Kingsport Renaissance Center
1200 East Center Street
Kingsport, TN 37660
(423) 392-8423
Fax: (423) 392-8428
E-mail: melissa@symphonyofthemountains.org
Web Site: www.symphonyofthemountains.org

FOUNDED: 1946

AREAS OF INTEREST:
Symphonic concerts and educational and social activities.

NAME(S) OF PROGRAMS:
- **Elizabeth Harper Vaughn Concerto Competition**

TYPE:
Awards/prizes. Cash prize and appearance with the Symphony of the Mountains Orchestra.

YEAR PROGRAM STARTED: 1969

PURPOSE:
To recognize excellence in music performance, with the potential for career advancement.

LEGAL BASIS:
Not-for-profit corporation.

ELIGIBILITY:
Open to musicians 25 years of age and under, with recommendation of private instructor.

FINANCIAL DATA:
Amount of support per award: $750.

Total amount of support: $750.

NO. MOST RECENT APPLICANTS: 10.

NO. AWARDS: 1.

APPLICATION INFO:
Requires recommendation of private instructor and CD or DVD of performance (full concerto or other appropriate musical arrangement with orchestral accompaniment).

Duration: One-time award.

Deadline: September 1.

PUBLICATIONS:
Posters, postcards, programs for subscription concerts.

IRS I.D.: 62-0534228

STAFF:
Cornelia Laemmli Orth, Music Director/Chief Operating Officer

ADDRESS INQUIRIES TO:
Cornelia Laemmli Orth
Music Director/Chief Operating Officer
(See address above.)

THE RICHARD TUCKER MUSIC FOUNDATION, INC. [780]

1790 Broadway
Suite 715
New York, NY 10019-1412
(212) 757-2218
Fax: (212) 757-2347
E-mail: info@richardtucker.org
Web Site: www.richardtucker.org

FOUNDED: 1975

AREAS OF INTEREST:
Financial aid to American opera singers and opera companies with development programs for American singers.

NAME(S) OF PROGRAMS:
- **Richard Tucker Award**
- **Richard Tucker Career Grants**
- **Sara Tucker Study Grants**

TYPE:
Awards/prizes.

YEAR PROGRAM STARTED: 1978

PURPOSE:
To help further the careers of young American singers.

LEGAL BASIS:
Tax-exempt, not-for-profit organization.

ELIGIBILITY:
Nominees must already be performing in opera. Open to males and females in all vocal categories. Singers cannot apply; they must be recommended by a professional in the field. Applicants must also be U.S.-born.

GEOG. RESTRICTIONS: United States.

FINANCIAL DATA:
Amount of support per award: Richard Tucker Award: $50,000. Richard Tucker Career Grants: Unrestricted grant of $10,000. Sara Tucker Study Grants: Unrestricted grant of $5,000.

Total amount of support: Approximately $105,000.

NO. MOST RECENT APPLICANTS: 100 to 120.

NO. AWARDS: Richard Tucker Award: 1. Richard Tucker Career Grants and Sara Tucker Study Grants: 3 to 5 each.

APPLICATION INFO:
Information on the nominating process for the awards is available on the web site or by telephoning the Foundation. Application is via a confidential anonymous nomination process.

Duration: Varies, but most of the awards are one-time awards.

Deadline: Recommendations are due December 31.

IRS I.D.: 23-7431029

BOARD OF DIRECTORS:
Jeffrey Manocherian, Chairman
Barry Tucker, President
Sherrill Milnes, Vice President
John A. Petts, Vice President
Samuel Ramey, Vice President
Robert S. Tucker, Vice President
Peter H. Carwell, Executive Director

ADDRESS INQUIRIES TO:
Peter H. Carwell, Executive Director
(See address above.)

THE VIOLIN SOCIETY OF AMERICA [781]

14070 Proton Road
Suite 100, LB9
Dallas, TX 75244
(972) 233-9107 ext. 204
Fax: (972) 490-4219
E-mail: info@vsaweb.org
Web Site: www.vsaweb.org

FOUNDED: 1973

AREAS OF INTEREST:
Making and restoring stringed instruments and their bows, the history of stringed instruments and performers, technique, performance practice, repertory and the acoustics of bowed stringed instruments. The Society also sponsors conventions that include lectures, demonstrations, symposia and concerts, biennial international competitions for new stringed instruments and their bows, a Music Fair and a periodical covering all aspects of bowed string instruments.

NAME(S) OF PROGRAMS:
- **Kaplan-Goodkind Memorial Scholarship Fund**
- **Kun Scholarship Fund**
- **Aram and Rose Nigogosian Fund**

TYPE:
Scholarships. Tuition grants to students of violin-making and bow-making enrolled in a full-time violin-making school.

YEAR PROGRAM STARTED: 1982

PURPOSE:
To bring together people from various fields to exchange ideas and skills and to help people learn about the making of bows and stringed instruments.

LEGAL BASIS:
Tax-exempt educational organization.

ELIGIBILITY:
Students must be U.S. citizens, have satisfactorily completed at least one full year of study in the program, have shown serious effort, talent and future promise, and have financial need.

GEOG. RESTRICTIONS: United States.

FINANCIAL DATA:
Tuition grants are made to the school in student's name.

Amount of support per award: $500 average.

Total amount of support: Varies.

NO. AWARDS: 8 to 12 annually.

APPLICATION INFO:
Apply by letter of recommendation from school to main office of VSA.

Duration: One-time tuition grant.

Deadline: Grants made on a continuing basis.

PUBLICATIONS:
The Journal, newsletter.

OFFICERS:
Lori Kirr, President
Fan Tao, President-Elect
Nicholas Lampo, Vice President
Richard Dodson, Treasurer
Ted White, Secretary

ADDRESS INQUIRIES TO:
Madeleine Crouch, Executive Director
(See address above.)

YOUNG CONCERT ARTISTS, INC. [782]

250 West 57th Street
Suite 1222
New York, NY 10107
(212) 307-6655
Fax: (212) 581-8894
E-mail: yca@yca.org
Web Site: www.yca.org

FOUNDED: 1961

AREAS OF INTEREST:
Young composers, young solo classical musicians (instruments and voice) and string quartets.

NAME(S) OF PROGRAMS:
- **Young Concert Artists International Auditions**

TYPE:
Awards/prizes. Artist management. YCA sponsors the Young Concert Artists Series in New York City at Carnegie's Zankel Hall, Lincoln Center's Alice Tully Hall, Kaufman Music Center's Merkin Hall, and in Washington, DC at the Kennedy Center; books concert engagements in the U.S. and abroad; offers career guidance and development; and provides all promotion and publicity materials, at no cost to the artists. YCA membership generally continues until the artists are signed by commercial management. The organization's work is made possible by contributions from corporations, foundations, individuals and government agencies.

YEAR PROGRAM STARTED: 1961

PURPOSE:
To discover and launch the careers of exceptional young musicians.

LEGAL BASIS:
Nonprofit, tax-exempt.

ELIGIBILITY:
Instrumentalists and singers must perform required repertoire and have letters of recommendation.

NO. MOST RECENT APPLICANTS: 289.

NO. AWARDS: Varies. Winners are selected only against a standard of excellence; any number can win who are selected by the jury.

APPLICATION INFO:
Auditions dates, application form and requirements are available online.

Duration: Each winner signs a multiyear renewable contract with Young Concert Artists, which may be extended by mutual consent.

Deadline: Contact the organization.

PUBLICATIONS:
Brochure.

IRS I.D.: 13-1951681

OFFICER:
Susan Wadsworth, Director

ADDRESS INQUIRIES TO:
Susan Wadsworth, Director

Auditions:
Mr. Erol Gurol
(See address above.)

YOUNG MUSICIANS FOUNDATION (YMF) [783]

244 South San Pedro Street
Fifth Floor, Suite 506
Los Angeles, CA 90012
(213) 617-7707
Fax: (213) 617-7706
E-mail: info@ymf.org
Web Site: www.ymf.org

FOUNDED: 1955

AREAS OF INTEREST:
Young musicians, ages four to 25, studying music fundamentals, as well as aspiring to careers in professional classical music.

NAME(S) OF PROGRAMS:
- **Arts Management Internship**
- **Chamber Music Series**
- **Debut Concerto Competition**
- **Debut Orchestra**
- **Music Director**
- **Music 360 Degrees**
- **Scholarship Program**
- **Teaching Artist Program**

TYPE:
Awards/prizes; Conferences/seminars; Fellowships; Scholarships. Mentor program. Financial assistance for private study and/or tuition at recognized musical institutions. Significant performance opportunity may be offered.

YEAR PROGRAM STARTED: 1955

PURPOSE:
To nurture the artistic and personal development of novice and advanced music students in their classical musical education.

LEGAL BASIS:
Nonprofit organization.

ELIGIBILITY:
Music students four to 25 years of age.

GEOG. RESTRICTIONS: Southern California.

FINANCIAL DATA:
Amount of support per award: $500 to $2,500.

Total amount of support: Over $15,000.

NO. MOST RECENT APPLICANTS: Approximately 80 for the year 2014-15.

NO. AWARDS: 32 for the year 2014-15.

APPLICATION INFO:
A complete application and financial information form must be accompanied by a letter of recommendation from applicant's music teacher. Applicants must audition in person for an adjudicating panel.

Duration: One year. Recipient must reapply for renewal.

Deadline: October; check online for exact date.

IRS I.D.: 95-2250007

EXECUTIVE OFFICERS:
Margot Smith Thomas, Chairperson of the Board
Walter Zooi, Executive Director

ADDRESS INQUIRIES TO:
Ko-Ni Choi, Programs Associate
(See address above.)

*PLEASE NOTE:
All eight programs are active. YMF currently serves 900 students.

YOUNG MUSICIANS FOUNDATION (YMF) [784]

244 South San Pedro Street
Fifth Floor, Suite 506
Los Angeles, CA 90012
(213) 617-7707
Fax: (213) 617-7706
E-mail: info@ymf.org
Web Site: www.ymf.org

FOUNDED: 1955

AREAS OF INTEREST:
Young musicians, ages 11 to 18, seeking training in chamber music.

NAME(S) OF PROGRAMS:
- **Chamber Music Series (CMS)**

TYPE:
Grants-in-aid; Scholarships. Each year, young musicians are selected through auditions to

receive a grant for a series of coaching sessions with leading professional musicians from the Los Angeles (CA) area.

YEAR PROGRAM STARTED: 1960

PURPOSE:
To promote chamber music training for young musicians.

LEGAL BASIS:
Nonprofit organization.

ELIGIBILITY:
The program is open to talented piano, string, harp, woodwind and brass players through age 18, and auditions are held annually in the fall. Each student receives a scholarship to pay for coaching sessions with one of Los Angeles' finest master teachers.

GEOG. RESTRICTIONS: Southern California.

NO. AWARDS: Approximately 24.

IRS I.D.: 95-2250007

ADDRESS INQUIRIES TO:
Ko-Ni Choi, Programs Associate
(See address above.)

THE LOREN L. ZACHARY SOCIETY FOR THE PERFORMING ARTS [785]

2250 Gloaming Way
Beverly Hills, CA 90210-1717
(310) 276-2731
Fax: (310) 275-8245
E-mail: infoz@zacharysociety.org
Web Site: www.zacharysociety.org

FOUNDED: 1972

AREAS OF INTEREST:
Performing arts, operatic vocal only.

NAME(S) OF PROGRAMS:
- **Annual Loren L. Zachary National Vocal Competition for Young Opera Singers**

TYPE:
Awards/prizes.

YEAR PROGRAM STARTED: 1973

PURPOSE:
To assist in the development of the careers of young opera singers through financial support and performance opportunities.

LEGAL BASIS:
Educational, tax-exempt, nonprofit corporation.

ELIGIBILITY:
Open to singers between the ages of 21 and 35, who have completed proper operatic training and are prepared to pursue professional stage careers. Awards are available only through participation in the annual vocal competition in New York and Los Angeles. All singers with completed applications are guaranteed an audition.

GEOG. RESTRICTIONS: United States and Canada.

FINANCIAL DATA:
Amount of support per award: Top five awards: $15,000, $10,000, $8,000, $6,000 and $4,500.

Total amount of support: Approximately $50,000 to $55,000.

NO. MOST RECENT APPLICANTS: 150.

NO. AWARDS: 10 for the year 2015.

APPLICATION INFO:
Application and rules are available at the web site, or submit a letter requesting audition information and applications in November. Singers must be present in Los Angeles and New York for all phases of the Competition. Recordings are not acceptable. No fax or e-mail requests.

For more information, contact the Competition Director at the phone number above.

Duration: February to May.

Deadline: January (for New York Auditions) and February (for Los Angeles Auditions); exact date varies each year.

PUBLICATIONS:
Application; guidelines.

IRS I.D.: 95-2800160

OFFICERS:
Nedra Zachary, President and Founder
Peter Hubner, Vice President
Allan J. Stephan, Vice President
Sharron Levey, Secretary
Joseph Givens, Treasurer

ADVISORY BOARD:
Tito Capobianco
John DeMain
Stephen De Maio
George Fritthum
Michael Hampe
Ioan Holender
Marilyn Horne
David Hulme
Mrs. George London
Peter Mark
Thea Musgrave
William Wiemhoff
Nedra Zachary

ADDRESS INQUIRIES TO:
Mrs. Nedra Zachary, Director of Competition
(See address above.)

Religion and theology

AMERICAN ACADEMY OF RELIGION [786]

825 Houston Mill Road, N.E.
Suite 300
Atlanta, GA 30329
(404) 727-3049
Fax: (404) 727-7959
E-mail: info@aarweb.org
Web Site: www.aarweb.org

FOUNDED: 1909

AREAS OF INTEREST:
Religion and theology.

NAME(S) OF PROGRAMS:
- **Collaborative Research Grants**
- **Individual Research Grants**
- **International Dissertation Research Grant**

TYPE:
Research grants. Collaborative Research Grants and Individual Research Grants provide support for important aspects of research such as travel to archives and libraries, research assistance, field work and released time. However, funds are not provided for dissertation research.

International Dissertation Research Grants support AAR student members whose dissertation research requires them to travel outside of the country in which their school or university is located. Grants are intended to help candidates complete their doctoral degrees by offsetting costs of travel, lodging, and other dissertation research-related expenses.

YEAR PROGRAM STARTED: 1989

PURPOSE:
To promote research and scholarship in the field of religion; to foster excellence in teaching in the field of religion; to support and encourage members' professional development; to develop programming and participation in AAR regional groups; to advance publication and scholarly communication in the field of religion; to contribute to the public understanding of religion; to welcome the various voices in the field of religion and to support and encourage diversity within the AAR; to help to advance and secure the future of the academic study of religion.

LEGAL BASIS:
501(c)(3).

ELIGIBILITY:
Applicants must be current AAR members who have been in good standing for the previous three years and have not received an AAR Research Award in the previous five years.

FINANCIAL DATA:
Amount of support per award: $500 to $5,000.

APPLICATION INFO:
Individual or Collaborative grant applicants should submit through the Academy's electronic system:
(1) cover page that includes the following: (a) name, (b) institutional affiliation, (c) title of the project and, (d) grant type - Individual or Collaborative;
(2) abstract of 50 words or fewer describing the project;
(3) project budget;
(4) two-page focused description of the research project that details its aims and significance and explains how the award would be used. Collaborative project descriptions should include brief descriptions of the scholarly role of each collaborator and a plan to have the research published and;
(5) curriculum vitae of no more than two pages.

International Dissertation Research Grant applicants must submit:
(1) letter of application (no longer than three pages) that describes their research project and how support for on-site research is critical for the completion of their dissertation;
(2) current curriculum vitae;
(3) proposed budget and project timeline and;
(4) letter of support from their dissertation supervisor.

Duration: Individual or Collaborative Grant: Research projects may be undertaken any time within that academic year and up to the end of the following calendar year. International Dissertation Research Grant: Funds must be expended by the end of the calendar year awarded.

Deadline: Individual or Collaborative Grant: August 1; International Dissertation Grant: December 1.

IRS I.D.: 25-6063005

STAFF:
Elizabeth Hardcastle, Service Coordinator

ADDRESS INQUIRIES TO:
Elizabeth Hardcastle, Service Coordinator
(See address above.)

AMERICAN ACADEMY OF RELIGION [787]

825 Houston Mill Road, N.E.
Suite 300
Atlanta, GA 30329
(404) 727-3049
Fax: (404) 727-7959
E-mail: dminor@aarweb.org
Web Site: www.aarweb.org

FOUNDED: 1909

AREAS OF INTEREST:
To support projects within the regions that promise to benefit the scholarly and professional life of AAR members and the work of the regions.

NAME(S) OF PROGRAMS:

- **Regional Development Grants**

TYPE:
Development grants. Workshops, special programs, training events and other innovative regional projects may be funded through this source.

PURPOSE:
To promote research and scholarship in the field of religion; to foster excellence in teaching in the field of religion; to support and encourage members' professional development; to develop programming and participation in AAR regional groups; to advance publication and scholarly communication in the field of religion; to contribute to the public understanding of religion; to welcome into our conversation the various voices in the field of religion and to support and encourage diversity within the AAR; to help to advance and secure the future of the academic study of religion.

LEGAL BASIS:
501(c)(3).

ELIGIBILITY:
Applicant must be a current member of AAR and maintain their membership throughout the grant period.

GEOG. RESTRICTIONS: United States.

FINANCIAL DATA:
Amount of support per award: Maximum $4,000.

Total amount of support: $10,000.

NO. MOST RECENT APPLICANTS: 15.

NO. AWARDS: 4.

APPLICATION INFO:
Applications should include a narrative description of the project, not to exceed two pages, detailing how the project promises to benefit the scholarly and professional life of AAR members and the work of the region. Please include comments on how these projects or activities may be adapted to other regional groups. The application should state the time period covered by the project and provide a detailed budget (office expenses, travel expenses, honoraria, stipend and other expenses).

Duration: One year.

Deadline: June 1.

IRS I.D.: 20-5478525

ADDRESS INQUIRIES TO:
Regional Coordinator

AMERICAN CATHOLIC HISTORICAL ASSOCIATION [788]

Fordham University, Dealy Hall, Room 637
441 East Fordham Road
Bronx, NY 10458
(718) 817-3830
Fax: (718) 817-5690
E-mail: acha@fordham.edu
Web Site: www.achahistory.org

FOUNDED: 1919

AREAS OF INTEREST:
The history of Catholicism from antiquity to the present.

NAME(S) OF PROGRAMS:

- **ACHA Graduate Student Summer Research Grant**
- **ACHA Junior Faculty Grant**
- **John Tracy Ellis Dissertation Award**
- **Graduate Student Travel Grant**

TYPE:
Awards/prizes; Challenge/matching grants; Conferences/seminars; Research grants; Travel grants. ACHA Graduate Student Summer Research Grant is awarded to an ACHA graduate student member who has completed all requirements for the Doctorate except the dissertation.

ACHA Junior Faculty Grant is awarded to an ACHA tenure-track scholar to assist in summer travel to conduct research.

John Tracy Ellis Dissertation Award memorializes the scholarship and teaching of Monsignor Ellis (1905-1992).

Graduate Student Travel Grant was created in 2010 by the Association from donations from former presidents.

PURPOSE:
To stimulate interest in the history of Catholicism among young scholars.

LEGAL BASIS:
Learned society.

ELIGIBILITY:
ACHA Graduate Student Summer Research Grant: Awarded to an ACHA graduate student member who has completed all requirements for the Doctorate except the dissertation and is attending an accredited institution of higher learning.

Graduate Student Travel Grant: Given on a competitive basis to two graduate students who are current members of the Association and who have papers accepted at either the Annual or Spring meetings.

FINANCIAL DATA:
Amount of support per award: ACHA Graduate Student Summer Research Grant and ACHA Junior Faculty Grant: $1,000 per award; John Tracy Ellis Dissertation Award: A purse of $1,500; Graduate Student Travel Grant: $500.

APPLICATION INFO:
Graduate Student Travel Grant: Applicants should provide a letter formally applying for the grant and detailing the content of his or her paper, a mini-curriculum vitae (one page), and a letter of recommendation from a faculty member (preferably the dissertation director).

Deadline: ACHA Graduate Student Summer Research Grant: Early 2016 (for applying), with notification no later than March 31; ACHA Junior Faculty Grant: Early 2016 (for applying); John Tracy Ellis Dissertation Award: September 30; Graduate Student Travel Grant: Applications should be submitted two months prior to either the Annual or Spring meeting.

ADDRESS INQUIRIES TO:
R. Bentley Anderson, S.J.
Executive Secretary-Treasurer
(See e-mail address above.)

AMERICAN CATHOLIC HISTORICAL ASSOCIATION [789]

Fordham University, Dealy Hall, Room 637
441 East Fordham Road
Bronx, NY 10458
(718) 817-3830
Fax: (718) 817-5690
E-mail: acha@fordham.edu
Web Site: www.achahistory.org

FOUNDED: 1919

AREAS OF INTEREST:
The history of Catholicism from antiquity to the present.

NAME(S) OF PROGRAMS:

- **The Msgr. Harry C. Koenig Award for Catholic Biography**

TYPE:
Awards/prizes. The Msgr. Harry C. Koenig Award for Catholic Biography is offered every two years (in even-numbered years) and recognizes outstanding biographies of members of the Catholic Church who have lived in any age or country.

ELIGIBILITY:
The Prize is awarded in even-numbered years to the author of the book deemed by the Prize Committee to be the best such work published in the two previous calendar years. Entries must have first been published in English.

FINANCIAL DATA:
Amount of support per award: $1,500.

APPLICATION INFO:
Application information is available on the web site.

Deadline: June 1, 2016. Prize is presented in January at the Association's annual meeting.

ADDRESS INQUIRIES TO:
R. Bentley Anderson, S.J.
Executive Secretary-Treasurer
(See e-mail address above.)

AMERICAN CATHOLIC HISTORICAL ASSOCIATION [790]

Fordham University, Dealy Hall, Room 637
441 East Fordham Road
Bronx, NY 10458
(718) 817-3830
Fax: (718) 817-5690
E-mail: acha@fordham.edu
Web Site: www.achahistory.org

FOUNDED: 1919

AREAS OF INTEREST:
The history of Catholicism from antiquity to the present.

NAME(S) OF PROGRAMS:

- **The Peter Guilday Prize**

TYPE:
Awards/prizes; Challenge/matching grants; Conferences/seminars; Travel grants. A prize awarded annually to the author whose article,

dealing with the history of the Catholic Church, is the first of his or her professional career and is judged to be the best of those in that category accepted for publication in any given year by the editors of the *Catholic Historical Review*.

YEAR PROGRAM STARTED: 1972

PURPOSE:
To stimulate interest in the history of Catholicism among young scholars.

LEGAL BASIS:
Learned society.

ELIGIBILITY:
The article must deal with some aspect of the history of the Catholic Church broadly considered. Anyone who has already published an historical book or an article in a learned journal will not be eligible for competition. Articles based on doctoral dissertations will be welcome, provided they are self-contained studies. Manuscripts must not exceed 30 typewritten pages (footnotes included). The author must be a citizen or permanent resident of the U.S. or Canada.

GEOG. RESTRICTIONS: United States and Canada.

FINANCIAL DATA:
Amount of support per award: $250.
Total amount of support: $250 per annum.

NO. MOST RECENT APPLICANTS: 3.

NO. AWARDS: 1 per annum.

APPLICATION INFO:
Inquiries and manuscripts should be sent to the address above.

ADDRESS INQUIRIES TO:
R. Bentley Anderson, S.J.
Executive Secretary-Treasurer
(See e-mail address above.)

AMERICAN CATHOLIC HISTORICAL ASSOCIATION [791]

Fordham University, Dealy Hall, Room 637
441 East Fordham Road
Bronx, NY 10458
(718) 817-3830
Fax: (718) 817-5690
E-mail: acha@fordham.edu
Web Site: www.achahistory.org

FOUNDED: 1919

AREAS OF INTEREST:
The history of Catholicism from antiquity to the present.

NAME(S) OF PROGRAMS:
- **The John Gilmary Shea Prize**

TYPE:
Awards/prizes. This Prize is given annually to the author of a book, published during a preceding 12-month period, which is judged by a committee of experts to have made the most original and distinguished contribution to knowledge of the history of the Catholic Church.

YEAR PROGRAM STARTED: 1945

PURPOSE:
To stimulate interest in the history of Catholicism among young scholars.

LEGAL BASIS:
Learned society.

ELIGIBILITY:
Any author who is a citizen or permanent resident of the U.S. or Canada is eligible to apply. The work submitted must have been published within the calendar year preceding the May 1 submission deadline.

GEOG. RESTRICTIONS: United States and Canada.

FINANCIAL DATA:
Amount of support per award: $1,500.
Total amount of support: $1,500 per annum.

NO. AWARDS: 1 per annum.

APPLICATION INFO:
No formal application is required. Publishers or authors may enter by sending three copies of the work to be considered. Write or e-mail to the above address for further details.
Deadline: The prize is presented each January at the Association's annual meeting.

ADDRESS INQUIRIES TO:
R. Bentley Anderson, S.J.
Executive Secretary-Treasurer
American Catholic Historical Association
(See e-mail address above.)

THE AMY FOUNDATION [792]

P.O. Box 16091
Lansing, MI 48901
(517) 323-6233
E-mail: amyawards@worldmag.com
Web Site: www.amyfound.org
www.worldmag.com/amyawards

FOUNDED: 1976

AREAS OF INTEREST:
Moral and spiritual renewal in America.

NAME(S) OF PROGRAMS:
- **Amy Writing Awards**

TYPE:
Awards/prizes. Program is designed to recognize creative, skillful writing that presents in a sensitive, thought-provoking manner the biblical position on issues affecting the world today.

PURPOSE:
To present biblical truth reinforced with scripture in secular, nonreligious publications.

ELIGIBILITY:
Submitted articles must be published in a secular, journalistic outlet such as a city or college newspaper, a local or national magazine, or a news web site. Articles from personal blogs, newsletters, or religious publications are ineligible, as are books, manuscripts, and works of poetry or fiction. World News Group is the final determiner of eligibility.

Submissions must be published during the calendar year and must contain at least one verse of scripture quoted from an accepted and popular edition of the Bible.

FINANCIAL DATA:
Amount of support per award: First prize: $10,000; second prize: $5,000; third prize: $4,000; fourth prize: $3,000; fifth prize: $2,000; up to 10 prizes of $1,000 each.
Total amount of support: $34,000.

APPLICATION INFO:
A PDF of the article, as published, must be submitted using the online submission form. The PDF must have the byline blacked out (redacted). Complete instructions are available online.
Deadline: Entries must be submitted on or before July 15 for the preceding January to June, and January 15 for the preceding July to December.

ADDRESS INQUIRIES TO:
See e-mail address above.

ATLANTIC SCHOOL OF THEOLOGY [793]

660 Francklyn Street
Halifax NS B3H 3B5 Canada
(902) 423-5592
Fax: (902) 492-4048
E-mail: academicoffice@astheology.ns.ca
Web Site: www.astheology.ns.ca

FOUNDED: 1971

AREAS OF INTEREST:
Any subject offered at the Atlantic School of Theology.

NAME(S) OF PROGRAMS:
- **The Evelyn Hilchie Betts Memorial Fellowship**

TYPE:
Assistantships; Awards/prizes; Conferences/seminars; Development grants; Endowments; Fellowships. The Atlantic School of Theology is an ecumenical university committed to excellence in graduate-level theological education and research. The school is also committed to the provision of training for Christian ministries, both lay and ordained, in church and society, primarily in Atlantic Canada.

PURPOSE:
To enable ordained clergy from the developing world to study at the school for one year and thereby to introduce persons from other Christian communities to the church and theological education in Canada and to share their context with the school.

ELIGIBILITY:
Applicants must be nominated by their denomination. Open to ordained clergy (male or female) from developing countries, who are interested in theological education in an ecumenical atmosphere and are able to speak and write in the English language.

Applicants must be interested in living and working in a Christian community and willing to share their work and experience with the Canadian church. Since the Atlantic School of Theology is a postgraduate school, applicants with university training are encouraged to apply.

FINANCIAL DATA:
Amount of support per award: Up to $18,000 for transportation, tuition, room and board.
Total amount of support: Varies.

NO. MOST RECENT APPLICANTS: 1.

NO. AWARDS: 1 award every two years.

APPLICATION INFO:
Applicants must submit a completed application form along with a letter of support.
Duration: One year.
Deadline: Varies.

ADDRESS INQUIRIES TO:
Academic Office
Atlantic School of Theology
(See address above.)

*SPECIAL STIPULATIONS:
Must return to own country after scholarship year.

THE CHATLOS FOUNDATION, INC. [794]

P.O. Box 915048
Longwood, FL 32791-5048
(407) 862-5077
E-mail: info@chatlos.org
Web Site: www.chatlos.org

FOUNDED: 1953

AREAS OF INTEREST:
Bible colleges, seminaries, religion, liberal arts colleges, medical and social concerns.

TYPE:
General operating grants; Project/program grants; Scholarships; Technical assistance; Training grants. Scholarships are not provided directly to individuals but rather to colleges and seminaries which in turn provide monies to the students of their choice.

YEAR PROGRAM STARTED: 1953

LEGAL BASIS:
Private foundation.

ELIGIBILITY:
The Foundation only funds nonprofit organizations which are tax-exempt for U.S. federal income tax purposes around the globe. Less emphasis on grant requests for bricks and mortar, endowments, conference and administrative expenses and multiyear grants. No grants for medical research, individual church congregations, primary/secondary schools, organizations in existence for less than two years, arts organizations or individuals. Contributions cannot be made to organizations which discriminate on the basis of race, color, sex, creed, age or national origin.

FINANCIAL DATA:
Amount of support per award: Bible colleges: $5,000 to $20,000; Religious causes and medical concerns: $5,000 to $15,000; Liberal arts colleges: $2,500 to $7,500; Social concerns: $2,000 to $5,000.

Initially, the Foundation tends to fund requests for amounts around $10,000.

Total amount of support: $2,261,650 in grants for the year 2015.

NO. MOST RECENT APPLICANTS: 836 for the year 2015.

NO. AWARDS: 322 grants for the year 2015.

APPLICATION INFO:
All requests must be submitted in writing and include the following:
(1) cover letter which includes the specific request amount and project description;
(2) complete proposal (kept brief);
(3) one copy of U.S. IRS tax-exempt status letter;
(4) most recent budget for the organization and;
(5) completed Chatlos Foundation application.

All requests are answered by the Foundation in writing.

Duration: Varies, although multiyear grants are rarely considered.

Deadline: Applications are accepted throughout the year.

PUBLICATIONS:
Application guideline brochure.

IRS I.D.: 13-6161425

BOARD OF DIRECTORS:

ADDRESS INQUIRIES TO:
Grants Administrator
(See address above.)

COLLEGEVILLE INSTITUTE FOR ECUMENICAL AND CULTURAL RESEARCH [795]

2475 Ecumenical Drive
Collegeville, MN 56321
(320) 363-3366
E-mail: staff@collegevilleinstitute.org
Web Site: www.collegevilleinstitute.org

FOUNDED: 1967

AREAS OF INTEREST:
Religion, ecumenism, faith and writing, faith and scholarship, faith and culture.

NAME(S) OF PROGRAMS:
- **Hoyt Fellowship**
- **Kilian McDonnell Fellowship**
- **Pastoral Fellowship**
- **Post-Doctoral Fellowship**
- **Resident Scholars Program**
- **Seminars on Vocation**
- **Summer Writing Workshops**

TYPE:
Awards/prizes; Conferences/seminars; Fellowships; Research grants; Residencies; Visiting scholars. Grant equivalencies are given in the form of living accommodations for Resident Scholars and their families in well-maintained apartments and excellent study facilities, privileges at Saint John's University and dialogue and community experience.

Post-Doctoral Fellowship offers a cash stipend.

YEAR PROGRAM STARTED: 1967

PURPOSE:
To facilitate constructive thought and research which bear upon Christianity, ecumenically understood, and its relation to the cultures of our world.

LEGAL BASIS:
Incorporated in Minnesota.

ELIGIBILITY:
Criteria include completion of graduate work and submission of a research or writing project proposal acceptable to the admissions committee. Award normally made to research scholars who already have the Doctorate, though persons writing doctoral dissertations can be considered. Oriented by tradition and conviction to Christian faith, the Institute welcomes people from other religions.

Applicant for Hoyt Fellowship must be a North American person of color who is writing a doctoral dissertation.

FINANCIAL DATA:
Residency fees include housing for self and family, utilities, spacious private study and Institute program. Fellowships cover residency fees, travel, research and, in some cases, living expenses.

Amount of support per award: Varies by program.

NO. MOST RECENT APPLICANTS: 45.

NO. AWARDS: 15.

APPLICATION INFO:
Applicants must include application form, three letters of recommendation and statement of project.

Duration: September to December semester, January to April semester or full academic year (September to April).

Deadline: Post-Doctoral Fellowship: January 15. All others: January 15. Announcement February 15.

PUBLICATIONS:
Bearings Magazine; annual report; application forms and provisions for Resident Scholars; informational brochures.

IRS I.D.: 41-6059644

STAFF:
Donald B. Ottenhoff, Executive Director

OFFICERS AND BOARD OF DIRECTORS:

ADDRESS INQUIRIES TO:
Carla Durand, Program Manager
(See address above.)

EPISCOPAL CHURCH FOUNDATION [796]

815 Second Avenue, Seventh Floor
New York, NY 10017
(212) 870-2847
(800) 697-2858
Fax: (212) 297-0142
E-mail: ecf@episcopalfoundation.org
Web Site: www.episcopalfoundation.org

FOUNDED: 1949

AREAS OF INTEREST:
Innovative programs in leadership development, education and philanthropy for the clergy and laity of the Episcopal Church.

CONSULTING OR VOLUNTEER SERVICES:
Capital campaigns, planned giving and endowment management services.

NAME(S) OF PROGRAMS:
- **ECF Fellowship Partners Program**

TYPE:
Fellowships. Religious studies. Fellowship Partners Program consists of two tracks: Academic Fellowships and Ministry Fellowships.

YEAR PROGRAM STARTED: 1964

PURPOSE:
To support doctoral study for Episcopalians planning teaching careers in theological education in the Episcopal Church in the U.S.

ELIGIBILITY:
Applications from both lay and ordained Episcopalians are welcome.

Academic Fellowship applicants on the academic track must be engaged in or embarking on a course of study at the graduate level, except for first professional degrees (e.g., M.Div., J.D., M.D.). Acceptable courses of study include doctoral- and Master's-level programs, as well as clinical study or training at the postundergraduate level.

Ministry Fellowship applicants will be asked to demonstrate how their ministry has the potential to transform community at the grassroots level, and special consideration will be given to programs in locations with limited resources or among underserved communities.

GEOG. RESTRICTIONS: United States.

FINANCIAL DATA:

Amount of support per award: Up to $15,000 per year.

Total amount of support: Approximately $100,000 annually.

NO. MOST RECENT APPLICANTS: 4.

NO. AWARDS: 3 to 4.

APPLICATION INFO:

Application information is available on the web site.

Duration: One year. Fellowship is renewable for two more years.

Deadline: March 15. Notification by May 15.

PUBLICATIONS:

ECF Vital Practices.

ADDRESS INQUIRIES TO:

Miguel Escobar, Managing Program Director
(See address above.)

EVANGELICAL LUTHERAN CHURCH IN AMERICA [797]

Congregation and Synodical Mission Unit
8765 West Higgins Road
Chicago, IL 60631-4101
(773) 380-2604
Fax: (773) 380-2750
E-mail: carol.josefowski@elca.org
Web Site: www.elca.org/Our-Work/Leadership/Seminaries/Educational-Grant-Program

FOUNDED: 1988

AREAS OF INTEREST:

Theological education.

NAME(S) OF PROGRAMS:

- **Educational Grant Program**

TYPE:

Scholarships. Educational grants for members of the Evangelical Lutheran Church in America in advanced academic theological education degrees with intent to teach in seminary or university.

YEAR PROGRAM STARTED: 1988

PURPOSE:

To provide support to members of the Evangelical Lutheran Church in America in graduate study that would prepare them to teach in a seminary or college department of religion.

LEGAL BASIS:

Nonprofit religious organization.

ELIGIBILITY:

Applicant church members must have been accepted into an accredited graduate institution, Ph.D. and Th.D. programs in theological areas appropriate to seminary teaching and research. Priority is given to women and Asians, Hispanics, Blacks and Native Americans preparing for leadership in the church and applicants with high potential for making substantial contributions to ministry in the Evangelical Lutheran Church in America.

FINANCIAL DATA:

Amount of support per award: $250 to $3,000.

APPLICATION INFO:

Educational Grant Program application is available online. Application is in the form of a downloadable PDF format. Please note that if applicant is a MAC user, he or she will have to print out the application and mail it to the Grant Administrator (or scan and e-mail it to the Grant Administrator) unless one uses Adobe Acrobat or Adobe Reader.

Duration: Up to five years. Must reapply each year.

Deadline: Late April. Contact Grant Administrator for exact date.

STAFF:

Jonathan Strandjord, Director for Seminaries

ADDRESS INQUIRIES TO:

Carol Josefowski, Grant Administrator
(See address above.)

GENERAL BOARD OF HIGHER EDUCATION AND MINISTRY, THE UNITED METHODIST CHURCH [798]

1001 19th Avenue South
Nashville, TN 37212
(615) 340-7338
Fax: (615) 340-7529
E-mail: mbigord@gbhem.org
Web Site: www.gbhem.org

AREAS OF INTEREST:

Religion.

NAME(S) OF PROGRAMS:

- **Georgia Harkness Scholarships**

TYPE:

Awards/prizes; Scholarships. Awards to encourage women over age 35 to prepare for ordained ministry as an Elder in the United Methodist Church as a second career. The scholarship is to be used for study toward the basic seminary degree in an accredited school of theology.

YEAR PROGRAM STARTED: 1975

PURPOSE:

To support and encourage women for ordained ministry as an Elder in the United Methodist Church.

LEGAL BASIS:

Nonprofit organization.

ELIGIBILITY:

An applicant must be a certified candidate for Elder in the United Methodist Church in the year they are applying. Women over age 35 who have received a Bachelor of Arts or equivalent degree, have been accepted in an accredited school of theology, and have affirmed a specific interest in preparation for ordination as an Elder in the United Methodist Church are eligible.

FINANCIAL DATA:

Amount of support per award: $5,000.

Total amount of support: $55,000 annually.

NO. MOST RECENT APPLICANTS: 60.

NO. AWARDS: 11.

APPLICATION INFO:

Applicants can access the application at the Board web site.

Duration: One year.

Deadline: March 5.

ADDRESS INQUIRIES TO:

Allyson Collinsworth
Director of Loans and Scholarships
(See address above.)

GENERAL COMMISSION ON ARCHIVES AND HISTORY OF THE UNITED METHODIST CHURCH [799]

36 Madison Avenue
Madison, NJ 07940
(973) 408-3189
Fax: (973) 408-3909
E-mail: atday@gcah.org
Web Site: www.gcah.org

FOUNDED: 1968

AREAS OF INTEREST:

History of the United Methodist Church and antecedent bodies.

NAME(S) OF PROGRAMS:

- **John Harrison Ness Memorial Award**

TYPE:

Awards/prizes. Awards to the students of accredited seminaries who submit the best papers on various aspects of United Methodist denominational history. In general, comprehensive subjects on the history of some phase of the denomination will be preferred, but papers on local church or annual conference subjects will be accepted if approved by the professor advising the project.

YEAR PROGRAM STARTED: 1979

PURPOSE:

To stimulate interest in history of the United Methodist Church.

LEGAL BASIS:

Private church-related organization.

ELIGIBILITY:

The paper must have been appraised by the professor of church history under whom the student has been studying and who will submit the paper. The paper must be properly annotated and be a minimum length of 3,000 words. It is desired that the project be undertaken only after the student has had a course in United Methodist history or at least during the enrollment in such.

FINANCIAL DATA:

Amount of support per award: First prize: $500; Second prize: $300.

Total amount of support: $800 annually.

NO. AWARDS: 2.

APPLICATION INFO:

Three copies of the paper will be submitted for judging, two of which will be retained by the Commission.

Duration: Annual. A recipient may resubmit if he or she is still in seminary.

Deadline: February 1. Announcement approximately three months later.

OFFICERS:

Rev. Alfred T. Day, III, General Secretary

ADDRESS INQUIRIES TO:

Rev. Alfred T. Day III, General Secretary
(See address above.)

THE STEWART HUSTON CHARITABLE TRUST [800]

50 South 1st Avenue
Coatesville, PA 19320
(610) 384-2666
Fax: (610) 384-3396
E-mail: admin@stewarthuston.org
Web Site: www.stewarthuston.org

FOUNDED: 1989

AREAS OF INTEREST:
Historic preservation, health and human services, civic and Protestant Christian organizations.

CONSULTING OR VOLUNTEER SERVICES:
General nonprofit organizational issues. Finance and fund-raising.

TYPE:
Capital grants; Challenge/matching grants; General operating grants; Matching gifts; Project/program grants.

YEAR PROGRAM STARTED: 1989

PURPOSE:
To provide funds, technical assistance and collaboration on behalf of nonprofit organizations engaged exclusively in religious, charitable or educational work; to extend opportunities to deserving needy persons.

LEGAL BASIS:
Private foundation.

ELIGIBILITY:
Applicants must be tax-exempt and address a particular community need. Grants are not awarded for scholarship support to individuals, endowment purposes, purchase of tickets or advertising for benefit purposes, coverage of continuing operating deficits, and document publication costs. Support is not provided to intermediate or pass-through organizations (other than United Way), groups such as fraternal organizations, political campaigns, veterans, labor or local civic groups, volunteer fire companies, and groups engaged in influencing legislation.

According to Stewart Huston's Indenture of Trust, 60% of distributions go to Trinitarian/Evangelical organizations as defined by the Chester County Orphans Court: "The grant applicant must be organized and operated exclusively to further religious and charitable activities carried on by Protestant churches, other than Unitarian churches, and affiliated or related organizations; grant proceeds must be used exclusively for one or both of the following two activities: dissemination of the Christian Gospel by preaching and conducting religious services, offering a Christian education, etc.; and promotion of Christian principles through charity."

The remaining 40% is to be distributed for secular purposes.

GEOG. RESTRICTIONS: Chester County, Pennsylvania and Savannah, Georgia areas.

FINANCIAL DATA:
Amount of support per award: Maximum grant: $50,000; Average $5,000 to $10,000.

Total amount of support: $733,300 in grants for the year ended December 31, 2015.

NO. MOST RECENT APPLICANTS: 103.

NO. AWARDS: 44.

REPRESENTATIVE AWARDS:
$35,000 to Calvary Day School; $20,000 to Christ Church; $50,000 to Episcopal Academy; $15,000 to Good Works; $4,000 to Habitat for Humanity of Chester County.

APPLICATION INFO:
Applications must be submitted online. Applicants are encouraged to call and discuss their project with the staff. The application form should be submitted with a grant proposal and include the following attachments:
(1) IRS tax-exemption letter;
(2) Pennsylvania charitable organizations registration certificate (any organization with gross revenue over $25,000, regardless of location). Churches exempt;
(3) by-laws;
(4) last independent financial audit;
(5) list of the organization's major public and private funding sources;
(6) list of the Board of Directors with their community/professional affiliations;
(7) agency's current operating budget;
(8) most recent Form 990 filed with the IRS;
(9) latest annual report;
(10) list of the public and private sources being solicited to fund the project;
(11) detailed project budget;
(12) statement that there has been no change in purpose, character or method of operation since the agency's IRS tax ruling was issued and;
(13) a few examples of media reviews about your agency program.

Duration: No multiyear commitments.

Deadline: April 1 for civic and health organizations; April 1 and October 1 for Protestant Christian organizations.

PUBLICATIONS:
Program announcement; guidelines; annual report.

IRS I.D.: 23-2612599

TRUSTEES:
Charles L. Huston, III
Elinor Lashley
Shelton Sanford

ADDRESS INQUIRIES TO:
Scott G. Huston, Executive Director
(See address above.)

IMMANUEL BIBLE FOUNDATION [801]

1301 South Fell Avenue
Normal, IL 61761
(309) 452-6710
Fax: (309) 862-4121
E-mail: immanuelbiblefoundation@yahoo.com
Web Site: www.ibfoundation.org

FOUNDED: 1944

AREAS OF INTEREST:
Local charities and youth-serving organizations.

TYPE:
General operating grants. Special needs grants.

YEAR PROGRAM STARTED: 1949

PURPOSE:
To promote the gospel and serve as a resource for the Christian community.

LEGAL BASIS:
Tax-exempt private foundation.

ELIGIBILITY:
Tax-exempt organizations, entirely local to the Foundation's immediate area. Out-of-state applications not accepted. No grants to individuals.

GEOG. RESTRICTIONS: McLean County, Illinois.

FINANCIAL DATA:
Amount of support per award: $500.

Total amount of support: Up to $7,500.

APPLICATION INFO:
By letter. Must get form and attach appropriate documentation.

Duration: Varies by need.

Deadline: Applications accepted January 1 to May 1. Announcement by September 1.

IRS I.D.: 37-0688539

ADDRESS INQUIRIES TO:
Annette Klinzing, Executive Director
(See address above.)

KOCH FOUNDATION, INC. [802]

4421 N.W. 39th Avenue
Suite 1-1
Gainesville, FL 32606
(352) 373-7491
Fax: (352) 337-1548
E-mail: staff@thekochfoundation.org
Web Site: www.thekochfoundation.org

FOUNDED: 1979

AREAS OF INTEREST:
Roman Catholic evangelization.

TYPE:
Fellowships; Grants-in-aid; Project/program grants; Training grants. Grants are made for direct evangelization programs, preparation of evangelists, resource-poor Catholic schools that are the principal means of evangelization in the community.

YEAR PROGRAM STARTED: 1979

PURPOSE:
To provide financial support for evangelization efforts to Catholic organizations throughout the world that propagate the Roman Catholic faith.

LEGAL BASIS:
Not-for-profit corporation.

ELIGIBILITY:
U.S. Catholic organizations must be 501(c)(3) and appear in the *Official Catholic Directory*. Non-U.S. Catholic organizations must have a fiscal agent in the U.S. who is willing to disburse grant funds for them, should a grant be awarded.

FINANCIAL DATA:
Amount of support per award: Varies depending on needs and nature of the request; typical grant $15,000.

Total amount of support: $7,205,344 in total support for fiscal year 2015-16.

NO. MOST RECENT APPLICANTS: 605.

NO. AWARDS: 556 approved grants.

APPLICATION INFO:
Application forms are available January 1 to May 1. Briefly describe the project when writing for a grant application. All requests must be in English to assure appropriate attention. Faxed requests are not accepted. Completed applications must be returned within 90 days. Applications must include a budget, a statement of the desired impact on evangelization and, if international, the country and diocese where the program will take place and the U.S. fiscal agent who will be responsible for distributing the funds. Applications for a continuing project must be accompanied by a six-month progress report or yearly evaluation.

Duration: Varies.

Deadline: August 31. Announcement in late March.

PUBLICATIONS:
Application guidelines.

IRS I.D.: 59-1885997

BOARD OF DIRECTORS:
William A. Bomberger, President
Inge L. Vraney, Vice President
Carolyn L. Bomberger, Treasurer
Lawrence E. Vraney, Jr., Assistant Treasurer
Rachel A. Bomberger, Secretary
Michelle H. Bomberger, Assistant Secretary
Matthew A. Bomberger
Charlotte L. Spacinsky
Jeffrey Vraney
Lori Vraney
Maura J. Vraney

ADDRESS INQUIRIES TO:
Executive Director
(See address above.)

LUTHERAN FOUNDATION OF ST. LOUIS [803]

8860 Ladue Road
Suite 200
St. Louis, MO 63124
(314) 231-2244
Fax: (314) 727-7688
E-mail: info@lutheranfoundation.org
Web Site: www.lutheranfoundation.org

FOUNDED: 1984

AREAS OF INTEREST:
Christian voluntarism, congregation social service outreach, Lutheran education, services to ex-offenders and their families, foreign-born populations, and older adults maintaining independence.

TYPE:
Project/program grants.

YEAR PROGRAM STARTED: 1984

PURPOSE:
To provide grant awards in the areas of Christian voluntarism, congregation social service outreach ministry, Lutheran education, prevention and early intervention in children's mental health, and services to prisoners, ex-offenders and their families.

LEGAL BASIS:
Religious foundation.

ELIGIBILITY:
Applicant must be a 501(c)(3), serve the St. Louis metropolitan area, address one or more of the funding focus areas, and complement the Foundation's core values.

The Foundation does not make grants to individuals.

GEOG. RESTRICTIONS: Metropolitan St. Louis, Missouri area.

FINANCIAL DATA:
Amount of support per award: Varies.

Total amount of support: $4,373,346 for the year 2015.

Matching fund requirements: Varies depending on the grant.

NO. AWARDS: 157 for the year 2014.

APPLICATION INFO:
Application information is available on the Foundation's web site.

Duration: Varies.

Deadline: June 1 and December 1. Announcement in August and February, respectively.

IRS I.D.: 43-1379359

BOARD OF DIRECTORS:
Bruce Pompe, Chairperson
Robert E. Beumer, Vice Chairperson
Elizabeth A. Goad, Secretary
Julie Bahr
Karl A. Dunajcik
Robert P. Ensor
Sarah A. Kramer
Cyril D. Loum
Linda L. Moen
Michael S. Murphy
Rev. Dr. Ronald D. Rall
Sharon Rohrbach
Jonathan D. Schultz
Rev. Dr. Scott K. Seidler
Ann L. Vazquez

ADDRESS INQUIRIES TO:
Program Director
(See address above.)

JACOB RADER MARCUS CENTER OF THE AMERICAN JEWISH ARCHIVES [804]

3101 Clifton Avenue
Cincinnati, OH 45220-2408
(513) 221-1875
Fax: (513) 221-7812
E-mail: kproffitt@huc.edu
Web Site: www.americanjewisharchives.org

FOUNDED: 1947

AREAS OF INTEREST:
American and western hemisphere Jewish history.

NAME(S) OF PROGRAMS:
- **The American Jewish Archives Fellowship Program**

TYPE:
Fellowships. The Marcus Center's Fellowship Program provides recipients with month-long fellowships for research and writing at The Jacob Rader Marcus Center of the American Jewish Archives. Fellowship stipends will be sufficient to cover transportation and living expenses while in residence. Applicants must be conducting serious research in some area relating to the history of North American Jewry.

YEAR PROGRAM STARTED: 1977

PURPOSE:
To collect, preserve and publish the history of the American Jewish experience.

LEGAL BASIS:
A division of the Hebrew Union College, Jewish Institute of Religion; tax-exempt.

ELIGIBILITY:
Doctoral and postdoctoral applicants working in the field are eligible.

FINANCIAL DATA:
Grant amount is based upon the individual's research. Fellowship stipends will be sufficient to cover transportation and living expenses while in residence in Cincinnati.

Amount of support per award: Varies.

Total amount of support: Varies.

REPRESENTATIVE AWARDS:
Dr. William Pencak, Pennsylvania State University, "Popular and Political Anti-Semitism in Early America;" Dr. Leonard W. Rogoff, Jewish Heritage Foundation of North Carolina, "A Tale of Two Cities: Race, Riots and Religion in North Carolina, 1898;" Dr. David Dalin, Ave Maria University, FL, "American Jewry and the Republican Party before 1932;" Dr. Raphael Medoff, The David Wyman Institute for Holocaust Studies, "American Jewish Efforts to Solve the Dilemma of Arab-Jewish Relations."

APPLICATION INFO:
In addition to a Fellowship application, Fellowship applicants must provide a research proposal (no more than five typewritten, double-spaced pages), and two recommendations, preferably from academic colleagues (for graduate and doctoral students, one of these recommendations must be from the candidate's dissertation advisor). Research must be done for one month on campus through the archives.

Application should not be made to individually named fellowship funds of the Center. Applicants will be considered for all available Center fellowships.

Prior to completion of the Fellowship applications, the Center strongly recommends that applicants familiarize themselves with its collection. The American Jewish Archives web site contains a list of holdings and a number of finding aids for applicant to peruse. An archivist can be contacted directly for information at the number above (ext. 403).

Duration: Up to one month.

Deadline: February 19.

PUBLICATIONS:
Program description.

STAFF:
Dr. Gary P. Zola, Executive Director
Kevin Proffitt, Program Director

ADDRESS INQUIRIES TO:
Kevin Proffitt
The Director of the Fellowship Program
(See e-mail address above.)

VERNE CATT MCDOWELL CORPORATION [805]

P.O. Box 1336
Albany, OR 97321-0440
(541) 924-0976

FOUNDED: 1963

AREAS OF INTEREST:
Graduate theological education.

NAME(S) OF PROGRAMS:
- **Verne Catt McDowell Scholarship**

TYPE:
Scholarships. Financial assistance for men and women attending an approved seminary to become ordained in the Christian Church (Disciples of Christ) denomination and work actively in that church.

YEAR PROGRAM STARTED: 1966

PURPOSE:
To train men and women to become pastors in the Christian Church (Disciples of Christ) Denomination.

LEGAL BASIS:
Private nonprofit corporation.

ELIGIBILITY:
A graduate from an accredited college and/or university who plans to enter an approved seminary of the Christian Church (Disciples of Christ) is eligible to apply. Study must take place in the U.S. Candidates must plan to be ordained in the Christian Church (Disciples of Christ) Denomination and work actively in that church.

Preference given to students from Oregon.

FINANCIAL DATA:
Amount of support per award: Varies. Approximately $200 to $400 per school month.

Total amount of support: Varies.

NO. MOST RECENT APPLICANTS: 4.

NO. AWARDS: 1 to 3 per year.

APPLICATION INFO:
Write for application and include eligibility and where information regarding program was found.

Duration: Varies with each student; continues support until completion of seminary.

Deadline: May 1. Awards are usually announced after annual meeting in June.

IRS I.D.: 93-6022991

OFFICERS:
Chet Houser, President
Nadine M. Wood, Business Manager

ADDRESS INQUIRIES TO:
Nadine M. Wood, Business Manager
(See address above.)

MEMORIAL FOUNDATION FOR JEWISH CULTURE [806]

50 Broadway, 34th Floor
New York, NY 10004
(212) 425-6606
Fax: (212) 425-6602
E-mail: office@mfjc.org
Web Site: www.mfjc.org

FOUNDED: 1964

AREAS OF INTEREST:
Support for Jewish cultural and educational programs all over the world, in cooperation with universities and established scholarly organizations. Also, annual scholarship and fellowship program.

NAME(S) OF PROGRAMS:
- **International Doctoral Scholarship for Studies Specializing in Jewish Fields**
- **International Fellowship in Jewish Studies and Jewish Culture**

TYPE:
Fellowships; Scholarships. Doctoral scholarships, post-rabbinic scholarships, Fellowships in Jewish culture and Jewish studies.

PURPOSE:
To help assure a creative Jewish future throughout the world by encouraging Jewish scholarship, Jewish education and Jewish cultural creativity; to support communities that are struggling to maintain their Jewish identity; to make possible the training of Jewish men and women for professional careers in communal service in Jewishly deprived communities.

LEGAL BASIS:
IRS Section 501(c)(3) charity; not a private foundation.

ELIGIBILITY:
Individual requirements vary according to the scholarship or fellowship.

FINANCIAL DATA:
Amount of support per award: Up to $10,000 per year. Scholarships and fellowships are given to individuals in amounts which vary according to the cost of living in the grantee's country of residence.

APPLICATION INFO:
Guidelines and application forms for scholarships and fellowships are available on written request to the Foundation at the address above.

Duration: One academic year.

Deadline: October 31 for doctoral scholarships and fellowships.

OFFICERS:
Jeni S. Friedman, Executive Vice President

ADDRESS INQUIRIES TO:
Jeni S. Friedman
Executive Vice President
(See address above.)

THE MUSTARD SEED FOUNDATION

7115 Leesburg Pike, Suite 304
Falls Church, VA 22043
(703) 524-5620
Fax: (703) 533-7340
E-mail: ljackson@msfdn.org
Web Site: www.msfdn.org

TYPE:
Fellowships.

See entry 1518 for full listing.

PONTIFICAL INSTITUTE OF MEDIAEVAL STUDIES

59 Queen's Park Crescent East
Toronto ON M5S 2C4 Canada
(416) 926-7142
Fax: (416) 926-7292
E-mail: allan.smith@utoronto.ca
Web Site: www.pims.ca

TYPE:
Fellowships.

See entry 619 for full listing.

PRESBYTERIAN CHURCH (U.S.A.) [807]

100 Witherspoon Street
Louisville, KY 40202-1396
(502) 569-5224
(800) 728-7228 ext. 5224
Fax: (502) 569-8766
E-mail: finaid@pcusa.org
Web Site: www.pcusa.org/financialaid

NAME(S) OF PROGRAMS:
- **Presbyterian Study Grants**

TYPE:
Grants-in-aid; Scholarships.

PURPOSE:
To assist graduate students who are communicant members of the Presbyterian Church (U.S.A.) in their preparation for professional church occupations.

ELIGIBILITY:
Applicants must demonstrate financial need, be enrolled on a full-time basis, be in good academic standing, be studying in a Presbyterian Church (U.S.A.) seminary, and must be studying in one of the two categories listed below:

(1) students preparing for ordination must be full-time M.Div. and must be enrolled as an inquirer with or received as a candidate by a Presbyterian Church (U.S.A.) presbytery for a church occupation or;

(2) students preparing for occupations as a Christian educator must be full-time M.A.C.E. students.

FINANCIAL DATA:
Grants are meant to be supplemental to other assistance a student has sought and is receiving from presbytery, seminary, home church, etc. Grants are not available for summer study, intern year or studying abroad.

Amount of support per award: Up to $4,000 for the academic year, depending upon demonstrated need and availability of funds.

Total amount of support: Varies.

APPLICATION INFO:
Detailed information and forms are available on the web site.

Duration: One academic year. Renewals possible (annually).

Deadline: Varies.

*SPECIAL STIPULATIONS:
No grants are available for doctoral study.

RASKOB FOUNDATION FOR CATHOLIC ACTIVITIES [808]

P.O. Box 4019
Wilmington, DE 19807
(302) 655-4440
Fax: (302) 655-3223
Web Site: www.rfca.org

FOUNDED: 1945

AREAS OF INTEREST:
Catholic activities.

TYPE:
Challenge/matching grants; Development grants; General operating grants; Project/program grants; Seed money grants; Training grants.

YEAR PROGRAM STARTED: 1945

PURPOSE:
To engage in such exclusively religious, charitable, literary and educational activities as will aid the Roman Catholic Church and institutions and organizations identified with it.

LEGAL BASIS:
Nonprofit foundation.

ELIGIBILITY:
Applicants must be Catholic organizations with nonprofit status.

FINANCIAL DATA:
Amount of support per award: $15,000 for the year 2013.

Total amount of support: $5,215,882 for the year 2013.

NO. MOST RECENT APPLICANTS: 948 for the year 2013.

NO. AWARDS: 302 for the year 2013.

APPLICATION INFO:
Process and requirements for Domestic and International Programs are available on the Foundation's web site.

Duration: Varies.

Deadline: Applications will only be accepted for the spring from December 8 to January 15 and for the fall from June 8 to July 15. Announcement follows May and November Board meetings.

PUBLICATIONS:
Application guidelines.

IRS I.D.: 51-0070060

STAFF:
L. Charles Rotunno, Jr., Executive Vice President-Grants and External Affairs
Theresa G. Robinson, Executive Vice President-Operations and Finance

ADDRESS INQUIRIES TO:
Janine Harlam, Grants Administrator
(See address above.)

DAVID AND SYLVIA STEINER CHARITABLE TRUST [809]

Steiner Equities Group
75 Eisenhower Parkway
Roseland, NJ 07068
(973) 228-5800
Fax: (973) 228-5817

FOUNDED: 1987

AREAS OF INTEREST:
Jewish organizations and higher education.

TYPE:
Project/program grants.

YEAR PROGRAM STARTED: 1987

LEGAL BASIS:
Private foundation.

ELIGIBILITY:
Applicants must be nonprofit entities. Grants are given to religious organizations and for religious education.

GEOG. RESTRICTIONS: New Jersey and New York.

FINANCIAL DATA:
Amount of support per award: Varies.

REPRESENTATIVE AWARDS:
$55,000 to United Jewish Appeal of Metrowest, East Orange, NJ; $20,000 to American Associates of Ben Gurion University of the Negev, New York, NY; $5,000 to National Council of Jewish Women, New York, NY.

APPLICATION INFO:
Applications should be in letter form and must include a statement of purpose, amount requested and a description of the organization.

Duration: One year.

ADDRESS INQUIRIES TO:
Robert Testa, Chief Financial Officer
(See address above.)

SUBCOMMITTEE ON THE HOME MISSIONS [810]

United States Conference of Catholic Bishops
3211 4th Street, N.E.
Washington, DC 20017-1194
(202) 541-5400
Fax: (202) 541-3473
E-mail: homemissions@usccb.org
Web Site: www.usccb.org

FOUNDED: 1924

AREAS OF INTEREST:
Catholic missions in America, including evangelization, catechesis, parish life and personnel training.

TYPE:
General operating grants; Project/program grants; Seed money grants; Training grants. Annual grants to fund home mission activities, such as evangelization through proclamation of the Word, pastoral services, personnel training and the formation of faith communities in the U.S. and its territories. Home mission activities may be centered at the national, regional, diocesan or local level and may address the country as a whole, a particular group of people or a particular place.

YEAR PROGRAM STARTED: 1924

ELIGIBILITY:
Eligible applicants may come from three sources, including (in order of priority) diocesan bishops of home mission dioceses for activities that serve to establish or strengthen the church in their dioceses, heads of national, regional or interdiocesan Catholic organizations for home mission activities that serve the church at a supra-diocesan level and provincials of religious institutes for home mission activities that form part of their apostolate. No funds are available for endowments or loans.

GEOG. RESTRICTIONS: United States and its Caribbean and Pacific territories.

FINANCIAL DATA:
Amount of support per award: Varies depending on needs and nature of the request.

Total amount of support: $9,000,000 for the year 2015.

APPLICATION INFO:
Application materials are available January of each year. Contact office for other requirements.

Duration: Grants are renewable.

Deadline: April 1. Announcement in October. Disbursements are made quarterly January to December.

PUBLICATIONS:
Annual report; guidelines; *Neighbors*, quarterly newsletter.

OFFICERS:
Most Rev. Peter F. Christensen, Chairman
Ms. Jessi Poré, Director

ADDRESS INQUIRIES TO:
Ms. Jessi Poré, Director
Tel: (202) 541-5400
(See e-mail address above.)

*PLEASE NOTE:
Currently considering grants from dioceses only.

UNITARIAN UNIVERSALIST ASSOCIATION OF CONGREGATIONS [811]

24 Farnsworth Street
Boston, MA 02210
(617) 742-2100
Fax: (617) 367-3237
E-mail: scarey@uua.org
Web Site: www.uua.org

FOUNDED: 1961

AREAS OF INTEREST:
Religious liberalism, philosophy, social change, child and family welfare, and ethics.

NAME(S) OF PROGRAMS:

- **Frederic G. Melcher Book Award**

TYPE:
Awards/prizes. Award for the book published in the U.S. during the last calendar year which is judged to make the most significant contribution to religious liberal thought.

YEAR PROGRAM STARTED: 1964

PURPOSE:
To encourage writing in liberal religion.

LEGAL BASIS:
Nonprofit association.

ELIGIBILITY:
Books must be published in the U.S. Any serious book-length publication in the tradition of free inquiry is eligible. Any publisher may submit a candidate. Entries are judged on the basis of scholarship, competence, responsibility and devotion to the ideals of religious liberalism which include freedom, reason and tolerance.

GEOG. RESTRICTIONS: United States.

FINANCIAL DATA:
Amount of support per award: $1,000 and a citation.

Total amount of support: $1,000.

NO. AWARDS: 1.

APPLICATION INFO:
Publishers should contact office for information.

Deadline: December 31.

ADDRESS INQUIRIES TO:
Stephanie Carey Maron
Executive Assistant for the
Office of the President
(See address above.)

*SPECIAL STIPULATIONS:
Recipient is expected to come to Boston to accept the award and make a public appearance, including a speech. Expenses paid.

UNITED JEWISH APPEAL-FEDERATION OF JEWISH PHILANTHROPIES OF NEW YORK [812]

130 East 59th Street
New York, NY 10022
(212) 980-1000
(212) 836-1321
Fax: (212) 836-1353
E-mail: feinsteinl@ujafedny.org
Web Site: www.ujafedny.org

FOUNDED: 1917

AREAS OF INTEREST:
Human services, Jewish identity and education, rescue and resettlement of Jewish communities in distress.

CONSULTING OR VOLUNTEER SERVICES:
Offers numerous opportunities to volunteer. Please call Resource Line: (212) 836-1447.

TYPE:
Awards/prizes; Block grants; Capital grants; Challenge/matching grants; Conferences/seminars; Demonstration grants; Development grants; Fellowships; General operating grants; Internships; Matching gifts; Project/program grants; Research grants; Scholarships; Technical assistance; Travel grants; Research contracts.

YEAR PROGRAM STARTED: 1917

PURPOSE:
To care for people in need; to inspire a passion for Jewish life and learning; to strengthen Jewish communities in New York, in Israel, and around the world.

LEGAL BASIS:
501(c)(3).

ELIGIBILITY:
No grants to individuals. Applicants must be 501(c)(3) organizations.

GEOG. RESTRICTIONS: New York including the five boroughs, Nassau, Suffolk and Westchester counties.

FINANCIAL DATA:
Amount of support per award: Varies depending upon needs and nature of the request.

Total amount of support: Approximately $135,300,000 for the year 2014-15.

APPLICATION INFO:
Application form required. Organizations must include documentation of IRS nonprofit status with their application.

Duration: One year. Renewal possible.

Deadline: January 15, 2017.

PUBLICATIONS:
Annual Report to the Community.

IRS I.D.: 51-0172429

STAFF:
Alex Bebeshko, Grant Manager

ADDRESS INQUIRIES TO:
E-mail: grants@ujafedny.org

UNITED METHODIST COMMUNICATIONS

810 12th Avenue South
Nashville, TN 37203-4704
(888) 278-4862
Fax: (615) 742-5423
E-mail: scholarships@umcom.org
Web Site: www.umcom.org

TYPE:
Fellowships. Assists one United Methodist student in postgraduate study at an accredited U.S. college or university who intends to pursue a career in religious journalism.

See entry 1900 for full listing.

THE WABASH CENTER FOR TEACHING AND LEARNING IN THEOLOGY AND RELIGION [813]

301 West Wabash Avenue
Crawfordsville, IN 47933
(765) 361-6047
Fax: (765) 361-6051
E-mail: wabashcenter@wabash.edu
Web Site: www.wabashcenter.wabash.edu

FOUNDED: 1995

AREAS OF INTEREST:
Teaching religion and theology, higher education pedagogy in theology and religion.

NAME(S) OF PROGRAMS:

- **Educational Environments**
- **Faculty Practices and Vocation**
- **Teaching and Learning Resources**

TYPE:
Conferences/seminars; Fellowships; Project/program grants; Research grants.

YEAR PROGRAM STARTED: 1995

PURPOSE:
To strengthen and enhance the teaching of religion and theology in North American theological schools, colleges and universities.

ELIGIBILITY:
Full-time faculty members in religion departments of colleges and universities in North America and in theological schools accredited by the Association of Theological Schools are eligible to apply for these grants.

GEOG. RESTRICTIONS: United States and Canada.

FINANCIAL DATA:
Amount of support per award: Up to $30,000.

NO. MOST RECENT APPLICANTS: 127.

NO. AWARDS: 70.

APPLICATION INFO:
Grant proposals should consist of an application form, project proposal (including budget) and letter of support. Specific format for grant proposals is explained in detail on the Center's web site.

Deadline: March 1 and October 1 annually.

PUBLICATIONS:
Teaching Theology and Religion, published quarterly by Wiley-Blackwell Publishers.

ADDRESS INQUIRIES TO:
Paul O. Myhre, Associate Director
(See address above.)

INTERNATIONAL AFFAIRS AND AREA STUDIES

International affairs and area studies

AMERICAN INSTITUTE OF PAKISTAN STUDIES [814]

University of Wisconsin-Madison
B488 Medical Sciences Center
1300 University Avenue
Madison, WI 53706
(608) 265-1471
Fax: (608) 265-3302
E-mail: aips@pakistanstudies-aips.org
Web Site: www.pakistanstudies-aips.org

FOUNDED: 1973

AREAS OF INTEREST:
All fields of humanities and social sciences if engaged in research on Pakistan and relations between Pakistan and other countries.

NAME(S) OF PROGRAMS:
- **AIPS Post Doctoral Fellowship**
- **AIPS Pre-Doctoral Fellowship**

TYPE:
Awards/prizes; Conferences/seminars; Fellowships; Travel grants; Visiting scholars. Awarded in several categories including predoctoral research, postdoctoral study, library service and professional development.

YEAR PROGRAM STARTED: 1973

PURPOSE:
To promote research on Pakistan.

ELIGIBILITY:
Applicants must be scholars and advanced graduate students who are American citizens and are engaged in research on Pakistan in ancient, medieval and modern times, in all fields of the humanities and social sciences. Research topics comparing aspects of Pakistan with other Muslim countries are especially encouraged.

Graduate student applicants must have fulfilled all residence, language and preliminary examination requirements for the Doctorate and have an approved dissertation topic.

FINANCIAL DATA:
The award will provide a maintenance allowance for the scholar and dependents, plus travel and other benefits.

Amount of support per award: Varies.

Total amount of support: $65,000.

NO. MOST RECENT APPLICANTS: 15.

NO. AWARDS: Varies.

APPLICATION INFO:
Predoctoral applications should include a proposal (five pages), curriculum vitae, a transcript, a letter from the dissertation advisor and contact information for two references. Postdoctoral applications should include a proposal (five pages), curriculum vitae, and contact information for two referees.

A nonrefundable processing fee of $30 must be included with the completed application form. Any forms that are incomplete will be returned without refund of the application fee.

Duration: Two to nine months.

Deadline: Varies.

STAFF:
Laura Hammond, U.S. Director

ADDRESS INQUIRIES TO:
Laura Hammond, U.S. Director
(See address above.)

THE KATHRYN AMES FOUNDATION [815]

c/o Pierson & Pierson
305 West Chesapeake Avenue, Suite 308
Towson, MD 21204
(410) 821-3006
Fax: (410) 821-3007
E-mail: info@kathrynames.org
Web Site: www.kathrynames.org

FOUNDED: 1993

AREAS OF INTEREST:
Israel, education, health care, poverty relief and pluralism.

TYPE:
General operating grants; Project/program grants.

YEAR PROGRAM STARTED: 1993

PURPOSE:
To benefit organizations located in Israel which are working for charitable and benevolent purposes.

LEGAL BASIS:
Private foundation.

ELIGIBILITY:
Eligible organizations must be nonprofit and located in Israel.

GEOG. RESTRICTIONS: Israel.

FINANCIAL DATA:
Amount of support per award: $5,000 to $40,000.

Total amount of support: $479,000 for the year 2014.

NO. AWARDS: 28 for the year 2014.

APPLICATION INFO:
Application form is available online.

Duration: Typically one year.

PUBLICATIONS:
Application guidelines.

ADDRESS INQUIRIES TO:
Lu Pierson, Grants Administrator
(See address above.)

ARCHAEOLOGICAL INSTITUTE OF AMERICA [816]

656 Beacon Street, 6th Floor
Boston, MA 02215
(617) 358-4184
Fax: (617) 353-6550
E-mail: fellowships@aia.bu.edu
Web Site: www.archaeological.org

FOUNDED: 1879

AREAS OF INTEREST:
Archaeological research and publication.

NAME(S) OF PROGRAMS:
- **The Archaeology of Portugal Fellowship**

TYPE:
Fellowships. The Fellowship supports projects pertaining to the archaeology of Portugal. These include, but are not limited to, research projects, colloquia, symposia, publication, research-related travel, or travel to academic meetings for the purpose of presenting papers on the archaeology of Portugal.

PURPOSE:
To promote archaeological studies pertaining to Portugal.

ELIGIBILITY:
Portuguese, American and other international scholars are invited to apply.

FINANCIAL DATA:
Amount of support per award: Award may vary based on the merit of the proposal. Typically $4,000.

Total amount of support: $4,000 to $8,000.

NO. MOST RECENT APPLICANTS: 11.

NO. AWARDS: 3.

APPLICATION INFO:
Application information is available on the web site.

Duration: One year; work to be conducted between July 1 of the award year and the following June 30.

Deadline: November 1. Announcement by February 1.

ADDRESS INQUIRIES TO:
Laurel Nilsen Sparks
Lecture and Fellowship Coordinator
(See address above.)

ASHBURN INSTITUTE INC. [817]

198 Okatie Village Drive
Suite 103, PMB 301
Bluffton, SC 29909
(703) 728-6482
Fax: (843) 705-7643
E-mail: info@ashburninstitute.org
Web Site: www.ashburninstitute.org

FOUNDED: 1940

AREAS OF INTEREST:
International relations, political science, Middle Eastern studies, and international security.

NAME(S) OF PROGRAMS:
- **Frank Educational Fund**

TYPE:
Research grants; Scholarships.

YEAR PROGRAM STARTED: 1991

PURPOSE:
To support the study of federalism and international integration at the graduate and postgraduate level.

ELIGIBILITY:
Open to graduate students of good academic standing working on a thesis or dissertation relating to international integration and federalism or doing coursework that places major weight on international integration and federalism. International (foreign institutions) graduate students are eligible, as well as U.S. students.

FINANCIAL DATA:
Amount of support per award: $1,000 to $2,000.

Total amount of support: $20,000 annually.

APPLICATION INFO:
Application information can be found on the Institute's web site. Please submit abstract paper for consideration at the International Conference.

Deadline: Determined by future conference dates.

ADDRESS INQUIRIES TO:
Frank Fund Manager
(See address above.)

AUSTRO-AMERICAN ASSOCIATION OF BOSTON [818]

67 Bridle Path
Sudbury, MA 01776
(978) 579-2191
E-mail: scholarship@austria-boston.org
Web Site: www.austria-boston.org

FOUNDED: 1944

AREAS OF INTEREST:
All aspects of Austrian society, especially culture; Austrian-American relations.

TYPE:
Research grants; Scholarships. Scholarship award provides support for a project relating to Austrian music, history, literature, science, art, architecture, contemporary life or other aspects of the Austrian contribution to culture.

YEAR PROGRAM STARTED: 1976

PURPOSE:
To further interest in Austrian culture.

LEGAL BASIS:
Organized and established as of July 6, 1970 by the Secretary of the Commonwealth.

ELIGIBILITY:
The project must be related to Austria.

Undergraduate or graduate students at New England colleges or universities are eligible. They must be willing to present the results of their project at an event of the Austro-American Association.

GEOG. RESTRICTIONS: New England.

FINANCIAL DATA:
The scholarship award does not support tuition or other expenses related to a course of study.

Amount of support per award: $3,000.

Total amount of support: $3,000.

NO. AWARDS: 1 per year (when funds are available).

APPLICATION INFO:
Applications should include a curriculum vitae, a detailed description of the proposed project and two letters of recommendation from faculty members well acquainted with the applicant's background and potential. Applicants will be invited to present the results of their project at a meeting of the Association. A personal interview will be required.

Deadline: March 4.

OFFICERS:
Traude Schieber-Acker, President
Marta Stasa, Vice President
Hana Sittler, Treasurer
Judy Zohn, Secretary

ADDRESS INQUIRIES TO:
Traude Schieber-Acker, President and Chairperson, Scholarship Panel
Austro-American Association of Boston, Inc.
(See address and e-mail above.)

*PLEASE NOTE:
E-mail correspondence and electronic submission are requested.

CENTER FOR INTERNATIONAL SECURITY AND COOPERATION (CISAC) [819]

Freeman Spogli Institute for International Studies
Stanford University
Encina Hall, C206-10, 616 Serra Street
Stanford, CA 94305-6165
(650) 725-5365
Fax: (650) 724-5683
E-mail: cisacfellowship@stanford.edu
Web Site: cisac.fsi.stanford.edu/docs/cisac_fellowships

FOUNDED: 1970

AREAS OF INTEREST:
CISAC fellows may focus on any of the following topics: nuclear weapons policy and nonproliferation; nuclear energy; cybersecurity, cyberwarfare, and the future of the Internet; biosecurity and global health; implications of geostrategic shifts; insurgency, terrorism, and homeland security; war and civil conflict; consolidating peace after conflict; as well as global governance, migration, and transnational flows, from norms to criminal trafficking. CISAC welcomes other research proposals on international security topics.

NAME(S) OF PROGRAMS:
- **Cybersecurity and International Security Fellowship**
- **Law and International Security Fellowship**
- **The MacArthur Foundation Nuclear Security Fellowship**
- **Natural Sciences or Engineering International Security Fellowship**
- **The William J. Perry Fellowship in International Security**
- **Social Sciences or Humanities International Security Fellowship**
- **The Stanton Nuclear Security Fellowship**

TYPE:
Fellowships.

PURPOSE:
To produce policy-relevant research on international security topics; to teach and train the next generation of security specialists; to influence policymaking in international security; to develop a more informed public discussion.

LEGAL BASIS:
University.

ELIGIBILITY:
Must be in Ph.D. program, have a Ph.D. or equivalent, or extraordinary professional experience.

FINANCIAL DATA:
Amount of support per award: Varies.

Total amount of support: Varies.

NO. MOST RECENT APPLICANTS: Over 200.

NO. AWARDS: 10 to 20.

APPLICATION INFO:
Application information is available on the CISAC web site.

Duration: Nine to 11 months.

Deadline: January 16.

ADDRESS INQUIRIES TO:
CISAC Fellowship Program
(See address above.)

CENTER FOR U.S. - MEXICAN STUDIES, UNIVERSITY OF CALIFORNIA, SAN DIEGO [820]

School of Global Policy and Strategy
9500 Gilman Drive, No. 0519
La Jolla, CA 92093-0519
(858) 822-1696
Fax: (858) 534-6447
E-mail: usmex@ucsd.edu
Web Site: usmex.ucsd.edu

FOUNDED: 1979

AREAS OF INTEREST:
The study of U.S. and Mexico relations and the study of Mexico within the social sciences and history.

NAME(S) OF PROGRAMS:
- **USMEX Visiting Fellows Program**

TYPE:
Fellowships; Professorships.

YEAR PROGRAM STARTED: 1980

PURPOSE:
To support the write-up of a Ph.D. dissertation or the write-up of a postdoctoral research project.

ELIGIBILITY:
Open to Mexican citizens, advanced graduate students, junior faculty and advanced faculty members from any campus of the University of California system, as well as other institutions.

GEOG. RESTRICTIONS: United States and Mexico.

FINANCIAL DATA:
Amount of support per award: Stipends average $22,500 for the academic year.

Total amount of support: $150,000.

APPLICATION INFO:
Applicants must submit a one-page letter of intent describing the work to be completed during residence. Letters are to be submitted by e-mail to Greg Mallinger, Fellows Coordinator, gmallinger@ucsd.edu.

Duration: Four to nine months. Former Visiting Fellows are eligible to apply again after five years.

Deadline: January.

ADDRESS INQUIRIES TO:
Greg Mallinger, Fellows Coordinator
(See address above.)

THE CHRISTENSEN FUND

487 Bryant Street
Second Floor
San Francisco, CA 94107
(415) 644-1630
Fax: (415) 644-1601
E-mail: info@christensenfund.org
Web Site: www.christensenfund.org

TYPE:
General operating grants; Project/program grants; Research grants.

See entry 64 for full listing.

COUNCIL FOR EUROPEAN STUDIES AT COLUMBIA UNIVERSITY [821]

420 West 118th Street, MC 3307
New York, NY 10027
(212) 854-4172
Fax: (212) 854-8808
E-mail: info@ces-europe.org
Web Site: councilforeuropeanstudies.org

FOUNDED: 1970

AREAS OF INTEREST:
The study of Europe.

NAME(S) OF PROGRAMS:
- **Book Award**
- **CES Small Event Grants**
- **Conference Travel Grants**
- **Council for European Studies Pre-Dissertation Research Fellowships**
- **European Studies Undergraduate Paper Prize**
- **First Article Prize in Humanities and Social Sciences**
- **Mellon-CES Dissertation Completion Fellowship in European Studies**

TYPE:
Awards/prizes; Conferences/seminars; Fellowships; Internships; Scholarships; Travel grants. The CES Book Award honors talented emerging scholars with an award for the best first book on any subject in European studies. The award is given every two years.

CES Conference Travel Grants support transcontinental travel for junior faculty and graduate students already scheduled to present at the Council's International Conference of Europeanists.

CES Small Event Grants support workshops, lectures, symposia and other small events that share research on Europe with a wider community.

Council for European Studies Pre-Dissertation Research Fellowships are intended to fund student's first major research project in Europe.

European Studies Undergraduate Paper Prize is designed to encourage interest in the field of European studies by rewarding talented undergraduates who have conducted original research in the field.

First Article Prize awards one prize to a scholar working in the humanities and one to a scholar working in the social sciences. These prizes will honor the writers of the best first articles on European studies published within a two-year period.

Mellon-CES Dissertation Completion Fellowships are intended to facilitate the timely completion of the doctoral degree by late-stage graduate students focused on topics in European studies.

YEAR PROGRAM STARTED: 1971

ELIGIBILITY:
Book Award: Must be scholar's first book on any subject in European studies. Books may be nominated by the author, a CES member, or by a publisher.

Pre-Dissertation Research Fellowships are limited to graduate students currently enrolled in a doctoral program at a university that is a member of the Council for European Studies Academic Consortium. Member universities and additional eligibility requirements can be found online.

First Article Prize nominees meet the following criteria:
(1) be the first article published by the nominee in the field of European studies in a peer-reviewed journal;
(2) be published between January 1, 2014 and December 31, 2015;
(3) be the work of one author only or be an article on which the nominee is the first author and;
(4) be authored by a member of the Council for European Studies or a faculty/student of an institution that is a member.
Nominations may be submitted by the publisher, editor, author, or admiring colleagues.

To be eligible for the Mellon-CES Dissertation Completion Fellowship, the applicant must be ABD, be enrolled at a higher education institution in the U.S., and can have no more than one full year of dissertation work remaining at the start of the fellowship year as certified by his or her dissertation advisor. The applicant must also have exhausted the dissertation completion funding normally provided by his or her academic department or university, and he or she must be working on a topic within or substantially overlapping European studies. To be eligible to receive the fellowship, applicants must also be enrolled in an institution that is a member of the CES Academic Consortium. However, students whose universities are not currently members of the CES consortium may apply, but they are encouraged to apply early in the application season so that every effort may be made to enroll the institution in the CES member consortium and, thus, establish the student's eligibility by the application deadline.

FINANCIAL DATA:
Book Award recipient receives a certificate, $1,000 and all-expenses-paid trip to International Conference and award ceremony. Fellowship recipients receive a stipend, travel support for attending and presenting at the CES International Conference of Europeanists, and the opportunity to publish in *Perspectives on Europe*.

Amount of support per award: Book Award: $1,000; CES Small Event Grants: $300 to $1,500; Conference Travel Grant: equivalent of $725, $500 cash grant and waiver of registration fee; European Studies Undergraduate Paper Prize and First Article Prize: $500; Mellon-CES Dissertation Completion Fellowship: $25,000 stipend to be paid in six bimonthly installments; Pre-Dissertation Research Fellowship: $4,000 stipend.

Total amount of support: Varies.

APPLICATION INFO:
Applications and guidelines are available online.

Deadline: Book Award: Early October; CES Small Event Grants: October and June; European Studies Undergraduate Paper Prize: Spring; First Article Prize: Nomination mid-April or before; Mellon-CES Dissertation Completion Fellowship and Pre-Dissertation Research Fellowship: January.

COUNCIL FOR INTERNATIONAL EXCHANGE OF SCHOLARS (CIES) [822]

1400 K Street, N.W.
Suite 700
Washington, DC 20005
(202) 686-6240
Fax: (202) 362-3442
E-mail: ckocinskimulder@iie.org
Web Site: www.cies.org/sir

FOUNDED: 1947

AREAS OF INTEREST:
Humanities or social sciences, or any field that will benefit from an international perspective.

NAME(S) OF PROGRAMS:
- **Fulbright Scholar-in-Residence Program**

TYPE:
Awards/prizes; Exchange programs; Visiting scholars. Grants support a visiting lecturer from outside the U.S. to teach regular courses or develop new ones, team teach or participate in special seminars or serve as a resource to faculty and students and, through outreach, to the community at large.

PURPOSE:
To initiate or develop international programs at colleges and universities by using a foreign scholar-in-residence to internationalize the curriculum, set up global studies or area-specific programs or otherwise expand contacts of students and faculty with other cultures and to strengthen or enrich existing international or area studies programs.

LEGAL BASIS:
Public Law 87-256, as amended, The Mutual Educational and Cultural Exchange Act of 1961.

ELIGIBILITY:
U.S. colleges and universities, including community colleges, are invited to submit proposals to obtain a foreign scholar-in-residence. Preference is given to proposals in the humanities or social sciences, although other fields focusing on international issues will be considered.

GEOG. RESTRICTIONS: United States.

FINANCIAL DATA:
Monthly stipend as well as round-trip international travel, excess baggage allowance, accident and sickness insurance, and allowances for books, professional development and dependents.

Amount of support per award: Approximately $2,710 to $3,145 per month, depending on the cost of living in the city where the scholar will reside.

Total amount of support: Over $1,000,000 for the year 2015.

Matching fund requirements: Some cost sharing by the host institution is encouraged, either supplementary funding or in-kind support, such as housing.

CO-OP FUNDING PROGRAMS: U.S. Department of State.

NO. AWARDS: 30 to 35.

APPLICATION INFO:
Guidelines are available in March. Application must be submitted online.

Duration: One semester to one academic year.

Deadline: October 15.

PUBLICATIONS:
Directory of Visiting Scholars; descriptive brochure; annual report.

ADDRESS INQUIRIES TO:
Cecilia Kocinski-Mulder, Program Officer
(See address above.)

COUNCIL FOR INTERNATIONAL EXCHANGE OF SCHOLARS (CIES) [823]

1400 K Street, N.W.
Suite 700
Washington, DC 20005-2403
(202) 686-6240
Fax: (202) 686-4029
E-mail: fulspec@iie.org
Web Site: www.cies.org/specialist

FOUNDED: 1947

AREAS OF INTEREST:
Scholarly exchange.

NAME(S) OF PROGRAMS:
- **Fulbright Specialist Program**

TYPE:
Exchange programs; Project/program grants. The Fulbright Specialist Program is designed to provide short-term project opportunities for U.S. faculty and professionals. Grant recipients have a chance to participate in a variety of new and exciting activities: collaborate with counterparts in other countries on curriculum and faculty development, assist in institutional planning, deliver a series of lectures or provide other expertise, etc.

YEAR PROGRAM STARTED: 2001

PURPOSE:
To promote mutual understanding and scholarship.

LEGAL BASIS:
Private, nonprofit organization that receives funding from the U.S. State Department.

ELIGIBILITY:
The Fulbright Specialist Program is open to qualified U.S. scholars and professionals in various fields. Applicants will be considered without regard to race, color, religion, sex, age, national origin and/or physical impairment.

Applicants must meet all of the following minimum eligibility requirements:
(1) U.S. citizen at the time of application; permanent resident status is not sufficient;
(2) for academics, a Ph.D. or equivalent professional/terminal degree at the time of application plus a minimum of five years of postdoctoral teaching or professional experience in the field in which person is applying;
(3) for professionals and artists outside academe, recognized professional standing and substantial professional accomplishments plus a minimum of five years of professional experience in the field in which person is applying;
(4) disclosure of prior conviction, current indictment or arrest for commission of a felony or misdemeanor (excluding minor traffic violations); prior conviction or current indictment may result in disqualification and;
(5) U.S. residency required at the time of selection for a grant.

In matching candidates with grant opportunities, preference will be given to candidates with the most relevant professional experience.

FINANCIAL DATA:
Grants awarded will include travel and per diem plus a $200 per day honorarium. Per diem costs, which are in-country costs for lodging, meals and in-country transportation, will be covered by the host institution.

Amount of support per award: Varies.

NO. MOST RECENT APPLICANTS: 600.

NO. AWARDS: Approximately 350 to 450 per year.

APPLICATION INFO:
Qualified U.S. scholars and professionals apply throughout the calendar year for candidacy on the Fulbright Specialists Roster. Peer review is conducted six times each year. CIES builds lists of qualified Specialist candidates for each eligible discipline and facilitates matching Specialist candidates with project requests. There is a two-tier application process for U.S. scholars.

Non-U.S. postsecondary degree-granting academic institutions and other eligible institutions with education-focused programming submit Specialist project requests through the appropriate Fulbright agency in their country. Once approved by the Fulbright Commission or U.S. Embassy, the Specialist project request is forwarded to the U.S. Department of State for final approval.

Duration: Two to six weeks.

ADDRESS INQUIRIES TO:
Cecilia Kocinski-Mulder, Program Officer
E-mail: ckocinskimulder@iee.org

COUNCIL FOR INTERNATIONAL EXCHANGE OF SCHOLARS (CIES)

1400 K Street, N.W.
Suite 700
Washington, DC 20005
(202) 686-4000
Fax: (202) 686-4029
E-mail: scholars@iie.org
Web Site: www.cies.org

TYPE:
Awards/prizes. There are approximately 40 distinguished chair awards in 18 countries. Awards available in a wide variety of disciplines.

See entry 1572 for full listing.

COUNCIL ON FOREIGN RELATIONS [824]

58 East 68th Street
New York, NY 10065
(212) 434-9740
Fax: (212) 434-9870
E-mail: fellowships@cfr.org
Web Site: www.cfr.org/fellowships

FOUNDED: 1921

AREAS OF INTEREST:
International relations, international affairs, Japan, U.S.-Japan relations, U.S.-Japan politics, Japanese studies, Japanese-American relations, foreign policy, policymaking, and public service.

NAME(S) OF PROGRAMS:
- **International Affairs Fellowship in Japan (IAF-J)**

TYPE:
Fellowships. The International Affairs Fellowship in Japan (IAF-J), sponsored by Hitachi, Ltd., provides a selected group of midcareer U.S. citizens the opportunity to expand their professional horizons by spending a period of research or other professional activity in Japan. Fellows are drawn from academia, business, government, media, NGOs and think tanks. In cooperation with the Council on Foreign Relations (CFR), the program's sponsor, Hitachi, Ltd., assists fellows in finding suitable host organizations in Japan.

YEAR PROGRAM STARTED: 1997

PURPOSE:
To strengthen mutual understanding and cooperation between the rising generations of leaders in the U.S. and Japan.

ELIGIBILITY:
The IAF-J is only open to U.S. citizens between the ages of 27 and 45. The program is intended primarily for those without substantial prior experience in Japan, although the selection committee has made exceptions when it considered that the fellowship would allow an individual to add a significant new dimension to his or her career. Knowledge of the Japanese language is not a requirement.

FINANCIAL DATA:
The program awards a stipend in yen, which covers travel and living expenses in Japan. Fellows are considered independent contractors rather than employees of CFR, and are not eligible for employment benefits, including health insurance.

CO-OP FUNDING PROGRAMS: Hitachi, Ltd.

NO. AWARDS: Approximately 3 to 5 per year.

APPLICATION INFO:
Interested candidates who meet the program's eligibility requirements can apply online via the CFR web site between June 1 and October 1 on an annual basis. Candidates who are selected as IAF-J finalists will be notified between December and January, with finalist interviews scheduled in Washington, DC, and New York, NY, between January and February. Official selections and announcement of IAF-J awards will be made between February and March.

Duration: Three to 12 months.

Deadline: October 31.

ADDRESS INQUIRIES TO:
See telephone or e-mail address above.

COUNCIL ON FOREIGN RELATIONS

58 East 68th Street
New York, NY 10065
(212) 434-9740
Fax: (212) 434-9870
E-mail: fellowships@cfr.org
Web Site: www.cfr.org/fellowships

TYPE:
Fellowships. The Edward R. Murrow Press Fellow spends nine months full-time in residence at the Council on Foreign Relations' (CFR) headquarters in New York. The program enables the fellow to engage in sustained analysis and writing, expand his or her intellectual and professional horizons, and extensively participate in CFR's active program of meetings and events. The Fellow will be part of the David Rockefeller Studies Program, CFR's think tank, alongside the program's full-time, adjunct and visiting fellows, whose expertise extends across the broad range of significant foreign policy issues facing the U.S. and the international community.

See entry 1869 for full listing.

COUNCIL ON FOREIGN RELATIONS [825]

58 East 68th Street
New York, NY 10065
(212) 434-9740
Fax: (212) 434-9800
E-mail: fellowships@cfr.org
Web Site: www.cfr.org/fellowships

FOUNDED: 1921

AREAS OF INTEREST:
International affairs, international relations, policymaking, U.S. foreign policy, foreign affairs, public service, government, and academia.

NAME(S) OF PROGRAMS:
- **International Affairs Fellowship (IAF)**

TYPE:
Fellowships. The International Affairs Fellowship (IAF) Program aims to strengthen career development by helping outstanding individuals acquire and apply foreign policy skills beyond the scope of their professional and scholarly achievements. The distinctive character of the IAF Program lies in the contrasting professional experiences fellows obtain through their 12-month appointment. Selected fellows from academia and the private sector spend fellowship tenures in public service and policy-oriented settings, while government officials spend their tenures in a scholarly atmosphere free from operational pressure.

YEAR PROGRAM STARTED: 1967

PURPOSE:
To assist midcareer scholars and professionals in advancing their analytic capabilities and broadening their foreign policy experience.

ELIGIBILITY:
The IAF Program is only open to U.S. citizens and permanent residents between the ages of 27 and 35 who are eligible to work in the U.S. CFR does not sponsor for visas. While a Ph.D. is not a requirement, selected fellows generally hold an advanced degree and possess a strong record of work experience as well as a firm grounding in the field of foreign policy. The program does not fund pre- or postdoctoral research, work toward a degree, or the completion of projects for which substantial progress has been made prior to the Fellowship period.

FINANCIAL DATA:
Fellows are considered independent contractors rather than employees of CFR, and are not eligible for employment benefits, including health insurance.

Amount of support per award: Stipend of $95,000.

NO. AWARDS: Approximately 10 annually.

APPLICATION INFO:
Interested candidates who meet the program's eligibility requirements can apply online via the Council web site between June 1 and October 1 on an annual basis. Candidates who are selected as IAF finalists will be notified between December and January, with finalist interviews scheduled in Washington, DC, and New York, NY, between January and February. Official selections and announcement of IAF awards will be made between February and March.

Duration: 12 months, preferably beginning in September. Though deferment is not an option, requests to do so, for up to one year only, will be considered on a case-by-case basis and under special circumstances.

Deadline: October 31.

ADDRESS INQUIRIES TO:
See telephone or e-mail address above.

COUNCIL ON FOREIGN RELATIONS [826]

58 East 68th Street
New York, NY 10065
(212) 434-9740
Fax: (212) 434-9870
E-mail: fellowships@cfr.org
Web Site: www.cfr.org/fellowships

FOUNDED: 1921

AREAS OF INTEREST:
Nuclear security, nuclear weapons, nuclear proliferation, nuclear terrorism, nuclear energy, nuclear arms, nuclear force posture, international relations, international affairs, foreign affairs, government, and public policy.

NAME(S) OF PROGRAMS:
- **International Affairs Fellowship in Nuclear Security (IAF-NS)**

TYPE:
Fellowships. The International Affairs Fellowship in Nuclear Security (IAF-NS), sponsored by the Stanton Foundation, offers university-based scholars valuable hands-on experience in the nuclear security policymaking field and places selected fellows in U.S. government positions or international organizations for a period of 12 months to work with practitioners. The Fellowships will be awarded on the basis of academic and professional accomplishments, and on the merits of the specific research projects proposed.

YEAR PROGRAM STARTED: 2011

PURPOSE:
To close the gap between research and practice and to enrich the teaching and scholarship of academics, while also benefiting policymakers by exposing them to cutting-edge scholarly research.

ELIGIBILITY:
The IAF-NS is only open to faculty members with tenure or on tenure-track lines at accredited universities and who propose to conduct policy-relevant research on nuclear security issues. Qualified candidates must be U.S. citizens or permanent residents who are eligible to work in the U.S. and be between the ages of 29 and 40. CFR does not sponsor for visas.

Potential topics appropriate for the Fellowship include nuclear terrorism, nuclear proliferation, nuclear weapons, nuclear force posture, and the security implications of nuclear energy.

FINANCIAL DATA:
Fellows are considered independent contractors rather than employees of CFR, and are not eligible for employment benefits, including health insurance.

Amount of support per award: Stipend of $125,000.

CO-OP FUNDING PROGRAMS: The Fellowship is sponsored by the Stanton Foundation.

NO. AWARDS: Approximately 2 fellowships annually.

APPLICATION INFO:
Interested candidates who meet the program's eligibility requirements must submit a cover letter, a curriculum vitae, and a proposal (maximum 1,000 words in length). Each applicant should arrange to have two letters of recommendation sent assessing the policy relevance of the applicant's proposed project as well as the applicant's qualifications for carrying it out.

All application materials must be submitted to the e-mail address above.

Duration: 12 months, preferably beginning in September.

Deadline: January 16.

ADDRESS INQUIRIES TO:
See telephone or e-mail address above.

COUNCIL ON FOREIGN RELATIONS [827]

58 East 68th Street
New York, NY 10065
(212) 434-9740
Fax: (212) 434-9870
E-mail: fellowships@cfr.org
Web Site: www.cfr.org/fellowships

FOUNDED: 1921

AREAS OF INTEREST:
Nuclear security, nuclear weapons, nuclear proliferation, nuclear terrorism, nuclear energy, nuclear force posture, nuclear arms, international relations, international affairs, foreign affairs, government, and public policy.

NAME(S) OF PROGRAMS:
- **Stanton Nuclear Security Fellowship Program (SNSF)**

TYPE:
Fellowships. The Stanton Nuclear Security Fellowship (SNSF) Program, made possible by a grant from the Stanton Foundation, offers younger scholars studying nuclear security issues the opportunity to spend a period of 12 months at the Council on Foreign Relations' (CFR) offices in New York or Washington, DC, conducting policy-relevant research. The Fellowships will be awarded on the basis of academic and professional accomplishments and promise, and on the merits of the specific research projects proposed.

YEAR PROGRAM STARTED: 2009

PURPOSE:
To stimulate the development of the next generation of thought leaders in nuclear security. The fellows could work on a wide range of issues, including nuclear terrorism, nuclear proliferation, nuclear weapons, nuclear force posture, and nuclear energy.

ELIGIBILITY:
Qualified candidates must be junior (non-tenured) faculty, postdoctoral fellows, or predoctoral candidates from any discipline who are working on a nuclear security-related issue. The program is only open to U.S. citizens and permanent residents who are eligible to work in the U.S. CFR does not sponsor for visas.

FINANCIAL DATA:
Payment will be made in 12 equal monthly installments. Fellows are considered independent contractors rather than employees of CFR, and are not eligible for employment benefits, including health insurance.

Amount of support per award: A stipend of $110,000 for junior (non-tenured) faculty and $80,000 for postdoctoral fellows.

CO-OP FUNDING PROGRAMS: The SNSF Program is made possible by a generous grant from the Stanton Foundation.

NO. AWARDS: 2 annually.

APPLICATION INFO:
Interested candidates who meet the program's eligibility requirements must submit an application form, a cover letter, a curriculum vitae, and a proposal outlining the work proposed to conduct (as specified on the CFR web site). Each applicant should arrange to have two letters of recommendation sent assessing the policy relevance of the applicant's proposed project as well as the applicant's qualifications for carrying it out.

All application materials must be sent to the e-mail address above.

Duration: 12 months, preferably beginning in September.

Deadline: December 15.

ADDRESS INQUIRIES TO:
See telephone or e-mail address above.

CULTURAL VISTAS [828]

440 Park Avenue South, 2nd Floor
New York, NY 10016
(212) 497-3510
Fax: (212) 497-3587
E-mail: alfa@cuturalvistas.org
Web Site: www.culturalvistas.org/alfa

FOUNDED: 2004

AREAS OF INTEREST:
Culture, business, law, politics, public policy, government, journalism, mass communications, finance and economics.

NAME(S) OF PROGRAMS:
- **Alfa Fellowship Program**

TYPE:
Exchange programs; Fellowships; Internships. A high-level professional development exchange program placing qualified American, British and German citizens in work assignments at leading organizations in Russia in the fields of business, economics, journalism, law and public policy. The program includes language training, seminar programs, and extended professional work experience. Fellows receive a stipend, travel, housing and insurance.

YEAR PROGRAM STARTED: 2004

PURPOSE:
To foster a new generation of future American, British and German leaders with in-depth practical experience in the modern business and public policy environment of the Russian Federation.

ELIGIBILITY:
Open to U.S., U.K. and German citizens with a graduate degree, work experience and professional interest or background in above fields. Russian language proficiency preferred, but not required.

Applicants must:
(1) have U.S., U.K. or German citizenship;
(2) be 25 to 35 years of age at time of application;
(3) have a graduate degree or equivalent training in business, economics, journalism, law or public policy and;
(4) have at least two years relevant work experience in their field of expertise.

Russian proficiency is preferred but not required at the time of application.

GEOG. RESTRICTIONS: United States, United Kingdom, Germany and Russia.

FINANCIAL DATA:
Monthly stipend, free accommodations in Russia, all in-country program-related travel, round-trip flight to Moscow, and limited international health, accident and liability insurance during the program in Russia.

Amount of support per award: Varies.

Total amount of support: Varies.

NO. MOST RECENT APPLICANTS: Approximately 150.

NO. AWARDS: 18.

APPLICATION INFO:
Candidates must submit application online with all supporting materials by the deadline.

Duration: 11 months, June to April.

Deadline: December 1, 2016 for 2017-18 program year.

ADDRESS INQUIRIES TO:
Melissa Graves, Program Director
(See address above.)

J.W. DAFOE FOUNDATION [829]

Department of Political Studies
University of Manitoba
University College, Room 351
Winnipeg MB R3T 2M8 Canada
(204) 474-6606
Fax: (204) 474-7645
E-mail: james.fergusson@ad.umanitoba.ca
Web Site: www.dafoefoundation.ca

AREAS OF INTEREST:
International relations, economics, history and political science.

TYPE:
Awards/prizes; Conferences/seminars; Fellowships; Project/program grants; Research grants. Fellowships for graduate study in international relations, economics, history or political studies.

PURPOSE:
To support graduate study in international relations, economics, history and political science.

LEGAL BASIS:
University association.

ELIGIBILITY:
Master's students enrolled at the University of Manitoba in the Departments of Economics, History, Political Studies, Faculty of Law or Conflict Resolution.

GEOG. RESTRICTIONS: Canada.

FINANCIAL DATA:
Amount of support per award: $10,000 (CAN).

Total amount of support: $10,000 (CAN); can be held in conjunction with other awards.

NO. AWARDS: 1 per year.

APPLICATION INFO:
Application information is available from the Awards Officer, Faculty of Graduate Studies, at the University of Manitoba.

Duration: Fellowships are for one year and are nonrenewable.

Deadline: February 28 for applications for tenure beginning with the fall term. The Award is announced following the Annual General Meeting of the Board in May.

*SPECIAL STIPULATIONS:
A submission fee of $50 per entry is required for the J.W. Dafoe Book Prize.

THE EAST-WEST CENTER [830]

1601 East West Road
Honolulu, HI 96848-1601
(808) 944-7735
Fax: (808) 944-7730 (Award Services Center)
E-mail: scholarships@eastwestcenter.org
Web Site: www.eastwestcenter.org/studentprograms

FOUNDED: 1960

AREAS OF INTEREST:
Economics; environmental change, vulnerability and governance; population and health; politics, governance and security, at a local, national and/or regional level in the Asia Pacific region.

NAME(S) OF PROGRAMS:
- **East-West Center Graduate Degree Fellowship**

TYPE:
Fellowships.

YEAR PROGRAM STARTED: 1960

PURPOSE:
To strengthen relations and understanding among the peoples and nations of Asia, the Pacific and the U.S.; to serve as a vigorous hub for cooperative research, education and dialogue on critical issues of common concern to the Asia Pacific region and the U.S.

LEGAL BASIS:
Public, nonprofit educational corporation established in Hawaii in 1960 by the U.S. Congress.

ELIGIBILITY:
Candidates must have obtained a four-year Bachelor's degree or its equivalent, must be a citizen or permanent resident of the U.S. or a country in Asia or the Pacific, and must come to the Center on the exchange visitor (J-1) visa.

Priority in the student selection process is given to applicants with a commitment to the Asia Pacific region seeking degrees in fields of study related to research themes at the East-West Center.

GEOG. RESTRICTIONS: Hawaii.

FINANCIAL DATA:
Award may include housing, stipend, tuition, health insurance, when relevant, and book allowance as approved. Costs may be shared by collaborating institutions.

Amount of support per award: Varies.

Total amount of support: Varies.

Matching fund requirements: Cost-sharing on any Center award is actively sought.

CO-OP FUNDING PROGRAMS: Funding for the Center comes from the U.S. government, with additional support provided by private agencies, individuals, foundations, corporations, and the governments of the region.

NO. MOST RECENT APPLICANTS: Over 300.

NO. AWARDS: Varies based on funding.

APPLICATION INFO:
Applications are available online.

Duration: Initially 12 months with possible renewal up to two years for Master's Degree or doctoral studies, contingent upon funding, performance and academic progress.

Deadline: November 1 for forwarding to the Award Services Office.

ADDRESS INQUIRIES TO:
Award Services Office
(See address above.)

*SPECIAL STIPULATIONS:
Study must be at the University of Hawaii at Manoa.

THE EAST-WEST CENTER [831]

1601 East West Road
Honolulu, HI 96848-1601
(808) 944-7744
Fax: (808) 944-7070 (Attn: APLP)
E-mail: aplp@eastwestcenter.org
Web Site: www.eastwestcenter.org/aplp

FOUNDED: 1960

AREAS OF INTEREST:
Issues related to the Asia Pacific region.

NAME(S) OF PROGRAMS:

- **Asia Pacific Leadership Program**

TYPE:
Fellowships. Links advanced and interdisciplinary analysis of emergent regional issues with experiential leadership learning.

YEAR PROGRAM STARTED: 2001

PURPOSE:
To create a network of action focused on building a peaceful, prosperous and just Asia Pacific community.

LEGAL BASIS:
Public, nonprofit educational corporation.

ELIGIBILITY:
Candidates must have at least a three-year Bachelor's degree or its equivalent from an accredited U.S. college or university or from a recognized institution of higher learning abroad.

Priority in the student selection process is given to candidates with professional work experience:
(1) international experience and aptitude, including overseas residence, language skills, intercultural and diversity exposure;
(2) leadership track record in professional, public and/or personal realms;
(3) volunteer and community service experience;
(4) Asia Pacific engagement and evidence of interest in the region, as well as commitment to its future prosperity; this might include classes taken at university, time spent in the region, languages spoken, membership and fellowships, specific projects, field studies and areas of research interest and;
(5) experience working collaboratively in small teams or in large groups.

GEOG. RESTRICTIONS: Hawaii.

FINANCIAL DATA:
Award includes program fees, living expenses, field study costs, and other academic expenses. Estimated value of $13,000.

Amount of support per award: Varies.

Total amount of support: Varies.

NO. AWARDS: 35 to 40 each year.

APPLICATION INFO:
Application form is available online.

Duration: Early August to early May.

Deadline: Priority Deadline: December 1. Final Deadline: March 1.

PUBLICATIONS:
Annual report.

ADDRESS INQUIRIES TO:
Award Services Office
(See address above.)

THE EISENHOWER INSTITUTE [832]

818 Connecticut Avenue, N.W.
Suite 800
Washington, DC 20006
(202) 628-4444
Fax: (202) 628-4445
E-mail: ei@gettysburg.edu
Web Site: www.eisenhowerinstitute.org

FOUNDED: 1983

AREAS OF INTEREST:
World affairs.

NAME(S) OF PROGRAMS:

- **Eisenhower Institute Scholarship Programs**

TYPE:
Conferences/seminars; Endowments; Fellowships; Internships; Scholarships.

PURPOSE:
To promote sound and forward-looking policies that lay the intellectual and civic groundwork for the next generation of opinion-leaders, policy-shapers and public servants.

ELIGIBILITY:
Open to American high school, undergraduate, and graduate students.

FINANCIAL DATA:
Amount of support per award: Scholarships and fellowships: $4,000 to $10,000.

APPLICATION INFO:
Application procedures are available online.

IRS I.D.: 52-1306218

ADDRESS INQUIRIES TO:
Ben Hill, Assistant Director
(See address above.)

GRADUATE INSTITUTE OF INTERNATIONAL AND DEVELOPMENT STUDIES [833]

Rue de Lausanne 132
P.O. Box 136
CH - 1211 Geneva 21 Switzerland
(41) 22 908 57 00
Fax: (41) 22 908 57 10
E-mail: info@graduateinstitute.ch
Web Site: graduateinstitute.ch

FOUNDED: 1927

AREAS OF INTEREST:
Development, anthropology and sociology of development, and international relations.

NAME(S) OF PROGRAMS:

- **Financial Aid for Study at The Graduate Institute of International and Development Studies**

TYPE:
Assistantships; Awards/prizes; Exchange programs; Fellowships; Residencies; Scholarships; Visiting scholars. Financial aid in advanced study in international relations including intensive research and study towards the Master's degree and the Ph.D. Tenable at the Institute.

PURPOSE:
To support the scientific study of contemporary international relations and development studies and the pursuit of advanced studies based on personal work and research.

LEGAL BASIS:
Foundation.

ELIGIBILITY:
Each year, financial assistance is awarded by the Institute in the form of scholarships covering the minimum needs of students. They are allocated on the basis of applicants' academic performance and financial needs.

Scholarships also awarded for young lecturers from the global south.

FINANCIAL DATA:
Scholars are exempted from Institute fees, but not from the obligatory fees of the University of Geneva which confers the Doctorate.

Amount of support per award: Full scholarship: CHF 18,000 per academic year.

NO. AWARDS: 250 scholarships annually.

APPLICATION INFO:
Applications are available upon request.

Duration: One year. Renewable.

Deadline: January 15.

PUBLICATIONS:
Annual report.

ADDRESS INQUIRIES TO:
E-mail: executive@graduateinstitute.ch

INSTITUTE OF CURRENT WORLD AFFAIRS [834]

1779 Massachusetts Avenue, N.W.
Suite 615
Washington, DC 20036
(202) 364-4068
E-mail: icwa@icwa.org
Web Site: www.icwa.org

FOUNDED: 1925

AREAS OF INTEREST:
Current world affairs.

TYPE:
Fellowships. Fellowships are not scholarships, and are not awarded to support work toward academic degrees or for collaborative research projects, or to write books.

YEAR PROGRAM STARTED: 1925

PURPOSE:
To provide talented and promising individuals with an opportunity to develop a deep understanding of an issue, country or region outside the U.S. and to share that understanding with a wider public.

ELIGIBILITY:
Fellowships are for self-designed independent study only. Applicants must have a good command of written and spoken English and be women and men under 36 years of age who demonstrate initiative, integrity, outstanding character, good communications skills, seriousness of purpose and enthusiasm for their chosen fields.

FINANCIAL DATA:
The Institute provides sufficient, though not unlimited, financial support for its fellows and their immediate families, allowing them to live in good health and reasonable comfort in order to fulfill the purposes of the fellowship.

Amount of support per award: Varies.

Total amount of support: Varies.

NO. AWARDS: 2.

APPLICATION INFO:

Applicants should write an initial letter of interest to the Executive Director explaining the personal background and professional experience that would qualify them for the fellowship they have in mind. They should describe the activities they would like to carry out during two years overseas and enclose a resume or curriculum vitae. Select candidates will be invited to submit a more detailed application.

Initial letter should be by e-mail, although regular mail will be accepted. Further information may be obtained from the Institute's web site.

Duration: Minimum period of two years.

Deadline: March 1 and September 1.

ADDRESS INQUIRIES TO:

Edward P. Joseph, Executive Director
(See address above.)

THE INTERNATIONAL FOUNDATION [835]

55 Lane Road
Fairfield, NJ 07004
(973) 406-3970
Fax: (973) 406-3969
E-mail: info@intlfoundation.org
Web Site: intlfoundation.org

FOUNDED: 1948

AREAS OF INTEREST:

Agriculture, health, education, social development, the environment and community development.

TYPE:

Development grants; Project/program grants; Seed money grants; Technical assistance; Training grants.

YEAR PROGRAM STARTED: 1948

PURPOSE:

To help people of the developing world in their endeavors to solve some of their problems, to attain a better standard of living, and to obtain a reasonable degree of self-sufficiency.

LEGAL BASIS:

Private foundation.

ELIGIBILITY:

The Foundation funds only projects of U.S.-based, IRS-certified philanthropies.

GEOG. RESTRICTIONS: United States.

FINANCIAL DATA:

Amount of support per award: Approximately $25,000.

NO. AWARDS: Approximately 100.

APPLICATION INFO:

Applications are to be submitted on the Foundation's web site. Proposals must include a statement from IRS of not-for-profit status, a brief overview of the proposal, amount of funds requested from The Foundation, a brief background of organization applying, a statement of the problem addressed by project, objectives of the project, plan of operation/method of achieving objectives, beneficiaries of the project, methods of project evaluation and report, project budget, sources of other funding applied for or received and date. All appropriate communications will be answered.

Duration: One year. Must reapply.

Deadline: Grant applications are reviewed twice monthly by the Grants Committee.

PUBLICATIONS:

Brochure, includes application guidelines.

IRS I.D.: 13-1962255

OFFICERS:

Frank H. Madden, President
John D. Carrico, Secretary and Treasurer
William M. McCormack, M.D., Grants Chairman

BOARD OF TRUSTEES:

John D. Carrico
Gary Dicovitsky
Edward A. Holmes, Ph.D.
Frank H. Madden
William M. McCormack, M.D.
Douglas P. Walker

IRISH AMERICAN CULTURAL INSTITUTE [836]

P.O. Box 1716
Morristown, NJ 07962
(973) 605-1991
Fax: (973) 605-8875
E-mail: info@iaci-usa.org
Web Site: www.iaci-usa.org

FOUNDED: 1962

AREAS OF INTEREST:

Irish studies.

NAME(S) OF PROGRAMS:

- **IACI Visiting Fellowship in Irish Studies at NUI-G**

TYPE:

Fellowships.

YEAR PROGRAM STARTED: 1992

PURPOSE:

To stimulate, develop and disseminate information pertinent to the Irish culture.

LEGAL BASIS:

Public foundation under IRS Code 501(c)(3).

ELIGIBILITY:

The Fellowship is tenable at NUI-G to scholars normally residents in the U.S. who wish to spend a semester (not less than four months) at NUI-G, and whose work relates to any aspect of Irish studies.

FINANCIAL DATA:

Fellowship includes transatlantic air transportation, office accommodation, and some access to departmental secretarial and other facilities.

Amount of support per award: Stipend $4,000.

NO. MOST RECENT APPLICANTS: Varies.

NO. AWARDS: 1.

APPLICATION INFO:

Application requirements and guidelines are available online.

Duration: Varies.

Deadline: December 31.

OFFICERS:

Peter Halas, Chairman
Brian Stack, Vice Chairman
Barbara Lyons, Treasurer
Edward F. Ginty, Secretary

THE JAPAN FOUNDATION, NEW YORK [837]

1700 Broadway
15th Floor
New York, NY 10019
(212) 489-0299
Fax: (212) 489-0409
E-mail: info@jfny.org
Web Site: www.jfny.org
www.cgp.org

FOUNDED: 1972

AREAS OF INTEREST:

Arts and cultural exchange, Japanese studies, intellectual exchange and grassroots exchange and education.

NAME(S) OF PROGRAMS:

- **CGP Grant Program - Grassroots Program**
- **CGP Grant Program - Intellectual Exchange**
- **Doctoral Fellowship**
- **Education Grants**
- **Exhibition Abroad Support Program**
- **Institutional Project Support Program for Japanese Studies**
- **Institutional Project Support Small Program for Japanese Studies**
- **JFNY Grant for Japanese Studies**
- **JFNY Grant Program - Arts and Culture**
- **Performing Arts Japan Program**
- **Research Fellowship**
- **Short-Term Research Fellowship**
- **Support Program for Translation and Publication on Japan**
- **U.S.-Southeast Asia-Japan Collaboration and Exchange Initiative**

TYPE:

Conferences/seminars; Fellowships; Professorships; Project/program grants; Research grants; Travel grants.

PURPOSE:

To conduct international cultural exchange; to assist Japanese studies programs in the U.S; to promote intellectual exchange, grassroots exchange and education programs in the U.S.

LEGAL BASIS:

Independent administrative institution.

ELIGIBILITY:

Varies according to program.

FINANCIAL DATA:

For Fellowships, the Foundation will provide a round-trip, economy-class airfare to and from Japan. The stipend is determined in accordance with the grantee's professional status.

Amount of support per award: Varies according to program.

Matching fund requirements: Varies according to program.

APPLICATION INFO:

Program announcements and application forms are available on the web site. Arts and Culture grant applications from Alaska, Arizona, California, Colorado, Hawaii, Idaho, Montana, Nevada, New Mexico, Oregon, Utah, Washington and Wyoming should be sent to the Japan Foundation, Los Angeles Office, 5700 Wilshire Boulevard, Suite 100, Los Angeles, CA 90036; Tel: (323) 761-7510; Fax: (323) 761-7517; E-mail: jflainfo@jflalc.org. Arts and Culture Grant applications from all other states should be sent directly to the Japan Foundation New York Office. Grant applications for all other

programs should be sent to the New York office to the section in charge of the grant program.

Duration: Varies according to program.

Deadline: Varies according to program.

PUBLICATIONS:
Annual report.

IRS I.D.: 13-2974222

STAFF:
Osamu Honda, Director General
Yoshihiro Wada, Deputy Director General
Miki Hotta, Program Director, Arts and Cultural Exchange
Ayumi Takita, Program Director, Intellectual Exchange
Takeshi Yoshida, Program Director, Japanese Studies, Grassroots Exchange and Education

ADDRESS INQUIRIES TO:
See e-mail address above.

JAPAN-U.S. FRIENDSHIP COMMISSION [838]

1201 15th Street, N.W.
Suite 330
Washington, DC 20005
(202) 653-9800
Fax: (202) 653-9802
E-mail: jusfc@jusfc.gov
Web Site: www.jusfc.gov

FOUNDED: 1976

AREAS OF INTEREST:
Cultural and educational activities between Japan and the U.S., including language and area studies, economic relations, media and public education.

TYPE:
Project/program grants. Programs of institutional support. Grants for projects of research, training and exchange with Japan.

YEAR PROGRAM STARTED: 1977

PURPOSE:
To enhance reciprocal people-to-people understanding and friendship between the U.S. and Japan.

LEGAL BASIS:
Independent agency of the U.S. government.

ELIGIBILITY:
Grants are offered to cultural and educational institutions in the U.S. and Japan.

GEOG. RESTRICTIONS: United States and Japan.

FINANCIAL DATA:
U.S. government trust fund of $40,000,000.

Amount of support per award: Varies.

Total amount of support: Varies.

CO-OP FUNDING PROGRAMS: NEA.

NO. MOST RECENT APPLICANTS: Varies by program.

NO. AWARDS: Approximately 30 annually.

APPLICATION INFO:
Application forms are available on the web site.

Duration: One year.

Deadline: July 1. Notification in October.

PUBLICATIONS:
Biennial report; program information/guidelines; application form.

OFFICERS:
Harry Hill, Chairman
Dr. Sheila Smith, Vice Chairman
Dr. Edward Lincoln
Dr. Patricia Maclachlan
Dr. Deanna Marcum
Rep. James McDermott
Dr. Anne Nishimura Morse
Hon. Lisa Murkowski
Dr. T.J. Pempel
Daniel Russel
Hon. Evan Ryan
Dr. Leonard J. Schoppa, Jr.
Dr. David Sneider

ADDRESS INQUIRIES TO:
Paige Cottingham-Streater, Executive Director
(See address above.)

*SPECIAL STIPULATIONS:
Institution grants only.

THE JAPANESE AMERICAN CITIZENS LEAGUE (JACL) [839]

Washington, DC Office
1629 K Street, N.W., Suite 400
Washington, DC 20006
(202) 223-1240
Fax: (202) 296-8082
E-mail: pouchida@jacl.org
Web Site: www.jacl.org

FOUNDED: 1929

AREAS OF INTEREST:
Cultural exchange.

NAME(S) OF PROGRAMS:
- **JACL Kakehashi Program**

TYPE:
Travel grants. The Kakehashi Program is a new international program, part of JACL's leadership development. It is for college students and consists of five webinars and a nine-day trip to Japan.

PURPOSE:
To strengthen cultural ties between Japan and the U.S.

ELIGIBILITY:
This Program is for college students in good standing between the ages of 18 and 25. Students are selected for their community service, leadership experience and academic accomplishments. Eligible students must be either of Japanese ancestry or Asian ancestry, and must be a U.S. citizen. Students who have previously participated in a program sponsored by the government of Japan are ineligible.

NO. AWARDS: 185 students are to be selected for the Program.

APPLICATION INFO:
Contact JACL.

ADDRESS INQUIRIES TO:
Priscilla Ouchida
Executive Director
(See e-mail address above.)

A.J. MUSTE MEMORIAL INSTITUTE

168 Canal Street, 6th Floor
New York, NY 10013
(212) 533-4335
E-mail: info@ajmuste.org
Web Site: www.ajmuste.org

TYPE:
Grants-in-aid. The Institute's regular grant fund annually funds international, national and local projects in the U.S. and around the world. It gives priority to those with small budgets and little chance of funding from more traditional sources. It also offers fiscal sponsorship. The Institute does not provide academic scholarships.

See entry 1457 for full listing.

THE NATIONAL COUNCIL FOR EURASIAN AND EAST EUROPEAN RESEARCH [840]

1828 L Street, N.W.
Suite 1200
Washington, DC 20036
(202) 572-9095
Fax: (866) 937-9872
E-mail: info@nceeer.org
Web Site: www.nceeer.org

FOUNDED: 1978

AREAS OF INTEREST:
The program is limited to research designed to contribute to knowledge of current developments and analysis of their significance in Eastern Europe and the successor states of the former Soviet Union.

TYPE:
Research grants; Research contracts. Institutional grants and research contracts and policy research scholarships and related activities, such as meetings and conferences, research-specific training, contact among scholars and specialists in government and private enterprise, development of databanks and other reference aids and dissemination of research data, methodology and findings, both in scholarly forms and through public media.

YEAR PROGRAM STARTED: 1978

PURPOSE:
To encourage and sustain high-quality research on Eastern Europe, the former Soviet Union and its successor states, in the social sciences (including geography, demography and environmental studies) and history.

LEGAL BASIS:
Incorporated, nonprofit, autonomous academic body.

ELIGIBILITY:
Limited to scholars at the postdoctoral level for academic participants and to an equivalent degree of maturity and professional employment for those from other fields. Applicant must be a U.S. citizen. Applications must be submitted to the Council by U.S. nonprofit institutions in the form of grant or contract proposals.

GEOG. RESTRICTIONS: United States.

FINANCIAL DATA:
Amount of support per award: Varies; normally not more than $70,000 for any individual project.

Matching fund requirements: Cost sharing at a minimum of 20% from non-federal funds is mandatory.

CO-OP FUNDING PROGRAMS: NEH Collaborative Research Fellowship; Carnegie Research Fellowship Program.

APPLICATION INFO:
Application guidelines, compliance with which is required, should be obtained from the Council, at the address above. Required documentation includes:
(1) identification form;
(2) one-page summary;
(3) detailed description of project;
(4) curriculum vitae and bibliographies for principal personnel;

(5) description of proposed written or other products and dissemination methods;
(6) budget and;
(7) letters of recommendation.

Duration: Varies.

Deadline: Spring of each year.

PUBLICATIONS:
Guidelines.

BOARD OF DIRECTORS:
Bruce Grant, Chairperson
Elizabeth Wood, Vice Chairperson
Maria Carlson
Richard Combs
Ted Gerber
Mary Kruger
Martha Lampland
Susan Linz
Mieke Meurs
Joanna Regulska
James Richter
Edward Schatz

ADDRESS INQUIRIES TO:
President
(See address above.)

NUCLEAR AGE PEACE FOUNDATION [841]

PMB 121
1187 Coast Village Road, Suite 1
Santa Barbara, CA 93108
(805) 965-3443
Fax: (805) 568-0466
E-mail: wagingpeace@napf.org
Web Site: www.wagingpeace.org

FOUNDED: 1982

AREAS OF INTEREST:
Achieving a nuclear weapon-free world, international law, international relations, liberty, justice, human dignity, human rights, nonviolence, responsible use of technology, peace education, and youth empowerment.

NAME(S) OF PROGRAMS:
- **Barbara Mandigo Kelly Peace Poetry Awards**

TYPE:
Awards/prizes; Internships. An annual series of awards to encourage poets to explore and illuminate positive visions of peace and the human spirit.

PURPOSE:
To play an important role in making the 21st century a time of peace and justice, and a time in which the rights of all individuals to peace, security and a healthy environment will be realized.

FINANCIAL DATA:
Amount of support per award: Adults: $1,000; Youth (13-18): $200; Youth (12 and under): $200.

Total amount of support: $1,400.

APPLICATION INFO:
Application information and guidelines are available at www.peacecontests.org.

Deadline: April 30.

ORGANIZATION OF AMERICAN STATES [842]

1889 F Street, N.W.
Seventh Floor
Washington, DC 20006
(202) 370-9771
Fax: (202) 458-3897
E-mail: scholarships@oas.org
Web Site: www.oas.org/scholarships

FOUNDED: 1890

AREAS OF INTEREST:
To promote the economic, social, scientific and cultural development of the Member States in order to achieve a stronger bond and better understanding among the peoples of the Americas through the advanced training of its citizens in the priority areas requested by the countries.

NAME(S) OF PROGRAMS:
- **Academic Studies**
- **Professional Development**

TYPE:
Fellowships; Scholarships; Technical assistance. Awarded for graduate academic studies and/or research, and last two years of undergraduate studies for students in the English-speaking Caribbean, for training in areas contributing to the economic, social, technical and cultural development of OAS member countries.

YEAR PROGRAM STARTED: 1958

PURPOSE:
Program of Scholarships and Training: to assist the member states with their domestic efforts in pursuit of integral development goals by supporting human resource development in the priority areas established by the member countries.

ELIGIBILITY:
Candidates must be citizens or permanent residents of an OAS member country, with a university degree in the case of academic studies, or who have demonstrated ability to pursue advanced training in the field chosen for professional development courses. Scholarships are for graduate or undergraduate studies, research, or professional training in any field, with the exception of the medical sciences and related areas and introductory language studies. Candidates must know the language of the study country. Studies must be undertaken at an institution in a member country of the OAS, with the exception of the country of which the candidate is a citizen or permanent resident.

Graduate scholarships are offered for study towards a Master's or Doctorate degree. They may also be used for research, if required by a specific academic program. Scholarships are awarded for an initial period of one academic year and may be extended subsequently for up to one additional year. Under the Self-Placed in an OAS Non-Consortium University, candidates apply directly for admission to the universities or educational institutions of their choice, and present their application for an OAS scholarship. Only one candidate per country will be awarded with this type of scholarship. In the Self-Placed in an OAS Consortium University, candidates apply directly to up to three programs in different universities, part of the OAS Consortium University, located in three different countries. Applying to this type of scholarship increases the applicant's chances of being offered an OAS scholarship. Undergraduate scholarships are available only to citizens of the English-speaking Caribbean member countries for the last two years of study for an undergraduate degree.

No fellowships will be awarded retroactively, and no benefits will be provided to the family of the fellowship holder.

FINANCIAL DATA:
Fellowship may include, depending upon the circumstances of each fellow, a round-trip ticket, tuition fees, study materials, health insurance, and partial subsistence allowance (which varies from country to country).

Amount of support per award: Not to exceed U.S. $30,000.

Matching fund requirements: Students are responsible for covering a portion of their subsistence costs.

APPLICATION INFO:
Application materials are available at the web site. Except for applicants in the U.S., applications must be presented to the National Liaison Offices (ONEs) of the applicant's country of origin or permanent residence. The ONE is the official channel identified by each government for submission of applications for OAS scholarships. U.S. citizens can send applications directly to the Organization's mailing address.

Duration: Fellowships are tenable for not less than one year nor more than two years.

Deadline: For presentation of applications to the National Liaison Office (ONE): Differs from country to country and should therefore be confirmed with the National Liaison Office (ONE) in the applicant's country of origin or permanent residence.

OFFICERS:
Marie Levens, Director

ADDRESS INQUIRIES TO:
Department of Human Development, Education and Employment
(See address above.)

*SPECIAL STIPULATIONS:
For countries other than the U.S., the fellowship form must be presented to the General Secretariat of the OAS in Washington, DC, through the official channels established by each government.

HERBERT SCOVILLE, JR., PEACE FELLOWSHIP [843]

322 Fourth Street, N.E.
Washington, DC 20002
(202) 446-1565
E-mail: info@scoville.org
Web Site: www.scoville.org

FOUNDED: 1987

AREAS OF INTEREST:
Arms control research and/or advocacy for disarmament, international security, nuclear and conventional arms control, peace building and peace organizations.

NAME(S) OF PROGRAMS:
- **Herbert Scoville Jr. Peace Fellowship Program**

TYPE:
Fellowships.

YEAR PROGRAM STARTED: 1987

PURPOSE:
To provide an opportunity for college graduates to gain practical knowledge and experience by contributing to the efforts of nonprofit, public-interest organizations working on peace and security issues.

LEGAL BASIS:
Nonprofit program.

ELIGIBILITY:
Prospective Fellows are expected to demonstrate excellent academic accomplishments and a strong interest in issues of peace and security. Graduate study,

a college major, course work, or substantial independent reading that reflects the substantive focus of the Fellowship is also a plus. Prior experience with public-interest activism or advocacy is highly desirable. It is preferred, but not required, that such activities be focused on peace and security issues.

Candidates are required to have completed a Baccalaureate degree by the time the Fellowship commences. Preference is given to U.S. citizens, although a Fellowship to a foreign national residing in the U.S. is awarded periodically based on availability of funding. The Scoville Fellowship is not intended for students or scholars interested in pursuing independent research in Washington, DC.

Preference will be given to individuals who have not had substantial prior public-interest or government experience in the Washington, DC area.

FINANCIAL DATA:

Amount of support per award: $2,900 per month, plus $1,000 in travel expenses to the Washington, DC area and health insurance.

Total amount of support: Varies.

NO. MOST RECENT APPLICANTS: 300 to 350.

NO. AWARDS: 6 to 8 per year.

APPLICATION INFO:

Information is available on the web site. All application materials must be submitted by e-mail to apply@scoville.org.

Duration: Six to nine months.

Deadline: Spring Fellowship: September 30; Fall Fellowship: January 6, 2017.

PUBLICATIONS:

Application guidelines; organization description.

ADDRESS INQUIRIES TO:

Paul Revsine, Program Director
(See address above.)

SOCIAL SCIENCE RESEARCH COUNCIL [844]

One Pierrepont Plaza
15th Floor
Brooklyn, NY 11201
(212) 377-2700 ext. 3672
Fax: (212) 377-2727
E-mail: japan@ssrc.org
Web Site: www.ssrc.org/fellowships/jsps-fellowship

FOUNDED: 1923

AREAS OF INTEREST:

Social sciences and humanities.

NAME(S) OF PROGRAMS:

- **SSRC/JSPS Long-Term Fellowship**
- **SSRC/JSPS Short-Term Fellowship**

TYPE:

Fellowships; Research grants. The Japan Society for the Promotion of Science (JSPS) Postdoctoral Fellowship for Foreign Researchers provides promising and highly qualified recent Ph.Ds. and ABDs with funding to conduct research in Japan. JSPS guidelines target the applicant who wishes to conduct cooperative research under the leadership of a host researcher, thereby advancing the Fellow's own research and at the same time stimulating Japanese academic circles through close collaboration with young Japanese researchers.

YEAR PROGRAM STARTED: 1967

PURPOSE:

To stimulate Japanese academic circles through close collaboration with young foreign researchers.

LEGAL BASIS:

Not-for-profit organization.

ELIGIBILITY:

Applicants must be U.S. citizens or permanent residents at the time of application and not be of Japanese descent. Citizens of other countries are eligible for short-term fellowships if they have completed a Master's or Ph.D. course at an institution of higher education in the U.S. and, upon completing the course, have for at least three continuous years conducted high-level research at a university in the U.S. Japanese nationals are not eligible for a fellowship regardless of current residency status. Applicants currently in Japan are not eligible for short-term fellowships.

Applicants for long-term fellowships must submit a copy of a Ph.D. diploma from a university outside Japan dated no more than six years prior to April 1, 2015.

Applicants for short-term fellowships must submit a copy of a Ph.D. diploma from a university outside Japan dated no more than six years prior to April 1, 2015 or a letter from their institution stating that the applicant is a Ph.D. candidate within two years of receiving a Ph.D.

Scholars who have previously received funding from JSPS for the Short-Term Fellowship are eligible to apply for the JSPS Long-Term Fellowship.

FINANCIAL DATA:

Grants are to be used for maintenance, travel and research expenses.

Amount of support per award: Varies based on length of research term and doctoral status.

Total amount of support: Varies.

NO. MOST RECENT APPLICANTS: Long-Term and Short-Term Fellowships: 45.

NO. AWARDS: Long-Term and Short-Term Fellowships: Up to 20 (10 in each category).

APPLICATION INFO:

Application information is available on the web site.

Duration: Long-Term Fellowships: 12 to 24 months; Short-Term Fellowships: One to 12 months.

Deadline: December 1.

PUBLICATIONS:

Annual report; *Items*, newsletter; *Fellowships and Grants for Training and Research*, brochure.

STAFF:

Nicole Restrick, Japan Program Coordinator
Paige Holt, Program Associate

ADDRESS INQUIRIES TO:

Paige Holt, Program Associate
Japan Program
Social Science Research Council
(See address above.)

SOCIAL SCIENCE RESEARCH COUNCIL [845]

One Pierrepont Plaza
15th Floor
Brooklyn, NY 11201
(212) 377-2700
Fax: (212) 377-2727
E-mail: idrf@ssrc.org
Web Site: www.ssrc.org/programs/idrf

FOUNDED: 1923

AREAS OF INTEREST:

Fellowships in the humanities and humanistic social sciences.

NAME(S) OF PROGRAMS:

- **International Dissertation Research Fellowship Program (IDRF)**

TYPE:

Fellowships. Support to graduate students in the humanities and humanistic social sciences who are enrolled in doctoral programs in the U.S. and conducting dissertation research outside of the U.S.

YEAR PROGRAM STARTED: 1997

PURPOSE:

To support the advancement of social science and humanistic research.

LEGAL BASIS:

Not-for-profit corporation.

ELIGIBILITY:

Applicants must be enrolled in a full-time doctoral program at a U.S. university. Research must be conducted outside of the U.S.

FINANCIAL DATA:

Amount of support per award: Average $20,000.

NO. MOST RECENT APPLICANTS: More than 1,000.

NO. AWARDS: 80.

APPLICATION INFO:

Application information is available on the web site.

Duration: Nine to 12 months.

Deadline: November 2015.

ADDRESS INQUIRIES TO:

See e-mail address above.

SOCIAL SCIENCE RESEARCH COUNCIL [846]

One Pierrepont Plaza
15th Floor
Brooklyn, NY 11201
(212) 377-2700 ext. 3672
Fax: (212) 377-2727
E-mail: abe@ssrc.org
Web Site: www.ssrc.org/fellowships/abe-fellowship

FOUNDED: 1923

AREAS OF INTEREST:

International multidisciplinary research on topics of pressing global concern.

NAME(S) OF PROGRAMS:

- **Abe Fellowship Program**

TYPE:

Fellowships; Research grants. The program encourages international multidisciplinary research on topics of pressing global concern and fosters the development of a new generation of researchers interested in policy-relevant topics of long-range

importance and willing to become key members of a bilateral and global research network built around such topics.

The Abe Fellowship Program administers an annual fellowship competition that provides scholars and nonacademic research professionals in the social sciences and related disciplines with support for research projects addressing one or more of three themes: (1) Threats to Personal, Societal and International Security; (2) Growth and Sustainable Development; (3) Social, Scientific and Cultural Trends and Transformations and; (4) Governance, Empowerment and Participation.

YEAR PROGRAM STARTED: 1991

PURPOSE:
To encourage international multidisciplinary research on topics of pressing global concern.

ELIGIBILITY:
Competition is open to citizens of the U.S. and Japan as well as to nationals of other countries who can demonstrate strong and serious long-term affiliations with research communities in Japan or the U.S. Applicants must hold the Ph.D. or the terminal degree in their field, or have attained an equivalent level of professional experience. Applications from researchers in professions other than academia are encouraged. Previous language training is not a prerequisite for this Fellowship. However, if the research project requires language ability, the applicant should provide evidence of adequate proficiency to complete the project. Projects proposing to address key policy issues or seeking to develop a concrete policy proposal must reflect nonpartisan positions.

GEOG. RESTRICTIONS: Japan and United States.

FINANCIAL DATA:
Awards may be used for maintenance, travel and research expenses.

Amount of support per award: Varies.

Total amount of support: Varies.

NO. AWARDS: 12 to 15.

APPLICATION INFO:
Applications must be submitted online at applications.ssrc.org.

Duration: Three to 12 months of full-time support over a 24-month period. Fellowship tenure must begin between April 1 and December 31 of a given year.

Deadline: Applications are available by early summer. Receipt of applications: September 1.

STAFF:
Nicole Levit, Associate Director
Paige Holt, Program Associate

ADDRESS INQUIRIES TO:
Abe Fellowship Program
Social Science Research Council
(See address above.)

SOCIETY FOR FRENCH HISTORICAL STUDIES

Department of History
University of Vermont
133 South Prospect Street
Burlington, VT 05405-0164
E-mail: steven.zdatny@uvm.edu
Web Site: www.societyforfrenchhistoricalstudies.net

TYPE:
Awards/prizes. The Chinard Prize is for a recent book on historical relations between France and the Americas.

Davis Graduate Student Award is given for the best paper presented by a graduate student at the Society's annual meeting.

Farrar Award is for dissertation research.

The Koren Prize is for a recent journal article written on French history.

The Pinkney Prize is for a recent book written on French history.

Research Travel Award is for recent recipients of doctorates (awarded jointly with Western Society for French History).

Wolf Travel Fellowship is for research travel pertaining to a dissertation.

See entry 624 for full listing.

SWEDISH WOMEN'S EDUCATIONAL ASSOCIATION INC. [847]

P.O. Box 4128
Fort Lauderdale, FL 33338-4128
E-mail: office@swea.org
Web Site: www.swea.org

AREAS OF INTEREST:
Sweden's culture, history and language.

NAME(S) OF PROGRAMS:

- **SWEA Scholarship in Literature, Language and Area Studies**

TYPE:
Scholarships. Funds may be used to study in Sweden. Previous trips to Sweden, or lack thereof, are of no consideration. Willingness to travel to Sweden for dissertation work is a plus, but not a requirement.

PURPOSE:
To promote and preserve the Swedish language, cultures and traditions.

ELIGIBILITY:
The applicant must:
(1) be a well-merited doctoral candidate, studying at a non-Swedish university and reside permanently outside of Sweden;
(2) have filed a dissertation topic and;
(3) have a good knowledge of the Swedish language (written and spoken).

FINANCIAL DATA:
Amount of support per award: $10,000.

Total amount of support: $10,000.

NO. AWARDS: 1.

APPLICATION INFO:
The applicant must submit an application, curriculum vitae, a detailed description of the dissertation project, a statement explaining how the scholarship money will be used, a presentation of himself or herself in Swedish, and three letters of recommendation. Applications are available online.

Duration: One year. Recipients may reapply.

Deadline: January 15.

ADDRESS INQUIRIES TO:
Administrator
(See address above.)

*SPECIAL STIPULATIONS:
There is no discrimination on the basis of gender, race, color, age, religion or nationality.

TINKER FOUNDATION INC. [848]

55 East 59th Street
New York, NY 10022
(212) 421-6858
Fax: (212) 223-3326
E-mail: tinker@tinker.org
Web Site: www.tinker.org

FOUNDED: 1959

AREAS OF INTEREST:
Institutional grants for projects addressing democratic governance, sustainable resource management, and education, with a geographic focus on the Spanish- and Portuguese-speaking countries of Latin America.

NAME(S) OF PROGRAMS:

- **Tinker Field Research Grants**

TYPE:
Travel grants. Travel grants (issued to universities) are to be used to support brief periods of individual research in Latin America by graduate students. There are also Institutional Grants for charitable organizations.

YEAR PROGRAM STARTED: 1979

PURPOSE:
To enable emerging scholars to work in the Spanish- and Portuguese-speaking countries of Latin America, enabling them to acquire a comprehensive knowledge of language, cultures and terrain, and to gather research data and develop contacts with scholars and institutions in their respective fields.

LEGAL BASIS:
Private foundation.

ELIGIBILITY:
Open to all recognized Centers or Institutes of Latin American Studies with graduate doctoral programs at accredited U.S. universities. Field Research Grants, awarded to individuals by the appropriate university institutes/centers, are to reflect the Foundation's broad areas of interest.

The Foundation's selection criteria include the quality of the overall graduate program in Latin American studies, the immediate benefits to the Latin American studies program that will result from the availability of Field Research Grants at the university and the level of general university support for Latin American studies as demonstrated by past commitments and future projects.

Institutional Grants: Open to any 501(c)(3) (or equivalent foreign) organization doing work in and on the Spanish- and Portuguese-speaking countries of Latin America.

GEOG. RESTRICTIONS: Latin America, excluding Puerto Rico.

FINANCIAL DATA:
Amount of support per award: $10,000 and $15,000. Institutional Grants: $50,000 to $150,000.

Total amount of support: Approximately $75,000 in new grants annually.

Matching fund requirements: Field Research Grant applicants are required to match the award on a 1:1 ratio.

NO. MOST RECENT APPLICANTS: 11.

NO. AWARDS: Up to 6 new annually; more than 6 annually for Institutional Grants.

APPLICATION INFO:
Application instructions and forms can be accessed via the web site.

Duration: Maximum of three years.

Deadline: Field Research Grants: October 1. Institutional Grants: March 1 and September 15.

STAFF:
Margaret J. Cushing, Associate Director
Jessica Tomb, Director of Administration and Finance
Karen Nassi, Program Officer
Rachel Fagiano, Program Assistant

DIRECTORS AND OFFICERS:
Alan Stoga, Chairman
Renate Rennie, President
Kathleen Waldron, Treasurer
Luis Rubio, Secretary
Sally Grooms Cowal
Arturo C. Porzecanski
Susan Segal
Bradford Smith

ADDRESS INQUIRIES TO:
Meg Cushing, Associate Director
(See address above.)

U.S. DEPARTMENT OF EDUCATION

International and Foreign Language Education (IFLE)
Advanced Training and Research Division
1990 K Street, N.W., Suite 6087
Washington, DC 20006-8521
(202) 502-7634
(202) 502-7700
Fax: (202) 502-7860
E-mail: ifle@ed.gov
Web Site: www.ed.gov/ope/iegps

TYPE:
Fellowships. The Foreign Language and Area Studies Fellowships program provides allocations of academic year and summer fellowships to institutions of higher education or consortia of institutions of higher education to assist meritorious undergraduate students and graduate students undergoing training in modern foreign languages and related international or area studies.

See entry 651 for full listing.

U.S. DEPARTMENT OF EDUCATION

International and Foreign Language Education (IFLE)
International Studies Division
Room 6084, 6th Floor
1990 K Street, N.W.
Washington, DC 20006-8521
(202) 502-7589
(202) 502-7700 (main office)
Fax: (202) 502-7860
E-mail: ddra@ed.gov
Web Site: www.ed.gov/programs/iegpsddrap/index.html

TYPE:
Fellowships. Fellowships to support doctoral dissertation research abroad in modern foreign languages and related area studies. For the purpose of these programs, area studies is defined as a program of comprehensive study of the aspects of a society or societies, including the study of their geography, history, culture, economy, politics, international relations and languages. The program is designed to develop research knowledge and capability in world areas not widely included in American curricula. Awards will not be available for projects focusing on Western Europe.

See entry 652 for full listing.

U.S. DEPARTMENT OF EDUCATION

Higher Education Programs
International and Foreign Language Education (IFLE)
National Resource Centers Program
1990 K Street, N.W., Room 6087
Mail Stop K-OPE-6-6078
Washington, DC 20006
(202) 502-7634
(202) 502-7700
Fax: (202) 502-7860
E-mail: IFLE@ed.gov
Web Site: www.ed.gov/ope/iegps

TYPE:
Project/program grants; Training grants. The NRC Program provides grants to institutions of higher education and consortia of institutions to establish, strengthen and operate comprehensive and undergraduate centers that will be national resources for:
(1) teaching of any modern foreign language;
(2) instruction in fields needed to provide full understanding of areas, regions or countries in which the modern foreign language is commonly used;
(3) research and training in international studies and the international and foreign language aspects of professional and other fields of study and;
(4) instruction and research on issues in world affairs that concern one or more countries.

See entry 653 for full listing.

U.S. DEPARTMENT OF EDUCATION [849]

International and Foreign Language Education (IFLE)
American Overseas Research Centers Program
1990 K Street, N.W., Room 6087
Mail Stop K-OPE-6-6078
Washington, DC 20006
(202) 502-7634
(202) 502-7700
Fax: (202) 502-7860
E-mail: cheryl.gibbs@ed.gov
Web Site: www.ed.gov/ope/iegps

AREAS OF INTEREST:
Area studies.

NAME(S) OF PROGRAMS:
- **American Overseas Research Centers (AORC) Program**

TYPE:
Project/program grants; Research grants; Training grants. The AORC Program provides grants to consortia of U.S. institutions of higher education to establish or operate an AORC that promotes postgraduate research, exchanges and area studies.

LEGAL BASIS:
Authorized under Section 609 of the Higher Education Act of 1965, as amended.

ELIGIBILITY:
Any American overseas research center can qualify that meets the following conditions:
(1) be a consortium of U.S. institutions of higher education that receives more than 50% of its funding from public or private U.S. sources;
(2) have a permanent presence in the country in which the center is located and;
(3) be an organization described in Section 501(c)(3) of the Internal Revenue Code of 1993, which is exempt from taxation under Section 501(a) of the Code.

FINANCIAL DATA:
AORC grants may be used to pay all or a portion of the cost of establishing or operating a center or program including:
(1) the cost of operation and maintenance of overseas facilities;
(2) the cost of organizing and managing conferences;
(3) the cost of teaching and research materials;
(4) the cost of acquisition, maintenance and preservation of library collections;
(5) the cost of bringing visiting scholars and faculty to the center to teach or to conduct research;
(6) the cost of faculty and staff stipends and salaries;
(7) the cost of faculty, staff and student travel and;
(8) the cost of publication and dissemination of materials for the scholarly and general public.
Amount of support per award: Average annual grant: $65,000.

APPLICATION INFO:
Duration: Up to 48 months.

ADDRESS INQUIRIES TO:
Cheryl E. Gibbs, Director
Advanced Training and Research Division
(See address above.)

*PLEASE NOTE:
The AORC Program competes every four years. New competition is anticipated in the spring of 2016.

U.S. INSTITUTE OF PEACE [850]

Jennings Randolph Fellowship
Programs for International Peace
2301 Constitution Avenue, N.W.
Washington, DC 20037-2900
(202) 429-4746
Fax: (202) 429-6063
E-mail: jrprogram@usip.org
Web Site: www.usip.org

FOUNDED: 1984

AREAS OF INTEREST:
Topics and disciplines related to international peace, conflict and conflict management.

NAME(S) OF PROGRAMS:
- **Jennings Randolph Fellowship Programs for International Peace**

TYPE:
Fellowships; Residencies. Program is generally residential, but may vary. The U.S. Institute of Peace is an independent, nonpartisan institution created by Congress to strengthen the nation's capacity to promote the peaceful resolution of international conflict.

Under the Jennings Randolph Fellowship Programs for International Peace, Senior Fellowships and Peace Scholar Dissertation Fellowships are awarded on a competitive basis.

Senior Fellowships are awarded annually to scholars and practitioners from a variety of professions, including college and university faculty, journalists, diplomats, writers, educators, military officers, international negotiators and lawyers, and staff of civil society organizations. Fellows are supported for varying periods of time to conduct research on themes defined by USIP's five centers in their Calls for Applications, which

will be published on USIP's web site, consult with staff and contribute to the ongoing work of the Institute. Some Senior Fellowships may be partially residential or possibly even nonresidential.

Peace Scholar program supports doctoral dissertations that explore the sources and nature of international conflict, and strategies to prevent or end conflict and to sustain peace. Peace Scholars work at their university or appropriate field research sites. Successful applicants must demonstrate that their work is relevant for policy and/or practice in the field of conflict analysis, prevention and management, and postconflict peacebuilding.

YEAR PROGRAM STARTED: 1987

PURPOSE:
To enable outstanding scholars, practitioners and doctoral students to focus their efforts on critical problems of international peace and conflict.

Fellows undertake research and education projects that will increase knowledge and spread awareness among the public and policymakers and the public about topics concerning the sources and nature of international conflict and the full range of ways to end or prevent conflict and to sustain peace.

LEGAL BASIS:
Independent, nonpartisan and educational institution created by the U.S. Congress.

ELIGIBILITY:
Senior Fellowships: The competition is open to citizens of all nations. Women and members of minorities are especially encouraged to apply. Fellowship topics will vary.

Peace Scholar Dissertation Fellowships: Citizens of all countries are eligible, but must be enrolled in an accredited college or university in the U.S. Applicants must have completed all requirements for the degree except the dissertation by the commencement of the award (September 1). Priority will be given to projects that contribute knowledge relevant to the formulation of policy or to understanding of best practices on international peace and conflict issues.

FINANCIAL DATA:
Senior Fellows receive a stipend that will vary according to the particular call for applications.

Amount of support per award: Senior Fellows can receive up to $100,000 each for a 10-month period. Peace Scholar Dissertation Fellows receive a $20,000 flat stipend, which may be used to support writing or field research.

Total amount of support: Varies each year.

NO. MOST RECENT APPLICANTS: 140 for Peace Scholar Awards.

NO. AWARDS: Senior Fellowships: Varies; Peace Scholar Awards: 5 to 7 per year.

APPLICATION INFO:
For application forms for either the Senior Fellowships or the Peace Scholar Dissertation Fellowships, please visit the Institute's web site or contact the Jennings Randolph Fellowship Programs at the address above. Please note that the applications for both competitions are online only.

Duration: Senior Fellowships: Varies; Peace Scholar Dissertation Fellowships: 10 months.

Deadline: Jennings Randolph Senior Fellowships: Varies. There may be up to four competitions per year. Peace Scholar Fellows: December 11, 2015.

PUBLICATIONS:
Program Description with guidelines; application form; brochure.

STAFF:
Elizabeth Cole, Ph.D., Senior Program Officer

ADDRESS INQUIRIES TO:
Jennings Randolph Fellowship Programs for International Peace
(See address above.)

*PLEASE NOTE:
Research on conflict within the U.S. may not be supported under the terms of the Institute's mandate.

*SPECIAL STIPULATIONS:
No phone calls please.

U.S. INSTITUTE OF PEACE [851]

2301 Constitution Avenue, N.W.
Washington, DC 20037
(202) 429-3842
Fax: (202) 833-1741
E-mail: grants@usip.org
Web Site: www.usip.org/grants-fellowships

FOUNDED: 1984

AREAS OF INTEREST:
International peace and conflict management and related fields. Topic areas of interest include, but are not restricted to, international conflict resolution, diplomacy, negotiation theory, functionalism and "track two" diplomacy, methods of third-party dispute settlement, international law, international organizations and collective security, deterrence and balance of power, arms control, psychological theories about international conflict, the role of nonviolence and nonviolent sanctions, moral and ethical thought about conflict and conflict resolution and theories about relationships among political institutions, human rights and conflict.

NAME(S) OF PROGRAMS:
- **U.S. Institute of Peace Grant Program**

TYPE:
Conferences/seminars; Project/program grants; Research grants; Research contracts. Support for research, education and training and the dissemination of information on international peace and conflict resolution.

YEAR PROGRAM STARTED: 1986

PURPOSE:
To carry out basic and applied research on the causes of war and other international conflicts; to develop curricula and texts for high school through postgraduate study and to conduct teacher-training institutes, workshops and seminars; to conduct training, symposia and continuing education programs for practitioners, policymakers, policy implementers and the public; to undertake public information efforts; to increase the store of information on international peace and conflict resolution.

LEGAL BASIS:
Independent, nonpartisan federal institution created and funded by the U.S. Congress.

ELIGIBILITY:
Grant applicants must be nonprofit organizations, official public institutions and individuals, both U.S. and foreign nationals, including the following: institutions of postsecondary, community and secondary education, public and private education, training or research institutions and libraries and public departments and agencies (including state and territorial departments of education and commerce).

Individuals requesting support for degree work are not eligible.

FINANCIAL DATA:
Amount of support per award: The amount of any grant is based on the proposed budget and on negotiations with successful applicants. Average $107,000.

Total amount of support: $5,217,462 for fiscal year 2014.

NO. AWARDS: 16 for the year 2014.

APPLICATION INFO:
Application information is available on the web site.

Duration: One to two years.

Deadline: Priority Grant Competition applications are accepted on an ongoing basis, or as advertised on the Institute's web site.

PUBLICATIONS:
Program announcement.

ADDRESS INQUIRIES TO:
The Grant Program
United States Institute of Peace
(See address above.)

*SPECIAL STIPULATIONS:
The Institute does not support funding for degree work.

U.S. INSTITUTE OF PEACE [852]

2301 Constitution Avenue, N.W.
Washington, DC 20037
(202) 457-1700
Fax: (202) 429-6063
E-mail: essaycontest@usip.org
Web Site: www.usip.org

FOUNDED: 1984

AREAS OF INTEREST:
International affairs, peace, conflict resolution, history, writing and research.

NAME(S) OF PROGRAMS:
- **National High School Essay Contest**

TYPE:
Awards/prizes; Scholarships. The National High School Essay Contest engages high school students in learning and writing about issues of peace and conflict. It encourages appreciation for diplomacy's role in building partnerships that can advance peacebuilding and protect national security.

YEAR PROGRAM STARTED: 1987

PURPOSE:
To have students research and write about issues dealing with international conflict resolution and peacemaking.

LEGAL BASIS:
Independent, nonpartisan institution created by the U.S. Congress.

ELIGIBILITY:
Open to students of U.S. citizenship in grades nine-12 from public and private high schools as well as home schools throughout the country, U.S. territories and overseas schools. Students whose parents are members of the Foreign Service are ineligible. Previous first-place winners and immediate

relatives of directors or staff of the American Foreign Service Association and Semester at Sea are not eligible to participate.

FINANCIAL DATA:
First-place winner receives an all-expense-paid, two-day trip to Washington, DC to meet the U.S. Secretary of State and tour the Institute, as well as a full-tuition-paid voyage with Semester at Sea upon his or her enrollment at an accredited university.

Runner-up receives a full scholarship to participate in the International Diplomacy Program of the National Student Leadership Conference, held annually in Washington, DC.

Amount of support per award: First-place winner: $2,500. Runner-up: $1,250.

CO-OP FUNDING PROGRAMS: The National High School Essay Contest is conducted in conjunction with the American Foreign Service Association.

APPLICATION INFO:
Up-to-date information and details can be found on the American Foreign Service Association's web site (www.afsa.org/essay-contest).

Duration: One-time award. This is an annual contest.

Deadline: Usually in the spring.

ADDRESS INQUIRIES TO:
Perri Green
Awards Coordinator
American Foreign Service Association
2101 E Street, N.W.
Washington, DC 20037
E-mail: green@afsa.org

UNITED STATES-JAPAN FOUNDATION [853]

145 East 32nd Street
12th Floor
New York, NY 10016
(212) 481-8753
(212) 481-8757
Fax: (212) 481-8762
E-mail: info@us-jf.org
Web Site: www.us-jf.org

FOUNDED: 1980

AREAS OF INTEREST:
Precollege education and policy studies, communication and public opinion.

NAME(S) OF PROGRAMS:
- **Grants**
- **Elgin Heinz Award**
- **U.S.-Japan Leadership Program**

TYPE:
Awards/prizes; General operating grants; Project/program grants; Research grants; Travel grants. In the area of Precollege Education, the Foundation supports the improvement and enhancement of instruction of Japan in the U.S. and on the U.S. in Japan in secondary and elementary schools through programs which foster the creative use of the Internet in education, teacher training, professional development, intensive study tours, and curriculum design. The Foundation also supports the improvement of Japanese language instruction.

In the area of Policy Studies, the Foundation supports joint policy research and has established several nongovernmental channels for ongoing discussions between small groups of prominent experts. Policy projects have been active in such fields as trade and international finance, the environment, multilateral crisis management, and Northeast Asian security.

The Foundation will consider communication/public opinion projects that not only raise awareness about Japan in the U.S. and of the U.S. in Japan, but also deal with concrete issues that affect the bilateral relationship. Using creative approaches, these programs should reach broad audiences to stimulate balanced, in-depth and quality media coverage of issues that are central to U.S.-Japan relations.

Projects that link civil society organizations in the two countries are also supported.

YEAR PROGRAM STARTED: 1980

PURPOSE:
To promote stronger ties between Americans and Japanese through education, communication, policy studies and similar activities that foster greater mutual knowledge and understanding regarding each other and issues of common concern.

LEGAL BASIS:
Not-for-profit private foundation.

ELIGIBILITY:
Certain types of programs fall outside the Foundation's current interests. These include undergraduate education, cultural performances or exhibitions, sports exchanges, publication subsidies, scientific research and research conferences. As a rule, grants cannot be made to individuals applying on their own behalf for independent study, research, travel or participation in meetings; grants also cannot be made to for-profit organizations.

Because the Foundation is interested primarily in supporting program activities, it does not award grants as contributions to capital campaigns, endowment funds or deficit operations. In addition, it does not award grants for the construction or maintenance of buildings or other physical premises or for the purchase of equipment.

The Foundation does not administer programs which it supports. Foundation grants may not be used to influence legislation or election to public office.

GEOG. RESTRICTIONS: United States or Japan.

FINANCIAL DATA:
Amount of support per award: $10,000 to $100,000.

Total amount of support: Approximately $2,000,000 annually.

NO. MOST RECENT APPLICANTS: 150 to 200.

NO. AWARDS: Approximately 40.

REPRESENTATIVE AWARDS:
Pre-College Education: $7,500 to Lincoln Memorial University, Harrogate, TN, to enable students from Kanto International Senior High School in Tokyo, Japan, to visit primary and secondary schools in Tennessee; Policy Studies: $75,103 to Pacific Forum CSIS, Honolulu, HI, to support the second year of a three-year focused policy dialogue on U.S.-Japan-China relations that will draw attention to the long-term strategic goals of the three countries, and how current policy positions and pronouncements on all three sides impact the realization of those goals; Communications/Public Opinion: $110,000 to Japan Society, New York, NY, to support the 11th year of an intensive fellowship program for American media professionals, allowing them to reside, study and work for six weeks in Japan, focused on research topic of their choice.

APPLICATION INFO:
Applicants should submit a preproposal letter of inquiry, including a brief description of the proposed project and its objectives, any necessary background information on the project and applicant, and a brief budget estimate. If there is interest, the applicant will be invited to prepare a full proposal.

Duration: 12 months. Annual renewal possible.

Deadline: Preproposals are accepted on a rolling basis.

OFFICERS AND STAFF:
Maria Cristina Manapat-Sims, Assistant Secretary, Treasurer of the Corporation
David P. Janes, Director of Foundation Grants
Kelly Nixon, Program Officer
Aya Tsujita, Program Officer, Tokyo Office
Tomoyuki Watanabe, Japan Representative

ADDRESS INQUIRIES TO:
David P. Janes
Director of Foundation Grants
(See address above.)

International studies and research abroad

AFS INTERCULTURAL PROGRAMS/USA [854]

120 Wall Street, 4th Floor
New York, NY 10005
(800) 237-4636
(212) 299-9000
Fax: (212) 299-9090
E-mail: afsinfo@afsusa.org
Web Site: www.afsusa.org

FOUNDED: 1947

AREAS OF INTEREST:
International exchange of high school students and secondary teachers who live with host families and attend local schools. Participants go to and from 55 countries, including the former Soviet Union and Eastern Europe.

CONSULTING OR VOLUNTEER SERVICES:
More than 100,000 volunteers around the world.

NAME(S) OF PROGRAMS:
- **AFS Cultural Studies Program**
- **AFS Faces of America Diversity Scholarship Program**
- **AFS Gap Year Program**
- **AFS Language Studies Program**
- **AFS Semester Program**

- **AFS Summer Home Stay Program**
- **AFS Volunteer Development Program**
- **AFS Year Program**

TYPE:
Exchange programs; Scholarships; Visiting scholars. U.S. students abroad. Scholarships are for AFS-run programs only.

YEAR PROGRAM STARTED: 1947

PURPOSE:
To provide cross-cultural learning experiences for young people in another environment.

LEGAL BASIS:
Incorporated under the Not-for-Profit Corporation Laws of the state of New York. Exempt from New York state, New York City and federal taxes.

ELIGIBILITY:
Age, health, academic background, motivation and personality are considered.

FINANCIAL DATA:
Amount of support per award: Varies depending on merit and need.

Total amount of support: Approximately $3,000,000.

NO. AWARDS: 40% of all participants receive financial aid. AFS deals with 4,400 students each year.

APPLICATION INFO:
Candidate must submit health record, school record, applicant essay, screening group recommendation, interview forms and parental essay.

Duration: Two to six weeks to one year. Nonrenewable.

Deadline: Dependent on program.

PUBLICATIONS:
Annual report; application forms; AFS program catalog; *Partnerships*, newsletter.

IRS I.D.: 39-1711417

ADDRESS INQUIRIES TO:
See e-mail address above.

ALBRIGHT INSTITUTE OF ARCHAEOLOGICAL RESEARCH (AIAR) [855]

Department of Art and Art History
Providence College
Providence, RI 02918
(401) 865-1789
Fax: (401) 865-2410
E-mail: jbranham@providence.edu
Web Site: www.aiar.org

FOUNDED: 1900

AREAS OF INTEREST:
Fellowships are open to those in Near Eastern studies from prehistory through the early Islamic period, including the fields of anthropology, archaeology, art history, Bible, epigraphy, historical geography, history, language, literature, philology and religion, and related disciplines.

NAME(S) OF PROGRAMS:

- **Fellowships at the Albright Institute of Archaeological Research in Jerusalem**

TYPE:
Fellowships; Professorships; Scholarships; Travel grants; Visiting scholars. Fellowships are for study at the Albright Institute in Jerusalem, Israel.

The ACLS Recent Doctoral Recipients Fellowship is available to awardees and alternates of the Mellon/ACLS Dissertation Completion Fellowships the prior year.

The Annual Professorship is awarded to postdoctoral scholars who are U.S. citizens.

The George A. Barton Fellowship is awarded for two months and is open to all doctoral students or recent Ph.D. recipients.

The Marcia and Oded Borowski Research Fellowship provides a two-month fellowship to doctoral and post-doctoral candidates of all nationalities.

The Council of American Overseas Research Centers (CAORC) Multi-Country Research Fellowships are open to U.S. doctoral candidates and scholars who have already earned their Ph.D. in fields in the humanities, social sciences, or allied natural sciences and wish to conduct research of regional or transregional significance. Fellowships require scholars to conduct research in more than one country, at least one of which hosts a participating American overseas research center. (Apply at www.caorc.org/programs/index.html.)

Educational and Cultural Affairs Fellowships (ECA): (1) Junior Research Fellowships consist of two fellowships of nine months each; these fellowships are open to doctoral students and recent Ph.D. recipients who are U.S. citizens and; (2) Associate Fellowships consist of 13 administrative fee awards for senior and junior fellows (one or two semesters).

Ernest S. Frerichs Fellow and Program Coordinator is for nine months and is open to doctoral and postdoctoral scholars of all nationalities. Recipient is expected to assist the Albright's Director in planning and implementing the Ernest S. Frerichs Program for Albright Fellows, which requires a working knowledge of living and traveling in Israel.

The Seymour Gitin Distinguished Professorship is open to internationally recognized senior scholars of all nationalities who have made significant contributions to their field of study.

Glassman Holland Research Fellowship is open to all European postdoctoral researchers who are permanently resident in Europe.

Carol and Eric Meyers Doctoral Dissertation Fellowship provides two months of study for doctoral students whose research involves the study of archaeology and society in the biblical or early postbiblical periods. Topics dealing with society at the household level are encouraged.

National Endowment for the Humanities (NEH) Fellowships are awarded for up to 12 months. Open to postdoctoral scholars who are U.S. citizens or alien residents in the U.S. for at least three years.

The Noble Group Fellowships are open to Chinese citizens who are doctoral students and postdoctoral candidates and are either studying or in residence in China or doing research at institutions in other countries.

The Lydie T. Shufro Summer Research Fellowship is for one month during the summer and open to scholars at all levels and nationalities.

YEAR PROGRAM STARTED: 1940

PURPOSE:
To help scholars undertake high-quality research and field projects in the Near East; to encourage interdisciplinary study and communication among scholars.

LEGAL BASIS:
Nonprofit, archaeological research corporation.

ELIGIBILITY:
Fellowships are open to those in Near Eastern studies from prehistoric through the early Islamic period, including the fields of archaeology, anthropology, art history, Bible, epigraphy, gender studies, historical geography, history, language, literature, philology and religion and related disciplines. The research period should be continuous, without frequent trips outside the country. Residence at the Albright is required. The option to accommodate dependents is subject to space available at the Albright.

FINANCIAL DATA:
Amount of support per award: Varies.

Total amount of support: $325,000 in fellowships and awards.

CO-OP FUNDING PROGRAMS: With various organizations and foundations, such as the NEH.

NO. AWARDS: 60 for all programs: 28 in fellowships and awards from the Institute; 32 Associate Fellows receive funding from other sources.

APPLICATION INFO:
All eligible persons are encouraged to apply for as many awards as they wish, but each awardee can hold only one AIAR award at a time. Persons who have received an award in one year can reapply for the same or other awards the following year, but new applicants will be given priority.

Duration: Up to one year.

Deadline: October 1 and January 15.

PUBLICATIONS:
Applications.

ADDRESS INQUIRIES TO:
Dr. Joan R. Branham, Chair
Albright Fellowship Committee
(See address above.)

THE AMERICAN ACADEMY IN BERLIN [856]

Am Sandwerder 17-19
D-14109 Berlin Germany
(49) 30 804 83 118
Fax: (49) 30 804 83 111
E-mail: cs@americanacademy.de
Web Site: www.americanacademy.de

FOUNDED: 1994

AREAS OF INTEREST:
History, political science, literature, economics, German studies, art history, musicology, anthropology, law, writing, journalism, religious studies and sociology.

NAME(S) OF PROGRAMS:

- **Berlin Prize Fellowship**

TYPE:
Fellowships; Research grants; Residencies. Academic semester fellowship in Berlin with residence at the Hans Arnhold Center.

YEAR PROGRAM STARTED: 1998

PURPOSE:
To further scholarly professional development; to foster greater understanding between the people of the U.S. and the people of Germany.

LEGAL BASIS:
Private, independent, nonprofit center.

ELIGIBILITY:
Must be either a U.S. citizen or permanent resident, and have completed their Doctorate or equivalent professional degree. Open to scholars, artists, and professionals who wish to engage in independent study in Berlin for an academic semester or, in rare cases, for an entire academic year. Candidates need not work on German topics, but their project descriptions should explain how a residency in Berlin will contribute to further professional development. Writers must have published at least one book at time of application.

FINANCIAL DATA:
Amount of support per award: Stipend of $5,000 per month, round-trip airfare, and an apartment and partial board at the Hans Arnhold Center.

NO. MOST RECENT APPLICANTS: 300 to 400.

NO. AWARDS: Approximately 20 to 23.

APPLICATION INFO:
General Application is available online from mid-May to the end of September.

Duration: One academic semester.

Deadline: September 30.

STAFF:
Carol Scherer, Manager of Fellows Selection

ADDRESS INQUIRIES TO:
Carol Scherer
Manager of Fellows Selection
(See address above.)

AMERICAN ACADEMY IN ROME

7 East 60th Street
New York, NY 10022-1001
(212) 751-7200
Fax: (212) 751-7220
E-mail: info@aarome.org
Web Site: www.aarome.org

TYPE:
Awards/prizes; Fellowships; Residencies. Fellowships for independent work in architecture, landscape architecture, design, musical composition, visual arts, historic preservation/conservation, ancient studies, medieval studies, renaissance and early modern studies, and modern Italian studies. Supported projects must be conducted at American Academy in Rome facilities.

See entry 334 for full listing.

AMERICAN ACADEMY IN ROME

7 East 60th Street
New York, NY 10022
(212) 751-7200
Fax: (212) 751-7220
E-mail: info@aarome.org
Web Site: www.aarome.org

TYPE:
Awards/prizes; Fellowships; Residencies. Provides a residential year at the American Academy in Rome for an American landscape architect for advanced study, travel and association with other fellows in the arts and humanities.

See entry 2099 for full listing.

AMERICAN CENTER OF ORIENTAL RESEARCH [857]

656 Beacon Street
5th Floor
Boston, MA 02215-2010
(617) 353-6571
Fax: (617) 353-6575
E-mail: acor@bu.edu
Web Site: www.bu.edu/acor

FOUNDED: 1968

AREAS OF INTEREST:
The study of humanistic disciplines, such as art and architecture, literature, philology, prehistory and topography, relating in particular to the Middle East from prehistoric times to the modern era. Projects involving Islamic studies are especially encouraged.

The American Center of Oriental Research in Amman, Jordan serves as a center of operations for scholars of all nationalities wishing to conduct research in Jordan.

NAME(S) OF PROGRAMS:
- **ACOR-CAORC Fellowship**
- **ACOR-CAORC Postgraduate Fellowships**
- **Pierre and Patricia Bikai Fellowship**
- **Bert and Sally de Vries Fellowship**
- **Jennifer C. Groot Fellowships in the Archaeology of Jordan**
- **Harrell Family Fellowship**
- **MacDonald/Sampson Fellowship**
- **National Endowment for the Humanities (NEH) Fellowship**
- **James A. Sauer Fellowship**

TYPE:
Fellowships; Research grants; Visiting scholars. ACOR-CAORC Fellowships are for M.A. and doctoral students. Fields of study include all areas of the humanities and the natural and social sciences. Topics should contribute to scholarship in Near Eastern studies; U.S. citizenship required.

ACOR-CAORC Postgraduate Fellowships are for postdoctoral scholars and scholars with a terminal degree in their field, pursuing research or publication projects in the natural and social sciences, humanities, and associated disciplines relating to the Near East; U.S. citizenship required.

Pierre and Patricia Bikai Fellowship is for a residency at ACOR in Amman and is open to enrolled graduate students of any nationality, except Jordanian citizens, participating in an archaeological project or conducting archaeological work in Jordan.

Bert and Sally de Vries Fellowship supports a student for participation on an archaeological project or research in Jordan. Senior project staff members whose expenses are being borne largely by the project are ineligible. Open to enrolled undergraduate or graduate students of any nationality except Jordanian citizens.

The Jennifer C. Groot Fellowships support beginners in archaeological fieldwork who have been accepted as team members on archaeological projects with ASOR/CAP affiliation in Jordan. Open to undergraduate or graduate students of U.S. or Canadian citizenship.

Harrell Family Fellowship supports a graduate student for participation on an archaeological project or research in Jordan. Senior project staff members whose expenses are being borne largely by the project are ineligible. Open to enrolled graduate students of any nationality except Jordanian citizens.

MacDonald/Sampson Fellowship is for a residency at ACOR for research in the fields of Ancient Near Eastern languages and history, archaeology, Bible studies, or comparative religion, or a travel grant to assist with participation in an archaeological field project in Jordan. Open to enrolled undergraduate or graduate students of Canadian citizenship or landed immigrant status.

The National Endowment for the Humanities (NEH) Fellowship is for scholars who have a Ph.D. or have completed their professional training. Fields of research include modern and classical languages, linguistics, literature, history, jurisprudence, philosophy, archaeology, comparative religion, ethics, and the history, criticism and theory of the arts. Social and political scientists are encouraged to apply. Applicants must be U.S. citizens or foreign nationals living in the U.S. three years immediately preceding the application deadline.

James A. Sauer Fellowship is open to enrolled graduate students of U.S. or Canadian citizenship participating on an archaeological project or research in Jordan.

YEAR PROGRAM STARTED: 1968

PURPOSE:
To help scholars undertake high-quality research and field projects in the Middle East; to encourage interdisciplinary study and communication among scholars.

LEGAL BASIS:
Nonprofit, archaeological research corporation.

ELIGIBILITY:
Most fellowships are restricted to U.S. or Canadian citizens.

CAORC, NEH, MacDonald/Sampson and Bikai Fellows will reside at the ACOR facility in Amman while conducting their research. Recipients are expected to participate actively in the formal and informal activities of the Center.

FINANCIAL DATA:
Amount of support per award:
ACOR-CAORC Fellowships: $22,600 maximum; ACOR-CAORC Postgraduate Fellowships: $31,800 maximum; Pierre and Patricia Bikai Fellowship: $600 monthly stipend plus room and board at ACOR; Bert and Sally de Vries Fellowship: $1,200; Groot Fellowships: $1,500; Harrell Family Fellowship: $1,800; MacDonald/Sampson Fellowship: $600 stipend, plus room and board at ACOR, or travel grant of $1,800 to help with any project-related expenses; National Endowment for the Humanities (NEH) Fellowship: $25,200 maximum (for six months); James A. Sauer Fellowship: Room and board at ACOR and a stipend of $400.

Total amount of support: Varies.

CO-OP FUNDING PROGRAMS: With various organizations and foundations, such as the NEH.

NO. MOST RECENT APPLICANTS: 45 for all programs.

NO. AWARDS: ACOR-CAORC Fellowships, ACOR-CAORC Postgraduate Fellowships and Groot Fellowships: 2 or more each; Bikai Fellowship and NEH Fellowship: 1 to

2 each; Bert and Sally de Vries, Harrell Family, MacDonald/Sampson and Sauer Fellowships: 1 each.

APPLICATION INFO:
Prospective applicants are encouraged to consult with the ACOR Administrative Director about application procedures, the competitiveness of their applications, or any other questions they might have about the awards program.

All eligible persons are encouraged to apply for as many awards as they wish, but each awardee can hold only one ACOR award at a time. Persons who have received an award in one year can reapply for the same or other awards the following year, but new applicants will be given priority.

Duration: ACOR-CAORC Fellowships/Postgraduate Fellowships: Two to six months; Bikai Fellowship: One to two months; National Endowment for the Humanities (NEH) Fellowship: Four to six months; Sauer Fellowship: One month.

Deadline: February 1.

PUBLICATIONS:
Program announcements.

IRS I.D.: 23-7084091

ADDRESS INQUIRIES TO:
ACOR Fellowship Committee
(See address above.)

AMERICAN FRIENDS OF THE ALEXANDER VON HUMBOLDT FOUNDATION [858]

1101 17th Street, N.W.
Suite 603
Washington, DC 20036
(202) 783-1907
E-mail: info@americanfriends-of-avh.org
Web Site: www.americanfriends-of-avh.org

FOUNDED: 1953

AREAS OF INTEREST:
Postgraduate research in Germany.

NAME(S) OF PROGRAMS:
- **Humboldt Research Fellowship for Experienced Researchers**

TYPE:
Fellowships; Research grants. This program allows a researcher to carry out a long-term research project (six to 18 months) at a research institution in Germany which the applicant has selected in cooperation with an academic host.

PURPOSE:
To support highly qualified scholars and scientists of all nationalities and disciplines so that they may carry out a long-term research project.

ELIGIBILITY:
Open to scientists and scholars from outside Germany with above-average qualifications, who:
(1) have completed their Doctorate less than 12 years ago;
(2) already have his or her own research profile and;
(3) are working at least at the level of Assistant Professor or Junior Research Group Leader or have a record of several years of independent academic work.

Fellowships are awarded on the basis of academic achievement, the quality and feasibility of the proposed research and the candidate's publications.

FINANCIAL DATA:
In addition to a monthly stipend, special allowances are available for accompanying family members, travel expenses, and German language instruction.

Amount of support per award: EUR 3,150 monthly stipend.

Total amount of support: Varies.

NO. AWARDS: Approximately 600.

APPLICATION INFO:
Those interested must use application documents which can be downloaded from www.humboldt-foundation.de.

Duration: Six to 18 months. Fellowships may be divided into a maximum of three visits of at least three months each.

Deadline: Applications may be submitted at any time to the Humboldt Foundation in Bonn, Germany. The review process takes four to seven months, and the selection committee meets three times a year to review applications.

ADDRESS INQUIRIES TO:
Program Coordination
(See address above.) or

Alexander von Humboldt Stiftung
Jean-Paul-Strasse 12
D-53173 Bonn
Germany
Tel: 49 (0228) 833-0
Fax: 49 (0228) 833-199
E-mail: info@avh.de

AMERICAN FRIENDS OF THE ALEXANDER VON HUMBOLDT FOUNDATION [859]

1101 17th Street, N.W.
Suite 603
Washington, DC 20036
(202) 783-1907
E-mail: info@americanfriends-of-avh.org
Web Site: www.americanfriends-of-avh.org

FOUNDED: 1953

AREAS OF INTEREST:
Intercultural exchange.

NAME(S) OF PROGRAMS:
- **German Chancellor Fellowship**

TYPE:
Exchange programs; Fellowships. Fellowship for one-year stay in Germany for professional development, study or research. Applicants design individual projects specific to Germany and decide at which institutions to pursue them.

YEAR PROGRAM STARTED: 1990

PURPOSE:
To strengthen ties between Germany and the U.S. through fellowship recipient's profession or studies.

ELIGIBILITY:
Intended for career-oriented individuals from any profession or field of study who show outstanding potential for U.S. leadership. Selected fellows represent the private, public, not-for-profit, cultural and academic sectors. Applicant must be from (and current national of) the U.S., Russia, China or Brazil. U.S. citizenship is required.

FINANCIAL DATA:
Stipend covers housing and living expenses. In addition, the Fellowship also covers travel expenses to and from Germany and the costs of a German language course, introductory seminar, study tour, and final meeting in Bonn.

Amount of support per award: Monthly stipend of EUR 2,150 to EUR 2,750, based on qualifications.

Total amount of support: Varies.

NO. MOST RECENT APPLICANTS: 30 (from U.S.).

NO. AWARDS: 10 annually (from U.S.).

APPLICATION INFO:
Applications must be submitted to the Foundation's Bonn, Germany office.

Duration: One year.

Deadline: October 15. Fellowship period begins the following year on September 1.

ADDRESS INQUIRIES TO:
Charlotte Johnson, Program Coordinator
(See address above.)

*SPECIAL STIPULATIONS:
Prior to submitting an application, applicants are expected to have established contact with a mentor in Germany who agrees to provide professional and/or scholarly assistance throughout the program year.

AMERICAN INSTITUTE FOR SRI LANKAN STUDIES (AISLS) [860]

155 Pine Street
Belmont, MA 02478
E-mail: rogersjohnd@aol.com
Web Site: www.aisls.org

FOUNDED: 1996

AREAS OF INTEREST:
The promotion of scholarly excellence in Sri Lankan studies.

NAME(S) OF PROGRAMS:
- **AISLS Fellowship Program**

TYPE:
Fellowships. Program supports research in Sri Lanka by U.S. citizens who already hold a Ph.D. or the equivalent at the time they begin their fellowship tenure.

PURPOSE:
To foster excellence in American research and teaching on Sri Lanka; to promote the exchange of scholars and scholarly information between the U.S. and Sri Lanka.

ELIGIBILITY:
Applicants must hold U.S. citizenship and a Ph.D. or equivalent academic degree, or show that they will hold such a degree before taking up the fellowship. Scholars at all ranks are eligible. Applicants must plan to spend at least two months in Sri Lanka and complete the fellowship within the time frame listed under eligibility guidelines. Projects in all fields in the social sciences and humanities are eligible.

FINANCIAL DATA:
Fellowship includes reimbursement up to $2,000 for round-trip airfare between the U.S. and Colombo via U.S. carriers, and a limited budget for research expenses, to be negotiated.

Amount of support per award: Stipend of $3,700 per month.

APPLICATION INFO:
The completed application should contain the following items:
(1) AISLS Fellowship Application Cover Sheet;
(2) curriculum vitae, not to exceed three pages;
(3) description of the proposed study, not to

exceed three single-spaced pages. This is the most important part of the application. It should cover the questions to be addressed by the project, the approach to be taken, work done to date, work to be accomplished during the fellowship period, the applicant's competence to carry out the project, how the project addresses the criteria of the competition, and a statement of other support received or being sought for the project and;
(4) one-page bibliography, including a selected list of publications by other scholars or primary sources that have been or will be used in the project.

Duration: Two to nine months.

Deadline: December 1.

ADDRESS INQUIRIES TO:
John Rogers, U.S. Director
(See address above.)

AMERICAN INSTITUTE FOR SRI LANKAN STUDIES (AISLS) [861]

155 Pine Street
Belmont, MA 02478
E-mail: rogersjohnd@aol.com
Web Site: www.aisls.org

FOUNDED: 1996

AREAS OF INTEREST:
The promotion of scholarly excellence in Sri Lankan studies.

NAME(S) OF PROGRAMS:
- **AISLS Dissertation Planning Grant**

TYPE:
Research grants. Grant to assist graduate students intending to do dissertation research in Sri Lanka.

YEAR PROGRAM STARTED: 2006

PURPOSE:
To enable graduate students to make a pre-dissertation visit to Sri Lanka to investigate the feasibility of their topic, to sharpen their research design, or to make other practical arrangements for future research.

ELIGIBILITY:
Applicants must be enrolled in a Ph.D. program (or equivalent) in a U.S. university. There are no citizenship requirements. Applicants should have completed most of their graduate coursework by the time they take up their grant. The grant is especially intended for students who are in the process of completing their dissertation proposals and preparing applications for funds to support their dissertation research, but other purposes may be proposed. Applicants should plan to spend at least six weeks in Sri Lanka.

GEOG. RESTRICTIONS: United States.

FINANCIAL DATA:
Grant includes reimbursement up to $2,000 for round-trip airfare between U.S. and Colombo, reimbursement for any visa fees paid to the Sri Lankan government, and a per diem for six to eight weeks.

Amount of support per award: Per diem of $525 per week.

APPLICATION INFO:
The completed application should contain the following items:
(1) AISLS Dissertation Planning Grant Application Cover Sheet;
(2) curriculum vitae, not to exceed two pages, which should include the name and e-mail address of the applicant's dissertation supervisor;
(3) copy of the applicant's graduate transcript. An unofficial copy is acceptable;
(4) project narrative, not to exceed two single-spaced pages. This is the most important part of the application and should contain a summary of the proposed dissertation project, or, if the purpose of the planning grant is to define a dissertation project, a summary of the more general questions the applicant hopes to address in his or her dissertation, a description of what the applicant intends to do during the grant period, and the applicant's competence to carry out his or her proposed project, including language training;
(5) one-page project bibliography, including a selected list of publications by other scholars or primary sources that have been or will be used in the project and;
(6) a confidential letter of recommendation from the applicant's dissertation supervisor. This letter should cover the applicant's academic record and be specific about the applicant's progress to date within the graduate program concerned. This letter should be sent directly to John Rogers at the address listed above.

Duration: Six to eight weeks.

Deadline: December 1. Early submission is encouraged.

ADDRESS INQUIRIES TO:
John Rogers, U.S. Director
(See address above.)

AMERICAN INSTITUTE FOR YEMENI STUDIES [862]

232 Bay State Road
Room 426
Boston, MA 02215
(202) 633-1599
Fax: (202) 633-3141
E-mail: aiys.us@aiys.org
Web Site: www.aiys.org

FOUNDED: 1977

AREAS OF INTEREST:
Study and research in or about Yemen.

NAME(S) OF PROGRAMS:
- **General Fellowship Program**

TYPE:
Fellowships. Fellowship program for graduate and postgraduate scholars for Arabic language study, feasibility studies or research projects in Yemen.

PURPOSE:
To foster research in and about Yemen; to utilize American academic talent to strengthen Yemeni scholarship; to promote U.S.-Yemeni understanding.

ELIGIBILITY:
Limited to U.S. citizens who are enrolled as full-time graduate students in recognized degree programs or who are postgraduate researchers. Awards are made on the basis of merit. Collaborative or group projects are eligible for funding. It is permissible to combine Arabic language study with a research or feasibility project.

FINANCIAL DATA:
Amount of support per award: Up to $10,000.

NO. AWARDS: Approximately 10.

APPLICATION INFO:
There is a $25 processing fee for applications to the U.S. fellowship program. The fee is waived for applicants who are individual AIYS members.

All applicants must submit the original, plus five copies, of each of the following:
(1) completed application form;
(2) curriculum vitae and;
(3) application narrative consisting of a short statement explaining their interest in Yemen and their background in Arabic language (for applicants of Arabic language training grants) or a project description, four to six double-spaced pages, plus a proposed budget and schedule (for all other applicants).

Three letters of recommendation, preferably on institutional stationery, must be sent directly to AIYS postmarked by the deadline. Predoctoral applicants must have both undergraduate and graduate transcripts sent; recent Ph.D. recipients are encouraged to provide a graduate transcript.

Duration: Two months minimum.

Deadline: January 31.

ADDRESS INQUIRIES TO:
Monica Clark, U.S. Director
(See address above.)

*SPECIAL STIPULATIONS:
If applicant is not an individual AIYS member, a $25 processing fee for application will apply. Named fellows must become AIYS members before starting their fellowship tenure.

AMERICAN INSTITUTE OF BANGLADESH STUDIES [863]

B488 Medical Sciences Center
1300 University Avenue
Madison, WI 53706
(608) 265-1471
Fax: (608) 265-3302
E-mail: aibs@southasia.wisc.edu
Web Site: www.aibs.net

FOUNDED: 1989

AREAS OF INTEREST:
Bangladesh culture and society.

NAME(S) OF PROGRAMS:
- **Junior Fellowship**
- **Pre-Dissertation Fellowships**
- **Seminar, Workshop and Conference Support**
- **Senior Fellowship**
- **Undergraduate Research Initiative**

TYPE:
Awards/prizes; Conferences/seminars; Fellowships; Research grants; Travel grants. Junior Fellowship is for those who are in the ABD phase of their Ph.D. program. Applicants must be prepared to commence field research at the start of the fellowship period.

Pre-Dissertation Fellowships are short-term grants offered to graduate students pursuing studies of Bangladesh. The grant provides a stay of between two and four months in Bangladesh that may be used for language study, resource assessment, or network building to aid the completion of a competitive dissertation proposal.

The Senior Fellowship is for those who have a Ph.D. They may already have research experience in Bangladesh or may be interested in developing a research area on Bangladesh.

YEAR PROGRAM STARTED: 1989

PURPOSE:
To improve the scholarly understanding of Bangladesh culture and society in the U.S. and to promote educational exchange between the U.S. and Bangladesh.

ELIGIBILITY:
Applicants must be U.S. citizens or permanent residents and have their Ph.D.

Pre-Dissertation Fellowship: At the time of application, students must have completed at least one year of graduate study in a recognized Ph.D.-granting institution.

GEOG. RESTRICTIONS: United States.

FINANCIAL DATA:
Amount of support per award: Junior Fellowship: $920 monthly allowance; Senior Fellowship: $1,150 plus research and dependents'allowances per month in non-convertible Bangladesh Taka. Round-trip air transportation will be provided via the most direct route and using the Bangladesh carrier whenever possible.

Total amount of support: Varies.

APPLICATION INFO:
Application forms and complete details are available online.

Duration: Junior Fellowship: Six to 10 months; Pre-Dissertation Fellowship: Two to four months; Senior Fellowship: Four to 12 months.

Deadline: Varies depending upon program.

ADDRESS INQUIRIES TO:
See e-mail address above.

AMERICAN INSTITUTE OF INDIAN STUDIES [864]

1130 East 59th Street
Chicago, IL 60637
(773) 702-8638
Fax: (773) 702-6636
E-mail: aiis@uchicago.edu
Web Site: www.indiastudies.org

FOUNDED: 1961

AREAS OF INTEREST:
Indian studies.

NAME(S) OF PROGRAMS:
- **AIIS Fellowships**

TYPE:
Fellowships; Research grants. Senior (postdoctoral) Research Fellowships are awarded to academic specialists in Indian studies who possess the Ph.D. or equivalent. While in India, each Senior Research Fellow will be formally affiliated with an Indian university.

Fellowships for Senior Scholarly Development are awarded to established scholars who have not previously specialized in Indian studies and to established professionals who have not previously worked or studied in India. Proposals in this category should have a substantial research or project component and the anticipated results should be clearly defined. While in India, each Fellow will be formally affiliated with an Indian university.

Junior (dissertation) Fellowships are awarded to graduate students from all academic disciplines whose dissertation research requires study in India. Junior Fellows will have formal affiliation with Indian universities and Indian research supervisors.

Senior Performing Arts Fellowships are awarded to accomplished practitioners of the performing arts of India who demonstrate that studying in India will enhance their skills, develop their capabilities to teach or perform in the U.S., enhance American involvement with India's artistic traditions and strengthen their links with peers in India.

YEAR PROGRAM STARTED: 1962

PURPOSE:
To support the advancement of knowledge and understanding of India, its people and culture, primarily through research conducted in India by American scholars.

LEGAL BASIS:
Cooperative, nonprofit organization of 47 American colleges and universities.

ELIGIBILITY:
U.S. citizens are eligible for AIIS grants, as are foreign nationals enrolled or teaching full-time at American colleges or universities. U.S. and Indian government employees are ineligible for AIIS grants. Eligible applicants who are unaffiliated or who are from nonmember institutions are encouraged to apply.

FINANCIAL DATA:
Fellowships include a maintenance allowance and international travel. Fellowships for four months or less have significant travel restrictions. Fellowships for six months or more may include limited dependent coverage if funds are available. Award funds are generally made available in foreign currency only. An administrative overhead charge will be assessed to each AIIS Fellowship; this is not an application fee and is incurred only when a fellowship is awarded.

CO-OP FUNDING PROGRAMS: Fellowship programs of the AIIS have been supported by foreign currency funds received from the Smithsonian Institution and the National Science Foundation. Funding was also provided by the U.S. Information Agency and the AIIS member institutions. Additionally, the Institute receives a continuing grant from the National Endowment for the Humanities (NEH).

NO. AWARDS: Determined by the amount of support received by AIIS.

APPLICATION INFO:
Application materials are available upon request from the address above.

Duration: Up to nine months for Senior Research Fellowships, Fellowships for Senior Scholarly Development and Senior Performing Arts Fellowships; up to 11 months for Junior Fellowships.

Deadline: July 1. Awards are announced the following spring or summer. Awards begin in July of the following year.

OFFICERS:
Frederick Asher, President
Elise Auerbach, Administrator

ADDRESS INQUIRIES TO:
Elise Auerbach, Administrator
(See address above.)

*PLEASE NOTE:
A limited number of Senior Fellows will be selected to receive $1,000 per month of their fellowship award in U.S. dollars (with the remainder of their award still being in Indian rupees) due to a grant from the National Endowment for the Humanities. Awards will be assigned to those scholars who appear most likely to carry out "distinguished work in the humanities" in India.

*SPECIAL STIPULATIONS:
All AIIS-sponsored research projects and programs must receive the approval of the Indian government.

AMERICAN INSTITUTE OF INDIAN STUDIES

1130 East 59th Street
Chicago, IL 60637
(773) 702-8638
Fax: (773) 702-6636
E-mail: aiis@uchicago.edu
Web Site: www.indiastudies.org

TYPE:
Fellowships. Awards for graduate studies in India in an Indian language.

See entry 642 for full listing.

THE AMERICAN JEWISH JOINT DISTRIBUTION COMMITTEE [865]

711 Third Avenue
New York, NY 10017-4104
(212) 687-6200
Fax: (212) 370-5467
E-mail: globalservice@jdcny.org
Web Site: www.jdcentwine.org

AREAS OF INTEREST:
International Jewish communal service.

NAME(S) OF PROGRAMS:
- **The Ralph I. Goldman Fellowship**

TYPE:
Fellowships. Premier leadership opportunity awarded to one person annually for a young rising star and a professional opportunity to live and work in locations where the Joint Distribution Committee is active.

YEAR PROGRAM STARTED: 1987

PURPOSE:
To provide young Jewish leaders with an insider's perspective on JDC's global programs, while also giving them the opportunity to participate in the life of international Jewish communities.

ELIGIBILITY:
Candidates should have the following credentials:
(1) Master's degree or equivalent and proven academic excellence;
(2) some work experience in the candidate's chosen career;
(3) demonstrated exceptional leadership skills;
(4) strong interest in international Jewish communal affairs and social welfare;
(5) knowledge of foreign language(s) is a plus, but not a requirement and;
(6) formal and/or informal Jewish education.

FINANCIAL DATA:
Amount of support per award: $45,000 stipend plus international travel expenses.

NO. AWARDS: 1 annually.

APPLICATION INFO:
Candidates should send an e-mail to the address above.

Duration: One year, beginning in January.

Deadline: Application: May 30.

AMERICAN RESEARCH CENTER IN EGYPT, INC. [866]

8700 Crownhill Boulevard, Suite 507
San Antonio, TX 78209
(210) 821-7000
Fax: (210) 821-7007
E-mail: info@arce.org
fellows@arce.org
Web Site: www.arce.org

FOUNDED: 1948

AREAS OF INTEREST:
Research on Egypt and in Egypt on all phases of Egyptian civilization and culture from earliest times to the present.

NAME(S) OF PROGRAMS:
- **Fellowships for Research in Egypt**

TYPE:
Fellowships. Fellowships awarded to doctoral students in the all-but-dissertation (ABD) stage as well as to postdoctoral scholars. Topics for research fellowship encompass the humanities, social sciences and art and archaeology and cover periods from ancient times to the present.

YEAR PROGRAM STARTED: 1974

PURPOSE:
To obtain a fresh and more profound knowledge of Egypt and the Near East through scholarly research; to train American specialists in Near Eastern Studies in academic disciplines which require familiarity with Egypt; to disseminate knowledge of Egypt and thus understanding of the whole Near East and promote American-Egyptian cultural relations.

LEGAL BASIS:
Nonprofit organization.

ELIGIBILITY:
Criteria for selections rest on the Committee's judgment of the applicant's intellectual capacity and maturity, fitness for field work in Egypt, the significance and relevance of the proposed topic and its potential contribution to scholarly research in Egypt. No special consideration is given to applicants from member institutions and candidates need not be members of the ARCE. Awards are open to all qualified candidates without regard to sex, race and religion. All applicants, pre- and postdoctoral, must be U.S. citizens due to funding guidelines. Under certain circumstances, funding is available through the NEH for non-U.S. postdoctoral scholars living in the U.S. for more than three consecutive years to receive funding. Therefore, it is advisable to contact fellows@arce.org for further clarification.

GEOG. RESTRICTIONS: Egypt.

FINANCIAL DATA:
Monthly per diem plus round-trip airfare between the U.S. and Cairo. Fellows may receive stipends only for the period of time during which they are present in Egypt. A small dependent allowance for accompanying family members is available.

Amount of support per award: $2,200 to $3,650 monthly per diem; NEH all-inclusive award: $4,200 per month.

Total amount of support: Varies.

CO-OP FUNDING PROGRAMS: NEH and CAORC/ECA.

NO. MOST RECENT APPLICANTS: 25 for the year 2015-16.

NO. AWARDS: 5.

APPLICATION INFO:
Electronic submission is preferred. Original letters of recommendation and transcripts, if applicable, may also be scanned and sent electronically.

All applicants must submit three letters of recommendation. Predoctoral applicants must submit a fourth recommendation attesting to their capacity in ancient or modern languages as related to their proposed research.

Duration: CAORC/ECA: Three to 12 months; NEH all-inclusive award: Four to 10 months.

Deadline: Mid-January.

PUBLICATIONS:
Annual report; application guidelines; journal; bulletin; e-newsletter.

IRS I.D.: 04-2319500

GOVERNING BOARD:
Melinda Hartwig, President
Emily Teeter, Vice President
Mary Jane Verette, Treasurer

ADDRESS INQUIRIES TO:
Djodi Deutsch
Academic Programs Coordinator
E-mail: fellows@arce.org

AMERICAN RESEARCH CENTER IN SOFIA (ARCS) - U.S. OFFICE [867]

The Field Museum
1400 South Lake Shore Drive
Chicago, IL 60605-2496
(312) 665-7478
E-mail: usadmin@arcsofia.org
Web Site: arcsofia.org

AREAS OF INTEREST:
Humanities and social sciences.

NAME(S) OF PROGRAMS:
- **Academic Program Fellowship Competition**

TYPE:
Fellowships. The American Research Center in Sofia (ARCS), Bulgaria, offers three programs with accompanying fellowships: a fall term program (September to November) focusing on the history and archaeology of Bulgaria and neighboring countries, from prehistory to the present; a spring term program (February to April) focusing on the history of religion in Bulgaria and neighboring countries; and a nine-month program (September to May) which incorporates the material of both fall and spring terms. The programs combine a formal academic curriculum with independent research. The Center hosts the programs' lectures and seminars, organizes related study trips, facilitates opportunities for taking Bulgarian and other Balkan language classes, and provides logistical support and access to local libraries, museums and other educational institutions. The Center engages the participants with eminent local scholars relevant to the field of their study and makes arrangements for specialized research at local institutions.

ELIGIBILITY:
Graduate students of any citizenship enrolled at North American academic institutions, or academic institutions accredited in North America, engaged in research in the humanities and/or social sciences with a focus on Bulgaria or the Balkan Peninsula (antiquity through modern day).

FINANCIAL DATA:
The Fellowship includes free housing in Sofia, Bulgaria, language instruction, travel expenses within the academic program, and travel expenses between North America and Bulgaria (up to $1,000).

Amount of support per award: $600 monthly stipend.

NO. AWARDS: 7 (3 for fall semester; 3 for spring semester; 1 full academic year).

APPLICATION INFO:
A complete application consists of the following:
(1) the ARCS application form;
(2) a project description, no more than 1,500 words, including significance of project, kinds of resources to be used, fieldwork to be pursued, and reason to conduct research at ARCS;
(3) a current curriculum vitae of no more than three pages;
(4) academic transcripts and;
(5) two letters of reference from scholars in the field commenting on the value and feasibility of the project.

Applications should be submitted to the Fellowship Committee at the e-mail address above.

Deadline: January.

ADDRESS INQUIRIES TO:
U.S. Office of ARCS:
Dr. Emil Nankov, Academic Director
E-mail: apo@arcsofia.org

AMERICAN RESEARCH INSTITUTE IN TURKEY, INC. [868]

c/o The University of Pennsylvania Museum
3260 South Street
Philadelphia, PA 19104-6324
(215) 898-3474
Fax: (215) 898-0657
E-mail: leinwand@sas.upenn.edu
Web Site: ccat.sas.upenn.edu/ARIT/ARITFellowships.html

FOUNDED: 1964

AREAS OF INTEREST:
Research and study in Turkey, including all fields of the humanities and social sciences.

NAME(S) OF PROGRAMS:
- **ARIT Fellowship Program**

TYPE:
Fellowships. ARIT offers a number of fellowships for research in Turkey in humanities and social sciences. Grants for tenures of up to one academic year will be considered; some preference is given to projects of shorter duration. ARIT operates hostel, research and study facilities for researchers in Turkey at its branch centers in Istanbul and Ankara.

YEAR PROGRAM STARTED: 1964

PURPOSE:
To support research in humanities and social sciences in Turkey.

LEGAL BASIS:
Funded in part by grants from U.S. Department of State, Bureau of Educational and Cultural Affairs.

ELIGIBILITY:
Scholars and advanced graduate students engaged in research on ancient, medieval or modern times in Turkey, in any field of the

humanities and social sciences, are eligible. Student applicants must have fulfilled all preliminary requirements for the Doctorate except the dissertation by June of the program year, and before beginning any ARIT-sponsored research. Non-U.S. applicants who currently reside in the U.S. or Canada are expected to maintain an affiliation with an educational institution in the U.S. or Canada. For questions of eligibility and procedures, please check with the ARIT office in Philadelphia.

FINANCIAL DATA:
Awards cover international travel to and from Turkey and provide a stipend based on Turkish living standards and the fellow's academic status.

Amount of support per award: $4,000 to $16,000.

Total amount of support: Varies.

CO-OP FUNDING PROGRAMS: The Fellowship program is supported in part by a grant from the U.S. Department of State, Bureau of Educational and Cultural Affairs.

NO. MOST RECENT APPLICANTS: 90 for the year 2014-15.

NO. AWARDS: 4 for the year 2014.

APPLICATION INFO:
Turkish law requires foreign scholars to obtain formal permission for any research to be carried out at institutions in Turkey. ARIT fellowship applicants are responsible for obtaining the appropriate research permissions and visas. In general, researchers should seek permission to carry out research directly from the director(s) of the institution(s) where they intend to work; this includes researchers who wish to work in libraries housed in Turkish museums. For archival and library research with tenures of less than three months, some foreign scholars may enter Turkey on a tourist visa and apply for the research permit and visa from within Turkey, or scholars may choose to procure a research visa from the Turkish embassy in advance of their arrival. Scholars wishing to carry out research in Turkey for terms longer than three months should apply for the research permit and in addition secure a research visa prior to entering Turkey. Non-U.S. researchers should consult the Turkish Consulate for specific procedures.

Researchers who wish to work with collections housed in the Turkish archaeological museums, however, should make their applications through the Ministry of Culture and Tourism, General Directorate for Cultural Heritage and Museums. In addition, if the material they wish to work with is part of an excavation, researchers must submit a letter with their application signed by the excavation director giving permission to carry out the research. The research permit application regulations and format for researchers are posted on the ARIT web site. ARIT reserves the right to withhold payment of fellowship stipends if appropriate research permission is not obtained.

Please include letters of reference with one's application. Graduate student applicants must provide a copy of their graduate transcript.

Duration: Stipends are provided for a period determined by each Fellow's research requirements, but not exceeding 12 months. Some preference will be given to projects of shorter duration.

Deadline: Applications and three letters of recommendation must be received by November 1 to ARIT, c/o University of Pennsylvania Museum.

OFFICERS:
A. Kevin Reinhart, President
Nick Cahill, Vice President
Maria de Jong Ellis, Treasurer

ADDRESS INQUIRIES TO:
Nancy W. Leinwand
(See telephone and e-mail above.)

AMERICAN RESEARCH INSTITUTE IN TURKEY, INC. [869]

c/o The University of Pennsylvania Museum
3260 South Street
Philadelphia, PA 19104-6324
(215) 898-3474
Fax: (215) 898-0657
E-mail: leinwand@sas.upenn.edu
Web Site: ccat.sas.upenn.edu/ARIT

FOUNDED: 1964

AREAS OF INTEREST:
Turkey.

NAME(S) OF PROGRAMS:
- **Bogazici University Summer Language Program for Intensive Advanced Turkish Language Study**

TYPE:
Fellowships. Bogazici University Summer Language Program: For summer study in Turkey. Also offer travel, stipend and tuition grants. This intensive program offers the equivalent of one full academic year of study in advanced Turkish language at the college level.

YEAR PROGRAM STARTED: 1981

PURPOSE:
To support the study of advanced Turkish language.

LEGAL BASIS:
Consortium of universities. Funding from the U.S. Department of Education.

ELIGIBILITY:
Full-time students and scholars affiliated at academic institutions are eligible to apply. To be a fellowship applicant, one must:
(1) be a citizen, national or permanent resident of the U.S.;
(2) be enrolled in an undergraduate- or graduate-level academic program, or be faculty;
(3) have a minimum B average in one's studies, if still a student and;
(4) perform at the high-intermediate level on a proficiency-based admissions examination.

FINANCIAL DATA:
Fellowships cover round-trip airfare to Istanbul, application and tuition fees, and a maintenance stipend.

CO-OP FUNDING PROGRAMS: Funded by U.S. Department of Education, Office of Post-Secondary Education.

NO. MOST RECENT APPLICANTS: Approximately 50.

NO. AWARDS: 17 for the year 2014.

APPLICATION INFO:
Application information is available on the web site.

Duration: Approximately eight weeks (late June through early August).

Deadline: Early February.

OFFICERS:
A. Kevin Reinhart, President
Nick Cahill, Vice President
Maria de Jong Ellis, Treasurer
Linda Darling, Secretary

ADDRESS INQUIRIES TO:
Dr. Sylvia Onder
Eastern Mediterranean Languages
Department of Arabic and Islamic Studies
Georgetown University
210 North Poulton Hall
1437 37th Street, N.W.
Washington, DC 20007
E-mail: aritfellowship@georgetown.edu or

Nancy Leinwand
American Research Institute in Turkey
(See address and e-mail above.)

AMERICAN RESEARCH INSTITUTE IN TURKEY, INC. [870]

c/o The University of Pennsylvania Museum
3260 South Street
Philadelphia, PA 19104-6324
(215) 898-3474
Fax: (215) 898-0657
E-mail: leinwand@sas.upenn.edu
Web Site: ccat.sas.upenn.edu/ARIT/

FOUNDED: 1964

AREAS OF INTEREST:
Turkey covering all periods of history in the general range of the humanities and including humanistically oriented aspects of the social sciences, prehistory, history, art, archaeology, literature and linguistics, as well as interdisciplinary aspects of cultural history.

NAME(S) OF PROGRAMS:
- **NEH Fellowships for Research in Turkey**

TYPE:
Fellowships. These advanced fellowships are made possible by support from the National Endowment for the Humanities. The fields of study cover all periods of history in the general range of the humanities and include humanistically oriented aspects of the social sciences, prehistory, history, art, archaeology, literature and linguistics, as well as interdisciplinary aspects of cultural history.

ARIT maintains two research institutes in Turkey. ARIT in Istanbul has a research library concentrated on Byzantine and Ottoman Turkey. The ARIT Ankara center focuses on art, archaeology, and ancient history in its library, and serves Turkish and American archaeologists through its programs. Both institutes have residential facilities for fellows and provide general assistance as well as introductions to colleagues, institutions and authorities in Turkey.

YEAR PROGRAM STARTED: 1991

PURPOSE:
To support long-term postdoctoral research in Turkey in the humanities.

LEGAL BASIS:
Consortium of universities. Funding from the National Endowment for the Humanities.

ELIGIBILITY:
Scholars who have completed their formal academic training by the application deadline and plan to carry out research in Turkey may apply. Applicants may be U.S. citizens or three-year residents of the U.S. Please

consult ARIT headquarters on questions of eligibility. Advanced scholars may also apply for ARIT Fellowships in the Humanities and Social Sciences.

FINANCIAL DATA:
Amount of support per award: $16,800 to $50,400 stipend, depending on individual proposals.

NO. MOST RECENT APPLICANTS: 15.

NO. AWARDS: 1 to 3 advanced fellowships for the 2015-16 academic year.

APPLICATION INFO:
Turkish law requires foreign scholars to obtain formal permission to carry out research at institutions in Turkey. ARIT fellowship applicants are responsible for obtaining the appropriate research permissions and visas. In general, researchers should seek permission to carry out research from the director(s) of the institution(s) where they intend to work; this includes researchers who wish to work in libraries housed in Turkish museums. For archival and library research with tenure of less than three months, some foreign scholars may enter Turkey on a tourist visa and apply for the research permit and visa from within Turkey; or they may choose to procure a research visa via the Turkish Embassy in advance of their arrival. Scholars wishing to carry out research in Turkey for terms longer than three months should apply for the research permit and in addition secure a research visa prior to entering Turkey. Non-U.S. researchers should consult the Turkish Consulate for specific procedures.

Researchers who wish to work with collections housed in the Turkish archaeological museums, however, should make their applications through the Ministry of Culture and Tourism, General Directorate for Cultural Heritage and Museums. In addition, if the material they wish to work with is part of an excavation, researchers must submit a letter with their application signed by the excavation director giving permission to carry out the research. The research permit application regulations and format for researchers are posted on the ARIT web site (ccat.sas.upenn.edu/ARIT/Research Permit.htm). ARIT reserves the right to withhold payment of fellowship stipends if appropriate research permission is not obtained.

Duration: Four to 12 continuous months.

Deadline: Applications and three letters of recommendation must be received by ARIT by November 1 for the following academic year. Please use the ARIT application format accessible on its web site and submit all materials to the above address. Applicants will be notified by the end of January of that following year.

PUBLICATIONS:
Program announcement.

OFFICERS:
A. Kevin Reinhart, President
Nick Cahill, Vice President
Maria de Jong Ellis, Treasurer
Linda Darling, Secretary

ADDRESS INQUIRIES TO:
Nancy W. Leinwand
(See telephone number above.)

THE AMERICAN-SCANDINAVIAN FOUNDATION [871]

58 Park Avenue
New York, NY 10016
(212) 879-9779
E-mail: grants@amscan.org
Web Site: www.amscan.org

FOUNDED: 1910

AREAS OF INTEREST:
Advanced study in Scandinavia.

NAME(S) OF PROGRAMS:
- **ASF Awards for Study in Scandinavia**

TYPE:
Fellowships; Research grants. Short-term project grants and long-term fellowships for advanced study in a field which may be pursued with particular merit in one of the Scandinavian countries (Denmark, Finland, Iceland, Norway or Sweden).

Fellowships are intended to support an academic year-long stay. Priority is given to candidates at the graduate level for dissertation-related study or research.

Grants are considered especially suitable for postgraduate scholars, professionals and candidates in the arts to carry out research or study visits of one to three months' duration.

YEAR PROGRAM STARTED: 1911

PURPOSE:
To advance cultural and intellectual understanding between the U.S. and Scandinavia, primarily through exchange programs, cultural programs and publications.

LEGAL BASIS:
Nonprofit educational institution qualifying under statutes 501(c)(3), 509(a)(1) and 170(c)(2) of the IRS code.

ELIGIBILITY:
Applicants must have a well-defined research or study project that makes a stay in Scandinavia essential. Applicants must be U.S. citizens or permanent residents who will have completed their undergraduate education by the start of their project in Scandinavia. Team projects are eligible, but each member must apply as an individual, submitting a separate, fully documented application. First priority will be given to applicants who have not previously received an ASF award. Only in exceptional cases will a third award be considered. The ASF considers it desirable that all candidates have at least some ability in the language of the host country, even if it is not essential for the execution of the research plan. For projects that require a command of one or more Scandinavian (or other) languages, candidates should defer application until they have the necessary proficiency. Evidence of a confirmed invitation or affiliation is an important factor in award consideration.

ASF does not fund the following:
(1) travel for attendance at professional meetings, conferences, seminars or conventions;
(2) performances or exhibitions;
(3) publication costs;
(4) equipment purchases, including personal computers, software and cell phones;
(5) research assistants;
(6) institutional overhead costs;
(7) tuition fees from U.S. home institution;
(8) foregone salary;
(9) supplementation of substantial sabbatical support;
(10) support for dependents;
(11) repayment of loans or other personal obligations;
(12) acquisition of language skills;
(13) study in programs especially designed for English-speaking students, or at English-language institutions;
(14) beginning studies in any subject or;
(15) retroactive program support.

Projects must be undertaken in Denmark, Finland, Iceland, Norway or Sweden.

GEOG. RESTRICTIONS: Scandinavia.

FINANCIAL DATA:
The awards support project-related costs, including maintenance, transatlantic round-trip travel, in-country travel, tuition and fees (where applicable) and materials expenditures (e.g., books, photocopying, art supplies).

Amount of support per award: Grants normally up to $5,000, especially suited for short visits of one to three months and fellowships of up to $23,000, intended for a full academic year of study or research.

Total amount of support: Varies annually. Over $300,000 is available for the 2015-16 competition.

NO. MOST RECENT APPLICANTS: 132.

NO. AWARDS: Varies each year according to total funds available. Awards were made to 25 Americans in the 2014-15 competition.

APPLICATION INFO:
Only applications on current official ASF forms will be considered. Such applications are available online. Incomplete applications cannot be processed. Unsuccessful applications will be discarded.

Applicants for Awards for Study in Scandinavia are urged to arrange their academic or professional affiliations as far in advance as possible. Applicants must secure these placements or affiliations on their own; the ASF cannot assist in establishing contacts. The ASF requires confirmation of invitation or affiliation from the institution or individuals detailed in the proposal. Since July and August are traditionally holiday months in Scandinavia, many people may not be available for consultation. Applicants are cautioned to plan their projects accordingly. Applicants are expected to devote full-time to their proposed study or research, and must justify the length of time needed to complete their project. Awards are based on the application submitted; subsequent changes in the proposal are discouraged and may not be considered.

Duration: Grants: One to three months. Fellowships: One academic year.

Deadline: November 1 for receipt of fully documented applications. Awards announced by the following April 15.

PUBLICATIONS:
Annual report; fellowship and grant application guidelines; *Scandinavian Review*; *Scan*, newsletter; *Study in Scandinavia*, guide.

ADMINISTRATION:
Edward P. Gallagher, President
Lynn Carter, Executive Vice President and Secretary
Matthew Walters, Director, Fellowships and Grants

ADDRESS INQUIRIES TO:
Fellowships and Grants
(See address above.)

*SPECIAL STIPULATIONS:
ASF awards may require supplementation from other sources, but they should not duplicate the benefits of additional awards (and vice versa). Candidates must notify the ASF if they have received other award offers. The ASF will not provide funds if, in its judgment, a proposal can be carried out without its assistance.

THE AMERICAN SCHOOL OF CLASSICAL STUDIES AT ATHENS [872]

6-8 Charlton Street
Princeton, NJ 08540-5232
(609) 683-0800
Fax: (609) 924-0578
E-mail: ascsa@ascsa.org (for information)
application@ascsa.org (to apply)
Web Site: www.ascsa.edu.gr

FOUNDED: 1881

AREAS OF INTEREST:
Classical studies.

NAME(S) OF PROGRAMS:
- **National Endowment for the Humanities Fellowships**

TYPE:
Fellowships. Fellowships for postdoctoral scholars and professionals in the humanities.

YEAR PROGRAM STARTED: 1881

LEGAL BASIS:
Graduate research and teaching center.

ELIGIBILITY:
Applicants must be U.S. citizens or foreign nationals who have been U.S. residents for three years prior to application deadline. Candidates must hold their Ph.D. or equivalent terminal degree at time of application.

School programs are generally open to qualified students and scholars at colleges or universities in the U.S. or Canada; restrictions may apply for specific fellowships and programs. The American School of Classical Studies at Athens does not discriminate on the basis of race, age, sex, sexual orientation, color, religion, ethnic origin, or disability when considering admission to any form of membership.

FINANCIAL DATA:
Amount of support per award: Stipend up to $21,000 (for a five-month project) and up to $42,000 (for a 10-month project). School fees are waived.

NO. MOST RECENT APPLICANTS: 21.

NO. AWARDS: 2 to 4.

APPLICATION INFO:
Correspondence about fellowships and admission to membership in the school should be directed to the address above. Applicants must submit an online application form and letters of reference.

Duration: Five to 10 months during academic year, September 1 to June 1.

Deadline: October 31.

STAFF:
James C. Wright, Director

ADDRESS INQUIRIES TO:
E-mail: ascsa@ascsa.org

*SPECIAL STIPULATIONS:
Membership application to the ASCSA must be made online on the web site at the same time one applies to any outside funding organization for work at the School.

THE AMERICAN SCHOOL OF CLASSICAL STUDIES AT ATHENS [873]

6-8 Charlton Street
Princeton, NJ 08540-5232
(609) 683-0800
Fax: (609) 924-0578
E-mail: ascsa@ascsa.org (for information)
application@ascsa.org (to apply)
Web Site: www.ascsa.edu.gr

FOUNDED: 1881

AREAS OF INTEREST:
Classical studies, archaeology, art history, post-classical, Byzantine and post-Byzantine, Late Antiquity and Modern Greek Studies.

NAME(S) OF PROGRAMS:
- **M. Alison Frantz Fellowship in Post-Classical Studies at the Gennadius Library**
- **The Jacob Hirsch Fellowship in Archaeology**

TYPE:
Fellowships. The M. Alison Frantz Fellowship and The Jacob Hirsch Fellowship are part of the Student Associate Program, which is open to advanced graduate students in the same fields as the Regular Academic Program (classical studies and ancient Mediterranean studies and related fields such as history of art, anthropology, prehistory, studies in postclassical Greece, etc.), who plan to pursue independent research projects and who do not wish to commit to the full Regular Academic Program.

The Jacob Hirsch Fellowship is also open to students from Israel.

YEAR PROGRAM STARTED: 1963

PURPOSE:
To provide financial assistance to advanced graduate students who plan to pursue independent research projects and who do not wish to commit to the American School's full Regular Academic Program.

LEGAL BASIS:
Graduate educational institution (non-degree granting).

ELIGIBILITY:
Frantz Fellowship: Awarded to Ph.D. candidates at a U.S. or Canadian institution or college or a recent Ph.D. from a U.S. or Canadian institution. Applicants must demonstrate their need to work in the Gennadius Library. Fields of study include late antiquity, Byzantine or modern Greek studies.

Hirsch Fellowship: Awarded to a Ph.D. candidate from U.S. or Israel (Israeli citizens) writing a dissertation, or a recent Ph.D. revising a dissertation for publication, for projects carried out in Greece.

School programs are generally open to qualified students and scholars at colleges or universities in the U.S. or Canada; restrictions may apply for specific fellowships and programs. The American School of Classical Studies at Athens does not discriminate on the basis of race, age, sex, sexual orientation, color, religion, ethnic origin, or disability when considering admission to any form of membership.

FINANCIAL DATA:
In addition to stipend, room and board is provided at the American School of Classical Studies in Athens.

Amount of support per award: Stipend of $11,500, plus room, board and waiver of School fees.

NO. MOST RECENT APPLICANTS: 24.

NO. AWARDS: 1 of each annually.

APPLICATION INFO:
Application must be made online on the ASCSA web site.

Frantz Fellowship: Applicants must submit a full curriculum vitae, a project description showing the need for using the Gennadius Library and three supporting letters from qualified scholars. Send application to Chairperson, Gennadius Library Committee.

Hirsch Fellowship: Online application for admission to the American School should be made in conjunction with application for the Hirsch Fellowship. Transcripts of record, three letters of recommendation and a detailed description of the project to be pursued in Greece should be submitted to Chair, Committee on Admissions and Fellowships.

Duration: One academic year (September to June).

Deadline: January 15, with announcement by March 15.

STAFF:
James C. Wright, Director

ADDRESS INQUIRIES TO:
Frantz Fellowship:
Chair,
Committee on Libraries and Archives
(See address above.)

Hirsch Fellowship:
Chair,
Committee on Admissions and Fellowships
(See address above.)

*SPECIAL STIPULATIONS:
Membership application to the ASCSA must be made online on the web site at the same time one applies to any outside funding organization for work at the School.

Hirsch and Frantz Fellowship recipients must maintain residence in Athens and work at the Gennadius Library during the full term of the Fellowship.

THE AMERICAN SCHOOL OF CLASSICAL STUDIES AT ATHENS [874]

6-8 Charlton Street
Princeton, NJ 08540-5232
(609) 683-0800
Fax: (609) 924-0578
E-mail: ascsa@ascsa.org (for information)
application@ascsa.org (to apply)
Web Site: www.ascsa.edu.gr

FOUNDED: 1881

AREAS OF INTEREST:
Classical studies, history of art, history of architecture, pottery, Mycenaean archaeology, Athenian architecture and archaeology.

NAME(S) OF PROGRAMS:
- **Advanced Fellowships**

TYPE:
Fellowships. Several Fellowships awarded by the School for the full academic year: the Samuel H. Kress Fellowship in art and architecture of antiquity; the Gorham Phillips Stevens Fellowship in the history of

architecture; the Ione Mylonas Shear Fellowship in Mycenaean archaeology or Athenian architecture and/or archaeology; the Homer A. and Dorothy B. Thompson Fellowship in the study of pottery. Additionally, three Fellowships are unrestricted as to field: the Edward Capps, the Doreen Canaday Spitzer, and the Eugene Vanderpool Fellowships.

PURPOSE:
To support work on a specific project by students who wish to study at the School for a year.

ELIGIBILITY:
Students who have completed the Regular Program or one year as a Student Associate Member at the ASCSA and plan to return to the School to pursue independent research, usually for the Ph.D. dissertation, may apply. Given only if candidates meet a standard acceptable to the Director and the Committee.

School programs are generally open to qualified students and scholars at colleges or universities in the U.S. or Canada; restrictions may apply for specific fellowships and programs. The American School of Classical Studies at Athens does not discriminate on the basis of race, age, sex, sexual orientation, color, religion, ethnic origin, or disability when considering admission to any form of membership.

GEOG. RESTRICTIONS: United States and Canada.

FINANCIAL DATA:
Amount of support per award: Stipend of $11,500, plus room, board and waiver of School fees.

NO. MOST RECENT APPLICANTS: 23.

NO. AWARDS: 7.

APPLICATION INFO:
Submit application form, curriculum vitae, transcripts, letters of recommendation and a detailed statement of the project to be pursued in Greece. Application must be made online on the ASCSA web site.

Duration: One year.

Deadline: February 15.

STAFF:
James C. Wright, Director

ADDRESS INQUIRIES TO:
Committee Chair
(See address above.)

*SPECIAL STIPULATIONS:
Membership application to the ASCSA must be made online on the web site at the same time one applies to any outside funding organization for work at the School.

THE AMERICAN SCHOOL OF CLASSICAL STUDIES AT ATHENS [875]

6-8 Charlton Street
Princeton, NJ 08540-5232
(609) 683-0800
Fax: (609) 924-0578
E-mail: ascsa@ascsa.org (for information)
application@ascsa.org (to apply)
Web Site: www.ascsa.edu.gr

FOUNDED: 1881

AREAS OF INTEREST:
Ancient Greek law.

NAME(S) OF PROGRAMS:
- **The Harry Bikakis Fellowship**

TYPE:
Fellowships. Research fellowship awarded periodically, but not more frequently than once a year.

PURPOSE:
To promote research.

ELIGIBILITY:
North American or Greek graduate students researching ancient Greek law, or Greek graduate students working on a School excavation.

School programs are generally open to qualified students and scholars at colleges or universities in the U.S. or Canada; restrictions may apply for specific fellowships and programs. The American School of Classical Studies at Athens does not discriminate on the basis of race, age, sex, sexual orientation, color, religion, ethnic origin, or disability when considering admission to any form of membership.

GEOG. RESTRICTIONS: North America.

FINANCIAL DATA:
Amount of support per award: $1,875. School fees are waived.

NO. MOST RECENT APPLICANTS: 2.

NO. AWARDS: 1.

APPLICATION INFO:
Submit Associate Member application, including an outline of the proposed project, and one letter of reference online on the ASCSA web site.

Deadline: January 15.

STAFF:
James C. Wright, Director

ADDRESS INQUIRIES TO:
Committee Chair
(See address above.)

*SPECIAL STIPULATIONS:
Membership application to the ASCSA must be made online on the web site at the same time one applies to any outside funding organization for work at the School.

THE AMERICAN SCHOOL OF CLASSICAL STUDIES AT ATHENS [876]

6-8 Charlton Street
Princeton, NJ 08540-5232
(609) 683-0800
Fax: (609) 924-0578
E-mail: ascsa@ascsa.org (for information)
application@ascsa.org (to apply)
Web Site: www.ascsa.edu.gr

FOUNDED: 1881

AREAS OF INTEREST:
Gennadeion collections.

NAME(S) OF PROGRAMS:
- **Cotsen Traveling Fellowship for Research in Greece**

TYPE:
Fellowships. Short-term travel-to-collections award.

PURPOSE:
To assist students and scholars in the pursuit of research topics requiring the use of Gennadeion collections.

ELIGIBILITY:
Senior scholars and graduate students for projects and research at the Gennadius Library. Requires residency in Athens of at least one month during the academic year from September 1 to June 1. The recipient is expected to take part in the activities of the Library and of the School in addition to pursuing research.

School programs are generally open to qualified students and scholars at colleges or universities in the U.S. or Canada; restrictions may apply for specific fellowships and programs. The American School of Classical Studies at Athens does not discriminate on the basis of race, age, sex, sexual orientation, color, religion, ethnic origin, or disability when considering admission to any form of membership.

FINANCIAL DATA:
Fellowship does not include costs for School trips, housing or board.

Amount of support per award: Grant of $2,000. School fees are waived.

NO. MOST RECENT APPLICANTS: 7.

NO. AWARDS: 1.

APPLICATION INFO:
Application must be made online and should include the following:
(1) curriculum vitae;
(2) letter (up to three pages) describing the project, proposed dates, budget, and explanation of the relation of the Gennadius Library's collection to the research project and;
(3) two letters of recommendation.

Deadline: January 15.

STAFF:
Dr. Maria Georgopoulou, Director, Gennadius Library

ADDRESS INQUIRIES TO:
Committee Chair, Libraries and Archives
(See address above.)

*SPECIAL STIPULATIONS:
Membership application to the ASCSA must be made online on the web site at the same time one applies to any outside funding organization for work at the School.

THE AMERICAN SCHOOL OF CLASSICAL STUDIES AT ATHENS [877]

6-8 Charlton Street
Princeton, NJ 08540-5232
(609) 683-0800
Fax: (609) 924-0578
E-mail: ascsa@ascsa.org (for information)
application@ascsa.org (to apply)
Web Site: www.ascsa.edu.gr

FOUNDED: 1881

AREAS OF INTEREST:
Medieval Greek language and philology.

NAME(S) OF PROGRAMS:
- **Medieval Greek Summer Session at the Gennadius Library**

TYPE:
Scholarships. Four-week program in intermediate-level Medieval Greek language and philology at the Gennadius Library, with site and museum trips. Seminar given every other year. Next seminar to be held in 2017.

YEAR PROGRAM STARTED: 2005

PURPOSE:
To promote the study of Medieval Greek language and philology.

ELIGIBILITY:
Graduate students and postdoctoral scholars in any field of late antiquity, post-antiquity, Byzantine or medieval studies at any university worldwide. The American School of Classical Studies at Athens does not discriminate on the basis of race, age, sex, sexual orientation, color, religion, ethnic origin, or disability when considering admission to any form of membership.

FINANCIAL DATA:
The Leventis scholarships cover tuition, travel within Greece, lodging but no meals.

NO. MOST RECENT APPLICANTS: 38.

NO. AWARDS: Up to 12 scholarships (pending funding).

APPLICATION INFO:
Application information is available on the web site. Application fee of $25 is required.

Duration: One full month.

Deadline: January 15.

STAFF:
Dr. Maria Georgopoulou, Director, Gennadius Library.

ADDRESS INQUIRIES TO:
Committee Chair, Libraries and Archives
(See address above.)

*SPECIAL STIPULATIONS:
Membership application to the ASCSA must be made online on the web site at the same time one applies to any outside funding organization for work at the School.

THE AMERICAN SCHOOL OF CLASSICAL STUDIES AT ATHENS [878]

6-8 Charlton Street
Princeton, NJ 08540-5232
(609) 683-0800
Fax: (609) 924-0578
E-mail: ascsa@ascsa.org (for information)
application@ascsa.org (to apply)
Web Site: www.ascsa.edu.gr

FOUNDED: 1881

AREAS OF INTEREST:
Skeletal, faunal, geoarchaeological, environmental studies and archaeological science.

NAME(S) OF PROGRAMS:
- **Wiener Laboratory Post-Doctoral Fellowship**
- **Wiener Laboratory Pre-Doctoral Fellowship**
- **Wiener Laboratory Research Associateships**
- **Wiener Laboratory Senior Fellowship**

TYPE:
Fellowships; Research grants. The Malcolm H. Wiener Laboratory for Archaeological Science at ASCSA provides funding for scholars pursuing interdisciplinary research on archaeological questions pertaining to the ancient Greek world and adjacent areas. Three different types of funding are offered: Post-Doctoral (three-year), Pre-Doctoral (two-year term), and Senior (five to 10 months). The School also offers shorter-duration, more focused Research Associate positions.

PURPOSE:
To promote laboratory research pertinent to the American School of Classical Studies at Athens.

ELIGIBILITY:
Applicants are welcome from any college or university worldwide. The American School of Classical Studies at Athens does not discriminate on the basis of race, age, sex, sexual orientation, color, religion, ethnic origin, or disability when considering admission to any form of membership or application for employment.

Post-Doctoral Fellowship: Eligibility limited to individuals who have received their Ph.D. within the last seven years.

Pre-Doctoral Fellowship: Eligibility limited to individuals actively enrolled in a graduate program who have passed all qualifying exams and have an approved Ph.D. proposal.

Research Associateships: Eligibility limited to individuals actively enrolled in a graduate program and individuals with a higher-level degree in a relevant discipline.

Senior Fellowship: Eligibility limited to individuals who received their Ph.Ds. at least five years previous to application.

FINANCIAL DATA:
Amount of support per award: Post-Doctoral Fellowship: Stipend of $35,000 per year; Pre-Doctoral Fellowship: Stipend up to $20,000 per year; Research Associateships: Stipend variable up to $7,000; Senior Fellowship: Stipend of $15,000 (five-month term) or $30,000 (10-month term).

NO. AWARDS: Varies.

APPLICATION INFO:
Application must be made online on the ASCSA web site.

Applicants for the Pre-Doctoral Fellowship must submit:
(1) cover sheet naming the applicant, current research interests, and title and brief summary of the proposed research project;
(2) project description including (a) objectives and expected significance, (b) background and relation to present state of knowledge, (c) research description and (d) timeframe;
(3) results of prior Wiener Laboratory research;
(4) references cited; facilities, equipment and other resources; permits;
(5) curriculum vitae following requested format;
(6) three letters of reference from scholars in the field and;
(7) expected contributions to and impact on the Wiener Laboratory and the ASCSA community.

Applicants for the Research Associateships must submit:
(1) cover sheet naming the applicant, current research interests, and title and brief summary of the proposed research project;
(2) project description including (a) objectives and expected significance, (b) background and relation to present state of knowledge, (c) research description and (d) timeframe;
(3) results of prior Wiener Laboratory research;
(4) references cited; budget; facilities, equipment and other resources; permits;
(5) curriculum vitae following requested format;
(6) one letter of reference from scholars in the field and;
(7) expected contributions to and impact on the Wiener Laboratory and the ASCSA community.

Applicants for the Senior Fellowship must submit:
(1) cover sheet naming the applicant, current research interests, and title and brief summary of the proposed research project;
(2) project description including (a) objectives and expected significance, (b) background and relation to present state of knowledge, (c) research description and (d) timeframe;
(3) results of prior Wiener Laboratory research;
(4) references cited; budget; facilities, equipment and other resources; permits;
(5) curriculum vitae following requested format;
(6) two letters of reference from scholars in the field and;
(7) expected contributions to and impact on the Wiener Laboratory and the ASCSA community.

Duration: Post-Doctoral Fellowship: Three-year term. Pre-Doctoral Fellowship: Two-year term. Research Associateships: Varies, up to nine months. Senior Fellowship: Terms of five to 10 months.

Deadline: Post-Doctoral Fellowship: Next competition for the 2017-18 academic-year Fellowship to be announced in the fall of 2016.

Pre-Doctoral Fellowship, Research Associateships and Senior Fellowship: Current competition begins in the fall for the next academic year, with a deadline for applications of January 15.

ADDRESS INQUIRIES TO:
Dr. Panagiotis Karkanas
Director, Wiener Laboratory
E-mail: TKarkanas@ascsa.edu.gr

*SPECIAL STIPULATIONS:
Membership application to the ASCSA must be made online on the web site at the same time one applies to any outside funding organization for work at the School.

THE AMERICAN SCHOOL OF CLASSICAL STUDIES AT ATHENS [879]

6-8 Charlton Street
Princeton, NJ 08540-5232
(609) 683-0800
Fax: (609) 924-0578
E-mail: application@ascsa.org
Web Site: www.ascsa.edu.gr

FOUNDED: 1881

AREAS OF INTEREST:
Research at the ASCSA excavations at Ancient Corinth in Greece.

NAME(S) OF PROGRAMS:
- **Henry S. Robinson Corinth Research Fellowship**

TYPE:
Fellowships. Fellowship for research on a doctoral dissertation or primary publication specifically on Corinth. Program is offered every other year. Robinson Fellowship for 2016-17 to be announced in the fall of 2015.

PURPOSE:
To revive field work at Corinth.

ELIGIBILITY:
Ph.D. candidate or recent Ph.D. (within five years), for research on a doctoral dissertation or primary publication specifically on Corinth, requiring the use of the resources,

archaeological site and collections at the ASCSA excavations at Ancient Corinth in Greece. Open to all nationalities.

FINANCIAL DATA:
The Fellowship does not allow travel costs (to and from country of origin or within Greece). Availability of rooms and work space is limited during the excavation season from April to June.

Amount of support per award: Stipend up to $4,000 for one or more individuals. School fees are waived. Funding is for research activities at Corinth, to be used to cover living expenses, including room, board, fees and other costs associated with the study, such as photography and drawings.

NO. AWARDS: 1 or more.

APPLICATION INFO:
Submit Associate Membership application online, including curriculum vitae and proposal statement, which should have the following items:
(1) project outline;
(2) explanation of goals;
(3) statement of the significance of the project;
(4) work completed to date;
(5) schedule for completion;
(6) dates for project;
(7) budget and;
(8) two letters of support, including one from dissertation advisor if applicant is a Ph.D. candidate.

Duration: Up to three months within the 12-month period July 1 to June 30. Nonrenewable.

Deadline: January 15. Announcement mid-March.

*SPECIAL STIPULATIONS:
The Robinson Fellowship may not be held concurrently with another School fellowship. Preference is given to candidates who have not previously held the Robinson Fellowship or received substantial ASCSA funding for the same project.

THE AMERICAN SCHOOL OF CLASSICAL STUDIES AT ATHENS [880]

6-8 Charlton Street
Princeton, NJ 08540-5232
(609) 683-0800
Fax: (609) 924-0578
E-mail: application@ascsa.org
Web Site: www.ascsa.edu.gr

FOUNDED: 1881

AREAS OF INTEREST:
Research in the art and architecture of antiquity.

NAME(S) OF PROGRAMS:
- **Kress Publication Fellowships**

TYPE:
Fellowships. Fellowships are aimed at supporting scholars who are assigned material for publication from the School's excavations at Ancient Corinth or the Athenian Agora.

ELIGIBILITY:
Senior postdoctoral scholars working on a Corinth or Agora publication assignment. Preference will be given to those working on a Corinth or Agora excavation volume and to those applicants who have not previously received the Kress Publications Fellowship. Applications from current staff of the School are not eligible.

FINANCIAL DATA:
School fees, travel costs, housing, board and other living expenses are to be paid out of the stipend by the recipient.

Total amount of support: Up to $30,000 per grant cycle, July 1 to June 30.

NO. AWARDS: Up to 3 per grant cycle.

APPLICATION INFO:
Application and requirements are available on the web site.

Duration: Three to nine months. No renewals.

Deadline: January 15.

THE AMERICAN SCHOOL OF CLASSICAL STUDIES AT ATHENS [881]

6-8 Charlton Street
Princeton, NJ 08540-5232
(609) 683-0800
Fax: (609) 924-0578
E-mail: application@ascsa.org
Web Site: www.ascsa.edu.gr

FOUNDED: 1881

AREAS OF INTEREST:
Modern Greek political and social history.

NAME(S) OF PROGRAMS:
- **The George Papaioannou Fellowship**

TYPE:
Fellowships. Research fellowship. Fellows are required to make use of and refer to the George Papaioannou Papers housed at the Archives of the Gennadius Library.

PURPOSE:
To honor George Papaioannou, leader of the Trichonis subdivision of EDES.

ELIGIBILITY:
Ph.D. candidates or recent Ph.Ds. researching Greece in the 1940s and the postwar period. Open to all nationalities.

FINANCIAL DATA:
The Fellowship does not include travel costs, housing, board and other living expenses.

Amount of support per award: Stipend of EUR 1,000. School fees are waived by the award for a maximum of two months.

APPLICATION INFO:
Submit application, curriculum vitae, project description (up to two pages) and two letters of reference online.

Duration: Up to two months. Nonrenewable.

Deadline: January 15. Announcement in mid-March.

*SPECIAL STIPULATIONS:
The recipient should not plan to work at the Archives of the Gennadius Library during the month of August.

AMERICAN SCHOOLS OF ORIENTAL RESEARCH (ASOR) [882]

656 Beacon Street, Fifth Floor
Boston, MA 02215
(617) 353-6570
Fax: (617) 353-6575
E-mail: asor@bu.edu
Web Site: www.asor.org

FOUNDED: 1900

AREAS OF INTEREST:
The study of humanistic disciplines, such as anthropology, archaeology, Biblical studies, epigraphy, history, history of art and architecture, literature, philology, prehistory and topography, relating in particular to the Middle East from prehistoric times to the modern era.

NAME(S) OF PROGRAMS:
- **William G. Dever Fellowship for Biblical Scholars**
- **Harris Grants**
- **Heritage Fellowships**
- **P.E. MacAllister Fellowships**
- **Member Supported Fellowships**
- **Mesopotamian Fellowship**
- **Meyers/Wright Fellowships**
- **Platt Fellowships**
- **Harva L. Sheeler Fellowships**

TYPE:
Conferences/seminars; Fellowships; Research grants; Scholarships; Travel grants.

YEAR PROGRAM STARTED: 1940

PURPOSE:
To encourage scholars to undertake study and research about the ancient Near East.

LEGAL BASIS:
Nonprofit, archaeological research corporation.

ELIGIBILITY:
The Fellowship is open to qualified students and scholars from any country. Applicants must be or become individual professional members of ASOR, or must be affiliated with an institution that is a member of ASOR.

FINANCIAL DATA:
Amount of support per award: Dever Fellowship: $7,000; Harris Grants: Varies; Heritage, MacAllister, Member-Supported, Meyers/Wright, Platt and Sheeler Fellowships: $2,000 each; Mesopotamian Fellowship: $9,000.

Total amount of support: Approximately $46,000 for the year 2015.

NO. MOST RECENT APPLICANTS: Varies.

NO. AWARDS: Dever and Mesopotamian Fellowships: 1 each; Harris Grants: 3; Heritage and MacAllister Fellowships: 6 each; Meyers/Wright Fellowships: 4; Member Supported Fellowships: 12; Platt Fellowships: 16; Sheeler Fellowships: 2.

APPLICATION INFO:
All eligible persons are encouraged to apply for as many fellowships and professorships as they wish, but a person can hold only one award at a time. Persons who have received an award in one year can reapply for the same or other awards the following year, but new applicants will have priority.

Deadline: Heritage, Meyers/Wright, Member Supported, MacAllister, Platt and Sheeler Fellowships: Mid-February. Mesopotamian Fellowships: November 1. Harris and Dever Fellowships: Mid-December.

STAFF:
Andrew Vaughn, Executive Director

ADDRESS INQUIRIES TO:
Office Coordinator
(See address above.)

*SPECIAL STIPULATIONS:
Applicants must be or become members of ASOR or attend an ASOR-affiliated institution.

THE AMERICAN SWEDISH INSTITUTE [883]

2600 Park Avenue
Minneapolis, MN 55407
(612) 871-4907
Fax: (612) 871-8682
E-mail: info@asimn.org
Web Site: www.asimn.org

FOUNDED: 1929

AREAS OF INTEREST:
Swedish culture.

NAME(S) OF PROGRAMS:
- **Lilly Lorénzen Scholarship**

TYPE:
Scholarships; Travel grants.

YEAR PROGRAM STARTED: 1980

PURPOSE:
To foster and preserve Swedish culture in America.

ELIGIBILITY:
Must be a Minnesota resident or a student attending a Minnesota school with working knowledge of the Swedish language that presents a creditable plan of study for the next academic year.

FINANCIAL DATA:
Amount of support per award: $1,000.
Total amount of support: $1,000.

NO. MOST RECENT APPLICANTS: 7.

NO. AWARDS: 1.

APPLICATION INFO:
Submit application form and college transcript. If transcript is not available, include a statement of professional and community achievement. Contact the Institute at the address above for an application, or visit the Institute web site.
Duration: One-time award.
Deadline: May 1.

ADDRESS INQUIRIES TO:
Karin Krull, Educational Programs and Special Events Coordinator
(See address above.)

THE AMERICAN SWEDISH INSTITUTE [884]

2600 Park Avenue
Minneapolis, MN 55407
(612) 871-4907
Fax: (612) 871-8682
E-mail: info@asimn.org
Web Site: www.asimn.org

FOUNDED: 1929

AREAS OF INTEREST:
Swedish culture.

NAME(S) OF PROGRAMS:
- **The Malmberg Scholarship for Study in Sweden**

TYPE:
Scholarships; Travel grants. The Malmberg Scholarship is awarded for up to one academic year of study in Sweden.

YEAR PROGRAM STARTED: 2005

PURPOSE:
To support intellectual connections between the U.S. and Sweden by providing grants to students and scholars.

ELIGIBILITY:
Enrolled undergraduate and graduate students and qualified scholars are eligible. The recipient must be a U.S. resident.

FINANCIAL DATA:
Amount of support per award: Up to $10,000.

NO. MOST RECENT APPLICANTS: 12.

NO. AWARDS: 1.

APPLICATION INFO:
Application forms are available on the web site.
Deadline: November 15.

ADDRESS INQUIRIES TO:
Karin Krull, Educational Programs and Special Events Coordinator
(See address above.)

BELGIAN AMERICAN EDUCATIONAL FOUNDATION, INC. [885]

195 Church Street
New Haven, CT 06510
(203) 785-4055
Fax: (203) 777-5765
E-mail: emile.boulpaep@yale.edu
Web Site: www.baef.us
www.baef.be

FOUNDED: 1920

AREAS OF INTEREST:
Educational exchange between the U.S. and Belgium.

NAME(S) OF PROGRAMS:
- **B.A.E.F. Fellowships for Study in Belgium**

TYPE:
Fellowships. Predoctoral and postdoctoral fellowships for advanced study in most fields of knowledge with supported work to be undertaken at a Belgian university or an institution of higher learning. Fellowships for Belgian students are also available.

YEAR PROGRAM STARTED: 1920

PURPOSE:
To allow American candidates to pursue independent study and research in Belgium on projects for which Belgium provides special advantages.

LEGAL BASIS:
Public foundation.

ELIGIBILITY:
The applicant must be a citizen or permanent resident of the U.S. and either have a Master's degree or equivalent degree, or be working towards a Ph.D. or equivalent degree. Preference is given to applicants under the age of 30. Knowledge of Dutch, French or German is optional.

FINANCIAL DATA:
Fellowships carry a fixed stipend for living expenses, travel and tuition, if any. This stipend is judged adequate for a single person, but additional funds must be provided from other sources if the fellow is to be accompanied by spouse or by spouse and family. Health insurance coverage is also provided.
Amount of support per award: $27,000 for 12 months.
Total amount of support: $3,675,000 for the academic year 2013-14.

NO. MOST RECENT APPLICANTS: 50 U.S. applicants per academic year.

NO. AWARDS: 9 awards to American students per academic year.

APPLICATION INFO:
Applicant shall furnish a completed application form with all its appropriate attachments. Application blanks are available on www.baef.us. Completed applications must be submitted electronically with attachments in PDF format to the e-mail address above.
Duration: 12 months preferred; no less than six months.
Deadline: October 31, for the following academic year. Fellowship starting as early as July 1 of that following year.

DIRECTORS:
Dr. Emile L. Boulpaep, President and Chairman
William S. Moody, Vice President
Olivier Trouveroy, Treasurer
L. Gilles Sion, Secretary
Maryan Ainsworth
Marcel Crochet
Jacques de Groote
Diego du Monceau
Susan Friberg
John H.F. Haskel, Jr.
Margaret Hoover
Andre Jacques
Daniel Janssen
Dirk Wauters
Jacques Willems

ADDRESS INQUIRIES TO:
Dr. Emile L. Boulpaep, President
(See address above.)

BRUCEBO FINE ART SCHOLARSHIP FOUNDATION

Studio Arts, EV Building
Sir George William Campus
Concordia University
1455 De Maisonneuve Boulevard West
Montreal QC H3G 1M8 Canada
(514) 848-2424 (University)
Fax: (514) 909-5115 (mobile)
E-mail: brucebosubmission@gmail.com
jessica@jessicaauer.com
Web Site: www.bruceboscholarships.ca

TYPE:
Development grants; Research grants; Residencies; Scholarships; Travel grants. Grant principally in the fields of fine arts, visual art and design. Grant is either for stay at the Brucebo Studio on the Island of Hanseatic Gotland, Sweden, in the Baltic Sea, for three months during the summer annually, or for undertaking a European Fine Art Travel-Study journey.

See entry 531 for full listing.

CANADIAN BUREAU FOR INTERNATIONAL EDUCATION (CBIE) [886]

220 Laurier Avenue West, Suite 1550
Ottawa ON K1P 5Z9 Canada
(613) 237-4820
Fax: (613) 237-1073
E-mail: scholarships-bourses@cbie.ca
Web Site: www.scholarships.gc.ca

FOUNDED: 1981

AREAS OF INTEREST:
All disciplines at the Master's, doctoral or postdoctoral levels.

NAME(S) OF PROGRAMS:
- **Foreign Government Awards**

TYPE:
Scholarships. Scholarships for study or research.

PURPOSE:
To provide opportunities for Canadians to pursue studies or research at institutions of higher education abroad.

ELIGIBILITY:
Candidates must be Canadian citizens by the competition deadline and must have obtained the equivalent of a Canadian Bachelor's degree from a recognized university. Studies must take place in Korea or Mexico.

FINANCIAL DATA:
Funding includes tuition and monthly living allowances, with additional benefits provided by varying countries. These scholarships are subject to the availability of funding.

Amount of support per award: Varies by geographical location.

NO. MOST RECENT APPLICANTS: 40.

NO. AWARDS: 2 to 15 per year, depending on geographical location.

APPLICATION INFO:
Further information and application forms are available on the web site above.

Duration: Varies depending on the program and level of study.

ADDRESS INQUIRIES TO:
Program Coordinator
International Scholarship Programs
(See address above.)

*SPECIAL STIPULATIONS:
Candidates may not hold other awards concurrently.

CANADIAN BUREAU FOR INTERNATIONAL EDUCATION (CBIE) [887]

220 Laurier Avenue West, Suite 1550
Ottawa ON K1P 5Z9 Canada
(613) 237-4820
Fax: (613) 237-1073
E-mail: scholarships-bourses@cbie.ca
Web Site: www.scholarships.gc.ca

AREAS OF INTEREST:
Higher education.

NAME(S) OF PROGRAMS:
- **Commonwealth Scholarship Plan**

TYPE:
Scholarships. Under the Commonwealth Scholarship and Fellowship Plan, scholarships are available for Canadians to pursue studies and/or research at higher education institutions in the Commonwealth.

PURPOSE:
To provide opportunities for candidates to pursue studies and/or research at higher education institutions in the Commonwealth.

ELIGIBILITY:
Candidates must be Canadian citizens by the competition deadline and must have obtained the equivalent of a Canadian Master's or Ph.D. degree from a recognized university. Studies must take place in India or New Zealand. Candidates studying in New Zealand must have a Ph.D. degree.

FINANCIAL DATA:
Funding includes tuition and monthly living allowances, with additional benefits provided by varying countries. These scholarships are subject to the availability of funding.

Amount of support per award: Varies by geographical location.

NO. MOST RECENT APPLICANTS: 150.

NO. AWARDS: 1 to 3.

APPLICATION INFO:
Further information and application forms are available on the web site above.

Duration: Up to five years.

ADDRESS INQUIRIES TO:
Program Coordinator
International Scholarship Programs
(See address above.)

CANADIAN INSTITUTE FOR ADVANCED LEGAL STUDIES

P.O. Box 43538, Leaside Post Office
1601 Bayview Avenue
Toronto ON M4G 4G8 Canada
(416) 429-3292
Fax: (416) 429-9805
E-mail: info@canadian-institute.com
Web Site: www.canadian-institute.com

TYPE:
Scholarships.

See entry 1911 for full listing.

CANADIAN INSTITUTE IN GREECE/L'INSTITUT CANADIEN EN GRECE

330 Albert Street
Waterloo ON N2L 3T8 Canada
(519) 886-4428
E-mail: gschaus@wlu.ca
Web Site: www.cig-icg.gr

TYPE:
Fellowships. Intended to support the graduate work of a person who needs to study in Greece.

See entry 345 for full listing.

WINSTON CHURCHILL FOUNDATION OF THE UNITED STATES [888]

600 Madison Avenue, Suite 1601
New York, NY 10022-1737
(212) 752-3200
Fax: (212) 246-8330
E-mail: info@churchillscholarship.org
Web Site: www.churchillscholarship.org

FOUNDED: 1959

AREAS OF INTEREST:
Science, math and engineering.

NAME(S) OF PROGRAMS:
- **Churchill Scholarship**

TYPE:
Scholarships. Scholarship for one year of graduate work at University of Cambridge. Churchill Scholarship may also include a Special Research Grant.

YEAR PROGRAM STARTED: 1963

PURPOSE:
To encourage Anglo-American cooperation and American scientific and technological talent.

LEGAL BASIS:
Public charity.

ELIGIBILITY:
Candidate must be a citizen of the U.S., have a Bachelor's degree from an accredited U.S. college or university and be enrolled at one of 108 participating American institutions.

FINANCIAL DATA:
Amount of support per award: Churchill Scholarship: Tuition, plus GBP 11,000 to GBP 13,900 living allowance, $1,500 travel allowance and reimbursement of visa application fees. Total individual package is approximately $50,000; Churchill Scholars may also receive a Special Research Grant of up to $2,000.

Total amount of support: Approximately $750,000 for the year 2015.

NO. MOST RECENT APPLICANTS: 100.

NO. AWARDS: 15 scholarships for the year 2015.

APPLICATION INFO:
Application forms are available from Foundation representatives at participating institutions. Information also available on Foundation's web site.

Duration: One year.

Deadline: Early November.

OFFICERS:
John L. Loeb, Jr., Chairman
Patrick A. Gerschel, President
Michael Morse, Executive Director
David D. Burrows, Treasurer
James A. Fitzpatrick, Jr., Secretary

ADDRESS INQUIRIES TO:
Michael Morse, Executive Director
(See address above.)

CORPUS CHRISTI COLLEGE [889]

Trumpington Street
Cambridge, CB2 1RH England
(44) 01223 338038
Fax: (44) 01223 765589
E-mail: graduate-tutor@corpus.cam.ac.uk
Web Site: www.corpus.cam.ac.uk

FOUNDED: 1352

AREAS OF INTEREST:
All subjects of postgraduate research at the University of Cambridge.

NAME(S) OF PROGRAMS:
- **Postgraduate Research at the University of Cambridge**

TYPE:
Scholarships.

PURPOSE:
To enable the candidate to pursue, as a member of the college, research in any subject leading to a research degree of Cambridge University.

LEGAL BASIS:
University College.

ELIGIBILITY:
Applicants must have a first degree from a recognized university and name Corpus Christi College as their college of first preference on GAF. Candidates must become registered as University of Cambridge graduate students.

FINANCIAL DATA:
Amount of support per award: Varies.

Matching fund requirements: It is a requirement that individuals who are eligible apply to other funding bodies, e.g. Cambridge Trusts.

APPLICATION INFO:
Application forms for graduate study are available from the Board of Graduate Studies, 4 Mill Lane, Cambridge CB2 1YP, England, or online at www.admin.cam.ac.uk/univ/gsprospectus.

Duration: Up to three years.

Deadline: November 15.

ADDRESS INQUIRIES TO:
Tutor for Advanced Students
(See e-mail address above.)

COUNCIL FOR INTERNATIONAL EXCHANGE OF SCHOLARS (CIES) [890]

1400 K Street, N.W.
Suite 700
Washington, DC 20005-2403
(202) 686-4000
Fax: (202) 686-4029
E-mail: scholars@iie.org
Web Site: www.cies.org

FOUNDED: 1947

AREAS OF INTEREST:
Fulbright Scholar grants to more than 125 countries for teaching, research or a combination of both.

NAME(S) OF PROGRAMS:
- **Fulbright Scholar Program**

TYPE:
Awards/prizes. Awards to university faculty and professionals outside academe for teaching and/or advanced research worldwide. Awards are available in 46 disciplines from agriculture to urban planning.

YEAR PROGRAM STARTED: 1947

PURPOSE:
To promote mutual understanding and scholarship.

LEGAL BASIS:
Private, nonprofit organization that receives funding from the U.S. State Department.

ELIGIBILITY:
Applicant must be a U.S. citizen at the time of application and hold a Ph.D. or equivalent professional/terminal degree. Recognized professional standing for artists and professionals outside of academe is required.

FINANCIAL DATA:
Amount of support per award: Award benefits vary by country. Usually a base stipend, in-country maintenance and travel.

Total amount of support: Varies.

NO. MOST RECENT APPLICANTS: Approximately 3,000.

NO. AWARDS: Approximately 800.

APPLICATION INFO:
Application forms and detailed awards information are available February 1 from the Council. Applications will be screened by CIES peer review committees. Recommendations will be made by the binational Fulbright Commissions or U.S. Information Service posts overseas, with final selection by the J. William Fulbright Foreign Scholarship Board.

Duration: Two to 10 months.

Deadline: August 3 for most programs. Rolling deadline for the short-term Fulbright Specialist Program.

PUBLICATIONS:
Annual awards; catalog; descriptive brochure; annual report.

ADDRESS INQUIRIES TO:
See e-mail address above.

COUNCIL OF AMERICAN OVERSEAS RESEARCH CENTERS (CAORC) [891]

P.O. Box 37012
MRC 178
Washington, DC 20013-7012
(202) 633-1599
Fax: (202) 786-2430
E-mail: fellowships@caorc.org
Web Site: www.caorc.org

FOUNDED: 1981

AREAS OF INTEREST:
Promoting the work of American overseas research centers.

NAME(S) OF PROGRAMS:
- **Multi-Country Research Fellowship Program**

TYPE:
Fellowships; Research grants. Requires scholars to conduct research in more than one country, at least one of which hosts a participating American overseas research center.

YEAR PROGRAM STARTED: 1993

PURPOSE:
To advance higher learning and scholarly research by providing a forum for communication and cooperation among American overseas advanced research centers; to provide general and continuing publicity about the importance and contributions of the centers; to exchange operational and administrative information among the centers; to exchange scholarly and research information among the centers; to encourage joint research projects.

LEGAL BASIS:
501(c)(3) organization.

ELIGIBILITY:
Program is open to U.S. doctoral candidates and scholars who have already earned their Ph.D. in fields in the humanities, social sciences, or allied natural sciences and wish to conduct research of regional or trans-regional significance. Must be U.S. citizen or permanent resident.

U.S. State Department travel restrictions apply. U.S. citizens may not travel to Afghanistan, Iraq, Yemen or Pakistan (senior scholars allowed only).

FINANCIAL DATA:
Amount of support per award: Up to $10,500.

NO. MOST RECENT APPLICANTS: 153.

NO. AWARDS: Ph.D./Postdoctoral: 8.

APPLICATION INFO:
A complete application consists of:
(1) application form;
(2) project description (1,500 words or less) describing the nature of the proposal and competence to carry out the required research;
(3) project bibliography/literature review (one page maximum);
(4) two signed letters of recommendation;
(5) curriculum vitae (three pages maximum) and;
(6) graduate transcripts (Ph.D. candidates only).

Applicants are urged to review the Application Instructions before submitting the application.

Duration: Ph.D./Postdoctoral: Minimum of 90 days.

Deadline: Mid-January.

ADDRESS INQUIRIES TO:
Program Manager
(See address above.)

*SPECIAL STIPULATIONS:
Fellows must complete their research within a specific time.

COUNCIL ON FOREIGN RELATIONS

58 East 68th Street
New York, NY 10065
(212) 434-9740
Fax: (212) 434-9870
E-mail: fellowships@cfr.org
Web Site: www.cfr.org/fellowships

TYPE:
Fellowships. The International Affairs Fellowship in Japan (IAF-J), sponsored by Hitachi, Ltd., provides a selected group of midcareer U.S. citizens the opportunity to expand their professional horizons by spending a period of research or other professional activity in Japan. Fellows are drawn from academia, business, government, media, NGOs and think tanks. In cooperation with the Council on Foreign Relations (CFR), the program's sponsor, Hitachi, Ltd., assists fellows in finding suitable host organizations in Japan.

See entry 824 for full listing.

CULTURAL SERVICES OF THE FRENCH EMBASSY [892]

972 Fifth Avenue
New York, NY 10075
(212) 439-1463
Fax: (212) 439-1455
E-mail: puf.scac@ambafrance-us.org
Web Site: face-foundation.org

NAME(S) OF PROGRAMS:
- **Partner University Fund**

TYPE:
Project/program grants; Research grants. Grants provided by this Fund support research and graduate education partnerships between French and American universities with emphasis placed on novel, innovative and interdisciplinary projects when relevant.

YEAR PROGRAM STARTED: 2007

PURPOSE:
To promote the exchange of ideas between France and the U.S.

ELIGIBILITY:
Grants are not given to individuals.

GEOG. RESTRICTIONS: United States and France.

FINANCIAL DATA:
Amount of support per award: Up to $100,000 (U.S.) per year per project in the humanities (up to 60% of the total cost of the project).

APPLICATION INFO:
There is an application form to complete. Details are available online.

Duration: Up to three years, with an annual review.

ADDRESS INQUIRIES TO:
Pauline Pedexes, Program Coordinator
(See address above.)

CULTURAL VISTAS [893]

440 Park Avenue South, 2nd Floor
New York, NY 10016
(212) 497-3522
Fax: (212) 497-3588
E-mail: cbyx@culturalvistas.org
Web Site: www.cbyx.info

FOUNDED: 1968

AREAS OF INTEREST:
All areas of culture, business, technical, and engineering.

NAME(S) OF PROGRAMS:
- **Congress-Bundestag Youth Exchange for Young Professionals**

TYPE:
Exchange programs; Fellowships; Internships; Scholarships; Work-study programs. Language learning. Scholarship program with a strong focus on cultural exchange. One-year scholarship for work/study program to Germany including German language training, academic semester in Germany and internship component.

YEAR PROGRAM STARTED: 1983

PURPOSE:
To give participants understanding for everyday life, education and professional training in Germany.

ELIGIBILITY:
Requirements include:
(1) U.S. citizenship or permanent residency;
(2) 18 to 24 years of age at start of program;
(3) at least high school diploma or equivalent and;
(4) clear career goals, a solid academic background, and relevant work experience or internships in field strongly preferred.

No German language proficiency requirements.

FINANCIAL DATA:
Funding provided for international airfare, language training and study costs, living expenses during study phases, all seminars, and sickness and accident insurance while abroad.

CO-OP FUNDING PROGRAMS: Funded in U.S. by the Bureau of Educational and Cultural Affairs of the Department of State and through the Administration of the Bundestag in Germany.

NO. MOST RECENT APPLICANTS: 650.

NO. AWARDS: 75.

APPLICATION INFO:
Electronic submission only.

Duration: One year (July to July).

Deadline: December 1 for the following program year.

ADDRESS INQUIRIES TO:
Congress-Bundestag Youth Exchange for Young Professionals
(See address above.)

*SPECIAL STIPULATIONS:
Must be U.S. citizens or permanent residents, 18 to 24 years of age at the start of the program. Previous recipients of Congress-Bundestag scholarships are not eligible for this program.

CULTURAL VISTAS [894]

440 Park Avenue South, 2nd Floor
New York, NY 10016
(212) 497-3500
Fax: (212) 497-3586
E-mail: bosch@culturalvistas.org
Web Site: www.culturalvistas.org

FOUNDED: 1968

AREAS OF INTEREST:
Business, economics, journalism, law and public policy.

NAME(S) OF PROGRAMS:
- **The Robert Bosch Foundation Fellowship Program**

TYPE:
Fellowships. Graduate fellowships for extended career training opportunities in Germany.

YEAR PROGRAM STARTED: 1984

PURPOSE:
To provide international professional experience through high-level work placements within German industry, business, government and media.

LEGAL BASIS:
Program funded by Robert Bosch Stiftung, a private German foundation.

ELIGIBILITY:
Applicants must be U.S. citizens under the age of 40 years old at the time of application deadline. Graduate degree is preferred and applicant should have a minimum of five years of relevant experience. Applicants must show evidence of outstanding professional performance and community involvement. German language is not required at the time of application.

FINANCIAL DATA:
Includes transatlantic flights, language training, three European seminars, travel, health, accident and liability insurance, etc.

Amount of support per award: EUR 3,000 stipend per month; monthly summer stipend EUR 1,000.

Total amount of support: Varies.

NO. MOST RECENT APPLICANTS: 600.

NO. AWARDS: 15 for the 2016-17 academic year.

APPLICATION INFO:
Candidates must submit an application form, personal statement, transcripts, letters of recommendation and resume.

Duration: Six to nine months.

Deadline: November 1.

PUBLICATIONS:
General information and applications.

STAFF:
Ruth Conkling, Program Officer

ADDRESS INQUIRIES TO:
See e-mail address above.

CYPRUS AMERICAN ARCHAEOLOGICAL RESEARCH INSTITUTE [895]

656 Beacon Street, 5th Floor
Boston, MA 02215
(617) 353-6571
Fax: (617) 353-6575
E-mail: caari@bu.edu
Web Site: www.caari.org

FOUNDED: 1900

AREAS OF INTEREST:
The study of humanistic disciplines, such as anthropology, archaeology, Biblical studies, epigraphy, history, history of art and architecture, literature, philology, prehistory and topography, relating in particular to the Middle East from prehistoric times to the modern era.

Cyprus American Archaeological Research Institute is the only residential archaeological institute on the island of Cyprus and serves as a center for the dissemination of information about the archaeology of Cyprus.

NAME(S) OF PROGRAMS:
- **The Anita Cecil O'Donovan Fellowship**
- **The Danielle Parks Memorial Fellowship**
- **The Helena Wylde Swiny and Stuart Swiny Fellowship**

TYPE:
Fellowships; Research grants; Residencies; Travel grants. There are a large variety of fellowships available through the Near Eastern Fellowship Program for the American Schools of Oriental Research and affiliated overseas research centers. Besides The Cyprus American Archaeological Research Institute in Nicosia, Cyprus (CAARI), there are also The American Center of Oriental Research in Amman, Jordan (ACOR) and the W.F. Albright Institute of Archaeological Research in Jerusalem, Israel (AIAR). Contact the American Schools of Oriental Research for full details.

The Anita Cecil O'Donovan Fellowship is an award to a graduate student of any nationality, enrolled in a graduate program in any nation, to pursue research on a project relevant to the archaeology and/or culture of Cyprus.

The Danielle Parks Memorial Fellowship is for a graduate student of any nationality who needs to work in Cyprus to further his or her research on a subject of relevance to Cypriot archaeology and culture.

The Helena Wylde Swiny and Stuart Swiny Fellowship is a grant to a graduate student of any nationality in a U.S. or Canadian university or college to pursue a research project relevant to an ongoing field project in Cyprus or that requires work on Cyprus itself.

YEAR PROGRAM STARTED: 1940

PURPOSE:
To help scholars undertake high-quality research and field projects in the Middle East; to encourage interdisciplinary study and communication among scholars.

LEGAL BASIS:
Nonprofit, archaeological research corporation.

ELIGIBILITY:
All ASOR awards are open to qualified students and scholars from any country. Applicants must be affiliated with an institution that is a member of the ASOR corporation or must be an individual professional member. Prime consideration is given to applicants whose projects are affiliated with ASOR.

ASOR does not conduct the competition nor take part in the selection process for the Fulbright Fellowships, but encourages qualified scholars to apply for these awards.

FINANCIAL DATA:
The Anita Cecil O'Donovan Fellowship and The Helena Wylde Swiny and Stuart Swiny Fellowship will be used to fund research time in residence at CAARI and to help defray costs of travel.

The Danielle Parks Memorial Fellowship covers travel to and living expenses in Cyprus.

Amount of support per award: $1,000 each.

Total amount of support: $3,000.

NO. MOST RECENT APPLICANTS: 11.

NO. AWARDS: 1 each.

APPLICATION INFO:
Application form is available on the Institute web site. All eligible persons are encouraged to apply for as many fellowships and professorships as they wish, but a person can hold only one award at a time. Persons who have received an award in one year can reapply for the same or other awards the following year, but new applicants will have priority.

Duration: One-time awards.

Deadline: December 15.

STAFF:
Donald Keller, Administrator

ADDRESS INQUIRIES TO:
See e-mail address above.

*SPECIAL STIPULATIONS:
For the O'Donovan, Parks and Swiny Fellowships, residence at CAARI is mandatory.

For the Danielle Parks Memorial Fellowship, the fellow is expected during his or her stay to give a presentation at CAARI on a subject related to his or her research. The fellow will periodically keep the Director of CAARI apprised of his or her research activities and will acknowledge CAARI and the Danielle Parks Memorial Fellowship in any publication that emerges from the research carried during the Fellowship.

THE LADY DAVIS FELLOWSHIP TRUST [896]

Hebrew University
Givat Ram
Jerusalem 91904 Israel
972-2-651-2306 (voice mail)
972-2-658-4723
Fax: 972-2-566-3848
E-mail: ld.fellows@mail.huji.ac.il
Web Site: ldft.huji.ac.il

FOUNDED: 1973

NAME(S) OF PROGRAMS:
- **Postdoctoral Researchers Fellowship**
- **Visiting Professorships Fellowship**

TYPE:
Fellowships.

YEAR PROGRAM STARTED: 1973

LEGAL BASIS:
University association.

ELIGIBILITY:
Postdoctoral Researchers: If applying for academic year 2015-16, must have received Doctorate no earlier than October 1, 2010.

Visiting Professorships: Must be a full or an associate professor.

FINANCIAL DATA:
The Trust pays round-trip airfare from the fellow's country of origin to Israel and half the medical insurance if purchased and paid for in Israel.

Amount of support per award: Visiting Professorships: $2,650 (per month); Associate Professor: $2,250 (per month); Postdoctoral Researchers: $5,404 (per month) for candidates who have held their Doctorates for less than two years before they take up the fellowship. Postdoctoral candidates who have their Doctorates for more than two years will receive $5,971 (per month) plus rental allowance.

APPLICATION INFO:
Prospective candidates must establish contact with the relevant department at the Hebrew University, and ensure that there is a faculty member willing to sponsor the application.

Duration: Postdoctoral researchers and doctoral students may request an extension of one year to their fellowships. There is no need to submit all the information again. A letter from the researcher/student explaining the request for the extension together with a supporting letter from the scholar, an updated curriculum vitae and an updated list of publications is sufficient.

Visiting professorships and associate professorships last from three to nine months during the academic year.

Deadline: Hebrew University: Visiting Professorships, November 30; Postdoctoral Researchers, December 31; Postdoctoral Researchers (one-year extension): February 25.

*SPECIAL STIPULATIONS:
Fellowships may not be deferred from one year to the next.

Fellows who have won another concurrent fellowship must disclose this to the Trust, whereupon the amount of the award will be reviewed.

A Fellow is expected to take up the Fellowship within the period of the academic year for which he has applied (in other words, between October 1 and September 30 in the following year). Attempts are made to be as elastic as possible should a Fellow expect to arrive before or after October 1.

FLANDERS HOUSE [897]

620 Eighth Avenue, 44th Floor
New York, NY 10018
(212) 584-2200 ext. 2004
E-mail: info@flandershouse.org
Web Site: www.flandershouse.org

AREAS OF INTEREST:
Belgium.

NAME(S) OF PROGRAMS:
- **Fellowship of the Flanders House**

TYPE:
Fellowships. Granted for study or research at universities, conservatories of music, or art academies recognized by the Flemish Community and encompasses the studies of art, music, humanities, social and political sciences, law, economics, sciences and medicine.

PURPOSE:
To assist American college students who wish to continue their postgraduate education in Flanders, Belgium.

ELIGIBILITY:
Open to U.S. citizens of no more than 35 years of age at the time of application deadline, who hold a Bachelor's or Master's degree, and who have no other Belgian sources of income. In cases of dual citizenship, proof is required.

FINANCIAL DATA:
Includes a monthly stipend, tuition fees at a Flemish institution, health insurance and public liability insurance in accordance with Belgian law. There is no reimbursement of travel expenses.

Amount of support per award: Monthly stipend approximately EUR 840; tuition fees maximum EUR 610.10. The amount of the stipend is subject to change without notice.

Total amount of support: Varies.

NO. AWARDS: 5.

APPLICATION INFO:
Application information is available on the web site.

Duration: 10 months.

Deadline: February 28.

ADDRESS INQUIRIES TO:
Nicolas Polet, Director of Communications and Public Affairs
(See address above.)

*PLEASE NOTE:
The academic year, for most institutes of higher learning in Flanders, starts at the end of September.

THE GARDEN CLUB OF AMERICA

14 East 60th Street, Third Floor
New York, NY 10022
(212) 753-8287
Fax: (212) 753-0134
E-mail: scholarshipapplications@gcamerica.org
Web Site: www.gcamerica.org/scholarships

TYPE:
Exchange programs; Fellowships. A graduate academic year in the U.S. for a British student and a work-study program for an American at universities and botanical gardens in the U.K. in fields related to horticulture, botany and landscape design.

See entry 2112 for full listing.

THE GARDEN CLUB OF AMERICA

14 East 60th Street, Third Floor
New York, NY 10022
(212) 753-8287
Fax: (212) 753-0134
E-mail: scholarshipapplications@gcamerica.org
Web Site: www.gcamerica.org/scholarships

TYPE:
Research grants. Financial assistance to college seniors and graduate students to study habitat-related issues that will benefit threatened or endangered bird species and lend useful information for land management decisions.

See entry 2113 for full listing.

GERMAN ACADEMIC EXCHANGE SERVICE [898]

871 United Nations Plaza, 14th Floor
New York, NY 10017
(212) 758-3223
Fax: (212) 755-5780
E-mail: daadny@daad.org
Web Site: www.daad.org

FOUNDED: 1925

AREAS OF INTEREST:
International exchanges in education, research in higher education, and academic teaching staff; scholarships to German and foreign students.

CONSULTING OR VOLUNTEER SERVICES:
DAAD serves on a consultancy service in the field of international academic mobility.

NAME(S) OF PROGRAMS:

- **DAAD Emigre Memorial German Internship Program (EMGIP-Bundestag)**
- **DAAD German Studies Research Grant**
- **DAAD Intensive Language Course Grant**
- **DAAD Research Internships in Science and Engineering (RISE)**
- **DAAD Research Stays for University Academics and Scientists**
- **DAAD RISE Professional**
- **DAAD Study Scholarship**
- **DAAD Undergraduate Scholarship**
- **DAAD University Summer Course Grant**
- **DAAD Visiting Professorship**

TYPE:
Awards/prizes; Conferences/seminars; Exchange programs; Fellowships; Internships; Professorships; Project/program grants; Research grants; Scholarships; Visiting scholars. The German Academic Exchange Service is the New York office of the Deutscher Akademischer Austausch Dienst (DAAD), a German organization with its head office in Bonn. DAAD offers a wide range of opportunities to students, scholars and higher education institutions of the U.S. and Canada, from undergraduate students to faculty, for study and research in Germany.

YEAR PROGRAM STARTED: 1971

PURPOSE:
To provide information on study and research opportunities in higher education at home and abroad; to promote international higher education and research through scholarships; to recruit and place German academic teaching staff from all disciplines at foreign institutions of higher education; to maintain a network of former scholarship holders abroad.

LEGAL BASIS:
Registered association under private law.

ELIGIBILITY:
DAAD grants are available to faculty and students in the U.S. and Canada to participate in a wide variety of academic activities. Funding is restricted to travel to Germany, including German higher education institutions, research institutions and archives in Germany.

GEOG. RESTRICTIONS: United States and Canada.

FINANCIAL DATA:
Amount of support per award: Varies.
Total amount of support: Varies.

APPLICATION INFO:
Application information is available on the web site.
Duration: Varies.
Deadline: Varies.

PUBLICATIONS:
Grants for Study and Research in Germany.

ADDRESS INQUIRIES TO:
Amra Dumisic
Program and Information Officer
(See address above.)

GERMAN HISTORICAL INSTITUTE

1607 New Hampshire Avenue, N.W.
Washington, DC 20009-2562
(202) 387-3355
Fax: (202) 387-6437
E-mail: fellowships@ghi-dc.org
Web Site: www.ghi-dc.org

TYPE:
Fellowships. The Institute awards short-term fellowships to German and American doctoral students as well as postdoctoral scholars/Habilitanden in the fields of German history, the history of German-American relations, and the role of Germany and the U.S. in international relations.

See entry 580 for full listing.

GRADUATE WOMEN INTERNATIONAL (GWI)

10, rue du Lac
CH 1207 Geneva Switzerland
(41) 22 731 23 80
Fax: (41) 22 738 04 40
Web Site: www.graduatewomen.org

TYPE:
Awards/prizes; Capital grants; Fellowships; Research grants; Training grants. IFUW fellowships and grants are awarded biennially to encourage and enable women graduates to undertake original research or obtain further training in the humanities, social sciences and natural sciences.

See entry 1062 for full listing.

THE HAGUE ACADEMY OF INTERNATIONAL LAW

Peace Palace
Carnegieplein 2
2517 KJ The Hague The Netherlands
(31) 70 3024242
E-mail: registration@hagueacademy.nl
Web Site: www.hagueacademy.nl

TYPE:
Project/program grants. Study programs. Residential scholarships for doctoral candidates from developing countries whose thesis, in private international law or public international law, is in the process of completion, who reside in their home country and who do not have access to scientific sources.

See entry 1914 for full listing.

THE HAGUE ACADEMY OF INTERNATIONAL LAW

Peace Palace
Carnegieplein 2
2517 KJ The Hague The Netherlands
(31) 70 3024242
E-mail: registration@hagueacademy.nl
Web Site: www.hagueacademy.nl

TYPE:
Project/program grants; Scholarships. Study programs. A limited number of scholarships are given to cover tuition and living expenses while studying at the three-week summer session of the Hague Academy of International Law. Because of the limited number, granting of scholarships to attendees from every country is not possible.

See entry 1915 for full listing.

THE HAGUE ACADEMY OF INTERNATIONAL LAW

Peace Palace
Carnegieplein 2
2517 KJ The Hague The Netherlands
(31) 70 3024242
E-mail: registration@hagueacademy.nl
Web Site: www.hagueacademy.nl

TYPE:
Project/program grants.

See entry 1916 for full listing.

THE HAGUE ACADEMY OF INTERNATIONAL LAW

Peace Palace
Carnegieplein 2
2517 KJ The Hague The Netherlands
(31) 70 3024242
E-mail: registration@hagueacademy.nl
Web Site: www.hagueacademy.nl

TYPE:
Project/program grants. External Programme is held each year, in turn in Africa, Asia and Latin America, upon the invitation of host governments or international organizations. It is designed for approximately 20 participants from the countries in the region (who are resident in their own country), whose traveling expenses are usually financed by the Academy and whose accommodation is financed by the government of the host state or organization. In addition, a number of participants come from the host state itself.

See entry 1917 for full listing.

HEINRICH HERTZ-STIFTUNG [899]

Ministry of Innovation, Science and Research des Landes Nordrhein-Westfalen
Heinrich Hertz-Stiftung
Voelklinger Strasse 49
D-40221 Duesseldorf Germany
(49) 211 896-4266
Fax: (49) 211 896-4407
E-mail: martina.schoeler@miwf.nrw.de
heinrich-hertz-stiftung@miwf.nrw.de
Web Site: www.heinrich-hertz-stiftung.de

FOUNDED: 1961

AREAS OF INTEREST:
International exchange of scientists.

TYPE:
Exchange programs; Scholarships. Scholarships to promote the sciences through the exchange of university teachers and young scientists (without special restrictions).

YEAR PROGRAM STARTED: 1962

PURPOSE:
To promote sciences.

LEGAL BASIS:
Public foundation.

ELIGIBILITY:
University teachers and young scientists are eligible. Non-German citizens should have a working knowledge of German and German citizens a working knowledge of the language of the host country.

GEOG. RESTRICTIONS: Land Nordrhine-Westphalia.

FINANCIAL DATA:
Amount of support per award: Award values are dependent upon individual needs.

Total amount of support: Varies.

NO. AWARDS: 26 for the year 2015.

APPLICATION INFO:
Applications should be submitted only by third persons. A curriculum vitae, examination record, two references and a full description of the planned project with a timetable are to be included. Further information may be obtained on request.

Duration: Dependent upon individual needs. Two years maximum.

PUBLICATIONS:
Hinweise auf die Antragstellung; *Die Heinrich Hertz-Stiftung*, booklet; Heinrich Hertz-Stiftung, folder.

STAFF:
Susanne Schneider-Salomon, Chief Executive Officer
Martina Schoeler, Head of Office

ADDRESS INQUIRIES TO:
Ministry of Innovation, Science and Research des Landes Nordrhein-Westfalen
Heinrich Hertz-Stiftung
E-mail: heinrich-hertz-stiftung@miwf.nrw.de

INSTITUTE FOR THE INTERNATIONAL EDUCATION OF STUDENTS (IES)

33 West Monroe Street
Suite 2300
Chicago, IL 60603-5405
(312) 944-1750
(800) 995-2300
Fax: (312) 944-1448
E-mail: info@IESabroad.org
Web Site: www.IESabroad.org

TYPE:
Awards/prizes; Scholarships. Boren and Gilman Scholarship Support Grants: This program offers recipients of these prestigious scholarships the opportunity to apply for additional financial support.

Disability Grants: This program's purpose is to enhance study abroad opportunities for students with disabilities. It offers grants to students whose disabilities may add significant costs to their study abroad experience.

Diversity Scholarships: This program offers one way to encourage and support students from a range of institutions and underrepresented populations. Underrepresented students include students from underrepresented racial and ethnic groups, first-generation-to-college students, students from low-income families and students with a history of overcoming adversity.

Donor Funded Scholarships: These scholarship opportunities have been created through the generosity of various donors who support the important mission of IES Abroad.

Need Based Aid (Early Aid Program): This program is available to students with demonstrated financial need. Priority is given to Pell Grant recipients.

Public University Grants: This program offers an automatic $2,000 credit toward a semester or academic year program.

See entry 1639 for full listing.

INSTITUTE OF INTERNATIONAL EDUCATION [900]

Fulbright U.S. Student Program
809 United Nations Plaza
New York, NY 10017-3580
(212) 984-5525
Fax: (212) 984-5523
Web Site: www.us.fulbrightonline.org

FOUNDED: 1919

AREAS OF INTEREST:
International educational and cultural exchange for graduate-level students and early career professionals.

NAME(S) OF PROGRAMS:
- **Fulbright U.S. Student Program**

TYPE:
Exchange programs; Scholarships. Grants for graduate study, research or English Teaching Assistantships abroad.

YEAR PROGRAM STARTED: 1946

PURPOSE:
To give U.S. students the opportunity to live, study, teach or do research in a foreign country for one academic year and to increase mutual understanding between the people of the U.S. and other countries through the exchange of persons, knowledge and skills.

LEGAL BASIS:
Nonprofit, as described under Internal Revenue Code 501(c)(3).

ELIGIBILITY:
The program is open to all disciplines and fields of study, except medical degree study. Candidates must possess U.S. citizenship, a Bachelor's degree by the beginning date of the grant, language proficiency sufficient to carry out the project overseas and good health. Preference in selecting candidates is for those who have had the majority of high school and undergraduate college education at educational institutions in the U.S and little experience living, studying or working in the country of application. Candidates may not hold a doctoral degree at the time of application.

FINANCIAL DATA:
Fulbright Grants provide round-trip transportation, orientation program, books, maintenance for one academic year and health benefits package. Some country programs may provide tuition and language study courses. The maintenance allowance is based on living costs in the host country and is sufficient to meet normal expenses of a single person at the graduate-study level. Dependents allowances vary by country.

Amount of support per award: Varies by country.

CO-OP FUNDING PROGRAMS: Funds from other scholarships, fellowships or grants in dollars or foreign currency received concurrently with a Fulbright Grant will be deducted if they duplicate the Fulbright benefits. No deduction is made if other grants are for assistance in meeting family expenses of grantees or other expenses not covered by the grant.

NO. MOST RECENT APPLICANTS: 11,150.

NO. AWARDS: Approximately 2,000 for the year 2016-17.

APPLICATION INFO:
Enrolled students should contact the Fulbright Program Adviser on their campus. Candidates who are not enrolled in an educational institution should contact IIE, U.S. Student Programs Division, at the address above.

Duration: One academic year.

Deadline: Enrolled students should submit their applications to their campus Fulbright Program Advisers by the dates set by them. At-large candidates must submit their applications to the IIE office in October.

ADDRESS INQUIRIES TO:
Jody Dudderar, Assistant Director of U.S. Student Programs
(See address above.)

INTERNATIONAL DEVELOPMENT RESEARCH CENTRE (IDRC)

150 Kent Street
Ottawa ON K1P 0B2 Canada
(613) 696-2098
Fax: (613) 236-4026
E-mail: awards@idrc.ca
Web Site: www.idrc.ca

TYPE:
Internships. Program provides training in research management and grant administration under the guidance of Centre program staff. Approximately 50% of the time spent on own research project.

See entry 1276 for full listing.

INTERNATIONAL RESEARCH & EXCHANGES BOARD (IREX) [901]

1275 K Street, N.W.
Suite 600
Washington, DC 20005
(202) 628-8188
Fax: (202) 628-8189
E-mail: irex@irex.org
Web Site: www.irex.org

FOUNDED: 1968

AREAS OF INTEREST:
Academic research exchanges and professional training programs in Europe, Eurasia, the Middle East and North Africa, and Asia.

NAME(S) OF PROGRAMS:
- **International Leaders in Education Program (ILEP)**

- **Regional Assistance Program (RAP)**
- **Teaching Excellence and Achievement Program (TEA)**

TYPE:
Conferences/seminars; Exchange programs; Fellowships; Project/program grants; Research grants; Training grants; Travel grants; Visiting scholars. ILEP: Grants to secondary teachers from around the globe to the U.S. to further develop expertise in their subject areas, enhance their teaching skills, and increase their knowledge about the U.S.

Regional Assistance Program (RAP) works with civil society organizations to advance political, social and economic reform across the Middle East and North Africa.

TEA: Grants to secondary-school teachers from Eurasia and South Asia with unique opportunities to develop expertise in their subject areas, enhance their teaching skills, and increase their knowledge about the U.S.

YEAR PROGRAM STARTED: 1968

PURPOSE:
To promote advanced field research and professional training programs between the U.S. and the countries of Europe, Eurasia, Asia and the Middle East and North Africa.

LEGAL BASIS:
Nonprofit organization.

GEOG. RESTRICTIONS: United States, Europe, Eurasia, the Middle East, Asia and North Africa.

FINANCIAL DATA:
Amount of support per award: Varies per program.

APPLICATION INFO:
Application information is available upon request.

PUBLICATIONS:
Policy papers, application materials.

ADDRESS INQUIRIES TO:
Program Coordinator
(See address above.)

ISTITUTO ITALIANO PER GLI STUDI STORICI

Via Benedetto Croce, 12
80134 Naples Italy
(39) 081 5517159
(39) 081 5512390
Fax: (39) 081 5514813
E-mail: info@iiss.it
Web Site: www.iiss.it

TYPE:
Awards/prizes; Conferences/seminars; Research grants; Scholarships. Awards for historical, literature and philosophical studies at the Istituto Italiano per gli Studi Storici in Naples.

Federico II Scholarship: Offered by the Universita di Napoli for graduates from Italian universities whose final thesis is in medieval studies.

See entry 588 for full listing.

JAPAN INFORMATION CENTER [902]

Consulate General of Japan
299 Park Avenue, 18th Floor
New York, NY 10171-0025
(212) 418-4452
Fax: (212) 371-1294
E-mail: scholarship@ny.mofa.go.jp
Web Site: www.ny.us.emb-japan.go.jp

FOUNDED: 1955

AREAS OF INTEREST:
Japanese language and cultural studies.

NAME(S) OF PROGRAMS:

- **Japanese Government (Monbukagakusho) Scholarships for Japanese Studies**

TYPE:
Scholarships. Undergraduate scholarships awarded to foreign students who wish to pursue Japanese language and cultural studies in Japan. The program offers students an intensive course of Japanese language and introduction to Japanese studies in various aspects.

YEAR PROGRAM STARTED: 1955

PURPOSE:
To provide funding for non-Japanese students who want to pursue a course of Japanese and cultural studies in Japan.

LEGAL BASIS:
Japanese government agency.

ELIGIBILITY:
Applicants must:
(1) be nationals of the country to which the scholarships are offered;
(2) be at least 18 years and less than 30 years of age as of April 1 of the year of application;
(3) be regular students who follow an undergraduate course at a university in their own country or a third country and who are mainly second- or third-year students or above in that course;
(4) be specializing in a field concerning Japanese language or Japanese culture at their university;
(5) have good knowledge of the Japanese language and;
(6) be in good health.

Applicants must have a background in Japanese studies to qualify. A written Japanese examination will be given to selected applicants before being considered by the government offices in Japan.

FINANCIAL DATA:
Amount of support per award: JPY 117,000 per month (subject to change), plus tuition, fees and round-trip transportation costs.

Total amount of support: Varies.

NO. AWARDS: Varies.

APPLICATION INFO:
Applicants should contact the appropriate Japanese consulate. Consulates General are located in Anchorage, Atlanta, Boston, Chicago, Denver, Detroit, Hagatna (Guam), Honolulu, Houston, Los Angeles, Miami, Nashville, New York City, Portland, Saipan, San Francisco and Seattle.

Duration: One academic year.

Deadline: Varies.

PUBLICATIONS:
Application guidelines.

ADDRESS INQUIRIES TO:
Local Japanese Consulate General

*PLEASE NOTE:
Placement of grantees to universities will be decided by Monbukagakusho after consultation with the universities concerned.

JAPAN INFORMATION CENTER [903]

Consulate General of Japan
299 Park Avenue, 18th Floor
New York, NY 10171-0025
(212) 371-8222
Fax: (212) 371-1294
E-mail: scholarship@ny.mofa.go.jp
Web Site: www.ny.us.emb-japan.go.jp

FOUNDED: 1955

AREAS OF INTEREST:
Humanities and social sciences: literature, history, aesthetics, law, politics, economics, commerce, pedagogy, psychology, sociology, music, fine arts, natural sciences, pure science, engineering, agriculture, fisheries, pharmacology, medicine, dentistry and home economics.

NAME(S) OF PROGRAMS:

- **Japanese Government (Monbukagakusho) Scholarships for Research Students**

TYPE:
Scholarships. Graduate scholarships awarded to foreign students who wish to study at Japanese universities as nondegree research students.

PURPOSE:
To help students wishing to pursue Japan-related studies.

LEGAL BASIS:
Japanese government agency.

ELIGIBILITY:
Applicants must:
(1) be nationals of the country to which the scholarships are offered;
(2) be under 35 years of age as of April 1 of the year of the award;
(3) be university or college graduates;
(4) be willing to study the Japanese language and to receive instruction in that language and;
(5) be in good health.

The study area must be in the same field as the applicant has studied (or is now studying) or a related one.

FINANCIAL DATA:
Amount of support per award: JPY 143,000 per month.

Total amount of support: Varies.

NO. AWARDS: Varies.

APPLICATION INFO:
Applicants should contact the appropriate Japanese consulate. Consulates General are located in Anchorage, Atlanta, Boston, Chicago, Denver, Detroit, Hagatna (Guam), Honolulu, Houston, Los Angeles, Miami, Nashville, New York City, Portland, Saipan, San Francisco and Seattle.

Duration: Up to two years, with possibility of extension.

Deadline: Varies.

PUBLICATIONS:
Application guidelines.

ADDRESS INQUIRIES TO:
Local Japanese Consulate General

*PLEASE NOTE:
Field of study must be one of those available at the Japanese universities and practical training given by factories or companies is excluded.

HERBERT D. KATZ CENTER FOR ADVANCED JUDAIC STUDIES [904]

420 Walnut Street
Philadelphia, PA 19106
(215) 238-1290
Fax: (215) 238-1540
E-mail: carrielo@sas.upenn.edu
Web Site: katz.sas.upenn.edu

AREAS OF INTEREST:
Advanced research in Judaic and related studies.

NAME(S) OF PROGRAMS:
- **Judaic and Related Studies Postdoctoral Fellowships**

TYPE:
Fellowships.

PURPOSE:
To support education in Judaic and related studies.

ELIGIBILITY:
Individuals are eligible to apply.

FINANCIAL DATA:
Amount of support per award: Up to $60,000.

NO. AWARDS: 20.

APPLICATION INFO:
Application information is available on the web site.

Duration: Up to one year. Fellowships are not renewable.

Deadline: Late October.

ADDRESS INQUIRIES TO:
Carrie Love
Fellowship Program Administrator
(See address above.)

MACKENZIE KING SCHOLARSHIP TRUST

c/o J. Blom, Faculty of Law
1822 East Mall, University of British Columbia
Vancouver BC V6T 1Z1 Canada
(604) 822-4564
Fax: (604) 822-8108
E-mail: mkingscholarships@law.ubc.ca
Web Site: www.mkingscholarships.ca

TYPE:
Scholarships. For graduate study, either in the U.S. or the U.K., in the field of international or industrial relations (including the international or industrial aspects of law, history, politics or economics).

See entry 1648 for full listing.

KOBE COLLEGE CORPORATION-JAPAN EDUCATION EXCHANGE [905]

540 West Frontage Road, Suite 3335
Northfield, IL 60093
(847) 386-7661
Fax: (847) 386-7662
E-mail: kccjee@comcast.net
Web Site: www.kccjee.org

AREAS OF INTEREST:
Japanese culture and language.

NAME(S) OF PROGRAMS:
- **The KCC-JEE High School Essay Contest**

TYPE:
Awards/prizes. The KCC-JEE High School Essay Contest includes a one-month trip to Japan. It incorporates intensive language study, college credit and a home stay with a Japanese family.

YEAR PROGRAM STARTED: 1995

PURPOSE:
To provide American high school students the opportunity to experience Japanese culture firsthand, enhancing their Japanese language skills and deepening their appreciation of Japanese culture and values by living in Japan for one month.

ELIGIBILITY:
Applicant must meet the following requirements:
(1) be an American citizen or permanent resident alien, 16 years of age by June 1 of the year contest is held;
(2) must have had at least one year of accredited Japanese language study;
(3) attend a public or private high school in the U.S. and;
(4) be available to study during the four weeks established for this program.

GEOG. RESTRICTIONS: United States.

FINANCIAL DATA:
Prize includes round-trip airfare, tuition, and room and board in a Japanese home.

Amount of support per award: Approximately $4,000.

NO. AWARDS: 1 award given annually.

APPLICATION INFO:
Application and complete information can be found online.

Duration: One summer month (typically July). Nonrenewable.

Deadline: February.

THE KOSCIUSZKO FOUNDATION, INC. [906]

15 East 65th Street
New York, NY 10065
(212) 734-2130
Fax: (212) 628-4552
E-mail: marykay@thekf.org
Web Site: www.thekf.org/kf/programs/teaching_english_in_poland

FOUNDED: 1925

AREAS OF INTEREST:
Educational and cultural exchange program in Poland.

NAME(S) OF PROGRAMS:
- **Teaching English in Poland**

TYPE:
Summer educational and cultural exchange program for American teachers and teaching assistants in Poland.

YEAR PROGRAM STARTED: 1991

PURPOSE:
To provide Polish students with English language experiences within an American cultural context; to familiarize Polish students with various aspects of American life and culture; to introduce American teachers and teaching assistants to Polish culture, history, traditions and people of Poland so that their knowledge and impressions will be shared.

LEGAL BASIS:
501(c)(3) not-for-profit organization.

ELIGIBILITY:
Experienced teachers/administrators certified in the U.S., educators with private/parochial school or other verifiable teaching experience, college/university faculty, and those engaged in student services (school nurse, social worker, guidance counselor, school psychologist, etc.) are eligible for participation. Group flight arrangements will be made by the Foundation. Participants are encouraged to travel to Poland with the group.

GEOG. RESTRICTIONS: United States.

FINANCIAL DATA:
Registration fee of $300 for teachers and $250 for teaching assistants and peer tutors. Medical insurance, required by The Kosciuszko Foundation, is covered. This is a volunteer opportunity. Applicant pays for airfare. Room and board during the teaching program as well as sightseeing in Poland after the program's end are covered by Polish hosts.

Amount of support per award: Varies.

Matching fund requirements: In-kind donations such as art and sport equipment towards the program are accepted.

CO-OP FUNDING PROGRAMS: Delta Kappa Gamma support in the amount of $14,000.

NO. MOST RECENT APPLICANTS: 120.

NO. AWARDS: 31.

APPLICATION INFO:
Applications must be completed on the Foundation's web site.

Duration: Two and one-half to four weeks.

Deadline: January 11.

PUBLICATIONS:
KF Newsletter; *Annual Report.*

IRS I.D.: 13-1628179

STAFF:
Mary Kay Pieski, Ph.D.

ADDRESS INQUIRIES TO:
Teaching English in Poland Program
315 Fawnwood Drive
Tallmadge, OH 44278

THE KOSCIUSZKO FOUNDATION, INC. [907]

15 East 65th Street
New York, NY 10065
(212) 734-2130 ext. 210
E-mail: addy@thekf.org
Web Site: www.thekf.org/programs/study

FOUNDED: 1925

AREAS OF INTEREST:
Strengthening of cultural and educational bonds between the U.S. and Poland through an exchange program to Poland for the purpose of Polish language, culture and history studies.

NAME(S) OF PROGRAMS:
- **Summer Study Abroad Programs**

TYPE:
Exchange programs; Scholarships. Summer programs. The Summer Study Abroad Programs offer a variety of courses from July through August at the Jagiellonian University in Krakow and at the John Paul II Catholic University of Lublin, Poland. Polish language, culture, history, art and many other subjects are available. The Foundation sponsors this program mainly for paying students; however, some scholarship awards are available for the program at the Jagiellonian University in Krakow.

YEAR PROGRAM STARTED: 1970

PURPOSE:
To enable American students to pursue a short-term course of Polish language, culture, history and art studies abroad.

LEGAL BASIS:
501(c)(3) not-for-profit organization.

ELIGIBILITY:
The Summer Study Abroad Programs are open to U.S. undergraduate and graduate students as well as graduating high school students who will be 18 years of age by the first day of the program.

Students of Polish descent can apply for funding to attend the Foundation's three-week program at the Jagiellonian University via the Foundation's Tomaszkiewicz-Florio Scholarship.

GEOG. RESTRICTIONS: United States.

FINANCIAL DATA:
Program fee includes tuition, course materials, cultural events and sightseeing trips, a language placement test, language classes, afternoon classes, shared dormitory room, three meals a day and assistance from Polish university students. The scholarships which are available cover program fees for three-week programs at the Jagiellonian University in Krakow.

Amount of support per award: Varies.

Total amount of support: $31,705 awarded towards Summer Studies in Krakow for the year 2014.

NO. MOST RECENT APPLICANTS: 59.

NO. AWARDS: 17 for the year 2014.

APPLICATION INFO:
Application materials and program details are available online. Application is available from January to May. When requesting forms and additional information via e-mail, please indicate "Summer Study Abroad Programs" in the subject line.

Duration: Two- to eight-week programs are available.

Deadline: April 15 for scholarship applicants. May 15 for students who wish to pay their own way.

PUBLICATIONS:
KF Newsletter; annual report.

IRS I.D.: 13-1628179

STAFF:
Dr. John S. Micgiel, President and Executive Director

ADDRESS INQUIRIES TO:
Addy Tymczyszyn, Coordinator
Summer Study Abroad Programs
(See address above.)

*PLEASE NOTE:
Students submit scholarship applications to the Foundation's chapters. Pay-to-go applicants must submit application materials to Kosciuszko Foundation's headquarters in New York City.

*SPECIAL STIPULATIONS:
Students who receive scholarships are required to submit a report upon completion of the program. The report is forwarded to the donors of the scholarship.

THE KOSCIUSZKO FOUNDATION, INC. [908]

15 East 65th Street
New York, NY 10065
(212) 734-2130 ext. 210
E-mail: addy@thekf.org
Web Site: www.thekf.org/scholarships/exchange-poland/year-abroad

FOUNDED: 1925

AREAS OF INTEREST:
Strengthening of cultural and educational bonds between the U.S. and Poland through an exchange program to Poland for the purpose of Polish language, culture and history studies.

NAME(S) OF PROGRAMS:
- **The Kosciuszko Foundation Year Abroad Program**

TYPE:
Exchange programs; Scholarships. The Year Abroad Program at the Center for Polish Language and Culture in the World, Jagiellonian University (Krakow) offers American students the opportunity to study Polish language, history, literature and culture for one academic year or one semester. This program allows students to spend their undergraduate junior or senior year in Poland. Undergraduate credit may be transferred. Students at the Master's level may also apply.

PURPOSE:
To enable American students to pursue an undergraduate course of Polish language, literature, history and culture at the Center for Polish Language and Culture, Jagiellonian University, Krakow.

LEGAL BASIS:
501(c)(3) not-for-profit organization.

ELIGIBILITY:
U.S. citizens enrolled at a U.S. college or university who will be entering their junior or senior year can apply. Graduate students, with the exception of those at the dissertation level, can also apply. Minimum grade point average of 3.0 is required.

Polish citizens are not eligible.

Scholarship does not cover second majors.

GEOG. RESTRICTIONS: United States.

FINANCIAL DATA:
Scholarship offers a tuition waiver, housing and a monthly stipend of 1,350 Polish zloty per month towards living expenses. Recipients also receive $900 per semester from the Foundation for living expenses. Transportation to and from Poland and other personal expenses are not included.

Amount of support per award: $900 per semester plus additional funding from the Polish Ministry in the amount of 1,350 Polish zloty per month of study.

Total amount of support: Varies.

NO. MOST RECENT APPLICANTS: 8.

NO. AWARDS: 5.

APPLICATION INFO:
Applications are available online from October to January 16. When requesting information and/or forms, please specify "Year Abroad Program" in the subject line of your e-mail. Applications and supporting materials must be accompanied by a nonrefundable $50 application fee.

Duration: One semester (October to February or February to June) or one academic year.

Deadline: January 15. Notification in June. Funding is for the following academic year.

PUBLICATIONS:
Guidelines; *KF Newsletter*; annual report.

IRS I.D.: 13-1628179

STAFF:
Dr. John S. Micgiel, President and Executive Director

ADDRESS INQUIRIES TO:
Year Abroad Program
(See address above.)

THE KOSCIUSZKO FOUNDATION, INC. [909]

15 East 65th Street
New York, NY 10065
(212) 734-2130 ext. 210
E-mail: addy@thekf.org
Web Site: www.thekf.org/scholarships/exchange-poland/research

FOUNDED: 1925

AREAS OF INTEREST:
Strengthening of cultural and educational bonds between the U.S. and Poland through an exchange program for graduate-level students and scholars who wish to conduct research programs in Poland.

NAME(S) OF PROGRAMS:
- **The Kosciuszko Foundation Graduate Studies and Research in Poland**

TYPE:
Exchange programs; Research grants; Scholarships; Visiting scholars. This program enables American students and scholars to pursue a course of graduate or postgraduate study and research in Poland. It is also open to university faculty who wish to spend a sabbatical conducting research in Poland.

Research may be conducted during the Polish academic year, October through June only. No funding during the summer months of July, August and September.

PURPOSE:
To assist Americans in continuing their graduate and postgraduate studies and research at institutions of higher learning in Poland.

LEGAL BASIS:
501(c)(3) not-for-profit organization.

ELIGIBILITY:
U.S. citizens with strong Polish language skills who wish to conduct research in Poland may apply. Funding is granted for research at institutions of higher learning in Poland which fall under the jurisdiction of the Polish Ministry of Education and Science.

Polish citizens are not eligible.

GEOG. RESTRICTIONS: United States.

FINANCIAL DATA:
Scholarship does not cover tuition costs. (Candidates who wish to attend classes must secure a tuition waiver prior to applying for funding.) Participants receive a stipend from the Polish government towards housing and living expenses. No provisions are made for dependents. Transportation to and from Poland is at the expense of the participant. The scholarship does not cover second majors. Personal expenses are not included.

Amount of support per award: $300 per month of approved study/research, plus 1,350 zloty per month from the Polish Ministry of National Education.

Total amount of support: Varies.

NO. MOST RECENT APPLICANTS: 8.

NO. AWARDS: 7.

APPLICATION INFO:

Applications are available online at the Foundation's web site from October through January 15. Nonrefundable application fee of $50 is required.

Applicants must submit a letter of invitation from the host university's International Student Office specifying terms of the research including start and end dates of the research project, whether dormitory housing will be provided to the candidate, and provisions for access to university libraries, archives, and/or equipment as needed. A letter from the professor or department chairperson with whom research is to be conducted indicating the feasibility of the research proposal, agreement to act as the candidate's Academic Advisor and provision for letters of introduction as may be necessary for the research proposal. The host institution must fall under jurisdiction of the Polish Ministry of Education and Science in order to be considered.

The Foundation does not accept faxed applications.

Duration: Maximum of nine months. Research may be conducted from October to June. No funding from July through September.

Deadline: January 15. Notification in June/July for funding in the following academic year.

PUBLICATIONS:

KF Newsletter; annual report.

IRS I.D.: 13-1628179

STAFF:

Dr. John S. Micgiel, President and Executive Director

ADDRESS INQUIRIES TO:

Studies and Research in Poland
(See address above.)

THE ROBERTO LONGHI FOUNDATION FOR THE STUDY OF THE HISTORY OF ART

Via Benedetto Fortini, 30
50125 Florence Italy
(39) 055 6580794
Fax: (39) 055 6580794
E-mail: longhi@fondazionelonghi.it
Web Site: www.fondazionelonghi.it

TYPE:

Fellowships.

See entry 542 for full listing.

MARSHALL AID COMMEMORATION COMMISSION [910]

ACU
Woburn House
20-24 Tavistock Square
London WC1H 9HF England
(44) 207 380 6704
(44) 207 380 6703
Fax: (44) 020 7387 2655
E-mail: apps@marshallscholarship.org
Web Site: www.marshallscholarship.org

FOUNDED: 1953

NAME(S) OF PROGRAMS:

- **Marshall Scholarships**

TYPE:

Scholarships. Tenable at any university in the U.K. in any subject leading to the award of a British university degree, which recipients are required to take.

Marshall Scholarships finance young Americans of high ability to study for a degree in the U.K. in a system of higher education recognized for its excellence. These grants have been established to express British gratitude for the European Recovery Program (the Marshall Plan) instituted by General of the Army George C. Marshall.

YEAR PROGRAM STARTED: 1954

PURPOSE:

To enable citizens of the U.S., both men and women who are graduates of U.S. colleges and universities, to study for a degree from a university in the U.K. for a period of at least one academic year.

LEGAL BASIS:

Programme established by British Parliamentary Act.

ELIGIBILITY:

Scholarships are offered to U.S. citizens for study in the U.K. Graduates of a degree-granting college or university who have graduated from their undergraduate college or university no more than three years before the year the award will be taken up are eligible (e.g., for awards tenable from October 2016, candidates must have graduated after April 2013). Candidates must be American citizens at the time of application and must have obtained a grade point average of not less than 3.7 (or A-). (Exceptions will be considered only on the specific recommendation of the sponsoring college.)

FINANCIAL DATA:

Scholarships include a personal allowance, tuition fees, grants for books, travel, thesis and fares to and from Britain.

Amount of support per award: Currently GBP 977 per month (GBP 1,208 for those registered within the London Metropolitan Police district) for 12 or 22 months, plus book grants and fares to/from the U.K.

Total amount of support: GBP 2,179,030 for the year ended March 31, 2014.

NO. MOST RECENT APPLICANTS: Approximately 800.

NO. AWARDS: Up to 40 awards annually.

APPLICATION INFO:

Application should be made to a British Consulate-General (in Atlanta, Boston, Chicago, Houston, Los Angeles, New York and San Francisco) or to the British Embassy in Washington, DC.

Duration: One to two years. May be extended for a third year.

Deadline: Early October of the year preceding the award.

OFFICERS:

John Kirkland, Executive Secretary
Mary C. Denyer, Assistant Secretary

COMMISSION MEMBERS:

Dr. John Hughes, Chairperson
Michael Birshan
Richard Dendy
Eliza Hermann
Timothy Hornsby
Ruth Kosmin
Janet Legrand
Prof. Simon Newman
Nigel Thrift

THE MATSUMAE INTERNATIONAL FOUNDATION [911]

4-14-46, Kamiogi, Suginami-ku
Tokyo 167-0043 Japan
(81) 3-3301-7600
Fax: (81) 3-3301-7601
E-mail: contact@mif-japan.org
Web Site: www.mif-japan.org

FOUNDED: 1979

AREAS OF INTEREST:

First priority: Natural sciences, engineering and medicine.

NAME(S) OF PROGRAMS:

- **Fellowship Program**

TYPE:

Fellowships; Research grants.

YEAR PROGRAM STARTED: 1980

PURPOSE:

To provide opportunity to foreign scientists to conduct research at Japanese institutions.

LEGAL BASIS:

Private foundation.

ELIGIBILITY:

Citizenship is unrestricted. Those of non-Japanese nationality who meet all of the following eligibility requirements are invited to submit the required application documents:
(1) Applicants must hold a Ph.D. degree, or be recognized by the Foundation as possessing equivalent academic qualifications;
(2) Applicants must be 49 years of age or under at the time of application;
(3) Applicants must have sufficient conversational ability in English or Japanese to prevent insurmountable difficulties during their research activities in Japan;
(4) Applicants should not have been in Japan in the past and/or in the present;
(5) Applicants should have firm positions and professions in their home countries and should return to their countries on completion of their fellowship stay by the Foundation and;
(6) Applicants must be of sound health and not physically handicapped in any way which would prevent them from carrying out research in Japan.

Fields of study such as natural science, engineering and medicine are given first priority.

FINANCIAL DATA:

Awards include stipend for research and stay, lump sum on arrival, round-trip travel and insurance.

Amount of support per award: Monthly stipend of JPY 220,000; lump sum on arrival of 120,000 JPY.

NO. MOST RECENT APPLICANTS: 147 from 45 countries for the year 2016.

NO. AWARDS: 31 from 26 countries for the year 2016. From 1980 to 2015, there have been 746 Research Fellows from 114 countries.

APPLICATION INFO:

Application form required. Applicants should obtain the current issue of the Fellowship Announcement from the Foundation. To obtain the announcement, write to the Foundation with name and address by postal mail, or by e-mail. The announcement can

also be downloaded from the web page of the Foundation; the Application Form must be printed out in PDF format or MS Word file.

Application must be submitted from the applicant's home country. Under no circumstances will an application be accepted from a person already in Japan. The Foundation does not accept applications by fax or e-mail.

All documents must be typewritten in English. The following documents (A4 in size) must be included and submitted on one occasion by the applicant:
(1) a photograph (taken within the last three months) along with the fully completed application form (signed and dated);
(2) a description of the research project by the applicant;
(3) complete list of publications;
(4) reprint of what the applicant considers to be his or her most important publication;
(5) a personal history (curriculum vitae);
(6) a letter of recommendation from the applicant's employer and/or supervisor testifying to academic ability and achievements and confirming the availability of study leave covering the grant period;
(7) a certified copy of the applicant's academic certificates (Ph.D., Master's, Bachelor's) issued by the university concerned (in English, or document with English translation attached) and;
(8) an invitation letter with signature from the host scientist confirming the period of stay, the research project, the availability of research facilities/materials and the arrangement of lodging accommodation under the Foundation Fellowship Program.

Submitted applications which do not contain all of the required documents will automatically be rejected.

The Foundation will not be responsible for costs incurred in submitting an application and reserves the right to request additional documents if necessary. All documents received become the property of the Foundation and will not be returned. The Foundation will not respond to individual inquiry concerning the status/arrival of application documents.

Contact the Foundation for full details.

Duration: Three to six months; extension/reduction of the granted period is not allowed.

Deadline: Applications must be received by the Foundation by August 31 for the following year's fellowship.

PUBLICATIONS:
Program announcement.

ADDRESS INQUIRIES TO:
Fellowship Program
(See address above.)

*PLEASE NOTE:
To promote deeper understanding of Japan, the Foundation organizes a Study Tour during the invitation period in Japan.

Each year, the Foundation issues a "Research Report" containing summaries of research activities or results which are kindly submitted by the Fellows.

In order to keep in touch with Fellows after their return home, the Foundation issues a "Newsletter" and "Fellowship Directory" annually.

MICHIGAN STATE UNIVERSITY [912]

Office of Study Abroad
International Center
427 North Shaw Lane, Room 109
East Lansing, MI 48824-1035
(517) 353-8920
Fax: (517) 432-2082
E-mail: studyabroad@isp.msu.edu
Web Site: www.studyabroad.msu.edu

NAME(S) OF PROGRAMS:
- **MSU Study Abroad Scholarships**

TYPE:
Scholarships. Academic study abroad scholarships for college-level credit. The program includes over 275 overseas study programs in more than 60 countries in a wide variety of academic fields.

PURPOSE:
To assist Michigan State University students who will benefit from study abroad.

LEGAL BASIS:
University.

ELIGIBILITY:
Applicants must be MSU students. Participation in study abroad program is:
(1) based on financial need. Applicant must have FAFSA application on file with MSU office of financial aid and have a minimum 2.5 grade point average and;
(2) based on academic performance. Applicant must have a minimum 3.5 grade point average and submit an essay explaining how study abroad would enhance the student's education.

FINANCIAL DATA:
Amount of support per award: $250 to $1,750 available per student.

Total amount of support: Approximately $400,000 annually.

NO. MOST RECENT APPLICANTS: Approximately 1,200.

NO. AWARDS: Approximately 400 per year.

APPLICATION INFO:
Application information is available on the web site.

Duration: Varies.

Deadline: October 15 and March 1.

STAFF:
Lynn Aguado, Study Abroad Program Coordinator

ADDRESS INQUIRIES TO:
Lynn Aguado
Study Abroad Program Coordinator
(See address above.)

THE NANSEN FUND, INC. [913]

5219 Pine Arbor Drive
Houston, TX 77066-2548
(281) 682-4327
Fax: (281) 587-9284
E-mail: anne-brith@nacchouston.org
Web Site: www.noram.no

FOUNDED: 1979

AREAS OF INTEREST:
International educational exchange, international relations, classics, political science and Norwegian culture.

NAME(S) OF PROGRAMS:
- **John Dana Archbold Fellowships**

TYPE:
Fellowships; Scholarships; Travel grants. Stipends for subsistence and quarters. One-year graduate fellowships for study at the University of Oslo in Norway, offered in even-numbered years; in odd-numbered years offered to Norwegians for study in the U.S.

YEAR PROGRAM STARTED: 1981

PURPOSE:
To promote better understanding among peoples for peace among nations and to support educational exchange between the U.S. and Norway.

LEGAL BASIS:
509(a)(2) organization.

ELIGIBILITY:
Fellowships are open to Norwegians and Americans for a year of graduate, postdoctoral or professional study and research. Eligibility is limited to persons 20 to 35 years old, in good health, of good character, and citizens of the U.S. or Norway. Qualified applicants must show evidence of real ability in their chosen field, indicate seriousness of purpose, and have a record of social adaptability. Undergraduate applicants must have a B.A. or B.S. degree (or equivalent) before their departure date.

GEOG. RESTRICTIONS: Norway and United States.

FINANCIAL DATA:
Maintenance stipend is sufficient to meet basic expenses for a single person. Some travel allowance.

Amount of support per award: Up to $10,000, depending on projected costs of tuition, maintenance, travel and rate of exchange.

Total amount of support: Up to $10,000.

CO-OP FUNDING PROGRAMS: The University of Oslo charges no tuition to fellows.

NO. MOST RECENT APPLICANTS: Average 6.

NO. AWARDS: 1 annually.

APPLICATION INFO:
Application forms are available from the address above until December 1 of the year preceding the award period. Completed applications require a statement of the proposed study, curriculum vitae, three academic references, foreign language report and transcripts, international relations, classics, political science and Norwegian culture.

Duration: One year, including Oslo International Summer School.

Deadline: February 1. Announcement by March 1.

PUBLICATIONS:
Program description.

IRS I.D.: 74-6043421

OFFICERS AND DIRECTORS:
Anne-Brith Berge

ADDRESS INQUIRIES TO:
For further information about the University of Oslo, contact:
Ms. Torild Homstad
The University of Oslo International Summer School
North American Branch Office
St. Olaf College
1520 St. Olaf Avenue
Northfield, MN 55057
Tel: (507) 786-3269 or (800) 639-0058
Fax: (507) 786-3732
E-mail: iss@stolaf.edu
Web site: www.uio.no/iss/

*SPECIAL STIPULATIONS:
Successful applicant(s) will be recommended to the University of Oslo by the Nansen Fund, but he or she must make application to, and be accepted by, the University as a graduate student in a particular department. The University of Oslo International Summer School offers orientation and Norwegian language courses for six weeks before the start of the regular academic year. For Americans, tuition is paid. Attendance is required.

NATIONAL SECURITY EDUCATION PROGRAM [914]

Boren Scholarships
Institute of International Education
1400 K Street, N.W., 7th Floor
Washington, DC 20005-2403
(800) 618-6737
Fax: (202) 326-7672
E-mail: boren@iie.org
Web Site: www.borenawards.org

FOUNDED: 1991

AREAS OF INTEREST:
Languages and cultures of world regions that are critical to U.S. interests and underrepresented in study abroad, including Africa, Asia, Central and Eastern Europe, Eurasia, Latin America, and the Middle East.

NAME(S) OF PROGRAMS:
- **Boren Scholarships**

TYPE:
Scholarships. Boren Scholarships provide funding for U.S. undergraduate students to study less commonly taught languages in world regions that are critical to U.S. interests and underrepresented in study abroad.

PURPOSE:
To provide American undergraduates with the resources and encouragement they need to acquire language skills and cultural experiences in areas of the world critical to national security, broadly defined. In exchange for funding, recipients commit to working in the federal government for a minimum of one year after graduation.

ELIGIBILITY:
Must be a U.S. citizen at the time of application. Open to high school graduates, or those who have earned a GED, and are matriculated as a freshman, sophomore, junior, or senior in a U.S. postsecondary institution, including universities, colleges, and community colleges. Applicant must plan to study abroad in Africa, Asia, Central and Eastern Europe, Eurasia, or the Middle East. The countries of Western Europe, Canada, Australia, and New Zealand are excluded. The study abroad program must meet home institution standards and end prior to graduation.

FINANCIAL DATA:
Amount of support per award: Summer: Up to $8,000; Semester: Up to $10,000; Full academic year: Up to $20,000.

NO. MOST RECENT APPLICANTS: 947.

NO. AWARDS: 161.

APPLICATION INFO:
Complete details and application information can be found on the Boren Awards web site.

Duration: Summer (minimum eight weeks), fall or spring semester, and full academic year.

Deadline: February 9, 2017.

ADDRESS INQUIRIES TO:
See e-mail address or phone number above.

*SPECIAL STIPULATIONS:
In exchange for funding, recipients agree to the National Security Education Program (NSEP) Service Requirement. The NSEP Service Requirement stipulates that an award recipient work for a minimum of one year in the federal government in a position with national security responsibilities. The Departments of Defense, Homeland Security, State, or any element of the Intelligence Community are priority agencies.

NATIONAL SECURITY EDUCATION PROGRAM [915]

Boren Fellowships
Institute of International Education
1400 K Street, N.W., 7th Floor
Washington, DC 20005-2403
(800) 618-6737
Fax: (202) 326-7672
E-mail: boren@iie.org
Web Site: www.borenawards.org

FOUNDED: 1991

AREAS OF INTEREST:
Boren Fellowships support study and research in areas of the world that are critical to U.S. interests, including Africa, Asia, Central and Eastern Europe, Eurasia, Latin America, and the Middle East.

NAME(S) OF PROGRAMS:
- **Boren Fellowships**

TYPE:
Fellowships. Fellowships for U.S. graduate students to provide support for overseas study or a combination of overseas and domestic study.

PURPOSE:
To encourage U.S. graduate students to add an important international and language component to their graduate education through specialization in area study, language study, or increased language proficiency; to support study and research in areas of the world that are critical to U.S. interests, including Africa, Asia, Central and Eastern Europe, Eurasia, Latin America, and the Middle East.

ELIGIBILITY:
Must be a U.S. citizen at the time of application. Applicants must be matriculated in or applying to a graduate degree program at an accredited U.S. college or university located within the U.S. Boren Fellows must remain matriculated in their graduate programs for the duration of the fellowship. Applicant must plan an overseas program that meets home institution standards in Africa, Asia, Central and Eastern Europe, Eurasia, Latin America, and the Middle East. The countries of Western Europe, Canada, Australia, and New Zealand are excluded.

FINANCIAL DATA:
Amount of support per award: Up to $24,000 for overseas study; Up to $30,000 for a combination of domestic and overseas study.

NO. MOST RECENT APPLICANTS: 526.

NO. AWARDS: 110.

APPLICATION INFO:
Complete details and application information can be found on the Boren Awards web site.

Duration: Maximum two years for domestic and overseas study. Minimum 12 weeks for overseas study. Preference will be given to programs of six to 12 months.

Deadline: Varies.

ADDRESS INQUIRIES TO:
See e-mail address or phone number above.

*SPECIAL STIPULATIONS:
In exchange for funding, recipients agree to the National Security Education Program (NSEP) Service Requirement. The NSEP Service Requirement stipulates that an award recipient work for a minimum of one year in the federal government in a position with national security responsibilities. The Departments of Defense, Homeland Security, State, or any element of the Intelligence Community are priority agencies.

THE PHI BETA KAPPA SOCIETY [916]

1606 New Hampshire Avenue, N.W.
Washington, DC 20009
(202) 745-3287
Fax: (202) 986-1601
E-mail: awards@pbk.org
Web Site: www.pbk.org

AREAS OF INTEREST:
French language, literature and culture.

NAME(S) OF PROGRAMS:
- **The Walter J. Jensen Fellowship for French Language, Literature and Culture**

TYPE:
Fellowships. Fellowship for at least six months of study in France. One award given annually.

YEAR PROGRAM STARTED: 2001

PURPOSE:
To help educators and researchers improve education in standard French language, literature and culture, and in the study of standard French in the U.S.

ELIGIBILITY:
Candidates must be U.S. citizens under 40 years of age who can demonstrate their career does or will involve active use of the French language. They must have earned a Baccalaureate degree from an accredited four-year institution, and have a 3.0 minimum grade point average in French language and literature as a major. They must demonstrate superior competence in French, according to the standards established by the American Association of Teachers of French. Preference may be given to members of Phi Beta Kappa and educators at the secondary school level or above.

GEOG. RESTRICTIONS: United States.

FINANCIAL DATA:
Includes single round-trip, economy-class ticket for travel to France.

Amount of support per award: $15,500 stipend.

NO. MOST RECENT APPLICANTS: 6.

NO. AWARDS: Minimum 1 annually.

APPLICATION INFO:
The application booklet contains:
(1) the Application for the Walter J. Jensen Fellowship;
(2) two Transcript Request forms and;
(3) the Letter of Recommendation Form.

Applicant must submit three complete sets of documents. The Letter of Recommendation and Transcript Request forms may be duplicated. Please indicate the Fellowship name on all correspondence.

Applicant should send the application, official transcripts, and confidential letters of recommendation (in sealed envelopes) to the Walter J. Jensen Fellowship Committee in care of the Phi Beta Kappa Society.

Duration: At least six months.

Deadline: October. Contact Society for exact date.

ADDRESS INQUIRIES TO:
Laura Hartnett
Program and Event Specialist
(See address above.)

THE ROTARY FOUNDATION OF ROTARY INTERNATIONAL [917]

One Rotary Center
1560 Sherman Avenue
Evanston, IL 60201-3698
(866) 976-8279
(847) 866-3000
Fax: (847) 556-2141
E-mail: rotarypeacecenters@rotary.org
Web Site: www.rotary.org/en/peace-fellowships

FOUNDED: 2002

AREAS OF INTEREST:
Higher education.

NAME(S) OF PROGRAMS:

- **Rotary Peace Fellowships**

TYPE:
Fellowships. The Rotary Peace Centers offer individuals committed to peace and cooperation the opportunity to pursue a one- to two-year Master's-level degree or a three-month professional certificate in international studies, peace studies and conflict resolution at one of the six Rotary Peace Centers. The university partners are: Duke University and the University of North Carolina at Chapel Hill (North Carolina, U.S.A.); International Christian University (Tokyo, Japan); University of Bradford (West Yorkshire, England); University of Queensland (Brisbane, Queensland, Australia); Uppsala University (Uppsala, Sweden); and Chulalongkorn University (Bangkok, Thailand).

YEAR PROGRAM STARTED: 2002

PURPOSE:
To further peace and international understanding.

LEGAL BASIS:
Incorporated not-for-profit foundation.

ELIGIBILITY:
Applicants must have:
(1) the academic background, training and work experience required for a Master's-level program at the partner universities;
(2) proficiency in more than one language (even if they propose to study in a country where their native language is spoken);
(3) excellent leadership skills;
(4) a demonstrated commitment to peace and international understanding through their personal and community service activities and/or academic and professional achievements and;
(5) endorsement of their local rotary district office.

Persons with disabilities and members of Rotaract clubs are eligible and encouraged to apply.

FINANCIAL DATA:
Fellowship will include funding for tuition and required fees, room and board, transportation, contingency expenses and other funding, including paid internship experience.

Amount of support per award: Master's Program: Average $75,000; Professional Development Certificate: Average $12,000.

Total amount of support: Varies.

NO. MOST RECENT APPLICANTS: 325.

NO. AWARDS: Approximately 100 each year.

APPLICATION INFO:
All Rotary districts around the world are invited to nominate an unlimited number of candidates for the world-competitive selection each year. Applications generally need to be completed approximately 18 months in advance of the planned study period. Applications are available from the Rotary web site. Interested applicants should contact their local Rotary club or district and inform them that they are applying for the fellowship. Applications are due to the Rotary district by May 31 of the year prior to the study period.

Duration: Master's Program: One to two years; Professional Development Certificate: Three months.

Deadline: July 1.

PUBLICATIONS:
Application; brochure.

ADDRESS INQUIRIES TO:
Local Rotary Club or Contact Center
(See e-mail address above.)

THE ROYAL SOCIETY OF EDINBURGH [918]

22-26 George Street
Edinburgh EH2 2PQ Scotland
(44) 0131 240 5000
(44) 0131 240 5013
Fax: (44) 0131 240 5024
E-mail: resfells@royalsoced.org.uk
afraser@royalsoced.org.uk
Web Site: www.royalsoced.org.uk

FOUNDED: 1783

AREAS OF INTEREST:
Physical, computational, biological, medical, natural and social disciplines.

NAME(S) OF PROGRAMS:

- **Royal Society of Edinburgh Personal Research Fellowships**

TYPE:
Awards/prizes; Fellowships; Research grants. Postdoctoral fellowships for research in science and technology disciplines in any Scottish higher education institution.

YEAR PROGRAM STARTED: 1983

PURPOSE:
To enhance the transfer of ideas and technology from the research community to wealth creation and improvement of the quality of life in Scotland.

ELIGIBILITY:
Applicants must possess a Doctorate, or equivalent higher education qualification, and should have two to six years of relevant postdoctoral academic research experience at the time of the application closing date. Only applicants who meet these criteria by the date of application will be considered. Applicants must show that they have an outstanding capacity for innovative research with a strong publication record relevant to their proposed field of study. Preference will be given to those not holding a permanent position in an academic or research institution.

Research fellows must be based in Scotland during the fellowship, but can travel outside the U.K. for up to one year.

FINANCIAL DATA:
Salary, national insurance and pension costs covered, plus GBP 10,000 support funds and up to GBP 8,000 for travel, attendance at approved meetings and cost of minor equipment.

Amount of support per award: Stipend approximately GBP 24,766 to GBP 37,382.

CO-OP FUNDING PROGRAMS: Fellowships are made with the support of the Scottish government.

NO. MOST RECENT APPLICANTS: 51.

NO. AWARDS: 3.

APPLICATION INFO:
Application form and guidelines are available from the Research Awards Officer and from the Royal Society of Edinburgh web site.

Duration: Up to five years.

Deadline: Mid-February.

OFFICERS:
Sir John Arbuthnott, President
Gerald Wilson, Treasurer

ADDRESS INQUIRIES TO:
Anne Fraser, Research and International Awards Manager
The Royal Society of Edinburgh
Tel: 44 0131 240 5013
E-mail: afraser@royalsoced.org.uk
(See address above.)

ST. ANDREW'S SOCIETY OF THE STATE OF NEW YORK [919]

150 East 55th Street, 3rd Floor
New York, NY 10022
(212) 223-4248
Fax: (212) 233-0748
E-mail: office@standrewsny.org
Web Site: www.standrewsny.org

FOUNDED: 1756

AREAS OF INTEREST:
Charitable support of needy persons of Scottish descent and scholarship program.

NAME(S) OF PROGRAMS:

- **Scholarship Program for Graduate Study in Scotland**

TYPE:
Scholarships. Scholarships for American students of Scottish descent for one year of graduate study in any Scottish university.

YEAR PROGRAM STARTED: 1956

PURPOSE:
To promote cultural interchange and goodwill between Scotland and the U.S.

LEGAL BASIS:
Tax-exempt charitable organization.

ELIGIBILITY:
An applicant must be in senior year of undergraduate study, exhibit financial need, possess an outstanding scholastic and activity record, provide evidence of Scottish descent, and reside within a 250-mile radius of New York state.

GEOG. RESTRICTIONS: New Jersey, New York, Pennsylvania and the New England states.

FINANCIAL DATA:
Award is to be used initially against tuition, then board, room, transportation and other expenses.

Amount of support per award: Up to $30,000.

Total amount of support: Varies each year.

NO. MOST RECENT APPLICANTS: 100.

NO. AWARDS: 2 per year (for U.S. applicants).

APPLICATION INFO:
The applicant must contact St. Andrew's Society in writing with a request for an application. When the application is completed, it should be submitted to the college/university from/at which the student graduated or is due to graduate. Each college or university is invited to send only one candidate forward to the St. Andrew's Society Selection Committee. Referral must be by president of the institution the applicant is attending.

Duration: One year. Nonrenewable.

Deadline: December 15. Announcement in early March.

PUBLICATIONS:
Quarterly newsletter.

IRS I.D.: 13-5602329

OFFICERS:
Thomas D. Halket, President
John A.D. Needham, Treasurer
David M. Murphy, Secretary
Heath McLendon, Chairman, Finance Committee

ADDRESS INQUIRIES TO:
Peter Lawrie, Scholarship Chairman
(See address above.)

*SPECIAL STIPULATIONS:
Candidates must be from northeastern U.S. and of Scottish descent, and must be U.S. citizens.

SCAC (FRENCH CULTURAL AND EDUCATIONAL OFFICE) [920]

4101 Reservoir Road, N.W.
Washington, DC 20007
(202) 944-6000
Fax: (202) 944-6268
E-mail: hss.coordinator@chateaubriand-fellowship.org
Web Site: frenchculture.org

FOUNDED: 1980

NAME(S) OF PROGRAMS:
- **Chateaubriand Humanities & Social Sciences (HSS) Fellowship Program**
- **Benjamin Franklin Travel Grant for Undergraduate Students**
- **Teaching Assistant Program in France**

TYPE:
Assistantships; Exchange programs; Fellowships; Grants-in-aid; Project/program grants; Research grants; Training grants; Travel grants. Chateaubriand Fellowship Program: Offered by the embassy of France in the U.S., each year this program allows doctoral students enrolled in American universities to conduct research in France for up to eight months.

Benjamin Franklin Travel Grant: Allows sophomore, junior and senior students enrolled in an American university, who are enrolled in a double major including one major in French and one major in another discipline, the opportunity to discover France. Consideration will also be given to students enrolled in a minor/certificate in French and majoring in another subject.

Teaching Assistant Program in France: The French Ministry of Education and the Cultural Services Department of the French Embassy in Washington, DC offer over 1,100 teaching assistantships each year for American citizens and permanent residents of the U.S. to teach English in French schools. Assistants may work in primary schools or secondary schools.

YEAR PROGRAM STARTED: 1980

PURPOSE:
To promote the exchange of ideas between France and the U.S.

LEGAL BASIS:
Embassy.

ELIGIBILITY:
Details are available online.

FINANCIAL DATA:
Amount of support per award: Chateaubriand Fellowship Program: EUR 1,500 monthly, a round-trip ticket to France and health insurance; Benjamin Franklin Travel Grant: One-time support stipend of $900 for airfare for travel; Teaching Assistant Program in France: EUR 790 per month.

NO. MOST RECENT APPLICANTS: Chateaubriand Fellowship Program: 120; Teaching Assistant Program in France: 2,350.

NO. AWARDS: Chateaubriand Fellowship Program: 15; Teaching Assistant Program in France: 1,100.

APPLICATION INFO:
Details are available online.

Duration: Chateaubriand Fellowship Program: Up to eight months (a full university year in France); Benjamin Franklin Travel Grant: Up to 90 days during the summer; Teaching Assistant Program in France: Seven months.

Deadline: Details are available online.

ADDRESS INQUIRIES TO:
Benjamin Franklin Travel Grant:
E-mail: benfranklin.travel.grant@gmail.com
Teaching Assistant Program in France:
E-mail: assistant.washington-amba@diplomatie.gouv.fr.

SCUOLA NORMALE SUPERIORE [921]

Piazza dei Cavalieri, 7
Palazzo D'Ancona
56126 Pisa Italy
(39) 050 509237
(39) 050 509111
Fax: (39) 050 563513
E-mail: mario.landucci@sns.it
phd@sns.it
Web Site: www.sns.it

FOUNDED: 1813

AREAS OF INTEREST:
Classical philology, linguistics and history, modern philology and linguistics, history, art history, philosophy, mathematics and physics and their applications in chemistry and biology.

NAME(S) OF PROGRAMS:
- **Graduate School Scholarships for Study in Italy**

TYPE:
Scholarships. Scholarships for study at the Scuola Normale Superiore, Pisa, Italy, for postgraduate study in the disciplinary areas of the humanities and of mathematics, physics and natural sciences listed above.

PURPOSE:
To promote research and study in Italy.

LEGAL BASIS:
State-owned university.

ELIGIBILITY:
Citizens of all countries who have an M.A. degree and know Italian may apply. Students over 30 at the time of application cannot be admitted to the graduate courses. Applicants may not be receiving other forms of assistance.

FINANCIAL DATA:
Amount of support per award:
Perfezionamento (Ph.D.): Study grant of EUR 14,187 per year.

NO. AWARDS: 86 for the year 2015-16.

APPLICATION INFO:
Information is available online. The new announcement appears around May to June each year.

Duration: Up to three years; fellowship may be extended for an additional year for justified academic and/or scientific reasons if possible within the budget.

Deadline: February 28 for spring session; August 31 for autumn session.

ADDRESS INQUIRIES TO:
Student Secretariat
Dott. Mario Landucci
(See address above.)

SHASTRI INDO-CANADIAN INSTITUTE (SICI) [922]

Room 1418, Education Tower
2500 University Drive, N.W.
Calgary AB T2N 1N4 Canada
(403) 220-7467
Fax: (403) 289-0100
E-mail: maldeen@ucalgary.ca
Web Site: www.sici.org

AREAS OF INTEREST:
Understanding of India in Canada.

NAME(S) OF PROGRAMS:
- **India Studies Fellowship Competition**

TYPE:
Fellowships. India Studies Fellowship Competition is intended to support candidates wishing to undertake research or training in India. The focus of study is subjects relating to India in the social sciences and humanities, including education, law, management, the arts, science, and technology.

YEAR PROGRAM STARTED: 1968

PURPOSE:
To promote understanding between Canada and India, mainly through facilitating academic activities.

ELIGIBILITY:
Applicants must be Canadian citizens or permanent residents.

FINANCIAL DATA:
Amount of support per award: Varies.

Total amount of support: Varies.

CO-OP FUNDING PROGRAMS: Department of Education, Ministry of Human Resources, Government of India.

NO. AWARDS: Approximately 32.

APPLICATION INFO:
Application information is available on the web site.

Duration: Three months to one year.

Deadline: Varies.

ADDRESS INQUIRIES TO:
See e-mail address above.

SOMMERHOCHSCHULE-UNIVERSITY OF VIENNA [923]

Alser Strasse 4/Hof 1/Tuer 1.16
1090 Vienna Austria
(43) 1-4277-24131
Fax: (43) 1-4277-9241
E-mail: sommerhochschule@univie.ac.at
Web Site: shs.univie.ac.at/shs

FOUNDED: 1949

AREAS OF INTEREST:
European Studies (with focus on the legal, economic, political and cultural aspects) taught in English; German Language Courses (A1, A2, B1, B2).

NAME(S) OF PROGRAMS:
- **International Summer Program (Summer Campus Strobl/St. Wolfgang/Austria)**

TYPE:
Scholarships. The European Studies courses focus on the political, economic and legal, but also historical and cultural, aspects of Europe and the EU. The German language courses are offered at four different levels of proficiency (beginners to advanced).

YEAR PROGRAM STARTED: 1949

PURPOSE:
To contribute to an increased understanding of the EU and its possible future shape and to create an environment which encourages intercultural and social exchange and favors mutual understanding among participants.

LEGAL BASIS:
A subcompany of the University of Vienna; nonprofit status; state supported.

ELIGIBILITY:
Applicants have to be at least 18 years old and must have completed at least two years of studies at college or university level in their countries of residence or have an educational background equivalent to one year at a European university before the beginning of the program.

FINANCIAL DATA:
A limited number of partial scholarships are available for the European Studies section of the program. The scholarships are awarded on the basis of academic excellence and financial need.

Amount of support per award: EUR 300 to 2,400.

Total amount of support: Approximately EUR 40,000 for the year 2013.

NO. MOST RECENT APPLICANTS: 80 to 100.

NO. AWARDS: Varies based on the size of the scholarships.

APPLICATION INFO:
Applicants must submit the following documents:
(1) completed application form;
(2) transcript of grades;
(3) two letters of recommendation (academic or professional);
(4) official proof of proficiency in English;
(5) statement of purpose (one page maximum);
(6) two passport-size photos taken within the past year and;
(7) application for financial assistance.

All documents have to be submitted either in original or as a certified copy and have to be translated into English or German.

Application material must be sent to the office of the Sommerhochschule (faxed or e-mailed applications cannot be accepted).

Duration: Four weeks, middle of July to middle of August.

Deadline: February 28 for scholarship applications; April 30 for regular applications.

PUBLICATIONS:
Annual brochures and leaflets for the International Summer Program of the Sommerhochschule.

OFFICERS:
Dr. Franz-Stefan Meissel, Director
Nina Gruber, Program Coordinator

ADDRESS INQUIRIES TO:
Nina Gruber, Program Coordinator
(See address above.)

U.S. DEPARTMENT OF EDUCATION [924]

International and Foreign Language Education
1990 K Street, N.W., 6th Floor
Mail Stop K-OPE-6-6078
Washington, DC 20006-8521
(202) 502-7626
(202) 502-7700
Fax: (202) 502-7860
E-mail: tanyelle.richardson@ed.gov
Web Site: www2.ed.gov/programs/iegpsgpa/index.html

FOUNDED: 1967

AREAS OF INTEREST:
Foreign languages and area studies.

NAME(S) OF PROGRAMS:
- **Fulbright-Hays Group Projects Abroad Program**

TYPE:
Exchange programs; Project/program grants; Seed money grants; Training grants; Travel grants. Also, study grants and grants for foreign language and area study programs of educational development for projects to be undertaken abroad. Grants are awarded to higher education institutions, nonprofit educational organizations, state department of education and consortium of such institutions, departments, organizations and institutions which, in turn, enable professors, college and elementary and secondary school teachers and advanced students to attend seminars abroad and to travel and study in foreign countries in order to strengthen the institution's programs in foreign languages, area studies and world affairs.

YEAR PROGRAM STARTED: 1967

PURPOSE:
To contribute to the development and improvement of the study of foreign languages and area studies in the U.S. by providing opportunities for faculty, teachers, upperclassmen and/or graduate students to travel to foreign countries in group projects for research, training and curriculum development.

LEGAL BASIS:
The Mutual Educational and Cultural Exchange Act of 1961, Public Law 87-256 (Fulbright Hays Act), Section 102(b)(6).

ELIGIBILITY:
Under the program, grants are awarded to institutions of higher education, state departments of education, private nonprofit educational organizations and consortiums of such institutions, departments and organizations to conduct overseas group projects in research, training and curriculum development, by groups of individuals engaged in a common endeavor.

A participant must be a citizen, national or permanent resident of the U.S. and either a faculty member in modern foreign languages or area studies, an experienced educator responsible for planning, conducting or supervising programs in modern foreign languages or area studies at the elementary, secondary or postsecondary levels, a graduate student or upperclassman who plans a teaching career in modern foreign languages or area studies.

The grant does not provide funds for project-related expenses within the U.S. Funds may be used only for a maintenance stipend based on 50% of the amount established in the U.S. Department of State publication, *Maximum Travel Per Diem Allowances for Foreign Areas*, round-trip international travel, a local travel allowance for necessary project-related transportation within the country of study, exclusive of the purchase of transportation equipment, the purchase of project-related artifacts, books and other teaching materials in the country of study, rent for instructional facilities in the country of study, and clerical and professional services performed by resident instructional personnel in the country of study.

FINANCIAL DATA:
Amount of support per award: $73,000 to $110,000 for the year 2014.

Total amount of support: $1,370,000 for the year 2014.

NO. AWARDS: 16 new grants for the year 2014.

APPLICATION INFO:
Application information is available on the web site.

Duration: Four weeks to one year. No renewal.

Deadline: March.

ADDRESS INQUIRIES TO:
Long-term Program:
Tanyelle Richardson
E-mail: tanyelle.richardson@ed.gov

Short-term Program:
Rhea Mallory
E-mail: rhea.mallory@ed.gov

U.S. DEPARTMENT OF EDUCATION [925]

Office of Postsecondary Education
International and Foreign Language Education
1990 K Street, N.W., 6th Floor
Washington, DC 20006-8521
(202) 502-7589
(202) 502-7700
Fax: (202) 502-7860
E-mail: stephanie.mckissic@ed.gov
Web Site: www2.ed.gov/programs/iegpsfra/index.html

NAME(S) OF PROGRAMS:
- **Fulbright-Hays Faculty Research Abroad Program**

TYPE:
Fellowships; Research grants. This program funds fellowships through institutions of higher education (IHEs) to faculty members who propose to conduct research abroad in modern foreign languages and area studies to improve their skill in language and their knowledge of the culture of the people of these countries.

YEAR PROGRAM STARTED: 1964

PURPOSE:
To strengthen college and university programs of international studies by helping key faculty members remain current in their specialties and by assisting institutions in updating curriculums and improving teaching methods and materials.

LEGAL BASIS:
U.S. Government agency.

ELIGIBILITY:
Faculty members must apply through their employing institution. A candidate must be a U.S. citizen, national or permanent resident, an educator experienced in foreign languages and/or area studies, must have engaged in teaching during the two years preceding the date of award and possess adequate skills in the language of the country or in a language germane to the project or region.

GEOG. RESTRICTIONS: United States.

APPLICATION INFO:
Applications must be submitted electronically using e-grants.ed.gov.

Duration: Three to 12 months.

Deadline: Late October of the year preceding the year of study.

PUBLICATIONS:
Guidelines.

ADDRESS INQUIRIES TO:
Program Officer
(See address above.)

UNIVERSITY OF BRISTOL [926]

Senate House
Tyndall Avenue
Bristol BS8 1TH England
(44) 0 117 928 9000
(44) 0 117 331 7972
Fax: (44) 0 117 331 7873
E-mail: student-funding@bristol.ac.uk
Web Site: www.bris.ac.uk

FOUNDED: 1909

AREAS OF INTEREST:
Faculties of arts, engineering, medical and veterinary sciences, medicine and dentistry, science, social sciences and law.

NAME(S) OF PROGRAMS:
- **Postgraduate Research Scholarships**

TYPE:
Scholarships. Postgraduate research scholarships for study toward the Ph.D. degree in one of the departments of the University of Bristol.

YEAR PROGRAM STARTED: 1989

PURPOSE:
To attract excellent research students.

LEGAL BASIS:
University.

ELIGIBILITY:
Scholarships are available for the U.K., Europe and overseas students.

APPLICATION INFO:
Information is available from the Student Funding Office at the University of Bristol or online.

Duration: Up to four years, subject to satisfactory academic progress and according to the particular discipline and training programme.

Deadline: Varies.

PUBLICATIONS:
Annual report; research prospectus.

STAFF:
Jane Fitzwalter, Student Funding Manager

ADDRESS INQUIRIES TO:
Student Funding Office
(See address above.)

UNIVERSITY OF ILLINOIS AT URBANA-CHAMPAIGN

College of Fine and Applied Arts
608 East Lorado Taft Drive, Suite 100
Champaign, IL 61820
(217) 333-1661
(217) 333-1660
Fax: (217) 244-8381
E-mail: faa@illinois.edu
Web Site: www.faa.illinois.edu/alumni-friends/kate-neal-kinley-memorial-fellowship

TYPE:
Fellowships. Awarded for advanced study in the fine arts in the U.S. or abroad, in an approved educational institution, with an approved private teacher or in independent study.

Three major Fellowships will be awarded:
(1) one in any field of music;
(2) one in architectural design and history, art and design, theatre, dance, or instrumental or vocal music and;
(3) one in art, architecture, dance, landscape architecture, theatre, or urban and regional planning.

See entry 560 for full listing.

THE UNIVERSITY OF MANCHESTER [927]

Manchester Doctoral College
Research Office, 2nd Floor
Christie Building
Manchester M13 9PL England
(44) 0161 275 8792
E-mail: mdc@manchester.ac.uk
Web Site: www.manchester.ac.uk/study/postgraduate-research/funding/

FOUNDED: 1824

AREAS OF INTEREST:
Arts, economic, social and legal studies, education, science, engineering, medicine and biological sciences.

NAME(S) OF PROGRAMS:
- **British Marshall Scholarships**
- **Fulbright - University of Manchester Award**
- **North American Foundation Awards**
- **President's Doctoral Scholar Award**

TYPE:
Assistantships; Awards/prizes; Block grants; Conferences/seminars; Endowments; Exchange programs; Fellowships; Research grants; Scholarships; Training grants; Travel grants; Visiting scholars. Research studentships for postgraduate-taught and research programmes in the fields above.
North American Foundation Awards are for postgraduate study at the University of Manchester (NAFUM).
The University of Manchester is also a recognized institution for the purpose of U.S. federal loans and Canadian student loans.

FINANCIAL DATA:
Studentships include payment of fees at U.K. level and/or maintenance allowance.

Amount of support per award: Varies.

ADDRESS INQUIRIES TO:
Student Services Centre
E-mail: ssc@manchester.ac.uk

UNIVERSITY OF OSLO INTERNATIONAL SUMMER SCHOOL [928]

Oslo International Summer School
c/o St. Olaf College
1520 St. Olaf Avenue
Northfield, MN 55057-1098
(507) 786-3269
(800) 639-0058
E-mail: iss@stolaf.edu
Web Site: www.uio.no/summerschool

FOUNDED: 1947

AREAS OF INTEREST:
The International Summer School offers undergraduate and graduate courses in the following areas:
General course offerings - Norwegian language, Norwegian art history, Norwegian architecture and design, Norwegian literature, history, political science, culture and society, international relations and gender equality in Nordic countries;
Graduate courses - special education, peace research, international development, media and communications, international community health, energy and sustainable development, human rights, and a changing Arctic.

TYPE:
Scholarships.

YEAR PROGRAM STARTED: 1947

PURPOSE:
To offer academic instruction to a gathering of many nationalities in the hope of a modest but concrete increase in understanding and goodwill among nations.

LEGAL BASIS:
Part of the University of Oslo.

ELIGIBILITY:
Scholarships awarded only to students accepted into the Oslo International Summer School program. Scholarship applicants must meet the entrance requirements of the International Summer School and must present evidence of attending or having attended a recognized university and have a good academic record. One year or more of

college or university is required. In addition, seriousness of academic purpose and personal qualities likely to make the applicant a good representative of his or her country.

FINANCIAL DATA:
Amount of support per award: Varies.

Total amount of support: Varies.

NO. MOST RECENT APPLICANTS: Approximately 30.

NO. AWARDS: Varies.

APPLICATION INFO:
A financial aid application form and the application for admission to the International Summer School and the supporting letters of recommendation are used by the Financial Aid Committee to choose financial aid recipients.

Duration: Six weeks during the summer, from late June to early August. No renewal possibilities.

Deadline: Papers are due by February 1. Results are announced the first week in April.

PUBLICATIONS:
ISS catalog.

ADMINISTRATION:
Einar Vannebo, Director, International Summer School Norwegian Office
Torild Homstad, Administrator, North American Admissions Office

ADDRESS INQUIRIES TO:
Non-North American students should request information from:
International Summer School
Postbox 1082
N-0317 Oslo, Norway
Tel: (011) 47 2285-6385
Fax: (011) 47 2285-4199

All other applicants can use the North American address above.

THE UNIVERSITY OF SYDNEY [929]

Scholarships Office
Level 5, Jane Foss Russell Building G02
The University of Sydney N.S.W. 2006
Australia
(02) 8627 8112
Fax: (02) 8627 8485
E-mail: scholarships.officer@sydney.edu.au
Web Site: www.sydney.edu.au/scholarships/research

FOUNDED: 1850

NAME(S) OF PROGRAMS:
- **Australian Postgraduate Awards (APA)**
- **International Postgraduate Research Scholarships (IPRS)**

TYPE:
Scholarships. Awarded for research leading to a higher degree. Tenable at the University of Sydney.

LEGAL BASIS:
University.

ELIGIBILITY:
The scholarships are awarded on academic merit and research ability to qualified candidates. Open to qualified foreign graduates from any country eligible to commence a higher degree by research. Australian and New Zealand citizens or permanent residents are not eligible.

APA candidates must be an Australian or a New Zealand citizen or an Australian permanent resident.

FINANCIAL DATA:
Amount of support per award: APA: $25,849 AUD per annum for the year 2015; IPRS: Tuition fees.

NO. AWARDS: 33 for the year 2013.

APPLICATION INFO:
Contact the International Office at the University of Sydney between mid-May and late-August.

Duration: Two years for a Master's research degree and three years for a Ph.D.

Deadline: APA: October 31 for semester one and June 5 for semester two. IPRS: July 31 for semester one commencement and December 15 for semester two commencement.

ADDRESS INQUIRIES TO:
International Office
Level 4, Jane Foss Russell Building G02
The University of Sydney
N.S.W. 2006 Australia
Web site: www.sydney.edu.au/scholarships/international

UNIVERSITY OF VIRGINIA [930]

120 Vincennes Road
Charlottesville, VA 22911
(434) 924-3192
(434) 977-1868
(434) 924-6932
Fax: (434) 924-3359
E-mail: al4u@virginia.edu

FOUNDED: 1976

AREAS OF INTEREST:
International law and politics, international economics, international institutions and international development.

NAME(S) OF PROGRAMS:
- **Gallatin Fellowships**

TYPE:
Exchange programs; Fellowships.

YEAR PROGRAM STARTED: 1976

PURPOSE:
To support advanced doctoral study in international affairs.

LEGAL BASIS:
University.

ELIGIBILITY:
Ph.D. students in international affairs at the dissertation stage of their work. Applicants must be U.S. citizens or permanent residents. Intended for students who plan to study at the Graduate Institute of International Studies, Geneva, Switzerland.

GEOG. RESTRICTIONS: United States.

FINANCIAL DATA:
Amount of support per award: $26,000 stipend plus transatlantic airfare up to $1,500.

Total amount of support: $55,000 to $60,000.

NO. MOST RECENT APPLICANTS: 7.

NO. AWARDS: 1 or more annually.

APPLICATION INFO:
Applicants should submit the following in five paper copies:
(1) personal data form;
(2) academic record to include a chronological list of all educational institutions attended above high school level, naming institutions, fields of study, years of study and degree, a transcript of graduate work completed, listing courses and grades, a list of published works, articles or topics of research papers undertaken during graduate study including a copy of a published work or research paper, a list of academic distinctions, fellowships, etc., including those currently held or applied for;
(3) international experience, which should consist of a list of the countries, other than the U.S., in which applicant has lived or traveled, with the dates, duration and purpose of these stays (business, education and/or pleasure) indicated and a description, of not more than 300 words, of any aspect of these experiences, or others, which is believed to have contributed notably to applicant's academic career or to their proposed professional interests, including language training;
(4) proficiency in foreign language, in which the applicant should list those foreign languages of which he or she has a speaking, reading and writing knowledge, indicating under each of these headings if knowledge is elementary, medium or advanced and provide among the references an individual who can be consulted on applicant's language competence;
(5) study program, which should consist of an essay of up to 1,500 words describing applicant's research program, showing how the Institute's curriculum of research, seminars, etc., as well as institutions located in Geneva, will contribute to it. Candidates are advised to study the Institute's catalogue in formulating their programs;
(6) career intentions, in which the applicant should briefly describe his or her professional objectives and how he or she sees their current studies and those proposed at the Institute contributing to them. Any professional work which applicant may have already undertaken in the international field should be described, including teaching assistantships, participation in research programs, publications and awards and;
(7) references, which should consist of the above information further supplemented by letters from four individuals who are familiar with the applicant's proposed research program, including thesis supervisor. If possible, one should be able to judge applicant's competence in the French language. These letters of reference should be sent directly to the address above when completed application is submitted. These letters should include the office addresses and telephone numbers of those sending them.

Duration: One academic year. Shorter term grants are also available.

Deadline: March 1.

PUBLICATIONS:
Application guidelines.

STAFF:
Allen C. Lynch, Supervisor, Gallatin Fellowship Program

ADDRESS INQUIRIES TO:
Allen C. Lynch, Supervisor
Gallatin Fellowship Program
(See address above.)

*SPECIAL STIPULATIONS:
Applicant must be engaged in the dissertation phase of Ph.D. work in international affairs.

VILLA I TATTI: THE HARVARD UNIVERSITY CENTER FOR ITALIAN RENAISSANCE STUDIES [931]

Via di Vincigliata, 26
50135 Florence Italy
(39) 055 603251
(39) 055 608909
Fax: (39) 055 603383
E-mail: info@itatti.harvard.edu
Web Site: www.itatti.harvard.edu/fellowships

FOUNDED: 1961

AREAS OF INTEREST:
All aspects of the Italian Renaissance: fine arts, literature, music, science, philosophy, religion and political, intellectual, economic and social history.

CONSULTING OR VOLUNTEER SERVICES:
Library, photographic collection and archive.

NAME(S) OF PROGRAMS:

- **Berenson Fellowship**
- **Fellowships for Independent Study on the Italian Renaissance**
- **Mellon Fellowship in the Digital Humanities**
- **Craig Hugh Smyth Fellowships**
- **David and Julie Tobey Fellowship**
- **Wallace Fellowship**

TYPE:
Fellowships. Stipendiary and nonstipendiary fellowships for the academic year July 1 through June 30 in residence in Florence for study on any aspect of the Italian Renaissance. There are also a limited number of short-term fellowships. Details are available online.

YEAR PROGRAM STARTED: 1961

PURPOSE:
To promote advanced interdisciplinary study in Renaissance fields.

LEGAL BASIS:
Part of Harvard University.

ELIGIBILITY:
I Tatti Fellowship applicants can be scholars of any nationality, and must be postdoctoral and in the earlier stages of their careers and free to devote full-time to study.

FINANCIAL DATA:
Stipends will be given in accord with the individual needs of the approved applicants and the availability of funds.

Amount of support per award: For a yearlong fellowship, the maximum stipend is $50,000.

Total amount of support: $893,500 for the yearlong fellowships for the year 2015-16.

CO-OP FUNDING PROGRAMS: Deborah Loeb Brice Fellowship, Committee to Rescue Italian Art, Francesco E. de Dombrowski Bequest, Florence Gould Foundation, Hanna Kiel Fellowship, Melville J. Kahn Fellowship Fund, Samuel H. Kress Foundation, Robert Lehman Fellowship, Jean Francois Malle Fellowship Fund, Andrew W. Mellon Foundation, Ahmanson Foundation, Lila Wallace - Reader's Digest Endowment Fund.

NO. MOST RECENT APPLICANTS: 115 for the year 2016-17.

NO. AWARDS: 15 for the 2016-17 academic year.

APPLICATION INFO:
Application forms are available online. Applications by fax are not accepted.

Duration: One year, July 1 to June 30.

Deadline: October 15. Notification made at the beginning of February.

IRS I.D.: 04-2103580

ADDRESS INQUIRIES TO:
Alina Payne, Director
(See address above.)

THOMAS J. WATSON FELLOWSHIP PROGRAM

11 Park Place, Suite 1503
New York, NY 10017
(212) 245-8859
Fax: (212) 245-8860
E-mail: tjw@tjwf.org
Web Site: watson.foundation

TYPE:
Fellowships. The Foundation provides Fellows an opportunity for a focused and disciplined "Wanderjahr" of their own devising or design-time in which to explore with thoroughness a particular interest, test their aspirations and abilities, view their lives and American society in greater perspective and concomitantly, to develop a more informed sense of international concern. The Fellowship experience is intended to provide Fellows an opportunity to immerse themselves in cultures other than their own for an entire year. The candidate's proposed project should involve investigation into an area of demonstrated concern and personal interest.

See entry 1593 for full listing.

WEIZMANN INSTITUTE OF SCIENCE [932]

Feinberg Graduate School of the
Weizmann Institute of Science
P.O. Box 26
234 Herzl Street
Rehovot 7610001 Israel
(972) 8-9343843
(972) 8-9342924
Fax: (972) 8-9344114
E-mail: FGS@weizmann.ac.il
Web Site: www.weizmann.ac.il/feinberg

FOUNDED: 1934

AREAS OF INTEREST:
Life sciences, chemistry, physics, mathematics, computer science and science teaching.

NAME(S) OF PROGRAMS:

- **Postdoctoral Fellowships Program at the Weizmann Institute of Science**

TYPE:
Fellowships. The Feinberg Graduate School of the Weizmann Institute of Science offers a limited number of postdoctoral fellowships in all areas of research in which the Weizmann Institute is engaged. The fellowships are offered in various fields of biology, chemistry, physics, biochemistry-biophysics, mathematics, computer science and science teaching.

YEAR PROGRAM STARTED: 1976

PURPOSE:
To train postgraduate research students to senior positions in academia, scientific research, medical research, industry, education, and government systems.

LEGAL BASIS:
Research institute.

ELIGIBILITY:
Postdoctoral fellowship applicants must have received a Ph.D. or equivalent degree within seven years of the start of the fellowship program. Candidates may be citizens of any country.

FINANCIAL DATA:
The annual stipend is adjusted periodically in accordance with living costs. Also offered is a small relocation allowance and a one-way, economy-class airfare (round-trip airfare in case the fellowship is extended to two years).

Amount of support per award:
Approximately $31,000 per year.

APPLICATION INFO:
Application forms and additional information may be obtained from the Feinberg Graduate School, Weizmann Institute of Science and from the web site.

Duration: 12 months. Possible renewal for a second and third year.

Deadline: Applications may be submitted year-round.

OFFICERS:
Prof. Daniel Zajfman, President
Prof. Michael Fainzilber, Head, Postdoctoral Fellowships Program

ADDRESS INQUIRIES TO:
Feinberg Graduate School
(See address above.)

YOUTH FOR UNDERSTANDING USA [933]

641 S Street, N.W.
Suite 200
Washington, DC 20001
(202) 774-5200
(800) 833-6243
Fax: (202) 588-7571
E-mail: admissions@yfu.org
Web Site: www.yfuusa.org

FOUNDED: 2002

AREAS OF INTEREST:
The exchange of U.S. and international high school students in more than 60 countries.

CONSULTING OR VOLUNTEER SERVICES:
Intercultural education and training and research.

NAME(S) OF PROGRAMS:

- **Adult Study Tours**
- **Americans Overseas Summer, Semester and Year Programs**
- **Congress-Bundestag Youth Exchange Program**
- **Corporate Scholarship Program**
- **Finland-U.S. Senate Youth Exchange Program**
- **International Semester and Year Programs**
- **Japan-U.S. Senate Youth Exchange Program**

TYPE:
Exchange programs; Grants-in-aid; Scholarships; Travel grants. Students on summer semester and year programs live with volunteer host families overseas. Students on semester and academic year programs also attend school. International students live and study at U.S. high schools or community colleges. Competitive, full and partial scholarships for Corporate, Finland-U.S. Senate, Japan-U.S. Senate Programs and Japan-America Friendship Scholars Program.

YEAR PROGRAM STARTED: 2002

PURPOSE:
To advance intercultural understanding, mutual respect and social responsibility through educational exchanges for youth, families and communities.

LEGAL BASIS:
Tax-exempt, 501(c)(3) international educational organization.

ELIGIBILITY:
Applicants must be U.S. or international high school students between the ages of 15 and 18. Full scholarships for special programs are awarded through merit competition. Partial scholarships (10 to 25%) are awarded on the basis of need.

FINANCIAL DATA:
Amount of support per award: From $500 to full support.

CO-OP FUNDING PROGRAMS: Funding sources for scholarships include a multitude of governments, corporations, foundations and individuals.

NO. AWARDS: Approximately 250.

APPLICATION INFO:
Applicants for programs involving full scholarships must complete special application materials. For corporate programs, applicants must meet special eligibility requirements. Applicants for partial scholarships must complete financial aid forms.

Duration: Scholarships awarded for the program period.

Deadline: Between September and March, depending on program. Announcement between February and April.

IRS I.D.: 02-0557010

OFFICERS:
Michael E. Hill, President and Chief Executive Officer
Heather Reynolds, Treasurer
Donna Schnaars, Secretary

BOARD OF TRUSTEES:
Daryl Weinert, Chairman
William Dant, Vice Chairman
Dianne Bradley
Ambassador Laurie S. Fulton
Benjamin Gutierrez
Magnus Karlberg
Martin Nichols
Jennifer N. Sigler
Andrew Towne
David Trads
James E. Waslawski
Ambassador Laurence Wohlers

ADDRESS INQUIRIES TO:
Alicia Kubert Smith, Communications Manager
(See address and toll-free telephone number above.)

Programs for foreign scholars

AMERICA-ISRAEL CULTURAL FOUNDATION [934]

1140 Broadway
Suite 304
New York, NY 10001
(212) 557-1600 ext. 801
Fax: (212) 557-1611
E-mail: admin@aicf.org
Web Site: www.aicf.org

FOUNDED: 1939

AREAS OF INTEREST:
Music, dance, theater, visual arts, film and television.

NAME(S) OF PROGRAMS:
- **Scholarship Program for Israelis**

TYPE:
Awards/prizes; Endowments; Fellowships; Project/program grants; Scholarships. For study in the arts of music, painting and sculpture, dance and drama, film and television, to be pursued either in Israel or in other countries.

YEAR PROGRAM STARTED: 1952

PURPOSE:
To further Israeli talent in the fields of music, visual arts, dance and drama, film and television.

ELIGIBILITY:
Only Israeli nationals that live and study in Israel are eligible to apply for domestic scholarships. Israeli nationals studying abroad are able to apply for scholarships to any international location of study.

FINANCIAL DATA:
Amount of support per award: $600 to $10,000.

Total amount of support: $1,300,000 per year.

NO. MOST RECENT APPLICANTS: Approximately 2,500.

NO. AWARDS: Approximately 600.

APPLICATION INFO:
Application materials are available upon request to America-Israel Cultural Foundation, 8 Shaul Hamelech Boulevard, Tel Aviv 64733, Israel.

Duration: Grants are awarded for one to two years of study. Teachers of the arts may also apply for up to six-month fellowships.

Deadline: Varies.

IRS I.D.: 13-1664048

ADDRESS INQUIRIES TO:
Scholarships: Inbal Grinberg
Executive Director
8 Shaul Hamelech Boulevard, Tel Aviv 64733, Israel

AMERICAN ASSOCIATION OF FAMILY AND CONSUMER SCIENCES (AAFCS) [935]

400 North Columbus Street
Suite 202
Alexandria, VA 22314-2752
(703) 706-4600
(800) 424-8080
Fax: (703) 706-4663
E-mail: awards@aafcs.org
Web Site: www.aafcs.org/awards/index.asp

FOUNDED: 1909

AREAS OF INTEREST:
Family and consumer sciences.

NAME(S) OF PROGRAMS:
- **National Fellowship**

TYPE:
Fellowships. AAFCS awards fellowships to individuals who have exhibited the potential to make contributions to the family and consumer sciences profession.

YEAR PROGRAM STARTED: 1962

PURPOSE:
To support graduate study in the field of family and consumer sciences.

LEGAL BASIS:
501(c)(3) nonprofit charity.

FINANCIAL DATA:
Amount of support per award: $5,000 fellowship, plus up to $1,000 of support.

Total amount of support: Varies.

NO. MOST RECENT APPLICANTS: 15.

NO. AWARDS: 1 to 5.

APPLICATION INFO:
Application information is available on the web site.

Duration: One academic year.

Deadline: Varies.

PUBLICATIONS:
Brochure.

ADDRESS INQUIRIES TO:
Sara Tantillo
Professional Development Manager
(See e-mail address above.)

AMERICAN ASSOCIATION OF UNIVERSITY WOMEN [936]

1111 Sixteenth Street, N.W.
Washington, DC 20036
(866) 795-4892
E-mail: aauw@applyists.com
Web Site: www.aauw.org

FOUNDED: 1888

AREAS OF INTEREST:
Advancement of educational and professional opportunities for women in the U.S. and around the globe.

NAME(S) OF PROGRAMS:
- **AAUW International Fellowships**

TYPE:
Fellowships. Awarded to women pursuing full-time graduate or postdoctoral study in the U.S. who are not U.S. citizens or permanent residents.

YEAR PROGRAM STARTED: 1917

PURPOSE:
To provide advanced study and training for non-American women (i.e., women who are not U.S. citizens or permanent residents) of outstanding academic ability who may be expected to give effective leadership in their homelands.

ELIGIBILITY:
International Fellowships are awarded for full-time study or research in the U.S. to women who are not U.S. citizens or permanent residents. Both graduate and postgraduate studies at accredited U.S. institutions are supported. Applicants must have earned the equivalent of a U.S. Bachelor's degree by September 30, 2015, and must have applied to their proposed institutions of study by the time of the application. Up to five International Master's/First Professional Degree Fellowships are renewable for a second year.

Recipients are selected for academic achievement and demonstrated commitment to women and girls. Recipients return to their home countries to become leaders in business, government, academia, community activism, the arts and sciences.

FINANCIAL DATA:
Amount of support per award: $18,000 to $30,000.

APPLICATION INFO:
Visit www.aauw.org/what-we-do/educational-funding-and-awards/selected-professions-fellowships for complete information.

Deadline: December 1.

ADDRESS INQUIRIES TO:
See e-mail address above.

THE AMERICAN SOCIETY OF MECHANICAL ENGINEERS AUXILIARY, INC.

2 Park Avenue, MS-RB
New York, NY 10016-5990
(212) 591-7650
Fax: (212) 591-7739
E-mail: bigleyr@asme.org
Web Site: go.asme.org/scholarships

TYPE:
Scholarships. Lucy and Charles W.E. Clarke Scholarship is for high school seniors participating on a FIRST team.

Baldwin, Cartwright, Farny, Kezios and Scharp Scholarships are for undergraduate students in mechanical engineering.

Parsons and Rothermel Scholarships are for graduate students with a degree in mechanical engineering, to be used to pursue a Master's degree in mechanical engineering.

Rice-Cullimore Scholarship is for foreign students at the graduate level.

Student Loan Fund is for juniors, seniors or graduate students enrolled as degree candidates in good standing.

See entry 2560 for full listing.

BELGIAN AMERICAN EDUCATIONAL FOUNDATION, INC.

195 Church Street
New Haven, CT 06510
(203) 785-4055
Fax: (203) 777-5765
E-mail: emile.boulpaep@yale.edu
Web Site: www.baef.us
www.baef.be

TYPE:
Fellowships. Predoctoral and postdoctoral fellowships for advanced study in most fields of knowledge with supported work to be undertaken at a Belgian university or an institution of higher learning. Fellowships for Belgian students are also available.

See entry 885 for full listing.

THE ENGLISH-SPEAKING UNION [937]

Dartmouth House
37 Charles Street
London W1J 5ED England
(44) 0 20 7529 1550
(44) 0 20 7529 1590
Fax: (44) 0 20 7495 6108
E-mail: education@esu.org
Web Site: www.esu.org

FOUNDED: 1918

AREAS OF INTEREST:
Education.

NAME(S) OF PROGRAMS:
- **The Chautauqua Institution Scholarships**
- **The Lindemann Trust Fellowships**
- **Walter Hines Page Scholarships**

TYPE:
Exchange programs; Fellowships; Scholarships; Travel grants.

YEAR PROGRAM STARTED: 1923

PURPOSE:
To enable teachers and students in Great Britain to observe teaching methods in the U.S. The same applies for U.S. and Canadian students spending time in the U.K.

LEGAL BASIS:
Educational charity.

ELIGIBILITY:
The Chautauqua Institution Scholarships are open to all qualified teachers. The award covers the cost of attendance at the Institution and includes lectures, classes, board, lodging, and entertainment for up to six weeks' stay.

The Lindemann Trust Fellowships are awarded for research in the U.S. to graduates of exceptional promise in both the pure and applied physical sciences, who have shown capacity for achieving original research.

Walter Hines Page Scholarships are awarded to teachers and educators from the U.K. and are intended to promote the exchange of educational ideas between Britain and America. Scholars travel to the U.S. to study a specific aspect of American education which interests them and which is relevant to their own professional responsibilities.

GEOG. RESTRICTIONS: Canada, United Kingdom and United States.

FINANCIAL DATA:
Amount of support per award: Varies.

Total amount of support: Varies.

CO-OP FUNDING PROGRAMS: Sponsored by the English-Speaking Union and various teaching unions.

NO. AWARDS: Chautauqua Institution Scholarships: 2; Lindemann Trust Fellowships and Walter Hines Page Scholarships: Varies.

APPLICATION INFO:
Applications must be made to the address above.

Duration: Chautauqua Institution Scholarships: Two to six weeks; Lindemann Trust Fellowships: One year; Walter Hines Page Scholarships: One academic year.

Deadline: Varies.

PUBLICATIONS:
Annual report; *Concord*, newsletter.

ADDRESS INQUIRIES TO:
Emma Coffey
Education Officer
(See address above.)

INTERNATIONAL ROAD FEDERATION [938]

500 Montgomery Street, Suite 525
Alexandria, VA 22314
(703) 535-1001
Fax: (703) 535-1007
E-mail: lmills@irfnews.org
info@irfnews.org
Web Site: www.irfnews.org

FOUNDED: 1948

AREAS OF INTEREST:
Highway engineering, management and policy.

NAME(S) OF PROGRAMS:
- **IRF Fellowship Program**

TYPE:
Fellowships; Scholarships. Annual awards for graduate study in highway and traffic engineering for graduate engineers and policymakers.

YEAR PROGRAM STARTED: 1949

PURPOSE:
To train personnel in the field of highways and highway transport.

LEGAL BASIS:
Private foundation.

ELIGIBILITY:
Open to non-U.S. graduate students. Qualified civil engineers must return to home country following completion of program.

FINANCIAL DATA:
Amount of support per award: $2,500 to $15,000 to defray partially one year of graduate study.

Total amount of support: Approximately $90,000 for the year 2013-14.

Matching fund requirements: Home country donors must make up differential.

NO. MOST RECENT APPLICANTS: 52 for the year 2015.

NO. AWARDS: 5 to 10.

APPLICATION INFO:
Applications must be submitted directly to the IRF web site during the open enrollment period.

Duration: One year.

Deadline: Around the end of September. Contact IRF for exact date.

PUBLICATIONS:
Annual Report; *Directory of Students*.

IRS I.D.: 52-0793883

STAFF:
C. Patrick Sankey, President and Chief Executive Officer

ADDRESS INQUIRIES TO:
Leslie Mills
Fellowship Program Coordinator
(See address above.)

THE KENNEDY MEMORIAL TRUST [939]

3 Birdcage Walk
Westminster
London SW1H 9JJ England
(020) 7222 1151
Fax: (020) 7222 7189
E-mail: annie@kennedytrust.org.uk
Web Site: www.kennedytrust.org.uk

FOUNDED: 1966

NAME(S) OF PROGRAMS:
- **Kennedy Scholarships**

TYPE:
Scholarships. Awarded for postgraduate work for one year at Harvard or the Massachusetts Institute of Technology (MIT). Field of study is unrestricted.

YEAR PROGRAM STARTED: 1966

LEGAL BASIS:
Private.

ELIGIBILITY:
Applications for awards tenable in 2017-18 are available on The Trust web site starting in mid- to late August and closing in late October 2016. In the same application season, candidates should make a separate and independent application to the programme(s) of their choice at Harvard and/or MIT.

Those applying for the Kennedy Scholarships must be all of the following:
(1) British citizens at the time of application;
(2) ordinarily resident in the U.K. and;
(3) wholly or mainly educated in the U.K.

All applicants must have spent at least two of the seven years prior to September 1, 2017 studying as an undergraduate at a U.K. university, taking their first degree not earlier than 2012. Those studying for a first or higher degree and due to graduate in the academic year 2016-17 are also eligible.

Awards will not be made to postdoctoral candidates wishing to pursue further research in their own field. Applications cannot be accepted from those already in the U.S. Marriage is not a bar to the award of a Kennedy Scholarship, but there is no extra funding for a spouse.

FINANCIAL DATA:
Full tuition and health insurance fees, plus a stipend for living costs and a grant for vacation travel within the U.S.

Amount of support per award: Minimum $25,500 stipend.

NO. MOST RECENT APPLICANTS: 298.

NO. AWARDS: 10 for the year 2014.

APPLICATION INFO:
Application information is available on The Trust's web site, and applications must be submitted online via The Trust's web site.

Duration: One year.

Deadline: Late October.

OFFICERS AND TRUSTEES:

ADDRESS INQUIRIES TO:
Secretary
(See address above.)

LASPAU [940]

25 Mount Auburn Street
Suite 203
Cambridge, MA 02138-6095
(617) 495-5255
Fax: (617) 495-8990
E-mail: laspau-webmaster@calists.harvard.edu
Web Site: www.laspau.harvard.edu

FOUNDED: 1964

AREAS OF INTEREST:
Designing and administering academic and professional exchange programs in Latin America, the Caribbean, Canada and the U.S.

CONSULTING OR VOLUNTEER SERVICES:
Specialized educational consulting services are offered by Laspau.

TYPE:
Conferences/seminars; Exchange programs; Fellowships; Project/program grants; Scholarships; Technical assistance; Training grants; Travel grants. Laspau administers school programs, institutional development programs through executive training, and graduate admission tests. Laspau is involved in these exchange areas: professional/business, students/educators and training.

YEAR PROGRAM STARTED: 1966

PURPOSE:
To strengthen human capital in Latin America and the Caribbean through educational and professional development opportunities.

LEGAL BASIS:
Nonprofit organization.

ELIGIBILITY:
In most cases, individuals wishing to apply for an award must be nominated through the program sponsor by a participating Latin American, Caribbean or other institution. (Similarly, all scholarship and loan recipients agree to return promptly to their home institutions.)

Laspau gives special priority to regional, socio-economic and ethnic diversity in order to broaden opportunities for underserved populations. Independent applications are accepted only for certain programs; details are available at the Programs section on the web site.

GEOG. RESTRICTIONS: Latin America and the Caribbean.

FINANCIAL DATA:
Laspau provides grantees and their sponsors with comprehensive financial services, disbursement of scholarship grants and regular reports to sponsoring agencies.

Amount of support per award: Varies.

Total amount of support: Approximately $13,000,000.

APPLICATION INFO:
Application procedures vary by program. Check the Programs section on the web site for details.

PUBLICATIONS:
eNewsletter, annual report; newsletter; brochures; grantee guides.

OFFICERS:
Angelica Natera, Executive Director
Cindy Bowen, Associate Director for Finance
Ester Ramirez, Clerk of the Corporation

TRUSTEES:

ADDRESS INQUIRIES TO:
Angelica Natera, Executive Director
(See address above.)

MEDICAL LIBRARY ASSOCIATION [941]

65 East Wacker Place
Suite 1900
Chicago, IL 60601-7246
(312) 419-9094
Fax: (312) 419-8950
E-mail: awards@mlahq.org
Web Site: www.mlanet.org

FOUNDED: 1898

AREAS OF INTEREST:
Health sciences librarianship.

NAME(S) OF PROGRAMS:
- **Cunningham Memorial International Fellowship**

TYPE:
Fellowships; Travel grants; Work-study programs. Work-study program for medical librarians from countries other than the U.S. or Canada for a time period of at least two weeks.

YEAR PROGRAM STARTED: 1972

PURPOSE:
To educate and train medical librarians from countries outside the continental U.S. and Canada in areas where improved medical library service is essential to the health and welfare of the people through the education of physicians and scientists.

LEGAL BASIS:
Nonprofit.

ELIGIBILITY:
Candidate must be working in a medical library or be preparing to work in one in his or her country and must have an undergraduate and a Master's-level library degree. (The latter requirement may be waived.) Candidate must have a statement from a responsible official of the institution where he or she is working or plans to work that he or she will be guaranteed a position in a medical library when he or she returns to his or her country; he or she must also pass the TOEFL exam to demonstrate competence in English and he or she must present three letters of recommendation and a health certificate. Past recipients of the Fellowship are ineligible.

FINANCIAL DATA:
The Fellowship pays a stipend toward living, travel and tuition expenses in the U.S. and Canada. These funds are for the fellow only. No support is provided for spouses or dependents. Payment for travel to and from the U.S. or Canada is the responsibility of the fellow.

Amount of support per award: Up to $4,000.

Matching fund requirements: Candidate may need additional resources during the period of his fellowship.

NO. AWARDS: 1 per year.

APPLICATION INFO:
Applicant must submit the following:
(1) three letters of reference, in English, from responsible persons who are familiar with the applicant's qualifications;
(2) a signed statement, in English, from a responsible official of the institution where he or she is working or plans to work, guaranteeing a position in a health sciences library upon his or her return;
(3) a TOEFL score of 500 or greater, except for applicants whose native language is

English or whose language of instruction at the university level was English;
(4) a project overview in accordance to the guidelines described in the "Project Goals" and;
(5) a certificate of good physical health, written in English, from a licensed physician.

Duration: At least two to three weeks.

Deadline: December 1. Announcement in March.

STAFF:
Maria Lopez, Grants, Scholarships and Awards Coordinator

ADDRESS INQUIRIES TO:
Coordinator
Grants, Scholarships and Awards
(See address above.)

NATIONAL INSTITUTES OF HEALTH

Division of International Services
31 Center Drive, B2BO7
MSC-2028
Bethesda, MD 20892-2028
(301) 496-6166
Fax: (301) 496-0847
E-mail: dis@mail.nih.gov
Web Site: www.training.nih.gov
www.ors.od.nih.gov

TYPE:
Exchange programs; Fellowships.

See entry 1418 for full listing.

ORGANIZATION OF AMERICAN STATES [942]

Department of Human Development, Education and Employment
1889 F Street, N.W., Seventh Floor
Washington, DC 20006
(202) 370-9760
Fax: (202) 458-3167
E-mail: rowefund@oas.org
Web Site: www.oas.org/en/rowefund

FOUNDED: 1948

AREAS OF INTEREST:
Education.

NAME(S) OF PROGRAMS:

- **The Leo S. Rowe Pan American Fund**

TYPE:
Assistantships; Awards/prizes; Scholarships; Visiting scholars. Loan program. The Leo S. Rowe Pan American Fund awards interest-free student loans to citizens from Latin America and the Caribbean countries, to help them finance their higher studies or research in accredited universities across the U.S. Program is available to foreign students and foreign scholars in U.S. universities.

YEAR PROGRAM STARTED: 1948

PURPOSE:
To provide a loan program to qualified citizens from Latin America and the Caribbean countries to help them finance their higher education or research at accredited institutions in the U.S. by awarding interest-free loans.

ELIGIBILITY:
Rowe Fund loans are granted to individuals currently studying or wishing to pursue graduate, postgraduate or the last two years of undergraduate studies. Additionally, professionals or university faculty who are currently pursuing, or wish to pursue, advanced training, research or technical certificates at accredited institutions in the U.S. are also eligible. This includes semester-abroad programs and professional development courses, with the exception of English-as-a-Second-Language courses. Most fields of study are accepted.

Candidates must:
(1) be nationals of a Latin American or Caribbean member state of the OAS (U.S. and Canadian citizens are not eligible);
(2) have an international student visa (F or J) allowing them to study full-time in the U.S.;
(3) be accepted as a full-time student in an accredited institution of higher learning in the U.S.;
(4) have adequate academic records (grade point average greater than or equal to 3.0);
(5) be able to demonstrate other sources of financing (such as savings, employment, fellowship, funds supplied by the university or relatives, etc.) to cover the greater portion of their academic expenses;
(6) ensure that loans are underwritten by a guarantor (citizen or permanent resident of the U.S.) and;
(7) promise that upon completion of his or her studies, he or she will repay the loan in full and return to his or her country; (if OPT is granted, the return date can be extended up to a year upon completion of studies).

FINANCIAL DATA:
Loans can be used to cover a portion of the tuition and other university fees, essential books and supplies, room and board and/or emergencies not covered by their principal source of funding. No application or processing fees. Funding is sent directly to the student after approval.

Amount of support per award: Up to U.S. $7,500 per academic period. Loan recipients may apply for additional loans for subsequent academic periods, providing the total amount of loans granted does not exceed U.S. $15,000 over the course of the studies for which the loan is granted.

Total amount of support: $15,000 (U.S.) per Rowe Fund recipient.

Matching fund requirements: The prospective applicant must demonstrate other sources of financing (such as savings, employment, a fellowship, funds supplied by the university or relatives, etc.), to cover the greater part of their academic expenses and must present a guarantor.

NO. AWARDS: Averaging 100.

APPLICATION INFO:
Applicants must be citizens of the following countries: Antigua and Barbuda, Argentina, Barbados, Belize, Bolivia, Brazil, Chile, Colombia, Costa Rica, Dominica (Commonwealth of), Dominican Republic, Ecuador, El Salvador, Grenada, Guatemala, Guyana, Haiti, Honduras, Jamaica, Mexico, Nicaragua, Panama, Paraguay, Peru, Saint Kitts and Nevis, Saint Lucia, Saint Vincent and the Grenadines, Suriname, The Bahamas (Commonwealth of), Trinidad and Tobago, Uruguay, Venezuela (Bolivarian Republic of).

Loan applications are usually submitted directly from students to the OAS-Rowe Fund Secretariat and are accepted and reviewed year-round at any time during the academic year in the U.S. Loan applications that comply with the eligibility requirements will be reviewed and evaluated by the Committee; however, this is not to be defined as automatic approval. The decision of the Committee, which is final, will be communicated to the applicant by the Secretariat of the Fund. Eligible candidates may find the application forms, eligibility requirement and FAQs at the web site, or may send an e-mail requesting the application forms to the e-mail address above.

Duration: Two years maximum.

Deadline: A person may apply for a Rowe Fund loan at any time.

STAFF:
Lina M. Sevillano, Program Manager

ADDRESS INQUIRIES TO:
Leo S. Rowe Pan American Fund
(See address above.)

*SPECIAL STIPULATIONS:
Repayment is deferred while the loan recipient is in school. Loan repayment is scheduled in 50 equal monthly payments starting three months after completion of studies.

These loans are made with the understanding that, upon completing those studies, loan recipients commit to repay the loan in full and return to their home countries within a year to apply their knowledge and training as well as continue fostering friendship and communication among the peoples of the Americas.

ORGANIZATION OF AMERICAN STATES

1889 F Street, N.W.
Seventh Floor
Washington, DC 20006
(202) 370-9771
Fax: (202) 458-3897
E-mail: scholarships@oas.org
Web Site: www.oas.org/scholarships

TYPE:
Fellowships; Scholarships; Technical assistance. Awarded for graduate academic studies and/or research, and last two years of undergraduate studies for students in the English-speaking Caribbean, for training in areas contributing to the economic, social, technical and cultural development of OAS member countries.

See entry 842 for full listing.

P.E.O. SISTERHOOD [943]

P.E.O. Executive Office
3700 Grand Avenue
Des Moines, IA 50312
(515) 255-3153
Fax: (515) 255-3820
E-mail: ips@peodsm.org
Web Site: www.peointernational.org

FOUNDED: 1869

NAME(S) OF PROGRAMS:

- **P.E.O. International Peace Scholarship**

TYPE:
Scholarships. Awards for selected women from countries other than the U.S. and Canada to pursue graduate study in the U.S. or Canada. Support is available for advanced study in any field except for research. No new applications at the dissertation level.

YEAR PROGRAM STARTED: 1949

PURPOSE:
To promote world peace and understanding through scholarship aid to selected women from other countries to further their education in the U.S. and Canada.

LEGAL BASIS:
Nonprofit organization.

ELIGIBILITY:
Prerequisites for applicants:
(1) Applicant must be qualified for admission to full-time graduate study, working toward a graduate degree in the accredited college or university she will attend in the U.S. or Canada;
(2) A copy of the applicant's confirmation of admission must be submitted with the application. This notice must specify the graduate degree program. No consideration will be given to applicants lacking evidence of admission and;
(3) Prerequisites 1 and 2 do not apply to the applicant who enrolls at Cottey College (Nevada, MO), which is owned and operated by the P.E.O. Sisterhood. The applicant shall present evidence of admission to Cottey.

In order to qualify for her first scholarship, an applicant must have a full year of coursework remaining and be enrolled and on campus for the entire school year. Doctoral students who have completed coursework and are working on dissertations only are not eligible as first-time applicants. Doctoral students in medicine or dentistry will be considered only in the final two years of coursework, internship or residency.

Upon completion of the degree program or Optional Practical Training, the applicant must promise to return to her home country or to a location outside the U.S. or Canada within 60 days, depending on visa status.

A student holding citizenship or permanent residency in the U.S. or Canada is ineligible. Scholarships are not given for online courses, research, internships or for practical training if not combined with coursework. Scholarships are not awarded for travel or repayment of past debt.

FINANCIAL DATA:
Scholarships to students studying in Canadian universities will be paid in Canadian dollars.

Amount of support per award: $10,000 maximum per year.

NO. MOST RECENT APPLICANTS: 400 to 600 per year.

NO. AWARDS: 160 to 200 per year.

APPLICATION INFO:
In order to be considered for an IPS Scholarship, a student must submit an eligibility form electronically through the P.E.O. International web site. Paper forms sent to the P.E.O. International office will not be accepted. The online eligibility form can be submitted from September 15 to December 15.

Duration: Initial support is for a period not to exceed one year (two semesters fall-spring), with one renewal possible. Not to exceed a total of two years.

Deadline: To establish eligibility: December 15. Final date to submit completed application materials from applicants already enrolled in the graduate program and school for which their scholarship is intended: March 1. Final date to submit completed application materials from applicants not yet enrolled in the graduate program or school for which the scholarship is intended: April 1. Last date to submit completed application materials for applicants who will be attending Cottey College: April 1. Notification of scholarships: May. Final date for student acceptance of scholarships: June 1.

No eligibility information will be accepted before September 15 or after December 15.

PUBLICATIONS:
Information sheet.

ADDRESS INQUIRIES TO:
Project Supervisor
(See address above.)

*SPECIAL STIPULATIONS:
Applicant must have round-trip or return travel expense guaranteed at the time of application.

THE UNIVERSITY OF SYDNEY [944]

Scholarships Office
Level 5, Jane Foss Russell Building G02
The University of Sydney N.S.W. 2006
Australia
(02) 8627 8112
Fax: (02) 8627 8485
E-mail: scholarships.officer@sydney.edu.au
Web Site: www.sydney.edu.au/scholarships/research

FOUNDED: 1850

NAME(S) OF PROGRAMS:
- **Walter Mersh Strong Scholarship**

TYPE:
Scholarships. Awarded for studies at postgraduate level. Tenable at the University of Sydney. The scholarship is available for a Master by coursework program in agriculture, education and social work, or public health.

PURPOSE:
To provide opportunities for graduate students from Papua New Guinea to attend the University of Sydney to undertake a Master by coursework program in agriculture, education and social work, or public health.

LEGAL BASIS:
University.

ELIGIBILITY:
Open to graduates from Papua New Guinea who qualify for admission to the University of Sydney.

GEOG. RESTRICTIONS: Papua New Guinea.

FINANCIAL DATA:
Amount of support per award: Tuition fees and living allowance of $25,849 AUD per annum for the year 2015.

NO. AWARDS: 1 for the year 2013.

APPLICATION INFO:
Application information is available on the web site.

Deadline: As advertised, when funds are available.

ADDRESS INQUIRIES TO:
The International Office
Level 4, Jane Foss Russell Building G02
The University of Sydney
N.S.W. 2006 Australia
Tel: (02) 8627 8302
Fax: (02) 8627 8387
E-mail: io.studentadvisers@sydney.edu.au

WENNER-GREN FOUNDATION FOR ANTHROPOLOGICAL RESEARCH, INC.

470 Park Avenue South
8th Floor
New York, NY 10016-6819
(212) 683-5000
Fax: (212) 532-1492
E-mail: internationalprograms@wennergren.org
Web Site: www.wennergren.org

TYPE:
Fellowships; Scholarships. Wadsworth International Fellowship is for scholars and students from developing countries undertaking study leading to a Ph.D. or equivalent doctoral degree at universities where they can receive international-level training in anthropology and its related subdisciplines. The main goals of these Fellowships are to expand and strengthen international ties and enhance anthropological infrastructure in countries where anthropology is underrepresented and where there are limited resources to send students overseas for training.

See entry 1964 for full listing.

Technical assistance and cooperative research

NATIONAL INSTITUTES OF HEALTH [945]

Division of International Relations
Fogarty International Center
Building 31, Room B2C39
31 Center Drive, MSC 2220
Bethesda, MD 20892-2220
(301) 496-4784
E-mail: tina.chung@nih.gov
mili.ferreira@nih.gov
Web Site: www.fic.nih.gov/programs/pages/japan-fellowships.aspx

AREAS OF INTEREST:
Biomedical and behavioral sciences.

NAME(S) OF PROGRAMS:
- **Japan Society for the Promotion of Science Postdoctoral Research Fellowships (Extramural)**

TYPE:
Fellowships. A limited number of postdoctoral research fellowships are provided by the Japan Science and Technology Agency (JSTA) to U.S. scientists to conduct research in Japan. Types of activity supported include collaboration in basic or clinical research and familiarization with or utilization of special techniques and equipment not otherwise available to the applicant.

YEAR PROGRAM STARTED: 1987

PURPOSE:
To provide a research experience in the biomedical, clinical and behavioral sciences in Japanese laboratories.

LEGAL BASIS:
Government agency.

ELIGIBILITY:
Applicants for the program must be U.S. citizens or permanent U.S. residents, hold a Doctorate in one of the clinical, behavioral or biomedical sciences and make prior arrangements with the appropriate Japanese host researcher as to the research plan.

The program does not provide support for activities that have as their principal purpose brief observational visits, attendance at scientific meetings or independent study.

NO. AWARDS: Up to 10 short-term, 5 long-term.

APPLICATION INFO:
Application information is available on the web site.

Duration: Short-term: Under 12 months; Long-term: 12 to 24 months.

Deadline: Varies.

ADDRESS INQUIRIES TO:
Tina Chung, M.P.H., Program Officer
(See address above.)

NORTH ATLANTIC TREATY ORGANIZATION [946]

Emerging Security Challenges Division (ESCD)
NATO HQ, Boulevard Leopold III
B-1110 Brussels Belgium
Fax: (32) 2 707 4232
E-mail: sps.info@hq.nato.int
Web Site: www.nato.int/science

FOUNDED: 1958

AREAS OF INTEREST:
Scientific cooperation between NATO Allies and partner countries.

NAME(S) OF PROGRAMS:

- **Science for Peace and Security (SPS) Programme**

TYPE:
Multiyear projects; workshops and training.

Offers grants to scientists in NATO and Partner countries to collaborate on priority research topics, which include NATO priorities and additional Partner country priorities.

In addition to activities funded by the NATO international budget, the Science for Peace and Security Programme also engages in activities funded directly by one or more nations. These consist of pilot studies, short-term projects and topical workshops which are aligned with NATO's Strategic Objectives and are in areas of priority to NATO or Partner countries. Any NATO or Partner country can initiate a new proposal. The initiating nation seeks the participation of other NATO and Partner nations and this participation is always voluntary. Support Grant Programme is open to experts from both NATO countries and those Partner countries eligible for support.

YEAR PROGRAM STARTED: 1960

PURPOSE:
To stimulate collaboration between laboratories in different countries and thus enhance the effectiveness of research.

GEOG. RESTRICTIONS: NATO countries: Albania, Belgium, Bulgaria, Canada, Croatia, Czech Republic, Denmark, Estonia, France, Germany, Greece, Hungary, Iceland, Italy, Latvia, Lithuania, Luxembourg, Netherlands, Norway, Poland, Portugal, Romania, Slovak Republic, Slovenia, Spain, Turkey, United Kingdom and United States.

FINANCIAL DATA:
Covering project-related costs, organizational costs, travel and living expenses.

Amount of support per award: EUR 5,000 to EUR 60,000 depending on the type of support mechanism.

APPLICATION INFO:
Applications should be presented on the official application forms that can be downloaded from the Science for Peace and Security web site. Applications should be submitted via e-mail to the Emerging Security Challenges/SPS Staff.

Duration: Depends on the mechanism. Up to three years for the multiyear projects.

Deadline: March 1, July 1 and October 1. Applications may be submitted at any time. Applications received later than this deadline date will be considered during the next evaluation cycle.

PUBLICATIONS:
NATO Science Series.

ADDRESS INQUIRIES TO:
See e-mail address above.

U.S.-ISRAEL BINATIONAL SCIENCE FOUNDATION (BSF) [947]

P.O. Box 45086 (Hamarpeh Street, No. 8)
Har Hotzvim
Jerusalem 91450 Israel
(972) 2-5828239
Fax: (972) 2-5828306
E-mail: bsf@bsf.org.il
Web Site: www.bsf.org.il

FOUNDED: 1972

AREAS OF INTEREST:
Science.

TYPE:
Research grants. Promotes cooperation between the countries in research concerned with science and technology for peaceful purposes through grants to cooperative research projects. Grants are for bilateral, cooperative research between U.S. and Israeli scientists for research conducted in either country.

YEAR PROGRAM STARTED: 1974

PURPOSE:
To strengthen U.S.-Israel science cooperation.

LEGAL BASIS:
Established by government-to-government agreement.

ELIGIBILITY:
Any scientist on the staff of a U.S. or Israel nonprofit research institution may apply by submitting a cooperative research proposal.

Eligible research areas are health sciences, life sciences, physics, chemistry, mathematical sciences, atmospheric and earth sciences, oceanography and limnology, materials research, environmental research, energy research, biomedical engineering, economics, sociology, social and developmental psychology, and computer sciences.

Submission of grant applications is on a split-program basis; namely, eligibility is limited, in alternate years, to either health and life sciences or to exact, natural and social sciences.

FINANCIAL DATA:
Awards are made to cover the direct cost of executing the approved research, i.e., salaries for research assistants, supplies, travel, etc. Salaries of principal investigators are not included.

Amount of support per award: Up to $230,000, for four years. Average $40,000 per year.

Total amount of support: Approximately $17,000,000.

APPLICATION INFO:
Proposals are unsolicited and should be submitted jointly by the collaborating scientists via the prospective grantee institution where the research will be performed. Proposals should be submitted via the BSF web site.

Duration: Up to four years.

Deadline: The completed application form must reach the BSF by November 15 for a grant to be awarded in the following year. Awards are made annually and are announced in July.

OFFICERS:
Dr. Yair Rotstein, Director
Dr. Rachel Haring, Assistant Director

ADDRESS INQUIRIES TO:
Dr. Yair Rotstein, Director
(See address above.)

SPECIAL POPULATIONS

Special Populations

THE ABLE TRUST [948]

3320 Thomasville Road
Suite 200
Tallahassee, FL 32308
(888) 838-2253
(850) 224-4493
Fax: (850) 224-4496
E-mail: info@abletrust.org
Web Site: www.abletrust.org

FOUNDED: 1991

AREAS OF INTEREST:
Disabilities and handicapped persons.

NAME(S) OF PROGRAMS:
- **Board Directed Initiative Grants**
- **General Support for Employment Placement Programs**
- **Strategic Employment Placement Initiatives**

TYPE:
Project/program grants. Board Directed Initiative Grants: This program is defined through an announcement by the Board of Directors for proposals that address a specific issue. The release of an Initiative Request is at the discretion of the Board and may occur at any time during a fiscal year. Funding parameters in this category will be described in the published Initiative Request and will correspond to the described objective of the Board Directed Initiative.

General Support for Employment Placement Programs: This program is for general support of employment programs for a grant year. Requests should result in employment placement for participating individuals with disabilities and could encompass equipment and/or staffing needs of an applicant organization to expand an existing program in a new way or create a new program. Awards for this category will occur twice a year at the Fall and Summer Board Meetings.

Strategic Employment Placement Initiatives: This is the primary grant program of The Foundation, and such proposals address the employment placement of Floridians with disabilities. Consideration for these large grants will occur at the Third Quarter Board Meeting of The Foundation.

YEAR PROGRAM STARTED: 1990

PURPOSE:
To be a key leader in providing Floridians with disabilities opportunities for successful employment.

LEGAL BASIS:
501(c)(3) public-private partnership foundation.

ELIGIBILITY:
Proposals will be accepted from Florida-based nonprofit organizations with 501(c)(3) status serving disabled Florida citizens. Each organization may have only one active grant in any one-year time period.

GEOG. RESTRICTIONS: Florida.

FINANCIAL DATA:
Amount of support per award: Average award is $50,000 for organizations. General Support for Employment Placement Programs: Up to $65,000. Strategic Employment Placement Initiatives: Up to $250,000.

Total amount of support: $1,767,000.

NO. MOST RECENT APPLICANTS: 100.

NO. AWARDS: 59.

APPLICATION INFO:
Application guidelines are available on the Trust web site.

Duration: Board Directed Initiative Grants and General Support for Employment Placement Programs: One year. Strategic Employment Placement Initiatives: Three years.

Deadline: General Support for Employment Placement Programs: April 5 and July 5. Strategic Employment Placement Initiatives: November 10.

IRS I.D.: 59-3052307

STAFF:
Dr. Susanne Homant, President and Chief Executive Officer

ADDRESS INQUIRIES TO:
Dr. Susanne Homant
President and Chief Executive Officer
(See address above.)

THE ACTUARIAL FOUNDATION

475 North Martingale Road
Suite 600
Schaumburg, IL 60173-2226
(847) 706-3535
Fax: (847) 706-3599
E-mail: Scholarships@ActFnd.org
Web Site: www.actuarialfoundation.org

TYPE:
Scholarships. The Actuarial Diversity Scholarship was formed in 1977 as a joint effort of the Casualty Actuarial Society and the Society of Actuaries. In 2008, the scholarship was transferred to The Actuarial Foundation.

The scholarship promotes diversity in the profession through an annual scholarship program for Black/African American, Hispanic, Native North American and Pacific Islander students. The scholarship award recognizes and encourages academic achievements by awarding scholarships to full-time undergraduate students pursuing a degree that may lead to a career in the actuarial profession.

See entry 2026 for full listing.

ALZHEIMER'S DRUG DISCOVERY FOUNDATION

57 West 57th Street
Suite 904
New York, NY 10019
(212) 901-8000
Fax: (212) 901-8010
E-mail: hfillit@alzdiscovery.org
Web Site: www.alzdiscovery.org

TYPE:
Awards/prizes; Conferences/seminars; Research grants.

See entry 2146 for full listing.

THE AMERICAN ACADEMY OF ESTHETIC DENTISTRY

225 West Wacker Drive
Suite 650
Chicago, IL 60606
(312) 981-6770
Fax: (312) 265-2908
E-mail: info@estheticacademy.org
Web Site: www.estheticacademy.org

TYPE:
Research grants.

See entry 2264 for full listing.

AMERICAN ASSOCIATION OF LAW LIBRARIES

105 West Adams Street
Suite 3300
Chicago, IL 60603
(312) 939-4764
Fax: (312) 431-1097
E-mail: membership@aall.org
Web Site: www.aallnet.org

TYPE:
Scholarships. Stipend for graduate study leading to a degree at an accredited school of library or information science or an accredited law school. Preference will be given to individuals with previous service to, or interest in, law librarianship.

See entry 700 for full listing.

AMERICAN BAR FOUNDATION [949]

750 North Lake Shore Drive
Fourth Floor
Chicago, IL 60611
(312) 988-6517
Fax: (312) 988-6579
E-mail: fellowships@abfn.org
Web Site: www.americanbarfoundation.org

FOUNDED: 1952

AREAS OF INTEREST:
Law and social science.

NAME(S) OF PROGRAMS:
- **Summer Research Diversity Fellowships in Law and Social Science for Undergraduate Students**

TYPE:
Fellowships; Internships.

YEAR PROGRAM STARTED: 1988

PURPOSE:
To interest undergraduate students from diverse backgrounds in pursuing graduate study in the social sciences; to introduce students to the rewards and demands of a research-oriented career in the field of law and social science.

LEGAL BASIS:
Private foundation.

ELIGIBILITY:
Must be a U.S. citizen or permanent resident. The program is open, but not limited to, persons who are African-American, Hispanic/Latino, Native American, or Puerto Rican. Applicants must be sophomores or juniors in college with a grade point average of at least 3.0 on a scale of 4.0 and must be moving toward an academic major in one of the social science or humanities disciplines.

GEOG. RESTRICTIONS: United States.

FINANCIAL DATA:
Amount of support per award: $3,600.

Total amount of support: $14,400.

NO. MOST RECENT APPLICANTS: 200.

NO. AWARDS: 4 each year.

APPLICATION INFO:
Application form is available online.

Duration: Eight weeks during the summer.

Deadline: Late March to April 15.

PUBLICATIONS:
Annual report, application guidelines and forms.

ADDRESS INQUIRIES TO:
Amanda Ehrhardt
(See address above.)

AMERICAN COUNCIL FOR POLISH CULTURE (ACPC)

27562 David Givens Avenue
Warren, MI 48092-3533
(586) 575-9279
E-mail: metyszka@sbcglobal.net
Web Site: www.polishcultureacpc.org

TYPE:
Scholarships.

See entry 1598 for full listing.

AMERICAN COUNCIL OF THE BLIND

2200 Wilson Boulevard, Suite 650
Arlington, VA 22201
(202) 467-5081
(800) 424-8666
Fax: (703) 465-5085
E-mail: info@acb.org
Web Site: www.acb.org

TYPE:
Assistantships; Awards/prizes; Internships; Scholarships. Scholarships for outstanding blind students enrolled in academic, vocational, technical or professional training programs beyond the high school level.

See entry 1599 for full listing.

AMERICAN FOUNDATION FOR THE BLIND, INC. [950]

1000 Fifth Avenue, Suite 350
Huntington, WV 25701
(212) 502-7600
(800) 232-5463
Fax: (888) 545-8331
TDD: (212) 502-7662
E-mail: afbinfo@afb.net
Web Site: www.afb.org/scholarships.asp

FOUNDED: 1921

AREAS OF INTEREST:
Blindness, education, vocational and social services, public education, consultation and publications related to blindness and visual impairment.

NAME(S) OF PROGRAMS:
- **Gladys C. Anderson Memorial Scholarship**
- **The Karen D. Carsel Memorial Scholarship**
- **The Delta Gamma Foundation Florence Margaret Harvey Memorial Scholarship**
- **The Rudolph Dillman Memorial Scholarship**
- **The R.L. Gillette Scholarship**
- **The Paul and Ellen Ruckes Scholarship**

TYPE:
Scholarships. Undergraduate and graduate scholarships for students who are legally blind.

The Gladys C. Anderson Memorial Scholarship is offered to a female undergraduate or graduate student studying classical or religious music.

The Karen D. Carsel Memorial Scholarship provides a grant to a full-time graduate student who is legally blind and who presents evidence of economic need.

The Delta Gamma Foundation Florence Margaret Harvey Memorial Scholarship is offered to an undergraduate or graduate student who is legally blind, has exhibited academic excellence, and is studying in the field of rehabilitation and/or education of persons who are visually impaired or blind.

The Rudolph Dillman Memorial Scholarship provides four grants to undergraduate or graduate students who are legally blind and studying in the field of rehabilitation and/or education of persons who are blind or visually impaired.

The R.L. Gillette Scholarship offers two scholarships to women who are legally blind and are enrolled in a four-year undergraduate degree program in literature or music.

The Paul and Ellen Ruckes Scholarship is offered to an undergraduate or graduate student who is legally blind and studying engineering, computer, physical or life sciences.

LEGAL BASIS:
Not-for-profit corporation.

ELIGIBILITY:
Applicants must be U.S. citizens or residents who are, by definition, legally blind. Other criteria vary depending on the specific scholarship.

GEOG. RESTRICTIONS: United States.

FINANCIAL DATA:
Amount of support per award: Gladys C. Anderson Memorial, Delta Gamma Foundation Florence Margaret Harvey Memorial and R.L. Gillette: $1,000 each; Karen D. Carsel Memorial Scholarship: $500; Rudolph Dillman Memorial Scholarship: $2,500; Paul and Ellen Ruckes Scholarships: $2,000.

Total amount of support: $18,500.

NO. AWARDS: 6 scholarships with 11 total awards.

APPLICATION INFO:
Applications must be submitted online. No paper applications will be accepted.

In general, applicants must submit a completed scholarship application form, evidence of legal blindness (or official letter from a state or private agency for the blind), official transcripts, proof of acceptance in a postsecondary school, proof of U.S. citizenship, two letters of reference and typewritten statement of educational and personal goals, the field of study applicant is pursuing and why he or she has chosen it, the applicant's work experience, extracurricular activities and how the award will be used.

Duration: One academic year.

Deadline: May 31.

OFFICERS:
Carl R. Augusto, President and Chief Executive Officer

ADDRESS INQUIRIES TO:
AFB Information Center
E-mail: tannis@afb.net
(See address above.)

THE AMERICAN GEOSCIENCES INSTITUTE (AGI)

4220 King Street
Alexandria, VA 22302-1502
(703) 379-2480 ext. 227
Fax: (703) 379-7563
E-mail: wallacescholarship@agiweb.org
Web Site: www.agiweb.org/scholarships/wallace

TYPE:
Scholarships. The Harriet Evelyn Wallace Scholarship is available for female students pursuing a Master's or Doctorate degree at an accredited institution of higher education in a recognized geoscience program.

See entry 2007 for full listing.

THE AMERICAN HELLENIC EDUCATIONAL PROGRESSIVE ASSOCIATION [951]

1909 Q Street, N.W.
Suite 500
Washington, DC 20009
(202) 232-6300
Fax: (202) 232-2140
E-mail: ahepa@ahepa.org
Web Site: www.ahepa.org

FOUNDED: 1922

AREAS OF INTEREST:
Culture, history, and issues relating to Greece and Cyprus.

TYPE:
Scholarships.

PURPOSE:
To promote, encourage, induce and advance education at the college, university and graduate school level.

ELIGIBILITY:
Applicants must be of Hellenic heritage, although their ancestry does not have to be 100% Greek. The applicant must be a member in good standing of AHEPA or affiliated organizations, demonstrate financial need and have no criminal record.

FINANCIAL DATA:
Amount of support per award: Up to $2,000.

Total amount of support: $100,000 for the year 2013.

NO. AWARDS: Varies.

APPLICATION INFO:
Scholarship application is posted online.

Duration: One year. Renewal possible.

Deadline: March 31.

ADDRESS INQUIRIES TO:
Basil Mossaidis, Executive Director
(See address above.)

THE AMERICAN INSTITUTE OF ARCHITECTS

1735 New York Avenue, N.W.
Washington, DC 20006-5292
(202) 626-7529
Fax: (202) 626-7399
E-mail: scholarships@aia.org
Web Site: www.aia.org

TYPE:
Scholarships. Awards to provide an opportunity for financially disadvantaged and/or minority groups to pursue a professional degree in architecture.

See entry 399 for full listing.

AMERICAN INSTITUTE OF CHEMICAL ENGINEERS (AICHE)

120 Wall Street, Floor 23
New York, NY 10005-4020
(646) 495-1384
Fax: (646) 495-1503
E-mail: awards@aiche.org
Web Site: www.aiche.org

TYPE:
Scholarships.

See entry 2548 for full listing.

AMERICAN PLANNING ASSOCIATION [952]

205 North Michigan Avenue
Suite 1200
Chicago, IL 60601
(312) 786-6363
E-mail: mgroh@planning.org
Web Site: www.planning.org

FOUNDED: 1909

AREAS OF INTEREST:
Urban and regional planning and the promotion of the art and science of planning.

NAME(S) OF PROGRAMS:

- **Judith McManus Fellowship**

TYPE:
Fellowships; Scholarships.

YEAR PROGRAM STARTED: 1970

PURPOSE:
To celebrate planning by providing partial funding for all women and minority (African American, Hispanic American or Native American) students.

LEGAL BASIS:
Private, nonprofit educational association.

ELIGIBILITY:
Applicants must be citizens of the U.S. and enrolled or accepted for enrollment in a planning program accredited by the Planning Accreditation Board (PAB). Applicants must document the need for financial assistance.

GEOG. RESTRICTIONS: United States.

FINANCIAL DATA:
Fellowship provides partial funding for tuition and living expenses. One-year student membership in the American Planning Association. Scholarship provides partial tuition funding.

Amount of support per award: Judith McManus Fellowship: $2,000 to $4,000.

Total amount of support: Varies.

NO. MOST RECENT APPLICANTS: 40.

NO. AWARDS: Varies.

APPLICATION INFO:
Contact the Association.

Duration: One academic year.

Deadline: April 30.

PUBLICATIONS:
Program announcement.

ADDRESS INQUIRIES TO:
Monica Groh, Director of Emerging Professionals
(See address above.)

AMERICAN POLITICAL SCIENCE ASSOCIATION

1527 New Hampshire Avenue, N.W.
Washington, DC 20036
(202) 483-2512
Fax: (202) 483-2657
E-mail: kmealy@apsanet.org
Web Site: www.apsanet.org

TYPE:
Fellowships; Grants-in-aid; Scholarships. Awards to aid prospective African American, Asian Pacific, Latino/Latina and Native American political science students beginning the doctoral study of political science.

See entry 1926 for full listing.

AMERICAN PSYCHOLOGICAL ASSOCIATION

Minority Fellowship Program/APA
750 First Street, N.E.
Washington, DC 20002-4242
(202) 336-6127
Fax: (202) 336-6012
E-mail: mfp@apa.org
Web Site: www.apa.org/pi/mfp

TYPE:
Fellowships. Fellowship is geared to those pursuing careers as practitioners specializing in the delivery of behavioral health services to ethnic minority populations. Students specializing in clinical, school and counseling psychology are encouraged to apply.

See entry 2488 for full listing.

AMERICAN PSYCHOLOGICAL ASSOCIATION

Minority Fellowship Program/APA
750 First Street, N.E.
Washington, DC 20002-4242
(202) 336-6127
Fax: (202) 336-6012
E-mail: mfp@apa.org
Web Site: www.apa.org/pi/mfp

TYPE:
Fellowships.

See entry 2486 for full listing.

AMERICAN SOCIETY FOR MICROBIOLOGY

Education Department
1752 N Street, N.W.
Washington, DC 20036
(202) 942-9283
Fax: (202) 942-9329
E-mail: fellowships@asmusa.org
Web Site: www.asm.org/cdcfellowship
www.asm.org/urc

TYPE:
Fellowships. ASM/CDC Postdoctoral Research Fellowship Program: The American Society for Microbiology and Centers for Disease Control and Prevention (ASM/CDC) Postdoctoral Research Fellowship Program is a comprehensive training program which provides opportunities to participate in interdisciplinary training on global public health issues. Fellows will perform research at one of the Centers for Disease Control and Prevention (CDC) locations.

Undergraduate Research Capstone Program: This fellowship encourages students to pursue careers or advanced degrees in the microbiological sciences by providing an opportunity to participate in a research project at their institution and gain experience in presenting their results. The fellowship allows students to conduct research in the summer with an ASM member faculty mentor and present the results at the ASM General Meeting the following year.

See entry 2074 for full listing.

AMERICAN SOCIETY FOR MICROBIOLOGY

Education Board
1752 N Street, N.W.
Washington, DC 20036
(202) 942-9283
Fax: (202) 942-9329
E-mail: fellowships@asmusa.org
Web Site: www.asm.org/watkins

TYPE:
Fellowships.

See entry 2075 for full listing.

AMERICAN SOCIOLOGICAL ASSOCIATION [953]

1430 K Street, N.W.
Suite 600
Washington, DC 20005
(202) 383-9005 ext. 322
Fax: (202) 638-0882
TDD: (202) 638-0981
E-mail: minority.affairs@asanet.org
Web Site: www.asanet.org

FOUNDED: 1905

AREAS OF INTEREST:
All areas of sociology.

NAME(S) OF PROGRAMS:

- **Minority Fellowship Program**

TYPE:
Fellowships. Predoctoral training fellowships for minority-group members studying sociology.

YEAR PROGRAM STARTED: 1974

PURPOSE:
To provide predoctoral students with financial support, academic and research training, and mentoring, in coordination with university graduate programs, in order to increase the talent pool of minority sociologists in the U.S.

LEGAL BASIS:
Nonprofit professional association.

ELIGIBILITY:
Applicants must be citizens, noncitizen nationals of the U.S. or have been lawfully admitted to the U.S. for permanent residence and have in their possession an Alien Registration Card, and they must be enrolled in (and have completed one full academic year) in a program that grants the Ph.D. in sociology.

In addition, applicants must be members of an underrepresented racial and ethnic group, including African Americans, Latinos (e.g., Mexican, Cuban, Puerto Rican), American Indians or Alaskan Natives and Asians (e.g., Chinese, Japanese, Korean, Southeast Asian) or Pacific Islanders (e.g., Hawaiian, Guamanian, Samoan, Filipino).

GEOG. RESTRICTIONS: United States.

FINANCIAL DATA:
Award includes stipend and some tuition assistance.

Amount of support per award: $18,000.

Total amount of support: Varies.

NO. MOST RECENT APPLICANTS: 100 for the 2015-16 Fellowship.

NO. AWARDS: Up to 5 annually.

APPLICATION INFO:
Applicants must submit completed application forms, transcripts, letters of recommendation and two essays. Selection is based upon evidence of scholarship, writing ability, research potential, financial need and racial and ethnic minority identification.

Duration: Fellowships are tenable for one calendar year.

Deadline: January 31. Announcement by April 30.

STAFF:
Jean H. Shin, Program Director
Beth Floyd, Program Coordinator

ADDRESS INQUIRIES TO:
Beth Floyd, Program Coordinator
(See address above.)

ARMENIAN GENERAL BENEVOLENT UNION

55 East 59th Street
New York, NY 10022-1112
(212) 319-6383
Fax: (212) 319-6507
E-mail: scholarship@agbu.org
Web Site: www.agbu-scholarship.org

TYPE:
Fellowships; Scholarships.

See entry 1608 for full listing.

ARMENIAN RELIEF SOCIETY OF EASTERN U.S.A., INC. [954]

80 Bigelow Avenue
Suite 200
Watertown, MA 02472
(617) 926-3801
Fax: (617) 924-7238
E-mail: arseastus@gmail.com
Web Site: www.arseastusa.org

FOUNDED: 1910

NAME(S) OF PROGRAMS:
- **A.R.S. Lazarian Graduate Scholarship**
- **A.R.S. Undergraduate Scholarship**

TYPE:
Awards/prizes; Scholarships. Scholarships to assist students of Armenian ancestry in their higher education studies.

PURPOSE:
To aid Armenian students residing in the U.S.

LEGAL BASIS:
Nonprofit organization.

ELIGIBILITY:
Undergraduate or graduate students of Armenian ancestry attending a four-year college or university may apply.

For the Undergraduate Scholarship, the applicant must:
(1) be an undergraduate student attending an accredited four-year college or university in the U.S. and;
(2) be a full-time matriculated student having completed at least one college semester and who is presently enrolled.
These Undergraduate Scholarships are awarded on the basis of financial need, merit and involvement in the Armenian community.

The Lazarian Graduate Scholarships are open to students who intend to pursue their studies at the Master's or Doctorate level in the fields of law, history, political science, international relations, journalism, government, economics, business administration, medicine and public service. Selection is based on scholastic qualifications, financial need and involvement in the Armenian community. Must have an undergraduate degree from an accredited university in the U.S.

FINANCIAL DATA:
Amount of support per award: Varies, according to donations.

NO. MOST RECENT APPLICANTS: Undergraduate: 25; Graduate: 20.

APPLICATION INFO:
To receive an application, send a self-addressed, stamped envelope to the ARS office, and state undergraduate or graduate status. Scholarships are awarded based on merit, need and involvement in the Armenian community.

For Undergraduate Scholarships, the following information must accompany the application:
(1) financial aid forms filed with a testing service or school's financial aid office or a copy of a recent income tax return of the applicant's parents;
(2) a recent official transcript of college grades with a raised seal (no faxes or copies will be accepted) and;
(3) three letters of recommendation from a college professor or advisor, affiliate(s) of Armenian organization(s) of which the student is a member, and a personal acquaintance other than a relative.

For the Lazarian Graduate Scholarship:
(1) applicants must be currently enrolled in a graduate program or provide proof of acceptance and entrance into a program within the coming six months;
(2) applicants must provide official, sealed transcripts as requested (unofficial, unsealed transcripts will not be accepted);
(3) applications and all required documents must be postmarked by April 1 to be considered;
(4) applicants will not be considered for a scholarship if they have already received it twice;
(5) applicants must provide a copy of the most recent income tax return and tuition bill to be considered for a scholarship;
(6) applications will not be considered without the required three recommendations (if from an institution/organization, it should be on official letterhead) and;
(7) incomplete applications will not be considered under any circumstance.

Deadline: April 1.

STAFF:
Vart Chiloyan, Executive Secretary

ADDRESS INQUIRIES TO:
Scholarship Committee
(See address above.)

ASTRAEA LESBIAN FOUNDATION FOR JUSTICE [955]

116 East 16th Street, 7th Floor
New York, NY 10003
(212) 529-8021
Fax: (212) 982-3321
Web Site: www.astraeafoundation.org

FOUNDED: 1977

AREAS OF INTEREST:
Racial, economic and gender justice for lesbian, gay, bisexual, transgender, and intersex (LGBTI) peoples in the global south and east.

NAME(S) OF PROGRAMS:
- **International Fund**

TYPE:
General operating grants; Grants-in-aid; Project/program grants.

PURPOSE:
To provide critically needed financial support to lesbian-led, LGBTI and progressive organizations striving to eliminate oppression based on race, age, sex, religion, sexual orientation, gender identity, economic exploitation, physical and mental ability, anti-semitism, and other such factors.

ELIGIBILITY:
Must be charitable nongovernmental organizations and meet the criteria used in determining 501(c)(3) status in the U.S. Those eligible to apply are:
(1) groups led by and/or for LGBTI communities;
(2) groups doing work towards social change on issues affecting LGBTI people;
(3) nongovernmental, not-for-profit groups with organizational budgets of $500,000 (U.S.) or less and;
(4) groups active for at least one year at the time of proposal.

Organizations applying must not have a budget of over $500,000 (U.S.).

GEOG. RESTRICTIONS: Africa, Asia and the Pacific, Eastern Europe/Commonwealth of Independent States, Latin America and the Caribbean, and the Middle East.

FINANCIAL DATA:
Amount of support per award: $5,000 to $30,000.

Total amount of support: Varies.

APPLICATION INFO:
Organizations must submit letter of interest. Full applications are by invitation only.

Duration: One year. Must reapply.

Deadline: Letter of interest: January 31 and July 31, for consideration in June and December respectively.

ADDRESS INQUIRIES TO:
Namita Chad, Program Officer
(See address above.)

ASTRAEA LESBIAN FOUNDATION FOR JUSTICE [956]

116 East 16th Street, 7th Floor
New York, NY 10003
(212) 529-8021
Fax: (212) 982-3321
Web Site: www.astraeafoundation.org

FOUNDED: 1977

AREAS OF INTEREST:
Social change organizations and projects (including film, video, media and cultural projects) that directly address the depth and complexity of critical issues in LGBTI communities.

NAME(S) OF PROGRAMS:
- **U.S. General Fund**

TYPE:
General operating grants; Grants-in-aid; Project/program grants.

PURPOSE:
To provide critically needed financial support to lesbian-led, LGBTI and progressive organizations striving to eliminate oppression based on race, age, sex, religion, sexual orientation, gender identity, economic exploitation, physical and mental ability, anti-semitism, and other such factors.

ELIGIBILITY:
501(c)(3) organizations. No grants to individuals.

GEOG. RESTRICTIONS: United States and its territories.

FINANCIAL DATA:
Amount of support per award: $5,000 to $30,000.

Total amount of support: Varies.

APPLICATION INFO:
Organizations must be invited to apply. Faxed proposals are not accepted. IRS letter certifying organization's or fiscal sponsor's nonprofit tax-exempt status is required.

Duration: One year. Must reapply.

ADDRESS INQUIRIES TO:
Namita Chad, Program Officer
(See address above.)

ASTRAEA LESBIAN FOUNDATION FOR JUSTICE [957]

116 East 16th Street, 7th Floor
New York, NY 10003
(212) 529-8021
Fax: (212) 982-3321
Web Site: www.astraeafoundation.org

FOUNDED: 1977

AREAS OF INTEREST:
Impactful art by LGBTQI people and organizations.

NAME(S) OF PROGRAMS:
- **Global Arts Fund**

TYPE:
Awards/prizes.

PURPOSE:
To recognize the work of LGBTQI artists and organizations by providing support to those who show artistic merit and whose art and perspective reflect a commitment to Astraea's mission and efforts to promote LGBTQI visibility and social justice in marginalized LGBTQI communities in the face of exploitations wrought by globalization, imperialism, and neocolonialism.

ELIGIBILITY:
LGBTQI people and organizations with limited access to resources are eligible. The Fund will consider submissions, requested through a nomination process, in many artistic expressions: video, film, poetry, fictional prose, photography, painting, performance, dance, theater, music and other interdisciplinary expressions.

GEOG. RESTRICTIONS: United States, the Global East and the Global South.

FINANCIAL DATA:
Amount of support per award: $5,000 to $30,000.

NO. AWARDS: 4 to 10.

APPLICATION INFO:
The Fund only considers submissions through a nomination process, nominators having been grantees.

Deadline: Varies.

ADDRESS INQUIRIES TO:
Namita Chad, Program Officer
(See address above.)

ALEXANDER GRAHAM BELL ASSOCIATION FOR THE DEAF AND HARD OF HEARING [958]

3417 Volta Place, N.W.
Washington, DC 20007
(202) 337-5220
Fax: (202) 337-8314
E-mail: financialaid@agbell.org
Web Site: www.agbell.org

FOUNDED: 1890

AREAS OF INTEREST:
All areas of study.

NAME(S) OF PROGRAMS:
- **Alexander Graham Bell College Scholarship Awards**

TYPE:
Scholarships.

YEAR PROGRAM STARTED: 1967

PURPOSE:
To assist students with pre-lingual, bilateral hearing loss, who use listening and spoken language, to attend mainstream colleges.

ELIGIBILITY:
Based on age of diagnosis, degree of hearing loss and grade point average.

FINANCIAL DATA:
Amount of support per award: $1,000 to $10,000.

Total amount of support: Varies.

NO. MOST RECENT APPLICANTS: Over 100 for the year 2015.

NO. AWARDS: 20 for the year 2015.

APPLICATION INFO:
Applicants should download the application (preferred) or request via e-mail. Photocopies are not accepted.

Duration: One year. Nonrenewable.

Deadline: Varies. Details posted online in December.

IRS I.D.: 53-0196644

ADDRESS INQUIRIES TO:
College Scholarships
(See address and e-mail above.)

BEN & JERRY'S FOUNDATION [959]

30 Community Drive
South Burlington, VT 05403-6828
(802) 846-1500
Fax: (802) 846-1610
E-mail: info@benandjerrysfoundation.org
Web Site: www.benandjerrysfoundation.org

FOUNDED: 1985

AREAS OF INTEREST:
Economic, environmental, social justice and grassroots organizing.

TYPE:
General operating grants; Project/program grants. Grants to nonprofit organizations which facilitate progressive social change by addressing the underlying conditions of societal and/or environmental problems using organizing as a strategy to create change.

YEAR PROGRAM STARTED: 1986

PURPOSE:
To support and encourage organizations that facilitate progressive social change by addressing the underlying conditions of societal and environmental problems.

LEGAL BASIS:
Private foundation.

ELIGIBILITY:
The Foundation generally funds organizations with budgets less than $500,000. Applicant must be a nonprofit 501(c)(3) organization or have a sponsoring agent that has this status. No grants to support basic services. Applicants need to demonstrate that their projects will lead to societal, institutional or environmental change, help ameliorate an unjust or destructive situation by empowering constituents and address the root causes of social and/or environmental problems.

No funding for discretionary or emergency requests, colleges or universities, individuals or scholarships, research projects, religious projects, state agencies, international or foreign programs or direct-service programs.

GEOG. RESTRICTIONS: United States and its territories.

FINANCIAL DATA:
Amount of support per award: $1,000 to $20,000.

Total amount of support: $2,600,000 for the year 2014.

REPRESENTATIVE AWARDS:
$10,000 to Ohio Valley Environmental Coalition to continue funding to support their work organizing broad-based opposition to mountaintop removal/valley fill coal mining practices as well as unsafe coal waste ponds; $10,000 to Little Village Environmental Justice Organization to continue funding for the People United for Dignity, Democracy and Justice project.

APPLICATION INFO:
Contact the Foundation.

Duration: One year. Must reapply.

Deadline: Pre-Applications: on or about January 15 and July 15.

PUBLICATIONS:
Annual report; application guidelines; grant recipients list.

IRS I.D.: 03-0300865

STAFF:
Lisa Pendolino, Managing Director
Rebecca Golden, Director of Programs

*PLEASE NOTE:
The Foundation does not accept mailed letters of interest. Please apply online.

JACOB AND HILDA BLAUSTEIN FOUNDATION [960]

One South Street
Suite 2900
Baltimore, MD 21202
(410) 347-7201
E-mail: info@blaufund.org
Web Site: www.blaufund.org

FOUNDED: 1957

AREAS OF INTEREST:
Jewish life and Israel, education, human rights, health and mental health.

TYPE:
General operating grants; Matching gifts; Project/program grants.

ELIGIBILITY:
Grants are made to organizations that have tax-exempt status under Section 501(c)(3) of the Internal Revenue Code. No grants are made to individuals.

GEOG. RESTRICTIONS: United States (primarily Baltimore, Maryland) and Israel.

FINANCIAL DATA:
Amount of support per award: Varies.

Total amount of support: $7,500,000 for the year 2014.

APPLICATION INFO:
Application information is available on the Foundation's web site.

Duration: Typically one to two years.

ADDRESS INQUIRIES TO:
Betsy F. Ringel
Executive Director
(See address above.)

CALIFORNIA LIBRARY ASSOCIATION

248 East Foothill Boulevard
Suite 101
Monrovia, CA 91016
(626) 239-1776
Fax: (626) 239-1776
E-mail: info@cla-net.org
Web Site: www.cla-net.org

TYPE:
Fellowships; Scholarships. Support for minority library school students. Support for graduate students in reference/information service librarianship.

See entry 707 for full listing.

CARING FOR MILITARY FAMILIES: THE ELIZABETH DOLE FOUNDATION [961]

600 New Hampshire Avenue, N.W.
Suite 1020
Washington, DC 20037
(202) 249-7170
E-mail: info@elizabethdolefoundation.org
Web Site: www.elizabethdolefoundation.org

FOUNDED: 2012

AREAS OF INTEREST:
Military and veteran caregivers.

NAME(S) OF PROGRAMS:
- **Innovation Grants Program**

TYPE:
Development grants; Project/program grants; Research grants. Innovation Grants Program provides grant money for specific products and initiatives that will enhance the quality of life for military caregivers, their care recipients and their families.

YEAR PROGRAM STARTED: 2012

PURPOSE:
To spur targeted support for military caregivers, providing funding to leading nonprofit organizations with an exemplary track record.

ELIGIBILITY:
The Innovation Grants Program does not give grants to individuals. Eligible organizations must have 501(c)(3) nonprofit status.

Applicant organizations must address an issue facing military caregivers with innovative programs and initiatives. The Foundation focuses on seven key issues facing caregivers:
(1) employment;
(2) financial and legal issues;
(3) community support;
(4) respite care;
(5) education/training;
(6) interfaith action/ministry and;
(7) mental and physical health.
Applicants are strongly encouraged to consider these areas of focus when applying and, if possible, to include one or more of these elements in their programming.

The Foundation gives preference to national programs that focus on the population as a whole, rather than programs limited to one area only. However, it will fund programs starting in a specific area if it sees them expanding nationally if the pilot program is successful.

FINANCIAL DATA:
Amount of support per award: Varies depending on the project.

REPRESENTATIVE AWARDS:
National Military Family Association; Military Officers Association of America; Military Child Education Coalition.

APPLICATION INFO:
Information may be obtained by contacting the Foundation at the e-mail address above.

Duration: Funding until completion of the specific project. Project duration is negotiated during the application process. Grant not renewable; however, organizations are allowed to apply more than once.

Deadline: Applications are accepted on a year-round basis.

ADDRESS INQUIRIES TO:
Laurel Rodewald
Foundation Programs Manager
(See address or e-mail above.)

*SPECIAL STIPULATIONS:
The program or project must support military caregivers directly. Programs supporting veterans, with incidental or tangential support for their caregivers, will not be considered.

THE CENTER FOR LGBTQ STUDIES [962]

The Graduate Center/CUNY
365 Fifth Avenue, Room 7115
New York, NY 10016
(212) 817-1958
E-mail: clagsfellowships@gmail.com
Web Site: www.clags.org

AREAS OF INTEREST:
Scholarly research on the lesbian, gay, bisexual, transgender, and queer experience.

NAME(S) OF PROGRAMS:
- **The Duberman-Zal Fellowship**

TYPE:
Awards/prizes; Fellowships. An endowed fellowship named for CLAGS founder and first executive director, Martin Duberman, and partner, Eli Zal.

PURPOSE:
To promote the study of historical, cultural, and political issues of vital concern to lesbian, gay, bisexual, and transgendered individuals.

ELIGIBILITY:
Graduate students, independent scholars, or adjunct from any country doing scholarly research on the lesbian/gay/bisexual/transgender/queer (LGBTQ) experience may apply. University affiliation is not necessary.

FINANCIAL DATA:
Amount of support per award: $2,500.

NO. AWARDS: 1.

APPLICATION INFO:
Applications must include the following:
(1) a cover letter with contact information (address, phone number, and e-mail), project title, names of recommenders, and the fellowship being applied for;
(2) a research proposal of seven to 10 pages (double-spaced) including references;
(3) a brief statement of how the funds will be used;
(4) a curriculum vitae and;
(5) two letters of recommendation.

All submissions must be sent electronically to the e-mail listed above.

Letters of recommendation should be electronically directly from recommenders to the e-mail listed above.

Deadline: Mid-November. Final decisions are made in Spring.

PUBLICATIONS:
Annual report.

ADDRESS INQUIRIES TO:
Noam Parness
Membership and Fellowships Coordinator
(See address above.)

*SPECIAL STIPULATIONS:
Fellowship recipient may be asked to participate in CLAG's programming the following academic year to present their research project.

CINTAS FOUNDATION

c/o MDC Museum of Art and Design
600 Biscayne Boulevard
Miami, FL 33132
(305) 237-7901
Fax: (305) 373-0056
E-mail: lescobar@mdc.edu
Web Site: www.cintasfoundation.org

TYPE:
Awards/prizes; Fellowships. Awarded to persons of Cuban citizenship or lineage residing outside Cuba for achievement of a creative nature in architecture, painting, sculpture, printmaking, music composition and literature.

See entry 426 for full listing.

THE CONSORTIUM FOR GRADUATE STUDY IN MANAGEMENT

229 Chesterfield Business Parkway
Chesterfield, MO 63005
(636) 681-5553
Fax: (636) 681-5499
Web Site: www.cgsm.org

TYPE:
Fellowships. Graduate fellowships for minority students interested in management careers in business.

See entry 1834 for full listing.

COUNCIL ON SOCIAL WORK EDUCATION [963]

1701 Duke Street, Suite 200
Alexandria, VA 22314-3457
(703) 683-8080
Fax: (703) 683-8099
E-mail: gmeeks@cswe.org
Web Site: www.cswe.org/mfp

FOUNDED: 1952

AREAS OF INTEREST:
Improvement of social services and mental health.

NAME(S) OF PROGRAMS:

- **The Mental Health and Substance Abuse Fellowship Program**

TYPE:
Fellowships. Awards for minority doctoral-level studies in social work, specializing in mental health and substance abuse-related education, research, policy and practice.

YEAR PROGRAM STARTED: 1974

PURPOSE:
To equip doctoral social work students for leadership in practice, teaching, research, administration, consultation and policy development in mental health and/or substance use services to ethnic/racial minority individuals and communities.

LEGAL BASIS:
Nonprofit organization.

ELIGIBILITY:
Applicants must be American citizens or noncitizen nationals of the U.S. or have permanent residence status, including but not limited to persons who are American Indian/Alaskan Native, Asian/Pacific Islander (e.g., Chinese, East Indian and other South Asians, Filipino, Hawaiian, Japanese, Korean, Samoan), Black and Hispanic (e.g., Mexican/Chicano, Cuban, Central or South American).

The Fellowship is open to students with a Master's degree in social work who will begin full-time study leading to a doctoral degree in social work or who are currently enrolled as full-time students in a doctoral social work program. Applicants should demonstrate potential for assuming leadership roles, potential for success in doctoral studies and commitment to a career in providing mental health and/or substance abuse services to ethnic/racial/social/cultural minority clients and communities.

FINANCIAL DATA:
Fellowship awards include a monthly stipend for one year to help meet living and doctoral study expenses.

Amount of support per award: Varies.

Total amount of support: Varies.

CO-OP FUNDING PROGRAMS: Funded by the Substance Abuse and Mental Health Services Administration (SAMHSA), Department of Health and Human Services.

NO. AWARDS: Up to 25.

APPLICATION INFO:
Complete information is available at the Council web site.

Duration: Three years maximum. Renewable each year subject to availability of funds and progress in program.

Deadline: February 28.

ADDRESS INQUIRIES TO:
E-mail: mfp@cswe.org
(See telephone number above.)

DARTMOUTH COLLEGE [964]

Office of Graduate Studies
Chavez/Eastman/Marshall
37 Dewey Field Road, Suite 6062, Room 437
Hanover, NH 03755-3526
(603) 646-2106
Fax: (603) 646-8762
E-mail: jane.b.seibel@dartmouth.edu
Web Site: graduate.dartmouth.edu/funding/fellowships/cem.html

FOUNDED: 1769

AREAS OF INTEREST:
Fellowships for underrepresented minority scholars (including African-American, Latina/o and Native American scholars) and other graduate scholars with a demonstrated commitment and ability to advance educational diversity.

NAME(S) OF PROGRAMS:

- **Chavez/Eastman/Marshall Dissertation Fellowships**

TYPE:
Exchange programs; Fellowships.

YEAR PROGRAM STARTED: 1991

PURPOSE:
To increase the number of underrepresented minority faculty in American higher education by supporting African-American, Latina/o, Native American and other scholars with a demonstrated commitment to the advancement of educational diversity.

LEGAL BASIS:
University.

ELIGIBILITY:
Applicants will be chosen on the basis of academic achievement and promise, membership in a racial or ethnic group that is currently underrepresented among faculty in the applicant's academic field, demonstrated commitment to increasing opportunities for underrepresented minorities and increasing cross-racial understanding, and potential for serving as an advocate and mentor for minority undergraduate and graduate students.

GEOG. RESTRICTIONS: United States and Canada.

FINANCIAL DATA:
Fellowship provides stipend, office space, library privileges and research assistance.

Amount of support per award: $36,000 stipend and $2,500 research assistance.

Total amount of support: $115,500 annually.

NO. AWARDS: 2.

APPLICATION INFO:
Application form required. Contact the Office of Graduate Studies. Supporting documentation includes abstract of dissertation prospectus, statement of academic career plan, curriculum vitae, transcripts and three letters of reference.

Duration: One year.

Deadline: February 1. Announcement April 1.

PUBLICATIONS:
Program announcement.

ADDRESS INQUIRIES TO:
Jane Seibel, Assistant Dean
(See address above.)

*SPECIAL STIPULATIONS:
Fellows are expected to complete the dissertation during the tenure of the Fellowship and may have the opportunity to participate in teaching, either as a primary instructor or as part of a team.

DAUGHTERS OF ITALY LODGE #2825

14 South Jupiter Avenue
Clearwater, FL 33755
(727) 447-6890
E-mail: vincenzad@verizon.net
Web Site: www.daughtersofitaly.com

TYPE:
Scholarships. Open to full-time students at a Florida-accredited junior college, college or university or students graduating from high school.

See entry 1621 for full listing.

DAUGHTERS OF PENELOPE FOUNDATION, INC. [965]

1909 Q Street, N.W., Suite 500
Washington, DC 20009
(202) 234-9741
Fax: (202) 483-6983
E-mail: president@dopfoundationinc.com
dophq@ahepa.org
Web Site: www.dopfoundationinc.com
www.daughtersofpenelope.org

FOUNDED: 1983

AREAS OF INTEREST:
Philanthropic, educational and cultural activities pertaining to Greek culture.

NAME(S) OF PROGRAMS:

- **Daughters of Penelope National Scholarship Awards**

TYPE:
Scholarships. Academic and Financial Need.

YEAR PROGRAM STARTED: 1984

PURPOSE:
To promote the social, ethical and intellectual interests of members; to perpetuate the study of American ideals and to encourage Hellenic study; to cultivate citizenship and patriotism.

ELIGIBILITY:
Applicant must be a woman and have a current member of their immediate family or legal guardian (court-appointed) in the Daughters of Penelope or the Order of Ahepa, in good standing for a minimum of two years, or be a member in good standing for two years in the Daughters of Penelope or the Maids of Athena.

FINANCIAL DATA:
Amount of support per award: $500 to $2,500 depending on scholarship.

NO. MOST RECENT APPLICANTS: Varies.

NO. AWARDS: Varies.

APPLICATION INFO:
Application is available on the Foundation web site.

Duration: One year.

Deadline: May 1.

ADDRESS INQUIRIES TO:
E-mail:
dopfoundationscholarship@gmail.com

EDUCATIONAL TESTING SERVICE

660 Rosedale Road
Princeton, NJ 08541
(609) 734-5543
Fax: (609) 734-5010
E-mail: internfellowships@ets.org
Web Site: www.ets.org/research/fellowships.html

TYPE:
Internships. Interns in this eight-week program participate in research under the guidance of a senior ETS staff member in one of the areas of interest listed above. Interns also participate in seminars and workshops on a variety of topics.

See entry 1495 for full listing.

LOIS AND RICHARD ENGLAND FAMILY FOUNDATION

P.O. Box 34-1077
Bethesda, MD 20827
(301) 657-7737
Fax: (301) 657-7738
E-mail: englandfamilyfdn@gmail.com
Web Site: fdnweb.org/england

TYPE:
Capital grants; Challenge/matching grants; Development grants; General operating grants; Matching gifts; Project/program grants; Seed money grants; Technical assistance; Training grants.

See entry 1101 for full listing.

EVANGELICAL LUTHERAN CHURCH IN AMERICA

Congregation and Synodical Mission Unit
8765 West Higgins Road
Chicago, IL 60631-4101
(773) 380-2604
Fax: (773) 380-2750
E-mail: carol.josefowski@elca.org
Web Site: www.elca.org/Our-Work/Leadership/Seminaries/Educational-Grant-Program

TYPE:
Scholarships. Educational grants for members of the Evangelical Lutheran Church in America in advanced academic theological education degrees with intent to teach in seminary or university.

See entry 797 for full listing.

FEDERAL HIGHWAY ADMINISTRATION

Technology Partnerships Programs
1310 North Court House Road, Suite 300
Arlington, VA 22201
(703) 235-0538
Fax: (703) 235-0593
E-mail: transportationedu@dot.gov
Web Site: www.fhwa.dot.gov/tpp/ddetfp.htm

TYPE:
Fellowships; Internships; Research grants. Dwight David Eisenhower Transportation Fellowship Program's objectives are to attract the nation's brightest minds to the field of transportation, to enhance the careers of transportation professionals by encouraging them to seek advanced degrees, and to retain top talent in the transportation industry of the U.S. This Program encompasses all areas of transportation. The Program has eight award categories:
(1) Eisenhower Graduate (GRAD) Fellowships enable students to pursue Master's degrees or Doctorates in transportation-related fields at the university of their choice;
(2) Eisenhower Grants for Research (GRF) Fellowships acquaint undergraduate and graduate students with transportation research, development and technology-transfer activities at the U.S. Department of Transportation facilities;
(3) Eisenhower Historically Black Colleges and Universities (HBCU) Fellowships provide HBCU students with additional opportunities to enter careers in transportation. The Fellowships also serve as a feeder for other Eisenhower fellowships;
(4) Eisenhower Hispanic Serving Institutions (HSI) Fellowships provide HSI students with additional opportunities to enter careers in transportation. The Fellowships also serve as a feeder for other Eisenhower fellowships;
(5) Eisenhower Tribal College and Universities Fellowships (TCU) provides students with additional opportunities to enter careers in transportation. The Fellowships also serve as a feeder for other Eisenhower fellowships;
(6) Eisenhower Intern Fellowships (EIF) provides students with opportunities to perform a wide range of transportation-related activities at public and private-sector transportation organizations;
(7) Eisenhower People with Disabilities (PWD) Fellowships provide additional opportunities for people with disabilities to enter careers in transportation. The Fellowships also serve as a feeder for other Eisenhower fellowships and;
(8) Eisenhower Community College Fellowships provide students at community colleges with opportunities to enter careers in transportation. The Fellowships also serve as a feeder for other Eisenhower fellowships.

See entry 2523 for full listing.

FEEA SCHOLARSHIP PROGRAM

3333 South Wadsworth Boulevard
Suite 300
Lakewood, CO 80227
(303) 933-7580
Fax: (303) 933-7587
E-mail: ngleason@feea.org
Web Site: www.feea.org

TYPE:
Scholarships. Merit-based scholarship competition program open exclusively to federal employees, their spouses and their children.

See entry 1626 for full listing.

FOUNDATION FOR SCIENCE AND DISABILITY [966]

503 N.W. 89th Street
Gainesville, FL 32607
(352) 374-5774
Fax: (352) 374-5781
E-mail: rmankin1@ufl.edu
Web Site: stemd.org

FOUNDED: 1978

AREAS OF INTEREST:
Science, mathematics, medicine, engineering and computer science.

TYPE:
Grants-in-aid; Research grants.

YEAR PROGRAM STARTED: 1978

PURPOSE:
To assist disabled students who are interested in obtaining a graduate degree in one of the above fields.

LEGAL BASIS:
Affiliate of American Association for Advancement of Science.

ELIGIBILITY:
Open to college seniors and graduate students who have some physical or sensory disability and who have been accepted to graduate or professional school. Selection is based on sincerity of purpose and scholarship and/or research ability.

FINANCIAL DATA:
Funds may be used for an assistive device or instrument, or as financial support to work with a professor on an individual research project, or for some other special need.

Amount of support per award: $1,000.

NO. MOST RECENT APPLICANTS: 5.

NO. AWARDS: Varies, depending on funds available.

APPLICATION INFO:
Application forms may be obtained by writing or e-mailing Dr. Richard Mankin, as listed above, or can be downloaded from the Foundation web site.

Applicants should submit a copy of college transcript, two letters of recommendation, 250-word summary of educational goals including what the funds will be used for, if awarded, and a copy of a U.S. birth or naturalization certificate.

Deadline: December 1.

ADDRESS INQUIRIES TO:
Dr. Richard Mankin, Chairperson
Science Student Grant Committee
(See address above.)

THE FOUNDATION OF THE AMERICAN COLLEGE OF HEALTHCARE EXECUTIVES

One North Franklin Street
Suite 1700
Chicago, IL 60606-3529
(312) 424-9400
Fax: (312) 424-9405
E-mail: contact@ache.org
Web Site: www.ache.org/scholarships

TYPE:
Scholarships. Offered annually, the Albert W. Dent and the Foster G. McGaw Graduate Student Scholarships are designated for students enrolled in their final year of classroom work in a health care management graduate program.

Albert W. Dent Graduate Student Scholarship is only available to minority students.

See entry 1395 for full listing.

4A'S [967]

1065 Avenue of the Americas, 16th Floor
New York, NY 10018
(212) 682-2500
Fax: (212) 867-8329
E-mail: maip@aaaa.org
Web Site: maip.aaaa.org

FOUNDED: 1917

AREAS OF INTEREST:
Advertising, media, marketing, data/analytics and design.

NAME(S) OF PROGRAMS:
- **Multicultural Advertising Intern Program (MAIP)**

TYPE:
Fellowships; Scholarships.

YEAR PROGRAM STARTED: 1973

PURPOSE:
To assist multicultural students in attaining skills and knowledge necessary for careers in advertising and to assist advertising agencies in recruiting multicultural persons for the professional level.

LEGAL BASIS:
Nonprofit organization.

ELIGIBILITY:
Open to any Black, Native Hawaiian or Pacific Islander, American Indian or Alaska Native, Asian, Hispanic, multiracial or multiethnic student. Students must be currently enrolled in an undergraduate or graduate program at any accredited, degree-granting college or university, or a student attending a participating 4A's portfolio school and have completed at least their junior year by the time of the internship. Applicants must have a grade point average minimum of 3.0 on a scale of 4.0 and must be citizens or permanent residents of the U.S. Applicants must be able to show their passion to launch an advertising career through their essays.

Students have the opportunity to work in one of the basic career areas of advertising including account management, media buying and planning, art direction, community management, copywriting, design, production, project management, public relations and strategy.

GEOG. RESTRICTIONS: United States.

FINANCIAL DATA:
Students who do not live in the metropolitan area of their host agency are housed in 4A's-arranged housing. MAIP fellows requesting travel/housing assistance will be responsible for paying $1,200 to the 4A's toward summer housing and transportation cost, payable in two installments during the internship period.

Amount of support per award: $12 per hour.

Total amount of support: Varies.

NO. MOST RECENT APPLICANTS: 325.

NO. AWARDS: 100 to 150.

APPLICATION INFO:
Candidates must submit an application, resume, letters of recommendation, school transcripts and supporting materials (such as artwork). $25 application fee required. Semi-finalists are interviewed before final selections are made.

Duration: 22 weeks (12-week online Spring Training and a 10-week internship).

Deadline: End of November.

ADDRESS INQUIRIES TO:
Carl Desir
Vice President, Talent Initiative
(See e-mail address above.)

THE GAMBLE FOUNDATION

1660 Bush Street, Suite 300
San Francisco, CA 94109
(415) 561-6540 ext. 226
Fax: (415) 561-5477
E-mail: elingren@pfs-llc.net
Web Site: www.pfs-llc.net/gamble/gamble.html
www.gamblefoundation.org

TYPE:
Project/program grants.

See entry 1500 for full listing.

GILL FOUNDATION [968]

2215 Market Street
Denver, CO 80205
(303) 292-4455
Fax: (303) 292-2155
E-mail: grantsmanager@gillfoundation.org
Web Site: www.gillfoundation.org

FOUNDED: 1994

AREAS OF INTEREST:
Lesbian, gay, bisexual, and transgender (LGBT).

NAME(S) OF PROGRAMS:
- **Gill Foundation General Fund**

TYPE:
Challenge/matching grants; Project/program grants.

YEAR PROGRAM STARTED: 1994

PURPOSE:
To secure equal opportunity for all people, regardless of sexual orientation or gender expression.

ELIGIBILITY:
Grants are by invitation only. Unsolicited grant requests will not be accepted. 501(c)(3) organizations with a copy of an official nondiscrimination policy for your organization including sexual orientation and gender expression and identity.

GEOG. RESTRICTIONS: United States.

FINANCIAL DATA:
Amount of support per award: Varies.

Total amount of support: $11,500,842 for the year 2014.

NO. MOST RECENT APPLICANTS: 254 for the year 2014.

NO. AWARDS: 254 for the year 2014.

APPLICATION INFO:
Contact the Foundation.

Duration: One year.

PUBLICATIONS:
Annual report.

IRS I.D.: 84-1264186

ADDRESS INQUIRIES TO:
Grants Department
(See address above.)

GRADUATE EDUCATION OPPORTUNITY PROGRAM [969]

Michigan State University, The Graduate School
Chittenden Hall, 466 West Circle Drive
East Lansing, MI 48824
(517) 353-3220
Fax: (517) 353-3355
E-mail: gradschool@grd.msu.edu
Web Site: grad.msu.edu

FOUNDED: 1855

AREAS OF INTEREST:
Higher education.

NAME(S) OF PROGRAMS:
- **Academic Achievement Graduate Assistantships**
- **Education Opportunity Fellowship**
- **University Distinguished Fellowships**
- **University Enrichment Fellowships**

TYPE:
Assistantships; Fellowships.

YEAR PROGRAM STARTED: 1970

PURPOSE:
To increase participation by all U.S. students in graduate programs leading to advanced degrees in fields that do not yet reflect the inclusive diversity of the U.S. population; to enhance their retention and degree completion.

LEGAL BASIS:
University.

ELIGIBILITY:
Candidates are considered for the Academic Achievement Graduate Assistantship if nominated by the academic unit of the graduate program. Candidates for the Education Opportunity Fellowship may apply directly upon admission into a graduate program.

Candidate must be admitted to or enrolled in a graduate/professional degree-granting program at Michigan State University. Some programs require a student to demonstrate financial need. To be considered for financial support under the Graduate Education Opportunity Programs (GEOP), all recipients must be able to prove U.S. citizenship or permanent residency. Funding based on financial need.

University Distinguished Fellowship and University Enrichment Fellowship are merit-based recruitment fellowships. Students must be nominated by a department/college.

GEOG. RESTRICTIONS: United States.

FINANCIAL DATA:
Amount of support per award: Academic Achievement Graduate Assistantship (AAGA): Level I, half-time, $13,032 to $23,361, plus nine credits (Fall/Spring), including health care; Education Opportunity Program (EOP): $1,500 per semester, plus $100 to $200 per dependent for each semester; University Distinguished Fellowships (UDF) and University Enrichment Fellowships (UEF): $27,000, plus six to 10 credits (Fall/Spring) or three to five credits (Summer), including health care.

Total amount of support: Education Opportunity Program: Approximately $270,000.

APPLICATION INFO:
Contact the Graduate Education Opportunity Program.

Duration: Five to 11 semesters.

Deadline: Academic Achievement Graduate Assistantship and Education Opportunity Program: April 15; University Distinguished and Enrichment Fellowships: Varies.

ADDRESS INQUIRIES TO:
Judith Stoddart
Interim Dean of the Graduate School
(See address above.)

*SPECIAL STIPULATIONS:
Students must be enrolled in a graduate/professional program at Michigan State University.

GSBA SCHOLARSHIP FUND [970]

400 East Pine Street, Suite 322
Seattle, WA 98122
(206) 363-9188
Fax: (206) 568-3123
E-mail: scholarship@thegsba.org
Web Site: www.thegsba.org

FOUNDED: 1991

AREAS OF INTEREST:
Leadership and service in the gay and lesbian community.

TYPE:
Awards/prizes; Scholarships. Scholarships are intended for college, creative study, vocational training and postsecondary education.

YEAR PROGRAM STARTED: 1991

PURPOSE:
To expand economic opportunities for the Lesbian, Gay, Bisexual and Transgender community and those who support equality for all.

LEGAL BASIS:
501(c)(3) nonprofit.

ELIGIBILITY:
Applicants must demonstrate proven leadership skills, strong academic achievement and a commitment to making a positive difference in the world. Applicant must be a current Washington state resident pursuing a postsecondary degree in the U.S.

GEOG. RESTRICTIONS: Washington state.

FINANCIAL DATA:
Amount of support per award: Up to $13,000.

Total amount of support: $350,000 for the year 2015.

NO. MOST RECENT APPLICANTS: 400 for the year 2016.

NO. AWARDS: 50 for the year 2016.

APPLICATION INFO:
Applicants must submit the online application form, letters of recommendation and transcripts.

Duration: One year. Renewable up to four years.

Deadline: January 15.

PUBLICATIONS:
Guide/Directory, business listing and resources; *Perspective*, monthly newsletter.

IRS I.D.: 94-3138514

STAFF:
Louise Chernin, President and Chief Executive Officer
Rachel Chernin, Director of Operations and Finance
Jason Dittmer, Director of Marketing
Mark Rosen, Director of Fund Development
Jessica Wootten, Director of Scholarships
Matt Landers, Public Policy Manager
Victoria Odell, Business Development Manager
Ari Rosen, Membership Services Manager

BOARD OF DIRECTORS:
Kevin Gaspari, Chairman
Drew Ness, Vice Chairman
Marci Flanery, Treasurer
Brandon Chun, Secretary
Stephanie Dallas, Scholarship Chairperson
Allan Aquila
Chris Befumo
Mariko Blakley
Kim Bogucki
Carrie Carson
Elaine G. DuCharme
Calvin Goings
Jenny Harding
David Hernandez
Freya Johnson
Jeff Kinney
Dena Levine
Linda Marzano
John Rubino
Kurt Sarchet
Carl Spence
John Sternlicht
Paul Villa
Barb Wilson
Beto Yarce

THE DONALD D. HAMMILL FOUNDATION [971]

8700 Shoal Creek Boulevard
Austin, TX 78757-6897
Fax: (512) 451-1888
E-mail: jvoress@hammillfoundation.org
Web Site: www.hammillfoundation.org

FOUNDED: 1987

AREAS OF INTEREST:
Financially disadvantaged, disabled people, chronically ill and aged.

NAME(S) OF PROGRAMS:
- **Organizational Grants**

TYPE:
General operating grants; Project/program grants. Fund nonprofit organizations that provide direct services to meet basic needs of clients in the Austin community.

YEAR PROGRAM STARTED: 1987

PURPOSE:
To improve the quality of life for people who have disabilities or who are financially disadvantaged, including those who are indigent, chronically ill, and aged.

LEGAL BASIS:
Private foundation.

GEOG. RESTRICTIONS: Austin, Texas.

FINANCIAL DATA:
Amount of support per award: Up to $15,000.

Total amount of support: $565,500 for the year 2015.

NO. MOST RECENT APPLICANTS: 78 for the year 2015.

NO. AWARDS: 69 for the year 2015.

REPRESENTATIVE AWARDS:
$15,000 to Capital Area Food Bank of Texas; $5,000 to Any Baby Can; $10,000 to Casa Marianella.

APPLICATION INFO:
Application by invitation only.

Deadline: March 15.

PUBLICATIONS:
Application guidelines.

IRS I.D.: 74-2499947

OFFICERS:
Judith K. Voress, Ph.D., President
Cindy Thigpen, Treasurer
Nils Pearson, Ph.D., Secretary

BOARD OF TRUSTEES:
Donald D. Hammill, Ed.D.
Robert Lum
Phyllis L. Newcomer, Ed.D.
Jim Patton, Ed.D.
Nils Pearson, Ph.D.
Judith K. Voress, Ph.D.

ADDRESS INQUIRIES TO:
Judith K. Voress, Ph.D., President
(See address above.)

*PLEASE NOTE:
Programs are only funded locally in Austin, TX. The Foundation does not fund directly to individuals.

MYRTLE E. AND WILLIAM G. HESS CHARITABLE TRUST [972]

c/o JPMorgan
480 Pierce Street, Second Floor
Birmingham, MI 48009
(248) 205-2172
E-mail: mark.r.andrews@jpmorgan.com
Web Site: www.jpmorgan.com/onlinegrants

FOUNDED: 1985

AREAS OF INTEREST:
Catholic charitable organizations located in Oakland County, MI; Catholic charitable, educational and scientific objectives.

TYPE:
Capital grants; Development grants; Endowments; General operating grants; Project/program grants.

YEAR PROGRAM STARTED: 1985

PURPOSE:
To provide funds in perpetuity for charitable purposes.

LEGAL BASIS:
Private foundation.

ELIGIBILITY:
Limited to Catholic organizations with charitable, educational and scientific objectives. Particular preference being given to such objectives within the confines of Waterford and White Lake Townships.

GEOG. RESTRICTIONS: Waterford and White Lake townships in Oakland County, Michigan.

FINANCIAL DATA:
Amount of support per award: $2,500 to $25,000.

Total amount of support: Varies.

NO. MOST RECENT APPLICANTS: 28.

NO. AWARDS: 26.

APPLICATION INFO:
Only online applications are accepted.

Duration: One year. Renewals possible.

Deadline: April 30.

ADDRESS INQUIRIES TO:
Mark Andrews, Trust Officer
(See address above.)

IMMUNE DEFICIENCY FOUNDATION [973]

110 West Road
Suite 300
Towson, MD 21204
(800) 296-4433
Fax: (410) 321-9165
E-mail: dantilla@primaryimmune.org
Web Site: www.primaryimmune.org

FOUNDED: 1980

AREAS OF INTEREST:
Immunodeficiency diseases.

NAME(S) OF PROGRAMS:
- **The Varun Bhaskaran (WAS) Scholarship Program of IDF**

TYPE:
Scholarships.

YEAR PROGRAM STARTED: 2013

ELIGIBILITY:
Scholarship for undergraduate or graduate students living with Wiskott-Aldrich Syndrome.

GEOG. RESTRICTIONS: United States.

FINANCIAL DATA:
Amount of support per award: Varies.
Total amount of support: Varies.

APPLICATION INFO:
Contact the Foundation for application procedures.
Duration: Renewable yearly based on financial need and academic participation.
Deadline: Usually February 1 to April 1.

ADDRESS INQUIRIES TO:
Dan Antilla, Program Manager
(See address above.)

INSTITUTE OF INDUSTRIAL AND SYSTEMS ENGINEERS (IISE)

3577 Parkway Lane
Building 5, Suite 200
Norcross, GA 30092
(770) 449-0461
Fax: (770) 441-3295
E-mail: bcameron@iienet.org
Web Site: www.iienet.org

TYPE:
Fellowships; Scholarships. The Institute supports the advancement of engineering education and research through scholarships and fellowships to recognize and support these types of endeavors.

See entry 2567 for full listing.

THE JAPANESE AMERICAN CITIZENS LEAGUE (JACL)

Washington, DC Office
1629 K Street, N.W., Suite 400
Washington, DC 20006
(202) 223-1240
Fax: (202) 296-8082
E-mail: pouchida@jacl.org
Web Site: www.jacl.org

TYPE:
Travel grants. The Kakehashi Program is a new international program, part of JACL's leadership development. It is for college students and consists of five webinars and a nine-day trip to Japan.

See entry 839 for full listing.

JEWISH COMMUNITY FOUNDATION OF LOS ANGELES

6505 Wilshire Boulevard
Suite 1200
Los Angeles, CA 90048
(323) 761-8700
(877) 363-6966
Fax: (323) 761-8720
E-mail: info@jewishfoundationla.org
Web Site: www.jewishfoundationla.org

TYPE:
Awards/prizes; Capital grants; Project/program grants; Seed money grants. Capital Grants: Construction and renovation projects for facilities that predominantly serve members of the Los Angeles Jewish community.

Cutting Edge Grants: New programs with the potential for transformative impact that address critical needs in the Los Angeles Jewish community.

General Community Grants: Programs by organizations outside of the Jewish community which address high-priority concerns in the Los Angeles community.

Israel Grants: Programs that have an impact on economic development and pluralistic Jewish identity in Israel.

See entry 1277 for full listing.

THE JOSEPH P. KENNEDY, JR. FOUNDATION [974]

1133 19th Street, N.W.
12th Floor
Washington, DC 20036-3604
(202) 393-1250

FOUNDED: 1946

AREAS OF INTEREST:
Public policy directed toward those with intellectual or developmental disabilities.

NAME(S) OF PROGRAMS:
- **Public Policy Fellowship**

TYPE:
Fellowships. During this one-year Fellowship, the successful applicant will learn how federal legislation is initiated, developed and passed by the U.S. Congress, as well as how programs are administered and regulations promulgated by federal agencies.

YEAR PROGRAM STARTED: 1980

PURPOSE:
To prepare both midcareer and more seasoned leaders to assume leadership in the public policy arena in their home states and/or nationally.

ELIGIBILITY:
Successful applicants will have outstanding experience in:
(1) state- or national-level advocacy for persons with intellectual and developmental disabilities and their families;
(2) practice, advocacy or research in health care, mental health care, employment, education, child care, child welfare, law, community organizing, financial management and financial issues impacting families, housing or development of inclusive community supports and services for people with intellectual and developmental disabilities;
(3) development of training programs for people with disabilities, families and communities and/or for the professionals who work with and for them and;
(4) development or improvements of family support services, programs focused on increasing individual's control of resources and decisions impacting their lives, technology in support of people with intellectual and developmental disabilities and any other area of focus important to these Americans.

FINANCIAL DATA:
The Program includes a stipend and modest relocation expenses.

APPLICATION INFO:
The sole method of application, letters and resume submission is via an online system listed on the Foundation web site.

Applicants should submit a letter of application between two to four pages (maximum) in length, single-spaced in 12-point font with one-inch margins, stating their background and history in the field of services and supports to people with intellectual disabilities, interests and accomplishments to date, as well as what they hope to do with the knowledge and experience gained from the Fellowship. They should also attach either a resume detailing their work and educational experience or a summary of their involvement in the field along with three letters of support from people familiar with their work. Applications should clearly show the candidate's name, address, telephone number(s) and e-mail address on the first page.

Letters of support should also be via a PDF file or a Word file. A hard copy on letterhead with the supporter's signature must follow in the mail only if it has been sent in any format other than PDF or Word. Please make sure that each letter clearly specifies the candidate for which the letter is being submitted.

Duration: One year, January through December.

Deadline: 5 P.M., October 31.

ADDRESS INQUIRIES TO:
Steven M. Eidelman
E-mail: Eidelman@jpkf.org

*SPECIAL STIPULATIONS:
Selected Fellows must be prepared to live in the Washington, DC area during their fellowship year and to devote themselves full-time to the Fellowship.

MARCUS AND THERESA LEVIE EDUCATION FUND

JVS Chicago
216 West Jackson Boulevard, Suite 700
Chicago, IL 60606-6921
(312) 673-3444
Fax: (312) 553-5544
TTY: (312) 444-2877
E-mail: jvsscholarship@jvschicago.org
Web Site: www.jvschicago.org

TYPE:
Awards/prizes; Scholarships. Awards to individuals for the academic year.

See entry 1653 for full listing.

THE LUCIUS N. LITTAUER FOUNDATION, INC. [975]

220 Fifth Avenue, 19th Floor
New York, NY 10001-7708
(646) 237-5158
E-mail: info@littauerfoundation.org
Web Site: www.littauerfoundation.org

FOUNDED: 1929

AREAS OF INTEREST:
Access to education and jobs for low-income and marginalized populations in New York and Israel, support for Jewish communal life in New York, and Judaica librairies and archives.

TYPE:
General operating grants; Project/program grants; Seed money grants; Training grants; Loan forgiveness programs.

YEAR PROGRAM STARTED: 1929

PURPOSE:
To support education, health care and social welfare in the Jewish world and beyond.

LEGAL BASIS:
Independent foundation.

ELIGIBILITY:
Funds are awarded to nonprofit 501(c)(3) institutions. No grants to individuals.

GEOG. RESTRICTIONS: New York, New York and Israel.

FINANCIAL DATA:
Amount of support per award: Varies.
Total amount of support: $3,000,000 for the year 2015.

NO. AWARDS: 175.

APPLICATION INFO:
All grant requests must be made online through the Foundation web site. Application includes a full description of project, budget request, timetable for completion, institution which will administer grant and contact person.
Duration: Varies. Renewal possible.
Deadline: Applications are accepted on a rolling basis.

PUBLICATIONS:
Guidelines.

IRS I.D.: 13-1688027

TRUSTEES AND OFFICERS:
Robert D. Frost, President
Geula R. Solomon, Treasurer
Noah Perlman, Secretary
Charles Berlin
Mark A. Bilski
George Harris
Sarah Levy
Henry A. Lowet
Peter J. Solomon

ADDRESS INQUIRIES TO:
Alan Divack, Program Director
(See address above.)

LUSO-AMERICAN EDUCATION FOUNDATION
7080 Donlon Way
Suite 200
Dublin, CA 94568
(925) 828-3883
Fax: (925) 828-4554
E-mail: education@luso-american.org
Web Site: www.luso-american.org/laef.php

TYPE:
Scholarships.
See entry 645 for full listing.

MARINE BIOLOGICAL LABORATORY
7 MBL Street
Woods Hole, MA 02543
(508) 289-7173
Fax: (508) 289-7934
E-mail: researchprograms@mbl.edu
Web Site: www.mbl.edu

TYPE:
Research grants.
See entry 2085 for full listing.

THURGOOD MARSHALL COLLEGE FUND (TMCF)
1770 St. James Place
Suite 414
Houston, TX 77056
(202) 507-4851
Fax: (202) 448-1017
E-mail: scholarships@tmcf.org
Web Site: www.tmcf.org

TYPE:
Scholarships. Program for underrepresented minority students who intend to enter the intellectual property law field, to attend law school.
See entry 1922 for full listing.

MAURICE J. MASSERINI CHARITABLE TRUST [976]
c/o Wells Fargo Private Bank
4365 Executive Drive, 18th Floor
San Diego, CA 92121
(858) 622-6866
Fax: (858) 622-6848
E-mail: grantadministration@wellsfargo.com
Web Site: www.wellsfargo.com/privatefoundationgrants/masserini

AREAS OF INTEREST:
Underprivileged children, the elderly, religious, human services, health, environment/animals, education, and arts and culture.

TYPE:
Project/program grants.

ELIGIBILITY:
Eligible organizations must be IRS 501(c)(3) tax-exempt and be located in San Diego County, CA. Start-up organizations or salaries are generally not supported.

GEOG. RESTRICTIONS: San Diego County, California.

FINANCIAL DATA:
Amount of support per award: Generally $5,000 to $20,000.
Total amount of support: Varies.

NO. AWARDS: More than 60 per year.

APPLICATION INFO:
Applications are submitted through an online application process.
Duration: One year. Renewable by reapplication.
Deadline: April 30, August 31 and December 31.

ADDRESS INQUIRIES TO:
Wells Fargo Philanthropic Services
(See e-mail address above.)

MEDICAL LIBRARY ASSOCIATION [977]
65 East Wacker Place
Suite 1900
Chicago, IL 60601-7246
(312) 419-9094
Fax: (312) 419-8950
E-mail: awards@mlahq.org
Web Site: www.mlanet.org

FOUNDED: 1898

AREAS OF INTEREST:
Health sciences librarianship.

NAME(S) OF PROGRAMS:
- **MLA Scholarship for Minority Students**

TYPE:
Awards/prizes; Scholarships. Awarded for study in health sciences librarianship.

YEAR PROGRAM STARTED: 1964

PURPOSE:
To contribute to the support of minority individuals who are qualified to make a contribution to health sciences librarianship.

LEGAL BASIS:
Nonprofit.

ELIGIBILITY:
Applicant must be:
(1) a member of a minority group. A minority group is defined as African-American, Asian, Hispanic, Aboriginal, North American Indian, Alaskan Native or Pacific Islander;
(2) entering a Master's program at an ALA-accredited graduate library school or must have completed no more than half of his or her graduate program academic requirements at the time the award is made and;
(3) a citizen of or have permanent residence status in the U.S. or Canada.

A past recipient of the MLA Scholarship or the MLA Scholarship for Minority Students is ineligible. Membership in MLA is not required.

FINANCIAL DATA:
Amount of support per award: Up to $5,000.

NO. AWARDS: 1 per year.

APPLICATION INFO:
Applicant must submit the following:
(1) a copy of the completed application;
(2) two letters of reference from persons not related to the applicant who are knowledgeable about the applicant's character, education and abilities;
(3) official transcript from each college or university attended, sent directly from the respective institution that grants either Baccalaureate degree or library study degree and;
(4) copy of catalog or web page of applicant's library school, which states the number of credits needed for applicant's degree.
Duration: One year.
Deadline: December 1.

STAFF:
Maria Lopez, Grants, Scholarships and Awards Coordinator

ADDRESS INQUIRIES TO:
Coordinator
Grants, Scholarships and Awards
(See address above.)

MITSUBISHI ELECTRIC AMERICA FOUNDATION
1300 Wilson Boulevard
Suite 210
Arlington, VA 22209
(703) 276-8240
E-mail: mea.foundation@meus.mea.com
Web Site: www.meaf.org

TYPE:
Demonstration grants; General operating grants; Internships; Matching gifts; Project/program grants; Seed money grants; Technical assistance; Training grants. Grants are offered to make a better world for all by

helping young people with disabilities to maximize their potential and participation in society.

See entry 1556 for full listing.

THE NATIONAL ACADEMIES OF SCIENCES, ENGINEERING, AND MEDICINE [978]

Fellowships Office
Ford Foundation Fellowship Programs
500 Fifth Street, N.W.
Washington, DC 20001
(202) 334-2872
E-mail: FordApplications@nas.edu
Web Site: www.nationalacademies.org/ford

FOUNDED: 1979

AREAS OF INTEREST:
Behavioral and social sciences, humanities, engineering, mathematics, physical sciences, biological sciences, education and interdisciplinary programs comprised of two or more eligible disciplines supported by the fellowship program.

NAME(S) OF PROGRAMS:
- **Ford Foundation Fellowship Programs**

TYPE:
Fellowships. Awards for study in research-based doctoral programs leading to the Ph.D. or Sc.D. degrees, as well as postdoctoral studies.

YEAR PROGRAM STARTED: 1986

PURPOSE:
To increase the diversity of the nation's college and university faculties and to encourage students to achieve their full potential as scholars who will inspire others to follow an academic career in teaching and research.

LEGAL BASIS:
Private foundation.

ELIGIBILITY:
Applicants to these Ford Foundation Fellowships must be citizens, permanent residents or nationals of the U.S. at the time of application.

Predoctoral Fellowships are intended for students who plan to work toward the Ph.D. or Sc.D. degree in selected academic disciplines that lead to careers in teaching and research at the college or university level, and who are at or near the beginning of their graduate study or Sc.D. program. They may be college seniors, or individuals who have completed undergraduate study, or who have completed some graduate study, or who have already enrolled in a Ph.D. or Sc.D. program.

Dissertation Fellowships are intended for Ph.D. or Sc.D. degree candidates who have finished all required course work and examinations except for the writing and defense of the dissertation. Fellowship support is intended for the final year of dissertation writing.

Predoctoral and Dissertation Fellowships: Persons holding a doctoral degree earned at any time and in any field are not eligible to apply. Applicants must be Ph.D. or Sc.D. degree candidates studying one of the fields in the behavioral sciences, humanities, social sciences, life sciences, chemistry, earth sciences, physics and astronomy, engineering, mathematics, or computer science. They must aspire to a teaching and research career. Awards are not made for work leading to degrees in such areas as business administration and management, health sciences, public health, home economics, library science, speech pathology and audiology, personnel and guidance, social work, fine arts and performing arts and education.

Postdoctoral Fellowships: Intended for fellows to engage in a year of postdoctoral research and scholarship in an environment free from the interference of their normal professional duties. Applicants are required to have earned a Ph.D. or Sc.D. degree from a U.S. educational institution within a specified time period. Only those individuals already engaged in a teaching and research career or those planning such a career are eligible to apply in this program. Previous Foundation postdoctoral fellows may not reapply. Awards will be made in research-based areas of the behavioral and social sciences, humanities, engineering, mathematics, physical sciences, life sciences, education, or for interdisciplinary programs composed of two or more eligible disciplines supported by the fellowship program.

FINANCIAL DATA:
Amount of support per award: Dissertation Fellowships: $25,000 for one year and expenses paid to attend one Conference of Ford Fellows; Predoctoral Fellowships: Annual $24,000 stipend, expenses paid to attend at least one Conference of Ford Fellows; Postdoctoral Fellowships: $45,000 stipend and expenses paid to attend one Conference of Ford Fellows.

CO-OP FUNDING PROGRAMS: Program funded by the Ford Foundation.

NO. MOST RECENT APPLICANTS: 2,165.

NO. AWARDS: Approximately 60 Predoctoral Fellowships, 36 Dissertation Fellowships, and 24 Postdoctoral Fellowships.

APPLICATION INFO:
Applications are to be submitted online.

Duration: Predoctoral Fellowships: Up to three years; Dissertation and Postdoctoral Fellowships: Nine or 12 months.

Deadline: Predoctoral Fellowships: November 17, 2016; Dissertation and Postdoctoral Fellowships: November 10, 2016.

PUBLICATIONS:
Program announcement.

NATIONAL ACTION COUNCIL FOR MINORITIES IN ENGINEERING, INC. (NACME) [979]

One North Broadway
Suite 601
White Plains, NY 10601
(914) 539-4010 ext. 222
Fax: (914) 539-4032
E-mail: scholars@nacme.org
Web Site: www.nacme.org

FOUNDED: 1974

CONSULTING OR VOLUNTEER SERVICES:
NACME communicates and cooperates with the precollege, college and industry communities that are involved in the minority engineering effort.

NAME(S) OF PROGRAMS:
- **NACME Pre-Engineering Student Scholarship**

TYPE:
Block grants; Endowments; Fellowships; Scholarships. NACME encourages students to consider engineering as a career and to pursue the requisite preparation in mathematics and science. It motivates high school students and channels them to engineering schools and provides scholarship support and leadership development seminars to its university scholars. The retention of minority students in engineering is a priority issue for NACME.

YEAR PROGRAM STARTED: 1975

PURPOSE:
To enhance awareness of the engineering profession among students, parents, teachers, and guidance counselors; to recognize high school graduating seniors who have achieved exemplary academic performance and have decided to pursue an engineering education.

LEGAL BASIS:
Nonprofit organization incorporated in New York.

ELIGIBILITY:
Selected graduating underrepresented minority high school seniors must satisfy the following criteria:
(1) be an African-American, Latino, or American Indian;
(2) be in the top 10 percent of the graduating class;
(3) have demonstrated leadership qualities both in and outside high school and;
(4) have been accepted as a full-time student to an ABET-accredited engineering program.

GEOG. RESTRICTIONS: United States.

FINANCIAL DATA:
Each NACME Pre-Engineering Student Scholarship winner receives a certificate of recognition and a $2,500 scholarship award to be used toward the cost of attending an engineering school.

Amount of support per award: $2,500.

NO. AWARDS: Approximately 1,000 annually.

APPLICATION INFO:
Each high school may submit one nomination per school year. Guidelines and nomination form are available on the Council's web site.

Duration: Students selected by participating schools for NACME awards will be funded until graduation or a maximum of five years.

Deadline: March 15.

ADDRESS INQUIRIES TO:
Melonia Simpson, Program Manager
(See address above.)

NATIONAL ASSOCIATION OF HISPANIC JOURNALISTS [980]

1050 Connecticut Avenue, N.W.
5th Floor
Washington, DC 20036
(202) 853-7760
E-mail: nahj@nahj.org
lafrank@nahj.org
Web Site: www.nahj.org

FOUNDED: 1984

AREAS OF INTEREST:
English or Spanish language print, photo, broadcast or online journalism.

NAME(S) OF PROGRAMS:
- **Ford Motor Scholarship**
- **Gannett Foundation Scholarship**
- **NAHJ General Scholarships (Ruben Salazar Fund)**

- **NBC Fellowship**
- **News Corporation Scholarship**
- **Soledad O'Brien Scholarship**
- **PepsiCo Scholarships/Internship**
- **Geraldo Rivera Scholarship**
- **Maria Elena Salinas Scholarship**

TYPE:
Awards/prizes; Conferences/seminars; Fellowships; General operating grants; Internships; Matching gifts; Project/program grants; Research grants; Scholarships; Seed money grants; Training grants; Travel grants.

YEAR PROGRAM STARTED: 1986

PURPOSE:
To encourage the study and practice of journalism and mass communications by Hispanics.

ELIGIBILITY:
Open to high school seniors, college undergraduates and first-year graduate students pursuing careers in print, photo, broadcast or online journalism.

Gannett Foundation Scholarship applicant must be Florida International University student.

GEOG. RESTRICTIONS: United States and Puerto Rico.

FINANCIAL DATA:
Amount of support per award: Ford Motor Scholarship: Up to $2,000; Gannett Foundation Scholarship, Soledad O'Brien Scholarship and Geraldo Rivera Scholarship: $5,000; NAHJ General Scholarships: $1,000 to $2,000; Maria Elena Salinas Scholarship: $2,000.

NO. MOST RECENT APPLICANTS: Approximately 230.

NO. AWARDS: 50 scholarships.

APPLICATION INFO:
Scholarship applications are available online in January of each year.

Duration: One year.

Deadline: March.

IRS I.D.: 95-3927141

ADDRESS INQUIRIES TO:
Scholarships Department
(See address above.)

NATIONAL FEDERATION OF THE BLIND [981]

NFB Scholarship Program
200 East Wells Street at Jernigan Place
Baltimore, MD 21230
(410) 659-9314 ext. 2415
E-mail: scholarships@nfb.org
Web Site: www.nfb.org/scholarships

FOUNDED: 1940

AREAS OF INTEREST:
Improving the quality of life for blind persons by creating opportunity and combating discrimination.

CONSULTING OR VOLUNTEER SERVICES:
Major programs in scholarships, promoting employment for the blind, civil rights litigation, helping parents of blind children, public education, etc.

NAME(S) OF PROGRAMS:
- **National Federation of the Blind Scholarship Program**

TYPE:
Scholarships. Awarded on the basis of academic excellence, service to the community and leadership. Provides a one-time grant plus a continuing program of mentors and seminars for blind college students.

PURPOSE:
To create opportunities for blind persons residing in and attending college or university in the U.S. or Puerto Rico.

LEGAL BASIS:
Nonprofit, tax-deductible, nationwide membership organization of the blind.

ELIGIBILITY:
Applicants residing in the U.S. or Puerto Rico must be legally blind and pursuing or planning to pursue a full-time postsecondary course of study in the upcoming fall semester in the U.S or Puerto Rico. One scholarship, however, may be given to a person working full-time while attending school part-time. In addition, some scholarships have been further restricted by the donor. Recipients of Federation scholarships need not be members of the National Federation of the Blind. International students are not eligible unless they reside in the U.S. or Puerto Rico.

GEOG. RESTRICTIONS: United States and Puerto Rico.

FINANCIAL DATA:
Scholarship includes financial assistance to attend the NFB Annual Convention and other gifts.

Amount of support per award: $3,000 to $12,000; other gifts vary in value.

NO. MOST RECENT APPLICANTS: 470.

NO. AWARDS: 30 (1 $12,000 scholarship, 1 $10,000 scholarship, 2 $7,000 scholarships, 4 $5,000 scholarships and 22 $3,000 scholarships).

APPLICATION INFO:
Application information is available on the web site. Those interested in applying should read the rules of eligibility, the timeline, the Submission Checklist and the Scholarship FAQ, then fill in the online Scholarship Application Form. Supply the required documents and complete one telephone interview with the NFB representative.

Duration: One year. Renewals possible upon reapplication.

Deadline: Scholarship applications are accepted from November 1 of the previous year to March 31 of the year in which the scholarship is to be awarded. All documentation and the interview request must be received by the deadline. Notification by June 1.

ADDRESS INQUIRIES TO:
Scholarship Committee
(See address above.)

*SPECIAL STIPULATIONS:
Applicants must be legally blind in both eyes. Winners are assisted to attend the NFB Annual Convention in July. Attendance is required and a part of the prize awarded to each winner.

THE NATIONAL GEM CONSORTIUM [982]

1430 Duke Street
Alexandria, VA 22314
(703) 562-3646
Fax: (202) 207-2518
E-mail: info@gemfellowship.org
Web Site: www.gemfellowship.org

FOUNDED: 1976

AREAS OF INTEREST:
Engineering at the Master's and Doctorate levels and science at the Doctorate level.

CONSULTING OR VOLUNTEER SERVICES:
Mentor/protege training, graduate study preparedness training, success training, programs and publications designed to promote graduate education in engineering and science.

NAME(S) OF PROGRAMS:
- **The GEM M.S. Engineering Fellowship**
- **The GEM Ph.D. Engineering Fellowship**
- **The GEM Ph.D. Science Fellowship**
- **Grad Lab**
- **Graduate and Faculty Development Program**

TYPE:
Fellowships; Internships. All-expense fellowship for graduate study (tuition and stipend) and paid summer work experience in a scientific or engineering environment.

YEAR PROGRAM STARTED: 1976

PURPOSE:
To increase the number of minorities with graduate degrees in engineering and science.

LEGAL BASIS:
Incorporated in the State of Indiana; 501(c)(3) tax-exempt.

ELIGIBILITY:
Must be a U.S. citizen or permanent resident and an American Indian, Black American, Mexican American or Hispanic American.

FINANCIAL DATA:
Amount of support per award: M.S. Fellowship: Tuition and fees, plus a $16,000 stipend over entire M.S. program. Master's-level students also are assigned to a paid internship. Ph.D. Fellowships: $16,000 stipend applied in one academic year. Additional stipend support from GEM University.

Total amount of support: Varies.

NO. MOST RECENT APPLICANTS: 1,000.

NO. AWARDS: 108 for the year 2016.

APPLICATION INFO:
Three recommendations, GRE scores, and unofficial transcript of all college work.

Duration: Average three semesters or four quarters for Master's; five years renewable for Doctorate.

Deadline: November 15. Announcement April 15.

PUBLICATIONS:
Annual report; application brochure.

OFFICERS:
Eric Evans, Ph.D., President

ADDRESS INQUIRIES TO:
Valerie Washington, Coordinator of Information
(See address above.)

NATIONAL INSTITUTE OF GENERAL MEDICAL SCIENCES

National Institutes of Health
45 Center Drive, MSC 6200
Bethesda, MD 20892-6200
(301) 496-7301
Fax: (301) 402-0224
E-mail: info@nigms.nih.gov
Web Site: www.nigms.nih.gov

TYPE:
Fellowships; Research grants; Training grants; Research contracts. The National Institute of General Medical Sciences (NIGMS) supports basic research that increases understanding of biological processes and lays the foundation for advances in disease diagnosis, treatment and prevention. NIGMS-funded scientists investigate how living systems work at a range of levels, from molecules and cells to tissues, whole organisms and populations. The Institute also supports research in certain clinical areas, primarily those that affect multiple organ systems. To assure the vitality and continued productivity of research enterprise, NIGMS provides leadership in training the next generation of scientists, in enhancing the diversity of scientific workforce, and in developing research capacities throughout the country.

See entry 2212 for full listing.

NATIONAL INSTITUTE OF GENERAL MEDICAL SCIENCES

Center for Research Capacity Building
45 Center Drive, Room 2AS-43
Bethesda, MD 20892
(301) 594-3900
Fax: (301) 480-2753
E-mail: zlotnikh@nigms.nih.gov
Web Site: www.nigms.nih.gov

TYPE:
Development grants; Research grants. Grants to assist eligible institutions to strengthen the institutions' biomedical research capabilities and provide opportunities to students to engage in biomedical or behavioral research and other activities in preparation for Ph.D. training in these areas.

See entry 2213 for full listing.

NATIONAL INSTITUTE ON MINORITY HEALTH AND HEALTH DISPARITIES [983]

6707 Democracy Boulevard, Suite 800
MSC 5465
Bethesda, MD 20892-5465
(301) 402-1366
Fax: (301) 480-6749
Web Site: www.nimhd.nih.gov

AREAS OF INTEREST:
Minority opportunities in biomedical and behavioral science.

NAME(S) OF PROGRAMS:
- **Minority Health and Health Disparities International Research Training Grant (MIRT)**

TYPE:
Research grants; Training grants. Awards to U.S. colleges and universities to encourage students to pursue careers and degrees in the biological sciences by broadening their undergraduate and graduate education through international experiences.

Award provides support for undergraduates to undertake research and course work for 10 to 12 weeks during the summer or one semester during the academic year.

YEAR PROGRAM STARTED: 1993

PURPOSE:
To provide research training opportunities for minority undergraduate students, minority graduate students and minority faculty members in biomedical and behavioral research; to support faculty members to conduct independent research abroad and to serve as mentors to students abroad.

ELIGIBILITY:
Minority participants must be from underrepresented minority groups including African Americans, Native Americans, Hispanic Americans, Alaskan Natives and Pacific Islanders.

Applicants must be undergraduate students pursuing life science curricula, students pursuing doctoral degrees in the biomedical or behavioral sciences and/or faculty members in the biomedical and behavioral sciences.

GEOG. RESTRICTIONS: United States and its territories.

FINANCIAL DATA:
Amount of support per award: Up to $250,000 in direct costs.

Total amount of support: Approximately $5,000,000 in grants annually.

NO. AWARDS: Up to 24.

APPLICATION INFO:
Contact the Institute.

Duration: Up to five years.

Deadline: Varies.

PUBLICATIONS:
Program announcement; guidelines.

ADDRESS INQUIRIES TO:
Richard Berzon
Health Services Administrator
(See address above.)

THE NATIONAL ITALIAN AMERICAN FOUNDATION

1860 19th Street, N.W.
Washington, DC 20009-5501
(202) 939-3116
Fax: (202) 483-2618
E-mail: scholarships@niaf.org
Web Site: www.niaf.org/scholarships

TYPE:
Scholarships. The National Italian American Foundation (NIAF) will award scholarships and grants to outstanding students for use during the following academic year. The awards will be made on the basis of academic merit and divided between two groups of students.

See entry 1663 for full listing.

NATIONAL MEDICAL FELLOWSHIPS, INC.

347 Fifth Avenue, Suite 510
New York, NY 10016
(212) 483-8880
Fax: (212) 483-8897
E-mail: scholarships@nmfonline.org
Web Site: www.nmfonline.org

TYPE:
Awards/prizes; Fellowships; Project/program grants; Research grants; Scholarships. Service learning. NMF supports underrepresented minority medical students as they matriculate. Awards are available to students M1 to M4/5. In addition to financial support, NMF provides opportunities for aspiring doctors to take their learning into the community.

See entry 2221 for full listing.

NATIONAL TAXIDERMISTS ASSOCIATION [984]

P.O. Box 384
Pocahontas, IL 62275
(618) 669-2929
Fax: (618) 669-2909
E-mail: info@NationalTaxidermists.com
Web Site: www.nationaltaxidermists.com

AREAS OF INTEREST:
Taxidermy and education.

NAME(S) OF PROGRAMS:
- **Charlie Fleming Scholarship**

TYPE:
Scholarships.

PURPOSE:
To promote higher education and taxidermy education.

ELIGIBILITY:
Students must be a member, spouse or dependent of the NTA for three consecutive years.

FINANCIAL DATA:
Amount of support per award: $1,500.

NO. AWARDS: 2 per year.

APPLICATION INFO:
Contact the Organization for application procedures.

Applicant must submit an essay incorporating the MTA mission statement, their personal desires and ambitions and the educator the applicant wishes to study under.

Duration: One year.

Deadline: May 15.

ADDRESS INQUIRIES TO:
Tim Thacker, Headquarters Manager
(See address above.)

NEW JERSEY OFFICE OF THE SECRETARY OF HIGHER EDUCATION

20 West State Street, Fourth Floor
P.O. Box 542
Trenton, NJ 08625-0542
(609) 984-2709
Fax: (609) 633-8420
E-mail: audrey.bennerson@oshe.nj.gov
Web Site: www.state.nj.us/highereducation/EOF/EOF_Description.shtml

TYPE:
Grants-in-aid. The Higher Education Student Assistance Authority (HESAA) is a New Jersey authority that provides students and families with the financial and informational resources for students to pursue their education beyond high school. With roots dating back to 1959, HESAA's singular focus has always been to benefit the students it serves. HESAA provides state supplemental loans, grants and scholarships. HESAA also administers the state's college savings plan.

Educational Opportunity Fund Grants (EOF) provide financial aid to eligible students from educationally and economically disadvantaged backgrounds at participating in-state institutions.

See entry 1674 for full listing.

ORDER SONS OF ITALY IN AMERICA, GRAND LODGE OF FLORIDA

1539 Fayetteville Drive
Spring Hill, FL 34609
(352) 799-5456
E-mail: gusguadagnino@gmail.com
Web Site: osiafl.org

TYPE:
Awards/prizes; Grants-in-aid; Scholarships. Scholarships are provided to high school students entering college.

Financial aid is given in support of charitable programs, such as Alzheimer's disease, Cooley's anemia, autism, and cancer.

See entry 1686 for full listing.

PEN AMERICAN CENTER

588 Broadway, Suite 303
New York, NY 10012-5246
(212) 334-1660
Fax: (212) 334-2181
E-mail: awards@pen.org
Web Site: www.pen.org

TYPE:
Awards/prizes. Invites submissions of book-length writings by authors of color, published during the calendar year.

See entry 674 for full listing.

PRIDE FOUNDATION [985]

2014 East Madison Street
Suite 300
Seattle, WA 98122
(206) 323-3318
Fax: (206) 323-1017
E-mail: grants@pridefoundation.org
Web Site: www.pridefoundation.org

FOUNDED: 1985

AREAS OF INTEREST:
Arts and recreation; education outreach and advocacy; HIV/AIDS; lesbian health; youth and family; and other health and community services.

TYPE:
Endowments; General operating grants; Project/program grants; Scholarships; Seed money grants.

YEAR PROGRAM STARTED: 1987

PURPOSE:
To strengthen the lesbian, gay, bisexual and transgender community today and build an endowment fund for tomorrow.

ELIGIBILITY:
Projects must support lesbian, gay, bisexual and transgender causes. Organizations applying for funds must have 501(c)(3) nonprofit tax status, or be affiliated with an organization that has 501(c)(3) status that will assume responsibility for administering all funds received and expended. Grants to individuals cannot be considered.

GEOG. RESTRICTIONS: Alaska, Idaho, Montana, Oregon and Washington.

FINANCIAL DATA:
Amount of support per award: Maximum $5,000; some rare special projects exceptions.

REPRESENTATIVE AWARDS:
$3,000 to Causa for LGBT Spanish language radio show; $4,200 to Youth Suicide Prevention Program for suicide and bias-based bullying prevention activities in Spokane, WA; $5,000 to Cedar River Clinics for training medical staff to create a safer, more culturally competent and compassionate environment for lesbians, bisexual women and transgendered people.

APPLICATION INFO:
Contact the Foundation.

Duration: One year.

Deadline: Varies.

PUBLICATIONS:
Newsletter.

IRS I.D.: 91-1325007

ADDRESS INQUIRIES TO:
Gunner Scott, Director of Programs
(See address above.)

PROSPANICA [986]

450 East John Carpenter Freeway
Suite 200
Irving, TX 75062
(214) 596-9338
(877) 467-4622
Fax: (214) 596-9325
E-mail: scholarship@prospanica.org
Web Site: www.nshmba.org

AREAS OF INTEREST:
Business administration.

NAME(S) OF PROGRAMS:

- **Prospanica Tuition Benefits Program**

TYPE:
Scholarships.

YEAR PROGRAM STARTED: 1989

PURPOSE:
To foster Hispanic leadership through graduate management education and professional development.

LEGAL BASIS:
501(c)(3) organization.

ELIGIBILITY:
Applicant must:
(1) be a member of Prospanica;
(2) express interest in the tuition benefit prior to first drop/add period. No current students are eligible for this benefit and;
(3) be admitted to and subsequently enroll in one of the designated programs.

GEOG. RESTRICTIONS: United States and Puerto Rico.

FINANCIAL DATA:
Amount of support per award: Up to $10,000.

APPLICATION INFO:
After being admitted to an affiliated tuition benefit program, applicant must inform admissions staff of their interest in the Prospanica scholarship. Applicant must submit proof of admission and a one-page essay on how this scholarship will help further their education to the e-mail address above.

The Prospanica Committee will review submissions and inform of their decision. If approved, the scholarship will be credited to the student's account throughout the length of the program.

Duration: One academic year.

THE RETIREMENT RESEARCH FOUNDATION [987]

8765 West Higgins Road
Suite 430
Chicago, IL 60631-4170
(773) 714-8080
Fax: (773) 714-8089
E-mail: info@rrf.org
Web Site: www.rrf.org

FOUNDED: 1950

AREAS OF INTEREST:
Aging.

NAME(S) OF PROGRAMS:

- **Grants Program**
- **Organizational Capacity Building**

TYPE:
Challenge/matching grants; Demonstration grants; Project/program grants; Research grants; Technical assistance; Training grants. For the Grants Program, awards are generally limited to projects directly related to the Foundation's interests.

Funding of service/service development projects which do not have potential for national or regional impact are limited to the six midwestern states (Illinois, Indiana, Iowa, Kentucky, Missouri, Wisconsin) and Florida. The Foundation has strong interest in serving the Chicago metropolitan area.

Organizational Capacity Building is designed to strengthen the effectiveness of Chicago-area nonprofit groups serving the elderly. Grants are available to help these organizations make long-term improvements in their management and governance, and by doing so, to sustain and enhance their services to the elderly.

YEAR PROGRAM STARTED: 1979

PURPOSE:
The Foundation is devoted exclusively to improving the quality of life for the nation's older population.

LEGAL BASIS:
Private foundation.

ELIGIBILITY:
To be eligible for support, organizations, congregations and institutions must qualify under the regulations of the IRS.

The Foundation's funding is directed to efforts that:
(1) improve the availability and quality of community-based and long-term services and supports;
(2) provide new and expanded opportunities for older adults to engage in meaningful roles in society;
(3) seek causes and solutions to significant problems of older adults and;
(4) increase the number of professionals and paraprofessionals adequately prepared to serve the elder population.

To achieve its goals, the Foundation supports education and training, advocacy, direct service, replications of evidence-based programs, models and practices, and applied clinical, policy and social science research.

The Foundation is particularly interested in innovative projects that develop and/or demonstrate new approaches to the problems of older Americans and that have the potential for national or regional impact.

The Foundation normally does not provide support for construction of facilities, general operating expenses, computers, endowment or developmental campaigns, scholarships or

loans, grants to individuals, projects outside the U.S., conferences, publications and travel unless components of a larger Foundation-funded project, dissertation research or the production of films and videos.

Requests for research, advocacy and training are considered from eligible organizations anywhere in the U.S.

GEOG. RESTRICTIONS: Direct-service grants limited to Florida, Illinois, Iowa, Kentucky, Michigan, Missouri and Wisconsin.

FINANCIAL DATA:
Assets of $132,000,000 for the year 2013.

Amount of support per award: $1,000 to $187,542; $46,800 average for the year 2013.

Total amount of support: $5,070,553 for the year 2013.

NO. MOST RECENT APPLICANTS: 248 for the year 2013.

NO. AWARDS: 97 for the year 2013.

REPRESENTATIVE AWARDS:
$75,000 to Brown University for research on the prevalence and impact of billing Medicare beneficiary stays as outpatient observation; $186,012 (over two years) to Easter Seals National Office for a training program to transform the culture of adult day services to deliver person-centered care; $40,000 to Swedish Covenant Hospital to expand a home telehealth monitoring program for congestive heart failure patients; $34,962 to Provena Mercy Medical Center for an Advance Practice Nurse to coordinate care and services to patients with dementia and their caregivers; $60,000 to the Center for Medicare Advocacy to train the National Medicare Alliance and to maintain an electronic searchable database of Medicare appeals decisions.

APPLICATION INFO:
The Foundation does not have a standard grant application form. Visit the Foundation web site to find information about submitting a proposal.

Deadline: February 1, May 1 and August 1, with award announcement three to six months after submission date.

TRUSTEES AND OFFICERS:

ADDRESS INQUIRIES TO:
See e-mail address above.

RIGHTEOUS PERSONS FOUNDATION [988]

400 South Beverly Drive, Suite 420
Beverly Hills, CA 90212
(310) 314-8393
Fax: (310) 314-8396
E-mail: grants@righteouspersons.org
Web Site: www.righteouspersons.org

FOUNDED: 1994

AREAS OF INTEREST:
Primarily Jewish organizations.

TYPE:
General operating grants; Matching gifts; Project/program grants; Seed money grants; Technical assistance.

PURPOSE:
To strengthen Jewish life in America.

LEGAL BASIS:
Nonprofit.

ELIGIBILITY:
Applicants must be tax-exempt organizations. Priority is given to national organizations and projects which create meaningful experiences for Jewish youth, promote Jewish learning, provide leadership training grounded in Jewish tradition, employ the arts and media to explore the relevance of modern Jewish identity, promote tolerance and understanding between Jews and non-Jews, and encourage Jews to participate in the work of social justice.

The Foundation does not make grants to individuals. Also, the Foundation does not support university faculty chairs, individual synagogues or day schools, research, the publication of books or magazines, or organizations or projects based outside of the U.S. In addition, the Foundation generally does not support endowments, capital campaigns, building funds, or social service projects.

GEOG. RESTRICTIONS: United States.

FINANCIAL DATA:
Amount of support per award: Varies.

Total amount of support: Varies.

APPLICATION INFO:
Applicants should submit a two- to three-page letter of inquiry including:
(1) a description of the proposed project including the issues the project will address and the target population(s);
(2) a brief description of the organization's mission, activities and history;
(3) the total amount of the organization's operating budget;
(4) the total amount requested from the Foundation;
(5) the name, mailing address and telephone number of a contact person;
(6) a detailed project budget;
(7) a list of the organization's board of directors;
(8) documentation of the organization's 501(c)(3) status;
(9) the total amount requested from the Foundation and;
(10) a list of the organization/project's primary sources of support over the last two years including names of foundations and amounts provided each year.

If there is a fiscal sponsor for the project, include a current copy of the sponsor's tax-exempt letter from the IRS as well as a letter of support from the sponsor acknowledging their responsibilities. Do not send full proposals or video or audio tapes unless otherwise requested. Faxed applications will not be considered.

Duration: Varies.

PUBLICATIONS:
Program announcement; guidelines.

STAFF:
Rachel Levin, Executive Director
Shayna Rose Triebwasser, Program Officer

BOARD OF DIRECTORS:

ADDRESS INQUIRIES TO:
Shayna Rose Triebwasser, Program Officer
(See address above.)

JACKIE ROBINSON FOUNDATION (JRF) [989]

75 Varick Street, 2nd Floor
New York, NY 10013-1917
(212) 290-8600
Fax: (212) 290-8081
E-mail: general@jackierobinson.org
Web Site: www.jackierobinson.org

FOUNDED: 1973

AREAS OF INTEREST:
Providing college education and a comprehensive set of support services for academically gifted, highly motivated students of color with financial need.

NAME(S) OF PROGRAMS:
- **Extra Innings Fellowship Program (EIF)**
- **Mentoring and Leadership Program**
- **Rachel Robinson International Fellowship Program (RRIF)**

TYPE:
Conferences/seminars; Fellowships; Scholarships. The Foundation Scholarship Program (Mentoring and Leadership Program) is designed to address the financial needs of college students and provide comprehensive mentoring services through its 42 Strategies for Success Curriculum.

The Fellowship programs are follow-up programs to the JRF Scholars program (Mentoring and Leadership Program).

The Extra Innings Fellowship Program helps highly motivated JRF Scholars to fund the cost of advanced professional or graduate training.

The Rachel Robinson International Fellowship Program promotes and supports international service and study opportunities for JRF Scholars.

PURPOSE:
To award four-year college scholarships to academically gifted students of color with financial need, enabling them to attend the college of their choice.

ELIGIBILITY:
Foundation Scholar applicants must meet all of the following criteria:
(1) have U.S. citizenship;
(2) be a minority student;
(3) be a high school senior enrolling in college in the coming fall;
(4) have a SAT score (combined math and critical reading sections) of 1,000 or above, an ACT of 21 or above;
(5) have leadership potential and;
(6) be in financial need.

FINANCIAL DATA:
JRF Scholars program includes financial sponsorship to attend JRF's annual, four-day "Mentoring and Leadership Conference " in New York City as well as other regional events throughout the year.

Amount of support per award: Scholarships: Up to $7,000 per year; maximum $28,000 over four years.

NO. MOST RECENT APPLICANTS: Scholarships: Approximately 5,000 per year.

NO. AWARDS: Scholarships: 40 to 60 per year.

APPLICATION INFO:
Application information is available at the Foundation web site. Scholarship application is available for online review on October 15, and goes live on November 1.

Duration: Four years.

Deadline: The application is due February 15. Applicants are notified of status April 30; final selection of Scholars is announced on June 15.

ADDRESS INQUIRIES TO:
Mentoring and Leadership Program
Jackie Robinson Foundation
(See address above.)

SANTA FE COMMUNITY FOUNDATION [990]

501 Halona Street
Santa Fe, NM 87505
(505) 988-9715
Fax: (505) 988-1829
E-mail: foundation@santafecf.org
Web Site: www.santafecf.org

FOUNDED: 1981

AREAS OF INTEREST:
Arts, animal welfare, education, economic opportunity, environment, health, human services, lesbian, gay, bisexual and transgender community and Native American.

NAME(S) OF PROGRAMS:
- **Community Leadership Fund**
- **Dollars 4 Schools**
- **Envision Fund**
- **Local Impact Investing Initiative**
- **MoGro**
- **Native American Advised Endowment Fund**
- **NM Health Equity Partnership**
- **Santa Fe Baby Fund**

TYPE:
General operating grants; Project/program grants.

YEAR PROGRAM STARTED: 1981

PURPOSE:
To promote charitable community outreaches.

LEGAL BASIS:
Community foundation.

ELIGIBILITY:
The Foundation awards grants to nonprofit organizations only. The Foundation does not award grants for religious or political purposes, capital outlay, endowment or to individuals.

GEOG. RESTRICTIONS: Santa Fe and northern New Mexico.

FINANCIAL DATA:
Amount of support per award: $5,000 to $15,000.

Total amount of support: $6,500,000 (including donor-advised funds) for the year 2015.

CO-OP FUNDING PROGRAMS: Hispanics in Philanthropy, Birth2Career, Law Enforcement Assisted Diversion, and Early Childhood Funders Network.

NO. MOST RECENT APPLICANTS: Approximately 200 for the year 2015.

NO. AWARDS: Approximately 50 for the year 2015.

APPLICATION INFO:
Applicants must submit proof of IRS 501(c)(3) status.

Duration: One year.

Deadline: Spring and Fall.

PUBLICATIONS:
Giving Together, catalogue; *Guide to Giving*.

IRS I.D.: 85-0303044

OFFICER:
Jerry Jones, Interim President and Chief Executive Officer

ADDRESS INQUIRIES TO:
Christa Coggins
Vice President for Community Philanthropy
(See address above.)

ALFRED P. SLOAN FOUNDATION [991]

630 Fifth Avenue
Suite 2200
New York, NY 10111
(212) 649-1649
Fax: (212) 757-5117
E-mail: boylan@sloan.org
Web Site: www.sloan.org

FOUNDED: 1934

AREAS OF INTEREST:
Multiple special purpose.

NAME(S) OF PROGRAMS:
- **Sloan Indigenous Graduate Partnership (SIGP)**

TYPE:
Fellowships; Scholarships. Offers substantial scholarship support to indigenous students (Native Americans, including American Indians, Native Alaskans and Native Hawaiians) who are beginning their Master's or doctoral work in sciences, technology, engineering and mathematics (STEM) fields in selected departments at selected U.S. universities.

YEAR PROGRAM STARTED: 2003

PURPOSE:
To increase the number of Master's and Ph.D. degrees among indigenous people.

ELIGIBILITY:
American Indians/Alaskan Natives/Hawaiian Natives. Candidates must first apply for and be accepted at one of the academic departments in their discipline at a university in the program. Those accepted qualify as a candidate for a Foundation scholarship.

GEOG. RESTRICTIONS: United States.

FINANCIAL DATA:
Amount of support per award: Varies.

Total amount of support: Varies.

Matching fund requirements: Universities must provide balance of support needed by students.

CO-OP FUNDING PROGRAMS: This program is administered by the National Action Council for Minorities in Engineering, Inc. (NACME).

NO. AWARDS: Varies.

APPLICATION INFO:
Duration: Varies.

ADDRESS INQUIRIES TO:
Program Director
Sloan Indigenous Graduate Partnership
(See address above.)

ALFRED P. SLOAN FOUNDATION [992]

630 Fifth Avenue
Suite 2200
New York, NY 10111
(212) 649-1649
Fax: (212) 757-5117
E-mail: boylan@sloan.org
Web Site: www.sloanphds.org

FOUNDED: 1934

AREAS OF INTEREST:
Multiple special purpose.

NAME(S) OF PROGRAMS:
- **Minority Ph.D. Program (MPHD)**

TYPE:
Fellowships; Scholarships. Offers substantial scholarship support to underrepresented minority (African American, Hispanic American or Native American) students who are U.S. citizens and who are beginning their doctoral work in engineering, natural science and mathematics in selected departments at selected U.S. universities.

YEAR PROGRAM STARTED: 1995

PURPOSE:
To increase the number of Ph.Ds. among underrepresented minorities.

ELIGIBILITY:
African Americans, Hispanic Americans and American Indians/Alaskan Natives. Candidates must first apply for and be accepted at one of the academic departments in their discipline supported by the Foundation. Those accepted qualify as a candidate for a Foundation scholarship.

GEOG. RESTRICTIONS: United States.

FINANCIAL DATA:
Amount of support per award: Varies.

Total amount of support: $3,500,000.

Matching fund requirements: Universities must provide balance of support needed by students.

CO-OP FUNDING PROGRAMS: This program is managed by the National Action Council for Minorities in Engineering, Inc. (NACME).

NO. AWARDS: Varies.

ADDRESS INQUIRIES TO:
Program Director
Minority Ph.D. Program
(See address above.)

SONS OF ITALY FOUNDATION [993]

219 E Street, N.E.
Washington, DC 20002
(202) 547-2900
Fax: (202) 546-8168
E-mail: scholarships@osia.org
Web Site: www.osia.org

FOUNDED: 1959

AREAS OF INTEREST:
Cultural preservation and advancement for Italian Americans; education.

NAME(S) OF PROGRAMS:
- **National Leadership Grant Competition**

TYPE:
Awards/prizes; Scholarships. The Foundation provides Italian language scholarships, study-abroad scholarships and merit-based higher education scholarships.

YEAR PROGRAM STARTED: 1959

PURPOSE:
To help educate Italian Americans and improve their lives.

LEGAL BASIS:
Public, tax-exempt organization as defined by Section 501(c)(3) and Section 509(a)(1) of the Internal Revenue Code.

ELIGIBILITY:
Open to high school seniors, undergraduate and graduate students. Applicants must be U.S. citizens of Italian heritage.

FINANCIAL DATA:
Amount of support per award: Scholarships: $4,000 to $20,000.

Total amount of support: Varies.

NO. MOST RECENT APPLICANTS: 1,000.

NO. AWARDS: 10 to 12.

APPLICATION INFO:
Contact the Foundation.

Duration: One year.

Deadline: February 28.

PUBLICATIONS:
Annual report; *Grant Priorities, Guidelines and Procedures*, booklet.

STAFF:
Philip R. Piccigallo, Ph.D., National Executive Director

OFFICERS OF THE TRUSTEES:
Vincent Sarno, President
Joseph DiTrapani, Chairman

ADDRESS INQUIRIES TO:
Laura Kelly, Scholarship Coordinator
(See address above.)

THE SPECIAL HOPE FOUNDATION [994]

2225 East Bayshore Road, Suite 200
Palo Alto, CA 94303
(650) 644-5376
Fax: (650) 320-1716
E-mail: info@specialhope.org
Web Site: www.specialhope.org

FOUNDED: 2002

AREAS OF INTEREST:
Health care access and health care research benefiting adults with developmental disabilities.

TYPE:
Challenge/matching grants; Conferences/seminars; General operating grants; Project/program grants; Research grants; Technical assistance.

YEAR PROGRAM STARTED: 2002

PURPOSE:
To provide financial support to organizations that promote the establishment of comprehensive health care for adults with developmental disabilities.

ELIGIBILITY:
Organizations must be nonprofit 501(c)(3). Only grant proposals consistent with the Foundation's mission statement will be eligible for funding. No grants are made to individuals.

GEOG. RESTRICTIONS: United States.

FINANCIAL DATA:
Amount of support per award: $20,000 to $50,000.

Matching fund requirements: By invitation only.

NO. MOST RECENT APPLICANTS: 50.

NO. AWARDS: 10.

APPLICATION INFO:
Pre-application questionnaire must be completed online.

Duration: One to three years.

ADDRESS INQUIRIES TO:
Shannon Cully, Director of Programs
(See address above.)

U.S. DEPARTMENT OF EDUCATION

Office of English Language Acquisition, Language Enhancement and Academic Achievement
LBJ Education Building, Room 5C-140, MS-6510
400 Maryland Avenue, S.W.
Washington, DC 20202
(202) 401-4300
Fax: (202) 205-1229
E-mail: libia.gill@ed.gov
Web Site: www.ed.gov/offices/oela

TYPE:
Formula grants. National Professional Development Program provides professional development activities intended to improve instruction for students with limited English proficiency (LEP) and assists education personnel working with such children to meet high professional standards.

Native American and Alaska Native Children in School Program provides grants to eligible entities that support language instruction education projects for limited English proficient (LEP) children from Native American, Alaska Native, native Hawaiian, and Pacific Islander backgrounds. The program is designed to ensure that LEP children master English and meet the same rigorous standards for academic achievement that all children are expected to meet. Funds may support the study of Native American languages.

See entry 1545 for full listing.

UCLA INSTITUTE OF AMERICAN CULTURES (IAC) [995]

2329 Murphy Hall, Box 957244
Los Angeles, CA 90095-7244
(310) 825-6815
Fax: (310) 825-3994
E-mail: iaccoordinator@conet.ucla.edu
Web Site: www.iac.ucla.edu

FOUNDED: 1969

AREAS OF INTEREST:
Advancing knowledge, strengthening and integrating interdisciplinary research and enriching instruction on African Americans, American Indians, Asian Americans and Chicanos.

NAME(S) OF PROGRAMS:

- **UCLA IAC Visiting Researcher and Visiting Scholar Program in Ethnic Studies**

TYPE:
Fellowships. Deals with arts and humanities, education and teacher training, fine arts, applied arts, law, social sciences, and sciences. The IAC, in cooperation with UCLA's four Ethnic Studies Research Centers (American Indian Studies Center, Asian American Studies Center, Bunche Center for African American Studies, and Chicano Studies Research Center), offers awards to visiting scholars to support research on African Americans, American Indians, Asian Americans and Chicanas/os.

PURPOSE:
To enable Ph.D. scholars wishing to work in association with the American Indian Studies Center, the Bunche Center for African American Studies, the Asian American Studies Center, and the Chicano Studies Research Center, in order to conduct research and publish books or manuscripts.

ELIGIBILITY:
Open to U.S. citizens or permanent residents of the U.S. who hold a Ph.D. from an accredited college or university (or, in the case of the arts, a terminal degree) in the appropriate field at the time of appointment. UCLA faculty, staff and currently enrolled students are not eligible to apply.

FINANCIAL DATA:
Amount of support per award: Up to $35,000 stipend and up to $4,000 in research support. Amount contingent upon rank, experience and date of completion of terminal degree.

NO. AWARDS: Up to 4.

APPLICATION INFO:
Applicants are encouraged to contact the Studies Research Center of interest prior to applying. Application process begins in November.

Duration: Up to one year.

Deadline: February.

ADDRESS INQUIRIES TO:
IAC Coordinator
(See address above.)

UNITED METHODIST COMMUNICATIONS [996]

810 12th Avenue South
Nashville, TN 37203-4744
(888) 278-4862
Fax: (615) 742-5777
E-mail: scholarships@umcom.org
Web Site: www.umcom.org

FOUNDED: 1948

AREAS OF INTEREST:
Religious communications.

NAME(S) OF PROGRAMS:

- **The Leonard M. Perryman Communications Scholarship for Ethnic Minority Students**

TYPE:
Fellowships; Scholarships. Award for junior or senior undergraduate study in religion journalism or mass communications. The term *communications* is meant to cover various media as audio-visual, electronic and print journalism.

PURPOSE:
To enable the recipient to continue his or her studies in communication; to promote a level of excellence in communication on the undergraduate level by an ethnic minority student.

ELIGIBILITY:
Applicants must be members of The United Methodist Church and must be racial ethnic minority undergraduate students, junior or senior, who have an intention to pursue a career in religion journalism or mass communications and are enrolled in an accredited U.S. college or university.

FINANCIAL DATA:

Amount of support per award: $2,500.

Total amount of support: $2,500 per academic year.

NO. AWARDS: 1.

APPLICATION INFO:

Applicant must submit:
(1) an application form (completed and submitted electronically or printed and mailed);
(2) official transcripts from the current institution of higher education and any others attended. Transcripts should be mailed by the school directly to the address listed in the application packet;
(3) three letters of recommendation, one from the local church pastor or a denominational official, one from the chairperson of the department in which the applicant is majoring as an undergraduate student, and one from an employer or supervisor in a position to evaluate the applicant's communications skills;
(4) an essay (no more than 500 words) about the applicant's commitment to the Christian faith and interest in communications, and how the applicant sees the two intersecting in their life presently and in the future;
(5) three examples of journalistic work (audiovisual, electronic, print). If requested in writing, these materials will be returned after the committee has completed its selection and;
(6) a recent photograph, preferably head and shoulders, suitable for publicity use if awarded the scholarship.

Duration: One academic year.

Deadline: March 15 (postmarked).

PUBLICATIONS:

Application guidelines.

ADDRESS INQUIRIES TO:

Scholarships Coordinator
(See address above.)

*SPECIAL STIPULATIONS:

Candidates must be in their junior or senior year to qualify.

UNIVERSITIES CANADA [997]

350 Albert Street, Suite 1710
Ottawa ON K1R 1B1 Canada
(613) 563-1236
(844) 567-1237
Fax: (613) 563-9745
E-mail: awards@univcan.ca
Web Site: www.univcan.ca

FOUNDED: 1911

AREAS OF INTEREST:

Financial aid for disabled students.

NAME(S) OF PROGRAMS:

- **Mattinson Scholarship Program for Students with Disabilities**

TYPE:

Scholarships. These scholarships are applicable towards full-time studies for applicants entering the first year or already enrolled in a first Bachelor's-degree program.

PURPOSE:

To encourage Canadian students with permanent disabilities to pursue university studies with the ultimate objective of obtaining a first university degree.

LEGAL BASIS:

Nonprofit association.

ELIGIBILITY:

All candidates must be Canadian citizens or permanent residents who have lived in Canada for at least two years and be diagnosed with a documented permanent disability that is the primary disability for which they are applying.

Eligible applicants must have a minimum cumulative average of 80% (or equivalent) over the last three semesters of available marks. Nonacademic courses such as career- or personal development-related courses will not be considered.

All disciplines are eligible. The program must be of a minimum three-year duration.

GEOG. RESTRICTIONS: Canada.

FINANCIAL DATA:

Amount of support per award: $2,500 (CAN).

Total amount of support: Varies.

NO. AWARDS: Up to 4 scholarships, distributed as follows: 1 in physical disability; 1 in sensory disability; and 2 in any of the categories of physical disability, sensory disability, mental health disability and learning disability.

APPLICATION INFO:

Eligible applicants must provide:
(1) an official transcript of the last three terms of available marks; if applicant was not enrolled in school during this time, he or she must provide marks for the last three available terms;
(2) two signed reference letters with the references' original signatures (one from a teacher and one from a person familiar with their volunteer/community involvement and/or extracurricular activities; the reference letters must come from two separate individuals and must be typewritten on letterhead, signed and include the reference's contact information);
(3) a 250-word essay describing their volunteer/community involvement and/or extracurricular activities and their future goals;
(4) the AUCC form listing the list of activities related to applicant's volunteer/community involvement and/or extracurricular activities (page 2 of the nomination form);
(5) nominee e-mail address (on first page of nomination) and;
(6) the nomination form completed and signed by a representative of the nominee's university disabilities' center.

Note that a transcript will be considered acceptable only if it meets the following criteria:
(1) it is presented on the official paper of the institution and;
(2) it bears the appropriate signature(s) and/or seal of the institution.

Duration: One academic year. Renewable upon reapplication.

Deadline: Postmarked paper application must be sent to the Association no later than May 15. Applicant is responsible for ensuring that the post office postmarks his or her envelope by the due date.

PUBLICATIONS:

Program announcement.

ADDRESS INQUIRIES TO:

Natalie Lapierre, Program Officer
(See address above.)

UNIVERSITY OF CALIFORNIA [998]

President's Postdoctoral Fellowship Program
104 California Hall
UC Berkeley
Berkeley, CA 94720-1500
(510) 643-8235
E-mail: ppfpinfo@berkeley.edu
Web Site: ppfp.ucop.edu/info

FOUNDED: 1869

AREAS OF INTEREST:

Education and research.

NAME(S) OF PROGRAMS:

- **University of California President's Postdoctoral Fellowship Program**

TYPE:

Fellowships. Awarded for research conducted under faculty sponsorship on any one of the University of California's 10 campuses.

YEAR PROGRAM STARTED: 1984

PURPOSE:

To encourage outstanding women and minority Ph.D. recipients to pursue academic careers at the University of California; to offer research fellowships to all qualified candidates who are committed to university careers in research, teaching and service that will enhance the diversity of the academic community at the University of California.

LEGAL BASIS:

University.

ELIGIBILITY:

Applicants must be U.S. citizens or permanent residents and must hold or receive a Ph.D. from an accredited university. Applicants should expect to have earned their Ph.D. degree by June 30 of the year for which they are applying.

The program will prefer candidates who have research interests focusing on underserved populations and understanding issues of racial or gender inequalities.

The program also prefers candidates with a record of leadership or significant experience teaching and mentoring students from groups that have been historically underrepresented in higher education.

FINANCIAL DATA:

The award includes salary, health, vision and dental benefits, and up to $5,000 for research-related and program travel expenses.

Amount of support per award: Approximately $45,000 per fellow, depending upon the field and level of experience, plus benefits for self and dependents.

NO. MOST RECENT APPLICANTS: 633 for the year 2015-16.

NO. AWARDS: 30 for the year 2015-16.

APPLICATION INFO:

Application consists of curriculum vitae, research proposal, dissertation abstract, personal statement, writing sample, mentor support letter and thesis advisor letter.

Duration: Initially one academic year beginning July 1. Renewal for a second year will be granted upon demonstration of academic productivity and participation in program events.

Deadline: November 1. Announcement of awardees in the spring.

STAFF:

Kimberly M. Adkinson, Assistant Director
Sarah E. Yee, Program Assistant

ADDRESS INQUIRIES TO:
Kimberly M. Adkinson, Assistant Director
President's Postdoctoral Fellowship Program
(See address above.)

UNIVERSITY OF CALIFORNIA, LOS ANGELES [999]

Asian American Studies Center
3230 Campbell Hall
405 Hilgard Avenue, Box 951546
Los Angeles, CA 90095-1546
(310) 825-2974
Fax: (310) 206-9844
E-mail: dkyoo@ucla.edu
Web Site: www.aasc.ucla.edu

FOUNDED: 1969

AREAS OF INTEREST:
Asian American studies, policy research on Asian Americans, and arts and humanities on Asian Americans.

NAME(S) OF PROGRAMS:
- **Ethnic Studies Fellowships**

TYPE:
Awards/prizes; Conferences/seminars; Fellowships; Research grants; Scholarships; Visiting scholars; Work-study programs. Support for visiting scholars and researchers.

YEAR PROGRAM STARTED: 1969

PURPOSE:
To provide funding for studies in the field of Asian American arts, humanities, social sciences and applied research.

LEGAL BASIS:
University.

ELIGIBILITY:
Applicants must have the Ph.D. in place at the time Fellowship is awarded. UCLA faculty members are not eligible for support.

FINANCIAL DATA:
Visiting Scholars may use the funds to supplement sabbatical support, though the total available will not exceed the maximum stipend levels, and when combined with sabbatical funds may not exceed the candidate's current institutional salary.

Visiting Scholars will be paid through their home institutions and will be expected to continue their health benefits through that source; Visiting Researchers receive health benefits and will be paid directly by UCLA. Awardees may receive up to $4,000 in research support (through reimbursements of research expenses).

Amount of support per award: Maximum stipend of $32,000 to $35,000, contingent upon rank, experience and date of completion of terminal degree.

Total amount of support: Varies.

NO. MOST RECENT APPLICANTS: 30.

NO. AWARDS: 1.

APPLICATION INFO:
Contact the University.

Duration: Nine months.

Deadline: February 2016.

STAFF:
Melany Dela Cruz-Viesca, Assistant Director/IAC Coordinator

ADDRESS INQUIRIES TO:
Melany Dela Cruz-Viesca
Assistant Director/IAC Coordinator
Asian American Studies Center
(See address above.)

UNIVERSITY OF SOUTHERN CALIFORNIA

USC Graduate School
3601 Watt Way, GFS 315
Los Angeles, CA 90089-1695
(213) 740-9033
Fax: (213) 740-9048
E-mail: gradfllw@usc.edu
Web Site: www.usc.edu/schools/GraduateSchool/

TYPE:
Fellowships. Merit fellowships. Fellowships will be combined with matching funds from individual schools to provide four or more years of funding toward the Ph.D.

See entry 1742 for full listing.

VIRGINIA POLYTECHNIC INSTITUTE AND STATE UNIVERSITY [1000]

MAOP Office
110 Femoyer Hall
Blacksburg, VA 24061
(540) 231-5023
Fax: (540) 231-2618
E-mail: maop@vt.edu
Web Site: www.maop.vt.edu

AREAS OF INTEREST:
Graduate programs particularly in science, math and technology.

NAME(S) OF PROGRAMS:
- **Multicultural Academic Opportunity Graduate Student Scholars Program**

TYPE:
Assistantships; Fellowships; Internships; Scholarships. The program assists with graduate school financing in exchange for assistance to MAOP administration. Graduate students assist with programming implementation such as mentoring to undergraduate students.

YEAR PROGRAM STARTED: 1973

PURPOSE:
To improve professional and educational opportunities for minority students in architecture, planning, public and international affairs, and landscape architecture.

ELIGIBILITY:
Grade point average of 3.0 during the last two years of undergraduate school is required along with an essay focusing upon their commitment to academic diversity at Virginia Tech and admission to the Graduate School. Scholars must maintain a 3.0 grade point average to remain qualified for the program.

FINANCIAL DATA:
Amount of support per award: Varies.

Total amount of support: Varies.

APPLICATION INFO:
Contact the Institute.

Duration: One year. Renewable.

Deadline: April 1.

ADDRESS INQUIRIES TO:
Dr. Jody Thompson-Marshall
Director, MAOP Office
(See address above.)

WIDENER MEMORIAL FOUNDATION IN AID OF HANDICAPPED CHILDREN [1001]

4060 Butler Pike
Suite 225
Plymouth Meeting, PA 19462
(610) 825-8900
Fax: (610) 825-8904
E-mail: jhagerty@erdixon.com

FOUNDED: 1912

AREAS OF INTEREST:
Handicapped children and education.

TYPE:
Capital grants.

PURPOSE:
To benefit orthopedically handicapped children.

LEGAL BASIS:
Special interest foundation.

ELIGIBILITY:
Applicants must be 501(c)(3) organizations that are not classified as private foundations. Organizations must benefit orthopedically handicapped children in some way.

GEOG. RESTRICTIONS: Greater Delaware Valley area (including the city of Philadelphia, Pennsylvania), and Bucks, Burlington, Camden, Chester, Delaware, Gloucester, Montgomery and Philadelphia counties.

FINANCIAL DATA:
Amount of support per award: Varies.

Total amount of support: Approximately $900,000 to $1,000,000 annually.

NO. MOST RECENT APPLICANTS: 26.

NO. AWARDS: 17.

APPLICATION INFO:
Applicant should include a letter describing the purpose for which grant would be used, persons who would benefit from the activity for which the grant is requested, specifically orthopedically handicapped children, and statements showing that the organization is exempt under 501(c)(3) of the Internal Revenue Code and also not classified as a private foundation.

Duration: Typically one year. Must reapply.

Deadline: May 15 and October 15. Board meets in May or June and November to approve grant requests.

IRS I.D.: 23-6267223

OFFICERS:
Edith D. Miller, President
Peter M. Mattoon, Esq., Vice President and Trustee
Edith R. Dixon, Treasurer and Trustee
George W. Dixon, Secretary
Bruce L. Castor, Esq., Trustee
Michael Clancy, M.D., Trustee
Mark S. DePillis, Esq., Trustee
Linda Grobman, Ed.D., Trustee
John Keleher, Trustee

ADDRESS INQUIRIES TO:
Edith D. Miller, President
P.O. Box 178
Lafayette Hill, PA 19444-0178

African-American

AFRICAN AMERICAN FUND OF NEW JERSEY [1002]

132 South Harrison Street
East Orange, NJ 07018
(908) 561-0123
Fax: (908) 561-4710
E-mail: lclark@aafnj.org
Web Site: www.aafnj.org

FOUNDED: 1980

AREAS OF INTEREST:
Primarily African-American communities in the state of New Jersey.

TYPE:
Conferences/seminars; Demonstration grants; General operating grants; Project/program grants; Seed money grants; Training grants. The African American Fund of New Jersey is a philanthropic organization that funds community-based agencies and programs in and for, but not limited to, African-American communities in the state of New Jersey.

The Fund supports social programs that are important to its donors. Its goal is to provide more extensive educational programs that cater to all age groups. The focus of the grants is to agencies that provide services in the following areas: Early Childhood and Youth Education, Healthcare, Teen Pregnancy Prevention, Substance Abuse, Aid to the Homeless, Adult Literacy, Child Abuse Prevention, AIDS Education, Recreation, Arts and Culture and Leadership Development.

YEAR PROGRAM STARTED: 1980

PURPOSE:
To develop and perpetuate the empowerment of the African-American community through fund-raising and volunteerism for the purpose of Black philanthropy.

LEGAL BASIS:
Private 501(c)(3).

ELIGIBILITY:
Applicants may be any 501(c)(3) nonprofit, tax-exempt organization, agency or community-based organization operating in the state of New Jersey.

GEOG. RESTRICTIONS: New Jersey.

FINANCIAL DATA:
Amount of support per award: $500 to $5,000.

Total amount of support: $60,000 to $100,000.

NO. MOST RECENT APPLICANTS: 60.

NO. AWARDS: 20.

APPLICATION INFO:
Request for Proposal (RFP) application required. Forms must be typed and complete. Information and/or technical assistance is available by contacting AAFNJ State Office at the address above.

Duration: One year.

Deadline: Letter of Intent: July; Request for Proposal: September.

PUBLICATIONS:
Annual report.

IRS I.D.: 22-2349446

BOARD OF DIRECTORS AND OFFICERS:
Sondra Clark, President and Chief Executive Officer
Robert T. Pickett, Chairperson
Hon. Charles Craig, Treasurer/Secretary

ADDRESS INQUIRIES TO:
Lisa Clark, Grants Coordinator
(See address above.)

CONGRESSIONAL BLACK CAUCUS FOUNDATION, INC. [1003]

1720 Massachusetts Avenue, N.W.
Washington, DC 20036
(202) 263-2800
Fax: (202) 263-0846
E-mail: fellowships@cbcfinc.org
Web Site: www.cbcfinc.org

FOUNDED: 1976

AREAS OF INTEREST:
Health policies and politics.

NAME(S) OF PROGRAMS:
- **The Louis Stokes Urban Health Policy Fellows Program**

TYPE:
Fellowships. The Louis Stokes Urban Health Policy Fellows Program is a 20-month policy training and leadership development program that targets early to mid-level policy professionals who are committed to eliminating health disparities nationally and globally. Fellows receive health policy training while working in a CBC Member's office as well as on a congressional committee. They spend 10 months working in a congressional Member's office and the remaining 10 months working on a congressional committee that focuses on health-related issues.

The program also includes educational enrichment opportunities through seminars on policy and politics.

YEAR PROGRAM STARTED: 2003

PURPOSE:
To increase the pool of qualified minority health policy professionals who are committed to eliminating health disparities in the U.S. and abroad.

ELIGIBILITY:
Applicants must be U.S. citizens or persons permitted to work in the U.S. for the duration of the program. Applicants must meet the following additional requirements:
(1) have a graduate or professional degree in a health-related field (behavioral sciences, social sciences, biological sciences and health professions) from an accredited institution completed prior to the fellowship start date;
(2) have a familiarity with the federal legislative process, Congress and the Congressional Black Caucus (CBC) and;
(3) have a demonstrated interest in public policy and a commitment to creating and implementing policy to improve the living conditions for underserved and underrepresented individuals.

Selection for the program is based on a combination of the following criteria:
(1) record of academic and professional achievement and;
(2) evidence of leadership skills and the potential for further growth.

FINANCIAL DATA:
Amount of support per award: $40,000 annual stipend.

NO. AWARDS: 2.

APPLICATION INFO:
Complete application details and guidelines are available on the web site.

Duration: 20 months.

ADDRESS INQUIRIES TO:
See e-mail address above.

*SPECIAL STIPULATIONS:
All Fellows must be able to participate for the full term of the program. If selected, applicants are expected to complete all professional qualifying exams. Participants must reside in or relocate to the Washington, DC, metropolitan area.

CONGRESSIONAL BLACK CAUCUS FOUNDATION, INC. [1004]

1720 Massachusetts Avenue, N.W.
Washington, DC 20036
(202) 263-2800
Fax: (202) 263-0846
E-mail: scholarships@cbcfinc.org
Web Site: www.cbcfinc.org

FOUNDED: 1976

NAME(S) OF PROGRAMS:
- **CBC Spouses-Heineken USA Performing Arts Scholarship**
- **CBC Spouses Visual Arts Scholarship**

TYPE:
Scholarships. CBC Spouses-Heineken USA Performing Arts Scholarship, developed in honor of the late Curtis Mayfield, is intended to ensure that students pursuing a career in the performing arts receive the financial assistance to achieve their goals.

CBC Spouses Visual Arts Scholarship was established for students who are pursuing a career in the visual arts.

PURPOSE:
To encourage education in the performing and visual arts among minority students.

ELIGIBILITY:
Applicant must:
(1) be a U.S. citizen or permanent U.S. resident;
(2) be preparing to pursue an undergraduate degree full-time, or be a current full-time student in good academic standing at a U.S. accredited college or university;
(3) have a minimum 2.5 grade point average and;
(4) exhibit leadership ability and participate in community service activities.

The scholarships do not have a residency requirement.

GEOG. RESTRICTIONS: United States.

FINANCIAL DATA:
Amount of support per award: $3,000.

Total amount of support: Up to $60,000.

NO. AWARDS: Up to 10 per scholarship annually.

APPLICATION INFO:
The Foundation utilizes an online application process.

Duration: One year. Must reapply.

Deadline: Late April to early May.

ADDRESS INQUIRIES TO:
Leadership Institute for Public Service
(See address or e-mail above.)

CONGRESSIONAL BLACK CAUCUS FOUNDATION, INC. [1005]

1720 Massachusetts Avenue, N.W.
Washington, DC 20036
(202) 263-2800
Fax: (202) 263-0846
E-mail: scholarships@cbcfinc.org
Web Site: www.cbcfinc.org

FOUNDED: 1976

AREAS OF INTEREST:
Promoting educational and leadership opportunities for African Americans.

NAME(S) OF PROGRAMS:
- **CBCS General Mills Health Scholarship**
- **CBC Spouses Education Scholarship**

TYPE:
Scholarships. The CBCS General Mills Health Scholarship is intended to increase the number of minority students pursuing degrees in the fields of medicine, engineering, technology, nutrition and other health-related professions.

The CBC Spouses Education Scholarship is a national program that awards scholarships to academically talented and highly motivated students who intend to pursue full-time undergraduate, graduate or doctoral degrees.

PURPOSE:
To support students who are pursuing majors related to health; to provide support to students, particularly African-Americans, who exhibit leadership skills, are involved in their community, and are pursuing higher education.

LEGAL BASIS:
Nonpartisan, nonprofit foundation.

ELIGIBILITY:
CBCS General Mills Health Scholarship is for students pursuing career in a health profession, who must reside or attend school in district represented by CBC member.

CBC Spouses Education Scholarship is for undergraduate or graduate students residing or attending school in district of CBC member.

FINANCIAL DATA:
Amount of support per award: CBCS General Mills Health Scholarship: $2,000; CBC Spouses Education Scholarship: Varies.

Total amount of support: Varies.

NO. AWARDS: CBCS General Mills Health Scholarship: 45 to 50; CBC Spouses Education Scholarship: Varies.

APPLICATION INFO:
CBCS General Mills Health Scholarship requires a paper application, which is available through a link on the Foundation web site.

CBC Spouses Education Scholarship: The Foundation utilizes an online application process.

Duration: One year. Must reapply.

Deadline: CBCS General Mills Health Scholarship: February 28. CBC Spouses Education Scholarship: End of May.

PUBLICATIONS:
Policy review; annual report.

IRS I.D.: 52-1160561

ADDRESS INQUIRIES TO:
Leadership Institute for Public Service
(See address or e-mail above.)

CONGRESSIONAL BLACK CAUCUS FOUNDATION, INC. [1006]

1720 Massachusetts Avenue, N.W.
Washington, DC 20036
(202) 263-2800
Fax: (202) 263-0846
E-mail: info@cbcfinc.org
internships@cbcfinc.org
Web Site: www.cbcfinc.org

AREAS OF INTEREST:
Promoting educational and leadership opportunities for African Americans.

NAME(S) OF PROGRAMS:
- **The CBCF Congressional Fellows Program**
- **The CBCF Congressional Internship Program**

TYPE:
Fellowships; Internships. The CBCF Congressional Fellows Program helps participants gain invaluable experience as they assist in the development of legislation and public policy initiatives while working as congressional staff for a year. This program targets early career policy professionals who have completed a professional and/or graduate degree and have demonstrated commitment to improving the lives and services for individuals living in underserved communities. Fellows work on Capitol Hill in the office of a Congressional Black Caucus member.

The CBCF Congressional Internship Program provides undergraduate students with an in-depth orientation to Capitol Hill and the legislative process through actual work experience in the offices of Congressional Black Caucus Members. In this way interns prepare to become decision makers in the policymaking process.

PURPOSE:
To increase the number of African Americans on congressional committees and subcommittees by providing students the opportunity to participate in all aspects of the legislative process.

LEGAL BASIS:
Nonpartisan, nonprofit foundation.

ELIGIBILITY:
Fellows Program applicants must have completed graduate coursework. Internship Program applicants must be college undergraduates.

FINANCIAL DATA:
Fellows are responsible for their own travel arrangements, expenses and housing accommodations. CBCF provides health and dental insurance coverage during term of fellowship. Interns receive a stipend and housing at a local university.

Amount of support per award: Fellows Program: $40,000 annual stipend; Internship Program: $3,000 stipend.

Total amount of support: Varies.

NO. AWARDS: 6 to 9 fellowships per year.

APPLICATION INFO:
Submit a completed application with detailed resume, certificate of academic standing and/or faculty certification, a writing sample of up to 10 pages, three letters of recommendation, one of which must be from the dean, department chairperson, faculty or advisor and an official transcript from each school attended.

Duration: Fellowships: 20 months; Internships: Nine weeks during the Summer.

Deadline: April.

IRS I.D.: 52-1160561

ADDRESS INQUIRIES TO:
Leadership Institute for Public Service
(See address above.)

FREDERICK DOUGLASS INSTITUTE FOR AFRICAN AND AFRICAN-AMERICAN STUDIES

311 Morey Hall
University of Rochester
P.O. Box 270440
Rochester, NY 14627-0440
(585) 276-5744
Fax: (585) 256-2594
E-mail: FDI@rochester.edu
Web Site: www.sas.rochester.edu/aas

TYPE:
Awards/prizes; Conferences/seminars; Fellowships.

See entry 1494 for full listing.

FLORIDA DEPARTMENT OF EDUCATION [1007]

Office of Student Financial Assistance
325 West Gaines Street, Suite 1314
Tallahassee, FL 32399-0400
(888) 827-2004
Fax: (850) 487-1809
E-mail: osfa@fldoe.org
Web Site: www.FloridaStudentFinancialAid.org/SSFAD/home/uamain.htm

NAME(S) OF PROGRAMS:
- **Rosewood Family Scholarship Program**

TYPE:
Scholarships. Financial assistance for descendants of the Rosewood family affected by the incidents of January 1923, to attend a state university, public community college or public postsecondary vocational-technical school.

PURPOSE:
To encourage and assist minority students to continue on to higher education.

LEGAL BASIS:
Governmental agency.

ELIGIBILITY:
To receive funding, the applying student must meet the following initial eligibility requirements:
(1) not owe a repayment or be in default under any state or federal grant, loan or scholarship program unless satisfactory arrangements to repay have been made;
(2) not have previously received a Baccalaureate degree;
(3) enroll full-time at an eligible participating postsecondary institution in a program of study leading to an undergraduate degree, a certificate or a diploma and;
(4) must provide copies of documents of ancestry by April 1; mail copies to Florida Department of Education, Office of Student Financial Assistance, State Scholarship and Grant Programs.

FINANCIAL DATA:
Amount of support per award: Varies.

Total amount of support: Varies.

NO. AWARDS: Up to 50.

APPLICATION INFO:
Detailed program information can be found on the web site.

Duration: Renewable for 100% of student's programs.

Deadline: April 1 for submitting a fully completed, error-free Florida Financial Aid Application. Florida residents must complete and submit the Free Application for Federal Student Aid (FAFSA) online in time to be processed error-free by the U.S. Department of Education on or before May 15. Florida nonresidents must complete and submit the FAFSA in time to receive the Student Aid Report (SAR) from the processor and postmark a copy of the SAR to OSFA by May 15.

ADDRESS INQUIRIES TO:
State Scholarship and Grant Programs
(See address above.)

THE JACK AND JILL OF AMERICA FOUNDATION [1008]

1930 17th Street, N.W.
Washington, DC 20009-6207
(202) 232-5290
Fax: (202) 232-1747
E-mail: administration@jackandjillfoundation.org
Web Site: www.jackandjillfoundation.org

FOUNDED: 1968

AREAS OF INTEREST:
African American families, education, and health and wellness.

CONSULTING OR VOLUNTEER SERVICES:
Volunteer services.

NAME(S) OF PROGRAMS:
- **National Community Investment**
- **Reading Corner Literacy Grant**
- **Teen Community Service Award**

TYPE:
Project/program grants; Scholarships. Volunteer opportunities.

YEAR PROGRAM STARTED: 1968

PURPOSE:
To influence the ongoing positive development of children.

LEGAL BASIS:
Public charity.

ELIGIBILITY:
National Community Investment Grant: Grants are made to 501(c)(3), 501(c)(4) and IRS charitable organizations.

GEOG. RESTRICTIONS: United States.

FINANCIAL DATA:
Amount of support per award: $2,000 to $25,000.

Total amount of support: Varies.

NO. MOST RECENT APPLICANTS: 500.

NO. AWARDS: Varies.

APPLICATION INFO:
Applicant should carefully read the Information for Grant Applicants on the Foundation web site before submitting an application on the designated form. Furthermore, answers on the application coversheet must be given in the space provided; no additional sheets can be attached. Type the application (using at least 10-point type). Applications may not be faxed. All signatures should be signed in blue ink. A complete application consists of an application coversheet along with the following materials:
(1) proposal;
(2) copy of IRS 501(c)(3) letter or documentation of 501(c)(4) status, whichever is applicable;
(3) most recent audited income statement or 990 tax return, if 501(c)(3) organization, or most recent year-end statement of income and expenses, if 501(c)(4) organization and;
(4) brief resume or bio of the organization's Project Director and other relevant supporting material.

Duration: One year.

Deadline: June 1.

PUBLICATIONS:
Newsletter; annual report; application guidelines.

IRS I.D.: 51-0224656

STAFF:
Pier A.H. Blake, Executive Director

ADDRESS INQUIRIES TO:
Pier A.H. Blake, Executive Director
(See address above.)

THE NAACP LEGAL DEFENSE AND EDUCATIONAL FUND, INC. [1009]

40 Rector Street
5th Floor
New York, NY 10006
(212) 965-2225
Fax: (212) 226-7592
E-mail: scholarships@naacpldf.org
mcorro@naacpldf.org
Web Site: www.naacpldf.org/scholarships

FOUNDED: 1964

AREAS OF INTEREST:
Financial assistance for African-American undergraduates and for law students with a demonstrable interest in civil rights.

NAME(S) OF PROGRAMS:
- **LDF Herbert Lehman Education Fund Scholarship Program**
- **LDF Earl Warren Legal Training Program**

TYPE:
Awards/prizes; Grants-in-aid; Internships; Scholarships. LDF Herbert Lehman Education Fund Scholarship Program: Scholarships for African-American high school seniors, high school graduates and college freshmen to attend four-year accredited colleges and universities.

LDF Earl Warren Legal Training Program: Scholarships for law students to attend three-year accredited law schools.

YEAR PROGRAM STARTED: 1964

PURPOSE:
To encourage students to continue the work of the Legal Defense Fund; to encourage young people to be involved in public service; to increase the presence of African-American students in colleges, universities and law schools in the U.S.

LEGAL BASIS:
501(c)(3) corporation.

ELIGIBILITY:
Applicants must be U.S. citizens. Candidates must have outstanding potential evidenced by their recommendations, high school academic records, test scores and essays. They must understand their educational goals and academic abilities. Candidates should have a clear commitment to working in the public service as exemplified by their community and school involvements. Candidates should have exceptional leadership potential with an ability to work well in diverse settings.

Law students already enrolled in law school are not eligible to apply for the LDF Earl Warren Legal Training Program.

GEOG. RESTRICTIONS: United States.

FINANCIAL DATA:
Amount of support per award: LDF Herbert Lehman Education Fund Scholarship Program: $3,000 to $5,000 per year; LDF Earl Warren Legal Training Program: Up to $10,000 per year.

NO. MOST RECENT APPLICANTS: Over 2,000.

NO. AWARDS: 50 to 100 annually.

APPLICATION INFO:
Applications will be available for online submission by November 1 of each year. Applicants who do not meet the basic criteria for eligibility or do not satisfy program requirements for the completion of applications will not be considered.

Duration: Up to four years depending upon availability of funds. Renewable during undergraduate career, if student remains in good standing with their college or university.

Deadline: May 1 for the Lehman Scholarship and June 1 for the Warren Legal Training Program. Notification normally takes place at the end of July, prior to the fall semester of the student's first academic year.

STAFF:
Maruja Corro, Program Assistant

ADDRESS INQUIRIES TO:
Maruja Corro, Program Assistant
(See address above.)

NATIONAL ASSOCIATION FOR EQUAL OPPORTUNITY IN HIGHER EDUCATION (NAFEO) [1010]

209 Third Street, S.E.
Washington, DC 20003
(202) 552-3300
Fax: (202) 552-3330
E-mail: admin@nafeo.org
Web Site: www.nafeointernships.net

FOUNDED: 1969

AREAS OF INTEREST:
Equal opportunity in higher education.

NAME(S) OF PROGRAMS:
- **NAFEO Internship Program**

TYPE:
Internships. NAFEO Internship Program offers full-time paid internships in the summer, spring and fall.

ELIGIBILITY:
Preference will be given to students enrolled in undergraduate or graduate programs at historically or predominantly black colleges and universities. A grade point average of 3.0 or above on a 4.0 scale is required. (Some internships require U.S. citizenship.)

FINANCIAL DATA:
Stipends are paid according to a student's classification at the time of application. Round-trip travel: Students selected for summer internships only who reside outside of the Washington, DC, metropolitan area will receive a travel allowance. A housing

stipend will be provided. Local travel: Interns receive an allowance to subsidize daily travel to and from their work assignments.

Amount of support per award: Undergraduate students, $11 per hour; graduate students, $13 per hour.

NO. AWARDS: Approximately 50.

APPLICATION INFO:
Application may be made online. Application requirements are as follows:
(1) U.S. citizen;
(2) complete application;
(3) current resume;
(4) unofficial transcript - by request only;
(5) official transcript - by request only and;
(6) two completed faculty recommendation forms - by request only.

In conjunction with NAFEO member institutions, NAFEO staff reviews applications to ensure that applicants are eligible and that the applications are complete. NAFEO staff then refers applications to employing agencies based on the academic disciplines they are seeking. Employing agencies review the applications, conduct interviews if necessary, and make all final selections.

Selected students will be notified by NAFEO staff and provided with an official internship offer.

Duration: Summer: 10 weeks; Fall and spring: 15 weeks.

Deadline: Varies.

ADDRESS INQUIRIES TO:
Internship Coordinator
(See address above.)

THE NATIONAL ASSOCIATION OF BLACK SOCIAL WORKERS [1011]

2305 Martin Luther King Jr. Avenue, S.E.
Washington, DC 20020
(202) 678-4570
Fax: (202) 678-4572
E-mail: officedirector@nabsw.org
Web Site: www.nabsw.org

FOUNDED: 1968

AREAS OF INTEREST:
Social work and community advocacy.

NAME(S) OF PROGRAMS:

- **Emma and Meloid Algood Tuition Scholarship (Undergraduate)**
- **Dr. Joyce Beckett Scholarship**
- **Selena Danette Brown Book Scholarship**
- **Stella Browne Book Scholarship**
- **Dr.Theresa L. Roberts Book Scholarship**
- **Cenie Jomo Williams Tuition Scholarship**

TYPE:
Scholarships.

YEAR PROGRAM STARTED: 1968

PURPOSE:
To promote the welfare, survival and liberation of communities of African ancestry.

LEGAL BASIS:
Nonprofit membership association.

ELIGIBILITY:
Student must:
(1) be an active paid member of NABSW;
(2) have a 2.5 grade point average on a 4.0 scale;
(3) express research interest in African Americans or those of African ancestry and;
(4) be enrolled for full-time study at an accredited U.S. social work program for the semester that the award will be granted.

GEOG. RESTRICTIONS: United States.

FINANCIAL DATA:
Amount of support per award: $250 to $2,000.

Total amount of support: Varies.

NO. AWARDS: Varies.

APPLICATION INFO:
Scholarship applications can be obtained from the National Office.

Duration: One-time award. May reapply for the Emma and Meloid Algood Tuition Scholarship.

Deadline: February 15.

PUBLICATIONS:
Quarterly newsletters.

IRS I.D.: 13-2779773

ADDRESS INQUIRIES TO:
Melanie Bryant, National Office Director
(See address above.)

NATIONAL BLACK MBA ASSOCIATION [1012]

400 West Peachtree Street, N.W.
Suite 203
Atlanta, GA 30308
(404) 260-5444
E-mail: scholarship@nbmbaa.org
Web Site: www.nbmbaa.org

AREAS OF INTEREST:
The economic and intellectual wealth of the black community.

NAME(S) OF PROGRAMS:

- **NBMBAA Undergraduate Scholarship Program**

TYPE:
Scholarships.

PURPOSE:
To help create economic and intellectual wealth for the Black community; to identify and increase the pool of Black talent for business, public, private and nonprofit sectors.

ELIGIBILITY:
Applicant must:
(1) be a student in their first, second, third or fourth year enrolled full-time at an accredited college or university at the time of award (September);
(2) be a financially active member of the National Black MBA Association;
(3) be a U.S. or Canadian citizen;
(4) submit an essay on provided topic;
(5) submit a current resume;
(6) have a grade point average of 3.0 or above;
(7) demonstrate academic excellence;
(8) demonstrate exceptional leadership potential;
(9) be actively involved in their local communities through service to others and;
(10) be recommended by faculty advisor.

GEOG. RESTRICTIONS: United States and Canada.

FINANCIAL DATA:
Amount of support per award: Up to $5,000 for the 2017-18 academic year.

APPLICATION INFO:
Applicant is strongly advised to contact the Association at the e-mail address above for up-to-date details.

The following application materials must be submitted:
(1) application (must be completed online);
(2) a 500-word essay completed on the selected topic (submitted online only);
(3) a current resume no more than two pages long;
(4) a copy uploaded of applicant's most recent official transcript(s) and;
(5) a professional headshot (photograph) in jpeg format (image should be at least 1024 x 768).

ADDRESS INQUIRIES TO:
See e-mail address above.

*SPECIAL STIPULATIONS:
Scholarship recipients are required to agree to participate in limited public relations activities.

NATIONAL BLACK NURSES ASSOCIATION, INC.

8630 Fenton Street
Suite 330
Silver Spring, MD 20910
(301) 589-3200
Fax: (301) 589-3223
E-mail: info@nbna.org
Web Site: www.nbna.org

TYPE:
Scholarships.

See entry 2413 for full listing.

NATIONAL SOCIETY OF BLACK ENGINEERS

205 Daingerfield Road
Alexandria, VA 22314
(703) 549-2207
Fax: (703) 683-5312
E-mail: scholarships@nsbe.org
Web Site: www.nsbe.org

TYPE:
Awards/prizes; Scholarships. The Society offers a variety of NSBE and corporate-sponsored scholarship and award opportunities to its precollege, collegiate undergraduate and graduate student members as well as technical professional members.

See entry 1668 for full listing.

NEED [1013]

The Law and Finance Building
429 Fourth Avenue, 20th Floor
Pittsburgh, PA 15219
(412) 566-2760
Fax: (412) 471-6643
E-mail: info@needld.org
Web Site: www.needld.org

FOUNDED: 1963

AREAS OF INTEREST:
Higher education, college access services.

CONSULTING OR VOLUNTEER SERVICES:
Counseling for postsecondary education; assistance to students and parents needing help with the completion of financial aid forms; mentoring services.

NAME(S) OF PROGRAMS:

- **Access to College and Career Education (ACE) Program**
- **African American Male Mentoring Initiative (AAMMI)**

- **Future NEED Scholars**
- **The NEED HBCU (Historically Black Colleges and Universities) Educational Tour**
- **Science Technology Engineering and Math (STEM) Female Mentoring Program**
- **Unmet NEED Grants and Scholarships**

TYPE:
Internships; Matching gifts; Scholarships. Supplemental grants for postsecondary education at colleges and business, trade and technical schools.

YEAR PROGRAM STARTED: 1963

PURPOSE:
To provide career and college access services which empower youth from the Pittsburgh region to aspire to, learn about, prepare for, and complete higher education.

LEGAL BASIS:
Incorporated nonprofit, tax-exempt.

ELIGIBILITY:
Applicant must be African American, with a high school diploma or GED, with a 3.0 grade point average, resident in Allegheny, Armstrong, Beaver, Butler, Fayette, Greene, Lawrence, Washington or Westmoreland counties in Pennsylvania and enrolled in or planning to enroll in a state-approved program.

GEOG. RESTRICTIONS: Allegheny, Armstrong, Beaver, Butler, Fayette, Greene, Lawrence, Washington and Westmoreland counties, Pennsylvania.

FINANCIAL DATA:
Amount of support per award: $1,000 to $1,500.

Total amount of support: $777,304 for the 2013-14 academic year.

NO. MOST RECENT APPLICANTS: 1,051 for the year 2014-15.

NO. AWARDS: 607 for the 2014-15 academic year.

APPLICATION INFO:
Applicant must submit:
(1) NEED application;
(2) high school, college or school transcript (whichever is most recent) and;
(3) photo.

Duration: Academic year. May reapply in subsequent years.

Deadline: May 31.

PUBLICATIONS:
Annual report.

OFFICERS:
TiAnda Blount, Chairperson of the Board

ADDRESS INQUIRIES TO:
Student Services Department
(See address above.)

SACHS FOUNDATION [1014]

90 South Cascade Avenue
Suite 1410
Colorado Springs, CO 80903
(719) 633-2353
Fax: (719) 633-3663
E-mail: lisa@sachsfoundation.org
Web Site: sachsfoundation.org

FOUNDED: 1931

AREAS OF INTEREST:
Education.

NAME(S) OF PROGRAMS:
- **Financial Aid for Education of Black Residents of Colorado**

TYPE:
Grants-in-aid; Scholarships.

YEAR PROGRAM STARTED: 1931

PURPOSE:
To promote education of Black residents of Colorado.

LEGAL BASIS:
Private foundation.

ELIGIBILITY:
Applicants must be U.S. citizens, Black, residents of the state of Colorado for five or more years and high school seniors with about a 3.0 grade point average or higher, on a 4.0 scale, depending on the number of applications. Awardees may attend any accredited college or university.

GEOG. RESTRICTIONS: Colorado.

FINANCIAL DATA:
Amount of support per award: $6,000 maximum per annum for undergraduates; $7,000 for graduate grants.

Total amount of support: Varies.

NO. MOST RECENT APPLICANTS: 400.

NO. AWARDS: 40 new for the year 2014.

APPLICATION INFO:
Application forms are only available online.

Duration: Four years for undergraduate and some graduate degrees, if requirements are met.

Deadline: March 15.

PUBLICATIONS:
Annual report; other printed materials available upon written request.

OFFICERS AND DIRECTORS:
Craig S. Ralston, President
Lisa M. Harris, Secretary/Treasurer
Wilton Cogswell, III, Director

TRUSTEE:
Wilton Cogswell, III
Thomas James

ADDRESS INQUIRIES TO:
Lisa M. Harris, Secretary/Treasurer
(See address above.)

*SPECIAL STIPULATIONS:
Must be Black Colorado resident for five years.

THE SCHOMBURG CENTER FOR RESEARCH IN BLACK CULTURE

515 Malcolm X Boulevard
New York, NY 10037-1801
(212) 491-2228
E-mail: sir@nypl.org
Web Site: schomburgcenter.org/scholarsinresidenceprogram

TYPE:
Fellowships. Awarded to scholars and professionals whose research in the Black experience can benefit from extended access to the Center's collections. Seminars, colloquia, forums, symposia and conferences complement the residency program.

See entry 387 for full listing.

UNITED NEGRO COLLEGE FUND (UNCF) [1015]

1805 Seventh Street, N.W.
Washington, DC 20001
(800) 331-2244
(202) 810-0258
E-mail: scholarships@uncf.org
Web Site: www.uncf.org

FOUNDED: 1944

TYPE:
Fellowships; Internships; Scholarships; Technical assistance. The Fund, since its founding, has raised money for 37 private, historically Black colleges and universities.

Faculty fellowship programs make it possible for hundreds of instructors to earn doctoral degrees.

Mentoring and internship opportunities are provided for hundreds of UNCF students.

Scholarships are offered to a pool of more than 60,000 talented students attending UNCF colleges and universities. The Fund oversees more than 450 scholarship programs in the following general categories:
(1) geographically based scholarships;
(2) scholarships based on academic major;
(3) scholarships based on merit and need and;
(4) financial aid for graduate study.

PURPOSE:
To provide low-cost quality education in an environment that enables students to excel.

FINANCIAL DATA:
Amount of support per award: Scholarships: $500 to $10,000.

APPLICATION INFO:
Contact the Fund for detailed information.

OFFICERS:
Michael L. Lomax, Ph.D, President and Chief Executive Officer

ADDRESS INQUIRIES TO:
Kimberly Hall, Director of Donor Relations
(See address above.)

Native American

AMERICAN INDIAN COLLEGE FUND [1016]

8333 Greenwood Boulevard
Denver, CO 80221
(303) 426-8900
Fax: (303) 426-1200
E-mail: scholarships@collegefund.org
Web Site: collegefund.org

FOUNDED: 1989

AREAS OF INTEREST:
Scholarship funding for Native American and Alaska Native students.

NAME(S) OF PROGRAMS:
- **Full Circle Scholarship Program**
- **TCU Scholarship Program**

TYPE:
Scholarships.

YEAR PROGRAM STARTED: 1989

PURPOSE:
To educate the mind and spirit of Native American communities by providing undergraduate and graduate Native student scholarships and programmatic support for the nation's 34 accredited tribal colleges and

universities to provide access to an affordable, quality higher education while preserving Native cultures and languages; to make scholarships available to undergraduate and graduate Native students at any accredited public or private (nonprofit) college.

ELIGIBILITY:
Minimum requirements for all American Indian College Fund Full Circle Scholarships include:
(1) U.S. citizenship;
(2) enrollment full-time in an accredited tribal, public or private (nonprofit) college or university;
(3) ability to trace Indian ancestry; registered as a member of a federal- or state-recognized tribe, or a descendant of at least one grandparent or parent who is an enrolled tribal member; Alaska Natives may use Native Corporation membership;
(4) minimum grade point average of 2.0 mandatory (many Full Circle Scholarships funded by Fund's partners are more competitive) and;
(5) submission of a completed online application.

Eligible organizations must be 501(c)(3) not-for-profit. No grants are made to religious organizations.

GEOG. RESTRICTIONS: United States.

FINANCIAL DATA:
Amount of support per award: Scholarships: $1,000 to $18,000 per year.

APPLICATION INFO:
Guidelines and application form are available on the web site.

Deadline: Applications accepted January 1 to May 31 each year.

ADDRESS INQUIRIES TO:
See e-mail address above.

AMERICAN INDIAN GRADUATE CENTER [1017]

3701 San Mateo Boulevard, N.E.
Suite 200
Albuquerque, NM 87110
(505) 881-4584
Fax: (505) 884-0427
E-mail: fellowships@aigcs.org
Web Site: www.aigcs.org

FOUNDED: 1969

AREAS OF INTEREST:
Graduate and undergraduate-level education in any field.

NAME(S) OF PROGRAMS:
- **Fellowships for American Indians or Alaskan Natives**

TYPE:
Fellowships; Grants-in-aid; Scholarships. Grants on an academic year basis. Summer funding available to continuing students only; these are students who are currently in the fellowship program.

YEAR PROGRAM STARTED: 1969

PURPOSE:
To help open doors to graduate education and help tribes obtain the educated professionals they need to become more self-sufficient and exercise their rights to self-determination.

LEGAL BASIS:
IRS status 501(c)(3), tax-exempt, incorporated in New Mexico.

ELIGIBILITY:
An applicant must be an enrolled member of a U.S. federally recognized American Indian tribe or Alaska Native group, or possess one-fourth degree Indian blood from a federally recognized tribe. Applicant must be pursuing a Master's, Doctorate or professional degree as a full-time graduate student at an accredited graduate school in the U.S. and must be in financial need. They must submit an essay as described in the application packet. Applicants must apply for federal financial and campus-based aid at the financial aid office of the university they plan to attend.

GEOG. RESTRICTIONS: United States.

FINANCIAL DATA:
Awards are based on each applicant's unmet financial need as verified by the applicant's college financial aid office. Fellowships are supplementary grants and are only a percentage of a student's total unmet financial need.

Amount of support per award: Varies.

Total amount of support: Varies.

Matching fund requirements: Universities are encouraged to provide assistance.

CO-OP FUNDING PROGRAMS: The organization works with other scholarship agencies to assure that there will be no overfunding of students.

NO. MOST RECENT APPLICANTS: Over 3,000 for the year 2015.

NO. AWARDS: Over 900 for the year 2015.

APPLICATION INFO:
Application must be submitted online.

Duration: One academic year at a time. Students may reapply each year.

Deadline: Varies depending on scholarship.

PUBLICATIONS:
Annual report; newsletter; brochure.

IRS I.D.: 85-0222386

STAFF:
Josh Lucio, Program Associate
Matthew Collins, Program Assistant

ADDRESS INQUIRIES TO:
See e-mail address above.

AMERICAN INDIAN SCIENCE AND ENGINEERING SOCIETY (AISES) [1018]

2305 Renard, S.E.
Suite 200
Albuquerque, NM 87106
(505) 765-1052 ext. 103
(720) 552-6123
Fax: (505) 765-5608
E-mail: kcristiano@aises.org
Web Site: www.aises.org/scholarships

FOUNDED: 1977

AREAS OF INTEREST:
American Indian education in the science and engineering fields.

NAME(S) OF PROGRAMS:
- **A.T. Anderson Memorial Scholarship**

TYPE:
Scholarships. AISES scholarships are intended to partially defray tuition and other educational expenses, thereby increasing access to higher education and improving college retention rates for AISES members.

AISES scholarships are made possible by corporations, government agencies, foundations, and individuals who wish to support the advancement of American Indians/Alaskan Natives. Scholarships are distributed in two disbursements and awarded for one academic year, unless otherwise specified. Recipients cannot receive more than one scholarship in any of the six programs.

Scholarships are also awarded to members of AISES who are American Indian/Alaskan Native college students who meet the eligibility requirements for each scholarship.

YEAR PROGRAM STARTED: 1983

PURPOSE:
To significantly increase the number of American Indian/Alaskan Native scientists and engineers, and develop knowledgeable leaders within native communities; to foster the building of community by bridging science and technology with traditional native values.

LEGAL BASIS:
Private, nonprofit corporation.

ELIGIBILITY:
Applicant must be a current member of AISES and a full-time undergraduate or graduate student at an accredited four-year college/university, or a full-time student at a two-year college enrolled in a program leading to an academic degree, with a 3.0 minimum, cumulative grade point average. Candidate must major in Math, Science, Engineering, Physical Science, Medicine, or Natural Resources. Candidate must be at least one-quarter American Indian/Alaskan Native or otherwise considered American Indian by a member with which affiliation is claimed.

GEOG. RESTRICTIONS: United States and Canada.

FINANCIAL DATA:
Amount of support per award: $1,000 undergraduate and $2,000 graduate per year.

Total amount of support: Varies.

NO. AWARDS: 20 to 40 for the year 2014-15.

APPLICATION INFO:
Guidelines and application are available on the web site after April 1, or can be requested from the Society.

Duration: One academic year.

Deadline: May 31 (postmark).

PUBLICATIONS:
AISES Scholarship Program brochure.

IRS I.D.: 73-1023474

STAFF:
Tina Farrenkopf, Director of Programs

ADDRESS INQUIRIES TO:
Katherine Cristiano, Programs Manager
American Indian Science
and Engineering Society
1225 Ken Pratt Boulevard, Suite 206
Longmont, CO 80501
Tel: (720) 552-6123

AMERICAN INDIAN SCIENCE AND ENGINEERING SOCIETY (AISES) [1019]

2305 Renard, S.E.
Suite 200
Albuquerque, NM 87106
(505) 765-1052
E-mail: info@aises.org
Web Site: www.aises.org/scholarships

FOUNDED: 1977

AREAS OF INTEREST:
American Indian education in the science, engineering and other related technical fields.

NAME(S) OF PROGRAMS:
- **AISES Google Scholarship**

TYPE:
Scholarships.

PURPOSE:
To aid in the education of American Indians and Alaskan Natives in the science, engineering fields and other related technical fields.

ELIGIBILITY:
Applicant must:
(1) be a current AISES member;
(2) be a member of an American Indian tribe, Alaska Native or Native Hawaiian or otherwise considered to be an American Indian by the tribe with which affiliation is claimed; or is at least one-fourth American Indian blood; or is at least one-fourth Alaskan Native or considered to be an Alaskan Native by an Alaskan Native group by which affiliation is claimed. Proof of tribal enrollment is required;
(3) be a full-time undergraduate or graduate student at an accredited four-year college or university, or in the second year at a two-year college leading to a four-year degree and have a minimum cumulative grade point average of 3.5 and;
(4) be majoring in one of the following disciplines: computer science or computer engineering.

GEOG. RESTRICTIONS: United States and Canada.

FINANCIAL DATA:
Amount of support per award: $10,000.
Total amount of support: $100,000 for the year 2012.

APPLICATION INFO:
Complete information is available online.
Duration: One year.
Deadline: March 31.

ADDRESS INQUIRIES TO:
Programs Officer
(See address above.)

AMERICAN PHILOSOPHICAL SOCIETY [1020]

104 South Fifth Street
Philadelphia, PA 19106-3387
(215) 440-3429
E-mail: lmusumeci@amphilsoc.org
Web Site: www.amphilsoc.org

FOUNDED: 1743

AREAS OF INTEREST:
Scholarly research.

NAME(S) OF PROGRAMS:
- **Phillips Fund for Native American Research**

TYPE:
Grants-in-aid; Research grants. Postgraduate grants for research in Native American linguistics, ethnohistory and the history of studies of Native Americans in the continental U.S. and Canada. The Committee prefers supporting the work of younger scholars/graduate students for research on Master's or doctoral dissertations. Grants are for travel costs, tapes, films and consultants' fees.

YEAR PROGRAM STARTED: 1940

LEGAL BASIS:
Nonprofit learned society.

ELIGIBILITY:
Open to graduate students and postdoctoral candidates.

The grants described above are for research in Native American linguistics and ethnohistory, as well as in the history of studies of Native Americans. There are no ethnic restrictions on applicants. Work must be on groups located north of the U.S.-Mexican border.

The Committee will seldom approve more than two awards to the same person within a five-year period. Grants are not made for projects in archaeology, ethnography, psycholinguistics, or for the preparation of pedagogical materials, general maintenance or purchase of permanent equipment (tape recorders, books, etc.).

FINANCIAL DATA:
The grants are intended for such extra costs as travel, tapes, films, consultants' fees, etc., but not for the purchase of permanent equipment (tape recorders, books, etc.)
Amount of support per award: Awards average $2,500; grants do not exceed $3,500.
Total amount of support: $56,600 for the year 2013.

NO. AWARDS: 18 for the year 2014.

APPLICATION INFO:
Application must be submitted electronically through the Society's online portal. Up to two additional pages may be submitted for the project statement.

Two letters of support are required.

The application and both letters of reference must be received by the deadline.
Duration: One year.
Deadline: March 1. Notification by May.

ADDRESS INQUIRIES TO:
Linda Musumeci
Director of Grants and Fellowships
(See address above.)

ASSOCIATION ON AMERICAN INDIAN AFFAIRS [1021]

966 Hungerford Drive, Suite 12-B
Rockville, MD 20850
(240) 314-7155
Fax: (240) 314-7159
E-mail: lw.aaia@indian-affairs.org
Web Site: www.indian-affairs.org

FOUNDED: 1922

AREAS OF INTEREST:
Advocates for the well-being of Indian people. Primary focus on cultural preservation, youth/education and sovereignty.

NAME(S) OF PROGRAMS:
- **David Risling Emergency Aid Scholarships**

TYPE:
Grants-in-aid; Scholarships. Emergency Aid Scholarships are for full-time graduate and undergraduate students who are seeking a degree in any curriculum. This program is limited by the availability of scholarship funds.

YEAR PROGRAM STARTED: 1922

PURPOSE:
To promote the welfare of American Indians and Alaska Natives by supporting efforts; to sustain and perpetuate their cultures and languages; to protect their sovereignty, constitutional, legal and human rights and natural resources; to improve their health, education and economic and community development.

ELIGIBILITY:
The applicant must meet the following basic requirements:
(1) be enrolled in one's tribe;
(2) be attending an accredited school full-time both fall and spring semesters and;
(3) be seeking an Associate's degree or higher.

Scholarship is open to college freshman, sophomores, juniors, seniors and graduate students from federally recognized tribes and tribes not recognized by the federal government. Funding is limited to eviction, utility disconnection, removal of children from daycare for nonpayment or some extreme car repairs for commuting students. Other extreme hardship may be considered on a case-by-case basis.

Expected expenses such as tuition, books and computers will not be funded. Expenses incurred over the summer months will not be funded.

GEOG. RESTRICTIONS: Continental United States and Alaska.

FINANCIAL DATA:
Amount of support per award: $100 to $400, pending availability and whether the emergency qualifies. Dollars and types of situations funded are very limited.

NO. AWARDS: Varies.

APPLICATION INFO:
Students must call AAIA's Director of Scholarship Programs in its Rockville, MD office prior to applying.
Deadline: Acceptance period is mid-October to early May, pending availability of funds. Turnaround time may be up to two weeks from time of first contacting AAIA office.

ADDRESS INQUIRIES TO:
Lisa Wyzlic
Director of Scholarship Programs
(See address above.)

ASSOCIATION ON AMERICAN INDIAN AFFAIRS [1022]

966 Hungerford Drive, Suite 12-B
Rockville, MD 20850
(240) 314-7155
Fax: (240) 314-7159
E-mail: lw.aaia@indian-affairs.org
Web Site: www.indian-affairs.org

FOUNDED: 1922

AREAS OF INTEREST:
Advocates for the well-being of Indian people. Primary focus on cultural preservation, youth/education and sovereignty.

NAME(S) OF PROGRAMS:
- **Graduate Scholarships**

TYPE:
Scholarships.

PURPOSE:
To promote the welfare of American Indians and Alaska Natives by supporting efforts to sustain and perpetuate their cultures and languages; to protect their sovereignty,

constitutional, legal and human rights and natural resources; to improve their health, education and economic and community development.

LEGAL BASIS:
Charitable nonprofit foundation.

ELIGIBILITY:
The applicant must meet the following basic requirements:
(1) be enrolled in one's tribe;
(2) be attending an accredited school full-time both fall and spring semesters and;
(3) be seeking a Master's degree in any curriculum, Ph.D., law degree or medical degree.

GEOG. RESTRICTIONS: Continental United States and Alaska.

FINANCIAL DATA:
Amount of support per award: $1,500.

NO. AWARDS: Varies.

APPLICATION INFO:
Application information is available on the web site each February.

Duration: One year.

Deadline: Acceptance period changes from year to year.

ADDRESS INQUIRIES TO:
Lisa Wyzlic
Director of Scholarship Programs
(See address above.)

ASSOCIATION ON AMERICAN INDIAN AFFAIRS [1023]

966 Hungerford Drive, Suite 12-B
Rockville, MD 20850
(240) 314-7155
Fax: (240) 314-7159
E-mail: lw.aaia@indian-affairs.org
Web Site: www.indian-affairs.org

FOUNDED: 1922

AREAS OF INTEREST:
Advocates for the well-being of Indian people. Primary focus on cultural preservation, youth/education and sovereignty.

NAME(S) OF PROGRAMS:
- **Undergraduate Scholarships**

TYPE:
Scholarships.

PURPOSE:
To promote the welfare of American Indians and Alaska Natives by supporting efforts to sustain and perpetuate their cultures and languages; to protect their sovereignty, constitutional, legal and human rights and natural resources; to improve their health, education and economic and community development.

ELIGIBILITY:
The applicant must meet the following basic requirements:
(1) be enrolled in one's tribe;
(2) be attending an accredited school full-time both fall and spring semesters and;
(3) be seeking an Associate's or Bachelor's degree.
These Scholarships are open to high school seniors who will be entering college in the fall, college freshman, sophomores, juniors and seniors.

GEOG. RESTRICTIONS: Continental United States and Alaska.

FINANCIAL DATA:
Amount of support per award: $1,500.

NO. AWARDS: Varies.

APPLICATION INFO:
Application information is available on the web site each February.

Duration: One year.

Deadline: Acceptance period changes from year to year.

PUBLICATIONS:
Brochure.

ADDRESS INQUIRIES TO:
Lisa Wyzlic
Director of Scholarship Programs
(See address above.)

ASSOCIATION ON AMERICAN INDIAN AFFAIRS [1024]

966 Hungerford Drive, Suite 12-B
Rockville, MD 20850
(240) 314-7155
Fax: (240) 314-7159
E-mail: lw.aaia@indian-affairs.org
Web Site: www.indian-affairs.org

FOUNDED: 1922

AREAS OF INTEREST:
Advocates for the well-being of Indian people. Primary focus on cultural preservation, youth/education and sovereignty.

NAME(S) OF PROGRAMS:
- **Allogan Slagle Memorial Scholarship**

TYPE:
Scholarships. Offered to American Indian and Alaskan Native graduate and undergraduate students in any curriculum who are members of tribes that are not federally recognized.

PURPOSE:
To promote the welfare of American Indians and Alaska Natives by supporting efforts to sustain and perpetuate their cultures and languages; to protect their sovereignty, constitutional, legal and human rights and natural resources; to improve their health, education and economic and community development.

ELIGIBILITY:
Applicants must be American Indian and Native Alaskan graduate or undergraduate students in any curriculum who are members of tribes that are not federally recognized. This Scholarship is open to high school seniors who will be entering college in the fall, college freshman, sophomores, juniors, seniors and graduate students.

The applicant must meet the following basic requirements:
(1) be enrolled in one's tribe;
(2) be attending an accredited school full-time both fall and spring semesters and;
(3) be seeking an Associate's degree or higher.

FINANCIAL DATA:
Amount of support per award: $1,500 ($750 each for fall and spring semesters).

NO. AWARDS: Varies.

APPLICATION INFO:
Application information is available on the web site.

Duration: One year. Students are eligible to apply on a yearly basis.

Deadline: Acceptance period changes from year to year.

ADDRESS INQUIRIES TO:
Lisa Wyzlic
Director of Scholarship Programs
(See address above.)

BNSF RAILWAY FOUNDATION [1025]

2650 Lou Menk Drive
Fort Worth, TX 76131-2830
(817) 867-6458
E-mail: bnsffoundation@bnsf.com
Web Site: www.bnsffoundation.org

NAME(S) OF PROGRAMS:
- **Native American Scholarship Program**

TYPE:
Scholarships. Awarded annually to outstanding Native American high school seniors from funds provided by the Foundation, for up to four years or until undergraduate degree requirements are completed, whichever occurs first. Scholarship winners may attend any accredited college (two-year leading to a four-year degree) or university in the U.S.

LEGAL BASIS:
Corporate foundation.

ELIGIBILITY:
High school seniors having one-fourth or more Indian blood are eligible. Applicants need not be related to Burlington Northern Santa Fe personnel to qualify. Two scholarships are provided exclusively for members of the Navajo Tribe and the other three are available to any Native American high school students residing in Arizona, California, Colorado, Kansas, Minnesota, Montana, New Mexico, North Dakota, Oklahoma, Oregon, South Dakota, or Washington.

Winners are selected on the basis of strong academic performance in high school, with award preference being given to the study of any of the sciences such as medicine, engineering, natural and physical sciences, as well as business, education and health administration.

GEOG. RESTRICTIONS: Arizona, California, Colorado, Kansas, Minnesota, Montana, New Mexico, North Dakota, Oklahoma, Oregon, South Dakota and Washington.

FINANCIAL DATA:
Amount of support per award: $1,000 to $2,500 annually for up to four years or until undergraduate degree requirements are completed, whichever occurs first (but not to exceed five years). Financial need determines the amount awarded.

NO. AWARDS: 5.

APPLICATION INFO:
The scholarship is administered by the American Indian Science and Engineering Society (AISES) and all winners are selected by the organization. Applications may be obtained by writing American Indian Science and Engineering Society, P.O. Box 9828, Albuquerque, NM 87119-9828. All correspondence and questions should be directed to AISES.

Duration: Up to four years or until undergraduate degree requirements are completed, whichever occurs first, but not to exceed five years.

ADDRESS INQUIRIES TO:
American Indian Science and Engineering Society
(See address above.)

BUREAU OF INDIAN AFFAIRS [1026]

Office of Indian Services
Division of Workforce Development
1849 C Street, N.W., Room 4520
Washington, DC 20240
(202) 513-7625
Fax: (202) 208-5113
E-mail: Terrence.Parks@bia.gov
Web Site: www.indianaffairs.gov

FOUNDED: 1824

AREAS OF INTEREST:
Vocational training, job placement, education, childcare and related services.

NAME(S) OF PROGRAMS:
- **Indian Employment Assistance**
- **Public Law 102-477**

TYPE:
Project/program grants; Training grants. Vocational training and job placement, advisory services and counseling, education, childcare and youth development programs.

YEAR PROGRAM STARTED: 1956

PURPOSE:
To provide individual grants for adult vocational training and job placement services for Indians.

LEGAL BASIS:
Public Law 67-85, The Snyder Act of November 2, 1921; Public Law 84-959, Indian Adult Vocational Training Act of August 3, 1956; Public Law 102-477.

ELIGIBILITY:
Applicant must be a member of a federally recognized tribe, band or group of Indians, whose residence is on or near an Indian reservation under the jurisdiction of BIA.

GEOG. RESTRICTIONS: United States.

FINANCIAL DATA:
Amount of support per award: $800 to $6,500 per year. $5,000 average.

Total amount of support: Over $100,000,000 annually.

CO-OP FUNDING PROGRAMS: Indian Education, Training and Employment.

APPLICATION INFO:
Applicants should make application to the nearest Agency or Tribal Employment Assistance. Contact tribal office nearest to place of residence.

Duration: One year. Renewal possible if continuing training.

STAFF:
Terrence Parks, Acting Chief

ADDRESS INQUIRIES TO:
Terrence Parks, Acting Chief
(See address above.)

BUREAU OF INDIAN AFFAIRS [1027]

Office of Indian Energy and Economic Development
Division of Energy and Mineral Development
13922 Denver West Parkway, Suite 200
Lakewood, CO 80401
(303) 969-5270
Fax: (303) 969-5273
E-mail: IEEDgrants@bia.gov
Web Site: www.indianaffairs.gov/WhoWeAre/AS-IA/IEED/index.htm

AREAS OF INTEREST:
Energy development; renewable energy; development capacity; oil, gas and coal development.

NAME(S) OF PROGRAMS:
- **Tribal Energy Development Capacity (TEDC) Grant**

TYPE:
Project/program grants.

PURPOSE:
To help tribes in assessing, developing or obtaining the managerial, organizational and technical capacity needed to develop energy resources on Indian land and to properly account for resulting energy production and revenues, as provided for in Title V, Section 503, of the Energy Policy Act.

LEGAL BASIS:
Public Law 67-85, The Snyder Act of November 2, 1921; The Energy Policy Act of 2005 (25 U.S.C. 3501 et seq.)

ELIGIBILITY:
Federally recognized Indian tribes and tribal energy resource development organizations.

GEOG. RESTRICTIONS: United States.

FINANCIAL DATA:
Amount of support per award: Approximately $155,000.

Total amount of support: Over $1,500,000.

NO. MOST RECENT APPLICANTS: 22.

NO. AWARDS: 10.

APPLICATION INFO:
Applicants should refer to the solicitation notice on www.Grants.gov.

Duration: 12 months; renewal possible.

STAFF:
Rebecca Naragon, IEED Grant Manager
Chandler Allen, TEDC Program Manager
Payton Batliner, TEDC Program Manager

ADDRESS INQUIRIES TO:
Jack Stevens, Acting Director
(See address above.)

BUREAU OF INDIAN AFFAIRS [1028]

Office of Indian Energy and Economic Development
Division of Energy and Mineral Development
13922 Denver West Parkway, Suite 200
Lakewood, CO 80401
(303) 969-5270
Fax: (303) 969-5273
E-mail: IEEDgrants@bia.gov
Web Site: www.indianaffairs.gov/WhoWeAre/AS-IA/IEED/index.htm

AREAS OF INTEREST:
Energy development; mineral development; feasibility study; renewable energy; oil, gas and coal development.

NAME(S) OF PROGRAMS:
- **Energy and Mineral Development Program (EMDP) Grant**

TYPE:
Project/program grants.

PURPOSE:
To promote energy and mineral development projects that explore for energy and mineral resources, inventory or assess known resources, or perform feasibility or market studies that tend to promote the use and development of known energy and mineral resources.

LEGAL BASIS:
Public Law 67-85, The Snyder Act of November 2, 1921; The Energy Policy Act of 2005 (25 U.S.C. 3501 et seq.)

ELIGIBILITY:
Federally recognized Indian tribes and tribal energy resource development organizations.

GEOG. RESTRICTIONS: "Indian land" within the United States.

FINANCIAL DATA:
Amount of support per award: Approximately $98,000.

Total amount of support: Over $5,000,000; total funds are contingent on annual appropriations.

NO. MOST RECENT APPLICANTS: 53.

NO. AWARDS: 34.

APPLICATION INFO:
Applicants should refer to the solicitation notice on www.Grants.gov.

Duration: 12 months; renewal possible.

STAFF:
Rebecca Naragon, IEED Grant Manager
Robert Anderson, EMDP Program Manager

ADDRESS INQUIRIES TO:
Jack Stevens, Acting Director
(See address above.)

BUREAU OF INDIAN AFFAIRS [1029]

Office of Indian Energy and Economic Development
1951 Constitution Avenue, N.W., MS-16-SIB
Washington, DC 20245
(202) 219-0740
Fax: (202) 208-4564
E-mail: IEEDgrants@bia.gov
rebecca.naragon@bia.gov
Web Site: www.indianaffairs.gov/WhoWeAre/AS-IA/IEED/index.htm

AREAS OF INTEREST:
Economic development, feasibility study.

NAME(S) OF PROGRAMS:
- **Native American Business Development Institute (NABDI)**

TYPE:
Project/program grants.

PURPOSE:
To study the viability of an economic development project or business or the practicality of a technology an eligible recipient may choose to pursue.

LEGAL BASIS:
Public Law 67-85, The Snyder Act of November 2, 1921.

ELIGIBILITY:
Federally recognized Indian tribes.

GEOG. RESTRICTIONS: United States.

FINANCIAL DATA:
Amount of support per award: Approximately $97,000.

Total amount of support: Over $1,300,000. Total funds are contingent on annual appropriations.

NO. MOST RECENT APPLICANTS: 45.

NO. AWARDS: 14.

APPLICATION INFO:
Applicants should refer to the solicitation notice on www.grants.gov.

Duration: 12 months; renewal possible.

STAFF:
Rebecca Naragon, IEED Grant Manager

ADDRESS INQUIRIES TO:
Jack Stevens, Acting Director
(See address above.)

BUREAU OF INDIAN EDUCATION [1030]

1849 C Street, N.W.
MS 3609 MIB
Washington, DC 20240
(202) 208-6123
Fax: (202) 208-3312
Web Site: www.bie.edu

FOUNDED: 1824

AREAS OF INTEREST:
Elementary and secondary education tribal colleges.

NAME(S) OF PROGRAMS:

- **Higher Education Grant Program for American Indians and Alaska Natives**

TYPE:
Fellowships; Scholarships.

YEAR PROGRAM STARTED: 1949

PURPOSE:
To provide financial aid to eligible Indian students enabling them to attend accredited institutions of higher education.

LEGAL BASIS:
Snyder Act.

ELIGIBILITY:
Applicant must be a member of a tribe eligible for services from the Bureau, enrolled or accepted for enrollment in an accredited college and have financial need as determined by the institution's financial aid office.

FINANCIAL DATA:
The grants are intended to supplement the financial aid package prepared by the educational institution's financial aid officer. The grant meets the unmet need portion of the package.

Amount of support per award: Varies.

Total amount of support: Varies.

Matching fund requirements: Meets the unmet need portion of the institution's financial aid package.

CO-OP FUNDING PROGRAMS: Other donor's funding programs are a part of the financial aid package.

NO. MOST RECENT APPLICANTS: 20,000.

NO. AWARDS: 15,000.

APPLICATION INFO:
Candidates should request an application from a home agency or tribal Higher Education Grant Program (HEGP). Contact the BIA/Tribal census office to obtain a Certificate of Degree of Indian Blood (CDIB) and tribal enrollment and submit with the application. Write to the admissions office of the chosen school for an application. Request a financial aid packet from the school's Financial Aid Officer, who will prepare a financial aid package based on the applicant's need. Then submit all these forms to the appropriate offices well in advance of the deadline.

Duration: One academic year. Must renew annually.

Deadline: Varies.

ADDRESS INQUIRIES TO:
Home agency or tribally administered Higher Education Grant Program

CATCHING THE DREAM [1031]

8200 Mountain Road, N.E.
Suite 103
Albuquerque, NM 87110
(505) 262-2351
Fax: (505) 262-0534
E-mail: NScholarsh@aol.com
Web Site: www.catchingthedream.org

FOUNDED: 1986

AREAS OF INTEREST:
Scholarships for Native college students and improvement of Indian schools and postsecondary education for Native American students in the fields of math, engineering, science, business, education and computers.

CONSULTING OR VOLUNTEER SERVICES:
The Fund assists Native American students who need help in locating other sources of funding and provides fund-raising, management training, conferences, and seminars.

NAME(S) OF PROGRAMS:

- **Math and Science Teaching (MAST)**
- **MESBEC (Math, Engineering, Science, Business, Education and Computers) Program**
- **Native American Leadership in Education (NALE) Program**
- **Reading Award Program (RAP)**
- **Tribal Business Management (TBM) Program**

TYPE:
Conferences/seminars; Development grants; Grants-in-aid; Scholarships; Technical assistance. CTD also works to improve Indian schools through a program of grants and technical assistance. This work has led to the development of 40 Exemplary Programs in Indian education since 1988. The annual Exemplary Institute is a meeting of these Exemplary Programs, where they teach other people how to develop similar programs.

MAST program makes grants of $5,000 to Indian high schools to improve their math and science teaching.

MESBEC Program consists of competitive scholarships for high-potential Native Americans studying in math, engineering, science, business, education and computers.

NALE Program consists of competitive scholarships for high-potential paraprofessional Native Americans who plan to complete their degrees and obtain credentials as teachers, counselors or administrators.

RAP makes grants to Indian schools to improve the reading ability of their students.

Tribal Business Management (TBM) Program consists of competitive scholarships for Native students in all fields of business.

YEAR PROGRAM STARTED: 1986

PURPOSE:
To help tribes prepare young people to work in the fields which are critical for economic, social, business and political development in Indian Country.

LEGAL BASIS:
Nonprofit organization.

ELIGIBILITY:
Applicants must be at least one-quarter blood member of a federally recognized, state recognized or terminated Indian tribe. They must have high potential for the field of study and work for which they are preparing. They must attend an accredited U.S. college or university. They must have clear goals in mind and have done some work toward accomplishing these goals. The goals must be related to the betterment of Indian people or the betterment of an Indian tribe or community. Progress toward accomplishing a goal may be demonstrated by study, by work, by volunteer work or by other means.

Students with no clear goals are discouraged from applying. Normally, successful applicants will plan to earn a four-year degree or a graduate degree. In a few cases, associate degrees are approved. Applicants must apply for all other sources of funding for which they are eligible, including private scholarship sources, corporate traineeships, federal funds, loans, jobs, grants and so forth.

Students can contact CTD up to three years in advance.

GEOG. RESTRICTIONS: United States.

FINANCIAL DATA:
Amount of support per award: $500 to $5,000.

Total amount of support: $304,000 for the year 2015-16.

NO. AWARDS: MAST: 6; RAP: 12; All other programs: 169 for the year 2015-16.

APPLICATION INFO:
Contact Catching the Dream.

Duration: Until completion of degree.

Deadline: March 15 for summer school. September 15 for winter quarter and spring semester. April 30 for fall semester.

PUBLICATIONS:
The National Indian Grant Directory; *Preparing Indian Students for College*; *Exemplary Programs in Indian Education*; *Reading for College*; *Racism in Indian Country*; *Modern American Indian Leaders*; *The Secret of No Face*; *Basics of Fund Raising*; *How to Write Winning Proposals*; *Literacy in Indian Country*.

IRS I.D.: 85-0360858

BOARD OF DIRECTORS:
James Lujan, President
Jodie Palmer, Secretary
Dr. Jerry Bread
Dr. Dean Chavers
Dr. Lester Sandoval
Ms. Lynn Okon Scholnick
John Tohtsoni, Jr.

CHEROKEE NATION [1032]

P.O. Box 948
Tahlequah, OK 74465
(918) 453-5000
(918) 453-5465
Fax: (918) 458-6286
E-mail: collegeresources@cherokee.org
Web Site: www.cherokee.org

FOUNDED: 1904

AREAS OF INTEREST:
Planning and development (individual and tribal), health, education and welfare.

CONSULTING OR VOLUNTEER SERVICES:
Tribal government administration consultants and volunteers in all interest areas available to eligible tribal members.

NAME(S) OF PROGRAMS:

- **College Resource Center**

TYPE:
Project/program grants; Scholarships; Technical assistance. Financial and other support through all programs to eligible tribal members.

YEAR PROGRAM STARTED: 1964

PURPOSE:
To serve its tribes and members in the areas indicated.

LEGAL BASIS:
Federally recognized Indian tribe.

ELIGIBILITY:
Tribal membership is required.

GEOG. RESTRICTIONS: Primarily northeast Oklahoma.

FINANCIAL DATA:
Tribe operates $300,000,000 in social and economic programs.

Amount of support per award: Varies.

Total amount of support: Varies.

APPLICATION INFO:
Guidelines and application form are available on the web site.

Duration: Varies.

Deadline: Varies.

ADDRESS INQUIRIES TO:
College Resource Center
(See e-mail address above.)

FIRST NATIONS DEVELOPMENT INSTITUTE [1033]

2432 Main Street, Second Floor
Longmont, CO 80501
(303) 774-7836
Fax: (303) 774-7841
E-mail: info@firstnations.org
Web Site: www.firstnations.org

FOUNDED: 1980

AREAS OF INTEREST:
Native American-owned business, small business development and capacity building.

CONSULTING OR VOLUNTEER SERVICES:
Yes.

NAME(S) OF PROGRAMS:
- **The Eagle Staff Fund**

TYPE:
Program development grants. First Nations works to improve economic conditions for Native Americans through technical assistance and training, advocacy and policy, and direct financial grants in the five key areas of Achieving Native Financial Empowerment, Investing in Native Youth, Strengthening Native Nonprofits, Native American Business and Asset Development and Nourishing Native Foods and Health.

YEAR PROGRAM STARTED: 1993

PURPOSE:
To strengthen American Indian economies to support healthy Native communities.

LEGAL BASIS:
Nonprofit organization.

ELIGIBILITY:
Eligible organizations include:
(1) tribal or Native government programs, entities, and enterprises;
(2) tribally or community-controlled development organizations;
(3) tribally or Native-controlled health, education, or other social programs or institutions;
(4) Native arts and crafts associations, co-ops and guilds;
(5) intertribal and regional tribal or Native groups;
(6) Native grassroots efforts and community programs and;
(7) Native nonprofit on or near Reservation.

Grants are not made to individuals for for-profit businesses, programs serving exclusively urban Native communities, programs serving Natives but not controlled by a majority of Natives, for-profit Native consulting firms, for-profit Native businesses except those associated with a nonprofit Native enterprise, or religious organizations (except for traditional Native American spiritual programs).

GEOG. RESTRICTIONS: United States and its territories.

FINANCIAL DATA:
Amount of support per award: Varies.

Total amount of support: Varies.

NO. AWARDS: Varies.

APPLICATION INFO:
Application must be made online. Complete information is available on the web site.

Duration: Typically one year.

PUBLICATIONS:
List of publications; annual report.

IRS I.D.: 54-1254491

ADDRESS INQUIRIES TO:
Marsha Whiting
Senior Grants and Program Officer
(See address above.)

HOLLAND & KNIGHT CHARITABLE FOUNDATION, INC. [1034]

100 North Tampa Street, Suite 4100
Tampa, FL 33602
(813) 227-8500
E-mail: nativewriters@hklaw.com
Web Site: foundation.hklaw.com
nativewriters.hklaw.com

AREAS OF INTEREST:
The development of Native American youth.

NAME(S) OF PROGRAMS:
- **Young Native Writers Essay Contest**

TYPE:
Awards/prizes; Scholarships. Young Native Writers Essay Contest is a writing contest for Native American high school students.

PURPOSE:
To encourage young Native Americans to write about their experience as a member of a Native American community and the culture that inspires them.

ELIGIBILITY:
Contest is open to Native American high school students currently enrolled in grades nine to 12 only. All students participating in Young Native Writers Essay Contest should have a significant and current relationship with a Native American tribal community.

FINANCIAL DATA:
The five First-Place Winners will each receive an all-expense-paid trip to Washington, DC, to visit the National Museum of the American Indian and other prominent sites. The winners will be accompanied by the teachers who inspired their entries into the contest. First-Place Winners will receive a special award for display at home or school.

Amount of support per award: Each First-Place Winner will receive a scholarship of $2,500 to be paid directly to the college or university of his or her choice.

NO. AWARDS: 5.

APPLICATION INFO:
All essays must be uploaded to the contest web. Essays sent by mail, faxed or e-mailed will be disqualified. The body of contestant's essay may be no more than 1,200 words. The essays must be written in English. Every student must also submit an entry form which he or she will be prompted to complete before he or she uploads his or her essay. Every essay must include a Bibliography, Works Cited or Reference Page (which are not to be included in the word count).

The Foundation will identify contestant's essay electronically through the entry form completed when entering the contest. Contestant must not include his or her name anywhere on any page of his or her essay.

Those entering this contest must read carefully the entire body of instructions on the contest web site.

Deadline: May 18.

*SPECIAL STIPULATIONS:
The winners of the essay contest must agree to participate in the entire trip to Washington, DC, in order to receive a scholarship. In the event that a winner is unable or unwilling to participate in the trip to Washington, DC, in its entirety, no substitution prize will be awarded.

NATIONAL SOCIETY DAUGHTERS OF THE AMERICAN REVOLUTION

1776 D Street, N.W.
Washington, DC 20006-5303
(202) 879-3263
Fax: (202) 879-3348
E-mail: scholarships@dar.org
Web Site: www.dar.org

TYPE:
Scholarships. Intended to help Native American college/university and technical school students at the undergraduate or graduate level.

See entry 1665 for full listing.

NATIONAL SOCIETY DAUGHTERS OF THE AMERICAN REVOLUTION

1776 D Street, N.W.
Washington, DC 20006-5303
(202) 879-3263
Fax: (202) 879-3348
E-mail: scholarships@dar.org
Web Site: www.dar.org

TYPE:
Scholarships. Intended to help Native American students enrolled full-time at a two- or four-year college or university.

See entry 1666 for full listing.

NATIVE AMERICAN COMMUNITY BOARD (NACB) [1035]

P.O. Box 572
Lake Andes, SD 57356-0572
(605) 487-7072
Fax: (605) 487-7964
E-mail: charon@charles-mix.com
Web Site: www.nativeshop.org

FOUNDED: 1986

AREAS OF INTEREST:
Civil rights, women's rights, reproductive justice, and a healthy environment.

NAME(S) OF PROGRAMS:

- **College Intern Program**

TYPE:
Internships.

PURPOSE:
To address pertinent issues of health, education, land and water rights, and economic development of Native American people.

ELIGIBILITY:
College juniors, seniors or graduate students interested in Native American rights and health issues. Priority will be given to those wishing to stay long-term (six months or longer).

FINANCIAL DATA:
Amount of support per award: $250 biweekly.
Total amount of support: Varies.

NO. AWARDS: 8.

APPLICATION INFO:
Contact the NACB for application procedures.
Duration: Three months to one year, with three months being the preferred minimum stay.
Deadline: Contact the NACB for openings.

ADDRESS INQUIRIES TO:
Charon Asetoyer, Executive Director
(See e-mail address above.)

THE NEWBERRY LIBRARY [1036]

Office of Research and Academic Programs
60 West Walton Street
Chicago, IL 60610
(312) 255-3666
E-mail: research@newberry.org
Web Site: www.newberry.org/fellowships

AREAS OF INTEREST:
Native American women, humanities and social sciences.

NAME(S) OF PROGRAMS:

- **Frances C. Allen Fellowships**

TYPE:
Fellowships; Visiting scholars. Allen fellows are expected to spend a significant part of their tenure in residence at Newberry's D'Arcy McNickle Center for American Indian and Indigenous Studies.

PURPOSE:
To encourage study by Native American women of the humanities and social sciences.

LEGAL BASIS:
Private research library.

ELIGIBILITY:
Applicants must be women of Native American heritage. While candidates for this award may be working on any graduate or pre-professional field related to the Newberry's collection, the particular goal of the Fellowship is to encourage Native American women in their studies of the humanities and social sciences.

FINANCIAL DATA:
Amount of support per award: $2,500 per month stipend; supplemental funding may be available.

NO. MOST RECENT APPLICANTS: 4.

NO. AWARDS: 1.

APPLICATION INFO:
Applications must be submitted through the online webform.
Duration: One to 12 months.
Deadline: December 15.

STAFF:
D. Bradford Hunt, Vice President for Research and Academic Programs

ADDRESS INQUIRIES TO:
See e-mail address above.

*SPECIAL STIPULATIONS:
Allen Fellows are expected to spend a significant part of their tenure in residence at the D'Arcy McNickle Center for American Indian and Indigenous Studies.

RUNNING STRONG FOR AMERICAN INDIAN YOUTH [1037]

8301 Richmond Highway
Alexandria, VA 22309
(703) 317-9881
(888) 491-9859
Fax: (703) 317-9690
E-mail: info@indianyouth.org
Web Site: www.indianyouth.org

FOUNDED: 1986

AREAS OF INTEREST:
Native Americans.

TYPE:
Capital grants; Challenge/matching grants; General operating grants; Project/program grants; Seed money grants.

YEAR PROGRAM STARTED: 1986

PURPOSE:
To help American Indian people meet their immediate survival needs - food, water and shelter - while implementing and supporting programs designed to create opportunities for self-sufficiency and self-esteem, particularly for tribal youth.

ELIGIBILITY:
No grants are made to individuals or fund-raising events. Grants made only to programs that support Native Americans.

GEOG. RESTRICTIONS: United States.

FINANCIAL DATA:
Amount of support per award: Up to $5,000 for new applicants.
Total amount of support: Varies.

NO. AWARDS: Varies.

APPLICATION INFO:
E-mail or call for grant guidelines.
Duration: Up to five years. Must reapply each year.

PUBLICATIONS:
Annual report; application guidelines.

IRS I.D.: 54-1594578

ADDRESS INQUIRIES TO:
Lauren Haas Finkelstein
Executive Director
(See address above.)

U.S. DEPARTMENT OF EDUCATION [1038]

Office of Indian Education
400 Maryland Avenue, S.W.
LBJ Building, 3W115
Washington, DC 20202-6335
(202) 260-3774
(202) 260-1454
E-mail: indian.education@ed.gov
Web Site: www.ed.gov

NAME(S) OF PROGRAMS:

- **Indian Education-Formula Grants to Local Education Agencies (LEAs)**

TYPE:
Formula grants. Grants to provide financial assistance to LEAs and tribal schools to develop and carry out elementary and secondary school programs specially designed to meet the special educational and culturally related educational needs of Indian children.

LEGAL BASIS:
Public Law 92-318, Title IV, Part A, as amended (25 U.S.C. 2601-2606, 2651).

ELIGIBILITY:
Local educational agencies which have at least 10 Indian children or in which Indians constitute at least 25% of the total enrollment may apply. However, these enrollment requirements do not apply to an LEA in Alaska, California or Oklahoma that serves Indian children or an LEA on, or in proximity to, an Indian reservation. An Indian tribe or an organization controlled or sanctioned by an Indian tribal government and that operates a school for children of that tribe is eligible if that school provides its students an educational program that meets the standards established by the Bureau of Indian Affairs (BIA) or is operated by that tribe or organization under a contract with the BIA.

FINANCIAL DATA:
Amount of support per award: Varies.
Total amount of support: Varies.

APPLICATION INFO:
Application instructions and forms are available upon request.

ADDRESS INQUIRIES TO:
Indian Education Programs
(See address above.)

U.S. DEPARTMENT OF HEALTH AND HUMAN SERVICES [1039]

HHS/ACF/ANA Aerospace Center
901 D Street, S.W., 2nd Floor West
Washington, DC 20447
(202) 690-7776
(877) 922-9262 (Help Desk)
Fax: (202) 690-8145; (202) 690-7441
E-mail: anacomments@acf.hhs.gov
Web Site: www.acf.hhs.gov

FOUNDED: 1974

AREAS OF INTEREST:
General community programming, training and technical assistance and research, demonstration and evaluation.

NAME(S) OF PROGRAMS:

- **Native American Programs**

TYPE:
Demonstration grants; Development grants; Project/program grants; Research grants; Seed money grants; Technical assistance; Training grants. Financial Assistance grants may be used for such purposes as, but not limited to, Governance Projects, development of codes and ordinances and status clarification activities; Economic Development Projects, to promote business starts for Native-owned businesses and improve Native American housing management; and Social Development Projects, to assume local control of planning and delivering social services in Native American communities, developing local models related to comprehensive planning and delivery of social services and developing or coordinating activities with state-funded projects in decreasing the incidence of child abuse, neglect and fetal alcohol syndrome.

YEAR PROGRAM STARTED: 1973

PURPOSE:
To support projects that improve social and economic conditions of Native Americans within their communities and increase the effectiveness of Indian Tribes and Native American organizations in meeting their economic and social goals.

LEGAL BASIS:
Native American Programs Act of 1974, as amended, Public Law 93-644; Older Americans Act Amendments of 1987, Title V, Public Law 100-175; Indian Reorganization Act Amendments, Section 215, Public Law 100-581; Older Americans Act Amendments of 1992, Title VIII, Public Law 102-375; 42 U.S.C. 2991 et. seq.

ELIGIBILITY:
Governing bodies of Indian tribes, Alaskan Native villages and regional associations established by the Alaska Native Claims Settlement Act, Indian and Alaska Native Organizations in urban or rural nonreservation areas, public and nonprofit agencies serving Native Hawaiians and other Native American Pacific Islanders which include the Native peoples from Guam, American Samoa, Palau or the Commonwealth of the Northern Mariana Islands. The populations served may be located on those islands or in the U.S.

GEOG. RESTRICTIONS: United States.

FINANCIAL DATA:
Amount of support per award: Approximately $125,000 average.

Total amount of support: Approximately $38,500,000 annually.

Matching fund requirements: A matching share of 20% is required unless waived in accordance with criteria which is published in 45 CFR, Part 1336.50. This program has maintenance of effort requirements.

APPLICATION INFO:
Nonprofit organizations which have not previously received ACF program support must submit proof of nonprofit status. The Administration for Native Americans will provide each applicant agency with the appropriate forms for applying for Federal Assistance and instructions for preparation of application for grants from Human Development Services programs.

Applications should be submitted to ACF Division of Grants Management Administration for Children and Families, Mail Stop AERO-6, OPS/ODG, 370 L'Enfant Promenade, S.W., Washington, DC 20447.

Duration: One year with possibility of multiyear funding.

Deadline: Varies.

STAFF:
Lillian Sparks, Commissioner

ADDRESS INQUIRIES TO:
Administration for Native Americans
(See address above.)

THE MORRIS K. UDALL AND STEWART L. UDALL FOUNDATION [1040]

130 South Scott Avenue
Tucson, AZ 85701
(520) 901-8561
Fax: (520) 670-5530
E-mail: khalil@udall.gov
Web Site: www.udall.gov

FOUNDED: 1992

AREAS OF INTEREST:
Educating young Americans in our nation's heritage, environmental studies, Native American affairs and public policy conflict resolution.

NAME(S) OF PROGRAMS:

- **Congressional Internships**

TYPE:
Internships. Congressional Internships: Native American college students work in congressional offices and the White House to gain a firsthand understanding of the federal government. They also take field trips and meet with congressional members, agency heads and cabinet secretaries.

YEAR PROGRAM STARTED: 1996

PURPOSE:
To educate a new generation of Americans to preserve and protect their national heritage through studies in the environment, Native American health and tribal policy and effective public policy conflict resolution.

LEGAL BASIS:
The Foundation is an executive branch agency. The President of the U.S. appoints its board of trustees with the advice and consent of the U.S. Senate.

ELIGIBILITY:
Interns will be selected by an independent committee. Applicants must demonstrate a commitment to learning about the federal government. They must be self-motivated and interested in taking advantage of the rich and diverse resources available to them in Washington, DC. Additionally, candidates for the internship program must:
(1) be an enrolled member of a recognized tribe or state-recognized tribe;
(2) be a college junior, senior, graduate student, law student or graduating from a tribal college;
(3) have a minimum 3.0 grade point average or a "B" average and;
(4) have an interest in tribal government and policy.

FINANCIAL DATA:
Interns are provided with airfare to and from Washington, DC, lodging convenient to Capitol Hill, and a daily allowance sufficient for meals, transportation and incidentals.

Amount of support per award: $1,200 educational stipend to be paid at the conclusion of the internship.

NO. MOST RECENT APPLICANTS: 50.

NO. AWARDS: 12.

APPLICATION INFO:
Application information is available on the web site.

Duration: 10 weeks.

Deadline: January 31 (postmark).

ADDRESS INQUIRIES TO:
Destiny Khalil, Internship Program Manager
(See address above.)

UNITED SOUTH AND EASTERN TRIBES, INC. [1041]

711 Stewarts Ferry Pike
Suite 100
Nashville, TN 37214
(615) 872-7900
Fax: (615) 872-7417
E-mail: mstephens@usetinc.org
Web Site: www.usetinc.org

FOUNDED: 1969

AREAS OF INTEREST:
Indian tribes.

TYPE:
Scholarships.

PURPOSE:
To enhance the development of Indian Tribes; to improve the capabilities of Tribal governments; to assist the member Tribes and their governments in dealing effectively with public policy issues and in serving the broad needs of Indian people.

ELIGIBILITY:
Supplemental monies are awarded to USET area Indian students who are enrolled members of USET member tribes.

Must be an Indian student that meets the following criteria:
(1) a demonstrated need for additional funding;
(2) satisfactory scholastic standing and;
(3) current enrollment or acceptance in a postsecondary educational institution.

FINANCIAL DATA:
Amount of support per award: Supplemental scholarships: $500.

APPLICATION INFO:
Contact the Organization for application procedures.

Duration: Annual supplemental scholarship. Must reapply for additional term.

Deadline: Postmark or delivery of applications: April 30.

ADDRESS INQUIRIES TO:
USET Scholarship Fund
(See address above.)

UNIVERSITY OF CALIFORNIA, LOS ANGELES [1042]

American Indian Studies Center
UCLA - 3220 Campbell Hall, Box 951548
Los Angeles, CA 90095-1548
(310) 825-7315
Fax: (310) 206-7060
E-mail: aisc@ucla.edu
Web Site: www.aisc.ucla.edu

FOUNDED: 1970

AREAS OF INTEREST:
American Indian studies and related topics in policy, education, economics, culture and community.

NAME(S) OF PROGRAMS:
- **Institute of American Cultures Grant**

TYPE:
Fellowships; Research grants; Visiting scholars.

YEAR PROGRAM STARTED: 1969

PURPOSE:
To conduct research in Native American Studies.

LEGAL BASIS:
University research organization; nonprofit organization.

ELIGIBILITY:
Applicants must be citizens or permanent residents of the U.S. and hold a Ph.D. from an accredited college or university (or, in the case of the arts, an appropriate terminal degree) in a relevant field at the time of appointment. UCLA faculty, staff and currently enrolled students are not eligible to apply.

FINANCIAL DATA:
Visiting Researchers may use funds to supplement sabbatical support for a total that does not exceed the candidate's current institutional salary. Visiting Researchers will be paid through their home institutions and will be expected to continue their health benefits through that source as well. Visiting Scholars will receive a stipend for living expenses and may be eligible for health benefits. Awardees may receive up to $4,000 in research support (through reimbursement of research expenses).

Amount of support per award: Maximum stipend $35,000.

Total amount of support: Varies.

APPLICATION INFO:
Application information is available on the web site.

Duration: Nine to 12 months. Nonrenewable.

Deadline: Varies.

PUBLICATIONS:
American Indian Culture and Research Journal; brochures; books.

IRS I.D.: 95-6006143

STAFF:
Mishuana Goeman, Interim Director
Pam Grieman, Managing Editor
Ken Wade, Librarian

ADDRESS INQUIRIES TO:
AISC Coordinator
(See address above.)

WASHINGTON HIGHER EDUCATION COORDINATING BOARD [1043]

American Indian Endowed Scholarship
917 Lakeridge Way
Olympia, WA 98502
(360) 753-7843
Fax: (360) 704-6243
E-mail: aies@wsac.wa.gov
annv@wsac.wa.gov
Web Site: www.wsac.wa.gov
www.rsg.org

AREAS OF INTEREST:
Student financial aid.

NAME(S) OF PROGRAMS:
- **American Indian Endowed Scholarship Program**

TYPE:
Scholarships.

YEAR PROGRAM STARTED: 1993

PURPOSE:
To create an educational opportunity for students with close social and cultural ties to the American Indian community to pursue undergraduate and graduate studies who might not be able otherwise to attend and graduate from higher education institutions in Washington state.

LEGAL BASIS:
Government agency.

ELIGIBILITY:
Applicants must be financially needy residents and students of an in-state institution with close social and cultural ties to the American Indian community in the state. Must have applied for financial aid via FAFSA. Applicant must intend to return service to the state Native American community. Academic merit is also a consideration.

FINANCIAL DATA:
Amount of support per award: $500 to $2,000.

Total amount of support: Varies.

APPLICATION INFO:
Application includes statement of commitment to return service to Washington American Indian communities, statement of close social and cultural ties, three letters of recommendation, completed application and release of information form and transcripts.

Duration: One year. Renewable for a maximum of four additional years.

Deadline: February 1. Announcement will be made by late Spring.

ADDRESS INQUIRIES TO:
Ann M. Voyles, Program Manager
American Indian Endowed Scholarship
P.O. Box 43430
Olympia, WA 98504-3430
E-mail: aies@wsac.wa.gov

Spanish-speaking

BNSF RAILWAY FOUNDATION [1044]

2650 Lou Menk Drive
Fort Worth, TX 76131-2830
(817) 867-6458
E-mail: bnsffoundation@bnsf.com
Web Site: www.bnsffoundation.org

NAME(S) OF PROGRAMS:
- **Hispanic American Scholarship Program**

TYPE:
Scholarships. Scholarships awarded to high school graduates of Hispanic origin through the Hispanic College Fund (HCF).

LEGAL BASIS:
Corporate foundation.

ELIGIBILITY:
Scholarships are awarded to high school graduates of Hispanic origin. All applicants must be U.S. citizens or legal residents and have already been accepted or enrolled in a college (two-year leading to a four-year degree) or university. Winners are selected by Hispanic Scholarship Fund (HSF) with scholarships to be awarded in each of the following Burlington Northern Santa Fe-served states: Arizona, California, Colorado, Illinois, Kansas, Missouri, New Mexico and Texas.

GEOG. RESTRICTIONS: Arizona, California, Colorado, Illinois, Kansas, Missouri, New Mexico and Texas.

FINANCIAL DATA:
Each Scholarship stipend is determined by HSF and funds are allocated from an annual $25,000 grant provided by the Foundation.

Amount of support per award: $500 to $2,500.

Total amount of support: $25,000 per academic year.

APPLICATION INFO:
Applications are available from Hispanic College Fund, Inc., 1301 K Street, N.W., Suite 450-A West, Washington, DC 20005.

Deadline: April 1.

ADDRESS INQUIRIES TO:
Hispanic College Fund, Inc.
1301 K Street, N.W.
Suite 450-A West
Washington, DC 20005

CONGRESSIONAL HISPANIC CAUCUS INSTITUTE [1045]

1128 16th Street, N.W.
Washington, DC 20036
(202) 543-1771
(202) 548-5864
Fax: (202) 546-2143
Web Site: www.chci.org

FOUNDED: 1978

AREAS OF INTEREST:
Leadership training in the legislative process for promising Latino undergraduates.

NAME(S) OF PROGRAMS:
- **CHCI Congressional Internship**

TYPE:
Internships. Internships provide college students with a paid work placement in a congressional office or federal agency for a period of 12 weeks (Spring and Fall Programs) or eight weeks (Summer Program).

PURPOSE:
To expose young Latinos to the legislative process and to strengthen their professional leadership skills, ultimately promoting the presence of Latinos on Capitol Hill and in federal agencies.

ELIGIBILITY:
Students must currently be enrolled full-time and working towards their undergraduate degree. Students must also be U.S. citizens or residents.

GEOG. RESTRICTIONS: United States.

FINANCIAL DATA:
Internship includes stipend, domestic round-trip transportation to Washington, DC, housing (all expenses covered) and academic credit if eligible.

Amount of support per award: Spring and Fall Programs: $3,750 stipend (12 weeks); Summer Program: $2,500 (eight weeks).

APPLICATION INFO:
A complete application consists of a one-page PDF resume, curriculum vitae, most recent unofficial transcript, and two letters of recommendation.

Duration: Spring and Fall Programs: 12 weeks; Summer Program: Eight weeks. Internships are not renewable.

Deadline: Spring Program: Early November. Fall Program: End of April. Summer Program: End of January.

CONGRESSIONAL HISPANIC CAUCUS INSTITUTE [1046]

1128 16th Street, N.W.
Washington, DC 20036
(202) 543-1771
(202) 548-8796
Fax: (202) 546-2143
Web Site: www.chci.org

FOUNDED: 1978

AREAS OF INTEREST:
Higher education, secondary education, health, housing, law, and public policy.

NAME(S) OF PROGRAMS:
- **CHCI Graduate Fellowship Program**
- **CHCI Public Policy Fellowship**

TYPE:
Fellowships. Graduate Fellowship Program offers exceptional Latinos who have earned a graduate degree or higher related to a chosen policy issue area within three years of program start date unparalleled exposure to hands-on experience in public policy.

Public Policy Fellowship offers talented Latinos who have earned a Bachelor's degree within two years of the program start date the opportunity to gain hands-on experience at the national level in public policy.

PURPOSE:
To help increase opportunities for Hispanics to participate in and contribute to the American policymaking process.

ELIGIBILITY:
Applicants must:
(1) demonstrate high academic achievement (preference of 3.0 grade point average or higher);
(2) show evidence of leadership skills and potential for leadership growth;
(3) demonstrate commitment to public service-oriented activities and;
(4) possess superior analytical skills, outstanding oral and written communication skills.

Graduate Fellowship Program applicants must have completed a Master's degree or postgraduate degree prior to the program start date.

Public Policy Fellowship applicants must have earned a Bachelor's degree within two years of the program start date.

Applicants must be U.S. citizens, lawful permanent residents, asylees, or individuals who are lawfully authorized to work full-time without restriction for any U.S. employer and who, at the time of application, possess lawful evidence of employment authorization.

GEOG. RESTRICTIONS: United States.

FINANCIAL DATA:
Amount of support per award: CHCI Graduate Fellowship Program: Initial stipend of approximately $2,900; biweekly stipend of approximately $1,160. CHCI Public Policy Fellowship: Initial stipend of approximately $2,400; biweekly stipend of approximately $960.

APPLICATION INFO:
A complete application consists of a one-page PDF resume, curriculum vitae, most recent unofficial transcript, and a letter of recommendation.

Duration: Nine months: Mid-August to mid-May.

Deadline: Mid-February.

CONGRESSIONAL HISPANIC CAUCUS INSTITUTE

1128 16th Street, N.W.
Washington, DC 20036
(202) 543-1771
Fax: (202) 546-2143
E-mail: scholarships@chci.org
Web Site: www.chci.org

TYPE:
Internships; Scholarships. CHCI Scholar-Intern Programs are designed to allow students to not only receive monetary support for their education, but also to gain hands-on experience in their chosen field through an internship. The program provides paid internship placements in a variety of fields including health care, human resource management, journalism, marketing and telecommunications.

See entry 1619 for full listing.

FLORIDA DEPARTMENT OF EDUCATION [1047]

Office of Student Financial Assistance
325 West Gaines Street, Suite 1314
Tallahassee, FL 32399-0400
(888) 827-2004
Fax: (850) 487-1809
E-mail: osfa@fldoe.org
Web Site: www.FloridaStudentFinancialAid.org/SSFAD/home/uamain.htm

NAME(S) OF PROGRAMS:
- **Jose Marti Scholarship Challenge Grant Fund**

TYPE:
Challenge/matching grants; Grants-in-aid. Jose Marti Scholarship Challenge Grant Fund is a need-based merit scholarship that provides financial assistance to eligible students of Hispanic origin who will attend Florida public or eligible private institutions.

YEAR PROGRAM STARTED: 1986

PURPOSE:
To provide financial assistance to Hispanic-American high school seniors and graduate students in Florida.

LEGAL BASIS:
Florida Department of Education.

ELIGIBILITY:
Applicants for undergraduate study must apply during their senior year of high school. Graduate students may apply; however, priority for the scholarship is given to graduating high school seniors.

For the applying student, initial eligibility requirements to receive funding are as follows:
(1) be a Florida resident and a U.S. citizen or eligible noncitizen; a student's residency and citizenship status are determined by the postsecondary institution; consult the financial aid office or admissions office of the institution the student plans to attend for questions;
(2) not owe a repayment or be in default under any state or federal grant, loan or scholarship program unless satisfactory arrangements to repay have been made;
(3) be of Spanish culture, born in or having a natural parent who was born in either Mexico, or a Hispanic country of the Caribbean, Central or South America, regardless of race;
(4) have earned, by the end of the seventh semester, a minimum unweighted cumulative grade point average of 3.0 on a 4.0 scale in high school for an undergraduate scholarship, or a 3.0 institutional cumulative grade point average for undergraduate college work if applying for a graduate-level scholarship and;
(5) enroll as a degree-seeking student at an eligible postsecondary institution and enroll each academic term for a minimum of 12 credit hours for undergraduate study or nine credit hours for graduate study.

GEOG. RESTRICTIONS: Florida.

FINANCIAL DATA:
Amount of support per award: Typically $2,000.

NO. AWARDS: 52 for the year 2014-15.

APPLICATION INFO:
Detailed program information can be found on the web site.

Deadline: For undergraduate study, submit a fully completed error-free Florida Financial Aid Application during the student's last year in high school by April 1. For graduate study, submit a fully completed error-free Florida Financial Aid Application by April 1 prior to the year of graduate study. Demonstrate sufficient financial need to receive a full $2,000 scholarship by completing and submitting the Free Application for Federal Student Aid (FAFSA) in time to be processed error-free by the U.S. Department of Education on or before May 15.

ADDRESS INQUIRIES TO:
State Scholarship and Grant Programs
(See address above.)

HISPANIC NATIONAL BAR FOUNDATION

1900 K Street, N.W.
Suite 100
Washington, DC 20006
(202) 496-7206
Fax: (202) 496-7756
E-mail: avilla@hnbf.org
Web Site: www.hnbf.org

TYPE:
Fellowships. The Law Fellows Program provides participating law students with the unique opportunity to join a corporation's legal department to focus on matters important to company business. The Law Fellows Program also includes a law firm component to expose the students to how law firms handle legal matters for their corporate clients. The Program includes training, professional development and work experience in Washington, DC, and in-house at the company's legal department.

See entry 1919 for full listing.

HISPANIC NATIONAL BAR FOUNDATION

1900 K Street, N.W.
Suite 100
Washington, DC 20006
(202) 496-7206
Fax: (202) 496-7756
E-mail: avilla@hnbf.org
Web Site: www.hnbf.org

TYPE:
Conferences/seminars; Training grants. Nine-day program held by the Foundation in Washington, DC which provides Latino high school students with the opportunity to learn more about the legal profession. The Law Camp offers students the chance to come to the nation's capital and learn more about the college application process, meet influential Latino leaders, and tour national monuments and various government agencies.

See entry 1920 for full listing.

HISPANIC SCHOLARSHIP FUND [1048]

1411 West 190th Street
Suite 700
Gardena, CA 90248
(877) 473-4636
(310) 975-3700
Fax: (310) 349-3328
E-mail: info@hsf.net
scholar1@hsf.net
Web Site: www.hsf.net

FOUNDED: 1975

AREAS OF INTEREST:
College scholarships for Hispanic American students.

NAME(S) OF PROGRAMS:
- **General College Scholarship Program**

TYPE:
Scholarships. Awarded to Hispanic community college, undergraduate and graduate students.

YEAR PROGRAM STARTED: 1975

PURPOSE:
To strengthen America by generating support for the educational advancement of Hispanics by increasing the rate of Hispanics earning a college degree.

LEGAL BASIS:
Nonprofit 501(c)(3) organization.

ELIGIBILITY:
Applicant must:
(1) be of Hispanic heritage;
(2) be a U.S. citizen or legal permanent resident;
(3) have a minimum 3.0 cumulative grade point average (on a 4.0 scale) and;
(4) apply for federal financial aid using FAFSA.

FINANCIAL DATA:
Amount of support per award: $1,000 to $15,000.

Total amount of support: Approximately $35,500,000 for the year 2015.

NO. MOST RECENT APPLICANTS: 56,000.

NO. AWARDS: 1,000.

APPLICATION INFO:
Electronic application only; forms available at the web site.

Duration: Students may reapply until they obtain a degree, providing they satisfy full-time enrollment.

Deadline: Early to mid-December.

PUBLICATIONS:
Annual report; newsletter.

IRS I.D.: 52-1051044

BOARD OF DIRECTORS:
Lisa Garcia-Quiroz, Chairperson
Gene Camarena, Vice Chairperson
Anthony Salcido, Treasurer
Margarita Flores, Secretary
Fidel A. Vargas, President and Chief Executive Officer
Linda Bagley
Michael J. Bender
Kimberly Casiano
Walter Dolhare
Dean William R. Fitzsimmons
Nely Galan
Juan Galarraga
Phillip Hyun
James McNamara
Angel Luis Morales
Diana Natalicio
Ida Nieto
Elizabeth Oliver-Farrow
Bea Perez
Adam Rodriguez
Gina Rodriguez
Maria Elena Salinas
Edgar A. Sandoval
Violeta Vera Seidell

UCLA CHICANO STUDIES RESEARCH CENTER [1049]

193 Haines Hall
Box 951544
Los Angeles, CA 90095
(310) 825-2363
Fax: (310) 206-1784
E-mail: csrcinfo@chicano.ucla.edu
Web Site: www.chicano.ucla.edu
www.iac.ucla.edu/

FOUNDED: 1969

AREAS OF INTEREST:
Chicano Studies and relevant fields.

NAME(S) OF PROGRAMS:
- **Institute of American Cultures Post Doctoral Fellowship Program**

TYPE:
Fellowships; Visiting scholars.

YEAR PROGRAM STARTED: 1976

PURPOSE:
To advance scholarship in the Chicano and Latino community in the U.S.

LEGAL BASIS:
University program.

ELIGIBILITY:
Applicants must possess a Ph.D. and a project proposal.

FINANCIAL DATA:
Amount of support per award: $32,000 to $35,000, health insurance, and $4,000 research grant, of which $1,000 can be used for relocation expenses.

Total amount of support: Up to $39,000 annually.

NO. MOST RECENT APPLICANTS: 16.

NO. AWARDS: 1.

APPLICATION INFO:
Application information available upon request.

Duration: One fiscal year, July 1 to June 30.

Deadline: February. Notification in April.

OFFICERS:
Chon A. Noriega, Director

ADDRESS INQUIRIES TO:
Grants and Fellowships Coordinator
(See address above.)

Women

THE ISABEL ALLENDE FOUNDATION [1050]

116 Caledonia Street
Sausalito, CA 94965
(415) 289-0992
Fax: (415) 332-4149
E-mail: lori@isabelallendefoundation.org
Web Site: www.isabelallendefoundation.org

FOUNDED: 1996

AREAS OF INTEREST:
Reproductive rights, healthcare, education, and protection from violence.

NAME(S) OF PROGRAMS:
- **Esperanza Grants**

TYPE:
Project/program grants. Promotes and preserves the fundamental rights of women and children to be empowered and protected.

PURPOSE:
To support nonprofits in California and Chile that provide vulnerable women and children access to reproductive rights, healthcare, education and protection from violence.

ELIGIBILITY:
Nonprofit 501(c)(3) grassroots organizations and equivalent international organizations that benefit the San Francisco Bay area and/or Chile are eligible to apply. No grants to individuals.

The Foundation does not fund capital campaigns, individual trips or tours, conferences or events, and projects that benefit political, religious, and/or military organizations.

Unsolicited requests are not accepted.

GEOG. RESTRICTIONS: San Francisco Bay area, California and Chile.

FINANCIAL DATA:
Amount of support per award: $3,000 to $8,000.

Total amount of support: Approximately $400,000.

APPLICATION INFO:
New organization proposals are not being accepted at this time. Current grantees may apply for renewal and will receive instructions from the Foundation on how to apply.

Duration: One year. Must submit report for renewal.

Deadline: January 1, April 1, July 1 and October 1.

ADDRESS INQUIRIES TO:
Lori Barra, Executive Director
(See address above.)

AMERICAN ASSOCIATION OF UNIVERSITY WOMEN [1051]

1111 Sixteenth Street, N.W.
Washington, DC 20036
(866) 795-4892
E-mail: aauw@applyists.com
Web Site: www.aauw.org

FOUNDED: 1888

AREAS OF INTEREST:
Advancement of educational and professional opportunities for women in the U.S.

NAME(S) OF PROGRAMS:
- **AAUW Selected Professions Fellowships**

TYPE:
Fellowships. Awarded to women who are U.S. citizens or permanent residents who are pursuing full-time study in a Master's or professional degree program in which women are underrepresented, including STEM, law, business and medicine.

PURPOSE:
To encourage women's participation in fields where they have been traditionally underrepresented.

ELIGIBILITY:
Selected Professions Fellowships are awarded for the following Master's programs:
(1) Architecture;
(2) Computer/information sciences;
(3) Engineering and;
(4) Mathematics/statistics.

Fellowships in the following degree programs are restricted to women of color, who have been underrepresented in these fields:
(1) Master's in business administration - applicants may apply for second year of study only;
(2) Law - applicants may apply for third year of study only and;
(3) Doctorate in medicine - applicants may apply for third or fourth year of study only.

GEOG. RESTRICTIONS: United States.

FINANCIAL DATA:
Amount of support per award: $5,000 to $18,000.

APPLICATION INFO:
Visit www.aauw.org/what-we-do/educational-funding-and-awards/selected-professions-fellowships for complete information.

Deadline: January 10.

AMERICAN ASSOCIATION OF UNIVERSITY WOMEN [1052]

1111 Sixteenth Street, N.W.
Washington, DC 20036
(866) 795-4892
E-mail: aauw@applyists.com
Web Site: www.aauw.org

FOUNDED: 1888

AREAS OF INTEREST:
Advancement of educational and professional opportunities for women in the U.S. and around the globe.

NAME(S) OF PROGRAMS:
- **American Fellowships**

TYPE:
Fellowships; Visiting scholars. Awarded to women who are U.S. citizens or permanent residents pursuing full-time study to complete dissertations, conducting postdoctoral research full-time, or preparing research for publication for eight consecutive weeks.

YEAR PROGRAM STARTED: 1888

PURPOSE:
To support women scholars who are completing dissertations, planning research leave from accredited institutions or preparing research for publication.

ELIGIBILITY:
Applicants must be citizens or permanent residents of the U.S. There are no restrictions as to place of study or age. Fellowship is open to women who will have completed all requirements for the Doctorate, except the writing of the dissertation, by November 15 preceding the fellowship year, July 1 to June 30, or who hold the Ph.D. at the time of application. Applicants are evaluated by academic professionals on the scholarly excellence of their proposals, quality and originality of project design, and experience teaching or mentoring female students. In addition, applicants will be asked to outline their commitment to helping women and girls through community service, service in their profession and/or service in their field of research.

GEOG. RESTRICTIONS: United States.

FINANCIAL DATA:
Amount of support per award: $6,000 to $30,000.

APPLICATION INFO:
Visit www.aauw.org/what-we-do/educational-funding-and-awards/american-fellowships for complete information.

Deadline: November 15.

AMERICAN ASSOCIATION OF UNIVERSITY WOMEN

1111 Sixteenth Street, N.W.
Washington, DC 20036
(866) 795-4892
E-mail: aauw@applyists.com
Web Site: www.aauw.org

TYPE:
Fellowships. Awarded to women pursuing full-time graduate or postdoctoral study in the U.S. who are not U.S. citizens or permanent residents.

See entry 936 for full listing.

AMERICAN ASSOCIATION OF UNIVERSITY WOMEN [1053]

1111 Sixteenth Street, N.W.
Washington, DC 20036
(866) 795-4892
E-mail: aauw@applyists.com
Web Site: www.aauw.org

FOUNDED: 1888

AREAS OF INTEREST:
Nontraditional fields.

NAME(S) OF PROGRAMS:
- **AAUW Career Development Grants**

TYPE:
Grants-in-aid. Awarded to women who are U.S. citizens or permanent residents pursuing a certificate or degree to advance their careers, change careers or re-enter the workforce and whose Bachelor's degree was received at least five years before the award period.

YEAR PROGRAM STARTED: 1972

PURPOSE:
To assist women who are continuing their self-development through higher education.

ELIGIBILITY:
Career Development Grants provide funding to women who hold a Bachelor's degree and are preparing to advance or change careers or re-enter the workforce. Primary consideration is given to women of color and women pursuing their first advanced degree or credentials in nontraditional fields.

Applicants must be U.S. citizens or permanent residents whose last degree was received before June 30, 2011. Funds are available for tuition, fees, books, supplies, local transportation and dependent care.

Grants provide support for course work beyond a Bachelor's degree, including a Master's degree, second Bachelor's degree, certification program or specialized training in technical or professional fields. Course work must be taken at an accredited two- or four-year college or university in the U.S. or at a technical school that is fully licensed or accredited by the U.S. Department of Education. Funds are not available for Doctorate-level work.

GEOG. RESTRICTIONS: United States.

FINANCIAL DATA:
Amount of support per award: $2,000 to $12,000.

APPLICATION INFO:
Visit www.aauw.org/what-we-do/educational-funding-and-awards/career-development-grants for complete information.

Deadline: December 15.

AMERICAN NUCLEAR SOCIETY (ANS)

555 North Kensington Avenue
LaGrange Park, IL 60526
(708) 352-6611
Fax: (708) 352-0499
E-mail: scholarships@ans.org
Web Site: www.ans.org

TYPE:
Scholarships. Delayed Education for Women Scholarship is designed for women in a nuclear-related field whose formal studies have been delayed or interrupted for at least one year.

Landis Scholarships are administered by the ANS NEED Committee, and are awarded to undergraduate and graduate students who have greater-than-average financial need.

See entry 2549 for full listing.

BERKSHIRE CONFERENCE OF WOMEN HISTORIANS

543 Bramhall Avenue
Jersey City, NJ 07304
(201) 521-9195
(201) 463-6749
E-mail: secretary@berksconference.org
Web Site: www.berksconference.org

TYPE:
Awards/prizes. One prize awarded annually for the best first book and one for the best article of historical scholarship published by a woman historian in any field of history during the preceding year.

See entry 569 for full listing.

BOSTON WOMEN'S FUND [1054]

14 Beacon Street
Suite 805
Boston, MA 02108
(617) 725-0035
E-mail: amy@bostonwomensfund.org
Web Site: www.bostonwomensfund.org

FOUNDED: 1984

AREAS OF INTEREST:
Women organized for social and economic change.

TYPE:
Grants-in-aid; Project/program grants; Seed money grants.

PURPOSE:
To pool funds from individuals; to channel money to support women's and girls' organizations for economic and social justice.

LEGAL BASIS:
Public foundation.

ELIGIBILITY:
Applicants or their fiscal agents must be 501(c)(3) organizations. Also funded are direct-service projects which have an organizing component. Groups just getting started are encouraged to apply, particularly those women who are most vulnerable and have the least access to other resources including women of color, low-income women, disabled women, lesbians, girls, older women, transgender people, immigrant and refugee women. Applicants with organizational budgets of less than $350,000 per year are preferred. No grants to individuals.

GEOG. RESTRICTIONS: Preference given to the Boston metropolitan area, and to selected outlying areas such as Brockton, Lawrence, Lowell and Worcester, Massachusetts.

FINANCIAL DATA:
Amount of support per award: Up to $20,000.

NO. MOST RECENT APPLICANTS: Varies.

NO. AWARDS: Varies.

APPLICATION INFO:
Download a Letter of Intent form at the web site, complete and submit to the Fund. Selected letters will be invited to submit a proposal.

Duration: One year.

PUBLICATIONS:
Application guidelines; donor contribution information in annual report.

ADDRESS INQUIRIES TO:
Amy Leung, Program Officer
(See address above.)

BROOKHAVEN WOMEN IN SCIENCE [1055]

P.O. Box 183
Upton, NY 11973
(631) 344-2425
Fax: (631) 344-5676
E-mail: bwisawards@bnl.gov
Web Site: www.bnl.gov/bwis/scholarships.php

FOUNDED: 1979

AREAS OF INTEREST:
Advancement of women in the natural sciences, engineering or mathematics fields.

NAME(S) OF PROGRAMS:
- **Renate W. Chasman Scholarship for Women**

TYPE:
Awards/prizes; Scholarships. These scholarships are offered to encourage women to resume their formal education in the natural sciences, engineering or mathematics.

YEAR PROGRAM STARTED: 1986

PURPOSE:
To encourage women to resume their formal education in a technical field.

LEGAL BASIS:
Tax-exempt, incorporated under the Educational Laws of New York state.

ELIGIBILITY:
Applicants must be:
(1) women;
(2) undergraduate seniors or graduate students at an accredited educational institution;
(3) performing research at Brookhaven National Laboratory in the STEM disciplines (science, technology, engineering or mathematics) and;
(4) receiving their degree not prior to May of the year of the award.

FINANCIAL DATA:
Amount of support per award: $1,000.

NO. AWARDS: 1 per year.

APPLICATION INFO:
Requests for application via mail must include a self-addressed, stamped envelope.

Duration: One-time award.

Deadline: All application materials - forms, transcripts, reference letters and goal statement - are due by November 30 for the following year's competition. The award will be presented in May.

ADDRESS INQUIRIES TO:
Chasman Scholarship Fund
Brookhaven Women in Science
(See address or e-mail above.)

CANADIAN FEDERATION OF UNIVERSITY WOMEN [1056]

331 Cooper Street, Suite 502
Ottawa ON K2P 0G5 Canada
(613) 234-8252
(888) 220-9606
Fax: (613) 234-8221
E-mail: fellowships@cfuw.org
Web Site: www.cfuw.org

FOUNDED: 1919

AREAS OF INTEREST:
Graduate education for women.

NAME(S) OF PROGRAMS:
- **Ruth Binnie Fellowship**
- **Canadian Home Economics Association (CHEA) Fellowship**
- **CFUW Aboriginal Women's Award (AWA)**
- **CFUW Bourse Georgette Lemoyne**
- **CFUW Dr. Alice E. Wilson Awards**
- **CFUW Dr. Margaret McWilliams Pre-Doctoral Fellowship**
- **CFUW Elizabeth Massey Award**
- **CFUW Linda Souter Humanities Award**
- **CFUW Memorial Fellowship**
- **CFUW 1989 Ecole Polytechnique Commemorative Awards**

TYPE:
Awards/prizes; Fellowships. The Ruth Binnie Fellowship is for Master's studies with a focus on one or more aspects of the field of home economics. The candidate may be studying abroad.

Canadian Home Economics Association Fellowship candidate must be studying one or more aspects in the field of home economics at the Master's or doctoral level in Canada.

CFUW Aboriginal Women's Award candidate must be a Canadian Aboriginal woman studying in Canada, who holds an undergraduate university degree or equivalent and has applied to be a full-time student in any year of an eligible program at a recognized or accredited Canadian post-secondary degree-granting institution.

CFUW Bourse Georgette Lemoyne Fellowship is for graduate study at a Canadian university. The candidate must be studying in French.

CFUW Dr. Alice E. Wilson Award is for graduate studies in any field, with special consideration given to candidates returning to study after at least three years.

CFUW Dr. Margaret McWilliams Pre-Doctoral Fellowship candidate must have completed at least one full calendar year as a full-time student in doctoral-level studies and be a full-time student in Canada or abroad at the time of application.

CFUW Elizabeth Massey Award is for postgraduate studies in the visual arts such as painting, sculpture or in music in Canada or abroad.

CFUW Linda Souter Humanities Award is for Master's or doctoral students studying in the area of the humanities including English language and literature, history, languages study, classics, philosophy, film studies, communication studies and culture studies.

CFUW Memorial Fellowship candidate must be enrolled in a Master's degree program in science, mathematics, or engineering in Canada or abroad.

CFUW 1989 Ecole Polytechnique Commemorative Award is for graduate studies in any field. The candidate must justify the relevance of her work to women.

YEAR PROGRAM STARTED: 1921

PURPOSE:
To support the education of women at the postgraduate level in Canada and abroad.

LEGAL BASIS:
Foundation of a nonprofit organization.

ELIGIBILITY:
Candidates must hold at least a Bachelor's degree or equivalent from a recognized university, have been accepted into the proposed program and place of study, and be a Canadian citizen or permanent resident.

GEOG. RESTRICTIONS: Canada.

FINANCIAL DATA:
Amount of support per award: $5,000 to $25,000 (CAN).

Total amount of support: Approximately $84,500 for the year 2015-16.

NO. MOST RECENT APPLICANTS: 234.

NO. AWARDS: 10 different categories, with 14 awards.

APPLICATION INFO:
Application form and guidelines are posted in May on the Federation's web site.

Duration: One year. Grants not renewable, except the CFUW Aboriginal Women's Award.

Deadline: November 1 (postmark). Announcement May 31.

PUBLICATIONS:
The Communicator; *CFUW Charitable Trust Annual Report*; *CFUW Fellowships and*

Awards, e-newsletter; *CFUW External Annual Report*; *CFUW News & Updates*; *CFUW Week in Review*.

ADDRESS INQUIRIES TO:
Betty Dunlop
Fellowships Program Manager
(See address above.)

THE COORDINATING COUNCIL FOR WOMEN IN HISTORY, INC. [1057]

6042 Blue Point Court
Clarksville, MD 21209
(805) 705-7097
E-mail: execdir@theccwh.org
Web Site: www.theccwh.org

FOUNDED: 1969

AREAS OF INTEREST:
Women's history.

NAME(S) OF PROGRAMS:
- **Catherine Prelinger Award**

TYPE:
Awards/prizes. The Catherine Prelinger Award is given to a scholar, with a Ph.D. or A.B.D., whose career has not followed a traditional academic path through secondary and higher education and whose work has contributed to women in the historical profession.

YEAR PROGRAM STARTED: 1998

PURPOSE:
To explore the diverse experiences and histories of all women; to honor scholars that have not followed a traditional academic path of uninterrupted and completed secondary, undergraduate, and graduate degrees leading into a tenured faculty position and whose work has contributed to women in the historical profession; to promote research and interpretation in areas of women's history; to recognize or to enhance the ability of the recipient to contribute significantly to women in history, whether in the profession in the present or in the study of women in the past.

ELIGIBILITY:
The applicant:
(1) must be a member in good standing of the Coordinating Council for Women in History;
(2) must hold either A.B.D. status or the Ph.D. at the time of application;
(3) shall be actively engaged in scholarship that is historical in nature, although the degree may be in related fields;
(4) shall have already contributed or shown potential for contributing significantly to women in history, whether in the profession in the present or in the study of women in the past and;
(5) has not followed a traditional academic path of uninterrupted and completed secondary, undergraduate and graduate degrees leading to a tenure-track faculty position.

FINANCIAL DATA:
Funds issued in U.S. dollars only.
Amount of support per award: $20,000.

NO. MOST RECENT APPLICANTS: 18.

NO. AWARDS: 1.

APPLICATION INFO:
Contact the organization.
Deadline: September 15.

ADDRESS INQUIRIES TO:
Sandra Trudgen Dawson, Executive Director
(See e-mail address above.)

*SPECIAL STIPULATIONS:
All recipients will be required to submit a final paper to CCWH on how the award was expended and summarizing the scholarly work completed.

THE COORDINATING COUNCIL FOR WOMEN IN HISTORY, INC.

6042 Blue Point Court
Clarksville, MD 21209
(805) 705-7097
E-mail: execdir@theccwh.org
Web Site: www.theccwh.org

TYPE:
Awards/prizes; Fellowships.

See entry 574 for full listing.

DALLAS WOMEN'S FOUNDATION [1058]

Campbell Centre II
8150 North Central Expressway, Suite 110
Dallas, TX 75206
(214) 965-9977
Fax: (214) 526-3633
E-mail: dwf@dallaswomensfdn.org
Web Site: www.dallaswomensfdn.org

FOUNDED: 1985

AREAS OF INTEREST:
Economic independence of women and girls.

TYPE:
General operating grants; Project/program grants.

YEAR PROGRAM STARTED: 1985

PURPOSE:
To promote women's philanthropy and raise money to support community programs that help women and girls realize their full potential.

LEGAL BASIS:
Community organization.

ELIGIBILITY:
Applicants must be 501(c)(3) organizations with 50% of the recipients residing in Dallas, Denton or Collin counties, TX. The applying program must serve at least 75% women and/or girls.

GEOG. RESTRICTIONS: Collin, Dallas and Denton counties, Texas.

FINANCIAL DATA:
Amount of support per award: Up to $30,000.
Total amount of support: $4,200,000 for fiscal year 2016.

APPLICATION INFO:
The guidelines and application form are available online.
Duration: One year.
Deadline: Varies.

IRS I.D.: 75-2048261

STAFF:
Roslyn Dawson Thompson, President and Chief Executive Officer
Mary Vares, Vice President-Finance and Operations
Dena L. Jackson, Vice President-Grants and Research
Mary Valadez, Senior Grants Director
Susan Walters, Development Operations Director

ADDRESS INQUIRIES TO:
Mary Valadez, Senior Grants Director
E-mail: mvaladez@dallaswomensfdn.org

DAUGHTERS OF PENELOPE FOUNDATION, INC. [1059]

1909 Q Street, N.W., Suite 500
Washington, DC 20009
(202) 234-9741
Fax: (202) 483-6983
E-mail: dophq@ahepa.org
Web Site: www.dopfoundationinc.com

FOUNDED: 1983

AREAS OF INTEREST:
Education, health and philanthropy.

NAME(S) OF PROGRAMS:
- **Paula J. Alexander Memorial Scholarship (Undergraduate)**
- **Helen J. Beldecos, Past Grand President, Scholarship (Undergraduate)**
- **The Big Five Graduate Scholarship**
- **Daughters of Penelope Past Grand Presidents Memorial Scholarship (Undergraduate)**
- **Daughters of Penelope Past Grand Presidents Undergraduate Scholarship**
- **Daughters of Penelope - St. Basil's Academy**
- **Eos #1 Mother Lodge Chapter Scholarship (Undergraduate)**
- **Joanne V. Hologgitas, Ph.D., Past Grand President, Scholarship (Undergraduate)**
- **Hopewell Agave Chapter #224 Scholarship (Undergraduate)**
- **Timothy Joannides Family Scholarship**
- **Mary Kandaras Memorial Scholarship (Undergraduate)**
- **Kottis Family Scholarship (Undergraduate)**
- **Dorothy Lillian Quincey Memorial Graduate Scholarship**
- **Alexandra Apostolides Sonenfeld Memorial Undergraduate Scholarship**
- **Sonja B. Stefanadis Graduate Student Scholarship**
- **Barbara Edith Quincey Thorndyke Memorial Undergraduate Scholarship**
- **Mary M. Verges, Past Grand President, Scholarship (Undergraduate)**
- **The Sotiri Zervoulias & Lea Soupata Scholarship (St. Basil's Academy)**

TYPE:
Scholarships.

YEAR PROGRAM STARTED: 1983

PURPOSE:
To support education for women of Greek descent.

LEGAL BASIS:
The Foundation is a recognized 501(c)(3) organization; tax-exempt.

ELIGIBILITY:
Scholarships are based on financial need or academic merit (or both). Contact the organization for full details.

GEOG. RESTRICTIONS: Canada, Greece and United States.

FINANCIAL DATA:
Amount of support per award: $500 to $2,500.

NO. AWARDS: 24 for the year 2016.

APPLICATION INFO:
Information and guidelines are available online.

Deadline: May 1.

PUBLICATIONS:
President's Bulletin, monthly publication.

IRS I.D.: 52-1346043

ADDRESS INQUIRIES TO:
Elena Saviolakis
Executive Director
(See address above.)

*SPECIAL STIPULATIONS:
Scholarship may not be deferred to be used at a later date. These awards are not renewable and must be used strictly for tuition and/or books. Application must be typewritten. All requirements must be met and all questions answered or applicant will be disqualified.

DAUGHTERS OF THE CINCINNATI

20 West 44th Street, Room 508
New York, NY 10036
(212) 991-9945
E-mail: scholarships@daughters1894.org
Web Site: www.daughters1894.org

TYPE:
Scholarships. Undergraduate scholarships.

See entry 1622 for full listing.

DREXEL UNIVERSITY COLLEGE OF MEDICINE [1060]

The Legacy Center:
Archives and Special Collections
2900 West Queen Lane
Philadelphia, PA 19129
(215) 991-8340
Fax: (215) 991-8172
E-mail: archives@drexelmed.edu
Web Site: archives.drexelmed.edu

FOUNDED: 1977

AREAS OF INTEREST:
Medicine as it relates to women in professional practice.

NAME(S) OF PROGRAMS:

- **M. Louise Gloeckner, M.D., Summer Research Fellowship**

TYPE:
Fellowships. For four to six weeks of research at The Legacy Center. Collections house the business and academic records of the Woman's Medical College of Pennsylvania, the Medical College of Pennsylvania, and Drexel University College of Medicine, the personal papers of women physicians, records of national and international women's medical organizations, schools, associations, hospitals and a historic photograph collection.

YEAR PROGRAM STARTED: 1985

PURPOSE:
To encourage the use of the institution's archival collections in the study of women in medicine, and history generally.

LEGAL BASIS:
University.

ELIGIBILITY:
Applicants must be either undergraduate or graduate students, medical students, faculty members or independent researchers. Preference is given to researchers with well-defined projects to be completed in one summer.

FINANCIAL DATA:
Total amount of support: $4,000.

NO. AWARDS: 1.

APPLICATION INFO:
Guidelines and application form are available on the web site.

Duration: Four to six weeks depending on project.

Deadline: March 1.

PUBLICATIONS:
Program announcement.

STAFF:
Joanne Murray, Historian and Director

ADDRESS INQUIRIES TO:
Joanne Murray, Historian and Director
(See address above.)

THE EDUCATIONAL FOUNDATION FOR WOMEN IN ACCOUNTING

136 South Keowee Street
Dayton, OH 45402-2241
(937) 424-3391
Fax: (937) 222-5794
E-mail: info@efwa.org
Web Site: www.efwa.org

TYPE:
Scholarships. Laurels Fund provides a one-year academic scholarship for women pursuing a Ph.D. in accounting.

Women in Need Scholarship is available to women in their third, fourth or fifth year of academic pursuit who need the financial support to complete their degrees. It is renewable annually upon satisfactory completion of course requirements.

Women in Transition Scholarship is intended for women returning to school as freshmen to earn a Bachelor's degree in accounting. It is renewable annually upon satisfactory completion of course requirements.

See entry 1837 for full listing.

GENERAL BOARD OF HIGHER EDUCATION AND MINISTRY, THE UNITED METHODIST CHURCH

1001 19th Avenue South
Nashville, TN 37212
(615) 340-7338
Fax: (615) 340-7529
E-mail: mbigord@gbhem.org
Web Site: www.gbhem.org

TYPE:
Awards/prizes; Scholarships. Awards to encourage women over age 35 to prepare for ordained ministry as an Elder in the United Methodist Church as a second career. The scholarship is to be used for study toward the basic seminary degree in an accredited school of theology.

See entry 798 for full listing.

GLOBAL FUND FOR WOMEN [1061]

800 Market Street, 7th Floor
San Francisco, CA 94102
(415) 248-4800
Fax: (415) 248-4801
E-mail: jsloan@globalfundforwomen.org
Web Site: www.globalfundforwomen.org

FOUNDED: 1987

AREAS OF INTEREST:
Female human rights, women's access to communications, economic autonomy of women, and girls' education.

TYPE:
Conferences/seminars; General operating grants; Seed money grants; Technical assistance; Training grants. The Global Fund for Women is a grantmaking foundation that brings together a worldwide network of women and men to strengthen women's rights around the world. Initiatives include promoting women's economic independence, girls' education, women's rights within religious and cultural tradition, and women's health and safety. The Fund also provides assistance to groups overseas that wish to establish philanthropic organizations designed to benefit women.

YEAR PROGRAM STARTED: 1987

PURPOSE:
To promote a world of equality and social justice; to provide the financial means to enable women to attain this vision.

LEGAL BASIS:
Nonprofit corporation, 501(c)(3) tax-exempt.

ELIGIBILITY:
The Global Fund does not make grants to individuals, groups based and working primarily or solely in the U.S., groups whose main or only purpose is to generate income for its members or the community or groups headed and managed by men and without women in important management functions.

The Global Fund considers support to groups which demonstrate a clear commitment to women's equality and female human rights, are governed and directed primarily by women, have defined plans to strengthen the work of the group over time and may be unlikely to obtain funding from other sources.

FINANCIAL DATA:
Amount of support per award: $5,000 to $30,000.

Total amount of support: Approximately $7,000,000 for fiscal year 2014-15.

NO. MOST RECENT APPLICANTS: Approximately 2,500 annually.

NO. AWARDS: Approximately 500 annually.

APPLICATION INFO:
Applicants may request and respond to grant request guidelines or send a letter describing the group and including contact information, organizational information and grant request information.

Duration: Varies depending on needs and nature of the request.

PUBLICATIONS:
Annual report; brochure; *Raising Our Voices*, newsletter.

IRS I.D.: 77-0155782

STAFF:
Deborah Holmes, Chief of Staff

Jane Sloane, Vice President Programs
Elizabeth Schaffer, Chief Financial and Operations Officer

GRADUATE WOMEN INTERNATIONAL (GWI) [1062]

10, rue du Lac
CH 1207 Geneva Switzerland
(41) 22 731 23 80
Fax: (41) 22 738 04 40
Web Site: www.graduatewomen.org

FOUNDED: 1919

AREAS OF INTEREST:
Secondary, tertiary, continuing and nontraditional education for girls and women, human rights, status of women.

CONSULTING OR VOLUNTEER SERVICES:
At the international level, IFUW has working relationships with a number of nongovernmental organizations, consultative status with ECOSOC, ILO and UNESCO, as well as periodic cooperation with other UN bodies. At the national level, affiliates in 61 countries work to accomplish IFUW's goals and to address issues of global concern, both through project work and interaction with their governments and other interested groups.

NAME(S) OF PROGRAMS:
- **CFUW/A. Vibert Douglas Fellowship**
- **Winifred Cullis Grant**
- **GWI Recognition Award**
- **Dorothy Leet Grant**
- **Ida Smedley MacLean Fellowship**
- **NZFGW Daphne Purves Grant**

TYPE:
Awards/prizes; Capital grants; Fellowships; Research grants; Training grants. IFUW fellowships and grants are awarded biennially to encourage and enable women graduates to undertake original research or obtain further training in the humanities, social sciences and natural sciences.

YEAR PROGRAM STARTED: 1919

PURPOSE:
To promote understanding and friendship among the university women of the world, irrespective of their race, nationality, religion or political opinions; to encourage international cooperation; to further the development of education; to represent university women in international organizations; to encourage the full application of members' skills to the problems which arise at all levels of public life, whether local, national, regional or worldwide; to encourage their participation in the solving of these problems.

LEGAL BASIS:
International nongovernmental organization, based in Geneva, Switzerland.

ELIGIBILITY:
Open to women graduates:
(1) who are members of IFUW enrolled in a Ph.D. programme of which they have completed the first year and;
(2) who are nonmembers and independent members of less than the nominated period of membership; these may apply subject to payment of an administrative fee.

Winifred Cullis Grants are open to women graduates who seek to obtain specialized training essential to their research, train in new techniques or carry out independent research, including completion of a piece of research well-advanced.

Dorothy Leet Grants are open to women graduates of countries with a comparatively low per capita income and to other women graduates who either wish to work as experts in these countries or whose research is of value to such countries. They are available for obtaining special training essential to research and survey work, training in new techniques in group research and further study and carrying out independent research or surveys, including completion of a project well-advanced at the time of the application. Special consideration will be given to applicants whose research or training will have a multiplier effect in their home country.

In the case of both Winifred Cullis and Dorothy Leet Grants, preference is given for work in a country other than that in which the candidate has received her education or habitually resides.

Applications are welcomed from the humanities, social sciences and natural sciences. Membership in a national association is also an eligibility factor.

FINANCIAL DATA:
Candidates must provide evidence of adequate budgetary provision to meet the costs of their studies over and above the amount requested for the GWI award.

Amount of support per award: Fellowships: CHF 8,000 to 10,000; Grants: CHF 3,000 to 6,000; GWI Recognition Award: CHF 1,000.

NO. MOST RECENT APPLICANTS: 70.

NO. AWARDS: 16 to 25 fellowships and grants are offered in each competition.

APPLICATION INFO:
All applications must be submitted electronically. Application forms are available on the web site. Members of one of GWI's national affiliates must submit applications when completed with required supporting documentation to their NFA. Independent members and nonmembers must submit their completed applications directly to the GWI Office in Geneva with any administrative fee that is required.

Duration: Fellowships are intended to cover eight to 12 months of work. Grants are awarded for a minimum of two months of work. The awards are not renewable.

Deadline: The final deadline for all applications to reach the IFUW Office in Geneva is 30 June.

ADDRESS INQUIRIES TO:
See e-mail address above.

*SPECIAL STIPULATIONS:
Women graduates only.

THE HAFIF FAMILY FOUNDATION [1063]

Claremont Professional Building
265 West Bonita Avenue
Claremont, CA 91711
(909) 625-7971
Fax: (909) 621-4851
E-mail: hffconcerts@gmail.com
Web Site: www.hafiffamilyfoundation.com

FOUNDED: 1987

AREAS OF INTEREST:
Drugs, gangs, battered women, children and youth, poverty and education.

TYPE:
Scholarships.

PURPOSE:
To serve the poorest of the poor.

LEGAL BASIS:
Private foundation.

ELIGIBILITY:
No capital projects; no large staffs; more volunteer work.

GEOG. RESTRICTIONS: The inland empire, California, and Los Angeles County.

FINANCIAL DATA:
Amount of support per award: Varies.
Total amount of support: $200,000 for the year 2014.

NO. AWARDS: Over 100.

APPLICATION INFO:
Contact the Foundation or visit its web site for guidelines.

Duration: One year. Nonrenewable.

ADDRESS INQUIRIES TO:
Burnis Simon, Executive Director
(See address above.)

KENTUCKY FOUNDATION FOR WOMEN [1064]

1215 Heyburn Building
332 West Broadway
Louisville, KY 40202-2184
(502) 562-0045
(866) 654-7564
Fax: (502) 561-0420
E-mail: team@kfw.org
Web Site: www.kfw.org

FOUNDED: 1985

AREAS OF INTEREST:
Arts, social change and feminism.

NAME(S) OF PROGRAMS:
- **Art Meets Activism**
- **Artist Enrichment**
- **Hopscotch House Artist Retreat Center**

TYPE:
Awards/prizes; Project/program grants; Residencies.

PURPOSE:
To promote positive social change through feminist expression in the arts.

ELIGIBILITY:
Individuals must be doing work focusing exclusively in Kentucky.

GEOG. RESTRICTIONS: Kentucky.

FINANCIAL DATA:
Amount of support per award: $1,000 to $7,500.
Total amount of support: $200,000 annually.

NO. MOST RECENT APPLICANTS: Varies.

NO. AWARDS: Varies.

APPLICATION INFO:
Contact the Foundation for guidelines and application form.

Duration: One year.

Deadline: Art Meets Activism: First Friday of March; Artist Enrichment: First Friday of September.

STAFF:
Sharon LaRue, Executive Director
Jenrose Fitzgerald, Grant Program Manager

ADDRESS INQUIRIES TO:
Sharon LaRue, Executive Director
(See address above.)

THE LALOR FOUNDATION, INC.

c/o GMA Foundations
77 Summer Street, Eighth Floor
Boston, MA 02110
(617) 426-7080
Fax: (617) 426-7087
E-mail: fellowshipmanager@gmafoundations.com
Web Site: www.lalorfound.org

TYPE:
Project/program grants.

See entry 2422 for full listing.

THE LEEWAY FOUNDATION [1065]

1315 Walnut Street
Suite 832
Philadelphia, PA 19107
(215) 545-4078
Fax: (215) 545-4021
E-mail: info@leeway.org
Web Site: www.leeway.org

FOUNDED: 1993

AREAS OF INTEREST:
Women and trans artists and art for social change.

NAME(S) OF PROGRAMS:
- **Art and Change Grant**
- **Leeway Transformation Award**

TYPE:
Awards/prizes; Project/program grants. Art and Change Grants provide project-based grants to fund art for social change projects.

Leeway Transformation Award is an unrestricted award (not project-based) for women and trans people demonstrating a commitment to art for social change work.

YEAR PROGRAM STARTED: 1998

PURPOSE:
To support women and trans artists who create art for social change.

ELIGIBILITY:
Women and trans artists living in the Delaware Valley region may apply. The Transformation Award is open to women and trans people working in any art form who create art and social change and have done so for the past five years or more, demonstrating a commitment to art for social change work.

GEOG. RESTRICTIONS: Camden County, New Jersey; Bucks, Chester, Delaware, Montgomery and Philadelphia counties, Pennsylvania.

FINANCIAL DATA:
Amount of support per award: Art and Change Grant: $2,500; Leeway Transformation Award: $15,000.

NO. MOST RECENT APPLICANTS: Varies.

NO. AWARDS: Varies.

APPLICATION INFO:
Contact the Foundation for application or download a copy of the current application and guideline procedures from the web site.

Deadline: Art and Change Grant: March 1 and September 1; Leeway Transformation Award: May 15.

STAFF:
Denise Brown, Executive Director

ADDRESS INQUIRIES TO:
Sara Zia Ebrahimi, Program Director
(See address above.)

MICHIGAN WOMEN'S FOUNDATION [1066]

333 West Fort Street
Suite 1920
Detroit, MI 48226
(313) 962-1920
Fax: (313) 962-1926
E-mail: grants@miwf.org
Web Site: www.miwf.org

FOUNDED: 1986

AREAS OF INTEREST:
Needs of women and girls.

NAME(S) OF PROGRAMS:
- **Young Women for Change**

TYPE:
General operating grants; Project/program grants; Seed money grants. Specific focus changes yearly and is determined by each of seven chapters.

YEAR PROGRAM STARTED: 1986

PURPOSE:
To develop young women through the process of philanthropy and grantmaking into successful, fiscally responsible and socially responsive women.

LEGAL BASIS:
Nonprofit 501(c)(3) organization.

ELIGIBILITY:
Eligible organizations must be IRS 501(c)(3) tax-exempt.

GEOG. RESTRICTIONS: Michigan.

FINANCIAL DATA:
Amount of support per award: $500 to $5,000.

Total amount of support: Varies.

APPLICATION INFO:
Guidelines and application form are available on the web site.

Duration: One year.

PUBLICATIONS:
Trillium, newsletter.

IRS I.D.: 38-2689979

STAFF:
Carolyn J. Cassin, President and Chief Executive Officer
Kate Spratt, Chief Financial Officer

ADDRESS INQUIRIES TO:
See e-mail address above.

MONEY FOR WOMEN/BARBARA DEMING MEMORIAL FUND, INC. [1067]

P.O. Box 717
Bearsville, NY 12409
E-mail: demingfund@gmail.com
Web Site: demingfund.org

FOUNDED: 1975

AREAS OF INTEREST:
Visual art, fiction, nonfiction and poetry.

NAME(S) OF PROGRAMS:
- **Individual Artist Support Grants**

TYPE:
Awards/prizes. Small grants awarded annually to individual feminists in the arts.

YEAR PROGRAM STARTED: 1975

PURPOSE:
To support feminists in the arts.

LEGAL BASIS:
Private foundation.

ELIGIBILITY:
Open to individual feminist women in the arts, in visual art, fiction (prose), nonfiction (prose) and poetry whose work addresses women's concerns and/or speaks for peace and justice from a feminist perspective. Applicants must be citizens with primary residence in the U.S. or Canada. No educational or study scholarships.

GEOG. RESTRICTIONS: United States and Canada.

FINANCIAL DATA:
Amount of support per award: $500 to $1,500.

Total amount of support: Varies.

NO. MOST RECENT APPLICANTS: 550.

NO. AWARDS: 20.

REPRESENTATIVE AWARDS:
Ana-Maurine Lara (poetry), Austin, TX, *Kohnjehr Woman*; Sarah Levine (nonfiction), Cambridge, MA, *What Hands Can Do*; Robin Parks (nonfiction), Bryn Mawr, PA, *Famished.*

APPLICATION INFO:
Visit the Fund web site to complete electronic application. Completed applications require an application/processing fee of $25.

Deadline: January 1 to January 31, 2017 for nonfiction and poetry. January 1 to January 31, 2018 for fiction and visual art. Announcement by May.

PUBLICATIONS:
Newsletter.

IRS I.D.: 51-0176956

BOARD OF DIRECTORS:
Maureen Brady
Martha Hughes
Lise Weil

ADDRESS INQUIRIES TO:
See e-mail address above.

MS. FOUNDATION FOR WOMEN [1068]

12 Metro Tech Center
26th Floor
Brooklyn, NY 11201
(212) 742-2300
Fax: (212) 742-1653
E-mail: info@ms.foundation.org
Web Site: www.forwomen.org

FOUNDED: 1972

AREAS OF INTEREST:
Economic justice, women's health, and safety.

NAME(S) OF PROGRAMS:
- **Economic Justice**
- **Women's Health**
- **Women's Safety**

TYPE:
Project/program grants; Technical assistance. General support. Capacity building.

YEAR PROGRAM STARTED: 1976

PURPOSE:
To support the efforts of women and girls to govern their own lives and influence the world around them; to champion an equitable society by effecting change in public

consciousness, law, philanthropy and social policy through its leadership, expertise and financial support.

LEGAL BASIS:
Public foundation.

ELIGIBILITY:
Funding is by invitation only. Within its funding priorities, the Foundation gives priority to:
(1) efforts that engage women and girls in crafting activist solutions to the particular challenges they face in their communities based on gender, race, ethnicity, class, age, disability, sexual orientation and culture and;
(2) national-, regional- or state-level public policy advocacy informed by local organizing work and undertaken by organizations with strong linkages to a grassroots constituency.

Special consideration is given to the organizations that:
(1) are pro-women's empowerment, proactively antiracist and working to dismantle heterosexism, class oppression and discrimination based on disability;
(2) address the particular challenges faced by low-income women and girls;
(3) clearly articulate and respond to issues of gender as related to class and race/ethnicity;
(4) are multi-issue and involved in a form of cross-constituency organizing and coalition work;
(5) encourage intergenerational work that empowers younger as well as older women;
(6) include in leadership positions those who are affected most directly by the issues addressed and;
(7) have limited access to other funding sources.

The Foundation does not fund direct-service projects, stand-alone cultural or media projects, publications, individuals, scholarships, religious institutions, conferences, university-based research or government agencies.

GEOG. RESTRICTIONS: United States.

FINANCIAL DATA:
Amount of support per award: Varies.
Total amount of support: Varies.

NO. AWARDS: 100.

APPLICATION INFO:
Applications are accepted by invitation only through targeted Requests for Proposals. From time to time, however, the Foundation will launch open calls for proposals, which will be posted on the Foundation web site.

Duration: Generally one-time grants. Some renewal funding.

Deadline: Varies per program.

PUBLICATIONS:
Annual report; application guidelines; most recent grants list.

BOARD OF DIRECTORS:
Heather Arnet, Chairperson
Susan Dickler, Vice Chairperson
Eve Ellis, Treasurer
Verna L. Williams, Secretary
Ashley Blanchard
Jenna Bussman-Wise
Lauren Embrey
Jocelyn Frye
Alicia Lara
Lynn Malerba
Cathy Raphael
Rene Redwood
Seth M. Rosen
Simone Sneed
Gail Wasserman
Tom Watson

NATIONAL FEDERATION OF REPUBLICAN WOMEN [1069]

124 North Alfred Street
Alexandria, VA 22314
(703) 548-9688
Fax: (703) 548-9836
E-mail: mail@nfrw.org
Web Site: www.nfrw.org

FOUNDED: 1938

AREAS OF INTEREST:
The political process.

NAME(S) OF PROGRAMS:
- **Dorothy Kabis Internship**
- **National Pathfinder's Scholarship**
- **Betty Rendel Scholarship**

TYPE:
Internships; Scholarships. Dorothy Kabis Internship includes a six-week internship in Washington, DC, housing, travel and stipend.

National Pathfinder's Scholarships are given to the best nominated candidates.

Betty Rendel Scholarships are given to undergraduate women who are majoring in political science, government or economics.

PURPOSE:
To involve more women in the political process and provide educational opportunities.

ELIGIBILITY:
National Pathfinder's Scholarship is open to young women seeking undergraduate or postgraduate degrees, college sophomores, juniors, seniors and students enrolled in a Master's program. Recent high school graduates and first-year college women are not eligible.

Betty Rendel Scholarship applicants must be undergraduate women who are majoring in political science, government or economics. Open only to women who have successfully completed two years of college work.

GEOG. RESTRICTIONS: United States.

FINANCIAL DATA:
Dorothy Kabis Internship includes a small stipend, housing and airfare.

Amount of support per award: National Pathfinder's Scholarship: $2,500; Betty Rendel Scholarship: $1,000.

NO. AWARDS: 3 per scholarship and 2 internships.

APPLICATION INFO:
All grant information, including a printable version of the application, can be found online.

Duration: One-time award.

Deadline: June 1 for the National Pathfinder's Scholarship and Betty Rendel Scholarship. December 1 for Dorothy Kabis Internship.

ADDRESS INQUIRIES TO:
Scholarship Coordinator
(See address above.)

*SPECIAL STIPULATIONS:
Applicants must be U.S. citizens and may only apply to one program in a given year. Winners may not reapply.

NATIVE AMERICAN COMMUNITY BOARD (NACB)

P.O. Box 572
Lake Andes, SD 57356-0572
(605) 487-7072
Fax: (605) 487-7964
E-mail: charon@charles-mix.com
Web Site: www.nativeshop.org

TYPE:
Internships.

See entry 1035 for full listing.

THE NEWBERRY LIBRARY

Office of Research and Academic Programs
60 West Walton Street
Chicago, IL 60610
(312) 255-3666
E-mail: research@newberry.org
Web Site: www.newberry.org/fellowships

TYPE:
Fellowships; Visiting scholars. Allen fellows are expected to spend a significant part of their tenure in residence at Newberry's D'Arcy McNickle Center for American Indian and Indigenous Studies.

See entry 1036 for full listing.

OPEN MEADOWS FOUNDATION [1070]

P.O. Box 150584
Brooklyn, NY 11215
E-mail: openmeadowsfdn@gmail.com
Web Site: www.openmeadows.org

FOUNDED: 1986

AREAS OF INTEREST:
Projects led by and benefiting women and girls, reflecting community diversity, building community power, and promoting racial, social, economic and environmental justice.

TYPE:
Development grants; Project/program grants; Training grants. International program for women and girls.

PURPOSE:
To fund projects that are led by and benefit women and girls.

ELIGIBILITY:
Applicant organization must be nonprofit 501(c)(3) or have a fiscal sponsor that is tax-exempt 501(c)(3). Small and start-up organizations are given priority. Proposals for projects that have limited financial access or have encountered obstacles in their search for funding are eligible to apply. Applicant's organizational budget should not exceed $75,000. Projects must be led by and benefit women and girls. No grants are made to individuals.

FINANCIAL DATA:
Amount of support per award: Up to $2,000.
Total amount of support: $60,000 per year.

NO. MOST RECENT APPLICANTS: 500.

NO. AWARDS: 40 per year.

APPLICATION INFO:
Proposals must be submitted via e-mail. Guidelines are available on the Foundation web site.

Duration: One year. Must reapply.

Deadline: February 15 and August 15 each year, 12 midnight.

ADDRESS INQUIRIES TO:
See e-mail address above.

P.E.O. SISTERHOOD

P.E.O. Executive Office
3700 Grand Avenue
Des Moines, IA 50312
(515) 255-3153
Fax: (515) 255-3820
E-mail: ips@peodsm.org
Web Site: www.peointernational.org

TYPE:
Scholarships. Awards for selected women from countries other than the U.S. and Canada to pursue graduate study in the U.S. or Canada. Support is available for advanced study in any field except for research. No new applications at the dissertation level.

See entry 943 for full listing.

THE PHI BETA KAPPA SOCIETY [1071]

1606 New Hampshire Avenue, N.W.
Washington, DC 20009
(202) 745-3287
Fax: (202) 986-1601
E-mail: awards@pbk.org
Web Site: www.pbk.org

FOUNDED: 1776

AREAS OF INTEREST:
French language, literature and culture; Greek language, literature and history.

NAME(S) OF PROGRAMS:

- **Mary Isabel Sibley Fellowship**

TYPE:
Fellowships. Grant to women scholars made in alternate years for advanced research dealing with Greek language, literature, history or archaeology (odd-numbered years) or with French language or literature (even-numbered years).

YEAR PROGRAM STARTED: 1939

PURPOSE:
To assist women scholars conducting original research.

LEGAL BASIS:
National scholarly honorary society.

ELIGIBILITY:
Unmarried women between 25 and 35 years of age (inclusive) are eligible to apply. They must hold the Doctorate or have fulfilled all requirements for the Doctorate except the dissertation. Applicants must have demonstrated ability to carry on original research and must plan to devote full-time work to research during the fellowship year. Eligibility is not restricted to members of the Society or to U.S. citizens.

FINANCIAL DATA:
The Fellowship carries a $20,000 stipend with one-half of the amount payable after July following announcement of the Fellowship and the balance after another six months have elapsed.

Amount of support per award: $20,000.

Total amount of support: $20,000.

NO. MOST RECENT APPLICANTS: 40.

NO. AWARDS: 1 each year.

APPLICATION INFO:
Official application materials are available upon request to the Awards Coordinator or on the web site. Fellowships are awarded alternately in the fields of Greek language, literature, history or archaeology (odd-numbered years) and French language or literature (even-numbered years). Send brief description of intended research project when requesting an application.

Duration: The Fellowship is tenable for one year.

Deadline: Applications must be filed in January for the Fellowship to be announced by the following May. Contact Society for exact date.

OFFICERS:
Catherine White Berheide, President
John Churchill, Secretary

ADDRESS INQUIRIES TO:
Mary Isabel Sibley Fellowship Committee
(See address above.)

ROCHESTER AREA COMMUNITY FOUNDATION [1072]

500 East Avenue
Rochester, NY 14607-1912
(585) 271-4100
Fax: (585) 271-4292
E-mail: lhall@racf.org
Web Site: www.racf.org

FOUNDED: 1972

AREAS OF INTEREST:
Women in poverty, organizational capacity building, aging, arts, the environment, civic engagement, youth and families, historical preservation, health, racial equity, concentrated poverty, academic and achievement gap.

TYPE:
Project/program grants; Scholarships.

PURPOSE:
To support community responsibility and leadership, healthy options for young people and their families, early childhood development and quality of life.

LEGAL BASIS:
Tax-exempt public charity.

GEOG. RESTRICTIONS: Genesee, Livingston, Monroe, Ontario, Orleans, Seneca, Wayne and Yates counties, New York.

FINANCIAL DATA:
$345,000,000 in grants since 1972.

Amount of support per award: Varies.

Total amount of support: $20,800,000 in grants for fiscal year 2013-14.

IRS I.D.: 23-7250641

ADDRESS INQUIRIES TO:
Grant inquiries to: LaKeya Hall
Program Assistant
All other inquiries to: Jennifer Leonard
President and Executive Director

SIGMA DELTA EPSILON/GRADUATE WOMEN IN SCIENCE

P.O. Box 240607
St. Paul, MN 55124-0607
(952) 236-9112
E-mail: gwised@mac.com
Web Site: www.gwis.org

TYPE:
Fellowships; Travel grants. Leadership Awards are given to Graduate Women in Science officers.

See entry 1785 for full listing.

SKILLBUILDERS FUND [1073]

4701 College Boulevard, Suite 214
Leawood, KS 66211
(913) 608-7545
E-mail: info@skillbuildersfund.org
Web Site: www.skillbuildersfund.org

FOUNDED: 1983

AREAS OF INTEREST:
Programs benefiting low-income women and girls.

TYPE:
Project/program grants. Programs that help women and girls with economic self-sufficiency. Matching gifts are for directors only. Scholarships are only given to organizations, not to individuals.

YEAR PROGRAM STARTED: 1984

PURPOSE:
To enhance the capabilities of women and girls of all ages in the Kansas City metropolitan area and to realize their full potential.

LEGAL BASIS:
Private foundation.

ELIGIBILITY:
Organizations must be IRS 501(c)(3) not-for-profit. Funding primarily is directed to 501(c)(3) organizations that specifically benefit women and girls. Individuals, businesses and other for-profit organizations do not qualify.

GEOG. RESTRICTIONS: Kansas City metropolitan area, including Cass, Clay, Jackson, Johnson, Leavenworth, Platte, Ray and Wyandotte counties.

FINANCIAL DATA:
Amount of support per award: $20,000 to $50,000.

Total amount of support: Varies.

NO. AWARDS: 3 to 9 annually.

APPLICATION INFO:
Application information is available on the web site. Applicants must include a copy of their IRS tax determination letter with the application.

Duration: One year.

Deadline: Varies from year to year.

PUBLICATIONS:
Information brochure with application procedures.

IRS I.D.: 48-0984713

ADDRESS INQUIRIES TO:
Jennifer Sullivan, Executive Assistant
(See address above.)

SOCIETY OF DAUGHTERS OF THE U.S. ARMY

11804 Grey Birch Place
Reston, VA 20191-4223

TYPE:
Scholarships.

See entry 1701 for full listing.

SOCIETY OF WOMEN ENGINEERS [1074]

203 North La Salle Street
Suite 1675
Chicago, IL 60601
(312) 596-5223
(877) 793-4636
Fax: (312) 596-5252
E-mail: scholarships@swe.org
Web Site: www.swe.org/scholarships

FOUNDED: 1950

AREAS OF INTEREST:
Engineering.

NAME(S) OF PROGRAMS:
- **Society of Women Engineers Scholarship Program**

TYPE:
Awards/prizes; Conferences/seminars; Scholarships. Support for undergraduate and graduate engineering studies including women who have been out of the engineering job market and out of school for a minimum of two years and who will return to school for an engineering program.

PURPOSE:
To encourage women to achieve their utmost in careers as professional engineers and as the leaders of tomorrow and to attain high levels of education.

LEGAL BASIS:
Nonprofit educational organization under IRS 501(c)(3) classification.

ELIGIBILITY:
Scholarships are open only to women studying an accredited engineering program in a school, college, or university. Candidate is evaluated on the basis of scholastic standing in high school and/or college and extracurricular activity. Students must be studying in the U.S. (or Mexico) in the upcoming year.

Some scholarships require applicant to be a U.S. citizen.

Additional criteria can be found on the Society web site.

FINANCIAL DATA:
Scholarship payments are made directly to academic institutions on the recipient's behalf.

Amount of support per award: $1,000 to $14,500.

Total amount of support: $667,000 awarded for the year 2015.

NO. MOST RECENT APPLICANTS: Over 3,000.

NO. AWARDS: 219 for the year 2015.

APPLICATION INFO:
Completed application form and letters of reference are required.

Duration: One year. Possible renewal.

Deadline: May 15 for freshmen. February 15 for sophomore, junior, senior and graduate. Announcement in late spring and summer, respectively, for use during the following academic year.

PUBLICATIONS:
Applications; *SWE* magazine.

IRS I.D.: 13-1947735

ADDRESS INQUIRIES TO:
See e-mail address above.

WASHINGTON UNIVERSITY

The Graduate School
One Brookings Drive
Campus Box 1186
St. Louis, MO 63130
(314) 935-6848
Fax: (314) 935-3929
E-mail: n.p.pope@wustl.edu
Web Site: pages.wustl.edu/olinfellowship

TYPE:
Fellowships. The Olin Fellowships are open to candidates for any of the following graduate and professional schools at Washington University: architecture, art, arts and sciences, business, engineering, medicine, and social work.

See entry 1747 for full listing.

WELLESLEY COLLEGE [1075]

Center for Work and Service
Green Hall 439A, 106 Central Street
Wellesley, MA 02481-8203
(781) 283-2347
Fax: (781) 283-3674
E-mail: cws-fellowships@wellesley.edu
Web Site: www.wellesley.edu/CWS

AREAS OF INTEREST:
Graduate education.

NAME(S) OF PROGRAMS:
- **Anne Louise Barrett Fellowship**
- **Margaret Freeman Bowers Fellowship**
- **The Eugene L. Cox Fellowship**
- **Professor Elizabeth F. Fisher Fellowship**
- **Ruth Ingersoll Goldmark Fellowship**
- **Horton-Hallowell Fellowship**
- **Peggy Howard Fellowship in Economics**
- **Edna V. Moffett Fellowship**
- **Alice Freeman Palmer Fellowship**
- **Kathryn Conway Preyer Fellowship**
- **Vida Dutton Scudder Fellowship**
- **Harriet A. Shaw Fellowship**
- **Mary Elvira Stevens Traveling Fellowship**
- **Maria Opasnov Tyler '52 Scholarship**
- **Sarah Perry Wood Medical Fellowship**
- **Fanny Bullock Workman Fellowship**

TYPE:
Fellowships; Research grants. The Anne Louise Barrett Fellowship is given preferably in music and primarily for study or research in musical theory, composition, or in the history of music, abroad or in the U.S.

The Margaret Freeman Bowers Fellowship is given for first year of study in the fields of social work, law, or policy/public administration, including MBA candidates with plans for a career in the field of social services.

The Eugene L. Cox Fellowship is for graduate study in medieval or renaissance history and culture abroad or in the U.S.

The Professor Elizabeth F. Fisher Fellowship is given for research or further study in geology or geography, including urban, environmental or ecological studies.

The Ruth Ingersoll Goldmark Fellowship is awarded for graduate study in English literature, English composition or in the classics.

The Horton-Hallowell Fellowship is awarded for graduate study in any field, preferably in the last two years of candidacy for the Ph.D. degree, or its equivalent, or for private research of equivalent standard.

The Peggy Howard Fellowship in Economics is given to provide financial aid for Wellesley students or alumnae continuing their study of economics. Administered by the economics faculty who may name one or two recipients depending on the income available.

The Edna V. Moffett Fellowship is given to a young alumna, preferably for a first year of graduate study in history.

The Alice Freeman Palmer Fellowship is awarded for study or research abroad or in the U.S.

The Kathryn Conway Preyer Fellowship is for advanced study in history.

The Vida Dutton Scudder Fellowship is given for study in the field of social science, political science or literature.

The Harriet A. Shaw Fellowship is given for study or research in music and the allied arts, in the U.S. or abroad.

Mary Elvira Stevens Traveling Fellowship is awarded for travel or study outside the U.S.

The Maria Opasnov Tyler '52 Scholarship is for graduate study in Russian studies.

The Sarah Perry Wood Medical Fellowship is awarded for the study of medicine at an accredited medical school approved by the American Medical Association.

The Fanny Bullock Workman Fellowship is given for graduate study in any field.

ELIGIBILITY:
Awards will be based on merit and financial need. Awards are usually made to applicants who plan full-time graduate study for the coming year. Preference in all cases, except for the Peggy Howard Fellowship, will be given to applicants who have not held one of these awards.

Alice Freeman Palmer Fellows must be no more than 26 years of age at the time of their appointment and unmarried throughout the whole of their tenure.

Preference for the Harriet A. Shaw Fellowship is given to music candidates; undergraduate work in history of art is required of other candidates.

Candidates for the Mary Elvira Stevens Traveling Fellowship must be at least 25 years of age in the year of application. Any scholarly, artistic, or cultural purpose may be considered.

Except under compelling circumstances, the Committee in recent years has not chosen to fund formal graduate study or Ph.D. dissertation research.

FINANCIAL DATA:
Amount of support per award: $3,000 to $76,000.

Total amount of support: Varies.

NO. MOST RECENT APPLICANTS: 160 for the academic year 2014-15.

NO. AWARDS: 25.

APPLICATION INFO:
Application forms for the Peggy Howard Fellowship may be obtained from the Economics Department at the College.

Deadline: Peggy Howard Fellowship: Early April. Mary Elvira Stevens Fellowship: Early December. All other awards: Early January.

PUBLICATIONS:
Program announcement.

*SPECIAL STIPULATIONS:
These fellowships are for study at institutions other than Wellesley College. Applicants must be graduating seniors or alumnae of Wellesley College for all fellowships.

WELLESLEY COLLEGE [1076]

Center for Work and Service
Green Hall 439A, 106 Central Street
Wellesley, MA 02481-8203
(781) 283-2347
Fax: (781) 283-3674
E-mail: cws-fellowships@wellesley.edu
Web Site: www.wellesley.edu/CWS

AREAS OF INTEREST:
Graduate study for women.

NAME(S) OF PROGRAMS:
- **Mary McEwen Schimke Scholarship**
- **M.A. Cartland Shackford Medical Fellowship**

TYPE:
Fellowships; Scholarships. Awards are made to female applicants who plan for full-time graduate study for the coming year.

The Mary McEwen Schimke Scholarship is a supplemental award given to afford relief from household and child care expenses while pursuing graduate study.

The M.A. Cartland Shackford Medical Fellowship is given for study of medicine with a view to general practice, not psychiatry.

ELIGIBILITY:
Applicant must be graduate woman of any American university.

The Mary McEwen Schimke Scholarship is made on the basis of scholarly expectation and identified need. The candidate must be over 30 years of age, have household and child care responsibilities, and be currently engaged in graduate study in literature and/or history. Preference is given to American Studies.

FINANCIAL DATA:
Amount of support per award: McEwen Scholarship: Up to $1,500; Shackford Medical Fellowship: Up to $11,000.

Total amount of support: Varies.

APPLICATION INFO:
Application information is available on the web site.

Duration: One year.

Deadline: Early January.

PUBLICATIONS:
Announcement.

THE WHO (WOMEN HELPING OTHERS) FOUNDATION [1077]

2121 Midway Road
Carrollton, TX 75006
(972) 458-0601 ext. 2060
(800) 946-4663
E-mail: who@whofoundation.org
Web Site: www.whofoundation.org

FOUNDED: 1993

AREAS OF INTEREST:
Women's and children's health, education and social services issues.

TYPE:
Development grants; Product donations; Project/program grants.

YEAR PROGRAM STARTED: 1993

PURPOSE:
To support community-focused charities that serve the overlooked needs of women, children and families.

LEGAL BASIS:
Tax-exempt, nonprofit foundation.

ELIGIBILITY:
Applicants must be nonpolitical charities and organizations that have been incorporated with 501(c)(3) status for a minimum of three years prior to application. No grants to individuals. Prefer requests dealing with projects and programs.

Volunteer service grant available for BeautiControl consultants only.

GEOG. RESTRICTIONS: United States and Puerto Rico.

FINANCIAL DATA:
Amount of support per award: $1,000 to $40,000.

NO. AWARDS: 8 for the year 2014.

APPLICATION INFO:
Application form required. Beauty Control consultant must provide a brief description of their affiliation with the organization and a brief description of the impact the organization has in their community. Also include the organization's IRS 501(c)(3) letter, the specific budget for which the grant is requested, and the prior year's organizational budget.

Duration: Varies.

Deadline: Usually June. Notification in July.

PUBLICATIONS:
Application; newsletters; cancer booklet for women.

IRS I.D.: 75-2504646

WOMEN IN DEFENSE [1078]

WID HORIZONS
2111 Wilson Boulevard, Suite 400
Arlington, VA 22201
(703) 522-1820
Fax: (703) 522-1885
E-mail: wid@ndia.org
Web Site: www.womenindefense.net

AREAS OF INTEREST:
Increasing women's participation in national security fields.

NAME(S) OF PROGRAMS:
- **Horizons Foundation Scholarship Program**

TYPE:
Scholarships. The Horizons Foundation Scholarship Program is supported by accredited colleges and universities. Awards are made on an annual basis. The Foundation selects all scholarship recipients based on criteria it sets. Scholarships are awarded to applicants who require financial assistance, demonstrate strong academic credentials and a commitment to a career in national security.

PURPOSE:
To encourage women to pursue careers related to the national security interests of the U.S.; to provide development opportunities to women who are already working in national security fields.

ELIGIBILITY:
Scholarship Program applicants should be pursuing studies in engineering, computer science, physics, mathematics, business, law, international relations, political science, operations research or economics. Other disciplines will be considered if the applicant can successfully demonstrate relevance to a career in the areas of national security or defense.

Scholarship Program applicants also must meet the following criteria (no exceptions will be considered):
(1) be currently enrolled at an accredited university or college, either full-time or part-time;
(2) undergraduate and graduate students are eligible; undergraduates must have attained at least junior-level status (60 credits);
(3) demonstrate interest in pursuing a career related to national security/national defense;
(4) demonstrate financial need;
(5) have a minimum grade point average of 3.25 and;
(6) be a citizen of the U.S.

Recipients of past awards may apply for future financial assistance.

FINANCIAL DATA:
Amount of support per award: Varies.

Total amount of support: Varies.

NO. MOST RECENT APPLICANTS: 99.

NO. AWARDS: 3 to 5 awards per year.

APPLICATION INFO:
Applications must be completed in full and include only the requested items (essays, recommendations and transcripts). Do not include copies of awards, certificates or photographs. Only students meeting eligibility requirements will be considered.

Deadline: July 1.

WOMEN IN FILM [1079]

6100 Wilshire Boulevard
Suite 710
Los Angeles, CA 90048
(323) 935-2211
Fax: (323) 935-2212
E-mail: mgreen@wif.org
Web Site: www.wif.org/programs/film-finishing-fund

FOUNDED: 1985

AREAS OF INTEREST:
Filmmaking.

NAME(S) OF PROGRAMS:
- **Women in Film Finishing Fund**

TYPE:
Project/program grants. Awards for completion of films on subjects that meet the stated guidelines of WIF on an annual basis.

YEAR PROGRAM STARTED: 1985

PURPOSE:
To increase employment and promote equal opportunities for women; to encourage individual creative projects by women; to enhance media images of women; to further the professional development of women; to influence prevailing attitudes and practices regarding and on behalf of women.

LEGAL BASIS:
Nonprofit organization.

ELIGIBILITY:
All independent producers and nonprofit corporations are eligible to submit proposals for completion funding on an existing film or video. Projects in development or pre-production will not be considered. No

student projects, graduate or undergraduate, will be considered. Applicants do not need to be members of Women In Film.

FINANCIAL DATA:
Amount of support per award: Up to $25,000 in cash and/or in-kind services.

Total amount of support: Varies.

NO. MOST RECENT APPLICANTS: Over 100.

NO. AWARDS: Approximately 7.

APPLICATION INFO:
Detailed guidelines and application form may be obtained from the Foundation's web site.

Duration: Varies.

Deadline: August 7.

ADDRESS INQUIRIES TO:
Morgan Green, Program Coordinator
(See e-mail address above.)

*SPECIAL STIPULATIONS:
Projects must be in post-production by the deadline. Filmmakers must submit a rough cut of their films to be considered.

WOMEN'S FOUNDATION OF MINNESOTA [1080]

105 Fifth Avenue South
Suite 300
Minneapolis, MN 55401-6050
(612) 337-5010
Fax: (612) 337-0404
E-mail: contactus@wfmn.org
Web Site: www.wfmn.org

FOUNDED: 1983

AREAS OF INTEREST:
Women and girls in Minnesota.

NAME(S) OF PROGRAMS:
- **girlsBEST Fund**
- **MN Girls Are Not For Sale Fund**
- **Ripley Memorial Foundation**
- **Social Change Fund**

TYPE:
Development grants; General operating grants; Project/program grants; Technical assistance. Start-up grants.

YEAR PROGRAM STARTED: 1986

PURPOSE:
To fund "social change" through our grantmaking; to make grants to programs that result in shifts in individual, cultural and community attitudes and behaviors, and shifts in institutions and policies that serve as barriers to gender equality.

LEGAL BASIS:
Public foundation.

ELIGIBILITY:
Must primarily benefit women and girls and be not-for-profit or informal not-for-profit. Foundation does not fund direct service programs.

GEOG. RESTRICTIONS: Minnesota.

FINANCIAL DATA:
Amount of support per award: $15,000 to $20,000.

Total amount of support: Over $2,200,000 total funding in all programs.

NO. MOST RECENT APPLICANTS: 500.

APPLICATION INFO:
Detailed instructions and guidelines are available from the Foundation.

Duration: One to three years.

Deadline: Varies.

PUBLICATIONS:
Annual report; equality report; brochure; grant guidelines; research/issue reports.

IRS I.D.: 41-1635761

ADDRESS INQUIRIES TO:
Saanii Hernandez-Mohr
(See address above.)

*SPECIAL STIPULATIONS:
Funds only in Minnesota. Does not fund individuals.

WOMEN'S FOUNDATION OF MINNESOTA [1081]

105 Fifth Avenue South
Suite 300
Minneapolis, MN 55401
(612) 337-5010
Fax: (612) 337-0404
E-mail: contactus@wfmn.org
Web Site: www.wfmn.org

FOUNDED: 1983

AREAS OF INTEREST:
Women and girls in Minnesota.

NAME(S) OF PROGRAMS:
- **girlsBEST**

TYPE:
Project/program grants. The girlsBEST program has four program tracks: Academic; Entrepreneurial; Employment Development and High-Paying/High-Skill Careers; Public Education and Advocacy.

YEAR PROGRAM STARTED: 2002

PURPOSE:
To increase financial resources available to programs and organizations by and for women and girls creating change on their own behalf; to increase future economic success for women and girls.

LEGAL BASIS:
Public foundation.

ELIGIBILITY:
Must primarily benefit women and girls and be not-for-profit or informal not-for-profit.

GEOG. RESTRICTIONS: Minnesota.

FINANCIAL DATA:
Amount of support per award: $10,000 to $15,000.

Total amount of support: Approximately $300,000 for the fiscal year 2016.

NO. MOST RECENT APPLICANTS: Approximately 100.

NO. AWARDS: 13 to 20.

REPRESENTATIVE AWARDS:
Entrepreneurial: $10,000 to Centro, Inc.; Academic: $12,000 to Laura Jeffrey Academy; Public Education and Advocacy: $11,000 to Crisis Center for Teens Against Dating Abuse.

APPLICATION INFO:
Application information is available on the web site.

Duration: Three years.

Deadline: May 2016. Contact Foundation for exact date.

ADDRESS INQUIRIES TO:
Andrea Satter, Program Officer
(See address above.)

*SPECIAL STIPULATIONS:
Funds only in Minnesota. Does not fund individuals.

WOMEN'S POLICY, INC. (WPI) [1082]

409 12th Street, S.W.
Suite 600
Washington, DC 20024
(202) 554-2323
Fax: (202) 554-2346
E-mail: webmaster@womenspolicy.org
Web Site: www.womenspolicy.org

FOUNDED: 1995

AREAS OF INTEREST:
Women's public policy issues.

NAME(S) OF PROGRAMS:
- **Congressional Fellowships on Women and Public Policy**

TYPE:
Fellowships.

YEAR PROGRAM STARTED: 1980

PURPOSE:
To encourage more effective participation by women in the formulation of policy options that recognize the needs of all people; to promote activities that encourage the translation of research into policy; to raise awareness that national and international issues concerning women are interdependent; to increase understanding that those issues often defined as women's issues are, in fact, human issues of equal importance to both women and men.

LEGAL BASIS:
501(c)(3) nonprofit organization.

ELIGIBILITY:
Applicants must be currently enrolled in, or have graduated within the last 18 months from, a graduate or professional degree program in the U.S. Preliminary selection is based on academic performance, writing skills, experience with community groups and interest in the analysis of gender differences as they affect federal laws and legislating. Candidates from all academic disciplines are considered. Final selection follows an interview by WPI.

FINANCIAL DATA:
Amount of support per award: Monthly stipends of $1,500, plus up to $1,500 for tuition and $500 health care allowance.

Total amount of support: $12,000 per awardee for academic year 2016.

NO. MOST RECENT APPLICANTS: Approximately 100.

NO. AWARDS: Approximately 5.

APPLICATION INFO:
Applications are available in early April. Applicants must submit all academic transcripts, three letters of recommendation, completed application form and an essay.

Duration: January to August. No renewals.

Deadline: June 1. Regional interviews of semi-finalists are held in June and awards made by July 31.

IRS I.D.: 52-1914894

STAFF:
Cindy Hall, President
Cheryl Williams, Vice President

ADDRESS INQUIRIES TO:
Cindy Hall, President
(See address above.)

*SPECIAL STIPULATIONS:
Foreign students at international universities are not eligible. Must come to Washington to work full-time in a congressional office from January until July/August.

WOMEN'S SPORTS FOUNDATION [1083]

Eisenhower Park
1899 Hempstead Turnpike, Suite 400
East Meadow, NY 11554
(516) 542-4700
(800) 227-3988
Fax: (516) 542-0095
E-mail: info@womenssportsfoundation.org
Web Site: www.womenssportsfoundation.org

FOUNDED: 1974

AREAS OF INTEREST:
The Foundation - the leading authority on the participation of women and girls in sports - advocates for equality, educates the public, conducts research and offers grants to promote sports and physical activity for girls and women.

NAME(S) OF PROGRAMS:
- **Travel & Training Fund**

TYPE:
Training grants; Travel grants.

YEAR PROGRAM STARTED: 1984

PURPOSE:
To advance the lives of girls and women through sports and physical activity; to provide direct financial assistance to aspiring female athletes with successful competitive records who have potential to achieve even higher performance levels and rankings.

LEGAL BASIS:
501(c)(3) nonprofit organization.

ELIGIBILITY:
Individual applicants and all members of a team must be female U.S. citizens or legal residents and be eligible to compete for a U.S. national team. Applicants must have amateur status.

GEOG. RESTRICTIONS: United States.

FINANCIAL DATA:
Amount of support per award: $2,500 to $10,000.

Total amount of support: Minimum $100,000 annually.

NO. AWARDS: Varies.

APPLICATION INFO:
Contact the Foundation for guidelines.

Duration: One year.

Deadline: Online applications must be submitted by 5 P.M. May 2. Grants will be disbursed during the fourth quarter of the year.

PUBLICATIONS:
Annual report; research reports; educational guides; educational curriculum.

IRS I.D.: 23-7380557

OFFICERS:
Deborah Slaner Larkin, Chief Executive Officer
Angela Hucles, President

ADDRESS INQUIRIES TO:
Elizabeth Flores, Program Officer
(See address above.)

*SPECIAL STIPULATIONS:
Applicants must demonstrate accomplishments and potential to be considered. No travel grants outside the U.S. An individual or team may be awarded only one grant per calendar year and a maximum of three grants in a lifetime.

ZONTA INTERNATIONAL FOUNDATION

1211 West 22nd Street, Suite 900
Oak Brook, IL 60523-3384
(630) 928-1400
Fax: (630) 928-1559
E-mail: programs@zonta.org
Web Site: www.zonta.org

TYPE:
Fellowships. Awarded annually to women for graduate study in aerospace-related sciences or aerospace-related engineering at any university or college offering accredited graduate courses and degrees.

See entry 1994 for full listing.

ZONTA INTERNATIONAL FOUNDATION

1211 West 22nd Street, Suite 900
Oak Brook, IL 60523-3384
(630) 928-1400
Fax: (630) 928-1559
E-mail: programs@zonta.org
Web Site: www.zonta.org

TYPE:
Awards/prizes; Scholarships. For women of any nationality pursuing degrees in business who demonstrate outstanding potential in the field of business.

See entry 1857 for full listing.

ZONTA INTERNATIONAL FOUNDATION [1084]

1211 West 22nd Street, Suite 900
Oak Brook, IL 60523-3384
(630) 928-1400
Fax: (630) 928-1559
E-mail: programs@zonta.org
Web Site: www.zonta.org

FOUNDED: 1919

AREAS OF INTEREST:
Encouraging women's involvement in public affairs.

NAME(S) OF PROGRAMS:
- **Young Women in Public Affairs Awards**

TYPE:
Awards/prizes.

YEAR PROGRAM STARTED: 1990

PURPOSE:
To encourage young women's involvement and interest in public affairs.

LEGAL BASIS:
Incorporated in the state of Illinois as a nonprofit organization.

ELIGIBILITY:
Women of ages 16 to 19 on April 1 of each year, living in a Zonta district/region, or a citizen of a Zonta country, who demonstrate evidence of the following, are eligible to apply:
(1) active commitment to volunteerism;
(2) experience in local government, student government or workplace leadership (paid or unpaid);
(3) volunteer leadership achievements;
(4) knowledge of Zonta International and its programs and;
(5) advocating for Zonta International's mission of advancing the status of women worldwide.

GEOG. RESTRICTIONS: Applicants from geographic areas within a Zonta district/region where no clubs are located will be considered and also eligible to apply for the district/region award.

FINANCIAL DATA:
Amount of support per award: District award recipients receive $1,000 (U.S.) from the Zonta International Foundation YWPA Fund. Districts may choose to add to this award amount. Also, 10 international award recipients are selected from district recipients and receive an additional $4,000 (U.S.)

Total amount of support: Varies.

NO. MOST RECENT APPLICANTS: 32.

NO. AWARDS: 32.

APPLICATION INFO:
The YWPA Awards program operates at the club, district and international levels of Zonta International and is managed by Zonta members. To apply, contact the Zonta Club within the applicant's district/region for deadlines and an address to mail application. (Such contact information is available on the web site.) Alternatively, one can e-mail one's name and contact information to the Young Women in Public Affairs Committee Chairman at ywpachairman@zonta.org.

Deadline: Must contact Zonta Club directly for deadline.

ADDRESS INQUIRIES TO:
Martina Gamboa, Programs Coordinator
(See e-mail address above.)

URBAN AND REGIONAL AFFAIRS

Children and youth

THE JOHN W. ALDEN TRUST [1085]

c/o Miki C. Akimoto, V.P., Market Philanthropic Dir.
Philanthropic Solutions, U.S. Trust
Bank of America Private Wealth Management
225 Franklin Street, MA1-225-04-02
Boston, MA 02110
(617) 951-1108
E-mail: susan.t.monahan@gmail.com
Web Site: www.cybergrants.com/alden

AREAS OF INTEREST:
Education and therapy for children who are blind, retarded, disabled, mentally or physically ill; medical and scientific research for the prevention and/or cure of the conditions.

TYPE:
Capital grants; Challenge/matching grants; Conferences/seminars; Demonstration grants; Development grants; Matching gifts; Project/program grants; Research grants; Scholarships; Seed money grants; Technical assistance; Training grants.

LEGAL BASIS:
Private foundation.

ELIGIBILITY:
Organizations must be IRS 501(c)(3) tax-exempt and serve residents of eastern Massachusetts.

FINANCIAL DATA:
Amount of support per award: Up to $20,000.

Total amount of support: $375,000 for fiscal year 2014.

Matching fund requirements: Determined on a case-by-case basis.

NO. AWARDS: 29 grants for the year 2014.

REPRESENTATIVE AWARDS:
$15,000 to Boston Health Care for the Homeless Program; $15,000 to Boston Children's Hospital; $15,000 to Boys and Girls Club of Dorchester, Inc.; $10,000 to Exceptional Lives Inc.; $50,000 to Root Cause Institute.

APPLICATION INFO:
All applications must be submitted online.

Duration: Varies.

Deadline: Approximately January 5, April 5, July 5 and October 5. Check web site.

PUBLICATIONS:
Guidelines.

TRUSTEES:
Miki Akimoto
Susan T. Monahan, Grants Coordinator

ADDRESS INQUIRIES TO:
Susan T. Monahan
Grants Coordinator and Trustee
(See e-mail address above.)

THE ISABEL ALLENDE FOUNDATION

116 Caledonia Street
Sausalito, CA 94965
(415) 289-0992
Fax: (415) 332-4149
E-mail: lori@isabelallendefoundation.org
Web Site: www.isabelallendefoundation.org

TYPE:
Project/program grants. Promotes and preserves the fundamental rights of women and children to be empowered and protected.

See entry 1050 for full listing.

AMERICAN ACADEMY OF CHILD AND ADOLESCENT PSYCHIATRY

3615 Wisconsin Avenue, N.W.
Washington, DC 20016-3007
(202) 966-7300 ext. 117
Fax: (202) 966-5894
E-mail: aarcher@aacap.org
Web Site: www.aacap.org

TYPE:
Conferences/seminars; Fellowships; Research grants; Travel grants. Educational Outreach Program is for both child and adolescent psychiatry residents and general psychiatry residents. It provides funding support to attend AACAP's Annual Meeting. Partnered with the Mentorship Program, these grants provide participants with networking opportunities, exposure to various specialties and interaction with a vibrant network of AACAP. This Program is instrumental in integrating residents into the field; 90% of general psychiatry residents who participate in the Program become child and adolescent psychiatrists.

Joshi International Scholars Award provides funding support for eligible international scholars to attend the Annual Meeting.

Junior Investigator Award is offered for one child and adolescent psychiatry junior faculty recipient (assistant professor level or equivalent).

Life Members Mentorship Grant for Medical Students provides funding support to attend AACAP's Annual Meeting. Partnered with the Mentorship Program, these grants provide participants with networking opportunities, exposure to various specialties and interaction with Life Members, along with a vibrant network of AACAP members.

Pilot Awards are offered for qualified residents and junior faculty who have an interest in beginning a career in child and adolescent mental health research.

Ülgür International Scholar Award recognizes a child psychiatrist or physician in the international community who has made significant contributions to the enhancement of mental health services for children and adolescents.

See entry 2481 for full listing.

AMERICAN ACADEMY OF CHILD AND ADOLESCENT PSYCHIATRY

3615 Wisconsin Avenue, N.W.
Washington, DC 20016-3007
(202) 966-7300 ext. 117
Fax: (202) 966-5894
E-mail: aarcher@aacap.org
Web Site: www.aacap.org

TYPE:
Awards/prizes; Conferences/seminars; Fellowships; Research grants; Travel grants. The Robinson-Cunningham Award recognizes a paper on some aspect of child and adolescent psychiatry started during residency and completed within three years of graduation.

Jeanne Spurlock Minority Medical Student Research Fellowship in Substance Abuse and Addiction provides support for research training in substance abuse and addiction under a mentor with experience in the type of research that is being proposed, and whose work includes children and adolescents participants.

Summer Medical Student Fellowship provides clinical or research training under a child and adolescent psychiatrist mentor.

See entry 2480 for full listing.

ANDRUS FAMILY FUND

330 Madison Avenue
30th Floor
New York, NY 10017
(212) 687-6975
Fax: (212) 687-6978
E-mail: info@affund.org
Web Site: www.affund.org

TYPE:
Project/program grants; Research grants.

See entry 1145 for full listing.

BAINUM FAMILY FOUNDATION [1086]

7735 Old Georgetown Road, Suite 1000
Bethesda, MD 20814
(240) 450-0000
Fax: (240) 450-4115
E-mail: vgentilcore@bainumfdn.org
Web Site: www.bainumfdn.org

FOUNDED: 1968

AREAS OF INTEREST:
Underserved children and youth; early childhood.

TYPE:
General operating grants; Project/program grants.

YEAR PROGRAM STARTED: 1968

PURPOSE:
To support educational programs assisting underserved children/youth.

LEGAL BASIS:
Private foundation.

ELIGIBILITY:
Eligible organizations must be IRS 501(c)(3) tax-exempt.

GEOG. RESTRICTIONS: Baltimore, Maryland and Washington, DC metropolitan areas.

NO. AWARDS: Awards to 80 organizations.

APPLICATION INFO:
Applications are accepted by invitation only.

ADDRESS INQUIRIES TO:
Jennifer Schauffler
Senior Grants Manager
(See address above.)

BASEBALL TOMORROW FUND [1087]

245 Park Avenue
New York, NY 10167
(212) 931-7991
Fax: (212) 949-5405
E-mail: btf@mlb.com
Web Site: www.baseballtomorrowfund.com

FOUNDED: 1999

AREAS OF INTEREST:
Youth baseball and softball.

TYPE:
Capital grants; Challenge/matching grants; Project/program grants. These grants are offered to promote and enhance the growth of youth baseball and softball in the U.S., Canada and throughout the world.

YEAR PROGRAM STARTED: 2000

PURPOSE:
To promote and enhance the growth of baseball in the U.S., Canada and throughout the world by funding programs, fields and equipment purchases, designed to encourage and maintain youth participation in the game.

ELIGIBILITY:
Grants are made to incremental programs and/or for facilities for youth baseball and softball. Organizations must be nonprofit or tax-exempt.

FINANCIAL DATA:
Amount of support per award: Approximately $40,000.

Total amount of support: $2,000,000 annually.

Matching fund requirements: 50% match required.

NO. MOST RECENT APPLICANTS: 200.

NO. AWARDS: Over 800 since inception.

APPLICATION INFO:
An online application is available on the web site.

Deadline: January 1, April 1, July 1 and October 1.

ADDRESS INQUIRIES TO:
Executive Director
(See address above.)

THE BOY SCOUTS OF AMERICA, NATIONAL EAGLE SCOUT ASSOCIATION [1088]

1325 West Walnut Hill Lane
P.O. Box 152079
Irving, TX 75015-2079
(972) 580-2000
E-mail: nesa@scouting.org
Web Site: www.nesa.org

AREAS OF INTEREST:
Scouting and youth.

NAME(S) OF PROGRAMS:
- **Hall/McElwain Merit Scholarships**

TYPE:
Scholarships.

PURPOSE:
To serve Eagle Scouts and through them, the entire movement of Scouting.

ELIGIBILITY:
Must be graduating high school seniors or an undergraduate college student no later than completion of their junior year. Applicant must have demonstrated leadership ability in scouting and a strong record of participation in activities outside of scouting.

Must supply Scout history and participation. Award is not based on financial need or grades.

FINANCIAL DATA:
Scholarships are for tuition, room, board and books.

Amount of support per award: $1,000 to $4,000.

Total amount of support: Varies.

NO. AWARDS: Varies, depending on funds available.

APPLICATION INFO:
Application process begins August 1. Information is available on the Association web site.

Duration: One-time award.

Deadline: October 31.

ADDRESS INQUIRIES TO:
Jeff Laughlin, Manager
(See address above.)

*PLEASE NOTE:
This scholarship is not available to students attending any of the U.S. military academies.

*SPECIAL STIPULATIONS:
Applicant must fill out new application each year.

THE BOY SCOUTS OF AMERICA, NATIONAL EAGLE SCOUT ASSOCIATION [1089]

1325 West Walnut Hill Lane
P.O. Box 152079
Irving, TX 75015-2079
(972) 580-2000
E-mail: nesa@scouting.org
Web Site: www.nesa.org

AREAS OF INTEREST:
Scouting and youth.

NAME(S) OF PROGRAMS:
- **Mabel and Lawrence S. Cooke Scholarship**
- **National Eagle Scout Scholarship Fund**
- **STEM Scholarship**

TYPE:
Scholarships.

PURPOSE:
To serve Eagle Scouts and through them, the entire movement of Scouting.

ELIGIBILITY:
For the Mabel and Lawrence S. Cooke Scholarship, applicant must register and maintain status as a full-time student at a college/university. The scholarship is not available to students attending any of the U.S. military academies, because the U.S. government pays expenses that are covered by NESA scholarships at these academies.

National Eagle Scout Scholarship Fund applicants must register and maintain status as a full-time student at a college/university.

FINANCIAL DATA:
Funds are for tuition, room, board, and books.

Amount of support per award: Mabel and Lawrence S. Cooke Scholarship: One scholarship of up to $48,000 (up to $12,000 per year for four years) and four $25,000 scholarships ($6,250 per year for four years) are given annually; National Eagle Scout Scholarship Fund: Varies each year, depending on the funds available; STEM Scholarship: Up to $50,000 for four years ($12,500 per year).

Total amount of support: Varies.

NO. AWARDS: Varies.

APPLICATION INFO:
Application information is available on the web site.

Duration: Up to four years.

Deadline: Applications open August 1; submit no later than October 31.

ADDRESS INQUIRIES TO:
Jeff Laughlin, Manager
(See address above.)

THE LOUIS CALDER FOUNDATION [1090]

125 Elm Street
New Canaan, CT 06840
(203) 966-8925
Fax: (203) 966-5785
E-mail: proposals@calderfdn.org
Web Site: www.louiscalderfoundation.org

FOUNDED: 1951

AREAS OF INTEREST:
Education.

TYPE:
Capital grants; Project/program grants. Curriculum development.

YEAR PROGRAM STARTED: 1951

PURPOSE:
To promote scholastic development of children and youth by improving elementary and secondary education through its support of charter and parochial schools.

LEGAL BASIS:
Private foundation.

ELIGIBILITY:
Nonprofit 501(c)(3) organizations.

Grants are not made to individuals, private foundations, governmental organizations or publicly operated educational institutions. The Foundation generally does not provide support to annual funds or special events.

GEOG. RESTRICTIONS: Continental United States.

FINANCIAL DATA:
Amount of support per award: $2,000 to $500,000.

REPRESENTATIVE AWARDS:
$100,000 to Public Preparatory Network for Curriculum Initiative; $100,000 to Relay Graduate School of Education for Undergraduate Teacher Pathways program; $200,000 to the Thomas B. Fordham Institute for core policy research and communications programs.

APPLICATION INFO:
The Foundation does not accept unsolicited proposals. Organizations unfamiliar to the Foundation, or those that are not current grantees, are encouraged to submit a letter of inquiry via the web site. If the organization's programming falls within the parameters of the current grantmaking strategy and is selected for further review, a full proposal will be requested.

Duration: Varies.

PUBLICATIONS:
Annual report.

IRS I.D.: 13-6015562

TRUSTEES:
Peter D. Calder
Frank E. Shanley

ADDRESS INQUIRIES TO:
Holly Nuechterlein
Grant Program Director
(See address and e-mail above.)

CAMPBELL FOUNDATION, INC. [1091]

705 York Road
Towson, MD 21204
(410) 828-1961
Fax: (410) 821-8814
E-mail: lsperato@stoycpa.com

AREAS OF INTEREST:
Social services, education, arts and cultural programs.

TYPE:
Capital grants; General operating grants; Project/program grants.

PURPOSE:
To provide support for cultural, educational and social services and institutions.

LEGAL BASIS:
Nonprofit foundation.

ELIGIBILITY:
Organization must have 501(c)(3) status.

GEOG. RESTRICTIONS: Maryland, primarily Baltimore.

FINANCIAL DATA:
Amount of support per award: Up to $1,500 general operating grant; $20,000 capital grant.

Total amount of support: Average $150,000 per year.

NO. AWARDS: 80.

APPLICATION INFO:
Organizations must submit a written proposal, up to two pages in length, including program specifications. Proof of 501(c)(3) status required.

Duration: One year. Renewal by reapplication.

Deadline: November 15.

ADDRESS INQUIRIES TO:
Virginia T. Campbell, President
(See address above.)

THE CARSON SCHOLARS FUND, INC.

305 West Chesapeake Avenue
Suite 310
Towson, MD 21204
(410) 828-1005
Fax: (410) 828-1007
E-mail: katie@carsonscholars.org
Web Site: carsonscholars.org

TYPE:
Scholarships. The Carson Scholars Fund awards college scholarships to students in grades 4-11 who excel academically and are dedicated to serving their communities.

See entry 1614 for full listing.

THOMAS AND AGNES CARVEL FOUNDATION [1092]

35 East Grassy Sprain Road
Yonkers, NY 10710
(914) 793-7300
Fax: (914) 793-7381
E-mail: tacarvelfoundation@gmail.com

AREAS OF INTEREST:
Children, youth, health and religion.

TYPE:
General operating grants; Grants-in-aid; Matching gifts; Project/program grants; Research grants.

ELIGIBILITY:
Applicants must be 501(c)(3) tax-exempt organizations. Grants may be given to religious organizations that meet geographic requirements. No grants to individuals.

GEOG. RESTRICTIONS: Connecticut, New Jersey and New York.

FINANCIAL DATA:
Amount of support per award: Varies, depending on needs and nature of the request.

APPLICATION INFO:
No application form required. Applicants must provide IRS tax-exempt documentation.

Duration: One year. Nonrenewable.

ADDRESS INQUIRIES TO:
Peter A. Smith, President
(See address above.)

CHILDREN'S BUREAU [1093]

Administration on Children, Youth and Families
330 C Street, S.W.
Washington, DC 20201
(202) 205-8172
E-mail: jan.shafer@acf.hhs.gov
Web Site: www.acf.hhs.gov/programs/cb

FOUNDED: 1974

AREAS OF INTEREST:
Prevention, identification, assessment and treatment of child abuse and neglect, sexual abuse, incidence of abuse and neglect.

NAME(S) OF PROGRAMS:

- **Child Abuse Prevention and Treatment Act (CAPTA) Research and Demonstration Grants**

TYPE:
Demonstration grants; Project/program grants; Research grants; Technical assistance; Training grants.

YEAR PROGRAM STARTED: 1974

PURPOSE:
To assist state, local and voluntary agencies and organizations to strengthen their capacities to prevent child abuse and neglect, identify and assess abused and neglected children and provide necessary ameliorative services to them and their families.

LEGAL BASIS:
Public Law 102-295, 45 CFR Subtitle B, part 1340.

ELIGIBILITY:
Grants for demonstration programs or projects and research projects may be made to states, public agencies, community-based organizations, or public or private organizations.

FINANCIAL DATA:
Amount of support per award: Average $400,000.

APPLICATION INFO:
Standard grant application forms provided by the agency must be used. Complete instructions and necessary forms are issued with each announcement or solicitation.

Duration: Normally 36 to 60 months.

Deadline: Varies.

ADDRESS INQUIRIES TO:
Jan Shafer, Director
Division of Program Innovation
(See address above.)

*SPECIAL STIPULATIONS:
Financial and program progress reports are required semiannually; a final report and an expenditure report are required no later than 90 days after the completion of the project. Audits conducted. Records must be maintained for three years.

ADOLPH COORS FOUNDATION [1094]

215 St. Paul Street, Suite 300
Denver, CO 80206
(303) 388-1636
Fax: (303) 388-1684
E-mail: info@acoorsfdn.org
Web Site: www.coorsfoundation.org

FOUNDED: 1975

AREAS OF INTEREST:
Primarily youth, job training, and self-sufficiency.

TYPE:
Capital grants; General operating grants; Project/program grants.

PURPOSE:
To build a stronger, healthier society.

ELIGIBILITY:
Organizations must be classified as 501(c)(3) and operate within the U.S. The Foundation does not consider grants to organizations that in policy or practice discriminate on the basis of race, creed or gender. No grants to religious organizations or individuals.

GEOG. RESTRICTIONS: Colorado.

FINANCIAL DATA:
Amount of support per award: Average: $10,000.

Total amount of support: $6,200,000.

APPLICATION INFO:
Applications may only be submitted online.

Duration: One year.

Deadline: March 1, July 1 and November 1.

ADDRESS INQUIRIES TO:
John Jackson, Executive Director
(See address above.)

THE CRAIL-JOHNSON FOUNDATION [1095]

461 West 6th Street
Suite 300
San Pedro, CA 90731
(310) 519-7413
Fax: (310) 519-7221
E-mail: rachelr@crail-johnson.org
Web Site: www.crail-johnson.org

FOUNDED: 1987

AREAS OF INTEREST:
Underserved children, youth and families in the areas of health, education and human services.

TYPE:
General operating grants; Project/program grants.

YEAR PROGRAM STARTED: 1987

PURPOSE:
To promote the well-being of children in need through effective application of human and financial resources.

LEGAL BASIS:
Private foundation.

ELIGIBILITY:
Applicants must be tax-exempt 501(c)(3) organizations. No grants to individuals.

GEOG. RESTRICTIONS: Los Angeles, California.

FINANCIAL DATA:
Amount of support per award: $5,000 to $30,000.

APPLICATION INFO:
Consult applications procedure page of web site.

Duration: Typically one year.

Deadline: Varies.

PUBLICATIONS:
Guidelines.

OFFICERS:
Craig C. Johnson, Chairman
Alan C. Johnson, President
Eric C. Johnson, Vice President
Byung Kim, Chief Financial Officer
John S. Peterson, General Counsel
Rachel Roth, Program Officer

ADDRESS INQUIRIES TO:
Rachel Roth, Program Officer
(See address above.)

MICHAEL AND SUSAN DELL FOUNDATION [1096]

P.O. Box 163867
Austin, TX 78716
Fax: (512) 600-5501
E-mail: info@msdf.org
Web Site: www.msdf.org

AREAS OF INTEREST:
Needs of children, health, education, safety, and youth development.

TYPE:
Project/program grants. Grants to support and initiate programs that directly serve the needs of children living in urban poverty.

PURPOSE:
To improve outcomes for children, living in urban poverty around the world, in a measurable way.

ELIGIBILITY:
Eligible organizations must be 501(c)(3) or have a fiscal sponsor which is 501(c)(3).

GEOG. RESTRICTIONS: United States, India and South Africa.

FINANCIAL DATA:
Foundation will not fund more than 25% of a project's budget or more than 10% of an organization's total annual operating expenses.

Amount of support per award: Varies.

Total amount of support: Varies.

APPLICATION INFO:
All grant requests should be submitted via online form.

Duration: Varies.

THE CLEVELAND H. DODGE FOUNDATION, INC. [1097]

420 Lexington Avenue, Suite 2331
New York, NY 10170
(212) 972-2800
Fax: (212) 972-1049
E-mail: chdodgefdn@aol.com
Web Site: www.chdodgefoundation.org

FOUNDED: 1917

AREAS OF INTEREST:
Educational institutions and welfare agencies serving the needs and training of young people.

TYPE:
Project/program grants.

YEAR PROGRAM STARTED: 1917

PURPOSE:
To help better mankind by providing funds for education and social welfare organizations.

LEGAL BASIS:
Private foundation.

ELIGIBILITY:
Grants are made to nonprofit, 501(c)(3) organizations in the Foundation's areas of interest. No grants are made to individuals.

GEOG. RESTRICTIONS: United States.

FINANCIAL DATA:
Amount of support per award: $5,000 to $500,000; average grant: $25,000.

Total amount of support: $2,044,000 for the year 2015.

NO. MOST RECENT APPLICANTS: 150.

NO. AWARDS: 75.

APPLICATION INFO:
Applicants must provide:
(1) a letter describing the organization and grant request, including budget;
(2) annual report and;
(3) proof of 501(c)(3) status.

Duration: One year. Some renewable.

Deadline: January 15, April 15 and September 15.

ADDRESS INQUIRIES TO:
Phyllis M. Criscuoli, Executive Director
(See address above.)

DUPONT PIONEER [1098]

7100 N.W. 62nd Avenue
Johnston, IA 50131
(515) 535-7719
(800) 247-6803 ext. 57719
Fax: (515) 535-4842
E-mail: community.investment@pioneer.com
Web Site: www.pioneer.com

AREAS OF INTEREST:
Education, food security and community betterment.

NAME(S) OF PROGRAMS:
- **Community Betterment**
- **Food Security**
- **PreK-12 Education**

TYPE:
General operating grants; Matching gifts; Project/program grants. Community outreach programs. Matching gifts are for educational institutions.

PURPOSE:
To help improve the quality of life in the communities in which customers and employees live and work.

LEGAL BASIS:
Corporation giving program.

ELIGIBILITY:
Must be an IRS tax-exempt 501(c)(3) organization. No grants to individuals or religious organizations that promote a particular doctrine.

FINANCIAL DATA:
Amount of support per award: Up to $5,000.

Total amount of support: $5,000,000 for the year 2015.

NO. AWARDS: Approximately 1,000 per year.

APPLICATION INFO:
Guidelines and application forms are available on the web site.

Duration: One year.

EAST TENNESSEE FOUNDATION [1099]

520 West Summit Hill Drive
Suite 1101
Knoxville, TN 37902
(865) 524-1223
(877) 524-1223
Fax: (865) 637-6039
E-mail: etf@etf.org
Web Site: www.easttennesseefoundation.org

FOUNDED: 1986

AREAS OF INTEREST:
Arts and culture, youth-at-risk, community development, affordable housing construction, and scholarships.

CONSULTING OR VOLUNTEER SERVICES:
A variety of technical assistance to applicants and grantees.

TYPE:
Project/program grants; Scholarships; Seed money grants; Technical assistance. The Foundation is comprised of 400 philanthropic funds and nine supporting organizations.

PURPOSE:
To make the region a better place today and for future generations.

LEGAL BASIS:
Community foundation; 501(c)(3) organization.

ELIGIBILITY:
Grants are awarded to 501(c)(3) public charities, units of government, or educational institutions. The Foundation does not make grants or loans to individuals.

GEOG. RESTRICTIONS: Counties in East Tennessee.

FINANCIAL DATA:
Amount of support per award: Funding support generally $500 to $10,000 per year for competitive grants and scholarships; $15,000 to $140,000 in Affordable Housing Trust Fund (AHTF) grants.

Total amount of support: $10,800,000 for the year 2014.

APPLICATION INFO:
Applications are accepted online.

Duration: Varies.

Deadline: Varies.

PUBLICATIONS:
Connections, *Funding Focus*, quarterly newsletter; annual reports; documents; brochures.

IRS I.D.: 62-0807696

STAFF:
Michael McClamroch, President and Chief Executive Officer
Carolyn Schwenn, Executive Vice President and Secretary
Sherri Alley, Vice President for Advancement
Jackie Lane, Vice President for Communications
Jan Elston, Vice President for Competitive Grant Program

ADDRESS INQUIRIES TO:
Michael McClamroch
President and Chief Executive Officer
(See address above.)

*PLEASE NOTE:
Organizations located outside of the Foundation's service area are not eligible for funding.

THE EISNER FOUNDATION [1100]

9401 Wilshire Boulevard
Suite 735
Beverly Hills, CA 90212
(310) 228-6808
E-mail: info@eisnerfoundation.org
Web Site: eisnerfoundation.org

FOUNDED: 1996

AREAS OF INTEREST:
After-school programs, learning differences, K-12 public education, and prevention and treatment of abused children.

TYPE:
Grants-in-aid.

PURPOSE:
To provide financial support to organizations working to create lasting positive changes in the lives of at-risk and disadvantaged seniors and children in the community; to fund programs that will make permanent changes in a child's life and give them tools to enable them to achieve their dreams and become productive adults.

LEGAL BASIS:
501(c)(3) organization.

ELIGIBILITY:
Grants are made to 501(c)(3) nonprofit organizations that serve Los Angeles County, California. Grants are not made to individuals.

GEOG. RESTRICTIONS: Los Angeles County, California.

FINANCIAL DATA:
Amount of support per award: Typically $100,000 to $300,000.

Total amount of support: Approximately $7,500,000 per year.

APPLICATION INFO:
Before submitting a Letter of Inquiry, organization must answer brief questions online to determine eligibility.

Deadline: Letters of Intent are reviewed on a rolling basis.

IRS I.D.: 95-4607191

ADDRESS INQUIRIES TO:
Trent Stamp, Executive Director
(See address above.)

LOIS AND RICHARD ENGLAND FAMILY FOUNDATION [1101]

P.O. Box 34-1077
Bethesda, MD 20827
(301) 657-7737
Fax: (301) 657-7738
E-mail: englandfamilyfdn@gmail.com
Web Site: fdnweb.org/england

FOUNDED: 1990

AREAS OF INTEREST:
Human services, education, Jewish life and causes, and after-school programs in Washington, DC.

TYPE:
Capital grants; Challenge/matching grants; Development grants; General operating grants; Matching gifts; Project/program grants; Seed money grants; Technical assistance; Training grants.

YEAR PROGRAM STARTED: 1994

PURPOSE:
To improve the lives of those in need in the Washington, DC metropolitan area; to strengthen Jewish life and institutions locally, nationally and in Israel.

LEGAL BASIS:
Private family foundation.

ELIGIBILITY:
Organizations must be classified by the IRS as public charities and tax-exempt under Section 501(c)(3) of the IRS Code of 1986. Unsolicited proposals are not considered. No grants to individuals.

GEOG. RESTRICTIONS: Washington, DC and Israel.

FINANCIAL DATA:
Amount of support per award: $5,000 to $50,000; average $15,000 to $25,000.

Total amount of support: $1,000,000.

NO. MOST RECENT APPLICANTS: 80.

NO. AWARDS: Approximately 50.

REPRESENTATIVE AWARDS:
Jewish Giving: $15,000 to American Jewish Committee. Washington, DC Giving: $25,000 to Heads Up. Discretionary Grants: $30,000 to Lymphoma Research Foundation.

APPLICATION INFO:
The Foundation does not accept unsolicited proposals. Any organization interested in applying should first contact the Foundation office via e-mail.

Duration: Annual grants.

Deadline: Educational and Youth Development grants: Spring; Jewish Community Life grants: Fall.

BOARD OF DIRECTORS:
Lois England, Vice President
Rick England, Treasurer
Larry Akman
Nonie Akman
Diana England

ADDRESS INQUIRIES TO:
Maggie Hudak, Program Manager
(See address above.)

FOSTER CARE TO SUCCESS

21351 Gentry Drive, Suite 130
Sterling, VA 20166
(571) 203-0270
Fax: (571) 203-0273
E-mail: scholarships@fc2success.org
Web Site: www.fc2success.org

TYPE:
Scholarships.

See entry 1498 for full listing.

H.B. FULLER COMPANY FOUNDATION [1102]

P.O. Box 64683
1200 Willow Lake Boulevard
St. Paul, MN 55164-0683
(651) 236-5900
Fax: (651) 236-5056
E-mail: hbfullerfoundation@hbfuller.com
Web Site: www.hbfuller.com/community

FOUNDED: 1974

AREAS OF INTEREST:
STEM education for youth (science, technology, engineering and math) and youth leadership development.

NAME(S) OF PROGRAMS:
- **Leadership Development for Youth**
- **STEM Education**

TYPE:
Matching gifts; Project/program grants. Leadership Development for Youth supports organizations and programs that operate in communities where the Company's employees live and work and that help young people become successful, productive adults.

STEM Education supports youth education initiatives in the areas of science, technology, engineering and math (STEM).

PURPOSE:
To support charitable activities of the company.

ELIGIBILITY:
Must be an eligible, tax-exempt 501(c)(3) organization. Projects must be aligned with the Company's focus areas and must aim to benefit people where employees live and work.

GEOG. RESTRICTIONS: Greater Atlanta, Georgia; Aurora, Illinois; Paducah, Kentucky; Grand Rapids, Michigan; Twin Cities metropolitan area, Minnesota; and Vancouver, Washington.

FINANCIAL DATA:
Amount of support per award: Varies. Individual grants typically are from $5,000 to $15,000.

Total amount of support: Varies.

APPLICATION INFO:
Online application process.

Duration: Typically one year.

Deadline: Minnesota STEM/Youth Leadership grants: Proposals accepted March 1 to 31 and August 1 to 31. All other North American grants: March 1 to October 1.

ADDRESS INQUIRIES TO:
H.B. Fuller Community Affairs
(See address above.)

THE GERBER FOUNDATION [1103]

4747 West 48th Street
Suite 153
Fremont, MI 49412
(231) 924-3175
Fax: (231) 924-7906
E-mail: tgf@gerberfoundation.org
Web Site: www.gerberfoundation.org

FOUNDED: 1952

AREAS OF INTEREST:
Enhancing the quality of life of infants and young children in nutrition, care and development.

TYPE:
Matching gifts; Research grants. Grants to ensure the continuity of scientific and educational research in infant nutrition and child health. Matching gifts to 501(c)(3) educational, health and human services institutions within the U.S.

YEAR PROGRAM STARTED: 1952

PURPOSE:
To enhance the quality of life of infants and young children.

LEGAL BASIS:
Private foundation.

ELIGIBILITY:
Must be 501(c)(3).

GEOG. RESTRICTIONS: United States.

FINANCIAL DATA:
Amount of support per award: $20,000 to $300,000.

Total amount of support: $3,658,972 for the year 2015.

NO. MOST RECENT APPLICANTS: 340 for the year 2015.

NO. AWARDS: 98 for the year 2015.

APPLICATION INFO:
Applicants should submit a two- to three-page letter of inquiry initially. If accepted, an application form will be provided.

Duration: One-time award with annual review.

Deadline: Letters of inquiry due June 1 and December 1. Grants made in May and November.

PUBLICATIONS:
Guidelines; application.

IRS I.D.: 38-6068090

OFFICERS:
Barbara J. Ivens, President
Fernando Flores-New, Vice President
Stan VanderRoest, Treasurer
Tracy Baker, Secretary

ADDRESS INQUIRIES TO:
Catherine Obits, Program Manager
(See address above.)

THE GRABLE FOUNDATION [1104]

650 Smithfield Street
Suite 240
Pittsburgh, PA 15222
(412) 471-4550
Fax: (412) 471-2267
E-mail: grable@grable.org
Web Site: www.grable.org

FOUNDED: 1976

AREAS OF INTEREST:
Education, youth, leadership and families.

TYPE:
Project/program grants. This grant is offered to support community efforts that create an environment in which children can achieve and succeed.

YEAR PROGRAM STARTED: 1976

PURPOSE:
To improve educational opportunities so that children can achieve their potential; to strengthen families so they can serve as the core support of children and society; to support community efforts that create an environment in which children can succeed.

LEGAL BASIS:
Private foundation.

ELIGIBILITY:
Organizations must be classified as 501(c)(3) and include copy of IRS letter of determination. Grants are not awarded to individuals. Focus of grant must be southwestern Pennsylvania.

GEOG. RESTRICTIONS: Southwestern Pennsylvania.

FINANCIAL DATA:
Amount of support per award: Varies.

Total amount of support: $12,394,935 for the year 2015.

NO. MOST RECENT APPLICANTS: 275 for the year 2015.

NO. AWARDS: 177 for the year 2015.

REPRESENTATIVE AWARDS:
$480,000 to Pittsburgh Public Schools to support the creation of STEAM-centered learning spaces at four Pittsburgh Public Schools, as well as district-wide STEAM-related professional development; $258,264 to the Smithsonian Institution to support training for Pittsburgh-area teachers in using digital resources in their classrooms; $105,000 to the Mattress Factory to support arts programming for K-12 teachers, students and families; $67,724 to the South Fayette Township School District to support a professional development institute that will provide instruction and support for regional school districts in utilizing innovative teaching models.

APPLICATION INFO:
All organizations applying to the Foundation should submit a one- to two-page letter of inquiry describing the project prior to submitting a full proposal.

Proposals must include:
(1) Grable inquiry sheet;
(2) one-page summary of the proposal;
(3) description of the applicant organization;
(4) statement of need for the project;
(5) project description, including a detailed listing of project activities;
(6) anticipated project outcomes and how they will be measured;
(7) project budget, detailing expenses, committed and anticipated revenues, and including a narrative;
(8) organization's current operating budget;
(9) explanation of how the project will be sustained after the grant has ended;
(10) list of board members;
(11) copy of IRS tax-exempt certification;
(12) current audited financial statements and;
(13) letters of support when appropriate, e.g., from collaborating organizations.

Duration: Funding for up to three years.

Deadline: Letters of inquiry: January 1, May 1 and September 1 of each year. Full proposals: February 1, June 1 and October 1 of each year.

PUBLICATIONS:
Program announcement; guidelines.

IRS I.D.: 25-1309888

STAFF:
Gregg S. Behr, Executive Director
Dana M. Lamenza, Financial Administrator
Mary Anne Mistick, Grants Administrator
D'Ann Swanson, Senior Program Officer
Kristen Burns, Program Officer
Tracey Reed Armant, Program Associate

BOARD OF TRUSTEES:
Charles R. Burke, Jr., Chairman
Jan Nicholson, President
Susan H. Brownlee
Patricia Grable Burke
William H. Isler
Robert Ivry
Barbara Nicholson McFayden

ADDRESS INQUIRIES TO:
Mary Anne Mistick, Grants Administrator
(See address above.)

THE WILLIAM T. GRANT FOUNDATION [1105]

570 Lexington Avenue
18th Floor
New York, NY 10022-6837
(212) 752-0071
Fax: (212) 752-1398
E-mail: info@wtgrantfdn.org
Web Site: www.wtgrantfoundation.org

FOUNDED: 1936

AREAS OF INTEREST:
Supporting research to improve the lives of young people in the U.S.

NAME(S) OF PROGRAMS:
- **William T. Grant Distinguished Fellows**
- **William T. Grant Scholars Program**
- **Research Grants Program**
- **Youth Service Improvement Grants Program**

TYPE:
Fellowships; Project/program grants; Research grants. William T. Grant Distinguished Fellows program gives influential midcareer researchers the opportunity to immerse themselves in practice or policy settings and conversely influential practitioners and policymakers the opportunity to work in research settings.

William T. Grant Scholars Program supports promising early career researchers from diverse disciplines. The award is intended to facilitate the professional development of early career scholars who have demonstrated success in conducting high-quality research and are seeking to further develop their skills and research program.

The Youth Service Improvement Grants Program supports activities conducted by community-based organizations in the five boroughs of New York City to improve the quality of services for young people ages 8 to 25.

YEAR PROGRAM STARTED: 1936

PURPOSE:
To help create a society that values young people and enables them to reach their full potential. In pursuit of this goal, the Foundation invests in research and in people and projects that use evidence-based approaches.

LEGAL BASIS:
Private foundation.

ELIGIBILITY:
Organization must have 501(c)(3) status. No grants to individuals.

GEOG. RESTRICTIONS: United States.

FINANCIAL DATA:
Amount of support per award: William T. Grant Distinguished Fellows: Up to $175,000, with up to $25,000 to fellowship site(s) to defray hosting costs; William T. Grant Scholars Program: $350,000; Research Grants: $100,000 to $600,000; Youth Service Improvement Grants Program: $25,000.

Total amount of support: Varies.

NO. AWARDS: William T. Grant Scholars Program: 4 to 6 annually; Youth Service Improvement Grants Program: Varies.

APPLICATION INFO:
Application, requirements and procedures are available online.

Duration: William T. Grant Distinguished Fellows: Six months to two years; William T. Grant Scholars Program: Five years; Investigator Initiated Grants: Two to three years.

Deadline: Varies.

PUBLICATIONS:
Annual report; guidelines; *William T. Grant Scholars*, brochure.

TRUSTEES:
Russell P. Pennoyer, Chairperson
Andres A. Alonso
Margaret R. Burchinal
Prudence L. Carter
Greg Duncan
Scott Evans
Adam Gamoran
Nancy Gonzales
Andrew C, Porter
Judson Reis
Estelle B. Richman
Noah Walley

STAFF:
Adam Gamoran, President
Deborah McGinn, Vice President, Finance and Administration
Vivian Tseng, Vice President, Programs
Julie Wong, Manager, Grantmaking Operations
Sharon Brewster, Grants Coordinator, Discretionary Grants
Nancy Rivera-Torres, Grants Coordinator, Major Grants
Irene Williams, Grants Coordinator, William T. Grant Scholars

ADDRESS INQUIRIES TO:
Mary Heglar, Communications Specialist
(See address above.)

HASBRO CHILDREN'S FUND [1106]

One Hasbro Place
Providence, RI 02903
(401) 727-5091
Fax: (401) 721-7275
Web Site: www.hasbro.org

FOUNDED: 2006

AREAS OF INTEREST:
The welfare and development of children.

NAME(S) OF PROGRAMS:
- **Community Grants**

TYPE:
Product donations; Project/program grants. Grants made by the Hasbro Children's Fund focus on three core principles:
(1) Programs which provide hope to children who need it most;
(2) Play for children who otherwise would not be able to experience that joy and;
(3) Empowerment of youth through service.

YEAR PROGRAM STARTED: 1985

PURPOSE:
To assist children in triumphing over critical life obstacles as well as bringing the joy of play into their lives.

ELIGIBILITY:
U.S.-based 501(c)(3) organizations who deliver programs to children in Springfield, MA; Rhode Island; Renton/Seattle, WA; or Los Angeles, CA.

FINANCIAL DATA:
Amount of support per award: Varies.

Total amount of support: Varies.

APPLICATION INFO:
All interested organizations are asked to apply through the Fund's online application system.

CHARLES HAYDEN FOUNDATION [1107]

140 Broadway, 51st Floor
New York, NY 10005
(212) 785-3677
Fax: (212) 785-3689
E-mail: fdn@chf.org
Web Site: www.charleshaydenfoundation.org

FOUNDED: 1937

AREAS OF INTEREST:
Education and youth agencies.

TYPE:
Capital grants; Challenge/matching grants; Project/program grants. Grant priorities focus on institutions and programs primarily serving youth at risk of not reaching their full potential, especially youth in low-income communities. Support is provided for youth development programs, charter schools, independent and parochial schools, and informal educational enrichment programs in institutions such as zoos, museums or libraries.

YEAR PROGRAM STARTED: 1937

PURPOSE:
To promote the mental, moral and physical development of children and youth five to 18 years of age in the New York and Boston metropolitan areas.

LEGAL BASIS:
Private foundation.

ELIGIBILITY:
Grants are restricted to institutions and organizations in the New York and Boston metropolitan areas, as defined by the Foundation. The Foundation focuses on those grants primarily serving youth, five to 18 years of age, that are most at-risk of not reaching their full potential, especially youth in low-income communities. Grants are available for capital and program support. Program grants must have clear goals to be met within the specified time frame. Program support goes mainly for new and expanded programs. No grants are awarded to individuals.

GEOG. RESTRICTIONS: New York and Boston, Massachusetts metropolitan areas.

FINANCIAL DATA:
Amount of support per award: Average $85,000.

Total amount of support: $14,000,000 in grants paid for the fiscal year ended June 30, 2015.

NO. MOST RECENT APPLICANTS: 273.

NO. AWARDS: 164.

APPLICATION INFO:
Applicants should submit a request online through the Foundation web site.

Interviews, if required or requested, are not arranged until the written grant application has been submitted and the preliminary review is completed.

Duration: Most grants are for one year. Grant renewals are sometimes considered.

IRS I.D.: 13-5562237

OFFICERS:
Dean H. Steeger, Chairman of the Board
Kenneth D. Merin, President and Chief Executive Officer
Kristen J. McCormack, Treasurer
Robert Andrews, Secretary
Maureen T. Fletcher, Assistant Secretary
Carol Van Atten, Assistant Secretary

BOARD OF TRUSTEES:
Robert Andrews
Jose Claxton
Robert Howitt
Kristen J. McCormack
Kenneth D. Merin
Dean H. Steeger

ADDRESS INQUIRIES TO:
Kenneth D. Merin
President and Chief Executive Officer
(See address above.)

*SPECIAL STIPULATIONS:
Institutions receiving capital support must wait two years before seeking additional assistance.

THE JACK AND JILL OF AMERICA FOUNDATION

1930 17th Street, N.W.
Washington, DC 20009-6207
(202) 232-5290
Fax: (202) 232-1747
E-mail: administration@jackandjillfoundation.org
Web Site: www.jackandjillfoundation.org

TYPE:
Project/program grants; Scholarships. Volunteer opportunities.

See entry 1008 for full listing.

KANSAS HEALTH FOUNDATION

309 East Douglas
Wichita, KS 67202
(316) 262-7676
(800) 373-7681
Fax: (316) 262-2044
E-mail: info@khf.org
Web Site: kansashealth.org

TYPE:
Project/program grants.

See entry 1409 for full listing.

THE KLINGENSTEIN THIRD GENERATION FOUNDATION

125 Park Avenue
Suite 1700
New York, NY 10017-5529
(212) 492-6179
Fax: (212) 492-7007
E-mail: info@ktgf.org
Web Site: www.ktgf.org

TYPE:
Fellowships; Research grants. The Foundation funds research and other programs related to childhood and adolescent ADHD and depression. All funding is directed towards three research fellowship programs (funding postdoctoral research in ADHD, depression and access to care) and the medical student training program. The Foundation does not accept general applications for project or research funding.

See entry 2500 for full listing.

THE AGNES M. LINDSAY TRUST [1108]

660 Chestnut Street
Manchester, NH 03104
(603) 669-1366
(866) 669-1366
E-mail: admin@lindsaytrust.org
proposals@lindsaytrust.org (for grants)
Web Site: www.lindsaytrust.org

FOUNDED: 1939

AREAS OF INTEREST:
Special community needs, including handicapped, elderly, children's homes, youth organizations, homeless shelters and food banks.

NAME(S) OF PROGRAMS:
- **Camp Scholarships**
- **Dental Health**
- **Health and Welfare**
- **Scholarships - Higher Education**

TYPE:
Capital grants; Scholarships. Awards grants for capital campaigns, capital items and renovation needs. Also, supports a number of health and welfare organizations, health projects, dental projects, special needs including blind, deaf and learning-disabled, elderly, children's hospitals, children's homes, youth organizations, youth and family services and summer camperships (summer enrichment programs). In addition, Trust supports colleges and universities and private secondary schools through scholarship aid.

YEAR PROGRAM STARTED: 1939

PURPOSE:
To support the education of poor and deserving students from rural communities; to relieve suffering through child welfare.

ELIGIBILITY:
Eligible organizations must be IRS 501(c)(3) tax-exempt and be located in the New England states of Maine, Massachusetts, New Hampshire and Vermont. The Trust does not fund in Connecticut or Rhode Island.

The Trust does not make grants to individuals.

The Trust rarely, if ever, approves grants for general operating funds, nor does it fund grant requests from public entities, municipalities, sectarian organizations, or individuals.

GEOG. RESTRICTIONS: Maine, Massachusetts, New Hampshire and Vermont.

FINANCIAL DATA:
$23,500,000 in assets for the year ended 2015.

Amount of support per award: $1,000 to $5,000.

Total amount of support: $1,088,496 in total grants for the year 2015.

NO. MOST RECENT APPLICANTS: 554 for the year 2015.

NO. AWARDS: 343 for the year 2015.

APPLICATION INFO:
Guidelines are available online. Proposals can be submitted electronically at proposals@lindsaytrust.org.

Duration: One year.

Deadline: Trustees meet monthly. It generally takes two months from time of submission of application to receipt of letter of decision.

IRS I.D.: 02-6004971

ADDRESS INQUIRIES TO:
Susan Bouchard, Administrative Director
(See address above.)

*PLEASE NOTE:
It is highly recommended that applicants review the information available online prior to submission of a grant proposal.

*SPECIAL STIPULATIONS:
If your organization is awarded a grant, the Trust requests that your organization wait one year before reapplying.

THE DR. JOHN T. MACDONALD FOUNDATION, INC. [1109]

1550 Madruga Avenue, Suite 215
Coral Gables, FL 33146
(305) 667-6017
Fax: (305) 667-9135
E-mail: info@jtmacdonaldfdn.org
Web Site: www.jtmacdonaldfdn.org

FOUNDED: 1992

AREAS OF INTEREST:
Health education, prevention and early detection of disease, children, economically disadvantaged, and medical rehabilitation.

TYPE:
Challenge/matching grants; Demonstration grants; General operating grants; Matching gifts; Project/program grants; Scholarships; Seed money grants.

YEAR PROGRAM STARTED: 1992

PURPOSE:
To provide funding for programs and projects designed to improve, preserve or restore the health and health care of people in Miami-Dade County, FL.

LEGAL BASIS:
Private.

ELIGIBILITY:
Tax-exempt organizations that are registered to solicit funds under Florida law. The Foundation funds projects for medical and health-related programs. The Foundation does not fund national projects, multiyear funding requests, for-profit organizations, political candidates or campaigns, religious projects, support for individuals, or other grantmaking foundations.

GEOG. RESTRICTIONS: Miami-Dade County, Florida.

FINANCIAL DATA:
Amount of support per award: $5,000 to $50,000.

Total amount of support: $2,600,000 per year.

NO. MOST RECENT APPLICANTS: 53 letters of inquiry in 2013.

NO. AWARDS: 18, plus 4 scholarships and awards; 2 major multimillion-dollar awards.

REPRESENTATIVE AWARDS:
Small Grants 2014: Lotus House Women's Shelter to support two counselor/resource coordinators for one year; Hearing Research Institute to support the purchase of more hearing testing equipment and hearing aids for needy children and adults.

2014 Scholarships: Florida International University College of Nursing and Health Sciences for the Dr. Frederick Poppe Scholarship.

Multi-year Million+ Signature Programs: Dr. John T. Macdonald Foundation School Health Initiative; Dr. John T. Macdonald Foundation Biomedical Nanotechnology Institute.

APPLICATION INFO:
All qualified, tax-exempt organizations which propose to conduct projects or programs related to the health needs of the citizens of Miami-Dade County and are seeking funding support from the Foundation should first submit a letter of inquiry on the Foundation web site. The Foundation will make an initial review. If the request is felt to be of interest, an organization will then be asked to submit a complete grant proposal for consideration by the Board of Directors.

General Online Instructions: When clicking on the "Apply Now" button for the first time, applicant will be asked to create an account. Once an account and a password are created, applicant will be able to log in using his or her e-mail address as well as the password he or she created. Questions during the application process should be directed through the Foundation e-mail address.

Deadline: Letters of inquiry are accepted February 1 to April 16.

PUBLICATIONS:
Program announcement; guidelines; application packet.

IRS I.D.: 59-0818918

ADDRESS INQUIRIES TO:
Kim Greene, Executive Director
(See address above.)

MAURICE J. MASSERINI CHARITABLE TRUST

c/o Wells Fargo Private Bank
4365 Executive Drive, 18th Floor
San Diego, CA 92121
(858) 622-6866
Fax: (858) 622-6848
E-mail: grantadministration@wellsfargo.com
Web Site: www.wellsfargo.com/privatefoundationgrants/masserini

TYPE:
Project/program grants.

See entry 976 for full listing.

R.J. MCELROY TRUST [1110]

425 Cedar Street, Suite 312
Waterloo, IA 50701-1351
(319) 287-9102
Fax: (319) 287-9105
E-mail: vangorp@mcelroytrust.org
Web Site: www.mcelroytrust.org

FOUNDED: 1965

AREAS OF INTEREST:
Education, children and youth.

TYPE:
Capital grants; Challenge/matching grants; General operating grants; Internships; Project/program grants; Scholarships; Seed money grants; Technical assistance.

PURPOSE:
To invest in nonprofit and public organizations that inspire and transform youth.

LEGAL BASIS:
Private.

ELIGIBILITY:
The Trust only supports programs, projects or endeavors that help young people. Applicant must be nonprofit or tax-exempt.

The Trust does not make grants to religious organizations for religious programming or to schools or school districts for one-to-one technology/computers for students.

GEOG. RESTRICTIONS: Allamakee, Black Hawk, Bremer, Buchanan, Butler, Chickasaw, Clayton, Delaware, Dubuque, Fayette, Floyd, Grundy, Howard, Tama and Winneshiek counties, Iowa.

FINANCIAL DATA:
Amount of support per award: Varies per project.

Total amount of support: Approximately $1,900,000 for the year 2015.

Matching fund requirements: The Trust seldom funds 100% of a project.

NO. AWARDS: Approximately 60 per year.

APPLICATION INFO:
Applicants must submit a one-page letter to the Trust describing the need for funding, which includes:
(1) contact information (address, phone and e-mail);
(2) organization's federal tax identification number;
(3) description of the project, program or endeavor and;
(4) funding request and total cost of the project.

Duration: One year. Renewal possible.

Deadline: Applications accepted on a rolling basis.

IRS I.D.: 42-6173496

TRUSTEES:
Dr. Raleigh D. Buckmaster
Kathy Flynn
Sally Hollis
Robert Smith, Jr.
James B. Waterbury
Mike Young
Rick Young

STAFF:
Dr. Stacy Van Gorp, Executive Director

ADDRESS INQUIRIES TO:
Dr. Stacy Van Gorp, Executive Director
(See address above.)

*PLEASE NOTE:
Contact the Executive Director before applying.

THE MCJ AMELIOR FOUNDATION [1111]

310 South Street
Morristown, NJ 07960
(973) 540-1946

AREAS OF INTEREST:
Youths at risk, children, community empowerment and mentoring.

TYPE:
Challenge/matching grants; General operating grants; Project/program grants; Seed money grants.

LEGAL BASIS:
Private foundation.

ELIGIBILITY:
Applicants must be 501(c)(3) organizations.

GEOG. RESTRICTIONS: Newark, New Jersey.

FINANCIAL DATA:
Amount of support per award: Varies.

Total amount of support: Varies.

APPLICATION INFO:
The Foundation does not accept unsolicited proposals.

Duration: Varies.

STAFF:
Suzanne Spero, Executive Director
Christine C. Gilfillan, President

ADDRESS INQUIRIES TO:
Suzanne Spero, Executive Director
(See address above.)

MEBANE CHARITABLE FOUNDATION, INC. [1112]

232 South Main Street
Mocksville, NC 27028
(336) 936-0041
Fax: (336) 936-0038
E-mail: lcolbourne@mebanefoundation.com
Web Site: www.mebanefoundation.com

FOUNDED: 1992

AREAS OF INTEREST:
Children's education.

NAME(S) OF PROGRAMS:
- **The Early Childhood Development Program**
- **Literacy Interventions K-5th Grades**
- **The Teacher Training and Professional Development Program**

TYPE:
Project/program grants.

PURPOSE:
To teach children first to read and to further their education at all levels of learning, thereby attempting to break the cycle of poverty.

ELIGIBILITY:
Organizations qualified for exemption under Section 501(c)(3) of the IRS Code and not private foundations as defined by Section 509(a).

GEOG. RESTRICTIONS: Mainly North Carolina, Southeast.

FINANCIAL DATA:
Amount of support per award: Varies.

Total amount of support: $2,212,000 for the year 2015.

APPLICATION INFO:
Organization must first complete a phone interview with the President to determine if their proposal is within the objectives and interest of the Foundation.

Duration: Varies.

Deadline: Application must be postmarked by July 1 for fall meeting of the board of directors, or by January 1 for spring meeting.

ADDRESS INQUIRIES TO:
Larry Colbourne, President
(See address above.)

THE MOYER FOUNDATION [1113]

One Penn Center
1617 JFK Boulevard, Suite 935
Philadelphia, PA 19103
(267) 687-7724
(206) 298-1217
Fax: (267) 687-7705; (206) 298-1207
E-mail: info@moyerfoundation.org
Web Site: www.moyerfoundation.org

FOUNDED: 2000

AREAS OF INTEREST:
Bereavement and grief services and support for children and teens; programming for children and teens impacted by drug and alcohol dependency.

NAME(S) OF PROGRAMS:
- **Camp Erin**
- **Camp Mariposa**

TYPE:
Grants-in-aid; Internships; Matching gifts.

YEAR PROGRAM STARTED: 2000

PURPOSE:
To empower children in distress by providing education and support, thereby helping them to live a healthy and inspired life.

LEGAL BASIS:
Public, 501(c)(3) nonprofit organization.

ELIGIBILITY:
501(c)(3) nonprofit organizations. Grants are not made to individuals.

GEOG. RESTRICTIONS: Pennsylvania and Washington state.

FINANCIAL DATA:
Amount of support per award: $1,000 to $10,000.

Total amount of support: $65,000 in grants awarded in the past year.

NO. MOST RECENT APPLICANTS: 100.

NO. AWARDS: 15.

APPLICATION INFO:
Application information is available on the web site.

Duration: Nonrenewable.

Deadline: August 14.

IRS I.D.: 91-2065051

ADDRESS INQUIRIES TO:
Director of Development and Communications
(See address above.)

NATIONAL FOOTBALL LEAGUE FOUNDATION

345 Park Avenue
New York, NY 10154
(212) 450-2000
Fax: (212) 847-1812
E-mail: alexia.gallagher@nfl.com
Web Site: www.nflfoundation.org

TYPE:
Awards/prizes; Challenge/matching grants; General operating grants; Project/program grants; Research grants; Seed money grants; Training grants.

See entry 1303 for full listing.

NATIONAL FOSTER PARENT ASSOCIATION [1114]

1102 Prairie Ridge Trail
Pflugerville, TX 78660
(512) 686-1948
(800) 557-5238
Fax: (888) 925-5634
E-mail: info@nfpaonline.org
Web Site: www.nfpaonline.org

FOUNDED: 1972

AREAS OF INTEREST:
Foster parents and children in foster care.

NAME(S) OF PROGRAMS:
- **NFPA Youth Scholarship**
- **Walk Me Home Program**

TYPE:
Conferences/seminars; Scholarships. Scholarships for youth living in foster families whose foster parents are members of NFPA.

Walk Me Home Program is a walk program to raise awareness of foster care and the need for more foster families, as well as to raise funds for recruitment and other activities.

YEAR PROGRAM STARTED: 1972

PURPOSE:
To support foster youth and children of foster parents that wish to further their education beyond high school, including college or university studies, vocational and job training, and correspondence courses, including the GED.

LEGAL BASIS:
Nonprofit, volunteer organization established in 1972, with tax-exempt status under Section 501(c)(3) of the Internal Revenue Code.

ELIGIBILITY:
Must be a foster youth or an adoptive or birth child of foster parent members who is a college- or university-bound senior or is 17 years of age (either in school or out) in pursuit of vocational/job training/correspondence GED/other educational advancement.

GEOG. RESTRICTIONS: United States and territories.

FINANCIAL DATA:
Amount of support per award: $500.
Total amount of support: $2,500.

NO. MOST RECENT APPLICANTS: 23.

NO. AWARDS: 5 scholarships; 3 to foster children and 2 to adoptive or birth children of foster parents.

APPLICATION INFO:
Application is available from the Association at the address above. A minimum of two letters of recommendation and a typewritten statement of 300 to 500 words on "Why I want to further my education and why I should be considered for a National Foster Parent Association Scholarship" is also required.
Duration: Possible renewal.
Deadline: Applications must be postmarked on or before March 15.

IRS I.D.: 06-0894870

ADDRESS INQUIRIES TO:
Irene Clements, Executive Director
(See address above.)

NATIONAL JEWISH COMMITTEE ON SCOUTING
1325 West Walnut Hill Lane, SUM 342
Irving, TX 75015
(972) 580-2425
Fax: (972) 580-2535
E-mail: gene.butler@scouting.org
Web Site: www.jewishscouting.org

TYPE:
Scholarships.

See entry 1664 for full listing.

ORLANDO MAGIC YOUTH FUND [1115]
8701 Maitland Summit Boulevard
Orlando, FL 32810
(407) 916-2400
Fax: (407) 916-2985
E-mail: omyf@orlandomagic.com
Web Site: www.omyf.org

FOUNDED: 1988

AREAS OF INTEREST:
Children and families at risk in central Florida in the areas of child and youth education, health and wellness with a specific focus on childhood obesity prevention, and homelessness.

NAME(S) OF PROGRAMS:
- **Orlando Magic Youth Fund, a McCormick Foundation Fund**

TYPE:
Development grants; General operating grants; Project/program grants.

PURPOSE:
To nourish the minds and bodies of children who need it most in central Florida.

ELIGIBILITY:
Organizations must be classified as 501(c)(3) or 170(c)(3) by the IRS and have a constituency open to all segments of the community with a focus on low income. The Fund does not typically provide funding for private schools, legal aid societies, political, lobbying or advocacy groups, or capital requests for building and/or major improvements, except those for equipment/supplies that are critical to the delivery of a program or service.

GEOG. RESTRICTIONS: Orange, Osceola and Seminole counties, Florida.

FINANCIAL DATA:
Amount of support per award: $10,000 to $100,000.
Total amount of support: $1,000,000 annually.
Matching fund requirements: The McCormick Foundation contributes $.50 for every dollar that the OMYF generates to supplement contributions in the partners' local communities.

NO. MOST RECENT APPLICANTS: 68.

NO. AWARDS: 18.

APPLICATION INFO:
Applicants are invited to submit Letter of Inquiry.
Duration: One year. May reapply.
Deadline: Letter of Inquiry: Late April.

LUCILE PACKARD FOUNDATION FOR CHILDREN'S HEALTH [1116]
400 Hamilton Avenue, Suite 340
Palo Alto, CA 94301
(650) 736-0675
(650) 497-8365
Fax: (650) 498-2619
E-mail: grants@lpfch.org
Web Site: www.lpfch-cshcn.org

FOUNDED: 1997

AREAS OF INTEREST:
Children's health.

TYPE:
Project/program grants.

YEAR PROGRAM STARTED: 2000

PURPOSE:
To promote the health and well-being of children through statewide and local partnerships; to improve the system of health care for children, especially those with chronic or complex health problems.

ELIGIBILITY:
Organizations must be 501(c)(3) nonprofit.

GEOG. RESTRICTIONS: California.

FINANCIAL DATA:
Amount of support per award: Varies.

NO. MOST RECENT APPLICANTS: 20.

NO. AWARDS: Varies.

APPLICATION INFO:
Application information is available on the web site.
Duration: Varies.

ADDRESS INQUIRIES TO:
Grants Manager
(See address above.)

PARENTS WITHOUT PARTNERS
1100-H Brandywine Boulevard
Zanesville, OH 43701
(740) 450-1332
Fax: (740) 452-2552
E-mail: intl.hq@parentswithoutpartners.org
Web Site: www.parentswithoutpartners.org

TYPE:
Scholarships.

See entry 1536 for full listing.

THE PINKERTON FOUNDATION [1117]
610 Fifth Avenue
Suite 316
New York, NY 10020
(212) 332-3385
Fax: (212) 332-3399
E-mail: pinkfdn@pinkertonfdn.org
Web Site: www.thepinkertonfoundation.org

FOUNDED: 1966

AREAS OF INTEREST:
After-school and summer learning, career readiness, education, youth and family justice.

TYPE:
General operating grants; Internships; Project/program grants. Support for programs that develop individual competencies, instill values and increase opportunities to participate in society.

Support for community-based programs with preference given to projects for children, youth and families that intervene before a pattern of failure has been established.

YEAR PROGRAM STARTED: 1968

PURPOSE:
To improve the lives of young people in poor neighborhoods throughout New York City.

LEGAL BASIS:
Not-for-profit corporation organized in the state of Delaware in 1966.

ELIGIBILITY:
Grant applicants must be nonprofit public charitable organizations which are tax-exempt under Section 501(c)(3) of the Internal Revenue Code. The Foundation does not make grants to individuals or give loans or emergency assistance, nor does it support medical research or the direct provision of health care or religious education. It

generally does not make grants to support conferences, publications, media or to building renovations or other capital projects, unless they are integrally related to the Foundation's program objectives or are an outgrowth of one of its grantee's programs.

GEOG. RESTRICTIONS: New York, New York.

FINANCIAL DATA:

Amount of support per award: $25,000 to $150,000; average $75,000.

Total amount of support: $35,100,000 for the year 2014.

NO. AWARDS: 295 for the year 2014.

APPLICATION INFO:

Letters of inquiry are welcome at any time. Grantmaking meetings are held by the Board of Trustees in May and December.

Duration: Usually up to three years.

Deadline: February 1 and September 1.

OFFICERS:
George J. Gillespie, III, Chairman
Richard Smith, President
Daniel Mosley, Treasurer
Marnie S. Pillsbury, Secretary

STAFF:
Laurie Dien, Vice President, Programs
Julie Peterson, Senior Program Officer
Jennifer Correa, Program Officer

ADDRESS INQUIRIES TO:
Julie Peterson, Senior Program Officer
(See address above.)

PRITCHETT TRUST [1118]

BMO Harris Bank
417 North Broadway
Pittsburg, KS 66762
(414) 287-7317
Fax: (414) 287-8580
E-mail: pritchett.foundation@bmo.com

AREAS OF INTEREST:
Children, families and youth.

TYPE:
Project/program grants; Seed money grants.

PURPOSE:
To promote projects that support children, youth and families.

LEGAL BASIS:
Private trust.

ELIGIBILITY:
Grants are made to organizations that have tax-exempt status under Section 501(c)(3) of the Internal Revenue Code. No grants are made to individuals.

GEOG. RESTRICTIONS: Southeast Kansas, with an emphasis on Crawford County.

FINANCIAL DATA:

Amount of support per award: Varies.

Total amount of support: $300,000 to $400,000.

APPLICATION INFO:

Applicants must submit a brief letter outlining the purpose of the grant.

Duration: One year. Renewal possible.

Deadline: May 31.

ADDRESS INQUIRIES TO:
Joseph Brzycki, Account Administrator
(See address above.)

RONALD MCDONALD HOUSE CHARITIES [1119]

One Kroc Drive
Oak Brook, IL 60523
(630) 623-8935
Fax: (630) 623-7488
E-mail: josephine.fazio@us.mcd.com
Web Site: www.rmhc.org

FOUNDED: 1984

AREAS OF INTEREST:
Primarily, the health and well-being of children.

NAME(S) OF PROGRAMS:

- **Africa and South Asia: Child and Maternal Health**
- **U.S. Grants: Children's Oral Health Care**

TYPE:
Challenge/matching grants; Grants-in-aid; Project/program grants; Training grants.

YEAR PROGRAM STARTED: 1984

PURPOSE:
To directly improve the health and well-being of children.

LEGAL BASIS:
Nonprofit, 501(c)(3) tax-exempt organization.

ELIGIBILITY:
Not-for-profit tax-exempt organizations, based in the U.S. but operating either domestically or internationally. Projects must be sustainable and measurable. Proposed projects must directly benefit children. No grants to individuals, political campaigns, secular religious activities, for salaries, travel or ongoing expenses, or capital expenses. Projects must include a "Train-the-Trainer" component in the methodology.

Grant requests from organizations more regional in nature will be referred to the closest local chapter.

FINANCIAL DATA:

Amount of support per award: $100,000 and up.

Total amount of support: Approximately $4,000,000.

NO. MOST RECENT APPLICANTS: 150.

NO. AWARDS: 11.

REPRESENTATIVE AWARDS:
$169,043 over two years to Curamericas, Liberia; $179,800 to Lwala Community Alliance, Kenya; $627,637 to Resurge, Nepal and India; $50,000 to Wyman Center, U.S.

APPLICATION INFO:

Application information is available on the web site.

Duration: One-year to multiyear funding.

PUBLICATIONS:
Application form; annual report; application guidelines.

BOARD OF TRUSTEES:
Steven Ramirez, Chairman of the Board
Sheila Musolino, President and Chief Executive Officer

ADDRESS INQUIRIES TO:
Josephine Fazio, Administrator/Supervisor
(See e-mail address above.)

*SPECIAL STIPULATIONS:
Applications only accepted online.

HENRY AND RUTH BLAUSTEIN ROSENBERG FOUNDATION

One South Street, Suite 2900
Baltimore, MD 21202
(410) 347-7201
Fax: (410) 347-7210
E-mail: info@blaufund.org
Web Site: www.blaufund.org

TYPE:
Capital grants; General operating grants; Project/program grants. Programs of benefit to the underserved community in the Baltimore, MD area.

See entry 1325 for full listing.

THE SAIGH FOUNDATION [1120]

7777 Bonhomme Avenue
Suite 2007
St. Louis, MO 63105
(314) 862-3055
Fax: (314) 862-9288
E-mail: joann@thesaighfoundation.org
Web Site: www.thesaighfoundation.org

FOUNDED: 2000

AREAS OF INTEREST:
Children and youth in the field of education and health care in the St. Louis metropolitan area.

TYPE:
Development grants; Endowments; General operating grants; Internships; Project/program grants; Research grants; Scholarships; Technical assistance; Training grants.

PURPOSE:
To enhance the quality of life in St. Louis metropolitan region through support for charitable projects and initiatives which primarily benefit children and youth through education and health care.

LEGAL BASIS:
501(c)(3).

GEOG. RESTRICTIONS: St. Louis, Missouri metropolitan area.

FINANCIAL DATA:

Amount of support per award: Varies.

Total amount of support: Varies.

NO. MOST RECENT APPLICANTS: Approximately 225.

APPLICATION INFO:

Applications are to be submitted using the Missouri Common Grant Application.

Deadline: January 15, April 15, July 15 and October 15.

STAFF:
JoAnn Hejna, Executive Director
Mary Kemp, Associate Executive Director

ADDRESS INQUIRIES TO:
JoAnn Hejna, Executive Director
(See address above.)

ST. LOUIS RAMS FOUNDATION [1121]

Community Outreach
One Rams Way
St. Louis, MO 63045
(314) 982-7267
Fax: (314) 770-9261; (314) 516-8888
E-mail: mmccarthy@rams.nfl.com
Web Site: www.stlouisrams.com/community

FOUNDED: 1997

AREAS OF INTEREST:
Youth health, fitness and character education.

TYPE:
General operating grants; Project/program grants.

YEAR PROGRAM STARTED: 1997

PURPOSE:
To support programs designed to engage youth in activities that promote health, fitness and character development.

ELIGIBILITY:
Grants are made to organizations that have tax-exempt status under Section 501(c)(3) of the Internal Revenue Code. No unsolicited grants are accepted.

GEOG. RESTRICTIONS: The Greater St. Louis area, Missouri.

FINANCIAL DATA:
Since 1997, the Foundation has donated more than $6,000,000 in cash, grants, merchandise and tickets to area charities.

Amount of support per award: Varies based on program or project scope.

Total amount of support: Up to $250,000 annually.

NO. AWARDS: 30 to 50.

REPRESENTATIVE AWARDS:
St. Louis Public Schools Foundation; Cooperating School Districts.

APPLICATION INFO:
Proposals are accepted by invitation only; however, letters and collateral material from potential grant recipients are welcome.

ADDRESS INQUIRIES TO:
Molly Higgins
Director of Community Outreach
(See address above.)

THE SCHUMANN FUND FOR NEW JERSEY [1122]

21 Van Vleck Street
Montclair, NJ 07042
(973) 509-9883

FOUNDED: 1988

AREAS OF INTEREST:
Children and youth, education, environment and public policy (statewide) as well as social services in Essex County, NJ.

TYPE:
Demonstration grants; General operating grants; Project/program grants. Priorities include early childhood development, supporting efforts to heighten the chances of academic and social success for young children, especially the urban poor. Other focus areas include environmental protection, public policy and local activities directed at solving community problems, with particular concern for families with young children and education.

YEAR PROGRAM STARTED: 1988

LEGAL BASIS:
Tax-exempt, private foundation.

ELIGIBILITY:
Organizations seeking grants must be designated 501(c)(3) by the IRS. No applications for capital campaigns, annual giving, endowment, direct support of individuals and local programs in counties other than Essex. Projects in the arts, health care and housing development normally fall outside the Schumann Fund priority areas.

GEOG. RESTRICTIONS: New Jersey, with special emphasis on Essex County.

FINANCIAL DATA:
Amount of support per award: $15,000 to $50,000.

Total amount of support: Approximately $1,000,000 to $1,500,000.

APPLICATION INFO:
There is no standard application form to be used in presenting a request to the Schumann Fund. The Fund, however, encourages the use of the New York/New Jersey Common Application Form. A written proposal should be submitted which includes a detailed description of the purpose for which assistance is desired and the plan for accomplishment. The proposal should be accompanied by a copy of the organization's latest financial statement, an expense budget which identifies all sources of income, the project's time frame and future funding plans, a list of the organization's Board of Directors, IRS documents confirming the organization's status as a 501(c)(3) tax-exempt organization and not a private foundation, and the most recent audit.

Duration: Usually one year. Multiyear grants possible.

Deadline: January 15, April 15, July 15 and October 15.

PUBLICATIONS:
Annual report.

IRS I.D.: 52-1556076

TRUSTEES:
Aubin Z. Ames
Anthony Cicatello
Leonard S. Coleman, Jr.
Christopher J. Daggett
Martha Day
Roger Pratt

STAFF:
Barbara Reisman, Executive Director
Annette B. Strickland, Program and Administrative Officer

ADDRESS INQUIRIES TO:
Barbara Reisman, Executive Director
(See address above.)

*PLEASE NOTE:
Grants are restricted to projects in New Jersey.

THE SEYBERT FOUNDATION [1123]

P.O. Box 1286
Doylestown, PA 18901
(215) 696-9336
E-mail: admin@seybertfoundation.org
Web Site: www.seybertfoundation.org

FOUNDED: 1914

AREAS OF INTEREST:
Operating support for nonprofit organizations serving disadvantaged children and youth who are residents of the city of Philadelphia. The Institution is limited under the terms of the will setting up the fund to disadvantaged boys and girls of the city of Philadelphia only.

TYPE:
General operating grants.

LEGAL BASIS:
501(c)(3) charitable foundation.

ELIGIBILITY:
Grants are limited to nonprofit organizations serving disadvantaged young people through the high school ages who are residents of the city of Philadelphia. Grants are made to qualifying tax-exempt organizations under Sections 501(c)(3) and 509(a) of the Internal Revenue Code. Priority is given to organizations with operating budgets of less than $1,500,000.

GEOG. RESTRICTIONS: Philadelphia, Pennsylvania.

FINANCIAL DATA:
Amount of support per award: Average: $3,500.

Total amount of support: $330,000 for the year 2013.

NO. MOST RECENT APPLICANTS: 180.

NO. AWARDS: 89.

REPRESENTATIVE AWARDS:
Anti-Violence Partnership, Juvenile Law Center, Taller Puertorriqueno.

APPLICATION INFO:
Guidelines are available on the Foundation web site.

Duration: One year. Renewal possible.

Deadline: March 15 and September 15. No more than one request will be considered per calendar year except under special circumstances.

PUBLICATIONS:
Application guidelines.

IRS I.D.: 23-6260105

OFFICERS AND BOARD OF DIRECTORS:
Dario Bellot, President
Aishah Miller, Vice President
Richardson Sedmak, Treasurer
Obinna I. Abara, Esq., Secretary
Julie Cousler-Emig
Landon Jones, Esq.
Deepa Vasudevan
Dwayne Wharton
Linda White

ADDRESS INQUIRIES TO:
Diana Loukedis Doherty, Manager
(See address above.)

*PLEASE NOTE:
Grants must benefit poor boys and girls of the city of Philadelphia.

SIERRA HEALTH FOUNDATION

1321 Garden Highway
Sacramento, CA 95833
(916) 922-4755
Fax: (916) 922-4024
E-mail: info@sierrahealth.org
Web Site: www.sierrahealth.org

TYPE:
Matching gifts; Project/program grants. Specific to funding opportunities - solicited.

See entry 1468 for full listing.

SILICON VALLEY COMMUNITY FOUNDATION

2440 West El Camino Real
Suite 300
Mountain View, CA 94040-1498
(650) 450-5400
Fax: (650) 450-5401
E-mail: info@siliconvalleycf.org
Web Site: www.siliconvalleycf.org

TYPE:
General operating grants; Project/program grants; Scholarships; Seed money grants.

Nonprofit organizations that provide services or programs related to the specific five grantmaking strategies in San Mateo and Santa Clara counties may be eligible to apply for funding from the Foundation's endowment. Scholarships for college-bound students are also open to application.

See entry 1340 for full listing.

SKY RANCH FOUNDATION [1124]

114 West 47th Street, 10th Floor
New York, NY 10036
(646) 743-0425
Fax: (646) 855-5463
E-mail: george.suttles@ustrust.com
Web Site: www.skyranchfoundation.org

FOUNDED: 2011

AREAS OF INTEREST:
Child and family welfare, youth development.

TYPE:
General operating grants; Project/program grants. Grants typically support specific programs targeting at-risk youth and families. The Foundation also provides general operating support to organizations that work with these populations.

PURPOSE:
To give at-risk youth a second chance by identifying and offering grants to efficient and effective programs focused on improving the quality of help available to these youth.

LEGAL BASIS:
Tax-exempt charitable organization.

ELIGIBILITY:
The Foundation supports 501(c)(3) organizations that work with at-risk youth and their families. The Foundation will consider grants operating throughout the U.S. The Foundation does not give grants to religious organizations or to individuals.

GEOG. RESTRICTIONS: United States.

FINANCIAL DATA:
Amount of support per award: $5,000 to $40,000.

APPLICATION INFO:
Organizations interested in applying to the Foundation for support should submit a brief two- to three-page Letter of Intent (LOI) that includes the following:
(1) contact information (contact person's name, title, e-mail and mailing addresses, phone and fax numbers);
(2) organizational information (brief statement of the organization's history and activities);
(3) description of the project/request (please identify the request amount, project purpose and timeline);
(4) financial information (estimated budgets both for the organization and the specific project);
(5) supporters (brief overview of the organization's sources of revenue and funders associated with the specific project);
(6) staff qualifications (brief background on the key personnel involved in the organization/project) and;
(7) organizations invited to submit a full application will be notified and will receive full proposal guidelines within three weeks of their LOI submission.

Organizations applying must submit Form 990 for IRS documentation.

Duration: One year. Grant is renewable.

Deadline: LOIs must be e-mailed by the first business day of October, February or May to be considered at the subsequent Board meeting.

ADDRESS INQUIRIES TO:
George Suttles
Foundation Officer
(See address above.)

*PLEASE NOTE:
Sky Ranch was formed in 1961. The Sky Ranch Foundation began in 2011.

STUART FOUNDATION [1125]

500 Washington Street
Eighth Floor
San Francisco, CA 94111
(415) 393-1551
Fax: (415) 568-9815
E-mail: info@stuartfoundation.org
Web Site: www.stuartfoundation.org

FOUNDED: 1985

NAME(S) OF PROGRAMS:
- **Education**

TYPE:
Development grants; General operating grants; Project/program grants; Research grants; Technical assistance; Training grants. Systematic change and collaborative service delivery.

YEAR PROGRAM STARTED: 1985

PURPOSE:
To provide a coordinated set of programs, activities, research, and policy analysis that improve opportunities for children and youth in California and Washington to become self-reliant, responsible and contributing members of their communities.

LEGAL BASIS:
Private foundation.

ELIGIBILITY:
No grants to individuals. The Foundation does not accept unsolicited requests for funding.

GEOG. RESTRICTIONS: California and Washington.

FINANCIAL DATA:
Amount of support per award: Average grant of $75,000.

Total amount of support: $16,800,000 in grants for the fiscal year 2016.

APPLICATION INFO:
Duration: Grants are approved for one year at a time, although projects can be funded for several years.

IRS I.D.: 20-0882784

BOARD MEMBERS:
Dwight L. Stuart, Jr., Chairman

ADDRESS INQUIRIES TO:
Grants Manager
(See address above.)

*PLEASE NOTE:
The Foundation does not accept unsolicited requests for funding.

SUBARU OF AMERICA FOUNDATION, INC.

2235 Route 70 West
Cherry Hill, NJ 08002
(856) 488-5099
Fax: (856) 488-3255
E-mail: foundation@subaru.com
Web Site: www.subaru.com/csr/soa-foundation.html

TYPE:
General operating grants; Project/program grants. Employee matching gift program.

See entry 1540 for full listing.

THE FRANK M. TAIT FOUNDATION [1126]

40 North Main Street
Suite 1530
Dayton, OH 45423
(937) 222-2401
Fax: (937) 224-6015
E-mail: taitfoundation@gmail.com

FOUNDED: 1955

AREAS OF INTEREST:
Early childhood development, youth development and cultural activities for underserved youth.

TYPE:
Project/program grants. Focus on youth development, particularly early childhood development.

YEAR PROGRAM STARTED: 1956

PURPOSE:
To provide programs that develop youth (particularly early childhood development programs); to provide cultural enrichment experiences for underserved youth.

LEGAL BASIS:
Ohio corporation, not for profit.

ELIGIBILITY:
Organizations must be exempt under 501(c)(3). No private foundations.

The Foundation does not fund:
(1) medical research or equipment;
(2) operating budgets or annual fund drives;
(3) emergency requests for crash programs;
(4) endowment funds;
(5) religious programs or activities or;
(6) lobbying or propaganda activities.

GEOG. RESTRICTIONS: Montgomery County, Ohio.

FINANCIAL DATA:
Amount of support per award: Typically $5,000 to $50,000.

Total amount of support: $317,500 for the year 2015.

APPLICATION INFO:
Must contact the Executive Director at the phone number above to discuss the prospective grant proposal and to obtain approval for its subsequent submission.

Duration: Usually one year. Reapply for renewal.

Deadline: Contact the Executive Director at the phone number above.

PUBLICATIONS:
Guidelines.

IRS I.D.: 31-6037499

ADDRESS INQUIRIES TO:
Jenni Roer, Executive Director
(See address above.)

TURRELL FUND [1127]

21 Van Vleck Street
Montclair, NJ 07042-2358
(973) 783-9358
Fax: (973) 783-9283
E-mail: turrell@turrellfund.org
Web Site: www.turrellfund.org

FOUNDED: 1935

AREAS OF INTEREST:
Agencies rendering direct services to at-risk children in the state of Vermont, and, primarily, in the New Jersey counties of Essex, Hudson, Passaic and Union; policy initiatives for the very young child. While there are exceptions, the Fund's emphasis is on programs serving children, from birth to five years of age, and advocacy programs which support children in the same age range.

TYPE:
General operating grants; Project/program grants.

YEAR PROGRAM STARTED: 1935

PURPOSE:
To financially and strategically support organizations which directly provide or foster the creation and delivery of high-quality, developmental and educational services to at-risk children, especially the youngest and their families in Vermont and designated areas of New Jersey.

LEGAL BASIS:
Tax-exempt private foundation.

ELIGIBILITY:
Tax-exempt 501(c)(3) organizations in New Jersey and Vermont only may apply. In New Jersey, emphasis is on northern urban areas centered in Essex, Hudson, Passaic and Union counties only. No grants are awarded for lobbying, endowments or research. No grants to individuals and most hospital work and health delivery services. Only organizations providing direct services and advocacy for children and youth are eligible.

GEOG. RESTRICTIONS: Essex, Hudson, Passaic and Union counties, New Jersey and Vermont.

FINANCIAL DATA:
Amount of support per award: $1,000 to $395,000; $16,000 average grant for the year 2014.

Total amount of support: $3,980,289 for the year 2014.

NO. MOST RECENT APPLICANTS: 410 for the year 2014.

NO. AWARDS: 286 awarded for the year 2014.

REPRESENTATIVE AWARDS:
Vermont Community Preschool Collaborative; St. Benedict's Preparatory School; Team Academy.

APPLICATION INFO:
Applications are accepted online only. Scanned into the proposal should be the following:
(1) a brief letter describing the project;
(2) a copy of the IRS letter granting tax exemption;
(3) operating and project budgets and;
(4) either a 990 form or audited statement from most recent year available.

The proposal should include:
(1) background information about the organization;
(2) identification of board members;
(3) staff qualifications;
(4) a financial report;
(5) current budget and;
(6) project costs.

Duration: One year.

Deadline: August 1 and February 1. Announcement in late June and late December.

PUBLICATIONS:
Annual report.

IRS I.D.: 22-1551936

OFFICERS:
S. Lawrence Prendergast, Chairman of the Board
Curtland E. Fields, Secretary
Kim Keiser, Assistant Secretary

TRUSTEES:
Robert E. Angelica
Elizabeth W. Christie
Curtland E. Fields
Rev. William S. Gannon
William H. Hammond, Jr.
Matthew E. Melmed
Dr. Julia A. Miller
Rev. Dr. John P. Mitchell
John Morning
S. Lawrence Prendergast
Mark Sustic

ADDRESS INQUIRIES TO:
Curtland E. Fields
President and Chief Executive Officer
(See address above.)

U.S. DEPARTMENT OF HEALTH AND HUMAN SERVICES [1128]

Administration for Children and Families
Office of Head Start
1250 Maryland Avenue, S.W., Suite 8000
Washington, DC 20024
(866) 763-6481
(202) 205-8573
Fax: (202) 205-9721
Web Site: www.acf.hhs.gov/programs/ohs

NAME(S) OF PROGRAMS:
- **Head Start**

TYPE:
Project/program grants. Grants for comprehensive programs focused primarily upon children from low-income families who have not reached the age of compulsory school attendance. Supported projects should involve:
(1) comprehensive health (including medical and dental examinations), nutritional, social, psychological, educational and mental health services;
(2) appropriate activities to encourage and provide opportunities for participation of parents and effective use of provided services and;
(3) other pertinent training, technical assistance, evaluation and follow-through activities.

YEAR PROGRAM STARTED: 1965

PURPOSE:
To promote school readiness for children in low-income families by offering educational, nutritional, health, social and other services.

LEGAL BASIS:
Omnibus Budget and Reconciliation Act of 1981 (Public Law 97-35).

ELIGIBILITY:
Public or private nonprofit organizations, including community-based and faith-based organizations, or for-profit agencies within a community that wish to compete for funds, are eligible to apply.

FINANCIAL DATA:
Federal funds may not exceed 80% except in certain limited situations where grantees may be relieved of all or part of the nonfederal share.

Amount of support per award: Varies.

Total amount of support: $7,782,420,000 (federal appropriation) for fiscal year 2014.

Matching fund requirements: Grantees are required to provide 20% of the total cost of the project.

APPLICATION INFO:
Applications from organizations which are not current grantees are accepted only in response to announcements in the *Federal Register*. Applicants for a Head Start grant should contact the Health and Human Services regional office in their area. Parents wishing to enroll their children should consult the local Head Start Program in their Community.

U.S. DEPARTMENT OF HEALTH AND HUMAN SERVICES [1129]

Administration for Children and Families
Family and Youth Services Bureau
Portals Building, Suite 800
1250 Maryland Avenue, S.W.
Washington, DC 20024
(301) 608-8098
Fax: (301) 587-4352
E-mail: ncfy@acf.hhs.gov
Web Site: www.acf.hhs.gov/programs/fysb

FOUNDED: 1974

AREAS OF INTEREST:
Crisis and referral services for runaway and homeless youth.

NAME(S) OF PROGRAMS:
- **Runaway and Homeless Youth (RHY) Programs**

TYPE:
Development grants; General operating grants; Project/program grants; Technical assistance. Title III of the Juvenile Justice and Delinquency Prevention Act of 1974, et seq., to authorize the Runaway and Homeless Youth Program.

Basic Center, Street Outreach, and Transitional Living are components of this Program.

Through Basic Center, the Bureau provides financial assistance to establish or strengthen community-based programs that address the immediate needs of runaway and homeless youth and their families. These programs are designed to provide youth with emergency shelter, food, clothing, counseling and referrals for health care.

Through Street Outreach, the Bureau awards grants to private, nonprofit agencies to conduct outreach designed to build relationships between grantee staff and street youth. These efforts are intended to help young people leave the streets.

Through Transitional Living, the Bureau supports projects that provide longer-term residential services to homeless youth, 16 to 21 years of age, for up to 18 months. Services are intended to help homeless youth make a successful transition to self-sufficient living. Transitional Living also supports youth maternity group home.

YEAR PROGRAM STARTED: 1974

PURPOSE:
To establish or strengthen locally controlled community programs that address the immediate needs of runaway and homeless youth and their families. Services must be provided outside of the law enforcement, juvenile justice system, child welfare or

mental health. The program is designed to alleviate problems of RHY youth, reunite youth with their families, and encourage the resolution of intrafamily problems through counseling and other services, strengthen family relationships and encourage stable living conditions for youth and help youth decide upon constructive courses of action.

ELIGIBILITY:
Grants are available to states, localities, nonprofit private agencies, coordinated networks and Indian Tribes.

GEOG. RESTRICTIONS: United States and its territories.

FINANCIAL DATA:
Amount of support per award: Maximum of $200,000 per year.

Total amount of support: Approximately $113,000,000 annually.

NO. MOST RECENT APPLICANTS: Varies.

APPLICATION INFO:
Guidelines available on the web site.

Duration: Three years for Basic Center and Street Outreach. Five years for Transitional Living.

Deadline: Varies.

ADDRESS INQUIRIES TO:
National Clearinghouse on Families and Youth
5515 Security Lane, Suite 800
North Bethesda, MD 20852

U.S. DEPARTMENT OF HEALTH AND HUMAN SERVICES [1130]

Administration for Children and Families
Children's Bureau
1250 Maryland Avenue, S.W.
Washington, DC 20024
(202) 205-8618
Fax: (202) 260-9345
Web Site: www.acf.hhs.gov/programs/cb

NAME(S) OF PROGRAMS:
- **Discretionary Grant Programs**
- **Promoting Safe and Stable Families**
- **State & Tribal Grant Programs**
- **State Formula Grants**

TYPE:
Formula grants; Project/program grants. Discretionary Grants are awarded for research and program development, through a competitive peer-review process, to State, Tribal and local agencies, faith-based and community-based organizations, and other nonprofit and for-profit groups.

Promoting Safe and Stable Families (PSSF) primarily aims to prevent the unnecessary separation of children from their families, improve the quality of care and services to children and their families, and ensure permanency for children by reuniting them with their parents, by adoption or by another permanent living arrangement.

State & Tribal Grant Programs provide matching funds to States and Tribes to help them operate every aspect of their child welfare systems - from prevention of child abuse and neglect to adoption - and the information systems necessary to support these programs.

State Formula Grants assist States and Territories in establishing, maintaining and expanding programs and projects to prevent family violence and to provide immediate shelter and related assistance for victims of family violence and their dependents.

PURPOSE:
To fund projects, programs and research that serve children, families or the community to states, territories and tribes.

ELIGIBILITY:
Discretionary Grants: States, local governments, tribes, public agencies or private agencies or organizations with expertise in providing technical assistance related to family preservation, family support, time-limited family reunification and adoption promotion and support.

Promoting Safe and Stable Families: Families and children who need services to assist them to stabilize their lives, strengthen family functioning, prevent out-of-home placement of children, enhance child development and increase competence in parenting abilities, facilitate timely reunification of the child and promote appropriate adoptions.

State & Tribal Grant Programs and State Formula Grants: States, territories and certain Indian Tribes are eligible.

FINANCIAL DATA:
Amount of support per award: Varies.

Total amount of support: Varies.

APPLICATION INFO:
ACF requires electronic submission of applications. Information on applying electronically is available at Grants.gov. Applicants who do not have an Internet connection or sufficient capacity to upload large files to the Internet may contact ACF for an exception that will allow these applicants to submit an application in paper format.

Duration: Discretionary Grants are generally for a 12-, 24- or 36-month period; some may be renewed for up to five years. Formula Grants: Awards will be made quarterly on a fiscal year basis through a letter of credit.

Deadline: Formula Grants: June 30. Contact the headquarters or regional office, as appropriate, for other application deadlines.

ADDRESS INQUIRIES TO:
Catherine Heath, Program Specialist
(See address above.)

U.S. DEPARTMENT OF JUSTICE

Office of Juvenile Justice and Delinquency Prevention
810 Seventh Street, N.W., 5th Floor
Washington, DC 20531
(202) 616-3807
Fax: (202) 307-2819
E-mail: eric.stansbury@usdoj.gov
ricco.hall@usdoj.gov
Web Site: www.ojjdp.gov

TYPE:
Block grants. Grants awarded on a formula basis to states. Funds are available for around 30 specific program purpose areas.

See entry 1378 for full listing.

U.S. DEPARTMENT OF JUSTICE

Office of Juvenile Justice and Delinquency Prevention
810 Seventh Street, N.W., 5th Floor
Washington, DC 20531
(202) 307-5911
Fax: (202) 307-2093
E-mail: nicki.polk@usdoj.gov
Web Site: www.ojjdp.gov

TYPE:
Block grants; Challenge/matching grants; Demonstration grants; Formula grants; Internships; Project/program grants; Research grants; Technical assistance; Training grants. Grants to increase the capacity of state and local governments to conduct effective juvenile justice and delinquency prevention programs as developed in the state comprehensive action plan.

See entry 1376 for full listing.

USDA FOOD AND NUTRITION SERVICE [1131]

Child Nutrition Service
3101 Park Center Drive, Room 628
Alexandria, VA 22302
(703) 305-2054
Fax: (703) 305-2879
Web Site: www.fns.usda.gov/cnd

FOUNDED: 1969

AREAS OF INTEREST:
Child nutrition.

NAME(S) OF PROGRAMS:
- **The Child and Adult Care Food Program**
- **The Fresh Fruit and Vegetable Program**
- **The National School Lunch Program**
- **The School Breakfast Program**
- **The Special Milk Program for Children**
- **The Summer Food Service Program for Children**

TYPE:
Formula grants; Grants-in-aid; Project/program grants. Reimbursement for the support of food service in schools, child and adult care institutions to improve nutrition.

The Child and Adult Care Food Program helps child care facilities and institutions serve nutritious meals and snacks to preschool and school-age children. To participate, facilities and institutions must be licensed or approved to provide child care services. They must also meet certain other eligibility requirements. The program operates in nonresidential day care centers, settlement houses, outside-school-hours care centers, family day care homes, institutions providing day care for handicapped children and others. Participating facilities and institutions get cash assistance, USDA-donated foods and technical guidance. In child care centers, the amount of cash assistance varies according to the family size and income of children served. In day care homes, the amount of cash assistance is based on a food service payment rate. Similar benefits are also now available to adult day care centers which serve functionally impaired adults or persons 60 years of age or older.

The Fresh Fruit and Vegetable Program introduces school children to a variety of produce that they otherwise might not have the opportunity to sample. The goal is to improve children's overall diet and create healthier eating habits to impact their present and future health.

The National School Lunch Program makes well-planned nutritious meals available to school children. Any public or nonprofit private schools of high school grade or under and licensed public or nonprofit private residential child care institutions are eligible to participate in the National School Lunch

and School Breakfast Programs. Schools that participate are required to provide free and reduced-price meals to children unable to pay the full price. Eligibility is based on application information submitted by a parent or guardian. The household income limit for free lunches is set at or below 130% of the federal poverty level and for reduced price lunches household income must be above 130% or at or below 185% of the federal poverty level. Children from households not eligible for free or reduced-price meals must pay the school's full price charge for lunch. Cash and donated commodities are provided to participating schools and institutions according to the number of meals served.

The School Breakfast Program makes nutritious breakfasts available to school children under the same eligibility guidelines and general requirements as the National School Lunch Program.

The Special Milk Program for Children makes it possible for all children attending a participating school or institution to purchase milk at a reduced price or receive it free, if they are eligible. Reimbursement is provided for each half-pint of milk served under the program. Schools and institutions that participate in other federal child nutrition programs authorized under the National School Lunch Act or the Child Nutrition Act of 1966 may not participate in the Special Milk Program for Children, except for split-session kindergarten programs conducted in schools in which the children do not have access to the other meal program.

The Summer Food Service Program for Children helps communities serve meals to needy children when school is not in session. The program is sponsored by public or private nonprofit school food authorities or local, municipal, county or state governments. Public or private nonprofit residential camps, other private nonprofit organizations, colleges and universities which participate in the National Youth Sports Program also may be sponsors. The program operates in areas in which at least 50% of the children meet the income criteria for free and reduced-price school meals. USDA reimburses sponsors for operating costs of food services up to a specified maximum rate for each meal served. In addition, sponsors receive some reimbursement for planning, operating and supervising expenses.

YEAR PROGRAM STARTED: 1946

PURPOSE:
To help safeguard the health and well-being of the nation's children and to encourage the domestic consumption of nutritious agricultural commodities and other foods.

LEGAL BASIS:
The National School Lunch Act as amended and the Child Nutrition Act of 1966, as amended.

ELIGIBILITY:
Family size and number of children based on income poverty levels.

GEOG. RESTRICTIONS: United States and its territories.

FINANCIAL DATA:
Amount of support per award: Varies.

Total amount of support: Varies.

Matching fund requirements: Varies.

APPLICATION INFO:
Official application materials are available upon request to state educational agencies or other state-designated agency. In states where education agencies do not administer the programs for nonprofit private schools, contact the appropriate Food and Nutrition Service Regional Office of the Department of Agriculture for more information.

Deadline: Applications are accepted throughout the year.

VETERANS OF FOREIGN WARS AUXILIARY

National Headquarters
406 West 34th Street, 10th Floor
Kansas City, MO 64111
(816) 561-8655
Fax: (816) 931-4753
E-mail: info@vfwauxiliary.org
Web Site: www.vfwauxiliary.org

TYPE:
Awards/prizes.

See entry 501 for full listing.

JOSEPH B. WHITEHEAD FOUNDATION [1132]

191 Peachtree Street, Suite 3540
Atlanta, GA 30303
(404) 522-6755
Fax: (404) 522-7026
E-mail: fdns@woodruff.org
Web Site: www.jbwhitehead.org

FOUNDED: 1937

AREAS OF INTEREST:
Human services, public education, children and youth services, and early childhood education.

TYPE:
Capital grants; General operating grants; Project/program grants.

LEGAL BASIS:
Private foundation.

GEOG. RESTRICTIONS: Metropolitan Atlanta, Georgia.

FINANCIAL DATA:
Amount of support per award: $100,000 to $1,000,000.

Total amount of support: $44,505,000 for the year 2014.

NO. AWARDS: 33.

APPLICATION INFO:
An application form is not required. Proposals should be made in letter form and should include the following information:
(1) a description of the organization, its purposes, programs, staffing and governing board;
(2) organization's latest financial statements, including the most recent report;
(3) a description of the proposed project and full justification for its funding;
(4) an itemized project budget, including other sources of support in hand anticipated and;
(5) evidence from the IRS of the organization's tax-exempt status and the applying organization itself is not a private foundation.

Deadline: February 1 and September 1.

TRUSTEES:
James B. Williams, Chairman
James M. Sibley, Vice Chairman
Charles H. McTier

OFFICERS:
P. Russell Hardin, President
Erik S. Johnson, Secretary and Treasurer

ADDRESS INQUIRIES TO:
P. Russell Hardin, President
(See address above.)

THE WHO (WOMEN HELPING OTHERS) FOUNDATION

2121 Midway Road
Carrollton, TX 75006
(972) 458-0601 ext. 2060
(800) 946-4663
E-mail: who@whofoundation.org
Web Site: www.whofoundation.org

TYPE:
Development grants; Product donations; Project/program grants.

See entry 1077 for full listing.

WIDENER MEMORIAL FOUNDATION IN AID OF HANDICAPPED CHILDREN

4060 Butler Pike
Suite 225
Plymouth Meeting, PA 19462
(610) 825-8900
Fax: (610) 825-8904
E-mail: jhagerty@erdixon.com

TYPE:
Capital grants.

See entry 1001 for full listing.

Community development and services

ABEL FOUNDATION [1133]

1815 Y Street
Lincoln, NE 68508
(402) 434-1212
Fax: (402) 434-1799
Web Site: www.abelfoundation.org

AREAS OF INTEREST:
Health and human services, higher education and community development programs.

TYPE:
Capital grants; Matching gifts; Project/program grants.

PURPOSE:
To improve the quality of life, particularly in communities where the company has facilities.

ELIGIBILITY:
Grants are made to organizations that have tax-exempt status under Section 501(c)(3) of the Internal Revenue Code. No grants are made to individuals.

GEOG. RESTRICTIONS: Nebraska, particularly Lincoln.

FINANCIAL DATA:
Amount of support per award: Varies.

Total amount of support: $617,825 for the year 2014.

APPLICATION INFO:
Applicants are requested to use the Lincoln/Lancaster County Grant Maker Common Application Form.

Duration: One year. Renewal possible.

Deadline: March 31, July 31 and October 31. Foundation meets in May, September and December, respectively, to review funding requests.

ADDRESS INQUIRIES TO:
J. Ross McCown, Vice President
(See address above.)

ADCO FOUNDATION

c/o AA Shareholders Service Company, LLC
1060 First Avenue, Suite 400
King of Prussia, PA 19406
(610) 768-8020

TYPE:
General operating grants; Project/program grants; Seed money grants.

See entry 1563 for full listing.

AKRON COMMUNITY FOUNDATION [1134]

345 West Cedar Street
Akron, OH 44307-2407
(330) 376-8522
Fax: (330) 376-0202
E-mail: jgarofalo@akroncf.org
Web Site: www.akroncf.org

FOUNDED: 1955

AREAS OF INTEREST:
Arts and culture, civic affairs, health and human services, and education.

TYPE:
Capital grants; General operating grants; Project/program grants; Scholarships; Seed money grants.

YEAR PROGRAM STARTED: 1955

PURPOSE:
To embrace and enhance the work of charitable people who make a permanent commitment to the good of the community.

LEGAL BASIS:
Community foundation.

ELIGIBILITY:
Organizations must be tax-exempt.

GEOG. RESTRICTIONS: Summit County, Ohio.

FINANCIAL DATA:
Assets of $185,000,000 for the year ended December 31, 2014.

Amount of support per award: Average $14,000 to $18,000.

Total amount of support: $7,849,147 for the year 2014.

CO-OP FUNDING PROGRAMS: City of Akron Neighborhood Partnership.

NO. MOST RECENT APPLICANTS: 1,147 for the year 2014.

NO. AWARDS: 1,052 for the year 2014.

APPLICATION INFO:
Applicants must contact the Foundation before submitting an application.

Deadline: Arts and Culture: April 1; Civic Affairs: July 1; Health and Human Services: October 1; Education: December 13.

PUBLICATIONS:
Guidelines.

IRS I.D.: 34-1087615

ADDRESS INQUIRIES TO:
John F. Garofalo
Vice President of Community Investment
(See address above.)

ALBION COMMUNITY FOUNDATION [1135]

P.O. Box 156
Albion, MI 49224-0156
(517) 629-3349
Fax: (517) 629-8027
E-mail: foundation@albionfoundation.org
Web Site: www.albionfoundation.org

FOUNDED: 1969

AREAS OF INTEREST:
Promoting philanthropy addressing community needs through grantmaking, and providing leadership on key community issues.

TYPE:
Capital grants; Challenge/matching grants; Development grants; Project/program grants.

PURPOSE:
To provide a favorable ratio between the amount of money requested and the number of people served, show innovation and creativity in addressing a community need that demonstrates careful planning that provides for successful completion of the project.

LEGAL BASIS:
501(c)(3).

GEOG. RESTRICTIONS: Greater Albion, Michigan area.

FINANCIAL DATA:
Amount of support per award: $250 to $5,000.

Total amount of support: Approximately $80,000 to $100,000 each year.

APPLICATION INFO:
One complete, hard copy of the application and attachments, with original signatures, must be sent to the Foundation at the address above. Complete details and application forms are available on the Foundation web site.

Deadline: Varies annually.

ALBUQUERQUE COMMUNITY FOUNDATION [1136]

624 Tijeras, N.W.
Albuquerque, NM 87102
(505) 883-6240
Fax: (505) 883-3629
E-mail: nancy@albuquerquefoundation.org
Web Site: www.albuquerquefoundation.org

FOUNDED: 1981

AREAS OF INTEREST:
Arts and culture, education, environmental and historic preservation, economic and workforce development, health and human services.

TYPE:
Challenge/matching grants; General operating grants; Project/program grants; Scholarships; Seed money grants; Technical assistance.

YEAR PROGRAM STARTED: 1983

PURPOSE:
To improve the quality of life in the greater Albuquerque area by providing support for projects and organizations that serve the community.

LEGAL BASIS:
Community foundation.

ELIGIBILITY:
Grants are made to nonprofit organizations. Foundation grants are generally not made to individuals, for political or religious purposes, to retire indebtedness, for the payment of interest or taxes, annual campaigns, endowments, emergency funding, to influence legislation or elections, to private foundations and other grantmaking organizations, or to organizations that discriminate on the basis of race, creed or sex.

GEOG. RESTRICTIONS: Albuquerque, New Mexico.

FINANCIAL DATA:
$66,000,000 in assets for fiscal year ended December 31, 2014.

Amount of support per award: Varies.

Total amount of support: $3,042,697 in grants and scholarships for fiscal year ended December 31, 2014.

APPLICATION INFO:
Current guidelines and criteria are available on the web site.

Duration: One year.

PUBLICATIONS:
Report to the Community.

IRS I.D.: 85-0295444

STAFF:
Randy Royster, President and Chief Executive Officer
Kelli Cooper, Vice President of Philanthropic Services
John Maes, Finance Director
Nancy Johnson, Grant Director
Andy Williams, Communications Associate

BOARD OF TRUSTEES:
Jennifer S. Thomas, Chairperson
Carl M. Alongi, Chairperson-elect
Julie Weaks-Gutierrez, Treasurer
Glenn Fellows, Secretary
Karen Bard
Beverly R. Bendicksen
William E. Ebel
Teri Giron-Gordon
Mark L. Gorham
Pam Hurd-Knief
Albert T. Jorgensen
Steve Keene
Bill Lang
Kenneth C. Leach
Steve Maestas
Bev McMillan
Marcus Mims, C.P.A.
Diane Harrison Ogawa
Deborah Peacock
Kathleen Raskob
Ron J. Rivera, C.P.A.
Jerrald J. Roehl
Walter E. Stern
Peter Touche
Kevin Yearout

ADDRESS INQUIRIES TO:
Nancy Johnson, Grant Director
(See address above.)

ALGER REGIONAL COMMUNITY FOUNDATION [1137]

P.O. Box 39
Munising, MI 49862
(906) 387-3900
Fax: (906) 387-2506
E-mail: algercf@yahoo.com
Web Site: www.algercf.com

FOUNDED: 1992

AREAS OF INTEREST:
Cultural arts, community service, education, the environment and conservation, health and human services, and youth.

TYPE:
Endowments.

YEAR PROGRAM STARTED: 1995

PURPOSE:
To provide support to organizations that enhance the quality of life in Alger County.

ELIGIBILITY:
Grants are made to organizations that have tax-exempt status under Section 501(c)(3) of the Internal Revenue Code. Nonsectarian religious programs may apply. Organizations must serve or be located in Alger County, MI. No grants are made to individuals.

GEOG. RESTRICTIONS: Alger County, Michigan.

FINANCIAL DATA:
Amount of support per award: Varies.

APPLICATION INFO:
Foundation staff members are available to talk with potential applicants who are interested in learning about opportunities and needs in the community.

IRS I.D.: 38-6189947

ADDRESS INQUIRIES TO:
Theresa Bray, Executive Director
(See address above.)

*SPECIAL STIPULATIONS:
Potential applicants must meet with the Executive Director before receiving the grant application(s).

ALLEGAN COUNTY COMMUNITY FOUNDATION [1138]

524 Marshall Street
Allegan, MI 49010-1632
(269) 673-8344
Fax: (269) 673-8745
E-mail: theresa.accf@gmail.com
Web Site: www.alleganfoundation.org

FOUNDED: 1965

AREAS OF INTEREST:
Education, health and human services, culture, community development, environmental issues and art.

TYPE:
General operating grants; Project/program grants; Scholarships; Technical assistance. Grants fall into the following categories: youth and general.

PURPOSE:
To positively impact the Allegan County community through the establishment of permanently endowed funds.

LEGAL BASIS:
Community foundation.

ELIGIBILITY:
Applications accepted from charitable organizations serving Allegan County, MI residents. No funding for individuals except for scholarships.

GEOG. RESTRICTIONS: Allegan County, Michigan.

FINANCIAL DATA:
Amount of support per award: $500 to $15,000.

Total amount of support: Varies.

NO. MOST RECENT APPLICANTS: 58 for the year 2014.

NO. AWARDS: 43 for the year 2014.

APPLICATION INFO:
Applications must include a copy of the IRS 501(c)(3) tax determination letter.

Duration: One year.

Deadline: TAG: November; Legacy: December.

ALTMAN FOUNDATION [1139]

8 West 40th Street
19th Floor
New York, NY 10018-2263
(212) 682-0970
Fax: (212) 682-1648
E-mail: info@altman.org
Web Site: www.altmanfoundation.org

FOUNDED: 1913

AREAS OF INTEREST:
Strengthening communities, health, education (independent and non-public schools), arts and culture.

TYPE:
Project/program grants.

YEAR PROGRAM STARTED: 1913

PURPOSE:
To support programs and organizations within the five boroughs of New York City working in the Foundation's four program areas.

LEGAL BASIS:
Private foundation.

ELIGIBILITY:
Must have a current IRS 501(c)(3) tax-exemption letter. No grants to individuals. No grants for bricks and mortar or capital equipment.

GEOG. RESTRICTIONS: Five boroughs of New York City.

FINANCIAL DATA:
Amount of support per award: Varies.

Total amount of support: $10,952,850 in grants authorized for the year 2013.

NO. MOST RECENT APPLICANTS: 326.

NO. AWARDS: 137 for the year 2013.

APPLICATION INFO:
Applicants should review material on the Foundation's web site regarding funding approach, guidelines, limitations and procedures.

Duration: One year. Renewal possible.

PUBLICATIONS:
Annual report.

IRS I.D.: 13-1623879

STAFF:
Karen L. Rosa, Vice President and Executive Director
Deborah Thompson Velazquez, Senior Program Officer
Megan McAllister, Program Officer
Rachael N. Pine, J.D., Program Officer

ADDRESS INQUIRIES TO:
Karen L. Rosa
Vice President and Executive Director
(See address above.)

AMARILLO AREA FOUNDATION [1140]

801 South Fillmore
Suite 700
Amarillo, TX 79101
(806) 376-4521
Fax: (806) 373-3656
E-mail: kathie@aaf-hf.org
Web Site: www.amarilloareafoundation.org

FOUNDED: 1957

AREAS OF INTEREST:
Community, arts and culture, education, health and human services, teen pregnancy prevention, youth-oriented programs and elderly services.

TYPE:
Project/program grants; Scholarships. Discretionary grants.

PURPOSE:
To exercise leadership on charitable issues, advance the cause of philanthropy throughout the region and promote efficient and effective delivery of services from nonprofit organizations.

LEGAL BASIS:
501(c)(3).

ELIGIBILITY:
No grants to individuals. Scholarships go to educational institutions.

GEOG. RESTRICTIONS: 26 northernmost counties in the Texas panhandle.

FINANCIAL DATA:
Amount of support per award: $20,000 to $250,000 for the year 2014.

Total amount of support: $4,900,000 for the year 2014.

APPLICATION INFO:
Contact Grants Coordinator for counseling prior to submitting application. Application is available online for download as a Word document.

Duration: Typically one year.

ADDRESS INQUIRIES TO:
Kathie Grant, Grants Coordinator
(See address above.)

AMERICAN PLANNING ASSOCIATION

205 North Michigan Avenue
Suite 1200
Chicago, IL 60601
(312) 786-6363
E-mail: mgroh@planning.org
Web Site: www.planning.org

TYPE:
Fellowships; Scholarships.

See entry 952 for full listing.

AMERICAN PLANNING ASSOCIATION [1141]

205 North Michigan Avenue
Suite 1200
Chicago, IL 60601
(312) 786-6363
E-mail: mgroh@planning.org
Web Site: www.planning.org

FOUNDED: 1909

AREAS OF INTEREST:
Urban and regional planning and promotion of the art and science of planning.

NAME(S) OF PROGRAMS:
- **Charles Abrams Scholarship Program**

TYPE:
Scholarships. For a student enrolled in a graduate planning program, leading to a Master's degree, who attends one of the following schools:
(1) Columbia University, Division of Urban Planning;
(2) Harvard University, Urban Planning Program, Harvard Graduate School of Design;
(3) Massachusetts Institute of Technology, Department of Urban Studies and Planning;
(4) New School University, Urban Policy Analysis and Management Program, Robert J. Milano Graduate School of Management and Urban Policy or;
(5) University of Pennsylvania, Department of City and Regional Planning.

PURPOSE:
To aid students who will pursue careers as practicing planners.

LEGAL BASIS:
Private, nonprofit educational association.

ELIGIBILITY:
An applicant must be a U.S. citizen and have been accepted into the graduate planning program of one of the five eligible schools. Incoming students are eligible. An applicant must be in need of financial assistance, as determined by a review of the applicant's financial needs. A nomination by the department chair is required.

FINANCIAL DATA:
Student also receives one-year membership in the American Planning Association.

Amount of support per award: $2,000 paid directly to the student's school to defray tuition costs.

Total amount of support: $2,000 each year.

NO. MOST RECENT APPLICANTS: 4.

NO. AWARDS: 1 each year.

APPLICATION INFO:
An eligible applicant should apply through one of the five designated schools on forms supplied to the participating university by APA. Applicant needs to be nominated by Department Chair.

Duration: One academic year.

Deadline: April 30.

OFFICERS:
Carol Rhea, FAICP, President
Jim Drinan, Executive Director

ADDRESS INQUIRIES TO:
Monica Groh, Director of Emerging Professionals
(See address above.)

THE ANDERSEN CORPORATE FOUNDATION [1142]

White Pine Building
342 Fifth Avenue North, Suite 200
Bayport, MN 55003
(651) 275-4450
Fax: (651) 439-9480
E-mail: andersencorpfdn@srinc.biz
Web Site: www.andersencorporation.com/corporate-responsibility/community-involvement

FOUNDED: 1941

AREAS OF INTEREST:
Education and youth development, health and safety, human services, civic support and affordable housing.

TYPE:
Capital grants; General operating grants; Project/program grants.

YEAR PROGRAM STARTED: 1941

PURPOSE:
To better people's lives and strengthen communities, focusing primarily where Andersen employees live and work.

LEGAL BASIS:
Private foundation.

ELIGIBILITY:
Qualified tax-exempt organizations. Primary focus on Washington County, MN and portions of western Wisconsin.

GEOG. RESTRICTIONS: Des Moines and Dubuque, Iowa; east metro area of St. Paul and Washington County, Minnesota; North Brunswick, New Jersey; Marion, Ohio; Page County, Virginia; and Menomonie and portions of western Wisconsin.

FINANCIAL DATA:
$45,000,000 in assets as of December 31, 2015.

Amount of support per award: $1,500 to $100,000.

Total amount of support: $2,124,800 for the year 2014-15.

NO. MOST RECENT APPLICANTS: 400.

NO. AWARDS: 150.

APPLICATION INFO:
Cover form and checklist are available online.

Duration: One year. Renewal by reapplication.

Deadline: October 15, February 15 and June 15 for board meetings in April, July and November, respectively.

PUBLICATIONS:
Application guidelines.

IRS I.D.: 41-6020912

OFFICERS AND BOARD OF DIRECTORS:
Keith Olson, President
Susan Roeder, Vice President
Phil Donaldson, Treasurer
Jay Lund
Jerry Redmond
Karen Richard

ADDRESS INQUIRIES TO:
Chloette Haley, Program Officer
(See address above.)

*PLEASE NOTE:
Foundation prefers that the proposal be sent to the address above.

FRED C. AND KATHERINE B. ANDERSEN FOUNDATION [1143]

P.O. Box 80
Bayport, MN 55003
(651) 264-7355
Fax: (651) 264-5537
E-mail: marygillstrom@sbcglobal.net

FOUNDED: 1959

AREAS OF INTEREST:
Education, youth, elderly and health programs.

TYPE:
Capital grants; Challenge/matching grants; General operating grants; Project/program grants. The Foundation supports four-year accredited colleges and universities that do not accept state or federal funding.

YEAR PROGRAM STARTED: 1959

PURPOSE:
To support organizations of higher learning that are four-year institutions that do not accept state or federal funding.

LEGAL BASIS:
Private foundation.

ELIGIBILITY:
Grants are made to organizations that have tax-exempt status under Section 501(c)(3) of the Internal Revenue Code. No grants are made to individuals. No grants for endowment.

GEOG. RESTRICTIONS: Washington County, Minnesota; Pierce, Polk and St. Croix counties, Wisconsin.

FINANCIAL DATA:
Total market value of $552,611,445 for the year 2015.

Amount of support per award: Varies by need.

Total amount of support: $25,897,586 for the year 2015.

APPLICATION INFO:
Organizations should submit a letter of intent to the Foundation.

Duration: One year. Must reapply for future grants.

Deadline: March 11, July 15 and October 14.

IRS I.D.: 41-6020920

ADDRESS INQUIRIES TO:
Mary Gillstrom, Vice President/Secretary
(See address above.)

HUGH J. ANDERSEN FOUNDATION [1144]

342 Fifth Avenue North, Suite 200
Bayport, MN 55003-1201
(651) 439-1557
Fax: (651) 439-9480
E-mail: hjafdn@srinc.biz
Web Site: www.srinc.biz/foundations/hugh-j-andersen-foundation

FOUNDED: 1962

AREAS OF INTEREST:
Humanities, arts/culture, elementary and secondary education, health care, human services, women and homelessness.

TYPE:
Capital grants; General operating grants; Project/program grants. Supports focused efforts that foster inclusivity, promotes equality, and lends to increased human independence, self-sufficiency and dignity.

PURPOSE:
To improve the quality of life in the St. Croix Valley.

LEGAL BASIS:
Private organization.

ELIGIBILITY:
Eligible organizations must be IRS 501(c)(3) tax-exempt.

GEOG. RESTRICTIONS: Primarily Washington County, Minnesota and Pierce, Polk, and St. Croix counties in Wisconsin, with secondary focus in St. Paul, Minnesota.

FINANCIAL DATA:
Amount of support per award: $500 to $75,000.

Total amount of support: $2,756,000 for fiscal year ended February 2016.

NO. AWARDS: 238.

APPLICATION INFO:
Applicant organizations must use the Foundation's application form and include a copy of the IRS tax-exempt determination letter.

Duration: One year. Renewal by reapplication.

Deadline: March 15, June 15, August 15 and November 15.

PUBLICATIONS:
Annual report; application guidelines.

ADDRESS INQUIRIES TO:
Brad Kruse, Philanthropy Director
(See address above.)

ANDRUS FAMILY FUND [1145]

330 Madison Avenue
30th Floor
New York, NY 10017
(212) 687-6975
Fax: (212) 687-6978
E-mail: info@affund.org
Web Site: www.affund.org

FOUNDED: 2000

AREAS OF INTEREST:
Juvenile justice and foster care.

NAME(S) OF PROGRAMS:
- **Foster Care Program**
- **Juvenile Justice Program**

TYPE:
Project/program grants; Research grants.

YEAR PROGRAM STARTED: 2000

PURPOSE:
To contribute to the body of knowledge and experience about what is necessary to create and sustain effective social change.

LEGAL BASIS:
501(c)(3).

ELIGIBILITY:
AFF does not fund endowments, capital improvements, fund-raising events/sponsorships, scholarships, or loans. Nor does AFF make grants to individuals. Presently, AFF does not fund international projects.

GEOG. RESTRICTIONS: United States.

FINANCIAL DATA:
Amount of support per award: $50,000 to $200,000.

Total amount of support: $3,500,000 to $4,000,000.

APPLICATION INFO:
Deadline: Grants are awarded by the trustees, who meet in September, February and May.

ADDRESS INQUIRIES TO:
Leticia Peguero, Executive Director
(See address above.)

*PLEASE NOTE:
The Fund is currently not accepting unsolicited grant requests.

ANN ARBOR AREA COMMUNITY FOUNDATION [1146]

301 North Main Street
Suite 300
Ann Arbor, MI 48104-1133
(734) 663-0401
Fax: (734) 663-3514
E-mail: info@aaacf.org
Web Site: www.aaacf.org

FOUNDED: 1963

AREAS OF INTEREST:
Environment, arts, health and human services, youth and seniors.

NAME(S) OF PROGRAMS:
- **The African American Endowment Fund**
- **The Anna Botsford Bach Fund**
- **Community Foundation of Plymouth**
- **Coordinated Funding**
- **Cultural Economic Development**
- **General Grantmaking**
- **Youth Council**
- **The Ypsilanti Area Community Fund**

TYPE:
Challenge/matching grants; Demonstration grants; Development grants; Project/program grants; Scholarships; Seed money grants; Technical assistance.

YEAR PROGRAM STARTED: 1963

PURPOSE:
To improve the quality of life in the Foundation's region.

ELIGIBILITY:
Eligible organizations must be nonprofit and located in the Ann Arbor, MI region.

GEOG. RESTRICTIONS: Plymouth and Washtenaw County, Michigan.

FINANCIAL DATA:
Amount of support per award: $500 to $20,000.

Total amount of support: More than $3,000,000 annually.

APPLICATION INFO:
A guideline on how to apply and application form are available on the Foundation web site.

Duration: One year.

Deadline: March and September. Contact the Foundation for exact dates.

ADDRESS INQUIRIES TO:
Patricia Walker, Chief Operating Officer
(See address above.)

THE ANNENBERG FOUNDATION

2000 Avenue of the Stars
Suite 1000 S
Los Angeles, CA 90067
(310) 209-4560
Fax: (310) 209-1631
E-mail: requests@annenberg.org
Web Site: www.annenbergfoundation.org

TYPE:
General operating grants; Grants-in-aid; Project/program grants; Technical assistance.

See entry 17 for full listing.

ARIZONA COMMUNITY FOUNDATION [1147]

2201 East Camelback Road
Suite 405-B
Phoenix, AZ 85016
(602) 381-1400
(800) 222-8221
Fax: (602) 381-1575
E-mail: info@azfoundation.org
Web Site: www.azfoundation.org

FOUNDED: 1978

AREAS OF INTEREST:
Children's mental health and prevention programs, economic development, arts and culture, youth agencies and health agencies.

NAME(S) OF PROGRAMS:
- **Communities for All Ages**

TYPE:
Project/program grants.

YEAR PROGRAM STARTED: 1978

PURPOSE:
To benefit the quality of life in the Phoenix, AZ community and the surrounding area.

LEGAL BASIS:
Community foundation.

ELIGIBILITY:
Tax-exempt, nonprofit organizations. No grants are made to individuals.

GEOG. RESTRICTIONS: Arizona.

FINANCIAL DATA:
Amount of support per award: $10,000 average.

APPLICATION INFO:
Application information is available on the web site.

Duration: Typically, one year.

PUBLICATIONS:
Annual report.

OFFICERS:
Ron Butler, Chairman

ADDRESS INQUIRIES TO:
Lora Golke, Senior Philanthropic Advisor
(See address above.)

ARKANSAS COMMUNITY FOUNDATION [1148]

1400 West Markham Street
Suite 206
Little Rock, AR 72201
(501) 372-1116
Fax: (501) 372-1166
E-mail: arcf@arcf.org
Web Site: www.arcf.org

FOUNDED: 1976

AREAS OF INTEREST:
Grants are made in all fields.

TYPE:
Project/program grants; Scholarships; Seed money grants.

PURPOSE:
To serve as a vehicle for Arkansans in carrying out their long-term philanthropic plans; to exercise stewardship in the investment of and grantmaking from both permanent and short-term charitable funds; to provide leadership to increase public understanding of emerging problems, issues and the importance of philanthropy to the future of the state.

LEGAL BASIS:
Community foundation.

ELIGIBILITY:
Applicants must be nonprofit organizations with projects to benefit Arkansans. Few unrestricted grants are made. Only Arkansas organizations need apply.

Most funds are restricted or designated for specific organizations. Very few unrestricted grants are made.

GEOG. RESTRICTIONS: Arkansas.

FINANCIAL DATA:
Total amount of support: $14,000,000 for fiscal year 2013-14.

APPLICATION INFO:
Application information is available on the web site.

Duration: One year.

PUBLICATIONS:
Annual report; newsletter.

IRS I.D.: 52-1055743

BOARD OF DIRECTORS:
Ted Belden, Chairperson
Carolyn Blakely, Vice Chairperson
Heather Larkin, President and Chief Executive Officer
Charlotte Brown
Mary Elizabeth Eldridge
Jackson Farrow
Dennis Hunt
Eric Hutchinson
Mahlon Maris
George E. McLeod
Steve Nipper
Sam Scruggs
Angela Shirey
Beth Sparks
Philip Tappan
Robert Thompson
Estella Tullgren
Robert Zunick

ADDRESS INQUIRIES TO:
Grants Coordinator
(See address above.)

THE AUSTIN COMMUNITY FOUNDATION FOR THE CAPITAL AREA [1149]

4315 Guadalupe, Suite 300
Austin, TX 78751
(512) 472-4483
Fax: (512) 472-4486
E-mail: info@austincf.org
Web Site: www.austincf.org

FOUNDED: 1977

AREAS OF INTEREST:
Arts and culture, community development, community service, education and training, environment, health and human services, recreation and animal-related services.

TYPE:
Project/program grants; Scholarships.

YEAR PROGRAM STARTED: 1977

PURPOSE:
To promote philanthropy in central Texas; to improve the quality of life now and in the future.

ELIGIBILITY:
Organizations must be 501(c)(3) or 170(b)(1)(a)(vi) and located in the central Texas area, including Travis and contiguous counties. Funds are not given to individuals.

GEOG. RESTRICTIONS: Central Texas.

FINANCIAL DATA:
Amount of support per award: Varies; average competitive grant is $17,500.

APPLICATION INFO:
Applications must include the IRS letter ruling 501(c)(3) status.

Duration: One year. Must reapply.

Deadline: Proposals are reviewed on an ongoing basis; four- to six-month process.

IRS I.D.: 74-1934031

ADDRESS INQUIRIES TO:
Meagan A. Longley
Director of Grants and Scholarships
(See address above.)

AUTRY FOUNDATION [1150]

4383 Colfax Avenue
Studio City, CA 91604
(818) 752-7770
Fax: (818) 752-7779

AREAS OF INTEREST:
Culture, education, children's and seniors' groups, hunger and health.

TYPE:
Project/program grants.

PURPOSE:
To offer assistance to communities in southern California.

LEGAL BASIS:
Private foundation.

ELIGIBILITY:
Eligible organizations must be IRS 501(c)(3) tax-exempt.

GEOG. RESTRICTIONS: Southern California.

FINANCIAL DATA:
Amount of support per award: Varies.

Total amount of support: Varies.

APPLICATION INFO:
Applicants should submit a letter and include a copy of the IRS tax determination letter.

Duration: Depends on project. Renewable.

ADDRESS INQUIRIES TO:
Maxine Hansen, Secretary
(See address above.)

BADGER METER FOUNDATION, INC. [1151]

4545 West Brown Deer Road
Milwaukee, WI 53223-2479
(414) 355-0400
Fax: (414) 371-5950

AREAS OF INTEREST:
Social services, education, conservation and community funds.

TYPE:
General operating grants; Research grants; Seed money grants.

PURPOSE:
To support education and community service organizations, health associations, the handicapped, the arts and conservation.

ELIGIBILITY:
Organizations classified as 501(c)(3) by the IRS can apply. No grants to individuals and religious organizations.

GEOG. RESTRICTIONS: Milwaukee area, Wisconsin.

FINANCIAL DATA:
Amount of support per award: Varies.

Total amount of support: Varies.

NO. AWARDS: 50.

APPLICATION INFO:
Request must be submitted on organization's letterhead paper.

Duration: One year. Grants are renewable.

ADDRESS INQUIRIES TO:
John Biever, Treasurer and Secretary
(See address above.)

BALTIMORE COMMUNITY FOUNDATION

2 East Read Street, 9th Floor
Baltimore, MD 21202
(410) 332-4171
Fax: (410) 837-4701
E-mail: info@bcf.org
Web Site: www.bcf.org

TYPE:
Scholarships. Neighborhood grants. Education grants.

See entry 30 for full listing.

BARAGA COUNTY COMMUNITY FOUNDATION [1152]

100 Hemlock Street
Baraga, MI 49908
(906) 353-7898
Fax: (906) 353-7896
E-mail: baragacf@up.net
Web Site: www.baragacountyfoundation.org

FOUNDED: 1994

AREAS OF INTEREST:
Arts and culture, community development, education, senior well-being, and youth development.

TYPE:
Capital grants; Challenge/matching grants; Endowments; Project/program grants; Scholarships; Seed money grants; Technical assistance. Community convening.

YEAR PROGRAM STARTED: 1994

PURPOSE:
To enhance the quality of life for the citizens of the community.

LEGAL BASIS:
501(c)(3).

ELIGIBILITY:
Grants are made to organizations that have tax-exempt status under Section 501(c)(3) of the Internal Revenue Code.

GEOG. RESTRICTIONS: Baraga County, Michigan.

FINANCIAL DATA:
Amount of support per award: Varies depending upon the needs and nature of the request; $1,500 common.

Total amount of support: Approximately $38,000.

NO. AWARDS: Varies.

APPLICATION INFO:
Application information is available upon request.

Duration: One year. Renewal possible.

Deadline: Varies.

IRS I.D.: 38-3198122

ADDRESS INQUIRIES TO:
Gordette Marie Leutz, Executive Director
(See address above.)

BARNES GROUP FOUNDATION [1153]

123 Main Street
Bristol, CT 06010
(860) 583-7070
Fax: (860) 589-7466
Web Site: www.bginc.com

AREAS OF INTEREST:
Cultural arts, education, and health and welfare.

TYPE:
General operating grants; Scholarships. Employee scholarship program.

PURPOSE:
To support higher education, cultural arts, and health and welfare.

ELIGIBILITY:
Organizations classified as 501(c)(3) by the IRS can apply. Individuals and religious organizations are ineligible.

GEOG. RESTRICTIONS: United States, with emphasis on Connecticut and New England.

FINANCIAL DATA:
Amount of support per award: Varies.
Total amount of support: Varies.

APPLICATION INFO:
Applicants must write to the Foundation for an application form.
Duration: One year. Grants are renewable.

ADDRESS INQUIRIES TO:
Tom Barnes, Secretary
(See address above.)

BARR FOUNDATION [1154]

The Pilot House, Lewis Wharf
Fourth Floor
Boston, MA 02110
(617) 854-3500
Fax: (617) 854-3501
E-mail: info@barrfoundation.org
Web Site: www.barrfoundation.org

FOUNDED: 1987

AREAS OF INTEREST:
Education, the environment, arts and cultural activities with a focus on Boston, MA.

TYPE:
Capital grants; Challenge/matching grants; Conferences/seminars; Demonstration grants; Development grants; Endowments; Fellowships; General operating grants; Matching gifts; Project/program grants; Technical assistance. The work of the Foundation focuses on three critical areas with a focus on Boston, MA:
(1) closing education opportunity gaps;
(2) mitigating climate change and;
(3) enhancing cultural vitality.

PURPOSE:
To enhance the quality of life for all of Boston's citizens.

ELIGIBILITY:
No unsolicited proposals.

GEOG. RESTRICTIONS: Boston, Massachusetts.

FINANCIAL DATA:
Amount of support per award: Varies.

APPLICATION INFO:
By invitation only.
Deadline: Quarterly, in conjunction with quarterly meeting.

IRS I.D.: 04-6579815

ADDRESS INQUIRIES TO:
Kerri Ann Hurley
Director of Grants Management
(See address above.)

NORWIN S. AND ELIZABETH N. BEAN FOUNDATION [1155]

40 Stark Street
Manchester, NH 03101
(603) 493-7257
E-mail: kcook@beanfoundation.org
Web Site: www.beanfoundation.org

FOUNDED: 1967

AREAS OF INTEREST:
Arts and humanities, education, environment, health, social and community services and development of the voluntary sector.

TYPE:
Capital grants; Challenge/matching grants. Grants to tax-exempt charitable organizations operating in Amherst or Manchester, NH, for broad charitable purposes. Generally, at least two-thirds of available funds are awarded as grants for programs undertaken by nonprofit organizations and public agencies. The remaining one-third is allocated for capital needs, including acquisition of equipment, renovation or construction of facilities and additions to endowment.

General operating support grants are not made to ongoing programs, nor are grants made to eliminate previously incurred deficits. Short-term operating support may be provided to new organizations or for new program initiatives of established organizations. Generally, grants are provided for expenditure over a period of one year.

YEAR PROGRAM STARTED: 1967

PURPOSE:
To promote the general welfare.

LEGAL BASIS:
Private foundation.

ELIGIBILITY:
Applications are accepted from nonprofit 501(c)(3) organizations, municipal and public agencies serving the communities of Amherst or Manchester, NH. Priority consideration is given to organizations operating primarily in those two communities. However, the Foundation will consider applications from statewide or regional organizations which provide a substantial and documented level of service to Manchester and Amherst. The Foundation does not make grants to individuals or provide scholarship aid.

GEOG. RESTRICTIONS: Amherst or Manchester, New Hampshire.

FINANCIAL DATA:
Amount of support per award: $1,000 to $50,000.
Total amount of support: $515,000 for fiscal year 2015.

NO. MOST RECENT APPLICANTS: 60.

NO. AWARDS: 37 for the year 2013.

REPRESENTATIVE AWARDS:
$30,000 to the capital campaign for a wildlife sanctuary and educational facility to be built by the Audubon Society of New Hampshire; $7,000 to Child and Family Services of New Hampshire to establish a volunteer management position; $3,000 to the Franco-American Centre for the preservation and cataloging of historic documents; $15,000 for the Manchester Families in Transition program; $2,000 to The Caregivers, Inc. for an improved development tracking system.

APPLICATION INFO:
Applications should include a completed cover letter sheet and proposal with appropriate enclosures explaining the purpose of the project, describing how the project will be accomplished, and indicating the amount of grant support sought.
Duration: Grants are usually awarded for a one-year period only. The Foundation does not consider multiyear grants except in very rare circumstances.
Deadline: April 1, September 1 and December 1 for decisions made in February, June and November, respectively.

PUBLICATIONS:
Guidelines.

TRUSTEES:
John F. Dinkel, Jr.
Thomas J. Donovan
William Dunlap
Cathryn E. Vaughn
Michael Whitney

STAFF:
Kathleen D. Cook, Grant Manager

ADDRESS INQUIRIES TO:
Kathleen D. Cook, Grant Manager
(See address above.)

BENTON FOUNDATION

1560 Sherman Avenue
Suite 440
Evanston, IL 60201
(847) 328-3049
Fax: (847) 328-3046
Web Site: www.benton.org

TYPE:
Technical assistance. Program is funded for preserving, protecting and strengthening the public benefits in America's media environment.
See entry 1861 for full listing.

BERKS COUNTY COMMUNITY FOUNDATION [1156]

237 Court Street
Reading, PA 19601
(610) 685-2223
Fax: (610) 685-2240
E-mail: info@bccf.org
Web Site: www.bccf.org

FOUNDED: 1994

AREAS OF INTEREST:
Community, health, energy, smart growth and public policy.

TYPE:
Project/program grants; Scholarships.

PURPOSE:
To promote philanthropy and improve the quality of life in Berks County; to encourage and nurture performing artists at critical points in their careers.

LEGAL BASIS:
501(c)(3).

ELIGIBILITY:
Tax-exempt or nonprofit organizations, individuals, associations and public or private agencies are eligible to apply. Grant must be used for charitable purposes only.

GEOG. RESTRICTIONS: Berks County, Pennsylvania.

FINANCIAL DATA:
$50,000,000 in assets.

Amount of support per award: Varies, depending on fund.

Total amount of support: Varies.

APPLICATION INFO:
Applicants must submit a letter of inquiry.

Duration: Varies.

PUBLICATIONS:
Annual report.

ADDRESS INQUIRIES TO:
See e-mail address above.

WILLIAM BLAIR AND COMPANY FOUNDATION [1157]

222 West Adams
Chicago, IL 60606
(312) 236-1600
Fax: (312) 236-3612

AREAS OF INTEREST:
Cultural programs, hospitals, education, social services, Jewish giving and Catholic giving.

TYPE:
Capital grants; Endowments; Fellowships; General operating grants.

ELIGIBILITY:
Organizations, including religious, must be classified as 501(c)(3) by the IRS. No grants to individuals. Limited to employees or clients of William Blair. Not open to the public.

FINANCIAL DATA:
Amount of support per award: $500 to $5,000.

Total amount of support: Varies.

APPLICATION INFO:
Contact the Foundation.

Duration: One year.

ADDRESS INQUIRIES TO:
E. David Coolidge, III, Vice Chairman
(See address above.)

BLOWITZ-RIDGEWAY FOUNDATION [1158]

1701 East Woodfield Road
Suite 201
Schaumburg, IL 60173-5127
(847) 330-1020
Fax: (847) 330-1028
E-mail: serena@blowitzridgeway.org
Web Site: www.blowitzridgeway.org

FOUNDED: 1984

AREAS OF INTEREST:
Health and human services.

TYPE:
Capital grants; General operating grants; Project/program grants; Scholarships. Scholarships are given through schools.

YEAR PROGRAM STARTED: 1984

PURPOSE:
To support advances in medical, psychiatric, psychological and/or residential care, and research programs in medicine, psychology, social science and education.

LEGAL BASIS:
Private independent foundation.

ELIGIBILITY:
Organizations classified as 501(c)(3) by the IRS can apply. Preference will be given to organizations in Illinois and to programs or services which benefit youth, seniors or individuals lacking sufficient resources to care for themselves. No grants to individuals, religious or political organizations, government agencies, organizations that subsist mainly on third-party funding nor for the production or writing of audio-visual materials.

GEOG. RESTRICTIONS: Illinois.

FINANCIAL DATA:
Assets of $23,400,000 for the year ended September 30, 2014.

Amount of support per award: Generally, $1,000 to $15,000; some larger grants.

Total amount of support: Approximately $1,100,000 for fiscal year 2014.

NO. MOST RECENT APPLICANTS: 232 for the year 2013.

NO. AWARDS: 109 grants for the year 2013.

APPLICATION INFO:
The Blowitz-Ridgeway application form must accompany all grant requests. If declined, applicants may reapply the next year.

Duration: One year. Grants are renewable.

PUBLICATIONS:
Annual report; application guidelines.

IRS I.D.: 36-2488355

ADDRESS INQUIRIES TO:
Serena Moy, Administrator
(See address above.)

BLUE MOUNTAIN COMMUNITY FOUNDATION [1159]

22 East Poplar Street
Suite 206
Walla Walla, WA 99362
(509) 529-4371
Fax: (509) 529-5284
E-mail: bmcf@bluemountainfoundation.org
Web Site: www.bluemountainfoundation.org

FOUNDED: 1984

AREAS OF INTEREST:
Social and community services, education, health, and the arts and humanities.

TYPE:
Endowments; Project/program grants; Scholarships. The Foundation administers and awards scholarships to local area students to enable them to attend college, graduate school or trade school.

PURPOSE:
To seek, steward and share charitable gifts in the Blue Mountain area.

ELIGIBILITY:
The Foundation awards grants to nonprofit, tax-exempt organizations in the Foundation's service area which includes the counties of Columbia, Garfield and Walla Walla in the state of Washington and the communities of Athena, Milton-Freewater and Weston in Umatilla County, OR. It strives to make awards to agencies and programs that meet community needs and bring the most benefit to people in the Blue Mountain area.

GEOG. RESTRICTIONS: Columbia, Garfield and Walla Walla counties in Washington, and the northern parts of Umatilla County in Oregon.

FINANCIAL DATA:
Amount of support per award: Varies.

Total amount of support: $1,500,000.

APPLICATION INFO:
Grant guidelines and application forms can be obtained through the Foundation's web site. Grant applicants should submit an original and nine copies each of the completed Summary of Applicant Organization form and a one-page description of the program/project or idea on the organization's letterhead. Upon review, the Foundation may request additional information, including but not limited to financial statements, project budgets, 501(c)(3) verification and a list of members of the governing board.

Duration: Typically one year.

Deadline: Grants: July 1; Scholarships: March 1.

THE BNY MELLON FOUNDATION OF SOUTHWESTERN PENNSYLVANIA [1160]

BNY Mellon Center, Room 1830
Pittsburgh, PA 15258-0001
(412) 234-2732
Fax: (412) 236-1662
E-mail: doreen.tumminello@bnymellon.com
Web Site: www.bnymellon.com

FOUNDED: 1974

AREAS OF INTEREST:
Basic needs provisions: food, clothing, and housing assistance; workforce development: access to employment through job training, education, mentoring and skills development.

TYPE:
Capital grants; General operating grants; Project/program grants; Technical assistance.

YEAR PROGRAM STARTED: 1974

PURPOSE:
To identify and support initiatives that improve the social and economic conditions of residents where the company does business and where employees live and work. Through powering potential, the company's strategic philanthropic investments will emphasize basic needs, provisions, and workforce development.

LEGAL BASIS:
Corporate foundation, part of BNY Mellon's Charitable Giving Program.

ELIGIBILITY:
Organizations requesting support must have 501(c)(3) tax-exempt charitable status and must be public charities as defined under Section 509(a)(1) of the Internal Revenue Code.

No support is available for loans or direct grants to individuals, religious programs of churches or other sectarian organizations and political parties, campaigns or candidates. As a general rule, support is not available for fraternal organizations, such as police or fire associations, scholarships, fellowships and travel grants, conference or seminar attendance, specialized health campaigns, endowment campaigns, individual United Way agencies which already benefit from the Corporation's gift to the United Way appeal, national organizations, projects or programs or those which operate outside the U.S. and multiyear commitments.

GEOG. RESTRICTIONS: Southwestern Pennsylvania.

FINANCIAL DATA:
Amount of support per award: $2,500 to $10,000 average.

Total amount of support: $4,066,000 for the year 2014.

NO. MOST RECENT APPLICANTS: 500.

NO. AWARDS: Approximately 125.

APPLICATION INFO:
Contact the Foundation.

Duration: One year.

Deadline: Requests are considered upon receipt.

PUBLICATIONS:
Annual report which contains contributions policy and application guidelines.

STAFF:
Kenya T. Boswell, President
Doreen Tumminello, Administrator

ADDRESS INQUIRIES TO:
Kenya T. Boswell, President
(See address above.)

BOSTON FOUNDATION [1161]

75 Arlington Street, 10th Floor
Boston, MA 02116-3936
(617) 338-1700
Fax: (617) 338-1604
E-mail: grantsinfo@tbf.org
Web Site: www.tbf.org

FOUNDED: 1915

AREAS OF INTEREST:
Health, welfare, educational, cultural, planning and housing needs of the Boston metropolitan area community.

TYPE:
General operating grants; Project/program grants; Technical assistance. Capacity building. Grants for new or experimental programs of both new and established institutions.

LEGAL BASIS:
Community foundation established in 1915 in Massachusetts by agreement and declaration of trust. Incorporated in 1917.

ELIGIBILITY:
Grants are made to organizations or for programs in the Boston standard metropolitan statistical area only. Organizations must have federal tax-exempt status or a fiscal nonprofit agent. No grants are made to individuals. Grants are not made for scholarship, travel, medical or scientific research, religious purposes, publications or films or for national/international organizations.

GEOG. RESTRICTIONS: Greater Boston, Massachusetts.

FINANCIAL DATA:
Amount of support per award: Averages approximately $50,000 to $75,000.

Total amount of support: Approximately $16,500,000 annually.

Matching fund requirements: Varies.

NO. MOST RECENT APPLICANTS: Approximately 300.

APPLICATION INFO:
The Foundation requires submission of a Letter of Inquiry. It will review only proposals that have been invited based on its review.

Duration: Up to five years.

PUBLICATIONS:
Annual report; application guidelines; quarterly newsletters.

OFFICERS:
Michael Keating, Chairman
Catherine D'Amato, Vice Chairperson
Alfred F. Van Ranst, Jr., Treasurer and Chief Financial Officer
Timothy Gassert, Secretary
George C. Wilson, Assistant Treasurer
Barbara Hindley, Assistant Secretary

BOARD MEMBERS:
Sandra M. Edgerley
Michael R. Eisenson
Grace Fey
Paul C. Gannon
Paul S. Grogan
Rev. Dr. Gregory G. Groover, Sr.
Paul LaCamera
Paul W. Lee
Claudio Martinez
Linda Mason
Jane Mendillo
Jack Meyer
Dr. Myechia Minter-Jordan
Peter Nessen
Ron O'Hanley
Greg Shell

ADDRESS INQUIRIES TO:
Grants Manager or Program Officer
(See address above.)

OTTO BREMER FOUNDATION [1162]

445 Minnesota Street, Suite 2250
St. Paul, MN 55101
(651) 227-8036
(888) 291-1123
Fax: (651) 312-3665
E-mail: obf@ottobremer.org
Web Site: www.ottobremer.org

AREAS OF INTEREST:
Community economic, civic, and social betterment.

TYPE:
Capital grants; Challenge/matching grants; General operating grants; Project/program grants.

PURPOSE:
To assist people in achieving full economic, civic and social participation in and for the betterment of their communities.

ELIGIBILITY:
Grants are restricted to private nonprofit or public tax-exempt organizations for purposes defined under Section 501(c)(3) of the Internal Revenue Code. Grants are only made to organizations whose beneficiaries are residents of Minnesota, North Dakota or Wisconsin. Grants are not made to individuals.

GEOG. RESTRICTIONS: Minnesota, North Dakota and Wisconsin.

FINANCIAL DATA:
Amount of support per award: $1,000 to $500,000; average $35,000.

Total amount of support: $38,000,000 for the year 2013.

APPLICATION INFO:
Application must be made online and must include copy of IRS 501(c)(3) letter of determination.

Duration: One year. Must reapply.

Deadline: Varies.

GLADYS BROOKS FOUNDATION [1163]

1055 Franklin Avenue
Suite 208
Garden City, NY 11530-2903
(516) 746-6103
Web Site: www.gladysbrooksfoundation.org

FOUNDED: 1981

AREAS OF INTEREST:
Libraries, education, hospitals and clinics.

TYPE:
Capital grants; Challenge/matching grants; Demonstration grants; Development grants; Endowments; Matching gifts; Project/program grants; Scholarships. Grants to private, not-for-profit publicly supported libraries, educational institutions, hospitals and clinics in the eastern U.S.

YEAR PROGRAM STARTED: 1981

PURPOSE:
To provide for the intellectual, moral and physical welfare of the people of this country by establishing and supporting nonprofit libraries, educational institutions, hospitals and clinics.

ELIGIBILITY:
Applicants must be publicly supported, not-for-profit tax-exempt organizations. Generally speaking, grant applications will only be considered where outside funding, including governmental, is not available. The project will be largely funded by the grant unless the grant request covers a discrete component of a larger project. The funds will be used for capital projects including equipment or endowments. Applications for direct salary support will not be accepted.

Grant applications will be considered only for major expenditures generally between $50,000 and $100,000 and greater or lesser amounts in certain circumstances.

GEOG. RESTRICTIONS: Connecticut, Delaware, District of Columbia, Florida, Indiana, Louisiana, Maine, Maryland, Massachusetts, New Hampshire, New Jersey, New York, Ohio, Pennsylvania, Rhode Island, Tennessee and Vermont.

FINANCIAL DATA:
Amount of support per award: $50,000 to $100,000.

APPLICATION INFO:
Foundation application form must be used and is available on the web site. Applications must be completed and postmarked and sent with all supporting documents to the Foundation within 45 days from the date the application is downloaded. The only exception to this is if the application is downloaded on or after April 17, in which case application materials must be postmarked with all supporting materials by May 31. Applicants must furnish audited financial statements and include a specific budget for the project; also an annual report or a brief description of applicant organization.

Electronic submissions are not acceptable.

Duration: One year.

Deadline: May 31.

PUBLICATIONS:
Annual report.

GOVERNING BOARD:
James J. Daly, Chairman
Christopher R. Hawkins
Thomas Q. Morris, M.D.

*PLEASE NOTE:
All grant awards are made on the condition that the entirety of the funds advanced shall be utilized in direct furtherance of the project and that no portion thereof shall be appropriated by the grantee as an administrative or processing fee, for overseeing the project or for its general overhead.

BRUNSWICK FOUNDATION, INC. [1164]

One Northfield Court
Lake Forest, IL 60045
(847) 735-4344
Fax: (847) 735-4330
E-mail: lisa.debartolo@brunswick.com

FOUNDED: 1957

AREAS OF INTEREST:
Organizations that support the company's products.

NAME(S) OF PROGRAMS:
- **Brunswick Employee Sons and Daughters Scholarship**
- **Dollars for Doers Volunteer Program**

TYPE:
General operating grants. Scholarships to employee's children.

PURPOSE:
To support causes and/or projects that are related to fitness activities.

LEGAL BASIS:
Private foundation.

ELIGIBILITY:
Organizations in areas of company operation classified as 501(c)(3) by the IRS will be considered. The Foundation does not have and is not able to donate equipment or products.

FINANCIAL DATA:
Amount of support per award: Dollars for Doers: $75 to $1,000.
Total amount of support: $220,000 for the year 2014.

NO. MOST RECENT APPLICANTS: 250.

NO. AWARDS: Varies.

APPLICATION INFO:
Applications are sent out by invitation only.
Duration: One year.
Deadline: Varies.

IRS I.D.: 36-6033576

STAFF:
Lisa DeBartolo, Coordinator

DIRECTORS:
Judith Zelisko, President
B. Russell Lockridge, Vice President
William L. Metzger, Treasurer
Marsha Vaughn, Secretary

ADDRESS INQUIRIES TO:
Lisa DeBartolo, Coordinator
(See address above.)

THE BUHL FOUNDATION [1165]

650 Smithfield Street
Suite 2300
Pittsburgh, PA 15222
(412) 566-2711
Fax: (412) 566-2714
E-mail: buhl@buhlfoundation.org
Web Site: www.buhlfoundation.org
www.onenorthsidepgh.org

FOUNDED: 1927

AREAS OF INTEREST:
Education, youth development, human services and economic and community development, particularly with regard to the Northside of Pittsburgh.

CONSULTING OR VOLUNTEER SERVICES:
Wide variety of community initiatives to improve quality of life in the greater Pittsburgh area in general, and the Northside of Pittsburgh in particular.

TYPE:
Demonstration grants; Development grants; Grants-in-aid; Project/program grants; Seed money grants; Training grants. Capacity building. Grants-in-aid, primarily to institutions in the Pittsburgh metropolitan area, Allegheny County and western Pennsylvania for developmental and innovative projects in education, children and youth, and community services. More recently, a place-based granting focus on the Northside of Pittsburgh.

YEAR PROGRAM STARTED: 1928

PURPOSE:
To support efforts that contribute to the vibrancy and well-being of the Northside and the Pittsburgh region, create learning environments so that young people will thrive and be prepared for adulthood, encourage innovation and entrepreneurial solutions to improve quality of life, and make a definitive difference in addressing persistent community challenges or unmet needs of at-risk neighborhoods.

LEGAL BASIS:
Independent private foundation established by will probated on June 20, 1927.

ELIGIBILITY:
Tax-exempt, nonprofit institutions with appropriate interests in southwestern Pennsylvania are eligible to apply. Emphasis is on grants to institutions in the Pittsburgh metropolitan area, with a particular focus on the Northside of Pittsburgh. Programs and projects which combine different professional interests and relate agencies in cooperative endeavors are often recognized as worthy of a grant. Grants are not made to individuals.

GEOG. RESTRICTIONS: Southwestern Pennsylvania, including Pittsburgh and Allegheny counties.

FINANCIAL DATA:
Total amount of support: $4,391,883 for the year ended June 30, 2015.

NO. MOST RECENT APPLICANTS: 166.

NO. AWARDS: 81.

REPRESENTATIVE AWARDS:
$500,000 to The Sprout Fund to implement a grant program on the Northside to encourage neighborhood and citizen participation in a unified vision for community improvement; $250,000 to Greater Pittsburgh Community Food Bank for support of a Northside-wide feeding program to alleviate hunger in school-aged children; $150,000 to Pittsburgh Parks Conservancy to restore Allegheny Commons fountain and surrounding landscape to its original design while incorporating best practices for modern-day use.

APPLICATION INFO:
Applicants must write a letter of inquiry to the President at the address above, followed, if requested, by a formal proposal. Interviews and other follow-up procedures are then initiated by staff. Applications must contain a statement of objectives and the proposed means of attaining these, a description of the program and budget as well as information regarding the applicant agency, its organization and structure, its tax status and its capacity to implement the project.
Duration: Usually one year. Some grants cover two or three years.

PUBLICATIONS:
Annual report; application procedures.

IRS I.D.: 25-0378910

OFFICERS:
Frederick W. Thieman, President
Diana A. Bucco, Vice President

TRUSTEES:
Peter F. Mathieson, Chairperson
Saleem H. Ghubril, Vice Chairperson
Kim Tillotson Fleming, Secretary and Treasurer
Quintin B. Bullock
Jean A. Robinson
Lara E. Washington

ADDRESS INQUIRIES TO:
Frederick W. Thieman, President
(See address above.)

PATRICK AND AIMEE BUTLER FAMILY FOUNDATION [1166]

2356 University Avenue West
Suite 420
St. Paul, MN 55114
(651) 222-2565
E-mail: bffinfo@visi.com
Web Site: www.butlerfamilyfoundation.org

FOUNDED: 1951

AREAS OF INTEREST:
Arts and culture, environment, and human services.

TYPE:
General operating grants; Project/program grants.

YEAR PROGRAM STARTED: 1951

PURPOSE:
To support solid progressive ideas in art and culture, the environment, social service and social change.

LEGAL BASIS:
Private foundation.

ELIGIBILITY:
Eligible organizations must be IRS 501(c)(3) tax-exempt. The Foundation does not fund criminal justice, economic development or education, employment or vocational programs, films or videos, health, hospitals or medical research, loans or grants to individuals, secondary or elementary education, theater or dance, or projects outside the U.S.

GEOG. RESTRICTIONS: Twin Cities Metropolitan area, Minnesota.

FINANCIAL DATA:
Amount of support per award: Average $20,000.
Total amount of support: $4,068,500 for the year 2013.

NO. MOST RECENT APPLICANTS: 96 for the year 2012.

NO. AWARDS: 118 for the year 2013.

APPLICATION INFO:
Application must include a copy of the IRS tax determination letter. Must apply online through web site link.

Duration: Two years.

Deadline: May 1.

PUBLICATIONS:
Guidelines.

TRUSTEES:
John K. Butler, President
Patrick Butler, Vice President
Peter M. Butler, Treasurer
Brigid M. Butler
Katherine Butler
Patricia M. Butler
Paul S. Butler
Sandra K. Butler
Suzanne A. LeFevour
Melanie Martinez
Temple Peterson

STAFF:
Robert Hybben, Director of Program Operations
JoAnne Peters, Manager of Community Grants
Kerrie Blevins, Senior Advisor for Program

ADDRESS INQUIRIES TO:
Robert Hybben
Director of Program Operations
(See address above.)

CALIFORNIA COMMUNITY FOUNDATION [1167]

221 South Figueroa Street, Suite 400
Los Angeles, CA 90012
(213) 413-4130
Fax: (213) 383-2046
E-mail: info@calfund.org
Web Site: www.calfund.org

FOUNDED: 1915

AREAS OF INTEREST:
Education, arts and culture, health prevention and treatment services, health care coverage expansion, college access, early childhood, immigrant integration, and affordable housing.

NAME(S) OF PROGRAMS:

- **Arts**
- **Civic Engagement**
- **Education**
- **Health Care**
- **Housing and Economic Development**
- **Immigrant Integration**
- **Scholarships**

TYPE:
Fellowships; General operating grants; Project/program grants; Scholarships. Program-related investments. Policy analysis and advocacy.

YEAR PROGRAM STARTED: 1915

PURPOSE:
To strengthen Los Angeles communities through effective philanthropy and civic engagement.

LEGAL BASIS:
Community foundation, designated a public charity by the IRS.

ELIGIBILITY:
The Foundation will consider applications that are consistent with current program priorities and goals. Eligible organizations are:
(1) nonprofit agencies with evidence of tax-exempt status under Section 501(c)(3) of the Internal Revenue Code and not classified as a private foundation;
(2) located within and primarily serving residents of Los Angeles County, with the exception of regional, statewide or national public policy efforts that may benefit a substantial portion of the local population and;
(3) operated and organized so that they do not discriminate in the hiring of staff or the provision of services on the basis of race, religion, gender, sexual orientation, age, national origin or disability.

GEOG. RESTRICTIONS: Los Angeles County, California.

FINANCIAL DATA:
Amount of support per award: Nonprofit Organization Grants: Generally $75,000 to $100,000; Scholarships: Generally $250 to $15,000; Fellowship for Visual Artists Awards: $15,000 to $20,000.

Total amount of support: $155,000,000 for the year 2015.

CO-OP FUNDING PROGRAMS: Building a Lifetime of Options and Opportunities for Men - BLOOM; Ford Extended Learning Time Partnership; Los Angeles Preschool Advocacy Initiative; One Los Angeles, One Nation Initiative.

NO. MOST RECENT APPLICANTS: 584.

NO. AWARDS: 224.

APPLICATION INFO:
Information about how to apply can be found on the web site.

Duration: Generally two years.

Deadline: Varies.

PUBLICATIONS:
Annual report; application form; application guidelines; philanthropic white papers; fund brochures.

IRS I.D.: 95-3510055

STAFF:
Antonia Hernandez, President and Chief Executive Officer
William C. Choi, General Counsel

BOARD OF DIRECTORS:
Tom Unterman, Chairperson
Gwen Baba
James Berliner
Louise Henry Bryson
William C. Choi
Dr. Patrick Dowling
Meloni M. Hallock
Antonia Hernandez
Preston L.C. Johnson
Joanne Corday Kozberg
Melvin D. Lindsey
Robert Lovelace
Thomas A. Saenz
Jean Bixby Smith
Melanie Staggs
Robert Sun
Peter J. Taylor
Cynthia Ann Telles, Ph.D.
Therese Tucker
Catherine L. Unger
Fidel Vargas
Sonia Marie De Leon de Vega
Ronald T. Vera

CALLAWAY FOUNDATION, INC. [1168]

209 Broome Street
LaGrange, GA 30240
(706) 884-7348
Fax: (706) 884-0201
E-mail: hsburdette@callawayfoundation.org
Web Site: www.callawayfoundation.org

FOUNDED: 1943

AREAS OF INTEREST:
Charitable, religious and educational interests.

TYPE:
Capital grants; Challenge/matching grants; Matching gifts. Matching grants focus on construction.

YEAR PROGRAM STARTED: 1943

PURPOSE:
To improve the quality of life in the city of LaGrange and Troup County, Georgia.

LEGAL BASIS:
Private foundation.

ELIGIBILITY:
Eligible organizations must be IRS 501(c)(3). Each application is considered on its merits.

GEOG. RESTRICTIONS: City of LaGrange and Troup County, Georgia.

FINANCIAL DATA:
Amount of support per award: Varies.

Total amount of support: Varies.

NO. MOST RECENT APPLICANTS: 100.

NO. AWARDS: Varies.

REPRESENTATIVE AWARDS:
$3,000,000 to LaGrange College; $450,000 to Downtown LaGrange Development Authority; $155,000 to Lafayette Society for Performing Arts.

APPLICATION INFO:
Applicants may submit a written proposal and must include a copy of the IRS tax determination letter. Application can be found on Foundation's web site.

Duration: Varies.

Deadline: March 31, June 30, September 30 and December 31.

PUBLICATIONS:
Annual report.

IRS I.D.: 58-0566147

ADDRESS INQUIRIES TO:
H. Speer Burdette, III
President and General Manager
(See address above.)

CAPITAL REGION COMMUNITY FOUNDATION [1169]

330 Marshall Street
Suite 300
Lansing, MI 48912
(517) 272-2870
Fax: (517) 272-2871
E-mail: ppasch@crcfoundation.org
Web Site: www.crcfoundation.org

FOUNDED: 1987

AREAS OF INTEREST:
Arts, education, environment, health care, human services, humanities and youth.

TYPE:
Capital grants; Challenge/matching grants; Development grants; General operating grants; Project/program grants; Scholarships.

YEAR PROGRAM STARTED: 1989

PURPOSE:
To build a permanent endowment; to meet charitable needs in the tri-county area.

LEGAL BASIS:
Community foundation.

ELIGIBILITY:
Eligible organizations must be IRS 501(c)(3) tax-exempt and be located in the tri-county area.

GEOG. RESTRICTIONS: Clinton, Eaton and Ingham counties, Michigan.

FINANCIAL DATA:
Amount of support per award: $2,000 to $15,000.

Total amount of support: Varies.

APPLICATION INFO:
Application information is available on the web site.

Duration: One year. No renewals.

Deadline: September 1.

PUBLICATIONS:
Annual report; grant guidelines.

IRS I.D.: 38-2776652

ADDRESS INQUIRIES TO:
Pauline Pasch, Senior Program Officer
(See address above.)

*PLEASE NOTE:
No grants are made to individuals. Do not apply for college scholarships.

THE CARPENTER FOUNDATION [1170]

824 East Main Street
Suite 102
Medford, OR 97504
(541) 772-5851
(541) 772-5732
Fax: (541) 773-3970
E-mail: pwilliams@carpenter-foundation.org
Web Site: www.carpenter-foundation.org

FOUNDED: 1958

AREAS OF INTEREST:
Arts, education, human services and public interest issues.

TYPE:
Capital grants; Challenge/matching grants; Demonstration grants; Development grants; General operating grants; Matching gifts; Project/program grants; Scholarships; Technical assistance; Training grants.

YEAR PROGRAM STARTED: 1958

PURPOSE:
To add opportunity, choice, inclusiveness, enrichment and a climate for change for those living in the Rogue Valley.

LEGAL BASIS:
Private family foundation.

ELIGIBILITY:
Grant applications will be accepted from tax-exempt agencies only. No grants are made to individuals. Only one grant per year to any agency is usually considered. The Foundation makes grants within Jackson and Josephine counties, with the exception of a few statewide public interest issues directly affecting persons living in these counties. The Foundation rarely makes multiyear grants, grants for historical applications, hospital construction or equipment, group or individual trips, or activities for religious purposes.

GEOG. RESTRICTIONS: Jackson and Josephine counties, Oregon.

FINANCIAL DATA:
Total assets of $19,156,454 for fiscal year ended June 30, 2015.

Amount of support per award: Varies.

Total amount of support: $740,268 in grants for fiscal year ended June 30, 2015.

CO-OP FUNDING PROGRAMS: The Foundation works in partnership with other agencies, organizations and public entities.

NO. MOST RECENT APPLICANTS: Approximately 100.

NO. AWARDS: 90.

REPRESENTATIVE AWARDS:
Human Services: $20,000 to Community Health Center, Medford, OR, for support of general operating costs; Education: $10,000 to Phoenix-Talent School District, Phoenix, OR, in support of a one-week residential program at SOU to encourage Latino students to attend college; Arts: $25,000 to Oregon Shakespeare Festival Association, Ashland, OR, to support special matinees and discount price performances for students and low-income residents; Public Interest: $12,000 to Southern Oregon Historical Society, Medford, OR, in support of staffing and funding a development office.

APPLICATION INFO:
Cover letter (no more than one page) from the applicant organization summarizing the scope of the project, the amount of the request, and the name, address, telephone number and e-mail address of the person to contact regarding the request is required.

Proposal information (no more than four pages) including:
(1) description of proposal or project, and the community needs or strengths that it addresses;
(2) review of the applicant agency, its purpose and services to the community, its staffing and use of volunteers;
(3) the project budget, showing specifically how the grant funds will be used, as well as other possible funding sources for this project;
(4) description of how the project will be funded in the future (if applicable);
(5) the planning process, staffing and timeline for the project;
(6) result expected and proposed evaluation method and;
(7) any recent independent board fund-raising efforts.

Required attachments (do not staple or clip):
(1) detailed budget for the agency's current year and the year for which the project is proposed (if different);
(2) income statement and balance sheet from the most recently completed fiscal year (or audit, if available); no 990s please;
(3) list of board of directors, occupations and addresses;
(4) approval of the application by the agency's board of directors and;
(5) copy of the IRS exemption letter under Section 501(c)(3).

Duration: One year.

Deadline: Applications are reviewed on a quarterly basis.

BOARD OF TRUSTEES:

ADDRESS INQUIRIES TO:
Polly Williams, Program Officer
Tel: (541) 772-5732
(See e-mail address above.)

CATERPILLAR FOUNDATION [1171]

100 N.E. Adams Street
Peoria, IL 61629-1480
(309) 675-1000
Web Site: www.caterpillar.com/foundation
www.togetherstronger.com

FOUNDED: 1952

AREAS OF INTEREST:
Poverty alleviation via programs with measurable outcomes in the areas of basic human needs, education and environment.

TYPE:
General operating grants; Project/program grants.

PURPOSE:
To support local and community activities where the company has a major manufacturing presence, as well as national and international organizations; to alleviate poverty and place people on the path to prosperity.

ELIGIBILITY:
Organizations in areas of company manufacturing operations and classified as 501(c)(3) by the IRS can apply. No grants to individuals and religious organizations.

FINANCIAL DATA:
Amount of support per award: Varies.

APPLICATION INFO:
Applicant must complete eligibility questionnaire. Grant application process is by invitation only.

Duration: One year. Grants are renewable.

CATHOLIC CAMPAIGN FOR HUMAN DEVELOPMENT [1172]

3211 4th Street, N.E.
Washington, DC 20017
(202) 541-3210
Fax: (202) 541-3399
E-mail: cchdgrants@usccb.org
Web Site: www.usccb.org/cchd

FOUNDED: 1970

AREAS OF INTEREST:
Humanitarianism.

NAME(S) OF PROGRAMS:
- **Community Development Grant**
- **Economic Development Grant**

TYPE:
Project/program grants.

YEAR PROGRAM STARTED: 1970

PURPOSE:
To address the root causes of poverty by nurturing solidarity between the poor and non-poor and facilitating the participation of people living in poverty.

LEGAL BASIS:
Roman Catholic Church-sponsored funding agency.

ELIGIBILITY:
To qualify for CCHD funds, applicant organizations must not promote, in any way, activities that work against Catholic values. CCHD's grants to local anti-poverty efforts are screened, awarded and monitored in close partnership with local Catholic dioceses. CCHD grants to groups in a local community require the explicit approval of the Bishop of that diocese.

GEOG. RESTRICTIONS: United States and territories.

FINANCIAL DATA:
Amount of support per award: $25,000 to $75,000.

Total amount of support: Up to $14,000,000 for the year 2014-15.

NO. MOST RECENT APPLICANTS: 650.

NO. AWARDS: 237.

APPLICATION INFO:
Contact CCHD for guidelines.

Duration: Community Development Grant: Six years; Economic Development Grant: Three years.

Deadline: Proposals accepted on a rolling basis.

ADDRESS INQUIRIES TO:
Grants Administrator
(See address above.)

CENTRAL INDIANA COMMUNITY FOUNDATION [1173]

615 North Alabama Street
Suite 119
Indianapolis, IN 46204
(317) 634-2423
Fax: (317) 684-0943
E-mail: info@cicf.org
Web Site: www.cicf.org

FOUNDED: 1997

AREAS OF INTEREST:
Arts, culture, civic affairs, education, environment, parks, and health and human services.

TYPE:
General operating grants; Project/program grants; Scholarships.

PURPOSE:
To strengthen Marion and Hamilton counties by attracting charitable endowments; to maximize benefits to donors; to make effective grants; to provide leadership to address community needs by developing productive citizens, building strong neighborhoods, embracing inclusiveness, and promoting community amenities.

LEGAL BASIS:
Community foundation.

ELIGIBILITY:
Grants are made to nonprofit charitable organizations exempt from federal taxation under Section 501(c)(3) of the Internal Revenue Code. Priority is given to programs and projects which expect to have a positive effect on Marion and Hamilton counties.

GEOG. RESTRICTIONS: Mostly Marion and Hamilton counties, Indiana.

FINANCIAL DATA:
Amount of support per award: $250 to $100,000.

Total amount of support: Varies.

APPLICATION INFO:
Application information is available on the web site.

Duration: Typically one year.

Deadline: Varies.

PUBLICATIONS:
Annual report; newsletter.

IRS I.D.: 35-1793630

ADDRESS INQUIRIES TO:
Julie Wright
Community Investment Coordinator
(See address above.)

CENTRAL MINNESOTA COMMUNITY FOUNDATION [1174]

101 7th Avenue South, No. 100
St. Cloud, MN 56301
(320) 253-4380
(877) 253-4380
Fax: (320) 240-9215
E-mail: slorenz@communitygiving.org
Web Site: www.communitygiving.org

FOUNDED: 1985

AREAS OF INTEREST:
Philanthropy to support arts and culture, education, environment, youth and families, and human services.

TYPE:
Challenge/matching grants; Conferences/seminars; General operating grants; Project/program grants; Scholarships; Seed money grants; Technical assistance.

PURPOSE:
To attract and administer funds to improve the quality of life for citizens of central Minnesota.

LEGAL BASIS:
Community foundation.

ELIGIBILITY:
Eligible organizations must be IRS 501(c)(3) tax-exempt and located within Benton, Sherburne and Stearns counties, Minnesota. Funding to religious organizations of a nonsectarian nature, which benefits the entire community. No grants to individuals.

GEOG. RESTRICTIONS: Benton, Sherburne and Stearns counties, Minnesota.

FINANCIAL DATA:
$112,000,000 in assets as of December 30, 2015.

Amount of support per award: Average: $5,000.

Total amount of support: $6,100,000 in grants paid as of June 30, 2015.

APPLICATION INFO:
Applicants should check web site for the online application and required documents, and must include a copy of the IRS 501(c)(3) tax determination letter.

Duration: One year.

Deadline: Varies.

PUBLICATIONS:
Annual report; application guidelines.

IRS I.D.: 36-3412544

ADDRESS INQUIRIES TO:
Susan Lorenz
Director of Community Programs
(See address above.)

CENTRAL NEW YORK COMMUNITY FOUNDATION [1175]

431 East Fayette Street
Suite 100
Syracuse, NY 13202-3314
(315) 422-9538
Fax: (315) 471-6031
E-mail: info@cnycf.org
Web Site: www.cnycf.org

FOUNDED: 1927

AREAS OF INTEREST:
Literacy, capacity building, sabbaticals for nonprofit executives, and classroom leadership.

TYPE:
Capital grants; Project/program grants; Seed money grants; Training grants. Grants to help provide training to develop leadership and grantwriting skills and to help build neighborhood stability. Grants also help participants learn from each other and become keenly aware of the level of need in the community.

PURPOSE:
To identify and initiate effective, creative actions which enrich the community by receiving, managing and disbursing charitable funds.

LEGAL BASIS:
Community foundation.

ELIGIBILITY:
Applicants must be tax-exempt, 501(c)(3) not-for-profit organizations in Madison and Onondaga counties which will fund innovative programs that address unmet community needs.

The Foundation encourages proposals that:
(1) suggest practical solutions to community problems;
(2) promote cooperation among not-for-profits without duplicating existing services;
(3) generate community support, both professional and volunteer;
(4) strengthen the organization's effectiveness or stability;
(5) demonstrate the organization's ability to secure realistic funding and;
(6) address prevention as well as remediation.

The Foundation does not make grants for annual operating budgets, endowments, sectarian purposes, loans or assistance to individuals, medical or academic research except when directed by donor, or activities that occurred before the Community Foundation's decision date.

GEOG. RESTRICTIONS: Madison and Onondaga counties, New York.

FINANCIAL DATA:
Amount of support per award: Varies.

APPLICATION INFO:
Standard application forms are available. Foundation staff is available to answer questions or discuss with any prospective applicant the appropriateness of a request.

Duration: Varies.

Deadline: July, September and April.

PUBLICATIONS:
Annual report.

OFFICERS:
Peter A. Dunn, President and Chief Executive Officer
Kim Sadowski, Chief Financial Officer
Gay M. Pomeroy, Esq., Counsel

ADDRESS INQUIRIES TO:
Peter Dunn, Chief Executive Officer
(See address above.)

THE CH FOUNDATION

6102 82nd Street
Suite 8A
Lubbock, TX 79424
(806) 792-0448
Fax: (806) 792-7824
E-mail: hhocker@chfoundation.com
Web Site: www.chfoundationlubbock.com

TYPE:
Capital grants; Project/program grants.

See entry 2053 for full listing.

HARRY CHAPIN FOUNDATION [1176]

16 Gerard Street
Huntington, NY 11743
(631) 423-7558
Fax: (631) 423-7596
E-mail: harrychapinfound@aol.com
Web Site: www.harrychapinfoundation.org

FOUNDED: 1981

AREAS OF INTEREST:
Community education, arts-in-education, agriculture and environment.

TYPE:
Challenge/matching grants; Project/program grants.

YEAR PROGRAM STARTED: 1981

PURPOSE:
To address the problems of the disadvantaged and promote educational programs that lead to a greater understanding of human suffering.

ELIGIBILITY:
Only programs operating in the U.S. will be funded. Applicants must be 501(c)(3) nonprofit. Complete description of focus areas is available on the Foundation web site. No grants to individuals.

GEOG. RESTRICTIONS: United States.

FINANCIAL DATA:
Amount of support per award: Up to $10,000.

NO. MOST RECENT APPLICANTS: 459.

NO. AWARDS: 23 for the year 2015.

APPLICATION INFO:
Application should be made in a brief written proposal to Ms. Leslie Ramme, Executive Director, at the HCF Office. HCF also accepts the New York/New Jersey Area Common Grant Application Form.

Duration: One year. Must reapply.

Deadline: Applications are accepted on an ongoing basis.

EXECUTIVE DIRECTOR:
Leslie Ramme

ADDRESS INQUIRIES TO:
Leslie Ramme, Executive Director
(See address above.)

CHARLESTON AREA CHARITABLE FOUNDATION [1177]

c/o Gilbert, Metzger & Madigan
P.O. Box 677
Charleston, IL 61920
(217) 345-2128
Fax: (217) 345-2315

AREAS OF INTEREST:
Community and education.

TYPE:
Grants-in-aid; Project/program grants.

PURPOSE:
To enhance and support the quality of life in Charleston, IL area.

ELIGIBILITY:
Grants are made to organizations that have tax-exempt status under Section 501(c)(3) of the Internal Revenue Code. No grants are made to individuals.

GEOG. RESTRICTIONS: Charleston, Illinois and surrounding area.

FINANCIAL DATA:
Amount of support per award: Grants vary in amount, depending upon the needs and nature of the request.

Total amount of support: Varies.

APPLICATION INFO:
Applicants must submit a brief letter outlining the purpose of the grant.

Duration: One-time grants.

Deadline: Quarterly; two weeks prior to Board meetings to be held in February, May, August and November.

ADDRESS INQUIRIES TO:
Michael Metzger, President
(See address above.)

THE CHAUTAUQUA REGION COMMUNITY FOUNDATION [1178]

418 Spring Street
Jamestown, NY 14701
(716) 661-3390
Fax: (716) 488-0387
E-mail: rsweeney@crcfonline.org
Web Site: www.crcfonline.org

FOUNDED: 1978

AREAS OF INTEREST:
Community.

NAME(S) OF PROGRAMS:

- **Axel W. Carlson Award**
- **John D. Hamilton Community Service Award**

TYPE:
Awards/prizes; Capital grants; Challenge/matching grants; Endowments; General operating grants; Matching gifts; Project/program grants; Scholarships; Seed money grants; Technical assistance; Training grants. Axel W. Carlson Award has been a tribute to the unsung heroes of our community. These individuals have made significant contributions through their efforts while neither receiving nor expecting reward or recognition.

The John D. Hamilton Community Service Award recognizes an individual's dedication, leadership and support in furthering community spirit and enhancing the quality of life in the Chautauqua Community.

YEAR PROGRAM STARTED: 1978

PURPOSE:
To enrich the quality of life in the Chautauqua region.

LEGAL BASIS:
501(c)(3).

ELIGIBILITY:
Grants are available to 501(c)(3) nonprofit organizations. Scholarships are provided to students for higher education.

GEOG. RESTRICTIONS: Chautauqua region, New York.

FINANCIAL DATA:
Amount of support per award: Varies.

Total amount of support: $2,500,000.

Matching fund requirements: Varies depending on the request.

NO. MOST RECENT APPLICANTS: 1,000.

NO. AWARDS: 850.

APPLICATION INFO:
Nominations are to be submitted by letter or e-mail, with the full name, address and detailed explanation of that person's contributions and accomplishments, along with an explanation of why the nominee is deserving of the award. If the nominator is uncertain if they should submit the nomination or has additional questions, please contact the office via telephone for clarification.

Duration: One calendar year.

Deadline: Carlson Award: March 1; Hamilton Award: April.

PUBLICATIONS:
Annual report; newsletters; scholarship booklet.

IRS I.D.: 16-1116837

STAFF:
Randall J. Sweeney, Executive Director
Sarah M. Marciniak, Communications Officer
Jacob S. Schrantz, Fiscal Officer
June C. Diethrick, Operations Officer
Lisa W. Lynde, Program Officer
Michelle Frederickson, Program Associate

ADDRESS INQUIRIES TO:
Randall J. Sweeney, Executive Director
(See address above.)

CHESTER COUNTY COMMUNITY FOUNDATION [1179]

28 West Market Street
West Chester, PA 19382
(610) 696-8211
Fax: (610) 696-8213
E-mail: info@chescocf.org
Web Site: www.chescocf.org

FOUNDED: 1994

AREAS OF INTEREST:
Quality of life in the Chester County, Pennsylvania area.

TYPE:
Capital grants; Challenge/matching grants; General operating grants; Grants-in-aid; Project/program grants; Scholarships.

YEAR PROGRAM STARTED: 1994

PURPOSE:
To improve the quality of life in communities within Chester County, PA.

LEGAL BASIS:
501(c)(3) public charity.

GEOG. RESTRICTIONS: Primarily Chester County, Pennsylvania.

FINANCIAL DATA:
$48,508,595 in assets.

Amount of support per award: $1,000 to $15,000.

Total amount of support: $2,000,097 for fiscal year 2015.

NO. MOST RECENT APPLICANTS: 150 for the year 2015.

NO. AWARDS: 701 for the year 2015.

APPLICATION INFO:
Information may be obtained from the Foundation web site.

Duration: One year. Renewal by reapplication.

Deadline: Proposals are accepted year-round.

ADDRESS INQUIRIES TO:
Beth Harper Briglia, Vice President of Donor Services and Grantmaking
(See address above.)

THE CHICAGO COMMUNITY TRUST [1180]

225 North Michigan Avenue
Suite 2200
Chicago, IL 60601
(312) 616-8000
Fax: (312) 616-7955
E-mail: sandy@cct.org
Web Site: www.cct.org

FOUNDED: 1915

AREAS OF INTEREST:
The well-being of the residents of Cook County, IL in the fields of health, basic human needs, community development, education, cultural arts, sustainability and the environment.

TYPE:
General operating grants; Project/program grants; Technical assistance. Grants to tax-exempt institutions and organizations for charitable purposes. Special initiatives are developed periodically.

YEAR PROGRAM STARTED: 1915

PURPOSE:
To provide for the broad charitable needs of the community in a manner which will assure response to the most pressing problems of the day.

LEGAL BASIS:
Community foundation.

ELIGIBILITY:
Applicants must be tax-exempt, 501(c)(3) organizations. Funded projects must benefit the residents of Cook County, IL. Some grants are made for the region.

GEOG. RESTRICTIONS: Cook County, Illinois.

FINANCIAL DATA:
Amount of support per award: Varies.

Total amount of support: $178,000,000 for the year 2014.

NO. MOST RECENT APPLICANTS: 700 to 800.

APPLICATION INFO:
Applicants must register through the online grant system. Paper letters of inquiry will not be accepted.

Duration: One year.

PUBLICATIONS:
Guidelines; annual report.

STAFF:
Terry Mazany, President and Chief Executive Officer

ADDRESS INQUIRIES TO:
Sandy Phelps, Director of Grants Management
(See address above.)

ROBERT STERLING CLARK FOUNDATION [1181]

135 East 64th Street
New York, NY 10065
(212) 288-8900
Fax: (212) 288-1033
E-mail: rscf@rsclark.org
Web Site: www.rsclark.org

FOUNDED: 1952

AREAS OF INTEREST:
Leadership and leadership development.

TYPE:
Project/program grants.

PURPOSE:
To support, encourage and invest in people and the nonprofit organizations that develop them in communities across New York City.

LEGAL BASIS:
501(c)(3).

ELIGIBILITY:
Applicants must be nonprofit organizations.

PUBLICATIONS:
Annual report; guidelines.

BOARD OF DIRECTORS:
James Allen Smith, Chairman
Philip Li, President
Julie Muraco, Treasurer
Paul Dolan
Clara Miller
John Hoyt Stookey

ADDRESS INQUIRIES TO:
Philip Li, President
(See address above.)

THE CLEVELAND FOUNDATION [1182]

1422 Euclid Avenue
Suite 1300
Cleveland, OH 44115-2001
(216) 861-3810
Fax: (216) 861-1729
E-mail: grantsmgmt@clevefdn.org
Web Site: www.clevelandfoundation.org

FOUNDED: 1914

AREAS OF INTEREST:
Economic development, public education reform, neighborhood and housing, human services and youth development strengthening the quality of life in early childhood, strengthening the arts and cultural community and greater university circle.

TYPE:
Project/program grants; Scholarships.

YEAR PROGRAM STARTED: 1914

PURPOSE:
To enhance the quality of life for all citizens of greater Cleveland, now and for generations to come, by building endowment, addressing needs through grantmaking and providing leadership on key community issues.

LEGAL BASIS:
Community foundation.

ELIGIBILITY:
Grantmaking is restricted to programs and services in the Greater Cleveland community, Cuyahoga, Geauga and Lake counties. Requests are considered from tax-exempt agencies in the following areas: civic affairs, economic development, education, health, social services, arts and culture, and environment. Careful consideration is given to such criteria as benefit the entire community and applicant's ability to successfully carry out the proposed activity. Applicant must be a nonprofit organization.

Giving is limited to the Greater Cleveland area unless specified by the donor. No grants to individuals or religious institutions for religious purposes. No support for community services such as fire and police protection, fund-raising campaigns, memberships and travel. No support for publications or audiovisual materials unless they are an integral part of a key program. Capital support for buildings, major equipment, land or renovation is only provided when there is strong evidence that the project has high priority for the community.

GEOG. RESTRICTIONS: Greater Cleveland, Cuyahoga, Geauga and Lake counties, Ohio.

FINANCIAL DATA:
Amount of support per award: $200 to $4,000,000; average $50,000.

Total amount of support: $98,000,000 annually.

Matching fund requirements: Depending upon proposal, grants may be authorized contingent upon receipt of matching funds from agency's own or other sources.

CO-OP FUNDING PROGRAMS: Neighborhood Connections Program.

APPLICATION INFO:
The Foundation requires organizations to submit inquiries and applications electronically. Guidelines can be found on the web site.

Duration: Usually one year.

PUBLICATIONS:
Annual report; *Giving Voice*, quarterly; Grantee e-newsletter.

IRS I.D.: 34-0714588

COASTAL COMMUNITY FOUNDATION OF SOUTH CAROLINA [1183]

635 Rutledge Avenue
Suite 201
Charleston, SC 29403
(843) 723-3635
Fax: (843) 577-3671
E-mail: info@coastalcommunityfoundation.org
Web Site: www.coastalcommunityfoundation.org

FOUNDED: 1974

AREAS OF INTEREST:
Community development, health, education, human needs, environment and arts.

TYPE:
Challenge/matching grants; Endowments; Project/program grants; Scholarships; Technical assistance; Training grants.

YEAR PROGRAM STARTED: 1974

PURPOSE:
To foster philanthropy for the lasting good of the community.

ELIGIBILITY:
Generally, applicants must be charitable 501(c)(3) organizations in Beaufort, Berkeley, Charleston, Colleton, Dorchester, Georgetown, Hampton, Horry and Jasper counties, South Carolina.

GEOG. RESTRICTIONS: Coastal South Carolina.

FINANCIAL DATA:
Amount of support per award: Generally $15,000 maximum.
Total amount of support: Varies.

APPLICATION INFO:
Application and instructions are available online.
Duration: Varies.
Deadline: Varies.

IRS I.D.: 23-7390313

THE COLUMBUS FOUNDATION [1184]

1234 East Broad Street
Columbus, OH 43205
(614) 251-4000
Fax: (614) 251-4009
E-mail: info@columbusfoundation.org
Web Site: www.columbusfoundation.org

FOUNDED: 1943

AREAS OF INTEREST:
Advancing philanthropy, arts and humanities, urban affairs, conservation, education, health and social services.

NAME(S) OF PROGRAMS:
- **Community Improvement Project**
- **Fund for Financial Innovation**
- **Fund for Innovative Operations**
- **Fund for Targeted Needs**

TYPE:
Capital grants; Development grants; Fellowships; General operating grants; Project/program grants; Scholarships. The Foundation awards competitive grants from the unrestricted and field-of-interest funds created by donors.

The Community Improvement Project supports a concentrated initiative to advance progress over a longer term in an identified area of community need.

The Fund for Financial Innovation will support nonprofit leaders and their organizations to adapt to the new economic reality.

The Fund for Innovative Operations addresses significant needs of local organizations through grants supporting continuous improvement, capacity-building, and arts and cultural efforts.

The Fund for Targeted Needs addresses basic needs, disadvantaged children, developmental disabilities (traditional grants program), as well as more narrow and specific grant programs.

YEAR PROGRAM STARTED: 1943

PURPOSE:
To provide a pool of charitable funds for the development of community programs and services and to offer various ways of giving for citizens who wish to benefit the community.

LEGAL BASIS:
Community foundation, exempt under Section 501(c)(3) of the Internal Revenue Code.

ELIGIBILITY:
Organizations in the central Ohio region having recognition under Section 501(c)(3) of the Internal Revenue Code. No grants are made to individuals.

GEOG. RESTRICTIONS: Primarily Franklin County and surrounding area.

FINANCIAL DATA:
Amount of support per award: $250 to $1,250,000.
Total amount of support: Varies.

NO. MOST RECENT APPLICANTS: 403.

NO. AWARDS: 292.

REPRESENTATIVE AWARDS:
Capacity Building and Leadership Grants: $6,000 to Jeanne B. McCoy Community Center for the Arts Corporation to support the fund-raising planning component of the business plan; Innovative Operations-Continuous Improvement: $273,500 to Ohio Association of Second Harvest Foodbanks to support overall operations; Basic Needs: $95,000 to Community Shelter Board to support general operating expenses to address homelessness.

APPLICATION INFO:
Those seeking grants may submit a Letter of Intent or a Full Proposal to the Foundation by accessing its online grant application system through its web site.
Duration: Typically one year.
Deadline: Varies.

PUBLICATIONS:
Annual yearbook; application guidelines.

IRS I.D.: 31-6044264

STAFF:
Douglas F. Kridler, President and Chief Executive Officer
Lisa S. Courtice, Ph.D., Executive Vice President, Community Research and Grants Management
Raymond J. Biddiscombe, Senior Vice President, Finance and Administration

ADDRESS INQUIRIES TO:
Melissa Neely
Grants Management Coordinator
(See address above.)

COLUMBUS JEWISH FOUNDATION [1185]

Robins Center for Philanthropy
1175 College Avenue
Columbus, OH 43209
(614) 338-2365
Fax: (614) 338-2361
E-mail: jjacobs@tcjf.org
Web Site: www.columbusjewishfoundation.org

FOUNDED: 1955

AREAS OF INTEREST:
Jewish education, Jewish leadership development and the preservation of the integrity of the Jewish family.

TYPE:
Challenge/matching grants; Demonstration grants; Seed money grants.

YEAR PROGRAM STARTED: 1955

PURPOSE:
To develop sustainable financial resources to fulfill the Foundation's mission to ensure continuity of Jewish life and to meet changing needs locally, in Israel, and in our worldwide community.

LEGAL BASIS:
Public charity.

ELIGIBILITY:
Applicants must be 501(c)(3) organizations. Money will be designated for pilot projects or as seed money only. Particular emphasis on central Ohio Jewish organizations.

No grants to individuals. No operating support.

FINANCIAL DATA:
Amount of support per award: Varies depending on needs and nature of the request.
Total amount of support: $488,160.

CO-OP FUNDING PROGRAMS: The Foundation prefers to set up networks for funding with other organizations.

NO. MOST RECENT APPLICANTS: 18.

NO. AWARDS: 13.

REPRESENTATIVE AWARDS:
$98,500 to Wexner Heritage Village for patient experience and outcome program; $30,050 to Jewish Day School for joint environmental project.

APPLICATION INFO:
Formal request forms are available from the Foundation.

PUBLICATIONS:
Annual report; guidelines.

IRS I.D.: 31-1384772

OFFICERS:
Jeffrey D. Meyer, President
Harlan W. Robins, Vice President
William Byers, Treasurer
Nevada Fine Smith, Secretary
Harlan S. Louis, Assistant Treasurer
Michael Schlonsky, Assistant Secretary

ADDRESS INQUIRIES TO:
Susan Tanur, Director of Grants
E-mail: stanur@tcjf.org
(See address above.)

COMMON COUNSEL FOUNDATION [1186]

1624 Franklin Street
Suite 1022
Oakland, CA 94612
(510) 834-2995
Fax: (510) 834-2998
E-mail: info@commoncounsel.org
Web Site: www.commoncounsel.org

FOUNDED: 1988

AREAS OF INTEREST:
Economic, environmental and social justice.

TYPE:
General operating grants; Training grants; Travel grants.

PURPOSE:
To offer strategic philanthropic advisory services to donors and family foundations while serving the community at large.

ELIGIBILITY:
501(c)(3) nonprofit organizations. Religious organizations must be working in interfaith coalitions. Grants are not made to individuals. Also, must involve low- and moderate-income members in grassroots community organizing to bring about long-term policy change. Organizational budget must be $400,000 or less except for the small Grassroots Exchange Fund (travel grants), which considers requests from organizations with budgets up to $1,000,000 (higher priority is given to those with budgets less than $750,000).

FINANCIAL DATA:
Amount of support per award: Travel and training grants: $500 to $1,000 with an average of approximately $800; General operating grants: $5,000 to $15,000.

CO-OP FUNDING PROGRAMS: Abelard Foundation West; Acorn Foundation; Penney Family Fund; Victor and Lorraine Honig Fund; Grassroots Exchange Fund; Social and Economic Justice Fund.

NO. MOST RECENT APPLICANTS: 280.

APPLICATION INFO:
Applicant should submit a letter of inquiry. Full proposals for most of the Funds are by invitation only.

Deadline: January 15 and June 15 (or February through November for Grassroots Exchange Fund).

THE COMMUNITY FOUNDATION [1187]

7501 Boulders View Drive, Suite 110
Richmond, VA 23225-4047
(804) 330-7400
Fax: (804) 330-5992
E-mail: info@tcfrichmond.org
Web Site: www.tcfrichmond.org

FOUNDED: 1968

AREAS OF INTEREST:
Children, families, communities, health care, education and arts.

NAME(S) OF PROGRAMS:
- **The Jenkins Foundation: Improving the Health of Greater Richmond**
- **Medarva Foundation Fund**
- **R.E.B. Awards for Teaching Excellence**
- **Sheltering Arms Fund**

TYPE:
Project/program grants; Scholarships. Competitive grants.

YEAR PROGRAM STARTED: 1968

PURPOSE:
To improve life for generations of children; to improve public education; to support innovative health care projects.

LEGAL BASIS:
Charitable trust.

ELIGIBILITY:
Proposals are accepted from charitable 501(c)(3) organizations serving residents of Greater Richmond and/or the Tri-Cities.

GEOG. RESTRICTIONS: Richmond and central Virginia.

FINANCIAL DATA:
Amount of support per award: Varies.

Total amount of support: Varies.

APPLICATION INFO:
Guidelines and application forms are available on the web site.

Duration: Typically one year.

Deadline: Varies per program.

PUBLICATIONS:
Annual report.

OFFICERS:
Thomas N. Chewning, Chairman
Thomas S. Gayner, Vice Chairman
Robert C. Sledd, Treasurer
Dee Ann Remo, Secretary

ADDRESS INQUIRIES TO:
Susan Hallett, Vice President, Programs
(See address above.)

COMMUNITY FOUNDATION FOR GREATER ATLANTA, INC. [1188]

191 Peachtree Street, N.E.
Suite 1000
Atlanta, GA 30303
(404) 688-5525
Fax: (404) 688-3060
E-mail: nbattle@cfgreateratlanta.org
Web Site: www.cfgreateratlanta.org

FOUNDED: 1951

AREAS OF INTEREST:
Operational grants to nonprofits serving a 23-county region in Georgia.

NAME(S) OF PROGRAMS:
- **A Place to Perform**
- **An Extra Wish**
- **Atlanta AIDS Fund**
- **Common Good Fund**
- **Clayton Fund**
- **Grants to Green**
- **Managing for Excellence**
- **Metropolitan Atlanta Arts Fund**
- **Morgan Fund**
- **Neighborhood Fund**
- **Newton Fund**
- **Nonprofit Toolbox**
- **Strategic Restructuring Fund**

TYPE:
General operating grants; Project/program grants; Scholarships; Technical assistance; Training grants. Project/program grants are for community development only.

YEAR PROGRAM STARTED: 1951

PURPOSE:
To provide quality services to donors and innovative leadership on community issues.

LEGAL BASIS:
501(c)(3) community foundation.

ELIGIBILITY:
Applicant organizations must have 501(c)(3) status. Project must be within the metropolitan Atlanta area. Request for funding may not exceed 10% of organization's operational budget. For general operation grants, organization must have an operating budget of $100,000.

Grant funds cannot be used for regranting, fund-raising or capital campaigns. No grants to individuals.

GEOG. RESTRICTIONS: 23 counties in the metropolitan Atlanta area.

FINANCIAL DATA:
Amount of support per award: Maximum $75,000.

NO. MOST RECENT APPLICANTS: 290 for discretionary monies.

APPLICATION INFO:
Grant application guidelines available from the Foundation. Initial approach by letter or phone.

Duration: No grants are awarded on a continuing basis. Generally, grants are one year. Common Good grants can be up to two years.

Deadline: Arts Fund and Common Good: May; Grants: February and October.

PUBLICATIONS:
Annual report; policy and application guidelines.

IRS I.D.: 58-1344646

OFFICERS:
Alicia Philipp, President
Diana Champ Davis, Vice President of Capacity
Benjamin T. White, Assistant Secretary and Legal Counsel

BOARD MEMBERS:
Suzanne E. Boas, Chairperson
John Reid, Vice Chairperson
Katy Barksdale
Becky Blalock
Robert L. Brown
Ann W. Cramer
Edward S. Croft, III
Patrice Greer
Dr. Sivan Hines
Tad Hutcheson
Jeffrey S. Muir
Joe Oesterling
Roger Chip Patterson, Jr.
Teresa Rivero
Joan King Salwen
Dave Stockert
Ramon Tome
Benjamin T. White, Legal Counsel

ADDRESS INQUIRIES TO:
Natasha Battle-Edwards, Grants Manager
(See address above.)

COMMUNITY FOUNDATION FOR GREATER BUFFALO [1189]

726 Exchange Street
Suite 525
Buffalo, NY 14210
(716) 852-2857
Fax: (716) 852-2861
E-mail: mail@cfgb.org
Web Site: www.cfgb.org

FOUNDED: 1919

TYPE:
Grants-in-aid; Scholarships. Grants to organizations in the eight counties of western New York state.

YEAR PROGRAM STARTED: 1919

PURPOSE:
To connect people, ideas and resources to improve lives in western New York state. The four community goals of the Foundation are:
(1) to improve educational achievement for students living in low-income households;
(2) to increase racial/ethnic equity;
(3) to enhance and leverage significant natural resources and;
(4) to strengthen the region as a center for architecture, arts and culture.

LEGAL BASIS:
Community trust; 501(c)(3) tax determination; public charity under Section 170(b)(1)(a)(vi).

ELIGIBILITY:
Programs and agencies must benefit residents of the eight counties of western New York state.

GEOG. RESTRICTIONS: 8 counties of western New York state.

FINANCIAL DATA:
Amount of support per award: $3,993 to $30,000 in 2015.

Total amount of support: $446,302.

NO. MOST RECENT APPLICANTS: 150 for the year 2015.

NO. AWARDS: 25.

REPRESENTATIVE AWARDS:
Child and Adolescent Treatment Services; Journey's End Refugee Services;

Massachusetts Avenue Project; Housing Opportunities Made Equal; Buffalo Niagara RiverKEEPER.

APPLICATION INFO:
Application information is available on the web site.

Deadline: For 2016, Letters of Intent accepted from January 1 to February 1. Selected Letters of Intent invited to submit a full proposal by May 20. Applicants notified by late August.

STAFF:
Clotilde Perez-Bode Dedecker, President/Chief Executive Officer
Gerald Reger, Chief Financial Officer/Chief Administrative Officer
Cara Matteliano, Vice President, Community Impact
Jean McKeown, Vice President, Community Impact
Myra Lawrence, Vice President, Finance
Betsy Constantine, Vice President, Giving Strategies
Colleen Becht, Controller
Kate Masiello, Director, Client Relations
Landrum Beard, Director, Communities of Giving Legacy Initiative
Adrienne Stanfill, Director, External Resources
Felicia Beard, Special Projects Director
Catie Stephenson, Associate Director, Communications and Branding
Holly Mergenhagen, Esq., Associate Director, Gift Planning
Darren Penoyer, Senior Program Officer
Clint McManus, Knowledge Management Officer
Linda Gallagher, Accounting Manager
Laura Schwamborn, Giving Strategies Manager
Anjuli Vecchies, Giving Strategies Manager
Mary Sheehan, Accountant
Emilie Rosenbluth, Giving Strategies Analyst
Ashley Swift, Special Projects Liason
Justine David, Communications Associate
Allie Urbanski, Community Impact Associate
Farhad Mustafa, Associate, Communities of Giving Legacy Initiative, AmeriCorps VISTA
Kristen K. Perry, Marketing Communications Associate
Aubrey Hammond, Scholarship Associate

BOARD OF DIRECTORS:
Melissa Baumgart
James Biltekoff
Gary Brost
Anne Conable
Bonnie R. Durand, Ph.D.
Ross Eckert
Larry Franco
Dottie Gallagher-Cohen
Danis J. Gehl, Ph.D.
Peter Grum
Alice Jacobs, J.D.
William Joyce
Alex Montante
Gary L. Mucci, Esq.
Alphonso O'Neil-White
Jennifer J. Parker, J.D.
Michael Piette, Esq.
Katie Schneider
Richard Stockton, Ph.D.
Marsha Joy Sullivan
Francisco Vasquez, Ph.D.
John Walsh, III

ADDRESS INQUIRIES TO:
Darren Penoyer, Senior Program Officer
(See address above.)

THE COMMUNITY FOUNDATION FOR GREATER NEW HAVEN [1190]

70 Audubon Street
New Haven, CT 06510-9755
(203) 777-2386
Fax: (203) 787-6584
E-mail: contactus@cfgnh.org
Web Site: www.cfgnh.org

FOUNDED: 1928

AREAS OF INTEREST:
Health, education, community development, regional and economic development, arts and culture, youth, environment, and food and shelter.

TYPE:
Capital grants; General operating grants; Matching gifts; Project/program grants; Scholarships. Capacity building grants. Support for youth and welfare agencies, social services, hospitals and health agencies, educational institutions, community funds and the humanities, including music and art, to organizations serving the residents of greater New Haven.

PURPOSE:
To create positive and sustainable change in greater New Haven, CT.

LEGAL BASIS:
Community foundation established in Connecticut by Resolution and Declaration of Trust.

ELIGIBILITY:
The Foundation welcomes grant requests from greater New Haven area organizations that are defined as tax-exempt under Section 501(c)(3) or any applicable statute of the Internal Revenue Code. While grants are occasionally made to governmental agencies, local nonprofits receive priority.

GEOG. RESTRICTIONS: Greater New Haven, Connecticut: Ansonia, Bethany, Branford, Cheshire, Derby, East Haven, Guilford, Hamden, Madison, Milford, New Haven, North Branford, North Haven, Orange, Oxford, Seymour, Shelton, Wallingford, West Haven, and Woodbridge.

FINANCIAL DATA:
Amount of support per award: Varies.

Total amount of support: Approximately $20,000,000 each year.

NO. MOST RECENT APPLICANTS: 1,188.

NO. AWARDS: 1,098.

REPRESENTATIVE AWARDS:
$35,000 to Housatonic Valley Association to support the stewardship manager position and to support the stream teams; $32,000 to Literacy Volunteers of Greater New Haven to support increasing the level of outreach to parents of school-age children in New Haven public schools and to provide literacy tutoring to at least 80 parents so they will participate more fully in their child's education; $18,000 to Downtown Evening Soup Kitchen to provide 28,000 free, nutritious meals to the homeless, unemployed, and working poor seven days a week, as well as to provide 4,000 bags of groceries to families on an emergency basis.

APPLICATION INFO:
Application information is available on the Foundation's web site.

Duration: One year with multiyears considered annually.

Deadline: Varies from year to year.

PUBLICATIONS:
Annual report; grant guidelines; newsletters.

IRS I.D.: 06-6032106

STAFF:
William W. Ginsberg, President and Chief Executive Officer
A.F. Drew Alden, Senior Vice President for Investments, Chief Financial Officer and Chief Compliance Officer

ADDRESS INQUIRIES TO:
Denise Canning, Grants Manager
(See address above.)

THE COMMUNITY FOUNDATION FOR MONTEREY COUNTY [1191]

2354 Garden Road
Monterey, CA 93940
(831) 375-9712
Fax: (831) 375-4731
E-mail: info@cfmco.org
Web Site: www.cfmco.org/grants

FOUNDED: 1945

AREAS OF INTEREST:
Animal welfare, arts and culture, community development, education, environment, health, human services, historic preservation and youth development.

NAME(S) OF PROGRAMS:
- **Community Impact Grants Program**
- **Opportunity Grants**
- **Organizational Development Grants**

TYPE:
Capital grants; General operating grants; Project/program grants; Scholarships; Technical assistance.

PURPOSE:
To inspire philanthropy and be a catalyst for strengthening communities throughout Monterey County.

LEGAL BASIS:
Community foundation.

ELIGIBILITY:
Community-based, nonprofit organizations whose programs benefit the residents of Monterey County, CA.

The Foundation does not make Community Impact Grants to support individuals, for normal operating costs usually covered by operating income, for endowment funds, to support sectarian religious programs, for annual campaigns, dinners, or special events, to pay off past debts or existing obligations, for scholarships, fellowships or travel grants, or for technical or specialized research.

GEOG. RESTRICTIONS: Monterey County, California.

FINANCIAL DATA:
Amount of support per award: $500 to $50,000.

Total amount of support: Varies.

APPLICATION INFO:
Detailed guidelines and application form can be obtained at the Foundation web site.

Duration: One year. Reapplication annually.

Deadline: Varies.

IRS I.D.: 94-1615897

ADDRESS INQUIRIES TO:
Senior Program Officer
(See address above.)

THE COMMUNITY FOUNDATION FOR NORTHEAST FLORIDA [1192]

245 Riverside Avenue
Suite 310
Jacksonville, FL 32202
(904) 356-4483
Fax: (904) 356-7910
E-mail: kshaw@jaxcf.org
Web Site: www.jaxcf.org

AREAS OF INTEREST:
Early childhood, seniors, and the arts.

TYPE:
Project/program grants.

PURPOSE:
To stimulate philanthropy to build a better community.

ELIGIBILITY:
Eligible organizations must be IRS 501(c)(3) tax-exempt.

GEOG. RESTRICTIONS: Baker, Clay, Duval, Nassau and St. Johns counties in northern Florida.

FINANCIAL DATA:
Amount of support per award: Varies.

Total amount of support: Varies.

APPLICATION INFO:
Application information is available on the web site.

Duration: Up to 24 months.

Deadline: Varies.

PUBLICATIONS:
Newsletter; annual report.

STAFF:
John Zell, Vice President, Development
Kathleen Shaw, Vice President, Programs

ADDRESS INQUIRIES TO:
Kathleen Shaw
Vice President, Programs
(See address above.)

COMMUNITY FOUNDATION FOR NORTHEAST GEORGIA [1193]

6500 Sugarloaf Parkway, Suite 220
Duluth, GA 30097
(770) 813-3380
Fax: (770) 813-3375
E-mail: rredner@cfneg.org
Web Site: www.cfneg.org

FOUNDED: 1985

AREAS OF INTEREST:
The quality of life in northeast Georgia.

TYPE:
Grants-in-aid.

PURPOSE:
To improve the quality of life throughout northeast Georgia.

ELIGIBILITY:
Grants can be made to tax-exempt private agencies that the IRS classifies as 501(c)(3) organizations, public charities and government agencies. The Foundation will consider organizations that serve people in the areas of education, health and human services, community service and the arts.

GEOG. RESTRICTIONS: Northeast Georgia.

FINANCIAL DATA:
Over $50,000,000 has been granted since inception.

Amount of support per award: Varies.

Total amount of support: $3,951,457 for the year 2015.

NO. AWARDS: 297 for the year 2015.

APPLICATION INFO:
The grant request must be completed according to the standard Grant Proposal Guidelines issued by the Foundation. Application can be downloaded from the web site.

Duration: Typically one year.

Deadline: March 1.

ADDRESS INQUIRIES TO:
Margaret Bugbee, Director of Finance
(See address above.)

COMMUNITY FOUNDATION FOR NORTHEAST MICHIGAN [1194]

100 North Ripley
Suite F
Alpena, MI 49707
(989) 354-6881
Fax: (989) 356-3319
E-mail: bfrantz@cfnem.org
Web Site: www.cfnem.org

FOUNDED: 1974

AREAS OF INTEREST:
Education, health, youth services, arts, community needs and issues important to women.

TYPE:
Conferences/seminars; Development grants; Endowments; Project/program grants; Scholarships; Seed money grants; Technical assistance; Training grants. Tobacco-related programs/projects. Women's Giving Circle for issues important to women. Youth-related programs/projects.

YEAR PROGRAM STARTED: 1974

PURPOSE:
To provide resources for community projects.

LEGAL BASIS:
Community foundation.

ELIGIBILITY:
Eligible organizations must be IRS 501(c)(3) tax-exempt, government schools or churches, providing the project is nonsectarian. No grants to individuals.

GEOG. RESTRICTIONS: Alcona, Alpena, Montmorency and Presque Isle counties, Michigan.

FINANCIAL DATA:
Amount of support per award: Community Impact Grant: Up to $5,000; Women's Giving Circle: Up to $2,000; Youth-related programs/projects: Up to $2,500.

Total amount of support: Over $179,000 in grants for fiscal year 2015.

CO-OP FUNDING PROGRAMS: Collaboration between organizations is encouraged.

NO. MOST RECENT APPLICANTS: 187.

NO. AWARDS: 157.

REPRESENTATIVE AWARDS:
Alpena Wildlife Sanctuary; Baby Basket Project; First Robotics Team; Lake Huron Discovery Tours; Water Supply Project.

APPLICATION INFO:
Applications must include a copy of the IRS 501(c)(3) determination documentation letter, except for schools, churches and government agencies.

Duration: One year, with the possibility of a six-month extension.

Deadline: Varies.

PUBLICATIONS:
Annual report; biannual newsletter; brochures; application guidelines.

IRS I.D.: 23-7384822

EXECUTIVE DIRECTOR:
Barbara Frantz

ADDRESS INQUIRIES TO:
For common general applications:
Julie Wiesen, Program Director

For youth-related grants:
Christine Hitch, Program Associate
(See address above.)

COMMUNITY FOUNDATION FOR PALM BEACH AND MARTIN COUNTIES [1195]

700 South Dixie Hwy
Suite 200
West Palm Beach, FL 33401-5854
(561) 659-6800
(888) 853-4438 (Florida only)
Fax: (561) 832-6542
E-mail: info@cfpbmc.org
Web Site: www.yourcommunityfoundation.org

FOUNDED: 1972

AREAS OF INTEREST:
Community development, arts and culture, hunger and capacity building, and environment.

TYPE:
Challenge/matching grants; Conferences/seminars; Development grants; Project/program grants; Scholarships; Technical assistance; Training grants.

PURPOSE:
To develop a shared vision of building a sense of community.

ELIGIBILITY:
501(c)(3) organizations are eligible to apply for grants.

GEOG. RESTRICTIONS: Martin and Palm Beach counties, Florida.

FINANCIAL DATA:
Amount of support per award: Varies.

Total amount of support: $9,900,000 for the year ended June 30, 2015.

Matching fund requirements: Varies.

NO. MOST RECENT APPLICANTS: Approximately 600 grant applicants and 600 scholarship applicants for the year ended June 30, 2015.

NO. AWARDS: 618 grants and scholarships for the year ended June 30, 2015.

APPLICATION INFO:
Applicants must complete a proposal summary and budget form. Check online for application and submission information.

Duration: Scholarships: Up to three years. Grants: Varies.

Deadline: Scholarships: February 1. Grants: Varies.

PUBLICATIONS:
Annual report; newsletter.

OFFICERS:
Bradley Herbert, President and Chief Executive Officer
Gloria O. Rex, Executive Vice President and Chief Financial Officer

ADDRESS INQUIRIES TO:
Daryl Houston, Community Investment Officer
(See address above.)

THE COMMUNITY FOUNDATION FOR THE GREATER CAPITAL REGION [1196]

6 Tower Place
Albany, NY 12203
(518) 446-9638
Fax: (518) 446-9708
E-mail: jmahoney@cfgcr.org
Web Site: www.cfgcr.org

FOUNDED: 1968

AREAS OF INTEREST:
Health, science, education, youth and environment.

NAME(S) OF PROGRAMS:
- **Capacity-Building Grant Initiative**
- **Regular Competitive Grants**

TYPE:
Capital grants; Challenge/matching grants; General operating grants; Matching gifts; Project/program grants; Research grants; Scholarships; Technical assistance. Small, flexible grants to support some of the costs associated with organizational capacity-building.

The Foundation creates networks of opportunity - opportunities to bring together interested donors and community service providers to address a particular problem or need in the local community served. It serves the Capital Region of New York state by funding creative, visionary and sensitive projects - often seed money for innovative programs - that address the evolving needs of the community. The Foundation also serves as a vehicle for individuals, families, corporations, private foundations and nonprofit organizations to use in carrying out their long-term philanthropic plans.

Homelessness: Grants are designed to eliminate homelessness in the Capital Region.

Disabilities: The purpose of these grants is to serve the needs of the mentally and/or physically disabled, including the hearing- and sight-impaired.

Health: Program and capital grants are available for health care organizations working to improve the health of residents of the four-county region around Albany, NY.

Science: This program makes grants to support and promote discovery and development in medicine, science and technology in the Capital District.

PURPOSE:
To support capacity-building efforts of organizations including projects that are designed to generate new thinking about ways to improve an organization's ability to serve the community, more effectively carry out its mission, and plan for the future.

LEGAL BASIS:
Classified by the Internal Revenue Code as a public charity.

ELIGIBILITY:
Grants are made to applicants that qualify under Section 501(c)(3) of the Internal Revenue Code as a nonprofit organization, or operate under the fiscal sponsorship of an organization that does, and serve residents and be located within the ten-county Greater Capital Region. No grants are made to individuals. Nonsectarian religious programs may apply.

The Foundation's competitive grants support organizations that do not discriminate in their employment practices, volunteer opportunities, or delivery of programs or services on the basis of race, color, religion, gender, national origin, ancestry, age, medical condition, disability, veteran status, marital status, sexual orientation, or any other characteristic protected by law.

GEOG. RESTRICTIONS: Albany, Columbia, Fulton, Greene, Montgomery, Rensselaer, Saratoga, Schenectady, Schoharie, or Washington counties, New York.

FINANCIAL DATA:
Assets of over $61,000,000.

Amount of support per award: $1,000 to $30,000.

Total amount of support: More than $4,200,000 in grants for the year 2014.

NO. AWARDS: 1,100 grants awarded for the year 2014.

APPLICATION INFO:
An application form is required and may be obtained online. Prospective applicants may discuss their plans with the Foundation's program staff prior to submitting an application. Applicants may submit only one application to the Foundation's regular competitive grantmaking program per year.

Duration: With the exception of operating grants, grant periods do not exceed one year in duration. Organizations that have been funded by the Foundation must wait one year from denial date until they can reapply.

Deadline: Varies.

PUBLICATIONS:
Grantmaking Guidelines.

ADDRESS INQUIRIES TO:
E-mail: info@cfgcr.org

COMMUNITY FOUNDATION OF ABILENE [1197]

500 Chestnut, Suite 1634
Abilene, TX 79604
(325) 676-3883
Fax: (325) 676-4206
E-mail: mparrish@cfabilene.org
Web Site: www.cfabilene.org

FOUNDED: 1986

AREAS OF INTEREST:
Human services, arts and culture, education, health, community development and civic affairs.

TYPE:
Capital grants; Challenge/matching grants; Project/program grants; Technical assistance.

PURPOSE:
To increase the quality of life in Abilene, TX; to increase the awareness of philanthropy in the area.

ELIGIBILITY:
Eligible organizations must be IRS 501(c)(3) tax-exempt and be located in the immediate Abilene, TX area.

GEOG. RESTRICTIONS: Abilene, Texas.

FINANCIAL DATA:
Amount of support per award: $1,000 to $25,000.

Total amount of support: Approximately $5,400,000.

NO. MOST RECENT APPLICANTS: 70.

NO. AWARDS: 50.

APPLICATION INFO:
Applicants must submit required documentation online.

Duration: One year.

Deadline: Spring and fall.

ADDRESS INQUIRIES TO:
Michelle Parrish, Grants Director
(See address above.)

COMMUNITY FOUNDATION OF COLLIER COUNTY [1198]

1110 Pine Ridge Road, Suite 300
Naples, FL 34108
(239) 649-5000
Fax: (239) 649-5337
E-mail: sbayata@cfcollier.org
Web Site: cfcollier.org

FOUNDED: 1985

AREAS OF INTEREST:
Health, human services, basic needs, education, civic affairs, environment, arts and humanities, women and girls, economic development and animal welfare.

NAME(S) OF PROGRAMS:
- **William D. Anderson Scholarship Fund**
- **The Cacho Family Fund**
- **The Daphne Scholarship Fund**
- **Frank and Ellen Daveler Educational Scholarship**
- **Joel A. Deifik Memorial Scholarship Fund**
- **Diano-Tougas Scholarship Fund**
- **Dorothy Edwards Vocational Scholarship Fund**
- **Carol Fedoryk Scholarship Fund**
- **Halie Guelfi Memorial Scholarship Fund**
- **Hispanic Council Foundation Scholarship**
- **Patricia and F. Craig Jilik Family Scholarship Fund**
- **David M. and Judy B. Jones Scholarship Fund**
- **Ashley Kelly Memorial Scholarship Fund**
- **MacNiven Family Fund**
- **John and Edith Meli Scholarship Fund**
- **Naples Junior Women's Club Scholarship Fund**
- **Doris Reynolds Naples Daily News Journalism Scholarship Fund**
- **Jimmy Schneeberger Scholarship Fund**
- **Richard M. Schulze Family Foundation Scholarship Program**
- **Marc Scialdo Scholarship Fund**
- **Michael J. Szwed Scholarship Legacy Fund - St. Ann Catholic School**
- **Michael J. Szwed Scholarship Legacy Fund - St. John Neumann Catholic High School**
- **Ray and Sara Thomas Technical College Fund**
- **Norman and Gail Thomson Scholarship Fund**
- **Lorenzo Walker Education Scholarship Fund**
- **Webster Scholarship Fund**
- **Working Republican Women's Scholarship Fund**

TYPE:
Development grants; Matching gifts; Project/program grants; Scholarships.

Capacity-building grants. Community Grant Programs in the area of professional development.

YEAR PROGRAM STARTED: 1985

PURPOSE:
To improve the quality of life in Collier County by connecting donors to community needs; to provide leadership on critical community issues.

LEGAL BASIS:
Public foundation.

ELIGIBILITY:
Eligible organizations must be IRS 501(c)(3) tax-exempt.

GEOG. RESTRICTIONS: Primarily Collier County, Florida.

FINANCIAL DATA:
Amount of support per award: Varies.

Total amount of support: Varies.

APPLICATION INFO:
Request guidelines two to three months prior to deadlines.

Duration: Varies.

Deadline: Scholarships: Postmarked March 1. Grants: Varies.

PUBLICATIONS:
Guidelines; annual report; newsletter; *Vital Signs*, report; *Donor Advised Fund Handbook*.

STAFF:
Eileen Connolly-Keesler, President and Chief Executive Officer
Mary George, Vice President of Community Grantmaking
Lisette Holmes, Chief Financial Officer

ADDRESS INQUIRIES TO:
Sharon Bayata
Grants and Scholarship Coordinator
(See address above.)

COMMUNITY FOUNDATION OF EASTERN CONNECTICUT [1199]

68 Federal Street
New London, CT 06320
(860) 442-3572
(877) 442-3572
Fax: (860) 442-0584
E-mail: jennob@cfect.org
Web Site: www.cfect.org

FOUNDED: 1982

AREAS OF INTEREST:
Arts, charity, civic affairs, community needs and development, culture, education, empower youth, promote basic needs and rights, preserve the environment, and advance animal welfare.

NAME(S) OF PROGRAMS:

- **Animal Welfare Grants**
- **Community Foundation Grants**
- **Community Foundation Scholarship Awards**
- **Environmental Grants**
- **Norwich Women and Girls Fund**
- **Norwich Youth Grants**
- **Southeastern General Grants**
- **Willimantic Welfare Bureau Grants**
- **Windham Women and Girls Fund**
- **Women and Girls Fund Northeast**
- **Women and Girls Fund Southeast**

TYPE:
General operating grants; Project/program grants; Scholarships.

YEAR PROGRAM STARTED: 1982

PURPOSE:
To connect the generosity of private donors with the changing needs of the residents of eastern Connecticut by promoting local philanthropy and funding local projects.

ELIGIBILITY:
Federally recognized 501(c)(3) organizations and most charitable, educational and civic institution organizations that serve the towns listed below.

GEOG. RESTRICTIONS: Towns of Ashford, Bozrah, Brooklyn, Canterbury, Chaplin, Colchester, Columbia, Coventry, Eastford, East Lyme, Franklin, Griswold, Groton, Hampton, Killingly, Lebanon, Ledyard, Lisbon, Lyme, Mansfield, Montville, New London, North Stonington, Norwich, Old Lyme, Plainfield, Pomfret, Preston, Putnam, Salem, Scotland, Sprague, Stafford, Sterling, Stonington, Thompson, Union, Voluntown, Waterford, Willington, Windham, and Woodstock, Connecticut.

FINANCIAL DATA:
Amount of support per award: Grants: $1,000 to $10,000; Scholarships: $500 to $5,000.

Total amount of support: Varies.

NO. MOST RECENT APPLICANTS: Grants: 200; Scholarships: Over 500.

NO. AWARDS: Grants: 100.

APPLICATION INFO:
Contact the Foundation for specific details on the various grant programs.

Duration: Typically one year.

Deadline: Varies by program.

ADDRESS INQUIRIES TO:
Jennifer O'Brien, Program Director
(See address above.)

THE COMMUNITY FOUNDATION OF FREDERICK COUNTY, MD, INC. [1200]

312 East Church Street
Frederick, MD 21701
(301) 695-7660
Fax: (301) 695-7775
E-mail: info@frederickcountygives.org
Web Site: www.frederickcountygives.org

FOUNDED: 1986

AREAS OF INTEREST:
Community development.

TYPE:
Project/program grants; Scholarships.

YEAR PROGRAM STARTED: 1986

PURPOSE:
To make charitable dreams come true by working with donors to establish funds that award grants and scholarships.

ELIGIBILITY:
Requirements can be found on the Foundation web site.

GEOG. RESTRICTIONS: Frederick County, Maryland.

FINANCIAL DATA:
Amount of support per award: Varies depending on need.

Total amount of support: Scholarships: Over $800,000 annually; Grants: Over $4,200,000 for fiscal year ended June 30, 2015.

NO. AWARDS: More than 371 scholarships to 276 individuals for the academic year 2015-16.

APPLICATION INFO:
Information may be found on the Foundation web site.

Duration: Varies.

Deadline: Varies.

PUBLICATIONS:
Annual report; newsletters; grant applications.

IRS I.D.: 52-1488711

ADDRESS INQUIRIES TO:
Pilar Olivo, Director of Community Impact
(See address above.)

THE COMMUNITY FOUNDATION OF GREATER CHATTANOOGA, INC. [1201]

1270 Market Street
Chattanooga, TN 37402
(423) 265-0586
Fax: (423) 265-0587
E-mail: rsuttles@cfgc.org
Web Site: www.cfgc.org

FOUNDED: 1963

AREAS OF INTEREST:
Nonprofit organizations.

TYPE:
Scholarships.

YEAR PROGRAM STARTED: 1963

PURPOSE:
To encourage giving and inspire action to improve lives in the Chattanooga area.

LEGAL BASIS:
501(c)(3).

ELIGIBILITY:
Each scholarship fund has specific eligibility criteria. Most funds require the applicant:
(1) be a graduating high school senior from a Hamilton County, TN high school;
(2) demonstrate financial need;
(3) applied to or have been accepted to attend a regionally accredited two- or four-year, technical, nonproprietary or community college or university and;
(4) have at least a cumulative grade point average of 2.5 or higher.

GEOG. RESTRICTIONS: Hamilton County, Tennessee.

FINANCIAL DATA:
Amount of support per award: Varies.

APPLICATION INFO:
Students must complete application and submit supplementary documents.

Duration: Varies.

Deadline: Varies.

IRS I.D.: 62-6045999

STAFF:
Meaghan Jones, President
Marty Robinson, Vice President of Donor Relations
Rebecca Suttles, Director of Scholarships

BOARD OF DIRECTORS:
Clif Cleaveland
Lakweshia Ewing
Tom Glenn
Tim Kelly
Barry Large
Travis Lytle
James McKissic
Ward Nelson
Gladys Pineda-Loher
Tiffanie Robinson
Michelle Ruest

Rachel Schulson
Julie Stowe
Elizabeth Williams

EXECUTIVE COMMITTEE:
Michelle Ruest, Chairperson
Clif Cleaveland, Vice Chairperson
Tim Kelly, Vice Chairperson
Julie Stowe, Treasurer
Ansley Moses, Corporate Secretary

ADDRESS INQUIRIES TO:
Rebecca Suttles
Director of Scholarships
(See address above.)

THE COMMUNITY FOUNDATION OF GREATER CHATTANOOGA, INC. [1202]

1270 Market Street
Chattanooga, TN 37402
(423) 265-0586 ext. 15
Fax: (423) 265-0587
E-mail: info@cfgc.org
Web Site: www.cfgc.org

FOUNDED: 1963

AREAS OF INTEREST:
Improving the quality of life in the Chattanooga, TN area.

NAME(S) OF PROGRAMS:
- **Fund for Chattanooga**

TYPE:
Capital grants; Project/program grants.

PURPOSE:
To encourage giving and to inspire action to improve lives in the Chattanooga area.

LEGAL BASIS:
501(c)(3).

ELIGIBILITY:
Organizations have to be 501(c)(3) public charities located in Hamilton County, TN and/or primarily serving Hamilton County.

GEOG. RESTRICTIONS: Hamilton County, Tennessee.

FINANCIAL DATA:
Approximately $116,000,000 in net assets as of December 31, 2013.
Amount of support per award: $2,000 to $20,000.
Total amount of support: Approximately $849,000 for fiscal year 2015.

NO. AWARDS: 70 for fiscal year 2015.

APPLICATION INFO:
Application information is available on the Foundation web site.
Duration: One year.
Deadline: January, May and September. Contact Foundation for exact date.

ADDRESS INQUIRIES TO:
Robin Posey
Director of Programs
(See address above.)

COMMUNITY FOUNDATION OF GREATER GREENSBORO [1203]

330 South Greene Street
Suite 100
Greensboro, NC 27401
(336) 379-9100
Fax: (336) 378-0725
E-mail: info@cfgg.org
Web Site: www.cfgg.org

FOUNDED: 1983

AREAS OF INTEREST:
Capacity-building for nonprofits serving the Greater Greensboro, NC area.

NAME(S) OF PROGRAMS:
- **College and University Scholarships**
- **Community Grants Program**
- **Pre-College Scholarships**

TYPE:
Challenge/matching grants; Conferences/seminars; Demonstration grants; Development grants; Endowments; General operating grants; Project/program grants; Scholarships. Recognition Awards.

ELIGIBILITY:
Grant applicant must be a 501(c)(3) nonprofit organization located in or serving the greater Greensboro area. No grants to individuals.

GEOG. RESTRICTIONS: Greater Greensboro, North Carolina area.

FINANCIAL DATA:
Amount of support per award: Average grant: $3,000 to $5,000. Scholarships: Varies.
Total amount of support: Varies.

APPLICATION INFO:
Applications and guidelines are available online.
Duration: Varies.
Deadline: Varies.

IRS I.D.: 56-1380249

ADDRESS INQUIRIES TO:
H. Walker Sanders, President
(See address above.)

COMMUNITY FOUNDATION OF GREATER ROCHESTER [1204]

P.O. Box 80431
Rochester, MI 48308-0431
(248) 608-2804
Fax: (248) 608-2826
E-mail: director@cfound.org
Web Site: www.cfound.org

FOUNDED: 1983

AREAS OF INTEREST:
Arts, conservation of natural resources, community needs and development, culture, education, environment, health, historic preservation and human services.

TYPE:
Endowments; Project/program grants; Scholarships; Travel grants. Community grants.

PURPOSE:
To enhance the quality of life for the citizens of Greater Rochester area by serving as a community endowment builder, grantmaker and leader.

ELIGIBILITY:
Grants are made to organizations that have tax-exempt status under Section 501(c)(3) of the Internal Revenue Code. Nonsectarian religious programs may apply.

GEOG. RESTRICTIONS: Greater Rochester, Michigan and surrounding area.

FINANCIAL DATA:
Amount of support per award: Varies.
Total amount of support: Varies.

APPLICATION INFO:
Contact the Foundation for application procedures.
Duration: Varies.
Deadline: Varies.

ADDRESS INQUIRIES TO:
Johanna Allen, Executive Director
(See address above.)

THE COMMUNITY FOUNDATION OF HERKIMER & ONEIDA COUNTIES, INC. [1205]

2608 Genesee Street
Utica, NY 13502
(315) 735-8212
(315) 731-3728
Fax: (315) 735-9363
E-mail: info@foundationhoc.org
Web Site: foundationhoc.org

FOUNDED: 1952

AREAS OF INTEREST:
Economic development, education, health, arts and culture.

TYPE:
Capital grants; Challenge/matching grants; Fellowships; Project/program grants; Scholarships; Seed money grants; Technical assistance; Training grants.

PURPOSE:
To improve the quality of life of the residents of Herkimer and Oneida counties in New York.

LEGAL BASIS:
Community foundation.

ELIGIBILITY:
Applications are entertained from organizations that are tax-exempt under Section 501(c)(3) of the Internal Revenue Code. Grants may be made for program or capital expenses. Operating funds will receive consideration on a short-term or emergency basis, with the understanding that applicants must submit a clear, realistic plan to secure alternative funding at the end of a specific time.

The Community Foundation does not make grants for religious purposes, nor does it provide financial assistance or scholarships directly to individuals, support for nonemergency expenses already incurred, requests over $100,000, or ongoing operating support.

GEOG. RESTRICTIONS: Herkimer and Oneida counties, New York.

FINANCIAL DATA:
Amount of support per award: $1,000 to $100,000; average $3,000 to $30,000.
Total amount of support: $4,700,716 for the year 2015.

APPLICATION INFO:
Applicants should call the Senior Community Investment Manager prior to submitting a written request.
Duration: One year.
Deadline: Grant requests are accepted on an ongoing basis.

PUBLICATIONS:
Annual report; newsletter; application guidelines; foundation brochure.

ADDRESS INQUIRIES TO:
Jan Squadrito
Senior Community Investment Manager
(See address above.)

COMMUNITY FOUNDATION OF JACKSON HOLE [1206]

245 East Simpson Street
Jackson, WY 83001
(307) 739-1026
Fax: (307) 734-2841
E-mail: info@cfjacksonhole.org
Web Site: www.cfjacksonhole.org

FOUNDED: 1989

AREAS OF INTEREST:
Art, education, environment, health and social services.

TYPE:
Development grants; General operating grants; Grants-in-aid; Project/program grants; Research grants.

PURPOSE:
To improve lives through philanthropic leadership.

LEGAL BASIS:
501(c)(3).

ELIGIBILITY:
Must be a 501(c)(3) corporation.

GEOG. RESTRICTIONS: Teton County, Wyoming.

APPLICATION INFO:
Application information is available on the web site.

IRS I.D.: 83-0308856

ADDRESS INQUIRIES TO:
Katharine Conover, President
(See address above.)

THE COMMUNITY FOUNDATION OF LORAIN COUNTY [1207]

9080 Leavitt Road
Elyria, OH 44035
(440) 984-7390
Fax: (440) 984-7399
E-mail: foundation@peoplewhocare.org
Web Site: www.peoplewhocare.org

FOUNDED: 1980

AREAS OF INTEREST:
Community of Lorain County, OH.

TYPE:
General operating grants; Project/program grants. Grants are given to improve the quality of life in Lorain County.

YEAR PROGRAM STARTED: 1980

PURPOSE:
To connect people who care with causes that matter.

ELIGIBILITY:
Organization or sponsor must be 501(c)(3). Funding must serve the people of Lorain County.

GEOG. RESTRICTIONS: Lorain County, Ohio.

FINANCIAL DATA:
Amount of support per award: Varies.
Total amount of support: Varies.

APPLICATION INFO:
Application can be downloaded at the web site.
Deadline: February 1 and July 1.

ADDRESS INQUIRIES TO:
Linda Styer, Senior Program Officer
E-mail: lstyer@peoplewhocare.org

COMMUNITY FOUNDATION OF NORTH CENTRAL WISCONSIN [1208]

500 First Street
Suite 2600
Wausau, WI 54403
(715) 845-9555
Fax: (715) 845-5423
E-mail: info@cfoncw.org
Web Site: www.cfoncw.org

FOUNDED: 1987

AREAS OF INTEREST:
Arts, education, health and human services, and resource preservation.

TYPE:
Capital grants; Development grants; Project/program grants; Scholarships; Seed money grants; Technical assistance.

YEAR PROGRAM STARTED: 1987

PURPOSE:
To enhance the quality of the greater Wausau (WI) area.

ELIGIBILITY:
Consideration is given primarily to those organizations that are tax-exempt under Section 501(c)(3) of the Internal Revenue Code.

GEOG. RESTRICTIONS: Greater Wausau area, Marathon County, Wisconsin.

FINANCIAL DATA:
Amount of support per award: $2,500 to $10,000.
Total amount of support: Varies.

CO-OP FUNDING PROGRAMS: Community Arts Grants are funded through the Wisconsin Arts Board; B.A. and Esther Greenheck Foundation and Community Foundation.

NO. MOST RECENT APPLICANTS: 72 for the year 2014.

NO. AWARDS: 39 for the year 2014.

REPRESENTATIVE AWARDS:
Performing Arts Foundation; Wausau Community Theatre; Wisconsin Institute for Public Policy and Service; Marathon County Historical Society; Stable Hands.

APPLICATION INFO:
Application information is available on the web site.
Duration: One year. Renewable upon reapplication.
Deadline: Applications are due the first business day of March, June, September and December.

STAFF:
Jean Tehan, Executive Director
Tammy Szekeress, Operations Director
Sue Nelson, Program Manager
Pauline Zweck, Accountant

ADDRESS INQUIRIES TO:
Jean Tehan, Executive Director
(See address above.)

COMMUNITY FOUNDATION OF SAINT JOSEPH COUNTY [1209]

P.O. Box 837
South Bend, IN 46624
(574) 232-0041
Fax: (574) 233-1906
E-mail: info@cfsjc.org
Web Site: www.cfsjc.org

AREAS OF INTEREST:
Arts and culture; community development and urban affairs; health and human services; parks, recreation, and environment; youth and education.

NAME(S) OF PROGRAMS:

- **African American Community Fund**
- **ArtsEverywhere Fund**
- **Leighton Award for Nonprofit Excellence**
- **Robert P. and Clara I. Milton Fund for Senior Housing**
- **Special Project Challenge Grant**

TYPE:
Capital grants; Challenge/matching grants; Project/program grants; Scholarships. Donor-advised grants.

PURPOSE:
To promote organizations whose programs benefit the residents of St. Joseph County; to assist existing agencies to better respond to the needs of the community.

ELIGIBILITY:
Grants are made to organizations that have tax-exempt status under Section 501(c)(3) of the Internal Revenue Code. No grants are made to individuals. Nonsectarian religious programs may apply. Funded projects should benefit a significant constituency within the community and the organization must exhibit the ability to raise the required matching funds, if applicable.

GEOG. RESTRICTIONS: Saint Joseph County, Indiana.

FINANCIAL DATA:
Amount of support per award: Varies per award.
Matching fund requirements: Some programs require matching funds.

APPLICATION INFO:
Application information is available on the web site.
Duration: Varies.
Deadline: Special Project Challenge Grant and African American Community Fund: March 1 and October 1; Robert P. and Clara I. Milton Fund and ArtsEverywhere Fund: May 1 and November 1; Leighton Award for Nonprofit Excellence: July 1 of odd-numbered years.

STAFF:
Rose Meissner, President

ADDRESS INQUIRIES TO:
Emily Slatt, Program Officer
(See address above.)

THE COMMUNITY FOUNDATION OF SHELBY COUNTY [1210]

Courtview Center, Suite 202
100 South Main Avenue
Sidney, OH 45365-2771
(937) 497-7800
Fax: (937) 497-7799
E-mail: info@commfoun.com
Web Site: www.commfoun.com

FOUNDED: 1952

AREAS OF INTEREST:
Arts and culture, family and community, education, environment, and health.

TYPE:
Capital grants; Scholarships; Seed money grants.

PURPOSE:
To improve the quality of life and to cultivate, administer and distribute legacy gifts for the benefit of its local community.

ELIGIBILITY:
Organizations must have 501(c)(3) status.

GEOG. RESTRICTIONS: Shelby County, Ohio.

FINANCIAL DATA:
Amount of support per award: Discretionary grants: $500 to $5,000.

Total amount of support: $30,000 in discretionary grants for the year 2015; approximately $1,400,000 in total grantmaking for fiscal year 2015.

NO. MOST RECENT APPLICANTS: Varies.

NO. AWARDS: Varies.

APPLICATION INFO:
Applicants must call the Executive Director of the Foundation to discuss the grant request idea and whether the project appears to fit within the Foundation's guidelines. Preliminary Grant Proposals and Full Proposals will not be accepted if they have not been requested by the Executive Director.

Applications for most of the scholarships are available online.

Deadline: Discretionary grants: February 1. Designated purpose grants: Varies.

ADDRESS INQUIRIES TO:
Marian Spicer, Executive Director
(See address above.)

THE COMMUNITY FOUNDATION OF SOUTH ALABAMA [1211]

212 St. Joseph Street
Mobile, AL 36602
(251) 438-5591
Fax: (251) 438-5592
E-mail: cmarston@communityfoundationsa.org
Web Site: www.communityfoundationsa.org

FOUNDED: 1976

AREAS OF INTEREST:
Arts and culture, economic opportunity, civic engagement, and health and wellness.

TYPE:
Project/program grants; Scholarships. Capacity-building grants. Special initiative grants.

PURPOSE:
To assemble and direct philanthropic assets to make Southwestern Alabama a better place.

LEGAL BASIS:
Alabama not-for-profit corporation/community foundation.

ELIGIBILITY:
Eligible organizations must be IRS 501(c)(3) tax-exempt and located in southwest Alabama.

GEOG. RESTRICTIONS: Southwestern Alabama (Baldwin, Choctaw, Clarke, Conecah, Escambia, Mobile, Monroe and Washington counties).

FINANCIAL DATA:
Amount of support per award: Varies.

Total amount of support: Varies.

APPLICATION INFO:
Guidelines and application form are available online.

Duration: One year. Renewal by reapplication.

Deadline: Varies.

PUBLICATIONS:
Annual report; newsletter; application guidelines; *Charitable Gift Annuity*; *Real Estate Gifts*.

IRS I.D.: 63-0695166

STAFF:
Rebecca Byrne, President and Chief Executive Officer
Linette Clausman, Chief Finance and Administrative Officer
Carolyn Marston, Director of Programs

ADDRESS INQUIRIES TO:
Carolyn Marston, Director of Programs
(See address above.)

COMMUNITY FOUNDATION OF THE EASTERN SHORE [1212]

1324 Belmont Avenue, Suite 401
Salisbury, MD 21804
(410) 742-9911
Fax: (410) 742-6638
E-mail: hmahler@cfes.org
Web Site: www.cfes.org

FOUNDED: 1984

AREAS OF INTEREST:
Arts, civic affairs, community needs, conservation, culture, education, health and historic preservation.

NAME(S) OF PROGRAMS:
- **Community Needs Grants**
- **Education Grants Program**
- **Richard A. Henson Award of Excellence**
- **Mini Grants**
- **Frank H. Morris Humanitarian Award**
- **Nonprofit Support Program**
- **Workforce Development Grants**

TYPE:
Awards/prizes; Challenge/matching grants; Demonstration grants; Project/program grants; Scholarships; Seed money grants; Technical assistance; Training grants.

YEAR PROGRAM STARTED: 1984

PURPOSE:
To improve the quality of life in the area by acting as a funding source for present and future generations.

ELIGIBILITY:
Grants are made to organizations that have tax-exempt status under Section 501(c)(3) of the Internal Revenue Code and not classified as a private foundation that is located or serves the residents of the counties. No grants are made to individuals. Nonsectarian religious programs may apply. Agencies must be operated and organized so that they do not discriminate in the hiring of staff on the basis of race, religion, gender, sexual orientation, age, national origin or disability.

GEOG. RESTRICTIONS: Somerset, Wicomico and Worcester counties, Maryland.

FINANCIAL DATA:
Amount of support per award: Community Needs: $2,000 to $5,000; Education Grants Program: $1,500 to $5,000; Henson and Morris Awards: Approximately $1,000; Mini Grants: $200 to $2,000.

Total amount of support: $5,300,000 in grants and scholarships for the year 2015.

APPLICATION INFO:
Application information is available on the web site.

Duration: One year.

Deadline: Community Needs: February and August; Education Grants Program: August; Henson and Morris Awards: Late August.

STAFF:
Heather Mahler, Program Director

ADDRESS INQUIRIES TO:
Heather Mahler, Program Director
(See address above.)

COMMUNITY FOUNDATION OF THE FOX RIVER VALLEY [1213]

111 West Downer Place
Suite 312
Aurora, IL 60506
(630) 896-7800
Fax: (630) 896-7811
E-mail: info@communityfoundationfrv.org
Web Site: www.communityfoundationfrv.org

AREAS OF INTEREST:
Education, health care, social services, the arts, and other charitable fields.

TYPE:
Capital grants; Scholarships.

PURPOSE:
To support worthwhile projects in the served communities.

ELIGIBILITY:
Grants are made to organizations that have tax-exempt status under Section 501(c)(3) of the Internal Revenue Code. No grants are made to individuals.

GEOG. RESTRICTIONS: Aurora, southern Kane County, and Kendall County, Illinois.

FINANCIAL DATA:
Amount of support per award: $1,000 to $10,000.

Total amount of support: $5,888,352 in 2015.

NO. MOST RECENT APPLICANTS: Scholarships: 608.

NO. AWARDS: Scholarships: 320.

APPLICATION INFO:
Applications may be obtained from the Foundation web site.
Duration: Varies.

Deadline: Grant proposals: First business day in April and October. Scholarships: January or February.

COMMUNITY FOUNDATION OF THE OZARKS [1214]

425 East Trafficway
Springfield, MO 65806
(417) 864-6199
Fax: (417) 864-8344
E-mail: jleeth@cfozarks.org
Web Site: cfozarks.org

AREAS OF INTEREST:
Health and social services; arts, culture and environment; education and community development.

TYPE:
Challenge/matching grants; Demonstration grants; Development grants; Endowments; Project/program grants; Scholarships. Initiative grants. Technical/Capacity-building grants.

PURPOSE:
To build a community endowment; to provide leadership; to prompt collaboration on

community issues; to improve the quality of life for citizens in Greene County, MO and the surrounding region.

LEGAL BASIS:
Community foundation.

ELIGIBILITY:
Eligible organizations must be IRS 501(c)(3) tax-exempt and located in Greene County, MO or counties represented by the Foundation's affiliate organizations which are located throughout the central and southern half of Missouri.

GEOG. RESTRICTIONS: Central and southern Missouri.

FINANCIAL DATA:
Amount of support per award: Grants: $1,500 to $25,000; Initiative Awards: $100,000 to $1,000,000.

Total amount of support: Discretionary Grants and Scholarships Programs: $2,000,000.

APPLICATION INFO:
Complete application information is available online.

Duration: Typically one year.

Deadline: Varies.

ADDRESS INQUIRIES TO:
Bridget Dierks, Grants Program Officer
(See address above.)

COMMUNITY FOUNDATION OF THE TEXAS HILL COUNTRY [1215]

301 Junction Highway, Suite 346-B
Kerrville, TX 78028
(830) 896-8811
Fax: (830) 792-5956
E-mail: paul@communityfoundation.net
Web Site: www.communityfoundation.net

FOUNDED: 1982

AREAS OF INTEREST:
Community development.

NAME(S) OF PROGRAMS:
- **Arts**
- **Children and Education**
- **Community**
- **Designated and Donor Advised Funds**
- **Healers**
- **Pass Through Grants**

TYPE:
Challenge/matching grants; Development grants; Grants-in-aid; Matching gifts; Project/program grants; Scholarships; Technical assistance.

PURPOSE:
To improve the quality of life in the Texas Hill Country of Texas.

LEGAL BASIS:
Corporation.

ELIGIBILITY:
Organization must be located in or provide services to Kerr County, the communities of Bandera, Comfort, Fredericksburg, Harper, Medina and Stonewall, TX, or their outlying areas. Grants are generally not awarded to individuals.

FINANCIAL DATA:
More than $17,000,000 in assets for the year ended December 31, 2015.

Amount of support per award: Varies.

Total amount of support: Varies.

NO. MOST RECENT APPLICANTS: 32.

NO. AWARDS: 26.

APPLICATION INFO:
Application information is available on the Foundation web site.

IRS I.D.: 74-2225369

STAFF:
Paul Urban, Executive Director
Amy Rector, Business Manager
Jayne Zirkel, Public Relations and Event Coordinator

ADDRESS INQUIRIES TO:
Paul Urban, Executive Director
(See address above.)

COMMUNITY FOUNDATION OF WEST TEXAS [1216]

6102 82nd Street, Suite 8B
Lubbock, TX 79424
(806) 762-8061
Fax: (806) 762-8551
E-mail: tami@communityfoundationofwesttexas.org
Web Site: communityofwesttexas.org

FOUNDED: 1981

AREAS OF INTEREST:
Charitable organizations and community development.

NAME(S) OF PROGRAMS:
- **Mini Grant for Teachers Program**

TYPE:
Project/program grants; Scholarships; Technical assistance. Responsiveness to changing or emerging community needs approach for solving community problems in South Plains area.

YEAR PROGRAM STARTED: 1981

PURPOSE:
To improve the quality of life in the South Plains area of Texas.

ELIGIBILITY:
Organizations must be 501(c)(3) not-for-profit.

GEOG. RESTRICTIONS: South Plains area of Texas.

FINANCIAL DATA:
Amount of support per award: Grant awards: Up to $5,000; Mini Grant for Teachers Program: Up to $1,000.

Total amount of support: Varies.

CO-OP FUNDING PROGRAMS: Affiliate Endowment Challenges, Community Endowment Challenge, Mini Grant for Teachers.

APPLICATION INFO:
Application information is available on the web site.

Duration: One year. Must reapply.

Deadline: Mini Grant for Teachers: June 15. All others: Varies.

ADDRESS INQUIRIES TO:
See e-mail address above.

COMMUNITY FOUNDATION OF WESTERN MASSACHUSETTS (CFWM) [1217]

1500 Main Street, Suite 2300
Springfield, MA 01115
(413) 732-2858
Fax: (413) 733-8565
E-mail: wmass@communityfoundation.org
Web Site: www.communityfoundation.org

FOUNDED: 1991

AREAS OF INTEREST:
Human services, economic development, education, arts and culture, health, housing and environment.

TYPE:
Capital grants; Challenge/matching grants; Project/program grants; Scholarships. Capacity building. Equipment.

YEAR PROGRAM STARTED: 1991

PURPOSE:
To enrich the quality of life of the people of our region.

ELIGIBILITY:
Grants are restricted to worthy public charities serving residents of Franklin, Hampden and Hampshire counties in Massachusetts.

GEOG. RESTRICTIONS: Franklin, Hampden and Hampshire counties, Massachusetts.

FINANCIAL DATA:
Amount of support per award: Maximum $25,000 per award.

Total amount of support: $9,900,000 for fiscal year 2015.

CO-OP FUNDING PROGRAMS: Informal linkages as well as funds established by family foundations within the community foundation.

NO. MOST RECENT APPLICANTS: 150 for the year 2015.

NO. AWARDS: 101 for the year 2015.

APPLICATION INFO:
Contact the Foundation for application procedures.

Duration: One year. Nonrenewable.

PUBLICATIONS:
Annual report; newsletter; brochures for donors and applicants.

STAFF:
Katie Allan Zobel, President and Chief Executive Officer
Janet Daisley, Vice President for Programs and Strategy

ADDRESS INQUIRIES TO:
Janet Daisley
Vice President for Programs and Strategy
(See address above.)

COMMUNITY FOUNDATIONS OF THE HUDSON VALLEY [1218]

80 Washington Street, Suite 201
Poughkeepsie, NY 12601
(845) 452-3077
Fax: (845) 452-3083
E-mail: mgallagher@cfhvny.org
Web Site: www.cfhvny.org

FOUNDED: 1969

AREAS OF INTEREST:
Health, education and social services.

NAME(S) OF PROGRAMS:
- **Community Response Grants**
- **Fund for Excellence in Education Grants**

TYPE:
Project/program grants; Scholarships; Training grants. Equipment to improve office operations.

PURPOSE:
To improve the quality of life in Dutchess, Putnam and Ulster counties, New York.

ELIGIBILITY:
Eligible organizations must be IRS 501(c)(3) tax-exempt or have a fiscal sponsor.

GEOG. RESTRICTIONS: Primarily Dutchess, Putnam and Ulster counties, New York.

FINANCIAL DATA:
Amount of support per award: Varies.
Total amount of support: $3,120,016 in fiscal year 2015.

NO. MOST RECENT APPLICANTS: 150.

NO. AWARDS: 50.

APPLICATION INFO:
Application information is available on the web site. Applications are submitted through the online application system.

PUBLICATIONS:
Annual report; newsletters.

IRS I.D.: 23-7026859

ADDRESS INQUIRIES TO:
March S. Gallagher, Esq.
President and Chief Executive Officer
(See address above.)

*SPECIAL STIPULATIONS:
Review web site, if possible, for grant information. Applicants may contact the organization for details of its grants.

CONNECTICUT COMMUNITY FOUNDATION [1219]

43 Field Street
Waterbury, CT 06702
(203) 753-1315
Fax: (203) 756-3054
E-mail: info@conncf.org
Web Site: www.conncf.org

FOUNDED: 1923

AREAS OF INTEREST:
Arts and culture, cradle to career (youth development/education), economic vitality, environment, grassroots engagement, healthy communities, older adults, technology and women's issues.

CONSULTING OR VOLUNTEER SERVICES:
Nonprofit advisor services available.

NAME(S) OF PROGRAMS:
- **Capacity Building Grants**
- **Nonprofit Assistance Initiative**
- **Program Grants**
- **Scholarships**
- **Training Programs**

TYPE:
Capital grants; Challenge/matching grants; Project/program grants; Scholarships; Seed money grants; Technical assistance. Sponsorships. Organizational development.

YEAR PROGRAM STARTED: 1923

PURPOSE:
To serve the people of the Greater Waterbury and Litchfield Hills to improve the quality of life.

LEGAL BASIS:
Community foundation.

ELIGIBILITY:
Applicant must:
(1) be a not-for-profit organization recognized under Section 501(c)(3) of the Internal Revenue Code, or a municipal entity seeking a grant for public purposes;
(2) have a board, representative of the community, of which a majority is neither employees nor relatives of employees;
(3) be located within and/or providing services to residents of the Foundation's 21-town service area: Beacon Falls, Bethlehem, Bridgewater, Cheshire, Goshen, Litchfield, Middlebury, Morris, Naugatuck, New Milford, Oxford, Prospect, Roxbury, Southbury, Thomaston, Warren, Washington, Waterbury, Watertown, Wolcott or Woodbury and;
(4) have a Nonprofit Registration to Solicit Funds (or exemption, if appropriate) from the Connecticut Department of Consumer Protection. Registration must be renewed annually.

Grant requests for political or religious purposes or for capital expenditures on buildings not owned by a nonprofit are not accepted. Religious organizations or municipalities are not eligible to apply for grants for buildings or expenses related to buildings. However, they may apply for equipment that is specifically part of an eligible programmatic request.

GEOG. RESTRICTIONS: Greater Waterbury and Litchfield Hills, Connecticut.

FINANCIAL DATA:
Amount of support per award: Varies.
Total amount of support: Approximately $4,000,000 in grants and scholarships for the year 2015.

NO. AWARDS: Over 900 grants and scholarships.

APPLICATION INFO:
Guidelines and application form may be obtained online.
Duration: One year. Multiyear funding should be applied for at the outset and is subject to review.

PUBLICATIONS:
Annual report.

IRS I.D.: 06-6038074

ADDRESS INQUIRIES TO:
Josh Carey, Director of Grants Management
(See address above.)

COOK FAMILY FOUNDATION [1220]

120 West Exchange Street, Suite 202
Owosso, MI 48867
(989) 725-1621
Fax: (989) 936-5910
E-mail: tom@cookfamilyfoundation.org
Web Site: www.cookfamilyfoundation.org

FOUNDED: 1978

AREAS OF INTEREST:
Community organizations, education and youth, environment, and University of Michigan.

TYPE:
Capital grants; Challenge/matching grants; Demonstration grants; Development grants; Matching gifts; Project/program grants; Scholarships; Seed money grants; Technical assistance. Educational support.

YEAR PROGRAM STARTED: 1978

PURPOSE:
To strengthen and invest in the future of community institutions in Shiawassee County; to support the University of Michigan.

LEGAL BASIS:
Family (private) foundation.

ELIGIBILITY:
Eligible organizations must be IRS 501(c)(3) tax-exempt. The Foundation does not give grants for religious purposes and upholds federal law which prohibits the expenditure of funds for political campaigns or direct lobbying activities. With the exception of scholarships, the Foundation does not give grants to individuals.

GEOG. RESTRICTIONS: Shiawassee County, Michigan.

FINANCIAL DATA:
Amount of support per award: Typically $5,000 to $50,000.
Total amount of support: Approximately $580,000 yearly.
Matching fund requirements: Varies based on grant; average 20% cash/in-kind.

APPLICATION INFO:
Applicants should submit a short letter of inquiry.
Deadline: None; however, first consideration will be given to grant applications submitted by April 1. Applications should be made no later than November 1.

STAFF:
Yvette Collard, Associate Director

ADDRESS INQUIRIES TO:
Thomas Cook, Executive Director
P.O. Box 278
Owosso, MI 48867

*PLEASE NOTE:
The Foundation establishes a total annual grant budget in January for that year and addresses applications on a first-come, first-served basis within that budget.

COOPERATIVE DEVELOPMENT FOUNDATION [1221]

1775 I Street, N.W.
Eighth Floor
Washington, DC 20006
(202) 442-2331
E-mail: equinn@cdf.coop
Web Site: www.cdf.coop
www.heroes.coop
seniors.coop

FOUNDED: 1944

AREAS OF INTEREST:
Community, economic and social development through cooperative enterprise.

TYPE:
Grants-in-aid. The Foundation makes grants and loans for cooperative development through its various funds.

PURPOSE:
To promote self-help and mutual aid in community, economic and social development through cooperative enterprise.

LEGAL BASIS:
501(c)(3) organization.

ELIGIBILITY:
The Foundation does not award grants for purely personal needs. It works only in the cooperative sector.

GEOG. RESTRICTIONS: Primarily the United States.

FINANCIAL DATA:
Amount of support per award: Varies.
Total amount of support: Varies.

NO. MOST RECENT APPLICANTS: Approximately 30.

NO. AWARDS: 27.

APPLICATION INFO:
Contact the Foundation after reviewing the various fund descriptions to determine if the proposed project fits within the Foundation's funding priorities. The Foundation supports cooperative development only.

PUBLICATIONS:
Annual report.

STAFF:
Leslie Mead, Executive Director
Ellen Quinn, Funds Manager
Cassandra Durand, Events Coordinator

ADDRESS INQUIRIES TO:
See e-mail address above.

*SPECIAL STIPULATIONS:
The Foundation supports cooperative development only.

ADOLPH COORS FOUNDATION

215 St. Paul Street, Suite 300
Denver, CO 80206
(303) 388-1636
Fax: (303) 388-1684
E-mail: info@acoorsfdn.org
Web Site: www.coorsfoundation.org

TYPE:
Capital grants; General operating grants; Project/program grants.

See entry 1094 for full listing.

CORPORATION FOR NATIONAL AND COMMUNITY SERVICE [1222]

250 E Street, S.W.
Washington, DC 20525
(202) 606-5000
(202) 606-6608
E-mail: VISTA@cns.gov
Web Site: www.NationalService.gov/VISTA

FOUNDED: 1965

AREAS OF INTEREST:
Anti-poverty or poverty-related activities.

NAME(S) OF PROGRAMS:

- **AmeriCorps VISTA**

TYPE:
Project/program grants. Provides full-time, full-year volunteers at the request of community groups to work on clearly defined tasks that lead to mobilization of the community's resources. The volunteers live among the people they serve at subsistence levels of support.

YEAR PROGRAM STARTED: 1965

PURPOSE:
To supplement efforts to eliminate poverty and poverty-related problems.

LEGAL BASIS:
Domestic Volunteer Service Act of 1973, as amended (P.L. 93-113).

ELIGIBILITY:
Sponsors applying for AmeriCorps VISTA must be nonprofit organizations. They may be public or private and include state and local governments.

GEOG. RESTRICTIONS: United States and its territories.

FINANCIAL DATA:
Volunteers receive a basic monthly subsistence allowance. An additional stipend is paid upon completion of service or the Segal AmeriCorps Educational Award.

Amount of support per award: Approximately $22,000 per volunteer service year.

Total amount of support: Varies.

NO. MOST RECENT APPLICANTS: Organizations: Approximately 6,000; Individuals: Approximately 70,000.

NO. AWARDS: Organizations: 1,300.

APPLICATION INFO:
Application information is available on the web site. Online tutorial on how to become a VISTA sponsor is available at www.vistacampus.gov/resources/vista-101-understanding-vista-0.

Duration: One to five years.

Deadline: Applications accepted on an ongoing basis.

ADDRESS INQUIRIES TO:
See e-mail address above.

THE DALLAS FOUNDATION [1223]

3963 Maple Avenue
Suite 390
Dallas, TX 75219
(214) 741-9898
Fax: (214) 741-9848
E-mail: mjalonick@dallasfoundation.org
Web Site: www.dallasfoundation.org

FOUNDED: 1929

AREAS OF INTEREST:
Arts, education, health and human services, and social services.

TYPE:
Capital grants; Project/program grants; Scholarships.

YEAR PROGRAM STARTED: 1929

PURPOSE:
To improve the quality of life for residents of the city and county of Dallas.

LEGAL BASIS:
Community foundation.

ELIGIBILITY:
Applicant organizations must be tax-exempt nonprofit focused on needs within Dallas County. Grants from the field of interest funds require a match between the purpose of the grant and the purpose of the available funds. Grants from the unrestricted funds may be given to any type of need within Dallas County.

Funds are not available from discretionary funds for individuals, endowments, research, debt retirement, annual campaigns, underwriting of fund-raising events, or for organizations that have received support within the preceding three to five years.

GEOG. RESTRICTIONS: City and county of Dallas, Texas.

FINANCIAL DATA:
Amount of support per award: Varies.

Total amount of support: Varies.

APPLICATION INFO:
The application form is available on the Foundation web site, or by request. Unrestricted funds must have a letter of inquiry submitted by August 1.

Duration: Varies.

Deadline: Interest funds: April 1 with announcement in June. Unrestricted funds: October 1 with announcement in December.

PUBLICATIONS:
Annual report; application guidelines.

ADDRESS INQUIRIES TO:
Helen Holman
Director of Community Philanthropy
(See address above.)

DANIELS FUND

101 Monroe Street
Denver, CO 80206-4467
(303) 393-7220
Fax: (720) 941-4110
E-mail: info@danielsfund.org
grantsinfo@danielsfund.org
Web Site: www.danielsfund.org

TYPE:
Capital grants; General operating grants; Project/program grants; Scholarships. Daniels Fund Grants Program supports highly effective nonprofit organizations in Colorado, New Mexico, Utah and Wyoming.

Daniels Fund Scholarship Program consists of the Daniels Scholarship Program and the Daniels Boundless Opportunity Scholarship Program. The Daniels Scholarship Program provides a comprehensive, four-year annually-renewable college scholarship for graduating high school seniors who demonstrate exceptional character, leadership, and a commitment to serving their communities, and applies toward the expense of attaining a Bachelor's degree at any nonprofit, accredited college or university in the U.S. The Daniels Boundless Opportunity Scholarship Program provides college scholarships for non-traditional students of all ages, awarded by select colleges and universities using funds provided by the Daniels Fund.

See entry 92 for full listing.

IRENE E. AND GEORGE A. DAVIS FOUNDATION [1224]

One Monarch Place
Suite 1300
Springfield, MA 01144-1300
(413) 734-8336
Fax: (413) 734-7845
E-mail: info@davisfdn.org
Web Site: www.davisfdn.org

FOUNDED: 1970

AREAS OF INTEREST:
Community, social services and early education.

TYPE:
Capital grants; Challenge/matching grants; General operating grants; Project/program grants.

PURPOSE:
To make strategically significant investments in organizations and projects that promise demonstrable long-range benefits improving the quality of life of citizens residing in Hampden County, MA.

LEGAL BASIS:
Private foundation.

ELIGIBILITY:
Grants are made to organizations that have tax-exempt status under Section 501(c)(3) of

the Internal Revenue Code. Catholic organizations may apply. No grants are made to individuals.

GEOG. RESTRICTIONS: Hampden County, Massachusetts.

FINANCIAL DATA:
Amount of support per award: Varies.
Total amount of support: Varies.

APPLICATION INFO:
Guidelines and application form are available on the Foundation web site. An initial Letter of Inquiry is required to determine the interest and appropriateness of a full proposal.
Duration: Typically one year.
Deadline: Proposals are accepted throughout the year.

ADDRESS INQUIRIES TO:
See telephone number above.

DEARBORN COMMUNITY FOUNDATION, INC. [1225]

322 Walnut Street
Lawrenceburg, IN 47025
(812) 539-4115
Fax: (812) 539-4119
E-mail: dsedler@dearborncf.org
Web Site: www.dearborncf.org

FOUNDED: 1997

AREAS OF INTEREST:
Art, culture and humanities, community and public benefit, education, environmental and animal protection, and human services and youth.

TYPE:
Capital grants; Challenge/matching grants; Development grants; General operating grants; Project/program grants; Scholarships; Seed money grants; Technical assistance; Training grants.

YEAR PROGRAM STARTED: 1997

PURPOSE:
To connect people who care with causes that improve the quality of life in the community by advancing cultural, educational and social opportunities, while preserving the community's heritage and helping donors create a permanent legacy in Dearborn County, IN.

ELIGIBILITY:
Grants are made to organizations that are tax-exempt under Section 501(c)(3) of the Internal Revenue Code and recognized by the state of Indiana as current and active not-for-profit organizations. No grants are made to individuals outside of scholarships and/or educational grants. Nonsectarian religious programs may apply.

GEOG. RESTRICTIONS: Dearborn County, Indiana.

FINANCIAL DATA:
Amount of support per award: Varies.
Total amount of support: Maximum $100,000.

APPLICATION INFO:
Application information is available on the web site. It is strongly suggested that all applicants consult DCF prior to submitting a grant application to ensure eligibility.
Duration: One year.
Deadline: Varies.

STAFF:
Fred McCarter, Executive Director
Denise Sedler, Program Director

ADDRESS INQUIRIES TO:
Denise Sedler, Program Director
(See address above.)

DELAWARE COUNTY FOUNDATION [1226]

3954 North Hampton Drive
Powell, OH 43065
(614) 764-2332
Fax: (614) 764-2333
E-mail: foundation@delawarecf.org
Web Site: www.delawarecf.org

FOUNDED: 1995

AREAS OF INTEREST:
Arts, civic affairs, community needs, culture, education, environment, health and human services.

NAME(S) OF PROGRAMS:
- **Designated Funds**
- **Donor Advised Funds**
- **Field of Interest Funds**
- **Organizational Endowment Funds**
- **Scholarship Funds**
- **Special Project Funds**
- **Unrestricted Funds**

TYPE:
Scholarships.

PURPOSE:
To enhance the quality of life for Delaware County residents.

ELIGIBILITY:
Grants are made to organizations that have tax-exempt status under Section 501(c)(3) of the Internal Revenue Code that serve Delaware County. No grants are made to individuals, religious programs, political groups or for deficit reduction.

GEOG. RESTRICTIONS: Delaware County, Ohio.

FINANCIAL DATA:
Amount of support per award: $500 to $100,000. Gooding Memorial Scholarships do not exceed $15,000.
Total amount of support: $1,300,000 in grants and scholarships for the year 2015.

NO. AWARDS: 131 grants and 131 scholarships for the year 2015.

APPLICATION INFO:
Information may be obtained from the Foundation web site.
Duration: Typically one year.
Deadline: Scholarships: Mid-April and mid-June. Grants: September 1.

STAFF:
Marlene A. Casini, President and Chief Executive Officer

ROGER L. AND AGNES C. DELL CHARITABLE TRUST [1227]

101 East Fifth Street, EP-MN-S14
St. Paul, MN 55101
(855) 452-4015
Fax: (651) 466-8742
E-mail: charitableservicesgroupmpls@usbank.com

AREAS OF INTEREST:
Arts and culture, education and youth in the Fergus Falls, MN region.

TYPE:
Capital grants; General operating grants; Project/program grants.

PURPOSE:
To improve the quality of life in Fergus Falls, MN and the surrounding area.

ELIGIBILITY:
Eligible organizations must be IRS 501(c)(3) tax-exempt.

GEOG. RESTRICTIONS: Fergus Falls, Minnesota and the surrounding area.

FINANCIAL DATA:
Amount of support per award: Varies.
Total amount of support: Varies.

APPLICATION INFO:
Application should be submitted in writing outlining the nature of the request.
Deadline: Varies.

ADDRESS INQUIRIES TO:
Matt McGovern
Pemberton Sorlie Rufer Kershner PLLP
110 North Mill Street
P.O. Box 866
Fergus Falls, MN 56538-0866

*SPECIAL STIPULATIONS:
Unsolicited proposals not accepted.

DEPAUW UNIVERSITY KEY CLUB INTERNATIONAL BONNER/WRIGHT SCHOLARSHIP [1228]

204 East Seminary Street
Greencastle, IN 46135
(765) 658-4030
(800) 447-2495
Fax: (765) 658-4137
E-mail: jenniecoy@depauw.edu
Web Site: www.keyclub.org

AREAS OF INTEREST:
Leadership and community service.

NAME(S) OF PROGRAMS:
- **Bonner Scholarship**
- **John Ellis Wright Award**

TYPE:
Scholarships.

PURPOSE:
To encourage youth to become actively involved in the community around them.

ELIGIBILITY:
Applicant must be a college-bound graduating high school senior with a grade point average of B or higher and have been an active Key Club member for two years, not serving as International Board member or governor.

Selection is based on academic achievement, commitment to community service, and leadership.

Women, ethnic minorities, and high-need students are encouraged to apply.

GEOG. RESTRICTIONS: United States.

FINANCIAL DATA:
Amount of support per award: Recipient receives $10,000 annual John Ellis Wright award and $2,500 Bonner Scholarship.

CO-OP FUNDING PROGRAMS: Corella and Bertram F. Bonner Foundation.

NO. AWARDS: Bonner Scholarship: 20 new annually; John Ellis Wright Award: 2.

APPLICATION INFO:
No special application is required. Applicants involved in Key Club will be identified via their admissions application.

Duration: Four years.

Deadline: March 1 for early consideration; however, applications will be received until all selections are made.

ADDRESS INQUIRIES TO:
DePauw University Office of Admission
Bonner/Wright Scholarship Program
Greencastle, IN 46135-1778

*SPECIAL STIPULATIONS:
Bonner scholars are expected to maintain good academic standing at DePauw (2.5 grade point average or better), participate in educational and enrichment activities, successfully complete the Bonner Program First-Year Student Seminar, as well as participate in community-service programs for an average of eight hours per week during the school year, and complete two summer internships consisting of 280 hours each.

RICHARD AND HELEN DEVOS FOUNDATION [1229]

P.O. Box 230257
Grand Rapids, MI 49523-0257
(616) 643-4700
Fax: (616) 774-0116

AREAS OF INTEREST:
Christian ministry and outreach and local community support.

TYPE:
General operating grants; Project/program grants.

PURPOSE:
To improve the quality of people's lives and to build a stronger community.

LEGAL BASIS:
Private foundation.

ELIGIBILITY:
Primarily, organizations that have prior affiliation with the family of DeVos and are located in western Michigan. Also, they must have evidence of tax-exempt status as an IRS 501(c)(3) public charity.

GEOG. RESTRICTIONS: Western Michigan.

FINANCIAL DATA:
Amount of support per award: Varies as to need and project.

Total amount of support: Varies.

APPLICATION INFO:
Organizations should submit a statement of purpose and history of organization, budget, sources of support, goals and specifics regarding the program to be funded, and annual report (if available).

Duration: One year. Renewal possible.

Deadline: Proposals are reviewed quarterly.

ADDRESS INQUIRIES TO:
Sue Volkers, Grants Manager
(See address above.)

DICKINSON AREA COMMUNITY FOUNDATION [1230]

333 South Stephenson Avenue
Suite 204
Iron Mountain, MI 49801
(906) 774-3131
Fax: (906) 774-7640
E-mail: dacf@uplogon.com
Web Site: www.
dickinsonareacommunityfoundation.org

FOUNDED: 1995

AREAS OF INTEREST:
Arts, community needs and development, culture, education, environment, health and human services.

TYPE:
Grants-in-aid; Scholarships.

PURPOSE:
To encourage philanthropic investment in Dickinson County and surrounding Wisconsin communities.

LEGAL BASIS:
501(c)(3) tax-exempt organization.

ELIGIBILITY:
Grants are made to organizations that have tax-exempt status under Section 501(c)(3) of the Internal Revenue Code. No grants are made to individuals. Nonsectarian religious programs may apply.

GEOG. RESTRICTIONS: Dickinson County, Michigan and surrounding Wisconsin and Michigan communities.

FINANCIAL DATA:
Amount of support per award: $200 to $5,000.

Total amount of support: Varies.

APPLICATION INFO:
When grants are available, application information is available on the web site.

Scholarship applicants can apply at their local schools.

Duration: One year.

Deadline: Scholaships: March 15. Grants: October 15.

PUBLICATIONS:
Brochures.

ADDRESS INQUIRIES TO:
Tamara Juul, Executive Director
(See address above.)

THE DIXON FOUNDATION [1231]

One Chase Corporate Center
Suite 400
Birmingham, AL 35244-7001
(205) 313-6501
Fax: (205) 313-6502
E-mail: diane@dixon-group.com

FOUNDED: 1986

AREAS OF INTEREST:
Local community.

TYPE:
General operating grants.

PURPOSE:
To support social services in northern Alabama and northern Georgia.

ELIGIBILITY:
Eligible organizations must be IRS 501(c)(3) tax-exempt. No funding to individuals.

GEOG. RESTRICTIONS: Central Alabama and northern Georgia.

FINANCIAL DATA:
Amount of support per award: Varies.

Total amount of support: Up to $50,000.

APPLICATION INFO:
Applicants should send in a brief summary, budget, and copy of IRS 501(c)(3) tax determination letter.

Duration: One year. Grants renewable by reapplication.

ADDRESS INQUIRIES TO:
Diane Gentry, Operations Manager
(See address above.)

THE JEAN AND LOUIS DREYFUS FOUNDATION, INC. [1232]

25 West 43rd Street
Suite 810
New York, NY 10036
(212) 599-1931
Fax: (212) 599-2956
E-mail: jk@jldreyfus.org
Web Site: www.jldreyfus.org

FOUNDED: 1979

AREAS OF INTEREST:
Aging and disadvantaged, arts-in-education, education and literacy, and social services.

TYPE:
Challenge/matching grants; General operating grants; Project/program grants. Funding to direct-service organizations and those projects which will produce systemic change.

PURPOSE:
To enhance the quality of life of New Yorkers, particularly the aging and disadvantaged.

ELIGIBILITY:
Nonprofit 501(c)(3) direct-service organizations focusing on enhancing the quality of life of New Yorkers.

GEOG. RESTRICTIONS: New York City (five boroughs), New York.

FINANCIAL DATA:
Total amount of support: $750,000 in grants for the year 2015.

APPLICATION INFO:
Initially, a one- to two-page letter of inquiry describing the grantee organization and outlining the project in question. Letters should be sent by mail to the attention of Ms. Edmee de M. Firth, Executive Director.

Letters of inquiry from organizations not previously funded are not being accepted at this time.

Duration: One year. Must reapply.

Deadline: Letter of Inquiry: January 15 and July 15.

ADDRESS INQUIRIES TO:
Edmee de M. Firth, Executive Director
(See address above.)

*PLEASE NOTE:
Letters of inquiry from organizations not previously funded are not being accepted at this time.

DULUTH SUPERIOR AREA COMMUNITY FOUNDATION [1233]

222 East Superior Street
Suite 302
Duluth, MN 55802
(218) 726-0232
Fax: (218) 726-0257
E-mail: grantsinfo@dsacommunityfoundation.com
Web Site: www.dsacommunityfoundation.com

FOUNDED: 1982

AREAS OF INTEREST:
Arts, community and economic development, education, environment and human services.

TYPE:
Challenge/matching grants; Development grants; Project/program grants; Scholarships; Seed money grants.

YEAR PROGRAM STARTED: 1983

PURPOSE:
To improve the quality of life in Duluth, Superior and surrounding counties.

LEGAL BASIS:
Community foundation.

ELIGIBILITY:
Eligible organizations must be IRS 501(c)(3) tax-exempt.

GEOG. RESTRICTIONS: Aitkin, Carlton, Cook, Itasca, Koochiching, Lake and St. Louis counties, Minnesota; Ashland, Bayfield and Douglas counties, Wisconsin.

FINANCIAL DATA:
Amount of support per award: Grants: $200 to $50,000.

Total amount of support: Varies.

APPLICATION INFO:
Information regarding the inquiry process is available online.

Duration: Grants: Usually one year. Nonrenewable. Scholarships: One year. Most are renewable.

Deadline: Varies according to program.

PUBLICATIONS:
Elements, newsletter; annual report.

ADDRESS INQUIRIES TO:
See e-mail address above.

THE JOHN G. DUNCAN TRUST [1234]

c/o Wells Fargo Bank, N.A.
1740 Broadway
MAC C7300-493
Denver, CO 80274
(720) 947-6766
Fax: (720) 947-6804
E-mail: kathy.cordova@wellsfargo.com
Web Site: www.wellsfargo.com/privatefoundationgrants/duncan

FOUNDED: 1955

AREAS OF INTEREST:
Animals, environment, culture and humanities, human services, health, education, religion and arts.

TYPE:
Project/program grants.

YEAR PROGRAM STARTED: 1956

PURPOSE:
To support education and health care, including dental care, food, children and youth, social, blind and aging services.

LEGAL BASIS:
Private foundation.

ELIGIBILITY:
501(c)(3) tax-exempt organizations in Colorado may apply. Grants are not made for individuals, general operating expenses, endowments, organizations outside of Colorado, or other grantmaking organizations.

Organizations receiving a grant are not eligible to apply for a grant in the following calendar year.

GEOG. RESTRICTIONS: Colorado.

FINANCIAL DATA:
Amount of support per award: Typically $5,000 to $10,000.

Total amount of support: Approximately $300,000 per year.

APPLICATION INFO:
Proposals should include standard summary and budget information, evidence of tax-exempt status, and written information deemed appropriate by the applicant organizations to be helpful in evaluating their proposal. Mission statement is required. Do not include audio or video materials.

Duration: No grants are made on a continuing basis.

Deadline: The last day of January, April, July and October.

ADDRESS INQUIRIES TO:
Kathy Cordova
(See e-mail address or phone number above.)

*PLEASE NOTE:
The Trust strongly discourages paper applications. If unable to apply online, contact Kathy Cordova at the telephone or e-mail address above.

THE EAST BAY COMMUNITY FOUNDATION [1235]

De Domenico Building
200 Frank H. Ogawa Plaza
Oakland, CA 94612
(510) 836-3223
Fax: (510) 836-7418
E-mail: grantmaking@eastbaycf.org
Web Site: www.ebcf.org

FOUNDED: 1928

AREAS OF INTEREST:
Preparing young people for success in the educational system and providing economic opportunities for the underprivileged and families.

TYPE:
Project/program grants. Building leadership capacity grants.

YEAR PROGRAM STARTED: 1928

PURPOSE:
To transform the lives of people in the East Bay with pressing needs.

LEGAL BASIS:
Public foundation.

ELIGIBILITY:
Eligible organizations must be IRS 501(c)(3) tax-exempt.

GEOG. RESTRICTIONS: Alameda and Contra Costa counties, California.

FINANCIAL DATA:
Amount of support per award: Varies.

Total amount of support: Approximately $1,000,000 annually.

APPLICATION INFO:
Guidelines and application are available online.

Duration: Varies.

PUBLICATIONS:
Guidelines.

EAST TEXAS COMMUNITIES FOUNDATION [1236]

315 North Broadway Avenue
Suite 210
Tyler, TX 75702-5712
(903) 533-0208
Fax: (903) 533-0258
E-mail: mlsmith@etcf.org
Web Site: www.etcf.org

FOUNDED: 1989

AREAS OF INTEREST:
Community development.

TYPE:
Grants-in-aid; Scholarships. The Foundation administers scholarship funds for donors, nonprofit organizations, civic clubs, service groups and businesses.

PURPOSE:
To promote charitable giving which enhances the quality of life for the people of east Texas.

ELIGIBILITY:
Grants are made to 501(c)(3) organizations. Scholarship applicants must be citizens or permanent residents of the U.S.

GEOG. RESTRICTIONS: East Texas.

FINANCIAL DATA:
Amount of support per award: Varies.

Total amount of support: Varies.

APPLICATION INFO:
Application information is available on the web site. Scholarship applications must be submitted electronically.

Duration: Varies.

Deadline: Varies.

ADDRESS INQUIRIES TO:
Mary Lynn Smith, Program Officer
(See address above.)

EAU CLAIRE COMMUNITY FOUNDATION [1237]

306 South Barstow Street, Suite 104
Eau Claire, WI 54701
(715) 552-3801
Fax: (715) 552-3802
E-mail: info@eccommunityfoundation.org
Web Site: www.eccommunityfoundation.org

FOUNDED: 1997

AREAS OF INTEREST:
Serving the charitable needs of the Eau Claire, WI area.

TYPE:
Project/program grants.

YEAR PROGRAM STARTED: 1997

PURPOSE:
To strengthen our community by offering donors opportunities to establish charitable legacies, by making grants, and by serving as a catalyst to address community needs.

LEGAL BASIS:
Nonprofit community foundation.

ELIGIBILITY:
Eligible organizations must have 501(c)(3) status. Grants are available to religious organizations when recipients of services are not required to profess membership or belief in the religious organization.

GEOG. RESTRICTIONS: Eau Claire County, Wisconsin.

FINANCIAL DATA:
Amount of support per award: Varies.
Total amount of support: $528,000 for the year 2015.

NO. MOST RECENT APPLICANTS: 60 for the year 2014.

NO. AWARDS: 40 for the year 2014.

REPRESENTATIVE AWARDS:
$1,500 to Literacy Volunteers-Chippewa Valley.

APPLICATION INFO:
Application must be submitted online.
Duration: One year.
Deadline: February 1.

STAFF:
Sue Bornick, Executive Director

ADDRESS INQUIRIES TO:
Sue Bornick, Executive Director
(See address above.)

ECOLAB FOUNDATION [1238]

370 North Wabasha Street, EUC/12
St. Paul, MN 55102
(651) 293-2923
Fax: (651) 225-3191
E-mail: ecolabfoundation@ecolab.com
Web Site: www.ecolab.com

FOUNDED: 1986

AREAS OF INTEREST:
Arts and culture, youth and education, environment and conservation, and civic and community development.

CONSULTING OR VOLUNTEER SERVICES:
501(c)(3) organizations.

TYPE:
General operating grants; Project/program grants. Employee matching gifts.

YEAR PROGRAM STARTED: 1986

PURPOSE:
To enrich the quality of life in communities where Ecolab operates.

LEGAL BASIS:
Corporate foundation.

ELIGIBILITY:
Eligible organizations must be IRS 501(c)(3) tax-exempt.

GEOG. RESTRICTIONS: City of Industry, California; McDonough, Georgia; Elk Grove Village, Joliet and Naperville, Illinois; Huntington, Indiana; Garyville, Louisiana; St. Paul, Minnesota; Columbus, Mississippi; Greensboro, North Carolina; Ellwood City, Pennsylvania; Corsicana, Fort Worth, Garland and Sugar Land, Texas; Martinsburg, West Virginia; and Beloit, Wisconsin.

FINANCIAL DATA:
Amount of support per award: $5,000 to $60,000.
Total amount of support: $10,564,500 total giving for the year 2014.
Matching fund requirements: Must be an Ecolab employee.

NO. MOST RECENT APPLICANTS: 300.

NO. AWARDS: 200.

APPLICATION INFO:
Application form is available online.
Duration: One year.
Deadline: December 1.

PUBLICATIONS:
Guidelines (on web site).

ADDRESS INQUIRIES TO:
Lisa Maloney-Vinz
Community Relations Program Manager
(See address above.)

EL PASO COMMUNITY FOUNDATION [1239]

333 North Oregon Street
2nd Floor
El Paso, TX 79901
(915) 533-4020
Fax: (915) 532-0716
E-mail: info@epcf.org
Web Site: www.epcf.org

FOUNDED: 1977

AREAS OF INTEREST:
Arts and humanities, education, economic development, health and disabilities, environment and animals, and human services.

TYPE:
General operating grants; Scholarships. A charitable fund established at the Foundation by individuals, corporations or organizations.

YEAR PROGRAM STARTED: 1972

PURPOSE:
To improve the quality of life in the El Paso region, TX.

LEGAL BASIS:
Permanent endowment.

ELIGIBILITY:
Grant request will be considered only from 501(c)(3) agencies located within or offering services to the community which includes far west Texas, southern New Mexico and northern Chihuahua, Mexico. Grants are not made to individuals or religious organizations.

GEOG. RESTRICTIONS: Far west Texas, southern New Mexico and northern Chihuahua, Mexico.

FINANCIAL DATA:
Amount of support per award: $4,000 to $40,000.
Total amount of support: $9,465,849 for the year 2014.

APPLICATION INFO:
The Foundation utilizes an online application process.
Duration: One year.
Deadline: Grants: February 1 and August 1.

ADDRESS INQUIRIES TO:
Bonita Johnson, Grants Manager
(See address above.)

FRED L. EMERSON FOUNDATION, INC. [1240]

5654 South Street Road
Auburn, NY 13021
(315) 253-9621
Fax: (315) 253-5235
E-mail: info@emersonfoundation.com
Web Site: www.emersonfoundation.com

FOUNDED: 1932

AREAS OF INTEREST:
Education (primarily private higher education), hospital and health programs, community agencies, cultural institutions, youth and community service programs, and social welfare agencies.

TYPE:
Capital grants; Challenge/matching grants; Endowments; Project/program grants; Research grants.

PURPOSE:
To improve the quality of life in Auburn, Cayuga County and upstate New York.

ELIGIBILITY:
Organizations must be tax-exempt. No grants are made to individuals or for-profit organizations. No sponsorship of fund-raising events or political activities. Proposals seeking support solely for recurring operating expenses of an organization are strongly discouraged.

GEOG. RESTRICTIONS: Focus on upstate New York with a concentration in the community of Auburn, Cayuga County and the surrounding region.

FINANCIAL DATA:
Amount of support per award: Varies.
Total amount of support: $3,407,783.86 for the year 2014.

APPLICATION INFO:
All proposals submitted for consideration must include the Emerson Foundation Grant Proposal Submission Form, which is available on the Foundation web site.
Duration: Varies.
Deadline: Proposals are accepted on an ongoing basis.

PUBLICATIONS:
Guidelines.

ADDRESS INQUIRIES TO:
Daniel J. Fessenden
Executive Director and Secretary
(See address above.)

ENTERPRISE COMMUNITY PARTNERS

334 Boylston Street, Suite 400
Boston, MA 02116
(781) 235-2006
(781) 591-4702
Fax: (781) 235-4011
E-mail: rosefellowship@enterprisecommunity.org
Web Site: www.enterprisecommunity.org

TYPE:
Fellowships.

See entry 403 for full listing.

ESSEX COUNTY COMMUNITY FOUNDATION [1241]

175 Andover Street
Suite 101
Danvers, MA 01923
(978) 777-8876 ext. 28
Fax: (978) 777-9454
E-mail: j.bishop@eccf.org
Web Site: www.eccf.org

FOUNDED: 1999

AREAS OF INTEREST:
Arts and culture, education, environment, health, social and community services and youth services.

CONSULTING OR VOLUNTEER SERVICES:
Nonprofit organizations in Essex County, MA.

NAME(S) OF PROGRAMS:
- **Emergency Fund**
- **First Jobs Fund**
- **Fund for Nonprofit Excellence**
- **Greater Lawrence Summer Fund**
- **Hardscrabble Education Fund**
- **The Hunger Relief Project**
- **Institute for Trustees**
- **Merrimack Valley General Fund**
- **North Shore Community Health Network**
- **Webster Family Fund**
- **The Women's Fund of Essex County**

TYPE:
Capital grants; Conferences/seminars; Endowments; General operating grants; Project/program grants; Scholarships; Technical assistance. Capacity-building grants. Various grantmaking funds. Mostly project/program grants. Agencies can establish endowment funds.

The Foundation has eight competitive grant funds and 25 scholarship programs. There are 120 donor-advised funds.

YEAR PROGRAM STARTED: 1999

PURPOSE:
To promote local philanthropy and to strengthen the nonprofit organizations of Essex County.

LEGAL BASIS:
Public 501(c)(3) charity.

ELIGIBILITY:
Organizations offering programs and services in Essex County (MA) communities, recognized as tax-exempt under Section 501(c)(3) of the Internal Revenue Code and, in some cases, to agencies of local or state government. Organizations with a qualified fiscal sponsor are also considered.

GEOG. RESTRICTIONS: Primarily Essex County, Massachusetts.

FINANCIAL DATA:
Approximately $40,000,000 in assets under management.

Amount of support per award: $2,000 to $20,000 for competitive grants; donor-advised funds may award larger grants.

Total amount of support: $4,400,000 for fiscal year 2015.

NO. AWARDS: 571 for fiscal year 2013.

REPRESENTATIVE AWARDS:
$9,000 to Elder Services of the Merrimack Valley, Inc., to support the financial literacy education program for elderly Spanish-speaking women; $15,000 to Pingree School, to support Prep@Pingree, an academic summer enrichment program for inner-city middle school students, to help sharpen their analytical, verbal and written skills.

APPLICATION INFO:
Application information for grants is available on the web site. Scholarship applicants should inquire at their local school.

Duration: Up to three years, depending on fund.

Deadline: Varies.

PUBLICATIONS:
Annual report; newsletter; brochure.

IRS I.D.: 04-3407816

STAFF:
Dave Edwards, President and Chief Executive Officer

ADDRESS INQUIRIES TO:
Julie Bishop, Vice President for Philanthropy
(See address above.)

FAIR OAKS FOUNDATION [1242]

726 Bell Avenue, Suite 301
Carnegie, PA 15106
(412) 456-4418
Fax: (412) 456-4436
E-mail: rhoover@ampcopgh.com

AREAS OF INTEREST:
United Way, universities and community funds.

TYPE:
Cash contributions.

PURPOSE:
To provide support for community funds and higher education.

ELIGIBILITY:
Organizations classified as 501(c)(3) by the IRS can apply. No grants to individuals.

GEOG. RESTRICTIONS: United States.

FINANCIAL DATA:
Amount of support per award: $250 to $1,000.

Total amount of support: $400,000 per year.

APPLICATION INFO:
Request should be in letter format.

Deadline: November 1.

ADDRESS INQUIRIES TO:
Rose Hoover, Secretary, Vice President and Trustee
(See address above.)

SAMUEL S. FELS FUND [1243]

1528 Walnut Street
Suite 1002
Philadelphia, PA 19102
(215) 731-9455
Fax: (215) 731-9457
E-mail: shanell@samfels.org
Web Site: www.samfels.org

FOUNDED: 1935

AREAS OF INTEREST:
Public education, community services and arts.

NAME(S) OF PROGRAMS:
- **Arts**
- **Community**
- **Education**
- **Internships in Community Service**
- **Memberships**

TYPE:
General operating grants; Project/program grants.

YEAR PROGRAM STARTED: 1936

PURPOSE:
To initiate and assist any activities or projects of a scientific, educational or charitable nature which tend to improve human daily life; to bring to the average person greater health, happiness, and a fuller understanding of the meaning and purposes of life.

LEGAL BASIS:
Private foundation.

ELIGIBILITY:
Applicants must be agencies located in the city of Philadelphia. Excluded from the Fund's program of grants are contributions to national organizations, capital campaigns, general support, scholarships, fellowships and grants-in-aid for travel, research and publication, or grants to individual day care or afterschool programs. No grants are made to individuals.

GEOG. RESTRICTIONS: Philadelphia, Pennsylvania.

FINANCIAL DATA:
Amount of support per award: $3,000 to $30,000.

Total amount of support: Approximately $3,000,000 for the year 2015.

NO. MOST RECENT APPLICANTS: Approximately 500.

NO. AWARDS: Approximately 200.

APPLICATION INFO:
Guidelines are available on the web site.

Duration: Primarily one year.

PUBLICATIONS:
Annual report; guidelines for applicants.

TRUSTEES:
Beverly Coleman, Chairperson
Sarah Martinez-Helfman, President
John H. Rice, Vice President
Pari Hashemi, Treasurer
Ida K. Chen
Helen Cunningham
Sandra Featherman
Gabriel Mandujano
Len Rieser
David H. Wice

STAFF:
Tim Murray, Grants Administrator

ADDRESS INQUIRIES TO:
Sarah Martinez-Helfman, President
(See telephone number above.)

FIRST HORIZON NATIONAL CORPORATION [1244]

P.O. Box 84
Memphis, TN 38101-0084
(901) 523-4444
(901) 523-4112
Fax: (901) 523-4354
E-mail: foundation@firsttennessee.com
Web Site: www.firsttennesseefoundation.com

FOUNDED: 1864

AREAS OF INTEREST:
Financial literacy and economic development, education and helping youth, health and human services, and arts and culture.

TYPE:
Capital grants; Challenge/matching grants; Development grants; General operating grants; Matching gifts; Project/program grants; Research grants; Scholarships.

YEAR PROGRAM STARTED: 1993

PURPOSE:
To generate economic development in core market; to preserve and enhance what is special about core market and its communities; to leverage additional resources for the community.

LEGAL BASIS:
Corporate contributions program.

ELIGIBILITY:
Grants are made to 501(c)(3) tax-exempt organizations whose activities meet the objectives outlined above. First Horizon National Corp. does not use corporate contributions to support individuals, charities sponsored solely by a single civic organization, charities which redistribute funds to other charitable organizations, except in the case of recognized united fund-type organizations, bank "clearing-house" organizations, agencies supported by United Way or united arts funds, religious, veteran, social, athletic or fraternal organizations, political organizations or those having the primary purpose of influencing legislation or promoting a particular ideological point of view, trips and tours, operating budget deficits, multiyear commitments of four years or more and/or endowments.

Grants are limited to communities where First Horizon National Corp. has a presence.

FINANCIAL DATA:
Amount of support per award: $1,000 and up.

Total amount of support: Approximately $5,000,000 annually.

APPLICATION INFO:
Details available on the web site.

Duration: Typically one year. Funding is not automatically renewed. Recipients desiring continued support should submit a request for review in the fall.

Deadline: December 1 prior to the year for which funds are being requested.

PUBLICATIONS:
Program guidelines and application procedures.

STAFF:
Alana Hu, Community Investment Manager, First Tennessee Foundation

ADDRESS INQUIRIES TO:
Alana Hu, Community Investment Manager
First Tennessee Foundation
(See address above.)

*PLEASE NOTE:
Impact reports are required following receipt of grants.

*SPECIAL STIPULATIONS:
Grants are limited to communities served by First Horizon National Corp.

THE FLINN FOUNDATION

1802 North Central Avenue
Phoenix, AZ 85004
(602) 744-6800
Fax: (602) 744-6815
E-mail: info@flinn.org
Web Site: www.flinn.org

TYPE:
Demonstration grants; Fellowships; Project/program grants; Scholarships; Seed money grants. The arts and culture grants program assists Arizona's large arts and culture organizations in generating capital through creative programming and fiscal planning.

The Foundation's biosciences grant projects aim to strengthen Arizona's biosciences infrastructure and thereby improve the state's capacity to compete nationally and internationally in the biosciences economy.

The Arizona Center for Civic Leadership seeks to strengthen civic leadership in Arizona.

The Flinn Scholars Program annually awards top Arizona high school graduates full scholarship support.

See entry 126 for full listing.

THE FOUNDATION FOR ENHANCING COMMUNITIES [1245]

200 North Third Street, 8th Floor
Harrisburg, PA 17108
(717) 236-5040
Fax: (717) 231-4463
E-mail: info@tfec.org
Web Site: www.tfec.org

FOUNDED: 1920

AREAS OF INTEREST:
Education, human services, arts and culture, children and youth, environment and community development.

CONSULTING OR VOLUNTEER SERVICES:
Consulting services available.

NAME(S) OF PROGRAMS:
- **Parents & Partners**
- **Women's Fund**

TYPE:
Challenge/matching grants; Conferences/seminars; Endowments; Internships; Matching gifts; Project/program grants; Scholarships; Seed money grants; Technical assistance. Management services.

YEAR PROGRAM STARTED: 1920

PURPOSE:
To stimulate philanthropy and enhance the quality of life in the community through accumulating, managing and disbursing financial assets and by serving as a catalyst and neutral convener to meet a wide range of community needs in south central Pennsylvania counties of Cumberland, Dauphin, Franklin, Lebanon and Perry.

LEGAL BASIS:
Community foundation.

ELIGIBILITY:
Eligible organizations must have 501(c)(3) status. No grants are made to individuals or religious organizations for religious purposes.

GEOG. RESTRICTIONS: Cumberland, Dauphin, Franklin, Lebanon and Perry counties, Pennsylvania.

FINANCIAL DATA:
Assets of $72,703,142 for the year ended December 31, 2015.

Amount of support per award: $2,000 average.

Total amount of support: $4,615,801 for the year ended December 31, 2015.

NO. AWARDS: 1,841.

APPLICATION INFO:
Applicants should:
(1) review the grantmaking guidelines for each regional foundation;
(2) contact the Program Officer to determine eligibility to apply and discuss the proposal and;
(3) submit a grant application according to the guidelines provided on the Foundation's web site.

Duration: One year. Nonrenewable.

PUBLICATIONS:
Annual report.

IRS I.D.: 01-0564355

STAFF:
Janice R. Black, President and Chief Executive Officer
Kirk C. Demyan, Chief Financial Officer
Jennifer Kuntch, Communications Officer
Jennifer Strechay, Program Officer for Community Investment
Allison Moesta, Asset Development and Scholarship Officer
Deborah Fulham-Winston, Asset Development Associate and Project Officer
Jennifer Doyle, Director of Development and Community Investment
Leslie Fick, Program Manager for Parents & Partners
Jeanne Predmore, Program Manager for Parents & Partners
Jim Martin, Senior Financial Services Associate
Brandon Tressler, Financial Services Associate
Faith Elmes, Scholarship Associate

ADDRESS INQUIRIES TO:
Director of Development and Community Investment
(See address above.)

*SPECIAL STIPULATIONS:
All discretionary grants must be awarded in the five-county region of Cumberland, Dauphin, Franklin, Lebanon and Perry counties.

FOUNDATION FOR THE CAROLINAS [1246]

220 North Tryon Street
Charlotte, NC 28202
(704) 973-4500
(704) 973-4556
(800) 973-7244
Fax: (704) 973-7244
E-mail: bcollier@fftc.org
Web Site: www.fftc.org

FOUNDED: 1958

AREAS OF INTEREST:
Education, human services, health and medical research, arts, environment and historical preservation, youth, senior programs and social capital.

TYPE:
Demonstration grants; General operating grants; Project/program grants; Scholarships; Seed money grants.

YEAR PROGRAM STARTED: 1958

PURPOSE:
To advance philanthropy by serving donors, increasing charitable giving and improving communities in its area of service.

LEGAL BASIS:
Community foundation.

ELIGIBILITY:
Grants will be made only to organizations recognized by the IRS as 501(c)(3) in the greater Charlotte area.

The Foundation generally does not fund capital campaigns and buildings, computers, vehicles and similar equipment, publication of books and production of videos, conferences and travel, grants to individuals or endowment funds.

GEOG. RESTRICTIONS: Greater Charlotte, 13-county region in North and South Carolina.

FINANCIAL DATA:
Amount of support per award: $2,500 to $100,000.
Total amount of support: $69,400,000 for the year 2015.

APPLICATION INFO:
Contact the Foundation.
Duration: One year.
Deadline: Varies.

BOARD OF DIRECTORS:
Chris Kearney, Chairperson
Kendall Alley
Gwin Barr
Catherine P. Bessant
Jesse Cureton
Al de Molina
Lynn Good
Venessa Harrison
Barnes Hauptfuhrer
Jewell D. Hoover
James Johnston
Howard Levine
Todd Mansfield
Fritz Nauck
Kevin Roche
Art Rogers
Geri Rucker
Lynne Scott Safrit

ADDRESS INQUIRIES TO:
Brian Collier, Executive Vice President
(See address above.)

FOUNDATION FOR THE MID SOUTH [1247]

134 East Amite Street
Jackson, MS 39201
(601) 355-8167
Fax: (601) 355-6499
E-mail: iallen@fndmidsouth.org
Web Site: www.fndmidsouth.org

FOUNDED: 1989

AREAS OF INTEREST:
Improving the quality of life for residents in the states of Arkansas, Louisiana and Mississippi, with a primary focus on education, community development, health and wellness, and wealth building.

NAME(S) OF PROGRAMS:
- **Community Development**
- **Education**
- **Health & Wellness**
- **Wealth Building**

TYPE:
Conferences/seminars; Fellowships; General operating grants; Internships; Training grants.

PURPOSE:
To nurture families and children; to improve schools; to build the economy for all people in the region.

ELIGIBILITY:
Applicants must be tax-exempt organizations under Section 501(c)(3) of the Internal Revenue Code.

GEOG. RESTRICTIONS: Arkansas, Louisiana and Mississippi.

FINANCIAL DATA:
Amount of support per award: Varies.
Total amount of support: Varies.

APPLICATION INFO:
The Foundation has an internal process for identifying and selecting grantees. Unsolicited grant proposals, inquiries or letters of intent are not accepted.
Duration: One to three years.
Deadline: Varies.

FOUNDATION FOR THE TRI-STATE COMMUNITY, INC. [1248]

855 Central Avenue
Suite 300
Ashland, KY 41101
(606) 324-3888
Fax: (606) 324-5961
E-mail: mwwiseman@tristatefoundation.org
Web Site: www.tristatefoundation.org

FOUNDED: 1972

AREAS OF INTEREST:
Arts and cultural programs, education, science and charity.

NAME(S) OF PROGRAMS:
- **21st Century Endowment Fund**

TYPE:
Challenge/matching grants; Project/program grants; Scholarships; Seed money grants; Technical assistance.

YEAR PROGRAM STARTED: 1980

PURPOSE:
To improve the quality of life in the tri-state area by encouraging, raising, administering and distributing gifts for charitable, cultural, educational and scientific purposes.

LEGAL BASIS:
Community foundation.

ELIGIBILITY:
Priority will be given to organizations which are 501(c)(3) and other organizations that meet the Foundation's special charitable grant guidelines. The Foundation does not fund sectarian activities or individuals.

GEOG. RESTRICTIONS: Boyd and Greenup counties, Kentucky; Lawrence County, Ohio; Cabell and Wayne counties, West Virginia.

FINANCIAL DATA:
Amount of support per award: $500 to $5,000.
Total amount of support: Typically, around $15,000 per quarter.

NO. AWARDS: 24 for the year 2015.

REPRESENTATIVE AWARDS:
$3,000 to River Valley Child Development Center to aid in the construction of a new playground for children six weeks to two years old; $3,000 to Greater Huntington Park and Recreation District to purchase cordless microphones; $3,000 to Southern Hills Garden Club to help create a permanent, interactive education exhibit in the Highlands Museum and Discovery Center's Science area.

APPLICATION INFO:
Contact Foundation for grant application and to discuss proposed project.
Duration: One-time award. Applicants may reapply after a one-year period.
Deadline: January 15, April 15, July 15 and October 15.

PUBLICATIONS:
Annual report; *How We've Grown*; grant guidelines; 35th anniversary report.

IRS I.D.: 61-0729266

STAFF:
Mary Witten Wiseman, President
Kathryn Davis Lamp, Vice President

ADDRESS INQUIRIES TO:
Mary Witten Wiseman, President
(See address above.)

THE FREMONT AREA COMMUNITY FOUNDATION [1249]

4424 West 48th Street
Fremont, MI 49412
(231) 924-5350
Fax: (231) 924-5391
E-mail: info@facommunityfoundation.org
Web Site: www.facommunityfoundation.org

FOUNDED: 1933

AREAS OF INTEREST:
Arts and culture, children, community and economic development, community health, education, environment and natural resources, family and youth.

TYPE:
Challenge/matching grants; Project/program grants.

YEAR PROGRAM STARTED: 1951

PURPOSE:
To bring community development to life in Newaygo County.

LEGAL BASIS:
Public community foundation.

ELIGIBILITY:
Eligible organizations must be IRS 501(c)(3) tax-exempt.

GEOG. RESTRICTIONS: Newaygo County, Michigan.

FINANCIAL DATA:
Total assets of $225,000,000 for the year 2017.
Amount of support per award: Varies.
Total amount of support: $8,295,577 in grants and $762,750 in scholarships for the year 2017.

APPLICATION INFO:
Applications are available from the Foundation and must include a copy of the IRS tax determination letter.
Duration: One year. Renewal by reapplication.
Deadline: General community grants: February 1 and September 1.

STAFF:
Carla A. Roberts, President and Chief Executive Officer

ADDRESS INQUIRIES TO:
Carla A. Roberts
President and Chief Executive Officer
(See address above.)

THE FRIST FOUNDATION [1250]

3100 West End Avenue, Suite 1200
Nashville, TN 37203
(615) 292-3868
Fax: (615) 292-5843
E-mail: askfrist@fristfoundation.org
Web Site: www.fristfoundation.org

FOUNDED: 1982

AREAS OF INTEREST:
Health, human services, education, technology, civic affairs and the arts.

NAME(S) OF PROGRAMS:
- **The Frist Foundation Awards of Achievement**
- **The Frist Foundation Technology Grants Program**

TYPE:
Capital grants; General operating grants; Project/program grants; Technical assistance. The Foundation makes direct grants to tax-exempt organizations in the greater Nashville area in the fields of health, human services, education, civic affairs and the arts, with a special emphasis on vulnerable populations.

In addition to conducting a grantmaking program responsive to external requests, the Frist Foundation actively seeks out and initiates programs addressing particular needs. Among these programs are the Center for Nonprofit Management, a community-wide effort to provide specialized management training and consulting to nonprofit community organizations.

Operating grants are given to organizations that offer management assistance, training, volunteers, goods or services to large numbers of Nashville agencies.

YEAR PROGRAM STARTED: 1983

PURPOSE:
To invest its resources in selected not-for-profit organizations in the greater Nashville area in ways that strengthen their ability to provide services; to enhance unique community assets in Nashville; to develop new sources of revenue through social enterprise.

LEGAL BASIS:
509(a) private foundation.

ELIGIBILITY:
Grantees must be tax-exempt under Section 501(c)(3) of the Internal Revenue Code and not private foundations as described in Section 509(a). The Foundation ordinarily does not make grants or provide support to:
(1) international, regional or local organizations outside the Nashville area;
(2) projects, programs or organizations that serve a limited audience or a relatively small number of people;
(3) hospitals, biomedical or clinical research, or disease-specific organizations seeking support for national projects and programs;
(4) organizations during their first three years of operation;
(5) endowments;
(6) social events, fund-raising activities or telethons;
(7) individuals or their projects;
(8) political activities;
(9) religious organizations for religious purposes;
(10) private foundations;
(11) advertising sponsorships or;
(12) schools below the college level, except for projects intended to serve the broader community.

Special emphasis is placed on organizations that provide services to vulnerable populations.

GEOG. RESTRICTIONS: Nashville, Tennessee area.

FINANCIAL DATA:
Amount of support per award: $500 to $100,000. Average $3,500.

Total amount of support: $10,287,040 for the year 2015.

NO. MOST RECENT APPLICANTS: 347 for the year 2015.

NO. AWARDS: 250 for the year 2015.

APPLICATION INFO:
If an organization wishes to apply for support, it should make contact by phone, by letter of inquiry, or by completing an application through the web site. If applying by mail, the letter should describe in no more than two pages:
(1) the organization and its record of accomplishment;
(2) the objectives of the program to be funded and whom it would benefit;
(3) the amount sought from the Foundation in relation to the total need;
(4) exactly how Foundation funds would be used and;
(5) the proposed method to evaluate the program's success.

The initial inquiry should also include an annual report, if available, and a copy of the IRS letter confirming that the organization is tax-exempt under Section 501(c)(3) of the Internal Revenue Code and not a private foundation as described in Section 509(a).

Duration: Up to three years. Renewals are not automatic. Applications from organizations supported in the past will be considered new requests.

IRS I.D.: 62-1134070

STAFF:
Peter F. Bird, Jr., President and Chief Executive Officer
Colette R. Easter, Treasurer
Barbara W. Baker, Program Assistant and Corporate Secretary

DIRECTORS:
Thomas F. Frist, Jr., Chairman
Peter F. Bird, Jr.
Frank F. Drowota, III
Patricia Frist Elcan
Patricia C. Frist
Thomas F. Frist, III
William R. Frist
Kenneth L. Roberts

ADDRESS INQUIRIES TO:
Peter F. Bird, Jr.
President and Chief Executive Officer
(See address above.)

THE GIFFORD FOUNDATION [1251]

100 Clinton Square
126 North Salina Street, 3rd Floor
Syracuse, NY 13202
(315) 474-2489
Fax: (315) 475-4983
E-mail: contact@giffordfoundation.org
dirk@giffordfoundation.org
Web Site: www.giffordfoundation.org

FOUNDED: 1954

AREAS OF INTEREST:
Youth development, education and job readiness, and capacity building.

TYPE:
Challenge/matching grants; Conferences/seminars; Demonstration grants; Development grants; General operating grants; Project/program grants; Research grants; Seed money grants; Training grants.

YEAR PROGRAM STARTED: 1954

PURPOSE:
To provide funds for general charitable purposes.

LEGAL BASIS:
Private.

ELIGIBILITY:
Only tax-exempt organizations may apply. Organizations must show evidence of problems to be solved and how proposed solution will benefit constituency and the community. No grants to individuals.

FINANCIAL DATA:
Amount of support per award: Varies.

Total amount of support: Varies.

APPLICATION INFO:
Application information is available on the web site.

Duration: One year.

PUBLICATIONS:
Application guidelines; statement of policies; mission statement.

STAFF:
Dirk E. Sonneborn, Executive Director
Lindsay McClung, Director of Community Grantmaking
Sheena Solomon, Director of Neighborhood Initiatives
Heidi Holtz, Director of Projects and Research

ADDRESS INQUIRIES TO:
Lindsay McClung
Director of Community Grantmaking
(See address above.)

LISA AND DOUGLAS GOLDMAN FUND [1252]

One Montgomery Street, Suite 3440
San Francisco, CA 94104
(415) 771-1717
E-mail: grantsmanager@ldgfund.org
Web Site: www.ldgfund.org

FOUNDED: 1992

AREAS OF INTEREST:
Jewish affairs, environment, democracy and civil liberties, health and recreation, literacy and education, and reproductive health and rights.

TYPE:
Capital grants; Project/program grants.

YEAR PROGRAM STARTED: 1992

PURPOSE:
To improve the quality of life, primarily in San Francisco.

LEGAL BASIS:
Private foundation.

ELIGIBILITY:
Eligible organizations must be IRS 501(c)(3) tax-exempt.

GEOG. RESTRICTIONS: Primarily San Francisco area, California.

FINANCIAL DATA:
Amount of support per award: $10,000 to $150,000.

Total amount of support: Generally $10,000,000.

APPLICATION INFO:
Online application process. Applicants must include a copy of the IRS tax determination letter. Letter of inquiry must be submitted before proposal.

Duration: Varies.

PUBLICATIONS:
Annual report; application guidelines.

ADDRESS INQUIRIES TO:
See e-mail address above.

GOLDSEKER FOUNDATION [1253]

1040 Park Avenue
Suite 310
Baltimore, MD 21201
(410) 837-5100
Fax: (410) 837-7927
E-mail: terri@goldsekerfoundation.org
Web Site: www.goldsekerfoundation.org

FOUNDED: 1973

AREAS OF INTEREST:
Community development and the nonprofit sector.

TYPE:
Challenge/matching grants; General operating grants; Matching gifts; Project/program grants; Technical assistance. Project grants and ongoing operating support.

The Foundation maintains a two-track grantmaking program that designates two priority areas, but retains the ability to initiate and respond to new ideas and opportunities within established program areas, namely community affairs, education, and human services. In each of the priority grant areas - community development and the nonprofit sector - the Foundation is a directly engaged and active partner. Grants include a mix of Foundation initiatives and projects submitted independently by potential grantees.

YEAR PROGRAM STARTED: 1976

PURPOSE:
To support programs which directly benefit the people of the Baltimore metropolitan area.

LEGAL BASIS:
Private, nonprofit.

ELIGIBILITY:
Qualified nonprofit, charitable and educational organizations as defined under federal and state laws as permissible grantees of private foundations. Support is limited to institutions in the Baltimore metropolitan area with special emphasis on disadvantaged persons, giving priority to programs intended to assist children and families and to strengthen neighborhoods.

No support for endowment, capital, deficits, annual giving, publications, religious purposes, arts and culture, specific diseases or disabilities or projects typically supported with public funds.

GEOG. RESTRICTIONS: Metropolitan Baltimore, Maryland.

FINANCIAL DATA:
No distribution in any calendar year to any single institution is to exceed five percent of the Foundation's net income for that year.

Amount of support per award: $1,500 to $205,000 for the year 2015.

Total amount of support: $4,100,000 for the year 2015.

Matching fund requirements: Varies with specific request.

NO. MOST RECENT APPLICANTS: 204 requests received in 2015.

NO. AWARDS: 123 approved in 2015.

REPRESENTATIVE AWARDS:
$75,000 to Impact Hub Baltimore; $115,000 to Southwest Partnership; $170,000 to Strong City Baltimore.

APPLICATION INFO:
Preliminary proposals submitted should include details as outlined in the Annual Report, available upon request. Program guidelines also available, and phone calls are welcomed.

Duration: Typically one year. Occasional multiyear grants.

Deadline: February 1, May 1 and September 1.

PUBLICATIONS:
Annual report; program guidelines.

IRS I.D.: 52-0983502

OFFICERS:
Sheldon Goldseker, Chairman
Simon Goldseker, Vice Chairman
Matthew D. Gallagher, President and Chief Executive Officer
Sheila L. Purkey, Vice President, Secretary, Treasurer, Controller

STAFF:
Laurie Latuda Kinkel, Program Officer

BOARD OF DIRECTORS:
Ana Goldseker
Deby Goldseker
Sharna Goldseker
Sheldon Goldseker
Simon Goldseker
Susan B. Katzenberg
Howard M. Weiss

ADDRESS INQUIRIES TO:
Program Officer
(See address above.)

*SPECIAL STIPULATIONS:
Grantmaking is limited to the metropolitan area of Baltimore, MD.

THE GRACO FOUNDATION [1254]

3501 North 4th Avenue
Sioux Falls, SD 57104
(605) 333-6767
Fax: (605) 333-4979
E-mail: kklee@graco.com
Web Site: www.graco.com

FOUNDED: 1956

AREAS OF INTEREST:
Education, workforce development, youth development and civic projects.

CONSULTING OR VOLUNTEER SERVICES:
Through established community programs.

NAME(S) OF PROGRAMS:
- **Financial Grants of Support**

TYPE:
Capital grants; Development grants; Scholarships. Grants for a variety of local programs concerning education and social problems. Emphasis is on support of local community programs.

YEAR PROGRAM STARTED: 1956

PURPOSE:
To provide financial support to well-screened and -evaluated community programs for making the community a better place in which to live.

LEGAL BASIS:
Established under the Minnesota Nonprofit Corporation Act as a nonprofit corporation under the provisions of Chapter 317, Minnesota Statutes 1953 and Acts amendatory thereof.

ELIGIBILITY:
Accredited institutions of higher education and other nonprofit organizations which have been validated by the IRS as charitable organizations under 501(c)(3) and not a private foundation as defined in 509(a) are eligible to apply. Must be located near Graco facilities. No grants are awarded to individuals or to churches and schools of religion.

FINANCIAL DATA:
Amount of support per award: Varies.

Total amount of support: $950,000 for the year 2015.

Matching fund requirements: Limited to educational institutions.

REPRESENTATIVE AWARDS:
$5,000 to Minneapolis Riverfront Corporation; $10,000 to Dunwoody College of Technology; $6,000 to FIRST Robotics.

APPLICATION INFO:
New applications by invitation only.

PUBLICATIONS:
Annual report/guidelines available on web site.

IRS I.D.: 41-6023537

BOARD OF DIRECTORS:
Patrick J. McHale, President
Karen P. Gallivan, Director
Janel W. French, Treasurer
Kristi K. Lee, Secretary

ADDRESS INQUIRIES TO:
Kristi Lee
Manager, Community Relations
(See address above.)

*PLEASE NOTE:
Unsolicited requests are not accepted.

GRAND HAVEN AREA COMMUNITY FOUNDATION [1255]

One South Harbor Drive
Grand Haven, MI 49417
(616) 842-6378
Fax: (616) 842-9518
E-mail: info@ghacf.org
Web Site: www.ghacf.org

FOUNDED: 1971

AREAS OF INTEREST:
Arts and culture, economic and community betterment, education, environment, and health and human services.

TYPE:
Project/program grants; Scholarships; Seed money grants. Pool of funds contributed by donors for the benefit of the Tri-Cities area.

YEAR PROGRAM STARTED: 1971

PURPOSE:
To enrich and enhance the quality of life in the Tri-Cities area; to link donors' interests with the needs of the community.

LEGAL BASIS:
Community foundation.

ELIGIBILITY:
Grant applicants must be charitable organizations recognized under Section 501(c)(3) of the Internal Revenue Code. Grants are also awarded to units of government, educational institutions and churches that are providing services which benefit the Tri-Cities community.

GEOG. RESTRICTIONS: Ferrysburg, Grand Haven and Spring Lake areas of western Michigan.

FINANCIAL DATA:
Amount of support per award: Varies depending on needs and nature of the request.

Total amount of support: Over $3,600,000 in competitive and donor-advised grants for the year 2014.

NO. MOST RECENT APPLICANTS: 1,190.

NO. AWARDS: 1,100.

REPRESENTATIVE AWARDS:
$7,000 to Wetland Watch for year-round environmental education project; $17,500 to Feeding America West Michigan to replace food trucks; $2,000 to Love Inc. for Love Links Bicycle Ministry.

APPLICATION INFO:
Applicant must submit Letter of Inquiry form online. Upon staff review and determination of project alignment with Foundation's priorities, applicant will be prompted to submit a full application.

Duration: Varies.

Deadline: Letter of Inquiry may be submitted at any time.

PUBLICATIONS:
Annual report; application.

STAFF:
Holly Johnson, President
Beth Larsen, Director of Grants and Nonprofit Services
Patty McDonald, Finance Director

BOARD OF TRUSTEES:
Kennard Creason, Chairperson
Mark Kleist, Vice Chairperson
Randy Hansen, Treasurer
Tammy Bailey, Secretary
Melinda Brink
Chad Bush
Sandy Huber
Steve Moreland
Gail Ringelberg
Monica Verplank
Kim Zevalkink

ADDRESS INQUIRIES TO:
Beth Larsen, Director of
Grants and Nonprofit Services
(See address above.)

THE GREATER CEDAR RAPIDS COMMUNITY FOUNDATION [1256]

324 Third Street, S.E.
Cedar Rapids, IA 52401
(319) 366-2862
Fax: (319) 366-2912
E-mail: grants@gcrcf.org
Web Site: www.gcrcf.org

FOUNDED: 1948

AREAS OF INTEREST:
Arts and culture, community development, education, environment, health and human services.

NAME(S) OF PROGRAMS:
- **Endowment Challenge Fund**
- **Linn County Fund**
- **Nonprofit Network**
- **Organizational Development Fund**
- **President's Fund**
- **Program Fund**

TYPE:
Demonstration grants; Project/program grants; Scholarships; Seed money grants; Technical assistance; Training grants.

YEAR PROGRAM STARTED: 1989

PURPOSE:
To enrich the quality of life in Linn County, IA.

LEGAL BASIS:
Community foundation.

ELIGIBILITY:
Eligible organizations must be IRS 501(c)(3) tax-exempt, public agencies/units of government or have a fiscal sponsor.

GEOG. RESTRICTIONS: Cedar Rapids and surrounding Linn County, Iowa.

FINANCIAL DATA:
Amount of support per award: $250 to $50,000 depending on fund.

Total amount of support: $8,000,000 for the year 2015.

CO-OP FUNDING PROGRAMS: A variety of donor advisors operate competitive funds.

NO. MOST RECENT APPLICANTS: Varies.

NO. AWARDS: 1,250 for the year 2015.

APPLICATION INFO:
Applications must be made online.

Duration: One to three years for most funds. Renewal by reapplication.

Deadline: Approximately February 15, June 15 and October 15.

PUBLICATIONS:
Annual report; "Community" newsletter; guidelines.

ADDRESS INQUIRIES TO:
See e-mail address above.

*SPECIAL STIPULATIONS:
The Foundation makes competitive grant awards only within Linn County, IA and its immediate vicinity.

THE GREATER CINCINNATI FOUNDATION [1257]

200 West 4th Street
Cincinnati, OH 45202-2602
(513) 241-2880
Fax: (513) 768-6122
E-mail: info@gcfdn.org
keetonj@gcfdn.org
Web Site: www.gcfdn.org

FOUNDED: 1963

AREAS OF INTEREST:
Addressing racial disparities and improving race relations, comprehensive community development, public education, economic development and strengthening the region's arts and cultural assets.

CONSULTING OR VOLUNTEER SERVICES:
General staff support provided by volunteers.

TYPE:
Capital grants; Development grants. Funds for capital improvements, one-time needs, demonstration projects, demands normally outside the reach of philanthropic budgets. Funds may not be used for operating budgets.

LEGAL BASIS:
Tax-exempt under Section 501(c)(3) of IRS code.

ELIGIBILITY:
Recipient must be a local agency in the Greater Cincinnati area and must be tax-exempt under Section 501(c)(3) of the IRS code.

GEOG. RESTRICTIONS: Greater Cincinnati, Ohio, northern Kentucky and southeast Indiana.

FINANCIAL DATA:
Amount of support per award: $5,000 to $100,000.

Total amount of support: Over $76,000,000 for the year 2014.

NO. MOST RECENT APPLICANTS: 75 for the year 2014.

REPRESENTATIVE AWARDS:
Dan Beard Council, Boy Scouts of America; Children's Protective Service, Cincinnati Association for the Blind.

APPLICATION INFO:
Application information is available on the web site.

Unsolicited proposals are not accepted under the Community Grants program.

Duration: Typically one year.

Deadline: Letter of Inquiry: June 30 and December 31. Proposals: August 15 and February 15.

IRS I.D.: 31-0669700

STAFF:
Ellen Katz, President and Chief Executive Officer
Elizabeth Reiter Benson, Vice President for Communications and Marketing
Shiloh Turner, Vice President for Community Investment
Scott McReynolds, Vice President for Finance and Administration
Amy Cheney, Vice President for Giving Strategies
Ronald C. Christian, Esq., Legal Counsel

GOVERNING BOARD:
Dianne M. Rosenberg, Chairperson
Christopher L. Fister, Vice Chairperson
Calvin D. Buford
Thomas D. Croft
Delores Hargrove-Young
Wijdan Jreisat, Esq.
Molly A. Katz, M.D.
Mike Keating
Uma R. Kotagal, M.D.
Ryan M. Rybolt
Charles R. Scheper
Ann M. Schwister
Patricia Mann Smitson, Esq.
Peter S. Strange
Ellen van der Horst

ADDRESS INQUIRIES TO:
Janine Keeton
Community Investment Coordinator
(See address above.)

GREATER GREEN BAY COMMUNITY FOUNDATION [1258]

320 North Broadway
Suite 260
Green Bay, WI 54303
(920) 432-0800
Fax: (920) 432-5577
Web Site: www.ggbcf.org

FOUNDED: 1991

AREAS OF INTEREST:
Improving the quality of life for the residents of the Greater Green Bay, WI area.

TYPE:
Project/program grants; Scholarships. Donor-advised funds.

YEAR PROGRAM STARTED: 1991

PURPOSE:
To connect people and resources to organizations and programs that strengthen the community, improve quality of life, and make northeastern Wisconsin a great place to live, work and play.

ELIGIBILITY:
Eligible organizations must have 501(c)(3) not-for-profit status. No grants are made to individuals.

GEOG. RESTRICTIONS: Brown, Kewaunee and Oconto counties, Wisconsin.

FINANCIAL DATA:
Amount of support per award: Varies by need.

NO. AWARDS: 400 to 500 annually.

APPLICATION INFO:
All applicants should share their ideas with the Foundation prior to the submission of a formal application.

Duration: Varies by grant program; usually one year.

Deadline: Varies by grant program.

ADDRESS INQUIRIES TO:
Vice President of Community Engagement
(See address above.)

THE GREATER KANAWHA VALLEY FOUNDATION [1259]

Huntington Square, Suite 1600
900 Lee Street East
Charleston, WV 25301
(304) 346-3620
Fax: (304) 346-3640
E-mail: sryder@tgkvf.org
Web Site: www.tgkvf.org

FOUNDED: 1962

AREAS OF INTEREST:
Education, health and leadership/civic engagement.

TYPE:
Project/program grants; Scholarships.

YEAR PROGRAM STARTED: 1964

PURPOSE:
To serve the greater Kanawha Valley and surrounding areas.

LEGAL BASIS:
501(c)(3).

ELIGIBILITY:
Grant applicant must be a 501(c)(3) nonprofit organization as determined by the IRS, a faith-based organization, or a government entity located in or directly benefiting residents of the Greater Kanawha Valley.

GEOG. RESTRICTIONS: Boone, Clay, Fayette, Kanawha, Lincoln and Putnam, West Virginia.

FINANCIAL DATA:
Amount of support per award: Grants: Varies; Scholarships: Usually $1,000.

Total amount of support: $1,385,992 in grants for the year ended December 31, 2013; $516,820 in scholarships for the academic year 2014-15.

Matching fund requirements: Must have a match, not a specific percent.

NO. MOST RECENT APPLICANTS: Varies.

NO. AWARDS: 398 scholarships for the academic year 2014-15.

APPLICATION INFO:
Applications are accepted online only.

Duration: Varies.

Deadline: Scholarships: January 11.

PUBLICATIONS:
Annual report.

IRS I.D.: 55-6024430

STAFF:
Sheri Ryder, Senior Program Officer
Susan Hoover, Scholarship Program Officer
Stephanie Hyre, Program Officer

ADDRESS INQUIRIES TO:
For grants:
Stephanie Hyre, Program Officer
E-mail: shyre@tgkvf.org
(See address above.)

For scholarships:
Susan Hoover, Scholarship Program Officer
E-mail: shoover@tgkvf.org
(See address above.)

THE GREATER KANSAS CITY COMMUNITY FOUNDATION AND AFFILIATED TRUSTS [1260]

1055 Broadway, Suite 130
Kansas City, MO 64105
(816) 842-0944
(866) 719-7886
(816) 627-3417
Fax: (816) 842-8079
E-mail: info@growyourgiving.org
Web Site: www.growyourgiving.org

FOUNDED: 1978

AREAS OF INTEREST:
Public education and life sciences.

CONSULTING OR VOLUNTEER SERVICES:
Grantmaking services.

TYPE:
Project/program grants; Scholarships. Grants in the areas of public education and life sciences and scholarships are given to make a positive support of the nonprofit sector and to promote philanthropy for the benefit of the community.

PURPOSE:
To improve the quality of life in greater Kansas City by increasing charitable giving, connecting donors to community needs they care about, and providing leadership on critical community issues.

LEGAL BASIS:
Public foundation.

ELIGIBILITY:
Unsolicited applications will not be accepted.

The Community Foundation does not ordinarily fund endowment campaigns, debt reduction, annual appeals and membership contributions, operating expenses and fund-raising projects of religious organizations, capital fund drives, including brick and mortar, land acquisition, equipment purchases, renovation or purchase of buildings, construction or the improvement of public spaces or financial assistance for individuals.

GEOG. RESTRICTIONS: Greater Kansas City, Missouri.

FINANCIAL DATA:
Amount of support per award: Varies.

Total amount of support: Approximately $212,000,000 annually.

NO. AWARDS: 20,000.

REPRESENTATIVE AWARDS:
$100,000 over three years to the University of Missouri-Kansas City Institute for Urban Education.

APPLICATION INFO:
Application information is available on the web site.

Duration: Typically one year.

Deadline: Varies.

IRS I.D.: 43-1152398

OFFICERS:
Deborah L. Wilkerson, President and Chief Executive Officer
Brenda Chumley, Senior Vice President of Foundation Relations and Operations
Katie Gray, Senior Vice President of Finance and Foundation Services

ADDRESS INQUIRIES TO:
See e-mail address above.

*PLEASE NOTE:
Unsolicited requests will not be accepted.

THE GREATER LANSING FOUNDATION [1261]

120 North Washington Square
Suite 650
Lansing, MI 48933
(517) 334-5299
Fax: (517) 334-5445
E-mail: info@crcfoundation.org

FOUNDED: 1947

AREAS OF INTEREST:
Arts, education, general charitable giving, handicapped and health.

NAME(S) OF PROGRAMS:
- **The Greater Lansing Foundation General Fund**

TYPE:
Capital grants; Development grants; Project/program grants; Scholarships; Seed money grants; Training grants; Work-study programs. General support for seed money and capital funds.

YEAR PROGRAM STARTED: 1947

PURPOSE:
To promote the well-being of the inhabitants of Clinton, Eaton and Ingham counties by distributing income to local charitable, public or educational institutions.

LEGAL BASIS:
Private foundation.

ELIGIBILITY:
Applicants must have a 501(c)(3) IRS exemption and be a public charity.

GEOG. RESTRICTIONS: Greater Lansing, Michigan counties.

FINANCIAL DATA:
Amount of support per award: Up to $10,000.

Total amount of support: Approximately $50,000 annually.

APPLICATION INFO:
Grant application requests should be made to:
Capital Region Community Foundation
c/o The Greater Lansing Foundation Fund
330 Marshall Street, Suite 300
Lansing, MI 48912
E-mail: info@crcfoundation.org
Tel: (517) 272-2870.

Duration: One year.

Deadline: April 1.

IRS I.D.: 38-6057513

ADDRESS INQUIRIES TO:
Steven J. Peters, Secretary
(See address above.)

*PLEASE NOTE:
The Foundation does not usually make grants to fund normal operating costs. The Committee prefers to consider grants in the nature of capital expenditures, expansion or improvement of existing programs or grants of a nonrecurring nature.

GREATER MILWAUKEE FOUNDATION [1262]

101 West Pleasant Street
Suite 210
Milwaukee, WI 53212
(414) 272-5805
Fax: (414) 272-6235
E-mail: info@greatermilwaukeefoundation.org
Web Site: www.greatermilwaukeefoundation.org

FOUNDED: 1915

AREAS OF INTEREST:
Unrestricted grantmaking in the areas of strengthening neighborhoods, strengthening education, increasing economic opportunities, and promoting equity and inclusion.

TYPE:
Awards/prizes; Capital grants; Challenge/matching grants; Demonstration grants; Development grants; Matching gifts; Professorships; Project/program grants; Research grants; Scholarships; Seed money grants; Technical assistance; Training grants. The Foundation's unrestricted grantmaking does not support general operations.

The Foundation operates as a community trust, a public nonprofit organization established to administer charitable funds for the benefit of the people of the community. It is composed of more than 1,200 funds, each created by donors to serve the charitable causes of their choice. Donors can make grants locally, nationally or around the world.

The component funds are of several types, depending upon the wishes of the donor expressed at the time the originating gift or bequest was made:
(1) Unrestricted funds are those in which the Foundation's Board is given full discretion in determining how income can best be disbursed each year for charitable purposes;
(2) Field of interest funds are administered with a particular charitable purpose in mind, such as support of the arts, child welfare or education;
(3) Designated funds have been established to favor specific charitable agencies and institutions; the income earned by this type of fund is paid annually to a particular agency or agencies named by the donor; grants are usually intended to provide general sustaining support for current agency operations and;
(4) Donor-advised funds are those established by gifts from individuals, foundations or corporations in which the original contributors make suggestions to the Foundation Board about grant distributions.

YEAR PROGRAM STARTED: 1915

PURPOSE:
To inspire philanthropy, serve donors, and strengthen communities now and for future generations.

LEGAL BASIS:
Public nonprofit organization exempt from federal taxation under Section 501(c)(3) of the Internal Revenue Code.

ELIGIBILITY:
The Greater Milwaukee Foundation Board welcomes grant applications from agencies serving the people of the greater Milwaukee community. Details regarding grantmaking criteria are available online.

The Foundation is committed to promoting equity and inclusion with a focus on racial equity in its community. This commitment applies to its grantmaking. Nonprofit board diversity is the first of many things it considers. Eligible nonprofits must have board membership that is at least 10% people of color (African Americans, Asian Americans, Hispanic/Latino Americans and all other persons not categorized as white by the U.S. Census).

GEOG. RESTRICTIONS: Greater Milwaukee, Wisconsin, including Milwaukee, Ozaukee, Washington and Waukesha counties.

FINANCIAL DATA:
The funds vary in size from $25,000 to $25,858,000.

Amount of support per award: $11,500 average.

Total amount of support: $44,869,000 for the year 2015.

CO-OP FUNDING PROGRAMS: Nonprofit Management Fund and Milwaukee Teen Pregnancy Prevention Initiative Collaborative Fund.

NO. AWARDS: 3,949 grants for the year 2015.

APPLICATION INFO:
To facilitate fair and equitable consideration, grant applicants are expected to use a prescribed proposal format. The application process is as follows:
(1) applicant organization should update (or add) its information on the Philanthropy Online database (see Grantseekers section of Foundation web site);
(2) organization must then submit a Letter of Inquiry to the Foundation (again, see Foundation web site);
(3) Foundation staff will then review applicant's proposal for merit;
(4) if encouraged by staff to apply, the applicant must complete a detailed online proposal;
(5) Foundation staff will thoroughly review the proposal;
(6) the Foundation Board's Community Investment Committee will review the proposal and make recommendations to the full Board, which must approve all grant awards and;
(7) each applicant will receive written notification of the Board's action; those selected for grants must adhere to the stipulated terms.

Grant seekers are strongly encouraged to consult with a program officer at the Foundation prior to submitting a Letter of Inquiry. Details for grant seekers are available online.

Duration: Generally, one year.

Deadline: Letters of Inquiry are accepted and reviewed quarterly. Funding decisions are made quarterly.

PUBLICATIONS:
Newsletters; magazine; annual report.

IRS I.D.: 39-6036407

STAFF:
Kenneth Robertson, Vice President and Chief Financial Officer
Kathryn Dunn, Vice President, Community Investment
Marcus White, Vice President, Community Partnerships
Tim Larson, Vice President, Development and Donor Services
Sonja Williams, Vice President, Human Resources and Organizational Learning
Laura Porfilio Glawe, Vice President, Marketing and Communications
Danae Davis, Executive Director, Milwaukee Succeeds

BOARD OF DIRECTORS:
Thomas L. Spero, Chairperson
David J. Lubar, Vice Chairperson
Wendy Reed Bosworth
Peter W. Bruce
David J. Drury
Ness Flores
Janine P. Geske
Cecelia Gore
Jacqueline Herd-Barber
Paul J. Jones
David J. Kundert
Gregory S. Marcus
Cory L. Nettles
Marie L. O'Brien

OFFICER:
Ellen M. Gilligan, President and Chief Executive Officer

ADDRESS INQUIRIES TO:
Laura Porfilio Glawe
Vice President, Marketing and Communications
(See address above.)

THE GREATER NEW ORLEANS FOUNDATION [1263]

K & B Plaza, Suite 100
1055 St. Charles Avenue
New Orleans, LA 70130
(504) 598-4663
Fax: (504) 598-4676
E-mail: richard@gnof.org
Web Site: www.gnof.org

AREAS OF INTEREST:
Housing, environment, health, workforce development, arts and culture, and children and youth.

TYPE:
Project/program grants. The Foundation provides start-up funds for promising new organizations or programs. It also funds demonstration grants to new or established organizations with innovative program models and offers transition grants to nonprofit organizations moving into a new state of organizational development.

PURPOSE:
To create a resilient, sustainable, vibrant community for all in the greater New Orleans region.

ELIGIBILITY:
The Foundation makes grants to nonprofit, tax-exempt organizations that serve the greater New Orleans area.

GEOG. RESTRICTIONS: Southeastern Louisiana and greater New Orleans region.

FINANCIAL DATA:
Amount of support per award: Varies.

Total amount of support: Varies.

APPLICATION INFO:
Guidelines are available online.

Duration: Typically one year. Renewal by reapplication.

Deadline: Varies.

PUBLICATIONS:
Guidelines.

*SPECIAL STIPULATIONS:
Upon completion of the funded project, or within one year, grant recipients must provide an end-of-grant report based on their proposed program evaluation.

THE GRUNDY FOUNDATION [1264]

680 Radcliffe Street
Bristol, PA 19007
(215) 788-5460
Fax: (215) 788-0915
E-mail: ejw@grundyfoundation.com
Web Site: www.grundyfoundation.com

FOUNDED: 1961

AREAS OF INTEREST:
Arts and culture, education and human services.

TYPE:
Capital grants. Capital grants for 501(c)(3) organizations throughout Bucks County, PA, primarily Lower Bucks County. Operating/programmatic support only for preselected organizations primarily in Bristol, PA and other parts of Lower Bucks County.

YEAR PROGRAM STARTED: 1961

PURPOSE:
To promote the well-being of the Commonwealth of Pennsylvania, with a particular emphasis in Bucks County.

LEGAL BASIS:
501(c)(3) private foundation.

ELIGIBILITY:
Applicants must be nonprofit organizations that have public charity status. No grants to individuals or for fellowships or loans.

GEOG. RESTRICTIONS: Primarily Lower Bucks County, Pennsylvania.

FINANCIAL DATA:
Amount of support per award: Excluding two impact grants each year, average grant $5,250 for the year 2014.

Total amount of support: $117,000 for the year 2015.

Matching fund requirements: Stipulated with specific programs.

NO. AWARDS: 4 for the year 2015.

APPLICATION INFO:
Applicants should use the Delaware Valley Grantmakers Common Grant Application form, which can be downloaded at www.dvg.org/?page=CGA.

Duration: No grants are awarded on a continuing basis.

PUBLICATIONS:
Application guidelines.

ADDRESS INQUIRIES TO:
Eugene J. Williams, Executive Director
(See address above.)

GULF COAST COMMUNITY FOUNDATION [1265]

601 Tamiami Trail South
Venice, FL 34285
(941) 486-4600
Fax: (941) 486-4699
E-mail: info@gulfcoastcf.org
Web Site: www.gulfcoastcf.org

FOUNDED: 1995

AREAS OF INTEREST:
Arts and culture, civic affairs, the environment, education, health and human services, and economic development.

TYPE:
Project/program grants.

YEAR PROGRAM STARTED: 1995

PURPOSE:
To improve the quality of life in communities the Foundation serves.

LEGAL BASIS:
Community foundation.

ELIGIBILITY:
Nonprofit organizations, 501(c)(3) tax-exempt, are eligible to apply.

GEOG. RESTRICTIONS: Charlotte, DeSoto, Lee, Manatee and Sarasota counties, Florida.

FINANCIAL DATA:
Amount of support per award: Varies.

Total amount of support: Varies.

Matching fund requirements: Varies.

REPRESENTATIVE AWARDS:
Charlotte County Homeless Coalition to provide first-year operating support for Safe House Shelter; Legal Aid of Manasota to provide free legal representation for southern Sarasota County homeowners facing foreclosure on their homes; United Way of Sarasota County to fund site coordinators who will facilitate the new Volunteer Income Tax Assistance Program.

APPLICATION INFO:
Application information is available on the web site.

Duration: Varies.

Deadline: Varies.

PUBLICATIONS:
Annual report; application guidelines.

ADDRESS INQUIRIES TO:
See e-mail address above.

HALL FAMILY FOUNDATION

P.O. Box 419580
Mail Drop 323
Kansas City, MO 64141-6580
(816) 274-8516
Fax: (816) 274-8547
Web Site: www.hallfamilyfoundation.org

TYPE:
Capital grants; Project/program grants; Technical assistance; Training grants.

See entry 150 for full listing.

HAMILTON COMMUNITY FOUNDATION [1266]

120 King Street West, Suite 700
Hamilton ON L8P 4V2 Canada
(905) 523-5600
Fax: (905) 523-0741
E-mail: grants@hamiltoncommunityfoundation.ca
Web Site: www.hamiltoncommunityfoundation.ca

FOUNDED: 1954

AREAS OF INTEREST:
Community development and services for Hamilton, ON.

TYPE:
Project/program grants.

YEAR PROGRAM STARTED: 1954

PURPOSE:
To foster the growth of community philanthropy; to build and prudently manage community endowments; to provide exceptional services to donors; to address needs through strategic grantmaking and organizational support; to provide leadership on key community issues.

LEGAL BASIS:
Community foundation.

GEOG. RESTRICTIONS: Community of Hamilton, Ontario, Canada.

FINANCIAL DATA:
Amount of support per award: Varies.

Total amount of support: $6,400,000 in grants and community leadership for the year 2014-15.

APPLICATION INFO:
Application information is available on the web site.

Duration: One year or multiyear grants.

STAFF:
Terry Cooke, President and Chief Executive Officer

ADDRESS INQUIRIES TO:
Matt Goodman, Vice President
Grants and Community Initiatives
(See address above.)

THE HAMPTON ROADS COMMUNITY FOUNDATION [1267]

101 West Main Street
Suite 4500
Norfolk, VA 23510
(757) 622-7951
Fax: (757) 622-1751
E-mail: grants@hamptonroadscf.org
Web Site: www.hamptonroadscf.org

FOUNDED: 1950

AREAS OF INTEREST:
Community development, education and social welfare.

TYPE:
Capital grants; Development grants; Project/program grants; Research grants; Seed money grants. Grants for nonprofit facilities, environment, arts and culture, education, health and human services, and special interests.

YEAR PROGRAM STARTED: 1950

PURPOSE:
To make grants that transform the quality of life and inspire philanthropy in southeastern Virginia.

LEGAL BASIS:
Nonprofit corporation.

ELIGIBILITY:
501(c)(3) nonprofit organizations that provide benefits to the residents.

GEOG. RESTRICTIONS: Southeastern Virginia.

FINANCIAL DATA:
Amount of support per award: $15,000 to $1,000,000.

Total amount of support: $19,000,000 for the year 2015.

NO. MOST RECENT APPLICANTS: 81.

NO. AWARDS: 52.

APPLICATION INFO:
Application information is available on the web site.

Duration: Grants: One year to multiyear; Scholarships: One to four years.

Deadline: Varies depending upon program.

PUBLICATIONS:
Annual report; application guidelines; quarterly newsletter.

IRS I.D.: 54-2035996

STAFF:
Deborah M. DiCroce, President and Chief Executive Officer
Robin Foreman, Vice President for Administration
Leigh Evans Davis, Vice President for Donor Engagement
Linda Rice, Vice President for Grantmaking and Community Engagement
Vivian Oden, Director of Donor Services
Amy Kurtz, Grants Specialist

ADDRESS INQUIRIES TO:
See e-mail address above.

*SPECIAL STIPULATIONS:
All discretionary grants are to charitable organizations for special purposes only.

HANCOCK COUNTY COMMUNITY FOUNDATION [1268]

312 East Main Street
Greenfield, IN 46140
(317) 462-8870
Fax: (317) 467-3330
E-mail: mgibble@giveHCgrowHC.org
Web Site: givehcgrowhc.org

FOUNDED: 1992

AREAS OF INTEREST:
Arts, civic affairs, culture, education, youth, and health and human services.

TYPE:
Project/program grants; Scholarships.

PURPOSE:
To build and improve the quality of life within the community.

LEGAL BASIS:
Nonprofit, public charity.

ELIGIBILITY:
Grants are made to organizations that have tax-exempt status under Section 501(c)(3) of the Internal Revenue Code. No grants are made to individuals. Nonsectarian religious programs may apply.

GEOG. RESTRICTIONS: Hancock County, Indiana.

FINANCIAL DATA:
Amount of support per award: Varies.

Total amount of support: Approximately $945,000 for the year 2013.

APPLICATION INFO:
Send a Letter of Intent, which outlines the request and projected request amount. Upon receiving the Letter of Intent, the Program Officer will follow up with the applicant organization to discuss the submission of a formal grant application.

Duration: One year. Extension possible.

ADDRESS INQUIRIES TO:
Kara Harrison, Grants Officer
E-mail: kharrison@giveHCgrowHC.org or
Kari Sisk, Scholarship Officer
E-mail: ksisk@giveHCgrowHC.org

HAWAII COMMUNITY FOUNDATION [1269]

827 Fort Street Mall
Honolulu, HI 96813
(808) 537-6333
(888) 731-3863 (Hawaii)
Fax: (808) 521-6286
E-mail: give@hawaiicommunityfoundation.org
Web Site: www.hawaiicommunityfoundation.org

FOUNDED: 1916

AREAS OF INTEREST:
Culture and art, natural resources conservation, education, health and medical research, human services, disability, mentoring and media, scholarships, neighbor island assistance, persons in need and the FLEX Program.

TYPE:
Development grants; Project/program grants; Scholarships; Seed money grants; Technical assistance; Training grants; Travel grants.

PURPOSE:
To build community among the people of Hawaii.

LEGAL BASIS:
Community foundation.

ELIGIBILITY:
Grantseeker must be a tax-exempt organization, either a unit of government or one classified by the IRS as a 501(c)(3) charity which is not a private foundation. The organization must serve Hawaii's people and environment and have leadership which represents the community served. It must make a request that is time-limited or has other source of future funding.

The Foundation supports innovative and creative programs that fit within specific areas. It also provides scholarships for college studies.

GEOG. RESTRICTIONS: Hawaii.

FINANCIAL DATA:
Foundation has more than $284,000,000 in charitable assets.

Amount of support per award: Varies.

Total amount of support: Varies.

APPLICATION INFO:
Applicant must submit a written proposal describing the proposed project.

Duration: Varies.

Deadline: Varies by program.

PUBLICATIONS:
Annual report.

ADDRESS INQUIRIES TO:
Lynelle Marble
Associate Director of Communications
(See address above.)

THE HEALTH FOUNDATION OF GREATER INDIANAPOLIS

429 East Vermont Street, Suite 400
Indianapolis, IN 46202-3698
(317) 630-1805
Fax: (317) 630-1806
E-mail: bwilson@thfgi.org
Web Site: www.thfgi.org

TYPE:
Project/program grants.

See entry 1444 for full listing.

THE HEALTHCARE FOUNDATION FOR ORANGE COUNTY

1505 East 17th Street
Suite 113
Santa Ana, CA 92705
(714) 245-1650
Fax: (714) 245-1653
E-mail: info@HFOC.org
Web Site: www.HFOC.org

TYPE:
Awards/prizes; Demonstration grants; Development grants; General operating grants; Project/program grants; Technical assistance; Training grants.

See entry 1403 for full listing.

HILLSDALE COUNTY COMMUNITY FOUNDATION [1270]

2 South Howell
Hillsdale, MI 49242-1634
(517) 439-5101
Fax: (517) 439-5109
E-mail: s.bisher@abouthccf.org
Web Site: www.abouthccf.org

FOUNDED: 1991

AREAS OF INTEREST:
Arts, education, community needs, scholarships and philanthropy.

TYPE:
Project/program grants; Scholarships.

YEAR PROGRAM STARTED: 1991

PURPOSE:
To improve the quality of life in Hillsdale County.

LEGAL BASIS:
Community foundation.

ELIGIBILITY:
For grants, organizations must be in and benefit Hillsdale County and be IRS 501(c)(3) tax-exempt. For scholarships, students must be graduates of Hillsdale County High School, residents of Hillsdale County and citizens of the U.S.

GEOG. RESTRICTIONS: Hillsdale County, Michigan.

FINANCIAL DATA:
Amount of support per award: $300 to $25,000.

Total amount of support: Varies.

NO. MOST RECENT APPLICANTS: 15 to 20.

NO. AWARDS: 10.

APPLICATION INFO:
Applications are available at the address above and must include all required documentation, completed application according to requirements, and a copy of the IRS 501(c)(3) tax determination letter.

Duration: One year.

Deadline: Foundation Grants: May 1 and November 1.

ADDRESS INQUIRIES TO:
Sharon Bisher, President and Chief Executive Officer
(See address above.)

THE HOME DEPOT FOUNDATION [1271]

2455 Paces Ferry Road, C-17
Atlanta, GA 30339
(770) 384-3889
(866) 593-7019
Fax: (770) 384-3908; (866) 593-7027
E-mail: hd_foundation@homedepot.com
Web Site: www.homedepotfoundation.org

FOUNDED: 1978

AREAS OF INTEREST:
Affordable housing, sustainable community development and community affairs.

CONSULTING OR VOLUNTEER SERVICES:
Team Depot volunteer program.

NAME(S) OF PROGRAMS:
- **Community Impact Grants Program**
- **Framing Hope Program**
- **Team Depot**
- **Veteran Housing Grants Program**

TYPE:
Challenge/matching grants; Development grants; Product donations; Project/program grants. Environmental research grants.

YEAR PROGRAM STARTED: 2002

PURPOSE:
To contribute to the development of affordable housing in communities where The Home Depot does business; to support employee participation in the community; to promote economic development in The Home Depot communities.

LEGAL BASIS:
Corporate giving program.

ELIGIBILITY:
Most grants are made in communities where The Home Depot operates stores. No grants to individuals, religious, fraternal, political, labor, athletic, social or veterans groups, fund-raising benefits, dinners, exhibits, conferences and sports events, charities sponsored solely by a single civic organization, courtesy or journal advertising campaigns, multiyear commitments, or organizations that are not 501(c)(3) or Revenue Canada-designated charities.

GEOG. RESTRICTIONS: United States, Canada and Mexico.

FINANCIAL DATA:
Amount of support per award: Varies depending on needs and nature of the request.

Total amount of support: Community Impact Grants: Up to $5,000; Veteran Housing Grants Program: $100,000 to $500,000.

Matching fund requirements: Employees making contributions to recognized nonprofits may apply for matching gifts up to $500 through The Home Depot Matching Gift Program.

APPLICATION INFO:
Contact the Foundation for application guidelines.

Duration: Varies.

Deadline: Varies according to program.

PUBLICATIONS:
Brochure; *Social Responsibility Report.*

ADDRESS INQUIRIES TO:
See e-mail address above.

HOUSING EDUCATION AND RESEARCH ASSOCIATION (HERA) [1272]

407 North 20th Avenue
Bozeman, MT 59718
(406) 994-3451
E-mail: heraballen@gmail.com
Web Site: www.housingeducators.org

AREAS OF INTEREST:
Housing education.

NAME(S) OF PROGRAMS:
- **Tessie Agan Award Competition**

TYPE:
Awards/prizes.

ELIGIBILITY:
Open to graduate and undergraduate students.

FINANCIAL DATA:
Amount of support per award: Graduate Award: $750 presented at the HERA Annual Meeting; Undergraduate Award: $250.

APPLICATION INFO:
Information and specific guidelines pertaining to all grants can be found online.

Duration: One-time award.

ADDRESS INQUIRIES TO:
Barbara Allen, Interim Executive Director
(See address above.)

*SPECIAL STIPULATIONS:
Award is contingent upon attending the meeting and presenting the paper. Conference registration fees are waived.

HUDSON-WEBBER FOUNDATION [1273]

333 West Fort Street
Suite 1310
Detroit, MI 48226-3134
(313) 963-7777
Fax: (313) 963-2818
Web Site: www.hudson-webber.org

FOUNDED: 1943

AREAS OF INTEREST:
The primary concern of the Foundation is the vitality of the metropolitan Detroit community. The Foundation's Trustees have defined four specific program missions in which they will concentrate their efforts and resources: the physical revitalization of downtown Detroit, the enhancement of major art and cultural resources in Detroit, the reduction of crime in Detroit and the economic development of Detroit, with emphasis on the creation of additional employment opportunities.

TYPE:
Project/program grants.

YEAR PROGRAM STARTED: 1943

PURPOSE:
To improve the vitality and quality of life of the metropolitan Detroit community.

LEGAL BASIS:
Private foundation.

ELIGIBILITY:
The Foundation assigns highest priority of support to programs in the city of Detroit. Programs outside of Detroit generally are not supported.

The Foundation does not make grants for endowments, fund-raising social events, conferences or exhibits. With the exception of the Foundation's program for Hudsonians, the Foundation does not make grants to individuals.

GEOG. RESTRICTIONS: Southeastern Michigan, specifically the city of Detroit.

FINANCIAL DATA:
Amount of support per award: $5,000 to $1,000,000.

Total amount of support: $7,587,354 for the year 2015.

NO. AWARDS: 64.

APPLICATION INFO:
Information may be obtained from the Foundation's web site.

Duration: One year.

BOARD OF TRUSTEES:

ADDRESS INQUIRIES TO:
Stephanie Armes, Grants Manager
(See address above.)

HUMBOLDT AREA FOUNDATION [1274]

363 Indianola Road
Bayside, CA 95524
(707) 442-2993
Fax: (707) 442-3811
E-mail: sarad@hafoundation.org
Web Site: www.hafoundation.org

FOUNDED: 1972

AREAS OF INTEREST:
Children, youth and families; community, economy and the environment; health and well-being; arts and humanities; native cultures.

NAME(S) OF PROGRAMS:
- **Community Grants**
- **Field of Interest Grant Program**
- **Native Cultures Fund**
- **Summer Youth Program**

TYPE:
Awards/prizes; Capital grants; Challenge/matching grants; General operating grants; Project/program grants; Scholarships; Seed money grants; Technical assistance.

YEAR PROGRAM STARTED: 1972

PURPOSE:
To improve the quality of life on the north coast of California.

ELIGIBILITY:
Eligible organizations must be IRS 501(c)(3) tax-exempt. Applications will be evaluated using the following criteria: need, planning and management, leadership and collaboration.

The Foundation will not fund projects outside of its service area, projects without sound planning and development, deferred

maintenance, annual operating costs, travel, scholarships and fellowships, or projects which violate the nonprofit public laws.

GEOG. RESTRICTIONS: Del Norte, Humboldt and Trinity counties, California.

FINANCIAL DATA:

Amount of support per award: Varies.

Total amount of support: Varies.

APPLICATION INFO:

Information, guidelines and applications are available online.

Duration: Varies.

Deadline: Varies.

PUBLICATIONS:

Guidelines.

ADDRESS INQUIRIES TO:

Sara Dronkers
Director of Grantmaking
(See address above.)

INTERNATIONAL DEVELOPMENT RESEARCH CENTRE (IDRC) [1275]

150 Kent Street
Ottawa ON K1P 0B2 Canada
(613) 696-2098
Fax: (613) 236-4026
E-mail: awards@idrc.ca
Web Site: www.idrc.ca

FOUNDED: 1970

NAME(S) OF PROGRAMS:

- **IDRC Doctoral Research Awards (IDRA)**

TYPE:

Awards/prizes. These awards are offered once a year and are intended for field research in one or more developing countries. Candidates must conduct their research in areas corresponding to IDRC's research priorities.

PURPOSE:

To support the field research of Canadian graduate students and developing country nationals enrolled in a Canadian university for doctoral research on a topic of relevance to sustainable and equitable development.

ELIGIBILITY:

Applicants must meet the following conditions for eligibility:
(1) hold Canadian citizenship (or permanent residency status), or hold citizenship of a developing country;
(2) be enrolled at a Canadian university at the doctoral level;
(3) research proposal is for a doctoral thesis and has been approved by the thesis supervisor;
(4) proposed field research must take place in one or more developing countries and be conducted for a doctoral dissertation;
(5) provide evidence of affiliation with an institution or organization in the developing-country region(s) in which the research will take place and;
(6) have completed course work and passed comprehensive examinations before taking up the award.

FINANCIAL DATA:

Total amount of support: Up to $20,000 (CAN).

NO. AWARDS: Approximately 20 per year.

APPLICATION INFO:

Applications are to be submitted online from the IDRC's grants page. Paper applications are not accepted.

Duration: Three to 12 months.

Deadline: Contact IDRC.

ADDRESS INQUIRIES TO:

IDRC Centre Awards
(See e-mail address above.)

INTERNATIONAL DEVELOPMENT RESEARCH CENTRE (IDRC) [1276]

150 Kent Street
Ottawa ON K1P 0B2 Canada
(613) 696-2098
Fax: (613) 236-4026
E-mail: awards@idrc.ca
Web Site: www.idrc.ca

FOUNDED: 1970

AREAS OF INTEREST:

Research for international development.

NAME(S) OF PROGRAMS:

- **IDRC Research Awards**

TYPE:

Internships. Program provides training in research management and grant administration under the guidance of Centre program staff. Approximately 50% of the time spent on own research project.

PURPOSE:

To provide exposure to research for international development through a program of training in research management and grant administration.

ELIGIBILITY:

Canadian citizens, permanent residents of Canada, and citizens of developing countries are eligible. Applicant must be registered in a Master's or Ph.D. program or have completed a Master's or Ph.D. degree in a recognized university.

NO. AWARDS: Approximately 10 per year.

APPLICATION INFO:

Applications must be submitted online from the IDRC's grants page.

Duration: One year.

Deadline: August.

ADDRESS INQUIRIES TO:

IDRC Centre Awards
(See e-mail address above.)

JEWISH COMMUNITY FOUNDATION OF LOS ANGELES [1277]

6505 Wilshire Boulevard
Suite 1200
Los Angeles, CA 90048
(323) 761-8700
(877) 363-6966
Fax: (323) 761-8720
E-mail: info@jewishfoundationla.org
Web Site: www.jewishfoundationla.org

FOUNDED: 1954

AREAS OF INTEREST:

Jewish life, community and health services, education, social services, arts and culture, and civic life.

CONSULTING OR VOLUNTEER SERVICES:

Center for Designed Philanthropy - consultation with family foundations and individual funders regarding the effectiveness of their grantmaking.

NAME(S) OF PROGRAMS:

- **Capital Grants**
- **Cutting Edge Grants**
- **General Community Grants**
- **Israel Grants**

TYPE:

Awards/prizes; Capital grants; Project/program grants; Seed money grants. Capital Grants: Construction and renovation projects for facilities that predominantly serve members of the Los Angeles Jewish community.

Cutting Edge Grants: New programs with the potential for transformative impact that address critical needs in the Los Angeles Jewish community.

General Community Grants: Programs by organizations outside of the Jewish community which address high-priority concerns in the Los Angeles community.

Israel Grants: Programs that have an impact on economic development and pluralistic Jewish identity in Israel.

YEAR PROGRAM STARTED: 1976

PURPOSE:

To provide endowment resources to enable the community to initiate model programs, assist agencies to address the diverse and demanding challenges to face emergencies and the needs of the Jewish community and the Los Angeles community at large.

LEGAL BASIS:

Jewish community foundation.

ELIGIBILITY:

Grants are made to nonprofit 501(c)(3) organizations.

GEOG. RESTRICTIONS: Primarily Los Angeles and Israel.

FINANCIAL DATA:

The Foundation currently manages assets of nearly $1 billion (as of December 31, 2014, unaudited).

Amount of support per award: Capital Grants: Up to $50,000. Cutting Edge Grants: Up to $250,000. General Community Grants: $10,000 to $25,000. Israel Grants: $100,000 to $250,000.

Total amount of support: In 2015 the Foundation and its donors distributed over $96,000,000 in grants.

NO. AWARDS: Grants to over 1,000 nonprofit organizations in 2014.

REPRESENTATIVE AWARDS:

$50,000 to Beit T'Shuvah for expanded treatment center; $200,000 to Chai Lifeline for i-Shrine; $200,000 to Tech-Career in Israel for Closing the Digital Gap-Empowering Ethiopian Israeli Young Adults.

APPLICATION INFO:

Application information is available on the web site.

Duration: One to three years. No renewals.

Deadline: Varies.

PUBLICATIONS:

Annual report.

OFFICERS:

Lawrence Rauch, Chairperson
Marvin I. Schotland, President and Chief Executive Officer
David Carroll, Senior Vice President, Finance and Administration/Chief Financial Officer
Daniel M. Rothblatt, Senior Vice President, Philanthropic Services

Elliot B. Kristal, Vice President, Charitable Gift Planning
Baruch S. Littman, Vice President, Development
Anthony Chanin, Vice President
William R. Feiler, Vice President
Abby L.T. Feinman, Vice President
Harold J. Masor, Vice President
Evan Schlessinger, Vice President
Michael G. Smooke, Vice President
Eugene Stein, Vice President
Adlai W. Wertman, Vice President
Scott H. Richland, Treasurer
Selwyn Gerber, Secretary

EXECUTIVE STAFF:
Marvin I. Schotland, President and Chief Executive Officer
David Carroll, Senior Vice President, Finance and Administration/Chief Financial Officer
Daniel M. Rothblatt, Senior Vice President, Philanthropic Services
Susan Mattisinko, Vice President and General Counsel
Elliot B. Kristal, Vice President, Charitable Gift Planning
Baruch S. Littman, Vice President, Development
Elana Wien, Director, Center for Designed Philanthropy
Lewis Groner, Director, Marketing and Communications

THE KANTZLER FOUNDATION [1278]

Pere Marquette Depot
1000 Adams Street, Suite 200
Bay City, MI 48708
(989) 893-4438
Fax: (989) 893-4448
E-mail: kaczer@charter.net

FOUNDED: 1974

AREAS OF INTEREST:
Education, science, arts, culture, human services, conservation, beautification and recreation projects in the Bay County area.

TYPE:
Capital grants; Development grants; Project/program grants.

YEAR PROGRAM STARTED: 1974

PURPOSE:
To provide financial support for charitable projects and programs that directly benefit the residents of Bay County, MI.

LEGAL BASIS:
Michigan nonprofit corporation.

ELIGIBILITY:
Organizations must be IRS 501(c)(3) tax-exempt. Priority is given to projects that will have a multiplier effect upon the community. The grants must be used to finance the cost of special projects and capital improvements and not to defray current operating expenses. The Foundation will not provide the entire support for a project and will expect that others will share the costs.

GEOG. RESTRICTIONS: Bay County area, Michigan.

FINANCIAL DATA:
Assets of approximately $6,000,000.
Amount of support per award: $1,000 to $250,000.
Total amount of support: Varies.

APPLICATION INFO:
Application can be obtained by telephone call to Kathy Czerwinski, Administrator, at (989) 213-1225.
Duration: Usually one year.
Deadline: Mid-March, early June, early September and late November.

PUBLICATIONS:
Brochure.

ADDRESS INQUIRIES TO:
Administrator for the Board of Trustees
(See address above.)

EDWARD BANGS KELLEY & ELZA KELLEY FOUNDATION, INC. [1279]

20 North Main Street
South Yarmouth, MA 02664
(508) 775-3117
Fax: (508) 775-3720
E-mail: contact@kelleyfoundation.org
Web Site: www.kelleyfoundation.org

FOUNDED: 1954

AREAS OF INTEREST:
Health, psychology, sociology, education, culture, and environment.

TYPE:
Capital grants; Challenge/matching grants; Development grants; Matching gifts; Project/program grants.

YEAR PROGRAM STARTED: 1954

PURPOSE:
To promote the health and welfare of the residents of Barnstable County.

LEGAL BASIS:
Private foundation.

ELIGIBILITY:
Applicants must be U.S. citizens, residents of Barnstable County, or organizations who serve Barnstable County. Grants must benefit health and welfare of Barnstable County (MA) residents.

GEOG. RESTRICTIONS: Barnstable County, Massachusetts.

FINANCIAL DATA:
Amount of support per award: Varies.
Total amount of support: $250,000.

CO-OP FUNDING PROGRAMS: Cape Cod Grantmakers Collaborative, other foundations.

APPLICATION INFO:
Grant applicants should contact Joel Crowell, President of the Foundation, for information and application forms. Additional information is available on the web site.
Duration: One year. Renewals by reapplication.

IRS I.D.: 04-6039660

ADDRESS INQUIRIES TO:
See e-mail address above.

THE KETTERING FUND [1280]

1480 Kettering Tower
Dayton, OH 45423
(937) 228-1021
E-mail: info@ketteringfamilyphilanthropies.org
Web Site: www.ketteringfamilyphilanthropies.org

FOUNDED: 1958

AREAS OF INTEREST:
The environment, medical research, teaching, the arts and higher education.

TYPE:
Capital grants; Challenge/matching grants; Development grants; Endowments; Matching gifts; Project/program grants; Research grants.

YEAR PROGRAM STARTED: 1958

PURPOSE:
To support scientific, medical, social and educational studies and research conducted by nonprofit, charitable organizations that are located in Ohio.

LEGAL BASIS:
Private foundation.

ELIGIBILITY:
Applicants must be tax-exempt 501(c)(3) nonprofit organizations. The Fund does not support individuals, partisan political causes or candidates, public elementary or secondary schools, scholarships or travel.

GEOG. RESTRICTIONS: Ohio.

FINANCIAL DATA:
Amount of support per award: Varies.

NO. AWARDS: 10.

REPRESENTATIVE AWARDS:
$40,000 to Ohio Arts Council; $20,000 to Ohio Foundation of Independent Colleges.

APPLICATION INFO:
The Kettering Fund requires a letter of inquiry, to be submitted online, as a preliminary step before an application is requested. Check online for availability of funding.
Duration: Varies with project.
Deadline: Letter of inquiry: Generally late January and July.

PUBLICATIONS:
Application guidelines.

ADDRESS INQUIRIES TO:
Judy Thompson, Executive Director
(See address above.)

KEWEENAW COMMUNITY FOUNDATION [1281]

236 Quincy Street
Hancock, MI 49930
(906) 482-9673
Fax: (906) 482-9679
E-mail: mail@k-c-f.org
Web Site: www.keweenawgives.org

FOUNDED: 1994

AREAS OF INTEREST:
Environment, health and youth.

TYPE:
Awards/prizes; Challenge/matching grants; Development grants; Endowments; Project/program grants; Scholarships.

YEAR PROGRAM STARTED: 1994

PURPOSE:
To inspire giving that invests in our community's quality of life.

ELIGIBILITY:
Grants are made to organizations that have tax-exempt status under Section 501(c)(3) of the Internal Revenue Code. No grants are made to individuals. Religious programs may apply. Grants can also be given to governmental units or eligible educational institutions.

GEOG. RESTRICTIONS: Houghton and Keweenaw counties, Michigan.

FINANCIAL DATA:

Amount of support per award: Grants vary in amount, depending upon the needs and nature of the request.

Total amount of support: Varies.

APPLICATION INFO:

Information is available on the web site.

Duration: One year. Renewal possible.

STAFF:

Kyle Krym, Head of Marketing and Communications

ADDRESS INQUIRIES TO:

Lisa Broemer, Office Manager
(See address above.)

KITSAP COMMUNITY FOUNDATION [1282]

9657 Levin Road, N.W.
Suite 260
Silverdale, WA 98383
(360) 698-3622
Fax: (360) 698-6043
E-mail: kcf@kitsapfoundation.org
Web Site: www.kitsapfoundation.org

FOUNDED: 1993

NAME(S) OF PROGRAMS:

- **Kitsap Center for Nonprofit Excellence**
- **Kitsap Great Give**
- **Kitsap Strong**

TYPE:

General operating grants; Project/program grants; Scholarships.

YEAR PROGRAM STARTED: 1999

PURPOSE:

To improve the quality of life in the community.

LEGAL BASIS:

501(c)(3).

ELIGIBILITY:

Grant support mostly for nonprofit organizations serving Kitsap County, WA and surrounding areas.

GEOG. RESTRICTIONS: Kitsap County, Washington and its surrounding areas.

FINANCIAL DATA:

$5,000,000 in assets as of December 2014.

Amount of support per award: $500 to $5,000.

Total amount of support: $500,000 in grants and scholarships for the year 2014.

NO. MOST RECENT APPLICANTS: 62.

NO. AWARDS: 25.

REPRESENTATIVE AWARDS:

Boys & Girls Clubs; Great Peninsula Conservancy; Kitsap Community Resources.

APPLICATION INFO:

Applications are to be submitted online at commongrantapplication.com.

Duration: One year.

Deadline: January 29.

PUBLICATIONS:

Newsletter; annual report.

IRS I.D.: 94-3205217

STAFF:

Kol Medina, Executive Director

ADDRESS INQUIRIES TO:

Kol Medina, Executive Director
(See address above.)

THE KROGER COMPANY FOUNDATION [1283]

1014 Vine Street
Cincinnati, OH 45202-1100
(513) 762-4000
Fax: (513) 762-1100
Web Site: www.thekrogerco.com/community/kroger-foundation

FOUNDED: 1987

AREAS OF INTEREST:

Education, human services, hunger relief and women's health.

TYPE:

General operating grants.

YEAR PROGRAM STARTED: 1987

PURPOSE:

To feed the hungry, support breast cancer and women's health initiatives, support and promote the advancement of women and minorities, provide disaster relief and assist local grassroots organizations.

LEGAL BASIS:

Corporate giving program.

ELIGIBILITY:

Only proposals from 501(c)(3) organizations located in communities where the Kroger Company has operations are considered.

The Foundation does not support international projects or national organizations, except when local chapter is active in a community served by the Kroger Company.

FINANCIAL DATA:

Amount of support per award: Typically $1,000 to $5,000.

APPLICATION INFO:

Eligible organizations may submit proposals at any time through the community relations department of the local retail division office. Proposals must include an IRS tax-exempt determination letter and should include a statement of the reason for the request.

PUBLICATIONS:

Program announcement; application guidelines.

ADDRESS INQUIRIES TO:

Foundation Administrator
(See address above.)

*SPECIAL STIPULATIONS:

Funding limited to organizations serving communities where Kroger operates.

LAWRENCE COUNTY COMMUNITY FOUNDATION [1284]

1324 K Street, Suite 150
Bedford, IN 47421
(812) 279-2215
Fax: (812) 279-1984
E-mail: lccf@cfpartner.org
Web Site: www.cfpartner.org

AREAS OF INTEREST:

Community improvement.

TYPE:

Endowments; Project/program grants; Scholarships. Collaborative projects. Classroom grants.

PURPOSE:

To be proactive in creating and growing an enduring source of charitable assets that will help to identify and respond to the emerging and changing needs of the community.

ELIGIBILITY:

Organizations and agencies who may or may not be tax-exempt according to Section 501(c)(3) of the Internal Revenue Code or for-profit entities interested in funding a charitable, not-for profit program are eligible. Population served by the program must be within Lawrence County, IN.

GEOG. RESTRICTIONS: Lawrence County, Indiana.

FINANCIAL DATA:

Amount of support per award: Varies.

Total amount of support: Varies.

APPLICATION INFO:

Application form can be requested from the Foundation or downloaded from the web site. Applicants must submit the following documents with the application form:
(1) concise summary of the proposed project, two or three paragraphs in length, stating the community need to be addressed by the project and why the organization is qualified to address the need, the target population and estimated number to be served, the organization's experience with similar projects, and a description of how the project will fit into and further the organization's overall mission;
(2) description of the activities or steps that will be taken to carry out the project, including project timeline;
(3) summary of funding details, including how the funds will be used, as well as other funding sources. Attach a detailed budget sheet showing projected income and expenses for the project;
(4) an explanation of how the success of this project will be evaluated. If the organization plans to continue the project, explain how will it be sustained after grant funding is expended and;
(5) list of names and amounts from sources contributing 10% or more of the organization's budget in the past two years. Also list affiliations with religious groups.

Application must be signed by the organization President or another nonpaid board officer. Staple or clip each grant application copy.

Duration: Funding for a multiyear project will usually be considered on an annual basis and not extend beyond three years.

ADDRESS INQUIRIES TO:

Hope Flores, Executive Director
(See address above.)

THE LEARY FIREFIGHTERS FOUNDATION [1285]

594 Broadway, Suite 409
New York, NY 10012-3234
(212) 343-0240
Fax: (212) 343-1762
E-mail: info@learyfirefighters.org
Web Site: www.learyfirefighters.org

FOUNDED: 2000

AREAS OF INTEREST:

Firefighting.

NAME(S) OF PROGRAMS:

- **The Jeremiah Lucey Grant Program**

TYPE:

Grants-in-aid; Project/program grants; Training grants. Grant program to assist professional fire departments.

YEAR PROGRAM STARTED: 2000

PURPOSE:
To provide funding and resources for fire departments to obtain the highest level of equipment, training and technology.

LEGAL BASIS:
Publicly funded tax-exempt organization under Section 501(c)(3) of the Internal Revenue Code.

ELIGIBILITY:
Fire departments with a financial need not covered by a municipal budget in order to maintain the highest level of public safety. Grants only to union-affiliated uniformed fire departments. No grants to individuals.

GEOG. RESTRICTIONS: Massachusetts; Detroit, Michigan; and New York.

FINANCIAL DATA:
Amount of support per award: Average grant: $25,000 to $50,000.

Total amount of support: Varies.

APPLICATION INFO:
Initial letter of inquiry, up to two pages, and project budget. Full details are available on the Foundation web site.

Duration: Varies.

IRS I.D.: 13-4125074

STAFF:
Sharon Badal, Development Associate

ADDRESS INQUIRIES TO:
Sharon Badal, Development Associate
(See address above.)

THE JOHN J. LEIDY FOUNDATION [1286]

c/o Pierson & Pierson
305 West Chesapeake Avenue, Suite 308
Towson, MD 21204
(410) 821-3006
Fax: (410) 821-3007
E-mail: info@leidyfoundation.org
Web Site: www.leidyfoundation.org

FOUNDED: 1957

AREAS OF INTEREST:
Education, health care, arts/culture, food services, human services, children and youth.

TYPE:
General operating grants; Project/program grants.

PURPOSE:
To improve the quality of life in the Baltimore area.

LEGAL BASIS:
Private foundation.

ELIGIBILITY:
Organizations must be IRS 501(c)(3) tax-exempt and be located in Maryland. The Foundation does not fund individuals.

GEOG. RESTRICTIONS: Baltimore metropolitan area.

FINANCIAL DATA:
Amount of support per award: $350 to $20,000.

Total amount of support: $499,086 for the year 2015.

NO. MOST RECENT APPLICANTS: 125.

NO. AWARDS: 73 for the year 2015.

APPLICATION INFO:
Applications must include the proposed budget and a copy of the IRS tax-exempt letter. Application submission via e-mail is preferred.

Duration: Typically one year.

PUBLICATIONS:
Application guidelines.

OFFICER:
Robert L. Pierson, President

ADDRESS INQUIRIES TO:
Lu Pierson, Grants Administrator
(See address above.)

LOCAL INITIATIVES SUPPORT CORPORATION [1287]

501 Seventh Avenue, 7th Floor
New York, NY 10018
(212) 455-9800
Fax: (212) 682-5929
E-mail: info@lisc.org
Web Site: www.lisc.org

FOUNDED: 1980

AREAS OF INTEREST:
Urban and rural community revitalization.

TYPE:
Project/program grants; Technical assistance. Equity. Organizational support.

YEAR PROGRAM STARTED: 1980

PURPOSE:
To support community development; to equip struggling communities with the capital, strategy and know-how to become places where people can thrive; to build sustainable communities, which are good places to work, do business and raise children.

ELIGIBILITY:
Nonprofit 501(c)(3) IRS status.

GEOG. RESTRICTIONS: United States.

FINANCIAL DATA:
Amount of support per award: Varies.

Total amount of support: Varies.

Matching fund requirements: A strict matching requirement, dollar-for-dollar of new money from local private sources.

APPLICATION INFO:
Contact LISC local offices or the Corporation.

Duration: Varies.

IRS I.D.: 13-3030229

BOARD OF DIRECTORS:
Robert E. Rubin, Chairman
Michael Rubinger, President and Chief Executive Officer

LONG ISLAND COMMUNITY FOUNDATION [1288]

900 Walt Whitman Road
Suite 205
Melville, NY 11747
(631) 991-8800 ext. 233
Fax: (631) 991-8801
E-mail: narnold@licf.org
Web Site: www.licf.org

FOUNDED: 1978

AREAS OF INTEREST:
Arts, education, community development, environment, health, mental health, hunger, technical assistance, youth development and progressive social change.

NAME(S) OF PROGRAMS:
- **Henry Phillip Kraft Memorial Fund-Environmental Grants**
- **LIUU Fund-Progressive Social Change Grants**

TYPE:
Project/program grants.

YEAR PROGRAM STARTED: 1978

PURPOSE:
To provide leadership in identifying current and future community needs, and building a permanent endowment to address these needs.

LEGAL BASIS:
501(c)(3) or fiscal agent.

ELIGIBILITY:
Programs and projects benefiting Long Island, NY. Nonprofit organizations headquartered outside of Nassau and Suffolk Counties may apply if the project benefits Nassau and Suffolk counties.

GEOG. RESTRICTIONS: Nassau and Suffolk counties, New York.

FINANCIAL DATA:
Amount of support per award: $10,000 to $25,000.

Total amount of support: Approximately $1,000,000.

NO. AWARDS: Over 50 annually.

APPLICATION INFO:
The Foundation has three grant cycles throughout the year. Detailed instructions are provided on the Foundation's web site. Applicants should review the instructions carefully before submitting an application.

Duration: One year.

STAFF:
Sol Marie Alfonso-Jones, Senior Program Officer
Mary Beth Guyther, Program Officer
Nancy Arnold, Grants Administrator

EXECUTIVE DIRECTOR:
David Okorn

ADDRESS INQUIRIES TO:
Nancy Arnold, Grants Administrator
(See address above.)

M & M AREA COMMUNITY FOUNDATION [1289]

1110 10th Avenue, Suite L-1
Menominee, MI 49858
(906) 864-3599
Fax: (906) 864-3657
E-mail: info@mmcommunityfoundation.org
Web Site: www.mmcommunityfoundation.org

FOUNDED: 1994

AREAS OF INTEREST:
Arts, charity, civic affairs, community development, culture, education, health, historic preservation and human services.

TYPE:
Project/program grants; Scholarships.

YEAR PROGRAM STARTED: 1997

PURPOSE:
To make people's lives better: more meaningful, secure, and safe.

ELIGIBILITY:
Grants are made to organizations that have tax-exempt status under Section 501(c)(3) of the Internal Revenue Code. No grants are made to individuals.

GEOG. RESTRICTIONS: Menominee County, Michigan and Marinette County, Wisconsin.

FINANCIAL DATA:
Amount of support per award: Varies.

Total amount of support: $300,000 in grants and $130,000 in scholarships in fiscal year 2015.

NO. AWARDS: 71 scholarships in fiscal year 2015.

APPLICATION INFO:
Applications must be submitted online.

Duration: Varies.

Deadline: Applications are accepted on a rolling basis.

ADDRESS INQUIRIES TO:
Paula Gruszynski
Executive Director
(See e-mail address above.)

MADISON COMMUNITY FOUNDATION [1290]

2 Science Court
Madison, WI 53711
(608) 232-1763
Fax: (608) 232-1772
E-mail: tlinfield@madisoncommunityfoundation.org
Web Site: www.madisoncommunityfoundation.org

FOUNDED: 1942

AREAS OF INTEREST:
Children and youth, arts and culture, community development, environment, elderly, learning and capacity building.

TYPE:
Capital grants; Project/program grants. Endowment challenge grants. Program grants support new programs or expansion of existing programs. Capital grants support the construction, acquisition and renovation of facilities and the purchase of equipment. Investments in technology are given to significantly enhance the organization's ability to operate or to improve services. Endowment grants are 1:2 or 1:3 challenge grants to grow agency endowment funds.

PURPOSE:
To enhance the quality of life for residents in Dane County.

LEGAL BASIS:
Community foundation.

ELIGIBILITY:
Organizations must be nonprofit IRS 501(c)(3) tax-exempt, serve the people of Dane County, employ a staff, elect a governing board, and conduct business without discrimination on the basis of race, religion, gender, sexual preference, age, marital status, disability or national origin.

Generally grants are not made for operating expenses, individuals, endowments, debt retirement, lobbying, annual campaigns, scholarships, religious organizations for religious purposes, conferences, fund-raising, celebrations or substance abuse treatment.

GEOG. RESTRICTIONS: Dane County, Wisconsin.

FINANCIAL DATA:
Approximately 25% of grant applications are funded at some level. The Foundation is rarely the sole funder of projects; other sources will be sought to accomplish project goals.

Amount of support per award: Program average: $35,000; Capital average: $55,000.

Total amount of support: Approximately $2,000,000 in unrestricted and field-of-interest grants for the year 2015.

NO. MOST RECENT APPLICANTS: 70 for the year 2014.

NO. AWARDS: 25 for the year 2014.

REPRESENTATIVE AWARDS:
Neighborhood Center STEM Project; Madison Public Library Capital Campaign; Madison Parks Foundation; Boys and Girls Club; Madison Opera.

APPLICATION INFO:
Guidelines and applications are available from the Foundation. Full proposals must be submitted in both paper and electronic form. Proposals by fax are not accepted. An online letter of inquiry (LOI) is required.

Duration: One to two years.

Deadline: Letter of Inquiry: January 15 and July 15. Those asked to submit a full proposal: March 1 and September 1.

PUBLICATIONS:
Grantmaking Guidelines.

ADDRESS INQUIRIES TO:
Tom Linfield
Vice President, Community Impact
(See address above.)

MARIETTA COMMUNITY FOUNDATION [1291]

100 Putnam Street
Marietta, OH 45750
(740) 373-3286
Fax: (740) 373-3937
E-mail: heather@mcfohio.org
Web Site: www.mcfohio.org

FOUNDED: 1974

AREAS OF INTEREST:
Civic affairs, the elderly, community needs and education.

TYPE:
Challenge/matching grants; Conferences/seminars; Development grants; Endowments; Grants-in-aid; Matching gifts; Scholarships; Seed money grants; Technical assistance; Training grants.

YEAR PROGRAM STARTED: 1974

PURPOSE:
To support philanthropy and the efforts of citizens to improve natural, human and civic resources.

LEGAL BASIS:
Community foundation.

ELIGIBILITY:
Must be a 501(c)(3) organization in or serving Washington County, OH.

GEOG. RESTRICTIONS: Greater Washington County, Ohio, and surrounding area.

FINANCIAL DATA:
Amount of support per award: $200 to $20,000.

Total amount of support: $150,000 unrestricted for the year 2016.

NO. MOST RECENT APPLICANTS: 60.

NO. AWARDS: 35.

APPLICATION INFO:
Organizations may either send a one-page letter of inquiry or submit a formal application form.

Duration: Varies.

Deadline: Proposals are accepted at any time during the year. To be considered in a particular quarter, the in-hand deadlines are April 1 and October 1. Applicants should allow 45 to 75 days for processing and response.

PUBLICATIONS:
Annual report; grant guidelines; memorial brochure.

FREDA MAYTAG-GRACE CRAWFORD TRUST

c/o JPMorgan Private Client Services
2200 Ross Avenue, Floor 5
Dallas, TX 75201
(214) 965-2296
Fax: (866) 337-8406
E-mail: kelly.t.adams@jpmorgan.com
Web Site: www.jpmorgan.com/onlinegrants

TYPE:
Project/program grants.

See entry 1412 for full listing.

LUTHER T. MCCAULEY CHARITABLE TRUST [1292]

c/o JPMorgan
370 17th Street, Suite 3200
Denver, CO 80202
(303) 607-7810
Fax: (303) 607-7761
E-mail: julie.golden@jpmorgan.com
Web Site: www.jpmorgan.com/onlinegrants

AREAS OF INTEREST:
Economically deprived, the socially disadvantaged, mentally and physically handicapped citizens, with preference made toward the youth of the community for their educational, social, recreational and medical needs.

TYPE:
Project/program grants.

ELIGIBILITY:
Qualifying charities, agencies and institutions which direct their attention to the economically deprived, the socially disadvantaged and the mentally and physically handicapped citizens of El Paso County, CO. No grants to individuals.

Organization must provide copy of current IRS determination letter showing tax-exempt status under Section 501(c)(3) and public charity status under Section 509(a).

GEOG. RESTRICTIONS: El Paso County, Colorado.

FINANCIAL DATA:
Total amount of support: Average: $7,500.

APPLICATION INFO:
Applications must be submitted online. No physical applications will be accepted.

Duration: One year. No renewals.

Deadline: November 1, 2016.

ADDRESS INQUIRIES TO:
Julie Golden, Trust Advisor
(See address above.)

RICHARD KING MELLON FOUNDATION [1293]

BNY/Mellon Center
500 Grant Street, Suite 4106
Pittsburgh, PA 15219-2502
(412) 392-2800
Fax: (412) 392-2837
E-mail: lreed@rkmf.org
Web Site: www.fdncenter.org/grantmaker/rkmellon

FOUNDED: 1947

AREAS OF INTEREST:
Conservation; regional economic development; education; human services and nonprofit capacity building.

TYPE:
Capital grants; Challenge/matching grants; Grants-in-aid; Project/program grants. Grant program for improving the quality of life in southwestern Pennsylvania.

PURPOSE:
To promote conservation, economic development, education, human services and programs in the public interest.

ELIGIBILITY:
Must be 501(c)(3) nonprofit organizations. Priority is given to projects and programs that have clearly defined outcomes and an evaluation component. Funding is almost exclusively committed to southwestern Pennsylvania. Preference is given for support of established organizations with specific objectives, and for partnering with other donors rather than solely underwriting the entire cost of projects.

GEOG. RESTRICTIONS: Southwestern Pennsylvania.

FINANCIAL DATA:
Amount of support per award: Varies.

Total amount of support: $113,694,928 in grants paid for the year 2015.

APPLICATION INFO:
Applications must be mailed; faxes are not accepted. Current IRS determination letter indicating 501(c)(3) tax-exempt status required.

Duration: Varies.

Deadline: Applications accepted on a rolling basis.

ADDRESS INQUIRIES TO:
Lisa Reed, Grant Manager
(See address above.)

EUGENE AND AGNES E. MEYER FOUNDATION [1294]

1250 Connecticut Avenue, N.W.
Suite 800
Washington, DC 20036
(202) 483-8294
Fax: (202) 328-6850
E-mail: jward@meyerfdn.org
Web Site: www.meyerfoundation.org

FOUNDED: 1944

AREAS OF INTEREST:
Housing, employment, education, financial security, and organizational effectiveness.

TYPE:
Capital grants; Challenge/matching grants; General operating grants; Project/program grants; Technical assistance. Grants for a wide variety of projects in the above areas of interest in the Washington, DC metropolitan area.

YEAR PROGRAM STARTED: 1944

PURPOSE:
To pursue and invest in solutions that build on equitable greater Washington, DC community in which economically vulnerable people thrive.

LEGAL BASIS:
Private foundation.

ELIGIBILITY:
The Foundation distributes its funds to and through tax-exempt nonprofit organizations. It does not make grants for projects that are primarily sectarian in character. Grants are seldom made for projects outside the geographical boundaries of Greater Washington and are never made to individuals. The Foundation does not support endowment drives, scientific or medical research, scholarship programs, seasonal programs, special or annual events or conferences.

GEOG. RESTRICTIONS: Montgomery and Prince George's counties, Maryland; Arlington, Fairfax and Prince William counties and the cities of Alexandria, Falls Church, Manassas and Manassas Park, Virginia; Washington, DC.

FINANCIAL DATA:
Amount of support per award: $1,000 to $500,000; $25,000 average.

Total amount of support: $8,233,000 in grants authorized for the year 2015.

CO-OP FUNDING PROGRAMS: Occasional joint funding.

NO. MOST RECENT APPLICANTS: Approximately 500.

NO. AWARDS: 205 grants for the year ended December 31, 2015.

APPLICATION INFO:
Applications must be submitted online via link on the Foundation's web site.

Duration: Generally one-year support from date of award.

PUBLICATIONS:
E-newsletter.

IRS I.D.: 53-0241716

STAFF:
Nicky Goren, President and Chief Executive Officer
Janice Thomas, Vice President of Finance and Administration
Richard L. Moyers, Vice President, Programs and Communications
Karen FitzGerald, Program Director
Julian A. Haynes, Program Officer
Amy Nakamoto, Program Officer
Maegan Scott, Program Officer
Leslie Bethke, Finance Manager
Jane Ward, Grants Manager
Andrew Brown, Grants Management Assistant
Kari Den Otter, Program and Communications Assistant
Sparkle Lonesome, Program Assistant
Shana Silver, Program Assistant

OFFICERS AND BOARD OF DIRECTORS:
Joshua Bernstein, Chairperson
Deborah Ratner Salzberg, Vice Chairperson and Treasurer
Nicky Goren, President and Chief Executive Officer
Lidia Soto-Harmon, Secretary
Charlene M. Dukes
William Dunbar
Michael N. Harreld
Bo Menkiti
James Sandman
Dr. Robert G. Templin, Jr.
Rajiv Vinnakota
Kerrie B. Wilson

ADDRESS INQUIRIES TO:
Nicky Goren, President and Chief Executive Officer
(See address above.)

MICHIGAN GATEWAY COMMUNITY FOUNDATION [1295]

111 Days Avenue
Buchanan, MI 49107-1609
(269) 695-3521
Fax: (269) 695-4250
E-mail: info@mgcf.org
Web Site: www.mgcf.org

FOUNDED: 1978

AREAS OF INTEREST:
Health, culture, education and community development.

TYPE:
Challenge/matching grants; Development grants; Project/program grants; Scholarships; Seed money grants.

YEAR PROGRAM STARTED: 1978

PURPOSE:
To address the changing needs of the community in Cass and South Berrien counties; to foster a community of philanthropy, for good, forever.

LEGAL BASIS:
501(c)(3) nonprofit foundation.

ELIGIBILITY:
Eligible organizations must be IRS 501(c)(3) tax-exempt.

GEOG. RESTRICTIONS: Cass and South Berrien counties, Michigan.

FINANCIAL DATA:
Amount of support per award: Varies.

Total amount of support: Varies.

REPRESENTATIVE AWARDS:
$2,500 over six weeks for Group Counseling "Life on a Tightrope" for High School Girls at risk for low self-esteem and peer pressure.

APPLICATION INFO:
Applicants may use the Common Grant Application Form of the Council of Michigan Foundations. Applications must include a copy of the IRS tax determination letter. Applications for grants and scholarships are available on the web site.

Applicants for grants are strongly encouraged to contact the Foundation for an appointment before completing an application.

Duration: One year. Most grants not renewable.

Deadline: Grants from unrestricted grant sources: February 1 and August 1.

PUBLICATIONS:
Annual report; scholarship programs.

IRS I.D.: 38-2180730

ADDRESS INQUIRIES TO:
Robert N. Habicht
President and Chief Executive Officer
(See address above.)

THE MINNEAPOLIS FOUNDATION [1296]

800 IDS Center
80 South Eighth Street
Minneapolis, MN 55402
(612) 672-3878
Fax: (612) 672-3846
E-mail: info@mplsfoundation.org
Web Site: www.minneapolisfoundation.org

FOUNDED: 1915

AREAS OF INTEREST:
Civic engagement, economic vitality, education.

CONSULTING OR VOLUNTEER SERVICES:
Philanthropic services for other foundations.

NAME(S) OF PROGRAMS:

- **Community Action Funds**
- **Field of Interest Funds**

TYPE:
General operating grants; Project/program grants.

PURPOSE:
To invest the Foundation's unrestricted resources towards specific results in order to achieve social, economic and racial equity for Minneapolis residents.

LEGAL BASIS:
Community foundation incorporated in Minnesota.

ELIGIBILITY:
Organizations must advance social, economic, and/or racial equity to be eligible for funding. The Foundation grants to 501(c)(3) organizations, some 501(c)(4) nonprofits, governmental or tribal organizations, and groups organized for nonprofit purposes (informal, emerging or collaborative groups).

The Foundation does not fund individuals, organizations/activities outside of Minnesota, conference registration fees, memberships, direct religious activities, political organizations or candidates' fund-raising efforts, conferences, events or sponsorships, financial deficits, replacement of public sector funds, emergency/safety net services, regranting/loans, production of housing units, or purchase or repair of vehicles.

GEOG. RESTRICTIONS: Primarily Minneapolis, Minnesota.

FINANCIAL DATA:
Amount of support per award: Competitive grants: $30,000 to $100,000; average approximately $50,000.

Total amount of support: $6,900,000 in competitive grants for fiscal year 2015-16.

NO. MOST RECENT APPLICANTS: Competitive Community Grants: 177 for fiscal year 2013-14.

NO. AWARDS: Competitive Community Grants: 64 for fiscal year 2013-14.

REPRESENTATIVE AWARDS:
$35,000 to African Development Center of Minnesota to produce affordable housing opportunities and support a more competitive workforce; $40,000 to State Voices to increase voter participation in communities of color; $50,000 to EMPOWER to recruit, prepare, train and mobilize a cohort of underserved and underrepresented low-income and communities of color across Minneapolis to advocate for high-quality educational options for all children.

APPLICATION INFO:
Application information and updates on the Foundation grantmaking cycle are available on the web site.

Duration: Annual. Must reapply for additional funding. No multiyear grants.

IRS I.D.: 41-6029402

OFFICERS:
R.T. Rybak, President and Chief Executive Officer
Jean Adams, Chief Operating Officer/Chief Financial Operator

ADDRESS INQUIRIES TO:
Community Grantmaking
(See address above.)

MIZUHO USA FOUNDATION, INC. [1297]

Mizuho Bank, Ltd.
1251 Avenue of the Americas
31st Floor
New York, NY 10020-1104
(212) 282-4192
E-mail: mizuho.usa.foundation@mizuhocbus.com
Web Site: www.mizuhocbk.com/americas/community/foundation/index.html

FOUNDED: 2003

AREAS OF INTEREST:
Community development, with a focus on affordable housing, economic development and workforce development.

NAME(S) OF PROGRAMS:

- **Fostering Economic Self-Sufficiency**
- **Mizuho Community Involvement Grants Program**
- **Mizuho Matching Gifts Program**
- **Promoting Economic Development**
- **Strengthening Affordable Housing**

TYPE:
Demonstration grants; Matching gifts; Project/program grants; Seed money grants. The Foundation awards grants to not-for-profit charitable organizations for community development programs that help sustain and revitalize economically distressed urban communities, and assist individuals who live in these neighborhoods.

Fostering Economic Self-Sufficiency funds programs that strengthen the workforce development field through the provision of technical assistance and/or training to not-for-profit organizations.

Mizuho Community Involvement Grants Program makes small grants available to the not-for-profit charitable organizations with which Mizuho Corporate Bank volunteer activities take place.

Mizuho Matching Gifts Program is for qualifying contributions made by eligible Mizuho Financial Group U.S. employees to qualifying not-for-profit charitable organizations in the areas of education, arts and culture, health and community affairs.

Promoting Economic Development supports programs that promote economic and commercial revitalization of communities by fostering small business development, entrepreneurship, job creation and job retention.

Strengthening Affordable Housing provides funding for programs that facilitate access to affordable housing for low- and moderate-income individuals and families.

YEAR PROGRAM STARTED: 2003

PURPOSE:
To provide grants to not-for-profit charitable organizations to support community development programs that contribute to the strength and vitality of urban neighborhoods; to serve as a catalyst for innovative programs in the U.S. that strengthen urban communities.

LEGAL BASIS:
Corporate foundation.

ELIGIBILITY:
Organizations applying to the Foundation must:
(1) be recognized as tax-exempt under Section 501(c)(3) of the Internal Revenue Code and classified as a public charity under Section 509(a)(1) or (2) of the Internal Revenue Code and not a supporting organization under Section 509(a)(3);
(2) present a proposal that satisfies the Foundation's guidelines;
(3) not discriminate against a person or group on the basis of age, race, national origin, ethnicity, gender, disability, sexual orientation, political affiliation or religious belief and;
(4) be in full compliance with U.S. anti-terrorism laws and regulations, including the USA Patriot Act and Executive Order 13224, pertaining to U.S.-based, not-for-profit charitable organizations conducting activities outside of the U.S.

The Foundation does not fund:
(1) general operating support;
(2) individuals;
(3) religious, sectarian, fraternal, veteran, athletic or labor groups;
(4) organizations or programs outside the U.S.;
(5) political organizations, political candidates or political activity;
(6) organizations whose primary purpose is to influence legislation;
(7) fund-raising activities such as charitable dinners or sporting events;
(8) advertising and;
(9) endowment or capital campaigns.

GEOG. RESTRICTIONS: New York City, New York.

FINANCIAL DATA:
Foundation's endowment is approximately $13,300,000 as of September 30, 2015.

Amount of support per award: $10,000 to $100,000; average $50,000.

Total amount of support: $575,679 in grants for the year 2015.

Matching fund requirements: Mizuho Matching Gifts Program: 1:1 match for qualifying contributions. Requests for matching gifts must come from eligible employees of the Mizuho Financial Group in the U.S.

CO-OP FUNDING PROGRAMS: Neighborhood Opportunities Fund (New York City, NY) and New York City Workforce Development Fund.

REPRESENTATIVE AWARDS:
$75,000 to WHEDco, New York, NY, for Childcare Improvement Project to expand the training component of a state-funded initiative to register unlicensed family day care providers in New York City; $10,000 to Los Angeles Neighborhood Housing Services for homeownership preservation and foreclosure prevention; $25,000 to Japan Center for International Exchange - USA for a new fund to support Japanese nongovernmental organizations and community associations working to rebuild communities in the aftermath of the Great East Japan Earthquake and tsunami.

APPLICATION INFO:
Qualifying organizations must submit a short concept paper of up to three pages for preliminary review. The concept paper should include:
(1) a brief description of the organization including its legal name, history, mission/goals, activities and web address;
(2) copy of the IRS determination letter indicating 501(c)(3) tax-exempt status and

509(1) public charity classification and;
(3) a description of the program for which funding is sought, including statement of need, goals and objectives of the program, expected outcomes and evaluation methods, projected time frame, population(s)/geographies served, grant amount requested, and a preliminary program budget, with projected expenses and revenues, including funding commitments received to date for the program as well as pending requests (may be provided in attachment form).

The Foundation staff will review all initial submissions and invite organizations on a selective basis to submit more detailed proposals. Each applicant will be notified of the Foundation's interest within eight weeks of the annual deadline. Selected proposals are presented to the Foundation's Board of Directors, which makes funding decisions each fall.

Duration: Usually one year; some multiyear grants may be awarded.

Deadline: First weekday in July, to be considered for funding in the same year.

PUBLICATIONS:
Brochure; application guidelines.

IRS I.D.: 13-3550008

OFFICERS:
John H. Higgs, Chairman
Minako Nakamoto, President
Paul Dankers, Treasurer
Mitsuhiro Kanazawa, Secretary
Lesley H. Palmer, Executive Director
Albert Scarola, Assistant Treasurer
Leah Markham, Program Officer

BOARD OF DIRECTORS:
Nancy Bercovici
John H. Higgs
Mitsuhiro Kanazawa
Minako Nakamoto
Hiroshi Suehiro

ADDRESS INQUIRIES TO:
Lesley H. Palmer, Executive Director
(See address above.)

MONTANA COMMUNITY FOUNDATION [1298]

One North Last Chance Gulch
Suite 1
Helena, MT 59601
(406) 443-8313
Fax: (406) 442-0482
E-mail: info@mtcf.org
Web Site: www.mtcf.org

FOUNDED: 1988

AREAS OF INTEREST:
General charitable purposes.

NAME(S) OF PROGRAMS:
- **Montana Community Foundation's Anti-Poverty Endowment**
- **Social Justice Montana**
- **Women's Foundation of Montana**

TYPE:
Grants-in-aid; Scholarships. The Foundation provides $2,000,000 yearly in grants and scholarships, almost all of that money is designated. It also has a large number of donor-advised and scholarship funds. The only competitive granting programs are the following:
Anti-Poverty Endowment: The mission of this endowment is to benefit rural communities, and grants given to projects/programs which identify assets, use inclusive decision-making, expand economic opportunities and enhance or develop community skills that design, lead and implement lasting change.
Social Justice Montana: The mission of this Fund is to promote tolerance and combat bigotry and discrimination, with a focus on youth, ages elementary through high school and;
Women's Foundation of Montana: Its mission is to promote economic self-sufficiency and a brighter future for women and girls.

PURPOSE:
To cultivate a culture of giving so Montana communities can flourish.

LEGAL BASIS:
501(c)(3) organization.

ELIGIBILITY:
Applicants must be 501(c)(3) tax-exempt organizations or an exempt government unit.

GEOG. RESTRICTIONS: Montana.

FINANCIAL DATA:
Assets of approximately $79,000,000 as of June 30, 2015.

Amount of support per award: Anti-Poverty Endowment: Varies. Social Justice Montana: Up to $5,000. Women's Foundation of Montana: Up to $10,000. Scholarships: Generally $500 to $5,000.

Total amount of support: $4,100,000 in grants and scholarships distributed in fiscal year 2016.

APPLICATION INFO:
Application information is posted online. Only one application per organization will be accepted.

Duration: Varies.

Deadline: Scholarships: March 18.

ADDRESS INQUIRIES TO:
Jessica Stewart-Kuntz
Operations and Grants Manager
(See address above.)

THE MORTON-KELLY CHARITABLE TRUST [1299]

c/o Jensen Baird Gardner & Henry
10 Free Street
Portland, ME 04101
(207) 775-7271
Fax: (207) 775-7935
E-mail: mquinlan@jbgh.com

FOUNDED: 1988

AREAS OF INTEREST:
The arts, education, environment and history.

TYPE:
Capital grants; Challenge/matching grants; Development grants; Project/program grants; Seed money grants. One-time cash award.

YEAR PROGRAM STARTED: 1988

PURPOSE:
To support organizations in the arts, education, environment and history.

LEGAL BASIS:
Private foundation.

ELIGIBILITY:
Organizations must be IRS 501(c)(3) tax-exempt and be located in Maine.

GEOG. RESTRICTIONS: Maine.

FINANCIAL DATA:
Amount of support per award: Varies.

Total amount of support: $826,100 for the year 2015.

NO. MOST RECENT APPLICANTS: 150 for the year 2015.

NO. AWARDS: 88 for the year 2015.

REPRESENTATIVE AWARDS:
$6,200 to Androscoggin River Watershed Council; $10,000 to Children's Museum & Theatre of Maine; $5,000 to Deer Isle-Stonington Historical Society; $5,000 to Friends of Casco Bay; $5,000 to Oratorio Chorale.

APPLICATION INFO:
Applicants may submit a written proposal and must include a copy of the IRS tax determination letter.

Duration: One year.

Deadline: October 1.

IRS I.D.: 01-0442078

ADDRESS INQUIRIES TO:
Michael J. Quinlan, Secretary
(See address above.)

*PLEASE NOTE:
Applications not accepted before July 1 each year.

CHARLES STEWART MOTT FOUNDATION [1300]

Mott Foundation Building
503 South Saginaw Street, Suite 1200
Flint, MI 48502-1851
(810) 238-5651
Fax: (810) 766-1753
E-mail: info@mott.org
Web Site: www.mott.org

FOUNDED: 1926

AREAS OF INTEREST:
Civil society, environment, education and Flint, MI area, besides exploratory interests.

TYPE:
Challenge/matching grants; Demonstration grants; General operating grants; Project/program grants; Seed money grants; Technical assistance; Training grants. Grants for improvement of the quality of living in the community through pilot ventures in a number of human service areas. Emphasis is on improving opportunity for the individual, partnership with the community, effectiveness of community systems and leadership.

PURPOSE:
To support efforts that promote a just, equitable and sustainable society.

LEGAL BASIS:
Private foundation.

ELIGIBILITY:
Applicants must be organizations and institutions with appropriate interests. No grants to individuals. Tax-exempt status is required.

FINANCIAL DATA:
Amount of support per award: $15,000 to $250,000.

Total amount of support: $101,365,342 for the year 2015.

NO. AWARDS: 400 grants for the year 2014.

APPLICATION INFO:
Information on application procedures is available online.

Duration: One year; occasionally multiyear.

PUBLICATIONS:
Annual report.

ADDRESS INQUIRIES TO:
Office of Proposal Entry
(See address above.)

MUSKINGUM COUNTY COMMUNITY FOUNDATION [1301]

534 Putnam Avenue
Zanesville, OH 43701
(740) 453-5192
Fax: (740) 453-5734
E-mail: giving@mccf.org (grants)
scholarshipcentral@mccf.org (scholarships)
Web Site: www.mccf.org

FOUNDED: 1985

AREAS OF INTEREST:
Improving the quality of life in Muskingum County, OH.

CONSULTING OR VOLUNTEER SERVICES:
Assistance to college-bound students, grantseekers and grantmakers in the Muskingum County, OH area.

NAME(S) OF PROGRAMS:
- **Scholarship Central**

TYPE:
Awards/prizes; Challenge/matching grants; Conferences/seminars; Development grants; Endowments; Project/program grants; Scholarships; Seed money grants; Technical assistance; Visiting scholars. Scholarships for Muskingum County, OH residents and others designated in fund agreements.

YEAR PROGRAM STARTED: 1985

PURPOSE:
To improve the quality of life and to serve the charitable needs of the community by attracting and administering charitable funds.

LEGAL BASIS:
Ohio nonprofit corporation classified by the IRS as a 501(c)(3) entity.

ELIGIBILITY:
Organization with primary or sole impact on Muskingum County, OH.

GEOG. RESTRICTIONS: Muskingum and contiguous counties, Ohio.

FINANCIAL DATA:
Assets of over $22,000,000.
Amount of support per award: Varies.
Total amount of support: Approximately $1,000,000 annually.

NO. AWARDS: Grants and scholarships: Over 100 yearly.

APPLICATION INFO:
Varies per grant or scholarship.
Duration: Grants and scholarships: Varies.
Deadline: Varies.

ADDRESS INQUIRIES TO:
Brian Wagner, Chief Executive Officer
(See address above.)

NATIONAL BLACK MBA ASSOCIATION [1302]

400 West Peachtree Street, N.W.
Suite 203
Atlanta, GA 30308
(404) 260-5444
E-mail: scholarship@nbmbaa.org
Web Site: www.nbmbaa.org

AREAS OF INTEREST:
The economic and intellectual wealth of the black community.

NAME(S) OF PROGRAMS:
- **NBMBAA Graduate Scholarship Program**

TYPE:
Scholarships.

PURPOSE:
To help create economic and intellectual wealth for the black community; to identify and increase the pool of Black talent for business, public, private and nonprofit sectors.

ELIGIBILITY:
Applicant must:
(1) be a financially active member of the National Black MBA Association;
(2) be a U.S. or Canadian citizen;
(3) be a student entering their first year (Fall 2017), or continuing in a full or part-time Master's program at an accredited college or university at the time of award (September 2017);
(4) have a 3.0 or above grade point average;
(5) demonstrate academic excellence;
(6) demonstrate exceptional leadership potential;
(7) be actively involved in their local communities through service to others and;
(8) be recommended by a faculty member or individual familiar with applicant's academic achievements or supervisor in a business workplace.

GEOG. RESTRICTIONS: United States and Canada.

FINANCIAL DATA:
The Association has awarded over $5,000,000 in scholarships to deserving youth and minority students (undergraduate, graduate and doctoral).
Amount of support per award: Up to $10,000.
Total amount of support: Over $500,000.

NO. MOST RECENT APPLICANTS: 550.

NO. AWARDS: Minimum of 25.

APPLICATION INFO:
Application materials include:
(1) application (must be completed online);
(2) essay (500 words on the selected topic, submitted online only);
(3) current resume no more than two pages long;
(4) copy of most recent official transcript(s) uploaded and;
(5) headshot in jpeg format (image should be at least 1024 x 768).
Deadline: June 6.

ADDRESS INQUIRIES TO:
Kenya Gray
E-mail: kenya.gray@uncf.org
Tel: (202) 810-0258

NATIONAL BLACK MBA ASSOCIATION

400 West Peachtree Street, N.W.
Suite 203
Atlanta, GA 30308
(404) 260-5444
E-mail: scholarship@nbmbaa.org
Web Site: www.nbmbaa.org

TYPE:
Scholarships.

See entry 1012 for full listing.

NATIONAL FOOTBALL LEAGUE FOUNDATION [1303]

345 Park Avenue
New York, NY 10154
(212) 450-2000
Fax: (212) 847-1812
E-mail: alexia.gallagher@nfl.com
Web Site: www.nflfoundation.org

FOUNDED: 1973

AREAS OF INTEREST:
Health and safety, youth football, and community.

NAME(S) OF PROGRAMS:
- **Field Grants**
- **Player Foundation Grants**
- **Pro Bowl Grants**
- **Youth Football Grants**

TYPE:
Awards/prizes; Challenge/matching grants; General operating grants; Project/program grants; Research grants; Seed money grants; Training grants.

YEAR PROGRAM STARTED: 1973

PURPOSE:
To support youth-oriented programs that promote education, physical fitness and the value of a healthy lifestyle.

LEGAL BASIS:
Private foundation.

ELIGIBILITY:
Grants will be awarded to organizations that focus on youth-centered educational and recreational programming on a national scale.

GEOG. RESTRICTIONS: United States.

FINANCIAL DATA:
Amount of support per award: Varies.
Total amount of support: Varies.

NO. MOST RECENT APPLICANTS: Approximately 1,200.

NO. AWARDS: Varies.

APPLICATION INFO:
Application information is available on the web site.

IRS I.D.: 23-7315236

ADDRESS INQUIRIES TO:
Alexia Gallagher, Director
(See address above.)

NATIONAL TRUST FOR HISTORIC PRESERVATION

2600 Virginia Avenue, N.W.
Suite 1100
Washington, DC 20037
(202) 588-6277
Fax: (202) 588-6223
E-mail: grants@savingplaces.org
Web Site: www.preservationnation.org/funding

TYPE:
Challenge/matching grants; Project/program grants; Seed money grants; Technical assistance; Training grants. Education program curricula. Project grants to support consultants with professional expertise in areas such as architecture, law, planning, economics, archeology and graphic design. Conferences that address subjects of particular importance to historic preservation also are funded. In addition, grants are made for curriculum development in preservation education directed at select audiences.

See entry 603 for full listing.

NBCC FOUNDATION, INC.

3 Terrace Way
Greensboro, NC 27403
(336) 232-0376
Fax: (336) 232-0010
E-mail: foundation@nbcc.org
Web Site: www.nbccf.org

TYPE:
Fellowships; Scholarships. Academic scholarships for individuals pursuing a graduate-level degree in professional counseling.

See entry 1670 for full listing.

NEW MEXICO COMMUNITY FOUNDATION [1304]

502 West Cordova Road, Suite 1
Santa Fe, NM 87505
(505) 820-6860
Fax: (505) 820-7860
E-mail: lmilbourn@nmcf.org
info@nmcf.org
Web Site: www.nmcf.org

FOUNDED: 1983

AREAS OF INTEREST:
New Mexico's communities and their people.

NAME(S) OF PROGRAMS:
- **Education and Leadership**
- **NewMexicoWomen.Org**
- **Philanthropic First Responder**
- **Rural Community Development**

TYPE:
Endowments; Grants-in-aid; Scholarships. New Mexico Community Foundation provides grants that help nonprofit organizations, community groups and charities statewide expand their efforts, increase their impact and advance their unique mission and vision to achieve success today and tomorrow. Although the Foundation does not have a regular open or revolving grant cycle, programmatic grant opportunities are available from time to time. It has the following program areas of focus:

Education and Leadership: Included in this program area are College Scholarships, which have originated through donor-advised funds and which assist high school graduates to pursue their academic goals; Fiscal Sponsorship Program, which enables new organizations to raise money for programs and provides guidance and oversight as needed to expand capacity and develop best practices; and Native American Preparatory Scholars Fund, an initiative and endowment fund of the Foundation that supports increasing the number of New Mexico Native American students who shall aspire to, be prepared for, and graduate from colleges and universities.

NewMexicoWomen.Org: A fund and initiative of the Foundation, which works to advance opportunities for women and girls statewide so that they can lead healthy, self-sufficient and empowered lives.

Philanthropic First Responder: Several emergency funds of the Foundation to respond to immediate emergency needs throughout the state.

Rural Community Development: A community-based approach to philanthropy which creates locally controlled assets and invests them to strengthen rural people and places.

GEOG. RESTRICTIONS: New Mexico.

FINANCIAL DATA:
Amount of support per award: Varies.

ADDRESS INQUIRIES TO:
Linda Milbourn
Grants and Fiscal Sponsorship Manager
(See address above.)

THE NORCLIFFE FOUNDATION

Wells Fargo Center
999 Third Avenue, Suite 1006
Seattle, WA 98104
(206) 682-4820
Fax: (206) 682-4821
E-mail: arline@thenorcliffefoundation.com
Web Site: www.thenorcliffefoundation.com

TYPE:
Capital grants; General operating grants; Project/program grants. Social service grants.

See entry 237 for full listing.

NORTHEAST AGRICULTURAL EDUCATION FOUNDATION

220 South Warren Street
9th Floor
Syracuse, NY 13202
(315) 671-0588
Fax: (315) 671-0589
E-mail: info@northeastagriculture.org
Web Site: www.northeastagriculture.org

TYPE:
Project/program grants.

See entry 2061 for full listing.

THE NORTHWEST MINNESOTA FOUNDATION [1305]

201 Third Street, N.W.
Bemidji, MN 56601
(218) 759-2057
Fax: (218) 759-2328
E-mail: nwmf@nwmf.org
Web Site: www.nwmf.org

FOUNDED: 1986

TYPE:
Challenge/matching grants; Demonstration grants; Project/program grants; Research grants; Scholarships; Seed money grants; Technical assistance.

YEAR PROGRAM STARTED: 1986

PURPOSE:
To improve the quality of life for the people of the region.

ELIGIBILITY:
Applicants must be a public agency or private nonprofit organization with a 501(c)(3) federal tax-exempt status. If an organization does not meet these criteria, it may work with an affiliated tax-exempt organization that may be the applicant and fiscal agent for the project. The affiliate must be a parent organization, provide similar services and/or define in writing its participation in project implementation. No grants are made to individuals.

GEOG. RESTRICTIONS: Beltrami, Clearwater, Hubbard, Kittson, Lake of the Woods, Mahnomen, Marshall, Norman, Pennington, Polk, Red Lake and Roseau counties, Minnesota.

FINANCIAL DATA:
Amount of support per award: Up to $25,000, depending on the grant type.
Total amount of support: Varies.
Matching fund requirements: 50% typically required.

NO. MOST RECENT APPLICANTS: 40.

NO. AWARDS: 25.

APPLICATION INFO:
A preproposal must be submitted on the NMF preproposal application form. Applicants are encouraged to contact NMF staff to discuss projects prior to submission. Once a project has been determined to be eligible, a full application is invited and NMF staff will explain the process for submitting additional information.
Duration: Up to two years; multiyear depending upon grant.
Deadline: Preproposals may be submitted at any time.

ADDRESS INQUIRIES TO:
Nate Dorr, Program Officer-Grants
(See address above.)

THE NORTHWESTERN MUTUAL FOUNDATION [1306]

720 East Wisconsin Avenue
Milwaukee, WI 53202
(414) 665-2200
Fax: (414) 665-2199
E-mail: foundationonline@northwesternmutual.com
Web Site: www.nmfoundation.com

FOUNDED: 1992

AREAS OF INTEREST:
Education, childhood cancer, building neighborhood capacity and volunteerism.

CONSULTING OR VOLUNTEER SERVICES:
MutualFriends is the name of the corporate employee volunteer program.

TYPE:
Project, program and capacity-building support, matching gifts, scholarships, disaster relief, United Way and UPAF support.

PURPOSE:
To inspire human potential through lifelong learning and community commitment.

ELIGIBILITY:
Organization must have tax-exempt classification under Section 501(c)(3) of the Internal Revenue Code. No grants to organizations that advocate, support or practice activities inconsistent with Northwestern Mutual's nondiscrimination policies.

GEOG. RESTRICTIONS: United States.

FINANCIAL DATA:
Amount of support per award: Varies.

Total amount of support: Approximately $17,000,000 for fiscal year ended June 30, 2013.

APPLICATION INFO:
Guidelines and deadlines are communicated annually in July on the Foundation web site. Foundation accepts online applications only through its web site.

Duration: One year. Must reapply.

OFFICER:
Eric Christophersen, President

ADDRESS INQUIRIES TO:
See e-mail address above.

OKLAHOMA CITY COMMUNITY FOUNDATION, INC. [1307]

P.O. Box 1146
Oklahoma City, OK 73101-1146
(405) 235-5603
Fax: (405) 235-5612
E-mail: info@occf.org
Web Site: www.occf.org

FOUNDED: 1969

AREAS OF INTEREST:
Beautification, education, the arts, social services and civic organizations.

TYPE:
Project/program grants; Scholarships. Support for philanthropic agencies designated by donors. Discretionary grants by the Foundation's trustees are relatively modest.

PURPOSE:
To serve the charitable purposes of its donors and the charitable needs of the Oklahoma City area through the development and administration of endowment and other charitable funds with the goal of preserving capital and enhancing value.

LEGAL BASIS:
Public foundation.

ELIGIBILITY:
Applicants can be any IRS 501(c)(3) organization.

GEOG. RESTRICTIONS: Oklahoma City, Oklahoma and surrounding area.

FINANCIAL DATA:
Assets of $833,000,000 for the year ended June 30, 2015.

Amount of support per award: Varies.

Total amount of support: $27,000,000 in grant distributions for fiscal year ended June 30, 2015.

APPLICATION INFO:
Application information is available on the web site.

Duration: Varies.

IRS I.D.: 23-7024262

ADDRESS INQUIRIES TO:
Nancy Anthony, President
(See address above.)

OMAHA COMMUNITY FOUNDATION

302 South 36th Street
Suite 100
Omaha, NE 68131
(402) 342-3458
Fax: (402) 342-3582
E-mail: tina@omahafoundation.org
Web Site: www.omahafoundation.org

TYPE:
Capital grants; Project/program grants; Scholarships. Donors can contribute through the Omaha Community Foundation to any nonprofit agency. The OCF also has four discretionary grant programs.

See entry 243 for full listing.

OMNOVA SOLUTIONS FOUNDATION [1308]

25435 Harvard Road
Beachwood, OH 44122-6201
(216) 682-7067
Fax: (216) 453-0113
E-mail: theresa.carter@omnova.com
Web Site: www.omnova.com

FOUNDED: 1999

AREAS OF INTEREST:
Support of educational, cultural and 501(c)(3) organizations in areas where OMNOVA Solutions has large concentrations of employment.

TYPE:
Capital grants; Development grants; Endowments; General operating grants; Matching gifts; Product donations; Project/program grants; Scholarships.

YEAR PROGRAM STARTED: 1999

PURPOSE:
To support education and other charitable organizations in the communities where OMNOVA Solutions has facilities.

LEGAL BASIS:
Nonprofit corporation, private foundation.

ELIGIBILITY:
Tax-exempt organizations are eligible.

GEOG. RESTRICTIONS: Georgia, Massachusetts, Mississippi, North Carolina, Ohio, Pennsylvania, South Carolina and Wisconsin.

FINANCIAL DATA:
Amount of support per award: $100 to $25,000. Average $5,000.

Total amount of support: $1,425,985 for the year 2015.

NO. AWARDS: 501 for the year 2015.

REPRESENTATIVE AWARDS:
American Red Cross; Akron Community Service Center and Urban League; E.J. Thomas Performing Arts Hall; United Way; Great Akron and Greater Cleveland Food Banks.

APPLICATION INFO:
A brief letter is required along with budget information, board of directors, 501(c)(3) form and recent annual report.

Duration: One-time grants. Renewable.

Deadline: Applications are reviewed and grants awarded throughout the year.

PUBLICATIONS:
Application guidelines; annual report.

IRS I.D.: 34-1909350

TRUSTEES:
Paul DeSantis, President
Christopher Weber, Treasurer
Sandi Noah
Charlotte Sideri
Ray Weinert

ADDRESS INQUIRIES TO:
Theresa Carter, President
(See address above.)

OPEN SOCIETY INSTITUTE - BALTIMORE [1309]

201 North Charles Street
Suite 1300
Baltimore, MD 21201
(410) 234-1091
Fax: (410) 234-2816
E-mail: osi.baltimore@opensocietyfoundations.org
Web Site: www.osibaltimore.org

AREAS OF INTEREST:
Drug addiction.

NAME(S) OF PROGRAMS:
- **The Drug Addiction Treatment Program**

TYPE:
Project/program grants. The Drug Addiction Treatment Program seeks to ensure universal access to treatment services for all in need regardless of income or insurance status.

YEAR PROGRAM STARTED: 1998

PURPOSE:
To focus on critical national urban issues as they are expressed locally.

LEGAL BASIS:
Foundation.

ELIGIBILITY:
Grants are made to organizations that have tax-exempt status under Section 501(c)(3) of the Internal Revenue Code. No grants are made to individuals. Nonsectarian religious programs may apply.

GEOG. RESTRICTIONS: Baltimore City, Maryland.

FINANCIAL DATA:
Amount of support per award: Varies.

Total amount of support: Varies.

APPLICATION INFO:
Applicants should submit a letter of inquiry of two to three pages which includes:
(1) a description of the program to be funded;
(2) the qualifications of the organization to carry out the program;
(3) the ways in which the program reflects the priorities of The Drug Addiction Treatment Program and;
(4) the amount requested.

Duration: Varies.

Deadline: Grant applications are accepted on an ongoing basis.

ADDRESS INQUIRIES TO:
Scott Nolen, Program Director
Drug Addiction Treatment
(See address above.)

THE ORDEAN FOUNDATION [1310]

501 Ordean Building
424 West Superior Street
Duluth, MN 55802
(218) 726-4785
Fax: (218) 726-4848
E-mail: smangan@ordean.org

FOUNDED: 1933

AREAS OF INTEREST:
Social services, education and health, services to low-income, mentally and physically handicapped, elderly, mentally ill, chemically dependent, prevention of delinquency, and scholarships for certain health-related majors at Duluth colleges.

TYPE:
Challenge/matching grants; Demonstration grants; General operating grants; Project/program grants; Scholarships.

YEAR PROGRAM STARTED: 1933

LEGAL BASIS:
Private foundation.

ELIGIBILITY:
Applicants must be nonprofit, tax-exempt IRS 501(c)(3) organizations located or providing services in Greater City of Duluth, MN.

GEOG. RESTRICTIONS: Greater City of Duluth, Minnesota.

FINANCIAL DATA:
Amount of support per award: $5,000 to $350,000.

Total amount of support: $2,000,000 for fiscal year 2013.

NO. AWARDS: Approximately 50.

REPRESENTATIVE AWARDS:
$350,000 to Lake Superior Community Health Center; $150,000 to Mentor Duluth to match caring adults with at-risk youths.

APPLICATION INFO:
Guidelines are available from the Foundation office at the address above. Minnesota Common Council grant applications also accepted.

Duration: One year. Renewal possible up to three years.

Deadline: The 15th of every month, for the next month's meeting agenda.

STAFF:
Stephen Mangan, Executive Director
Joe Everett, Program Director

BOARD OF DIRECTORS:
Mary Beth Santori, Chairperson
Ann Niedringhaus, Vice Chairperson
Marge Bray, Treasurer
Ben Stromberg, Secretary
Carl Crawford
Jon Nelson
Dr. Tom Patnoe
Jim Vizanko
Chuck Walt

ADDRESS INQUIRIES TO:
Joe Everett, Program Director
(See address above.)

THE OREGON COMMUNITY FOUNDATION [1311]

1221 S.W. Yamhill Street, Suite 100
Portland, OR 97205-2108
(503) 227-6846
Fax: (503) 274-7771
E-mail: info@oregoncf.org
Web Site: www.oregoncf.org

FOUNDED: 1973

AREAS OF INTEREST:
Health and well-being, education, arts and culture, economic vitality, and community livability, environment and engagement.

NAME(S) OF PROGRAMS:

- **Community Grants Program**

TYPE:
Capital grants; Challenge/matching grants; Matching gifts; Project/program grants; Scholarships.

YEAR PROGRAM STARTED: 1974

PURPOSE:
To strengthen the social fabric of our communities by awarding grants that build civic leadership and engagement and address evolving, community-identified needs.

LEGAL BASIS:
Community foundation.

ELIGIBILITY:
Applicants for programs must be nonprofit, tax-exempt organizations in Oregon.

Applicants must have received a community grant only once during the previous 12 months and must have completed evaluation reports for all prior grants. The Foundation gives preference to projects that demonstrate strong local support and promise tangible benefits or means of solving community problems or concerns.

GEOG. RESTRICTIONS: Oregon.

FINANCIAL DATA:
Amount of support per award: $5,000 to $50,000. Average grant $20,000.

Total amount of support: $90,000,000 in grants, including $9,000,000 in scholarships and $6,900,000 for the Community Grants Program for the year 2015.

Matching fund requirements: Varies.

NO. MOST RECENT APPLICANTS: 700 to 1,000 annually.

NO. AWARDS: 300 to 350 annually.

APPLICATION INFO:
Application information is available on the web site. Application must be submitted via the online system.

Duration: Small grants: One year; Large grants: One to three years.

Deadline: Community Grants Program: January 15 and July 15.

IRS I.D.: 23-7315673

STAFF:
Sheila Murty, Vice President of Operations

ADDRESS INQUIRIES TO:
Megan Schumaker, Senior Program Officer
(See address above.)

*SPECIAL STIPULATIONS:
Generally funds only in Oregon.

OUTER BANKS COMMUNITY FOUNDATION [1312]

13 Skyline Road
Southern Shores, NC 27949
(252) 261-8839
Fax: (252) 261-0371
E-mail: info@obcf.org
Web Site: www.obcf.org

FOUNDED: 1982

AREAS OF INTEREST:
Outer Banks, from Corolla to Ocracoke Island.

TYPE:
Project/program grants; Scholarships. 40 different scholarship funds available to local students. Grants available for local nonprofit programs and projects.

YEAR PROGRAM STARTED: 1982

PURPOSE:
To help meet local needs in the Outer Banks of North Carolina, from Corolla to Ocracoke Island.

LEGAL BASIS:
501(c)(3).

GEOG. RESTRICTIONS: Corolla area of Currituck County, Dare County and Ocracoke Island in Hyde County, North Carolina.

FINANCIAL DATA:
Amount of support per award: Varies.

Total amount of support: Varies.

APPLICATION INFO:
Application information is available on the web site.

Deadline: Varies.

IRS I.D.: 58-1516313

ADDRESS INQUIRIES TO:
Lorelei Costa, Executive Director
(See address above.)

PERMIAN BASIN AREA FOUNDATION [1313]

200 North Loraine, Suite 500
Midland, TX 79701
(432) 682-4704
Fax: (432) 704-5276
E-mail: gmccrary@pbaf.org
Web Site: www.pbaf.org

FOUNDED: 1989

AREAS OF INTEREST:
Community development.

TYPE:
Grants-in-aid; Scholarships.

PURPOSE:
To enrich the quality of life for the communities of the Permian Basin area of Texas.

LEGAL BASIS:
501(c)(3) organization.

GEOG. RESTRICTIONS: Communities of the Permian Basin region of Texas.

FINANCIAL DATA:
The Foundation has awarded nearly $70,500,000 in grants and scholarships since inception.

Amount of support per award: Grants: Average $15,000; Scholarships: $1,000 to $2,500.

APPLICATION INFO:
Organizations wishing to apply for a grant must fully complete and submit one copy of the Pre-Application Summary (SF-1). Organizations that have received funding during a previous grant cycle must also complete and submit the Grant Award Follow-up Form (SF-FW). Do not include a cover letter with the application.

A full application will be complete when one copy of the appropriate Standard Forms and additional documents indicated on the Standard Form Checklist are completed and submitted to the Foundation by the full application due date. (The list of required forms differs depending on the purpose of the grant request.) Upon receiving a full application, the Foundation will conduct a full application review which may include an applicant interview, a site visit, and/or a request for additional information.

All scholarship applications must contain the following:
(1) transcript with fall semester grades;
(2) college transcript if student is enrolled in concurrent college courses and;
(3) at least one letter of recommendation, but not more than three.

Some applications require an essay. Check the individual scholarship criteria to determine if an essay is required and the designated topic.

Duration: Grants: Typically one year. Can reapply every two years.

Deadline: Grant proposals: April 1 for Spring and October 1 for Fall.

ADDRESS INQUIRIES TO:
Kenda Prather, Grants and Administration
(See address above.)

PETOSKEY-HARBOR SPRINGS AREA COMMUNITY FOUNDATION [1314]

616 Petoskey Street, Suite 203
Petoskey, MI 49770
(231) 348-5820
Fax: (231) 348-5883
E-mail: info@phsacf.org
Web Site: www.phsacf.org

FOUNDED: 1992

AREAS OF INTEREST:
Arts, education, environment, health, human service and community development.

TYPE:
Grants-in-aid; Scholarships. Grants are given for scholarships or for charitable needs.

YEAR PROGRAM STARTED: 1992

PURPOSE:
To build an endowment to serve community needs.

LEGAL BASIS:
Community foundation.

ELIGIBILITY:
Grants must be for charitable purposes, but not for individuals.

GEOG. RESTRICTIONS: Emmet County, Michigan.

FINANCIAL DATA:
Over $30,000,000 in assets.

Amount of support per award: $500 to $10,000.

Total amount of support: Varies.

APPLICATION INFO:
Applications are available at the address above and must include a copy of the IRS tax determination letter. Call before you apply.

Duration: One year.

Deadline: March 1 and October 1.

PUBLICATIONS:
Annual report; application guidelines.

ADDRESS INQUIRIES TO:
Program Officer
(See address above.)

THE PHILADELPHIA FOUNDATION [1315]

1234 Market Street
Suite 1800
Philadelphia, PA 19107
(215) 563-6417
Fax: (215) 563-6882
E-mail: info@philafound.org
Web Site: www.philafound.org

FOUNDED: 1918

AREAS OF INTEREST:
Arts, culture, humanities, education, environment, health, human services and public/community development.

TYPE:
General operating grants; Scholarships. Capacity building grants. The Philadelphia Foundation's grantmaking strategies are sensitive to the needs of diverse population groups in the community and reflect a commitment to stabilizing the infrastructure of nonprofit organizations.

YEAR PROGRAM STARTED: 1918

PURPOSE:
To serve as a vehicle and resource for philanthropy in Bucks, Chester, Delaware, Montgomery and Philadelphia counties, PA; to develop, manage and allocate community resources in partnership with donors and grantees to build on community assets, to respond to the needs of the entire community, and to promote empowerment, leadership, and civic participation among underserved groups; to practice and encourage diversity, equity, and inclusiveness as fundamental values of community life.

LEGAL BASIS:
Community foundation established in Pennsylvania by bank resolution.

ELIGIBILITY:
Organization must be IRS 501(c)(3), located in five-county area of southeastern Pennsylvania.

GEOG. RESTRICTIONS: Bucks, Chester, Delaware, Montgomery, and Philadelphia counties, Pennsylvania.

FINANCIAL DATA:
Amount of support per award: $3,000 to $50,000 (but not more than 10% of an organization's budget).

Total amount of support: $25,000,000 annually.

CO-OP FUNDING PROGRAMS: The Nonprofit Repositioning Fund.

NO. AWARDS: 1,000 annually.

APPLICATION INFO:
The Foundation encourages applicants to address:
(1) empowering people and groups;
(2) building community assets or;
(3) managing current issues or preparing for future trends when submitting grant requests.

Additional information is available from the Foundation through its web site.

Duration: Usually one year.

Deadline: Applications are accepted on a rolling basis.

PUBLICATIONS:
Newsletters; annual report.

OFFICERS:
Pedro A. Ramos, President
Patricia Meller, Vice President for Finance and Administration

ADDRESS INQUIRIES TO:
Grantmaking Services Department
E-mail: grantmakingservices@philafound.org
(See address above.)

PIEDMONT HEALTH FOUNDATION

P.O. Box 9303
Greenville, SC 29604
(864) 370-0212
Fax: (864) 370-0212
E-mail: katysmith@piedmonthealthfoundation.org
Web Site: www.piedmonthealthfoundation.org

TYPE:
Demonstration grants; Project/program grants; Research grants; Seed money grants.

See entry 1420 for full listing.

THE PITTSBURGH FOUNDATION [1316]

5 PPG Place
Suite 250
Pittsburgh, PA 15222
(412) 391-5122
Fax: (412) 391-7259
E-mail: email@pghfdn.org
Web Site: www.pittsburghfoundation.org

FOUNDED: 1945

AREAS OF INTEREST:
Education, family life, economic development, health care and the arts.

TYPE:
Capital grants; General operating grants; Project/program grants; Research grants; Scholarships. The Foundation promotes and champions the betterment of the greater Pittsburgh community and the quality of life for all its citizens by helping a wide variety of donors fulfill significant community needs and providing a vehicle to make giving easy, personally satisfying and effective. The Foundation awards grants through restricted and unrestricted funds. Purposes for which unrestricted grants are awarded include: organizational capacity building; systemic change; improved service delivery; planning and program development; capital and equipment (in limited and special circumstances) through one targeted fund; operating (in very limited and defined circumstances); research (in special circumstances).

Scholarships and medical research grants are awarded from specific funds established for this purpose.

PURPOSE:
To achieve educational excellence and equity; to support families; to foster economic development; to eliminate disparities in health outcomes; to advance the arts.

LEGAL BASIS:
Community foundation established in Pennsylvania by bank resolution and declaration of trust.

ELIGIBILITY:
Grant applicants must be tax-exempt, public charitable organizations and institutions located in Pittsburgh or Allegheny County. Generally, grants are nonrecurring and are not granted for operating budgets and not made to individuals.

GEOG. RESTRICTIONS: Pittsburgh and Allegheny County, Pennsylvania.

FINANCIAL DATA:
Amount of support per award: Varies.

Total amount of support: Approximately $9,000,000 in unrestricted funds; $9,000,000 in restricted funds.

NO. MOST RECENT APPLICANTS: 2,581.

NO. AWARDS: 2,255.

APPLICATION INFO:
Applicants must submit grant application and IRS tax-exemption letter. Prior to sending a full proposal, applicants are encouraged to send a letter of inquiry that includes a brief

statement about the organization, the proposed project, its intended results, and a general idea of costs.

Duration: Up to three years.

PUBLICATIONS:
Annual report; newsletter; donor information; application guidelines; scholarship brochure.

IRS I.D.: 25-0965466

STAFF:
Maxwell King, President and Chief Executive Officer
Jonathan Brelsford, Vice President of Finance and Investments

BOARD OF DIRECTORS:
Edith L. Shapira, M.D., Chairperson
John C. Harmon, Esq., Vice Chairperson
Kim Tillotson Fleming, Treasurer
Walter H. Smith, Jr., Ph.D., Secretary
Dr. Morton Coleman
Edward J. Donnelly, III, M.D.
Patrick Dowd, Ph.D.
Lee B. Foster, II
Evan Frazier
David McL. Hillman
Anne Lewis
Claudette R. Lewis
Gail Malloy
Vincent J. Quatrini, Jr.
James C. Roddey
Dr. Howard Slaughter, Jr.
William Strickland

ADDRESS INQUIRIES TO:
Maxwell King
President and Chief Executive Officer
(See address above.)

PRINCETON AREA COMMUNITY FOUNDATION [1317]

15 Princess Road
Lawrenceville, NJ 08648
(609) 219-1800
Fax: (609) 219-1850
E-mail: info@pacf.org
Web Site: www.pacf.org

FOUNDED: 1991

AREAS OF INTEREST:
Connecting people who care with causes that matter across central New Jersey.

NAME(S) OF PROGRAMS:
- **The Fund for Women and Girls**
- **Greater Mercer Grants**

TYPE:
General operating grants; Project/program grants; Scholarships. The Fund for Women and Girls supports organizations that improve the lives of girls and the women who raise them.

Greater Mercer Grants focus support on current priorities with the greatest impact within Mercer County, NJ. There are two grant categories: one provides program and/or operating support for nonprofit organizations addressing the needs of low-income individuals and families; the other provides program support for building community within and among municipalities in Mercer County, NJ.

PURPOSE:
To connect people who care with causes that matter across central New Jersey.

LEGAL BASIS:
A public benefit (nonprofit) organization.

ELIGIBILITY:
Eligible organizations must have 501(c)(3) status.

GEOG. RESTRICTIONS: Trenton, the 12 other Mercer County (New Jersey) municipalities and surrounding communities in Burlington, Hunterdon, Middlesex, Monmouth and Somerset counties.

FINANCIAL DATA:
Since its founding, the Foundation has granted nearly $18,000,000 to its community area of service.

Amount of support per award: Varies.

Total amount of support: Fund for Women and Girls: $117,000 in grants in 2015. Greater Mercer Grants: Over $1,000,000 in 2014. In 2014, 1,714 grants, totaling nearly $10,000,000, were made from the 330 funds held by the Community Foundation.

APPLICATION INFO:
Application information is available on the web site.

Duration: One year. Renewable.

STAFF:
Jeffrey M. Vega, President and Chief Executive Officer
Elizabeth B. Wagner, Vice President of Development
Laura J. Longman, MBA, Chief Financial Officer
Myriam Padro, Administrator

ADDRESS INQUIRIES TO:
Grants and Programs
Princeton Area Community Foundation
(See address above.)

PROLITERACY WORLDWIDE [1318]

104 Marcellus Street
Syracuse, NY 13204
(315) 422-9121
Fax: (315) 422-6369
E-mail: asuskin@proliteracy.org
Web Site: www.proliteracy.org

FOUNDED: 1955

AREAS OF INTEREST:
Literacy, adult basic education, English as a second language, and family literacy.

NAME(S) OF PROGRAMS:
- **National Book Fund (NBF)**

TYPE:
Project/program grants; Technical assistance.

YEAR PROGRAM STARTED: 1995

PURPOSE:
To provide grants for books and other materials local programs can use to expand their current volunteer literacy programs; to develop, promote and expand literacy programs in the U.S. that target the needs of women.

LEGAL BASIS:
Nonprofit organization.

ELIGIBILITY:
Adult literacy and adult basic education programs only.

GEOG. RESTRICTIONS: United States.

FINANCIAL DATA:
Amount of support per award: Typically $500 to $2,000.

Matching fund requirements: Up to 20% match required.

NO. MOST RECENT APPLICANTS: 86 for the year 2015.

NO. AWARDS: 70 for the year 2015.

APPLICATION INFO:
Application information is available on the web site.

Duration: One year. NBF grantee eligible again in three years.

Deadline: April 15.

PUBLICATIONS:
Guidelines.

IRS I.D.: 16-1214734

ADDRESS INQUIRIES TO:
Alicia Suskin
National Book Fund Program Director
(See address above.)

RANCHO SANTA FE FOUNDATION [1319]

162 South Rancho Santa Fe Road
Suite B-30
Encinitas, CA 92024
(858) 756-6557
Fax: (858) 756-6561
E-mail: christy@rsffoundation.org
Web Site: www.rsffoundation.org

FOUNDED: 1981

AREAS OF INTEREST:
Seniors, military.

NAME(S) OF PROGRAMS:
- **The Patriots Connection**
- **Rancho Santa Fe Women's Fund**
- **Senior Connections**

TYPE:
Challenge/matching grants; Development grants; Endowments; General operating grants; Project/program grants; Scholarships.

YEAR PROGRAM STARTED: 1981

PURPOSE:
To connect donors with regional and global needs through visionary community leadership, personalized service and effective grantmaking.

LEGAL BASIS:
Community foundation.

ELIGIBILITY:
San Diego County organizations who have been asked to submit a grant request are eligible for support.

Organizations must have tax-exempt status under Section 501(c)(3) of the Internal Revenue Code.

FINANCIAL DATA:
Amount of support per award: $500 to $250,000.

Total amount of support: $450,000 in grants from designated and discretionary funds. Nearly $7,000,000 from donor-advised funds.

APPLICATION INFO:
The Foundation accepts the San Diego Grantmakers Common Grant Application, by invitation only. The Foundation does not accept unsolicited grant requests, except for the Rancho Santa Fe Women's Fund. Women's Fund application process opens August 1.

Duration: Typically one year.

Deadline: Varies. Women's Fund: September 1.

PUBLICATIONS:
Annual report.

IRS I.D.: 95-3709639

STAFF:
Christina P. Wilson, Executive Director
Debbie Anderson, Programs Director
Dan Beals, Finance Director
Susan Pyke, Marketing Director
Nancy Hashim, Administrative Manager, Women's Fund

ADDRESS INQUIRIES TO:
Christina P. Wilson, Executive Director
(See address above.)

RBC FOUNDATION - U.S.A. [1320]

RBC Plaza
60 South Sixth Street
Minneapolis, MN 55402-4422
(612) 371-2936
Fax: (612) 371-7933
E-mail: fndapplications@rbc.com
Web Site: www.rbcwm-usa.com/communityinvolvement

AREAS OF INTEREST:
Arts and culture, civic programs, education, health and human services.

NAME(S) OF PROGRAMS:
- **After School Grants/Education/Financial Literacy**
- **Children's Mental Health**
- **Emerging Artists/Art Access for Diverse Populations**
- **Human Services**

TYPE:
Project/program grants. In the area of education, the Foundation supports after school grants programs, structured, supervised academic mentoring or college preparatory activities and programs, or youth financial literacy programs.

In the area of arts and culture, the Foundation's emphasis is on emerging artists project programs and programs providing arts access for diverse populations.

PURPOSE:
To improve the quality of life in communities where the company has facilities.

LEGAL BASIS:
Corporate foundation.

ELIGIBILITY:
Organizations must have tax-exempt status according to Internal Revenue Code 501(c)(3). Grants are made to organizations where RBC Wealth Management has employees actively involved.

FINANCIAL DATA:
Total amount of support: $2,200,000 for fiscal year 2012.

APPLICATION INFO:
Guidelines and application forms are available on the web site.

Duration: One year.

Deadline: Varies.

ADDRESS INQUIRIES TO:
Julie Allen
E-mail: julie.allen@rbc.com

THE REINBERGER FOUNDATION [1321]

30000 Chagrin Boulevard, Suite 300
Cleveland, OH 44124
(216) 292-2790
Fax: (216) 292-4466
E-mail: info@reinbergerfoundation.org
Web Site: www.reinbergerfoundation.org

FOUNDED: 1968

AREAS OF INTEREST:
Arts, education, health care and social service.

NAME(S) OF PROGRAMS:
- **Arts, Culture and Humanities**
- **Education**
- **Human Service Health**
- **Human Service - Other**

TYPE:
Capital grants; Challenge/matching grants; General operating grants; Matching gifts; Project/program grants; Research grants; Scholarships.

PURPOSE:
To enhance quality of life for individuals from all walks of life.

LEGAL BASIS:
Private foundation.

ELIGIBILITY:
Eligible organizations must be IRS 501(c)(3) tax-exempt.

GEOG. RESTRICTIONS: Northeast Ohio or greater Columbus area.

FINANCIAL DATA:
Since its beginning, the Foundation has provided more than $100,000,000 in funding support to the community.

Amount of support per award: $5,000 to $500,000.

Total amount of support: $3,159,592 for the year 2014.

NO. MOST RECENT APPLICANTS: 306 for the year 2014.

NO. AWARDS: 116 for the year 2014.

APPLICATION INFO:
Online application is available on the web site.

Duration: Up to seven years.

Deadline: March, June, September and December.

ADDRESS INQUIRIES TO:
Karen L. Hooser, President
(See address above.)

LUTHER I. REPLOGLE FOUNDATION [1322]

1720 N Street, N.W.
Washington, DC 20036-2907
(202) 679-0677
Fax: (202) 580-6579
E-mail: info@lirf.org
Web Site: www.lirf.org

FOUNDED: 1966

AREAS OF INTEREST:
At-risk youth and children, educational opportunities for inner-city children, and affordable and supportive housing.

TYPE:
Challenge/matching grants; General operating grants; Project/program grants; Seed money grants. The Foundation supports programs that:
(1) address the needs of youth and children living in, or at risk of, long-term poverty, especially children of inner-city residents. Of particular interest are programs for teen pregnancy prevention, counseling, broad-spectrum social services, and other programs that help young people improve their own lives;
(2) improve educational opportunities for inner-city children, including enrichment programs in the arts and sciences, alternative schools, after-school tutoring and mentoring, and scholarship programs and;
(3) provide for affordable and supportive housing that reaches people frequently left out of traditional shelter programs, including single mothers and families with children, the elderly, ex-offenders, and youth. An emphasis is placed on programs that enable individuals to help themselves and become self-sufficient over the long-term.

PURPOSE:
To address the needs of youth and children living in, or at risk of, long-term poverty; to improve educational opportunities for inner-city children; to support programs for affordable and supportive housing that reach groups of people frequently left out of traditional shelter programs.

ELIGIBILITY:
Organizations must be not-for-profit 501(c)(3). Grants are given to religious organizations only for social services programs, not for religious programs, buildings or bibles. No grants to individuals.

GEOG. RESTRICTIONS: Washington, District of Columbia; Chicago, Illinois; Minneapolis, Minnesota.

FINANCIAL DATA:
Amount of support per award: Usually $5,000 to $10,000.

Total amount of support: $504,000 for the year 2015.

APPLICATION INFO:
Applicants meeting the grant criteria through the online eligibility quiz will be prompted to complete the Letter of Inquiry form.

Duration: Renewable if grantee sends report.

Deadline: March 15 and September 15.

IRS I.D.: 36-6141697

ADDRESS INQUIRIES TO:
Gwenn H.S. Gebhard, Executive Director
(See address above.)

ROCHESTER AREA FOUNDATION [1323]

12 Elton Hills Drive, N.W.
Rochester, MN 55901
(507) 282-0203
Fax: (507) 282-4938
E-mail: raf-info@rochesterarea.org
Web Site: www.rochesterarea.org

FOUNDED: 1944

AREAS OF INTEREST:
General grants to benefit residents of the Greater Rochester area.

TYPE:
Capital grants; Challenge/matching grants; Project/program grants; Scholarships; Seed money grants.

YEAR PROGRAM STARTED: 1944

PURPOSE:
To use its resources to improve the quality of life, promote greater equality of opportunities and to support development of effective methods to assist those in need in the Greater Rochester area.

LEGAL BASIS:
Community foundation.

ELIGIBILITY:
Applicants must be 501(c)(3) organizations or units of government agencies or

government-created public agencies located in or serving the Greater Rochester area. Grants are not given to individuals.

GEOG. RESTRICTIONS: Greater Rochester, Minnesota.

FINANCIAL DATA:
Amount of support per award: Varies.
Total amount of support: $1,853,336 for the year 2015.

NO. AWARDS: 559.

APPLICATION INFO:
Pre-approved and approved application forms are required. Applicant organizations must include an IRS letter of tax determination.
Duration: One-time grants.
Deadline: January 1 and August 1.

PUBLICATIONS:
Annual report with consolidated financials.

ADDRESS INQUIRIES TO:
E-mail: jane@rochesterarea.org

ROSE COMMUNITY FOUNDATION [1324]

600 South Cherry Street
Suite 1200
Denver, CO 80246-1712
(303) 398-7400
(303) 398-7446
Fax: (303) 398-7430
E-mail: grantsmanager@rcfdenver.org
Web Site: www.rcfdenver.org

FOUNDED: 1995

AREAS OF INTEREST:
Child and family development, education, the elderly, health of the community, Jewish life, human service, transportation (aging only), early childhood education, family self-sufficiency, health preventive, low-income health access and health policy leadership.

TYPE:
Capital grants; Challenge/matching grants; General operating grants; Project/program grants; Seed money grants; Technical assistance. Capacity-building grants.

YEAR PROGRAM STARTED: 1995

PURPOSE:
To enhance the quality of life of the greater Denver community through leadership, resources, traditions and values.

ELIGIBILITY:
Applicants must be charitable, nonprofit organizations classified as 501(c)(3) by the IRS or be a tax-supported institution, such as a school or government agency. New or emerging organizations are permitted to apply through a sponsoring tax-exempt organization. Applicants (including university departments) may have only one proposal pending at any given time.

The Foundation will not support grants to individuals or endowments, including academic chairs, grants to one organization to be passed to another, annual appeals or membership drives, fund-raising events, or political candidates.

GEOG. RESTRICTIONS: Denver metropolitan area, specifically Adams, Arapahoe, Boulder, Broomfield, Denver, Douglas and Jefferson counties, Colorado.

FINANCIAL DATA:
Amount of support per award: Varies depending on needs and nature of the request.
Total amount of support: $14,787,000 in grants for the year 2014.
Matching fund requirements: Varies by nature of award.

NO. AWARDS: 762 grants for the year 2015.

APPLICATION INFO:
It is recommended to speak with a Program Officer prior to submitting an application to discuss the program, project or organization.
Duration: Varies.

IRS I.D.: 84-0920862

STAFF:
Sheila Bugdanowitz, President and Chief Executive Officer
Cheryl McDonald, Grants Manager

ADDRESS INQUIRIES TO:
Cheryl McDonald, Grants Manager
(See address above.)

HENRY AND RUTH BLAUSTEIN ROSENBERG FOUNDATION [1325]

One South Street, Suite 2900
Baltimore, MD 21202
(410) 347-7201
Fax: (410) 347-7210
E-mail: info@blaufund.org
Web Site: www.blaufund.org

AREAS OF INTEREST:
Arts and culture, youth development, adult self-sufficiency, and health.

TYPE:
Capital grants; General operating grants; Project/program grants. Programs of benefit to the underserved community in the Baltimore, MD area.

PURPOSE:
To promote arts and culture, youth development, and adult self-sufficiency within the underserved community.

ELIGIBILITY:
501(c)(3) nonprofit organizations. No grants to individuals.

GEOG. RESTRICTIONS: Baltimore, Maryland.

FINANCIAL DATA:
Amount of support per award: $5,000 to $25,000.
Total amount of support: Approximately $1,400,000.

APPLICATION INFO:
Send two- to three-page letter of intent or application. IRS tax status determination letter is required. Faxed and e-mailed letters of intent are not accepted.
Duration: One to two years. Prior grantee organizations may be renewable.

ADDRESS INQUIRIES TO:
Betsy F. Ringel, Executive Director
(See address above.)

ROSS FOUNDATION [1326]

202 South Fifth Street
Arkadelphia, AR 71923
(870) 246-9881
Fax: (870) 246-9674
E-mail: info@rossfoundation.us
Web Site: www.rossfoundation.us

FOUNDED: 1966

AREAS OF INTEREST:
Education, culture, conservation and community activities.

TYPE:
Project/program grants.

LEGAL BASIS:
Private foundation.

ELIGIBILITY:
Applicants must be IRS 501(c)(3) organizations located in Clark County or Arkadelphia, AR. No grants to individuals.

GEOG. RESTRICTIONS: Clark County or Arkadelphia, Arkansas.

FINANCIAL DATA:
Amount of support per award: Generally $500 to $25,000.
Total amount of support: $617,852 for the year 2015.

NO. MOST RECENT APPLICANTS: Approximately 50 for the year 2015.

NO. AWARDS: 44 for the year 2015.

APPLICATION INFO:
Application form is available online.
Duration: Typically one year.
Deadline: Proposals are reviewed March, July and October.

ADDRESS INQUIRIES TO:
Mary Elizabeth Eldridge
Director of Programs or
Amanda Fenocchi, Assistant Grants Officer
(See address above.)

THE RUSSELL FAMILY FOUNDATION [1327]

3025 Harborview Drive
Gig Harbor, WA 98335
(253) 858-5050
Fax: (253) 851-0460
E-mail: info@trff.org
Web Site: www.trff.org

FOUNDED: 1999

AREAS OF INTEREST:
Elimination of poverty, healthy educational and extracurricular activities for youth, and social justice.

NAME(S) OF PROGRAMS:
- **Jane's Fellowship Program**

TYPE:
Fellowships. Fellowship program for individuals who plan to work in the Foundation's areas of interest.

YEAR PROGRAM STARTED: 2004

PURPOSE:
To support grassroots leaders in Pierce County and Tacoma, WA.

ELIGIBILITY:
Must be a grassroots leader who has demonstrated exceptional creativity, courage and commitment in serving diverse needs in Tacoma and countywide.

GEOG. RESTRICTIONS: Pierce County and Tacoma, Washington.

FINANCIAL DATA:
Amount of support per award: Varies.
Total amount of support: Varies.

APPLICATION INFO:
Application information is available on the web site.
Duration: Two years. Nonrenewable.
Deadline: Every two years.

SAGINAW COMMUNITY FOUNDATION [1328]

One Tuscola Street, Suite 100
Saginaw, MI 48607
(989) 755-0545
Fax: (989) 755-6524
E-mail: brian@saginawfoundation.org
Web Site: www.saginawfoundation.org

FOUNDED: 1984

AREAS OF INTEREST:
Arts, community development, culture, education, health, youth and human services.

CONSULTING OR VOLUNTEER SERVICES:
Seminars, group presentations and one-on-one consultation.

TYPE:
Grants-in-aid; Project/program grants; Scholarships.

YEAR PROGRAM STARTED: 1984

PURPOSE:
To fulfill donor wishes and enable community initiatives to come to life, now and forever; to provide strategic leadership in the community; to practice impactful grantmaking in the areas of youth development, early education, and community improvement; to provide stewardship of the Foundation's resources, human and financial.

ELIGIBILITY:
Grants are made to organizations that have tax-exempt status under Section 501(c)(3) of the Internal Revenue Code, local units of government and religious institutions to support projects or programs benefiting the citizens and communities of Saginaw County. Except for scholarships, no grants are made to individuals. Nonsectarian religious programs may apply.

GEOG. RESTRICTIONS: Saginaw County, Michigan.

FINANCIAL DATA:
Amount of support per award: Grants vary in amount, depending upon the needs and nature of the request.

Total amount of support: $1,919,083 for the year 2015.

Matching fund requirements: Varies by program.

NO. MOST RECENT APPLICANTS: 6,800.

NO. AWARDS: 627.

APPLICATION INFO:
Application information is available on the web site.

ADDRESS INQUIRIES TO:
Program Officer
(See address above.)

ST. CROIX VALLEY FOUNDATION [1329]

516 Second Street, Suite 214
Hudson, WI 54016
(715) 386-9490
Fax: (715) 386-1250
E-mail: info@scvfoundation.org
Web Site: www.scvfoundation.org

FOUNDED: 1995

AREAS OF INTEREST:
Arts, civic affairs, community needs and development, environment, health and human services, and education.

NAME(S) OF PROGRAMS:
- **Health and Wellness Grant**
- **Music Education Grant**
- **Valley Arts Initiative Grant**

TYPE:
Project/program grants; Scholarships. Environmental and humane grants.

YEAR PROGRAM STARTED: 1995

PURPOSE:
To advance the quality of life in the St. Croix Valley of Wisconsin and Minnesota.

LEGAL BASIS:
501(c)(3).

ELIGIBILITY:
Grants are made to organizations that have tax-exempt status under Section 501(c)(3) of the Internal Revenue Code or serving the St. Croix Valley of Wisconsin and Minnesota. Nonsectarian religious programs may apply.

GEOG. RESTRICTIONS: Typically Burnett, Pierce, Polk and St. Croix counties in St. Croix Valley, Wisconsin; Chisago and Washington counties in Minnesota.

FINANCIAL DATA:
Amount of support per award: Grants: $2,250 average; Scholarships: $2,000.

Total amount of support: $1,500,000 in grants for fiscal year ended June 30, 2015.

APPLICATION INFO:
For full guidelines, refer to the Foundation web site.

Duration: Varies depending on the field of interest. One year for the Valley Arts Initiative Grant. Grants are renewable upon review.

Deadline: Health and Wellness Grant: Spring; Music Education Grant and Valley Arts Initiative Grant: Fall.

IRS I.D.: 41-1817315

STAFF:
Sally Hermann, Program Associate

ADDRESS INQUIRIES TO:
Jane Hetland Stevenson, President
(See address above.)

SAINT-GOBAIN CORPORATION FOUNDATION [1330]

20 Moores Road
Malvern, PA 19355
(610) 893-5484
Fax: (855) 639-6629
E-mail: SGNorthAmericaInfo@saint-gobain.com
Web Site: www.saint-gobain-northamerica.com

FOUNDED: 2001

AREAS OF INTEREST:
Education, energy conservation, environmental concerns and insulation/weatherization of homes.

NAME(S) OF PROGRAMS:
- **Direct Grants Program**

TYPE:
Project/program grants.

PURPOSE:
To play a vital role in the economic, social and educational development of the community.

LEGAL BASIS:
Corporation foundation.

ELIGIBILITY:
Eligible organizations must be IRS 501(c)(3) tax-exempt and be located in areas where Saint-Gobain Corporation has manufacturing locations.

GEOG. RESTRICTIONS: Massachusetts and Pennsylvania.

FINANCIAL DATA:
Amount of support per award: Varies.

Total amount of support: Varies.

APPLICATION INFO:
Applications are available from the Foundation.

Duration: Typically one year.

Deadline: Applications must be submitted by end of February for April Board Meeting and by end of July for September Board Meeting.

ADDRESS INQUIRIES TO:
See e-mail address above.

SAN ANGELO AREA FOUNDATION [1331]

221 South Irving Street
San Angelo, TX 76903
(325) 947-7071
Fax: (325) 947-7322
E-mail: infosaaf@saafound.org
Web Site: www.saafound.org

FOUNDED: 2002

AREAS OF INTEREST:
Community development.

TYPE:
Grants-in-aid; Scholarships. To build a legacy of philanthropy by attracting and prudently managing endowed gifts in order to match donor interests with community needs of the area.

PURPOSE:
To improve the quality of life in the San Angelo, TX area.

LEGAL BASIS:
Community foundation.

ELIGIBILITY:
Must be a 501(c)(3) nonprofit organization. Grant funds must be used within and for the benefit of residents and communities of the 17 counties of the San Angelo area.

GEOG. RESTRICTIONS: San Angelo area, Texas.

FINANCIAL DATA:
Amount of support per award: Varies.

Total amount of support: Varies.

APPLICATION INFO:
Application and proposal forms are available online.

Duration: Grants: Typically one year. Scholarships: One to eight semesters.

Deadline: Grants: September 1 for Executive Summary. Scholarships: March 1.

ADDRESS INQUIRIES TO:
Matt Lewis, President and
Chief Executive Officer
(See address above.)

SAN ANTONIO AREA FOUNDATION [1332]

303 Pearl Parkway
Suite 114
San Antonio, TX 78215
(210) 225-2243
Fax: (210) 225-1980
E-mail: info@saafdn.org
Web Site: www.saafdn.org

FOUNDED: 1964

AREAS OF INTEREST:
Animal services, arts and culture, biomedical research, community and human services, high school completion, strengthening nonprofits, children and youth, seniors, and medicine and health care.

NAME(S) OF PROGRAMS:
- **Discretionary Grant Process**
- **San Antonio Area African-American Community Fund**
- **South Texas Hispanic Fund**
- **Women and Girls Development Fund**

TYPE:
Capital grants; General operating grants; Project/program grants; Research grants; Scholarships; Seed money grants; Technical assistance.

YEAR PROGRAM STARTED: 1964

PURPOSE:
To help donors achieve their charitable goals for the greater benefit of the community.

LEGAL BASIS:
Community foundation.

ELIGIBILITY:
Eligible organizations must be IRS 501(c)(3) tax-exempt and located in Bexar County or surrounding counties. Endowments and debt reduction will not be funded. The Foundation does not provide grants to individuals.

GEOG. RESTRICTIONS: Bexar County and surrounding counties, Texas.

FINANCIAL DATA:
Amount of support per award: Varies.
Total amount of support: Donor-advised, $18,000,000 (2014); Competitive Grants: $8,500,000 (2015); Scholarships: $3,200,000 (2015).

APPLICATION INFO:
Application and guidelines are available on the web site.
Duration: One year. Must reapply for additional funding.
Deadline: Varies.

PUBLICATIONS:
Newsletter; annual report.

IRS I.D.: 74-6065414

ADDRESS INQUIRIES TO:
Lydia Saldana
Program Officer, Community and Research Grants
(See address above.)

*SPECIAL STIPULATIONS:
The Foundation does not fund statewide; only in Bexar County and surrounding counties.

THE SAN DIEGO FOUNDATION [1333]

2508 Historic Decatur Road
Suite 200
San Diego, CA 92106-6138
(619) 235-2300
Fax: (619) 239-1710
E-mail: info@sdfoundation.org
Web Site: www.sdfoundation.org

FOUNDED: 1975

AREAS OF INTEREST:
Civil society, economic/employment development, education, health and human services, environment, arts and culture, capacity building, science and technology.

TYPE:
Awards/prizes; Capital grants; Challenge/matching grants; Demonstration grants; Development grants; Fellowships; General operating grants; Matching gifts; Project/program grants; Research grants; Scholarships; Seed money grants; Technical assistance; Training grants.

YEAR PROGRAM STARTED: 1975

PURPOSE:
To improve the quality of life for all San Diegans through effective responsible philanthropy.

LEGAL BASIS:
Community foundation.

ELIGIBILITY:
Applicant organizations must be IRS 501(c)(3).

GEOG. RESTRICTIONS: San Diego County, California.

FINANCIAL DATA:
Amount of support per award: Varies.
Total amount of support: Over $40,000,000 annually.
Matching fund requirements: On a case-by-case basis.

NO. AWARDS: 2,800.

APPLICATION INFO:
Requests for proposals in the area of Community Partnerships must include a project budget, organization budget, and letter of qualification.
Duration: Generally, one year.
Deadline: Varies.

PUBLICATIONS:
Annual report; newsletters.

IRS I.D.: 95-2942582

OFFICERS:
Bob Kelly, President and Chief Executive Officer

*SPECIAL STIPULATIONS:
Most grants made only in San Diego region.

THE SAN FRANCISCO FOUNDATION [1334]

One Embarcadero Center
Suite 1400
San Francisco, CA 94111
(415) 733-8500
Fax: (415) 477-2783
E-mail: info@sff.org
Web Site: www.sff.org

FOUNDED: 1948

AREAS OF INTEREST:
Societal and civic issues, health and environment, and arts and humanities.

NAME(S) OF PROGRAMS:
- **Community Leadership Awards**

TYPE:
Awards/prizes.

PURPOSE:
To recognize individuals and organizations whose leadership has made a significant impact in the Bay Area.

LEGAL BASIS:
Community foundation.

ELIGIBILITY:
Organizations must be 501(c)(3).

GEOG. RESTRICTIONS: Alameda, Contra Costa, Marin, San Francisco and San Mateo counties, California.

FINANCIAL DATA:
Amount of support per award: Individual leaders: $10,000; Organizations: $20,000.
Total amount of support: Varies.

NO. MOST RECENT APPLICANTS: 275.

NO. AWARDS: Varies.

APPLICATION INFO:
Details are available online at the web site.
Deadline: Varies.

ADDRESS INQUIRIES TO:
Community Leadership Award Program
E-mail: cla@sff.org

SANTA BARBARA FOUNDATION [1335]

1111 Chapala Street, Suite 200
Santa Barbara, CA 93101
(805) 963-1873
Fax: (805) 966-2345
E-mail: info@sbfoundation.org
Web Site: www.sbfoundation.org

FOUNDED: 1928

AREAS OF INTEREST:
Arts and culture expression, living and dying with dignity, lifelong learning, safety, civic engagement and sustainable protection of environment/historic places.

NAME(S) OF PROGRAMS:
- **Community Learning Sponsorships**
- **Express Grants**
- **Opportunity Grants**

TYPE:
Challenge/matching grants; Development grants; General operating grants; Project/program grants.

YEAR PROGRAM STARTED: 1928

PURPOSE:
To enrich the lives of the people of Santa Barbara County, CA.

LEGAL BASIS:
Community foundation incorporated in California.

ELIGIBILITY:
501(c)(3) organizations only. Funds must be used to benefit the people of Santa Barbara County, CA.

GEOG. RESTRICTIONS: Santa Barbara County, California.

FINANCIAL DATA:
Amount of support per award: Community Learning Sponsorships: Up to $2,500; Express Grants: Up to $5,000; Opportunity Grants: Up to $50,000.
Total amount of support: Approximately $6,000,000 in discretionary grants for the year ended December 31, 2014.
Matching fund requirements: Varies.

APPLICATION INFO:
Application information is available on the web site.
Duration: One year. No guarantee for continuation.
Deadline: Community Learning Sponsorships and Express Grants: Applications are accepted on a rolling basis through November 2, 2015. Opportunity Grants: Applications are accepted periodically throughout the year.

PUBLICATIONS:
Annual report; application guidelines; quarterly newsletter.

IRS I.D.: 95-1866094

STAFF:
Ron Gallo, President and Chief Executive Officer
Jan Campbell, Senior Vice President of Philanthropic Services, Communications and Marketing
Dee Jennings, Senior Vice President of Finance and Administration/Chief Financial Officer
Al Rodriguez, Vice President of Community Investments

ADDRESS INQUIRIES TO:
Grants Associate
(See address above.)

CHARLES AND LYNN SCHUSTERMAN FAMILY FOUNDATION [1336]

110 West Seventh Street, Suite 2000
Tulsa, OK 74119
(918) 879-0290
Fax: (918) 392-9724
E-mail: ahughes@schusterman.org
Web Site: www.schusterman.org

FOUNDED: 1987

AREAS OF INTEREST:
Child advocacy, Jewish life, education, and community service.

TYPE:
Capital grants; General operating grants; Project/program grants.

PURPOSE:
To fund projects of interest to the Foundation including, but not limited to, those working with education, community life and Jewish affairs.

LEGAL BASIS:
Family foundation.

ELIGIBILITY:
Tax-exempt U.S. and international organizations that enhance Jewish life and nonsectarian Oklahoma-based organizations focused on child advocacy, education and youth leadership through service are eligible.

FINANCIAL DATA:
Amount of support per award: Varies.

Total amount of support: Varies.

NO. MOST RECENT APPLICANTS: 582 requests received, January 1, 2013 to December 31, 2013.

NO. AWARDS: 494 requests approved, January 1, 2013 to December 31, 2013.

APPLICATION INFO:
Grants are by invitation only.

Duration: One year; seldom more than three years. Must reapply for renewal based on performance.

Deadline: Applications are received on a rolling basis.

ADDRESS INQUIRIES TO:
Alana Hughes, Chief Operating Officer
(See address above.)

SCRANTON AREA FOUNDATION [1337]

615 Jefferson Avenue, Suite 102
Scranton, PA 18510
(570) 347-6203
Fax: (570) 347-7587
E-mail: safinfo@safdn.org
Web Site: www.safdn.org

FOUNDED: 1954

AREAS OF INTEREST:
The people and community of the city of Scranton and Lackawanna County, PA.

TYPE:
Challenge/matching grants; Demonstration grants; Grants-in-aid; Project/program grants; Scholarships; Seed money grants; Training grants.

PURPOSE:
To strengthen the local community; to enrich the lives of the people of Scranton and Lackawanna County, PA.

ELIGIBILITY:
Grants to 501(c)(3) nonprofits serving Lackawanna County, PA.

GEOG. RESTRICTIONS: The city of Scranton and Lackawanna County, Pennsylvania.

FINANCIAL DATA:
Amount of support per award: Varies.

Total amount of support: Approximately $481,000 for the year 2013.

APPLICATION INFO:
Before a grant application is submitted to the Foundation, it is strongly recommended that the applicant submit a letter of intent (one to two pages maximum).

Duration: Varies.

Deadline: Typically March, June, August and November.

THE SELF FAMILY FOUNDATION [1338]

120 Main Street
Greenwood, SC 29646
(864) 941-4011
Fax: (864) 941-4091
E-mail: fwideman@selffoundation.org
Web Site: www.selffoundation.org

FOUNDED: 1942

AREAS OF INTEREST:
Community wellness, education, with emphasis on early childhood development and youth, and health with emphasis on prevention.

TYPE:
Challenge/matching grants; Project/program grants. Project grants in areas of the Foundation's interest.

YEAR PROGRAM STARTED: 1942

PURPOSE:
To help people to help themselves in South Carolina.

LEGAL BASIS:
Tax-exempt, private foundation.

ELIGIBILITY:
Applicants must be tax-exempt organizations in South Carolina only. No grants are awarded directly to individuals.

GEOG. RESTRICTIONS: South Carolina, with preference to Greenwood.

FINANCIAL DATA:
Amount of support per award: $1,000 to $500,000. Typical grant: $25,000.

Total amount of support: $1,130,042 for the year 2014.

Matching fund requirements: Stipulated with specific programs.

NO. MOST RECENT APPLICANTS: 65.

NO. AWARDS: 34.

REPRESENTATIVE AWARDS:
$50,000 to Greenwood Community Children's Center; $75,230 to Independent Colleges and Universities of South Carolina; $7,500 to Ed Venture Children's Museum; $15,000 to Greater Greenwood United Ministries.

APPLICATION INFO:
There is no application form. Applicants are requested to submit a written proposal, leadership list, a description of the organization's activities and objectives and a description of the purpose for which funding is sought. Include copy of IRS tax determination letter, expense budget of the organization and copy of latest financial statement.

Duration: No grants on a continuing basis.

Deadline: February 1, June 1, September 1 and November 1. Announcements in March, July, October and December.

IRS I.D.: 57-0400594

OFFICERS:
W.M. Self, Chairman
Frank J. Wideman, III, President
J.C. Self, III, Treasurer
Dr. Sally E. Self, Secretary

TRUSTEES:
J. Welborn Adams
Virginia Self Goldsmith
Jon Holloway
Cade Jackson
Furman C. Self
J.C. Self, III
Dr. Sally E. Self
W.M. Self
W.M. Self, Jr.
Mary Andrews Self Whittington

ADDRESS INQUIRIES TO:
Mamie Nicholson, Program Officer
(See address above.)

SHASTA REGIONAL COMMUNITY FOUNDATION [1339]

1335 Arboretum Drive, Suite B
Redding, CA 96003
(530) 244-1219
Fax: (530) 244-0905
E-mail: amanda@shastarcf.org
Web Site: www.shastarcf.org

FOUNDED: 2000

AREAS OF INTEREST:
Arts and culture, community development, education, health and human services.

NAME(S) OF PROGRAMS:
- **The McConnell Fund**
- **Redding Rancheria Community Fund**

TYPE:
Project/program grants.

PURPOSE:
To enhance the quality of life of Shasta and Siskiyou communities through philanthropy, education and information.

ELIGIBILITY:
To be eligible for funding, the applicant must be a nonprofit 501(c)(3) organization or

public agency and provide specific and direct benefits to residents of Shasta and/or Siskiyou counties, primarily, or to Modoc, Tehama or Trinity counties.

GEOG. RESTRICTIONS: Primarily Shasta and Siskiyou counties, California. Limited funding to Modoc, Tehama and Trinity counties, California.

FINANCIAL DATA:
Net investment assets of $23,700,000 in 2015.

Amount of support per award: Varies.

Total amount of support: $1,900,757 in grants awarded in 2015; $98,350 in scholarships awarded in 2015.

NO. AWARDS: Scholarships to 79 students in 2015.

APPLICATION INFO:
Consult the Foundation web site.

Duration: Varies.

Deadline: Varies.

ADDRESS INQUIRIES TO:
Grants:
Amanda Hutchings, Program Officer
(See e-mail address above.)

Scholarships:
Miriam Leal, Program Associate
(See phone number above.)

SILICON VALLEY COMMUNITY FOUNDATION [1340]

2440 West El Camino Real
Suite 300
Mountain View, CA 94040-1498
(650) 450-5400
Fax: (650) 450-5401
E-mail: info@siliconvalleycf.org
Web Site: www.siliconvalleycf.org

FOUNDED: 2007

AREAS OF INTEREST:
This community foundation utilizes five grantmaking strategies: economic security; education (closing the middle school achievement gap in mathematics); immigrant integration; regional planning (land use and transportation planning); and a community opportunity fund currently focused on safety-net services of food and shelter.

TYPE:
General operating grants; Project/program grants; Scholarships; Seed money grants. Nonprofit organizations that provide services or programs related to the specific five grantmaking strategies in San Mateo and Santa Clara counties may be eligible to apply for funding from the Foundation's endowment. Scholarships for college-bound students are also open to application.

YEAR PROGRAM STARTED: 2008

PURPOSE:
To advance philanthropic solutions to challenging problems, engaging donors to make our region and world a better place for all.

LEGAL BASIS:
Community foundation.

ELIGIBILITY:
To be eligible for a grant, an organization should have current evidence of tax-exempt status under Section 501(c)(3) from the IRS, be a public entity or have a fiscal sponsor with tax-exempt status.

In general, the Foundation does not make grants from its endowment for or to:
(1) activities not directly benefiting the residents of San Mateo and Santa Clara counties;
(2) organizations that are discriminatory;
(3) individuals (contact the Foundation for exceptions to this rule);
(4) costs already incurred;
(5) fraternal organizations, unless sponsoring a specific program open to the entire community;
(6) religious purposes; however, organizations with religious affiliations will be considered for grants if their programs seek to address the needs of the wider community without regard to religious beliefs;
(7) fund-raising events such as walk-a-thons, tournaments and fashion shows and general fund-raising solicitations;
(8) organizations and programs designed to elect candidates to public office or;
(9) out-of-area travel.

GEOG. RESTRICTIONS: San Mateo and Santa Clara counties only.

FINANCIAL DATA:
Amount of support per award: $10,000 to $250,000, with average grant size less than $100,000. Grant size varies according to the type of project, needs of the organization, and the Foundation's annual giving budget and program concentration.

Total amount of support: Dependent on the Foundation's annual giving budget.

NO. MOST RECENT APPLICANTS: 360.

APPLICATION INFO:
The first step for any potential applicant is to learn the specific components of the grantmaking strategies. If the potential applicant's organization does work or plans to do work related to one of the grantmaking strategies and a Request for Proposal (RFP) regarding that strategy is open for application, then a representative should attend a grant information session. This will give the potential applicant an opportunity to learn more about the grantmaking strategy, the RFP process and talk with a program officer.

Step two would be to submit a proposal with all the required information outlined in the RFP application checklist. The Foundation encourages submission of proposals via e-mail and accepts proposals postmarked and submitted electronically by the respective deadline date.

Duration: Grants are usually for one year, and should not be considered a source of ongoing support.

Deadline: Contact the Foundation for the appropriate grantmaking strategy application.

PUBLICATIONS:
Annual report; RFP guidelines; research papers; *One Magazine*.

IRS I.D.: 20-5205488

BOARD OF DIRECTORS:
Thomas J. Friel, Chairperson
C.S. Park, Vice Chairperson
Jayne Battey
Gloria Brown
Emmett D. Carson, Ph.D.
Gregory M. Gallo
Nancy H. Handel
John F. Hopkins
Samuel Johnson, Jr.
Robert A. Keller
Daniel Lewin
David P. Lopez, Ed.D.
Anne F. Macdonald
Catherine A. Molnar
Ivonne Montes de Oca
Eduardo Rallo
Sanjay Vaswani
Thurman V. White, Jr.
Gordon Yamate

ADDRESS INQUIRIES TO:
Manuel J. Santamaria
Director of Grantmaking
(See address above.)

*SPECIAL STIPULATIONS:
Please note the geographical restriction (above).

SOUTHWEST FLORIDA COMMUNITY FOUNDATION [1341]

8771 College Parkway
Building 2, Suite 201
Fort Myers, FL 33919
(239) 274-5900
Fax: (239) 274-5930
E-mail: info@floridacommunity.com
Web Site: www.floridacommunity.com

FOUNDED: 1977

AREAS OF INTEREST:
Arts, animal welfare and rights, community needs and development, culture, education, and health and human services.

TYPE:
Capital grants; Challenge/matching grants; Demonstration grants; Project/program grants; Scholarships; Seed money grants; Technical assistance; Training grants.

PURPOSE:
To connect donors and their philanthropic aspirations with evolving community needs.

LEGAL BASIS:
501(c)(3).

ELIGIBILITY:
Grants are made to organizations that have tax-exempt status under Section 501(c)(3) of the Internal Revenue Code. No grants are made to individuals. Nonsectarian religious programs may apply. Must serve the needs of the communities listed below.

GEOG. RESTRICTIONS: Charlotte, Collier, Glades, Hendry and Lee counties, Florida.

FINANCIAL DATA:
Amount of support per award: $5,000 to $25,000; Initiative Grant Awards: Up to $100,000.

Total amount of support: $2,500,000 for fiscal year ended June 30, 2013.

NO. MOST RECENT APPLICANTS: 1,200.

NO. AWARDS: 300.

APPLICATION INFO:
Contact the Foundation for application procedures.

Duration: One year.

Deadline: Varies per program.

PUBLICATIONS:
Annual report; quarterly newsletter.

IRS I.D.: 59-6580974

ADMINISTRATORS:
Sarah Owen, President and Chief Executive Officer

ADDRESS INQUIRIES TO:
Anne Douglas, Director of Programs
(See address above.)

STARK COMMUNITY FOUNDATION [1342]

400 Market Avenue North
Suite 200
Canton, OH 44702-2107
(330) 454-3426
Fax: (330) 454-5855
E-mail: info@starkcf.org
Web Site: www.starkcommunityfoundation.org

FOUNDED: 1963

AREAS OF INTEREST:
Advancement of the health, social welfare, education, culture or civic improvement of the community.

TYPE:
Capital grants; Challenge/matching grants; Demonstration grants; Development grants; General operating grants; Matching gifts; Project/program grants; Research grants; Scholarships; Seed money grants; Technical assistance; Training grants; Loan forgiveness programs.

YEAR PROGRAM STARTED: 1965

LEGAL BASIS:
Community foundation.

ELIGIBILITY:
Organizations with 501(c)(3) status serving Stark County, OH, are eligible. The Foundation will not support operating expenses of well-established organizations, deficit programs, or capital expenditures, endowment funds, religious organizations or religious purposes, annual appeal or membership contributions, conferences or recognition events.

GEOG. RESTRICTIONS: Stark County, Ohio.

FINANCIAL DATA:
Total assets $203,000,000 as of January 31, 2013.

Amount of support per award: $1,000 to $225,000.

Total amount of support: Approximately $110,000,000 annually.

Matching fund requirements: No general requirements.

NO. MOST RECENT APPLICANTS: Approximately 200.

NO. AWARDS: 130 Discretionary Field of Interest and 60 Pro-Active Initiatives.

APPLICATION INFO:
Application information is available on the web site.

Duration: One year.

Deadline: January 5. August 1 for discretionary funds.

PUBLICATIONS:
Annual report; guidelines and policies; *Community and Commitment*, newsletter.

STAFF:
Mark Samolczyk, President

ADDRESS INQUIRIES TO:
Mark Samolczyk, President
(See address above.)

THE STEELE-REESE FOUNDATION [1343]

32 Washington Square West
New York, NY 10011
(212) 674-4039
Fax: (212) 286-8513
E-mail: charles@steele-reese.org
Web Site: www.steele-reese.org

FOUNDED: 1955

AREAS OF INTEREST:
Education, health, social welfare, the humanities and the environment.

TYPE:
General operating grants; Project/program grants. Funding is only provided for rural projects of interest to the Foundation. The projects must serve people in the geographic area served by the Foundation.

YEAR PROGRAM STARTED: 1955

LEGAL BASIS:
Private foundation.

ELIGIBILITY:
Funding is provided to nonprofit organizations servicing communities in Appalachian Kentucky and the western states of Idaho and Montana.

All organizations seeking funds must demonstrate additional local community support for their programming.

GEOG. RESTRICTIONS: Appalachian Kentucky, Idaho and Montana.

FINANCIAL DATA:
Amount of support per award: Typically $5,000 to $50,000. Larger grants are typically for multiyear support.

Total amount of support: $1,984,000 for the year 2013.

Matching fund requirements: Some grants require that an organization raise a specific matching amount.

NO. MOST RECENT APPLICANTS: 200 to 250.

NO. AWARDS: Approximately 60.

APPLICATION INFO:
The Foundation welcomes proposals that are accurately aimed. The Foundation's policies and guidelines in detail are available for review online. All applicants must submit proposal materials electronically through the Foundation's web site.

Duration: Grants payable over one to three years. Absolutely no renewals.

Deadline: March 1 for consideration during the current fiscal year.

PUBLICATIONS:
Annual report.

ADDRESS INQUIRIES TO:
For general inquiries about Foundation policies:
William T. Buice, Trustee
The Steele-Reese Foundation
(See address above.) or

Charles U. Buice, Trustee
The Steele-Reese Foundation
123 Fort Greene Place
Brooklyn, NY 11217
(See e-mail address above.)

For Kentucky:
Judy Owens, Appalachian Director
2613 Clubside Court
Lexington, KY 40513
Tel & Fax: (859) 313-5225
E-mail: jkowensjd@aol.com

For Idaho or Montana:
Linda Tracy, Western Program Director
P.O. Box 8311
Missoula, MT 59807-8311
Tel: (406) 207-7984
Fax: (207) 470-3872
E-mail: linda@steele-reese.org

THE ABBOT AND DOROTHY H. STEVENS FOUNDATION [1344]

P.O. Box 111
North Andover, MA 01845
(978) 688-7211
E-mail: grantprocess@stevensfoundation.com

AREAS OF INTEREST:
Education, community welfare, arts and youth programs.

TYPE:
Capital grants; General operating grants; Project/program grants.

PURPOSE:
To improve the quality of life in greater Lawrence and Merrimack Valley.

ELIGIBILITY:
Eligible organizations must be IRS 501(c)(3) tax-exempt.

GEOG. RESTRICTIONS: Greater Lawrence and Merrimack Valley, Massachusetts.

FINANCIAL DATA:
Amount of support per award: $8,000 average.

Total amount of support: Varies.

APPLICATION INFO:
Applicants must include a copy of their IRS 501(c)(3) tax determination letter.

Duration: One year.

Deadline: Trustees meet monthly with the exception of July and August.

PUBLICATIONS:
Guidelines.

ADDRESS INQUIRIES TO:
Joshua Miner, Administrator
(See address above.)

THE NATHANIEL AND ELIZABETH P. STEVENS FOUNDATION [1345]

P.O. Box 111
North Andover, MA 01845
(978) 688-7211
E-mail: grantprocess@stevensfoundation.com

AREAS OF INTEREST:
Education, community welfare, arts and youth programs.

TYPE:
Capital grants; General operating grants; Project/program grants.

PURPOSE:
To improve the quality of life in the greater Lawrence and Merrimack Valley.

ELIGIBILITY:
Eligible organizations must be IRS 501(c)(3) tax-exempt.

GEOG. RESTRICTIONS: Greater Lawrence and Merrimack Valley, Massachusetts.

FINANCIAL DATA:
Amount of support per award: $8,000 average.

Total amount of support: Varies.

APPLICATION INFO:
Applications must include a copy of the IRS 501(c)(3) tax determination letter.

Duration: One year.

Deadline: Trustees meet monthly with the exception of July and August.

PUBLICATIONS:
Guidelines.

ADDRESS INQUIRIES TO:
Joshua Miner, Administrator
(See address above.)

H. CHASE STONE TRUST

c/o JPMorgan
370 17th Street, Suite 3200
Denver, CO 80202
(303) 607-7810
Fax: (303) 607-7761
E-mail: julie.golden@jpmorgan.com
Web Site: www.jpmorgan.com/onlinegrants

TYPE:
Project/program grants.

See entry 491 for full listing.

SUDBURY FOUNDATION [1346]

326 Concord Road
Sudbury, MA 01776
(978) 443-0849
Fax: (978) 579-9536
E-mail: contact@sudburyfoundation.org
Web Site: www.sudburyfoundation.org

FOUNDED: 1952

AREAS OF INTEREST:
Scholarships, environment, and charitable grants for communities in the Sudbury area; children, youth and families.

NAME(S) OF PROGRAMS:
- **The Atkinson Scholarship Program**
- **Children, Youth and Families Program**
- **The Environmental Program**
- **The Sudbury Program**

TYPE:
Project/program grants; Scholarships. Capacity-building grants.

YEAR PROGRAM STARTED: 1952

PURPOSE:
To improve the quality of life in Sudbury and the surrounding communities.

ELIGIBILITY:
Eligible organizations must be IRS 501(c)(3) tax-exempt. The Foundation funds projects in Sudbury and the 10 communities surrounding Sudbury that address the issues of Youth Development and Opportunity, Community Building, Preservation of Community Character and Assets, and/or Organizational Capacity and Effectiveness.

The Environmental Program focuses on food and local farm initiatives in Massachusetts.

The Atkinson Scholarship Program provides college financial aid to students connected to Sudbury, MA.

GEOG. RESTRICTIONS: Sudbury, Massachusetts and surrounding areas.

FINANCIAL DATA:
Scholarships are administered to the schools earmarked for specific students.

Amount of support per award: Scholarships: Up to $5,000 annually; Grants: $5,000 to $50,000.

Total amount of support: Varies.

NO. AWARDS: Scholarships: 15 new awards per year; Grants to nonprofits: 35 per year.

APPLICATION INFO:
Refer to the web site.

Duration: Typically one year.

Deadline: Varies.

ADDRESS INQUIRIES TO:
Marilyn Martino, Executive Director
(See address above.)

*SPECIAL STIPULATIONS:
Scholarship program open to local high school seniors only for undergraduate education.

THE SUMMERLEE FOUNDATION [1347]

5556 Caruth Haven Lane
Dallas, TX 75225
(214) 363-9000
Fax: (214) 363-1941
E-mail: info@summerlee.org
Web Site: www.summerlee.org

FOUNDED: 1988

AREAS OF INTEREST:
Animal protection and Texas history.

NAME(S) OF PROGRAMS:
- **Animal Protection Program**
- **Texas History**

TYPE:
Project/program grants; Research grants; Technical assistance.

YEAR PROGRAM STARTED: 1988

PURPOSE:
To promote animal protection and the prevention of cruelty to animals; to research and document all facts of Texas history.

LEGAL BASIS:
Charitable foundation.

ELIGIBILITY:
No grants are made for religious purposes or to individuals. Must be 501(c)(3).

FINANCIAL DATA:
Amount of support per award: $5,000 to $10,000.

NO. MOST RECENT APPLICANTS: Approximately 200.

NO. AWARDS: 84.

APPLICATION INFO:
Consult the web site.

Duration: Generally one year; occasionally multiyear.

Deadline: The Foundation meets quarterly to review grant proposals.

IRS I.D.: 75-2252355

OFFICERS:
John W. Crain, President
Melanie K. Anderson, Vice President and Program Director-Animal Protection
Ron Tyler, Ph.D., Vice President
Hon. Nikki DeShazo, Treasurer
Hon. David D. Jackson, Secretary

BOARD OF DIRECTORS:
Melanie K. Anderson
Jim Bruseth, Ph.D.
Joan Casey
John W. Crain
Hon. Nikki DeShazo
Ron Tyler, Ph.D.
Mary Volcansek, Ph.D.

ADDRESS INQUIRIES TO:
Melanie K. Anderson
Program Director-Animal Protection or
Gary N. Smith
Program Director-Texas History
(See address above.)

THE SUMMIT FOUNDATION [1348]

111 A Lincoln Street
Breckenridge, CO 80424
(970) 453-5970
Fax: (970) 453-1423
E-mail: tsfdirector@summitfoundation.org
Web Site: www.summitfoundation.org

FOUNDED: 1984

AREAS OF INTEREST:
Art and culture, health and human service, education, environment and sports.

TYPE:
Capital grants; Challenge/matching grants; Endowments; General operating grants; Project/program grants; Scholarships; Technical assistance. The Foundation supports scholarship programs at Summit High School and neighboring community high schools. Scholarships are available to graduating seniors each year.

YEAR PROGRAM STARTED: 1984

PURPOSE:
To improve the quality of life for residents and guests of Summit County and neighboring communities.

LEGAL BASIS:
Community foundation.

ELIGIBILITY:
Grants are made to organizations that have tax-exempt status under Section 501(c)(3) of the Internal Revenue Code. No grants are made to individuals.

GEOG. RESTRICTIONS: Summit County and neighboring communities of Alma, Fairplay, Kremmling and Leadville, Colorado.

FINANCIAL DATA:
Amount of support per award: Varies.

Total amount of support: Approximately $2,339,730 for the year 2013.

NO. MOST RECENT APPLICANTS: 97.

NO. AWARDS: 91.

APPLICATION INFO:
Contact the Foundation for specific details on the various grant programs.

Deadline: Typically April and October.

IRS I.D.: 74-2341399

ADDRESS INQUIRIES TO:
Lee Zimmerman, Executive Director
(See address above.)

THOMAS THOMPSON TRUST [1349]

c/o Rackemann, Sawyer & Brewster
160 Federal Street, 15th Floor
Boston, MA 02110-1700
(617) 951-1108
Fax: (617) 542-7437
E-mail: smonahan@rackemann.com
Web Site: www.thomasthompsontrust.org

AREAS OF INTEREST:
Education, health/mental health, social services and cultural.

TYPE:
Capital grants; Challenge/matching grants; Conferences/seminars; Demonstration grants; Development grants; Endowments; Professorships; Project/program grants; Seed money grants; Technical assistance; Training grants; Research contracts. Support for special programs, capital support, new construction, renovation and equipment.

PURPOSE:
To promote health, education, or general social and civic betterment.

LEGAL BASIS:
Private foundation.

ELIGIBILITY:
Eligible organizations must be in operation for three consecutive years prior to submitting an application.

GEOG. RESTRICTIONS: Dutchess County, New York, particularly in Rhinebeck; and Windham County, Vermont, particularly in Brattleboro.

FINANCIAL DATA:
Amount of support per award: $5,000 to $15,000.

Total amount of support: $523,975 for fiscal year 2012.

Matching fund requirements: Determined on case-by-case basis.

NO. AWARDS: 39 for fiscal year 2012.

REPRESENTATIVE AWARDS:
Brattleboro Boys and Girls Club; Windham Housing Trust; Young Rhinebeck.

APPLICATION INFO:
Applications must be submitted online.

Duration: Varies.

PUBLICATIONS:
Application guidelines.

ADDRESS INQUIRIES TO:
Susan T. Monahan
Grants Coordinator and Trustee
(See address or e-mail above.)

TIDES FOUNDATION [1350]

P.O. Box 29198
San Francisco, CA 94129-0198
(415) 561-6400
Fax: (415) 561-6401
E-mail: info@tides.org
Web Site: www.tides.org

FOUNDED: 1976

AREAS OF INTEREST:
Civic participation, economic development, economic and racial justice, environment, environmental justice, LGBTIQ communities, HIV/AIDS, native communities, progressive media, arts and culture, violence prevention, women's empowerment and reproductive health, and youth organizing and development.

NAME(S) OF PROGRAMS:
- **Colin Higgins Youth Courage Awards**
- **Jane Bagley Lehman Awards for Excellence in Public Advocacy**
- **Antonio Pizzigati Prize for Software in the Public Interest**

TYPE:
General operating grants; Project/program grants.

YEAR PROGRAM STARTED: 1976

PURPOSE:
To partner with donors to increase and organize resources for social change.

LEGAL BASIS:
Public foundation.

FINANCIAL DATA:
Amount of support per award: Varies.

Total amount of support: $128,800,000 in grants (U.S. and international) in 2014.

NO. AWARDS: 3,381 total grants in 2014.

APPLICATION INFO:
The Fund does not accept unsolicited grant requests.

IRS I.D.: 51-0198509

ADDRESS INQUIRIES TO:
Grants Manager
(See address above.)

TOLEDO COMMUNITY FOUNDATION [1351]

300 Madison Avenue, Suite 1300
Toledo, OH 43604
(419) 241-5049
Fax: (419) 242-5549
E-mail: toledocf@toledocf.org
Web Site: www.toledocf.org

FOUNDED: 1973

AREAS OF INTEREST:
Education, social services, physical and mental health, neighborhood and urban affairs, natural resources and the arts.

TYPE:
Challenge/matching grants; Project/program grants; Seed money grants. The Foundation has a particular interest in providing seed money for new programs designed to meet emerging community needs or to expand existing successful programs. Emphasis is placed on programs that will:
(a) create safe, positive living environments;
(b) enable families to develop the skills/resources needed to support and nurture each member and;
(c) foster the development of responsible young people who are capable of achieving their fullest potential.

PURPOSE:
To enrich the quality of life for individuals and families in the greater Toledo, OH service area.

ELIGIBILITY:
Grants are awarded only to nonprofit, charitable organizations that are IRS 501(c)(3) tax-exempt. The Foundation usually will not make grants from its unrestricted funds to support general operating budgets (or budget deficits) of established organizations, annual campaigns, capital campaigns, purchase of equipment such as computer hardware/software or motor vehicles, production of films, videos, television programs, etc., or for sectarian activities of religious organizations.

GEOG. RESTRICTIONS: Northwest Ohio and southeast Michigan, with particular emphasis on the greater Toledo, Ohio area.

FINANCIAL DATA:
Amount of support per award: Varies.

APPLICATION INFO:
Online grant application must be completed. No hard copies accepted.

Duration: Varies.

Deadline: January 15 and September 15.

PUBLICATIONS:
Guidelines.

ADDRESS INQUIRIES TO:
Anneliese Grytafey, Senior Program Officer
(See address above.)

THE TRULL FOUNDATION [1352]

404 Fourth Street
Palacios, TX 77465
(361) 972-5241
Fax: (361) 972-1109
E-mail: info@trullfoundation.org
Web Site: www.trullfoundation.org

FOUNDED: 1967

AREAS OF INTEREST:
Children, substance abuse problems, Texas coastal environment, and The Palacios, Matagorda County area.

CONSULTING OR VOLUNTEER SERVICES:
Assists local projects and organizations in Texas, with a priority to rural Texas.

TYPE:
Challenge/matching grants; Development grants; General operating grants; Project/program grants; Scholarships.

YEAR PROGRAM STARTED: 1948

PURPOSE:
To support charitable and educational programs.

LEGAL BASIS:
Private (family) foundation.

ELIGIBILITY:
Applicants must have federal tax-exemption letter from IRS.

GEOG. RESTRICTIONS: Primarily in rural Texas.

FINANCIAL DATA:
Amount of support per award: $2,000 to $5,000 average.

Total amount of support: $2,221,295 for the year 2013.

NO. MOST RECENT APPLICANTS: 412 for the year 2012.

NO. AWARDS: 288 for the year 2013.

REPRESENTATIVE AWARDS:
$3,000 to Children's Discovery Museum, Victoria, TX; $5,000 to Central Texas Library System, Inc., Austin, TX; $4,000 to Pines and Prairies Land Trust, Bastrop, TX; $2,000 to Devereux Texas Treatment Network, Victoria, TX; $5,000 to Child Welfare Alliance of Calhoun County, Port Lavaca, TX.

APPLICATION INFO:
Each applicant should submit the following:
(1) cover letter (two-page maximum);
(2) proposal fact sheet (two-page maximum);
(3) current agency budget (one to three pages), including sources of income;
(4) one-page project budget, if different from operating budget;
(5) documentation of IRS status 501(c)(3). If there is any matter which might affect the IRS status to cause the revocation of the exemption, include information about this matter and;
(6) selected additional material or information (limit five pages) (optional).

Proposals sent by fax or e-mail are not accepted.

The Foundation may request additional information if there is an interest in the proposal.

Duration: Usually no more than three years per project.

Deadline: Announcement within two months after receipt of proposal.

PUBLICATIONS:
Biennial report; application guidelines; proposal fact sheet.

IRS I.D.: 23-7423943

ADDRESS INQUIRIES TO:
E. Gail Purvis, Executive Director
(See address above.)

U.S. BANCORP FOUNDATION [1353]

BC-MN-H21B
800 Nicollet Mall
Minneapolis, MN 55402
(612) 303-4000
Web Site: www.usbank.com/communityrelations

FOUNDED: 1979

AREAS OF INTEREST:
Arts and culture, education, affordable housing and economic opportunity.

TYPE:
Capital grants; Development grants; General operating grants; Matching gifts; Project/program grants.

PURPOSE:
To improve the quality of life in communities where U.S. Bancorp employees live and work.

LEGAL BASIS:
Corporate foundation.

ELIGIBILITY:
Organizations must be IRS 501(c)(3) tax-exempt and must be located in communities where United States Bank operates.

The Foundation charitable contributions program will not provide funding for:
(1) organizations not tax-exempt under Internal Revenue Code Section 501(c)(3);
(2) fraternal organizations, merchant associations, chamber memberships or programs, or 501(c)(4) or (6) organizations;
(3) fund-raising events or sponsorships, "pass through" organizations or private foundations;
(4) organizations outside U.S. Bancorp communities;
(5) programs operated by religious organizations for religious purposes;
(6) political organizations or organizations designed primarily to lobby;
(7) individuals;
(8) travel and related expenses;
(9) endowment campaigns;
(10) deficit reduction;
(11) organizations receiving primary funding from the United Way or;
(12) organizations whose practices are not in keeping with the Company's equal opportunity policy.

GEOG. RESTRICTIONS: Communities where United States Bank has operations.

FINANCIAL DATA:
Amount of support per award: Varies.

Total amount of support: Varies.

APPLICATION INFO:
Application and guidelines are available online.

Duration: One year.

Deadline: Varies.

PUBLICATIONS:
Guidelines; Corporate Citizenship Report.

IRS I.D.: 41-1359579

U.S. DEPARTMENT OF HEALTH AND HUMAN SERVICES [1354]

Administration on Intellectual and Developmental Disabilities
One Massachusetts Avenue
Washington, DC 20201
(202) 401-4541
Fax: (202) 205-8037
Web Site: www.acl.gov/programs/AIDD

AREAS OF INTEREST:
Developmental disabilities.

NAME(S) OF PROGRAMS:
- **Projects of National Significance for Persons with Developmental Disabilities**

TYPE:
Demonstration grants; Technical assistance; Training grants. Model demonstration grants. Support for persons with developmental disabilities.

YEAR PROGRAM STARTED: 1975

PURPOSE:
To support policy development and awards funding that enhance the independence, productivity, inclusion and integration of people with developmental disabilities and their families.

LEGAL BASIS:
Government agency.

ELIGIBILITY:
Applicants must be nonprofit organizations, state agencies, or consortia.

GEOG. RESTRICTIONS: United States and its territories.

FINANCIAL DATA:
Amount of support per award: Varies.

Total amount of support: $8,857,000 for the year 2015.

Matching fund requirements: 25% local match.

NO. AWARDS: Approximately 20 for the year 2013.

APPLICATION INFO:
Application information is available on the web site.

Duration: 12 to 60 months.

Deadline: Varies.

OFFICERS:
Aaron Bishop, Commissioner, Administration on Intellectual and Developmental Disabilities

ADDRESS INQUIRIES TO:
Ophelia McLain, Director
(See address above.)

U.S. DEPARTMENT OF HOUSING AND URBAN DEVELOPMENT [1355]

451 7th Street, S.W.
Room 7286
Washington, DC 20410
(202) 708-3587 (Office of Block Grant Assistance)
(202) 708-1577 (Entitlement Division)
(202) 708-1322 (State/Small Cities Division)
Fax: (202) 401-2044
Web Site: www.hudexchange.info

FOUNDED: 1974

AREAS OF INTEREST:
Community development.

NAME(S) OF PROGRAMS:
- **Community Development Block Grant Program: Entitlement Communities Program**
- **State Community Development Block Grant Program**

TYPE:
Block grants; Project/program grants. Acquisition, construction of certain public works, facilities and improvements, clearance, housing rehabilitation, relocation and demolition, public services (limited), activities relating to conservation and renewable energy resources, neighborhood revitalization and economic development projects, including assistance to micro enterprises.

YEAR PROGRAM STARTED: 1975

PURPOSE:
To develop viable urban communities, including decent housing and a suitable living environment and expand economic opportunities, principally for persons of low and moderate income.

LEGAL BASIS:
Units of general local government under Title I of the Housing and Community Development Act of 1974 (PL 93-383).

ELIGIBILITY:
The following units of general local government and states are all entitled to receive block grants from the CDBG Entitlement Communities Program and State and Small Cities Program. Grant amounts are determined by a statutory formula:
(1) principal cities of Metropolitan Statistical Areas (MSAs);
(2) other metropolitan cities with a population of at least 50,000 and;
(3) qualified urban counties, as defined in the Act, with populations of at least 200,000 (excluding the population of entitled cities).

Under the State CDBG Program, HUD provides grant assistance to 49 states and Puerto Rico that in turn award grants to units of general local government not eligible to receive grants from the Entitlement Communities Program. Grant amounts to states are determined by statutory formula.

Under the HUD Administered Small Cities Program, HUD directly awards grants to non-entitled units of general local government within the state of Hawaii by formula. The total value of grants awarded through this Program is determined by statutory formula.

FINANCIAL DATA:
Amount of support per award: Varies from city to city.

Total amount of support: Approximately $3.03 billion for fiscal year 2014.

APPLICATION INFO:

For the CDBG Entitlement Communities Program, a grantee must develop and submit to HUD its consolidated plan, which is a jurisdiction's comprehensive planning document and application for funding under the Community Planning and Development formula grant programs: CDBG, HOME, Emergency Shelter Grants (ESG) and Housing Opportunities for Persons with AIDS (HOPWA). In its consolidated plan, the jurisdiction must identify its goals for these community planning and development programs, as well as for housing programs. These goals will serve as the criteria against which HUD will evaluate a jurisdiction's plan and its performance under the plan. In addition, the consolidated plan must include required certifications, including that not less than 70% of the CDBG funds expended over a one-, two- or three-year period specified by the grantee, will be used for activities that benefit low- and moderate-income persons. A consolidated plan submission will be approved by HUD unless the plan (or a portion of it) is inconsistent with the purposes of the National Affordable Housing Act or it is substantially incomplete.

Under the State CDBG Program, to receive a grant from HUD, a state must certify that it:
(1) is following a detailed citizen participation plan and that each funded unit of general local government is following a detailed citizen participation plan;
(2) has consulted with affected units of general local government in the nonentitled area in determining the method of distribution of funding; it engages or will engage in planning for community development activities; it will provide assistance to units of general local government; it will not refuse to distribute funds to any unit of general local government based on the particular eligible activity chosen by the unit of general local government, except that a state is not prevented from establishing priorities based on the activities selected;
(3) has a consolidated plan that identifies community development and housing needs and short-term and long-term community development objectives;
(4) will conduct its program in accordance with the Civil Rights Act of 1964 and the Fair Housing Act of 1988 and will affirmatively further fair housing;
(5) will set forth a method of distribution that ensures that each of the funded activities will meet one or more of the program's three broad, national objectives (grant maximum feasible priority to activities which benefit low- and moderate-income families, aid in the prevention or elimination of slums or blight or, in unique circumstances, meet urgent community development needs) and at least 70% of the amount expended for activities over a period of one, two or three consecutive program years will benefit low- and moderate-income families, and that the state will not attempt to recover any capital costs of public improvements assisted with CDBG funds, except for certain exceptions found in 24 CFR 91.325(b)(4);
(6) will require units of general local government to certify that they are adapting and enforcing laws to prohibit the use of excessive force against nonviolent civil rights demonstrations, and they will enforce laws against barring entrance and exit from facilities that are the targets of nonviolent civil rights demonstrations in their jurisdiction and;
(7) will comply with Title I of the HCD Act and all other applicable laws.

Under the HUD Administered Small Cities Program, to receive a grant, the counties of Hawaii, Maui and Kauai in Hawaii must prepare and submit a consolidated plan to HUD.

ADDRESS INQUIRIES TO:
Office of Block Grant Assistance
(See address above.)

*SPECIAL STIPULATIONS:
Block grants made to states and local governments, not individuals.

THE UNITY FOUNDATION OF LAPORTE COUNTY [1356]

115 East Fourth Street
Michigan City, IN 46360
(219) 879-0327
Fax: (219) 210-3881
E-mail: unity@uflc.net
Web Site: www.uflc.net

FOUNDED: 1992

AREAS OF INTEREST:
Community development in LaPorte County, IN.

CONSULTING OR VOLUNTEER SERVICES:
Technical assistance to nonprofits and donors.

NAME(S) OF PROGRAMS:
- **Community Fund**

TYPE:
Challenge/matching grants; Grants-in-aid; Project/program grants; Scholarships; Technical assistance. Community Fund makes grants to education, the arts, health and human services, and the environment to the whole community. Grants are based on what the community needs at a given time.

YEAR PROGRAM STARTED: 1992

PURPOSE:
To improve the quality of life in LaPorte County, IN.

LEGAL BASIS:
Indiana corporation 501(c)(3).

ELIGIBILITY:
Nonprofits serving people of LaPorte County, IN.

GEOG. RESTRICTIONS: LaPorte County, Indiana.

FINANCIAL DATA:
Amount of support per award: Community grants: Up to $3,000.

Total amount of support: More than $700,000 in community grants and more than $130,000 in scholarships each year.

NO. MOST RECENT APPLICANTS: Grants: 75.

NO. AWARDS: 53.

APPLICATION INFO:
Applications should follow the format outlined in the online directions. The following information is required:
(1) narrative describing the program or specific need to be addressed, its significance to the community and its particular benefit to those living in the LaPorte County area, and the names and qualifications of those persons who will carry it out;
(2) complete budget for the project, including funding plan, amount of the request, and names of other funding sources the organization has applied to for assistance and;
(3) description of applicant organization(s) including the name, address, telephone and fax number of the contact person, a list of the officers and board members, a copy of the IRS letter designating the organization as 501(c)(3) federal tax-exempt, latest annual financial report, and any descriptive brochures or promotional literature.

Deadline: Community Grants: Mid-July; Community Scholarships: April 1.

PUBLICATIONS:
Report to Community.

STAFF:
Maggi Spartz, President

ADDRESS INQUIRIES TO:
Maggi Spartz, President
(See address above.)

VAN LOEBENSELS/REMBEROCK FOUNDATION [1357]

131 Steuart Street
Suite 301
San Francisco, CA 94105
(415) 512-0500
Fax: (415) 371-0227
E-mail: info@vlsrr.org
Web Site: www.vlsrr.org

FOUNDED: 1964

AREAS OF INTEREST:
Legal services.

TYPE:
General operating grants; Project/program grants; Seed money grants.

YEAR PROGRAM STARTED: 1964

PURPOSE:
To support projects that will test potentially useful innovations in the areas of public interest law.

LEGAL BASIS:
Private independent foundation.

ELIGIBILITY:
Grants are restricted to northern California. Grants are not ordinarily made for projects requiring medical, scientific or other technical knowledge for evaluation, operating budgets of well-established organizations, capital expenditures, to national organizations unless for a specific local project, to individuals or for scholarships.

GEOG. RESTRICTIONS: Northern California.

FINANCIAL DATA:
Amount of support per award: Average grant: $15,000.

Total amount of support: $2,068,000 for the year 2015.

NO. AWARDS: 80 for the year 2015.

REPRESENTATIVE AWARDS:
$35,000 to East Bay Community Law Center.

APPLICATION INFO:
Application information is available on the web site.

Duration: Most grants are awarded on a single-year basis, but may be renewed if warranted.

Deadline: Proposals are considered every two to three months. Announcement several days after Board meetings.

BOARD OF DIRECTORS:
Toni Rembe, President
Dan Corsello, Treasurer
Julie Divola, Secretary

Thomas C. Layton
Brian Wong

EXECUTIVE DIRECTOR:
Nancy Wiltsek

ADDRESS INQUIRIES TO:
Toni Rembe, President
(See address above.)

VENTURA COUNTY COMMUNITY FOUNDATION [1358]

4001 Mission Oaks Boulevard
Suite A
Camarillo, CA 93012
(805) 988-0196
Fax: (805) 484-2700
E-mail: vccf@vccf.org
Web Site: www.vccf.org

FOUNDED: 1987

AREAS OF INTEREST:
Community needs and development, culture, education, health, human services, women's issues and Latino issues.

TYPE:
Project/program grants; Scholarships.

YEAR PROGRAM STARTED: 1987

PURPOSE:
To promote and enable philanthropy to improve our community, for good, forever.

ELIGIBILITY:
Must qualify under the Internal Revenue Code Section 501(c)(3) as a nonprofit organization, or operate under the fiscal sponsorship of an organization that does, and serve residents of Ventura County, CA.

GEOG. RESTRICTIONS: Ventura County, California.

FINANCIAL DATA:
Amount of support per award: Varies.
Total amount of support: Varies.

NO. AWARDS: 802.

APPLICATION INFO:
Applications accepted only in response to an open request for proposals.
Duration: Varies per program.

ADDRESS INQUIRIES TO:
Appropriate program officer, as outlined in the Request for Proposals.

VICTORIA FOUNDATION, INC. [1359]

31 Mulberry Street, Fifth Floor
Newark, NJ 07102
(973) 792-9200
Fax: (973) 792-1300
E-mail: info@victoriafoundation.org
Web Site: www.victoriafoundation.org

FOUNDED: 1924

AREAS OF INTEREST:
Education, neighborhood revitalization, youth and families in Newark, NJ, as well as statewide environmental issues.

TYPE:
Capital grants; Challenge/matching grants; General operating grants; Project/program grants. The focus in Education includes after-school programs, educational enrichment, teacher training and curriculum development.

Neighborhood Revitalization includes community development, employment training, housing programs and community organizing.

The focus in Youth and Families includes youth development programs and efforts to strengthen families.

The concentration in Environment includes open space preservation in New Jersey, particularly in the Highlands and Pinelands.

YEAR PROGRAM STARTED: 1924

PURPOSE:
To promote education, urban environment, neighborhood development and urban revitalization, and youth and families in the city of Newark; to preserve and conserve resources including land and water in the state of New Jersey and within the city of Newark.

LEGAL BASIS:
Independent foundation.

ELIGIBILITY:
Organizations must be nonprofit per Internal Revenue Code 501(c)(3) and must address the Foundation's interests. No grants are made to individuals or for programs dealing with specific diseases, afflictions or geriatric needs. Proposals from arts organizations will be considered only if they directly bear on education.

General programs are focused within Newark, NJ. Environmental programs encompass the state of New Jersey.

GEOG. RESTRICTIONS: New Jersey.

FINANCIAL DATA:
Amount of support per award: Varies.
Total amount of support: $10,130,000 in total grants paid for the year ended December 31, 2015.

NO. MOST RECENT APPLICANTS: 229.

NO. AWARDS: 188 for the year ended December 31, 2015.

REPRESENTATIVE AWARDS:
$75,000 to New Jersey Symphony Orchestra to support the Newark Early Strings Program, which provides Suzuki violin instruction to over 500 elementary school children; $130,000 to Ironbound Community Corporation towards general operating support.

APPLICATION INFO:
Application information is available on the web site.
Duration: One year. Renewal based upon careful trustee and staff review of subsequent proposal submissions.
Deadline: Current grantees: January 15 and July 15; New applicants: February 1 and August 1; School applications: February 1; Summer camp: September 1. Announcements in late June and December.

PUBLICATIONS:
Annual report.

IRS I.D.: 22-1554541

OFFICERS:
Frank Alvarez, President
Margaret H. Parker, Vice President
Gary Wingens, Treasurer
Irene Cooper-Basch, Executive Officer and Secretary

TRUSTEES:
Frank Alvarez
Henry Amoroso
Charles M. Chapin, III
Percy Chubb, III
Sally Chubb
Sara Chubb-Sauvayre
Robert Holmes
Robert L. Johnson, M.D.
Franklin Parker, IV
John E. Parker
Margaret H. Parker
Grizel Ubarry
Gary Wingens
A. Zachery Yamba

ADDRESS INQUIRIES TO:
Irene Cooper-Basch, Executive Officer
(See address above.)

THE WACO FOUNDATION [1360]

1227 North Valley Mills Drive
Suite 235
Waco, TX 76710
(254) 754-3404
(254) 752-9457 (MAC Program)
Fax: (254) 753-2887
E-mail: info@wacofoundation.org
Web Site: www.wacofoundation.org

FOUNDED: 1958

AREAS OF INTEREST:
Residents of McLennan County, TX.

NAME(S) OF PROGRAMS:
- **MAC College Money Program**

TYPE:
Scholarships. Intended to promote postsecondary educational opportunities in the community, and thereby promote greater employment opportunities for those of working age.

YEAR PROGRAM STARTED: 1995

PURPOSE:
To make a positive difference in the lives and future of the people who live in Waco and McLennan County through grantmaking, promotion of community philanthropy, and support of the not-for-profit sector.

ELIGIBILITY:
Must have graduated from McLennan County high schools and have family income of less than $50,000.

GEOG. RESTRICTIONS: McLennan County, Texas.

FINANCIAL DATA:
Amount of support per award: Varies.
Total amount of support: $500,000 in contributions annually.

APPLICATION INFO:
High school seniors must submit completed application form and FAFSA.
Duration: Two years. Renewable for two years.
Deadline: May 1 of student's senior year of high school.

ADDRESS INQUIRIES TO:
Robbie Stabeno, Director of Scholarships
(See address above.)

DENNIS & PHYLLIS WASHINGTON FOUNDATION [1361]

P.O. Box 16630
Missoula, MT 59808
(406) 523-1300
Fax: (406) 523-1399
E-mail: info@dpwfoundation.org
Web Site: www.dpwfoundation.org

FOUNDED: 1987

AREAS OF INTEREST:
Youth-focused programs in arts and culture, community service, health and human services and education.

TYPE:
Project/program grants; Scholarships. Scholarship monies awarded to Montana's nine colleges and universities and seven Indian reservations.

YEAR PROGRAM STARTED: 1987

PURPOSE:
To invest in people to improve the quality of their lives.

LEGAL BASIS:
Private foundation.

ELIGIBILITY:
Eligible organizations must be IRS 501(c)(3) tax-exempt. Low administrative costs.

GEOG. RESTRICTIONS: Montana and communities where Washington has services.

FINANCIAL DATA:
Amount of support per award: Average grant: $9,600.

Total amount of support: Varies.

APPLICATION INFO:
Grant applicants must complete the online application process which includes reading grant guidelines and completion of a short eligibility review. If qualified, the organization will be invited to submit a full application online.

Scholarship applicants can review application guidelines on the Foundation's web site.

Duration: One year. Renewals are possible upon reapplication.

ADDRESS INQUIRIES TO:
Mike Halligan, Executive Director
(See address above.)

WASHINGTON FORREST FOUNDATION [1362]

2407 Columbia Pike, Suite 200
Arlington, VA 22204
(703) 920-3688
Fax: (703) 920-0130
E-mail: allison@washingtonforrest.org

FOUNDED: 1968

AREAS OF INTEREST:
Health and human services, education, religion and the arts.

TYPE:
Capital grants; Challenge/matching grants; General operating grants; Matching gifts; Project/program grants; Scholarships; Seed money grants.

PURPOSE:
To improve and enhance the quality of life in Arlington and especially South Arlington, VA.

LEGAL BASIS:
Public foundation.

ELIGIBILITY:
Eligible organizations must be IRS 501(c)(3) tax-exempt and be located in northern Virginia.

GEOG. RESTRICTIONS: Arlington and northern Virginia.

FINANCIAL DATA:
Amount of support per award: $500 to $25,000.

APPLICATION INFO:
Applicants should first call the Foundation to discuss the proposal. Applications must include a copy of the IRS tax determination letter.

Duration: One year. Renewal by reapplication.

Deadline: August 1, November 1, February 1 and May 1.

ADDRESS INQUIRIES TO:
Allison A. Erdle, Executive Director
(See address above.)

WEGE FOUNDATION [1363]

99 Monroe Avenue, N.W.
Suite 902
Grand Rapids, MI 49503
(616) 957-0480
Fax: (616) 957-0616
E-mail: tmccarthy@wegefoundation.org
Web Site: www.wegefoundation.org

FOUNDED: 1968

AREAS OF INTEREST:
Education, environment, health care, human services and the arts in west Michigan.

TYPE:
Capital grants; Endowments; General operating grants; Project/program grants.

YEAR PROGRAM STARTED: 1968

PURPOSE:
To assist programs and projects in the areas of education, environment, health care, arts and culture, and human services.

ELIGIBILITY:
Grants are made to tax-exempt, nonprofit organizations which meet the Foundation's current program priorities and are located in the west Michigan area.

GEOG. RESTRICTIONS: Grand Rapids and west Michigan.

FINANCIAL DATA:
Amount of support per award: $500 to $40,000.

Total amount of support: Approximately $10,000,000 annually.

NO. MOST RECENT APPLICANTS: 110.

NO. AWARDS: 68.

APPLICATION INFO:
Applications must be submitted through the Foundation's web site.

Duration: One year. Renewal possible.

Deadline: Proposals are accepted twice per year for Spring and Fall grant review.

BOARD OF DIRECTORS AND TRUSTEES:
Peter M. Wege, II, Chairman
Ellen Satterlee, Chief Executive Officer
W. Michael Van Haren, Secretary
Mary Goodwillie Nelson
Johanna Osman
Diana Wege Sherogan
Christopher Wege
Jonathan Wege

ADDRESS INQUIRIES TO:
Terri McCarthy
Vice President of Programs
(See address above.)

THE HARRY AND JEANETTE WEINBERG FOUNDATION, INC. [1364]

7 Park Center Court
Owings Mills, MD 21117
(410) 654-8500
Fax: (410) 654-3943
Web Site: www.hjweinbergfoundation.org

FOUNDED: 1959

NAME(S) OF PROGRAMS:
- **Basic Human Needs & Health**
- **Disabilities**
- **Education**
- **General Community Support**
- **Older Adults**
- **Veterans**
- **Workforce Development**

TYPE:
Capital grants; Challenge/matching grants; General operating grants; Matching gifts; Project/program grants.

ELIGIBILITY:
Grants are made to nonprofit 501(c)(3) organizations that provide direct services to low-income and vulnerable individuals and families, primarily in the U.S. and Israel. Grants are focused on meeting basic needs and enhancing an individual's ability to meet those needs with emphasis on older adults, the Jewish community and the hometown communities of Maryland, northeastern Pennsylvania and Hawaii.

Religious organizations are eligible to apply.

The Foundation does not give grants to individuals.

GEOG. RESTRICTIONS: The Foundation administers most of its funds in what it considers its "hometown" communities: Hawaii, Maryland, northeastern Pennsylvania, the Former Soviet Union and Israel.

FINANCIAL DATA:
Total amount of support: Approximately $100,000,000 annually in grants.

APPLICATION INFO:
Refer to the web site.

Deadline: Grant requests are accepted throughout the year.

THOMAS H. WHITE FOUNDATION [1365]

1422 Euclid Avenue, Suite 966
Cleveland, OH 44115-1952
(216) 696-7273
Fax: (216) 621-8198
E-mail: kmccullough@fmscleveland.com
Web Site: www.fmscleveland.com/thomaswhite

FOUNDED: 1913

AREAS OF INTEREST:
Early childhood education, middle school to high school education, high school to higher education, and human services.

TYPE:
Project/program grants. The Foundation will focus its grantmaking in two major areas: Education and Human Services. Specifically, the Foundation is interested in supporting programs that address four critical areas:
(1) Workforce readiness: programs that emphasize science and technology education, adequate employment preparation, support systems and the relationship to earning potential;
(2) School retention: programs that emphasize the critical transition issues that

occur during early teenage years and affect family relationships and school attendance;
(3) Early childhood enrichment: programs which enhance the learning environment; provide support, training and ancillary services to parents; and/or enhance the recruitment and training of day care providers and;
(4) Programs that support education in science, technology, engineering and math.

Organizations and programs that contribute generally to the quality of life in Greater Cleveland may also be considered at the Foundation's discretion.

YEAR PROGRAM STARTED: 1913

PURPOSE:
To improve educational resources and support charitable purposes in the city of Cleveland, OH.

LEGAL BASIS:
Private foundation.

ELIGIBILITY:
Grants awarded to tax-exempt, nonprofit charitable and educational institutions located within Cuyahoga County, OH, if such organizations, and their services and facilities, primarily serve residents of the city of Cleveland.

Applicants are discouraged from submitting requests for endowment, general operating support, research, symposia or seminars. No grants are awarded to individuals. The Foundation does not respond to general solicitations or annual fund-raising campaigns.

GEOG. RESTRICTIONS: Cuyahoga County, Ohio; primarily the city of Cleveland.

FINANCIAL DATA:
Amount of support per award: $1,000 to $100,000.

Total amount of support: Approximately $1,000,000 in grants approved for the year 2014.

Matching fund requirements: Stipulated with individual programs.

NO. MOST RECENT APPLICANTS: 125 for the year 2014.

NO. AWARDS: 96.

REPRESENTATIVE AWARDS:
$5,000 to Cleveland Music School Settlement for the planning and development of an early childhood education classroom; $17,500 to Scranton Road Ministries Community Development Corporation for the Youth Jobs Partnership Program; $75,000 to Cleveland Metropolitan School District for upgrades to the fabrication laboratories at the MC2 STEM High School; $10,000 to Burten, Bell, Carr Development, Inc. for the Bridgeport Market and Community Kitchen.

APPLICATION INFO:
Applications will only be accepted online and must contain the following:
(1) a brief history of the organization;
(2) explanation of request;
(3) evaluation plan and future funding plan;
(4) its total budget, other funding sources and its importance to the people of Cleveland;
(5) the amount requested;
(6) the organization's tax-exempt status;
(7) a list of the organization's trustees and;
(8) the proposal, plus one copy.

Foundation staff is available to assist applicants and/or to further clarify the Foundation's grantmaking policies and procedures.

Duration: Most grants are made for one year only. Two- to three-year grants are made occasionally.

Deadline: December 1, April 1 and August 1, respectively, for meetings which are held in February, May and September. Announcement is made within three weeks of meeting.

ADDRESS INQUIRIES TO:
Kara McCullough, Consultant
(See address above.)

*SPECIAL STIPULATIONS:
Local giving only.

WICHITA COMMUNITY FOUNDATION [1366]

301 North Main Street
Suite 100
Wichita, KS 67202
(316) 264-4880
Fax: (316) 264-7592
E-mail: wcf@wichitacf.org
Web Site: www.wichitacf.org

FOUNDED: 1986

AREAS OF INTEREST:
Arts, conservation, education, environmental health, humanities and social services.

TYPE:
Project/program grants; Scholarships; Seed money grants.

PURPOSE:
To provide a permanent resource for building community philanthropy.

LEGAL BASIS:
Community foundation.

ELIGIBILITY:
Grants are made to organizations that have tax-exempt status under Section 501(c)(3) of the Internal Revenue Code. No grants are made to individuals.

GEOG. RESTRICTIONS: Sedgwick County, Kansas.

FINANCIAL DATA:
Amount of support per award: $10,000 to $100,000.

Total amount of support: Approximately $3,400,000 for the year ended June 30, 2014.

APPLICATION INFO:
Grant application information is available on the web site. High school students may apply for scholarships online.

Duration: Typically one year.

Deadline: Grant applications are accepted throughout the year; deadlines vary. Scholarship applications: March 15.

ADDRESS INQUIRIES TO:
Holly Landon
Director of Philanthropic Services
(See address above.)

HARVEY RANDALL WICKES FOUNDATION [1367]

4800 Fashion Square Boulevard
Suite 472
Saginaw, MI 48604
(989) 799-1850
Fax: (989) 799-3327
E-mail: hrwickes@att.net

FOUNDED: 1945

AREAS OF INTEREST:
Arts, health, education, recreation, civic improvement and human services.

TYPE:
Matching gifts; Project/program grants.

YEAR PROGRAM STARTED: 1945

PURPOSE:
To improve the quality of life in Saginaw County.

ELIGIBILITY:
Eligible organizations must be IRS 501(c)(3) tax-exempt. No grants to individuals.

GEOG. RESTRICTIONS: Saginaw County, Michigan.

FINANCIAL DATA:
Amount of support per award: $10,000 average grant.

Total amount of support: $1,779,264 for the year 2013.

NO. AWARDS: 59 for the year 2013.

APPLICATION INFO:
Applicants may send a written proposal and must include a copy of the IRS tax determination letter.

Duration: One year. Renewal possible by reapplication.

Deadline: Two weeks prior to board meetings, which are held on the second Tuesday in March, June and September and the first Tuesday in December.

PUBLICATIONS:
Annual report; grant guidelines.

IRS I.D.: 38-6061470

ADDRESS INQUIRIES TO:
Hugo E. Braun, Jr., President
(See address above.)

THE WINSTON-SALEM FOUNDATION [1368]

751 West Fourth Street
Suite 200
Winston-Salem, NC 27101-2702
(336) 725-2382
Fax: (336) 727-0581
E-mail: info@wsfoundation.org
Web Site: www.wsfoundation.org

FOUNDED: 1919

AREAS OF INTEREST:
Human services, education, arts, culture, health, environment, animal welfare, community and economic development, public interest, and recreation.

NAME(S) OF PROGRAMS:
- **Black Philanthropy Grants**
- **Community Grants**
- **Elkin/Tri-County Grants**
- **Sosnik Fund Grants**
- **Student Aid Grants, Scholarship, and Loans**
- **Teacher Grants**
- **Victim Assistance Grants**
- **Women's Fund Grants**
- **Youth Philanthropy Grants**

TYPE:
Capital grants; Challenge/matching grants; Development grants; Endowments; Project/program grants; Scholarships; Seed money grants; Training grants. Discretionary grants given to organizations providing benefit to citizens within the greater Forsyth County, NC area, subject to limitations on program areas expressed by the donor of the source fund. Student aid primarily for Forsyth County residents.

YEAR PROGRAM STARTED: 1919

PURPOSE:
To help agencies initiate, innovate and experiment, as well as to provide other types of support as appropriate.

LEGAL BASIS:
Community foundation.

ELIGIBILITY:
Applicants must be charitable organizations and publicly supported charities. No grants are made to individuals.

GEOG. RESTRICTIONS: Forsyth County, North Carolina and contiguous counties.

FINANCIAL DATA:
Amount of support per award: $500 to $200,000; average $25,000.

Total amount of support: $20,965,432 for the year 2013.

NO. MOST RECENT APPLICANTS: 175.

NO. AWARDS: 100.

APPLICATION INFO:
Application information is available on the web site.

Duration: Generally, grants are for one year.

Deadline: Preliminary applications accepted on the first business day of odd-numbered months.

PUBLICATIONS:
Annual report; guidelines for donors and grantseekers; newsletters.

IRS I.D.: 56-6037615

STAFF:
Scott F. Wierman, President
Lisa Purcell, Executive Vice President

ADDRESS INQUIRIES TO:
Latonya Wright, Grants Manager
(See address above.)

WOODS CHARITABLE FUND, INC. [1369]

1248 O Street, Suite 1130
Lincoln, NE 68508
(402) 436-5971
E-mail: twoods@woodscharitable.org
Web Site: www.woodscharitable.org

FOUNDED: 1941

AREAS OF INTEREST:
Children, youth and families, education, community development and housing, arts and humanities.

TYPE:
Challenge/matching grants; Demonstration grants; General operating grants; Project/program grants; Seed money grants; Technical assistance. Grants to support organizations and projects located in and directly serving the residents of Lincoln, NE.

YEAR PROGRAM STARTED: 1941

PURPOSE:
To strengthen the community by improving opportunities and life outcomes for all people in Lincoln, NE.

LEGAL BASIS:
Private foundation.

ELIGIBILITY:
Grants are made only to tax-exempt organizations described in Section 501(c)(3) of the IRS Code and which have a written ruling from the IRS that they also qualify under 509(a)(1), (2) or (3) of the Code (publicly supported organizations and their affiliates).

Geographically, grants are limited to organizations in Lincoln. Occasionally, the Fund reviews proposals from outside the city if the proposed activities have statewide impact and a significant Lincoln component. While the Fund makes grants in very diverse fields, fund-raising benefits or program advertising, individual needs, endowments, scholarships or fellowships are not eligible for grant review.

GEOG. RESTRICTIONS: Lincoln, Nebraska.

FINANCIAL DATA:
Amount of support per award: Average payment: $24,727 for the year 2015.

Total amount of support: $1,360,000 grants paid for the year 2015.

NO. MOST RECENT APPLICANTS: 146 for the year 2015.

NO. AWARDS: 55 for the year 2015.

REPRESENTATIVE AWARDS:
$40,000 (over two years) to The Bridge Behavioral Health, Inc. for a new Licensed Alcohol and Drug Counselor position specializing in treatment of alcoholism and drug addiction; $30,000 (over two years) to Lincoln Lancaster County Child Advocacy Center for staffing support for a new Training and Prevention Director position that provides a safe, neutral location for conducting forensic interviews of victims of child abuse; $65,000 (over three years) to University of Nebraska-Lincoln Department of Psychology for Project SAFE, a clinical research and treatment program for sexually abused children and their families that works collaboratively with the Lincoln Lancaster County Child Advocacy Center.

APPLICATION INFO:
Guidelines are available on the Fund web site. Before submitting a full proposal, applicants should contact the Fund with a two-page summary request and budget or a phone call. If the request appears suitable, a full proposal will be requested.

Deadline: April 15 to 30 for November Board Meeting. October 15 to 31 for May Board Meeting. Proposals that arrive well before the deadline have a better chance for careful review.

IRS I.D.: 47-6032847

STAFF:
Tom Woods, President and Secretary
Kathy Steinauer Smith, Community Investment Director
Angie Zmarzly, Community Investment Director
Joan Stolle, Operations Manager

DIRECTORS:
Donna W. Woods, Chairperson
Orville Jones, III, Vice Chairperson
Hank Woods, Treasurer
Michael J. Tavlin, Assistant Treasurer
Ernesto Castillo, Jr.
Carl Eskridge
Candice Howell
Nelle Woods Jamison

ADDRESS INQUIRIES TO:
Tom Woods, President
(See address above.)

WOODS FUND OF CHICAGO [1370]

35 East Wacker Drive
Suite 1760
Chicago, IL 60601
(312) 782-2698
Fax: (312) 782-4155
E-mail: application@woodsfund.org
Web Site: www.woodsfund.org

FOUNDED: 1941

AREAS OF INTEREST:
Arts and social justice, community organizing, intersection of community organizing and public policy, and public policy.

TYPE:
General operating grants; Project/program grants; Training grants. Small training grants.

PURPOSE:
To increase opportunities for less advantaged people and communities in the metropolitan area, including the opportunity to contribute to decisions affecting them.

LEGAL BASIS:
Nonprofit.

ELIGIBILITY:
Grants are made to cultural organizations that have tax-exempt status under Section 501(c)(3) of the Internal Revenue Code. No grants are made to individuals.

GEOG. RESTRICTIONS: Metropolitan Chicago, Illinois.

FINANCIAL DATA:
Amount of support per award: $10,000 to $35,000.

Total amount of support: Typically $3,400,000 in grants annually.

APPLICATION INFO:
The Woods Fund requires that prospective grantees first submit a completed Inquiry Form. If the Fund responds positively, applicants will be asked to submit a full application. Form and application instructions are available at the Fund web site.

Duration: One to three years.

Deadline: For March grants, letter of inquiry should be received by the first Friday in December. For September grants, letter of inquiry should be received by the last business day in May.

ADDRESS INQUIRIES TO:
Grant Processing
(See e-mail address above.)

*PLEASE NOTE:
Contact program officer prior to applying for grant.

WYOMING ARTS COUNCIL

2301 Central Avenue
Barrett Building, 2nd Floor
Cheyenne, WY 82002
(307) 777-7742
Fax: (307) 777-5499
Web Site: wyoarts.state.wy.us

TYPE:
Awards/prizes; Capital grants; Development grants; Fellowships; Formula grants; General operating grants; Project/program grants; Technical assistance. Blanchan/Doubleday Fellowships, Individual Artist Grants, Literary Arts Fellowships, Performing Arts Fellowships and Visual Arts Fellowships are for individual artists.

See entry 513 for full listing.

Crime prevention

INTERNATIONAL CENTRE FOR COMPARATIVE CRIMINOLOGY [1371]

University of Montreal
C.P. 6128, Succursale Centre-Ville
Montreal QC H3C 3J7 Canada
(514) 343-7065
Fax: (514) 343-2269
E-mail: cicc@umontreal.ca
Web Site: www.cicc.umontreal.ca

FOUNDED: 1969

AREAS OF INTEREST:
Sociology of crime and deviance, comparative studies on criminal justice, police, courts, prisons, victims, national and international research, terrorism and counterterrorism.

CONSULTING OR VOLUNTEER SERVICES:
In all the fields of criminal justice.

NAME(S) OF PROGRAMS:
- **Research Fieldwork**

TYPE:
Conferences/seminars; Exchange programs; Fellowships. Postdoctoral scholarship. The Centre brings visiting professors and specialists to confer on projects and cooperate on research investigation and invites graduate and postgraduate students to do fieldwork at the Centre.

YEAR PROGRAM STARTED: 1969

PURPOSE:
To provide funding to encourage continued study in the field of crime and criminal justice.

LEGAL BASIS:
University.

ELIGIBILITY:
Applicants must have a Ph.D. from any country.

FINANCIAL DATA:
Amount of support per award: Postdoctoral scholarships: $35,000 (CAN) per year. Fixed sum for living expenses.

NO. MOST RECENT APPLICANTS: 6.

NO. AWARDS: Postdoctoral scholarships: 1 or 2 per year.

APPLICATION INFO:
Submit research project, curriculum vitae, three letters from researchers who know the candidate and an abstract of the Ph.D. thesis.

Duration: One year.

Deadline: June 30.

PUBLICATIONS:
Annual report; Revue *Criminologie.*

OFFICERS:
Benoit Dupont, Director

ADDRESS INQUIRIES TO:
See e-mail address above.

NATIONAL INSTITUTE OF JUSTICE, U.S. DEPARTMENT OF JUSTICE [1372]

810 Seventh Street, N.W.
Washington, DC 20531
(202) 307-2942
E-mail: support@grants.gov
Web Site: www.nij.gov

FOUNDED: 1968

AREAS OF INTEREST:
Criminal justice research and evaluation, program development, dissemination of research-based criminal justice, and fellowships.

NAME(S) OF PROGRAMS:
- **Research Grants**

TYPE:
Research grants. Grants and contracts related to topics in criminal justice and social science, physical science, and forensic science, including those for evaluative research; research and development grants and contracts in science and technology for criminal justice applications.

The focus of NIJ research is on generating information that is useful to state and local public officials in developing policies related to crime reduction.

YEAR PROGRAM STARTED: 1968

PURPOSE:
To increase knowledge of the causes, prevention, and control of crime, the effectiveness and efficiency of the criminal justice system, and the responsiveness of the nation's law enforcement and justice administration systems; to disseminate this knowledge to the federal, state, and local policymakers.

LEGAL BASIS:
Omnibus Crime Control and Safe Streets Act of 1968; Homeland Security Act of 2002.

ELIGIBILITY:
NIJ awards grants to or enters into cooperative agreements with educational institutions, nonprofit organizations, public agencies, individuals, and profit-making organizations that are willing to waive their fees. Special eligibility criteria are indicated in NIJ's solicitations for proposals.

GEOG. RESTRICTIONS: United States.

FINANCIAL DATA:
All NIJ awards must be used to supplement existing funds, not to replace those already appropriated for the same purpose.

Amount of support per award: $10,000 to more than $1,000,000.

Total amount of support: $233,536,728 for fiscal year 2014.

Matching fund requirements: Units of state and local governments are encouraged to contribute matching funds and other applicants are encouraged to seek matching contributions from government agencies or private organizations.

NO. AWARDS: 418 for the year 2014.

APPLICATION INFO:
Guidelines, applications, and information about specific solicitations for proposals are available on the web site.

Duration: Normally two years maximum. Renewal possible.

Deadline: Varies.

ADDRESS INQUIRIES TO:
National Criminal Justice Reference Service
P.O. Box 6000
Rockville, MD 20849-6000
Tel: (800) 851-3420

GARDINER HOWLAND SHAW FOUNDATION [1373]

355 Boylston Street
Boston, MA 02116
(617) 247-3500
Fax: (617) 247-3505
E-mail: admin@shawfoundation.org
Web Site: shawfoundation.org

FOUNDED: 1959

AREAS OF INTEREST:
Criminal justice, the study, prevention, correction and alleviation of crime and delinquency and the rehabilitation of juvenile and adult offenders.

CONSULTING OR VOLUNTEER SERVICES:
Technical assistance to grantees and other human service agencies on request.

NAME(S) OF PROGRAMS:
- **Grantee Workshops**
- **Shaw Foundation Grants**

TYPE:
Conferences/seminars; Demonstration grants; General operating grants; Project/program grants; Seed money grants; Technical assistance. Priorities for funding include programs which can effectively divert court-involved youth and juvenile offenders from escalating involvement in the criminal justice system, programs which promote the use and acceptance of alternatives to incarceration and intermediate criminal sanctions, innovative and effective approaches to rehabilitation for detained and incarcerated juvenile and adult offenders, methods which improve the administration of justice and the quality of services for individuals appearing before the criminal court, and initiatives which can impact current public policy in the field of criminal justice through education, training and effective advocacy. Added weight will be given to proposals which clearly demonstrate the ability to utilize Shaw Foundation support to attract new public and private resources to the field of criminal justice.

YEAR PROGRAM STARTED: 1959

PURPOSE:
To aid the study, prevention, correction and alleviation of crime and delinquency and the rehabilitation of adult and juvenile offenders.

LEGAL BASIS:
Private foundation.

ELIGIBILITY:
Applicant must have tax-exempt public charitable status from the IRS and must operate within Massachusetts. The Foundation does not support capital requests, the arts, endowments, grants to individuals or scholarships.

GEOG. RESTRICTIONS: Massachusetts.

FINANCIAL DATA:
Amount of support per award: Average $15,000 to $20,000.

Total amount of support: $629,200 for fiscal year ended April 30, 2013.

CO-OP FUNDING PROGRAMS: The Shaw Foundation does, from time to time, work with other sources for the purpose of cooperative fundings.

NO. MOST RECENT APPLICANTS: 87.

NO. AWARDS: 41.

REPRESENTATIVE AWARDS:
$30,000 to Criminal Justice Policy Coalition for public education; $10,000 to Advocacy

City Mission Society for prison services program; $20,000 to Span Inc., service for ex-offenders in transition from prison to the community.

APPLICATION INFO:
Potential applicants are encouraged to telephone the Foundation to discuss their ideas prior to submitting a proposal. All new applicants should also submit a concept paper describing their organization and the purposes for which funds are being sought, along with a budget and evidence of tax-exempt status. The applicant will be informed if the work being proposed fits with the current interests of the Foundation.

Duration: Typically, the Foundation will provide support up to three years, with renewal dependent upon grantee performance and program need.

Deadline: February 1. Decision by May.

PUBLICATIONS:
Annual report; guidelines.

TRUSTEES:

ADDRESS INQUIRIES TO:
Thomas E. Coury, Executive Director
(See address above.)

U.S. DEPARTMENT OF JUSTICE [1374]

Bureau of Justice Statistics
810 7th Street, N.W.
Washington, DC 20531
(202) 307-0765
Fax: (202) 616-1351
E-mail: devon.adams@usdoj.gov
Web Site: bjs.ojp.usdoj.gov

FOUNDED: 1969

AREAS OF INTEREST:
Statistics on crime, victims of crime, criminal offenders and operations of justice systems at all levels of government throughout the U.S.

NAME(S) OF PROGRAMS:
- **State Justice Statistics for Statistical Analysis Centers**

TYPE:
Development grants; Research grants. Cooperative agreements for the development of statistical methods and techniques and the aggregation and analysis of statistical information on crime and criminal justice in the states.

YEAR PROGRAM STARTED: 1972

PURPOSE:
To develop and enhance the capabilities of the states in gathering, analyzing and using statistical information pertaining to crime and the criminal justice system and to obtain selected types of data for multistate aggregation.

LEGAL BASIS:
Government agency formed under the Justice System Improvement Act of 1979.

ELIGIBILITY:
Applicants must be state agencies whose activities include statistical analysis at the state level.

FINANCIAL DATA:
Amount of support per award: $60,000 to $210,000.

Total amount of support: Varies.

NO. MOST RECENT APPLICANTS: 43.

APPLICATION INFO:
Contact the U.S. Department of Justice.

Duration: 12 months.

Deadline: Varies.

ADDRESS INQUIRIES TO:
Devon Adams, Chief of Criminal History Improvement Program Section
(See address above.)

U.S. DEPARTMENT OF JUSTICE [1375]

Office of Juvenile Justice and Delinquency Prevention
810 Seventh Street, N.W., 5th Floor
Washington, DC 20531
(202) 307-5911
Fax: (202) 307-2093
E-mail: nicki.polk@usdoj.gov
Web Site: www.ojjdp.gov

FOUNDED: 1975

AREAS OF INTEREST:
Delinquency prevention research, juvenile gangs, serious violent juvenile offenders and juvenile justice statistics.

NAME(S) OF PROGRAMS:
- **Juvenile Justice and Delinquency Prevention Program**

TYPE:
Conferences/seminars; Development grants; Fellowships; Internships; Project/program grants; Research grants; Residencies; Visiting scholars; Research contracts. Grants to conduct research, evaluation and development on juvenile justice and delinquency prevention activities, including the development of new or improved approaches, techniques, systems and program models to conduct behavioral research on the causes of juvenile crime, means of, intervention and prevention, and to evaluate juvenile programs and procedures.

YEAR PROGRAM STARTED: 1975

PURPOSE:
To encourage, coordinate and conduct research and evaluation of juvenile justice and delinquency prevention activities; to provide a clearinghouse and information center for collecting, publishing and distributing information on juvenile delinquency; to conduct a national training program; to establish standards for the administration on juvenile justice. Current emphasis is work in the area of serious and violent juvenile crime, drug involvement by youth and missing children.

LEGAL BASIS:
Juvenile Justice and Delinquency Prevention Act of 1974, Public Law 93-415, 42 U.S.C. 5601, as amended.

ELIGIBILITY:
Public or private agencies, organizations, including institutions of higher learning, or individuals.

GEOG. RESTRICTIONS: United States and its territories.

FINANCIAL DATA:
Amount of support per award: Varies.

Total amount of support: Varies.

NO. MOST RECENT APPLICANTS: 100.

NO. AWARDS: 80.

REPRESENTATIVE AWARDS:
Law Enforcement Agencies Policies Regarding Missing Children; School Crime and Discipline Research and Discipline; Causes and Correlates of Delinquency.

APPLICATION INFO:
Contact the U.S. Department of Justice.

Duration: Generally one to three years.

Deadline: Varies.

PUBLICATIONS:
Annual report; annual program plan; various project reports.

ADDRESS INQUIRIES TO:
Juvenile Justice Clearinghouse
National Criminal Justice Reference Service
P.O. Box 6000
Rockville, MD 20849-6000
Tel: (800) 851-3420
Fax: (301) 240-5830

U.S. DEPARTMENT OF JUSTICE [1376]

Office of Juvenile Justice and Delinquency Prevention
810 Seventh Street, N.W., 5th Floor
Washington, DC 20531
(202) 307-5911
Fax: (202) 307-2093
E-mail: nicki.polk@usdoj.gov
Web Site: www.ojjdp.gov

AREAS OF INTEREST:
Juvenile justice, delinquency prevention and child protection.

NAME(S) OF PROGRAMS:
- **Juvenile Justice and Delinquency Prevention Allocation to States**

TYPE:
Block grants; Challenge/matching grants; Demonstration grants; Formula grants; Internships; Project/program grants; Research grants; Technical assistance; Training grants. Grants to increase the capacity of state and local governments to conduct effective juvenile justice and delinquency prevention programs as developed in the state comprehensive action plan.

YEAR PROGRAM STARTED: 1974

LEGAL BASIS:
Juvenile Justice and Delinquency Prevention Act of 1974, Public Law 93-415, 42 U.S.C. 5601 as amended (JJDP Act).

ELIGIBILITY:
All states as defined by Section 103(7) of the JJDP Act and meeting the requirements of Section 223 of the Act.

GEOG. RESTRICTIONS: United States and its territories.

FINANCIAL DATA:
Amount of support per award: Varies.

Total amount of support: Varies.

Matching fund requirements: Formula is based upon population of people under age 18. No match is required except for construction programs, where the match is 50%. Seven and one half percent administrative funds are matched 100%.

NO. MOST RECENT APPLICANTS: 60.

NO. AWARDS: 60.

APPLICATION INFO:
Contact the U.S. Department of Justice.

Duration: One to three years from the fiscal year of awards.

Deadline: Varies.

ADDRESS INQUIRIES TO:
Juvenile Justice Clearinghouse
National Criminal Justice
Reference Service
P.O. Box 6000
Rockville, MD 20849-6000
Tel: (800) 851-3420
Fax: (301) 240-5830

U.S. DEPARTMENT OF JUSTICE [1377]

Office of Juvenile Justice and
Delinquency Prevention
810 Seventh Street, N.W., 5th Floor
Washington, DC 20531
(202) 307-5911
(202) 514-5655
Fax: (202) 307-2819
Web Site: www.ojjdp.gov

FOUNDED: 1974

AREAS OF INTEREST:
Juvenile justice, delinquency prevention and child protection.

NAME(S) OF PROGRAMS:
- **Enforcing the Underage Drinking Laws Program**

TYPE:
Block grants; Demonstration grants.

YEAR PROGRAM STARTED: 1998

PURPOSE:
To support state and local efforts to prevent juvenile delinquency, to improve the juvenile system response to delinquency, and to protect children from victimization.

LEGAL BASIS:
Government grant program.

ELIGIBILITY:
Applicants are limited to states (including territories) units of local government as determined by the Secretary of the Interior, nonprofit and for-profit organizations and institutions of higher education.

GEOG. RESTRICTIONS: United States and its territories.

FINANCIAL DATA:
Amount of support per award: Varies.

APPLICATION INFO:
Applicants must register at Grants.gov prior to submitting an application.
Deadline: Varies.

U.S. DEPARTMENT OF JUSTICE [1378]

Office of Juvenile Justice and
Delinquency Prevention
810 Seventh Street, N.W., 5th Floor
Washington, DC 20531
(202) 616-3807
Fax: (202) 307-2819
E-mail: eric.stansbury@usdoj.gov
ricco.hall@usdoj.gov
Web Site: www.ojjdp.gov

FOUNDED: 1974

AREAS OF INTEREST:
Accountability-based programs, graduated sanctions, reentry, drug courts, and judiciary and prosecutorial staffing and training.

NAME(S) OF PROGRAMS:
- **Juvenile Accountability Block Grants Program**

TYPE:
Block grants. Grants awarded on a formula basis to states. Funds are available for around 30 specific program purpose areas.

YEAR PROGRAM STARTED: 1986

PURPOSE:
To provide states and units of local government with funds to develop programs to promote greater accountability in the juvenile justice system.

LEGAL BASIS:
The Omnibus Safe Streets and Crime Control Act of 2002.

ELIGIBILITY:
In order to receive JABG funds, the chief executive officer of the state must designate the appropriate agency.

GEOG. RESTRICTIONS: United States and its territories.

FINANCIAL DATA:
Amount of support per award: Varies.
Total amount of support: Approximately $20,000,000 for the year 2013.
Matching fund requirements: The state or local government recipient of a JABG award must contribute (in the form of a cash match) 10% of the total program cost (other than costs of construction of permanent corrections facilities, which require a 50% match).

APPLICATION INFO:
Contact the U.S. Department of Justice.
Duration: Three years.

ADDRESS INQUIRIES TO:
Eric Stansbury, JABG Coordinator or
Ricco Hall, JABG Coordinator
(See address above.)

Public health

AAA FOUNDATION FOR TRAFFIC SAFETY [1379]

607 14th Street, N.W.
Suite 201
Washington, DC 20005
(202) 638-5944 ext. 7
Fax: (202) 638-5943
E-mail: jgrabowski@aaafoundation.org
Web Site: www.aaafoundation.org

FOUNDED: 1947

AREAS OF INTEREST:
Traffic safety.

TYPE:
Demonstration grants; Project/program grants; Research grants; Research contracts.

YEAR PROGRAM STARTED: 1947

PURPOSE:
To save lives and reduce injuries by preventing traffic crashes; to reduce injuries when crashes do occur.

LEGAL BASIS:
Publicly supported not-for-profit 501(c)(3).

ELIGIBILITY:
Foundation grants to organizations only.

The Foundation does not fund research to develop new devices, grants for community action initiatives or other purely local traffic safety programs, or projects outside the field of traffic safety.

GEOG. RESTRICTIONS: Primarily United States and Canada.

FINANCIAL DATA:
Amount of support per award: $5,000 to $1,000,000.
Total amount of support: Approximately $5,000,000.
Matching fund requirements: Encourage co-funding, but not required.

NO. MOST RECENT APPLICANTS: 125.

NO. AWARDS: 12.

APPLICATION INFO:
Contact the Foundation for application procedures.
Duration: Six months to five years.
Deadline: May 15.

PUBLICATIONS:
Annual report.

IRS I.D.: 52-0794368

ADDRESS INQUIRIES TO:
Jurek Grabowski, Director of Research
(See address above.)

ABMRF/THE FOUNDATION FOR ALCOHOL RESEARCH [1380]

1200-C Agora Drive
Suite 310
Bel Air, MD 21014
(800) 688-7152
E-mail: grantinfo@abmrf.org
Web Site: www.abmrf.org

FOUNDED: 1982

AREAS OF INTEREST:
Medical research on the effects of alcohol on health and behavior.

TYPE:
Project/program grants; Research grants; Seed money grants. Major research interests include factors influencing transitions in drinking patterns and behavior, the effects of moderate use of alcohol on health and well-being, mechanisms underlying the behavioral and biomedical effects of alcohol and biobehavioral/interdisciplinary research on the etiology of alcohol misuse.

YEAR PROGRAM STARTED: 1982

PURPOSE:
To provide support for scientific studies on the use, and prevention of misuse, of alcohol.

LEGAL BASIS:
Private foundation.

ELIGIBILITY:
Applicants must be U.S., Canadian or South African institutions. Nonresearch activities such as education projects, public awareness efforts and treatment or referral services are not eligible for support.

GEOG. RESTRICTIONS: United States, Canada and South Africa.

FINANCIAL DATA:
Approximately $2,000,000 (U.S.) is available each year to fund newly approved applications and continuation of previously funded projects. Funds may be requested in U.S. or Canadian currency for a period of up to two years. Funding of the second year depends on the availability of funds and satisfactory research progress during the first year.
Amount of support per award: Up to $50,000 (U.S.) per year.

NO. MOST RECENT APPLICANTS: 142.

NO. AWARDS: 23 new projects funded.

REPRESENTATIVE AWARDS:
$50,000 (for the second of two years) to M. Scott Bowers, Ph.D., Virginia Commonwealth University, "Role of rat nucleus accumbens astrocytes in alcoholism;" $50,000 (for the second of two years) to Dingcai Cao, Ph.D., The University of Chicago, "Alcohol effects on visual processing in at-risk social-drinkers;" $50,000 (for the second of two years) to Tara Chaplin, Ph.D., Yale University, "Responses during parent-child interactions and alcohol-use behaviors in adolescents;" $50,000 (for the second of two years) to Cedrick D. Dotson, Ph.D., University of Florida College of Medicine, "Hormonal signaling by GLP-1 glucagon and leptin modulates the taste of alcohol."

APPLICATION INFO:
Application is available on the Foundation web site.

Duration: One year. Two years if justified.

Deadline: February 15.

PUBLICATIONS:
Annual report; application guidelines.

IRS I.D.: 52-1234277

OFFICERS:
Mack C. Mitchell, Jr., M.D., President

ADDRESS INQUIRIES TO:
Grants Program Director
(See address above.)

AGENCY FOR HEALTHCARE RESEARCH AND QUALITY (AHRQ) [1381]

Office of Communications
and Knowledge Transfer
540 Gaither Road, 2nd Floor
Rockville, MD 20850
(301) 427-1104 (specify funding area)
(301) 427-1450
E-mail: support@grants.gov
Web Site: www.ahrq.gov

FOUNDED: 1968

AREAS OF INTEREST:
AHRQ is the primary source of federal support for research on problems related to the quality and delivery of health services.

NAME(S) OF PROGRAMS:
- **AHRQ Research Grants**

TYPE:
Conferences/seminars; Development grants; Fellowships; Project/program grants; Research grants; Training grants. Dissertation support highlighting primary care, market forces, cost containment, managed care, the cost of treating AIDS, the improvement of treatment for persons with HIV, rural health care, infant mortality, medical liability, malpractice reform, health care of the aged and disabled and policy studies.

YEAR PROGRAM STARTED: 1969

PURPOSE:
To develop knowledge concerning cost, quality, effectiveness, access and distribution of health services.

LEGAL BASIS:
AHCPR Research Grants: Section 304, 5, 7, 8, of the Public Health Service Act.

ELIGIBILITY:
Any academic institution, agency of a state or local government, nonprofit organization or individual is eligible to submit grant proposals under this program. For-profit entities are not eligible.

FINANCIAL DATA:
Amount of support per award: Varies according to the project type and nature of the individual research proposal.

Total amount of support: Varies.

APPLICATION INFO:
Contact the Agency.

Duration: One to five years.

Deadline: Varies.

STAFF:
Kishna Wadhwani, Scientific Review Division

ADDRESS INQUIRIES TO:
Office of Communications and Knowledge Transfer
(See address above.)

THE AMERICAN FOUNDATION FOR SUICIDE PREVENTION

120 Wall Street
29th Floor
New York, NY 10005
(212) 363-3500 ext. 2015
Fax: (212) 363-6237
E-mail: grantsmanager@afsp.org
Web Site: www.afsp.org/research/research-grant-information

TYPE:
Research grants.

See entry 1473 for full listing.

THE AMERICAN FOUNDATION FOR SUICIDE PREVENTION

120 Wall Street
29th Floor
New York, NY 10005
(212) 363-3500 ext. 2015
Fax: (212) 363-6237
E-mail: grantsmanager@afsp.org
Web Site: www.afsp.org/research/research-grant-information

TYPE:
Fellowships; Research grants.

See entry 1474 for full listing.

THE AMERICAN FOUNDATION FOR SUICIDE PREVENTION

120 Wall Street
29th Floor
New York, NY 10005
(212) 363-3500 ext. 2015
Fax: (212) 363-6237
E-mail: grantsmanager@afsp.org
Web Site: www.afsp.org/research/research-grant-information

TYPE:
Research grants.

See entry 1475 for full listing.

THE AMERICAN FOUNDATION FOR SUICIDE PREVENTION

120 Wall Street
29th Floor
New York, NY 10005
(212) 363-3500 ext. 2015
Fax: (212) 363-6237
E-mail: grantsmanager@afsp.org
Web Site: www.afsp.org/research/research-grant-information

TYPE:
Research grants. Standard Research Grants are awarded to individual investigators. An additional annual stipend is available for mentors on Young Investigator Awards in which the investigator is at the level of Assistant Professor or lower.

See entry 1476 for full listing.

AMERICAN MEDICAL WOMEN'S ASSOCIATION, INC.

12100 Sunset Hills Road
Suite 130
Reston, VA 20190
(703) 234-4069
Fax: (703) 435-4390
E-mail: associatedirector@amwa-doc.org
Web Site: www.amwa-doc.org

TYPE:
Awards/prizes; Conferences/seminars; General operating grants; Project/program grants; Training grants; Travel grants. Support for clinics serving the poor in medically underserved areas, scholarships and loans to qualifying women medical students, and continuing medical education for physicians in areas related to women's health.

See entry 2160 for full listing.

AMERICAN PSYCHOLOGICAL ASSOCIATION

Government Relations Office
Public Interest Directorate
750 First Street, N.E.
Washington, DC 20002-4242
(202) 336-5935
Fax: (202) 336-6063
E-mail: mhaskell-hoehl@apa.org
Web Site: www.apa.org/about/gr/fellows

TYPE:
Fellowships. Program provides trained scientists and practitioners an opportunity for enhanced understanding of and involvement in the federal policymaking process by serving as congressional staff in Washington, DC.

See entry 2487 for full listing.

AMERICAN SOCIETY FOR HEALTHCARE RISK MANAGEMENT [1382]

155 North Wacker Drive
Suite 400
Chicago, IL 60606
(312) 422-3980
Fax: (312) 422-4580
E-mail: khoarle@aha.org
Web Site: www.ashrm.org

FOUNDED: 2004

AREAS OF INTEREST:
Health care risk management.

TYPE:
Awards/prizes; Conferences/seminars; Development grants; Fellowships; Project/program grants; Research grants; Scholarships; Training grants. Education grants.

YEAR PROGRAM STARTED: 2004

PURPOSE:
To help facilitate the advancement of the health care risk management profession by funding education, research and scholarship programs; to promote professional development of hospital risk managers; to provide educational resources and programs on health care risk management; to address risk management issues affecting the health care industry; to foster research and innovation among professionals and graduate students; to identify and reward exemplary writing in the *Journal of Healthcare Risk Management* and encourage other members to write in it.

ELIGIBILITY:
Open to individual professionals in risk management or a related field, as well as graduate students in health care risk management, health law, or health administration programs that wish to develop original research studies that enhance the profession of health care risk management. Must be original work related to health care risk management research and innovation for consideration.

FINANCIAL DATA:
Since inception, the Society has awarded more than $90,000.

Amount of support per award: Education Grants: Up to $1,500; Scholarship Grants: Up to $3,000; Research Grants: Up to $14,500.

APPLICATION INFO:
Contact the Society.

Duration: One year. Must reapply.

Deadline: Early July.

ADDRESS INQUIRIES TO:
Kim Hoarle, Executive Director
(See address above.)

ARCHSTONE FOUNDATION [1383]

401 East Ocean Boulevard
Suite 1000
Long Beach, CA 90802
(562) 590-8655
Fax: (562) 495-0317
E-mail: archstone@archstone.org
Web Site: www.archstone.org

FOUNDED: 1985

AREAS OF INTEREST:
Aging in community, depression in late life, family caregiving, and workforce development.

TYPE:
Challenge/matching grants; Conferences/seminars; Demonstration grants; Development grants; Project/program grants; Technical assistance; Training grants.

YEAR PROGRAM STARTED: 1985

PURPOSE:
To contribute toward the preparation of society in meeting the needs of an aging population.

ELIGIBILITY:
501(c)(3) organizations. Individuals may not apply. No funding available for capital expenditures, fund-raisers or research.

GEOG. RESTRICTIONS: Southern California.

FINANCIAL DATA:
Limited indirect costs to 10%.

Amount of support per award: $15,000 to $400,000.

Total amount of support: $101,832,844 since inception.

NO. MOST RECENT APPLICANTS: 113.

NO. AWARDS: 72 for fiscal year ended June 30, 2014.

APPLICATION INFO:
Application forms and reporting guidelines are available on the Foundation's web site.

Duration: One year. May be renewed for up to three years.

IRS I.D.: 33-0133359

BOARD OF DIRECTORS:
Rocky Suares, C.F.P., Chairman
Joseph F. Prevratil, President and Chief Executive Officer
Diana M. Bonta, Dr.P.H., R.N.
Hon. Lynn Daucher
Amye L. Leong, MBA
Hon. Renee B. Simon, M.S., M.L.S.
Mark D. Smith, M.D., MBA
Peter C. Szutu, M.P.H.

ADDRESS INQUIRIES TO:
Tanisha Davis, Grants Manager
(See address above.)

MAX BELL FOUNDATION [1384]

1201 5th Street, S.W.
Suite 380
Calgary AB T2R 0Y6 Canada
(403) 215-7310
E-mail: white@maxbell.org
Web Site: www.maxbell.org

FOUNDED: 1972

AREAS OF INTEREST:
Health, education and environment.

TYPE:
Challenge/matching grants; Development grants; Internships; Project/program grants.

YEAR PROGRAM STARTED: 1972

PURPOSE:
To develop innovative ideas that impact public policies and practices.

LEGAL BASIS:
Private foundation.

ELIGIBILITY:
Organizations must have a registered Canadian charitable number issued by Revenue Canada. Grants are not made for conferences and workshops, scholarships, individuals, sabbaticals, equipment purchases, capital campaigns, fund-raising drives or annual charitable appeals.

GEOG. RESTRICTIONS: Canada.

FINANCIAL DATA:
Amount of support per award: Varies.

Total amount of support: Approximately $1,200,000 (CAN).

Matching fund requirements: Varies.

APPLICATION INFO:
For Internship Grants: Interested applicants should initiate the process by outlining:
(1) tentative details, including objectives, intended output/deliverables, and summary work plan showing activities and outputs by month;
(2) process by which applicant would search for and hire an intern and;
(3) budget with line items for intern stipend, administration/overhead and mentoring/supervision.

This information should be forwarded by post or fax to Allan Northcott, Senior Program Officer.

Applicants for Project/Program Grants should submit a letter of intent to Alida White, Office Administrator.

Applications for Development and Project Grants must be submitted online through the Foundation's web site.

Duration: One to three years. Nonrenewable.

OFFICERS:
Dr. David Elton, President
Allan Northcott, Vice President
Alida White, Administrator

STAFF:
Alida White, Administrator
Margaret Herriman, Program Officer

BOARD OF DIRECTORS:
Carolyn Hursh, Chairman
Ken Marra, Vice Chairman
Dr. Paul Boothe
Brenda Eaton
Jim Gray
Carol Hill
Provost Christopher Manfredi

ADDRESS INQUIRIES TO:
Allan Northcott, Vice President
(See address above.)

BRIGHAM AND WOMEN'S HOSPITAL [1385]

75 Francis Street
Boston, MA 02115
(617) 732-8422
Fax: (617) 582-6112
E-mail: bwhdeland@partners.org
Web Site: www.brighamandwomens.org/about_bwh/delandfellowship

AREAS OF INTEREST:
Health care.

NAME(S) OF PROGRAMS:
- **Deland Fellowship Program in Health Care and Society**

TYPE:
Fellowships.

PURPOSE:
To train outstanding future leaders in health care.

ELIGIBILITY:
It is anticipated that candidates will come from a variety of careers and educational backgrounds including business, law, economics, public policy, medicine and nursing. Candidates are required to have an advanced degree from a U.S. accredited institution.

NO. MOST RECENT APPLICANTS: 100 for the year 2014.

NO. AWARDS: 2 annually.

APPLICATION INFO:
Complete applications must be submitted to the e-mail address listed above by the deadline and must include the following items:
(1) completed application form;
(2) copy of curriculum vitae;
(3) list of three references and;
(4) candidates statement (application provides additional information).

Duration: One year.

Deadline: First Monday in October. Notification in November.

ADDRESS INQUIRIES TO:
Director, Deland Fellowship Program
(See e-mail address above.)

BRIGHT FOCUS FOUNDATION [1386]

22512 Gateway Center Drive
Clarksburg, MD 20871
(301) 948-3244
Fax: (301) 948-4403
E-mail: researchgrants@brightfocus.org
Web Site: www.brightfocus.org

FOUNDED: 1997

AREAS OF INTEREST:
Macular degeneration.

NAME(S) OF PROGRAMS:
- **Macular Degeneration Research Program**

TYPE:
Research grants.

YEAR PROGRAM STARTED: 1998

PURPOSE:
To fund research on and educate the public about macular degeneration.

LEGAL BASIS:
501(c)(3) nonprofit charitable organization.

ELIGIBILITY:
Grants are awarded on the basis of the proposal's scientific merit and its relevance to understanding the diseases studied. No funds for large equipment, institutional overhead cost, construction or building expenses.

The Foundation is particularly interested in receiving letters from new investigators and from established investigators seeking to explore new directions in macular degeneration research.

FINANCIAL DATA:
Amount of support per award: $160,000 over two years..
Total amount of support: Varies.

APPLICATION INFO:
Must send initial letter of intent. Subsequent proposal by invitation.
Duration: Up to two years.

PUBLICATIONS:
Annual report; newsletters; clinical brochures.

ADDRESS INQUIRIES TO:
E-mail: researchgrants@brightfocus.org

THE CALIFORNIA ENDOWMENT [1387]

1000 North Alameda Street
Los Angeles, CA 90012
(213) 928-8645
(800) 449-4149
Fax: (213) 928-8818
E-mail: destrada@calendow.org
Web Site: www.calendow.org

FOUNDED: 1996

AREAS OF INTEREST:
Health care access, disparities in health, public health, multicultural health, health and well-being, cultural competency and work force diversity.

NAME(S) OF PROGRAMS:
- **Building Healthy Communities Initiative**

TYPE:
Challenge/matching grants; General operating grants; Matching gifts; Project/program grants.

YEAR PROGRAM STARTED: 1998

PURPOSE:
To improve access to affordable, quality health care for underserved individuals and communities; to promote fundamental improvements in the health status of the people of California; to improve the health of Californians through community-based programs, collaborations and partnerships that strengthen leadership, stimulate policy development and contribute to systems change.

ELIGIBILITY:
Grants are awarded to tax-exempt organizations only. No grants to individuals.

GEOG. RESTRICTIONS: California.

FINANCIAL DATA:
Amount of support per award: Varies.

NO. MOST RECENT APPLICANTS: 1,112 for fiscal year ended March 31, 2014.

NO. AWARDS: 1,648 for fiscal year ended March 31, 2014.

APPLICATION INFO:
Applications by invitation only.

IRS I.D.: 95-4523232

CALIFORNIA HEALTHCARE FOUNDATION [1388]

1438 Webster Street
Suite 400
Oakland, CA 94612
(510) 238-1040
Fax: (510) 238-1388
E-mail: info@chcf.org
Web Site: www.chcf.org

FOUNDED: 1996

AREAS OF INTEREST:
Advancing meaningful, measurable improvements in the way the health care delivery system provides care to the people of California.

NAME(S) OF PROGRAMS:
- **Health Innovation Fund**
- **HighValue Care**
- **Improving Access**
- **Informing Decision-Makers**

TYPE:
Project/program grants.

PURPOSE:
To commission research and analysis; to publish and disseminate information; to convene stakeholders and fund development of programs and models aimed at improving the health care delivery and financing systems.

GEOG. RESTRICTIONS: California.

FINANCIAL DATA:
Amount of support per award: Varies.
Total amount of support: Varies.

APPLICATION INFO:
Letters of inquiry are preferred for unsolicited projects with description, timeline and estimated budget.
Duration: Varies.

ADDRESS INQUIRIES TO:
Lisa Kang
Director, Grants Administration
(See address above.)

THE CALIFORNIA WELLNESS FOUNDATION [1389]

6320 Canoga Avenue
Suite 1700
Woodland Hills, CA 91367-7111
(818) 702-1900
Fax: (818) 702-1999
E-mail: grants@calwellness.org
info@calwellness.org
Web Site: www.calwellness.org

FOUNDED: 1991

AREAS OF INTEREST:
Diversity in the health professions, environmental health, healthy aging, mental health, violence prevention, women's health, and work and health.

NAME(S) OF PROGRAMS:
- **Advancing Wellness Grants Program**

TYPE:
Conferences/seminars; Demonstration grants; General operating grants; Project/program grants; Seed money grants.

YEAR PROGRAM STARTED: 1992

PURPOSE:
To improve the health of the people of California by making grants for health promotion, wellness education and disease prevention.

LEGAL BASIS:
Private foundation.

ELIGIBILITY:
Applicants must be nonprofit organizations that are exempt under Section 501(c)(3) of the IRS and are defined as "not a private foundation" under Section 509(a)(1). The Foundation also funds government agencies.

The Foundation does not fund Section 509(a)(3) Type III non-functionally integrated supporting organizations and does not provide international funding or fund organizations located outside of the U.S. Grants are not made for annual fund drives, building campaigns, major equipment, biomedical research or to activities that exclusively benefit members of sectarian or religious organizations.

GEOG. RESTRICTIONS: California.

FINANCIAL DATA:
Amount of support per award: Varies depending on needs and nature of the request.
Total amount of support: Approximately $12,000,000 for the year 2014.

NO. MOST RECENT APPLICANTS: More than 1,300 for the year 2013.

NO. AWARDS: 115 for the year 2014.

APPLICATION INFO:
Applicant must submit a Letter of Interest through Cal Wellness' Grants Portal. If asked to submit a full proposal, guidance will be provided about how to submit the proposal.
Duration: Varies.

PUBLICATIONS:
Annual report; brochure; quarterly newsletter.

IRS I.D.: 95-4292101

STAFF:
Fatima Angeles, Vice President of Programs
Amy B. Scop, Director of Grants Management
Crystal D. Crawford, Program Director
Earl Lui, Program Director
Julio Marcial, Program Director
Padmini Parthasarathy, Program Director

ADMINISTRATIVE STAFF:
Margaret W. Minnich, Chief Operating and Financial Officer
David B. Littlefield, Manager of Communications Grants

EXECUTIVE STAFF:
Judy Belk, President and Chief Executive Officer

ADDRESS INQUIRIES TO:
Amy B. Scop
Director of Grants Management
(See address above.)

CENTER FOR SCIENCE IN THE PUBLIC INTEREST

1220 L Street, N.W.
Suite 300
Washington, DC 20005
(202) 332-9110
Fax: (202) 265-4954
E-mail: coday@cspinet.org
Web Site: www.cspinet.org

TYPE:
Internships. These unpaid internships allow interns to work on specific projects under the direction of a Project Director or the Executive Director.

See entry 2586 for full listing.

CHICAGO BOARD OF TRADE FOUNDATION [1390]

141 West Jackson Boulevard
Suite 1404
Chicago, IL 60604
(312) 789-8225
Fax: (312) 789-8255
E-mail: cbotfoundation@hctech.com
Web Site: www.cbotfoundation.org

AREAS OF INTEREST:
Youth, education, seniors, wildlife, social and human services.

TYPE:
General operating grants; Project/program grants.

PURPOSE:
To assist children in need, seniors, people with disabilities, social and human services within the Chicago community.

ELIGIBILITY:
Organizations classified as 501(c)(3) by the IRS can apply. Individuals and religious organizations are ineligible. Must be nondiscriminatory in its practices and may not give funds to ancillary organizations.

GEOG. RESTRICTIONS: Greater Chicago, Illinois metropolitan area.

FINANCIAL DATA:
Amount of support per award: $1,000 to $20,000.

NO. MOST RECENT APPLICANTS: 50 for the year 2015.

NO. AWARDS: 30 for the year 2015.

APPLICATION INFO:
Applicant must submit a copy of proposal, 501(c)(3), (4) or (10) documentation, and a recent financial statement.

Duration: One year. Grants are renewable.

ADDRESS INQUIRIES TO:
Dawn Andersen
(See address above.)

THE COLORADO TRUST [1391]

1600 Sherman Street
Denver, CO 80203-1604
(303) 837-1200
(888) 847-9140
Fax: (303) 839-9034
E-mail: gwyn@coloradotrust.org
Web Site: www.coloradotrust.org

FOUNDED: 1985

AREAS OF INTEREST:
Policies and information related to advancing health equity, as well as projects that address health equity in partnership with communities throughout Colorado.

NAME(S) OF PROGRAMS:

- **Community Partnerships**
- **Data and Information**
- **Health Equity Advocacy**
- **Health Equity Learning Series**

TYPE:
General operating grants; Project/program grants; Research grants; Technical assistance.

YEAR PROGRAM STARTED: 1985

PURPOSE:
To advance the health and well-being of the people of Colorado.

LEGAL BASIS:
Private foundation.

GEOG. RESTRICTIONS: Colorado.

FINANCIAL DATA:
Amount of support per award: Varies.

Total amount of support: $13,100,000 in total grantmaking for fiscal year 2014.

CO-OP FUNDING PROGRAMS: Supporting the Colorado School of Public Health, along with Caring for Colorado, The Colorado Health Foundation, Kaiser Permanente and Rose Community Foundation; Supporting the Colorado Fresh Food Financing Fund, along with the Colorado Health Foundation and the Colorado Housing and Finance Authority.

APPLICATION INFO:
Applications are accepted following the release of Requests for Proposals issued by The Colorado Trust. Application requirements are detailed specifically in Requests for Proposals.

Duration: Varies.

PUBLICATIONS:
Annual report; community connections blog; evaluation reports; program reports.

IRS I.D.: 84-0994055

ADDRESS INQUIRIES TO:
Gwyn Barley, Director of Community Partnerships and Grants
(See address and e-mail above.)

CONGRESSIONAL BLACK CAUCUS FOUNDATION, INC.

1720 Massachusetts Avenue, N.W.
Washington, DC 20036
(202) 263-2800
Fax: (202) 263-0846
E-mail: fellowships@cbcfinc.org
Web Site: www.cbcfinc.org

TYPE:
Fellowships. The Louis Stokes Urban Health Policy Fellows Program is a 20-month policy training and leadership development program that targets early to mid-level policy professionals who are committed to eliminating health disparities nationally and globally. Fellows receive health policy training while working in a CBC Member's office as well as on a congressional committee. They spend 10 months working in a congressional Member's office and the remaining 10 months working on a congressional committee that focuses on health-related issues.

The program also includes educational enrichment opportunities through seminars on policy and politics.

See entry 1003 for full listing.

THE CULLEN TRUST FOR HEALTH CARE [1392]

601 Jefferson, Suite 4000
Houston, TX 77002
(713) 651-8860
Fax: (713) 651-8993
E-mail: julie@werinterests.com
Web Site: www.cullentrust.org

FOUNDED: 1978

AREAS OF INTEREST:
Health care.

TYPE:
Capital grants; Development grants; Endowments; General operating grants; Project/program grants. Clinical-based research grants.

YEAR PROGRAM STARTED: 1978

PURPOSE:
To provide financial assistance and to benefit institutions providing health care.

LEGAL BASIS:
Charitable trust.

ELIGIBILITY:
Applicants must be tax-exempt 501(c)(3).

GEOG. RESTRICTIONS: Primarily Houston, Texas area.

FINANCIAL DATA:
Amount of support per award: Average $50,000.

Total amount of support: Varies.

APPLICATION INFO:
Applications are only accepted through the Trust web site.

Duration: One to five years.

Deadline: February 1 and September 1.

ADDRESS INQUIRIES TO:
Gina McEvily, Executive Administrator
(See address above.)

RAY EDWARDS MEMORIAL TRUST [1393]

101 East Fifth Street, EP-MN-S14
St. Paul, MN 55101
(855) 452-4015
Fax: (651) 466-8742
E-mail: charitableservicesgroupmpls@usbank.com

FOUNDED: 1961

AREAS OF INTEREST:
Hospital-based health care delivery and direct health care services to indigent.

TYPE:
Capital grants; General operating grants; Project/program grants.

YEAR PROGRAM STARTED: 1961

PURPOSE:
To provide hospital-based health care services for those who are in greatest financial need and are enduring or experiencing serious illnesses.

LEGAL BASIS:
Private foundation.

ELIGIBILITY:
Eligible organizations must be IRS 501(c)(3) tax-exempt.

GEOG. RESTRICTIONS: Greater St. Paul, Minnesota and the metropolitan area to the east.

FINANCIAL DATA:
Amount of support per award: $1,000 to $150,000.

Total amount of support: Up to $845,000 annually.

NO. MOST RECENT APPLICANTS: Approximately 200.

NO. AWARDS: 15 to 25.

REPRESENTATIVE AWARDS:
$30,000 ($15,000 per year for two years) to Children's Hospitals and Clinics.

APPLICATION INFO:
Applications must include four copies of the following:
(1) one-page cover letter signed by Chief Executive Officer or Board Chair;
(2) Minnesota Common Grant Application (cover page only);
(3) audited financial statement from most recent fiscal year;
(4) IRS tax-exempt determination letter;
(5) Board of Directors listing and;
(6) report describing use and impact of any recent grants from the Trust.

The Foundation does not accept letters of inquiry.

Duration: Typically one year. Capital projects: Multiyear.

Deadline: May 1.

PUBLICATIONS:
Application guidelines.

ADDRESS INQUIRIES TO:
See e-mail address above.

*SPECIAL STIPULATIONS:
No inquiry letters. Submit proposals only.

FIRST CANDLE/SIDS ALLIANCE

9 Newport Drive, Suite 200
Forest Hill, MD 21050
(443) 640-1049
Fax: (443) 640-1031
E-mail: info@firstcandle.org
Web Site: www.firstcandle.org

TYPE:
Conferences/seminars; Research grants. Professional medical research for SIDS, stillbirths and related issues.

See entry 2449 for full listing.

THE FOUNDATION FOR SPIRITUALITY AND MEDICINE [1394]

13500 Fork Road
Baldwin, MD 21013
(410) 592-3583
Fax: (410) 592-3583 (Call ahead)
E-mail: smdcdaneker@comcast.net
Web Site: www.foundationspiritmed.org

FOUNDED: 1981

AREAS OF INTEREST:
Health, health education and spirituality.

TYPE:
Challenge/matching grants; Conferences/seminars; Demonstration grants; Development grants; General operating grants; Project/program grants; Research grants; Seed money grants; Training grants.

YEAR PROGRAM STARTED: 1995

PURPOSE:
To promote the integration of spirituality into health care.

ELIGIBILITY:
Grants are given to any nonprofit organization whose mission is the training of professionals in the healing arts, the delivery of health care, or the provision of spiritual services. Preference may be given to applicants who demonstrate matching funds by their organization or from other sources.

GEOG. RESTRICTIONS: Primarily Maryland.

FINANCIAL DATA:
Net worth as of December 31, 2015: $1,723,000.

Amount of support per award: Maximum $25,000 per year.

Total amount of support: $144,750 for the year 2015.

Matching fund requirements: Matching funds are preferred.

NO. MOST RECENT APPLICANTS: 9 for the year 2014.

NO. AWARDS: 6 for the year 2014.

REPRESENTATIVE AWARDS:
Mobile medical clinic operations; Program for teens with development disabilities; Clinical pastoral education; Religious-oriented psych counseling program; Telephone chaplaincy program; Research project on spiritual healing path for victims of human sex trafficking.

APPLICATION INFO:
Applications must be no more than 10 pages in length (double-spaced) and should include the following:
(1) description and history of the project;
(2) description of organization and personnel;
(3) rationale for proposed project;
(4) goals and objectives of the project;
(5) short-term and long-term benefits expected from the project;
(6) plans for a continuation of the project;
(7) timetable and;
(8) budget.

Grantees must meet Foundation requirements for regular financial and project reporting, and submit an annual and final written report. An oral presentation to the board of directors of the Foundation may be requested as part of the application process and/or as part of the report.

Submit three copies of application, if possible.

Duration: Two years.

Deadline: January 15 and July 15. Announcements April 1 and October 1.

PUBLICATIONS:
Brochure.

IRS I.D.: 52-1238713

ADDRESS INQUIRIES TO:
David C. Daneker, Chairman
(See address above.)

THE FOUNDATION OF THE AMERICAN COLLEGE OF HEALTHCARE EXECUTIVES [1395]

One North Franklin Street
Suite 1700
Chicago, IL 60606-3529
(312) 424-9400
Fax: (312) 424-9405
E-mail: contact@ache.org
Web Site: www.ache.org/scholarships

FOUNDED: 1933

AREAS OF INTEREST:
Health care management.

NAME(S) OF PROGRAMS:
- **Albert W. Dent Graduate Student Scholarship**
- **Foster G. McGaw Graduate Student Scholarship**

TYPE:
Scholarships. Offered annually, the Albert W. Dent and the Foster G. McGaw Graduate Student Scholarships are designated for students enrolled in their final year of classroom work in a health care management graduate program.

Albert W. Dent Graduate Student Scholarship is only available to minority students.

YEAR PROGRAM STARTED: 1969

PURPOSE:
To provide financial aid, increase the enrollment in health care management graduate programs and to encourage students to obtain positions in the middle and upper levels of health care management.

ELIGIBILITY:
An applicant must:
(1) be a full-time student entering the final year of classroom work in a health care management graduate program;
(2) be able to demonstrate financial need;
(3) be a U.S. or Canadian citizen;
(4) have not been a previous recipient of the scholarship and;
(5) be a minority if applying for the Albert W. Dent Graduate Student Scholarship.

GEOG. RESTRICTIONS: United States and Canada.

FINANCIAL DATA:
Amount of support per award: $5,000.

Total amount of support: Varies.

CO-OP FUNDING PROGRAMS: The initial gift for the McGaw Student Scholarship was from the Foster G. McGaw Charitable Fund. Additional gifts were made by Mr. McGaw from his personal funds before his death in 1986.

NO. MOST RECENT APPLICANTS: 200 to 250.

NO. AWARDS: Up to 20 scholarships awarded per year.

APPLICATION INFO:
Application is submitted online via the Foundation web site.

Duration: One year. Renewal by reapplication.

Deadline: March 31.

ADDRESS INQUIRIES TO:
Scholarship Committee
Division of Member Services
(See address above.)

THE DAVID GEFFEN FOUNDATION [1396]

12011 San Vicente Boulevard
Suite 606
Los Angeles, CA 90049
(310) 581-5955
Fax: (310) 581-5949
E-mail: ddishman@geffenco.com

FOUNDED: 1986

AREAS OF INTEREST:
AIDS/HIV, civil liberties, health and health care, the arts and issues of concern to the Jewish community.

TYPE:
General operating grants; Project/program grants.

PURPOSE:
To support the arts, health care, issues of concern to the Jewish community, HIV/AIDS and civil liberties.

LEGAL BASIS:
Private foundation.

ELIGIBILITY:
Applicants must be 501(c)(3) organizations. No grants for documentaries, audio-visual programming or publications. No grants to individuals.

GEOG. RESTRICTIONS: Primarily New York City and Los Angeles, California.

FINANCIAL DATA:
Amount of support per award: Varies depending on needs and nature of the request.

Total amount of support: $29,440,605.

APPLICATION INFO:
No application form. Proposals should include summary and description of the project or program, background information of the organization, description of key staff, list of Board of Directors, IRS letter confirming tax-exempt status and financial information including annual operating and project budgets. Applicants should not send videotapes or additional materials unless otherwise requested.

Duration: One-time grant and multiyear support. Renewal possible.

Deadline: Applications accepted throughout the year. Each request may take up to three months to evaluate.

PUBLICATIONS:
Application guidelines.

IRS I.D.: 95-4085811

STAFF:
J. Dallas Dishman, Ph.D., Executive Director

ADDRESS INQUIRIES TO:
J. Dallas Dishman, Ph.D., Executive Director
(See address above.)

HCR MANORCARE FOUNDATION [1397]

333 North Summit Street
Toledo, OH 43604
(419) 252-5989
Fax: (419) 252-5521
E-mail: gives@hcr-manorcare.com
Web Site: www.hcr-manorcare.com
www.hcrgives.org

FOUNDED: 1997

AREAS OF INTEREST:
Community service and outreach, hospice-related programs, research and public education for diseases and disorders that affect the elderly, those requiring post-acute services and those requiring hospice or end-of-life care.

TYPE:
Challenge/matching grants; Project/program grants.

YEAR PROGRAM STARTED: 1997

PURPOSE:
To support organizations involved in research and public education about diseases and disorders affecting the elderly, and organizations which provide community service and outreach to such individuals; to provide support to programs addressing end-of-life care; to provide support for hospice.

LEGAL BASIS:
Corporate foundation.

ELIGIBILITY:
Preference is given to organizations in states where HCR ManorCare Corporation has strategic operations. Organizations must be IRS 501(c)(3) tax-exempt and have one other source of support.

HCR ManorCare will not fund advertising or fund-raising events, individuals, for-profit organizations, building or capital campaigns, endowments, organizations with primary service areas in non-HCR ManorCare states, multiyear commitments, research projects with overhead fees in excess of 10% or organizations that have applied for funding within the last 12 months.

GEOG. RESTRICTIONS: United States.

FINANCIAL DATA:
Amount of support per award: Varies.

Total amount of support: Varies.

NO. MOST RECENT APPLICANTS: 300.

NO. AWARDS: 150.

APPLICATION INFO:
The Foundation does not accept unsolicited applications. Grants are only given through HCR ManorCare Corporation locations.

Duration: One year.

IRS I.D.: 52-2031975

ADDRESS INQUIRIES TO:
Bill White, Executive Director
(See address above.)

HEALTH EFFECTS INSTITUTE (HEI) [1398]

75 Federal Street
Suite 1400
Boston, MA 02110-1817
(617) 488-2338
Fax: (617) 488-2335
E-mail: jrutledge@healtheffects.org
Web Site: www.healtheffects.org

FOUNDED: 1980

AREAS OF INTEREST:
Health effects of air pollution.

NAME(S) OF PROGRAMS:

- **Health Effects of Air Pollution**
- **Walter A. Rosenblith New Investigator Award**

TYPE:
Research contracts.

YEAR PROGRAM STARTED: 1980

PURPOSE:
To provide high-quality, impartial, and relevant science on the health effects of air pollution.

LEGAL BASIS:
Public/Private partnership.

ELIGIBILITY:
Requirements vary according to program.

FINANCIAL DATA:
Amount of support per award: Health Effects of Air Pollution: Up to $400,000 per study; Rosenblith New Investigator Award: $150,000 per year.

Total amount of support: Varies.

APPLICATION INFO:
Application information is available online.

Duration: Health Effects of Air Pollution: Up to two or two and one-half years. Rosenblith New Investigator Award: Up to three years.

Deadline: Health Effects of Air Pollution: February 1 for Preliminary Application and September 1 for Full Application. Rosenblith New Investigator Award: February 1 for Letter of Intent and April 1 for Full Application.

ADDRESS INQUIRIES TO:
For Health Effects:
Dr. Katy Walker
Tel: (617) 488-2310
For Walter A. Rosenblith New Investigator Award:
Dr. Annemoon van Erp
Tel: (617) 488-2346
(See address above.)

THE HEALTH FOUNDATION OF GREATER INDIANAPOLIS, INC. [1399]

429 East Vermont Street, Suite 400
Indianapolis, IN 46202-3698
(317) 630-1805
Fax: (317) 630-1806
E-mail: info@thfgi.org
Web Site: www.thfgi.org

FOUNDED: 1985

AREAS OF INTEREST:
Childhood obesity, school-based health and HIV/AIDS.

NAME(S) OF PROGRAMS:

- **Indiana AIDS Fund**

TYPE:
Grants-in-aid.

PURPOSE:
To serve the community's most vulnerable citizens by funding health-related projects and organizations not easily supported by other means.

ELIGIBILITY:
Any Indiana-based nonprofit 501(c)(3) group, organization or agency that provides HIV/AIDS-related programs or services to local constituencies may apply for funding.

GEOG. RESTRICTIONS: Indiana.

FINANCIAL DATA:
Amount of support per award: Varies.
Total amount of support: $800,000 for the year 2015.

NO. AWARDS: Varies.

APPLICATION INFO:
Submit one master copy of the proposal with all attachments and 10 copies of the proposal without attachments. Proposal must contain the following elements:
(1) the provided Proposal Cover Sheet;
(2) brief description of the organization and its qualifications for this project, no longer than two pages;
(3) proposal narrative which should describe need, target population, geographic area served by this project, project objectives and prospects for future funding, no longer than five pages;
(4) budget statement and justification, no longer than three pages, which should include form provided;
(5) evaluation component, no longer than two pages, which describes the behavior change evaluation component, explains what it will measure, lists the expected outcomes, and explains the rationale for choosing this component and;
(6) attachments.
Duration: One year.
Deadline: Varies.

ADDRESS INQUIRIES TO:
Jason Grisell, MBA
Program Director
(See address above.)

HEALTH FOUNDATION OF SOUTH FLORIDA [1400]

One Biscayne Tower
2 South Biscayne Boulevard, Suite 1710
Miami, FL 33131
(305) 374-7200
Fax: (305) 374-7003
E-mail: pwood@hfsf.org
Web Site: www.hfsf.org

FOUNDED: 1993

AREAS OF INTEREST:
Primary care, healthy eating active communities, oral health, preventative health measures, and healthy aging.

TYPE:
Challenge/matching grants; General operating grants; Project/program grants; Technical assistance; Training grants.

PURPOSE:
To promote charitable, scientific and educational purposes in order to advance the health and well-being of the people of Broward, Miami-Dade and Monroe counties, FL; to facilitate and support efforts at the neighborhood, county and regional levels to improve the health status of underserved individuals and families.

ELIGIBILITY:
Eligible organizations must be IRS 501(c)(3) tax-exempt and be located in south Florida.

GEOG. RESTRICTIONS: South Florida counties of Broward, Miami-Dade and Monroe.

FINANCIAL DATA:
Amount of support per award: Typically $20,000 to $160,000.
Total amount of support: $3,500,000.

NO. MOST RECENT APPLICANTS: 200 for the year 2015.

NO. AWARDS: 55.

APPLICATION INFO:
Preliminary proposal must be submitted electronically through the Foundation's web site.
Duration: One to two years.
Deadline: Preliminary proposals: July and December. Full proposals: September and January.

ADDRESS INQUIRIES TO:
Peter N. Wood
Vice President of Programs
and Community Investments
(See address above.)

THE HEALTH TRUST [1401]

3180 Newberry Drive
Suite 200
San Jose, CA 95118
(408) 513-8700
Fax: (408) 448-4055
E-mail: grants@healthtrust.org
Web Site: www.healthtrust.org

FOUNDED: 1996

AREAS OF INTEREST:
Public health.

NAME(S) OF PROGRAMS:
- **Event Grants**

TYPE:
Project/program grants.

YEAR PROGRAM STARTED: 1996

PURPOSE:
To lead the Silicon Valley community to advance wellness.

LEGAL BASIS:
Nonprofit, public charity, qualifying as IRS 501(c)(3) organization.

ELIGIBILITY:
The organization must be tax-exempt and nonprofit. Health services must be provided within Santa Clara County and the following three zip codes of San Benito County: 95045, 95023 and 95024.

GEOG. RESTRICTIONS: Santa Clara and northern San Benito counties, California.

FINANCIAL DATA:
Amount of support per award: $250 to $5,000.
Total amount of support: Varies.

NO. MOST RECENT APPLICANTS: Approximately 110.

APPLICATION INFO:
Guidelines are available on the Trust web site. Event Grant application must be submitted online.
Duration: One year.
Deadline: Applications are accepted on a rolling basis.

STAFF:
Carla Freeman, Program Officer

ADDRESS INQUIRIES TO:
Grants Administrator
(See address above.)

THE HEALTH TRUST [1402]

3180 Newberry Drive
Suite 200
San Jose, CA 95118
(408) 513-8700
Fax: (408) 448-4055
E-mail: grants@healthtrust.org
Web Site: www.healthtrust.org

FOUNDED: 1996

AREAS OF INTEREST:
Public health.

NAME(S) OF PROGRAMS:
- **Health Partnership Grants**

TYPE:
Project/program grants.

PURPOSE:
To make grants to programs and projects that advance specific strategies under three initiatives: Healthy Living, Healthy Aging and Healthy Communities.

LEGAL BASIS:
Nonprofit, public charity.

ELIGIBILITY:
Organization must be tax-exempt and nonprofit. Health services must be provided within Santa Clara County and the following three zip codes of San Benito County: 95045, 95023 and 95024.

GEOG. RESTRICTIONS: Santa Clara and northern San Benito counties, California.

FINANCIAL DATA:
Amount of support per award: Varies.
Total amount of support: Varies.

APPLICATION INFO:
Applications must be submitted online.
Duration: Varies.
Deadline: Varies.

ADDRESS INQUIRIES TO:
Grants Administrator
(See address above.)

THE HEALTHCARE FOUNDATION FOR ORANGE COUNTY [1403]

1505 East 17th Street
Suite 113
Santa Ana, CA 92705
(714) 245-1650
Fax: (714) 245-1653
E-mail: info@HFOC.org
Web Site: www.HFOC.org

FOUNDED: 1996

AREAS OF INTEREST:
Health care and community health.

CONSULTING OR VOLUNTEER SERVICES:
Some training and technical assistance.

NAME(S) OF PROGRAMS:
- **Gold Fund for Health**
- **Partnership for a Healthy Orange County**

TYPE:
Awards/prizes; Demonstration grants; Development grants; General operating grants; Project/program grants; Technical assistance; Training grants.

YEAR PROGRAM STARTED: 1999

PURPOSE:
To promote health and support health care for the benefit of the people of Orange County, CA; to improve the health of the neediest and most underserved residents of the county.

LEGAL BASIS:
Private 501(c)(3) foundation.

ELIGIBILITY:
Grants are made to nonprofit organizations that are exempt from taxation under Section 501(c)(3) of the Internal Revenue Code and that are defined as "not a private foundation" under Section 509(a). Government agencies may also be funded.

Grants are not generally awarded for annual fund drives, building campaigns, major equipment or biomedical research. Activities that exclusively benefit the members of a religious or fraternal organization are not funded.

GEOG. RESTRICTIONS: Primarily Anaheim, Orange, Santa Ana and Tustin, California.

FINANCIAL DATA:
Amount of support per award: Gold Fund for Health: $70,000; Partnership for a Healthy Orange County: $650,000.

Total amount of support: Approximately $700,000 per year.

CO-OP FUNDING PROGRAMS: Health Funders Partnership.

NO. MOST RECENT APPLICANTS: Approximately 39.

NO. AWARDS: Approximately 10.

REPRESENTATIVE AWARDS:
$290,652 to St. Joseph Hospital of Orange, for children and families' community oral health; $88,600 to Children's Hospital of Orange County for behavioral health prevention and intervention services.

APPLICATION INFO:
Requests for proposals may be obtained from the Foundation.

Duration: One year; multiyear funding at the Board's discretion.

Deadline: October.

IRS I.D.: 33-0644620

ADDRESS INQUIRIES TO:
Foundation Coordinator
(See address above.)

HUGOTON FOUNDATION [1404]

900 Park Avenue, Suite 17E
New York, NY 10075
(212) 734-5447
Fax: (212) 734-5447

AREAS OF INTEREST:
Patient care and health.

TYPE:
Project/program grants.

PURPOSE:
To improve patient care.

LEGAL BASIS:
Nonprofit organization.

ELIGIBILITY:
Eligible organizations must be IRS 501(c)(3) tax-exempt and be located in Miami, FL or the borough of Manhattan, NY.

GEOG. RESTRICTIONS: Miami, Florida and borough of Manhattan, New York.

FINANCIAL DATA:
Amount of support per award: $1,000 to $100,000.

APPLICATION INFO:
Application should be made by letter and include a copy of the IRS tax determination letter.

Duration: One year. Nonrenewable.

ADDRESS INQUIRIES TO:
Joan K. Stout, President
(See address above.)

IRVINE HEALTH FOUNDATION [1405]

18301 Von Karman Avenue
Suite 440
Irvine, CA 92612-0120
(949) 253-2959
E-mail: info@ihf.org
Web Site: www.ihf.org

FOUNDED: 1986

AREAS OF INTEREST:
Technology-enabled healthy living, with a focus on the veteran and senior populations of Orange County, CA.

TYPE:
Focus grants by invitation only.

YEAR PROGRAM STARTED: 1987

PURPOSE:
To intensify focus on approaches that improve individual healthy behaviors, especially those using technologies that provide broader access to effective health practices; to highlight systems that bolster the well-being of Orange County's seniors and veterans.

LEGAL BASIS:
Independent, nonprofit foundation.

ELIGIBILITY:
Applicants must be qualified tax-exempt charitable organizations recognized as such by the IRS. To receive favorable consideration, a project or program must be economically viable, provide effective management and serve a legitimate purpose which avoids duplicating work performed by other organizations.

The Foundation is accelerating its efforts to form new partnerships with technology companies, academic and philanthropy organizations, investors, innovators, and the development of nontraditional approaches.

GEOG. RESTRICTIONS: Orange County, California.

FINANCIAL DATA:
Amount of support per award: Varies.

Total amount of support: Varies.

Matching fund requirements: Varies.

APPLICATION INFO:
Application information is available on the Foundation's web site.

Duration: Varies.

STAFF:
Edward B. Kacic, CAIA, President
Patricia A. Meredith, Vice President, Administration and Programs

BOARD OF DIRECTORS:
Timothy L. Strader, Chairman
Carol Mentor McDermott, Vice Chairman
Jeffrey E. Flocken, Treasurer
Thomas C. Cesario, M.D., Secretary
Douglas M. Mancino, Esq., Director
Margarita Pereyda, M.D., Director

*SPECIAL STIPULATIONS:
Funding requests are by invitation only. Unsolicited inquiries are not accepted.

THE JENKINS FOUNDATION [1406]

7501 Boulders View Drive, Suite 110
Richmond, VA 23225
(804) 330-7400
Fax: (804) 330-5992
E-mail: info@tcfrichmond.org
Web Site: www.jenkinsfoundation-va.org

FOUNDED: 1995

AREAS OF INTEREST:
Health care services for the uninsured and underserved, violence prevention and substance abuse prevention in the greater Richmond, VA area.

TYPE:
General operating grants; Project/program grants.

YEAR PROGRAM STARTED: 1996

PURPOSE:
To expand access to community-based health care programs and improved health care in the greater Richmond area.

LEGAL BASIS:
Supporting organization of The Community Foundation Serving Richmond and Central Virginia.

ELIGIBILITY:
Eligible organizations must be IRS 501(c)(3) tax-exempt and serve the greater Richmond, VA area.

GEOG. RESTRICTIONS: Richmond and the counties of Chesterfield, Goochland, Hanover, Henrico and Powhatan, Virginia.

FINANCIAL DATA:
Amount of support per award: Up to $50,000.

Total amount of support: Approximately $1,600,000 for the year 2013.

APPLICATION INFO:
Application forms are available online.

Duration: Annually. May reapply.

Deadline: May 5 and November 5.

PUBLICATIONS:
Guidelines; annual report (online).

ADDRESS INQUIRIES TO:
Elaine Summerfield
Vice President of Programs
(See address above.)

THE JEWISH HEALTHCARE FOUNDATION OF PITTSBURGH [1407]

Centre City Tower, Suite 2400
650 Smithfield Street
Pittsburgh, PA 15222
(412) 594-2550
Fax: (412) 232-6240
E-mail: info@jhf.org
Web Site: www.jhf.org

FOUNDED: 1990

AREAS OF INTEREST:
Health care.

CONSULTING OR VOLUNTEER SERVICES:
Research, planning, convening and technical assistance.

TYPE:
Challenge/matching grants; Demonstration grants; Fellowships; Project/program grants; Research grants; Seed money grants; Technical assistance; Training grants.

YEAR PROGRAM STARTED: 1991

PURPOSE:
To provide for the health care needs of the Jewish and general community in southwestern Pennsylvania.

LEGAL BASIS:
Public charity.

ELIGIBILITY:
Applicants must be 501(c)(3) organizations. No grants to programs without a health care component, general operations, endowments, capital campaigns, retirement of debt, scholarships, fellowships, travel or individual research grants.

GEOG. RESTRICTIONS: Western Pennsylvania.

FINANCIAL DATA:
Amount of support per award: Average $50,000.

Total amount of support: $6,800,879 for the year ended December 31, 2014.

NO. MOST RECENT APPLICANTS: 40.

NO. AWARDS: 50.

REPRESENTATIVE AWARDS:
Pittsburgh Regional Health Initiative; Brandeis University; University of Pittsburgh Graduate School of Public Health.

APPLICATION INFO:
Send letter of intent (not to exceed six pages), including program objectives, timetable, long-term plans, board of directors list, budget, documentation of 501(c)(3) status and most recent financial statements.

The Foundation also accepts the common grant application designed by Grantmakers of Western Pennsylvania.

Duration: Varies.

Deadline: Applications accepted on a continual basis.

PUBLICATIONS:
Annual report; *Roots*, reports; *Branches*, periodical.

IRS I.D.: 25-1624347

STAFF:
Karen Wolk Feinstein, Ph.D., President and Chief Executive Officer
Nancy D. Zionts, MBA, Chief Operating Officer and Chief Program Officer

ADDRESS INQUIRIES TO:
Nancy D. Zionts, Chief Operating Officer and Chief Program Officer
(See address above.)

THE JOHNS HOPKINS CENTER FOR ALTERNATIVES TO ANIMAL TESTING [1408]

Johns Hopkins University
615 North Wolfe Street, Room W7032
Baltimore, MD 21205
(410) 614-4990
Fax: (410) 614-2871
E-mail: altweb@jhsph.edu
jderita1@jhu.edu
Web Site: altweb.jhsph.edu

FOUNDED: 1981

AREAS OF INTEREST:
Health and safety.

TYPE:
Development grants; Research grants.

YEAR PROGRAM STARTED: 1982

PURPOSE:
To develop innovative non-whole animal methods to evaluate fully commercial and/or therapeutic products to ensure the health and safety of the public. CAAT accomplishes this goal by funding research which will lead to the refinement, replacement or reduction of animals in toxicity testing and by disseminating scientifically correct information about these methods and their applications.

LEGAL BASIS:
University research program.

ELIGIBILITY:
Grants are made to institutions which have an established mechanism for handling private funding. Grant proposals should provide the fundamental knowledge base to develop alternative methods to whole animals for the safety evaluation of commercial products. CAAT encourages the development of in vitro approaches to toxicity evaluation including, but not limited to, methods using human cells/cell lines and studies in the areas of skin hypersensitivity/toxicity, phototoxicity, target organ toxicity (e.g., neurotoxicity) and structure-activity relationships.

FINANCIAL DATA:
Amount of support per award: $25,000 maximum per year, including 15% overhead or actual costs, whichever is less.

APPLICATION INFO:
Applicants must submit and receive approval of preproposal by deadline date using CAAT preproposal form.

Duration: Up to two years.

Deadline: May 16 for preproposal abstracts.

PUBLICATIONS:
CAAT Newsletter; technical reports; *Alternatives in Toxicology*, book series.

IRS I.D.: 52-0595110

ADDRESS INQUIRIES TO:
Jamie DeRita-Rodriguez, Grants Coordinator
(See address above.)

KANSAS HEALTH FOUNDATION [1409]

309 East Douglas
Wichita, KS 67202
(316) 262-7676
(800) 373-7681
Fax: (316) 262-2044
E-mail: info@khf.org
Web Site: kansashealth.org

FOUNDED: 1985

AREAS OF INTEREST:
Health equity and civic health.

NAME(S) OF PROGRAMS:
- **Recognition Grants**

TYPE:
Project/program grants.

YEAR PROGRAM STARTED: 1994

PURPOSE:
To improve the health of all Kansans.

ELIGIBILITY:
Applicants must be tax-exempt under Section 501(c)(3), a government entity, or a church (with certain exclusions), located within the state, and not a previous recipient of a Recognition Grant within the calendar year.

GEOG. RESTRICTIONS: Kansas.

FINANCIAL DATA:
Amount of support per award: Up to $25,000 per organization.

Total amount of support: Up to $2,000,000 annually in two cycles per year.

NO. AWARDS: Varies.

APPLICATION INFO:
Applications are to be submitted using the Online Recognition Grant Application Form.

Letters of Inquiry are accepted from organizations that believe they have a project fitting the Foundation's funding priorities.

Duration: One year.

Deadline: September 15 and March 15. Announcement December 1 and June 1, respectively.

PUBLICATIONS:
Grant announcement press release.

IRS I.D.: 48-0873431

ADDRESS INQUIRIES TO:
Chan Brown, Program Officer
(See address above.)

LA84 FOUNDATION [1410]

2141 West Adams Boulevard
Los Angeles, CA 90018
(323) 730-4600
Fax: (323) 730-9637
E-mail: info@la84.org
Web Site: www.la84.org

FOUNDED: 1984

AREAS OF INTEREST:
Youth sports.

TYPE:
Capital grants; Project/program grants. Field of play activities.

PURPOSE:
To promote and enhance youth sports opportunities in southern California.

LEGAL BASIS:
Private nonprofit foundation.

ELIGIBILITY:
Grants are made only to organizations with nonrestrictive membership operating open to all, regardless of race, creed, sex, sexual orientation, religious affiliation, or nationality. No grants to individuals. Grants are discouraged for endowments, travel outside of southern California, general operating expenses, land purchases, or debt recovery and liability. Grants are need-based.

GEOG. RESTRICTIONS: Imperial, Los Angeles, Orange, Riverside, San Bernardino, San Diego, Santa Barbara and Ventura counties, California.

FINANCIAL DATA:
Amount of support per award: Small grants: Generally $10,000 or less. Other grants: Average $25,000 to $50,000.

Total amount of support: Approximately $4,000,000 per year.

NO. AWARDS: Approximately 80 per year.

REPRESENTATIVE AWARDS:
$23,563 to Beat The Streets-Los Angeles, Inc. for mats and uniforms; $20,000 to Girls Incorporated of Greater Santa Barbara for personnel and equipment for the gymnastics program; $326,000 to Kids in Sports for

personnel, equipment, athlete expenses, venue and administrative expenses for sports leagues.

APPLICATION INFO:
Application guidelines will be posted on the Foundation web site in October or later.

Duration: One year.

Deadline: Applications are accepted year-round.

PUBLICATIONS:
Biannual report.

IRS I.D.: 95-3792725

OFFICERS:
Renata Simril, President and Chief Executive Officer
Wayne Wilson, Vice President, Education Services
Marcia Suzuki, Treasurer

STAFF:
Oscar Delgado, Director, Partnerships and Development
Gabby Tovar, Manager, Grants and Programs

ADDRESS INQUIRIES TO:
Renata Simril
President and Chief Executive Officer
E-mail: rsimril@la84.org

LIVINGSTON MEMORIAL FOUNDATION [1411]

c/o Musick, Peeler and Garrett
2801 Townsgate Road, Suite 200
Westlake Village, CA 91361-5842
(805) 418-3115
Fax: (805) 418-3101
E-mail: l.mcavoy@mpglaw.com
Web Site: www.livingstonmemorialfoundation.org

FOUNDED: 1974

AREAS OF INTEREST:
Medical and health care in Ventura County, CA.

NAME(S) OF PROGRAMS:
- **Operational Program Grants**
- **Special Project Grants**

TYPE:
Capital grants; General operating grants; Project/program grants. Capital grants are for medical and health care services.

Operational grants support well-established programs that continue to provide positive results.

Special project grants support those agencies and institutions that can demonstrate the need for assistance in funding a special project or with the cost of medical equipment that promises significant positive results.

YEAR PROGRAM STARTED: 1976

PURPOSE:
To promote medical and health-related services of benefit to the underserved and uninsured people of Ventura County, CA.

ELIGIBILITY:
Grant applications are assessed according to criteria that include giving preferential treatment to programs or projects that offer measurable medical benefits, are patient-specific or involve hands-on care.

Grants are not usually made to individuals, for projects or programs normally financed from government sources, conferences, seminars, workshops, exhibits, travel, or publishing activities.

GEOG. RESTRICTIONS: Ventura County, California.

FINANCIAL DATA:
Amount of support per award: $1,000 to $171,500 for the year 2015-16.

Total amount of support: $375,000 for the year 2016.

NO. MOST RECENT APPLICANTS: 27 for the year 2015-16.

NO. AWARDS: 25.

APPLICATION INFO:
Organizations should first submit a brief introductory letter, not to exceed three pages. The letter should include a concise statement of the need for the funds, the amount requested, pertinent factual information, and state the desired type of grant. Current verification of tax-exempt status should also be included. After review, eligible organizations may be invited to submit a formal grant application.

Duration: One year.

Deadline: Formal applications are received in late December. Awards are announced in April of each year.

PUBLICATIONS:
Brochure.

IRS I.D.: 23-7364623

DIRECTORS AND OFFICERS:
Laura K. McAvoy, Esq., President and Chairman
Richard M. Loft, M.D., Vice President and Vice Chairman
Thomas P. Pecht, Vice President, Vice Chairman and Assistant Secretary
Kathleen F. Deutschman, Secretary
Marcia L. Donlon, Assistant Secretary
John R. Walters, M.D., Chief Financial Officer
Charles M. Hair, M.D., Director

ADDRESS INQUIRIES TO:
Laura K. McAvoy, Esq.
President and Chairman
(See address above.)

THE DR. JOHN T. MACDONALD FOUNDATION, INC.

1550 Madruga Avenue, Suite 215
Coral Gables, FL 33146
(305) 667-6017
Fax: (305) 667-9135
E-mail: info@jtmacdonaldfdn.org
Web Site: www.jtmacdonaldfdn.org

TYPE:
Challenge/matching grants; Demonstration grants; General operating grants; Matching gifts; Project/program grants; Scholarships; Seed money grants.

See entry 1109 for full listing.

FREDA MAYTAG-GRACE CRAWFORD TRUST [1412]

c/o JPMorgan Private Client Services
2200 Ross Avenue, Floor 5
Dallas, TX 75201
(214) 965-2296
Fax: (866) 337-8406
E-mail: kelly.t.adams@jpmorgan.com
Web Site: www.jpmorgan.com/onlinegrants

AREAS OF INTEREST:
Tuberculosis and other respiratory diseases; preservation of a clean and healthy environment.

TYPE:
Project/program grants.

PURPOSE:
To provide medical and nursing care for individuals in the Colorado Springs community who are afflicted with tuberculosis or other respiratory diseases.

ELIGIBILITY:
Grants to 501(c)(3) nonprofit organizations. No grants to individuals.

GEOG. RESTRICTIONS: Colorado Springs, CO.

FINANCIAL DATA:
Amount of support per award: Varies.

APPLICATION INFO:
Application and guidelines are available online.

Duration: Varies.

Deadline: March 20, June 20, September 20 and December 20.

ADDRESS INQUIRIES TO:
Kelly Adams, Trust Officer
(See address above.)

MT. SINAI HEALTH CARE FOUNDATION [1413]

11000 Euclid Avenue
Cleveland, OH 44106-1714
(216) 421-5500
Fax: (216) 421-5633
E-mail: msb12@case.edu
Web Site: www.mtsinaifoundation.org

FOUNDED: 1996

AREAS OF INTEREST:
Urban health, Jewish community, health policy, academic medicine and bioscience.

TYPE:
Challenge/matching grants; Demonstration grants; Development grants; Project/program grants; Seed money grants.

YEAR PROGRAM STARTED: 1997

PURPOSE:
To improve the health of the citizens in the greater Cleveland, OH area.

LEGAL BASIS:
Public charity.

ELIGIBILITY:
Eligible organizations must be IRS 501(c)(3) tax-exempt.

GEOG. RESTRICTIONS: Greater Cleveland, Ohio.

FINANCIAL DATA:
Amount of support per award: Varies.

Total amount of support: $6,400,000 for the year 2016.

APPLICATION INFO:
Application information may be obtained by contacting the Foundation or visiting the web site listed above.

Duration: Varies.

Deadline: January 1, April 1, July 1 and October 1.

PUBLICATIONS:
Guidelines; annual report; *Legacy*, newsletter.

IRS I.D.: 34-1777878

ADDRESS INQUIRIES TO:
Mitchell Balk, President
(See address above.)

NATIONAL HEALTH SERVICE CORPS (NHSC) [1414]

U.S. Department of Health and Human Services
Health Resources and Services Administration
5600 Fishers Lane
Rockville, MD 20857
(800) 221-9393
E-mail: CallCenter@hrsa.gov (grants information)
Web Site: www.hrsa.gov

AREAS OF INTEREST:
Competitive scholarships for students enrolled in schools of osteopathic and allopathic medicine, family nurse practitioner, nurse midwifery and physician assistant training programs and dental school.

NAME(S) OF PROGRAMS:
- **National Health Service Corps Scholarship Program**

TYPE:
Scholarships. The scholarship award includes the payment of a monthly stipend, an amount for other reasonable educational expenses, tuition and required fees. Recipients owe one year of professional clinical service in a health professional shortage area (HPSA) for each year of support, with a two-year service minimum.

YEAR PROGRAM STARTED: 1973

PURPOSE:
To provide the National Health Service Corps with an adequate supply of trained health professionals to serve in health professional shortage areas.

ELIGIBILITY:
All applicants must be citizens or nationals of the U.S. at the time they apply, enrolled or accepted for enrollment in an accredited health professions education program.

GEOG. RESTRICTIONS: United States.

FINANCIAL DATA:
Scholarship recipients receive a monthly stipend, one annual payment for other reasonable educational expenses, and payment to the school, on their behalf, of tuition and required fees. The stipend is taxable only for certain scholarships.

Amount of support per award: Based on costs for every student in the program.

Total amount of support: Varies.

CO-OP FUNDING PROGRAMS: Educational benefits from the Veterans Administration (G.I. Bill) may continue along with Scholarship Program funds since these benefits were earned by prior active duty in a uniformed service.

NO. MOST RECENT APPLICANTS: 1,844 for the year 2014.

NO. AWARDS: Approximately 177 for the year 2015.

APPLICATION INFO:
Complete information is available on the web site.

Duration: The scholarship award is only for the year(s) that the contract is signed with a two-year minimum service obligation.

Deadline: Varies.

PUBLICATIONS:
Applicant information bulletin.

ADDRESS INQUIRIES TO:
See e-mail or telephone number above.

*SPECIAL STIPULATIONS:
Recipients must serve where needed in a designated Health Professional Shortage Area (HPSA).

NATIONAL INSTITUTE ON AGING [1415]

Division of Extramural Activities
31 Center Drive, MSC 2292
Bethesda, MD 20892
(301) 496-9322
Fax: (301) 402-2945
E-mail: barrr@mail.nih.gov
Web Site: www.nia.nih.gov

FOUNDED: 1975

AREAS OF INTEREST:
Biology of aging research, geriatrics and gerontology research, neuroscience and neuropsychology of aging research, behavioral and social research on aging.

NAME(S) OF PROGRAMS:
- **Aging Research**

TYPE:
Conferences/seminars; Fellowships; Grants-in-aid; Project/program grants; Research grants; Technical assistance; Training grants; Research contracts. Loan repayment programs.

PURPOSE:
To support biomedical, clinical, social, neuroscience, neuropsychology and behavioral research and research training directed toward greater understanding of the aging process and the needs and problems of older people. The primary goal is to improve the health and well-being of older people through the development of new knowledge.

LEGAL BASIS:
Government agency.

ELIGIBILITY:
Grants and contracts are available to universities, colleges, medical, dental and nursing schools, schools of public health, laboratories, hospitals, state and local health departments and other public or private profit or nonprofit institutions.

NRSA awards are provided for individual postdoctoral and institutional pre-and postdoctoral research training in health and health-related areas which are periodically specified by the National Institutes of Health. Individuals with a professional or scientific degree are eligible. Applicants must be citizens of the U.S. or be admitted for permanent residency.

GEOG. RESTRICTIONS: United States.

FINANCIAL DATA:
Amount of support per award: Average: $392,500 for research project grants.

Total amount of support: Varies.

NO. MOST RECENT APPLICANTS: 2,000.

NO. AWARDS: 1,400.

APPLICATION INFO:
Contact the Institute.

Duration: One year to multiyear.

Deadline: Varies.

OFFICERS:
Robin A. Barr, D.Phil., Director

ADDRESS INQUIRIES TO:
Division of Extramural Activities
(See address above.)

NATIONAL INSTITUTE ON ALCOHOL ABUSE AND ALCOHOLISM [1416]

Office of Extramural Activities
5635 Fishers Lane
MSC 9304
Bethesda, MD 20892-9304
(301) 443-9737
Fax: (301) 443-6077
E-mail: bautista@mail.nih.gov
Web Site: www.niaaa.nih.gov

FOUNDED: 1971

NAME(S) OF PROGRAMS:
- **Academic Career Awards (K07)**
- **Career Enhancement Award for Stem Cell Research (K18)**
- **Independent Scientist Awards (K02)**
- **Mentored Patient-Oriented Research Career Development Award (K23)**
- **Mentored Quantitative Research Career Development Award (K25)**
- **Midcareer Investigator Award in Patient-Oriented Research (K24)**
- **NIH Pathway to Independence Award (K99/R00)**
- **Scientist Development Awards for Mentored Clinical (K08)**
- **Scientist Development Awards for Mentored Research (K01)**

TYPE:
Research grants. Support for full-time research on a long-term (five years) basis for research scientists.

Academic Career Awards (K07) support development of clinical faculty in clinical research and teaching related to alcohol problems. Developmental award only.

Career Enhancement Award for Stem Cell Research (K18) is to encourage investigators to obtain the training they need to appropriately use stem cells in their research.

Independent Scientist Awards (K02) support advanced research experience.

NIH Pathway to Independence (PI) Award (K99/R00) will provide up to five years of support consisting of two phases. The PI award is limited to postdoctoral trainees.

Scientist Development Awards for Mentored Research (K01) and Scientist Development Awards for Mentored Clinical (K08) support individuals with one to four years of postdoctoral training or experience, but no extensive research experience.

PURPOSE:
To provide salary support to talented investigators so that they can engage in full-time research on a long-term basis and develop their full research potential.

LEGAL BASIS:
PHS Act, Section 301 as amended (42 U.S.C. 241).

ELIGIBILITY:
Applicants can either be public or nonprofit private organizations and institutions located in the U.S. or its territories and possessions or U.S. citizens or permanent residents. Citizenship is mandatory for renewal beyond the initial five-year award.

FINANCIAL DATA:
Amount of support per award: Varies.

Total amount of support: Varies.

APPLICATION INFO:
Application kits are available at most institutional offices of sponsored research and may be obtained from the Grants Information Office.

Duration: Generally five years. Renewal possible.

Deadline: February 12, June 12 and October 12.

PUBLICATIONS:
NIAAA additional information to the NIH Career Development Program Announcements (K Awards).

ADDRESS INQUIRIES TO:
Dr. Bob Huebner, Acting Director
Division of Treatment
and Recovery Research
Tel: (301) 443-4344 or

Dr. Ralph Hingson, Director
Division of Epidemiology
and Prevention Research
Tel: (301) 443-1274 or

Dr. Gary Murray
Division of Metabolism
and Health Effects
Tel: (301) 443-9940 or

Dr. Antonio Noronha
Division of Neuroscience and Behavior
Tel: (301) 443-7722
(See address above.)

NATIONAL INSTITUTE ON ALCOHOL ABUSE AND ALCOHOLISM [1417]

Division of Metabolism and Health Effect
5635 Fishers Lane, Room 2021
MSC 9304
Bethesda, MD 20892-9304
(301) 443-8744
Fax: (301) 594-0673
E-mail: kathy.jung@nih.gov
Web Site: www.niaaa.nih.gov

FOUNDED: 1971

AREAS OF INTEREST:
Pharmaceuticals, diagnostic instruments, and the prevention and treatment of alcoholism and alcohol abuse.

NAME(S) OF PROGRAMS:

- **Small Business Innovation Research Program**

TYPE:
Research grants; Research contracts. Separate grant applications are awarded for Phase I and Phase II of the program. Phase I is designed to establish the feasibility of the technological innovation and determine the quality of performance. The objective of Phase II is to further demonstrate the efficacy of the product for commercial exploitation. Only funded applicants from Phase I are eligible to apply for Phase II.

YEAR PROGRAM STARTED: 1983

PURPOSE:
To stimulate technological innovation in the alcohol field, increase private-sector commercialization of innovations derived from federal research and development and foster and encourage participation by minority and disadvantaged firms in technological innovation.

LEGAL BASIS:
The Small Business Innovation Development Act, P.L. 97-219.

ELIGIBILITY:
Each organization must qualify as a small business in accordance with the stipulations set forth in the Omnibus Solicitation of the PHS Small Business Innovation Research Program. In general, the organization must be independently owned and operated, must be located in the U.S. and at least 51% of the ownership must be by U.S. citizens or lawfully admitted permanent resident aliens. The primary employment of the principal investigator must be with the firm at the time of award and during the conduct of the proposed project. The performance site must be in the U.S.

GEOG. RESTRICTIONS: United States.

FINANCIAL DATA:
Amount of support per award: May not exceed $150,000 for both direct and indirect costs, for a maximum period of six months, for Phase I. May not exceed $1,000,000 for two years in total costs for Phase II. If costs exceed these amounts, contact the program officer named in the solicitation or the SBIR coordinator.

APPLICATION INFO:
The electronic submission process is multi-step. Details on applying can be found at sbir.nih.gov.

Duration: Six months for Phase I. Two years for Phase II.

Deadline: Contracts: Early November; Grants: April 5, September 5 and January 5.

PUBLICATIONS:
Omnibus solicitation for SBIR grant applications.

ADDRESS INQUIRIES TO:
Kathy Jung, SBIR Coordinator
Division of Metabolism and Health Effect
(See address above.)

NATIONAL INSTITUTES OF HEALTH [1418]

Division of International Services
31 Center Drive, B2BO7
MSC-2028
Bethesda, MD 20892-2028
(301) 496-6166
Fax: (301) 496-0847
E-mail: dis@mail.nih.gov
Web Site: www.training.nih.gov
www.ors.od.nih.gov

FOUNDED: 1950

AREAS OF INTEREST:
Biomedical and behavioral sciences.

NAME(S) OF PROGRAMS:

- **The NIH Visiting Program**

TYPE:
Exchange programs; Fellowships.

YEAR PROGRAM STARTED: 1950

PURPOSE:
To provide talented scientists throughout the world an opportunity to participate in the varied research activities of the National Institutes of Health. Two categories of Visiting Program participants include Visiting Fellows for obtaining research training experience and Visiting Scientists for conducting health-related research.

LEGAL BASIS:
Government agency.

ELIGIBILITY:
Visiting Fellows must have a doctoral degree or its equivalent and not more than five years of relevant postdoctoral research experience when the fellowship begins. Visiting Fellows may be resident or nonresident aliens. U.S. citizens are not eligible for the Visiting Fellow award.

Visiting Scientists must have a doctoral degree or its equivalent and more than three years of postdoctoral research experience.

All Visiting Program participants must be proficient in the use and understanding of the English language, both written and spoken.

FINANCIAL DATA:
Visiting Fellows receive a monthly stipend during the award period to cover living expenses. The stipend level is determined by the number of years of relevant postdoctoral research experience. Visiting Scientists receive a salary based on the candidate's qualifications and several of the benefits available to employees of the U.S. Government.

Amount of support per award: Visiting Fellows: $41,200 to $78,700. Visiting Scientists start at $45,461. Funding may be increased annually by $1,500 to $2,000 per year.

NO. AWARDS: 1,700.

APPLICATION INFO:
Individuals interested in a Visiting Program fellowship award or appointment should visit the NIH web site for application information.

Duration: Generally, two years. Renewable for a total of five years, based upon merit and depending on visa restrictions.

Deadline: Applications are accepted on a rolling basis.

PUBLICATIONS:
Program description.

ADDRESS INQUIRIES TO:
Candelario Zapata, Director
(See address above.)

NATIONAL INSTITUTES OF HEALTH

Division of International Relations
Fogarty International Center
Building 31, Room B2C39
31 Center Drive, MSC 2220
Bethesda, MD 20892-2220
(301) 496-4784
E-mail: tina.chung@nih.gov
mili.ferreira@nih.gov
Web Site: www.fic.nih.gov/programs/pages/japan-fellowships.aspx

TYPE:
Fellowships. A limited number of postdoctoral research fellowships are provided by the Japan Science and Technology Agency (JSTA) to U.S. scientists to conduct research in Japan. Types of activity supported include collaboration in basic or clinical research and familiarization with or utilization of special techniques and equipment not otherwise available to the applicant.

See entry 945 for full listing.

LUCILE PACKARD FOUNDATION FOR CHILDREN'S HEALTH

400 Hamilton Avenue, Suite 340
Palo Alto, CA 94301
(650) 736-0675
(650) 497-8365
Fax: (650) 498-2619
E-mail: grants@lpfch.org
Web Site: www.lpfch-cshcn.org

TYPE:
Project/program grants.

See entry 1116 for full listing.

THE PATRON SAINTS FOUNDATION [1419]

260 South Los Robles Avenue, No. 201
Pasadena, CA 91101
(626) 564-0444
Fax: (626) 564-0444
E-mail: patronsaintsfdn@sbcglobal.net
Web Site: www.patronsaintsfoundation.org

FOUNDED: 1986

AREAS OF INTEREST:
Health care.

TYPE:
Capital grants; Project/program grants; Research grants. Limited operating support will be awarded at the discretion of the Board of Directors.

YEAR PROGRAM STARTED: 1986

PURPOSE:
To improve the health of individuals residing in the West San Gabriel Valley through health care programs that are consistent with the moral and religious teachings of the Roman Catholic Church.

LEGAL BASIS:
Private foundation.

ELIGIBILITY:
Organizations must be IRS 501(c)(3) tax-exempt.

GEOG. RESTRICTIONS: West San Gabriel Valley, California.

FINANCIAL DATA:
Amount of support per award: $5,000 to $15,000.

Total amount of support: $470,130 for fiscal year ended June 30, 2014.

NO. MOST RECENT APPLICANTS: 37.

NO. AWARDS: 30 for fiscal year ended June 30, 2014.

APPLICATION INFO:
Two copies of the application (not to exceed three pages, no less than 11-point type, one stapled and one paper-clipped) must be mailed to the Foundation, along with other required documents including financial statements, copy of the organization's 501(c)(3) determination letter and IRS Form 990.

Duration: One year. Renewal by reapplication.

Deadline: First Friday in March and first Friday in October.

PUBLICATIONS:
Grant guidelines; grant application form; brochure.

IRS I.D.: 95-3484257

EXECUTIVE DIRECTOR:
Kathleen T. Shannon

ADDRESS INQUIRIES TO:
Kathleen T. Shannon, Executive Director
(See address above.)

PIEDMONT HEALTH FOUNDATION [1420]

P.O. Box 9303
Greenville, SC 29604
(864) 370-0212
Fax: (864) 370-0212
E-mail: katysmith@piedmonthealthfoundation.org
Web Site: www.piedmonthealthfoundation.org

FOUNDED: 1985

AREAS OF INTEREST:
Health.

TYPE:
Demonstration grants; Project/program grants; Research grants; Seed money grants.

YEAR PROGRAM STARTED: 1986

PURPOSE:
To improve health in Greenville County, SC.

LEGAL BASIS:
Private foundation.

ELIGIBILITY:
Organizations must be nonprofit 501(c)(3). No grants to individuals.

GEOG. RESTRICTIONS: Greenville, South Carolina.

FINANCIAL DATA:
Amount of support per award: Grants typically $2,000 to $15,000.

Total amount of support: Approximately $100,000 for the year 2015.

NO. AWARDS: 5 for the year 2015.

REPRESENTATIVE AWARDS:
$11,500 to Greenville Free Medical Clinic; $7,000 to Triune Mercy Center; $4,000 to United Ministries.

APPLICATION INFO:
Application information is available on the web site.

Duration: One year.

Deadline: February 10, April 10, July 10 and October 10.

OFFICERS:
Addy Matney, Chairman
Peggy Baxter, Vice Chairman
Frances Patterson, Treasurer
Bob Coleman, P.E., Secretary

ADDRESS INQUIRIES TO:
Katy Pugh Smith, Executive Director
(See address above.)

THE DOROTHY RIDER POOL HEALTH CARE TRUST [1421]

645 West Hamilton Street
Suite 202
Allentown, PA 18101
(610) 770-9346
Fax: (610) 770-9361
E-mail: info@pooltrust.org
Web Site: www.pooltrust.org

FOUNDED: 1975

AREAS OF INTEREST:
Community health, health services research, leadership development and medical education, recruitment and retention of outstanding health care providers, access to care, health studies, and clinical innovation.

TYPE:
Awards/prizes; Challenge/matching grants; Development grants; Endowments; Fellowships; Project/program grants. Grants addressing at least one of the key components of the Trust's Philanthropic Agenda: improved health status of the citizens of the region, recruitment and retention of outstanding health care providers, clinical innovation, access to care, medical education, community health and health service research.

PURPOSE:
To serve as a resource that enables Lehigh Valley Hospital to be a superior regional hospital and improve the health of the citizens of the region it serves.

ELIGIBILITY:
The Trust considers proposals from nonprofit organizations and institutions within the Trust's interest areas.

GEOG. RESTRICTIONS: Allentown, Pennsylvania and surrounding area.

FINANCIAL DATA:
Amount of support per award: Varies.

Total amount of support: $5,939,022 for the year 2015.

REPRESENTATIVE AWARDS:
$600,000 to Lehigh Valley Health Network for Youth Engagement Program (Building 21, Allentown School District); $200,000 to Lehigh Valley Health Network for Street Medicine; $150,000 for Community Development Collaborative and Community Based Action Learning Initiative (Collective Impact Fellowship 2015-16).

APPLICATION INFO:
Funding requests should be initiated with a letter of intent from the applicant. The letter should be two to four pages summarizing the need, objective, strategy, evaluation, budget and duration.

Electronic application process is available on the web site.

Duration: Varies.

PUBLICATIONS:
Annual report.

IRS I.D.: 23-6627932

TRUSTEES:
Denise M. Gargan
John P. Jones, III
Peter M. Leibold, Esq.
Mary D. Naylor, Ph.D., R.N.
James O. Wolliscroft, M.D.

STAFF:
Edward F. Meehan, M.P.H., Executive Director
Ronald C. Dendas, M.S., Program Officer
Joseph J. Napolitano, Ph.D., M.P.H., Program Officer
Bridget I. Rassler, Manager, Finance and Administration
Regina M. Marks, Program Secretary
Brenda C. Schoenberger, Secretary

ADDRESS INQUIRIES TO:
Edward F. Meehan, M.P.H., Executive Director
(See address above.)

QUANTUM FOUNDATION [1422]

2701 North Australian Avenue, Suite 200
West Palm Beach, FL 33407
(561) 832-7497
Fax: (561) 832-5794
E-mail: randy@quantumfnd.org
Web Site: www.quantumfnd.org

FOUNDED: 1995

AREAS OF INTEREST:
Health access, health education, health workforce, and basic needs to support health.

TYPE:
Capital grants; Challenge/matching grants; Demonstration grants; Matching gifts; Project/program grants; Seed money grants.

YEAR PROGRAM STARTED: 1997

PURPOSE:
To inspire and fund bold initiatives that improve the health of our communities.

LEGAL BASIS:
Private foundation.

ELIGIBILITY:
Eligible organizations must be IRS 501(c)(3) tax-exempt and defined as a public charity under Section 509(a)(1), (2) or (3), an accredited school or university, or a unit of government or public agency, typically tax-exempt under Section 107(c)(1) or Section 511(a)(2)(B), providing services in Palm Beach County.

GEOG. RESTRICTIONS: Palm Beach County, Florida.

FINANCIAL DATA:
Amount of support per award: Varies.

Total amount of support: Approximately $7,500,000 annually.

APPLICATION INFO:
Submit a Letter of Inquiry at the Foundation's web site.

Duration: One to three years.

Deadline: Varies.

STAFF:
Randy Scheid, Vice President of Programs
Shannon Hawkins, Senior Program Officer

ADDRESS INQUIRIES TO:
Randy Scheid, Vice President of Programs
(See e-mail address above.)

RESEARCH MANITOBA [1423]

205 - 445 Ellice Avenue
Winnipeg MB R3B 3P5 Canada
(204) 775-1096
Fax: (204) 786-5401
E-mail: info@researchmb.ca
Web Site: researchmanitoba.ca

FOUNDED: 1980

AREAS OF INTEREST:
Basic research in health, natural and social sciences, engineering and the humanities in the province of Manitoba.

CONSULTING OR VOLUNTEER SERVICES:
The Council advises the provincial Minister of Health on matters relating to health research, as the Minister may refer to the Council for its consideration.

TYPE:
Awards/prizes; Fellowships; General operating grants; Project/program grants; Research grants; Travel grants. Establishment grants. Postdoctoral Fellowships are meant to allow recent doctoral degree recipients, with considerable research training and accomplishments, to further their training to allow them to become independent investigators.

Graduate Studentships are offered to qualified graduate students who are undertaking full-time Master's or doctoral programs in the province of Manitoba.

Ph.D. Dissertation Awards are for graduate students in population and health-related social sciences fields.

New Investigator Operating Grants are for investigators who have held an academic appointment at the rank of assistant professor or above (or equivalent) in Manitoba for a period of not more than five years. They are for new investigators only.

Mid-Career Operating Grants are for investigators who are within 10 years post-Associate Professor appointment in North America.

Bridge Funding awards are intended to allow investigators who have recently lost funding, after a sustained period of support from a major agency, to maintain their research program while attempting to regain their funding by reapplication.

Travel grants are for fellowship awards only.

Manitoba Partnership Program is intended to support operating grant applications that are judged to be of high scientific merit through peer review, but are below the funding capacity of CIHR's base budget, to increase their chances of success in their next submission.

YEAR PROGRAM STARTED: 1981

PURPOSE:
To provide support for health-related research in the Province of Manitoba.

LEGAL BASIS:
Established by an Act of the Provincial Legislature and provincially funded.

ELIGIBILITY:
Grants are awarded to individuals in the Province of Manitoba.

GEOG. RESTRICTIONS: Manitoba, Canada.

FINANCIAL DATA:
Amount of support per award: Dissertation Awards: Up to $5,000; Fellowships: $36,750; Manitoba Partnership Program: Up to $65,000 per year; Operating Grants: Varies; Studentships: $17,850.

Total amount of support: Varies.

Matching fund requirements: For Bridge Funding, MMSF Awards, Partnered Chair and Regional Partnership Grants.

APPLICATION INFO:
Applications must be made on the appropriate Research Manitoba forms online.

Duration: Operating Grants: Up to two years.

Deadline: Clinical Fellows, Fellowships and Studentships: February 1. Operating Grants: March 1. Manitoba Partnership Fund: February 28.

PUBLICATIONS:
Annual report; awards guide; EGMS user guide.

STAFF:
Christina Weise, Chief Executive Officer
Liz Ford, Financial and Administrative Officer
Kristen Hooper, Communications Officer
Ted Catalla, Evaluation and Policy Analyst
Shannon Rogalski, Director of Programs
Necole Sommersell, Manager, Funding Programs

BOARD MEMBERS:
Dr. Brian Postl, Chairperson
Dr. Digvir Jayas, Vice-Chairperson
Bob Brennan, Secretary-Treasurer
Dr. Sylvie Albert
Donald J. Boitson
Dr. Jino Distasio
Hugh Eliasson
Hugh Fearon
Karen Herd
Rick Jensen
Chris Johnson
Dr. John Langstaff
Dr. Susan McClement
Dr. Peter Nickerson
Cathy Nieroda
Dr. Laura Saward
Dr. Barbara Triggs-Raine
Arlene Wilgosh

ADDRESS INQUIRIES TO:
See e-mail address above.

JOSEPHINE G. RUSSELL TRUST [1424]

9 Bartlet Street, Suite 343
Andover, MA 01810
E-mail: russelltrust@yahoo.com

FOUNDED: 1933

AREAS OF INTEREST:
Education, health care, poverty and social services.

TYPE:
General operating grants; Project/program grants; Scholarships.

PURPOSE:
To provide care, healing and nursing of the sick and injured; to provide relief and aid to the poor; to provide training and education of the young; to assist in any other manner of social service in the City of Lawrence.

LEGAL BASIS:
Private charitable trust.

ELIGIBILITY:
Eligible organizations must be IRS 501(c)(3) tax-exempt and serve the Lawrence area. No grants to individuals. No grants are made for endowments, equipment, capital campaigns, construction or renovations of buildings and facilities. No matching gifts.

Organizations intending to submit applications for funds must be able to demonstrate that, if funds are awarded by the Trust, the program will confer a direct benefit to Lawrence residents who are sick, injured or poor; or for education or in any other manner of social services upon the people of the city of Lawrence, MA.

GEOG. RESTRICTIONS: Lawrence, Massachusetts.

FINANCIAL DATA:
Amount of support per award: Minimum $2,000.

Total amount of support: $447,000 for the year 2015.

NO. MOST RECENT APPLICANTS: 45.

NO. AWARDS: 39.

APPLICATION INFO:
Applicants may submit a written proposal and must include a copy of the IRS tax determination letter, budget and list of trustees in the organization.

Once application is completed, individual copies must be sent to all designated trustees.

Contact the Trust for complete guidelines.

Duration: One year. Renewal possible.

Deadline: January 31.

PUBLICATIONS:
Guidelines.

STAFF:
Marsha E. Rich, Managing Trustee

ADDRESS INQUIRIES TO:
See e-mail address above.

EUNICE KENNEDY SHRIVER NATIONAL INSTITUTE OF CHILD HEALTH AND HUMAN DEVELOPMENT [1425]

Division of Extramural Research (DER)
6710B Rockledge Drive
Room 2314, MSC 7002
Bethesda, MD 20817
(800) 370-2943
Fax: (866) 760-5947
E-mail: NICHDInformationResourceCenter@mail.nih.gov
Web Site: www.nichd.nih.gov/about/org/der/branches/Pages/index.aspx

FOUNDED: 1963

AREAS OF INTEREST:
All health sciences pertaining to mothers and children.

NAME(S) OF PROGRAMS:
- **Child Development and Behavior Branch (CDBB)**
- **Contraception Research Branch (CRB)**
- **Developmental Biology and Structural Variation Branch (DBSVB)**
- **Fertility and Infertility (FI) Branch**
- **Gynecologic Health and Disease Branch (GHDB)**
- **Intellectual and Developmental Disabilities Branch (IDDB)**
- **Maternal and Pediatric Infectious Disease Branch (MPIDB)**
- **Obstetric and Pediatric Pharmacology and Therapeutics Branch (OPPTB)**
- **Pediatric Growth and Nutrition Branch (PGNB)**
- **Pediatric Trauma and Critical Illness Branch (PTCIB)**
- **Population Dynamics Branch (PDB)**
- **Pregnancy and Perinatology Branch (PPB)**

TYPE:
Conferences/seminars; Development grants; Fellowships; General operating grants; Project/program grants; Training grants; Research contracts. Project grants and research contracts to expand the health and well-being of individuals from the moment of conception and extending through the later teenage years.

PURPOSE:
To discover new knowledge through research.

LEGAL BASIS:
Public Health Service Act, Sections 301(c), 444 and 472.

ELIGIBILITY:
Universities, colleges, medical, dental and nursing schools, schools of public health, laboratories, hospitals, state and local health departments, other public or private nonprofit institutions and commercial organizations are eligible. Individuals may apply for grants for academic and research training. They must have a professional or scientific degree and be citizens or permanent residents of the U.S.

FINANCIAL DATA:
Amount of support per award: Varies.

APPLICATION INFO:
Contact the Institute.

Duration: One year to multiyear funding.

ADDRESS INQUIRIES TO:
See e-mail address above.

SICKKIDS FOUNDATION [1426]

525 University Avenue, 14th Floor
Toronto ON M5G 2L3 Canada
(416) 813-6166 ext. 2354
(800) 661-1083
Fax: (416) 813-4912
E-mail: national.grants@sickkidsfoundation.com
Web Site: www.sickkidsfoundation.com/about-us/grants

FOUNDED: 1973

AREAS OF INTEREST:
Healthier children; a better world.

NAME(S) OF PROGRAMS:
- **Community Conference Grants Program**
- **New Investigator Research Grants**

TYPE:
Awards/prizes; Conferences/seminars; Project/program grants; Research grants. Community Conference Grants program brings together families with researchers and clinicians for medical presentations and family-oriented discussions. It helps ensure knowledge exchange with families so that they are able to access the most up-to-date information about their children's health.

New Investigator Research Grants program focus is to ensure that there continues to be well-trained researchers across the country working to address the most pressing childhood diseases and conditions.

YEAR PROGRAM STARTED: 1974

PURPOSE:
To promote quality programs in child health, research and public health education in the field.

LEGAL BASIS:
Public foundation with charitable registration.

ELIGIBILITY:
Grants are paid to recognized Canadian charitable organizations. Institutions, agencies and other groups working in the field of child health in Canada may apply. Applications are subjected to peer assessment as to the merits of the project, feasibility, and significance for child health and study design criteria as appropriate.

GEOG. RESTRICTIONS: Canada.

FINANCIAL DATA:
Amount of support per award: $5,000 to $100,000 per year.

Total amount of support: Varies.

NO. MOST RECENT APPLICANTS: 100 for the year 2011-12.

NO. AWARDS: 15 for the year 2011-12.

APPLICATION INFO:
Application guidelines are available online. To discuss eligibility, contact grants office directly.

Duration: Maximum of three years with annual review of progress. No renewals.

Deadline: Community Conference Grants: January 31, May 31 and September 30. New Investigator Research Grant: Mid-January.

ADDRESS INQUIRIES TO:
See e-mail address above.

SISTERS OF ST. JOSEPH HEALTHCARE FOUNDATION [1427]

440 South Batavia
Orange, CA 92868-3998
(714) 633-8121 ext. 7109
Fax: (714) 744-3135
E-mail: rfox@csjorange.org
Web Site: www.csjorange.org

FOUNDED: 1992

AREAS OF INTEREST:
Health care and health access.

TYPE:
General operating grants; Project/program grants. The Foundation sponsors or supports long-term efforts which are closely identified with the Sisters of St. Joseph of Orange and their mission of bringing unity and healing where divisiveness and oppression exist.

PURPOSE:
To fund programs which directly serve the needs of the underserved, especially families and children at risk.

LEGAL BASIS:
Public foundation.

ELIGIBILITY:
Applicants must be nonprofit organizations operating in Humbolt County, southern California and San Francisco Bay area which have programs that directly serve the needs of the underserved, especially families and children at risk, as well as programs of education and advocacy which are directed at improving health and access to health care. Religious organizations also receive support. A Sister of St. Joseph of Orange endorsement or Vice President for Mission Integration endorsement and/or involvement is required. Capital projects will not be considered.

The Foundation supports the concept of Healthy Communities, and desires to fund programs and organizations that:
(1) provide direct health-related services;
(2) support and transform the individual, social, economic, institutional, and cultural aspects of communities;
(3) provide change within larger societal systems to benefit low-income and at-risk populations and;
(4) develop the leadership and capacity for self-determination of those served by the Foundation's funding.

GEOG. RESTRICTIONS: Southern California, Humbolt County and San Francisco Bay area.

NO. MOST RECENT APPLICANTS: 106.

APPLICATION INFO:
Contact the Foundation.

Duration: One year.

Deadline: Contact Foundation for exact dates.

ADDRESS INQUIRIES TO:
Sister Regina Fox, S.S.N.D.
Program Director
(See address above.)

GERTRUDE E. SKELLY CHARITABLE FOUNDATION

4600 North Ocean Boulevard
Suite 206
Boynton Beach, FL 33435
(561) 276-1008
Fax: (561) 272-2793
E-mail: skelly@hhk.com

TYPE:
Challenge/matching grants; Conferences/seminars; Internships; Project/program grants; Research grants; Scholarships; Training grants. Emergency grants for continued education.

See entry 1586 for full listing.

THE CHRISTOPHER D. SMITHERS FOUNDATION, INC. [1428]

P.O. Box 67
Mill Neck, NY 11765
(516) 676-0067
Fax: (516) 676-0323
E-mail: info@smithersfoundation.org
Web Site: www.smithersfoundation.org

FOUNDED: 1952

AREAS OF INTEREST:
Education and prevention of alcoholism.

TYPE:
Conferences/seminars; Project/program grants; Research grants; Technical assistance; Training grants.

YEAR PROGRAM STARTED: 1952

PURPOSE:
To prevent alcoholism through education.

APPLICATION INFO:
Grant proposal must include:
(1) brief description of the program and grant amount requested (budget);
(2) copy of 501(c)(3) nonprofit status and;
(3) copy of most recent annual report.

PUBLICATIONS:
Annual report.

OFFICERS:
Adele C. Smithers, President
Christopher B. Smithers, Vice President
Richard Esposito, Vice President/Treasurer
Nikki Smithers, Secretary

DIRECTORS:
Stacia Murphy
Nicholas A. Pace, M.D.
M. Elizabeth Brothers, Honorary Director

ARTEMAS W. STEARNS TRUST [1429]

9 Bartlet Street, Suite 343
Andover, MA 01810
E-mail: stearnstrust@yahoo.com

FOUNDED: 1896

AREAS OF INTEREST:
The aged and poor, health care in the Lawrence area, social services and education.

TYPE:
General operating grants; Project/program grants; Scholarships. Elder and infirm support.

YEAR PROGRAM STARTED: 1896

PURPOSE:
To pay income to such nonprofit and charitable homes, nursing homes, convalescent homes, retirement homes, sanitaria, homes for the aged, hospitals, agencies and such other similar institutions, organizations and agencies as may provide for or care, in whole or in part, for the indigent aged people of both sexes; to provide relief of the deserving poor of the City of Lawrence, without distinction of nationality or religious belief.

LEGAL BASIS:
Private charitable trust.

ELIGIBILITY:
Eligible organizations must be IRS 501(c)(3) tax-exempt. No grants to individuals. No grants are made for endowments, equipment, capital campaigns, construction or renovations of buildings and facilities.

Organizations intending to submit applications for funds must be able to demonstrate that, if funds are awarded by the Trust, the program will confer a direct benefit upon the indigent aged people or to the deserving poor of the city of Lawrence, MA exclusively.

GEOG. RESTRICTIONS: Lawrence, Massachusetts.

FINANCIAL DATA:
Amount of support per award: Minimum $1,000.
Total amount of support: $187,000 for the year 2013.

NO. MOST RECENT APPLICANTS: 33.

NO. AWARDS: 28.

APPLICATION INFO:
Guidelines are sent upon request. Applicants may submit a written proposal and must include a copy of the IRS tax determination letter, budget and list of trustees in the organization.

Once application is completed, individual copies must be sent to all designated trustees. Contact the Trust for complete guidelines.

Duration: One year. Renewal possible.

Deadline: January 31.

PUBLICATIONS:
Application guidelines.

STAFF:
Marsha E. Rich, Managing Trustee

ADDRESS INQUIRIES TO:
See e-mail address above.

U.S. DEPARTMENT OF HEALTH AND HUMAN SERVICES [1430]

Health Resources and Services Administration
Bureau of Primary Health Care
Parklawn Building, 5600 Fishers Lane
Room 1874
Rockville, MD 20857
(301) 594-4300
(301) 594-4110
Fax: (301) 594-4997
Web Site: www.hrsa.gov
www.bphc.hrsa.gov

FOUNDED: 1976

AREAS OF INTEREST:
Assisting communities located in medically underserved areas to develop needed primary health care services.

CONSULTING OR VOLUNTEER SERVICES:
Information and technical assistance is available from U.S. Public Health Service Regional Office staff.

NAME(S) OF PROGRAMS:
- **The Health Center Program**

TYPE:
Project/program grants. Grants may be made for planning and development of a community health center and for operations.

YEAR PROGRAM STARTED: 1975

PURPOSE:
To provide primary health care in ambulatory care settings located in severely medically underserved areas and to develop a network of services involving as many other health programs and facilities operating in the area as possible; to arrange for other federal programs not operating in the area to establish services within the federally funded primary care center whenever possible.

LEGAL BASIS:
Government agency.

ELIGIBILITY:
Grants may be made to public or private not-for-profit entities. Area to be served must be medically underserved. Priority will be given to areas of highest need.

GEOG. RESTRICTIONS: United States.

FINANCIAL DATA:
Amount of support per award: Approximately $650,000.
Matching fund requirements: The applicant must assume part of the project costs determined on a case-by-case basis.

CO-OP FUNDING PROGRAMS: Funding along with other federal programs, such as Migrant Health Centers, National Health Service Corps, MCH, or Mental Health Alcohol and Drug Abuse is encouraged, as well as cooperation with state and local programs.

APPLICATION INFO:
Information available from HRSA Grant Application Center, 901 Russell Avenue, Suite 450, Gaithersburg, MD 20879, or call (877) 477-2123.

Duration: Project periods may be up to three years, with annual budget periods.

PUBLICATIONS:
Application guidelines.

STAFF:
Jim Macrae, Associate Administrator to Bureau of Primary Health Care Director

U.S. DEPARTMENT OF HEALTH AND HUMAN SERVICES [1431]

Centers for Medicare and Medicaid Services
7500 Security Boulevard
Baltimore, MD 21244-1850
(410) 786-3000
(877) 267-2323
Fax: (410) 786-1008
Web Site: www.cms.gov

FOUNDED: 1967

NAME(S) OF PROGRAMS:
- **Medicaid**

TYPE:
Formula grants. Financial assistance to states for in- and outpatient hospital services, other laboratory services, home health care, family planning, physicians' services and early diagnosis and treatment for persons who are medically needy.

LEGAL BASIS:
Title XIX, Social Security Act as amended; Public Law 89-97; Public Law 90-248; Public Law 91-56; 42 U.S.C. 1396, et seq. Public Law 92-223; Public Law 92-603.

ELIGIBILITY:
State and local welfare agencies operating under an approved Medicaid plan are eligible for support.

GEOG. RESTRICTIONS: United States.

FINANCIAL DATA:
Amount of support per award: Varies.
Total amount of support: Varies.

APPLICATION INFO:
Application forms are available from the address above or from regional or local offices of the Medical Services Administration to whom applications should be submitted.

Duration: Quarterly.

Deadline: States must submit quarterly estimates of funds no later than May 15, August 15, November 15 and February 15 in order to receive quarterly grant awards.

UNITED HOSPITAL FUND OF NEW YORK [1432]

1411 Broadway, 12th Floor
New York, NY 10018
(212) 494-0761
Fax: (212) 494-0801
E-mail: hholmes@uhfnyc.org
Web Site: www.uhfnyc.org

FOUNDED: 1879

AREAS OF INTEREST:
Expanding health insurance coverage, improving quality of care, and redesigning health care services.

NAME(S) OF PROGRAMS:

- **Health Care Improvement Grant Program**

TYPE:
Project/program grants; Seed money grants.

YEAR PROGRAM STARTED: 1938

PURPOSE:
To provide support to innovative projects by nonprofit hospitals and health care and other organizations to improve the quality of health care for all New Yorkers.

LEGAL BASIS:
Public charity.

ELIGIBILITY:
Nonprofit 501(c)(3) tax-exempt organizations in or to the benefit of New York City are eligible for support. No grants to individuals, capital or endowment campaigns or general operating grants.

GEOG. RESTRICTIONS: Primarily New York, New York, including the five boroughs.

FINANCIAL DATA:
Amount of support per award: $50,000 to $125,000.

Total amount of support: Approximately $1,000,000 for the year 2014-15.

NO. MOST RECENT APPLICANTS: 60.

NO. AWARDS: 15 for the year 2014.

REPRESENTATIVE AWARDS:
$75,000 to Community Service Society of New York; $75,000 to Young Invincibles; $125,000 to Greater New York Hospital Association; $40,000 (over 15 months) to New York-Presbyterian Morgan Stanley Children's Hospital; $65,000 to Memorial Sloan Kettering Cancer Center/Immigrant Health and Cancer Disparities Service.

APPLICATION INFO:
Applicants must submit Letter of Intent prior to submitting proposal. Proposals are accepted by invitation only.

Duration: One to two years. Nonrenewable.

Deadline: Letters of Inquiry: July 15 and October 15.

PUBLICATIONS:
Annual report; application guidelines.

OFFICERS:
J. Barclay Collins, II, Chairman
James R. Tallon, Jr., President
Sheila M. Abrams, Senior Vice President and Treasurer
Andrea G. Cohen, Senior Vice President
Sally J. Rogers, Senior Vice President
Patricia S. Levinson, Vice Chairman
John C. Simmons, Vice Chairman
Frederick W. Telling, Ph.D., Vice Chairman
Anne-Marie J. Audet, M.D., M.Sc., Vice President
Deborah E. Halper, Vice President
Amanda A. Williams, Corporate Secretary

BOARD OF DIRECTORS:
Michelle A. Adams
Stephen Berger
Lori Evans Bernstein
Jo Ivey Boufford, M.D.
Rev. John E. Carrington
Derrick D. Cephas
Dale C. Christensen, Jr.
J. Barclay Collins, II
Michael R. Golding, M.D.
Cary Kravet
Josh N. Kuriloff
Patricia S. Levinson
David Levy, M.D.
Howard P. Milstein
Susana R. Morales, M.D.
Robert C. Osborne
Peter J. Powers
John C. Simons
Michael A. Stocker, M.D.
James R. Tallon, Jr.
Frederick W. Telling, Ph.D.
Mary Beth C. Tully

ADDRESS INQUIRIES TO:
Hollis Holmes, Grants Manager
(See address above.)

US COMMUNITY PARTNERSHIPS [1433]

GSK
5 Moore Drive
Research Triangle Park, NC 27709
E-mail: us.communitypartnerships@gsk.com
Web Site: us.gsk.com

AREAS OF INTEREST:
Education, health and human services, arts and culture, and civic and community.

TYPE:
Project/program grants.

PURPOSE:
To support innovative health and education programs that foster healthy communities across the U.S.

LEGAL BASIS:
Corporate foundation.

ELIGIBILITY:
Applicants must be nonprofit organizations with proposals consistent with guidelines and interest areas. No grants for capital projects, operating expenses, conferences, symposia, publications, fund-raising events, lobbying to influence legislation, religious organizations, sporting events, universities, free-standing research centers, scholar aid, expeditions or individuals.

GEOG. RESTRICTIONS: United States.

FINANCIAL DATA:
Amount of support per award: Varies depending on needs and nature of the request.

APPLICATION INFO:
Applicants must first register on the U.S. Community Partnerships Charitable Grant Request System. Once registration is approved (approximately 10 days), organization may be required to submit additional information including:
(1) copy of 501(c)(3) or 501(c)(1), if a public school, IRS letter of determination;
(2) member list for the Board of Directors;
(3) program literature;
(4) program evaluation (if an ongoing program for three or more years);
(5) most recent audited financials and;
(6) additional information as required per Impact Awards or Impact Grants programs.

Duration: Typically one year.

Deadline: Applications accepted throughout the year.

THE WHITEHORSE FOUNDATION [1434]

IBM Building
1200 Fifth Avenue, Suite 1300
Seattle, WA 98101-3151
(206) 515-2131
(206) 622-2294
Fax: (206) 622-7673
E-mail: c.erickson@seattlefoundation.org
Web Site: www.seattlefoundation.org

FOUNDED: 1990

AREAS OF INTEREST:
Preventative human services to improve the lives of children, youth and families.

TYPE:
Capital grants; Development grants; Project/program grants; Training grants. Program development.

YEAR PROGRAM STARTED: 1990

PURPOSE:
To fund comprehensive preventive social service programs in Snohomish County, WA.

LEGAL BASIS:
Community foundation.

ELIGIBILITY:
Applicant organizations must be IRS 501(c)(3) tax-exempt. No grants to individuals.

GEOG. RESTRICTIONS: Snohomish County, Washington.

FINANCIAL DATA:
Amount of support per award: Varies.

NO. MOST RECENT APPLICANTS: 10.

NO. AWARDS: 5.

APPLICATION INFO:
Applications guidelines are available on the web site.

Duration: Up to several years.

STAFF:
Ceil Erickson, Program Director

ADDRESS INQUIRIES TO:
Ceil Erickson, Program Director
(See address above.)

MR. AND MRS. P.A. WOODWARD'S FOUNDATION [1435]

1055 West Hastings Street, Suite 300
Vancouver BC V6E 2E9 Canada
(604) 682-8116
E-mail: pawoodwardfoundation@gmail.com
Web Site: www.woodwardfoundation.ca

FOUNDED: 1951

AREAS OF INTEREST:
Health care.

TYPE:
The Foundation supports those projects which affect the people of the Province of British Columbia where there is clear indication of the health benefit anticipated. The Foundation is charged with aiding in the purchase of the latest medical equipment of proven performance that provides direct benefit to the patient. A preference was expressed to fund items with direct patient benefit, as contrasted to that done in the laboratory with uncertain or delayed benefits.

PURPOSE:
To assist in projects which could contribute to better health care.

LEGAL BASIS:
Charitable foundation.

ELIGIBILITY:
Organizations applying for funding must be domiciled within the Province of British Columbia. All individuals and organizations applying must be in possession of a Charitable Gift Registration Number as issued by the Department of National Revenue of Canada.

The Foundation will consider applications in the following general areas:
(1) health care equipment of proven effectiveness and;
(2) special projects which will benefit the health of British Columbians.

The Foundation will not support routine operational budgets, fundamental research not directly related to patient care, conferences or annual meetings, endowments or capital building costs.

GEOG. RESTRICTIONS: British Columbia, Canada.

FINANCIAL DATA:
Amount of support per award: Grants vary in amount, depending upon the needs and nature of the request.

NO. AWARDS: Up to 30.

APPLICATION INFO:
Applications will be received by invitation only. Organizations must e-mail a Letter of Intent indicating what they would like to apply for. Organizations may then be invited to submit a full application.

Deadline: Beginning of February for March Board meeting; beginning of May for June Board meeting; Middle of September for October Board meeting. Actual dates are posted on the Foundation web site.

OFFICERS:
Christopher C. Woodward, President
Jill Leversage, Treasurer
Leo P. Sauve, Secretary
Mark Cullen

MEMBERS AND DIRECTORS:
E. Wallace Campbell
Mark Cullen
Jill Leversage
Gregory J.D. McKinstry
Hon. Madam Justice Mary V. Newbury
David Ostrow
Leo P. Sauve
Christopher C. Woodward

ADDRESS INQUIRIES TO:
Dr. J. Wm. Ibbott, Medical Advisor
(See address above.)

Social welfare

THE ABELARD FOUNDATION-EAST [1436]

P.O. Box 148
Lincoln, MA 01773
E-mail: eastabel@aol.com
Web Site: foundationcenter.org/grantmaker/abelardeast/

AREAS OF INTEREST:
Progressive social change, community organizing, civil and human rights.

TYPE:
General operating grants; Project/program grants.

PURPOSE:
To support local progressive social change activities that expand and protect civil liberties and civil and human rights, and promote and strengthen community involvement in, and control over, the decisions that affect their lives.

ELIGIBILITY:
Applicants must represent or be associated with a nonprofit, 501(c)(3) tax-exempt organization. Priority is given to projects that are in their first years of development and have budgets less than $300,000.

GEOG. RESTRICTIONS: Eastern United States, east of the Mississippi River.

FINANCIAL DATA:
Amount of support per award: Average $10,000.

Total amount of support: Approximately $140,000 annually.

APPLICATION INFO:
Applicants should submit one copy of a proposal (no more than seven to 10 pages) which includes:
(1) background of the organization;
(2) description of the work for which funds are being sought;
(3) explanation of need and;
(4) impact the project will have.

Proposals prepared in a "common application" format will also be accepted.

Applying organizations must include IRS 501(c)(3) determination letter.

Duration: One year. Up to two renewals possible.

Deadline: Applications mailed by March 15 will be reviewed for the spring meeting, and applications mailed by September 15 will be reviewed for the fall meeting.

ADDRESS INQUIRIES TO:
Susan Collins, Trustee
The Abelard Foundation-East
(See address above.)

EMMA J. ADAMS MEMORIAL FUND, INC. [1437]

328 Eldert Lane
Brooklyn, NY 11208
(347) 789-6717
Fax: (347) 789-6717

FOUNDED: 1933

AREAS OF INTEREST:
Geriatric institutions, welfare, elderly, and needy, mostly through organizations.

TYPE:
Grants-in-aid. Financial support and organized aid to geriatric, needy and/or elderly institutional agencies and occasionally to referred respectable, aged indigent persons in financial difficulty through no fault of their own, in the greater New York City area.

YEAR PROGRAM STARTED: 1936

PURPOSE:
To aid elderly, needy and indigent people and geriatric institutions.

LEGAL BASIS:
Nonprofit corporation.

ELIGIBILITY:
Most grants are awarded to operating geriatric institutions.

No scholarships, program grants, administrative expenses, and no brick-and-mortar grants.

GEOG. RESTRICTIONS: Greater New York area.

FINANCIAL DATA:
Amount of support per award: $450 average.

Total amount of support: Average $60,000 per year.

NO. MOST RECENT APPLICANTS: Over 200.

NO. AWARDS: Approximately 15.

APPLICATION INFO:
Application forms available upon request. The letter must indicate the referral source. No telephone requests honored.

Duration: Varies.

Deadline: September 1.

IRS I.D.: 13-6116503

DIRECTORS:
Jill Arkwright
Rev. Bruce Forbes
Rev. Elizabeth Jacks
Betsy Rowe
Sally Saran
Carolyn Swayze

ADDRESS INQUIRIES TO:
Sally Saran, President
(See address above.)

JUDD S. ALEXANDER FOUNDATION [1438]

500 First Street, Suite 10
Wausau, WI 54403
(715) 845-4556
Fax: (715) 843-9018
E-mail: office@alexanderprop.org
Web Site: juddsalexanderfoundation.org

FOUNDED: 1978

AREAS OF INTEREST:
Education, recreation, human services, children's services and economic development.

TYPE:
Capital grants; Challenge/matching grants; Project/program grants; Seed money grants. Support is provided for capital building and emergency funds.

YEAR PROGRAM STARTED: 1978

LEGAL BASIS:
Private foundation.

ELIGIBILITY:
Organizations classified as 501(c)(3) by the IRS can apply. The Foundation does not make grants to individuals or private businesses.

GEOG. RESTRICTIONS: Marathon County, Wisconsin.

FINANCIAL DATA:
Amount of support per award: Varies.
Total amount of support: Varies.

APPLICATION INFO:
Five copies, unbound, of the proposal should be submitted. Proposal material should not be placed in protective covers or other presentation formats. Videos and other supplementary materials are not encouraged and will not be returned to applicants. A fully reviewable proposal will include:
(1) a cover page with the exact name and location of the proposed grant recipient, along with the name, title, address and phone number of an individual at the organization;
(2) a project overview, which includes a description of the organization's main activities and whether it is a public, private or not-for-profit entity, a description of the project or activity for which funding is requested, and specific outcomes and goals and;
(3) a project budget which includes revenue and expense pages and a budget narrative.

The following items must also be attached:
(1) the organization's current annual operating budget, including revenues and expenses;
(2) a list of the organization's governing body and its officers, showing business, professional and/or community affiliations, along with officers' financial contributions to the organization;
(3) letters of support and letters from other agencies indicating their intent to collaborate (as appropriate);
(4) other documents to supplement the above information, provided it is not duplicative of other material or information contained in the narratives or budget presentation;
(5) the most recent audited financial statements and;
(6) the most recent IRS determination letter.

The Foundation does not accept proposals by fax or e-mail.

Duration: Typically one year. Must reapply.

ADDRESS INQUIRIES TO:
Gary W. Freels, President
(See address above.)

THE ALLSTATE FOUNDATION [1439]

2775 Sanders Road
Suite F-4
Northbrook, IL 60062
E-mail: grants@allstate.com
Web Site: www.allstatefoundation.org

FOUNDED: 1952

AREAS OF INTEREST:
Teen safe driving and economic empowerment for domestic abuse survivors.

TYPE:
Matching gifts; Project/program grants. Program support in the Foundation's areas of focus; matching gifts for higher education only.

YEAR PROGRAM STARTED: 1952

PURPOSE:
To assist deserving organizations serving the fields of teen safe drivers and economic empowerment for domestic abuse survivors.

LEGAL BASIS:
Corporate foundation.

ELIGIBILITY:
Grants are made only to nonprofit 501(c)(3) organizations, if invited to apply.

GEOG. RESTRICTIONS: United States.

FINANCIAL DATA:
Amount of support per award: National programs: $100,000; Local/regional grants: $5,000 to $20,000.
Total amount of support: $29,000,000 for the year 2013.
Matching fund requirements: For colleges and universities.

APPLICATION INFO:
Information and guidelines are available online.
Duration: One year. Renewal based on program outcome and results.

PUBLICATIONS:
Guidelines.

IRS I.D.: 36-6116535

ADDRESS INQUIRIES TO:
See e-mail address above.

*PLEASE NOTE:
Unsolicited requests will not be accepted in 2015.

*SPECIAL STIPULATIONS:
Funding for domestic programs only.

THE CALIFORNIA ENDOWMENT

1000 North Alameda Street
Los Angeles, CA 90012
(213) 928-8645
(800) 449-4149
Fax: (213) 928-8818
E-mail: destrada@calendow.org
Web Site: www.calendow.org

TYPE:
Challenge/matching grants; General operating grants; Matching gifts; Project/program grants.

See entry 1387 for full listing.

CAMPBELL FOUNDATION, INC.

705 York Road
Towson, MD 21204
(410) 828-1961
Fax: (410) 821-8814
E-mail: lsperato@stoycpa.com

TYPE:
Capital grants; General operating grants; Project/program grants.

See entry 1091 for full listing.

CATHOLIC CHARITIES USA [1440]

2050 Ballenger Avenue, Suite 400
Alexandria, VA 22314
(703) 549-1390
Fax: (703) 549-1656
E-mail: info@catholiccharitiesusa.org
Web Site: www.catholiccharitiesusa.org

AREAS OF INTEREST:
The aged, community services, homeless, emergency relief and family services.

TYPE:
Assistantships; Project/program grants.

PURPOSE:
To provide service to those in need and to advocate justice in societal structures.

LEGAL BASIS:
Nonprofit organization.

ELIGIBILITY:
Grants are only offered to the 1,700 Catholic Charities member agencies. Any organization which is not affiliated with Catholic Charities is ineligible for support.

GEOG. RESTRICTIONS: United States.

FINANCIAL DATA:
Amount of support per award: Varies depending on project and need of the geographic area being served.
Total amount of support: Varies.

APPLICATION INFO:
Organizations should contact their local or diocesan chapters of Catholic Charities for application information and materials.
Duration: Up to five years.

THE COMMONWEALTH FUND [1441]

One East 75th Street
New York, NY 10021
(212) 606-3800
Fax: (212) 606-3500
E-mail: grants@cmwf.org
Web Site: www.commonwealthfund.org

FOUNDED: 1918

AREAS OF INTEREST:
Supporting independent research on health care issues, and making grants to improve health care practice and policy.

NAME(S) OF PROGRAMS:
- **Breakthrough Health Care Opportunities**
- **Health Care Coverage and Access**
- **Health Care Delivery System Reform**
- **International Health Policy and Practice Innovations**

TYPE:
Project/program grants; Research grants; Research contracts.

YEAR PROGRAM STARTED: 1918

PURPOSE:
To promote a high-performing health care system that achieves better access, improved quality, and greater efficiency, particularly for society's most vulnerable, including low-income people, the uninsured, minority Americans, young children and elderly adults.

The Fund carries out this mandate by supporting independent research on health care issues and making grants to improve health care practice and policy. An international program in health policy is designed to stimulate innovative policies and practices in the U.S. and other industrialized countries.

LEGAL BASIS:
Private foundation.

ELIGIBILITY:
The Fund makes grants only to tax-exempt organizations and public agencies. No grants to individuals.

FINANCIAL DATA:
Amount of support per award: Varies.
Total amount of support: Projected $21,200,000 in grants for fiscal year 2016-17.

NO. MOST RECENT APPLICANTS: 870.

NO. AWARDS: 186.

REPRESENTATIVE AWARDS:
$258,582 to Harvard University to analyze the relationship between quality and efficiency in hospital care; $72,936 to Massachusetts General Hospital to assess the role of pay-for-performance in reducing racial and ethnic inequalities in health care.

APPLICATION INFO:
The Fund requests letters of inquiry to initiate the grant application process. Applicants are encouraged to submit letters of inquiry using the online form. While the Fund will continue to accept letters of inquiry via regular mail and fax, such submissions will take longer to process than those received online. Letters of inquiry are acknowledged when received. Applicants are typically advised of the results of an initial staff review within two months. Program staff will contact applicants if more detailed information is required.

Duration: Typically one year, although some multiyear funding available.

Deadline: Applications may be submitted at any time.

IRS I.D.: 13-1635260

STAFF:
David Blumenthal, M.D., President
Kathleen Regan, Executive Vice President and Chief Operating Officer
Donald Moulds, Executive Vice President for Programs
Eric C. Schneider, M.D., Senior Vice President for Policy and Research
Barry A. Scholl, Senior Vice President for Communications and Publishing
Robin Osborn, Vice President and Director, International Program in Health Policy and Innovation
Andrea Landes, Vice President of Grants Management

BOARD OF DIRECTORS:
Benjamin K. Chu, M.D., Chairman
Cristine Russell, Vice Chairman
Maureen Bisognano
David Blumenthal, M.D.
Sheila P. Burke, R.N.
Michael V. Drake, M.D.
Julio Frenk, M.D.
Kathryn D. Haslanger
Jane E. Henney, M.D.
Robert C. Pozen
Mark D. Smith, M.D.
Simon Stevens
William Y. Yun

ADDRESS INQUIRIES TO:
Andrea Landes
Vice President of Grants Management
(See address above.)

COMMUNITY FOUNDATION OF THE VERDUGOS [1442]

111 East Broadway, Suite 200
Glendale, CA 91205
(818) 241-8040
Fax: (818) 241-8045
E-mail: info@cfverdugos.org
Web Site: www.cfverdugos.org

FOUNDED: 1956

AREAS OF INTEREST:
Arts and culture, children, education, health, homeless services, human services, senior services and environment.

TYPE:
Capital grants; Development grants; Project/program grants; Scholarships.

YEAR PROGRAM STARTED: 1956

PURPOSE:
To meet current and changing needs in the community; to provide grants that create impact on the community.

LEGAL BASIS:
Community foundation.

ELIGIBILITY:
Eligible organizations must be schools or IRS 501(c)(3) tax-exempt.

GEOG. RESTRICTIONS: Burbank, Glendale, La Canada/Flintridge, La Crescenta, Montrose and Verdugo City, California.

FINANCIAL DATA:
Amount of support per award: Varies; $40,000 each grant cycle; $80,000 annually.

Total amount of support: Approximately $400,000 to $500,000 annually.

CO-OP FUNDING PROGRAMS: Through restricted, donor-advised funds within the Foundation.

REPRESENTATIVE AWARDS:
$10,000 to The Salvation Army for ZONE after-school program; $15,000 to Glendale Adventist Medical Center toward cost of Omni Giraffe Bed for NICU; $10,000 to College View School toward cost of playground equipment for developmentally disabled children.

APPLICATION INFO:
Guidelines and application form are available on the Foundation web site.

Duration: One year. Agency can reapply one year after the grant ends.

Deadline: February 1, May 15 and August 1.

PUBLICATIONS:
Annual report; quarterly newsletters.

IRS I.D.: 95-6068137

ADDRESS INQUIRIES TO:
Chief Executive Officer
(See address above.)

CORPORATION FOR NATIONAL AND COMMUNITY SERVICE [1443]

250 E Street, S.W.
Washington, DC 20024
(202) 606-6850
Fax: (202) 606-3475
E-mail: info@cns.gov
Web Site: www.nationalservice.gov
www.seniorcorps.gov

FOUNDED: 1971

AREAS OF INTEREST:
Volunteer service.

NAME(S) OF PROGRAMS:

- **Foster Grandparent Program**
- **Retired and Senior Volunteer Program (RSVP)**
- **Senior Companion Program**

TYPE:
Demonstration grants; General operating grants; Grants-in-aid; Project/program grants; Technical assistance. Grants to provide meaningful opportunities for low-income persons age 55 years and over, specifically providing person-to-person service to children with special needs as Foster Grandparents and providing services to adults with special needs as Senior Companions. The Retired and Senior Volunteer Program helps people 55 and older put their skills and life experience to work in their communities.

PURPOSE:
To provide volunteer service opportunities for older Americans.

LEGAL BASIS:
Federal agency.

ELIGIBILITY:
State and local public agencies, private nonprofit organizations, and tribal entities may apply.

GEOG. RESTRICTIONS: United States and territories.

FINANCIAL DATA:
Amount of support per award: Foster Grandparent Program: $328,000 average. Retired Senior Volunteer Program: $77,000 average. Senior Companion Program: $204,000 average.

Matching fund requirements: 10% for Foster Grandparent Program and Senior Companion Program. For Retired Senior Volunteer Program, 10-20-30%.

CO-OP FUNDING PROGRAMS: Local public and private nonprofit agencies receive grants to sponsor and operate FGP, RSVP and SCP.

APPLICATION INFO:
Contact the Corporation.

Duration: Three years with opportunity to amend annually.

Deadline: Varies.

PUBLICATIONS:
Grant application; guidelines.

IRS I.D.: 53-0260397

CARL M. FREEMAN FOUNDATION

31556 Winterberry Parkway
Selbyville, DE 19975
(302) 436-3015
E-mail: info@freemanfoundation.org
Web Site: www.carlfreemanfoundation.org

TYPE:
Capital grants; Challenge/matching grants; General operating grants.

See entry 438 for full listing.

THE HEALTH FOUNDATION OF GREATER INDIANAPOLIS [1444]

429 East Vermont Street, Suite 400
Indianapolis, IN 46202-3698
(317) 630-1805
Fax: (317) 630-1806
E-mail: bwilson@thfgi.org
Web Site: www.thfgi.org

FOUNDED: 1985

AREAS OF INTEREST:
Childhood obesity, school-based health and HIV/AIDS.

TYPE:
Project/program grants.

PURPOSE:
To serve the community's most vulnerable citizens by funding health-related projects and organizations not easily supported by other means.

ELIGIBILITY:
Applicant must be a 501(c)(3) group, organization or agency that provides health-related programs or services within Marion and the seven contiguous counties. Must also function without discrimination or segregation based on race, gender, age,

religion, national origin, sexual orientation, disability, military or marital status in hiring, termination, assignment and promotion of staff, selection of board members or provisions of services. No grants are made to individuals. Nonsectarian religious programs may apply.

GEOG. RESTRICTIONS: Marion County, Indiana and the seven contiguous counties.

FINANCIAL DATA:

Amount of support per award: Varies.

Total amount of support: Approximately $1,400,000 for the year 2015.

NO. MOST RECENT APPLICANTS: 15.

NO. AWARDS: 11.

APPLICATION INFO:

The Foundation does not accept unsolicited proposals. The Board of Directors identify relevant health issues and direct the staff to connect organizations to one another.

Duration: One year.

Deadline: Varies.

ADDRESS INQUIRIES TO:
Jason Grisell, Program Director
(See address above.)

VICTOR AND LORRAINE HONIG FUND [1445]

1624 Franklin Street
Suite 1022
Oakland, CA 94612
(510) 834-2995
Fax: (510) 834-2998
E-mail: info@commoncounsel.org
Web Site: www.commoncounsel.org

AREAS OF INTEREST:

Social change, community development, environment, public policy and empowerment.

TYPE:

General operating grants; Project/program grants.

PURPOSE:

To support community organizations that are working to advance equality, opportunity, justice and civil rights for low-income communities and communities of color in the San Francisco Bay area and beyond; to support organizations that connect local social justice efforts with national and international movements for peace and justice.

LEGAL BASIS:

Family foundation.

ELIGIBILITY:

Grants made only to IRS 501(c)(3) tax-exempt organizations. No grants are made to social service programs offering ongoing or direct delivery of services, medical, educational or cultural institutions, emergency funding, scholarship funds or other aids to individuals, organizations which have sophisticated fund-raising capabilities, capital expenditure, construction or renovation programs or programs undertaken at government initiative. Priority is given to grassroots community organizations in low-income areas.

GEOG. RESTRICTIONS: California.

FINANCIAL DATA:

Amount of support per award: $1,000 to $25,000.

Total amount of support: Varies.

NO. MOST RECENT APPLICANTS: 50 to 100.

NO. AWARDS: Varies.

APPLICATION INFO:

Letters of Inquiry and Proposals are by invitation only.

Duration: Most grants are for one year.

ADDRESS INQUIRIES TO:
Grants Administrator
(See address above.)

A.V. HUNTER TRUST, INC. [1446]

650 South Cherry Street
Suite 535
Glendale, CO 80246
(303) 399-5450
Fax: (303) 399-5499
E-mail: barbarahowie@avhuntertrust.org
Web Site: avhuntertrust.org

FOUNDED: 1924

AREAS OF INTEREST:

Disabled, seniors, youth, indigent, and individuals with medical needs.

NAME(S) OF PROGRAMS:

- **Direct Operating Grants**

TYPE:

General operating grants. Grants to Colorado-based organizations in the priority areas listed above.

YEAR PROGRAM STARTED: 1924

PURPOSE:

To give aid, comfort, support or assistance to children or aged persons or indigent adults.

LEGAL BASIS:

Private foundation.

ELIGIBILITY:

Applicants must be organizations classified as 501(c)(3) by the IRS. The Trust will consider only one request from an organization during any 12-month period. Institutions or organizations supported by tax-derived monies, including those which have lost governmental funding, will not be considered. The Trustees will not consider grants or loans to individuals, developmental or start-up funds, research, publications, films or other media projects, capital campaigns or acquisitions, including construction and renovations, education or scholarship aid, grants to cover deficits or retirement of debt, purchase of memberships or blocks of tickets, endowments, recruiting and training of staff or gathering and disseminating information.

GEOG. RESTRICTIONS: Colorado.

FINANCIAL DATA:

Amount of support per award: $5,000 to $30,000. Average: $15,000.

Total amount of support: $2,000,000 annually.

NO. AWARDS: 212 grants to organizations and 461 grants to individuals for the year 2014.

REPRESENTATIVE AWARDS:

$20,000 to Boys & Girls Clubs of San Luis Valley; $10,000 to Greeley Transitional Housing; $15,000 to Senior Support Services, Inc.

APPLICATION INFO:

Detailed application information can be obtained at the Trust web site or by calling the telephone number listed above.

STAFF:
Barbara L. Howie, Executive Director
Charlotte A. Gillespie, Senior Program Officer

BOARD OF TRUSTEES:
W. Robert Alexander, President
Bruce K. Alexander, Vice President
Allan B. Adams, Treasurer
Mary K. Anstine
George C. Gibson

ADDRESS INQUIRIES TO:
Barbara L. Howie, Executive Director
(See address above.)

THE STEWART HUSTON CHARITABLE TRUST

50 South 1st Avenue
Coatesville, PA 19320
(610) 384-2666
Fax: (610) 384-3396
E-mail: admin@stewarthuston.org
Web Site: www.stewarthuston.org

TYPE:

Capital grants; Challenge/matching grants; General operating grants; Matching gifts; Project/program grants.

See entry 800 for full listing.

THE HYAMS FOUNDATION, INC. [1447]

50 Federal Street, 9th Floor
Boston, MA 02110
(617) 426-5600
Fax: (617) 426-5696
E-mail: info@hyamsfoundation.org
Web Site: www.hyamsfoundation.org

FOUNDED: 1921

AREAS OF INTEREST:

Low-income and underserved populations; low-income youth.

TYPE:

General operating grants; Project/program grants; Technical assistance. General operating, multiyear pledges, special projects, technical assistance/consulting, unrestricted grants in the following program areas:
(1) Affordable Housing: Public policy/community organizing;
(2) Civic Engagement: Grassroots leadership development, including teen organizing, public policy/community organizing, voter engagement and;
(3) Teen Development: Public policy/community organizing.

PURPOSE:

To increase economic and social justice and power within low-income communities in Boston and Chelsea, MA.

LEGAL BASIS:

Nonprofit foundation.

ELIGIBILITY:

Applicants must be Massachusetts charitable corporations, tax-exempt under Section 501(c)(3) and designated as not a private foundation under Section 509(a). No grants will be made to one organization for the programs of another organization which has not itself received both such determinations. The Foundation ordinarily will consider only one application from an organization in any given 12-month period. However, a single application may include a request for more than one program or purpose.

Grants are not given to individuals, educational institutions for standard educational or capital programs, any municipal, state or federal agency, hospital capital campaigns, endowments and religious organizations for sectarian religious purposes.

Grants are rarely made for curriculum development, conferences, film production, scholarships or to national or international organizations.

GEOG. RESTRICTIONS: Boston and Chelsea, Massachusetts.

FINANCIAL DATA:

Total assets (unaudited) of approximately $134,000,000 as of December 31, 2015.

Total amount of support: $5,509,820 in grants in 2015.

NO. AWARDS: Funding provided to 158 local nonprofit organizations in 2015.

APPLICATION INFO:

Application form required. Organizations which are unsure about whether they meet the Foundation's funding priorities and criteria are encouraged to submit a one-page letter of interest to the Foundation. This letter should describe the reason for seeking support and the geographic area(s) and population(s) to be served.

Application form is available online.

Duration: Typically one year. Multiyear grants also given.

Deadline: March 1, September 1 and December 1.

TRUSTEES:

Martella Wilson-Taylor, Chairperson
Adam D. Seitchik, Treasurer
Iris Gomez, Clerk
Willma H. Davis, Assistant Treasurer
Penn S. Loh, Assistant Clerk
Lucas H. Guerra
Rahsaan D. Hall
Karen L. Mapp
Omar Simmons

STAFF:

Elizabeth B. Smith, Executive Director
Angela Brown, Director of Programs
R. Shani Pankam, Grants Manager
Maria Mulkeen, Program Officer, Affordable Housing
David Moy, Program Officer, Civic Engagement
Nahir Torres, Program Officer, Teen Development

ADDRESS INQUIRIES TO:

R. Shani Pankam, Grants Manager
(See address above.)

ITTLESON FOUNDATION, INC. [1448]

15 East 67th Street
New York, NY 10065
(212) 794-2008
Fax: (212) 794-0351
Web Site: www.ittlesonfoundation.org

FOUNDED: 1932

AREAS OF INTEREST:

Mental health, environment and AIDS.

TYPE:

Demonstration grants; Project/program grants; Seed money grants. Seed money for the start-up of innovative programs that will improve the social welfare of citizens of the U.S.

In the area of AIDS, the Foundation supports cutting-edge prevention efforts. It is also particularly interested in new model, pilot, and demonstration efforts which address the needs of underserved at-risk populations, respond to the challenges facing community-based AIDS service organizations, provide meaningful school-based sex education, make treatment information accessible, available, and easily understandable to those in need of it, and address the psycho-social needs of those infected and affected by AIDS, especially adolescents.

In the area of environment, the Foundation supports innovative pilot, model and demonstration projects that will help move individuals, communities and organizations from environmental awareness to environmental activism. The Foundation seeks to support the present generation of environmental activists, educate and engage the next generation, strengthen the infrastructure of the environmental movement with a particular focus on efforts at the grassroots and statewide levels, and activate new constituencies.

In the area of mental health, the Foundation continues to support efforts to address the needs of underserved populations. It also seeks pilot, model and demonstration projects which fight the stigma associated with mental illness, utilize new knowledge and current technological advances to improve programs and services for people with mental illness, bring the full benefits of this new knowledge and technology to those who presently do not have access to them, and advance preventative mental health efforts, especially those targeted to youth and adolescents.

PURPOSE:

To launch innovative projects in the areas of mental health, AIDS and the environment.

ELIGIBILITY:

Grants are available to nonprofit organizations within the U.S. Preference is given to pilot projects, test and demonstration projects and applied research which ideally should inform public policy, if successful. The Foundation also supports dissemination projects.

The Foundation does not usually support capital building projects, endowments, grants to individuals, scholarships or internships (except as part of a program), or continuing support to existing programs. Moreover, the Foundation does not support programs of direct service to individuals with only a local focus or constituency. The Foundation does not make international grants.

GEOG. RESTRICTIONS: United States.

FINANCIAL DATA:

Amount of support per award: Average $20,000 to $70,000.

Total amount of support: $639,500 for the year 2014.

NO. MOST RECENT APPLICANTS: Approximately 500.

APPLICATION INFO:

There are no application forms. Applicants should write a brief letter to the Executive Director describing the basic organization and the work for which funds are being sought, along with a budget and evidence of tax-exempt status. If the activity falls within the current scope of the Foundation's interests, the applicant will be asked to supply additional information as required. Applicant should consult web site for current year's focus.

Duration: Generally one year. Multiyear when appropriate. No renewals.

Deadline: Letters of inquiry must be received by September 1 for December meeting.

OFFICERS AND DIRECTORS:

H. Anthony Ittleson, Chairman and President
Pamela Syrmis, Vice President and Director
H. Davison, Treasurer
Anthony C. Wood, Secretary and Executive Director
Andrew Auchincloss, Director
H. Philip Ittleson, Director
Stephanie Ittleson, Director
Christina Ittleson Smith, Director
Victor Syrmis, M.D., Director

ADDRESS INQUIRIES TO:

Anthony C. Wood, Executive Director
(See address above.)

JACKSONVILLE JAGUARS FOUNDATION

One EverBank Field Drive
Jacksonville, FL 32202
(904) 633-5437
Fax: (904) 633-5683
Web Site: www.jaguars.com/foundation-community/index.html

TYPE:

General operating grants; Project/program grants. Limited capital grants that target economically and socially "at-risk" youths in northeast Florida.

See entry 169 for full listing.

THE CARL W. AND CARRIE MAE JOSLYN CHARITABLE TRUST [1449]

c/o JPMorgan Private Client Services
2200 Ross Avenue, Floor 5
Dallas, TX 75201
(866) 836-6818
E-mail: kelly.t.adams@jpmorgan.com
Web Site: www.jpmorgan.com/onlinegrants

FOUNDED: 1975

AREAS OF INTEREST:

Children, elderly and handicapped persons of El Paso County, CO.

TYPE:

Project/program grants. Small project grants and general operating support.

YEAR PROGRAM STARTED: 1975

LEGAL BASIS:

Tax-exempt charitable trust.

ELIGIBILITY:

Organizations and individuals serving children, the elderly and handicapped persons in El Paso County, CO, are eligible to apply.

GEOG. RESTRICTIONS: El Paso County, Colorado.

FINANCIAL DATA:

Amount of support per award: $500 to $15,000.

Total amount of support: Approximately $55,000 to $65,000 annually.

NO. MOST RECENT APPLICANTS: 150.

NO. AWARDS: 30.

APPLICATION INFO:

Application must be made online; paper applications will not be accepted.

Duration: One year. Nonrenewable.

Deadline: November 1.

ADDRESS INQUIRIES TO:
Kelly Adams, Trust Officer
JPMorgan
(See address above.)

LIBERTY HILL FOUNDATION [1450]

6420 Wilshire Boulevard
Suite 700
Los Angeles, CA 90048
(323) 556-7200
Fax: (323) 556-7240
E-mail: info@libertyhill.org
Web Site: www.libertyhill.org

FOUNDED: 1976

AREAS OF INTEREST:
Economic justice, environmental justice and LGBTQ justice.

NAME(S) OF PROGRAMS:

- **Brothers, Sons, Selves**
- **Fund for Change**
- **Wally Marks Leadership Institute for Change**

TYPE:
General operating grants; Project/program grants; Scholarships; Seed money grants; Technical assistance. The Brothers, Sons, Selves program is a coalition of community-based organizations from across Los Angeles County that are organizing and working with African-American, Latino and Asian-Pacific Islander youth in low-income communities to address inequities through grassroots policy campaigns and leadership development.

Fund for Change supports high-impact social change through cultivating effective community leaders, seeding emerging organizations, and developing a base of grassroots activists within the areas of economic and racial justice, environmental justice and LGBTQ justice.

The Wally Marks Leadership Institute for Change invests in community leaders at the front lines of change with intensive on-the-job training for community organizers.

YEAR PROGRAM STARTED: 1976

PURPOSE:
To advance social change through a strategic combination of grants, leadership training and campaigns.

LEGAL BASIS:
Public foundation.

ELIGIBILITY:
Fund for Change: The Foundation considers applications from nonprofit 501(c)(3) organizations, or those organizations having a fiscal sponsorship agreement with a nonprofit organization which complies with Liberty Hill's policy on fiscal sponsorship, in Los Angeles County, CA, that actively work toward a more just distribution of resources and power, develop grassroots activism and leadership, are building their organizational infrastructure and promote a society free from discrimination.

The Foundation does not fund capital campaigns for land or buildings, individual efforts, films or video projects, profit-making ventures, direct union organizing, electioneering for candidates in public office, one-time events or conferences that are not linked to social change organizing strategies, or projects that only serve communities outside Los Angeles County.

GEOG. RESTRICTIONS: Primarily Los Angeles County, California.

FINANCIAL DATA:
Amount of support per award: Fund for Change: $10,000 to $50,000.

CO-OP FUNDING PROGRAMS: Donor-advised program.

APPLICATION INFO:
Letter of Inquiry for Fund for Change must be submitted electronically. Submissions by fax will not be accepted.

Unsolicited proposals will not be accepted.

Duration: One to two years.

Deadline: Letter of Inquiry: Varies.

PUBLICATIONS:
Guidelines; newsletter.

IRS I.D.: 51-0181191

STAFF:
Shane Goldsmith, President and Chief Executive Officer
Margarita Ramirez, Deputy Director of Grantmaking

ADDRESS INQUIRIES TO:
See e-mail address above.

*PLEASE NOTE:
Applicants must submit a Letter of Inquiry. Unsolicited proposals will not be accepted.

THE AGNES M. LINDSAY TRUST

660 Chestnut Street
Manchester, NH 03104
(603) 669-1366
(866) 669-1366
E-mail: admin@lindsaytrust.org
proposals@lindsaytrust.org (for grants)
Web Site: www.lindsaytrust.org

TYPE:
Capital grants; Scholarships. Awards grants for capital campaigns, capital items and renovation needs. Also, supports a number of health and welfare organizations, health projects, dental projects, special needs including blind, deaf and learning-disabled, elderly, children's hospitals, children's homes, youth organizations, youth and family services and summer camperships (summer enrichment programs). In addition, Trust supports colleges and universities and private secondary schools through scholarship aid.

See entry 1108 for full listing.

LUTHERAN FOUNDATION OF ST. LOUIS

8860 Ladue Road
Suite 200
St. Louis, MO 63124
(314) 231-2244
Fax: (314) 727-7688
E-mail: info@lutheranfoundation.org
Web Site: www.lutheranfoundation.org

TYPE:
Project/program grants.

See entry 803 for full listing.

M & M AREA COMMUNITY FOUNDATION

1110 10th Avenue, Suite L-1
Menominee, MI 49858
(906) 864-3599
Fax: (906) 864-3657
E-mail: info@mmcommunityfoundation.org
Web Site: www.mmcommunityfoundation.org

TYPE:
Project/program grants; Scholarships.

See entry 1289 for full listing.

RODERICK MACARTHUR FOUNDATION [1451]

9333 North Milwaukee Avenue
Niles, IL 60714
(847) 966-0143
Fax: (847) 581-8730

FOUNDED: 1976

AREAS OF INTEREST:
Protecting and encouraging freedom of expression, human rights, civil liberties and social justice.

TYPE:
Project/program grants. Project budgets, litigation and special projects.

YEAR PROGRAM STARTED: 1976

PURPOSE:
To support those working on programs and projects of interest to the Foundation, especially to maintain individual freedoms of expression and correct social injustices.

LEGAL BASIS:
Independent private foundation.

FINANCIAL DATA:
Amount of support per award: Varies.

Total amount of support: $4,712,500 for the year ended December 31, 2014.

NO. MOST RECENT APPLICANTS: 10.

NO. AWARDS: 4 for the year ended December 31, 2014.

REPRESENTATIVE AWARDS:
$4,712,500 to Harper's Magazine Foundation.

APPLICATION INFO:
Board-initiated only. Unsolicited requests are not accepted.

Duration: Varies according to project.

PUBLICATIONS:
Grants list.

IRS I.D.: 51-0214450

STAFF:
Marylou Bane, Administrator and Treasurer

BOARD OF DIRECTORS:
John R. MacArthur, Chairman
Robert Cordova, Vice Chairman
James Liggett, Director

ADDRESS INQUIRIES TO:
Marylou Bane
Administrator and Treasurer
(See address above.)

MAINE INITIATIVES [1452]

P.O. Box 66
Brunswick, ME 04011
(207) 607-4070
E-mail: info@maineinitiatives.org
Web Site: www.maineinitiatives.org

FOUNDED: 1993

AREAS OF INTEREST:
Supporting social change in Maine.

NAME(S) OF PROGRAMS:
- **Felder Fund for Art and Action**
- **Grants for Change**
- **Public Life Program**
- **Rapid Response "Lightning" Grants**

TYPE:
General operating grants; Seed money grants; Technical assistance. Grants provide funding to Maine groups advancing social, economic, and environmental justice at the grassroots level.

YEAR PROGRAM STARTED: 1994

PURPOSE:
To cultivate social, economic and environmental justice through grants and other support to grassroots organizations in Maine communities.

ELIGIBILITY:
Organization must be tax-exempt. Religious organizations are eligible but not for religious purposes.

GEOG. RESTRICTIONS: Maine.

FINANCIAL DATA:
Amount of support per award: Grants for Change: Up to $25,000 per year.
Total amount of support: Varies.

NO. MOST RECENT APPLICANTS: Grants for Change: 50.

NO. AWARDS: 5 to 10.

APPLICATION INFO:
Copies of IRS 501(c)(3) designation letters are requested. Contact the organization for application.
Duration: Grants for Change: Up to three years.
Deadline: Grants for Change: July 15. Rapid Response Grants are reviewed on an ongoing basis.

PUBLICATIONS:
Newsletter; annual report.

IRS I.D.: 01-0484310

STAFF:
Phil Walsh, Executive Director

ADDRESS INQUIRIES TO:
See e-mail address above.

MAZON: A JEWISH RESPONSE TO HUNGER [1453]
10495 Santa Monica Boulevard
Suite 100
Los Angeles, CA 90025
(310) 442-0020
Fax: (310) 442-0030
E-mail: mazonmail@mazon.org
Web Site: www.mazon.org

FOUNDED: 1986

AREAS OF INTEREST:
Anti-hunger advocacy pertaining to local, state and federal nutrition safety-net services.

TYPE:
Demonstration grants; General operating grants; Internships; Project/program grants.

YEAR PROGRAM STARTED: 1986

PURPOSE:
To prevent and alleviate hunger among people of all faiths and backgrounds.

GEOG. RESTRICTIONS: United States and Israel.

FINANCIAL DATA:
Amount of support per award: Varies.
Total amount of support: Varies.

NO. MOST RECENT APPLICANTS: 240.

NO. AWARDS: 190.

APPLICATION INFO:
All MAZON applications are by invitation only.
Duration: One year.

PUBLICATIONS:
Program announcement; guidelines.

ADDRESS INQUIRIES TO:
Daniel Rosove, Program Director
Sara Hahn, Program Officer
(See address above.)

THE MCKNIGHT FOUNDATION [1454]
710 South Second Street
Suite 400
Minneapolis, MN 55401
(612) 333-4220
Fax: (612) 332-3833
E-mail: info@mcknight.org
Web Site: www.mcknight.org

FOUNDED: 1953

AREAS OF INTEREST:
Early literacy, region and communities, arts, international, environment, and research and applied sciences.

NAME(S) OF PROGRAMS:
- **Arts Program**
- **Education and Learning**
- **International**
- **Midwest Climate and Energy**
- **Mississippi River**
- **Neuroscience**
- **Region and Communities**

TYPE:
General operating grants; Project/program grants.

YEAR PROGRAM STARTED: 1953

LEGAL BASIS:
Family foundation.

GEOG. RESTRICTIONS: Minnesota, with emphasis on the Minneapolis-St. Paul area, Mississippi River Corridor, and select international areas of work.

FINANCIAL DATA:
Total amount of support: $88,357,232 (unaudited) for the year 2014.

NO. MOST RECENT APPLICANTS: 1,055.

NO. AWARDS: 440 for the year 2014.

APPLICATION INFO:
Applications are available online.
Deadline: Initial Inquiry - Arts and Region and Communities: October 15, January 15, April 15 and July 15; Mississippi River: November 1, February 1, May 1 and August 1.

PUBLICATIONS:
Annual report, including grants list; grantmaking guidelines for all programs.

OFFICERS:
Kate Wolford, President
Richard J. Scott, Vice President of Finance and Compliance

DIRECTORS:
Meghan Binger Brown, Chairperson
Anne Binger
Erika Binger
Robert Bruininks
David Crosby
Phyllis Goff
Bill Gregg
Debby Landesman
Perry Moriearty
Roger Sit
Ted Staryk
Robert J. Struyk

ADDRESS INQUIRIES TO:
Stephanie Duffy
Director of Grants Administration
(See address above.)

MARIETTA MCNEILL MORGAN AND SAMUEL TATE MORGAN, JR. FOUNDATION [1455]
U.S. Trust, Philanthropic Solutions
1111 East Main Street, 12th Floor
Richmond, VA 23219
(804) 887-8773
Fax: (804) 887-8854
E-mail: va.grantmaking@ustrust.com
Web Site: www.bankofamerica.com/grantmaking

FOUNDED: 1965

AREAS OF INTEREST:
Specific capital projects of organizations only in the Commonwealth of Virginia.

TYPE:
Capital grants. Grants for capital only. No grants to individuals, for endowment funds or operating funds.

LEGAL BASIS:
Private foundation.

ELIGIBILITY:
Nonprofit organizations in the Commonwealth of Virginia who are classified by IRS as tax-exempt and are not private foundations.

GEOG. RESTRICTIONS: Virginia.

FINANCIAL DATA:
Amount of support per award: $5,000 to $35,000 dispersed in a single payment; average $25,000.
Total amount of support: Varies.

CO-OP FUNDING PROGRAMS: Other funding sources encouraged.

APPLICATION INFO:
Applicant should write to the Foundation, requesting guidelines for application.
Duration: One year.
Deadline: May 1 and November 1. Award announcements late June and early February.

ADDRESS INQUIRIES TO:
Sarah D. Kay
(See address above.)

MRG FOUNDATION [1456]
1235 S.E. Morrison, Suite A
Portland, OR 97214
(503) 234-2338
(800) 489-6743
Fax: (503) 232-1731
E-mail: info@mrgfoundation.org
Web Site: www.mrgfoundation.org

FOUNDED: 1976

AREAS OF INTEREST:
Community-based groups working for progressive social, racial, economic and environmental justice change.

NAME(S) OF PROGRAMS:
- **Capacity Building Grants**
- **Critical Response Grants**
- **General Fund Grants**
- **Travel Grants**

TYPE:
General operating grants; Project/program grants; Seed money grants; Travel grants. Funds special project grants and general support.

Critical Response Grants provide community-based groups with the additional capacity needed to organize a progressive response to an unexpected crisis or opportunity for organizing.

Travel Grants help MRG grantees make national and regional connections and develop the leadership and skills needed for effective organizational development and organizing.

YEAR PROGRAM STARTED: 1976

PURPOSE:
To empower those impacted by injustice; to promote social change.

LEGAL BASIS:
Nonprofit, tax-exempt 501(c)(3) public foundation.

ELIGIBILITY:
Organizations must do tax-exempt activities in the state of Oregon and fit criteria of social change work listed in fields of interest. No grants to individuals. The Foundation does not fund food co-ops, health centers, schools or social services.

Travel Grants: Group applicant must have received an MRG General Fund grant within the prior two years.

Grant applicants for the Critical Response Grant and the Travel Grant must have an organizational budget under $500,000 to be eligible.

GEOG. RESTRICTIONS: Oregon.

FINANCIAL DATA:
Amount of support per award: Critical Response Grants: Up to $2,000; General Fund: $2,000 to $20,000; Travel Grants: Up to $1,000.

Total amount of support: $470,000.

NO. MOST RECENT APPLICANTS: 100.

NO. AWARDS: 40.

REPRESENTATIVE AWARDS:
Center for Intercultural Organizing; Community Alliance of Tenants; Salem/Keizer Coalition for Equality.

APPLICATION INFO:
Application forms and information are available upon request.

Duration: Six to 12 months.

Deadline: Critical Response Grants and Travel Grants have no application deadline, but are subject to exhaustion of annual funding monies. General Fund: August and February.

PUBLICATIONS:
Applying for a Grant from MRG.

OFFICERS:
Sirius Bonner, Chairperson

ADDRESS INQUIRIES TO:
Cris Lira, Grants Program Director
(See address above.)

*PLEASE NOTE:
Formerly known as the McKenzie River Gathering Foundation.

A.J. MUSTE MEMORIAL INSTITUTE [1457]

168 Canal Street, 6th Floor
New York, NY 10013
(212) 533-4335
E-mail: info@ajmuste.org
Web Site: www.ajmuste.org

FOUNDED: 1974

AREAS OF INTEREST:
Peace and disarmament, social and economic justice, racial and gender equality, human rights, and the labor movement.

TYPE:
Grants-in-aid. The Institute's regular grant fund annually funds international, national and local projects in the U.S. and around the world. It gives priority to those with small budgets and little chance of funding from more traditional sources. It also offers fiscal sponsorship. The Institute does not provide academic scholarships.

YEAR PROGRAM STARTED: 1974

PURPOSE:
To promote peace and disarmament, social and economic justice, racial and sexual equality, and the labor movement.

ELIGIBILITY:
The Institute funds projects which seek to advance nonviolent grassroots education and action for social and economic justice. The Institute does not make grants for general support of ongoing operations. It does not generally accept proposals from organizations with annual budgets over $500,000 or for projects with budgets over $50,000. It will also not accept a new request from a previously funded group for two years after a grant. Grants are not made to individuals and generally not to religious organizations or development projects.

FINANCIAL DATA:
Amount of support per award: Average grant: $5,000; reviewed in quarterly cycles.

Total amount of support: Varies.

NO. AWARDS: Varies.

APPLICATION INFO:
Complete information is available on the Institute web site.

Duration: Varies.

Deadline: Varies according to program.

ADDRESS INQUIRIES TO:
Jane Guskin, Program Manager
(See address above.)

NATIONAL COUNCIL ON FAMILY RELATIONS [1458]

1201 West River Parkway
Suite 200
Minneapolis, MN 55454
(763) 781-9331
Fax: (763) 781-9348
E-mail: info@ncfr.org
Web Site: www.ncfr.org

FOUNDED: 1938

AREAS OF INTEREST:
Social work, family life education, child development, family science, sociology, psychology, family health, human ecology and religion.

NAME(S) OF PROGRAMS:
- **Affiliate Councils Award for Meritorious Service**
- **Margaret E. Arcus Outstanding Family Life Educator Award**
- **Felix Berardo Mentoring Award**
- **Jessie Bernard Outstanding Contribution to Feminist Scholarship Paper**
- **Jessie Bernard Outstanding Research Proposal**
- **Ernest W. Burgess Award**
- **Czaplewski Fellowship Award**
- **Reuben Hill Award**
- **Ruth Jewson Award**
- **John L. and Harriet P. McAdoo Award**
- **NCFR Student Award**
- **Ernest G. Osborne Award**
- **Marie Peters Award**
- **Anselm Straus Award for Qualitative Family Research**
- **Jan Trost Award**
- **Cindy Winter Award**

TYPE:
Awards/prizes. Awards given for contributions to the area of family science. All of the awards, except the Reuben Hill Award and the Jessie Bernard initiatives, require NCFR membership. The Reuben Hill Award is a juried award.

YEAR PROGRAM STARTED: 1938

PURPOSE:
To support contributions in teaching, research and distinguished service in the area of family relations.

LEGAL BASIS:
501(c)(3) education and research association.

FINANCIAL DATA:
Amount of support per award: $200 to $1,500.

Total amount of support: Varies.

NO. AWARDS: 1 award each annually.

APPLICATION INFO:
Application information is available on the web site.

Duration: One year.

Deadline: May 1 for most awards; April 15 for Jessie Bernard.

PUBLICATIONS:
Journal of Marriage and the Family; *Family Relations*; *Journal of Family Theory and Review*.

OFFICERS:
William D. Allen, President

ADDRESS INQUIRIES TO:
Jeanne Strand
Director of Governance and Operations
(See address above.)

OPEN SOCIETY INSTITUTE - BALTIMORE [1459]

201 North Charles Street
Suite 1300
Baltimore, MD 21201
(410) 234-1091
Fax: (410) 234-2816
E-mail: osi.baltimore@opensocietyfoundations.org
Web Site: www.osibaltimore.org

AREAS OF INTEREST:
Criminal rehabilitation.

NAME(S) OF PROGRAMS:
- **Criminal and Juvenile Justice Program**

TYPE:
Project/program grants. The Criminal and Juvenile Justice Program seeks to reduce the use of incarceration and its social and economic costs without compromising public safety, and promote justice systems that are fair, are used as a last resort, and offer second chances. The Program supports advocacy, public education, research, grassroots organizing, litigation and demonstration projects that focus on reforming racial and social inequities at critical stages of the criminal and juvenile justice systems - from arrest to re-entry into the community.

YEAR PROGRAM STARTED: 1998

PURPOSE:
To reduce Maryland's overuse of incarceration and its social and economic costs without compromising public safety.

LEGAL BASIS:
Foundation.

ELIGIBILITY:
Grants are made to organizations that have tax-exempt status under Section 501(c)(3) of the Internal Revenue Code. No grants are made to individuals.

GEOG. RESTRICTIONS: Baltimore City, Maryland.

FINANCIAL DATA:
Amount of support per award: Varies.
Total amount of support: Varies.

APPLICATION INFO:
Applicants should submit a letter of inquiry of two to three pages which includes:
(1) a description of the program to be funded;
(2) the qualifications of the organization to carry out the program;
(3) the ways in which the program reflects the priorities of the Criminal and Juvenile Justice Program;
(4) the amount of the budget and the funds requested and;
(5) a copy of the IRS letter stating the organization's tax-exempt status.

Duration: Varies.

Deadline: Grant applications are accepted on an ongoing basis.

ADDRESS INQUIRIES TO:
Tara Huffman, Program Director
Criminal and Juvenile Justice Program
(See address above.)

PASADENA COMMUNITY FOUNDATION [1460]

301 East Colorado Boulevard
Suite 810
Pasadena, CA 91101
(626) 796-2097
Fax: (626) 583-4738
E-mail: jdevoll@pasadenacf.org
Web Site: www.pasadenacf.org

FOUNDED: 1954

AREAS OF INTEREST:
Charitable organizations (Pasadena area only), children, youth and family, community development, environment education, arts and the humanities, health and people with special needs.

TYPE:
Capital grants; Project/program grants. Grants for non-recurring capital needs, such as equipment, building repairs and vehicles.

YEAR PROGRAM STARTED: 1954

PURPOSE:
To support charitable organizations in the Pasadena area.

LEGAL BASIS:
Nonprofit public benefit corporation.

ELIGIBILITY:
Applicants must be 501(c)(3) organizations. No personal grants to individuals, churches or schools. No grants out of the Pasadena area.

GEOG. RESTRICTIONS: Greater Pasadena area, California.

FINANCIAL DATA:
Amount of support per award: Capital grants: Up to $25,000; Project/program grants: Up to $30,000.

NO. MOST RECENT APPLICANTS: 50.

NO. AWARDS: 35.

REPRESENTATIVE AWARDS:
$8,000 to Bishop Gooden Home for kitchen improvements; $25,000 to Rosemary Children's Center for passenger van; $10,000 to College Access Plan.

APPLICATION INFO:
Guidelines are available on the Foundation web site.

Duration: One year.

Deadline: Early February.

PUBLICATIONS:
Application guidelines; formal application form; newsletter.

IRS I.D.: 20-0253310

ADDRESS INQUIRIES TO:
Mike deHilster, Program Officer
E-mail: mdehilster@pasadenacf.org

JAY AND ROSE PHILLIPS FAMILY FOUNDATION OF MINNESOTA [1461]

615 1st Avenue, N.E.
Suite 330
Minneapolis, MN 55413-3061
(612) 623-1654
Fax: (612) 623-1653
E-mail: info@phillipsfamilymn.org
Web Site: www.phillipsfamilymn.org

FOUNDED: 1944

AREAS OF INTEREST:
Human services, education, employment, housing, transit, programs to combat discrimination, and programs to help people in poverty attain economic stability.

TYPE:
Project/program grants. Grants to improve organizational effectiveness.

YEAR PROGRAM STARTED: 1944

PURPOSE:
To provide support for organizations and projects that address unmet human and social needs; to help people in poverty attain economic stability.

LEGAL BASIS:
Private foundation.

ELIGIBILITY:
Grants are made to organizations that have tax-exempt status under Section 501(c)(3) of the Internal Revenue Code. No grants are made to individuals.

During times of severe economic hardship and financial distress, the Foundation's primary concern is in providing support for projects addressing unmet human and social needs.

Additional Funding Considerations: The Foundation's preference is to support projects that represent new thinking about community needs and innovative efforts that have the potential for long-term solutions to the problems being addressed.

GEOG. RESTRICTIONS: Minnesota, primarily the seven-county Twin Cities central region.

FINANCIAL DATA:
Amount of support per award: $15,000 to $50,000.
Total amount of support: Varies.

NO. AWARDS: Varies.

APPLICATION INFO:
Application information is available on the web site.

Duration: Typically one year.

Deadline: By invitation only.

PUBLICATIONS:
Annual report; application guidelines.

IRS I.D.: 27-4196509

ADDRESS INQUIRIES TO:
Tracy Lamparty
Grants and Operations Manager
(See address above.)

*SPECIAL STIPULATIONS:
Unsolicited requests are not accepted.

PLOUGH FOUNDATION [1462]

62 North Main, Suite 201
Memphis, TN 38103
(901) 521-2779
Fax: (901) 529-4063
E-mail: mail@ploughfoundation.org
Web Site: www.ploughfoundation.org

FOUNDED: 1960

AREAS OF INTEREST:
Families in crisis, public education and youth, crime, health and economic development.

TYPE:
Capital grants; Challenge/matching grants; Seed money grants.

YEAR PROGRAM STARTED: 1960

PURPOSE:
To make payments or distributions to charitable organizations or for charitable purposes which will benefit the greatest number of people in the City of Memphis and/or Shelby County, TN.

LEGAL BASIS:
Private, independent foundation.

ELIGIBILITY:
No grants for assistance to address a crisis management situation caused by poor initial planning, individuals and projects outside the Memphis/Shelby County (TN) area. No grants for funding for private schools K-12, public charter schools, funding for annual fund-raising, or to individuals.

GEOG. RESTRICTIONS: Shelby County, Tennessee.

FINANCIAL DATA:
Amount of support per award: Varies.
Total amount of support: Varies.

REPRESENTATIVE AWARDS:
University of Memphis; Memphis Child Advocacy Center; Memphis College of Art; Memphis Shelby Crime Commission.

APPLICATION INFO:
Application information can be found on the Foundation's web site.

Duration: One to three years.

Deadline: Concept letter must be received by January 1, April 1, July 1 and October 1 for review at quarterly board meetings.

PUBLICATIONS:
Brochure.

IRS I.D.: 23-7175983

BOARD OF TRUSTEES:

ADDRESS INQUIRIES TO:
Courtney Leon, Program Officer
(See address above.)

PRITCHETT TRUST

BMO Harris Bank
417 North Broadway
Pittsburg, KS 66762
(414) 287-7317
Fax: (414) 287-8580
E-mail: pritchett.foundation@bmo.com

TYPE:
Project/program grants; Seed money grants.

See entry 1118 for full listing.

KATE B. REYNOLDS CHARITABLE TRUST [1463]

128 Reynolda Village
Winston-Salem, NC 27106-5123
(336) 397-5500
Fax: (336) 723-7765
E-mail: allen@kbr.org
Web Site: www.kbr.org

FOUNDED: 1947

AREAS OF INTEREST:
Human services and health care for the financially disadvantaged.

NAME(S) OF PROGRAMS:
- **Health Care Division**
- **Poor and Needy Division**

TYPE:
Capital grants; Challenge/matching grants; Conferences/seminars; Demonstration grants; Fellowships; Project/program grants; Seed money grants; Technical assistance; Training grants; Research contracts. Capacity building. Through the Health Care Division, the Trust responds to health and wellness needs and invests in solutions that improve the quality of health for financially needy residents of North Carolina. This Division seeks impact through two program areas: Supporting Prevention and Providing Treatment.

Through the Poor and Needy Division, the Trust responds to basic life needs and invests in solutions that improve the quality of life for financially needy residents of Forsyth County. This Division seeks impact through two program areas: Increasing Self Reliance and Providing Basic Needs.

YEAR PROGRAM STARTED: 1947

PURPOSE:
To improve the quality of life and quality of health for the financially needy of North Carolina; to accelerate positive movement on critical community issues and to effect enduring systemic change.

LEGAL BASIS:
Private foundation.

ELIGIBILITY:
Organizations eligible for grants are those that have qualified for exemption under Section 501(c)(3) and are not private foundations or a Type III supporting organization. Grants are not made to individuals or for medical research. Advance consultations are required prior to accepting an application.

GEOG. RESTRICTIONS: North Carolina.

FINANCIAL DATA:
Amount of support per award: Average $20,000 to $200,000.

APPLICATION INFO:
The Trust requires prospective applicants to call for an advance consultation prior to submitting an application. Applications are only accepted electronically.

Duration: Generally one to three years.

Deadline: Second Tuesday in February and August.

PUBLICATIONS:
Annual report; *CATALYST*, newsletter.

IRS I.D.: 56-6036515

STAFF:
Allen J. Smart, Interim President and Vice President of Programs
Joel T. Beeson, Director, Operations
Lori V. Fuller, Director, Evaluation and Learning
Joe D. Crocker, Director, Poor and Needy Division
Alan G. Welch, Information Systems Manager

ADDRESS INQUIRIES TO:
Health Care Division:
Allen J. Smart, Vice President of Programs
(See address above.)

RURITAN NATIONAL FOUNDATION

5451 Lyons Road
Dublin, VA 24084
(540) 674-5431
(877) 787-8727
Fax: (540) 674-2304
E-mail: foundation@ruritan.org
Web Site: www.ruritan.org

TYPE:
Grants-in-aid; Matching gifts. These programs allow Ruritan clubs to increase their financial assistance to a student of the club's choice. Ruritan clubs contribute $300 to the Foundation and, in turn, the Foundation will add to this amount for grants.

See entry 1538 for full listing.

RURITAN NATIONAL FOUNDATION [1464]

5451 Lyons Road
Dublin, VA 24084
(540) 674-5431
(877) 787-8727
Fax: (540) 674-2304
E-mail: foundation@ruritan.org
Web Site: www.ruritan.org

AREAS OF INTEREST:
Disaster relief.

NAME(S) OF PROGRAMS:
- **Operation We Care**

TYPE:
Project/program grants.

PURPOSE:
To provide aid to victims of situations officially declared disasters by the state and federal governments.

ELIGIBILITY:
Available to individuals in areas that are officially declared disasters by the state and federal governments. This program fills in the gap of assistance when other relief agencies have no more to give.

GEOG. RESTRICTIONS: United States.

FINANCIAL DATA:
Amount of support per award: Grants vary in amount, depending upon the needs and nature of the request.

Total amount of support: Varies.

APPLICATION INFO:
Application must be made to the local Ruritan District Governor.

ADDRESS INQUIRIES TO:
Michael Chrisley, Executive Director
(See address above.)

SAILORS' SNUG HARBOR OF BOSTON [1465]

c/o GMA Foundations
77 Summer Street, 8th Floor
Boston, MA 02110-1006
(617) 391-3092
Fax: (617) 426-7087
E-mail: eraskopf@gmafoundations.com
Web Site: www.sailorssnugharbor.org

FOUNDED: 1852

AREAS OF INTEREST:
Elderly and fishing families.

TYPE:
General operating grants; Project/program grants.

PURPOSE:
To help current and former Massachusetts fishing families achieve sustainable self-sufficiency during the current transition period in their industry; to help Greater Boston's low-income elderly population live independently.

LEGAL BASIS:
Private foundation.

ELIGIBILITY:
Grants are made to organizations that have tax-exempt status under Section 501(c)(3) of the Internal Revenue Code. No grants are made to individuals. Nonsectarian religious programs may apply.

GEOG. RESTRICTIONS: Massachusetts.

FINANCIAL DATA:
Amount of support per award: $5,000 to $25,000; typical grant $10,000.

Total amount of support: Varies.

CO-OP FUNDING PROGRAMS: Fishing Communities Initiative of Island Foundation.

NO. MOST RECENT APPLICANTS: 60.

NO. AWARDS: 30 to 40.

APPLICATION INFO:
Applications must be submitted online.

Duration: One year. Renewal by reapplication.

Deadline: Late August for programs with a fishing communities focus and mid-December for programs with an elderly focus.

ADDRESS INQUIRIES TO:
Gracelaw Simmons, Foundation Administrator
(See address above.)

GEORGE J. AND EFFIE L. SEAY MEMORIAL TRUST [1466]

Bank of America
1111 East Main Street, 12th Floor
Richmond, VA 23219
(804) 887-8763
Fax: (804) 887-8854

FOUNDED: 1959

AREAS OF INTEREST:
General philanthropic purposes with emphasis on direct-service projects in Virginia.

TYPE:
Project/program grants. Grants for specific needs.

PURPOSE:
To enhance the quality of life in the Commonwealth of Virginia.

LEGAL BASIS:
Private foundation.

ELIGIBILITY:
Nonprofit organizations only in the Commonwealth of Virginia. No grants to individuals or to endowment funds.

GEOG. RESTRICTIONS: Virginia.

FINANCIAL DATA:
Amount of support per award: $5,000 to $15,000.

Total amount of support: Varies.

Matching fund requirements: Stipulated for specific grants.

CO-OP FUNDING PROGRAMS: Other funding sources are encouraged.

APPLICATION INFO:
Applicants should write to the Trust for application guidelines.

Duration: Single payment grants made for one year.

Deadline: May 1 and November 1. Award announcement made in late June and early February.

PUBLICATIONS:
Application guidelines.

ADDRESS INQUIRIES TO:
Elizabeth D. Seaman, Advisor
(See address above.)

*SPECIAL STIPULATIONS:
Grants made only to organizations in Virginia.

SHARE OUR STRENGTH [1467]

1030 15th Street, N.W.
Suite 1100 W
Washington, DC 20005
(800) 969-4767
Fax: (202) 347-5868
E-mail: grants@strength.org
Web Site: www.strength.org
www.nokidhungry.org

FOUNDED: 1984

AREAS OF INTEREST:
Domestic childhood hunger, hunger prevention and alleviation limited to summer meals, after-school meals, school breakfast and nutrition education.

NAME(S) OF PROGRAMS:
- **No Kid Hungry**

TYPE:
Project/program grants. Grants are focused on increasing participation in the federal nutrition programs, including summer meals, after-school meals, school breakfast, and on nutrition education.

YEAR PROGRAM STARTED: 1984

PURPOSE:
To end childhood hunger in the United States.

LEGAL BASIS:
Nonprofit organization.

ELIGIBILITY:
Applicants must be 501(c)(3) organizations, schools/school districts, churches/faith-based organizations or other organizations/agencies eligible to receive grants.

Grants are made by invitation only.

GEOG. RESTRICTIONS: United States.

FINANCIAL DATA:
Amount of support per award: Varies.

Total amount of support: $7,200,000.

NO. AWARDS: 765.

APPLICATION INFO:
Applications will be accepted by invitation or in response to an RFP only.

Duration: One year. Renewal possible.

Deadline: Varies.

PUBLICATIONS:
Annual report.

ADDRESS INQUIRIES TO:
Grants Team
(See e-mail address above.)

SIERRA HEALTH FOUNDATION [1468]

1321 Garden Highway
Sacramento, CA 95833
(916) 922-4755
Fax: (916) 922-4024
E-mail: info@sierrahealth.org
Web Site: www.sierrahealth.org

FOUNDED: 1984

AREAS OF INTEREST:
Improving health outcomes and reducing health disparities.

NAME(S) OF PROGRAMS:
- **Conference and Convening Program**
- **Grizzly Creek Ranch Camp and Conference Center**
- **Health Leadership Program**
- **Healthy Sacramento Coalition**
- **Responsive Grants Program**
- **Sacramento Region Health Care Partnership**
- **Youth Pathways to Health**

TYPE:
Matching gifts; Project/program grants. Specific to funding opportunities - solicited.

YEAR PROGRAM STARTED: 1984

PURPOSE:
To invest in and serve as a catalyst for ideas, partnerships and programs that improve health and quality of life in northern California through convening, educating and strategic grantmaking.

LEGAL BASIS:
Private foundation.

ELIGIBILITY:
Applicant must be a public entity or designated 501(c)(3) organization by the IRS with 509(a)(1) or 509(a)(2) status. No grants to individuals, endowments or activities which exclusively benefit members of private or religious organizations.

GEOG. RESTRICTIONS: Northern California counties.

FINANCIAL DATA:
Amount of support per award: $1,000 to $100,000. Average $10,000.

Total amount of support: Approximately $12,300,000 in direct grants, in-kind support and operating expenses in 2014.

PUBLICATIONS:
Healthy Youth Healthy Regions; *Renewing Juvenile Justice*.

IRS I.D.: 68-0050036

OFFICERS:
Chet Hewitt, President and Chief Executive Officer
Gil Alvarado, Vice President of Administration and Chief Financial Officer
Diane Littlefield, Vice President of Programs and Partnerships

BOARD OF DIRECTORS:
Jose Hermocillo, M.D., Chairman
David W. Gordon, Vice Chairman
Chet Hewitt
Nancy P. Lee
Robert Petersen, C.P.A.
Dr. Claire Pomeroy
Dr. Earl Washburn
Carol Whiteside

ADDRESS INQUIRIES TO:
See e-mail address above.

SOCIAL JUSTICE FUND NORTHWEST [1469]

1904 Third Avenue, Suite 806
Seattle, WA 98101
(206) 624-4081
Fax: (206) 382-2640
E-mail: info@socialjusticefund.org
Web Site: www.socialjusticefund.org

FOUNDED: 1978

AREAS OF INTEREST:
Funding community-based groups to promote social justice activities and organizations attempting to establish a society that is politically and economically democratic, equitable and environmentally sound.

CONSULTING OR VOLUNTEER SERVICES:
Facilitates regional networking and general foundation information.

TYPE:
General operating grants; Project/program grants; Seed money grants; Technical assistance; Training grants.

YEAR PROGRAM STARTED: 1978

PURPOSE:
To be a resource for organizations working for social justice in the states of Idaho, Montana, Oregon, Washington and/or Wyoming attempting to establish a society that is politically and economically democratic, equitable and environmentally just.

LEGAL BASIS:
Nonprofit, 501(c)(3), public foundation.

ELIGIBILITY:
Applicant must address fundamental issues facing Northwest/Northern Rockies or any organizations that work in and have a direct impact on the people of Idaho, Montana, Oregon, Washington and/or Wyoming. Considered are organizations that are led by the people most impacted.

GEOG. RESTRICTIONS: Idaho, Montana, Oregon, Washington and Wyoming.

FINANCIAL DATA:
Amount of support per award: Average grant: $10,000.

Total amount of support: Approximately $530,000 for the year 2013.

APPLICATION INFO:
Application information is available on the web site.

Duration: Typically one year.

Deadline: Varies.

PUBLICATIONS:
Guidelines; monthly e-mail newsletter; annual report.

IRS I.D.: 91-1036971

BOARD OF DIRECTORS:
Molly Chidsey
Sashya Clark
Dina Flores-Breyer
Ubax Gardheere
Esther Handy
Jessan Hutchison-Quillian
Alice Ito
Michael McGinn
Burke Stansbury
Rich Stolz
Joaquin Uy
Abel Valladares

ADDRESS INQUIRIES TO:
Yasmeen Perez, Program Director
(See address above.)

THE STODDARD CHARITABLE TRUST [1470]

370 Main Street
Suite 1250
Worcester, MA 01608
(508) 798-8621
Fax: (508) 791-6454

FOUNDED: 1939

AREAS OF INTEREST:
General charitable activities.

TYPE:
Capital grants. Grants to support activities in the Trustees' areas of interest.

YEAR PROGRAM STARTED: 1939

PURPOSE:
To provide funding to worthy causes in the Worcester, MA area and to help that community during times of need.

LEGAL BASIS:
Private, charitable foundation.

ELIGIBILITY:
Nonprofit organizations.

GEOG. RESTRICTIONS: Worcester, Massachusetts.

FINANCIAL DATA:
Amount of support per award: $5,000 to $2,000,000; average grant $10,000.

Total amount of support: $3,000,000 annually.

APPLICATION INFO:
Submit requests for application procedures to the address above.

Duration: One year.

Deadline: March 1, June 1, September 1 and December 1.

OFFICERS AND TRUSTEES:
Warner S. Fletcher, Chairman
Judith S. King, Treasurer
Valerie S. Loring, Secretary

TRUSTEE:
Allen W. Fletcher, Trustee

ADDRESS INQUIRIES TO:
Warner S. Fletcher, Chairman
(See address above.)

THE SUMMIT FOUNDATION

111 A Lincoln Street
Breckenridge, CO 80424
(970) 453-5970
Fax: (970) 453-1423
E-mail: tsfdirector@summitfoundation.org
Web Site: www.summitfoundation.org

TYPE:
Capital grants; Challenge/matching grants; Endowments; General operating grants; Project/program grants; Scholarships; Technical assistance. The Foundation supports scholarship programs at Summit High School and neighboring community high schools. Scholarships are available to graduating seniors each year.

See entry 1348 for full listing.

SUNNEN FOUNDATION [1471]

7910 Manchester Avenue
St. Louis, MO 63143
(314) 781-2100

FOUNDED: 1953

AREAS OF INTEREST:
Grants for specific goal-oriented activities to protect reproductive and First Amendment rights and for youth and family services.

TYPE:
Capital grants; Challenge/matching grants; Development grants; Matching gifts; Project/program grants.

YEAR PROGRAM STARTED: 1953

LEGAL BASIS:
Private foundation.

ELIGIBILITY:
Limited to those organizations having tax-exempt status. No scholarship, research or travel grants are made to or for specific individuals.

GEOG. RESTRICTIONS: St. Louis, Missouri.

FINANCIAL DATA:
Assets of $13,864,000 (unaudited) as of December 31, 2015.

Amount of support per award: $2,500 to $100,000 for the year 2015.

Total amount of support: $735,000 for the year 2015.

NO. MOST RECENT APPLICANTS: Approximately 30.

NO. AWARDS: 14 for the year 2015.

REPRESENTATIVE AWARDS:
$150,000 to Planned Parenthood Agencies.

APPLICATION INFO:
The Sunnen Foundation has no formal application form. Proposal should include:
(1) summary page that describes the project and amount of funds requested;
(2) organizational background that includes mission, history, types of programs offered and constituencies served;
(3) project description that justifies the need, outlines specific goals, objectives and activities planned to meet the goals and objectives, a project timeline and specific methods of evaluation;
(4) project budget that notes anticipated expenses, including details of how the Sunnen Foundation funds will be used and anticipated income, including information about other grantmakers approached for funding;
(5) organizational budget that notes the current year budget and proposed budget for project year(s) showing income and expenses, the organization's most recent audited financial statement and public and private sources of funds and;
(6) supporting documents that should include a list of current board members, annual report and evidence of 501(c)(3) status.

Five copies of the proposal should be submitted.

Duration: Varies.

Deadline: August 1. Proposals should be submitted in June or July.

PUBLICATIONS:
Guidelines.

IRS I.D.: 43-6029156

OFFICERS:
Kurt J. Kallaus, President and Director
Matthew S. Kreider, Vice President and Director
Susan S. Brasel, Treasurer and Director
Ruth Cardinale, Secretary and Director
Helen S. Sly, Director

ADDRESS INQUIRIES TO:
Kurt J. Kallaus, President
(See address above.)

TIDES FOUNDATION

P.O. Box 29198
San Francisco, CA 94129-0198
(415) 561-6400
Fax: (415) 561-6401
E-mail: info@tides.org
Web Site: www.tides.org

TYPE:
General operating grants; Project/program grants.

See entry 1350 for full listing.

UNITED JEWISH APPEAL-FEDERATION OF JEWISH PHILANTHROPIES OF NEW YORK

130 East 59th Street
New York, NY 10022
(212) 980-1000
(212) 836-1321
Fax: (212) 836-1353
E-mail: feinsteinl@ujafedny.org
Web Site: www.ujafedny.org

TYPE:
Awards/prizes; Block grants; Capital grants; Challenge/matching grants; Conferences/seminars; Demonstration grants; Development grants; Fellowships; General operating grants; Internships; Matching gifts; Project/program grants; Research grants; Scholarships; Technical assistance; Travel grants; Research contracts.

See entry 812 for full listing.

UNITED METHODIST HEALTH MINISTRY FUND [1472]

100 East First Street
Hutchinson, KS 67501
(620) 662-8586
Fax: (620) 662-8597
E-mail: healthfund@healthfund.org
Web Site: www.healthfund.org

FOUNDED: 1986

AREAS OF INTEREST:
Health care.

NAME(S) OF PROGRAMS:

- **Access to Health Care-System Change and Advocacy**
- **Healthy Congregations Program**
- **Healthy Nutrition and Physical Activity for Young Children**
- **Mental Health for Young Children**

TYPE:
Challenge/matching grants; Conferences/seminars; Demonstration grants; General operating grants; Project/program grants; Seed money grants; Technical assistance; Training grants.

YEAR PROGRAM STARTED: 1986

PURPOSE:
To advance health, healing and wholeness for persons within and beyond the bounds of the former Kansas West Conference of the United Methodist Church.

LEGAL BASIS:
Church foundation.

ELIGIBILITY:
Grants are made:
(1) to organizations exempt from income tax under Section 501(c)(3) of the IRS Code;
(2) to governmental entities;
(3) for health care services and;
(4) for projects located in Kansas.

GEOG. RESTRICTIONS: Kansas.

FINANCIAL DATA:
Amount of support per award: Average grant $19,353 for the year 2014.
Total amount of support: $2,070,821 for the year 2014.

NO. MOST RECENT APPLICANTS: 129 for the year 2014.

NO. AWARDS: 107 for the year 2014.

REPRESENTATIVE AWARDS:
$250,000 to Enroll America to support expanded outreach efforts-Affordable Care Act enrollment; $150,400 to Prairie View, Inc., Newton, IL, for a Tri-County Mental Health Project to improve and increase mental health services.

APPLICATION INFO:
Application information is available by contacting the Fund.
Duration: Varies.
Deadline: January, March, July and October. Contact Fund for exact dates.

PUBLICATIONS:
Annual report; special publications.

IRS I.D.: 48-1019578

STAFF:
Kim Moore, President
Aaron Walker, Vice President for Strategic Development
Katie Schoenhoff, Program Officer

ADDRESS INQUIRIES TO:
Aaron Walker
Vice President for Strategic Development
(See address above.)

*SPECIAL STIPULATIONS:
Preference for United Methodist Churches and agencies in Kansas.

WICHITA COMMUNITY FOUNDATION

301 North Main Street
Suite 100
Wichita, KS 67202
(316) 264-4880
Fax: (316) 264-7592
E-mail: wcf@wichitacf.org
Web Site: www.wichitacf.org

TYPE:
Project/program grants; Scholarships; Seed money grants.

See entry 1366 for full listing.

EDUCATION

Educational projects and research (general)

THE AMERICAN FOUNDATION FOR SUICIDE PREVENTION [1473]

120 Wall Street
29th Floor
New York, NY 10005
(212) 363-3500 ext. 2015
Fax: (212) 363-6237
E-mail: grantsmanager@afsp.org
Web Site: www.afsp.org/research/research-grant-information

FOUNDED: 1987

AREAS OF INTEREST:
Suicide prevention.

NAME(S) OF PROGRAMS:
- **Pilot Grant**

TYPE:
Research grants.

PURPOSE:
To enable established investigators to pursue promising leads that emerge from their investigations and help develop preliminary data for the submission of larger funding requests to granting agencies.

ELIGIBILITY:
Grants are awarded to individuals affiliated with not-for-profit institutions or organizations in the U.S. and abroad. Grant applications are not accepted from for-profit organizations. Grant payments are made to the grantee institution and not the individual investigator.

FINANCIAL DATA:
Amount of support per award: Up to $30,000.

NO. MOST RECENT APPLICANTS: 30.

NO. AWARDS: Varies.

APPLICATION INFO:
Applications must be submitted online at the Foundation web site.

Duration: One or two years.

Deadline: November 16, 2015.

ADDRESS INQUIRIES TO:
Carl Niedzielski, Research Grants Manager
(See address above.)

THE AMERICAN FOUNDATION FOR SUICIDE PREVENTION [1474]

120 Wall Street
29th Floor
New York, NY 10005
(212) 363-3500 ext. 2015
Fax: (212) 363-6237
E-mail: grantsmanager@afsp.org
Web Site: www.afsp.org/research/research-grant-information

FOUNDED: 1987

AREAS OF INTEREST:
Suicide prevention.

NAME(S) OF PROGRAMS:
- **Postdoctoral Research Fellowships**

TYPE:
Fellowships; Research grants.

YEAR PROGRAM STARTED: 1987

PURPOSE:
To sponsor full-time training projects by investigators who have recently received a Ph.D. degree.

ELIGIBILITY:
Postdoctoral Research Fellowships are awarded for full-time training projects by investigators who have received an M.D. or Ph.D. degree within the preceding six years and have not had more than three years of fellowship support.

FINANCIAL DATA:
Amount of support per award: Up to $104,000 (stipend $46,000 per year and $6,000 per year institutional allowance).

NO. MOST RECENT APPLICANTS: 15.

NO. AWARDS: Varies.

APPLICATION INFO:
Applications must be submitted online at the Foundation web site.

Duration: Two years.

Deadline: November 16, 2015.

ADDRESS INQUIRIES TO:
Carl Niedzielski, Research Grants Manager
(See address above.)

THE AMERICAN FOUNDATION FOR SUICIDE PREVENTION [1475]

120 Wall Street
29th Floor
New York, NY 10005
(212) 363-3500 ext. 2015
Fax: (212) 363-6237
E-mail: grantsmanager@afsp.org
Web Site: www.afsp.org/research/research-grant-information

FOUNDED: 1987

AREAS OF INTEREST:
Suicide prevention.

NAME(S) OF PROGRAMS:
- **Distinguished Investigator Award**

TYPE:
Research grants.

YEAR PROGRAM STARTED: 1987

PURPOSE:
To advance knowledge of suicide and the ability to prevent it; to fund new directions and initiatives in suicidology.

ELIGIBILITY:
Applicant must be an associate professor or higher with a proven history of research in the area of suicide.

FINANCIAL DATA:
Amount of support per award: $125,000 ($62,500 per year).

NO. MOST RECENT APPLICANTS: 10.

NO. AWARDS: Varies.

APPLICATION INFO:
Applications must be submitted online at the Foundation web site.

Duration: Up to two years.

Deadline: November 16, 2015.

ADDRESS INQUIRIES TO:
Carl Niedzielski, Research Grants Manager
(See address above.)

THE AMERICAN FOUNDATION FOR SUICIDE PREVENTION [1476]

120 Wall Street
29th Floor
New York, NY 10005
(212) 363-3500 ext. 2015
Fax: (212) 363-6237
E-mail: grantsmanager@afsp.org
Web Site: www.afsp.org/research/research-grant-information

FOUNDED: 1987

AREAS OF INTEREST:
Suicide prevention.

NAME(S) OF PROGRAMS:
- **Standard Research Grants**
- **Young Investigator Grants**

TYPE:
Research grants. Standard Research Grants are awarded to individual investigators. An additional annual stipend is available for mentors on Young Investigator Awards in which the investigator is at the level of Assistant Professor or lower.

YEAR PROGRAM STARTED: 1987

PURPOSE:
To advance the knowledge of suicide and the ability to prevent it; to promote the study of clinical, biological and psychosocial aspects of suicide.

ELIGIBILITY:
Grants are awarded to not-for-profit organizations.

FINANCIAL DATA:
Amount of support per award: Up to $100,000 for a Standard Research Grant or $85,000 over two years with a mentor on Young Investigator Grant.

NO. MOST RECENT APPLICANTS: Standard Research Grants: 80; Young Investigator Grants: 30.

NO. AWARDS: Varies.

APPLICATION INFO:
Applications must be submitted online at the Foundation web site.

Duration: Two years.

Deadline: November 16, 2015.

ADDRESS INQUIRIES TO:
Carl Niedzielski, Research Grants Manager
(See address above.)

AMERICAN HONDA FOUNDATION [1477]

1919 Torrance Boulevard
Torrance, CA 90501
(310) 781-4090
Fax: (310) 781-4270
E-mail: ahf@ahm.honda.com
Web Site: www.foundation.honda.com

FOUNDED: 1984

AREAS OF INTEREST:
Youth education in the areas of science, technology, engineering, mathematics, environment, job training and literacy.

TYPE:
Challenge/matching grants; General operating grants; Project/program grants.

YEAR PROGRAM STARTED: 1984

PURPOSE:
To fund programs which strive to educate communities in the process of problem solving and planning; to educate minority youth in the areas of science and math.

LEGAL BASIS:
501(c)(3) corporate foundation.

ELIGIBILITY:
Applicants must be 501(c)(3) organizations, national in scope, impact and outreach and focused on youth and scientific education. To be considered for possible funding, programs related to youth and scientific education should be dedicated to improving the human condition of all mankind, soundly managed and administered by enthusiastic and dedicated individuals who approach their jobs in a youthful way, look to the future or foresightful programs, innovative and creative programs that propose untried methods which ultimately may result in providing solutions to the complex cultural, educational, scientific and social concerns currently facing American society, broad in scope, intent, impact and outreach, possess a high potential for success with a relatively low incidence of duplication of effort, operate from a position of financial soundness, in urgent need of funding from a priority basis (not necessarily financial need), i.e., the relative importance of the program or project to the public and represent a minimal risk in terms of venture capital investment.

Grants are not given to individuals or for scholarships, politics, fund-raising activities, religious activities, arts and culture, medical or educational research, sponsorships for nonprofit, or disaster relief.

No in-kind contributions from the Foundation. No donations of Honda products.

GEOG. RESTRICTIONS: United States.

FINANCIAL DATA:
Amount of support per award: $20,000 to $75,000 per year; $30,000 to $50,000 average.

Total amount of support: $1,800,000 for fiscal year 2015.

APPLICATION INFO:
Grant application is accessible online. Grant requests should include:
(1) a description of the program for which the grant will be used;
(2) a copy of the IRS determination letter, 501(c)(3), designating the organization as a nonprofit, tax-exempt, public-supported charity;
(3) a copy of the organization's most recent Form 990 to the IRS;
(4) a list of the Board of Directors and a resolution from the Board which authorizes the request for a grant;
(5) a copy of the current budget for the entire organization, with comparisons to the last previous budget;
(6) a proposed budget utilizing the grant funds requested with line-item detail;
(7) audited financial statements for the last two years;
(8) a list of current contributions, with giving levels, particularly of other corporate sponsors and/or corporate foundations;
(9) a three- to five-year plan from the organization and;
(10) support materials (i.e., annual reports, press kits, brochures, flyers, press clippings, photos, etc.).

Duration: One year.

Deadline: February 1 and August 1 for organizations that have never received funding from the Foundation. May 1 for organizations that have received at least one year of funding support in the last 10 years.

ADDRESS INQUIRIES TO:
See e-mail address above.

*SPECIAL STIPULATIONS:
One proposal per year, per grant seeker.

AMERICAN INSTITUTE OF CERTIFIED PUBLIC ACCOUNTANTS (AICPA) [1478]

220 Leigh Farm Road
Durham, NC 27707
(919) 402-2161
Fax: (919) 419-4705
E-mail: scholarships@aicpa.org
Web Site: www.thiswaytocpa.com

AREAS OF INTEREST:
Accounting.

NAME(S) OF PROGRAMS:
- **AICPA Scholarship for Minority Accounting Students**

TYPE:
Scholarships.

YEAR PROGRAM STARTED: 1969

PURPOSE:
To provide financial assistance to minority students who show significant potential to become CPAs.

ELIGIBILITY:
An applicant must meet the following requirements:
(1) be an underrepresented minority in the accounting profession (e.g., Black or African American, Hispanic or Latino, Native American or Asian American);
(2) enrolled as a full-time undergraduate (12 semester-hours or equivalent) or a full-time graduate-level student (nine semester-hours or equivalent) for the 2015-16 academic year; an exception may be granted if the student plans to participate in an internship;
(3) pursuing an undergraduate- or graduate-level degree in an "accounting-related" major ("accounting-related" shall be as determined by Sponsor in Sponsor's sole discretion);
(4) planning to pursue the C.P.A. licensure but not presently be a C.P.A.;
(5) completed at least 30 semester-hours (or equivalent) of college coursework, including at least six semester-hours (or equivalent) in accounting, by end of spring 2015;
(6) applied to or been accepted into a public or private, 501(c) four-year college or university located in the U.S. or its territories; the business program must be accredited by the AACSB and/or ACBSP;
(7) maintained an overall and major grade point average of at least 3.0 (on a 4.0 scale);
(8) be an AICPA student affiliate member (or have submitted a new member application); those interested can apply on the web site at no cost;
(9) be a U.S. citizen or permanent resident (green card holder) and;
(10) have some financial need (i.e., not receiving a full or partial scholarship(s) and/or grant(s) that cover and/or exceed one's educational expenses).
Note: AICPA staff and their family members are not eligible to receive this scholarship.

GEOG. RESTRICTIONS: United States and its territories.

FINANCIAL DATA:
Amount of support per award: $1,000 to $5,000.

Total amount of support: Approximately $400,000 for the academic year 2014-15.

NO. AWARDS: Up to 80 per academic year.

APPLICATION INFO:
Information is available online.

Duration: One year. Renewable.

Deadline: April 1.

ADDRESS INQUIRIES TO:
AICPA Scholarship for
Minority Accounting Students Program
(See e-mail address above.)

*SPECIAL STIPULATIONS:
Students selected to receive an AICPA scholarship must participate in the AICPA Legacy Scholars program, which includes performing at least eight hours of community service per semester to advocate for the CPA profession. Through their community service efforts, AICPA Legacy Scholars enhance their leadership and communication skills by building relationships with both aspiring and seasoned CPAs.

AMERICAN INSTITUTE OF CERTIFIED PUBLIC ACCOUNTANTS (AICPA)

220 Leigh Farm Road
Durham, NC 27707
(919) 402-4682
Fax: (919) 419-4705
E-mail: scholarships@aicpa.org
Web Site: www.aicpa.org

TYPE:
Fellowships. Awarded annually to full-time minority accounting scholars who demonstrate significant potential to become accounting educators.

See entry 1601 for full listing.

THE AMERICAN SOCIETY FOR NONDESTRUCTIVE TESTING, INC. [1479]

1711 Arlingate Lane
Columbus, OH 43228
(614) 274-6003
(800) 222-2768 ext. 233 (U.S. and Canada)
Fax: (614) 274-6899
E-mail: jvandervort@asnt.org
Web Site: www.asnt.org

FOUNDED: 1997

AREAS OF INTEREST:
Promotion of nondestructive testing.

NAME(S) OF PROGRAMS:
- **ASNT Faculty Grant Award**

TYPE:
Development grants. The Society sponsors an annual award that will provide grants to foster the development of nondestructive testing and evaluation courses (NDT & NDE) as an integral part of its engineering curricula.

PURPOSE:
To support research and education in nondestructive testing; to increase public awareness of nondestructive testing's critical role in ensuring the safety and well-being of mankind.

LEGAL BASIS:
501(c)(3) corporation.

ELIGIBILITY:
Faculty members from ABET-accredited engineering programs are encouraged to submit proposals for this award.

FINANCIAL DATA:
Amount of support per award: $8,000.
Total amount of support: Up to $16,000.

NO. AWARDS: Up to 2.

APPLICATION INFO:
Guidelines for submitting proposals are available online. Contact the ASNT administrative assistant for an application.
Duration: One year.
Deadline: December 1. Funding will begin the following July.

ADDRESS INQUIRIES TO:
Michelle Thomas, ASNT Administrative Assistant
(See address above.)

THE KATHRYN AMES FOUNDATION
c/o Pierson & Pierson
305 West Chesapeake Avenue, Suite 308
Towson, MD 21204
(410) 821-3006
Fax: (410) 821-3007
E-mail: info@kathrynames.org
Web Site: www.kathrynames.org

TYPE:
General operating grants; Project/program grants.

See entry 815 for full listing.

ARCHAEOLOGICAL INSTITUTE OF AMERICA
656 Beacon Street, 6th Floor
Boston, MA 02215
(617) 358-4184
Fax: (617) 353-6550
E-mail: fellowships@aia.bu.edu
Web Site: www.archaeological.org

TYPE:
Fellowships. The Fellowship supports projects pertaining to the archaeology of Portugal. These include, but are not limited to, research projects, colloquia, symposia, publication, research-related travel, or travel to academic meetings for the purpose of presenting papers on the archaeology of Portugal.

See entry 816 for full listing.

ARIZONA STATE UNIVERSITY [1480]
P.O. Box 870901
Tempe, AZ 85287-0901
(480) 965-5292
Fax: (480) 965-6712
E-mail: jameson.root@asu.edu
Web Site: www.students.asu.edu/lsp

AREAS OF INTEREST:
Leadership.

NAME(S) OF PROGRAMS:
- **ASU Leadership Scholarship Program**

TYPE:
Scholarships.

PURPOSE:
To recognize outstanding high school graduating seniors who have achieved excellence in leadership.

ELIGIBILITY:
Must have demonstrated leadership abilities, responsibilities, and potential in Key Club leadership and high school activities.

FINANCIAL DATA:
Amount of support per award: In-state: $9,000 per year; Out-of-state: $13,000 per year.

NO. AWARDS: 25 per year.

APPLICATION INFO:
Guidelines are available on the University web site.
Duration: Eight consecutive semesters.
Deadline: December.

ADDRESS INQUIRIES TO:
Jameson Root, Assistant Director
(See address above.)

AXE-HOUGHTON FOUNDATION
c/o Foundation Source
55 Walls Drive, 3rd Floor
Fairfield, CT 06824
(800) 839-1754
Fax: (800) 421-6579
Web Site: www.foundationcenter.org/grantmaker/axehoughton

TYPE:
Project/program grants.

See entry 643 for full listing.

BAT CONSERVATION INTERNATIONAL [1481]
P.O. Box 162603
Austin, TX 78716
(512) 327-9721
Fax: (512) 327-9724
E-mail: cwoodruff@batcon.org
grants@batcon.org
Web Site: www.batcon.org

FOUNDED: 1982

AREAS OF INTEREST:
Mammals, ecology, conservation and biology; specifically bats.

NAME(S) OF PROGRAMS:
- **BCI Student Research Scholarships**
- **Global Grassroots Grants**

TYPE:
Research grants; Scholarships. Support graduate students in research.

YEAR PROGRAM STARTED: 1990

PURPOSE:
To conserve bats and their habitat worldwide; to support research that specifically provides for bat conservation progress.

ELIGIBILITY:
Must be currently enrolled in a degree-granting program.

FINANCIAL DATA:
Amount of support per award: Varies.

NO. MOST RECENT APPLICANTS: 77.

NO. AWARDS: 24 for the year 2012.

APPLICATION INFO:
Open Requests for Proposals are posted online.
Duration: One year.
Deadline: Varies.

IRS I.D.: 74-2553144

ADDRESS INQUIRIES TO:
Chris Woodruff
Global Conservation Program Manager
(See address above.)

BATON ROUGE AREA FOUNDATION
402 North Fourth Street
Baton Rouge, LA 70802
(225) 387-6126
Fax: (225) 387-6153
E-mail: jcarpenter@braf.org
Web Site: www.braf.org

TYPE:
Capital grants; Challenge/matching grants; Conferences/seminars; Demonstration grants; Development grants; Matching gifts; Project/program grants; Scholarships; Seed money grants; Technical assistance; Training grants; Visiting scholars.

See entry 423 for full listing.

THE BAY AND PAUL FOUNDATIONS [1482]
17 West 94th Street, 1st Floor
New York, NY 10025
(212) 663-1115
Fax: (212) 932-0316
E-mail: info@bayandpaulfoundations.org
Web Site: www.bayandpaulfoundations.org

FOUNDED: 1962

AREAS OF INTEREST:
Arts in education and educational reform.

TYPE:
Challenge/matching grants; General operating grants; Project/program grants.

YEAR PROGRAM STARTED: 1962

PURPOSE:
To support a variety of programs that empower students through democracy, environmental stewardship, meaningful community service and the arts.

LEGAL BASIS:
Private foundation.

ELIGIBILITY:
Grants are made to organizations that have tax-exempt status under Section 501(c)(3) of the Internal Revenue Code. No grants are made to individuals and no grants are made to building campaigns or sectarian religious programs.

Additional information can be found on the Foundations web site.

FINANCIAL DATA:
Amount of support per award: Varies.
Total amount of support: $4,000,000.

NO. AWARDS: 70 to 80.

APPLICATION INFO:
Proposals are accepted by invitation only. Online funding inquiries may be submitted through the Foundation's web site.
Duration: One year; some multiyear.

IRS I.D.: 13-1991717

STAFF:
Gail F. Stone, Director of Finance and Human Resources
Michelle Graham, Senior Program Officer and Chief Program Administrator

BOARD OF DIRECTORS:
Frederick Bay, President and Chief Executive Officer
Rebecca Adamson, Director
David Bury, Director
Kenneth Hurwitz, Director
Corinne Steel, Director
Khalif Williams, Director

*PLEASE NOTE:
Unsolicited requests are not accepted.

BAYER USA FOUNDATION

100 Bayer Road
Pittsburgh, PA 15205
(800) 422-9374
Fax: (412) 778-4413
E-mail: bayerusafoundation@bayer.com
Web Site: www.bayer.us

TYPE:
General operating grants; Project/program grants.

See entry 1762 for full listing.

BETHESDA LUTHERAN COMMUNITIES, INC. [1483]

600 Hoffmann Drive
Watertown, WI 53094
(920) 206-4428
Fax: (920) 206-7706 (Attn.: Chris Dovnik)
E-mail: chris.dovnik@mailblc.org
Web Site: bethesdalutherancommunities.org

AREAS OF INTEREST:
Developmental disabilities.

NAME(S) OF PROGRAMS:
- **Developmental Disabilities Scholastic Achievement Scholarships**

TYPE:
Scholarships.

PURPOSE:
To encourage Lutheran youth to develop God-pleasing attitudes and actions toward people with individual differences, and to consider careers in the field of developmental disabilities services.

ELIGIBILITY:
Must be an active communicant member of a Lutheran church, have achieved sophomore status at a college or university, have a minimum 3.0 overall grade point average and have a career objective in the field of developmental disabilities services.

GEOG. RESTRICTIONS: United States and Canada.

FINANCIAL DATA:
Amount of support per award: $3,000.
Total amount of support: $6,000.

NO. MOST RECENT APPLICANTS: 21.

APPLICATION INFO:
The application process includes a short, relevant essay, 100 hours of paid or volunteer work in the field of developmental disabilities, services, and letters of reference.
Deadline: April 16.

ADDRESS INQUIRIES TO:
Chris Dovnik, Coordinator
(See address above.)

BIBLIOGRAPHICAL SOCIETY OF AMERICA [1484]

P.O. Box 1537
Lenox Hill Station, NY 10021
(212) 734-2500
Fax: (212) 452-2710
E-mail: bsa@bibsocamer.org
Web Site: www.bibsocamer.org

FOUNDED: 1904

AREAS OF INTEREST:
Study of books and manuscripts.

NAME(S) OF PROGRAMS:
- **BSA Fellowship Program**

TYPE:
Fellowships. Stipend in support of travel, living and research expenses.

YEAR PROGRAM STARTED: 1983

PURPOSE:
To support bibliographical inquiry as well as research in the history of the book trades and in publishing history.

ELIGIBILITY:
Open to doctorates, postdoctorates and postgraduates. Applicants of any nationality can apply. Eligible topics may concentrate on books and documents in any field, but should focus on the book or manuscript (the physical object) as historical evidence. Such topics may include establishing a text or studying the history of book production, publication, distribution, collecting, or reading. Enumerative listings do not fall within the scope of this program.

FINANCIAL DATA:
Amount of support per award: Up to $2,000.

APPLICATION INFO:
Instructions on how to apply and application form are available on the Society's web site.
Duration: Nonrenewable.
Deadline: December 15.

ADDRESS INQUIRIES TO:
Michele Randall, Executive Director
(See address above.)

THE BROWARD EDUCATION FOUNDATION, INC. [1485]

KC Wright Administration Building, 1st Floor
600 S.E. Third Avenue
Fort Lauderdale, FL 33301
(754) 321-2030
Fax: (754) 321-2706
E-mail: befinfo@browardschools.com
Web Site: www.browardedfoundation.org

FOUNDED: 1983

AREAS OF INTEREST:
Education.

NAME(S) OF PROGRAMS:
- **Broward Advisors for Continuing Education (BRACE) Scholarship Fund**
- **The Florida Prepaid College Tuition Program**
- **Impact Teacher Grants**
- **Tools for Schools Broward**

TYPE:
Grants-in-aid; Scholarships. Broward Advisors for Continuing Education (BRACE) Scholarship Fund awards last-dollar scholarships to qualifying students who have exhausted all avenues for financial aid and still fall short of their monetary need to pursue a postsecondary education, including community college, university and vocational school.

The Florida Prepaid College Tuition Program purchases prepaid contracts through the state of Florida's Prepaid College Foundation. It provides a defined benefit college tuition contract for state universities, community colleges, and vocational/technical centers.

YEAR PROGRAM STARTED: 1983

PURPOSE:
To provide resources for students, teachers and other employees to help them achieve educational success.

LEGAL BASIS:
501(c)(3) education foundation.

GEOG. RESTRICTIONS: Broward County, Florida.

FINANCIAL DATA:
Amount of support per award: Varies.
Total amount of support: $2,000,000.

NO. MOST RECENT APPLICANTS: 1,300.

APPLICATION INFO:
Contact the Foundation for specific application forms.
Duration: Varies.
Deadline: Varies.

PUBLICATIONS:
Financial report.

STAFF:
Tom Severino, Chief Executive Officer and President

ADDRESS INQUIRIES TO:
Coco Burns, Program Coordinator
(See address above.)

THE BROWN FOUNDATION, INC. [1486]

P.O. Box 130646
Houston, TX 77219-0646
(713) 523-6867
Fax: (713) 523-2917
E-mail: bfi@brownfoundation.org
Web Site: www.brownfoundation.org

FOUNDED: 1951

AREAS OF INTEREST:
Education, arts and humanities, civic/public affairs, medicine and science, and human services.

TYPE:
Assistantships; Capital grants; Challenge/matching grants; Fellowships; General operating grants; Matching gifts; Professorships; Project/program grants; Seed money grants.

YEAR PROGRAM STARTED: 1951

PURPOSE:
To distribute funds for public charitable purposes, principally for the support, encouragement and assistance to education, the arts and community service.

LEGAL BASIS:
Private foundation.

ELIGIBILITY:
Funding given to 501(c)(3) nonprofit institutions only. No grants to individuals.

GEOG. RESTRICTIONS: Primarily Texas.

FINANCIAL DATA:
Amount of support per award: Varies.
Total amount of support: $74,424,847 for fiscal year ended June 30, 2014.

APPLICATION INFO:
Grant proposals must include the purpose of the organization requesting funds, tax-exempt determination letter, audited financial statement, summary of proposed project, budget and letter of approval from a chief administrator. Applications will not be processed until all required information is included.
Duration: Typically one year.

PUBLICATIONS:
Application guidelines.

OFFICERS AND TRUSTEES:
Nancy Negley, Chairman
Herman L. Stude, President

Louisa Sarofim, Secretary
Andrew Abendshein
Nancy Abendshein
Holbrook Dorn
Isabel Lunnis
Will Mathis
Alexander McAllister
Christopher B. Sarofim

ADDRESS INQUIRIES TO:
Katy Hays, Chief Grants Officer
(See address above.)

FRITZ B. BURNS FOUNDATION [1487]

21800 Oxnard Street
Suite 490
Woodland Hills, CA 91367
(818) 313-8818
Fax: (818) 313-8821

FOUNDED: 1955

AREAS OF INTEREST:
Education.

TYPE:
Capital grants; Scholarships. Grants are educational in nature. The emphasis is on buildings, equipment, endowments (not for operational expenses), scholarships, faculty fellowships, hospitals and hospital equipment and medical research.

YEAR PROGRAM STARTED: 1955

LEGAL BASIS:
Private foundation.

ELIGIBILITY:
Eligible organizations must have IRS 501(c)(3) not-for-profit status. Grants are not made to individuals or to religious organizations.

GEOG. RESTRICTIONS: Southern California, primarily Los Angeles County.

FINANCIAL DATA:
Amount of support per award: $500 to $100,000.
Total amount of support: Varies.

APPLICATION INFO:
Applicant organizations must provide IRS 501(c)(3) documentation. Financial statements and a list of the organization's board of directors must be included with the application.
Duration: One year.
Deadline: September 30.

OFFICER:
Rex Rawlinson, President

ADDRESS INQUIRIES TO:
Rex Rawlinson, President
(See address above.)

BUSINESS SOLUTIONS ASSOCIATION EDUCATIONAL FOUNDATION [1488]

3601 East Joppa Road
Baltimore, MD 21234
(410) 931-8100
Fax: (410) 931-8111
E-mail: info@businesssolutionsassociation.com
Web Site: www.businesssolutionsassociation.com

AREAS OF INTEREST:
Education.

NAME(S) OF PROGRAMS:
- **Business Solutions Association Educational Foundation Scholarships**

TYPE:
Scholarships.

PURPOSE:
To assist students that are working in the office products industry with educational needs.

ELIGIBILITY:
Open to students that are already at college or starting in the fall, who are:
(1) employed by Business Solutions Association member company;
(2) a relative of an employee of Business Solutions Association member company;
(3) a member of a group affiliated with the office products industry or;
(4) a relative of a member of a group affiliated with the office products industry.

FINANCIAL DATA:
Amount of support per award: Up to $5,000.
Total amount of support: Varies.

APPLICATION INFO:
Applicant must complete a Scholarship Application Form and mail it, along with attachments, to the address above. Form is available on the web site. The attachments which must accompany the completed form are:
(1) transcript of grades and credits through the most recent grading period (high school applicants) or transcripts covering a minimum of the previous two scholastic years;
(2) letter of recommendation from a person employed by a firm in the office products industry. This person should hold an executive or managerial position and;
(3) letter of recommendation from a teacher, professor or other educational professional.
Duration: One year. Renewal possible.
Deadline: March 17. Announcement in June.

ADDRESS INQUIRIES TO:
Paula Kreuzburg, Executive Director
(See address above.)

CEMALA FOUNDATION [1489]

330 South Greene Street, Suite 101
Greensboro, NC 27401
(336) 274-3541
Fax: (336) 272-8153
E-mail: cemala@cemala.org
Web Site: www.cemala.org

FOUNDED: 1986

AREAS OF INTEREST:
Education, arts, job creation, human services, environment and public interest.

TYPE:
Capital grants; Challenge/matching grants; Conferences/seminars; Development grants; Fellowships; Grants-in-aid; Project/program grants; Seed money grants; Technical assistance; Training grants.

PURPOSE:
To better the quality of life for the citizens of Greensboro, NC.

LEGAL BASIS:
Private foundation.

ELIGIBILITY:
Eligible organizations must be IRS 501(c)(3) tax-exempt.

GEOG. RESTRICTIONS: Primarily Greensboro, North Carolina.

FINANCIAL DATA:
Amount of support per award: Varies.
Total amount of support: Varies.

NO. MOST RECENT APPLICANTS: 46.

NO. AWARDS: 39.

APPLICATION INFO:
The Cemala Foundation is no longer accepting unsolicited grant proposals. It is making strategic investments in projects compatible with the Foundation's vision. Consult its web site for additional information.
Duration: Typically one year. Renewal possible.
Deadline: March 1 and September 1.

STAFF:
Susan Schwartz, Executive Director
Melissa Burroughs, Assistant Treasurer

THE COCA-COLA FOUNDATION, INC. [1490]

P.O. Box 1734
Atlanta, GA 30301
(404) 676-2121
E-mail: cocacolacommunityrequest@coca-cola.com
Web Site: www.cocacolacommunityrequest.com

FOUNDED: 1984

AREAS OF INTEREST:
Water stewardship, healthy and active lifestyles, community recycling, and education.

TYPE:
Project/program grants.

PURPOSE:
To help develop and maintain vibrant, sustainable and local communities; to support initiatives and programs that respond in a meaningful way to community needs and priorities.

LEGAL BASIS:
Corporate foundation.

ELIGIBILITY:
Grants are made only to nonprofit 501(c)(3) or equivalent organizations. No grants to individuals, religious organizations or endeavors, or political, legislative, lobbying or fraternal organizations.

FINANCIAL DATA:
Amount of support per award: Varies.
Total amount of support: Varies.

APPLICATION INFO:
Detailed instructions and application form are available online.
Duration: Typically one year.
Deadline: Requests accepted and reviewed on a year-round basis.

PUBLICATIONS:
Annual report.

THE COMMUNITY FOUNDATION FOR THE GREATER CAPITAL REGION [1491]

6 Tower Place
Albany, NY 12203
(518) 446-9638
Fax: (518) 446-9708
E-mail: jcuilla@cfgcr.org
Web Site: www.cfgcr.org

AREAS OF INTEREST:
Education.

TYPE:
Scholarships.

YEAR PROGRAM STARTED: 1968

PURPOSE:
To assist outstanding students who plan to pursue postsecondary education in college and vocational programs.

LEGAL BASIS:
Community foundation.

ELIGIBILITY:
Eligible students must be high school seniors enrolling in a full-time undergraduate course of study at an accredited college, university, or vocational-technical school.

GEOG. RESTRICTIONS: Varies according to scholarship opportunity.

FINANCIAL DATA:
Amount of support per award: Varies.
Total amount of support: Varies.

NO. AWARDS: Over 50 for the year 2015.

APPLICATION INFO:
Applications are posted online as they become available.
Duration: One year.
Deadline: Generally March to May.

ADDRESS INQUIRIES TO:
Jenna Cuilla, Donor Relations Manager
(See telephone or e-mail address above.)

COMMUNITY FOUNDATION OF THE LOWCOUNTRY, INC. [1492]

4 Northridge Drive, Suite A
Hilton Head Island, SC 29926
(843) 681-9100
Fax: (843) 681-9101
E-mail: foundation@cf-lowcountry.org
Web Site: www.cf-lowcountry.org

FOUNDED: 1994

TYPE:
Community impact grants. Investment grants. Organization development grants.

PURPOSE:
To maintain and enhance the educational, social, culture, health, civic and environmental resources of the community.

LEGAL BASIS:
501(c)(3) and SC Secretary of State annual registration.

ELIGIBILITY:
501(c)(3) organizations.

GEOG. RESTRICTIONS: Hilton Head area, South Carolina.

FINANCIAL DATA:
Amount of support per award: Community Impact Grants: $5,000 to $50,000; Community Investment Grants: $50,000 to $150,000; Organizational Development Grants: Not to exceed $5,000.
Total amount of support: Approximately $4,000,000 for fiscal year 2014-15.

APPLICATION INFO:
Applicants must attend a grants information session and register on the Giving Marketplace. In order to determine project eligibility, applicants are then required to meet with the Vice President for Grantmaking. Those eligible are invited to apply.
Duration: One year.
Deadline: April 1, August 1 and December 1.

ADDRESS INQUIRIES TO:
Denise K. Spencer
President and Chief Executive Officer
(See address above.)

COUNCIL ON TECHNOLOGY AND ENGINEERING TEACHER EDUCATION (CTETE) [1493]

Department of Sustainable Technology and the Built Environment
Appalachian State University, Katherine Harper Hall
Boone, NC 28608
(828) 262-3122
E-mail: hoepflmc@appstate.edu
Web Site: ctete.net

FOUNDED: 1950

AREAS OF INTEREST:
Technology and engineering teacher education.

CONSULTING OR VOLUNTEER SERVICES:
NCATE state guideline preparation found on web site.

NAME(S) OF PROGRAMS:
- **International Travel Award**
- **Outstanding Research Award**

TYPE:
Challenge/matching grants; Conferences/seminars; Project/program grants; Research grants; Travel grants; Research contracts. Field study support and curriculum development.

YEAR PROGRAM STARTED: 1996

PURPOSE:
To discover philosophical rationales, theoretical models, principles and/or practices that potentially increase the effectiveness and efficiency of pre-service or in-service engineering and technology teacher education.

LEGAL BASIS:
Special-interest foundation.

ELIGIBILITY:
Applicants must be members of the Council on Technology and Engineering Teacher Education.

FINANCIAL DATA:
Amount of support per award: Average $1,000.
Total amount of support: Varies.

NO. AWARDS: Varies.

APPLICATION INFO:
Contact the Council for guidelines.
Duration: Typically one year.
Deadline: December 1.

ADDRESS INQUIRIES TO:
Dr. Marie Hoepfl, Past President
(See address above.)

THE DANA FOUNDATION

505 Fifth Avenue, Sixth Floor
New York, NY 10017
(212) 223-4040
Fax: (212) 317-8721
E-mail: kaguirre@dana.org
Web Site: www.dana.org

TYPE:
Awards/prizes; Research grants. For the decade of the 1990s, the Foundation focused on brain research. Grants in these areas are made principally through competitive Clinical Hypotheses Programs in immuno-imaging, neuroimaging and brain-cardiovascular system interactions. These competitive grants programs support pilot testing of experimental and innovative ideas that in immunology and neuroscience research have the potential of advancing clinical applications. The Foundation also supports an invitational program in which leading scientists are invited to compete for research grants designed to improve immune system responses to biological agents.

The Foundation has supported advances in education throughout its history. Its current interest is focused primarily on professional development programs that foster improved teaching of the performing arts in public schools. Programs emphasize innovative training projects that are exported from, or imported to, New York City, Washington, DC, Los Angeles and their surrounding areas. Letters of intent are accepted on a rolling basis. Grantees are selected through a competitive process.

See entry 2183 for full listing.

FREDERICK DOUGLASS INSTITUTE FOR AFRICAN AND AFRICAN-AMERICAN STUDIES [1494]

311 Morey Hall
University of Rochester
P.O. Box 270440
Rochester, NY 14627-0440
(585) 276-5744
Fax: (585) 256-2594
E-mail: FDI@rochester.edu
Web Site: www.sas.rochester.edu/aas

FOUNDED: 1986

AREAS OF INTEREST:
African and African-American studies and graduate education through advanced research at the University of Rochester.

NAME(S) OF PROGRAMS:
- **FDI Postdoctoral Fellowship**
- **FDI Predoctoral Dissertation Fellowship**

TYPE:
Awards/prizes; Conferences/seminars; Fellowships.

PURPOSE:
To promote the development of African and African-American studies and graduate education through advanced research at the University of Rochester; specifically, to support the completion of a project (FDI Postdoctoral Fellowship) and to support the completion of a dissertation (FDI Predoctoral Dissertation Fellowship).

ELIGIBILITY:
FDI Postdoctoral Fellowship: Open to scholars who hold a Ph.D. degree in a field related to African and African-American studies.

FDI Predoctoral Dissertation Fellowship: Open to graduate students of any university whose degree contributes to the scholarship in the field of African and African-American studies.

FINANCIAL DATA:
Amount of support per award: Postdoctoral Fellowship: Annual stipend of $40,000 and a $3,000 fund for research-related activities; Predoctoral Dissertation Fellowship: Annual

stipend of $26,000 plus Institute-offered research funds to support the fellow's research.

NO. MOST RECENT APPLICANTS: Approximately 30 to 40.

NO. AWARDS: 1 of each Fellowship annually.

APPLICATION INFO:
Applicants to the Postdoctoral Fellowship must submit the following information online via www.rochester.edu/fort/fdi_postdoc:
(1) a completed FDI fellowship application form;
(2) a curriculum vitae;
(3) a three- to five-page description of the project (plus a short bibliography);
(4) a sample of published or unpublished writing on a topic related to the proposal and;
(5) three letters of recommendation that comment upon the value and feasibility of the work proposed, to be sent by the referees.

Applicants to the Predoctoral Dissertation Fellowship must submit the following information online via www.rochester.edu/fort/fdi_predoc:
(1) a completed FDI fellowship application form;
(2) a curriculum vitae;
(3) an official transcript showing completion of all preliminary coursework and qualifying examinations;
(4) the dissertation prospectus;
(5) a sample chapter from the dissertation and;
(6) three letters of recommendation to be sent out by the referees, including one from the dissertation supervisor, assessing the candidate's prospects for completing the project within a year.

Duration: September 1 to May 31.

Deadline: December 31.

ADDRESS INQUIRIES TO:
Ghislaine Radegonde-Eison
Program Manager
(See e-mail address above.)

EDUCATIONAL TESTING SERVICE [1495]

660 Rosedale Road
Princeton, NJ 08541
(609) 734-5543
Fax: (609) 734-5010
E-mail: internfellowships@ets.org
Web Site: www.ets.org/research/fellowships.html

FOUNDED: 1947

AREAS OF INTEREST:
Validity, including design and development, fairness, score meaning, interpretation and reporting, and consequences; games, simulation and collaboration.

NAME(S) OF PROGRAMS:
- **Summer Internship Program for Graduate Students**

TYPE:
Internships. Interns in this eight-week program participate in research under the guidance of a senior ETS staff member in one of the areas of interest listed above. Interns also participate in seminars and workshops on a variety of topics.

YEAR PROGRAM STARTED: 1963

PURPOSE:
To provide research opportunities to individuals enrolled in a doctoral program in the fields described above; to increase the number of underrepresented minority professionals conducting research in educational measurement and related fields.

LEGAL BASIS:
Not-for-profit organization.

ELIGIBILITY:
Graduate students who are currently enrolled in a full-time doctoral program in one of the areas listed above and who have completed a minimum of two years of coursework toward their Ph.D. or Ed.D. prior to the program start date are eligible to apply.

GEOG. RESTRICTIONS: Princeton, New Jersey.

FINANCIAL DATA:
Amount of support per award: $6,000 salary and transportation allowance for relocating to and from the Princeton area; housing will be provided for interns commuting more than 50 miles.

NO. MOST RECENT APPLICANTS: Average of 200.

NO. AWARDS: Approximately 15 to 20.

APPLICATION INFO:
The application process opens in November. Applicants must complete the electronic application form.

Duration: Eight weeks in June and July.

Deadline: February 1. Applicants will be notified by April 1.

PUBLICATIONS:
Program announcement.

STAFF:
Georgiana Weingart, Fellowship Program Administrator

ADDRESS INQUIRIES TO:
See e-mail address above.

FEDERATION OF AMERICAN CONSUMERS AND TRAVELERS [1496]

318 Hillsboro Avenue
P.O. Box 104
Edwardsville, IL 62025
(618) 656-0454
Fax: (618) 656-5369
E-mail: vrolens@usafact.org
Web Site: www.usafact.org

FOUNDED: 1984

AREAS OF INTEREST:
Education.

NAME(S) OF PROGRAMS:
- **Classroom and Community Grants**
- **Continuing Education Scholarships**

TYPE:
Project/program grants; Scholarships.

PURPOSE:
To help provide supplies or to otherwise support a classroom project for which funds may not be readily available somewhere else; to improve the teacher's ability to teach and the students' opportunity to learn.

ELIGIBILITY:
Classroom Grants: Any dues-paying member of FACT may nominate any teacher to apply for a grant. Only one nomination per year per member.

Continuing Education Scholarships: All applicants must be FACT members, their children or grandchildren.

Scholarships available to:
(1) current high school seniors;
(2) people who graduated from high school four or more years ago and are now planning to enroll in an undergraduate college, university or trade school program;
(3) students currently enrolled in an undergraduate college or university and;
(4) people who wish to attend a trade school or technical college.

GEOG. RESTRICTIONS: United States.

FINANCIAL DATA:
Amount of support per award: Classroom and Continuing Grants: $100 to $2,500; Continuing Education Scholarships: One $10,000 and one $2,500 award available in each of the four categories of eligibility for scholarships.

Total amount of support: Classroom and Community Grants: Approximately $140,000 since 1999; Continuing Education Scholarships: $909,000 since 1992.

APPLICATION INFO:
Contact the Federation for guidelines.

Duration: Annual awards.

Deadline: Classroom and Community Grants: January, April, July and October; Continuing Education Scholarships: January 15 and June 15.

ADDRESS INQUIRIES TO:
Vicki Rolens, Managing Director
(See address above.)

FLORIDA EDUCATION FUND [1497]

201 East Kennedy Boulevard
Suite 1525
Tampa, FL 33602
(813) 272-2772 ext. 203
Fax: (813) 272-2784
E-mail: fef.jackson@verizon.net
mdf@fefonline.org
Web Site: www.fefonline.org

FOUNDED: 1984

AREAS OF INTEREST:
Arts and sciences, mathematics, business, engineering, health sciences, nursing, higher education, visual and performing arts.

NAME(S) OF PROGRAMS:
- **McKnight Doctoral Fellowship**

TYPE:
Fellowships.

YEAR PROGRAM STARTED: 1984

PURPOSE:
To address the underrepresentation of African American and Hispanic faculty at colleges and universities in the state of Florida by increasing the pool of citizens qualified with Ph.D. degrees to teach at the college and university levels, thus expanding employment opportunities in the industry.

LEGAL BASIS:
Corporation.

ELIGIBILITY:
Applicants must be African American or Hispanic, U.S. citizens, and hold a minimum of a Bachelor's degree from a regionally accredited college or university. The Fellowship will be awarded only to persons who intend to seek the Ph.D. degree in one of the disciplines in the arts and sciences, mathematics, business or engineering.

FINANCIAL DATA:
Fellowships include a $12,000 stipend, plus up to $5,000 for tuition and fees. Any tuition and fees over $5,000 are waived.

Amount of support per award: $17,000 per year.

Total amount of support: Approximately $850,000.

NO. MOST RECENT APPLICANTS: 300.

NO. AWARDS: Up to 50 per academic year.

APPLICATION INFO:
Online application is available at the web site.

Duration: Three years, with fourth and fifth years supported by the institution if necessary.

Deadline: January 15.

PUBLICATIONS:
Annual report.

ADDRESS INQUIRIES TO:
Charles Jackson, Program Manager
(See address above.)

FOSTER CARE TO SUCCESS [1498]

21351 Gentry Drive, Suite 130
Sterling, VA 20166
(571) 203-0270
Fax: (571) 203-0273
E-mail: scholarships@fc2success.org
Web Site: www.fc2success.org

FOUNDED: 1981

AREAS OF INTEREST:
Foster children.

NAME(S) OF PROGRAMS:
- **FCS Scholarship Fund**

TYPE:
Scholarships.

YEAR PROGRAM STARTED: 1986

PURPOSE:
To recognize outstanding scholarship and community service by a college student who has no family supporting their goals and efforts.

LEGAL BASIS:
501(c)(3), nonprofit organization.

ELIGIBILITY:
Applicants must:
(1) have been in public or private foster care for the 12 consecutive months leading up to and including their 18th birthday, or have been adopted or placed into legal guardianship from foster care after their 16th birthday, or they must have been orphaned for at least one year at the time of their 18th birthday;
(2) have been accepted into or expect to be accepted into an accredited, Pell-eligible college or other postsecondary school;
(3) be under the age of 25 on March 31 of the year in which they apply if they have not previously received scholarship funding from FC2S and;
(4) have been in foster care or orphaned while living in the U.S.

U.S. citizenship is not required.

GEOG. RESTRICTIONS: United States.

FINANCIAL DATA:
Funds may be used for tuition, books, and approved living expenses.

Amount of support per award: $1,500 to $6,000.

Total amount of support: Varies.

NO. MOST RECENT APPLICANTS: 2,200.

NO. AWARDS: 75 new; 300 repeat recipients.

APPLICATION INFO:
Information may be obtained from the address above or online from January 1 to March 31.

Duration: One academic year. Renewable up to five years if student remains eligible.

Deadline: March 31 for online application and postmark no later than April 15 for submission of additional materials required of applicant.

IRS I.D.: 52-1238437

EXECUTIVE DIRECTOR:
Eileen McCaffrey

ADDRESS INQUIRIES TO:
Tina Raheem, Director of Scholarships and Grants
(See address above.)

FOUNDATION FOR TECHNOLOGY AND ENGINEERING EDUCATION [1499]

1914 Association Drive
Suite 201
Reston, VA 20191-1539
(703) 860-2100
Fax: (703) 860-0353
E-mail: iteea@iteea.org
Web Site: www.iteea.org

FOUNDED: 1939

AREAS OF INTEREST:
Technology education.

NAME(S) OF PROGRAMS:
- **Maley/FTEE Scholarship Technology and Engineering Teacher Professional Development**

TYPE:
Scholarships.

PURPOSE:
To support teachers in their preparation to increase the positive outcomes of technology and engineering education.

ELIGIBILITY:
Applicant must be a technology and engineering teacher at any grade level who is beginning or continuing graduate study. Criteria includes evidence of teaching success, plans for action research, recommendations, plans for professional development, and the applicant's needs. Applicant must be a member of the International Technology and Engineering Educators Association.

FINANCIAL DATA:
Amount of support per award: $1,000.

NO. AWARDS: 1.

APPLICATION INFO:
Applicant must send an application package, which is to include the following required items:
(1) letter of application explaining plans for graduate study, plans for action research, the applicant's need and the school's name, address, telephone, grade level, and home address;
(2) resume (not to exceed four pages) describing current position, professional activities and achievements;
(3) official college transcript(s);
(4) documentation of acceptance into graduate school and;
(5) three letters of recommendation from among the following: undergraduate faculty, graduate faculty and school administration.

Deadline: December 1.

ADDRESS INQUIRIES TO:
Maley/FTEE Scholarship
Foundation for Technology and Engineering Education
(See address above.)

*SPECIAL STIPULATIONS:
Applicant must be a member of the ITEEA.

THE GAMBLE FOUNDATION [1500]

1660 Bush Street, Suite 300
San Francisco, CA 94109
(415) 561-6540 ext. 226
Fax: (415) 561-5477
E-mail: elingren@pfs-llc.net
Web Site: www.pfs-llc.net/gamble/gamble.html
www.gamblefoundation.org

FOUNDED: 1968

AREAS OF INTEREST:
Disadvantaged children and youth.

TYPE:
Project/program grants.

YEAR PROGRAM STARTED: 1968

PURPOSE:
To support academic enrichment programs and environmental education for disadvantaged youths; to promote a healthy and productive lifestyle.

LEGAL BASIS:
Private foundation.

ELIGIBILITY:
Grants are made to organizations that have tax-exempt status under Section 501(c)(3) of the Internal Revenue Code. No grants are made to individuals.

GEOG. RESTRICTIONS: San Francisco, Marin and Napa counties, California.

FINANCIAL DATA:
Amount of support per award: $10,000 to $25,000.

Total amount of support: Varies.

APPLICATION INFO:
Application must be made online. The Foundation encourages submission of proposals and attachments by e-mail. Additional instructions, such as required attachments, are available on the Foundation web site.

Duration: One to four years.

Deadline: See Foundation web site.

ADDRESS INQUIRIES TO:
Grants Manager
(See address above.)

THE GOODRICH FOUNDATION [1501]

4 Coliseum Centre
2730 West Tyvola Road
Charlotte, NC 28217-4578
(704) 423-7000
Web Site: utcaerospacesystems.com/Company/Pages/goodrich-foundation.aspx

FOUNDED: 1988

AREAS OF INTEREST:
STEM education, community revitalization, health and social services, arts and culture, building sustainable cities, and veteran's and military causes.

TYPE:
Development grants; General operating grants; Grants-in-aid; Matching gifts; Project/program grants; Technical assistance.

YEAR PROGRAM STARTED: 1988

PURPOSE:
To provide support to charitable organizations serving the public where UTC Aerospace Systems employees live and work.

LEGAL BASIS:
Corporate foundation.

ELIGIBILITY:
Grant applicants must be tax-exempt 501(c)(3) organizations as defined by the IRS. No grants to individuals.

GEOG. RESTRICTIONS: United States.

FINANCIAL DATA:
Amount of support per award: $5,000 to $50,000.

NO. MOST RECENT APPLICANTS: 350 for the year 2015.

NO. AWARDS: 65 for the year 2015.

APPLICATION INFO:
Online application only.

Duration: Varies depending on project.

Deadline: March 1 and August 1.

ADDRESS INQUIRIES TO:
Community Affairs
(See address above.)

HAMILTON FAMILY FOUNDATION [1502]

200 Eagle Road
Suite 308
Wayne, PA 19087
(610) 293-2225
Fax: (610) 293-0967
E-mail: nwingo@218enterprises.com
Web Site: www.hamiltonfamilyfoundation.org

FOUNDED: 1992

AREAS OF INTEREST:
Education, youth and literacy-based education programs for underserved children and youth.

TYPE:
Challenge/matching grants; General operating grants; Project/program grants.

YEAR PROGRAM STARTED: 1996

PURPOSE:
To promote quality programs of education for economically underserved youth.

LEGAL BASIS:
Private foundation.

ELIGIBILITY:
Grants are made to organizations that have tax-exempt status under Section 501(c)(3) of the Internal Revenue Code. No grants are made to individuals.

GEOG. RESTRICTIONS: Philadelphia, Pennsylvania and surrounding counties.

FINANCIAL DATA:
Amount of support per award: $5,000 to $100,000.

APPLICATION INFO:
Application form and guidelines are available on the Foundation web site.

Duration: One calendar year.

Deadline: November 1, February 1, May 1 and August 1.

STAFF:
Nancy Wingo, Executive Director

ADDRESS INQUIRIES TO:
Nancy Wingo, Executive Director
(See address above.)

HANNAFORD CHARITABLE FOUNDATION [1503]

145 Pleasant Hill Road
Scarborough, ME 04074
(207) 885-3834
Fax: (207) 885-3051
Web Site: www.hannaford.com

AREAS OF INTEREST:
Education, health through healthy communities and food security.

TYPE:
Capital grants. Employee scholarships. Long-term project/program grants.

YEAR PROGRAM STARTED: 1994

PURPOSE:
To provide financial support to nonprofit organizations dedicated to improving the communities where Hannaford operates.

LEGAL BASIS:
Private foundation.

ELIGIBILITY:
Preference for funding is given to organizations or programs that involve Hannaford associates and are located in Hannaford's marketing area, and have the potential to provide ongoing services to Foundation customers.

The Foundation does not offer support to individuals, tax-supported institutions or scholarship (employee) programs outside of their marketing area.

GEOG. RESTRICTIONS: Maine, Massachusetts, New Hampshire, New York and Vermont.

FINANCIAL DATA:
Amount of support per award: Varies.

Total amount of support: $1,300,000 for the year 2014.

NO. AWARDS: Varies.

APPLICATION INFO:
Instructions and requirements are available on the Foundation web site.

Duration: Typically one year.

HARBUS FOUNDATION [1504]

Harvard Business School
Gallatin Hall D
Boston, MA 02163
(617) 495-6528
Fax: (617) 495-8619
E-mail: info@harbusfoundation.org
Web Site: www.harbus.org/tag/harbus-foundation

FOUNDED: 1997

AREAS OF INTEREST:
Education, journalism and literacy.

TYPE:
Project/program grants. The Foundation, which was formed by the student-run Harbus News Corporation at Harvard Business School, seeks to give back to the community by supporting programs of educational development in the communities where students live and learn.

PURPOSE:
To support small, community-based organizations, individuals, or local schools with limited resources to establish and sustain new and innovative programs in the areas of literacy, journalism, and/or education.

ELIGIBILITY:
Proposals will be accepted from individuals and tax-exempt organizations as defined by Section 501(c)(3) of the Internal Revenue Code for purposes to be carried out within the greater Boston area.

The Foundation does not fund scholarships and fellowships, religious organizations for religious purposes, city or state governments, capital campaigns, for-profit organizations or purely personal needs.

GEOG. RESTRICTIONS: Greater Boston, Massachusetts area with priority given to the communities of Allston and Brighton.

FINANCIAL DATA:
Amount of support per award: $10,000.

Total amount of support: Varies.

APPLICATION INFO:
Application for funding is by invitation only. However, if one's organization aligns with the Foundation mission, send e-mail with a brief description of this organization and desired use of the Foundation resources.

Duration: One year. Renewal possible by reapplication for a maximum of three years.

Deadline: December 1.

PUBLICATIONS:
Brochure.

ADDRESS INQUIRIES TO:
Connie Chen and/or
Soyoon Sung
Co-Trustees
(See address above.)

THE PHIL HARDIN FOUNDATION [1505]

2750 North Park Drive
Meridian, MS 39305
(601) 483-4282
Fax: (601) 483-5665
E-mail: info@philhardin.org
Web Site: www.philhardin.org

FOUNDED: 1964

AREAS OF INTEREST:
Education with special (but not exclusive) emphasis on preK-12th grade.

TYPE:
Challenge/matching grants; Conferences/seminars; Endowments; Internships; Matching gifts; Project/program grants. Foundation's current primary focus is improving student achievement for preK-12th grade.

YEAR PROGRAM STARTED: 1964

PURPOSE:
To improve teaching and learning for Mississippians from grades preK-12.

LEGAL BASIS:
Tax-exempt, private foundation.

ELIGIBILITY:
Tax-exempt organizations in and out of Mississippi for projects to improve the education of Mississippians. No individual grants.

GEOG. RESTRICTIONS: Mississippi.

FINANCIAL DATA:
Amount of support per award: $2,000 to $500,000.

Total amount of support: $1,900,000 per year for all programs.

Matching fund requirements: Stipulated with specific program.

CO-OP FUNDING PROGRAMS: Economic Development Administration, Kresge Foundation, Mississippi Governor's Office of Job Development and Training, Texas Educational Association, Chisholm Foundation and CREATE.

NO. AWARDS: 25 to 30.

APPLICATION INFO:
Proposals are to be based on current research and best practices. If not available, then prior approval to submit proposal must be obtained. Applications must be submitted online and include the following:
(1) IRS tax-exempt determination letter;
(2) list of board members, affiliations and contact information;
(3) most recent audited financial statement, including 990;
(4) copy of operating budget and;
(5) list of past and present funders.

The Foundation does not accept videotapes, faxed or e-mailed proposals.

Duration: One-time, one-year or multiyear grants. Some renewals possible.

OFFICERS:
Robert Ward, President and Chairperson
R.B. Deen, Jr., Senior Vice President
Marty Davidson, Vice President for Investments
Steve Moore, Treasurer
Ronnie L. Walton, Secretary and General Counsel

DIRECTORS:
Dr. J.S. Covington
Marty Davidson
R.B. Deen, Jr.
Jim McGinnis
Steve Moore
Ronnie L. Walton
Robert Ward

ADDRESS INQUIRIES TO:
Sheryl Feltenstein
Administrative Assistant
(See address above.)

HEALTH RESOURCES AND SERVICES ADMINISTRATION [1506]

5600 Fishers Lane, Room 9-105
Rockville, MD 20857
(301) 443-4776
Fax: (301) 443-0846
E-mail: dpolicy@hrsa.gov
Web Site: www.hrsa.gov

AREAS OF INTEREST:
Health professions and nursing education.

NAME(S) OF PROGRAMS:
- **Scholarships for Disadvantaged Students**

TYPE:
Scholarships. Funds made available to eligible schools for the purpose of providing scholarships to full-time financially needy students from disadvantaged backgrounds. Students must apply at the financial aid office of school where enrolled or admitted for enrollment.

YEAR PROGRAM STARTED: 1991

PURPOSE:
To improve and expand health care services for underserved people.

LEGAL BASIS:
Government agency.

ELIGIBILITY:
Must be a citizen or permanent resident of the U.S. enrolled in a health profession or nursing program and be from a disadvantaged background.

GEOG. RESTRICTIONS: United States.

FINANCIAL DATA:
Amount of support per award: Varies.

Total amount of support: Varies.

NO. MOST RECENT APPLICANTS: 403.

NO. AWARDS: 99.

APPLICATION INFO:
Contact student financial aid office at the school attended for application procedure.

Duration: Four years. Must reapply for additional funding after four years.

WILLIAM G. AND MYRTLE E. HESS CHARITABLE TRUST [1507]

c/o JPMorgan
480 Pierce Street, Second Floor
Birmingham, MI 48009
(248) 205-2172
E-mail: mark.r.andrews@jpmorgan.com
Web Site: www.jpmorgan.com/onlinegrants

FOUNDED: 1969

AREAS OF INTEREST:
Science, education and charity.

TYPE:
General operating grants; Grants-in-aid; Project/program grants.

YEAR PROGRAM STARTED: 1969

PURPOSE:
To benefit organizations in Michigan.

ELIGIBILITY:
Eligible organizations must be nonprofit, 501(c)(3) tax-exempt. Grants are not given to individuals or for religious or political purposes.

GEOG. RESTRICTIONS: Michigan.

FINANCIAL DATA:
Amount of support per award: $1,000 to $10,000.

Total amount of support: Varies.

APPLICATION INFO:
Applications are to be submitted online.

Duration: Typically one year.

Deadline: August 15. Decisions on grant requests made annually in September.

ADDRESS INQUIRIES TO:
Mark Andrews, Trust Officer
(See address above.)

*PLEASE NOTE:
Applications received late will be held until the following year.

HUTCHINSON COMMUNITY FOUNDATION

One North Main Street
Suite 501
Hutchinson, KS 67501
(620) 663-5293
Fax: (620) 663-9277
E-mail: info@hutchcf.org
Web Site: www.hutchcf.org

TYPE:
Project/program grants; Seed money grants.

See entry 445 for full listing.

INTERNATIONAL ASSOCIATION OF ICE CREAM DISTRIBUTORS AND VENDORS (IAICDV) [1508]

3601 East Joppa Road
Baltimore, MD 21234
(410) 931-8100
Fax: (410) 931-8111
E-mail: info@iaicdv.org
Web Site: www.iaicdv.org

FOUNDED: 1969

AREAS OF INTEREST:
The ice cream vending and distributing industries.

NAME(S) OF PROGRAMS:
- **IAICDV Annual Scholarship**

TYPE:
Scholarships.

YEAR PROGRAM STARTED: 1990

PURPOSE:
To award deserving applicants who are determined to further their profession, and our industry, through advanced education.

ELIGIBILITY:
The following criteria apply:
(1) Applicant must be an owner of a member company, employee of a member company or a dependent (natural or adopted) of a member company; the member company must be in good standing with the IAICDV;
(2) Applicant must be or have been working in the ice cream industry during the award year and;
(3) Applicant must use the scholarship for their postsecondary education, including university, college or trade school.

FINANCIAL DATA:
Amount of support per award: $3,000.

Total amount of support: $3,000.

NO. MOST RECENT APPLICANTS: 10.

NO. AWARDS: 1.

APPLICATION INFO:
Contact the Association for detailed guidelines.

Duration: One-time award.

Deadline: October 1.

ADDRESS INQUIRIES TO:
IAICDV Scholarship Program
(See address above.)

INTERNATIONAL LITERACY ASSOCIATION (ILA) [1509]

800 Barksdale Road
Newark, DE 19711-3204
(800) 336-7323 (U.S. and Canada)
(302) 731-1600 (all other countries)
Fax: (302) 731-1057
E-mail: exec@reading.org
Web Site: www.literacyworldwide.org

FOUNDED: 1956

AREAS OF INTEREST:
Reading and literacy through professional development, advocacy, partnership, research, and global literacy development.

NAME(S) OF PROGRAMS:
- **ILA Jerry Johns Outstanding Teacher Educator in Reading Award**
- **ILA Regie Routman Teacher Recognition Grant**

TYPE:
Awards/prizes; Research grants; Travel grants. ILA Jerry Johns Outstanding Teacher Educator in Reading Award: Honors an outstanding college or university teacher of reading methods or reading-related courses. Nominees must be Association members, affiliated with a college or a university, and engaged in teacher preparation in reading at the undergraduate and/or graduate levels.

ILA Regie Routman Teacher Recognition Grant: Honors an outstanding mainstream, elementary classroom teacher dedicated to improving the teaching and learning of reading and writing, across the curriculum in real-world contexts in grades K-6 (ages 5-12). The grant may not be used for purchase of commercial programs.

PURPOSE:
To promote literacy worldwide.

FINANCIAL DATA:
Amount of support per award: Jerry Johns: $1,000. Regie Routman: $2,500.

APPLICATION INFO:
Forms and guidelines can be obtained at the Association web site.

Deadline: January 15.

ADDRESS INQUIRIES TO:
E-mail: committees@reading.org

INTERNATIONAL LITERACY ASSOCIATION (ILA) [1510]

800 Barksdale Road
Newark, DE 19711-3204
(800) 336-7323 (U.S. and Canada)
(302) 731-1600 (all other countries)
Fax: (302) 731-1057
E-mail: research@reading.org
Web Site: www.literacyworldwide.org

FOUNDED: 1956

AREAS OF INTEREST:
Reading and literacy through professional development, advocacy, partnership, research, and global literacy development.

NAME(S) OF PROGRAMS:
- **Jeanne S. Chall Research Fellowship**
- **Dina Feitelson Research Award**
- **Elva Knight Research Grant**
- **Helen M. Robinson Grant**
- **Steven A. Stahl Research Grant**
- **Teacher as Researcher Grant**

TYPE:
Awards/prizes; Fellowships; Grants-in-aid; Research grants. Jeanne S. Chall Research Fellowship encourages and supports reading research by promising scholars. Its special emphasis is to support research efforts in the areas of beginning reading, readability, reading difficulty, stages of reading development, the relation of vocabulary to reading, and diagnosing and teaching adults with limited reading ability.

Dina Feitelson Research Award recognizes an outstanding empirical study published in English in a refereed journal. The work should report on one or more aspects of literacy acquisition, such as phonemic awareness, the alphabetic principle, bilingualism, home influences on literacy development, or cross-cultural studies of beginning reading. Works may be submitted by the author or anyone else.

Elva Knight Research Grant provides research in reading and literacy. Projects should be completed within two years and may be carried out using any research method or approach so long as the focus of the project is on research in reading or literacy.

Helen M. Robinson Grant is given annually to assist doctoral students at the early stages of their dissertation research in the areas of reading and literacy.

Steven A. Stahl Research Grant encourages and supports promising graduate students in their research. The grant will be awarded annually to a recipient with at least three years of teaching experience who is conducting classroom research (including action research) focused on improving reading instruction and children's reading achievement.

Teacher as Researcher Grant supports classroom teachers who undertake action research inquiries about literacy and instruction.

PURPOSE:
To promote reading by continuously advancing the quality of literacy instruction and research worldwide.

FINANCIAL DATA:
Amount of support per award: Jeanne S. Chall: $5,000; Dina Feitelson: $500; Elva Knight: $5,000; Helen M. Robinson: $1,200; Steven A. Stahl: $1,000; Teacher as Researcher: $5,000.

Total amount of support: Varies.

NO. AWARDS: 1 each annually. Research grants vary.

APPLICATION INFO:
Application guidelines are available online.

Deadline: January 15.

PUBLICATIONS:
Application guidelines.

ADDRESS INQUIRIES TO:
Marcella Moore, Project Manager
Research Division
P.O. Box 8139
Newark, DE 19714-8139

JELLISON BENEVOLENT SOCIETY [1511]

P.O. Box 145
Junction City, KS 66441-0145
(785) 762-5566
E-mail: s_williams1948@yahoo.com

FOUNDED: 1947

AREAS OF INTEREST:
Higher education.

TYPE:
Scholarships.

PURPOSE:
To aid area students in pursuit of higher education.

LEGAL BASIS:
Private foundation.

ELIGIBILITY:
Must be a high school senior or older, preferably a resident of Geary County, KS.

GEOG. RESTRICTIONS: Typically Geary County, Kansas.

FINANCIAL DATA:
Amount of support per award: $500 to $1,500 per semester.

Total amount of support: Varies.

NO. MOST RECENT APPLICANTS: 75.

NO. AWARDS: 71.

APPLICATION INFO:
Contact the Society for guidelines.

Duration: One year. Renewable by supplying copy of grades above 2.0.

Deadline: June 20 and November 20.

IRS I.D.: 48-6106092

STAFF:
Dale Ann Clore, President
Susan E. Williams, Secretary

ADDRESS INQUIRIES TO:
Susan E. Williams, Secretary
(See address above.)

JPRO NETWORK (JEWISH PROFESSIONAL RESOURCE ORGANIZATION) [1512]

25 Broadway, Suite 1700
New York, NY 10004
(212) 284-6945
Fax: (212) 284-6566
E-mail: info@jpro.org
Web Site: www.jpro.org

FOUNDED: 1899

AREAS OF INTEREST:
Jewish communal services.

NAME(S) OF PROGRAMS:
- **Norman Edell Scholarship**
- **Graduate Student Network**
- **Local Groups Network**
- **Mandelkorn Distinguished Service Award**
- **Professional Development Programs**
- **Young Professional Award**

TYPE:
Awards/prizes; Conferences/seminars; Internships. Support of local groups of Jewish professionals.

YEAR PROGRAM STARTED: 1899

PURPOSE:
To enrich Jewish education in the communal service field; to connect and enhance professionals working on behalf of the Jewish community.

LEGAL BASIS:
Nonprofit corporation.

GEOG. RESTRICTIONS: United States and Canada.

FINANCIAL DATA:
Amount of support per award: Varies.

NO. AWARDS: 5.

APPLICATION INFO:
Contact JPRO Network through its web site for application procedures.

PUBLICATIONS:
Journal of Jewish Communal Service; monthly newsletter.

EXECUTIVE DIRECTOR:
Brenda D. Gevertz, Executive Director

ADDRESS INQUIRIES TO:
Brenda D. Gevertz, Executive Director
(See e-mail address above.)

WILLIAM R. KENAN, JR. CHARITABLE TRUST [1513]

360 Kenan Center Drive, Floor 5
Chapel Hill, NC 27599
(919) 391-7222
Fax: (919) 962-3331
E-mail: dzinn@kenancharitabletrust.org
Web Site: www.kenancharitabletrust.org

FOUNDED: 1965

AREAS OF INTEREST:
Education.

TYPE:
Project/program grants.

PURPOSE:
To support educational programs of interest to the Trust.

LEGAL BASIS:
Private foundation.

ELIGIBILITY:
The Foundation does not accept unsolicited proposals.

GEOG. RESTRICTIONS: United States.

FINANCIAL DATA:
Amount of support per award: Varies.
Total amount of support: Varies.

APPLICATION INFO:
Trustee's statement of guidelines, areas of interest and required procedures are available on request.
Duration: Varies.

ADDRESS INQUIRIES TO:
Executive Director
William R. Kenan, Jr. Charitable Trust
P.O. Box 3858
Chapel Hill, NC 27515-3858

*PLEASE NOTE:
The Trust does not accept unsolicited proposals.

CHARLES G. KOCH CHARITABLE FOUNDATION [1514]

1320 North Courthouse Road
Suite 500
Arlington, VA 22201
(703) 875-1770
Fax: (703) 875-1766
E-mail: grants@charleskochfoundation.org
Web Site: www.charleskochfoundation.org

FOUNDED: 1980

AREAS OF INTEREST:
Higher education, research, and professional education programs.

TYPE:
Project/program grants; Research grants; Seed money grants.

YEAR PROGRAM STARTED: 1980

PURPOSE:
To advance an understanding of how economic freedom improves the well-being of people around the world.

LEGAL BASIS:
Private foundation.

ELIGIBILITY:
The Foundation primarily makes grants to Section 501(c)(3) public charities. The Foundation does not support for-profit corporations or individuals. Grant proposals for capital construction, debt reduction, or general fund-raising drives or events are discouraged. The Foundation does not make grants intended to support lobbying activities or candidates for political office, and rarely funds endowments.

GEOG. RESTRICTIONS: United States.

FINANCIAL DATA:
Amount of support per award: Varies depending on program.

APPLICATION INFO:
Organizations seeking grants must submit a proposal online. If the proposal meets the initial requirements, it is reviewed to assess whether it fits within the Foundation's priorities. Prospective grantees may be contacted for further information.
Duration: Varies depending on needs and nature of the request.
Deadline: Proposals are evaluated on a rolling basis.

STAFF:
Brian Hooks, President
Vonda Holliman, Secretary and Treasurer
Matthew Brown, Policy Research Director
Elizabeth Brannen, Human Resource Coordinator
Christopher Cardiff, Program Officer
Ryan Stowers, Program Officer

ADDRESS INQUIRIES TO:
Grants Administrator
(See address above.)

THE JEAN AND E. FLOYD KVAMME FOUNDATION [1515]

P.O. Box 2494
Saratoga, CA 95070
(408) 395-2829
Fax: (408) 354-0804

AREAS OF INTEREST:
Arts, charitable and cultural, education, health, medical research and Christian religious organizations.

TYPE:
Capital grants; Development grants; General operating grants; Project/program grants. Medical grants are given primarily in the areas of Alzheimers, leukemia, arthritis, and spondylitis; however, grants for research in other areas are considered.

PURPOSE:
To support organizations and institutes that promote arts, cultural, education, health, medical, scientific and social advancement of the international communities.

LEGAL BASIS:
Corporate contributions.

ELIGIBILITY:
Grants are made to organizations that have tax-exempt status under Section 501(c)(3) of the Internal Revenue Code and international Christian organizations. No grants are made to individuals.

GEOG. RESTRICTIONS: Artistic and educational grants: Northern California.

FINANCIAL DATA:
Amount of support per award: Varies.
Total amount of support: Varies.

APPLICATION INFO:
Applicants must submit a brief (one-page) letter of intent with a brief description of the project, dollar amount and verification of 501(c)(3) status.
Duration: One year.

TRUSTEE:
Jean Kvamme

ADDRESS INQUIRIES TO:
Jean Kvamme, Trustee
(See address above.)

LEARNING FOR LIFE [1516]

1329 West Walnut Hill Lane
P.O. Box 152252
Irving, TX 75015-2225
(972) 580-2418
Fax: (972) 580-2137; (214) 256-4078
E-mail: anissa.hicks@lflmail.org
Web Site: www.learningforlife.org/exploring

AREAS OF INTEREST:
Career opportunities, life skills, service learning, character education and leadership experience.

NAME(S) OF PROGRAMS:
- **Exploring Program**

TYPE:
Awards/prizes; Scholarships.

PURPOSE:
To provide experiences to help young people mature and to prepare them to become responsible and caring adults; to provide an opportunity for youth to investigate the meaning of interdependence in their personal relationships and communities.

ELIGIBILITY:
Young men and women 15 to 20 years old or 14 years old, if they have completed the eighth grade. Must be a participant in the Learning for Life Exploring Program to receive scholarship.

FINANCIAL DATA:
Amount of support per award: Varies per award.
Total amount of support: Varies.

APPLICATION INFO:
Guidelines are available on the web site.
Duration: One year. Must reapply.
Deadline: Varies per program.

ADDRESS INQUIRIES TO:
Anissa Hicks
Project Coordinator
(See address above.)

MARSHALL COMMUNITY FOUNDATION [1517]

614 Homer Road
Marshall, MI 49068
(269) 781-2273
Fax: (269) 781-9747
E-mail: info@marshallcf.org
Web Site: www.marshallcf.org

FOUNDED: 1970

AREAS OF INTEREST:
Arts and education, culture, environment, health and well-being, human services, youth and seniors, and community/economic development.

TYPE:
Project/program grants; Scholarships.

YEAR PROGRAM STARTED: 1985

PURPOSE:
To support projects that promote the educational, recreational, environmental and cultural development of the Marshall area and Calhoun County.

LEGAL BASIS:
Community foundation.

ELIGIBILITY:
Grants are made to organizations that have tax-exempt status under Section 501(c)(3) and 509(a)(1) or (2) of the Internal Revenue Code. Nonsectarian religious programs meeting a general community need may apply. No grants are made to individuals.

GEOG. RESTRICTIONS: Calhoun County, Michigan.

FINANCIAL DATA:
Amount of support per award: Varies.
Total amount of support: Varies.

APPLICATION INFO:
Application information is available online.
Duration: One year.
Deadline: January 1, April 1, July 1 and October 1.

ADDRESS INQUIRIES TO:
Shannon Tiernan, Executive Director
(See address above.)

THE MUSTARD SEED FOUNDATION [1518]

7115 Leesburg Pike, Suite 304
Falls Church, VA 22043
(703) 524-5620
Fax: (703) 533-7340
E-mail: ljackson@msfdn.org
Web Site: www.msfdn.org

FOUNDED: 1983

AREAS OF INTEREST:
Education and religion.

NAME(S) OF PROGRAMS:
- **Harvey Fellows Program**

TYPE:
Fellowships.

YEAR PROGRAM STARTED: 1992

PURPOSE:
To encourage students who are committed to Jesus Christ to pursue vocations that are culturally influential and to pursue vocational credentials in the most prestigious graduate programs; to validate exceptional abilities in academics and leadership as gifts from God worthy of cultivation and development.

LEGAL BASIS:
Nonprofit.

ELIGIBILITY:
The Harvey Fellows must be Christian graduate students and attend a graduate school program that is considered to be one of the top five in a given subject area or specialty in the world.

FINANCIAL DATA:
Amount of support per award: $12,000.
Total amount of support: Varies.

NO. AWARDS: Varies.

APPLICATION INFO:
The application process has two stages. First, the application must be completed and submitted through the online application system. No paper applications are accepted. The online application does not need to be completed all at once. Secondly, specific required materials must be submitted via mail (e.g., official transcripts, letters of recommendation, test scores). All required materials must be collected by the applicant, bundled, and sent directly to the Foundation. A complete list of the required documents can be found on the Foundation's web site.
Duration: One year. Optional renewal up to three years.
Deadline: November 1.

ADDRESS INQUIRIES TO:
See e-mail address above.

THE NAACP LEGAL DEFENSE AND EDUCATIONAL FUND, INC.

40 Rector Street
5th Floor
New York, NY 10006
(212) 965-2225
Fax: (212) 226-7592
E-mail: scholarships@naacpldf.org
mcorro@naacpldf.org
Web Site: www.naacpldf.org/scholarships

TYPE:
Awards/prizes; Grants-in-aid; Internships; Scholarships. LDF Herbert Lehman Education Fund Scholarship Program: Scholarships for African-American high school seniors, high school graduates and college freshmen to attend four-year accredited colleges and universities.

LDF Earl Warren Legal Training Program: Scholarships for law students to attend three-year accredited law schools.

See entry 1009 for full listing.

THE NATIONAL ACADEMY OF EDUCATION [1519]

500 Fifth Street, N.W.
Washington, DC 20001
(202) 334-2093
Fax: (202) 334-2350
E-mail: info@naeducation.org
Web Site: www.naeducation.org

FOUNDED: 1965

AREAS OF INTEREST:
All aspects of educational research.

NAME(S) OF PROGRAMS:
- **National Academy of Education/Spencer Dissertation Fellowship**
- **National Academy of Education/Spencer Postdoctoral Fellowship**

TYPE:
Fellowships. The Dissertation Fellowship seeks to encourage a new generation of scholars from a wide range of disciplines and professional fields to undertake research relevant to the improvement of education. These fellowships support individuals whose dissertations show potential for bringing fresh and constructive perspectives to the history, theory or practice of formal or informal education anywhere in the world.

The Postdoctoral Fellowship is nonresidential and funds proposals that make significant scholarly contributions to the field of education. The program also develops the careers of its recipients through professional development activities involving National Academy of Education members.

PURPOSE:
To support early career scholars working in critical areas of education research.

LEGAL BASIS:
Private operating foundation.

ELIGIBILITY:
Dissertation Fellowship: The basic selection criteria are the importance of the research question to education, the quality of the research approach and feasibility of the work plan, and the applicant's future potential as a researcher and interest in educational research.

Postdoctoral Fellowship: Primary criterion for selection is promise as an educational research scholar, with special emphasis on potential to make a significant contribution to our understanding of education. Applicant must have received Ph.D., Ed.D. or equivalent degree in the past five years.

FINANCIAL DATA:
Dissertation Fellowship: The Fellowship funding is to support the writing of the dissertation only. The Fellowship funding must not be spent on data collection.

Postdoctoral Fellowship: Terms of the award do not permit institutional overhead. If the scholar transfers institutions, the grant transfers with him or her. The money may be spent toward any salary, supplies, etc., that aid the grantee in pursuing research described in the Fellowship application.
Amount of support per award: Dissertation Fellowship: $27,500 for one year. Postdoctoral Fellowship: $70,000 over one year, 18 months or two years.

NO. MOST RECENT APPLICANTS: Dissertation Fellowship: Approximately 500 each year. Postdoctoral Fellowship: Approximately 300 each year.

NO. AWARDS: Dissertation Fellowship: 35. Postdoctoral Fellowship: 30.

APPLICATION INFO:
Application material is available in August.
Duration: Dissertation Fellowship: One or two years. Postdoctoral Fellowship: Up to two years.
Deadline: Dissertation Fellowship: Early October. Postdoctoral Fellowship: Early November.

NATIONAL CENTER FOR LEARNING DISABILITIES [1520]

32 Laight Street, 2nd Floor
New York, NY 10013
(212) 545-7510
Fax: (212) 545-9665
Web Site: www.ncld.org/scholarships-and-awards

FOUNDED: 1977

AREAS OF INTEREST:
Education and learning disabilities.

NAME(S) OF PROGRAMS:
- **Bill Ellis Teacher Preparation Award**

TYPE:
Awards/prizes.

YEAR PROGRAM STARTED: 1996

PURPOSE:
To recognize and award excellence in teaching by a general education teacher committed to helping all students, including those with learning disabilities, to learn

successfully; to increase opportunities for all individuals with learning disabilities to achieve their potential.

LEGAL BASIS:
Nonprofit organization.

ELIGIBILITY:
Applicants must be general educators who would not otherwise be able to participate in professional meetings that focus on the needs of individuals with learning disabilities.

GEOG. RESTRICTIONS: United States.

NO. AWARDS: 1.

APPLICATION INFO:
Information is available on the Center's web site.

Duration: One-time award.

ADDRESS INQUIRIES TO:
Natalie Tamburello
Learning Resources and Research
E-mail: ntamburello@ncld.org

NATIONAL CENTER FOR LEARNING DISABILITIES [1521]

32 Laight Street, 2nd Floor
New York, NY 10013
(646) 616-1211
Fax: (212) 545-9665
E-mail: afscholarship@ncld.org
Web Site: www.ncld.org/scholarships-and-awards

FOUNDED: 2001

AREAS OF INTEREST:
Education and learning disabilities.

NAME(S) OF PROGRAMS:
- **Anne Ford Scholarship**
- **Allegra Ford Thomas Scholarship**

TYPE:
Awards/prizes; Scholarships. Anne Ford Scholarship is a four-year scholarship granted to a graduating high school senior with a documented learning disability who will be enrolled in a full-time Bachelor's degree program.

Allegra Ford Thomas Scholarship is a one-time scholarship awarded to a graduating high school senior with a documented learning disability who will be enrolled in a two-year community college, a vocational or technical training program, or a specialized program for students with LD.

YEAR PROGRAM STARTED: 2001

PURPOSE:
To support a high school senior of high merit with an identified learning disability, who is pursuing an undergraduate degree.

LEGAL BASIS:
Nonprofit organization.

ELIGIBILITY:
Anne Ford Scholarship applicant must:
(1) be a graduating high school senior who will be attending a four-year Bachelor's degree program;
(2) have an overall grade point average of 3.0 or higher on a four-point scale (or equivalent);
(3) provide most current documentation of an identified learning disability and;
(4) be a U.S. citizen.

Allegra Ford Thomas Scholarship applicant must:
(1) be a graduating high school senior who will be attending a two-year community college, a vocational/technical training program, or specialized program for students with LD;
(2) demonstrate financial need;
(3) provide most current documentation of an identified learning disability and;
(4) be a U.S. citizen.

GEOG. RESTRICTIONS: United States.

FINANCIAL DATA:
Amount of support per award: Anne Ford Scholarship: $10,000 ($2,500 per year over four years). Allegra Ford Thomas Scholarship: $2,500.

NO. AWARDS: 1 of each award per year.

APPLICATION INFO:
Application information is available on the web site.

Duration: Anne Ford Scholarship: Four years. Allegra Ford Thomas Scholarship: One-time scholarship.

Deadline: Varies. Check web site for specific dates.

ADDRESS INQUIRIES TO:
Natalie Tamburello
Learning Resources and Research
(See e-mail address above.)

*PLEASE NOTE:
For both scholarships:
Attention-Deficit/Hyperactivity Disorder alone is not considered to be a learning disability; eligible candidates with AD/HD must also provide documentation of a specific learning disability.

*SPECIAL STIPULATIONS:
The scholars will be required to submit annual reports detailing their progress in school and describing their insights about their personal growth.

NATIONAL CENTER FOR LEARNING DISABILITIES [1522]

32 Laight Street, 2nd Floor
New York, NY 10013
(212) 545-7510
Fax: (212) 545-9665
Web Site: www.ncld.org/scholarships-and-awards

FOUNDED: 2000

AREAS OF INTEREST:
Education and learning disabilities.

NAME(S) OF PROGRAMS:
- **Rozelle Founders Award**

TYPE:
Awards/prizes.

YEAR PROGRAM STARTED: 1977

PURPOSE:
To recognize a school or school-related program that addresses the educational and social/emotional needs of all children, including those with learning disabilities. The award will allow for expanded programmatic and staff development opportunities that focus on incorporating effective research-based practices into classroom and schoolwide practice with preference given to programs that serve underprivileged and underserved communities, or programs that have demonstrated unique impact for students with learning disabilities.

LEGAL BASIS:
Nonprofit organization.

GEOG. RESTRICTIONS: United States.

NO. AWARDS: 1.

APPLICATION INFO:
Contact the Center for application procedures.

Deadline: End of August to early September.

ADDRESS INQUIRIES TO:
Natalie Tamburello
Learning Resources and Research
E-mail: ntamburello@ncld.org

NATIONAL COALITION OF BLACK MEETING PLANNERS (NCBMP) [1523]

700 North Fairfax Street
Suite 510
Alexandria, VA 22314
(571) 527-3110
Fax: (571) 527-3105
E-mail: info@ncbmp.org
Web Site: www.ncbmp.com

FOUNDED: 1983

AREAS OF INTEREST:
Professional meeting planning and hospitality management.

TYPE:
Conferences/seminars; Scholarships.

YEAR PROGRAM STARTED: 1983

PURPOSE:
To be the preeminent organization in educating the African American meeting planner in all aspects of the meeting planning profession; to improve the meetings, conferences, exhibitions, and convocations that African Americans manage.

ELIGIBILITY:
Students seeking careers in meeting planning and enrolled in a hospitality management program.

GEOG. RESTRICTIONS: United States.

FINANCIAL DATA:
Amount of support per award: $1,000 to $2,500.

Total amount of support: $3,000 annually.

NO. AWARDS: 3.

APPLICATION INFO:
Contact the Coalition for application procedures.

Duration: One-time award.

Deadline: November.

ADDRESS INQUIRIES TO:
Monica Robinson, Executive Director
(See address above.)

NATIONAL COUNCIL FOR THE SOCIAL STUDIES

8555 16th Street, Suite 500
Silver Spring, MD 20910
(301) 588-1800 ext. 107
Fax: (301) 588-2049
E-mail: excellence@ncss.org
Web Site: www.socialstudies.org

TYPE:
Awards/prizes; Grants-in-aid.

See entry 1805 for full listing.

NATIONAL COUNCIL FOR THE SOCIAL STUDIES

8555 16th Street, Suite 500
Silver Spring, MD 20910
(301) 588-1800 ext. 107
Fax: (301) 588-2049
E-mail: excellence@ncss.org
Web Site: www.socialstudies.org/fasse

TYPE:
Project/program grants. The grants are intended to support collaborative projects that demonstrate potential to enhance international relationships and global perspectives in social studies education. Funded projects will hold promise for enhancing international and cross-cultural understanding (e.g., through global or international education, human rights education, a focus on global issues, global citizenship, etc.)

See entry 1804 for full listing.

NATIONAL COUNCIL FOR THE SOCIAL STUDIES

8555 16th Street, Suite 500
Silver Spring, MD 20910
(301) 588-1800 ext. 107
Fax: (301) 588-2049
E-mail: excellence@ncss.org
Web Site: www.socialstudies.org

TYPE:
Awards/prizes. Annual award for projects representing excellence and innovation in social studies education and having the potential of serving as a model for other teachers.

See entry 1806 for full listing.

NATIONAL COUNCIL FOR THE SOCIAL STUDIES

8555 16th Street, Suite 500
Silver Spring, MD 20910
(301) 588-1800 ext. 107
Fax: (301) 588-2049
E-mail: excellence@ncss.org
Web Site: www.socialstudies.org

TYPE:
Awards/prizes. Annual award honoring the outstanding performance of teachers, researchers, and other worthy individuals and programs.

See entry 1807 for full listing.

NATIONAL COUNCIL FOR THE SOCIAL STUDIES

8555 16th Street, Suite 500
Silver Spring, MD 20910
(301) 588-1800 ext. 107
Fax: (301) 588-2049
E-mail: excellence@ncss.org
Web Site: www.socialstudies.org

TYPE:
Awards/prizes.

See entry 1808 for full listing.

NATIONAL COUNCIL OF TEACHERS OF ENGLISH RESEARCH FOUNDATION [1524]

1111 West Kenyon Road
Urbana, IL 61801
(217) 328-3870 ext. 3670
Fax: (217) 328-0977
E-mail: jmay@ncte.org
Web Site: www.ncte.org/research-foundation

FOUNDED: 1911

AREAS OF INTEREST:
Materials, methods, curriculum patterns in English and studies related to the teaching of English.

TYPE:
Research grants. Support for individuals and groups engaged in theoretical, basic or applied research that has significance for the teaching or learning of English/Language Arts or related fields.

YEAR PROGRAM STARTED: 1960

PURPOSE:
To encourage research, experimentation and investigation in the teaching of English.

LEGAL BASIS:
Separate entity within nonprofit, tax-exempt organization.

ELIGIBILITY:
Applicants must be members of NCTE.

GEOG. RESTRICTIONS: United States.

FINANCIAL DATA:
Funds are not available for travel costs or subsidies for loss of salary unless cooperating agencies are willing to bear a substantial part of the cost.

Amount of support per award: Up to $5,000.

NO. MOST RECENT APPLICANTS: 25.

APPLICATION INFO:
Applicant must submit an application cover sheet, grant proposal and one-page resume.

Duration: Generally one year. Applicants may reapply to Trustees for extension.

Deadline: June 15. Notification by mid-August.

PUBLICATIONS:
Application guidelines.

ADDRESS INQUIRIES TO:
Julie May, Meeting Planner
(See address above.)

*PLEASE NOTE:
Research grants are awarded in alternating years. Next grant cycle is 2017.

NATIONAL EMERGENCY MEDICINE ASSOCIATION [1525]

P.O. Box 1039
Edgewood, MD 21040
(443) 922-7533
Fax: (888) 682-7947
E-mail: info@nemahealth.org
Web Site: www.nemahealth.org

FOUNDED: 1982

AREAS OF INTEREST:
Emergency medicine.

NAME(S) OF PROGRAMS:

- **Kids Do Matter (KDM)**
- **National Alzheimer's Council (NAC)**
- **National Heart Council (NHC)**
- **National Stroke Council (NSC)**

TYPE:
Awards/prizes; Capital grants; Project/program grants; Research grants.

YEAR PROGRAM STARTED: 1982

PURPOSE:
To prevent injury or illness by addressing health and social issues through education, applied research, technology, and equipment.

LEGAL BASIS:
Educational nonprofit 501(c)(3).

ELIGIBILITY:
The granting of funds to applicants is considered according to the following priorities:
(1) first consideration to grants relating to coronary trauma and heart wellness program;
(2) second consideration to grants relating to all other types of trauma, vehicular trauma and strokes and;
(3) third consideration to grants relating to trauma prevention and the cause of trauma.

GEOG. RESTRICTIONS: United States.

FINANCIAL DATA:
Amount of support per award: Varies.

NO. MOST RECENT APPLICANTS: 5.

NO. AWARDS: 1.

REPRESENTATIVE AWARDS:
St. Agnes Hospital, Catonsville, MD, for Chest Pain Emergency Clinic; National Institute of Health, Bethesda, MD, for research into coronary ischemia; Beth Israel Medical Center, New York, NY, for research in reversing effects of heart disease.

APPLICATION INFO:
The proposal should be written in clear, concise language with all technical terms defined and should give a full description of the project. The proposal should also include:
(1) purpose and services;
(2) a history of other similar projects and their results;
(3) activities, benefits and desired results;
(4) amount requested, anticipated costs, budget, and funding sources;
(5) annual report, financial statements and background information of the sponsoring organization;
(6) proof of tax-exempt status;
(7) qualifications of staff;
(8) list of Board members and;
(9) a plan for how information on the project will be communicated to the public and how NEMA will be credited.

Duration: Varies.

Deadline: Applications considered as received.

PUBLICATIONS:
Five Minute Guide to Heart Attack Prevention and Survival; *Five Minute Guide to Stroke (Brain Attack) Prevention and Survival*; wallet cards for Heart, Stroke and Alzheimer's.

IRS I.D.: 52-1257429

OFFICERS:
Kelly Herzog, President/Chief Executive Officer

ADDRESS INQUIRIES TO:
Kelly Herzog
President/Chief Executive Officer
(See address above.)

NATIONAL FOSTER PARENT ASSOCIATION

1102 Prairie Ridge Trail
Pflugerville, TX 78660
(512) 686-1948
(800) 557-5238
Fax: (888) 925-5634
E-mail: info@nfpaonline.org
Web Site: www.nfpaonline.org

TYPE:
Conferences/seminars; Scholarships. Scholarships for youth living in foster families whose foster parents are members of NFPA.

Walk Me Home Program is a walk program to raise awareness of foster care and the need for more foster families, as well as to raise funds for recruitment and other activities.

See entry 1114 for full listing.

NATIONAL INSTITUTE ON DRUG ABUSE [1526]

6001 Executive Boulevard, Room 4244
MSC 9550
Bethesda, MD 20892-9550
(301) 402-1918
E-mail: ghimm@mail.nih.gov
Web Site: www.nida.nih.gov/researchtraining

AREAS OF INTEREST:
Drug abuse and addiction.

TYPE:
Awards/prizes. The Institute supports a variety of training and career development grant awards for all career stages.

PURPOSE:
To support research training and/or career development at predoctoral, postdoctoral (including postresident or research-track resident), and junior faculty levels.

ELIGIBILITY:
Specific eligibility criteria vary based on the award.

FINANCIAL DATA:
Amount of support per award: Varies.

ADDRESS INQUIRIES TO:
Mimi Ghim, Ph.D.
Coordinator of Research Training
(See address above.)

NATIONAL MOLE DAY FOUNDATION

3896 Leaman Court
Freeland, MI 48623
(989) 964-8020
E-mail: moleday@hotmail.com
Web Site: www.moleday.org

TYPE:
Grants-in-aid. The George Hague Memorial Travel Award is given to financially support a young chemistry instructor (with two to five years of chemistry experience) in attending a biennial ChemEd conference.

The Maury Award is given to teachers to support student-centered Mole Day activities (promoting chemistry education).

The National Mole of the Year Award (MOTY) is given to a member of the National Mole Day Foundation who has contributed the most to furthering the cause of Mole Day and chemistry education.

See entry 2003 for full listing.

NATIONAL OCEANIC AND ATMOSPHERIC ADMINISTRATION [1527]

NOAA Chesapeake Bay Office
410 Severn Avenue, Suite 207-A
Annapolis, MD 21403
(410) 267-5660
Fax: (410) 267-5666
E-mail: kevin.schabow@noaa.gov
Web Site: chesapeakebay.noaa.gov

FOUNDED: 1985

AREAS OF INTEREST:
Stock assessment, multispecies, and ecosystem-based fisheries research in Chesapeake Bay.

NAME(S) OF PROGRAMS:
- **Chesapeake Bay Fisheries Research Program**

TYPE:
Project/program grants; Research grants; Research contracts.

YEAR PROGRAM STARTED: 1985

PURPOSE:
To support stock assessment, multispecies and ecosystem-based fisheries research in Chesapeake Bay.

LEGAL BASIS:
Government agency.

ELIGIBILITY:
Individuals who are U.S. citizens or residents and organizations, including religious, classified as 501(c)(3) by the IRS can apply.

GEOG. RESTRICTIONS: United States, with a focus on Chesapeake Bay/mid-Atlantic.

FINANCIAL DATA:
Amount of support per award: $400,000 average.

NO. MOST RECENT APPLICANTS: 26.

NO. AWARDS: 17.

APPLICATION INFO:
Application information is available on the web site. RFPs released between December and February.

Duration: Multiyear.

Deadline: March/April time frame; varies each year.

PUBLICATIONS:
Application guidelines; annual report.

ADDRESS INQUIRIES TO:
Kevin Schabow, Grants Manager
National Marine Fisheries Service
(See address above.)

NATIONAL SCIENCE FOUNDATION

Directorate for Education and Human Resources
Division of Research on Learning in Formal and Informal Settings
4201 Wilson Boulevard, Suite 885 S
Arlington, VA 22230
(703) 292-8620
(703) 570-1975
Fax: (703) 292-9044; (703) 292-9046
E-mail: acarroll@nsf.gov
Web Site: www.nsf.gov

TYPE:
Conferences/seminars; Demonstration grants; Development grants; Project/program grants; Research grants; Training grants. With an emphasis on two-year colleges, the Advanced Technological Education (ATE) program focuses on the education of technicians for the high-technology fields that drive the nation's economy.

Discovery Research K-12 (DR K12) funds research, development and evaluation activities through knowledge generation and application to improve K-12 learning and teaching.

Informal Science Education (ISE) program invests in projects that develop and implement informal learning experiences designed to increase interest, engagement and understanding of science, technology, engineering and mathematics (STEM) by individuals of all ages and backgrounds, as well as projects that advance knowledge and practice of informal science education.

Innovative Technology Experiences for Students and Teachers (ITEST) is designed to increase the opportunities for students and teachers to learn about, experience, and use information technologies within the context of science, technology, engineering and mathematics (STEM), including Information Technology (IT) courses. It is in direct response to the concern about shortages of information technology workers in the U.S.

Research and Evaluation on Education in Science and Engineering (REESE) supports basic and applied research and evaluation that enhances science, technology, engineering and mathematics (STEM) learning and teaching.

See entry 1557 for full listing.

NATIVE AMERICAN COMMUNITY BOARD (NACB) [1528]

P.O. Box 572
Lake Andes, SD 57356-0572
(605) 487-7097
(605) 487-7072
Fax: (605) 487-7964
E-mail: charon@charles-mix.com
Web Site: www.nativeshop.org

AREAS OF INTEREST:
Native American women.

NAME(S) OF PROGRAMS:
- **NACB Internship Program**

TYPE:
Internships. Internships at the Native American Women's Health Education Resource Center and the Women's Lodge.

PURPOSE:
To support young women interested in learning about indigenous issues and willing to serve indigenous communities.

LEGAL BASIS:
Nonprofit tax-exempt 501(c)(3) organization.

ELIGIBILITY:
Internships are open to college and graduate students or recent graduates looking for some work experience. Applicants need to be interested in Native American rights and health issues and have a desire to actively promote civil rights, women's rights and a healthy environment. Priority will be given to those wishing to stay six months or longer.

GEOG. RESTRICTIONS: United States.

FINANCIAL DATA:
Internship includes free room at the shelter and partial board from the Resource Center's food pantry.

Amount of support per award: $500 per month.

Total amount of support: Varies.

APPLICATION INFO:
A resume with references is required, and the Board needs to know the time frame in which the intern expects to serve. Applicant should mail personal resume to the Internship Coordinator; Native American Women's

Health Education Resource Center; at the mailing address above, send it to the fax number above or e-mail it to the address above.

Duration: Three months to one year.

Deadline: Internship positions are available all year-round.

ADDRESS INQUIRIES TO:
Charon Asetoyer, Executive Director
(See e-mail address above.) or

The Native American Women's
Health Education Resource Center
(See phone numbers above.)

*PLEASE NOTE:
Each intern will be assigned to the Resource Center and to the Domestic Violence Shelter, which is located nearby. After arrival and an orientation period, assignments will be given out based on the individual's experience, strengths, interests and, if necessary, academic requirements.

THE NEA FOUNDATION [1529]

1201 16th Street, N.W., Suite 416
Washington, DC 20036
(202) 822-7840
Fax: (202) 822-7779
E-mail: NEAF@neafoundation.org
Web Site: www.neafoundation.org

AREAS OF INTEREST:
Public education.

TYPE:
Awards/prizes. Recognizes and awards the excellence demonstrated by educators nationwide.

PURPOSE:
To advance student achievement, through the unique strength of the Foundation's partnership with educators, by investing in public education that will prepare each of America's children to learn and thrive in a rapidly changing world.

GEOG. RESTRICTIONS: United States.

FINANCIAL DATA:
Amount of support per award: State level: $650 gift to teacher's school and travel to Annual Salute to Excellence in Education Gala. Five finalists from the state level: $10,000 courtesy of the Horace Mann Educators Corporation. National awardee: $25,000 total from NEA Member Benefits Company.

APPLICATION INFO:
Applicants must complete proposals through the Foundation's online grant system.

Deadline: May 1.

THE NEA FOUNDATION [1530]

1201 16th Street, N.W., Suite 416
Washington, DC 20036-3207
(202) 822-7840
Fax: (202) 822-7779
E-mail: NEAF@neafoundation.org
Web Site: www.neafoundation.org

FOUNDED: 1969

AREAS OF INTEREST:
Education.

NAME(S) OF PROGRAMS:
- **NEA Foundation Learning and Leadership Grants**
- **NEA Foundation Student Achievement Grants**

YEAR PROGRAM STARTED: 1999

PURPOSE:
To improve the academic achievement of students in U.S. public schools and public higher education institutions in any subject area(s); to support public school teachers, public education support professionals, and/or faculty and staff in public institutions of higher education.

ELIGIBILITY:
Applicants must be practicing U.S. public school teachers in grades PreK-12, public school education support professionals, or faculty or staff at public higher education institutions.

Applicants must be members of the National Education Association. The NEA Foundation encourages grant applications from education support professionals.

Learning and Leadership Grant: All professional development must improve practice, curriculum, and student achievement. Decisions regarding the content of the professional growth activities must be based upon an assessment of student work undertaken with colleagues, and must be integrated into the institutional planning process. Funds may not be used to pursue degrees, pay direct costs, grant administration fees, or salaries, or support travel costs or conference fees for more than one person.

Student Achievement Grant: The proposed work should engage students in critical thinking and problem solving that deepens their knowledge of standards-based subject matter. The work should also improve students' habits of inquiry, self-directed learning, and critical reflection. Proposals for work resulting in low-income and minority student success with honors, advanced placement, or other challenging curricula are particularly encouraged. Funds may be used for resource materials, supplies, equipment, transportation, software, or scholars-in-residence. Although some funds may be used to support the professional development necessary to implement the project, the majority of grant funds must be spent on materials or educational experiences for students.

GEOG. RESTRICTIONS: United States.

FINANCIAL DATA:
Amount of support per award: Learning and Leadership Grants: $2,000 (individuals) and $5,000 (groups engaged in collegial study); Student Achievement Grants: $2,000 and $5,000.

NO. MOST RECENT APPLICANTS: 950.

NO. AWARDS: 170.

APPLICATION INFO:
All proposals must be submitted through the Foundation's online grant system.

Duration: Annual. Nonrenewable.

Deadline: February 1, June 1 and October 15.

ADDRESS INQUIRIES TO:
Jesse Graytock, Grants Manager
(See address above.)

NELLIE MAE EDUCATION FOUNDATION [1531]

1250 Hancock Street, Suite 205N
Quincy, MA 02169-4331
(781) 348-4200
Fax: (617) 472-4089
E-mail: info@nmefoundation.org
Web Site: www.nmefoundation.org

FOUNDED: 1998

AREAS OF INTEREST:
Systems change and student-centered learning.

TYPE:
Matching gifts; Research grants.

YEAR PROGRAM STARTED: 1998

PURPOSE:
To promote accessibility, quality and effectiveness of education, especially for underserved populations in the six New England states.

LEGAL BASIS:
Public charity.

ELIGIBILITY:
Organizations must be 501(c)(3) or public schools. No grants are made to individuals.

GEOG. RESTRICTIONS: Connecticut, Maine, Massachusetts, New Hampshire, Rhode Island and Vermont.

FINANCIAL DATA:
Amount of support per award: Varies.

Total amount of support: Varies.

APPLICATION INFO:
Application information is available online.

Duration: Varies.

Deadline: Varies.

ADDRESS INQUIRIES TO:
See e-mail address above.

NICSA [1532]

8400 Westpark Drive, 2nd Floor
McLean, VA 22102
(508) 485-1500
Fax: (508) 485-1560
E-mail: info@nicsa.org
Web Site: www.nicsa.org

FOUNDED: 1962

AREAS OF INTEREST:
Education.

NAME(S) OF PROGRAMS:
- **The NICSA/William T. Blackwell Scholarship Fund**

TYPE:
Scholarships.

PURPOSE:
To provide leadership and innovation in educational programming and information exchange within the operations sector of the mutual fund industry worldwide; to recognize outstanding students of the NICSA Family with financial support for postsecondary education.

ELIGIBILITY:
Applicants must be dependent children of full-time employees of NICSA member companies and be enrolled in or planning to pursue a full-time course of study leading to a Bachelor's degree from an accredited four-year college or university.

FINANCIAL DATA:
Amount of support per award: $2,000 to $5,000.

Total amount of support: Maximum of $40,000 annually.

APPLICATION INFO:
Application information is available on the web site in the fall.

Duration: One-time award.

Deadline: January.

ADDRESS INQUIRIES TO:
The NICSA/William T. Blackwell Scholarship Fund
Scholarship Management Services
One Scholarship Way, P.O. Box 297
St. Peter, MN 56082
Tel: (507) 931-1682

NORTH CAROLINA GLAXOSMITHKLINE FOUNDATION [1533]

5 Moore Drive
P.O. Box 13398
Research Triangle Park, NC 27709
(919) 483-2140
Fax: (919) 315-3015
E-mail: info@ncgskfoundation.org
Web Site: www.ncgskfoundation.org

FOUNDED: 1986

AREAS OF INTEREST:
Science, health and education at all educational and professional levels.

NAME(S) OF PROGRAMS:
- **Child Health Recognition Awards**
- **Ribbon of Hope**
- **Traditional Grants**
- **Women in Science Scholars Program**

TYPE:
Support for activities which help meet the educational and health needs of today's society and future generations.

Child Health Recognition Awards program honors local health departments, public health staff, and individuals for innovative, collaborative programs that improve the lives of North Carolina's children.

Ribbon of Hope provides one-time grants to nonprofits for projects furthering health, science and education in their communities.

The Traditional Grants program provides for larger grants that may be multiyear in nature, to support programs advancing health, science and education throughout the state of North Carolina.

Women in Science Scholars Program offers an educational opportunity to young women by coupling college scholarships with a mentoring program.

YEAR PROGRAM STARTED: 1986

PURPOSE:
To provide programs that emphasize the understanding and applications of science, health and education at all academic and professional levels.

LEGAL BASIS:
Foundation.

ELIGIBILITY:
Ribbon of Hope: North Carolina community-based nonprofit, charitable organizations and institutions exempt under Section 501(c)(3) of the Internal Revenue Code are eligible to apply. Individuals may not apply. Nonprofits with proposals pertaining to science, health and education as well as collaborative partnerships between several community-based organizations are encouraged to apply.

Traditional Grants: Grant applicants must be nonprofit, charitable organizations and institutions exempt under Section 501(c)(3) of the Internal Revenue Code. No grants are made to individuals, for construction or restoration projects, or for international programs. The primary focus of the Foundation is to provide seed funds for new and worthwhile educational programs. This policy does not preclude the consideration and possible funding of ongoing projects.

GEOG. RESTRICTIONS: North Carolina.

FINANCIAL DATA:
Amount of support per award: Ribbon of Hope: $25,000; Traditional Grants: $25,000 and up.

Total amount of support: Approximately $3,000,000 paid out annually.

REPRESENTATIVE AWARDS:
Ribbon of Hope: NC Institute for Child Development Professionals, Orange County, to develop a Child Care Health Consultant tiered certification process to merge consultants' health education, continuing education and child care technical assistance skills; Graham Children's Health Services, Yancey County, to expand its offering of physical fitness programs in schools and the community; Heart Tutoring, Mecklenburg County, for a math tutoring intervention program working with high-poverty elementary schools.

Traditional Grants: $1,000,000 to The University of North Carolina General Administration to support the Bronco STAR program at Fayetteville State University to assist students who struggle to learn because they learn differently; $350,000 to the Museum of Life and Science to build two new exhibits, Hideaway Woods and Earth Moves; $1,760,000 to North Carolina A & T State University to develop a STEM Center of Excellence for Active Learning; $160,000 to North Carolina Center for Public Policy Research to conduct a project to examine key issues affecting the rapidly growing aging population in the state.

APPLICATION INFO:
Refer to the web site.

Duration: Ribbon of Hope: One-time grant; Traditional Grants: Up to five years.

Deadline: Child Health Recognition Awards: May 31. Ribbon of Hope: April 1 and October 1. Traditional Grants: January 1, April 1, July 1 and October 1.

PUBLICATIONS:
Annual report; application; brochure.

IRS I.D.: 58-1698610

STAFF:
Marilyn E. Foote-Hudson, Executive Director

BOARD OF DIRECTORS:
Robert A. Ingram, Chairman
Margaret B. Dardess, President
Paul A. Holcombe, Jr., Secretary

ADDRESS INQUIRIES TO:
See e-mail address above.

OAK GROVE SCHOOL FOUNDATION [1534]

P.O. Box 150
South China, ME 04358
(207) 445-3333
(207) 872-5908
Fax: (207) 445-4477
E-mail: nrshed@gmail.com
austinlaw@fairpoint.net
Web Site: www.ogsfoundation.org

FOUNDED: 1989

AREAS OF INTEREST:
Education, secondary school curriculum augmenting, limited secondary school scholarships, and some not-for-profits.

NAME(S) OF PROGRAMS:
- **Grants Program**
- **Tuition Assistance**

TYPE:
Demonstration grants; General operating grants; Grants-in-aid; Project/program grants; Scholarships. Scholarships are for Quaker high schools.

YEAR PROGRAM STARTED: 1991

PURPOSE:
To foster secondary education innovation in proximate geographic area; to provide tuition assistance.

LEGAL BASIS:
Private foundation.

ELIGIBILITY:
Secondary schools and 501(c)(3) organizations in Central Maine. For tuition assistance, candidates may be either currently enrolled or accepted for enrollment in a Quaker secondary school and must be a resident of Maine or children or grandchildren of Oak Grove School or Oak Grove-Coburn School alumni/ae. In addition, children and grandchildren of former Oak Grove or Oak Grove-Coburn faculty and staff are eligible applicants.

GEOG. RESTRICTIONS: Central Maine.

FINANCIAL DATA:
Amount of support per award: Grants: $1,000 to $5,000. Scholarships: Varies.

Total amount of support: Approximately $130,000 yearly.

NO. MOST RECENT APPLICANTS: Approximately 150.

NO. AWARDS: Approximately 100 yearly.

APPLICATION INFO:
Application forms are available from the Foundation web site.

Duration: Grants: One year; possibly renewable upon review for up to two more years.

Deadline: Large grants: April 1. Small grants: Early October.

IRS I.D.: 01-0211537

ADDRESS INQUIRIES TO:
Austin Law
(See address above.)

PANASONIC FOUNDATION, INC. [1535]

2 Riverfront Plaza, 11th Floor
Newark, NJ 07102
(201) 392-4132
(201) 271-3367
E-mail: info@foundation.us.panasonic.com
Web Site: www.panasonicfoundation.net

FOUNDED: 1984

AREAS OF INTEREST:
Pre-collegiate education and school reform.

NAME(S) OF PROGRAMS:
- **Collaboration for Innovation**
- **New Jersey Network of Superintendents**
- **Panasonic Foundation Partnership Program for School Reform**

TYPE:
Technical assistance. Collaboration for Innovation is an online community of practice serving 16 school districts all across the U.S.

The New Jersey Network of Superintendents, established December 2008, supports monthly meetings of district superintendents focused on improving teaching and learning for all students.

The Partnership Program was established with urban school districts serving large proportions of disadvantaged youth. The Foundation does not make grants, but rather it provides technical assistance to school districts with which it has formed a partnership.

YEAR PROGRAM STARTED: 1987

PURPOSE:
To partner with selected public school districts and their communities to break the links between race, poverty and educational outcomes by improving the academic and social success of all students: all means all!.

LEGAL BASIS:
Corporate foundation.

GEOG. RESTRICTIONS: United States.

FINANCIAL DATA:
Amount of support per award: $35,000 to $70,000 per site.

Matching fund requirements: Districts in the Panasonic Partnership Program participate in the Foundation Leadership Associates Program, which requires the district to assume the travel and lodging of at least four participants in two three-day-long events.

PUBLICATIONS:
Newsletter; brochure.

OFFICERS:
Michael Riccio, Treasurer
Gordon Kyvik, Assistant Treasurer
Stephen Weingarten, Secretary

STAFF:
Larry Leverett, Executive Director
Scott Thompson, Assistant Executive Director
Daniel Meaney, Financial Manager
Kathleen Archetti, Planning Coordinator

BOARD OF DIRECTORS:
Milton Chen, Chairman
Andres Alonso
Damien Atkins
Patricia Gandara
Megan Lee
Kent McGuire
Sophie Sa

ADDRESS INQUIRIES TO:
Larry Leverett, Executive Director
(See address above.)

PARENTS WITHOUT PARTNERS [1536]

1100-H Brandywine Boulevard
Zanesville, OH 43701
(740) 450-1332
Fax: (740) 452-2552
E-mail: intl.hq@parentswithoutpartners.org
Web Site: www.parentswithoutpartners.org

FOUNDED: 1957

AREAS OF INTEREST:
Education of children of single parents belonging to the organization.

NAME(S) OF PROGRAMS:
- **Parents Without Partners International Scholarship**

TYPE:
Scholarships.

PURPOSE:
To provide single parents and their children with an opportunity for enhancing personal growth, self-confidence, and sensitivity towards others by offering an environment for support, friendship and the exchange of parenting techniques.

LEGAL BASIS:
Nonprofit.

ELIGIBILITY:
Applicants must be dependent children, up to 25 years of age, of PWP members. Also, must be either in the senior class of any high school and planning to enter and have applied to a school of higher education for the following year, or be an undergraduate student at a college or trade school.

GEOG. RESTRICTIONS: United States and Canada.

FINANCIAL DATA:
Amount of support per award: Varies.

Total amount of support: Varies.

APPLICATION INFO:
Contact PWP for guidelines.

Duration: One year. Nonrenewable. Must reapply.

ADDRESS INQUIRIES TO:
See e-mail address above.

THE MABEL LOUISE RILEY FOUNDATION [1537]

77 Summer Street, Eighth Floor
Boston, MA 02110
(617) 399-1850
Fax: (617) 399-1851
E-mail: info@rileyfoundation.com
Web Site: www.rileyfoundation.com

FOUNDED: 1972

AREAS OF INTEREST:
Emphasis on priority needs in social services and education, especially for youth, community development including cultural, housing and urban environmental programs.

TYPE:
Capital grants; Challenge/matching grants; Development grants; Project/program grants; Seed money grants; Training grants.

LEGAL BASIS:
Private foundation.

ELIGIBILITY:
Requests are considered only from corporations organized under the laws of Massachusetts for purposes to be carried out within Massachusetts and those who have a 501(c)(3) IRS determination.

GEOG. RESTRICTIONS: Greater Boston area, with a primary focus on the city of Boston, Massachusetts.

FINANCIAL DATA:
Amount of support per award: $50,000 to $100,000.

Total amount of support: $3,248,520 for the year 2014.

APPLICATION INFO:
Applicants are required to submit a brief summary (LOI) of their proposal, not more than two pages, without a cover letter before submitting a formal grant request. This summary should briefly describe the purposes and objectives of the proposal, a brief history of the applicant and the amount requested from the Foundation. In addition to the two-page summary, a copy of the IRS 501(c)(3) Determination Letter and a program budget relative to the request should be included.

The Foundation will notify the applicant if the submission of a formal grant request is invited. Formal grant proposal must be made using the Common Proposal Form of the Associated Grant Makers.

Duration: One year. Renewals possible. Two-year waiting period is requested before applying again for those who have been awarded a grant.

Deadline: Meetings are held in March, June, September and December with deadlines for receipt of full grant proposals set 60 days prior to each meeting.

PUBLICATIONS:
Guidelines.

IRS I.D.: 04-6278857

TRUSTEES:
Grace Fey
Robert W. Holmes, Jr.

CORPORATE TRUSTEE:
BNY Mellon

ADDRESS INQUIRIES TO:
Nancy A. Saunders, Administrator
(See address above.)

ROSS FOUNDATION

202 South Fifth Street
Arkadelphia, AR 71923
(870) 246-9881
Fax: (870) 246-9674
E-mail: info@rossfoundation.us
Web Site: www.rossfoundation.us

TYPE:
Project/program grants.

See entry 1326 for full listing.

RURITAN NATIONAL FOUNDATION [1538]

5451 Lyons Road
Dublin, VA 24084
(540) 674-5431
(877) 787-8727
Fax: (540) 674-2304
E-mail: foundation@ruritan.org
Web Site: www.ruritan.org

AREAS OF INTEREST:
Education.

NAME(S) OF PROGRAMS:
- **Build Your Dollars Grant**
- **Educational Grant Program**

TYPE:
Grants-in-aid; Matching gifts. These programs allow Ruritan clubs to increase their financial assistance to a student of the club's choice. Ruritan clubs contribute $300 to the Foundation and, in turn, the Foundation will add to this amount for grants.

PURPOSE:
To manage and maintain a trust for the encouragement, promotion, and financing of the charitable, educational, and benevolent principles and activities of Ruritan Clubs and of Ruritan National.

ELIGIBILITY:
Must be sponsored by a local Ruritan Club and have the endorsement of two members. Applicant should be pursuing a postsecondary education. Selection is based on financial need, character, scholarship and applicant's desire for higher education.

GEOG. RESTRICTIONS: United States.

FINANCIAL DATA:
Amount of support per award: Varies.
Total amount of support: Varies.

APPLICATION INFO:
Applications for grant programs are available online.
Duration: Applicants must reapply each year.
Deadline: April 1.

ADDRESS INQUIRIES TO:
Michael Chrisley, Executive Director
(See address above.)

GEORGE J. AND EFFIE L. SEAY MEMORIAL TRUST

Bank of America
1111 East Main Street, 12th Floor
Richmond, VA 23219
(804) 887-8763
Fax: (804) 887-8854

TYPE:
Project/program grants. Grants for specific needs.

See entry 1466 for full listing.

SMITHSONIAN ENVIRONMENTAL RESEARCH CENTER (SERC)

647 Contees Wharf Road
Edgewater, MD 21037
(443) 482-2217
Fax: (443) 482-2380
E-mail: gustafsond@si.edu
Web Site: www.serc.si.edu

TYPE:
Fellowships; Internships. The Internship Program enables undergraduates, recent graduates and graduate students to work on specific projects under the direction of the Center's professional staff and is tailored to provide the maximum educational benefit to each participant. Graduate students and undergraduates may conduct independent projects with the approval of the staff member with whom they plan to study.

Subject matter of the projects includes terrestrial and estuarine environmental research within the disciplines of mathematics, chemistry, microbiology, botany, zoology, and environmental education.

Fellowships are offered annually at the postdoctoral, predoctoral and graduate levels.

Internships are offered three times per year at the undergraduate levels, recent graduate, or beginning Master's student.

See entry 2132 for full listing.

SPENCER FOUNDATION [1539]

625 North Michigan Avenue
Suite 1600
Chicago, IL 60611
(312) 337-7000
Fax: (312) 337-0282
E-mail: abrinkman@spencer.org
Web Site: www.spencer.org

FOUNDED: 1962

AREAS OF INTEREST:
Research on education as approached from scholars in the sciences, social sciences and humanities.

TYPE:
Research grants. Grants for research to expand knowledge and understanding of the problems and processes of education.

YEAR PROGRAM STARTED: 1970

PURPOSE:
To support research that gives promise of yielding new knowledge leading to the improvement of education, broadly defined.

LEGAL BASIS:
Independent foundation.

ELIGIBILITY:
The Foundation is interested in a wide variety of disciplinary and interdisciplinary approaches to the study of education. The principal investigator ordinarily must have an earned Doctorate in an academic discipline or in the field of education and must have an affiliation with a nonprofit organization such as a college or university, a research facility, or a cultural institution.

FINANCIAL DATA:
Amount of support per award: Varies.
Total amount of support: Approximately $20,000,000 annually.

NO. MOST RECENT APPLICANTS: Approximately 1,500.

NO. AWARDS: 150.

REPRESENTATIVE AWARDS:
$40,000 (over one year) to Mary Haywood Metz, University of Wisconsin-Madison, for "Models of School Organization: Comparing Understandings of School Organization Grounded in Ethnographics, Survey Research and the Federal 'No Child Left Behind Act';" $300,000 (over two years) to Jill V. Hamm et al., University of North Carolina at Chapel Hill, for "Correlations and Consequences of Growth in Mathematics Conceptual Understanding in Middle and High School."

APPLICATION INFO:
Application procedures differ by program. Researchers seeking support should view the Foundation's web site for general program information.
Duration: Varies.

PUBLICATIONS:
Annual report.

OFFICERS:
Michael McPherson, President

BOARD OF DIRECTORS:
Deborah Loewenberg Ball, Chairperson
Carl Cohen
Pamela Grossman
Michael McPherson
Richard Murnane
Na'ilah Suad Nasir
Stephen Raudenbush
Cybele Raver
Mario Small
Dennis Sullivan
Mark Vander Ploeg

ADDRESS INQUIRIES TO:
Annie Brinkman, Grants Manager
(See address above.)

SUBARU OF AMERICA FOUNDATION, INC. [1540]

2235 Route 70 West
Cherry Hill, NJ 08002
(856) 488-5099
Fax: (856) 488-3255
E-mail: foundation@subaru.com
Web Site: www.subaru.com/csr/soa-foundation.html

FOUNDED: 1984

AREAS OF INTEREST:
Education for children and youth and environmental stewardship for youth.

TYPE:
General operating grants; Project/program grants. Employee matching gift program.

YEAR PROGRAM STARTED: 1984

PURPOSE:
To make a difference in the lives of young people by offering them enrichment and educational programs that support their academic needs.

LEGAL BASIS:
Corporate foundation.

ELIGIBILITY:
Consideration will be given primarily to nonprofit 501(c)(3) organizations in the communities located in and around National Headquarters and in the immediate surrounding areas of regional offices.

The Foundation does not permit contributions to religious, fraternal, veterans' or political associations, individual schools, charter schools or special events, nor does it make grants to individuals, fund organizations outside the U.S., programs that benefit residents outside the U.S., or consider donation of vehicles.

GEOG. RESTRICTIONS: Only proposals serving the geographic locations listed will be considered:
Corporate Headquarters: southern New Jersey (mainly Camden and Burlington counties); and Philadelphia, Pennsylvania;
Eastern Region: Washington, District of Columbia; Orlando, Florida; Atlanta, Georgia; Frederick, Howard, Montgomery and Prince Georges counties in Maryland; Westhampton, New Jersey; and Fairfax, Loudon and Prince William counties in Virginia;
Central Region: Chicago and Itasca, Illinois; Minneapolis, Minnesota; Columbus, Ohio; and Dallas, Texas;
Western Region: Phoenix, Arizona; Los Angeles, San Diego and San Francisco, California; Denver, Colorado; Portland, Oregon; and Seattle, Washington.

FINANCIAL DATA:
Amount of support per award: Varies.

Matching fund requirements: Contributions for the matching gift program must be made by Subaru of America employees at a $25 minimum or $2,000 maximum per employee per fiscal year.

APPLICATION INFO:
Application form is available online as a Word document. Grant application and all required supporting documentation must be submitted at the same time as one package and should be mailed to the address above to arrive by the deadline (not postmarked by the deadline). Grant applications with missing information or documentation will not be considered.

Deadline: Grant spring funding cycle: Applications due February 15. Grant fall funding cycle: Applications due August 15.

IRS I.D.: 22-2531774

STAFF:
Sandra E. Capell, Philanthropy and Corporate Responsibility Manager

ADDRESS INQUIRIES TO:
Sandra E. Capell
Philanthropy and Corporate Responsibility Manager
(See address above.)

TAILHOOK EDUCATIONAL FOUNDATION [1541]

9696 Business Park Avenue
San Diego, CA 92131
(858) 689-9223
Fax: (858) 578-8839
E-mail: tag@tailhook.net
Web Site: www.tailhook.net

FOUNDED: 1992

AREAS OF INTEREST:
Education.

NAME(S) OF PROGRAMS:
- **Tailhook Educational Foundation Scholarship Award**

TYPE:
Scholarships. The Foundation awards merit-based scholarships.

YEAR PROGRAM STARTED: 1992

PURPOSE:
To support dependents of the Naval Aviation community with their educational needs.

LEGAL BASIS:
501(c)(3).

ELIGIBILITY:
The applicant or the applicant's parent/grandparent/guardian must have served in the U.S. Navy, U.S. Marine Corps, or U.S. Coast Guard as a Naval Aviator, Naval Flight Officer, or Designated Naval Aircrewman, or served on board a U.S. Navy aircraft carrier in any capacity as a member of ship's company or assigned air wing.

GEOG. RESTRICTIONS: United States.

FINANCIAL DATA:
Amount of support per award: $2,000 to $15,000.

NO. MOST RECENT APPLICANTS: 485 for the year 2015.

NO. AWARDS: 92 for the year 2015.

APPLICATION INFO:
Application information is available on the web site.

Duration: One year. Must reapply.

Deadline: March 15.

IRS I.D.: 33-0487778

ADDRESS INQUIRIES TO:
The Tailhook Educational Foundation
P.O. Box 26626
San Diego, CA 92196-0626

TRIANGLE COMMUNITY FOUNDATION [1542]

324 Blackwell Street, Suite 1220
Durham, NC 27701
(919) 474-8370
Fax: (919) 941-9208
E-mail: libby@trianglecf.org
Web Site: www.trianglecf.org

AREAS OF INTEREST:
Projects of excellence.

TYPE:
Grants-in-aid; Scholarships. General grantmaking.

YEAR PROGRAM STARTED: 1984

PURPOSE:
To expand philanthropy.

ELIGIBILITY:
Organizations, including religious, classified as 501(c)(3) by the IRS can apply. No grants to individuals.

GEOG. RESTRICTIONS: Chatham, Durham, Orange and Wake counties, North Carolina.

FINANCIAL DATA:
Amount of support per award: Minimum $250.

Total amount of support: Varies.

APPLICATION INFO:
Application available online.

Duration: Grants are not renewable.

PUBLICATIONS:
Annual report.

ADDRESS INQUIRIES TO:
Libby Richards
Senior Community Programs Officer
(See address above.)

U.S. DEPARTMENT OF EDUCATION [1543]

Institute of Education Sciences, Room 600E
555 New Jersey Avenue, N.W.
Washington, DC 20208
(202) 219-0644
Fax: (202) 219-1402
E-mail: ies@ed.gov
ellie.pelaez@ed.gov
Web Site: ies.ed.gov

FOUNDED: 1972

AREAS OF INTEREST:
Basic and applied research, evaluations and analyses in education practice and policy.

NAME(S) OF PROGRAMS:
- **Education Research**

TYPE:
Project/program grants; Research grants. Grants competitions.

The Institute supports research on a diverse set of student outcomes including: school readiness for prekindergarten; academic outcomes in kindergarten through Grade 12 that include learning, achievement, and higher order thinking in the core academic content areas of reading, writing, mathematics, and science measured by specific assessments (e.g., researcher-developed assessments, standardized tests, grades, end of course exams, exit exams) as well as course completion, grade retention, high school graduation and dropout rates; social skills, dispositions, and behaviors that support academic outcomes for students from prekindergarten through high school; access to, retention in, and completion of postsecondary education; and reading, writing, and mathematics skills for adult learners (i.e., students at least 16 years old and outside of the K-12 system). The Institute supports research from prekindergarten through Grade 12 for the typically developing student. For postsecondary and adult learners the Institute supports research on typically developing students and students with disabilities. The Institute supports research on students with disabilities from birth through high school through a different grant program run by the Institute's National Center for Special Education Research.

LEGAL BASIS:
Public Law 92-318, as amended.

ELIGIBILITY:
Applicants must be colleges, universities, state departments of education, local education agencies, other public or private profit and nonprofit agencies, organizations, groups and individuals. Support is restricted to basic and applied research, planning studies, evaluations, investigations, experiments and developmental activities directly related to research in the field of education.

Most funds provide continuing support for long-term research and development programs. The remaining funds are used for new projects, announced as Grants Competitions in specific areas of interest.

FINANCIAL DATA:
Amount of support per award: Varies.

Total amount of support: Varies.

APPLICATION INFO:
Application information is available on the web site.

Duration: Varies.

Deadline: Specific date changes each year, but application deadlines generally fall between June and September.

U.S. DEPARTMENT OF EDUCATION [1544]

Office of Career, Technical and Adult Education
550 12th Street, S.W., 11th Floor
Washington, DC 20202-7100
(202) 245-7700
Fax: (202) 245-7838
E-mail: octae@ed.gov
Web Site: www2.ed.gov/about/offices/list/ovae

FOUNDED: 1965

AREAS OF INTEREST:
Adult basic education, basic literacy skills, English as a second language and adult secondary education.

CONSULTING OR VOLUNTEER SERVICES:
Technical assistance is provided to state educational agencies.

TYPE:
Grants-in-aid. The program provides grants to states to fund local programs of adult

education and literacy services, including workplace literacy services, family literacy services, English language learning and integrated English literacy/civics education programs. Basic grants to all states including the District of Columbia as well as the Virgin Islands, American Samoa, Guam, Northern Mariana Islands and Palau.

YEAR PROGRAM STARTED: 1965

PURPOSE:
To provide educational opportunities for educationally disadvantaged adults.

LEGAL BASIS:
The Adult Education and Family Literacy Act (AEFLA), enacted as Title II of the Workforce Investment Act (WIA) of 1998, is the principal source of federal support for adult basic and literacy education programs for adults who lack basic skills, a high school diploma, or proficiency in English.

ELIGIBILITY:
Individuals and local providers cannot receive grant money directly from the Office of Vocational and Adult Education (OVAE).

Adult education and literacy programs are funded through federal grants to the states. The amount each state receives is based on a formula established by Congress. States, in turn, distribute funds to local eligible entities to provide adult education and literacy services.

The Division provides assistance to states to improve program quality and capacity.

GEOG. RESTRICTIONS: United States and its territories.

FINANCIAL DATA:
AEFLA funds are distributed by formula to states using census data on the number of adults (ages 16 and older) in each state who lack a high school diploma and who are not enrolled in school. States must match 25% of the federal contribution with state or local funds, but many states contribute considerably more.

Amount of support per award: Varies.

Matching fund requirements: 25% of grant award.

NO. MOST RECENT APPLICANTS: 57.

NO. AWARDS: 57.

APPLICATION INFO:
Applicants interested in participating in the State-Administered Program should contact the appropriate state educational agency for information.

Duration: One year and continuing based on appropriations.

ADDRESS INQUIRIES TO:
Office of Career, Technical and
Adult Education
Adult Education and Literacy Division
400 Maryland Avenue, S.W.
Washington, DC 20202-7100

U.S. DEPARTMENT OF EDUCATION [1545]

Office of English Language Acquisition, Language Enhancement and Academic Achievement
LBJ Education Building, Room 5C-140, MS-6510
400 Maryland Avenue, S.W.
Washington, DC 20202
(202) 401-4300
Fax: (202) 205-1229
E-mail: libia.gil1@ed.gov
Web Site: www.ed.gov/offices/oela

AREAS OF INTEREST:
English language acquisition, language enhancement and academic achievement for Limited English Proficient (LEP) children.

NAME(S) OF PROGRAMS:
- **National Professional Development Program**
- **Native American and Alaska Native Children in School Program**

TYPE:
Formula grants. National Professional Development Program provides professional development activities intended to improve instruction for students with limited English proficiency (LEP) and assists education personnel working with such children to meet high professional standards.

Native American and Alaska Native Children in School Program provides grants to eligible entities that support language instruction education projects for limited English proficient (LEP) children from Native American, Alaska Native, native Hawaiian, and Pacific Islander backgrounds. The program is designed to ensure that LEP children master English and meet the same rigorous standards for academic achievement that all children are expected to meet. Funds may support the study of Native American languages.

YEAR PROGRAM STARTED: 1968

LEGAL BASIS:
Elementary and Secondary Education Act of 1965, as amended by No Child Left Behind Act of 2001.

ELIGIBILITY:
National Professional Development Program: Institutions of higher education in consortia with local education agencies or state education agencies may apply.

Native American and Alaska Native Children in School Program: Entities that operate the following kinds of elementary, secondary and postsecondary schools primarily for Native American children (including Alaska Native children) are eligible applicants under this program:
(1) Indian tribes;
(2) tribally sanctioned educational authorities;
(3) Native Hawaiian or Native American Pacific Islander native language educational organizations;
(4) elementary schools or secondary schools that are operated or funded by the Bureau of Indian Education (BIE), or a consortium of such schools;
(5) elementary schools or secondary schools operated under a contract with or grant from the BIE in consortium with another such school or a tribal or community organization and;
(6) elementary schools or secondary schools operated by the BIE and an institution of higher education (IHE), in consortium with elementary schools or secondary schools operated under a contract with or a grant from the BIE or a tribal or community organization.

GEOG. RESTRICTIONS: United States and its Commonwealths and territories.

STAFF:
Libia Gil, Assistant Deputy Director

ADDRESS INQUIRIES TO:
National Professional Development Program:
Samuel Lopez
Tel: (202) 401-1423

Native American and Alaska Native Children in School Program:
Trinidad Torres-Carrion
Tel: (202) 401-1445

U.S. DEPARTMENT OF STATE, FULBRIGHT DISTINGUISHED AWARDS IN TEACHING PROGRAM [1546]

c/o Institute of International Education
1400 K Street, N.W., Suite 700
Washington, DC 20005
(202) 326-7778
E-mail: fulbrightdat@iie.org
Web Site: www.fulbrightteacherexchange.org

FOUNDED: 1946

AREAS OF INTEREST:
All subjects, including mathematics, science, English, English as a Second Language (ESL), foreign language and history.

NAME(S) OF PROGRAMS:
- **Fulbright Distinguished Awards in Teaching Program**

TYPE:
Exchange programs; Travel grants.

YEAR PROGRAM STARTED: 1946

PURPOSE:
To increase mutual understanding between the people of the U.S. and the people of other countries through the funding of K-12 educator exchanges.

LEGAL BASIS:
Mutual Educational and Cultural Exchange Act (Fulbright Hays Act) of 1961.

ELIGIBILITY:
Applicants must meet the following general requirements:
(1) be a U.S. citizen or hold citizenship and be a resident in one of the participating countries;
(2) be fluent in English;
(3) hold a Master's degree or higher (for U.S. educators; international applicant requirements vary);
(4) be employed full-time at an accredited school in the U.S., its territories, or in one of the participating countries;
(5) spend at least 50% of their time teaching or working directly with students and;
(6) have taught for at least five years.

FINANCIAL DATA:
In most cases, the U.S. educator secures a leave of absence with or without pay from his or her home institution (as does the foreign teacher). Exchange grants include a summer orientation program and round-trip transportation for grantee only.

Amount of support per award: Varies.

Total amount of support: Varies.

APPLICATION INFO:
Applications are available online.

Duration: U.S. Educators: Three to six months; International Educators: Four months.

Deadline: November of the year preceding the grant year.

STAFF:
Judy Gibson, Program Director

ADDRESS INQUIRIES TO:
See e-mail address above.

*PLEASE NOTE:
All programs are tentative and are subject to the availability of funds.

UNIVERSITY OF MANITOBA [1547]

Faculty of Graduate Studies
500 University Centre
Winnipeg MB R3T 2N2 Canada
(204) 474-9836
Fax: (204) 474-7553
E-mail: rowena.krentz@umanitoba.ca
Web Site: umanitoba.ca/graduate_studies

AREAS OF INTEREST:
Teaching and cutting-edge research.

NAME(S) OF PROGRAMS:
- **University of Manitoba Graduate Fellowships**

TYPE:
Fellowships. Any discipline taught at graduate level at the university.

PURPOSE:
To reward academic excellence.

ELIGIBILITY:
At the time of application, students do not need to have been accepted by the department or faculty, but at the time of taking up the award must be regular full-time graduate students who have been admitted to and registered in advanced degree programmes, e.g., Master's or Ph.D., but not pre-Master's in any field of study or faculty of the University of Manitoba. Students beyond the second year in the Master's programme or beyond the fourth year in the Ph.D. programme are not eligible to apply for or hold a University of Manitoba Fellowship.

FINANCIAL DATA:
Amount of support per award: $18,000 for Ph.D.; $14,000 for Master's.

APPLICATION INFO:
Applicant must request information from the department to which he or she is applying at the University of Manitoba.

ADDRESS INQUIRIES TO:
Rowena Krentz, Awards Officer
(See address above.)

VIETNOW NATIONAL [1548]

1835 Broadway
Rockford, IL 61104
(815) 227-5100
(800) 837-8669
Fax: (815) 227-5127
E-mail: nationalhq@vietnow.com
Web Site: www.vietnow.com

AREAS OF INTEREST:
Veterans.

TYPE:
Scholarships.

PURPOSE:
To provide financial assistance to college students of VietNow members.

ELIGIBILITY:
Applicant must be a VietNow member or a dependent of a VietNow member or deceased member who has been in good standing for one year. Dependent is defined as a child, grandchild, stepchild, adopted or foster child.

FINANCIAL DATA:
Amount of support per award: Up to $2,000.
Total amount of support: Varies.

APPLICATION INFO:
Contact the Organization for application procedures.

Duration: One year. Renewal by reapplication.

Deadline: April 1.

ADDRESS INQUIRIES TO:
Shawn Conrad, Office Manager or Scholarship Committee
(See address above.)

DENNIS & PHYLLIS WASHINGTON FOUNDATION

P.O. Box 16630
Missoula, MT 59808
(406) 523-1300
Fax: (406) 523-1399
E-mail: info@dpwfoundation.org
Web Site: www.dpwfoundation.org

TYPE:
Project/program grants; Scholarships. Scholarship monies awarded to Montana's nine colleges and universities and seven Indian reservations.

See entry 1361 for full listing.

FRED B. AND RUTH B. ZIGLER FOUNDATION [1549]

P.O. Box 986
Jennings, LA 70546-0986
(337) 824-2413
Fax: (337) 824-2414
E-mail: frzigler@bellsouth.net
Web Site: www.ziglerfoundation.org

FOUNDED: 1956

AREAS OF INTEREST:
Education.

TYPE:
Project/program grants; Scholarships.

PURPOSE:
To benefit Jefferson-Davis Parish area.

LEGAL BASIS:
Private foundation.

ELIGIBILITY:
Grants are made to organizations that have tax-exempt status under Section 501(c)(3) of the Internal Revenue Code. No grants are made to individuals.

GEOG. RESTRICTIONS: Jefferson-Davis Parish area, Louisiana.

FINANCIAL DATA:
Amount of support per award: $12,000.

Total amount of support: Approximately $400,000.

NO. AWARDS: Approximately 30 each year.

APPLICATION INFO:
Applicants must submit a brief letter outlining the purpose of the grant.

Duration: Up to four years.

Deadline: 30 days prior to the Board meeting. The Board meets every other month starting in January.

ADDRESS INQUIRIES TO:
Julie G. Berry, President
(See address above.)

Elementary and secondary education

ALTMAN FOUNDATION

8 West 40th Street
19th Floor
New York, NY 10018-2263
(212) 682-0970
Fax: (212) 682-1648
E-mail: info@altman.org
Web Site: www.altmanfoundation.org

TYPE:
Project/program grants.

See entry 1139 for full listing.

THE BELK FOUNDATION [1550]

2801 West Tyvola Road
Charlotte, NC 28217-4500
(704) 426-8396
Fax: (704) 357-1896
E-mail: mandy@belkfoundation.org
Web Site: www.belkfoundation.org

FOUNDED: 1928

AREAS OF INTEREST:
Education.

TYPE:
General operating grants; Project/program grants; Research grants; Training grants. Core achievement in grades K-3; Teacher and Leader development.

PURPOSE:
To invest in schools and organizations that work aggressively to ensure all students graduate from high school and continue on an intentional path toward college, career and life.

ELIGIBILITY:
Charitable organizations, with 501(c)(3) status, located in communities where Belk associates live and work, with particular emphasis on Birmingham, AL; Atlanta, GA; and Charlotte, NC.

No grants made to individuals, private elementary or secondary schools, international programs and/or organizations, and organizations for the primary purpose of fund-raising.

GEOG. RESTRICTIONS: Birmingham, Alabama; Atlanta, Georgia; and Charlotte, North Carolina.

FINANCIAL DATA:
Amount of support per award: $5,000 to $500,000.

Total amount of support: Varies.

APPLICATION INFO:
Applicant must complete online Eligibility Quiz. If prompted, applicant will submit Letter of Inquiry.

Deadline: April 1 and October 1.

STAFF:
Johanna Anderson, Executive Director
Carol Shinn, Program Associate

*PLEASE NOTE:
The Foundation dedicates its resources to two areas:
(1) Teaching and Leading and;
(2) K-3 Achievement.

*SPECIAL STIPULATIONS:
Currently the Foundation is only accepting Letters of Inquiry from organizations serving the communities of Birmingham, AL; Atlanta, GA; and Charlotte, NC.

THE LOUIS CALDER FOUNDATION

125 Elm Street
New Canaan, CT 06840
(203) 966-8925
Fax: (203) 966-5785
E-mail: proposals@calderfdn.org
Web Site: www.louiscalderfoundation.org

TYPE:
Capital grants; Project/program grants. Curriculum development.

See entry 1090 for full listing.

SAMUEL N. AND MARY CASTLE FOUNDATION [1551]

733 Bishop Street, Suite 1275
Honolulu, HI 96813
(808) 522-1101
Fax: (808) 522-1103
E-mail: snandmarycastle@hawaii.rr.com
Web Site: fdnweb.org/castle/

FOUNDED: 1894

AREAS OF INTEREST:
Early education and care, cultural arts, human services for children, teacher training, and some maternal/child health support.

CONSULTING OR VOLUNTEER SERVICES:
Castle colleagues training for directors of early childhood centers.

TYPE:
Scholarships; Technical assistance; Training grants.

YEAR PROGRAM STARTED: 1894

PURPOSE:
To support training for early childhood education professionals; to support early education, preschools, scholarships, and select higher education programs in teacher training; to support early education.

LEGAL BASIS:
Private family foundation.

GEOG. RESTRICTIONS: Hawaii.

FINANCIAL DATA:
Amount of support per award: Typically $5,000 to $100,000.

Total amount of support: $2,099,363 for the year 2015.

Matching fund requirements: Varies.

NO. MOST RECENT APPLICANTS: 400.

NO. AWARDS: 65.

REPRESENTATIVE AWARDS:
$75,000 to Catholic Charities for families with children; $125,000 to Chaminade University for student scholarships; $150,000 to University of Hawaii for scholarships.

APPLICATION INFO:
The applicant organization should review the Foundation's priorities and policies to determine whether it is eligible to be considered for funding and whether the type of activity proposed is in one of the Foundation's funding areas. Applicants are required to contact the Foundation's Executive Director by letter, e-mail, phone or personal visit before making fund application.

Proposals may be hand delivered or mailed and should include the following:
(1) proposal (one copy);
(2) one copy of each of the additional materials as defined on the Foundation's web site (e.g., IRS determination letter, audited financial statements);
(3) one- to two-page executive summary (two copies);
(4) budget (two copies) and;
(5) Board of Directors list (two copies).

Organizations which have submitted their charters, bylaws and 501(c)(3) may submit complete applications by e-mail attachment.

Applicant organizations should not bind their proposals or submit videos or other items which have not been requested by the Foundation.

Duration: One year. Renewal possible up to three years.

Deadline: February 1, June 1 and September 15.

OFFICERS:
Dr. Robert Peters, President
Dr. Kittredge A. Baldwin, Vice President
Alfred L. Castle, Treasurer and Executive Director
Cynthia Quisenberry, Secretary

ADDRESS INQUIRIES TO:
Alfred L. Castle, Executive Director
(See address above.)

*SPECIAL STIPULATIONS:
All applicants must be prescreened before applying.

HUGH AND HAZEL DARLING FOUNDATION

520 South Grand Avenue, Suite 395
Los Angeles, CA 90071
(213) 683-5200
Fax: (213) 627-7795

TYPE:
Block grants; Capital grants; Challenge/matching grants; Matching gifts; Scholarships; Training grants.

See entry 1573 for full listing.

FIRSTENERGY [1552]

76 South Main Street
Akron, OH 44308
(330) 384-5022
Fax: (330) 245-5566
E-mail: delores.jones@firstenergycorp.com
Web Site: www.firstenergycorp.com/community

AREAS OF INTEREST:
Science, technology, engineering and mathematics education.

NAME(S) OF PROGRAMS:
- **STEM Grants Program**

TYPE:
Project/program grants. Project/program grants in the classroom setting.

YEAR PROGRAM STARTED: 1985

PURPOSE:
To support classroom projects and teacher professional development initiatives focusing on science, technology, engineering and mathematics.

ELIGIBILITY:
Educators (grades preK-12) and youth group leaders in the service areas of FirstEnergy and communities where FirstEnergy has facilities are encouraged to apply. Any creative project dealing with science, technology, engineering and mathematics is eligible. Projects that involve students directly, incorporate matching funds, community resources, interdisciplinary or team-teaching and involve various age groups are highly favored. Teacher training projects are highly favored. Completed projects or those previously funded are not eligible.

GEOG. RESTRICTIONS: Maryland, New Jersey, Ohio, Pennsylvania and West Virginia.

FINANCIAL DATA:
Grants may be used to compensate experts who come to work with the students, but not to pay teachers or staff.

Amount of support per award: Up to $1,000.

Total amount of support: Varies.

APPLICATION INFO:
Application can be downloaded and completed electronically.

Duration: One school year.

Deadline: Usually third week in September.

PUBLICATIONS:
Bright Ideas for Educators.

ADDRESS INQUIRIES TO:
Community Involvement Department
(See address above.)

*SPECIAL STIPULATIONS:
Grants are only available to schools or groups in the FirstEnergy service area or in communities where it has facilities.

CHARLES HAYDEN FOUNDATION

140 Broadway, 51st Floor
New York, NY 10005
(212) 785-3677
Fax: (212) 785-3689
E-mail: fdn@chf.org
Web Site: www.charleshaydenfoundation.org

TYPE:
Capital grants; Challenge/matching grants; Project/program grants. Grant priorities focus on institutions and programs primarily serving youth at risk of not reaching their full potential, especially youth in low-income communities. Support is provided for youth development programs, charter schools, independent and parochial schools, and informal educational enrichment programs in institutions such as zoos, museums or libraries.

See entry 1107 for full listing.

INVESTED [1553]

911 Eighth Avenue North
Seattle, WA 98109
(206) 352-1199
Fax: (206) 352-1203
E-mail: dcushing@invested.org
Web Site: www.invested.org

FOUNDED: 1963

AREAS OF INTEREST:
Secondary education and immediate needs for disadvantaged students.

NAME(S) OF PROGRAMS:
- **InvestED School Fund Program**

TYPE:
Grants-in-aid; Matching gifts.

YEAR PROGRAM STARTED: 1963

PURPOSE:
To support middle and senior high school aid program providing for grants to both accredited public and private schools (grades 6-12) within the state of Washington to enable these schools to assist individual students who have needs their families cannot afford.

LEGAL BASIS:
Public charity.

ELIGIBILITY:
Grants are restricted to a program aiding students in Washington state secondary schools.

School must submit year-end report May 1 to June 30 to be eligible for grant the following year.

GEOG. RESTRICTIONS: Washington state.

FINANCIAL DATA:
Amount of support per award: $200 to $2,900 in initial funding; up to $1,000 matching if donations are received.

Total amount of support: $268,650 initial funding and $88,845 additional matching for the year 2013-14.

APPLICATION INFO:
Contact the Organization for guidelines.

Duration: One year. Renewable.

Deadline: June 30.

IRS I.D.: 23-7189670

DIRECTORS:
Thomas E. Gleason, President
Paul G. Condrat, Vice President
Michael Dunn, Ed.D., Vice President
Jim Ivers, Treasurer
Pamela J. Hughes, Secretary
David Andra
Dan Barritt
Emory Bundy
Shirley Gordon
Tom Horton
Sam Howard
Martin J. Neeb
Roger Percy
Tom Rath
Lisa Schaures
Kerry Swanson
Jason Edward Wax
Debbie Williams

ADDRESS INQUIRIES TO:
Executive Director
(See address above.)

MARTHA HOLDEN JENNINGS FOUNDATION [1554]

The Halle Building
1228 Euclid Avenue, Suite 710
Cleveland, OH 44115-1811
(216) 589-5700
Fax: (216) 589-5730
Web Site: www.mhjf.org

FOUNDED: 1959

AREAS OF INTEREST:
Ohio elementary and secondary education.

NAME(S) OF PROGRAMS:
- **Grants-to-Educators Program**
- **Open Grants**

TYPE:
Project/program grants. Project/program grants are for education only. Support to aide the improvement of elementary and secondary public school education in Ohio.

YEAR PROGRAM STARTED: 1959

PURPOSE:
To foster the development of individual capabilities of young people to the maximum extent through improving the quality of teaching in secular primary and secondary schools; to provide a means for greater accomplishment on the part of Ohio's teachers by encouraging creativity in teaching and bringing greater recognition to the teaching profession.

LEGAL BASIS:
Nonprofit foundation.

ELIGIBILITY:
For Grants-to-Educators, applicants must be teachers or public school administrators and are intended for classroom, schoolwide or districtwide projects. For other grants, applicants must be tax-exempt with 501(c)(3) status from the IRS.

Open Grants are available to any public school district, nonreligious private school working with public schools, or tax-exempt organization that assists elementary and secondary schools in Ohio. No grants for capital improvements or graduate study, and generally no grants for equipment or travel.

GEOG. RESTRICTIONS: Ohio.

FINANCIAL DATA:
Amount of support per award:
Grants-to-Educators: Up to $3,000; Open Grants: Varies depending on needs and nature of the request. Average: $15,000.

Total amount of support: $3,017,870 for the year 2013.

NO. AWARDS: 249 for the year 2015.

REPRESENTATIVE AWARDS:
$15,000 to Invent Now, Inc., North Canton, OH, for Camp Invention Program; $22,000 to Idea Stream, Cleveland, OH, for News Depth Program; $7,750 to Botkins' Local Schools, Botkins, OH, for Balanced Literacy Program; $12,516 to Osnaburg Local Schools, Osnaburg, OH, for STEM Robotics.

APPLICATION INFO:
There are two funding categories within the Grants-to-Educators and Open Grants programs: Excellent Teaching and Deep Learning. Applicants need to understand the rationale behind these grant categories before completing a proposal. Applicants must indicate the category or categories for which they are seeking funds within each program.

All grant requests must be submitted online at the Foundation web site.

Duration: One year. Proposal may be resubmitted for a second or third year.

Deadline: Proposals must be submitted by the 15th of the month preceding the month in which they are to be considered. If the 15th falls on a weekend or a holiday, requests must be submitted on the previous business day.

Grants-to-Educators: The Distribution Committee meets ten months a year (not in July or December).

Open Grants: The Board of Directors does not meet in February, July, October or December. Decisions on grant applications are generally communicated within two months of submission.

PUBLICATIONS:
Guidelines; *Pro-Excellentia.*

STAFF:
Dr. Daniel J. Keenan, Executive Director

KLINGENSTEIN CENTER FOR INDEPENDENT SCHOOL LEADERSHIP [1555]

Teachers College, Columbia University
525 West 120th Street, Box 125
New York, NY 10027-6696
(212) 678-3156
Fax: (212) 678-3156
E-mail: klingenstein@tc.columbia.edu
Web Site: www.klingenstein.org

FOUNDED: 1977

AREAS OF INTEREST:
Leadership development for independent and international education.

NAME(S) OF PROGRAMS:
- **Klingenstein Heads Program**
- **Klingenstein Summer Institute for Early Career Teachers**
- **Master's Degree in Educational Independent Leadership**

TYPE:
Scholarships. The Klingenstein Heads Program gathers heads of independent and international schools from throughout the nation and the world for two weeks of intensive study among professional peers.

The Klingenstein Summer Institute gathers teachers in the beginning years of their careers for an exploration of teaching styles, educational philosophies and issues, and personal development.

The Master's Degree in Private School Leadership, with a focus in independent and international school leadership, gathers independent school teachers and administrators for a rigorous degree program. The Two Summers Master's Program is the two-summer version of the full-year degree program. Either program can be paired with an MBA from either Columbia Business School or INSEAD in France or Singapore to earn an M.A./MBA dual degree. The majority of students get generous tuition scholarships.

YEAR PROGRAM STARTED: 1978

PURPOSE:
To draw attention to outstanding leadership.

LEGAL BASIS:
Private foundation.

ELIGIBILITY:
Teachers and administrators working in an independent or international school with a nondiscriminatory admissions policy are eligible to apply. All programs are open to international applicants.

FINANCIAL DATA:
All programs offer tuition funding. The Heads of School Program and the Summer Institute for Early Career Teachers are fully-funded fellowships. Students in Master's programs are eligible for financial aid and scholarships.

Amount of support per award: Varies.

Total amount of support: Varies.

APPLICATION INFO:
Applicant must submit application, transcripts, autobiographical information and recommendations from sponsoring school. Master's program applicants must submit GMAT or GRE scores.

Duration: Varies.

Deadline: Klingenstein Heads of Schools Program: May 1; Summer Institute and Master's Degree: January 15; Two Summers Master's Program: November 1 of even-numbered years.

PUBLICATIONS:
Klingbrief.

ADDRESS INQUIRIES TO:
Assistant Director
(See address above.)

MEBANE CHARITABLE FOUNDATION, INC.

232 South Main Street
Mocksville, NC 27028
(336) 936-0041
Fax: (336) 936-0038
E-mail: lcolbourne@mebanefoundation.com
Web Site: www.mebanefoundation.com

TYPE:
Project/program grants.

See entry 1112 for full listing.

MITSUBISHI ELECTRIC AMERICA FOUNDATION [1556]

1300 Wilson Boulevard
Suite 210
Arlington, VA 22209
(703) 276-8240
E-mail: mea.foundation@meus.mea.com
Web Site: www.meaf.org

FOUNDED: 1991

AREAS OF INTEREST:
People with disabilities, including education, employment, independence and community inclusion.

TYPE:
Demonstration grants; General operating grants; Internships; Matching gifts; Project/program grants; Seed money grants; Technical assistance; Training grants. Grants are offered to make a better world for all by helping young people with disabilities to maximize their potential and participation in society.

YEAR PROGRAM STARTED: 1991

PURPOSE:
To help young people with disabilities maximize their potential and participation in society.

LEGAL BASIS:
Foundation.

ELIGIBILITY:
Applicants must meet criteria as stated in Foundation guidelines. Priority given to applicants in communities where MEUS facilities are located.

GEOG. RESTRICTIONS: United States.

FINANCIAL DATA:
Amount of support per award: Average: $60,000.

Total amount of support: $612,400 for the year 2015.

Matching fund requirements: Mitsubishi Electric employee must submit a request to match for qualified organizations.

CO-OP FUNDING PROGRAMS: $240,000 Matching Fund Program with The HSC Foundation to support Youth Transitions Collaborative member programming.

NO. MOST RECENT APPLICANTS: 130.

NO. AWARDS: 10 for the year 2015.

REPRESENTATIVE AWARDS:
$187,500 to support the Autistic Self-Advocacy Network Autism Campus Inclusion Program; $150,000 to the University of Pittsburgh to support the Advancing Inclusive Manufacturing (AIM) Program; $150,000 to the U.S. Business Leadership Network to support the Career Link Mentoring Program.

APPLICATION INFO:
Submit a two-page concept paper (click on the "How to Apply" tab on the Foundation web site) including a budget summary and description of the need and objectives for the funds requested. Instructions for full proposals will be sent after initial screening. Concept papers are reviewed throughout the year.

Applicants are requested not to telephone the Foundation during the application process.

Duration: One to three years. Renewal possible on a case-by-case basis.

Deadline: June 1 to be considered for following year funding.

BOARD OF DIRECTORS:
Mike Corbo
Mike DeLano
Kiyoshi Furukawa
Chris Gerdes
Chatham Gongola
Jack Greaf
Shinji Harada
Brian Heery
Perry Pappous
David Rebmann
Alex Stephens, V
Dr. Richard C. Waters
Kenichiro Yamanishi

ADDRESS INQUIRIES TO:
Kevin R. Webb, Senior Director
(See address above.)

NATIONAL ENDOWMENT FOR THE HUMANITIES

The Constitution Center
400 7th Street, S.W.
Washington, DC 20001
(202) 606-8424
Fax: (202) 606-8240
E-mail: info@neh.gov
Web Site: www.neh.gov

TYPE:
Conferences/seminars. Grants support summer seminars and national institutes in the humanities for college and school teachers. These faculty development activities are conducted at colleges and universities across the country. Lists of pending seminars and institutes are available from the program.

See entry 369 for full listing.

NATIONAL SCIENCE FOUNDATION [1557]

Directorate for Education and Human Resources
Division of Research on Learning in Formal and Informal Settings
4201 Wilson Boulevard, Suite 885 S
Arlington, VA 22230
(703) 292-8620
(703) 570-1975
Fax: (703) 292-9044; (703) 292-9046
E-mail: acarroll@nsf.gov
Web Site: www.nsf.gov

FOUNDED: 1950

AREAS OF INTEREST:
Science, mathematics, technology education content; pedagogy; applied research; development of resources and tools for instruction, assessment, evaluation and informal science.

NAME(S) OF PROGRAMS:
- **Advanced Technological Education (ATE)**
- **Discovery Research K-12 (DR K12)**
- **Informal Science Education (ISE) (AISL)**
- **Innovative Technology Experiences for Students and Teachers (ITEST)**
- **Research and Evaluation on Education in Science and Engineering (REESE)**

TYPE:
Conferences/seminars; Demonstration grants; Development grants; Project/program grants; Research grants; Training grants. With an emphasis on two-year colleges, the Advanced Technological Education (ATE) program focuses on the education of technicians for the high-technology fields that drive the nation's economy.

Discovery Research K-12 (DR K12) funds research, development and evaluation activities through knowledge generation and application to improve K-12 learning and teaching.

Informal Science Education (ISE) program invests in projects that develop and implement informal learning experiences designed to increase interest, engagement and understanding of science, technology, engineering and mathematics (STEM) by individuals of all ages and backgrounds, as well as projects that advance knowledge and practice of informal science education.

Innovative Technology Experiences for Students and Teachers (ITEST) is designed to increase the opportunities for students and teachers to learn about, experience, and use information technologies within the context of science, technology, engineering and mathematics (STEM), including Information Technology (IT) courses. It is in direct response to the concern about shortages of information technology workers in the U.S.

Research and Evaluation on Education in Science and Engineering (REESE) supports basic and applied research and evaluation that enhances science, technology, engineering and mathematics (STEM) learning and teaching.

PURPOSE:
To promote quality programs of education in mathematics, science and technology for all the nation's youth, and informal learning opportunities in these fields for youth and adults.

LEGAL BASIS:
The National Science Foundation Act of 1950, Public Law 81-507, as amended.

GEOG. RESTRICTIONS: United States.

FINANCIAL DATA:
Amount of support per award: Grants vary in amount, depending upon the needs and nature of the request and availability of funds.

Total amount of support: $180,000,000.

APPLICATION INFO:
Application information is available on the Foundation's web site.

Duration: One to five years.

Deadline: Varies.

THE RADIANT PEACE FOUNDATION INTERNATIONAL, INC. [1558]

P.O. Box 40822
St. Petersburg, FL 33743-0822
(727) 343-8212
Fax: (727) 343-8212
E-mail: radiantpeaceintl@gmail.com
Web Site: www.radiantpeace.org

FOUNDED: 1986

NAME(S) OF PROGRAMS:
- **Radiant Peace Education Awards**

TYPE:
Awards/prizes. Recognizes and awards children, teachers and schools for Radiant Peace essays, art, projects, and videos.

YEAR PROGRAM STARTED: 1990

PURPOSE:
To inspire, promote and encourage Radiant Peace worldwide.

LEGAL BASIS:
A 501(c)(3) nonprofit educational organization.

ELIGIBILITY:
All students grades one-12 including home schools and youth groups.

FINANCIAL DATA:
Amount of support per award: $25 to $500.

Total amount of support: Varies by year.

NO. AWARDS: Varies.

APPLICATION INFO:
Invitations and guidelines posted online.

Deadline: December and April.

ADDRESS INQUIRIES TO:
Office Manager
(See address above.)

THOMAS B. AND ELIZABETH M. SHERIDAN FOUNDATION [1559]

Executive Plaza II, Suite 704
11350 McCormick Road
Hunt Valley, MD 21031
(410) 771-0475

FOUNDED: 1962

AREAS OF INTEREST:
Education and cultural arts.

TYPE:
Development grants; General operating grants; Project/program grants. Grants to private secondary schools and the cultural arts in the Baltimore area.

PURPOSE:
To support private secondary schools and cultural organizations.

ELIGIBILITY:
Organizations, including parochial schools, classified as 501(c)(3) by the IRS can apply. No grants to individuals.

GEOG. RESTRICTIONS: Baltimore area, Maryland.

FINANCIAL DATA:
$16,159,232 in assets (market value) for the year ended December 31, 2012.

Amount of support per award: $50 to $310,000 for the year ended December 31, 2012.

Total amount of support: $770,050 for the year ended December 31, 2012.

NO. AWARDS: 12 for the year ended December 31, 2012.

SONY USA FOUNDATION, INC. [1560]

550 Madison Avenue, 33rd Floor
New York, NY 10022-3211
(212) 833-6851
E-mail: erin_amaty@sonyusa.com
Web Site: www.sony.com/sca/corporate-responsibility

FOUNDED: 1972

AREAS OF INTEREST:
Arts, culture and technology, with primary focus in education; environmental issues; civic affairs; health and welfare.

TYPE:
General operating grants; Matching gifts; Product donations; Project/program grants.

YEAR PROGRAM STARTED: 1972

PURPOSE:
To meet the needs of the communities where Sony has a presence; to support national organizations which extend into Sony presence areas.

LEGAL BASIS:
Corporate foundation.

ELIGIBILITY:
No grants to individuals, political or religious organizations, labor unions, endowments, capital campaigns, lobbying groups, testimonial dinners, for-profit publications seeking advertisements and foreign or non-U.S. organizations.

GEOG. RESTRICTIONS: United States.

FINANCIAL DATA:
Amount of support per award: Varies.

Total amount of support: Varies.

Matching fund requirements: Sony matches contributions made by full-time employees to educational institutions, hospitals and cultural organizations.

APPLICATION INFO:
Send brief letter describing organization, amount requested, objectives of organization, recent audited financial statement and proof of tax-exempt status. Phone calls not accepted, only written requests.

Duration: One year. Must reapply for continued support.

Deadline: Requests accepted throughout the year. Notification within three months.

PUBLICATIONS:
Contribution guidelines.

OFFICERS:
Mark Khalil, President

ADDRESS INQUIRIES TO:
Erin Amaty
Public Affairs Administrator
(See address above.)

STATE LIBRARY AND ARCHIVES OF FLORIDA

R.A. Gray Building
500 South Bronough Street
Tallahassee, FL 32399-0250
(850) 245-6620
Fax: (850) 245-6643
E-mail: marian.deeney@dos.myflorida.com
Web Site: info.florida.gov/services-for-libraries/grants/lsta/

TYPE:
Project/program grants. Project grants congruent with the state long-range plan.

See entry 728 for full listing.

W. CLEMENT & JESSIE V. STONE FOUNDATION [1561]

1100 Lake Street, Suite 202
Oak Park, IL 60301
(800) 288-4859
E-mail: jeff@wcstonefnd.org
Web Site: www.wcstonefnd.org

FOUNDED: 1958

AREAS OF INTEREST:
Education, early childhood and youth development.

TYPE:
Demonstration grants; Development grants; General operating grants; Project/program grants; Technical assistance; Training grants.

YEAR PROGRAM STARTED: 1958

PURPOSE:
To make the world a better place by supporting programs in education, early childhood and youth development.

ELIGIBILITY:
Grants are made to organizations that have tax-exempt status under Section 501(c)(3) of the Internal Revenue Code. Nonsectarian religious programs may apply. No grants are made to individuals.

GEOG. RESTRICTIONS: San Francisco Bay area, California; Chicago, Illinois; Boston, Massachusetts; New York City, New York; and Philadelphia, Pennsylvania.

FINANCIAL DATA:
Amount of support per award: $10,000 to $100,000, depending upon the program.

Total amount of support: $4,400,000 for the year 2013.

NO. AWARDS: 100.

REPRESENTATIVE AWARDS:
$70,000 to Youth Radio; $75,000 to Partners for School Innovation; $100,000 to Strategies for Children.

APPLICATION INFO:
The Foundation does not accept unsolicited proposals. Organizations may call if they feel there is a strong match between their work and the Foundation's grantmaking priorities.

Duration: Typically one year.

IRS I.D.: 36-2498125

OFFICERS AND DIRECTORS:
Norman C. Stone, Chairman
Sandra Stone, President
Steven M. Stone, Treasurer
Michael A. Stone, Secretary

Tony Smith, Executive Director
Alex Knecht
Amy Stone
Barbara Stone
David Stone
Debbie Stone
Jamison Stone
Jennifer Stone
Norah Stone
Sara Stone
Chad Tingley

ADDRESS INQUIRIES TO:
Tony Smith, Executive Director
(See address above.)

TOSHIBA AMERICA FOUNDATION [1562]

1251 Avenue of the Americas, 41st Floor
New York, NY 10020
(212) 596-0620
E-mail: foundation@tai.toshiba.com
Web Site: www.taf.toshiba.com

FOUNDED: 1990

AREAS OF INTEREST:
Mathematics and science education for grades K-12.

TYPE:
Project/program grants.

YEAR PROGRAM STARTED: 1990

PURPOSE:
To improve science and math education at the pre-college level (grades K-12 only).

LEGAL BASIS:
Corporate foundation.

ELIGIBILITY:
Grants are made to private or public schools. Preference is given to programs or projects that take place in science or math classrooms. The Foundation does not fund grants for general operating costs, endowments, scholarships, conferences, summer programs, purchase of equipment (product or donations), sponsorships, or individuals.

GEOG. RESTRICTIONS: United States.

FINANCIAL DATA:
Amount of support per award: $1,000 to $20,000.
Total amount of support: Approximately $500,000.

NO. AWARDS: 150 annually.

APPLICATION INFO:
Applications are available on the Foundation's web site.
Duration: One year.
Deadline: Grades K-5: October 1. Grades 6-12: February 1 and August 1 for requests more than $5,000.

IRS I.D.: 13-3596612

ADDRESS INQUIRIES TO:
Program Officer
(See address above.)

U.S. DEPARTMENT OF EDUCATION

Office of Indian Education
400 Maryland Avenue, S.W.
LBJ Building, 3W115
Washington, DC 20202-6335
(202) 260-3774
(202) 260-1454
E-mail: indian.education@ed.gov
Web Site: www.ed.gov

TYPE:
Formula grants. Grants to provide financial assistance to LEAs and tribal schools to develop and carry out elementary and secondary school programs specially designed to meet the special educational and culturally related educational needs of Indian children.

See entry 1038 for full listing.

U.S. DEPARTMENT OF EDUCATION

Office of Postsecondary Education
Federal TRIO Programs
1990 K Street, N.W., Suite 7000
Washington, DC 20006-8510
(202) 502-7586
(202) 502-7600
Fax: (202) 502-7857
E-mail: OPE_TRIO@ed.gov
Web Site: www.ed.gov/ope/trio

TYPE:
Project/program grants. There are three types of grants under the Upward Bound program: Regular Upward Bound Grants, Veterans Upward Bound Grants, and Upward Bound Math and Science Grants.

The Regular Upward Bound projects are designed to generate in participants the skills and motivation necessary for success in education beyond secondary school. The Veterans Upward Bound projects are designed to assist veterans in preparing for a program of postsecondary education. The Upward Bound Math and Science projects are designed to prepare high school students for postsecondary education programs that lead to careers in the fields of math and science.

See entry 1588 for full listing.

YOUTH FOR UNDERSTANDING USA

641 S Street, N.W.
Suite 200
Washington, DC 20001
(202) 774-5200
(800) 833-6243
Fax: (202) 588-7571
E-mail: admissions@yfu.org
Web Site: www.yfuusa.org

TYPE:
Exchange programs; Grants-in-aid; Scholarships; Travel grants. Students on summer semester and year programs live with volunteer host families overseas. Students on semester and academic year programs also attend school. International students live and study at U.S. high schools or community colleges. Competitive, full and partial scholarships for Corporate, Finland-U.S. Senate, Japan-U.S. Senate Programs and Japan-America Friendship Scholars Program.

See entry 933 for full listing.

Higher education projects and research

ABEL FOUNDATION

1815 Y Street
Lincoln, NE 68508
(402) 434-1212
Fax: (402) 434-1799
Web Site: www.abelfoundation.org

TYPE:
Capital grants; Matching gifts; Project/program grants.

See entry 1133 for full listing.

ADCO FOUNDATION [1563]

c/o AA Shareholders Service Company, LLC
1060 First Avenue, Suite 400
King of Prussia, PA 19406
(610) 768-8020

AREAS OF INTEREST:
Higher education, communications, civic affairs, community funds, health and mental health.

TYPE:
General operating grants; Project/program grants; Seed money grants.

PURPOSE:
To promote higher education, physical and mental health.

ELIGIBILITY:
Grants are made to organizations that have tax-exempt status under Section 501(c)(3) of the Internal Revenue Code. No grants are made to individuals.

GEOG. RESTRICTIONS: Primarily New Jersey, New York and Pennsylvania.

FINANCIAL DATA:
Amount of support per award: $500 to $12,000.
Total amount of support: $52,000 for the year 2013.

NO. AWARDS: 4 for the year 2013.

APPLICATION INFO:
Send a letter of inquiry to the Foundation, outlining the organization's goal and purposes, and the intended use and amount of the grant requested.
Duration: One year. Renewal possible.
Deadline: November 30.

ADDRESS INQUIRIES TO:
Barry Doney, Administrator
(See address above.)

AMERICAN FLORAL ENDOWMENT

1601 Duke Street
Alexandria, VA 22314
(703) 838-5211
Fax: (703) 838-5212
E-mail: afe@endowment.org
Web Site: endowment.org

TYPE:
Internships; Project/program grants; Research grants; Scholarships. The Endowment funds research and educational development in floriculture and environmental horticulture designed to produce solutions to industry needs and promote the growth and improvement of the floral industry for the benefit of the grower, wholesale, retail, allied segments and the general public.

The Endowment supports educational programs focused on attracting young people to the industry, and educational endeavors to identify and solve industry needs and/or challenges. The programs are divided into two major areas:
(1) paid floriculture internships/scholarships for full-time college students and;
(2) general educational grants to national programs.

See entry 2050 for full listing.

AMERICAN FOUNDATION FOR PHARMACEUTICAL EDUCATION (AFPE)

6076 Franconia Road, Suite C
Alexandria, VA 22310-1758
(703) 875-3095
Fax: (703) 875-3098
E-mail: info@afpenet.org
Web Site: www.afpenet.org

TYPE:
Fellowships.

See entry 2457 for full listing.

AMERICAN FOUNDATION FOR PHARMACEUTICAL EDUCATION (AFPE) [1564]

6076 Franconia Road, Suite C
Alexandria, VA 22310-1758
(703) 875-3095
Fax: (703) 875-3098
E-mail: info@afpenet.org
Web Site: www.afpenet.org

FOUNDED: 1942

AREAS OF INTEREST:
Education.

NAME(S) OF PROGRAMS:

- **AFPE Predoctoral Fellowships in the Pharmaceutical Sciences**

TYPE:
Fellowships.

YEAR PROGRAM STARTED: 1942

PURPOSE:
To encourage an outstanding pharmacy school graduate to pursue an advanced degree in the pharmaceutical sciences; to identify and support students who have the potential to become leaders in the pharmaceutical profession.

ELIGIBILITY:
Eligible applicants must meet the following criteria:
(1) be a U.S. citizen or permanent resident;
(2) be a full-time student enrolled in a graduate Ph.D. program in pharmaceutical science administered by or officially affiliated with a U.S. college of pharmacy accredited by ACPE;
(3) have at least three semesters of study completed in the current Ph.D. program;
(4) have no more that three and a half years remaining to obtain the Ph.D. degree and;
(5) may be a joint Pharm.D./Ph.D. student who has completed the equivalent of three full semesters of graduate credit toward the Ph.D. and will be awarded the Ph.D. degree within three additional years.

GEOG. RESTRICTIONS: United States.

FINANCIAL DATA:
The Fellowship stipend may be used for a purpose decided by the awardee and college that will enable the student to make progress in their pursuit of the Ph.D., such as student stipend, laboratory supplies, books, materials, travel, etc. None of the funds shall be used for indirect costs by the institution.

Amount of support per award: $10,000 stipend.

Total amount of support: Varies.

NO. MOST RECENT APPLICANTS: 150.

NO. AWARDS: 42.

APPLICATION INFO:
Application and guidelines are available online.

Duration: One year, September to August. Renewable.

AMERICAN FRIENDS OF THE ALEXANDER VON HUMBOLDT FOUNDATION [1565]

1101 17th Street, N.W.
Suite 603
Washington, DC 20036
(202) 783-1907
E-mail: info@americanfriends-of-avh.org
Web Site: www.americanfriends-of-avh.org

FOUNDED: 1953

AREAS OF INTEREST:
Postgraduate research in Germany.

NAME(S) OF PROGRAMS:

- **Humboldt Research Fellowship for Postdoctoral Researchers**

TYPE:
Fellowships. This program supports highly qualified scholars and scientists of all nationalities and disciplines so that they may carry out long-term research projects that the applicant has selected in cooperation with an academic host the applicant has selected at a research institution in Germany.

PURPOSE:
To support highly qualified scholars and scientists of all nationalities and disciplines so that they may carry out long-term research projects in Germany.

ELIGIBILITY:
Open to scientists and scholars who completed a doctoral degree within four years prior to the application submission date.

Fellowships are awarded on the basis of academic achievement, the quality and feasibility of the proposed research and the candidate's publications.

FINANCIAL DATA:
In addition to a monthly stipend, special allowances are available for accompanying family members, travel expenses and German language instruction.

Amount of support per award: EUR 2,650 monthly.

Total amount of support: Varies.

NO. AWARDS: Approximately 600 total fellowships for postdoctoral researchers and experienced researchers each year.

APPLICATION INFO:
Application information is available on the web site.

Duration: Six to 24 months in Germany.

Deadline: Continuous. The review process takes several months, and the selection committee meets three times a year to review applications.

ADDRESS INQUIRIES TO:
Program Coordination
(See address above.) or

Alexander von Humboldt Stiftung
Jean-Paul-Strasse 12
D-53173 Bonn
Germany
Tel: 49 (0228) 833-0
Fax: 49 (0228) 833-199
E-mail: info@avh.de

AMERICAN LIBRARY ASSOCIATION (ALA) [1566]

50 East Huron Street
Chicago, IL 60611-2795
(312) 280-4279
(800) 545-2433 ext. 4279
Fax: (312) 280-3256
E-mail: scholarships@ala.org
Web Site: www.ala.org/educationcareers/scholarships

AREAS OF INTEREST:
Library science.

NAME(S) OF PROGRAMS:

- **ALA/Century Scholarship**
- **ALSC/Bound-to-Stay-Bound Books Scholarship**
- **ALSC/Frederic G. Melcher Scholarship**
- **David H. Clift Scholarship**
- **Tom and Roberta Drewes Scholarship**
- **Mary V. Gaver Scholarship**
- **Miriam L. Hornback Scholarship**
- **Christopher J. Hoy/ERT Scholarship**
- **Tony B. Leisner Scholarship**
- **LITA/Christian Larew Memorial Scholarship**
- **LITA/LSSI Minority Scholarship**
- **LITA/OCLC Minority Scholarship**
- **Peter Lyman Memorial/SAGE Scholarships**
- **Spectrum Initiative Scholarship Program**

TYPE:
Scholarships. ALA Century Scholarship is for an individual with a disability entering a Master's degree or Ph.D. program.

ALSC and Gaver Scholarships are for a youth services librarian.

Clift and Hoy/ERT are general scholarships.

Drewes, Hornback and Leisner Scholarships are for paid library support staff currently working in a library.

LITA/Christian Larew Memorial, LITA/LSSI Minority and LITA/OCLC Minority Scholarships are for librarians entering a Master's degree program.

SAGE Scholarship is for a new media services librarian.

YEAR PROGRAM STARTED: 1996

PURPOSE:
To support library staff education.

ELIGIBILITY:
Applicants must be U.S. or Canadian citizens, or permanent residents thereof.

Applicants must demonstrate academic excellence, leadership qualities and evidence of commitment to a career in library service.

Applicants may not have completed more than 12 semester hours or the equivalent towards a Master's degree in library science prior to June 1.

GEOG. RESTRICTIONS: United States and Canada.

FINANCIAL DATA:
Amount of support per award: Varies.
Total amount of support: Varies.

NO. MOST RECENT APPLICANTS: 559 for the year 2014.

NO. AWARDS: 68 for the year 2014.

APPLICATION INFO:
Application information is available on the web site.
Deadline: March 1.

STAFF:
Kimberly Redd, Program Officer

ADDRESS INQUIRIES TO:
Kimberly Redd, Program Officer
(See address above.)

THE AMERICAN-SCANDINAVIAN FOUNDATION [1567]

58 Park Avenue
New York, NY 10016
(212) 879-9779
E-mail: grants@amscan.org
Web Site: www.amscan.org

FOUNDED: 1910

AREAS OF INTEREST:
Cross-cultural exchange at an academic level.

NAME(S) OF PROGRAMS:
- **Visiting Lectureships**

TYPE:
Exchange programs. The Foundation invites U.S. colleges and universities to apply for funding to host a visiting lecturer from Norway or Sweden. Lectureships should be in the area of contemporary studies with an emphasis in one of the following areas: (1) public policy; (2) conflict resolution; (3) environmental studies; (4) multiculturalism and; (5) health care.

PURPOSE:
To promote international understanding through educational and cultural exchange between the U.S. and Scandinavia.

ELIGIBILITY:
The competition is open to all American colleges and universities. The award is appropriate for any department or interdisciplinary program with an interest in incorporating a Scandinavian focus. The lecturer must be a Norwegian or Swedish citizen and a scholar or expert in a field appropriate to the host department or program.

FINANCIAL DATA:
Amount of support per award: $20,000 teaching/research stipend plus a $5,000 travel stipend for lecture appearances outside home institution. Award also includes a J-1 visa sponsorship as a short-term scholar (up to six months) through the ASF Visitor Exchange Program.

APPLICATION INFO:
Application and instructions are available on the Foundation web site.
Duration: One semester.
Deadline: February 15. Announcement April 15.

*SPECIAL STIPULATIONS:
The selected lecturer is expected to teach one course (undergraduate or graduate-level) and perform modest public activities (lectures, etc.) for which he or she will receive $20,000.

ARCHAEOLOGICAL INSTITUTE OF AMERICA [1568]

656 Beacon Street, 6th Floor
Boston, MA 02215
(617) 358-4184
Fax: (617) 353-6550
E-mail: fellowships@aia.bu.edu
Web Site: www.archaeological.org

FOUNDED: 1879

AREAS OF INTEREST:
Archaeological research and publication.

NAME(S) OF PROGRAMS:
- **Helen M. Woodruff Fellowship of the AIA and the American Academy in Rome**

TYPE:
Fellowships. A predoctoral or postdoctoral fellowship for study of archaeology and classical studies established by the Institute at the American Academy in Rome. Award supports a Rome Prize.

PURPOSE:
To promote the study of archaeology and classical studies.

ELIGIBILITY:
Applicant must be a citizen or permanent resident of the U.S.

GEOG. RESTRICTIONS: United States.

FINANCIAL DATA:
Amount of support per award: $10,000.
Total amount of support: $10,000.

NO. AWARDS: 1.

APPLICATION INFO:
Applications must be sent to the American Academy in Rome; 7 East 60th Street; New York, NY 10022.
Duration: One year.
Deadline: November 1.

ADDRESS INQUIRIES TO:
Fellowship Coordinator
(See e-mail address above.)

ARCHITECTURAL LEAGUE OF NEW YORK

594 Broadway, Suite 607
New York, NY 10012
(212) 753-1722
Fax: (212) 486-9173
E-mail: info@archleague.org
Web Site: www.archleague.org

TYPE:
Travel grants. The Deborah J. Norden Fund, established in 1995 in memory of architect and arts administrator Deborah Norden, awards travel/study grants to students and recent graduates in the field of architecture, architectural history, and urban studies.

See entry 401 for full listing.

ARCTIC INSTITUTE OF NORTH AMERICA [1569]

The University of Calgary
2500 University Drive, N.W., ES 1040
Calgary AB T2N 1N4 Canada
(403) 220-7515
Fax: (403) 282-4609
E-mail: arctic@ucalgary.ca
Web Site: www.arctic.ucalgary.ca

FOUNDED: 1945

AREAS OF INTEREST:
Arctic natural and social sciences.

NAME(S) OF PROGRAMS:
- **AINA Grants-in-Aid**

TYPE:
Grants-in-aid; Scholarships.

YEAR PROGRAM STARTED: 1945

PURPOSE:
To provide funding to young investigators, especially graduate students, to augment their research.

ELIGIBILITY:
Proposed projects can include field, library or office-intensive investigations. Although there is no limitation on the area of investigation, the Institute encourages applications focused on the natural sciences and social sciences, including anthropology and economics, in the North.

FINANCIAL DATA:
Funding can be used for travel, supplies, equipment and services, but not for salary or wages.
Amount of support per award: $1,000.
Total amount of support: Varies each year, depending on number of applications received.

NO. MOST RECENT APPLICANTS: 80.

NO. AWARDS: Varies.

APPLICATION INFO:
Applications must be mailed to:
Arctic Institute of North America
University of Alaska, Rasmuson Library
P.O. Box 6808
Fairbanks, AK 99775-6808.
Deadline: February 1 (postmark).

PUBLICATIONS:
Arctic Journal.

ADDRESS INQUIRIES TO:
Arctic Institute of North America
(See e-mail address above.)

BARNES GROUP FOUNDATION

123 Main Street
Bristol, CT 06010
(860) 583-7070
Fax: (860) 589-7466
Web Site: www.bginc.com

TYPE:
General operating grants; Scholarships. Employee scholarship program.

See entry 1153 for full listing.

ROY J. CARVER CHARITABLE TRUST [1570]

202 Iowa Avenue
Muscatine, IA 52761-3733
(563) 263-4010
Fax: (563) 263-1547
E-mail: info@carvertrust.org
Web Site: www.carvertrust.org

FOUNDED: 1982

AREAS OF INTEREST:
Biomedical and scientific research; elementary, secondary and higher education; youth recreation.

TYPE:
Capital grants; Challenge/matching grants; Professorships; Project/program grants; Research grants; Scholarships.

YEAR PROGRAM STARTED: 1982

PURPOSE:
To support medical and scientific research, scholarships, general education and programs addressing the needs of youth.

LEGAL BASIS:
Trust.

ELIGIBILITY:
Eligible organizations must be IRS 501(c)(3) tax-exempt.

GEOG. RESTRICTIONS: Iowa and portions of western Illinois.

FINANCIAL DATA:
Amount of support per award: Varies.
Total amount of support: Varies.

APPLICATION INFO:
Detailed information is available online.
Duration: Varies.
Deadline: February 15, May 15, August 15 and November 15.

ADDRESS INQUIRIES TO:
Troy K. Ross, Ph.D.
Executive Administrator
(See address above.)

CENTER FOR CALIFORNIA STUDIES, CAPITAL FELLOWS PROGRAMS

California State University, Sacramento
6000 J Street
Sacramento, CA 95819-6081
(916) 278-6906
Fax: (916) 278-5199
E-mail: calstudies@csus.edu
Web Site: www.csus.edu/calst/assembly_fellowship_program.html

TYPE:
Fellowships. Jointly sponsored by the Center for California Studies at California State University, Sacramento and the California State Assembly. Full-time fellowships for 18 fellows, 11 months and units of graduate study through California State University, Sacramento.

See entry 1931 for full listing.

CENTER FOR CALIFORNIA STUDIES, CAPITAL FELLOWS PROGRAMS

California State University, Sacramento
6000 J Street
Sacramento, CA 95819-6081
(916) 278-6906
Fax: (916) 278-5199
E-mail: calstudies@csus.edu
Web Site: www.csus.edu/calst/judicial

TYPE:
Fellowships. Jointly sponsored by the Center for California Studies at California State University, Sacramento and the California Judicial Council. Full-time fellowships for 10 fellows, 10 months and graduate units earned from California State University, Sacramento.

See entry 1928 for full listing.

CENTER FOR CALIFORNIA STUDIES, CAPITAL FELLOWS PROGRAMS

California State University, Sacramento
6000 J Street
Sacramento, CA 95819-6081
(916) 278-6906
Fax: (916) 278-5199
E-mail: calstudies@csus.edu
Web Site: www.csus.edu/calst/senate

TYPE:
Fellowships. Jointly sponsored by the Center for California Studies at California State University, Sacramento and the California State Senate. Full-time fellowships for 18 fellows, 11 months and graduate units earned from California State University, Sacramento.

See entry 1929 for full listing.

CENTER FOR CALIFORNIA STUDIES, CAPITAL FELLOWS PROGRAMS

California State University, Sacramento
6000 J Street
Sacramento, CA 95819-6081
(916) 278-6906
Fax: (916) 278-5199
E-mail: calstudies@csus.edu
Web Site: www.csus.edu/calst/executive

TYPE:
Fellowships. Jointly sponsored by the Center for California Studies at California State University, Sacramento and the California governor. Full-time fellowships for 18 fellows, 10 months and six units of graduate study through California State University, Sacramento.

See entry 1930 for full listing.

CORNELL UNIVERSITY

Society for the Humanities
A.D. White House
27 East Avenue
Ithaca, NY 14853-1101
(607) 255-9274
(607) 255-4086
Fax: (607) 255-1422
E-mail: humctr-mailbox@cornell.edu
Web Site: www.arts.cornell.edu/sochum

TYPE:
Fellowships. Postdoctoral teaching-research fellowships in the humanities, each awarded for a two-year period. While in residence at Cornell, postdoctoral fellows hold department affiliation and have limited teaching duties and the opportunity for scholarly work.

See entry 353 for full listing.

COUNCIL FOR INTERNATIONAL EXCHANGE OF SCHOLARS (CIES) [1571]

1400 K Street, N.W.
Suite 700
Washington, DC 20005-2403
(202) 686-4000
Fax: (202) 686-4029
E-mail: scholars@iie.org
Web Site: www.cies.org/iea

FOUNDED: 1947

AREAS OF INTEREST:
Scholarly exchange.

NAME(S) OF PROGRAMS:
- **Fulbright International Education Administrators Program**

TYPE:
Conferences/seminars; Exchange programs; Project/program grants; Research grants; Travel grants. Through its short-term seminars, the Fulbright International Education Administrators Program can help U.S. higher education administrators establish lasting connections within the social, cultural and education systems of other countries. Selected administrators have the opportunity to gain in-depth knowledge about the host country's higher education system as well as to establish networks of U.S. and international colleagues. Grantees return home with enhanced ability to serve international students and encourage prospective study-abroad students.

YEAR PROGRAM STARTED: 1947

PURPOSE:
To promote mutual understanding between people of the U.S. and people of other nations.

LEGAL BASIS:
Public Law 87-256, as amended, The Mutual Educational and Cultural Exchange Act of 1961.

ELIGIBILITY:
Applicants must be U.S. citizens.

U.S.-India and U.S.-France IEA Programs are open to experienced international education administrators and senior administrators responsible for enhancing the international dimensions of their institutions.

U.S.-Japan IEA Program is open to experienced international education administrators and senior administrators responsible for enhancing the international dimensions of their institutions. Preference is given to applicants who have not had significant professional visits to Japan in the last five years and who indicate an institutional interest in increasing the number of Japanese students on their campus.

U.S.-Korea IEA Program is open to experienced international education administrators and senior administrators responsible for enhancing the international dimensions of their institutions. Preference is given to applicants who have an existing population of Korean students on campus.

U.S.-Germany IEA Program is open to experienced administrators in international exchanges, foreign admissions, study-abroad, international education, career services, alumni affairs and development/fund-raising.

Applicants to any of these IEA programs are not required to hold a Ph.D.

GEOG. RESTRICTIONS: United States.

FINANCIAL DATA:
Amount of support per award: Varies.

NO. MOST RECENT APPLICANTS: Approximately 75.

NO. AWARDS: U.S.-France IEA: Up to 12; U.S.-Germany IEA: Up to 20; U.S.-India IEA: Up to 10; U.S.-Japan IEA: Up to 10; U.S.-Korea IEA: Up to 8.

APPLICATION INFO:
Applicants must submit:
(1) adapted application form;
(2) project statement (not to exceed five single-spaced pages);

(3) institutional statement (one to two pages);
(4) curriculum vitae (not to exceed six pages) and;
(5) three references.

Duration: U.S.-India IEA: Two weeks in March; U.S.-Japan and U.S.-Korea IEA: Two weeks in June; U.S.-France and U.S. Germany IEA: Two weeks in October.

Deadline: U.S.-Japan IEA and U.S.-Korea IEA: November 1; U.S.-France IEA and U.S.-Germany IEA: February 1; U.S.-India IEA: August 3.

PUBLICATIONS:
Descriptive brochure; annual awards catalog; annual report.

ADDRESS INQUIRIES TO:
Fulbright International Education Administrators Program
(See e-mail and address above.)

COUNCIL FOR INTERNATIONAL EXCHANGE OF SCHOLARS (CIES) [1572]

1400 K Street, N.W.
Suite 700
Washington, DC 20005
(202) 686-4000
Fax: (202) 686-4029
E-mail: scholars@iie.org
Web Site: www.cies.org

FOUNDED: 1947

AREAS OF INTEREST:
Distinguished chair lecturing awards.

NAME(S) OF PROGRAMS:

- **Fulbright Distinguished Chairs**

TYPE:
Awards/prizes. There are approximately 40 distinguished chair awards in 18 countries. Awards available in a wide variety of disciplines.

PURPOSE:
To promote mutual understanding and scholarship.

ELIGIBILITY:
Applicants must have a Ph.D. or equivalent professional degree; a terminal degree is required. Applicants should have a record of prominent scholarly achievement. U.S. citizenship required. Lecturing is in English.

FINANCIAL DATA:
Award benefits vary by country and generally include a monthly stipend, travel, and housing.

Amount of support per award: Varies.

Total amount of support: Varies.

APPLICATION INFO:
Application must be submitted online.

Duration: Varies.

Deadline: August.

ADDRESS INQUIRIES TO:
See e-mail address above.

HUGH AND HAZEL DARLING FOUNDATION [1573]

520 South Grand Avenue, Suite 395
Los Angeles, CA 90071
(213) 683-5200
Fax: (213) 627-7795

FOUNDED: 1987

AREAS OF INTEREST:
Education.

TYPE:
Block grants; Capital grants; Challenge/matching grants; Matching gifts; Scholarships; Training grants.

YEAR PROGRAM STARTED: 1987

PURPOSE:
To support education in California, with principle emphasis on legal education.

LEGAL BASIS:
Private foundation.

ELIGIBILITY:
Grants are made only to tax-exempt 501(c)(3) organizations. No grants are made to individuals.

GEOG. RESTRICTIONS: California.

FINANCIAL DATA:
Amount of support per award: Varies.

Total amount of support: Varies.

NO. MOST RECENT APPLICANTS: 100.

NO. AWARDS: 46 for the year 2015.

REPRESENTATIVE AWARDS:
$15,000 to Azusa Pacific University for scholarships; $100,000 to Loyola Law School for scholarships; $25,000 to Pepperdine Law School for clinical program; $30,000 to Federalist Society for student program.

APPLICATION INFO:
Send letter and literature.

Deadline: Applications accepted throughout the year.

OFFICERS:
Richard L. Stack, Trustee

ADDRESS INQUIRIES TO:
Richard L. Stack, Trustee
(See address above.)

DELOITTE FOUNDATION [1574]

695 East Main Street
Stamford, CT 06901
(203) 761-3413
Fax: (203) 423-6413
E-mail: plevine@deloitte.com
Web Site: www.deloitte.com/us/df

FOUNDED: 1928

AREAS OF INTEREST:
Higher education, specializing in accounting and business.

TYPE:
Conferences/seminars; Fellowships; Matching gifts; Professorships; Research grants.

YEAR PROGRAM STARTED: 1956

PURPOSE:
To support education through a variety of initiatives that help develop the talent of the future and their influencers and promote excellence in teaching, research and curriculum innovation.

LEGAL BASIS:
Foundation.

ELIGIBILITY:
Doctoral Fellowship Program applicants must be doctoral candidates pursuing a Ph.D. in accounting at U.S. colleges and universities.

GEOG. RESTRICTIONS: United States.

FINANCIAL DATA:
Amount of support per award: Doctoral Fellowship Program: $25,000.

Total amount of support: Fellowship: $250,000 each year.

NO. MOST RECENT APPLICANTS: Approximately 50.

NO. AWARDS: Doctoral Fellowship Program: Up to 10.

APPLICATION INFO:
Application required only for Doctoral Fellowship Program and can be obtained through head of university accounting program. Send letter for other grant requests.

Duration: Doctoral Fellowship Program: Up to two years.

Deadline: Doctoral Fellowships: October 15. Announcement in late January or early February. No deadline for Research Grants.

PUBLICATIONS:
Information brochure.

BOARD OF DIRECTORS:
Mike Fucci, Chairman
Carol Lindstrom, President
David Williams, Secretary and Treasurer

ADDRESS INQUIRIES TO:
Peg Levine, Specialist
(See address above.)

HALBERT CENTRE FOR CANADIAN STUDIES [1575]

Canadian Friends of the Hebrew University
3080 Yonge Street, Suite 3020
P.O. Box 65
Toronto ON M4N 3N1 Canada
(416) 485-8000
(888) 432-7398 (Canada only)
Fax: (416) 485-8565
E-mail: info@cfhu.org
Web Site: www.cfhu.org

FOUNDED: 1944

AREAS OF INTEREST:
Canadian studies.

NAME(S) OF PROGRAMS:

- **Halbert Centre for Canadian Studies Visiting Professors Program**

TYPE:
Professorships; Research grants; Visiting scholars.

YEAR PROGRAM STARTED: 1945

PURPOSE:
To build bridges and strengthen ties between Canadian and Israeli scholars.

LEGAL BASIS:
Nonprofit.

ELIGIBILITY:
Applicants should hold university teaching positions in the social sciences, humanities or law. Applicants will be expected to combine broad teaching and research experience in their field with an ability to emphasize Canadian content. An expression of interest in participating in cooperative work to emphasize the development of joint Israel-Canada research will be of advantage to the applicant.

GEOG. RESTRICTIONS: Canada.

FINANCIAL DATA:
Remuneration includes up to $1,500 (CAN) for economy-class return airfare.

Amount of support per award: $2,800 (CAN) per month, plus $400 (CAN) stipend toward accommodation.

Total amount of support: Varies.

NO. AWARDS: 2 for the academic year 2015-16.

APPLICATION INFO:
Application should include the following: (1) curriculum vitae (not to exceed two pages) and short biography detailing the candidate's academic merit and teaching ability and experience;
(2) proposed course topic and syllabus and:
(3) a letter from the hosting department in support of the applicant, as well as justification for why and how the department would benefit from the inclusion of such a course in their curriculum.

Duration: One semester (10 weeks) or short visit of one to four weeks.

PUBLICATIONS:
Program announcement.

ADDRESS INQUIRIES TO:
Merle Goldman, Executive Vice President
Canadian Friends of
the Hebrew University
(See address above.)

THE HALLETT CHARITABLE TRUSTS [1576]

P.O. Box 39045
Edina, MN 55439
(952) 946-1229
E-mail: info@hallettrusts.org
Web Site: www.hallettrusts.org

AREAS OF INTEREST:
Higher education, social services, children's services, health, economic and cultural services.

TYPE:
Project/program grants.

PURPOSE:
To directly impact the population of the community in a manner that will measurably enrich its educational, health, economic and cultural opportunities.

ELIGIBILITY:
Grants are made to organizations that have tax-exempt status under Section 501(c)(3) of the Internal Revenue Code. No grants are made to individuals.

GEOG. RESTRICTIONS: Cuyuna Range area, Minnesota.

FINANCIAL DATA:
Amount of support per award: Varies.

Total amount of support: $1,000,000 annually.

APPLICATION INFO:
Application information is available on the web site.

Duration: Trustees may make multiyear commitments for grants.

Deadline: November 1.

ADDRESS INQUIRIES TO:
Margaret M. Poley, Executive Director
(See address above.)

HALLIBURTON FOUNDATION, INC. [1577]

10200 Bellaire Boulevard
Houston, TX 77072-5206
(281) 575-3558
Fax: (281) 575-3570
E-mail: brinda.maxwell@halliburton.com
Web Site: www.halliburton.com

AREAS OF INTEREST:
Higher education and elementary/secondary education.

TYPE:
Matching gifts; Project/program grants.

LEGAL BASIS:
Corporate giving program.

ELIGIBILITY:
Direct grant process is by invitation. Applicants are accredited junior colleges, colleges and universities or accredited elementary/secondary schools.

No grants are awarded for building programs, financial assistance to students or support of student activities and organizations.

GEOG. RESTRICTIONS: United States.

FINANCIAL DATA:
Amount of support per award: Varies.

Total amount of support: Varies.

Matching fund requirements: Contributions of directors, officers and employees of the Halliburton companies to accredited junior colleges, colleges/universities and elementary/secondary schools are matched 2.25:1 under certain conditions.

NO. AWARDS: Over 500.

APPLICATION INFO:
Requests for support should be mailed to the address listed above. Lengthy proposals are not required.

Duration: One year.

PUBLICATIONS:
Guidelines.

ADDRESS INQUIRIES TO:
Brinda Maxwell, Administrator
(See address above.)

THE HOROWITZ FOUNDATION FOR SOCIAL POLICY

P.O. Box 7
Rocky Hill, NJ 08553-0007
(732) 445-2280
E-mail: info@horowitz-foundation.org
Web Site: www.horowitz-foundation.org

TYPE:
Awards/prizes; Research grants. Grants to doctoral candidates at the dissertation level with emphasis on policy-related studies.

See entry 1800 for full listing.

THE GEORGE A. AND ELIZA GARDNER HOWARD FOUNDATION [1578]

346 Brook Street
Marston Hall, Room B-9
Providence, RI 02912
(401) 863-2640
Fax: (401) 863-6280
E-mail: howard_foundation@brown.edu
Web Site: www.brown.edu/Howard_Foundation

FOUNDED: 1952

TYPE:
Fellowships. The Foundation awards a limited number of fellowships each year for independent projects in fields selected on a rotational basis.

YEAR PROGRAM STARTED: 1952

PURPOSE:
To aid the personal development of promising individuals at the crucial middle stages of their careers.

LEGAL BASIS:
Private foundation.

ELIGIBILITY:
Nominees should normally have the rank of assistant or associate professor or their nonacademic equivalents. Support is intended to augment paid sabbatical leaves, making it financially possible for grantees to have time off in which to pursue their projects, free of any other professional responsibilities. Accepted nominees should therefore be eligible for sabbaticals or other leave with guaranteed additional support.

The project undertaken by a Howard Fellow should also be comprehensible to persons outside the immediate field of specialization. Candidates, regardless of their country of citizenship, must be professionally based in the U.S. either by affiliation with an institution or by residence.

GEOG. RESTRICTIONS: United States.

FINANCIAL DATA:
Amount of support per award: $33,000 for the year 2016-17.

Total amount of support: Approximately $330,000.

NO. MOST RECENT APPLICANTS: 100.

NO. AWARDS: Approximately 10 per year.

APPLICATION INFO:
Application information is available on the web site.

Duration: One academic year, July 1 to June 30.

Deadline: November 1.

ADMINISTRATION:
Christina Paxson, President of the University
Prof. William C. Crossgrove, Administrative Director
Peter Weber, Dean of the Graduate School
Prof. Sheila Bonde
Prof. John Cayley
Prof. Mary Gluck
Prof. Massimo Riva

BOARD OF TRUSTEES:
Karen Binder
Jane G. Gurzenda
Robert W. Kenyon
William W. Kenyon
Arthur H. Parker

ADDRESS INQUIRIES TO:
Prof. William C. Crossgrove
Administrative Director
George A. and Eliza
Gardner Howard Foundation
Box 1945
Brown University
Providence, RI 02912

THE FLETCHER JONES FOUNDATION [1579]

117 East Colorado Boulevard
Suite 600
Pasadena, CA 91105
(626) 535-9506
Fax: (626) 535-9508
E-mail: chris@fletcherjonesfdn.org
Web Site: www.fletcherjonesfdn.org

FOUNDED: 1969

AREAS OF INTEREST:
Primarily, support to private independent colleges and universities in California.

TYPE:
Capital grants; Endowments; Fellowships; Grants-in-aid; Internships; Professorships; Project/program grants; Scholarships. Equipment grants. Academic programs.

YEAR PROGRAM STARTED: 1969

PURPOSE:
To assist private higher education in California.

LEGAL BASIS:
Private foundation.

ELIGIBILITY:
Grants are made to nonprofit, 501(c)(3) organizations. 90% of grants are for private colleges and universities in California. Grants are not made to carry on propaganda, to influence legislation or elections, to promote voter registration, to political candidates, to political campaigns, or to organizations engaged in such activities. Grants are not made to individuals.

The Foundation generally does not favor requests for projects which should be financed by government agencies, nor does it normally make grants to operating funds, elementary or secondary schools, deficit financing, or contingencies.

GEOG. RESTRICTIONS: California.

FINANCIAL DATA:
Amount of support per award: Varies.

NO. AWARDS: 14 regular grants and 72 Trustee discretionary grants.

REPRESENTATIVE AWARDS:
$1,000,000 to Pomona College; $300,000 to Biola University.

APPLICATION INFO:
A qualified, nonprofit organization which believes it meets the Foundation's criteria for a grant may wish to contact the Executive Director. Link to online application must be provided by the Executive Director after preliminary consultation.

Deadline: Applications are accepted throughout the year and reviewed quarterly.

IRS I.D.: 23-7030155

STAFF:
Christine Sisley, Executive Director and Treasurer

OFFICERS AND TRUSTEES:
Peter K. Barker, President
John D. Pettker, Vice President and Secretary
Samuel P. Bell, Vice President
Patrick C. Haden, Vice President
Parker S. Kennedy, Vice President
Robert W. Kummer, Jr., Vice President
Daniel E. Lungren, Vice President
Donald E. Nickelson, Vice President
Hon. Rockwell Schnabel, Vice President
Stewart R. Smith, Vice President

ADDRESS INQUIRIES TO:
Christine Sisley
Executive Director and Treasurer
(See address above.)

ALICE AND JULIUS KANTOR CHARITABLE TRUST

809 North Bedford Drive
Beverly Hills, CA 90210
(310) 360-7541

TYPE:
Development grants; Project/program grants; Research grants.

See entry 175 for full listing.

LUMINA FOUNDATION [1580]

30 South Meridian Street, Suite 700
Indianapolis, IN 46204-3503
(317) 951-5300
(800) 834-5756
Fax: (317) 951-5063
E-mail: newinquiry@luminafoundation.org
Web Site: www.luminafoundation.org

FOUNDED: 2000

AREAS OF INTEREST:
Promoting educational improvements and access. Focus beginning in 2013: Mobilizing to reach Goal 2025 and designing and building a 21st-century higher education system.

TYPE:
Project/program grants; Research contracts. The Foundation has worked with and made grants to many colleges, universities, peer foundations, associations and other organizations that work to improve student access and outcomes across the nation.

PURPOSE:
To help people achieve their potential by expanding access to and success in education beyond high school. Specific goal: To increase the proportion of Americans with high-quality college degrees, certificates and credentials to 60% by 2025.

ELIGIBILITY:
Organizations that are classified as tax-exempt under Section 501(c)(3) of the Internal Revenue Code and as public charities under Section 509(a)(1), (2) or (3) or to public organizations that are designated under Section 170(c) of the Code, not individuals. Grants will not be made to supporting organizations controlled by disqualified persons to Lumina or Type III supporting organizations that are not functionally integrated Type III supporting organizations (as defined in the Internal Revenue Code).

GEOG. RESTRICTIONS: United States and its territories.

FINANCIAL DATA:
Amount of support per award: Average grant amount: $200,000.

Total amount of support: More than $45,000,000 for the year 2014.

APPLICATION INFO:
All unsolicited inquiries should be submitted as formal Letters of Inquiry (LOI) so that Foundation staff may carefully review the request. Preference is submission online. Full information can be found on the web site. Full proposals are by invitation.

Duration: One to three years. Grant is not renewable.

Deadline: End of September for Letter of Inquiry.

ADDRESS INQUIRIES TO:
Candace Brandt, Grants Management Officer
P.O. Box 1806
Indianapolis, IN 46206-1806

MONROE-BROWN FOUNDATION [1581]

7950 Moorsbridge Road
Portage, MI 49024
(269) 324-5586
Fax: (269) 324-0686
E-mail: jbaker@monroebrown.org
Web Site: www.monroebrown.org

FOUNDED: 1984

AREAS OF INTEREST:
Higher education and economic development.

TYPE:
Development grants; Internships; Project/program grants; Scholarships.

PURPOSE:
To advance the public well-being through higher education and economic development.

LEGAL BASIS:
Private foundation.

ELIGIBILITY:
Organizations must qualify as a nonprofit under Section 501(c)(3) of the Internal Revenue Code.

GEOG. RESTRICTIONS: Kalamazoo, Michigan.

FINANCIAL DATA:
Amount of support per award: Varies.

Total amount of support: Varies.

APPLICATION INFO:
Application information is available on the web site.

Duration: Varies.

Deadline: March 15, June 15, September 15 and December 15.

ADDRESS INQUIRIES TO:
Jane Baker, Director
(See address above.)

NATIONAL ASSOCIATION OF SCHOLARS [1582]

8 West 38th Street
Suite 503
New York, NY 10018
(917) 551-6770
E-mail: contact@nas.org
Web Site: www.nas.org

NAME(S) OF PROGRAMS:
- **The Barry R. Gross Memorial Award**
- **The Sidney Hook Memorial Award**
- **The Peter Shaw Memorial Award**

TYPE:
Awards/prizes. The Barry R. Gross Memorial Award rewards an NAS member for outstanding service to the cause of academic reform.

The Sidney Hook Memorial Award is given to an individual for distinguished contributions to the defense of academic freedom and the integrity of academic life.

The Peter Shaw Memorial Award recognizes exemplary writing on issues pertaining to higher education and American intellectual culture.

PURPOSE:
To enrich the substance and strengthen the integrity of scholarship and teaching.

ELIGIBILITY:
Candidates must be chosen by the Association.

FINANCIAL DATA:
Award includes a plaque and travel expenses to attend the Association's National Conference and present a speech.

Amount of support per award: Gross and Shaw Memorial Awards: $1,000; Hook Memorial Award: $2,500.

*PLEASE NOTE:
Awards are not given on an annual basis, but only when the Association holds a National Conference.

NATIONAL WILDLIFE FEDERATION

11100 Wildlife Center Drive
Reston, VA 20190-5362
(703) 438-6265
Fax: (703) 438-6468
E-mail: fellows@nwf.org
Web Site: www.nwf.org

TYPE:
Fellowships.

See entry 2123 for full listing.

THE SAMUEL ROBERTS NOBLE FOUNDATION, INC. [1583]

2510 Sam Noble Parkway
Ardmore, OK 73401
(580) 224-6213
Fax: (580) 224-6212
E-mail: granting@noble.org
Web Site: www.noble.org

FOUNDED: 1945

AREAS OF INTEREST:
Higher education (primarily in Oklahoma), capital funding for higher education, health research, health delivery systems, and social services and community.

TYPE:
Capital grants; Challenge/matching grants; General operating grants; Project/program grants; Research grants. Focus on capital funding for higher education and on health research and delivery systems.

YEAR PROGRAM STARTED: 1946

PURPOSE:
To advance agricultural science and practice by conducting field and laboratory research, and by providing consultations to farmers, ranchers, and land managers in the Southern Great Plains; to foster sustainable agricultural practices; to support worthy charities through a program of grants with the aim of building stronger communities.

LEGAL BASIS:
Private foundation.

ELIGIBILITY:
Organizations must be classified as 501(c)(3) by the IRS and are primarily located in Oklahoma. No loans or grants are made to individuals.

GEOG. RESTRICTIONS: Oklahoma.

FINANCIAL DATA:
Amount of support per award: Varies.

Total amount of support: Varies.

NO. MOST RECENT APPLICANTS: 199 grant requests for the year 2015.

NO. AWARDS: 31 grants approved for the year 2015.

APPLICATION INFO:
Applicant organizations must send a letter of request summarizing the project prior to making a formal grant application. This letter should be addressed to Mary Kate Wilson, Director of Philanthropy, Engagement and Project Management, at the address above.

Deadline: Letters of inquiry will be accepted January 1 through June 1.

IRS I.D.: 73-0606209

STAFF:
Mary Kate Wilson, Director of Philanthropy, Engagement and Project Management
Samantha Ephgrave, Program Associate
Julie Barrick, Project Management Associate

ADDRESS INQUIRIES TO:
Mary Kate Wilson, Director of Philanthropy, Engagement and Project Management
(See address above.)

NORTH CAROLINA ASSOCIATION OF EDUCATORS [1584]

NCAE Center for Instructional Advocacy
700 South Salisbury Street
Raleigh, NC 27601
(919) 832-3000 ext. 227
(800) 662-7924 ext. 227
Fax: (919) 829-1626
E-mail: elic.senter@ncae.org
Web Site: www.ncae.org

FOUNDED: 1970

AREAS OF INTEREST:
Teaching.

NAME(S) OF PROGRAMS:

- **Mary Morrow/Edna Richards Scholarship Fund**

TYPE:
Scholarships. To be used for college expenses in senior year.

YEAR PROGRAM STARTED: 1994

PURPOSE:
To aid worthy students who plan to teach in North Carolina after graduation.

LEGAL BASIS:
Nonprofit organization.

ELIGIBILITY:
The applicant must be in their junior year in a North Carolina college or university, planning to teach and willing to teach in the public schools of North Carolina for at least two years following graduation. Selection is based on character, personality, scholastic achievement, evidence of promise as a teacher and financial need.

GEOG. RESTRICTIONS: North Carolina.

FINANCIAL DATA:
Amount of support per award: $1,000 per year.

Total amount of support: Varies.

NO. MOST RECENT APPLICANTS: Varies.

NO. AWARDS: Varies.

APPLICATION INFO:
Application forms are mailed in Fall to the heads of the department of education in colleges in North Carolina, both state-supported and private. The department head is requested to give the application forms to two juniors of his or her selection.

Duration: One year.

Deadline: January 30 (postmark).

STAFF:
Elic A. Senter, Manager

ADDRESS INQUIRIES TO:
Elic A. Senter, Manager
NCAE Center for Instructional Advocacy
P.O. Box 27347
Raleigh, NC 27611
(See e-mail address above.)

RADCLIFFE INSTITUTE FOR ADVANCED STUDY, HARVARD UNIVERSITY [1585]

Radcliffe Institute Fellowship Program
Byerly Hall
8 Garden Street
Cambridge, MA 02138
(617) 496-1324
Fax: (617) 495-8136
E-mail: fellowships@radcliffe.harvard.edu
Web Site: www.radcliffe.harvard.edu

FOUNDED: 1960

NAME(S) OF PROGRAMS:

- **Radcliffe Institute Fellowship Program**

TYPE:
Fellowships. The Radcliffe Institute for Advanced Study is a scholarly community where individuals pursue advanced work across a wide range of academic disciplines, professions or creative arts. Within this broad purpose, and in recognition of Radcliffe's historic contributions to the education of women and to the study of issues related to women, the Radcliffe Institute sustains a continuing commitment to the study of women, gender and society, although applicants' projects need not focus on gender.

Radcliffe Institute Fellowships are designed to support scholars, scientists, artists and writers of exceptional promise and demonstrated accomplishment who wish to pursue independent work in academic and professional fields, and in the creative arts.

YEAR PROGRAM STARTED: 1961

PURPOSE:
To offer support to The Radcliffe Institute for Advanced Study Fellowship programs for a scholarly community where individuals pursue advanced work across a wide range of academic disciplines, professions and creative arts.

LEGAL BASIS:
Department of Harvard University, nonprofit.

ELIGIBILITY:
For all programs, residence in the Boston area and participation in the Institute community are required during the fellowship appointment.

FINANCIAL DATA:
Additional funds provided for project expenses. Some support for relocation expenses provided when relevant. If so directed, Radcliffe will pay stipend to home institution if the institution is U.S.-based.

Amount of support per award: Stipends up to $75,000 for one year.

NO. MOST RECENT APPLICANTS: Over 1,200.

NO. AWARDS: Up to 50 fellowships.

APPLICATION INFO:
Applications are available online in late Spring.

Duration: September 1 to May 31.

Deadline: Humanities and Social Sciences and Creative Arts: September 15. Natural Sciences and Mathematics: October 6.

STAFF:
Alison Ney, Administrator of Fellowships

ADDRESS INQUIRIES TO:
See e-mail address above.

*SPECIAL STIPULATIONS:
Fellows are expected to present their work-in-progress and to attend other fellows' events.

THE NELL J. REDFIELD FOUNDATION

P.O. Box 61
Reno, NV 89504
(775) 323-1373
Fax: (775) 323-4476
E-mail: redfieldfoundation@yahoo.com

TYPE:
Capital grants; Challenge/matching grants; Development grants; Matching gifts; Project/program grants. Grants for higher education. Medical and social welfare for disadvantaged children and seniors.

See entry 266 for full listing.

GERTRUDE E. SKELLY CHARITABLE FOUNDATION [1586]

4600 North Ocean Boulevard
Suite 206
Boynton Beach, FL 33435
(561) 276-1008
Fax: (561) 272-2793
E-mail: skelly@hhk.com

FOUNDED: 1991

AREAS OF INTEREST:
Nursing education and medical care for indigents.

TYPE:
Challenge/matching grants; Conferences/seminars; Internships; Project/program grants; Research grants; Scholarships; Training grants. Emergency grants for continued education.

YEAR PROGRAM STARTED: 1991

PURPOSE:
To provide scholarships for individuals to obtain educational opportunities and/or medical care.

LEGAL BASIS:
Private foundation.

ELIGIBILITY:
Eligible applicants are colleges and universities, and other IRS 501(c)(3) tax-exempt organizations. No grants are given to agencies which do not provide direct services or scholarships.

GEOG. RESTRICTIONS: United States.

FINANCIAL DATA:
Amount of support per award: Up to $50,000.

Total amount of support: $750,000 for the year 2013.

Matching fund requirements: Tailored to specific projects.

NO. MOST RECENT APPLICANTS: 85.

NO. AWARDS: 50.

APPLICATION INFO:
Write to the address above for application guidelines.

Duration: One year.

Deadline: June 30. Award announcement the following January.

TRUSTEES:
Erik Edward Joh

ADDRESS INQUIRIES TO:
Erik Edward Joh, Trustee
(See address above.)

TARAKNATH DAS FOUNDATION [1587]

South Asia Institute
Columbia University
606 West 122nd Street, Room 213
New York, NY 10027
(212) 666-4282
Web Site: www.columbia.edu/cu/sai/tdas.html

FOUNDED: 1930

AREAS OF INTEREST:
Indian national graduate students studying any field in a U.S. university.

TYPE:
Grants-in-aid.

YEAR PROGRAM STARTED: 1935

PURPOSE:
To promote friendly relations and cultural cooperation between the U.S. and India.

LEGAL BASIS:
Special interest foundation.

ELIGIBILITY:
Applicants are not limited by discipline or subject area. Applicants must be Indian nationals (holding Indian passports) and must have completed at least one year of graduate study in the U.S.

FINANCIAL DATA:
Amount of support per award: $3,000 to $8,000.

Total amount of support: Approximately $25,000.

NO. MOST RECENT APPLICANTS: 20.

NO. AWARDS: About 4 annually.

APPLICATION INFO:
Applicants must submit all application materials together. Only complete applications will be judged for the awards. Complete applications include:
(1) completed application form;
(2) transcript from most recent academic institution;
(3) three sealed letters of recommendation, including one from the applicant's academic advisor;
(4) academic plans of applicant and;
(5) photocopy of applicant's passport.

Duration: One year.

Deadline: September 1. Award announcement in late October.

ADDRESS INQUIRIES TO:
Leonard Gordon, Director
(See address above.)

U.S. DEPARTMENT OF EDUCATION

Centers for International Business Education
1990 K Street, N.W., 6th Floor
Washington, DC 20006-8521
(202) 502-7622
Fax: (202) 502-7858
E-mail: timothy.duvall@ed.gov
Web Site: www2.ed.gov/programs/iegpscibe/index.html

TYPE:
Project/program grants. The program provides grants to eligible institutions of higher education or combinations of these institutions for planning, establishing and operating Centers for International Business Education.

See entry 1854 for full listing.

U.S. DEPARTMENT OF EDUCATION [1588]

Office of Postsecondary Education
Federal TRIO Programs
1990 K Street, N.W., Suite 7000
Washington, DC 20006-8510
(202) 502-7586
(202) 502-7600
Fax: (202) 502-7857
E-mail: OPE_TRIO@ed.gov
Web Site: www.ed.gov/ope/trio

AREAS OF INTEREST:
Education for low-income youth.

NAME(S) OF PROGRAMS:
- **Upward Bound**

TYPE:
Project/program grants. There are three types of grants under the Upward Bound program: Regular Upward Bound Grants, Veterans Upward Bound Grants, and Upward Bound Math and Science Grants.

The Regular Upward Bound projects are designed to generate in participants the skills and motivation necessary for success in education beyond secondary school. The Veterans Upward Bound projects are designed to assist veterans in preparing for a program of postsecondary education. The Upward Bound Math and Science projects are designed to prepare high school students for postsecondary education programs that lead to careers in the fields of math and science.

YEAR PROGRAM STARTED: 1966

PURPOSE:
To generate participation skills and the motivation necessary for success in education beyond school.

LEGAL BASIS:
Title IV of the Higher Education Act of 1965, as amended.

GEOG. RESTRICTIONS: United States.

FINANCIAL DATA:
Amount of support per award: Average $325,036 for fiscal year 2014.

Total amount of support: Estimated $265,357,000 for fiscal year 2015.

NO. MOST RECENT APPLICANTS: 61,458.

NO. AWARDS: 814.

APPLICATION INFO:
Official application materials are available from the address above.

Duration: Five-year grant award cycles.

ADDRESS INQUIRIES TO:
Kenneth Waters, Program Specialist
(See address above.)

U.S. DEPARTMENT OF EDUCATION [1589]

International and Foreign Language Education Office
1990 K Street, N.W., Sixth Floor
Washington, DC 20006-8521
(202) 502-7626
Fax: (202) 502-7860
E-mail: tanyelle.richardson@ed.gov
Web Site: www.ed.gov/ope/iegps

NAME(S) OF PROGRAMS:
- **Undergraduate International Studies and Foreign Language Program**

TYPE:
Project/program grants; Seed money grants. Grants to plan, develop, and carry out a program to strengthen and improve

undergraduate instruction in international studies and foreign languages. Projects primarily focus on curriculum and faculty development. Institutions of higher education and public and private nonprofit agencies and organizations may apply for funds to develop projects which have the potential for making an especially significant contribution to the improvement of undergraduate instruction in international and foreign language studies in the U.S.

YEAR PROGRAM STARTED: 1972

PURPOSE:
To assist institutions to internationalize the curriculum. Applicants may propose to initiate a global studies program or a program focusing on a single world area and its languages; to develop a program which focuses on issues or topics, such as environmental studies or international business; to combine the teaching of international studies with professional or preprofessional training; to integrate undergraduate studies with Master's degree programs; to combine international studies with teacher training programs.

LEGAL BASIS:
Title VI, section 604A, Higher Education Act, as amended in 1986.

ELIGIBILITY:
Proposals are invited from institutions of higher education, including universities and two- to four-year colleges, and consortia of such institutions. The proposed program should include plans to initiate new or revised courses in international studies or area studies, and to improve or expand instruction in foreign languages. The program should be comparative or interdisciplinary in nature and strengthen linkages among disciplines and professional fields.

GEOG. RESTRICTIONS: United States.

FINANCIAL DATA:
Amount of support per award: Single Institutions: Average $89,000 per year; Organizations, Associations and Institutional Consortia: Average $140,000 per year.

Total amount of support: $2,900,000 available for fiscal year 2015.

Matching fund requirements: Dollar-for-dollar primarily within in-kind contributions.

NO. MOST RECENT APPLICANTS: 92.

NO. AWARDS: Approximately 30.

APPLICATION INFO:
Applications are required to be submitted electronically using the grants.gov system.

Duration: Single Institutions: Up to two years; Organizations, Associations and Institutional Consortia: Up to three years.

STAFF:
Tanyelle Richardson, Senior Program Officer

ADDRESS INQUIRIES TO:
Tanyelle Richardson, Senior Program Officer
(See address above.)

*PLEASE NOTE:
Request program materials and project abstracts at the web site. If there are additional questions after consulting web site, call (202) 502-7626.

U.S. DEPARTMENT OF EDUCATION

Higher Education Programs
International and Foreign Language Education (IFLE)
Language Resource Centers Program
1990 K Street, N.W., 6th Floor
Mail Stop K-OPE-6-6078
Washington, DC 20006
(202) 502-7589
Fax: (202) 502-7860
E-mail: stephanie.mckissic@ed.gov
Web Site: www.ed.gov/ope/iegps

TYPE:
General operating grants. Language Resource Centers Program provides grants for establishing, strengthening and operating centers that serve as resources for improving the nation's capacity for teaching and learning foreign languages through teacher training, research, materials development and dissemination projects.

See entry 654 for full listing.

UCLA INSTITUTE OF AMERICAN CULTURES (IAC)

2329 Murphy Hall, Box 957244
Los Angeles, CA 90095-7244
(310) 825-6815
Fax: (310) 825-3994
E-mail: iaccoordinator@conet.ucla.edu
Web Site: www.iac.ucla.edu

TYPE:
Fellowships. Deals with arts and humanities, education and teacher training, fine arts, applied arts, law, social sciences, and sciences. The IAC, in cooperation with UCLA's four Ethnic Studies Research Centers (American Indian Studies Center, Asian American Studies Center, Bunche Center for African American Studies, and Chicano Studies Research Center), offers awards to visiting scholars to support research on African Americans, American Indians, Asian Americans and Chicanas/os.

See entry 995 for full listing.

THE UNIVERSITY OF CALGARY [1590]

Faculty of Graduate Studies
MacKimmie Library Tower, Room 213
2500 University Drive, N.W.
Calgary AB T2N 1N4 Canada
(403) 220-4938
Fax: (403) 289-7635
E-mail: gsaward@ucalgary.ca
Web Site: www.grad.ucalgary.ca/awards

AREAS OF INTEREST:
Management.

NAME(S) OF PROGRAMS:
- **Robert A. Willson Doctoral Management Scholarship**

TYPE:
Awards/prizes; Scholarships.

PURPOSE:
To produce a noteworthy leader in management teaching and research who has a broad appreciation of management's role in society, both nationally and internationally.

ELIGIBILITY:
Open to candidates who, at the time of tenure, are registered in a full-time program leading to a doctoral degree in Management at the University of Calgary, Haskayne School of Business. While academic excellence is essential, candidates should also present evidence of leadership in their academic or professional background. Students with international experience and orientation will be particularly considered.

FINANCIAL DATA:
Amount of support per award: $10,000.

Total amount of support: $10,000.

CO-OP FUNDING PROGRAMS: The donor of this scholarship program is the Haskayne School of Business.

NO. AWARDS: 1 per annum.

APPLICATION INFO:
No application is required. The Haskayne School of Business will recommend a recipient on the basis of academic and professional leadership. The Graduate Coordinator will submit recommendations to the Graduate Scholarship Office. The recommendation is subject to final approval of the Graduate Scholarship Committee.

Duration: One year.

Deadline: May 15.

PUBLICATIONS:
Academic calendar.

ADDRESS INQUIRIES TO:
Graduate Scholarship Office
(See address above.)

UNIVERSITY OF CALIFORNIA

President's Postdoctoral Fellowship Program
104 California Hall
UC Berkeley
Berkeley, CA 94720-1500
(510) 643-8235
E-mail: ppfpinfo@berkeley.edu
Web Site: ppfp.ucop.edu/info

TYPE:
Fellowships. Awarded for research conducted under faculty sponsorship on any one of the University of California's 10 campuses.

See entry 998 for full listing.

UNIVERSITY OF TEXAS AT AUSTIN [1591]

LBJ School of Public Affairs
P.O. Box Y
Austin, TX 78713-8925
(512) 471-4292
Fax: (512) 471-8455
E-mail: lbjadmit@austin.utexas.edu
Web Site: www.utexas.edu/lbj

AREAS OF INTEREST:
Public policy.

NAME(S) OF PROGRAMS:
- **Lyndon B. Johnson School of Public Affairs**

TYPE:
Assistantships; Fellowships. Merit fellowships are available to assist graduate students with financial support for education at the Master's and doctoral level.

ELIGIBILITY:
Applicants must be graduate students enrolled in Lyndon B. Johnson School of Public Affairs.

FINANCIAL DATA:
Amount of support per award: $4,000 to $60,000.

NO. AWARDS: 150.

APPLICATION INFO:
Contact the University for application procedures.

Duration: One to two years. Grants not renewable.

Deadline: December 1.

ADDRESS INQUIRIES TO:
Office of Student and Alumni Programs
(See address above.)

THE WABASH CENTER FOR TEACHING AND LEARNING IN THEOLOGY AND RELIGION

301 West Wabash Avenue
Crawfordsville, IN 47933
(765) 361-6047
Fax: (765) 361-6051
E-mail: wabashcenter@wabash.edu
Web Site: www.wabashcenter.wabash.edu

TYPE:
Conferences/seminars; Fellowships; Project/program grants; Research grants.

See entry 813 for full listing.

JEANNETTE K. WATSON FELLOWSHIP [1592]

11 Park Place, Suite 1503
New York, NY 10007
(212) 655-0201
Fax: (212) 843-0370
E-mail: jkw@watson.foundation
Web Site: watson.foundation

TYPE:
Fellowships. The program offers 15 students each year, from 12 New York City colleges, the opportunity for paid internships for three consecutive summers. The internships offer closely supervised, challenging work from which the student can learn. The expectation is that three summers in different sectors (nonprofit organizations, public service and for-profit firms) in New York City and overseas will make fellows more compelling candidates for national fellowships, graduate admissions and good jobs.

YEAR PROGRAM STARTED: 2000

PURPOSE:
To develop talent, leadership and motivation for service.

ELIGIBILITY:
Applicant must:
(1) be enrolled at one of the invited colleges (Baruch College, Brooklyn College, City College, College of Staten Island, Hunter College, John Jay College, Lehman College, Long Island University-Brooklyn Campus, Marymount Manhattan College, Pace University-Manhattan Campus, Queens College, and St. John's University);
(2) be a second-semester freshman or a sophomore;
(3) not be older than 25 on March 1 of application year;
(4) be enrolled in a liberal arts program;
(5) be a U.S. citizen or a "green card" holder and;
(6) be willing to participate in three successive summer internships and their collateral summer and term-time seminars.

FINANCIAL DATA:
Amount of support per award: $5,000 for the first summer; $6,000 for each of the second and third summers.

Total amount of support: $255,000 annually.

APPLICATION INFO:
Application information is available on the web site.

Duration: Three consecutive summer internships of 10 weeks plus year-round activities.

Deadline: February.

STAFF:
Chris Kasabach, Foundation Executive Director

THOMAS J. WATSON FELLOWSHIP PROGRAM [1593]

11 Park Place, Suite 1503
New York, NY 10017
(212) 245-8859
Fax: (212) 245-8860
E-mail: tjw@tjwf.org
Web Site: watson.foundation

FOUNDED: 1968

AREAS OF INTEREST:
Independent study outside of the U.S. for graduating college seniors.

TYPE:
Fellowships. The Foundation provides Fellows an opportunity for a focused and disciplined "Wanderjahr" of their own devising or design-time in which to explore with thoroughness a particular interest, test their aspirations and abilities, view their lives and American society in greater perspective and concomitantly, to develop a more informed sense of international concern. The Fellowship experience is intended to provide Fellows an opportunity to immerse themselves in cultures other than their own for an entire year. The candidate's proposed project should involve investigation into an area of demonstrated concern and personal interest.

YEAR PROGRAM STARTED: 1968

PURPOSE:
To give exceptional college graduates the freedom to engage in a year of independent study, purposeful exploration and travel outside of the U.S. in order to enhance their capacity for resourcefulness, imagination, openness and leadership, and to foster their humane and effective participation in the world community.

LEGAL BASIS:
Private foundation.

ELIGIBILITY:
The Foundation welcomes applicants from a diverse range of backgrounds and academic disciplines. Only graduating seniors at participating institutions are eligible for nomination by their institution.

GEOG. RESTRICTIONS: United States.

FINANCIAL DATA:
Amount of support per award: $30,000.

Total amount of support: Varies.

NO. MOST RECENT APPLICANTS: 180.

NO. AWARDS: 50 each year.

APPLICATION INFO:
Students must first be nominated by their college or university, and then compete on a national level. Application form required.

Duration: One year.

Deadline: Nominations and nominees' completed applications should arrive by first Tuesday in November. Announcement made in mid-March.

PUBLICATIONS:
Guidelines.

IRS I.D.: 13-6038151

STAFF:
Sneha Subramanian, Program Manager

*SPECIAL STIPULATIONS:
All Fellows are required to maintain contact with the fellowship office during their year abroad. In addition to quarterly progress reports, they must submit a final evaluation of the Fellowship year together with a financial accounting of the expenditure of Fellowship funds. The Fellowship is taxable and must be reported by recipients as income. Taxes are not withheld by the Foundation.

TODD WEHR FOUNDATION [1594]

555 East Wells Street
Suite 1900
Milwaukee, WI 53202-3819
(414) 273-2100
Fax: (414) 223-5000

FOUNDED: 1954

AREAS OF INTEREST:
Education and inner-city Milwaukee capital projects for the benefit of children.

TYPE:
Capital grants.

ELIGIBILITY:
Organizations must have 501(c)(3) tax-exempt status. No grants to individuals.

GEOG. RESTRICTIONS: Wisconsin, with emphasis on Milwaukee.

FINANCIAL DATA:
Amount of support per award: $10,000 to $50,000.

NO. AWARDS: 1 to 10.

APPLICATION INFO:
Send brief letter of inquiry along with full proposal.

Duration: One to 10 years.

Deadline: Applications accepted throughout the year.

ADDRESS INQUIRIES TO:
Allan E. Iding, President
(See address above.)

Scholar aid programs (all disciplines)

ALABAMA COMMISSION ON HIGHER EDUCATION [1595]

100 North Union Street
Montgomery, AL 36104-3702
(334) 242-2273
Fax: (334) 242-2269
E-mail: cheryl.newton@ache.alabama.gov
Web Site: www.ache.alabama.gov

FOUNDED: 1977

AREAS OF INTEREST:
Continuing higher education.

NAME(S) OF PROGRAMS:

- **Senior Adult Scholarship Program**

TYPE:
Grants-in-aid; Scholarships. A free tuition program for senior citizens who meet the admission requirements.

ELIGIBILITY:
Alabama residents who are 60 years of age or older and who attend public two-year postsecondary educational institutions in Alabama are eligible to apply.

GEOG. RESTRICTIONS: Alabama.

APPLICATION INFO:
Applications can be obtained by contacting the financial aid office at any public two-year postsecondary educational institution in Alabama.

ADDRESS INQUIRIES TO:
Cheryl B. Newton, Grants Coordinator
(See address above.)

ALABAMA COMMISSION ON HIGHER EDUCATION [1596]

100 North Union Street
Montgomery, AL 36104-3702
(334) 242-2273
Fax: (334) 242-2269
E-mail: cheryl.newton@ache.alabama.gov
Web Site: www.ache.alabama.gov

FOUNDED: 1977

AREAS OF INTEREST:
Higher education.

NAME(S) OF PROGRAMS:
- **Alabama National Guard Educational Assistance Program**

TYPE:
Awards/prizes. An award to be used for tuition, educational fees and books/supplies for Alabama National Guard members to attend a public or private postsecondary educational institution in Alabama.

YEAR PROGRAM STARTED: 1984

ELIGIBILITY:
Students who are active members in good standing with a federally recognized unit of the Alabama National Guard are eligible to apply. Participants may receive federal veterans benefits, but must show a cost-less-aid amount of at least $100. Awards are based on need.

GEOG. RESTRICTIONS: Alabama.

FINANCIAL DATA:
Amount of support per award: Awards are limited to $1,000 per term and no more than $2,000 per year.

NO. AWARDS: 363 for the year 2014-15.

APPLICATION INFO:
Application forms are available from Alabama National Guard Units. Funds are limited, so students who are Guard members are encouraged to apply early. Forms must be signed by a representative of the Alabama Military Department and the financial aid officer at the college or university the student plans to attend. All applicants must have the Free Application for Federal Student Aid (FAFSA) on file.

ADDRESS INQUIRIES TO:
Cheryl B. Newton, Grants Coordinator
(See address above.)

ALABAMA COMMISSION ON HIGHER EDUCATION [1597]

100 North Union Street
Montgomery, AL 36104-3702
(334) 242-2273
Fax: (334) 242-2269
E-mail: cheryl.newton@ache.alabama.gov
Web Site: www.ache.alabama.gov

FOUNDED: 1977

AREAS OF INTEREST:
Higher education.

NAME(S) OF PROGRAMS:
- **Alabama Student Assistance Program**
- **Alabama Student Grant Program**

TYPE:
Awards/prizes; Grants-in-aid; Scholarships. The Alabama Student Assistance Program is a need-based, state grant. Awards are limited to undergraduate work.

The Alabama Student Grant Program is an award of grant assistance at an eligible independent Alabama college or university. Award is not based on need. Maximum amount available only when sufficient funds are available.

ELIGIBILITY:
Applicants for the Alabama Student Assistance Program must be undergraduate students who are Alabama residents attending eligible Alabama institutions. 55 Alabama institutions participate in the program.

Applicants for the Alabama Student Grant Program must be undergraduate students either half-time or full-time who are Alabama residents attending Amridge University, Birmingham-Southern College, Concordia College, Faulkner University, Huntington College, Judson College, Miles College, Oakwood College, Samford University, South University, Spring Hill College, Stillman College, U.S. Sports Academy or the University of Mobile.

GEOG. RESTRICTIONS: Alabama.

FINANCIAL DATA:
Amount of support per award: Student Assistance Program: $300 to $5,000; Student Grant Program: Up to $1,200.

Total amount of support: ASAP: $2,619,980; ASGP: $1,996,350 for the year 2014-15.

NO. AWARDS: ASAP: 4,112; ASGP: 5,145 for the year 2014-15.

APPLICATION INFO:
Application forms are available at the institution that the applicant is planning on attending.

ADDRESS INQUIRIES TO:
Cheryl B. Newton, Grants Coordinator
(See address above.)

AMERICAN ASSOCIATION OF UNIVERSITY WOMEN

1111 Sixteenth Street, N.W.
Washington, DC 20036
(866) 795-4892
E-mail: aauw@applyists.com
Web Site: www.aauw.org

TYPE:
Fellowships. Awarded to women who are U.S. citizens or permanent residents who are pursuing full-time study in a Master's or professional degree program in which women are underrepresented, including STEM, law, business and medicine.

See entry 1051 for full listing.

AMERICAN COUNCIL FOR POLISH CULTURE (ACPC) [1598]

27562 David Givens Avenue
Warren, MI 48092-3533
(586) 575-9279
E-mail: metyszka@sbcglobal.net
Web Site: www.polishcultureacpc.org

NAME(S) OF PROGRAMS:
- **ACPC Scholarship, Summer Studies in Poland**
- **Pulaski Scholarships for Advanced Studies**
- **Louis and Nellie Skalny Scholarships for Polish Studies**

TYPE:
Scholarships.

ELIGIBILITY:
ACPC Scholarship, Summer Studies in Poland: American of Polish descent entering junior or senior year at accredited college or university. Must have an ACPC affiliation.

Pulaski Scholarships for Advanced Studies: Applicant must be of Polish heritage and have completed at least two years in advanced studies at a U.S. university.

Skalny Scholarships for Polish Studies: Intended for students pursuing some Polish studies (major may be in other fields) at universities in the U.S. who have completed at least two years of college or university work. Scholarships awarded for the fall term.

FINANCIAL DATA:
Amount of support per award: ACPC Scholarship, Summer Studies in Poland: $2,000 toward transportation and tuition. Pulaski Scholarships for Advanced Studies: $5,000. Skalny Scholarships for Polish Studies: $3,000.

APPLICATION INFO:
Instructions and application form, if required, are available online.

Deadline: ACPC Scholarship, Summer Studies in Poland: April 1. Pulaski Scholarships for Advanced Studies: March 15. Skalny Scholarships for Polish Studies: May 15.

ADMINISTRATION:
Mary Ellen Tyszka, President

ADDRESS INQUIRIES TO:
ACPC Scholarship, Summer Studies in Poland:
Alice Lech Laning
E-mail: laning@verizon.net

Pulaski Scholarships for Advanced Studies:
Mr. Marion W. Winters
Tel: (508) 949-0160
E-mail: mvwinters@charter.net

Skalny Scholarships for Polish Studies:
Deborah M. Majka
Tel: (215) 627-1391
E-mail: dziecko2@comcast.net

AMERICAN COUNCIL OF THE BLIND [1599]

2200 Wilson Boulevard, Suite 650
Arlington, VA 22201
(202) 467-5081
(800) 424-8666
Fax: (703) 465-5085
E-mail: info@acb.org
Web Site: www.acb.org

FOUNDED: 1961

AREAS OF INTEREST:
The needs, interests and concerns of blind and visually impaired people on the local, state and national level.

CONSULTING OR VOLUNTEER SERVICES:
The Council offers the following services:
(1) information and referral on all aspects of blindness;
(2) legal consultation and representation;
(3) support to consumer advocates working on issues related to visual handicaps;
(4) assistance in chapter development;
(5) assistance in program development;
(6) employment opportunities information;
(7) speaker referral;
(8) monitoring of existing service delivery systems, with advocacy for improvement when necessary;
(9) representation on boards and advisory committees, both governmental and private;
(10) consultation and assistance in technological research and;
(11) national legislative hotline.

NAME(S) OF PROGRAMS:
- **American Council of the Blind Scholarships**

TYPE:
Assistantships; Awards/prizes; Internships; Scholarships. Scholarships for outstanding blind students enrolled in academic, vocational, technical or professional training programs beyond the high school level.

YEAR PROGRAM STARTED: 1982

PURPOSE:
To assist blind postsecondary students with educational expenses.

LEGAL BASIS:
Nonprofit membership organization.

ELIGIBILITY:
Applicants must be legally blind persons admitted or under consideration for admission to postsecondary training programs for the next school year, who are U.S. citizens or resident aliens and who have submitted a completed application and the required supporting materials.

GEOG. RESTRICTIONS: United States.

FINANCIAL DATA:
Amount of support per award: $500 to $3,000.

Total amount of support: $35,000.

NO. MOST RECENT APPLICANTS: 300.

NO. AWARDS: 20.

APPLICATION INFO:
Applications must be submitted online. Applicant must submit completed application, certified transcript, autobiographical sketch, letter of recommendation from instructor, proof of acceptance by postsecondary school and proof of legal blindness.

Duration: One academic year. Nonrenewable, but recipient may reapply.

Deadline: Postmarked by March 1. Announcement June 1.

PUBLICATIONS:
Annual report; *Braille Forum*; *Student Advocate*.

IRS I.D.: 58-0914436

OFFICERS:
Kim Charlson, President
Jeff Thom, First Vice President
Marlaina Lieberg, Second Vice President

ADDRESS INQUIRIES TO:
Scholarship Coordinator
(See address above.)

AMERICAN FRIENDS OF THE ALEXANDER VON HUMBOLDT FOUNDATION [1600]

1101 17th Street, N.W.
Suite 603
Washington, DC 20036
(202) 783-1907
E-mail: info@americanfriends-of-avh.org
Web Site: www.americanfriends-of-avh.org

FOUNDED: 1953

AREAS OF INTEREST:
Scholarly research and academic cooperation through provision of awards and fellowships. All countries and all disciplines.

NAME(S) OF PROGRAMS:
- **Humboldt Research Awards for Foreign Scholars**

TYPE:
Awards/prizes; Fellowships. Research awards for outstanding achievements in the fields of humanities and social sciences, natural sciences, medicine and engineering sciences providing for visits to German research institutes.

YEAR PROGRAM STARTED: 1972

PURPOSE:
To strengthen scientific cooperation between foreign and German researchers.

LEGAL BASIS:
Government agency run according to private law.

ELIGIBILITY:
Open to internationally renowned scientists and scholars having full professor or equivalent standing.

FINANCIAL DATA:
Amount of support per award: Up to EUR 60,000, plus travel expenses for awardee and accompanying family members.

Total amount of support: Varies.

NO. AWARDS: Varies.

APPLICATION INFO:
Awards are made by nomination and by eminent German scholars only. No direct applications are allowed.

Duration: Visits to German institutes from six to 12 months. No renewal of the award is possible, but recipient may be invited to Germany again.

Deadline: Nominations may be submitted at any time.

ADDRESS INQUIRIES TO:
See e-mail address above.

AMERICAN INDIAN COLLEGE FUND

8333 Greenwood Boulevard
Denver, CO 80221
(303) 426-8900
Fax: (303) 426-1200
E-mail: scholarships@collegefund.org
Web Site: collegefund.org

TYPE:
Scholarships.

See entry 1016 for full listing.

AMERICAN INDIAN GRADUATE CENTER

3701 San Mateo Boulevard, N.E.
Suite 200
Albuquerque, NM 87110
(505) 881-4584
Fax: (505) 884-0427
E-mail: fellowships@aigcs.org
Web Site: www.aigcs.org

TYPE:
Fellowships; Grants-in-aid; Scholarships. Grants on an academic year basis. Summer funding available to continuing students only; these are students who are currently in the fellowship program.

See entry 1017 for full listing.

AMERICAN INDIAN SCIENCE AND ENGINEERING SOCIETY (AISES)

2305 Renard, S.E.
Suite 200
Albuquerque, NM 87106
(505) 765-1052 ext. 103
(720) 552-6123
Fax: (505) 765-5608
E-mail: kcristiano@aises.org
Web Site: www.aises.org/scholarships

TYPE:
Scholarships. AISES scholarships are intended to partially defray tuition and other educational expenses, thereby increasing access to higher education and improving college retention rates for AISES members.

AISES scholarships are made possible by corporations, government agencies, foundations, and individuals who wish to support the advancement of American Indians/Alaskan Natives. Scholarships are distributed in two disbursements and awarded for one academic year, unless otherwise specified. Recipients cannot receive more than one scholarship in any of the six programs.

Scholarships are also awarded to members of AISES who are American Indian/Alaskan Native college students who meet the eligibility requirements for each scholarship.

See entry 1018 for full listing.

AMERICAN INSTITUTE OF CERTIFIED PUBLIC ACCOUNTANTS (AICPA)

220 Leigh Farm Road
Durham, NC 27707
(919) 402-2161
Fax: (919) 419-4705
E-mail: scholarships@aicpa.org
Web Site: www.thiswaytocpa.com

TYPE:
Scholarships.

See entry 1478 for full listing.

AMERICAN INSTITUTE OF CERTIFIED PUBLIC ACCOUNTANTS (AICPA) [1601]

220 Leigh Farm Road
Durham, NC 27707
(919) 402-4682
Fax: (919) 419-4705
E-mail: scholarships@aicpa.org
Web Site: www.aicpa.org

AREAS OF INTEREST:
Accounting/doctoral program.

NAME(S) OF PROGRAMS:
- **AICPA Fellowship for Minority Doctoral Students**

TYPE:
Fellowships. Awarded annually to full-time minority accounting scholars who demonstrate significant potential to become accounting educators.

PURPOSE:
To ensure that C.P.As. of diverse backgrounds are visible in college and university classrooms; to increase the number of minority C.P.As. who serve as role models and mentors to young people in the academic environment.

ELIGIBILITY:
To be considered, applicants must meet the following requirements:
(1) have applied to a doctoral program and awaiting word on acceptance, or have been accepted into a doctoral program or already matriculated in a doctoral program and pursuing appropriate coursework;
(2) have earned a Master's degree and/or completed a minimum of three years of full-time experience in the practice of accounting;
(3) be a minority student of Black or African American, Hispanic or Latino, or Native American ethnicity;
(4) attend school on a full-time basis and plan to remain enrolled full-time until attaining one's doctoral degree;
(5) agree not to work full-time in a paid position or accept responsibility for teaching more than one course per semester as a teaching assistant, or dedicate more than one quarter of the time as a research assistant;
(6) be a C.P.A. or plan to pursue the C.P.A. credential and;
(7) be a U.S. citizen or permanent resident (green card holder).

GEOG. RESTRICTIONS: United States and its territories.

FINANCIAL DATA:
Amount of support per award: $12,000.
Total amount of support: Approximately $264,000 for the academic year 2013-14.

NO. AWARDS: 21 to 22.

APPLICATION INFO:
Instructions are available online, or send an e-mail to the Institute.
Duration: One year. Renewable.
Deadline: May 15.

ADDRESS INQUIRIES TO:
AICPA Minority Doctoral Fellowship Program
(See address and e-mail above.)

AMERICAN LEGION AUXILIARY - DEPARTMENT OF WISCONSIN [1602]

2930 American Legion Drive
Portage, WI 53901
(608) 745-0124
Fax: (608) 745-1947
E-mail: alawi@amlegionauxwi.org
Web Site: www.amlegionauxwi.org

FOUNDED: 1921

AREAS OF INTEREST:
Scholar aid programs for children of Veterans.

NAME(S) OF PROGRAMS:
- **American Legion Auxiliary Badger Girls State Scholarships**
- **American Legion Auxiliary National Scholarships**
- **Child Welfare Scholarship**
- **Health Careers Scholarships**
- **Eileen Knox Memorial Scholarship**
- **Harry and Shirley Kuehl Foundation Scholarship**
- **H.S. and Angeline Lewis Scholarships**
- **Merit and Memorial Scholarships**
- **State President's Scholarships**
- **Della Van Deuren Scholarships**

TYPE:
Scholarships.

PURPOSE:
To enable students to secure Baccalaureate degrees.

ELIGIBILITY:
(1) Applicant must be a daughter, son, stepdaughter, stepson, wife or widow of a veteran;
(2) Granddaughters, grandsons, great-granddaughters, great-grandsons, step-granddaughters, step-grandsons, step-great-granddaughters, step-great-grandsons of a Wisconsin American Legion Auxiliary member may also apply;
(3) If the applicant is a member of a Wisconsin American Legion Auxiliary Unit, a Wisconsin American Legion Post or a Wisconsin Sons of The American Legion Squadron, they do not need to reside in Wisconsin;
(4) Applicant must be in need of financial help to continue their education;
(5) Applicant must have at least a 3.5 grade point average on a 4.0 grade base and;
(6) Applicant must be a resident of Wisconsin, except as noted in (3) above.

Applicant may apply for more than one scholarship, but can only receive one scholarship from the American Legion Auxiliary-Department of Wisconsin, awarded on a one-time only basis, nonrenewable. School selected to attend must be an accredited school, but need not be located in Wisconsin. Judges reserve the right to determine the type of scholarship awarded and their decision is final.

GEOG. RESTRICTIONS: Wisconsin.

FINANCIAL DATA:
Amount of support per award: Varies depending on available funds.
Total amount of support: $25,000 for the year 2015.

NO. MOST RECENT APPLICANTS: Approximately 200.

NO. AWARDS: 28 for the year 2015.

APPLICATION INFO:
Applicants must use only the application form designated for the year that they are applying for. For the Lewis, State President's, Merit and Memorial, Child Welfare, Health Careers and Registered Nurse Scholarships, one application form may be used regardless of how many programs an applicant may be eligible for.
Duration: One year.
Deadline: March 15.

ADDRESS INQUIRIES TO:
Bonnie Dorniak
Executive Secretary/Treasurer
(See address above.)

AMERICAN MEDICAL ASSOCIATION FOUNDATION [1603]

330 North Wabash Avenue
Suite 39300
Chicago, IL 60611-5885
(312) 464-4200
Fax: (312) 464-4142
E-mail: amafoundation@ama-assn.org
Web Site: www.amafoundation.org

FOUNDED: 1950

AREAS OF INTEREST:
Public health and medical education.

NAME(S) OF PROGRAMS:
- **Excellence in Medicine**
- **Joan F. Giambalvo Memorial Scholarship**
- **Healthy Communities/Healthy America**
- **Healthy Living Grant Program**
- **Minority Scholars Award**
- **Physicians of Tomorrow Scholarship**
- **Seed Grant Research Program**
- **Arthur N. Wilson, M.D. Scholarship**

TYPE:
Awards/prizes; Project/program grants; Research grants; Scholarships; Seed money grants. Excellence in Medicine Awards are given to recognize physicians and medical students who are improving the health of their communities and the lives of those who are most in need.

The Joan F. Giambalvo Memorial Scholarship is presented in conjunction with the AMA's Women Physicians Congress to provide a research grant to help researchers advance the progress of women in the medical profession and identify and address the needs of women physicians and medical students.

Healthy Communities/Healthy America awards grants to existing, physician-led free clinics that provide free or low-cost medical care to underserved and uninsured populations.

Healthy Living Grant Program provides grants to support healthy lifestyle projects in various categories such as prescription medical safety and cancer prevention awareness.

The Minority Scholars Awards are given in collaboration with the AMA Minority Affairs Section to first- and second-year medical students from historically underrepresented minority groups in the medical profession.

The Physicians of Tomorrow Scholarships are awarded to rising fourth-year medical students based on financial need and academic excellence.

The Seed Grant Research Program provides medical students, physician residents and fellows with grants to help them conduct basic science, applied or clinical research projects.

The Arthur N. Wilson, M.D. Scholarship is awarded to a medical student who is a graduate of a high school in southeast Alaska.

PURPOSE:
To bring together physicians and communities to improve our nation's health.

LEGAL BASIS:
Public foundation.

GEOG. RESTRICTIONS: United States.

FINANCIAL DATA:
Amount of support per award: Joan F. Giambalvo Fund for the Advancement of Women, Minority Scholars Award and Physicians of Tomorrow Award: $10,000; Healthy Communities/Healthy America and Healthy Living Grant Program: Varies each year; Arthur N. Wilson, M.D. Scholarship: $5,000; Seed Grant Research Program: $2,500 to $5,000.

PUBLICATIONS:
Brochure; program announcement; e-newsletter; quarterly newsletter.

ADDRESS INQUIRIES TO:
Emily Demko, Program Asoociate
(See address above.)

AMERICAN OSTEOPATHIC FOUNDATION

142 East Ontario Street, Suite 1450
Chicago, IL 60611-2864
(312) 202-8235
Fax: (312) 202-8216
E-mail: info@aof.org
Web Site: www.aof.org

TYPE:
Awards/prizes; Scholarships. Grants.

See entry 2443 for full listing.

THE AMERICAN SOCIETY FOR NONDESTRUCTIVE TESTING, INC. [1604]

1711 Arlingate Lane
Columbus, OH 43228
(614) 274-6003
(800) 222-2768
Fax: (614) 274-6899
E-mail: jvandervort@asnt.org
Web Site: www.asnt.org

FOUNDED: 1941

AREAS OF INTEREST:
Nondestructive testing and engineering.

NAME(S) OF PROGRAMS:
- **Engineering Undergraduate Award**
- **Robert B. Oliver Scholarship**

TYPE:
Scholarships.

YEAR PROGRAM STARTED: 1998

PURPOSE:
To support research and education in nondestructive testing and to increase public awareness of nondestructive testing's critical role in ensuring the safety and well-being of mankind.

LEGAL BASIS:
501(c)(3) corporation.

ELIGIBILITY:
Engineering Undergraduate Award: Students must be enrolled in an engineering program of a university accredited by ABET or its equivalent and choosing NDT as their field of specialization.

Oliver Scholarship: Students must be officially enrolled in an undergraduate degree, associate degree, or postsecondary certificate program, which includes studies in NDT.

FINANCIAL DATA:
Amount of support per award: Engineering Undergraduate Award: $3,000; Oliver Scholarship: $2,500.

Total amount of support: Engineering Undergraduate Award: $9,000; Oliver Scholarship: $7,500.

NO. AWARDS: Up to 3 per year per award.

APPLICATION INFO:
Information and application are available online.

Duration: One year.

Deadline: Engineering Undergraduate Award: December 15. Oliver Scholarship: February 15.

ADDRESS INQUIRIES TO:
Michelle Thomas
ASNT Administrative Assistant
(See address above.)

AMERICAN SOCIETY OF HEMATOLOGY

2021 L Street, N.W.
Suite 900
Washington, DC 20036
(202) 776-0544
E-mail: awards@hematology.org
Web Site: www.hematology.org

TYPE:
Awards/prizes; Fellowships; Research grants; Scholarships.

See entry 2163 for full listing.

THE AMERICAN SWEDISH INSTITUTE

2600 Park Avenue
Minneapolis, MN 55407
(612) 871-4907
Fax: (612) 871-8682
E-mail: info@asimn.org
Web Site: www.asimn.org

TYPE:
Scholarships; Travel grants. The Malmberg Scholarship is awarded for up to one academic year of study in Sweden.

See entry 884 for full listing.

AMVETS [1605]

4647 Forbes Boulevard
Lanham, MD 20706-4380
(301) 683-4030
(877) 726-8387
E-mail: scholarships@amvets.org
Web Site: www.amvets.org

FOUNDED: 1944

NAME(S) OF PROGRAMS:
- **AMVETS National Scholarship Program: Entering College Freshman Scholarship**
- **AMVETS National Scholarship Program: JROTC Scholarship**

TYPE:
Scholarships. National scholarship program for high school seniors who are children or grandchildren of veterans.

PURPOSE:
To make the goal of postsecondary education more attainable for the children and grandchildren of veterans by assisting deserving students who might not otherwise have the financial means to achieve their educational goals.

ELIGIBILITY:
Applicant must:
(1) be a graduating high school senior entering at the college freshman level in the upcoming fall or be an active JROTC cadet and currently a high school senior;
(2) have a minimum grade point average of 3.0 (or documented evidence of extenuating circumstances that caused a lower grade point average);
(3) be the child or grandchild of a U.S. veteran who is an AMVETS member, or if deceased, would have been eligible for AMVETS membership;
(4) be a U.S. citizen;
(5) demonstrate academic promise and financial need and;
(6) agree to authorize AMVETS to publicize their scholarship award, if they are selected.

GEOG. RESTRICTIONS: United States.

FINANCIAL DATA:
Amount of support per award: Entering College Freshman Scholarship: $4,000 ($1,000 per year of a four-year program); JROTC Scholarship: $1,000.

NO. AWARDS: Entering College Freshman Scholarship: 6; JROTC Scholarship: 1.

APPLICATION INFO:
Application information is available online. Applications must be sent via regular mail.

Duration: One to four years. Nonrenewable.

Deadline: April 30.

ADDRESS INQUIRIES TO:
Hazel Moon
E-mail: hmoon@amvets.org

AMVETS [1606]

4647 Forbes Boulevard
Lanham, MD 20706-4380
(301) 683-4030
(877) 726-8387
E-mail: scholarships@amvets.org
Web Site: www.amvets.org

FOUNDED: 1944

NAME(S) OF PROGRAMS:
- **AMVETS/University of Phoenix Scholarship**

TYPE:
Scholarships. For U.S. veterans, active-duty service members, reservists, Guardsmen and their family members.

YEAR PROGRAM STARTED: 2007

PURPOSE:
To enable members of the active military, veterans, and their families to be successful and have a better quality of life for themselves and their families, starting with education.

ELIGIBILITY:
All veterans, service members, and family members are eligible to apply. Applicant must be a current member of the active military or an honorably discharged veteran, spouse or child of these two groups and not be receiving 100% tuition reimbursement.

GEOG. RESTRICTIONS: United States.

FINANCIAL DATA:
Scholarships in the form of a noncash credit to the awardee's University Account to be used for tuition and fees only.

NO. AWARDS: Approximately 20 annually.

APPLICATION INFO:
Applicants must submit a complete essay on one of the listed topics. All materials must be submitted online. Recipients will be selected

by the Scholarship Committee, consisting of representatives from the University of Phoenix and AMVETS.

Duration: Varies. Nonrenewable.

Deadline: September 8.

ADDRESS INQUIRIES TO:
E-mail: scholarships@phoenix.edu

ARCHAEOLOGICAL INSTITUTE OF AMERICA [1607]

656 Beacon Street, 6th Floor
Boston, MA 02215
(617) 358-4184
Fax: (617) 353-6550
E-mail: fellowships@aia.bu.edu
Web Site: www.archaeological.org

FOUNDED: 1879

AREAS OF INTEREST:
Archaeological research and publication.

NAME(S) OF PROGRAMS:
- **The AIA Publication Subvention Program**
- **Samuel H. Kress Grants for Research and Publication in Classical Art and Architecture**

TYPE:
Grants-in-aid. The AIA Publication Subvention Program offers subventions from the AIA's Bothmer Publication Fund in support of new book-length publications in the field of Greek, Roman, and Etruscan archaeology and art history.

Samuel H. Kress Grants for Research and Publication in Classical Art and Architecture funds publication preparation or research leading to publication undertaken by professional members of the AIA.

PURPOSE:
To support the scholarly publication of archaeological works.

ELIGIBILITY:
Applicants must be members of the AIA.

FINANCIAL DATA:
Amount of support per award: AIA Publication Subvention Program: Up to $10,000; average $3,000 to $5,000. Samuel H. Kress Grants: $3,000.

Total amount of support: Varies.

NO. MOST RECENT APPLICANTS: AIA Publication Subvention Program: 5; Samuel H. Kress Grants: 3.

NO. AWARDS: AIA Publication Subvention Program: 4; Samuel H. Kress Grants: 3.

APPLICATION INFO:
Applications must be completed online. Full details are available on the Institute web site.

Duration: Typically one year.

Deadline: March 1 and November 1.

ADDRESS INQUIRIES TO:
Laurel Nilsen Sparks
Lecture and Fellowship Coordinator
(See address above.)

ARMENIAN GENERAL BENEVOLENT UNION [1608]

55 East 59th Street
New York, NY 10022-1112
(212) 319-6383
Fax: (212) 319-6507
E-mail: scholarship@agbu.org
Web Site: www.agbu-scholarship.org

AREAS OF INTEREST:
Education.

NAME(S) OF PROGRAMS:
- **A.G.B.U. Scholarship Program**
- **Fellowship for U.S.-Based Study**
- **International Scholarships**
- **Performing Arts Fellowship**
- **Religious Studies Fellowship**

TYPE:
Fellowships; Scholarships.

PURPOSE:
To provide financial assistance to students of Armenian descent.

ELIGIBILITY:
Students must be of Armenian descent enrolled in college or university.

FINANCIAL DATA:
Amount of support per award: $1,500 to $7,500, depending on category.

Total amount of support: Approximately $1,000,000 annually.

NO. MOST RECENT APPLICANTS: Over 1,000.

NO. AWARDS: Over 500.

APPLICATION INFO:
Applications are available online.

Deadline: U.S. Fellowship: April 30; Performing Arts and Religious Studies Fellowships: May 31; International Scholarship: June 1 for study in Syria and France, September 15 for study in all other countries.

ADDRESS INQUIRIES TO:
Scholarship Program
(See address above.)

ASIAN AMERICAN JOURNALISTS ASSOCIATION [1609]

5 Third Street
Suite 1108
San Francisco, CA 94103
(415) 346-2051 ext. 107
Fax: (415) 346-6343
E-mail: justins@aaja.org
Web Site: www.aaja.org

FOUNDED: 1981

AREAS OF INTEREST:
Journalism.

NAME(S) OF PROGRAMS:
- **Stanford Chen Grant**
- **Sam Chu Lin Broadcast News Internship Grant**
- **Lloyd LaCuesta Broadcast News Internship Grant**
- **William Woo Print & Online News Grant**

TYPE:
Awards/prizes; Grants-in-aid; Scholarships.

YEAR PROGRAM STARTED: 1981

PURPOSE:
To encourage Asian-American students to pursue journalism careers.

ELIGIBILITY:
Must be a full-time college student or high school senior pursuing journalism as a major.

GEOG. RESTRICTIONS: United States.

FINANCIAL DATA:
Amount of support per award: Stanford Chen Grant: $1,750; Sam Chu Lin Broadcast News Internship Grant: $500; Lloyd LaCuesta Broadcast News Internship Grant and Print & Online News Grant: $1,000.

Total amount of support: Varies.

NO. MOST RECENT APPLICANTS: 50.

NO. AWARDS: 7.

APPLICATION INFO:
Application information is available on the web site.

Duration: One-time award. No renewals.

Deadline: Stanford Chen Grant: April 12. Sam Chu Lin Broadcast News Internship Grant, Lloyd LaCuesta Broadcast News Internship Grant and William Woo Printing & Online News Grant: April 19.

IRS I.D.: 95-3755203

STAFF:
Justin Seiter, Program Associate

ADDRESS INQUIRIES TO:
Justin Seiter, Program Associate
(See address above.)

ASSOCIATION ON AMERICAN INDIAN AFFAIRS

966 Hungerford Drive, Suite 12-B
Rockville, MD 20850
(240) 314-7155
Fax: (240) 314-7159
E-mail: lw.aaia@indian-affairs.org
Web Site: www.indian-affairs.org

TYPE:
Scholarships.

See entry 1023 for full listing.

ASSOCIATION ON AMERICAN INDIAN AFFAIRS

966 Hungerford Drive, Suite 12-B
Rockville, MD 20850
(240) 314-7155
Fax: (240) 314-7159
E-mail: lw.aaia@indian-affairs.org
Web Site: www.indian-affairs.org

TYPE:
Grants-in-aid; Scholarships. Emergency Aid Scholarships are for full-time graduate and undergraduate students who are seeking a degree in any curriculum. This program is limited by the availability of scholarship funds.

See entry 1021 for full listing.

ASSOCIATION ON AMERICAN INDIAN AFFAIRS

966 Hungerford Drive, Suite 12-B
Rockville, MD 20850
(240) 314-7155
Fax: (240) 314-7159
E-mail: lw.aaia@indian-affairs.org
Web Site: www.indian-affairs.org

TYPE:
Scholarships.

See entry 1022 for full listing.

ASSOCIATION ON AMERICAN INDIAN AFFAIRS

966 Hungerford Drive, Suite 12-B
Rockville, MD 20850
(240) 314-7155
Fax: (240) 314-7159
E-mail: lw.aaia@indian-affairs.org
Web Site: www.indian-affairs.org

TYPE:
Scholarships. Offered to American Indian and Alaskan Native graduate and undergraduate students in any curriculum who are members of tribes that are not federally recognized.

See entry 1024 for full listing.

ALEXANDER GRAHAM BELL ASSOCIATION FOR THE DEAF AND HARD OF HEARING

3417 Volta Place, N.W.
Washington, DC 20007
(202) 337-5220
Fax: (202) 337-8314
E-mail: financialaid@agbell.org
Web Site: www.agbell.org

TYPE:
Scholarships.

See entry 958 for full listing.

BNSF RAILWAY FOUNDATION

2650 Lou Menk Drive
Fort Worth, TX 76131-2830
(817) 867-6458
E-mail: bnsffoundation@bnsf.com
Web Site: www.bnsffoundation.org

TYPE:
Scholarships. Awarded annually to outstanding Native American high school seniors from funds provided by the Foundation, for up to four years or until undergraduate degree requirements are completed, whichever occurs first. Scholarship winners may attend any accredited college (two-year leading to a four-year degree) or university in the U.S.

See entry 1025 for full listing.

BNSF RAILWAY FOUNDATION

2650 Lou Menk Drive
Fort Worth, TX 76131-2830
(817) 867-6458
E-mail: bnsffoundation@bnsf.com
Web Site: www.bnsffoundation.org

TYPE:
Scholarships. Scholarships awarded to high school graduates of Hispanic origin through the Hispanic College Fund (HCF).

See entry 1044 for full listing.

THE LYNDE AND HARRY BRADLEY FOUNDATION, INC. [1610]

1241 North Franklin Place
Milwaukee, WI 53202-2901
(414) 291-9915
Fax: (414) 291-9991
Web Site: www.bradleyfdn.org

FOUNDED: 1942

AREAS OF INTEREST:
Humanities, social sciences and law.

NAME(S) OF PROGRAMS:
- **Bradley Fellowship Program**

TYPE:
Fellowships. To strengthen America's "intellectual infrastructure" at a higher-education level, providing useful assistance to young scholars during a critical phase in their education.

YEAR PROGRAM STARTED: 1986

PURPOSE:
To assist candidates to complete their studies, prepare manuscripts for publication, conduct research, and enhance their competitiveness in the job market.

ELIGIBILITY:
Selected candidates must be intelligent doctoral and postdoctoral fellows within the discretion of participating professors or nominators. The principal consideration is excellence and merit. Candidates must also be U.S. citizens or residents.

GEOG. RESTRICTIONS: United States.

FINANCIAL DATA:
Amount of support per award: Up to $25,000 per academic year.

APPLICATION INFO:
Recipients must be nominated by participating professors or nominators.

Duration: One year.

ADDRESS INQUIRIES TO:
Dianne Sehler, Director of Academic, International and Cultural Programs
(See address above.)

BROADCAST EDUCATION ASSOCIATION

1771 N Street, N.W.
Washington, DC 20036-2891
(202) 602-0587
Fax: (202) 609-9940
E-mail: Help@beaweb.org
Web Site: www.beaweb.org

TYPE:
Scholarships. BEA is the professional development association for professors, industry professionals and students involved in teaching and research related to radio, television and other electronic media. BEA administers scholarships annually, to honor broadcasters and the entire electronic media profession.

John Bayliss and Abe Voron Awards: Study toward a career in radio.

BEA Founders, Richard Eaton and Vincent T. Wasilewski Awards: Study in any electronic media area. (Wasilewski Award is for graduate students only.)

Library of American Broadcasting Foundation Award is for graduate students with a demonstrated research interest in broadcast history.

For the BEA Founders Award, preference is given to students enrolled in a BEA Two-Year/Small College Member Institution or graduates of these programs now enrolled in a BEA Four-Year Institution.

All other scholarships are awarded to juniors, seniors and graduate students at BEA Member institutions.

See entry 1862 for full listing.

BUREAU OF INDIAN EDUCATION

1849 C Street, N.W.
MS 3609 MIB
Washington, DC 20240
(202) 208-6123
Fax: (202) 208-3312
Web Site: www.bie.edu

TYPE:
Fellowships; Scholarships.

See entry 1030 for full listing.

CALIFORNIA STUDENT AID COMMISSION [1611]

P.O. Box 419026
Rancho Cordova, CA 95741-9026
(888) 224-7268
Fax: (916) 464-8002
E-mail: studentsupport@csac.ca.gov
Web Site: www.csac.ca.gov

FOUNDED: 1955

NAME(S) OF PROGRAMS:
- **Cal Grants A, B and C**

TYPE:
Assistantships; Grants-in-aid. Grant A will help pay for tuition and fees at public and private colleges, and some private career colleges. Grant B provides low-income students with a living allowance and assistance with tuition and fees. Most five-year students receive an allowance for books and living expenses. Grant C helps pay for tuition and training costs at occupational or career technical schools.

YEAR PROGRAM STARTED: 1956

PURPOSE:
To assist with tuition and books for students attending college in California.

LEGAL BASIS:
California Education Code.

ELIGIBILITY:
Student must be a U.S. citizen or eligible noncitizen and a California resident.

GEOG. RESTRICTIONS: California.

FINANCIAL DATA:
Amount of support per award: Grants A and B: Varies by type of college; Grant C: Up to $2,462 for tuition and fees and $547 for books, tools and equipment.

NO. MOST RECENT APPLICANTS: 350,000.

NO. AWARDS: 75,000.

APPLICATION INFO:
Students should submit the Free Application for Federal Student Aid (FAFSA) or the California Dream Act Application and a verified Cal Grant grade point average. The FAFSA is available online.

Duration: Up to four years.

Deadline: March 2. California Community College students: March 2 and September 2.

PUBLICATIONS:
Fund Your Future; *Financial Aid for Students*, booklet.

CALIFORNIA STUDENT AID COMMISSION [1612]

P.O. Box 419029
Rancho Cordova, CA 95741-9029
(888) 224-7268 Option 5
Fax: (916) 464-8002
E-mail: specialized@csac.ca.gov
Web Site: www.csac.ca.gov

FOUNDED: 1955

AREAS OF INTEREST:
Dependents of law enforcement personnel.

NAME(S) OF PROGRAMS:
- **Law Enforcement Personnel Dependents' Grant Program (LEPD)**

TYPE:
Grants-in-aid. The program provides need-based educational grants to dependents and spouses of California peace officers (Highway Patrol, marshals, sheriffs, police officers), Department of Corrections and California Youth Authority employees and permanent/full-time firefighters, employed by public entities who have been killed in the performance of duty or totally disabled as a result of an accident or injury caused by external violence or physical force incurred in the performance of duty.

Grant awards are for attendance at WASC-accredited colleges in California.

YEAR PROGRAM STARTED: 1969

LEGAL BASIS:
California Labor Code, Section 4709. State agency.

ELIGIBILITY:
Dependents and spouses of California peace officers, Department of Corrections and California Youth Authority employees and permanent/full-time firefighters employed by public entities killed or totally disabled in the performance of duty.

GEOG. RESTRICTIONS: California.

FINANCIAL DATA:
Amount of support per award: $100 to $12,192.

Total amount of support: Varies.

NO. MOST RECENT APPLICANTS: 9.

APPLICATION INFO:
Eligible students must file the following documents with the Specialized Programs Branch:
(1) a Law Enforcement Personnel Dependent's Grant application;
(2) a copy of the Student Aid Report (SAR), which is generated after filing a FAFSA;
(3) birth certificate (not required for spouse);
(4) the death certificate of the parent or spouse and the coroner's report (if appropriate), police report, and any other documentation that shows evidence that the death or total disability was caused by external violence or physical force incurred in the line of duty (for peace and law enforcement officers), by the direct action of an inmate (for officers and employees of the Department of Corrections and Rehabilitation), or in the performance of duty (for firefighters);
(5) findings of the Workers' Compensation Appeals Board or other evidence that the fatality or 100% disabling accident or injury was compensable under Division 4.0 and 4.5 (commencing with Section 6100) of the Labor Code and;
(6) proof of enrollment at a California postsecondary institution as described above for the applicable academic year.

Duration: Up to four years.

PUBLICATIONS:
Financial Aid for Students, booklet.

STAFF:
Lupita Cortez Alcala, Executive Director

ADDRESS INQUIRIES TO:
Lupita Cortez Alcala, Executive Director
(See address above.)

CANADIAN FRIENDS OF THE HEBREW UNIVERSITY [1613]

P.O. Box 65
3080 Yonge Street, Suite 3020
Toronto ON M4N 3N1 Canada
(416) 485-8000
(888) 432-7398 (Canada only)
Fax: (416) 485-8565
E-mail: mgoldman@cfhu.org
info@cfhu.org
Web Site: www.cfhu.org

FOUNDED: 1944

AREAS OF INTEREST:
Law, dentistry, social sciences, economics, humanities, the sciences, medicine and computer science.

TYPE:
Awards/prizes; Scholarships. The Canadian Friends of the Hebrew University sponsors Canadian college or university students who participate in programs at the Hebrew University of Jerusalem.

YEAR PROGRAM STARTED: 1944

PURPOSE:
To give the financial support necessary for Canadian students to study at Hebrew University in Jerusalem, Israel; to raise funds in support of the Hebrew University research programs.

LEGAL BASIS:
Nonprofit.

ELIGIBILITY:
Applicants must be Canadian citizens or landed immigrants. Awards are given based on need. Some scholarships are designated for Israeli students.

GEOG. RESTRICTIONS: Canada.

FINANCIAL DATA:
Amount of support per award: $1,000 to $10,000.

Total amount of support: Varies.

NO. AWARDS: Varies.

APPLICATION INFO:
Contact the Office of Academic Affairs at the address above.

Duration: At least one year.

Deadline: May 1.

STAFF:
Rami Kleinmann, Chief Executive Officer and President

ADDRESS INQUIRIES TO:
Merle Goldman, Executive Vice President
(See address above.)

THE CARSON SCHOLARS FUND, INC. [1614]

305 West Chesapeake Avenue
Suite 310
Towson, MD 21204
(410) 828-1005
Fax: (410) 828-1007
E-mail: katie@carsonscholars.org
Web Site: carsonscholars.org

FOUNDED: 1994

AREAS OF INTEREST:
Education.

NAME(S) OF PROGRAMS:
- **Carson Scholarships**

TYPE:
Scholarships. The Carson Scholars Fund awards college scholarships to students in grades 4-11 who excel academically and are dedicated to serving their communities.

YEAR PROGRAM STARTED: 1994

PURPOSE:
To operate on the principle that if children could be taught early to excel, they would stay motivated and have a higher chance of educational success later in life.

ELIGIBILITY:
Students must be nominated by the principal at his or her school. Only one student from each school is able to apply. Carson Scholars must have a grade point average of 3.75 and display humanitarian qualities through community service. Scholarships are awarded solely on the basis of academic achievements and humanitarian qualities, without regard to financial need or ethnicity. Carson Scholars must be U.S. citizens or residents.

GEOG. RESTRICTIONS: United States.

FINANCIAL DATA:
Scholarship winners receive the honor of being named "Carson Scholars" and are awarded an Olympic-sized medal and a trophy for their school. Winners receive a recognition package and an invitation to attend an awards banquet.

Amount of support per award: $1,000.

NO. AWARDS: 626 in 2016.

APPLICATION INFO:
Students must be nominated by the principal of his or her school to compete. Only one student from each school is able to apply. Complete information is on the web site.

Duration: One-time award.

Deadline: Nominations open in October and close the beginning of January. Notification is made in March.

ADDRESS INQUIRIES TO:
Katie Damaroda, Scholarship Director
(See e-mail address above.)

CATCHING THE DREAM

8200 Mountain Road, N.E.
Suite 103
Albuquerque, NM 87110
(505) 262-2351
Fax: (505) 262-0534
E-mail: NScholarsh@aol.com
Web Site: www.catchingthedream.org

TYPE:
Conferences/seminars; Development grants; Grants-in-aid; Scholarships; Technical assistance. CTD also works to improve Indian schools through a program of grants and technical assistance. This work has led to the development of 40 Exemplary Programs in Indian education since 1988. The annual Exemplary Institute is a meeting of these Exemplary Programs, where they teach other people how to develop similar programs.

MAST program makes grants of $5,000 to Indian high schools to improve their math and science teaching.

MESBEC Program consists of competitive scholarships for high-potential Native Americans studying in math, engineering, science, business, education and computers.

NALE Program consists of competitive scholarships for high-potential paraprofessional Native Americans who plan to complete their degrees and obtain credentials as teachers, counselors or administrators.

RAP makes grants to Indian schools to improve the reading ability of their students.

Tribal Business Management (TBM) Program consists of competitive scholarships for Native students in all fields of business.

See entry 1031 for full listing.

CHATHAM UNIVERSITY [1615]

Woodland Road
Berry Hall
Pittsburgh, PA 15232
(412) 365-1825
Fax: (412) 365-1609
E-mail: admission@chatham.edu
Web Site: www.chatham.edu/admission/aid/undergraduate/firstyear.cfm

FOUNDED: 1869

AREAS OF INTEREST:
Providing scholarship opportunities to students who have shown academic promise during their high school career and who are enrolled at Chatham University.

NAME(S) OF PROGRAMS:
- **The Chatham University Merit Scholarship Programs**

TYPE:
Awards/prizes; Endowments; Formula grants; General operating grants; Grants-in-aid; Internships; Scholarships. The Chatham University Merit Scholarship Programs include the Presidential, Trustee, Dean, and Founder, as well as Chatham Grants.Additional scholarship opportunities include the S-STEM Scholarship, the Heffer Family Scholarship, the Girl Scout Gold Scholarship, the Minna Kaufmann Ruud Music Scholarship, the Eden Hall Scholarship for Sustainability, the AFS/YFU/Rotary International Scholarship, the Visual Arts Scholarship, the Interior Architecture Scholarship, the Girl Scout Leadership Award, the Legacy Award, the Family Heritage Award, the Phi Theta Kappa Scholarship, and the Rachel Carson Book Award.

YEAR PROGRAM STARTED: 1978

PURPOSE:
To attract outstanding students to Chatham University and to provide recognition of their academic performance.

ELIGIBILITY:
Chatham University Merit Scholars are chosen based on their performance in high school, grades, and SAT or ACT scores.

Grants are based strictly on need; many of the scholars are from families for whom the choice of a college such as Chatham would not be possible without this support.

FINANCIAL DATA:
Presidential Scholarship pays full tuition.

Amount of support per award: Other Scholarships are from $1,000 per year to $16,000 per year (renewable based on minimum grade point average requirements and full-time enrollment).

Total amount of support: Varies.

NO. MOST RECENT APPLICANTS: 1,000 for the year 2016.

APPLICATION INFO:
All applicants must complete an application for admission to Chatham University which includes SAT or ACT scores, high school transcript, and application.

First-year students who choose not to submit the SAT/ACT will be required to submit a graded writing sample and resume or list of activities as well as complete an interview. Applicants will also have the option to submit a portfolio or special project/activity.

Duration: Four years of the undergraduate career, provided the high academic criteria expected of such scholars is maintained. Renewable annually based on grade point average of 3.0 or higher for Presidential Scholarship and 2.0 or higher for the other scholarships, and full-time enrollment.

Deadline: March 1.

STAFF:
Amy Becher, Vice President for Enrollment Management
Dr. Jennifer Burns, Director of Financial Aid

ADDRESS INQUIRIES TO:
Office of Enrollment Management
(See address above.)

CHINESE AMERICAN MEDICAL SOCIETY

265 Canal Street
Suite 515
New York, NY 10013
(212) 334-4760
Fax: (646) 304-6373
E-mail: jlove@camsociety.org
Web Site: www.camsociety.org

TYPE:
Fellowships; Scholarships.

See entry 2182 for full listing.

THE CLARK FOUNDATION [1616]

One Rockefeller Plaza
New York, NY 10020
(607) 547-9927 (Cooperstown)
(212) 977-6900 (New York City)
Fax: (607) 547-8598

FOUNDED: 1931

NAME(S) OF PROGRAMS:
- **Clark Foundation Scholarship Program**

TYPE:
Scholarships. Undergraduate college scholarships.

YEAR PROGRAM STARTED: 1961

PURPOSE:
To assist Cooperstown area students in their pursuit of higher education.

LEGAL BASIS:
Nonprofit foundation.

ELIGIBILITY:
Individual undergraduate college scholarships are awarded to graduates of Central School, Cooperstown, NY and nine surrounding rural central school districts.

GEOG. RESTRICTIONS: Cooperstown and the nine surrounding New York rural central school districts of Cherry Valley-Springfield, Edmeston, Laurens, Milford, Mount Markham, Richfield Springs, Schenevus, Worcester and Owen D. Young.

FINANCIAL DATA:
Amount of support per award: Approximately $3,800.

Total amount of support: $3,726,000.

NO. MOST RECENT APPLICANTS: 331.

NO. AWARDS: 193.

APPLICATION INFO:
Students are recommended by their respective schools.

Duration: One year. Possible renewal each year for duration of undergraduate education.

Deadline: First week in February.

OFFICERS:
Jane Forbes Clark, President
Kevin S. Moore, Treasurer
Douglas Bauer, Executive Director and Secretary

ADDRESS INQUIRIES TO:
Gary Kuch, Director
Clark Foundation Scholarship Office
P.O. Box 427
Cooperstown, NY 13326

COCA-COLA SCHOLARS FOUNDATION [1617]

P.O. Box 442
Atlanta, GA 30301-0442
(800) 306-2653
Fax: (404) 733-5439
E-mail: scholars@coca-cola.com
Web Site: www.coca-colascholars.org

FOUNDED: 1986

AREAS OF INTEREST:
Enhancing educational opportunities in the U.S.

NAME(S) OF PROGRAMS:
- **Coca-Cola Scholars Program**

TYPE:
Scholarships. Awards based on leadership, academics and community service.

YEAR PROGRAM STARTED: 1989

PURPOSE:
To enhance educational opportunities in the U.S. through scholarship awards and enrichment programs for young people who demonstrate, through academic excellence and leadership in their communities, their capacity for and commitment to making a difference in the world.

ELIGIBILITY:
Current high school (or home-schooled) seniors attending school in the U.S. (or select DoD schools). Applicant must not graduate prior to deadline.

GEOG. RESTRICTIONS: United States.

FINANCIAL DATA:
Program has awarded over $56,000,000 in scholarships since inception.

Amount of support per award: $20,000.

Total amount of support: Over $3,000,000 annually.

NO. MOST RECENT APPLICANTS: 50,000 to 100,000 annually.

NO. AWARDS: 150 annually.

APPLICATION INFO:
Application must be submitted online.

Duration: Four to 10 years.

Deadline: October 31.

ADDRESS INQUIRIES TO:
See e-mail address above.

CONCORDIA UNIVERSITY [1618]

1455 de Maisonneuve Boulevard West
Graduate Awards Office, Room S-GM 930.00
Montreal QC H3G 1M8 Canada
(514) 848-2424 ext. 3809
(514) 848-2424 ext. 3801
Fax: (514) 848-2812
E-mail: graduate-awards@concordia.ca
Web Site: www.concordia.ca/offices/sgs.html

FOUNDED: 1974

AREAS OF INTEREST:
All disciplines.

NAME(S) OF PROGRAMS:
- **Concordia University Graduate Fellowships**

TYPE:
Assistantships; Awards/prizes; Conferences/seminars; Endowments; Fellowships; Scholarships. Postgraduate full-time fellowships.

PURPOSE:
To recruit highly qualified graduate students to Master's and doctoral programs.

ELIGIBILITY:
Candidates must be planning to pursue full-time Master's or doctoral studies at Concordia University. Academic merit is the prime consideration in the granting of the award.

All new admissions will be considered for awards.

GEOG. RESTRICTIONS: Canada.

FINANCIAL DATA:
Amount of support per award: $5,000 (CAN) to $45,000 (CAN) for three years.

NO. MOST RECENT APPLICANTS: Over 1,000.

NO. AWARDS: 100 or more.

APPLICATION INFO:
Applicants must submit a completed application form, statement of purpose, three letters of recommendation, and official transcripts of all university studies.

Duration: One to three years.

CONGRESSIONAL HISPANIC CAUCUS INSTITUTE [1619]

1128 16th Street, N.W.
Washington, DC 20036
(202) 543-1771
Fax: (202) 546-2143
E-mail: scholarships@chci.org
Web Site: www.chci.org

FOUNDED: 1978

AREAS OF INTEREST:
Postsecondary education for Latino students.

NAME(S) OF PROGRAMS:
- **Scholar-Intern Programs**

TYPE:
Internships; Scholarships. CHCI Scholar-Intern Programs are designed to allow students to not only receive monetary support for their education, but also to gain hands-on experience in their chosen field through an internship. The program provides paid internship placements in a variety of fields including health care, human resource management, journalism, marketing and telecommunications.

YEAR PROGRAM STARTED: 2009

PURPOSE:
To ensure the benefits of a postsecondary education are available to Latino students for whom the cost of community college, a four-year college or graduate school would otherwise be out of reach.

ELIGIBILITY:
Opportunities are afforded to low- and moderate-income students who have a history of performing public service-oriented activities in their communities and demonstrate a desire to continue their civic engagement in the future. Selection is based on a combination of criteria.

Students who are seeking consideration under the Deferred Action for Childhood Arrival (DACA) policy are welcome to apply. Student must possess an Employment Authorization Document at the time of application.

GEOG. RESTRICTIONS: United States.

FINANCIAL DATA:
Scholarship awards are intended to provide assistance with tuition, room and board, textbooks, and other educational expenses associated with college enrollment.

Amount of support per award: Upon completion of their internship, scholar-interns receive a one-year scholarship of $1,000 to $5,000, depending on the program.

Total amount of support: Varies.

NO. AWARDS: Varies.

APPLICATION INFO:
Internship placement depends on the partner organization. Applicant should review the CHCI web site to see the various partner organizations and job descriptions for each scholar-intern program.

Duration: Internship: Varies. Scholarship: One year.

Deadline: Varies by program.

COOK FAMILY FOUNDATION

120 West Exchange Street, Suite 202
Owosso, MI 48867
(989) 725-1621
Fax: (989) 936-5910
E-mail: tom@cookfamilyfoundation.org
Web Site: www.cookfamilyfoundation.org

TYPE:
Capital grants; Challenge/matching grants; Demonstration grants; Development grants; Matching gifts; Project/program grants; Scholarships; Seed money grants; Technical assistance. Educational support.

See entry 1220 for full listing.

JACK KENT COOKE FOUNDATION [1620]

44325 Woodridge Parkway
Lansdowne, VA 20176-5297
(703) 723-8000
E-mail: scholarships@jkcf.org
Web Site: www.jkcf.org

FOUNDED: 2000

AREAS OF INTEREST:
Education.

NAME(S) OF PROGRAMS:
- **College Scholarship Program**
- **Undergraduate Transfer Scholarship**
- **Young Scholars Program**

TYPE:
Fellowships; Scholarships. College Scholarship Program is available to high-performing high school seniors with financial need who seek to attend and graduate from the nation's best four-year colleges and universities.

Undergraduate Transfer Scholarship honors excellence by supporting outstanding community college students with financial need to transfer to and complete their Bachelor's degrees at the nation's top four-year colleges and universities.

Young Scholars Program seeks high-achieving, low- to moderate-income seventh-grade students, and cultivates their talents and abilities throughout high school by providing the personalized advising and financial support needed to secure challenging academic opportunities.

PURPOSE:
To help students of exceptional promise reach their full potential through education.

GEOG. RESTRICTIONS: United States.

FINANCIAL DATA:
Total assets of $710,694,000 for year ended May 31, 2014.

Amount of support per award: College Scholarship Program and Undergraduate Transfer Scholarship: Up to $40,000 per year. Young Scholars Program: Varies.

Total amount of support: $25,100,000 for year ended May 31, 2014.

APPLICATION INFO:
An application form needs to be completed. Application information is available on the web site.

Duration: College Scholarship Program: Up to four years. Undergraduate Transfer Scholarship: Two to three years.

Deadline: College Scholarship Program: Opens September; closes early November. Undergraduate Transfer Scholarship: Opens October; closes December. Young Scholars Program: Opens January; closes April.

DARTMOUTH COLLEGE

Office of Graduate Studies
Chavez/Eastman/Marshall
37 Dewey Field Road, Suite 6062, Room 437
Hanover, NH 03755-3526
(603) 646-2106
Fax: (603) 646-8762
E-mail: jane.b.seibel@dartmouth.edu
Web Site: graduate.dartmouth.edu/funding/fellowships/cem.html

TYPE:
Exchange programs; Fellowships.

See entry 964 for full listing.

DAUGHTERS OF ITALY LODGE #2825 [1621]

14 South Jupiter Avenue
Clearwater, FL 33755
(727) 447-6890
E-mail: vincenzad@verizon.net
Web Site: www.daughtersofitaly.com

AREAS OF INTEREST:
Furtherance of education of Floridian students of Italian descent.

NAME(S) OF PROGRAMS:
- **Daughters of Italy Lodge #2825 Scholarship**

TYPE:
Scholarships. Open to full-time students at a Florida-accredited junior college, college or university or students graduating from high school.

PURPOSE:
To benefit worthy students of Italian descent that display academic excellence, leadership qualities and a financial need.

ELIGIBILITY:
Applicant must:
(1) be a Florida resident of Italian descent and a U.S. citizen;

(2) have a minimum grade point average of 3.0 (unweighted) and a minimum SAT total score of 1100, or must have an ACT Composite Score of 23 and;
(3) be a full-time student at a Florida-accredited junior college, college or university or a student graduating from high school.

GEOG. RESTRICTIONS: Florida.

FINANCIAL DATA:
Scholarship funds will not be released to any school until the Daughters of Italy Lodge 2825 Scholarship Chairperson receives a letter of acceptance from an accredited school and the recipient notifies the Chairperson in writing of her/his intent to enroll in the fall semester.

Amount of support per award: $1,000.

NO. AWARDS: 3.

APPLICATION INFO:
Application, checklist and procedures may be accessed online. Applicants must include a 500-word essay on student's current and futuristic academic goals.

Duration: One year. Not renewable.

Deadline: End of March; exact date available online.

DAUGHTERS OF PENELOPE FOUNDATION, INC.

1909 Q Street, N.W., Suite 500
Washington, DC 20009
(202) 234-9741
Fax: (202) 483-6983
E-mail: dophq@ahepa.org
Web Site: www.dopfoundationinc.com

TYPE:
Scholarships.

See entry 1059 for full listing.

DAUGHTERS OF THE CINCINNATI [1622]

20 West 44th Street, Room 508
New York, NY 10036
(212) 991-9945
E-mail: scholarships@daughters1894.org
Web Site: www.daughters1894.org

FOUNDED: 1894

NAME(S) OF PROGRAMS:
- **Daughters of the Cincinnati Scholarship Program**

TYPE:
Scholarships. Undergraduate scholarships.

YEAR PROGRAM STARTED: 1906

PURPOSE:
To assist high school seniors entering college with financial aid (annually for the four years).

LEGAL BASIS:
Nonprofit, tax-exempt organization.

ELIGIBILITY:
Applicant must be a senior in high school who is the daughter of a career officer commissioned in the regular Army, Navy, Air Force, Coast Guard or Marine Corps (active, retired or deceased). The daughters of officers in the Reserves, National Guard and State Militia are not eligible to apply for this scholarship.

FINANCIAL DATA:
Aid for tuition and/or living expense.

Amount of support per award: Average $3,000 to $5,000 annually.

Total amount of support: Varies.

NO. MOST RECENT APPLICANTS: Approximately 200.

NO. AWARDS: Approximately 4 annually.

APPLICATION INFO:
The application is accessible from the web site after supplying the parent's branch of service and rank.

Duration: Four years, or as long as the student attends college up to that length of time. Reviewed annually.

Deadline: Postmarked by March 15. Announcement in mid-May.

PUBLICATIONS:
Information sheet.

ADDRESS INQUIRIES TO:
Scholarship Administrator
(See address above.)

DAVIDSON INSTITUTE [1623]

9665 Gateway Drive, Suite B
Reno, NV 89521
(775) 852-3483
E-mail: tmoessner@davidsongifted.org
Web Site: www.DavidsonGifted.org/Fellows

FOUNDED: 1999

AREAS OF INTEREST:
Encouraging the development of academically gifted students.

NAME(S) OF PROGRAMS:
- **Davidson Fellows**

TYPE:
Scholarships.

YEAR PROGRAM STARTED: 2001

PURPOSE:
To award students working at the college graduate level on projects that have the potential to benefit society.

ELIGIBILITY:
Students must be 18 or younger as of October 1 of the year of application, must be U.S. citizens or permanent residents residing in the U.S. and must have completed a significant piece of work.

FINANCIAL DATA:
Amount of support per award: Scholarships of $10,000, $25,000 or $50,000 to be used at an accredited college or university.

Total amount of support: More than $6,200,000 has been awarded to 266 brilliant young people through the Davidson Fellows Scholarship.

APPLICATION INFO:
Application categories are Science, Technology, Engineering, Mathematics, Literature, Music, Philosophy and Outside the Box. The application is completely online. Students must submit a project, two essays and a video; they must also have two nominators.

Duration: The scholarship is available for 10 years and is not renewable.

Deadline: The first Wednesday in February.

ADDRESS INQUIRIES TO:
Tacie Moessner, Manager
Davidson Fellows Scholarship Program
(See e-mail address above.)

MICHAEL AND SUSAN DELL FOUNDATION [1624]

P.O. Box 163867
Austin, TX 78716-3867
(800) 294-2039
Fax: (512) 600-5501
E-mail: info@msdf.org
Web Site: www.msdf.org
www.dellscholars.org

NAME(S) OF PROGRAMS:
- **Dell Scholars Program**

TYPE:
Scholarships. Need-based scholarship that recognizes academic potential in lower-income and underserved students. Applicants must demonstrate a drive to succeed while overcoming personal obstacles.

PURPOSE:
To assist students who have worked hard to prepare themselves for higher education yet may have lower grade point averages and test scores because of adverse personal situations or surroundings.

ELIGIBILITY:
Applicants must:
(1) be high school seniors who have participated in a Michael and Susan Dell Foundation-approved college readiness program;
(2) be a U.S. citizen or legal permanent resident;
(3) have financial need confirmed through eligibility for a Federal Pell Grant;
(4) have a minimum 2.4 grade point average on a 4.0 scale and;
(5) be planning to enroll full-time in a Bachelor's degree program at an accredited higher education institution in the fall directly after high school graduation.

Scholarship may be used at any accredited two- or four-year institution in the U.S. where credits can be earned towards a Baccalaureate degree, including community and junior colleges. Technical colleges and vocational programs are not eligible.

GEOG. RESTRICTIONS: United States.

FINANCIAL DATA:
Award may be applied to any cost of acquiring an education. Also provide other means of support, such as mentoring.

Amount of support per award: $20,000 over a maximum of six years.

Total amount of support: Varies.

NO. AWARDS: 300 annually.

APPLICATION INFO:
All applications must be completed online. No paper applications will be accepted.

Duration: Up to six years.

Deadline: Application process opens in November and closes the following January 15.

THE EBELL OF LOS ANGELES [1625]

743 South Lucerne Boulevard
Los Angeles, CA 90005-3707
(323) 931-1277 ext. 184
Fax: (323) 937-0272
E-mail: Scholarship@ebellofIosangeles.com
Web Site: www.ebellla.org

FOUNDED: 1894

AREAS OF INTEREST:
Higher education.

NAME(S) OF PROGRAMS:
- **Ebell/Flint Scholarship**

TYPE:
Scholarships.

YEAR PROGRAM STARTED: 1921

PURPOSE:
To support scholarships for qualified college students.

LEGAL BASIS:
Private foundation.

ELIGIBILITY:
To be eligible for an Ebell scholarship, applicants must:
(1) be a U.S. citizen; if naturalized citizen, send copy of official documentation;
(2) be a permanent resident of Los Angeles County;
(3) be a full-time student attending an accredited Los Angeles County educational institution;
(4) achieve at least a 3.25 cumulative grade point average;
(5) demonstrate community commitment and;
(6) be available for an in-person interview with the Ebell Scholarship Committee on the Ebell campus.

GEOG. RESTRICTIONS: Los Angeles County, California.

FINANCIAL DATA:
Amount of support per award: Four-year colleges: $5,000 per year (12 months) paid semiannually in September and February; Two-year colleges: $3,000 per year.

Total amount of support: Over $200,000 annually.

NO. MOST RECENT APPLICANTS: 162.

NO. AWARDS: 58.

APPLICATION INFO:
Guidelines and application form are available on the web site.

Duration: Three years or when the student attains Bachelor's degree, whichever comes first.

Deadline: April 1.

IRS I.D.: 23-7049580

ADDRESS INQUIRIES TO:
See e-mail address above.

THE EISENHOWER FOUNDATION

200 S.E. 4th Street
Abilene, KS 67410
(785) 263-4751
(877) 746-4453
Fax: (785) 263-6715
E-mail: info@eisenhowerfoundation.net
Web Site: www.eisenhowerfoundation.net
www.eisenhower.archives.gov

TYPE:
Travel grants. Travel grants are awarded to individual researchers on a competitive basis to cover a portion of expenses while in Abilene, KS, using the presidential library.

See entry 1935 for full listing.

FEEA SCHOLARSHIP PROGRAM [1626]

3333 South Wadsworth Boulevard
Suite 300
Lakewood, CO 80227
(303) 933-7580
Fax: (303) 933-7587
E-mail: ngleason@feea.org
Web Site: www.feea.org

AREAS OF INTEREST:
Education.

NAME(S) OF PROGRAMS:
- **Scholarship Program**

TYPE:
Scholarships. Merit-based scholarship competition program open exclusively to federal employees, their spouses and their children.

PURPOSE:
To financially aid hard-working federal employees, their spouses and their children in their college education.

ELIGIBILITY:
Must be a U.S. citizen and current civilian federal and/or postal employee (with at least three years of federal service), or their spouses or their children. Applicant must be a current high school senior who will be a college freshman by the fall of application or college student working toward an accredited degree and enrolled in a two- or four-year undergraduate, graduate or postgraduate program. All applicants must have a 3.0 cumulative grade point average unweighted on a 4.0 scale.

Current college freshmen must have a minimum 3.0 grade point average for the fall semester. Applicants who are dependents must be full-time students. Applicants who are federal employees may be part-time students.

GEOG. RESTRICTIONS: United States.

FINANCIAL DATA:
Amount of support per award: $500 to $5,000.

NO. MOST RECENT APPLICANTS: 3,548.

NO. AWARDS: 372.

APPLICATION INFO:
Application may be downloaded. Complete details may be viewed online. Applications should be submitted to the address above in a 9" x 12" (or larger) envelope, materials unbound and unfolded.

Duration: One year. Must reapply for renewal.

Deadline: End of March.

ADDRESS INQUIRIES TO:
Niki Gleason
(See e-mail address above.)

*PLEASE NOTE:
Top student applicants have the opportunity to win one of two additional awards.

THE JAMES MARSTON FITCH CHARITABLE FOUNDATION

c/o The Neighborhood Preservation Center
232 East 11th Street
New York, NY 10003
(212) 252-6809
Fax: (212) 471-9987
E-mail: cpena@fitchfoundation.org
Web Site: www.fitchfoundation.org

TYPE:
Research grants. Richard L. Blinder Award was created to promote studies that explore the architecture of cultural buildings which integrate historic preservation and new construction - past, present and future; presented biennially.

Mid-Career Fellowship: This grant is the primary mission and the signature grant of this Foundation. The grants are intended to support projects of innovative original research or creative design that advance the practice of historic preservation in the U.S.

See entry 404 for full listing.

FLORIDA DEPARTMENT OF EDUCATION

Office of Student Financial Assistance
325 West Gaines Street, Suite 1314
Tallahassee, FL 32399-0400
(888) 827-2004
Fax: (850) 487-1809
E-mail: osfa@fldoe.org
Web Site: www.FloridaStudentFinancialAid.org/SSFAD/home/uamain.htm

TYPE:
Scholarships. Financial assistance for descendants of the Rosewood family affected by the incidents of January 1923, to attend a state university, public community college or public postsecondary vocational-technical school.

See entry 1007 for full listing.

FLORIDA DEPARTMENT OF EDUCATION [1627]

Office of Student Financial Assistance
325 West Gaines Street, Suite 1314
Tallahassee, FL 32399-0400
(888) 827-2004
Fax: (850) 487-1809
E-mail: osfa@fldoe.org
Web Site: www.FloridaStudentFinancialAid.org/SSFAD/home/uamain.htm

AREAS OF INTEREST:
Financial aid for Florida undergraduate students.

NAME(S) OF PROGRAMS:
- **Access to Better Learning and Education Grant Program (ABLE)**
- **Mary McLeod Bethune Scholarship Program (MMB)**
- **First Generation Matching Grant Program (FGMG)**
- **Florida Resident Access Grant (FRAG)**
- **Florida Student Assistance Grant Program (FSAG)**
- **Florida Work Experience Program (FWEP)**
- **Scholarships for Children and Spouses of Deceased or Disabled Veterans (CSDDV)**

TYPE:
Challenge/matching grants; Grants-in-aid; Scholarships. The Access to Better Learning and Education (ABLE) Grant Program provides tuition assistance to Florida undergraduate students enrolled in degree programs at eligible private Florida colleges or universities. ABLE is a decentralized program, and each participating institution determines application procedures, deadlines and student eligibility.

The Mary McLeod Bethune Scholarships (MMB) are awarded to undergraduate students who meet scholastic requirements attending Bethune-Cookman University, Edward Waters College, Florida A&M University, or Florida Memorial University.

The First Generation Matching Grant Program (FGMG) provides need-based grants to degree-seeking, resident, undergraduate students who demonstrate financial need, are

enrolled in participating postsecondary institutions, and whose parents have not earned Baccalaureate or higher degrees.

Florida Resident Access Grants (FRAG) are provided to full-time Florida undergraduates attending an eligible private, nonprofit Florida college or university.

The Florida Student Assistance Grant Program (FSAG) is a need-based grant program available to degree-seeking and certificate-seeking, resident, undergraduate students who demonstrate substantial financial need and are enrolled in participating postsecondary institutions.

The Florida Work Experience Program (FWEP) provides eligible Florida students the opportunity to secure work experiences that will complement and reinforce the students' educational and career goals.

Scholarships for Children and Spouses of Deceased or Disabled Veterans (CSDDV) provides scholarships for dependent children and unremarried spouses of Florida veterans who died as a result of service-connected injuries, diseases, or disabilities sustained while on active duty or have been certified by the Florida Department of Veterans' Affairs as having service-connected 100% total and permanent disabilities.

PURPOSE:
To provide financial assistance to Florida students continuing their education.

LEGAL BASIS:
State agency.

GEOG. RESTRICTIONS: Florida.

FINANCIAL DATA:
Amount of support per award: Varies per program.

Total amount of support: Varies.

APPLICATION INFO:
Detailed program information can be found on the web site.

ADDRESS INQUIRIES TO:
See e-mail and phone number above.

FLORIDA DEPARTMENT OF EDUCATION [1628]

Office of Student Financial Assistance
325 West Gaines Street, Suite 1314
Tallahassee, FL 32399-0400
(888) 827-2004
Fax: (850) 487-1809
E-mail: osfa@fldoe.org
Web Site: www.FloridaStudentFinancialAid.org/SSFAD/bf/bfmain.htm

NAME(S) OF PROGRAMS:
- **Florida Bright Futures Scholarship Program**

TYPE:
Scholarships. The Florida Bright Futures Scholarship Program is the umbrella program for three state-funded scholarships based on academic achievement in high school: Florida Academic Scholars (FAS) Award, Florida Medallion Scholars (FMS) Award and Florida Gold Seal Vocational Scholars (GSV) Award.

YEAR PROGRAM STARTED: 1997

PURPOSE:
To reward Florida's high school graduates who merit recognition of high academic achievement.

LEGAL BASIS:
State agency.

ELIGIBILITY:
Initial eligibility requirements to receive funding are as follows:
(1) be a Florida resident and a U.S. citizen or eligible noncitizen; student's residency and citizenship status are determined by the postsecondary institution; consult the financial aid office or admissions office of the institution one plans to attend;
(2) meet specific coursework, volunteer service hours, and minimum grade point average and test score requirements and;
(3) not be found guilty of, or pled nolo contendere to, a felony charge, unless the student has been granted clemency by the Governor and Cabinet sitting as the Executive Office of Clemency.

GEOG. RESTRICTIONS: Florida.

FINANCIAL DATA:
Total amount of support: Varies.

NO. AWARDS: 166,751 for the year 2014-15.

APPLICATION INFO:
Detailed program information can be found on the web site.

Duration: One year; renewable up to five years from high school graduation or a first Baccalaureate degree, whichever comes first.

Deadline: High school graduation.

ADDRESS INQUIRIES TO:
State Scholarship and Grant Programs
(See address above.)

FLORIDA DEPARTMENT OF EDUCATION

Office of Student Financial Assistance
325 West Gaines Street, Suite 1314
Tallahassee, FL 32399-0400
(888) 827-2004
Fax: (850) 487-1809
E-mail: osfa@fldoe.org
Web Site: www.FloridaStudentFinancialAid.org/SSFAD/home/uamain.htm

TYPE:
Challenge/matching grants; Grants-in-aid. Jose Marti Scholarship Challenge Grant Fund is a need-based merit scholarship that provides financial assistance to eligible students of Hispanic origin who will attend Florida public or eligible private institutions.

See entry 1047 for full listing.

FOUNDATION FOR TECHNOLOGY AND ENGINEERING EDUCATION [1629]

1914 Association Drive
Suite 201
Reston, VA 20191-1539
(703) 860-2100
Fax: (703) 860-0353
E-mail: iteea@iteea.org
Web Site: www.iteea.org

FOUNDED: 1939

AREAS OF INTEREST:
Technology education.

NAME(S) OF PROGRAMS:
- **FTEE Undergraduate Scholarship**

TYPE:
Scholarships. The scholarship is for an undergraduate student majoring in technology and engineering education teacher preparation.

PURPOSE:
To support teacher preparation in technology and engineering education.

ELIGIBILITY:
Applicant must be a member of the International Technology and Engineering Educators Association and be a current, full-time undergraduate majoring in technology and engineering education teacher preparation. Applicant must not be a senior by application deadline.

FINANCIAL DATA:
Amount of support per award: $1,000.

NO. AWARDS: 1.

APPLICATION INFO:
Applicants must submit the application package, which is to include the following required items:
(1) letter of transmittal that includes a statement about personal interest in teaching technology and engineering and applicant's address with day and evening telephone numbers;
(2) resume or vitae which indicate career goals, current professional and college activities and achievements (maximum three pages);
(3) photocopy of college transcript (required 2.5 grade point average on 4.0 scale) and;
(4) three faculty letters of recommendation from among his or her professors and/or advisor.

Application may be submitted electronically to the e-mail address listed above.

Deadline: December 1.

ADDRESS INQUIRIES TO:
FTEE Undergraduate Scholarship
Foundation for Technology and Engineering Education
(See address above.)

*SPECIAL STIPULATIONS:
Applicant must be a member of the ITEEA.

FOUNDATION FOR TECHNOLOGY AND ENGINEERING EDUCATION [1630]

1914 Association Drive
Suite 201
Reston, VA 20191-1539
(703) 860-2100
Fax: (703) 860-0353
E-mail: iteea@iteea.org
Web Site: www.iteea.org

FOUNDED: 1939

AREAS OF INTEREST:
Technology education.

NAME(S) OF PROGRAMS:
- **Litherland/FTEE Scholarship Undergraduate Major in Technology and Engineering Education**

TYPE:
Scholarships.

PURPOSE:
To assist an undergraduate student majoring in technology education and engineering teacher preparation.

ELIGIBILITY:
Applicant must be member of the International Technology and Engineering Educators Association and a current, full-time undergraduate majoring in technology education and engineering teacher preparation. The student must not be a senior by application deadline. The award is based upon interest in teaching, academic ability, need and faculty recommendations.

FINANCIAL DATA:
Amount of support per award: $1,000.

NO. AWARDS: 1.

APPLICATION INFO:
Applicants must submit an application package, which is to include the following required items:
(1) a letter of transmittal that includes a statement about his or her personal interest in teaching technology and engineering and applicant's address with day and evening telephone numbers;
(2) resume or vitae identifying career goals, current professional activities and achievements;
(3) photocopy of college transcript and;
(4) three faculty letters of recommendation from among his or her professors and/or advisor.

Deadline: December 1.

ADDRESS INQUIRIES TO:
Litherland/FTEE Scholarship
Foundation for Technology and Engineering Education
(See address above.)

*SPECIAL STIPULATIONS:
Applicant must be a member of the ITEEA.

FREEDOM ALLIANCE [1631]

22570 Markey Court, Suite 240
Dulles, VA 20166
(703) 444-7940
(800) 475-6620
Fax: (703) 444-9893
E-mail: info@fascholarship.com
Web Site: www.fascholarship.com

FOUNDED: 1990

AREAS OF INTEREST:
Scholarship aid to the children of American military personnel who have been killed or injured in military service.

NAME(S) OF PROGRAMS:
- **Freedom Alliance Scholarship Fund**

TYPE:
Scholarships. Freedom Alliance Scholarship Fund provides college scholarships to the sons and daughters of America's military heroes - those who sacrifice life or limb in defense of America's freedom.

YEAR PROGRAM STARTED: 1990

PURPOSE:
To honor the bravery and dedication exhibited by Americans in the U.S. armed forces who have sacrificed life and limb by providing educational scholarships to their children.

LEGAL BASIS:
501(c)(3) educational and charitable foundation.

ELIGIBILITY:
Students must be a dependent child of a service member who was killed or was permanently disabled (100% rating) in the line of duty, or who is currently certified as POW or MIA. The applicant must also be a senior in high school, a high school graduate, or enrolled in an institution of higher learning, including colleges, universities or vocational schools.

FINANCIAL DATA:
Amount of support per award: Varies.

NO. AWARDS: 301 for the year 2015.

APPLICATION INFO:
Eligible students seeking a Freedom Alliance scholarship must first complete an application form. Applications will not be considered by the scholarship committee unless all required materials listed below accompany the application package:
(1) certificate of death/disability or proof of POW/MIA status as defined in the instructions;
(2) proof of dependency as defined in the instructions;
(3) 500-word essay as explained in the instructions;
(4) official transcripts from high school and all post-high school educational institutions;
(5) photo of applicant and;
(6) photo of parent.

DD Form 214 is also required in the case of a student whose parent is permanently disabled, in addition to the VA rating letter demonstrating permanent disability in the application packet.

Duration: Scholarships are awarded annually and are renewable for a total of four scholarships.

STAFF:
Thomas Kilgannon, President
Calvin Coolidge, Executive Director

BOARD OF DIRECTORS:
Hon. Ralph Smith, Chairman
Thomas Cook, Treasurer
Michael Mason
Jerry Morris
Rita Scott

FOUNDERS:
Lt Col Oliver L. North, USMC (Ret.), Honorary Chairman
Lt Gen Edward J. Bronars, USMC

ADDRESS INQUIRIES TO:
Wanda Cruz, Program Assistant
(See address above.)

*PLEASE NOTE:
No graduate scholarships are provided.

GOLDEN KEY INTERNATIONAL HONOUR SOCIETY, INC. [1632]

1040 Crown Pointe Parkway
Suite 900
Atlanta, GA 30338
(678) 689-2200
(800) 377-2401
Fax: (678) 689-2297
E-mail: awards@goldenkey.org
Web Site: www.goldenkey.org

AREAS OF INTEREST:
Nonprofit academic honors organization that recognizes the top 15% of juniors and seniors in all undergraduate fields.

NAME(S) OF PROGRAMS:
- **Advisor Professional Development Grant**
- **Alumni Professional Development Grant**
- **Chartering Officer Scholarship**
- **Community Service Award**
- **Education Debt Reduction Award**
- **Education Development Grant**
- **Emerging Scholar Award**
- **GEICO Life Scholarship**
- **The Golden Key Graduate Scholarship Award**
- **Golden Key Research Grants**
- **Living the Mission Award**
- **Military Service Scholarship**
- **Joan Nelson Study Abroad Scholarship**
- **Study Abroad Scholarships**
- **Undergraduate Achievement Scholarship**

TYPE:
Awards/prizes; Scholarships; Travel grants. Advisor Professional Development Grant allows current Golden Key chapter advisors the ability to attend professional development conferences or pursue research within their academic disciplines.

Alumni Professional Development Grant allows Golden Key alumni to attend professional development conferences or pursue research.

Chartering Officer Scholarship recognizes members who have chartered or re-chartered their local chapter in the previous academic year.

Community Service Award: Recognizes one member for outstanding service to the community.

Education Debt Reduction Award assists members with the repayment of student loans.

Education Development Grant allows current members the ability to attend professional development conferences or research conferences within their academic disciplines. Additionally, this grant may be used to attend Golden Key conferences.

Emerging Scholar Award recognizes outstanding sophomore members who have made a difference in their chapter.

GEICO Life Scholarship: Recognizes outstanding members who achieve academic excellence while balancing additional commitments such as family and/or career.

The Golden Key Graduate Scholar Award: Golden Key's premier scholarship program. Supports members' post-Baccalaureate study at accredited universities anywhere in the world.

Golden Key Research Grants: Allow members to conduct thesis research and/or present their research at professional conferences or student research symposia.

Living the Mission Award recognizes a member that lives out the values of the Society in all that they do.

Military Service Scholarship recognizes and awards members who are actively engaged in the military or public service.

Joan Nelson Study Abroad Scholarship assists members who are going to participate in a study abroad program.

Study Abroad Scholarships: Assists members who participate in a study abroad program.

Undergraduate Achievement Scholarship recognizes members for their excellence throughout their undergraduate careers.

PURPOSE:
To enable members to realize their potential.

ELIGIBILITY:
Open to Golden Key members.

FINANCIAL DATA:
Amount of support per award: $1,000 to $10,000.

Total amount of support: $1,000,000 annually.

APPLICATION INFO:
Golden Key's scholarships and awards require a formal application. Each scholarship has a unique submission deadline and application process. Details about each of the scholarship programs can be found under the Scholarship and Award Listing on the web site. All scholarship submissions must be written in English.

ADDRESS INQUIRIES TO:
Scholarship Program Manager
(See address above.)

*SPECIAL STIPULATIONS:
Only Golden Key members may apply for these scholarships and awards.

GRADUATE EDUCATION OPPORTUNITY PROGRAM

Michigan State University, The Graduate School
Chittenden Hall, 466 West Circle Drive
East Lansing, MI 48824
(517) 353-3220
Fax: (517) 353-3355
E-mail: gradschool@grd.msu.edu
Web Site: grad.msu.edu

TYPE:
Assistantships; Fellowships.

See entry 969 for full listing.

THE GREATER KANAWHA VALLEY FOUNDATION

Huntington Square, Suite 1600
900 Lee Street East
Charleston, WV 25301
(304) 346-3620
Fax: (304) 346-3640
E-mail: sryder@tgkvf.org
Web Site: www.tgkvf.org

TYPE:
Project/program grants; Scholarships.

See entry 1259 for full listing.

THE HIGHER EDUCATION STUDENT ASSISTANCE AUTHORITY [1633]

P.O. Box 540
Trenton, NJ 08625-0540
(609) 588-3300
E-mail: Client_Services@hesaa.org
Web Site: www.hesaa.org

FOUNDED: 1959

AREAS OF INTEREST:
State financial assistance for college students.

NAME(S) OF PROGRAMS:
- **Tuition Aid Grant (TAG)**

TYPE:
Grants-in-aid. The Higher Education Student Assistance Authority (HESAA) is a New Jersey authority that provides students and families with the financial and informational resources for students to pursue their education beyond high school. With roots dating back to 1959, HESAA's singular focus has always been to benefit the students it serves. HESAA provides state supplemental loans, grants and scholarships. HESAA also administers the state's college savings plan.

YEAR PROGRAM STARTED: 1969

PURPOSE:
To provide financial assistance to needy students attending approved New Jersey institutions. This is calculated by estimating what a family can contribute from income and assets plus a contribution from the student's earnings and savings. The amount and type of aid will depend upon program eligibility, available funds and the degree of need.

LEGAL BASIS:
New Jersey Higher Education Tuition Aid Act.

ELIGIBILITY:
Applicants must be New Jersey residents for at least 12 consecutive months prior to receiving an award, and will be enrolled in an approved New Jersey institution. Student must be a U.S. citizen or eligible noncitizen and be registered with the Selective Service, if applicable. Grants are renewable annually based upon satisfactory academic progress and continued financial need. Students who have received a Baccalaureate degree are not eligible.

GEOG. RESTRICTIONS: New Jersey.

FINANCIAL DATA:
Amount of support per award: Award amounts are based on the student's New Jersey Eligibility Index, tuition charged and appropriated funds.

NO. AWARDS: Based upon appropriations.

APPLICATION INFO:
Applicants must file the Free Application for Federal Student Aid (FAFSA), including the additional New Jersey questions.

Duration: Renewable for four years of undergraduate study providing eligibility continues and an application is filed.

Deadline: October 1 for fall and spring terms. March 1 for spring term only. Renewals June 1 for fall and spring terms.

PUBLICATIONS:
State and Federal Financial Aid Programs for New Jersey Students, brochure.

THE HIGHER EDUCATION STUDENT ASSISTANCE AUTHORITY [1634]

P.O. Box 540
Trenton, NJ 08625-0540
(609) 588-3300
E-mail: Client_Services@hesaa.org
Web Site: www.hesaa.org

FOUNDED: 1959

AREAS OF INTEREST:
State financial assistance for college students.

NAME(S) OF PROGRAMS:
- **Law Enforcement Officer Memorial Scholarship**
- **New Jersey Governor's Industry Vocations Scholarship for Women and Minorities (NJ-GIVS)**
- **New Jersey Student Tuition Assistance Reward Scholarship (NJ STARS)**
- **New Jersey Student Tuition Assistance Reward Scholarship II (NJ STARS II)**
- **New Jersey World Trade Center Scholarship**
- **NJBEST Scholarship**
- **Survivor Tuition Benefits Program**

TYPE:
Scholarships. Law Enforcement Officer Memorial Scholarship provides financial aid for eligible children of law enforcement officers killed in the line of duty.

New Jersey Governor's Industry Vocations Scholarship for Women and Minorities pays for an eligible certificate or degree-granting program in a construction-related field at one of New Jersey's eligible institutions.

New Jersey Student Tuition Assistance Reward Scholarship provides access to higher education for the state's highest achieving students.

New Jersey Student Tuition Assistance Reward Scholarship II enables successful NJ STARS scholars to transfer to a New Jersey four-year college or university and earn a Bachelor's degree.

New Jersey World Trade Center Scholarship benefits dependent children and surviving spouses of New Jersey residents who were killed in or who died of the terrorist attacks against the U.S. on September 11, 2001.

NJBEST Scholarship is a one-time scholarship to beneficiaries in the NJBEST 529 college savings plan, who are enrolled at least half-time in his or her first year, first semester of postsecondary education at a New Jersey institution.

Survivor Tuition Benefits Program benefits dependent children and surviving spouses of New Jersey firefighters, emergency service workers or law enforcement officers who were killed in the line of duty.

PURPOSE:
To provide financial assistance to college students demonstrating academic proficiency, and/or need.

ELIGIBILITY:
Student must be a U.S. citizen or eligible noncitizen and registered with the Selective Service. For some programs, New Jersey residency and a current-year FAFSA are required. Application deadlines, years of eligibility and payment limits apply to all programs. Contact HESAA for details.

GEOG. RESTRICTIONS: New Jersey.

FINANCIAL DATA:
Amount of support per award: New Jersey Governor's Industry Vocations Scholarship for Women and Minorities: Up to $2,000 per year or up to the cost of tuition, less any federal, state or institutional aid. NJBEST Scholarship: Varies depending upon the number of years open and level of contributions. Survivor Tuition Benefits Program: Covers the cost of tuition at any New Jersey public college or university. Students enrolled at an independent New Jersey college or university may receive up to the highest tuition charges at a New Jersey public institution.

APPLICATION INFO:
Application information as well as applications are available on the HESAA web site. Some programs require a FAFSA to be filed before applying.

Deadline: All programs have deadline dates for fall and spring terms. Contact HESAA for application deadline dates.

STAFF:
Larry Sharp, Director, Grants and Scholarships

HISPANIC SCHOLARSHIP FUND

1411 West 190th Street
Suite 700
Gardena, CA 90248
(877) 473-4636
(310) 975-3700
Fax: (310) 349-3328
E-mail: info@hsf.net
scholar1@hsf.net
Web Site: www.hsf.net

TYPE:
Scholarships. Awarded to Hispanic community college, undergraduate and graduate students.

See entry 1048 for full listing.

HOLLAND & KNIGHT CHARITABLE FOUNDATION, INC.

100 North Tampa Street, Suite 4100
Tampa, FL 33602
(813) 227-8500
E-mail: nativewriters@hklaw.com
Web Site: foundation.hklaw.com
nativewriters.hklaw.com

TYPE:
Awards/prizes; Scholarships. Young Native Writers Essay Contest is a writing contest for Native American high school students.

See entry 1034 for full listing.

THE HONOR SOCIETY OF PHI KAPPA PHI [1635]

7576 Goodwood Boulevard
Baton Rouge, LA 70806
(225) 388-4917 ext. 235
(800) 804-9880 ext. 235
Fax: (225) 388-4900
E-mail: kpartin@phikappaphi.org
Web Site: www.phikappaphi.org

FOUNDED: 1897

AREAS OF INTEREST:
Scholastic excellence in all academic fields.

NAME(S) OF PROGRAMS:
- **The Phi Kappa Phi Fellowship**

TYPE:
Fellowships. Support for the first year of graduate or professional school.

YEAR PROGRAM STARTED: 1932

PURPOSE:
To stimulate members of Phi Kappa Phi to go to graduate or professional school.

LEGAL BASIS:
Honor Society incorporated in Michigan, May 20, 1972. Authorized to operate in Louisiana, September 1978. Tax-exempt under IRS 501(c)(3). Companion organization, the Phi Kappa Phi Foundation, incorporated in California, December 17, 1969, as a Public Benefit Foundation, tax-exempt under IRS 501(c)(3).

ELIGIBILITY:
Applicant must be a member of Phi Kappa Phi, maintain high scholastic standing and be recommended by a chapter of Phi Kappa Phi.

GEOG. RESTRICTIONS: United States.

FINANCIAL DATA:
Amount of support per award: $5,000 or $15,000.

Total amount of support: $345,000.

CO-OP FUNDING PROGRAMS: Awards made through Phi Kappa Phi Foundation, a companion organization to the Society.

NO. MOST RECENT APPLICANTS: 170.

NO. AWARDS: 57 (51 valued at $5,000 and 6 valued at $15,000) for the year 2015.

APPLICATION INFO:
Completed application packet must be returned to the local chapter on or before the deadline.

Duration: One academic year. Nonrenewable.

IRS I.D.: 95-1856406

STAFF:
Kelli Partin, Programs Coordinator

ADDRESS INQUIRIES TO:
Kelli Partin, Programs Coordinator
(See address above.)

HORTICULTURAL RESEARCH INSTITUTE, INC. [1636]

2130 Stella Court
Columbus, OH 43215
(614) 487-1117
Fax: (614) 487-1216
E-mail: jenniferg@americanhort.org
Web Site: www.hriresearch.org

AREAS OF INTEREST:
Nursery, landscape research and horticulture.

NAME(S) OF PROGRAMS:
- **Carville M. Akehurst Memorial Scholarship**
- **Timothy Bigelow and Palmer W. Bigelow, Jr. Scholarship**
- **Bryan A. Champion Memorial Scholarship**
- **Muggets Scholarship**
- **Spring Meadow Nursery Scholarship**
- **Usrey Family Scholarship**
- **Susie and Bruce Usrey Education Scholarship**

TYPE:
Scholarships.

YEAR PROGRAM STARTED: 1988

PURPOSE:
To aid students seeking a career in the horticulture industry.

LEGAL BASIS:
Nonprofit organization.

ELIGIBILITY:
Varies.

GEOG. RESTRICTIONS: Varies.

FINANCIAL DATA:
Amount of support per award: $500 to $4,000.

Total amount of support: Varies.

NO. MOST RECENT APPLICANTS: 110.

NO. AWARDS: 7.

APPLICATION INFO:
Applications are available online.

Deadline: May 31.

IRS I.D.: 52-1052547

ADDRESS INQUIRIES TO:
See e-mail address above.

ILLINOIS RESTAURANT ASSOCIATION EDUCATIONAL FOUNDATION [1637]

33 West Monroe, Suite 250
Chicago, IL 60603
(312) 787-4000
Fax: (312) 845-1956
E-mail: ksummers@illinoisrestaurants.org
Web Site: www.illinoisrestaurants.org

FOUNDED: 1973

AREAS OF INTEREST:
Foodservice/restaurant/hospitality.

NAME(S) OF PROGRAMS:
- **IRA Educational Foundation Scholarship Program**

TYPE:
Scholarships.

YEAR PROGRAM STARTED: 1973

PURPOSE:
To build the Illinois hospitality workforce through the ProStart® curriculum, career exploration, workforce development and scholarships for high school students.

LEGAL BASIS:
Not-for-profit organization.

ELIGIBILITY:
Applicants must be permanent residents of the state of Illinois who are applying to or enrolled in an accredited culinary school, college or university and who are enrolled full-time or substantial part-time, taking a minimum of nine credit hours each term, majoring in a culinary restaurant management or foodservice-related program.

GEOG. RESTRICTIONS: Illinois.

FINANCIAL DATA:
Scholarships provide assistance toward tuition and materials.

Amount of support per award: Minimum $1,000.

NO. MOST RECENT APPLICANTS: 65.

NO. AWARDS: 61.

APPLICATION INFO:
Application forms are available on the web site.

Duration: One academic year. Renewal is not automatic.

Deadline: April 29.

IRS I.D.: 36-3271510

ADDRESS INQUIRIES TO:
Betty Roland
Tel: 312-380-4117
Fax: 312-787-4792
(See address above.)

INDIANA COMMISSION FOR HIGHER EDUCATION, DIVISION OF STUDENT FINANCIAL AID [1638]

101 West Ohio Street
Suite 300
Indianapolis, IN 46204-4206
(317) 464-4400
(888) 528-4719
Fax: (317) 232-3260
E-mail: awards@che.in.gov
Web Site: www.in.gov/che/4498.htm

FOUNDED: 1965

AREAS OF INTEREST:
Student financial aid.

NAME(S) OF PROGRAMS:
- **William A. Crawford Minority Teacher Scholarship**
- **Mitch Daniels Early Graduation Scholarship**
- **EARN Indiana (State Work Study)**
- **National Guard Supplemental Grant**
- **The Frank O'Bannon Grant**
- **Earlene S. Rodgers Student Teaching Stipend for Minorities**
- **Student Teaching Stipend for High-Needs Fields**
- **21st Century Scholars Program**

TYPE:
Grants-in-aid; Project/program grants; Scholarships; Work-study programs. Monetary grants awarded annually toward the cost of tuition.

The Crawford Minority Teacher Scholarship was created to address the critical shortage of Black and Hispanic teachers in Indiana.

The Rodgers Student Teaching Stipend for Minorities is for minority students (defined as Black and Hispanic) who plan to teach.

Student Teaching Stipend for High-Needs Fields is for students who plan to teach in "high-need" fields, which means a teaching specialty that affects the economic vitality of Indiana and in which there is a shortage of candidates.

21st Century Scholars Program was created as Indiana's way of raising the educational aspirations of low- and moderate-income families.

YEAR PROGRAM STARTED: 1971

PURPOSE:
To provide financial assistance to students attending colleges within the state of Indiana.

LEGAL BASIS:
Indiana Scholarship Act, I.C. 20-12-21. I.C. 20-12-21.1.

ELIGIBILITY:
An applicant must be an Indiana resident, a U.S. citizen or eligible noncitizen and must attend an eligible institution located within the state of Indiana as a full-time undergraduate student (12 to 15 hours per term).

GEOG. RESTRICTIONS: Indiana.

FINANCIAL DATA:
Total amount of support: Varies.

Matching fund requirements: Only in EARN Indiana.

APPLICATION INFO:
Free Application for Federal Student Aid (FAFSA) must be received by deadline for The Frank O'Bannon Grant.

21st Century Scholars Program: Must sign and submit pledge affirmation before March 10. File for state and federal financial aid by completing the FAFSA on time. Apply for admission and institutional financial aid at the Indiana college attending by the deadline for each college. Enroll as a full-time college student and maintain Indiana residency.

Duration: Four years. Reapplication required annually.

Deadline: Mitch Daniels Early Graduation and Minority Teacher Scholarships: September 4. EARN Indiana, The Frank O'Bannon Grant and 21st Century Scholars Program: March 10. Student Teaching Stipend: Fall term October 4 and spring term January 31.

PUBLICATIONS:
Application guidelines.

ADDRESS INQUIRIES TO:
State Student Assistance Commission
(See address above.)

INSTITUTE FOR THE INTERNATIONAL EDUCATION OF STUDENTS (IES) [1639]

33 West Monroe Street
Suite 2300
Chicago, IL 60603-5405
(312) 944-1750
(800) 995-2300
Fax: (312) 944-1448
E-mail: info@IESabroad.org
Web Site: www.IESabroad.org

FOUNDED: 1950

AREAS OF INTEREST:
International education (JYA).

NAME(S) OF PROGRAMS:
- **Boren and Gilman Scholarship Support Grants**
- **Disability Grants**
- **Diversity Scholarships**
- **Donor Funded Scholarships**
- **Need Based Aid (Early Aid Program)**
- **Public University Grants**

TYPE:
Awards/prizes; Scholarships. Boren and Gilman Scholarship Support Grants: This program offers recipients of these prestigious scholarships the opportunity to apply for additional financial support.

Disability Grants: This program's purpose is to enhance study abroad opportunities for students with disabilities. It offers grants to students whose disabilities may add significant costs to their study abroad experience.

Diversity Scholarships: This program offers one way to encourage and support students from a range of institutions and underrepresented populations. Underrepresented students include students from underrepresented racial and ethnic groups, first-generation-to-college students, students from low-income families and students with a history of overcoming adversity.

Donor Funded Scholarships: These scholarship opportunities have been created through the generosity of various donors who support the important mission of IES Abroad.

Need Based Aid (Early Aid Program): This program is available to students with demonstrated financial need. Priority is given to Pell Grant recipients.

Public University Grants: This program offers an automatic $2,000 credit toward a semester or academic year program.

YEAR PROGRAM STARTED: 1950

PURPOSE:
To provide study opportunities abroad for qualified undergraduate students from U.S. colleges and universities.

LEGAL BASIS:
Not-for-profit educational organization organized under the laws of Illinois.

ELIGIBILITY:
All aid categories require applicants to be accepted to and attend an IES Abroad standard program. (Customized programs are not eligible for IES Abroad aid.)

Some aid categories require that applicants attend a college or university that is part of the IES Abroad Consortium and that transfers at least 75% of institutional aid for study abroad expenses.

FINANCIAL DATA:
Amount of support per award: Boren and Gilman Scholarship Support Grants: $500 for summer program; $1,000 for fall or spring program. Disability Grants: $500. Diversity Scholarships: Up to $5,000 depending on category. Donor Funded Scholarships: Award amounts vary by category. Need Based Aid (Early Aid Program): Up to $5,000 (fall or spring programs); up to $1,000 (summer programs). Public University Grants: $2,000.

Total amount of support: Boren and Gilman Scholarship Support Grants: $35,500. Disability Grants: $1,500. Diversity Scholarships: $75,000. Donor Funded Scholarships: $114,500. Need Based Aid (Early Aid Program): $845,150. Public University Grants: $1,629,500.

NO. AWARDS: Boren and Gilman Scholarship Support Grants: 42. Disability Grants: 3. Diversity Scholarships: 36. Donor Funded Scholarships: 52. Need Based Aid (Early Aid Program): 520. Public University Grants: 1,062.

APPLICATION INFO:
Applications may be submitted online.

Duration: Academic year, one semester, or summer (need-based only). Nonrenewable.

Deadline: May 1 for fall semester and academic year; November 1 for spring semester; April 1 for summer.

PUBLICATIONS:
Annual report; IES Abroad Alumni Exchange Newsletter; IES Abroad catalogs; IES MAP©.

IRS I.D.: 36-2251912

GOVERNING BOARD:
Ezio Vergani, Chairperson
Dr. Loren J. Anderson
Mary Cahillane
Susan Carty
James Crawford
Debora de Hoyos
Dr. Pamela Brooks Gann
John J. Gearen
Rhonda Jordan
Dr. Raynard Kington
Thomas McDonald
Robert McNeill
Dr. Marla Salmon
Alan Schwartz
Clayton Spencer
Sheila A. Stamps
Peter E. Sundman
Monica Vachher
Dr. C. James Yeh

ADDRESS INQUIRIES TO:
Joseph Sevigny, Associate Vice President of Enrollment Management
(See address above.)

INTERNATIONAL ASSOCIATION OF FIRE CHIEFS FOUNDATION, INC. [1640]

4025 Fair Ridge Drive
Suite 300
Fairfax, VA 22033-2868
(703) 273-0911
Fax: (703) 273-9363
E-mail: foundation@iafc.org
Web Site: www.iafcf.org

FOUNDED: 1974

NAME(S) OF PROGRAMS:
- **International Association of Fire Chiefs Foundation Scholarship Program**

TYPE:
Scholarships. Scholarships for advanced study in fire science, fire department administration and operation, public administration or any fire-related program.

YEAR PROGRAM STARTED: 1974

PURPOSE:
To aid in better fire service administration and to support training in this area.

ELIGIBILITY:
Under the regulations, any member of the fire service who is an active member of U.S. or Canadian Fire Service in a state, county, provincial, municipal, community, industrial or federal fire department, and who has demonstrated proficiency as a member, is eligible to apply for a scholarship to a recognized institution of higher education of his or her choice. Applicants must have the approval of their department chiefs. Dependents are not eligible.

GEOG. RESTRICTIONS: United States.

FINANCIAL DATA:
Amount of support per award: Generally $500 to $2,000, providing a maximum of this dollar amount toward tuition costs.

Total amount of support: Approximately $36,000 per year.

NO. MOST RECENT APPLICANTS: Approximately 60.

NO. AWARDS: Approximately 21 awards annually.

APPLICATION INFO:
Application information is available on the web site.

Duration: One year.

Deadline: June 1.

PUBLICATIONS:
Application guidelines.

ADDRESS INQUIRIES TO:
Terry Monroe
Association Manager for Foundation
(See address above.)

INTERNATIONAL DEVELOPMENT RESEARCH CENTRE (IDRC)

150 Kent Street
Ottawa ON K1P 0B2 Canada
(613) 696-2098
Fax: (613) 236-4026
E-mail: awards@idrc.ca
Web Site: www.idrc.ca

TYPE:
Awards/prizes. These awards are offered once a year and are intended for field research in one or more developing countries. Candidates must conduct their research in areas corresponding to IDRC's research priorities.

See entry 1275 for full listing.

IODE [1641]

40 Orchard View Boulevard, Suite 219
Toronto ON M4R 1B9 Canada
(416) 487-4416
Fax: (416) 487-4417
E-mail: iodecanada@bellnet.ca
Web Site: www.iode.ca

FOUNDED: 1900

AREAS OF INTEREST:
Education, social service and citizenship.

NAME(S) OF PROGRAMS:
- **War Memorial Scholarships**

TYPE:
Scholarships. Postgraduate scholarships tenable in any university in Canada and the Commonwealth.

YEAR PROGRAM STARTED: 1920

PURPOSE:
To provide scholarships for educational purposes as a memorial to Canadian men and women who gave their lives in defense of freedom during World Wars I and II.

LEGAL BASIS:
Charitable organization.

ELIGIBILITY:
Candidates must be Canadian citizens. At the time of application, candidates must be enrolled in at least the second year of a doctoral program.

GEOG. RESTRICTIONS: Canada and the Commonwealth.

FINANCIAL DATA:
Amount of support per award: $15,000 (CAN) for study in Canada and for study overseas within the Commonwealth.

NO. AWARDS: 5 annually.

APPLICATION INFO:
A candidate must apply to the War Memorial Convener in the province in which the first degree was obtained. The names of Conveners change from year to year, but appear in the scholarship folder. Check web site for the application.

Duration: One year.

Deadline: Applications must reach the Convener of the province from which the first degree was obtained by November 1.

OFFICERS:
Hazel MacLeod, National War Memorial Officer

TRUSTEES:
E. Anne Mason, National President

THE JAPAN FOUNDATION, LOS ANGELES [1642]

5700 Wilshire Boulevard
Suite 100
Los Angeles, CA 90036
(323) 761-7510
Fax: (323) 761-7517
E-mail: culture@jflalc.org
Web Site: www.jflalc.org

FOUNDED: 1983

AREAS OF INTEREST:
Japanese arts, culture and language education.

NAME(S) OF PROGRAMS:
- **Arts & Culture Grants**
- **J-LEAP**
- **Japanese Language Grants**

TYPE:
Conferences/seminars; Exchange programs; Fellowships; Grants-in-aid; Product donations; Project/program grants; Research grants; Training grants; Visiting scholars.

PURPOSE:
To support grants that promote Japanese arts, culture, language and education.

ELIGIBILITY:
Candidates must be citizens or permanent residents of the U.S.

GEOG. RESTRICTIONS: United States.

FINANCIAL DATA:
Amount of support per award: Varies.

Total amount of support: Varies.

APPLICATION INFO:
Guidelines are available online.

Duration: One year. No renewals.

Deadline: Varies.

THE JAPANESE AMERICAN CITIZENS LEAGUE (JACL) [1643]

1765 Sutter Street
San Francisco, CA 94115
(415) 345-1075
E-mail: pwada@jacl.org
Web Site: www.jacl.org

FOUNDED: 1929

AREAS OF INTEREST:
Education, cultural preservation, and civil rights.

NAME(S) OF PROGRAMS:
- **JACL National Scholarship and Awards Program**

TYPE:
Scholarships. JACL offers more than 30 scholarships and student aid awards (financial aid).

Scholarship categories: Entering Freshman (High School Senior), Undergraduate, Graduate, Law, Creative and Performing Arts, and Financial Aid.

YEAR PROGRAM STARTED: 1946

PURPOSE:
To recognize education as a key to greater opportunities for its members.

ELIGIBILITY:
Applicant must be an active National JACL member at either an individual or student/youth level. Applicants must be planning to attend full-time an institution of higher learning within the U.S. at the undergraduate or graduate school level. Applicants may apply under only one scholarship category. Entering freshman applicants must be high school seniors. Creative and performing arts applicants cannot be professional artists.

JACL membership is open to everyone of any ethnic background.

FINANCIAL DATA:
Amount of support per award: $1,000 to $5,000.

Total amount of support: Over $70,000 in scholarships.

APPLICATION INFO:
Information brochure and applications are posted on the JACL web site annually in November.

Freshman applications must be postmarked and mailed to the local JACL chapter to which the applicant belongs. All other applications must be postmarked and mailed to the JACL National Scholarship Committee, c/o Central California District Council (address listed on the application).

Duration: One year. Limited to a total of two awards.

Deadline: March 1 (freshman applications); April 1 (all other applications).

ADDRESS INQUIRIES TO:
Patty Wada
Scholarships Department
(See phone number or e-mail address above.)

JEWISH FAMILY AND CHILDREN'S SERVICES [1644]

2150 Post Street
San Francisco, CA 94115
(415) 449-1226
Fax: (415) 848-7012
TDD: (415) 567-1044
E-mail: michellel@jfcs.org
Web Site: www.jfcs.org

FOUNDED: 1850

AREAS OF INTEREST:
Jewish individuals and their families, college tuition and expenses, vocational training and loans for business and professional endeavors.

NAME(S) OF PROGRAMS:

- **Educational Loans and Grants Program**

TYPE:
Grants-in-aid. Need-based loans and grants.

PURPOSE:
To provide educational loans and grants to Jewish students.

LEGAL BASIS:
Nonprofit.

ELIGIBILITY:
Applicants must be students of Jewish descent who have demonstrated academic achievement (generally demonstrated by a 3.0 grade point average on a 4.0 scale), financial need, broad-based extracurricular activities and in-depth community involvement and acceptance to an accredited college, university or vocational school.

GEOG. RESTRICTIONS: Marin, San Francisco, San Mateo, Santa Clara, or Sonoma counties, California.

FINANCIAL DATA:
Amount of support per award: Need-based grants: $500 to $1,500; Loans: $1,000 to $6,000.

Total amount of support: Up to $6,000 per student, per year.

NO. MOST RECENT APPLICANTS: 110.

NO. AWARDS: Varies per year.

APPLICATION INFO:
Application information is available on the web site. Contact the organization's Director of Financial Aid Center for more information.

Duration: One academic year.

Deadline: Priority deadline: October 31. Applications will be accepted until funding is exhausted.

PUBLICATIONS:
Program announcement.

ADDRESS INQUIRIES TO:
Michelle Lamphere
Director, JFCS Financial Aid Center
(See address above.)

KANSAS BOARD OF REGENTS [1645]

1000 S.W. Jackson, Suite 520
Topeka, KS 66612-1368
(785) 296-4749
Fax: (785) 296-0983
E-mail: dlindeman@ksbor.org
Web Site: www.kansasregents.org

FOUNDED: 1925

AREAS OF INTEREST:
Higher education.

NAME(S) OF PROGRAMS:

- **Kansas Comprehensive Grant**

TYPE:
Grants-in-aid. Grant-in-aid is available to students with demonstrated financial need attending the four-year public and independent colleges and universities in Kansas.

YEAR PROGRAM STARTED: 1999

PURPOSE:
To provide access and choice for needy students attending either public or independent four-year colleges and universities in the state.

ELIGIBILITY:
Students must be U.S. citizens or residents and Kansas resident undergraduates, attending either a four-year public or independent college/university, and have demonstrated financial need as determined by the Free Application for Federal Student Aid (FAFSA) need analysis.

GEOG. RESTRICTIONS: Kansas.

FINANCIAL DATA:
Amount of support per award: Eligible students attending four-year public colleges and universities may be awarded up to $1,500 annually. Eligible students attending four-year independent colleges and universities may be awarded up to $3,500 annually.

Total amount of support: $16,283,907 for the 2015-16 academic year.

APPLICATION INFO:
No application other than the FAFSA.

Duration: Annual award. Students need to file their FAFSA annually.

Deadline: Priority deadline is April 1 annually.

ADDRESS INQUIRIES TO:
Diane Lindeman
Director of Student Financial Assistance
(See address above.)

KENTUCKY HIGHER EDUCATION ASSISTANCE AUTHORITY (KHEAA) [1646]

P.O. Box 798
Frankfort, KY 40602-0798
(800) 928-8926
Fax: (502) 696-7373
E-mail: studentaid@kheaa.com
Web Site: www.kheaa.com

FOUNDED: 1966

AREAS OF INTEREST:
Postsecondary student financial assistance.

NAME(S) OF PROGRAMS:

- **College Access Program (CAP)**
- **Early Childhood Development Scholarship**
- **Go Higher Grant**
- **Kentucky Educational Excellence Scholarship (KEES)**
- **Kentucky Tuition Grant (KTG)**

TYPE:
Grants-in-aid; Scholarships. Need-based or incentive-based student aid; College Access Program helps Kentucky's financially needy undergraduate students attend eligible public and private Kentucky colleges, universities, proprietary schools and technical colleges.

Early Childhood Development Scholarship provides financial aid to Kentucky students pursuing a degree or credential in early childhood education.

Go Higher Grant provides assistance to help financially needy adult students attend a participating Kentucky college.

Kentucky Educational Excellence Scholarship awards scholarships to Kentucky high school students based on grade point average and ACT/SAT scores to encourage them to attend a college or university in Kentucky. Low-income students may earn additional awards based on Advanced Placement (AP) or International Baccalaureate (IB) exam scores.

Kentucky Tuition Grant provides a tuition equalization grant to help Kentucky residents attend eligible Kentucky private colleges.

ELIGIBILITY:
Applicant must be a U.S. citizen or resident.

College Access Program: Student must reside in Kentucky, demonstrate financial need, attend an eligible college or university, have no past due financial obligations to KHEAA or any Title IV program, and be enrolled at least half-time in a program of study at least two years in length.

Early Childhood Development Scholarship: Student must be a Kentucky resident, enrolled no more than nine credit hours per term in an approved curriculum at a participating school and maintain satisfactory academic progress. Student must be employed at least 20 hours weekly in a participating early childhood facility, have no past due financial obligations to KHEAA or any Title IV program, and not be eligible for state or federal training funds through Head Start, a public preschool program, or First Steps.

Go Higher Grant: Student must be a Kentucky resident, age 24 or older, demonstrate financial need, attend an eligible college or university, have no past due financial obligations to KHEAA or any Title IV program, and be seeking first undergraduate degree.

Kentucky Educational Excellence Scholarship: Student must earn at least a 2.5 grade point average in any year of high school in Kentucky while meeting Kentucky Educational Excellence Scholarship curriculum requirements. Student must reside in Kentucky and attend and graduate from a certified Kentucky high school. Student must have an ACT composite score of 15 or higher for ACT bonus. Convicted felons will be disqualified.

Kentucky Tuition Grant: Student must reside in Kentucky, demonstrate financial need, attend an eligible college or university, have no past due financial obligations to KHEAA or any Title IV program, and be enrolled full-time in an Associate or Bachelor's degree program.

For the Early Childhood Development Scholarship, Go Higher Grant and Kentucky Educational Excellence Scholarship, applicant must be a U.S. citizen, national or permanent resident.

FINANCIAL DATA:

Amount of support per award: College Access Program: $1,900 per academic year; Early Childhood Development Scholarship: $1,800 per academic year; Go Higher Grant: $1,000 per academic year; Kentucky Educational Excellence Scholarship: Varies by student; Kentucky Tuition Grant: Up to $3,000 per academic year.

APPLICATION INFO:

College Access Program and Kentucky Tuition Grant : Applicant must complete the Free Application for Federal Student Aid (FAFSA) (available at www.fafsa.ed.gov). Early Childhood Development Scholarship: Applicant must complete the FAFSA form and the Early Childhood Development Scholarship application (available at KHEAA web site). Go Higher Grant: Applicant must complete the FAFSA form and the Go Higher Grant application (available at the KHEAA web site).

Duration: College Access Program, Go Higher Grant, and Kentucky Tuition Grant: Awarded on an annual basis. Nonrenewable. Early Childhood Development Scholarship: Awarded by academic term. Nonrenewable. Kentucky Educational Excellence Scholarship: Funds awarded based on high school academic performance. Renewal requirements must be met annually once the student is in college.

Deadline: College Access Program, Go Higher Grant and Kentucky Tuition Grant: End of FAFSA processing year, which is the end of the academic year. Early Childhood Development Scholarship: July 15 for fall term; November 15 for spring term; April 15 for summer term.

ADDRESS INQUIRIES TO:

Customer Care
Kentucky Higher Education
Assistance Authority
(See address or phone number above.)

KENTUCKY HIGHER EDUCATION ASSISTANCE AUTHORITY (KHEAA) [1647]

P.O. Box 798
Frankfort, KY 40602-0798
(800) 928-8926
Fax: (502) 696-7373
E-mail: studentaid@kheaa.com
Web Site: www.kheaa.com

FOUNDED: 1966

AREAS OF INTEREST:

Postsecondary student financial assistance.

NAME(S) OF PROGRAMS:

- **Coal County Scholarship for Pharmacy Students**
- **Kentucky Coal County College Completion Scholarship (KC4S)**
- **Kentucky National Guard Tuition Award Program**
- **Osteopathic Medicine Scholarship**
- **Teacher Scholarship Program**

TYPE:

Scholarships. Need-based student aid; Conversion scholarship/loan; Military service grant; Coal County Scholarship for Pharmacy Students provides financial aid to Kentucky residents who plan to work as certified pharmacists in Kentucky coal-producing counties.

Kentucky Coal County College Completion Scholarship provides financial assistance for residents of Kentucky's coal-producing counties to complete a Bachelor's degree.

Kentucky National Guard Tuition Award Program provides tuition assistance for active members of the Kentucky National Guard to attend a Kentucky college or university.

Osteopathic Medicine Scholarship provides financial aid to Kentucky students pursuing a degree at the Kentucky College of Osteopathic Medicine at the University of Pikeville.

Teacher Scholarship Program provides financial aid to Kentucky students pursuing initial teacher certification at participating Kentucky colleges.

ELIGIBILITY:

Applicants must be U.S. citizens or residents.

Coal County Scholarship for Pharmacy Students: Student must be a resident of a Kentucky coal-producing county, enrolled or accepted for enrollment at an accredited school of pharmacy in Kentucky, and work one year as a full-time, licensed pharmacist in a Kentucky coal-producing county for each year the scholarship is received, or repay the scholarship plus interest if the program is not completed or the service requirement is not met.

Kentucky Coal County College Completion Scholarship: Student must be a permanent resident of a Kentucky coal-producing county. Student must have earned at least 60 credit hours toward a Bachelor's degree, be enrolled at least half-time in a Bachelor's degree program in good academic standing, and have no past due financial obligations to KHEAA or any Title IV program.

Kentucky National Guard Tuition Award Program: Student must be an active member of the Kentucky National Guard, maintain all minimum eligibility standards, be eligible for all positive personnel actions, and have completed basic training or its equivalent.

Osteopathic Medicine Scholarship: Student must be a Kentucky resident and practice one year in Kentucky in a qualifying field for each year the scholarship is received, or repay the scholarship plus interest if the service requirement is not met. Teacher Scholarship Program: Student must be Kentucky resident demonstrating financial need. Student must be admitted into a teacher education program, attend an eligible college or university, be enrolled full-time in a teacher certification program and maintain satisfactory academic progress, and teach one semester in Kentucky for each semester the scholarship is received, or repay the scholarship plus interest if the program is not completed or recipient does not teach in Kentucky.

FINANCIAL DATA:

Amount of support per award: Coal County Scholarship for Pharmacy Students: Varies. Kentucky Coal County College Completion Scholarship: Up to $6,800 per year at a nonprofit, independent institution located in a coal-producing county; up to $2,300 per year at a public university extension campus located in a coal-producing county; up to $3,400 per year at a Kentucky college or university whose main campus is located in a county that is not coal-producing. Kentucky National Guard Tuition Award Program: Up to in-state tuition for full- or part-time study at a Kentucky public university. Osteopathic Medicine Scholarship: Varies; equal to the difference between the average amount charged for in-state tuition at Kentucky medical schools and the tuition rate at the Kentucky College of Osteopathic Medicine. Teacher Scholarship Program: Up to $2,500 per semester.

APPLICATION INFO:

Coal County Scholarship for Pharmacy Students: Application is available at the KHEAA web site. Kentucky Coal County College Completion Scholarship: Complete the Free Application for Federal Student Aid (FAFSA) at www.fafsa.ed.gov and the Kentucky Coal County College Completion Scholarship application available at the KHEAA web site. Kentucky National Guard Tuition Award Program: Application available online (https://ky.ngb.army.mil/tuitionstudent) or contact the Boone National Guard at (502) 607-1039. Osteopathic Medicine Scholarship: Contact Teresa Jones at the Kentucky College of Osteopathic Medicine. Teacher Scholarship Program: Complete the FAFSA form and the Teacher Scholarship application at the KHEAA web site.

Duration: Coal County Scholarship for Pharmacy Students, Kentucky National Guard Tuition Award Program, Osteopathic Medicine Scholarship and Teacher Scholarship Program: Awards are made on an annual basis. Nonrenewable. Kentucky Coal County College Completion Scholarship: Awards are made on an annual basis; application is required annually regardless of renewal status.

Deadline: Coal County Scholarship for Pharmacy Students, Kentucky Coal County College Completion Scholarship and Teacher Scholarship Program: Application is available from January 1 to May 1. Kentucky National Guard Tuition Award Program: April 1 for Fall term; October 1 for Spring term.

ADDRESS INQUIRIES TO:

Student Aid
Kentucky Higher Education
Assistance Authority
(See address or phone number above.)

MACKENZIE KING SCHOLARSHIP TRUST [1648]

c/o J. Blom, Faculty of Law
1822 East Mall, University of British Columbia
Vancouver BC V6T 1Z1 Canada
(604) 822-4564
Fax: (604) 822-8108
E-mail: mkingscholarships@law.ubc.ca
Web Site: www.mkingscholarships.ca

FOUNDED: 1950

AREAS OF INTEREST:

Industrial and international relations.

NAME(S) OF PROGRAMS:

- **The Mackenzie King Traveling Scholarships**

TYPE:

Scholarships. For graduate study, either in the U.S. or the U.K., in the field of international or industrial relations (including the international or industrial aspects of law, history, politics or economics).

YEAR PROGRAM STARTED: 1950

LEGAL BASIS:
Private charitable trust.

ELIGIBILITY:
Applicants must be graduates of any Canadian university.

FINANCIAL DATA:
Amount of support per award: Approximately $10,500 (CAN).

Total amount of support: Approximately $42,000 (CAN).

NO. MOST RECENT APPLICANTS: 150 for the 2011-12 academic year.

NO. AWARDS: 4 annually.

APPLICATION INFO:
Applicants must submit completed application forms, all official transcripts and three letters of reference to the Canadian university from which they received their most recent degree, c/o the Faculty of Graduate Studies.

Deadline: February 1.

*SPECIAL STIPULATIONS:
Award may not be accepted if total scholarship support, including the award, exceeds expected tuition expense plus $17,000 (CAN).

MACKENZIE KING SCHOLARSHIP TRUST [1649]

c/o J. Blom, Faculty of Law
1822 East Mall, University of British Columbia
Vancouver BC V6T 1Z1 Canada
(604) 822-4564
Fax: (604) 822-8108
E-mail: mkingscholarships@law.ubc.ca
Web Site: www.mkingscholarships.ca

FOUNDED: 1950

AREAS OF INTEREST:
Graduate studies.

NAME(S) OF PROGRAMS:
- **The Mackenzie King Open Scholarship**

TYPE:
Scholarships. For full-time graduate studies in Canada or elsewhere, in any field.

YEAR PROGRAM STARTED: 1950

PURPOSE:
To assist graduates of Canadian universities pursue graduate study in any discipline anywhere in the world.

LEGAL BASIS:
Private charitable trust.

ELIGIBILITY:
Applicants must be graduates of any Canadian university.

FINANCIAL DATA:
Amount of support per award: Approximately $8,500 (CAN).

Total amount of support: Approximately $8,500 (CAN) available annually.

NO. MOST RECENT APPLICANTS: 300 for 2011-12 academic year.

NO. AWARDS: Generally 1.

APPLICATION INFO:
Applicants must submit completed application forms, all official transcripts and three letters of reference to the Canadian university from which they received their most recent degree, c/o Faculty of Graduate Studies.

Duration: Scholarships are tenable for one year.

Deadline: February 1.

*SPECIAL STIPULATIONS:
Award may not be accepted if total scholarship support, including the award, exceeds expected tuition expense plus $17,000 (CAN).

KNIGHTS OF COLUMBUS [1650]

P.O. Box 1670
New Haven, CT 06507-0901
(203) 752-4332
Fax: (203) 752-4103
Web Site: www.kofc.org/scholarships

AREAS OF INTEREST:
Educational support.

NAME(S) OF PROGRAMS:
- **Educational Trust Scholarships**
- **Bishop Charles P. Greco Graduate Fellowships**
- **John W. McDevitt (Fourth Degree) Scholarships**
- **Pro Deo and Pro Patria Scholarships**

TYPE:
Fellowships; Project/program grants; Scholarships. Scholarships and fellowships are awarded to members of The Knights of Columbus in good standing, a son or daughter of such a member or deceased member, or to a member of the Columbian Squires.

The Educational Trust provides scholarships to sons and daughters of members who died or became permanently and totally disabled while serving in the military during a period of conflict or who died as a result of criminal violence directed against them while performing duties of full-time law enforcement officers or full-time firemen. The awards are for undergraduate studies in a four-year program leading to a Bachelor's degree at a Catholic college and include the amount not covered by other financial aid for tuition up to $25,000 per year.

The Bishop Greco Graduate Fellowships are for full-time graduate study leading to a Master's degree in a program for classroom teachers of persons with intellectual disabilities.

The John W. McDevitt (Fourth Degree) Scholarships are awarded to students entering the freshman class of undergraduate study at a Catholic college or university in the U.S.

For the Pro Deo and Pro Patria Scholarships, students must be entering the freshman class in a college program leading to a Bachelor's degree. Scholarships are available at The Catholic University of America in Washington, DC and to students entering other Catholic colleges in the U.S.

PURPOSE:
To provide support for community activities, education, the elderly, poor, disabled and victims of disasters; to provide financial assistance to children of members in good standing.

ELIGIBILITY:
For Educational Trust Scholarships, applicants must be:
(1) Children of a member in good standing who, while serving in the military forces of his country in a combat zone, specifically designated as such by the Board of Directors, is killed by hostile action or wounded by hostile action resulting within two years thereof in permanent and total disability; an application must be filed within two years of the death or determination of total and permanent disability of the member or;
(2) Children of a member in good standing who, while in the lawful performance of his duties as a full-time law enforcement officer or full-time firefighter, died as the result of criminal violence directed at him; an application must be filed within two years of the date of the death of the member.
A candidate for benefits is required to submit documents to establish eligibility.

For Bishop Greco Graduate Fellowships, applicants must be enrolled in a graduate study program leading to a Master's degree in a program designed for the preparation of classroom teachers of persons with intellectual disabilities. Membership requirements as listed for the scholarship above also apply for this award.

For McDevitt (Fourth Degree) Scholarships, applicants must be members in good standing of the Knights of Columbus or the wife, widow, son or daughter of such a member or deceased member.

For Pro Deo and Pro Patria Scholarships, applicants must be students entering in the freshman class in a Catholic college program leading to a Bachelor's degree. An applicant must be a member in good standing of the Knights of Columbus or the son or daughter of such a member, a deceased member or a member in good standing of the Columbian Squires.

GEOG. RESTRICTIONS: United States.

FINANCIAL DATA:
Amount of support per award: Bishop Greco Graduate Fellowships: $1,000 maximum per year; Educational Trust Scholarships: Up to $25,000 per year; McDevitt (Fourth Degree) Scholarships: $1,500; Pro Deo and Pro Patria Scholarships: $1,500 per year.

APPLICATION INFO:
Application form required. Candidates are required to submit supporting documents to substantiate eligibility.

Duration: Pro Deo and Pro Patria and Educational Trust Scholarships: Up to four years. Greco Graduate Fellowship: Up to two years.

Deadline: May 1 for filing fellowship applications for the Bishop Greco Graduate Fellowships. March 1 for filing scholarship applications for the Pro Deo and Pro Patria Scholarships and McDevitt (Fourth Degree) Scholarships.

ADDRESS INQUIRIES TO:
Department of Scholarships
(See address above.)

*SPECIAL STIPULATIONS:
Candidates for Educational Trust Fund scholarships will be required to submit supporting documents to substantiate the claim.

THE KOSCIUSZKO FOUNDATION, INC. [1651]

15 East 65th Street
New York, NY 10065
(212) 734-2130
E-mail: addy@thekf.org
Web Site: www.thekf.org/scholarships/tuition/

FOUNDED: 1925

AREAS OF INTEREST:
Scholarships and grant support for Americans of Polish descent and to Americans whose

majors focus on Polish language, history and culture; funding for graduate-level studies in the U.S.

NAME(S) OF PROGRAMS:
- **The Kosciuszko Foundation Tuition Scholarship**

TYPE:
Scholarships. Offers funding to American citizens of Polish descent and to Polish citizens who have permanent residency status in the U.S. Scholarships are for Master's and Ph.D. students for full-time studies only. Undergraduate seniors may apply for a scholarship towards their first year of Master's-level studies. Americans (non-Polish descent) are eligible for graduate-level studies when majoring in Polish language, history or culture.

All majors are supported. However, the Kosciuszko Foundation has special funding allocated in the following areas:
law and engineering studies at DePaul University and nonpublic colleges and universities in the Chicagoland area and nonpublic Midwest colleges and universities (Illinois, Indiana, Iowa, Kansas, Michigan, Minnesota, Missouri, Nebraska, North Dakota, Ohio, South Dakota, and Wisconsin);
Bayonne, NJ residents;
residents of Connecticut, particularly Fairfield and New Haven counties; Amsterdam, NY, Chicopee, MA and New Hampshire and;
for violin and piano.

Contact Foundation for additional funding opportunities.

YEAR PROGRAM STARTED: 1950

PURPOSE:
To promote higher education of Americans of Polish descent and Polish studies.

LEGAL BASIS:
501(c)(3) not-for-profit organization which is engaged in educational and cultural relations between the U.S. and Poland.

ELIGIBILITY:
Applicants must:
(1) be U.S. citizens of Polish descent or;
(2) be Polish citizens who have legal permanent residency status in the U.S. or;
(3) be Americans of non-Polish descent who are pursuing Polish majors and;
(4) have a minimum grade point average of 3.0.

Scholarships are awarded on the basis of academic excellence and evidence of identification with the Polish-American community. Financial need is taken into consideration. Scholarships are for full-time graduate study in the U.S. and certain programs in Poland.

Within the parameters of the scholarship program are special opportunities for studies in journalism, nursing, teaching, business, piano performance, law, arts, social sciences and education.

GEOG. RESTRICTIONS: United States and Poland.

FINANCIAL DATA:
Funding for tuition and educational expenses such as books and fees associated with attendance at colleges and universities.

Amount of support per award: $1,000 to $7,000. Average: $3,100.

Total amount of support: $320,140 for the academic year 2015.

NO. MOST RECENT APPLICANTS: Over 100.

NO. AWARDS: 91.

APPLICATION INFO:
Applications are available online. Application materials include:
(1) application form;
(2) financial information form;
(3) statement of purpose;
(4) official transcripts of credit (three years of academic work);
(5) two letters of recommendation from professors or teachers discussing applicant's academic performance;
(6) copy of acceptance letter for Master's program of applicant's choice;
(7) proof of Polish descent and;
(8) two passport-size photos.

Completed applications must be accompanied by a nonrefundable $35 application fee. Faxed applications and supporting materials are not accepted. Applications posted to the Internet in October are available through the deadline date.

Duration: One academic year. Possible renewal for a second year upon reapplication.

Deadline: January 15. Notification in May. Funding for the following academic year.

PUBLICATIONS:
Guidelines; *KF Newsletter*; grants brochure; annual report.

IRS I.D.: 13-1628179

STAFF:
Dr. John S. Micgiel, President and Executive Director

ADDRESS INQUIRIES TO:
Tuition Scholarship Program
(See address above.)

*SPECIAL STIPULATIONS:
Scholarship checks are issued upon proof of full-time status.

THE KOSCIUSZKO FOUNDATION, INC. [1652]

15 East 65th Street
New York, NY 10065
(212) 734-2130 ext. 210
E-mail: addy@thekf.org
Web Site: www.thekf.org/kf/programs/study/wsips

AREAS OF INTEREST:
Strengthening of cultural and educational bonds between the U.S. and Poland through an exchange program to Poland for the purpose of Polish language and culture studies.

NAME(S) OF PROGRAMS:
- **Wisconsin Study in Poland (WSIP)**

TYPE:
Scholarships. The Wisconsin Study in Poland scholarship offers a four-week Polish language and culture program at the Jagiellonian University in Krakow during the summer session.

PURPOSE:
To enable Wisconsin residents of Polish descent the opportunity to pursue a short-term course of Polish language and culture studies abroad.

LEGAL BASIS:
501(c)(3) not-for-profit organization.

ELIGIBILITY:
Applicant must meet all requirements for the Summer Study Abroad Program. Applicant must be a Wisconsin resident of Polish descent. Consideration may also be given to nonresident Wisconsin students of Polish descent if they are attending Wisconsin college or university. Candidate must have a cumulative grade point average of 3.0 or higher.

Previous knowledge of the Polish language is not required.

FINANCIAL DATA:
Scholarship covers the cost of program fees, including tuition, course materials and textbooks, a shared room, three meals per day, and complementary programs such as sightseeing. Scholarship recipients will be responsible for their own transportation, health care coverage and all other costs.

NO. AWARDS: 2 for the year 2016.

APPLICATION INFO:
Student must complete the Summer Study Abroad online application form and submit the following supporting materials:
(1) a completed financial information form;
(2) three passport-size photos with name printed on the reverse side (electronic photos will be accepted);
(3) official transcript(s) for the past three years;
(4) academic letters of reference from two teachers or professors submitted on university/school letterhead. Letters may be sent by U.S. Post or e-mail to the address listed above;
(5) an essay or statement of purpose (two pages, double-spaced, printed on one side of page only) and;
(6) a $35 nonrefundable scholarship application fee.

Duration: Four weeks, to begin in July.

Deadline: Mid-April. E-mail notification in May.

PUBLICATIONS:
KF Newsletter; annual report.

IRS I.D.: 13-1628179

STAFF:
John S. Micgiel, President and Executive Director

ADDRESS INQUIRIES TO:
Addy Tymczyszyn, Coordinator
Wisconsin Study in Poland
(See telephone number and e-mail address above.)

*PLEASE NOTE:
Students who receive scholarship funding will be required to submit a $95 nonrefundable registration fee, as well as additional application materials.

MARCUS AND THERESA LEVIE EDUCATION FUND [1653]

JVS Chicago
216 West Jackson Boulevard, Suite 700
Chicago, IL 60606-6921
(312) 673-3444
Fax: (312) 553-5544
TTY: (312) 444-2877
E-mail: jvsscholarship@jvschicago.org
Web Site: www.jvschicago.org

FOUNDED: 1959

AREAS OF INTEREST:
Higher education for Jewish students in full-time academic programs in the helping professions, legally domiciled in the metropolitan Chicago (IL) area.

TYPE:
Awards/prizes; Scholarships. Awards to individuals for the academic year.

YEAR PROGRAM STARTED: 1959

PURPOSE:
To provide financial support to Jewish men and women for their full-time academic programs.

LEGAL BASIS:
Tax-exempt private foundation.

ELIGIBILITY:
Scholarships are awarded on the basis of financial need. Applicants must be full-time students of Jewish background, legally domiciled in the metropolitan Chicago area. Applicants must have demonstrated career promise. Assistance is available for the fields listed below, including but not limited to:
(1) the helping professions such as medicine, dentistry, social work, education, psychology, the rabbinate and noncorporate areas of law;
(2) mathematics, engineering and other sciences and;
(3) communications within the College of Media at the University of Illinois at Urbana-Champaign.

Additional requirements:
(1) undergraduates entering or who have entered the junior year in career-specific programs which require no postgraduate education for professional-level employment in one of the professional areas mentioned above or;
(2) students entering or who have entered a graduate or professional school in a helping profession described above or;
(3) students in a vocational training program with a specific educational goal in the helping professions.

Newcomers who are refugees or asylees are encouraged to apply. Citizenship is not a prerequisite.

FINANCIAL DATA:
Total amount of support: Approximately $400,000 per year.

CO-OP FUNDING PROGRAMS: Program is administered by the Jewish Vocational Service.

NO. MOST RECENT APPLICANTS: 150 for the year 2014.

NO. AWARDS: 89.

APPLICATION INFO:
Application submission must include application form, budget worksheet, personal and financial data, IRS Form 1040, proof of (Cook County) legal domicility, two reference letters, autobiography and official academic transcript. Applicants must be available for a personal interview at Jewish Vocational Service offices located throughout the Chicago metropolitan area prior to April 20.

Applications are available in the fall and can be downloaded from the Jewish Vocational Service web site. (Click on "Scholarship Services.").

Duration: One academic year. Recipients may reapply for renewal.

Deadline: February 1 for submission of applications.

OFFICERS:
Sally Yarberry, Scholarship Administrator

ADDRESS INQUIRIES TO:
Scholarship Administrator
(See address and phone number above.)

*SPECIAL STIPULATIONS:
All applicants must be available for a personal interview at the Jewish Vocational Service offices located throughout the Chicago metropolitan area.

LORAN SCHOLARS FOUNDATION [1654]

460 Richmond Street West, Suite 502
Toronto ON M5V 1Y1 Canada
(416) 646-2120
Fax: (416) 646-0846
E-mail: info@loranscholar.ca
Web Site: www.loranscholar.ca

FOUNDED: 1988

AREAS OF INTEREST:
Higher education.

NAME(S) OF PROGRAMS:
- **Loran Awards**

TYPE:
Scholarships. Grants for graduating high school students about to enter a university in Canada.

PURPOSE:
To identify and support talented students who show promise of leadership and a strong commitment to service in the community; to fund these citizens to study on Canadian campuses, to the benefit of their future and ours.

ELIGIBILITY:
Applicant must:
(1) be in the graduating year of uninterrupted full-time studies in high school or CEGEP. Exceptions may be considered for those who have undertaken a gap year for academic pursuits or community service-based activities;
(2) present a minimum cumulative average of 85% and;
(3) hold Canadian citizenship or permanent resident status.

GEOG. RESTRICTIONS: Canada.

FINANCIAL DATA:
Amount of support per award: Up to $100,000 for four years.

Total amount of support: $3,200,000 (CAN).

NO. AWARDS: 110 annually.

APPLICATION INFO:
Applications are available early September and can be completed online. Students should speak to their guidance counselor about their school's nomination process.

Duration: Up to four years.

Deadline: Varies.

ADDRESS INQUIRIES TO:
See e-mail address above.

*PLEASE NOTE:
Loran Award Finalist and Provincial Awards are tenable at any public university in Canada. Loran Awards are tenable at participating Canadian consortium universities only.

LOUISIANA DIVISION OF THE ARTS, DEPARTMENT OF CULTURE, RECREATION AND TOURISM

1051 North Third Street, Room 420
Baton Rouge, LA 70802
(225) 342-8200
Fax: (225) 342-8173
E-mail: arts@crt.state.la.us
Web Site: www.crt.state.la.us/arts

TYPE:
General operating grants; Technical assistance. Grants in a variety of programs are offered to arts organizations across the state.

General operating support grants are offered in three levels of operating support to nonprofit arts organizations.

See entry 454 for full listing.

MARINE CORPS SCHOLARSHIP FOUNDATION, INC. [1655]

909 North Washington Street
Suite 400
Alexandria, VA 22314
(703) 549-0060
Fax: (703) 549-9474
E-mail: scholarship@mcsf.org
Web Site: www.mcsf.org

FOUNDED: 1962

AREAS OF INTEREST:
Scholarships to children of Marines and children of veteran Marines.

TYPE:
Scholarships. Scholarships are for higher education (post-high school) college, trade or vocational school.

YEAR PROGRAM STARTED: 1962

PURPOSE:
To provide financial resources and the support of an extended community, ensuring that the children of Marines and eligible Navy Corpsmen have the opportunity to attend college and successfully achieve their goals.

LEGAL BASIS:
Nonprofit, tax-exempt corporation.

ELIGIBILITY:
Sons or daughters of Marines or children of veteran Marines. College or trade school. No graduate study.

Scholarships are for children of active duty, reserve, and honorably discharged Marines and Navy Corpsmen that serve with Marines. Applicants must be planning to attend, or already attending, an accredited college or vocational/technical institution, have a grade point average of at least 2.0, and pursuing their first degree or technical certificate. An income requirement must be met. Special funding is available for children of those who were wounded or killed in combat.

FINANCIAL DATA:
The Scholarship Foundation has provided over 33,000 scholarships valued at nearly $100,000,000 since 1962.

Amount of support per award: $1,500 to $10,000 per year; average $3,000.

Total amount of support: Over $6,800,000 for the 2015-16 academic year.

NO. MOST RECENT APPLICANTS: 2,643 for the 2015-16 academic year.

NO. AWARDS: 2,306 for the 2015-16 academic year.

APPLICATION INFO:
Application available online beginning January 1.

Duration: One year. Renewable for up to three years. Recipients must reapply.

Deadline: March 1.

PUBLICATIONS:
Annual report; guidelines; yearbook; trifold; newsletter.

IRS I.D.: 22-1905062

STAFF:
Steven D. Peterson, Chief Operating Officer
Jeanna Adams, Assistant Director, Scholarship Programs
Matthew Rosales, Scholarship Programs Coordinator

ADDRESS INQUIRIES TO:
Director of Scholarship Programs
(See address above.)

*SPECIAL STIPULATIONS:
Cannot violate civil or campus law.

THURGOOD MARSHALL COLLEGE FUND (TMCF) [1656]

1770 St. James Place
Suite 414
Houston, TX 77056
(202) 507-4851
Fax: (202) 448-1017
E-mail: scholarships@tmcf.org
Web Site: www.tmcf.org

FOUNDED: 1987

NAME(S) OF PROGRAMS:
- **TMCF Scholarships**

TYPE:
Scholarships. Scholarship for full-time students pursuing a degree at one of the 47 TMCF "member schools."

ELIGIBILITY:
Students must:
(1) have a minimum cumulative grade point average of 3.0 on a 4.0 scale;
(2) apply for financial aid using the Free Application for Federal Student Aid;
(3) attend one of the 47 TMCF member-schools (unless otherwise stated on the application);
(4) be a U.S. citizen or legal permanent resident with a valid permanent resident card or passport stamped;
(5) demonstrate leadership qualities and service experience and;
(6) be recommended by a faculty or staff member of one's current school.

Awards are merit-based.

GEOG. RESTRICTIONS: United States.

FINANCIAL DATA:
TMCF scholarships are restricted for payment of tuition, on-campus room and board, and books and fees.

Amount of support per award: Usually $6,200 split into two semesters: fall $3,100; spring $3,100.

Total amount of support: Varies.

NO. AWARDS: Nearly 500 scholarships per year.

APPLICATION INFO:
Apply online only.

Duration: Usually one academic year.

Deadline: Varies.

ADDRESS INQUIRIES TO:
Deshuandra Walker
Manager of Student Support Programs
E-mail: deshuandra.walker@tmcf.org

MARYLAND HIGHER EDUCATION COMMISSION [1657]

Office of Student Financial Assistance (OSFA)
6 North Liberty Street
Baltimore, MD 21201
(410) 767-3301
(410) 767-3300
(800) 974-0203 (toll-free)
Fax: (410) 332-0250; (410) 332-0252
TTY: (800) 735-2258
E-mail: osfamail.mhec@maryland.gov
Web Site: www.mhec.state.md.us

FOUNDED: 1961

NAME(S) OF PROGRAMS:
- **Maryland State Scholarships**

TYPE:
Grants-in-aid; Scholarships; Loan forgiveness programs. The Howard P. Rawlings Program of Educational Excellence Awards is the state's largest need-based program. It has two components: the Educational Assistance Grant and the Guaranteed Access Grant. The Educational Assistance Grant is targeted to low- to moderate-income families and is based on financial need (40% of calculated financial need for four-year institutions, 60% for community colleges). The Guaranteed Access Grant is for very low-income high school students and requires a 2.5 high school grade point average (100% of student need up to a maximum of $17,900).

The Part-Time Grant supports part-time, degree-seeking, undergraduate students.

The Graduate and Professional School Scholarship provides support to full-time and part-time graduate and professional students in nursing, pharmacy, dentistry, law, medicine, veterinary science, and social work.

Senatorial Scholarships: Each member of the state senate may award scholarships each year.

Delegate Scholarships: Each member of the House of Delegates may award scholarships to students attending approved Maryland postsecondary institutions.

Maryland also offers a number of career/occupational and unique population financial assistance programs.

LEGAL BASIS:
Government agency.

ELIGIBILITY:
Candidate must be a resident of the state and generally enrolled or intending to enroll in a college or university in Maryland.

GEOG. RESTRICTIONS: Maryland.

FINANCIAL DATA:
Amount of support per award: Educational Assistance Grant: $400 to $3,000; Guaranteed Access Grant: Up to $17,900; Part-Time Grant: Up to $2,000; Graduate and Professional School Scholarship: Up to $5,000; Senatorial Scholarships: $400 to $11,250 annually per member of the state senate; Delegate Scholarships: $200 minimum award per member of the House of Delegates.

Total amount of support: $108,962,935 for all aid programs (including loan repayment programs) for the 2014-15 award year. Educational Assistance Grant: $61,251,035; Guaranteed Access Grant: $18,253,550; Part-Time Grant: $5,035,853; Graduate and Professional School Scholarship: $1,165,665; Senatorial Scholarships: $7,335,721; Delegate Scholarships: $5,648,498.

APPLICATION INFO:
Use the Free Application for Federal Student Aid (FAFSA) or special program application.

Duration: Up to four years. Renewable.

Deadline: March 1 for state-administered, need-based aid program; other deadlines vary throughout the year.

PUBLICATIONS:
A Quick Guide to Cash for College and How to Get it; Student Guide to Higher Education and Financial Aid In Maryland; 6 Steps to Choosing the Right School.

ADDRESS INQUIRIES TO:
See e-mail address above.

MASSACHUSETTS MEDICAL SOCIETY (MMS) [1658]

860 Winter Street
Waltham Woods Corporate Center
Waltham, MA 02451-1411
(781) 893-4610
(800) 322-2303
Fax: (781) 893-8009
E-mail: info@massmed.org
Web Site: www.massmed.org

FOUNDED: 1954

NAME(S) OF PROGRAMS:
- **Massachusetts Medical Society International Health Studies Grant Program**
- **Massachusetts Medical Society (MMS) Annual Scholars Program**
- **MMS Medical Information Technology Awards**
- **MMS Student Section Community Service Grants**

TYPE:
Awards/prizes; Grants-in-aid; Research grants; Scholarships. Massachusetts Medical Society International Health Studies Grant Program: Grants to defray the costs of study abroad.

Massachusetts Medical Society (MMS) Annual Scholars Program: Awarded to four students from each of the four Massachusetts medical schools.

MMS Medical Information Technology Awards: Given annually to one medical student and one resident physician.

MMS Student Section Community Service Grants: Funding for each of two service projects per medical school chapter of the Section, per calendar year.

PURPOSE:
To advance medical knowledge; to develop and maintain the highest professional and ethical standards of medical practice and health care; to promote medical institutions formed on liberal principles for the health, benefit, and welfare of the citizens of the Commonwealth.

ELIGIBILITY:
Massachusetts Medical Society International Health Studies Grant Program: MMS medical student or resident; preference given to applicants planning a career serving underprivileged populations. Massachusetts Medical Society (MMS) Annual Scholars Program: MMS member; fourth-year medical students expected to graduate each year and enrolled in a Massachusetts medical school.

MMS Medical Information Technology Awards: MMS member; medical students, residents or fellows enrolled in one of the four Massachusetts Medical Schools or a Massachusetts hospital or training program. MMS Student Section Community Service Grants: Current medical student members of the MMS whose projects meet objectives in community and social service, public health activism and education or volunteer mentorship activities.

FINANCIAL DATA:
Amount of support per award: Massachusetts Medical Society International Health Studies Grant Program: Up to $2,000. Massachusetts Medical Society (MMS) Annual Scholars Program: $10,000. MMS Medical Information Technology Awards: $3,000 annually. MMS Student Section Community Service Grants: Up to $250.

NO. AWARDS: Massachusetts Medical Society International Health Studies Grant Program: 5 to 7. Massachusetts Medical Society (MMS) Annual Scholars Program: 16. MMS Medical Information Technology Awards: 1 medical student and 1 resident physician. MMS Student Section Community Service Grants: 2 service projects per medical school chapter of the Section, per calendar year.

APPLICATION INFO:
Application information is available on the web site.

Deadline: Massachusetts Medical Society International Health Studies Grant Program: September 15. Massachusetts Medical Society (MMS) Annual Scholars Program: January 13. MMS Medical Information Technology Awards: mid-November. MMS Student Section Community Service Grants: Accepted on a rolling deadline basis.

PUBLICATIONS:
Application guidelines.

ADDRESS INQUIRIES TO:
Linda Howard, Regional Manager
Massachusetts Medical Society (MMS)
(See address above.)

MMS International Health Studies Grant Program:
Jennifer Day, MMS and Alliance Charitable Foundation Director
Tel: (781) 434-7044
E-mail: jday@mms.org.

MMS Annual Scholars Program:
Applicant's Office of Student Affairs or
Thelma Tatten, Program Coordinator
MMS Department of Continuing Education and Certification
Tel: (781) 434-7305
E-mail: ttatten@mms.org

MMS Medical Information Technology Awards
Leon Q. Barzin, MMS Technical Program Portfolio Director
Tel: (800) 322-2303 ext. 7048
E-mail: lbarzin@mms.org

MMS Student Section Community Service Grants:
Colleen Hennessey, Academic Administrator
Tel: (781) 434-7315
E-mail: chennessey@mms.org

MASSACHUSETTS OFFICE OF STUDENT FINANCIAL ASSISTANCE [1659]

Office of Student Financial Assistance
454 Broadway, Suite 200
Revere, MA 02151
(617) 391-6070
Fax: (617) 727-0667
E-mail: cmccurdy@osfa.mass.edu
osfa@osfa.mass.edu
Web Site: www.osfa.mass.edu

FOUNDED: 1980

AREAS OF INTEREST:
Financial assistance to Massachusetts students.

NAME(S) OF PROGRAMS:
- **Massachusetts Cash Grant**
- **Massachusetts Gilbert Matching Student Grant Program**
- **MASSGrants**

TYPE:
Grants-in-aid. Massachusetts Cash Grant is intended to assist needy students in meeting institutionally held charges such as mandatory fees and non-state-supported tuition. Designed as an offset of the Tuition Waiver Program, these grants provide financial support to those individuals who would otherwise be denied the opportunity for higher education.

Massachusetts Gilbert Matching Student Grant Program is based on financial need and awarded to Massachusetts residents enrolled in nonprofit private colleges.

MASSGrants are state grants in all undergraduate fields, based solely on financial need, renewable for up to four years of undergraduate study. State grants must be used at accredited institutions in Massachusetts and reciprocal states.

PURPOSE:
To assist those who are unable to meet the costs of postsecondary education.

ELIGIBILITY:
For Massachusetts Cash Grant, applicant must be a permanent legal resident of Massachusetts for one year prior to the academic year for which the grant is awarded, be a U.S. citizen or eligible noncitizen, and be in compliance with applicable laws. For Massachusetts Gilbert Matching Student Grant Program, applicants must be permanent Massachusetts residents for at least one year, attending full-time in Massachusetts. MASSGrant applicants may attend school in Massachusetts, Pennsylvania, Vermont or Washington, DC.

GEOG. RESTRICTIONS: Primarily Massachusetts.

FINANCIAL DATA:
Amount of support per award: Massachusetts Cash Grant: Varies; Massachusetts Gilbert Matching Student Grant Program: $200 to $2,500 per academic year; MASSGrant: Varies.

Total amount of support: Massachusetts Cash Grant: $26,391,254; Massachusetts Gilbert Matching Student Grant Program: $16,500,800; MASSGrant: $41,534,205.

APPLICATION INFO:
Applicants must file the Free Application for Federal Student Aid (FAFSA) after January 1.

Deadline: Massachusetts Cash Grant: May 1. Massachusetts Gilbert Matching Student Grant Program is determined by college. MASSGrant: FAFSA by May 1. FAFSA must be completed by May 1 each year for the MASSGrant. Students must meet the FAFSA priority date for Massachusetts Cash Grant, Massachusetts Gilbert Matching Student Grant Program and other state financial aid programs that are awarded directly by the college.

PUBLICATIONS:
Guidelines.

ADDRESS INQUIRIES TO:
Clantha McCurdy
Senior Deputy Commissioner
(See address above.)

MISSOURI DEPARTMENT OF HIGHER EDUCATION (MDHE) [1660]

P.O. Box 1469
Jefferson City, MO 65102-1469
(573) 751-2361
(800) 473-6757 option 4
Fax: (573) 751-6635
E-mail: info@dhe.mo.gov
Web Site: www.dhe.mo.gov

FOUNDED: 1986

NAME(S) OF PROGRAMS:
- **Missouri Higher Education Academic Scholarship Program ("Bright Flight")**

TYPE:
Scholarships. Provides undergraduate student financial aid to qualified Missouri students who wish to attend qualified Missouri institutions of higher education, both public and private.

PURPOSE:
To enable qualified full-time students to attend a participating postsecondary institution (public and private).

LEGAL BASIS:
RSMO Supp. 173.250. Government agency.

ELIGIBILITY:
Applicant must be a resident of Missouri and a U.S. citizen or permanent resident and enrolled in an eligible Missouri institution, be a high school senior who plans to enroll as a first-time, full-time student and have a composite score on the American College Testing Program (ACT) or the Scholastic Aptitude Test (SAT) in the top five percent of all Missouri students taking the tests.

Student must take the ACT or SAT assessment and receive the required test score on or before the June test date of their senior year. GED and home-schooled students may also qualify. The Missouri Department of Higher Education will obtain the ACT or SAT assessment records, whichever the student has taken, and will notify students, high schools and postsecondary institutions of scholarship awards. Scholarships may not be used for theology for divinity studies.

GEOG. RESTRICTIONS: Missouri.

FINANCIAL DATA:
Amount of support per award: Statutory maximum award for an academic year is $3,000 for the top three percent and $1,000 for the fourth/fifth percentile.

Total amount of support: $17,972,366 for the 2014-15 academic year.

NO. AWARDS: 6,283 awards for the 2014-15 academic year.

APPLICATION INFO:
Contact the Department.

Duration: One academic year. Renewable annually until students have obtained a Baccalaureate degree or completed a total of 10 semesters.

Deadline: Student applicant has to achieve the qualified score by the June test date.

ADDRESS INQUIRIES TO:
Information Center
(See address above.)

MISSOURI DEPARTMENT OF HIGHER EDUCATION (MDHE) [1661]

P.O. Box 1469
Jefferson City, MO 65102-1469
(573) 751-2361
(800) 473-6757 option 4
Fax: (573) 751-6635
E-mail: info@dhe.mo.gov
Web Site: www.dhe.mo.gov

FOUNDED: 1986

NAME(S) OF PROGRAMS:

- **Access Missouri Financial Assistance Program**

TYPE:
Grants-in-aid. Undergraduate student financial aid to qualified Missouri students who wish to attend qualified Missouri institutions of higher education, both public and private.

YEAR PROGRAM STARTED: 2007

PURPOSE:
To enable full-time students to attend a participating postsecondary institution (public and private).

LEGAL BASIS:
Section 173.1101-173.1107, RSMo. Government agency.

ELIGIBILITY:
Initially, applicants must meet the following requirements:
(1) have a FAFSA on file by April 1;
(2) have any FAFSA corrections made by July 31 (if one is eligible, school choices may be added until September 30 by contacting the MDHE);
(3) be a U.S. citizen or permanent resident and a Missouri resident;
(4) be an undergraduate student enrolled full-time at a participating Missouri school (students with documented disabilities who are enrolled in at least six credit hours may be considered to be enrolled full-time);
(5) have an Expected Family Contribution (EFC) of $12,000 or less;
(6) not be pursuing a degree or certificate in theology or divinity and;
(7) not have received the first Bachelor's degree, completed the required hours for a Bachelor's degree, or completed 150 semester credit hours.

Renewal students must continue to meet the eligibility requirements for initial students and additionally:
(1) continue to meet the eligibility requirements for initial students;
(2) maintain a minimum cumulative grade point average of 2.5 and otherwise maintain satisfactory academic progress as defined by the applicant's school (if this is the first academic year in which one has received an Access Missouri payment, this requirement does not apply) and;
(3) not have received an Access Missouri award for a maximum of five semesters at a two-year school or 10 semesters at any combination of two-year or four-year schools, whichever occurs first.
If Charles Gallagher or Missouri College Guarantee awardee in past semesters, those semesters are counted in the 10-semester limit, along with any semester in which the applicant has received an Access Missouri award.

GEOG. RESTRICTIONS: Missouri.

FINANCIAL DATA:
Amount of support per award: Award amounts are based on the type of school one is attending when award is received. If applicant transfers to a different school, his or her award amount may change based on the type of school to which he or she transfers. Public two-year: $300 to $1,300. Public four-year and State Technical College of Missouri: $1,500 to $2,850. Private: $1,500 to $2,850. (Note: Maximum award amounts may be less than these figures; it depends on the amount of funding that is available for the program.)

Total amount of support: Varies; $59,200,000 for the 2014-15 academic year.

NO. AWARDS: 51,367 for the 2014-15 academic year.

APPLICATION INFO:
Contact the Department or consult the web site.

Duration: One academic year. Renewable.

Deadline: FAFSA on file by April 1.

ADDRESS INQUIRIES TO:
Information Center
(See address above.)

NATIONAL FEDERATION OF THE BLIND

NFB Scholarship Program
200 East Wells Street at Jernigan Place
Baltimore, MD 21230
(410) 659-9314 ext. 2415
E-mail: scholarships@nfb.org
Web Site: www.nfb.org/scholarships

TYPE:
Scholarships. Awarded on the basis of academic excellence, service to the community and leadership. Provides a one-time grant plus a continuing program of mentors and seminars for blind college students.

See entry 981 for full listing.

NATIONAL INSTITUTE FOR LABOR RELATIONS RESEARCH [1662]

5211 Port Royal Road
Suite 510
Springfield, VA 22151
(703) 321-9606 ext. 2231
Fax: (703) 321-7143
E-mail: clj@nrtw.org
Web Site: www.nilrr.org

FOUNDED: 1975

AREAS OF INTEREST:
Organization of public opposition to compulsory unionism in the education community.

NAME(S) OF PROGRAMS:

- **Applegate/Jackson Parks Future Teacher Scholarship**

TYPE:
Scholarships. Scholarship awarded annually to the education student who exemplifies dedication to principle and high professional standards.

YEAR PROGRAM STARTED: 1989

PURPOSE:
To promote awareness of compulsory unionism.

LEGAL BASIS:
Nonprofit 501(c)(3) organization.

ELIGIBILITY:
Applicants are limited to undergraduates and graduate students majoring in education in institutions of higher learning throughout the U.S. Applicants who will be considered must demonstrate potential for successful completion of educational requirements in a college or university Department of Education program and the potential of successful application for a teaching license and demonstrate, by means of a written essay, an understanding of the individual freedom issue as it applies to the problem of compulsory unionism in the education community.

GEOG. RESTRICTIONS: United States.

FINANCIAL DATA:
Amount of support per award: $1,000 per scholarship.

Total amount of support: $1,000.

NO. MOST RECENT APPLICANTS: Approximately 212.

NO. AWARDS: 1.

APPLICATION INFO:
Applications may be submitted electronically. A total application will consist of a completed application form and a typewritten essay of approximately 500 words clearly demonstrating an interest in and a knowledge of the Right to Work principle as it applies to educators. All applicants will be requested to submit an official copy of his or her most recent transcript of grades.

Duration: One year. Nonrenewable.

Deadline: Applications must be postmarked on or by December 31 of calendar year.

ADDRESS INQUIRIES TO:
Cathy Jones, Scholarship Administrator
(See address above.)

*SPECIAL STIPULATIONS:
Applicant must be an education major attending college or have been admitted to an institution of higher learning in the U.S.

THE NATIONAL ITALIAN AMERICAN FOUNDATION [1663]

1860 19th Street, N.W.
Washington, DC 20009-5501
(202) 939-3116
Fax: (202) 483-2618
E-mail: scholarships@niaf.org
Web Site: www.niaf.org/scholarships

NAME(S) OF PROGRAMS:

- **NIAF Scholarship Program**

TYPE:
Scholarships. The National Italian American Foundation (NIAF) will award scholarships and grants to outstanding students for use during the following academic year. The awards will be made on the basis of academic merit and divided between two groups of students.

PURPOSE:
To assist Italian American students or those interested in Italian studies.

ELIGIBILITY:
Italian Americans studying any field, or students of any ethnic background studying Italian or Italian studies.

Italian American students who demonstrate outstanding potential and high academic achievements. The area of study is open.

Students from any ethnic background majoring or minoring in Italian language, Italian studies, Italian American studies or a related field, who demonstrate outstanding potential and high academic achievements.

GEOG. RESTRICTIONS: United States.

FINANCIAL DATA:
Each scholarship award can only cover tuition and university-provided room and board. Scholarship monies not used during one academic year are not transferable to the following academic year.

Amount of support per award: $2,000 to $10,000.

Total amount of support: Varies.

APPLICATION INFO:
In order to be complete, an application must include the following:
(1) completed student application submitted online;
(2) Teacher Evaluation Form submitted online;
(3) an official school transcript submitted by mail and;
(4) FAFSA Financial Aid Form submitted by mail (optional).

Duration: One academic year.

Deadline: March 1.

PUBLICATIONS:
Scholarship brochure.

ADDRESS INQUIRIES TO:
See e-mail address above.

NATIONAL JEWISH COMMITTEE ON SCOUTING [1664]

1325 West Walnut Hill Lane, SUM 342
Irving, TX 75015
(972) 580-2425
Fax: (972) 580-2535
E-mail: gene.butler@scouting.org
Web Site: www.jewishscouting.org

NAME(S) OF PROGRAMS:
- **Rick Arkans Eagle Scout Scholarship**
- **Chester M. Vernon Memorial Eagle Scout Scholarship**
- **Frank L. Weil Memorial Eagle Scout Scholarship**

TYPE:
Scholarships.

PURPOSE:
To promote Boy Scouting among Jewish youth; to help Jewish institutions and local council Jewish committees to provide Scouting opportunities for Jewish youth; to promote Jewish values in Scouting.

ELIGIBILITY:
Applicants must:
(1) be a registered, active member of a Boy Scout troop, Varsity Scout team, or Venturing crew;
(2) have received the Eagle Scout Award;
(3) be an active member of a synagogue and must have received the Ner Tamid or Etz Chaim religious emblem;
(4) have demonstrated practical citizenship in his synagogue, school, Scouting unit, and community and;
(5) be enrolled in an accredited high school and in his final year at the time of selection, except Scouts whose Eagle Scout boards of review are held the same year of their high school graduation may apply in that calendar year. They may receive a scholarship one time only.

Applicants for Rick Arkans and Chester M. Vernon Memorial Eagle Scout Scholarships must also demonstrate financial need.

GEOG. RESTRICTIONS: United States.

FINANCIAL DATA:
Amount of support per award: Rick Arkans Eagle Scout Scholarship: $1,000; Chester M. Vernon Memorial Eagle Scout Scholarship: $1,000 per year for four years; Frank L. Weil Memorial Eagle Scout Scholarship: $1,000 first place award and two $500 second place awards.

NO. AWARDS: 6.

APPLICATION INFO:
Applicants for the Arkans and Vernon Scholarships must submit a copy of the Free Application for Federal Student Assistance (FAFSA).

All sections of the scholarship application should be completed with as much information as possible. However, except for the required letter of recommendation (and FAFSA), no additional pages may be attached.

Duration: One year. Chester M. Vernon Memorial Eagle Scout Scholarship: Up to four years.

Deadline: Application submitted no later than February 28. Announcements by June 1.

ADDRESS INQUIRIES TO:
Gene Butler, Staff Advisor
(See address above.)

NATIONAL SOCIETY DAUGHTERS OF THE AMERICAN REVOLUTION [1665]

1776 D Street, N.W.
Washington, DC 20006-5303
(202) 879-3263
Fax: (202) 879-3348
E-mail: scholarships@dar.org
Web Site: www.dar.org

FOUNDED: 1890

AREAS OF INTEREST:
Furthering the education of Native Americans.

NAME(S) OF PROGRAMS:
- **American Indian Scholarship**

TYPE:
Scholarships. Intended to help Native American college/university and technical school students at the undergraduate or graduate level.

PURPOSE:
To provide scholarship assistance to Native American students of any age or tribe, in any state, striving to get an education.

ELIGIBILITY:
Applicants must:
(1) be Native Americans (proof required by letter or proof papers) in financial need;
(2) be U.S. citizens/residents and;
(3) have a grade point average of 3.25 or higher.

Graduate students are eligible; however, undergraduate students are given preference.

GEOG. RESTRICTIONS: United States.

FINANCIAL DATA:
Amount of support per award: $4,000.

Total amount of support: Varies.

NO. AWARDS: Up to 5.

APPLICATION INFO:
No phone or fax inquiries. Application may be made online.

Duration: One-time award.

Deadline: February 15.

NATIONAL SOCIETY DAUGHTERS OF THE AMERICAN REVOLUTION [1666]

1776 D Street, N.W.
Washington, DC 20006-5303
(202) 879-3263
Fax: (202) 879-3348
E-mail: scholarships@dar.org
Web Site: www.dar.org

FOUNDED: 1890

AREAS OF INTEREST:
Furthering the education of Native Americans.

NAME(S) OF PROGRAMS:
- **Frances Crawford Marvin American Indian Scholarship**

TYPE:
Scholarships. Intended to help Native American students enrolled full-time at a two- or four-year college or university.

PURPOSE:
To provide scholarship assistance to Native American students.

ELIGIBILITY:
Applicants must:
(1) be enrolled full-time at a two- or four-year college or university;
(2) be Native Americans (proof required by letter or proof papers);
(3) be U.S. citizens/residents;
(4) demonstrate financial need and academic achievement and;
(5) have a grade point average of 3.25 or higher.

A recipient may reapply and be considered along with members of the applicant pool.

GEOG. RESTRICTIONS: United States.

FINANCIAL DATA:
Amount of support per award: Varies.

NO. AWARDS: 1.

APPLICATION INFO:
No phone or fax inquiries. Application may be made online.

Duration: Renewable upon reapplication.

Deadline: February 15.

NATIONAL SOCIETY OF ACCOUNTANTS SCHOLARSHIP FOUNDATION [1667]

1330 Braddock Place
Suite 540
Alexandria, VA 22314
(703) 549-6400
(800) 966-6679
Fax: (703) 549-2984
E-mail: members@nsacct.org
Web Site: www.nsacct.org

AREAS OF INTEREST:
Accounting.

NAME(S) OF PROGRAMS:
- **The Stanley H. Stearman Award**

TYPE:
Scholarships.

PURPOSE:
To provide financial encouragement to students who select accounting as a career.

LEGAL BASIS:
501(c)(3) charitable organization.

ELIGIBILITY:
Must be an undergraduate accounting major who is a U.S. or Canadian citizen that attends a U.S.-accredited school and maintains a "B" or better overall grade point average. Also, must be the spouse, son, daughter, grandchild, niece, nephew, daughter-in-law or son-in-law of an active or retired NSA living or deceased member. The member must have held membership for at least one year prior to the annual distribution of applications in October.

GEOG. RESTRICTIONS: United States.

FINANCIAL DATA:
Amount of support per award: $2,000 per year.

NO. AWARDS: 1.

APPLICATION INFO:
Duration: Not to exceed three years. This renewable award may extend through graduate studies.

Deadline: March 31 (postmark).

NATIONAL SOCIETY OF BLACK ENGINEERS [1668]

205 Daingerfield Road
Alexandria, VA 22314
(703) 549-2207
Fax: (703) 683-5312
E-mail: scholarships@nsbe.org
Web Site: www.nsbe.org

FOUNDED: 1975

AREAS OF INTEREST:
All areas of engineering.

TYPE:
Awards/prizes; Scholarships. The Society offers a variety of NSBE and corporate-sponsored scholarship and award opportunities to its precollege, collegiate undergraduate and graduate student members as well as technical professional members.

PURPOSE:
To increase the number of culturally responsible Black engineers who excel academically, succeed professionally and positively impact the community.

ELIGIBILITY:
For scholarships, applicant must be an active, paid NSBE member.

FINANCIAL DATA:
Amount of support per award: $500 to $10,000.

Total amount of support: Approximately $400,000 given annually in scholarships.

NO. AWARDS: Approximately 250 scholarships annually.

APPLICATION INFO:
Application information is available on the web site. Application must be submitted online.

Duration: One year. Nonrenewable.

Deadline: Applications open in April with a deadline of June 30 and August with a deadline of December 31.

*SPECIAL STIPULATIONS:
Each scholarship recipient cannot be awarded more than two scholarships in a given program year. Members that apply for more than one scholarship that has an internship requirement must rank acceptance of scholarship for awarding, if selected as a recipient. (A member cannot accept both internships for a given time period; thus he or she must decide prior to selection which scholarship/internship they would want to accept in priority order.)

NATSO FOUNDATION [1669]

1330 Braddock Place
Suite 501
Alexandria, VA 22314
(703) 549-2100
Fax: (703) 684-4525
E-mail: foundation@natso.com
Web Site: www.natso.com

FOUNDED: 1989

AREAS OF INTEREST:
Research, scholarships and public outreach.

NAME(S) OF PROGRAMS:
- **Bill Moon Scholarships**

TYPE:
Scholarships.

PURPOSE:
To aid travel plaza employees and their dependents with educational expenses.

ELIGIBILITY:
Must be an employee or a dependent of an employee of a travel plaza facility.

FINANCIAL DATA:
Amount of support per award: $5,000.

Total amount of support: Varies.

NO. MOST RECENT APPLICANTS: 30.

NO. AWARDS: 5.

APPLICATION INFO:
Must submit application including transcript, essay, letter(s) of recommendation, and demonstration of need.

Duration: One semester.

Deadline: Mid-May.

NBCC FOUNDATION, INC. [1670]

3 Terrace Way
Greensboro, NC 27403
(336) 232-0376
Fax: (336) 232-0010
E-mail: foundation@nbcc.org
Web Site: www.nbccf.org

FOUNDED: 2005

AREAS OF INTEREST:
Philanthropy, mental health care, professional counseling, credentialing, scholarships and grant funding.

NAME(S) OF PROGRAMS:
- **ACS Training Award**
- **BCC Training Award**
- **CCE Professional Development Award**
- **Doctoral Minority Fellowship**
- **GCDF Scholarship**
- **Master's Youth Addictions Minority Fellowship**
- **Master's Youth Minority Fellowship**
- **NBCC Foundation Military Scholarship**
- **NBCC Foundation Rural Scholarship**

TYPE:
Fellowships; Scholarships. Academic scholarships for individuals pursuing a graduate-level degree in professional counseling.

YEAR PROGRAM STARTED: 2009

PURPOSE:
To increase the availability of counselors in underserved areas, with the current priority areas of minority, rural and military communities. Military Scholarship: To increase the number of counselors available to serve active duty service members and veterans. Minority Fellowship: To increase counseling resources available to underserved minority populations. Rural Scholarship: To increase access to needed counseling services in remote areas.

ELIGIBILITY:
For the ACS Training Award, the applicant must:
(1) currently hold the NCC certification maintained with no ethical holds or missed payments for a minimum of one year;
(2) have extensive clinical experience in providing mental health or substance abuse counseling services and;
(3) commit to applying for the ACS credential within one year of the award.

For the BCC Training Award, the applicant must:
(1) not be currently or previously certified as a BCC;
(2) commit to applying for the BCC and;
(3) demonstrate exceptional coaching potential through one or more of the following: having access to the population in need of coaching or working in a setting conducive to coaching; having a background in leadership; and holding or pursuing a degree from a relevant program.

For the CCE Professional Development Award, applicant must:
(1) currently hold a CCE credential maintained in good standing for a minimum of one year and;
(2) promote their CCE credential or contribute to the related field through one or more of the following: providing credential-related training for others; bringing programs that promote the credential to their campus or organization; delivering a presentation at a relevant conference; conducting relevant research; writing for a relevant publication; holding leadership positions in relevant groups or associations; and mentoring another who is pursuing the credential.

For the Doctoral Minority Fellowship, the applicant must:
(1) be a U.S. citizen or have permanent resident status;

(2) not receive any other federal funds (except for federal loans) or work for a federal agency;
(3) must currently hold the National Certified Counselor (NCC) certification and be in good standing or document all of the following: a full state license as a professional counselor; a passing score on the National Counselor Examination for Licensure and Certification (NCE) or the National Clinical Mental Health Counseling Examination (NCMHCE); and a commitment to obtain the NCC certification within three months if awarded a fellowship;
(4) be enrolled full-time and be in good standing in a CACREP-accredited, doctoral-level counseling program;
(5) have demonstrated knowledge and experience with racially and ethnically diverse populations and;
(6) commit to provide mental health and substance abuse services to underserved minority populations in the private nonprofit and public sectors through direct practice or the training of direct practitioners.
African Americans, Alaska Natives, American Indians, Asian Americans, Hispanics/Latinos, Native Hawaiians and Pacific Islanders are especially encouraged to apply.

For the GCDF Scholarship, the applicant must:
(1) (if a U.S. applicant) hold an active GCDF credential in good standing and be enrolled in a Master's-level program accredited by the Council for Accreditation of Counseling & Related Educational Programs (CACREP);
(2) (if an international applicant) either hold an active GCDF credential in good standing and be enrolled in an advanced education program in counseling or be a student currently enrolled in both a GCDF training program and a post-Bachelor's counseling program, as appropriate to their country and;
(3) commit to providing career counseling services for two years.

For the Master's Youth Addictions Minority Fellowship, the applicant must:
(1) be a U.S. citizen or have permanent resident status;
(2) not receive any other federal funds (except for federal student loans) or work for a federal agency;
(3) be entering their last year of study in the upcoming fall academic year;
(4) be enrolled full-time in either an accredited addictions counseling Master's program or a CACREP-accredited Master's program with a concentration in addictions counseling;
(5) demonstrate knowledge of and experience with racially and ethnically diverse populations;
(6) commit to applying for the National Certified Counselor (NCC) certification prior to graduation and to completing the application process;
(7) commit to providing addictions counseling services to underserved minority transition-age youth (16 to 25) populations for two years.
African Americans, Alaska Natives, American Indians, Asian Americans, Hispanics/Latinos, Native Hawaiians and Pacific Islanders are especially encouraged to apply.

For the Master's Youth Minority Fellowship, the applicant must:
(1) be a U.S. citizen or have permanent resident status;
(2) not receive any other federal funds (except for federal student loans) or work for a federal agency;
(3) be enrolled full-time in a CACREP-accredited counseling Master's program;
(4) must demonstrate knowledge of and experience with racially and ethnically diverse populations;
(5) must commit to applying for the National Certified Counselor (NCC) certification prior to graduation and to completing the application process and;
(6) must commit to providing mental health services to underserved minority transition-age youth (16 to 25) populations for two years.
African Americans, Alaska Natives, American Indians, Asian Americans, Hispanics/Latinos, Native Hawaiians and Pacific Islanders are especially encouraged to apply.

For the Military Scholarship, the applicant must:
(1) be enrolled full-time in a CACREP-accredited counseling Master's program;
(2) be former or current active duty U.S. military service members or spouses of a military service member whose service was within the past five years; veterans must have served in the military within the past five years and have received an honorable discharge;
(3) commit to applying for the National Certified Counselor (NCC) certification prior to graduation and to completing the application process and;
(4) commit to providing mental health services to service members and/or veterans for at least two years.

For the Rural Scholarship, the applicant must:
(1) be enrolled full-time in a CACREP-accredited counseling Master's program;
(2) reside in a rural area as defined by the Health Resources and Services Administration (HRSA);
(3) commit to applying for the National Certified Counselor (NCC) certification prior to graduation and to completing the application process and;
(4) commit to providing mental health services in a rural area for at least two years.

FINANCIAL DATA:
Awards go directly to recipients for any expenses associated with educational pursuit.

Amount of support per award: ACS Training Award: $500. BCC Training Award: Up to $3,000. CCE Professional Development Award: $500. Doctoral Minority Fellowship: Up to $20,000. GCDF Scholarship: $5,000. Master's Youth Addictions Minority Fellowship: Up to $11,000. Master's Youth Minority Fellowship: Up to $8,000. Military and Rural Scholarships: $5,000 (subject to change upon annual review).

APPLICATION INFO:
Application information is available on the web site.

Duration: One-time scholarship award. Not renewable.

Deadline: Varies from year to year.

ADDRESS INQUIRIES TO:
Program Coordinator
(See address above.)

NEBRASKA'S COORDINATING COMMISSION FOR POSTSECONDARY EDUCATION [1671]

140 North 8th Street, Suite 300
Lincoln, NE 68508
(402) 471-2847
Fax: (402) 471-2886
E-mail: Ritchie.Morrow@nebraska.gov
Web Site: www.ccpe.nebraska.gov

FOUNDED: 1991

AREAS OF INTEREST:
Higher education in Nebraska.

NAME(S) OF PROGRAMS:
- **Nebraska Opportunity Grant**

TYPE:
Scholarships. Nebraska Opportunity Grant is a need-based aid program to assist Nebraska students working on an undergraduate degree.

ELIGIBILITY:
Applicant must be a Nebraska resident who has not earned a Bachelor's, Master's or professional degree. He or she must complete Free Application for Federal Student Aid (FAFSA) and have an Expected Family Contribution (EFC) equal to or less than the yearly maximum.

GEOG. RESTRICTIONS: Nebraska.

FINANCIAL DATA:
Amount of support per award: Varies.

APPLICATION INFO:
Must complete the FAFSA. Institutions may have additional application requirements.

Duration: Up to one academic year. Renewable.

Deadline: Applications are accepted on a rolling basis.

ADDRESS INQUIRIES TO:
J. Ritchie Morrow, M.S.Ed.
Financial Aid Officer
Nebraska's Coordinating Commission for Postsecondary Education
P.O. Box 95005
Lincoln, NE 68509-5005
(See phone number above.)

NEED

The Law and Finance Building
429 Fourth Avenue, 20th Floor
Pittsburgh, PA 15219
(412) 566-2760
Fax: (412) 471-6643
E-mail: info@needld.org
Web Site: www.needld.org

TYPE:
Internships; Matching gifts; Scholarships. Supplemental grants for postsecondary education at colleges and business, trade and technical schools.

See entry 1013 for full listing.

NEW JERSEY DEPARTMENT OF MILITARY AND VETERANS AFFAIRS [1672]

DVS-VBB
P.O. Box 340
Trenton, NJ 08625-0340
(609) 530-6854
Fax: (609) 530-6970
E-mail: patty.richter@dmava.nj.gov
Web Site: www.state.nj.us/military

FOUNDED: 1959

AREAS OF INTEREST:
State financial assistance for postsecondary students.

NAME(S) OF PROGRAMS:
- **Veterans Tuition Credit Program (VTCP)**

TYPE:
Grants-in-aid. Tuition assistance grant for attendance at any eligible undergraduate, graduate or vocational institution in the U.S.

YEAR PROGRAM STARTED: 1977

PURPOSE:
To provide tuition assistance to U.S. veterans of the Armed Forces of the U.S. who served on active duty between December 31, 1960 and May 7, 1975 who were, or are, eligible for federal veterans' educational assistance (G.I. Bill).

LEGAL BASIS:
Entitlement.

ELIGIBILITY:
Applicant must be a veteran of the armed forces of the U.S. who is or was eligible for veterans educational assistance pursuant to federal law and served on active duty in the armed forces of the U.S. between December 31, 1960 and May 7, 1975. Applicant must have been a legal New Jersey resident at the time of induction into the armed forces, or at the time of discharge from active duty or for at least one year prior to the time of application, excluding the time spent in active duty. If a veteran was not a New Jersey resident at time of induction or separation, veteran must provide documentation reflecting residency – copy of NJ Income Tax Return, letter from postmaster, home mortgage or apartment lease. Applicant must be currently enrolled in an approved state approving agency course of study at any eligible academic, professional or vocational institution in the U.S.

GEOG. RESTRICTIONS: New Jersey.

FINANCIAL DATA:
Amount of support per award: Eligible veterans may receive a maximum award of $400 a year for full-time attendance or $200 a year for half-time attendance as provided by regulations and available appropriations.

NO. MOST RECENT APPLICANTS: 17.

NO. AWARDS: Based upon appropriations.

APPLICATION INFO:
Applications are available at campus Veterans Affairs offices or by calling the New Jersey Department of Military and Veterans Information Number, Tel: (888) 865-8387, available from any location in New Jersey, Monday through Friday, 8:30 A.M. to 4:30 P.M.

Duration: Eligible veterans may receive up to four academic years of payment.

Deadline: October 1 for fall and spring terms. March 1 for spring term only.

OFFICERS:
Carl Lang, Director, Fiscal Operations

ADDRESS INQUIRIES TO:
Patricia Richter, Bureau Chief, VBB
(See address above.)

NEW JERSEY DEPARTMENT OF MILITARY AND VETERANS AFFAIRS [1673]

DVS-VBB
P.O. Box 340
Trenton, NJ 08625-0340
(609) 530-6854
Fax: (609) 530-6970
E-mail: patty.richter@dmava.nj.gov
Web Site: www.state.nj.us/military

FOUNDED: 1959

AREAS OF INTEREST:
State financial assistance for college students, 16 to 21 years of age.

NAME(S) OF PROGRAMS:
- **Prisoner of War/Missing in Action (POW/MIA) Program**

TYPE:
Grants-in-aid; Scholarships.

YEAR PROGRAM STARTED: 1978

LEGAL BASIS:
Entitlement.

ELIGIBILITY:
Applicants must be dependent children (any child born before, during or after the period of time its parent was a POW/MIA) of military service personnel who were officially declared "Prisoner of War" or "Person Missing in Action" after January 1, 1960. The POW or MIA must have been a resident of New Jersey at the time he or she entered the Armed Forces of the U.S. or whose official residence is New Jersey.

GEOG. RESTRICTIONS: New Jersey.

FINANCIAL DATA:
Amount of support per award: Full tuition costs will be paid on behalf of the eligible dependent to any New Jersey public or independent college or university upon certification of full-time enrollment.

APPLICATION INFO:
Applications are available by contacting the New Jersey Department of Military and Veterans Affairs, Veterans Service Office, located in Mercer County.

Deadline: October 1 for fall and spring term benefits. March 1 for spring term benefits only.

OFFICERS:
Carl Lang, Director, Fiscal Operations

ADDRESS INQUIRIES TO:
Patricia Richter, Bureau Chief, VBB
(See address above.)

NEW JERSEY OFFICE OF THE SECRETARY OF HIGHER EDUCATION [1674]

20 West State Street, Fourth Floor
P.O. Box 542
Trenton, NJ 08625-0542
(609) 984-2709
Fax: (609) 633-8420
E-mail: audrey.bennerson@oshe.nj.gov
Web Site: www.state.nj.us/highereducation/EOF/EOF_Description.shtml

FOUNDED: 1968

AREAS OF INTEREST:
State financial assistance for low-income, first-generation college students.

NAME(S) OF PROGRAMS:
- **The New Jersey Educational Opportunity Fund (EOF) Program**

TYPE:
Grants-in-aid. The Higher Education Student Assistance Authority (HESAA) is a New Jersey authority that provides students and families with the financial and informational resources for students to pursue their education beyond high school. With roots dating back to 1959, HESAA's singular focus has always been to benefit the students it serves. HESAA provides state supplemental loans, grants and scholarships. HESAA also administers the state's college savings plan.

Educational Opportunity Fund Grants (EOF) provide financial aid to eligible students from educationally and economically disadvantaged backgrounds at participating in-state institutions.

YEAR PROGRAM STARTED: 1968

PURPOSE:
To ensure meaningful access to higher education for those who come from backgrounds of economic and educational disadvantage.

LEGAL BASIS:
New Jersey Educational Opportunity Act of 1968.

ELIGIBILITY:
Applicants must be New Jersey residents for at least 12 consecutive months prior to receiving an award. Applicants must be full-time, matriculated students in an approved New Jersey college or university in an approved program of study. Household income cannot exceed established guidelines. The amount of the grant varies based on financial need, cost of attendance and available funding.

GEOG. RESTRICTIONS: New Jersey.

FINANCIAL DATA:
Amount of support per award: Dependent upon annual appropriations, financial need and cost of attendance.

Public four-year institution: $700 a semester for a resident student; $575 a semester for a commuter student. County/community college: $525 a semester. Independent college/university: $1,250 a semester.

Total amount of support: $26,019,000.

NO. AWARDS: 13,136 unduplicated.

APPLICATION INFO:
All applicants for New Jersey grant assistance must file the Free Application for Federal Student Aid (FAFSA). EOF applicants must also file an admissions application with a New Jersey college or university that participates in the EOF Program. Applications are available at high school guidance and college financial aid offices or by calling this toll-free phone number: (800) 792-8670, available from any location in New Jersey, Monday through Friday, 9 A.M. to 5 P.M.

Duration: Financial assistance is renewable for four years of undergraduate study providing student is making satisfactory academic progress, demonstrates unmet need, and an application is filed.

Deadline: October 1 for fall term and March 1 for spring term.

PUBLICATIONS:
State and Federal Financial Aid Programs for New Jersey Students, brochure.

ADDRESS INQUIRIES TO:
Audrey Bennerson
EOF Executive Director

Office of the Secretary
of Higher Education
(See address above.)

NEW YORK STATE EDUCATION DEPARTMENT [1675]

Scholarships and Grants
Education Building, Room 505 West
Albany, NY 12234
(518) 474-3719
Fax: (518) 474-7468
E-mail: scholar@nysed.gov
Web Site: www.highered.nysed.gov/kiap/scholarships

NAME(S) OF PROGRAMS:

- **Regents Physician Loan Forgiveness Award Program**
- **Scholarships for Academic Excellence**

TYPE:
Scholarships. Regents Physician Loan Forgiveness Award Program: Designed to increase the number of physicians practicing in areas of New York state designated by the Regents as having a shortage of physicians. Emphasis is placed on primary care.

Scholarships for Academic Excellence: For use only at colleges and universities within New York state. Students are nominated by their high schools for this award.

PURPOSE:
To encourage specially talented youth to continue their education.

GEOG. RESTRICTIONS: New York state.

FINANCIAL DATA:
Amount of support per award: Regents Physician Loan Forgiveness Award Program: Up to $10,000 per year for two years, then reapply for up to two more years at same amount; Scholarships for Academic Excellence: $500 to $1,500.

Total amount of support: Varies.

NO. AWARDS: Regents Physician Loan Forgiveness Award Program: Minimum of 80; Scholarships for Academic Excellence; 2,000 $1,500 scholarships, 6,000 $500 scholarships.

APPLICATION INFO:
Regents Physician Loan Forgiveness Award Program: Consult the Department web site. Scholarships for Academic Excellence: Available through the student's high school.

Duration: Regents Physician Loan Forgiveness Award Program: Two years, after which the physician must reapply; physician then may be able to get two more years of funding. Scholarships for Academic Excellence: Four years.

Deadline: Regents Physician Loan Forgiveness Award Program: June 1. Scholarships for Academic Excellence: February 15.

ADDRESS INQUIRIES TO:
See e-mail or phone number above.

NEW YORK STATE HIGHER EDUCATION SERVICES CORPORATION [1676]

99 Washington Avenue
Albany, NY 12255
(888) 697-4372
(518) 473-1574
Fax: (518) 474-3749
E-mail: barbara.hochberg@hesc.ny.gov
Web Site: www.hesc.ny.gov

FOUNDED: 1975

AREAS OF INTEREST:
Postsecondary student financial aid.

NAME(S) OF PROGRAMS:

- **Military Service Recognition Scholarship (MSRS)**
- **NYS Memorial Scholarships**

TYPE:
Grants-in-aid; Scholarships. Military Service Recognition Scholarship (MSRS) provides financial aid to children, spouses and financial dependents of members of the armed forces of the U.S. or of a state-organized militia who, at any time on or after August 2, 1990, while a New York state resident, died or became severely and permanently disabled while engaged in hostilities or training for hostilities. It is for study in New York state.

NYS Memorial Scholarships (NYS Memorial Scholarships for Families of Deceased Firefighters, Volunteer Firefighters, Police Officers, Peace Officers, and Emergency Medical Service Workers) provides financial aid to children, spouses and financial dependents of deceased members of these branches of public service who have died as the result of injuries sustained in the line of duty in service to the state of New York. It is for study in New York state.

The Corporation administers more than 25 grant, scholarship, award and other programs providing college financial aid for New York state residents.

YEAR PROGRAM STARTED: 2004

PURPOSE:
To provide special financial assistance for postsecondary study for children in certain categories.

LEGAL BASIS:
Article 13 of the Education Law. New York state agency.

ELIGIBILITY:
Students must:
(1) study at an approved postsecondary institution in New York state;
(2) have graduated from high school in the U.S., earned a GED, or passed a federally approved "Ability to Benefit" test as defined by the Commissioner of the State Education Department;
(3) be enrolled as a full-time student taking 12 or more credits per semester;
(4) be matriculated in an approved program of study and be in good academic standing;
(5) have at least a cumulative "C" average after receipt of two annual payments and;
(6) not be in default on a student loan guaranteed by HESC or any repayment of state awards.

GEOG. RESTRICTIONS: New York state.

FINANCIAL DATA:
Amount of support per award: Varies.

Total amount of support: Varies.

APPLICATION INFO:
Applicants must complete and submit either the Military Service Recognition Scholarship Web Supplement or the NYS Memorial Scholarship Web Supplement. Be sure to print the Web Supplement confirmation, sign the supplement, and submit it along with the required documentation according to the instructions. FAFSA must be completed after eligibility is established and applicant has been assigned an account number.

Duration: Four years of full-time undergraduate study or five years of undergraduate study if the student is enrolled in an approved five-year program.

Deadline: June 30.

NEW YORK STATE HIGHER EDUCATION SERVICES CORPORATION [1677]

99 Washington Avenue
Albany, NY 12255
(888) 697-4372
(518) 473-1574
Fax: (518) 474-3749
E-mail: danielle.freeman@hesc.ny.gov
Web Site: www.hesc.ny.gov

FOUNDED: 1975

AREAS OF INTEREST:
Postsecondary student financial aid.

NAME(S) OF PROGRAMS:

- **NYS Aid for Part-Time Study (APTS)**

TYPE:
Grants-in-aid. College-based program providing grant assistance for eligible part-time students enrolled in approved undergraduate studies.

YEAR PROGRAM STARTED: 1984

PURPOSE:
To help pay tuition for eligible students enrolled in approved certificate or degree programs.

LEGAL BASIS:
State agency.

ELIGIBILITY:
To be considered for an award, a student must enroll part-time in a degree or an approved certificate program at a degree-granting institution, meet specific income limits, be a New York state resident, be either a U.S. citizen or eligible noncitizen, have a tuition charge of at least $100 per year, and not have used up Tuition Assistance Program (TAP) eligibility.

For this program, part-time study means being enrolled for at least three, but less than 12, semester-hours per semester, or four, but less than eight, credit hours per trimester. A participating college selects recipients from among eligible students.

GEOG. RESTRICTIONS: New York state.

FINANCIAL DATA:
Award amount is based on the student's need and the amount of money available at the institution.

Amount of support per award: Up to $2,000 per year.

APPLICATION INFO:
Awards are made through each college offering the program. Students should contact the college financial aid office to find out how to apply at their school.

Duration: Renewable up to four years.

Deadline: Varies.

OFFICERS:
Angela Van Decker, Chairman

NEW YORK STATE HIGHER EDUCATION SERVICES CORPORATION [1678]

99 Washington Avenue
Albany, NY 12255
(888) 697-4372
(518) 473-1574
Fax: (518) 474-3749
E-mail: barbara.hochberg@hesc.ny.gov
Web Site: www.hesc.ny.gov

FOUNDED: 1975

AREAS OF INTEREST:
Postsecondary student financial aid.

NAME(S) OF PROGRAMS:
- **New York State Tuition Assistance Program (TAP)**

TYPE:
Grants-in-aid. New York's largest grant program, the Tuition Assistance Program helps eligible New York residents attending in-state postsecondary institutions pay for tuition. TAP grants are based on the applicant's and his or her family's New York state net taxable income.

YEAR PROGRAM STARTED: 1976

PURPOSE:
To partially defray tuition charges to students.

LEGAL BASIS:
Article 13 of the Education Law.

ELIGIBILITY:
Legal New York state residents who are U.S. citizens or eligible noncitizens, who are full-time students at an approved postsecondary institution in New York state, and who meet income eligibility limitations are eligible to apply.

GEOG. RESTRICTIONS: New York state.

FINANCIAL DATA:
Grant varies according to New York net taxable income of the applicant and the family. Student must attend an institution charging at least $200 annual tuition.

Amount of support per award: Up to $5,165.

Total amount of support: Varies.

NO. AWARDS: Unlimited.

APPLICATION INFO:
Student must complete the annual FAFSA online application; from there he or she can proceed via online link to the HESC TAP application, which must also be completed. The TAP application is also available by accessing the HESC web site (above).

Duration: Up to four or five years of undergraduate study if the student is enrolled in an approved five-year program.

Deadline: June 30 of the current school year.

BOARD OF TRUSTEES:
Alan M. Klinger, Chairman

ADDRESS INQUIRIES TO:
Student Information
(See address above.)

THE CHARLOTTE W. NEWCOMBE FOUNDATION [1679]

35 Park Place
Princeton, NJ 08542-6918
(609) 924-7022
Fax: (609) 252-1773
E-mail: info@newcombefoundation.org
Web Site: www.newcombefoundation.org

FOUNDED: 1979

AREAS OF INTEREST:
College scholarship funds to colleges and universities.

NAME(S) OF PROGRAMS:
- **Newcombe Fellowships**
- **Newcombe Scholarships for Mature Women**
- **Newcombe Scholarships for Students with Disabilities**
- **Special Scholarship Endowment Grants**

TYPE:
Challenge/matching grants; Endowments; Fellowships; Internships; Scholarships. Endowment challenges build up current Newcombe Scholarship Endowments at colleges in a Newcombe program.

Newcombe Fellowships are designed to encourage original and significant study of ethical and religious values in all areas of human endeavor. The selection process and all administration for this continuing fellowship program are handled by the Woodrow Wilson National Fellowship Foundation of Princeton, NJ. All doctoral requirements except the dissertation must be completed by November of the year preceding the Fellowship award. Student must be attending a graduate school in the U.S.

Newcombe Scholarships for Students with Disabilities are intended to recognize the extraordinary expenses these students incur because of their disabilities and to supplement other sources of aid. The Newcombe Foundation offers special disability expense scholarships, internship scholarships and partial tuition scholarships through the counseling offices of colleges which provide excellent support services for disabled students. Preference in this program is given to four-year colleges which render exceptional service to large numbers of disabled students. Eight colleges are in the Newcombe Program.

Newcombe Scholarships for Mature Women are for women age 25 and older who have completed half the credits required for their Bachelor's degrees. These scholarships are available at selected colleges which offer support services for mature women. Preference in this program is given to four-year colleges with excellent support services for mature women students. It is Foundation policy not to provide grants in this program to professional schools, including theological seminaries and those training health care professionals; 31 colleges are in this program.

Special Scholarship Endowment Grants are awarded to selected institutions to benefit students from a specified economically disadvantaged population that the institution serves.

The Foundation makes no awards to individual students. All grants are made to colleges, universities and other institutions of higher education.

YEAR PROGRAM STARTED: 1981

PURPOSE:
To provide selected colleges and universities with scholarship funds for specifically targeted groups of students.

LEGAL BASIS:
Private.

ELIGIBILITY:
No grants to individuals. Scholarship aid only. No funds for program development staffing or support. The Foundation provides grants to colleges, universities and foundations to create scholarships for designated undergraduate and graduate students. No aid is available for postdoctoral fellowships.

GEOG. RESTRICTIONS: Scholarships for Disabled Students and Mature Women Scholarships are limited to Colleges in Delaware, Maryland, New Jersey, New York City, Pennsylvania and Washington, DC.

FINANCIAL DATA:
Amount of support per award: In three scholarship programs: $12,500 to $63,500 for the year 2014-15.

Total amount of support: $2,338,661 for the year 2014-15.

Matching fund requirements: Varies.

NO. MOST RECENT APPLICANTS: 43 (by invitation).

NO. AWARDS: 43.

REPRESENTATIVE AWARDS:
$61,000 to Misericordia University; $50,000 to Gwynedd-Mercy College; $61,000 to LaSalle University; $25,000 to Brooklyn College.

APPLICATION INFO:
For Newcombe Fellowships, contact Woodrow Wilson National Fellowship Foundation, P.O. Box 5281, Princeton, NJ 08543-5281 for application materials. Tel: (609) 452-7007. Web site: www.woodrow.org.

For Newcombe Scholarships for Mature Women and Students with Disabilities, colleges within geographic area should contact the Foundation for applications. Individuals should contact their college of choice for availability of these scholarships.

Duration: Varies.

Deadline: Inquiries are accepted on an ongoing basis. Proposals by invitation.

PUBLICATIONS:
Annual report.

IRS I.D.: 23-2120614

STAFF:
Thomas N. Wilfrid, Executive Director
Diane C. Wilfrid, Program Officer
Jean Woodman, Administrative Associate
James H. Stocking, Financial and Technical Associate

BOARD OF TRUSTEES:
Robert M. Adams
Dale Robinson Anglin
Elizabeth T. Frank
Louise U. Johnson
J. Barton Luedeke

ADDRESS INQUIRIES TO:
Thomas N. Wilfrid, Executive Director
(See address above.)

*PLEASE NOTE:
No grants to individuals.

*SPECIAL STIPULATIONS:
Grants are made to colleges and universities exclusively for student scholarships. Two programs (Mature Women and Students with Disabilities) are limited to colleges in Delaware, Maryland, New Jersey, New York City, Pennsylvania, and Washington, DC.

NORTH CAROLINA STATE EDUCATION ASSISTANCE AUTHORITY/COLLEGE FOUNDATION OF NORTH CAROLINA [1680]

P.O. Box 13663
Research Triangle Park, NC 27709-3663
(800) 700-1775
(866) 866-2362
Fax: (919) 248-6686
E-mail: programinformation@cfnc.org
Web Site: www.cfnc.org

AREAS OF INTEREST:
Financial aid for North Carolina students.

TYPE:
Grants-in-aid; Scholarships.

PURPOSE:
To provide access to higher education and information for the citizens of North Carolina.

ELIGIBILITY:
Varies with program. All applicants must be North Carolina residents and intend to use funds for tuition purposes only.

GEOG. RESTRICTIONS: North Carolina.

FINANCIAL DATA:
Amount of support per award: Varies.
Total amount of support: Varies.

APPLICATION INFO:
Applications may be obtained online or by telephone request.
Duration: Varies.
Deadline: Varies.

ADDRESS INQUIRIES TO:
NCSEAA Grants Training and Outreach
(See address above.)

NORTHERN CHAUTAUQUA COMMUNITY FOUNDATION [1681]

212 Lake Shore Drive West
Dunkirk, NY 14048
(716) 366-4892
Fax: (716) 366-3905
E-mail: nccf@nccfoundation.org
Web Site: www.nccfoundation.org

FOUNDED: 1986

AREAS OF INTEREST:
Youth development and economic development.

TYPE:
Challenge/matching grants; Project/program grants; Scholarships. Youth Development and Economic Development grants.

YEAR PROGRAM STARTED: 1986

PURPOSE:
To enhance the northern Chautauqua community.

LEGAL BASIS:
Community foundation.

ELIGIBILITY:
Applicants must be registered 501(c)(3) organizations that serve the northern Chautauqua County community.

GEOG. RESTRICTIONS: Northern Chautauqua County, New York.

FINANCIAL DATA:
Amount of support per award: $25 to $10,000.
Total amount of support: Approximately $400,000.

APPLICATION INFO:
Call the Foundation for information.
Deadline: Grants: March 1 and September 1.

PUBLICATIONS:
Annual report; Spring and Fall newsletters.

IRS I.D.: 16-1271663

STAFF:
Diane E. Hannum, Executive Director
Eileen Dunn, Program Coordinator
Ida Klahn, Community Relations and Development Coordinator
Nancy Mosier, Administrative Scholarship Coordinator

ADDRESS INQUIRIES TO:
Eileen Dunn, Program Coordinator
(See address above.)

*SPECIAL STIPULATIONS:
Scholarships to northern Chautauqua County residents only.

THE NRA [1682]

11250 Waples Mill Road
Fairfax, VA 22030
(703) 267-1087
Fax: (703) 267-1083
E-mail: jebrayscholarship@nrahq.org
Web Site: nra.org

NAME(S) OF PROGRAMS:
- **Jeanne E. Bray Memorial Scholarship**

TYPE:
Scholarships. For children of peace officers.

YEAR PROGRAM STARTED: 1988

PURPOSE:
To assist children of peace officers, who are current NRA members, in furthering their education.

ELIGIBILITY:
Must be an adult or junior member of the NRA and the son or daughter of a currently serving, full-time/deceased, full-time/retired, full-time, or disabled and retired commissioned peace officer who is also a current NRA member or was at the time of death. Eligible students can be senior high school students through senior college students. Applicants must have a satisfactory academic record and be enrolled full-time. Must be U.S. citizens or residents.

GEOG. RESTRICTIONS: United States.

FINANCIAL DATA:
Amount of support per award: Up to $10,000 or four years, whichever comes first.

NO. AWARDS: Varies.

APPLICATION INFO:
Applicant will need to contact Chandra Bolland to receive the personal reference forms.
Duration: Up to four years.
Deadline: November 15.

ADDRESS INQUIRIES TO:
Chandra Bolland
Jeanne E. Bray Memorial Scholarship Committee
(See address above.)

OHIO BOARD OF REGENTS [1683]

Office of Financial Aid
25 South Front Street
Columbus, OH 43215
(614) 466-6000
Fax: (614) 752-5903
E-mail: wo_admin@regents.state.oh.us
Web Site: www.ohiohighered.org/ohio-war-orphans

NAME(S) OF PROGRAMS:
- **Ohio War Orphans Scholarship**

TYPE:
Scholarships. Full-time undergraduate scholarships.

YEAR PROGRAM STARTED: 1954

PURPOSE:
To enable children of disabled or deceased Ohio war veterans or children of Vietnam conflict MIAs or POWs to attend college.

LEGAL BASIS:
State agency.

ELIGIBILITY:
Applicant must be 16 to 25 years of age and a child of disabled or deceased Ohio war veteran or child of Vietnam conflict MIA or POW. Veteran parent must have at least a 60% combined disability rating. Applicant must also be enrolled as a full-time student in an eligible institution of higher education.

GEOG. RESTRICTIONS: Ohio.

FINANCIAL DATA:
Students attending Ohio nonprofit and profitmaking institutions of higher education will receive amounts no greater than the average amount paid for students attending public institutions; tuition coverage at public institutions varies each year.
Amount of support per award: Varies.
Total amount of support: $5,588,674 for the year 2014.

NO. AWARDS: 826 for the year 2014.

APPLICATION INFO:
Student must submit a completed application form.
Duration: Scholarships are automatically renewable for up to five years of undergraduate education.
Deadline: July 1. Announcements in early August.

STAFF:
Amber Brady, Program Manager

ADDRESS INQUIRIES TO:
Amber Brady, Program Manager
(See address above.)

*SPECIAL STIPULATIONS:
This program is not for graduate students.

OHIO BOARD OF REGENTS [1684]

Office of Financial Aid
25 South Front Street
Columbus, OH 43215
(614) 466-6000
Fax: (614) 752-5903
E-mail: ocog_admin@regents.state.oh.us
Web Site: www.ohiohighered.org/ocog

FOUNDED: 1963

NAME(S) OF PROGRAMS:
- **Ohio College Opportunity Grant Program (OCOG)**

TYPE:
General operating grants. Grants for college-bound students or current undergraduate students.

YEAR PROGRAM STARTED: 2006

PURPOSE:
To assist in achieving the goals of access and choice for low-income and middle-income students.

LEGAL BASIS:
State agency.

ELIGIBILITY:
Applicant must be an Ohio resident, demonstrate financial need, and be seeking an Associate's degree, a Bachelor's degree, or nursing diploma at an eligible institution.

GEOG. RESTRICTIONS: Ohio and Pennsylvania.

FINANCIAL DATA:
Amount of support per award: Varies.

Total amount of support: $80,855,553 for the year 2014.

NO. AWARDS: 86,435 for the year 2014.

APPLICATION INFO:
Student must submit a Free Application for Federal Student Aid (FAFSA).

Duration: One academic year. Renewable for a maximum of five years of full-time study.

Deadline: October 1.

ADDRESS INQUIRIES TO:
Tamika Braswell, Program Manager
(See address above.)

*SPECIAL STIPULATIONS:
This program is not for graduate students.

OHIO NATIONAL GUARD SCHOLARSHIP PROGRAM [1685]

The Adjutant General's Department
Attention: NGOH-ONG-SP (SGT Burdiss)
2825 West Dublin Granville Road
Columbus, OH 43235-2789
(614) 336-7143
(614) 336-7053
(888) 400-6484
Fax: (614) 336-7318
E-mail: ng.oh.oharng.mbx.ong-scholarship@mail.mil
Web Site: www.ong.ohio.gov/information/education/scholarship_index.html

FOUNDED: 1977

AREAS OF INTEREST:
Associate or undergraduate general education.

TYPE:
Scholarships. Grants for undergraduate students attending three credit hours or more.

YEAR PROGRAM STARTED: 1978

PURPOSE:
To encourage enlistment in Ohio National Guard.

LEGAL BASIS:
Ohio Revised Code. Nonprofit.

ELIGIBILITY:
Applicants must possess a high school diploma or a GED certificate and enlist, re-enlist or extend their current enlistment in a valid authorized or required MTOE/TDA (ARNG) or UMD (ANG) position for enlistment in Selective Reserve duty in the Ohio National Guard.

GEOG. RESTRICTIONS: Ohio.

FINANCIAL DATA:
Instructional and general fees paid 100% for student attending public institution.

Amount of support per award: Private Institution: $4,714 maximum per semester; $3,143 maximum per quarter. Public Institution: Varies.

Total amount of support: $16,000,000 annually.

NO. MOST RECENT APPLICANTS: 3,500.

APPLICATION INFO:
An applicant must apply each term so that the application is received in the Scholarship Program Office no later than the established deadlines, which are no later than the close of business (4:30 P.M.).

Duration: Scholarships are renewable for up to four years of undergraduate education. Grants provide two years tuition assistance with three-year enlistment or four years tuition assistance with six-year enlistment.

Deadline: July 1 for fall; November 1 for winter/quarter, semester, trimester/spring semester; February 1 for spring quarter; April 1 for summer.

PUBLICATIONS:
Regulation AGOR 621-1(Army); *35-1*(Air).

STAFF:
Angela L. Bailey, Education Services Officer
Angela Wallace, Grants Coordinator

ADDRESS INQUIRIES TO:
Afrika Alsup, Administrator
(See address above.)

*SPECIAL STIPULATIONS:
Applicant must enlist in Ohio National Guard for not less than three years. Must enroll minimum three credit hours in degree-granting program.

ORDER SONS OF ITALY IN AMERICA, GRAND LODGE OF FLORIDA [1686]

1539 Fayetteville Drive
Spring Hill, FL 34609
(352) 799-5456
E-mail: gusguadagnino@gmail.com
Web Site: osiafl.org

FOUNDED: 1953

AREAS OF INTEREST:
Culture, charity and education.

TYPE:
Awards/prizes; Grants-in-aid; Scholarships. Scholarships are provided to high school students entering college.

Financial aid is given in support of charitable programs, such as Alzheimer's disease, Cooley's anemia, autism, and cancer.

YEAR PROGRAM STARTED: 1988

PURPOSE:
To share and help those in need; to support high school students entering college; to support charitable programs.

ELIGIBILITY:
Scholarship program: Applying student must be a U.S. citizen or resident who resides in the states of Florida or Georgia, be of Italian heritage, and achieve high scholastic grades.

Applying organizations must have 501(c)(3) not-for-profit status. No grants are made to religious organizations.

FINANCIAL DATA:
Amount of support per award: Scholarship program: $1,000 per student.

NO. MOST RECENT APPLICANTS: 42.

NO. AWARDS: Scholarship program: Varies with funding; 9 scholarships in 2014.

APPLICATION INFO:
Scholarship application form can be obtained on the web site or at applying student's local high school. Completed application materials must be submitted to the State Scholarship Chairperson.

Duration: One-time awards. Grants are not renewable.

Deadline: March 31.

ADDRESS INQUIRIES TO:
Gustave Guadagnino, State Scholarship Chairperson
(See e-mail address above.)

PENNSYLVANIA HIGHER EDUCATION ASSISTANCE AGENCY [1687]

1200 North Seventh Street
Harrisburg, PA 17102-1398
(717) 720-2800
(800) 692-7392 (Pennsylvania only)
Fax: (717) 720-3786
E-mail: granthelp@pheaa.org
Web Site: www.pheaa.org

FOUNDED: 1964

NAME(S) OF PROGRAMS:

- **Pennsylvania State Grant Program**

TYPE:
Grants-in-aid. The Pennsylvania State Grant Program allows eligible Pennsylvania residents to obtain financial assistance for undergraduate study at any PHEAA-approved institution of higher education. The Free Application for Federal Student Aid (FAFSA) serves as the program's application.

YEAR PROGRAM STARTED: 1964

PURPOSE:
To assist needy students in obtaining higher education.

LEGAL BASIS:
Government agency.

ELIGIBILITY:
The student applying for Pennsylvania State Grants must:
(1) meet criteria for financial need;
(2) be enrolled on at least a half-time basis in a PHEAA-approved undergraduate program of study and not already have a four-year (or more) undergraduate degree;
(3) be a high school graduate or the recipient of a GED;
(4) demonstrate academic progress (for continued aid) and;
(5) be a Pennsylvania resident (domiciliary).

Summer school students may also qualify for State Grant funds.

GEOG. RESTRICTIONS: Pennsylvania.

FINANCIAL DATA:
Amount of support per award: Varies annually.

Total amount of support: Varies annually due to appropriations, number of applicants, and financial strength of applying families.

NO. AWARDS: Approximately 185,000.

APPLICATION INFO:
Submit the Free Application for Federal Student Aid (FAFSA). For faster processing,

those applying can find out what they need to fill out the FAFSA and how to complete it by going online.

Duration: One academic year. Renewal contingent upon continued eligibility and financial need.

Deadline: Varies.

EXECUTIVE OFFICERS:
James L. Preston, President and Chief Executive Officer
Christine Zuzack, Vice President of State Grants and Special Programs

ADDRESS INQUIRIES TO:
Christine Zuzack, Vice President of State Grants and Special Programs
(See address above.)

THE PHI BETA KAPPA SOCIETY [1688]

1606 New Hampshire Avenue, N.W.
Washington, DC 20009
(202) 745-3287
Fax: (202) 986-1601
E-mail: awards@pbk.org
Web Site: www.pbk.org

AREAS OF INTEREST:
Philosophy.

NAME(S) OF PROGRAMS:
- **The Romanell-Phi Beta Kappa Professorship in Philosophy**

TYPE:
Fellowships. Professorship awarded to scholars in the field of philosophy, without restriction to any one school of philosophical thought.

YEAR PROGRAM STARTED: 1983

PURPOSE:
To recognize not only distinguished achievement, but also the recipient's contribution or potential contribution to public understanding of philosophy.

ELIGIBILITY:
Scholar need not be a member of Phi Beta Kappa, but must be on the faculty of an institution sheltering a chapter of Phi Beta Kappa and must be nominated by that chapter.

GEOG. RESTRICTIONS: United States.

FINANCIAL DATA:
Amount of support per award: $7,500 stipend.

NO. AWARDS: 1 annually.

APPLICATION INFO:
Recipient must be nominated by the chapter of Phi Beta Kappa at the institution in which they are on faculty.

Duration: One year. Nonrenewable.

STAFF:
Laura Hartnett, Program and Event Specialist

ADDRESS INQUIRIES TO:
Laura Hartnett
Program and Event Specialist
(See address above.)

*SPECIAL STIPULATIONS:
Recipient will be expected to give a series of three special lectures during the year of the Professorship. Such lectures are to be given at the sheltering institution and to be open to the general public as well as to the academic community.

PI GAMMA MU, INTERNATIONAL HONOR SOCIETY IN SOCIAL SCIENCE [1689]

1001 Millington, Suite B
Winfield, KS 67156
(620) 221-3128
Fax: (620) 221-7124
E-mail: executivedirector@pigammamu.org
Web Site: www.pigammamu.org

FOUNDED: 1924

AREAS OF INTEREST:
Economics, history, political science, sociology, anthropology, international relations, social work, psychology, social philosophy, history of education and criminal justice, law and human/cultural geography.

NAME(S) OF PROGRAMS:
- **Pi Gamma Mu Scholarships**

TYPE:
Scholarships. Awarded for graduate study.

YEAR PROGRAM STARTED: 1951

PURPOSE:
To promote scholarship in the Society's areas of interest.

LEGAL BASIS:
Nonprofit.

ELIGIBILITY:
Applicants must be a member of Pi Gamma Mu.

FINANCIAL DATA:
Amount of support per award: $1,000 or $2,000.

Total amount of support: $13,000 annually.

NO. MOST RECENT APPLICANTS: Approximately 47.

NO. AWARDS: 10.

APPLICATION INFO:
Resume, personal statement, transcript and three letters of recommendation required.

Duration: One year.

Deadline: February 15. Announcement May 1.

PUBLICATIONS:
Application guidelines.

OFFICERS:
Dr. C. Laurence Heck, President
Dr. Susan Kinsella, First Vice President
Dr. Clara Small, Second Vice President
Dr. Janet Adamski, Secretary and Treasurer
Dr. Charles Hartwig, Chancellor
J.L. Kemp, Chancellor
Allison G.S. Knox, Chancellor
Dr. Yongsheng Wang, Chancellor

MINNIE STEVENS PIPER FOUNDATION [1690]

1250 N.E. Loop 410, Suite 810
San Antonio, TX 78209-1539
(210) 525-8494
Fax: (210) 341-6627
E-mail: mspf@mspf.org
Web Site: www.mspf.org

FOUNDED: 1950

NAME(S) OF PROGRAMS:
- **Piper Professor Program**
- **Piper Scholar Program**
- **Student Loan Program**

TYPE:
Awards/prizes; Scholarships. Piper Professor Program: Annual awards to professors for superior teaching at the college level.

Piper Scholars: Four-year scholarships awarded to academically promising and superior high school seniors in amounts that assist them in attending the college or university of their choice within the state of Texas.

Student Loan Program: Loans to worthy and needy students at the junior, senior, undergraduate or graduate college level.

PURPOSE:
To support charitable, scientific, or educational undertakings by providing for, or contributing toward, the education of financially limited but worthy students; to assist young men and women residents of Texas, attending or wishing to attend colleges and universities in the state of Texas, to complete their education and obtain degrees; to contribute to community chests; to support any other nonprofit organization or activity dedicated to promoting the general welfare within the state of Texas.

LEGAL BASIS:
Private foundation with Letter Ruling under Section 4945 of the Tax Reform Act of 1969.

ELIGIBILITY:
Piper Professor Program: Candidates must be U.S. citizens and nominated through college/university President's office.

Piper Scholar Program: Participation is by invitation only to high schools in certain geographic areas. Student must be nominated by their high school counselor.

Student Loan Program: Must be full-time status. Restricted to Texas residents attending a college or university within the state of Texas.

GEOG. RESTRICTIONS: Texas.

FINANCIAL DATA:
Amount of support per award: Piper Professor Program: $5,000.

NO. AWARDS: Piper Professor Program: 10; Piper Scholar Program: 25.

APPLICATION INFO:
Contact the Foundation.

Duration: Piper Scholar Program: Four years.

ADDRESS INQUIRIES TO:
Joyce M. Ellis, Executive Director
(See address above.)

*SPECIAL STIPULATIONS:
Piper Professor and Piper Scholars Programs are by invitation only.

THE PLANNING AND VISUAL EDUCATION PARTNERSHIP [1691]

4651 Sheridan Street, Suite 470
Hollywood, FL 33021
(954) 241-4800
(954) 241-4834
Fax: (954) 893-8375
E-mail: pave@paveinfo.org
Web Site: www.paveinfo.org

FOUNDED: 1992

AREAS OF INTEREST:
Retail design planning, industrial design and visual merchandising.

TYPE:
Awards/prizes; Capital grants; Conferences/seminars; Product donations; Project/program grants; Scholarships. Student educational support. Mentorships.

PURPOSE:
To encourage students to study in the field of retail design and planning and visual merchandising.

FINANCIAL DATA:
Amount of support per award: PAVE Global Shop Design Project: $14,500; Student Aid Program: $55,000; Student Design Competition: $5,000 for first place, $2,500 for second place, $1,500 for third place and $500 for honorable mention.

Total amount of support: $150,000 for the year 2014-15.

NO. AWARDS: 13.

ADDRESS INQUIRIES TO:
Dash Nagel, Managing Director
(See address above.)

PRESBYTERIAN CHURCH (U.S.A.) [1692]

100 Witherspoon Street
Louisville, KY 40202-1396
(888) 728-7228 ext. 5224
Fax: (502) 569-8766
E-mail: finaid@pcusa.org
Web Site: www.pcusa.org/financialaid

AREAS OF INTEREST:
Majors in health services/sciences, religious studies, sacred music, social services and social sciences.

NAME(S) OF PROGRAMS:
- **Student Opportunity Scholarship**

TYPE:
Scholarships. Need-based.

YEAR PROGRAM STARTED: 1956

PURPOSE:
To assist undergraduate sophomores, juniors and seniors already in college, with preference to racial ethnic students.

ELIGIBILITY:
Scholarship preference to African Americans, Asian Americans, Middle Eastern Americans and Hispanic Americans. Applicants must:
(1) demonstrate financial need;
(2) be a member of the Presbyterian Church (U.S.A.);
(3) be a sophomore, junior or senior already in college and;
(4) have a 2.5 grade point average to get in the program and a 2.5 grade point average to stay in.

GEOG. RESTRICTIONS: United States and Puerto Rico.

FINANCIAL DATA:
Amount of support per award: Up to $2,000 per academic year.

Total amount of support: Approximately $160,000 annually.

NO. MOST RECENT APPLICANTS: 120.

NO. AWARDS: 80.

APPLICATION INFO:
Applications can be downloaded from the web site, beginning April 1.

Duration: Renewable up to three years depending on need and maintenance of a 2.5 grade point average.

Deadline: May 15 for "getting started" part; June 15 for financial information.

PUBLICATIONS:
Financial Aid Programs.

ADDRESS INQUIRIES TO:
Financial Aid for Service
(See address above.)

PRESBYTERIAN CHURCH (U.S.A.) [1693]

100 Witherspoon Street
Louisville, KY 40202-1396
(888) 728-7228 ext. 5224
Fax: (502) 569-8766
E-mail: finaid@pcusa.org
Web Site: www.pcusa.org/financialaid

NAME(S) OF PROGRAMS:
- **Samuel Robinson Essay Contest**

TYPE:
Awards/prizes. Essay contest, awarded to junior or senior undergraduate students enrolled full-time in one of the colleges/universities related to the Presbyterian Church (U.S.A.).

YEAR PROGRAM STARTED: 1940

PURPOSE:
To instill an interest in the work of the Presbyterian Church throughout the U.S.

LEGAL BASIS:
Nonprofit.

ELIGIBILITY:
Must be a member of the Presbyterian Church (U.S.A.) and a junior or senior attending a Presbyterian-related college or university.

GEOG. RESTRICTIONS: United States.

FINANCIAL DATA:
Amount of support per award: $1,500 to $5,000.

Total amount of support: Varies.

NO. MOST RECENT APPLICANTS: 2.

NO. AWARDS: Up to 10.

APPLICATION INFO:
Applications by request only November 15 to March 15. Contact the Presbyterian Church (U.S.A.).

Duration: One-time award.

Deadline: April 1.

ADDRESS INQUIRIES TO:
Financial Aid for Service
(See address above.)

*SPECIAL STIPULATIONS:
Open to Presbyterian students attending a Presbyterian-related school.

THE PRESS CLUB OF METROPOLITAN ST. LOUIS AND JOURNALISM FOUNDATION OF METROPOLITAN ST. LOUIS [1694]

c/o The Press Club of Metropolitan St. Louis
P.O. Box 410522
St. Louis, MO 63141
(314) 449-8029
Fax: (314) 317-0031
E-mail: info@stlpressclub.org
Web Site: stlpressclub.org

FOUNDED: 1956

AREAS OF INTEREST:
Journalism.

NAME(S) OF PROGRAMS:
- **Enterprise Investigative Journalism Grants**
- **Journalism Foundation Scholarships**
- **Press Club Fellowship Program**
- **Press Club Internship Scholarships**
- **Press Club Journalism Scholarship**
- **Press Club Martin P. Quigley Journalism Scholarship**
- **Press Club Media Summer Internship Scholarships**
- **Press Club Neiman Marcus Media Scholarship**

TYPE:
Capital grants; Fellowships; Internships; Project/program grants; Scholarships.

YEAR PROGRAM STARTED: 1970

PURPOSE:
To award scholarships to those entering sophomore, junior and senior years of college or graduate school preparing for journalism/communications careers at recognized schools, majoring in journalism, broadcasting, English or related fields; to award fellowships for journalists to do investigative stories for publication.

LEGAL BASIS:
Incorporated as nonprofit organization in state of Missouri.

ELIGIBILITY:
Applicants for scholarships must be currently enrolled as full-time students who are intending to pursue a career in journalism, media communications or a related field; graduate students must carry at least six hours. Press Club Fellowship Program: Journalists with an investigative project concerning the St. Louis region.

GEOG. RESTRICTIONS: St. Louis, Missouri and counties of Franklin, Jefferson, Lincoln, St. Charles, St. Louis and Warren, and Illinois counties of Bond, Clinton, Jersey, Madison, Monroe and St. Clair.

FINANCIAL DATA:
Amount of support per award:
Fellowship/Grants Program: Up to $10,000.
Scholarships: $1,000 to $2,500.

CO-OP FUNDING PROGRAMS: Grants from member organizations.

NO. MOST RECENT APPLICANTS: 24.

NO. AWARDS: Fellowship/Grants: 2.
Scholarships: 14.

APPLICATION INFO:
Consult the Press Club web site.

Deadline: May 13 for scholarships.

PUBLICATIONS:
Courier, newsletter.

IRS I.D.: 43-1489003

STAFF:
Glenda Partlow, Executive Director
Laura Schnarr, Development and Social Media Coordinator

ADDRESS INQUIRIES TO:
Glenda Partlow
Executive Director, Press Club
(See address above.)

RONALD REAGAN PRESIDENTIAL FOUNDATION [1695]

40 Presidential Drive
Simi Valley, CA 93065
(805) 522-2977
Fax: (805) 520-9702
E-mail: info@reaganfoundation.org
Web Site: www.reaganfoundation.org/scholarships

FOUNDED: 1987

NAME(S) OF PROGRAMS:

- **GE-Reagan Foundation Scholarship Program**

TYPE:
Scholarships. The GE-Reagan Foundation Scholarship Program rewards college-bound students who demonstrate exemplary leadership, drive, integrity and citizenship with financial assistance to pursue higher education.

PURPOSE:
To honor the legacy and character of America's 40th president.

ELIGIBILITY:
Open to current high school seniors.

GEOG. RESTRICTIONS: United States.

FINANCIAL DATA:
Amount of support per award: $10,000 for each scholarship.

NO. AWARDS: Up to 20 new scholarships each year.

APPLICATION INFO:
Application information is available on the web site.

Duration: One academic year; renewable for up to three additional years.

Deadline: Application is available in the fall and is due the first week of January. The scholarship will then be awarded for the next full academic year. Contact the Foundation for exact details.

ADDRESS INQUIRIES TO:
E-mail: ge-reagan@scholarshipamerica.org
Tel: (844) 402-0354

SID RICHARDSON MEMORIAL FUND [1696]

309 Main Street
Fort Worth, TX 76102
(817) 336-0494
Fax: (817) 332-2176
E-mail: mkuykendall@sidrichardson.org
Web Site: www.sidrichardsonmemorialfund.org

FOUNDED: 1965

AREAS OF INTEREST:
Academic and vocational scholarships.

TYPE:
Scholarships. Scholarships are for both academic and vocational studies.

YEAR PROGRAM STARTED: 1965

LEGAL BASIS:
Tax-exempt.

ELIGIBILITY:
Limited funds are available to assist in defraying the cost of college education or of vocational training. These scholarships are awarded on a competitive basis according to academic achievement and/or financial need.

Those eligible to apply for a Sid Richardson Memorial Fund scholarship are direct descendants (children or grandchildren) of persons who qualified for Early Retirement, Normal Retirement, Disability Retirement, or Death Benefits from The Bass Retirement Plan (formerly The Retirement Plan For Employees of Bass Enterprises Production Co.), Retirement Plan for Employees of Barbnet/San Jose Cattle Co., Retirement Plan for Employees of City Center Development Co., City Club Retirement Plan, Retirement Plan for Employees of Richardson Aviation, G.P., Retirement Plan for Employees of Sid W. Richardson Foundation, or Retirement Plan for Employees of Sundance Square. Those eligible also include direct descendants (children or grandchildren) of persons presently employed with a minimum of three years' full-time service (as of March 31) with any of the following employers: Barbnet Investment Co., BBT Capital Management, LLC, BEPCO, L.P., BOPCO, L.P., City Club of Fort Worth, Richardson Aviation, San Jose Cattle Co., SHSM Partners, L.P., Sid Richardson Carbon Co. (SRCE, L.P.), Sid W. Richardson Foundation, and Sundance Square Management, L.P.

FINANCIAL DATA:
Amount of support per award: $1,000 to $10,000 per student per academic year.

Total amount of support: Approximately $405,000.

NO. MOST RECENT APPLICANTS: Varies.

NO. AWARDS: Varies.

APPLICATION INFO:
Application request may be submitted via the Fund's web site. Follow "How to Apply" tab. You may also direct a written request for an application to Mary Kuykendall, Sid Richardson Memorial Fund, at the address, e-mail or fax number listed above. Include the student name, address, e-mail and phone number, as well as the qualifying employee's name, last 4-digits of Social Security Number, qualifying company name and dates of employment, as well as relationship to the student.

Duration: Considered for renewal annually if a 2.0 grade point average is maintained for each semester.

Deadline: Completed applications must be postmarked no later than March 31 annually for the following academic year. Announcement of awards by May 31.

IRS I.D.: 75-1220266

OFFICERS:
Pete Geren, Executive Director
Shanda Ranelle, Treasurer
Mary Kuykendall, Secretary

BOARD OF DIRECTORS:
Thomas White, Chairman
William Jones, Vice President
Ken McCarty, Vice President
Mitchell Roper, Vice President

ADDRESS INQUIRIES TO:
Mary Kuykendall, Scholarship Coordinator
(See address above.)

JACKIE ROBINSON FOUNDATION (JRF)

75 Varick Street, 2nd Floor
New York, NY 10013-1917
(212) 290-8600
Fax: (212) 290-8081
E-mail: general@jackierobinson.org
Web Site: www.jackierobinson.org

TYPE:
Conferences/seminars; Fellowships; Scholarships. The Foundation Scholarship Program (Mentoring and Leadership Program) is designed to address the financial needs of college students and provide comprehensive mentoring services through its 42 Strategies for Success Curriculum.

The Fellowship programs are follow-up programs to the JRF Scholars program (Mentoring and Leadership Program).

The Extra Innings Fellowship Program helps highly motivated JRF Scholars to fund the cost of advanced professional or graduate training.

The Rachel Robinson International Fellowship Program promotes and supports international service and study opportunities for JRF Scholars.

See entry 989 for full listing.

THE ROTARY CLUB OF BRYN MAWR [1697]

P.O. Box 84
Bryn Mawr, PA 19010
(484) 254-6377
E-mail: rbcuff@verizon.net
Web Site: www.brynmawrrotary.org

FOUNDED: 1969

AREAS OF INTEREST:
To serve others and satisfy Rotary principles.

NAME(S) OF PROGRAMS:

- **Harry H. Cabell Scholarship Program**

TYPE:
Awards/prizes; Scholarships.

YEAR PROGRAM STARTED: 1985

PURPOSE:
To recognize and reward college students who meet trust requirements.

LEGAL BASIS:
Not-for-profit society.

ELIGIBILITY:
Financial need, high academic standards and leadership qualities, service to others and achievement qualities are important factors in the decision process. Applicants must be in an area college or university.

GEOG. RESTRICTIONS: Metropolitan Philadelphia and surrounding counties.

FINANCIAL DATA:
Amount of support per award: $1,500 to $2,000.

Total amount of support: Varies.

NO. AWARDS: 2 to 4.

APPLICATION INFO:
Application form must include recommendation from faculty, statement of good standing from dean, transcript of grades and 300-word essay.

Duration: One year. No renewals.

Deadline: Early March. Announcement approximately April 30.

ADDRESS INQUIRIES TO:
Richard Cuff, Scholarship Committee
Harry H. Cabell Scholarship Awards
(See address above.)

SACHS FOUNDATION

90 South Cascade Avenue
Suite 1410
Colorado Springs, CO 80903
(719) 633-2353
Fax: (719) 633-3663
E-mail: lisa@sachsfoundation.org
Web Site: sachsfoundation.org

TYPE:
Grants-in-aid; Scholarships.

See entry 1014 for full listing.

SCHOOL FOR ADVANCED RESEARCH [1698]

P.O. Box 2188
Santa Fe, NM 87504-2188
(505) 954-7237
Fax: (505) 954-7214
E-mail: scholar@sarsf.org
Web Site: www.sarweb.org

FOUNDED: 1907

AREAS OF INTEREST:
Anthropology and allied disciplines in the humanities and social sciences.

NAME(S) OF PROGRAMS:

- **Summer Scholar Fellowships**

TYPE:
Fellowships. Eight-week summer residency program.

PURPOSE:
To promote the pursuit of research or writing projects that promote understanding of human behavior, culture, society, and the history of anthropology.

ELIGIBILITY:
Scholars in anthropology and related disciplines are invited to apply in order to pursue research or writing projects. Scholars whose projects relate to anthropological linguistics or to the history of anthropology are especially encouraged to apply. Both humanistically and scientifically oriented scholars are encouraged to apply.

FINANCIAL DATA:
Scholars are provided with a small stipend, free housing and office space, an allowance account, library support and other benefits.

Amount of support per award: Stipend up to $1,000 and an allowance up to $160.

CO-OP FUNDING PROGRAMS: Ethel-Jane Westfeldt Bunting Foundation and the William Y. and Nettie K. Adams Fellowship in the History of Anthropology.

NO. MOST RECENT APPLICANTS: 64 for the year 2015.

NO. AWARDS: 6.

APPLICATION INFO:
Applicants should submit the following:
(1) cover sheet;
(2) letter describing the project, its significance, the status of the research, and what will be accomplished during the residency and;
(3) curriculum vitae.

Duration: Up to eight weeks.

Deadline: Second Monday in January each year. Awards will be announced within two months.

ADDRESS INQUIRIES TO:
Maria Spray
Scholar Programs Coordinator
(See address above.)

For overnight delivery:
660 Garcia Street
Santa Fe, NM 87505

SHASTRI INDO-CANADIAN INSTITUTE (SICI)

Room 1418, Education Tower
2500 University Drive, N.W.
Calgary AB T2N 1N4 Canada
(403) 220-7467
Fax: (403) 289-0100
E-mail: maldeen@ucalgary.ca
Web Site: www.sici.org

TYPE:
Fellowships. India Studies Fellowship Competition is intended to support candidates wishing to undertake research or training in India. The focus of study is subjects relating to India in the social sciences and humanities, including education, law, management, the arts, science, and technology.

See entry 922 for full listing.

SIMON FRASER UNIVERSITY [1699]

Maggie Benston Student
Services Centre 1100
8888 University Drive
Burnaby BC V5A 1S6 Canada
(778) 782-3042
Fax: (778) 782-3080
E-mail: gradstudies@sfu.ca
Web Site: www.sfu.ca/dean-gradstudies.html

FOUNDED: 1966

NAME(S) OF PROGRAMS:

- **SFU Teaching Assistantships**

TYPE:
Assistantships. The SFU Teaching Assistantships are for the various faculties/schools/departments/programs, etc. of the University. A full list of these is available from the University.

PURPOSE:
To provide financial support to the University's students enrolled in a Master's or Ph.D. program.

ELIGIBILITY:
Applicants must have already been accepted into Master's or Ph.D. program. Most teaching assistantships are available to visa students, as well as Canadian citizens and residents. There are entrance awards.

FINANCIAL DATA:
Amount of support per award: $2,500 to $50,000 (CAN).

NO. MOST RECENT APPLICANTS: 5,000.

APPLICATION INFO:
Contact the University.

Duration: Varies by department, program and award.

Deadline: Varies by department.

ADDRESS INQUIRIES TO:
Specific Department of Enrollment
Simon Fraser University
(Request specific department's address.)

HORACE SMITH FUND [1700]

1441 Main Street, 6th Floor
Suite 620
Springfield, MA 01103
(413) 739-4222
Fax: (413) 739-1108
E-mail: info@horacesmithfund.org
Web Site: www.horacesmithfund.org

FOUNDED: 1899

AREAS OF INTEREST:
Education, scholarships and fellowships.

TYPE:
Fellowships; Scholarships.

YEAR PROGRAM STARTED: 1899

PURPOSE:
To help students obtain scholarships and fellowships.

ELIGIBILITY:
For scholarships, students must have graduated from a high school in Hampden County. For fellowships, students must be legal residents of Hampden County.

GEOG. RESTRICTIONS: Hampden County, Massachusetts.

FINANCIAL DATA:
Amount of support per award: Scholarships: $2,500 per year for four years; Fellowships: $4,000 per year for up to three years.

Total amount of support: Scholarships: $360,000; Fellowships: $60,000.

APPLICATION INFO:
Applications are available in September.

Duration: One year. Scholarships renewable up to four years; Fellowships up to three years.

Deadline: February 1.

PUBLICATIONS:
Annual report; contributions policy; application guidelines.

ADDRESS INQUIRIES TO:
Josephine Sarnelli, Executive Director
(See address above.)

*SPECIAL STIPULATIONS:
Hampden County, Massachusetts residents only.

SOCIETY OF DAUGHTERS OF THE U.S. ARMY [1701]

11804 Grey Birch Place
Reston, VA 20191-4223

FOUNDED: 1928

NAME(S) OF PROGRAMS:

- **Society of Daughters of the United States Army Scholarships**

TYPE:
Scholarships.

PURPOSE:
To help daughters or granddaughters (including adopted or step) of career warrant and commissioned Army officers (Warrant Officers through General) who are on active duty, retired after at least 20 years of active service, were medically retired, or died while on active duty or after eligible retirement.

LEGAL BASIS:
Nonprofit corporation.

ELIGIBILITY:
For the Roberts, Wagner, Prickett, Simpson and DUSA Scholarships, applicants must be a daughter or granddaughter (including step or adopted) of a career warrant (WO 1-5) or commissioned (2nd & 1st LT, CPT, MAJ, LTC, COL and BG, MG, LT or full General) officer of the U.S. Army who either:
(1) is currently on active duty;
(2) retired after at least 20 years of active service;
(3) was medically retired before 20 years of active service;
(4) died while on active duty or;
(5) died after retiring with 20 or more years of active service.

U.S. Army must have been the officer's primary occupation. These scholarships are for undergraduate study only and cover academic expenses only. Minimum grade point average is 3.0.

FINANCIAL DATA:
Amount of support per award: $1,000 per year.

NO. MOST RECENT APPLICANTS: 50.

NO. AWARDS: 10.

APPLICATION INFO:

Mail one request with the officer's name, rank, component (active, reserve, retired), inclusive dates of active duty, and the relationship to the applicant, along with a stamped, self-addressed envelope, to the Scholarship Chairman. Do not send any documentation. Requests for applications must be postmarked between November 1 and March 1 for awards in the next academic year. Office is closed between March 2 and October 31. Application is not available when office is closed. Application will not be sent without qualifying information.

Do not send by registered/certified or commercial mail; delivery will be delayed. All application submissions become the property of DUSA.

Duration: One year. The scholarships may be renewed annually for four years, provided a student maintains eligibility.

Deadline: March 1.

STAFF:

Mary P. Maroney, Chairman, Memorial and Scholarship Funds

ADDRESS INQUIRIES TO:

Mary P. Maroney, Scholarship Chairman
Daughters of the United States Army
(See address above.)

SOCIETY OF PHYSICS STUDENTS [1702]

One Physics Ellipse
College Park, MD 20740-3843
(301) 209-3007
Fax: (301) 209-0839
E-mail: sps@aip.org
Web Site: www.spsnational.org

FOUNDED: 1968

AREAS OF INTEREST:

Physics.

NAME(S) OF PROGRAMS:

- **Society of Physics Students Leadership Scholarship**

TYPE:

Scholarships. Award made to physics majors in the latter stages of their undergraduate careers.

YEAR PROGRAM STARTED: 1985

PURPOSE:

To encourage the study of physics and the pursuit of high scholarship.

LEGAL BASIS:

Not-for-profit, 501(c)(3).

ELIGIBILITY:

Applicants must be a junior according to their institution's definition and plan to be enrolled as an undergraduate for at least one more semester. Only Society of Physics Students members are eligible. Scholarship is awarded on the basis of academic performance and leadership in the Society of Physics Students.

GEOG. RESTRICTIONS: United States.

FINANCIAL DATA:

Amount of support per award: $2,000 to $5,000.

APPLICATION INFO:

Completed application form, official transcript of grades, and two letters of recommendation required. Applications are accepted through the online application system only.

Duration: One year. No renewals.

Deadline: February 15.

STAFF:

Daniel Golombek, Assistant Director

ADDRESS INQUIRIES TO:

Daniel Golombek, Assistant Director
(See address above.)

*SPECIAL STIPULATIONS:

Applicant must be an active member of the Society of Physics Students.

THE PAUL & DAISY SOROS FELLOWSHIPS FOR NEW AMERICANS [1703]

224 West 57th Street
New York, NY 10019
(212) 547-6926
Fax: (212) 548-4605
E-mail: pdsoros@sorosny.org
Web Site: www.pdsoros.org

FOUNDED: 1997

AREAS OF INTEREST:

Financial aid for New Americans.

TYPE:

Fellowships.

PURPOSE:

To provide opportunities for continuing generations of able and accomplished New Americans to achieve leadership in their chosen fields.

ELIGIBILITY:

A New American is defined as an individual who:
(1) is a resident alien (i.e., holds a Green Card);
(2) is a DACA (Deferred Action for Childhood Arrivals) recipient;
(3) has been naturalized as a U.S. citizen or;
(4) is the child of parents born abroad as non-U.S. citizens.

The applicant must either have a Bachelor's degree or be in his or her final year of undergraduate study.

Upper age limit is 30 years by deadline.

GEOG. RESTRICTIONS: United States.

FINANCIAL DATA:

Amount of support per award: Fellow receives maintenance grant of $25,000 and a tuition grant of one-half tuition cost of U.S. graduate program attended, up to a maximum of $20,000 per annum.

Total amount of support: $90,000 over two years.

NO. MOST RECENT APPLICANTS: 1,400.

NO. AWARDS: 30 per year.

APPLICATION INFO:

Applications must be submitted via the online application system.

Duration: Up to two years.

Deadline: November 1.

ADDRESS INQUIRIES TO:

Yulian Ramos, Deputy Director
(See address above.)

*SPECIAL STIPULATIONS:

Must be 30 years old or younger by deadline in order to be eligible.

SOUTH CAROLINA HIGHER EDUCATION TUITION GRANTS COMMISSION [1704]

115 Atrium Way
Suite 102
Columbia, SC 29223
(803) 896-1120
Fax: (803) 896-1126
E-mail: info@sctuitiongrants.org
Web Site: www.sctuitiongrants.org

FOUNDED: 1970

AREAS OF INTEREST:

Undergraduate student financial aid to eligible South Carolina residents attending in-state, independent colleges on a full-time basis.

CONSULTING OR VOLUNTEER SERVICES:

Assistance to South Carolina high schools and colleges with questions and problems pertaining to student financial aid.

NAME(S) OF PROGRAMS:

- **South Carolina Tuition Grants Program**

TYPE:

Grants-in-aid.

YEAR PROGRAM STARTED: 1970

PURPOSE:

To increase the level of college attendance in South Carolina and to better utilize the existing educational resources of the state; to give students a choice of attending the college that best meets their academic needs.

LEGAL BASIS:

Established by state statute.

ELIGIBILITY:

Applicant must be a South Carolina resident, demonstrate good moral character, be accepted by or enrolled full-time in an eligible South Carolina private college and have financial need. Incoming freshmen must rank in the upper three-quarters of their class or score 900 or higher on the re-centered SAT. Renewal applicants must complete at least 24 semester-hours per year.

GEOG. RESTRICTIONS: South Carolina.

FINANCIAL DATA:

Awards cannot exceed tuition and fees at the institution, the need of the student and the average per-pupil expenditure by the state at a public college.

Amount of support per award: $100 to $3,200 per year. Average grant $2,710 for the year 2015-16.

Total amount of support: $36,095,796 total state appropriations for the 2014-15 academic year.

NO. MOST RECENT APPLICANTS: 34,301 for the year 2014-15.

NO. AWARDS: 13,350 for the year 2014-15.

APPLICATION INFO:

Application available online.

Duration: One year. Renewable if need continues for up to eight semesters. Must reapply each year.

Deadline: June 30.

PUBLICATIONS:

Annual report; general brochure.

GRANTS COMMITTEE:

Beth Dinndorf, Chairperson
Dr. Nayef Samhat, Vice Chairperson
Dr. Maurice Scherrens, Secretary
Scott Cochran
Dr. Jairy Hunter

Dr. Randall Pannell
Robert Staton
Dr. Todd Voss

ADDRESS INQUIRIES TO:
Earl L. Mayo, Jr.
(See address above.)

STATE COUNCIL OF HIGHER EDUCATION FOR VIRGINIA [1705]

James Monroe Building, 10th Floor
101 North 14th Street
Richmond, VA 23219
(804) 225-2600
Fax: (804) 225-2604
E-mail: communications@schev.edu
Web Site: www.schev.edu

FOUNDED: 1956

AREAS OF INTEREST:
Statewide coordination of higher education.

NAME(S) OF PROGRAMS:
- **Virginia Tuition Assistance Grant Program (VTAG)**

TYPE:
Grants-in-aid.

YEAR PROGRAM STARTED: 1972

PURPOSE:
To assist Virginia residents who attend accredited private, nonprofit colleges and universities in Virginia for other than religious training or theological education.

LEGAL BASIS:
State agency. Program mandated by state law.

ELIGIBILITY:
Recipients must be domiciliary residents of Virginia who are enrolled full-time at an approved private college or university within the state. Not available at Virginia public institutions, for-profit institutions or non-Virginia institutions. Awards are not based on financial need. Students may not be enrolled in a program of religious training or theological education.

GEOG. RESTRICTIONS: Virginia.

FINANCIAL DATA:
Funding is specified biennially by the Appropriations Act.

Amount of support per award: Up to $3,200 for Undergraduate and $1,600 for Graduate for the academic year 2016-17, depending on amount of appropriation and number of recipients.

Total amount of support: $65,800,000 for the academic year 2015-16.

NO. AWARDS: Approximately 22,000 for the academic year 2015-16.

APPLICATION INFO:
Application is available from participating private colleges or universities in Virginia, or may be downloaded from the web site above.

Duration: Nine months (academic year). Renewals are reviewed by the institutions.

Deadline: July 31. December 1 for late applications.

ADDRESS INQUIRIES TO:
Applicants should contact the financial aid officer at the private Virginia college or university they plan to attend.

STATE OF IDAHO BOARD OF EDUCATION [1706]

650 West State Street, No. 307
Boise, ID 83720-0037
(208) 332-1595
Fax: (208) 334-2632
E-mail: scholarshiphelp@osbe.idaho.gov
Web Site: www.boardofed.idaho.gov/scholarship/scholarship_jump.asp

FOUNDED: 1891

AREAS OF INTEREST:
Idaho education.

NAME(S) OF PROGRAMS:
- **Idaho Governor's Cup Scholarship**
- **Idaho Opportunity Scholarship**

TYPE:
Scholarships. Scholarships are available for high school and college students.

YEAR PROGRAM STARTED: 2009

PURPOSE:
To provide scholarships for Idaho citizens who have graduated from an Idaho high school or earned their GED in Idaho.

LEGAL BASIS:
Idaho Code Title 33, Chapter 43 (33-4303).

ELIGIBILITY:
The following scholarship application requirements apply:
(1) Idaho residency;
(2) graduation from an Idaho high school;
(3) grade point average of 3.0;
(4) demonstration of need by completion of Free Application for Federal Student Aid (FAFSA) and;
(5) U.S. citizenship or residency.

GEOG. RESTRICTIONS: Idaho.

FINANCIAL DATA:
Scholarship award cannot exceed cost of attendance.

Amount of support per award: $100 to $3,000.

Total amount of support: $5,129,790 for the year 2015-16.

NO. MOST RECENT APPLICANTS: 4,611.

NO. AWARDS: 1,163.

APPLICATION INFO:
An application form needs to be completed. Apply online at the web site address above from December 1 to March 1 of the following year.

Duration: Four years. Scholarship grant is renewable.

Deadline: March 1.

STAFF:
Joy Miller, Scholarships Program Manager

ADDRESS INQUIRIES TO:
Scholarships Program Manager
(See address above.)

STATE OF MICHIGAN DEPARTMENT OF TREASURY [1707]

P.O. Box 30462
Lansing, MI 48909
(888) 447-2687
Fax: (517) 241-5835
E-mail: ssg@michigan.gov
Web Site: www.michigan.gov/mistudentaid
www.michigan.gov/ssg

AREAS OF INTEREST:
Promoting and aiding student higher education in the state of Michigan.

NAME(S) OF PROGRAMS:
- **Children of Veterans Tuition Grant (CVTG)**
- **Dual Enrollment**
- **Fostering Futures**
- **Michigan Competitive Scholarship (MCS)**
- **Michigan Nursing Scholarship (MSN)**

TYPE:
Grants-in-aid; Scholarships.

ELIGIBILITY:
All state of Michigan programs require:
(1) high school diploma, certificate of completion, or GED;
(2) Michigan residency of at least one year prior to enrollment;
(3) U.S. citizenship, permanent residency or approved refugee status;
(4) at least half-time enrollment at an approved Michigan college or university;
(5) student not being in default on a federal student loan and;
(6) the student meeting Satisfactory Academic Progress (SAP) standards as set by the institution.

Children of Veterans Tuition Grant: Student must be the natural or adopted child of a Michigan veteran who is totally and permanently disabled, deceased or missing in action. Student must be at least 16 and less than 26 years old and must maintain a cumulative grade point average of 2.25 for renewal.

Dual Enrollment: Students attending a private high school are determined eligible by the Michigan Department of Education (MDE).

Fostering Futures: Student must have been in foster care after the 13th birthday. There is no upper age limit and student can receive funding at any age. Student must be attending a Michigan public or private four-year college/university or a community college. Funding can be used along with the Education Training Voucher.

Michigan Competitive Scholarship: Student must have a qualifying ACT score of at least 23 (composite) or 90 (scaled score) and cannot be attending an institution whose primary purpose is to prepare students for ordination or appointment as a member of the clergy of a church, denomination or religious sect. Student must maintain a minimum cumulative 2.0 grade point average.

Michigan Nursing Scholarship: A non-need award available to Michigan residents enrolled at least half-time at an eligible institution in a program leading to a Licensed Practical Nurse (LPN) certification, Associate Degree in Nursing (ADN), Bachelor of Science in Nursing (B.S.N.) or Master's of Science in Nursing (M.S.N).

FINANCIAL DATA:
Fostering Futures provides eligible foster youth with scholarship funds for tuition, fees, room/board, books and supplies/equipment required for enrollment. Michigan Competitive Scholarship program is both merit- and need-based. Limited to tuition and mandatory fees.

Amount of support per award: Children of Veterans Tuition Grant: Up to $2,800 per academic year (award limited to tuition and mandatory fees). Dual Enrollment: Varies. Michigan Competitive Scholarship: $676 for the year 2014-15. Michigan Nursing Scholarship: $4,000 per academic year for

full-time students, but cannot exceed the cost of attendance minus other grants and scholarships.

APPLICATION INFO:

Fostering Futures: Application must be submitted with copies of student financial aid award letter, most recent transcripts, and documentation supporting any off-campus expenses requested.

Duration: Children of Veterans Tuition Grant: Up to four academic years. Michigan Competitive Scholarship: Limited to 10 semesters or 15 terms.

ADDRESS INQUIRIES TO:

State of Michigan
Student Scholarships and Grants
(See address and e-mail above.)

*SPECIAL STIPULATIONS:

Michigan Nursing Scholarship (MSN): Students receiving a full-time scholarship award must agree to work as a direct patient-care nurse in an eligible Michigan facility, or as a teacher of nursing at an eligible Michigan postsecondary institution, one year for each year of assistance. If the work commitment is not fulfilled, the scholarship becomes a loan that must be repaid.

STATE OF MICHIGAN DEPARTMENT OF TREASURY [1708]

P.O. Box 30462
Lansing, MI 48909
(888) 447-2687
Fax: (517) 241-5835
E-mail: ssg@michigan.gov
Web Site: www.michigan.gov/mistudentaid
www.michigan.gov/ssg

NAME(S) OF PROGRAMS:

- **Michigan Merit Award**
- **Michigan Tuition Grant (MTG)**
- **Police Officer's and Fire Fighter's Survivor Tuition Grant (STG)**
- **Tuition Incentive Program (TIP)**

TYPE:

Grants-in-aid.

ELIGIBILITY:

Michigan Merit Award: Available only for students with military extensions until 2017.

Michigan Tuition Grant: Program is need-based. Student must be enrolled at an approved independent, degree-granting Michigan institution. However, student cannot be enrolled in a course of study leading to a degree in theology, divinity or religious education.

Police Officer's and Fire Fighter's Survivor Tuition Grant: For children and surviving spouses of Michigan police officers and firefighters killed in the line of duty. Must provide satisfactory proof. Child must be less than 21 at the time of the police officer's or firefighter's death and must apply before age 26. Award recipient must enroll at least half-time in a program leading to a certificate or degree at an approved Michigan community college or public university. Applicant must, excluding death benefits, be below 400% of the federal poverty level (must demonstrate financial need).

Tuition Incentive Program: Student must have received Medicaid coverage, as determined by The Michigan Department of Human Services (DHS), for 24 months within any 36 consecutive months between the ages of 9 and high school graduation. Awardee must begin using program within four years from high school graduation. Eligibility ends after 10 years from the date of high school graduation.

FINANCIAL DATA:

Police Officer's and Fire Fighter's Survivor Tuition Grant: Award limited to tuition only. Tuition Incentive Program: Award limited to tuition and mandatory fees; eligible mandatory fees cannot exceed $250 per semester or term.

Amount of support per award: Michigan Merit Award: Up to $3,000. Michigan Tuition Grant: $1,626; award limited to tuition and mandatory fees.

APPLICATION INFO:

Duration: Michigan Tuition Grant: Limited to 10 semesters or 15 terms. Police Officer's and Fire Fighter's Survivor Tuition Grant: Limited to 9 semesters or 13 terms (124 semester- or 180 term-credits). Tuition Incentive Program: Pays up to 24 semester- or 36 term-credits per academic year; cannot exceed 80 semester- or 120 term-credits.

Deadline: Michigan Tuition Grant: Federal processor must receive Free Application for Federal Student Aid (FAFSA) by June 30.

ADDRESS INQUIRIES TO:

State of Michigan
Student Scholarships and Grants
(See address and e-mail above.)

SUDBURY FOUNDATION

326 Concord Road
Sudbury, MA 01776
(978) 443-0849
Fax: (978) 579-9536
E-mail: contact@sudburyfoundation.org
Web Site: www.sudburyfoundation.org

TYPE:

Project/program grants; Scholarships. Capacity-building grants.

See entry 1346 for full listing.

SYRACUSE UNIVERSITY [1709]

Enrollment Management
212 Bowne Hall
Syracuse, NY 13244-1200
(315) 443-4492
Fax: (315) 443-3423
E-mail: gradawd@syr.edu
Web Site: www.syr.edu

AREAS OF INTEREST:

Student work/study programs.

NAME(S) OF PROGRAMS:

- **Syracuse University Graduate Assistantships**

TYPE:

Assistantships. Syracuse University Graduate Assistantships are of a teaching or research nature.

FINANCIAL DATA:

Amount of support per award: $14,780 minimum stipend plus up to 24 credit hours of tuition scholarship for the year 2016-17. Majority of stipends are greater than the minimum.

NO. AWARDS: Approximately 1,300 annually.

APPLICATION INFO:

Applicants must apply through departments.

Duration: One year. Renewable, depending upon student's performance and departmental need.

Deadline: Varies by program and is dependent upon admission deadline.

ADDRESS INQUIRIES TO:

Academic department of interest.

SYRACUSE UNIVERSITY [1710]

Enrollment Management
212 Bowne Hall
Syracuse, NY 13244-1200
(315) 443-4492
Fax: (315) 443-3423
E-mail: gradawd@syr.edu
Web Site: www.syr.edu

AREAS OF INTEREST:

Graduate university education.

NAME(S) OF PROGRAMS:

- **African American Graduate Fellowship**
- **Hursky Fellowship**
- **McNair Graduate Fellowship**
- **STEM Doctoral Fellowships**
- **Syracuse University Fellowship**

TYPE:

Fellowships.

PURPOSE:

To provide a full support package during a student's term of study.

ELIGIBILITY:

African American Graduate Fellowships: Awarded annually to new and continuing students across disciplines whose work supports that of the African American Studies Program.

Hursky Fellowship: Open to graduate students with a Ukrainian background whose area of study is the Ukraine or includes topics related to the Ukraine.

McNair Graduate Fellowship: Students must be either from an underrepresented group (African American, Hispanic or Native American) or a McNair Scholar at their undergraduate institution. Preference will be given to those in doctoral programs. Students will have already been admitted into a Syracuse University graduate program and must be formally nominated by their department for the award.

STEM Doctoral Fellowships: Science, technology, engineering and math disciplines. Open to members of an underrepresented group who are U.S. citizens or permanent residents.

Syracuse University Fellowships: Open to nationals of any country.

FINANCIAL DATA:

Fellowships include up to 30 credits of tuition.

Amount of support per award: African American Graduate Fellowship, McNair Graduate Fellowship and Syracuse University Fellowship: $14,825 for Master's stipend plus full tuition; $24,795 for Ph.D. stipend plus full tuition; Hursky Fellowship: $15,000 stipend; STEM Doctoral Fellowships: $24,795.

NO. AWARDS: African American Graduate Fellowship: 6 new per year; Hursky Fellowship: 1 new per year; McNair Graduate Fellowship: Up to 6 new per year; STEM Doctoral Fellowships: Up to 5 new per year; Syracuse University Fellowship: Number of awards determined by each academic college, varies yearly.

APPLICATION INFO:
Applicants must apply through admission application.

Duration: Varies by fellowship type, one to five years.

Deadline: January 1, unless earlier date determined by specific department.

ADDRESS INQUIRIES TO:
See e-mail address above.

TAMPA BAY TIMES FUND, INC. [1711]

490 First Avenue South
St. Petersburg, FL 33701
(727) 893-8765
E-mail: tbtschls@gmail.com
Web Site: www.tampabay.com/scholarships

FOUNDED: 1953

AREAS OF INTEREST:
Journalism.

NAME(S) OF PROGRAMS:

- **Career Journalism Scholarship**

TYPE:
Scholarships.

YEAR PROGRAM STARTED: 1990

PURPOSE:
To identify worthy students who need additional resources to support their education in pursuing a journalism major in college and career after graduation.

ELIGIBILITY:
High school seniors in the Times' circulation area.

GEOG. RESTRICTIONS: Citrus, Hernando, Hillsborough, Pasco and Pinellas counties, Florida.

FINANCIAL DATA:
Amount of support per award: $2,500 annually.

Total amount of support: Average $10,000.

NO. MOST RECENT APPLICANTS: 12.

NO. AWARDS: Average 3 annually.

APPLICATION INFO:
Application information is online. Applicant must submit:
(1) completed Questionnaire (two pages);
(2) short essay (500 to 800 words) describing journalism experience; if applicant does not have such experience, explain why interested in journalism as a career; also provide, on another sheet of paper, resume of achievements/awards;
(3) letter detailing which college applicant plans to attend, total cost of education for that institution, other financial aid applied for or known to be received, and anything else pertinent to family's financial situation;
(4) portfolio of work (or link to web site). No more than six examples and do not send originals; if applicant has no previous experience, send three samples of writing for class assignments and;
(5) three letters of recommendation, written and signed by teachers or others for whom applicant has done a substantial amount of writing, discussing the applicant's writing ability, strengths as a student, character, areas for improvement, and how applicant has demonstrated interest in journalism; each letter should have, at the top, applicant's name, teacher's name and teacher's phone number.

Duration: Up to four years. Must reapply annually.

Deadline: January 5.

ADDRESS INQUIRIES TO:
Nancy Waclawek, Scholarships Administrator
(See address above.)

TAMPA BAY TIMES FUND, INC. [1712]

490 First Avenue South
St. Petersburg, FL 33701
(727) 893-8765
E-mail: tbtschls@gmail.com
Web Site: www.tampabay.com/scholarships

FOUNDED: 1953

AREAS OF INTEREST:
Education, arts, social services and journalism.

NAME(S) OF PROGRAMS:

- **Barnes Scholarship**

TYPE:
Scholarships.

YEAR PROGRAM STARTED: 1999

PURPOSE:
To provide assistance to college-bound teens who have overcome significant obstacles in their lives while remaining committed to academic achievement and community involvement.

ELIGIBILITY:
Applicants must be U.S. citizens or permanent residents, high school seniors in public or private schools in specific counties of Florida. Preference will be given to students whose parents have not graduated from a college or university and also to students who are applying to schools outside of Florida.

GEOG. RESTRICTIONS: Citrus, Hernando, Hillsborough, Pasco and Pinellas counties, Florida.

FINANCIAL DATA:
Amount of support per award: Up to $15,000 per year.

Total amount of support: Up to $60,000.

NO. AWARDS: 4 annually.

APPLICATION INFO:
Application information is online. There are three parts to the application:

The first part includes basic information about the applicant, e.g., addresses of applicant and parents or guardians, phone numbers, e-mails, test scores, high school information, and colleges to which applicant has applied to or intends to apply.

The second part is a resume providing information about academic honors, classes taken, community service performed, extracurricular activities, employment, awards, athletics, and other activities that have been key in forming the applicant's life experience thus far.

The third part is an essay (250 to 1,000 words) describing the applicant's greatest obstacle in life and how it has been overcome.

Duration: Up to four years.

Deadline: October 15.

ADDRESS INQUIRIES TO:
Nancy Waclawek, Scholarships Administrator
(See address above.)

TENNESSEE STUDENT ASSISTANCE CORPORATION [1713]

404 James Robertson Parkway
Parkway Towers, Suite 1510
Nashville, TN 37243-0820
(615) 741-1346
(800) 342-1663
Fax: (615) 741-6101
E-mail: tsac.aidinfo@tn.gov
Web Site: www.tn.gov/collegepays

FOUNDED: 1974

NAME(S) OF PROGRAMS:

- **Dependent Children Scholarship Program**
- **Graduate Nursing Loan-Forgiveness Program**
- **Ned McWherter Scholars Program**
- **Minority Teaching Fellows Program**
- **Tennessee Education Lottery Scholarship Program**
- **Tennessee Math & Science Teachers Loan Forgiveness Program**
- **Tennessee Student Assistance Award**
- **Tennessee Teaching Scholars Program**

TYPE:
Grants-in-aid; Scholarships; Loan forgiveness programs. Need-based grants for undergraduate Tennessee residents enrolled in an eligible Tennessee institution.

Dependent Children Scholarship Program provides aid for Tennessee residents who are dependent children of a Tennessee law enforcement officer, fireman or an emergency medical service technician who has been killed or totally and permanently disabled while performing duties within the scope of such employment.

Graduate Nursing Loan-Forgiveness Program is designed to encourage Tennessee residents who are nurses to become teachers and administrators in Tennessee nursing education programs. Participants in this program incur an obligation to enter a faculty or administrative position in a nursing education program, in Tennessee, immediately upon completion of the education program.

The Ned McWherter Scholars Program is intended to encourage academically superior Tennessee high school graduates to attend college in Tennessee.

Minority Teaching Fellows Program is intended to encourage talented minority Tennesseans to enter the teaching field in Tennessee.

Tennessee Education Lottery Scholarship Program is for those who have been a Tennessee resident for one year by September 1 of the year of application date.

Tennessee Math & Science Teachers Loan Forgiveness Program provides financial assistance to Tennessee public school teachers seeking an advanced degree in a math or a science, or a certification to teach a math or a science. Loan forgiveness requires employment in a Tennessee public school system two years for each year of the loan funding received.

Tennessee Student Assistance Award provides nonrepayable financial assistance to financially needy undergraduate students who are residents of Tennessee.

Tennessee Teaching Scholars Program is intended to encourage exemplary students to enter the teaching field in Tennessee.

YEAR PROGRAM STARTED: 1976

PURPOSE:
To provide grants based on financial need for Tennessee residents.

LEGAL BASIS:
State agency.

ELIGIBILITY:
Applicants for the Ned McWherter Scholars Program must be high school seniors with a 3.5 grade point average, a GED score of 570 and 29 ACT or 1280 SAT, and planning to attend an eligible Tennessee institution.

Applicants for the Minority Teaching Fellows Program are preferably high school seniors with a 2.75 grade point average and 18 ACT or be at the top 25% of their graduating class. Undergraduate applicants must have a 2.5 college grade point average.

Applicants for the Tennessee Education Lottery Scholarship Program must:
(1) be entering freshmen who are Tennessee residents for one year prior to application;
(2) enroll in a Tennessee public college/university or enroll in a Tennessee private college/university that is accredited by the Southern Association of Colleges and Schools and;
(3) be enrolled full-time (part-time prorated), leading to a certificate in the Tennessee Technology Centers or degree in approved colleges and universities. Satisfactory academic progress required.

Applicants for the Tennessee Teaching Scholars Program must be college juniors or seniors or post-Baccalaureate students admitted to teacher education programs in Tennessee colleges or universities and U.S. citizens.

GEOG. RESTRICTIONS: Tennessee.

FINANCIAL DATA:
Amount of support per award: Varies.

Matching fund requirements: For Ned McWherter Scholars Program, the institution must match $3,000.

NO. MOST RECENT APPLICANTS: Ned McWherter Scholars: 900; Minority Teaching Fellows: 150; Tennessee Teaching Scholars: 400.

NO. AWARDS: Ned McWherter Scholars: 50; Minority Teaching Fellows: 29; Tennessee Education Lottery Scholarship Program: 40,000; Tennessee Teaching Scholars: 160.

APPLICATION INFO:
Detailed information is available online.

Duration: Renewable each academic year.

Deadline: Ned McWherter Scholars: February 15; Minority Teaching Fellows: April 15; Tennessee Education Lottery Scholarship Program: September 1 for fall term, February 1 for spring and summer terms; Tennessee Teaching Scholars: April 15.

ADDRESS INQUIRIES TO:
See telephone numbers above.

*SPECIAL STIPULATIONS:
Loan Forgiveness Programs, Tennessee Teaching Scholars and Minority Teaching Fellows: Recipients agree to teach one year for each year of funding in a public Tennessee grades K-12 school or appropriate learning institution or repayment will be required.

TOURISM CARES [1714]

275 Turnpike Street
Suite 307
Canton, MA 02021
(781) 821-5990
Fax: (781) 821-8949
E-mail: amandad@tourismcares.org
Web Site: www.tourismcares.org

FOUNDED: 2005

AREAS OF INTEREST:
Travel and tourism, hospitality and sustainable tourism.

NAME(S) OF PROGRAMS:
- **Graduate Research Scholarships**
- **High School Scholarships**
- **Professional Development Scholarship Program**
- **Undergraduate or Graduate Scholarships**

TYPE:
Internships; Scholarships. Academic and Professional Development.

YEAR PROGRAM STARTED: 2005

PURPOSE:
To benefit society by preserving the travel experience for future generations by awarding academic and professional scholarships, internships, volunteering and mentoring opportunities to students of travel, tourism, and hospitality; by giving grants to cultural, historic and natural tourism-related sites worldwide; and by organizing volunteer efforts to restore tourism-related sites in need of care and rejuvenation.

LEGAL BASIS:
Nonprofit, tax-exempt 501(c)(3) public charity.

FINANCIAL DATA:
Amount of support per award: $300 to $5,000.

Total amount of support: More than $1,000,000 cumulative total since the beginning of the program.

NO. MOST RECENT APPLICANTS: 300.

NO. AWARDS: Varies.

APPLICATION INFO:
Application process, FAQs and access to online-only applications are available at the web site.

Deadline: Varies.

PUBLICATIONS:
e-newsletter.

ADDRESS INQUIRIES TO:
Tourism Cares Scholarship Department
(See e-mail address above.)

TUSKEGEE UNIVERSITY

1200 West Montgomery Road
Tuskegee, AL 36088
(334) 727-8201 (Financial Aid)
E-mail: faid@mytu.tuskegee.edu
Web Site: www.tuskegee.edu

TYPE:
Fellowships.

See entry 1979 for full listing.

TWO TEN FOOTWEAR FOUNDATION [1715]

1466 Main Street
Waltham, MA 02451
(800) 346-3210 ext. 1512
Fax: (781) 736-1555; (781) 736-1554
E-mail: contactus@applyists.com
Web Site: www.twoten.org

AREAS OF INTEREST:
Footwear design.

NAME(S) OF PROGRAMS:
- **Two Ten Footwear Foundation Design Scholarship Program**

TYPE:
Scholarships. Intended for students who are interested in pursuing a career in footwear design.

PURPOSE:
To provide financial aid to those studying footwear design.

ELIGIBILITY:
Applicant must:
(1) demonstrate an interest and commitment to a career in footwear design;
(2) be a U.S. citizen or eligible noncitizen;
(3) display financial need as calculated by the federal method of need analysis and the Design Scholarship Selection Committee (applicant can estimate Expected Family Contribution at www.finaid.com) and;
(4) attend or plan to attend an approved postsecondary institution.

GEOG. RESTRICTIONS: United States.

FINANCIAL DATA:
Amount of support per award: Varies.

Total amount of support: Varies.

NO. AWARDS: Varies.

APPLICATION INFO:
Applicants for consideration must submit a portfolio. Interested candidates must contact the director of scholarship for further information.

Duration: Up to four years.

Deadline: Varies.

ADDRESS INQUIRIES TO:
International Scholarship and Tuition Services (ISTS)
Tel: (855) 670-4787
(See e-mail address above.)

TWO TEN FOOTWEAR FOUNDATION [1716]

Scholarship Department
1466 Main Street
Waltham, MA 02451
(800) 346-3210
Fax: (781) 736-1555; (781) 736-1554
E-mail: contactus@applyists.com
Web Site: www.twoten.org

FOUNDED: 1939

AREAS OF INTEREST:
Footwear industry.

NAME(S) OF PROGRAMS:
- **Two Ten Footwear Foundation College Scholarship Program**

TYPE:
Scholarships. Offered to students affiliated with the footwear, leather or allied industries.

YEAR PROGRAM STARTED: 1969

PURPOSE:
To provide financial assistance to people in the footwear, leather and allied industries.

LEGAL BASIS:
Private foundation.

ELIGIBILITY:
Scholarship applicant must be affiliated with the footwear, leather or allied industries:
(1) either the student must be employed in the above industries, or have a parent (natural, step or adopted) who must be employed in these industries for a minimum of two years prior to January 1 (student must be considered a dependent);
(2) student must display financial need for college costs as calculated by the federal method of need analysis and the Two Ten Selection Committee;
(3) student must be a U.S. citizen or eligible noncitizen and;
(4) student must enroll at an accredited college, university, nursing or vocational/technical school, earning a two- or four-year undergraduate degree.

FINANCIAL DATA:
Amount of support per award: Generally, up to $3,000. There are also several larger awards available, as well as one super scholarship award of up to $15,000 of unmet need annually.

Total amount of support: $865,000 in scholarships for the year 2015.

NO. AWARDS: Over 300 for the year 2015.

APPLICATION INFO:
Contact the Foundation.

Duration: Up to four years.

Deadline: April 1.

ADDRESS INQUIRIES TO:
International Scholarship and Tuition Services (ISTS)
(See e-mail address above.)

*SPECIAL STIPULATIONS:
Eligible companies must do at least 50% of their business in footwear, or applicant or parent must work in a specific footwear division.

U.S. DEPARTMENT OF EDUCATION [1717]

Federal Student Aid Programs
830 First Street, N.E.
Washington, DC 20202
(800) 433-3243
(319) 337-5665
TTY: (800) 730-8913
E-mail: studentaid@ed.gov
Web Site: www.studentaid.gov

AREAS OF INTEREST:
Student financial aid.

NAME(S) OF PROGRAMS:
- **Federal Work-Study**

TYPE:
Work-study programs. Federal Work-Study program provides part-time jobs for undergraduate and graduate students with financial need. This allows them to earn money to help pay education expenses. Jobs can be on- or off-campus and are available to full-time or part-time students. Students are paid at least federal minimum wage. The money earned does not have to be repaid. The program is administered by schools participating in the Federal Work-Study Program. Interested students should check with their school's financial aid office to determine if their school does participate.

PURPOSE:
To enable students to earn a part of educational expenses.

LEGAL BASIS:
Government agency.

ELIGIBILITY:
In general, the aid recipient must:
(1) show financial need;
(2) be a U.S. citizen or eligible noncitizen with a valid Social Security number (SSN);
(3) be working toward a degree or certificate in an eligible program;
(4) demonstrate one is qualified to obtain a postsecondary education;
(5) register (if not already done so) with the Selective Service, if one is a male between the ages of 18 and 25 and;
(6) maintain satisfactory academic progress once in school.

FINANCIAL DATA:
Federal Work-Study wages will be at least the current federal minimum wage, but may be higher, depending on the type of work and the skills required. The total Federal Work-Study award depends on when a student applies, one's level of need, and the funding level of one's school.

Amount of support per award: Varies.

Total amount of support: Varies.

APPLICATION INFO:
The interested student should consult with his or her school's financial aid office.

Duration: One year. Renewable.

PUBLICATIONS:
Funding Your Education: The Guide to Federal Student Aid.

ADDRESS INQUIRIES TO:
Federal Student Aid Programs
P.O. Box 84
Washington, DC 20044

U.S. DEPARTMENT OF EDUCATION [1718]

Federal Student Aid Programs
830 First Street, N.E.
Washington, DC 20202
(800) 433-3243
TTY: (800)-730-8913
E-mail: studentaid@ed.gov
Web Site: www.studentaid.gov

AREAS OF INTEREST:
Student financial aid.

NAME(S) OF PROGRAMS:
- **Pell Grant**

TYPE:
Grants-in-aid. Student aid grants for higher education. Available almost exclusively to undergraduates. Grant does not have to be repaid.

YEAR PROGRAM STARTED: 1973

PURPOSE:
To help undergraduates pay for education after high school.

LEGAL BASIS:
Title IV, Higher Education Act of 1965, as amended.

ELIGIBILITY:
In general, the aid recipient must:
(1) show financial need;
(2) enroll as a regular student in an eligible degree or certificate program;
(3) be a U.S. citizen or eligible noncitizen and;
(4) meet the school's satisfactory academic progress standards in his or her course of study.

The student also must register with the Selective Service, if required.

FINANCIAL DATA:
Amount of support per award: Depends on student's financial need, the cost of attendance (COA) at the student's school, status as full-time or part-time student and how long the student will be enrolled in the academic year in question. The financial aid office at student's college or career school will determine how much financial aid he or she is eligible to receive.

APPLICATION INFO:
Applicants should contact the financial aid office at each school they are considering attending to determine which forms must be submitted. Students can request a copy of the *Student Guide* at the toll-free phone number.

Duration: One year. Renewable. Student can receive Federal Pell Grant for no more than 12 semesters or the equivalent (roughly six years).

PUBLICATIONS:
Funding Education Beyond High School: The Guide to Federal Student Aid.

ADDRESS INQUIRIES TO:
Federal Student Aid Programs
P.O. Box 84
Washington, DC 20044

*PLEASE NOTE:
Applicant may receive only one Pell Grant in an award year, and may not receive Pell Grant funds from more than one school at a time.

U.S. DEPARTMENT OF EDUCATION [1719]

Federal Student Aid Programs
830 First Street, N.E.
Washington, DC 20202
(800) 433-3243
TTY: (800) 730-8913 (for hearing-impaired)
E-mail: studentaid@ed.gov
Web Site: www.studentaid.gov

AREAS OF INTEREST:
Student financial aid.

NAME(S) OF PROGRAMS:
- **Federal Supplemental Educational Opportunity Grant (FSEOG)**

TYPE:
Grants-in-aid. Federal Supplemental Educational Opportunity Grant (FSEOG) is a grant for undergraduate students with exceptional financial need. This grant does not need to be repaid. The program is administered directly by the financial aid office at each participating school and is therefore called "campus-based" aid. Not all schools participate.

PURPOSE:
To help undergraduates with exceptional financial need.

ELIGIBILITY:
FSEOG is awarded to undergraduate students who have exceptional financial need and who have not earned a Bachelor's or graduate degree. Federal Pell Grant recipients receive priority.

FINANCIAL DATA:
Amount of support per award: $100 to $4,000 a year, depending on student's

financial need, when student applied, the amount of other aid student has received, and the availability of funds at student's school.

APPLICATION INFO:
Student should check with his or her school's financial aid office to ascertain if the school offers the FSEOG.

Deadline: Each school sets its own deadlines for campus-based funds.

*PLEASE NOTE:
Each participating school receives a certain amount of FSEOG funds each year from the U.S. Department of Education's office of Federal Student Aid. Once the full amount of the school's FSEOG funds has been awarded to students, no more FSEOG awards can be made for that year.

U.S. DEPARTMENT OF EDUCATION [1720]

Federal Student Aid Programs
830 First Street, N.E.
Washington, DC 20202
(800) 433-3243
TTY: (800) 730-8913 (for hearing-impaired)
E-mail: studentaid@ed.gov
Web Site: www.studentaid.gov

AREAS OF INTEREST:
Student financial aid.

NAME(S) OF PROGRAMS:
- **Teacher Education Assistance for College and Higher Education (TEACH) Grant**

TYPE:
Grants-in-aid. Grant does not have to be repaid unless recipient fails to carry out the service obligation.

PURPOSE:
To help undergraduate, post-Baccalaureate and graduate students with financial need.

ELIGIBILITY:
The TEACH Grant is intended for undergraduate, post-Baccalaureate and graduate students who plan to become elementary or secondary teachers. Recipient must sign Agreement to Serve saying he or she will teach full-time in a high-need field for four complete years (within eight years of completing the academic program) at an elementary school, secondary school or educational service agency serving children from low-income families. Grant recipient must attend a participating college and meet certain academic achievement requirements. Failure to complete the teaching service commitment will result in the grant being converted to a Direct Unsubsidized Loan that must be repaid.

FINANCIAL DATA:
Amount of support per award: Up to $4,000 per year.

THE MORRIS K. UDALL AND STEWART L. UDALL FOUNDATION [1721]

130 South Scott Avenue
Tucson, AZ 85701
(520) 901-8564
Fax: (520) 901-8570
E-mail: randler@udall.gov
Web Site: www.udall.gov

FOUNDED: 1992

AREAS OF INTEREST:
Environment, including policy, engineering, science, education, urban planning and renewal, business, justice and economics; Native American health care and tribal public policy, including policy, engineering, science, education and business.

NAME(S) OF PROGRAMS:
- **Udall Scholarship**

TYPE:
Scholarships. The Udall Foundation seeks future leaders across a wide spectrum of environmental fields, including policy, engineering, science, education, urban planning and renewal, business, justice and economics.

The Udall Foundation also seeks future Native American and Alaska Native leaders in Native American health care and tribal public policy. Tribal policy includes fields related to tribal sovereignty, tribal governance, tribal law, Native American education, Native American justice, natural resource management, cultural preservation and revitalization, Native American economic development and other areas affecting Native American communities. Native American health care includes health care administration, social work, medicine and research into health conditions affecting Native American communities.

YEAR PROGRAM STARTED: 1996

PURPOSE:
To educate a new generation of Americans to preserve and protect their national heritage through studies in the environment, Native American health and tribal policy, and effective public policy conflict resolution.

LEGAL BASIS:
The Foundation is an executive branch agency. The President of the U.S. appoints its board of trustees with the advice and consent of the U.S. Senate.

ELIGIBILITY:
Citizens, nationals or permanent residents of the U.S. are eligible to apply. The scholarship awards are made on the basis of merit to two groups of students:
(1) those who are college sophomores or juniors in the current academic year, have outstanding potential and who study the environment and related fields and;
(2) Native American and Alaska Native students who are college sophomores or juniors in the current academic year, have outstanding potential and are in fields related to health care or tribal public policy.

FINANCIAL DATA:
Amount of support per award: Up to $5,000.

Total amount of support: Varies.

NO. MOST RECENT APPLICANTS: 490 for the year 2014.

NO. AWARDS: 50.

APPLICATION INFO:
Application information is available on the web site.

Duration: One year.

Deadline: Approximately early March each year.

STAFF:
Paula Randler, Program Manager

ADDRESS INQUIRIES TO:
Paula Randler, Program Manager
(See address above.)

*SPECIAL STIPULATIONS:
Students must have support from a faculty or staff member at their college.

UNICO NATIONAL, INC. [1722]

271 U.S. Highway 46 West
Suite F-103
Fairfield, NJ 07004
(973) 808-0035
Fax: (973) 808-0043
E-mail: uniconational@unico.org
Web Site: www.unico.org

FOUNDED: 1922

NAME(S) OF PROGRAMS:
- **Basilone Postgraduate Scholarship**
- **Cottone Postgraduate Scholarship (Medical Only)**
- **William C. Davini Scholarship**
- **DiMattio Celli Undergraduate Study Abroad Program**
- **Major Don S. Gentile Scholarship**
- **Ella Grasso Literary Scholarship**
- **Guglielmo Marconi Engineering Scholarship**
- **Theodore Mazza Scholarship**
- **Alphonse A. Miele Scholarship**
- **Robert J. Tarte Scholarship for Italian Studies**
- **Bernard and Carolyn Torraco Nursing Scholarships**
- **Louise Torraco Memorial Scholarship for Science**
- **Ralph J. Torraco Fine Arts Scholarship**
- **Ralph J. Torraco Scholarship**

TYPE:
Scholarships. Postgraduate scholarships and undergraduate scholarships.

PURPOSE:
To give financial aid to students of outstanding merit so they may complete their education.

ELIGIBILITY:
Candidates must reside in the home state of an active chapter of UNICO National. Candidates must also meet the eligibility requirements stated on each of the respective applications. Online degree programs are not eligible for UNICO scholarships.

Scholarship candidates must, in general, be of Italian heritage, i.e., must have one parent or grandparent of Italian heritage. The extent to which a candidate has contributed to the life and welfare of school and/or community will be taken into account in the assessment of merit. UNICO member's children are eligible. Each chapter of UNICO National may submit applications for each of the UNICO Foundation scholarships.

A candidate for the undergraduate scholarships must be a citizen of the U.S. and have Italian heritage. An applicant must be a graduating senior at a public or private secondary school.

The Basilone Scholarship requires that the applicant be a senior in college or a graduate beginning postgraduate studies.

The Cottone Scholarship requires that a candidate be a college senior or graduate who is beginning postgraduate studies in the field of medicine or is currently enrolled in an accredited medical school in the U.S.

A candidate for either postgraduate program (Basilone or Cottone Scholarship) must be a U.S. citizen of Italian heritage.

A candidate for the Guglielmo Marconi Engineering Scholarship must be a sophomore, junior or senior student enrolled full-time, in an accredited college/university program in the U.S. majoring in engineering. Applicant must be a U.S. citizen of Italian heritage.

A candidate for the Robert J. Tarte Scholarship for Italian Studies must be a student enrolled full-time in an accredited college/university program in the U.S. pursuing Italian Studies. That candidate must hold U.S. citizenship. The program is open to applicants of all ethnicities.

A candidate for the Bernard and Carolyn Torraco Memorial Nursing Scholarship must currently be enrolled in an accredited nursing degree program in the U.S., completing core nursing courses, at one of the following: An Associate Degree School of Nursing; A Collegiate School of Nursing; A Diploma School of Nursing. Proof of enrollment must be provided. The candidate must have a minimum grade point average of 3.0 or B to qualify. Preference will be given to applicants demonstrating financial need. Program is open to nursing students of all ethnicities.

A candidate for the Louise Torraco Memorial Scholarship for Science must be enrolled full-time in an accredited college/university program in the U.S. pursuing study in the physical sciences or life sciences. Nominee must hold U.S. citizenship. Program is open to applicants of all ethnicities.

Ralph J. Torraco Fine Arts Scholarship is given to students enrolled full-time in an accredited college/university program in the U.S. pursuing a degree in the fine arts. A nominee must hold U.S. citizenship. Program is open to applicants of all ethnicities. pursuing the study of music. Nominee must hold U.S. citizenship.

Ralph J. Torraco Scholarship requires students to be enrolled full-time, in an accredited college/university program in the U.S. pursuing a degree. Nominees must hold U.S. citizenship. Program is open to applicants of all ethnicities.

FINANCIAL DATA:
Amount of support per award: Undergraduate and Basilone Postgraduate Scholarships: $1,500 per year; Cottone Postgraduate Scholarship: $5,000; DiMattio Celli Program and Guglielmo Marconi Engineering Scholarship: $1,250; Ella Grasso Scholarship and Robert J. Tarte Scholarship for Italian Studies: $1,000; Torraco Nursing Scholarship, Louise Toracco Memorial Scholarship, Ralph J. Torraco Fine Arts Scholarship and Ralph J. Torraco Scholarship: $2,500.

Total amount of support: Varies.

APPLICATION INFO:
Applications for scholarships are available and must be acquired from and submitted through a State Chapter, the District Governor or the UNICO National Office. Applicants may access the UNICO National web site and click on Find a Chapter.

Applicants for all of the Torraco Scholarships are required to submit the current FAFSA Student Aid Report (SAR) or the tax return from the previous year.

Duration: Undergraduate and Basilone Postgraduate Scholarships: Maximum of four years; Cottone Postgraduate Scholarship: One-time only.

Deadline: DiMattio Celli Undergraduate Study Abroad Program: March 1. All others: April 15.

ADDRESS INQUIRIES TO:
UNICO National Scholarship Director
(See address above.)

UNITED NEGRO COLLEGE FUND (UNCF)

1805 Seventh Street, N.W.
Washington, DC 20001
(800) 331-2244
(202) 810-0258
E-mail: scholarships@uncf.org
Web Site: www.uncf.org

TYPE:
Fellowships; Internships; Scholarships; Technical assistance. The Fund, since its founding, has raised money for 37 private, historically Black colleges and universities.

Faculty fellowship programs make it possible for hundreds of instructors to earn doctoral degrees.

Mentoring and internship opportunities are provided for hundreds of UNCF students.

Scholarships are offered to a pool of more than 60,000 talented students attending UNCF colleges and universities. The Fund oversees more than 450 scholarship programs in the following general categories:
(1) geographically based scholarships;
(2) scholarships based on academic major;
(3) scholarships based on merit and need and;
(4) financial aid for graduate study.

See entry 1015 for full listing.

UNIVERSITIES CANADA [1723]

350 Albert Street, Suite 1710
Ottawa ON K1R 1B1 Canada
(613) 563-1236
Fax: (613) 563-9745
E-mail: awards@univcan.ca
Web Site: www.univcan.ca

FOUNDED: 1911

AREAS OF INTEREST:
Undergraduate education at a Canadian university.

NAME(S) OF PROGRAMS:
- **C.D. Howe Scholarships**

TYPE:
Scholarships. Applicable towards full-time studies for applicants entering the first year of a first Bachelor's degree program. There are no restrictions on the program of study or discipline. The program must be of a minimum three-year duration. Canadian educational institutions which have provincial degree-granting powers, or their affiliates, are eligible for this program.

YEAR PROGRAM STARTED: 1987

PURPOSE:
To assist Canadian students from Thunder Bay and the former federal constituency of Port Arthur to pursue an undergraduate degree in any field at a Canadian university.

LEGAL BASIS:
Nonprofit foundation.

ELIGIBILITY:
Each applicant must be a Canadian citizen or permanent resident and must be a resident of Thunder Bay or the former federal constituency of Port Arthur.

The Thunder Bay area includes the following school boards:
(1) Thunder Bay Catholic District School Board;
(2) Red Lake Combined Roman Catholic Separate School Board and;
(3) Superior North Catholic District School Board.

The former constituency of Port Arthur includes the following school boards:
(1) Lakehead District School Board;
(2) Superior Greenstone District School Board and;
(3) Conseil scolaire de district catholique des Aurores Boreales.
In most cases, applicant will be a student in the school boards mentioned above.

Applicant must also have a minimum cumulative average of 80% (or equivalent) over the last three semesters of available marks. Nonacademic courses such as career- or personal development-related courses will not be considered.

To be considered for renewal, scholarship recipients must maintain a full-time status, as defined by the educational institution, and must pass all courses and maintain a B average (or equivalent). They must also send the Association an official transcript at the end of each academic year. Students must complete and return the *Renewal Report* provided by the Association. Any changes of personal or academic status must also be transmitted to Universities Canada.

GEOG. RESTRICTIONS: Canada.

FINANCIAL DATA:
Payment will be made by Universities Canada to the universities attended. Payment by the university will be according to the usual practice of the university.

Amount of support per award: $5,500 (CAN) annually.

Total amount of support: $11,000 (CAN) annually.

NO. AWARDS: Up to 2 entrance scholarships: one to a Thunder Bay student and one to a student from C.D. Howe's former constituency of Port Arthur.

APPLICATION INFO:
Each applicant must provide:
(1) an official transcript of the last three semesters of available marks;
(2) two signed reference letters with the references' original signatures (one from a teacher and one from a person familiar with their volunteer/community involvement and/or extracurricular activities) and;
(3) one page (maximum 250 words) describing their volunteer/community involvement and/or extracurricular activities.

Note that a transcript will be considered acceptable only if it meets the following criteria:
(1) it is presented on the official paper of the institution and;
(2) it bears the appropriate signature(s) and/or seal of the institution.

Duration: Maximum of four years or until first degree is obtained, whichever occurs first.

PUBLICATIONS:
Program announcement.

ADDRESS INQUIRIES TO:
Higher Education Scholarships
Universities Canada

Ref: C.D. Howe Scholarship Endowment Fund-Thunder Bay/Port Arthur Scholarship Program
(See address or e-mail above.)

THE UNIVERSITY OF BRITISH COLUMBIA [1724]

Faculty of Graduate and Postdoctoral Studies
170-6371 Crescent Road
Vancouver BC V6T 1Z2 Canada
(604) 822-2848
Fax: (604) 822-5802
E-mail: killam.fellowships@ubc.ca
Web Site: www.postdocs.ubc.ca

NAME(S) OF PROGRAMS:
- **Izaak Walton Killam Memorial Postdoctoral Research Fellowships**

TYPE:
Fellowships. Offered to allow researchers holding a Ph.D. to undertake full-time research at the University of British Columbia.

YEAR PROGRAM STARTED: 1967

LEGAL BASIS:
University.

ELIGIBILITY:
Open to persons who have shown superior ability in research and have obtained, within two academic years of the anticipated commencement date of the Fellowship, a Ph.D. at a university other than the University of British Columbia and who wish to pursue further study.

Fellowships are tenable only at the University of British Columbia. People holding faculty positions at universities or colleges are not eligible to apply.

Killam Postdoctoral Research Fellows are permitted to undertake teaching or other academic duties up to the equivalent of one six-credit (two-term) course over the two-year term of the Fellowship.

Citizens of any country may apply.

FINANCIAL DATA:
Amount of support per award: Stipend of up to $50,000 per annum plus a research/travel allowance of $4,000 over two years.

Total amount of support: Approximately $350,000 per year.

NO. MOST RECENT APPLICANTS: 150.

NO. AWARDS: 4 to 6 per year.

APPLICATION INFO:
Applicant must first contact department of interest. Fellowships are awarded on the basis of applications submitted to UBC departments.

Duration: Fellowships are granted for two years, subject to review at the end of the first year.

Deadline: Mid-October to early November.

ADDRESS INQUIRIES TO:
See e-mail address above.

THE UNIVERSITY OF BRITISH COLUMBIA [1725]

Faculty of Graduate and Postdoctoral Studies
170-6371 Crescent Road
Vancouver BC V6T 1Z2 Canada
(604) 822-2848
Fax: (604) 822-5802
E-mail: graduate.awards@ubc.ca
Web Site: www.grad.ubc.ca/awards

AREAS OF INTEREST:
All areas of advanced study.

NAME(S) OF PROGRAMS:
- **Affiliated Fellowships**

TYPE:
Fellowships. For postgraduate studies leading to a Master's or Doctorate degree at the University of British Columbia.

PURPOSE:
To allow outstanding students to devote full-time to research and study leading to a Master's or Doctorate degree.

LEGAL BASIS:
University.

ELIGIBILITY:
Citizens of any country may apply. Applicants must have outstanding academic records.

FINANCIAL DATA:
Amount of support per award: $1,000 to $30,000 (CAN) per annum.

Total amount of support: Approximately $600,000 (CAN) per annum.

NO. MOST RECENT APPLICANTS: Approximately 800.

NO. AWARDS: 50 per year.

APPLICATION INFO:
Fellowships are awarded on the basis of applications submitted to graduate programs.

Duration: One or two years.

Deadline: Mid- to late September.

ADDRESS INQUIRIES TO:
See e-mail address above.

THE UNIVERSITY OF BRITISH COLUMBIA [1726]

Faculty of Graduate and Postdoctoral Studies
170-6371 Crescent Road
Vancouver BC V6T 1Z2 Canada
(604) 822-2848
Fax: (604) 822-5802
E-mail: graduate.awards@ubc.ca
Web Site: www.grad.ubc.ca/awards

AREAS OF INTEREST:
Research-based Master's and doctoral studies.

NAME(S) OF PROGRAMS:
- **Graduate Student Initiative**

TYPE:
Scholarships.

YEAR PROGRAM STARTED: 2008

PURPOSE:
To provide funding for graduate students through entrance scholarships, multiyear funding packages, tuition awards, and scholarship top-ups.

LEGAL BASIS:
University.

ELIGIBILITY:
Citizens of any country may apply.

FINANCIAL DATA:
Amount of support per award: Set by graduate programs.

Total amount of support: $6,700,000.

APPLICATION INFO:
Student should submit research proposal and academic record to the graduate department of interest.

Duration: Up to four years.

Deadline: Inquiry to graduate program of interest accepted throughout the year. Most funding decisions are made January to March.

ADDRESS INQUIRIES TO:
See e-mail address above.

THE UNIVERSITY OF BRITISH COLUMBIA [1727]

Faculty of Graduate and Postdoctoral Studies
170-6371 Crescent Road
Vancouver BC V6T 1Z2 Canada
(604) 822-2848
Fax: (604) 822-5802
E-mail: graduate.awards@ubc.ca
Web Site: www.grad.ubc.ca/awards

AREAS OF INTEREST:
Doctoral study in all disciplines.

NAME(S) OF PROGRAMS:
- **Four Year Doctoral Fellowships**

TYPE:
Fellowships.

YEAR PROGRAM STARTED: 2009

PURPOSE:
To attract and retain outstanding doctoral students by offering stable, base-level funding for four years of their Ph.D. studies and research.

ELIGIBILITY:
Open to doctoral students in any discipline. Citizens of any country may apply.

FINANCIAL DATA:
Ensures student receives financial support of at least $18,000 (CAN) per year plus tuition.

Total amount of support: Approximately $14,000,000.

NO. AWARDS: 200 new fellowships offered by graduate programs each year.

APPLICATION INFO:
Applicant must first contact graduate program of interest. Fellowships are awarded on basis of nomination made by graduate program.

Duration: Four years.

Deadline: Most funding decisions made in January to March.

ADDRESS INQUIRIES TO:
See e-mail address above.

THE UNIVERSITY OF CALGARY [1728]

Faculty of Graduate Studies
MacKimmie Library Tower, Room 213
2500 University Drive, N.W.
Calgary AB T2N 1N4 Canada
(403) 220-4938
Fax: (403) 289-7635
E-mail: gsaward@ucalgary.ca
Web Site: www.grad.ucalgary.ca/awards

FOUNDED: 1966

AREAS OF INTEREST:
Petroleum industry.

NAME(S) OF PROGRAMS:
- **The Archibald Waynne Dingman Memorial Graduate Scholarship**

TYPE:
Awards/prizes; Scholarships. Graduate scholarship for study in all areas relevant to the petroleum industry. Tenable at The University of Calgary. Award endowed through a bequest of the late Corinne Patteson.

ELIGIBILITY:
Open to qualified graduates of any recognized university who are registered in or admissible to a program leading to a Master's or doctoral degree at The University of Calgary.

FINANCIAL DATA:
Amount of support per award: $2,800 (CAN).

Total amount of support: $2,800 (CAN).

NO. AWARDS: 1.

APPLICATION INFO:
Students should consult the Graduate Award Competition Guidelines and Application available online.

Duration: One year.

Deadline: February 1 to candidate's Graduate Program Office, unless program has an earlier deadline.

ADDRESS INQUIRIES TO:
Graduate Scholarship Office
(See address above.)

THE UNIVERSITY OF CALGARY [1729]

Faculty of Graduate Studies
MacKimmie Library Tower, Room 213
2500 University Drive, N.W.
Calgary AB T2N 1N4 Canada
(403) 220-4938
Fax: (403) 289-7635
E-mail: gsaward@ucalgary.ca
Web Site: www.grad.ucalgary.ca/awards

FOUNDED: 1966

NAME(S) OF PROGRAMS:

- **Queen Elizabeth II Graduate Scholarships**

TYPE:
Awards/prizes; Fellowships; Scholarships. Graduate scholarships and fellowships in all fields of study tenable at The University of Calgary.

ELIGIBILITY:
Open to qualified graduate students who are or will be, at the time of tenure, registered in a full-time Master's or doctoral program in the Faculty of Graduate Studies. Candidates must be either Canadian citizens or permanent residents and a resident of Alberta. Students whose awards begin in May are expected to carry out a full-time research program during the summer months.

This award cannot be held in addition to funding from a major award.

FINANCIAL DATA:
Amount of support per award: Master's level: Up to $10,800 (CAN); Doctoral level: Up to $15,000 (CAN).

NO. AWARDS: Varies.

APPLICATION INFO:
Students should consult with their Graduate Program Office for application information.

Duration: One year.

Deadline: Students should consult with their Graduate Program Office for deadline information.

ADDRESS INQUIRIES TO:
Graduate Scholarship Office
(See address above.)

THE UNIVERSITY OF CALGARY [1730]

Faculty of Graduate Studies
MacKimmie Library Tower, Room 213
2500 University Drive, N.W.
Calgary AB T2N 1N4 Canada
(403) 220-4938
Fax: (403) 289-7635
E-mail: gsaward@ucalgary.ca
Web Site: www.grad.ucalgary.ca/awards

FOUNDED: 1966

AREAS OF INTEREST:
Medical sciences.

NAME(S) OF PROGRAMS:

- **William H. Davies Medical Research Scholarships**

TYPE:
Awards/prizes; Scholarships. Awards for study in the medical sciences. Tenable at The University of Calgary. Award endowed through a bequest of the late William H. Davies.

ELIGIBILITY:
Open to qualified graduates of any recognized university who will be registered full-time in the Cumming School of Medicine at The University of Calgary. Successful candidates must contact their research program within the Faculty of Medicine; others cannot be considered. Awards are made solely on the basis of academic excellence.

FINANCIAL DATA:
Amount of support per award: $3,000 to $11,000 (CAN), depending upon the candidate's qualifications, experience and graduate program.

NO. AWARDS: Varies.

APPLICATION INFO:
Information is available from the Faculty of Graduate Studies. Candidates should apply to the Associate Dean, Graduate Science Education, Faculty of Medicine. Recommendations from the Faculty of Medicine will be submitted for approval to the Graduate Scholarship Committee.

Duration: One year.

Deadline: June 15.

ADDRESS INQUIRIES TO:
Graduate Scholarship Office
(See address above.)

THE UNIVERSITY OF CALGARY [1731]

Faculty of Graduate Studies
MacKimmie Library Tower, Room 213
2500 University Drive, N.W.
Calgary AB T2N 1N4 Canada
(403) 220-4938
Fax: (403) 289-7635
E-mail: gsaward@ucalgary.ca
Web Site: www.grad.ucalgary.ca/awards

FOUNDED: 1966

NAME(S) OF PROGRAMS:

- **Izaak Walton Killam Predoctoral Scholarships**

TYPE:
Awards/prizes; Scholarships.

YEAR PROGRAM STARTED: 1967

PURPOSE:
To encourage advanced study, to increase the scientific and scholastic attainment of Canadians and to promote sympathetic understanding between Canadians and the peoples of other countries. Those receiving scholarships would likely contribute to the advancement of learning or win distinction in their profession.

ELIGIBILITY:
Scholarships are normally awarded to students who will be in their first, second, third or fourth year of Ph.D. studies during the tenure of the award. The recipients must be registered full-time in a doctoral program at the University of Calgary. Applicants must have completed at least one year of graduate study before taking up an award.

GEOG. RESTRICTIONS: Canada.

FINANCIAL DATA:
$3,000 of this award (a Killam Research Scholarship) is reserved to cover costs associated with special equipment, conferences and/or travel in direct connection with the Ph.D. research.

Amount of support per award: $36,000 (CAN).

Total amount of support: Varies.

NO. AWARDS: Varies.

APPLICATION INFO:
In order to receive the Killam Research Scholarship portion of the award, the student must submit a letter outlining the proposed use of funds. This statement must be signed by the supervisor approving the use. No receipts are required.

Duration: One year. Renewable once upon presentation of evidence of satisfactory progress.

Deadline: February 1, unless candidate's graduate program office has an earlier deadline.

ADDRESS INQUIRIES TO:
Graduate Scholarship Office
(See address above.)

THE UNIVERSITY OF CALGARY [1732]

Faculty of Graduate Studies
MacKimmie Library Tower, Room 213
2500 University Drive, N.W.
Calgary AB T2N 1N4 Canada
(403) 220-4938
Fax: (403) 289-7635
E-mail: gsaward@ucalgary.ca
Web Site: www.grad.ucalgary.ca/awards

FOUNDED: 1966

AREAS OF INTEREST:
Cellular, molecular, microbial and biochemical biology.

NAME(S) OF PROGRAMS:

- **Bettina Bahlsen Memorial Graduate Scholarship**

TYPE:
Awards/prizes; Scholarships. Award for study in the fields of cellular, molecular, microbial or biochemical biology. Tenable at The University of Calgary, Department of Biological Sciences.

ELIGIBILITY:
Open to full-time graduate students entering or enrolled in a doctoral program in the Department of Biological Sciences. Selection will be based on academic excellence. Preference will be accorded to an international student and, if possible, to a student entering the first year of graduate studies.

FINANCIAL DATA:
Amount of support per award: $15,500 (CAN).
Total amount of support: $15,500 (CAN).

NO. AWARDS: 1.

APPLICATION INFO:
Students should consult the Department of Biological Sciences. A recommendation will be forwarded to the Graduate Scholarship Office. The recommendation is subject to final approval of the Graduate Scholarship Committee.
Duration: One year. Possible renewal in open competition.
Deadline: February 1.

ADDRESS INQUIRIES TO:
Graduate Scholarship Office
(See address above.)

THE UNIVERSITY OF CALGARY [1733]

Faculty of Graduate Studies
MacKimmie Library Tower, Room 213
2500 University Drive, N.W.
Calgary AB T2N 1N4 Canada
(403) 220-4938
Fax: (403) 289-7635
E-mail: gsaward@ucalgary.ca
Web Site: www.grad.ucalgary.ca/awards

FOUNDED: 1966

AREAS OF INTEREST:
Business and management.

NAME(S) OF PROGRAMS:
- **John Labatt Limited Scholarship**
- **ScotiaMcLeod Scholarship**

TYPE:
Awards/prizes; Scholarships. Awards for study in the fields of business, management and related areas. Tenable at the University of Calgary. Awards are endowed through gifts from John Labatt Limited and ScotiaMcLeod Inc. Matching grants provided from the Province of Alberta's Advanced Education Endowment Fund.

ELIGIBILITY:
Open to qualified graduate students who are registered in or admissible to the MBA program at The University of Calgary. Awardees must be engaged in full-time study during the tenure of the award.

FINANCIAL DATA:
Amount of support per award: Labatt Scholarship: $2,600 (CAN); ScotiaMcLeod Scholarship: $2,800 (CAN).

NO. AWARDS: 1 per award.

APPLICATION INFO:
Duration: One year.
Deadline: May 15.

ADDRESS INQUIRIES TO:
Graduate Scholarship Office
(See address above.)

THE UNIVERSITY OF CALGARY [1734]

Faculty of Graduate Studies
MacKimmie Library Tower, Room 213
2500 University Drive, N.W.
Calgary AB T2N 1N4 Canada
(403) 220-4938
Fax: (403) 289-7635
E-mail: gsaward@ucalgary.ca
Web Site: www.grad.ucalgary.ca/awards

AREAS OF INTEREST:
Natural resources, energy and environmental law.

NAME(S) OF PROGRAMS:
- **Faculty of Law Graduate Scholarship**

TYPE:
Awards/prizes; Scholarships.

ELIGIBILITY:
Open to students entering or enrolled in a full-time graduate program in the Faculty of Law. If, in the opinion of the University of Calgary Graduate Scholarship Selection Committee, no suitable applications are received, no awards will be made.

FINANCIAL DATA:
Amount of support per award: $8,700.
Total amount of support: $8,700.

CO-OP FUNDING PROGRAMS: Endowed through contributions made to the Focus on Natural Resources Law Campaign; matching grant provided from the Province of Alberta.

NO. AWARDS: 1.

APPLICATION INFO:
Application forms available from the Director, Graduate Programme, Faculty of Law. Awards will be recommended by a committee of the Faculty of Law based upon academic excellence. The Graduate Coordinator, Law, will submit recommendations to the Graduate Scholarship Office. The recommendation is subject to final approval of the Graduate Scholarship Committee.
Duration: One year. Nonrenewable.
Deadline: December 15.

PUBLICATIONS:
Academic calendar.

ADDRESS INQUIRIES TO:
Graduate Scholarship Office
(See address above.)

THE UNIVERSITY OF CALGARY [1735]

Faculty of Graduate Studies
MacKimmie Library Tower, Room 213
2500 University Drive, N.W.
Calgary AB T2N 1N4 Canada
(403) 220-4938
Fax: (403) 289-7635
E-mail: gsaward@ucalgary.ca
Web Site: www.grad.ucalgary.ca/awards

FOUNDED: 1966

NAME(S) OF PROGRAMS:
- **The University of Calgary Silver Anniversary Graduate Fellowships**

TYPE:
Awards/prizes; Fellowships. Graduate fellowships in all fields of study tenable in The Faculty of Graduate Studies at The University of Calgary. Award endowed by an anonymous donor and matched by the Province of Alberta.

ELIGIBILITY:
Open to qualified graduates of any recognized university who are registered in or admissible to a doctoral program at The University of Calgary. Candidates must be residents of Canada. Awards are granted on the basis of academic standing and demonstrated potential for advanced study and research.

FINANCIAL DATA:
Amount of support per award: $16,000 to $20,000.
Total amount of support: Varies.

NO. AWARDS: Varies depending on funds.

APPLICATION INFO:
Contact the University.
Duration: One year. Renewable once upon presentation of evidence of satisfactory progress.
Deadline: February 1, unless specific program has an earlier deadline.

ADDRESS INQUIRIES TO:
Graduate Scholarship Office
(See address above.)

THE UNIVERSITY OF CALGARY [1736]

Faculty of Graduate Studies
MacKimmie Library Tower, Room 213
2500 University Drive, N.W.
Calgary AB T2N 1N4 Canada
(403) 220-4938
Fax: (403) 289-7635
E-mail: gsaward@ucalgary.ca
Web Site: www.grad.ucalgary.ca/awards

FOUNDED: 1966

AREAS OF INTEREST:
Creative writing in English, English literature, and related literary fields.

NAME(S) OF PROGRAMS:
- **The A.T.J. Cairns Memorial Scholarship**

TYPE:
Awards/prizes; Scholarships. Graduate scholarship tenable at The University of Calgary. Award endowed through the estate of the late A.T.J. Cairns, with a matching grant provided by the Province of Alberta's Advanced Education Endowment Fund.

ELIGIBILITY:
Candidates must be registered in or admissible to a Master's or doctoral degree program in the Department of English.

FINANCIAL DATA:
Amount of support per award: $1,000 to $5,000.
Total amount of support: Varies.

NO. AWARDS: Determined annually.

APPLICATION INFO:
Students interested in the award should apply to the Department of English in the first instance. Recommendations from the Department will be considered by the University Graduate Scholarship Committee.
Duration: One year.
Deadline: April 30.

ADDRESS INQUIRIES TO:
Graduate Scholarship Office
(See address above.)

THE UNIVERSITY OF CALGARY [1737]

Faculty of Graduate Studies
MacKimmie Library Tower, Room 213
2500 University Drive, N.W.
Calgary AB T2N 1N4 Canada
(403) 220-4938
Fax: (403) 289-7635
E-mail: gsaward@ucalgary.ca
Web Site: www.grad.ucalgary.ca/awards

FOUNDED: 1966

NAME(S) OF PROGRAMS:

- **Graduate Faculty Council Scholarship**

TYPE:
Awards/prizes; Scholarships. Graduate scholarship in all fields of study tenable at The University of Calgary. Award endowed by The University of Calgary Graduate Faculty Council.

ELIGIBILITY:
Open to qualified full-time graduate students who are or will be, at the time of tenure, registered in a thesis-based doctoral program in the Faculty of Graduate Studies.

FINANCIAL DATA:
Amount of support per award: $10,000 per annum.

Total amount of support: Varies depending on funds available.

NO. AWARDS: Varies.

APPLICATION INFO:
Students should consult their Graduate Program Officer for application information.

Duration: One year.

Deadline: February 1, unless specific program has an earlier deadline.

ADDRESS INQUIRIES TO:
Graduate Scholarship Office
(See address above.)

THE UNIVERSITY OF CALGARY [1738]

Faculty of Graduate Studies
MacKimmie Library Tower, Room 213
2500 University Drive, N.W.
Calgary AB T2N 1N4 Canada
(403) 220-4938
Fax: (403) 289-7635
E-mail: gsaward@ucalgary.ca
Web Site: www.grad.ucalgary.ca/awards

FOUNDED: 1966

AREAS OF INTEREST:
Humanities.

NAME(S) OF PROGRAMS:

- **Peter C. Craigie Memorial Scholarship**

TYPE:
Awards/prizes; Scholarships. Graduate scholarship tenable at The University of Calgary. Award endowed by friends, family and colleagues of Peter Craigie, who was Vice President (Academic) at the University; matching grant provided from the Province of Alberta's Advanced Education Endowment Fund.

ELIGIBILITY:
Open to full-time registrants who are registered in and have completed one term of study in a program of studies leading to a Master's degree in a department in the Faculty of Humanities. The recipient must have an outstanding scholastic record and have been or be involved in activities contributing to the general welfare of the University community.

FINANCIAL DATA:
Amount of support per award: $3,700.

Total amount of support: $3,700.

NO. AWARDS: 1.

APPLICATION INFO:
Application information is available at the web site address.

Duration: One year.

Deadline: February 1, unless the program has an earlier deadline.

ADDRESS INQUIRIES TO:
Graduate Scholarship Office
(See address above.)

THE UNIVERSITY OF CALGARY [1739]

Faculty of Graduate Studies
MacKimmie Library Tower, Room 213
2500 University Drive, N.W.
Calgary AB T2N 1N4 Canada
(403) 220-4938
Fax: (403) 289-7635
E-mail: gsaward@ucalgary.ca
Web Site: www.grad.ucalgary.ca/awards

FOUNDED: 1966

AREAS OF INTEREST:
Economics, geoscience, engineering and management.

NAME(S) OF PROGRAMS:

- **Canadian Natural Resources Limited Graduate Scholarship**

TYPE:
Awards/prizes; Scholarships. Graduate scholarship tenable at the University of Calgary. This Scholarship recognizes the importance training and education play in helping students take advantage of the career and economic prospects available in the oil and gas industry.

ELIGIBILITY:
Open to candidates who at the time of tenure will be registered full-time in a thesis-based program in the Faculty of Graduate Studies at the University of Calgary.

FINANCIAL DATA:
Amount of support per award: $7,200.

Total amount of support: $7,200.

CO-OP FUNDING PROGRAMS: Endowed by Canadian Natural Resources Ltd (formerly Sceptre Resources Limited); matching grant provided from the Province of Alberta's Advanced Education Endowment Fund.

NO. AWARDS: 1.

APPLICATION INFO:
Students should consult the Graduate Award Competition Guidelines. Application information is available at the web site address.

Duration: One year.

Deadline: February 1 to the candidate's graduate program office, unless the program has an earlier deadline.

ADDRESS INQUIRIES TO:
Graduate Scholarship Office
(See address above.)

UNIVERSITY OF KANSAS CHILD LANGUAGE DOCTORAL PROGRAM [1740]

1000 Sunnyside Avenue
Room 3031, Dole Center
Lawrence, KS 66045-7555
(785) 864-4570
Fax: (785) 864-4571
E-mail: childlang@ku.edu
Web Site: www.clp.ku.edu

AREAS OF INTEREST:
Early childhood education and language research.

NAME(S) OF PROGRAMS:

- **Child Language Doctoral Program**

TYPE:
Conferences/seminars; Research grants; Scholarships.

PURPOSE:
To train individuals on language impairment across the life span.

ELIGIBILITY:
Applicants must have U.S. citizenship or permanent residency status, admission to the Child Language Doctoral Program or Intercampus Program in Speech-Language-Hearing or a related program, submission of a significant research plan of high quality, demonstrated high academic achievements and potential, and research interests congruent with those of one or more of the training program faculty members.

FINANCIAL DATA:
Amount of support per award: $21,180 per year predoctoral award.

APPLICATION INFO:
Applicants must submit:
(1) a curriculum vitae;
(2) a list of all courses taken in relevant areas such as language impairment of children, linguistics, psychology, special education, and speech and hearing sciences;
(3) a research plan describing the applicant's plans for research on language impairments of children;
(4) two official transcripts;
(5) names and phone numbers of three references who can evaluate the applicant's research potential;
(6) scores from the Graduate Record Examinations and;
(7) letter of intent stating willingness to participate in continuous research practicum.

Duration: One year.

Deadline: Beginning of February.

STAFF:
Dr. Mabel L. Rice, Director
Linda Mann, Program Assistant

ADDRESS INQUIRIES TO:
Dr. Mabel L. Rice, Director
(See address above.)

UNIVERSITY OF SOUTHERN CALIFORNIA [1741]

3720 South Flower Street, Third Floor
CUB 303
Los Angeles, CA 90089-0701
(213) 740-8336
Fax: (213) 740-6070
E-mail: jeri.muniz@usc.edu
Web Site: www.usc.edu/research/dcg

AREAS OF INTEREST:
Art history.

TYPE:
Fellowships; Grants-in-aid.

PURPOSE:
To support graduate education in art history at USC.

ELIGIBILITY:
Admission to Ph.D. program in art history.

GEOG. RESTRICTIONS: California.

FINANCIAL DATA:
Amount of support per award: Varies.

APPLICATION INFO:
Applicants must submit the Graduate School Application and the Supplemental

Application form along with Graduate Record Exam (GRE) scores and letters of recommendation.

Duration: One year. Renewal possible based on academic progress.

Deadline: January.

ADDRESS INQUIRIES TO:
Contracts and Grants
(See address above.)

UNIVERSITY OF SOUTHERN CALIFORNIA [1742]

USC Graduate School
3601 Watt Way, GFS 315
Los Angeles, CA 90089-1695
(213) 740-9033
Fax: (213) 740-9048
E-mail: gradfllw@usc.edu
Web Site: www.usc.edu/schools/GraduateSchool/

NAME(S) OF PROGRAMS:
- **Annenberg Graduate Fellowship Program**
- **Global Ph.D. Fellowship**
- **Provost's Ph.D. Fellowship Program**
- **Rose Hills Ph.D. Fellowship**

TYPE:
Fellowships. Merit fellowships. Fellowships will be combined with matching funds from individual schools to provide four or more years of funding toward the Ph.D.

YEAR PROGRAM STARTED: 1982

PURPOSE:
To allow outstanding students to devote full-time to research and study at USC leading to a career in university teaching and research.

LEGAL BASIS:
University.

ELIGIBILITY:
Excellent incoming Ph.D. applicants who show outstanding promise for academic careers in research and training.

FINANCIAL DATA:
Amount of support per award: $30,000 plus tuition and mandatory fees.

NO. AWARDS: Up to 150 for the 2012-13 academic year.

APPLICATION INFO:
Nomination by department only.

Duration: Two years, awarded annually with at least two years subsequent departmental/school support, based upon continued superior performance.

Deadline: Varies.

PUBLICATIONS:
Program announcements.

ADDRESS INQUIRIES TO:
Kate Tegmeyer, Fellowship Coordinator
(See address above.)

UNIVERSITY OF SOUTHERN CALIFORNIA [1743]

USC Undergraduate Programs
3601 Trousdale Parkway, STU 300
Los Angeles, CA 90089-0896
(213) 740-1741
E-mail: ugp@usc.edu
Web Site: www.usc.edu/programs/ugprograms/ugresearch/rose_hill.shtml

AREAS OF INTEREST:
Science and engineering.

NAME(S) OF PROGRAMS:
- **Rose Hills Summer Research Fellowships**

TYPE:
Fellowships. Summer fellowship for undergraduate students at USC supporting full-time research in science or engineering.

PURPOSE:
The Rose Hills Foundation, which supports nonprofit organizations for the benefit of the people of southern California, has generously provided funding for a limited number of students who would like to obtain science and engineering fellowships.

ELIGIBILITY:
Applicant must be enrolled at USC during the fall as a junior or senior in a program leading to an undergraduate degree in the life or natural sciences or engineering. USC cumulative grade point average of 3.0 or better is required. (Preference will be given to students whose USC cumulative grade point average is 3.5 or better.) U.S. citizenship is required, with residency in southern California. (A resident of southern California is defined as a student whose permanent address is south of the Tehachapi Mountains.)

GEOG. RESTRICTIONS: Southern California.

FINANCIAL DATA:
Amount of support per award: Stipend of $5,000.

NO. AWARDS: Average of 42 annually.

APPLICATION INFO:
Students must submit an online application and faculty recommendation form to be considered for funding.

Duration: Eight weeks, mid-May through mid-August.

Deadline: End of March. Announcement before mid-April.

ADDRESS INQUIRIES TO:
Dr. David Glasgow
Director, Office of Undergraduate Programs
Tel: (213) 740-6146
E-mail: dglasgow@usc.edu

THE UNIVERSITY OF SOUTHERN MISSISSIPPI

118 College Drive
Box 5148
Hattiesburg, MS 39406
(601) 266-4349
Fax: (601) 266-6269
E-mail: ellen.ruffin@usm.edu
Web Site: www.lib.usm.edu/degrummond/research/fellowships.html

TYPE:
Fellowships. Rey Fellowship is awarded to hire translators (French, German, Portuguese or Russian) for the purpose of translating the H.A. and Margret Rey documents into English to further facilitate use in research, as needed. Funds may also be used for the preservation and conservation of the Rey documents or to provide funding for an individual conducting research on the life and work of the Reys.

See entry 732 for full listing.

VERMONT STUDENT ASSISTANCE CORPORATION [1744]

10 East Allen Street
Winooski, VT 05404-2601
(800) 642-3177 (continental U.S.)
(802) 655-9602 (Burlington area)
Fax: (802) 654-3765
TDD: (800) 281-3341
E-mail: info@vsac.org
Web Site: www.vsac.org

FOUNDED: 1965

AREAS OF INTEREST:
Students in need.

NAME(S) OF PROGRAMS:
- **Vermont Incentive Grants and Scholarships**
- **Vermont Outreach Programs**

TYPE:
Conferences/seminars; Grants-in-aid; Scholarships. Grants and loans for students enrolled in approved postsecondary institutions.

YEAR PROGRAM STARTED: 1965

PURPOSE:
To ensure that all Vermonters have the necessary financial and informational resources to pursue their educational goals beyond high school.

LEGAL BASIS:
Nonprofit, public corporation.

ELIGIBILITY:
For Incentive Grant, applicant must be a Vermont resident, enrolled full-time at an approved postsecondary institution, and must meet need test.

For Part-Time Grant, applicant must be a Vermont resident, taking fewer than 12 credit hours, have not received a Bachelor's degree, and must meet need test.

For Non-Degree Grant, applicant must be a Vermont resident, not matriculated, and must meet need test.

GEOG. RESTRICTIONS: Vermont.

FINANCIAL DATA:
Amount of support per award: Incentive Grant: $1,692 average; Part-Time Grant: $458 average; Non-Degree Grant: $1,678 average for fiscal year 2015.

Total amount of support: $19,217,511 for fiscal year 2015.

NO. MOST RECENT APPLICANTS: 23,750 for fiscal year 2015.

NO. AWARDS: 13,608 for fiscal year 2015.

APPLICATION INFO:
Incentive grant application is required.

Duration: One academic year. Renewal possible under annual reapplication.

Deadline: Applications accepted on a rolling basis for all grants.

ADDRESS INQUIRIES TO:
VSAC Research Department
(See address above.)

VERTICAL FLIGHT FOUNDATION

2701 Prosperity Avenue, Suite 210
Fairfax, VA 22031
(703) 684-6777
Fax: (703) 739-9279
E-mail: bchen@vtol.org
Web Site: www.vtol.org/vff

TYPE:
Awards/prizes; Scholarships. Annual scholarships to undergraduate senior, Master's or Ph.D. students interested in pursuing careers in some technical aspect of helicopter or vertical flight engineering.

See entry 2545 for full listing.

WASHINGTON STUDENT ACHIEVEMENT COUNCIL [1745]

917 Lakeridge Way, S.W.
Olympia, WA 98504-3430
(360) 753-7847
Fax: (360) 704-6204
E-mail: carlai@wsac.wa.gov
health@wsac.wa.gov
Web Site: www.wsac.wa.gov/health

AREAS OF INTEREST:
Primary health care.

NAME(S) OF PROGRAMS:
- **Health Professional Loan Repayment and Scholarship Programs**

TYPE:
Scholarships; Loan forgiveness programs.

YEAR PROGRAM STARTED: 1991

PURPOSE:
To encourage health professionals to work in rural or underserved urban areas of the state of Washington by providing scholarships and loan repayment.

LEGAL BASIS:
Government agency.

ELIGIBILITY:
Scholarship applicants must be accepted in or enrolled in designated health profession training leading to licensure as a health professional in the state of Washington.

GEOG. RESTRICTIONS: Washington state.

FINANCIAL DATA:
Amount of support per award: Loan Repayment: $70,000 to $75,000 with a three-year service commitment; Scholarships: Varies, but cannot exceed cost of attendance.

APPLICATION INFO:
Application form required.

Duration: Completion of training program. Maximum of five years.

Deadline: Approximately April 30.

PUBLICATIONS:
Application form; brochure.

STAFF:
Carla Idohl-Corwin, Associate Director of Workforce Programs
Chris Wilkins, Program Manager

ADDRESS INQUIRIES TO:
Chris Wilkins, Program Manager
(See address above.)

*SPECIAL STIPULATIONS:
Must commit to employment in Washington state.

WASHINGTON STUDENT ACHIEVEMENT COUNCIL [1746]

917 Lakeridge Way, S.W.
Olympia, WA 98502
(360) 753-7861
Fax: (855) 480-8718
E-mail: sws@wsac.wa.gov
Web Site: www.wsac.wa.gov

FOUNDED: 1969

AREAS OF INTEREST:
Postsecondary education planning and policy development, advisory board.

NAME(S) OF PROGRAMS:
- **Washington State Need Grant Program**
- **Washington State Work-Study Program**

TYPE:
Work-study programs. Subsidized employment opportunities.

YEAR PROGRAM STARTED: 1974

PURPOSE:
To provide financial assistance to needy students attending eligible postsecondary institutions in the state of Washington by stimulating and promoting their employment and to provide such needy students, wherever possible, with employment related to their academic pursuits.

LEGAL BASIS:
State agency.

ELIGIBILITY:
Applicants must demonstrate financial need, be enrolled or accepted for enrollment as at least half-time undergraduate, graduate or professional students and be capable, in the opinion of the institution, of maintaining good standing in a course of study while employed under the program.

GEOG. RESTRICTIONS: Washington state.

FINANCIAL DATA:
Amount of support per award: Varies.

Total amount of support: Approximately $7,500,000 for the 2015-16 academic year.

NO. AWARDS: 4,400 for the academic year 2013-14.

APPLICATION INFO:
There is no separate application for this program. Students are awarded automatically by their school on the basis of their financial need as evidenced from their Free Application for Federal Student Aid (FAFSA) results.

Duration: Renewable.

STAFF:
Marlena Rae Robbins, Program Associate

ADDRESS INQUIRIES TO:
Financial Aid Office at the college or Washington Student Achievement Council (See address above.)

WASHINGTON UNIVERSITY [1747]

The Graduate School
One Brookings Drive
Campus Box 1186
St. Louis, MO 63130
(314) 935-6848
Fax: (314) 935-3929
E-mail: n.p.pope@wustl.edu
Web Site: pages.wustl.edu/olinfellowship

FOUNDED: 1974

AREAS OF INTEREST:
Anthropology, architecture, art history, archaeology, audiology, biology, biomedical sciences, business administration, chemistry, Chinese, classics, comparative literature, creative writing, dance, earth and planetary sciences, economics, education, engineering, English, German, history, Japanese, law, materials science, mathematics, medicine, movement science, music, occupational therapy, philosophy, physics, physical therapy, political science, psychology, public health, romance languages, social work, statistics, and visual arts.

NAME(S) OF PROGRAMS:
- **Mr. and Mrs. Spencer T. Olin Fellowships for Women**

TYPE:
Fellowships. The Olin Fellowships are open to candidates for any of the following graduate and professional schools at Washington University: architecture, art, arts and sciences, business, engineering, medicine, and social work.

YEAR PROGRAM STARTED: 1974

PURPOSE:
To encourage women of exceptional promise to prepare for careers in higher education and the professions; to continue and extend the historically important contributions of Monticello College to the education of women; to extend the influence of Washington University by assisting in the advanced education of outstanding young women who are likely to make significant contributions to higher education and the professions.

LEGAL BASIS:
Joint program of a private foundation (The Monticello College Foundation) and of Washington University in St. Louis.

ELIGIBILITY:
Any female graduate of a Baccalaureate institution in the U.S. who plans to prepare for a career in higher education or the professions by full-time advanced study at Washington University is eligible to apply. Applicants are considered without regard to age, handicap, religious creed, race, sexual orientation or national origin and only with regard to the excellence of their qualifications. Applicants must meet the admission requirements of the graduate or professional school of Washington University. Preference will be given to those who wish to study for the highest earned degree in their chosen field.

FINANCIAL DATA:
The Olin Fellowships are tenable only at Washington University. They carry awards which compare favorably in each discipline with the most attractive financial aid offers available in that discipline at Washington University.

NO. MOST RECENT APPLICANTS: 302.

NO. AWARDS: 11.

APPLICATION INFO:
Application and instructions are available at https://gradapply.wustl.edu/apply/fellowship.

Duration: Given satisfactory academic achievement, awards are renewable for a period of four years or until the completion of the program of academic degree study, whichever is first.

Deadline: Applications, with all supporting documents, must be submitted online no later than January 25 preceding the academic year for which application has been made.

STAFF:
Nancy P. Pope, Ph.D., Director
Cecily Stewart Hawksworth, Fellowship Assistant

ADDRESS INQUIRIES TO:
Cecily Stewart Hawksworth
(See address above.)

WASHINGTON UNIVERSITY [1748]

The Graduate School
One Brookings Drive
Campus Box 1187
St. Louis, MO 63130-4899
(314) 935-6831
Fax: (314) 935-4887
E-mail: snotaro@wustl.edu
Web Site: pages.wustl.edu/cgfp

FOUNDED: 1853

AREAS OF INTEREST:
Anthropology, architecture, art history, archaeology, biology, biomedical sciences, business administration, chemistry, Chinese/Japanese and comparative literature, creative writing, earth and planetary sciences, economics, education, engineering, English, fine arts, German, history, material science and engineering, mathematics, movement science, music, philosophy, physics, political science, psychology, romance languages, statistics, social work, and visual arts.

NAME(S) OF PROGRAMS:
- **The Chancellor's Graduate Fellowship Program at Washington University in St. Louis**

TYPE:
Fellowships; Research grants; Scholarships; Travel grants.

YEAR PROGRAM STARTED: 1991

PURPOSE:
To facilitate training for students interested in becoming college or university professors, and who can contribute to diversity on the Washington University campus.

LEGAL BASIS:
University.

ELIGIBILITY:
Open to students who are admissible into any of Washington University's Ph.D. programs in Arts and Sciences, Business, Engineering or Social Work. Also eligible are students admissible to other Washington University programs providing final disciplinary training for prospective college professors (e.g., M.F.A. in Creative Writing, M.F.A. in Art). Students must be able to contribute to the diversity on the Washington University campus.

Applicants must be in the process of receiving, or will receive, an undergraduate degree from a four-year institution in the U.S. International students may apply, as long as they meet all admissions criteria.

FINANCIAL DATA:
Amount of support per award: Doctoral candidates are provided stipends and allowances of $31,944 per twelve-month year for five years, plus full tuition scholarships, with a total value in excess of $120,000. This combines a fellowship stipend of $30,444 and a $1,500 educational allowance.

CO-OP FUNDING PROGRAMS: Fellows will meet as a community on a regular basis to discuss trends and activities within their various disciplines. Scholars will lead discussions on a multitude of topics and the fellows will participate in an annual conference.

NO. MOST RECENT APPLICANTS: 186.

NO. AWARDS: 9.

APPLICATION INFO:
Application information is available on the web site.

Duration: Five years for doctoral candidates, contingent upon satisfactory academic progress. Two years for graduate students in MFA (in Writing, Visual Art and Dance) and M.Arch. (Master of Architecture) programs. Three years for J.D. in Law.

Deadline: January 15 for application to a degree program. January 25 for application for Chancellor's Program.

PUBLICATIONS:
Program announcement.

ADDRESS INQUIRIES TO:
Sheri R. Notaro, Associate Dean
The Graduate School
(See address above.)

WELLESLEY COLLEGE

Center for Work and Service
Green Hall 439A, 106 Central Street
Wellesley, MA 02481-8203
(781) 283-2347
Fax: (781) 283-3674
E-mail: cws-fellowships@wellesley.edu
Web Site: www.wellesley.edu/CWS

TYPE:
Fellowships; Research grants. The Anne Louise Barrett Fellowship is given preferably in music and primarily for study or research in musical theory, composition, or in the history of music, abroad or in the U.S.

The Margaret Freeman Bowers Fellowship is given for first year of study in the fields of social work, law, or policy/public administration, including MBA candidates with plans for a career in the field of social services.

The Eugene L. Cox Fellowship is for graduate study in medieval or renaissance history and culture abroad or in the U.S.

The Professor Elizabeth F. Fisher Fellowship is given for research or further study in geology or geography, including urban, environmental or ecological studies.

The Ruth Ingersoll Goldmark Fellowship is awarded for graduate study in English literature, English composition or in the classics.

The Horton-Hallowell Fellowship is awarded for graduate study in any field, preferably in the last two years of candidacy for the Ph.D. degree, or its equivalent, or for private research of equivalent standard.

The Peggy Howard Fellowship in Economics is given to provide financial aid for Wellesley students or alumnae continuing their study of economics. Administered by the economics faculty who may name one or two recipients depending on the income available.

The Edna V. Moffett Fellowship is given to a young alumna, preferably for a first year of graduate study in history.

The Alice Freeman Palmer Fellowship is awarded for study or research abroad or in the U.S.

The Kathryn Conway Preyer Fellowship is for advanced study in history.

The Vida Dutton Scudder Fellowship is given for study in the field of social science, political science or literature.

The Harriet A. Shaw Fellowship is given for study or research in music and the allied arts, in the U.S. or abroad.

Mary Elvira Stevens Traveling Fellowship is awarded for travel or study outside the U.S.

The Maria Opasnov Tyler '52 Scholarship is for graduate study in Russian studies.

The Sarah Perry Wood Medical Fellowship is awarded for the study of medicine at an accredited medical school approved by the American Medical Association.

The Fanny Bullock Workman Fellowship is given for graduate study in any field.

See entry 1075 for full listing.

WELLESLEY COLLEGE

Center for Work and Service
Green Hall 439A, 106 Central Street
Wellesley, MA 02481-8203
(781) 283-2347
Fax: (781) 283-3674
E-mail: cws-fellowships@wellesley.edu
Web Site: www.wellesley.edu/CWS

TYPE:
Fellowships; Scholarships. Awards are made to female applicants who plan for full-time graduate study for the coming year.

The Mary McEwen Schimke Scholarship is a supplemental award given to afford relief from household and child care expenses while pursuing graduate study.

The M.A. Cartland Shackford Medical Fellowship is given for study of medicine with a view to general practice, not psychiatry.

See entry 1076 for full listing.

WEST VIRGINIA HIGHER EDUCATION POLICY COMMISSION [1749]

1018 Kanawha Boulevard East, Suite 700
Charleston, WV 25301
(304) 558-4016
Fax: (304) 558-5719
E-mail: brian.weingart@wvhepc.edu
Web Site: www.wvhepc.edu

FOUNDED: 1969

AREAS OF INTEREST:
Education.

NAME(S) OF PROGRAMS:
- **West Virginia Higher Education Grant Program**

TYPE:
Grants-in-aid. Monetary grants awarded to undergraduate students attending approved institutions of higher education.

YEAR PROGRAM STARTED: 1968

PURPOSE:
To guarantee that the most able and needy students are given the opportunity to continue their program of self-improvement at the postsecondary level by assisting in the removal of financial barriers through monetary awards.

LEGAL BASIS:
West Virginia Higher Education Grant Program is a government program administered under the authority of West Virginia Code 18-C-5-1.

ELIGIBILITY:
An applicant must be a citizen of the U.S., have been a resident of West Virginia for at least one year immediately preceding the date of application for a grant or renewal of a grant, require financial assistance to pursue a college education, possess academic promise

or be making satisfactory progress and enroll as a full-time undergraduate in an approved educational institution.

Grants are restricted to approved educational institutions located in West Virginia and Pennsylvania.

GEOG. RESTRICTIONS: West Virginia and Pennsylvania.

FINANCIAL DATA:

Amount of support per award: Up to $2,700.

Total amount of support: $40,619,864 total funding for student awards for academic year 2016-17 in state-appropriated funds, special fee revenues allocated by the governing Board.

NO. MOST RECENT APPLICANTS: Approximately 83,000 for academic year 2015-16.

NO. AWARDS: Approximately 31,500 for academic year 2015-16.

APPLICATION INFO:

Applicants must submit the Free Application for Federal Student Aid (FAFSA).

Duration: Total of eight semesters or 12 quarters. The eight semesters do not have to be consecutive. Receipt of a grant in a given year does not guarantee its continuance in a subsequent year even though eligibility may be maintained. Students must reapply each year.

Deadline: April 15 for priority consideration.

IRS I.D.: 55-0517092

STAFF:

Matt Turner, Vice Chancellor for Administration
Brian Weingart, Senior Director of Financial Aid

ADDRESS INQUIRIES TO:

Brian Weingart
Senior Director of Financial Aid
(See address above.)

THE WOODROW WILSON NATIONAL FELLOWSHIP FOUNDATION [1750]

5 Vaughn Drive
Princeton, NJ 08540
(609) 452-7007 ext. 310
E-mail: newcombe@woodrow.org
Web Site: www.woodrow.org

FOUNDED: 1945

AREAS OF INTEREST:

Higher education.

NAME(S) OF PROGRAMS:

- **Charlotte W. Newcombe Doctoral Dissertation Fellowships**

TYPE:

Awards/prizes; Fellowships; Scholarships. Awards to support and encourage original and significant study of ethical and/or religious values in the humanities and social sciences.

YEAR PROGRAM STARTED: 1981

PURPOSE:

To encourage study of ethical or religious values.

LEGAL BASIS:

Publicly supported charity.

ELIGIBILITY:

Doctoral candidates enrolled in a U.S. university, located in the U.S., working on topics of religious or ethical values in the Humanities or Social Sciences may apply.

FINANCIAL DATA:

Amount of support per award: $25,000 for 12 months of dissertation writing.

CO-OP FUNDING PROGRAMS: Program made available by funds from the Charlotte W. Newcombe Foundation.

NO. MOST RECENT APPLICANTS: 520.

NO. AWARDS: Minimum of 22.

APPLICATION INFO:

Applications are accepted beginning September 1 and must be submitted electronically.

Duration: Tenure of the award is for the academic year following the announcement of the winners.

Deadline: November 15.

OFFICERS:

Arthur Levine, President

ADDRESS INQUIRIES TO:

See e-mail address above.

*SPECIAL STIPULATIONS:

Fellowship is for humanities and social sciences. Applicants in highly quantitative fields should not apply.

WOMEN IN DEFENSE

WID HORIZONS
2111 Wilson Boulevard, Suite 400
Arlington, VA 22201
(703) 522-1820
Fax: (703) 522-1885
E-mail: wid@ndia.org
Web Site: www.womenindefense.net

TYPE:

Scholarships. The Horizons Foundation Scholarship Program is supported by accredited colleges and universities. Awards are made on an annual basis. The Foundation selects all scholarship recipients based on criteria it sets. Scholarships are awarded to applicants who require financial assistance, demonstrate strong academic credentials and a commitment to a career in national security.

See entry 1078 for full listing.

YOUNG MUSICIANS FOUNDATION (YMF)

244 South San Pedro Street
Fifth Floor, Suite 506
Los Angeles, CA 90012
(213) 617-7707
Fax: (213) 617-7706
E-mail: info@ymf.org
Web Site: www.ymf.org

TYPE:

Awards/prizes; Conferences/seminars; Fellowships; Scholarships. Mentor program. Financial assistance for private study and/or tuition at recognized musical institutions. Significant performance opportunity may be offered.

See entry 783 for full listing.

YOUNG MUSICIANS FOUNDATION (YMF)

244 South San Pedro Street
Fifth Floor, Suite 506
Los Angeles, CA 90012
(213) 617-7707
Fax: (213) 617-7706
E-mail: info@ymf.org
Web Site: www.ymf.org

TYPE:

Grants-in-aid; Scholarships. Each year, young musicians are selected through auditions to receive a grant for a series of coaching sessions with leading professional musicians from the Los Angeles (CA) area.

See entry 784 for full listing.

SCIENCES (multiple disciplines)

Sciences (multiple disciplines)

THE ACADEMY OF NATURAL SCIENCES OF PHILADELPHIA [1751]

1900 Benjamin Franklin Parkway
Philadelphia, PA 19103-1101
(215) 299-1065
Fax: (215) 299-1079
E-mail: kepics@ansp.org
Web Site: www.ansp.org/research

FOUNDED: 1812

AREAS OF INTEREST:
Research, exhibition and education in natural sciences.

NAME(S) OF PROGRAMS:

- **John J. and Anna H. Gallagher Fellowship**

TYPE:
Fellowships; Project/program grants; Research grants; Residencies; Training grants; Visiting scholars. The Gallagher Fellowship provides support for original postdoctoral or sabbatical research on the systematics of microscopic invertebrates, with priority for the study of rotifers.

YEAR PROGRAM STARTED: 1990

LEGAL BASIS:
Private, nonprofit natural science museum.

ELIGIBILITY:
Candidates must have a Ph.D. in zoology or in ecology, evolution and biodiversity from a major university. Applicants must provide a research proposal involving microscopic freshwater invertebrate animals, including development of expertise in one or more taxonomic groups and the names of three references who are acknowledged scholars in the field. Preference will be given to candidates specializing in Rotifera.

Work must take place primarily at the Academy of Natural Sciences of Philadelphia and/or in the field and should emphasize utilization of the Academy's collections of literature and specimens. Projects should be scaled for completion during the one-year duration of the fellowship.

FINANCIAL DATA:
Fellowship includes salary, benefits, travel expenses, field and laboratory supplies.

Total amount of support: $30,000 to $50,000.

NO. MOST RECENT APPLICANTS: 9.

NO. AWARDS: 1.

APPLICATION INFO:
Research proposal should include:
(1) curriculum vitae;
(2) statement of research interests;
(3) a three- to five-page description of the project (including salary request, research project costs and a timeline) and;
(4) names and contact information of three references.

Duration: Up to 12 months.

Deadline: Proposals are accepted on a rolling basis.

ADDRESS INQUIRIES TO:
Kristen Kepics, Department Administrator
(See e-mail address above.)

ALABAMA ACADEMY OF SCIENCE, INC. [1752]

University of Alabama at Birmingham
Department of Chemistry, CHEM-201
Birmingham, AL 35294
(205) 934-8017
Fax: (205) 934-2543
E-mail: krannich@uab.edu
Web Site: www.alabamaacademyofscience.org

FOUNDED: 1924

AREAS OF INTEREST:
Chemistry, biology, archaeology, earth science, forestry, geography, conservation, physics, industry, economics, mathematics, computer science, anthropology, engineering, psychology, behavioral and social sciences, physical sciences, health sciences and ecology.

CONSULTING OR VOLUNTEER SERVICES:
Visiting Scientist Speaker Program for elementary schools, high schools and colleges.

NAME(S) OF PROGRAMS:

- **Gorgas Scholarship**
- **Mason Science Teaching Fellowships**
- **Student Research Grants**
- **Student Travel Awards**

TYPE:
Assistantships; Awards/prizes; Conferences/seminars; Fellowships; Project/program grants; Research grants; Scholarships; Travel grants; Visiting scholars. Grants to college and university students for small research projects and for travel to scientific meetings to present papers.

Fellowships are for teaching science for Alabama teachers.

The Gorgas Scholarships are awarded to high school senior students who were Alabama Science Scholar Search entrants for any Alabama college or university.

YEAR PROGRAM STARTED: 1924

PURPOSE:
To stimulate student science study and research; to promote the development of interested scientific matter in the state; to render public service in scientific matters.

LEGAL BASIS:
Tax-exempt membership organization.

ELIGIBILITY:
Open to individuals committed to the purpose of the Academy.

GEOG. RESTRICTIONS: Alabama.

FINANCIAL DATA:
Amount of support per award: MST Fellowship: $1,000 for teacher and $50 to $100 per award for student research; Student Research Grants: $250; Student Travel Awards: $50; $10,000 in scholarships to high school seniors.

Total amount of support: Up to $13,000 annually.

CO-OP FUNDING PROGRAMS: Gorgas Scholarship Program is supported by the Alabama Power Foundation, Inc. All other programs are funded by membership dues, meeting registrations, exhibits, contributions and university memberships.

NO. MOST RECENT APPLICANTS: 12.

NO. AWARDS: MST Fellowship: 1 teacher award; Student Research Grants: 3 or 4; Student Travel Awards: 4 or 5.

APPLICATION INFO:
Contact the Academy.

Duration: One year.

Deadline: Approximately February 1. Award announcement at annual meeting in March.

PUBLICATIONS:
Journal of the Alabama Academy of Sciences.

IRS I.D.: 63-6050246

OFFICERS:
Akshaya Kumar, President
Malia Fincher, Treasurer
Bettina Riley, Secretary

BOARD OF TRUSTEES:

ADDRESS INQUIRIES TO:
Larry K. Krannich, Ph.D.
Executive Director
(See address above.)

ALBERTA INNOVATES - HEALTH SOLUTIONS

Suite 1500
10104 - 103 Avenue, N.W.
Edmonton AB T5J 4A7 Canada
(780) 423-5727
Fax: (780) 429-3509
E-mail: health@aihealthsolutions.ca
Web Site: www.aihealthsolutions.ca

TYPE:
Awards/prizes; Block grants; Conferences/seminars; Development grants; Fellowships; General operating grants; Project/program grants; Research grants; Scholarships; Training grants. Interdisciplinary team grants. Awards for conferences and workshops.

See entry 2145 for full listing.

ALTERNATIVES RESEARCH AND DEVELOPMENT FOUNDATION [1753]

801 Old York Road, Suite 316
Jenkintown, PA 19046
(215) 887-8076
Fax: (215) 887-0771
E-mail: grants@ardf-online.org
Web Site: www.ardf-online.org

FOUNDED: 1993

AREAS OF INTEREST:
Development, validation and adoption of non-animal methods in biomedical research, product testing and education.

NAME(S) OF PROGRAMS:

- **Alternatives Research Grant Program**
- **William and Eleanor Cave Award**

TYPE:
Awards/prizes; Research grants.

YEAR PROGRAM STARTED: 1993

PURPOSE:
To fund and promote the development, validation and adoption of non-animal methods in biomedical research, product testing and education.

ELIGIBILITY:
Nonsectarian religious programs may apply. Preference is given to universities and research institutions in the U.S. No grants are made to individuals.

FINANCIAL DATA:
Amount of support per award: Up to $40,000.

Total amount of support: Varies.

APPLICATION INFO:
Primary grant application should be no more than 15 pages, including the Alternatives Research Grant Program Application Form. ADRF encourages electronic submission via dropbox.com. If submitting by mail, send five copies of the primary grant application and supplemental material.

Primary grant application is composed of:
(1) abstract (not to exceed 200 words) that describes the proposed research project and includes an explanation of how the work will contribute to reducing or replacing current uses of laboratory animals in biomedical research, product safety testings, or educational demonstrations;
(2) proposal that presents a clear research plan and includes sections on materials and methods, expected results, and a list of relevant references;
(3) description of how the proposed research will lead to a significant reduction or replacement of laboratory animals;
(4) detailed budget and justification for equipment and supplies;
(5) description of additional sources of funding for the project currently available or applied for. Also supply information about previous grant support in this project area during the past two years and;
(6) curriculum vitae for the principal investigator.

Supplemental material includes previous publications which directly support the current grant application and curriculum vitae (one page each) for up to three personnel involved other than the principal investigator.

Duration: One year.

Deadline: April 30.

ADDRESS INQUIRIES TO:
Sue Leary, President
(See address above.)

AMERICAN ASSOCIATION FOR CLINICAL CHEMISTRY (AACC) [1754]

1850 K Street, N.W., Suite 625
Washington, DC 20006-2213
(202) 857-0717
(800) 892-1400 ext. 8710
Fax: (202) 887-5093
E-mail: kblake@aacc.org
Web Site: www.aacc.org

AREAS OF INTEREST:
Clinical laboratory science and study of outcomes of point-of-care testing (POCT).

NAME(S) OF PROGRAMS:
- **AACC Critical and Point-of-Care Testing Research Grant**

TYPE:
Research grants; Travel grants. AACC Critical and Point-of-Care Testing Research Grant is targeted to clinical laboratorians who need limited research funds to explore new ideas in areas where funds are not normally available.

PURPOSE:
To encourage and support deserving clinical laboratory scientists and students throughout the world.

FINANCIAL DATA:
Amount of support per award: $5,000.

APPLICATION INFO:
Application information is available on the web site.

Deadline: March 15.

ADDRESS INQUIRIES TO:
Kelsey Blake, Education Coordinator
(See e-mail address and phone number above.)

AMERICAN ASSOCIATION FOR THE ADVANCEMENT OF SCIENCE

1200 New York Avenue, N.W.
Washington, DC 20005
(202) 326-6645
Fax: (202) 371-9849
E-mail: drossite@aaas.org
Web Site: www.aaas.org/MassMedia

TYPE:
Fellowships; Internships. Fellowships to primarily support graduate students in the fields of social, natural and physical sciences, mathematics, and engineering during the summer as intern reporters, researchers or production assistants in mass media organizations nationwide. Fellows will have the opportunity to observe and participate in the process by which events and ideas become news, improve their communication skills by learning to describe complex technical subjects in a manner understandable to the lay public, and increase their understanding of editorial decision making and the way in which information is effectively disseminated.

Each fellow will work for a specific media organization. Some will work for newspapers or magazines on news and feature writing assignments. Others may be involved in television or radio production.

See entry 1858 for full listing.

AMERICAN INSTITUTE OF CHEMICAL ENGINEERS (AICHE) [1755]

120 Wall Street, Floor 23
New York, NY 10005-4020
(203) 702-7660
(646) 495-1348
Fax: (212) 591-8890
E-mail: awards@aiche.org
Web Site: www.aiche.org

AREAS OF INTEREST:
Chemical engineering.

NAME(S) OF PROGRAMS:
- **Food, Pharmaceutical and Bioengineering Division Award in Chemical Engineering**

TYPE:
Awards/prizes.

YEAR PROGRAM STARTED: 1970

PURPOSE:
To recognize an individual's outstanding chemical engineering contribution in the food, pharmaceutical and/or bioengineering industry.

LEGAL BASIS:
Professional association.

ELIGIBILITY:
Grants given to individuals. Contribution may have been made in industry, government, or academic areas, or with other organizations.

FINANCIAL DATA:
Amount of support per award: $4,000.

Total amount of support: $4,000.

NO. AWARDS: 1 annually.

APPLICATION INFO:
Contact the Institute.

Deadline: May 15.

ADDRESS INQUIRIES TO:
Dr. Eleftherios Terry Papoutsakis, Director
Eugene DuPont Chair of Chemical Engineering
Delaware Biotechnology Institute
University of Delaware
15 Innovation Way
Newark, DE 19711
Tel: (302) 831-8376

THE AMERICAN MUSEUM OF NATURAL HISTORY [1756]

Richard Gilder Graduate School
Central Park West at 79th Street
New York, NY 10024-5192
(212) 769-5017
Fax: (212) 769-5257
E-mail: fellowships-rggs@amnh.org
mrios@amnh.org
Web Site: www.amnh.org/our-research/richard-gilder-graduate-school

FOUNDED: 1869

AREAS OF INTEREST:
Anthropology, paleontology and zoology.

NAME(S) OF PROGRAMS:
- **Collection Study Grants**
- **Lerner-Gray Grants for Marine Research**
- **Theodore Roosevelt Memorial Grants**

TYPE:
Grants-in-aid; Research grants. Collection Study Grants enable predoctoral and recent postdoctoral investigators to study any of the scientific collections at the American Museum in the departments of anthropology, earth and planetary sciences, entomology, herpetology, ichthyology, invertebrates, mammalogy, ornithology, and vertebrate paleontology.

The Lerner-Gray Grants for Marine Research provide support to highly qualified persons starting careers in marine zoology.

The Theodore Roosevelt Memorial Grants support research on North American fauna in wildlife conservation or natural history.

YEAR PROGRAM STARTED: 1976

PURPOSE:
To provide modest short-term awards to advanced graduate students and postdoctoral researchers who are commencing their careers in the fields of zoology, paleontology and anthropology.

ELIGIBILITY:
Applicants should be advanced graduate students and postdoctoral researchers who are beginning their careers in the interest areas listed above. Research projects need not be carried out at the American Museum.

FINANCIAL DATA:
Amount of support per award: $500 to $3,500.

Total amount of support: Varies.

NO. AWARDS: Average 45 per program.

APPLICATION INFO:
Application information is available on the web site.

Duration: One year.

Deadline: Varies by grant.

ADDRESS INQUIRIES TO:
Maria Rios, Assistant Director
Fellowships and Student Affairs
(See address above.)

THE AMERICAN MUSEUM OF NATURAL HISTORY [1757]

Richard Gilder Graduate School
Central Park West at 79th Street
New York, NY 10024-5192
(212) 769-5017
Fax: (212) 769-5257
E-mail: fellowships-rggs@amnh.org
mrios@amnh.org
Web Site: www.amnh.org/our-research/richard-gilder-graduate-school

FOUNDED: 1869

AREAS OF INTEREST:
Vertebrate and invertebrate zoology, paleozoology, anthropology, earth and planetary sciences.

NAME(S) OF PROGRAMS:
- **Postdoctoral Research Fellowship Program**

TYPE:
Fellowships.

YEAR PROGRAM STARTED: 1960

PURPOSE:
To advance the training of recent postdoctoral investigators and established scientists.

LEGAL BASIS:
Nonprofit.

ELIGIBILITY:
Provides training to postdoctoral investigators and established scientists to carry out a specific project, which must fit into the Museum's areas of interest. Postdoctoral Fellows are expected to be in residence at the Museum.

FINANCIAL DATA:
Limited relocation, research, and publication support is provided.

APPLICATION INFO:
Applications require a project description with bibliography, budget, curriculum vitae including a list of publications, and letters of recommendation.

Duration: Up to two years.

Deadline: November 15.

PUBLICATIONS:
Grants and Fellowships of the American Museum of Natural History, booklet.

ADDRESS INQUIRIES TO:
Maria Rios, Assistant Director
Fellowships and Student Affairs
(See address above.)

AMERICAN TINNITUS ASSOCIATION (ATA) [1758]

522 S.W. 5th Avenue
Suite 825
Portland, OR 97204
(503) 248-9985
(800) 634-8978
Fax: (503) 248-0024
E-mail: tinnitus@ata.org
Web Site: www.ata.org

FOUNDED: 1971

AREAS OF INTEREST:
Tinnitus.

NAME(S) OF PROGRAMS:
- **ATA Student Research Grant Program**
- **ATA Tinnitus Research Grant Program**

TYPE:
Research grants; Seed money grants. Financially supports scientific studies about tinnitus.

YEAR PROGRAM STARTED: 1980

PURPOSE:
To identify the mechanisms of tinnitus or to improve tinnitus treatments.

LEGAL BASIS:
501(c)(3) nonprofit association.

ELIGIBILITY:
Tinnitus Research Grant: Postdoctorate. Student Grant: Doctorate or medical student. ATA will consider the subject of research, quality of its design, potential for significant advances in basic knowledge or clinical application, available facilities and personnel at the institution and qualifications of investigators. Facility must be nonprofit.

GEOG. RESTRICTIONS: United States.

FINANCIAL DATA:
Amount of support per award: Tinnitus Research Grant: Up to $150,000 ($50,000 per year); Student Grant: $10,000.

APPLICATION INFO:
In addition to the application form, applicants must submit a concisely written research proposal containing detailed descriptions of the following elements:
(1) introduction, statement of the problem and specific aims of the research;
(2) background and significance of the issue;
(3) relevant preliminary or pilot studies;
(4) the facility that will house the study and/or administer the funds;
(5) discussion of relevant literature and, where appropriate, standardized tinnitus measures;
(6) outline of intended study procedures including study design, sampling and measurement data to be used, and description of analysis and evaluation plan and;
(7) outcomes expected from the study and the study's use.

Duration: Tinnitus Research Grant: Up to three years. Student Grant: One year.

Deadline: November 1.

STAFF:
Cara James, Executive Director

ADDRESS INQUIRIES TO:
Cara James, Executive Director
(See address above.)

AMFAR, THE FOUNDATION FOR AIDS RESEARCH [1759]

120 Wall Street, 13th Floor
New York, NY 10005-3908
(212) 806-1600
Fax: (212) 806-1601
E-mail: grants@amfar.org
Web Site: www.amfar.org

FOUNDED: 1985

AREAS OF INTEREST:
Research relevant to HIV/AIDS and projects that extend the benefits of HIV/AIDS research.

NAME(S) OF PROGRAMS:
- **Mathilde Krim Fellowships in Basic Biomedical Research**
- **Research Grants**

TYPE:
Fellowships; Project/program grants; Research grants. Mathilde Krim Fellowships are grants made to support two years of original research on any biomedical topic relevant to HIV conducted by outstanding postdoctoral scientists and facilitate transition to an independent position in HIV/AIDS research.

Research Grants provide one to four years of support for HIV/AIDS research relevant to achieving a cure for HIV. Investigators must hold a degree and be affiliated with a nonprofit research institution. Specific requirements are detailed in RFPs issued for each research grant program.

YEAR PROGRAM STARTED: 1985

PURPOSE:
To end the global AIDS epidemic through innovative research; to respond quickly to emerging areas of scientific promise; to accelerate the pace of HIV/AIDS research and achieve real breakthroughs; to increase understanding of HIV and help lay the groundwork for major advances in the study and treatment of HIV/AIDS.

LEGAL BASIS:
Not-for-profit public benefit corporation.

ELIGIBILITY:
Varies by program.

FINANCIAL DATA:
Since 1985, amfAR has invested more than $388,000,000 in its mission and has awarded more than 3,300 grants to research teams worldwide.

Amount of support per award: Krim Fellowships: Up to $150,000; Research Grants: $180,000 to $2,000,000, depending on program.

APPLICATION INFO:
The Foundation does not accept unsolicited grant applications or requests. Open Requests for Proposals and directions for proposal submission are posted on the web site.

Duration: Krim Fellowships: Two years; Research Grants: Two to four years, depending on program.

Deadline: Varies.

STAFF:
Rowena Johnston, Ph.D., Vice President, Research
Kent Cozad, Director, Grants Administration and Compliance
Jonathan Miller, Grants Administrator, Research

ADDRESS INQUIRIES TO:
Grants Administration
(See address above.)

ARGONNE NATIONAL LABORATORY [1760]

Communications, Education and Public Affairs Division
9700 South Cass Avenue
Argonne, IL 60439-4845
(630) 252-4114
Fax: (630) 252-3193
E-mail: lisareed@anl.gov
Web Site: www.dep.anl.gov

FOUNDED: 1968

AREAS OF INTEREST:
Basic physical and life sciences, mathematics, computer science, engineering, applied research relating to coal, conservation, environmental impact and technology, fission and fusion energy.

NAME(S) OF PROGRAMS:
- **Science Undergraduate Laboratory Internships**

TYPE:
Internships.

PURPOSE:
To encourage the further study of science.

LEGAL BASIS:
Research center of the U.S. Department of Energy.

ELIGIBILITY:
Applicants must be U.S. citizens or permanent resident aliens who are full-time students at accredited U.S. colleges or universities. In addition to their research activities, participants are expected to attend a series of seminars and tours dealing with current topics in science and engineering.

GEOG. RESTRICTIONS: United States.

FINANCIAL DATA:
Amount of support per award: $500 per week.
Total amount of support: Varies.

NO. MOST RECENT APPLICANTS: 100.

APPLICATION INFO:
Applications must be submitted at the Department of Energy web site.
Duration: 10 weeks during the summer; 15 weeks during fall or spring.
Deadline: Summer: January 10. Fall: Approximately May 30. Spring: October 30.

ADDRESS INQUIRIES TO:
Lisa Reed, Program Coordinator
(See address above.)

ARGONNE NATIONAL LABORATORY [1761]

Communications, Education and Public Affairs Division
9700 South Cass Avenue
Argonne, IL 60439-4845
(630) 252-4114
Fax: (630) 252-3193
E-mail: lisareed@anl.gov
Web Site: www.dep.anl.gov

FOUNDED: 1946

AREAS OF INTEREST:
Basic physical and life sciences, mathematics, computer science and engineering, applied research relating to coal, conservation, environmental science and energy technologies and fission and fusion energy.

NAME(S) OF PROGRAMS:
- **Laboratory-Graduate Program**
- **Thesis Parts Program**

TYPE:
Fellowships. Laboratory Graduate Program provides support for thesis research in residence at Argonne.
Thesis Parts Program provides support for partial dissertation research or to satisfy practicum requirements at Argonne.

YEAR PROGRAM STARTED: 1968

PURPOSE:
To encourage the advanced study of science.

LEGAL BASIS:
Research center of the U.S. Department of Energy.

ELIGIBILITY:
U.S. citizens or permanent residents are eligible. Appointments are made to graduate students who have completed all requirements for their Master's or doctoral degrees except for the dissertation. The research must require resources not available on campus.

GEOG. RESTRICTIONS: United States.

FINANCIAL DATA:
Amount of support per award: Laboratory-Graduate Program provides stipend, plus up to $10,500 per year tuition. Thesis Parts Program provides per diem amount.
Total amount of support: Varies.

NO. AWARDS: 15.

APPLICATION INFO:
Applications must be submitted electronically.
Duration: Laboratory-Graduate Program: Up to one year. Renewable for a total of three years.

ADDRESS INQUIRIES TO:
Lisa Reed, Program Coordinator
(See address above.)

BAYER USA FOUNDATION [1762]

100 Bayer Road
Pittsburgh, PA 15205
(800) 422-9374
Fax: (412) 778-4413
E-mail: bayerusafoundation@bayer.com
Web Site: www.bayer.us

FOUNDED: 1953

AREAS OF INTEREST:
Education and workforce development, environment and sustainability, health and social services.

TYPE:
General operating grants; Project/program grants.

PURPOSE:
To take an active role in business communities; to enhance the quality of life for Bayer employees and neighbors.

LEGAL BASIS:
Corporate giving program.

ELIGIBILITY:
Proposed projects must impact at least one of Bayer Corporation's business locations. No grants to organizations without IRS 501(c)(3) status, United Way-affiliated agencies for general operating support, charitable dinners and events, individuals, political organizations, endowment funds, deficit reduction, religious organizations, student trips or exchange programs, community advertising, athletic sponsorships or telephone solicitations.

GEOG. RESTRICTIONS: United States and its territories.

FINANCIAL DATA:
Amount of support per award: Varies depending on needs and nature of the request.

APPLICATION INFO:
Applications must be submitted online. Applicants will receive confirmation when an application is received. Grant applications will be reviewed on a regular basis, and grant seekers with approved proposals will be contacted. If applicant does not hear from the Foundation, his or her proposal does not meet the strategic interests of the company.
Deadline: Varies by location.

ADDRESS INQUIRIES TO:
See e-mail address above.

BROOKHAVEN WOMEN IN SCIENCE

P.O. Box 183
Upton, NY 11973
(631) 344-2425
Fax: (631) 344-5676
E-mail: bwisawards@bnl.gov
Web Site: www.bnl.gov/bwis/scholarships.php

TYPE:
Awards/prizes; Scholarships. These scholarships are offered to encourage women to resume their formal education in the natural sciences, engineering or mathematics.

See entry 1055 for full listing.

CARNEGIE INSTITUTION FOR SCIENCE [1763]

1530 P Street, N.W.
Washington, DC 20005
(202) 939-1120
Fax: (202) 939-1120
E-mail: tmcdowell@carnegiescience.edu
Web Site: www.carnegiescience.edu

FOUNDED: 1902

AREAS OF INTEREST:
Astronomy, physics, chemistry, earth sciences, materials science, plant biology, developmental biology and global ecology.

NAME(S) OF PROGRAMS:
- **Predoctoral and Postdoctoral Fellowships at the Carnegie Institution**

TYPE:
Fellowships; Internships; Technical assistance; Visiting scholars; Research contracts. Predoctoral and Postdoctoral fellowships for research training in the fields of astronomy, geophysics, physics and related sciences, plant biology, genetics and developmental biology in residence at one of the Carnegie Institution's six operating centers.

YEAR PROGRAM STARTED: 1938

PURPOSE:
To encourage in the broadest and most liberal manner investigation, research and discovery and the application of knowledge to the improvement of mankind.

LEGAL BASIS:
Exempt under Section 501(c)(3) of the Internal Revenue Code.

ELIGIBILITY:
Qualified scientists who have obtained the doctoral degree or are in the process are eligible. Candidates are evaluated on the basis of academic record, recommendations of professors and associates and the complementing nature of their research to work in progress at the Carnegie department. Women and minorities are encouraged to apply.

FINANCIAL DATA:
Fellowships provide direct financial support and the use of the Institution's laboratory and observational facilities, including special equipment when needed. Travel funds may be included where long-distance travel is required to reach the Institution.

Amount of support per award: Varies by department.

APPLICATION INFO:
Fellowship applications should be made to the Directors of the Departments of Carnegie Institution at the addresses listed below.

Duration: Fellowships are usually awarded for one year with the possibility of renewal for another year.

Deadline: Varies.

PUBLICATIONS:
Newsletter.

OFFICERS:
Matthew P. Scott, President
Timothy Doyle, Chief Operating Officer

DIRECTORS:
Yixian Zheng, Acting Director, Department of Embryology
Christopher Field, Director, Department of Global Ecology
Sue Rhee, Director, Department of Plant Biology
Richard Carlson, Director, Department of Terrestrial Magnetism
George Cody, Acting Director, Geophysical Laboratory
John Mulchaey, Acting Director, Observatories of Carnegie

ADDRESS INQUIRIES TO:
Call first to determine to whom inquiry should be directed.

Dr. Yixian Zheng
Acting Director, Department of Embryology
3520 San Martin Drive
Baltimore, MD 21218 or

Dr. Christopher Field
Director, Department of Global Ecology
260 Panama Street
Stanford, CA 94305
Tel: (650) 462-1047 or

Dr. Sue Rhee
Director, Department of Plant Biology
260 Panama Street
Stanford, CA 94305 or

Dr. Richard Carlson
Director, Department of Terrestrial Magnetism
5241 Broad Branch Road, N.W.
Washington, DC 20015 or

Dr. George Cody
Acting Director, Geophysical Laboratory
5251 Broad Branch Road, N.W.
Washington, DC 20015 or

Dr. John Mulchaey
Acting Director, The Observatories of the Carnegie Institution
813 Santa Barbara Street
Pasadena, CA 91101

*SPECIAL STIPULATIONS:
Fellowships are tenable only at one of the Institution's facilities. No extracurricular grants.

EARTHWATCH INSTITUTE [1764]

114 Western Avenue
Boston, MA 02134
(800) 776-0188
Fax: (978) 450-1200
E-mail: research@earthwatch.org
Web Site: earthwatch.org/scientific-research

FOUNDED: 1971

AREAS OF INTEREST:
Scientific field research that can utilize highly motivated nonspecialist volunteers, also called citizen scientists (recruited by Earthwatch), to collect data. Earthwatch focuses on research areas that address response to global change in urban, freshwater, terrestrial and ocean ecosystems.

NAME(S) OF PROGRAMS:

- **Earthwatch Funding for Field Research**

TYPE:
Assistantships; Exchange programs; Fellowships; General operating grants; Internships; Project/program grants; Research grants; Training grants. Financial support for field research projects. Earthwatch works on a system of participant-based funding whereby volunteers pay to directly assist scientists with their work in the field. Typically, projects have the need for 30 to 60 volunteers per fielding season, distributed over multiple teams. For example, during a given year a Principal Investigator may run four to eight teams of five to 12 volunteers per team. Most projects have teams that do field work for approximately eight to 15 days each.

YEAR PROGRAM STARTED: 1971

PURPOSE:
To engage people worldwide in scientific field research and education to promote the understanding and action necessary for a sustainable environment.

LEGAL BASIS:
Incorporated as a nonprofit, tax-exempt organization, 501(c)(3) of the IRS Code.

ELIGIBILITY:
All Principal Investigators must have a Ph.D. and an affiliation with a university, government agency or not-for-profit organization. Earthwatch strongly encourages graduate student participation in projects as co-Principal Investigators and is particularly interested in helping support emerging scientists from developing nations.

Proposals may be submitted by researchers of any nationality. Participation of host-country researchers or staff is strongly encouraged.

GEOG. RESTRICTIONS: Due to safety concerns, Earthwatch is not able to support any research projects in certain regions of the world. More information is provided during the application process.

FINANCIAL DATA:
Amount of support per award: Field grants vary based on project needs. Typical field grants average approximately $20,000 to $80,000 per year per project.

Total amount of support: $57,000,000.

NO. MOST RECENT APPLICANTS: 400.

APPLICATION INFO:
Application information is available on the web site. Click on "Scientist Opportunities" under "Scientific Research."

Duration: Earthwatch supports long-term projects that plan to run for at least three years.

Deadline: Projects are developed 18 months in advance of fielding.

PUBLICATIONS:
Earthwatch, magazine; *Project Briefings*; proposal guidelines; grants list.

OFFICERS:
Mark Chandler, International Director of Research

ADDRESS INQUIRIES TO:
Research Department
(See address above.)

EARTHWATCH INSTITUTE [1765]

114 Western Avenue
Boston, MA 02134
(800) 776-0188
Fax: (978) 461-2332
E-mail: fellowshipawards@earthwatch.org
Web Site: www.earthwatch.org/education

FOUNDED: 1971

AREAS OF INTEREST:
Promoting a sustainable environment.

NAME(S) OF PROGRAMS:

- **Earthwatch Educator Program**
- **Earthwatch Teach Earth USA Program**

TYPE:
Fellowships. Teachers in grades K-12 apply for seven- to 10-day Earthwatch expedition fellowships that take place during the summer. Earthwatch selects over 50 teachers from all subject areas across the U.S. to assist scientists on expeditions by collecting data on climate change and sustainable resource management. Funding for these fellowships comes from a variety of donors, e.g., individuals, corporations, family foundations, community organizations and nonprofits. On their return from the field, these teachers must develop a lesson or action plan that ties their experience back to their classroom or community.

YEAR PROGRAM STARTED: 1971

PURPOSE:
To inspire young people to become environmental ambassadors by engaging educators and empowering them to be role models regarding environmental issues and science research; to accomplish this, the Teach Earth USA Fellowship program focuses on engaging teachers from all subject areas and grade levels to assist scientists with research on climate change and sustainable resource management.

LEGAL BASIS:
Incorporated as a nonprofit, tax-exempt organization, 501(c)(3) of the IRS Code.

ELIGIBILITY:
All U.S. teachers that currently teach grades K-12. These teachers must be passionate about teaching, looking to learn more about environmental issues, are interested in how scientific research is conducted, excited to collaborate with a team of teachers, and committed to engaging students and the community outside the classroom.

Earthwatch searches for evidence of passionate teaching that stretches beyond the basics of the classroom and engages professionals who may not identify as science experts but are willing to learn and do more.

GEOG. RESTRICTIONS: United States.

FINANCIAL DATA:
Fellowship covers the full cost of the assigned expedition including meals and accommodations and on-site transportation. The fellowship also includes a travel award to offset out-of-pocket travel expenses to and from the expedition.

Amount of support per award: $6,500.

Total amount of support: $377,006.

NO. MOST RECENT APPLICANTS: 156.

NO. AWARDS: 50.

APPLICATION INFO:
Contact Earthwatch for application details.

Duration: Seven- to 10-day expedition.

Deadline: Applications are sent out during the fall. Deadline is mid-January to mid-February.

PUBLICATIONS:
Earthwatch, magazine; Project Briefings; proposal guidelines; grants list.

THE ELECTROCHEMICAL SOCIETY [1766]

65 South Main Street, Building D
Pennington, NJ 08534-2839
(609) 737-1902 ext. 124
Fax: (609) 737-2743
E-mail: marcelle.austin@electrochem.org
Web Site: www.electrochem.org/awards

FOUNDED: 1902

AREAS OF INTEREST:
Advancement of the theory and practice of electrochemical and solid-state science and technology, and allied subjects.

NAME(S) OF PROGRAMS:

- **Edward Goodrich Acheson Award**
- **Allen J. Bard Award**
- **Vittorio de Nora Award**
- **Henry B. Linford Award for Distinguished Teaching**
- **Gordon E. Moore Medal for Outstanding Achievement in Solid State Science and Technology**
- **Olin Palladium Award**
- **Charles W. Tobias Young Investigator Award**
- **Carl Wagner Memorial Award**

TYPE:
Awards/prizes. Edward Goodrich Acheson Award is for distinguished contributions to the advancement of any of the objects, purposes or activities of The Electrochemical Society.

Allen J. Bard Award recognizes distinguished contributions to electrochemical science.

Vittorio de Nora Award is for contributions to the field of electrochemical engineering and technology.

Henry B. Linford Award for Distinguished Teaching recognizes excellence in teaching in subject areas of interest to the Society.

Gordon E. Moore Medal for Outstanding Achievement in Solid State Science and Technology is for distinguished contributions to the field of solid state science.

Olin Palladium Award is for distinguished contributions to the field of electrochemical or corrosion science.

Charles W. Tobias Young Investigator Award recognizes outstanding scientific and/or engineering work in fundamental or applied electrochemistry or solid-state science and technology by a young scientist or engineer.

Carl Wagner Memorial Award recognizes a midcareer achievement and excellence in research areas of interest of the Society, and significant contributions in the teaching or guidance of students or colleagues in education, industry or government.

PURPOSE:
To advance the theory and practice of electrochemical and solid-state science and technology, and allied subjects.

ELIGIBILITY:
Varies by award.

FINANCIAL DATA:
Amount of support per award: Edward Goodrich Acheson Award: Gold medal, wall plaque, and prize of $10,000. Allen J. Bard Award: Wall plaque with glass carbon medal, prize of $7,500, ECS Life Membership, and a complimentary meeting registration to accept the Award. Vittorio de Nora Award: Gold medal, wall plaque and prize of $7,500. Henry B. Linford Award for Distinguished Teaching: Silver medal, wall plaque and prize of $2,500. Olin Palladium Award: Palladium medal, wall plaque and prize of $7,500. Gordon E. Moore Medal for Outstanding Achievement in Solid State Science and Technology: Silver medal, wall plaque and prize of $7,500. Charles W. Tobias Young Investigator Award: Framed scroll, prize of $5,000, ECS Life Membership and travel assistance to the meeting of the award presentation (up to $1,000). Carl Wagner Memorial Award: ECS Life Membership, certificate, sterling silver medal, travel assistance to the meeting of award presentation (up to $1,000).

NO. MOST RECENT APPLICANTS: 5 to 10.

NO. AWARDS: Only 1 winner per award given in any of the award cycles.

APPLICATION INFO:
Application information is available on the web site.

Deadline: Varies by award.

ADDRESS INQUIRIES TO:
E-mail: awards@electrochem.org

THE ELECTROCHEMICAL SOCIETY [1767]

65 South Main Street, Building D
Pennington, NJ 08534-2839
(609) 737-1902
(609) 737-1902 ext. 111
Fax: (609) 737-2743
E-mail: awards@electrochem.org
tammi.doerflier@electrochem.org
Web Site: www.electrochem.org

FOUNDED: 1902

AREAS OF INTEREST:
Advancement of the theory and practice of electrochemistry, electrometallurgy, solid-state science, electrothermics and allied subjects.

NAME(S) OF PROGRAMS:

- **ECS Summer Fellowships**

TYPE:
Awards/prizes; Conferences/seminars; Development grants; Fellowships; Grants-in-aid; Project/program grants; Research grants; Training grants; Travel grants. Four summer fellowships granted annually for study in a college or university.

YEAR PROGRAM STARTED: 1928

PURPOSE:
To stimulate and encourage participation and education in the fields of electrochemical science and technology as well as other interests to the Society.

LEGAL BASIS:
Scientific, educational, nonprofit, tax-exempt organization.

ELIGIBILITY:
For Fellowships, the applicant must be a graduate student (between B.S. and Ph.D.) in a college or university who will continue studies following the summer months the award is given.

No limitations on sex, race, nationality or religion.

FINANCIAL DATA:
Amount of support per award: Varies upon approval from the Board of Directors; usually $5,000 each.

Total amount of support: Varies.

NO. MOST RECENT APPLICANTS: 50.

NO. AWARDS: Up to 4 Summer Fellowships annually.

APPLICATION INFO:
Submit a brief statement of educational objectives, work accomplished on thesis, work planned, transcript of undergraduate and graduate work, two letters of recommendation and a letter of agreement not to hold other appointments or fellowships simultaneously.

Deadline: Fellowships: January 15. Notification for Fellowships will be made on or before March 15.

PUBLICATIONS:
Interface Magazine.

STAFF:
Ericka Robinson, Human Resources and Operations Specialist

ADDRESS INQUIRIES TO:
The Electrochemical Society
Awards/ECS
(See address above.)

FATS AND PROTEINS RESEARCH FOUNDATION, INC. [1768]

500 Montgomery Street
Suite 310
Alexandria, VA 22314
(703) 683-2633
Fax: (703) 683-2626
E-mail: dmeeker@nationalrenderers.com
Web Site: www.fprf.org

FOUNDED: 1962

AREAS OF INTEREST:
Use of rendered product in animal nutrition; feed safety and biosecurity of processes.

TYPE:
Research grants; Research contracts.

YEAR PROGRAM STARTED: 1962

PURPOSE:
To promote scientific and technological research into new and expanded uses for fats

and proteins from animal by-products and processing technology; to encourage cooperative studies.

LEGAL BASIS:
Nonprofit foundation, 501(c)(6).

ELIGIBILITY:
Colleges, universities and research institutes with appropriate interests and capabilities are eligible to apply.

FINANCIAL DATA:
Amount of support per award: Average $35,000.

Total amount of support: $180,000 to $250,000 annually.

CO-OP FUNDING PROGRAMS: Encouraged.

NO. MOST RECENT APPLICANTS: 15.

NO. AWARDS: 6 for the year 2013.

APPLICATION INFO:
Request proposal format from the above address or visit the web site. Prospective applicants should submit a brief outline of the proposed project (including background information, objectives, scope and mode of approach) along with a statement of the required budget and a brief biographical sketch of personnel to be involved in the research.

Duration: Varies.

Deadline: March 15 and September 15 for review of applications.

PUBLICATIONS:
Annual report; contributions policy; application guidelines.

IRS I.D.: 39-2497869

DIRECTORS:
Erika Weltzien, Chairman
Duane Anderson, Vice Chairman
Nancy Cook, President

ADDRESS INQUIRIES TO:
Dr. David L. Meeker, Research Director
(See address above.)

FLORIDA EDUCATION FUND

201 East Kennedy Boulevard
Suite 1525
Tampa, FL 33602
(813) 272-2772 ext. 203
Fax: (813) 272-2784
E-mail: fef.jackson@verizon.net
mdf@fefonline.org
Web Site: www.fefonline.org

TYPE:
Fellowships.

See entry 1497 for full listing.

FOUNDATION FOR SCIENCE AND DISABILITY

503 N.W. 89th Street
Gainesville, FL 32607
(352) 374-5774
Fax: (352) 374-5781
E-mail: rmankin1@ufl.edu
Web Site: stemd.org

TYPE:
Grants-in-aid; Research grants.

See entry 966 for full listing.

HARVARD TRAVELLERS CLUB, PERMANENT FUND [1769]

P.O. Box 190
Canton, MA 02021
(781) 821-0400
Fax: (781) 828-4254
E-mail: gpbates@shieldpackaging.com
Web Site: www.travellersfund.org

FOUNDED: 1937

AREAS OF INTEREST:
Various scientific fields.

TYPE:
Project/program grants; Research grants. Small grants for research projects.

YEAR PROGRAM STARTED: 1937

PURPOSE:
To foster research and/or exploration which involves travel.

LEGAL BASIS:
501(c)(3) nonprofit organization.

ELIGIBILITY:
Applicants must have ability to make a competent contribution in the field of research. The Fund does not pay travel expenses unless it is intimately involved with the research and/or exploration. Preference is given to applicants working on advanced degrees.

FINANCIAL DATA:
Amount of support per award: Up to $4,000.

Total amount of support: Varies.

NO. MOST RECENT APPLICANTS: 15.

NO. AWARDS: 2.

APPLICATION INFO:
Applicants should submit an explanation of goals, an indication of ability, and a resume.

Duration: Usually one-time grant.

Deadline: End of March, for travel during the following summer.

IRS I.D.: 04-6115589

TRUSTEES:
George P. Bates
Jesse R. Page

ADDRESS INQUIRIES TO:
George P. Bates, Trustee
(See address above.)

*SPECIAL STIPULATIONS:
No scholarships for study at educational institutions.

THE HERB SOCIETY OF AMERICA, INC.

9019 Kirtland Chardon Road
Kirtland, OH 44094
(440) 256-0514
Fax: (440) 256-0541
E-mail: herbs@herbsociety.org
Web Site: www.herbsociety.org

TYPE:
Research grants.

See entry 2057 for full listing.

HISTORY OF SCIENCE SOCIETY

440 Geddes Hall
University of Notre Dame
Notre Dame, IN 46556
(574) 631-1194
Fax: (574) 631-1533
E-mail: info@hssonline.org
Web Site: www.hssonline.org

TYPE:
Awards/prizes. The Davis Prize honors books in the history of science directed to a wide public and was established through a long-term pledge from Miles and Audrey Davis.

The Joseph H. Hazen Education Prize recognizes excellence in teaching in the history of science.

The Levinson Prize is awarded in even-numbered years to an outstanding book in the life sciences and natural history.

The Pfizer Prize honors the best English-language work related to the history of science published in the preceding three years.

The Nathan Reingold Prize is given for an original essay in the history of science and its cultural influences. Essay must be no more than 8,000 words in length and thoroughly documented.

The Margaret W. Rossiter History of Women in Science Prize honors an outstanding book, or in even-numbered years an article, published in the preceding four years.

See entry 586 for full listing.

HISTORY OF SCIENCE SOCIETY

440 Geddes Hall
University of Notre Dame
Notre Dame, IN 46556
(574) 631-1194
Fax: (574) 631-1533
E-mail: info@hssonline.org
Web Site: www.hssonline.org

TYPE:
Awards/prizes. Prize for the best scholarly article published in *Isis* during the past three years.

See entry 585 for full listing.

ILLINOIS STATE ACADEMY OF SCIENCE [1770]

c/o Research and Collections Center
1011 East Ash Street
Springfield, IL 62703
(217) 524-0497
Fax: (217) 782-1254
E-mail: rmyers@museum.state.il.us
Web Site: ilacadofsci.com

FOUNDED: 1907

AREAS OF INTEREST:
Promotion of science in the state of Illinois.

NAME(S) OF PROGRAMS:

- **Scientific Research Grants/Proposal Writing Contest**

TYPE:
Awards/prizes; Grants-in-aid; Project/program grants; Research grants; Seed money grants. Cash grants and certificates to Illinois college or junior college students for writing a scientific proposal and conducting the proposed research.

YEAR PROGRAM STARTED: 1981

PURPOSE:
To promote science in the state of Illinois.

LEGAL BASIS:
Nonprofit organization.

ELIGIBILITY:
All public or private college or junior college students in the state of Illinois who are

sponsored by a signing instructor are eligible. ISAS membership is required. Proposals do not have to be original. They can be a spin-off of a lab experiment from class or something the student is interested in as a hobby.

GEOG. RESTRICTIONS: Illinois.

FINANCIAL DATA:
Total amount of support: Varies each year.

NO. AWARDS: Varies.

APPLICATION INFO:
Students must submit application electronically through the Academy's web site.

Duration: One-time award. Renewable.

Deadline: November 1.

PUBLICATIONS:
Transactions of the Illinois State Academy of Science.

IRS I.D.: 37-6043007

ADDRESS INQUIRIES TO:
Robyn Myers, Executive Secretary
(See address above.)

INSTITUTE OF FOOD TECHNOLOGISTS FOUNDATION

525 West Van Buren Street
Suite 1000
Chicago, IL 60607
(312) 782-8424
Fax: (312) 416-7919
E-mail: feedingtomorrow@ift.org
Web Site: www.ift.org/scholarships

TYPE:
Scholarships. Freshman Scholarships and Undergraduate Scholarships encourage undergraduate enrollment in food science and technology. Graduate Scholarships support advanced study in the field of food science and technology.

See entry 2526 for full listing.

INTERNATIONAL FOUNDATION FOR ETHICAL RESEARCH, INC. [1771]

53 West Jackson Boulevard, Suite 1552
Chicago, IL 60604
(312) 427-6025
Fax: (312) 427-6524
E-mail: podonovan@navs.org
ifer@navs.org
Web Site: www.ifer.org

FOUNDED: 1985

AREAS OF INTEREST:
Scientifically valid alternatives to the use of animals in research, product testing, and education.

TYPE:
Fellowships. Graduate Fellowships in Animal Welfare support research in, but not limited to, tissue, cell and organ cultures, clinical studies using animals or humans, epidemiological studies, enhanced use of extensive tissue repositories and patient databases, public education, and computer modeling.

YEAR PROGRAM STARTED: 1997

PURPOSE:
To provide monetary assistance to graduate students whose programs of study seem likely to have impact on animal welfare.

LEGAL BASIS:
Nonprofit.

ELIGIBILITY:
Application is open to students enrolled in Master's and Ph.D. programs in the sciences, humanities, psychology, and journalism.

GEOG. RESTRICTIONS: United States.

FINANCIAL DATA:
Amount of support per award: Up to $12,500 stipend, plus up to $2,500 for supplies per year.

APPLICATION INFO:
Information and preproposal guidelines are available from the Foundation.

Duration: The fellowships are renewable for up to three years.

Deadline: Preproposal: Usually March 15. Awards announced October.

PUBLICATIONS:
Newsletter.

IRS I.D.: 22-2628153

STAFF:
Peter O'Donovan, Executive Director

ADDRESS INQUIRIES TO:
Peter O'Donovan, Executive Director
(See address above.)

INVENT NOW [1772]

3701 Highland Park, N.W.
North Canton, OH 44720-4535
(800) 968-4332 (option 5)
E-mail: collegiate@invent.org
Web Site: www.collegiateinventors.org

AREAS OF INTEREST:
Creative invention: science, engineering, mathematics, technology and related fields.

NAME(S) OF PROGRAMS:
- **Collegiate Inventors Competition**

TYPE:
Awards/prizes. National competition in the U.S. that recognizes and rewards innovations, discoveries, and research by college and university students and their faculty advisors.

YEAR PROGRAM STARTED: 1990

PURPOSE:
To promote exploration in invention, science, engineering, technology, and other creative endeavors and provide a window on the future technologies from which society will benefit in the future.

ELIGIBILITY:
Open to students who are enrolled (or have been enrolled) full-time in any U.S. college or university at least part of the 12-month period prior to the date the entry is submitted. In the case of a team (maximum of four students), at least one member must meet the full-time eligibility criteria.

Entry must be the original idea and work product of the student/advisor team, and must not have been:
(1) made available to the public as a commercial product or process or;
(2) patented or published more than one year prior to the date of competition submission.

Entries must be written in English.

GEOG. RESTRICTIONS: United States.

FINANCIAL DATA:
Up to 12 finalists will win an all-expense-paid trip in the fall to present their work to a panel of expert judges.

Academic advisors of each of the top winning teams will also receive a cash award.

Amount of support per award: Up to $15,000.

Total amount of support: Up to $100,000.

NO. MOST RECENT APPLICANTS: Average 100.

NO. AWARDS: 6.

APPLICATION INFO:
All entries must be submitted on the official application form, which is available online.

Deadline: Mid-June.

ADDRESS INQUIRIES TO:
Collegiate Inventors Competition
(See e-mail address above.)

THE LALOR FOUNDATION, INC. [1773]

c/o GMA Foundations
77 Summer Street, Eighth Floor
Boston, MA 02110-1006
(617) 426-7080
Fax: (617) 426-7087
E-mail: fellowshipmanager@gmafoundations.com
Web Site: www.lalorfound.org

FOUNDED: 1935

AREAS OF INTEREST:
Basic postdoctoral research in mammalian reproductive physiology and biochemistry bearing on sterilization and/or prevention or termination of pregnancy.

NAME(S) OF PROGRAMS:
- **The Lalor Foundation Postdoctoral Fellowship Program**

TYPE:
Fellowships. Fellowships to institutions for basic postdoctoral research in mammalian reproductive biology as related to the regulation of fertility.

YEAR PROGRAM STARTED: 1937

PURPOSE:
To promote intensive research in mammalian reproductive biology.

LEGAL BASIS:
Tax-exempt philanthropic foundation.

ELIGIBILITY:
Domestic institutions must be exempt from federal income taxes under Section 501(c)(3) of the Internal Revenue Code. Domestic and foreign institutions must qualify under Section 509(a)(1), (2) or (3). Individuals who are nominated by the applicant institution may be citizens of any country and should have training and experience at least equal to the Ph.D. or M.D. level. Potential fellows may not have held the doctoral degree more than two years.

The applicant institution may make its nomination of a fellow from among its own personnel or elsewhere, but, qualifications being equal, candidates from other than the proposing institution itself may carry modest preference. The application must name the institution's nominee for fellowship and include his or her performance record.

FINANCIAL DATA:
Grants for coverage of fellowship stipend and institutional expenses.

Amount of support per award: $50,000 (U.S.).

Total amount of support: Fellowships: $700,000 for fiscal year 2015.

NO. MOST RECENT APPLICANTS: 32 for fiscal year 2015.

NO. AWARDS: 15 for fiscal year 2015.

APPLICATION INFO:
One reference letter, two reviews from independent experts, and a letter from the sponsor-mentor are requested. Full application information is available on the web site.

Duration: One year. Renewable under some circumstances.

Deadline: January 15. Notification by April 15.

IRS I.D.: 51-6000153

OFFICERS:
Cynthia B. Patterson, President
Christopher Burdick, Vice President
Lalor Burdick, Secretary and Treasurer

BOARD OF TRUSTEES:
Christopher Burdick
Lalor Burdick
Carol Chandler, Esq.
Marnie Cochran
Cynthia B. Patterson
Sally H. Zeckhauser

ADDRESS INQUIRIES TO:
Fellowship Manager
(See address above.)

LOS ALAMOS NATIONAL LABORATORY [1774]

P.O. Box 1663
MS-P125
Los Alamos, NM 87545
(505) 664-6947 ext. 05004
Fax: (505) 606-5901
E-mail: hrstaffing-postdocs@lanl.gov
Web Site: www.lanl.gov/science/postdocs

FOUNDED: 1943

AREAS OF INTEREST:
Biosciences, chemistry, computing, Earth and space science, engineering, materials science, mathematics and physics.

NAME(S) OF PROGRAMS:
- **Richard P. Feynman Postdoctoral Fellowship in Theory and Computing**
- **J. Robert Oppenheimer Postdoctoral Fellowship**
- **Frederick Reines Postdoctoral Fellowship in Experimental Sciences**

TYPE:
Fellowships. The Distinguished Postdoctoral Fellowships provide the opportunity for the recipients to collaborate with LANL scientists and engineers on staff-initiated research. Candidates for these awards must display extraordinary ability in scientific research and show clear and definite promise of becoming outstanding leaders in the research they pursue.

YEAR PROGRAM STARTED: 1960

ELIGIBILITY:
Candidates must have a doctoral degree within the last five years or will have completed all Ph.D. requirements by commencement of their appointment. The Feynman and Reines Fellowships require the ability to obtain a DOE "Q" clearance, which normally requires U.S. citizenship.

Every candidate must be sponsored by a technical staff member before being reviewed by the Postdoctoral Committee.

FINANCIAL DATA:
A generous and comprehensive salary and benefits package is provided, including incoming relocation.

Amount of support per award: Feynman, Oppenheimer and Reines Postdoctoral Fellowships provide a starting salary of $108,000.

NO. AWARDS: Up to 2 in each fellowship category.

APPLICATION INFO:
Details are available online.

Duration: Appointments are for three years.

Deadline: January.

ADDRESS INQUIRIES TO:
See e-mail address above.

MICHIGAN SOCIETY OF FELLOWS

University of Michigan
0540 Rackham Building
915 East Washington Street
Ann Arbor, MI 48109-1070
(734) 763-1259
E-mail: society.of.fellows@umich.edu
Web Site: www.societyoffellows.umich.edu

TYPE:
Fellowships. Fellows are appointed as Assistant Professors in appropriate departments and as Postdoctoral Scholars in the Michigan Society of Fellows. They are expected to be in residence in Ann Arbor during the academic years of the fellowship, to teach for the equivalent of one academic year, to participate in the informal intellectual life of the Society, and to devote time to their independent research or artistic projects.

See entry 365 for full listing.

MICRON TECHNOLOGY FOUNDATION, INC.

P.O. Box 6
Boise, ID 83707-0006
(208) 363-3675
Fax: (208) 368-4435
E-mail: mtf@micron.com
Web Site: www.micron.com/foundation

TYPE:
Matching gifts; Professorships; Project/program grants; Research grants.

See entry 2031 for full listing.

MICROSCOPY SOCIETY OF AMERICA [1775]

12100 Sunset Hills Road
Suite 130
Reston, VA 20190
(703) 234-4115
(800) 538-3672
Fax: (703) 435-4390
E-mail: associationmanagement@microscopy.org
Web Site: www.microscopy.org

FOUNDED: 1942

AREAS OF INTEREST:
Microscopy.

NAME(S) OF PROGRAMS:
- **Undergraduate Research Scholarship Program**

TYPE:
Scholarships.

PURPOSE:
To foster educational and research potential in full-time undergraduate students intent on pursuing microscopy as a career or major research tool.

LEGAL BASIS:
Nonprofit society.

ELIGIBILITY:
The applicant must be a full-time undergraduate student and must have achieved junior or senior standing by the time the work is initiated. Research must be completed prior to graduation. Scholarship funds must be expended within one year of award date.

Applicants may receive only one scholarship and may perform research at an institution other than the one in which the applicant is enrolled. Successful applicants must agree to furnish MSA with an abstract for publication in the Society Journal, *Microscopy & Microanalysis*, describing the results and status of their project within two months after the conclusion of the award period, to acknowledge the award in all resulting publications, and to provide reprints of any other resulting publications to the Society.

FINANCIAL DATA:
Amount of support per award: Up to $3,000.

Total amount of support: Varies.

NO. MOST RECENT APPLICANTS: 20.

NO. AWARDS: Average 5.

APPLICATION INFO:
Required application form should include:
(1) a research proposal not to exceed three pages in length, including a brief introduction, a short methods section and description and itemized goals of the study;
(2) a budget indicating how the awarded funds will be expended;
(3) two letters of reference from scientists or university faculty familiar with the applicant's capabilities;
(4) a letter from the laboratory supervisor where the proposed research will be performed, confirming that the applicant and research project are acceptable;
(5) a curriculum vitae detailing previous education and/or training in microscopy and a brief statement of career goals and;
(6) a letter of recommendation from an MSA member.

An original and four copies of a completed application form and attachments are required, unless all materials are being submitted electronically to the e-mail address above.

Duration: One year. No renewals.

Deadline: December 31. Award announcement April 1.

PUBLICATIONS:
Program announcement.

ADDRESS INQUIRIES TO:
Dr. Ralph Albrecht
Animal Sciences
University of Wisconsin
1675 Observatory Drive
Madison, WI 53706
Tel: (608) 263-3952/4162
Fax: (608) 262-5157
E-mail: albrecht@ansci.wisc.edu

MICROSCOPY SOCIETY OF AMERICA [1776]

12100 Sunset Hills Road
Suite 130
Reston, VA 20190
(703) 234-4115
(800) 538-3672
Fax: (703) 435-4390
E-mail: associationmanagement@microscopy.org
Web Site: www.microscopy.org

FOUNDED: 1942

AREAS OF INTEREST:
All phases of microscopy.

NAME(S) OF PROGRAMS:
- **Microscopy & Microanalysis (M & M) Student Award**

TYPE:
Awards/prizes; Conferences/seminars. Awards are given to outstanding students selected on the basis of the quality and originality of their research abstracts submitted for the Annual MSA Scientific Program. The award consists of free registration for the meeting, a copy of *Proceedings*, and an invitation to the Sunday social event.

PURPOSE:
To promote student interest in microscopy and exchange of information.

LEGAL BASIS:
Nonprofit.

ELIGIBILITY:
Applicants must be bona fide students at a recognized college or university at the time of the meeting. Awards are based on the quality of the paper submitted for presentation at the meeting and the applicant must be the submitted paper's first author. Successful applicants must present their papers personally at the meeting in order to receive the award. They are expected to attend and participate in the entire meeting. Candidates should be juniors or seniors at the time the work is initiated. Former winners are ineligible.

FINANCIAL DATA:
Awardees will be reimbursed up to $1,000 for travel (round-trip, lowest-fare, continental U.S.) and complimentary full-meeting registration to the Microscopy & Microanalysis meeting, and invitation to the Presidential Reception.

Amount of support per award: Varies.

Total amount of support: Average $10,000.

APPLICATION INFO:
Applications consist of a completed Advanced Reservation Form, payment for student registration, a supporting letter from a member of MSA, preferably a research advisor, attesting to the applicant's status, and a scientific paper for presentation accompanied by a completed Data Form.

Deadline: February 15.

PUBLICATIONS:
The MSA Proceedings.

ADDRESS INQUIRIES TO:
See e-mail address above.

NATIONAL CENTER FOR ATMOSPHERIC RESEARCH [1777]

1850 Table Mesa Drive
Boulder, CO 80305
(303) 497-1328
Fax: (303) 497-1646
E-mail: paulad@ucar.edu
Web Site: www.asp.ucar.edu

FOUNDED: 1960

AREAS OF INTEREST:
Research in atmospheric sciences, including such topics as atmospheric dynamics (on all scales) and models, climate science, cloud physics, atmospheric chemistry and radiation, turbulence, upper-atmosphere physics, solar and solar-terrestrial physics (including ionospheric studies and aeronomy), oceanography and atmospheric technology. Also included are studies of the interaction of the atmosphere with the oceans, the cryosphere, the Earth's surface and human society and application of biology, ecology, geology, economics and political science skills to atmospheric issues.

NAME(S) OF PROGRAMS:
- **Postdoctoral Fellowships at NCAR**

TYPE:
Fellowships. The fellowships cover a year's appointment, with a likely extension to two years, at NCAR to take advantage of its educational programs and/or research facilities in the broad field of atmospheric sciences.

YEAR PROGRAM STARTED: 1964

PURPOSE:
To provide an opportunity for talented scientists who have recently received their Ph.Ds. to continue to pursue their research interests and to develop expertise in new areas; to enrich the research talent in the atmospheric sciences by offering an opportunity for highly qualified Ph.D. physicists, chemists, applied mathematicians, engineers and specialists from other disciplines such as biology, geology, science education, economics and geography, as well as atmospheric science, to apply their training to research in the atmospheric sciences.

LEGAL BASIS:
Research institution operated by the nonprofit University Corporation for Atmospheric Research (UCAR) under sponsorship of the National Science Foundation (NSF).

ELIGIBILITY:
Interested scientists who have received their Ph.D. (or equivalent) are eligible. NCAR encourages applications from women and minorities. There are no restrictions for foreign applicants.

Primary criteria in selection of postdoctoral appointees are the applicant's scientific capability and potential, originality and independence, and the ability to take advantage of the research opportunities at NCAR.

Appointments are tenable only in residence in Boulder, CO.

FINANCIAL DATA:
All appointees are eligible for life and health insurance in addition to excellent retirement benefits. Travel expenses to NCAR will be reimbursed for the fellow and his or her family. A small allowance for moving and storage is provided. Scientific travel and conference registration that costs up to $3,500 each year is normally available.

Amount of support per award: Basic stipend of $62,000 for the first year and $63,500 for the second year.

NO. MOST RECENT APPLICANTS: 122.

NO. AWARDS: 7 to 9.

APPLICATION INFO:
Contact the Center.

Duration: Two years.

Deadline: January 5, to be considered for fellowship awards to begin the following summer or fall. Selections announced in March.

PUBLICATIONS:
Program announcement.

ADDRESS INQUIRIES TO:
Paula Fisher, Coordinator
Advanced Study Program
(See address above.)

*SPECIAL STIPULATIONS:
Appointments are tenable only in residence at the National Center for Atmospheric Research.

NATIONAL OCEANIC AND ATMOSPHERIC ADMINISTRATION [1778]

NOAA/Sea Grant, R/SG
1315 East-West Highway, SSMC-3, 11th Floor
Silver Spring, MD 20910
(301) 734-1066
(301) 734-1071
Fax: (301) 713-1031; (301) 713-0799
E-mail: sgweb@noaa.gov
Web Site: www.seagrant.noaa.gov

FOUNDED: 1966

AREAS OF INTEREST:
Marine resource development.

NAME(S) OF PROGRAMS:
- **National Sea Grant College Program**

TYPE:
Research grants. Grants for research, education and outreach in oceanography, fisheries science and environmental studies; marine commerce and engineering and marine biotechnology; economic, legal and sociological considerations related to the management and development of natural resources in the marine environment; and development, conservation and economic utilization of resources in the marine environment.

The grant provides training and advisory service activities in order to increase the understanding, development and wise use of ocean, coastal and Great Lakes resources. The Secretary of Commerce, through NOAA, awards grants on a competitive basis for these purposes.

The program is carried out through a network of 30 Sea Grant programs, located in coastal and Great Lakes states, involving hundreds of universities nationwide.

YEAR PROGRAM STARTED: 1966

PURPOSE:
To promote wise utilization of marine and coastal resources.

LEGAL BASIS:
The National Sea Grant College and Program Act of 1966, Public Law 89-688, as amended. (33 U.S.C. 1121, et seq.)

ELIGIBILITY:
Universities and colleges, junior colleges, technical schools, institutes, laboratories and other public or private agencies with appropriate interests are eligible to apply.

FINANCIAL DATA:
Amount of support per award: Varies.

Total amount of support: Approximately $62,000,000 in grant funds per year.

APPLICATION INFO:
Detailed information is available on the web site.

Duration: Generally two years.

Deadline: Varies.

ADDRESS INQUIRIES TO:
Jonathan Pennock, Director
(See address above.)

NATIONAL RESEARCH COUNCIL OF CANADA [1779]

1200 Montreal Road, Building M-55
Room 369A
Ottawa ON K1A 0R6 Canada
(613) 949-4655
Fax: (613) 990-1286
E-mail: info@nrc-cnrc.gc.ca
racoordinator.hrb@nrc-cnrc.gc.ca
Web Site: www.nrc-cnrc.gc.ca

FOUNDED: 1916

AREAS OF INTEREST:
Science and engineering.

NAME(S) OF PROGRAMS:
- **National Research Council Research Associate Program**

TYPE:
Associateships. Research Associate Program provides promising scientists and engineers with the opportunity to work in a challenging research environment during the early stages of their career. Applicants will be selected competitively and must demonstrate the ability to perform original, high-quality research in their chosen field.

Research Associates will be offered appointments to the staff of the National Research Council on a term basis and will be offered salaries and benefits currently available to Research Officers.

YEAR PROGRAM STARTED: 1975

PURPOSE:
To undertake, assist or promote scientific and engineering research to further Canada's economic and social development and to give promising scientists and engineers an opportunity to work on challenging research problems.

LEGAL BASIS:
Federal government agency.

ELIGIBILITY:
Applicant must possess a Ph.D. in natural science or engineering or a Master's degree in an engineering field earned within the last five years, or expect to obtain the degree within six months. Applicant must have a demonstrated ability to perform original high-quality research in their chosen field.

Although preference will be given to Canadian citizens and permanent residents, Associateships are open to nationals of all countries. The offer of an Associateship does not ensure foreign nationals permanent residency in Canada. Non-Canadian candidates should apply for non-immigrant status (i.e., temporary status) and an employment visa.

FINANCIAL DATA:
Salaries commensurate with experience are taxable and subject to other deductions.

Amount of support per award: Current annual Ph.D. recruiting rate is $54,351.

Total amount of support: Varies.

NO. MOST RECENT APPLICANTS: 400.

NO. AWARDS: Varies.

APPLICATION INFO:
Applicants must apply online. All applicants must submit university transcripts, two letters of recommendation and resume. Application is valid for one year.

Duration: Two years. Renewal to a maximum of five years.

ADDRESS INQUIRIES TO:
Research Associates Program Coordinator
(See address above.)

NATIONAL SCIENCE FOUNDATION [1780]

Directorate for Education and Human Resources
Division of Graduate Education
4201 Wilson Boulevard, Suite 875
Arlington, VA 22230
(703) 292-8694
(866) 673-4737
Fax: (703) 292-9048
E-mail: grfp@nsf.gov
info@nsfgrfp.org
Web Site: www.nsf.gov/grfp (official program information)
www.nsfgrfp.org (application assistance)

FOUNDED: 1950

AREAS OF INTEREST:
Science, math and engineering.

NAME(S) OF PROGRAMS:
- **NSF Graduate Research Fellowship Program**

TYPE:
Fellowships. Awarded for graduate study leading to research-based Master's and doctoral degrees in science and engineering.

YEAR PROGRAM STARTED: 1952

PURPOSE:
To help ensure the vitality and diversity of the scientific and engineering workforce in the U.S. The program recognizes and supports outstanding graduate students who are pursuing research-based Master's and doctoral degrees in science and engineering. The GRFP provides three years of support for the graduate education of individuals who have demonstrated their potential for significant achievements in science and engineering. The ranks of NSF Fellows include individuals who have made transformative breakthrough discoveries in science and engineering, become leaders in their chosen careers and been honored as Nobel laureates.

LEGAL BASIS:
Government agency.

ELIGIBILITY:
Applicants for the GRFP are generally allowed to have completed no more than 12 months of full-time graduate study or its equivalent by August. Additional information is available on the Foundation web site.

GEOG. RESTRICTIONS: United States.

FINANCIAL DATA:
Amount of support per award: $138,000 per award; $46,000 annually (includes $34,000 stipend to the Fellow and $12,000 cost of education allowance to the institution), with up to three years of support.

NO. MOST RECENT APPLICANTS: 16,000.

NO. AWARDS: 2,000.

APPLICATION INFO:
Application must be completed online.

The following material is required from all applicants:
(1) personal, relevant background and future goals statement;
(2) graduate research plan statement;
(3) three reference letters and;
(4) academic transcripts.

Duration: Normal tenure is 12 months for each fellowship year. Availability of the second and third years of a three-year award is contingent upon certification by the fellowship institution that progress is being made and availability of appropriated funds.

ADDRESS INQUIRIES TO:
Graduate Research Fellowship Program
(See address above.)

*PLEASE NOTE:
Program eligibility requirements subject to change each year.

NATIONAL SCIENCE FOUNDATION [1781]

4201 Wilson Boulevard, Room 990
Arlington, VA 22230
(703) 292-7283
Fax: (703) 292-9068
E-mail: fkronz@nsf.gov
Web Site: www.nsf.gov

FOUNDED: 1950

AREAS OF INTEREST:
Research that uses historical, philosophical, or social scientific methods to investigate the intellectual, material, or social facets of STEM (Science, Technology, Engineering and Mathematics), including medical science. It encompasses a broad spectrum of topics including interdisciplinary studies of ethics, equity, governance, and policy issues closely related to STEM disciplines.

NAME(S) OF PROGRAMS:
- **Science, Technology and Society**

TYPE:
Conferences/seminars; Fellowships; Project/program grants; Research grants; Training grants. Grants support research and educational projects, national meetings, dissemination efforts, cross-disciplinary study, dissertation research, small group training activities, dissertation improvement grants for graduate students, and postdoctoral fellowships. The proposals that are considered for support use methods from a variety of disciplines including anthropology, communications, history, philosophy, political science, and sociology to investigate STEM theory and practice with regards to their history, socio-cultural formation, philosophical underpinnings, and impacts on quality of life, culture, and society.

YEAR PROGRAM STARTED: 1976

PURPOSE:
To provide educational opportunities for graduate students.

LEGAL BASIS:
Government agency.

ELIGIBILITY:
Individuals, universities, colleges and nonprofit organizations.

FINANCIAL DATA:
Amount of support per award: Generally, $12,000 to $500,000.

Total amount of support: Approximately $6,200,000.

CO-OP FUNDING PROGRAMS: National Institutes of Health; Department of Energy.

NO. MOST RECENT APPLICANTS: 400.

NO. AWARDS: 80.

APPLICATION INFO:
Proposers should consult the Science, Technology and Society (STS) Announcement 15-506 and appropriate NSF brochures such as Grant Proposal Guide, available from the address above.

Duration: One to five years.

Deadline: February 2 and August 3.

ADDRESS INQUIRIES TO:
Frederick Kronz, Program Director
(See address above.)

NATIONAL SCIENCE FOUNDATION [1782]

Division of Polar Programs
4201 Wilson Boulevard, Suite 755 S
Arlington, VA 22230
(703) 292-8014
Fax: 703-292-9081
E-mail: dfriscic@nsf.gov
Web Site: www.nsf.gov

FOUNDED: 1950

AREAS OF INTEREST:
Antarctic natural sciences.

NAME(S) OF PROGRAMS:
- **U.S. Antarctic Research Program**

TYPE:
Fellowships; Project/program grants; Research grants. Grants for research projects in all fields of science pertinent to the Antarctic, including both field work in the Antarctic and study in the U.S. of already gathered data and specimens. Support is provided for research projects in astronomy, astrophysics, the behavioral sciences, biology, cartography, geology, glaciology, meteorology, oceanography, solid earth geophysics, upper atmospheric physics and magnetospheric physics. Logistics and support in Antarctica are arranged by the Foundation.

YEAR PROGRAM STARTED: 1959

PURPOSE:
To fund, coordinate and arrange for support of research in all fields of science pertinent to Antarctica.

LEGAL BASIS:
Federal agency under the National Science Foundation Act of 1950, Public Law 81-507, as amended. Also White House memo 6646 dated February 5, 1982.

ELIGIBILITY:
U.S. universities and colleges are the primary participants in the program. Other eligible participants include nonacademic research institutions, profit or nonprofit, and unaffiliated scientists or scientists employed by other federal agencies.

GEOG. RESTRICTIONS: United States.

FINANCIAL DATA:
Amount of support per award: Varies with need.

Total amount of support: Varies.

Matching fund requirements: Grantee institutions are generally required to share in project costs by a contribution to any cost element in the project, direct or indirect.

NO. AWARDS: Approximately 50.

APPLICATION INFO:
Applications are submitted in the form of a proposal with a detailed research plan and budget. Information concerning proposal preparation is available in the PAPPG, NSF 11-1, *Grant Proposal Guide, Antarctic Research Program Announcement and Proposal Guide* and NSF 11-532, *Antarctic Conservation Act of 1978*. Information regarding guidelines for the Division of Polar Programs can be found on the web site under the tab "Geosciences."

Duration: Average of two to four years depending on the quality of submissions and the availability of funds.

Deadline: Applications should be submitted by April 17, 2017.

ADDRESS INQUIRIES TO:
David Friscic, Tech Information Specialist
(See address above.)

NATIONAL SCIENCE FOUNDATION [1783]

Division of Polar Programs
4201 Wilson Boulevard, Suite 755 S
Arlington, VA 22230
(703) 292-8014
Fax: (703) 292-9081
E-mail: dfriscic@nsf.gov
Web Site: www.nsf.gov

FOUNDED: 1950

AREAS OF INTEREST:
Arctic natural sciences, social sciences, Arctic system science, and Arctic observing network.

NAME(S) OF PROGRAMS:
- **Arctic Research Program**

TYPE:
Conferences/seminars; Research grants; Research contracts. Grants and contracts to support scientific research projects relating to the Arctic as well as the subsequent analysis of data. Research may be concerned with problems of marine research, including the polar pack ice; terrestrial biology, including analysis of the ecosystem; meteorology; solar-terrestrial physics; glaciology, including permafrost; geology and geophysics; social sciences; and data and information.

YEAR PROGRAM STARTED: 1971

PURPOSE:
To increase man's knowledge of the Arctic environment and its dynamic parameters; to increase cooperation in research with other agencies and nations having Arctic interests.

LEGAL BASIS:
The National Science Foundation Act of 1950, Public Law 81-507, as amended; Arctic Research and Policy Act of 1984.

ELIGIBILITY:
Proposals may be submitted by U.S. colleges and universities and by academically related nonprofit research organizations. Industry and other organizations are also eligible for support.

GEOG. RESTRICTIONS: United States.

FINANCIAL DATA:
Amount of support per award: Varies.

Total amount of support: Approximately $25,000,000 per year, depending on availability of funds.

Matching fund requirements: Cost sharing is not required.

NO. AWARDS: 75 per year, pending availability of funds.

APPLICATION INFO:
Application information may be requested from the Foundation. Information regarding guidelines for the Division of Polar Programs can be found on the web site under the tab "Geosciences."

Because of far-reaching scientific, logistic and international implications of Arctic research projects, it is essential that scientists specify all field needs when submitting proposals. Special procedures and a longer lead time apply to research proposed for Greenland. Proposers should also consult the Foundation's *Proposal and Award Procedures Guide* (PAPPG) (NSF 11-1).

Duration: Three years or more depending on the scientific merit and requirements of the project.

Deadline: October 18.

ADDRESS INQUIRIES TO:
David Friscic, Tech Information Specialist
(See address above.)

THE ROYAL SOCIETY OF CANADA [1784]

Walter House
282 Somerset Street West
Ottawa ON K2P 0J6 Canada
(613) 998-9920
Fax: (613) 991-6996
E-mail: nominations@rsc-src.ca
Web Site: www.rsc-src.ca/en/fellows/medals-awards

FOUNDED: 1883

AREAS OF INTEREST:
Arts and humanities, social sciences and science.

NAME(S) OF PROGRAMS:
- **The Konrad Adenauer Research Award**
- **The Bancroft Award**
- **The Pierre Chauveau Medal**
- **The Flavelle Medal**
- **Ursula Franklin Award in Gender Studies**
- **The Innis-Gérin Medal**
- **The McLaughlin Medal**
- **The McNeil Medal**
- **Willet G. Miller Medal**
- **The Lorne Pierce Medal**
- **The Miroslaw Romanowski Medal**
- **The Rutherford Memorial Medals**
- **The John L. Synge Award**
- **The Henry Marshall Tory Medal**
- **The J.B. Tyrrell Historical Medal**
- **The Alice Wilson Award**

TYPE:
Awards/prizes. The Konrad Adenauer Research Award is intended to promote academic collaboration between Canada and the Federal Republic of Germany.

The Bancroft Award is given for publication, instruction and research in the earth sciences that have conspicuously contributed to public understanding and appreciation of the subject.

The Pierre Chauveau Medal is awarded for a distinguished contribution to knowledge in the humanities.

The Flavelle Medal is awarded for an outstanding contribution to biological science during the preceding 10 years or for significant additions to a previous outstanding contribution to biological science.

The Ursula Franklin Award in Gender Studies is intended to recognize significant contributions by a Canadian scholar in the humanities and social sciences to furthering our understanding of issues concerning gender.

The Innis-Gérin Medal is presented for a distinguished and sustained contribution to the literature of the social sciences.

The McLaughlin Medal is awarded for important research of sustained excellence in any branch of the medical sciences.

The McNeil Medal for the Public Awareness of Science is awarded to a candidate who has demonstrated outstanding ability to promote and communicate science to students and the public (in the broadest sense of the latter term) within Canada.

The Willet G. Miller Medal is given for outstanding research in any branch of earth sciences.

The Lorne Pierce Medal is awarded for an achievement of special significance and conspicuous merit in imaginative or critical literature written in either English or French (critical literature dealing with Canadian subjects has priority over critical literature of equal merit that does not deal with Canadian subjects).

The Miroslaw Romanowski Medal is awarded for significant contributions to the resolution of scientific aspects of environmental problems or for important improvements to the quality of an ecosystem in all aspects - terrestrial, atmospheric and aqueous - brought about by scientific means.

The Rutherford Memorial Medals are awarded for outstanding research in any branch of physics and chemistry.

The John L. Synge Award is given to acknowledge outstanding research in any of the branches of the mathematical sciences.

The Henry Marshall Tory Medal is given for outstanding research in any branch of astronomy, chemistry, mathematics, physics or an allied science.

The J.B. Tyrrell Historical Medal is awarded for outstanding work in the history of Canada.

The Alice Wilson Award is given to three women of outstanding academic qualifications in the arts and humanities, social sciences or science who are entering a career in scholarship or research at the postdoctoral level.

YEAR PROGRAM STARTED: 1955

PURPOSE:
To annually recognize Canadian citizens for contributions to Canadian academic excellence in various branches.

LEGAL BASIS:
Nonprofit.

ELIGIBILITY:
Awarded to Canadian citizens or those who have had status for at least three years as Canadian Permanent Residents.

GEOG. RESTRICTIONS: Canada.

FINANCIAL DATA:
Amount of support per award: Varies with every medal.

APPLICATION INFO:
Open call for nominations takes place September 1 to March 1.

Duration: The Bancroft Award, The Chauveau Medal, The Flavelle Medal, Ursula Franklin Award in Gender Studies, The Innis-Gérin Medal, Willet G. Miller Medal, The Lorne Pierce Medal, The John L. Synge Award, The Henry Marshall Tory Medal and The J.B. Tyrrell Historical Medal: Every two years. The Konrad Adenauer Research Award, McLaughlin, McNeil, Romanowski and Rutherford Memorial Medals and The Wilson Award: Every year.

Deadline: March 1.

ADDRESS INQUIRIES TO:
Marie-Lyne Renaud
Manager, Fellowship and Recognition
(See address above.)

SIGMA DELTA EPSILON/GRADUATE WOMEN IN SCIENCE [1785]

P.O. Box 240607
St. Paul, MN 55124-0607
(952) 236-9112
E-mail: gwised@mac.com
Web Site: www.gwis.org

FOUNDED: 1922

AREAS OF INTEREST:
Science and research.

CONSULTING OR VOLUNTEER SERVICES:
A great deal of volunteering is provided by 22 chapters of the organization (e.g., science fair judges, girl scout support in science, etc.).

NAME(S) OF PROGRAMS:
- **SDE Fellowship Program**

TYPE:
Fellowships; Travel grants. Leadership Awards are given to Graduate Women in Science officers.

YEAR PROGRAM STARTED: 1941

PURPOSE:
To increase knowledge in the fundamental sciences; to encourage research careers in the sciences by women.

ELIGIBILITY:
Applicants must be enrolled as a graduate student or engaged in postdoctoral or early-stage academic research.

FINANCIAL DATA:
Applications are vetted for scientific expertise and financial need.

Amount of support per award: Up to $10,000.

Total amount of support: Varies.

NO. MOST RECENT APPLICANTS: 211 for the year 2012-13.

NO. AWARDS: 10.

APPLICATION INFO:
Information about the application process is available online.

Duration: One year. No renewals.

Deadline: January 15.

PUBLICATIONS:
GWIS Bulletin; *GWIS e-news*, monthly electronic newsletter.

IRS I.D.: 24-0825560

ADDRESS INQUIRIES TO:
Ms. Dee M. McManus
National Executive Director
(See address above.)

SIGMA XI: THE SCIENTIFIC RESEARCH SOCIETY [1786]

3200 East NC Highway 54
Suite 300
Research Triangle Park, NC 27709
(919) 549-4691 ext. 206
Fax: (919) 549-0090
E-mail: giar@sigmaxi.org
Web Site: www.sigmaxi.org

FOUNDED: 1886

AREAS OF INTEREST:
The sciences, physical sciences, engineering, social, behavioral and life sciences.

NAME(S) OF PROGRAMS:
- **Grants-in-Aid of Research**

TYPE:
Grants-in-aid; Project/program grants; Research grants; Travel grants. Grants-in-aid to support research projects in any field of scientific investigation. Assistance is available for such research-related activities as travel to research location or supplies.

YEAR PROGRAM STARTED: 1922

PURPOSE:
To encourage scientific research.

LEGAL BASIS:
Nonprofit organization.

ELIGIBILITY:
Graduate and undergraduate students with proposals for specific research projects are eligible to apply. Student faculty advisor (first recommender) should be a full, active member of Sigma Xi to compete for Sigma Xi funds. NAS funds in the program are unrestricted and cover the physical, life and medical sciences (excluding the social sciences).

Grants do not cover overhead costs. No grants for publication/presentation costs, travel to meetings or stipends. Will fund travel to a research site.

FINANCIAL DATA:
Amount of support per award: Up to $1,000 for all areas of the sciences and engineering; Up to $5,000 for astronomy; Up to $2,500 for eye/vision research.

Total amount of support: Approximately $300,000.

CO-OP FUNDING PROGRAMS: National Academy of Sciences.

APPLICATION INFO:
Contact the Society for details.

Duration: Applicants may apply for a second grant after submitting a report on the outcome of the project supported by a first grant.

Deadline: Applications and supporting letters must be received by March 15 or October 15. Awards are announced within 12 weeks.

PUBLICATIONS:
Annual report; application guidelines.

ADDRESS INQUIRIES TO:
Janelle Simmons, Manager of Programs
E-mail: jsimmons@sigmaxi.org

ALFRED P. SLOAN FOUNDATION

630 Fifth Avenue
Suite 2200
New York, NY 10111
(212) 649-1649
Fax: (212) 757-5117
E-mail: boylan@sloan.org
Web Site: www.sloan.org

TYPE:
Fellowships; Scholarships. Offers substantial scholarship support to indigenous students (Native Americans, including American Indians, Native Alaskans and Native Hawaiians) who are beginning their Master's or doctoral work in sciences, technology, engineering and mathematics (STEM) fields in selected departments at selected U.S. universities.

See entry 991 for full listing.

ALFRED P. SLOAN FOUNDATION

630 Fifth Avenue
Suite 2200
New York, NY 10111
(212) 649-1649
Fax: (212) 757-5117
E-mail: boylan@sloan.org
Web Site: www.sloanphds.org

TYPE:
Fellowships; Scholarships. Offers substantial scholarship support to underrepresented minority (African American, Hispanic American or Native American) students who are U.S. citizens and who are beginning their doctoral work in engineering, natural science and mathematics in selected departments at selected U.S. universities.

See entry 992 for full listing.

SMITHSONIAN INSTITUTION [1787]

Office of Fellowships and Internships
470 L'Enfant Plaza, S.W., Suite 7102
MRC 902, P.O. Box 37012
Washington, DC 20013-7012
(202) 633-7070
Fax: (202) 633-7069
E-mail: siofi@si.edu
Web Site: www.smithsonianofi.com

FOUNDED: 1846

AREAS OF INTEREST:
Animal behavior, ecology and environmental science, including an emphasis on the tropics; anthropology, including archaeology; astrophysics and astronomy; earth sciences and paleobiology; evolutionary and systematic biology; history of science and technology; history of art, especially American, contemporary, African and Asian art; 20th-century American crafts and decorative arts; social and cultural history of the U.S.; and folklore.

NAME(S) OF PROGRAMS:
- **Smithsonian Graduate Student Fellowships**
- **Smithsonian Postdoctoral Fellowships**
- **Smithsonian Predoctoral Fellowships**
- **Smithsonian Senior Fellowships**

TYPE:
Fellowships. Offered to qualified scholars for research to be conducted in residence at the Smithsonian in association with the staff, using collections and research facilities.

YEAR PROGRAM STARTED: 1964

PURPOSE:
To provide students and scholars in the sciences, arts and humanities with an opportunity for research utilizing the unique collections and facilities of the Smithsonian, while working with the institution's research staff.

LEGAL BASIS:
Act of Congress approved August 10, 1846; 20 U.S.C. 41 et seq.

ELIGIBILITY:
Smithsonian Fellowships are open to both U.S. citizens and foreign nationals. Fluency in English is required.

For the graduate fellowships, students must be formally enrolled and engaged in a graduate program of study at a degree-granting institution, have completed at least one semester and have not yet been advanced to candidacy if in a Ph.D. program.

For the predoctoral fellowships, students must be enrolled in a university as candidates for the Ph.D. or equivalent. At the time of appointment, the university must approve the undertaking of dissertation research at the Smithsonian and indicate that requirements for the Doctorate, other than the dissertation, have been met.

For the postdoctoral fellowships, applicants must have received the Ph.D., or equivalent, within seven years of the program deadline and must have completed the degree or certificate at the time the fellowship commences.

For the senior fellowships, applicants must have received the Ph.D., or equivalent, seven or more years before the program deadline.

Research must be conducted while in residence at the Smithsonian.

The Smithsonian Institution does not offer financial assistance for degree-granting programs at academic institutions. All forms of financial assistance are to support research in residence at the Smithsonian and its facilities.

FINANCIAL DATA:
Stipends are offered per calendar year and are prorated for terms of less than one year. Pre, Post and Senior Postdoctoral Fellows also receive research and travel allowances.

Amount of support per award: Graduate Fellowships: $7,000; Predoctoral Fellowships: $32,700; Postdoctoral and Senior Postdoctoral Fellowships: $48,000; Earth and Planetary Sciences Senior and Postdoctoral Fellowships: up to $53,000.

APPLICATION INFO:
Official application materials are available upon request. Specify the fellowship corresponding to your academic level.

Duration: Graduate Fellowships: Ten weeks; Predoctoral, Postdoctoral and Senior Fellowships: Three to 12 months.

Deadline: December 1. Research appointments with or without fellowships may be conducted at any time during the year.

PUBLICATIONS:
Smithsonian Opportunities for Research and Study.

OFFICER:
Eric Woodard, Director

ADDRESS INQUIRIES TO:
Office of Fellowships and Internships
(See address above.)

SOCIETY FOR SCIENCE AND THE PUBLIC [1788]

1719 N Street, N.W.
Washington, DC 20036
(202) 785-2255
E-mail: sts@societyforscience.org
Web Site: www.societyforscience.org
student.societyforscience.org

FOUNDED: 1942

AREAS OF INTEREST:
Sciences, mathematics, engineering and medicine.

NAME(S) OF PROGRAMS:
- **Intel Science Talent Search**

TYPE:
Awards/prizes. Competition for high school seniors excelling in science, math and engineering.

YEAR PROGRAM STARTED: 1942

PURPOSE:
To discover at the high school senior year level, those who have the potential to become the scientists, mathematicians and engineers of the future; to make the public aware of the impact that a quality science, mathematics or engineering education has on our future and the future of our nation.

LEGAL BASIS:
Nonprofit educational institution.

ELIGIBILITY:
Student must be in the last year of secondary school in the U.S., Puerto Rico, Guam, Virgin Islands, American Samoa, Wake and Midway Islands, the Marianas, DOD Schools or American schools abroad or for citizens studying abroad.

FINANCIAL DATA:
Amount of support per award: National Semifinalists receive $1,000 and their schools receive $1,000. Prize is awarded in three categories: Basic Research, Global Good, and Innovation. 1st place: $150,000; 2nd place: $75,000; 3rd place: $35,000; remaining finalists receive $7,500.

Total amount of support: $1,612,500, including $300,000 awarded to semifinalist schools.

NO. AWARDS: 300 National Semifinalists; 40 Finalists.

APPLICATION INFO:
Entries in the Intel Science Talent Search are submitted via an online application, with the exception of school transcripts, which must be mailed. Additional information is available on the Society web page.

Deadline: November.

ADDRESS INQUIRIES TO:
Caitlin Sullivan, Program Manager
(See address above.)

THE SOCIETY FOR THE SCIENTIFIC STUDY OF SEXUALITY [1789]

881 Third Street, Suite B-5
Whitehall, PA 18052
(610) 443-3100
Fax: (610) 443-3105
E-mail: thesociety@sexscience.org
Web Site: www.sexscience.org

FOUNDED: 1957

AREAS OF INTEREST:
Sex research, sex therapy and sex education.

NAME(S) OF PROGRAMS:
- **Grants-in-Aid Project**
- **Student Research Grants**

TYPE:
Grants-in-aid; Research grants. Grants-in-Aid Project supports scientific sexuality research in areas not likely to receive support from other sources.

Student Research Grant supports an SSSS student member who is doing human sexuality research.

YEAR PROGRAM STARTED: 1985

PURPOSE:
To assist with the development of quality research projects in the area of sex research.

LEGAL BASIS:
Tax-exempt, private, not-for-profit corporation.

ELIGIBILITY:
Grants-in-Aid Project is open to all professionals conducting research related to human sexuality.

Student Research Grants are open to students who are enrolled in a degree-granting program and student members of SSSS.

FINANCIAL DATA:
Amount of support per award: $1,000.

Total amount of support: $2,000.

NO. MOST RECENT APPLICANTS: 25.

NO. AWARDS: Grants-in-Aid Project: Varies; Student Research Grants: 1 in the Spring and 1 in the Fall.

APPLICATION INFO:
Applications and additional information can be found at fsssonline.org/grants.

Deadline: Grants-in-Aid Project: Proposals may be submitted at any time during the year. Student Research Grants: February 1 and June 1.

PUBLICATIONS:
Application guidelines.

IRS I.D.: 13-2642753

ADDRESS INQUIRIES TO:
Mandy Peters, Executive Director
(See address above.)

SYSTEMS PLUS, INC.

One Research Court
Rockville, MD 20850
(301) 948-4232
E-mail: afsffp@sysplus.com
Web Site: afsffp.sysplus.com

TYPE:
Fellowships. Research fellowship.

See entry 2578 for full listing.

TOURETTE ASSOCIATION OF AMERICA, INC.

42-40 Bell Boulevard
Suite 205
Bayside, NY 11361-2820
(718) 224-2999
Fax: (718) 279-9596
E-mail: support@tourette.org
Web Site: www.tourette.org

TYPE:
Fellowships; General operating grants; Research grants; Seed money grants; Technical assistance. Research grants available for Ph.D. and M.D. researchers in the following categories:
(1) proposals in basic neuroscience specifically relevant to Tourette Syndrome and;
(2) clinical studies related to the etiology, pathophysiology and treatment of Tourette Syndrome.

Fellowships provide one-year postdoctoral training.

See entry 2405 for full listing.

U.S. ARMY RESEARCH OFFICE [1790]

4300 South Miami Boulevard
Research Triangle Park, NC 27703
(919) 549-0641
Fax: (919) 549-4310
E-mail: patricia.j.fox8.civ@mail.mil
Web Site: www.arl.army.mil

FOUNDED: 1951

AREAS OF INTEREST:
Biosciences, chemistry, electronics, engineering, environmental sciences, materials sciences, mathematical and computer sciences and physics.

TYPE:
Conferences/seminars; Research grants; Research contracts. Grants and contracts for scientific research in such areas of interest to the U.S. Army as chemistry, engineering, biology, mathematics, metallurgy and materials, physics, electronics and environmental sciences. Support is also provided for symposia on particular aspects of scientific investigation, the results of which further Department of the Army objectives.

YEAR PROGRAM STARTED: 1951

PURPOSE:
To increase knowledge of natural phenomena and environment in an attempt to solve problems in the physical, engineering, environmental and life sciences.

LEGAL BASIS:
Government agency.

ELIGIBILITY:
Organizations with appropriate interests are eligible to apply.

FINANCIAL DATA:
Amount of support per award: Grants and contracts vary in amount, depending upon the needs and nature of the request; $136,000 yearly average.

Total amount of support: $500,000,000 to $550,000,000 including both grants and contracts.

NO. MOST RECENT APPLICANTS: Approximately 550.

NO. AWARDS: Approximately 350.

APPLICATION INFO:
Research awards are selected from proposals submitted in response to an open-ended Broad Agency Announcement (BAA). Contractors interested in submitting proposals should go to the ARL web site and download the ARO BAA.

Duration: One to three years. Continuations possible if work has not been completed.

Deadline: Varies.

ADDRESS INQUIRIES TO:
Patty Fox, Chief
RDECOM Acquisitions Center
(See address above.)

U.S. DEPARTMENT OF ENERGY

3610 Collins Ferry Road
P.O. Box 880
Morgantown, WV 26507-0880
(304) 285-4784
Web Site: www.netl.doe.gov

TYPE:
Assistantships; Project/program grants; Research grants.

See entry 2580 for full listing.

U.S. DEPARTMENT OF THE NAVY [1791]

Office of Naval Research, One Liberty Center
875 North Randolph Street, Suite 1425
Arlington, VA 22203-1995
(703) 696-4111
Fax: (703) 696-5940
E-mail: onrpao@onr.navy.mil
Web Site: www.onr.navy.mil

FOUNDED: 1946

AREAS OF INTEREST:
Advanced materials, ocean sciences, mathematics, information sciences, physics, electronics, chemistry, mechanics, cognitive and neural sciences.

NAME(S) OF PROGRAMS:
- **Basic Research Challenge Program**
- **University Research Initiative**
- **Young Investigator Program**

TYPE:
Research grants; Research contracts. ONR sponsors long-range scientific research, applied research and advanced technology development which offer potential for advancement and improvement of naval operations. Programs include physics, electronic and solid state sciences, mathematics, operations research, statistics and probability, information science, fluid dynamics, physiology, biochemistry, biophysics, microbiology, naval biology, cognitive and neural sciences research, personnel and training research, Arctic research, coastal sciences, earth and environmental physics, atmospheric sciences, metallurgy and ceramics research, chemistry, energy research, structural mechanics, physical and chemical oceanography, marine geology and geophysics, ocean biology, ocean acoustics and ocean engineering.

YEAR PROGRAM STARTED: 1946

PURPOSE:
To support research in various scientific fields including ocean science and physics.

LEGAL BASIS:
Public Law 588, as amended and Public Law 85-934, as amended.

ELIGIBILITY:
Nonprofit institutions of higher education and organizations whose primary purpose is the conduct of scientific research may apply for contracts or grants. Nonprofit and profit-making institutions, organizations or industrial establishments, as well as qualified individuals, are eligible for contract support.

FINANCIAL DATA:
Amount of support per award: Varies, depending upon the needs and nature of the request.

Total amount of support: Varies.

NO. MOST RECENT APPLICANTS: Approximately 4,000 inquiries.

NO. AWARDS: Approximately 2,500 annually.

APPLICATION INFO:
Before submitting a proposal, interested individuals are encouraged to assess the relevance of their research interests to Navy research priorities by consulting the ONR web page and talking to the relevant ONR Program Manager. Applications are submitted in the form of a proposal which should include:
(1) general statement requesting consideration of the proposal;
(2) brief review of the scientific background of the proposed research;
(3) technical description of the project, including statement of objectives and scientific methods to be employed;
(4) description of available facilities;
(5) background of principal investigator(s) and associates;
(6) bibliography of pertinent publications;
(7) proposed duration of project and annual itemized budget;
(8) other research projects currently undertaken by the principal investigator;
(9) other agencies to whom the proposal is being submitted for possible financial support and;
(10) cost breakdown by year.

WEIZMANN INSTITUTE OF SCIENCE

Feinberg Graduate School of the Weizmann Institute of Science
P.O. Box 26
234 Herzl Street
Rehovot 7610001 Israel
(972) 8-9343843
(972) 8-9342924
Fax: (972) 8-9344114
E-mail: FGS@weizmann.ac.il
Web Site: www.weizmann.ac.il/feinberg

TYPE:
Fellowships. The Feinberg Graduate School of the Weizmann Institute of Science offers a limited number of postdoctoral fellowships in all areas of research in which the Weizmann Institute is engaged. The fellowships are offered in various fields of biology, chemistry, physics, biochemistry-biophysics, mathematics, computer science and science teaching.

See entry 932 for full listing.

THE HELEN HAY WHITNEY FOUNDATION [1792]

20 Squadron Boulevard
Suite 630
New City, NY 10956-5247
(845) 639-6799
Fax: (845) 639-6798
E-mail: hhwf@earthlink.net
Web Site: www.hhwf.org

FOUNDED: 1947

AREAS OF INTEREST:
Biomedical sciences.

NAME(S) OF PROGRAMS:
- **Early Postdoctoral Research Fellowship Program in Biomedical Sciences**

TYPE:
Fellowships. Postdoctoral research fellowships.

YEAR PROGRAM STARTED: 1957

PURPOSE:
To provide beginning postdoctoral research training to young M.Ds. and Ph.Ds. to further their careers in research in biomedical sciences.

LEGAL BASIS:
Independent foundation.

ELIGIBILITY:
Candidates living in North America or foreign nationals that pursue their fellowship in the U.S., who hold the M.D., Ph.D. or equivalent degree, who are seeking beginning postdoctoral training in basic biomedical research and have no more than one year postdoctoral experience by July 1 are eligible. U.S. citizenship is not a requirement, but fellowships to resident noncitizens are awarded only for training in the U.S. Citizens may train abroad.

Applications from established scientists or advanced fellows will not be considered. Applicants who have already had one year's postdoctoral laboratory training at the time of deadline will not be considered for a Whitney Fellowship.

FINANCIAL DATA:
Amount of support per award: Fellowships provide stipends as follows: $51,000 for the first year, $52,000 for the second year and $53,000 for the third year, plus a $1,500 research allowance to the department for each year of tenure, travel to fellowship location and annual meeting of all fellows. Additionally, there is a dependent child allowance of $1,500 per each dependent child.

NO. MOST RECENT APPLICANTS: 500.

APPLICATION INFO:
Online application is available at the Foundation web site.

Duration: Three years. Contingent upon satisfactory performance.

Deadline: Applications accepted April 1 to July 1. Fellowships begin the following April 1 through September 1.

PUBLICATIONS:
Annual report.

WOODS HOLE OCEANOGRAPHIC INSTITUTION [1793]

Clark Laboratory
360 Woods Hole Road
Education Office, MS #31
Woods Hole, MA 02543-1541
(508) 289-2200
Fax: (508) 457-2188
E-mail: education@whoi.edu
Web Site: www.whoi.edu

FOUNDED: 1930

AREAS OF INTEREST:
Research in biological oceanography, marine chemistry and geochemistry, marine geology and geophysics, applied ocean physics and engineering, physical oceanography and marine policy.

NAME(S) OF PROGRAMS:
- **Summer Student Fellowship Program in Oceanography**

TYPE:
Fellowships. Awards for independent research in oceanography/ocean engineering and marine policy projects pursued under the guidance of a member of the research staff of the Woods Hole Oceanographic Institution. Fellowship is for a 10- to 12-week summer study at Woods Hole Oceanographic Institution.

YEAR PROGRAM STARTED: 1954

PURPOSE:
To give a small group of qualified undergraduate science and engineering students experience that will enable them to determine whether they wish to devote lifetime careers to studying the oceans.

LEGAL BASIS:
Charter under the Commonwealth of Massachusetts.

ELIGIBILITY:
Applicant must be an undergraduate (junior) studying at a college or university in any fields of science or engineering with at least a tentative interest in oceanography.

FINANCIAL DATA:
Award includes weekly stipend, travel and housing allowance for WHOI housing.

Amount of support per award: Stipend of $562.50 per week.

Total amount of support: Varies.

APPLICATION INFO:
Applications must be submitted online. A complete application should include an application form, transcripts of college and university records, at least three personal references, a concise statement of the applicant's research plans and interests, future education and career plans, and reasons for applying to the Institution.

Duration: 10 to 12 weeks.

Deadline: February 15. Notification by March 15.

STAFF:
Dr. James A. Yoder, Dean

ADDRESS INQUIRIES TO:
See e-mail address above.

SOCIAL SCIENCES

Social sciences (general)

AGENCY FOR HEALTHCARE RESEARCH AND QUALITY (AHRQ)

Office of Communications
and Knowledge Transfer
540 Gaither Road, 2nd Floor
Rockville, MD 20850
(301) 427-1104 (specify funding area)
(301) 427-1450
E-mail: support@grants.gov
Web Site: www.ahrq.gov

TYPE:
Conferences/seminars; Development grants; Fellowships; Project/program grants; Research grants; Training grants. Dissertation support highlighting primary care, market forces, cost containment, managed care, the cost of treating AIDS, the improvement of treatment for persons with HIV, rural health care, infant mortality, medical liability, malpractice reform, health care of the aged and disabled and policy studies.

See entry 1381 for full listing.

AMERICAN BAR FOUNDATION

750 North Lake Shore Drive
Fourth Floor
Chicago, IL 60611
(312) 988-6517
Fax: (312) 988-6579
E-mail: fellowships@abfn.org
Web Site: www.americanbarfoundation.org

TYPE:
Fellowships; Internships.

See entry 949 for full listing.

AMERICAN BAR FOUNDATION

750 North Lake Shore Drive
Fourth Floor
Chicago, IL 60611-4403
(312) 988-6517
Fax: (312) 988-6579
E-mail: fellowships@abfn.org
Web Site: www.americanbarfoundation.org

TYPE:
Fellowships. Residential fellowships at the ABF.

The American Bar Foundation is committed to developing the next generation of scholars in the field of law and social science. Since 1987, the Foundation has supported the dissertation research of a diverse group of graduate students from all social science disciplines and, in 1996, added a postdoctoral component to its fellowship program.

See entry 1909 for full listing.

BRETT FAMILY FOUNDATION [1794]

1123 Spruce Street
Boulder, CO 80302
(303) 442-1200
Fax: (303) 442-1221
E-mail: info@brettfoundation.org
Web Site: www.brettfoundation.org

FOUNDED: 2000

AREAS OF INTEREST:
Social justice, equal rights and access to opportunity for individuals and families.

NAME(S) OF PROGRAMS:
- **Nonprofit Media Grant Program**
- **Social Justice Grant Program**

TYPE:
General operating grants.

PURPOSE:
To promote caring communities by investing in organizations throughout Colorado working for social justice and nonprofit media.

ELIGIBILITY:
By invitation only.

GEOG. RESTRICTIONS: Colorado.

FINANCIAL DATA:
Amount of support per award: $2,500 to $10,000.

Total amount of support: Over $500,000 in total grants for the year 2015.

REPRESENTATIVE AWARDS:
$5,000 to 9to5 National Association of Working Women, Colorado Chapter for strengthening economic justice for women; $5,000 to Chalkbeat Colorado for presenting detailed and balanced analysis of education policymaking; $2,000 to Alternatives for Youth/iThrive for providing early intervention for teens struggling with substance abuse.

APPLICATION INFO:
By invitation only.

Duration: One year. Must reapply.

Deadline: Social Justice: Letter of Inquiry, January 15. Full proposals, March 1.

ADDRESS INQUIRIES TO:
Senior Advisor
(See address above.)

CANADIAN FEDERATION FOR THE HUMANITIES AND SOCIAL SCIENCES [1795]

275 Bank Street, Suite 300
Ottawa ON K2P 2L6 Canada
(613) 238-6112 ext. 352
Fax: (613) 238-6114
E-mail: aspp-paes@ideas-idees.ca
Web Site: www.ideas-idees.ca

FOUNDED: 1941

AREAS OF INTEREST:
Social sciences and humanities.

NAME(S) OF PROGRAMS:
- **Awards to Scholarly Publications Program**

TYPE:
Grants-in-aid. Grants to support the publication of scholarly books in the social sciences and humanities.

YEAR PROGRAM STARTED: 1941

PURPOSE:
To assist the publication of books of advanced scholarship in the humanities and social sciences that make an important contribution to knowledge.

LEGAL BASIS:
NGO, nonprofit.

ELIGIBILITY:
Scholarly works in English or French of at least 40,000 words in length authored by Canadian citizens or permanent residents of Canada. The following works are not eligible: unrevised theses, conference proceedings, scholarly journals or articles, textbooks, technical reports, concordances, memoires and autobiographies. Approved works must be published in Canada by ASPP-approved publishers.

GEOG. RESTRICTIONS: Canada.

FINANCIAL DATA:
Grants are paid following publication directly to the publisher.

Amount of support per award: Publication Grant: $8,000. Translation Grant: $12,000.

NO. MOST RECENT APPLICANTS: 260.

NO. AWARDS: 180 Publication Grants and 5 Translation Grants per year.

APPLICATION INFO:
Publishers usually apply on the behalf of authors, though authors may also apply directly. Visit the program web site to download the most up-to-date guidelines and application forms.

PUBLICATIONS:
Application guidelines; application forms.

ADDRESS INQUIRIES TO:
Program Officer, ASPP
(See address above.)

*SPECIAL STIPULATIONS:
Non-Canadians may be eligible for ASPP support if their work is on a Canadian subject and is based on Canadian sources.

CANADIAN INSTITUTE OF UKRAINIAN STUDIES

University of Alberta
430 Pembina Hall
Edmonton AB T6G 2H8 Canada
(780) 492-2972
Fax: (780) 492-4967
E-mail: cius@ualberta.ca
Web Site: www.cius.ca

TYPE:
Fellowships; Research grants; Scholarships.

See entry 571 for full listing.

COUNCIL FOR EUROPEAN STUDIES AT COLUMBIA UNIVERSITY

420 West 118th Street, MC 3307
New York, NY 10027
(212) 854-4172
Fax: (212) 854-8808
E-mail: info@ces-europe.org
Web Site: councilforeuropeanstudies.org

TYPE:
Awards/prizes; Conferences/seminars; Fellowships; Internships; Scholarships; Travel grants. The CES Book Award honors talented emerging scholars with an award for the best first book on any subject in European studies. The award is given every two years.

CES Conference Travel Grants support transcontinental travel for junior faculty and graduate students already scheduled to present at the Council's International Conference of Europeanists.

CES Small Event Grants support workshops, lectures, symposia and other small events that share research on Europe with a wider community.

Council for European Studies Pre-Dissertation Research Fellowships are intended to fund student's first major research project in Europe.

European Studies Undergraduate Paper Prize is designed to encourage interest in the field of European studies by rewarding talented undergraduates who have conducted original research in the field.

First Article Prize awards one prize to a scholar working in the humanities and one to a scholar working in the social sciences. These prizes will honor the writers of the best first articles on European studies published within a two-year period.

Mellon-CES Dissertation Completion Fellowships are intended to facilitate the timely completion of the doctoral degree by late-stage graduate students focused on topics in European studies.

See entry 821 for full listing.

CROSSROADS FUND [1796]

3411 West Diversey Avenue, Suite 20
Chicago, IL 60647-1245
(773) 227-7676
Fax: (773) 227-7790
E-mail: info@crossroadsfund.org
Web Site: www.crossroadsfund.org

FOUNDED: 1981

AREAS OF INTEREST:
Social change.

TYPE:
General operating grants; Project/program grants; Seed money grants; Technical assistance.

PURPOSE:
To support grassroots organizations working to alleviate underlying causes of social ills.

LEGAL BASIS:
Public foundation.

ELIGIBILITY:
Projects must be run by community organizations or nonprofits. No individuals. The Foundation only funds groups with annual expenses under $300,000.

GEOG. RESTRICTIONS: Chicago, Illinois metropolitan area and northwestern Indiana.

FINANCIAL DATA:
Amount of support per award: Up to $10,000.

Total amount of support: $600,000 for the year 2014.

APPLICATION INFO:
Application information is available on the web site.

Duration: One year.

Deadline: February 15.

PUBLICATIONS:
Application guidelines; newsletter; brochure; annual report.

ADDRESS INQUIRIES TO:
Jane Kimondo, Program Director
(See address above.)

THE HARRY FRANK GUGGENHEIM FOUNDATION [1797]

25 West 53rd Street
16th Floor
New York, NY 10019-5401
(646) 428-0971
Fax: (646) 428-0981
E-mail: info@hfg.org
Web Site: www.hfg.org

FOUNDED: 1929

AREAS OF INTEREST:
Scholarly research on aggression and violence.

NAME(S) OF PROGRAMS:

- **The Harry Frank Guggenheim Foundation Dissertation Fellowship**

TYPE:
Fellowships. Awarded to individuals who will complete the writing of the dissertation within the award year. Support is for projects which seek to advance and coordinate creative breakthroughs in the social and biological sciences relating to the study of violence and aggression.

YEAR PROGRAM STARTED: 1990

PURPOSE:
To further understanding of human social problems related to violence and aggression.

LEGAL BASIS:
Private foundation.

ELIGIBILITY:
Fellowships are for students in the final year of their doctoral programs. They are designed to support the write-up stage of the dissertation. They are available to citizens of any country in the world.

Recipients of the Dissertation Fellowship must submit a copy of the dissertation, approved and accepted by their institution, within six months after the end of the award year. Any papers, books, articles, or other publications based on the research should also be sent to the Foundation.

FINANCIAL DATA:
Amount of support per award: $20,000.

Total amount of support: $200,000 each year.

NO. MOST RECENT APPLICANTS: Average 225.

NO. AWARDS: 10 or more.

REPRESENTATIVE AWARDS:
Amy Chasteen for "Constructing Rape;" James Hogue for "Bayonet Rule: Five Street Battles in New Orleans and the Rise and Fall of Radical Reconstruction;" David LeMarquand for "Tryptophan Depletion, Aggression, and Passive Avoidance Learning in Nonalcoholic Young Men with Paternal Family Histories of Alcoholism."

APPLICATION INFO:
Guidelines and application forms are available on the web site.

Duration: Dissertation Fellowships are one-time awards and are not renewable.

Deadline: February 1.

PUBLICATIONS:
Guidelines and Report.

OFFICERS:
Josiah Bunting, III, President
Deirdre Hamill, Treasurer and Secretary
Karen Colvard, Program Director
Joel Wallman, Senior Program Officer

ADDRESS INQUIRIES TO:
Dissertation Fellowship
(See address above.)

THE HARRY FRANK GUGGENHEIM FOUNDATION [1798]

25 West 53rd Street
16th Floor
New York, NY 10019-5401
(646) 428-0971
Fax: (646) 428-0981
E-mail: info@hfg.org
Web Site: www.hfg.org

FOUNDED: 1929

AREAS OF INTEREST:
Research on dominance, aggression and violence.

NAME(S) OF PROGRAMS:

- **The Harry Frank Guggenheim Foundation Research Grant**

TYPE:
Research grants. Support for projects which seek to advance and coordinate creative breakthroughs in the social and biological sciences relating to the study of dominance, violence and aggression.

YEAR PROGRAM STARTED: 1972

PURPOSE:
To further understanding of human social problems related to dominance, violence and aggression.

LEGAL BASIS:
Private, operating foundation.

ELIGIBILITY:
The Foundation awards research grants to individuals (or a few principal investigators at most) for individual projects and does not award grants to institutions for institutional programs.

Applicants for a research grant may be citizens of any country. While almost all recipients of a Foundation research grant possess a Ph.D., M.D., or equivalent degree, there are no formal degree requirements for the grant. The grant, however, may not be used to support research undertaken as part of the requirements for a graduate degree. Applicants need not be affiliated with an institution of higher learning, although most are college or university professors.

FINANCIAL DATA:
Amount of support per award: Usually $15,000 to $40,000 per year.

Total amount of support: Grants and Fellowships: $400,000 to $500,000.

NO. MOST RECENT APPLICANTS: 175.

NO. AWARDS: Approximately 10.

APPLICATION INFO:
Guidelines and application form are available at the Foundation web site.

Duration: Usually one to two years. Renewal is possible if requested in original application, but not guaranteed.

Deadline: August 1 (received, not postmarked).

PUBLICATIONS:
Guidelines; Annual Report.

OFFICERS:
Josiah Bunting, III, President
Deirdre Hamill, Secretary-Treasurer
Karen Colvard, Program Director
Joel Wallman, Senior Program Officer

ADDRESS INQUIRIES TO:
Research Grants
(See address above.)

THE JOHN RANDOLPH HAYNES AND DORA HAYNES FOUNDATION [1799]

888 West Sixth Street, Suite 1150
Los Angeles, CA 90017-2737
(213) 623-9151
Fax: (213) 623-3951
E-mail: info@haynesfoundation.org
Web Site: www.haynesfoundation.org

FOUNDED: 1926

AREAS OF INTEREST:
Public policy for Los Angeles.

TYPE:
Fellowships; Research grants.

YEAR PROGRAM STARTED: 1926

PURPOSE:
To strengthen research in the social sciences into issues of the Los Angeles region.

LEGAL BASIS:
Independent private foundation.

ELIGIBILITY:
501(c)(3) organizations only.

No grants are made to individuals.

GEOG. RESTRICTIONS: California, specifically Los Angeles, Orange, Riverside, San Bernardino, and Ventura counties.

FINANCIAL DATA:
Amount of support per award: $5,000 to $250,000.

Total amount of support: Up to $3,000,000.

NO. MOST RECENT APPLICANTS: 50.

NO. AWARDS: 12.

REPRESENTATIVE AWARDS:
$50,000 to Center for the Study of Political Graphics; $30,000 to KPCC Southern California Public Radio; $18,800 to Los Angeles City Historical Society.

APPLICATION INFO:
Application information is available on the web site.

Duration: One to two years.

Deadline: Varies.

PUBLICATIONS:
Annual report.

IRS I.D.: 95-1644020

ADDRESS INQUIRIES TO:
See e-mail address above.

THE HOROWITZ FOUNDATION FOR SOCIAL POLICY [1800]

P.O. Box 7
Rocky Hill, NJ 08553-0007
(732) 445-2280
E-mail: info@horowitz-foundation.org
Web Site: www.horowitz-foundation.org

FOUNDED: 1997

AREAS OF INTEREST:
Social sciences, including anthropology, area studies, economics, political science, psychology, sociology, urban studies, as well as newer areas such as evaluation research.

TYPE:
Awards/prizes; Research grants. Grants to doctoral candidates at the dissertation level with emphasis on policy-related studies.

YEAR PROGRAM STARTED: 1997

PURPOSE:
To support the advancement of research and understanding in the major fields of the social sciences.

ELIGIBILITY:
Awards are only open to aspiring Ph.Ds. at the dissertation level whose project has received approval from their appropriate department head/university. Applicants are not required to be U.S. citizens or U.S. residents.

Preference will be given to projects that deal with contemporary issues in the social sciences and issues of policy relevance.

Awards are not allocated so as to insure a representative base of disciplines, but are approved solely on merit.

FINANCIAL DATA:
Amount of support per award: $7,500 plus additional special grants; Additional $5,000 for best overall project.

CO-OP FUNDING PROGRAMS: Determined on a case-by-case basis.

NO. MOST RECENT APPLICANTS: 535 for the year 2015.

NO. AWARDS: Approximately 15 annually.

APPLICATION INFO:
Application guidelines and eligibility criteria can be found at the Foundation web site. Applications must be submitted through the online system. All materials must be submitted, in English, prior to the closing date.

Duration: One year. Nonrenewable.

Deadline: January 31.

IRS I.D.: 31-1612153

ADDRESS INQUIRIES TO:
Mary E. Curtis
Chairman and Trustee
(See address above.)

INSTITUTE FOR ADVANCED STUDY [1801]

One Einstein Drive
Princeton, NJ 08540
(609) 734-8250
Fax: (609) 951-4457
E-mail: donne@ias.edu
Web Site: www.sss.ias.edu

FOUNDED: 1930

AREAS OF INTEREST:
Economics, political science, sociology, education, anthropology and history.

NAME(S) OF PROGRAMS:

- **School of Social Science Fellowships**

TYPE:
Fellowships; Residencies. Postdoctoral research fellowships at the School of Social Science.

YEAR PROGRAM STARTED: 1970

PURPOSE:
To support fundamental research and scholarship in the social sciences and humanities.

LEGAL BASIS:
Private, nonprofit research center.

ELIGIBILITY:
Scholars of any nationality who have obtained their highest degree and whose work is relevant to any aspect of the social sciences are urged to apply.

FINANCIAL DATA:
Amount of support per award: Approximately $35,000 to $70,000.

Total amount of support: Varies.

Matching fund requirements: Institute strongly encourages applicants to apply for outside funds as well.

NO. MOST RECENT APPLICANTS: 220.

NO. AWARDS: 24.

APPLICATION INFO:
Applications must be submitted online.

Duration: One academic year.

Deadline: November 1.

PUBLICATIONS:
Annual report.

STAFF:
Donne Petito, Administrative Officer

ADDRESS INQUIRIES TO:
School of Social Science
(See address above.)

*SPECIAL STIPULATIONS:
This is a residential (on-site) fellowship.

INSTITUTE FOR QUANTITATIVE SOCIAL SCIENCE, HARVARD UNIVERSITY [1802]

Henry A. Murray Research Archive
CGIS Knafel Building, Room 318
Cambridge, MA 02138
(617) 496-6528
Fax: (617) 496-5149
E-mail: support@dataverse.org
Web Site: www.murray.harvard.edu

FOUNDED: 1976

AREAS OF INTEREST:
Social sciences, psychology and human development, and education.

NAME(S) OF PROGRAMS:

- **Jeanne Humphrey Block Dissertation Award**

TYPE:
Awards/prizes. The Block Dissertation Award is offered by the Henry A. Murray Research Archive.

YEAR PROGRAM STARTED: 1990

PURPOSE:
To support research that best embodies Henry A. Murray's commitment to the in-depth study of individuals in context, over time and from a variety of perspectives.

LEGAL BASIS:
University or research association.

ELIGIBILITY:
Applicant must be a Harvard Ph.D. candidate (third year or above) in the social sciences.

FINANCIAL DATA:
Amount of support per award: $2,500.
Total amount of support: $2,500.

NO. AWARDS: 1.

APPLICATION INFO:
Detailed information and application guidelines are available upon request to the Institute or can be found on its web site.
Duration: One year.
Deadline: March 13.

PUBLICATIONS:
Program announcement.

IRS I.D.: 04-2103589

ADDRESS INQUIRIES TO:
E-mail: funding@iq.harvard.edu

*SPECIAL STIPULATIONS:
Dissertation must utilize data archived in the Harvard Dataverse.

KAPPA OMICRON NU HONOR SOCIETY
1749 Hamilton Road
Suite 106
Okemos, MI 48864
(517) 351-8335
Fax: (517) 351-8336
E-mail: info@kon.org
Web Site: www.kon.org

TYPE:
Fellowships; Project/program grants; Research grants; Scholarships. Awarded to members for graduate or postgraduate study and research in human sciences or one of its specializations at colleges or universities with strong research programs and supporting disciplines for the chosen major or topic.
See entry 2589 for full listing.

MADDIE'S FUND [1803]
6150 Stoneridge Mall Road
Suite 125
Pleasanton, CA 94588
(925) 310-5450
E-mail: grants@maddiesfund.org
Web Site: www.maddiesfund.org

AREAS OF INTEREST:
Animal welfare.

TYPE:
Project/program grants.

PURPOSE:
To revolutionize the status and well-being of companion animals.

GEOG. RESTRICTIONS: United States.

APPLICATION INFO:
Contact the Fund for guidelines.
Duration: Varies by program.

ADDRESS INQUIRIES TO:
Shelly Thompson, Grants Manager
(See address above.)

THE NATIONAL ASSOCIATION OF BLACK SOCIAL WORKERS
2305 Martin Luther King Jr. Avenue, S.E.
Washington, DC 20020
(202) 678-4570
Fax: (202) 678-4572
E-mail: officedirector@nabsw.org
Web Site: www.nabsw.org

TYPE:
Scholarships.
See entry 1011 for full listing.

NATIONAL COUNCIL FOR THE SOCIAL STUDIES [1804]
8555 16th Street, Suite 500
Silver Spring, MD 20910
(301) 588-1800 ext. 107
Fax: (301) 588-2049
E-mail: excellence@ncss.org
Web Site: www.socialstudies.org/fasse

AREAS OF INTEREST:
Social studies education.

NAME(S) OF PROGRAMS:
- **FASSE-IA International Understanding Grants**

TYPE:
Project/program grants. The grants are intended to support collaborative projects that demonstrate potential to enhance international relationships and global perspectives in social studies education. Funded projects will hold promise for enhancing international and cross-cultural understanding (e.g., through global or international education, human rights education, a focus on global issues, global citizenship, etc.)

PURPOSE:
The Fund for the Advancement of Social Studies Education (FASSE) was created by the National Council for the Social Studies to support research and classroom application projects that improve social studies education and promote engaged, effective citizens. The International Assembly (IA) was founded upon a commitment to build international understanding and to share the activities and scholarship of global social studies educators.

ELIGIBILITY:
Members of NCSS from all geographic locations (i.e., U.S.-based and international) are encouraged to submit proposals. The primary grantee must be a member of NCSS. Upon awarding of the grant, he or she will be expected to join the International Assembly.

Grants are not made to individuals.

FINANCIAL DATA:
The International Assembly and the Fund for the Advancement of Social Studies Education will award up to three International Understanding Grants. The total of the three grants will not exceed $5,000.
Amount of support per award: Varies.
Total amount of support: $5,000.

NO. AWARDS: Up to 3 annually.

APPLICATION INFO:
Complete application information and form are available on the web site.
Duration: Typically, one year.
Deadline: End of May or early June.

NATIONAL COUNCIL FOR THE SOCIAL STUDIES [1805]
8555 16th Street, Suite 500
Silver Spring, MD 20910
(301) 588-1800 ext. 107
Fax: (301) 588-2049
E-mail: excellence@ncss.org
Web Site: www.socialstudies.org

FOUNDED: 1921

AREAS OF INTEREST:
Social studies education.

NAME(S) OF PROGRAMS:
- **Exemplary Research in Social Studies**
- **Jean Dresden Grambs Distinguished Career in Social Studies**
- **The Larry Metcalf Exemplary Dissertation Award**
- **Outstanding Social Studies Teacher of the Year Awards**
- **Carter G. Woodson Book Awards**

TYPE:
Awards/prizes; Grants-in-aid.

PURPOSE:
To provide leadership, service and support for all social studies educators.

GEOG. RESTRICTIONS: United States.

FINANCIAL DATA:
Amount of support per award: Up to $3,000.
Total amount of support: Varies.

APPLICATION INFO:
Applications must be submitted through the online system.
Deadline: May 31.

NATIONAL COUNCIL FOR THE SOCIAL STUDIES [1806]
8555 16th Street, Suite 500
Silver Spring, MD 20910
(301) 588-1800 ext. 107
Fax: (301) 588-2049
E-mail: excellence@ncss.org
Web Site: www.socialstudies.org

FOUNDED: 1921

AREAS OF INTEREST:
Social studies education.

NAME(S) OF PROGRAMS:
- **Christa McAuliffe Reach for the Stars Award**

TYPE:
Awards/prizes. Annual award for projects representing excellence and innovation in social studies education and having the potential of serving as a model for other teachers.

YEAR PROGRAM STARTED: 1986

PURPOSE:
To help a social studies educator make his or her dream of innovative social studies a reality; to assist classroom teachers in developing and implementing imaginative, innovative, and illustrative social studies teaching strategies; to assist classroom teachers in supporting student implementation of innovative social studies, citizenship projects, field experiences, and community connections.

ELIGIBILITY:
NCSS membership is required. Applicant must be a full-time social studies teacher or social studies teacher educator currently engaged with K-12 students.

GEOG. RESTRICTIONS: United States.

FINANCIAL DATA:
Amount of support per award: $2,500.

NO. MOST RECENT APPLICANTS: 10.

NO. AWARDS: 1.

APPLICATION INFO:
Applications must be submitted through the online system. No mail-in copies will be

allowed. A complete proposal contains the following:
(1) cover page;
(2) 50- to 150-word project proposal abstract;
(3) project proposal and narrative description;
(4) professional resume (including current teaching assignment);
(5) two letters of support from applicant's supervisor acknowledging teaching status and support for the project (one letter may be from state or local social studies council);
(6) publicity outreach, including name, contact name, title and e-mail for a major local/community newspaper (up to two), district superintendent, and direct supervisor and;
(7) information release statement.

The project proposal and narrative description must include the following information:
(1) clear, concise statement of the project objectives;
(2) brief summary of project activities and timeline for completion;
(3) identification of population served, including relevant demographic information;
(4) budget showing how the funds will be used and if additional funds are being sought from other sources;
(5) brief explanation of how the award can facilitate the project;
(6) brief explanation of how the success of the project will be evaluated;
(7) description of the specific plan for sharing the project with local or state councils and with NCSS and;
(8) brief explanation of how the project can serve as a model for other teachers.

Deadline: End of May to early June.

NATIONAL COUNCIL FOR THE SOCIAL STUDIES [1807]

8555 16th Street, Suite 500
Silver Spring, MD 20910
(301) 588-1800 ext. 107
Fax: (301) 588-2049
E-mail: excellence@ncss.org
Web Site: www.socialstudies.org

FOUNDED: 1921

AREAS OF INTEREST:
Social studies education.

NAME(S) OF PROGRAMS:
- **Grant for the Enhancement of Geographic Literacy**

TYPE:
Awards/prizes. Annual award honoring the outstanding performance of teachers, researchers, and other worthy individuals and programs.

PURPOSE:
To promote geography education in the schools; to enhance the geographic literacy of students at the classroom, district, or statewide level; to encourage integration of geography into the social studies curriculum/classroom.

ELIGIBILITY:
Programs, not individuals, individual lessons or units, which will enhance the geographic literacy of students at the classroom, district, or statewide levels. Recipients may be individuals or groups in school districts, public institutions, or universities.

GEOG. RESTRICTIONS: United States.

FINANCIAL DATA:
Amount of support per award: $2,500.

NO. MOST RECENT APPLICANTS: 10 to 12.

NO. AWARDS: 1.

APPLICATION INFO:
Applicants must complete the online application and be prepared to upload the following documents within the application. Links to external websites are not acceptable, and will be disregarded by the selection committee. Maximum file size to be uploaded for each nontext box item is one megabyte. File types accepted are: pdf, doc and docx. The proposal should be five pages, double-spaced (maximum), and include:
(1) concise rationale statement;
(2) complete program description that highlights specific geography skills and knowledge that will be introduced or reinforced;
(3) number of teachers and students served;
(4) specific criteria for and means of evaluating program effectiveness;
(5) statement of potential program impact after the first year;
(6) specific line-item budget for grant (funds may not be used for indirect costs);
(7) vitae or professional resume for key persons involved in the implementation of the grant (maximum of six);
(8) publicity outreach, including name, contact name, title and e-mail for a major local/community newspaper (up to two), district superintendent, and direct supervisor and;
(9) information release statement.

Deadline: End of May to early June.

NATIONAL COUNCIL FOR THE SOCIAL STUDIES [1808]

8555 16th Street, Suite 500
Silver Spring, MD 20910
(301) 588-1800 ext. 107
Fax: (301) 588-2049
E-mail: excellence@ncss.org
Web Site: www.socialstudies.org

FOUNDED: 1921

AREAS OF INTEREST:
Social studies education.

NAME(S) OF PROGRAMS:
- **Award for Global Understanding**

TYPE:
Awards/prizes.

PURPOSE:
To recognize a social studies educator (or a team of educators) who has made notable contributions in helping social studies students increase their understanding of the world.

ELIGIBILITY:
NCSS membership is required. Anyone may nominate. Nominees must be social studies educators who are affecting the global understanding of preK-12 students.

FINANCIAL DATA:
Amount of support per award: $2,000 cash award, up to $700 in transportation/lodging reimbursement, a complimentary NCSS conference registration, publicity for a session to present at the NCSS annual conference, and a commemorative gift.

NO. MOST RECENT APPLICANTS: 10.

NO. AWARDS: 1 annually.

APPLICATION INFO:
Applicants must complete the online application and be prepared to upload required documents within the application. Maximum file size to be uploaded for each nontext box item is one megabyte. File types accepted are: pdf, doc and docx. Applicant must include:
(1) a description of the activity/activities of which he or she is most proud that exemplify two to three of the award criteria in his or her social studies teaching for global understanding (limit 500 words);
(2) a description of his or her approach to teaching social studies for global understanding, which can include, but is not limited to, interaction with students and parents, pedagogical approaches, integration of technology, differentiation of curriculum to accommodate learning styles and abilities and views on assessment (limit 500 words);
(3) a curriculum vitae or resume (two-page maximum);
(4) applicant/nominee lesson plan including a social studies unit or lesson plan that integrates global perpectives and cross-cultural understanding elements (per award selection criteria) that was created and successfully taught (not to exceed 500 words, double-spaced);
(5) a letter of support from the nominator (maximum 250 words), four letters total;
(6) a letter from his or her immediate supervisor (two-page maximum);
(7) a letter from professional colleague (teacher, professor, district supervisor, etc.) (two-page maximum);
(8) a letter from a parent or student that highlights teacher effectiveness, unique abilities memorable experiences, etc. (two-page maximum);
(9) publicity outreach, including name, contact name, title and e-mail for a major local/community newspaper (up to two), district superintendent and direct supervisor and;
(10) information release statement.
Preference will be given to nominees directly affecting the global understanding of P-12 social studies students.

Deadline: End of May to early June.

NATIONAL COUNCIL ON FAMILY RELATIONS

1201 West River Parkway
Suite 200
Minneapolis, MN 55454
(763) 781-9331
Fax: (763) 781-9348
E-mail: info@ncfr.org
Web Site: www.ncfr.org

TYPE:
Awards/prizes. Awards given for contributions to the area of family science. All of the awards, except the Reuben Hill Award and the Jessie Bernard initiatives, require NCFR membership. The Reuben Hill Award is a juried award.

See entry 1458 for full listing.

NATIONAL INSTITUTE OF MENTAL HEALTH [1809]

Division of Translational Research (DTR)
6001 Executive Boulevard, Room 7111, MSC 9632
Bethesda, MD 20892-9632
(301) 443-9232
E-mail: ftuma@nih.gov
Web Site: www.nimh.nih.gov/about/organization/dtr/index.shtml

AREAS OF INTEREST:
Traumatic stress, violence (both perpetrators and victims) and disaster within the scope of the biological, behavioral, clinical, applied and psychosocial sciences.

NAME(S) OF PROGRAMS:
- **Traumatic Stress Research Program**

TYPE:
Fellowships; Project/program grants; Research grants; Technical assistance; Training grants; Visiting scholars; Research contracts.

YEAR PROGRAM STARTED: 1969

PURPOSE:
To plan, support and administer programs of research, research training and resource development aimed at understanding the pathophysiology of mental illness and hastening the translation of behavioral science and neuroscience advances into innovations in clinical care.

LEGAL BASIS:
Section 301 of the Public Health Service Act, as amended; Public Law 78-410, 42 U.S.C. 241.

ELIGIBILITY:
Applicants can be any public or nonprofit institution such as a university, college, hospital or a community agency, unit of state or local government, an authorized unit of the federal government or a for-profit institution and/or entity.

GEOG. RESTRICTIONS: United States and its territories.

FINANCIAL DATA:
Amount of support per award: Funding amounts vary by grant type.

NO. MOST RECENT APPLICANTS: 60.

NO. AWARDS: 20.

APPLICATION INFO:
Forms and instructions are available online.

Duration: Average three to five years.

NATIONAL SCIENCE FOUNDATION

4201 Wilson Boulevard, Room 990
Arlington, VA 22230
(703) 292-7283
Fax: (703) 292-9068
E-mail: fkronz@nsf.gov
Web Site: www.nsf.gov

TYPE:
Conferences/seminars; Fellowships; Project/program grants; Research grants; Training grants. Grants support research and educational projects, national meetings, dissemination efforts, cross-disciplinary study, dissertation research, small group training activities, dissertation improvement grants for graduate students, and postdoctoral fellowships. The proposals that are considered for support use methods from a variety of disciplines including anthropology, communications, history, philosophy, political science, and sociology to investigate STEM theory and practice with regards to their history, socio-cultural formation, philosophical underpinnings, and impacts on quality of life, culture, and society.

See entry 1781 for full listing.

NATIONAL SOCIETY DAUGHTERS OF THE AMERICAN REVOLUTION [1810]

1776 D Street, N.W.
Washington, DC 20006-5303
(202) 879-3263
Fax: (202) 879-3348
E-mail: scholarships@dar.org
Web Site: www.dar.org

FOUNDED: 1895

AREAS OF INTEREST:
Political science, history, government and economics.

NAME(S) OF PROGRAMS:
- **Enid Hall Griswold Memorial Scholarship**

TYPE:
Scholarships. Undergraduate scholarships awarded to a deserving junior or senior accepted or enrolled in an accredited college or university in the U.S. who is majoring in either political science, history, government or economics.

YEAR PROGRAM STARTED: 1982

PURPOSE:
To provide ways and means to aid students to attain higher education.

LEGAL BASIS:
Incorporated historical society.

ELIGIBILITY:
Scholarships are awarded without regard to race, religion, sex or national origin. Candidates must be U.S. citizens and must attend an accredited college or university in the U.S. No affiliation or relationship to DAR is required for qualification. Awards are judged on the basis of academic excellence, commitment to field of study, as required, and financial need.

Candidate must major in political science, history, government or economics.

GEOG. RESTRICTIONS: United States.

FINANCIAL DATA:
Amount of support per award: Varies.

Total amount of support: Varies.

NO. AWARDS: Varies.

APPLICATION INFO:
Application information is available online.

Duration: One academic year. Nonrenewable.

Deadline: February 15.

PUBLICATIONS:
American Spirit, magazine.

ADDRESS INQUIRIES TO:
Office of the Reporter General
DAR Scholarship Committee
(See address above.)

PI GAMMA MU, INTERNATIONAL HONOR SOCIETY IN SOCIAL SCIENCE

1001 Millington, Suite B
Winfield, KS 67156
(620) 221-3128
Fax: (620) 221-7124
E-mail: executivedirector@pigammamu.org
Web Site: www.pigammamu.org

TYPE:
Scholarships. Awarded for graduate study.

See entry 1689 for full listing.

POVERTY & RACE RESEARCH ACTION COUNCIL [1811]

1200 18th Street, N.W.
Suite 200
Washington, DC 20036
(202) 906-8023
Fax: (202) 842-2885
E-mail: ptegeler@prrac.org
Web Site: www.prrac.org

FOUNDED: 1991

AREAS OF INTEREST:
Poverty and race.

TYPE:
Research grants. Research on the intersection of race and poverty must support an advocacy plan.

YEAR PROGRAM STARTED: 2000

PURPOSE:
To generate, gather and disseminate information and resources regarding the intersection of race and poverty in the U.S.; to promote the development and implementation of policies and practices that alleviate conditions caused by the interaction of race and poverty.

LEGAL BASIS:
Nonprofit organization.

ELIGIBILITY:
Must be an advocate or social science researcher and be a tax-exempt 501(c)(3) organization or have a tax-exempt fiscal sponsor.

GEOG. RESTRICTIONS: United States.

FINANCIAL DATA:
Amount of support per award: $10,000 maximum.

Total amount of support: Varies.

APPLICATION INFO:
Applicants must submit a brief letter outlining the purpose of the grant. Further information is available online.

Duration: One-time. Must reapply.

PUBLICATIONS:
Poverty & Race, bimonthly newsletter; journal; annual report; application guidelines.

IRS I.D.: 52-1705073

ADDRESS INQUIRIES TO:
Philip Tegeler, Executive Director
(See address above.)

*SPECIAL STIPULATIONS:
Research must support planned advocacy agenda.

SMITH RICHARDSON FOUNDATION, INC. [1812]

60 Jesup Road
Westport, CT 06880
(203) 222-6222
Fax: (203) 222-6282
E-mail: jhollings@srf.org
Web Site: www.srf.org

FOUNDED: 1935

AREAS OF INTEREST:
Improvement of public policy in the fields of social welfare, economic and regulatory schemes and education issues; improvement of American foreign policy, particularly as it relates to national security.

NAME(S) OF PROGRAMS:
- **Domestic Public Policy Program**
- **International Security and Foreign Policy Program**

TYPE:
Conferences/seminars; Project/program grants; Research grants. The Domestic Policy Program primarily supports research on ways to improve public policy in the fields of social welfare, economic and regulatory schemes and education issues. The program has a particular interest in research that examines the effectiveness of institutions which serve children and families at-risk.

The Foreign Policy Program supports projects in national security and defense policy, in military history and strategy, in the political, military and economic affairs of Eastern Europe and the states of the former Soviet Union, economic and security developments in the Asia Pacific, and also in international economic issues of vital interest to American policymakers. The program aims to define the nature of the post-cold war security environment.

YEAR PROGRAM STARTED: 1935

PURPOSE:
To support and promote a vigorous and free society.

LEGAL BASIS:
Private foundation.

ELIGIBILITY:
Organizations sponsoring projects appropriate to the Foundation's interests are eligible. The Foundation originates many of the grant commitments which are made, and the vast majority of unsolicited requests for funding must be rejected. Because of fund limitations, no grants are available for deficit funding of previously established operations, projects relating to building construction (i.e., "brick and mortar"), programs related to the arts, historic restoration projects, or research in the physical sciences. No grants are made directly to individuals or to advocacy organizations. The Foundation does not provide support for the operating costs of direct-service programs or charities. The Foundation rarely provides general support for any organization or funding for conferences and documentaries.

The Foundation awards grants for policy research with national implications. Some small grants are available to support innovative service and educational programs in Connecticut and North Carolina which assist children and families at-risk. Nearly all such local grants are solicited by the staff and the Board of the Foundation. Service programs in states other than Connecticut and North Carolina are ineligible for funding.

GEOG. RESTRICTIONS: Connecticut and North Carolina.

FINANCIAL DATA:
Amount of support per award: Median grant: $120,000.

APPLICATION INFO:
The Foundation has a rigorous proposal review process. The first step in the process is the submission of a concept paper (not to exceed five pages).

If the staff determines that a project warrants further consideration under the Foundation's guidelines, an applicant will be asked to submit a full proposal that conforms to a proposal template provided by the Foundation.

Upon receipt of a grant application, the Foundation will either mail or e-mail a confirmation of receipt to the grant applicant. The Foundation will respond to all grant requests in a timely manner. However, given the large number of grant proposals that it receives, it cannot guarantee a response within a specific time frame.

Requests for grants greater than $50,000 and for multiyear grant support are made at one of its regular board meetings. Requests for grants of $50,000 or less are reviewed on an ongoing basis and are handled as promptly as possible.

Duration: Typically one year. Nonrenewable.

Deadline: Grants are reviewed on an ongoing basis.

PUBLICATIONS:
Annual report.

IRS I.D.: 56-0611550

STAFF:
Dr. Nadia Schadlow, Senior Program Officer
Allan Song, Senior Program Officer
Mark Steinmeyer, Senior Program Officer
Olga Ramous, Grants Coordinator
Dale Stewart, Records Coordinator

OFFICERS AND TRUSTEES:
Peter L. Richardson, Chairman of the Board
Marin J. Strmecki, Ph.D., Senior Vice President, Director of Programs
Ross F. Hemphill, Vice President and Chief Financial Officer
Arvid R. Nelson, Ph.D., Secretary
W. Winburne King, III, General Counsel
Adele Richardson Ray
Stuart S. Richardson

ADDRESS INQUIRIES TO:
Domestic Policy or Foreign Policy Program
(See address above.)

THE ROYAL TOWN PLANNING INSTITUTE [1813]

41 Botolph Lane
London EC3R 8DL England
(020) 7929-9494
Fax: (020) 7929-9490
E-mail: ellie.green@rtpi.org.uk
Web Site: www.rtpi.org.uk

FOUNDED: 1914

AREAS OF INTEREST:
Urban and regional planning, land use, transport and housing, industrial strategy on planning, rural planning, conservation and recreational planning.

NAME(S) OF PROGRAMS:
- **George Pepler International Award**

TYPE:
Travel grants. This biennial award is made to individuals under 30 years of age, who wish to visit Britain or, as residents of Britain, desire to visit another country for a short period to study the theory and practice of town and country planning or some particular aspect of planning.

YEAR PROGRAM STARTED: 1964

PURPOSE:
To provide an international travelling award for young people of any nationality who wish to visit another country in order to study town planning or a related subject.

LEGAL BASIS:
Charitable trust.

ELIGIBILITY:
Young people of any nationality under the age of 30 are eligible to apply. Professional qualifications are not necessary. Each applicant is required to complete a prescribed application form and submit to a panel of advisers a statement showing the nature of the study and suggested itinerary.

FINANCIAL DATA:
Amount of support per award: GBP 1,500 paid in two installments.

NO. MOST RECENT APPLICANTS: 15.

NO. AWARDS: 1.

APPLICATION INFO:
Contact the Institute through its e-mail address for an entry form and details. Application and information can be found online.

Duration: Three to four weeks.

Deadline: June 27.

ADDRESS INQUIRIES TO:
Ellie Green
Events and Marketing Assistant
(See address above.)

RUSSELL SAGE FOUNDATION [1814]

112 East 64th Street
New York, NY 10065
(212) 750-6000
Fax: (212) 371-4761
E-mail: info@rsage.org
Web Site: www.russellsage.org

FOUNDED: 1907

AREAS OF INTEREST:
Research in the future of work, cultural contact, immigration to the U.S. and social inequality.

TYPE:
Conferences/seminars; Research grants; Visiting scholars. Research awards. The Foundation currently pursues three principal programs:
(1) a program of research on the future of work, concerned principally with the causes and consequences of changes in the quality of low-wage work in the U.S. and other advanced economies;
(2) a program of research on current U.S. immigration focused on the adaptation of the second generation to American society and;
(3) a program on cultural contact that focuses on understanding and improving relations between racial and ethnic groups in schools, workplaces and neighborhood settings.

YEAR PROGRAM STARTED: 1907

PURPOSE:
To improve social and living conditions in the U.S. by conducting and supporting social science research relevant to public policy issues.

LEGAL BASIS:
Private operating foundation.

ELIGIBILITY:
The Foundation supports focused, empirical research projects under the direction of a principal investigator. Under the terms of the contract, the research must be coordinated through a fiscal agency (university, college or 501(c)(3) organization under the Internal Revenue Code).

The Foundation's awards are restricted to support for basic social science research within its announced programs. These currently include research on the future of work, immigration and the social psychology of social contact.

The Foundation conducts a Visiting Scholar program under which persons working in the areas of current interest to the Foundation join the staff for one year to consult and continue their own research and writing.

GEOG. RESTRICTIONS: United States.

FINANCIAL DATA:

Total amount of support: Approximately $6,500,000.

APPLICATION INFO:

Applications for awards should be preceded by a letter of inquiry to the Foundation. Guidelines and other details are available on the web site.

Duration: Varies.

Deadline: Eight weeks prior to Board meetings to be held March, June and November.

PUBLICATIONS:

Biennial report; scholarly books.

IRS I.D.: 13-1635303

OFFICERS:

Sheldon Danziger, President
Claire Gabriel, Secretary

ADDRESS INQUIRIES TO:

E-mail: programs@rsage.org

SOCIAL SCIENCES AND HUMANITIES RESEARCH COUNCIL OF CANADA [1815]

350 Albert Street
Ottawa ON K1P 6G4 Canada
(613) 943-7777
Fax: (613) 943-1329
E-mail: fellowships@sshrc-crsh.gc.ca
Web Site: www.sshrc-crsh.gc.ca

FOUNDED: 1977

AREAS OF INTEREST:

The development and support of research and research training in the social sciences and humanities.

NAME(S) OF PROGRAMS:

- **Doctoral Awards**

TYPE:

Awards/prizes; Fellowships; Scholarships. Through its Doctoral Awards program, SSHRC offers two types of funding for doctoral students:
(1) SSHRC Doctoral Fellowships and;
(2) Joseph-Armand Bombardier (JAB) Canada Graduate Scholarships (CGS) program - Doctoral Scholarships.

YEAR PROGRAM STARTED: 1977

PURPOSE:

To develop research skills and assist in the training of highly qualified personnel by supporting students who demonstrate a high standard of scholarly achievement in undergraduate and graduate studies in the social sciences and humanities.

LEGAL BASIS:

Government agency.

ELIGIBILITY:

Applicants must be Canadian citizens or permanent residents of Canada. SSHRC Doctoral Fellowships are tenable at any recognized university in Canada, or abroad, in which case the award holder has to have at least one previous degree from a Canadian university.

Joseph-Armand Bombardier Canada Graduate Scholarships-Doctoral Scholarships are tenable only at Canadian universities.

FINANCIAL DATA:

Amount of support per award: SSHRC Doctoral Fellowships: $20,000 (CAN) per year; Joseph-Armand Bombardier Canada Graduate Scholarships-Doctoral Scholarships: $35,000 (CAN) per year.

NO. MOST RECENT APPLICANTS: 4,969 total applicants from Canadian universities for the year 2011-12.

NO. AWARDS: SSHRC Doctoral Fellowships: 525; Joseph-Armand Bombardier Canada Graduate Scholarships-Doctoral Scholarships: 460 for the year 2011-12.

APPLICATION INFO:

On university campuses, information may be obtained from the Dean or Faculty of Graduate Studies, the Office of Research Administration, the Registrar, or the Student Awards Office. Inquiries may also be addressed directly to the Research Training Portfolio of the Council, at the address above. Detailed program and application information is available online.

Duration: SSHRC Doctoral Fellowships: From six months to four years; Joseph-Armand Bombardier Canada Graduate Scholarships-Doctoral Scholarships: Three years.

Deadline: For applicants registered at a Canadian university, in the fall on the date set by the university; for other applicants, usually in early November.

OFFICERS AND STAFF:

Ted Hewitt, President
Dr. Brent Herbert-Copley, Executive Vice President
Gordana Krcevinac, Director, Research Training

ADDRESS INQUIRIES TO:

Research Training Portfolio
(See address above.)

SOCIAL SCIENCES AND HUMANITIES RESEARCH COUNCIL OF CANADA [1816]

350 Albert Street
Ottawa ON K1P 6G4 Canada
(613) 943-7777
Fax: (613) 943-1329
E-mail: fellowships@sshrc-crsh.gc.ca
Web Site: www.sshrc-crsh.gc.ca

FOUNDED: 1977

AREAS OF INTEREST:

The development and support of research, research training, and scholarly activities in the social sciences and humanities.

NAME(S) OF PROGRAMS:

- **SSHRC Postdoctoral Fellowships**

TYPE:

Fellowships. For Canadian citizens or permanent residents of Canada, to support postdoctoral research in the humanities and social sciences.

YEAR PROGRAM STARTED: 1977

PURPOSE:

To support promising new scholars in the social sciences and humanities and to assist them in establishing a research base at an important time in their research careers.

LEGAL BASIS:

Government agency.

ELIGIBILITY:

Competition is open to persons who have been awarded an earned Doctorate within the two years preceding competition closing date (or up to five years if the applicant's career was interrupted or delayed for the purpose of maternity, childrearing, illness or health-related family responsibilities). Applicants must demonstrate that all doctoral requirements will be completed before the proposed starting date of tenure. Awards are for postdoctoral study or research within a university or research institution.

Applicants must be Canadian citizens or permanent residents of Canada at the time of application.

Contact the Council for complete details.

FINANCIAL DATA:

Amount of support per award: $40,500 (CAN) per year for up to two years.

Total amount of support: Up to $81,000 (CAN).

NO. MOST RECENT APPLICANTS: 877 for the year 2011-12.

NO. AWARDS: 175 for the year 2011-2012.

APPLICATION INFO:

Fellowships are tenable only at universities or other recognized research institutions in Canada or abroad. Applicants must present a significant and feasible program of postdoctoral research. Fellowships may not be used to obtain a degree. Fellows may be allowed to assume limited teaching duties, equivalent to one course per year. Detailed program and application information is available online.

Duration: Period of tenure is from 12 up to 24 months.

Deadline: Usually in mid-September. Announcement in February.

OFFICERS AND STAFF:

Ted Hewitt, President
Dr. Brent Herbert-Copley, Executive Vice President
Gordana Krcevinac, Director, Research Training

ADDRESS INQUIRIES TO:

Research Training Portfolio
(See address or e-mail above.)

SOCIAL SCIENCES AND HUMANITIES RESEARCH COUNCIL OF CANADA [1817]

350 Albert Street
Ottawa ON K1P 6G4 Canada
(613) 943-7777
Fax: (613) 943-1329
E-mail: vanier@cihr-irsc.gc.ca
fellowships@sshrc-crsh.gc.ca
Web Site: www.vanier.gc.ca
www.sshrc-crsh.gc.ca

FOUNDED: 2008

AREAS OF INTEREST:

The development and support of research and research training in the social sciences and humanities.

NAME(S) OF PROGRAMS:

- **Vanier Canada Graduate Scholarships (CGS)**

TYPE:

Awards/prizes; Fellowships; Scholarships. For full-time doctoral students in the humanities and social sciences.

YEAR PROGRAM STARTED: 2008

PURPOSE:
To attract and retain world-class doctoral students by supporting students who demonstrate both leadership skills and a high standard of scholarly achievement in graduate studies in social sciences and humanities, natural sciences and engineering, and health.

LEGAL BASIS:
Government agency.

ELIGIBILITY:
Applicants can be citizens or permanent residents of Canada, as well as international students.

GEOG. RESTRICTIONS: Canada.

FINANCIAL DATA:
Amount of support per award: $50,000 (CAN) per year.

Total amount of support: Varies.

NO. MOST RECENT APPLICANTS: 206 for the year 2011-2012.

NO. AWARDS: Up to 167 annually.

APPLICATION INFO:
On university campuses, information may be obtained from the Dean or Faculty of Graduate Studies, the Office of Research Administration, the Registrar, or the Student Awards Office. Inquiries may also be addressed directly to the Research Training Portfolio of the Council at the address above.

Duration: Three years. Nonrenewable.

Deadline: Nomination deadline is set by the university. SSHRC's deadline for nominations submitted by the universities is usually early November.

OFFICERS AND STAFF:
Ted Hewitt, President
Dr. Brent Herbert-Copley, Executive Vice President
Gordana Krcevinac, Director, Research Training

ADDRESS INQUIRIES TO:
E-mail: vanier@cihr-irsc.gc.ca

SOCIAL SCIENCES AND HUMANITIES RESEARCH COUNCIL OF CANADA [1818]

350 Albert Street
Ottawa ON K1P 6G4 Canada
(613) 943-7777
Fax: (613) 943-1329
E-mail: fellowships@sshrc-crsh.gc.ca
Web Site: www.sshrc-crsh.gc.ca

FOUNDED: 2010

AREAS OF INTEREST:
The development and support of research, research training and scholarly activities in the social sciences and humanities.

NAME(S) OF PROGRAMS:
- **Banting Postdoctoral Fellowships**

TYPE:
Fellowships. For Canadian citizens, permanent residents of Canada and foreign citizens to support postdoctoral research in the humanities and social sciences.

YEAR PROGRAM STARTED: 2010

PURPOSE:
To support promising new scholars in the social sciences and humanities and to assist them in establishing a research base at an important time in their research careers.

LEGAL BASIS:
Government agency.

ELIGIBILITY:
Competition is open to persons who have been awarded an earned Doctorate within the three years preceding competition and applicants can be citizens or permanent residents of Canada, as well as international students.

Without exception, the Banting Postdoctoral Fellowships:
(1) are tenable only at the institution which supported the original application for the program;
(2) must be taken up no earlier than April 1 and no later than October 1 of the year following the application deadline and;
(3) are for two years from the date of up-take.

FINANCIAL DATA:
Amount of support per award: $70,000 (CAN) per year for two years.

NO. MOST RECENT APPLICANTS: 105 for the year 2011-12.

NO. AWARDS: 23.

APPLICATION INFO:
On university campuses, information may be obtained from the Dean or Faculty of Graduate Studies, the Office of Research Administration, the Registrar, or the Student Awards Office.

Duration: Period of tenure is 24 months. Nonrenewable.

Deadline: Usually mid-September. Announcement usually at end of January.

OFFICERS AND STAFF:
Ted Hewitt, President
Dr. Brent Herbert-Copley, Executive Vice President
Gordana Krcevinac, Director, Research Training

ADDRESS INQUIRIES TO:
Research Training Portfolio
(See address above.)

SOCIAL SCIENCES AND HUMANITIES RESEARCH COUNCIL OF CANADA [1819]

350 Albert Street
Ottawa ON K1P 6G4 Canada
(613) 943-7777
Fax: (613) 943-1329
E-mail: fellowships@sshrc-crsh.gc.ca
Web Site: www.sshrc-crsh.gc.ca

FOUNDED: 1977

AREAS OF INTEREST:
The development and support of research and research training in the social sciences and humanities.

NAME(S) OF PROGRAMS:
- **Joseph-Armand Bombardier Canada Graduate Scholarships Program - Master's Scholarships**
- **Master's Awards**

TYPE:
Awards/prizes; Fellowships; Scholarships.

YEAR PROGRAM STARTED: 2003

PURPOSE:
To develop research skills and assist in the training of highly qualified personnel by supporting students who demonstrate a high standard of scholarly achievement in undergraduate and graduate studies in the social sciences and humanities.

LEGAL BASIS:
Government agency.

ELIGIBILITY:
Applicants must be Canadian citizens or permanent residents of Canada.
Joseph-Armand Bombardier Canada Graduate Scholarships-Master's Scholarships are tenable only at Canadian universities.

FINANCIAL DATA:
Amount of support per award:
Joseph-Armand Bombardier Canada Graduate Scholarships - Master's Scholarships: $17,500 (CAN).

NO. MOST RECENT APPLICANTS: 1,494 applicants from Canadian universities for the year 2011-12.

NO. AWARDS: 1,300 Joseph-Armand Bombardier Canada Graduate Scholarships - Master's Scholarships.

APPLICATION INFO:
On university campuses, information may be obtained from the Dean or Faculty of Graduate Studies, the Office of Research Administration, the Registrar, or the Student Awards Office. Inquiries may also be addressed directly to the Research Training Portfolio of the Council at the address above. Detailed program and application information is available online.

Duration: One year. Nonrenewable.

Deadline: For applicants registered at a Canadian university, in the fall on the date set by the university; for other applicants, usually December 1.

OFFICERS AND STAFF:
Ted Hewitt, President
Dr. Brent Herbert-Copley, Executive Vice President
Jean Francois Fortin, Director, Research Training

ADDRESS INQUIRIES TO:
Research Training Portfolio
(See address above.)

THE SOCIETY FOR THE PSYCHOLOGICAL STUDY OF SOCIAL ISSUES (SPSSI) [1820]

208 I Street, N.E.
Washington, DC 20002-4340
(202) 675-6956
(877) 310-7778
Fax: (202) 675-6902
E-mail: awards@spssi.org
Web Site: www.spssi.org

FOUNDED: 1936

AREAS OF INTEREST:
Social issues and psychology.

NAME(S) OF PROGRAMS:
- **Awards for Outstanding Teaching and Mentoring**

TYPE:
Awards/prizes. SPSSI confers one or two annual awards for outstanding teaching and mentoring in areas related to the psychological study of social issues. The award recognizes teaching excellence in a variety of contexts.

PURPOSE:
To recognize outstanding teaching in areas related to the psychological study of social issues.

LEGAL BASIS:
Independently incorporated society.

ELIGIBILITY:
Nominees should be SPSSI members who have made substantial contributions to students in the psychological study of social issues. To be eligible, individuals must have been teaching and/or mentoring students for at least five years full-time since the doctoral degree. Nominees may teach at graduate degree-granting institutions, Bachelor's degree universities and colleges, or two-year and community colleges. Self-nominations are encouraged.

FINANCIAL DATA:
Amount of support per award: $1,000 plus a plaque.

NO. AWARDS: 1 or 2 annually.

APPLICATION INFO:
Application information is available on the web site.

Deadline: March 15.

PUBLICATIONS:
Application guidelines.

ADDRESS INQUIRIES TO:
Anila Balkissoon
Program Director
E-mail: abalkissoon@spssi.org

THE SOCIETY FOR THE PSYCHOLOGICAL STUDY OF SOCIAL ISSUES (SPSSI) [1821]

208 I Street, N.E.
Washington, DC 20002-4340
(202) 675-6956
(877) 310-7778
Fax: (202) 675-6902
E-mail: awards@spssi.org
Web Site: www.spssi.org

FOUNDED: 1936

AREAS OF INTEREST:
Social psychology research.

NAME(S) OF PROGRAMS:
- **Gordon Allport Intergroup Relations Prize**

TYPE:
Awards/prizes. The Gordon Allport Intergroup Relations Prize honors the memory of the late Dr. Gordon W. Allport, a founder and past president of SPSSI.

LEGAL BASIS:
Independently incorporated society.

ELIGIBILITY:
Entries must be papers published during the calendar year preceding the year of submission. For the Award, submissions are limited to articles, chapters or other works published in their primary form (e.g., appearing in print for print journals or books or online for online-only journals or other volumes) with a formal publication date of the prior year. An individual or group may only submit one paper to SPSSI awards (including the Allport, Klineberg and Dissertation Awards) per award year (January 1 to December 31).

The award is given to "the best paper or article of the year on intergroup relations." Originality of the contribution, whether theoretical or empirical, will be given special weight. The research area of intergroup relations includes such dimensions as age, gender, and socioeconomic status, as well as ethnicity.

FINANCIAL DATA:
Amount of support per award: $1,000.

CO-OP FUNDING PROGRAMS: The Award is sponsored by The Gordon W. Allport Memorial Fund of Harvard University and SPSSI.

APPLICATION INFO:
Online submissions are the preferred method. Limit the number and size of files uploaded when applying online.

For hard-copy submissions, send five copies to SPSSI.

Duration: Annual award.

Deadline: Applications must be received by June 15.

ADDRESS INQUIRIES TO:
Anila Balkissoon
Program Director
E-mail: abalkissoon@spssi.org

THE SOCIETY FOR THE PSYCHOLOGICAL STUDY OF SOCIAL ISSUES (SPSSI) [1822]

208 I Street, N.E.
Washington, DC 20002-4340
(202) 675-6956
(877) 310-7778
Fax: (202) 675-6902
E-mail: awards@spssi.org
Web Site: www.spssi.org

FOUNDED: 1936

AREAS OF INTEREST:
Social psychology research.

NAME(S) OF PROGRAMS:
- **Innovative Teaching Award**

TYPE:
Awards/prizes. SPSSI confers an annual award for innovative teaching in areas related to the psychological study of social issues. This award recognizes effective courses, assignments or classroom activities addressing social issues.

ELIGIBILITY:
Nominees should be SPSSI members who have developed innovative pedagogical products that aid in teaching the psychological study of social issues. Nominees may teach at graduate degree-granting institutions, Bachelor's-degree universities and colleges, two-year and community colleges, or as contingent or adjunct faculty.

FINANCIAL DATA:
Recipients will be recognized in the Teaching and Learning column in the SPSSI *Forward* newsletter. Honorable Mention awardees will receive one year of free SPSSI membership.

Amount of support per award: $1,000 and a plaque.

APPLICATION INFO:
Application instructions are available on the web site.

Deadline: March 15 for receipt of materials.

ADDRESS INQUIRIES TO:
Anila Balkissoon
Program Director
E-mail: abalkissoon@spssi.org

THE SOCIETY FOR THE PSYCHOLOGICAL STUDY OF SOCIAL ISSUES (SPSSI) [1823]

208 I Street, N.E.
Washington, DC 20002-4340
(202) 675-6956
(877) 310-7778
Fax: (202) 675-6902
E-mail: awards@spssi.org
Web Site: www.spssi.org

FOUNDED: 1936

AREAS OF INTEREST:
Social psychology research.

NAME(S) OF PROGRAMS:
- **SPSSI Grants-in-Aid**

TYPE:
Grants-in-aid.

YEAR PROGRAM STARTED: 1956

PURPOSE:
To support scientific research in social problem areas related to the basic interests and goals of SPSSI and particularly those that are not likely to receive support from traditional sources.

LEGAL BASIS:
Independently incorporated society.

ELIGIBILITY:
The applicant must be a member of SPSSI. Applicants may submit only one application per deadline. If an applicant has applied to the Clara Mayo Grant in the same award year (July 1 to June 30), he or she is not eligible to apply for Grants-in-Aid. Individuals may submit a joint application.

The SPSSI Committee on Grants-in-Aid especially encourages proposals involving:
(1) unique and timely research opportunities;
(2) underrepresented institutions, graduate students and junior scholars;
(3) volunteer research teams and;
(4) actual, not pilot, projects.

SPSSI's Grants-in-Aid program will include grants earmarked especially in support of research related to SPSSI's current policy priorities: interpersonal violence, marriage equality, and immigration reform. Proposals within these priorities will receive special consideration, though submissions are not limited to these areas of focus.

FINANCIAL DATA:
Funds are normally not provided for travel to conventions, travel or living expenses while conducting research, stipends of principal investigators, costs associated with manuscript preparation, or the indirect costs of institutions.

Amount of support per award: Usually, up to $2,000 for postdoctoral work and up to $1,000 for predoctoral work.

Total amount of support: Varies.

Matching fund requirements: Applicant is required to submit evidence of a request to match amount offered.

NO. MOST RECENT APPLICANTS: 35.

NO. AWARDS: 20.

APPLICATION INFO:
Application information is available on the web site.

Duration: One year.

Deadline: Spring round May 15, with announcement by July 20. Fall round October 15, with announcement by December 5.

PUBLICATIONS:
Application guidelines.

ADDRESS INQUIRIES TO:
Anila Balkissoon
Program Director
E-mail: abalkissoon@spssi.org

THE SOCIETY FOR THE PSYCHOLOGICAL STUDY OF SOCIAL ISSUES (SPSSI) [1824]

208 I Street, N.E.
Washington, DC 20002-4340
(202) 675-6956
(877) 310-7778
Fax: (202) 675-6902
E-mail: awards@spssi.org
Web Site: www.spssi.org

FOUNDED: 1936

AREAS OF INTEREST:
Intergroup relations, social issues and psychology.

NAME(S) OF PROGRAMS:
- **The Applied Social Issues Internship Program**

TYPE:
Internships.

PURPOSE:
To encourage research that is conducted in cooperation with a community or government organization, public interest group or other not-for-profit entity that will benefit directly from the project.

LEGAL BASIS:
Independently incorporated society.

ELIGIBILITY:
College seniors, graduate students and first-year postdoctorates in psychology, applied social science, and related disciplines are eligible. Applicant must be an SPSSI member.

FINANCIAL DATA:
Amount of support per award: $300 to $2,500 to cover research costs, community organizing and, in unusual cases, a stipend for the intern.

CO-OP FUNDING PROGRAMS: Cost sharing by sponsoring department or organization is desirable.

NO. MOST RECENT APPLICANTS: 20.

APPLICATION INFO:
Application information may be obtained from the web site.

Deadline: April 15. Announcement by June 1.

ADDRESS INQUIRIES TO:
Anila Balkissoon
Program Director
E-mail: abalkissoon@spssi.org

THE SOCIETY FOR THE PSYCHOLOGICAL STUDY OF SOCIAL ISSUES (SPSSI) [1825]

208 I Street, N.E.
Washington, DC 20002-4340
(202) 675-6956
(877) 310-7778
Fax: (202) 675-6902
E-mail: awards@spssi.org
Web Site: www.spssi.org

FOUNDED: 1936

AREAS OF INTEREST:
Intergroup relations, social issues and psychology.

NAME(S) OF PROGRAMS:
- **Clara Mayo Grants**

TYPE:
Research grants. Supports Master's theses and predissertation research on sexism, racism or prejudice, with preference given to students enrolled in a terminal Master's program.

PURPOSE:
To support Master's theses or predissertation research on aspects of sexism, racism or prejudice, with preference given to students enrolled in a terminal Master's program. Studies of the application of theory or the design of interventions or treatments to address these problems are welcome.

LEGAL BASIS:
Independently incorporated society.

ELIGIBILITY:
Individuals who are SPSSI members and who have matriculated in graduate programs in psychology, applied social science and related disciplines are eligible to apply. Self-nominations are encouraged. A student who is applying for the Grants-In-Aid program may not apply for the Clara Mayo award in the same award year. Applicants may submit only one Mayo application per calendar year.

Studies of the application of theory or the design of interventions or treatments to address these problems are welcome. Proposals that include a college or university agreement to match the amount requested will be favored, but proposals without matching funds will also be considered.

FINANCIAL DATA:
Amount of support per award: $1,000 maximum.

NO. MOST RECENT APPLICANTS: Approximately 20 per cycle.

NO. AWARDS: Up to 6 each cycle (12 per year).

APPLICATION INFO:
Application information is available on the web site.

Duration: One to two years.

Deadline: Spring round May 15, with announcement by July 15. Fall round October 10, with announcement by December 10.

ADDRESS INQUIRIES TO:
Anila Balkissoon
Program Director
E-mail: abalkissoon@spssi.org

THE SOCIETY FOR THE PSYCHOLOGICAL STUDY OF SOCIAL ISSUES (SPSSI) [1826]

208 I Street, N.E.
Washington, DC 20002-4340
(202) 675-6956
(877) 310-7778
Fax: (202) 675-6902
E-mail: awards@spssi.org
Web Site: www.spssi.org

FOUNDED: 1936

AREAS OF INTEREST:
Intergroup relations, social issues and psychology.

NAME(S) OF PROGRAMS:
- **The SAGES Program**

TYPE:
Research grants. Program to encourage retired members to apply their knowledge to helping solve social problems or to assist policymakers to solve social problems. Proposals are invited that use social science research findings to address social problems through direct action projects, consulting with not-for-profit groups, or through preparing reviews of existing social science literature that could be used by policymakers.

LEGAL BASIS:
Independently incorporated society.

ELIGIBILITY:
Applicants must be retired SPSSI members. Members nearing retirement may be considered. Proposals will be evaluated in terms of how well they build on existing social science research and theory, the feasibility of the project, and the importance of the project.

FINANCIAL DATA:
Funding can be submitted for direct costs related to the project. This can be spent over a two-year period. Money can be used for hiring staff (including clerical assistance), computing fees, travel, telephone, or other justifiable expenses. Funding cannot be used as a stipend for the applicant.

Amount of support per award: $1,000 to $10,000.

NO. MOST RECENT APPLICANTS: 5.

NO. AWARDS: 2 to 3 annually.

APPLICATION INFO:
Application information may be obtained from the web site.

Duration: Up to two years.

Deadline: April 15. Announcement by June 15.

ADDRESS INQUIRIES TO:
Anila Balkissoon
Program Director
E-mail: abalkissoon@spssi.org

THE SOCIETY FOR THE PSYCHOLOGICAL STUDY OF SOCIAL ISSUES (SPSSI) [1827]

208 I Street, N.E.
Washington, DC 20002-4340
(202) 675-6956
(877) 310-7778
Fax: (202) 675-6902
E-mail: awards@spssi.org
Web Site: www.spssi.org

FOUNDED: 1936

AREAS OF INTEREST:
Intergroup relations, social issues and psychology.

NAME(S) OF PROGRAMS:
- **The Louise Kidder Early Career Award**

TYPE:
Awards/prizes. This award is named in honor of Louise Kidder for her early career accomplishments and contributions to SPSSI.

PURPOSE:
To recognize social issues researchers who have made substantial contributions to the field early in their careers.

LEGAL BASIS:
Independently incorporated society.

ELIGIBILITY:
Nominees should be investigators who have made substantial contributions to social issues research within 10 years of receiving a graduate degree and who have demonstrated the potential to continue such contributions. Nominees need not be current Society members. Applicants must be scholars who are within 10 years of obtaining their doctoral degree.

FINANCIAL DATA:
Amount of support per award: $500 and plaque.

NO. MOST RECENT APPLICANTS: 10.

NO. AWARDS: 1.

APPLICATION INFO:
Application information may be obtained from the web site.

Deadline: June 1. Decisions announced by August 1.

ADDRESS INQUIRIES TO:
Anila Balkissoon
Program Director
E-mail: abalkissoon@spssi.org

THE SOCIETY FOR THE PSYCHOLOGICAL STUDY OF SOCIAL ISSUES (SPSSI) [1828]

208 I Street, N.E.
Washington, DC 20002-4340
(202) 675-6956
(877) 310-7778
Fax: (202) 675-6902
E-mail: awards@spssi.org
Web Site: www.spssi.org

FOUNDED: 1936

AREAS OF INTEREST:
Intergroup relations, social issues and psychology.

NAME(S) OF PROGRAMS:

- **The Social Issues Dissertation Award**

TYPE:
Awards/prizes. The Social Issues Dissertation Award is given for the best psychological dissertation concerned with social issues. It is judged upon scientific excellence and potential application to social problems.

PURPOSE:
To award dissertations that best demonstrate scientific excellence and potential application to social problems.

LEGAL BASIS:
Independently incorporated society.

ELIGIBILITY:
Any doctoral dissertation in psychology (or in a social science with psychological subject matter) accepted between March 1 of the previous year and up to the deadline of the current year is eligible. Applicants must have successfully defended their dissertation prior to the current year's award deadline. An individual or group may only submit one paper to one SPSSI award (including the Allport, Klineberg and Dissertation Awards) per award year. Applicants may not submit to the Dissertation Prize more than one time.

FINANCIAL DATA:
Amount of support per award: First prize $1,000; Second prize $500.

APPLICATION INFO:
Online applications are the preferred method. Limit the number and size of files uploaded when applying online. For hard-copy submissions, mail the complete application to SPSSI, at the address above; Attn: Social Issues Dissertation.

The application should include a 500-word summary of the dissertation. The summary should include title, rationale, methods, and results of dissertation, as well as its implications for social problems. Please also include a cover sheet that states the title of one's dissertation, applicant's name, postal and e-mail addresses, phone number and university granting the degree.

Deadline: May 1. Announcement of finalist status by July 1.

PUBLICATIONS:
Application guidelines.

ADDRESS INQUIRIES TO:
Anila Balkissoon
Program Director
E-mail: abalkissoon@spssi.org

STIFTELSEN RIKSBANKENS JUBILEUMSFOND

Kungstradgardsg. 18
SE-114 86 Stockholm Sweden
(46) 08-50 62 64 00
Fax: (46) 08-50 62 64 31
E-mail: rj@rj.se
Web Site: www.rj.se

TYPE:
Conferences/seminars; Research grants.

See entry 389 for full listing.

U.S. ARMY RESEARCH INSTITUTE FOR BEHAVIORAL AND SOCIAL SCIENCES [1829]

Building 1464
6000 6th Street
Ft. Belvoir, VA 22060-5586
(703) 545-2410
E-mail: gerald.f.goodwin.civ@mail.mil

FOUNDED: 1940

AREAS OF INTEREST:
Leadership, interactive training and simulation, individual performance and information comprehension, and social structures affecting army performance.

TYPE:
Fellowships; Research grants; Visiting scholars; Work-study programs.

PURPOSE:
To contribute to the cumulative knowledge base in behavioral science, with an eye to building new technologies capable of improving the effectiveness of Army personnel and their units.

LEGAL BASIS:
Government agency.

ELIGIBILITY:
Both single-investigator and collaborative research efforts will be considered, and multidisciplinary approaches to a central problem are encouraged. Collaborative efforts may involve researchers at a single institution or in cooperating institutions and joint university/industry partnerships are welcomed. Interest is welcomed from the widest range of institutions, including historically Black colleges and universities and minority institutions.

No consideration will be given to applied research or investigations whose primary focus is on physiological or chemical mechanisms or psychopathology. Another consideration determining support for the research is the judgment that findings have the potential for feeding into development of new behavioral technologies capable of improving the effectiveness of Army personnel and their units.

FINANCIAL DATA:
Amount of support per award: Grant amounts vary according to funds available and Army requirements. Generally $100,000 to $800,000. Average $300,000 per year.

Total amount of support: $5,300,000 for the year 2015.

APPLICATION INFO:
Interested individuals should seek ARI's Broad Agency Announcement, issued annually between January and June. Preliminary concept papers (three to five pages) as well as formal proposals may be submitted. Concept papers should describe the problem to be addressed, justify the effort's theoretical significance and uniqueness, briefly describe the approach to the problem and state potential benefits to the Army. An estimated budget and project duration should be included, along with brief vitae of the principal investigators.

Concept papers will be reviewed within ARI for their relevance to Army priorities, theoretical significance and technical merit. Offers of highly rated concept papers will be invited to submit formal proposals.

Duration: Maximum five years. Average three years.

Deadline: Varies.

PUBLICATIONS:
Program announcement.

STAFF:
Dr. Jay Goodwin, Ph.D., Chief of Foundational Science Research Unit

ADDRESS INQUIRIES TO:
Dr. Jay Goodwin, Ph.D.
Chief of Foundational Science Research Unit
(See address above.)

U.S. DEPARTMENT OF JUSTICE

Office of Juvenile Justice and Delinquency Prevention
810 Seventh Street, N.W., 5th Floor
Washington, DC 20531
(202) 307-5911
Fax: (202) 307-2093
E-mail: nicki.polk@usdoj.gov
Web Site: www.ojjdp.gov

TYPE:
Conferences/seminars; Development grants; Fellowships; Internships; Project/program grants; Research grants; Residencies; Visiting scholars; Research contracts. Grants to conduct research, evaluation and development on juvenile justice and delinquency prevention activities, including the development of new or improved approaches, techniques, systems and program models to conduct behavioral research on the causes of juvenile crime, means of, intervention and prevention, and to evaluate juvenile programs and procedures.

See entry 1375 for full listing.

WOODROW WILSON INTERNATIONAL CENTER FOR SCHOLARS
One Woodrow Wilson Plaza
1300 Pennsylvania Avenue, N.W.
Washington, DC 20004-3027
(202) 691-4170
Fax: (202) 691-4001
E-mail: fellowships@wilsoncenter.org
Web Site: www.wilsoncenter.org

TYPE:
Fellowships; Research grants; Residencies; Scholarships; Visiting scholars. The Center seeks to commemorate, through its residential fellowship program of advanced research, both the scholarly depth and the public concerns of Woodrow Wilson. The Center welcomes outstanding project proposals in the social sciences and humanities on global issues - topics that intersect with questions of public policy or provide the historical framework to illume policy issues of contemporary importance. The Center especially welcomes projects likely to foster communication between the world of ideas and the world of public affairs.

Projects should have relevance to the world of public policy. Fellows should be prepared to interact with policymakers in Washington and with the Center's staff working on similar areas.

Fellowships are tenable in residence only at the Woodrow Wilson International Center for Scholars. The Center will not provide support for research to be carried out elsewhere. Fellows devote their full time to research and writing.

See entry 393 for full listing.

CARTER G. WOODSON INSTITUTE FOR AFRICAN-AMERICAN AND AFRICAN STUDIES
University of Virginia
McCormick Road, 108 Minor Hall
Charlottesville, VA 22903
(434) 924-3109
Fax: (434) 924-8820
E-mail: woodson@virginia.edu
Web Site: woodson.virginia.edu

TYPE:
Fellowships. The Woodson Institute offers residential fellowships to predoctoral and postdoctoral scholars. These fellowships are designed to facilitate the completion of works in progress by providing scholars with unencumbered leave.

Afro-American and African Studies is considered to cover Africa, Africans and peoples of African descent in North, Central and South America and the Caribbean, past and present.

See entry 395 for full listing.

Business and economics

THE ACTUARIAL FOUNDATION
475 North Martingale Road
Suite 600
Schaumburg, IL 60173-2226
(847) 706-3535
Fax: (847) 706-3599
E-mail: Scholarships@ActFnd.org
Web Site: www.actuarialfoundation.org

TYPE:
Scholarships.

See entry 2027 for full listing.

AMERICAN INSTITUTE OF CERTIFIED PUBLIC ACCOUNTANTS (AICPA) [1830]
220 Leigh Farm Road
Durham, NC 27707
(919) 402-2161
Fax: (919) 419-4705
E-mail: scholarships@aicpa.org
Web Site: www.thiswaytocpa.com

AREAS OF INTEREST:
Accounting.

NAME(S) OF PROGRAMS:
- **John L. Carey Scholarship**

TYPE:
Scholarships.

YEAR PROGRAM STARTED: 2013

PURPOSE:
To provide financial assistance to liberal arts or other nonbusiness-related degree holders pursuing graduate studies in accounting and the C.P.A. designation; to encourage students with little or no previous accounting education to consider professional accounting careers.

ELIGIBILITY:
An applicant must meet the following requirements:
(1) have obtained a liberal arts or other nonbusiness undergraduate degree from a regionally accredited institution in the U.S. prior to enrolling in a graduate accounting program;
(2) have not earned more than 12 credits in accounting or business during his or her undergraduate program;
(3) planning to pursue the C.P.A. licensure but not presently be a C.P.A.;
(4) planning to pursue a graduate-level degree in an "accounting-related" major ("accounting-related" shall be as determined by Sponsor in Sponsor's sole discretion); this program will enable a student to sit for the C.P.A. exam;
(5) applied to or been accepted into a public or private, 501(c) four-year college or university located in the U.S. or its territories; the business program must be accredited by the AACSB and/or ACBSP;
(6) not actively participating in a graduate accounting program;
(7) enrolled as a full-time graduate-level student (nine semester-hours or equivalent) for the 2015-16 academic year; an exception may be granted if one plans to participate in an internship program;
(8) be an AICPA student affiliate member (or have submitted a new member application) by the beginning of the 2015-16 academic year; those interested can apply on the web site at no cost;
(9) be a U.S. citizen or permanent resident (green card holder) and;
(10) have some financial need (i.e., not already be receiving a full or partial scholarship(s) that covers or exceeds one's educational expenses).
Note: AICPA staff and their family members are not eligible to receive this scholarship.

GEOG. RESTRICTIONS: United States and its territories.

FINANCIAL DATA:
Amount of support per award: $5,000.
Total amount of support: Up to $25,000 annually.

NO. AWARDS: Up to 5.

APPLICATION INFO:
Guidelines are available on the web site.
Duration: One year. Nonrenewable.
Deadline: April 1.

ADDRESS INQUIRIES TO:
See e-mail address above.

*SPECIAL STIPULATIONS:
Students selected to receive an AICPA scholarship must participate in the AICPA Legacy Scholars program, which includes performing at least eight hours of community service per semester to advocate for the C.P.A. profession. Through their community service efforts, AICPA Legacy Scholars enhance their leadership and communication skills by building relationships with both aspiring and seasoned C.P.As.

AMERICAN INSTITUTE OF CERTIFIED PUBLIC ACCOUNTANTS (AICPA) [1831]
220 Leigh Farm Road
Durham, NC 27707
(919) 402-2161
Fax: (919) 419-4705
E-mail: scholarships@aicpa.org
Web Site: www.thiswaytocpa.com

AREAS OF INTEREST:
Accounting, finance and information systems.

NAME(S) OF PROGRAMS:
- **AICPA Accountemps Student Scholarship**

TYPE:
Scholarships. Awarded to accounting majors to encourage them to become a C.P.A.

PURPOSE:
To provide financial assistance to students who are currently majoring in accounting, finance or information systems; to encourage students to consider careers in accounting and business.

ELIGIBILITY:
An applicant must meet the following requirements:
(1) pursuing an undergraduate- or graduate-level degree in an "accounting-related" major ("accounting-related" shall be as determined by Sponsors in Sponsors' sole discretion);
(2) planning to pursue the C.P.A. licensure but not presently be a C.P.A.;
(3) applied to or been accepted into a public or private, 501(c) four-year college or university located in the U.S. or its territories; the business program must be accredited by the AACSB and/or ACBSP;
(4) completed at least 30 semester-hours (or equivalent) of college coursework, including at least six semester-hours (or equivalent) in accounting, by end of spring 2015;

(5) maintained an overall and major grade point average of at least 3.0 (on a 4.0 scale);
(6) enrolled as a full-time undergraduate (12 semester-hours or equivalent) or a full-time graduate-level student (nine semester-hours or equivalent) for the 2015-16 academic year; an exception may be made if one plans to participate in an internship program;
(7) be an AICPA student affiliate member (or have submitted a new member application); those interested can apply on the web site at no cost;
(8) be a U.S. citizen or permanent resident (green card holder) and;
(9) have some financial need (i.e., not receiving a full or partial scholarship(s) and/or grant(s) that cover and/or exceed one's educational expenses).
Note: AICPA and RHI/Accountemps staff and their family members are not eligible to receive this scholarship.

GEOG. RESTRICTIONS: United States and its territories.

FINANCIAL DATA:
Amount of support per award: $10,000.

NO. AWARDS: 4.

APPLICATION INFO:
Guidelines are available on the web site.
Duration: One year. Nonrenewable.
Deadline: April 1.

ADDRESS INQUIRIES TO:
See e-mail address above.

*SPECIAL STIPULATIONS:
Students selected to receive an AICPA scholarship must participate in the AICPA Legacy Scholars program, which includes performing at least eight hours of community service per semester to advocate for the C.P.A. profession. Through their community service efforts, AICPA Legacy Scholars enhance their leadership and communication skills by building relationships with both aspiring and seasoned C.P.As.

AMERICAN INSTITUTE OF CERTIFIED PUBLIC ACCOUNTANTS (AICPA) [1832]

220 Leigh Farm Road
Durham, NC 27707
(919) 402-2161
Fax: (919) 402-4705
E-mail: scholarships@aicpa.org
Web Site: www.thiswaytocpa.com

AREAS OF INTEREST:
Accounting, finance and information systems.

NAME(S) OF PROGRAMS:
- **AICPA Foundation Two-Year Transfer Scholarship**

TYPE:
Scholarships. AICPA Foundation Two-Year Transfer Scholarship provides financial assistance to students who have earned an Associate's degree in business, accounting, finance or economics with a declared intent to major in accounting at a four-year college or university.

PURPOSE:
To provide financial assistance to students who are currently majoring in accounting, finance or information systems; to encourage students to consider careers in accounting and business.

ELIGIBILITY:
An eligible applicant must be/have:
(1) earned an Associate's degree in business, accounting, finance or economics with a declared intent to major in accounting or an "accounting-related field" at a four-year college or university ("accounting-related" shall be as determined by Sponsors in Sponsors' sole discretion);
(2) planning to pursue the C.P.A. licensure but not presently be a C.P.A.;
(3) proof of acceptance into a public or private, not-for-profit 501(c) four-year college or university located in the U.S. states or territories for the full upcoming academic year; the business program must be accredited by the AACSB and/or ACBSP; (exception may be granted, but not guaranteed, at the discretion of Sponsor; inquire at the e-mail address above if one is unsure of one's eligibility);
(4) maintained an overall and major grade point average of at least 3.0 (on a 4.0 scale);
(5) enrolled as a full-time undergraduate (12 semester hours or equivalent); an exception may be made if one plans to participate in an internship program;
(6) an AICPA student affiliate member (or have submitted a new member application); one can apply online at no cost at the web site above;
(7) a U.S. citizen or permanent resident (green card holder) and;
(8) some financial need (i.e., not receiving a full or partial scholarship(s) and/or grant(s) that cover and/or exceed one's educational expenses).
Note: AICPA staff and their family members are not eligible to receive this scholarship.

FINANCIAL DATA:
Scholarship aid may be used only for the payment of expenses that directly relate to obtaining an accounting education (e.g., tuition, fees, room and board and/or books and materials only). Scholarship payments are sent directly to the student's financial aid office on behalf of the student.
Amount of support per award: $3,000.

NO. AWARDS: 15.

APPLICATION INFO:
Guidelines are available on the web site.
Duration: One academic year. Awards are nonrenewable, and past recipients may not reapply.
Deadline: April 1.

ADDRESS INQUIRIES TO:
See e-mail address above.

*SPECIAL STIPULATIONS:
Students selected to receive an AICPA scholarship must participate in the AICPA Legacy Scholars program, which includes performing at least eight hours of community service per semester to advocate for the C.P.A. profession. Through their community service efforts, AICPA Legacy Scholars enhance their leadership and communication skills by building relationships with both aspiring and seasoned C.P.As.

APICS SUPPLY CHAIN COUNCIL

8430 West Bryn Mawr Avenue
Suite 1000
Chicago, IL 60631-3439
(773) 867-1758
Fax: (773) 659-3058
E-mail: saspacher@apics.org
Web Site: www.apics.org/education/erfoundation

TYPE:
Awards/prizes; Conferences/seminars; Fellowships; Project/program grants; Research grants. Plossl Doctoral Dissertation Fellowship is in the area of operations management.

See entry 2515 for full listing.

APPRAISAL INSTITUTE EDUCATION TRUST [1833]

200 West Madison Street
Suite 1500
Chicago, IL 60606
(312) 335-4133
Fax: (312) 335-4134
E-mail: educationtrust@appraisalinstitute.org
Web Site: www.aiedtrust.org

NAME(S) OF PROGRAMS:
- **Appraisal Institute Education Trust Scholarship**

TYPE:
Scholarships. Graduate and undergraduate scholarships to help worthy and qualified students finance the cost of college work leading to a degree in the fields of real estate appraisal, land economics, real estate and allied fields.

PURPOSE:
To help finance the educational endeavors of individuals concentrating their studies in real estate appraisal, land economics, real estate or allied fields.

ELIGIBILITY:
Applicants must be citizens of the U.S., attending a full-time college, U.S. university or community college, and have the expressed intention of majoring in real estate evaluation and related subjects. Related subjects may include land economics, economics, economic geography, and others similarly related. Levels of education for the scholarship must be sophomore, junior, senior and graduate year of college.

Preference will be given to those applicants whose previous training and whose future course of study indicate that they intend to follow a field of endeavor which comes within the scope of the objectives of the Appraisal Institute. Applicants must also demonstrate qualities of leadership and scholarly attainments.

GEOG. RESTRICTIONS: United States.

FINANCIAL DATA:
Amount of support per award: Graduate: $2,000; Undergraduate: $1,000.

NO. AWARDS: Approximately 50 per year.

APPLICATION INFO:
Scholarship applications are available on the web site.
Duration: One academic year.
Deadline: April 15 for the following academic year.

OFFICERS:
Fred Grubbe, Chief Executive Officer

ADDRESS INQUIRIES TO:
Scholarship Committee
(See address above.)

THE CONSORTIUM FOR GRADUATE STUDY IN MANAGEMENT [1834]

229 Chesterfield Business Parkway
Chesterfield, MO 63005
(636) 681-5553
Fax: (636) 681-5499
Web Site: www.cgsm.org

FOUNDED: 1966

NAME(S) OF PROGRAMS:
- **Consortium Fellowship**
- **Fellowships for Under-Represented Minorities in Management**

TYPE:
Fellowships. Graduate fellowships for minority students interested in management careers in business.

YEAR PROGRAM STARTED: 1967

PURPOSE:
To hasten the entry of minorities into management positions in business.

LEGAL BASIS:
Not-for-profit, IRS 501(c)(3) status.

ELIGIBILITY:
U.S. citizenship and permanent residence in the U.S. is required. Applicant must present evidence of their commitment to the Consortium's mission of promoting the inclusion of African Americans, Hispanic Americans and Native Americans in American Business. The undergraduate degree need not be in business or economics.

Fellowships are awarded only by Consortium institutions, including University of California-Berkeley, Carnegie-Mellon University, Dartmouth College, Emory University, Indiana University (Bloomington), New York University, University of Michigan (Ann Arbor), University of North Carolina (Chapel Hill), University of Rochester, University of Southern California, University of Texas (Austin), University of Virginia, University of Wisconsin (Madison) and Washington University (St. Louis).

There are no fellowships awarded for part-time study.

FINANCIAL DATA:
The fellowship includes full tuition and required fees.

Total amount of support: $31,000,000 for fiscal year 2015.

NO. MOST RECENT APPLICANTS: 1,250.

NO. AWARDS: 425.

APPLICATION INFO:
Guidelines and application form are available on the web site.

Duration: Fellowships are awarded for a maximum of four semesters of full-time study.

Deadline: November 15 and January 5.

IRS I.D.: 43-0962198

STAFF:
Peter Aranda, Chief Executive Officer
Glenn Wilen, Vice President of Finance and Administration

DECA INC. [1835]

1908 Association Drive
Reston, VA 20191
(703) 860-5000
Fax: (703) 860-4013
E-mail: cindy_allen@deca.org
Web Site: www.deca.org

FOUNDED: 1946

AREAS OF INTEREST:
Marketing education, management and entrepreneurship.

TYPE:
Scholarships.

YEAR PROGRAM STARTED: 1962

PURPOSE:
To prepare emerging leaders and entrepreneurs in marketing, finance, hospitality and management in high schools and colleges around the globe.

LEGAL BASIS:
Nonprofit association.

ELIGIBILITY:
Applicant must be a current member of DECA.

GEOG. RESTRICTIONS: United States.

FINANCIAL DATA:
Amount of support per award: Varies.

Total amount of support: Over $300,000 in scholarships provided at the International Career Development Conference (ICDC) each year.

NO. MOST RECENT APPLICANTS: 6,660.

NO. AWARDS: 150.

APPLICATION INFO:
Information is available at the web site.

Duration: One year. Renewals are considered. Must reapply.

Deadline: January 15, 2017.

ADDRESS INQUIRIES TO:
Cindy Allen
Corporate and External Affairs Department
(See e-mail address above.)

ECONOMIC HISTORY ASSOCIATION [1836]

Department of Economics, University of Arizona
McClelland Hall, 401 GG
1130 East Helen Street
Tucson, AZ 85721
(520) 621-4421
Fax: (520) 621-8450
E-mail: fishback@email.arizona.edu
Web Site: www.eh.net/eha

FOUNDED: 1940

AREAS OF INTEREST:
Economic history.

NAME(S) OF PROGRAMS:
- **Arthur H. Cole Grants-in-Aid**

TYPE:
Grants-in-aid. Grants for advanced research in any aspect of economic history.

YEAR PROGRAM STARTED: 1972

PURPOSE:
To support individual research in the field of economic history.

LEGAL BASIS:
Nonprofit.

ELIGIBILITY:
Applicants must have completed their Ph.D. and must be members of the Economic History Association. Preference is given to recent Ph.D. recipients.

FINANCIAL DATA:
Amount of support per award: Up to $5,000.

Total amount of support: $15,000 to $20,000.

NO. MOST RECENT APPL

NO. AWARDS: 4.

APPLICATION INFO:
Application informati
Association web site.

Duration: One year.

Deadline: March 1.

PUBLICATIONS:
Annual newsletter; *The Journal of Economic History.*

IRS I.D.: 13-6128711

THE EDUCATIONAL FOUNDATION FOR WOMEN IN ACCOUNTING [1837]

136 South Keowee Street
Dayton, OH 45402-2241
(937) 424-3391
Fax: (937) 222-5794
E-mail: info@efwa.org
Web Site: www.efwa.org

FOUNDED: 1966

AREAS OF INTEREST:
Women in the accounting field.

NAME(S) OF PROGRAMS:
- **Laurels Fund**
- **Michelle L. McDonald Scholarship**
- **Moss Adams LLP Scholarship**
- **Seattle ASWA Chapter Scholarship**
- **Women in Need Scholarship**
- **Women in Transition Scholarship**

TYPE:
Scholarships. Laurels Fund provides a one-year academic scholarship for women pursuing a Ph.D. in accounting.

Women in Need Scholarship is available to women in their third, fourth or fifth year of academic pursuit who need the financial support to complete their degrees. It is renewable annually upon satisfactory completion of course requirements.

Women in Transition Scholarship is intended for women returning to school as freshmen to earn a Bachelor's degree in accounting. It is renewable annually upon satisfactory completion of course requirements.

YEAR PROGRAM STARTED: 1966

PURPOSE:
To support the advancement of women in the accounting profession through the funding of education, research, career literature, publications and other projects; to encourage and enable women to enter the accounting profession and empower them to achieve equal opportunities and equal rewards.

LEGAL BASIS:
501(c)(3) organization.

ELIGIBILITY:
Women who are pursuing accounting degrees at the undergraduate, graduate and postgraduate levels.

GEOG. RESTRICTIONS: United States.

FINANCIAL DATA:
Amount of support per award: Varies.

Total amount of support: Varies.

NO. AWARDS: Vary annually.

APPLICATION INFO:
Applications are available on the web site.

...ation: Laurels Fund, Michelle L. ...cDonald, Moss Adams LLP and Seattle ASWA Chapter Scholarships: One year; Women in Need Scholarship: Two years; Women in Transition Scholarship: Four years.

Deadline: Laurels Fund: May 30. All others: May 1.

IRS I.D.: 36-6149364

ADDRESS INQUIRIES TO:
Kimberly Fantaci, Foundation Administrator
(See address above.)

ERNST & YOUNG FOUNDATION [1838]

200 Plaza Drive
Secaucus, NJ 07094
(201) 872-5686
(201) 872-2200
Fax: (866) 855-4960
E-mail: ellen.glazerman@ey.com
Web Site: www.ey.com

FOUNDED: 1937

AREAS OF INTEREST:
Higher education, with specific interests in accounting and business.

TYPE:
Fellowships; Matching gifts; Scholarships.

YEAR PROGRAM STARTED: 1937

PURPOSE:
To support higher education.

LEGAL BASIS:
Public charity.

ELIGIBILITY:
No grants to individuals. No cold requests.

GEOG. RESTRICTIONS: United States and its territories.

FINANCIAL DATA:
Amount of support per award: Varies.

Total amount of support: Varies.

Matching fund requirements: Ernst & Young Foundation will only match contributions to an accredited college, junior college, community college, university, graduate school or professional school.

APPLICATION INFO:
Contact the Foundation for details.

Duration: Varies.

Deadline: Grant requests are reviewed continuously.

ADDRESS INQUIRIES TO:
Ellen Glazerman, Executive Director
(See address and e-mail above.)

FEDERATION OF AMERICAN CONSUMERS AND TRAVELERS [1839]

318 Hillsboro Avenue
P.O. Box 104
Edwardsville, IL 62025
(618) 656-0454
(800) 872-3228
Fax: (618) 656-5369
E-mail: vrolens@usafact.org
Web Site: www.usafact.org

NAME(S) OF PROGRAMS:
- **Community and Business Project Grants**

TYPE:
Project/program grants; Seed money grants.

PURPOSE:
To support civic club, church, and community projects that are nominated by members.

ELIGIBILITY:
Projects are nominated by members.

GEOG. RESTRICTIONS: United States.

FINANCIAL DATA:
Amount of support per award: $100 to $2,500, based on funding availability and the needs of the specific proposal.

Total amount of support: Varies.

APPLICATION INFO:
Contact the Federation for guidelines.

Duration: One-time award.

Deadline: January, April, July and October.

ADDRESS INQUIRIES TO:
Vicki Rolens, Managing Director
(See address above.)

*SPECIAL STIPULATIONS:
Applicant must be a FACT member or have been nominated by a FACT member.

4A'S

1065 Avenue of the Americas, 16th Floor
New York, NY 10018
(212) 682-2500
Fax: (212) 867-8329
E-mail: maip@aaaa.org
Web Site: maip.aaaa.org

TYPE:
Fellowships; Scholarships.

See entry 967 for full listing.

HAGLEY MUSEUM AND LIBRARY

Center for the History of
Business, Technology and Society
298 Buck Road
Wilmington, DE 19807
(302) 658-2400 ext. 243
Fax: (302) 655-3188
E-mail: clockman@hagley.org
Web Site: www.hagley.org

TYPE:
Fellowships; Research grants; Travel grants; Visiting scholars. Grants to support short-term research in the imprint, manuscript, pictorial and artifact collections of the Hagley Museum and Library.

The Henry Belin du Pont Dissertation Fellowship in Business, Technology, and Society supports research and writing by candidates for doctoral degrees. Projects should demonstrate superior intellectual quality and make substantial use of Hagley's collections.

Henry Belin du Pont Research Grants support research in the collections of the museum and library.

Hagley Exploratory Research Grant supports a one-week visit by scholars who believe that their project will benefit from Hagley research collections, but need the opportunity to explore them on-site to determine if a Henry Belin du Pont research grant application is warranted.

See entry 581 for full listing.

THE S.S. HUEBNER FOUNDATION FOR INSURANCE EDUCATION [1840]

Department of Risk Management and Insurance
Georgia State University
35 Broad Street, Room 1135
Atlanta, GA 30303
(404) 413-7462
Fax: (404) 413-7499
E-mail: cciccotello@gsu.edu
Web Site: www.huebnerfoundation.org

FOUNDED: 1940

AREAS OF INTEREST:
Insurance and risk management.

TYPE:
The Foundation's program goals are:
(1) to support the Ph.D. program at Georgia State University that is training the next generation of scholars who will conduct academic research on insurance economics specifically and the efficient allocation of risk in the economy more generally;
(2) to sponsor a periodic summer symposium or occasional lecture series facilitated by leading scholars designed to build collaborative research relationships among young researchers at Georgia State University and elsewhere who are interested in risk-related topics and;
(3) to provide assistance for professionals who seek to develop the research skills necessary to address contemporary insurance and risk problems in such areas as regulation, policy or industry practice.

YEAR PROGRAM STARTED: 1940

PURPOSE:
To advance university-level risk management and insurance scholarship and learning.

APPLICATION INFO:
Contact the Foundation for guidelines.

IRS I.D.: 23-6297325

ADDRESS INQUIRIES TO:
Conrad Ciccotello, J.D., Ph.D.
Executive Director
(See address above.)

INSTITUTE FOR SUPPLY MANAGEMENT [1841]

2055 East Centennial Circle
Tempe, AZ 85284-1802
(480) 752-6276
(800) 888-6276
Fax: (480) 752-7890
E-mail: nneibergall@instituteforsupplymanagement.org
Web Site: www.instituteforsupplymanagement.org

FOUNDED: 1915

AREAS OF INTEREST:
Purchasing/supply management.

NAME(S) OF PROGRAMS:
- **ISM Doctoral Dissertation Grant Program**

TYPE:
Research grants. A limited number of grants are available to doctoral candidates interested in pursuing advanced study in procurement, supply management and supply chain management.

YEAR PROGRAM STARTED: 1984

PURPOSE:
To encourage and develop doctoral students interested in procurement, supply

management and supply chain management to pursue and complete their dissertation research in these fields of study.

LEGAL BASIS:
501(c)(3) nonprofit educational and research organization.

ELIGIBILITY:
The following general requirements apply:
(1) Previous awardees are ineligible;
(2) Candidates must be enrolled in an accredited university; candidates from outside of the U.S. are eligible to participate; all grants will be made in U.S. funds;
(3) The Institute reserves the right to make all final decisions regarding the awards;
(4) Candidates have three years from the time of award to complete their dissertation; candidates who do not successfully complete their dissertation will not receive the second half of the research grant.

FINANCIAL DATA:
The award recipient will receive one-half of the grant upon award (to be delivered no later than August 1) and one-half upon successful completion of his or her dissertation.

Amount of support per award: One top award of $20,000; two runner-up awards of $5,000.

NO. AWARDS: Up to 3 in 2016.

APPLICATION INFO:
Application guidelines are available at the web site.

Duration: Must be complete within three years.

Deadline: March 31. Announcement on or about May 15.

PUBLICATIONS:
Brochure.

ADDRESS INQUIRIES TO:
Nora Neibergall
Senior Vice President
Doctoral Grant Committee
(See address above.)

THE CALVIN K. KAZANJIAN ECONOMICS FOUNDATION, INC. [1842]

P.O. Box 300
Dallas, PA 18612-0330
(570) 690-4629
E-mail: director@kazanjian.org
Web Site: www.kazanjian.org

FOUNDED: 1947

AREAS OF INTEREST:
Promoting the understanding of economics and addressing the issue of economic illiteracy.

TYPE:
Grants-in-aid. Grants for economic education.

PURPOSE:
To aid in bringing greater happiness and prosperity to all through a better understanding of economics.

ELIGIBILITY:
The Foundation will only give serious consideration to those projects which directly advance its immediate purposes and meet its guidelines. It will only support nonprofit 501(c)(3) organizations and will not support overhead or indirect costs.

GEOG. RESTRICTIONS: United States.

FINANCIAL DATA:
Amount of support per award: Varies; average grant: approximately $22,000.

Total amount of support: Approximately $350,000.

APPLICATION INFO:
Guidelines and criteria are found on the web site. Applicants must include:
(1) copy of an IRS nonprofit determination letter;
(2) latest audited financial statement;
(3) list of board of directors;
(4) annual budget and;
(5) project budget.

Duration: Varies.

Deadline: September 15 for November/December review. February 15 for May/June review.

ADDRESS INQUIRIES TO:
Dr. Michael MacDowell, Managing Director
(See address above.)

*PLEASE NOTE:
The Foundation does not give scholarships.

KPMG FOUNDATION [1843]

3 Chestnut Ridge Road
Montvale, NJ 07645-0435
(201) 307-7932
Fax: (201) 624-7763
E-mail: tperino@kpmg.com
Web Site: www.kpmgfoundation.org

FOUNDED: 1968

AREAS OF INTEREST:
Academic research, education and professional development in the area of business.

NAME(S) OF PROGRAMS:
- **The PhD Project**

TYPE:
Conferences/seminars; Matching gifts; Professorships; Project/program grants. Special grants, made on the recommendations of the Firm's college relations partners, are for specific projects that create new educational opportunities.

YEAR PROGRAM STARTED: 1968

PURPOSE:
To recognize outstanding achievement in accounting education and research; to recognize academic excellence and community achievement; to help minority students obtain careers in business and industry; to promote research that will benefit the profession now and in the future.

LEGAL BASIS:
Private foundation.

ELIGIBILITY:
The Foundation restricts grants to educational purposes related to its firm's functional areas, including accounting, auditing and tax.

GEOG. RESTRICTIONS: United States.

FINANCIAL DATA:
Matching fund requirements: The Matching Gift Program only matches employee/partner gifts to colleges and universities from which the donors are alumni or where KPMG recruits. Minimum $50 for employees and maximum $7,500 per institution per fiscal year.

PUBLICATIONS:
Annual report.

IRS I.D.: 13-6262199

ADDRESS INQUIRIES TO:
Tara Perino, Director
(See address above.)

LIBRA FUTURE FUND [1844]

3 Canal Plaza, Suite 500
Portland, ME 04101
(207) 879-6280
Fax: (207) 879-6281
E-mail: erik@librafoundation.org
Web Site: www.librafoundation.org/libra-future-fund

FOUNDED: 2005

AREAS OF INTEREST:
Economic development and job opportunities in Maine.

NAME(S) OF PROGRAMS:
- **Libra Future Fund Young Adult Grant Program**

TYPE:
Project/program grants. To promote economic development and create job opportunities in Maine.

YEAR PROGRAM STARTED: 2005

PURPOSE:
To capitalize upon the energy and creativity that Maine's young people embody; to combat youth out-migration by supporting initiatives that increase the number of Maine-based professional opportunities.

ELIGIBILITY:
Applicants must be 18 to 29 years of age, reside in Maine at least eight months per year, or be originally from Maine, but attending school out of state.

GEOG. RESTRICTIONS: Maine.

FINANCIAL DATA:
Amount of support per award: $3,000 to $5,000.

Total amount of support: Approximately $30,000 for the year 2015.

APPLICATION INFO:
Complete instructions can be found on the Fund's web site.

Duration: One-time grant.

Deadline: January 23, April 23, July 23, and October 23.

ADDRESS INQUIRIES TO:
Erik Hayward, President
(See address above.)

THE GERALD LOEB AWARDS
UCLA Anderson School of Management
110 Westwood Plaza
Gold Hall, Suite B307
Los Angeles, CA 90095-1481
(310) 825-4478
Fax: (310) 825-4479
E-mail: loeb@anderson.ucla.edu
Web Site: www.loeb.anderson.ucla.edu

TYPE:
Awards/prizes. Awards to recognize business and financial journalists for important contributions to the understanding of business, finance and the economy.

See entry 1880 for full listing.

LOGISTICS & TRANSPORTATION ASSOCIATION OF NORTH AMERICA (LTNA) [1845]
P.O. Box 426
Union, WA 98592
(877) 858-8627 (continental U.S.)
(877) 858-8628 (Canada)
E-mail: executive.director@ltna.org
Web Site: www.ltna.org

NAME(S) OF PROGRAMS:
- **Hooper Memorial Scholarship**
- **Denny Lydic Scholarship**
- **Texas Transportation Scholarship**
- **Alice Glaisyer Warfield Scholarship**
- **Charlotte Woods Memorial Scholarship**

TYPE:
Scholarships. Texas Transportation Scholarship is awarded to a student who has been enrolled in a school in Texas during some phase of his or her education (elementary, secondary or high school.)

Charlotte Woods Memorial Scholarship is awarded to a student who is an LTNA member or a dependent of a member.

PURPOSE:
To encourage advanced vocational, undergraduate and graduate study in the field of transportation and traffic management.

ELIGIBILITY:
LTNA awards scholarships to graduating high school seniors and college undergraduate students accepted to or currently enrolled at accredited institutions of higher learning in degree programs in the fields of transportation logistics, supply-chain management, traffic management, transportation safety and/or related transportation industry operations and services.

In addition to the acceptance, enrollment and field of study requirements described above, the basis for awarding LTNA scholarships includes a calculated review and assessment of each applicant's academic record, character, potential and professional interest as revealed through the applicant's application and specified supporting documents.

GEOG. RESTRICTIONS: United States and Canada.

APPLICATION INFO:
In addition to a completed application form, supporting documents include:
(1) certified transcript directly from applicant's college/university;
(2) three letters of recommendation;
(3) current four- by six-inch color photograph (to be used for publication) and;
(4) 500-word essay explaining why the applicant has chosen transportation logistics or an allied field as a career path, and outlining the objectives. Essay should be composed separately in Microsoft Word file only. Application form is available at the web site.

All application documents must be mailed to the Executive Director at the address above.

Deadline: Postmarked by May 31 (no exceptions).

ADDRESS INQUIRIES TO:
Katie Dejonge, Executive Director
(See address above.)

MARKETING EDGE [1846]
1333 Broadway, Suite 301
New York, NY 10018
(212) 790-1510
Fax: (212) 790-1561
E-mail: admin@marketingedge.org
Web Site: www.marketingedge.org

FOUNDED: 1966

NAME(S) OF PROGRAMS:
- **Collegiate ECHO Marketing Challenge**
- **Collegiate Summit**
- **Direct/Interactive Marketing Research Summit**
- **Robert Kestnbaum Research Program**
- **Marketing EDGE Scholarship Program**
- **Professor's Institute**
- **Shankar-Spiegel Award for the Best Dissertation Proposal in Direct/Interactive Marketing**
- **Student Career Forums**

TYPE:
Awards/prizes; Conferences/seminars; Internships; Research grants; Scholarships; Research contracts. Collegiate ECHO Marketing Challenge provides students worldwide with experiential learning, crafting an integrated marketing plan.

Collegiate Summit is an annual conference focused on digital and database marketing for undergraduate students.

Direct/Interactive Marketing Research Summit provides a forum for digital, social media, database and direct/interactive marketing topics in the areas of research and teaching.

Robert Kestnbaum Research Program is intended to generate leading-edge academic research to impact the future of direct/interactive marketing.

Marketing EDGE Scholarship Program provides education funding support to undergraduate and graduate students nationwide.

Professor's Institute is an invitation-only conference that brings marketing academics and practitioners together to engage in thought-provoking conversations that have the potential to influence marketing curricula and current marketing practice.

Shankar-Spiegel Award for the Best Dissertation Proposal in Direct/Interactive Marketing recognizes doctoral candidates with the best dissertation proposal in direct/interactive marketing. Doctoral students from accredited doctoral programs are eligible to receive this award.

Student Career Forums provides opportunity for college students to meet and network with marketing professionals.

YEAR PROGRAM STARTED: 1966

PURPOSE:
To educate, develop, grow and employ college students in the marketing field - expanding and enriching the pool of trained, market-ready talent.

LEGAL BASIS:
Nonprofit, tax-exempt organization.

ELIGIBILITY:
Varies by program.

GEOG. RESTRICTIONS: United States.

FINANCIAL DATA:
Amount of support per award: $1,000 to $5,000.

CO-OP FUNDING PROGRAMS: Corporate Leadership Program.

APPLICATION INFO:
Form and guidelines available online.

PUBLICATIONS:
Annual report; conference materials; *Journal of Interactive Marketing®*.

IRS I.D.: 13-6222757

STAFF:
Terri L. Bartlett, President
Marie Adolphe, Vice President, Program Development

ADDRESS INQUIRIES TO:
André Roggy, Administration Manager
(See address above.)

THE BURTON D. MORGAN FOUNDATION [1847]
22 Aurora Street
Hudson, OH 44236
(330) 655-1660
Fax: (330) 655-1673
E-mail: admin@bdmorganfdn.org
Web Site: www.bdmorganfdn.org

FOUNDED: 1967

AREAS OF INTEREST:
Entrepreneurship education, economic development and free enterprise system.

TYPE:
Challenge/matching grants; Conferences/seminars; Endowments; General operating grants; Project/program grants.

YEAR PROGRAM STARTED: 1967

PURPOSE:
To champion the entrepreneurial spirit.

LEGAL BASIS:
Private foundation.

ELIGIBILITY:
Grants are made to organizations recognized as public charities under the Internal Revenue Code Section 501(c)(3). The Foundation does not usually make multiyear grants and does not ordinarily consider grants to annual fund drives, units of government, or organizations and institutions which are primarily tax-supported, including state universities. Grants are not made to individuals.

GEOG. RESTRICTIONS: Primarily northeastern Ohio.

FINANCIAL DATA:
Amount of support per award: Varies.
Total amount of support: Varies.

CO-OP FUNDING PROGRAMS: Blackstone LaunchPad Program; Northeast Ohio Collegiate Entrepreneurship Program.

REPRESENTATIVE AWARDS:
$75,500 to Invent Now; $80,000 to Junior Achievement of North Central Ohio; $80,000 to Entrepreneurship Education Consortium; $56,000 to Northeast Ohio Technology Coalition; $40,000 to ideastream.

APPLICATION INFO:
Before submitting a full proposal, organizations should send a letter of inquiry to the Foundation regarding the request. All letters of inquiry and applications must be submitted online through the Foundation's web site.

Duration: One year.

Deadline: Letter of Inquiry: February 1, May 1 and September 1. Full Proposal: March 1, June 1 and October 1.

PUBLICATIONS:
E-Spirit, newsletter; *Pipeline*, Foundation newsletter; *Venture Adventure*, e-newsletter.

IRS I.D.: 34-6598971

OFFICER:
Deborah D. Hoover, President and Chief Executive Officer

ADDRESS INQUIRIES TO:
Diane Rafferty, Executive Assistant
(See address above.)

THE NASDAQ EDUCATIONAL FOUNDATION, INC. [1848]

805 King Farm Boulevard
Rockville, MD 20850
(301) 978-8738
(800) 842-0356
Fax: (301) 978-8472
E-mail: foundation@nasdaq.com
Web Site: www.business.nasdaq.com

FOUNDED: 1994

AREAS OF INTEREST:
Financial markets literacy.

TYPE:
Development grants; Fellowships; Project/program grants; Research grants; Seed money grants. The Foundation offers grants in the following areas:
(1) academic study or research;
(2) Ph.D. dissertation fellowships;
(3) curriculum development and;
(4) educational projects or programs.

PURPOSE:
To promote learning about capital formation, financial markets and entrepreneurship through innovative educational programs.

ELIGIBILITY:
The Foundation will accept proposals from educational institutions and organizations designated as tax-exempt according to Section 501(c)(3) of the Internal Revenue Code.

In limited cases, proposals from highly and specifically qualified individuals, only for the purpose of conducting independent academic study or research on financial markets, are accepted.

FINANCIAL DATA:
Amount of support per award: Varies.

Total amount of support: Varies.

APPLICATION INFO:
Applicants must submit a letter of inquiry and be invited to submit a proposal.

Duration: One year, unless otherwise specified.

Deadline: Varies.

ADDRESS INQUIRIES TO:
Joan C. Conley, Senior Vice President and Corporate Secretary or
Angela Henson, Project Coordinator
(See address above.)

NATIONAL ENDOWMENT FOR FINANCIAL EDUCATION (NEFE) [1849]

1331 17th Street, Suite 1200
Denver, CO 80202
(303) 741-6333
Fax: (303) 220-0838
E-mail: nefegrantrequest@nefe.org
Web Site: www.nefe.org

FOUNDED: 1997

AREAS OF INTEREST:
Financial education for the American public.

NAME(S) OF PROGRAMS:
- **NEFE Research Funding Program**

TYPE:
Fellowships; Research grants. NEFE Research Funding Program recruits qualified individuals from diverse backgrounds who share a common interest in working on projects within NEFE's broad scope of activities and in gaining nonprofit operations and management experience. The program also awards grants for research projects that will expand the body of knowledge in the field of financial literacy.

YEAR PROGRAM STARTED: 1998

PURPOSE:
To help all Americans acquire the information and gain the skills necessary to take control of their personal finances.

ELIGIBILITY:
To be considered for a fellowship opportunity, candidates must be:
(1) in good standing with their academic institution and;
(2) a currently registered graduate degree-seeking student.

Grants are awarded to organizations that have been designated tax-exempt status according to Internal Revenue Code Section 501(c)(3) or its equivalent for colleges and universities. Grants are not awarded to:
(1) individuals;
(2) organizations that have not been designated tax-exempt under Section 501(c)(3) or its equivalent;
(3) organizations that discriminate on the basis of age, color, disability, marital status, nationality, race, religion, sex, sexual orientation, or veteran status;
(4) organizations and/or project principals and team members who fail to meet NEFE's Strategy Statement and Procedures requirements concerning the U.S.A. Patriot Act and related regulations;
(5) foreign organizations;
(6) international programs or projects or;
(7) organizations whose projects include re-grant of NEFE funding.

GEOG. RESTRICTIONS: United States.

FINANCIAL DATA:
Amount of support per award: Fellowships: $3,000 per semester; Grants: Generally $100,000 up.

Total amount of support: Varies.

NO. MOST RECENT APPLICANTS: 28.

NO. AWARDS: 3.

APPLICATION INFO:
Fellowship Program does not accept unsolicited applications. Applicants to the Grant Program must first submit a Letter of Inquiry. Those projects appearing to have strong potential will move to a proposal phase; applicants for those selected projects will be given further instruction at that time.

Duration: Varies.

Deadline: Varies.

PUBLICATIONS:
NEFE Digest.

IRS I.D.: 84-0632115

ADDRESS INQUIRIES TO:
Grants Manager
(See address above.)

THE NATIONAL RESTAURANT ASSOCIATION EDUCATIONAL FOUNDATION [1850]

2055 L Street, N.W.
Washington, DC 20036
(800) 424-5156
E-mail: scholars@nraef.org
Web Site: www.nraef.org/scholarships

FOUNDED: 1987

AREAS OF INTEREST:
Foodservice education and training.

NAME(S) OF PROGRAMS:
- **Professional Development for Educators Scholarship**

TYPE:
Training grants; Travel grants.

PURPOSE:
To support foodservice educators earning their Certified Secondary Educators Foodservice certification; to provide financial support to attend an NRA Summer Institute or participate in a "hands-on" industry work experience.

ELIGIBILITY:
Must be an educator of a restaurant and/or foodservice-related program in a secondary school and submit a signed letter of recommendation on school letterhead that also verifies employment by an immediate supervisor or program director. Applicants must be U.S. citizens/residents.

GEOG. RESTRICTIONS: United States.

FINANCIAL DATA:
Amount of support per award: $1,750.

Total amount of support: Varies.

NO. AWARDS: Varies.

APPLICATION INFO:
Application information is available online.

Duration: Varies.

THE NATIONAL RESTAURANT ASSOCIATION EDUCATIONAL FOUNDATION

2055 L Street, N.W.
Washington, DC 20036
(800) 424-5156
E-mail: scholars@nraef.org
Web Site: www.nraef.org/scholarships

TYPE:
Scholarships. Provides scholarships for students who are pursuing an education and career in the foodservice industry.

See entry 2592 for full listing.

PHI CHI THETA EDUCATIONAL FOUNDATION [1851]

1508 East Beltline Road, Suite 104
Carrollton, TX 75006
(972) 245-7202
E-mail: foundationinfo@phichitheta.org
Web Site: www.phichitheta.org/foundation

FOUNDED: 1999

AREAS OF INTEREST:
Business and economics.

NAME(S) OF PROGRAMS:
- **Educational and Scholastic Advancement Programs**

TYPE:
Scholarships. Grants.

YEAR PROGRAM STARTED: 2000

PURPOSE:
To provide scholarships and grants to members of the Phi Chi Theta Fraternity.

LEGAL BASIS:
Public charity, 501(c)(3) organization.

ELIGIBILITY:
Open to students who are members of Phi Chi Theta in approved courses in colleges and universities in the U.S. leading to Bachelor's, Master's or doctoral degrees in the fields of business administration and/or economics. Applicants must have completed at least one semester of college-level study. Selection is based on scholastic achievement, motivation, leadership potential and financial need.

GEOG. RESTRICTIONS: United States.

FINANCIAL DATA:
Amount of support per award: $500 to $1,000.
Total amount of support: Varies.

NO. MOST RECENT APPLICANTS: Over 20.

NO. AWARDS: Varies.

APPLICATION INFO:
Applicants must submit an official transcript and two letters of recommendation.
Duration: One year. Nonrenewable.
Deadline: May 1.

PUBLICATIONS:
Application guidelines.

IRS I.D.: 31-1672618

OFFICERS:
Frances Q. Spencer, President
Mary Ellen Lewis, Treasurer

PROSPANICA

450 East John Carpenter Freeway
Suite 200
Irving, TX 75062
(214) 596-9338
(877) 467-4622
Fax: (214) 596-9325
E-mail: scholarship@prospanica.org
Web Site: www.nshmba.org

TYPE:
Scholarships.

See entry 986 for full listing.

S&P GLOBAL

55 Water Street, 46th Floor
New York, NY 10041
(212) 438-1273
E-mail: louise.raymond@spglobal.com
Web Site: www.spglobal.com

TYPE:
Matching gifts; Project/program grants. Employee Giving Programs including Matching Gift, Employee Volunteer Grants, Signature Volunteer Program (Community Impact Month), and Direct Grants that focus on women entrepreneurs and STEM.

See entry 276 for full listing.

CHARLES SCHWAB FOUNDATION [1852]

211 Main Street, SF211 MN-16-205
San Francisco, CA 94105-1905
(877) 408-5438
Fax: (415) 667-1593
E-mail: charlesschwabfoundation@schwab.com
Web Site: www.aboutschwab.com/community

FOUNDED: 1993

AREAS OF INTEREST:
Financial education.

NAME(S) OF PROGRAMS:
- **Schwab Moneywise™**

TYPE:
General operating grants; Matching gifts; Project/program grants. The Charles Schwab Foundation awards strategic financial support through direct grants to selected nonprofit organizations that respond to local cultural and social needs or support Schwab's commitment to financial literacy. These grants provide employees with a voice and role in supporting the community groups they care about most.

YEAR PROGRAM STARTED: 1993

PURPOSE:
To give back to communities by supporting employee-selected causes and fostering financial literacy through funding, involvement and expertise.

LEGAL BASIS:
Corporate foundation.

ELIGIBILITY:
The Foundation provides direct grants to select nonprofit organizations that support Schwab's commitment to financial literacy and respond to local cultural and social needs.

Applicants must meet at least one of the following selection criteria:
(1) be recommended by a Schwab employee who is an active volunteer in the organization;
(2) be performing community work that corresponds to the Foundation's initiatives or;
(3) promote financial capability.

Greater consideration will be given to those organizations that already have Schwab employee volunteer involvement. The more employees involved, the greater the opportunity to be considered for a direct grant.

To qualify for a direct grant, an organization must:
(1) be based in the U.S. or one of its territories;
(2) be recognized as a tax-exempt public charity under Section 501(c)(3) of the U.S. Internal Revenue Code (per Section 170) and;
(3) (if an educational institution) be accredited by a regional accrediting association or by a recognized independent accrediting group.

GEOG. RESTRICTIONS: United States.

FINANCIAL DATA:
Total amount of support: More than $4,000,000 given annually to directly support nonprofit organizations; $3,270,000 given in employee gifts and matching donations in 2014; approximately $150,000 given in employee board-service grants in 2014.

NO. AWARDS: More than 2,200 nonprofit organizations received financial support in 2014.

APPLICATION INFO:
The Foundation is currently accepting grant requests by invitation only.
Deadline: Proposals are reviewed on a quarterly basis.

PUBLICATIONS:
Program brochure with application guidelines.

IRS I.D.: 94-1737782

ADDRESS INQUIRIES TO:
Direct Grant Program
(See address above.)

SIMON FRASER UNIVERSITY [1853]

Maggie Benston Student Services Centre 1100
8888 University Drive
Burnaby BC V5A 1S6 Canada
(778) 782-8499
Fax: (778) 782-3080
E-mail: gradstudies@sfu.ca
Web Site: www.sfu.ca/dean-gradstudies.html

NAME(S) OF PROGRAMS:
- **SFU Graduate Fellowships**

TYPE:
Fellowships.

PURPOSE:
To offer financial support to the University's students enrolled in a Master's or Ph.D. program.

ELIGIBILITY:
Open to current or entering Master's or Ph.D. program students with a grade point average of 3.5 or above.

FINANCIAL DATA:
Amount of support per award: $3,250 to $6,500 (CAN).

APPLICATION INFO:
Contact the University.
Duration: One semester or more. Must reapply.
Deadline: April 15.

ADDRESS INQUIRIES TO:
Specific Department of Enrollment
Simon Fraser University
(Request specific department's address.)

SOCIETY OF ACTUARIES (SOA)

475 North Martingale Road
Suite 600
Schaumburg, IL 60173-2226
(847) 706-3509
Fax: (847) 273-8605
E-mail: ttatsumi@soa.org
Web Site: www.soa.org/education/resources/academic-initiatives/soa-doc-stipend.aspx

TYPE:
Awards/prizes; Scholarships. Society of Actuaries' James C. Hickman Scholar Doctoral Stipend Program is designed to

provide stipends to doctoral students who will, through their studies, address research and education needs of the profession, including both the theoretical and practical aspects.

See entry 2032 for full listing.

SOCIETY OF ACTUARIES (SOA)

475 North Martingale Road
Suite 600
Schaumburg, IL 60173-2226
(847) 706-3509
Fax: (847) 273-8605
E-mail: ttatsumi@soa.org
Web Site: www.soa.org/education/resources/edu-institution-grant/default.aspx

TYPE:
Awards/prizes; Development grants; General operating grants; Project/program grants; Research grants; Scholarships; Travel grants. Grants to educational institutions.

See entry 2033 for full listing.

U.S. DEPARTMENT OF EDUCATION [1854]

Centers for International Business Education
1990 K Street, N.W., 6th Floor
Washington, DC 20006-8521
(202) 502-7622
Fax: (202) 502-7858
E-mail: timothy.duvall@ed.gov
Web Site: www2.ed.gov/programs/iegpscibe/index.html

AREAS OF INTEREST:
International business education.

CONSULTING OR VOLUNTEER SERVICES:
Offers technical assistance.

NAME(S) OF PROGRAMS:

- **Centers for International Business Education Program**

TYPE:
Project/program grants. The program provides grants to eligible institutions of higher education or combinations of these institutions for planning, establishing and operating Centers for International Business Education.

YEAR PROGRAM STARTED: 1989

PURPOSE:
To provide funding to schools of business for curriculum development, research, and training on issues of importance to U.S. trade and competitiveness.

LEGAL BASIS:
Government agency.

ELIGIBILITY:
An applicant must be an institution of higher education or a combination of such institutions that establishes a Center Advisory Council prior to the date that federal assistance is received. The Center Advisory Council shall conduct extensive planning prior to the establishment of the Center for International Business Education concerning the scope of the Center's activities and the design of its programs. Programs and activities to be conducted by Centers for International Business Education must meet the programmatic requirements listed above.

FINANCIAL DATA:
Grant funds may be used to pay the federal share of costs of faculty and staff travel in foreign areas, regions or countries, teaching and research materials, curriculum planning and development, bringing visiting scholars and faculty to the center to teach or to conduct research, training and improvement of the staff for the purpose of and subject to such conditions as the Secretary finds necessary for carrying out the objectives of this program and other costs consistent with planning, establishing or operating a center.

Amount of support per award: $285,000 for the fiscal year 2015.

Total amount of support: $4,571,400 for the fiscal year 2015.

NO. MOST RECENT APPLICANTS: Approximately 50 in fiscal year 2015.

NO. AWARDS: Approximately 16 for fiscal year 2015.

APPLICATION INFO:
The Department of Education provides an application package upon request to the Office of Postsecondary Education. Applications become available in May.

Duration: Four years.

Deadline: June. Competition held every four years.

PUBLICATIONS:
Application guidelines; abstracts of grantees.

ADDRESS INQUIRIES TO:
Tim Duvall, Ph.D.
(See address above.)

THE UNIVERSITY OF CALGARY

Faculty of Graduate Studies
MacKimmie Library Tower, Room 213
2500 University Drive, N.W.
Calgary AB T2N 1N4 Canada
(403) 220-4938
Fax: (403) 289-7635
E-mail: gsaward@ucalgary.ca
Web Site: www.grad.ucalgary.ca/awards

TYPE:
Awards/prizes; Scholarships. Awards for study in the fields of business, management and related areas. Tenable at the University of Calgary. Awards are endowed through gifts from John Labatt Limited and ScotiaMcLeod Inc. Matching grants provided from the Province of Alberta's Advanced Education Endowment Fund.

See entry 1733 for full listing.

UNIVERSITY OF NEBRASKA AT OMAHA [1855]

Mammel Hall, Room 300
6708 Pine Street
Omaha, NE 68182-0048
(402) 554-2303
Fax: (402) 554-3747
E-mail: mba@unomaha.edu
Web Site: cba.unomaha.edu/mba

AREAS OF INTEREST:
UNO MBA Program and MS Economics.

NAME(S) OF PROGRAMS:

- **UNO Graduate Assistantships**

TYPE:
Assistantships. Graduate, MBA scholarships in all subjects.

ELIGIBILITY:
Graduate assistantships are available for qualified students who are enrolled in a graduate degree program in the College of Business Administration.

FINANCIAL DATA:
Amount of support per award: Waiver of tuition costs up to 12 semester-hours of graduate credit per semester.

NO. MOST RECENT APPLICANTS: 25.

NO. AWARDS: 5 for the academic year 2015-16.

APPLICATION INFO:
Applicants should complete the Graduate Assistantship application that is available on the web site and submit it with a resume and letters of recommendation prior to the application deadline.

Deadline: July 1.

THE DEAN WITTER FOUNDATION [1856]

57 Post Street, Suite 510
San Francisco, CA 94104
(415) 981-2966
Fax: (415) 981-5218
E-mail: admin@deanwitterfoundation.org
Web Site: www.deanwitterfoundation.org

FOUNDED: 1952

AREAS OF INTEREST:
Research and higher education in finance, wildlife research and conservation projects, and K-12 education.

TYPE:
Challenge/matching grants; Fellowships; General operating grants; Internships; Matching gifts; Professorships; Project/program grants; Research grants; Scholarships; Seed money grants.

YEAR PROGRAM STARTED: 1952

PURPOSE:
To help fund research and higher education in areas of special interest to the Foundation, as well as K-12 education.

LEGAL BASIS:
Private foundation.

ELIGIBILITY:
Grants are made to tax-exempt 501(c)(3) institutions. No grants are made to individuals.

GEOG. RESTRICTIONS: Northern California.

FINANCIAL DATA:
Amount of support per award: $10,000 to $25,000.

Total amount of support: Approximately $950,000 for fiscal year ended June 30, 2014.

NO. MOST RECENT APPLICANTS: 100 for fiscal year ended June 30, 2014.

NO. AWARDS: 40 for fiscal year ended June 30, 2014.

APPLICATION INFO:
Applicants should first submit a brief letter to the Consultant, explaining their program and its merits with estimated budget, personnel, time required to carry out the proposal, evidence of tax-exempt status, and a brief explanation of any other sources of support for the project, such as volunteer workers and matching funds commitments. If the project, program or institution falls within the priorities, interests and available funds of the Foundation, a more detailed proposal will be requested.

Duration: One year. Renewal possible.

OFFICERS AND TRUSTEES:

ADDRESS INQUIRIES TO:
Kenneth J. Blum, Administrative Director
(See address above.)

ZONTA INTERNATIONAL FOUNDATION [1857]

1211 West 22nd Street, Suite 900
Oak Brook, IL 60523-3384
(630) 928-1400
Fax: (630) 928-1559
E-mail: programs@zonta.org
Web Site: www.zonta.org

FOUNDED: 1919

AREAS OF INTEREST:
Financial support for women of any nationality pursuing degrees in business leading to a business management career.

NAME(S) OF PROGRAMS:
- **Jane M. Klausman Women in Business Scholarships**

TYPE:
Awards/prizes; Scholarships. For women of any nationality pursuing degrees in business who demonstrate outstanding potential in the field of business.

YEAR PROGRAM STARTED: 1998

PURPOSE:
To provide financial support for women of any nationality pursuing degrees in business leading to a business management career.

LEGAL BASIS:
Incorporated in the state of Illinois as a nonprofit organization.

ELIGIBILITY:
Applicant must meet the following minimum requirements:
(1) be undertaking a business and/or business-related program at an accredited university, college or institute;
(2) be enrolled in at least the second year of an undergraduate program through the final year of a Master's program at the time the application is submitted (applicants must still be attending school to receive this award in November);
(3) have achieved an outstanding academic record during her academic studies, including business-related subjects;
(4) have demonstrated initiative, ambition and commitment to pursuing a career in business and;
(5) be living or studying in a Zonta region/district.

FINANCIAL DATA:
The scholarship award may be used for tuition, books or living expenses at any university, college or institution offering accredited business courses and degrees.

Amount of support per award: $1,000 at the District Level and 12 scholarships for $7,000.

Total amount of support: Varies.

NO. MOST RECENT APPLICANTS: Varies.

NO. AWARDS: 32.

APPLICATION INFO:
Applications must be completed in English. English translations must accompany all non-English documents. The Jane M. Klausman Women in Business Scholarship program operates at the club, district and international levels of Zonta International. To apply, contact the Zonta Club within the applicant's district/region for deadlines and an address to mail application. (Such contact information is also available on the web site.) Alternatively, one can e-mail one's name and contact information to Zonta International Headquarters at the address above.
Applicants must be nominated by a local Zonta Club first.

Deadline: Must contact Zonta Club for deadlines.

ADDRESS INQUIRIES TO:
Martina Gamboa, Programs Coordinator
(See e-mail address above.)

Communications

AMERICAN ASSOCIATION FOR THE ADVANCEMENT OF SCIENCE [1858]

1200 New York Avenue, N.W.
Washington, DC 20005
(202) 326-6645
Fax: (202) 371-9849
E-mail: drossite@aaas.org
Web Site: www.aaas.org/MassMedia

FOUNDED: 1848

AREAS OF INTEREST:
Science-related issues in the media and public understanding and appreciation of science technology.

NAME(S) OF PROGRAMS:
- **Mass Media Science and Engineering Fellows Program**

TYPE:
Fellowships; Internships. Fellowships to primarily support graduate students in the fields of social, natural and physical sciences, mathematics, and engineering during the summer as intern reporters, researchers or production assistants in mass media organizations nationwide. Fellows will have the opportunity to observe and participate in the process by which events and ideas become news, improve their communication skills by learning to describe complex technical subjects in a manner understandable to the lay public, and increase their understanding of editorial decision making and the way in which information is effectively disseminated.

Each fellow will work for a specific media organization. Some will work for newspapers or magazines on news and feature writing assignments. Others may be involved in television or radio production.

YEAR PROGRAM STARTED: 1974

PURPOSE:
To strengthen the relationship between science and technology and the media and to enhance coverage of science-related issues in the media in order to improve public understanding and appreciation of science and technology.

LEGAL BASIS:
Nonprofit association.

ELIGIBILITY:
Applicants must be American-born, naturalized citizens, or permanent residents. Non-U.S. citizens must have a valid work visa.

FINANCIAL DATA:
Fellowships include a weekly stipend, travel costs to and from the media site, and travel and expenses to attend a presummer orientation in Washington, DC, along with a wrap-up session.

Amount of support per award: $5,000 for a 10-week report.

NO. MOST RECENT APPLICANTS: Over 130.

NO. AWARDS: Typically 20.

APPLICATION INFO:
In addition to the completed application form, candidates must submit a current resume, two writing samples, transcripts of undergraduate and graduate work, and three letters of recommendation. Transcripts and letters of recommendation must be submitted directly to the program. Applicants should be available for a telephone interview in March and be able to accept assignments anywhere in the U.S.

Duration: 10 weeks in the summer.

Deadline: January 15. Announcement in April.

STAFF:
Dione Rossiter, Ph.D., Director, Mass Media Science and Engineering Fellows Program

ADDRESS INQUIRIES TO:
Dione Rossiter, Ph.D.
Director, Mass Media Science and Engineering Fellows Program
(See address above.)

AMERICAN ASSOCIATION FOR THE ADVANCEMENT OF SCIENCE [1859]

1200 New York Avenue, N.W.
Washington, DC 20005
(202) 326-6431
Fax: (202) 789-0455
E-mail: elane@aaas.org
Web Site: www.aaas.org/sjawards

FOUNDED: 1848

AREAS OF INTEREST:
Science and engineering.

NAME(S) OF PROGRAMS:
- **AAAS Kavli Science Journalism Awards**

TYPE:
Awards/prizes. U.S. awards for stories of life, physical and social sciences, engineering and mathematics, excluding the field of medicine, published in newspapers, general magazines, aired on radio and television, and online. Entries should be intended for general, nontechnical audiences. There is also an award open to journalists worldwide, recognizing excellence in science news reporting for children.

YEAR PROGRAM STARTED: 1945

PURPOSE:
To encourage newspaper, magazine, radio, television and online science writing.

LEGAL BASIS:
Nonprofit scientific organization.

ELIGIBILITY:
Qualified individuals may apply with appropriate single stories or series published in U.S. newspapers or general circulation magazines, or aired on radio and television. Reporters for international media outlets are eligible for the award for reporting on science for children. Awards may not be presented to the same entrant in any two

consecutive years, and individuals who have already won three of the annual awards are no longer eligible to apply.

Must be published by a U.S.-based news outlet, with the exception of the international award for reporting on science for children.

FINANCIAL DATA:
Amount of support per award: $3,000.
Total amount of support: $24,000.

CO-OP FUNDING PROGRAMS: Sponsored by The Kavli Foundation.

NO. MOST RECENT APPLICANTS: 606.

NO. AWARDS: 8 for the 2015 contest year. Seven awards in the U.S., one each for outstanding science writing in a newspaper with less than 100,000 circulation, a newspaper with over 100,000 daily circulation, in a general circulation magazine, on radio, television (two awards) and online. In addition, an international award for excellence in science news reporting for children, across all news media.

APPLICATION INFO:
Online application information and FAQ can be found at the web site.
Deadline: August 1.

PUBLICATIONS:
Application guidelines.

OFFICERS:
Dr. Rush Holt, Chief Executive Officer

ADDRESS INQUIRIES TO:
Earl Lane, AAAS Kavli Science Journalism Awards Administrator
(See address above.)

AMERICAN POLITICAL SCIENCE ASSOCIATION

1527 New Hampshire Avenue, N.W.
Washington, DC 20036
(202) 483-2512
Fax: (202) 483-2657
E-mail: cfp@apsanet.org
Web Site: www.apsanet.org/cfp

TYPE:
Fellowships. Awards to political science professors and journalists in early-career to midcareer status; the award provides an opportunity for support as a full-time aide to a member of the House or Senate or as a staff member for a Congressional committee.

See entry 1925 for full listing.

ART DIRECTORS CLUB, INC. [1860]

106 West 29th Street
New York, NY 10001
(212) 643-1440
Fax: (212) 643-4266
E-mail: info@adcglobal.org
Web Site: www.adcglobal.org

FOUNDED: 1920

AREAS OF INTEREST:
Art and graphic design, advertising, visual communications and media arts, art direction, creative arts, computer graphics, art and design education, industrial and environmental design and publication planning.

NAME(S) OF PROGRAMS:
- **ADC National Scholarships**

TYPE:
Awards/prizes; Conferences/seminars; Scholarships. Programs include the annual competition, exhibitions, publications, symposia, workshops, scholarships and other special events.

PURPOSE:
To promote excellence in the fields of visual communications through the support of young and aspiring talent nationwide.

LEGAL BASIS:
Not-for-profit association with an international membership.

ELIGIBILITY:
Applicants must be students at their sophomore or junior level enrolled in an accredited undergraduate program or in their last semester or quarter in a portfolio program and must be enrolled in schools in the U.S.

FINANCIAL DATA:
Amount of support per award: $2,500 to $3,500.
Total amount of support: Varies.

NO. AWARDS: Varies.

APPLICATION INFO:
Students are required to submit five images of recent work (to be submitted online), a statement of purpose, a resume, a letter of recommendation from their professor, and an application.
Duration: One year.
Deadline: Late June to early July.

ADDRESS INQUIRIES TO:
Brendan Watson, Director of Education
(See address above.)

BENTON FOUNDATION [1861]

1560 Sherman Avenue
Suite 440
Evanston, IL 60201
(847) 328-3049
Fax: (847) 328-3046
Web Site: www.benton.org

FOUNDED: 1948

AREAS OF INTEREST:
The use of media and information technology in solving social problems and strengthening communities.

NAME(S) OF PROGRAMS:
- **Media Policy and Public Service Media**

TYPE:
Technical assistance. Program is funded for preserving, protecting and strengthening the public benefits in America's media environment.

PURPOSE:
To articulate a public-interest vision for the digital age and to demonstrate the value of communications for solving social problems; to leverage media and technology in innovative ways as a means to strengthen communities.

LEGAL BASIS:
501(c)(3) private foundation.

FINANCIAL DATA:
Amount of support per award: $500 to $5,000.
Total amount of support: $250,000 for the year 2013.

APPLICATION INFO:
By invitation only. The Foundation does not accept unsolicited grant applications.
Deadline: Varies.

ADDRESS INQUIRIES TO:
Adrianne Benton Furniss, Executive Director
(See address above.)

BROADCAST EDUCATION ASSOCIATION [1862]

1771 N Street, N.W.
Washington, DC 20036-2891
(202) 602-0587
Fax: (202) 609-9940
E-mail: Help@beaweb.org
Web Site: www.beaweb.org

FOUNDED: 1923

AREAS OF INTEREST:
Electronic media.

NAME(S) OF PROGRAMS:
- **John Bayliss Scholarship Award**
- **BEA Founders Award**
- **Richard Eaton Foundation Award**
- **Library of American Broadcasting Foundation Award**
- **Abe Voron Award**
- **Vincent T. Wasilewski Award**

TYPE:
Scholarships. BEA is the professional development association for professors, industry professionals and students involved in teaching and research related to radio, television and other electronic media. BEA administers scholarships annually, to honor broadcasters and the entire electronic media profession.

John Bayliss and Abe Voron Awards: Study toward a career in radio.

BEA Founders, Richard Eaton and Vincent T. Wasilewski Awards: Study in any electronic media area. (Wasilewski Award is for graduate students only.)

Library of American Broadcasting Foundation Award is for graduate students with a demonstrated research interest in broadcast history.

For the BEA Founders Award, preference is given to students enrolled in a BEA Two-Year/Small College Member Institution or graduates of these programs now enrolled in a BEA Four-Year Institution.

All other scholarships are awarded to juniors, seniors and graduate students at BEA Member institutions.

YEAR PROGRAM STARTED: 1962

PURPOSE:
To secure mutual advantages that flow from a continuing relationship between broadcasters and institutions of higher learning which offer a high standard of training and guidance for those who plan to enter the electronic media.

LEGAL BASIS:
Private association.

ELIGIBILITY:
Scholarships will be awarded for full-time degree work for the full academic year. One-semester grants are not made. Scholarships must be used exclusively for tuition, student fees, university bookstore course purchases, dormitory and related items eligible to be charged to a student's official campus account. Current scholarship holders are not eligible to reapply in the year following their award. All scholarships must be applied to study at a campus where at least one department is a BEA institutional member. Applicant can visit the Association

web site (click on "Scholarship") or phone (at the number above) to verify that one's campus is a member.

The applicant should be able to show substantial evidence of superior academic performance and potential to be an outstanding electronic media professional. There should be compelling evidence that the applicant possesses high integrity and a well-articulated sense of personal and professional responsibility.

FINANCIAL DATA:
Amount of support per award: John Bayliss and Richard Eaton Foundation Awards: $2,500 each; BEA Founders Award: $1,500 each; Library of American Broadcasting Foundation and Voron Awards: $3,000 each; Wasilewski Award: $4,000.

Total amount of support: Varies.

NO. AWARDS: Bayliss, Eaton, Library of American Broadcasting Foundation and Wasilewski Awards: 1 each; BEA Founders Award: 2; Voron Award: 3.

APPLICATION INFO:
Scholarship applicants can obtain the official application forms from their campus faculty or can download them from the Association web site (under Scholarships). The forms ask for personal and academic data and transcripts, broadcast and other experience, a written statement of goals and supportive statements from two references, one of which must be an electronic media faculty member. The completed application should contain:
(1) four completed and collated copies of the main application form;
(2) waiver sheet (four copies);
(3) two letters of reference (at least one from an electronic media professor; the other from either a professor or an industry professional); both mailed directly to Dr. Orlik and both submitted on the reference's letterhead; check with one's references to make sure these letters reach Dr. Orlik by the deadline) and;
(4) college transcripts (one from each institution attended).
Do not send disk, tapes, resumes, photos, etc. These will not be considered by the committee. No faxed or e-mailed material will be accepted.

Completed applications should be sent to:
Dr. Peter B. Orlik, Scholarships, BEA
344 Moore Hall
Central Michigan University
Mount Pleasant, MI 48859.

Duration: One academic year.

Deadline: All application forms and materials must be received by Dr. Orlik by the close of business on October 4, 2016.

PUBLICATIONS:
Journal of Broadcasting & Electronic Media; *Journal of Education Media*; *Journal of Radio Studies*.

ADDRESS INQUIRIES TO:
Dr. Peter B. Orlik, Scholarships
Central Michigan University
E-mail: orlik1pb@cmich.edu
(See address above.)

*PLEASE NOTE:
Due to the large volume of scholarship-related business, phone calls cannot be returned.

*SPECIAL STIPULATIONS:
All scholarships must be applied to study at a campus where at least one department is a BEA institutional member. Applications listing ineligible schools will be disqualified.

COLUMBIA JOURNALISM SCHOOL [1863]

2950 Broadway, Room 709
New York, NY 10027-7004
(212) 854-6468
Fax: (212) 854-7701; (212) 854-3800
E-mail: cm3443@columbia.edu
Web Site: www.journalism.columbia.edu

FOUNDED: 1960

NAME(S) OF PROGRAMS:
- **Mike Berger Award**

TYPE:
Awards/prizes. A newspaper competition, covering the previous calendar year, open to reporters nationwide.

YEAR PROGRAM STARTED: 1960

PURPOSE:
To honor distinguished newspaper reporting in the tradition of the late Meyer Berger of the New York Times.

LEGAL BASIS:
University.

ELIGIBILITY:
All newspaper reporters across the country are eligible whether they report for dailies, weeklies, monthlies, newspaper magazines, radio broadcast, digital reporting or online publications. Members of the ethnic press should submit copies of original stories with an English translation.

FINANCIAL DATA:
Winners receive a cash award along with a certificate and hotel and travel expenses to New York.

Amount of support per award: $1,500.

NO. AWARDS: 1 annually.

APPLICATION INFO:
Nominations are solicited from the editors of all daily newspapers across the country, as well as ethnic, weekly and online publications. Judges request that a nominating exhibit include two copies of a letter from the editor, a brief biographical resume of the reporter, and two copies of not more than five clippings.

Deadline: Early March. Notification in the spring. Presented at Columbia University in May.

ADDRESS INQUIRIES TO:
Caroline Martinet
Program Manager
(See address above.)

COLUMBIA UNIVERSITY [1864]

709 Pulitzer Hall
2950 Broadway
New York, NY 10027
(212) 854-3841
Fax: (212) 854-3342
E-mail: pulitzer@pulitzer.org
Web Site: www.pulitzer.org

FOUNDED: 1917

AREAS OF INTEREST:
Excellence in journalism, books, drama and music.

NAME(S) OF PROGRAMS:
- **Pulitzer Fellowships**
- **Pulitzer Prizes**

TYPE:
Awards/prizes; Fellowships. Awards in journalism, books and music.

Pulitzer Prizes in Journalism are awarded based on material appearing in a text-based U.S. newspaper or news site that publishes at least once a week during the year. Awards given for:
(1) meritorious public service by a newspaper through the use of its journalistic resources which may include editorials, cartoons, photographs, graphics and online material;
(2) local reporting of breaking news;
(3) investigative reporting by an individual or team, presented as a single article or series;
(4) explanatory journalism that illuminates a significant or complex subject, demonstrating mastery of the subject, lucid writing and clear presentation;
(5) local reporting;
(6) reporting on national affairs;
(7) reporting on international affairs, including United Nations correspondence;
(8) feature writing giving prime consideration to high literary quality and originality;
(9) commentary;
(10) criticism;
(11) editorial writing;
(12) cartoon or portfolio of cartoons;
(13) breaking news photography in black and white or color, which may consist of a photograph or photographs, a sequence or an album and;
(14) feature photography in black and white or color with the same stipulations as above.

Prizes in Letters are restricted to works first published in the U.S. during the year in book form and available for purchase by the general public. Awards given for:
(1) fiction by an American author, preferably dealing with American life;
(2) a play by an American author, preferably original in its source and dealing with American life, produced in the U.S. January 1 to December 31;
(3) appropriately documented book on the history of the U.S.;
(4) appropriately documented biography or autobiography by an American author;
(5) volume of original verse by an American author and;
(6) appropriately documented book of nonfiction by an American author that is not eligible for consideration in any other category.

A prize in music is given for distinguished musical composition by an American that has had its first performance in the U.S. during the year.

Four fellowships enable outstanding graduates to travel, report and study abroad. One fellowship is given to an outstanding graduate who wishes to specialize in drama, music, literary, film or television criticism.

YEAR PROGRAM STARTED: 1917

PURPOSE:
To recognize excellence in journalism, letters, drama and music.

LEGAL BASIS:
University.

ELIGIBILITY:
Competition for prizes is limited to work done during the calendar year ending December 31.

FINANCIAL DATA:
Amount of support per award: $10,000.
Total amount of support: $210,000.

NO. AWARDS: Fellowships: 5; Prizes in Drama: 1; Prizes in Journalism: 14; Prizes in Music: 1.

APPLICATION INFO:
Application form and $50 handling fee required with entries.
Duration: One-time awards. Previous winners are eligible for consideration each year for any award.
Deadline: Prizes in Books: June 15 and October 1; Prizes in Drama and Prize in Music: December 31; Prizes in Journalism: January 25.

PUBLICATIONS:
Award announcement; brochure.

BOARD:

ADDRESS INQUIRIES TO:
The Pulitzer Prize Board
(See address above.)

COLUMBIA UNIVERSITY [1865]

Graduate School of Journalism
2950 Broadway, Mail Code 3850
New York, NY 10027
(212) 854-2711
Fax: (212) 854-3900
E-mail: tat5@columbia.edu
Web Site: www.jrn.columbia.edu/knight-bagehot

FOUNDED: 1975

AREAS OF INTEREST:
Economics and business journalism for midcareer journalists.

NAME(S) OF PROGRAMS:
- **Knight-Bagehot Fellowship in Economics and Business Journalism**

TYPE:
Awards/prizes; Fellowships. Awarded to midcareer professional journalists to study business and economics at Columbia University.

YEAR PROGRAM STARTED: 1975

PURPOSE:
To improve the quality of business and economics journalism.

LEGAL BASIS:
University-affiliated fellowship program.

ELIGIBILITY:
Applicants must have at least four years' experience in journalism.

FINANCIAL DATA:
The Fellowship includes free tuition plus a stipend to cover living expenses.
Amount of support per award: $55,000.

NO. AWARDS: 10.

APPLICATION INFO:
Application information is available online.
Duration: One academic year.
Deadline: March 1.

PUBLICATIONS:
Annual report.

ADDRESS INQUIRIES TO:
Terri Thompson, Director
Knight-Bagehot Fellowship
(See address above.)

COLUMBIA UNIVERSITY GRADUATE SCHOOL OF JOURNALISM [1866]

2950 Broadway
New York, NY 10027
(212) 854-5047
Fax: (212) 854-3148
E-mail: awright@columbia.edu
lm3105@columbia.edu
Web Site: www.journalism.columbia.edu

AREAS OF INTEREST:
Journalism and inter-American relations.

NAME(S) OF PROGRAMS:
- **Maria Moors Cabot Prizes**

TYPE:
Awards/prizes. The prize program recognizes distinguished journalistic contributions to inter-American understanding. Prizes are awarded annually by the Trustees of Columbia University on recommendations made by the Dean of the Graduate School of Journalism and the Cabot Board.

YEAR PROGRAM STARTED: 1938

PURPOSE:
To recognize sustained and distinguished contributions of journalists to the advancement of understanding among the peoples of the Western Hemisphere.

LEGAL BASIS:
University.

ELIGIBILITY:
Although awards have been made to publishers or others in managerial positions, the board is particularly interested in working journalists throughout the Americas whose writings or broadcasts have contributed to mutual understanding and freedom of the press over a period of time.

GEOG. RESTRICTIONS: Western Hemisphere.

FINANCIAL DATA:
Amount of support per award: $5,000 and a Cabot medal, plus round-trip transportation to Columbia University for the award ceremonies.

NO. AWARDS: 4 for the year 2014.

APPLICATION INFO:
The Committee appreciates the submission of at least five, but no more than 10, newspaper or magazine articles, television or radio programs or Internet stories that are representative of the nominee's work. Complete nomination instructions are available online.
Deadline: March 16.

ADDRESS INQUIRIES TO:
Lauren Meregildo-Santos
Program Coordinator
(See address above.)

COLUMBIA UNIVERSITY GRADUATE SCHOOL OF JOURNALISM [1867]

2950 Broadway
New York, NY 10027
(212) 854-6468
Fax: (212) 854-3148
E-mail: cm3443@columbia.edu
Web Site: www.journalism.columbia.edu

FOUNDED: 1960

AREAS OF INTEREST:
Environmental journalism.

NAME(S) OF PROGRAMS:
- **John B. Oakes Award**

TYPE:
Awards/prizes. Awarded for distinguished excellence in environmental journalism.

YEAR PROGRAM STARTED: 1993

ELIGIBILITY:
To be considered for this Award, submitted articles must have been written between January 1 and December 31 of previous year. The article must have been published in a U.S.-based publication. An online publication is acceptable.

GEOG. RESTRICTIONS: United States.

FINANCIAL DATA:
Amount of support per award: $5,000 and a plaque.

NO. AWARDS: 1 award yearly.

APPLICATION INFO:
Nomination instructions are available online. Entry fee of $50 required for each nomination (non-refundable).
Duration: Recipients of the Oakes Award can win it a second time.
Deadline: January 31.

ADDRESS INQUIRIES TO:
Caroline Martinet
Program Manager, Oakes Award
(See address above.)

COUNCIL FOR THE ADVANCEMENT OF SCIENCE WRITING, INC. [1868]

P.O. Box 910
Hedgesville, WV 25427
(304) 754-6786
E-mail: diane@casw.org
Web Site: www.casw.org

FOUNDED: 1959

AREAS OF INTEREST:
Writing about science, medicine, health, technology, energy, the environment, etc., for the general public via the mass media (distinct from technical writing or technical journalism).

NAME(S) OF PROGRAMS:
- **The Victor Cohn Prize for Excellence in Medical Science Reporting**
- **Rennie Taylor/Alton Blakeslee Fellowships for Graduate Study in Science Writing**

TYPE:
Awards/prizes; Fellowships. The Victor Cohn Prize salutes general excellence in medical science writing for the mass media. The prize, to be given annually, seeks to honor a writer for a body of work published or broadcast within the last five years which, for

reasons of uncommon clarity, accuracy, breadth of coverage, enterprise, originality, insight and narrative power, has made a profound and lasting contribution to public awareness and understanding of critical advances in medical science and their impact on human health and well-being.

Rennie Taylor/Alton Blakeslee Fellowships support graduate students in science journalism and experienced reporters who wish to study science writing at the graduate level.

PURPOSE:
To increase public understanding of science by upgrading the quality and quantity of science and medical writing and by improving relationships between scientists and the press.

LEGAL BASIS:
Nonprofit 501(c)(3).

ELIGIBILITY:
The Victor Cohn Prize: Editors, colleagues, scientists and others familiar with the candidate's body of work may proffer nominations. Individuals may nominate themselves.

Rennie Taylor/Alton Blakeslee Fellowships: Journalists with two years of experience who wish to specialize in science writing will receive priority selection. Such applicants should be employed by daily newspapers, wire services, news magazines, radio stations, or television stations or networks. Students must have undergraduate degrees in science or journalism and prove to the satisfaction of a selection committee that they have the motivation and ability to pursue a career in science writing. Fellows may attend school full- or part-time.

Fellowships are not available to those who are pursuing or plan to pursue careers in public relations or public information work.

GEOG. RESTRICTIONS: United States.

FINANCIAL DATA:
Amount of support per award: The Victor Cohn Prize: $3,000 and a framed certificate; Rennie Taylor/Alton Blakeslee Fellowships: $2,000 to $5,000.

NO. MOST RECENT APPLICANTS: Rennie Taylor/Alton Blakeslee Fellowships: 30.

NO. AWARDS: The Victor Cohn Prize: 1; Rennie Taylor/Alton Blakeslee Fellowships: 4.

APPLICATION INFO:
Applicants must apply on the Council web site.

Duration: One academic year. Nonrenewable.

Deadline: The Victor Cohn Prize: July 31. Rennie Taylor/Alton Blakeslee Fellowships: March 29.

PUBLICATIONS:
Guide to Careers in Science Writing.

IRS I.D.: 13-1953314

OFFICERS AND DIRECTORS:
Alan Boyle, President
Deborah Blum, Vice President
Tom Siegfried, Treasurer
Charles Petit, Secretary
Rosalind Reid, Executive Director
Lewis Cope
Barbara J. Culliton
Richard Harris
Maggie Koerth-Baker
Robin Lloyd
Betsy Mason
Miles O'Brien
Joann Rodgers
Cristine Russell
Carl Zimmer

ADDRESS INQUIRIES TO:
Rosalind Reid, Executive Director
(See address above.)

*SPECIAL STIPULATIONS:
U.S. citizens only.

COUNCIL ON FOREIGN RELATIONS [1869]

58 East 68th Street
New York, NY 10065
(212) 434-9740
Fax: (212) 434-9870
E-mail: fellowships@cfr.org
Web Site: www.cfr.org/fellowships

FOUNDED: 1921

AREAS OF INTEREST:
International relations, international news, foreign policy, journalism, international journalism, war reporting, foreign affairs, international affairs, and international media.

NAME(S) OF PROGRAMS:
- **Edward R. Murrow Press Fellowship**

TYPE:
Fellowships. The Edward R. Murrow Press Fellow spends nine months full-time in residence at the Council on Foreign Relations' (CFR) headquarters in New York. The program enables the fellow to engage in sustained analysis and writing, expand his or her intellectual and professional horizons, and extensively participate in CFR's active program of meetings and events. The Fellow will be part of the David Rockefeller Studies Program, CFR's think tank, alongside the program's full-time, adjunct and visiting fellows, whose expertise extends across the broad range of significant foreign policy issues facing the U.S. and the international community.

YEAR PROGRAM STARTED: 1949

PURPOSE:
To promote the quality of responsible and discerning journalism that exemplified the work of Edward R. Murrow.

ELIGIBILITY:
The program is only open to applicants who have distinguished credentials in the field of journalism and who have covered international news as a working journalist for print, broadcast or online media widely available in the U.S. Applicants are limited to those individuals who are authorized to work in the U.S. and who will continue to be authorized for the duration of the Fellowship. CFR does not sponsor for visas.

FINANCIAL DATA:
The Fellow is considered an independent contractor rather than an employee of CFR, and is not eligible for employment benefits, including health insurance.

Amount of support per award: A stipend of $65,000, as well as a modest travel grant.

CO-OP FUNDING PROGRAMS: CBS Foundation and Ford Foundation.

NO. AWARDS: 1 per year.

APPLICATION INFO:
Interested candidates who meet the program's eligibility requirements can apply online between January 1 and March 1 on an annual basis.

Duration: Nine months, preferably beginning in September.

Deadline: March 1. Official selections and announcement will be made in April.

ADDRESS INQUIRIES TO:
See e-mail address or phone number above.

THE DOW JONES NEWS FUND [1870]

4300 Route One North
South Brunswick, NJ 08852
(609) 452-2820
Fax: (609) 520-5804
E-mail: djnf@dowjones.com
Web Site: www.newsfund.org

FOUNDED: 1958

AREAS OF INTEREST:
Journalism.

NAME(S) OF PROGRAMS:
- **Business Reporting Interns, Juniors, Seniors and Graduate Students**
- **Editing Intern Program for College Juniors, Seniors and Graduate Students**

TYPE:
Internships. Editing intern program for juniors, seniors and graduate college students who successfully complete a summer of work as beginning copy editors at newspapers.

PURPOSE:
To encourage students to consider careers in copy-editing.

LEGAL BASIS:
Nonprofit foundation.

ELIGIBILITY:
Applicants must be juniors, seniors or graduate students at any college who have a sincere interest in professional copy-editing news work. Working on a school publication is not a stated requirement, but highly recommended. Applicants must also be U.S. citizens or have a working Visa permitting them to work in the U.S.

GEOG. RESTRICTIONS: United States.

FINANCIAL DATA:
Interns will receive regular wages (minimum $350 per week) from the newspapers for which they work. After the summer of work, a $1,000 scholarship check is awarded to the intern's college, but only if that intern returns to school following the internship.

Amount of support per award: $1,000.

Total amount of support: $200,000 to $300,000, depending on number of interns selected and cost of pre-training course.

NO. MOST RECENT APPLICANTS: 900.

NO. AWARDS: Up to 125.

APPLICATION INFO:
Applications available online September 1 to November 1.

Duration: Full summer.

Deadline: November 1.

OFFICERS:
Richard J. Levine, President
Paul Schmidt, Treasurer
Diana Mitsuklos, Secretary

STAFF:
Linda Shockley, Managing Director
Diane Cohn, Finance and Administration Manager
Heather Taylor, Digital Media and Programs Manager

DIRECTORS:
Don E. Carter
Thomas E. Engleman
Ken Herts
Richard S. Holden
Diana Mitsu Klos
Neal Lipschutz
Mark Musgrave
Laurence G. O'Donnell
Dr. Reginald Owens
Dr. Russell G. Todd

ADDRESS INQUIRIES TO:
Internship Coordinator
Editing Intern Programs
(See address above.)

FUND FOR INVESTIGATIVE JOURNALISM [1871]

529 14th Street, N.W.
13th Floor
Washington, DC 20045
(202) 662-7564
E-mail: fundfij@gmail.com
Web Site: www.fij.org

FOUNDED: 1969

AREAS OF INTEREST:
Promoting the work of investigative journalism.

TYPE:
Project/program grants. The Fund gives grants to investigative reporters working outside the protection and backing of major news organizations.

PURPOSE:
To provide funding for reporters engaged in investigative journalism.

ELIGIBILITY:
Projects on domestic and international issues are eligible. Entries must be written in English.

FINANCIAL DATA:
Amount of support per award: Average grant: $5,000.
Total amount of support: Varies.

APPLICATION INFO:
Applications are to be submitted online. Applicant must write a proposal letter outlining the story, what he or she expects to prove, how this will be done, and the sources for the proof. For projects, include the anticipated completion date.

The letter must be supported by a resume, a detailed budget to justify the size of the grant, no more than two writing samples or one sample chapter in the case of a book applicant, and a letter of commitment from an editor or publisher or an executive of a broadcast news operation or online news outlet stating that the project will be published or broadcast if completed according to the proposal.

A letter of commitment is required for all applicants and is a nonnegotiable requirement. In the case of individuals seeking grants for books, a signed copy of a contract with a publisher is required and should be substituted for the commitment letter.

Deadline: Varies.

ADDRESS INQUIRIES TO:
Sandy Bergo, Executive Director
(See address above.)

RUTH HANCOCK SCHOLARSHIP FOUNDATION [1872]

c/o Broadcast Executives Society
Box 75150-20 Bloor Street East
Toronto ON M4W 3T3 Canada
(647) 985-0880
E-mail: bob.reaume@gmail.com
Web Site: www.bes.ca

FOUNDED: 1926

AREAS OF INTEREST:
Communications and marketing.

NAME(S) OF PROGRAMS:
- **Ruth Hancock Scholarships**

TYPE:
Awards/prizes; Scholarships. Scholarships to encourage talented, hard-working students to pursue careers in Canadian broadcasting.

PURPOSE:
To encourage talented, hard working students to pursue careers in Canadian broadcasting or broadcast sales/marketing.

LEGAL BASIS:
Private.

ELIGIBILITY:
Applicants must be Canadian students enrolled in a recognized communications or marketing course in Canada who are seriously interested in a career in Canadian broadcasting or broadcast sales/marketing.

GEOG. RESTRICTIONS: Canada.

FINANCIAL DATA:
Amount of support per award: $1,500.
Total amount of support: $4,500.

NO. AWARDS: 3.

APPLICATION INFO:
Signed recommendation from course director or professor and a 500-word essay must be submitted with the application form to the Ruth Hancock Memorial Scholarships; c/o Broadcast Executives Society, at the address above.

Duration: One year. Recipients can reapply.
Deadline: June 30. Announcement in the fall.

ADDRESS INQUIRIES TO:
Bob Reaume
c/o Broadcast Executives Society
(See address above.)

WILLIAM RANDOLPH HEARST FOUNDATION [1873]

90 New Montgomery Street, Suite 1212
San Francisco, CA 94105
(415) 908-4560
(800) 841-7048 ext. 4565
Fax: (415) 243-0760
E-mail: jwatten@hearstfdn.org
Web Site: www.hearstawards.org

FOUNDED: 1948

AREAS OF INTEREST:
Writing, photojournalism and broadcast journalism.

NAME(S) OF PROGRAMS:
- **Journalism Awards Program**

TYPE:
Awards/prizes; Scholarships. Awards to the top 10 winners of 13 monthly competitions: six writing, three photo, two broadcast (TV and radio) and multimedia. Entrants must be journalism majors attending one of the 105 accredited schools of journalism. The schools receive a matching grant.

YEAR PROGRAM STARTED: 1960

PURPOSE:
To provide support, encouragement and assistance to education in journalism at the undergraduate college level.

LEGAL BASIS:
Nonprofit foundation.

ELIGIBILITY:
Participation in the program is open only to journalism majors who are undergraduates at the colleges and universities that are members of the Association of Schools of Journalism and Mass Communication.

GEOG. RESTRICTIONS: United States.

FINANCIAL DATA:
Amount of support per award: $1,000 to $5,000, depending upon placement of winners.
Total amount of support: Over $500,000 for the year 2015-16.

NO. MOST RECENT APPLICANTS: 1,200.

NO. AWARDS: 150 scholarships and grants.

APPLICATION INFO:
Full application information may be obtained through individual departments of journalism at participating schools. A list of accredited schools is available at Hearst Foundation's San Francisco address.

Duration: Varies.
Deadline: Monthly during academic year.

STAFF:
Dino Dinovitz, Executive Director
Jan C. Watten, Program Director
Yasi Haerizadeh, Program Assistant

BOARD OF DIRECTORS:
William R. Hearst, III, President
James Asher
Annissa Balson
David Barrett
Frank A. Bennack, Jr.
John G. Conomikes
Ron Doerfler
George R. Hearst, Jr.
John R. Hearst, Jr.
Harvey Lipton
Gilbert C. Maurer
Mark Miller
Virginia Randt

ADDRESS INQUIRIES TO:
Jan C. Watten, Program Director
(See address above.)

THE SIDNEY HILLMAN FOUNDATION, INC. [1874]

12 West 31st Street
12th Floor
New York, NY 10001
(646) 448-6413
E-mail: alex@hillmanfoundation.org
Web Site: www.hillmanfoundation.org

FOUNDED: 1950

AREAS OF INTEREST:
Civil liberties, race relations, labor movement, social welfare, housing, economic security and international understanding.

NAME(S) OF PROGRAMS:
- **Hillman Prizes in Journalism**
- **Sidney Awards**

TYPE:
Awards/prizes. Monetary awards presented annually for outstanding contributions in the

fields of daily or periodical journalism, nonfiction, radio and television, blogs and commentary.

YEAR PROGRAM STARTED: 1950

PURPOSE:
To recognize outstanding contributions to the field of journalism dealing with themes relating to the ideals which Sidney Hillman held throughout his life, including the protection of individual civil liberties, improved race relations, a strengthened labor movement, the advancement of social welfare, housing and economic security, greater world understanding and related problems.

LEGAL BASIS:
Private foundation.

ELIGIBILITY:
Only work published in English in the previous calendar year and distributed in the U.S. and Canada is eligible for consideration. Radio and television contributions must have been produced under professional auspices in the previous calendar year.

GEOG. RESTRICTIONS: United States and Canada.

FINANCIAL DATA:
Amount of support per award: Hillman Prize: $5,000; Sidney Award: $500.

NO. MOST RECENT APPLICANTS: 600.

NO. AWARDS: Hillman Prizes: 7; Sidney Awards: 12.

APPLICATION INFO:
Material may be submitted by the author, his or her publication or publisher, or by anyone connected with it. The submission must be accompanied by a brief cover letter.

Deadline: Hillman Prizes: January 30. Sidney Awards: Last day of each month.

STAFF:
Alexandra Lescaze, Executive Director
Lindsay Beyerstein, Lead Writer

ADDRESS INQUIRIES TO:
Alexandra Lescaze, Executive Director
(See address above.)

INTER AMERICAN PRESS ASSOCIATION (IAPA) [1875]

3511 N.W. 94th Avenue
Miami, FL 33172
(305) 634-2465
Fax: (305) 860-4264
E-mail: rtrottie@sipiapa.org
Web Site: www.sipiapa.org

FOUNDED: 1942

AREAS OF INTEREST:
Press freedom.

NAME(S) OF PROGRAMS:
- **IAPA Scholarship Fund**

TYPE:
Exchange programs; Fellowships; Scholarships. Scholarships for American and Canadian working journalists, journalism graduates or journalism students to study in Latin America and for journalists who are citizens or residents of countries outside the U.S. or Canada to study in the U.S. or Canada.

YEAR PROGRAM STARTED: 1954

PURPOSE:
To support the exchange of journalists and journalism students between countries of the Western Hemisphere.

LEGAL BASIS:
Nonprofit association, tax-exempt under Internal Revenue Code 501(c)(3).

ELIGIBILITY:
Journalists or journalism school seniors or graduates between 21 and 35 years of age with a good command of the language they are to use. Students must have completed their degree before beginning the scholarship year.

Language ability for U.S. and Canadian candidates must be confirmed by a recognized authority in Spanish or Portuguese. Latin American candidates must take a TOEFL (Test of English as a Foreign Language).

FINANCIAL DATA:
U.S. and Canadian scholars will receive $20,000 for the duration of their stay abroad. Latin American and Caribbean scholars will receive $20,000 and a one-time round-trip airfare for the year.

NO. MOST RECENT APPLICANTS: 95.

NO. AWARDS: 4.

APPLICATION INFO:
Application is available on the web site or by writing to the Association.

Duration: One academic year.

Deadline: January 2017.

STAFF:
Ricardo Trotti, Executive Director
Mauricio J. Montaldo, Coordinator of Scholarship Fund

ADDRESS INQUIRIES TO:
Mauricio J. Montaldo
Coordinator of Scholarship Fund
(See address above.)

INTERNATIONAL DOCUMENTARY ASSOCIATION

3470 Wilshire Boulevard
Suite 980
Los Angeles, CA 90010
(213) 232-1660
Fax: (213) 232-1669
E-mail: toni.b@documentary.org
Web Site: www.documentary.org

TYPE:
Awards/prizes; Internships. IDA Documentary Awards celebrate the best nonfiction films and programs of the year. Prize awarded in seven categories: feature, short, episodic series, curated series, short film series, limited series, and the David L. Wolper Student Documentary Award.

IDA/David L. Wolper Student Documentary Achievement Award recognizes exceptional achievement in nonfiction film and video production at the university level and brings greater public and industry awareness to the work of students in the documentary field.

The Pare Lorentz Award is awarded for films that reflect the spirit and tradition of Pare Lorentz's work. The film should demonstrate one or more of Lorentz's central concerns (the appropriate use of the natural environment, justice for all, and the illumination of pressing social problems) presented as a compelling story by skillful filmmaking.

Pare Lorentz Documentary Fund supports full-length documentary films that reflect the spirit and nature of Pare Lorentz's work, exhibiting objective research, artful storytelling, strong visual style, high production values, artistic writing and outstanding music composition, as well as skillful direction, camerawork and editing.

Los Angeles County Arts Commission Internships are offered to undergraduate students who currently reside or are enrolled in a college or university located in Los Angeles County, CA. Those interested should consult the Association web site for up-to-date details.

See entry 449 for full listing.

INVESTIGATIVE REPORTERS AND EDITORS [1876]

141 Neff Annex
Missouri School of Journalism
Columbia, MO 65211
(573) 882-6668
Fax: (573) 882-5431
E-mail: rescntr@ire.org
Web Site: www.ire.org

FOUNDED: 1975

AREAS OF INTEREST:
Journalism across all media.

NAME(S) OF PROGRAMS:
- **Investigative Reporters and Editors Contest**

TYPE:
Awards/prizes; Fellowships. Investigative Reporters and Editors Contest is an annual investigative reporting contest. The Tom Renner Award (one of the 17 categories of this Contest) is given to the best investigative reporting in print, broadcast or book form, covering crime and its impact on society.

IRE also offers fellowships to minority journalism students and professionals to attend IRE national or regional conferences. There are also fellowships available for small newspaper staffers and for journalism students.

PURPOSE:
To promote high-quality, in-depth journalism.

LEGAL BASIS:
University.

ELIGIBILITY:
Individual journalists and news organizations may submit entries for the Renner Award. No more than 10 stories can be entered. Entries that disregard the rules will be disqualified. Qualifications for IRE minority fellowships include financial need, references and answers to essay questions.

FINANCIAL DATA:
Amount of support per award: Renner Award: $500; Student Award: $250.

Total amount of support: Varies.

NO. MOST RECENT APPLICANTS: 550.

NO. AWARDS: 17.

APPLICATION INFO:
All entry materials are entered online through the IRE Award contest platform. There is no limit on the number of entries allowed from individual journalists.

Deadline: Mid-January. Deadline for fellowships depends on conference dates.

PUBLICATIONS:
Program announcement; entry form.

IRS I.D.: 51-0166741

ADDRESS INQUIRIES TO:
Lauren Grandestaff, Contest Coordinator
(See address above.)

JOURNAL OF THE AMERICAN MEDICAL ASSOCIATION [1877]

330 North Wabash Avenue
Suite 39300
Chicago, IL 60611
(312) 464-4334
Fax: (312) 464-5824
E-mail: robert.golub@jama-archives.org
Web Site: www.jama.com

FOUNDED: 1847

AREAS OF INTEREST:
Public health, physician and health care personnel education and medical publications.

NAME(S) OF PROGRAMS:
- **Morris Fishbein Fellowship in Medical Editing**

TYPE:
Fellowships. Award granted to physicians exclusively as a one-year, full-time editorial fellowship with *The Journal of the American Medical Association*. The successful candidate will work with the editorial and production staff in all facets of editing and publishing a major weekly medical journal. At the completion of the program, it is expected that the candidate will be proficient in all aspects of manuscript selection, peer review, issue makeup, copy editing and styling, issue planning and managing, in addition to the many other elements of medical journal publication.

YEAR PROGRAM STARTED: 1978

PURPOSE:
To provide physicians with an opportunity to learn the editorial functions of a major medical journal.

LEGAL BASIS:
Not-for-profit organization serving members in the medical profession.

ELIGIBILITY:
Applicants must be physicians. Candidates also must have proven writing ability at the time of application because they will be required during the course of the year to prepare articles for publication. Although the fellow will work under the supervision of a physician-editor, ability to work independently is a must. Ability to use a resource library is a strong plus.

Fellow must live in Chicago during the 12-month full-time fellowship (July to June).

FINANCIAL DATA:
Amount of support per award: $54,000.
Total amount of support: $54,000 annually.

NO. MOST RECENT APPLICANTS: 12.

NO. AWARDS: 1 annually.

APPLICATION INFO:
Application forms may be obtained from the address or e-mail listed above.
Duration: One year.
Deadline: Early January.

ADDRESS INQUIRIES TO:
Robert Golub, M.D., Deputy Editor
(See e-mail and address above.)

KAPPA TAU ALPHA [1878]

76 Gannett Hall
School of Journalism
University of Missouri
Columbia, MO 65211-1200
(573) 882-7685
Fax: (573) 884-1720
E-mail: umcjourkta@missouri.edu
Web Site: www.kappataualpha.org

FOUNDED: 1910

AREAS OF INTEREST:
Journalism research and mass communication.

NAME(S) OF PROGRAMS:
- **Frank Luther Mott KTA Research/Book Award**

TYPE:
Awards/prizes. Annual award for a published book concerned with journalism and mass communications research.

YEAR PROGRAM STARTED: 1944

PURPOSE:
To recognize the top book published in the field of journalism and mass communications research; to promote interest in Kappa Tau Alpha among students and faculty.

LEGAL BASIS:
National society honoring scholarship in journalism and mass communication.

ELIGIBILITY:
Qualified individuals may apply for the award with an appropriate book published during the year.

FINANCIAL DATA:
Amount of support per award: $1,000 and a plaque.

NO. MOST RECENT APPLICANTS: 14.

NO. AWARDS: 1 annually.

APPLICATION INFO:
Interested applicants should submit six copies of the published work to be considered.
Deadline: Typically first Monday in December.

OFFICERS:
Andrew Mendelson, President
Jeff Fruit, Vice President
Dr. Keith P. Sanders, Executive Director

JUDGES:
Jeff Fruit
Andrew Mendelson
Dr. Keith P. Sanders

ADDRESS INQUIRIES TO:
Dr. Keith P. Sanders, Executive Director
(See address above.)

LIVINGSTON AWARDS [1879]

Wallace House, University of Michigan
620 Oxford Road
Ann Arbor, MI 48104
(734) 998-7575
Fax: (734) 998-7979
E-mail: livawards@umich.edu
Web Site: wallacehouse.umich.edu/livingston-awards

AREAS OF INTEREST:
Broadcast, print and online journalism.

NAME(S) OF PROGRAMS:
- **Livingston Awards for Young Journalists**

TYPE:
Awards/prizes.

YEAR PROGRAM STARTED: 1981

PURPOSE:
To recognize the best young journalists; to support the work of young journalists; to create modern role models for the next generation of news consumers; to advance excellence in journalism.

LEGAL BASIS:
Foundation.

ELIGIBILITY:
Entries must be directly related to current events or include new information about old events. Features and commentary are eligible. There are no awards for still photography.

Journalists who are 34 years old or younger as of December 31 and whose work appears in print, broadcast or online media may apply.

Submissions must consist of materials prepared in the ordinary course of the journalist's professional production. One entry per individual. Individuals may apply on their own, or be entered by their organization. Multiple bylines are eligible, but all must meet age criteria. Materials prepared by journalists specifically for submission to the Livingston Awards will not qualify and may not be considered. Student media are not eligible.

All entries will be judged on the basis of either a single piece, or in the case of series, a maximum of three related pieces.

FINANCIAL DATA:
Amount of support per award: $10,000.
Total amount of support: $30,000.

NO. AWARDS: 3.

APPLICATION INFO:
Detailed information is available online.
Deadline: February 1. Announcement in June.

PUBLICATIONS:
Program brochure.

STAFF:
Melissa Riley, Administrator

ADDRESS INQUIRIES TO:
See e-mail address above.

THE GERALD LOEB AWARDS [1880]

UCLA Anderson School of Management
110 Westwood Plaza
Gold Hall, Suite B307
Los Angeles, CA 90095-1481
(310) 825-4478
Fax: (310) 825-4479
E-mail: loeb@anderson.ucla.edu
Web Site: www.loeb.anderson.ucla.edu

FOUNDED: 1957

AREAS OF INTEREST:
Business, economic and financial news writing and journalism.

TYPE:
Awards/prizes. Awards to recognize business and financial journalists for important contributions to the understanding of business, finance and the economy.

YEAR PROGRAM STARTED: 1957

PURPOSE:
To recognize journalists who make significant contributions to the understanding of business and finance.

LEGAL BASIS:
University.

ELIGIBILITY:
Entries submitted must have been published or broadcast for the first time during the previous calendar year in the U.S.

FINANCIAL DATA:
Amount of support per award: $2,000; $500 Honorable Mention.

APPLICATION INFO:
Application must be submitted online.

PUBLICATIONS:
Entry brochure.

ADDRESS INQUIRIES TO:
Jonathan Daillak, Deputy Director of Administration and Development
(See address above.)

MASSACHUSETTS INSTITUTE OF TECHNOLOGY [1881]

MIT E19-623
77 Massachusetts Avenue
Cambridge, MA 02139-4307
(617) 253-3442
Fax: (617) 258-8100
E-mail: knight-info@mit.edu
Web Site: ksj.mit.edu

AREAS OF INTEREST:
Science journalism.

NAME(S) OF PROGRAMS:
- **Knight Science Journalism Fellowships**

TYPE:
Fellowships. Nine months access to courses, laboratories and researchers.

YEAR PROGRAM STARTED: 1983

PURPOSE:
To recognize excellence in explaining science, medicine, technology and the environment to the public; to provide a deeper familiarity with the processes of research and development to widen the fellows' acquaintance with leading engineers, scientists and medical researchers experienced in explaining complex issues.

LEGAL BASIS:
University.

ELIGIBILITY:
Applicants must be full-time journalists, whether they are on staff or freelance. They must have at least three years of full-time experience covering science, technology, medicine or environment. Candidates may be reporters, writers, editors, producers, illustrators, filmmakers or photojournalists. They may work for newspapers, magazines, television, radio, the Web or other media. Journalists from all countries are eligible to apply.

FINANCIAL DATA:
Fellowship includes stipend. During their residence, fellows may join an MIT affiliates health plan.

Amount of support per award: $70,000 stipend.

CO-OP FUNDING PROGRAMS: Sponsored by the John S. and James L. Knight Foundation.

NO. AWARDS: 10 annually.

APPLICATION INFO:
Online submission only.

Duration: Nine months, September to May.

Deadline: February 28. Interviews will begin in April with public announcement in early May.

ADDRESS INQUIRIES TO:
Bianca Sinausky
Program Administrator
400 Main Street, Suite 623
Cambridge, MA 02123
E-mail: singleta@mit.edu

NATIONAL ASSOCIATION OF BROADCASTERS [1882]

1771 N Street, N.W.
Washington, DC 20036-2800
(202) 429-5300
E-mail: nab@nab.org
Web Site: www.nab.org

NAME(S) OF PROGRAMS:
- **Grants for Research in Broadcasting**

TYPE:
Research grants. Grants are intended to stimulate interest in broadcast research, especially research on economic, business, social or policy issues of importance to the U.S. commercial broadcast industry.

YEAR PROGRAM STARTED: 1967

PURPOSE:
To attract qualified personnel into the field of broadcast research; to facilitate the training of broadcast researchers; to assist individuals already working in this area; to make high-quality academic research available to industry practitioners as well as other academics.

LEGAL BASIS:
Nonprofit association.

ELIGIBILITY:
The competition is open to all academic personnel and graduate students. Senior undergraduates are invited to submit proposals.

FINANCIAL DATA:
Monies are not to be used for overhead or benefits.

Amount of support per award: Average $5,000. More can be awarded if the project merits additional funds.

Total amount of support: Up to $10,000.

NO. MOST RECENT APPLICANTS: 50.

NO. AWARDS: 4 to 6 annually.

APPLICATION INFO:
Official application materials are available upon request.

Duration: One year.

Deadline: Late January. Award notification by April 1.

ADDRESS INQUIRIES TO:
Vice President
Research and Information
(See address above.)

NATIONAL ASSOCIATION OF FARM BROADCASTING FOUNDATION [1883]

1100 Platte Falls Road
Platte City, MO 64079
(816) 431-4032
Fax: (816) 431-4087
E-mail: susan@nafb.com
Web Site: www.nafbfoundation.com

AREAS OF INTEREST:
Agricultural journalism and communications.

NAME(S) OF PROGRAMS:
- **Glenn Kummerow Memorial Scholarship**
- **The George Logan Scholarship**
- **Orion Samuelson Scholarship**

TYPE:
Scholarships. Since 1977, the NAFB Foundation has provided financial support and educational opportunities in the form of college scholarships to assist students in pursuit of careers in agricultural communications. Currently the NAFB Foundation offers three annual college scholarships. These scholarships are recognized at the National NAFB Convention.

YEAR PROGRAM STARTED: 1975

PURPOSE:
To provide financial support and educational opportunities for students in pursuit of careers in agricultural communications.

ELIGIBILITY:
Must be at least junior-year college students, enrolled in an agricultural journalism/agricultural communications curriculum, or plan to transfer to a university which offers a designated professional program of study in agricultural radio-television broadcasting. Selection is by application and is based on agricultural communications aptitude and leadership achievements, academic record and career plans.

FINANCIAL DATA:
Winners receive an expense-paid trip to attend the convention as part of the award.

Amount of support per award: $5,000 each scholarship.

Total amount of support: $15,000.

NO. AWARDS: 1 per award.

APPLICATION INFO:
Applications are available in April on the Foundation web site.

Duration: One school year.

Deadline: June 6.

ADDRESS INQUIRIES TO:
NAFB Member Services Manager
(See address above.)

NATIONAL ASSOCIATION OF HISPANIC JOURNALISTS

1050 Connecticut Avenue, N.W.
5th Floor
Washington, DC 20036
(202) 853-7760
E-mail: nahj@nahj.org
lafrank@nahj.org
Web Site: www.nahj.org

TYPE:
Awards/prizes; Conferences/seminars; Fellowships; General operating grants; Internships; Matching gifts; Project/program grants; Research grants; Scholarships; Seed money grants; Training grants; Travel grants.

See entry 980 for full listing.

NATIONAL ASSOCIATION OF SCIENCE WRITERS, INC. [1884]

P.O. Box 7905
Berkeley, CA 94707
(510) 647-9500
E-mail: director@nasw.org
Web Site: www.nasw.org

FOUNDED: 1934

AREAS OF INTEREST:
Dissemination of scientific and medical information to a general lay audience and professional development for science writers.

NAME(S) OF PROGRAMS:
- **Science in Society Awards**

TYPE:
Conferences/seminars; Fellowships; Project/program grants; Seed money grants; Training grants; Travel grants. Separate monetary prizes and awards for writers in five categories:
(1) books;
(2) commentary or opinion;
(3) science reporting;
(4) science reporting for a local or regional market and;
(5) longform science reporting.

YEAR PROGRAM STARTED: 1972

PURPOSE:
To recognize investigative or interpretive reporting about the sciences and their impact on society.

LEGAL BASIS:
Professional membership organization.

ELIGIBILITY:
Any writer (or team) is eligible to submit not more than one entry in each category. Material may be single article or broadcast or a series. Books with a copyright date of 2016 are eligible. Works must be written or spoken, in English, intended for the layperson and published or broadcast in North America between January 1, 2016 and December 31, 2016.

GEOG. RESTRICTIONS: North America.

FINANCIAL DATA:
Amount of support per award: $2,500 and Certificates of Recognition in each category.
Total amount of support: Varies.

NO. MOST RECENT APPLICANTS: 200.

NO. AWARDS: 5 annually.

APPLICATION INFO:
Details are available online.
Deadline: February 1.

ADDRESS INQUIRIES TO:
Tinsley Davis, Executive Director
(See address above.)

NATIONAL ASSOCIATION OF SCIENCE WRITERS, INC. [1885]

P.O. Box 7905
Berkeley, CA 94707
(510) 647-9500
E-mail: director@nasw.org
Web Site: www.nasw.org

FOUNDED: 1934

AREAS OF INTEREST:
Dissemination of scientific and medical information to a general audience and professional development for science writers.

NAME(S) OF PROGRAMS:
- **NASW Idea Grants**

TYPE:
Project/program grants. Grants to support projects or programs designed to help science writers in their professional lives and/or benefit the field of science writing.

YEAR PROGRAM STARTED: 2010

PURPOSE:
To award the creativity and initiative of science writers; to create projects and programs that benefit the field and the writers in it.

LEGAL BASIS:
Professional membership organization.

ELIGIBILITY:
Individuals or groups are eligible to apply. Proposals can serve non-members, as well as members. Creative thinking is encouraged.

GEOG. RESTRICTIONS: North America.

FINANCIAL DATA:
Amount of support per award: $1,000 to $40,000.
Total amount of support: Varies.

APPLICATION INFO:
Details are available online.
Deadline: Varies.

ADDRESS INQUIRIES TO:
Tinsley Davis, Executive Director
(See address above.)

NATIONAL ENDOWMENT FOR THE HUMANITIES [1886]

The Constitution Center
400 7th Street, S.W.
Washington, DC 20506
(202) 606-8269
Fax: (202) 606-8557
E-mail: publicpgms@neh.gov
Web Site: www.neh.gov

FOUNDED: 1965

AREAS OF INTEREST:
Scholarship, research, education and public programs in the humanities. In the act that established the Endowment, the term humanities includes, but is not limited to, the study of history, philosophy, languages, linguistics, literature, archaeology, jurisprudence, the history, theory and criticism of the arts, ethics, comparative religion and those aspects of the social sciences that employ historical or philosophical approaches.

NAME(S) OF PROGRAMS:
- **Public Humanities Projects**

TYPE:
Project/program grants. Public Humanities Projects grants support projects that bring the ideas and insights of the humanities to life for general audiences. Projects must engage humanities scholarship to illuminate significant themes in disciplines such as history, literature, ethics and art, or to address challenging issues in contemporary life. NEH encourages projects that involve members of the public in collaboration with humanities scholars or that invite contributions from the community in the development and delivery of humanities programming. The grant program supports a variety of forms of audience engagement:
Community Conversations: This format supports one- to three-year-long series of community-wide public discussions in which diverse residents creatively address community challenges, guided by the perspectives of the humanities;
Exhibitions: This format supports permanent exhibitions that will be on view for at least three years, or traveling exhibitions that will be available to public audiences in at least two venues in the U.S. (including the originating location) and;
Historic Places: This format supports the interpretation of historic sites, houses, neighborhoods and regions, which might include living history presentations, guided tours, exhibitions and public programs.

YEAR PROGRAM STARTED: 1969

PURPOSE:
To create an understanding and appreciation of the humanities among the general public.

LEGAL BASIS:
The National Foundation on the Arts and Humanities Act of 1965, Public Law 89-209, as amended.

ELIGIBILITY:
Any U.S. nonprofit organization with IRS tax-exempt status is eligible, as are state and local governmental agencies and federally recognized Indian tribal governments.

GEOG. RESTRICTIONS: United States.

FINANCIAL DATA:
Amount of support per award: Planning: Mostly up to $40,000, with a maximum of $75,000 for complex projects that will reach large national audiences. Implementation: Typically up to $400,000 ($460,000 for projects requesting a Position in Public Humanities); up to $1,000,000 for Chairman's Special Awards.
Total amount of support: Varies.

APPLICATION INFO:
All applications must be submitted via Grants.gov. Applications should follow the parameters set out in one of the three formats listed above. See www.neh.gov for details.
Deadline: August 10. NEH strongly recommends that applicant complete or verify one's Grants.gov registration at least two weeks before the application deadline, as it takes time to process one's registration.

PUBLICATIONS:
Annual report; *Grant Programs*; *Humanities Magazine.*

IRS I.D.: 52-1098584

ADDRESS INQUIRIES TO:
Division of Public Programs
(See e-mail or phone number above.)

NATIONAL INSTITUTE FOR LABOR RELATIONS RESEARCH [1887]

5211 Port Royal Road
Suite 510
Springfield, VA 22151
(703) 321-9606 ext. 2231
Fax: (703) 321-7143
E-mail: CLJ@nrtw.org
Web Site: www.nilrr.org

FOUNDED: 1985

AREAS OF INTEREST:
Research and analysis exposing the economic and social inequities of compulsory unionism.

NAME(S) OF PROGRAMS:
- **The William B. Ruggles Journalist Scholarship**

TYPE:
Scholarships. Unrestricted scholarship awarded annually to the student who exemplifies the dedication to principle and high journalistic standards of the late William B. Ruggles, the well-known and respected Texas journalist who contributed significantly to the Right to Work movement.

YEAR PROGRAM STARTED: 1974

PURPOSE:
To honor the late William B. Ruggles, former editorial page editor of *The Dallas Morning News*.

LEGAL BASIS:
Nonpartisan coalition of citizens.

ELIGIBILITY:
Applicants are limited to graduate or undergraduate students majoring in journalism in institutions of higher learning throughout the U.S. Graduating high school seniors may apply, if accepted to a journalism or communications school. To be considered, applicants must demonstrate the potential for a successful completion of educational requirements in an accredited journalism program and an understanding of voluntarism and of the problems of compulsory unionism.

GEOG. RESTRICTIONS: United States.

FINANCIAL DATA:
Amount of support per award: $2,000.

Total amount of support: $2,000 each year.

NO. MOST RECENT APPLICANTS: 50.

NO. AWARDS: 1 annually.

APPLICATION INFO:
A total application will consist of a completed formal application form, available from the address above, an official grade transcript from essay finalists and a typewritten essay of approximately 500 words clearly demonstrating an interest in and a knowledge of the Right to Work principle. Application may be submitted electronically or by mail. Online applications are encouraged.

Deadline: Postmark by December 31. Announcement in April.

OFFICERS:
Mark Mix, Executive Vice President and Treasurer

ADDRESS INQUIRIES TO:
Cathy Jones, Scholarship Administrator
(See address above.)

NATIONAL PRESS FOUNDATION [1888]

1211 Connecticut Avenue, N.W.
Suite 310
Washington, DC 20036
(202) 663-7280
E-mail: npf@nationalpress.org
Web Site: www.nationalpress.org

AREAS OF INTEREST:
Journalism.

NAME(S) OF PROGRAMS:

- **Clifford K. and James T. Berryman Award for Editorial Cartoons**
- **Capitol Hill Issues Briefings**
- **Everett McKinley Dirksen Award**
- **The Feddie Award**
- **Paul Miller Washington Reporting Fellowship**
- **National Issues Programs**
- **Thomas L. Stokes Award**

TYPE:
Awards/prizes; Fellowships. International programs. The Everett McKinley Dirksen Award is intended to recognize individuals whose work shows thoughtful appraisal and insight in to the workings of the U.S. Congress.

The Feddie Award recognizes coverage of the impact of federal laws on local communities.

Paul Miller Washington Reporting Fellowship provides free professional development opportunities to nine, day-long monthly seminars to reporters new to covering Washington. Agency visits, briefings from officials and presentations by experts enable journalists to add depth and insight to topics they cover.

National Issues Programs offer free, all-expenses-paid fellowships to one- to four-day seminars on a variety of topics including Alzheimer's disease, cancer, and retirement.

PURPOSE:
To help journalists better understand the issues about which they write and broadcast.

ELIGIBILITY:
Clifford K. and James T. Berryman Award for Editorial Cartoons is open to editorial cartoonists in the U.S. for work that exhibits power to influence public opinion, plus good drawing and striking effect.

Thomas L. Stokes Award is for the best writing on the subject of energy. The subject may be any form of energy - oil, gas, coal, nuclear, water, solar, etc. The writing may be reporting, analysis or commentary and can consist of one to three articles on unrelated subjects, or one series of articles or a project on a related subject. Journalists from print, online and broadcast are welcome to apply.

FINANCIAL DATA:
Amount of support per award: Berryman Award: $2,500; Dirksen and Feddie Awards: $5,000; Stokes Award: $1,000 and citation.

APPLICATION INFO:
Application information is available on the Foundation's web site.

Deadline: Berryman and Feddie Awards: October 1; Stokes Award: January 31.

STAFF:
Sandy Johnson, President

NEW YORK STATE SENATE

Student Programs Office
80 South Swan Street, Suite 1426
Albany, NY 12247
(518) 455-2611
Fax: (518) 426-6827
E-mail: students@nysenate.gov
Web Site: www.nysenate.gov/student-programs

TYPE:
Fellowships. These fellowships are intended for the graduate/postgraduate/midcareer level. Stipends are for bipartisan opportunities to train in government while on-site in Albany, NY. Fellows spend almost a year immersed in the work of the Senate, learning techniques associated with policymaking and legislative process. Placement is usually to the office of an elected Senate member. The Senate Legislative Fellows Program, Biggane Fellowship, Roth Journalism Fellowship and Wiebe Public Service Fellowship constitute the Senate Graduate/Post-Graduate/Mid-Career Fellowships.

See entry 1947 for full listing.

THE NEWSGUILD-CWA (TNG-CWA) [1889]

501 Third Street, N.W.
Washington, DC 20001-2797
(202) 434-1162
Fax: (202) 434-1472
E-mail: jhartman@cwa-union.org
Web Site: www.newsguild.org/heywood-broun-award

FOUNDED: 1933

AREAS OF INTEREST:
Representing journalists and other media workers in the traditional and digital news industry in the U.S., Canada and Puerto Rico. Areas of interest include all matters involving the news media; freedom of the press and other First Amendment issues; and workers' rights.

NAME(S) OF PROGRAMS:

- **Heywood Broun Award**

TYPE:
Awards/prizes. The Heywood Broun Award is given in name and tradition of the famed early 20th-century New York City columnist and NewsGuild founder whose journalism righted wrongs, fought injustice and championed the underdog. The total award package consists of a Top award and two lesser Substantial Distinction awards.

YEAR PROGRAM STARTED: 1941

PURPOSE:
To encourage and recognize individual journalistic achievement in this spirit by members of the working press, particularly if it helps right a wrong or correct an injustice, or shows an "abiding concern for the underdog and the underprivileged."

LEGAL BASIS:
Labor union.

ELIGIBILITY:
All journalists working for professional mass media in the U.S., Canada and Puerto Rico are eligible, whether or not they are Guild members. Entries can be from newspapers, web sites, nonprofit news organizations, magazines, television and radio - any type of professional news broadcast or publication, print or digital.

Entries on behalf of an entire staff of a publication or employer are not eligible. While team entries are eligible, and have been Broun winners, judges are instructed to give more weight to entries by individuals or pairs of journalists.

Entries written or reported by managers are not eligible.

GEOG. RESTRICTIONS: United States, Puerto Rico and Canada.

FINANCIAL DATA:
Amount of support per award: Top award: $5,000 and engraved plaque. Substantial Distinction awards: $1,000 and framed citation.

Total amount of support: $7,000.

NO. MOST RECENT APPLICANTS: 80.

NO. AWARDS: 1 Top award and 2 Substantial Distinction awards annually.

APPLICATION INFO:
Consult the web site address above for details.

Deadline: Last Friday in January.

OFFICERS:
Bernard J. Lunzer, President
Marian Needham, Vice President

ADDRESS INQUIRIES TO:
Broun Award Committee
(See address above.)

THE NEWSGUILD-CWA (TNG-CWA) [1890]

501 Third Street, N.W.
Washington, DC 20001-2797
(202) 434-7177
Fax: (202) 434-1472
E-mail: dedmondson@cwa-union.org
Web Site: www.newsguild.org/david-s-barr-award-student-journalism

FOUNDED: 1933

AREAS OF INTEREST:
Representing journalists and other media workers in the traditional and digital news industry in the U.S., Canada and Puerto Rico. Areas of interest include all matters involving the news media; freedom of the press and other First Amendment issues; and workers' rights.

NAME(S) OF PROGRAMS:
- **David S. Barr Award**

TYPE:
Awards/prizes; Scholarships.

YEAR PROGRAM STARTED: 1999

PURPOSE:
To inspire a new generation of journalists by recognizing work that contributes to the pursuit of justice and fairness; to promote issues of importance to working people; to serve as a lasting memorial and tribute to David S. Barr.

ELIGIBILITY:
The contest is open to:
(1) high school students, including those enrolled in vocational, technical or special education programs and;
(2) part-time or full-time college students, including those in community colleges and in graduate programs.

Students who have worked or are working as professional journalists - excluding internships - are not eligible to enter.

FINANCIAL DATA:
Amount of support per award: $1,000 for high school winner; $1,500 for college winner.

NO. MOST RECENT APPLICANTS: 180.

NO. AWARDS: High School and College: 1 each.

APPLICATION INFO:
Application form is available at the Guild web site. Entry must be mailed to TNG-CWA, along with four copies and the application form. Applicant must refer to the web site for complete details.

Duration: One-time award.

Deadline: Last Friday of January (postmark).

ADDRESS INQUIRIES TO:
Dominique Edmondson, Secretary to Collective Bargaining Department
David S. Barr Award
(See address above.)

NIEMAN FOUNDATION FOR JOURNALISM AT HARVARD [1891]

Walter Lippmann House
One Francis Avenue
Cambridge, MA 02138
(617) 496-8511
Fax: (617) 495-8976
E-mail: samantha_henry@harvard.edu
Web Site: www.nieman.harvard.edu

FOUNDED: 1938

AREAS OF INTEREST:
Journalism and investigative reporting.

NAME(S) OF PROGRAMS:
- **Worth Bingham Prize for Investigative Journalism**

TYPE:
Awards/prizes. Honors investigative reporting of stories of national significance where the public interest is being ill-served. These stories may involve state, local or national government, lobbyists or the press itself wherever there exists an "atmosphere of easy tolerance" that journalist Worth Bingham himself once described in his reporting on the nation's capital. The investigative reporting may cover actual violations of the law, rule or code; lax or ineffective administration or enforcement; or activities which create conflicts of interest, entail excessive secrecy or otherwise raise questions of propriety.

YEAR PROGRAM STARTED: 1967

PURPOSE:
To honor exceptional investigative reporting of stories of national significance where the public interest is being ill-served.

ELIGIBILITY:
All submissions must have been published in a U.S. newspaper or magazine or on the newspaper or magazine's web site during the calendar year. Web-based news organizations that follow a strict code of journalistic ethics and publish original reporting on a regular basis may also submit entries. No broadcast-only entries are allowed.

Entries may include a single story, a related series of stories, or up to three unrelated stories. Columns and editorials are eligible. Individuals are encouraged to submit their own entries. In the case of a series, at least half the individual stories must have been published during the contest year.

Winners in any one year will be eligible for future awards without restriction.

GEOG. RESTRICTIONS: United States.

FINANCIAL DATA:
Amount of support per award: $20,000 annually.

NO. AWARDS: 1.

APPLICATION INFO:
Application must be made online, and application fee must be paid online as well.

Duration: Prize given annually.

Deadline: January 22.

ADDRESS INQUIRIES TO:
Samantha Henry
Assistant Director for Programming and Special Projects
(See address above.)

NIEMAN FOUNDATION FOR JOURNALISM AT HARVARD [1892]

Walter Lippmann House
One Francis Avenue
Cambridge, MA 02138
(617) 496-6333
Fax: (617) 495-8976
E-mail: christine_kaye@harvard.edu
Web Site: www.nieman.harvard.edu

FOUNDED: 1938

AREAS OF INTEREST:
Journalism.

NAME(S) OF PROGRAMS:
- **Taylor Family Award for Fairness in Journalism**

TYPE:
Awards/prizes. Established through gifts for an endowment by members of the Taylor family, which published *The Boston Globe* from 1872 to 1999.

YEAR PROGRAM STARTED: 2001

PURPOSE:
To encourage fairness in news coverage by America's journalists and news organizations.

ELIGIBILITY:
Nominations are for a single article, editorial, commentary, photograph, or a series of stories, photographs, editorials, commentaries, or a body of work by an individual journalist. The work must have been published in a U.S. newspaper or magazine or on the newspaper or magazine's web site during the previous calendar year.

GEOG. RESTRICTIONS: United States.

FINANCIAL DATA:
Amount of support per award: $10,000, plus two $1,000 finalist awards.

Total amount of support: $12,000.

APPLICATION INFO:
All entries must be submitted online using the Foundation's online application form.

Deadline: January 22.

ADDRESS INQUIRIES TO:
Christine Kaye, Event Manager
(See address above.)

NIEMAN FOUNDATION FOR JOURNALISM AT HARVARD [1893]

Walter Lippmann House
One Francis Avenue
Cambridge, MA 02138
(617) 495-2238
Fax: (617) 495-8976
E-mail: nieman_applications@harvard.edu
Web Site: www.nieman.harvard.edu

FOUNDED: 1938

AREAS OF INTEREST:
Journalism.

NAME(S) OF PROGRAMS:
- **Nieman Fellowships in Journalism**

TYPE:
Fellowships. Provides journalists with the opportunity to spend a year of study at Harvard University. Awards are for U.S. and international journalists.

The Foundation also offers short-term Knight Visiting Nieman Fellowships to journalists and other professionals working on projects to advance journalism. Contact the Foundation for further details.

YEAR PROGRAM STARTED: 1938

PURPOSE:
To provide an opportunity for journalists to deepen their knowledge in a field of specialty, broaden their knowledge in several areas, or prepare for a new journalistic assignment.

LEGAL BASIS:
A foundation of Harvard University.

ELIGIBILITY:
Print, broadcast and online reporters, editors, photographers, producers, editorial writers, columnists, filmmakers and cartoonists with at least five years of full-time, professional experience in the news media are invited to apply.

During the two years prior to applying, an applicant should not have participated in a fellowship or taken a leave of absence from work that lasted for four months or longer. There are no age limits or academic prerequisites, and a college degree is not required.

All prospective fellows must speak, read and write English fluently.

FINANCIAL DATA:
Nieman Fellows receive a stipend plus housing, child care and health insurance allowance, if appropriate.

Amount of support per award: $65,000 stipend.

NO. AWARDS: Approximately 24 annually (up to 12 to journalists from the U.S. and up to 12 to journalists from other countries).

APPLICATION INFO:
Contact the Foundation.

Duration: Nine months.

Deadline: U.S. applications due January 31 for the academic year beginning in August. International applications are due December 1 for the academic year beginning the following August.

PUBLICATIONS:
Nieman Reports.

STAFF:
Nicole Arias, Fellowship Administrator

ADDRESS INQUIRIES TO:
Nicole Arias, Fellowship Administrator
(See address above.)

THE ALICIA PATTERSON FOUNDATION [1894]

1100 Vermont Avenue, N.W.
Suite 900
Washington, DC 20005
(202) 393-5995
Fax: (301) 951-8512
E-mail: info@aliciapatterson.org
Web Site: www.aliciapatterson.org

FOUNDED: 1961

AREAS OF INTEREST:
Journalism.

NAME(S) OF PROGRAMS:

- **Fellowship Program for Journalists**

TYPE:
Fellowships. Awarded to working print journalists for six months or one year of travel and inquiry. On leave from their normal writing, editing or photographing duties, Fellows examine their chosen subjects (areas or problems of significant interest, foreign or domestic) and write quarterly articles for the *APF Reporter.* These articles may be reprinted.

YEAR PROGRAM STARTED: 1965

PURPOSE:
To foster, promote, sustain and improve the best traditions of American journalism; to provide a few talented and promising American journalists with the opportunity to pursue independent projects.

LEGAL BASIS:
Section 501(c)(3) of the IRS Code and Not For Profits Corporation Law: New York State.

ELIGIBILITY:
The program is open to U.S. citizens who are full-time print journalists or to non-U.S. citizens who work full-time for U.S. print publication, either in America or abroad.

GEOG. RESTRICTIONS: United States.

FINANCIAL DATA:
Amount of support per award: $20,000 stipend for six months or $40,000 stipend for the year.

Total amount of support: Varies.

NO. MOST RECENT APPLICANTS: Varies.

NO. AWARDS: 7 to 10 per year.

REPRESENTATIVE AWARDS:
"The Impact of Budget Cuts on Civil Justice in America;" "Northeast India: Creatures and Cultures in Collision."

APPLICATION INFO:
Application forms are available in June. Information may be requested from the address above throughout the year.

Duration: Fellowships support a one-year or six-month leave of absence. The fellowship typically begins within the first three months of the calendar year.

Deadline: October 1 (postmark).

PUBLICATIONS:
APF Reporter, quarterly magazine.

IRS I.D.: 13-6092124

ADDRESS INQUIRIES TO:
Margaret Engel, Executive Director
(See address above.)

THE PRESS CLUB OF METROPOLITAN ST. LOUIS AND JOURNALISM FOUNDATION OF METROPOLITAN ST. LOUIS

c/o The Press Club of Metropolitan St. Louis
P.O. Box 410522
St. Louis, MO 63141
(314) 449-8029
Fax: (314) 317-0031
E-mail: info@stlpressclub.org
Web Site: stlpressclub.org

TYPE:
Capital grants; Fellowships; Internships; Project/program grants; Scholarships.

See entry 1694 for full listing.

PULLIAM JOURNALISM FELLOWSHIP [1895]

Indiana Star
130 South Meridian Street
Indianapolis, IN 46225
(317) 444-6001
E-mail: russell.pulliam@indystar.com
Web Site: www.indystar.com/pjf

FOUNDED: 1974

AREAS OF INTEREST:
Journalism awards.

TYPE:
Fellowships. Cash awards and on-the-job study at *The Indianapolis Star* or *The Arizona Republic*, which are owned by Gannett Co.

YEAR PROGRAM STARTED: 1974

PURPOSE:
To offer on-the-job experience, plus seminars and writing criticism, to college students seriously pursuing a newspaper journalism career.

LEGAL BASIS:
Corporate-sponsored.

ELIGIBILITY:
Applicants are generally college journalism majors or liberal arts majors with part-time newspaper experience, outstanding character references, proven writing ability and a solid academic record.

GEOG. RESTRICTIONS: United States.

FINANCIAL DATA:
Amount of support per award: $6,500 ($650 per week for 10-week program).

NO. MOST RECENT APPLICANTS: 200.

NO. AWARDS: 25.

APPLICATION INFO:
Brochures are available from the address above. View the instructions and download the application at the web site.

Duration: 10 weeks, June to August. No renewals.

Deadline: November 1.

PUBLICATIONS:
Brochure.

ADDRESS INQUIRIES TO:
Russ Pulliam, Director
(See address above.)

QUILL AND SCROLL FOUNDATION [1896]

School of Journalism and Mass Communication
The University of Iowa
100 Adler Journalism Building, Room E346
Iowa City, IA 52242-2004
(319) 335-3321
(319) 335-3457
Fax: (319) 335-3989
E-mail: quill-scroll@uiowa.edu
Web Site: www.quillandscroll.org

FOUNDED: 1926

AREAS OF INTEREST:
Journalism, high school media, media law and ethics, and scholastic journalism education.

CONSULTING OR VOLUNTEER SERVICES:
Coordinate judging of K-12 writing, journalism and media contests.

TYPE:
Research grants; Scholarships; Training grants. Grants for research projects in the field of high school journalism and school media.

YEAR PROGRAM STARTED: 1964

PURPOSE:
To improve the quality of secondary school journalism.

LEGAL BASIS:
Nonprofit special-interest foundation.

ELIGIBILITY:
Qualified scholars or educational departments with appropriate interests are eligible to apply.

GEOG. RESTRICTIONS: Primarily United States.

FINANCIAL DATA:
Support may be provided to cover partial or complete project costs.

Amount of support per award: $500 to $1,000.

Total amount of support: $6,000 for the year 2014-15.

NO. MOST RECENT APPLICANTS: 45 for the year 2014-15.

NO. AWARDS: 8 for the year 2014-15.

APPLICATION INFO:
Prospective grant applicants should submit a letter describing the proposed project in terms of scope, objectives and financial need. Also include a letter of support from project, thesis adviser.

Scholarship applications are available online.

Duration: One-time award.

Deadline: May 10.

PUBLICATIONS:
Application guidelines.

IRS I.D.: 42-0795095

OFFICER:
Vanessa Shelton, Executive Director

ADDRESS INQUIRIES TO:
Vanessa Shelton, Executive Director
(See address above.)

RADIO TELEVISION DIGITAL NEWS FOUNDATION [1897]

The National Press Building
529 14th Street, N.W., Suite 1240
Washington, DC 20045
(202) 536-8356
Fax: (202) 223-4007
E-mail: karenh@rtdna.org
Web Site: www.rtdna.org

FOUNDED: 1946

AREAS OF INTEREST:
Electronic journalism.

NAME(S) OF PROGRAMS:

- **N.S. Biestock Fellowship**
- **Ed Bradley Scholarship**
- **Michele Clark Fellowship**
- **George Foreman Tribute to Lyndon B. Johnson**
- **Jacque I. Minnotte Fellowship**
- **Vada and Barney Oldfield Fellowship for National Security Reporting**
- **Lou and Carole Prato Sports Reporting Scholarship**
- **The President's Scholarships**
- **Mike Reynolds Journalism Scholarship**
- **Carole Simpson Scholarship**
- **Pete Wilson Scholarship**

TYPE:
Fellowships; Scholarships. Awards for one year of undergraduate and/or graduate study in broadcast journalism.

YEAR PROGRAM STARTED: 1967

PURPOSE:
To aid in advanced learning of electronic journalism.

LEGAL BASIS:
Incorporated.

ELIGIBILITY:
For scholarships, applicants must be officially enrolled in college and have at least one full academic year remaining, must be a fully enrolled college sophomore or higher, may apply for only one scholarship, and may be enrolled in any major so long as their career intent is television or radio news. Fellowships are available to young professionals with fewer than 10 years in the field. U.S. citizens and international applicants are eligible.

International applicants must have a U.S. Taxpayer ID Number (TIN).

FINANCIAL DATA:
Amount of support per award: Scholarships: $1,000 to $10,000; Fellowships: $1,000 and $2,500.

NO. MOST RECENT APPLICANTS: 500.

NO. AWARDS: Undergraduate: 7; Fellowships: 4.

APPLICATION INFO:
Application must be submitted online.

Duration: Scholarships: One year.

Deadline: Varies.

PUBLICATIONS:
Annual report.

IRS I.D.: 38-1860090

ADDRESS INQUIRIES TO:
Karen Hansen, Program Coordinator
(See address above.)

REPORTERS COMMITTEE FOR FREEDOM OF THE PRESS [1898]

1156 15th Street, N.W.
Suite 1250
Washington, DC 20005
(202) 795-9306
Fax: (202) 795-9310
E-mail: rcfp@rcfp.org
Web Site: www.rcfp.org

FOUNDED: 1970

AREAS OF INTEREST:
First Amendment interests of the news media.

NAME(S) OF PROGRAMS:

- **The Reporters Committee Legal Fellowships**

TYPE:
Fellowships. Legal fellows monitor significant developments in First Amendment media law, assist with legal defense requests from reporters, prepare legal memoranda, amicus briefs and other special projects. The Fellowship focuses on media law.

YEAR PROGRAM STARTED: 1987

PURPOSE:
To protect the right to gather and distribute news; to keep government accountable by ensuring access to public records, meetings and courtrooms; to preserve the principles of free speech and unfettered press, as guaranteed by the First Amendment of the U.S. Constitution.

ELIGIBILITY:
Candidates must have received a law degree by August of the year the Fellowship begins. Strong legal research and writing skills are required, and a background in news reporting is very strongly preferred.

FINANCIAL DATA:
Fellowship includes fully paid health benefits.

Amount of support per award: Minimum of $43,000.

NO. AWARDS: 2 to 4 annually.

APPLICATION INFO:
Contact the Committee.

Duration: One year, September to August.

Deadline: November 3.

PUBLICATIONS:
News Media & the Law.

ADDRESS INQUIRIES TO:
E-mail: fellowship@rcfp.org

KURT SCHORK MEMORIAL FUND [1899]

4441 MacArthur Boulevard, N.W.
Washington, DC 20007
(202) 333-2545
E-mail: enquiries@ksmfund.org
Web Site: www.ksmfund.org

FOUNDED: 2001

AREAS OF INTEREST:
International journalism.

NAME(S) OF PROGRAMS:

- **Kurt Schork Awards in International Journalism**

TYPE:
Awards/prizes. Awards for print reporters whose stories shed new light on controversial issues. Two prizes are awarded each year, one to a local reporter in a developing country or nation in transition, and the other to a freelance journalist covering international news.

The awards are underwritten by the Kurt Schork Memorial Fund and Reuters, and administered by the Columbia University Graduate School of Journalism.

YEAR PROGRAM STARTED: 2002

PURPOSE:
To honor Kurt Schork, an American freelance journalist, killed in a military ambush while on assignment for Reuters on May 24, 2000 in Sierra Leone.

ELIGIBILITY:
Local Reporter: Print journalists employed by a local news outlet and residing in a developing country or nation in transition (non-OECD or EU countries), whose work has been published in a local publication, are eligible.

Freelance Journalist: All freelance print journalists and those contracted by news organizations are eligible.

Eligible Media: Entries are welcomed from all types of print-based media including newspapers and magazines and established online publications.

FINANCIAL DATA:
Amount of support per award: $5,000.

Total amount of support: $10,000 annually.

NO. AWARDS: 2.

APPLICATION INFO:
Complete information may be found on the Fund web site (above).

Deadline: May 31.

ADDRESS INQUIRIES TO:
See e-mail address above.

UNITED METHODIST COMMUNICATIONS [1900]

810 12th Avenue South
Nashville, TN 37203-4704
(888) 278-4862
Fax: (615) 742-5423
E-mail: scholarships@umcom.org
Web Site: www.umcom.org

FOUNDED: 1948

AREAS OF INTEREST:
Religion communications.

NAME(S) OF PROGRAMS:

- **The Stoody-West Fellowship**

TYPE:
Fellowships. Assists one United Methodist student in postgraduate study at an accredited U.S. college or university who intends to pursue a career in religious journalism.

YEAR PROGRAM STARTED: 1964

PURPOSE:
To enable the recipient to continue graduate studies in religion journalism; to promote a level of excellence in communication at the graduate level.

LEGAL BASIS:
Nonprofit.

ELIGIBILITY:
Applicant must be a member of The United Methodist Church who intends to pursue a career in religion journalism and is enrolled in graduate study at an accredited U.S. college or university (includes electronic and broadcast media as well as print). Employees of United Methodist Communications and members of the General Commission on Communication are not eligible for the Fellowship.

FINANCIAL DATA:
Amount of support per award: $6,000.

Total amount of support: $6,000.

NO. AWARDS: 1 annually.

APPLICATION INFO:
Application forms are available online.

Applicant must submit:
(1) completed application form;
(2) official transcripts of schools attended, including evidence of enrollment as a graduate student in the journalism or communications department of a duly accredited college or university in the U.S.;
(3) three letters of recommendation;
(4) statement of interest and plans;
(5) three writing samples and;
(6) recent personal photograph.

If materials must be mailed, use the following address:
Stoody-West Fellowship Committee
United Methodist Communications
P.O. Box 320
Nashville, TN 37202-0320.

If submitting by FedEx or UPS, send to: Stoody-West Fellowship Committee, United Methodist Communications, at the street address above.

Duration: One academic year.

Deadline: March 15 (postmark).

PUBLICATIONS:
Application guidelines.

ADDRESS INQUIRIES TO:
Communications Ministry
(See address above.)

*PLEASE NOTE:
Religious journalism is interpreted to include news writing for secular press, church press and for church institutions. Appropriate news and journalism forms will be considered, including electronic and broadcast media, as well as print.

UNITED METHODIST COMMUNICATIONS

810 12th Avenue South
Nashville, TN 37203-4744
(888) 278-4862
Fax: (615) 742-5777
E-mail: scholarships@umcom.org
Web Site: www.umcom.org

TYPE:
Fellowships; Scholarships. Award for junior or senior undergraduate study in religion journalism or mass communications. The term *communications* is meant to cover various media as audio-visual, electronic and print journalism.

See entry 996 for full listing.

UNIVERSITY FILM AND VIDEO ASSOCIATION [1901]

Northern Illinois University
Communications
396 Kingsbury Drive
DeKalb, IL 60115
E-mail: lvazquez@niu.edu
Web Site: www.ufva.org

AREAS OF INTEREST:
Film, video and multimedia production.

NAME(S) OF PROGRAMS:

- **Carole Fielding Student Grants**

TYPE:
Block grants; Capital grants; Development grants; General operating grants; Project/program grants; Research grants; Seed money grants. Annual support for student projects in film, video and multimedia productions or research activities in historical, critical, theoretical or experimental studies in film or video.

YEAR PROGRAM STARTED: 1993

PURPOSE:
To support and promote student film and video makers.

LEGAL BASIS:
UFVA membership funded.

ELIGIBILITY:
An applicant must be a graduate or undergraduate student at the time the application is made, be sponsored by a faculty member who is an active member of the University Film and Video Association and agree to present, or have presented by his or her representative, a report on the project or production at the next annual meeting of the Association.

The judges reserve the right not to make an award if quality or quantity of submissions so justify.

FINANCIAL DATA:
Amount of support per award: Varies.

Total amount of support: $5,000 per year.

NO. MOST RECENT APPLICANTS: 90.

APPLICATION INFO:
Applicants should submit materials online. The proposal must include a one-page description of the production or project which includes a statement of purpose, an indication of the resources available to complete the work and a summary of the proposed film, video production or study. If a narrative film is proposed, submit a copy of the script. A documentary proposal should include a short treatment. An experimental or animated film proposal should include a treatment (or script) and/or story boards. Also include a one-page budget, indicating what portion of the total project will be supported by this grant and a statement by a faculty member who is an active member of the University Film and Video Association assessing the feasibility of the project or production and indicating his or her willingness to serve as faculty supervisor or consultant.

Deadline: December 15. Announcements by March 31.

OFFICERS:
Francisco Menendez, President
Jennifer Machiorlatti, Executive Vice President
Joe Brown, Editorial Vice President

ADDRESS INQUIRIES TO:
Laura Vazquez, UFVA Grants Office
(See e-mail address above.)

THE UNIVERSITY OF CALGARY [1902]

Faculty of Graduate Studies
MacKimmie Library Tower, Room 213
2500 University Drive, N.W.
Calgary AB T2N 1N4 Canada
(403) 220-4938
Fax: (403) 289-7635
E-mail: gsaward@ucalgary.ca
Web Site: www.grad.ucalgary.ca/awards

FOUNDED: 1966

AREAS OF INTEREST:
Communications studies.

NAME(S) OF PROGRAMS:

- **Cogeco Inc. Graduate Scholarship**

TYPE:
Awards/prizes; Scholarships.

LEGAL BASIS:
University scholarship program.

ELIGIBILITY:
Applicants must be students admissible to or registered in a Master's program (either thesis-based or course-based) in the Communications Studies Programme at the University of Calgary. Awards will be made on the basis of academic excellence.

FINANCIAL DATA:
Amount of support per award: $7,200.

Total amount of support: $7,200.

CO-OP FUNDING PROGRAMS: Scholarship is financed by Cogeco Inc.

NO. AWARDS: 1 each year.

APPLICATION INFO:
Candidates should apply to the Master of Communications Studies Programme in the first instance. Recommendations from the

Programme will be submitted to the University of Calgary Graduate Scholarship Office for approval. The recommendation is subject to final approval of the Graduate Scholarship Committee.

Duration: One year.

Deadline: February 1.

ADDRESS INQUIRIES TO:
Graduate Scholarship Office
(See address above.)

UNIVERSITY OF MICHIGAN [1903]

Knight-Wallace Fellows
Wallace House
620 Oxford Road
Ann Arbor, MI 48104-2635
(734) 998-7666
Fax: (734) 998-7979
E-mail: kwfellows@umich.edu
Web Site: www.kwfellows.org

AREAS OF INTEREST:
Arts, sciences and professions.

NAME(S) OF PROGRAMS:

- **Knight-Wallace Fellows**

TYPE:
Fellowships.

YEAR PROGRAM STARTED: 1973

PURPOSE:
To offer a full academic year in any field or fields at the University of Michigan.

LEGAL BASIS:
A part of the Provost's office at the University of Michigan.

ELIGIBILITY:
Status of eligibility extends to all full-time print, broadcast, online, photo and film journalists with five years' experience whose work appears regularly in U.S.-controlled news organizations. Freelancers are included. Work may be related or unrelated to professional objectives.

FINANCIAL DATA:
Fellowship also includes tuition and fees, plus travel expenses for our international news tours.

Amount of support per award: $70,000 stipend.

NO. MOST RECENT APPLICANTS: 120.

NO. AWARDS: 12 National.

APPLICATION INFO:
Application form, a leave of absence (if possible) for the period of the Fellowship, and a support letter from direct supervisor is required. Two statements, an intellectual autobiography, and a proposed program of study must be included. Do not submit more than five examples of applicant's work.

Duration: Eight-month academic year, September to April.

Deadline: February 1. Announcement in May.

PUBLICATIONS:
Wall House Journal.

ADDRESS INQUIRIES TO:
Birgit Rieck, Assistant Director
(See address above.)

Labor

IMAGINE AMERICA FOUNDATION [1904]

12001 Sunrise Valley Drive
Suite 203
Reston, VA 20191
(571) 267-3015
Fax: (866) 734-5812
E-mail: studentservices@imagine-america.org
Web Site: www.imagine-america.org

FOUNDED: 1982

AREAS OF INTEREST:
Private career education.

NAME(S) OF PROGRAMS:

- **Imagine America Adult Excellence Award**
- **Imagine America Adult Skills Education Program (ASEP)**
- **Imagine America High School Scholarship Program**
- **Imagine America LDRSHIP Award**
- **Imagine America Military Award Program (MAP)**
- **Imagine America Promise Scholarship Program**

TYPE:
Awards/prizes; Scholarships; Research contracts. Sponsorships. Three scholarships are given to each high school listed on the Foundation web site above.

YEAR PROGRAM STARTED: 1982

PURPOSE:
To provide research, scholarship and training for America's career colleges.

LEGAL BASIS:
501(c)(3) nonprofit organization.

ELIGIBILITY:
Applicants must be graduating high school seniors. Applicants for Imagine America MAP must be honorably discharged, active duty, reservist or retired military.

GEOG. RESTRICTIONS: United States and Puerto Rico.

FINANCIAL DATA:
Amount of support per award: Varies.

Total amount of support: $110,000,000.

NO. AWARDS: More than 35,000.

PUBLICATIONS:
Imagine America's Guide to Career Colleges; *Imagine America's Student's Guide*; *A Profile of Career Colleges and Universities.*

ADDRESS INQUIRIES TO:
Lee Doubleday
Student Services Representative
(See address above.)

NATIONAL INSTITUTE OF STANDARDS AND TECHNOLOGY [1905]

U.S. Department of Commerce, NIST
100 Bureau Drive, Mail Stop 4800
Gaithersburg, MD 20899-4800
(301) 975-6544
(301) 975-5020
Fax: (301) 840-5976
E-mail: mfg@nist.gov
Web Site: www.nist.gov/mep

FOUNDED: 1901

AREAS OF INTEREST:
Advanced manufacturing technology.

NAME(S) OF PROGRAMS:

- **Manufacturing Extension Partnership**

TYPE:
Project/program grants.

YEAR PROGRAM STARTED: 1988

PURPOSE:
To establish, maintain and support manufacturing extension centers and services, the functions of which are to accelerate the usage of appropriate manufacturing technology by smaller U.S.-based manufacturing firms, and partner with the states in developing such technical assistance programs and services for their manufacturing base.

LEGAL BASIS:
Ominibus Trade and Competitiveness Act of 1988, Public Law 100-148, American Technology Preeminence Act of 1991.

ELIGIBILITY:
For extension services, eligible applicants should be U.S.-based nonprofit institutions or organizations or groups thereof. For extension service planning and pilot services agreements, eligible applicants shall be state governments and state-affiliated nonprofit organizations. For multistate regional planning and pilot services agreements, eligible applicants shall be state and local governments, representing either themselves or a consortium of states, and appropriate private or public nonprofit organizations, operating on behalf of a consortium of states or as a representative of states. Beneficiary shall be U.S.-based manufacturing firms, especially smaller companies.

FINANCIAL DATA:
Amount of support per award: Awards for manufacturing extension centers: $7,000,000 annually. Individual awards for extension service planning and pilot testing agreements: $25,000 to $100,000.

Total amount of support: Varies.

Matching fund requirements: Applicants must provide at least 50% of the capital, annual operating and maintenance funds required to create and maintain the center. Funds may be provided by any nonfederal source. A minimum of 50% of the applicant's share must be as cash of full-time personnel.

APPLICATION INFO:
An applicant should consult the office or official designated as the single point of contact in his or her state for information on the process the state requires to be followed in applying for assistance, if the state has selected the program for review. For manufacturing extension centers, no formal preapplication is required, although applicants are advised to discuss their proposal during the early stages of development with NIST MEP regional managers. This portion of the program is excluded from coverage under E.O. 12372.

A *Federal Register* notice announcing the request for proposals from qualified organizations will be published when funds are available.

Duration: One year for extension service planning and pilot-testing agreements. Six years maximum for manufacturing extension centers. Agreements are renewed annually based upon positive evaluation and availability of funds.

Deadline: Notice of availability of funds and deadlines are published on cfda.gov.

U.S. DEPARTMENT OF HEALTH AND HUMAN SERVICES/ADMINISTRATION FOR CHILDREN AND FAMILIES/OFFICE OF FAMILY ASSISTANCE [1906]

370 L'Enfant Promenade S.W.
5th Floor East
Washington, DC 20447
(202) 401-9275
Fax: (202) 205-5887
E-mail: rachel.gwilliam@acf.hhs.gov
Web Site: www.acf.hhs.gov/programs/ofa

FOUNDED: 1996

AREAS OF INTEREST:
Education, employment and support services, and financial assistance.

NAME(S) OF PROGRAMS:
- **Temporary Assistance for Needy Families (TANF)**

TYPE:
Block grants; Internships; Technical assistance. Block grants to states, the District of Columbia, territories, and federally recognized Indian tribes and Alaska Native Organizations for education, employment, training and supportive services to help eligible families move to work and self-sufficiency.

YEAR PROGRAM STARTED: 1996

PURPOSE:
To help needy families achieve self-sufficiency.

LEGAL BASIS:
Social Security Act, Title IV-A and Title IV-F, as amended (42 USC 602-603, 681-687 and 1302) and Public Law 100-485.

ELIGIBILITY:
Grants are awarded to states, the District of Columbia, territories, and federally recognized Indian tribes and Alaska Native Organizations based on a complete TANF plan. Statute precludes any grantees other than those stated above.

FINANCIAL DATA:
Amount of support per award: Calculated share of federal block grant.

Total amount of support: $16.5 billion.

PUBLICATIONS:
TANF Annual Report to Congress; policy announcements; program instructions; information memoranda.

ADDRESS INQUIRIES TO:
Rachel Gwilliam, Program Specialist
(See address above.)

U.S. DEPARTMENT OF LABOR [1907]

Office of Apprenticeship
Room N-5311
200 Constitution Avenue, N.W.
Washington, DC 20210
(202) 693-2796
Fax: (202) 692-3799
E-mail: oa.administrator@dol.gov
Web Site: www.dol.gov/apprenticeship

FOUNDED: 1937

AREAS OF INTEREST:
Apprenticeship, skill and technical training.

CONSULTING OR VOLUNTEER SERVICES:
Provides technical assistance at no cost.

NAME(S) OF PROGRAMS:
- **National Apprenticeship System**

TYPE:
Technical assistance. Management and labor, along with government and the education system, work together at the national, state and local levels to formulate and promote effective apprenticeship programs. The program must be an organized, written plan embodying training and supervision of one or more apprentices in an apprenticeable occupation, as defined in 29 CFR 29.4 and subscribed to by a sponsor who has undertaken to carry out the apprenticeship program.

YEAR PROGRAM STARTED: 1937

PURPOSE:
To formulate, promote and publish labor standards necessary to safeguard the welfare of apprentices, encourage the inclusion of such standards in apprenticeship contracts, bring together employers and labor to create apprenticeship programs, cooperate with state agencies in formulating and promoting apprenticeship standards, and cooperate with the U.S. Department of Education on vocational education and related instruction in apprenticeship.

LEGAL BASIS:
National Apprenticeship Act of 1937 (P.L. 308-75); Title 29, CFR Part 30; Title 29, CFR Part 29.

ELIGIBILITY:
To be eligible as a sponsor, apprenticeship programs must meet the basic standards and established criteria set forth by the Secretary of Labor and may be registered upon request of the program sponsor. Registration of programs and apprentices in states having apprenticeship agencies recognized by the U.S. Department of Labor is performed by the state apprenticeship agencies. Programs in states not having recognized apprenticeship agencies will be registered by the Bureau of Apprenticeship and Training.

To be eligible as a beneficiary, applicants for apprenticeship must be at least 16 years of age. They must have the ability and aptitude to master the occupations and sufficient education to complete satisfactorily the required hours of related theoretical instruction.

GEOG. RESTRICTIONS: United States.

FINANCIAL DATA:
The Department of Labor does not finance apprenticeships. Program sponsors bear the expenses of the program.

NO. MOST RECENT APPLICANTS: 100,000.

APPLICATION INFO:
Notices for accepting applications are published locally by apprenticeship program sponsors. Information may be obtained from local One Stop Centers or may be requested by contacting regional, state or area offices of the Office of Apprenticeship, U.S. Department of Labor, or the ETA Grants Office.

PUBLICATIONS:
Apprenticeship Past and Present; *National Apprenticeship Program.*

ADDRESS INQUIRIES TO:
Grants Department
Division of Grants and Contracts
(See address above.)

W.E. UPJOHN INSTITUTE FOR EMPLOYMENT RESEARCH [1908]

300 South Westnedge Avenue
Kalamazoo, MI 49007-4686
(269) 343-5541
Fax: (269) 343-3308
E-mail: communications@upjohn.org
Web Site: www.upjohn.org

FOUNDED: 1945

AREAS OF INTEREST:
Policy-relevant research on employment and unemployment at the international, national, state and local levels. The Institute is also receptive to international studies for the purpose of drawing lessons for U.S. policy. Topics of interest include job creation, job stabilization, matching of jobs and people, alleviation of unemployment hazards, the political science of manpower programs and the quality of work life.

CONSULTING OR VOLUNTEER SERVICES:
Both consulting and volunteer services are available, though the latter are limited.

NAME(S) OF PROGRAMS:
- **Early Career Research Awards**

TYPE:
Conferences/seminars; Research grants; Visiting scholars; Research contracts. Early Career Research Awards are intended to provide resources to junior faculty (untenured and within six years of earning the Ph.D.) to carry out policy-related research on labor market issues. The Institute supports and encourages research on all issues related to labor markets and public workforce policy.

YEAR PROGRAM STARTED: 1976

PURPOSE:
To conduct research into the causes and effects of unemployment and measures for the alleviation of unemployment at the national, state and local levels.

LEGAL BASIS:
Public nonprofit organization.

ELIGIBILITY:
Award proposals will be evaluated according to the following criteria:
(1) contribution to important labor market policy issues and to the professional literature;
(2) technical merit and;
(3) professional qualifications.

FINANCIAL DATA:
The Institute does not pay indirect costs but will entertain any legitimate research expense as part of the budget. Acceptable items include costs for professional, technical, and support personnel, data acquisition, materials and supplies, computer services, and travel. The Institute does not fund dissertation research although it does have a Dissertation Award program. Grant payments are made to the individual upon award.

Amount of support per award: Up to $5,000.

NO. MOST RECENT APPLICANTS: 37.

NO. AWARDS: 15.

APPLICATION INFO:
Applicants should submit a proposal of up to 1,200 words (approximately four double-spaced pages) describing the proposed research and its relevance to labor market policy. The proposal should include an abstract and a brief budget. Applications must also include a current curriculum vitae.

Applications submitted via regular mail are to be addressed to: Institute Grant Committee, W.E. Upjohn Institute for Employment Research, at the address above. Submissions by e-mail are accepted at the Institute's e-mail address.

Duration: Ordinarily one year, which includes research and writing of paper to be submitted to a scholarly journal.

Deadline: Applications: January 31. Announcement: March 1.

PUBLICATIONS:
Program announcement; proposal guidelines.

IRS I.D.: 38-1360419

TRUSTEES:

ADDRESS INQUIRIES TO:
Randall W. Eberts, President
(See address above.)

*PLEASE NOTE:
Awards are essentially performance-based contracts. Applications and all work submitted under Early Career Research Awards become the property of the Institute. It is Institute policy to require submission of the research paper to its working paper series. Unaccepted proposals and rejected research papers will be returned upon request, without restrictions on further use by others. It is also Institute policy to encourage publication of the sponsored research in scholarly journals following submission of the research paper to the Institute. Submission of any material waives all rights to make any claim because of any use thereof by the W.E. Upjohn Unemployment Trustee Corporation, its agents and employees.

*SPECIAL STIPULATIONS:
Award recipients are expected to write a research paper based on the funded work for submission to the Institute's working paper series, submit the paper to a peer-reviewed journal, and prepare a synopsis of the research for possible publication in the Institute's newsletter, *Employment Research.*

Law

AMERICAN ASSOCIATION OF LAW LIBRARIES

105 West Adams Street
Suite 3300
Chicago, IL 60603
(312) 939-4764
Fax: (312) 431-1097
E-mail: membership@aall.org
Web Site: www.aallnet.org

TYPE:
Scholarships. For study of law or librarianship, with support intended for prospective law librarians.

See entry 699 for full listing.

AMERICAN BAR FOUNDATION [1909]

750 North Lake Shore Drive
Fourth Floor
Chicago, IL 60611-4403
(312) 988-6517
Fax: (312) 988-6579
E-mail: fellowships@abfn.org
Web Site: www.americanbarfoundation.org

FOUNDED: 1952

AREAS OF INTEREST:
Socio-legal research. Current research interests include: professionalism and the transformation of the legal profession in the U.S. and abroad, the impact of civil rights law on the economic progress of minorities, hate speech and its regulation, the influence of family and environmental factors on juvenile delinquency, the impact of public policy on the spread of the Internet, jury decision-making, historical analyses of labor and regulatory law, public interest lawyering and social reform, and sentencing judgement and the effect of victim impact evidence.

NAME(S) OF PROGRAMS:
- **ABF Fellowships in Law and Social Science**

TYPE:
Fellowships. Residential fellowships at the ABF.

The American Bar Foundation is committed to developing the next generation of scholars in the field of law and social science. Since 1987, the Foundation has supported the dissertation research of a diverse group of graduate students from all social science disciplines and, in 1996, added a postdoctoral component to its fellowship program.

YEAR PROGRAM STARTED: 1987

PURPOSE:
To encourage original and significant research on law, the legal profession and legal institutions.

LEGAL BASIS:
Private foundation.

ELIGIBILITY:
Applications are invited from outstanding students who are candidates for Ph.D. degrees in the social sciences, or who have completed their Ph.D. within the past two years. Proposed research must be in the general area of sociolegal studies or in social scientific approaches to law, the legal profession or legal institutions. The research must address significant issues in the field and show promise of a major contribution to social scientific understanding of law and legal processes. Applicants must, at a minimum, have been admitted to candidacy for the Ph.D. before the commencement of the fellowship.

Minority applicants are especially encouraged.

In exceptional circumstances, candidates with a J.D. who have substantial social science training may also be considered.

GEOG. RESTRICTIONS: United States.

FINANCIAL DATA:
Fellows will receive a stipend for 12 months. Fellows may also request up to $1,500 each fellowship year for research support, including travel to conferences at which papers are presented. Relocation expenses of up to $2,500 may be reimbursed upon application.

Amount of support per award: $30,000 stipend.

NO. MOST RECENT APPLICANTS: 100.

NO. AWARDS: 2.

APPLICATION INFO:
Applications must include:
(1) letter of application;
(2) statement describing research interests and achievements to date and plans for the fellowship period;
(3) two letters of reference;
(4) curriculum vitae;
(5) transcript of graduate record;
(6) sample of written work (conference paper, dissertation chapter or published article) and;
(7) Ph.D. candidates should include a copy of their dissertation proposal.

Duration: One year. Renewable for a second year subject to satisfactory progress and participation.

Deadline: December.

ADDRESS INQUIRIES TO:
Amanda Ehrhardt
Administrative Associate for Academic Affairs
(See address above.)

*PLEASE NOTE:
Fellowships are held in residence at the American Bar Foundation. Appointments to fellowships are full-time. Fellows are expected to participate fully in the academic life of the ABF so that they may develop close collegial ties with other scholars in residence.

AMERICAN COLLEGE OF LEGAL MEDICINE

9700 Bryn Mawr Avenue
Rosemont, IL 60018
(847) 447-1713
(651) 265-7846
Fax: (847) 447-1150
E-mail: lauriek@ewald.com
Web Site: www.aclm.org

TYPE:
Awards/prizes. The Hirsh Award is awarded to a law, dentistry, podiatry, nursing, pharmacy, health science, health care administration, or public health student.

See entry 2154 for full listing.

THE CANADIAN BAR ASSOCIATION [1910]

500-865 Carling Avenue
Ottawa ON K1S 5S8 Canada
(613) 237-2925
(800) 267-8860
Fax: (613) 237-0185
E-mail: info@cba.org
Web Site: www.cba.org

FOUNDED: 1914

AREAS OF INTEREST:
Law and the administration of justice, promoting access to justice and promotion of equality in the professional justice system.

NAME(S) OF PROGRAMS:
- **Viscount Bennett Fellowship**

TYPE:
Awards/prizes; Fellowships. Award is paid to one law student for legally oriented graduate study in an institution of higher learning anywhere, to be approved by selection committee.

YEAR PROGRAM STARTED: 1946

PURPOSE:
To encourage a high standard of legal education, training and ethics.

ELIGIBILITY:
Canadian citizens who have graduated from an approved law school in Canada or who, at the time of application, are pursuing final-year studies as undergraduate students at such approved law school. All applicants must be CBA members in good standing. Candidates must have completed and filed an application for graduate studies with the institution of higher learning of their choice before submitting the fellowship application to the CBA.

GEOG. RESTRICTIONS: Canada.

FINANCIAL DATA:
Amount of support per award: $40,000 (CAN) paid in two equal installments.

Total amount of support: $40,000 (CAN).

NO. MOST RECENT APPLICANTS: 27.

NO. AWARDS: 1 annually.

APPLICATION INFO:
Each applicant must submit a Viscount Bennett Application Form with relevant attachments. Applications must be accompanied by:
(1) a birth or citizenship certificate;
(2) a certified copy of all law school transcripts;
(3) a one-page synopsis highlighting pertinent information from university transcripts;
(4) a synopsis of extracurricular activities during postsecondary studies;
(5) a statement of the course of study to be pursued and;
(6) three letters of reference.

Completed application forms must be submitted to the address above:
Viscount Bennett Fellowship
c/o Senior Director of Communications and Marketing.

Duration: One year. Nonrenewable.

Deadline: November 15 (postmark).

ADDRESS INQUIRIES TO:
Marie Josee Lapointe, Senior Director of Communications and Marketing
(See address above.)

*SPECIAL STIPULATIONS:
As a condition of the Fellowship, recipient(s) of the Viscount Bennett Fellowship must submit a written report at midterm and at the end of the year of graduate study, and must submit a copy of their final thesis at year end.

CANADIAN INSTITUTE FOR ADVANCED LEGAL STUDIES [1911]

P.O. Box 43538, Leaside Post Office
1601 Bayview Avenue
Toronto ON M4G 4G8 Canada
(416) 429-3292
Fax: (416) 429-9805
E-mail: info@canadian-institute.com
Web Site: www.canadian-institute.com

FOUNDED: 1979

AREAS OF INTEREST:
Law.

NAME(S) OF PROGRAMS:
- **French Language Scholarship**
- **The Right Honourable Paul Martin, Sr. Scholarship**

TYPE:
Scholarships.

YEAR PROGRAM STARTED: 1983

PURPOSE:
French Language Scholarship: To study for the equivalent of a Master's or doctoral degree from a Canadian university at a European university where instruction is given in French.

The Right Honourable Paul Martin, Sr. Scholarship: To study for an L.L.M. at the University of Cambridge.

ELIGIBILITY:
French Language Scholarship: The Institute annually awards a scholarship for graduate studies in law toward a second-cycle or third-cycle diploma (the equivalent of a Master's or doctoral degree from a Canadian university) at a European university where instruction is given in French, to a person who has (in the four years before the candidate will commence the proposed studies) been awarded a Bachelor's degree in law from a Canadian university. An applicant must be accepted into a French-language European university for graduate studies in law in order to receive this Scholarship, although such acceptance need not be confirmed at the time of the application for the Scholarship or at the time that the Institute provides the candidate with notice that he or she has been selected to receive the Scholarship.

The Right Honourable Paul Martin, Sr. Scholarship: The Institute annually awards two full scholarships for graduate studies in law at the University of Cambridge (Cambridge, England) to candidates who have been awarded a law degree from a three- or four-year program at a faculty of law in a Canadian university in the four years before the candidate will commence his or her studies at the University of Cambridge (supported by The Right Honourable Paul Martin Sr. Scholarship). An applicant must be accepted into the University of Cambridge and a College of the University of Cambridge for graduate studies in law in order to receive this Scholarship, although such acceptance need not be confirmed at the time of the application for the Scholarship nor at the time that the Institute provides the candidate with notice that he or she has been selected to receive the Scholarship.

FINANCIAL DATA:
French Language Scholarship: Scholarship includes full tuition and includes an allowance to cover a portion of living expenses and reasonable travel expenses to and from the European university, subject to any other awards received by the successful candidate. The Institute determines each year the maximum amount of the Scholarship, up to an amount of $20,000 for the 2014-15 academic year, and in so doing will take into account the tuition fees as well as the anticipated living expenses and travel expenses of the successful candidate.

The Right Honourable Paul Martin, Sr. Scholarship: Scholarships include tuition and college fees.

Total amount of support: French Language Scholarship: Approximately $20,000 (CAN). The Right Honourable Paul Martin, Sr. Scholarship: Approximately $25,000 (CAN).

NO. MOST RECENT APPLICANTS: French Language Scholarship: 4. The Right Honourable Paul Martin, Sr. Scholarship: 25.

NO. AWARDS: French Language Scholarship: 1. The Right Honourable Paul Martin, Sr. Scholarship: 2.

APPLICATION INFO:
French Language Scholarship: Applications must include:
(1) curriculum vitae;
(2) a personal statement indicating why the applicant wishes to undertake graduate studies in law and why the applicant is suited to undertake such studies;
(3) a copy of transcripts for undergraduate and graduate studies, for studies in law or for a Bar Admission Course, as applicable;
(4) a maximum of three letters of reference and;
(5) a statement of tuition fees and anticipated living and travel expenses.

The Right Honourable Paul Martin, Sr. Scholarship: Applications must include:
(1) curriculum vitae;
(2) a personal statement indicating why the applicant wishes to undertake graduate studies in law at the University of Cambridge and why the applicant is suited to undertake such studies;
(3) a copy of transcripts for undergraduate and graduate studies, for studies in law and for a Bar Admissions Course, as applicable, and;
(4) a maximum of three letters of reference.

Applications may be submitted by mail, fax or electronic mail.

Duration: One year.

Deadline: The Right Honourable Paul Martin, Sr. Scholarship: Applications must be received no later than December 31 each year.

ADDRESS INQUIRIES TO:
See e-mail address above.

ENVIRONMENTAL LAW INSTITUTE [1912]

1730 M Street, N.W.
Suite 700
Washington, DC 20036
(202) 939-3800
Fax: (202) 939-3868
E-mail: law@eli.org
Web Site: www.eli.org

FOUNDED: 1969

AREAS OF INTEREST:
Environmental law, management and policy, including economic and scientific aspects and protection of natural areas.

CONSULTING OR VOLUNTEER SERVICES:
Variety of services including tuition scholarships to continuing legal education programs, consulting services and technical assistance.

NAME(S) OF PROGRAMS:
- **Continuing Legal Education Scholarship Program**

TYPE:
Scholarships. Tuition scholarships to annual Environmental Law Course.

YEAR PROGRAM STARTED: 1970

PURPOSE:
To provide access to education on environmental law and policy; to improve the level of practice and raise the quality of debate on key legal/policy questions.

LEGAL BASIS:
Nonprofit corporation, 501(c)(3).

ELIGIBILITY:
Open to public interest lawyers, attorneys doing substantial pro bono work, and state and local government attorneys involved in environmental law.

FINANCIAL DATA:
Amount of support per award: Approximately $800 to $900 per scholarship applicant approved.

Total amount of support: Approximately $25,000 annually.

CO-OP FUNDING PROGRAMS: Environmental Law Conference with ALI-CLE.

NO. MOST RECENT APPLICANTS: Approximately 25.

NO. AWARDS: Approximately 25.

APPLICATION INFO:
Send letter of application stating need and expected benefit.

PUBLICATIONS:
Annual report; *Environmental Law Reporter*; *The Environmental Forum*; *National Wetlands Newsletter*.

IRS I.D.: 52-0901863

OFFICERS:
Scott Fulton, President

ADDRESS INQUIRIES TO:
See e-mail address above.

FOOD AND DRUG LAW INSTITUTE (FDLI) [1913]

1155 15th Street, N.W., Suite 910
Washington, DC 20005-2706
(202) 371-1420
Fax: (202) 371-0649
E-mail: comments@fdli.org
Web Site: www.fdli.org/resources/academics/h-thomas-austern-memorial-writing-competition

FOUNDED: 1949

AREAS OF INTEREST:
Food and drug law issues.

NAME(S) OF PROGRAMS:
- **H. Thomas Austern Memorial Writing Competition**

TYPE:
Awards/prizes. The subject matter of the competition is an in-depth analysis of a current issue relevant to the food and drug field, including a relevant case law, legislative history and other authorities, particularly where the U.S. Food and Drug Administration is involved.

YEAR PROGRAM STARTED: 1978

PURPOSE:
To encourage law students interested in the areas of law affecting foods, drugs, devices, cosmetics and biologics; to provide a marketplace for discussing food and drug law issues.

LEGAL BASIS:
Nonprofit educational association.

ELIGIBILITY:
The level of study is postgraduate. Entrants must currently be enrolled in a J.D. program at any of the U.S. ABA-accredited law schools.

GEOG. RESTRICTIONS: United States.

FINANCIAL DATA:
Amount of support per award: $5,000 first prize; $3,000 second prize; $2,000 third prize.

Total amount of support: $10,000.

NO. MOST RECENT APPLICANTS: 50.

NO. AWARDS: 5 for the year 2015.

APPLICATION INFO:
Applicants must submit all materials electronically. Instructions can be found on the web site.

PUBLICATIONS:
Food and Drug Law Journal.

THE HAGUE ACADEMY OF INTERNATIONAL LAW [1914]

Peace Palace
Carnegieplein 2
2517 KJ The Hague The Netherlands
(31) 70 3024242
E-mail: registration@hagueacademy.nl
Web Site: www.hagueacademy.nl

FOUNDED: 1923

AREAS OF INTEREST:
Private and public international law.

NAME(S) OF PROGRAMS:
- **Doctoral Scholarships in International Law**

TYPE:
Project/program grants. Study programs. Residential scholarships for doctoral candidates from developing countries whose thesis, in private international law or public international law, is in the process of completion, who reside in their home country and who do not have access to scientific sources.

YEAR PROGRAM STARTED: 1923

PURPOSE:
To facilitate the completion of the theses through the use of the Academy, especially from the directors of studies and the use of the resources of the Library of the Peace Palace.

LEGAL BASIS:
Government agency.

ELIGIBILITY:
The candidates' doctoral thesis should be in the process of completion. Applicant should be a national of a developing country who is a resident in their own country.

FINANCIAL DATA:
Help in the form of a contribution towards travelling expenses may be granted to participants, taking into account the distance of their country of normal residence.

Amount of support per award: EUR 2,250 plus half of the traveling expenses, up to a maximum of EUR 910.

NO. MOST RECENT APPLICANTS: 30.

NO. AWARDS: 4.

APPLICATION INFO:
Application online only. Applications should be accompanied by a recommendation from the professor under whose direction the thesis is being written which mentions the title of the thesis. It should also contain a CV, a copy of the highest degree certificate (translated in French or English) and a short letter giving reasons for application.

Duration: Two months from July 1 onward.

Deadline: February 1.

PUBLICATIONS:
Programme de la Session; *Collected Courses*, series of published lectures.

ADDRESS INQUIRIES TO:
Registration Office
(See address above.)

*SPECIAL STIPULATIONS:
The Academy will verify that recipients of scholarships are effectively resident in The Hague without interruption and that they use the Peace Palace Library on a regular basis.

No person may receive more than one scholarship.

THE HAGUE ACADEMY OF INTERNATIONAL LAW [1915]

Peace Palace
Carnegieplein 2
2517 KJ The Hague The Netherlands
(31) 70 3024242
E-mail: registration@hagueacademy.nl
Web Site: www.hagueacademy.nl

FOUNDED: 1923

AREAS OF INTEREST:
Private and public international law.

NAME(S) OF PROGRAMS:
- **Hague Academy of International Law Summer Courses**

TYPE:
Project/program grants; Scholarships. Study programs. A limited number of scholarships are given to cover tuition and living expenses while studying at the three-week summer session of the Hague Academy of International Law. Because of the limited number, granting of scholarships to attendees from every country is not possible.

YEAR PROGRAM STARTED: 1923

PURPOSE:
To support personal and effective participation of members in scientific work related to international law and international affairs.

ELIGIBILITY:
Candidates must have completed at least four years of university studies, which must have included lectures on International Law, or must hold a three-year law degree on the date of the opening of the courses.

FINANCIAL DATA:
Amount of support per award: EUR 1,200 (including registration fees of EUR 650) covering general expenses incurred during the three weeks of one of the teaching periods. Travelling expenses will be partially reimbursed either by the relevant donor or by the Academy.

NO. MOST RECENT APPLICANTS: 680.

NO. AWARDS: 100.

APPLICATION INFO:
Application for scholarship should be made through the online registration form. The application must contain an identity photograph, a curriculum vitae, a copy of the highest degree certificate (translated in English or French), a short letter giving reason for the application and a recommendation from a professor of international law, sent separately. Candidates must possess a satisfactory knowledge of either French or English, the working languages of the Academy.

Duration: Three weeks in public international law; three weeks in private international law.

Deadline: Complete files of scholarship candidates should be in the possession of the Secretariat before February 1.

PUBLICATIONS:
Collected Courses, series of published lectures.

OFFICERS:
Prof. Yves Daudet, Secretary-General of the Academy

ADDRESS INQUIRIES TO:
Registration Office
(See address above.)

*SPECIAL STIPULATIONS:
No person may receive more than one scholarship for the Summer Courses. Recipients of scholarships are required to attend the Academy's courses throughout the session.

THE HAGUE ACADEMY OF INTERNATIONAL LAW [1916]

Peace Palace
Carnegieplein 2
2517 KJ The Hague The Netherlands
(31) 70 3024242
E-mail: registration@hagueacademy.nl
Web Site: www.hagueacademy.nl

FOUNDED: 1923

AREAS OF INTEREST:
Public and private international law.

NAME(S) OF PROGRAMS:
- **Centre for Studies and Research in International Law and International Relations**

TYPE:
Project/program grants.

YEAR PROGRAM STARTED: 1957

PURPOSE:
To bring together young international lawyers of a high standard from all over the world, to undertake original research on a common general theme which is determined each year by the Academy.

ELIGIBILITY:
The program is open to academics or lawyers of a high standard. Applications are open only to those persons who hold advanced university degrees (a Doctorate or the Academy's diploma) or to those who provide evidence of their actual involvement, for at least three years, in international legal matters. Candidates must have real practical experience and an ability to undertake research. There are between 20 and 24 participants, half in the English-speaking section and half in the French-speaking section.

FINANCIAL DATA:
All participants receive a daily allowance of EUR 35 according to the length of the stay and the reimbursement of half of the travel expenses, up to a maximum of EUR 910.

NO. MOST RECENT APPLICANTS: 70.

NO. AWARDS: 10.

APPLICATION INFO:
Candidates should upload to the online registration form a curriculum vitae with, if applicable:
(1) a list of the publications;
(2) a copy of the law diplomas, translated into one of the two languages of the Academy (English or French);
(3) a short letter giving reasons for the application and;
(4) a recommendation letter from a professor of international law sent separately.

Duration: Three weeks.

Deadline: End of March.

PUBLICATIONS:
Books of the Centre for Studies and Research - Hague Academy of International Law.

OFFICERS:
Prof. Yves Daudet, Secretary General

ADDRESS INQUIRIES TO:
Registration Office
(See address above.)

*PLEASE NOTE:
The research work undertaken at the Centre may be included in a collective work published by the Academy.

*SPECIAL STIPULATIONS:
In principle, no person may participate more than once in the Centre's activities. Each participant must write a report on a subject arising out of the general theme of the year, which will be determined by the director of studies. This report must be sent to the relevant director of studies, by mid-November at the latest.

THE HAGUE ACADEMY OF INTERNATIONAL LAW [1917]

Peace Palace
Carnegieplein 2
2517 KJ The Hague The Netherlands
(31) 70 3024242
E-mail: registration@hagueacademy.nl
Web Site: www.hagueacademy.nl

FOUNDED: 1923

AREAS OF INTEREST:
Public and private international law.

NAME(S) OF PROGRAMS:
- **External Programme**

TYPE:
Project/program grants. External Programme is held each year, in turn in Africa, Asia and Latin America, upon the invitation of host governments or international organizations. It is designed for approximately 20 participants from the countries in the region (who are resident in their own country), whose traveling expenses are usually financed by the Academy and whose accommodation is financed by the government of the host state or organization. In addition, a number of participants come from the host state itself.

YEAR PROGRAM STARTED: 1969

ELIGIBILITY:
This programme is aimed at persons having studied international law (young university teachers and young civil servants from the ministry of foreign affairs or other ministries), selected by the Secretary General in the name of the Curatorium on exclusively scientific criteria. Candidates should come from countries in the region of the host country. A list of the eligible nationalities is published every year.

FINANCIAL DATA:
Regional participants receive a daily allowance of $35 (U.S.) according to the length of the stay and the reimbursement of their travel expenses. The accommodation is provided by the host country.

NO. MOST RECENT APPLICANTS: 50.

NO. AWARDS: 20.

APPLICATION INFO:
Candidates should apply online with the following:
(1) a curriculum vitae with, if applicable, a list of publications;
(2) a copy of candidate's highest degree certificate or an official document from candidate's university certifying candidate is preparing to obtain a degree. If the original document is not in English or French, please add a translation;
(3) indication of the number of hours of international law courses attended, together with the results and marks obtained;
(4) a short letter giving reasons for the application (one to two pages);
(5) a recommendation letter from a professor of international law sent separately;
(6) a copy of candidate's valid passport or ID and;
(7) an identity photograph.

Duration: Eight days.

Deadline: July 31, 0:00 hours.

OFFICERS:
Prof. Yves Daudet, Secretary General

ADDRESS INQUIRIES TO:
Registration Office
(See address above.)

*SPECIAL STIPULATIONS:
One is not allowed to participate more than once in the External Programme. Candidates should reside in their home country when applying.

THE HISPANIC BAR ASSOCIATION OF D.C. FOUNDATION [1918]

1341 G Street, N.W.
Suite 500
Washington, DC 20005
(202) 466-8585
Fax: (202) 463-4803
E-mail: foundation@hbadc.org
Web Site: www.hbadc.org

FOUNDED: 1995

AREAS OF INTEREST:
Law and public interest.

NAME(S) OF PROGRAMS:
- **The HBA-DC Foundation Fellowship**

TYPE:
Fellowships.

PURPOSE:
To provide students with valuable work experience and exposure to an area of public interest law.

ELIGIBILITY:
First- and second-year law students attending accredited law schools in the District of Columbia metropolitan area are eligible to apply, once having obtained a job offer from a sponsoring organization.

GEOG. RESTRICTIONS: District of Columbia and the metropolitan area.

FINANCIAL DATA:
Amount of support per award: $5,000.
Total amount of support: Varies.

NO. AWARDS: 5.

APPLICATION INFO:
Application information is available on the web site. Completed application must be submitted by e-mail to fellowships@hbadc.org.

Duration: One year.

Deadline: May.

ADDRESS INQUIRIES TO:
See e-mail address above.

HISPANIC NATIONAL BAR FOUNDATION [1919]

1900 K Street, N.W.
Suite 100
Washington, DC 20006
(202) 496-7206
Fax: (202) 496-7756
E-mail: avilla@hnbf.org
Web Site: www.hnbf.org

FOUNDED: 1985

AREAS OF INTEREST:
Promoting the legal education of persons of Hispanic heritage throughout the U.S. and Puerto Rico.

NAME(S) OF PROGRAMS:
- **Law Fellows Program**

TYPE:
Fellowships. The Law Fellows Program provides participating law students with the unique opportunity to join a corporation's legal department to focus on matters important to company business. The Law Fellows Program also includes a law firm component to expose the students to how law firms handle legal matters for their corporate clients. The Program includes training, professional development and work experience in Washington, DC, and in-house at the company's legal department.

PURPOSE:
To increase the number of Hispanic lawyers practicing in corporate legal departments; to promote diversity in the legal profession.

LEGAL BASIS:
Section 501(c)(3) organization dedicated to charitable and educational purposes.

ELIGIBILITY:
The Foundation selects first-year law students to participate in the Law Fellows Program.

FINANCIAL DATA:
Each Law Fellow receives a weekly stipend for participating in the program. Transportation cost from the student's home to Washington, DC may be covered by the Foundation as well as transportation cost from Washington, DC to the company site, if necessary.

APPLICATION INFO:
Duration: Six to eight weeks in the summer.

Deadline: June 1.

ADDRESS INQUIRIES TO:
Alba Lucero Villa
Executive Director
(See address above.)

HISPANIC NATIONAL BAR FOUNDATION [1920]

1900 K Street, N.W.
Suite 100
Washington, DC 20006
(202) 496-7206
Fax: (202) 496-7756
E-mail: avilla@hnbf.org
Web Site: www.hnbf.org

FOUNDED: 1985

AREAS OF INTEREST:
Promoting the legal education of persons of Hispanic heritage throughout the U.S. and Puerto Rico.

NAME(S) OF PROGRAMS:
- **Future Latino Leaders Law Camp**

TYPE:
Conferences/seminars; Training grants. Nine-day program held by the Foundation in Washington, DC which provides Latino high school students with the opportunity to learn more about the legal profession. The Law Camp offers students the chance to come to the nation's capital and learn more about the college application process, meet influential Latino leaders, and tour national monuments and various government agencies.

YEAR PROGRAM STARTED: 2005

PURPOSE:
To provide tools and resources necessary to ensure full and equal opportunity for Hispanics to become leaders in the global community, thereby ensuring a brighter future for all.

LEGAL BASIS:
Section 501(c)(3) organization dedicated to charitable and educational purposes.

ELIGIBILITY:
Applicants must meet the following criteria:
(1) be a high school student entering the sophomore, junior or senior year, or be a recent graduate;
(2) have an interest in learning about law school and becoming a lawyer;
(3) be a U.S. citizen, legal permanent resident or be a legal U.S. visitor with a valid visa and passport and;
(4) have a demonstrated interest in helping one's community and building one's leadership skills.

FINANCIAL DATA:
There is no cost to participate in the Law Camp. However, accepted students must pay a $50 application fee, unless a waiver of this fee is requested and granted. Students are also responsible for arranging transportation to Washington, DC. The cost of transportation should not deter one from applying. Upon acceptance to the program, the Foundation is committed to working with the attendee and his or her family in order to ensure that person's ability to attend.

Amount of support per award: Valued at over $3,000 per person.

NO. AWARDS: 38 for the year 2015.

APPLICATION INFO:
Application process begins mid-January. Application can be completed online or sent by mail and must include:
(1) Applicant Information Form;
(2) Rules and Regulations Form;
(3) essays;
(4) two letters of recommendation (from teachers, counselors or employers);
(5) resume (may include community service, leadership positions or civic activities);
(6) certified copy of academic record from high school and;
(7) $50 application fee or fee waiver approval.

Duration: Nine days.

Deadline: April 1.

ADDRESS INQUIRIES TO:
E-mail: hnbflawcamp@hnbf.org

JOHN M. LLOYD FOUNDATION [1921]

11777 San Vicente Boulevard
Suite 745
Los Angeles, CA 90049
(310) 622-1050
Fax: (424) 625-0740
E-mail: info@johnmlloyd.org
Web Site: www.johnmlloyd.org

FOUNDED: 1991

AREAS OF INTEREST:
Criminal justice reform primarily in Los Angeles County, CA.

TYPE:
General operating grants; Project/program grants.

YEAR PROGRAM STARTED: 1992

PURPOSE:
To promote one just criminal justice system in Los Angeles County, CA, a system centered on strong communities and practical resources, not prisons; to help Los Angeles County become a leader in a movement toward true justice nationwide.

LEGAL BASIS:
Private, family foundation.

ELIGIBILITY:
The Foundation does not accept unsolicited requests for funding at this time.

GEOG. RESTRICTIONS: Primarily Los Angeles County, California.

FINANCIAL DATA:
Amount of support per award: Varies; most grants are about $25,000.

Total amount of support: $300,000.

NO. MOST RECENT APPLICANTS: 14.

NO. AWARDS: 10.

REPRESENTATIVE AWARDS:
Dignity and Power Now; Youth Justice Coalition; Healing Dialogue and Action.

APPLICATION INFO:
Unsolicited formal proposals will not be considered.

Duration: One year.

IRS I.D.: 36-3766003

BOARD OF DIRECTORS:
James Anderson
Eliot Estrin
Jesse Estrin
Mary Lloyd Estrin
Robert L. Estrin
Zoe Lloyd Estrin
Griff Foxley
Trish Devine Karlin
Linda Dorn Klein
Heidi Mage Lloyd

ADDRESS INQUIRIES TO:
Melanie Havelin, Executive Director
(See e-mail address above.)

*SPECIAL STIPULATIONS:
Unsolicited formal proposals will not be considered.

THURGOOD MARSHALL COLLEGE FUND (TMCF) [1922]

1770 St. James Place
Suite 414
Houston, TX 77056
(202) 507-4851
Fax: (202) 448-1017
E-mail: scholarships@tmcf.org
Web Site: www.tmcf.org

NAME(S) OF PROGRAMS:
- **The Sidney B. Williams, Jr. Intellectual Property Law Scholarship**

TYPE:
Scholarships. Program for underrepresented minority students who intend to enter the intellectual property law field, to attend law school.

PURPOSE:
To significantly increase the number of underrepresented minorities working as intellectual property law lawyers in both private and corporate practice.

ELIGIBILITY:
Applicant must:
(1) be a U.S. citizen;
(2) be a member of an underrepresented minority group;
(3) be currently enrolled in or have been accepted to an ABA-accredited law school;
(4) have a demonstrated commitment to developing a career in intellectual property law and;
(5) be in need of financial assistance.

GEOG. RESTRICTIONS: United States.

FINANCIAL DATA:
Amount of support per award: $10,000 per school year.
Total amount of support: Varies.

CO-OP FUNDING PROGRAMS: This Scholarship is administered by the Thurgood Marshall College Fund (TMCF), and it is offered through a partnership between the TMCF and the American Intellectual Property Law Education Foundation.

NO. AWARDS: Varies.

APPLICATION INFO:
Contact TMCF.
Duration: Up to three academic years. Must reapply each year.
Deadline: Mid-March. Check online for exact date.

ADDRESS INQUIRIES TO:
Deshuandra Walker
Student Support Programs Manager
Tel: (713) 955-1073
(See address and e-mail above.)

MCGILL UNIVERSITY [1923]
Chancellor Day Hall
3644 Peel Street
Montreal QC H3A 1W9 Canada
(514) 398-6666
Fax: (514) 398-4659
E-mail: staffappointments.law@mcgill.ca
Web Site: www.mcgill.ca/law

AREAS OF INTEREST:
Law, especially pertaining to the Canadian legal system and legal community.

NAME(S) OF PROGRAMS:
- **Maxwell Boulton Q.C. Fellowship**

TYPE:
Fellowships.

PURPOSE:
To provide younger scholars with an opportunity to pursue a major research project or to complete the research requirement for a higher degree.

ELIGIBILITY:
Open to candidates who have completed residency requirements for a doctoral degree in law.

FINANCIAL DATA:
Amount of support per award: $35,000 to $40,000 (CAN) per year.

NO. MOST RECENT APPLICANTS: 13.

NO. AWARDS: 1.

APPLICATION INFO:
Information is available on the web site.
Duration: One year.
Deadline: February 1.

ADDRESS INQUIRIES TO:
See e-mail address above.

REPORTERS COMMITTEE FOR FREEDOM OF THE PRESS
1156 15th Street, N.W.
Suite 1250
Washington, DC 20005
(202) 795-9306
Fax: (202) 795-9310
E-mail: rcfp@rcfp.org
Web Site: www.rcfp.org

TYPE:
Fellowships. Legal fellows monitor significant developments in First Amendment media law, assist with legal defense requests from reporters, prepare legal memoranda, amicus briefs and other special projects. The Fellowship focuses on media law.

See entry 1898 for full listing.

RHODE ISLAND STATE INTERNSHIP PROGRAM
State House, Room 8AA
Providence, RI 02903
(401) 222-6782
Fax: (401) 222-4447
E-mail: intern@rilegislature.gov
Web Site: www.rilin.state.ri.us

TYPE:
Internships. Funding through General Assembly is also available. Internship opportunities for graduate and undergraduate students in the state government operation. Students are involved in executive, legislative and judicial assignments. The internship is viewed as an extension of the classroom and is seen as complementing and building upon the educational opportunities available on campuses.

This program has established a Summer Internship section, open to Rhode Island residents only, that begins in late June and concludes in August.

See entry 1951 for full listing.

THE UNIVERSITY OF CALGARY [1924]
Faculty of Graduate Studies
MacKimmie Library Tower, Room 213
2500 University Drive, N.W.
Calgary AB T2N 1N4 Canada
(403) 220-4938
Fax: (403) 289-7635
E-mail: gsaward@ucalgary.ca
Web Site: www.grad.ucalgary.ca/awards

FOUNDED: 1966

AREAS OF INTEREST:
Law.

NAME(S) OF PROGRAMS:
- **The Honourable N.D. McDermid Graduate Scholarship in Law**

TYPE:
Awards/prizes; Scholarships. Graduate scholarships in law tenable at The University of Calgary. Awards endowed by the McDermid Law Fund in memory of the late Honourable Neil Douglas McDermid, Q.C., who was a prominent member of the legal profession of Alberta and the Calgary community for many years.

PURPOSE:
To financially assist students who want to study law at the university.

LEGAL BASIS:
University.

ELIGIBILITY:
Graduate students entering or enrolled on a full-time basis in the graduate program in the Faculty of Law at The University of Calgary. If, in the opinion of the Faculty of Graduate Studies Scholarships Selection Committee, no suitable applications are received, no awards will be made.

GEOG. RESTRICTIONS: Canada.

FINANCIAL DATA:
Amount of support per award: $10,000 (award may be divided further to $5,000).
Total amount of support: $20,000.

NO. AWARDS: 2.

APPLICATION INFO:
Application forms are available from the Dean's Office, Faculty of Law. Applications will be reviewed by a Committee of the Faculty of Law based upon academic excellence. The Graduate Coordinator, Law will submit recommendations to the Graduate Scholarship Office. The recommendation is subject to final approval of the Graduate Scholarship Committee.
Duration: One year. Nonrenewable.
Deadline: December 15.

ADDRESS INQUIRIES TO:
Graduate Scholarship Office
(See address above.)

THE UNIVERSITY OF CALGARY
Faculty of Graduate Studies
MacKimmie Library Tower, Room 213
2500 University Drive, N.W.
Calgary AB T2N 1N4 Canada
(403) 220-4938
Fax: (403) 289-7635
E-mail: gsaward@ucalgary.ca
Web Site: www.grad.ucalgary.ca/awards

TYPE:
Awards/prizes; Scholarships.

See entry 1734 for full listing.

Political science

AMERICAN POLITICAL SCIENCE ASSOCIATION [1925]
1527 New Hampshire Avenue, N.W.
Washington, DC 20036
(202) 483-2512
Fax: (202) 483-2657
E-mail: cfp@apsanet.org
Web Site: www.apsanet.org/cfp

FOUNDED: 1903

AREAS OF INTEREST:
Political science.

NAME(S) OF PROGRAMS:
- **Congressional Fellowship Program**

TYPE:
Fellowships. Awards to political science professors and journalists in early-career to midcareer status; the award provides an opportunity for support as a full-time aide to a member of the House or Senate or as a staff member for a Congressional committee.

YEAR PROGRAM STARTED: 1953

PURPOSE:
To equip outstanding young political scientists and journalists with a better understanding of the national legislative process.

LEGAL BASIS:
Nonprofit association.

ELIGIBILITY:
Open to U.S. political scientists and journalists. Political scientists must have completed their Ph.D. within the last 15 years or will have defended a dissertation by the start of the fellowship year. Applicant journalists must have a Bachelor's degree and between two and 10 years of full-time professional experience in newspaper, magazine, radio or television work. Special fellowships are available for Ph.D.-level scholars of any discipline or journalists with demonstrated professional interest in telecommunications.

FINANCIAL DATA:
Amount of support per award: $50,000 stipend plus travel.

NO. MOST RECENT APPLICANTS: Varies.

NO. AWARDS: Varies.

APPLICATION INFO:
Official application materials are available on the web site.

Duration: 10 months, November to August.

Deadline: December 1.

ADDRESS INQUIRIES TO:
Kara Abramson, Director
(See address above.)

AMERICAN POLITICAL SCIENCE ASSOCIATION [1926]

1527 New Hampshire Avenue, N.W.
Washington, DC 20036
(202) 483-2512
Fax: (202) 483-2657
E-mail: kmealy@apsanet.org
Web Site: www.apsanet.org

FOUNDED: 1903

AREAS OF INTEREST:
Political science.

NAME(S) OF PROGRAMS:
- **APSA Minority Fellows Program**

TYPE:
Fellowships; Grants-in-aid; Scholarships. Awards to aid prospective African American, Asian Pacific, Latino/Latina and Native American political science students beginning the doctoral study of political science.

YEAR PROGRAM STARTED: 1969

PURPOSE:
To increase the number of minority scholars in the discipline; to assist minority students in completing their doctorates by concentrating not only on the recruitment of minorities, but also on the retention of these groups within the profession.

LEGAL BASIS:
Nonprofit association.

ELIGIBILITY:
Applicants must:
(1) be minority students applying to enter a doctoral program in political science for the first time;
(2) be members of one of the following racial/ethnic minority groups: African Americans, Asian Pacific Americans, Latinos/Latinas, and Native Americans (federal and state recognized tribes);
(3) demonstrate an interest in teaching and potential for research in political science and;
(4) be a U.S. citizen at time of award.

FINANCIAL DATA:
Amount of support per award: $4,000, disbursed in two $2,000 payments, one at the end of their first graduate year and one at the end of their second, provided that they remain in good academic standing.

Total amount of support: $48,000.

NO. MOST RECENT APPLICANTS: 30.

NO. AWARDS: 17 for the year 2015-16.

APPLICATION INFO:
Forms can be downloaded from the web site.

Duration: One year.

ADDRESS INQUIRIES TO:
Kimberly Mealy, Program Director
(See address above.)

AMERICAN POLITICAL SCIENCE ASSOCIATION [1927]

1527 New Hampshire Avenue, N.W.
Washington, DC 20036
(202) 483-2512
Fax: (202) 483-2657
E-mail: researchgrants@apsanet.org
Web Site: www.apsanet.org

AREAS OF INTEREST:
Political science.

NAME(S) OF PROGRAMS:
- **Small Research Grant Program**

TYPE:
Project/program grants; Research grants; Seed money grants; Technical assistance; Travel grants. The Association Small Research Grant Program supports research in all fields of political science.

PURPOSE:
To support the research of political scientists who are not employed at Ph.D.-granting institutions and to help further the careers of these scholars.

ELIGIBILITY:
Applicants must be Association members at the time of application and when the funds are dispersed. The principal investigator and any coauthor must be one of the following:
(1) a faculty member at a college or university that does not award a Ph.D. in political science, public administration, public policy, international relations, government or politics and whose primary appointment is in one of these departments or;
(2) a political scientist not affiliated with an academic institution who is unemployed or working in a research organization such as a think tank.

This grant does not provide support for dissertation research or writing. Graduate students are not eligible to apply. Applicants do not have to be U.S. citizens or residents.

FINANCIAL DATA:
Funds may be used for such research activities as:
(1) travel to archives;
(2) travel to conduct interviews;
(3) administration and coding of instruments;
(4) research assistance and;
(5) purchase of data-sets.

The following activities are excluded from funding:
(1) travel to professional meetings;
(2) secretarial costs except for preparation of the final manuscripts for publication and;
(3) salary support for the principal investigator.
Overhead or indirect costs are not allowable expenses.

Amount of support per award: Up to $2,500.

APPLICATION INFO:
Complete proposal and application procedures as well as sample proposals can be found on the web site. Applicant should send seven collated and stapled hard copies to the address above (Attn: Small Research Grant Competition).

Duration: One year. Nonrenewable.

Deadline: February 1.

*SPECIAL STIPULATIONS:
Funds must be expended between the time they are received (usually in May) and the end of the following fiscal year (June 30).

ASHBURN INSTITUTE INC.

198 Okatie Village Drive
Suite 103, PMB 301
Bluffton, SC 29909
(703) 728-6482
Fax: (843) 705-7643
E-mail: info@ashburninstitute.org
Web Site: www.ashburninstitute.org

TYPE:
Research grants; Scholarships.

See entry 817 for full listing.

CENTER FOR CALIFORNIA STUDIES, CAPITAL FELLOWS PROGRAMS [1928]

California State University, Sacramento
6000 J Street
Sacramento, CA 95819-6081
(916) 278-6906
Fax: (916) 278-5199
E-mail: calstudies@csus.edu
Web Site: www.csus.edu/calst/judicial

FOUNDED: 1982

AREAS OF INTEREST:
California judicial system.

NAME(S) OF PROGRAMS:
- **Judicial Administration Fellowship Program**

TYPE:
Fellowships. Jointly sponsored by the Center for California Studies at California State University, Sacramento and the California Judicial Council. Full-time fellowships for 10 fellows, 10 months and graduate units earned from California State University, Sacramento.

YEAR PROGRAM STARTED: 1997

PURPOSE:
To enable fellows to conduct research, advocate on behalf of the judiciary, develop and implement programs, seek grants, and engage in educational outreach, strategic planning, and policy analysis.

ELIGIBILITY:
Must be 20 years of age by September 1 of fellowship year and have a minimum four-year Bachelor's degree with graduation by September 1 of fellowship year. Graduate, postgraduate and midcareer applicants are welcome.

FINANCIAL DATA:
Fellowship includes monthly stipend plus health, vision and dental benefits.

Amount of support per award: $2,627 monthly stipend.

APPLICATION INFO:
Applications will only be accepted online. Applicants must submit all transcripts, three letters of recommendation (minimum) and two essays.

Duration: 10 months.

Deadline: Early February. Interviews in Los Angeles and Sacramento in April/May. Fellowship announcement in May.

ADDRESS INQUIRIES TO:
Megan Thorall, Program Director
(See address above.)

*SPECIAL STIPULATIONS:
International fellows must have a valid work visa.

CENTER FOR CALIFORNIA STUDIES, CAPITAL FELLOWS PROGRAMS [1929]

California State University, Sacramento
6000 J Street
Sacramento, CA 95819-6081
(916) 278-6906
Fax: (916) 278-5199
E-mail: calstudies@csus.edu
Web Site: www.csus.edu/calst/senate

FOUNDED: 1982

AREAS OF INTEREST:
California state government.

NAME(S) OF PROGRAMS:
- **California Senate Fellows Program**

TYPE:
Fellowships. Jointly sponsored by the Center for California Studies at California State University, Sacramento and the California State Senate. Full-time fellowships for 18 fellows, 11 months and graduate units earned from California State University, Sacramento.

PURPOSE:
To provide participants with insight into the legislative process, including exposing people with diverse life experiences and backgrounds to the legislative process and providing research and other professional staff assistance to the Senate.

ELIGIBILITY:
Must be 20 years of age by September 1 of fellowship year and have a minimum four-year Bachelor's degree with graduation by September 1 of fellowship year. Graduate, postgraduate and midcareer applicants are welcome. Applicants need not be California residents; however, preference will be given to candidates who demonstrate knowledge of and commitment to the state.

FINANCIAL DATA:
Fellowship includes monthly stipend plus full health, vision and dental benefits.

Amount of support per award: $2,627 monthly stipend.

APPLICATION INFO:
Applications will only be accepted online. Applicants must submit all transcripts, three letters of recommendation (minimum), and essay.

Duration: 11 months.

Deadline: Early February. Interviews in Los Angeles and Sacramento in April/May. Fellowship announcement in May.

ADDRESS INQUIRIES TO:
David Pacheco, Program Director
(See address above.)

*SPECIAL STIPULATIONS:
International fellows must have a valid work visa.

CENTER FOR CALIFORNIA STUDIES, CAPITAL FELLOWS PROGRAMS [1930]

California State University, Sacramento
6000 J Street
Sacramento, CA 95819-6081
(916) 278-6906
Fax: (916) 278-5199
E-mail: calstudies@csus.edu
Web Site: www.csus.edu/calst/executive

FOUNDED: 1982

AREAS OF INTEREST:
California state government.

NAME(S) OF PROGRAMS:
- **Executive Fellowship Program**

TYPE:
Fellowships. Jointly sponsored by the Center for California Studies at California State University, Sacramento and the California governor. Full-time fellowships for 18 fellows, 10 months and six units of graduate study through California State University, Sacramento.

YEAR PROGRAM STARTED: 1986

PURPOSE:
To provide an experiential learning opportunity in California state government, whereby Fellows gain valuable insight and experience in the realm of public policy and politics.

ELIGIBILITY:
Must be 20 years of age by September 1 of the fellowship year and have a minimum four-year Bachelor's degree with graduation by September 1 of the fellowship year. Graduate, postgraduate and midcareer applicants are welcome.

FINANCIAL DATA:
Fellowship includes monthly stipend plus medical, vision and dental benefits. Recipients also earn units of graduate credit.

Amount of support per award: $2,627 per month stipend.

APPLICATION INFO:
Applications will only be accepted online. Applicants must submit all transcripts, three letters of recommendation (minimum), a policy statement and a personal statement of interest.

Duration: 10 months.

Deadline: Early February. Interviews in Los Angeles and Sacramento, CA in April/May. Fellowship announced in May.

ADDRESS INQUIRIES TO:
Brian Aguilar, Program Director
(See address above.)

*SPECIAL STIPULATIONS:
International fellows must have a valid work visa.

CENTER FOR CALIFORNIA STUDIES, CAPITAL FELLOWS PROGRAMS [1931]

California State University, Sacramento
6000 J Street
Sacramento, CA 95819-6081
(916) 278-6906
Fax: (916) 278-5199
E-mail: calstudies@csus.edu
Web Site: www.csus.edu/calst/assembly_fellowship_program.html

FOUNDED: 1982

AREAS OF INTEREST:
California state government.

NAME(S) OF PROGRAMS:
- **Jesse M. Unruh Assembly Fellowship Program**

TYPE:
Fellowships. Jointly sponsored by the Center for California Studies at California State University, Sacramento and the California State Assembly. Full-time fellowships for 18 fellows, 11 months and units of graduate study through California State University, Sacramento.

PURPOSE:
To provide educational and governmental experience and assistance for legislators.

LEGAL BASIS:
University/government program funded by State Budget-General Budget Fund.

ELIGIBILITY:
Must be 20 years of age by September 1 of fellowship year and have a minimum four-year Bachelor's degree with graduation by September 1 of fellowship year. Graduate, postgraduate and midcareer applicants are welcome.

FINANCIAL DATA:
In addition to the stipend, full medical, vision and dental benefits are provided.

Amount of support per award: $2,627 per month stipend.

APPLICATION INFO:
Applicants must submit all transcripts, three letters of recommendation (minimum), and two essays.

Duration: 11 months.

Deadline: Late February. Interviews in Los Angeles and Sacramento in May. Fellowship announcement in May.

ADDRESS INQUIRIES TO:
Pam Chueh, Program Director
(See address above.)

*SPECIAL STIPULATIONS:
International fellows must have a valid work visa.

CITY OF NEW YORK [1932]

Department of Citywide Administrative Services
One Centre Street, Room 2425
New York, NY 10007
(212) 386-0058
Fax: (212) 669-3688
E-mail: urbanfellows@dcas.nyc.gov
Web Site: www.nyc.gov/fellowships

FOUNDED: 1969

AREAS OF INTEREST:
City government and New York City government.

NAME(S) OF PROGRAMS:
- **New York City Urban Fellows Program**

TYPE:
Fellowships. Stipend for full-time work in New York City government agencies. Fellows work closely with city officials on long- and short-term projects and attend weekly seminars to get an academic perspective on the workings and problems of local government. Assignments range over fields such as urban planning, housing, health and social sciences, economic and financial administration, youth service, intergovernmental relations, criminal justice, cultural affairs and innumerable others. Positions are at relatively high levels as assistants to administrators and staff within the various city agencies.

YEAR PROGRAM STARTED: 1969

PURPOSE:
To attract qualified college graduates to participate in a management training program in New York City government.

LEGAL BASIS:
City Government agency.

ELIGIBILITY:
As of September of the program year, applicants must be recent college graduates (no more than two full years out of college). Fellows participate on a full-time basis. Applicants must be able to demonstrate their eligibility to work in the U.S. after graduation and for the entire fellowship period.

FINANCIAL DATA:
A choice of paid health insurance plans is provided.

Amount of support per award: Currently $30,000 for nine-month duration (annualized to $40,000).

NO. MOST RECENT APPLICANTS: Approximately 350.

NO. AWARDS: 25 annually.

APPLICATION INFO:
Application information is available on the web site.

Duration: Nine months, September to May.

Deadline: Second Friday in January.

PUBLICATIONS:
Application guidelines.

ADDRESS INQUIRIES TO:
New York City Urban Fellows Program
(See address above.)

CONGRESSIONAL BLACK CAUCUS FOUNDATION, INC.

1720 Massachusetts Avenue, N.W.
Washington, DC 20036
(202) 263-2800
Fax: (202) 263-0846
E-mail: scholarships@cbcfinc.org
Web Site: www.cbcfinc.org

TYPE:
Scholarships. The CBCS General Mills Health Scholarship is intended to increase the number of minority students pursuing degrees in the fields of medicine, engineering, technology, nutrition and other health-related professions.

The CBC Spouses Education Scholarship is a national program that awards scholarships to academically talented and highly motivated students who intend to pursue full-time undergraduate, graduate or doctoral degrees.

See entry 1005 for full listing.

CONGRESSIONAL BLACK CAUCUS FOUNDATION, INC.

1720 Massachusetts Avenue, N.W.
Washington, DC 20036
(202) 263-2800
Fax: (202) 263-0846
E-mail: info@cbcfinc.org
internships@cbcfinc.org
Web Site: www.cbcfinc.org

TYPE:
Fellowships; Internships. The CBCF Congressional Fellows Program helps participants gain invaluable experience as they assist in the development of legislation and public policy initiatives while working as congressional staff for a year. This program targets early career policy professionals who have completed a professional and/or graduate degree and have demonstrated commitment to improving the lives and services for individuals living in underserved communities. Fellows work on Capitol Hill in the office of a Congressional Black Caucus member.

The CBCF Congressional Internship Program provides undergraduate students with an in-depth orientation to Capitol Hill and the legislative process through actual work experience in the offices of Congressional Black Caucus Members. In this way interns prepare to become decision makers in the policymaking process.

See entry 1006 for full listing.

CONGRESSIONAL HISPANIC CAUCUS INSTITUTE

1128 16th Street, N.W.
Washington, DC 20036
(202) 543-1771
(202) 548-5864
Fax: (202) 546-2143
Web Site: www.chci.org

TYPE:
Internships. Internships provide college students with a paid work placement in a congressional office or federal agency for a period of 12 weeks (Spring and Fall Programs) or eight weeks (Summer Program).

See entry 1045 for full listing.

CONGRESSIONAL HISPANIC CAUCUS INSTITUTE

1128 16th Street, N.W.
Washington, DC 20036
(202) 543-1771
(202) 548-8796
Fax: (202) 546-2143
Web Site: www.chci.org

TYPE:
Fellowships. Graduate Fellowship Program offers exceptional Latinos who have earned a graduate degree or higher related to a chosen policy issue area within three years of program start date unparalleled exposure to hands-on experience in public policy.

Public Policy Fellowship offers talented Latinos who have earned a Bachelor's degree within two years of the program start date the opportunity to gain hands-on experience at the national level in public policy.

See entry 1046 for full listing.

THE DIRKSEN CONGRESSIONAL CENTER [1933]

2815 Broadway
Pekin, IL 61554
(309) 347-7113
Fax: (309) 347-6432
E-mail: fmackaman@dirksencenter.org
Web Site: www.dirksencongressionalcenter.org

FOUNDED: 1963

AREAS OF INTEREST:
U.S. Congress and its leaders.

NAME(S) OF PROGRAMS:
- **Congressional Research Grants**

TYPE:
Research grants; Seed money grants; Travel grants. Financial awards to individuals conducting research about the U.S. Congress and its leaders.

YEAR PROGRAM STARTED: 1978

PURPOSE:
To foster study of Congress in order to enhance public understanding and appreciation of the legislative branch of the federal government.

LEGAL BASIS:
Independent, nonpartisan, not-for-profit research and educational organization.

ELIGIBILITY:
Open to anyone with a serious interest in studying Congress. The Center seeks applications specifically from political scientists, historians, biographers, scholars of public administration or American studies or journalists. Graduate students may also apply.

The program does not fund undergraduates or pre-Ph.D. study. Organizations are not eligible. No institutional overhead or indirect costs will be covered.

FINANCIAL DATA:
Amount of support per award: Up to $3,500.

Total amount of support: $35,000 for the year 2016.

NO. MOST RECENT APPLICANTS: 70 or more.

NO. AWARDS: Approximately 12 per year.

APPLICATION INFO:
Details on application are available on the web site.

Duration: Usually one year.

Deadline: March 1. Announcement in April.

IRS I.D.: 36-6132816

BOARD OF DIRECTORS AND OFFICERS:
William T. Fleming, President
Louis Miller, Vice President
Dr. Michael D. Danner, Treasurer
Sue Ann Kortkamp, Secretary
John A. Barra
Tim Butler
Christopher Deverman
Barbara E. Drake
David E. Glassman
Lincoln C. Hobson
Carla J. Schaefer
Timmothy J. Schwartz
Kay Sutton
Leslie K. Weyhrich
Ed Whitaker

ADDRESS INQUIRIES TO:
Frank H. Mackaman
(See address above.)

*SPECIAL STIPULATIONS:
This program does not fund tuition.

DONNER CANADIAN FOUNDATION [1934]

8 Prince Arthur Avenue, 3rd Floor
Toronto ON M5R 1A9 Canada
(416) 920-6400
Fax: (416) 920-5577
E-mail: mclean@donner.ca
Web Site: www.donnerfoundation.org

FOUNDED: 1950

AREAS OF INTEREST:
Local and municipal government, school reform, environmental education and provincial fiscal policy.

TYPE:
Project/program grants.

PURPOSE:
To determine how government handles public assets in delivering public services.

LEGAL BASIS:
Private foundation.

ELIGIBILITY:
The Foundation only makes grants to charitable organizations under the Income Tax Act of Canada. Grants are usually made for specific projects. The Foundation does not make grants for ongoing expenses, the acquisition of capital (equipment, buildings, land, etc.), endowments, fund-raising drives or to cover budget deficits. The Foundation does not accept unsolicited proposals.

GEOG. RESTRICTIONS: Canada.

FINANCIAL DATA:
Amount of support per award: Varies.

Total amount of support: Approximately $3,000,000.

APPLICATION INFO:
The Foundation does not regularly respond to letters of inquiry or unsolicited requests for funding. Charitable organizations may send the Foundation's Executive Director a two- to three-page description of their goals and programs and if there is a potential match between this work and the interests of the Foundation, staff will contact the charity for more information.

Duration: One year.

EXECUTIVE DIRECTOR:
Helen McLean

ADDRESS INQUIRIES TO:
Helen McLean, Executive Director
(See address above.)

*PLEASE NOTE:
The Foundation only provides support to organizations recognized as charitable by the Canada Revenue Agency.

THE EISENHOWER FOUNDATION [1935]

200 S.E. 4th Street
Abilene, KS 67410
(785) 263-4751
(877) 746-4453
Fax: (785) 263-6715
E-mail: info@eisenhowerfoundation.net
Web Site: www.eisenhowerfoundation.net
www.eisenhower.archives.gov

AREAS OF INTEREST:
Scholarly research in the fields of history, government, economics, communications and international affairs.

NAME(S) OF PROGRAMS:
- **Travel Grants**

TYPE:
Travel grants. Travel grants are awarded to individual researchers on a competitive basis to cover a portion of expenses while in Abilene, KS, using the presidential library.

PURPOSE:
To assist scholars' research of primary sources in such fields as history, government, economics, communications and international affairs so they may provide informed leadership in American national life.

ELIGIBILITY:
Applicants must be graduate-level students.

FINANCIAL DATA:
Grants are not retroactive and travel must occur within one year of award.

Amount of support per award: Up to $1,000, dependent upon the distance traveled and duration of stay in Abilene.

Total amount of support: Varies.

APPLICATION INFO:
Applications may be accessed online.

Deadline: Varies.

*SPECIAL STIPULATIONS:
If grantee's research results in a thesis, dissertation, book or article, a copy of the final product must be submitted to the Eisenhower Library for its holdings.

GERALD R. FORD PRESIDENTIAL LIBRARY [1936]

1000 Beal Avenue
Ann Arbor, MI 48109
(734) 205-0555
Fax: (734) 205-0571
E-mail: ford.library@nara.gov
Web Site: www.fordlibrarymuseum.gov

AREAS OF INTEREST:
Domestic issues, foreign policy and politics of the 1970s.

NAME(S) OF PROGRAMS:
- **Research Travel Grant Program**

TYPE:
Research grants; Travel grants. Research Travel Grants are awarded biannually to scholars to help defray the expenses of travel to conduct archival research in the collections of the Ford Library. Library collections focus on federal policies, foreign relations, and politics in the 1970s.

PURPOSE:
To promote research in the holdings of the Ford Library.

ELIGIBILITY:
Overseas applicants are welcome to apply, but they are responsible for costs of travel from their home country to North America.

FINANCIAL DATA:
Amount of support per award: Up to $2,200.

Total amount of support: Approximately $45,000 annually.

NO. AWARDS: Varies.

APPLICATION INFO:
Before applying, contact the Library for information about holdings related to your project. Applicants should submit the application form, a curriculum vitae, and a two- or three-page project proposal to the Library. The proposal should provide both a description of the project and the ways in which Ford Library resources can advance the research. Three professional references must submit supporting letters of recommendation.

Duration: Research to be conducted within one year notice of award.

Deadline: March 15 and September 15 (postmark).

ADDRESS INQUIRIES TO:
Grants Coordinator
(See address above.)

*SPECIAL STIPULATIONS:
The Gerald R. Ford Foundation expects acknowledgment of its support in resulting publication(s) and a donated copy of same to the Gerald R. Ford Presidential Library.

GERALD R. FORD PRESIDENTIAL LIBRARY [1937]

1000 Beal Avenue
Ann Arbor, MI 48109
(734) 205-0555
Fax: (734) 205-0571
E-mail: ford.library@nara.gov
Web Site: www.fordlibrarymuseum.gov

FOUNDED: 1981

AREAS OF INTEREST:
The U.S. political process, broadly defined, since circa 1970. Of special interest is the role and analysis of public opinion in that process.

NAME(S) OF PROGRAMS:
- **Gerald R. Ford Scholar Award (Dissertation Award) in Honor of Robert M. Teeter**

TYPE:
Awards/prizes; Research grants. Annual award to a doctoral student doing dissertation research and writing on an aspect of the U.S. political process during the latter part of the 20th century. Robert Teeter spent over 30 years as a leader in public opinion analysis and campaign strategy, including the 1976 campaign of President Gerald R. Ford. The majority of written materials from Teeter's career are part of the Gerald R. Ford Presidential Library collections. The Robert M. Teeter Papers document public opinion analysis and political campaign strategy from 1972 to 2004. They also include NBC News and *Wall Street Journal* National Public Opinion Surveys from 1989 to 2004.

PURPOSE:
To promote research regarding the U.S. political process during the latter part of the 20th century.

ELIGIBILITY:
Applicants must have completed all requirements for the Ph.D. program (coursework and examinations) by the application deadline, except for the dissertation.

FINANCIAL DATA:
The Library will present the award when the recipient arrives at the Library to conduct research. The recipient determines use of the award money, including, but not limited to, travel, paper and audiovisual reproductions and administrative costs, and other research and writing expenses.

Amount of support per award: $5,000.

CO-OP FUNDING PROGRAMS: The Award has been made possible by the generous support of the Teeter family and friends, and the United Parcel Service.

APPLICATION INFO:
Applicants must submit each of the following:
(1) an abstract describing the dissertation (no longer than 150 words);
(2) a five- to 10-page proposed plan of research;
(3) three letters of recommendation from individuals who can attest to the applicant's qualifications for the Award (one must be from their academic director that includes a statement approving the dissertation topic);
(4) unofficial transcripts from all graduate schools attended and;
(5) a curriculum vitae.

Deadline: March 31 annually. Awards are made each spring. Applications may be submitted at any time, but those received after the deadline will automatically be entered for the following year's award.

ADDRESS INQUIRIES TO:
Gerald R. Ford Scholar Award
in Honor of Robert M. Teeter
(See address above.)

THE FUND FOR AMERICAN STUDIES [1938]

1706 New Hampshire Avenue, N.W.
Washington, DC 20009
(202) 986-0384
Fax: (202) 986-8930
E-mail: jhollingsworth@tfas.org
Web Site: www.tfas.org/novak

FOUNDED: 1990

AREAS OF INTEREST:
Advancement of constitutional principles, a democratic society and a vibrant free enterprise system.

NAME(S) OF PROGRAMS:
- **Robert Novak Journalism Fellowship Program**

TYPE:
Fellowships. One-year writing project on a topic of applicant's choosing, focusing on journalism supportive of American culture and a free society.

YEAR PROGRAM STARTED: 1994

PURPOSE:
To award grants to working print and online journalists who share the Foundation's mission.

ELIGIBILITY:
Applicants must be U.S. citizens and working journalists with less than 10 years of professional experience in print and online journalism and who share the mission to advance constitutional principles, a democratic society and a vibrant free enterprise system.

FINANCIAL DATA:
Amounts include funds for reimbursement of fellowship-related expenses.

Amount of support per award: $50,000 full-time gold fellowship and $25,000 part-time silver fellowship.

Total amount of support: Varies.

NO. AWARDS: Varies, depending upon funding available and the number of qualified applicants.

APPLICATION INFO:
Contact the Foundation.

Duration: One year.

Deadline: February 9.

IRS I.D.: 13-6223604

ADDRESS INQUIRIES TO:
Vanessa Henderson, Executive Assistant
E-mail: vhenderson@tfas.org

HOOVER PRESIDENTIAL FOUNDATION [1939]

302 Parkside Drive
West Branch, IA 52358
(319) 643-5327
Fax: (319) 643-2391
E-mail: info@hooverassociation.org
Web Site: www.hooverassociation.org

FOUNDED: 1954

NAME(S) OF PROGRAMS:
- **Herbert Hoover Presidential Travel Grant Program**

TYPE:
Travel grants. Money is only available for travel to the Hoover Presidential Library in West Branch, IA. The program seeks to encourage scholarly use of the holdings of the Herbert Hoover Presidential Library. It is specifically intended to promote the study of subjects of interest and concern to Herbert Hoover, Lou Henry Hoover, their associates and other public figures as reflected in the Library's 150 manuscript collections.

YEAR PROGRAM STARTED: 1978

PURPOSE:
To encourage graduate and postdoctoral scholarship consistent with Program objectives.

LEGAL BASIS:
Tax-exempt, privately supported educational foundation.

ELIGIBILITY:
Open on a competitive basis to all scholars whose research projects are consistent with Program objectives. Qualified nonacademic researchers are also encouraged to apply. The program is also open to qualified undergraduates and independent scholars/researchers.

FINANCIAL DATA:
Amount of support per award: Up to $1,500. The Association will consider larger requests for extended graduate and postgraduate research at the Library.

Total amount of support: Varies.

NO. MOST RECENT APPLICANTS: 8.

NO. AWARDS: 6.

APPLICATION INFO:
Application materials are available on the web site or upon request from the Association. Applicants must consult with the archival staff concerning their topic prior to submitting a request for funding.

Duration: No grants made on a continuing basis. Reapplications for consecutive support periods are accepted. No more than two grants are allowed within a five-year period.

Deadline: March 1. Announcement April 30.

PUBLICATIONS:
Historical Materials in the Herbert Hoover Presidential Library.

ADDRESS INQUIRIES TO:
Delene W. McConnaha
Academic Programs Manager
(See address above.)

INSTITUTE FOR HUMANE STUDIES (IHS) [1940]

3434 Washington Boulevard, MS 1C5
Arlington, VA 22201
(703) 993-4880
Fax: (703) 993-4890
E-mail: funding@theihs.org
Web Site: www.theihs.org

AREAS OF INTEREST:
Individual liberty.

NAME(S) OF PROGRAMS:
- **Humane Studies Fellowships**

TYPE:
Fellowships; Research grants. Humane Studies Fellowships cover the fields of the social sciences and humanities.

PURPOSE:
To assist graduate students worldwide with a special interest in individual liberty.

ELIGIBILITY:
Graduate students in a Ph.D. program at a college or university may apply. Applicant must have a research interest that contributes to liberty-advancing scholarship. Past attendance at an IHS program or event required.

FINANCIAL DATA:
Amount of support per award: Up to $15,000 per year.

Total amount of support: Varies.

NO. AWARDS: 170 in fiscal year 2015.

APPLICATION INFO:
Application information is available on the web site.

Duration: One academic year. Renewable.

Deadline: February 8.

ADDRESS INQUIRIES TO:
See e-mail address above.

THE INTERCOLLEGIATE STUDIES INSTITUTE [1941]

3901 Centerville Road
Wilmington, DE 19807
(302) 652-4600
(800) 526-7022
Fax: (302) 652-1760
E-mail: awards@isi.org
Web Site: www.isifellowships.org

FOUNDED: 1953

AREAS OF INTEREST:
Education.

NAME(S) OF PROGRAMS:
- **Renshaw Fellowship**
- **Salvatori Fellowship**
- **Richard M. Weaver Fellowship**

TYPE:
Awards/prizes; Fellowships; Scholarships.

PURPOSE:
To convey to successive generations of college students a better understanding of the values and institutions that sustain a free society.

LEGAL BASIS:
A nonprofit, nonpartisan, tax-exempt educational organization.

ELIGIBILITY:
Applicant must be a member of the Intercollegiate Studies Institute. Applicant must also engage in graduate studies for the purpose of teaching at the college level (Renshaw Fellowship: or seeking to become a superintendent or curriculum developer). Those attending preprofessional schools (such as law, business, medicine and divinity) are ineligible. Applicants must be U.S. citizens who will be enrolled in a full-time graduate program for the upcoming academic year. Applicants may apply for more than one fellowship in any given academic cycle.

The Renshaw Fellowship is granted to current graduate students or applicants to graduate schools in doctoral study in education.

The Salvatori Fellowship is granted to current graduate students in a field related to the American Founding.

The Weaver Fellowship is granted to students who intend to use their advanced degree to teach.

FINANCIAL DATA:
Amount of support per award: Renshaw Fellowship: $12,000 grant; Salvatori Fellowship: $10,000 grant; Weaver Fellowship: five at $15,000 each, three at $10,000 each, and seven at $5,000 each.

Total amount of support: Varies.

NO. AWARDS: Salvatori Fellowship: 2; Weaver Fellowship: 15.

APPLICATION INFO:
Application information is available on the web site.

Deadline: January 23.

ADDRESS INQUIRIES TO:
Academic Program Officer
Program and Fellowships
(See address above.)

THE JAPANESE AMERICAN CITIZENS LEAGUE (JACL) [1942]

Washington, DC Office
1629 K Street, N.W., Suite 400
Washington, DC 20006
(202) 223-1240
E-mail: pouchida@jacl.org
Web Site: www.jacl.org

FOUNDED: 1929

AREAS OF INTEREST:
Public service leadership development.

NAME(S) OF PROGRAMS:
- **Mike M. Masaoka Fellowship Fund Congressional Program**

TYPE:
Fellowships. Congressional fellowship established to help understand the importance of public service at the national level. The Masaoka fellow serves in the Washington, DC office of a member of Congress in either the U.S. House of Representatives or the U.S. Senate.

YEAR PROGRAM STARTED: 1988

PURPOSE:
To develop leaders for public service.

ELIGIBILITY:
Candidates must be U.S. citizens who are graduating college seniors or students in graduate or professional programs. Preference will be given to those who have demonstrated commitment to Asian American and Pacific Islander (AAPI) issues, particularly those affecting the Japanese American community. Membership in the JACL is required. Communication skills, especially in writing, are important.

GEOG. RESTRICTIONS: United States.

FINANCIAL DATA:
Fellowship includes round-trip airfare from fellow's home to Washington, DC.

Amount of support per award: $2,500 monthly stipend.

Total amount of support: Up to $30,000 per fellow.

NO. AWARDS: Up to 4 annually.

APPLICATION INFO:
Completed application materials may be sent via e-mail to pouchida@jacl.org.

Duration: Six to eight months.

Deadline: 11:59 P.M., July 31.

ADDRESS INQUIRIES TO:
Priscilla Ouchida, Executive Director
(See address above.)

THE LYNDON BAINES JOHNSON FOUNDATION [1943]

2313 Red River Street
Austin, TX 78705-5702
(512) 232-2266
Fax: (512) 232-2285
E-mail: grants@lbjfoundation.org
Web Site: www.lbjfoundation.org

FOUNDED: 1969

AREAS OF INTEREST:
Support for the LBJ Presidential Library and the LBJ School of Public Affairs at The University of Texas.

NAME(S) OF PROGRAMS:
- **Middleton Fellowship in Presidential Studies**
- **Moody Research Grants**

TYPE:
Fellowships; Research grants.

YEAR PROGRAM STARTED: 1972

PURPOSE:
To defray living, travel and related expenses incurred while conducting research at the LBJ Library during the period for which the grant is awarded.

LEGAL BASIS:
Nonprofit organization.

ELIGIBILITY:
In accepting a grant, an applicant must agree to the following conditions:
(1) that the product of the research which is made possible through these funds will not be used for any political purpose;
(2) that the funds are for the purpose of helping to defray expenses incurred while conducting research at the Johnson Library;
(3) that the grant must be used in the grant period in which it is awarded and;
(4) that the LBJ Foundation will be promptly provided with a copy of any publication, paper, article or book resulting from research made possible by this grant.

FINANCIAL DATA:
Amount of support per award: Middleton Fellowship: $5,000; Moody Research Grants: $600 to $3,000.

Total amount of support: Moody Research Grants: Approximately $30,000 per grant period.

NO. MOST RECENT APPLICANTS: 5 Middleton Fellowships and 28 Moody Research Grants for Spring 2014.

NO. AWARDS: Middleton Fellowship: 1; Moody Research Grants: 15.

APPLICATION INFO:
Application forms must be accompanied by a written proposal. Candidates should state clearly and precisely how the holdings of the LBJ Library will contribute to the completion of the project.

Middleton Fellowship applicants are also required to submit three letters of recommendation.

Duration: Eight months for spring grant period. Six months for fall grant period.

Deadline: September 15 for January to August grant period. March 15 for June to December grant period.

IRS I.D.: 74-1774063

STAFF:
Amy Barbee, Executive Director
Samantha Stone, Deputy Director

ADDRESS INQUIRIES TO:
Samantha Stone, Deputy Director
Tel: (512) 232-2280
(See e-mail address above.)

THE JOSEPH P. KENNEDY, JR. FOUNDATION

1133 19th Street, N.W.
12th Floor
Washington, DC 20036-3604
(202) 393-1250

TYPE:
Fellowships. During this one-year Fellowship, the successful applicant will learn how federal legislation is initiated, developed and passed by the U.S. Congress, as well as how programs are administered and regulations promulgated by federal agencies.

See entry 974 for full listing.

NATIONAL ENDOWMENT FOR DEMOCRACY [1944]

1025 F Street, N.W.
Suite 800
Washington, DC 20004
(202) 378-9700
Fax: (202) 378-9407
E-mail: info@ned.org
Web Site: www.ned.org/grantseekers

FOUNDED: 1983

AREAS OF INTEREST:
Democracy throughout the world.

NAME(S) OF PROGRAMS:
- **National Endowment for Democracy Grants**

TYPE:
Project/program grants.

PURPOSE:
To strengthen democratic institutions throughout the world.

ELIGIBILITY:
Individuals and religious organizations are ineligible.

FINANCIAL DATA:
Amount of support per award: Average $50,000.

Total amount of support: Varies.

NO. MOST RECENT APPLICANTS: Over 6,000.

NO. AWARDS: Approximately 1,500.

APPLICATION INFO:
Application information is available on the web site.

Duration: One year. Renewable.

Deadline: 10 to 12 weeks prior to board meetings held in January, March, June and September.

NATIONAL FEDERATION OF REPUBLICAN WOMEN

124 North Alfred Street
Alexandria, VA 22314
(703) 548-9688
Fax: (703) 548-9836
E-mail: mail@nfrw.org
Web Site: www.nfrw.org

TYPE:
Internships; Scholarships. Dorothy Kabis Internship includes a six-week internship in Washington, DC, housing, travel and stipend.

National Pathfinder's Scholarships are given to the best nominated candidates.

Betty Rendel Scholarships are given to undergraduate women who are majoring in political science, government or economics.

See entry 1069 for full listing.

NEW YORK STATE ASSEMBLY INTERN COMMITTEE [1945]

Legislative Office Building, Room 104A
Albany, NY 12248
(518) 455-4704
Fax: (518) 455-4705
E-mail: intern@assembly.state.ny.us
Web Site: www.assembly.state.ny.us/internship

FOUNDED: 1971

AREAS OF INTEREST:
Government.

NAME(S) OF PROGRAMS:
- **Assembly Session Internships**

TYPE:
Internships. Program provides firsthand knowledge of the legislative process and functions. The interns are assigned research and administrative responsibilities in an Assembly office. They receive a practical educational experience and attend weekly classes. The Assembly benefits from the new ideas and fresh perspectives of the interns. All intern placements are in Albany, NY.

YEAR PROGRAM STARTED: 1971

PURPOSE:
To encourage talented students from all fields to learn about and get involved in state government.

LEGAL BASIS:
Government legislature.

ELIGIBILITY:
Applicants must be matriculated in a U.S. college or university degree program as juniors or seniors. Applications are welcome from students in any academic field. Colleges generally award a full semester of credit for participation. International students should have academic requirements in the U.S. to be eligible.

FINANCIAL DATA:
Session interns receive a stipend and semester of college credit.

Amount of support per award: $5,025 session term.

NO. MOST RECENT APPLICANTS: 200.

NO. AWARDS: 150.

APPLICATION INFO:
Applications are available from an Intern Program liaison officer on college campuses. Applications and all supporting documents must be submitted to the Intern Committee in a complete package.

The following documents must be included with the application:
(1) personal statement;
(2) official transcripts of all college courses completed and in progress;
(3) two letters of recommendation;
(4) a letter from an appropriate college official endorsing the student's participation and indicating the amount of credit to be granted by the college and;
(5) a concise writing sample.

Duration: January to mid-May.

Deadline: November 1.

STAFF:
Kathleen McCarty, Director, Assembly Intern Committee

ADDRESS INQUIRIES TO:
Kathleen McCarty, Director
Assembly Intern Committee
(See address above.)

NEW YORK STATE ASSEMBLY INTERN COMMITTEE [1946]

Legislative Office Building, Room 104A
Albany, NY 12248
(518) 455-4704
Fax: (518) 455-4705
E-mail: intern@assembly.state.ny.us
Web Site: www.assembly.state.ny.us/internship

FOUNDED: 1971

AREAS OF INTEREST:
Government.

TYPE:
Internships. Assignments designed to provide up to 10 graduate students with full-time work placements as Assembly researchers and policy analysts with all the responsibilities and expectations of such positions. The work placements are with Assembly leaders. The interns will have the opportunity to develop a better understanding of the legislative process while contributing new ideas and fresh perspectives to the legislative decision making process.

YEAR PROGRAM STARTED: 1976

PURPOSE:
To bring the expertise and thinking of the state's best graduate students into the legislative process.

LEGAL BASIS:
Government.

ELIGIBILITY:
All students matriculated in or who have recently completed a graduate degree program may apply. Students with expertise in a variety of public policy issues are being sought. Issues include public finance, education, environmental conservation, etc. Students must work full-time in the Assembly. International students should have academic requirements in the U.S. to be eligible. Credit can often be arranged by the school.

GEOG. RESTRICTIONS: New York state.

FINANCIAL DATA:
Amount of support per award: $15,000 per year.

NO. MOST RECENT APPLICANTS: 50.

NO. AWARDS: Up to 10 each year.

APPLICATION INFO:
Applications are available from graduate schools, directly from the Assembly Intern Committee, or on the web site. Applications must include two letters of recommendation, a letter from graduate program dean or director, official transcripts, a writing sample and a personal statement.

Duration: Six months (January to June). Nonrenewable.

Deadline: October 30. Selection by December 1.

STAFF:
Kathleen McCarty, Director

ADDRESS INQUIRIES TO:
Kathleen McCarty, Director
(See address above.)

NEW YORK STATE SENATE [1947]

Student Programs Office
80 South Swan Street, Suite 1426
Albany, NY 12247
(518) 455-2611
Fax: (518) 426-6827
E-mail: students@nysenate.gov
Web Site: www.nysenate.gov/student-programs

FOUNDED: 1965

AREAS OF INTEREST:
New York state government and education which includes improved public access to and understanding of government, resulting in enhanced citizenship, career staffing, government administration and leadership.

CONSULTING OR VOLUNTEER SERVICES:
Placement in staff support roles in senate offices, ordinarily in the office of a senator. Also, host or travel to inform interested citizens, students and faculty; host or travel to government offices responsible for development or administration of similar programs.

NAME(S) OF PROGRAMS:
- **James L. Biggane Fellowship in Finance**
- **New York State Senate Legislative Fellows Program**
- **Richard J. Roth Journalism Fellowship**
- **Richard A. Wiebe Public Service Fellowship**

TYPE:
Fellowships. These fellowships are intended for the graduate/postgraduate/midcareer level. Stipends are for bipartisan opportunities to train in government while on-site in Albany, NY. Fellows spend almost a year immersed in the work of the Senate, learning techniques associated with policymaking and legislative process. Placement is usually to the office of an elected Senate member. The Senate Legislative Fellows Program, Biggane Fellowship, Roth Journalism Fellowship and Wiebe Public Service Fellowship constitute the Senate Graduate/Post-Graduate/Mid-Career Fellowships.

YEAR PROGRAM STARTED: 1965

PURPOSE:
To provide an opportunity for career experience and learning for graduate assistants, career recruitment among superior fellows, and citizenship training in general.

LEGAL BASIS:
Legislative authority.

ELIGIBILITY:
Graduate/Postgraduate/Mid-Career Fellowships: In most cases, Fellows must be full-time matriculating graduate students in an accredited university during the immediately previous spring and fall semesters. Fellowships are open to all majors. Training in the history/politics/government of New York state is not required.

The Biggane Fellow may be a person in midcareer. Biggane applicants need not be currently enrolled in graduate-level study, but must have either obtained a previous graduate-level degree or be working toward the completion of an advanced degree. Legislative Fellows will be talented and skilled graduate/postgraduate students from a variety of academic disciplines.

The Roth Fellow may be a student with experience and/or intentions in the fields of communications, journalism and/or public relations.

The Wiebe Fellow may be a student with legal training and a variety of other backgrounds.

Applicants must be U.S. citizens. Students are not required to presently reside in New York state or attend school in New York state.

FINANCIAL DATA:
The stipend is distributed in biweekly installments prorated from the first day to the last day of enrollment. Some benefit options are available (health, dental, vision, life insurance, and the retirement program). Fellows are not Senate employees; they do not earn vacation or personal leave.

All Senate Fellowships are on-site in Albany, NY. Fellowships are not financial aid for academic work, on-campus or classroom study. Housing in Albany is the responsibility of the Fellow.

Amount of support per award: Grant-in-Study stipend of $33,000 for the fellowship year September 2016 to July 2017.

NO. MOST RECENT APPLICANTS: 65.

NO. AWARDS: Approximately 16 fellowships each year. Legislative Fellows Program: Up to 13; Biggane, Roth and Wiebe Fellowships: 1 each.

APPLICATION INFO:
Applications must include the following:
(1) course work-in-progress list signed by campus official (if not on transcript);
(2) calling of Office of Student Programs to indicate one's intent to apply;
(3) policy proposal;
(4) rebuttal of policy proposal;
(5) statement of purpose;
(6) writing sample essay;
(7) resume or curriculum vitae;
(8) all official transcripts (graduate and undergraduate) and;
(9) three letters of reference from persons familiar with the applicant's character, academic and/or professional abilities (at least two from faculty members).

Duration: Approximately one year, September through mid-July. No renewals.

Deadline: April 28.

PUBLICATIONS:
Program announcement.

ADDRESS INQUIRIES TO:
Director, Office of Student Programs
New York State Senate
Legislative Office Building, Suite 1426
Albany, NY 12247

NEW YORK STATE SENATE [1948]

80 South Swan Street, Suite 1426
Albany, NY 12247
(518) 455-2611
Fax: (518) 426-6827
E-mail: students@nysenate.gov
Web Site: www.nysenate.gov/student-programs

FOUNDED: 1978

AREAS OF INTEREST:
State government internships for undergraduates.

NAME(S) OF PROGRAMS:
- **Undergraduate Session Assistants Program**

TYPE:
Internships. Annual undergraduate internship running second Thursday in January to third Wednesday in April.

YEAR PROGRAM STARTED: 1978

PURPOSE:
To provide on-site experience at the New York State Senate, Albany, NY.

ELIGIBILITY:
Each applicant must be a U.S. citizen matriculating full-time in an accredited, undergraduate degree program on a campus in New York state. The program is intended and designed for college juniors and seniors; exceptional sophomores may occasionally be selected. Freshmen are ineligible.

The Senate welcomes majors in all accredited disciplines. Training in the history/politics/government of New York is neither a prerequisite of nor an advantage to selection. Skill and ability, initiative, eagerness to learn, discretion and mature flexibility are essential for success.

Each student should demonstrate a 3.0 grade point average and meet the campus/departmental standard for off-campus study; full-time enrollment in the immediately previous spring (not summer) and current fall semester/previous two trimesters. Each standard is to be certified by the Campus Liaison Officer (CLO), student's academic advisor, chairman, dean, or other duly authorized campus official.

Placements are ordinarily to the offices of individual senators. Students may observe, participate in, and/or acquire experience with state government procedures. Combined participation in the program and legislative placement is for a minimum of 35 hours per week. Longer hours are possible and should be expected.

Each applicant must be able to earn campus-awarded credit for participation in the program to be eligible. On-campus faculty is responsible for academic advisement, evaluation, grading and granting of credit for their student participant(s) enrolled in this Senate program.

GEOG. RESTRICTIONS: New York state.

FINANCIAL DATA:
Arrangement of housing in Albany is the responsibility of the individual enrollee.

Amount of support per award: A stipend of $5,025 to offset costs of moving to and living in Albany.

NO. MOST RECENT APPLICANTS: Approximately 60.

NO. AWARDS: Approximately 30.

APPLICATION INFO:
Enrollment is on-site at the New York State Senate in Albany, NY. Applications are available on campus, from the Student Programs Office, or at the web site.

If there is no CLO on campus, contact Nicholas J. Parrella, Director of Student Programs, at the address listed above.

Duration: Approximately four months.

Deadline: The last Friday in October. Expect an earlier on-campus deadline if one's school has a Campus Liaison Officer (CLO). Announcement of selections is approximately mid-November.

STAFF:
Nicholas J. Parrella, Director of Student Programs
Kimberly Burke, Confidential Assistant

ADDRESS INQUIRIES TO:
Nicholas J. Parrella
Director of Student Programs
New York State Senate
Legislative Office Building, Suite 1426
Albany, NY 12247

PIPER FUND [1949]

15 Research Drive
Suite B
Amherst, MA 01002
(413) 256-0349
E-mail: grantsmanager@proteusfund.org
Web Site: www.proteusfund.org

AREAS OF INTEREST:
Campaign finance reform in the American political system.

TYPE:
General operating grants; Project/program grants.

PURPOSE:
To help meet the needs of the growing movement for campaign finance reform in America.

GEOG. RESTRICTIONS: United States.

FINANCIAL DATA:
Amount of support per award: $10,000 to $50,000.

Total amount of support: Approximately $25,000,000 since inception. Over $2,500,000 for the year 2015.

APPLICATION INFO:
Guidelines are available on the web site.

Duration: One year.

ADDRESS INQUIRIES TO:
Beery Adams-Jimenez, Grants Manager
(See address above.)

*SPECIAL STIPULATIONS:
Grants are by invitation only.

PRESIDENT'S COMMISSION ON WHITE HOUSE FELLOWSHIPS [1950]

712 Jackson Place, N.W.
Washington, DC 20503
(202) 395-4522
Fax: (202) 395-6179
E-mail: whitehousefellows@whf.eop.gov
Web Site: www.whitehouse.gov/fellows

FOUNDED: 1964

AREAS OF INTEREST:
Leadership and public service for young professionals.

NAME(S) OF PROGRAMS:
- **White House Fellowships**

TYPE:
Fellowships. The White House Fellows program is America's most prestigious program for leadership and public service. White House Fellowships offer exceptional young men and women firsthand experience working at the highest levels of the federal government.

White House Fellows typically spend a year working as full-time, paid special assistants to senior White House staff, the Vice President, cabinet secretaries and other top-ranking government officials. Fellows also participate in an education program consisting of roundtable discussions with renowned leaders from the private and public sectors, and trips to study U.S. policy in action both domestically and internationally. Fellowships are awarded on a strictly nonpartisan basis.

PURPOSE:
To give those who participate in the program firsthand, high-level experience with the workings of the federal government and to increase their sense of participation in national affairs.

ELIGIBILITY:
The following criteria apply:
(1) applicants must be U.S. citizens and not hold any foreign citizenships;
(2) employees of the federal government are not eligible unless they are career military personnel;
(3) applicants should be finished with their undergraduate education and working in their chosen professions and;
(4) there are no formal age restrictions; however, the fellowship program was created to give selected Americans the experience of government service early in their careers.

The Commission awards fellowships on a strict nonpartisan basis and encourages balance and diversity in all aspects of the program.

GEOG. RESTRICTIONS: United States.

FINANCIAL DATA:
Fellows are eligible to purchase health insurance through the Federal Employee Health Benefit Plans.

Total amount of support: Approximately $100,000 for the year 2013-14. Military personnel maintain their current salary and benefits.

NO. MOST RECENT APPLICANTS: Up to 1,000.

NO. AWARDS: 11 to 19 fellowships per year.

APPLICATION INFO:
Application must be submitted online and is available beginning in the Fall.

Deadline: Mid-January.

RHODE ISLAND STATE INTERNSHIP PROGRAM [1951]

State House, Room 8AA
Providence, RI 02903
(401) 222-6782
Fax: (401) 222-4447
E-mail: intern@rilegislature.gov
Web Site: www.rilin.state.ri.us

FOUNDED: 1969

NAME(S) OF PROGRAMS:
- **Rhode Island State Internship Program**

TYPE:
Internships. Funding through General Assembly is also available. Internship opportunities for graduate and undergraduate students in the state government operation. Students are involved in executive, legislative and judicial assignments. The internship is viewed as an extension of the classroom and is seen as complementing and building upon the educational opportunities available on campuses.

This program has established a Summer Internship section, open to Rhode Island residents only, that begins in late June and concludes in August.

YEAR PROGRAM STARTED: 1969

PURPOSE:
To provide a link between the public and state government; to open a channel for the potential recruitment of personnel for state government internship; to supplement college and university course offerings in state and local government; to enable students to develop a knowledge of the structure and procedure of state government.

LEGAL BASIS:
Chapter 47, General Laws, state of Rhode Island.

ELIGIBILITY:
Spring semester interns are chosen by members of the faculties of 11 participating Rhode Island colleges and universities. Students must have junior or senior status. Summer applicants can be out-of-state students who are Rhode Island residents.

FINANCIAL DATA:
Academic credit, up to a maximum of six credits, is available. For the Summer Internship, a student is required to work 35 hours per week and receives a monthly stipend.

Amount of support per award: Summer: $20 for every seven hours of work.

APPLICATION INFO:
Interns are selected by the academic committee and referred to Intern Staff.

Duration: 12 weeks in the spring (one school semester) and eight weeks (July and August) for Summer Internship.

Deadline: November 15. May 15 for Summer Internship. Announcement by the end of May.

ADDRESS INQUIRIES TO:
Robert W. Gemma, Executive Director
(See address above.)

FRANKLIN D. ROOSEVELT LIBRARY AND MUSEUM

4079 Albany Post Road
Hyde Park, NY 12538
(845) 486-7770
E-mail: grants.fdr@nara.gov
Web Site: fdrlibrary.org/research-grants

TYPE:
Grants-in-aid; Research grants. The Roosevelt Institute - the Library's nonprofit partner - supports a program of small grants-in-aid, in support of research on the "Roosevelt years" or clearly related subjects.

See entry 622 for full listing.

SARAH SCAIFE FOUNDATION, INC. [1952]

One Oxford Centre, Suite 3900
301 Grant Street
Pittsburgh, PA 15219-6401
(412) 392-2900
Web Site: www.scaife.com

FOUNDED: 1941

AREAS OF INTEREST:
Domestic and international public policy issues.

TYPE:
Challenge/matching grants; Fellowships; General operating grants; Project/program grants; Seed money grants.

YEAR PROGRAM STARTED: 1941

PURPOSE:
To direct money to programs that address major domestic and international issues.

LEGAL BASIS:
Private foundation.

ELIGIBILITY:
The Foundation's grant program is directed primarily toward public policy programs that address major domestic and international issues. The Foundation does not make grants to individuals for any purpose or to nationally organized fund-raising groups.

FINANCIAL DATA:
Amount of support per award: Average $25,000 to $200,000.

REPRESENTATIVE AWARDS:
$200,000 to American Civil Rights Institute; $125,000 to Foundation for Individual Rights in Education, Inc.; $60,000 to New England Legal Foundation.

APPLICATION INFO:
Initial inquiries to the Foundation should be in letter form signed by the organization's chief executive officer or authorized representative and have the approval of the organization's Board of Directors. The letter should include a concise description of the purpose for which funds are requested, along with the related budget.

Applicant must also provide:
(1) latest audited financial statements and annual report;
(2) current annual budget;
(3) list of officers and directors and their major affiliations and;
(4) copy of current determination letter from the IRS evidencing tax-exempt status under Section 501(c)(3).

Duration: One year.

Deadline: Board meets quarterly in February, May, September and November. Notification within two to four weeks.

PUBLICATIONS:
Annual report.

OFFICERS:
Richard M. Scaife, Chairman
Michael W. Gleba, President

Barbara L. Slaney, Vice President and Treasurer
R. Daniel McMichael, Secretary

ADDRESS INQUIRIES TO:
Michael W. Gleba, President
(See address above.)

THE SOCIETY FOR THE PSYCHOLOGICAL STUDY OF SOCIAL ISSUES (SPSSI) [1953]

208 I Street, N.E.
Washington, DC 20002-4340
(202) 675-6956
(877) 310-7778
Fax: (202) 675-6902
E-mail: awards@spssi.org
Web Site: www.spssi.org

FOUNDED: 1936

AREAS OF INTEREST:
Public policy, social issues, psychology and international relations.

NAME(S) OF PROGRAMS:

- **Otto Klineberg Intercultural and International Relations Award**

TYPE:
Awards/prizes. The Klineberg Award is given for the best paper or article of the year on intercultural or international relations.

PURPOSE:
To award the best paper or article of the year on intercultural or international relations.

LEGAL BASIS:
Independently incorporated society.

ELIGIBILITY:
Entries can be either unpublished manuscripts, in press papers, book chapters, or journal articles published no more than 18 months prior to the submission deadline. Entries cannot be returned. The competition is open to nonmembers and members of SPSSI. Graduate students are especially urged to submit papers. Submissions from across the social sciences are encouraged, however the paper must clearly demonstrate its relevance for psychological theory and research in the domain of intercultural and international relations.

FINANCIAL DATA:
Amount of support per award: $1,000.

NO. MOST RECENT APPLICANTS: 15.

NO. AWARDS: 1.

APPLICATION INFO:
Online submissions are the preferred method. Please limit the number and size of files uploaded when applying online. For hard-copy submissions, send five (5) copies to the address listed above, "Attn: Klineberg Award."

Deadline: Applications must be received by March 5.

PUBLICATIONS:
Program announcement; application guidelines.

ADDRESS INQUIRIES TO:
Anila Balkissoon
Program Director
E-mail: abalkissoon@spssi.org

HATTON W. SUMNERS FOUNDATION [1954]

325 North St. Paul Street
Suite 3920
Dallas, TX 75201
(214) 220-2128
Fax: (214) 953-0737
E-mail: info@hattonsumners.org
Web Site: www.hattonsumners.org

FOUNDED: 1949

AREAS OF INTEREST:
Self-government, political science and democracy.

TYPE:
Challenge/matching grants; Conferences/seminars; Endowments; Fellowships; Internships; Project/program grants; Scholarships. Scholarship programs at selected universities and grants to support other educational activities for both students and adults, which are designed to create an appreciation and understanding for the U.S. executive, legislative and judicial processes.

YEAR PROGRAM STARTED: 1949

PURPOSE:
To encourage the study, teaching and research into the science and art of self-government so that the American people may understand the fundamental principles of democracy and be guided thereby in shaping governmental policies.

LEGAL BASIS:
Private charitable foundation.

GEOG. RESTRICTIONS: Arkansas, Kansas, Louisiana, Missouri, Nebraska, New Mexico, Oklahoma and Texas.

FINANCIAL DATA:
Amount of support per award: Varies.

Total amount of support: $2,400.000 for the year 2012.

NO. AWARDS: 47.

REPRESENTATIVE AWARDS:
$25,000 to Bill of Rights Institute, Arlington, VA, for constitutional seminars in Oklahoma and New Mexico; $35,000 to Project Vote Smart, Philipsburg, MT, for National Key Votes Database Project; $45,000 to Law Focused Education, Austin, TX, for Texas Citizen Bee Competition.

APPLICATION INFO:
Grant applications must be in writing, but do not need to be formal. The Foundation does not accept applications via fax or e-mail.

Duration: One year. Occasional multiyear funding.

Deadline: August 1. Decision in October.

PUBLICATIONS:
Annual report.

STAFF:
Hugh C. Akin, Executive Director

ADDRESS INQUIRIES TO:
Hugh C. Akin, Executive Director
(See address above.)

HARRY S. TRUMAN LIBRARY INSTITUTE [1955]

500 West U.S. Highway 24
Independence, MO 64050
(816) 268-8248
Fax: (816) 268-8299
E-mail: sullivan.hstli@gmail.com
Web Site: www.trumanlibraryinstitute.org

FOUNDED: 1957

AREAS OF INTEREST:
Harry S. Truman and the Truman administration.

NAME(S) OF PROGRAMS:

- **Dissertation Year Fellowships**
- **Research Grant**
- **Scholar's Award**
- **Harry S. Truman Book Award**

TYPE:
Awards/prizes; Fellowships; Grants-in-aid; Research grants; Travel grants. The Dissertation Year Fellowships are given to encourage historical scholarship of the public career of Harry S. Truman or the Truman era. Support is given annually to one or two graduate students who have completed the dissertation research and are in the writing stage. Preference will be given to projects based on extensive research at the Truman Library. Successful applicants will be expected to deposit one copy of their completed dissertation, or any publication resulting therefrom, with the Truman Library.

Research Grants are intended to enable graduate students as well as postdoctoral scholars to come to the Library for one to three weeks to use its archival facilities.

The Scholar's Award is given every other year, even-numbered years only, to a scholar engaged in a study of either the public career of Harry S. Truman or some aspect of the history of the Truman administration or of the U.S. during that administration. The scholar's work must be based on extensive research at the Truman Library and must be designed to result in the publication of a book-length manuscript. One copy of such book (and/or any other publication resulting from work done under this award) shall be deposited by the author with the Harry S. Truman Library.

The Harry S. Truman Book Award is given in even years for the best book dealing with some aspect of history of the U.S. between April 12, 1945 and January 20, 1953 or with the public career of Harry S. Truman.

YEAR PROGRAM STARTED: 1959

PURPOSE:
To encourage study of the history of the Truman administration and the public career of Harry S. Truman; to promote the use of the Truman Library as a national center for historical scholarship.

ELIGIBILITY:
Undergraduate students, doctoral candidates and postdoctoral scholars with appropriate interests are eligible for support. Applicants must be competent researchers with viable topics for which pertinent materials are available at the Truman Library.

FINANCIAL DATA:
Amount of support per award: Dissertation Year Fellowships: $16,000 payable in two installments; Research Grants: Up to $2,500; Scholar's Award: Up to $30,000; Truman Book Award: $2,500.

REPRESENTATIVE AWARDS:
Alonzo Hamby for "Man of the People: A Life of Harry S. Truman;" Richard B. Frank for "Downfall: The End of the Japanese Imperial Empire;" Kari Frederickson for "The Dixiecrat Revolt and the End of Solid South, 1932-1968;" Stephen C. Schlesinger for "Act of Creation: The Founding of the United Nations;" John Lewis Gaddis for "The Cold War: A New History."

APPLICATION INFO:
Applicants for the Scholar's Award should submit an application and proposal for preliminary screening. If selected, applicants must submit further information including a list of Truman files already utilized or planned to be utilized, a projected timeline for completion, and projected income for the academic year in which the award will be announced. Applicants for Research Grants may receive no more than two grants in this category in any one five-year period.

For the Harry S. Truman Book Award, six copies of each book entered must be submitted to the Book Award Administrator.

Duration: Research Grants: One to three weeks.

Deadline: Dissertation Year Fellowships: February 1. Announcement first week of April. Research Grants: April 1 and October 1. Results announced six weeks later. Scholar's Award: December 15 for preliminary screening. Decision by February 1. If selected, further information will be requested with announcement by April 15. Harry S. Truman Book Award: Books must be received by January 20 in even-numbered years.

PUBLICATIONS:
Program announcement; *Whistle Stop*, newsletter.

OFFICERS:
John J. Sherman, Chairman of the Board
Clyde F. Wendel, Vice Chairperson
John A. MacDonald, Treasurer
Herb M. Kohn, Secretary

BOARD OF DIRECTORS:
Clifton Truman Daniel, Honorary Chairperson
Carol Anderson
Alan Atterbury
Alex Burden
Kirk Carpenter
John A. Dillingham
Robert P. Dunn
Susie S. Evans
Charles M. Foudree
Mary Ann Heiss
Mary Hunkeler
Allen L. Lefko
Thomas R. McGee, Jr.
John P. McMeel
Larry L. McMullen
James B. Nutter, Jr.
Carol P. Powell
Page Branton Reed
Elizabeth T. Solberg
Charles S. Sosland
Jeannine Strandjord
David Von Drehle
Maurice A. Watson
David Williams

ADDRESS INQUIRIES TO:
Grants Administrator
(See address above.)

THE HARRY S. TRUMAN SCHOLARSHIP FOUNDATION [1956]

712 Jackson Place, N.W.
Washington, DC 20006-4901
(202) 395-4831
Fax: (202) 395-6995
E-mail: office@truman.gov
Web Site: www.truman.gov

FOUNDED: 1975

AREAS OF INTEREST:
Local, state and national government service.

NAME(S) OF PROGRAMS:
- **Harry S. Truman Scholarship Program**

TYPE:
Awards/prizes. Awards for undergraduate students who demonstrate outstanding leadership potential, plan to pursue careers in government or elsewhere in public service and wish to attend graduate school to help prepare for their careers. At least one Truman Scholar is selected each year from each state, the District of Columbia, Puerto Rico and, considered as a single entity, Guam, the Virgin Islands, American Samoa and the Commonwealth of the Northern Mariana Islands. Scholars may attend graduate schools in the U.S. or in foreign countries.

YEAR PROGRAM STARTED: 1975

PURPOSE:
To develop increased opportunities for young Americans to prepare for and pursue careers in public service, whether it be at the local, county, state or national level, through an educational scholarship program. The Foundation defines public service as employment in government at any level, including uniformed services, public-interest organizations, non-governmental research and/or educational organizations and public-service oriented nonprofit organizations such as those whose primary purposes are to help needy or disadvantaged persons or to protect the environment.

LEGAL BASIS:
Authorized by Congress in 1975; the sole Federal memorial to President Harry S. Truman.

ELIGIBILITY:
To be considered for nomination as a Truman Scholar, a student must be:
(1) a full-time student as a junior at a four-year institution pursuing a Bachelor's degree;
(2) enrolled in a four-year accredited institution of higher education;
(3) committed to a career in government or in public service as defined above;
(4) in the upper quarter of his or her class and;
(5) a U.S. citizen or, in the case of nominees from American Samoa or the Commonwealth of the Northern Mariana Islands, a U.S. national.

FINANCIAL DATA:
The award may only be used for tuition, fees, books, room and board and other specifically approved expenses in graduate school.

Amount of support per award: Up to $30,000.

NO. MOST RECENT APPLICANTS: 772.

NO. AWARDS: 60 for the year 2016.

APPLICATION INFO:
All candidates for scholarships are nominated by their institutions of higher education. The Foundation neither solicits nor accepts direct candidate applications. Each participating institution must appoint a faculty representative to serve as liaison between the institution and the Foundation. The Foundation's nomination and supporting information forms are available from faculty representatives.

Duration: Up to four years.

Deadline: February 7, 2017.

THE MORRIS K. UDALL AND STEWART L. UDALL FOUNDATION

130 South Scott Avenue
Tucson, AZ 85701
(520) 901-8561
Fax: (520) 670-5530
E-mail: khalil@udall.gov
Web Site: www.udall.gov

TYPE:
Internships. Congressional Internships: Native American college students work in congressional offices and the White House to gain a firsthand understanding of the federal government. They also take field trips and meet with congressional members, agency heads and cabinet secretaries.

See entry 1040 for full listing.

WOMEN'S POLICY, INC. (WPI)

409 12th Street, S.W.
Suite 600
Washington, DC 20024
(202) 554-2323
Fax: (202) 554-2346
E-mail: webmaster@womenspolicy.org
Web Site: www.womenspolicy.org

TYPE:
Fellowships.

See entry 1082 for full listing.

Sociology and anthropology

AMERICAN SOCIOLOGICAL ASSOCIATION

1430 K Street, N.W.
Suite 600
Washington, DC 20005
(202) 383-9005 ext. 322
Fax: (202) 638-0882
TDD: (202) 638-0981
E-mail: minority.affairs@asanet.org
Web Site: www.asanet.org

TYPE:
Fellowships. Predoctoral training fellowships for minority-group members studying sociology.

See entry 953 for full listing.

L.S.B. LEAKEY FOUNDATION [1957]

1003B O'Reilly Avenue
San Francisco, CA 94129-1359
(415) 561-4646
Fax: (415) 561-4647
E-mail: grants@leakeyfoundation.org
Web Site: www.leakeyfoundation.org

FOUNDED: 1968

AREAS OF INTEREST:
Human evolution, including research into the environments, archaeology and human paleontology of the Miocene, Pliocene and Pleistocene, into the behavior, morphology and ecology of the great apes and other primate species when it contributes to the development or testing of models of human evolution and into the ecology and adaptations of living hunter-gatherer peoples.

NAME(S) OF PROGRAMS:
- **Leakey Foundation Grants**

TYPE:
Research grants. The General Research Grants priority is normally given to the exploratory phase of promising new projects that most closely meet the stated purpose of the Foundation.

YEAR PROGRAM STARTED: 1968

PURPOSE:
To conduct research related to human origins.

LEGAL BASIS:
Public foundation 501(c)(3).

ELIGIBILITY:
Grants are made to senior scientists and postdoctoral students with professional qualifications and demonstrated capability in the area of human evolution. Graduate students must be advanced to candidacy (ABD) in order to be considered.

FINANCIAL DATA:
Amount of support per award: General Research Grants are awarded up to $15,000 for Ph.D. candidate students (ABD), and up to $25,000 for senior scientists and postdoctoral students.

Total amount of support: Approximately $900,000 per year.

NO. AWARDS: Approximately 40 to 60 per year.

APPLICATION INFO:
Guidelines and application forms are available on the Foundation's web site. Applications are submitted and accepted online only.

All applications must be for research projects related to understanding human evolution.

Duration: One year.

Deadline: Session One (Fall): July 15, with notification in mid-December. Session Two (Spring): January 10, with notification in May.

PUBLICATIONS:
Application guidelines; newsletter.

IRS I.D.: 95-2536475

ADDRESS INQUIRIES TO:
E-mail: grants@leakeyfoundation.org

NATIONAL SCIENCE FOUNDATION [1958]

4201 Wilson Boulevard
Arlington, VA 22230
(703) 292-7315
Fax: (703) 292-9068
E-mail: dwinslow@nsf.gov
Web Site: www.nsf.gov

FOUNDED: 1950

AREAS OF INTEREST:
Scientific research on the causes and consequences of human social and cultural variability.

NAME(S) OF PROGRAMS:
- **Cultural Anthropology Program**

TYPE:
Conferences/seminars; Grants-in-aid; Project/program grants; Research grants. The program supports a broad portfolio of research by both senior scholars and by graduate students.

YEAR PROGRAM STARTED: 1952

PURPOSE:
To support basic scientific research on the causes, consequences, and complexities of human social and cultural variability.

LEGAL BASIS:
National Science Foundation Act of 1950.

ELIGIBILITY:
The program does not fund research that takes as its primary goal improved clinical practice or applied policy.

Applicants may be colleges and universities on behalf of their staff members, nonprofit, U.S. nonacademic research institutions, such as independent museums, observatories, research laboratories, stock centers and similar organizations, private profit organizations, in exceptional circumstances, rarely, foreign institutions utilizing U.S. currency, and under special circumstances, unaffiliated U.S. scientists.

FINANCIAL DATA:
Support may cover salaries, research assistantships, staff benefits related directly to purpose, permanent equipment, travel, publication costs, computer costs and certain other direct and indirect costs.

Amount of support per award: $5,000 to $300,000; average $150,000.

Total amount of support: Approximately $3,000,000.

APPLICATION INFO:
Application must be submitted online at FastLane or Grants.gov.

Duration: Up to 60 months, depending on the scientific merit and requirements of the project.

Deadline: August 15 and January 15.

STAFF:
Jeffrey Mantz, Program Director
Deborah Winslow, Ph.D., Program Director

ADDRESS INQUIRIES TO:
Deborah Winslow, Ph.D., Program Director
(See address above.)

NATIONAL SCIENCE FOUNDATION [1959]

Division of Behavioral and Cognitive Sciences
4201 Wilson Boulevard
Arlington, VA 22230
(703) 292-8759
Fax: (703) 292-9068
E-mail: jyellen@nsf.gov
Web Site: www.nsf.gov

NAME(S) OF PROGRAMS:
- **Archaeology Program**
- **Archaeometry Program**

TYPE:
Conferences/seminars; Grants-in-aid; Project/program grants; Research grants. The programs provide support for anthropologically relevant archaeological research at both a "senior" and doctoral-dissertation level. It also funds anthropologically significant archaeometric research and high-risk exploratory research proposals.

FINANCIAL DATA:
Maximum of $20,000 in direct costs to meet expenses associated with doctoral dissertation research.

Amount of support per award: Varies.

Total amount of support: Approximately $8,437,095 for the year 2015.

NO. AWARDS: Approximately 50 annually.

APPLICATION INFO:
Instructions and application form are available on the web site above.

Duration: One to five years.

Deadline: Target dates: Archaeology: July 1 and December 20; Archaeometry: December 1.

STAFF:
Dr. John E. Yellen, Program Director

ADDRESS INQUIRIES TO:
Dr. John E. Yellen, Program Director
(See address above.)

*PLEASE NOTE:
All proposals must be submitted online.

SCHOOL FOR ADVANCED RESEARCH [1960]

P.O. Box 2188
Santa Fe, NM 87504-2188
(505) 954-7237
Fax: (505) 954-7214
E-mail: scholar@sarsf.org
seminar@sarsf.org
Web Site: www.sarweb.org

FOUNDED: 1907

AREAS OF INTEREST:
Anthropology and allied disciplines in the humanities and social sciences.

NAME(S) OF PROGRAMS:
- **Advanced Seminar Program**
- **Resident Scholar Fellowships**

TYPE:
Conferences/seminars; Fellowships; Residencies. Advanced Seminars promote in-depth communication among scholars who are at a critical stage of research on a common topic and whose interaction has the potential to move the discipline of anthropology forward with new insights into human evolution, behavior, culture or society, including critical contemporary issues. Each consists of up to 10 scholars who meet at SAR's Santa Fe campus for five days of intense discussion on a topic that provides new insights into human evolution, behavior, society or culture. Support is also available for two- and three-day short seminars, including a program funded by the National Science Foundation for research team seminars. Participants appraise ongoing research, assess recent innovations in theory and methods, and share data relevant to broad problems in anthropology and related disciplines.

Resident Scholar Fellowships are awarded each year to scholars in anthropology and related disciplines who have completed their research and who need time to prepare book-length manuscripts or doctoral dissertations on topics important to the understanding of humankind.

YEAR PROGRAM STARTED: 1973

PURPOSE:
To support advanced research in anthropology and related disciplines.

LEGAL BASIS:
Private, nonprofit.

ELIGIBILITY:
Proposals are sought for the Advanced Seminar Program.

Resident Scholar Program: Applications are evaluated on the basis of the overall excellence and significance of the proposed

project, clarity of presentation and the applicant's academic accomplishments relative to subdiscipline and career stage. The program supports scholars whose work is broad, synthetic and interdisciplinary and promises to yield significant advances in understanding human culture, behavior, evolution or critical contemporary issues. Projects that are narrowly focused geographically and theoretically or that are primarily methodological seldom receive strong consideration. Each year the program supports a mix of scholars with scientific and humanistic orientations. Preference is given to applicants whose research and analysis are complete and who need time to prepare manuscripts. Applicants for postdoctoral fellowships must have their Ph.D. in hand at time of application. Immediate dissertation rewrites are not encouraged.

FINANCIAL DATA:
Advanced Seminars: SAR provides round-trip coach airfare within the U.S., lodging and all meals. Overseas airfare for up to two participants may also be offered.

Resident scholars are provided with an office, low-cost housing, a stipend, library assistance and other benefits during a nine-month tenure, from September through the following May. Books written by scholars may be considered for publication by SAR Press.

Amount of support per award: Resident Scholar Program: Maximum stipend of $40,000.

Total amount of support: Varies.

CO-OP FUNDING PROGRAMS: Funding for the Resident Scholar Program is provided by the Weatherhead Foundation, the Katrin H. Lamon Endowment for Native American Art and Education, the Anne Ray Charitable Trust, the Andrew H. Mellon Foundation and the Vera R. Campbell Foundation.

NO. MOST RECENT APPLICANTS: 158 for the year 2016.

NO. AWARDS: Advanced Seminars: 2 to 3 seminars annually (10 per seminar); Resident Scholar Fellowships: 5 to 6 annually.

APPLICATION INFO:
Submissions must be made via online application process. Guidelines and application form are available on the web site.

Duration: Advanced Seminars: Five days; Resident Scholar Fellowships: Nine months, September 1 through May 31.

Deadline: Resident Scholar Program: November 1. Announcement in April.

PUBLICATIONS:
Application guidelines.

OFFICERS:
Dr. Michael Brown, President and Chief Executive Officer
Nicole Taylor, Director of Scholar Programs

ADDRESS INQUIRIES TO:
Maria Spray, Program Coordinator
(See address above.)

SCHOOL FOR ADVANCED RESEARCH [1961]

P.O. Box 2188
Santa Fe, NM 87504-2188
(505) 954-7237
Fax: (505) 954-7214
E-mail: staley@sarsf.org
Web Site: www.sarweb.org

FOUNDED: 1907

AREAS OF INTEREST:
Anthropology and related disciplines in the humanities and social sciences.

NAME(S) OF PROGRAMS:
- **J.I. Staley Prize**

TYPE:
Awards/prizes. Prize awarded annually to a living author of a ground-breaking book that exemplifies outstanding scholarship and writing in anthropology. The award recognizes innovative works that add new dimensions to the understanding of the human species.

YEAR PROGRAM STARTED: 1988

PURPOSE:
To acknowledge those innovative works that have gone beyond traditional frontiers and dominant schools of thought in anthropology and given new dimensions to our understanding of the human species; to honor books that cross subdisciplinary boundaries within anthropology and reach out in new and expanded interdisciplinary directions.

LEGAL BASIS:
Private, nonprofit.

ELIGIBILITY:
To be considered, a book must be currently in print and must have been in publication at least two years, but not more than eight years. Co-authored books may be nominated, but edited volumes and textbooks may not. The nomination must clearly be for a single book. The award is for one outstanding and influential publication, not for an author's lifetime achievement.

Nominated books are evaluated according to the following criteria:
(1) significant contribution to our understanding of humankind;
(2) innovative and rigorous thinking in terms of theory, research methods and/or application of findings;
(3) superior integration of subdisciplinary and/or interdisciplinary perspectives;
(4) exemplary writing and clarity of expression and;
(5) demonstrated or anticipated impact on the field of anthropology.

FINANCIAL DATA:
Amount of support per award: Cash award of $10,000.

Total amount of support: $10,000.

NO. MOST RECENT APPLICANTS: 35 for the year 2016.

NO. AWARDS: 1 annually.

REPRESENTATIVE AWARDS:
2013: Joao Biehl, "Vita: Life in a Zone of Social Abandonment;" 2014: Joseph Masco, "The Nuclear Borderlands: The Manhattan Project in Post-Cold War New Mexico;" 2015: William F. Hanks, "Converting Words: Maya in the Age of the Cross."

APPLICATION INFO:
Detailed information is available on the web site.

Duration: One-time award.

Deadline: Nominations may be submitted at any time throughout the year. Nominations received by October 1 will be considered for next year's prize.

OFFICERS:
Dr. Michael Brown, President and Chief Executive Officer
Nicole Taylor, Director of Scholar Programs

ADDRESS INQUIRIES TO:
Maria Spray, Program Coordinator
(See address above.)

THE AMAURY TALBOT FUND [1962]

Royal Anthropological Institute
50 Fitzroy Street
London W1T 5BT England
(020) 7387 0455
Fax: (020) 7388 8817
E-mail: admin@therai.org.uk
Web Site: www.therai.org.uk/awards/prizes/the-amaury-talbot-prize-for-african-anthropology/

FOUNDED: 1948

AREAS OF INTEREST:
Nigeria or West Africa.

NAME(S) OF PROGRAMS:
- **Amaury Talbot Prize for African Anthropology**

TYPE:
Awards/prizes. Prize for a significant book, article or work of anthropological research relating to West Africa.

YEAR PROGRAM STARTED: 1948

PURPOSE:
To recognize and support valuable works dealing with African anthropological research.

LEGAL BASIS:
Created under the terms of the will of Mrs. Miriam Winifred Florence Talbot.

ELIGIBILITY:
Works of anthropological research concerning Africa which were published during a calendar year, to be received no later than March 31 in succeeding year, are eligible for the prize. Although works relating to any region of Africa may be submitted, preference is given first to works focusing on Nigeria, then to those dealing with any other section of West Africa or to publications relating to West Africa in general.

FINANCIAL DATA:
The amount of the prize is determined by income from investments and is therefore not constant.

Amount of support per award: Approximately GBP 750 per annum.

NO. MOST RECENT APPLICANTS: 10.

NO. AWARDS: 1.

APPLICATION INFO:
No official application form is required, but copies of the prospectus are available upon request to the Coordinator at the address above. Entries must be accompanied by three copies of the book, article or work in question. Entries will not be returned.

Deadline: March 31 in the year following publication.

ADDRESS INQUIRIES TO:
Amaury Talbot Prize Coordinator
Royal Anthropological Institute
(See address above.)

WENNER-GREN FOUNDATION FOR ANTHROPOLOGICAL RESEARCH, INC. [1963]

470 Park Avenue South
8th Floor
New York, NY 10016-6819
(212) 683-5000
Fax: (212) 532-1492
E-mail: inquiries@wennergren.org
Web Site: www.wennergren.org

FOUNDED: 1941

AREAS OF INTEREST:
All branches of anthropology, including cultural/social anthropology, ethnology, biological/physical anthropology, archaeology and anthropological linguistics, and closely related disciplines concerned with human origins, development and variation.

NAME(S) OF PROGRAMS:
- **Individual Research Grants**

TYPE:
Awards/prizes; Research grants. The Foundation offers Dissertation Fieldwork Grants, Post-Ph.D. Research Grants, and Hunt Postdoctoral Fellowships. Awards are available for basic research in all branches of anthropology. Grants are made to cover expenses or phases of a research project. The Foundation particularly invites projects employing comparative perspectives or integrating two or more subfields of anthropology.

The Hunt Postdoctoral Fellowship is awarded to scholars within 10 years of receipt of the Doctorate to aid the write-up of research results for publication.

Dissertation Fieldwork Grants are awarded to individuals to aid doctoral dissertation or thesis research.

Post-Ph.D. Research Grants are awarded to individual scholars holding the Doctorate or equivalent qualification in anthropology or a related discipline.

YEAR PROGRAM STARTED: 1941

PURPOSE:
To support anthropological research.

LEGAL BASIS:
Private operating foundation.

ELIGIBILITY:
Qualified scholars are eligible without regard to nationality or institutional affiliation for Dissertation Fieldwork, Post-Ph.D. Research Grants and Hunt Postdoctoral Fellowships.

Application for grants may be made by the scholar. Predoctoral grants application must be made jointly with a thesis advisor.

Dissertation Fieldwork Grants are for individuals enrolled in a doctoral program. These grants are contingent upon the applicant's successful completion of all requirements for the degree other than the dissertation/thesis.

Post-Ph.D. Research Grants are for individual scholars holding the Doctorate or equivalent qualification in anthropology or a related discipline.

Hunt Postdoctoral Fellowships are available to all scholars regardless of institutional affiliation and nationality. Applicants must have their Ph.D. in hand to apply and be within 10 years of receipt of their Doctorate.

FINANCIAL DATA:
Individual Research Grants, except for the Hunt Fellowship, are primarily for basic research. Grants cover research expenses directly related and essential to the project (i.e., travel, living expenses during fieldwork, equipment, supplies, research assistance and other relevant expenditures). Aid is not provided for salary and/or fringe benefits of applicant, tuition, nonproject personnel, travel to meetings, institutional overhead or institutional support. Expenses incurred prior to the effective date of an award will not be covered.

Amount of support per award: Dissertation Fieldwork Grants and Post Ph.D. Research Grants: Up to $20,000; May apply for a supplementary award, maximum $5,000. Hunt Fellowship: $40,000.

Total amount of support: Approximately $5,000,000.

NO. AWARDS: 142 for the year 2014.

APPLICATION INFO:
Applicants are required to submit a formal application. Application forms must be submitted online through the Foundation's web site beginning three months prior to the application deadline.

Duration: Hunt Postdoctoral Fellowship: Up to one year (12 continuous months of full-time writing). Nonrenewable; Research Grants: Duration of the project.

Deadline: May 1 for funding during first half of the year. November 1 for projects scheduled to begin July or later. Announcement within six to eight months.

PUBLICATIONS:
Program announcement.

IRS I.D.: 13-1813827

OFFICERS:
Seth J. Masters, Chairman of the Board
Dr. John Immerwahr, Vice-Chairman
Dr. Leslie C. Aiello, President
Lauren Meserve, Treasurer
Maugha Kenny, Vice-President for Finance and Secretary

WENNER-GREN FOUNDATION FOR ANTHROPOLOGICAL RESEARCH, INC. [1964]

470 Park Avenue South
8th Floor
New York, NY 10016-6819
(212) 683-5000
Fax: (212) 532-1492
E-mail: internationalprograms@wennergren.org
Web Site: www.wennergren.org

FOUNDED: 1941

AREAS OF INTEREST:
All branches of anthropology, including cultural/social anthropology, ethnology, biological/physical anthropology, archaeology and anthropological linguistics, and closely related disciplines concerned with human origins, development and variation.

NAME(S) OF PROGRAMS:
- **Wadsworth International Fellowships**

TYPE:
Fellowships; Scholarships. Wadsworth International Fellowship is for scholars and students from developing countries undertaking study leading to a Ph.D. or equivalent doctoral degree at universities where they can receive international-level training in anthropology and its related subdisciplines. The main goals of these Fellowships are to expand and strengthen international ties and enhance anthropological infrastructure in countries where anthropology is underrepresented and where there are limited resources to send students overseas for training.

YEAR PROGRAM STARTED: 1980

PURPOSE:
To support anthropological study.

LEGAL BASIS:
Private operating foundation.

ELIGIBILITY:
Wadsworth International Fellowships are available only to students from countries where anthropology is underrepresented and where there are limited resources to send students overseas for training. Students must be in the early stages of their doctoral programs. Priority is given to applicants who have not already begun graduate training abroad, and who are likely to return to an academic position in their home country upon completion of their degree.

The applicant must have a Home Sponsor who is a member of the institution with which he or she is affiliated in the home country and a Host Sponsor who is a member of the institution in which the candidate plans to pursue training. The Host Sponsor must be willing to assume responsibility for overseeing the candidate's training.

FINANCIAL DATA:
Fellowships may be used to cover travel, living expenses, tuition, student fees, income taxes, research expenses, insurance, books and any other relevant categories of expenditure. Aid is not provided for salary and/or fringe benefits of applicant, family expenses or institutional overhead.

Amount of support per award: Up to $17,500 per year.

Total amount of support: Varies.

Matching fund requirements: Because the fellowship is intended as a partnership with the host institution in providing the fellow's training, it is expected that candidates will also be offered support by the institution.

NO. AWARDS: Approximately 5 per year.

APPLICATION INFO:
The Foundation operates an online application submission procedure. Application forms and guidelines for completing these forms are available three months before each application deadline. Two printed copies of the application materials must also be mailed to the Foundation. Applications and supporting materials must be in English. The application asks for the following categories of information:
(1) general information about the applicant, the home institution and sponsor, and the host institution and sponsor;

(2) answers to three questions about the proposed plan of study, research interests, and professional goals and plans;
(3) a detailed budget;
(4) copies of official transcripts from the home institution (provide a translation if they are not in English);
(5) where applicable, the applicant must provide evidence of competency in the language of the country in which he/she will be pursuing training;
(6) curriculum vitae of the applicant and host sponsor and;
(7) the applicant should request letters from both the home sponsor and the host sponsor, to be sent directly to the Foundation. These letters must clearly identify the applicant by their full legal name. Applications cannot be processed unless both letters of recommendation are received by the application deadline.

Duration: One year. Possibility of renewal up to three additional years.

Deadline: March 1. Final decisions are made by May 1.

PUBLICATIONS:
Program announcement.

IRS I.D.: 13-1813827

OFFICERS:
Seth J. Masters, Chairman of the Board
Dr. Leslie C. Aiello, President

ADDRESS INQUIRIES TO:
International Program Office
(See address and e-mail above.)

WENNER-GREN FOUNDATION FOR ANTHROPOLOGICAL RESEARCH, INC. [1965]

470 Park Avenue South
8th Floor
New York, NY 10016-6819
(212) 683-5000
Fax: (212) 532-1492
E-mail: lobbink@wennergren.org
Web Site: www.wennergren.org

FOUNDED: 1941

AREAS OF INTEREST:
All branches of anthropology, including cultural/social anthropology, ethnology, biological/physical anthropology, archaeology, anthropological linguistics, and closely related disciplines concerned with human origins, development and variation.

NAME(S) OF PROGRAMS:
- **Conference and Workshop Grants**
- **Wenner-Gren Symposium Program**

TYPE:
Conferences/seminars. Workshops.

PURPOSE:
To support anthropological research.

LEGAL BASIS:
Private operating foundation.

ELIGIBILITY:
The Foundation provides conference support in two forms. Conference and workshop grants are made to the organizer(s). Priority is given to public conferences sponsored by international scholarly organizations (e.g., the IUAES and EASA) that serve as their annual or periodic meetings and to working conferences that address broad research issues in anthropology and provide for intensive interaction among participants. Funds are not normally provided for panels or sessions that are part of larger meetings. Exceptions may be made for organizers who are applying for funds to aid the participation of scholars from developing countries.

The Foundation also sponsors and directly administers a limited number of conferences each year under the Wenner-Gren Symposium Program. These symposia are intended for topics of broad significance for anthropology. They are planned jointly by the organizer(s) and the Foundation president and follow a specific format developed by the Foundation.

Requests by individuals to support their own travel to meetings are not accepted.

FINANCIAL DATA:
The Foundation pays all costs related to the Wenner-Gren Symposium and actively manages it, including sending out invitations and making travel arrangements.

Amount of support per award: Conference and Workshop Grants: $20,000.

Total amount of support: Varies.

NO. MOST RECENT APPLICANTS: 60.

NO. AWARDS: 30.

APPLICATION INFO:
Consult the Foundation web site for application procedures. Guidelines include the following:
(1) Proposals for symposia should be received by the Foundation no less than 18 months before the proposed date for the symposium;
(2) Symposia must aim to make major theoretical or methodological interventions in current issues within anthropology, broadly construed;
(3) Symposia must also advance the Foundation's goal of fostering an international community of anthropologists by drawing participants from around the world;
(4) The Foundation prefers two organizers for the symposium, ideally from two different countries;
(5) The objectives of the symposium should be to coalesce and advance knowledge on the issue, to present and address divergent viewpoints, and to mark out directions for future research;
(6) Symposia should show the relevance of basic research in anthropology to analyzing the human condition, past and/or present and;
(7) Organizers choose the location from a list of suggested sites provided by the Foundation.

Duration: Length of particular conference.

Deadline: Conference and Workshop Grants: June 1 and December 1.

PUBLICATIONS:
Annual report.

IRS I.D.: 13-1813827

OFFICERS:
Seth J. Masters, Chairman
Dr. Leslie C. Aiello, President

ADDRESS INQUIRIES TO:
Laurie Obbink
Conference Program Associate
(See address above.)

WHATCOM MUSEUM [1966]

121 Prospect Street
Bellingham, WA 98225
(360) 778-8968
Fax: (360) 778-8931
E-mail: jgrant@cob.org
Web Site: www.whatcommuseum.org

AREAS OF INTEREST:
Linguistics.

NAME(S) OF PROGRAMS:
- **Jacobs Research Funds Small Grants Program**

TYPE:
Research grants. Grants are given for work on problems in language, social organization, political organization, religion, mythology, music and other arts, psychology and folk science.

YEAR PROGRAM STARTED: 1973

PURPOSE:
To support anthropological and linguistics research on the indigenous peoples of Canada, mainland U.S. and Mexico, with a focus on the Pacific Northwest.

ELIGIBILITY:
Formal academic credentials are not required. Applicants who are inexperienced in research should arrange for the collaboration or supervision of an appropriate and experienced research scholar.

GEOG. RESTRICTIONS: Canada, Mexico, United States and Pacific Northwest.

FINANCIAL DATA:
Amount of support per award: Individuals: $3,000; Group Grant: $6,000; Kinkade Grant: $9,000.

NO. MOST RECENT APPLICANTS: 35.

NO. AWARDS: 25.

APPLICATION INFO:
Two letters in support of the applicant and the project are required. Applications are also accepted online.

Duration: One year. Must reapply for renewal.

Deadline: February 15.

ADDRESS INQUIRIES TO:
Amy Geise, Museum Representative
(See address above.)

PHYSICAL SCIENCES

Physical sciences (general)

AMERICAN CHEMICAL SOCIETY [1967]

1155 16th Street, N.W.
Washington, DC 20036
(202) 872-6092
(800) 227-5558
Fax: (202) 872-6319
E-mail: prfinfo@acs.org
Web Site: www.acsprf.org

FOUNDED: 1944

AREAS OF INTEREST:
Fundamental research in chemistry, engineering and earth sciences which may impact the petroleum field.

NAME(S) OF PROGRAMS:
- **The Petroleum Research Fund**

TYPE:
Grants-in-aid; Research grants. The project may be in any field of pure science which may afford a basis for subsequent research directly connected with the petroleum field.

YEAR PROGRAM STARTED: 1944

PURPOSE:
To support advanced scientific education and fundamental research in the petroleum field.

LEGAL BASIS:
Private trust established in 1944 with contributions of seven petroleum companies.

ELIGIBILITY:
Grants are made to nonprofit scientific or educational institutions, such as universities, on behalf of projects of their regularly appointed faculty.

FINANCIAL DATA:
Amount of support per award: Up to $100,000 per year, depending upon the grant program.

Total amount of support: Varies.

Matching fund requirements: Varies.

APPLICATION INFO:
Application information is available on the web site.

Duration: Up to two years.

Deadline: Five months prior to each scheduled meeting held in May and September.

PUBLICATIONS:
Annual report.

ADDRESS INQUIRIES TO:
Gayle Peterman, Director
(See address above.)

AMERICAN INDIAN SCIENCE AND ENGINEERING SOCIETY (AISES)

2305 Renard, S.E.
Suite 200
Albuquerque, NM 87106
(505) 765-1052
E-mail: info@aises.org
Web Site: www.aises.org/scholarships

TYPE:
Scholarships.

See entry 1019 for full listing.

AMERICAN SOCIETY FOR MASS SPECTROMETRY [1968]

2019 Galisteo Street
Building I-1
Santa Fe, NM 87505
(505) 989-4517
Fax: (505) 989-1073
E-mail: office@asms.org
Web Site: www.asms.org

FOUNDED: 1969

AREAS OF INTEREST:
Mass spectrometry.

NAME(S) OF PROGRAMS:
- **ASMS Research Awards in Mass Spectrometry**

TYPE:
Project/program grants; Research grants.

YEAR PROGRAM STARTED: 1985

PURPOSE:
To promote academic research in mass spectrometry by young scientists.

LEGAL BASIS:
Nonprofit corporation.

ELIGIBILITY:
Grant applicants must be academic scientists within four years of joining the tenure track faculty or equivalent in a North American university for research in mass spectrometry.

Applicants must be members of ASMS.

GEOG. RESTRICTIONS: North America.

FINANCIAL DATA:
Grants are made to the university in the name of the selected individual.

Amount of support per award: $35,000.

Total amount of support: $70,000 annually.

NO. MOST RECENT APPLICANTS: 15.

NO. AWARDS: 2.

APPLICATION INFO:
Applicants should submit applications electronically in a PDF format including a curriculum vitae, list of current research support, three-page proposal, one-page fiscal proposal and justification, and two letters of recommendation. Proposals are ranked primarily on scientific merit and secondarily on effectiveness of proposed use of funds.

Duration: Varies.

Deadline: November 30.

IRS I.D.: 23-7050068

ADDRESS INQUIRIES TO:
See e-mail address above.

AMERICAN SOCIETY OF NAVAL ENGINEERS (ASNE)

1452 Duke Street
Alexandria, VA 22314-3458
(703) 836-6727
Fax: (703) 836-7491
E-mail: nlackey@navalengineers.org
Web Site: www.navalengineers.org

TYPE:
Scholarships. Stipend for tuition, fees and expenses to follow a full-time or co-op program of study that applies to naval engineering, such as naval architecture, marine engineering, ocean engineering, mechanical engineering, structural engineering, electrical engineering, electronic engineering and the physical sciences, as well as other programs leading to careers with civilian and military maritime organizations supporting and developing work and life at sea.

See entry 2561 for full listing.

ASPRS - THE IMAGING AND GEOSPATIAL INFORMATION SOCIETY [1969]

5410 Grosvenor Lane
Suite 210
Bethesda, MD 20814-2160
(301) 493-0290 ext. 101
Fax: (301) 493-0208
E-mail: scholarships@asprs.org
Web Site: www.asprs.org

FOUNDED: 1934

AREAS OF INTEREST:
Geospatial sciences, photogrammetry, remote sensing, geographic information systems (GIS) and Lidar supporting technologies.

NAME(S) OF PROGRAMS:
- **Robert E. Altenhofen Memorial Scholarship**
- **DigitalGlobe Foundation Award**
- **William A. Fischer Memorial Scholarship**
- **Ta Liang Memorial Award**
- **Paul R. Wolf Memorial Scholarship**
- **Z/I Imaging Scholarship**

TYPE:
Assistantships; Awards/prizes; Fellowships; Internships; Scholarships; Travel grants. Robert E. Altenhofen Memorial Scholarship is for undergraduate or graduate study in photogrammetry.

The DigitalGlobe Foundation Award is a grant of digital satellite imagery open to full-time undergraduate or graduate students at an accredited college or university in the U.S. or Canada with image processing facilities appropriate for conducting the proposed work.

William A. Fischer Memorial Scholarship is open to students pursuing graduate-level studies in remote sensing at an accredited institution.

Ta Liang Memorial Award is awarded to a graduate student in remote sensing to be used for research-related travel.

The Paul R. Wolf Memorial Scholarship is designed for prospective teachers in the general area of surveying, mapping or photogrammetry.

Z/I Imaging Scholarship is for a student who is currently pursuing graduate-level studies or who plans to enroll for graduate studies in a recognized college or university in the U.S. or elsewhere, and is designed to facilitate graduate-level studies and career goals adjudged to address new and innovative uses of signal processing, image processing techniques and the application of photogrammetry to real-world techniques within earth-imaging industry.

YEAR PROGRAM STARTED: 1960

PURPOSE:
To advance knowledge and improve understanding of mapping sciences; to promote the responsible applications of photogrammetry, remote sensing, geographic information systems (GIS) and supporting technologies.

LEGAL BASIS:
501(c)(3) organization.

ELIGIBILITY:
Applicant must be enrolled in an accredited college or university and in most cases be an active or student member of ASPRS.

FINANCIAL DATA:
Amount of support per award: Robert E. Altenhofen Memorial Scholarship, William A. Fischer Memorial Scholarship, Ta Liang Memorial Award and Z/I Imaging Award: $2,000; DigitalGlobe Foundation Award: Potential value of up to $20,000; Paul R. Wolf Memorial Scholarship: $4,000.

NO. AWARDS: 1 per award.

APPLICATION INFO:
Application information is available on the web site.

Duration: One year.

Deadline: All complete applications, including reference letters and transcripts, must be received at ASPRS no later than midnight, October 16, 2015.

PUBLICATIONS:
ASPRS Foundation Awards & Scholarships booklet.

STAFF:
Michael Hauck, Executive Director
Jesse Winch, Scholarship Administrator

ADDRESS INQUIRIES TO:
Awards and Scholarships
(See address and e-mail above.)

ASPRS - THE IMAGING AND GEOSPATIAL INFORMATION SOCIETY [1970]

5410 Grosvenor Lane
Suite 210
Bethesda, MD 20814-2160
(301) 493-0290 ext. 101
Fax: (301) 493-0208
E-mail: scholarships@asprs.org
Web Site: www.asprs.org

FOUNDED: 1934

AREAS OF INTEREST:
Geospatial sciences, photogrammetry, remote sensing, geographic information systems (GIS) and supporting technologies.

NAME(S) OF PROGRAMS:
- **Abraham Anson Memorial Scholarship**
- **John O. Behrens Institute for Land Information (ILI) Memorial Scholarship**
- **Robert N. Colwell Memorial Fellowship**
- **Francis H. Moffitt Memorial Scholarship**
- **The Kenneth J. Osborn Memorial Scholarship**

TYPE:
Fellowships; Scholarships; Travel grants. Abraham Anson Memorial Scholarship is designed to encourage undergraduate students who have an exceptional interest in pursuing scientific research or education in geospatial science or technology related to photogrammetry, remote sensing, surveying and mapping to enter a professional field where they can use the knowledge of their discipline to excel in their profession.

John O. Behrens Institute for Land Information (ILI) Memorial Scholarship is an undergraduate award established by the Institute for Land Information to encourage those who have an exceptional interest in pursuing scientific research or education in geospatial science or technology or land information systems/records to enter a professional field where they can use the knowledge of this discipline.

Robert N. Colwell Memorial Fellowship is made to a graduate student (Master's or Ph.D. level) currently enrolled or intending to enroll in a college or university in the U.S. or Canada, who is pursuing a program of study aimed at starting a professional career where expertise is required in remote sensing or other related geospatial information technologies.

Francis H. Moffitt Memorial Scholarship is for students currently enrolled or intending to enroll in a college or university in the U.S. or Canada, who are pursuing a program of study in surveying or photogrammetry leading to a career in the geospatial mapping profession.

The Kenneth J. Osborn Memorial Scholarship is made to an undergraduate student currently enrolled or intending to enroll in a college or university in the U.S., who is pursuing a program of study in preparation for entering the profession in the general area of surveying, mapping, photogrammetry or geospatial information and technology, and shows good collaboration skills.

PURPOSE:
To advance knowledge and improve understanding of mapping sciences; to promote the responsible applications of photogrammetry, remote sensing, geographic information systems (GIS) and supporting technologies.

LEGAL BASIS:
501(c)(3) organization.

ELIGIBILITY:
Requirements vary with the program. Applicant must be enrolled in an accredited college or university and in most cases be an active or student member of ASPRS.

FINANCIAL DATA:
Amount of support per award: Anson Memorial Scholarship, Behrens Memorial Scholarship and Osborn Memorial Scholarship: $2,000; Colwell Memorial Fellowship: $6,500; Moffitt Memorial Scholarship: $6,500.

NO. MOST RECENT APPLICANTS: 100.

NO. AWARDS: 1 for each award.

APPLICATION INFO:
Application information is available on the web site. All complete applications, including reference letters and transcripts, must be submitted electronically.

Duration: One year.

Deadline: Contact the Society for dates.

PUBLICATIONS:
ASPRS Awards and Scholarships booklet (including application form).

STAFF:
Michael Hauck, Executive Director

ADDRESS INQUIRIES TO:
See e-mail address above.

BUILDING AND FIRE RESEARCH LABORATORY [1971]

National Institute of Standards and Technology
100 Bureau Drive, Stop 8660
Gaithersburg, MD 20899-8660
(301) 975-6598
Fax: (301) 975-4052
Web Site: www.nist.gov/el/fire_grants.cfm

FOUNDED: 1974

AREAS OF INTEREST:
Exploratory fire research, furnishing flammability, fire performance and validation, smoke hazard calculation, fire growth and extinction, compartment fire models and fire safety performance.

NAME(S) OF PROGRAMS:
- **Fire Research Grants Program**

TYPE:
Research grants. The program includes the following: Fire Fighting Technology Group, Engineered Fire Safety Group, Flammability Reduction Group, Wildland Urban Interface Fire Group and National Fire Research Laboratory.

YEAR PROGRAM STARTED: 1981

PURPOSE:
To conduct research in the areas of fire analysis and prediction, fire metrology, fire fighting technology, integrated performance assessment, and materials and products.

LEGAL BASIS:
Public Law 93-498; Section 18.

ELIGIBILITY:
Institutions of higher education, hospitals, nonprofit organizations, commercial organizations, state, local, and Indian tribal governments, foreign governments, organizations under the jurisdiction of foreign governments, and international organizations are eligible. Joint programs with participation by more than one eligible entity are possible.

GEOG. RESTRICTIONS: United States.

FINANCIAL DATA:
Amount of support per award: Typically $50,000 to $100,000 per award.

NO. MOST RECENT APPLICANTS: 30.

NO. AWARDS: 3 to 5 annually.

APPLICATION INFO:
Electronic filing is accepted through www.grants.gov.

Duration: Up to three years.

Deadline: As listed in *Federal Register* notice.

COOPERATIVE INSTITUTE FOR RESEARCH IN ENVIRONMENTAL SCIENCES (CIRES)

CIRES Building, Room 318
University of Colorado
Boulder, CO 80309-0216
(303) 492-1143
Fax: (303) 492-1149
E-mail: info@cires.colorado.edu
karen.dempsey@colorado.edu
Web Site: cires.colorado.edu

TYPE:
Fellowships. The program provides opportunities for interactions between CIRES scientists and visiting fellows to pursue common research interests. CIRES research includes theoretical studies, laboratory experimentation, and field investigations which may affect the enhancement of air and water quality and prediction of weather climate fluctuations.

See entry 2107 for full listing.

JILA [1972]

440 UCB
University of Colorado at Boulder
Boulder, CO 80309-0440
(303) 492-7789
Fax: (303) 492-5235
E-mail: kim.monteleone@jila.colorado.edu
Web Site: jila.colorado.edu

FOUNDED: 1962

AREAS OF INTEREST:
Atomic and molecular physics, chemical physics, laser physics, astrophysics, optical physics, precision measurements, geophysical measurement and other closely related areas.

NAME(S) OF PROGRAMS:

- **Postdoctoral Research Associateships**
- **Visiting Fellowships**

TYPE:
Assistantships; Fellowships. Postdoctoral Research Associateships provide advanced research experience in the years immediately after the Ph.D. degree. Visiting Fellowships support research and study for experienced scientists.

YEAR PROGRAM STARTED: 1963

PURPOSE:
To further scientific exchange.

LEGAL BASIS:
Jointly sponsored by the University of Colorado at Boulder and the National Institute of Standards and Technology.

ELIGIBILITY:
Postdoctoral Research Associateships are awarded on the basis of the applicants' scholarly qualifications, promise as research scientists, and research interests and experience in relation to those specific ongoing research programs for which financial support is available. There are no restrictions as to citizenship except as may be imposed by conditions of individual contracts. Ph.D. required.

Visiting Fellowships are available to scientists with extensive research experience beyond the doctoral degree, although younger persons with significant scientific achievements are also encouraged to apply. Awards are based on the fields of scientific interest and the scholarly achievements or promise of the applicants. There are no restrictions as to citizenship.

APPLICATION INFO:
Application information is available on the web site.

Deadline: Varies.

ADDRESS INQUIRIES TO:
Kim Monteleone, Coordinator
Visiting Scientists Program
(See address above.)

LINK FOUNDATION [1973]

c/o Binghamton University Foundation
P.O. Box 6005
Binghamton, NY 13902-6005
(607) 777-2210
Fax: (607) 777-2533
Web Site: www.linkfoundation.org

FOUNDED: 1953

AREAS OF INTEREST:
Energy, oceanographic, aerospace simulation research and fellowships.

NAME(S) OF PROGRAMS:

- **Energy Fellowship Program**
- **Oceanography Engineering Fellowship Program**
- **Simulation Fellowship Program**

TYPE:
Fellowships. Grants for research, development and training related to the mastery of air, sea and energy resources.

YEAR PROGRAM STARTED: 1953

PURPOSE:
To promote the general welfare through the advancement of scientific, technological and general educational projects.

ELIGIBILITY:
Nonprofit educational institutions and organizations with appropriate interests are eligible to apply. Grants are not awarded directly to individuals.

FINANCIAL DATA:
Amount of support per award: $3,000 to $28,500.

APPLICATION INFO:
Information on applying for fellowships may be obtained from the administrators for the individual programs. Proof of an organization's tax-exempt status must accompany the application if not listed in the publication Cumulative List of Organizations described in Section 170(c) of the Internal Revenue Code.

The following documents must be submitted in the order indicated or they will not be accepted:
(1) cover sheet specific to the individual program;
(2) 500-word description of the project that places the research in the context of current activities in the field;
(3) two letters of recommendation, as specified for the individual program;
(4) two additional letters of reference (professional or educational);
(5) project objectives, timeline and projected budget (projected budget only for Energy Program) and;
(6) current resume.

Duration: Subject to annual review.

Deadline: January.

TRUSTEES:

ADDRESS INQUIRIES TO:
Dr. Thomas F. Kelly, Chairman
(See address above.)

NATIONAL RESEARCH COUNCIL OF THE NATIONAL ACADEMIES [1974]

Fellowship and Research Associateship Programs
500 Fifth Street, N.W.
Washington, DC 20001
(202) 334-2760
E-mail: rap@nas.edu
Web Site: www.nationalacademies.org/rap

AREAS OF INTEREST:
All fields in science and engineering.

NAME(S) OF PROGRAMS:

- **NRC Graduate, Postdoctoral and Senior Research Associateship Programs**

TYPE:
Research scientists. Fellowships at the graduate, postdoctoral and senior levels for research-in-residence at U.S. federal laboratories and affiliated institutions.

YEAR PROGRAM STARTED: 1954

PURPOSE:
To provide research opportunities for qualified personnel.

LEGAL BASIS:
Not-for-profit agency.

ELIGIBILITY:
Citizens of the U.S. and foreign nationals may apply. Must have or expect to receive Ph.D., Sc.D. or other earned equivalent research Doctorate. Program also available for graduate-level applicants.

Awards are tenable only at participating U.S. federal laboratories and affiliated institutions.

GEOG. RESTRICTIONS: United States.

FINANCIAL DATA:
Research Associateship awards include stipend, support for relocation and professional travel and health insurance.

Amount of support per award: Annual stipend for recent Ph.D. recipients: $45,000 to $80,000, with higher stipend for additional experience. Annual entry-level stipend for graduate awards: $30,000, with higher stipend for additional experience.

Total amount of support: Varies.

NO. MOST RECENT APPLICANTS: 1,000.

NO. AWARDS: 275.

APPLICATION INFO:
Application information is available on the web site.

Duration: One to three years.

Deadline: February 1, May 1, August 1 and November 1.

STAFF:
Dr. H. Ray Gamble, Director of Fellowships and Associateships

ADDRESS INQUIRIES TO:
Research Associateship Programs
(See address above.)

NATIONAL SCIENCE FOUNDATION [1975]

Division of Atmospheric and Geospace Sciences
4201 Wilson Boulevard, Room 775S
Arlington, VA 22230
(703) 292-8520
Fax: (703) 292-9022
E-mail: trozell@nsf.gov
Web Site: www.nsf.gov

FOUNDED: 1950

AREAS OF INTEREST:
The Atmospheric Sciences program supports research to add new understanding of the behavior of the Earth's atmosphere and its interactions with the Sun. Included are studies of the physics, chemistry and dynamics of the Earth's upper and lower atmosphere and its space environment, research on climate processes and variations and studies to understand the natural global cycles of gases and particles in the Earth's atmosphere.

TYPE:
Conferences/seminars; Research grants.

YEAR PROGRAM STARTED: 1962

PURPOSE:
To continue to build a base of fundamental knowledge of the atmospheres of the Earth and other planets and of the Sun.

LEGAL BASIS:
Government agency.

ELIGIBILITY:
Proposals may be submitted by academic institutions, nonacademic and nonprofit research organizations, profitmaking and private research organizations and individuals. Occasionally, NSF sponsors efforts by other government agencies, particularly for field programs.

GEOG. RESTRICTIONS: United States and its territories.

FINANCIAL DATA:
Amount of support per award: Varies.

Total amount of support: Varies.

APPLICATION INFO:
Application information is available on the web site.

Duration: Varies.

Deadline: Varies.

PUBLICATIONS:
NSF Guide to Programs.

ADDRESS INQUIRIES TO:
Tracy L. Rozell, Program Support Manager
(See address above.)

OAK RIDGE INSTITUTE FOR SCIENCE AND EDUCATION (ORISE)

MC-100-36
P.O. Box 117
Oak Ridge, TN 37831-0117
(865) 574-7798
(865) 576-3424
Fax: (865) 576-1609
E-mail: science.education@orau.org
Web Site: orise.orau.gov/science-education

TYPE:
Fellowships; Internships; Scholarships. ORISE administers a broad range of internships, scholarships, fellowships and research experiences. ORISE programs include research experiences at Department of Energy national laboratories as well as other federal agencies with research facilities located across the country as well as some positions outside the U.S.

See entry 2575 for full listing.

RESEARCH CORPORATION FOR SCIENCE ADVANCEMENT [1976]

4703 East Camp Lowell Drive
Suite 201
Tucson, AZ 85712-1281
(520) 571-1111
Fax: (520) 571-1119
E-mail: awards@rescorp.org
Web Site: www.rescorp.org

FOUNDED: 1912

AREAS OF INTEREST:
University research and education in physics, chemistry and astronomy.

NAME(S) OF PROGRAMS:
- **Cottrell Scholar Awards**
- **Scialog**

TYPE:
Awards/prizes; Conferences/seminars; Research grants; Seed money grants. Cottrell Scholar Awards recognize early-career faculty in Ph.D.-granting universities and in primarily undergraduate institutions.

Scialog provides seed funding for early-career academic scientists that work in highly innovative cross-disciplinary teams. Programs have included solar energy conversion research and cell biology and theoretical physics collaborations.

PURPOSE:
To promote excellence in both research and teaching in science departments in colleges and universities.

LEGAL BASIS:
Operating foundation.

ELIGIBILITY:
Cottrell Scholar Awards: Applicants must be tenure-track assistant professors in a Ph.D.-granting or primarily undergraduate institution in a department of astronomy, chemistry or physics. Additionally, they must be in their third academic year during the calendar year of application.

Scialog: Faculty in U.S. colleges and universities may apply.

GEOG. RESTRICTIONS: United States.

FINANCIAL DATA:
Cottrell Scholar and Scialog Awards: Grant awards can be used at discretion of awardee for most direct costs.

Amount of support per award: Cottrell Scholar Award: $100,000; Scialog: Varies, with typical award $100,000.

Total amount of support: Varies.

APPLICATION INFO:
Application information is available on the web site.

Duration: Two years with a possible one-year no-cost extension.

PUBLICATIONS:
Annual report; newsletter; occasional publications and guidelines.

IRS I.D.: 13-1963407

OFFICERS:
Jack Pladziewicz, Interim President

BOARD OF DIRECTORS:
Lars Bildsten, Ph.D.
G. Scott Clemons
Peter K. Dorhout, Ph.D.
Jonathan Hook, MBA
Brent L. Iverson, Ph.D.
Gayle P.W. Jackson, Ph.D.
Elizabeth McCormack, Ph.D.
David L. Wenner
Joan B. Woodard, Ph.D.

ADDRESS INQUIRIES TO:
Science Advancement Program
(See address above.)

ALFRED P. SLOAN FOUNDATION [1977]

630 Fifth Avenue
Suite 2200
New York, NY 10111
(212) 649-1649
E-mail: researchfellows@sloan.org
Web Site: www.sloan.org/fellowships

FOUNDED: 1934

AREAS OF INTEREST:
Science, technology, mathematics, computer science, economics, ocean sciences, neuroscience, physics, chemistry and computational and molecular biology.

NAME(S) OF PROGRAMS:
- **Sloan Research Fellowships**

TYPE:
Awards/prizes; Fellowships. Research fellowships are awarded to young scholars in chemistry, computational and evolutionary molecular biology, computer science, economics, mathematics, neuroscience, physics, and ocean sciences. The Fellow need not pursue a specified research project and is free to change the direction of his or her research at any time.

YEAR PROGRAM STARTED: 1955

PURPOSE:
To identify and support promising young scientists at an early stage.

LEGAL BASIS:
Private foundation.

ELIGIBILITY:
Candidates are required to hold a Ph.D. (or equivalent) in chemistry, physics, mathematics, computer science, economics, computational and evolutionary molecular biology, neuroscience, or ocean sciences, and must be members of the regular faculty of a U.S. or Canadian college or university. They may be no more than six years from completion of the most recent Ph.D. or equivalent as of the year of their nomination, unless special circumstances are involved such as military service, a change of field, child rearing or for less than two years they have held a faculty appointment.

Applicant must be employed at a U.S. or Canadian institution.

GEOG. RESTRICTIONS: United States and Canada.

FINANCIAL DATA:
Each fellowship is administered by the Fellow's institution and is designed to allow the greatest possible freedom and flexibility in its use. The award may be used for equipment, technical assistance, professional travel, or any other activity directly related to the Fellow's research.

Amount of support per award: $60,000 over a two-year term.

Total amount of support: $7,560,000 for fiscal year 2017.

NO. MOST RECENT APPLICANTS: 800.

NO. AWARDS: 126 fellowships: 23 for physics, 23 for chemistry, 20 for mathematics, 16 for neuroscience, 16 for computer science, 8 for economics, 8 for ocean science, and 12 for computational and evolutionary molecular biology.

APPLICATION INFO:
Candidates may not apply directly, but must be nominated by a department head or other senior researcher. The nominator should submit a letter describing the candidate's qualifications and must see that the Foundation receives three supporting letters directly from other researchers, preferably not all from the same institution. A curriculum vitae, a list of scientific publications plus one copy of two representative publications, and a one-page statement by the candidate describing his or her significant scientific work and immediate research plans should accompany the nomination form and letter. Strong evidence in submitted publications and supporting

letters of the nominee's independent creativity is one of the most important considerations in the review process.

Duration: Two years. One two-year extension is permitted on request.

Deadline: Selections are made in February. Nominations must be received no later than September 15 for awards to begin the following September.

PUBLICATIONS:
Brochure; annual report.

ADMINISTRATIVE OFFICERS AND STAFF:
Paul L. Joskow, President
Leisle Lin, Financial Vice President and Secretary
Christopher T. Sia, Controller

ADDRESS INQUIRIES TO:
Gayle K. Myerson
Grants Coordinator
(See e-mail address above.)

SOCIETY FOR THE STUDY OF AMPHIBIANS AND REPTILES [1978]

Department of Biological Sciences
University of Wisconsin-Whitewater
Whitewater, WI 53190
(262) 472-1069
E-mail: kapferj@uww.edu
Web Site: www.ssarherps.org/pages/GIH.php

AREAS OF INTEREST:
Herpetology.

NAME(S) OF PROGRAMS:
- **Grants in Herpetology**

TYPE:
Awards/prizes; Research grants. Awards are given in six categories: Conservation of Amphibians and/or Reptiles, Field Research, Laboratory Research, Herpetological Education, Travel and International Research.

PURPOSE:
To advance research, conservation, and education concerning amphibians and reptiles; to provide financial support for deserving individuals or organizations involved in herpetological research, education, or conservation.

ELIGIBILITY:
Applicants must be students and members of the SSAR with the exception of those applying for educational grants.

FINANCIAL DATA:
Amount of support per award: $500.

Total amount of support: $3,000.

NO. AWARDS: 6.

APPLICATION INFO:
Applicants may only apply for one category and must designate to which of the six their proposal is submitted. Each proposal must include the following:
(1) title page;
(2) background and objects of the proposed project;
(3) methods of carrying out the project;
(4) complete project budget;
(5) brief resume or curriculum vitae of the applicant or project coordinator and;
(6) letter of support.

Duration: One-time award.

Deadline: December 15.

ADDRESS INQUIRIES TO:
Dr. Joshua M. Kapfer, Chairperson
(See address above.)

TUSKEGEE UNIVERSITY [1979]

1200 West Montgomery Road
Tuskegee, AL 36088
(334) 727-8201 (Financial Aid)
E-mail: faid@mytu.tuskegee.edu
Web Site: www.tuskegee.edu

FOUNDED: 1881

AREAS OF INTEREST:
Postgraduate education in the sciences.

NAME(S) OF PROGRAMS:
- **Master's Program in Material Science and Engineering**
- **Ph.D. Program in Material Science and Engineering**

TYPE:
Fellowships.

YEAR PROGRAM STARTED: 1944

PURPOSE:
To enable students who might otherwise be unable to pursue Master's and doctoral degrees at Tuskegee University.

LEGAL BASIS:
University.

FINANCIAL DATA:
Amount of support per award: Master's Program: $18,000 stipend plus tuition and other fees for U.S. citizens; $15,000 stipend plus tuition and other fees for international students. Ph.D. Program: Up to $54,000 per year ($25,000 to $30,000 stipend plus tuition and other fees up to $24,000) for U.S. citizens; $20,000 to $25,000 stipend plus tuition and other fees for international students.

Total amount of support: Varies.

NO. AWARDS: Varies.

APPLICATION INFO:
Application form is available online.

Duration: Three to five years, depending upon student's performance.

Deadline: February 1.

ADDRESS INQUIRIES TO:
Office of Graduate Studies and Research
John A. Kenney Hall
Suite 44-320, Tuskegee University
Tuskegee, AL 36088
(See e-mail address above.)

WILLIAM P. WHARTON TRUST [1980]

c/o Choate, Hall & Stewart
2 International Place
Boston, MA 02110
(617) 248-5000
Fax: (617) 248-4000
E-mail: williampwhartontrust@choate.com
Web Site: www.williampwhartontrust.org

AREAS OF INTEREST:
Conservation and nature.

TYPE:
Project/program grants.

YEAR PROGRAM STARTED: 1976

PURPOSE:
To support projects that directly promote the study, conservation and appreciation of nature.

ELIGIBILITY:
Organizations must be 501(c)(3) tax-exempt. No funding for individuals.

GEOG. RESTRICTIONS: United States and Canada.

FINANCIAL DATA:
Amount of support per award: Usually $2,500 to $15,000. The Trust's Trustees and Advisors are willing to make larger multiyear grants for important acquisitions of land for conservation purposes.

Total amount of support: Approximately $175,000 annually.

NO. AWARDS: Approximately 30.

APPLICATION INFO:
Complete application instructions are available on the Trust web site.

Duration: Varies.

Astronomy and aerospace science

AMERICAN ASTRONOMICAL SOCIETY [1981]

2000 Florida Avenue, N.W.
Suite 400
Washington, DC 20009-1231
(202) 328-2010
Fax: (202) 234-2560
E-mail: marvel@aas.org
Web Site: www.aas.org

FOUNDED: 1899

AREAS OF INTEREST:
The advancement of astronomy and closely related branches of science.

NAME(S) OF PROGRAMS:
- **Chrétien International Research Grant**

TYPE:
Research grants. Research grant(s) with preference given to individuals of high promise who are otherwise unfunded.

YEAR PROGRAM STARTED: 1982

PURPOSE:
To further international collaborative projects in observational astronomy, with emphasis on long-term international visits and the development of close working relationship with astronomers in other countries.

LEGAL BASIS:
Nonprofit, scientific corporation.

ELIGIBILITY:
Astronomers with a Ph.D. or equivalent are eligible. Graduate students are not eligible.

FINANCIAL DATA:
Amount of support per award: Up to $20,000.

Total amount of support: $20,000 each year.

NO. MOST RECENT APPLICANTS: 18.

NO. AWARDS: 1.

APPLICATION INFO:
Application and all supporting materials should be submitted electronically to Kelly Clark at grants@aas.org. Applications should include:
(1) a description of the research project (less than three pages in length), including an assessment of its importance to that particular subfield of astronomy and a statement enumerating all the aspects of international collaboration;
(2) a statement of the candidate's ability to do the proposed research, with special emphasis on international collaboration and foreign visits which have been arranged,

including facilities available and observing time allocations, if any;
(3) the proposed budget, with brief justification for the amount requested;
(4) a description of other financial resources available;
(5) the candidate's curriculum vitae and bibliography of recent papers;
(6) two letters of reference from astronomers who know the candidate's work and;
(7) any special circumstances which might help in the decision process.

Duration: One year.

Deadline: Application due April 1. Announcement the following September.

ADDRESS INQUIRIES TO:
Kelly Clark
E-mail: grants@aas.org

AMERICAN ASTRONOMICAL SOCIETY [1982]

2000 Florida Avenue, N.W.
Suite 400
Washington, DC 20009-1231
(202) 328-2010
Fax: (202) 234-2560
E-mail: marvel@aas.org
Web Site: www.aas.org/grants/awards.html

FOUNDED: 1899

AREAS OF INTEREST:
Astronomy and closely related branches of science.

NAME(S) OF PROGRAMS:
- **Newton Lacy Pierce Prize in Astronomy**

TYPE:
Awards/prizes. Given to recognize outstanding achievement during the five years preceding the award in observational astronomical research based on measurements of radiation from an astronomical object. A monetary prize and certificate are awarded annually.

YEAR PROGRAM STARTED: 1974

LEGAL BASIS:
Nonprofit, scientific corporation.

ELIGIBILITY:
Applicants must be residents of North America (including Hawaii or Puerto Rico) or a member of a North American institution stationed abroad. Applicants should also be under 36 years of age.

FINANCIAL DATA:
Amount of support per award: $1,500.

Total amount of support: $1,500.

NO. AWARDS: 1.

APPLICATION INFO:
Contact the Society regarding application materials and requirements.

PUBLICATIONS:
Program announcement.

ADDRESS INQUIRIES TO:
Dr. G. Fritz Benedict, Secretary
American Astronomical Society
University of Texas-Austin
McDonald Observatory
Austin, TX 78712-1083

ASTRONOMICAL SOCIETY OF THE PACIFIC [1983]

390 Ashton Avenue
San Francisco, CA 94112
(415) 337-1100
Fax: (415) 337-5205
E-mail: awards@astrosociety.org
Web Site: www.astrosociety.org

FOUNDED: 1889

AREAS OF INTEREST:
Astronomy and science education.

NAME(S) OF PROGRAMS:
- **Maria and Eric Muhlmann Award**

TYPE:
Awards/prizes.

YEAR PROGRAM STARTED: 1995

PURPOSE:
To improve significant observational research, possibly through advances in astronomical instrumentation, software or support infrastructure.

ELIGIBILITY:
Award is available to individuals. Applicants do not have to be U.S. citizens or residents.

FINANCIAL DATA:
Amount of support per award: $500 and plaque.

Total amount of support: $500 each year.

NO. MOST RECENT APPLICANTS: Varies.

NO. AWARDS: 1.

APPLICATION INFO:
Sponsors should submit a two-page nomination giving strong support to the choice.

Duration: One-time award.

Deadline: January 1.

ADDRESS INQUIRIES TO:
Dr. Linda Shore, Executive Director
(See address above.)

ASTRONOMICAL SOCIETY OF THE PACIFIC [1984]

390 Ashton Avenue
San Francisco, CA 94112
(415) 337-1100
Fax: (415) 337-5205
E-mail: lshore@astrosociety.org
Web Site: www.astrosociety.org

AREAS OF INTEREST:
Astronomy.

NAME(S) OF PROGRAMS:
- **Klumpke-Roberts Award**

TYPE:
Awards/prizes.

PURPOSE:
To recognize outstanding contributions to the public understanding and appreciation of astronomy.

ELIGIBILITY:
There are no restrictions on nominations for this award. The contributions may be in the form of popular books and articles; lectures; radio, TV or movie productions; or service to public education in astronomy of any other nature.

FINANCIAL DATA:
Award includes travel reimbursement and hotel accommodation to annual meeting.

Amount of support per award: $500 and plaque.

NO. MOST RECENT APPLICANTS: Varies.

NO. AWARDS: 1.

APPLICATION INFO:
Nominations only. Self-nominations are not accepted.

Deadline: January 1.

ADDRESS INQUIRIES TO:
Dr. Linda Shore, Executive Director
(See e-mail address above.)

ASTRONOMICAL SOCIETY OF THE PACIFIC [1985]

390 Ashton Avenue
San Francisco, CA 94112
(415) 337-1100
Fax: (415) 337-5205
E-mail: lshore@astrosociety.org
Web Site: www.astrosociety.org

AREAS OF INTEREST:
Astronomy.

NAME(S) OF PROGRAMS:
- **Thomas Brennan Award for Outstanding Contributions to the Teaching of Astronomy in Grades 9-12**

TYPE:
Awards/prizes.

PURPOSE:
To recognize exceptional achievement related to the teaching of astronomy at the high school level.

ELIGIBILITY:
Nominees must reside in North America.

GEOG. RESTRICTIONS: North America.

FINANCIAL DATA:
Award includes travel reimbursement and hotel accommodation to annual meeting.

Amount of support per award: $500 and plaque.

NO. MOST RECENT APPLICANTS: Varies.

NO. AWARDS: 1.

APPLICATION INFO:
Nominations must be made on the Brennan Award form, available on the web site. Neither self-nominations nor nomination by a family member will be accepted.

Deadline: January 1.

ADDRESS INQUIRIES TO:
Dr. Linda Shore, Executive Director
(See e-mail address above.)

ASTRONOMICAL SOCIETY OF THE PACIFIC [1986]

390 Ashton Avenue
San Francisco, CA 94112
(415) 337-1100
Fax: (415) 337-5205
E-mail: lshore@astrosociety.org
Web Site: www.astrosociety.org

AREAS OF INTEREST:
Astronomy and amateur astronomy.

NAME(S) OF PROGRAMS:
- **Amateur Achievement Award**
- **Las Cumbres Amateur Outreach Award**

TYPE:
Awards/prizes. Amateur Achievement Award recognizes significant observational or technological contributions to astronomy or amateur astronomy.

Las Cumbres Amateur Outreach Award honors outstanding educational outreach by an amateur astronomer to K-12 children and the interested lay public.

PURPOSE:
To award outstanding contribution or educational outreach in the field of astronomy or amateur astronomy.

ELIGIBILITY:
Amateur Achievement Award: Nominees must not be employed as professional astronomers.

Las Cumbres Amateur Outreach Award: Nominee must not receive compensation (other than expenses) for their activitiy and not receive the majority of their income from a profession in astronomy.

FINANCIAL DATA:
Awards include travel reimbursement and hotel accommodation to annual meeting.

Amount of support per award: $500 and plaque.

NO. MOST RECENT APPLICANTS: Varies.

NO. AWARDS: 1 per award.

APPLICATION INFO:
Nominations are made from the ASP Amateur Advisory Committee and by members of the astronomical community. Self-nominations or nomination by a family member will not be accepted. Letters of support are required.

Deadline: January 1. Announcements in spring.

ADDRESS INQUIRIES TO:
Dr. Linda Shore, Executive Director
(See e-mail address above.)

LUNAR AND PLANETARY INSTITUTE [1987]

3600 Bay Area Boulevard
Houston, TX 77058
(281) 486-2159
Fax: (281) 486-2127
E-mail: explorationintern@lpi.usra.edu
Web Site: www.lpi.usra.edu

FOUNDED: 1968

AREAS OF INTEREST:
Study of lunar exploration, planetary remote sensing and spectroscopy, image processing, planetary geology and surface processes, impact studies, geophysical data analysis and modeling, physics and chemistry of planetary atmospheres, meteorites and sample analysis, interplanetary dust and presolar grains, minerology/petrology and astrobiology.

NAME(S) OF PROGRAMS:

- **Exploration Science Summer Intern Program**

TYPE:
Conferences/seminars; Internships; Scholarships; Travel grants.

YEAR PROGRAM STARTED: 1969

PURPOSE:
To promote and assist in the analysis and interpretation of lunar and planetary data.

ELIGIBILITY:
College graduate students in geology, planetary science, and related programs are eligible. Applicants will be considered for appointment without regard to race, creed, color, sex, national origin, age, handicap status or other non-merit factors.

Due to security issues, citizens of U.S. State Department designated countries are not eligible. See link under "ECP Notices" at oiir.hq.nasa.gov/nasaecp.

FINANCIAL DATA:
Amount of support per award: Selected interns will receive a $5,675 stipend to cover the costs associated with being in Houston for the duration of the program. Additionally, U.S. citizens will receive up to $1,000 in travel expense reimbursement and foreign nationals will receive up to $1,500 in travel expense reimbursement.

Total amount of support: Varies.

APPLICATION INFO:
Applications are only accepted using the electronic application form found on the Institute web site.

Duration: 10-week program, May through July.

Deadline: January.

ADDRESS INQUIRIES TO:
See e-mail address above.

MCDONNELL CENTER FOR THE SPACE SCIENCES

Washington University, Campus Box 1105
One Brookings Drive
St. Louis, MO 63130-4899
(314) 935-5332
E-mail: trecia@physics.wustl.edu
Web Site: mcss.wustl.edu

TYPE:
Fellowships. These fellowships are funded by a gift from the McDonnell Douglas Foundation to Washington University and provide tuition remission plus stipend for graduate students interested in pursuing research in the space sciences who are enrolled in the Washington University Departments of Physics or Earth and Planetary Sciences.

See entry 2538 for full listing.

NATIONAL CENTER FOR ATMOSPHERIC RESEARCH [1988]

High Altitude Observatory
P.O. Box 3000
Boulder, CO 80307-3000
(303) 497-1598
Fax: (303) 497-1589
E-mail: mdelaney@ucar.edu
Web Site: www2.hao.ucar.edu

FOUNDED: 1940

AREAS OF INTEREST:
Solar physics, solar-terrestrial physics and related astrophysics. Specific research interests include coronal and interplanetary physics, solar activity and magnetic fields, the solar interior and terrestrial interactions.

NAME(S) OF PROGRAMS:

- **Newkirk Graduate Research Fellowship**

TYPE:
Fellowships.

PURPOSE:
To promote cooperative research between HAO and academic institutions by providing support for aspiring young scientists at formative stages in their careers.

ELIGIBILITY:
Applicants must be full-time graduate students enrolled in a university program leading to the Ph.D. Students must declare their intention of working on their thesis in cooperation with an HAO staff member and should expect to spend a significant fraction of their time in residence at HAO.

FINANCIAL DATA:
Amount of support per award: Varies.

Total amount of support: Varies.

APPLICATION INFO:
Application includes transcripts of undergraduate and graduate courses, brief statement of goals and three letters of recommendation.

Duration: One-year term with possibility of renewals until completion of the Ph.D. degree.

PUBLICATIONS:
Brochure.

ADDRESS INQUIRIES TO:
Megan Delaney, HAO Visitor Committee
(See address above.)

*PLEASE NOTE:
Fellowship award is dependent upon funding.

NATIONAL RADIO ASTRONOMY OBSERVATORY [1989]

520 Edgemont Road
Charlottesville, VA 22903-2475
(434) 296-0237
Fax: (434) 296-0278
E-mail: jutley@nrao.edu
Web Site: www.nrao.edu

FOUNDED: 1957

AREAS OF INTEREST:
Ground-based radio astronomy. Current areas of research include cosmology, theoretical and observational studies of radio sources, the interstellar and intergalactic medium, structure and dynamics of galactic and extragalactic sources, physics of HII regions, stars, solar system objects and astrometry.

NAME(S) OF PROGRAMS:

- **Jansky Fellowships at the NRAO**

TYPE:
Fellowships. Research appointments. Postdoctoral appointments with liberal support for research travel, data reduction and publication. Jansky Fellows may or may not be residents at NRAO sites.

YEAR PROGRAM STARTED: 1960

LEGAL BASIS:
Federally funded research organization.

ELIGIBILITY:
Fellows must have received their Ph.D. prior to beginning the appointment. Preference is given to recent Ph.D. recipients.

FINANCIAL DATA:
Vacation accrual, health insurance, a moving allowance and other benefits available.

Amount of support per award: Annual salary $64,260, plus $10,000 travel budget per year.

NO. MOST RECENT APPLICANTS: 98.

NO. AWARDS: 3 for the year 2015-16.

APPLICATION INFO:
Application should include a curriculum vitae and a statement of the type of research activity to be undertaken at the NRAO. The applicant should request letters of recommendation from three references. These letters should be sent directly to the NRAO.

Duration: Two years. Possibility of renewal for a third year if mutually agreeable.

Deadline: On or around November 1 of each year.

PUBLICATIONS:
Program announcement.

ADDRESS INQUIRIES TO:
Jessica Utley
Science Support and Research
(See address above.)

NATIONAL SCIENCE FOUNDATION [1990]

Division of Astronomical Sciences
4201 Wilson Boulevard, Room 1045
Arlington, VA 22230
(703) 292-8820
Fax: (703) 292-9034
E-mail: julvesta@nsf.gov
Web Site: www.nsf.gov

FOUNDED: 1950

NAME(S) OF PROGRAMS:

- **Astronomy and Astrophysics Research Grants**

TYPE:
Awards/prizes; Challenge/matching grants; Conferences/seminars; Fellowships; Project/program grants; Research grants; Seed money grants; Travel grants; Research contracts. Broad base of support for fundamental research directed at explaining celestial objects and the cosmos in terms of physical principles.

Basic research support is provided under the following grant programs:

Planetary Astronomy - Objects studied in this program include the planets and their satellites, the asteroids and the comets. Ground-based observations are indispensable to the complete understanding of their structure, composition and origin.

Stellar Astronomy and Astrophysics - This program supports studies of the physical and chemical characteristics of the Sun and other stars, especially as they relate to the stars' past and future evolution. These studies make use of observations at many wavelengths, as well as laboratory measurements and theoretical modeling.

Galactic Astronomy - The topics studied in this program are the spatial and kinematics characteristics of the stars in our galaxy and the properties and distribution of the interstellar medium.

Extragalactic Astronomy and Cosmology - The objective of this program is the description of the nature, structure and evolution of external galaxies and quasars, as well as the implications of these data for the birth, expansion rate and future of the universe.

Advanced Technologies and Instrumentation - This program provides support for development of astronomical equipment at universities. In addition to supporting the acquisition of telescopes and auxiliary instrumentation, this program also supports the reduction of astronomical data by providing funds for minicomputers. Particular emphasis is being placed on the use of advanced technology detectors at radio, infrared and optical wavelengths.

PURPOSE:
To support research and education in astronomy and astrophysics.

LEGAL BASIS:
Government agency.

ELIGIBILITY:
NSF eligibility criteria apply.

GEOG. RESTRICTIONS: United States.

FINANCIAL DATA:
Amount of support per award: Varies.

Total amount of support: Varies.

APPLICATION INFO:
Application information is available on the Foundation web site.

Duration: Varies.

PUBLICATIONS:
Guide to Programs; *Grants for Scientific and Engineering Research.*

OFFICERS:
Jim Ulvestad, Division Director

ADDRESS INQUIRIES TO:
Jim Ulvestad, Division Director
(See address and e-mail above.)

SMITHSONIAN ASTROPHYSICAL OBSERVATORY [1991]

60 Garden Street
Mail Stop 67
Cambridge, MA 02138
(617) 495-7103
Fax: (617) 496-7589
E-mail: predoc@cfa.harvard.edu
Web Site: www.cfa.harvard.edu/opportunities/fellowships/predoc

FOUNDED: 1890

AREAS OF INTEREST:
Astrophysical research, including the fields of astronomy, astrophysics and planetary sciences.

NAME(S) OF PROGRAMS:

- **Predoctoral Research Fellowships**

TYPE:
Exchange programs; Fellowships; Internships. Predoctoral fellowships for thesis research. Fellowships are designed to allow students from other institutions throughout the world to do all or part of their thesis research at the Observatory. A wide variety of research projects may be proposed. About 300 scientific staff conduct research in observation, theory and instrumentation, and in nearly all areas related to astronomy.

YEAR PROGRAM STARTED: 1985

ELIGIBILITY:
Applicants must be enrolled in a Ph.D. program in appropriate fields (i.e., astronomy or astrophysics) and have completed all course work and examinations.

Applicants must be ready to begin dissertation research at the time of the award. They must have the approval of their department head at their home institution to conduct their thesis research at the Observatory. Students from any country are eligible.

FINANCIAL DATA:
Some funds may be available for relocation, travel and other expenses.

Amount of support per award: $34,200 for the year 2016.

NO. MOST RECENT APPLICANTS: 13 for the year 2014.

NO. AWARDS: 13 for the year 2016.

APPLICATION INFO:
Application forms are available on the web site.

Duration: Six months. Renewable up to three years.

Deadline: Proposals are reviewed on an ongoing basis.

STAFF:
Charles R. Alcock, Director

ADDRESS INQUIRIES TO:
Christine Crowley
Fellowship Program Coordinator
(See address above.)

SMITHSONIAN ASTROPHYSICAL OBSERVATORY [1992]

60 Garden Street
Mail Stop 67
Cambridge, MA 02138
(617) 495-7103
Fax: (617) 496-7589
E-mail: postdoc@cfa.harvard.edu
Web Site: www.cfa.harvard.edu/opportunities/postdocs.html

FOUNDED: 1973

AREAS OF INTEREST:
Astrophysics, including the areas of theory, observation, instrumentation and/or laboratory research. Research programs at the Center are organized into seven divisions including atomic and molecular physics, high energy astrophysics, optical and infrared astronomy, radio and geoastronomy, solar, stellar and planetary sciences, theoretical astrophysics, and science education.

NAME(S) OF PROGRAMS:

- **Clay Postdoctoral Fellowship**

TYPE:
Fellowships. Postdoctoral fellowships for research in the Center's areas of interest.

YEAR PROGRAM STARTED: 1974

ELIGIBILITY:
Open to recent Ph.D. recipients with interests in any of the areas above.

FINANCIAL DATA:
Amount of support per award: Stipends of approximately $68,000; annual research budget of approximately $16,000 per appointee for the year 2015-16.

NO. MOST RECENT APPLICANTS: 277.

NO. AWARDS: 1.

APPLICATION INFO:
Application forms are available online.

Duration: Two years. Renewal possible for a third year.

Deadline: October 30.

PUBLICATIONS:
Observatory reports issue of the *Bulletin of the American Astronomical Society.*

STAFF:
Charles R. Alcock, Director

SPACE TELESCOPE SCIENCE INSTITUTE [1993]

3700 San Martin Drive
Baltimore, MD 21218
(410) 338-4425
(410) 338-2474
Fax: (410) 338-4976
E-mail: hfinquiry@stsci.edu
Web Site: www.stsci.edu

FOUNDED: 1990

AREAS OF INTEREST:
Astronomy, astrophysics and related disciplines.

NAME(S) OF PROGRAMS:
- **Hubble Fellowship Program**

TYPE:
Fellowships. Provides a limited number of recent postdoctoral scientists of unusual promise and ability with the opportunity to pursue research of their choice at a participating U.S. astronomical institution designated as host institution by the scientist.

YEAR PROGRAM STARTED: 1990

PURPOSE:
To expand and strengthen the research work of the astronomical community.

ELIGIBILITY:
Applicants must have earned a Doctorate degree, three years prior to application, in physics, astronomy or a related discipline. Applicants can be any nationality. Candidates are selected on the basis of their research proposal, publications and academic achievement. No more than one fellow per year is approved for any one academic location.

Fellowships must be held at U.S. institutions.

FINANCIAL DATA:
Amount of support per award: Annual stipend of approximately $67,500, plus $16,000 per year for research expenses.

Total amount of support: Varies.

CO-OP FUNDING PROGRAMS: Funded by the National Aeronautics and Space Administration (NASA).

NO. MOST RECENT APPLICANTS: 272 for the year 2016.

NO. AWARDS: 17.

APPLICATION INFO:
Application information is available on the web site.

Duration: One year and two annual renewals contingent on satisfactory performance and availability of NASA funds.

Deadline: First week in November.

ADDRESS INQUIRIES TO:
Program Director
Hubble Fellowship Program
(See address above.)

ZONTA INTERNATIONAL FOUNDATION [1994]

1211 West 22nd Street, Suite 900
Oak Brook, IL 60523-3384
(630) 928-1400
Fax: (630) 928-1559
E-mail: programs@zonta.org
Web Site: www.zonta.org

FOUNDED: 1919

AREAS OF INTEREST:
Aerospace-related sciences or aerospace-related engineering.

NAME(S) OF PROGRAMS:
- **Amelia Earhart Fellowship**

TYPE:
Fellowships. Awarded annually to women for graduate study in aerospace-related sciences or aerospace-related engineering at any university or college offering accredited graduate courses and degrees.

YEAR PROGRAM STARTED: 1938

PURPOSE:
To encourage and support the study and research of women scientists and engineers throughout the world and to improve the status of women.

LEGAL BASIS:
Incorporated in the state of Illinois as a nonprofit organization.

ELIGIBILITY:
Women of any nationality who must meet the following minimum requirements:
(1) be registered in an accredited Ph.D./doctoral program in a qualifying area of science or engineering closely related to advanced studies in aerospace-related science or aerospace-related engineering; a letter of acceptance or verification of enrollment must be submitted with the application;
(2) demonstrate a superior academic record at a recognized university or college with accredited courses in aerospace-related studies as verified by transcripts and recommendations;
(3) provide evidence of a well-defined research program in aerospace-related science or aerospace-related engineering as described in the application essay, research and publications;
(4) clearly demonstrate the relationship of their research to aerospace and furnish verification of their research program through at least one of the reference letters required with the application (i.e., research supervisor or advisor must be one of the referees) and;
(5) be registered in a Ph.D./Doctorate program when funds are received in September and will not graduate before April 2017.

The Fellowship may be used at any university or college offering accredited graduate courses and degrees in aerospace studies. Fellowship may be renewed for an additional year by a current Fellow and will undergo the same application and evaluation procedures as first-time applicants. Fellows may accept additional grants and scholarships from other sources.

Defense-related and postdoctoral research programs are not eligible for the Fellowship.

FINANCIAL DATA:
Fellowship awards may be used for tuition, books, fees or living expenses.

Amount of support per award: $10,000 annually.

Total amount of support: $350,000.

NO. MOST RECENT APPLICANTS: 145.

NO. AWARDS: 35 per year.

APPLICATION INFO:
Applications can be secured from the Foundation web site. Elements to be included are biographical information, list of schools attended and degrees received, transcripts of grades and school verification form (on Foundation web site), employment history, plans for intended study, essay on academic and professional goals, and three recommendations from teachers or supervisors. Information other than transcripts and recommendations must be limited to the space provided. Attachments will not be considered.

The application must be completed in English. In addition, international applicants must provide English translations for all non-English documents.

Duration: One academic year. Recipient may reapply for a second year.

Deadline: November 15.

AWARDS COMMITTEE:
Holly Anderson, Chairman

ADDRESS INQUIRIES TO:
Program Department
(See address above.)

Chemistry

AMERICAN CHEMICAL SOCIETY [1995]

1155 16th Street, N.W.
Washington, DC 20036-4800
(202) 872-6283
Fax: (202) 776-8008
E-mail: awards@acs.org
Web Site: www.acs.org/nationalawards

FOUNDED: 1876

AREAS OF INTEREST:
Chemical.

CONSULTING OR VOLUNTEER SERVICES:
Volunteer services.

NAME(S) OF PROGRAMS:
- **Nakanishi Prize**

TYPE:
Awards/prizes. Award presented in the U.S. in odd years and Japan in even years.

YEAR PROGRAM STARTED: 1995

PURPOSE:
To recognize and stimulate significant work that extends chemical and spectroscopic methods to the study of important biological phenomena.

LEGAL BASIS:
Nonprofit association.

ELIGIBILITY:
Individuals can apply. There are no limits on age or nationality.

FINANCIAL DATA:
Amount of support per award: $5,000, plus up to $2,500 travel allowance, medallion with presentation box and certificate.

NO. MOST RECENT APPLICANTS: 6 for the year 2015.

NO. AWARDS: 1.

APPLICATION INFO:
Application procedures are available online.

Duration: Nomination renewable.

Deadline: November 1.

ADDRESS INQUIRIES TO:
Office of Awards
(See address above.)

*SPECIAL STIPULATIONS:
Special consideration will be given for work that has contributed broadly on an international scope.

AMERICAN CHEMICAL SOCIETY [1996]

1155 16th Street, N.W.
Washington, DC 20036-4800
(202) 872-6283
Fax: (202) 776-8008
E-mail: awards@acs.org
Web Site: www.acs.org/awards

FOUNDED: 1876

AREAS OF INTEREST:
Research in industrial and engineering chemistry and chemical engineering principles.

NAME(S) OF PROGRAMS:
- **E.V. Murphree Award in Industrial and Engineering Chemistry**

TYPE:
Awards/prizes.

YEAR PROGRAM STARTED: 1955

PURPOSE:
To stimulate fundamental research in industrial and engineering chemistry, the development of chemical engineering principles and their application to industrial processes.

LEGAL BASIS:
Nonprofit association.

ELIGIBILITY:
Individuals can apply. Nominee must have accomplished outstanding research of theoretical or experimental nature in fields of industrial chemistry or chemical engineering. There are no limits on age or nationality.

FINANCIAL DATA:
Amount of support per award: $5,000, certificate, and up to $1,000 travel expenses.

NO. MOST RECENT APPLICANTS: 15 for the year 2015.

NO. AWARDS: 1.

APPLICATION INFO:
Application procedures are available online.

Duration: One year. Nominations renewable.

Deadline: November 1.

ADDRESS INQUIRIES TO:
Office of Awards
(See address above.)

AMERICAN NUCLEAR SOCIETY (ANS) [1997]

555 North Kensington Avenue
LaGrange Park, IL 60526
(708) 352-6611
Fax: (708) 352-0499
E-mail: scholarships@ans.org
Web Site: www.ans.org

FOUNDED: 1954

AREAS OF INTEREST:
Radioanalytical chemistry or analytical applications of nuclear science.

NAME(S) OF PROGRAMS:
- **James R. Vogt Radiochemistry Scholarship**

TYPE:
Scholarships. Scholarship award to recognize one outstanding undergraduate student or one graduate student pursuing a career in radioanalytical chemistry or analytical applications of nuclear science.

YEAR PROGRAM STARTED: 1987

ELIGIBILITY:
U.S. and non-U.S. applicants must be ANS student members. Applicants must have completed a minimum of two years in an accredited undergraduate program and be enrolled in a four-year college or university in the U.S. Undergraduates in their junior and senior years are eligible to apply as are graduate students in their first or second year of graduate study.

Student must be engaged in proposing to undertake graduate or undergraduate research in radioanalytical chemistry or its applications.

Applicants must be U.S. citizens or hold permanent resident visa at the time of application.

FINANCIAL DATA:
Scholarship funds may be used by the student to defray any bona fide education costs including tuition, fees, books, room and board.

Amount of support per award: $3,000.

NO. AWARDS: 1 annually.

APPLICATION INFO:
Applications must be submitted online. Applicant should include interest in radioanalytical chemistry and its applications in their Personal Statement of Future Plans.

Duration: One year. Nonrenewable.

Deadline: February 1.

ADDRESS INQUIRIES TO:
Scholarship Coordinator
(See address above.)

AMERICAN OIL CHEMISTS SOCIETY [1998]

2710 South Boulder Drive
Urbana, IL 61802-6996
(217) 359-2344
Fax: (217) 351-8091
E-mail: awards@aocs.org
Web Site: www.aocs.org

FOUNDED: 1909

AREAS OF INTEREST:
Lipid chemistry, biochemistry, fats, oils and related materials, surfactants and detergents, and personal care products.

NAME(S) OF PROGRAMS:
- **Stephen S. Chang Award**
- **Schroepfer Medal Award**
- **Supelco AOCS Research Award**

TYPE:
Awards/prizes.

YEAR PROGRAM STARTED: 1982

PURPOSE:
To annually recognize scientists, technologists or engineers who have made substantial accomplishments in lipid chemistry, either by one major breakthrough or by an accumulation of publications.

LEGAL BASIS:
Professional society.

ELIGIBILITY:
Nominations are accepted. Preference shall be given to individuals who are actively associated with research and who have made discoveries that have influenced their fields of endeavor.

FINANCIAL DATA:
Amount of support per award: Varies.

NO. MOST RECENT APPLICANTS: 18.

NO. AWARDS: Chang Award and Supelco Award: 1 of each annually. Schroepfer Medal: 1 biennially in even-numbered years.

APPLICATION INFO:
Nominations for the Chang Award must include a letter from the nominator describing the nominee's distinguished accomplishments in basic research and how they have been utilized by industry to help improve or develop products related to lipids. The nomination must include at least three letters of recommendation and biographical information, including the curriculum vitae.

Nominations for the Supelco Award consist of the same supporting documentation as the Chang Award.

Nominations for the Schroepfer Medal should include a 300- to 1,000-word summary describing the significance of the nominee's accomplishments in the steriod field, a current curriculum vitae including a full list of publications, and two supporting letters.

Duration: One-time awards.

Deadline: October 15 for the Chang Award and Schroepfer Medal; November 1 for the Supelco Award.

PUBLICATIONS:
INFORM: International News on Fats, Oils, and Related Materials; *JAOCS: Journal of the American Oil Chemists' Society*; *Lipids*; *Journal of Surfactants and Detergents*.

ADDRESS INQUIRIES TO:
Membership Department
(See address above.)

CANADIAN SOCIETY FOR CHEMICAL TECHNOLOGY [1999]

222 Queen Street
Suite 400
Ottawa ON K1P 5V9 Canada
(613) 232-6252 ext. 223
Fax: (613) 232-5862
E-mail: awards@cheminst.ca
Web Site: www.cheminst.ca/awards

AREAS OF INTEREST:
Chemistry, biochemistry, chemical engineering technology or chemical technology.

NAME(S) OF PROGRAMS:
- **Norman and Marion Bright Memorial Award**

TYPE:
Awards/prizes.

YEAR PROGRAM STARTED: 1980

PURPOSE:
To reward an individual who has made an outstanding contribution in Canada to the furtherance of chemical technology.

ELIGIBILITY:
The person honored must be either a chemical sciences technologist or a person from outside the field who had made a significant or noteworthy contribution to its advancement.

GEOG. RESTRICTIONS: Canada.

FINANCIAL DATA:
Amount of support per award: $500.

NO. AWARDS: 1.

APPLICATION INFO:
Applicants must complete a nomination form.

Deadline: December 1.

ADDRESS INQUIRIES TO:
Gale Thirlwall, Awards Manager
(See address above.)

CANADIAN SOCIETY FOR CHEMISTRY [2000]

222 Queen Street
Suite 400
Ottawa ON K1P 5V9 Canada
(613) 232-6252 ext. 223
Fax: (613) 232-5862
E-mail: awards@cheminst.ca
Web Site: www.cheminst.ca/awards

AREAS OF INTEREST:
Biochemistry, organic and bioorganic chemistry.

NAME(S) OF PROGRAMS:
- **CCUCC Chemistry Doctoral Award**

TYPE:
Awards/prizes. CCUCC Chemistry Doctoral Award recognizes outstanding achievement and potential in research by a graduate student.

PURPOSE:
To recognize outstanding contributions by chemists for their research in a wide variety of fields.

ELIGIBILITY:
CCUCC Chemistry Doctoral Award is intended to recognize outstanding achievement and potential in research by a graduate student whose Ph.D. thesis in chemistry was formally accepted by a Canadian university in the 12-month period preceding the nomination deadline.

FINANCIAL DATA:
Amount of support per award: CCUCC Chemistry Doctoral Award: $2,000.

Total amount of support: Varies.

NO. AWARDS: CCUCC Chemistry Doctoral Award: 1.

APPLICATION INFO:
Nominations for the CCUCC Chemistry Doctoral Award should include:
(1) letter of support by nominator;
(2) curriculum vitae (using NSERC guidelines);
(3) brief synopsis of doctoral thesis (10 pages double-spaced maximum) and;
(4) copy of the official thesis appraisal.
There is an online submission of the nomination.

Deadline: CCUCC Chemistry Doctoral Award: September 15.

PUBLICATIONS:
Program announcement.

ADDRESS INQUIRIES TO:
Gale Thirlwall, Awards Manager
(See address above.)

GEORGETOWN UNIVERSITY [2001]

Department of Chemistry
Box 571227
Washington, DC 20057-1227
(202) 687-6073
Fax: (202) 687-6209
E-mail: chemad@georgetown.edu
Web Site: chemistry.georgetown.edu

FOUNDED: 1789

AREAS OF INTEREST:
Graduate education in chemistry.

NAME(S) OF PROGRAMS:
- **Doctoral Program in Chemistry**

TYPE:
Assistantships; Awards/prizes; Conferences/seminars; Exchange programs; Fellowships; General operating grants; Professorships; Research grants; Scholarships; Visiting scholars; Work-study programs.

YEAR PROGRAM STARTED: 1924

PURPOSE:
To enable graduate students to earn a Ph.D. degree in chemistry, inorganic, organic, analytical, physical or theoretical chemistry, organometallic, synthetic, or nano-chemistry, biochemistry, or structural crystallography.

LEGAL BASIS:
University.

ELIGIBILITY:
Fellowships are open to nationals of any country. Bachelor's degree or the equivalent is required.

FINANCIAL DATA:
Amount of support per award: $29,350 stipend, full-time tuition coverage and comprehensive individual medical insurance.

NO. MOST RECENT APPLICANTS: 95.

NO. AWARDS: 10.

APPLICATION INFO:
Application information is available on the web site.

Duration: Nine months to one year. Renewable for as long as student continues good progress toward the degree.

Deadline: Although applications will be accepted at any time, priority deadline is January 15.

PUBLICATIONS:
Graduate Studies in Chemistry, booklet.

DIRECTORS:
Dr. YuYe J. Tong, Professor and Chairperson
Dr. Diana Glick, Professor
Dr. Steven Metallo, Professor

ADDRESS INQUIRIES TO:
Dr. YuYe J. Tong
Professor and Chairperson
(See address above.)

THE HAMNER INSTITUTES FOR HEALTH SCIENCES [2002]

6 Davis Drive
Research Triangle Park, NC 27709
(919) 558-1200
Fax: (919) 558-1430
E-mail: koverman@thehamner.org
Web Site: www.thehamner.org

FOUNDED: 1974

AREAS OF INTEREST:
All areas of human health and related risk assessment.

NAME(S) OF PROGRAMS:
- **Postdoctoral Fellowship at The Hamner Institutes for Health Sciences**

TYPE:
Conferences/seminars; Fellowships; Internships; Visiting scholars.

YEAR PROGRAM STARTED: 1976

PURPOSE:
To train toxicologists and computational biologists.

LEGAL BASIS:
Nonprofit, 501(c)(3) organization.

ELIGIBILITY:
Candidate must have completed a doctoral degree in a bioscience or related field.

FINANCIAL DATA:
Amount of support per award: $40,000 to $44,000.

NO. MOST RECENT APPLICANTS: Over 30.

NO. AWARDS: 20 ongoing awards.

APPLICATION INFO:
Application information is available on the web site.

Duration: One to three years. Renewal for second and third year contingent on satisfactory performance the first year.

PUBLICATIONS:
Annual report; *The Hamner Activities*, monthly; Index of The Hamner publications available on request.

BOARD OF DIRECTORS:
Charles Hamner, Chairman

ADDRESS INQUIRIES TO:
Human Resources Department
(See address above.)

NATIONAL MOLE DAY FOUNDATION [2003]

3896 Leaman Court
Freeland, MI 48623
(989) 964-8020
E-mail: moleday@hotmail.com
Web Site: www.moleday.org

FOUNDED: 1991

AREAS OF INTEREST:
Chemistry education.

NAME(S) OF PROGRAMS:
- **The George Hague Memorial Travel Award**
- **The Maury Award**
- **National Mole of the Year Award (MOTY)**

TYPE:
Grants-in-aid. The George Hague Memorial Travel Award is given to financially support a young chemistry instructor (with two to five years of chemistry experience) in attending a biennial ChemEd conference.

The Maury Award is given to teachers to support student-centered Mole Day activities (promoting chemistry education).

The National Mole of the Year Award (MOTY) is given to a member of the National Mole Day Foundation who has contributed the most to furthering the cause of Mole Day and chemistry education.

PURPOSE:
To support Mole Day activities in classrooms, schools or communities.

ELIGIBILITY:
Must be a member of the National Mole Day Foundation and be involved with chemical education. Those receiving grants are not eligible again for the following three years.

FINANCIAL DATA:
Amount of support per award: The George Hague Memorial Travel Award: Up to $750; The Maury Award: Up to $200; National Mole of the Year Award (MOTY): $250.

APPLICATION INFO:
Application information is available on the web site.

Deadline: Hague Award: March 1. Maury Award: June 1. National Mole of the Year Award: May 1 of odd-numbered years.

ADDRESS INQUIRIES TO:
Rebecca Talik, Executive Director
(See address above.)

THE UNIVERSITY OF SYDNEY [2004]

Scholarships Office
Level 5, Jane Foss Russell Building G02
The University of Sydney N.S.W. 2006
Australia
(02) 8627 8112
Fax: (02) 8627 8485
E-mail: scholarships.officer@sydney.edu.au
Web Site: www.sydney.edu.au/scholarships/research

FOUNDED: 1850

AREAS OF INTEREST:
Chemistry in relation to agriculture and industry.

NAME(S) OF PROGRAMS:
- **Henry Bertie and Florence Mabel Gritton Postgraduate Research Scholarships/Fellowships**

TYPE:
Fellowships; Scholarships. Scholarships are awarded for research leading to a higher degree. Fellowships are available for postdoctoral research.

PURPOSE:
To promote the knowledge and study of chemistry in relation to industry and agriculture, including chemistry connected with electrical engineering, metallurgical chemistry and chemistry in its application to mining and the winning and treatment of minerals and natural products of the soil.

LEGAL BASIS:
University.

ELIGIBILITY:
Open to graduates of universities which are members of the Association of Commonwealth Universities or to graduates of any university who are either citizens of a Commonwealth country or who are permanent residents of Australia. Candidates for scholarships must hold at least a first class honours degree. Candidates for Fellowships must hold a Ph.D. degree.

Tenable at the University of Sydney.

FINANCIAL DATA:
Scholarship does not cover tuition fees payable by international students.

Amount of support per award: Scholarships: $25,849 AUD per annum for the year 2015; Fellowships: $78,252 to $83,998 AUD per annum.

NO. AWARDS: 6 scholarships for the year 2013.

APPLICATION INFO:
Application information is available on the web site.

Duration: Scholarships: Two years for a Master's research degree and three years for a Ph.D.; Fellowships: Tenable for two years.

Deadline: Scholarships: Second week in January and early in July. Fellowships: As vacancy occurs.

THE ROBERT A. WELCH FOUNDATION [2005]

5555 San Felipe
Suite 1900
Houston, TX 77056-2730
(713) 961-9884
Fax: (713) 961-5168
E-mail: info@welch1.org
Web Site: www.welch1.org

FOUNDED: 1954

AREAS OF INTEREST:
Basic research in chemistry.

NAME(S) OF PROGRAMS:
- **Departmental Grants**
- **Research Grants**
- **Welch Summer Scholar Program**

TYPE:
Research grants. Grants to support long-range fundamental research in the broad domain of chemistry.

The Welch Foundation supports chemical research at educational institutions within the state of Texas.

LEGAL BASIS:
Corporate.

ELIGIBILITY:
Full-time regular faculty members at Texas colleges or universities, who are tenured or on the tenured track, are eligible to apply for research grants.

GEOG. RESTRICTIONS: Texas.

FINANCIAL DATA:
Amount of support per award: Minimum $60,000 per year.

Total amount of support: Varies.

NO. AWARDS: Varies.

APPLICATION INFO:
Application information is available on the web site.

Duration: Two years. Renewable.

Deadline: February 1.

IRS I.D.: 76-0343128

Earth sciences

AMERICAN ASSOCIATION OF PETROLEUM GEOLOGISTS FOUNDATION [2006]

1444 South Boulder
Tulsa, OK 74119
(855) 302-2743
Fax: (918) 560-2642
E-mail: foundation@aapg.org
Web Site: foundation.aapg.org

FOUNDED: 1917

AREAS OF INTEREST:
The science of geology, especially as it relates to the search and development of hydrocarbons and economic sedimentary minerals and/or to environmental geology as it pertains to the petroleum industry.

NAME(S) OF PROGRAMS:
- **AAPG Foundation Grants-in-Aid**

TYPE:
Grants-in-aid; Research grants.

YEAR PROGRAM STARTED: 1956

PURPOSE:
To foster research in the geosciences by providing support to graduate students in the earth sciences whose research has application to the search for and development of petroleum and energy mineral resources, and to related environmental geology issues.

LEGAL BASIS:
Special-interest foundation.

ELIGIBILITY:
Graduate students in the geological sciences are eligible to apply. Factors weighed in selection of successful applicants include qualifications of the applicant as indicated by past performance, originality and imagination of the proposed project, support of the department in which the work is being done and perceived significance of the project to science and industry. The program focuses on support of qualified Master's candidates. Qualified doctoral candidates with expenses outside the usual scope of funding by other agencies are also encouraged to apply.

Grants are based on merit and, in part, on the financial needs of the applicant.

Applicants are eligible to receive awards twice as long as they remain qualified graduate students.

FINANCIAL DATA:
Grants are to be applied to selected expenses of graduate study such as a summer of field work, etc. Funds may not be used for tuition, room and board, capital expenses, to pay salaries or attend conferences.

Amount of support per award: Grants not to exceed $3,000.

Total amount of support: $207,750 for the year 2014-15.

NO. MOST RECENT APPLICANTS: Over 375 for the year 2014-15.

NO. AWARDS: Approximately 91 for the year 2014-15.

APPLICATION INFO:
Applications must be submitted electronically. A completed application includes:
(1) applicant name and contact information;
(2) academic and employment history;
(3) a project summary;
(4) description of the research project (limited to 300 words);
(5) project budget and funding request;
(6) disclose if applicant has been a previous recipient of an AAPG Foundation grant;
(7) name and e-mail address for two separate references qualified to endorse the applicant and project and;
(8) official academic transcripts from the last two years (or equivalent).

Duration: One year.

Deadline: January 31. Announcement in early April.

PUBLICATIONS:
Explorer, magazine; annual report; application guidelines.

IRS I.D.: 73-1298684

OFFICER:
David Curtiss, Executive Director
David Lange, Deputy Executive Director

ADDRESS INQUIRIES TO:
Tamra Campbell, Program Coordinator
(See address above.)

*PLEASE NOTE:
This program is intended for support of individuals only in earth sciences related to the petroleum industry.

THE AMERICAN GEOSCIENCES INSTITUTE (AGI) [2007]

4220 King Street
Alexandria, VA 22302-1502
(703) 379-2480 ext. 227
Fax: (703) 379-7563
E-mail: wallacescholarship@agiweb.org
Web Site: www.agiweb.org/scholarships/wallace

FOUNDED: 1948

AREAS OF INTEREST:
Major study in the fields of geology, geophysics, geochemistry, hydrology, meteorology, physical oceanography, planetary geology and earth-science education.

NAME(S) OF PROGRAMS:
- **Harriet Evelyn Wallace Scholarship**

TYPE:
Scholarships. The Harriet Evelyn Wallace Scholarship is available for female students pursuing a Master's or Doctorate degree at an accredited institution of higher education in a recognized geoscience program.

YEAR PROGRAM STARTED: 2013

PURPOSE:
To increase the participation of female students in the geosciences by providing financial support.

LEGAL BASIS:
Nonprofit, tax-exempt scientific federation.

ELIGIBILITY:
The successful applicant will be a thesis-based, full-time student and must be a U.S. citizen or permanent resident. Applicants will be evaluated on their probability of successfully completing a geoscience graduate program and transitioning into the geoscience profession following graduation. The successful applicant will have an undergraduate grade point average of 3.25 or higher and a graduate grade point average of 3.0 or higher. In addition, all applicants must be active members of at least one of AGI's professional member societies.

GEOG. RESTRICTIONS: United States.

FINANCIAL DATA:
Amount of support per award: $5,000 per year.

CO-OP FUNDING PROGRAMS: Funding for the Wallace Scholarship is from a bequest by Harriet Evelyn Wallace, a founding member of the Geoscience Information Society of AGI.

NO. AWARDS: 2 per year.

APPLICATION INFO:
Applications may be submitted beginning October. Applicants must submit unofficial Graduate Record Examination scores, all postsecondary unofficial academic transcripts, unofficial graduate academic transcripts (if applicable), curriculum vitae or resume, and a 500-word abstract about their research interests. If the applicant is intending on pursuing graduate school, she will need to send proof of acceptance in the program before the award is funded.

Duration: Up to two years.

Deadline: January 4, 2016.

ADDRESS INQUIRIES TO:
Workforce Development, Education, Outreach and Scholarship Coordinator
The American Geosciences Institute (AGI)
(See address above.)

*PLEASE NOTE:
Only women pursuing a doctoral degree will be considered for the 2016-17 scholarship.

AMERICAN METEOROLOGICAL SOCIETY

45 Beacon Street
Boston, MA 02108-3693
(617) 226-3907
Fax: (617) 742-8718
E-mail: dfernandez@ametsoc.org
Web Site: www.ametsoc.org

TYPE:
Fellowships; Scholarships. AMS Freshman Undergraduate Scholarship Program awards funding to high school seniors entering their freshman year of undergraduate study in the fall.

AMS Graduate Fellowship in the History of Science is awarded to a student wishing to complete a dissertation on the history of the atmospheric and related oceanic or hydrologic sciences.

AMS Graduate Fellowships are designed to attract students entering their first year of graduate study in the fall who wish to pursue advanced degrees in the atmospheric and related oceanic and hydrologic sciences.

AMS Minority Scholarship awards funding to high school minority students who have been traditionally underrepresented in the sciences, especially Hispanic, Native American and Black/African American students.

AMS Named Scholarships are directed to students entering their final year of undergraduate study in the fall.

The Father James B. Macelwane Annual Awards in Meteorology are intended to stimulate interest in meteorology among college students through the submission of original student papers concerned with some phase of the atmospheric sciences. The student must be enrolled as an undergraduate at the time the paper was written.

See entry 2535 for full listing.

THE ASSOCIATION OF AMERICAN GEOGRAPHERS [2008]

1710 16th Street, N.W.
Washington, DC 20009
(202) 234-1450
Fax: (202) 234-2744
E-mail: grantsawards@aag.org
Web Site: www.aag.org

FOUNDED: 1904

NAME(S) OF PROGRAMS:
- **AAG-IGIF Graduate Research Awards**
- **AAG-IGIF Student Paper Awards**
- **AAG-IGIF Student Travel Grants**

TYPE:
Research grants; Travel grants. AAG International Geographic Information Fund offers three types of awards:

Graduate Research Awards support research in any area of spatial analysis or geographic information science or systems.

Student Paper Awards are given in recognition of outstanding papers in any area of spatial analysis or geographic information science or systems that were given at a national and international conference or specialized meeting sponsored by recognized professional organizations.

Student Travel Grant supports travel to national and international symposia or specialized meetings sponsored by recognized professional organizations.

PURPOSE:
To support college and university student career development in the academic areas of applied spatial data analysis or geographic information systems (GIS).

ELIGIBILITY:
Full-time students currently registered in undergraduate or graduate degree programs providing a degree or explicit specialization in some area of applied spatial data analysis or GIS study at a duly accredited and recognized college, university or other educational institution located within the U.S.

FINANCIAL DATA:
Amount of support per award: Graduate Research Award: Up to $500; Student Paper Award: Up to $200; Student Travel Grant: Approximately $500.

APPLICATION INFO:
Digital submissions are required for all applications.

For the Graduate Research Award, applicant must submit a proposal of no more than five pages which includes:
(1) an abstract of research intent;
(2) statement of problem and relevancy;
(3) context of proposed research in the literature;
(4) methodology/research design;
(5) anticipated results and significance of such results;
(6) schedule of research;
(7) budget and;
(8) a letter of recommendation from a faculty member.

For the Student Paper Award, applicant must submit:
(1) a copy of the full paper presented at the conference or event;
(2) a letter requesting consideration for the award and indicating the applicant's present status as a student and;
(3) in the case of papers already presented, evidence of the presentation of the paper or, in the case of papers yet to be presented, evidence of acceptance of the paper to the specific event selected by the applicant for presentation of the paper, clearly identifying the name and dates of the conference.

For the Student Travel Grant, applicants must submit:
(1) a letter of no more than three pages in length specifically addressing how the grant funds will be used, the career goals of the student and how these funds will assist in meeting those goals. This may be supplemented, if necessary, by no more than two pages of supporting illustrations;
(2) a letter from the student's faculty advisor including an endorsement from the chairperson of the applicable department or program;
(3) a brief curriculum vitae of the applicant and;
(4) a copy of the applicant's most recent transcript.

Deadline: December 31.

ADDRESS INQUIRIES TO:
See e-mail address above.

THE ASSOCIATION OF AMERICAN GEOGRAPHERS [2009]

1710 16th Street, N.W.
Washington, DC 20009
(202) 234-1450
Fax: (202) 234-2744
E-mail: grantsawards@aag.org
Web Site: www.aag.org

FOUNDED: 1904

NAME(S) OF PROGRAMS:

- **AAG Research Grant**

TYPE:
Research grants. Small grant to support research and fieldwork.

PURPOSE:
To support research and fieldwork proposals which offer the prospect of obtaining substantial subsequent support from private foundations or federal agencies and that address questions of major importance to the discipline.

ELIGIBILITY:
Must be an AAG member for at least two years at the time of application. Grants can be used only for direct expenses of research; salary and overhead costs are not allowed. The committee will not approve awards for Master's or doctoral dissertation research.

FINANCIAL DATA:
Amount of support per award: Up to $1,000.

APPLICATION INFO:
Digital submissions are required.

Deadline: December 31.

ADDRESS INQUIRIES TO:
See e-mail address above.

THE ASSOCIATION OF AMERICAN GEOGRAPHERS [2010]

1710 16th Street, N.W.
Washington, DC 20009
(202) 234-1450
Fax: (202) 234-2744
E-mail: grantsawards@aag.org
Web Site: www.aag.org

FOUNDED: 1904

NAME(S) OF PROGRAMS:

- **AAG Dissertation Research Grants**

TYPE:
Research grants.

PURPOSE:
To provide financial assistance to candidates preparing doctoral dissertations in geography.

ELIGIBILITY:
Must be an AAG member for at least one year at the time of application, must not have a Doctorate at the time of the award, and have completed all Ph.D. requirements except the dissertation by the end of the semester or term following approval of the award. Dissertation supervisor must certify eligibility. The Paul Vouras Fund gives preference to minority student applicants.

FINANCIAL DATA:
Amount of support per award: Up to $500.

APPLICATION INFO:
Digital submissions are required.

Deadline: December 31.

THE ASSOCIATION OF AMERICAN GEOGRAPHERS [2011]

1710 16th Street, N.W.
Washington, DC 20009
(202) 234-1450
Fax: (202) 234-2744
E-mail: grantsawards@aag.org
Web Site: www.aag.org

FOUNDED: 1904

NAME(S) OF PROGRAMS:

- **AAG Globe Book Award for Public Understanding of Geography**
- **AAG Meridian Book Award for the Outstanding Scholarly Work in Geography**

TYPE:
Awards/prizes. AAG Globe Book Award is awarded annually to a book that conveys most powerfully the nature and importance of geography to the nonacademic world.

AAG Meridian Book Award is awarded annually to a book that makes an unusually important contribution to advancing the science and art of geography.

PURPOSE:
To award outstanding geographic authors.

ELIGIBILITY:
Books must be written or co-authored by a geographer. Books published in the previous calendar year are eligible.

FINANCIAL DATA:
Amount of support per award: $1,000.

APPLICATION INFO:
Nomination statements (two-page maximum) should provide full contact information for the author(s) and the nominator(s), including e-mail addresses, and should document the ways the nominated work conveys the nature and importance of geography to the nonacademic world (Globe Book Award) or contributes to advancing the science and art of geography (Meridian Book Award). Nomination statements and four copies of each nominated book should be submitted.

Deadline: December 31.

ADDRESS INQUIRIES TO:
Attn: Globe Book Award or
Attn: Meridian Book Award
(See address and e-mail above.)

THE GEOLOGICAL SOCIETY OF AMERICA, INC. [2012]

P.O. Box 9140
Boulder, CO 80301-9140
(303) 357-1060
Fax: (303) 357-1070
E-mail: shollister@geosociety.org
awards@geosociety.org
Web Site: www.geosociety.org

FOUNDED: 1888

AREAS OF INTEREST:
Geoscience.

NAME(S) OF PROGRAMS:

- **GSA Research Grants**

TYPE:
Grants-in-aid; Project/program grants; Research grants. Grants for projects contributing to the science of geology.

YEAR PROGRAM STARTED: 1933

PURPOSE:
To provide partial support of Master's and doctoral thesis research in earth science for graduate students.

LEGAL BASIS:
Private membership association.

ELIGIBILITY:
Qualified investigators with appropriate interests are eligible to apply. Graduate students apply for support of Master's or doctoral thesis work. The GSA strongly encourages women, minorities and persons with disabilities to participate in this grants program.

Applicants must be members of GSA.

GEOG. RESTRICTIONS: North and Central America.

FINANCIAL DATA:
Funds are intended as an aid to the research project and not to sustain entire research costs.

Amount of support per award: Grants vary in amount, depending upon the needs and nature of the request.

NO. MOST RECENT APPLICANTS: 699.

NO. AWARDS: 359.

APPLICATION INFO:
Official application materials are available online.

Duration: One year.

Deadline: Applications must be submitted electronically by February 1 for consideration at the spring review meeting.

PUBLICATIONS:
Annual report; application guidelines.

OFFICERS:
Vicki McConnell, Executive Officer

ADDRESS INQUIRIES TO:
Program Manager
Grants, Awards and Recognition
(See address above.)

INTERNATIONAL WOMEN'S FISHING ASSOCIATION SCHOLARSHIP TRUST [2013]

P.O. Box 460387
Fort Lauderdale, FL 33346-0387
E-mail: scholarship@iwfa.org
Web Site: www.iwfa.org

FOUNDED: 1965

AREAS OF INTEREST:
Marine science.

NAME(S) OF PROGRAMS:

- **IWFA Scholarship Trust**

TYPE:
Scholarships. For postgraduate educational expense including tuition, supplies and books.

YEAR PROGRAM STARTED: 1965

PURPOSE:
To aid needy students who are seeking postgraduate degrees in marine science.

LEGAL BASIS:
501(c)(3) nonprofit organization.

ELIGIBILITY:
Applicant must be a graduate student in marine science. Student must be matriculated at a school in the U.S.

FINANCIAL DATA:
Amount of support per award:
Approximately $1,000 per award.

Total amount of support: $30,500 for the year 2015.

NO. MOST RECENT APPLICANTS: 28.

NO. AWARDS: 22.

APPLICATION INFO:
Application form may be downloaded from the Scholarship page on the web site above or obtained by sending written request to the Association.

Duration: One year.

Deadline: March 1.

ADDRESS INQUIRIES TO:
IWFA Scholarship Trustees
(See address above.)

*SPECIAL STIPULATIONS:
For graduate students in the Marine Science field only.

LUNAR AND PLANETARY INSTITUTE

3600 Bay Area Boulevard
Houston, TX 77058
(281) 486-2159
Fax: (281) 486-2127
E-mail: explorationintern@lpi.usra.edu
Web Site: www.lpi.usra.edu

TYPE:
Conferences/seminars; Internships; Scholarships; Travel grants.

See entry 1987 for full listing.

THE MINERALOGICAL SOCIETY OF AMERICA [2014]

3635 Concorde Parkway, Suite 500
Chantilly, VA 20151-1110
(703) 652-9950
Fax: (703) 652-9951
E-mail: business@minsocam.org
Web Site: www.minsocam.org

FOUNDED: 1919

AREAS OF INTEREST:
Crystallography, mineralogy and petrology.

NAME(S) OF PROGRAMS:
- **Research Grant in Crystallography, Mineral Physics or Chemistry and Mineralogy**
- **Student Research Grant in Mineralogy and Petrology**

TYPE:
Research grants. Grants supported through endowment funds.

YEAR PROGRAM STARTED: 1973

PURPOSE:
To encourage research in mineralogy, crystallography, geochemistry, and petrology.

LEGAL BASIS:
501(c)(3) organization and Virginia corporation.

ELIGIBILITY:
For the crystallography grant, applicant must have reached his or her 25th birthday, but not yet have reached his or her 36th birthday, in the year the grant proposal is submitted, and must be an MSA Counselor. The mineralogy/petrology grant is limited to students.

FINANCIAL DATA:
The grant is for research-related expenses only. Travel to meetings, conferences, short courses, nonresearch field trips, tuition, nonresearch living (room and board) expenses, etc., are not suitable uses of the money. Neither should the money be used for salary or wages for the researcher.

Amount of support per award: $5,000.

Total amount of support: $15,000.

NO. MOST RECENT APPLICANTS: 56.

NO. AWARDS: 3.

APPLICATION INFO:
Proposal submissions are to be made online.

Duration: One year.

Deadline: June 1.

IRS I.D.: 52-6044250

ADDRESS INQUIRIES TO:
Dr. J. Alex Speer, Executive Director
(See address above.)

NATIONAL ASSOCIATION OF GEOSCIENCE TEACHERS [2015]

c/o Science Education Resource Center
200 Division Street, Suite 210
Northfield, MN 55057
(507) 222-4545
Fax: (507) 222-5175
E-mail: cmanduca@carleton.edu
Web Site: www.nagt.org

FOUNDED: 1938

AREAS OF INTEREST:
Earth sciences.

NAME(S) OF PROGRAMS:
- **Scholarships for Field Study**
- **Dottie Stout Professional Development Grants**

TYPE:
Development grants; Scholarships. Scholarships for Field Study: Cash award to undergraduate students to facilitate their study of field geoscience.

Dottie Stout Professional Development Grants will be awarded in support of the following activities:
(1) participation in earth science classes or workshops;
(2) attendance at professional scientific or science education meetings;
(3) participation in earth science field trips and;
(4) purchase of earth science materials for classroom use.

YEAR PROGRAM STARTED: 1970

PURPOSE:
To further geological education at the undergraduate level.

LEGAL BASIS:
Tax-exempt corporation.

ELIGIBILITY:
Scholarships for Field Study: Applicants must be full-time students with a geology major. The chief criterion for selection is advanced students with distinguished academic records within the major.

Dottie Stout Professional Development Grants: Community college faculty and K-12th grade teachers who teach one or more earth science courses and community college students actively pursuing a career in the earth sciences are encouraged to apply for these awards.

FINANCIAL DATA:
Amount of support per award: Scholarships for Field Study: $750; Dottie Stout Professional Development Grants: $750 each to a community college faculty member, a community college student and a K-12th grade educator.

Total amount of support: Varies.

NO. MOST RECENT APPLICANTS: Scholarships for Field Study: 80; Dottie Stout Professional Development Grants: 10.

NO. AWARDS: Scholarships for Field Study: 18; Dottie Stout Professional Development Grants: 3.

APPLICATION INFO:
Application information is available at the web site.

Deadline: Scholarships for Field Study: February 14; Dottie Stout Professional Development Grants: April 15.

PUBLICATIONS:
Journal of Geoscience Education; *In The Trenches*, magazine.

IRS I.D.: 74-6068050

OFFICERS:
Randy Richardson, President
Cathy Manduca, Executive Director

NATIONAL CENTER FOR ATMOSPHERIC RESEARCH

1850 Table Mesa Drive
Boulder, CO 80305
(303) 497-1328
Fax: (303) 497-1646
E-mail: paulad@ucar.edu
Web Site: www.asp.ucar.edu

TYPE:
Fellowships. The fellowships cover a year's appointment, with a likely extension to two years, at NCAR to take advantage of its educational programs and/or research facilities in the broad field of atmospheric sciences.

See entry 1777 for full listing.

NATIONAL GEOGRAPHIC SOCIETY [2016]

Committee for Research and Exploration
1145 17th Street, N.W.
Washington, DC 20036
(202) 857-7000
Fax: (202) 429-5729
E-mail: cre@ngs.org
Web Site: www.nationalgeographic.com/field/grants-programs

FOUNDED: 1888

AREAS OF INTEREST:
Sciences pertinent to geography, including anthropology, archeology, astronomy, biology, botany, geography, geology, oceanography, paleontology and zoology.

NAME(S) OF PROGRAMS:
- **National Geographic Society Committee for Research and Exploration**

TYPE:
Grants-in-aid; Research grants; Seed money grants. Grants-in-aid for basic research in the sciences pertinent to geography (including, but not limited to, projects in geography). Support may also be provided for projects in these fields that depend on exploration. The Society is currently emphasizing multidisciplinary projects that address environmental issues.

YEAR PROGRAM STARTED: 1890

PURPOSE:
To support scientific field research and exploration through its Committee for Research and Exploration.

LEGAL BASIS:
Nonprofit.

ELIGIBILITY:
Applicants are expected to have advanced degrees (Ph.D. or equivalent) and be associated with an educational organization or institution. Independent researchers or those pursuing a Ph.D.-level degree may apply, but competition is keen and awards to non-Ph.D. applicants are rare. As a general rule, all applicants are expected to have published a minimum of three articles in peer-reviewed scientific journals. Individuals between the ages of 18 and 25 are invited to apply to the Young Explorers Program. These applicants are not expected to have advanced degrees but should have a record of prior experience as it pertains to their proposed project. Citizens of any country are eligible.

Grants normally are made only for field research. Laboratory work is supported only to the extent that it may be a necessary follow-up to Society-funded field research.

Grants are awarded on the basis of the project's scientific merit. All proposed projects must have both a geographical dimension and relevance to other scientific fields and be of broad scientific interest. The Committee pays special attention to the significance of the research proposal in terms of its relationship to major scientific questions or problems. The Committee's priorities favor research that relates to environmental concerns and has relevance to global geographic issues.

FINANCIAL DATA:
Society funds may be used for transportation, supplies, and daily subsistence. Capital equipment (generally defined as any item costing more than U.S. $500) must be individually justified. Laboratory expenses are acceptable, provided the laboratory work is a logical extension of the field research.

Amount of support per award: $15,000 to $20,000 per year.

Total amount of support: $3,000,000 budgeted for research program annually.

Matching fund requirements: National Geographic Society funds are intended to function as complementary support. The committee strongly encourages applicants to seek additional, concurrent funding from other agencies.

NO. MOST RECENT APPLICANTS: 976.

NO. AWARDS: Approximately 250 per year.

APPLICATION INFO:
Prior to applying for a grant, each potential investigator must submit a preapplication, available on the web site, with a 500-word maximum length outlining the significance of the research and describing who will conduct the research and where it will occur. Also, a fieldwork schedule should be projected. Anticipated budgetary expenses must be itemized and, if necessary, justified. A curriculum vitae for each principal investigator, along with a list of his or her scholarly publications, should also be included.

A link to the full application will be e-mailed to those individuals whose project(s) are deemed appropriate for further formal review. Previous Society research grant recipients must comply with all grant obligations from past awards and must be up-to-date with any outstanding reports and/or financial accounting requirements before submitting applications for additional support.

Duration: One year.

Deadline: Applications may be submitted at any time.

PUBLICATIONS:
Program description; National Geographic Index 1888-1988.

*PLEASE NOTE:
Applicants are encouraged to confirm program online for recent changes.

NATIONAL OCEANIC AND ATMOSPHERIC ADMINISTRATION [2017]

1315 East West Highway, 12th Floor
Silver Spring, MD 20910-5603
(301) 734-1206
Fax: (301) 713-0517
E-mail: cpogrants@noaa.gov
diane.brown@noaa.gov
Web Site: www.cpo.noaa.gov

FOUNDED: 1966

AREAS OF INTEREST:
Climate and atmospheric research.

NAME(S) OF PROGRAMS:
- **Climate Program**

TYPE:
Challenge/matching grants; Conferences/seminars; Formula grants. Grant activities are organized within four programs:
(1) Climate Observation Division designs, deploys, and maintains an integrated global in situ network of oceanic and atmospheric observing instruments to produce continuous records and analyses of a range of ocean and atmosphere parameters. Climate Observation coordinates observing efforts across NOAA, collaborates with federal agencies, and has strong international partnerships.
(2) Earth System Science (ESS) Program aims to provide process-level understanding of the climate system through observation, modeling, research analysis and field studies to support the development of improved climate models and predictions in support of NOAA's mission. ESS-sponsored research is carried out at NOAA and other federal laboratories, NOAA Cooperative Institutes, and academic institutions and is coordinated with major national and international scientific bodies including the World Climate Research Programme, the International Geosphere-Biosphere Programme, and the U.S. Global Change Research Program.
(3) Modeling, Analysis, Predictions, and Projections (MAPP) Program aims to enhance the Nation's capability to predict variability and changes in Earth's climate system. The MAPP Program focuses on the coupling, integration, and application of Earth system models and analyses across NOAA, among partner agencies, and with the external research community. The MAPP Program includes targeted infrastructure support, competitive grants programs, and mechanisms to support transferring research findings into NOAA's operations.
(4) Climate and Societal Interactions (CSI) Program provides leadership and support for research, assessments and climate services development activities designed to bring sound, interdisciplinary science to bear on climate-sensitive resource management and adaptation challenges in key sectors and regions.

PURPOSE:
To develop the knowledge required to establish a predictive capability for short- and long-term climate fluctuations and trends.

LEGAL BASIS:
Government agency.

ELIGIBILITY:
Applicants may be institutions of higher education, other nonprofits, commercial organizations, international organizations, state, local and Indian tribal governments. Federal agencies or institutions are ineligible.

FINANCIAL DATA:
Grants may be used for research and development, advisory services and operational systems as they relate to specific programs.

Amount of support per award: Up to $200,000.

Total amount of support: Approximately $15,500,000 for the year 2015.

NO. AWARDS: Approximately 100 new awards for the year 2015.

APPLICATION INFO:
Applications are to be submitted through grants.gov.

Duration: One to three years.

Deadline: Varies.

ADDRESS INQUIRIES TO:
Diane Brown
Grants Administration Team Leader
Climate Program Office
(See address above.)

NATIONAL OCEANIC AND ATMOSPHERIC ADMINISTRATION [2018]

National Marine Fisheries Service
263 13th Avenue South
St. Petersburg, FL 33701
(727) 824-5324
Fax: (727) 824-5364
E-mail: dax.ruiz@noaa.gov
robert.sadler@noaa.gov
kelly.donnelly@noaa.gov
Web Site: sero.nmfs.noaa.gov

AREAS OF INTEREST:
Southeast region.

NAME(S) OF PROGRAMS:
- **Cooperative Research Program Grants**
- **Marine Fisheries Initiative Grants**

TYPE:
Development grants; Research grants.

YEAR PROGRAM STARTED: 2003

PURPOSE:
To support research and development.

ELIGIBILITY:
Cooperative Research Program Grants: Applicants who are not commercial or recreational fishermen must have commercial or recreational fishermen participating in their project. There must be a written agreement with a fisherman describing the involvement in the project activity. Eligible applicants include institutions of higher education, other nonprofits, commercial organizations, state, local and Indian tribal governments and individuals. Federal agencies or institutions are not eligible. Foreign governments, organizations under the jurisdiction of foreign

governments, and international organizations are excluded for purposes of this solicitation since the objective of the CRP is to optimize research and development benefits from U.S. marine fishery resources.

Marine Fisheries Initiative Grants are available to institutions of higher education, other nonprofits, commercial organizations, state, local and Indian tribal governments. Federal agencies or institutions are not eligible. Foreign governments, organizations under the jurisdiction of foreign governments, and international organizations are excluded for purposes of this solicitation since the objective of the MARFIN program is to optimize research and development benefits from U.S. marine fishery resources.

FINANCIAL DATA:
Amount of support per award: $25,000 to $175,000.

Total amount of support: $2,800,000 for the year 2016.

Matching fund requirements: Cost sharing is not required.

NO. AWARDS: 8 to 10.

APPLICATION INFO:
Applications are available on grants.gov. New applicants should contact the National Marine Fisheries Service Office.

Duration: Cooperative Research Program Grants: One year; Marine Fisheries Initiative Grants: One to three years.

Deadline: Announced in NOAA solicitation and grant opportunities index.

PUBLICATIONS:
Annual report.

ADDRESS INQUIRIES TO:
Cooperative Research Program Grants:
Dax Ruiz, Federal Grants Program Officer

Marine Fisheries Initiative Grants:
Robert Sadler or Kelly Donnelly
Federal Grants Program Officers
(See address above.)

NATIONAL OCEANIC AND ATMOSPHERIC ADMINISTRATION [2019]

Ocean Exploration and Research Program
SSMC3, R/OER, Room 10210
1315 East-West Highway
Silver Spring, MD 20910
(301) 734-1014
(301) 734-1023
Fax: (301) 713-1967
E-mail: john.mcdonough@noaa.gov
oceanexplorer@noaa.gov
Web Site: oceanexplorer.noaa.gov
explore.noaa.gov

AREAS OF INTEREST:
Marine research.

NAME(S) OF PROGRAMS:
- **Ocean Exploration and Research Program**

TYPE:
Project/program grants; Research grants.

ELIGIBILITY:
Eligible applicants are U.S. institutions of higher education, not-for-profit institutions, and federal, state, and local governments. Federal agencies may not charge salary or overhead.

GEOG. RESTRICTIONS: United States.

FINANCIAL DATA:
Amount of support per award: $50,000 to $1,500,000 projected for fiscal year 2016.

Total amount of support: Approximately $3,000,000 projected for fiscal year 2016.

NO. AWARDS: 3 to 10 projected for fiscal year 2016.

APPLICATION INFO:
Each National Undersea Research Center has its own proposal forms and guidelines. Specific locations and instructions are available online.

Duration: One year.

Deadline: Varies by center.

ADDRESS INQUIRIES TO:
John McDonough, Deputy Director
(See address above.)

NATIONAL OCEANIC AND ATMOSPHERIC ADMINISTRATION [2020]

Center for Satellite Applications and Research
National Environmental Satellite Data
and Information Services
5830 University Research Court E/RA1, Suite 2600, Room 2623
College Park, MD 20740
(301) 683-3512
E-mail: erica.rosier@noaa.gov
Web Site: www.nesdis.noaa.gov

AREAS OF INTEREST:
Environmental sciences, application, data and education.

NAME(S) OF PROGRAMS:
- **Research in Remote Sensing of the Earth and Environment Grants**

TYPE:
Research grants.

PURPOSE:
To advance and promote applied research and technology development in satellite remote sensing of the earth and the atmosphere in support of national operational needs.

ELIGIBILITY:
Applicant must be any state university, college, institute or laboratory, public or private nonprofit, tax-exempt institution or consortium. No grants to individuals.

GEOG. RESTRICTIONS: United States.

FINANCIAL DATA:
Amount of support per award: $25,000 to $300,000.

Total amount of support: Varies.

Matching fund requirements: Varies.

APPLICATION INFO:
Applications are available on grants.gov.

Duration: One to three years. Renewals possible.

Deadline: Posted online or published in *Federal Register*.

ADDRESS INQUIRIES TO:
Erica Rosier, Administrator
(See address above.)

NATIONAL SCIENCE FOUNDATION [2021]

Division of Earth Sciences, Room 785
4201 Wilson Boulevard
Arlington, VA 22230
(703) 292-8550
Fax: (703) 292-9025
Web Site: www.nsf.gov

FOUNDED: 1950

AREAS OF INTEREST:
Earth sciences.

TYPE:
Research grants. The Division of Earth Sciences supports proposals for research geared toward improving the understanding of the structure, composition, and evolution of the Earth and the processes that govern the formation and behavior of the Earth's materials.

YEAR PROGRAM STARTED: 1950

PURPOSE:
To create a better understanding of the Earth's changing environments and the natural distribution of its mineral, water and energy resources; to provide methods for predicting and mitigating the effects of geologic hazards such as earthquakes, volcanic eruptions, floods and landslides.

LEGAL BASIS:
Federal agency.

ELIGIBILITY:
Scientists and engineers, especially college and university faculty members, are eligible to apply.

GEOG. RESTRICTIONS: United States and its territories.

FINANCIAL DATA:
Amount of support per award: Varies.

Total amount of support: Varies.

NO. MOST RECENT APPLICANTS: 1,600.

NO. AWARDS: 500.

APPLICATION INFO:
Application information is available on the web site.

Duration: One to five years.

PUBLICATIONS:
Grant proposal guide (NSF 04-23).

NATIONAL SCIENCE FOUNDATION [2022]

Division of Ocean Sciences, Room 725 N
4201 Wilson Boulevard
Arlington, VA 22230
(703) 292-8580
Fax: (703) 292-9085
E-mail: rwmurray@nsf.gov
Web Site: www.nsf.gov

FOUNDED: 1950

NAME(S) OF PROGRAMS:
- **Ocean Section**

TYPE:
Research grants. Support for fundamental research in marine science, including physical oceanography and limnology, chemical oceanography, biological oceanography and marine geology, geophysics and ocean technology, with the objective of increasing knowledge and enhancing our understanding of the marine environment.

Most of the research supported is basic in character, although some applied research is also supported. This program also supports research workshops, symposia and conferences and purchases of scientific equipment related to projects supported.

YEAR PROGRAM STARTED: 1980

PURPOSE:
To improve understanding of the nature of the ocean and its influence on human activities and of human impacts on the marine environment.

LEGAL BASIS:
Government agency.

ELIGIBILITY:
Program is primarily for support of scientists in basic research in ocean sciences and instrumentation and the facilities to support it.

FINANCIAL DATA:
Amount of support per award: Varies.

Total amount of support: Varies.

APPLICATION INFO:
Application information is available at the web site.

Duration: Varies.

Deadline: Proposals may be submitted at any time. Approximately six months are required for review and processing. Target dates are February 15 and August 15.

OFFICERS:
Richard W. Murray, Division Director
David L. Garrison, Program Director, Biological Oceanography
Eric Itsweire, Program Director, Physical Oceanography

ADDRESS INQUIRIES TO:
Richard W. Murray, Division Director
(See address above.)

NATIONAL SOCIETY OF PROFESSIONAL SURVEYORS (NSPS)

5119 Pegasus Court
Suite Q
Frederick, MD 21704
(240) 439-4615 ext. 105
Fax: (240) 439-4952
E-mail: trisha.milburn@nsps.us.com
Web Site: www.nsps.us.com

TYPE:
Scholarships. Berntsen International Scholarship in Surveying: Annual scholarship award for undergraduate study in four-year degree programs in surveying or in closely related degree programs such as geomatics or surveying engineering.

Berntsen International Scholarship in Surveying Technology: For students enrolled in two-year degree programs in surveying technology. Scholarship awarded in even years only.

See entry 2571 for full listing.

NATIONAL SOCIETY OF PROFESSIONAL SURVEYORS (NSPS)

5119 Pegasus Court
Suite Q
Frederick, MD 21704
(240) 439-4615 ext. 105
Fax: (240) 439-4952
E-mail: trisha.milburn@nsps.us.com
Web Site: www.nsps.us.com

TYPE:
Scholarships. For students enrolled in four-year degree programs in surveying or in closely related degree programs such as geomatics or surveying engineering.

See entry 2570 for full listing.

NATIONAL SOCIETY OF PROFESSIONAL SURVEYORS (NSPS)

5119 Pegasus Court
Suite Q
Frederick, MD 21704
(240) 439-4615 ext. 105
Fax: (240) 439-4952
E-mail: trisha.milburn@nsps.us.com
Web Site: www.nsps.us.com

TYPE:
Scholarships.

See entry 2572 for full listing.

NATIONAL SOCIETY OF PROFESSIONAL SURVEYORS (NSPS) AMERICAN ASSOCIATION FOR GEODETIC SURVEYING (AAGS)

5119 Pegasus Court
Suite Q
Frederick, MD 21704
(240) 439-4615 ext. 105
Fax: (240) 439-4952
E-mail: trisha.milburn@nsps.us.com
Web Site: www.aagsmo.org
www.nsps.us.com

TYPE:
Fellowships. Annual fellowship award to support graduate study in a program with a significant focus on geodetic surveying or geodesy at a school of the recipient's choice.

See entry 2573 for full listing.

NATIONAL SOCIETY OF PROFESSIONAL SURVEYORS (NSPS) AMERICAN ASSOCIATION FOR GEODETIC SURVEYING (AAGS)

5119 Pegasus Court
Suite Q
Frederick, MD 21704
(240) 439-4615 ext. 105
Fax: (240) 439-4952
E-mail: trisha.milburn@nsps.us.com
Web Site: www.aagsmo.org
www.nsps.us.com

TYPE:
Scholarships. The award is intended for students enrolled in four-year degree programs in surveying or in closely related degree programs.

See entry 2574 for full listing.

V. KANN RASMUSSEN FOUNDATION [2023]

475 Riverside Drive, Suite 900
New York, NY 10115
(212) 812-4268
Fax: (212) 812-4299
E-mail: ikrarup@vkrf.org
Web Site: www.vkrf.org

FOUNDED: 1991

AREAS OF INTEREST:
Climate change, unsustainable consumption, and loss of biodiversity.

TYPE:
Challenge/matching grants; Project/program grants.

PURPOSE:
To support the transition to a more environmentally resilient, stable and sustainable planet.

LEGAL BASIS:
Private foundation.

ELIGIBILITY:
Eligible organizations must be IRS 501(c)(3) tax-exempt.

GEOG. RESTRICTIONS: United States.

FINANCIAL DATA:
Amount of support per award: Varies.

Total amount of support: Approximately $5,000,000 for the year ended June 30, 2016.

APPLICATION INFO:
Application procedures can be found on the Foundation web site.

Duration: One to two years.

Deadline: Varies.

IRS I.D.: 22-3101266

STAFF:
Irene Krarup, Executive Director and Head of Programs

ADDRESS INQUIRIES TO:
Irene Krarup, Executive Director and Head of Programs
(See address above.)

THE PERCY SLADEN MEMORIAL FUND

c/o The Linnean Society of London
Burlington House, Piccadilly
London W1J 0BF England
(44) 020 7434 4479
Fax: (44) 020 7287 9364
E-mail: info@linnean.org
gina@linnean.org
Web Site: www.linnean.org

TYPE:
Awards/prizes; Project/program grants; Research grants; Travel grants. Field work grants in life and earth sciences (excludes any projects which are part of further education, e.g., a Doctorate or a Master's course).

See entry 2045 for full listing.

SOCIETY OF EXPLORATION GEOPHYSICISTS [2024]

8801 South Yale Avenue
Suite 500
Tulsa, OK 74137
(918) 497-5549
Fax: (918) 497-5560
E-mail: scholarships@seg.org
Web Site: www.seg.org/foundation
www.seg.org/scholarships

FOUNDED: 1956

AREAS OF INTEREST:
Applied geophysics.

NAME(S) OF PROGRAMS:

- **SEG Scholarship Program**

TYPE:
Scholarships. Undergraduate and graduate scholarships for the study of geophysics.

YEAR PROGRAM STARTED: 1956

PURPOSE:
To assist young people in pursuing careers in the field of applied geophysics.

LEGAL BASIS:
Nonprofit society.

ELIGIBILITY:
Applicant must intend to pursue a college course directed toward a career in applied geophysics and must have an interest in and aptitude for physics, mathematics, and geology. Applicant must be:
(1) a high school student with above-average grades planning to enter college the next fall term;
(2) an undergraduate college student whose grades are above average or;
(3) a graduate college student whose studies are directed toward a career in applied geophysics in operations, teaching or research.

FINANCIAL DATA:
Amount of support per award: $500 to $10,000 per academic year, averaging $3,500 per academic year.

Total amount of support: $680,210 for the academic year 2015.

NO. AWARDS: 140 for the academic year 2015.

APPLICATION INFO:
Application must be submitted electronically. Transcripts and letters of recommendation may be submitted online or sent via regular mail. Results of aptitude tests are not required but should be included if taken.

Duration: One year. Renewable at the discretion of the SEG Scholarship Committee, subject to student's maintenance of satisfactory grades, funds available and continued study leading to a career in geophysics.

Deadline: March 1.

ADDRESS INQUIRIES TO:
Scholarship Administrator
(See address above.)

*SPECIAL STIPULATIONS:
Certain scholarships carry additional qualifications specified by the scholarships' donors.

THE UNIVERSITY OF CALGARY [2025]

Faculty of Graduate Studies
MacKimmie Library Tower, Room 213
2500 University Drive, N.W.
Calgary AB T2N 1N4 Canada
(403) 220-4938
Fax: (403) 289-7635
E-mail: gsaward@ucalgary.ca
Web Site: www.grad.ucalgary.ca/awards

NAME(S) OF PROGRAMS:
- **Harry and Laura Jacques Graduate Scholarship**

TYPE:
Scholarships.

ELIGIBILITY:
Open to candidates who at the time of tenure will be registered full-time in a thesis-based graduate program at the University of Calgary.

FINANCIAL DATA:
Amount of support per award: $3,700.

Total amount of support: $3,700.

NO. AWARDS: 1.

APPLICATION INFO:
Students should consult the Graduate Award Competition Guidelines and Application available at the web site.

Duration: One year.

Deadline: February 1 to the candidate's graduate program office, unless the program has an earlier deadline.

ADDRESS INQUIRIES TO:
Graduate Scholarship Office
(See address above.)

Mathematics

THE ACTUARIAL FOUNDATION [2026]

475 North Martingale Road
Suite 600
Schaumburg, IL 60173-2226
(847) 706-3535
Fax: (847) 706-3599
E-mail: Scholarships@ActFnd.org
Web Site: www.actuarialfoundation.org

FOUNDED: 1994

AREAS OF INTEREST:
Actuarial science, a branch of mathematics based on calculus, probability and statistics, as well as business economics.

NAME(S) OF PROGRAMS:
- **Actuarial Diversity Scholarship**

TYPE:
Scholarships. The Actuarial Diversity Scholarship was formed in 1977 as a joint effort of the Casualty Actuarial Society and the Society of Actuaries. In 2008, the scholarship was transferred to The Actuarial Foundation.

The scholarship promotes diversity in the profession through an annual scholarship program for Black/African American, Hispanic, Native North American and Pacific Islander students. The scholarship award recognizes and encourages academic achievements by awarding scholarships to full-time undergraduate students pursuing a degree that may lead to a career in the actuarial profession.

LEGAL BASIS:
Private- and corporate-funded.

ELIGIBILITY:
Each applicant must fulfill all of the following requirements:
(1) must have at least one birth parent who is a member of one of the following minority groups: Black/African American, Hispanic, Native North American, or Pacific Islander;
(2) enrolled as a full-time undergraduate student at a U.S.-accredited educational institution during the application academic year;
(3) minimum grade point average of 3.0 (on a 4.0 scale), emphasis on math or actuarial courses;
(4) entering college freshmen must have a minimum ACT math score of 28 or SAT math score of 600 and;
(5) intent on pursuing a career in the actuarial profession.

GEOG. RESTRICTIONS: United States.

FINANCIAL DATA:
Amount of support per award: $1,000 for freshmen, $2,000 for sophomores, $3,000 for juniors, and $4,000 for seniors.

Total amount of support: $105,000 for the year 2015.

NO. MOST RECENT APPLICANTS: 54 for the year 2015.

NO. AWARDS: 39 for the year 2015.

APPLICATION INFO:
Applications are posted in early January. Application and guidelines are available online.

Duration: One academic year. Renewable based on academic performance.

Deadline: May.

IRS I.D.: 36-2136422

ADDRESS INQUIRIES TO:
Scholarship Coordinator
(See address above.)

*PLEASE NOTE:
Applicants must intend to pursue a career in the actuarial profession.

THE ACTUARIAL FOUNDATION [2027]

475 North Martingale Road
Suite 600
Schaumburg, IL 60173-2226
(847) 706-3535
Fax: (847) 706-3599
E-mail: Scholarships@ActFnd.org
Web Site: www.actuarialfoundation.org

FOUNDED: 1994

AREAS OF INTEREST:
Actuarial science.

NAME(S) OF PROGRAMS:
- **Actuary of Tomorrow - Stuart A. Robertson Memorial Scholarship**

TYPE:
Scholarships.

YEAR PROGRAM STARTED: 2006

PURPOSE:
To recognize and encourage the academic achievements of undergraduate students pursuing a career in actuarial science.

ELIGIBILITY:
Applicant must:
(1) be a full-time undergraduate student entering as a sophomore, junior or senior in the fall term;
(2) have a minimum cumulative grade point average of 3.0 (on a 4.0 scale);
(3) have successfully completed two actuarial exams;
(4) attach a current unofficial copy of transcripts from attending college/university;
(5) provide a letter of recommendation supporting academic achievement, leadership and communication skills from professor or advisor;
(6) provide a letter of recommendation from an employer or previous employer and;
(7) submit a personal essay of approximately 500 words, focusing on why you want to be an actuary.

GEOG. RESTRICTIONS: United States.

FINANCIAL DATA:
Amount of support per award: $9,000.

NO. MOST RECENT APPLICANTS: 33 for the year 2015.

NO. AWARDS: 2 for the year 2015.

APPLICATION INFO:
Application is available online. Applicant should meet the eligibility requirements.

Deadline: June 1. Notification by mail after August 1.

ADDRESS INQUIRIES TO:
Scholarship Coordinator
(See address and e-mail above.)

*SPECIAL STIPULATIONS:
Scholarships are awarded directly to the college/university of choice in the recipients' name.

AMERICAN MATHEMATICAL SOCIETY [2028]

201 Charles Street
Providence, RI 02904-2294
(800) 321-4267 ext. 4130
(401) 455-4101
Fax: (401) 455-4004
E-mail: prof-serv@ams.org
Web Site: www.ams.org

FOUNDED: 1888

AREAS OF INTEREST:
Research mathematics.

NAME(S) OF PROGRAMS:

- **American Mathematical Society Centennial Fellowship**

TYPE:
Fellowships. The AMS Centennial Research Fellowship Program makes awards annually to outstanding mathematicians to help further their careers in research.

YEAR PROGRAM STARTED: 1974

PURPOSE:
To help outstanding mathematicians further their careers in research.

LEGAL BASIS:
Nonprofit corporation.

ELIGIBILITY:
The primary selection criterion for the Centennial Fellowship is the excellence of the candidate's research. Preference will be given to candidates who have not had extensive fellowship support in the past. Recipients may not hold the Centennial Fellowship concurrently with another research fellowship such as a Sloan Fellowship, NSF Postdoctoral Fellowship, or Career Award. Under normal circumstances, the fellowship cannot be deferred. A recipient of the fellowship shall have held his or her doctoral degree for at least three years and not more than 12 years at the inception of the award. Applications will be accepted from those currently holding a tenured, tenure-track, postdoctoral, or comparable (at the discretion of the selection committee) position at an institution in North America.

GEOG. RESTRICTIONS: North America.

FINANCIAL DATA:
Amount of support per award: Approximately $89,000, plus about $8,900 for expenses for the academic year 2016-17.

Total amount of support: Varies.

CO-OP FUNDING PROGRAMS: The Society has a matching program so that funds for at least one fellowship are guaranteed.

NO. AWARDS: Usually 1 per academic year.

APPLICATION INFO:
Applications should include a cogent plan indicating how the fellowship will be used. The plan should include travel to at least one other institution and should demonstrate that the fellowship will be used for more than reduction of teaching at the candidate's home institution. The selection committee will consider the plan in addition to the quality of the candidate's research, and will try to award the fellowship to those for whom the award would make a real difference in the development of their research careers. Work in all areas of mathematics, including interdisciplinary work, is eligible.

Application forms can be accessed at the web site. For questions, contact the Membership and Programs Department, American Mathematical Society, at the address or e-mail above, or phone (401) 455-4096.

Duration: One year. Nonrenewable.

Deadline: December 1. Announcement in February, or earlier if possible.

PUBLICATIONS:
Application guidelines.

OFFICERS:
Robert L. Bryant, President
Jane Hawkins, Treasurer
Zbigniew Nitecki, Associate Treasurer

ADDRESS INQUIRIES TO:
Associate Executive Director
(See address above.)

*SPECIAL STIPULATIONS:
Acceptance of the Fellowship cannot be postponed.

CONFERENCE BOARD OF THE MATHEMATICAL SCIENCES [2029]

1529 18th Street, N.W.
Washington, DC 20036
(410) 730-1426
E-mail: rosier@georgetown.edu
Web Site: www.cbmsweb.org

FOUNDED: 1960

AREAS OF INTEREST:
Mathematical sciences.

NAME(S) OF PROGRAMS:

- **NSF-CBMS Regional Conferences in the Mathematical Sciences**

TYPE:
Conferences/seminars. Grants given jointly by NSF and the Conference Board for five-day conferences in the mathematical sciences.

YEAR PROGRAM STARTED: 1969

PURPOSE:
To stimulate interest and activity in mathematical research.

LEGAL BASIS:
A nonprofit professional society.

ELIGIBILITY:
Colleges or universities with at least some research competence in the field of the proposal are eligible to apply. Since a major goal of these conferences is to attract new researchers into the field of the conference and to stimulate new research activity, institutions that are interested in upgrading or improving their research efforts are especially encouraged to apply.

FINANCIAL DATA:
Grants may include travel and lodging costs, director's and secretary's salaries, announcement costs and other miscellaneous expenses.

Amount of support per award: $35,000 per conference.

CO-OP FUNDING PROGRAMS: Grants are given jointly with NSF.

NO. AWARDS: Up to 10.

APPLICATION INFO:
Proposals must be submitted electronically via Fastlane to the Division of Mathematical Sciences (DMS) at NSF.

Duration: Five days during the summer or during a recess in the academic year.

Deadline: Mid- to late April. Announcement in October.

PUBLICATIONS:
Monographs of the conferences are available from the American Mathematical Society, the Society for Industrial and Applied Mathematics, the Institute of Mathematical Statistics and the American Statistical Association.

IBM THOMAS J. WATSON RESEARCH CENTER [2030]

Department of Business Solutions and Mathematical Sciences
1101 Kitchawan Road, Route 134
Yorktown Heights, NY 10598
(914) 945-1614
E-mail: goldpost@us.ibm.com
Web Site: www.research.ibm.com/goldstine

AREAS OF INTEREST:
Research in pure and applied mathematics and in theoretical and exploratory computer science.

NAME(S) OF PROGRAMS:

- **IBM Herman Goldstine Memorial Postdoctoral Fellowship for Research in Mathematical and Computer Sciences**

TYPE:
Fellowships.

YEAR PROGRAM STARTED: 1972

PURPOSE:
To provide scientists of outstanding ability an opportunity to advance their scholarship as resident department members at the IBM Thomas J. Watson Research Center.

ELIGIBILITY:
Applicant must have a Ph.D. in science, engineering or mathematics received within the last five years, or must expect to receive one before the fellowship commences in the second half of the year (usually in September).

FINANCIAL DATA:
Allowance provided for moving expenses.

Amount of support per award: Approximately $105,000 to $130,000 per year, depending on the length of experience.

NO. AWARDS: Up to 2 per year.

APPLICATION INFO:
Applications accepted via e-mail only.

Applicants are also responsible for arranging for three or more letters of recommendation, including one from the thesis advisor, that must also be e-mailed to the address above. Consult the web site address above for details.

Duration: One year. Renewable for a second year if of mutual interest.

Deadline: Applications accepted November to January (exact dates vary).

ADDRESS INQUIRIES TO:
See e-mail address above.

MICRON TECHNOLOGY FOUNDATION, INC. [2031]

P.O. Box 6
Boise, ID 83707-0006
(208) 363-3675
Fax: (208) 368-4435
E-mail: mtf@micron.com
Web Site: www.micron.com/foundation

FOUNDED: 1999

AREAS OF INTEREST:
Education with an emphasis on STEM (science, technology, engineering and mathematics).

TYPE:
Matching gifts; Professorships; Project/program grants; Research grants.

YEAR PROGRAM STARTED: 2000

PURPOSE:
To advance education and local communities; to partner with educators to spark a passion in youth for science, technology, engineering and mathematics; to engineer the future for students; to enrich the communities through strategic giving where team members live, work and volunteer.

LEGAL BASIS:
Private corporate foundation.

ELIGIBILITY:
Micron will consider projects or programs:
(1) which address an educational need, especially those which advance math and science;
(2) which impact a large number of people;
(3) which have long-term benefits and;
(4) which are in a geographic area where Micron has operations.

Micron generally does not address individual sponsorships or donations, requests for assistance with travel or lodging expenses, religious organizations requesting funds for purposes other than nondenominational education or organizations located in areas where Micron has no operations.

GEOG. RESTRICTIONS: Boise, Idaho and Manassas, Virginia.

FINANCIAL DATA:
Amount of support per award: Varies.

Total amount of support: Varies.

Matching fund requirements: Micron may match employee donations at a 1:1 ratio, K-12 and higher education grants up to $250 per employee per calendar year to qualified educational institutions.

NO. AWARDS: Varies.

REPRESENTATIVE AWARDS:
Boise School District Educational Foundation; Boise State University; University of Idaho; University of Washington; Virginia Tech.

APPLICATION INFO:
Paper applications are no longer accepted. Applicants for K-12 grants and nonprofit community grants must apply online on the web site.

Higher education grants by invitation only.

Duration: Varies.

IRS I.D.: 82-0516178

ADDRESS INQUIRIES TO:
Micron Technology Foundation, M/S 407
Community and Academic Relations
8000 South Federal Way, P.O. Box 6
Boise, ID 83707-0006

SOCIETY OF ACTUARIES (SOA) [2032]

475 North Martingale Road
Suite 600
Schaumburg, IL 60173-2226
(847) 706-3509
Fax: (847) 273-8605
E-mail: ttatsumi@soa.org
Web Site: www.soa.org/education/resources/academic-initiatives/soa-doc-stipend.aspx

FOUNDED: 1949

AREAS OF INTEREST:
Actuarial science, a branch of mathematics based on calculus, probability and statistics, as well as business economics.

NAME(S) OF PROGRAMS:
- **Society of Actuaries' James C. Hickman Scholar Doctoral Stipend Program**

TYPE:
Awards/prizes; Scholarships. Society of Actuaries' James C. Hickman Scholar Doctoral Stipend Program is designed to provide stipends to doctoral students who will, through their studies, address research and education needs of the profession, including both the theoretical and practical aspects.

YEAR PROGRAM STARTED: 2009

PURPOSE:
To increase the number of academic actuaries who hold a Ph.D. and an actuarial designation, and who intend to pursue academic careers in the U.S. or Canada.

LEGAL BASIS:
Society-funded.

ELIGIBILITY:
Individuals who meet the following requirements may apply:
(1) enrolled full-time, have recently been admitted or are currently applying to a qualifying doctoral program in the U.S. or Canada; a qualifying doctoral program is one in actuarial science or a field related to actuarial science (e.g., business, demography, economics, financial economics, insurance, mathematics, risk management, statistics); applicants may apply at the same time they are applying for a doctoral program; if selected, these applicants will be awarded the stipend conditional upon enrollment in a qualifying doctoral program;
(2) hold a fellowship-level actuarial credential or are pursuing Associateship or Fellowship membership of an accrediting actuarial organization (i.e., CAS, CIA, FA, IA, IAA, SOA); applicants who are already Associate members (including those awarded the CERA designation) will be expected to pursue a Fellowship credential and;
(3) all applicants must have at least two actuarial exams passed.

While U.S. or Canadian citizenship is not expressly required, the applicant will attest to citizenship status on the application. An applicant's citizenship status may be used to evaluate the likelihood that the applicant will pursue an academic career in the U.S. or Canada.

FINANCIAL DATA:
The stipend is to be used at the discretion of the Ph.D. candidate for appropriate expenses related to the completion of the Ph.D. and the actuarial credential if not yet attained. Applicants should be aware that stipend funds are provided for qualified expenses (tuition, books, fees, etc.). Qualified expenses do not include room and board. Stipend funds not used for qualified expenses may be taxable. Please consult one's tax advisor if one has any questions.

Amount of support per award: Generally $20,000 per academic year.

Total amount of support: Varies.

NO. MOST RECENT APPLICANTS: 23.

NO. AWARDS: Varies.

APPLICATION INFO:
Applicants must submit an application and supporting documentation that includes the following:
(1) Applicants currently applying to doctoral programs must provide the names of the schools/programs to which they have applied, and the intended field of study in each school/program. (If a stipend is awarded, it will be conditional on enrollment in the specified program and for the field of study proposed in the application.);
(2) Applicants already enrolled in a doctoral program will indicate how many years they have been studying, and approximately how many more years they believe they need to complete their Doctorate. They will also provide a statement from their supervisor or program director attesting to progess in their doctoral program and;
(3) Applicant must submit a Statement of Interest. This may be the same statement submitted for the doctoral program, but additional language should be added for this application to clearly explain their goals regarding teaching, research and contributions to the actuarial profession.

Duration: One academic year. Renewable up to four times based on satisfactory progress.

Deadline: Completed application forms and supporting materials must be received at the Society no later than February 15. Recipients will be announced April 15. Recipients must notify the Society of acceptance of the stipend by May 15.

PUBLICATIONS:
Application guidelines.

OFFICERS:
Craig W. Reynolds, FSA, M.A.A.A., President

ADDRESS INQUIRIES TO:
SOA James C. Hickman Scholar Doctoral Stipend Program
(See address above.)

SOCIETY OF ACTUARIES (SOA) [2033]

475 North Martingale Road
Suite 600
Schaumburg, IL 60173-2226
(847) 706-3509
Fax: (847) 273-8605
E-mail: ttatsumi@soa.org
Web Site: www.soa.org/education/resources/edu-institution-grant/default.aspx

FOUNDED: 1949

AREAS OF INTEREST:
Actuarial science, a branch of mathematics based on calculus, probability and statistics, as well as business economics.

NAME(S) OF PROGRAMS:
- **Society of Actuaries Educational Institution Grant**

TYPE:
Awards/prizes; Development grants; General operating grants; Project/program grants; Research grants; Scholarships; Travel grants. Grants to educational institutions.

YEAR PROGRAM STARTED: 1991

PURPOSE:
To provide financial support for the promotion and development of educational and research programs in actuarial science; to recognize the added value professional actuarial qualifications offer to actuarial teaching and research.

LEGAL BASIS:
Society-funded.

ELIGIBILITY:
A full-time faculty member at the applying institution must attain Associateship (ASA) status or Fellowship (FSA) status to qualify the institution for a grant.

Full-time faculty are defined as individuals employed by a college or university who are considered to be full-time members of the regular faculty by their employer. This does not include visiting faculty, adjuncts, graduate students or teaching assistants.

The institution must appear on the Universities and Colleges Actuarial Programs (UCAP) list at the time the ASA or FSA designation is earned, or within one year from the date the designation is earned, and must continue on the list through the time of application.

FINANCIAL DATA:
Amount of support per award: $5,000 one-time grant to an educational institution when a full-time faculty member attains ASA status; $7,500 one-time grant to an educational institution when a full-time faculty member attains FSA status.

Total amount of support: Varies.

NO. MOST RECENT APPLICANTS: 8.

NO. AWARDS: Varies.

APPLICATION INFO:
Application form and details are available online.

Deadline: Applications for institution grants must be received within three years of the date the faculty member attains FSA or ASA status as indicated on the FSA or ASA diploma.

PUBLICATIONS:
Application guidelines.

OFFICERS:
Craig W. Reynolds, FSA, M.A.A.A., President

ADDRESS INQUIRIES TO:
Educational Institution Grants (ASA/FSA Grants)
(See address above.)

Physics

AMERICAN INSTITUTE OF PHYSICS [2034]

One Physics Ellipse
College Park, MD 20740-3843
(301) 209-3099
Fax: (301) 209-0846
E-mail: writing@aip.org
Web Site: www.aip.org/aip/writing

FOUNDED: 1931

AREAS OF INTEREST:
The advancement and diffusion of the knowledge of physics and its application to human welfare.

NAME(S) OF PROGRAMS:
- **American Institute of Physics Science Writing Award in Physics and Astronomy**

TYPE:
Awards/prizes. Four writing awards, one to a physicist, astronomer or member of an AIP society, one to a journalist for noteworthy writing about physics and astronomy in the print media, one to a journalist for noteworthy writing about physics and astronomy for broadcast media, and one for science writing aimed at children.

PURPOSE:
To stimulate distinguished reporting and writing that will improve public understanding of physics and astronomy.

ELIGIBILITY:
Entries must have been printed in any recognized international, national or local medium of communication such as newspapers, magazines or books. The media should normally be available to, and intended for, the general public. Purely scientific, technical and trade publications are excluded.

Entries must have been published or translated into English during the period one year immediately prior to the deadline date. No more than three entries may be submitted by any one individual. Persons other than the author may submit entries on behalf of an author in accordance with the rules.

FINANCIAL DATA:
Amount of support per award: $3,000.

Total amount of support: $9,000.

NO. MOST RECENT APPLICANTS: 75.

NO. AWARDS: 3.

APPLICATION INFO:
Application information is available on the web site.

OFFICERS:
H. Frederick Dylla, Executive Director and Chief Executive Officer
Richard Baccante, Treasurer and Chief Financial Officer
Benjamin Snavely, Secretary
John Haynes, Senior Vice President, Publishing
Theresa C. Braun, Vice President, Human Resources
Catherine O'Riordan, Vice President, Physics Resource Center

ADDRESS INQUIRIES TO:
Marissa Nielsen, Programs Coordinator
(See address above.)

AMERICAN VACUUM SOCIETY (AVS) [2035]

125 Maiden Lane, Room 1501
New York, NY 10038-4714
(212) 248-0200
Fax: (212) 248-0245
E-mail: avsnyc@avs.org
Web Site: www.avs.org

FOUNDED: 1953

AREAS OF INTEREST:
Vacuum science and technology, thin film research, vacuum metallurgy, surface physics, electronic materials and processing, plasma science and technology and applied surface science.

NAME(S) OF PROGRAMS:
- **Graduate Research Awards**
- **Russell and Sigurd Varian Award**
- **Nellie Yeoh Whetten Award**

TYPE:
Awards/prizes; Fellowships. Cash awards and a one-year fellowship in recognition of scientific promise or excellence in graduate studies in vacuum science.

The Whetten Award is offered to encourage and recognize participation by women in science and engineering.

PURPOSE:
To recognize and encourage excellence in graduate studies in the sciences and technologies of interest to the Society.

LEGAL BASIS:
Nonprofit 501(c)(3) organization.

ELIGIBILITY:
All awards are open to students engaged in graduate studies in major fields of the organization's interest at accredited graduate schools in North America.

For the Whetten Award, the nominee must be a registered female graduate student in an accredited academic institution at the time when the applications are due. Criteria for selection of the awardee are research and academic excellence.

FINANCIAL DATA:
Amount of support per award: Graduate Research Awards: $1,000 per award; $1,500 each for the Whetten Award and for the Varian Award, plus reimbursed travel support (up to $750 maximum) to attend the International Symposium.

Total amount of support: Varies.

NO. MOST RECENT APPLICANTS: 11.

NO. AWARDS: Graduate Research Awards: Approximately 3 annually; Varian Award and Whetten Award: 1 each per year.

ADDRESS INQUIRIES TO:
Angela Klink, Program Administrator
E-mail: angela@avs.org

MCDONNELL CENTER FOR THE SPACE SCIENCES

Washington University, Campus Box 1105
One Brookings Drive
St. Louis, MO 63130-4899
(314) 935-5332
E-mail: trecia@physics.wustl.edu
Web Site: mcss.wustl.edu

TYPE:
Fellowships. These fellowships are funded by a gift from the McDonnell Douglas Foundation to Washington University and provide tuition remission plus stipend for graduate students interested in pursuing research in the space sciences who are enrolled in the Washington University Departments of Physics or Earth and Planetary Sciences.

See entry 2538 for full listing.

NATIONAL SCIENCE FOUNDATION [2036]

Division of Physics
4201 Wilson Boulevard
Arlington, VA 22230
(703) 292-8890
Fax: (703) 292-9078
E-mail: dcalwel@nsf.gov
Web Site: www.nsf.gov

AREAS OF INTEREST:
Nuclear, theoretical, atomic and molecular, gravitational, and elementary particles, education and interdisciplinary research, physics of living systems, particle and nuclear astrophysics.

NAME(S) OF PROGRAMS:
- **Physics Research Grants**

TYPE:
Research grants.

ELIGIBILITY:
As specified in the NSF Grant Proposal Guidelines.

FINANCIAL DATA:
Amount of support per award: Varies.
Total amount of support: Varies.

APPLICATION INFO:
Application information is available on the web site.
Duration: Typically one to five years. Renewals by reapplication.
Deadline: Varies according to program.

ADDRESS INQUIRIES TO:
Cognizant Program Director
Division of Physics
(See address above.)

SOCIETY OF PHYSICS STUDENTS [2037]

American Institute of Physics
One Physics Ellipse
College Park, MD 20740
(301) 209-3007
Fax: (301) 209-0839
E-mail: sps@aip.org
Web Site: www.spsnational.org/programs/awards/research.htm

AREAS OF INTEREST:
Physics.

NAME(S) OF PROGRAMS:
- **SPS Award for Outstanding Undergraduate Research**

TYPE:
Awards/prizes.

PURPOSE:
To promote interest in physics among students and the general public.

LEGAL BASIS:
Nonprofit.

ELIGIBILITY:
Must participate in annual competition and must be SPS national member. Applicants must be undergraduate students at the time the application is due. Winners are chosen based on their research, letters of recommendation and SPS participation from among qualified applicants.

FINANCIAL DATA:
Award pays expenses for winner to attend and present a paper at the annual International Association of Physics Students (IAPS), which is usually held in Europe.
Amount of support per award: $500 honorarium for winner and $500 for the SPS chapter.
Total amount of support: Varies.

NO. AWARDS: 1 or more annually.

APPLICATION INFO:
Consult the web site.
Duration: One year.
Deadline: March 15.

STAFF:
Daniel Golombek, Assistant Director

SOCIETY OF PHYSICS STUDENTS [2038]

One Physics Ellipse
College Park, MD 20740
(301) 209-3007
Fax: (301) 209-0839
E-mail: sps@aip.org
Web Site: www.spsnational.org

FOUNDED: 1968

AREAS OF INTEREST:
Physics.

NAME(S) OF PROGRAMS:
- **Future Faces of Physics Awards**

TYPE:
Awards/prizes.

YEAR PROGRAM STARTED: 2011

PURPOSE:
To promote interest in physics.

LEGAL BASIS:
Not-for-profit, 501(c)(3).

ELIGIBILITY:
Applicant must be a Society of Physics Students member.

FINANCIAL DATA:
Amount of support per award: Up to $300.
Total amount of support: Approximately $1,500 per year.

NO. MOST RECENT APPLICANTS: 5.

NO. AWARDS: 5.

APPLICATION INFO:
Application information is available on the web site.
Duration: One year.
Deadline: November 15. Announcement January 1.

STAFF:
Sean Bentley, Director

*SPECIAL STIPULATIONS:
Only one proposal may be submitted by an SPS chapter.

SOCIETY OF PHYSICS STUDENTS [2039]

One Physics Ellipse
College Park, MD 20740
(301) 209-3007
Fax: (301) 209-0839
E-mail: sps@aip.org
Web Site: www.spsnational.org

FOUNDED: 1968

AREAS OF INTEREST:
Physics.

NAME(S) OF PROGRAMS:
- **Marsh W. White Awards**

TYPE:
Awards/prizes. Awards are made to SPS chapters to support projects designed to promote interest in physics among students and the general public.

YEAR PROGRAM STARTED: 1975

PURPOSE:
To promote interest in physics.

LEGAL BASIS:
Not-for-profit, 501(c)(3).

ELIGIBILITY:
Applicants must be SPS chapters in good standing with the SPS national organization. The project leader must be a student that is a member of the SPS national organization.

FINANCIAL DATA:
Amount of support per award: Up to $500.

APPLICATION INFO:
Consult the web site.
Duration: One year.
Deadline: November 15.

STAFF:
Daniel Golombek, Assistant Director

ADDRESS INQUIRIES TO:
E-mail: SPS-Programs@aip.org

*SPECIAL STIPULATIONS:
Only one proposal may be submitted by an SPS chapter.

SOCIETY OF PHYSICS STUDENTS

One Physics Ellipse
College Park, MD 20740-3843
(301) 209-3007
Fax: (301) 209-0839
E-mail: sps@aip.org
Web Site: www.spsnational.org

TYPE:
Scholarships. Award made to physics majors in the latter stages of their undergraduate careers.

See entry 1702 for full listing.

LIFE SCIENCES

Life sciences (general)

DJ & T FOUNDATION [2040]

9201 Wilshire Boulevard, Suite 204
Beverly Hills, CA 90210
(310) 278-1160
Fax: (310) 275-6202
E-mail: will@prappascompany.com
Web Site: www.djtfoundation.org

FOUNDED: 1995

AREAS OF INTEREST:
Animal population control.

TYPE:
Grants-in-aid. Fund grants to organizations that operate low-cost spay/neuter clinics.

YEAR PROGRAM STARTED: 1995

PURPOSE:
To fund nonprofit, low-cost spay and neuter clinics.

LEGAL BASIS:
Private foundation.

ELIGIBILITY:
Eligible organizations must be IRS 501(c)(3) tax-exempt.

GEOG. RESTRICTIONS: United States.

FINANCIAL DATA:
Amount of support per award: Varies.
Total amount of support: Varies.

NO. MOST RECENT APPLICANTS: Approximately 80.

NO. AWARDS: 30 to 40.

APPLICATION INFO:
Applications are available at the web site and must include a copy of the IRS tax determination letter.
Duration: Varies.

ADDRESS INQUIRIES TO:
DJ & T Foundation
(See address above.)

THE HAMNER INSTITUTES FOR HEALTH SCIENCES

6 Davis Drive
Research Triangle Park, NC 27709
(919) 558-1200
Fax: (919) 558-1430
E-mail: koverman@thehamner.org
Web Site: www.thehamner.org

TYPE:
Conferences/seminars; Fellowships; Internships; Visiting scholars.

See entry 2002 for full listing.

THE HASTINGS CENTER [2041]

21 Malcolm Gordon Road
Garrison, NY 10524
(845) 424-4040
Fax: (845) 424-4545
E-mail: visitors@thehastingscenter.org
Web Site: www.thehastingscenter.org

FOUNDED: 1969

AREAS OF INTEREST:
Ethical issues in medicine, health care and the life sciences. Recent research topics include biotechnology, death and dying, aging, neonatal care, allocation of resources, occupational health, health professional-patient relationships, chronic illness, rehabilitation medicine, AIDS, surrogate motherhood and artificial reproduction, organ transplantation, prospective payment systems, deinstitutionalization, nursing homes, animal experimentation, environmental protection, civic education and the professions and the public good.

NAME(S) OF PROGRAMS:
- **Visiting Scholars Program**

TYPE:
Residencies; Visiting scholars. Independent study.

YEAR PROGRAM STARTED: 1969

PURPOSE:
To permit scholars and practitioners in the humanities or the sciences to conduct productive research on ethical issues in medicine, the life sciences and the professions.

LEGAL BASIS:
Nonprofit independent research association.

ELIGIBILITY:
Visiting Scholars Program is open to persons with a degree in the humanities, sciences, law or medicine and that are prepared to pursue their own independent research project in the Center's areas of interest.

NO. MOST RECENT APPLICANTS: 35.

NO. AWARDS: 14.

APPLICATION INFO:
Application information is available on the web site.
Duration: Two to eight weeks.

PUBLICATIONS:
Annual report; application guidelines; *Hastings Center Report*; *Hastings Center Books in Print*; *IRB: Ethics and Human Research*; *Bioethics Forum*.

ADDRESS INQUIRIES TO:
Visiting Scholars Program
(See address above.)

THOMAS F. AND KATE MILLER JEFFRESS MEMORIAL TRUST [2042]

Bank of America–Philanthropic Management
VA 2-300-12-92
1111 East Main Street, 12th Floor
Richmond, VA 23219
E-mail: sarah.kay@ustrust.com
Web Site: www.hria.org/tmfgrants/jeffress

FOUNDED: 1981

AREAS OF INTEREST:
Astronomy, biosciences, chemistry, computer sciences, engineering, environmental sciences, material science, mathematics and physics.

NAME(S) OF PROGRAMS:
- **Jeffress Trust Awards Program in Interdisciplinary Research**

TYPE:
Seed money grants. Administered by The Medical Foundation, this awards program supports high-impact, innovative one-year projects that integrate computational and quantitative scientific methodologies across a broad range of scientific disciplines.

YEAR PROGRAM STARTED: 1982

PURPOSE:
To support basic research in chemical, medical, or other scientific fields at educational and research institutions in the Commonwealth of Virginia.

LEGAL BASIS:
Trust.

ELIGIBILITY:
Grants are made to tax-exempt institutions and organizations which are operated exclusively for charitable, scientific purposes. Grants are not made to private foundations.

GEOG. RESTRICTIONS: Virginia.

FINANCIAL DATA:
Amount of support per award: $100,000.
Total amount of support: Up to $1,200,000.

NO. MOST RECENT APPLICANTS: 41 for the year 2015.

NO. AWARDS: Up to 12 annually.

APPLICATION INFO:
Grant procedures and guidelines are available at the web site above.
Duration: One year.
Deadline: January 15.

PUBLICATIONS:
Guidelines.

ADDRESS INQUIRIES TO:
Jeanne Brown, Program Officer
E-mail: jbrown@hria.org
Tel: (617) 279-2240 ext. 709

*PLEASE NOTE:
The Trust grants funds only in Virginia.

NATIONAL DAIRY COUNCIL

10255 West Higgins Road
Suite 900
Rosemont, IL 60018-5616
(847) 627-3232
Fax: (847) 803-2077
E-mail: elieke.demmer@dairy.org
Web Site: researchsubmission.
nationaldairycouncil.org

TYPE:
Research contracts. The National Dairy Council is the nutrition research, education and communications arm of Dairy Management Inc. On behalf of U.S. dairy farmers, the National Dairy Council provides science-based nutrition information to, and in collaboration with, a variety of stakeholders committed to fostering a healthier society, including health professionals, educators, school nutrition directors, academia, industry, consumers and media. The National Dairy Council comprises a staff of nutrition science researchers, registered dietitians and communications experts dedicated to educating the public on the health benefits of consuming milk and milk products throughout a person's lifespan.

See entry 2591 for full listing.

NATIONAL EYE INSTITUTE

National Institutes of Health
5635 Fishers Lane, Suite 1300
Bethesda, MD 20892
(301) 451-2020
Fax: (301) 496-2267
E-mail: wujekjer@mail.nih.gov
Web Site: www.nei.nih.gov

TYPE:
Conferences/seminars; Fellowships; Research grants; Training grants. Research Project Grants support individual investigators whose work is aimed at discovering means of

improving the prevention, diagnosis and treatment of blinding and disabling eye and vision disorders.

Small Business Innovation Research Awards aim to stimulate technological innovations, to use small business to meet federal research-development needs that may ultimately lead to commercial products or services and to foster and encourage participation by minority and disadvantaged persons in technological innovations.

Areas of study include vision research, retinal diseases, corneal diseases, cataract, glaucoma, low vision and blindness rehabilitation, visual impairment and its rehabilitation, strabismus, amblyopia and visual processing.

See entry 2440 for full listing.

NATIONAL EYE INSTITUTE

National Institutes of Health
5635 Fishers Lane, Suite 1300
Bethesda, MD 20892
(301) 451-2020
Fax: (301) 402-0528
E-mail: esl@nei.nih.gov
Web Site: www.nei.nih.gov

TYPE:
Research grants.

See entry 2441 for full listing.

NATIONAL RESEARCH COUNCIL OF THE NATIONAL ACADEMIES

Fellowship and Research Associateship Programs
500 Fifth Street, N.W.
Washington, DC 20001
(202) 334-2760
E-mail: rap@nas.edu
Web Site: www.nationalacademies.org/rap

TYPE:
Research scientists. Fellowships at the graduate, postdoctoral and senior levels for research-in-residence at U.S. federal laboratories and affiliated institutions.

See entry 1974 for full listing.

PFD RESEARCH FOUNDATION [2043]

2025 M Street, N.W., Suite 800
Washington, DC 20036
(202) 367-1167
Fax: (202) 367-2167
E-mail: info@augs.org
Web Site: www.pfdresearch.org

AREAS OF INTEREST:
Incontinence and pelvic dysfunctions.

NAME(S) OF PROGRAMS:
- **June Allyson Award**

TYPE:
Research grants.

PURPOSE:
To provide research training and experience for a candidate who exhibits significant evidence of talent and dedication to research.

ELIGIBILITY:
Applicant must:
(1) be an active, life, honorary or allied health member of the PFD Research Foundation;
(2) be a current fellow in either an accredited or nonaccredited fellowship program;
(3) have a senior research mentor or mentoring team. Mentors or co-investigators need not be members of the PFD Research Foundation and;
(4) funding must remain at the same institution for the period of the research project.

FINANCIAL DATA:
The award may be used for purchases of equipment and supplies, laboratory tests, technician/research assistant salaries, Institutional Review Board costs, and/or statistical report. Salary support for the applicant is not allowed.

Amount of support per award: Up to $25,000.

Total amount of support: $25,000.

NO. MOST RECENT APPLICANTS: Average 20 per year.

NO. AWARDS: 1.

APPLICATION INFO:
Application requirements are available online.

Duration: One year.

Deadline: March 1.

ADDRESS INQUIRIES TO:
Tristan Wood, Senior Coordinator
(See e-mail address above.)

KENNETH A. SCOTT CHARITABLE TRUST [2044]

c/o KeyBank Nonprofit Services
100 Public Square, Suite 600
Cleveland, OH 44113
(216) 752-3301
E-mail: director@kennethscottcharitabletrust.org
Web Site: www.kennethscottcharitabletrust.org

FOUNDED: 1995

AREAS OF INTEREST:
Animal welfare.

TYPE:
Project/program grants. Grants are available for animal welfare and humane education projects of national scope or significance in the U.S. Grants are available for localized projects of shelters and humane groups in Ohio and other Great Lakes states (only).

YEAR PROGRAM STARTED: 1995

PURPOSE:
To prevent cruelty to animals and promote the humane treatment of animals, particularly companion animals (dogs, cats) and other species commonly kept as household pets. Requests related to wildlife and animals in other settings may also be considered.

LEGAL BASIS:
Private foundation.

ELIGIBILITY:
Eligible organizations must be IRS 501(c)(3) tax-exempt. No grants to individuals.

GEOG. RESTRICTIONS: Ohio. Some grants in other Great Lakes states.

FINANCIAL DATA:
Amount of support per award: $14,606 average.

Total amount of support: $978,575 for the year 2015.

NO. AWARDS: 67 for the year 2015.

APPLICATION INFO:
A letter of inquiry, e-mail or phone call to the Trust is required before submitting the application.

Duration: One year.

Deadline: March 15 and September 15 for Ohio proposals. December 15 and June 15 for National and Great Lakes proposals.

IRS I.D.: 34-7034544

ADDRESS INQUIRIES TO:
Dr. H. Richard Obermanns
Executive Director
(See address above.)

THE PERCY SLADEN MEMORIAL FUND [2045]

c/o The Linnean Society of London
Burlington House, Piccadilly
London W1J 0BF England
(44) 020 7434 4479
Fax: (44) 020 7287 9364
E-mail: info@linnean.org
gina@linnean.org
Web Site: www.linnean.org

FOUNDED: 1904

AREAS OF INTEREST:
Natural sciences, with a focus of support on field work in the life and earth sciences, both through expeditions and individual research projects overseas.

NAME(S) OF PROGRAMS:
- **Percy Sladen Memorial Fund Grants**

TYPE:
Awards/prizes; Project/program grants; Research grants; Travel grants. Field work grants in life and earth sciences (excludes any projects which are part of further education, e.g., a Doctorate or a Master's course).

YEAR PROGRAM STARTED: 1904

PURPOSE:
To support field work away from usual country of residence.

LEGAL BASIS:
Registered charity.

ELIGIBILITY:
There are no restrictions in award of grants based on nationality, age, sex or prior qualifications. No grants for field work undertaken as part of a higher degree or general support for undergraduate expeditions.

FINANCIAL DATA:
Grants may be used toward a portion of total costs or for specific items of equipment.

Amount of support per award: Generally, less than GBP 1,000.

APPLICATION INFO:
Application form and referees reports are available from the Secretary to the Trustees at the address above.

Duration: Grant must be taken up within one year of receipt.

Deadline: January 30 and September 30.

ADDRESS INQUIRIES TO:
Gina Douglas
Secretary to the Trustees
(See address above.)

*SPECIAL STIPULATIONS:
No support for course work. No undergraduate expeditions. No grants for field work for completion of dissertations or higher degrees.

SOCIETY FOR THE STUDY OF AMPHIBIANS AND REPTILES

Department of Biological Sciences
University of Wisconsin-Whitewater
Whitewater, WI 53190
(262) 472-1069
E-mail: kapferj@uww.edu
Web Site: www.ssarherps.org/pages/GIH.php

TYPE:
Awards/prizes; Research grants. Awards are given in six categories: Conservation of Amphibians and/or Reptiles, Field Research, Laboratory Research, Herpetological Education, Travel and International Research.

See entry 1978 for full listing.

ROB AND BESSIE WELDER WILDLIFE FOUNDATION [2046]

10429 Welder Wildlife
Sinton, TX 78387
(361) 364-2643
Fax: (361) 364-2650
E-mail: tblankenship@welderwildlife.org
Web Site: www.welderwildlife.org

FOUNDED: 1954

AREAS OF INTEREST:
Wildlife conservation, wildlife ecology, wildlife science and higher education (graduate level only).

TYPE:
Fellowships. Graduate research fellowships only in fields of wildlife ecology and management.

YEAR PROGRAM STARTED: 1956

PURPOSE:
To encourage and sponsor wildlife research and education.

LEGAL BASIS:
Private, nonprofit foundation.

ELIGIBILITY:
Graduate students at accredited universities seeking advanced degrees in the above-designated fields are eligible to apply. Undergraduates need not apply.

GEOG. RESTRICTIONS: Continental United States.

FINANCIAL DATA:
Fellowships are generally $1,600 (M.S.) to $1,800 (Ph.D.) per month, plus some funds for field supplies and travel. Living quarters are available for students doing research on the Foundation's refuge area near Sinton, TX, including utilities.

Amount of support per award: Normally $20,000 per calendar year.

Total amount of support: $100,000 available for the year 2015.

CO-OP FUNDING PROGRAMS: The Foundation participates in cooperative funding for approvable proposals not adequately financed through other sources, if and when surplus funds are available.

NO. MOST RECENT APPLICANTS: Over 20.

NO. AWARDS: 5 to 6.

APPLICATION INFO:
Initial contact with the Foundation may be submitted in an abbreviated outline of the research problem, a preliminary estimate of expenses, and letter signed by a qualified member of the faculty at the parent university. If the Foundation staff thereafter entertains the matter further, a more complete proposal will be requested along with material concerning the proposed fellowship recipient.

Duration: One year. May be renewed if progress is satisfactory.

Deadline: October 1.

PUBLICATIONS:
Biennial report of staff and student activities.

IRS I.D.: 74-1381321

OFFICERS:
Terry Blankenship, Ph.D., Director
Selma Glasscock, Ph.D., Assistant Director

ADDRESS INQUIRIES TO:
Terry Blankenship, Ph.D., Director
(See address above.)

*SPECIAL STIPULATIONS:
Priority will be given to research proposals involving studies on the Foundation's refuge area and/or in south Texas.

THE WILEY FOUNDATION, INC. [2047]

111 River Street
Hoboken, NJ 07030-5773
(201) 748-6000
E-mail: wileyfoundation@wiley.com
Web Site: www.wileyfoundation.org

FOUNDED: 2001

AREAS OF INTEREST:
Biomedical sciences.

NAME(S) OF PROGRAMS:
- **Wiley Prize in Biomedical Sciences**

TYPE:
Awards/prizes. The annual Wiley Prize in Biomedical Sciences has recognized breakthrough research in pure or applied life science research.

YEAR PROGRAM STARTED: 2002

PURPOSE:
To honor research that is distinguished by its excellence, originality and impact on the understanding of biological systems and processes.

ELIGIBILITY:
The Foundation invites and encourages the nomination of exceptional scientists or research teams whose work has achieved an impressive level of excellence.

GEOG. RESTRICTIONS: The Foundation encourages international nominations.

FINANCIAL DATA:
Amount of support per award: $35,000 prize and a luncheon in honor of the recipient.

APPLICATION INFO:
Each nomination should be submitted by someone other than the nominee. More than one nomination can be made from the same organization.

Duration: Annual award.

Deadline: September 30.

Agriculture, land resources, rural development

AGRICULTURAL HISTORY SOCIETY

MSU History Department
P.O. Box H
Mississippi State, MS 39762
(662) 268-2247
E-mail: jgiesen@history.msstate.edu
Web Site: www.aghistorysociety.org

TYPE:
Awards/prizes. The Everett E. Edwards Award is presented to the graduate student who submits the best manuscript on any aspect of agricultural history and rural studies during the current calendar year.

The Gilbert C. Fite Dissertation Award will be presented to the author of the best dissertation on any aspect of agricultural history completed during the current calendar year.

The Wayne D. Rasmussen Award is given to the author of the best article on agricultural history published by a journal other than *Agricultural History* during the current calendar year.

The Theodore Saloutos Book Award is presented to the author of a book on any aspect of agricultural history in the U.S. within the current year, broadly interpreted.

The Henry A. Wallace Award is presented to the author of a book on any aspect of agricultural history outside of the U.S. within the current year, broadly interpreted.

See entry 562 for full listing.

THE AMERICAN CHESTNUT FOUNDATION [2048]

50 North Merrimon Avenue
Suite 115
Asheville, NC 28804
(828) 281-0047
Fax: (828) 253-5373
E-mail: lisa@acf.org
Web Site: www.acf.org

FOUNDED: 1983

AREAS OF INTEREST:
Chestnut research.

TYPE:
Research grants.

YEAR PROGRAM STARTED: 1983

PURPOSE:
To restore the American chestnut to Eastern forests.

ELIGIBILITY:
Grants are reviewed on a case-by-case basis.

GEOG. RESTRICTIONS: United States.

FINANCIAL DATA:
Amount of support per award: $1,000 to $10,000.

Total amount of support: Approximately $30,000 for the year 2015.

APPLICATION INFO:
Send a letter of inquiry letter form, outlining the goal and purpose, the intended use, and amount of the grant requested.

Duration: Up to one year.

Deadline: Varies.

ADDRESS INQUIRIES TO:
Samantha Bowers, Grants Manager
(See address above.)

AMERICAN FARM BUREAU FOUNDATION FOR AGRICULTURE [2049]

600 Maryland Avenue, S.W.
Suite 1000 West
Washington, DC 20024
(800) 443-8456
Fax: (202) 314-5121
E-mail: foundation@fb.org
Web Site: www.agfoundation.org

AREAS OF INTEREST:
Agricultural, consumer education, classroom, consumer and farm safety programs.

NAME(S) OF PROGRAMS:

- **White-Reinhardt Fund for Education**

TYPE:
Conferences/seminars; Project/program grants; Research contracts. Teacher Scholarships to National Conference.

YEAR PROGRAM STARTED: 1967

PURPOSE:
To provide travel expense funds to educators employed by a school system or to active agricultural literacy volunteers to attend the national conference.

GEOG. RESTRICTIONS: United States.

FINANCIAL DATA:
Amount of support per award: Up to $1,500 for reimbursement of expenses not covered by other funding source.

Total amount of support: Varies.

APPLICATION INFO:
Mini-grant applications must be completed and submitted to the State Farm Bureau president, Agriculture in the Classroom coordinator or administrator for signature. All applications will be pre-screened for compliance with grant proposal guidelines. Any grant not meeting guidelines will be eliminated from the judging process prior to examination by judges.

Duration: One year.

Deadline: November 1.

ADDRESS INQUIRIES TO:
Julia Recko, Assistant Director
(See address above.)

AMERICAN FLORAL ENDOWMENT [2050]

1601 Duke Street
Alexandria, VA 22314
(703) 838-5211
Fax: (703) 838-5212
E-mail: afe@endowment.org
Web Site: endowment.org

FOUNDED: 1961

AREAS OF INTEREST:
Floricultural/environmental horticulture research and development funding in the U.S.

TYPE:
Internships; Project/program grants; Research grants; Scholarships. The Endowment funds research and educational development in floriculture and environmental horticulture designed to produce solutions to industry needs and promote the growth and improvement of the floral industry for the benefit of the grower, wholesale, retail, allied segments and the general public.

The Endowment supports educational programs focused on attracting young people to the industry, and educational endeavors to identify and solve industry needs and/or challenges. The programs are divided into two major areas:
(1) paid floriculture internships/scholarships for full-time college students and;
(2) general educational grants to national programs.

YEAR PROGRAM STARTED: 1961

PURPOSE:
To further the advancement of education and science in the field of floriculture through funding research and studies in the floriculture field, the results of which will be published; to finance scholarships and internships to students interested in floriculture.

LEGAL BASIS:
Not-for-profit, nongovernmental organization.

GEOG. RESTRICTIONS: United States.

FINANCIAL DATA:
Amount of support per award: Varies.

Total amount of support: Varies.

APPLICATION INFO:
Contact the Endowment.

Duration: Typically one year; research grants can be multiyear.

Deadline: Varies.

PUBLICATIONS:
Update, quarterly newsletter; annual report.

AMERICAN SOCIETY FOR ENOLOGY AND VITICULTURE [2051]

1784 Picasso Avenue, Suite D
Davis, CA 95618-0551
(530) 753-3142
Fax: (530) 753-3318
E-mail: society@asev.org
Web Site: www.asev.org

FOUNDED: 1951

AREAS OF INTEREST:
A scientific society of enologists, viticulturists and others in the fields of wine and grape production, promoting technical advancement and integrated research in science and industry.

TYPE:
Scholarships. Awards for undergraduate or graduate students enrolled in enology or viticulture or in a curriculum which emphasizes a science basic to the wine and grape industry and who intend to pursue a career in research for the wine or grape industry after graduation from college or university.

PURPOSE:
To support education and research in enology, viticulture or related fields.

LEGAL BASIS:
Professional, scientific association.

ELIGIBILITY:
Undergraduate and graduate students who have been accepted at an accredited college or university in North America, are enrolled in an appropriate field of study and reside in North America may apply. Applicants must be at least junior level in academic status (60 quarter units or 45 semester units). Undergraduate students must have a minimum 3.0 overall grade point average on a scale of 4.0. Graduate students must have a minimum 3.2 overall grade point average on a scale of 4.0.

FINANCIAL DATA:
Amount of support per award: Varies each academic year.

Total amount of support: Varies each academic year.

APPLICATION INFO:
Applications can be downloaded from the web site.

Duration: One academic year. Renewable in open competition.

Deadline: All completed forms, letters and transcripts must be received by March 1.

ADDRESS INQUIRIES TO:
Scholarship Committee
P.O. Box 1855
Davis, CA 95617-1855

CENTER FOR PLANT CONSERVATION [2052]

San Diego Zoo
15600 San Pasqual Valley Road
Escondido, CA 92027-7000
(760) 796-5686
E-mail: cpc@sandiegozoo.org
Web Site: saveplants.org

FOUNDED: 1984

AREAS OF INTEREST:
Education.

NAME(S) OF PROGRAMS:

- **Catherine H. Beattie Fellowship for Conservation Horticulture**

TYPE:
Fellowships.

YEAR PROGRAM STARTED: 1984

PURPOSE:
To aid students who pursue research in the area of rare plant conservation.

LEGAL BASIS:
501(c)(3) nonprofit organization.

ELIGIBILITY:
Open to graduate students in biology, horticulture, or a related field. Preference is given to students whose projects focus on the endangered flora of the Carolinas and southeastern U.S.

FINANCIAL DATA:
Amount of support per award: Up to $4,500.

NO. MOST RECENT APPLICANTS: 6.

NO. AWARDS: 1.

APPLICATION INFO:
Applicants should submit the following:
(1) a two- to three-page proposal, which includes a description of the research project and how it relates to the student's academic and professional development;
(2) an itemized budget for the funds requested;
(3) a current resume;
(4) a letter of endorsement by an academic advisor from the institution where the student is pursuing graduate studies;
(5) the names of three additional persons qualified to describe the student's character and ability and;
(6) official transcripts for both undergraduate and graduate academic records.

Applicant should be prepared to write an article for CPC Newsletter, *Plant Conservation*.

Duration: Varies.

Deadline: November 30. Notification by March 31.

PUBLICATIONS:
Plant Conservation, newsletter.

THE CH FOUNDATION [2053]

6102 82nd Street
Suite 8A
Lubbock, TX 79424
(806) 792-0448
Fax: (806) 792-7824
E-mail: hhocker@chfoundation.com
Web Site: www.chfoundationlubbock.com

FOUNDED: 1976

AREAS OF INTEREST:
Agriculture, arts, community development, cultural education, health, ranching, research, social services and youth.

TYPE:
Capital grants; Project/program grants.

YEAR PROGRAM STARTED: 1991

PURPOSE:
To support programs that meet the needs of and improve the quality of life.

ELIGIBILITY:
Grants are limited to organizations whose services benefit the Lubbock area of Texas. Grants are made to organizations that have tax-exempt status under Section 501(c)(3) of the Internal Revenue Code. No grants are made to individuals or political organizations.

GEOG. RESTRICTIONS: Lubbock, Texas and surrounding counties.

APPLICATION INFO:
Contact the Foundation to determine the interest and appropriateness of a full proposal.

Duration: One year. Renewal possible.

Deadline: May 1. Disbursements are made in December.

PUBLICATIONS:
Application guidelines.

IRS I.D.: 75-1534816

ADDRESS INQUIRIES TO:
Heather Hocker, Grants Administrator
(See address above.)

FARM AID [2054]

501 Cambridge Street
Third Floor
Cambridge, MA 02141
(617) 354-2922
Fax: (617) 354-6992
E-mail: grants@farmaid.org
Web Site: www.farmaid.org

FOUNDED: 1985

AREAS OF INTEREST:
Supporting organizations that help farm families stay on their land, build local markets, confront the threat of corporate control of agriculture, train new farmers and support farmer-to-farmer programs for more sustainable agricultural practices. Emergency and disaster assistance for farm families.

TYPE:
General operating grants; Project/program grants. Grants fall within three broad categories which make it possible for organizations to build long-term solutions to the problems farmers face.

Grant Categories:
(1) Growing the Good Food Movement: These grants fund organizations or projects that seek to strengthen what Farm Aid calls the Good Food Movement, the growing number of Americans reaching for and demanding family farm-identified, local, organic or humanely raised food. These grants build connections between farmers and consumers, creating new markets for family farmers.
(2) Helping Farmers Thrive: These grants fund organizations or projects that assist farmers in transitioning to more sustainable and profitable farming practices, finding alternative markets, or starting a new farming operation as well as providing support services to farm families in crisis. These organizations are the core of the Farmer Resource Network which responds to individual farmers as well as regional events such as natural disasters. (See www.farmaid.org/ideas.)
(3) Taking Action to Change the System: These grants fund organizations or projects that promote fair farm policies and organize grassroots campaigns to defend and bolster family farm-centered agriculture. These grants enable advocates to strengthen the voices of family farmers and promote their interests on a local, regional and national level.

YEAR PROGRAM STARTED: 1985

LEGAL BASIS:
Tax-exempt, charitable and educational organization.

ELIGIBILITY:
Applicants must be IRS 501(c)(3) nonprofit organizations and include a copy of their IRS 501(c)(3) tax-exempt verification letter. If organization does not have 501(c)(3) status, it must include the IRS 501(c)(3) letter and authorization from the organization acting as its fiscal agent.

The following types of projects are not eligible for Farm Aid funding:
(1) grants or loans to individuals;
(2) grants or loans to support commercial operation of a farming enterprise;
(3) production of book, film, television or radio projects;
(4) projects outside the U.S.;
(5) projects directed or substantially funded by government bodies (federal, state or local), including Resource Conservation & Development Councils (RC & Ds);
(6) legal defense funds;
(7) capital campaigns, equipment purchases, endowments or deficit financing;
(8) historic preservation of farmland or buildings;
(9) lobbying to influence elections or legislation and;
(10) conferences, publications or research projects unless they are directly connected to ongoing program activities.

GEOG. RESTRICTIONS: United States.

FINANCIAL DATA:
Amount of support per award: Grants typically from $3,000 to $20,000; mostly $5,000 to $7,500.

Total amount of support: Varies.

NO. MOST RECENT APPLICANTS: 150.

NO. AWARDS: 45 or more.

APPLICATION INFO:
Up-to-date application information is available on the web site.

Deadline: Letter of Inquiry: May 1. Grants are awarded in December.

PUBLICATIONS:
Newsletter.

IRS I.D.: 36-3383233

ADDRESS INQUIRIES TO:
Grant Program
(See address above.)

THE GARDEN CLUB OF AMERICA [2055]

14 East 60th Street, Third Floor
New York, NY 10022
(212) 753-8287
Fax: (212) 753-0134
E-mail: scholarshipapplications@gcamerica.org
Web Site: www.gcamerica.org/scholarships

FOUNDED: 1913

AREAS OF INTEREST:
Public horticulture.

NAME(S) OF PROGRAMS:

- **The Garden Club of America Hope Goddard Iselin Fellowship in Public Horticulture**

TYPE:
Fellowships. Garden Club of America Hope Goddard Iselin Fellowship in Public Horticulture: Funds one or more students annually for practical research and training at a recognized public garden, botanic garden, arboretum or other institution directly engaged with connecting people, plants and gardening within the U.S.

YEAR PROGRAM STARTED: 1981

PURPOSE:
To further the study of public horticulture through experiential learning that takes place at a recognized public garden, botanic garden, arboretum or other closely aligned public horticulture institution within the U.S.

LEGAL BASIS:
Nonprofit national organization.

ELIGIBILITY:
Open to students enrolled in a graduate-level university program to study public horticulture. Student applicant must confirm ability to conduct research or otherwise utilize facility where study will be undertaken.

FINANCIAL DATA:
Amount of support per award: $5,000.

NO. AWARDS: 1 or more.

APPLICATION INFO:
Applications are available online and must be sent to the American Public Gardens Association (see address below).

Duration: One year.

Deadline: January 1 preceding the period of study.

PUBLICATIONS:
Program announcement.

ADDRESS INQUIRIES TO:
Ms. Kate Tyrawski
American Public Gardens Association
351 Longwood Road
Kennett Square, PA 19348
Tel: (610) 708-3010
Email: ktyrawski@publicgardens.org
Web Site: www.publicgardens.org

*PLEASE NOTE:
Only one GCA scholarship, fellowship or award may be applied for annually.

THE FRED C. GLOECKNER FOUNDATION, INC. [2056]

550 Mamaroneck Avenue
Suite 510
Harrison, NY 10528-1609
(914) 698-2300
Fax: (914) 698-0848
E-mail: thutter@fredgloeckner.com
Web Site: www.gloecknerfoundation.org

FOUNDED: 1960

AREAS OF INTEREST:
Floriculture and related fields such as plant pathology, plant breeding, agricultural engineering, agricultural economics, entomology and plant physiology related to floriculture.

TYPE:
Assistantships; Project/program grants; Research grants.

YEAR PROGRAM STARTED: 1961

PURPOSE:
To support floriculture research and education.

LEGAL BASIS:
Nonprofit educational corporation.

ELIGIBILITY:
Grants are awarded to nonprofit institutions, primarily colleges and universities, for research and education projects in the above fields. Research in basic plant physiology unrelated to floriculture is not considered. Grants may include assistantships for qualified graduate students seeking an M.S. or Ph.D. in the above fields. Grants are not made directly to students.

GEOG. RESTRICTIONS: United States.

FINANCIAL DATA:
Amount of support per award: $2,000 to $12,000.

Total amount of support: Varies.

NO. MOST RECENT APPLICANTS: 45.

NO. AWARDS: 20.

REPRESENTATIVE AWARDS:
$8,000 to Miller B. McDonald, Ohio State University, for the development of seed quality tests for monitoring flower seed vigor and deterioration; $6,000 to Merriam Karlsson, University of Alaska, Fairbanks, for day and night temperature requirements for flowering and development of cyclamen; $9,700 to Bernard Rubinstein, University of Massachusetts, Amherst, for use of heat shock to preserve flowers not affected by ethylene; $2,000 to Andrew Senesac, Cornell University, for preemergent weed control for transplanted field-grown cutflowers.

APPLICATION INFO:
Applications are available from the Foundation office, or can be downloaded from the web site.

Duration: One year. Renewals possible.

Deadline: April 1.

PUBLICATIONS:
Annual report; application guidelines.

OFFICERS:
Paul L. Daum, President
Dr. Richard Craig, Vice President
Martin D. Kortjohn, Treasurer
Joseph A. Simone, Secretary

DIRECTORS:
Dr. Richard Craig
Margery Daughtery
Paul L. Daum
Dr. Paul Allen Hammer
J. Michael Klesa
Martin D. Kortjohn
Andrew Lee
Jay Sheely
Joseph A. Simone

ADDRESS INQUIRIES TO:
Theresa Hutter, Administrator
(See address above.)

THE HERB SOCIETY OF AMERICA, INC. [2057]

9019 Kirtland Chardon Road
Kirtland, OH 44094
(440) 256-0514
Fax: (440) 256-0541
E-mail: herbs@herbsociety.org
Web Site: www.herbsociety.org

FOUNDED: 1933

AREAS OF INTEREST:
Furthering the knowledge and use of herbs and contributing the results of the experience and research of its members to the records of horticulture, science, literature, history, art or economics.

CONSULTING OR VOLUNTEER SERVICES:
Volunteer services including maintenance of public gardens and workshops.

TYPE:
Research grants.

YEAR PROGRAM STARTED: 1971

PURPOSE:
To promote the knowledge, use and delight of herbs through educational programs, research, and sharing the experiences of its members with the community.

LEGAL BASIS:
Tax-exempt, nonprofit corporation under IRS 501(c)(3).

ELIGIBILITY:
Students, professionals and individuals engaged in research on the horticultural, scientific and/or social applications or use of herbs throughout history.

Funding does not cover indirect costs, purchase or maintenance of durable computer, laboratory or office equipment, expenses related to tuition, textbooks, or conference attendance, private garden development, or travel to/from research site.

FINANCIAL DATA:
Total amount of support: Up to $5,000.

NO. MOST RECENT APPLICANTS: 30.

NO. AWARDS: Varies.

APPLICATION INFO:
Applications should include the following:
(1) application form;
(2) professional vitae, not to exceed two pages, listing qualifications for the project, academic degrees and honors;
(3) explanation, not to exceed 500 words, describing how the project will be completed, where the work will be done, and what facilities and equipment are available;
(4) detailed listing of all anticipated costs and;
(5) specific timeline for the project.

Successful applicants will be required to sign a Grant Acceptance Form prior to the award of a grant.

Duration: One year. No renewals.

Deadline: January 31. Announcement May 1.

PUBLICATIONS:
The Herbarist; newsletter; grant guidelines.

IRS I.D.: 34-1596261

ADDRESS INQUIRIES TO:
Katrinka Morgan, Executive Director
(See address above.)

*SPECIAL STIPULATIONS:
Under the terms of the grant, periodic progress reports are to be sent to the Research Grant Chairman. At the termination of the project, The Herb Society expects a complete copy of the finished product for the Herb Society Library and a summary of the work for publication in the Society's publication, *The Herbarist*. The Society reserves the right to reject or accept credit in any publication resulting from the grant.

HORTICULTURAL RESEARCH INSTITUTE, INC. [2058]

2130 Stella Court
Columbus, OH 43215
(614) 487-1117
Fax: (614) 487-1216
E-mail: jenniferg@americanhort.org
Web Site: www.hriresearch.org

FOUNDED: 1962

AREAS OF INTEREST:
Nursery and landscape research.

NAME(S) OF PROGRAMS:
- **HRI Competitive Grants Program**

TYPE:
Grants-in-aid; Research grants; Scholarships; Seed money grants; Research contracts.

YEAR PROGRAM STARTED: 1974

PURPOSE:
To direct, fund, promote and communicate research which increases the quality and value of plants, improves the productivity and profitability of the nursery and landscape industry and protects and enhances the environment.

LEGAL BASIS:
501(c)(3).

ELIGIBILITY:
Proposals are evaluated on the basis of their relevance to the nursery industry.

GEOG. RESTRICTIONS: North America.

FINANCIAL DATA:
Amount of support per award: $5,000 to $35,000 for the year 2017.

Total amount of support: Varies.

Matching fund requirements: Not required, but preferred.

NO. MOST RECENT APPLICANTS: 65.

NO. AWARDS: 5 for the year 2016.

APPLICATION INFO:
Completed proposals must be submitted using HRI's online application process. No hard copies or e-mailed applications will be accepted.

Deadline: May 31. Announcement in late January/early February.

PUBLICATIONS:
Application guidelines.

IRS I.D.: 52-1052547

ADDRESS INQUIRIES TO:
Jennifer Gray
Research Programs Administrator
(See address above.)

HORTICULTURAL RESEARCH INSTITUTE, INC.

2130 Stella Court
Columbus, OH 43215
(614) 487-1117
Fax: (614) 487-1216
E-mail: jenniferg@americanhort.org
Web Site: www.hriresearch.org

TYPE:
Scholarships.

See entry 1636 for full listing.

LAND O'LAKES FOUNDATION

4001 Lexington Avenue North
Arden Hills, MN 55126
(651) 375-2470
E-mail: landolakesfoundation@landolakes.com
Web Site: www.foundation.landolakes.com

TYPE:
Scholarships. John Brandt Memorial Scholarship Program is a $25,000 scholarship available to graduate students pursuing dairy-related degrees. One or two scholarships are awarded annually to deserving candidates who have demonstrated exceptional commitment and aptitude toward their field of study.

See entry 197 for full listing.

NATIONAL ASSOCIATION OF FARM BROADCASTING FOUNDATION

1100 Platte Falls Road
Platte City, MO 64079
(816) 431-4032
Fax: (816) 431-4087
E-mail: susan@nafb.com
Web Site: www.nafbfoundation.com

TYPE:
Scholarships. Since 1977, the NAFB Foundation has provided financial support and educational opportunities in the form of college scholarships to assist students in pursuit of careers in agricultural communications. Currently the NAFB Foundation offers three annual college scholarships. These scholarships are recognized at the National NAFB Convention.

See entry 1883 for full listing.

NATIONAL CATTLEMAN'S BEEF ASSOCIATION

9110 East Nichols Avenue
Centennial, CO 80112-3450
(830) 569-0046
Fax: (303) 770-6921
E-mail: smcneill@beef.org
Web Site: www.beefresearch.org

TYPE:
Grants-in-aid; Research grants; Research contracts. Research contracts and grants-in-aid for experimental projects in the areas of:
(1) beef as part of a balanced diet;
(2) parity studies;
(3) health benefits of beef lipids and;
(4) contribution of beef nutrients to total diet.

Proposals solicited via specific RFPs (request for proposals).

See entry 2590 for full listing.

NATIONAL DAIRY SHRINE [2059]

P.O. Box 725
Denmark, WI 54208
(920) 863-6333
Fax: (920) 863-6333
E-mail: info@dairyshrine.org
Web Site: www.dairyshrine.org

FOUNDED: 1949

AREAS OF INTEREST:
Dairy production, research, milk products, milk marketing, genetics and education.

NAME(S) OF PROGRAMS:
- **National Dairy Shrine Student Recognition Program**
- **NDS Graduate Production Award**
- **NDS Progressive Commercial Manager Grant**
- **NDS/Core Scholarship**
- **NDS/DMI Milk Marketing Scholarships**
- **NDS/Iager Scholarship**
- **NDS/Kildee Scholarships**
- **NDS/Klussendorf Scholarship**
- **NDS/McCullough Scholarships**
- **NDS/McKown Scholarship**

TYPE:
Awards/prizes; Scholarships; Training grants. Awards made annually to students interested in careers in the dairy industry. Majors can include dairy science, animal science, agricultural economics, agricultural communications, agriculture education, food and nutrition.

YEAR PROGRAM STARTED: 1951

PURPOSE:
To encourage students to pursue careers in the dairy industry.

LEGAL BASIS:
Nonprofit corporation.

ELIGIBILITY:
National Dairy Shrine Student Recognition Program: Graduating seniors planning a career related to dairy-production agriculture who have demonstrated leadership skills, academic ability and interest in dairy cattle.

NDS/Core Scholarship: Applicants must be outstanding freshman college students at a four-year agricultural college.

NDS/DMI Milk Marketing Scholarships: Available to undergraduate students (except previous winners) during his or her sophomore or junior year with an explicit interest in dairy products marketing. The applicants must have at least a cumulative 2.5 grade point average on a 4.0 scale.

NDS Graduate Production Award: Available to a two- or four-year college graduate to finance replacement animals. Must have graduated four years prior.

NDS/Iager Scholarship: Open to outstanding second-year college dairy students in a two-year agricultural college.

NDS/Kildee Scholarships: Applicants must have placed in Top 25 at National Intercollegiate or National 4-H Dairy Judging Contests. Platinum winners in the last three National Dairy Challenge Contests may apply for Kildee Graduate Study Scholarships.

NDS/Klussendorf Scholarship: Open to students successfully completing their first, second or third years at a two- or four-year college or university in Dairy/Animal Science.

NDS/McCullough Scholarships: The applicant must be a high school graduating senior planning to enter a four-year college or university with intent to major in Dairy/Animal Science with a Communications emphasis or Agricultural Journalism with a Dairy/Animal Science emphasis and be a U.S. citizen.

NDS/McKown Scholarship: Open to students successfully completing their first, second or third year at a four-year college or university in Dairy/Animal Science.

NDS Progressive Commercial Manager Grant: Applicant must be 21 to 50 years of age and demonstrate leadership in the dairy industry.

GEOG. RESTRICTIONS: United States.

FINANCIAL DATA:
Amount of support per award: National Dairy Shrine Student Recognition Program: $5,000 to $7,500; NDS/Core Scholarship and NDS/Iager Scholarship: $1,000; NDS/DMI Milk Marketing Scholarships: $1,500 and $1,000; NDS Graduate Production Award: $2,500; NDS/Kildee Scholarships: $6,000 graduate and $1,000 undergraduate; NDS/Klussendorf Scholarships: $3,500; NDS/McCullough Scholarships: $2,000 and $1,500; NDS/McKown Scholarship: $4,000; NDS Progressive Commercial Manager Grant: $2,000 each for educational travel.

Total amount of support: Over $40,000.

NO. MOST RECENT APPLICANTS: 125.

NO. AWARDS: National Dairy Shrine Student Recognition Program: 7 to 10; NDS/Core Scholarship and NDS Graduate Production Award: 2; NDS/DMI Milk Marketing Scholarships: 5 or 8 awards of $1,000 and 1 award of $1,500; NDS/Iager Scholarship: 2 or more; NDS/Kildee Scholarships: 2 graduate and 1 undergraduate; NDS/Klussendorf Scholarships and NDS/McKown Scholarship: 7; NDS/McCullough Scholarships: 1 award of $2,500 and 1 award of $1,000; NDS Progressive Commercial Manager Grant: 2.

APPLICATION INFO:
All NDS scholarships and awards require the submission of a completed application form with additional requirements for some scholarships. Forms are available at the web site above. All requirements for the scholarship application and submission deadlines must be followed.

Duration: One year.

Deadline: Applications accepted March 1 to April 15 (postmarked). Announcements by July 1.

PUBLICATIONS:
Application form.

EXECUTIVE DIRECTOR:
David Selner

ADDRESS INQUIRIES TO:
David Selner, Executive Director
(See address above.)

*SPECIAL STIPULATIONS:
The second half of each scholarship will be awarded after successful completion of next year. Recipients will be asked to submit their

most recent grade transcript and proof of enrollment in the first term of the following year.

NATIONAL FARMER'S ORGANIZATION [2060]

528 Billy Sunday Road
Suite 100
Ames, IA 50010
(515) 292-2000
Fax: (866) 629-4853
E-mail: nfo@nfo.org
Web Site: www.nfo.org

AREAS OF INTEREST:
Agricultural careers.

NAME(S) OF PROGRAMS:

- **Farm Kids for College Scholarships**

TYPE:
Scholarships.

PURPOSE:
To assist students planning careers in agriculture and farming.

ELIGIBILITY:
Must be a high school senior that will major in an agricultural field at an accredited college or university.

GEOG. RESTRICTIONS: United States.

FINANCIAL DATA:
Amount of support per award: $1,000.
Total amount of support: $3,000.

NO. AWARDS: 3.

APPLICATION INFO:
Application information is available on the web site.
Duration: One year.
Deadline: Late February to early March.

ADDRESS INQUIRIES TO:
Helene Bergren
National Scholarship Coordinator
(See address above.)

NATIONAL PARK FOUNDATION

1110 Vermont Avenue, N.W.
Suite 200
Washington, DC 20005
(202) 796-2500
Fax: (202) 796-2509
E-mail: ask-npf@nationalparks.org
Web Site: www.nationalparks.org

TYPE:
Block grants; Challenge/matching grants; Research grants; Scholarships. Grants range from small seed or start-up programs to larger ones which continue successful projects. Grants enable the parks to obtain additional cash and in-kind contributions, such as products, service or volunteer time.

The Albright-Wirth Employee Development Fund underwrites advanced skills training, graduate education and other professional development programs for Park Service employees.

The Harry Yount National Park Ranger Award recognizes a Ranger for leadership, exemplary skills and dedication to the Park Ranger profession.

See entry 2122 for full listing.

NORTHEAST AGRICULTURAL EDUCATION FOUNDATION [2061]

220 South Warren Street
9th Floor
Syracuse, NY 13202
(315) 671-0588
Fax: (315) 671-0589
E-mail: info@northeastagriculture.org
Web Site: www.northeastagriculture.org

FOUNDED: 1966

AREAS OF INTEREST:
Agriculture, civic and community.

TYPE:
Project/program grants.

PURPOSE:
To support nonprofit organizations dedicated to serving the interests of farmers and rural communities in the Northeast.

LEGAL BASIS:
Private foundation.

ELIGIBILITY:
Grants are made to nonprofit organizations that have tax-exempt status under Section 501(c)(3) of the Internal Revenue Code. No grants are made to individuals.

GEOG. RESTRICTIONS: Primarily northeastern United States.

FINANCIAL DATA:
Amount of support per award: Varies.
Total amount of support: Varies.

APPLICATION INFO:
Complete Grant Summary Sheet and provide supporting documents. Full grant application package is available on web site.
Duration: Varies.
Deadline: Applications are accepted on a rolling basis. Grant requests should be submitted at least 90 to 120 days prior to date funding is needed.

PUBLICATIONS:
Background and application guidelines; application requirements; grant request summary.

ADDRESS INQUIRIES TO:
Craig Buckhout, Administrator
(See address above.)

*SPECIAL STIPULATIONS:
The Foundation does not fund recurring operating costs unless it is for programmatic start-up.

NORTHEASTERN LOGGERS' ASSOCIATION, INC. [2062]

3311 State Route 28
Old Forge, NY 13420-0069
(315) 369-3078
Fax: (315) 369-3736
E-mail: mona@northernlogger.com
Web Site: www.northernlogger.com

FOUNDED: 1952

AREAS OF INTEREST:
Forestry, wood science and technology.

NAME(S) OF PROGRAMS:

- **NELA Annual Scholarship Contest**

TYPE:
Scholarships. Essay scholarship contest.

YEAR PROGRAM STARTED: 1975

PURPOSE:
To provide support for students and employees of members.

LEGAL BASIS:
501(c)(6) giving program.

ELIGIBILITY:
Scholarships are available to the immediate families of individual members, or the immediate families of employees of Industrial and Associate Members of the Northeastern Loggers' Association. Applicants must be bound for or engaged in post-high school education and must be either seniors in high school graduating in the current year, students in two-year Associate's degree or technical school programs or juniors/seniors in four-year Bachelor's degree programs.

GEOG. RESTRICTIONS: United States.

FINANCIAL DATA:
Amount of support per award: $500 to $1,000.
Total amount of support: $6,000.

NO. MOST RECENT APPLICANTS: 17.

NO. AWARDS: Up to 8 annually.

APPLICATION INFO:
Applicants must prepare a 1,000-word essay (about four pages double-spaced) on the topic: "What It Means to Grow Up in the Forest Industry." The essay must be typed and the quality of the essay will be the primary determining factor for the award. Applicant must submit with the essay a completed application form, grade transcript, and report card information before the application deadline.

Application forms and additional information are also available on the Association web site.
Duration: One year.
Deadline: March 31. Notification in May.

ADDRESS INQUIRIES TO:
Mona Lincoln
Director, Safety and Training
(See address and e-mail above.)

JESSIE SMITH NOYES FOUNDATION

122 East 42nd Street
Suite 2501
New York, NY 10168
(212) 684-6577
Fax: (212) 689-6549
E-mail: noyes@noyes.org
Web Site: www.noyes.org

TYPE:
General operating grants; Project/program grants. Grants to tax-exempt institutions in the connected and overlapping areas of sustainable agriculture, toxics, reproductive rights, and New York City environment in order to achieve the Foundation's overall goal, which is to promote a sustainable and just social and natural system by supporting grassroots organizations and movements committed to this goal.

See entry 2125 for full listing.

RURAL HOUSING SERVICE [2063]

1400 Independence Avenue, S.W.
Room 5014
Washington, DC 20250
(202) 690-1533
Fax: (202) 720-6895
Web Site: www.rurdev.usda.gov

FOUNDED: 1949

AREAS OF INTEREST:
Rural development.

NAME(S) OF PROGRAMS:
- **Rural Housing Grants (Section 504)**

TYPE:
Grants-in-aid; Project/program grants. Grants to assist elderly, very low-income owner-occupants in rural areas to repair or improve their dwellings to make such dwellings safe and sanitary and remove hazards.

RHS is the credit agency for rural development in USDA. RHS has offices at the state, district and county levels which serve every county or parish in the 50 states, plus the western Pacific areas, Guam, Puerto Rico and the Virgin Islands.

YEAR PROGRAM STARTED: 1961

PURPOSE:
To assist applicants who are unable to repay a loan amortized at one percent over 20 years.

LEGAL BASIS:
42 U.S.C. 1474.

ELIGIBILITY:
Open to counties and towns or places of 10,000 or less within SMA's and towns or places of up to 20,000 outside SMA's. Areas classified as rural prior to October 1, 1990, with a population in excess of 10,000 are eligible if the area population is 25,000 or less.

Applicants must own and occupy houses in rural areas that need repair to remove health or safety hazards. Grant recipients must be 62 years of age or older, very low-income households (under 50% of median income) owner-occupants, and unable to pay for that cost of repair with a loan.

FINANCIAL DATA:
Amount of support per award: Lifetime assistance cannot exceed $7,500.

APPLICATION INFO:
Applicants must apply at the local county Rural Development (RD) office. Awards are approved by Community Development Manager.

TREE RESEARCH & EDUCATION ENDOWMENT FUND (TREE FUND) [2064]

552 South Washington Street
Suite 109
Naperville, IL 60540
(630) 369-8300
Fax: (630) 369-8382
E-mail: treefund@treefund.org
Web Site: www.treefund.org

FOUNDED: 1975

AREAS OF INTEREST:
Research in areas of urban tree care, preservation and arboriculture education.

NAME(S) OF PROGRAMS:
- **Arboriculture Education Grant**
- **John Duling Grant**
- **Robert Felix Memorial Scholarship**
- **Hyland Johns Grant**
- **Jack Kimmel International Grant**
- **Ohio Chapter ISA Education Grant**
- **Research Fellowship**
- **Horace M. Thayer Scholarship**
- **Fran Ward Women in Arboriculture Scholarship**
- **John Wright Memorial Scholarship**

TYPE:
Fellowships; Research grants; Scholarships; Seed money grants. Grants to further research relating to arboriculture. Scholarships are for arboriculture and horticulture students.

YEAR PROGRAM STARTED: 1976

PURPOSE:
To initiate and foster scientific investigation of problems concerned with the practice of arboriculture.

LEGAL BASIS:
Tax-exempt public-supported corporation, 501(c)(3) classification.

ELIGIBILITY:
Qualified persons who have a B.S. degree and are planning on graduate study for a Master's or Doctorate in a related field are eligible to apply for scholarship program. Scholarships available for undergraduate study focusing on arboriculture or horticulture.

GEOG. RESTRICTIONS: United States.

FINANCIAL DATA:
Grants do not pay for overhead expenses.

Amount of support per award: John Duling Grant: Up to $25,000; Education Grants: $5,000; Fellowship: $100,000; Hyland Johns Grant: Up to $50,000; Jack Kimmel Grant: Up to $10,000; Scholarships: Up to $3,000.

Matching fund requirements: 10% match or in-kind.

NO. MOST RECENT APPLICANTS: Varies.

NO. AWARDS: Varies.

APPLICATION INFO:
Applications are to be completed online. Before applying for a grant, carefully read the Grant Guidelines. Applications that do not contain all the requested information may be denied.

Duration: John Duling Grant: One to three years; Education Grants: One year; Hyland Johns and Jack Kimmel Grants: Multiyear; Research Fellowship: Multiyear.

Deadline: John Duling and Jack Kimmel Grants: October 1; Education Grants: March 1; Hyland Johns Grant: April 1; Research Fellowship: Varies.

PUBLICATIONS:
Application guidelines.

IRS I.D.: 37-1018692

STAFF:
J. Eric Smith, President and Chief Executive Officer
Mary DiCarlo, Director of Philanthropy
Karen Lindell, Community Engagement Manager

ADDRESS INQUIRIES TO:
Barbara Duke, Office Manager
E-mail: bduke@treefund.org

*SPECIAL STIPULATIONS:
No part of grant can be used for overhead expenses.

U.S. DEPARTMENT OF AGRICULTURE

1400 Independence Avenue, S.W.
Stop 0513
Washington, DC 20250-0510
(202) 720-6221
Fax: (202) 720-4619
E-mail: matthewponish@wdc.usda.gov
Web Site: www.fsa.usda.gov

TYPE:
Grants-in-aid. Cost-share assistance with agricultural producers to rehabilitate agricultural lands damaged by natural disasters. Assistance may also be provided for carrying out emergency water conservation measures during periods of severe drought.

See entry 2136 for full listing.

U.S.-ISRAEL BINATIONAL AGRICULTURE RESEARCH AND DEVELOPMENT FUND (BARD) [2065]

P.O. Box 6
Bet Dagan 50250 Israel
(972) 3-9683834
(972) 3-9683366
Fax: (972) 3-9662506
E-mail: nitsan@bard-isus.com
Web Site: www.bard-isus.com

FOUNDED: 1977

AREAS OF INTEREST:
Agriculture.

NAME(S) OF PROGRAMS:
- **Graduate Student Fellowship Program**
- **Senior Research Fellowship Program**
- **Vaadia-BARD Postdoctoral Fellowship Program**

TYPE:
Fellowships; Research grants; Visiting scholars.

YEAR PROGRAM STARTED: 1977

PURPOSE:
To promote cooperative agriculture research between the U.S. and Israel; to provide BARD with input into new research areas; to enhance scientific competence in these areas.

LEGAL BASIS:
Nonprofit organization. Governmental Associations in U.S. and Israel.

ELIGIBILITY:
Citizens of the U.S. or Israel who are established research scientists, Ph.D. students and young scientists from American or Israeli nonprofit research institutions, universities, or federal or state agencies are eligible.

GEOG. RESTRICTIONS: United States and Israel.

FINANCIAL DATA:
Amount of support per award: Graduate Student Fellowship: $1,500 per month, plus $2,000 to cover travel costs. Postdoctoral Fellowship: $37,000, plus $8,000 for fellows with dependents. Research Grant: Approximately $320,000 over three years. Senior Research Fellowship: $3,000 per month, plus one-time allocation of $2,000 for travel.

Total amount of support: $8,000,000 per year.

NO. MOST RECENT APPLICANTS: 100.

NO. AWARDS: 25.

APPLICATION INFO:
For application information, consult with BARD office in Israel.

Duration: Graduate Student Fellowship: Three to six months. Postdoctoral Fellowship: One year; second year possible with agreement from mentor and shared on a matching basis between BARD and host lab. Research awards: Three years. Senior Research Fellowship: Two to 12 months.

Deadline: Research awards: Mid-September. Postdoctoral Fellowship, Senior Fellowship Program, and Graduate Student Fellowship Program: January 15.

PUBLICATIONS:
Application guidelines.

OFFICERS:
Edo Chalutz, Executive Director
Miriam Green, Controller

THE UNIVERSITY OF SYDNEY [2066]

Scholarships Office
Level 5, Jane Foss Russell Building G02
The University of Sydney N.S.W. 2006
Australia
(02) 8627 8112
Fax: (02) 8627 8485
E-mail: scholarships.officer@sydney.edu.au
Web Site: www.sydney.edu.au/scholarships/research

FOUNDED: 1850

AREAS OF INTEREST:
Veterinary science.

NAME(S) OF PROGRAMS:
- **F.H. Loxton Postgraduate Studentships**

TYPE:
Scholarships. Awarded for research leading to a higher degree. Tenable at the University of Sydney.

PURPOSE:
To enable a male graduate of any university to engage in postgraduate research at the University of Sydney, within the Faculty of Veterinary Science.

LEGAL BASIS:
University.

ELIGIBILITY:
Open only to male graduates of any university enrolled in a higher degree by research in the Faculty of Veterinary Science.

FINANCIAL DATA:
Award does not cover tuition fees payable by international students. Relocation allowance within Australia and thesis allowance available.

Amount of support per award: $25,849 AUD per annum for the year 2015.

NO. AWARDS: Offered as vacancies occur. Awarded annually depending on the availability of funds in the area of Agriculture and Environment.

APPLICATION INFO:
Particulars are available from the Faculty of Veterinary Science, The University of Sydney.

Duration: Master's research degree: Two years; Ph.D. degree: Three years.

Deadline: Varies.

ADDRESS INQUIRIES TO:
The Faculty of Veterinary Science
The University of Sydney
N.S.W. 2006 Australia
E-mail: vetsci@vetsci.usyd.edu.au

THE UNIVERSITY OF SYDNEY [2067]

Scholarships Office
Level 5, Jane Foss Russell Building G02
The University of Sydney N.S.W. 2006
Australia
(02) 8627 8112
Fax: (02) 8627 8485
E-mail: scholarships.officer@sydney.edu.au
Web Site: www.sydney.edu.au/scholarships/research

FOUNDED: 1850

AREAS OF INTEREST:
Any subject in the Faculty of Agriculture.

NAME(S) OF PROGRAMS:
- **Thomas Lawrance Pawlett Scholarship**

TYPE:
Scholarships. Awarded for postgraduate research. Tenable at the University of Sydney.

PURPOSE:
To encourage and promote scientific study in agriculture at the University of Sydney.

LEGAL BASIS:
University.

ELIGIBILITY:
Open to University of Sydney graduates, graduands, or persons holding equivalent qualification who are eligible for admission to candidature for a higher degree by research and thesis and who enroll as full-time candidates in the Faculty of Agriculture and Environment.

Scholarships may not be held concurrently with other awards or salaried position, except with the approval of the Faculty of Agriculture and Environment.

FINANCIAL DATA:
No assistance with travel costs of scholars taking up award from outside Australia. Award does not cover tuition fees payable by international students.

Amount of support per award: $25,849 AUD per annum for the year 2015.

NO. AWARDS: Offered as funds available.

APPLICATION INFO:
Contact the University.

Duration: Tenable for two years for Master's candidate. Tenable for three years with the possibility of a six-month extension for Ph.D. candidate.

Deadline: October 31.

ADDRESS INQUIRIES TO:
The Faculty of Agriculture and Environment
The University of Sydney
N.S.W. 2006 Australia
Tel: (02) 8627 1002
E-mail: fae.pgscholarships@sydney.edu.au

USDA - RURAL UTILITIES SERVICE [2068]

1400 Independence Avenue, S.W.
Stop 1548
Washington, DC 20250
(202) 690-2670
Fax: (202) 720-0718
Web Site: www.usda.gov/rus/water

FOUNDED: 1935

AREAS OF INTEREST:
Rural areas and towns that have a population of up to 10,000.

NAME(S) OF PROGRAMS:
- **Water and Waste Disposal Systems for Rural Communities**

TYPE:
Capital grants; Development grants; Project/program grants. Loans.

YEAR PROGRAM STARTED: 1965

PURPOSE:
To provide financial assistance for water and waste disposal facilities in rural areas and towns.

LEGAL BASIS:
Government agency.

ELIGIBILITY:
Only rural areas and cities and towns with populations under 10,000 are eligible.

Applicants must:
(1) be a public entity, nonprofit corporation or Indian tribe;
(2) be unable to obtain needed funds from other sources at reasonable rates and terms;
(3) have legal capacity and;
(4) have adequate security for loans.

FINANCIAL DATA:
Amount of support per award: Varies.

CO-OP FUNDING PROGRAMS: Can cooperate with any other federal, state, local or private credit source.

APPLICATION INFO:
Applicants must submit Form SF-424, application for federal assistance and state intergovernmental review comments and recommendations.

Deadline: Applications accepted throughout the year.

ADDRESS INQUIRIES TO:
Jacqueline M. Ponti-Lazaruk
Assistant Administrator
Water and Environmental Programs
(See address above.)

WOMAN'S NATIONAL FARM & GARDEN ASSOCIATION, INC. [2069]

32500 Susanne Drive
Franklin, MI 48025
E-mail: SBTfellowship@aol.com
Web Site: www.wnfga.org

FOUNDED: 1914

NAME(S) OF PROGRAMS:
- **Sarah Bradley Tyson Memorial Fellowship**

TYPE:
Fellowships; Internships; Scholarships. Awards for advanced study in the fields of agriculture, horticulture and allied subjects.

YEAR PROGRAM STARTED: 1928

PURPOSE:
To encourage better living around the world.

ELIGIBILITY:
Open to properly qualified young women (now including men) who have proven their ability by several years of experience. Awards have been made in recognition of leadership in cooperative extension work and initiative in scientific research.

The Fellowship is to be used for advanced study (Master's or Doctorate) at an educational institution of recognized standing within the U.S. It is to be chosen by the candidate and with the approval of the Fellowship Committee.

FINANCIAL DATA:
Amount of support per award: $1,000. Checks are made out to the student's university and mailed to the student.

APPLICATION INFO:
There are no application forms. A letter of application should be sent to the Chairman of the Committee. The letter of application should contain:
(1) an account of the applicant's educational training;
(2) a statement, in full, of the object in view and the plan of study;
(3) a certificate (transcript) from the registrar of the school, college or university awarding the degree or degrees received by the applicant;
(4) testimonials as to character, ability, personality and scholarship;
(5) theses, papers or reports of investigations, published or unpublished, if available; these will be returned if postage is sent for that purpose; confidential letters sent to the Committee are retained;
(6) a health certificate; (a doctor's handwritten and signed note on prescription paper, verifying good health of the student, will suffice;) and;
(7) a small recent photograph.

Duration: One year.

Deadline: Applications and recommendations for the Fellowship must be received not later than April 15 of the year to be awarded.

IRS I.D.: 52-6073829

OFFICERS:
Molly Hammerle, President
Mary Pat Ford, Vice President
Lenore Treba, A & O Treasurer
Susan Hunt, E & C Treasurer
Audrey Ehrler, Corresponding Secretary
Kathy Beveridge, Recording Secretary
Julia Siefker, Advisor

ADDRESS INQUIRIES TO:
Mrs. Harold L. Matyn
Chairman, Fellowship Committee
Woman's National Farm
& Garden Association, Inc.
3801 Riverview Terrace, South
East China Township, MI 48054
E-mail: matynjm@att.net

*SPECIAL STIPULATIONS:
The acceptance of the Fellowship implies the obligation on the part of the student to devote herself or himself unreservedly to study or research as outlined in her or his application, and to submit any proposed change in her or his plan to the Chairman for approval.

Biology

THE ACADEMY OF NATURAL SCIENCES OF PHILADELPHIA [2070]

1900 Benjamin Franklin Parkway
Philadelphia, PA 19103-1195
(215) 299-1065
Fax: (215) 299-1079
E-mail: kepics@ansp.org
Web Site: www.ansp.org/research/jessupinfo.html

FOUNDED: 1812

AREAS OF INTEREST:
Research, exhibition and education in natural sciences.

NAME(S) OF PROGRAMS:
- **Jessup Fellowship**
- **McHenry Fellowship**

TYPE:
Fellowships. The Jessup Fellowship is for research support in any specialty in which the curatorial staff of the Academy have expertise. The McHenry Fellowship is for botanical research support.

PURPOSE:
To promote research in the natural sciences.

ELIGIBILITY:
The Jessup Fellowships are awarded competitively to students wishing to conduct studies at the postgraduate, doctoral and postdoctoral levels under the supervision or sponsorship of a member of the curatorial staff of the Academy. The Fellowships are not available for undergraduate study. These Fellowships are restricted to those who wish to conduct their study at the Academy and are intended to assist predoctoral and postdoctoral students within several years of receiving their Ph.Ds.

FINANCIAL DATA:
Round-trip travel costs up to a total of $500 for North American (including Mexico and the Caribbean) applicants and $1,000 for applicants from other parts of the world may be available, but cannot be guaranteed. The provision of scientific supplies and equipment is the responsibility of the student and the sponsoring curator.

Amount of support per award: Stipend for subsistence of $375 per week. (Method of distribution subject to change.)

APPLICATION INFO:
Applicant is responsible to submit his or her application in time and to be sure that the three letters of recommendation also reach the Fund Chairman in time. One of these letters of recommendation must be from the Academy curator overseeing or sponsoring the student.

Application form and supporting information should be sent to Dr. Edward Daeschler, Jessup-McHenry Fund Committee, using the address above.

Duration: Two to 16 weeks.

Deadline: Applications for grants will be considered in March and October of each year. Applicants wishing to do their research between April 1 and October 31 should apply by March 1; those wishing to work between November 1 and March 31 should apply by October 1.

ADDRESS INQUIRIES TO:
Kristen Kepics, Department Administrator
(See e-mail address above.)

*SPECIAL STIPULATIONS:
Fellowship awardees are expected to give a seminar after their arrival and are encouraged to publish at least some of their work accomplished at the Academy.

AMERICAN ASSOCIATION OF ZOO KEEPERS [2071]

8476 East Speedway
Suite 204
Tucson, AZ 85710-1728
(520) 298-9688
Fax: (520) 298-9688
E-mail: ed.hansen@aazk.org
Web Site: www.aazk.org

FOUNDED: 1968

AREAS OF INTEREST:
Animal care and the promotion of animal keeping as a profession.

NAME(S) OF PROGRAMS:
- **Bowling for Rhinos Conservation Resource Grant (BFR CRG)**
- **Conservation, Preservation and Restoration (CPR) Grant**
- **Polar Bear International (PBI) Conservation Grant**
- **Polar Bear International (PBI) Research Grant**
- **Professional Development Grant**
- **Research Grant**
- **Trees for You and Me (TFYM) Reforestation Grant**

TYPE:
Challenge/matching grants; Conferences/seminars; Grants-in-aid; Research grants; Scholarships; Training grants; Travel grants. Grants in the area of zoology, with emphasis on contributions to improving animal management.

YEAR PROGRAM STARTED: 1980

PURPOSE:
To provide funds for original keeper-initiated research of behavioral and/or biomedical topics and general zoological park management principles.

LEGAL BASIS:
Nonprofit corporation.

ELIGIBILITY:
Candidates must be full-time, permanent keepers in the zoo and aquarium profession and must be AAZK professional members in good standing.

GEOG. RESTRICTIONS: United States and Canada.

FINANCIAL DATA:
Amount of support per award: Up to $1,000.
Total amount of support: $2,000 per year.

NO. MOST RECENT APPLICANTS: 5.

NO. AWARDS: 4 annually.

APPLICATION INFO:
Applications consist of an application form, brief research proposal and resume. Application materials and further information are available from the Committee chairperson or can be downloaded from the web site.

Duration: One year. One-year extension is possible with status report and Committee approval.

Deadline: March 1. Successful applicants are notified within three months of the deadline.

PUBLICATIONS:
Application guidelines.

IRS I.D.: 23-7274856

BOARD OF DIRECTORS:
Penny Jolly, President
Wendy Lenhart, Vice President
Bethany Bingham
Mary Ann Cisneros
Rachael Ruffino
Bill Steele

ADDRESS INQUIRIES TO:
Ed Hansen, Chief Executive Officer/Chief Financial Officer
(See address above.)

*SPECIAL STIPULATIONS:
Research results must be presented to the AAZK membership by either an oral presentation at an AAZK conference, a paper published in *Animal Keepers' Forum* or a research summary report published in *Animal Keepers' Forum.*

THE AMERICAN MUSEUM OF NATURAL HISTORY [2072]

Richard Gilder Graduate School
Central Park West at 79th Street
New York, NY 10024-5192
(212) 769-5017
Fax: (212) 769-5257
E-mail: mrios@amnh.org
info-rggs@amnh.org
Web Site: www.amnh.org/our-research/richard-gilder-graduate-school

FOUNDED: 1869

AREAS OF INTEREST:
Education of Ph.D. candidates in scientific disciplines.

NAME(S) OF PROGRAMS:
- **Graduate Student Fellowship Program**

TYPE:
Fellowships. An educational partnership with selected universities dedicated to the training of Ph.D. candidates. The university exercises educational jurisdiction over the program and awards the degree. The museum curator serves as a graduate advisor, co-major professor, or major professor. The student benefits by having the staff and facilities of both the university and the museum in order to carry on his or her training and research programs. Joint programs are with the following universities:
(1) Columbia University in vertebrate and invertebrate paleontology, earth and planetary sciences, and evolutionary biology;
(2) Cornell University in entomology;
(3) City University of New York in evolutionary biology and the biological anthropology programs and;
(4) New York University in molecular biology.

PURPOSE:
To encourage bright and promising students to enter the fields of science in which the museum participates.

ELIGIBILITY:
Applicants must have a Bachelor's degree and be able to fulfill university admission requirements, including TOEFL and Graduate Record Examinations. The program is not open to candidates for the Master's degree.

FINANCIAL DATA:
Fellowships cover stipend, tuition and health insurance.

Amount of support per award: Varies.

Total amount of support: Varies.

APPLICATION INFO:
All applications are to be completed online only. All materials, including reference letters, must be submitted electronically, using the forms provided on the web site. Complete instructions are available on the web site.

Duration: One year. Renewable annually for up to four years.

Deadline: December 15.

PUBLICATIONS:
Program announcement; application.

ADDRESS INQUIRIES TO:
Maria Rios, Assistant Director
Fellowships and Student Affairs
(See address above.)

AMERICAN ORCHID SOCIETY [2073]

Fairchild Tropical Botanic Garden
10901 Old Cutler Road
Coral Gables, FL 33156
(305) 740-2010
E-mail: theaos@aos.org
Web Site: www.aos.org

FOUNDED: 1921

AREAS OF INTEREST:
Orchid research.

NAME(S) OF PROGRAMS:
- **American Orchid Society Grants for Orchid Research**

TYPE:
Awards/prizes; Block grants; Capital grants; Development grants; Grants-in-aid; Research grants. Grants and research contracts for experimental projects and applied and fundamental research pertaining to orchids and grants-in-aid to graduate students engaged in research on orchids. Support is given in such areas relevant to orchids as biological research (including taxonomy, anatomy, genetics, physiology development, tissue culture and pathology), conservation and education.

YEAR PROGRAM STARTED: 1966

PURPOSE:
To advance the scientific study of orchids in every aspect; to assist in the publication of scholarly and popular scientific literature on orchids.

LEGAL BASIS:
Corporation.

ELIGIBILITY:
Qualified personnel associated with accredited institutions or appropriate institutes or organizations may apply for grants. Support is not restricted to individuals or institutions within the U.S. The salaries of established scientists is not supported. Qualified graduate students with appropriate interests may apply for grants in support of their research. If justified, their salary may be supported.

In general, travel to collect orchids is not supported. Other types of travel may be supported on a case-by-case basis. Projects that involve commercial sales of plants are generally not supported.

FINANCIAL DATA:
Amount of support per award: Grants and research contracts vary in amount, depending upon the needs and nature of the request and the potential for securing additional funds from other sources.

APPLICATION INFO:
As a first step, prospective applicants should submit a brief letter outlining the objectives and general plans of the project. If appropriate, an application form and project outline for request of a grant will then be supplied to provide the applicant with further detailed information.

Duration: Although the duration of each grant depends upon the particular project, most grants are awarded for one year with the possibility of renewal. In all cases, the maximum grant period is three years.

Deadline: January 1 for spring consideration; August 1 for fall consideration.

PUBLICATIONS:
Application guidelines.

ADDRESS INQUIRIES TO:
Ron McHatton, Director of Education
(See address above.)

*SPECIAL STIPULATIONS:
Research application must involve orchids.

AMERICAN SOCIETY FOR MICROBIOLOGY [2074]

Education Department
1752 N Street, N.W.
Washington, DC 20036
(202) 942-9283
Fax: (202) 942-9329
E-mail: fellowships@asmusa.org
Web Site: www.asm.org/cdcfellowship
www.asm.org/urc

FOUNDED: 1899

AREAS OF INTEREST:
Biological research.

NAME(S) OF PROGRAMS:
- **ASM/CDC Postdoctoral Research Fellowship Program**
- **Undergraduate Research Capstone Program**

TYPE:
Fellowships. ASM/CDC Postdoctoral Research Fellowship Program: The American Society for Microbiology and Centers for Disease Control and Prevention (ASM/CDC) Postdoctoral Research Fellowship Program is a comprehensive training program which provides opportunities to participate in interdisciplinary training on global public health issues. Fellows will perform research at one of the Centers for Disease Control and Prevention (CDC) locations.

Undergraduate Research Capstone Program: This fellowship encourages students to pursue careers or advanced degrees in the microbiological sciences by providing an opportunity to participate in a research project at their institution and gain experience in presenting their results. The fellowship allows students to conduct research in the summer with an ASM member faculty mentor and present the results at the ASM General Meeting the following year.

PURPOSE:
To promote study and research in microbiology; to fulfill the later stages of undergraduate professional development for underrepresented minority students completing doctoral degrees in microbiology.

LEGAL BASIS:
Private, nonprofit science organization.

ELIGIBILITY:
ASM/CDC Postdoctoral Research Fellowship Program: Applicant must have earned their doctorate degree or completed a primary residency within three years of their proposed start date.

Undergraduate Research Capstone Program: Applicants must:
(1) be a U.S. citizen or permanent U.S. resident;

(2) be enrolled as full-time matriculating undergraduate student during the 2015-2016 academic years;
(3) be from an underrepresented minority group (African-American, Hispanic, Native American, Alaskan Native and Pacific Islander), a community college, a minority serving institution, a first generation college student or non-traditional student;
(4) have conducted research in the microbiological sciences at a U.S. institution (host mentor is not required to be an ASM member, but recommended);
(5) have a strong interest in obtaining a research career and postgraduate training in research within the microbiological sciences and;
(6) be accepted to present a poster or oral presentation at the ASM General Meeting.

Preference will be given to juniors and seniors.

GEOG. RESTRICTIONS: United States.

FINANCIAL DATA:
Amount of support per award: ASM/CDC Postdoctoral Research Fellowship Program: Up to $46,106 annual stipend, up to $3,000 annually in health benefits for a maximum of two years, up to $500 for relocation benefits, and up to $2,000 annually for professional development for a maximum of two years; Undergraduate Research Capstone Program: A two-year ASM student membership, and up to $1,500 travel support to attend the ASM General Meeting.

Total amount of support: Varies.

APPLICATION INFO:
Application information is available on the web site.

Duration: ASM/CDC Postdoctoral Research Fellowship Program: Two years; Undergraduate Research Capstone Program: Minimum 12 weeks.

Deadline: ASM/CDC Postdoctoral Research Fellowship Program: January 15; Undergraduate Research Capstone Program: January 20.

PUBLICATIONS:
Application guidelines.

ADDRESS INQUIRIES TO:
See e-mail address above.

AMERICAN SOCIETY FOR MICROBIOLOGY [2075]

Education Board
1752 N Street, N.W.
Washington, DC 20036
(202) 942-9283
Fax: (202) 942-9329
E-mail: fellowships@asmusa.org
Web Site: www.asm.org/watkins

FOUNDED: 1899

AREAS OF INTEREST:
Microbiology.

NAME(S) OF PROGRAMS:
- **ASM Robert D. Watkins Graduate Research Fellowships**

TYPE:
Fellowships.

YEAR PROGRAM STARTED: 1980

PURPOSE:
To help increase the number of underrepresented groups completing doctoral degrees in the microbiological sciences.

LEGAL BASIS:
Private, nonprofit science organization.

ELIGIBILITY:
Fellowships are available to graduate students enrolled in a full-time Ph.D. program in microbiology at an accredited U.S. institution of higher learning who are from an underrepresented group including African-Americans, Hispanics, Native Americans, Alaskan Natives, and Pacific Islanders. Applicants must be U.S. citizens or permanent residents, ASM student members, been formally admitted and have successfully completed the first year as a doctoral candidate.

GEOG. RESTRICTIONS: United States.

FINANCIAL DATA:
Funds cannot be used for tuition and fees.

Amount of support per award: $63,000 ($21,000 annual stipend).

Total amount of support: Varies.

NO. AWARDS: 6 for the year 2013.

APPLICATION INFO:
Applications are available online. Students must apply electronically.

Duration: Up to three years.

Deadline: May 1.

PUBLICATIONS:
Application guidelines.

ADDRESS INQUIRIES TO:
See e-mail address above.

ATLANTIC SALMON FEDERATION [2076]

P.O. Box 5200
St. Andrews NB E5B 3S8 Canada
(506) 529-1385
Fax: (506) 529-4985
E-mail: jcarr@asf.ca
Web Site: www.asf.ca

FOUNDED: 1948

AREAS OF INTEREST:
Conservation of Atlantic salmon and its habitat through programs in education, research, enhancement, restoration and international cooperation.

NAME(S) OF PROGRAMS:
- **Olin Fellowships**

TYPE:
Awards/prizes; Block grants; Capital grants; Demonstration grants; Fellowships; General operating grants; Grants-in-aid; Internships; Project/program grants; Research grants; Scholarships; Training grants; Travel grants; Visiting scholars; Work-study programs. Fellowships are offered to individuals seeking to improve their knowledge or skills in advanced fields while looking for solutions to current problems in Atlantic salmon biology, management or conservation.

YEAR PROGRAM STARTED: 1971

PURPOSE:
To further salmon conservation.

LEGAL BASIS:
Tax-exempt, nonprofit organization.

ELIGIBILITY:
Applicants must be legal residents of the U.S. or Canada. The Fellowships are tenable at any accredited university or research laboratory or in an active management program and may be applied toward a wide range of endeavors including salmon management, graduate study and research. Applicants need not be enrolled in a degree program.

FINANCIAL DATA:
Amount of support per award: Olin Fellowships: $1,000 to $3,000.

Total amount of support: Varies.

NO. AWARDS: Olin Fellowships: Up to 3.

APPLICATION INFO:
Information and application forms may be obtained from the address above, from Atlantic Salmon Federation, P.O. Box 807, Calais, ME 04619 or from the web site.

Duration: One year. May be renewed.

Deadline: Applications must be received at the St. Andrews office by March 15. Applicants will be advised of awards by May 15.

PUBLICATIONS:
Atlantic Salmon Journal; annual report.

OFFICERS:
Bill Taylor, President
Hon. M.A. Meighen, Q.C., Chairman, ASF (Canada)
Christopher Buckley, Chairman, ASF (U.S.)

ADDRESS INQUIRIES TO:
Shawna Wallace, Research Assistant
(See address above.)

CALIFORNIA ACADEMY OF SCIENCES [2077]

Department of Invertebrate Zoology and Geology
55 Music Concourse Drive
San Francisco, CA 94118
(415) 379-5270
E-mail: rmooi@calacademy.org
ssi-bi@calacademy.org
Web Site: www.calacademy.org/scientists
www.calacademy.org/summer-systematics-institute

FOUNDED: 1853

AREAS OF INTEREST:
Biology, anthropology, aquatic biology, botany, entomology, geology, herpetology, ichthyology, invertebrate zoology, mammalogy, ornithology and paleontology.

NAME(S) OF PROGRAMS:
- **Summer Systematics Institute**

TYPE:
Internships. Matches students with Academy scientists to work on specific research projects. May include laboratory and molecular components.

YEAR PROGRAM STARTED: 1995

PURPOSE:
To allow students to gain hands-on experience in the labs and collections archive.

ELIGIBILITY:
Applicants must be undergraduates who are U.S. citizens or alien residents with an excellent academic record and demonstrated participation in a wide range of campus activities.

FINANCIAL DATA:
Travel costs up to $450 to San Francisco will be reimbursed and a subsistence allowance of $2,500 is given for housing and food. Research costs, publication costs, and travel to return to CAS or to a conference are supported.

Amount of support per award: $4,200 stipend for the internship period.

Total amount of support: Varies.

NO. MOST RECENT APPLICANTS: 150.

NO. AWARDS: 7 to 10.

APPLICATION INFO:
Application information is available online.

Duration: Full-time (40 hours per week) for eight weeks (mid-June to mid-August).

Deadline: Mid-February.

PUBLICATIONS:
Program announcement.

IRS I.D.: 94-1156258

STAFF:
Dr. Rich Mooi, REU Site Director

ADDRESS INQUIRIES TO:
Dr. Rich Mooi, REU Site Director
(See address above.)

COLUMBIA UNIVERSITY [2078]

College of Physicians and Surgeons
630 West 168th Street, Box 37b
New York, NY 10032
(212) 305-7970
E-mail: horwitzprize@columbia.edu
Web Site: www.cumc.columbia.edu/research/horwitz-prize

FOUNDED: 1754

NAME(S) OF PROGRAMS:
- **The Louisa Gross Horwitz Prize**

TYPE:
Awards/prizes. An annual prize designed to honor a major scientific contribution in basic research to the fields of biology or biochemistry.

YEAR PROGRAM STARTED: 1967

PURPOSE:
To honor a scientific investigator, or group of investigators, whose contributions to knowledge in either of these fields are deemed worthy of special recognition.

ELIGIBILITY:
The prize is open to scientists for outstanding basic research in the fields of biology or biochemistry.

NO. AWARDS: 1.

APPLICATION INFO:
Nomination must include the name, title, mailing address and e-mail address of the nominee and nominator, along with the following supporting documents:
(1) curriculum vitae;
(2) biographical sketch;
(3) 500-word research summary;
(4) 500-word research significance and;
(5) key publications list.

Deadline: January 31.

ADDRESS INQUIRIES TO:
See e-mail address above.

THE ENTOMOLOGICAL FOUNDATION [2079]

3 Park Place, Suite 307
Annapolis, MD 21401
(301) 731-4535 ext. 3012
Fax: (301) 731-4538
E-mail: cstelzig@entsoc.org
Web Site: entfdn.weebly.com/kids_scifair.html

FOUNDED: 1991

AREAS OF INTEREST:
Entomology.

NAME(S) OF PROGRAMS:
- **Science Fair Project Contest**

TYPE:
Awards/prizes. Award given to children who submit good science fair projects.

FINANCIAL DATA:
Amount of support per award: $100.

APPLICATION INFO:
Application information is available on the web site.

Deadline: Entries must be received between May 1 through August 31.

ADDRESS INQUIRIES TO:
Chris Stelzig
Entomological Society of America
Director of Strategic Initiatives
(See address above.)

THE ENTOMOLOGICAL FOUNDATION [2080]

3 Park Place, Suite 307
Annapolis, MD 21401
(301) 731-4535 ext. 3012
Fax: (301) 731-4538
E-mail: cstelzig@entsoc.org
Web Site: www.entsoc.org/awards/professional/educational

FOUNDED: 1991

AREAS OF INTEREST:
Entomology.

NAME(S) OF PROGRAMS:
- **President's Prize for Outstanding Achievement in Primary and Secondary Education**

TYPE:
Awards/prizes. This is a professional award for educators who use insects in the classroom.

YEAR PROGRAM STARTED: 1996

FINANCIAL DATA:
Value of package totals $1,600.

NO. AWARDS: 1 for primary school educators (grades K-6); 1 for secondary school educators (grades 7-12).

APPLICATION INFO:
Application information is available on the Foundation web site.

Deadline: July 1.

ADDRESS INQUIRIES TO:
Chris Stelzig
Entomological Society of America
Director of Strategic Initiatives
(See address above.)

THE HARRY FRANK GUGGENHEIM FOUNDATION

25 West 53rd Street
16th Floor
New York, NY 10019-5401
(646) 428-0971
Fax: (646) 428-0981
E-mail: info@hfg.org
Web Site: www.hfg.org

TYPE:
Fellowships. Awarded to individuals who will complete the writing of the dissertation within the award year. Support is for projects which seek to advance and coordinate creative breakthroughs in the social and biological sciences relating to the study of violence and aggression.

See entry 1797 for full listing.

THE HARRY FRANK GUGGENHEIM FOUNDATION

25 West 53rd Street
16th Floor
New York, NY 10019-5401
(646) 428-0971
Fax: (646) 428-0981
E-mail: info@hfg.org
Web Site: www.hfg.org

TYPE:
Research grants. Support for projects which seek to advance and coordinate creative breakthroughs in the social and biological sciences relating to the study of dominance, violence and aggression.

See entry 1798 for full listing.

HUMAN FRONTIER SCIENCE PROGRAM ORGANIZATION [2081]

12 Quai St. Jean
BP 10034
67000 Strasbourg Cedex France
(33) 3-88-21-51-26 (Grants)
(33) 3-88-21-51-27 (Fellowships)
Fax: (33) 3-88-32-88-97
E-mail: grant@hfsp.org
fellow@hfsp.org
Web Site: www.hfsp.org

FOUNDED: 1989

AREAS OF INTEREST:
Interdisciplinary research into the complex mechanisms of biological functions.

NAME(S) OF PROGRAMS:
- **Career Development Award**
- **Cross-Disciplinary Fellowships**
- **Long-Term Fellowships**
- **Program Grants**
- **Young Investigator Grants**

TYPE:
Fellowships; Project/program grants; Research grants. Career Development Awards are to help former HFSP Fellows set up their own independent laboratories in the home country or another HFSP member country.

Long-Term Fellowships are for young scientists within three years of obtaining their Ph.D. who wish to broaden their scientific experience in a foreign laboratory.

Cross-Disciplinary Fellowships are modeled on the Long-Term Fellowships but are specifically for scientists with Ph.Ds. in nonbiological disciplines who seek training in the life sciences.

Program Grants are collaborative research projects for interdisciplinary teams of researchers in different countries at any stage of their career.

Young Investigator Grants are collaborative research projects for interdisciplinary teams of young researchers who are within the first five years of their first independent positions and located in different countries.

YEAR PROGRAM STARTED: 1989

PURPOSE:
To foster international collaboration and postdoctoral training at the frontiers of the life sciences.

LEGAL BASIS:
Not-for-profit association.

ELIGIBILITY:
Scientists from all countries can apply, but with some restrictions. The principal investigator of grants must be from a member country. Fellowship candidates from nonmember countries can only apply to work in a member country.

Career Development Award competition is only open to former HFSP fellows.

FINANCIAL DATA:
Amount of support per award: Varies, depending upon the size of the grant team or the host country of the fellowship.

NO. MOST RECENT APPLICANTS: Career Development Awards: 57; Cross-Disciplinary Fellowships: 54; Long-Term Fellowships: 643; Young Investigator Grants and Program Grants: 871 letters of intent, 87 full applications.

NO. AWARDS: Career Development Awards: 8; Cross-Disciplinary Fellowships: 6; Long-Term Fellowships: 69; Program Grants: 25; Young Investigator Grants: 7.

APPLICATION INFO:
Application information is available on the web site.

Duration: Up to three years.

PUBLICATIONS:
Annual report.

ADDRESS INQUIRIES TO:
For fellowships: fellow@hfsp.org
For grants: grant@hfsp.org

INTERNATIONAL CRANE FOUNDATION, INC. [2082]

E-11376 Shady Lane Road
Baraboo, WI 53913
(608) 356-9462
Fax: (608) 356-9465
E-mail: cranes@savingcranes.org
Web Site: www.savingcranes.org

FOUNDED: 1973

AREAS OF INTEREST:
Aviculture, crane ecology and conservation education.

CONSULTING OR VOLUNTEER SERVICES:
Work with individuals who have specific questions regarding crane propagation, restoration of natural habitats, or conservation education on an informal basis and as the need arises.

TYPE:
Internships. Formal stipended internship programs in the fields of aviculture, crane ecology and conservation education.

YEAR PROGRAM STARTED: 1980

PURPOSE:
To act as the world center for the study and preservation of cranes and their natural habitats.

LEGAL BASIS:
Nonprofit corporation.

ELIGIBILITY:
College sophomores through recent college graduates in biology, zoology, botany or education who have a willingness to work at a variety of tasks and can work in a self-directed manner.

FINANCIAL DATA:
Amount of support per award: $560 stipend per month, plus housing.

NO. MOST RECENT APPLICANTS: Approximately 80.

NO. AWARDS: 11.

APPLICATION INFO:
Letter of application indicating interest, relevant coursework and experience, plus three references. An interview will be required, although a phone interview may suffice.

Duration: Six to nine months. Must submit additional application for renewal.

IRS I.D.: 39-1187711

ADDRESS INQUIRIES TO:
See e-mail address above.

THE JACKSON LABORATORY [2083]

600 Main Street
Bar Harbor, ME 04609
(207) 288-6906
Fax: (207) 288-6697
E-mail: education@jax.org
Web Site: www.jax.org

FOUNDED: 1929

AREAS OF INTEREST:
Mammalian genetics and genomic medicine.

NAME(S) OF PROGRAMS:
- **Postdoctoral Program of the Jackson Laboratory**

TYPE:
Fellowships. Research participation at the postdoctoral level in cancer genetics, developmental genetics, hematology and immunology and other fields of mammalian biology, genomic medicine and computational biology. Support is for research training at the Jackson Laboratory.

PURPOSE:
To support postdoctoral research training in mammalian genetics and genomic medicine.

LEGAL BASIS:
Private institution.

ELIGIBILITY:
An applicant must be a recipient of the Ph.D., M.D., D.V.M. or equivalent degree. An applicant for a training grant appointment must be either a citizen of the U.S. or a foreign national holding a visa permitting permanent residence in the U.S.

FINANCIAL DATA:
Program includes full benefits.

Amount of support per award: $43,692 to $57,504 in stipends, depending upon years of postdoctoral experience.

Total amount of support: Varies.

APPLICATION INFO:
Applications must include a curriculum vitae, cover letter and three letters of recommendation.

Duration: Appointments are for one year. Renewable for up to two years.

Deadline: Applications accepted throughout the year.

ADMINISTRATIVE OFFICERS:
Dr. Thomas Litwin, Vice President for Education

ADDRESS INQUIRIES TO:
Dr. Thomas Litwin
Vice President for Education
(See address above.)

LIFE SCIENCES RESEARCH FOUNDATION (LSRF) [2084]

Lewis Thomas Laboratory
Princeton University
Washington Road
Princeton, NJ 08544
E-mail: direnzo@lsrf.org
sdirenzo@princeton.edu
Web Site: www.lsrf.org

FOUNDED: 1984

AREAS OF INTEREST:
Biological sciences.

NAME(S) OF PROGRAMS:
- **Three-Year Postdoctoral Fellowships**

TYPE:
Fellowships.

YEAR PROGRAM STARTED: 1984

PURPOSE:
To offer research support for aspiring scientists.

LEGAL BASIS:
Private organization.

ELIGIBILITY:
Individuals who have held a Ph.D. or M.D. degree for more than five years at the time of application are not eligible for an LSRF fellowship.

FINANCIAL DATA:
Stipend includes salary, fringe benefits, travel to the host institution and to the annual meeting and research expenses.

Amount of support per award: $60,000 per year.

NO. MOST RECENT APPLICANTS: 1,000.

NO. AWARDS: 25.

APPLICATION INFO:
Applications are to be completed online and must contain all three components: Application Info, Research Proposal, and Letters of Reference and Support.

Duration: Three years.

Deadline: October 1.

ADDRESS INQUIRIES TO:
Susan DiRenzo, Assistant Director
(See address above.)

MARINE BIOLOGICAL LABORATORY [2085]

7 MBL Street
Woods Hole, MA 02543
(508) 289-7173
Fax: (508) 289-7934
E-mail: researchprograms@mbl.edu
Web Site: www.mbl.edu

FOUNDED: 1888

AREAS OF INTEREST:
Cellular and molecular physiology, molecular biology, developmental biology, neurobiology, innate immunity, ecology, parasitology, microbiology, pharmacology, toxicology, cancer biology, regenerative biology, aging, molecular evolution, microbial biology, sensory physiology, aquaculture, metabolic diseases, environmental science, climate change, and plant physiology.

NAME(S) OF PROGRAMS:
- **Marine Biological Laboratory Research Awards**

TYPE:
Research grants.

PURPOSE:
To provide funding to scientists interested in conducting research projects in various scientific areas.

LEGAL BASIS:
Nonprofit organization.

ELIGIBILITY:
Applicants must be independent investigators. Working scientists must be willing to come to the Laboratory for a minimum six-week stay to conduct independent research in areas of interest to the Laboratory. Sabbaticals are encouraged.

FINANCIAL DATA:
Amount of support per award: Varies.

Total amount of support: Varies.

Matching fund requirements: Strongly encouraged from home institution.

CO-OP FUNDING PROGRAMS: APA, ASCB and HHMI.

NO. AWARDS: Varies.

APPLICATION INFO:
Application information is available on the web site.

Duration: Varies.

Deadline: December 15.

IRS I.D.: 04-2104690

ADDRESS INQUIRIES TO:
Division of Research
(See address above.)

MICROSCOPY SOCIETY OF AMERICA [2086]

12100 Sunset Hills Road
Suite 130
Reston, VA 20190-3221
(703) 234-4115
(800) 538-3672
Fax: (703) 435-4390
E-mail: associationmanagement@microscopy.org
Web Site: www.microscopy.org/awards

FOUNDED: 1942

AREAS OF INTEREST:
Microscopy.

NAME(S) OF PROGRAMS:
- **MSA Professional Technical Staff Awards**

TYPE:
Awards/prizes; Conferences/seminars.

PURPOSE:
To stimulate attendance for those who ordinarily might not participate; to encourage supervisors to support their staff in professional activities.

LEGAL BASIS:
Special interest society.

ELIGIBILITY:
Applicants must be regular, current members of MSA at the time of submission. Awards are based on the quality of the paper submitted for presentation at the meeting. Abstracts will be judged by the MSA Technologist's Forum. The applicant must be the first author of the submitted paper.

Successful applicants must present their papers personally at the meeting in order to receive the award. They are expected to attend and participate in the entire meeting. Former winners will not be eligible for another award.

FINANCIAL DATA:
Amount of support per award: The award consists of complimentary full registration for the Microscopy and Microanalysis meeting including proceedings and the social event ticket. In addition, MSA will reimburse awardees up to $1,000 for travel, lodging and meeting expenses.

Total amount of support: Varies.

NO. AWARDS: Up to 4.

APPLICATION INFO:
Applications shall consist of a copy of the abstract and data form to be sent to the Technologist's Forum Committee and a supporting letter from the applicant's employer, manager or supervisor, attesting to the applicant's status as a full-time, professional staff member.

Duration: One-time award.

Deadline: February 8.

STAFF:
Bob Dziuban, Managing Director
Ashley Carey, Program Manager

ADDRESS INQUIRIES TO:
See e-mail address above.

MUSEUM OF COMPARATIVE ZOOLOGY [2087]

Harvard University, OEB Administration
26 Oxford Street, Room 108
Cambridge, MA 02138
(617) 495-2460
Fax: (617) 496-8308
E-mail: grants@oeb.harvard.edu
Web Site: www.mcz.harvard.edu/grants_and_funding/ernst-mayr-travel.html

FOUNDED: 1858

AREAS OF INTEREST:
Comparative zoology.

NAME(S) OF PROGRAMS:
- **Ernst Mayr Grants in Animal Systematics**

TYPE:
Awards/prizes; Research grants; Travel grants.

YEAR PROGRAM STARTED: 1984

PURPOSE:
To enable animal systematists to make short visits to museums for research needed to complete taxonomic revisions and monographs; to stimulate taxonomic work on neglected taxa, including those with numerous poorly described species, genera and families known to have many undescribed species in institutional collections, taxa for which it is unknown what proportion of the nominal species are synonyms, and difficult genera without keys.

ELIGIBILITY:
Preference is given to studies that use the Museum of Comparative Zoology collections, although applications to work at other museums also will be considered.

FINANCIAL DATA:
Grants may cover travel, lodging and meals for up to a few months while conducting research at the museums, services purchased from the host institution, research supplies, etc.

Amount of support per award: $1,000 average.

Total amount of support: Varies.

NO. MOST RECENT APPLICANTS: 42.

NO. AWARDS: 24.

APPLICATION INFO:
Proposals should consist of an application form which includes a short project description and explicit statement of the goals of the research, itinerary, and budget, a curriculum vitae, and three letters of support. All applications should be written in English. Proposals may be submitted through standard mail to the address above or electronically to the e-mail listed above. Submissions through standard mail must include five copies of the proposal materials and must be received by the deadline.

Duration: Must be used within one year.

Deadline: April 1 and October 15. Announcements typically within two months following the application deadline.

STAFF:
Melissa Aja, Museum Projects Coordinator

ADDRESS INQUIRIES TO:
Melissa Aja
Museum Projects Coordinator
(See address and e-mail above.)

*SPECIAL STIPULATIONS:
Each grantee is required to submit a written report summarizing the scientific accomplishments achieved with the award within one month of travel completion.

MYCOLOGICAL SOCIETY OF AMERICA [2088]

P.O. Box 1897
Lawrence, KS 66044
(785) 865-9402
(800) 627-0326
Fax: (785) 843-6153
E-mail: msa@allenpress.com
Web Site: msafungi.org/msa-awards/

FOUNDED: 1932

AREAS OF INTEREST:
The study of fungi.

NAME(S) OF PROGRAMS:
- **Backus Award**
- **Salomon Bartnicki-Garcia Award**
- **Forest Fungal Ecology Award**
- **International Travel Awards**
- **Martin-Baker Research Awards**
- **Mentor Student Travel Awards**
- **MSA Graduate Fellowship**
- **NAMA Memorial Graduate Fellowship**
- **John W. Rippon Research Award**
- **Clark T. Rogerson Research Award**
- **Alexander H. and Helen V. Smith Research Fund**

TYPE:
Awards/prizes; Conferences/seminars; Fellowships; Travel grants. Supplementary grant for an outstanding candidate awarded in addition to any fellowship, scholarship or assistantship support from other sources to further graduate studies in the field of mycology.

LEGAL BASIS:
Nonprofit organization.

ELIGIBILITY:
Applicants must be student members of the Mycological Society of America. In selecting the recipient of the Fellowship, consideration is given to scholastic merit, research ability and promise shown as a future mycologist.

FINANCIAL DATA:
Amount of support per award:
Approximately $2,000 per fellowship; $1,000 for Backus Award.

Total amount of support: Approximately $15,000 annually.

APPLICATION INFO:
Application information is available on the web site.

Duration: One year. Nonrenewable.

Deadline: February 15.

PUBLICATIONS:
Mycologia, research journal; *Inoculum*, newsletter.

ADDRESS INQUIRIES TO:
Backus Award, MSA Graduate and NAMA Memorial Graduate Fellowships:
Dr. Tim James, Chairperson
Student Awards Committee
E-mail: tyjames@umich.edu

Bartnicki-Garcia and
Forest Fungal Ecology Awards,
Martin-Baker Research,
John W. Rippon Research
Clark T. Rogerson Research Awards, and
Smith Research Fund:
Dr. David Geiser, Chairperson
Research Awards Committee
E-mail: dgeiser@psu.edu

International Travel Awards:
Maria P. Martin-Esteban, Chairperson
International Committee
E-mail: maripaz@rjb.csic.es

Mentor Student Travel Awards:
Dr. Brian Perry, Chairperson
Mentor Travel Awards Committee
E-mail: brian.perry@csueastbay.edu

NATIONAL ALOPECIA AREATA FOUNDATION [2089]

65 Mitchell Boulevard
San Rafael, CA 94903
(415) 472-3780
Fax: (415) 480-1800
E-mail: info@naaf.org
Web Site: www.naaf.org

FOUNDED: 1981

AREAS OF INTEREST:
Baldness, hair loss and alopecia areata.

TYPE:
Research grants.

YEAR PROGRAM STARTED: 1985

PURPOSE:
To support research to find an acceptable treatment and studies that will lead to an eventual cure for alopecia areata.

ELIGIBILITY:
Must be an Institute Review Board-approved researcher who has submitted a proposal about alopecia areata or hair biology. No funding for established investigators.

FINANCIAL DATA:
Salaries only fellows, assistants, residents and technicians.

Amount of support per award: $10,000 to $50,000.

Total amount of support: Over $6,000,000 since inception of program.

CO-OP FUNDING PROGRAMS: Joint grants with other organizations.

NO. MOST RECENT APPLICANTS: Varies.

NO. AWARDS: Varies.

APPLICATION INFO:
Contact the Foundation for application procedures.

Duration: One year.

ADDRESS INQUIRIES TO:
Jeanne Rappoport, Vice President
Administration and Meetings
(See address above.)

NATIONAL SCIENCE FOUNDATION [2090]

Division of Molecular and Cellular Biosciences (BIO/MCB)
4201 Wilson Boulevard, Room 655 S
Arlington, VA 22230
(703) 292-8440
(800) 381-1532
Fax: (703) 292-9061
E-mail: rgov@nsf.gov
Web Site: www.nsf.gov

FOUNDED: 1950

AREAS OF INTEREST:
Molecular biophysics, cellular dynamics and function, genetic mechanisms, and systems and synthetic biology.

NAME(S) OF PROGRAMS:
- **Division of Molecular and Cellular Biosciences Programs**

TYPE:
Conferences/seminars; Project/program grants; Research grants; Seed money grants. The Division of Molecular and Cellular Biosciences at the National Science Foundation has the following clusters:

Molecular Biophysics, which encourages proposals such as the following areas of research:
(1) general principles of the relationship between structure, dynamics and function of biomolecules and;
(2) fundamental principles governing biomolecular interactions and mechanisms.

Cellular Dynamics and Function, which encourages proposals such as the following areas of research:
(1) predictive understanding of the behavior of living cells through integration of modeling and experimentation;
(2) integrative cellular function across broad spatiotemporal scales, from single molecules to whole cells and;
(3) origin, evolution and function of cells, organelles and microcompartments.

Genetic Mechanisms, which encourages proposals such as the following areas of research:
(1) gene expression, including epigenetics and RNA-mediated regulation;
(2) chromosome dynamics, DNA replication, repair, recombination and inheritance and;
(3) evolution of genes and genomes.

Systems and Synthetic Biology, which encourages proposals such as the following areas of research:
(1) systems-level, theory-driven analysis of regulatory, signaling and metabolic networks;
(2) synthetic biology to address fundamental biological questions including the origin of life, minimal cell, emergent behavior in complex systems, robustness in design and organization and;
(3) tool development to facilitate systems and synthetic biology studies.

YEAR PROGRAM STARTED: 1992

PURPOSE:
To increase our store of knowledge in these fields and enhance our understanding of the scientific aspects of major problems confronting the nation.

LEGAL BASIS:
National Science Foundation Act of 1950, Public Law 81-507, as amended.

ELIGIBILITY:
The principal recipients of scientific research project support are academic institutions and nonprofit research institutions. Grants may also be awarded to other types of institutions and to individuals. In these cases, preliminary inquiry should be made to the cognizant program officer before a proposal is submitted. Support may be provided to projects involving a single scientist or to projects covering the activities of a number of scientists. Awards are made for projects confined to a single disciplinary area and for projects which cross or merge disciplinary interests. Clinically oriented research is not supported.

FINANCIAL DATA:
Amount of support per award: Varies.

Total amount of support: Varies.

APPLICATION INFO:
Application information is available on the web site.

Duration: Varies.

Deadline: Contact Foundation for specific dates.

PUBLICATIONS:
Brochures.

DIRECTORS:
Linda Hyman, Division Director

ADDRESS INQUIRIES TO:
Cognizant Program Officer

NATIONAL SCIENCE FOUNDATION [2091]

Division of Environmental Biology
4201 Wilson Boulevard, Room 635N
Arlington, VA 22230
(703) 292-8480
Fax: (703) 292-9064
E-mail: atessier@nsf.gov
Web Site: www.nsf.gov/bio/deb/about.jsp

FOUNDED: 1950

AREAS OF INTEREST:
Population and community, ecology, ecosystem science, population and systematic biology, biodiversity inventories cluster and evolution processes.

NAME(S) OF PROGRAMS:
- **Division of Environmental Biology**

TYPE:
Conferences/seminars; Research grants; Training grants; Travel grants.

PURPOSE:
To increase our store of knowledge in these fields and enhance our understanding of the scientific aspects of major problems confronting the nation.

LEGAL BASIS:
National Science Foundation Act of 1950, Public Law 81-507, as amended.

ELIGIBILITY:
The principal recipients of scientific research project support are academic institutions and nonprofit research institutions. Grants may also be awarded to other types of institutions and to individuals. In these cases, preliminary inquiry should be made to the cognizant program officer before a proposal is submitted. Support may be provided to

projects involving a single scientist or to projects covering the activities of a number of scientists. Awards are made for projects confined to a single disciplinary area and for projects which cross or merge disciplinary interests.

FINANCIAL DATA:
Amount of support per award: $108,000 average.

NO. MOST RECENT APPLICANTS: 2,500.

NO. AWARDS: 500.

APPLICATION INFO:
Application information is available on the web site.

Duration: 12 to 60 months, depending on the scientific merit and requirements of the project.

Deadline: Varies.

PUBLICATIONS:
Awards list; program description.

ADDRESS INQUIRIES TO:
Alan Tessier, Deputy Division Director
(See address above.)

SOCIETY FOR DEVELOPMENTAL BIOLOGY [2092]

9650 Rockville Pike
Bethesda, MD 20814-3998
(301) 634-7815
Fax: (301) 634-7825
E-mail: sdb@sdbonline.org
Web Site: www.sdbonline.org

FOUNDED: 1939

AREAS OF INTEREST:
Developmental biology.

NAME(S) OF PROGRAMS:
- **Edwin G. Conklin Medal**
- **Developmental Biology-SDB Lifetime Achievement Award**
- **John Doctor Best Education Poster Award**
- **Viktor Hamburger Outstanding Educator Prize**
- **Non-SDB Education Activities Grant**
- **Non-SDB Meeting Grants**
- **SDB Boot Camp for New Faculty**
- **SDB Emerging Models Grant**
- **SDB Innovation Grant**
- **SDB International Scholarships**
- **SDB Travel Awards**
- **Teaching and Junior Faculty Travel Grants**

TYPE:
Awards/prizes; Conferences/seminars; Scholarships.

PURPOSE:
To further the study of development in all organisms and at all levels; to represent and promote communication among students of development; to promote the field of developmental biology.

ELIGIBILITY:
Must be a student or investigator studying in the field of developmental biology.

FINANCIAL DATA:
Amount of support per award: John Doctor Best Education Poster Award: $1,000; SDB International Scholarships: $2,000; Student/Postdoctoral Travel Awards: Varies; Teaching and Junior Faculty Travel Grants: $500.

Total amount of support: Varies.

APPLICATION INFO:
Nomination instructions and application guidelines may be obtained from the Society's web site.

Duration: One-time award. Reapplication possible for grants and scholarships.

Deadline: Varies.

ADDRESS INQUIRIES TO:
Ida Chow, Executive Officer
(See address above.)

SOCIETY FOR THE STUDY OF AMPHIBIANS AND REPTILES

Department of Biological Sciences
University of Wisconsin-Whitewater
Whitewater, WI 53190
(262) 472-1069
E-mail: kapferj@uww.edu
Web Site: www.ssarherps.org/pages/GIH.php

TYPE:
Awards/prizes; Research grants. Awards are given in six categories: Conservation of Amphibians and/or Reptiles, Field Research, Laboratory Research, Herpetological Education, Travel and International Research.

See entry 1978 for full listing.

THE UNIVERSITY OF CALGARY

Faculty of Graduate Studies
MacKimmie Library Tower, Room 213
2500 University Drive, N.W.
Calgary AB T2N 1N4 Canada
(403) 220-4938
Fax: (403) 289-7635
E-mail: gsaward@ucalgary.ca
Web Site: www.grad.ucalgary.ca/awards

TYPE:
Awards/prizes; Scholarships. Award for study in the fields of cellular, molecular, microbial or biochemical biology. Tenable at The University of Calgary, Department of Biological Sciences.

See entry 1732 for full listing.

THE WETLANDS INSTITUTE [2093]

1075 Stone Harbor Boulevard
Stone Harbor, NJ 08247-1424
(609) 368-1211
Fax: (609) 368-3871
E-mail: research@wetlandsinstitute.org
Web Site: www.wetlandsinstitute.org

FOUNDED: 1969

AREAS OF INTEREST:
Environmental education and conservation research.

NAME(S) OF PROGRAMS:
- **Coastal Conservation Research Program**
- **Environmental Education Internship**

TYPE:
Internships. Coastal Conservation Research Program offers 10-week summer internships for field research on mid-Atlantic coastal organisms and environments at the Wetlands Institute.

Environmental Education Internships are for undergraduate students with an interest in environmental or outdoor education and/or classroom science education.

YEAR PROGRAM STARTED: 1969

PURPOSE:
To involve undergraduate students in a wide variety of research projects pertaining to the environment.

LEGAL BASIS:
Nonprofit organization that conducts research and education.

ELIGIBILITY:
Coastal Conservation Research Program applicants should be completing their sophomore, junior or senior year at a college or university and be interested in biological research as a career.

Environmental Education Internship applicants must have completed at least two years of college.

A science or education major is desired, but not required.

GEOG. RESTRICTIONS: United States.

FINANCIAL DATA:
Amount of support per award: Varies with project.

Total amount of support: Varies.

NO. MOST RECENT APPLICANTS: Over 100.

NO. AWARDS: 10.

APPLICATION INFO:
Contact the Institute for guidelines.

Duration: Late May to early August.

Deadline: March 1.

IRS I.D.: 23-7046783

ADDRESS INQUIRIES TO:
Coastal Conservation Research Program
E-mail: research@wetlandsinstitute.org

Environmental Education Internship
E-mail: education@wetlandsinstitute.org

WHITEHALL FOUNDATION, INC. [2094]

125 Worth Avenue
Suite 220
Palm Beach, FL 33480
(561) 655-4474
Fax: (561) 655-1296
E-mail: email@whitehall.org
Web Site: www.whitehall.org

FOUNDED: 1937

AREAS OF INTEREST:
Exclusive focus on assisting basic research in vertebrate (excluding clinical) and invertebrate neurobiology in the U.S.

TYPE:
Grants-in-aid; Research grants. Grants are available to established scientists of all ages working at accredited institutions in the U.S.

YEAR PROGRAM STARTED: 1937

PURPOSE:
To assist scholarly research in the life sciences; to assist those dynamic areas of basic biological research that are not heavily supported by federal agencies or other foundations with specialized missions.

LEGAL BASIS:
Not-for-profit corporation.

ELIGIBILITY:
Applications will be judged on the scientific merit and innovative aspects of the proposal, as well as on past performance and evidence of the applicant's continued productivity.

The Foundation does not award funds to investigators who have substantial existing or potential support (even if it is for an

unrelated purpose), and applications may be held in abeyance until the results of other funding decisions are determined. In general, the Foundation currently defines "substantial" as approximately $200,000 per year (including both direct and indirect expense but excluding the principal investigator's salary). The principal investigator must hold no less than the position of assistant professor, or the equivalent, in order to make application.

GEOG. RESTRICTIONS: United States.

FINANCIAL DATA:
Amount of support per award: Research Grants: Up to $75,000 per year; Grants-in-aid: Up to $30,000.

APPLICATION INFO:
The first step in the proposal process is the submission of a Letter of Intent, which includes the following:
(1) cover page on institutional letterhead including investigator's full name, academic rank and institutional affiliation, complete U.S. mail and e-mail addresses, telephone and fax numbers, title of the project (not to exceed 60 characters), type of grant requested, and a table of all current and pending funding including grant title, source, total amount of direct and indirect costs per year, length in years, percent effort expended on the project and notification date if the application is still pending and;
(2) research abstract of the proposed research project (not to exceed two pages or 600 words). Investigator's last name must be placed on the top right corner of each page. Do not include any reprints, curriculum vitaes, or letters of reference.

On the basis of this letter, the Whitehall Foundation's scientific advisory staff will determine whether or not the proposed research project will continue to the application process.

Letters of Intent will not be accepted via e-mail.

Duration: Grants-in-aid: One year. Research Grants: Up to three years; a renewal grant with a maximum of two years is possible, but it will be awarded on a competitive basis.

IRS I.D.: 13-5637595

ADDRESS INQUIRIES TO:
Whitehall Foundation, Inc.
P.O. Box 3423
Palm Beach, FL 33480

*PLEASE NOTE:
The Foundation encourages the use of electronic mail. All correspondence and reports should be sent to the e-mail address above. The Letter of Intent must be submitted in hard copy on institutional letterhead.

THE WILEY FOUNDATION, INC.
111 River Street
Hoboken, NJ 07030-5773
(201) 748-6000
E-mail: wileyfoundation@wiley.com
Web Site: www.wileyfoundation.org

TYPE:
Awards/prizes. The annual Wiley Prize in Biomedical Sciences has recognized breakthrough research in pure or applied life science research.

See entry 2047 for full listing.

WILSON ORNITHOLOGICAL SOCIETY [2095]
Museum of Zoology
University of Michigan
1109 Geddes Avenue
Ann Arbor, MI 48109-1079
(734) 764-0457
E-mail: wos@salve.edu
Web Site: www.wilsonsociety.org/awards/wosawards.html

FOUNDED: 1888

AREAS OF INTEREST:
Ornithology.

NAME(S) OF PROGRAMS:
- **Louis Agassiz Fuertes Award**
- **George A. Hall/Harold Mayfield Award**
- **Paul A. Stewart Award**
- **Student Travel Awards**
- **Alexander Wilson Student Presentation Award**

TYPE:
Grants-in-aid. Fuertes, Hall/Mayfield and Stewart Awards provide for the promotion and encouragement of field research on birds. A research proposal is required.

Student Travel Awards provide funds for students to attend the annual meeting.

Alexander Wilson Student Presentation Award is given to the best student paper presented at the annual meeting.

YEAR PROGRAM STARTED: 1947

PURPOSE:
To promote the scientific study of birds.

LEGAL BASIS:
Corporation.

ELIGIBILITY:
Each award requires a willingness of the awardee to report results of the research as an oral or poster paper at an annual meeting of the Wilson Ornithological Society.

Louis Agassiz Fuertes Award: Available to all ornithologists, although graduate students and young professionals are preferred. Any avian research is eligible.

George A. Hall/Harold Mayfield Award: Limited to independent researchers without access to funds and facilities available at colleges, universities or governmental agencies, and is restricted to nonprofessionals, including high school students. Any kind of avian research is eligible.

Paul A. Stewart Awards: Preference will be given to proposals for studies of bird movements based on banding, analysis of recoveries and returns of banded birds, with an emphasis on economic ornithology.

Student Travel Awards: Students presenting an oral paper or poster at WOS Annual Meeting are invited to apply.

FINANCIAL DATA:
Amount of support per award: Fuertes Award: $2,500; Hall/Mayfield Award: $1,000; Stewart Award: $500.

NO. MOST RECENT APPLICANTS: Approximately 100.

NO. AWARDS: Fuertes Award: 1; Hall/Mayfield Award: 1; Stewart Award: 8.

APPLICATION INFO:
Requirements and application instructions are available on the Society web site.

Duration: One-time grant. Nonrenewable.

Deadline: February 1.

PUBLICATIONS:
Wilson Journal of Ornithology; Wilson Bulletin; Guide to Graduate Programs in Ornithology; Manual of Ornithology.

Environment

ACORN FOUNDATION [2096]
c/o Common Counsel Foundation
405 14th Street, Suite 809
Oakland, CA 94612
(510) 834-2995
Fax: (510) 834-2998
E-mail: info@commoncounsel.org
grantsadmin@commoncounsel.org
Web Site: www.commoncounsel.org

FOUNDED: 1978

AREAS OF INTEREST:
A sustainable ecological future and a healthy global environment.

TYPE:
General operating grants.

YEAR PROGRAM STARTED: 1978

PURPOSE:
To advance community-based organizations working for environmental conservation, sustainability and environmental justice.

ELIGIBILITY:
The Foundation makes grants to grassroots organizations. Organizational budget must be $600,000 or less. The Foundation is particularly interested in small and innovative community-based projects that engage in community organizing in order to:
(1) preserve and restore habitats supporting biological diversity and wildlife;
(2) advocate for environmental justice, particularly in low-income and indigenous communities and;
(3) prevent or remedy toxic pollution.

GEOG. RESTRICTIONS: Western and southern United States and Appalachia.

FINANCIAL DATA:
Amount of support per award: $5,000 to $10,000.

NO. MOST RECENT APPLICANTS: More than 100.

NO. AWARDS: 10 to 14 per year.

APPLICATION INFO:
Organizations that meet the eligibility and funding criteria are encouraged to submit a letter of inquiry form.

Duration: 12 months.

Deadline: January 15 and June 15 for spring and fall grantmaking meetings.

ADDRESS INQUIRIES TO:
Grants Administrator
(See address above.)

ALASKA CONSERVATION FOUNDATION [2097]
911 West Eighth Avenue
Suite 300
Anchorage, AK 99501
(907) 276-1917
Fax: (907) 274-4145
E-mail: grants@alaskaconservation.org
Web Site: www.alaskaconservation.org

FOUNDED: 1980

AREAS OF INTEREST:
Conservation, ecosystem and lands protection, marine conservation, linking conservation with the economy and organizational effectiveness.

NAME(S) OF PROGRAMS:
- **Alaska Native Fund**
- **Organizational Capacity Grants**

TYPE:
General operating grants; Internships; Project/program grants.

YEAR PROGRAM STARTED: 1980

PURPOSE:
To build strategic leadership and support for Alaskan efforts to take care of wild lands, water and wildlife, which sustain diverse cultures, healthy communities and prosperous economies.

LEGAL BASIS:
501(c)(3) public foundation.

ELIGIBILITY:
Incorporate, tax-exempt organizations, non-incorporated organizations and individuals may apply for funding.

Alaska Native Fund: Must perform work that aligns with the priority environmental issues and core strategies supported by the Fund and be an Alaska Native individual, Tribe or other Alaska Native nonprofit organization (with Alaska Native majority on the Council or Board of Directors).

To be considered for an Organizational Capacity Grant, an organization must already demonstrate a commitment to achieve more robust environmental policies, enduring conservation impact, and a more influential conservation movement through implementation of the Foundation's favored conservation strategies. Only organizations whose work strongly aligns with two or more of these strategies should consider submitting an application.

GEOG. RESTRICTIONS: Alaska.

FINANCIAL DATA:
Amount of support per award: Alaska Native Fund: $10,000 to $20,000; Organizational Capacity Grants: $20,000.

NO. AWARDS: Organizational Capacity Grants: 6 for the year 2015.

APPLICATION INFO:
Submit proposals via e-mail only. ACF will invite full proposals to appropriate projects.

Duration: Varies.

Deadline: Varies.

IRS I.D.: 92-0061466

EXECUTIVE DIRECTOR:
Ann Rothe

ADDRESS INQUIRIES TO:
See e-mail address above.

*SPECIAL STIPULATIONS:
ACF funds only in Alaska.

ALASKA CONSERVATION FOUNDATION [2098]

911 West Eighth Avenue
Suite 300
Anchorage, AK 99501
(907) 276-1917
Fax: (907) 274-4145
E-mail: grants@alaskaconservation.org
Web Site: www.alaskaconservation.org

AREAS OF INTEREST:
Conservation, ecosystem and lands protection, marine conservation, linking conservation with the economy and organizational effectiveness.

NAME(S) OF PROGRAMS:
- **Rapid Response Grant**

TYPE:
Awards/prizes; General operating grants; Internships; Project/program grants.

YEAR PROGRAM STARTED: 1977

PURPOSE:
To allow for a timely response to fast-breaking, unforeseen environmental threats of statewide or national significance.

ELIGIBILITY:
Applicants for Rapid Response Grants must meet the following criteria:
(1) be a nonprofit organization engaged in Alaska conservation advocacy;
(2) be based in Alaska, or have an Alaska-based program;
(3) if a current ACF grantee, be in good standing with required grants reports;
(4) grant must address an unforeseen opportunity for action and;
(5) issue must be a statewide concern or have statewide impact.

GEOG. RESTRICTIONS: Alaska.

FINANCIAL DATA:
Amount of support per award: $2,500 to $10,000.

Total amount of support: $3,500,000 for the year 2013.

APPLICATION INFO:
Submit Letter of Inquiry via the Foundation's online application system. ACF will invite full proposals to appropriate projects. Rapid Response projects must address an issue of statewide or national importance. If invited, proposals to the Rapid Response Fund should provide a compelling narrative/justification, a clear timeline, a detailed budget, and have a good chance for success.

Duration: Up to six months.

EXECUTIVE DIRECTOR:
Ann Rothe

ADDRESS INQUIRIES TO:
See e-mail address above.

AMERICAN ACADEMY IN ROME [2099]

7 East 60th Street
New York, NY 10022
(212) 751-7200
Fax: (212) 751-7220
E-mail: info@aarome.org
Web Site: www.aarome.org

FOUNDED: 1894

AREAS OF INTEREST:
Landscape architecture.

NAME(S) OF PROGRAMS:
- **The Rome Prize Fellowship in Landscape Architecture**

TYPE:
Awards/prizes; Fellowships; Residencies. Provides a residential year at the American Academy in Rome for an American landscape architect for advanced study, travel and association with other fellows in the arts and humanities.

YEAR PROGRAM STARTED: 1920

PURPOSE:
To provide American landscape architects with a special opportunity for advanced study in Rome.

LEGAL BASIS:
Nonprofit, national organization.

ELIGIBILITY:
Applicants must hold an accredited degree in landscape architecture, or equivalent experience.

GEOG. RESTRICTIONS: United States.

FINANCIAL DATA:
Award consists of stipend, plus housing and meals allowance.

Amount of support per award: $15,000 for six-month fellowship; $28,000 for 11-month fellowship.

Total amount of support: $90,000.

NO. MOST RECENT APPLICANTS: 20.

NO. AWARDS: 2 annually.

APPLICATION INFO:
Applications are submitted electronically.

Duration: Six months or 11 months.

Deadline: November 1. Announcement in April.

PUBLICATIONS:
Program announcement.

STAFF:
Mark Robbins, President
Shawn Miller, Program Director

ADDRESS INQUIRIES TO:
Program Director
(See address above.)

AMERICAN ALPINE CLUB [2100]

710 10th Street
Suite 100
Golden, CO 80401
(303) 384-0110
Fax: (303) 384-0111
E-mail: grants@americanalpineclub.org
jmiller@americanalpineclub.org
Web Site: www.americanalpineclub.org

FOUNDED: 1902

AREAS OF INTEREST:
Mountaineering, mountain environment and polar regions.

NAME(S) OF PROGRAMS:
- **McNeill-Nott Climbing Award**
- **Mountain Fellowship**
- **Research Grants**
- **Lyman Spitzer Cutting Edge Climbing Award**

TYPE:
Project/program grants; Research grants; Travel grants. Grants to support research in Arctic and alpine environments. Funds may also be used to assist in publication or other dissemination of the results of such research.

The Mountain Fellowship encourages young American climbers under 26 years of age to go into remote areas and seek out climbs more difficult than they might ordinarily be able to do.

YEAR PROGRAM STARTED: 1945

PURPOSE:
To encourage and broaden scientific research in mountains and the polar regions.

LEGAL BASIS:
Membership organization.

ELIGIBILITY:
Individuals engaged in appropriate research are eligible to apply.

FINANCIAL DATA:
Amount of support per award: Varies.

Total amount of support: Over $50,000 annually.

APPLICATION INFO:
Application information is available on the web site.

Duration: One-time grant. New application required for ongoing projects.

Deadline: McNeill-Nott Climbing Award: January 1. Lyman Spitzer Cutting Edge Climbing Award: December 1. Research Grants: January 15.

PUBLICATIONS:
Application guidelines.

ADDRESS INQUIRIES TO:
Janet Miller, Grants Manager
E-mail: jmiller@americanalpineclub.org

AMERICAN WATER RESOURCES ASSOCIATION [2101]
4 West Federal Street
Middleburg, VA 20117
(540) 687-8390
Fax: (540) 687-8395
E-mail: info@awra.org
Web Site: www.awra.org

FOUNDED: 1964

AREAS OF INTEREST:
Water resources.

NAME(S) OF PROGRAMS:
- **Richard A. Herbert Memorial Educational Fund**

TYPE:
Scholarships.

YEAR PROGRAM STARTED: 1980

PURPOSE:
To advance multidisciplinary water resources management and research.

ELIGIBILITY:
Applicant must be a national AWRA member who is enrolled in a program related to water resources. May be a full-time undergraduate student working towards an undergraduate degree or a full-time graduate student.

The undergraduate scholarship will be awarded to the student most qualified by academic performance. Measures of academic performance include the cumulative grade point average, relevance of the student's curriculum to water resources, and leadership in extracurricular activities related to water resources. The graduate scholarship will be awarded to the student most qualified by academic and/or research performance.

FINANCIAL DATA:
Amount of support per award: $2,000.

Total amount of support: $7,300.

NO. MOST RECENT APPLICANTS: 10 undergraduate and 10 graduate applications.

NO. AWARDS: 6.

APPLICATION INFO:
Application must be submitted electronically as one document to the e-mail listed above. File cannot be greater that five MB in size to ensure delivery. A complete application includes a title page and summary of academic interests and achievements, extracurricular interests, and career goals as they relate to the selection criteria. Summaries must be limited to two pages. Include three letters of reference, a transcript of all college courses (undergraduate and graduate), and the applicant's full name, permanent mailing address, e-mail address, and a phone number at which applicant may be reached.

Duration: One year.

Deadline: April 22.

ADDRESS INQUIRIES TO:
AWRA Scholarship Coordinator
(See e-mail address above.)

BEN & JERRY'S FOUNDATION
30 Community Drive
South Burlington, VT 05403-6828
(802) 846-1500
Fax: (802) 846-1610
E-mail: info@benandjerrysfoundation.org
Web Site: www.benandjerrysfoundation.org

TYPE:
General operating grants; Project/program grants. Grants to nonprofit organizations which facilitate progressive social change by addressing the underlying conditions of societal and/or environmental problems using organizing as a strategy to create change.

See entry 959 for full listing.

BONNEVILLE ENVIRONMENTAL FOUNDATION [2102]
240 S.W. First Avenue
Portland, OR 97204-3503
(503) 248-1905
Fax: (503) 248-1908
E-mail: info@b-e-f.org
Web Site: www.b-e-f.org

FOUNDED: 1998

AREAS OF INTEREST:
Environmental conservation and the development of new sources of renewable energy.

NAME(S) OF PROGRAMS:
- **Model Watershed Program**
- **Renewable Energy Program**

TYPE:
Grants-in-aid. Model Watershed Program is intended to restore ecological integrity and native fish populations in watersheds across the western U.S.

Renewable Energy Program supports school solar projects and other renewable energy technologies that are taken up by utility and community-based renewable energy projects.

PURPOSE:
To support watershed restoration programs; to develop new sources of renewable energy.

ELIGIBILITY:
The Foundation does not fund residential projects.

FINANCIAL DATA:
Amount of support per award: Varies.

Total amount of support: Varies.

APPLICATION INFO:
Complete application information is available on the Foundation web site.

Duration: Varies.

STAFF:
Angus Duncan, President
Dick Wanderscheid, Vice President for Renewable Energy Program
Todd Reeve, Chief Executive Officer
Robert Warren, Director, Model Watershed Program

BRAINERD FOUNDATION [2103]
1601 Second Avenue
Suite 610
Seattle, WA 98101
(206) 448-0676
Fax: (206) 448-7222
E-mail: info@brainerd.org
Web Site: www.brainerd.org

FOUNDED: 1995

AREAS OF INTEREST:
Environment.

NAME(S) OF PROGRAMS:
- **Grassroots Fund Grants**
- **Opportunity Fund Grants**

TYPE:
General operating grants; Matching gifts; Project/program grants; Training grants.

YEAR PROGRAM STARTED: 1995

PURPOSE:
To protect the environment of the Northwest and build broad citizen support for conservation.

ELIGIBILITY:
Organizations must be nonprofit classified as 501(c)(3) public charities by the IRS or Canadian organizations deemed equivalent by the Foundation.

GEOG. RESTRICTIONS: British Columbia, Canada; Alaska, Idaho, Montana, Oregon and Washington, United States.

FINANCIAL DATA:
Grants may be used to cover costs associated with, but not limited to, grassroots outreach, media strategies, litigation, scientific and economic studies, communications, and organizational capacity building.

Amount of support per award: Program Grants: $15,000 to $50,000; Grassroots Fund Grants: Up to $10,000; Opportunity Fund Grants: Up to $3,000.

Total amount of support: Varies.

APPLICATION INFO:
Proposals by invitation only. One- to three-page letters of inquiry are accepted on a rolling basis. Each inquiry is weighed on its merits and strategic value, and on how it fits with guidelines. If a program officer invites a full proposal, a specific deadline will be given.

Duration: One to two years. Occasionally three.

STAFF:
Ann Krumboltz, Co-Director
Keiki Kehoe, Co-Director

BRUNSWICK PUBLIC FOUNDATION [2104]
One Northfield Court
Lake Forest, IL 60045
(847) 735-4344
Fax: (847) 735-4330
E-mail: services@brunswick.com
Web Site: www.brunswick.com

FOUNDED: 1998

AREAS OF INTEREST:
Environmental waterways.

TYPE:
Project/program grants.

PURPOSE:
To support community development primarily through contributions to preselected local United Way organizations; to support organizations that enhance the country's water resources for the recreational use by the public through proposals invited by the Foundation trustees.

ELIGIBILITY:
Grants are made to organizations that have tax-exempt status under Section 501(c)(3) of the Internal Revenue Code. Nonsectarian religious programs may apply. No grants are made to individuals.

FINANCIAL DATA:
Amount of support per award: $5,000 to $80,000.

Total amount of support: $360,000 for the year 2014.

NO. AWARDS: 25.

APPLICATION INFO:
Contact the Foundation for guidelines.

Duration: One year.

Deadline: March 15, July 15 and October 15.

IRS I.D.: 36-4195390

STAFF:
Lisa DeBartolo, Coordinator

BOARD OF DIRECTORS:
Kevin Grodzki
Jim Hubbard
David Knight

ADDRESS INQUIRIES TO:
Lisa DeBartolo, Coordinator
(See address above.)

*SPECIAL STIPULATIONS:
By invitation only.

THE BULLITT FOUNDATION [2105]

1501 East Madison, Suite 600
Seattle, WA 98122
(206) 343-0807
Fax: (206) 343-0822
E-mail: info@bullitt.org
Web Site: www.bullitt.org

FOUNDED: 1952

AREAS OF INTEREST:
Environment.

NAME(S) OF PROGRAMS:
- **Deep Green Buildings**
- **Energy, Climate and Materials**
- **Regional Ecosystem Health**
- **Resilient Cities, Healthy Communities**
- **Thought Leadership and Innovation**

TYPE:
Awards/prizes; Matching gifts; Project/program grants.

YEAR PROGRAM STARTED: 1952

PURPOSE:
To safeguard the natural environment by promoting responsible human activities and sustainable communities in the Pacific Northwest.

LEGAL BASIS:
Private foundation.

ELIGIBILITY:
Applicants must be organizations that have nonprofit tax status with clear, significant and achievable goals, as well as a cogent strategy to realize them. The trustees favor projects that avoid excessive reliance on any one source of funding. The Foundation cannot fund political elections or lobbying activities involving specific legislation. The Foundation does not fund university overhead costs or capital projects.

GEOG. RESTRICTIONS: Emerald Corridor: Vancouver, British Columbia to Portland, Oregon.

FINANCIAL DATA:
Amount of support per award: Grants: $5,000 to $100,000; $35,000 average.

Total amount of support: $5,200,000 in grants for the year 2014.

Matching fund requirements: Employee and trustee donations will be matched.

NO. MOST RECENT APPLICANTS: 200.

NO. AWARDS: Approximately 125 annually.

REPRESENTATIVE AWARDS:
$50,000 to Justice Alliance Education Fund; $100,000 to Climate Solutions; $30,000 to Duwamish River Cleanup Coalition; $25,000 to Ecotrust.

APPLICATION INFO:
An organization must first submit a proposal inquiry via the web site. Complete application information is available online.

Duration: One year.

Deadline: Proposal inquiry: March 15 and September 15.

PUBLICATIONS:
Guidelines.

IRS I.D.: 91-6027795

TRUSTEES AND OFFICERS:
Doug Raff, Chairperson
Harriet Bullitt, Vice Chairperson
Sallie Anderson, Treasurer
Howard Frumkin, Secretary
Michael Allen
Rod Brown
Maud Daudon
Erin Gomez
Frank Greer
Denis Hayes
Martha Kongsgaard
Michael Parham
Bill Ruckelshaus

ADDRESS INQUIRIES TO:
Program Officer
(See e-mail or address above.)

LIZ CLAIBORNE ART ORTENBERG FOUNDATION [2106]

1385 Broadway
23rd Floor
New York, NY 10018
(212) 333-2536
E-mail: lcaof@lcaof.org
Web Site: www.lcaof.org

FOUNDED: 1984

AREAS OF INTEREST:
Integration of conservation and development in the rural landscape.

TYPE:
Challenge/matching grants; Development grants; General operating grants; Project/program grants; Research grants; Seed money grants.

PURPOSE:
To conserve nature and relieve human distress; to redress the breakdown in the processes linking nature and humanity.

ELIGIBILITY:
The Foundation funds modest, carefully designed field projects, primarily in developing countries. No funding for general support or to underwrite institutional overhead. Local people should have a substantial proprietary interest in the project.

GEOG. RESTRICTIONS: Northern Rockies region of the United States.

FINANCIAL DATA:
Amount of support per award: $10,000 to $100,000.

Total amount of support: $4,200,000 for fiscal year 2014.

REPRESENTATIVE AWARDS:
$142,000 to African Conservation Centre for Amboseli Research and Conservation Program in Kenya and Tanzania; $49,030 to Wildlife Conservation Society for Tiger Conservation Program in Cambodia; $90,000 to Panthera Corporation for Jaguar Conservation Program in Brazil.

APPLICATION INFO:
Contact the Foundation for guidelines.

Duration: One year.

PUBLICATIONS:
The View from Airlie; *MONTANA: People and the Economy*; brochure; *Next Year Country-View from Red Lodge*; *9 Case Studies on the Interior West of U.S.*

TRUSTEES:
Victor Kovner
Alison Richard

DIRECTORS:
Douglas Chadwick
William Conway
William deBuys
Ullas Karanth
Grant Parker
George Schaller
David Western

ADDRESS INQUIRIES TO:
James Murtaugh, Program Director
Lori Cohen, Program Coordinator
(See address above.)

*PLEASE NOTE:
The Foundation is not accepting unsolicited proposals at this time.

COLUMBIA UNIVERSITY GRADUATE SCHOOL OF JOURNALISM

2950 Broadway
New York, NY 10027
(212) 854-6468
Fax: (212) 854-3148
E-mail: cm3443@columbia.edu
Web Site: www.journalism.columbia.edu

TYPE:
Awards/prizes. Awarded for distinguished excellence in environmental journalism.

See entry 1867 for full listing.

COOPERATIVE INSTITUTE FOR RESEARCH IN ENVIRONMENTAL SCIENCES (CIRES) [2107]

CIRES Building, Room 318
University of Colorado
Boulder, CO 80309-0216
(303) 492-1143
Fax: (303) 492-1149
E-mail: info@cires.colorado.edu
karen.dempsey@colorado.edu
Web Site: cires.colorado.edu

FOUNDED: 1967

AREAS OF INTEREST:
Physics, chemistry and dynamics of the earth system; global and regional environmental change; climate system monitoring, diagnostics, and modeling; development and application of remote sensing and in-situ measurement techniques for the earth and its atmosphere, cryosphere, ecosystems, and oceans.

NAME(S) OF PROGRAMS:
- **CIRES Visiting Fellowship Program in Environmental Sciences**

TYPE:
Fellowships. The program provides opportunities for interactions between CIRES scientists and visiting fellows to pursue common research interests. CIRES research includes theoretical studies, laboratory experimentation, and field investigations which may affect the enhancement of air and water quality and prediction of weather climate fluctuations.

YEAR PROGRAM STARTED: 1968

PURPOSE:
To provide support for scientists from around the world to visit CIRES and collaborate in a variety of research projects.

LEGAL BASIS:
Sponsored jointly by the University of Colorado and National Oceanic and Atmospheric Administration.

ELIGIBILITY:
Applicants must be Ph.D. scientists at all levels; faculty planning sabbatical leave and recent Ph.D. recipients are especially encouraged to apply. Priority is given to candidates with research experience at institutions outside the Boulder scientific community. The program is open to scientists of all countries. The University of Colorado is committed to diversity and equality in education and employment.

FINANCIAL DATA:
Amount of support per award: Stipend is flexible based on research experience.

NO. AWARDS: Up to 15.

APPLICATION INFO:
Applicant must send a resume, publications list and a brief (two- to four-page) description of the proposed research. In addition, candidates should request three letters of recommendation, to be sent directly to CIRES, from persons familiar with their qualifications. Postdoctoral-level applicants must also submit undergraduate and graduate transcripts.

Duration: Postdoctoral: One year. Possible extension to two years. Senior Scientist: Three to 12 months.

Deadline: December 31. Selection the following March.

ADDRESS INQUIRIES TO:
Karen Dempsey
Human Resources Coordinator
(See address above.)

THE ENERGY FOUNDATION [2108]

301 Battery Street, 5th Floor
San Francisco, CA 94111
(415) 561-6700
Fax: (415) 561-6709
E-mail: grants@ef.org
Web Site: www.ef.org

FOUNDED: 1991

AREAS OF INTEREST:
Energy efficiency and renewable energy.

NAME(S) OF PROGRAMS:
- **Buildings Program**
- **Climate Program**
- **Energy Foundation China**
- **Power Program**
- **Public Engagement Program**
- **Transportation Program**

TYPE:
Project/program grants. Promotes energy efficiency and renewable energy.

Buildings Program supports policies to increase the efficiency of U.S. homes and businesses and to reduce carbon emissions and utility bills.

Climate Program has a goal of putting the U.S. on a path to meet or exceed its stated target of reducing greenhouse gas emissions by 17 percent below 2005 levels by 2020.

Energy Foundation China, with an emphasis on both national policy and regional implementation, assists agencies, experts and entrepreneurs in solving that country's energy challenges.

Power Program seeks to move the U.S. toward cleaner, more affordable sources of energy.

Public Engagement Program seeks to build national and state support for clean energy and strong climate policies.

Transportation Program works to reduce energy use and carbon pollution through policies that improve vehicle efficiency and promote clean fuels.

YEAR PROGRAM STARTED: 1991

PURPOSE:
To assist in a national, and ultimately a global, transition to a sustainable future by promoting energy efficiency and renewable energy.

LEGAL BASIS:
Public charity 501(c)(3).

ELIGIBILITY:
501(c)(3) organizations only. No grants to individuals or for-profit organizations. Projects must have broad regional or national implications. No grants to religious organizations, political parties or for development of technology. No research and development or demonstration grants.

GEOG. RESTRICTIONS: United States and China.

FINANCIAL DATA:
Amount of support per award: Varies.

Total amount of support: Approximately $75,000,000 in grant payments for the year 2014.

APPLICATION INFO:
Program officers identify funding opportunities in accordance with program strategies. The Foundation does not accept unsolicited proposals or letters of inquiry.

Duration: Typically one year. Renewal possible.

PUBLICATIONS:
Annual report.

IRS I.D.: 94-3126848

BOARD OF DIRECTORS:
Philip R. Sharp, Chairperson
Mark Burget
Robert Crane
Stephen Harper
Eric Heitz
Khee Poh Lam
Rose McKinney-James
David Nieh
Bill Ritter, Jr.
William Ruckelshaus
Sue Tierney
Hongjun Zhang

ADDRESS INQUIRIES TO:
Jason Mark, Senior Vice President and Director of U.S. Programs
(See address above.)

ENVIRONMENTAL LAW INSTITUTE

1730 M Street, N.W.
Suite 700
Washington, DC 20036
(202) 939-3800
Fax: (202) 939-3868
E-mail: law@eli.org
Web Site: www.eli.org

TYPE:
Scholarships. Tuition scholarships to annual Environmental Law Course.

See entry 1912 for full listing.

FISHAMERICA FOUNDATION [2109]

1001 North Fairfax Street, Suite 501
Alexandria, VA 22314
(703) 519-9691
Fax: (703) 519-1872
E-mail: fafgrants@asafishing.org
Web Site: www.fishamerica.org

FOUNDED: 1983

AREAS OF INTEREST:
Environment and conservation.

NAME(S) OF PROGRAMS:
- **Fisheries Conservation and Research Projects**

TYPE:
Challenge/matching grants; Project/program grants; Research grants; Seed money grants.

YEAR PROGRAM STARTED: 1983

PURPOSE:
To provide funding for on-the-ground projects aimed at enhancing fish populations, restoring fish habitat, improving water quality and advancing fisheries research to improve sportfishing success.

LEGAL BASIS:
Public foundation, 501(c)(3).

ELIGIBILITY:
Any nonprofit tax-exempt organization including conservation organizations, sporting clubs, civic groups, and local and state agencies can apply.

GEOG. RESTRICTIONS: United States and Canada.

FINANCIAL DATA:

Amount of support per award: Average $15,000 per grant.

Matching fund requirements: 1:1.

NO. MOST RECENT APPLICANTS: 162.

NO. AWARDS: 22.

REPRESENTATIVE AWARDS:

$20,000 to Mississippi Fish and Wildlife Foundation to improve water quality within the Bayou Pierre River and its tributaries; $50,000 to Toe River Valley Watch to implement the stream restoration project and greenway along Grassy Creek; $5,000 to New Hampshire B.A.S.S. Nation for the bass research project.

APPLICATION INFO:

Applicants should submit application, letter of support from the appropriate state resource agency biologist, and evidence of nonprofit status.

Duration: One year.

PUBLICATIONS:

Guidelines and application.

IRS I.D.: 36-3219015

BOARD OF DIRECTORS:

Dave Bulthuis, Chairman
Kirk Immens, Vice Chairman
Jim Hubbard, Treasurer
Louis Chemi, Secretary
Thomas Dammrich
Martin MacDonald
Chris Megan
Dave Pfeiffer
Jeff Pontius
Gary Remensnyder
Paul Schluter
Aledia Hunt Tush
K.C. Walsh
Nick Wiley
Gregg Wollner
Gary Zurn

ADDRESS INQUIRIES TO:

Grants Manager
(See address above.)

THE GARDEN CLUB OF AMERICA [2110]

14 East 60th Street, Third Floor
New York, NY 10022
(212) 753-8287
Fax: (212) 753-0134
E-mail: scholarshipapplications@gcamerica.org
Web Site: www.gcamerica.org/scholarships

FOUNDED: 1913

AREAS OF INTEREST:

Conservation, historic preservation and plant conservation.

NAME(S) OF PROGRAMS:

- **GCA Awards for Summer Environmental Studies**

TYPE:

Scholarships.

YEAR PROGRAM STARTED: 1964

PURPOSE:

To encourage studies and careers in the environmental field.

LEGAL BASIS:

Nonprofit, national organization.

ELIGIBILITY:

Open to qualified undergraduates entering a summer program following the freshman, sophomore, and junior years.

FINANCIAL DATA:

Amount of support per award: $2,000.

NO. AWARDS: 4 or more.

APPLICATION INFO:

Application guidelines and form are available online.

Deadline: February 10.

PUBLICATIONS:

Program announcement.

ADDRESS INQUIRIES TO:

Danielle Bartolone, Administrator
(See address above.)

THE GARDEN CLUB OF AMERICA [2111]

14 East 60th Street, Third Floor
New York, NY 10022
(212) 753-8287
Fax: (212) 753-0134
E-mail: scholarshipapplications@gcamerica.org
Web Site: www.gcamerica.org/scholarships

FOUNDED: 1913

AREAS OF INTEREST:

Conservation, historic preservation and plant conservation, and tropical plant study.

NAME(S) OF PROGRAMS:

- **The Garden Club of America Award in Coastal Wetland Studies**

TYPE:

Fellowships. Funds one graduate student annually to support field-based wetlands research. A student may propose a wetlands program of his or her choice at a leading educational institution within the U.S. that specializes in wetlands studies. For the purposes of this scholarship, coastal wetlands are defined as those tidal or nontidal wetlands found within coastal states, including the Great Lakes.

YEAR PROGRAM STARTED: 1983

PURPOSE:

To promote wetlands conservation through the support of young scientists in their field work and research.

LEGAL BASIS:

Nonprofit, national organization.

ELIGIBILITY:

Graduate students pursuing advanced degrees in coastal wetlands science.

GEOG. RESTRICTIONS: United States.

FINANCIAL DATA:

Amount of support per award: $5,000.

NO. AWARDS: 1 annually.

APPLICATION INFO:

Guidelines and application form are available online.

Duration: One year.

Deadline: January 15 preceding the year of study.

PUBLICATIONS:

Program announcement.

ADDRESS INQUIRIES TO:

Danielle Bartolone, Administrator
The Garden Club of America
(See address above.)

*PLEASE NOTE:

Only one GCA scholarship, fellowship or award may be applied for annually.

THE GARDEN CLUB OF AMERICA [2112]

14 East 60th Street, Third Floor
New York, NY 10022
(212) 753-8287
Fax: (212) 753-0134
E-mail: scholarshipapplications@gcamerica.org
Web Site: www.gcamerica.org/scholarships

FOUNDED: 1913

AREAS OF INTEREST:

Horticulture, botany, landscape architecture and environmental studies.

NAME(S) OF PROGRAMS:

- **The GCA and The Royal Horticultural Society Interchange Fellowships**

TYPE:

Exchange programs; Fellowships. A graduate academic year in the U.S. for a British student and a work-study program for an American at universities and botanical gardens in the U.K. in fields related to horticulture, botany and landscape design.

YEAR PROGRAM STARTED: 1948

PURPOSE:

To foster British-American relations through the interchange of scholars in horticulture, botany, landscape architecture and environmental studies.

LEGAL BASIS:

Nonprofit, national organization.

ELIGIBILITY:

Open to men or women who are American citizens at the time of application. Applicants must have earned a B.A. or B.S. degree prior to the start of the Fellowship.

GEOG. RESTRICTIONS: United States.

FINANCIAL DATA:

The Fellowship covers the cost of tuition, travel expenses, board, lodging and incidental college expenses. It also provides an allowance for personal needs.

Amount of support per award: Varies.

CO-OP FUNDING PROGRAMS: Sponsored jointly by The Garden Club of America and The Royal Horticultural Society.

NO. AWARDS: 2 annually.

APPLICATION INFO:

Application form must be accompanied by:
(1) one essay describing the applicant, including biographical data, how the applicant first became interested in horticulture, hobbies and special interests, travel in the U.S. and abroad, and applicant's ability to speak a foreign language;
(2) one essay stating the reasons for applying for this scholarship, the specific field to be studied while in England, and what the applicant expects to gain and contribute, should he or she be awarded this scholarship;
(3) copy of official college transcript and;
(4) four letters of recommendation, including one from a college professor who knows the applicant well, and one from a personal reference (not a member of the applicant's family and not connected with the applicant's academic career). Please furnish names and addresses of those who are writing these recommendations.

Duration: 10-month program.

Deadline: January 15.

PUBLICATIONS:
Program announcement.

ADDRESS INQUIRIES TO:
The Garden Club of America
Danielle Bartolone, Administrator
GCA/RHS Interchange Fellowships
(See address above.)

THE GARDEN CLUB OF AMERICA [2113]

14 East 60th Street, Third Floor
New York, NY 10022
(212) 753-8287
Fax: (212) 753-0134
E-mail: scholarshipapplications@gcamerica.org
Web Site: www.gcamerica.org/scholarships

FOUNDED: 1913

AREAS OF INTEREST:
Plant preservation and tropical botany.

NAME(S) OF PROGRAMS:

- **The Frances M. Peacock Scholarship for Native Bird Habitat**

TYPE:
Research grants. Financial assistance to college seniors and graduate students to study habitat-related issues that will benefit threatened or endangered bird species and lend useful information for land management decisions.

YEAR PROGRAM STARTED: 1983

PURPOSE:
To study areas in the U.S. that provide winter or summer habitat for threatened or endangered native birds and to tend useful information for land-management decisions.

LEGAL BASIS:
Nonprofit, national organization.

ELIGIBILITY:
College seniors and graduate students only. (Second-semester juniors may apply for their senior year.)

GEOG. RESTRICTIONS: United States.

FINANCIAL DATA:
Amount of support per award: $4,500 annually. In special instances, because of two unusually fine candidates or two candidates working on one project, the award may be divided between two candidates.

NO. AWARDS: 1 to 2.

APPLICATION INFO:
Applications should include:
(1) a curriculum vitae for the student, including graduate and undergraduate transcripts;
(2) a two-page outline of the proposed research and a letter of recommendation from the advisor, which should include an evaluation of the student's progress to date and plans for the future and;
(3) evidence of foreign language capability, if necessary for country of research.

Duration: One year.

Deadline: January 15 preceding the proposed period of study.

PUBLICATIONS:
Program announcement.

STAFF:
Danielle Bartolone, Administrator

ADDRESS INQUIRIES TO:
Frances M. Peacock Scholarship:
Prof. Irby Lovette
Cornell Lab of Ornithology
159 Sapsucker Woods Road
Ithaca, NY 14850-1999
E-mail: ijl2@cornell.edu
Web Site: www.birds.cornell.edu

*PLEASE NOTE:
Only one GCA scholarship, fellowship or award may be applied for annually.

GREAT LAKES PROTECTION FUND [2114]

1560 Sherman Avenue
Suite 1370
Evanston, IL 60201
(847) 425-8150
Fax: (847) 424-9832
E-mail: info@glpf.org
Web Site: www.glpf.org

FOUNDED: 1989

AREAS OF INTEREST:
To identify, demonstrate and promote regional action to enhance the health of the Great Lakes ecosystem.

NAME(S) OF PROGRAMS:

- **Great Lakes Protection Fund**

TYPE:
Demonstration grants; Development grants; Seed money grants.

YEAR PROGRAM STARTED: 1990

PURPOSE:
To support projects that identify, demonstrate and promote regional action to enhance the health of the Great Lakes ecosystem.

LEGAL BASIS:
Nonprofit, multi-state endowment.

ELIGIBILITY:
The Great Lakes Protection Fund can support a wide variety of applicants. Nonprofit organizations (including environmental organizations, trade associations, and universities), for-profit businesses, government agencies, and individuals are eligible for Fund support. Successful applicants must maintain open access to certain project data, records and information.

All applicants must comply with the Fund's guidelines, show that the proposed work has clear public benefit to the Great Lakes basin, and that any related financial benefits will accrue to the public good. Government agencies must show that Fund support is not being used to replace or duplicate public funds.

FINANCIAL DATA:
Since inception, the Great Lakes Protection Fund has awarded more than $73,000,000 to support 260 projects with the goal of improving the health of the Great Lakes ecosystem.

Amount of support per award: Varies.

Total amount of support: Varies.

REPRESENTATIVE AWARDS:
$435,000 over 24 months to the Delta Institute to develop a series of tools to track and measure the full extent of the environmental impacts associated with specific reduction actions. Working with 13 facilities in Michigan, the team expects to reduce water use by over 15 million gallons per day, to eliminate almost 3 million tons of solid waste, reduce CO2 emissions by over 11,000 tons, reduce emissions of criteria air pollutants by 150,000 pounds, and reduce hazard chemical use by over 200,000 gallons each year. The tools developed will provide a more accurate account of how on-site energy efficiency actions translate into "real" air pollutant reductions at a power generating facility. In conjunction with a panel of Sustainability Institute Fellows, the team will verify these ecosystem impacts and identify third-party transactions to retire the benefits.

APPLICATION INFO:
The first step is the submission of a brief proposal that summarizes the proposed project. The following documents must be included:
(1) completed applicant cover sheet;
(2) preproposal document, no more than three pages, describing the environmental outcome, proposed work, key personnel and financial plan and;
(3) a resume of the project's manager (no more than two pages).

Preproposal documents can be submitted by e-mail to preproposal@glpf.org or send six copies addressed to Preproposal Application, Great Lakes Protection Fund, at the address above.

Duration: Multiyear.

PUBLICATIONS:
Annual report; guidelines for funding; summary papers.

STAFF:
Russell Van Herik, Executive Director
Drew Pfeifer, Director of Finance and Investment
J. David Rankin, Program Director
Amy Elledge, Communications Manager
Stephanie Lindloff, Project Development Manager
Shannon Donley, Project Implementation Manager
Janis Post, Business Manager

BOARD MEMBERS:
Michael Batchelor
Patty Birkholz
Vita DeMarchi
Matthew Driscoll
Frederick Duddерar, Jr.
Patricia Glaza
Peter Gove
Richard Hylant
Jeffrey Logan
Richard Meeusen
Dan T. Moore
Kevin Shafer
Debra Shore

ADDRESS INQUIRIES TO:
E-mail: startaconversation@glpf.org (initial inquiry)
preproposal@glpf.org (preproposal submission)

THE JACOB AND TERESE HERSHEY FOUNDATION [2115]

3212 Smith Street
Suite 202
Houston, TX 77006
(713) 529-7611
Fax: (713) 529-7613
E-mail: judithboyce@jthershey.org

FOUNDED: 1961

AREAS OF INTEREST:
Animal protection, conservation, environmental, open space and parks, environmental education, land acquisition and human population control.

TYPE:
Capital grants; Conferences/seminars; Development grants; General operating grants; Matching gifts; Project/program grants; Seed money grants. Land acquisition for conservation.

YEAR PROGRAM STARTED: 1961

PURPOSE:
To promote preservation and conservation of land, forests, streams, wetlands and habitat existing in a natural state and the defense of such resources; to establish, conserve and preserve parks and open space for public use; to help provide care facilities for animals and birds, both domestic and wild; to aid education efforts to promote environmental literacy and comprehension of the complexities of the web of life, particularly in museums and through citizen nonprofit organizations with similar purpose; to promote efforts toward population control.

LEGAL BASIS:
Private foundation.

ELIGIBILITY:
Grants are made to organizations that have tax-exempt status under Section 501(c)(3) of the Internal Revenue Code. Grants are not made to medical or religious institutions or groups, or to individuals. No grants for galas or parties. Multiple funding sources are encouraged.

GEOG. RESTRICTIONS: Southwestern Colorado; Austin and Houston, Texas areas.

FINANCIAL DATA:
Amount of support per award: $2,000 to $10,000.

Total amount of support: $200,000 to $400,000.

NO. MOST RECENT APPLICANTS: 100.

NO. AWARDS: 85.

APPLICATION INFO:
Submit written applications only. No general solicitations or bulk mailings. Keep the application simple. One copy only.

Contact the Foundation for one-page grant guidelines.

Duration: One year. May reapply.

Deadline: April 15 and September 15. Applicant will receive an acknowledgement of receipt of application, as well as the date of the meeting at which it will be considered.

IRS I.D.: 74-6039126

EXECUTIVE DIRECTOR:
Judith Boyce

ADDRESS INQUIRIES TO:
Judith Boyce, Executive Director
(See address above.)

THE HUDSON RIVER FOUNDATION [2116]

17 Battery Place, Suite 915
New York, NY 10004
(212) 483-7667
Fax: (212) 924-8325
E-mail: info@hudsonriver.org
Web Site: www.hudsonriver.org

FOUNDED: 1981

AREAS OF INTEREST:
Environmental, ecological and public policy aspects of the Hudson River estuary.

NAME(S) OF PROGRAMS:

- **Hudson River Fund**
- **Hudson River Improvement Fund**
- **New York City Environmental Fund**
- **New York-New Jersey Harbor & Estuary Program**

TYPE:
Capital grants; Fellowships; Research grants; Travel grants. The Hudson River Fund was created to meet the critical need for an independent institution to sponsor scientific research programs that would contribute to the development of sound public policy concerning the River's ecological system. The Hudson River Fund makes grants in five categories: Hudson River Research Grants, Travel Grants, Expedited Grants, Mark B. Baine Graduate Fellowship, and Tibor T. Polgar Fellowships.

The Hudson River Improvement Fund supports projects to enhance public use and enjoyment of the Hudson River's natural, scenic and cultural resources. The emphasis of the Improvement Fund is on physical projects requiring capital construction, development, or improvement.

The New York City Environmental Fund proposes to foster "restoration, care, public enjoyment of, and education about New York City's natural resources."

YEAR PROGRAM STARTED: 1983

PURPOSE:
To make science integral to decision-making with regard to the Hudson River and its watershed; to support competent stewardship of this extraordinary resource.

LEGAL BASIS:
Private foundation.

ELIGIBILITY:
Research must be focused on Hudson River.

FINANCIAL DATA:
Amount of support per award: Graduate Fellowships: Up to $11,000 for one year, plus up to $1,000 toward supplies (Master's students); up to $15,000 for one year, plus up to $1,000 for supplies (doctoral students). Polgar Fellowships: $3,800, plus $1,000 for equipment and supplies.

Total amount of support: Varies.

NO. MOST RECENT APPLICANTS: 60 for research grants.

NO. AWARDS: 15.

APPLICATION INFO:
Guidelines are available online.

Duration: One to two years for fellowships.

Deadline: Contact the Foundation.

PUBLICATIONS:
Annual Program Plan; *Hudson River Fund: Call for Proposals.*

EXECUTIVE DIRECTOR:
Clay Hiles

ILLINOIS CLEAN ENERGY COMMUNITY FOUNDATION [2117]

2 North LaSalle Street, Suite 1140
Chicago, IL 60602
(312) 372-5191
Fax: (312) 372-5190
E-mail: dobrien@illinoiscleanenergy.org
Web Site: www.illinoiscleanenergy.org

FOUNDED: 1999

AREAS OF INTEREST:
Improving the environmental quality of life in the state of Illinois and natural habitat preservation.

TYPE:
Grants-in-aid; Project/program grants. The Foundation provides financial support in two principal ways:
(1) Grantmaking: The Foundation provides grants on a competitive basis, in response to proposals submitted by organizations in accord with the Foundation's announced strategic priorities and the application process described below. The Foundation can provide several different types of financial support, including grants.
(2) Direct Initiatives: The Foundation identifies strategic opportunities to undertake large-scale, high-impact projects and special initiatives that further its program objectives in energy efficiency, renewable energy and natural areas conservation.

YEAR PROGRAM STARTED: 2001

PURPOSE:
To invest in clean energy development and land preservation efforts, working with communities and citizens to improve environmental quality in Illinois.

LEGAL BASIS:
Independent, nonprofit grantmaking institution.

ELIGIBILITY:
The Foundation provides funding to tax-exempt organizations, including governmental entities. The Foundation will not provide funding for remediation of environmentally impaired properties, technology research, promotion of proprietary products, reoccurring operating costs, political campaigns or lobbying, capital campaigns or support for an organization's endowment, or projects undertaken by individuals.

GEOG. RESTRICTIONS: Illinois.

FINANCIAL DATA:
Amount of support per award: Varies.

Total amount of support: Approximately $13,000,000 in total grants awarded for the year 2013.

APPLICATION INFO:
Guidelines available on the web site.

Duration: One to two years.

ADDRESS INQUIRIES TO:
Gabriela Martin, Program Officer
(See address above.)

INTERNATIONAL CRANE FOUNDATION, INC.

E-11376 Shady Lane Road
Baraboo, WI 53913
(608) 356-9462
Fax: (608) 356-9465
E-mail: cranes@savingcranes.org
Web Site: www.savingcranes.org

TYPE:
Internships. Formal stipended internship programs in the fields of aviculture, crane ecology and conservation education.

See entry 2082 for full listing.

LANDSCAPE ARCHITECTURE FOUNDATION [2118]

1129 20th Street, N.W.
Suite 202
Washington, DC 20036
(202) 331-7070 ext. 14
Fax: (202) 331-7079
E-mail: scholarships@lafoundation.org
Web Site: www.lafoundation.org/scholarship

FOUNDED: 1966

AREAS OF INTEREST:
The profession of landscape architecture.

NAME(S) OF PROGRAMS:
- **ASLA Council of Fellows Scholarship**
- **EDSA Minority Scholarship**
- **Hawaii Chapter/David T. Woolsey Scholarship**
- **Steven G. King Play Environments Scholarship**
- **Landscape Forms Design for People Scholarship**
- **Olmsted Scholars Program**
- **Courtland Paul Scholarship**
- **Peridian International Inc./Rae L. Price, FASLA Scholarship**
- **Rain Bird Intelligent Use of Water Scholarship**
- **Douglas Dockery Thomas Fellowship in Garden History and Design**

TYPE:
Fellowships; Scholarships. Awards for undergraduate and graduate students pursuing an education in landscape architecture.

PURPOSE:
To assist students enrolled in programs of landscape architecture.

LEGAL BASIS:
Nonprofit, tax-exempt foundation.

ELIGIBILITY:
Open to undergraduate and graduate students currently enrolled in a professional degree program in landscape architecture. Available to students in financial need who show promise and commitment to the profession.

GEOG. RESTRICTIONS: United States and Canada.

FINANCIAL DATA:
Amount of support per award: Olmsted Scholars Program: $25,000 for graduate winner and $15,000 for undergraduate winner; $1,000 for finalist. All others: $2,000 to $5,000.

Total amount of support: $85,000.

NO. MOST RECENT APPLICANTS: 228 for the academic year 2015-16.

NO. AWARDS: 22 for the academic year 2015-16.

APPLICATION INFO:
Application information is available on the web site.

Duration: One academic year.

Deadline: Douglas Dockery Thomas Fellowship: February 1. All others: February 15.

PUBLICATIONS:
Guidelines.

ADDRESS INQUIRIES TO:
Program Manager
(See address and e-mail above.)

THE LEF FOUNDATION

P.O. Box 382066
Cambridge, MA 02238-2066
(617) 492-5333
Fax: (617) 868-5603
E-mail: sara@lef-foundation.org
gen@lef-foundation.org
Web Site: www.lef-foundation.org

TYPE:
The Foundation gives grants for preproduction, production and post production of nonfiction film and video.

See entry 406 for full listing.

MARSHALL COMMUNITY FOUNDATION

614 Homer Road
Marshall, MI 49068
(269) 781-2273
Fax: (269) 781-9747
E-mail: info@marshallcf.org
Web Site: www.marshallcf.org

TYPE:
Project/program grants; Scholarships.

See entry 1517 for full listing.

MONSANTO FUND [2119]

800 North Lindbergh Boulevard, A2N
St. Louis, MO 63167
(314) 694-4391
Fax: (314) 694-7658
E-mail: monsanto.fund@monsanto.com
Web Site: www.monsantofund.org

FOUNDED: 1964

AREAS OF INTEREST:
Strengthening both farming communities and the communities where company employees live and work.

TYPE:
Project/program grants.

PURPOSE:
To improve the Earth's ecosystem - including clean water, clean air, productive land and thriving biodiversity - and the well-being of her people by supporting projects in the focus areas.

ELIGIBILITY:
Applicants must be nonprofit 501(c)(3) or units of government 170(c)(1). Proposed projects must fit within one of the focus areas. Must be an experienced, established and reputable organization (not a start-up organization), financially sound with a diverse funding base, and be audited annually.

Grants are not given to religious organizations.

FINANCIAL DATA:
Amount of support per award: $2,500 to $250,000.

Total amount of support: Varies.

APPLICATION INFO:
Application information is available online.

Duration: One to two years.

Deadline: Varies.

NATIONAL FISH AND WILDLIFE FOUNDATION [2120]

1133 15th Street, N.W.
Suite 1100
Washington, DC 20005
(202) 857-0166
Fax: (202) 857-0162
E-mail: info@nfwf.org
Web Site: www.nfwf.org

FOUNDED: 1984

AREAS OF INTEREST:
Conservation of natural resources including fish, wildlife, plants and habitat.

TYPE:
Challenge/matching grants; Formula grants; Matching gifts; Project/program grants; Scholarships.

YEAR PROGRAM STARTED: 1986

PURPOSE:
To conserve natural resources through habitat protection, environmental education, natural resource management, species conservation and leadership training for conservation professionals.

LEGAL BASIS:
Private 501(c)(3) organization.

ELIGIBILITY:
Must be a 501(c)(3) organization. No grants to individuals.

GEOG. RESTRICTIONS: Primarily United States.

FINANCIAL DATA:
Amount of support per award: Varies.

Total amount of support: More than $378,000,000 in on-the-ground conservation impact for the year 2015.

Matching fund requirements: At least 1:1, preference for higher leverage.

NO. MOST RECENT APPLICANTS: Varies.

NO. AWARDS: Varies.

REPRESENTATIVE AWARDS:
$100,000 to Iowa Department of Natural Resources to restore 1,254 acres of bottomland hardwood forest in northeast Iowa on former agricultural lands. The project is working to reduce forest fragmentation, enhance water quality, and improve critical habitat for neo-tropical birds and other wildlife; $400,000 to Conservation Fund to reduce nutrient and sediment runoff entering Rockymarsh Run – a tributary to the Potomac River and ultimately the Chesapeake Bay.

APPLICATION INFO:
Application information may be obtained online.

Duration: Support usually lasts for one year. Renewals are on a case-by-case basis.

PUBLICATIONS:
Annual report; application guidelines.

IRS I.D.: 52-1384129

STAFF:
Lila Helms, Executive Vice President, External Affairs
Jeff Trandahl, Executive Director/Chief Executive Officer
Holly Bamford, Chief Conservation Officer

BOARD OF DIRECTORS:
John V. Faraci, Jr., Chairman
Patsy Ishiyama, Vice Chairperson
Paul Tudor Jones, II, Vice Chairperson
Carl R. Kuehner, III, Vice Chairperson
Charles D. McCrary, Vice Chairperson
Don J. McGrath, Vice Chairperson

Dan Ashe
Michael L. Campbell
J. Michael Cline
John Dane, III
Caroline Getty
J.J. Healy
George C. (Tim) Hixon
Christopher M. James
Sydney McNiff Johnson
Eaddo H. Kiernan
Reuben Mark
R. King Milling
Jennifer Mull
Trina Overlock
David Perkins
Chad Pike
Amy Robbins Towers
Edwin Rodriguez, Jr.
Thomas L. Strickland
Kathryn D. Sullivan
John A. Tomke
Victoria J. Tschinkel
John E. von Schlegell
Steven A. Williams

ADDRESS INQUIRIES TO:
Appropriate Partnership Office Director
(See address above.)

NATIONAL INSTITUTE OF ENVIRONMENTAL HEALTH SCIENCES [2121]

Division of Extramural Research and Training
MD K3-05
111 T.W. Alexander Drive
Research Triangle Park, NC 27709
(919) 541-3289
Fax: (919) 541-2843
E-mail: mastin@niehs.nih.gov
Web Site: www.niehs.nih.gov

FOUNDED: 1966

AREAS OF INTEREST:
Research on environmental agents and chemicals and their effects on human health.

NAME(S) OF PROGRAMS:
- **Environmental Health Sciences Research and Training Grants**

TYPE:
Conferences/seminars; Demonstration grants; Development grants; Fellowships; Project/program grants; Research grants; Training grants. NIEHS pursues its mission by supporting basic and applied research on the consequences of the exposure of humans to potentially toxic or harmful agents in the environment.

Research of interest encompasses studies that relate to the biological effects of environmental chemicals and physical factors including such agents as hazardous gases, suspended particles, aerosols, industrial by-products and intermediates, heavy metals, trace elements, food additives, adulterants and pesticides. Physical factors include noise, light, heat, microwaves and other forms of nonionizing radiation.

Research Training Programs support individuals at both the predoctoral and postdoctoral levels in the areas of environmental toxicology, environmental pathology, environmental mutagenesis and environmental epidemiology.

YEAR PROGRAM STARTED: 1966

PURPOSE:
To support research and research training in environmental health.

LEGAL BASIS:
Government agency authorized under Section 301(d), Public Health Services Act; 42 U.S.C. 241; 42 C.F.R. 52.

ELIGIBILITY:
Universities, research institutes and other public or private institutions may apply on behalf of qualified researchers. Small businesses may apply for SBIR grants.

GEOG. RESTRICTIONS: United States.

FINANCIAL DATA:
Funds are provided, as available, for all allowable expenses associated with approved research projects.

Amount of support per award: Varies.

Total amount of support: Varies.

APPLICATION INFO:
Guidelines are available on the web site.

Duration: Total grant project periods may not exceed five years and are renewable on a competitive basis at the end of the project period. Average project period length is currently four years.

Deadline: Varies with the specific grant.

PUBLICATIONS:
Fact book; special announcements.

STAFF:
Dr. Carol Shreffler, Health Science Administrator

ADDRESS INQUIRIES TO:
J. Patrick Mastin, Ph.D.
Deputy Director
(See address above.)

NATIONAL PARK FOUNDATION [2122]

1110 Vermont Avenue, N.W.
Suite 200
Washington, DC 20005
(202) 796-2500
Fax: (202) 796-2509
E-mail: ask-npf@nationalparks.org
Web Site: www.nationalparks.org

FOUNDED: 1967

NAME(S) OF PROGRAMS:
- **Active Trails**
- **Albright-Wirth Grants Program**
- **America's Best Idea**
- **The Junior Ranger Program**
- **Parks Climate Challenge**
- **Parks Stewards Program**
- **Transportation Scholars**
- **Harry Yount National Park Ranger Award**

TYPE:
Block grants; Challenge/matching grants; Research grants; Scholarships. Grants range from small seed or start-up programs to larger ones which continue successful projects. Grants enable the parks to obtain additional cash and in-kind contributions, such as products, service or volunteer time.

The Albright-Wirth Employee Development Fund underwrites advanced skills training, graduate education and other professional development programs for Park Service employees.

The Harry Yount National Park Ranger Award recognizes a Ranger for leadership, exemplary skills and dedication to the Park Ranger profession.

YEAR PROGRAM STARTED: 1967

PURPOSE:
To help fund important conservation, preservation, and education efforts on-the-ground in the National Parks.

LEGAL BASIS:
Nonprofit organization.

ELIGIBILITY:
All grants are made directly for projects in the national park system. Grants will fund educational projects, field training for volunteers and interns, resource conservation, historic preservation, interpretation programs for park visitors, outreach programs, and park projects conducted by park friends, cooperating associations or academic institutions.

The grants program will not fund the purchase of vehicles or maintenance equipment, new construction or large-scale improvements to buildings, infrastructure construction or maintenance of roads and utilities, base salaries of full-time NPS staff, advocacy or litigation, or the start-up costs of friends groups.

FINANCIAL DATA:
Amount of support per award: $5,000 to $50,000.

Total amount of support: Varies.

Matching fund requirements: Varies.

APPLICATION INFO:
Applications accepted only from national park units. Complete information is available online.

Duration: Usually one year. Renewal applications permitted.

Deadline: Varies.

PUBLICATIONS:
Annual report.

IRS I.D.: 52-1086761

OFFICERS:
Hon. Sally Jewell, Chairman and Secretary of the Interior
Ellen S. Alberding, Vice Chairman
Brien O'Brien, Treasurer
John Jarvis, Secretary, Director National Park Service

STAFF:
Will Shafroth, President and Chief Executive Officer
Mandeep Singh, Chief Financial Officer

ADDRESS INQUIRIES TO:
See e-mail address above.

NATIONAL WILDLIFE FEDERATION [2123]

11100 Wildlife Center Drive
Reston, VA 20190-5362
(703) 438-6265
Fax: (703) 438-6468
E-mail: fellows@nwf.org
Web Site: www.nwf.org

FOUNDED: 1936

AREAS OF INTEREST:
Global warming impacts and solutions.

NAME(S) OF PROGRAMS:
- **Campus Ecology Fellowships**
- **Emerging Leaders Fellowships**

TYPE:
Fellowships.

YEAR PROGRAM STARTED: 1973

PURPOSE:
To give well-qualified and highly motivated individuals substantive practical experience.

LEGAL BASIS:
Nonprofit organization able to carry on a defined amount of lobbying.

ELIGIBILITY:
Campus Ecology Fellowships: Undergraduate or graduate students from any college or university in the U.S. may apply. Applications are invited from students in all disciplines and are not limited to environmental studies majors. Current and former employees of National Wildlife Federation and former NWF Campus Ecology Fellows are ineligible to apply. Former NWF interns are eligible to apply following one year from their final work date. The applicant must be enrolled in school throughout the duration of the grant period.

Emerging Leaders Fellowships are open to postgraduate, young professionals (ages 21 to 35) interested in career development and leadership opportunities within the conservation movement.

GEOG. RESTRICTIONS: United States.

FINANCIAL DATA:
Amount of support per award: Campus Ecology Fellowships: Up to $2,000 to offset project expenses for undergraduates; Up to $5,000 for graduates. Emerging Leaders Fellowships: Up to $3,000 stipend.

Total amount of support: Varies.

CO-OP FUNDING PROGRAMS: Kendeda Sustainability Fund of the Tides Foundation, Kendeda Fund, Nathan Cummings Foundation, Town Creek Foundation.

NO. MOST RECENT APPLICANTS: Approximately 400.

NO. AWARDS: Varies.

APPLICATION INFO:
Information is available on the web site.

Duration: Varies.

Deadline: Varies.

PUBLICATIONS:
Program description.

OFFICERS:
Colin O'Mara, President and Chief Executive Officer

ADDRESS INQUIRIES TO:
See e-mail address above.

NEW YORK SEA GRANT [2124]

125 Nassau Hall
Stony Brook University
Stony Brook, NY 11794-5001
(631) 632-6905
Fax: (631) 632-6917
E-mail: nyseagrant@stonybrook.edu
Web Site: www.nyseagrant.org

FOUNDED: 1971

AREAS OF INTEREST:
Coastal resource management, fisheries biology, contaminants and environmental quality, environmental processes and marine economics, seafood use and technology, recreation and tourism, human dimensions, marine aquaculture, youth education, biotech, and coastal processes.

TYPE:
Awards/prizes; Conferences/seminars; Development grants; Endowments; Fellowships; Internships; Project/program grants; Research grants; Scholarships; Technical assistance; Travel grants. Principally grants for laboratory and field studies, publications and communication and curriculum development.

YEAR PROGRAM STARTED: 1971

PURPOSE:
To foster the wise use and development of coastal resources through research, education and training.

LEGAL BASIS:
A cooperative research and education activity of the State University of New York and Cornell University, as well as NOAA's National Sea Grant College Program.

ELIGIBILITY:
Applicant must be a member of the faculty of an institution of higher learning or of a nonprofit organization. Projects must address issues relevant to New York state. In most cases, applicants are affiliated with New York institutions.

FINANCIAL DATA:
Amount of support per award: Varies.

Total amount of support: $1,000,000.

Matching fund requirements: Matching funds equal to 50% of funds requested must be provided by applicant from non-federal sources.

NO. MOST RECENT APPLICANTS: Around 100 for most biennial solicitations.

NO. AWARDS: Approximately 10 per year.

APPLICATION INFO:
Application information is available on the web site.

Duration: One year. Continuation possible.

Deadline: Biennial with occasional out-of-cycle.

OFFICERS:
William Wise, Interim Director

ADDRESS INQUIRIES TO:
William Wise, Interim Director
(See address above.)

JESSIE SMITH NOYES FOUNDATION [2125]

122 East 42nd Street
Suite 2501
New York, NY 10168
(212) 684-6577
Fax: (212) 689-6549
E-mail: noyes@noyes.org
Web Site: www.noyes.org

FOUNDED: 1947

AREAS OF INTEREST:
Sustainable agriculture, toxics, reproductive rights, environmental justice, and environment in New York City.

TYPE:
General operating grants; Project/program grants. Grants to tax-exempt institutions in the connected and overlapping areas of sustainable agriculture, toxics, reproductive rights, and New York City environment in order to achieve the Foundation's overall goal, which is to promote a sustainable and just social and natural system by supporting grassroots organizations and movements committed to this goal.

PURPOSE:
To support programs that promote a sustainable and just social and natural system.

LEGAL BASIS:
Family foundation.

ELIGIBILITY:
The Foundation makes grants to tax-exempt organizations with 501(c)(3) classification from the IRS for work within the U.S. to individuals. It will not consider requests for endowments, capital construction, general fund-raising, deficit financing or scholarships, fellowships, loans or grants to individuals. The Foundation does not make grants for research or give support to conferences, seminars, media events, or workshops, unless they are an integral part of a broader program, does not generally make grants for college- and university-based programs, and does not provide support for the production and development of television and media programming.

GEOG. RESTRICTIONS: United States.

FINANCIAL DATA:
Amount of support per award: Varies.

NO. MOST RECENT APPLICANTS: Approximately 350 letters of inquiry received each year.

NO. AWARDS: Approximately 100 per year.

REPRESENTATIVE AWARDS:
$45,000 to Alaska Community Action on Toxics, Anchorage, AK; $20,000 to Hunger Action Network of New York State, Albany, NY; $25,000 to Young Women United, Albuquerque, NM.

APPLICATION INFO:
The first step should be a letter of inquiry of no more than three pages. The Foundation welcomes the opportunity to meet with prospective grantees, but prefers to wait until after it receives a letter to determine if the meeting will be useful.

Letters of inquiry are reviewed by the program staff who determine if requests meet the Foundation's funding priorities. Those not meeting the priorities are declined. Requests that meet the priorities are given further consideration and a full proposal may be requested. Proposals should be submitted to the Foundation only upon request.

Duration: Varies.

Deadline: Letters of inquiry are accepted at any time. If a proposal is requested, it is assigned to one of the Foundation's three board meetings.

IRS I.D.: 13-5600408

OFFICERS:
Genaro Lopez-Rendon, President

STAFF:
Millie Buchanan, Program Director for Environmental Justice
Wilma Montanez, Program Director for Reproductive Rights
Margaret Segall, Director of Administration

ADDRESS INQUIRIES TO:
Genaro Lopez-Rendon, President
(See address above.)

PATAGONIA INC. [2126]

259 West Santa Clara Street
Ventura, CA 93001
(805) 643-8616
Fax: (805) 643-2367
E-mail: inquiries@patagonia.com
Web Site: www.patagonia.com/enviro

AREAS OF INTEREST:
Preservation and protection of the natural environment.

NAME(S) OF PROGRAMS:

- **Environmental Grant Program**

TYPE:
General operating grants; Product donations; Project/program grants. Funds to help local groups working to protect local habitats and to force the government to abide by its own laws in regards to biodiversity and ecosystem protection.

YEAR PROGRAM STARTED: 1987

PURPOSE:
To assist groups who strive to preserve and restore the natural environment.

LEGAL BASIS:
Private corporation giving program.

ELIGIBILITY:
Applicants must be 501(c)(3) tax-exempt organizations. Support is given to small, grassroots, activist organizations with provocative direct-action agendas, working on multipronged campaigns to preserve and protect the environment. No grants for more general environmental education efforts. Contact Patagonia Inc. for complete details.

GEOG. RESTRICTIONS: Argentina, Australia, Austria, Belgium, Canada, Chile, Czech Republic, Denmark, France, Germany, Ireland, Italy, Japan, Luxembourg, The Netherlands, Norway, Spain, Sweden, Switzerland, United Kingdom and United States.

FINANCIAL DATA:
Company pledges one percent of sales to grassroots environmental groups.

Amount of support per award: Up to $12,000.

Total amount of support: $6,200,000 in cash donations in fiscal year 2015.

NO. AWARDS: Donations to 741 grassroots environmental groups in 18 countries in fiscal year 2015.

APPLICATION INFO:
Application information is available on the web site.

Duration: One year. Applicants must reapply for continued funding.

Deadline: Proposals must be submitted no later than April 30 or August 31. Applications receive a response by the end of August and January, respectively.

PUBLICATIONS:
Program guidelines.

ADDRESS INQUIRIES TO:
Lisa Myers
Environmental Grants Manager
(See address above.)

*PLEASE NOTE:
Phone calls are discouraged.

PEW FELLOWS PROGRAM IN MARINE CONSERVATION [2127]

Pew Environment Group
901 E Street, N.W., 10th Floor
Washington, DC 20004
(202) 540-6850
Web Site: www.pewtrusts.org/en/projects/marine-fellows

FOUNDED: 1988

AREAS OF INTEREST:
Marine conservation.

TYPE:
Fellowships.

YEAR PROGRAM STARTED: 1990

PURPOSE:
To support innovative, applied projects aimed at developing and implementing solutions to critical challenges facing the world's oceans.

LEGAL BASIS:
Public trust.

ELIGIBILITY:
Applicant must work in the field of research, education, communications, advocacy or policy, and must be nominated.

FINANCIAL DATA:
Amount of support per award: $150,000 over three years, to be applied to a specific project.

Total amount of support: $750,000 per year.

NO. MOST RECENT APPLICANTS: Approximately 35.

NO. AWARDS: 5 individuals or teams.

APPLICATION INFO:
Applications are by nomination only. Unsolicited applications are not accepted.

Duration: Three years.

Deadline: Varies.

PUBLICATIONS:
Program guidelines; newsletter.

ADDRESS INQUIRIES TO:
Polita Glynn, Program Director
(See address above.)

*SPECIAL STIPULATIONS:
The Foundation does not accept unsolicited proposals.

RESOURCES FOR THE FUTURE [2128]

1616 P Street, N.W., Suite 600
Washington, DC 20036-1436
(202) 328-5000
Fax: (202) 939-3460
E-mail: info@rff.org
Web Site: www.rff.org

AREAS OF INTEREST:
Economics, policy sciences or issues relating to the environment and natural resources of energy.

NAME(S) OF PROGRAMS:

- **Joseph L. Fisher Doctoral Dissertation Fellowships**
- **The Walter O. Spofford, Jr., Memorial Internship**

TYPE:
Awards/prizes; Fellowships; Internships. Joseph L. Fisher Dissertation Fellowships are in support of doctoral dissertation research on issues related to the environment, natural resources or energy.

The Walter O. Spofford, Jr., Memorial Internship is a paid internship for graduate students.

PURPOSE:
Joseph L. Fisher Dissertation Fellowships: To support graduate students in the final year of their dissertation research. The Walter O. Spofford, Jr., Memorial Internship: To offer a paid resident internship for graduate students with a special interest in Chinese environmental issues.

ELIGIBILITY:
Joseph L. Fisher Doctoral Dissertation Fellowships: Candidates must have completed the preliminary examinations for the Doctorate prior to the application deadline. Applicants are expected to complete all requirements for their Doctorate by the end of the summer of the academic year of their fellowship (e.g., end of summer 2017 for 2016-17 academic year). Resources for the Future particularly encourages women and members of minority groups to apply. RFF's primary research disciplines are economics and other social sciences. Proposals originating in these fields will have the greatest likelihood of success. Proposals from the physical or biological sciences must have an immediate and obvious link to environmental policy matters.

The Walter O. Spofford, Jr., Memorial Internship: Candidates should be highly motivated and in the first or second year of graduate training in the social or natural sciences. Candidates should also have outstanding policy analysis and writing skills. They should also have a special interest in Chinese environmental issues.

Both programs are open to both U.S. and non-U.S. citizens, provided that the latter have proper work and residency documentation. Chinese students are particularly encouraged to apply for the Spofford Memorial Internship.

FINANCIAL DATA:
Under the Tax Reform Act of 1986, most, if not all, of this stipend will probably be taxable income. This Fellowship is intended to be the principal source of support for graduate students in the final year of their dissertation research. The Fellowship will be reduced dollar-for-dollar by the amount of any other financial assistance other than tuition support. However, the Fellowship will still pay a minimum stipend of $2,000 to awardees whose stipends would otherwise be reduced below that amount. All other financial assistance must be disclosed to RFF; it is expected that fellowship recipients will not engage in full-time employment during the period of fellowship tenure.

Amount of support per award: Joseph L. Fisher Doctoral Dissertation Fellowships: $18,000 stipend for the academic year.

Walter O. Spofford, Jr. Memorial Internship: $375 stipend per week; no housing assistance is provided.

NO. AWARDS: 3 Fisher Fellowships for 2015-16; 1 Spofford Internship for 2015-16 .

APPLICATION INFO:
Joseph L. Fisher Doctoral Dissertation Fellowships: Graduate students interested in applying should submit the following materials through RFF's online application system:
(1) a cover letter;
(2) a resume/curriculum vitae;
(3) for non-U.S. citizens, proof of eligibility to be employed in the U.S.;
(4) a one-page abstract of the dissertation and;
(5) a technical summary of the dissertation not to exceed 2,500 words (not including the bibliography) that clearly describes the aim of the dissertation, its significance in relation to the existing literature, and the research methods and data to be used.
Candidates should also submit the following by e-mail to fisher-award@rff.org with the name of the applicant in the subject field:
(1) a graduate transcript; (2) a letter from the department chair or other university official certifying the student's doctoral candidacy and;

(3) two letters of recommendation from faculty members on the student's dissertation committee.
RFF cannot provide written evaluations of proposals.

The Walter O. Spofford, Jr., Memorial Internship: Students should submit the following materials through RFF's online application system:
(1) a cover letter describing their areas of interest;
(2) a resume/curriculum vitae and;
(3) for non-U.S. citizens, proof of eligibility to be employed in the U.S.
Candidates should also submit the following by e-mail to spofford-award@rff.org with the name of the applicant in the subject field:
(1) a recent transcript and;
(2) one letter of recommendation from a faculty member should be sent directly by the professor to RFF.

Duration: Joseph L. Fisher Doctoral Dissertation Fellowships: Up to one year; The Walter O. Spofford, Jr., Memorial Internship: Three months during the summer.

Deadline: Both awards: All application materials must be received by February 20; awards announced in April.

RESOURCES FOR THE FUTURE [2129]

1616 P Street, N.W., Suite 600
Washington, DC 20036-1436
(202) 328-5000
Fax: (202) 939-3460
E-mail: info@rff.org
Web Site: www.rff.org

FOUNDED: 1952

AREAS OF INTEREST:
Research and public education in development, conservation, economics, the use of natural resources and in the quality of the environment.

NAME(S) OF PROGRAMS:
- **Gilbert F. White Postdoctoral Fellowship Program**

TYPE:
Awards/prizes; Fellowships; Internships; Research grants; Residencies; Visiting scholars. Resident fellowships in honor of Gilbert F. White, internationally known statesman of science, for postdoctoral research related to natural resources, energy or the environment.

YEAR PROGRAM STARTED: 1980

PURPOSE:
To support research in areas related to natural resources, energy, or the environment.

LEGAL BASIS:
Private, nonprofit research organization.

ELIGIBILITY:
Open to individuals in any discipline who will have completed their doctoral requirements by the beginning of the academic year for which they are applying. Selection criteria include the nature of the applicant's proposed research program and how it will fit with RFF work in progress. Teaching and/or research experience at the postdoctoral level is preferred, though not essential. Individuals holding positions in government, as well as at academic institutions, are eligible.

The program is open to both U.S. and non-U.S. citizens, provided that the latter have proper work and residency documentation.

FINANCIAL DATA:
Fellows receive an annual stipend based upon their current salary, plus research support, office facilities at RFF, and an allowance of up to $1,000 for moving or living expenses. This stipend may be supplemented from other sources if the supplement does not divert the fellow from his or her research. Fellowships do not provide medical insurance or other RFF fringe benefits. Neither Social Security nor tax payments are deducted from the stipend.

Amount of support per award: Varies.

Total amount of support: Varies.

NO. AWARDS: 2 for the academic year 2015-16.

APPLICATION INFO:
Candidates should submit the following through RFF's online application system:
(1) a cover letter;
(2) a curriculum vitae including educational background, professional experience, honors/awards received, list of publications and description of significant completed unpublished research;
(3) a project budget and;
(4) statement of proposed research (not more than 10 double-spaced pages) with main hypothesis or major objective of the research, methods to be used, explanation of anticipated benefit and importance of the results; proposal should also contain a discussion of how the work fits with the current RFF research and how an association would be mutually beneficial.

Candidates should also submit by e-mail to white-award@rff.org three letters of recommendation from fellow faculty members or colleagues. (Insert the name of the applicant in the subject field.)

Duration: 11 months.

Deadline: February 21. Announcement in April.

PUBLICATIONS:
Guidelines.

IRS I.D.: 53-0220900

OFFICERS:
Philip R. Sharp, President

ADDRESS INQUIRIES TO:
Coordinator for Academic Programs
(See address above.)

RESOURCES FOR THE FUTURE [2130]

1616 P Street, N.W., Suite 600
Washington, DC 20036-1436
(202) 328-5000
Fax: (202) 939-3460
E-mail: info@rff.org
Web Site: www.rff.org

AREAS OF INTEREST:
Economics, policy sciences or issues relating to the environment and natural resources of energy.

NAME(S) OF PROGRAMS:
- **John V. Krutilla Research Stipend**

TYPE:
Research grants. Stipend can be used for summer salary support, to pay for research assistance, or for any other legitimate research expenses.

PURPOSE:
To provide research assistance.

ELIGIBILITY:
Open to young scholars who have a recently awarded doctoral degree (no more than five years beyond receipt of Ph.D.). The focus of the award is on research related to environmental and natural resource economics. Special attention will be given to applications that seek to pursue research into one or more of the areas pioneered by John Krutilla, after whom the award is named.

The program is open to both U.S. and non-U.S. citizens, provided that the latter have proper work and residency documentation.

FINANCIAL DATA:
Amount of support per award: $5,500.

NO. AWARDS: 1 per academic year.

APPLICATION INFO:
Individuals interested in applying should submit the following materials through RFF's online application system:
(1) a short description of the proposed research (no more than five typed pages, double-spaced; references do not count in the page total) and;
(2) a resume/curriculum vitae.

Candidates should also submit one letter of recommendation that comments on the candidate's past research and proposed project in specific terms by e-mail to krutilla-award@rff.org. (Insert the name of the applicant in the subject field.)

Duration: One year.

Deadline: All application materials must be received by February 20. Announcement in April.

THE RUSSELL FAMILY FOUNDATION [2131]

3025 Harborview Drive
Gig Harbor, WA 98335
(253) 858-5050
Fax: (253) 851-0460
E-mail: info@trff.org
Web Site: www.trff.org

FOUNDED: 1999

AREAS OF INTEREST:
Environmental sustainability.

TYPE:
General operating grants; Project/program grants. Grants focused on environmental education for grades five to 12 in King, Kitsap, Pierce and Thurston counties.

PURPOSE:
To implement strategies that raise awareness and understanding of our environment and the importance of protecting it.

ELIGIBILITY:
Organizations must be 501(c)(3) or nonprofit entities such as public schools and school districts, and must be located in and/or provide services within the Puget Sound region. No grants to individuals.

GEOG. RESTRICTIONS: Western Washington state (King, Kitsap, Pierce and Thurston counties).

FINANCIAL DATA:
Amount of support per award: Average grant: $30,000.

APPLICATION INFO:
Submit letter of inquiry through Foundation's online grantmaking system. Full proposals are accepted by invitation only.

Duration: One year. Renewal by reapplication.

Deadline: Letter of inquiry: January, July and October.

ADDRESS INQUIRIES TO:
Linsey Sauer, Grants Manager
(See address above.)

SMITHSONIAN ENVIRONMENTAL RESEARCH CENTER (SERC) [2132]

647 Contees Wharf Road
Edgewater, MD 21037
(443) 482-2217
Fax: (443) 482-2380
E-mail: gustafsond@si.edu
Web Site: www.serc.si.edu

FOUNDED: 1965

AREAS OF INTEREST:
Environmental research and environmental education.

NAME(S) OF PROGRAMS:

- **Professional Training**

TYPE:
Fellowships; Internships. The Internship Program enables undergraduates, recent graduates and graduate students to work on specific projects under the direction of the Center's professional staff and is tailored to provide the maximum educational benefit to each participant. Graduate students and undergraduates may conduct independent projects with the approval of the staff member with whom they plan to study.

Subject matter of the projects includes terrestrial and estuarine environmental research within the disciplines of mathematics, chemistry, microbiology, botany, zoology, and environmental education.

Fellowships are offered annually at the postdoctoral, predoctoral and graduate levels.

Internships are offered three times per year at the undergraduate levels, recent graduate, or beginning Master's student.

YEAR PROGRAM STARTED: 1972

PURPOSE:
To offer undergraduate and graduate-level students a unique opportunity to gain exposure to and experience in environmental research.

LEGAL BASIS:
Research unit of the Smithsonian Institution.

ELIGIBILITY:
Applicants must be qualified students from academic institutions in the U.S. or abroad. The SERC will accept applications from interested individuals who are in a position to commit themselves fully to the completion of a project. Selection is based upon the student's academic credentials, extent of relevant training or experience, letters of recommendation and the congruence of the student's expressed goals with those of the Professional Training Program.

FINANCIAL DATA:
Dorm space is available for $105 per week and does not include board. Space is limited.

Amount of support per award: Interns receive $500 per week.

Total amount of support: $48,000 postdoctoral/senior stipend; $32,500 predoctoral stipend; $7,000 graduate student; research allowances are additional.

NO. MOST RECENT APPLICANTS: 36 fellowship applicants and 400 internship applicants for the year 2016.

NO. AWARDS: 3 to 5 fellowships and 35 to 50 internships for the year 2016.

APPLICATION INFO:
Application materials and additional information regarding fellowships can be obtained from the Smithsonian Institution Office of Fellowships and Grants, E-mail: siofg@ofg.si.edu.

Applicants must use the Smithsonian On-Line Academic Appointment (SOLAA) web site for application submittal: https://solaa.si.edu/solaa/solaahome.html.

Duration: Intern Appointments: Generally 12 to 16 weeks; Fellowships: One year, with renewal.

Deadline: Winter/Spring Session: November 15; Summer Session: February 1; Fall Session: June 1; Fellowships: January 15.

PUBLICATIONS:
Application guidelines.

STAFF:
Anson H. Hines, Director
Patrick Megonigal, Associate Director of Research
Daniel E. Gustafson, Jr., Professional Training Coordinator

ADDRESS INQUIRIES TO:
Daniel E. Gustafson, Jr.
Professional Training Coordinator
(See address above.)

SOIL AND WATER CONSERVATION SOCIETY [2133]

945 S.W. Ankeny Road
Ankeny, IA 50023-9764
(515) 289-2331
Fax: (515) 289-1227
E-mail: swcs@swcs.org
Web Site: www.swcs.org

AREAS OF INTEREST:
Soil, water and related natural resource management.

NAME(S) OF PROGRAMS:

- **Kenneth E. Grant Research Scholarship**

TYPE:
Research grants. Provides financial aid to members of the Society for graduate-level research on a specific conservation topic that will help the Society carry out its mission of fostering the science and the art of soil, water, and related natural resource management to achieve sustainability.

PURPOSE:
To foster the science and the art of soil, water and related natural resource management to achieve sustainability; to promote and practice an ethic recognizing the interdependence of people and the environment.

ELIGIBILITY:
Open to members of the Society who have demonstrated integrity, ability and competence to complete the specified study topic. Applicants must be eligible for graduate work at an accredited institution and show reasonable need for financial assistance. Must be members of the Society for at least one year.

FINANCIAL DATA:
Amount of support per award: $300.

NO. AWARDS: 1.

APPLICATION INFO:
Applicants must submit a proposal and evidence of their ability to meet eligibility requirements. There are no specific application forms.

Duration: One year.

Deadline: February 12.

ADDRESS INQUIRIES TO:
Christine Rhodes, Corporate Relations
E-mail: christine.rhodes@swcs.org

THE ROBERT & PATRICIA SWITZER FOUNDATION [2134]

P.O. Box 293
Belfast, ME 04915-0293
(207) 338-5654
Fax: (207) 338-5655
E-mail: erin@switzernetwork.org
Web Site: www.switzernetwork.org

FOUNDED: 1987

AREAS OF INTEREST:
Environment.

NAME(S) OF PROGRAMS:

- **Switzer Environmental Fellowship Program**

TYPE:
Fellowships; Project/program grants. Annual fellowship to recognize environmental leaders who have the ability and determination to make a significant impact on environmental quality.

YEAR PROGRAM STARTED: 1987

PURPOSE:
To support highly talented graduate students in California and New England whose studies are directed toward improving environmental quality and who demonstrate leadership in their field.

ELIGIBILITY:
Applicants must meet the following criteria:
(1) be a U.S. citizen;
(2) be enrolled in an accredited institution in California or New England and;
(3) have strong academic qualifications.

Master's degree candidates must have completed at least one semester of course work.

Ph.D. candidates must have completed at least three years of doctoral work or passed their qualifying exams.

GEOG. RESTRICTIONS: California and New England.

FINANCIAL DATA:
Amount of support per award: $15,000, paid in two equal installments, the first in June and the second in late January or early February.

Total amount of support: $300,000.

NO. MOST RECENT APPLICANTS: 300.

NO. AWARDS: 20 annually; 10 in California and 10 in New England.

APPLICATION INFO:
Application information is available on the web site.

Duration: One year.

Deadline: January 10.

ADDRESS INQUIRIES TO:
Erin Lloyd, Program Officer
(See address above.)

TOWN CREEK FOUNDATION, INC. [2135]

121 North West Street
Easton, MD 21601
(410) 763-8171
Fax: (410) 763-8172
E-mail: info@towncreekfdn.org
Web Site: www.towncreekfdn.org

FOUNDED: 1981

AREAS OF INTEREST:
The environment and climate change.

TYPE:
Challenge/matching grants; Conferences/seminars; General operating grants; Matching gifts; Project/program grants.

YEAR PROGRAM STARTED: 1981

PURPOSE:
To seek a healthy natural and sustainable environment, through public education, citizen action and advocacy.

LEGAL BASIS:
Private, tax-exempt foundation.

ELIGIBILITY:
501(c)(3) tax-exempt organizations are eligible for support. The Foundation does not make grants to individuals, organizations considered to be "private foundations," primary and secondary schools, hospitals or health care institutions, religious organizations or capital and building fund campaigns. It does not make grants to colleges or universities except when some aspect of their work is an integral part of a program supported by the Foundation. It does not fund research, scholarship programs, conferences not part of a program supported by the Foundation, or publication of books and periodicals, or visual or performing arts.

GEOG. RESTRICTIONS: United States, Mid-Atlantic region.

FINANCIAL DATA:
Amount of support per award: Average: $40,000 to $50,000.

Total amount of support: $6,428,500 for the year 2013.

NO. MOST RECENT APPLICANTS: 136.

NO. AWARDS: 90 grants for the year 2014.

REPRESENTATIVE AWARDS:
$80,000 to Nanticoke Watershed Alliance; $100,000 to Climate Central; $100,000 to Smart Growth America.

APPLICATION INFO:
Online application required. Guidelines are available on the Foundation web site.

Duration: One year.

Deadline: Spring: Letter of Intent/Inquiry: November. Invited Proposals: December.

Summer: Letter of Intent/Inquiry: March. Invited Proposals: April.

IRS I.D.: 52-1227030

TRUSTEES AND OFFICERS:

*PLEASE NOTE:
Town Creek Foundation is in the process of spending out its endowment. The plan is to close in 2021.

U.S. DEPARTMENT OF AGRICULTURE [2136]

1400 Independence Avenue, S.W.
Stop 0513
Washington, DC 20250-0510
(202) 720-6221
Fax: (202) 720-4619
E-mail: matthewponish@wdc.usda.gov
Web Site: www.fsa.usda.gov

FOUNDED: 1933

AREAS OF INTEREST:
The conservation of the nation's soil, forest and water resources.

CONSULTING OR VOLUNTEER SERVICES:
Technical assistance is provided by federal and state agencies cooperating with this program.

NAME(S) OF PROGRAMS:
- **Emergency Conservation Program (ECP)**

TYPE:
Grants-in-aid. Cost-share assistance with agricultural producers to rehabilitate agricultural lands damaged by natural disasters. Assistance may also be provided for carrying out emergency water conservation measures during periods of severe drought.

YEAR PROGRAM STARTED: 1957

PURPOSE:
To provide emergency funding and technical assistance for farmers and ranchers to rehabilitate farmland damaged by natural disasters and for carrying out emergency water conservation measures in periods of severe drought.

LEGAL BASIS:
Government agency, authorized by P.L. 95-334, August 1978.

ELIGIBILITY:
Applicants are limited to agricultural producers, such as owners, landlords, tenants or sharecroppers of farms or ranches used to produce grains, row crops, livestock, vegetables, hay, orchards, vineyards, seed crops or other agricultural commodities commercially.

All landowners, regardless of race, sex, religion, marital status, disability, color, age or national origin, may apply for cost-sharing.

GEOG. RESTRICTIONS: United States.

FINANCIAL DATA:
Amount of support per award: Maximum of $200,000 per person.

Matching fund requirements: Producers are required to contribute the difference between the cost-share amount and the total cost of each ECP practice.

ADDRESS INQUIRIES TO:
Contact the nearest FSA County Office where your land is located.

U.S. ENVIRONMENTAL PROTECTION AGENCY [2137]

Office of Enforcement and Compliance Assurance
1200 Pennsylvania Avenue, N.W.
Washington, DC 20460
(202) 564-2280
Fax: (202) 564-0085
E-mail: chow,emily@epa.gov
Web Site: www.epa.gov/enforcement

FOUNDED: 1970

AREAS OF INTEREST:
Pesticides enforcement.

NAME(S) OF PROGRAMS:
- **Pesticide Enforcement Cooperative Agreements**

TYPE:
Grants-in-aid; Project/program grants.

YEAR PROGRAM STARTED: 1977

PURPOSE:
To develop and maintain comprehensive pesticide programs that address all aspects of pesticide enforcement and special pesticide initiatives; to sponsor cooperative surveillance monitoring and analytical procedures; to encourage regulatory activities within the states and tribes.

LEGAL BASIS:
Federal Insecticide, Fungicide and Rodenticide Act, as amended; P.L. 92-516; 7 U.S.C. 136 et seq. as amended by P.L. 94-140, Section 23(a) and 95-396.

ELIGIBILITY:
State agencies having pesticide enforcement responsibilities in each state, territory and possession of the U.S., including the District of Columbia and Indian tribes.

The applicant must supply evidence of legal authority to conduct pesticide enforcement activities and a workable program adopted for the agency.

Each application will be reviewed according to the following criteria:
(1) the need for the development, improvement and/or maintenance of a comprehensive pesticides enforcement program within the state;
(2) the relative amount of pesticide production, formulation and use in the state and the potential risk to human health and the environment from pesticide misuse or abuse;
(3) the potential of the cooperative agreement to have a long-term beneficial impact on human health and the environment resulting from the comprehensive enforcement program and;
(4) the past level and effectiveness of the state pesticide regulatory program.

FINANCIAL DATA:
Amount of support per award: Varies by state, territory and tribe.

Matching fund requirements: 15% state match.

NO. AWARDS: Approximately 75.

APPLICATION INFO:
It is advisable to preapply by having an informal meeting with the regional program office concerning program preparation. Prior to approval of any grants, the official State Pesticides Regulatory Agency must coordinate local pesticide enforcement efforts. The standard application forms furnished by the federal agency and OMB Circular No. A-102 must be used for this program. Completed applications and other required forms should be submitted to the appropriate EPA Regional Office.

Duration: Usually 12 months.

ADDRESS INQUIRIES TO:
Emily Chow
(See address above.)

U.S. ENVIRONMENTAL PROTECTION AGENCY [2138]

Office of Superfund Remediation and Technology Innovation (5204P)
1200 Pennsylvania Avenue, N.W.
Washington, DC 20460
(703) 603-8835
Fax: (703) 603-9104
E-mail: singer.yolanda@epa.gov
Web Site: www.epa.gov/superfund

FOUNDED: 1970

AREAS OF INTEREST:
Cleanup of hazardous waste releases into the environment.

NAME(S) OF PROGRAMS:
- **Superfund State and Indian Tribe Core Program Cooperative Agreements**
- **Superfund State, Political Subdivision, and Indian Tribe Site-Specific Cooperative Agreements**

TYPE:
Project/program grants. Superfund State and Indian Tribe Core Program Cooperative Agreements: This program seeks to effectively implement the statutory requirements of the Comprehensive Environmental Response, Compensation, and Liability Act (CERCLA), Section 121(f) for state involvement. It is intended to provide funds to conduct CERCLA activities which are not assignable to specific sites, but support a recipient's site-specific response program.

Superfund State, Political Subdivision, and Indian Tribe Site-Specific Cooperative Agreements: This program proposes to:
(1) conduct site characterization activities at potential or confirmed hazardous waste sites;
(2) undertake response planning and implementation actions at sites on the National Priorities List (NPL) to clean up the hazardous waste sites that are found to pose hazards to human health and;
(3) effectively implement the statutory requirements of CERCLA 121(f) which mandates substantial and meaningful state involvement.

YEAR PROGRAM STARTED: 1981

PURPOSE:
To undertake removal actions at NPL and non-NPL sites to protect the public from the release of hazardous materials; to conduct preremedial activities to determine if sites require listing on the NPL; to perform remedial planning and remedial implementation actions in response to releases on the NPL; to clean up the hazardous waste sites that are found to pose the most imminent threat to human health; to support state involvement in the Superfund program.

LEGAL BASIS:
Comprehensive Environmental Response, Compensation and Liability Act of 1980 (Superfund) (P.L. 96-510), as amended by The Superfund Amendments and Reauthorization Act of 1986 (SARA) (P.L. 99-499), The Small Business Liability Relief and Brown Fields Revitalization Act (PL 107-118).

ELIGIBILITY:
States (and political subdivisions thereof), commonwealths, U.S. territories and possessions, and federally recognized Indian tribal governments, including intertribal consortia.

GEOG. RESTRICTIONS: United States and its territories.

FINANCIAL DATA:
Amount of support per award: Superfund State and Indian Tribe Core Program Cooperative Agreements: $8,000 to $400,000; average: $122,574 for the year 2014. Superfund State, Political Subdivision, and Indian Tribe Site-Specific Cooperative Agreements: $188,000 to $3,500,000; average: $308,157.

ADDRESS INQUIRIES TO:
Yolanda Singer, Environmental Scientist
Site Assessment Remedy Decisions Branch
(See address above.)

U.S. SOCIETY ON DAMS

1616 17th Street, Suite 483
Denver, CO 80202
(303) 628-5430
Fax: (303) 628-5431
E-mail: stephens@ussdams.org
Web Site: www.ussdams.org

TYPE:
Scholarships.

See entry 2581 for full listing.

UNIVERSITY OF PITTSBURGH [2139]

Pymatuning Laboratory of Ecology
13142 Hartstown Road
Linesville, PA 16424
(814) 273-0416
Fax: (814) 683-2302
E-mail: pymlab@pitt.edu
Web Site: www.pitt.edu/~biology/pymatuning.htm

FOUNDED: 1949

AREAS OF INTEREST:
Ecology research.

NAME(S) OF PROGRAMS:
- **Leasure K. Darbaker Prize in Botany**
- **McKinley Research Fund**
- **Pape Research Fund**

TYPE:
Research grants. The Leasure K. Darbaker Prize in Botany is an annual award available for support of botanically related studies at the graduate or postdoctoral level.

The G. McKinley Research Fund and the Pape Research Fund of the Pittsburgh Foundation provide grants for support of graduate and postdoctoral research in ecology. Several are awarded each summer.

LEGAL BASIS:
Department of the University of Pittsburgh.

ELIGIBILITY:
Proposals are welcome at all academic graduate and postdoctoral levels for research in any area of ecology.

Awards are granted for work to be carried out at the facility in northwestern Pennsylvania.

FINANCIAL DATA:
Funds for travel, equipment, supplies, assistants and room and board at the laboratory may be included.

Amount of support per award: Up to $3,500 per award.

Total amount of support: Approximately $14,000 annually.

NO. AWARDS: 6 for the year 2014.

APPLICATION INFO:
Application information can be found at the web site.

Deadline: February 7.

PUBLICATIONS:
Application guidelines.

ADDRESS INQUIRIES TO:
Chris Davis, Assistant Director
(See address above.)

THE UNIVERSITY OF SYDNEY [2140]

Scholarships Office
Level 5, Jane Foss Russell Building G02
The University of Sydney N.S.W. 2006
Australia
(02) 8627 8112
Fax: (02) 8627 8485
E-mail: scholarships.officer@sydney.edu.au
Web Site: www.sydney.edu.au/scholarships/research

FOUNDED: 1850

AREAS OF INTEREST:
Water conservation.

NAME(S) OF PROGRAMS:
- **Richard Claude Mankin Scholarship**

TYPE:
Scholarships. Postdoctoral award for research and postgraduate for research leading to a higher degree. Tenable at the University of Sydney.

YEAR PROGRAM STARTED: 1973

PURPOSE:
To promote research related to water conservation at the University of Sydney.

LEGAL BASIS:
University.

ELIGIBILITY:
Candidates may be of postgraduate or postdoctoral standing at the University of Sydney.

FINANCIAL DATA:
The scholarship does not cover tuition fees payable by international students.

Amount of support per award: $25,849 AUD per annum for the year 2015.

NO. AWARDS: 1 offered as vacancy occurs and funds are available.

APPLICATION INFO:
Application information is available on the web site.

Duration: Two years for Master's candidate. Up to three-and-one-half years for Ph.D. candidate.

Deadline: Second week in January and early in July.

VIRGINIA ENVIRONMENTAL ENDOWMENT [2141]

919 East Main Street, Suite 1070
Richmond, VA 23219
(804) 644-5000
Fax: (804) 644-0603
E-mail: info@vee.org
Web Site: www.vee.org

FOUNDED: 1977

AREAS OF INTEREST:
Environmental improvement.

NAME(S) OF PROGRAMS:
- **Kanawha and Ohio River Valleys Program**
- **Virginia Program**

TYPE:
Challenge/matching grants; Demonstration grants; Project/program grants; Research grants; Seed money grants; Research contracts. Provides grants to projects that demonstrate feasibility, innovation and appropriateness to the Endowment's purpose and priorities. Improvement of the quality of the environment in the Commonwealth of Virginia, especially water quality research and monitoring; land conservation; Chesapeake Bay conservation, research and education; and environmental education. Programs addressing water quality and the effects of water pollution on public health and the environment in the Kanawha River and Ohio River valleys of Kentucky and West Virginia.

YEAR PROGRAM STARTED: 1977

PURPOSE:
To improve the quality of the environment by using its capital to encourage all sectors to work together to prevent pollution, conserve natural resources and promote environmental literacy.

LEGAL BASIS:
Tax-exempt, grantmaking organization 501(c)(4).

ELIGIBILITY:
The Endowment makes grants to nonprofit, tax-exempt, charitable organizations and institutions, and occasionally to governmental agencies. It encourages requests for specific projects that promise measurable results to improve the environment. Applicants should describe specifically how they propose to measure the success of a grant project. Grant funds are not provided for general support, overhead, indirect costs, capital projects, land purchases, building construction or renovation, endowments, lawsuits or to individuals.

GEOG. RESTRICTIONS: The state of Virginia and the Kanawha and Ohio River valleys of Kentucky and West Virginia.

FINANCIAL DATA:
Reviewed asset value: $16,884,918 as of March 31, 2013.

Amount of support per award: Varies.

Total amount of support: $287,366 for fiscal year ended March 31, 2014.

Matching fund requirements: At least a 1:1 match is normally required.

CO-OP FUNDING PROGRAMS: The Endowment welcomes opportunities for collaboration.

NO. AWARDS: 16 for fiscal year ended March 31, 2014.

APPLICATION INFO:
Two copies of the complete proposal, signed by the organization's chief executive officer or board chairman, must be received by the deadline date. The Endowment does not review or comment on preliminary proposals.

Each proposal must include the following information:
(1) a cover letter identifying the applicant, project title, grant request, matching funds, project schedule, and whether the proposal is being submitted to the Virginia Program or the Kanawha and Ohio River Valleys Program;
(2) a project description, limited to five pages, clearly stating the need for the project, goals and objectives and how they will be achieved, how project results will be measured, and relationship to other work being done in the field;
(3) a description of the organization, names and qualifications of key project staff, a list of the members of the governing board, the current operating budget, and a copy of the current tax-exempt ruling from the IRS, if applicable;
(4) a line-item budget for the proposed project showing total project costs, the amount and proposed allocation of grant funds requested from the Endowment, and all sources and amounts of matching funds, which must equal or exceed the requested grant;
(5) the project schedule, with specific beginning and ending dates for requested grant support and;
(6) a detailed plan for evaluating and disseminating project results, for continuing project activities, and for raising future financial support.

Proposals may not be submitted by facsimile or by e-mail.

For delivery by U.S. Mail, address to Joseph Maroon, Executive Director, Virginia Environmental Endowment, P.O. Box 790, Richmond, VA 23218-0790.

Duration: Stipulated with specific projects. One year preferred.

Deadline: Kanawha and Ohio River Valleys Program: June 15; Virginia Program: June 15 and December 1. Proposals must be received by 5 P.M. Board decisions about proposals are normally made in April and October.

PUBLICATIONS:
Annual report, including guidelines.

IRS I.D.: 54-1041973

STAFF:
Joseph Maroon, Executive Director

DIRECTORS:
Robin D. Baliles
Dixon M. Butler
Landon Hilliard
Lawrence Kochard
Nina Randolph
Nancy N. Rogers
Robert B. Smith, Jr.

ADDRESS INQUIRIES TO:
Joseph Maroon, Executive Director
(See address above.)

*SPECIAL STIPULATIONS:
No preliminary proposal reviews are provided; full proposals are required.

WEEDEN FOUNDATION [2142]

35 Adams Street
Bedford Hills, NY 10507
(914) 864-1375
Fax: (914) 864-1377
E-mail: weedenfdn@weedenfdn.org
Web Site: www.weedenfdn.org

FOUNDED: 1963

AREAS OF INTEREST:
Biodiversity, population and environment, natural resource conservation and consumption.

NAME(S) OF PROGRAMS:
- **Consumption**
- **Domestic Biodiversity**
- **International Biodiversity**
- **Population**

TYPE:
General operating grants; Project/program grants.

YEAR PROGRAM STARTED: 1963

PURPOSE:
To address the adverse impact of exploding human population and overuse of natural resources on the biological fabric of the planet.

LEGAL BASIS:
Nonprofit, family foundation.

ELIGIBILITY:
Applicants must be nonprofit, tax-exempt organizations with 501(c)(3) status or international equivalent.

GEOG. RESTRICTIONS: Bolivia, Central Siberia, Chile and the Pacific Northwest.

FINANCIAL DATA:
Amount of support per award: Average: $15,000 to $25,000.

Total amount of support: Varies.

NO. MOST RECENT APPLICANTS: 100 for the year 2014.

NO. AWARDS: 80 for the year 2014.

REPRESENTATIVE AWARDS:
$20,000 to IPAS; $20,000 to Center for a New American Dream; $20,000 to Forest Ethics.

APPLICATION INFO:
Applicants should submit a letter of inquiry. Foundation will request a full proposal, if interested.

Duration: One year. Renewal possible.

Deadline: Varies.

IRS I.D.: 94-6109313

STAFF:
Donald A. Weeden, Executive Director
Emily Rodriguez, Research Assistant

BOARD OF DIRECTORS:
Norm Weeden, Ph.D., President
Bob Weeden, Treasurer
Leslie Weeden, Secretary
Barbara Daugherty
Christina Roux
Alan Weeden
Donald E. Weeden
Jack D. Weeden
John D. Weeden
William Weeden

ADDRESS INQUIRIES TO:
Donald A. Weeden, Executive Director
(See address above.)

THE WILDLIFE CONSERVATION SOCIETY [2143]

2300 Southern Boulevard
Bronx, NY 10460
(718) 220-5100
Fax: (718) 364-4275
E-mail: fellowship@wcs.org
Web Site: programs.wcs.org/grants
www.wcs.org

FOUNDED: 1895

AREAS OF INTEREST:
Wildlife conservation, wildlands, communities, threatened wildlife and ecosystems.

NAME(S) OF PROGRAMS:
- **Research Fellowship Program**

TYPE:
Awards/prizes; Fellowships; Project/program grants; Research grants. Awards small grants to field research projects leading to the conservation of threatened wildlife and wildlife habitat.

YEAR PROGRAM STARTED: 1993

PURPOSE:
To support individual research projects that lead to concrete advances in the understanding and conservation of wildlife or wildlands.

LEGAL BASIS:
Nonprofit organization.

ELIGIBILITY:
Research project should focus on addressing a conservation issue relevant to the Society's priorities. Project should have direct relevance to the conservation objective and to improving conservation management. Projects that do not serve to answer questions and solve problems will be given low priority.

Awards are for direct support of research activities, but cannot be used for conference attendance, expeditions, travel to scientific meetings, legal actions, construction of permanent field stations, tuition expenses, salary for principal investigator, overhead costs, costly laboratory analyses, gene storage, vehicle purchases, computer purchases or captive breeding (except in projects directory working on recovery species).

Preference will be given to applicants enrolled in Master's and Ph.D. level programs, however applications will be accepted from all conservationists in the early stages of their careers.

Applicants must be citizens of developing countries. An exception is made for applicants who are Native American or First Nations, Metis or Inuit. Applicants cannot be current WCS employees and must not have received a WCS research fellowship program grant in the past.

Organizations or teams are not eligible.

FINANCIAL DATA:
Amount of support per award: Maximum $15,000.

APPLICATION INFO:
All applications, including curriculum vitae, any permits or letters of endorsement, and a letter of recommendation must be submitted electronically. Applications are accepted in English, French and Spanish.

Duration: One year.

Deadline: July 31.

PUBLICATIONS:
Application guidelines.

THE DEAN WITTER FOUNDATION

57 Post Street, Suite 510
San Francisco, CA 94104
(415) 981-2966
Fax: (415) 981-5218
E-mail: admin@deanwitterfoundation.org
Web Site: www.deanwitterfoundation.org

TYPE:
Challenge/matching grants; Fellowships; General operating grants; Internships; Matching gifts; Professorships; Project/program grants; Research grants; Scholarships; Seed money grants.

See entry 1856 for full listing.

Medicine (multiple disciplines)

A-T CHILDREN'S PROJECT [2144]

5300 West Hillsboro Boulevard
Suite 105
Coconut Creek, FL 33073
(954) 481-6611
Fax: (954) 725-1153
E-mail: grants@atcp.org
info@atcp.org
Web Site: www.atcp.org

FOUNDED: 1993

AREAS OF INTEREST:
Projects that, while drawing on basic discoveries, apply innovative and novel strategies for suggesting, developing and evaluating specific disease-modifying and symptomatic interventions for ataxia-telangiectasia (A-T); clinical studies for A-T.

NAME(S) OF PROGRAMS:
- **A-T Postdoctoral Fellowship Award**
- **A-T Research Grant Program**

TYPE:
Research grants.

YEAR PROGRAM STARTED: 1993

PURPOSE:
To accelerate first-rate, international scientific research in an attempt to help find a cure or life-improving therapies for children with ataxia-telangiectasia.

ELIGIBILITY:
Open to all ages and nationalities. Proposal for grant must have direct relevance to ataxia-telangiectasia.

Applicants should be aware that meritorious proposals may be rejected if:
(1) the proposed research is too far from being relevant to a therapeutic intervention;
(2) the A-T Children's Project's scientific advisors find the research redundant and in no need of validation;
(3) the proposed research is likely to happen anyway, without the A-T Children's Project's support and;
(4) the research cannot realistically be achieved with the proposed budget.

FINANCIAL DATA:
Amount of support per award: Up to $75,000 per year.

Total amount of support: Varies.

APPLICATION INFO:
Detailed information can be found on the organization web site. A Letter of Intent (LOI) is required prior to submission of a full-length proposal. An LOI form can be downloaded from the web site.

Duration: One to two years.

Deadline: Letter of Intent: August 1 for September 1 deadline and February 1 for March 1 deadline. Full proposal: March 1 and September 1.

ADDRESS INQUIRIES TO:
Dr. Cynthia Rothblum-Oviatt
Science Coordinator
E-mail: cynthia@atcp.org

ALBERTA INNOVATES - HEALTH SOLUTIONS [2145]

Suite 1500
10104 - 103 Avenue, N.W.
Edmonton AB T5J 4A7 Canada
(780) 423-5727
Fax: (780) 429-3509
E-mail: health@aihealthsolutions.ca
Web Site: www.aihealthsolutions.ca

FOUNDED: 2010

AREAS OF INTEREST:
Supporting biomedical and health research at Alberta universities, affiliated institutions, and other medical and technology-related institutions.

NAME(S) OF PROGRAMS:
- **AIHS Collaborative Research and Innovation Opportunities**
- **AIHS Community Engagement and Conference Grant**
- **AIHS Industry Partnered Translational Fund**
- **AIHS Sustainability Funding Opportunity**
- **AIHS Training and Early Career Development Programs**
- **AIHS Translational Health Chairs**
- **Knowledge-to-Action Grant**
- **Partnership for Research and Innovation in the Health System (PRIHS)**

TYPE:
Awards/prizes; Block grants; Conferences/seminars; Development grants; Fellowships; General operating grants; Project/program grants; Research grants; Scholarships; Training grants. Interdisciplinary team grants. Awards for conferences and workshops.

YEAR PROGRAM STARTED: 2010

PURPOSE:
To promote research in medical and health sciences and implement means of using the scientific resources of the medical sciences in Alberta.

LEGAL BASIS:
Funding agency created by an act of the Alberta legislature.

ELIGIBILITY:
Most awards tenable only in Alberta.

GEOG. RESTRICTIONS: Alberta.

FINANCIAL DATA:
Grants are made on a year-round basis from interest revenue earned on an original endowment of $300,000,000.

Amount of support per award: Stipulated with individual awards.

Total amount of support: Approximately $70,000,000 for the fiscal year 2015-16.

Matching fund requirements: Stipulated with applicable awards.

APPLICATION INFO:
Application forms and guidelines are available from the Research Services Offices of Alberta universities and on the AIHS web site.

Duration: Varies by program.

Deadline: Varies by program.

PUBLICATIONS:
Guidelines for Grants and Awards.

ADDRESS INQUIRIES TO:
Carla Weyland, Lead Industry and Technology Initiatives
(See address above.)

*SPECIAL STIPULATIONS:
Awards are to be held in Alberta, or if held outside Alberta, are to be sponsored by an Alberta university.

THE JOHN W. ALDEN TRUST

c/o Miki C. Akimoto, V.P., Market Philanthropic Dir.
Philanthropic Solutions, U.S. Trust
Bank of America Private Wealth Management
225 Franklin Street, MA1-225-04-02
Boston, MA 02110
(617) 951-1108
E-mail: susan.t.monahan@gmail.com
Web Site: www.cybergrants.com/alden

TYPE:
Capital grants; Challenge/matching grants; Conferences/seminars; Demonstration grants; Development grants; Matching gifts; Project/program grants; Research grants; Scholarships; Seed money grants; Technical assistance; Training grants.

See entry 1085 for full listing.

ALZHEIMER'S DRUG DISCOVERY FOUNDATION [2146]

57 West 57th Street
Suite 904
New York, NY 10019
(212) 901-8000
Fax: (212) 901-8010
E-mail: hfillit@alzdiscovery.org
Web Site: www.alzdiscovery.org

FOUNDED: 2004

AREAS OF INTEREST:
Drug discovery and development for Alzheimer's disease, related dementias and cognitive decline.

NAME(S) OF PROGRAMS:
- **ADDF/Belfer ApoE Therapeutics Innovation Program**
- **ADDF/NIH**
- **Preclinical Drug Discovery**
- **Program to Accelerate Clinical Trials (PACT)**

TYPE:
Awards/prizes; Conferences/seminars; Research grants.

PURPOSE:
To promote the research and development of therapies to identify, treat and prevent cognitive decline, Alzheimer's disease and related dementias.

LEGAL BASIS:
Nonprofit Delaware corporation 501(c)(3) public charity.

ELIGIBILITY:
Applicant must be a university medical center or early-stage biotechnology company.

FINANCIAL DATA:
Amount of support per award: $150,000 to $300,000 per year for preclinical projects. Budget requests up to $1,500,000 are accepted for clinical trial submissions.

Total amount of support: Varies.

NO. MOST RECENT APPLICANTS: Approximately 450 for the year 2014.

NO. AWARDS: 39 for the year 2014.

APPLICATION INFO:
Complete instructions are available on the Foundation web site.

Duration: One to two years.

Deadline: Letters of intent accepted on an ongoing basis. Applications due quarterly.

ADDRESS INQUIRIES TO:
Danielle Popow, Grants Coordinator
E-mail: dpopow@alzdiscovery.org

AMERICAN ACADEMY OF FACIAL PLASTIC AND RECONSTRUCTIVE SURGERY (AAFPRS) [2147]

Educational and Research Foundation for the AAFPRS
310 South Henry Street
Alexandria, VA 22314
(703) 299-9291 ext. 234
Fax: (703) 299-8898
E-mail: info@aafprs.org
Web Site: www.aafprs.org

AREAS OF INTEREST:
Facial plastic and reconstructive surgery.

NAME(S) OF PROGRAMS:
- **Community Service Award**
- **John Dickinson Teacher of the Year Award**
- **Sir Harold Delf Gillies Award**
- **F. Mark Rafaty Memorial Award**
- **Residency Travel Award**
- **John Orlando Roe Award**
- **Ben Shuster Memorial Award**
- **Ira Tresley Research Award**
- **William K. Wright Award**

TYPE:
Awards/prizes; Fellowships; Travel grants. Community Service Award may be presented annually to an AAFPRS member who has distinguished himself/herself by providing and/or making possible free medical service to the poor in his or her community.

John Dickinson Teacher of the Year Award honors an AAFPRS fellow member for sharing knowledge about facial plastic and reconstructive surgery with the effective use of audiovisuals in any one year.

Sir Harold Delf Gillies Award is presented each year to the graduate fellow who submits the best basic science research paper written during fellowship.

The F. Mark Rafaty Memorial Award may be presented each year to an AAFPRS member who has made outstanding contributions to facial plastic and reconstructive surgery.

The Residency Travel Award is presented to the most outstanding paper in facial plastic and reconstructive surgery, primarily authored by a resident or medical student in training. The paper must be submitted by February 1 for consideration, and to be presented at the Annual Fall Meeting.

The John Orlando Roe Award is presented each year to the graduate fellow who submits the best clinical research paper written during fellowship.

The Ben Shuster Memorial Award is presented for the most outstanding research paper by a resident or fellow in training on any clinical work or research in facial plastic and reconstructive surgery delivered at a national meeting (or its equivalent) between March 1 and the following February 28. Each entrant must be the sole or senior author and an AAFPRS member.

The Ira Tresley Research Award recognizes the best original research in facial plastic surgery by an AAFPRS member who has been board-certified for at least three years. Papers presented at a national meeting (or its equivalent) between March 1 and the following February 28 are eligible for this award.

William Wright Award may be presented each year to an AAFPRS member who has made outstanding contributions to facial plastic and reconstructive surgery.

PURPOSE:
To support research in facial and reconstructive plastic surgery.

LEGAL BASIS:
Foundation.

ELIGIBILITY:
Applicants must be AAFPRS members, except medical students may apply for Resident Travel Award.

GEOG. RESTRICTIONS: United States.

FINANCIAL DATA:
Amount of support per award: $1,000; Residency Travel Award: $500.

Total amount of support: $5,000.

NO. AWARDS: Residency Travel Award: Up to 2; All others: 1.

APPLICATION INFO:
Contact AAFPRS for application information.

Deadline: February 1.

PUBLICATIONS:
Application form.

STAFF:
Stephen C. Duffy, Executive Vice President
Ann K. Jenne, Director, Development and Humanitarian Programs
Rita Chua Magness, Director, Marketing and Publications
Fatima E. El-Porter, Manager, Fellowship Programs
Ollie Edwards, Manager, Meetings and Exhibits
Maria Atkins, Manager, Membership Services

ADDRESS INQUIRIES TO:
Awards Coordinator
(See address above.)

AMERICAN ACADEMY OF FACIAL PLASTIC AND RECONSTRUCTIVE SURGERY (AAFPRS) [2148]

Educational and Research Foundation for the AAFPRS
310 South Henry Street
Alexandria, VA 22314
(703) 299-9291
Fax: (703) 299-8284
E-mail: ksloat@aafprs.org
Web Site: www.aafprs.org

FOUNDED: 1964

AREAS OF INTEREST:
Physician education in cosmetic and reconstructive surgery of the face, head and neck.

CONSULTING OR VOLUNTEER SERVICES:
Combined Otolaryngology Research Efforts (C.O.R.E.).

NAME(S) OF PROGRAMS:

- **Leslie Bernstein Resident Research Grants**

TYPE:
Research grants; Seed money grants. Cash award toward research by a resident member in facial plastic and reconstructive surgery.

YEAR PROGRAM STARTED: 1983

PURPOSE:
To stimulate resident research in projects that are well conceived and scientifically valid.

LEGAL BASIS:
Professional association of independent members.

ELIGIBILITY:
Applicant must be an AAFPRS member. Residents at any level may apply, even if the research work will be done during their fellowship year.

FINANCIAL DATA:
Grant money must be used for direct costs; only 10% of monies can be used for indirect cost.

Amount of support per award: $5,000.

Total amount of support: $10,000.

NO. MOST RECENT APPLICANTS: 15.

NO. AWARDS: Up to 2.

APPLICATION INFO:
Applicants must submit a letter of intent. Guidelines are available from AAFPRS.

Duration: One to two years.

Deadline: January 15. Announcement in August.

PUBLICATIONS:
Guidelines; application form.

IRS I.D.: 36-2952891

ADDRESS INQUIRIES TO:
Karen Sloat, Senior Project Consultant
(See address above.)

AMERICAN ACADEMY OF FACIAL PLASTIC AND RECONSTRUCTIVE SURGERY (AAFPRS) [2149]

Educational and Research Foundation
for the AAFPRS
310 South Henry Street
Alexandria, VA 22314
(703) 299-9291
Fax: (703) 299-8284
E-mail: ksloat@aafprs.org
Web Site: www.aafprs.org

FOUNDED: 1964

AREAS OF INTEREST:
Physician education in cosmetic and reconstructive surgery of the face, head and neck.

CONSULTING OR VOLUNTEER SERVICES:
Combined Otolaryngology Research Efforts (C.O.R.E.).

NAME(S) OF PROGRAMS:

- **Leslie Bernstein Investigator Development Grant**

TYPE:
Project/program grants; Research grants; Seed money grants. Support for the work of a young faculty member conducting significant clinical or laboratory research in facial plastic surgery and training resident surgeons in research. Funded by a donation from Leslie Bernstein, M.D., D.D.S., to the AAFPRS Foundation.

YEAR PROGRAM STARTED: 1983

PURPOSE:
To support work of a young faculty member in Facial Plastic Surgery conducting significant clinical or laboratory research and involved in the training of resident surgeons in research.

LEGAL BASIS:
Professional association of independent members.

ELIGIBILITY:
Applicants must be Academy members. Research proposals are subject to the following conditions:
(1) a sponsor, either an Academy Fellow or the investigator's department chairman, is required;
(2) the parent institution must provide professional support and;
(3) the research plan must incorporate a resident or residents in the research activities.

FINANCIAL DATA:
Grant monies must be used for direct costs; only 10% can be used for indirect cost.

Amount of support per award: $15,000.

Total amount of support: $15,000.

NO. MOST RECENT APPLICANTS: 2.

NO. AWARDS: 1.

APPLICATION INFO:
Applicants must submit a letter of intent. The official entry form must be completed and submitted with the proposal. Failure to comply with the particular requirements and format outlined in the guidelines may result in disqualification.

Duration: Three years.

Deadline: January 15 each year. Announcement in August.

PUBLICATIONS:
Grants and awards brochure.

IRS I.D.: 36-2952891

ADDRESS INQUIRIES TO:
Karen Sloat, Senior Project Consultant
(See address above.)

AMERICAN ACADEMY OF FACIAL PLASTIC AND RECONSTRUCTIVE SURGERY (AAFPRS) [2150]

Educational and Research Foundation
for the AAFPRS
310 South Henry Street
Alexandria, VA 22314
(703) 299-9291
Fax: (703) 299-8284
E-mail: ksloat@aafprs.org
Web Site: www.aafprs.org

FOUNDED: 1964

AREAS OF INTEREST:
Physician education in cosmetic and reconstructive surgery of the face, head and neck.

CONSULTING OR VOLUNTEER SERVICES:
Combined Otolaryngology Research Efforts (C.O.R.E.).

NAME(S) OF PROGRAMS:

- **Leslie Bernstein Research Grant**

TYPE:
Project/program grants; Research grants; Seed money grants. Research award for Academy members, funded by income from a donation by Leslie Bernstein, M.D., D.D.S., to the Academy's Foundation.

YEAR PROGRAM STARTED: 1988

PURPOSE:
To encourage original research projects which will advance facial plastic and reconstructive surgery.

LEGAL BASIS:
Professional association of independent members.

ELIGIBILITY:
Applicants must be AAFPRS members undertaking research that will advance facial plastic and reconstructive surgery. The primary criteria are that the research be original and have direct application to facial plastic surgery.

FINANCIAL DATA:
Grants may be used as seed money for research projects.

Amount of support per award: $25,000.

Total amount of support: $25,000.

NO. AWARDS: 1.

APPLICATION INFO:
Proposals should be typed (double-spaced) and include the following information:
(1) investigator's curriculum vitae;
(2) brief statement of the specific aims of the investigator's research project, not to exceed 150 words;
(3) brief review of the significance of the work performed by the investigator and/or others, not to exceed two pages;
(4) a detailed description of research procedures including the experimental design, justification of sample size, outcome measures and methods of analysis including justification of each item;
(5) budget for the research award;
(6) description of facilities;
(7) certification of institutional conformity to the U.S. Government Guidelines for Human and Animal Experimentation and;
(8) application must be submitted through C.O.R.E. program.

Duration: Three years.

Deadline: January 15 for review. Announcement in August.

PUBLICATIONS:
Grants and awards brochure.

IRS I.D.: 36-2952891

ADDRESS INQUIRIES TO:
Karen Sloat, Senior Project Consultant
(See address above.)

AMERICAN ACADEMY OF FAMILY PHYSICIANS FOUNDATION [2151]

11400 Tomahawk Creek Parkway
Leawood, KS 66211
(913) 906-6000
Fax: (913) 906-6095
E-mail: shunt@aafp.org
Web Site: www.aafpfoundation.org

FOUNDED: 1958

AREAS OF INTEREST:
Family physician practice and training.

NAME(S) OF PROGRAMS:

- **Joint Grant Awards Program**

TYPE:
Awards/prizes; Research grants; Scholarships; Seed money grants; Training grants. The Joint Grant Awards Program supports research that poses questions of high relevance to family medicine. The program gives funding to new researchers or to those who mentor new investigators on the research team.

PURPOSE:
To strengthen research in family medicine.

LEGAL BASIS:
Foundation.

ELIGIBILITY:
The Joint Grant Awards Program seeks proposals requesting grant support for family medicine research. Those eligible to receive a grant include individual family physicians, family medicine organizations or associations, family medicine residency programs, departments of family medicine and educational and health care institutions or organizations which will use the program support exclusively for research projects directly involving and impacting on family medicine.

The principal investigator must be a family medicine researcher (a clinician or Ph.D.). The principal investigator or one of the co-investigators must be a member of the AAFP. Priority is given to the new researchers or those who mentor new investigators on the research team.

GEOG. RESTRICTIONS: United States.

FINANCIAL DATA:
Amount of support per award: Up to $50,000.

NO. AWARDS: Varies.

APPLICATION INFO:
Instructions and application are available online.

Duration: Varies.

Deadline: January 7 and July 7.

PUBLICATIONS:
Program announcement; application packet.

OFFICERS:
Jason E. Marker, M.D., President
S. Hughes Melton, M.D., Vice President
Craig Doane, Executive Director

ADDRESS INQUIRIES TO:
Sharon Hunt, Program Strategist
(See address above.)

AMERICAN AGING ASSOCIATION [2152]

1700 K Street, N.W., Suite 740
Washington, DC 20006
(202) 293-2856
Fax: (202) 955-8394
E-mail: contact@americanagingassociation.org
Web Site: www.americanagingassociation.org

FOUNDED: 1970

AREAS OF INTEREST:
Biomedical gerontology.

NAME(S) OF PROGRAMS:
- **Paul Glenn Award**
- **Walter Nicolai Award in Biomedical Gerontology**

TYPE:
Awards/prizes; Conferences/seminars; Travel grants. One first prize and one runner-up for each award annually.

Paul Glenn Award: For meritorious research in the area of biomedical gerontology by a postdoctoral fellow.

Walter Nicolai Award: For meritorious basic biologic aging research by a graduate or medical student.

PURPOSE:
To promote biological aging research.

ELIGIBILITY:
Nominees must be graduate or medical students. Each nomination must have a sponsor. A nomination may be made by any member of a society associated with aging research. The sponsor may reside in the U.S., Canada or Mexico.

GEOG. RESTRICTIONS: North America.

FINANCIAL DATA:
Awards include a citation and cash prize.

Amount of support per award: $500 for first place and $250 for each runner-up.

Total amount of support: $1,500 annually.

NO. AWARDS: 2 per award.

APPLICATION INFO:
Nominations should include four copies of a six- to 10-page report of the research being nominated, sponsor's letter commenting on the significance of the work and candidate's curriculum vitae with current address.

Duration: One-time award.

Deadline: March 1.

PUBLICATIONS:
AGE, the Journal of the American Aging Association, quarterly; *Age News Quarterly*.

IRS I.D.: 23-7364654

ADDRESS INQUIRIES TO:
Kate Reinert, Administrator
(See address above.)

AMERICAN ASSOCIATION FOR HAND SURGERY [2153]

500 Cummings Center
Suite 4550
Beverly, MA 01915
(978) 927-8330
Fax: (978) 524-8890
E-mail: contact@handsurgery.org
Web Site: www.handsurgery.org

FOUNDED: 1970

AREAS OF INTEREST:
Hand surgery and hand therapy.

TYPE:
Research grants. International hand therapy outreach.

YEAR PROGRAM STARTED: 1970

PURPOSE:
To promote education and research; to foster creativity and innovation in basic and/or clinical research in all areas pertinent to hand surgery and hand therapy.

ELIGIBILITY:
Applications are open to AAHS members and candidates for membership. Residents and fellows sponsored by an AAHS member are also eligible to apply. One of the co-investigators must be an Active or Affiliate AAHS member. AAHS therapist and surgeon members are eligible to apply for the Vargas International Hand Therapy Teaching Award.

FINANCIAL DATA:
Amount of support per award: AAHS/PSF Combined Pilot Research Grant and AAHS Research Grant: Up to $10,000; Vargas International Hand Therapy Teaching Award: Up to $5,000 in reimbursement for mission expenses.

CO-OP FUNDING PROGRAMS: Match grant with Plastic Surgery Foundation.

APPLICATION INFO:
Application information is available on the web site.

Duration: One year.

ADDRESS INQUIRIES TO:
See e-mail address above.

AMERICAN COLLEGE OF LEGAL MEDICINE [2154]

9700 Bryn Mawr Avenue
Rosemont, IL 60018
(847) 447-1713
(651) 265-7846
Fax: (847) 447-1150
E-mail: lauriek@ewald.com
Web Site: www.aclm.org

FOUNDED: 1960

AREAS OF INTEREST:
Legal medicine.

NAME(S) OF PROGRAMS:
- **American College of Legal Medicine's Student Writing Competition in Law, Medicine and Bioethics**

TYPE:
Awards/prizes. The Hirsh Award is awarded to a law, dentistry, podiatry, nursing, pharmacy, health science, health care administration, or public health student.

PURPOSE:
To promote interdisciplinary cooperation and an understanding of issues where law and medicine converge.

ELIGIBILITY:
Must be a student at an accredited school of law, medicine, dentistry, podiatry, nursing, pharmacy, health science, health care, administration, or public health that has written an outstanding original paper on Legal Medicine.

FINANCIAL DATA:
Amount of support per award: Hirsh Award: $1,000 first prize, $500 second prize and $250 third prize.

Total amount of support: $1,750.

NO. MOST RECENT APPLICANTS: 12 to 14.

NO. AWARDS: 3.

APPLICATION INFO:
Contact the College.

Deadline: January 1. Announcements in August.

ADDRESS INQUIRIES TO:
Laurie Krueger, Executive Director
(See address above.)

AMERICAN FEDERATION FOR AGING RESEARCH (AFAR) [2155]

55 West 39th Street
16th Floor
New York, NY 10018
(212) 703-9977
(888) 582-2327
Fax: (212) 997-0330
E-mail: grants@afar.org
Web Site: www.afar.org

FOUNDED: 1981

AREAS OF INTEREST:
Aging research.

NAME(S) OF PROGRAMS:

- **Rosalinde and Arthur Gilbert Foundation/AFAR New Investigator Awards in Alzheimer's Disease**

TYPE:
Awards/prizes; Research grants. New Investigator Awards support research in areas in which more scientific investigation is needed to improve the prevention, diagnosis and treatment of Alzheimer's Disease.

PURPOSE:
To support basic biomedical research that promotes healthier aging and advances the understanding of the aging process and its associated diseases and disorders; to encourage the training of new scientists and physicians in geriatric research and in the practice of geriatric medicine.

LEGAL BASIS:
Private foundation.

ELIGIBILITY:
Junior faculty in the U.S. and Israel who conduct research on Alzheimer's Disease or healthy brain aging.

GEOG. RESTRICTIONS: United States and Israel.

FINANCIAL DATA:
Amount of support per award: $100,000.

NO. MOST RECENT APPLICANTS: 50.

NO. AWARDS: Up to 3.

APPLICATION INFO:
Required application form is available on the web site.

Duration: One to two years.

Deadline: Mid-December.

PUBLICATIONS:
Program announcement.

STAFF:
Stephanie Lederman, Executive Director
Odette van der Willik, Director, Grant Programs
Hattie Herman, Program Officer
Catherine Cullar, Administrative Manager

ADDRESS INQUIRIES TO:
Hattie Herman, Program Officer
(See address above.)

AMERICAN FEDERATION FOR AGING RESEARCH (AFAR) [2156]

55 West 39th Street
16th Floor
New York, NY 10018
(212) 703-9977
(888) 582-2327
Fax: (212) 997-0330
E-mail: grants@afar.org
Web Site: www.afar.org

FOUNDED: 1981

AREAS OF INTEREST:
Biomedical aging research.

NAME(S) OF PROGRAMS:

- **Glenn/AFAR Scholarships for Research in the Biology of Aging**

TYPE:
Scholarships.

PURPOSE:
To support basic biomedical research that promotes healthier aging and advances the understanding of the aging process and its associated diseases and disorders; to encourage the training of new scientists and physicians in geriatric research and in the practice of geriatric medicine.

LEGAL BASIS:
Private foundation.

ELIGIBILITY:
Open to graduate students enrolled in M.D., D.O., Ph.D. or combined-degree programs.

GEOG. RESTRICTIONS: United States.

FINANCIAL DATA:
Amount of support per award: $5,000.
Total amount of support: $50,000.

NO. MOST RECENT APPLICANTS: 52.

NO. AWARDS: 10.

APPLICATION INFO:
Application form is available on the web site.

Duration: Three- to six-month research project.

Deadline: Mid-January.

STAFF:
Stephanie Lederman, Executive Director
Shelly Binder, Director, Development
Odette van der Willik, Director, Grant Programs
Hattie Herman, Program Officer
Catherine Cullar, Administrative Manager

ADDRESS INQUIRIES TO:
Hattie Herman, Program Officer
(See address above.)

AMERICAN FEDERATION FOR AGING RESEARCH (AFAR) [2157]

55 West 39th Street
16th Floor
New York, NY 10018
(212) 703-9977
(888) 582-2327
Fax: (212) 997-0330
E-mail: grants@afar.org
Web Site: www.afar.org

FOUNDED: 1981

AREAS OF INTEREST:
Biomedical aging research.

NAME(S) OF PROGRAMS:

- **AFAR Research Grants**
- **Paul Beeson Career Development Awards in Aging Research Program**
- **Glenn/AFAR Breakthroughs in Gerontology Awards**
- **Medical Student Training in Aging Research Program (MSTAR)**

TYPE:
Fellowships; Research grants; Scholarships; Training grants. The AFAR Research Grants are given to provide one to two years of support for junior faculty to do research that will serve as the basis for longer-term research efforts.

The Paul Beeson Career Development Awards in Aging Research Program is intended to bolster the current and severe shortage of academic physicians who have the combination of medical, academic and scientific training relative to caring for older people.

The Glenn/AFAR Breakthroughs in Gerontology Awards are to provide timely support to a small number of pilot research programs that may be of relatively high risk but which offer significant promise of yielding transforming discoveries in the fundamental biology of aging.

Medical Student Training in Aging Research Program (MSTAR) provides medical students, early in their training, with an enriching experience in aging-related research and geriatrics, under the mentorship of top experts in the field. Students participate in an eight- to 12-week structured research, clinical and didactic program in geriatrics.

PURPOSE:
To support basic biomedical research that promotes healthier aging and advances the understanding of the aging process and its associated diseases and disorders; to encourage the training of new scientists and physicians in geriatric research and in the practice of geriatric medicine.

LEGAL BASIS:
Private foundation.

ELIGIBILITY:
For the AFAR Research Grants, applicants must be junior faculty (M.Ds. and Ph.Ds.).

Paul Beeson Career Development Awards in Aging Research Program applicants are clinically trained individuals who are pursuing research careers in aging.

For the Glenn/AFAR Breakthroughs in Gerontology Awards, qualified applicants must be full-time faculty members at the rank of assistant professor or higher who can demonstrate a strong record of independence.

The Medical Student Training in Aging Research Program (MSTAR) is intended for medical students and is built on the Medical Student Geriatric Scholars Program.

GEOG. RESTRICTIONS: United States.

FINANCIAL DATA:
Amount of support per award: AFAR Research Grants: Up to $100,000; Paul Beeson Career Development Awards in Aging Research: $200,000 per year; Glenn/AFAR Breakthroughs in Gerontology Awards: Up to $200,000.

NO. MOST RECENT APPLICANTS: AFAR Research Grants: 132; Paul Beeson Career Development Awards in Aging Research: Varies; Glenn/AFAR Breakthroughs in Gerontology Awards: 75.

NO. AWARDS: AFAR Research Grants: Up to 10; Paul Beeson Career Development Awards in Aging Research: Up to 10; Glenn/AFAR Breakthroughs in Gerontology Awards: 2.

APPLICATION INFO:
Required application form is available on the web site.

Duration: One to two years. Up to five years for Beeson Award.

Deadline: AFAR Research Grants and Glenn/AFAR: Mid-December. Paul Beeson: Varies.

PUBLICATIONS:
Program announcement.

STAFF:
Stephanie Lederman, Executive Director
Odette van der Willik, Director, Grant Programs
Hattie Herman, Program Officer
Catherine Cullar, Administrative Manager

ADDRESS INQUIRIES TO:
Hattie Herman, Program Officer
(See address above.)

AMERICAN KIDNEY FUND [2158]

11921 Rockville Pike, Suite 300
Rockville, MD 20852
(800) 638-8299
(866) 300-2900 (Spanish/English HelpLine)
Fax: (301) 881-0898
E-mail: helpline@kidneyfund.org
Web Site: www.kidneyfund.org

FOUNDED: 1971

AREAS OF INTEREST:
Treatment, prevention and cure of kidney disease.

NAME(S) OF PROGRAMS:
- **Clinical Scientist in Nephrology (CSN)**

TYPE:
Fellowships.

YEAR PROGRAM STARTED: 1988

PURPOSE:
To improve the quality of care provided to kidney patients; to promote clinical research in nephrology.

ELIGIBILITY:
Applicant must be a nephrologist in a current academic setting.

GEOG. RESTRICTIONS: United States and its territories.

FINANCIAL DATA:
Amount of support per award: Up to $80,000 per year.
Total amount of support: Up to $160,000.

NO. MOST RECENT APPLICANTS: 11.

NO. AWARDS: 1.

APPLICATION INFO:
Complete application information may be found on the web site.
Duration: One to two years.
Deadline: December 1.

ADDRESS INQUIRIES TO:
Michael Spigler, Vice President of Patient Services and Kidney Disease Education
(See address above.)

AMERICAN KIDNEY FUND [2159]

11921 Rockville Pike, Suite 300
Rockville, MD 20852
(800) 638-8299
(866) 300-2900 (Spanish/English HelpLine)
Fax: (301) 881-0898
E-mail: helpline@kidneyfund.org
Web Site: www.kidneyfund.org

FOUNDED: 1971

AREAS OF INTEREST:
Treatment, prevention and cure of kidney disease.

NAME(S) OF PROGRAMS:
- **Patient Services Grants: Safety Net Grant Program**

TYPE:
Grants-in-aid; Product donations. Medical Grants. Provides financial assistance to qualified dialysis patients who are referred by their physicians and social workers for treatment-specific expenses such as transportation, over-the-counter medicines, medication co-payments, kidney donor expenses, mobility aids and nutritional supplements.

YEAR PROGRAM STARTED: 1971

PURPOSE:
To provide aid in the treatment, prevention, and cure of kidney disease.

ELIGIBILITY:
Based on financial need. Kidney dialysis and transplant patients living in the U.S. are eligible. Additional requirements are available online.

GEOG. RESTRICTIONS: United States and its territories.

FINANCIAL DATA:
Amount of support per award: $100 per year.

APPLICATION INFO:
Applications must be submitted online via Grants Management System. Applications must be completed by the patient and a dialysis or transplant renal professional. Paper applications will no longer be accepted.
Duration: Renewable 12 months from the check date of the last grant.

IRS I.D.: 23-7124261

ADDRESS INQUIRIES TO:
Patient Services Department
Tel: (800) 795-3226
(See address above.)

AMERICAN MEDICAL ASSOCIATION FOUNDATION

330 North Wabash Avenue
Suite 39300
Chicago, IL 60611-5885
(312) 464-4200
Fax: (312) 464-4142
E-mail: amafoundation@ama-assn.org
Web Site: www.amafoundation.org

TYPE:
Awards/prizes; Project/program grants; Research grants; Scholarships; Seed money grants. Excellence in Medicine Awards are given to recognize physicians and medical students who are improving the health of their communities and the lives of those who are most in need.

The Joan F. Giambalvo Memorial Scholarship is presented in conjunction with the AMA's Women Physicians Congress to provide a research grant to help researchers advance the progress of women in the medical profession and identify and address the needs of women physicians and medical students.

Healthy Communities/Healthy America awards grants to existing, physician-led free clinics that provide free or low-cost medical care to underserved and uninsured populations.

Healthy Living Grant Program provides grants to support healthy lifestyle projects in various categories such as prescription medical safety and cancer prevention awareness.

The Minority Scholars Awards are given in collaboration with the AMA Minority Affairs Section to first- and second-year medical students from historically underrepresented minority groups in the medical profession.

The Physicians of Tomorrow Scholarships are awarded to rising fourth-year medical students based on financial need and academic excellence.

The Seed Grant Research Program provides medical students, physician residents and fellows with grants to help them conduct basic science, applied or clinical research projects.

The Arthur N. Wilson, M.D. Scholarship is awarded to a medical student who is a graduate of a high school in southeast Alaska.

See entry 1603 for full listing.

AMERICAN MEDICAL WOMEN'S ASSOCIATION, INC. [2160]

12100 Sunset Hills Road
Suite 130
Reston, VA 20190
(703) 234-4069
Fax: (703) 435-4390
E-mail: associatedirector@amwa-doc.org
Web Site: www.amwa-doc.org

FOUNDED: 1915

AREAS OF INTEREST:
Women physicians, women medical students and women's health.

NAME(S) OF PROGRAMS:
- **American Women's Hospitals Service (AWHS)**

TYPE:
Awards/prizes; Conferences/seminars; General operating grants; Project/program grants; Training grants; Travel grants. Support for clinics serving the poor in medically underserved areas, scholarships and loans to qualifying women medical students, and continuing medical education for physicians in areas related to women's health.

YEAR PROGRAM STARTED: 1915

PURPOSE:
To advance women in medicine and improve women's health through advocacy, leadership, education, expertise and mentoring, and strategic alliances.

LEGAL BASIS:
AMWA: 501(c)(6) corporation. AWHS: 501(c)(3) foundation.

ELIGIBILITY:
Open to women who are enrolled in accredited medical schools in the U.S.

GEOG. RESTRICTIONS: United States.

BOARD OF DIRECTORS:
Theresa Rohr-Kirchgraber, M.D., President

ADDRESS INQUIRIES TO:
Katherine He
(See address above.)

THE AMERICAN PORPHYRIA FOUNDATION [2161]

4900 Woodway Drive
Suite 780
Houston, TX 77056-1837
(713) 266-9617
Fax: (713) 840-9552
E-mail: porphyrus@aol.com
Web Site: www.porphyriafoundation.com

AREAS OF INTEREST:
Porphyria.

TYPE:
Research grants.

PURPOSE:
To improve the health and well-being of individuals and families affected by porphyria.

ELIGIBILITY:
Qualified investigators involved in porphyria research.

FINANCIAL DATA:
Amount of support per award: $5,000 to $10,000.

Total amount of support: Varies.

APPLICATION INFO:
Send a two-page summary of proposed research and research experience to the Foundation.

Duration: Typically one year.

PUBLICATIONS:
Newsletters.

ADDRESS INQUIRIES TO:
Desiree H. Lyon, Executive Director
(See address above.)

AMERICAN ROENTGEN RAY SOCIETY [2162]

44211 Slatestone Court
Leesburg, VA 20176
(703) 729-3353
Fax: (703) 729-4839
E-mail: info@arrs.org
Web Site: www.arrs.org

FOUNDED: 1900

AREAS OF INTEREST:
Diagnostic radiology.

NAME(S) OF PROGRAMS:

- **ARRS Annual Scholarship Program**

TYPE:
Scholarships.

YEAR PROGRAM STARTED: 1992

PURPOSE:
To provide resources needed to acquire knowledge, skills and training in the areas that are vital to radiology but have traditionally been outside the scope of diagnostic radiology.

ELIGIBILITY:
Candidates must have earned an M.D. or D.O. from an accredited institution. Also, must have completed all residencies or fellowship training or equivalent, full-time appointment as instructor, assistant professor or equivalent for no more than five years beyond training. Appointment must be in a department of radiology, nuclear medicine, ultrasound or radiation oncology.

Scholar may choose a one-year program requiring a minimum 80% time commitment, or a two-year program requiring a minimum 50% time commitment.

FINANCIAL DATA:
Funds distributed to individual's institution.

Amount of support per award: $140,000.

Total amount of support: Varies.

NO. AWARDS: 1.

APPLICATION INFO:
Submission of a curriculum vitae, summary of qualifications, goals and purposes of the study, estimated budget, and a statement from department regarding applicant's goals and commitment ensuring applicant's return to faculty upon completion.

Duration: One or two years.

Deadline: November.

ADDRESS INQUIRIES TO:
Nazish Khaliq
Education Administrative Assistant
(See address above.)

AMERICAN SOCIETY OF HEMATOLOGY [2163]

2021 L Street, N.W.
Suite 900
Washington, DC 20036
(202) 776-0544
E-mail: awards@hematology.org
Web Site: www.hematology.org

FOUNDED: 1985

AREAS OF INTEREST:
Hematology, basic and clinical/translational research.

NAME(S) OF PROGRAMS:

- **Fellow Scholar Award**
- **Junior Faculty Scholar Award**

TYPE:
Awards/prizes; Fellowships; Research grants; Scholarships.

PURPOSE:
To support hematologists who have chosen a career in research.

ELIGIBILITY:
Applicants must be a citizen of, or hold a visa in, the U.S. or Canada. Research must be conducted within the U.S. and Canada. Applicants are required to be members of ASH in good standing at the time of the Letter of Intent submission, and for the duration of the Scholar Award Program. Consideration will be given if membership application is pending at the time of the application deadline.

For the Fellow Scholar Award, Ph.D. or M.D./Ph.D. applicants must have fewer than five years of research experience after completion of their Ph.D. (including research performed during fellowship, but excluding clinical fellowship time). M.D. applicants should have more than three but fewer than five years of research experience (including research performed during fellowship, but excluding clinical fellowship time). M.D. applicants with fewer than three years research experience (inclusive of fellowship research time) should consider applying for the Senior RTAF award.

For the Junior Faculty Scholar Awards, applicant must hold an M.D., Ph.D. or M.D./Ph.D. and have more than five but fewer than 10 years of research experience after completion of their Ph.D. (including research performed during fellowship, but excluding clinical fellowship time).

Applicants with the title of Assistant Professor or equivalent must apply for the Junior Faculty Award, regardless of research experience.

GEOG. RESTRICTIONS: United States and Canada.

FINANCIAL DATA:
Amount of support per award: $150,000 for a Junior Faculty Scholar Award or $100,000 for a Fellow Scholar Award. These awards can be spread over two or three years with an annual maximum not to exceed $75,000 for junior faculty and $50,000 for fellows.

Total amount of support: Approximately $3,800,000.

APPLICATION INFO:
A letter of intent is required before submission of full proposal. Contact the Society for details.

Duration: Two to three years.

Deadline: Mandatory Letter of Intent: May 1.

ADDRESS INQUIRIES TO:
Lisa Diop
Awards and Diversity Programs Manager
(See address above.)

AMERICAN SOCIETY OF HEMATOLOGY [2164]

2021 L Street, N.W.
Suite 900
Washington, DC 20036
(202) 776-0544
Fax: (888) 724-0513
E-mail: training@hematology.org
Web Site: www.hematology.org

AREAS OF INTEREST:
Hematology.

NAME(S) OF PROGRAMS:

- **HONORS (Hematology Opportunities for the Next Generation of Research Scientists)**

TYPE:
Awards/prizes. Each scholarship provides the medical school with funds to cover the expenses for students to complete a program and travel support for students to attend the ASH annual meetings.

PURPOSE:
To provide medical students and residents with an introduction to the specialty of hematology by encouraging them to take time during their medical school curriculum to work on a project with a hematologist.

ELIGIBILITY:
Medical students and residents in the United States, Mexico and Canada.

GEOG. RESTRICTIONS: United States, Mexico and Canada.

FINANCIAL DATA:
Amount of support per award: $5,000 cash award and $1,000 travel stipend for each of the two annual meetings.

Total amount of support: $200,000 for the year 2014.

APPLICATION INFO:
The institution is responsible for selecting student participants. Contact the Society for additional application information.

Duration: Varies.

Deadline: Mid-February.

ADDRESS INQUIRIES TO:
Joe Basso, Training Manager
(See address above.)

AMERICAN SOCIETY OF HEMATOLOGY [2165]

2021 L Street, N.W.
Suite 900
Washington, DC 20036
(202) 776-0544
Fax: (888) 724-0513
E-mail: training@hematology.org
Web Site: www.hematology.org

AREAS OF INTEREST:
Hematology.

NAME(S) OF PROGRAMS:
- **Physician-Scientist Career Development Award**
- **Research Training Award for Fellows**

TYPE:
Awards/prizes. Physician-Scientist Career Development Award allows medical students to gain knowledge and perform research in between their first, second and third year of school.

Research Training Award for Fellows allows protected time for research.

PURPOSE:
To help medical students gain experience in hematology research; to encourage research in hematology, hematology/oncology, or other hematology-related training programs.

ELIGIBILITY:
Physician-Scientist Career Development Award applicant must:
(1) be a medical student member of ASH;
(2) be a first-, second- or third-year medical student actively enrolled in an M.D. or D.O. medical program in an LCME or AOA COCA (or its equivalent) accredited medical school in the U.S. or Canada. Applicant must be in good standing relative to their course work at the time of application and be between their first and second, second and third, or third and fourth year of medical school at the time the research is done;
(3) not be currently enrolled in a combined M.D.-Ph.D. program;
(4) be planning an investigative career in laboratory, translational, or clinical hematology research;
(5) have a mentor who is an active ASH member at the time of application and;
(6) not have any other concurrent funding for a similar experience.

Research Training Award for Fellows applicant must be a second-, third-, fourth- or fifth-year student at the time of the award, who is not yet eligible for the ASH Scholar Awards. Applicant must:
(1) possess an M.D. or D.O.;
(2) continue to maintain ASH membership and remain a member in good standing for the duration of the award term;
(3) plan to pursue an investigative career in hematology research;
(4) have a mentor who is an ASH member at the time the application is submitted and;
(5) not hold a position as an Assistant Professor.

FINANCIAL DATA:
Amount of support per award: Physician-Scientist Award: $42,000; Research Training Award: $55,000.

NO. AWARDS: Physician-Scientist Award: Up to 5; Research Training Award: Up to 6.

APPLICATION INFO:
Guidelines are available on the Society's web site.

Duration: One year.

Deadline: Physician-Scientist Award: September; Research Training Award: January.

ADDRESS INQUIRIES TO:
Joe Basso, Training Manager
(See address above.)

AMERICAN SOCIETY OF HYPERTENSION [2166]

45 Main Street
Suite 712
Brooklyn, NY 11201
(212) 696-9099
Fax: (347) 916-0267
E-mail: awards@ash-us.org
Web Site: www.ash-us.org

AREAS OF INTEREST:
Hypertension and related cardiovascular disease.

TYPE:
Awards/prizes; Research grants.

PURPOSE:
To organize and conduct educational activities designed to promote and encourage the development, advancement, and exchange of scientific information in all aspects of research, diagnosis, and treatment of hypertension and related cardiovascular diseases.

GEOG. RESTRICTIONS: North America.

FINANCIAL DATA:
Amount of support per award: $500 to $10,000.

Total amount of support: Varies.

APPLICATION INFO:
Contact the Society.

Duration: Typically one year.

STAFF:
Ashley Buron, Program Coordinator
Scientific Meetings and Professional Affairs

ADDRESS INQUIRIES TO:
Ashley Buron, Program Coordinator
Scientific Meetings and Professional Affairs
(See address above.)

AMERICAN SOCIETY OF REGIONAL ANESTHESIA AND PAIN MEDICINE

4 Penn Center West
Suite 401
Pittsburgh, PA 15276
(412) 471-2718
Fax: (412) 471-7503
E-mail: asraassistant@asra.com
Web Site: www.asra.com

TYPE:
Research grants.

See entry 2459 for full listing.

AMERICAN VETERINARY MEDICAL ASSOCIATION [2167]

AVMA Governmental Relations Division
1910 Sunderland Place, N.W.
Washington, DC 20036
(202) 289-3208
Fax: (202) 842-4360
E-mail: fellowship@avma.org
Web Site: www.avma.org/fellowship

AREAS OF INTEREST:
Veterinary medicine.

NAME(S) OF PROGRAMS:
- **AVMA Fellowship**

TYPE:
Fellowships.

YEAR PROGRAM STARTED: 1988

PURPOSE:
To support AVMA members to serve as a congressional fellow for one year in a personal or committee office of the U.S. Congress.

LEGAL BASIS:
Association.

ELIGIBILITY:
Applicants must be AVMA members and U.S. citizens who demonstrate special competence in an area of veterinary medicine, possess a broad professional background and exhibit an interest in applying scientific knowledge to solve societal/public policy problems.

Applicants must be articulate, literate, adaptable and capable of working on a wide range of policy issues.

Fellows must serve in Washington, DC.

FINANCIAL DATA:
Amount of support per award: Approximately $80,000 plus expenses and up to $6,000 in health insurance premiums.

NO. MOST RECENT APPLICANTS: 21 for the year 2014-15.

NO. AWARDS: 3 for the year 2014-15.

APPLICATION INFO:
Applicants must submit:
(1) a letter of intent;
(2) a curriculum vitae;
(3) two letters of reference from professional colleagues;
(4) a letter of support from the applicant's local, state, specialty or allied veterinary medical organization and;
(5) a personal statement (not to exceed 750 words) describing the applicant's qualifications, commitment to veterinary medicine and why the fellowship is desired.

Duration: One year.

Deadline: Usually second Friday in February.

PUBLICATIONS:
Program announcement.

IRS I.D.: 36-6117739

ADDRESS INQUIRIES TO:
See e-mail address above.

ANIMAL ASSISTANCE FOUNDATION [2168]

405 Urban Street
Suite 340
Lakewood, CO 80228
(303) 744-8396
Fax: (303) 744-7065
E-mail: rogerhaston@aaf-fd.org
Web Site: www.aaf-fd.org

FOUNDED: 1975

AREAS OF INTEREST:
Companion animal overpopulation, operational optimization, adoption and permanent homes, cruelty prevention and intervention, innovation and ingenuity and companion animals and unwanted horse issues.

TYPE:
Capital grants; General operating grants; Project/program grants. Operating and service grants. The Foundation offers charitable support through its grantmaking program to organizations located within the state of Colorado or an agency that has a direct impact on animals and their owners in Colorado. Direct impact on animals and their

owners in Colorado applies to institutions conducting studies that result in new science, practice or knowledge significantly affecting animals living in Colorado.

YEAR PROGRAM STARTED: 1975

PURPOSE:
To provide leadership and support to make Colorado the Model State for animal welfare through philanthropy toward animals.

LEGAL BASIS:
Private foundation.

ELIGIBILITY:
In considering grant requests, the Foundation values proposals that:
(1) are located in Colorado or that have a direct impact on animals and their owners in Colorado;
(2) have a measurable impact on animal welfare;
(3) fit within the key focus areas for AAF and;
(4) include additional funding from other sources.

Grants are not given to individuals. Eligible applicants must be a unit of government or recognized as an IRS 501(c)(3) tax-exempt organization and must propose an activity compatible with the Foundation's mission. (Groups designated by the IRS as Type III supporting organizations, however, are not eligible to apply.) Religious organizations are not eligible.

The Foundation does not fund individuals, pets of individuals, debt retirement, indirect administrative costs, start-up costs, endowments or political campaigns.

GEOG. RESTRICTIONS: Colorado.

FINANCIAL DATA:
Amount of support per award: Varies.

Total amount of support: More than $1,000,000 in grants for the year 2014.

Matching fund requirements: Varies.

NO. MOST RECENT APPLICANTS: 100.

NO. AWARDS: 80.

REPRESENTATIVE AWARDS:
$5,000 to Fort Collins Cat Rescue; $10,000 to Humane Society of Weld County.

APPLICATION INFO:
Application information is available on the Foundation web site.

Duration: One to two years. Renewable with reapplication.

Deadline: Last Friday in April and September.

PUBLICATIONS:
Annual report.

IRS I.D.: 84-0715412

ADDRESS INQUIRIES TO:
Letters of inquiry and formal proposals should be addressed to:
Grant Committee: Application and Information
Animal Assistance Foundation
E-mail: info@aaf-fd.org
(See address or phone number above.)

*SPECIAL STIPULATIONS:
Eligible organizations are asked to submit only one proposal per year. If funded, programs are eligible to request a second year's funding.

APLASTIC ANEMIA AND MDS INTERNATIONAL FOUNDATION [2169]

100 Park Avenue, Suite 108
Rockville, MD 20850
(301) 279-7202
(800) 747-2820
Fax: (301) 279-7205
E-mail: help@aamds.org
Web Site: www.aamds.org

FOUNDED: 1983

AREAS OF INTEREST:
Aplastic anemia, myelodysplastic syndrome (MDS) and paroxysmal nocturnal hemoglobinuria (PNH).

NAME(S) OF PROGRAMS:
- **AA&MDSIF Research Grant Program**

TYPE:
Research grants.

YEAR PROGRAM STARTED: 1989

PURPOSE:
To support research related to aplastic anemia, myelodysplastic syndrome (MDS) and paroxysmal nocturnal hemoglobinuria (PNH).

ELIGIBILITY:
Qualified investigators affiliated with appropriate institutions are eligible to apply.

FINANCIAL DATA:
Amount of support per award: $30,000 per year.

Total amount of support: $60,000.

APPLICATION INFO:
Applications must be submitted electronically.

Duration: Two years. Second-year funding pending approval by Medical Board.

Deadline: February 28.

STAFF:
Alice Houk, Director of Health Professional Programs
Ellen Salkeld, Senior Director of Research and Health Professional Programs

ADDRESS INQUIRIES TO:
Ellen Houlk, Senior Director of Research and Health Professional Programs
(See address above.)

ARTHRITIS NATIONAL RESEARCH FOUNDATION (ANRF) [2170]

5354 East Second Street, Suite 201
Long Beach, CA 90803
(800) 588-2873
(562) 437-6808
E-mail: hbelisle@curearthritis.org
Web Site: www.curearthritis.org

FOUNDED: 1952

AREAS OF INTEREST:
Research related to arthritis.

NAME(S) OF PROGRAMS:
- **ANRF Arthritis Research Grants**

TYPE:
Research grants; Travel grants. ANRF Arthritis Research Grants are intended to support basic and clinical research focusing on rheumatic and related autoimmune diseases, such as osteoarthritis and rheumatoid arthritis.

YEAR PROGRAM STARTED: 1952

PURPOSE:
To support basic and clinical research related to arthritis.

ELIGIBILITY:
Applicants must hold an M.D. and/or Ph.D. degree or equivalent. Applicants need not be U.S. citizens, but must conduct their research at U.S. nonprofit institutions.

FINANCIAL DATA:
No overhead expenses funded.

Amount of support per award: $50,000 to $100,000.

Total amount of support: $1,250,000 for fiscal year 2015-16.

CO-OP FUNDING PROGRAMS: American Federation for Aging Research (AFAR) and National Psoriasis Foundation.

NO. MOST RECENT APPLICANTS: 86 for fiscal year 2016-17.

NO. AWARDS: 12 for fiscal year 2016-17.

REPRESENTATIVE AWARDS:
$100,000 to study the role of autoantibodies in pulmonary manifestations of inflammatory arthritis.

APPLICATION INFO:
A standard cover sheet and budget page are required and provided on the Foundation's web site. Application must be submitted online. Hard copies are not accepted.

Duration: One year. May apply for second year of funding.

Deadline: January 15 or next business day.

IRS I.D.: 95-6043953

STAFF:
Helene Belisle, Executive Director

ADDRESS INQUIRIES TO:
See e-mail address above.

ASCP [2171]

33 West Monroe, Suite 1600
Chicago, IL 60603
(312) 541-4110
E-mail: membership@ascp.org
Web Site: www.ascp.org/scholarships

FOUNDED: 1922

AREAS OF INTEREST:
Laboratory medicine.

NAME(S) OF PROGRAMS:
- **Siemens - ASCP Scholarships**

TYPE:
Scholarships.

PURPOSE:
To recognize students for outstanding academic performance.

LEGAL BASIS:
Professional society.

ELIGIBILITY:
Siemens - ASCP Scholarship awards of $1,000 are available for students in their final year of study in one of the following NAACLS-accredited programs:
(1) Cytogenetics Technologist (CG);
(2) Cytotechnologist (CT);
(3) Histotechnician (HT);
(4) Histotechnologist (HTL);
(5) Molecular Biology Technologist (MB);
(6) Medical Laboratory Technician/Clinical Laboratory Technician (MLT/CLT);
(7) Medical Laboratory Scientist/Medical Technologist/Clinical Laboratory Scientist (MLS/MT/CLS) and;
(8) Pathologists' Assistants (PA).

ASCP Phlebotomy Scholarships of $500 each will be awarded to students enrolled in or recent (within the past nine months) graduates of an approved phlebotomy training program.

Siemens Legacy Scholarships of $2,000 are available to 10 students who are a child, grandchild, sibling or niece/nephew of a certified MT/CLS/MLS and are enrolled in their final year of education in a Medical Technology (MT), Clinical Laboratory Science (CLS), Medical Laboratory Science (MLS), Medical Laboratory Technician (MLT) or Clinical Laboratory Technician (CLT) program.

Siemens Graduate Scholarships of $1,000 each are available to five students who are currently pursuing a graduate degree in the area of medical laboratory science.

GEOG. RESTRICTIONS: United States.

FINANCIAL DATA:
Amount of support per award: $500 to $2,000. ASCP Phlebotomy Scholarships: $500. Siemens - ASCP Scholarship: $1,000. Siemens Graduate Scholarships: $1,000. Siemens Legacy Scholarships: $2,000.

Total amount of support: Approximately $150,000 per year.

CO-OP FUNDING PROGRAMS: ASCP and Siemens Healthcare Diagnostics have partnered to provide theSiemens - ASCP Scholarship Program.

NO. MOST RECENT APPLICANTS: Over 350.

NO. AWARDS: 153 for the year 2014. Siemens Graduate Scholarships: 5. Siemens Legacy Scholarships: 10.

APPLICATION INFO:
Application form required. Contact ASCP.

Duration: One year. Nonrenewable.

Deadline: December 2015.

PUBLICATIONS:
Announcement.

ADDRESS INQUIRIES TO:
ASCP Scholarship Committee
c/o Angela Papaleo
(See address above.)

*SPECIAL STIPULATIONS:
Membership is required for ASCP and Siemens - ASCP Scholarships. More details are available online.

AUTISM SPEAKS [2172]

1060 State Road, 2nd Floor
Princeton, NJ 08540
(609) 228-7313
E-mail: jnew@autismspeaks.org
Web Site: www.autismspeaks.org

FOUNDED: 1994

AREAS OF INTEREST:
Autism.

NAME(S) OF PROGRAMS:
- **Family Services Local Grants**
- **Fellowship Training Grants**
- **Suzanne and Bob Wright Trailblazer**

TYPE:
Fellowships; Project/program grants; Research grants. Research grants that are in line with Autism Speaks research priorities.

Fellowship Training Grants provide predoctoral and postdoctoral research grants in response to periodical requests for applications.

YEAR PROGRAM STARTED: 1994

PURPOSE:
To fund global biomedical research into the causes, prevention, treatment and cure for autism; to raise public awareness about autism and its effects on individuals, families and society.

LEGAL BASIS:
National nonprofit, tax-exempt organization.

ELIGIBILITY:
Science grants: Open to investigators at established research institutions.

GEOG. RESTRICTIONS: Family Services Local Grants are restricted to United States.

FINANCIAL DATA:
Amount of support per award: Varies.

Total amount of support: Varies.

NO. MOST RECENT APPLICANTS: Family Services: More than 500; Science: Approximately 150 for the year 2015.

NO. AWARDS: Varies.

APPLICATION INFO:
All proposals must be submitted online via Autism Speaks grants administration site.

Duration: Varies.

Deadline: Varies.

IRS I.D.: 20-2329938

ADDRESS INQUIRIES TO:
Joan New, Grants Manager
(See address above.)

Family Services:
Serena Selkin, Grants Manager
E-mail: sselkin@autismspeaks.org

BATTEN DISEASE SUPPORT AND RESEARCH ASSOCIATION [2173]

1175 Dublin Road
Columbus, OH 43215
(614) 973-6011
(800) 448-4570
Fax: (866) 648-8718
E-mail: mfrazier@bdsra.org
Web Site: www.bdsra.org

FOUNDED: 1987

AREAS OF INTEREST:
Batten Disease, NCL and Kufs Disease.

NAME(S) OF PROGRAMS:
- **Batten Disease Research Grant**

TYPE:
Fellowships; Research grants; Seed money grants.

YEAR PROGRAM STARTED: 1994

PURPOSE:
To maximize the opportunities of victims of Batten to lead as normal lives as possible; to provide a parent communication network, information and emotional support to families of persons with Batten Disease; to educate lay persons and professionals about the special needs of victims and their families; to act as a national registry for NCL researchers throughout the world.

ELIGIBILITY:
Applications will be reviewed based upon the quality of the proposed science, the probability of achieving the specific aims proposed and the likelihood of securing federal funding for continued research.

APPLICATION INFO:
Write or call the Foundation to determine the interest and appropriateness of a full proposal.

Duration: One to two years.

Deadline: May 15.

IRS I.D.: 91-1397792

STAFF:
Margie Frazier, Executive Director

ADDRESS INQUIRIES TO:
Margie Frazier, Executive Director
(See address above.)

*SPECIAL STIPULATIONS:
Grants must not be used to cover indirect or overhead costs.

BRIGHAM AND WOMEN'S HOSPITAL

75 Francis Street
Boston, MA 02115
(617) 732-8422
Fax: (617) 582-6112
E-mail: bwhdeland@partners.org
Web Site: www.brighamandwomens.org/about_bwh/delandfellowship

TYPE:
Fellowships.

See entry 1385 for full listing.

BURROUGHS WELLCOME FUND [2174]

21 T.W. Alexander Drive
Research Triangle Park, NC 27709
(919) 991-5100
Fax: (919) 991-5160
E-mail: info@bwfund.org
Web Site: www.bwfund.org

FOUNDED: 1955

AREAS OF INTEREST:
Biomedical research.

NAME(S) OF PROGRAMS:
- **Career Awards at the Scientific Interface**
- **Career Awards for Medical Scientists**
- **Institutional Program Unifying Population and Laboratory Based Sciences**
- **Investigators in the Pathogenesis of Infectious Disease**
- **Preterm Birth Initiative**

TYPE:
Awards/prizes; Conferences/seminars; Research grants. Career Awards at the Scientific Interface bridge advanced postdoctoral training and the first three years of faculty service. These awards are intended to foster the early career development of researchers with backgrounds in the physical/mathematical/computational sciences whose work addresses biological questions.

Career Awards for Medical Scientists provide funds to bridge advanced postdoctoral/fellowship training and the early years of faculty service. This award addresses the ongoing problem of increasing the number of physician scientists and will help facilitate the transition to a career in research.

Institutional Program Unifying Population and Laboratory Based Sciences provides funds to unite the population and computational sciences and the laboratory-based biological sciences. The award supports the training of researchers

working between existing research concentrations in population approaches to human health and in basic biological sciences.

Investigators in the Pathogenesis of Infectious Disease provides awards for opportunities for accomplished investigators at the assistant professor level to study pathogenesis, with a focus on the intersection of human and microbial biology. The program is intended to shed light on the overarching issues of how human hosts handle infectious challenge.

Preterm Birth Initiative brings together a diverse interdisciplinary group with expertise in genetics/genomics, immunology, microbiology and proteomics along with the more traditional areas of parturition research such as maternal fetal medicine, obstetrics and pediatrics to address the scientific issues related to preterm birth.

PURPOSE:
To advance the biomedical sciences by supporting research and other scientific and educational activities; to help scientists early in their careers develop as independent investigators; to advance fields in the basic biomedical sciences that are undervalued or in need of particular encouragement.

LEGAL BASIS:
Private foundation.

GEOG. RESTRICTIONS: United States and Canada.

FINANCIAL DATA:
Amount of support per award: Career Awards at the Scientific Interface: $500,000; Career Awards for Medical Scientists: $700,000; Institutional Program Unifying Population and Laboratory Based Sciences: $500,000; Investigators in Pathogenesis of Infectious Disease: $500,000; Preterm Birth Initiative: Up to $600,000.

Total amount of support: Approximately $25,000,000 in grants awarded annually.

APPLICATION INFO:
Contact the Fund.

Duration: Preterm Birth Initiative: Four years. All others: Five years.

Deadline: Varies.

PUBLICATIONS:
FOCUS, newsletter; *Career Development Guides*, annual report.

IRS I.D.: 23-7225395

ADDRESS INQUIRIES TO:
Burroughs Wellcome Fund
P.O. Box 13901
Research Triangle Park, NC 27709-3901

CANADIAN BLOOD SERVICES [2175]

1800 Alta Vista Drive
Ottawa ON K1G 4J5 Canada
(613) 739-2408
Fax: (613) 739-2201
E-mail: cilla.perry@blood.ca
Web Site: www.blood.ca

AREAS OF INTEREST:
Research in transfusion science.

NAME(S) OF PROGRAMS:
- **Canadian Blood Services Trainee Awards Graduate Fellowship Program**
- **Canadian Blood Services Trainee Awards Postdoctoral Fellowship**

TYPE:
Fellowships.

PURPOSE:
To attract and support young investigators to initiate or continue training in the field of transfusion science; to foster careers related to transfusion science in Canada.

ELIGIBILITY:
Graduate Fellowship: Open to graduate students who are undertaking full-time research training leading to a Ph.D. degree. Students registering solely for a Master's degree will not be considered.

Postdoctoral Fellowship: Candidates must hold a recent Ph.D., M.D., D.D.S., D.V.M. or equivalent.

GEOG. RESTRICTIONS: Canada.

FINANCIAL DATA:
Amount of support per award: Graduate Fellowship: $25,000 per annum (CIHR guidelines); Postdoctoral Fellowship: $40,000 per annum (CIHR guidelines).

Total amount of support: Graduate Fellowship: Approximately $300,000; Postdoctoral Fellowship: Approximately $200,000.

NO. MOST RECENT APPLICANTS: 8 Graduate Fellowship and 9 Postdoctoral Fellowship for the year 2014.

NO. AWARDS: 8 Graduate Fellowships and 5 Postdoctoral Fellowships for the year 2014.

APPLICATION INFO:
Candidates are required to submit application form GFP-01 for Graduate Fellowship or RD40 for Postdoctoral Fellowship.

Duration: Two years. Renewal to maximum of four years for Graduate Fellowship and three years for Postdoctoral Fellowship.

Deadline: Graduate Fellowship Program: May and November; Postdoctoral Fellowship: July.

ADDRESS INQUIRIES TO:
Cilla Perry
Manager, Center for Innovation
(See address above.)

*SPECIAL STIPULATIONS:
Awards must be held in Canada.

CANADIAN INSTITUTES OF HEALTH RESEARCH (CIHR) [2176]

160 Elgin Street, 9th Floor
Address Locator 4809A
Ottawa ON K1A 0W9 Canada
(613) 954-1968
(888) 603-4178 (press 1)
Fax: (613) 954-1800
E-mail: info@cihr-irsc.gc.ca
Web Site: www.cihr-irsc.gc.ca

FOUNDED: 2000

AREAS OF INTEREST:
Basic, applied and clinical research in Canada in the health sciences.

NAME(S) OF PROGRAMS:
- **Canada Graduate Scholarships-Master's Program**

TYPE:
Awards/prizes; Scholarships. Intended to provide special recognition and support to students who are pursuing a Master's degree in a health-related field in Canada. These candidates are expected to have an exceptionally high potential for future research achievement and productivity.

YEAR PROGRAM STARTED: 2003

PURPOSE:
To help ensure a reliable supply of highly qualified personnel to meet the needs of Canada's knowledge economy.

LEGAL BASIS:
Government agency.

ELIGIBILITY:
The program is open to Canadian citizens and permanent residents. At the time of the CIHR deadline for application, candidates must have completed or be in the last year of a Bachelor's degree or have been registered for no more than 10 months as a full-time student in a Master's program. Only those students engaged in full-time Master's programs in which research is a major component are eligible for support. Awards will take effect only after the recipient has registered in a full-time Master's program.

Persons with a health professional degree who seek support for Master's research training are eligible to apply, but should also consult the guidelines for the CIHR Fellowships program. Those eligible for both have the option of applying to either program but not to both in the same year (i.e., September through August).

GEOG. RESTRICTIONS: Canada.

FINANCIAL DATA:
Amount of support per award: $17,500 (CAN).

Total amount of support: Varies.

CO-OP FUNDING PROGRAMS: This program is part of the Tri-Agency Harmonization of the Canada Graduate Scholarships, involving the Canadian Institutes of Health Research, the Natural Sciences and Engineering Research Council of Canada and the Social Sciences and Humanities Research Council of Canada.

APPLICATION INFO:
Contact the Institutes.

Duration: One year. Nonrenewable.

Deadline: December 1, 2015.

ADDRESS INQUIRIES TO:
Program Delivery Coordinator
Canada Graduate Scholarships-Master's Program
(See address above.)

*SPECIAL STIPULATIONS:
Awards must be taken up between July 1 and October 1 following the offer of award and must commence at the beginning of the semesters, September 1 and January 1.

CANADIAN INSTITUTES OF HEALTH RESEARCH (CIHR) [2177]

160 Elgin Street, 9th Floor
Address Locator 4809A
Ottawa ON K1A 0W9 Canada
(613) 954-1968
(888) 603-4178 (press 1)
Fax: (613) 954-1800
E-mail: info@cihr-irsc.gc.ca
Web Site: www.cihr-irsc.gc.ca

FOUNDED: 1969

AREAS OF INTEREST:
Basic, applied and clinical research in Canada in the health sciences.

NAME(S) OF PROGRAMS:
- **Frederick Banting and Charles Best Canada Graduate Scholarships Doctoral Awards (CGS-D)**

TYPE:
Scholarships.

PURPOSE:
To provide special recognition and support to students who are pursuing a doctoral degree in a health-related field in Canada.

ELIGIBILITY:
The program is open to Canadian citizens and permanent residents of Canada. Only those students engaged in full-time research training in a Canadian graduate school are eligible for support.

GEOG. RESTRICTIONS: Canada.

FINANCIAL DATA:
Amount of support per award: $30,000 (CAN) annual stipend, plus an annual research allowance of $5,000.

Total amount of support: Varies.

NO. MOST RECENT APPLICANTS: 1,365.

NO. AWARDS: 180.

APPLICATION INFO:
Application information is available on the web site.

Duration: Three years.

Deadline: October.

ADDRESS INQUIRIES TO:
Deputy Director
Doctoral Research Awards
(See address above.)

CANADIAN INSTITUTES OF HEALTH RESEARCH (CIHR) [2178]

160 Elgin Street, 9th Floor
Address Locator 4809A
Ottawa ON K1A 0W9 Canada
(613) 954-1968
(888) 603-4178 (press 1)
Fax: (613) 954-1800
E-mail: info@cihr-irsc.gc.ca
Web Site: www.cihr-irsc.gc.ca

FOUNDED: 1969

AREAS OF INTEREST:
Health research sciences, natural sciences, engineering, social sciences and humanities.

NAME(S) OF PROGRAMS:
- **Banting Postdoctoral Fellowships Program**

TYPE:
Fellowships. Postdoctoral fellowships.

YEAR PROGRAM STARTED: 1969

PURPOSE:
To provide support for highly qualified candidates to add to their experience by engaging in research either in Canada or abroad.

LEGAL BASIS:
Government agency.

ELIGIBILITY:
Applicants can be Canadian citizens, permanent residents of Canada or foreign citizens. Applicants research must be in the area of health, natural sciences and/or engineering, or social science and/or humanities.

Contact CIHR for full details.

FINANCIAL DATA:
Amount of support per award: $70,000 (CAN) per year (taxable).

Total amount of support: Varies.

APPLICATION INFO:
Application information is available on the web site.

Duration: Two years. Nonrenewable.

PUBLICATIONS:
Annual Report of the President; Grants and Awards Guide.

ADDRESS INQUIRIES TO:
Project Officer
Banting Postdoctoral Fellowships Program
(See address above.)

CANADIAN LIVER FOUNDATION [2179]

3100 Steeles Avenue East
Suite 801
Markham ON L3R 8T3 Canada
(416) 491-3353
(800) 563-5483 (within Canada and U.S.)
Fax: (905) 752-1540
E-mail: clf@liver.ca
Web Site: www.liver.ca

FOUNDED: 1969

AREAS OF INTEREST:
Research and education into the causes, diagnosis, prevention and treatment of diseases of the liver.

NAME(S) OF PROGRAMS:
- **Canadian Liver Foundation Graduate Studentships**

TYPE:
Scholarships.

PURPOSE:
To enable academically superior students to undertake full-time studies in a Canadian university in a discipline relevant to the Foundation's objectives.

LEGAL BASIS:
Registered Canadian charity.

ELIGIBILITY:
Candidates must be accepted into a full-time university graduate science program in a medically related discipline related to a Master's or doctoral degree and hold a record of superior academic performance in studies relevant to the proposed training.

Candidates must be sponsored by a faculty supervisor with a record of productive medical research and sufficient, competitively acquired research funding to ensure the satisfactory conduct of the student's research during the term of the award.

GEOG. RESTRICTIONS: Canada.

FINANCIAL DATA:
Amount of support per award: $20,000 (CAN) per year.

NO. MOST RECENT APPLICANTS: 2 for the year 2014.

NO. AWARDS: 1 for the year 2014.

APPLICATION INFO:
Contact the Foundation.

Duration: Two academic years. Nonrenewable.

Deadline: March 31, for awards to become tenable the following September 1.

PUBLICATIONS:
Program description and guidelines.

STAFF:
Billie Potkonjak, Research Grants Administrator

ADDRESS INQUIRIES TO:
Billie Potkonjak
Research Grants Administrator
(See address above.)

CANADIAN LIVER FOUNDATION

3100 Steeles Avenue East
Suite 801
Markham ON L3R 8T3 Canada
(416) 491-3353
(800) 563-5483 (within Canada and U.S.)
Fax: (905) 752-1540
E-mail: clf@liver.ca
Web Site: www.liver.ca

TYPE:
Research grants.

See entry 2339 for full listing.

CANADIAN LIVER FOUNDATION [2180]

3100 Steeles Avenue East
Suite 801
Markham ON L3R 8T3 Canada
(416) 491-3353
(800) 563-5483 (within Canada and U.S.)
Fax: (905) 752-1540
E-mail: clf@liver.ca
Web Site: www.liver.ca

FOUNDED: 1969

AREAS OF INTEREST:
Research and education into the causes, diagnosis, prevention and treatment of diseases of the liver.

NAME(S) OF PROGRAMS:
- **Summer Studentships**

TYPE:
Scholarships.

PURPOSE:
To provide an opportunity for a limited number of well-motivated students with records of strong academic performance to participate in liver-related research in Canada.

LEGAL BASIS:
Registered Canadian charity.

ELIGIBILITY:
Applicants must be registered at a Canadian institution in an undergraduate degree program.

GEOG. RESTRICTIONS: Canada.

FINANCIAL DATA:
Amount of support per award: $4,000 (CAN) for any three summer months (May through August).

NO. MOST RECENT APPLICANTS: 4 for the year 2015.

NO. AWARDS: 3 for the year 2015.

APPLICATION INFO:
Guidelines and application forms are available in hospitals and universities through the office of Research Administration, on the Foundation web site, or from the address above.

Duration: Each award will be for any three summer months (May to August).

Deadline: March 31, for awards to become tenable the following June 1.

PUBLICATIONS:
Program description and guidelines.

STAFF:
Billie Potkonjak, Research Grants Administrator

ADDRESS INQUIRIES TO:
Billie Potkonjak
Research Grants Administrator
(See address above.)

CANADIAN SOCIETY FOR MEDICAL LABORATORY SCIENCE [2181]

33 Wellington Street North
Hamilton ON L8R 1M7 Canada
(905) 528-8642
(800) 263-8277
Fax: (905) 528-4968
E-mail: awards@csmls.org
Web Site: www.csmls.org

FOUNDED: 1937

AREAS OF INTEREST:
Continuing education and medical research.

TYPE:
Scholarships. Available to students involved in the clinical phase of their medical lab technology training program. Students must be enrolled in general medical laboratory technology, cytotechnology, or clinical genetics studies leading to CSMLS certification.

YEAR PROGRAM STARTED: 1937

ELIGIBILITY:
Applicants must be enrolled with the CSMLS as a student member and be a Canadian citizen or permanent resident.

GEOG. RESTRICTIONS: Canada.

FINANCIAL DATA:
Amount of support per award: $500 (CAN).
Total amount of support: $2,000 (CAN).

CO-OP FUNDING PROGRAMS: Program is made possible by the generous support of Cowan Insurance Brokers and Becton Dickinson Canada Inc.

NO. MOST RECENT APPLICANTS: 5 for the year 2014.

NO. AWARDS: 2 for the year 2014.

APPLICATION INFO:
Contact the Society.
Duration: Varies depending on award. Generally nonrenewable.
Deadline: October 1.

ADDRESS INQUIRIES TO:
CSMLS Grants, Scholarships and Awards Committee
(See e-mail address above.)

*SPECIAL STIPULATIONS:
Must be a student enrolled in an accredited training program in Canada.

CHINESE AMERICAN MEDICAL SOCIETY [2182]

265 Canal Street
Suite 515
New York, NY 10013
(212) 334-4760
Fax: (646) 304-6373
E-mail: jlove@camsociety.org
Web Site: www.camsociety.org

FOUNDED: 1963

AREAS OF INTEREST:
Medicine.

NAME(S) OF PROGRAMS:
- **CAMS Scholarship Program**
- **Medical Student Summer Research Fellowship**

TYPE:
Fellowships; Scholarships.

YEAR PROGRAM STARTED: 1973

PURPOSE:
To promote the scientific association of medical professionals of Chinese descent; to advance medical knowledge and scientific research with emphasis on aspects unique to the Chinese; to establish scholarships to medical and dental students and to provide endowments to medical schools and hospitals of good standing; to promote the health status of Chinese Americans.

LEGAL BASIS:
A nonprofit, charitable, educational, and scientific society.

ELIGIBILITY:
Candidates must currently be in their first, second or third year of medical or dental school in a U.S.-accredited medical or dental school when applying. Candidates must reside in the U.S. at the time of application either as an alien student or citizen of the U.S. Students who have just been accepted into medical or dental school at the time of application are not eligible.

FINANCIAL DATA:
Amount of support per award: Scholarships: $5,000; Research Fellowships: $3,200 to $4,000.
Total amount of support: $10,000 to $15,000.

NO. AWARDS: Scholarships: 4 to 6; Research Fellowships: Up to 3.

APPLICATION INFO:
Contact the Society.
Duration: One-time award.
Deadline: April 30.

STAFF:
Ms. Jamie Love, Administrator

ADDRESS INQUIRIES TO:
Warren W. Chin, M.D.
Executive Director
(See address above.)

COLLEGE OF PHYSICIANS OF PHILADELPHIA

Francis Clark Wood Institute
for the History of Medicine
19 South 22nd Street
Philadelphia, PA 19103-3097
(215) 399-2305
Fax: (215) 575-3499
E-mail: blander@collegeofphysicians.org
Web Site: www.collegeofphysicians.org

TYPE:
Travel grants; Visiting scholars. This program allows scholars to conduct short-term research in the College's Library and/or Mutter Museum.

See entry 572 for full listing.

CUREPSP FOUNDATION FOR PSP/CBD AND RELATED BRAIN DISEASES

404 Fifth Avenue, Third Floor
New York, NY 10018
(347) 294-2871
Fax: (410) 785-7009
E-mail: caruana@curepsp.org
Web Site: www.curepsp.org

TYPE:
Research grants.

See entry 2383 for full listing.

THE DANA FOUNDATION [2183]

505 Fifth Avenue, Sixth Floor
New York, NY 10017
(212) 223-4040
Fax: (212) 317-8721
E-mail: kaguirre@dana.org
Web Site: www.dana.org

FOUNDED: 1950

AREAS OF INTEREST:
Science, health and education, with a current focus on neuroscience research.

NAME(S) OF PROGRAMS:
- **Clinical Neuroscience Research**
- **David Mahoney Neuro-Imaging Program**

TYPE:
Awards/prizes; Research grants. For the decade of the 1990s, the Foundation focused on brain research. Grants in these areas are made principally through competitive Clinical Hypotheses Programs in immuno-imaging, neuroimaging and brain-cardiovascular system interactions. These competitive grants programs support pilot testing of experimental and innovative ideas that in immunology and neuroscience research have the potential of advancing clinical applications. The Foundation also supports an invitational program in which leading scientists are invited to compete for research grants designed to improve immune system responses to biological agents.

The Foundation has supported advances in education throughout its history. Its current interest is focused primarily on professional development programs that foster improved teaching of the performing arts in public schools. Programs emphasize innovative training projects that are exported from, or imported to, New York City, Washington, DC, Los Angeles and their surrounding areas. Letters of intent are accepted on a rolling basis. Grantees are selected through a competitive process.

YEAR PROGRAM STARTED: 1950

PURPOSE:
To strengthen and improve the quality of science, health and education.

LEGAL BASIS:
Private, independent philanthropic foundation.

ELIGIBILITY:
The Foundation, in general, makes its grants in accordance with the following policies:
(1) it supports programs in science, health and education; carefully defined objectives in each field guide its grantmaking;
(2) in many cases, it requires grantee institutions to share the cost of a project;
(3) it makes no grants directly to individuals;
(4) it does not support annual operating budgets of organizations, deficit reduction, capital campaigns or individual sabbaticals and;
(5) it does not schedule meetings with applicants, other than by specific invitation initiated by the Foundation.

GEOG. RESTRICTIONS: United States.

FINANCIAL DATA:
Amount of support per award: $200,000 to $300,000.
Total amount of support: Varies by program.

NO. MOST RECENT APPLICANTS: 120.

NO. AWARDS: Varies.

APPLICATION INFO:
Application details can be found on the web site.

Duration: Up to three years. Renewals are rare.

Deadline: Clinical Neuroscience Research Program applications are accepted on a rolling basis.

PUBLICATIONS:
Annual report; *Dana Report*, newsletter; application guidelines.

IRS I.D.: 06-6036761

BOARD OF DIRECTORS:
Edward F. Rover, Chairman
Edward Bleier
Wallace L. Cook
Charles A. Dana, III
Steven E. Hyman, M.D.
LaSalle D. Leffall, Jr., M.D.
Hildegarde E. Mahoney
Ann McLaughlin-Korologos
Herbert J. Siegel

ADMINISTRATION:
Edward F. Rover, President
Barbara E. Gill, Vice President, Communications
Burton M. Mirsky, Vice President, Finance

ADDRESS INQUIRIES TO:
Kevin Aguirre, Grant Officer
(See address above.)

DERMATOLOGY FOUNDATION [2184]

1560 Sherman Avenue
Suite 500
Evanston, IL 60201-4808
(847) 328-2256
Fax: (847) 328-0509
E-mail: dfgen@dermatologyfoundation.org
Web Site: www.dermatologyfoundation.org

FOUNDED: 1964

AREAS OF INTEREST:
Cancer and other diseases of the skin, hair and nails.

TYPE:
Fellowships; Project/program grants; Research grants. Research funding in the form of career development grants, fellowships, project/program grants and research grants for academic investigators in the early stages of their careers.

There are 12 research award categories. Career development awards include Physician Scientist, Dermatologic Surgery, Health Care Policy, Medical Dermatology, Psoriasis, Science of Human Appearance and Women's Health Issues. Dermatologist Investigator and Pediatric Dermatology Fellowships. Various Patient-Directed and Research Grants available.

YEAR PROGRAM STARTED: 1964

PURPOSE:
To advance the research careers of young individuals in dermatology and cutaneous biology, with the emphasis on research benefiting the dermatology community at large.

LEGAL BASIS:
Nonprofit charitable organization.

GEOG. RESTRICTIONS: United States.

FINANCIAL DATA:
Amount of support per award: Career development awards: Average $55,000; Fellowships: Average $30,000; Grants: Average $20,000.

Total amount of support: $3,100,000 in research funding for the year 2013.

NO. AWARDS: 70.

APPLICATION INFO:
Forms are available only on the Foundation web site.

Duration: One year. Renewal possibilities vary.

Deadline: October 15. Announcement midwinter at the annual meeting of the American Academy of Dermatology.

PUBLICATIONS:
Annual report; *Dermatology Focus*, scientific publication.

IRS I.D.: 04-6115524

OFFICERS:
Bruce U. Wintroub, M.D., Chairman, Board of Trustees
Michael D. Tharp, M.D., President
Stuart R. Lessin, M.D., Vice President
Elizabeth I. McBurney, M.D., Secretary/Treasurer

ADDRESS INQUIRIES TO:
Sandra R. Benz, Executive Director
(See address above.)

EMERGENCY MEDICINE FOUNDATION [2185]

1125 Executive Circle
Irving, TX 75038-2522
(800) 798-1822 ext. 3217
Fax: (972) 580-2816
E-mail: csingh@acep.org
Web Site: www.emfoundation.org

FOUNDED: 1972

AREAS OF INTEREST:
Emergency medicine research.

NAME(S) OF PROGRAMS:
- **Emergency Medicine Research**

TYPE:
Research grants; Technical assistance. Policy-based research awards in emergency medicine.

YEAR PROGRAM STARTED: 1972

PURPOSE:
To promote education and research in emergency medicine.

LEGAL BASIS:
501(c)(3) nonprofit.

ELIGIBILITY:
Must be an emergency medicine researcher.

GEOG. RESTRICTIONS: United States.

FINANCIAL DATA:
Amount of support per award: $5,000 to $150,000.

Total amount of support: Varies.

NO. AWARDS: 19 for the year 2015.

APPLICATION INFO:
Contact the Foundation.

Duration: One year.

Deadline: Varies.

IRS I.D.: 75-2331221

STAFF:
Robert Heard, MBA, Executive Director

ADDRESS INQUIRIES TO:
Cynthia Singh
Director of Grant Development
(See address above.)

FOUNDATION FOR ANESTHESIA EDUCATION AND RESEARCH [2186]

1061 American Lane
Schaumburg, IL 60173-4973
(847) 268-9214
Fax: (847) 825-2085
E-mail: FAER@faer.org
Web Site: www.faer.org

AREAS OF INTEREST:
Anesthesiology, critical care, pain, and all areas of perioperative medicine.

NAME(S) OF PROGRAMS:
- **FAER Health Services Research Grant**
- **FAER Mentored Research Training Grant**
- **FAER Research Education Grant**
- **FAER Research Fellowship Grant**
- **FAER Transition to Independence Grant**

TYPE:
Fellowships; Research grants; Training grants. These grants are designed to create opportunities for physicians to excel in an exceedingly competitive environment and to eventually acquire NIH funding.

PURPOSE:
To provide research grant funding for promising investigators to train in clinical, basic science and translational anesthesiology research.

ELIGIBILITY:
FAER Mentored Research Training Grant: Applicants must be instructors or assistant professors who are within 10 years of their initial appointment.

FAER Research Education Grant: Open to anesthesiology residents or faculty.

FAER Research Fellowship Grant: Open to anesthesiology residents after CA-1 training and six months of clinical scientist track.

A 20-member committee consisting of both clinical and basic science anesthesiologists reviews proposals. Clinical and outcomes projects are encouraged.

GEOG. RESTRICTIONS: United States.

FINANCIAL DATA:
Amount of support per award: $50,000 to $175,000.

Total amount of support: $2,000,000 annually.

NO. MOST RECENT APPLICANTS: 57.

NO. AWARDS: 22 for the year 2015.

APPLICATION INFO:
Contact the Foundation.

Deadline: February 15 and August 15.

IRS I.D.: 52-1494164

ADDRESS INQUIRIES TO:
Jody Clikeman, Programs Specialist
(See address above.)

THE FOUNDATION OF THE AMERICAN SOCIETY OF NEURORADIOLOGY [2187]

800 Enterprise Drive, Suite 205
Oak Brook, IL 60523
(630) 574-0220
Fax: (630) 574-0661
E-mail: jgantenberg@asnr.org
Web Site: foundation.asnr.org

FOUNDED: 1995

AREAS OF INTEREST:
Neuroradiology.

TYPE:
Research grants.

PURPOSE:
To promote education and research in the field of neuroradiology and the development of new ideas for clinical practice.

ELIGIBILITY:
Applicant must be a member in good standing of the American Society of Neuroradiology with an M.D. or D.O. degree and must be board-certified or board-eligible in radiology by the American Board of Radiology or the Royal College of Physicians and Surgeons of Canada.

FINANCIAL DATA:
Amount of support per award: Up to $60,000.

Total amount of support: Approximately $250,000 in grants annually.

NO. AWARDS: Varies.

APPLICATION INFO:
Award prospectus and information on applying is posted on the Foundation web site in October. Applicants must submit a letter of intent and a one-page abstract of the research proposal. Those selected will receive a follow-up e-mail invitation.

Duration: One year. Some renewals.

Deadline: Varies.

PUBLICATIONS:
American Journal of Neuroradiology.

ADDRESS INQUIRIES TO:
James B. Gantenberg, Executive Director
(See address above.)

THE MICHAEL J. FOX FOUNDATION FOR PARKINSON'S RESEARCH [2188]

Grand Central Station
P.O. Box 4777
New York, NY 10163-4777
(212) 509-0995
(800) 708-7644
Fax: (212) 509-2390
E-mail: research@michaeljfox.org
Web Site: www.michaeljfox.org

FOUNDED: 2000

AREAS OF INTEREST:
Medical research and Parkinson's disease.

TYPE:
Conferences/seminars; Research grants.

YEAR PROGRAM STARTED: 2000

PURPOSE:
To find a cure for Parkinson's disease through an aggressively funded research agenda; to ensure the development of improved therapies for those living with Parkinson's today.

LEGAL BASIS:
501(c)(3).

ELIGIBILITY:
Varies depending on research program.

FINANCIAL DATA:
Amount of support per award: Varies.

Total amount of support: Varies.

APPLICATION INFO:
The Foundation has implemented an electronic grant submission and review system that will enable research to be funded quickly and efficiently. Applicants should consult the Foundation web site for information.

Duration: Varies.

Deadline: Varies.

PUBLICATIONS:
Accelerating the Cure, newsletter; *Fox Flash*, e-newsletter; annual report; progress report.

IRS I.D.: 13-4141945

STAFF:
Deborah W. Brooks, Co-Founder and Executive Vice Chairman
Todd Sherer, Ph.D., Chief Executive Officer
Brian Fiske, Senior Vice President of Research Programs
Mark Frasier, Senior Vice President of Research Programs
Claire Meunier, Vice President of Research Engagement

ADDRESS INQUIRIES TO:
Brian Fiske, Senior Vice President of Research Programs
(See address above.)

THE PARKER B. FRANCIS FELLOWSHIP PROGRAM [2189]

8427 S.E. 35th Street
Mercer Island, WA 98040
(206) 240-7121
E-mail: dsnapp@uw.edu
Web Site: www.francisfellowships.org

FOUNDED: 1951

AREAS OF INTEREST:
Research related to lung biology, critical illness and control of breathing.

TYPE:
Fellowships. Awarded to scientists embarking on careers in clinical, laboratory or translational science in pulmonary, critical care and sleep medicine.

YEAR PROGRAM STARTED: 1975

PURPOSE:
To exert a favorable and lasting influence on the field of pulmonary medicine by providing the means to support promising young physicians and scientists for a period of training in research.

LEGAL BASIS:
Private foundation.

ELIGIBILITY:
Eligibility and evaluation criteria can be found on the Foundation's web site.

GEOG. RESTRICTIONS: United States and Canada.

FINANCIAL DATA:
Funds to be used for stipends and fringe benefits, with up to $2,000 per year as a travel allowance.

Amount of support per award: $156,000 over three years.

NO. MOST RECENT APPLICANTS: 60.

NO. AWARDS: 10 to 13.

APPLICATION INFO:
Contact the Program.

Duration: Three years.

Deadline: October of each year.

STAFF:
Deborah Snapp, Administrator

ADDRESS INQUIRIES TO:
Deborah Snapp
PBF Fellowship Program Administrator
(See e-mail address above.)

FRAXA RESEARCH FOUNDATION [2190]

10 Prince Place
Newburyport, MA 01950
(978) 462-1866
E-mail: info@fraxa.org
Web Site: www.fraxa.org

FOUNDED: 1994

AREAS OF INTEREST:
Medical research aimed at the treatment of Fragile X Syndrome.

NAME(S) OF PROGRAMS:
- **FRAXA Grants and Fellowships**

TYPE:
Fellowships; Research grants; Research contracts.

YEAR PROGRAM STARTED: 1994

PURPOSE:
To promote research aimed at finding a specific treatment for Fragile X Syndrome; to provide funds for postdoctoral fellowships and investigator-initiated grants.

FINANCIAL DATA:
Amount of support per award: Up to $45,000 per year for fellowships. No limit on grants.

APPLICATION INFO:
Application form, plus a one-page initial inquiry letter.

Duration: One year. Renewable.

Deadline: February 1.

PUBLICATIONS:
Newsletter; e-mail updates.

IRS I.D.: 04-3222167

OFFICER:
Katherine Clapp, President

ADDRESS INQUIRIES TO:
Michael Tranfaglia, Chief Scientific Officer
E-mail: mtranfaglia@fraxa.org and
Katherine Clapp, President
E-mail: kclapp@fraxa.org

FSH SOCIETY, INC. [2191]

450 Bedford Street
Lexington, MA 02420
(781) 301-6060
Fax: (781) 862-1116
E-mail: june.kinoshita@fshsociety.org
Web Site: www.fshsociety.org

FOUNDED: 1991

AREAS OF INTEREST:
Facioscapulohumeral Muscular Dystrophy.

TYPE:
Conferences/seminars; Fellowships; Project/program grants; Research grants; Seed money grants; Travel grants.

YEAR PROGRAM STARTED: 1998

PURPOSE:
To promote research on and disperse information on Facioscapulohumeral Muscular Dystrophy.

LEGAL BASIS:
501(c)(3) organization.

ELIGIBILITY:
Applications may be submitted by domestic or foreign for-profit and nonprofit organizations, public and private, such as universities, colleges, hospitals, laboratories, units of state and local governments, and eligible agencies of the federal government.

FINANCIAL DATA:
Amount of support per award: Average grant: $45,500.

NO. MOST RECENT APPLICANTS: 9.

NO. AWARDS: 4 new and 1 renewal for the year 2015.

APPLICATION INFO:
Contact the Society.

Duration: One year.

Deadline: February 28 and August 31.

PUBLICATIONS:
FSH Watch Newsletter; patient information on FSHD (English and Spanish).

IRS I.D.: 52-1762747

STAFF:
Daniel Paul Perez, President
June Kinoshita, Executive Director

ADDRESS INQUIRIES TO:
June Kinoshita, Executive Director
(See address above.)

GLAUCOMA RESEARCH FOUNDATION

251 Post Street, Suite 600
San Francisco, CA 94108
(415) 986-3162
Fax: (415) 986-3763
E-mail: research@glaucoma.org
Web Site: www.glaucoma.org

TYPE:
Research grants.

See entry 2436 for full listing.

THE GRAYSON-JOCKEY CLUB RESEARCH FOUNDATION [2192]

821 Corporate Drive
Lexington, KY 40503
(859) 224-2850
Fax: (859) 224-2853
E-mail: ebowen@jockeyclub.com
Web Site: www.grayson-jockeyclub.org

FOUNDED: 1940

AREAS OF INTEREST:
Race horses, veterinary medicine and research for all horses.

TYPE:
Fellowships; Project/program grants; Research grants. Supports research relevant to equine health and performance.

YEAR PROGRAM STARTED: 1940

PURPOSE:
To promote research in veterinary medicine and in the breeding, raising and handling of horses.

LEGAL BASIS:
Nonprofit foundation.

ELIGIBILITY:
The principal investigator should have some professional rank and salary from the institution involved, or hold some grade of Research Professorship with salary from the institution. Research interest must be relevant to the equine, particularly in regard to, but not limited to, cardiopulmonary disorders, infectious diseases, musculoskeletal disorders, and reproduction.

FINANCIAL DATA:
Amount of support per award: Average $71,000.

Total amount of support: Approximately $1,000,000 annually.

NO. MOST RECENT APPLICANTS: 70.

NO. AWARDS: 19 for the year 2016.

APPLICATION INFO:
The Foundation will only accept the online application. See web site for complete information.

Duration: One or two years.

Deadline: October 1. Announcement April 1.

PUBLICATIONS:
Application; guidelines; *Research Today*, newsletter.

IRS I.D.: 61-6031750

OFFICERS:
Dell Hancock, Chairman
A. Gary Lavin, D.V.M., Vice Chairman
Edward L. Bowen, President
Nancy C. Kelly, Vice President of Development/Secretary
Laura Barillaro, Treasurer

STAFF:
Garrett Gleeson, Director of Development and Major Gifts

ADDRESS INQUIRIES TO:
Edward L. Bowen, President
(See address above.)

HEALTH RESOURCES AND SERVICES ADMINISTRATION [2193]

Bureau of Health Workforce
Division of Medicine and Dentistry
5600 Fishers Lane, Room 9A-27
Rockville, MD 20857
(301) 443-8437
E-mail: aanyanwu@hrsa.gov
Web Site: bhpr.hrsa.gov/grants/medicine

NAME(S) OF PROGRAMS:

- **Primary Care Training and Enhancement (PCTE)**

TYPE:
Residencies; Training grants. Grants to strengthen the primary care workforce by supporting enhanced training for future primary care clinicians, teachers, and researchers and promoting primary care practice in rural and underserved areas. This grant focuses on producing primary care providers who will be well prepared to practice in and lead transforming health care systems aimed at improving access, quality of care, and cost effectiveness.

YEAR PROGRAM STARTED: 1972

PURPOSE:
To improve and expand access to quality health care for all.

LEGAL BASIS:
Section 747(a) of the PHS Act, as amended by the Health Professions Education Extension Amendments of 1992, Public Law 102-408.

ELIGIBILITY:
Applicants for the PCTE program must focus on training for transforming health care systems, particularly enhancing the clinical training experience of trainees.

Eligible applicants are accredited health professions schools and programs, including schools of allopathic or osteopathic medicine, academically affiliated physician assistant training programs, accredited public or nonprofit private hospitals, and public or nonprofit private entity capable of carrying out the grant.

GEOG. RESTRICTIONS: United States.

NO. AWARDS: Varies.

APPLICATION INFO:
Applicants are required to apply for this funding opportunity electronically through www.grants.gov.

All applications are competitively reviewed and evaluated.

Duration: One to three years. Renewal permitted.

HEALTHY MINDS CANADA

1920 Yonge Street
3rd Floor
Toronto ON M4S 3E2 Canada
(416) 351-7757
E-mail: admin@healthymindscanada.ca
Web Site: www.healthymindscanada.ca/awards/

TYPE:
Awards/prizes; Conferences/seminars; Project/program grants; Research grants.

See entry 2498 for full listing.

THE LARRY L. HILLBLOM FOUNDATION, INC. [2194]

755 Baywood Drive, Suite 180
Petaluma, CA 94954
(707) 762-6691
Fax: (707) 762-6694
E-mail: petaluma@llhf.org
Web Site: www.llhf.org

FOUNDED: 1996

AREAS OF INTEREST:
Medical research on diabetes mellitus and diseases associated with aging.

NAME(S) OF PROGRAMS:

- **Fellowship Research Grants**
- **Network Grants**
- **Start-Up Research Grants**

TYPE:
Assistantships; Block grants; Endowments; Fellowships. Fellowship Research Grants are intended to enable qualified institutions to provide postdoctoral research fellowship training to qualified applicants in one of the two areas of stated interest to the Foundation.

Network Grants facilitate interaction between a network of researchers. It is anticipated these investigators will be independently funded and have demonstrated productivity in their own field.

Start-Up Research Grants are offered to qualified institutions to enable them to select and assist qualified researchers to initiate independent research careers.

YEAR PROGRAM STARTED: 2000

PURPOSE:
To provide philanthropic support exclusively for charitable, religious, scientific, literary and educational purposes.

ELIGIBILITY:
Eligible organizations must have 501(c)(3) status.

GEOG. RESTRICTIONS: Primarily, California.

FINANCIAL DATA:
Amount of support per award: Fellowship Grants: Up to $60,000 per year; Network Grants: $300,000 per year; Start-Up Grants: $70,000 per year.

Total amount of support: Varies.

NO. MOST RECENT APPLICANTS: Varies.

NO. AWARDS: Varies.

APPLICATION INFO:
Contact the Foundation.

Duration: Fellowship Grants and Start-Up Grants: Up to three years; Network Grants: Four years.

Deadline: Fellowship Grants and Start-Up Grants: January. Notification by June. Network Grants: January 30 for Letters of Inquiry; July 17 for full application.

HIMSS FOUNDATION [2195]

33 West Monroe Street, Suite 1700
Chicago, IL 60603-5616
(312) 915-9515
(312) 664-4467
Fax: (312) 664-6143
E-mail: scholarships@himss.org
Web Site: www.himss.org

FOUNDED: 1961

AREAS OF INTEREST:
Health care information and management systems.

NAME(S) OF PROGRAMS:
- **HIMSS Foundation Scholarship Program**

TYPE:
Awards/prizes; Conferences/seminars; Fellowships; Internships; Research grants; Scholarships.

YEAR PROGRAM STARTED: 1986

PURPOSE:
To recognize students who have the potential to be future leaders in the health care information management systems industry.

ELIGIBILITY:
Applicant must be a student in an accredited degree-granting institution, a junior when the scholarship is awarded, and a student member of the Healthcare Information and Management Systems Society. Previous winners are not eligible, although the undergraduate winner is eligible if pursuing a graduate degree.

FINANCIAL DATA:
An all-expense-paid trip to the HIMSS annual conference is awarded in addition to grant.

Amount of support per award: $5,000.

Total amount of support: Varies.

NO. MOST RECENT APPLICANTS: 95.

NO. AWARDS: 7 for the year 2016.

APPLICATION INFO:
Call for applications is posted on the Foundation web site in early July.

Duration: One year.

Deadline: Applications are accepted annually early July to August.

ADDRESS INQUIRIES TO:
Maggie Van Vossen
Manager, Career Services
Tel: (312) 915-9245
(See address above.)

THE MAXIMILIAN E. & MARION O. HOFFMAN FOUNDATION, INC. [2196]

970 Farmington Avenue, Suite 203
West Hartford, CT 06107
(860) 521-2949
Fax: (860) 561-5082

AREAS OF INTEREST:
Education, medicine and the arts.

TYPE:
Project/program grants.

PURPOSE:
To provide funding to 501(c)(3) nonprofits conducting projects in education, medicine, and the arts.

LEGAL BASIS:
Nonprofit private foundation.

ELIGIBILITY:
Applicants must be 501(c)(3). No grants to individuals.

GEOG. RESTRICTIONS: United States, with preference to Connecticut.

FINANCIAL DATA:
Amount of support per award: Varies depending on needs and nature of the request.

APPLICATION INFO:
Submit Letter of Inquiry with copy of 501(c)(3).

Duration: One year. Some multiyear grants. Renewal possible by reapplication.

Deadline: The Board of Directors meets four to six times a year to consider requests.

PUBLICATIONS:
Application form.

ADDRESS INQUIRIES TO:
Marion Barrak, President
(See address above.)

HOWARD HUGHES MEDICAL INSTITUTE [2197]

Medical Research Fellows Program
4000 Jones Bridge Road
Chevy Chase, MD 20815
(800) 448-4882 ext. 6708
Fax: (240) 497-2314
E-mail: medfellows@hhmi.org
Web Site: www.hhmi.org/medfellowships

FOUNDED: 1953

AREAS OF INTEREST:
Fundamental biomedical research.

NAME(S) OF PROGRAMS:
- **Medical Research Fellows Program**

TYPE:
Fellowships.

YEAR PROGRAM STARTED: 1989

PURPOSE:
To strengthen and expand the pool of medically trained researchers.

LEGAL BASIS:
Medical research organization.

ELIGIBILITY:
Applicant must attend a medical, dental or veterinary school located in the U.S., not in a Ph.D. or M.D./Ph.D. or other combined professional degree/Ph.D. program. Applicant must have laboratory research experience and plan to spend a year full-time in fundamental biomedical research.

FINANCIAL DATA:
Amount of support per award: $30,000 stipend, $5,500 research allowance, and $5,500 Fellow's allowance.

NO. MOST RECENT APPLICANTS: 195 for the year 2016.

NO. AWARDS: 66 for the year 2016.

APPLICATION INFO:
Online application requires the following information:
(1) educational background;
(2) prior research experience;
(3) research plan;
(4) mentor's endorsement and reference letters and;
(5) undergraduate academic transcript data.

Duration: One year.

Deadline: January 11. Announcement at the end of March.

IRS I.D.: 59-0735717

ADDRESS INQUIRIES TO:
Melanie Daub, Program Officer
(See e-mail address above.)

IMMUNE DEFICIENCY FOUNDATION

110 West Road
Suite 300
Towson, MD 21204
(410) 321-6647
Fax: (410) 321-9165
E-mail: tcaulder@primaryimmune.org
Web Site: usidnet.org
primaryimmune.org

TYPE:
Travel grants; Visiting scholars.

See entry 2262 for full listing.

INTERNATIONAL ANESTHESIA RESEARCH SOCIETY (IARS) [2198]

44 Montgomery Street
Suite 1605
San Francisco, CA 94104
(415) 296-6900
Fax: (415) 296-6901
E-mail: awards@iars.org
Web Site: www.iars.org

FOUNDED: 1922

AREAS OF INTEREST:
Anesthesia.

NAME(S) OF PROGRAMS:
- **Anesthesiology Teaching Recognition Awards**
- **Frontiers in Anesthesia Research Award**
- **IARS Mentored Research Awards**

TYPE:
Research grants. Education awards.

YEAR PROGRAM STARTED: 1983

ELIGIBILITY:
Applicant must be a member of the IARS.

FINANCIAL DATA:
Amount of support per award: Anesthesiology Teaching Recognition Awards: $1,000 and $15,000 Innovation in Education grant; Frontiers in Anesthesia Research Award: $750,000, in three annual installments; IARS Mentored Research Awards: $150,000.

NO. MOST RECENT APPLICANTS: Anesthesiology Teaching Recognition Awards: 2; Frontiers in Anesthesia Research Award: 30; IARS Mentored Research Awards: 30 for the year 2015-16.

NO. AWARDS: Anesthesiology Teaching Recognition Awards: 2 annually; Frontiers in Anesthesia Research Award: 1 triennially; IARS Mentored Research Awards: 4 annually.

APPLICATION INFO:
Interested applicants should visit the IARS web site. Applications can be submitted online.

Duration: Anesthesiology Teaching Recognition Awards: One year; Frontiers in Anesthesia Research Award: Three years; IARS Mentored Research Awards: Two years.

Deadline: Anticipated December 2016 for the 2016-17 cycle. Contact IARS for exact date.

PUBLICATIONS:
Anesthesia & Analgesia, journal; *Anesthesia & Analgesia Case Reports*, online journal.

ADDRESS INQUIRIES TO:
Tom Cooper, Executive Director
(See address above.)

INTERNATIONAL COLLEGE OF SURGEONS (ICS) [2199]

1516 North Lakeshore Drive
Chicago, IL 60610-1694
(312) 560-5006
Fax: (312) 787-1683
E-mail: max@icsglobal.org
Web Site: www.icsglobal.org

AREAS OF INTEREST:
Medical research and surgery.

NAME(S) OF PROGRAMS:
- **ICS Scholarship**

TYPE:
Scholarships. ICS makes grants available to surgeons who wish to enhance their surgical skills through postgraduate training.

PURPOSE:
To support education and research.

ELIGIBILITY:
Open to surgeons around the world traveling to developed nations to further their education.

FINANCIAL DATA:
Amount of support per award: Varies.

Total amount of support: Varies.

NO. MOST RECENT APPLICANTS: Varies.

NO. AWARDS: Varies.

APPLICATION INFO:
Send request to ICS.

Duration: Varies.

ADDRESS INQUIRIES TO:
Max C. Downham, Executive Director
(See address above.)

INTERNATIONAL MYELOMA FOUNDATION (IMF) [2200]

12650 Riverside Drive, Suite 206
North Hollywood, CA 91607-3421
(818) 487-7455
Fax: (818) 487-7454
E-mail: theimf@myeloma.org
Web Site: www.myeloma.org

FOUNDED: 1990

AREAS OF INTEREST:
Myeloma.

NAME(S) OF PROGRAMS:
- **Brian D. Novis Research Grants**

TYPE:
Internships; Research grants; Travel grants.

YEAR PROGRAM STARTED: 1995

PURPOSE:
To promote research into better treatments, management, prevention and a cure for myeloma.

LEGAL BASIS:
Nonprofit organization.

ELIGIBILITY:
Open to junior researchers or senior researchers working in the field of multiple myeloma. Junior researchers must have completed postdoctoral studies or clinical fellowships no later than August 1 of the application year and must have the ability to devote a minimum of 50% of his or her time to research during the award year. Also, must provide a completed application with evidence of a meritorious research project.

FINANCIAL DATA:
Amount of support per award: Junior researchers: $50,000; Senior researchers: $80,000.

Total amount of support: Varies each year.

APPLICATION INFO:
Applications can be downloaded from the Foundation's web site.

Duration: One year. Renewable upon reapplication.

Deadline: August 1 (postmarked) for the following year's program.

PUBLICATIONS:
Myeloma Today, newsletter.

IRS I.D.: 95-4296919

STAFF:
Susie Novis, President
Lisa Paik, Senior Vice President of Clinical Education and Research Initiatives

ADDRESS INQUIRIES TO:
Lisa Paik, Senior Vice President of Clinical Education and Research Initiatives or Amirah Limayo, Research Project Coordinator
(See address above.)

ROBERT WOOD JOHNSON FOUNDATION [2201]

Route One and College Road East
Princeton, NJ 08543-2316
(877) 843-7953
Fax: (609) 627-7582
E-mail: lryba@rwjf.org
Web Site: www.rwjf.org

FOUNDED: 1972

AREAS OF INTEREST:
Health leadership, health systems, healthy communities, healthy kids/healthy weight.

TYPE:
Project/program grants; Research grants.

YEAR PROGRAM STARTED: 1972

PURPOSE:
To build a national culture of health; to raise the health of everyone in the U.S. to the level a great nation deserves by placing well-being at the center of every aspect of life.

LEGAL BASIS:
Private foundation.

ELIGIBILITY:
Preference is given to tax-exempt, public agencies under Section 501(c)(3). The Foundation does not fund general operating expenses or existing deficits, endowments or capital costs, basic biomedical research, drug therapies or devices research, direct support of individuals, or lobbying of any kind.

Additionally, the Foundation rarely makes grants for conferences, unless they relate clearly to the Foundation's goals, or for publications and media projects, except those that grow out of one of the Foundation's grant programs.

GEOG. RESTRICTIONS: United States.

FINANCIAL DATA:
Amount of support per award: Median award approximately $200,000 for the year 2015.

Total amount of support: $375,000,000 for the year 2015.

Matching fund requirements: Varies; only a limited number of awards include matching fund requirements.

NO. MOST RECENT APPLICANTS: 3,386 for the year 2015.

NO. AWARDS: 737 individual awards for the year 2015.

REPRESENTATIVE AWARDS:
$300,000 to New Jersey YMCA State Alliance Inc., Trenton, NJ, to support a collaborative effort to expand the Healthy Corner Store Initiative in New Jersey to increase the sale and marketing of nutritious food; $119,741 to University of Edinburgh, College of Medicine, Edinburgh, U.K., to conduct an international landscape analysis of the disaggregation of health data by racial/ethnic groups to complement and inform U.S.-based work; $255,000 to Cooper's Ferry Partnership, Inc., Camden, NJ, to implement strategies for changes in policy and the environment to improve the quality of life of Camden, NJ residents; $99,381 to Prevention Institute, Oakland, CA, to reach multiple audiences with recommendations for research and practice to counter the production of health inequities.

APPLICATION INFO:
Funding is awarded through targeted calls for proposals. The Foundation will accept brief proposals for funding of new and creative approaches to building a culture of health.

Duration: Varies.

STAFF:
Risa Lavizzo-Mourey, M.D., M.B.A., President and Chief Executive Officer
James Marks, M.D., M.P.H., Executive Vice President, Programs
Katherine Hatton, J.D., Vice President, General Counsel and Secretary
David L. Waldman, Vice President, Human Resources and Administration
Margaret Einhorn, MBA, Chief Financial Officer
Brian S. O'Neil, MBA, C.F.A., Chief Investment Officer

Stephen Downs, Chief Technology and Strategy Officer
Robin Mockenhaupt, Chief of Staff

ADDRESS INQUIRIES TO:
Lydia Ryba, Senior Manager
Office of Proposal Management
P.O. Box 2316
Princeton, NJ 08543-2316

THE JACOB AND VALERIA LANGELOTH FOUNDATION [2202]

275 Madison Avenue, 33rd Floor
New York, NY 10016
(212) 687-1133
Fax: (212) 687-8877
E-mail: info@langeloth.org
Web Site: www.langeloth.org

AREAS OF INTEREST:
Health care.

TYPE:
Demonstration grants; Project/program grants; Research grants.

PURPOSE:
To promote and support effective and creative programs, practices and policies related to healing from illness, accident, physical, social or emotional trauma; to extend the availability of programs that promote healing to underserved populations.

ELIGIBILITY:
Grants are made to organizations that have tax-exempt status under Section 501(c)(3) of the Internal Revenue Code and that are health care providers, academic research institutions or community-based organizations. Grants are made nationwide, with a specific interest in New York state.

GEOG. RESTRICTIONS: Primarily New York state.

FINANCIAL DATA:
$94,618,709 in assets for fiscal year ended November 30, 2015.

Amount of support per award: Varies.

Total amount of support: $4,780,466 for fiscal year ended November 30, 2015.

APPLICATION INFO:
Applications must be submitted online. Organizations may submit more than one application, but each project requires a separate registration and user name. The process involves the following steps:
(1) project registration;
(2) letter of intent invitation;
(3) letter of intent submission;
(4) proposal invitation and;
(5) proposal submission.

Applicants will be notified via e-mail at each step.

Duration: Up to three years.

Deadline: April 7 and October 7.

STAFF:
Scott Moyer, President
Andrea Fionda, Program Officer
Melissa Houston, Grants and Office Administrator

ADDRESS INQUIRIES TO:
Scott Moyer, President
(See address above.)

*SPECIAL STIPULATIONS:
Foundation does not accept unsolicited proposals.

LEUKEMIA RESEARCH FOUNDATION

191 Waukegan Road
Suite 105
Northfield, IL 60093
(847) 424-0600
Fax: (847) 424-0606
E-mail: info@lrfmail.org
Web Site: www.allbloodcancers.org

TYPE:
Research grants. The goal of the grant program is to support new investigators. It funds scientists and physicians around the world.

See entry 2366 for full listing.

LOVELACE RESPIRATORY RESEARCH INSTITUTE

2425 Ridgecrest Drive, S.E.
Albuquerque, NM 87108
(505) 348-9400
Fax: (505) 348-8567
E-mail: info@lrri.org
Web Site: www.lrri.org

TYPE:
Fellowships. Training program in respiratory tract disease caused by environmental agents.

See entry 2263 for full listing.

LOWE SYNDROME ASSOCIATION [2203]

P.O. Box 417
Chicago Ridge, IL 60415
(216) 630-7723
E-mail: info@lowesyndrome.org
Web Site: www.lowesyndrome.org

FOUNDED: 1982

AREAS OF INTEREST:
Medical research pertaining to Lowe Syndrome.

NAME(S) OF PROGRAMS:
- **The Leland McSpadden Memorial Fund for Medical and Scientific Research**

TYPE:
Research grants. Supports research leading to a better understanding of the metabolic basis of Lowe Syndrome, to better treatments of the major complications of Lowe Syndrome, to the prevention of Lowe Syndrome, and/or to a cure for Lowe Syndrome.

YEAR PROGRAM STARTED: 1983

PURPOSE:
To improve the lives of persons with Lowe Syndrome and their families through fostering communication, providing education and supporting research so that individuals can attain their highest potential.

ELIGIBILITY:
Researchers of all types are invited to send applications, including but not limited to, universities, hospitals, and other nonprofit organizations with interest in research in areas specified by the Association.

FINANCIAL DATA:
Amount of support per award: Up to $25,000.

NO. MOST RECENT APPLICANTS: 1.

APPLICATION INFO:
Contact the Association.

Duration: One year.

Deadline: Receipt of research proposals: When RFPs are issued.

ADDRESS INQUIRIES TO:
Lisa Waldbaum, President
(See address above.)

LUPUS FOUNDATION OF AMERICA, INC. [2204]

2000 L Street, N.W., Suite 410
Washington, DC 20036
(202) 349-1155
(202) 212-6771
(800) 875-2562 (customer support)
E-mail: pcsupport@altum.com
Web Site: www.lupus.org/finzifellowships

FOUNDED: 1977

AREAS OF INTEREST:
Lupus research.

NAME(S) OF PROGRAMS:
- **Gina M. Finzi Memorial Student Summer Fellowship Program**

TYPE:
Summer Fellowship. The Gina M. Finzi Memorial Student Summer Fellowship Program proposes to foster an interest among students in the areas of basic, clinical, translational, epidemiological or behavioral research relevant to lupus under the sponsorship and supervision of an established, tenure-track Principal Investigator who directs a laboratory dedicated at least in part to the investigation of lupus at a U.S. or Canadian academic, medical or research institution.

YEAR PROGRAM STARTED: 1984

FINANCIAL DATA:
The Finzi Student Summer Fellowship provides financial support for a summer research project, opportunities for professional training, enrichment and mentorship, lifetime professional association with LFA network, and access to LFA professional resources.

Amount of support per award: $4,000.

APPLICATION INFO:
Applicants should check the Foundation web site in January for the next competition. Paper or e-mailed Letters of Intent or Proposals will not be accepted under any circumstances.

Duration: One summer.

Deadline: March annually.

ADDRESS INQUIRIES TO:
Anita Roach, M.S.
Research Program Manager
(See address above.)

JOSIAH MACY JR. FOUNDATION [2205]

44 East 64th Street
New York, NY 10065
(212) 486-2424
Fax: (212) 644-0765
E-mail: info@macyfoundation.org
Web Site: www.macyfoundation.org

FOUNDED: 1930

AREAS OF INTEREST:
Health care, health professions and medical education.

NAME(S) OF PROGRAMS:
- **Board Grants**
- **Macy Faculty Scholars**
- **President's Grants**

TYPE:
Conferences/seminars; Demonstration grants; Development grants; Matching gifts; Project/program grants. Major interest in education for careers in medicine or medical science. Special programs on preparation of minority groups for health professions and teamwork among and between health professions.

YEAR PROGRAM STARTED: 1930

PURPOSE:
To fund activities in medical and other health professional education.

LEGAL BASIS:
Private foundation.

ELIGIBILITY:
Applicants must be qualified not-for-profit institutions with appropriate interests. No grants are made directly to individuals, nor for building, annual fund appeals or medical research.

GEOG. RESTRICTIONS: United States.

FINANCIAL DATA:
Amount of support per award: Board Grants and Macy Faculty Scholars: Varies based on need; President's Grants: Up to $35,000, including overhead.

Total amount of support: Varies.

Matching fund requirements: Foundation matches gifts from full-time employees, directors and officers only to charitable organizations.

APPLICATION INFO:
Complete application information can be found on the Foundation web site.

Duration: Board Grants: May be multiyear. President's Grants: One year.

PUBLICATIONS:
Annual report; conference proceedings.

STAFF:
George E. Thibault, M.D., President
Peter Goodwin, MBA, Chief Operating Officer and Treasurer
Karen Butler, Assistant Treasurer
Eric Hoffman, Program Assistant
Yasmine R. Legendre, MPA, Program Associate
Stephen C. Schoenbaum, M.D., M.P.H., Special Advisor to the President

BOARD OF DIRECTORS:
William H. Wright, II, Chairman
George E. Thibault, M.D., President
David Blumenthal, M.D., M.P.P.
George Campbell, Jr., Ph.D.
Francisco G. Cigarroa, M.D.
Linda Cronenwett, Ph.D., R.N.
Linda P. Fried, M.D., M.P.H.
Terry Fulmer, Ph.D., R.N.
Henry P. Johnson, MBA
Howard K. Koh, M.D., M.P.H.
Paul G. Ramsey, M.D.
George Erik Rupp, Ph.D.
Steven M. Safyer, M.D.
Gregory H. Warner, MBA

ADDRESS INQUIRIES TO:
See e-mail address above.

MARCH OF DIMES FOUNDATION [2206]

1275 Mamaroneck Avenue
White Plains, NY 10605
(914) 997-4555
Fax: (914) 997-4560
E-mail: researchgrants@marchofdimes.org
Web Site: www.marchofdimes.org
researchgrants.marchofdimes.org (online application system)

FOUNDED: 1938

AREAS OF INTEREST:
Prevention of birth defects, premature birth and infant mortality.

NAME(S) OF PROGRAMS:
- **Basil O'Connor Starter Scholar Research Award**

TYPE:
Research grants. The March of Dimes defines a birth defect as any abnormality of structure or function, whether inherited or acquired in utero and presenting in infancy or early childhood. Deviations from reproductive health of women and men as an underlying basis of birth defects (i.e., preconceptional events, perinatal course and premature births) are appropriate subjects for research support.

The applicants' research interests should be in agreement with those of the mission of the March of Dimes: to improve the health of babies by preventing birth defects, premature birth and infant mortality.

Relevance is interpreted broadly to include fundamental cell biology (embryogenesis, cell lineage, differentiation), genetics and genomics, fundamental cellular and clinical pathogenesis of disorders of importance to mothers and infants, biomedical engineering and imaging, and social and behavioral aspects.

YEAR PROGRAM STARTED: 1973

PURPOSE:
To support young scientists just embarking on their independent research careers.

LEGAL BASIS:
Tax-exempt 501(c)(3) organization.

ELIGIBILITY:
Award is intended to be an initial independent grant to young investigators. Eligibility is thus restricted.

Each application should be accompanied by a Letter of Support from a Nominator. The Nominator should first vouch for a candidate's having an unrestricted faculty position and lab space. Ph.D. applicants should be no more than eight years past their degree. Successful applicants have traditionally had four to six years of postdoctoral training or other faculty-mentored work, but not more than eight years. For M.D. or M.D./Ph.D. applicants, the same four- to eight-year timeline applies, but begins upon completion of the last year of clinical training required for medical specialty board certification. Requests for exceptions (e.g., pregnancy and maternity leave) should be directed to the Senior Vice President for Research and Global Programs.

March of Dimes takes into account the purpose of the research program and plan submitted, qualifications, experience and abilities of the persons who are to supervise and participate in the proposed program and the facilities available.

FINANCIAL DATA:
The budget covers salary support for technical help and a portion of the Principal Investigator's salary, which may not exceed 10% of the total direct costs of the grant.

Amount of support per award: $75,000 per year for two years.

NO. MOST RECENT APPLICANTS: 94 for the year 2014.

NO. AWARDS: 28 for the year 2014.

REPRESENTATIVE AWARDS:
$150,000 to Gregory Charles Rogers, Ph.D., University of Arizona, Arizona Cancer Center, for "Cellular Control of Centriole Assembly: Elucidating the Mechanisms of Polo-like Kinase 4 Activity;" $150,000 to Craig Thomas Miller, Ph.D., University of California at Berkeley, for "Genetic Analysis of Craniofacial Patterning in Sticklebacks;" $150,000 to Yi Xing, Ph.D., University of Iowa, for "Genomic Signatures of Gene Expression and Alternative Splicing in Preterm Labor."

APPLICATION INFO:
The entire process must be completed online via the March of Dimes online application system.

The following information is required from the candidate:
(1) title of the proposed research project;
(2) candidate's name, academic appointment, mailing address, telephone and fax numbers and e-mail address;
(3) candidate's curriculum vitae in NIH format and;
(4) Letter of Intent (template provided) for the proposed research.

This Letter of Intent must include the following information in this order:
(1) title of proposal;
(2) hypothesis;
(3) preliminary data;
(4) précis of specific aims and methods of procedure;
(5) plan for evaluating results and;
(6) current financial support: list each current grant or contract for the conduct of this research; if there is no other support, state "NONE."
NOTE: Items 1-6 should not exceed three pages.

Information required from the Nominator: Deans, Chairpersons of Departments or Directors of Institutes/Centers may submit nominations for this award, addressed to the Senior Vice President for Research and Global Programs. Included should be the Nominator's name, academic appointment, mailing address, telephone and fax numbers and e-mail address. The Letter of Nomination should be submitted via the online application system. It should explicitly contain information about the candidate's faculty appointment, independence, and facilities available, including his or her laboratory space.

Letters of Intent will be reviewed initially by the Senior Vice President for Research and Global Programs for adherence to eligibility. Those eligible will be subjected to a preliminary selection process to identify a pool suitable for a committee to analyze critically. Those selected will then be invited to submit a full application. The scientific advisory committee will then conduct its review of the proposals.

Duration: Awards are approved for two years.

Deadline: Nominations: March 15. Proposals: By July 15. Reviewed in November for February 1 funding cycle.

PUBLICATIONS:
Program announcement and grants list.

NATIONAL OFFICERS:
Gary Dixon, Chairperson
Jennifer L. Howse, Ph.D., President
Edward R.B. McCabe, M.D., Ph.D., Senior Vice President and Chief Medical Officer
Lisa Bellsey, Esq., Executive Vice President/Chief Operating Officer
Deidra Merriwether, Treasurer
Monica Luechtefeld, M.D., Secretary
David Horne, Assistant Treasurer

ADDRESS INQUIRIES TO:
Susan Rauh, Research Program Coordinator
E-mail: srauh@marchofdimes.org

*PLEASE NOTE:
The Foundation does not accept applications dealing with infertility.

*SPECIAL STIPULATIONS:
Basil O'Connor applicants may not be recipients of a major grant (e.g., an R01, or other grant exceeding $200,000 a year) at the time of the application. If an application for such other grant is under review, eligibility for Basil O'Connor remains so long as it has not been awarded at the time of March of Dimes review. Applicants who have transition faculty-mentored awards (e.g., K99/R00) are welcome, if they have completed the mentored portion. If not, application should be deferred. Candidates may not simultaneously submit an application for any other March of Dimes research program. Those who have previously submitted an application to the March of Dimes are not eligible for a Basil O'Connor Award unless permission has been explicitly given; however, application for a regular research grant is welcomed.

MARCH OF DIMES FOUNDATION [2207]

1275 Mamaroneck Avenue
White Plains, NY 10605
(914) 997-4555
Fax: (914) 997-4560
E-mail: researchgrants@marchofdimes.org
Web Site: www.marchofdimes.org
researchgrants.marchofdimes.org (online application system)

FOUNDED: 1938

AREAS OF INTEREST:
Prevention of birth defects, premature birth and infant mortality.

NAME(S) OF PROGRAMS:

- **Research Grants Program**

TYPE:
Research grants. Grants for research in human birth defects.

The March of Dimes defines a birth defect as any abnormality of structure or function, whether inherited or acquired in utero and presenting in infancy or early childhood. Deviations from reproductive health of women and men as an underlying basis of birth defects (i.e., preconceptional events, perinatal course and premature births) are appropriate subjects for research support. The Foundation does not accept applications dealing with infertility.

YEAR PROGRAM STARTED: 1974

PURPOSE:
To support programs designed to gain new knowledge about the mechanisms that cause birth defects and to find ways of controlling or preventing them.

LEGAL BASIS:
Tax-exempt 501(c)(3) organization.

ELIGIBILITY:
In considering grant applications, the March of Dimes takes into account purpose of the research program and plan of study, qualifications, experience and abilities of the persons who are to supervise and participate in the proposed program, and facilities available.

Qualified scientists, with faculty appointments or equivalent, at universities, hospitals and research institutions (not-for-profit or for-profit) are invited to submit applications for research grants relevant to the Foundation's mission. This encompasses basic biological processes governing differentiation and development, genetics and genomics of these processes, clinical studies, reproductive health and environmental toxicology, and social and behavioral studies concerning cognitive and behavioral risks that affect outcomes of pregnancy, the perinatal period, and subsequent child development.

Applications will be directed to one of three committees whose respective foci are:
(1) cell lineage and differentiation, developmental biology;
(2) gene discovery, biological mechanisms, translational medicine and;
(3) social and behavioral sciences involving family units; this includes genes, toxicants, social determinants that adversely affect language or behavior, especially if involving premature infants or children with birth defects.

FINANCIAL DATA:
The budget covers salary support for technical help and a portion of the Principal Investigator's salary, which may not exceed 10% of the total direct costs of the grant.

Amount of support per award: Approximately $100,000 per year for a three-year grant.

NO. MOST RECENT APPLICANTS: 282 for the year 2014.

NO. AWARDS: 40 for the year 2014.

REPRESENTATIVE AWARDS:
$314,965 to Michael Fant, M.D., Ph.D., University of South Florida, College of Medicine, for "PLAC1 in Placental Development and Function;" $292,508 to Mark K. Abe, M.D., University of Chicago, for "Mitogen Activated Protein Kinase p38alpha in Lung Branching Morphogenesis;" $294,093 to Emily Feinberg, Sc.D., C.P.N.P., Boston University School of Public Health, for "Reducing Risk After An Adverse Pregnancy Outcome: Addressing Maternal Depression During Internatal Periods."

APPLICATION INFO:
Potential applicants should electronically submit the required administrative information and a Letter of Intent addressed to the Senior Vice President for Research and Global Programs via the Foundation's online application system. The Letter of Intent must include the following information in this order:
(1) title of proposal;
(2) hypothesis;
(3) preliminary data;
(4) précis of specific aims and methods of procedure;
(5) plan for evaluating results;
NOTE: Items 1-5 should not exceed three pages;
(6) current financial support: list each current grant or contract for the conduct of this research; if there is no other support, state "NONE" and;
(7) if the applicant is already a recipient of a current March of Dimes research grant or a Basil O'Connor Starter Scholar Research Award, include a summary of its progress (not to exceed one page).

The Letters of Intent will be evaluated by a scientific advisory committee, and full applications will be invited from those whom the committee recommends.

Duration: Grants are usually awarded for a three-year period, but may be made for a lesser time if it is appropriate.

Deadline: The online Letter of Intent process must be completed by April 30. The scientific advisory committee's selection will be transmitted no later than July 15. Complete application (from those selected): September 15. Applicants will be informed of the decisions regarding these applications no later than the following April 30. Funding initiated June 1.

PUBLICATIONS:
Program announcement; grants list.

ADDRESS INQUIRIES TO:
Geraldine Tamburro
Senior Research Program Coordinator
E-mail: gtamburro@marchofdimes.org

*PLEASE NOTE:
The Foundation does not accept applications dealing with infertility.

Please adhere to the instructions precisely. Any letter that does not follow this precise format will not be included in the review process.

MAYO CLINIC [2208]

Mayo School of Graduate Medical Education
200 First Street, S.W.
Rochester, MN 55905
(507) 538-6453
Fax: (507) 538-3267
E-mail: pathologyeducation@mayo.edu
Web Site: www.mayo.edu/msgme

AREAS OF INTEREST:
Surgical and medical pathology, including bone and soft tissue pathology, cardiovascular pathology, cytopathology, GI/liver pathology, breast pathology, and renal pathology.

NAME(S) OF PROGRAMS:

- **Surgical Pathology Fellowships**

TYPE:
Fellowships. Available subspecialty fellowships include bone and soft tissue pathology, breast pathology, cardiovascular pathology, cytopathology, gastrointestinal pathology, hematopathology, molecular genetic pathology, neuropathology, pulmonary pathology, renal pathology, special coagulation, and surgical pathology. Each fellowship will give ample opportunity to diagnose and work with a large diverse volume of tissue specimens. Fellows will assist Mayo's staff consultants with projects and will be encouraged to initiate and participate in clinical pathology and basic research studies for publication and

presentation at national meetings. Fellows will also develop and present studies at conferences and seminars and may assist in teaching pathology residents, medical students and fellows from other departments. Each specialty fellowship consists of a one-year program except neuropathology, which is a two-year appointment. Combined fellowships are also possible.

PURPOSE:
To promote the belief that physicians need to work together, teach and learn from others and conduct research to provide sustained, excellent patient care.

LEGAL BASIS:
Hospital.

ELIGIBILITY:
Applicants must have a medical degree with U.S. or Canadian specialty training in anatomic pathology for all specialty fellowships.

FINANCIAL DATA:
Fellows will be permitted 15 days each year for vacation. Fellows will also receive a stipend and benefits package including a comprehensive medical care plan, short-term disability insurance, voluntary family life insurance, dental assistance plan, professional liability coverage and excess personal liability insurance.

Amount of support per award: Varies depending on experience and fellowship.

NO. AWARDS: 1 in each specialty except for surgical pathology, which has 9 fellows.

APPLICATION INFO:
Applications are to be submitted through the Apply Yourself link:
app.applyyourself.com/?id=mayo-fp.
Completed online application must include:
(1) three letters of recommendation (one must be from applicant's current program director or supervisor);
(2) curriculum vitae;
(3) personal statement of professional goals;
(4) copy of graduate school and/or medical school diploma;
(5) dean's letter;
(6) official final transcripts;
(7) official test transcripts for all applicable examinations (USMLE, LMCC, COMLEX, NBOME, FMGEMS, FLEX, NBME);
(8) valid ECFMG certificate (if applicable) and;
(9) copy of completion certification from each of applicant's prior residency and/or fellowship training programs.

There is a $15 application fee.

If an applicant is considered for an appointment, they will be asked to visit Mayo Clinic Rochester for an interview with the program director and selected faculty. Interviews are conducted October and November of each year.

Duration: One year for specialties and two years for neuropathology.

Deadline: October 1 of the year preceding appointment.

BENJAMIN AND MARY SIDDONS MEASEY FOUNDATION [2209]

P.O. Box 258
Media, PA 19063
(610) 566-5800
Fax: (610) 566-8197

FOUNDED: 1958

AREAS OF INTEREST:
Medical education in Philadelphia area processed through Philadelphia medical schools only.

NAME(S) OF PROGRAMS:
- **Medical Education Grants**

TYPE:
Challenge/matching grants; Fellowships; Grants-in-aid.

YEAR PROGRAM STARTED: 1958

PURPOSE:
To advance medical education of physicians.

LEGAL BASIS:
1958 Trust Document.

ELIGIBILITY:
Grants are made through accredited medical schools in the immediate Philadelphia, PA area. Individual applications are not accepted by the Foundation; institutions only.

GEOG. RESTRICTIONS: Philadelphia, Pennsylvania area.

FINANCIAL DATA:
Amount of support per award: $7,500 to $500,000.

Total amount of support: $2,000,000 for the year 2014.

NO. MOST RECENT APPLICANTS: 10.

APPLICATION INFO:
Application is by letter. Organizations must provide 501(c)(3) tax-exempt information.

Duration: One year. Nonrenewable.

Deadline: Two weeks prior to quarterly meetings held in March, June, September and December.

IRS I.D.: 23-6298781

STAFF:
James C. Brennan, Esq., Manager
M.S. Donaldson, Esq., Secretary

ADDRESS INQUIRIES TO:
James C. Brennan, Esq., Manager and Counsel
(See address above.)

*SPECIAL STIPULATIONS:
No applications to Foundation directly.

MEDICAL LIBRARY ASSOCIATION

65 East Wacker Place
Suite 1900
Chicago, IL 60601-7246
(312) 419-9094
Fax: (312) 419-8950
E-mail: awards@mlahq.org
Web Site: www.mlanet.org

TYPE:
Fellowships; Scholarships. Awarded for study and doctoral work in health sciences librarianship.

Thomson Reuters/MLA Doctoral Fellowship is awarded biennially (in even-numbered years). It was established by the Institute for Scientific Information (ISI) and is administered by the MLA.

See entry 718 for full listing.

NATIONAL ALOPECIA AREATA FOUNDATION

65 Mitchell Boulevard
San Rafael, CA 94903
(415) 472-3780
Fax: (415) 480-1800
E-mail: info@naaf.org
Web Site: www.naaf.org

TYPE:
Research grants.

See entry 2089 for full listing.

NATIONAL BRAIN TUMOR SOCIETY [2210]

55 Chapel Street
Suite 200
Newton, MA 02458
(617) 924-9997
Fax: (617) 924-9998
E-mail: research@braintumor.org
Web Site: www.braintumor.org

FOUNDED: 1981

AREAS OF INTEREST:
Brain tumor research and public policy.

CONSULTING OR VOLUNTEER SERVICES:
Research, advocacy/public policy, and patient engagement.

NAME(S) OF PROGRAMS:
- **Defeat GBM Research Collaborative**
- **Project Impact: Defeat Pediatric Brain Tumors**

TYPE:
Awards/prizes; Project/program grants; Research grants.

YEAR PROGRAM STARTED: 1981

PURPOSE:
To provide information and support for brain tumor patients, family members, and health care professionals; to support innovative research into better treatment options and a cure for brain tumors.

ELIGIBILITY:
For clinical grants, applicants must be qualified research investigators with a Ph.D. or higher level practicing neuroscience at U.S. or international medical centers.

Grant monies cannot be used for general administrative costs, debt reduction, or indirect costs of the project.

APPLICATION INFO:
Contact the Society for information and guidelines.

Current grants are tied to long-term, existing research initiatives. Open RFAs are limited, but do occur.

IRS I.D.: 94-2876985

ADDRESS INQUIRIES TO:
Ann Kingston, Director of Research
(See address above.)

NATIONAL HEART, LUNG AND BLOOD INSTITUTE (NHLBI)

National Institutes of Health
Grants Operations Branch, Room 7160
6701 Rockledge Drive, MSC 7926
Bethesda, MD 20892-7926
(301) 435-0166
Fax: (301) 451-5462
E-mail: lombardr@nhlbi.nih.gov
Web Site: www.nhlbi.nih.gov/research/funding

TYPE:
Conferences/seminars; Fellowships; Project/program grants; Research grants; Training grants; Loan forgiveness programs. Career awards and other grant mechanisms to foster research on heart, vascular and lung diseases, and to develop scientists in these areas. Also, small business grants. Loan forgiveness programs are for research.

See entry 2317 for full listing.

THE NATIONAL HEMOPHILIA FOUNDATION [2211]

7 Penn Plaza
370 Seventh Avenue, Suite 1204
New York, NY 10001
(212) 328-3767
Fax: (212) 328-3766
E-mail: awang@hemophilia.org
Web Site: www.hemophilia.org

FOUNDED: 1948

AREAS OF INTEREST:
Biochemistry, genetics, hematology, microbiology, orthopedics, psychiatry and other disciplines related to hemophilia and other bleeding disorders.

NAME(S) OF PROGRAMS:
- **Judith Graham Pool Postdoctoral Research Fellowships in Bleeding Disorders**

TYPE:
Development grants; Fellowships; Research grants. Support for research in clinical and/or basic sciences in areas relating to problems in hemophilia and other bleeding disorders.

Judith Graham Pool Postdoctoral Research Fellowships are designed to support research studies of high scientific merit and relevance to bleeding disorders. They are awarded through professional and graduate schools, or research institutions.

YEAR PROGRAM STARTED: 1972

PURPOSE:
To encourage and support hemophilia-related and other bleeding disorders research.

LEGAL BASIS:
Voluntary, nonprofit health organization.

ELIGIBILITY:
Applicants must have completed doctoral training and must enter the fellowship program from a doctoral, postdoctoral, internship or residency training program.

Individuals with more than six years of experience since completing doctoral training are not eligible to apply. Established investigators or faculty members are also not eligible.

GEOG. RESTRICTIONS: United States.

FINANCIAL DATA:
Amount of support per award: $42,000 per year.

Total amount of support: Varies.

NO. AWARDS: Varies depending on award.

APPLICATION INFO:
Interested candidates must submit a Letter of Intent. This should be a brief letter identifying the researcher, their mentor, institution, and a description of the proposed research project. Letters of Intent should include an NIH-style curriculum vitae or biosketch for both candidate and mentor. After review, candidates may be invited to submit a full application.

Duration: Up to two years. Continuation for second year is based upon progress report and continuation application.

STAFF:
Angelina Wang, Director of Research and Medical Information

ADDRESS INQUIRIES TO:
Angelina Wang, Director of Research and Medical Information
(See address above.)

NATIONAL INSTITUTE OF ENVIRONMENTAL HEALTH SCIENCES

Division of Extramural Research and Training
MD K3-05
111 T.W. Alexander Drive
Research Triangle Park, NC 27709
(919) 541-3289
Fax: (919) 541-2843
E-mail: mastin@niehs.nih.gov
Web Site: www.niehs.nih.gov

TYPE:
Conferences/seminars; Demonstration grants; Development grants; Fellowships; Project/program grants; Research grants; Training grants. NIEHS pursues its mission by supporting basic and applied research on the consequences of the exposure of humans to potentially toxic or harmful agents in the environment.

Research of interest encompasses studies that relate to the biological effects of environmental chemicals and physical factors including such agents as hazardous gases, suspended particles, aerosols, industrial by-products and intermediates, heavy metals, trace elements, food additives, adulterants and pesticides. Physical factors include noise, light, heat, microwaves and other forms of nonionizing radiation.

Research Training Programs support individuals at both the predoctoral and postdoctoral levels in the areas of environmental toxicology, environmental pathology, environmental mutagenesis and environmental epidemiology.

See entry 2121 for full listing.

NATIONAL INSTITUTE OF GENERAL MEDICAL SCIENCES [2212]

National Institutes of Health
45 Center Drive, MSC 6200
Bethesda, MD 20892-6200
(301) 496-7301
Fax: (301) 402-0224
E-mail: info@nigms.nih.gov
Web Site: www.nigms.nih.gov

FOUNDED: 1962

AREAS OF INTEREST:
Basic biomedical research.

NAME(S) OF PROGRAMS:
- **Center for Research Capacity Building**
- **Division of Biomedical Technology, Bioinformatics, and Computational Biology**
- **Division of Cell Biology and Biophysics**
- **Division of Genetics and Developmental Biology**
- **Division of Pharmacology, Physiology, and Biological Chemistry**
- **Division of Training, Workforce Development, and Diversity**

TYPE:
Fellowships; Research grants; Training grants; Research contracts. The National Institute of General Medical Sciences (NIGMS) supports basic research that increases understanding of biological processes and lays the foundation for advances in disease diagnosis, treatment and prevention. NIGMS-funded scientists investigate how living systems work at a range of levels, from molecules and cells to tissues, whole organisms and populations. The Institute also supports research in certain clinical areas, primarily those that affect multiple organ systems. To assure the vitality and continued productivity of research enterprise, NIGMS provides leadership in training the next generation of scientists, in enhancing the diversity of scientific workforce, and in developing research capacities throughout the country.

YEAR PROGRAM STARTED: 1962

PURPOSE:
To support basic biomedical research that lays the foundation for advances in disease diagnosis, treatment, and prevention; to help provide the most critical element of good research: well-prepared scientists.

LEGAL BASIS:
Part of a government agency under the PHS Act, various sections, and various public laws.

ELIGIBILITY:
For Research Grants, applicants must be academic institutions, teaching hospitals, public agencies, nonprofit organizations and for-profit corporations.

National Research Service Awards for the above areas may be made to individuals for postdoctoral training or nonprofit institutions for the training of individuals at the predoctoral and postdoctoral level.

For Small Business Innovative Research Program, applicants must be qualified small businesses to stimulate technological innovation in areas of interest to the Institute.

FINANCIAL DATA:
Total amount of support: $2.5 billion for fiscal year 2016.

NO. AWARDS: 4,768 NIGMS-funded research grants for fiscal year 2016.

APPLICATION INFO:
The appropriate application forms and instructions may be obtained from and submitted to:
The Division of Extramural Outreach and Information Resources
Office of Extramural Research
National Institutes of Health, Room 6207
6701 Rockledge Drive, MSC 7910
Bethesda, MD 20892-7910
Tel: (301) 435-0714
E-mail: grantsinfo@nih.gov.

Duration: Varies.

Deadline: Varies by program.

STAFF:
Ann Dieffenbach, Chief, Office of Communications and Public Liaison

ADDRESS INQUIRIES TO:
Office of Communications and Public Liaison
(See address above.)

NATIONAL INSTITUTE OF GENERAL MEDICAL SCIENCES [2213]

Center for Research Capacity Building
45 Center Drive, Room 2AS-43
Bethesda, MD 20892
(301) 594-3900
Fax: (301) 480-2753
E-mail: zlotnikh@nigms.nih.gov
Web Site: www.nigms.nih.gov

FOUNDED: 1972

NAME(S) OF PROGRAMS:

- **Minority Biomedical Research Support**
- **Support of Competitive Research Awards**

TYPE:
Development grants; Research grants. Grants to assist eligible institutions to strengthen the institutions' biomedical research capabilities and provide opportunities to students to engage in biomedical or behavioral research and other activities in preparation for Ph.D. training in these areas.

YEAR PROGRAM STARTED: 1972

PURPOSE:
To increase the number of faculty, students, and investigators who are members of groups underrepresented in the biomedical and behavioral sciences who are engaged in research in these fields.

LEGAL BASIS:
Public Health Service Act of 1944 as amended, Section 301(c); U.S.C. 241.d.

ELIGIBILITY:
Applicant must be located in a state, the District of Columbia or a U.S. territory, and be a public or private university, four-year college or other institution offering undergraduate, graduate or health professional degrees with more than 50% minority enrollment, a public or private nonprofit four-year college or other institution offering undergraduate, graduate or health professional degrees, with a significant enrollment (but not necessarily more than 50%) derived from ethnic minorities, if the secretary of DHHS determines that the institution is committed to encouragement and assistance to ethnic minority faculty, students and investigators, or an Indian tribe with a recognized governing body which performs substantial government functions or an Alaska Regional Corporation (ARC) as defined in the Alaska Native Claims Settlement Act and located in a state, the District of Columbia, Puerto Rico, the Virgin Islands, the Canal Zone, Guam, American Samoa or the Trust Territory of the Pacific Islands.

GEOG. RESTRICTIONS: United States and its territories.

FINANCIAL DATA:
Amount of support per award: $75,000 to $250,000 direct costs.

CO-OP FUNDING PROGRAMS: Co-funding with other NIH Institutes.

APPLICATION INFO:
Detailed information is available from the Branch Chief.

Duration: Typically three to four years.

ADDRESS INQUIRIES TO:
Dr. Hinda Zlotnik, Program Director
(See address above.)

NATIONAL INSTITUTE OF GENERAL MEDICAL SCIENCES [2214]

Natcher Building, MSC 6200
45 Center Drive, 2AS-13C
Bethesda, MD 20892-6200
(301) 594-0828
Fax: (301) 480-2004
E-mail: preuschp@nigms.nih.gov
Web Site: www.nigms.nih.gov

AREAS OF INTEREST:
Basic biomedical research.

NAME(S) OF PROGRAMS:

- **Medical Scientist Training Program**

TYPE:
Grants-in-aid; Training grants. The goal of this program is to prepare its graduates to function independently in both clinical practice and scientific research. MSTP has over 40 participating programs.

YEAR PROGRAM STARTED: 1964

PURPOSE:
To support research training leading to the combined M.D.-Ph.D. degree.

ELIGIBILITY:
Applicants must be U.S. domestic institutions.

GEOG. RESTRICTIONS: United States.

FINANCIAL DATA:
Many institutions supplement the basic stipend provided by the MSTP grant. Trainees incur no payback obligation.

Amount of support per award: $23,376 stipend, plus tuition allowance of up to $21,000, travel allowance of $300, and $4,200 for equipment, supplies and health care for the year 2016.

Total amount of support: Varies.

NO. AWARDS: 978 for the year 2015.

APPLICATION INFO:
Individuals who wish to enter the program should contact the program office at the participating institution(s) of their choice directly for curriculum information and admission requirements. Interested institutions should contact the NIGMS program director. Institutions should include the standard Form 424.

Applications guidelines are available online.

Duration: Maximum six years, although the course of study for the combined degree may take longer. Continued support conditional upon annual review and availability of funds to the institution.

Deadline: January 25, May 25 and September 25. Grant awarded only once per year.

NATIONAL INSTITUTES OF HEALTH [2215]

Office of Extramural Research (OER)
9000 Rockville Pike
Bethesda, MD 20892
(301) 435-0714
TTY: (301) 451-5936
E-mail: grantsinfo@nih.gov
Web Site: grants.nih.gov/funding/index.htm

FOUNDED: 1930

AREAS OF INTEREST:
Biomedical research and improvement of human health.

NAME(S) OF PROGRAMS:

- **Ruth L. Kirschstein National Research Service Awards (NRSA) for Individual Postdoctoral Fellows (Parent F32)**

TYPE:
Fellowships; Research grants; Training grants. This individual postdoctoral research training fellowship is to enhance training of promising postdoctoral candidates who have the potential to become productive, independent investigators in scientific health-related research fields relevant to the missions of the participating NIH Institutes and Centers.

PURPOSE:
To help ensure that a diverse pool of highly trained scientists is available in appropriate scientific disciplines to address the nation's biomedical, behavioral and clinical research needs.

ELIGIBILITY:
Eligible organizations: Higher education institutions, nonprofits other than institutions of higher education, for-profit organizations, governments and other (non-U.S.) entities.

Eligible Individuals: Applicant - Project Director/Principal Investigator (PD/PI) - must be a citizen or a permanent resident of the U.S. and must have received a research doctoral degree from an accredited domestic or foreign institution.

Before the award can be activated, the candidate must have received a Ph.D., M.D., D.O., D.C., D.D.S., D.V.M., O.D., D.P.M., Sc.D., Eng.D., Dr.P.H., DNSc., N.D., Pharm.D., D.S.W., Psy.D., or equivalent doctoral degree from an accredited domestic or foreign institution.

GEOG. RESTRICTIONS: United States and its territories.

FINANCIAL DATA:
Award budgets are composed of stipends, tuition and fees, and institutional allowance. NIH does not separately reimburse indirect costs (also known as Facilities and Administrative - or F and A - Costs) for fellowships. Costs for administering fellowships are part of institutional allowance.

NO. AWARDS: Varies.

APPLICATION INFO:
Guidelines and detailed information are available on the NIH web site. Applicants are encouraged to apply early to allow adequate time to make any corrections to errors found in the application during the submission process by the due date. Paper applications will not be accepted.

Applicants are strongly urged to check the NIH web site for the most up-to-date information.

Duration: Varies; up to three years for individuals.

*SPECIAL STIPULATIONS:
Conformance to all requirements (both in the Application Guide and the Funding Opportunity Announcement (FOA)) is required and strictly enforced.

At the time of award, individuals are required to pursue their research training on a full-time basis, normally defined as 40 hours per week or as specified by the sponsoring institution in accordance with its own policies.

NATIONAL INSTITUTES OF HEALTH [2216]

Office of Extramural Research (OER)
9000 Rockville Pike
Bethesda, MD 20892
(301) 435-0714
TTY: (301) 451-5936
E-mail: grantsinfo@nih.gov
Web Site: grants.nih.gov/funding/index.htm

FOUNDED: 1887

AREAS OF INTEREST:
Biomedical and behavioral research and improvement of human health.

NAME(S) OF PROGRAMS:

- **Mentored Clinical Scientist Research Career Development Award (Parent K08)**

TYPE:
Research grants. This program prepares qualified individuals for careers that have a significant impact on the health-related research needs of the nation.

PURPOSE:
To help ensure that a diverse pool of highly trained scientists are available in appropriate scientific disciplines to address the nation's biomedical, behavioral and clinical research needs.

LEGAL BASIS:
Public Health Service Act, Section 301(c).

ELIGIBILITY:
Eligible organizations include higher education institutions, nonprofits other than institutions of higher education, for-profit organizations, different domestic levels of government, Native American tribal organizations and faith-based or community-based organizations.

Eligible individuals (program director/principal investigator) must be a citizen or a noncitizen national of the U.S. or have been lawfully admitted for permanent residence. They must have a clinical doctoral degree (e.g., M.D., D.D.S., D.M.D., D.O., D.C., O.D., N.D., D.V.M., Pharm.D., or, in certain clinical disciplines, Ph.D.). The K08 award may be used by candidates with different levels of prior research training and at different stages in their mentored career development.

GEOG. RESTRICTIONS: United States.

NO. AWARDS: Varies.

APPLICATION INFO:
Applications must be submitted electronically. Paper applications will not be accepted.

Applicants are strongly urged to check the NIH web site for the most up-to-date information.

Duration: Up to five years.

NATIONAL INSTITUTES OF HEALTH [2217]

Office of Extramural Research (OER)
9000 Rockville Pike
Bethesda, MD 20892
(301) 435-0714
TTY: (301) 451-5936
E-mail: grantsinfo@nih.gov
Web Site: grants.nih.gov/funding/index.htm

FOUNDED: 1930

AREAS OF INTEREST:
Biomedical research and improvement of human health.

NAME(S) OF PROGRAMS:

- **Ruth L. Kirschstein National Research Service Awards (NRSA) for Individual Senior Fellows (Parent F33)**

TYPE:
Fellowships. This program awards senior individual research training fellowships to experienced scientists who wish to make major changes in the direction of their research careers or who wish to broaden their scientific background by acquiring new research capabilities as independent investigators in research fields relevant to the missions of the participating NIH Institutes and Centers.

PURPOSE:
To help ensure that a diverse pool of highly trained scientists is available in appropriate scientific disciplines to address the nation's biomedical, behavioral and clinical research needs.

LEGAL BASIS:
An agency of the U.S. Public Health Service.

ELIGIBILITY:
Eligible organizations: Higher education institutions, nonprofits other than institutions of higher education, for-profit organizations, governments and other (non-U.S.) entities.

Eligible Individuals: The Project Director/Principal Investigator must have had at least seven subsequent years of relevant research or professional experience and will have established an independent research career. By the time of the award, that individual must be a citizen or permanent resident of the U.S.

GEOG. RESTRICTIONS: United States.

FINANCIAL DATA:
Award budgets are composed of stipends, tuition and fees, and institutional allowance. NIH does not separately reimburse indirect costs (also known as Facilities and Administrative - or F and A - Costs) for fellowships. Costs for administering fellowships are part of institutional allowance.

NO. AWARDS: Varies.

APPLICATION INFO:
Guidelines and detailed information are available on the NIH web site. Applicants are encouraged to apply early to allow adequate time to make any corrections to errors found in the application during the submission process by the due date. Paper applications will not be accepted.

Applicants are strongly urged to check the NIH web site for the most up-to-date information.

Duration: Typically, up to two years.

*SPECIAL STIPULATIONS:
Conformance to all requirements (both in the Application Guide and the Funding Opportunity Announcement (FOA)) is required and strictly enforced.

At the time of award, individuals are required to pursue their research training on a full-time basis, normally defined as 40 hours per week or as specified by the sponsoring institution in accordance with its own policies.

NATIONAL INSTITUTES OF HEALTH [2218]

Office of Research Infrastructure Programs
6701 Democracy Boulevard
Room 958, Building One
Bethesda, MD 20892
(301) 435-0772
Fax: (301) 480-3659
E-mail: sig@mail.nih.gov
Web Site: dpcpsi.nih.gov/orip/diic/shared_instrumentation

FOUNDED: 1930

AREAS OF INTEREST:
Biomedical research and improvement of human health.

NAME(S) OF PROGRAMS:

- **Shared Instrumentation Grant Program**

TYPE:
Project/program grants.

YEAR PROGRAM STARTED: 1982

PURPOSE:
To provide research institutions the opportunity to obtain expensive (over $50,000 per item) commercially available instruments to be shared by groups of NIH-funded investigators.

LEGAL BASIS:
An agency of the U.S. Public Health Service.

ELIGIBILITY:
Federal agencies, foreign institutions and for-profit institutions are not eligible.

GEOG. RESTRICTIONS: United States.

FINANCIAL DATA:
Amount of support per award: Maximum award is $600,000.

Total amount of support: $42,000,000 for fiscal year 2015.

NO. AWARDS: Varies.

APPLICATION INFO:
Contact the National Institutes of Health.

Duration: One year. No renewals.

Deadline: Mid- to late May. Check NIH guide.

ADDRESS INQUIRIES TO:
Shared Instrumentation Grant Program
(See address above.)

NATIONAL INSTITUTES OF HEALTH [2219]

9000 Rockville Pike
Bethesda, MD 20892
(301) 435-0714
E-mail: grantsinfo@od.nih.gov
Web Site: grants.nih.gov/funding/index.htm

NAME(S) OF PROGRAMS:

- **Research Project Grant Program (R01)**

TYPE:
Project/program grants; Research grants. Research Project Grant (R01) is an award made to support a discrete, specified, circumscribed project to be performed by the named investigator(s) in an area representing the investigator's specific interest and competencies, based on the mission of the NIH. The Research Project Grant (R01) is the original and historically oldest grant mechanism used by NIH. The R01 provides support for health-related research and development based on the mission of the NIH.

LEGAL BASIS:
Government agency.

FINANCIAL DATA:
The following are allowable costs:
(1) salary and fringe benefits for Principal Investigator, key personnel and other essential personnel;
(2) equipment and supplies;
(3) consultant costs;
(4) alterations and renovations;
(5) publications and miscellaneous costs;
(6) contract services;
(7) consortium costs;
(8) facilities and administrative costs (indirect costs) and;
(9) travel expenses.

APPLICATION INFO:
Applicants may find it helpful to seek advice from an experienced investigator and to contact the Institute or Center most likely to fund their application.

Applicants are strongly urged to check the NIH web site for the most up-to-date information.

Duration: Investigator-initiated grants: Normally one to five years.

Deadline: Varies.

NATIONAL INSTITUTES OF HEALTH [2220]

9000 Rockville Pike
Bethesda, MD 20892
(301) 435-0714 (grants information)
(800) 518-4726 (customer support)
E-mail: GrantsInfo@od.nih.gov (grants information)
support@grants.gov (customer support)
Web Site: grants.nih.gov/grants/guide

NAME(S) OF PROGRAMS:
- **Small Research Grant Program (Parent R03)**

TYPE:
Research grants. This program supports different types of projects including pilot and feasibility studies; secondary analysis of existing data; small, self-contained research projects; development of research methodology; and development of new research technology.

PURPOSE:
To support small research projects that can be carried out in a short period of time with limited resources.

ELIGIBILITY:
The Small Research Grant Program supports discrete, well-defined projects that realistically can be completed in two years and that require limited levels of funding.

Higher education institutions, other nonprofits, for-profit organizations, governments, other institutions, and foreign institutions are eligible to apply.

Any individual(s) with the skills, knowledge and resources necessary to carry out the proposed research as the Program Director(s)/Principal Investigator(s) (PD(s)/PI(s)) is invited to work with his or her organization to develop an application for support. Individuals from underrepresented racial and ethnic groups as well as individuals with disabilities are always encouraged to apply for NIH support.

FINANCIAL DATA:
This grant support mechanism provides money, property or both to an eligible entity to carry out an approved project or activity.

Amount of support per award: Up to $50,000 in direct costs per year.

NO. AWARDS: Varies depending on NIH appropriations and the submission of a sufficient number of meritorious applications.

APPLICATION INFO:
Deadline: Up to two years.

ADDRESS INQUIRIES TO:
See phone numbers or e-mail addresses above.

NATIONAL MEDICAL FELLOWSHIPS, INC. [2221]

347 Fifth Avenue, Suite 510
New York, NY 10016
(212) 483-8880
Fax: (212) 483-8897
E-mail: scholarships@nmfonline.org
Web Site: www.nmfonline.org

FOUNDED: 1946

AREAS OF INTEREST:
Minority medical students and the health care of low-income and minority communities.

NAME(S) OF PROGRAMS:
- **Aetna Foundation/NMF Healthcare Leadership Program**
- **Hugh J. Andersen Scholarship**
- **California Community Service-Learning Program**
- **Emergency Scholarship Fund**
- **GE-NMF Primary Care Leadership Program (PCLP)**
- **Monash/Scott Medical Student Scholarship Program**
- **United Health Foundation/Diverse Medical Scholars Program**

TYPE:
Awards/prizes; Fellowships; Project/program grants; Research grants; Scholarships. Service learning. NMF supports underrepresented minority medical students as they matriculate. Awards are available to students M1 to M4/5. In addition to financial support, NMF provides opportunities for aspiring doctors to take their learning into the community.

YEAR PROGRAM STARTED: 1946

PURPOSE:
To improve the health of low-income and minority communities by increasing the number of minority physicians and addressing the special needs of these communities.

LEGAL BASIS:
Nonprofit corporation.

ELIGIBILITY:
Varies by program.

FINANCIAL DATA:
Amount of support per award: Varies.

Total amount of support: Varies.

NO. MOST RECENT APPLICANTS: Varies.

NO. AWARDS: Varies.

APPLICATION INFO:
Guidelines and official application materials are available on the organization web site.

Duration: Varies by program.

Deadline: Varies by program.

BOARD OF DIRECTORS:
Daniel T. McGowan, Chairman
Paula Madison, Vice Chairman
Ester R. Dyer, M.L.S., D.L.S., President and Chief Executive Officer
Stephen N. Keith, M.D., M.S.P.H., Treasurer and Secretary

ADDRESS INQUIRIES TO:
Franca Gaudio, Chief Operating Officer
Thaina Mondefir, Program Assistant or
Tamekia Jackson, Program Consultant
(See address above.)

THE NATIONAL ORGANIZATION FOR RARE DISORDERS (NORD) [2222]

55 Kenosia Avenue
Danbury, CT 06810
(203) 744-0100
Fax: (203) 798-2291
E-mail: research@rarediseases.org
Web Site: www.rarediseases.org

FOUNDED: 1983

AREAS OF INTEREST:
Rare "orphan" disease.

NAME(S) OF PROGRAMS:
- **Research Grant Program**

TYPE:
Research grants; Seed money grants. The Research Grant Program provides seed money grants to academic scientists for translational or clinical studies related to development of potential new diagnostics or treatments for rare disease.

PURPOSE:
To promote the diagnosis, treatment and cure of rare disorders through programs of education, advocacy, service and research.

ELIGIBILITY:
Must be an academic scientist. IRB approval and a copy of informed consent is necessary if the study involves human, and NIH Recombinant DNA Advisory Committee review or waiver of review if human gene therapy is involved.

FINANCIAL DATA:
Overhead and indirect costs are not awarded.

Amount of support per award: Minimum $33,500.

Total amount of support: Varies.

NO. MOST RECENT APPLICANTS: Approximately 25.

NO. AWARDS: 5 to 10.

APPLICATION INFO:
Submit a letter of intent, curriculum vitae, one-page abstract, and a brief budget. Full proposals by invitation only. Requests for proposals announcements typically posted online.

Duration: One to two years.

Deadline: April/May for preliminary proposals; July/August for full proposals from finalists.

ADDRESS INQUIRIES TO:
Research Program Administrator
(See address above.)

*SPECIAL STIPULATIONS:
Reports and communication must be written in English and adhere to the most recent guidelines set forth by the National Institutes of Health.

NATIONAL SOCIETY DAUGHTERS OF THE AMERICAN REVOLUTION [2223]

1776 D Street, N.W.
Washington, DC 20006-5303
(202) 879-3263
Fax: (202) 879-3348
E-mail: scholarships@dar.org
Web Site: www.dar.org

FOUNDED: 1895

AREAS OF INTEREST:
Medicine and psychiatric nursing.

NAME(S) OF PROGRAMS:
- **Irene and Daisy MacGregor Memorial Scholarship**

TYPE:
Scholarships.

YEAR PROGRAM STARTED: 1991

PURPOSE:
To provide ways and means to aid students in attaining higher education.

LEGAL BASIS:
Incorporated historical society.

ELIGIBILITY:
Scholarships are awarded without regard to race, religion, sex or national origin. All four-year scholarships must be for consecutive years and are renewable only upon review and approval of annual transcript. Candidates must be U.S. citizens and must attend or plan to attend an accredited college or university in the U.S. No affiliation or relationship to DAR is required for qualification, but candidate must be sponsored by a local DAR Chapter. Awards are judged on the basis of academic excellence, commitment to field of study, as required, and financial need.

The MacGregor Memorial Scholarship is awarded to students of high scholastic standing and character who have been accepted into or are pursuing an approved course of study to become a medical doctor (not pre-med) at an approved, accredited medical school.

This MacGregor Memorial Scholarship is also available to students who have been accepted into or who are pursuing an approved course of study in the field of psychiatric nursing, graduate level, at medical schools, colleges or universities. There is a preference to females "if equally qualified."

GEOG. RESTRICTIONS: United States.

FINANCIAL DATA:
Amount of support per award: $5,000 annually.

APPLICATION INFO:
Application information is available online. All scholarship applicants are required to have a letter of sponsorship from a chapter. Individuals interested in obtaining a letter of sponsorship from a local chapter are encouraged to contact the DAR State Chairman.

Duration: Up to four consecutive years possible, depending upon availability of funds. Annual transcript review required for renewal and award.

Deadline: February 15.

PUBLICATIONS:
American Spirit, magazine.

ADDRESS INQUIRIES TO:
Office of the Reporter General
DAR Scholarship Committee
(See address above.)

NORTH AMERICAN SPINE SOCIETY (NASS) [2224]

8320 St. Moritz Drive
Spring Grove, IL 60081
(630) 230-3691
Fax: (630) 230-3791
E-mail: kjames@spine.org
Web Site: www.spine.org

FOUNDED: 1985

AREAS OF INTEREST:
Disorders and functions of the human spine.

NAME(S) OF PROGRAMS:
- **Clinical Traveling Fellowship**
- **Research Grant**
- **Research Traveling Fellowship**
- **Young Investigator Grants**

TYPE:
Awards/prizes; Fellowships; Research grants. Clinical Traveling Fellowship: At least one month to be spent in three to five different medical centers studying spine techniques.

Research Traveling Fellowship: At least five months at one medical center, other than the one in which the applicants currently practice. This Fellowship primarily covers the cost of travel and housing.

Research Grant: This grant is for investigative, basic, clinical and translational research on the spine.

Young Investigator Grant: This grant is for projects in basic science, clinical or translational.

YEAR PROGRAM STARTED: 1989

PURPOSE:
To advance quality spine care through education, research and advocacy; to encourage and support basic and clinical science that is performed with integrity and with a goal towards improving quality spine care for patients and understanding underlying disorders.

ELIGIBILITY:
Qualified investigators are eligible to apply.

FINANCIAL DATA:
Amount of support per award: $50,000.

Total amount of support: Varies.

NO. MOST RECENT APPLICANTS: 158.

NO. AWARDS: Fellowships: 2; Research Grants: 3.

APPLICATION INFO:
Contact the Organization for application procedures. Budget restrictions are available when requesting an application.

Duration: Two years.

Deadline: Letters of Proposals for Grants: First week in February. Invited Grants and Fellowships: First week in May.

ADDRESS INQUIRIES TO:
Karen James, Manager of Research and Quality Improvement
(See address above.)

ORTHOPAEDIC RESEARCH AND EDUCATION FOUNDATION [2225]

9400 West Higgins Road
Suite 215
Rosemont, IL 60018-4975
(847) 698-9980
Fax: (847) 698-7806
E-mail: barnes@oref.org
marino@oref.org
Web Site: www.oref.org

FOUNDED: 1955

AREAS OF INTEREST:
Orthopaedic research.

NAME(S) OF PROGRAMS:
- **Career Development Grants**

TYPE:
Research grants. Grants for scientific research in orthopaedic surgery.

YEAR PROGRAM STARTED: 1984

PURPOSE:
To encourage a commitment to scientific research in orthopaedic surgery.

LEGAL BASIS:
501(c)(3) special-interest foundation.

ELIGIBILITY:
Candidates must have completed residency in orthopaedic surgery and have demonstrated a sustained interest in research, as well as excellence in clinical training. Letters of nomination and support must offer convincing evidence of the candidate's potential to develop as an investigator.

GEOG. RESTRICTIONS: United States.

FINANCIAL DATA:
Amount of support per award: Up to $75,000 per year. Budget may include salary support.

Total amount of support: Varies.

APPLICATION INFO:
Contact the Foundation.

Duration: Up to three years, conditional upon annual review.

Deadline: September. Announcement the following March.

PUBLICATIONS:
Annual report; application guidelines.

ADDRESS INQUIRIES TO:
Mary Marino, Grants Manager
(See address above.)

*SPECIAL STIPULATIONS:
Applicant must be working in the U.S. only.

ORTHOPAEDIC RESEARCH AND EDUCATION FOUNDATION [2226]

9400 West Higgins Road
Suite 215
Rosemont, IL 60018-4975
(847) 698-9980
Fax: (847) 698-7806
E-mail: barnes@oref.org
Web Site: www.oref.org

FOUNDED: 1955

AREAS OF INTEREST:
Orthopaedic surgery research.

NAME(S) OF PROGRAMS:
- **Resident Clinician Scientist Training Grant**

TYPE:
Research grants. Grants to prepare residents for a career with research as a major component.

YEAR PROGRAM STARTED: 1961

PURPOSE:
To encourage the research interests and meritorious projects of residents and fellows in approved orthopaedic programs.

LEGAL BASIS:
501(c)(3) special-interest foundation.

ELIGIBILITY:
Candidates must be residents or fellows in approved orthopaedic programs.

GEOG. RESTRICTIONS: United States.

FINANCIAL DATA:
Grants provide funds for supplies and expenses, but not for resident salary or travel.

Amount of support per award: $20,000.

Total amount of support: Varies.

APPLICATION INFO:
Applications are available on the web site from May until September.

Duration: One year.

Deadline: Mid-September. Announcement the following February or March.

PUBLICATIONS:
Annual report; application guidelines.

ADDRESS INQUIRIES TO:
Ponda Barnes, M.P.H., C.R.A.
Vice President of Grants
(See address above.)

*SPECIAL STIPULATIONS:
Resident must be working in the U.S.

ORTHOPAEDIC RESEARCH AND EDUCATION FOUNDATION [2227]

9400 West Higgins Road
Suite 215
Rosemont, IL 60018-4975
(847) 430-5109
Fax: (847) 698-7806
E-mail: barnes@oref.org
Web Site: www.oref.org

FOUNDED: 1955

AREAS OF INTEREST:
Musculoskeletal research.

NAME(S) OF PROGRAMS:
- **OREF Clinical Research Award**

TYPE:
Awards/prizes.

YEAR PROGRAM STARTED: 1996

PURPOSE:
To award outstanding research related to clinical musculoskeletal disease or injury.

LEGAL BASIS:
Special-interest foundation, 501(c)(3).

ELIGIBILITY:
Individual applicants must be members of the AAOS, ORS, Canadian Orthopaedic Association, Canadian ORS or sponsored by a member.

FINANCIAL DATA:
Amount of support per award: $20,000.

Total amount of support: $20,000.

NO. MOST RECENT APPLICANTS: 6.

NO. AWARDS: 1.

APPLICATION INFO:
Submission guidelines are available on the web site.

Duration: One-time award.

Deadline: July 1.

PUBLICATIONS:
Annual report; application guidelines.

ADDRESS INQUIRIES TO:
Ponda Barnes, M.P.H., C.R.A.
Vice President of Grants
(See address above.)

OSTEOGENESIS IMPERFECTA FOUNDATION [2228]

804 West Diamond Avenue
Suite 210
Gaithersburg, MD 20878
(301) 947-0083
(844) 889-7579
Fax: (301) 947-0456
E-mail: bonelink@oif.org
Web Site: www.oif.org

FOUNDED: 1970

AREAS OF INTEREST:
Osteogenesis imperfecta medical research.

NAME(S) OF PROGRAMS:
- **Clinical Seed Grants**
- **Michael Geisman Fellowships**
- **Seed Grants**

TYPE:
Fellowships; Research grants; Seed money grants. Clinical Seed Grants are designed to study people with osteogenesis imperfecta and their families.

Michael Geisman Fellowships: Applicants must be in academic institutions and the work must be done under the supervision of a mentor with training and experience in osteogenesis imperfecta (OI) or a related field.

Seed Grants are for basic or clinical studies with relevance to OI.

YEAR PROGRAM STARTED: 1970

PURPOSE:
To expand understanding and identify improved treatments for osteogenesis imperfecta.

LEGAL BASIS:
Nonprofit organization.

ELIGIBILITY:
Applicants for the fellowship must be postdoctoral fellows in academic institutions and the work must be done under the supervision of a mentor with appropriate training and experience in this or related field.

FINANCIAL DATA:
Amount of support per award: Clinical Seed Grants: Up to $120,000; Michael Geisman Fellowships: Up to $50,000 per year ($35,000 toward the investigator's salary and up to $15,000 per year for supplies); Seed Grants: Up to $60,000.

APPLICATION INFO:
Applicants should submit an original application with 10 copies. The application should include an abstract for a lay audience, budget, education, previous research experience, professional training, publications and a research plan. Electronic submissions are accepted.

Duration: Clinical Seed Grants: One-time funding for two years; Michael Geisman Fellowships: One year with possible renewal; Seed Grants: One-time funding for one year.

Deadline: December 1.

PUBLICATIONS:
Annual report; application guidelines; bimonthly newsletter.

IRS I.D.: 23-7076021

ADDRESS INQUIRIES TO:
OIF Research Department
(See address above.)

OXALOSIS AND HYPEROXALURIA FOUNDATION [2229]

201 East 19th Street, Suite 12-E
New York, NY 10003
(212) 777-0470
(800) 643-8699
Fax: (212) 777-0471
E-mail: info@ohf.org
kimh@ohf.org
Web Site: www.ohf.org

FOUNDED: 1989

AREAS OF INTEREST:
Hyperoxaluria and oxalosis.

NAME(S) OF PROGRAMS:
- **OHF Research Grant**

TYPE:
Research grants. The Research Grant program assists investigators, new or established, who have research projects for which they need support.

PURPOSE:
To fund grants which will increase the understanding of hyperoxaluria and oxalosis and improve the clinical management and treatment of these diseases.

ELIGIBILITY:
Applications are accepted from anywhere in the world. There are no citizenship requirements.

FINANCIAL DATA:
Funds may be used for salaries for the investigators, technical assistance, special equipment, animals, supplies and travel.

Amount of support per award: Up to $200,000.

Total amount of support: Varies.

APPLICATION INFO:
All applications must be made on the OHF forms. OHF prefers that applications be submitted electronically as an attachment and e-mailed to grantapp@ohf.org. Appendices, if included, may also be submitted electronically. Additionally, one original paper copy of the application must be submitted to the OHF Office address listed above. Applications or supporting material received after the deadline will not be considered, regardless of the date of postmark.

Duration: Up to two years.

Deadline: 12:00 A.M., October 23.

ADDRESS INQUIRIES TO:
Kim Hollander, Executive Director
(See address above.)

OXNARD FOUNDATION [2230]

5 Royal St. George Road
Newport Beach, CA 92660
(949) 644-4160
Fax: (949) 644-4171
E-mail: covlineage@gmail.com

AREAS OF INTEREST:
General medical research.

TYPE:
Matching gifts; Research grants.

PURPOSE:
To help continue medical research in the areas of concern for the Foundation.

ELIGIBILITY:
IRS 501(c)(3) tax-exempt organizations, schools and hospitals.

GEOG. RESTRICTIONS: California, New Mexico and Tennessee.

FINANCIAL DATA:
Amount of support per award: $35,000 to $50,000.

Total amount of support: Varies.

APPLICATION INFO:
Applicants should first send a letter and include a copy of the IRS tax determination letter.

Duration: One to three years.

Deadline: Applications are reviewed at Board meetings in February, June and November.

ADDRESS INQUIRIES TO:
Christopher Veitch, President
(See address above.)

PHARMACEUTICAL RESEARCH AND MANUFACTURERS OF AMERICA FOUNDATION, INC. [2231]

950 F Street, N.W.
Suite 300
Washington, DC 20004
(202) 572-7756
E-mail: foundation@phrma.org
Web Site: www.phrmafoundation.org

FOUNDED: 1965

AREAS OF INTEREST:
Health outcomes.

NAME(S) OF PROGRAMS:
- **Post Doctoral Fellowship in Health Outcomes**

TYPE:
Fellowships. This program provides stipend to well-trained graduates from Pharm.D., M.D., and Ph.D. programs who seek to further develop and refine research skills through formal postdoctoral training.

YEAR PROGRAM STARTED: 2002

PURPOSE:
To encourage graduates from Ph.D. programs in health outcomes to continue their research skills through formal postdoctoral training.

LEGAL BASIS:
501(c)(3) organization.

ELIGIBILITY:
Applicant must be a graduate from Pharm.D., M.D. or Ph.D. program.

Before an individual is eligible to apply for a PhRMA Foundation award, he or she must first have a firm commitment from a sponsor/mentor at an accredited U.S. university. Applications must be submitted by an accredited school in the U.S. and all applicants should either be a U.S. citizen or permanent resident. Applicants are encouraged to apply at the earliest point possible in their postdoctoral research.

GEOG. RESTRICTIONS: United States.

FINANCIAL DATA:
Amount of support per award: Maximum $110,000 ($55,000 per year).

NO. AWARDS: 1 budgeted.

APPLICATION INFO:
Contact the Foundation.

Duration: Two years.

Deadline: Information will be available online along with announcement date.

PUBLICATIONS:
Brochure.

IRS I.D.: 52-6063009

ADDRESS INQUIRIES TO:
Postdoctoral Fellowship in Health Outcomes
(See address above.)

PHARMACEUTICAL RESEARCH AND MANUFACTURERS OF AMERICA FOUNDATION, INC.

950 F Street, N.W.
Suite 300
Washington, DC 20004
(202) 572-7756
E-mail: foundation@phrma.org
Web Site: www.phrmafoundation.org

TYPE:
Project/program grants; Research grants; Seed money grants. Starter grants to support research in the fields of pharmacology, clinical pharmacology, drug toxicology, pharmaceutics, informatics and health outcomes. The grants offer financial support to individuals beginning independent research careers at the faculty level.

See entry 2463 for full listing.

PHARMACEUTICAL RESEARCH AND MANUFACTURERS OF AMERICA FOUNDATION, INC. [2232]

950 F Street, N.W.
Suite 300
Washington, DC 20004
(202) 572-7756
E-mail: foundation@phrma.org
Web Site: www.phrmafoundation.org

AREAS OF INTEREST:
Health outcomes and pharmaceutical research.

NAME(S) OF PROGRAMS:
- **Pre Doctoral Fellowships in Health Outcomes**

TYPE:
Fellowships.

YEAR PROGRAM STARTED: 2002

PURPOSE:
To support promising students during their advanced stages of training and thesis research.

ELIGIBILITY:
Full-time, in-residence Ph.D. candidates in the fields of health outcomes enrolled in U.S. schools of medicine, pharmacy, dentistry, or schools of public health are eligible to apply. Students must have completed two years of study and start their thesis research by the time the award is activated. Applicants must be U.S. citizens or permanent residents. Applications must be submitted by an accredited U.S. college or university.

GEOG. RESTRICTIONS: United States.

FINANCIAL DATA:
Award is made to the university on behalf of the fellow. Annual stipend payable monthly for one to two years. $1,000 per year may be used for incidentals directly associated with thesis research preparation.

Amount of support per award: Maximum $50,000 ($25,000 per year).

NO. AWARDS: 2 budgeted.

APPLICATION INFO:
Contact the Foundation.

Duration: Two years.

Deadline: Available online along with announcement date.

PUBLICATIONS:
Brochure.

BOARD OF DIRECTORS:
Michael Rosenblatt, M.D., Chairman
Thomas O. Daniel, M.D.
Mikael Dolsten, M.D., Ph.D.
Betsy Garofalo, M.D.
Jan M. Lundberg, Ph.D.
Andrew Plump, M.D., Ph.D.
Alfred W. Sandrock, M.D., Ph.D.
Moncef Slaoui, Ph.D.
Joanne Waldstreicher, M.D.
Elias Zerhouni, M.D.

ADVISORY COMMITTEE:
Bill Chin, M.D.
Darrell R. Abernethy, M.D., Ph.D., Chairman
Terry L. Bowlin, Ph.D.
Jean Paul Gagnon, Ph.D.
Michael J. Hageman, Ph.D.
Michael N. Liebman, Ph.D.

ADDRESS INQUIRIES TO:
Predoctoral Fellowships in Health Outcomes
(See address above.)

PHARMACEUTICAL RESEARCH AND MANUFACTURERS OF AMERICA FOUNDATION, INC. [2233]

950 F Street, N.W.
Suite 300
Washington, DC 20004
(202) 572-7756
E-mail: foundation@phrma.org
Web Site: www.phrmafoundation.org

AREAS OF INTEREST:
Informatics.

NAME(S) OF PROGRAMS:
- **Post Doctoral Fellowships in Informatics**

TYPE:
Fellowships.

YEAR PROGRAM STARTED: 2002

PURPOSE:
To support postdoctoral career development activities of individuals preparing to engage in research that will bridge the gap between experimental and computational approaches in genomic and biomedical studies.

ELIGIBILITY:
Applicants must hold a Ph.D. degree in the field of study logically or functionally related to the proposed postdoctoral activities, or expect to receive the Ph.D. before activating the award. Must also have firm commitment from a sponsor/mentor at an accredited U.S. university and be a U.S. citizen or permanent resident.

GEOG. RESTRICTIONS: United States.

FINANCIAL DATA:
Annual stipend made to the institution on behalf of the fellow.

Amount of support per award: Maximum $80,000 ($40,000 per year).

NO. AWARDS: 2 budgeted.

APPLICATION INFO:
Applications are to be submitted at the Foundation web site.

Duration: One to two years.

Deadline: September 1. Announcement December 15.

PUBLICATIONS:
Brochure.

ADDRESS INQUIRIES TO:
Postdoctoral Fellowships in Informatics
(See address above.)

*SPECIAL STIPULATIONS:
Second year contingent upon progress report approved by the Foundation and submission of a financial report.

PHARMACEUTICAL RESEARCH AND MANUFACTURERS OF AMERICA FOUNDATION, INC. [2234]

950 F Street, N.W.
Suite 300
Washington, DC 20004
(202) 572-7756
E-mail: foundation@phrma.org
Web Site: www.phrmafoundation.org

AREAS OF INTEREST:
Health outcomes, informatics, pharmacology/toxicology and pharmaceutics.

NAME(S) OF PROGRAMS:

- **Sabbatical Fellowships in Health Outcomes**
- **Sabbatical Fellowships in Informatics**
- **Sabbatical Fellowships in Pharmaceutics**
- **Sabbatical Fellowships in Pharmacology/Toxicology**

TYPE:
Fellowships.

YEAR PROGRAM STARTED: 2002

PURPOSE:
To provide support for individuals engaged in a multidisciplinary research training program that will create or extend their credentials in the fields of health outcomes, informatics, pharmacology/toxicology or pharmaceutics.

ELIGIBILITY:
Varies by program. All applicants must be U.S. citizens or permanent residents.

GEOG. RESTRICTIONS: United States.

FINANCIAL DATA:
Amount of support per award: $40,000.

Matching fund requirements: Matching funds must be provided by the institution.

NO. AWARDS: 1 budgeted for each program.

APPLICATION INFO:
Applications are to be submitted at the Foundation web site.

Duration: Up to one year.

Deadline: Health Outcomes: February 1. All others: September 1.

PUBLICATIONS:
Brochure.

ADDRESS INQUIRIES TO:
Sabbatical Fellowships
(See address above.)

PHARMACEUTICAL RESEARCH AND MANUFACTURERS OF AMERICA FOUNDATION, INC. [2235]

950 F Street, N.W.
Suite 300
Washington, DC 20004
(202) 572-7756
E-mail: foundation@phrma.org
Web Site: www.phrmafoundation.org

AREAS OF INTEREST:
Pharmacology and toxicology.

NAME(S) OF PROGRAMS:

- **Post Doctoral Fellowship in Pharmacology/Toxicology**

TYPE:
Fellowships.

YEAR PROGRAM STARTED: 2002

PURPOSE:
To support postdoctoral career development activities of individuals prepared (or preparing) to engage in research that integrates information on molecular or cellular mechanisms of action with information on the effects of an agent observed in the intact organism, in experimental animal or clinical studies or both.

ELIGIBILITY:
Applicants must hold a Ph.D. degree or appropriate terminal research Doctorate in a field of study logically or functionally related to the proposed postdoctoral activities, or expect to receive the Ph.D. before activating the award. They must also have a firm commitment from a sponsor/mentor at an accredited U.S. university and be a U.S. citizen or permanent resident.

GEOG. RESTRICTIONS: United States.

FINANCIAL DATA:
Stipend is made to the institution on behalf of the fellow.

Amount of support per award: Maximum $80,000 ($40,000 per year).

NO. AWARDS: 2 budgeted.

APPLICATION INFO:
Applications are to be submitted at the Foundation web site.

Duration: Two years.

Deadline: September 1. Announcement by December 15.

PUBLICATIONS:
Brochure.

ADDRESS INQUIRIES TO:
Postdoctoral Fellowship in Pharmacology/Toxicology
(See address above.)

*SPECIAL STIPULATIONS:
Second year is contingent upon a progress report approved by the Foundation and submission of a financial report.

DR. AND MRS. ARTHUR WILLIAM PHILLIPS CHARITABLE TRUST [2236]

P.O. Box 316
Oil City, PA 16301-0316
(814) 676-2736
E-mail: bwinters_pct@comcast.net

FOUNDED: 1979

AREAS OF INTEREST:
Primarily medical centers, research and education.

TYPE:
Project/program grants; Scholarships.

PURPOSE:
To support many varied projects.

ELIGIBILITY:
Organizations must be:
(1) IRS 501(c)(3) tax-exempt;
(2) located in northwestern Pennsylvania;
(3) able to raise the balance of necessary funding from other sources and;
(4) able to show evidence of financial responsibility that will insure the completion and success of the project.

GEOG. RESTRICTIONS: Northwestern Pennsylvania.

FINANCIAL DATA:
Amount of support per award: Varies.

Total amount of support: Approximately $500,000.

NO. MOST RECENT APPLICANTS: 35.

NO. AWARDS: 25.

APPLICATION INFO:
Applications should be made in triplicate and include a short history of the organization, the need for the project, the annual budget for the project, other helpful financial budgetary information and a copy of their 501(c)(3).

Duration: Typically one year.

Deadline: March 15 for spring meeting; July 31 for fall meeting.

IRS I.D.: 25-6201015

TRUSTEES:
Larry S. Adams
Edith Gilmore Letcher
Robert W. McFate

ADDRESS INQUIRIES TO:
Robert W. McFate, Trustee
(See address above.)

PLASTIC SURGERY FOUNDATION (PSF) [2237]

ASPS/PSF
444 East Algonquin Road
Arlington Heights, IL 60005
(847) 228-9900
E-mail: research@plasticsurgery.org
Web Site: www.thepsf.org/research/grant-applications

AREAS OF INTEREST:
Basic/translational research, clinical, or health services research.

NAME(S) OF PROGRAMS:

- **ASE/PSF Combined Research Grant**
- **Combined Pilot Research Grants**
- **National Endowment for Plastic Surgery**
- **Pilot Research Grant**
- **The PSF/MTF Dermal Tissue Grant**
- **Research Fellowship**

TYPE:
Awards/prizes. ASE/PSF Combined Research Grant: The PSF and the Association for Surgical Education (ASE) recognize the importance of fostering the development of surgeon scientists that yield improvements in patient care in surgery. The ASE/PSF Combined Research Grant is intended to fund

a research project that will advance the scientific knowledge and aim to develop and validate new methods of surgical care.

PSF/MTF Dermal Tissue Grant: This grant is intended to provide support for one-year research projects focused on dermal allografts, transplant science, and the biologic reconstruction of tissues using grafts derived from dermal tissues.

National Endowment for Plastic Surgery: This grant is designed to support projects that address clinically relevant, immediate issues facing the practice of plastic surgery. The Endowment encourages the specialty to be proactive in identifying research opportunities; it also quickly responds to changing demands within the field of plastic surgery. Sponsoring institutions, as well as individuals, are encouraged to apply for this specific type of funding.

Pilot Research Grant: This program is designed to promote advancement and innovation in plastic surgery. These grants provide "seed" funding and allow researchers to conduct preliminary studies related to plastic surgery science; they also set the stage for investigators to apply for external funding sources. The PSF also has Combined Pilot Research Grants with the following organizations: AAHS, AAPS, ACAPS, ASMS, ASPN, ASRM and PSRC.

Research Fellowship: These grants encourage research and academic career development in plastic surgery. This program is designed for those who wish to supplement one year of clinical training for a research experience and can be utilized for training in any area of plastic surgery. Fellowship to be used for salary support only.

ELIGIBILITY:

ASE/PSF Combined Research Grant: Applicants must be M.D., D.O. or Ph.D. and hold a full-time clinical or research position in a U.S. or Canadian institution where the research will be conducted. Applicants must be an active or candidate member of ASPS or obtain sponsorship from an active ASPS member at one's institution. Additional eligibility criteria may apply.

Combined Pilot Research and Pilot Research Grants: Applicants must be M.D., D.O. or Ph.D. and hold a full-time clinical or research position in a U.S. or Canadian institution where the research will be conducted. Applicants must be an active or candidate member of ASPS or obtain sponsorship from an active ASPS member at one's institution. Additional eligibility criteria may apply for the Combined Pilot Research Grant.

National Endowment for Plastic Surgery: Applicants must be M.D., D.O. or Ph.D. and hold a full-time clinical or research position in a U.S. or Canadian institution where the research will be conducted. Applicants must be an active or candidate member of ASPS or obtain sponsorship from an active ASPS member at one's institution.

The PSF/MTF Dermal Tissue Grant: Applicants must be an M.D., D.O. or Ph.D. and hold a full-time clinical or research position in a U.S. or Canadian institution where the research will be conducted. Applicants must be an active or candidate member of ASPS or obtain sponsorship from an active ASPS member at one's institution.

Research Fellowship: Applicants must be an M.D. or D.O. and hold a full-time clinical or research position in a U.S. or Canadian institution where the research will be conducted. Applicants must be a resident or within five years of an initial faculty appointment and must be an active or candidate member of ASPS or obtain sponsorship from an active ASPS member at one's institution.

FINANCIAL DATA:

Amount of support per award: ASE/PSF Combined Research Grant: Up to $15,000. Combined Pilot Research Grants: Up to $10,000. The PSF/MTF Dermal Tissue Research Grant: Up to $50,000. National Endowment for Plastic Surgery Grant: Up to $50,000; Pilot Research Grant: Up to $10,000; Research Fellowship: Up to $50,000.

Total amount of support: The Foundation awarded nearly $690,000 in grant funding in 2014.

NO. AWARDS: 32 research grants in 2014.

APPLICATION INFO:

Application instructions can be found on The Foundation web site.

Duration: One year.

Deadline: December 1, 2015.

POST-POLIO HEALTH INTERNATIONAL [2238]

4207 Lindell Boulevard
Suite 110
St. Louis, MO 63108-2930
(314) 534-0475
Fax: (314) 534-5070
E-mail: director@post-polio.org
Web Site: www.post-polio.org

FOUNDED: 1995

AREAS OF INTEREST:

Neuromuscular respiratory diseases and post-poliomyelitis.

NAME(S) OF PROGRAMS:

- **The Research Fund**

TYPE:

Research grants; Seed money grants. The Research Fund supports the work of researchers investigating the late effects of poliomyelitis and/or neuromuscular respiratory disease through one of two grants:

The Thomas Wallace Rogers Memorial Respiratory Research Grant: To study the cause(s) and treatment of neuromuscular respiratory insufficiency and the effects of long-term home mechanical ventilation.

The Post-Poliomyelitis Research Grant: This grant is to study the cause(s), treatment and management of the problem of the late effects of polio.

The award is for two years. The next call for proposals will be in 2016.

YEAR PROGRAM STARTED: 2000

PURPOSE:

To help support researchers, scientists, and clinicians worldwide to investigate the cause, treatment, and management of post-poliomyelitis and neuromuscular respiratory disease; to seek scientific information leading to eventual amelioration of the consequences of poliomyelitis and/or neuromuscular respiratory diseases.

LEGAL BASIS:

Not-for-profit organization.

ELIGIBILITY:

Applicants must be affiliated with an institution or organization. Citizens of all countries may apply. Applications, however, must be in English. Proposals will not be accepted via fax. The research may be quantitative and/or qualitative and follow sound and appropriate research standards relevant to the subject matter. The research findings must relate to improving the quality of life for people with disabilities. Preference will be given to innovative or original research.

FINANCIAL DATA:

Funding does cover indirect costs to a maximum of $3,000 per year.

Amount of support per award: $50,000 per year; maximum $100,000.

NO. MOST RECENT APPLICANTS: 11.

NO. AWARDS: 1.

APPLICATION INFO:

Contact the organization.

Duration: Up to two years.

IRS I.D.: 34-0961952

ADDRESS INQUIRIES TO:

Joan L. Headley, Executive Director
(See address above.)

THE ELISABETH SEVERANCE PRENTISS FOUNDATION [2239]

c/o PNC Bank
1900 East Ninth Street
Mailstop B7-YB13-03-1
Cleveland, OH 44114
(216) 222-2760
Fax: (216) 781-6744
E-mail: john.baco@pnc.com
Web Site: www.esprentissfoundation.org

FOUNDED: 1944

AREAS OF INTEREST:

Medical research, public health, hospital assistance for capital improvements, operation, management and administration.

TYPE:

Capital grants; Project/program grants. Project grants, educational support grants and building improvement grants in related medical areas.

YEAR PROGRAM STARTED: 1944

PURPOSE:

To promote and improve medical services, especially within Cuyahoga County (OH) for all individuals.

LEGAL BASIS:

Charitable foundation.

ELIGIBILITY:

Grant request must fall within restrictions of general purpose requirements, must not be for individuals for scholarships, fellowships, grants-in-aid or other personal purposes and must not be for redistribution by national foundations. Most favorable consideration will be given to those requests from applicants for purposes within the Cuyahoga County (OH) area. The Foundation strongly favors grant requests for specific projects over those requesting general operating support.

GEOG. RESTRICTIONS: Greater Cleveland, Ohio.

FINANCIAL DATA:

Total assets of $86,521,123 as of December 31, 2013.

Total amount of support: $3,180,812 for the year ended December 31, 2013.

APPLICATION INFO:
There is no set form, but sufficient information and facts with supporting data should be given in the application to permit the Board of Managers to make a fair decision based on full and complete information. Applicant should also include six copies of each pertinent document being sent.

Duration: Support will continue, with annual installments, until requested grant has been satisfied. Grants are renewable.

Deadline: April 15 and October 15. Announcement after May and November semiannual board meetings.

ADDRESS INQUIRIES TO:
Richard Mack, Secretary
(See address above.)

PULMONARY FIBROSIS FOUNDATION [2240]

230 East Ohio Street
Suite 304
Chicago, IL 60611
(888) 733-6741
Fax: (866) 587-9158
E-mail: grants@pulmonaryfibrosis.org
Web Site: www.pulmonaryfibrosis.org

AREAS OF INTEREST:
Research of and treatment for pulmonary fibrosis.

NAME(S) OF PROGRAMS:
- **PFF Research Fund To Cure PF**

TYPE:
Matching gifts; Research grants. Supports postdoctoral research for studies in the clinical investigation of pulmonary fibrosis.

YEAR PROGRAM STARTED: 2000

PURPOSE:
To improve the quality of life of those affected by pulmonary fibrosis; to provide funding for research and treatment of pulmonary fibrosis.

ELIGIBILITY:
Researchers by invitation only.

FINANCIAL DATA:
Amount of support per award: Varies.

Total amount of support: Over $4,000,000 over the last 10 years.

IRS I.D.: 84-1558631

ADDRESS INQUIRIES TO:
Zoe Bubany, Vice President of Board and External Relations
(See address above.)

RADIOLOGICAL SOCIETY OF NORTH AMERICA RESEARCH AND EDUCATION FOUNDATION [2241]

820 Jorie Boulevard
Oak Brook, IL 60523-2251
(630) 571-7816
Fax: (630) 571-7837
E-mail: swalter@rsna.org
Web Site: www.rsna.org/foundation

FOUNDED: 1984

AREAS OF INTEREST:
Radiology.

NAME(S) OF PROGRAMS:
- **RSNA Research Scholar Grant**

TYPE:
Research grants.

PURPOSE:
To support junior faculty members who have completed the conventional resident/fellowship training programs but have not yet been recognized as independent investigators.

ELIGIBILITY:
Any area of research related to the radiologic sciences is eligible for Research Scholar Grant support. Applicants must be nominated by their department chair (one new application per department per year). Contact the Foundation for full details.

GEOG. RESTRICTIONS: North America.

FINANCIAL DATA:
Amount of support per award: $150,000 ($75,000 per year).

Total amount of support: Varies.

NO. MOST RECENT APPLICANTS: Foundation generally funds approximately 25% of the applications received.

NO. AWARDS: 10 for the year 2015.

APPLICATION INFO:
Applications must be submitted online.

Duration: Two years.

Deadline: January 15.

ADDRESS INQUIRIES TO:
Scott Walter
Assistant Director, Grant Administration
(See address above.)

*SPECIAL STIPULATIONS:
Applicant must commit to devoting 40% of time to granted project.

RADIOLOGICAL SOCIETY OF NORTH AMERICA RESEARCH AND EDUCATION FOUNDATION [2242]

820 Jorie Boulevard
Oak Brook, IL 60523-2251
(630) 571-7816
Fax: (630) 571-7837
E-mail: swalter@rsna.org
Web Site: www.rsna.org/foundation

FOUNDED: 1984

AREAS OF INTEREST:
Radiology.

NAME(S) OF PROGRAMS:
- **Research Resident/Fellow Grant**

TYPE:
Research grants. Grants will be awarded for diverse types of projects in the radiologic sciences including basic science and clinical research studies. This program is not intended to fund Ph.D. postdoctoral projects, nor to support those whose primary aim is to obtain practical experience in clinical radiology.

PURPOSE:
To provide young investigators not yet professionally established in the radiologic sciences an opportunity to gain further insight into scientific investigation and to develop competence in research techniques and methods.

ELIGIBILITY:
At the time of application, the applicant must:
(1) be an RSNA member (at any level);
(2) be (if an applicant within North American educational institutions) a resident or fellow in a department of radiology, radiation oncology or nuclear medicine; applicants from outside North America must already be accepted into a one- or two-year Fellowship position at a North American education institution at the time of the grant application;
(3) have completed the internship year (PGY-1) and at least six months of specialty training in the radiologic sciences (PGY-2) for the resident grant, or be in the last year of, or have completed, the prescribed residency training for the fellow grant. (If awarded the latter, recipient must be in a fellowship position during the period of grant support);
(4) be certified by the American Board of Radiology, or on track for certification;
(5) not have been principal investigator on external/extramural grant/contract amounts totaling more than $60,000 in a single calendar year (includes support from single or combined grants or contracts from any source including government, private or industrial/commercial sources);
(6) not be agent(s) of any for-profit, commercial company in the radiologic sciences (applies to applicant/co-principal investigator);
(7) not submit more than one research or education grant application to the RSNA Research and Education Foundation per year;
(8) not have concurrent RSNA grants and;
(9) devote at least 50% of applicant's time to granted project under the guidance of a scientific advisor/mentor.

Supplementation of funding from other grant sources must be approved by Foundation staff if not described in the original research plan. Awards from other sources may be approved by Foundation staff if the investigator submits a satisfactory plan to address any budgetary overlap.

Contact the Foundation for full details.

FINANCIAL DATA:
Funds may be used for salary and/or nonpersonnel research expenses.

Amount of support per award: $50,000 salary support for one-year Research Fellow project or $30,000 salary support for one-year Research Resident project.

Total amount of support: Varies.

NO. MOST RECENT APPLICANTS: Foundation generally funds approximately 25% of the applications received.

NO. AWARDS: 23 for the year 2015.

APPLICATION INFO:
Applications are completed online using the Online Grant Application System.

Duration: One year; however, residents may opt for a six-month, full-time research project.

Deadline: January 15.

ADDRESS INQUIRIES TO:
Scott Walter
Assistant Director, Grant Administration
(See address above.)

RADIOLOGICAL SOCIETY OF NORTH AMERICA RESEARCH AND EDUCATION FOUNDATION [2243]

820 Jorie Boulevard
Oak Brook, IL 60523-2251
(630) 571-7816
Fax: (630) 571-7837
E-mail: swalter@rsna.org
Web Site: www.rsna.org/foundation

FOUNDED: 1984

AREAS OF INTEREST:
Radiology.

NAME(S) OF PROGRAMS:
- **Research Seed Grant**

TYPE:
Seed money grants. Research Seed Grant support is available for any area of research related to the radiologic sciences.

PURPOSE:
To enable investigators to gain experience in defining objectives and testing hypotheses in preparation for major grant applications to corporations, foundations and governmental agencies.

ELIGIBILITY:
Applications are accepted from individuals throughout the world. Applicants must be RSNA members at the time of application. Contact the Foundation for full details.

FINANCIAL DATA:
Research Seed Grant is to support the preliminary or pilot phase of scientific projects, not to supplement major funding already secured. No salary support for the principal investigator will be provided.

Amount of support per award: Up to $40,000.

Total amount of support: Varies.

NO. MOST RECENT APPLICANTS: Foundation generally funds approximately 25% of the applications received.

NO. AWARDS: 11 for the year 2015.

APPLICATION INFO:
Applications are completed using the online Grant Application System.

Duration: One year.

Deadline: January 15.

ADDRESS INQUIRIES TO:
Scott Walter
Assistant Director, Grant Administration
(See address above.)

RADIOLOGICAL SOCIETY OF NORTH AMERICA RESEARCH AND EDUCATION FOUNDATION [2244]

820 Jorie Boulevard
Oak Brook, IL 60523-2251
(630) 571-7816
Fax: (630) 571-7837
E-mail: swalter@rsna.org
Web Site: www.rsna.org/foundation

FOUNDED: 1984

AREAS OF INTEREST:
Radiology.

NAME(S) OF PROGRAMS:
- **Research Medical Student Grant**

TYPE:
Research grants. Research Medical Student Grant is for any area of research related to the radiologic sciences.

PURPOSE:
To make radiology research opportunities possible for medical students and to encourage them, early in their medical careers, to consider academic radiology as an important option for their future.

ELIGIBILITY:
Applicants must be RSNA members at the time of application and be full-time medical students at an accredited North American medical school. The scientific advisor or one of the co-investigators must also be a dues-paying RSNA member. Contact the Foundation for full details.

FINANCIAL DATA:
Funds are intended to secure protected time for the recipient and may not be used for nonpersonnel research expenses.

Amount of support per award: $3,000 stipend.

Total amount of support: Approximately $75,000.

Matching fund requirements: $3,000 to be matched by the sponsoring department ($6,000 total) as a stipend for the medical student.

NO. AWARDS: 25 for the year 2015.

APPLICATION INFO:
Applications are completed using the online Grant Application System.

Duration: 10 weeks full-time (or equivalent).

Deadline: February 1.

ADDRESS INQUIRIES TO:
Scott Walter
Assistant Director, Grant Administration
(See address above.)

RADIOLOGICAL SOCIETY OF NORTH AMERICA RESEARCH AND EDUCATION FOUNDATION [2245]

820 Jorie Boulevard
Oak Brook, IL 60523-2251
(630) 571-7816
Fax: (630) 571-7837
E-mail: swalter@rsna.org
Web Site: www.rsna.org/foundation

FOUNDED: 1984

AREAS OF INTEREST:
Radiology.

NAME(S) OF PROGRAMS:
- **Education Scholar Grant**

TYPE:
Training grants. Any area of education related to the radiologic sciences.

PURPOSE:
To fund individuals in radiology or related disciplines who are seeking an opportunity to develop their expertise in radiologic education; to develop teachers in radiology who can share their knowledge with the radiology community.

ELIGIBILITY:
Applications are accepted from individuals throughout the world. Applicants must be RSNA members (at any level) at the time of application. Contact the Foundation for full details.

FINANCIAL DATA:
Education Scholar Grant to be used for salary support and/or other project costs.

Amount of support per award: Up to $75,000.

NO. MOST RECENT APPLICANTS: Foundation generally funds approximately 25% of the applications received.

NO. AWARDS: 7 for the year 2015.

APPLICATION INFO:
Applications are completed using the online Grant Application System.

Duration: One year. In exceptional cases, grants for up to two years will be considered.

Deadline: January 11.

ADDRESS INQUIRIES TO:
Scott Walter
Assistant Director, Grant Administration
(See address above.)

RADIOLOGICAL SOCIETY OF NORTH AMERICA RESEARCH AND EDUCATION FOUNDATION [2246]

820 Jorie Boulevard
Oak Brook, IL 60523-2251
(630) 571-7816
Fax: (630) 571-7837
E-mail: swalter@rsna.org
Web Site: www.rsna.org/foundation

FOUNDED: 1984

AREAS OF INTEREST:
Radiology.

NAME(S) OF PROGRAMS:
- **RSNA/AUR/APDR/SCARD Radiology Education Research Development Grant**

TYPE:
Research grants.

PURPOSE:
To encourage innovation and improvement in health sciences education by providing research opportunities to individuals in pursuit of advancing the science of radiology education; to help in building a critical mass of radiology education researchers and promote the careers of persons advancing the science of radiology education.

ELIGIBILITY:
Applications are accepted from individuals throughout the world. Grants are awarded to any person, at any level of career development, who have a primary appointment in a radiology department. Applicants must be members of one or more of the sponsoring organizations. Contact the Foundation for full details.

FINANCIAL DATA:
Grants can be used to help cover the costs of research materials, research assistant support and limited primary investigator salary support (no more than half of grant award).

Amount of support per award: Up to $10,000.

Total amount of support: Varies.

CO-OP FUNDING PROGRAMS: Co-sponsored by the Radiological Society of North America (RSNA), Association of University Radiologists (AUR), Association of Program Directors in Radiology (APDR), and Society of Chairmen of Academic Radiology Departments (SCARD).

NO. MOST RECENT APPLICANTS: Foundation generally funds approximately 25% of the applications received.

NO. AWARDS: 3 for the year 2015.

APPLICATION INFO:
Applications must be submitted online.

Duration: One year.

Deadline: January 11.

ADDRESS INQUIRIES TO:
Scott Walter
Assistant Director, Grant Administration
(See address above.)

V. KANN RASMUSSEN FOUNDATION

475 Riverside Drive, Suite 900
New York, NY 10115
(212) 812-4268
Fax: (212) 812-4299
E-mail: ikrarup@vkrf.org
Web Site: www.vkrf.org

TYPE:
Challenge/matching grants; Project/program grants.

See entry 2023 for full listing.

SAVOY FOUNDATION [2247]

230 Foch Street
St.-Jean-sur-Richelieu QC J3B 2B2 Canada
(450) 358-9779
Fax: (450) 346-1045
E-mail: epilepsy@savoy-foundation.ca
Web Site: www.savoy-foundation.ca

FOUNDED: 1971

AREAS OF INTEREST:
Epilepsy and medical research.

TYPE:
Fellowships; Research grants; Scholarships.

PURPOSE:
To promote research on epilepsy.

ELIGIBILITY:
Studentships will be awarded to meritorious applicants wishing to acquire training and pursue research in a biomedical discipline, the health sciences or social sciences related to epilepsy. To be eligible, the candidate must have a good university record (B.Sc., M.D. or equivalent diploma) and have ensured that a qualified researcher affiliated to a university and/or hospital will supervise his or her work. Concomitant registration in a graduate program (M.Sc. or Ph.D.) is encouraged.

Post-Doctoral and Clinical Research Fellowships will be awarded to scientists or medical specialists (Ph.D. or M.D.) wishing to carry out a full-time research project in the field of epilepsy.

Research Grants are available to clinicians and/or established scientists working on epilepsy or related subjects.

Studentships, fellowships, and grants are available to Canadian researchers, to foreign nationals or for projects conducted in Canada.

GEOG. RESTRICTIONS: Canada.

FINANCIAL DATA:
Amount of support per award: Studentships: $15,000 (CAN) per year. An annual sum of $1,000 will be allocated to the laboratory or institution as additional support for the research project. Postdoctoral and Clinical Research Fellowships: $30,000. Research Grants: Up to $23,000.

Total amount of support: More than $250,000 (CAN) per year.

NO. MOST RECENT APPLICANTS: 63.

NO. AWARDS: 16.

APPLICATION INFO:
Application information is available on the web site.

Duration: Studentships: One year. Renewable for a maximum duration of four years; Post-Doctoral and Clinical Research Fellowships: One year. Nonrenewable; Research grants generally are not renewable.

Deadline: January 15 (postmark). If January 15 falls on a weekend or holiday, the Foundation will consider the next working day as the deadline.

EXECUTIVE COMMITTEE:
George M. Savoy, President
Caroline Savoy, Vice President/Secretary
Alain Barbeau, Secretary and Treasurer

ADDRESS INQUIRIES TO:
Caroline Savoy, Secretary
(See address above.)

SCLERODERMA FOUNDATION [2248]

300 Rosewood Drive, Suite 105
Danvers, MA 01923
(978) 463-5843 ext. 248
(800) 722-4673
Fax: (978) 463-5809
E-mail: tsperry@scleroderma.org
Web Site: www.scleroderma.org

FOUNDED: 1998

AREAS OF INTEREST:
Scleroderma.

NAME(S) OF PROGRAMS:
- **Scleroderma Foundation Research Grants**

TYPE:
Research grants.

YEAR PROGRAM STARTED: 1998

PURPOSE:
To support research in the area of scleroderma.

ELIGIBILITY:
Applicants must be principal investigators.

GEOG. RESTRICTIONS: United States for new and established investigators; international for established investigators only.

FINANCIAL DATA:
Amount of support per award: $150,000.

Total amount of support: Average $1,000,000 annually.

NO. MOST RECENT APPLICANTS: 39.

NO. AWARDS: Average 7.

APPLICATION INFO:
Applicants must use the application form following NIH guidelines.

Duration: Established investigators: Two years; New investigators: Three years.

Deadline: September 15 annually. Deadline is subject to change. Call or visit the web site to verify deadline date.

PUBLICATIONS:
Quarterly magazine; literature.

IRS I.D.: 52-1375827

STAFF:
Tracey O'Connell Sperry, National Director of Development and Research

ADDRESS INQUIRIES TO:
Tracey O'Connell Sperry
National Director of
Development and Research
(See address above.)

SCLERODERMA FOUNDATION [2249]

300 Rosewood Drive, Suite 105
Danvers, MA 01923
(978) 463-5843 ext. 248
(800) 722-4673
Fax: (978) 463-5809
E-mail: tsperry@scleroderma.org
Web Site: www.scleroderma.org

FOUNDED: 1998

AREAS OF INTEREST:
Scleroderma.

NAME(S) OF PROGRAMS:
- **Scleroderma Foundation Multi-Center Collaborative Research Grant**

TYPE:
Research grants.

PURPOSE:
To support and enhance collaborations between two or more scleroderma centers to advance significant research on scleroderma.

ELIGIBILITY:
Applicants must be principal investigators.

GEOG. RESTRICTIONS: United States.

FINANCIAL DATA:
Amount of support per award: $500,000.

Total amount of support: $500,000.

NO. MOST RECENT APPLICANTS: 6.

NO. AWARDS: 1.

APPLICATION INFO:
Contact the Foundation.

Duration: Two years.

Deadline: Letter of Intent: September 2. Application: September 15.

PUBLICATIONS:
Quarterly magazine; literature.

IRS I.D.: 52-1375827

STAFF:
Tracey O'Connell Sperry, National Director of Development and Research

ADDRESS INQUIRIES TO:
Tracey O'Connell Sperry
National Director of
Development and Research
(See address above.)

SMITH FAMILY AWARDS PROGRAM FOR EXCELLENCE IN BIOMEDICAL RESEARCH [2250]

95 Berkeley Street, Second Floor
Boston, MA 02116
(617) 279-2240 ext. 702
E-mail: glockwood@hria.org
Web Site: www.tmfgrants.org/smith

FOUNDED: 1991

AREAS OF INTEREST:
Basic biomedical science including physics, chemistry and engineering with a focus on biomedical research.

TYPE:
Research grants.

YEAR PROGRAM STARTED: 1991

PURPOSE:
To provide research grants for newly independent junior faculty.

ELIGIBILITY:
Detailed information is available on the web site.

GEOG. RESTRICTIONS: Massachusetts, Yale University and Brown University.

FINANCIAL DATA:
Amount of support per award: $300,000 over three years.

Total amount of support: $1,500,000 for five new awards each year.

CO-OP FUNDING PROGRAMS: Principal funding provided by the Richard and Susan Smith Family Foundation with contributing support from other donors.

NO. MOST RECENT APPLICANTS: 53 for the year 2015.

NO. AWARDS: 6 for funding cycle 2015-18.

REPRESENTATIVE AWARDS:
"Maintenance of Genome Stability by the Hippo Tumor Suppressor Pathway;" "Neuro-molecular Mechanisms Underlying Alcoholism;" "Micro-Environmental Regulation of Network State and Drug Sensitivity in Triple-Negative Breast Cancer."

APPLICATION INFO:
Information and forms are available on the web site.

Duration: Three years. Nonrenewable.

Deadline: Late August.

PUBLICATIONS:
Application guidelines; directory of grant recipients (online); summaries of current and previous funded projects.

ADDRESS INQUIRIES TO:
Senior Program Officer
(See address above.)

THE SOCIETY FOR INVESTIGATIVE DERMATOLOGY [2251]

526 Superior Avenue East
Suite 540
Cleveland, OH 44114-1999
(216) 579-9300
Fax: (216) 579-9333
E-mail: sid@sidnet.org
Web Site: www.sidnet.org

FOUNDED: 1938

AREAS OF INTEREST:
Skin biology, skin disease, and publication and results of skin research.

CONSULTING OR VOLUNTEER SERVICES:
Advocacy for biomedical research.

NAME(S) OF PROGRAMS:
- **Albert M. Kligman Fellowship Fund Award**

TYPE:
Awards/prizes; Conferences/seminars; Fellowships; Research grants; Travel grants. Awards will be used to support resident, fellow and medical student travel to the Society's annual meetings to present their scientific work.

YEAR PROGRAM STARTED: 1973

PURPOSE:
To encourage trainees to become skin scientists; to encourage the best and brightest young scholars to become members of the research community in dermatology and to participate in the activities of the Society.

LEGAL BASIS:
Tax-exempt.

ELIGIBILITY:
Applicants must hold the M.D. or Ph.D. Project must be skin-/skin disease-related. Preceptor is required. One year of work minimum.

FINANCIAL DATA:
No indirect costs.

Amount of support per award: $25,000.

NO. AWARDS: Approximately 20.

APPLICATION INFO:
Information on application can be obtained from the address above.

Duration: One year.

Deadline: Contact the Society for exact dates.

IRS I.D.: 23-1361165

OFFICERS:
Mark Udey, M.D., Ph.D., President
Anthony Gaspari, M.D., Vice President

SOCIETY OF CARDIOVASCULAR ANESTHESIOLOGISTS

8735 West Higgins Road
Suite 300
Chicago, IL 60631
(855) 658-2828
Fax: (847) 375-6323
E-mail: info@scahq.org
Web Site: www.scahq.org

TYPE:
Research grants.

See entry 2321 for full listing.

SOCIETY OF CRITICAL CARE MEDICINE [2252]

500 Midway Drive
Mount Prospect, IL 60056
(847) 827-6869
Fax: (847) 493-6441
E-mail: splenner@sccm.org
Web Site: www.sccm.org

AREAS OF INTEREST:
Critical care medicine.

NAME(S) OF PROGRAMS:
- **SCCM-Weil Research Grant**

TYPE:
Research grants. Recipients receive financial rewards, prestige and recognition within the field of critical care medicine.

PURPOSE:
To promote excellence in critical care teaching and research for the improved care of the critically ill and injured.

ELIGIBILITY:
SCCM membership is required for research grants. Entries are judged by a committee with expertise in the field.

FINANCIAL DATA:
Amount of support per award: $50,000.

Total amount of support: $50,000 per award.

NO. AWARDS: 2.

APPLICATION INFO:
Contact the Society for guidelines.

ADDRESS INQUIRIES TO:
Sharon Plenner, Education Specialist
(See e-mail address above.)

SOCIETY OF NUCLEAR MEDICINE AND MOLECULAR IMAGING (SNMMI) [2253]

1850 Samuel Morse Drive
Reston, VA 20190-5316
(703) 326-1194
Fax: (703) 708-9015
E-mail: mmcmahon@snmmi.org
Web Site: www.snmmi.org/grants

FOUNDED: 1969

AREAS OF INTEREST:
Nuclear medicine.

NAME(S) OF PROGRAMS:
- **Mitzi & William Blahd, M.D. Pilot Research Grant**
- **Bradley-Alavi Student Fellowship**

TYPE:
Awards/prizes; Fellowships; Research grants; Seed money grants. Mitzi & William Blahd, M.D. Pilot Research Grant: This grant is designed to help a basic or clinical scientist in the early stages of his or her career conduct research that may lead to further funding.

Bradley-Alavi Student Fellowship: This program is designed to provide an introduction to, and to stimulate students' interest in, molecular imaging and nuclear medicine by supporting awardees' full-time participation in clinical or basic research activities for three months (or less).

YEAR PROGRAM STARTED: 1969

PURPOSE:
To advance excellence in health care through education and research in nuclear medicine by the provision of grants and awards.

LEGAL BASIS:
Tax-exempt, nonprofit organization.

ELIGIBILITY:
For the Mitzi & William Blahd, M.D. Pilot Research Grant, all candidates must be active members of SNMMI. In addition, the following applicant requirements apply:
(1) basic or clinical scientists with an advanced degree, such as M.D., Ph.D. or equivalent;
(2) awardee must hold a full-time position in an educational/training institution when the award starts (faculty and trainees are eligible);
(3) applicant must be no more than five years post-nuclear medicine/-molecular imaging training (training can include residency, M.D./Ph.D. training or postdoctoral training);
(4) the research may be done in any country;
(5) applicant must not have served as the principal investigator of a peer-reviewed grant for more than $50,000 in a single calendar year and;
(6) preference will be given to individuals who have demonstrated great potential for a research career in the field of nuclear medicine/molecular imaging and whose research focuses on translational in vivo studies that include radionuclide imaging or therapy.

Bradley-Alavi Student Fellowship: An applicant from any country may apply, and must:
(1) be enrolled in a medical, pharmacy or graduate school, or be an undergraduate

student demonstrating outstanding interest in nuclear medicine and/or molecular imaging research and;
(2) carry out fellowship during a three-month period between May 1 and December 31, 2016.

FINANCIAL DATA:
This grant may be used for salary support of the principal investigator, as well as direct costs of supplies and equipment. Support is not provided for salaries of other research personnel, or for indirect costs.

Amount of support per award: Mitzi & William Blahd, M.D. Pilot Research Grant: $25,000; Bradley-Alavi Student Fellowship: $3,000 each over three months.

CO-OP FUNDING PROGRAMS: Mitzi & William Blahd, M.D. Pilot Research Grant is made possible by support from the Education and Research Foundation for Nuclear Medicine and Molecular Imaging.

The Bradley-Alavi Student Fellowship program is made possible through a grant from the Education and Research Foundation for Nuclear Medicine and Molecular Imaging.

NO. MOST RECENT APPLICANTS: Mitzi & William Blahd, M.D. Pilot Research Grant: 8. Bradley-Alavi Student Fellowship: 15.

NO. AWARDS: Mitzi & William Blahd, M.D. Pilot Research Grant: 1. Bradley-Alavi Student Fellowship: Up to 3.

APPLICATION INFO:
Mitzi & William Blahd, M.D. Pilot Research Grant: The application must be completed in its entirety and submitted along with:
(1) principal investigator's current curriculum vitae;
(2) a research abstract and a detailed research proposal not to exceed 10 pages, excluding references;
(3) one letter of recommendation from the program director or research supervisor;
(4) one letter of recommendation from a professional colleague and;
(5) applicant must be a member of SNMMI at the time of award.

Bradley-Alavi Student Fellowship: The application must be completed in its entirety and submitted along with:
(1) a current curriculum vitae;
(2) a detailed research proposal not to exceed two pages, excluding references;
(3) a completed evaluation from the nuclear medicine faculty advisor overseeing the research (preceptor) and;
(4) at least one (preferably two) support letters from others involved in the applicant's educational/research experience; the applicant's preceptor may submit a letter of support; however, it must not be the sole letter received; letters of support must be received by the application deadline in order to be accepted.

Duration: Mitzi & William Blahd, M.D. Pilot Research Grant: One year. Bradley-Alavi Student Fellowship: Three months or less.

Deadline: Mitzi & William Blahd, M.D. Pilot Research Grant: February 3. Bradley-Alavi Student Fellowship: February 28.

OFFICERS:
Virginia Pappas, Chief Executive Officer

ADDRESS INQUIRIES TO:
Mary McMahon
Director of Development
(See telephone or e-mail address above.)

*SPECIAL STIPULATIONS:
Mitzi & William Blahd, M.D. Pilot Research Grant: No grantee may receive more than one research grant in any one year. Likewise no other grant request will be considered until a satisfactory summary of an earlier grant is received.

SOCIETY OF NUCLEAR MEDICINE AND MOLECULAR IMAGING (SNMMI) [2254]

1850 Samuel Morse Drive
Reston, VA 20190-5316
(703) 326-1194
Fax: (703) 708-9015
E-mail: mmcmahon@snmmi.org
Web Site: www.snmmi.org/grants

FOUNDED: 1969

AREAS OF INTEREST:
Nuclear medicine.

NAME(S) OF PROGRAMS:
- **Susan C. Weiss Clinical Advancement Scholarship**

TYPE:
Scholarships. Susan C. Weiss Clinical Advancement Scholarship: Named in honor of Susan C. Weiss, SNMMI-TS former President and former Executive Director of the Education and Research Foundation for SNMMI, this program supports a certified nuclear medicine technologist (CNMTs) who is pursuing clinical advancement through a didactic educational program.

PURPOSE:
To advance excellence in health care through education and research in nuclear medicine by the provision of grants and awards.

LEGAL BASIS:
Tax-exempt, nonprofit organization.

ELIGIBILITY:
Candidates for the Weiss Clinical Advancement Scholarship must:
(1) be an active member of the Society of Nuclear Medicine and Molecular Imaging;
(2) be currently enrolled in a didactic educational program(s) (ex. CT, MR, DEXA, EKG, tomography, sonography, exercise physiology, physics, statistics) which is/are college/continuing education credit-eligible and;
(3) complete the said class or program; it is not required that class/program completion results in a degree.

FINANCIAL DATA:
Amount of support per award: $500.

CO-OP FUNDING PROGRAMS: Susan C. Weiss Clinical Advancement Scholarship is made possible through a grant from the Education and Research Foundation for Nuclear Medicine and Molecular Imaging (ERF).

NO. AWARDS: 1.

APPLICATION INFO:
Applications for the Weiss Clinical Advancement Scholarship are submitted through the above web site. Applicants must provide:
(1) a current resume or curriculum vitae;
(2) a professional reference letter as either a signed original on institution letterhead or a scanned copy of the signed original;
(3) an applicant statement not to exceed one page that details applicant's activity level in the SNMMI Technologist Section (SNMMI-TS) and states applicant's career and educational goals and the type of help the applicant expects from the course/program in order to achieve these goals.
This scholarship program is for serious applicants only.

Duration: One year.

Deadline: January 13.

OFFICERS:
Virginia Pappas, Chief Executive Officer

ADDRESS INQUIRIES TO:
Mary McMahon
Director of Development
(See telephone or e-mail address above.)

SOCIETY OF RADIOLOGISTS IN ULTRASOUND [2255]

1891 Preston White Drive
Reston, VA 20191
(703) 858-9210
Fax: (703) 880-0295
E-mail: info@sru.org
Web Site: www.sru.org

AREAS OF INTEREST:
Diagnostic ultrasound.

TYPE:
Research grants.

PURPOSE:
To fund clinical ultrasound research projects.

ELIGIBILITY:
Applicants must be members of the Society of Radiologists in Ultrasound. Membership requirements include board certification in diagnostic radiology with majority of the member's practice being in diagnostic ultrasound.

FINANCIAL DATA:
Funds are made payable to applicant's institution.

Total amount of support: Up to $25,000.

NO. MOST RECENT APPLICANTS: 4.

NO. AWARDS: 1.

APPLICATION INFO:
Submit a curriculum vitae, a five-page summary of proposed project and a proposed budget.

Duration: Varies.

ADDRESS INQUIRIES TO:
Susan Roberts, Executive Director
(See address above.)

TASTE AND SMELL CLINIC [2256]

Center for Molecular Nutrition and Sensory Disorders
5125 MacArthur Boulevard, N.W., Suite 20
Washington, DC 20016
(202) 364-4180
Fax: (202) 364-9727
E-mail: doc@tasteandsmell.com
Web Site: www.tasteandsmell.com

FOUNDED: 1969

AREAS OF INTEREST:
Taste and smell, clinical treatment of patients with taste and smell disorders, growth factors in relationship to stem cell maturation and development, saliva, salivary diagnostics, salivary proteins, functional magnetic imaging of the brain, transcranial magnetic stimulation of the brain, nasal mucus physiology and pathology, and nasal mucus diagnostics.

CONSULTING OR VOLUNTEER SERVICES:
The Taste and Smell Dysfunction Foundation.

NAME(S) OF PROGRAMS:
- **Taste and Smell Disorders Internship Program**

TYPE:
Internships; Training grants. The Taste and Smell Disorders Internship Program is offered to provide internships and programs to evaluate and treat patients with taste and smell dysfunctions.

YEAR PROGRAM STARTED: 1975

PURPOSE:
To provide internships and other programs to evaluate and treat patients with taste and smell dysfunctions; to study salivary and nasal mucus proteins; to support biochemists and physicians interested in cognitive neurology who want to come work with the clinic.

LEGAL BASIS:
Private organization.

ELIGIBILITY:
Preference to individuals from the Washington, DC metropolitan area.

GEOG. RESTRICTIONS: Washington, DC region.

FINANCIAL DATA:
Stipend commensurate with best academic and/or clinical achievement.

Amount of support per award: Varies depending on need and tasks required.

Total amount of support: $20,000 to $60,000 per year.

CO-OP FUNDING PROGRAMS: Taste and Smell Dysfunction Foundation.

NO. MOST RECENT APPLICANTS: 3.

NO. AWARDS: 1.

APPLICATION INFO:
Resume and three letters of recommendation from scientific mentors are required.

Duration: One year. Renewable for second and third year.

Deadline: June 30.

STAFF:
R.I. Henkin, Director
S. Holen, Staff Scientist
S.J. Potolicchio, Senior Scientist in Neurology

ADDRESS INQUIRIES TO:
R.I. Henkin, Director
(See address above.)

*SPECIAL STIPULATIONS:
Work limited to Washington, DC region.

U.S. DEPARTMENT OF THE NAVY [2257]

Navy Bureau of Medicine and Surgery
NM Accessions Department
8955 Wood Road, Suite 13154
Bethesda, MD 20889-5628
(301) 319-4059
(301) 295-9950
E-mail: usn.ohstudent@mail.mil
Web Site: www.med.navy.mil/Accessions/Pages/default.aspx

FOUNDED: 1972

AREAS OF INTEREST:
Medicine, dentistry, optometry, and clinical psychology.

CONSULTING OR VOLUNTEER SERVICES:
Navy Recruiting Command.

NAME(S) OF PROGRAMS:
- **Navy Health Professions Scholarship Program (HPSP)**

TYPE:
Scholarships. This is an educational support program for individuals pursuing graduate degrees in professional medical programs and who have a desire to serve in the U.S. Navy following graduation.

YEAR PROGRAM STARTED: 1972

PURPOSE:
To provide officers for the Navy who are trained in these disciplines.

LEGAL BASIS:
Authorized by Public Law 92-426.

ELIGIBILITY:
Applicants must be:
(1) U.S. citizens (dual citizenship not permitted);
(2) physically qualified for a commission in the U.S. Navy and;
(3) accepted into an accredited school in the U.S. or Puerto Rico.

Eligible degree programs include medicine-allopathic (M.D.) or osteopathic (D.O.), dentistry (D.D.S. or D.M.D.), optometry (O.D.), and APA-accredited Ph.D. and Psy.D. degree programs.

GEOG. RESTRICTIONS: United States and Puerto Rico.

FINANCIAL DATA:
Amount of support per award: Scholarship includes full tuition (no upper limit) and allowable fees, reimbursement for all required books, supplies and equipment (some limits apply), $20,000 signing bonus (medicine and dentistry only), monthly stipend of $2,229.30 (taxable), full pay and allowances of an ensign (O-1) for 45 days per year (about $4,500), and reimbursement for student's health insurance if required by school.

Total amount of support: Over $125,000,000 in tuition and stipends. Part of annual Congressional appropriation.

NO. MOST RECENT APPLICANTS: 500 for medical; 200 for dental.

NO. AWARDS: 330.

APPLICATION INFO:
Must apply through Navy Recruiting Command.

Duration: Two to four years, according to year level upon entry. Acceptance of the program requires continuous participation until graduation. Dental scholarships are the same as medical scholarships.

Deadline: Rolling acceptance for medical, dental and optometry. Clinical psychology applications: January.

STAFF:
Dr. Sandra Yerkes, Program Manager

ADDRESS INQUIRIES TO:
See e-mail address above.

*SPECIAL STIPULATIONS:
For Scholarship awardees, one year of active duty (not in training) is required for each year of the Scholarship, with a three-year minimum.

THE UNIVERSITY OF CALGARY

Faculty of Graduate Studies
MacKimmie Library Tower, Room 213
2500 University Drive, N.W.
Calgary AB T2N 1N4 Canada
(403) 220-4938
Fax: (403) 289-7635
E-mail: gsaward@ucalgary.ca
Web Site: www.grad.ucalgary.ca/awards

TYPE:
Awards/prizes; Scholarships. Awards for study in the medical sciences. Tenable at The University of Calgary. Award endowed through a bequest of the late William H. Davies.

See entry 1730 for full listing.

THE UNIVERSITY OF SYDNEY [2258]

Scholarships Office
Level 5, Jane Foss Russell Building G02
The University of Sydney N.S.W. 2006
Australia
(02) 8627 8112
Fax: (02) 8627 8145
E-mail: scholarships.officer@sydney.edu.au
Web Site: www.sydney.edu.au/scholarships/research

FOUNDED: 1850

AREAS OF INTEREST:
Medicine.

NAME(S) OF PROGRAMS:
- **Sydney Medical School Postgraduate Research Scholarships**

TYPE:
Scholarships. For research leading to a higher degree. Tenable in the Sydney Medical School at the University of Sydney.

PURPOSE:
To promote and encourage research in the medical sciences at the University of Sydney.

LEGAL BASIS:
University.

ELIGIBILITY:
Available to full-time research candidates, normally Ph.D., in any department or research unit associated with the Sydney Medical School at the University of Sydney. Applicants must be either Australian citizens or permanent residents.

GEOG. RESTRICTIONS: Australia.

FINANCIAL DATA:
Amount of support per award: $25,849 AUD per annum for the year 2015.

NO. AWARDS: Varies according to availability of funds.

APPLICATION INFO:
Contact the University for guidelines.

Duration: One year. Renewal for second and third year subject to satisfactory progress.

ADDRESS INQUIRIES TO:
Scholarships Officer
Sydney Medical School (A27)
The University of Sydney
N.S.W. 2006 Australia
E-mail: scholarships@med.usyd.edu.au

*PLEASE NOTE:
Very few awards are available and competition for them is extremely keen. They are awarded strictly on academic merit and only graduates with First Class Honours or equivalent qualifications (e.g., graduation magna cum laude) will be considered.

THE VALLEY FOUNDATION [2259]
226 Airport Parkway
Suite 350
San Jose, CA 95110
(408) 358-4545
Fax: (408) 358-4548
E-mail: info@valley.org
Web Site: www.valley.org

FOUNDED: 1984

AREAS OF INTEREST:
Medical services and health care for lower-income households, the arts, senior citizens, education and research.

TYPE:
Project/program grants.

YEAR PROGRAM STARTED: 1984

PURPOSE:
To provide funding for nonprofit organizations in Santa Clara County, CA, with an emphasis in the medical field.

LEGAL BASIS:
Nonprofit foundation.

ELIGIBILITY:
Qualified 501(c)(3) charitable organizations. No individuals or political organizations.

GEOG. RESTRICTIONS: Santa Clara County, California.

FINANCIAL DATA:
The Foundation prefers to avoid grants which provide more than one-half of an organization's total budget in a 12-month period, usually expecting community and applicant commitment to a project through local cost sharing.

Amount of support per award: $10,000 to $1,000,000.

REPRESENTATIVE AWARDS:
$100,000 to Opera San Jose to fund artist salaries for the inaugural season at the California Theatre; $100,000 to Walden West School Foundation to fund Science Learning Center project; $25,000 to Diabetes Society of Santa Clara Valley to fund diabetes educational camps.

APPLICATION INFO:
Guidelines are available on the Foundation web site.

Duration: Varies, but multiple-year requests are discouraged. Organizations which have received funding must wait at least one full year before submitting another application. Organizations that did not make it to the full LOI full proposal cycle can reapply on the anniversary of their first LOI submission.

Deadline: February 20, May 20, August 20 and November 20.

PUBLICATIONS:
Application guidelines.

IRS I.D.: 94-1584547

ADDRESS INQUIRIES TO:
See e-mail address above.

Allergy, immunology, infectious diseases

AMERICAN ACADEMY OF ALLERGY ASTHMA & IMMUNOLOGY [2260]
555 East Wells Street, Suite 1100
Milwaukee, WI 53202-3823
(414) 272-6071
Fax: (414) 272-6070
E-mail: info@aaaai.org
Web Site: www.aaaai.org

FOUNDED: 1943

AREAS OF INTEREST:
Allergy and immunology.

NAME(S) OF PROGRAMS:
- **Travel Grant Awards**

TYPE:
Travel grants. Travel funds to attend the Academy's annual scientific meeting.

PURPOSE:
To advance the knowledge and practice of allergy by discussion at meetings, by fostering the education of students and the public, by encouraging union and cooperation among those engaged in this field and by promoting and stimulating research and study in allergy.

LEGAL BASIS:
Nonprofit.

ELIGIBILITY:
Travel grants for the annual meeting are awarded to member fellows-in-training in the field of allergy and immunology. The grants will be awarded on the basis of merit as judged by the committee. Individuals with a faculty appointment will not be considered.

GEOG. RESTRICTIONS: United States and Canada.

FINANCIAL DATA:
Amount of support per award: Up to $800 for travel to the annual meeting for first- and second-year fellows-in-training; up to $650 for third- or fourth-year fellows-in-training; up to $1,100 for applicants who submit an abstract which is accepted for presentation.

APPLICATION INFO:
Application information is available online.

ADDRESS INQUIRIES TO:
Mari Duran, Program Manager
(See address above.)

ARTHRITIS NATIONAL RESEARCH FOUNDATION (ANRF)
5354 East Second Street, Suite 201
Long Beach, CA 90803
(800) 588-2873
(562) 437-6808
E-mail: hbelisle@curearthritis.org
Web Site: www.curearthritis.org

TYPE:
Research grants; Travel grants. ANRF Arthritis Research Grants are intended to support basic and clinical research focusing on rheumatic and related autoimmune diseases, such as osteoarthritis and rheumatoid arthritis.

See entry 2170 for full listing.

CANCER RESEARCH INSTITUTE
One Exchange Plaza
55 Broadway, Suite 1802
New York, NY 10006
(212) 688-7515
(800) 992-2623
Fax: (212) 832-9376
E-mail: grants@cancerresearch.org
Web Site: www.cancerresearch.org

TYPE:
Fellowships; Research grants; Training grants.

See entry 2358 for full listing.

DYSTROPHIC EPIDERMOLYSIS BULLOSA RESEARCH ASSOCIATION OF AMERICA, INC. (DEBRA) [2261]
75 Broad Street
Suite 300
New York, NY 10004
(212) 868-1573 ext. 110
Fax: (212) 868-9296
E-mail: staff@debra.org
Web Site: www.debra.org

FOUNDED: 1980

AREAS OF INTEREST:
Research into the causes, treatment and cure of EB and other genetic disorders of the skin.

NAME(S) OF PROGRAMS:
- **debra International Research Grants**

TYPE:
Research grants. Financial aid for EB families in crisis.

YEAR PROGRAM STARTED: 1980

PURPOSE:
To provide opportunity to advance research into the effects, causes, treatments and cure for epidermolysis bullosa.

ELIGIBILITY:
Peer-reviewed grants made to full-time or part-time researchers.

FINANCIAL DATA:
Amount of support per award: Varies.

Total amount of support: Varies.

APPLICATION INFO:
Guidelines may be obtained from the organization at the address above.

Duration: One to three years.

IRS I.D.: 11-2519726

ADDRESS INQUIRIES TO:
Brett Kopelan, Executive Director
(See address above.)

IMMUNE DEFICIENCY FOUNDATION [2262]
110 West Road
Suite 300
Towson, MD 21204
(410) 321-6647
Fax: (410) 321-9165
E-mail: tcaulder@primaryimmune.org
Web Site: usidnet.org
primaryimmune.org

AREAS OF INTEREST:
Immunodeficiency diseases.

NAME(S) OF PROGRAMS:
- **U.S. Immunodeficiency Network**

TYPE:
Travel grants; Visiting scholars.

YEAR PROGRAM STARTED: 2003

PURPOSE:
To improve the diagnosis and treatment of patients with primary immunodeficiency diseases through research and education.

ELIGIBILITY:
Open to researchers whose work focuses on identifying the causes and treatment of primary immunodeficiency diseases.

GEOG. RESTRICTIONS: United States.

FINANCIAL DATA:
Amount of support per award: Generally up to $2,200.

Total amount of support: $1,500,000.

NO. MOST RECENT APPLICANTS: 11.

NO. AWARDS: 4 to 6 per year.

APPLICATION INFO:
Contact the Foundation for guidelines.

Duration: Travel grants (reimbursement) for one- to two-week training visits.

Deadline: Applications accepted on a rolling basis.

ADDRESS INQUIRIES TO:
Tara Caulder
USIDNET Project Director
(See address above.)

MAGIC JOHNSON FOUNDATION, INC.

9100 Wilshire Boulevard
Suite 700, East Tower
Beverly Hills, CA 90212
(310) 246-4400
Fax: (310) 786-8796
Web Site: www.magicjohnson.org

TYPE:
Project/program grants; Scholarships; Technical assistance.

See entry 172 for full listing.

LOVELACE RESPIRATORY RESEARCH INSTITUTE [2263]

2425 Ridgecrest Drive, S.E.
Albuquerque, NM 87108
(505) 348-9400
Fax: (505) 348-8567
E-mail: info@lrri.org
Web Site: www.lrri.org

FOUNDED: 1947

AREAS OF INTEREST:
Respiratory diseases.

NAME(S) OF PROGRAMS:
- **Postdoctoral Training Program**

TYPE:
Fellowships. Training program in respiratory tract disease caused by environmental agents.

YEAR PROGRAM STARTED: 1947

PURPOSE:
To provide research into prevention, treatment and cure of respiratory disease.

LEGAL BASIS:
Private biomedical research organization.

ELIGIBILITY:
Programs are tailored to individuals. Laboratory research or pathogenesis of disease can focus on one of several disciplinary areas, including cell biology, molecular biology, biochemistry, immunology, pathology, physiology, radiobiology or aerosol science, depending on interests and qualifications. Applicants must be U.S. citizens or permanent residents or eligible for a visa.

GEOG. RESTRICTIONS: United States.

FINANCIAL DATA:
Fellowship includes stipend and health insurance, relocation allowance, tuition and fees.

Amount of support per award: Varies.

Total amount of support: Varies.

NO. MOST RECENT APPLICANTS: 26.

NO. AWARDS: Varies.

APPLICATION INFO:
Application form required. Contact Institute for application guidelines.

Duration: One year. Renewable for second and third year.

Deadline: Varies.

ROBERT MAPPLETHORPE FOUNDATION, INC.

477 Madison Avenue, 15th Floor
New York, NY 10022-5835
(212) 755-3025
Fax: (212) 941-4764
E-mail: joree@mapplethorpe.org
Web Site: www.mapplethorpe.org

TYPE:
Project/program grants. Funds medical research in the fight against AIDS and HIV infection and supports the promotion of photography as a fine art, embracing exhibitions, acquisitions, and publications.

See entry 457 for full listing.

Dentistry

THE AMERICAN ACADEMY OF ESTHETIC DENTISTRY [2264]

225 West Wacker Drive
Suite 650
Chicago, IL 60606
(312) 981-6770
Fax: (312) 265-2908
E-mail: info@estheticacademy.org
Web Site: www.estheticacademy.org

FOUNDED: 1975

AREAS OF INTEREST:
Dentistry.

NAME(S) OF PROGRAMS:
- **AAED Esthetic Dentistry Research Grants**

TYPE:
Research grants.

YEAR PROGRAM STARTED: 1993

PURPOSE:
To promote the integration of dental esthetics into the total spectrum of oral health care.

ELIGIBILITY:
Applicant must be a graduate student or young untenured faculty at the instructor or assistant professor level at an accredited dental school.

GEOG. RESTRICTIONS: United States, Canada and Puerto Rico.

FINANCIAL DATA:
Amount of support per award: Up to $3,000.

NO. MOST RECENT APPLICANTS: 8.

NO. AWARDS: 1 per year.

APPLICATION INFO:
Contact the Academy for application procedures.

Duration: One year.

Deadline: End of May.

ADDRESS INQUIRIES TO:
Joe Jackson, Executive Director
(See address above.)

AMERICAN ACADEMY OF IMPLANT DENTISTRY (AAID) FOUNDATION [2265]

211 East Chicago Avenue
Suite 750
Chicago, IL 60611
(312) 335-1550
Fax: (312) 335-9090
E-mail: afshin@aaid.com
Web Site: www.aaid.com

FOUNDED: 1979

AREAS OF INTEREST:
Dental implant research.

NAME(S) OF PROGRAMS:
- **Humanitarian Project Support**
- **Research Award**
- **Student Research Grant**
- **Wish a Smile**

TYPE:
Awards/prizes; Project/program grants; Research grants. Humanitarian Project Support is available to those 501(c)(3) organizations who support the handicapped or disabled and medically-at-risk in need of dental implant.

Research Award provides limited support for meritorious dental implant research projects which determine the feasibility of a larger research project. This may be described as the conduct of pilot studies or venture research to develop and test new techniques and procedures, to carry out a small clinical or animal research project and to analyze existing data.

Student Research Grant is available for all graduate dental students. Research must be related to dental implant.

Wish a Smile, a partnership between the AAID Foundation, Dental Lifeline Network, Implant and Bone Grafting corporate sponsors and volunteer dentists, aims to provide free dental service to patients who have congenitally missing teeth and are financially disadvantaged. The AAIDF and DLN would seek to get all needed restorative supplies and services donated in addition to implant.

YEAR PROGRAM STARTED: 1981

PURPOSE:
To provide limited support for meritorious dental implant research projects; to provide a humanitarian service to the public; to increase public awareness of the AAID Foundation, AAID, AAID's members and Dental Lifeline Network.

LEGAL BASIS:
Research foundation.

ELIGIBILITY:
Investigators from any scientific discipline and at any stage of their career may apply for a Research Award. These awards are

appropriated for new investigators and those changing areas of research or resuming research careers.

Student Research Grant is available to postgraduate dental students for implant-related research studies.

Wish a Smile requires applicants to meet the following criteria:
(1) be 16 to 29 years old at the time of application;
(2) be congenitally missing one to three teeth with no more than three teeth requiring replacement;
(3) be medically healthy and a nonsmoker and;
(4) have a patient or family gross income (if patient is a dependent minor) that is low or displays significant need.

FINANCIAL DATA:
Grants may be used for supplies, small items of equipment and salary for technical and support personnel.

Amount of support per award: Humanitarian Project Support: Varies; Small Research Award: Up to $25,000 (total project costs); Student Research Grant: Up to $2,500 per year.

Total amount of support: $78,000.

NO. MOST RECENT APPLICANTS: 36.

NO. AWARDS: Research Award: 1 to 3; Student Research Grant: Up to 8.

APPLICATION INFO:
Required documentation includes abstract of research plan, budget estimate, explanation of the project, including its specific aims, significance, experimental design and methods, sequence of events and time schedule and a complete bibliography, curriculum vitae and a list of all co-investigators and consultants.

Duration: Student Research Grant: Up to two years. Nonrenewable.

Deadline: Research Award: August 1. Student Research Grant: May 1.

PUBLICATIONS:
Guidelines.

OFFICERS:
Jaime Lozada, D.D.S., Chairman
Sharon Bennett, Chief Executive Officer

ADDRESS INQUIRIES TO:
F. Afshin Alavi, Chief Financial Officer
(See address above.)

AMERICAN ASSOCIATION FOR DENTAL RESEARCH [2266]

1619 Duke Street
Alexandria, VA 22314-3406
(703) 548-0066
Fax: (703) 548-1883
E-mail: sherren@iadr.org
Web Site: www.aadr.org

AREAS OF INTEREST:
Dental research.

NAME(S) OF PROGRAMS:
- **AADR Hatton Competition**

TYPE:
Awards/prizes. For junior investigators (junior, senior and postdoctoral) who exhibit potential for a productive career in dental research.

PURPOSE:
To advance research and increase knowledge for the improvement of oral health; to support and represent the oral health research community; to facilitate the communication and application of research findings.

ELIGIBILITY:
Applicants must be U.S. citizens or noncitizen nationals of the U.S. (or who have been lawfully admitted for permanent residence at the time of submission of the abstract - those with a "green card") or persons of other nationalities whose research is performed in the U.S. Must be an AADR member. There is no age limit for entrants in the AADR competition.

FINANCIAL DATA:
Amount of support per award: First prize: $1,000; Second prize: $500.

Total amount of support: $4,500.

NO. AWARDS: 3 First Prizes and 3 Second Prizes.

APPLICATION INFO:
Details of the abstract to be submitted are available on the web site.

Deadline: October 13, 2016.

ADDRESS INQUIRIES TO:
Sheri S. Herren
Strategic Programs Manager
(See address above.)

AMERICAN ASSOCIATION FOR DENTAL RESEARCH [2267]

1619 Duke Street
Alexandria, VA 22314-3406
(703) 548-0066
Fax: (703) 548-1883
E-mail: sherren@iadr.org
Web Site: www.aadr.org

AREAS OF INTEREST:
Basic and clinical research related to oral health.

NAME(S) OF PROGRAMS:
- **Student Research Fellowships**

PURPOSE:
To advance research and increase knowledge for the improvement of oral health; to support and represent the oral health research community; to facilitate the communication and application of research findings.

ELIGIBILITY:
Applicant must be enrolled in an accredited D.D.S./D.M.D. or hygiene program in a dental institution and must be sponsored by a faculty member. Students should not have received their degree, nor should they in the year of award. Applicant may have an advanced degree in a basic science subject. Must be an AADR member.

GEOG. RESTRICTIONS: United States.

FINANCIAL DATA:
Amount of support per award: $2,700.

Total amount of support: Varies.

NO. AWARDS: 16 for the year 2016.

APPLICATION INFO:
Proposals will follow the general format of the Public Health Service Grant Application Form PHS 398, which is to be used only as a guideline. Each proposal must include the following:
(1) objectives, describing what the research is intended to accomplish and the hypothesis to be tested;
(2) research strategy, including significance, innovation and approach;
(3) facilities and equipment to be used for the research project;
(4) other support for applicant and sponsor and;
(5) for those projects involving Recombinant DNA/Recombinant DNA Molecules, an indication that the project adheres to the current NIH Guidelines for Research Involving Recombinant DNA Molecules.

The following documents must also be included:
(1) cover letter from the applicant's sponsor, indicating the dental school's and the sponsor's support of the proposed research;
(2) cover letter from the applicant explaining student's motivations and reasons to have the Fellowship experience and what plans are after completion of this phase of their education;
(3) curriculum vitae, not to exceed two pages, outlining the student's career up to the time of application;
(4) sponsor's biographical sketch in NIH format, not to exceed two pages;
(5) literature cited and;
(6) documentation that the project has been approved by the Institutional Review Board for projects involving human subjects or vertebrate animals.

Proposals longer than four pages (PDF) and/or 1,400 words will not be considered.

Deadline: January 19.

ADDRESS INQUIRIES TO:
Sheri S. Herren
Strategic Programs Manager
(See address above.)

AMERICAN ASSOCIATION FOR DENTAL RESEARCH [2268]

1619 Duke Street
Alexandria, VA 22314-3406
(703) 548-0066
Fax: (703) 548-1883
E-mail: sherren@iadr.org
Web Site: www.aadr.org

AREAS OF INTEREST:
Clinical research in periodontology.

NAME(S) OF PROGRAMS:
- **William B. Clark Fellowship in Clinical Research**

TYPE:
Fellowships.

PURPOSE:
To advance research and increase knowledge for the improvement of oral health; to support and represent the oral health research community; to facilitate the communication and application of research findings.

ELIGIBILITY:
Applicant must have completed first professional degree, should be appointed at an accredited dental school or academic research center in U.S., and must be a member of AADR.

GEOG. RESTRICTIONS: United States.

FINANCIAL DATA:
Amount of support per award: $5,000.

Total amount of support: $5,000.

APPLICATION INFO:
Applicants must submit the following:
(1) letter stating their interest in applying for the award;
(2) curriculum vitae;
(3) three- to four-page (double-spaced) overview of their proposed areas of training, including how the experience will affect

future research to be conducted by the applicant;
(4) brief description of the facility which will provide the training and;
(5) letter of support from the proposed mentor.

Deadline: October 13, 2016.

ADDRESS INQUIRIES TO:
Sheri S. Herren
Strategic Programs Manager
(See address above.)

AMERICAN ASSOCIATION FOR DENTAL RESEARCH [2269]

1619 Duke Street
Alexandria, VA 22314-3406
(703) 548-0066
Fax: (703) 548-1883
E-mail: sherren@iadr.org
Web Site: www.aadr.org

AREAS OF INTEREST:
Dental research.

NAME(S) OF PROGRAMS:
- **William J. Gies Award**

TYPE:
Awards/prizes. For the best paper published in the *Journal of Dental Research* during the preceding year.

PURPOSE:
To advance research and increase knowledge for the improvement of oral health; to support and represent the oral health research community; to facilitate the communication and application of research findings.

FINANCIAL DATA:
Amount of support per award: $1,000.

Total amount of support: $1,000.

APPLICATION INFO:
Information on the nomination process is available on the web site.

Deadline: October 13, 2016.

ADDRESS INQUIRIES TO:
Sheri S. Herren
Strategic Programs Manager
(See address above.)

AMERICAN ASSOCIATION OF WOMEN DENTISTS [2270]

7794 Grow Drive
Pensacola, FL 32514
(850) 484-9987
(800) 920-2293
Fax: (850) 484-8762
E-mail: info@aawd.org
Web Site: www.aawd.org

FOUNDED: 1921

AREAS OF INTEREST:
Dentistry.

NAME(S) OF PROGRAMS:
- **Colgate Research Scholarship**
- **Procter & Gamble Research Award for Postdoctoral Students**
- **Smiles for Success Program**

TYPE:
Awards/prizes; Scholarships. Colgate Research Scholarships support AAWD member/junior or senior dental students who are involved in dental research.

Proctor & Gamble Research Award for Postdoctoral Students provides a scholarship for research projects involving women's oral health.

Smiles for Success Program helps women in transition from welfare to work by providing low- or no-cost dental work.

PURPOSE:
To encourage women dental students who contribute to the school, to dentistry or dental health who are in need of financial assistance.

ELIGIBILITY:
Applicants must be dentists or junior/senior dental students.

FINANCIAL DATA:
Amount of support per award: Varies.

Total amount of support: Varies.

CO-OP FUNDING PROGRAMS: Scholarships are donated by Colgate Company and other organizations and members.

APPLICATION INFO:
Contact the Association for detailed guidelines.

Duration: One year.

Deadline: Applications for Colgate Research Scholarship are accepted January to April. Applications for Proctor and Gamble Research Award are accepted April to August. Smiles for Success Program applications are accepted year-round.

PUBLICATIONS:
Chronicle; *Women's Dental Journal.*

ADDRESS INQUIRIES TO:
Donna Deans, Executive Director
(See address above.)

AMERICAN DENTAL ASSISTANTS ASSOCIATION [2271]

140 North Bloomingdale Road
Bloomingdale, IL 60108
(630) 994-4247
Fax: (630) 351-8490
E-mail: jaykasper@adaausa.org
Web Site: www.adaausa.org

FOUNDED: 1923

AREAS OF INTEREST:
Dental assisting.

NAME(S) OF PROGRAMS:
- **Juliette A. Southard/Oral-B Laboratories Scholarship Program**

TYPE:
Scholarships. Tuition scholarships awarded to dental assisting students interested in furthering their education.

YEAR PROGRAM STARTED: 1946

PURPOSE:
To provide financial assistance for highly qualified applicants pursuing dental assisting education.

LEGAL BASIS:
Nonprofit professional organization.

ELIGIBILITY:
Applicants must be high school graduates or equivalent and enrolled in a dental assisting program. Candidates will be considered on the basis of academic achievement, ability, interest in dentistry and personal attributes. Must be a member of the ADAA.

GEOG. RESTRICTIONS: United States.

FINANCIAL DATA:
Amount of support per award: Up to $750, a congratulatory letter and one year active membership with the ADAA.

NO. MOST RECENT APPLICANTS: 7 for the year 2014.

NO. AWARDS: Up to 10 for the year 2014.

APPLICATION INFO:
Applicants must submit academic transcripts (high school and/or college), proof of acceptance into an accredited program and a letter of intent to pursue a long-range career in dental assisting. Two letters of reference are also required.

Duration: One year.

Deadline: March 15.

STAFF:
John Kasper, Executive Director

ADDRESS INQUIRIES TO:
Scholarship Committee
(See address above.)

AMERICAN DENTAL HYGIENISTS' ASSOCIATION INSTITUTE FOR ORAL HEALTH [2272]

444 North Michigan Avenue
Suite 3400
Chicago, IL 60611
(312) 440-8900 ext. 261 or 770
(800) 735-4916
Fax: (312) 467-1806
E-mail: institute@adha.net
Web Site: www.adha.org/institute-for-oral-health

FOUNDED: 1927

AREAS OF INTEREST:
Dental hygiene.

NAME(S) OF PROGRAMS:
- **ADHA Institute Dental Hygiene Scholarships**

TYPE:
Scholarships. The Graduate Scholarship Program awards licensed dental hygienists who are, or will be, enrolled as graduate students in a program leading to a Master's or doctoral degree in dental hygiene or dental hygiene education. There is also an undergraduate scholarship program.

YEAR PROGRAM STARTED: 1986

PURPOSE:
To invest in the future careers of dental hygiene students by ensuring that they will be of exceptional quality and dedication.

LEGAL BASIS:
501(c)(3) public charity, as described in Sections 509(1)(1)-170(b)(1)(A)(vi) of the Internal Revenue Code.

ELIGIBILITY:
Applicant must be an undergraduate or graduate student in an accredited dental hygiene program in the U.S.

GEOG. RESTRICTIONS: United States.

FINANCIAL DATA:
Amount of support per award: $1,000 to $2,000.

Total amount of support: $60,000 for the year 2014.

NO. MOST RECENT APPLICANTS: 115.

NO. AWARDS: 55.

APPLICATION INFO:
Applications can only be downloaded from the web site.

Duration: Scholarships are awarded for a period of one academic year.

Deadline: February 1.

PUBLICATIONS:
Annual report.

ADDRESS INQUIRIES TO:
John Brazas, IOH Development Manager
(See address above.)

HISPANIC DENTAL ASSOCIATION FOUNDATION [2273]

3910 South IH-35, Suite 245
Austin, TX 78704
(512) 904-0252
Fax: (512) 904-0254
E-mail: support@hdassoc.org
Web Site: www.hdassoc.org

FOUNDED: 1990

AREAS OF INTEREST:
Oral health careers.

NAME(S) OF PROGRAMS:

- **A-dec Scholarship**
- **Colgate-Palmolive Scholarship**
- **Hispanic Dental Association Scholarship**
- **Procter & Gamble Scholarship**
- **Dr. Esperanza Rodriguez Scholarship**
- **Dr. Juan D. Villarreal Scholarship**

TYPE:
Awards/prizes; Conferences/seminars; Internships; Product donations; Scholarships.

YEAR PROGRAM STARTED: 1990

PURPOSE:
To encourage entry of Hispanics into oral health careers.

ELIGIBILITY:
Students must have permanent resident status in the U.S., be current student members of the Hispanic Dental Association, and attending U.S. dental schools.

Colgate-Palmolive Scholarships are open to student members of the Association who have been accepted into or are currently enrolled in an accredited Master's program in a dentistry-related field. Students must have an undergraduate or graduate degree in an oral health-related field (dental hygienist, dentistry, etc.) from the U.S. or abroad.

Dr. Esperanza Rodriguez Scholarship is open to second- or third-year dental students.

Dr. Juan D. Villarreal Scholarships are open to student members of the Association who have been accepted into or are currently enrolled in an accredited dental school or dental hygiene program in the state of Texas. The student may be at any stage of the undergraduate program, first through fourth years.

GEOG. RESTRICTIONS: Dr. Juan D. Villareal Scholarship: Texas; United States for all others.

FINANCIAL DATA:
Amount of support per award: Colgate-Palmolive Scholarships: $4,000; Hispanic Dental Association Scholarship: $1,500 for Dental students and $750 for Dental Hygiene students; Procter & Gamble Scholarships: $2,000 for Dental students and $1,000 for Dental Hygiene students; Dr. Esperanza Rodriguez Scholarship: $1,000; Dr. Juan D. Villarreal Scholarships: $1,000 for Dental students and $500 for Dental Hygiene student.

Total amount of support: Varies.

NO. MOST RECENT APPLICANTS: Approximately 90.

NO. AWARDS: Colgate-Palmolive Scholarships: Varies; Hispanic Dental Association Scholarships and Procter & Gamble Scholarships: 6; Dr, Esperanza Rodriguez Scholarships: 1; Dr. Juan D. Villarreal Scholarships: 2 for Dental students and 1 for Dental Hygiene student.

APPLICATION INFO:
Application can be downloaded from the web site.

Duration: One year. Renewal possible by reapplication.

Deadline: September 15.

STAFF:
Jessica Chihuahua, Membership and Communications Coordinator

ADDRESS INQUIRIES TO:
See e-mail address above.

INTERNATIONAL ASSOCIATION FOR DENTAL RESEARCH (IADR) [2274]

1619 Duke Street
Alexandria, VA 22314-3406
(703) 548-0066
Fax: (703) 548-1883
E-mail: sherren@iadr.org
Web Site: www.iadr.org

AREAS OF INTEREST:
Original research in the area of oral health, basic, clinical and applied studies.

NAME(S) OF PROGRAMS:

- **IADR Colgate Research in Prevention Travel Awards**

TYPE:
Awards/prizes; Travel grants. These Awards are for young investigators who have submitted an abstract which has a preventive component for a travel award to support their attendance at the IADR General Session.

Contact IADR for the full range of awards.

PURPOSE:
To advance research and increase knowledge for the improvement of oral health; to support and represent the oral health research community; to facilitate the communication and applications of research findings.

ELIGIBILITY:
Applicants must be IADR members. Young investigators (up to five years postgraduation from dental, dental hygiene, specialty training or pre-Ph.D.) are eligible to apply for a travel award. (No persons who have already obtained a Ph.D. are eligible to apply.) Entrants must provide a verification letter of their educational status and can only receive this Award once.

FINANCIAL DATA:
Amount of support per award: $2,000.

Total amount of support: $2,000.

NO. AWARDS: 1 for North America (Canada, U.S. and Mexico). There are also Awards for other geographic regions.

APPLICATION INFO:
In applying for this Award, candidates must submit their abstract as well as a separate and more detailed overview of their projects (two pages, double-spaced). This overview must include brief details of their material and methods, the results of the research including details of statistical analysis and a brief discussion including how the research will affect the prevention of the condition stated.

Deadline: October 13, 2016.

ADDRESS INQUIRIES TO:
Sheri S. Herren
Grants and Awards Manager
(See e-mail address above.)

NATIONAL INSTITUTE OF DENTAL AND CRANIOFACIAL RESEARCH (NIDCR) [2275]

National Institutes of Health
6701 Democracy Boulevard, Room 688
Bethesda, MD 20892
(301) 496-4263
Fax: (301) 402-7033
E-mail: friedenla@nidcr.nih.gov
Web Site: www.nidcr.nih.gov/careersandtraining

FOUNDED: 1948

AREAS OF INTEREST:
Dental, craniofacial health and research.

NAME(S) OF PROGRAMS:

- **Individual NRSA Postdoctoral Fellowships (F-32)**

TYPE:
Fellowships. Provides up to three years of support for trainees at academic institutions to broaden their scientific background or extend their potential for research in health-related areas.

YEAR PROGRAM STARTED: 1974

PURPOSE:
To develop individuals for careers in oral health research.

LEGAL BASIS:
Public Health Service Act as amended, Section 301c; 42 CFR 61; 42 U.S.C. 288a.

ELIGIBILITY:
Applicants must be citizens, non-citizen nationals or permanent residents of the U.S. at the time of the award and have a Ph.D., M.D., D.D.S., D.O., D.V.M. or equivalent degree prior to the beginning date of the proposed fellowship.

GEOG. RESTRICTIONS: United States.

FINANCIAL DATA:
Stipend level is based on number of years of postdoctoral experience. Additional funds are available for other training-related expenses.

Amount of support per award: Stipend levels are $43,692 to $57,504. Up to $8,850 per 12 months for institutional allowances.

Total amount of support: Varies.

APPLICATION INFO:
Detailed information can be obtained from the Institute.

Duration: One, two or three years.

Deadline: April 8, August 8 and December 8.

ADDRESS INQUIRIES TO:
Leslie Frieden
Extramural Training Officer
(See address above.)

NATIONAL INSTITUTE OF DENTAL AND CRANIOFACIAL RESEARCH (NIDCR) [2276]

National Institutes of Health
31 Center Drive, Room 5B-55
MSC 2190
Bethesda, MD 20892-2190
(301) 496-4261
Fax: (301) 496-9988
E-mail: nidcrinfo@mail.nih.gov
Web Site: www.nidcr.nih.gov

FOUNDED: 1948

AREAS OF INTEREST:
Multiple areas of research with the goal of improving dental, oral and craniofacial health.

NAME(S) OF PROGRAMS:
- **AIDS and Immunosuppression**
- **Behavioral & Social Science Research**
- **Career Development**
- **Clinical Research & Clinical Trials**
- **Computational Science**
- **Craniofacial and Dental Developmental Disorders**
- **Dental Materials & Biomaterials**
- **Epidemiology**
- **Gene Discovery**
- **Genomics & Multi-omics Analysis**
- **Health Disparities**
- **Immunopathology & Immunotherapy**
- **Oral Immunology**
- **Oral Microbiology & Metagenomics**
- **Oral, Oropharyngeal & Salivary Gland Cancers**
- **Orofacial Pain**
- **Salivary Biology & Dysfunction**
- **Small Business Innovation Research (SBIR)**
- **Small Business Technology Transfer (STTR)**
- **Statistical Analysis & Data Science**
- **Technology Development**
- **Temporomandibular Joint Disorder & Neurobiology**
- **Tissue Engineering and Regenerative Medicine**
- **Training & Fellowships**

TYPE:
Conferences/seminars; Project/program grants; Research grants; Research contracts. Grants for the support of basic and clinical research.

YEAR PROGRAM STARTED: 1948

PURPOSE:
To develop methods for preventing and treating oral diseases and conditions through research related to oral and craniofacial health.

LEGAL BASIS:
Public Health Service Act as amended, Section 301c; 42 CFR 61; 42 U.S.C. 288a.

ELIGIBILITY:
Open to scientists at universities, hospitals, laboratories and other public, nonprofit or profit institutions. Applications are competitively rated on the basis of scientific merit and grants must be approved by the National Advisory Dental and Craniofacial Research Council.

FINANCIAL DATA:
Amount of support per award: Varies.

APPLICATION INFO:
Varies by program. Visit the NIDCR web site above for detailed information.

Duration: Varies.

OFFICERS:
Martha J. Somerman, D.D.S., Ph.D., Director

NATIONAL INSTITUTE OF DENTAL AND CRANIOFACIAL RESEARCH (NIDCR) [2277]

National Institutes of Health
6701 Democracy Boulevard, Room 688
Bethesda, MD 20892
(301) 496-4263
Fax: (301) 402-7033
E-mail: friedenla@nidcr.nih.gov
Web Site: www.nidcr.nih.gov/careersandtraining

FOUNDED: 1948

AREAS OF INTEREST:
Biomedical and behavioral research.

NAME(S) OF PROGRAMS:
- **Individual NRSA Senior Fellowship Award (F-33)**

TYPE:
Fellowships. Provides health research training for experienced scientists, enabling them to update their skills or make changes in the direction of their career.

YEAR PROGRAM STARTED: 1979

PURPOSE:
To provide opportunities for experienced scientists to make major changes in the direction of their research careers, to enlarge their scientific background, to acquire new research capabilities, or to enlarge their command of an allied research field.

LEGAL BASIS:
Section 472 of the Public Health Service Act as amended (42 U.S.C. 2981-1).

ELIGIBILITY:
Applicants must be citizens, non-citizen nationals or permanent residents of the U.S. at the time of the award. Applicants must be at least seven years beyond the qualifying doctoral degree and have a sponsoring institution and mentor.

GEOG. RESTRICTIONS: United States.

FINANCIAL DATA:
A stipend is provided. Additional funds are available for other training-related expenses.

Amount of support per award: Varies based on experience.

Total amount of support: Varies.

NO. AWARDS: 3.

APPLICATION INFO:
Detailed information can be obtained from the Institute.

Duration: Up to two years.

Deadline: April 8, August 8 and December 8.

ADDRESS INQUIRIES TO:
Leslie Frieden
Extramural Training Officer
(See address above.)

Internal medicine

A.S.P.E.N. RHOADS RESEARCH FOUNDATION

8630 Fenton Street
Suite 412
Silver Spring, MD 20910
(301) 587-6315
Fax: (301) 587-2365
E-mail: aspen@nutritioncare.org
Web Site: www.nutritioncare.org

TYPE:
Research grants. Annual support for nutritional research.

See entry 2322 for full listing.

AMERICAN SOCIETY OF HEMATOLOGY [2278]

2021 L Street, N.W.
Suite 900
Washington, DC 20036
(202) 776-0544
E-mail: ashabstracts@hematology.org
Web Site: www.hematology.org

AREAS OF INTEREST:
Scientific abstracts.

NAME(S) OF PROGRAMS:
- **Abstract Achievement Award**
- **Outstanding Abstract Achievement Award**

TYPE:
Awards/prizes; Travel grants.

PURPOSE:
To offer need- and merit-based awards to select individuals in order to help defray annual meeting travel expenses.

ELIGIBILITY:
Abstract Achievement Award: Applicants must be undergraduate students, medical students, graduate students, resident physicians, and postdoctoral fellows who are both first author and presenter of an abstract.

Outstanding Abstract Achievement Award: Awards are offered to the first authors/presenters of abstracts that receive the highest score in the categories of undergraduate student, medical student, graduate student, resident physician, and postdoctoral fellow (M.D. or Ph.D.).

FINANCIAL DATA:
Amount of support per award: $500.

Total amount of support: Varies.

APPLICATION INFO:
Contact the Society for application procedures.

Duration: One-time award.

Deadline: Early August.

ADDRESS INQUIRIES TO:
Lisa Diop
Awards and Diversity Programs Manager
(See address above.)

AMERICAN SOCIETY OF NEPHROLOGY [2279]

1510 H Street, N.W.
Suite 800
Washington, DC 20005
(202) 640-4660
Fax: (202) 478-2117
E-mail: grants@asn-online.org
Web Site: www.asn-online.org

AREAS OF INTEREST:
Nephrology.

NAME(S) OF PROGRAMS:
- **ASN Research Fellowships**

TYPE:
Fellowships. ASN Research Fellowships: The Society especially encourages applications from women and members of underrepresented minorities.

PURPOSE:
To fund fellows to conduct original, meritorious research projects, fostering, under the direction of a sponsor, the training of fellows who are highly motivated to make contributions to the understanding of kidney biology and disease.

ELIGIBILITY:
To apply for an ASN Research Fellowship, a candidate:
(1) must hold an M.D., D.O., Ph.D. or the equivalent degree;
(2) may not have completed more than three years of research training after the completion of the M.D. or D.O. degree or equivalent, or one year of postdoctoral research training after the Ph.D. degree (at the time of the activation of the award);
(3) cannot have or have had at any time a faculty position at any academic institution;
(4) must complete research under the direction and mentorship of a sponsor;
(5) must be a member of ASN at the time of the fellowship application; the sponsor of the candidate must also be an ASN member at the time of the fellowship application;
(6) cannot hold another full fellowship award such as another foundation fellowship or grant or a postdoctoral research fellowship from the National Institutes of Health; however, a candidate's institutions may supplement the support provided by ASN;
(7) must be working in North or Central America during the fellowship period and;
(8) must commit a minimum of 75% time to research during the fellowship period.

GEOG. RESTRICTIONS: North America.

FINANCIAL DATA:
Funds must be used for salary support (including fringe benefits) and cannot be used for project costs, travel expenses or overhead costs.

Amount of support per award: $50,000 per year for up to two years.

Total amount of support: Varies.

NO. AWARDS: Approximately 10.

APPLICATION INFO:
Only online applications will be accepted.

Duration: Up to two years. Second-year funding is contingent on a satisfactory progress report.

Deadline: Mid-December.

AMERICAN SOCIETY OF NEPHROLOGY [2280]

1510 H Street, N.W.
Suite 800
Washington, DC 20005
(202) 640-4660
Fax: (202) 478-2117
E-mail: grants@asn-online.org
Web Site: www.asn-online.org

AREAS OF INTEREST:
Nephrology.

NAME(S) OF PROGRAMS:
- **William and Sandra Bennett Clinical Scholars Program**
- **NephCure Kidney International - ASN Foundation for Kidney Research Grant**
- **OHF - ASN Foundation for Kidney Research Grant**

TYPE:
Project/program grants; Research grants. William and Sandra Bennett Clinical Scholars Program supports aspiring nephrology educators to conduct a project to advance all facets of nephrology education and teaching.

NephCure Kidney International - ASN Foundation for Kidney Research Grant supports investigations of glomerular disease.

OHF - ASN Foundation for Kidney Research Grant supports research on topics relevant to oxalosis, primary hyperoxaluria and related stone diseases.

FINANCIAL DATA:
Amount of support per award: William and Sandra Bennett Clinical Scholars Program: $50,000 annually. NephCure Kidney International - ASN Foundation for Kidney Research Grant and OHF - ASN Foundation for Kidney Research Grant: $100,000 annually.

NO. AWARDS: 1 of each award annually.

APPLICATION INFO:
Only online applications will be accepted.

Duration: Two years.

Deadline: Mid-December.

ADDRESS INQUIRIES TO:
E-mail: grants@asn-online.org

AMERICAN SOCIETY OF NEPHROLOGY [2281]

1510 H Street, N.W.
Suite 800
Washington, DC 20005
(202) 640-4660
Fax: (202) 478-2117
E-mail: grants@asn-online.org
Web Site: www.asn-online.org

AREAS OF INTEREST:
Nephrology.

NAME(S) OF PROGRAMS:
- **Carl W. Gottschalk Research Scholar Grant**
- **John Merrill Grant in Transplantation**
- **Norman Siegel Research Scholar Grant**

TYPE:
Research grants. The Gottschalk, Merrill and Siegel Grants are part of the Career Development Grant program.

PURPOSE:
To enhance and assist the study and practice of nephrology; to provide a forum for the promulgation of research; to meet the professional and continuing education needs of its members; to foster the independent careers of young investigators in biomedical research related to nephrology and transplantation.

ELIGIBILITY:
Merrill and Gottschalk Grants: Applicants must be active ASN members and hold an M.D., Ph.D., or equivalent degree. At the time of submission, the applicant's membership must be current and their dues paid. Appointment to full-time faculty must be confirmed in writing by the department chair, indicating the date of first full-time faculty appointment, and providing assurance that the department will provide needed resources for conducting independent research. Additionally, applicants will be considered ineligible should they submit more than one ASN grant application during any particular grants cycle.

GEOG. RESTRICTIONS: North America.

FINANCIAL DATA:
Amount of support per award: $100,000 per year.

APPLICATION INFO:
Only online applications will be accepted.

Duration: Two years.

Deadline: Mid-December.

ADDRESS INQUIRIES TO:
E-mail: grants@asn-online.org

CANCER FEDERATION, INC. [2282]

711 West Ramsey Street
Banning, CA 92220
(951) 849-4325
Fax: (951) 849-0156
E-mail: info@cancerfed.org
Web Site: www.cancerfed.org

FOUNDED: 1977

AREAS OF INTEREST:
Cancer.

TYPE:
Awards/prizes; Research grants; Scholarships; Seed money grants. The Federation has five basic programs: research, biology, scholarships, publishing (books, a magazine, a newsletter, and other materials) and patient aid.

YEAR PROGRAM STARTED: 1977

PURPOSE:
To fund research in cancer immunology and scholarships; to serve cancer patients and their families; to provide patient aid.

LEGAL BASIS:
Member-supported charity.

ELIGIBILITY:
Candidates must major in biology or natural sciences.

FINANCIAL DATA:
Total amount of support: $600,000.

NO. AWARDS: 60 scholarships.

APPLICATION INFO:
Scholar is chosen by institution.

Duration: One year. Renewal possible by reapplication. Scholarships are one-time only.

Deadline: Varies according to sponsoring institution.

PUBLICATIONS:
Challenge, magazine; *CF Newsletter*; *Four Women Against Cancer*; and several others.

IRS I.D.: 95-3133568

ADDRESS INQUIRIES TO:
Lya Cole, Executive Director
P.O. Box 1298
Banning, CA 92220

CHILDREN'S TUMOR FOUNDATION [2283]

120 Wall Street
16th Floor
New York, NY 10005
(212) 344-6633
Fax: (212) 747-0004
E-mail: slarosa@ctf.org
Web Site: www.ctf.org

AREAS OF INTEREST:
Neurofibromatosis research.

NAME(S) OF PROGRAMS:
- **Clinical Research Awards**
- **Drug Discovery Initiative Award**
- **NF Clinic Network (CTF-NFCN)**
- **Young Investigator Awards**

TYPE:
Conferences/seminars; Research grants; Seed money grants; Travel grants; Research contracts. Clinic support grants.

PURPOSE:
To improve the health and well-being of individuals and families affected by neurofibromatosis.

ELIGIBILITY:
Clinical Research Award: Preclinical/clinical collaborative studies, pilot clinical trials, and clinical enabling studies are considered for support.

Drug Discovery Initiative Award: Applicants should have an M.D., Ph.D., or equivalent degree and access to all resources needed. Applicants from academia and the private sector are welcome, and partnerships between the two are encouraged. Applications are welcomed from all qualified individuals worldwide.

NF Clinic Network: Any clinic in the U.S. that sees NF patients may apply to be a CTF-NFCN Affiliate Clinic.

Young Investigator Award: Open to graduate students, postdoctoral fellows and young investigators no more than four years past completion of their M.D./Ph.D. training. The Investigator can be a graduate student or postdoctoral fellow associated with the laboratory of a more senior researcher, who acts as the research sponsor.

FINANCIAL DATA:
Amount of support per award: Clinical Research Award: Up to $150,000; Drug Discovery Initiative Award: Up to $85,000; NF Clinic Network: Up to $6,000 per year; Young Investigator Award: Commensurate with experience.

Total amount of support: Young Investigator Award: $64,000 to $110,000.

NO. MOST RECENT APPLICANTS: Young Investigator Award: Approximately 25.

NO. AWARDS: Clinical Research Award: Up to 3; Young Investigator Award: Approximately 8.

APPLICATION INFO:
Application information is available on the web site. Applications may be submitted online.

Clinical Research Award: Letter of Inquiry required. Based on review, applicant may be invited to submit full application.

Duration: Clinical Research Award: 18 to 24 months; Drug Discovery Initiative: One year; Young Investigator Award: Up to two years.

Deadline: Young Investigator Award: January to February.

IRS I.D.: 13-2298956

STAFF:
Vidya Dhote, Basic Science Manager

ADDRESS INQUIRIES TO:
Salvatore La Rosa
Vice President of Research
(See address above.)

CYSTIC FIBROSIS CANADA [2284]

2323 Yonge Street
Suite 800
Toronto ON M4P 2C9 Canada
(416) 485-9149
(800) 378-2233 (Canada only)
Fax: (416) 485-0960
E-mail: info@cysticfibrosis.ca
Web Site: www.cysticfibrosis.ca

FOUNDED: 1960

AREAS OF INTEREST:
Cystic fibrosis.

NAME(S) OF PROGRAMS:
- **Early Career Investigator**

TYPE:
Awards/prizes; Fellowships; General operating grants; Grants-in-aid; Research grants; Training grants; Travel grants. Studentships; Summer studentships.

A limited number of competitive fellowships are offered by the Organization each year for basic or clinical research training in areas of the biomedical or behavioral sciences pertinent to cystic fibrosis.

Research grants are intended to facilitate the scientific investigation of all aspects of cystic fibrosis.

Early Career Investigator awards provide salary support for a limited number of exceptional investigators, offering them an opportunity to develop outstanding cystic fibrosis research programs, unhampered by heavy teaching or clinical loads.

A limited number of competitive studentships are offered by the Organization each year to:
(1) highly qualified graduate students who are registered for a higher degree, and who are undertaking full-time research training in areas of the biomedical or behavioral sciences relevant to cystic fibrosis or;
(2) highly qualified students who are registered in a joint M.D./M.Sc. or M.D./Ph.D. program.

YEAR PROGRAM STARTED: 1961

PURPOSE:
To further research on cystic fibrosis.

LEGAL BASIS:
Nonprofit organization.

ELIGIBILITY:
Research Grants: A principal investigator should hold a recognized, full-time faculty appointment in a relevant discipline at a Canadian university or hospital. Under exceptional circumstances, and at the discretion of the Scientific Review Panel, research grant applications from other individuals may be evaluated on a case-by-case basis, with significant emphasis placed on the degree of independence of the applicant, and on the institutional commitments to this individual.

Early Career Investigator awards applications are restricted to candidates who have received their first faculty appointment within the preceding five calendar years. Applicants must hold an M.D. or Ph.D. degree, and must be sponsored by the chairman of the appropriate department and by the dean of the faculty. A commitment should be provided by the nominating institution, stating that the institution intends to continue to support the Early Career Investigator following the completion of the award.

Fellowships: Individuals who hold M.D. or Ph.D. degrees are eligible to apply. Medical graduates should have already completed basic residency training, and must be eligible for Canadian licensure. Applications for clinical fellowships must have a strong research component in the proposed program. Fellowships are not awarded for residency-type clinical training. Applicants who have already completed six or more years of postgraduate study or training are not eligible for Cystic Fibrosis Canada fellowships.

Studentships are awarded for studies at the Master's or doctoral level. If a student receiving support for studies leading to a Master's degree elects to continue to a Doctorate degree, he or she must reapply for an initial Cystic Fibrosis Canada studentship at the doctoral level. Students are expected to spend at least 75% of their time on the research training described in their application.

GEOG. RESTRICTIONS: Canada.

FINANCIAL DATA:
Fellowship and Studentship awards follow prevailing Canadian rates.

Amount of support per award: Varies.

Total amount of support: Varies.

CO-OP FUNDING PROGRAMS: CIHR Partnerships, CFC-UBC Clinician Scientist at Saint Paul's, CFC-SMH Adult CF Research Chair.

NO. MOST RECENT APPLICANTS: 99.

NO. AWARDS: 24.

APPLICATION INFO:
Copies of the Organization's Grants and Awards Guide are available. Applications should be submitted on the forms provided by the Organization. The guidelines and application forms must be closely followed.

Duration: Varies.

Deadline: Varies.

PUBLICATIONS:
Annual report; *Grants and Awards Guide*, English/French booklet; application guidelines.

ADDRESS INQUIRIES TO:
See e-mail address above.

CYSTIC FIBROSIS CANADA [2285]

2323 Yonge Street
Suite 800
Toronto ON M4P 2C9 Canada
(416) 485-9149
(800) 378-2233 (Canada only)
Fax: (416) 485-0960
E-mail: info@cysticfibrosis.ca
Web Site: www.cysticfibrosis.ca

FOUNDED: 1960

AREAS OF INTEREST:
Cystic fibrosis.

NAME(S) OF PROGRAMS:
- **Clinic Incentive Grants**

TYPE:
Grants-in-aid; Seed money grants. Clinic Incentive Grants are intended to enhance the standard of clinical care available to Canadians with cystic fibrosis, by providing funds to initiate a comprehensive program for cystic fibrosis patient care, research and teaching, or to strengthen an existing program.

YEAR PROGRAM STARTED: 1961

PURPOSE:
To help establish a comprehensive program for patient care, research, and teaching in cystic fibrosis.

LEGAL BASIS:
Nonprofit organization.

ELIGIBILITY:
Grants may be made to medical schools or hospitals in Canada. Program potential, regional need, relative need of the institution for assistance and special medical and technical advantages will be considered.

GEOG. RESTRICTIONS: Canada.

FINANCIAL DATA:
Grant payments will be made at the beginning of each quarter. Limited funding is available for related travel.

Total amount of support: Varies.

APPLICATION INFO:
Application information is available on the web site.

Duration: One year. Grants are to be renegotiated annually.

Deadline: October 1.

ADDRESS INQUIRIES TO:
Ian D. McIntosh
Program Director, Healthcare
(See address above.)

HISTIOCYTOSIS ASSOCIATION [2286]

332 North Broadway
Pitman, NJ 08071
(856) 589-6606
Fax: (856) 589-6614
E-mail: grants@histio.org
Web Site: www.histio.org

FOUNDED: 1986

AREAS OF INTEREST:
Histiocytosis, hemophagocytic lymphohistiocytosis, Langerhans cell histiocytosis, and histiocytic disorders.

NAME(S) OF PROGRAMS:
- **Research Grant Program**

TYPE:
Project/program grants; Research grants; Seed money grants.

YEAR PROGRAM STARTED: 1989

PURPOSE:
To fund worthy scientific research projects; to educate physicians and scientists; to encourage and support symposia into histiocytic disorders; to directly participate in research projects; to encourage publication of scientific information.

ELIGIBILITY:
Must be a tax-exempt, nonprofit medical research organization with researchers working in the field of histiocytosis research.

FINANCIAL DATA:
Amount of support per award: Up to $50,000 for one-year grants.

Total amount of support: Varies.

NO. MOST RECENT APPLICANTS: 21.

NO. AWARDS: 6.

APPLICATION INFO:
Application must be submitted online.

Duration: Up to one year.

Deadline: July 1.

IRS I.D.: 22-2827069

STAFF:
Jeffrey Toughill, President and Chief Executive Officer

ADDRESS INQUIRIES TO:
Heather Fullerton
Research Grants Administrator
(See address above.)

THE LEUKEMIA & LYMPHOMA SOCIETY [2287]

3 International Drive
Suite 200
Rye Brook, NY 10573
(203) 988-6235
E-mail: James.Kasper@lls.org
Web Site: www.lls.org

AREAS OF INTEREST:
Medicinal chemistry and/or drug target screening in hematological malignancies.

NAME(S) OF PROGRAMS:
- **Screen to Lead Program (SLP)**

TYPE:
Research grants. Research grant is for new laboratories/projects to participate in a model of collaboration whereby the Society, grantee, sponsoring institution and appropriate contract service organizations (CROs) or core facilities at academic institutions work together to develop compounds with the potential to change the standard of care for patients with blood cancer.

PURPOSE:
To provide drug discovery support specifically directed towards medicinal chemistry and/or drug target screening in hematological malignancies.

ELIGIBILITY:
Investigators at academic laboratories are eligible to apply. Projects previously funded through SLP are ineligible to apply. Investigators must demonstrate that their research environment is equipped and suitable for aspects of the work plan that would be carried out at their institution rather than at a CRO. Collaborations between multiple investigators to strengthen the work proposed will be considered favorably but are not a requirement. Applicants need not be U.S. citizens nor associated with a U.S.-based institution. Applicants should hold a Ph.D., M.D., D.V.M. or equivalent degree.

FINANCIAL DATA:
The budget ceiling includes all costs associated with the grant including CRO and indirects. For any budgeted line items that are specifically related to the Principal Investigator, for work conducted in their laboratory, indirect costs will be capped at 11.1%.

Amount of support per award: Up to $1,000,000 for the two years of the grant.

APPLICATION INFO:
Application may be obtained at the following web site: lls.fluxx.io under Screen to Lead Program.

Duration: One to two years. Second-year funding is contingent on demonstrating suitable progress toward the aims of the proposal, at the sole discretion of the Society.

Deadline: Call for Proposals: July 1. Deadline: August 29. Notification: November. Funding start date: July 1 of the following year.

ADDRESS INQUIRIES TO:
James Kasper, Senior Director
(See e-mail address above.)

THE LEUKEMIA & LYMPHOMA SOCIETY [2288]

1311 Mamaroneck Avenue
Suite 310
White Plains, NY 10605
(914) 821-8301
Fax: (914) 821-3290
E-mail: researchprograms@lls.org
Web Site: www.lls.org

AREAS OF INTEREST:
Leukemia, lymphoma and myeloma.

NAME(S) OF PROGRAMS:
- **Career Development Program**

TYPE:
Fellowships; Research grants; Scholarships. The Career Development Program provides awards intended to meet the specific needs of investigators at different stages of their research careers. The five awards, Fellow, Scholar, Scholar in Clinical Research, Special Fellow and Special Fellow in Clinical Research, provide stipends to investigators, allowing them to devote themselves to research bearing on leukemia, lymphoma and myeloma.

YEAR PROGRAM STARTED: 1949

PURPOSE:
To cure leukemia, lymphoma, Hodgkin's disease and myeloma; to improve the quality of life of patients and their families; to support individuals pursuing careers in basic or clinical research in leukemia, lymphoma and myeloma.

ELIGIBILITY:
Qualified investigators affiliated with appropriate institutions are eligible to apply. Applicants must have the approval of the institution and recommendation of the department head where the research training will be conducted. Ph.D. or M.D. status is required.

FINANCIAL DATA:
Amount of support per award: $165,000 for three years for Fellows; $550,000 for five years for Scholars and Scholars in Clinical Research; $195,000 for three years for Special Fellows and Special Fellows in Clinical Research.

APPLICATION INFO:
Guidelines are available on the web site.

Duration: Renewable for up to five years at the level of Scholar and three years at the level of Special Fellow and Fellow.

Deadline: Letter of Intent: September 1. Full application: October 1.

ADDRESS INQUIRIES TO:
Erik Nelson
Director of Research Programs
(See address above.)

THE LEUKEMIA & LYMPHOMA SOCIETY [2289]

3 International Drive
Suite 200
Rye Brook, NY 10573
(914) 821-8301
E-mail: researchprograms@lls.org
Web Site: www.lls.org

AREAS OF INTEREST:
Leukemia, lymphoma and myeloma.

NAME(S) OF PROGRAMS:

- **Translational Research Program**

TYPE:
Research grants. Translational Research Program is intended to encourage and provide support for new and novel clinical research. The goal of the program is to accelerate transfer of findings from the laboratory to clinical application.

YEAR PROGRAM STARTED: 1996

PURPOSE:
To encourage and provide early-stage support for clinical research in leukemia, lymphoma, and myeloma, with the intention of developing innovative approaches to treatment, diagnosis or prevention; to support projects that translate laboratory findings to clinical application.

ELIGIBILITY:
Ph.D. or M.D. status is required. Candidates must be affiliated with a nonfederal public or private nonprofit institution engaged in cancer-related research.

FINANCIAL DATA:
Amount of support per award: $200,000 annually.

CO-OP FUNDING PROGRAMS: National Career Institutes; Academic, Public, Private, Partnership Program (AP4).

APPLICATION INFO:
Guidelines are available on the web site.

Duration: Three years. In special cases these may be renewed for two years.

Deadline: Preliminary application: January 25. Full application: March 1.

ADDRESS INQUIRIES TO:
See e-mail address above.

THE LEUKEMIA & LYMPHOMA SOCIETY [2290]

3 International Drive
Suite 200
Rye Brook, NY 10573
(914) 821-8301
E-mail: researchprograms@lls.org
Web Site: www.lls.org

AREAS OF INTEREST:
Leukemia, lymphoma, Hodgkin's disease and myeloma.

NAME(S) OF PROGRAMS:

- **Marshall A. Lichtman Specialized Center of Research Program**

TYPE:
Research grants. The core program intends to bring together distinguished investigators from one or several institutions to develop a focused research center, foster new interactions and cooperation, and enhance disciplinary research among the participants to understand the causes of hematological malignancies and ultimately develop effective treatments for cancer patients.

PURPOSE:
To support research programs that are focused on any aspect of leukemia, lymphoma, Hodgkin's disease and myeloma in order to foster interactions, cooperation, and to enhance interdisciplinary research among the participants.

ELIGIBILITY:
Applications may be submitted by individuals holding an M.D., Ph.D., or equivalent degree, working in domestic or foreign nonprofit organizations, such as universities, colleges, hospitals or laboratories. Applications may be multi-institutional in nature. Applicants need not be U.S. citizens, and there are no restrictions on applicant age, race, gender or creed.

FINANCIAL DATA:
Expenses for administrative staff (including secretarial) costs cannot exceed one full-time equivalent for the Center per year. Travel costs for all investigators cannot exceed $10,000 per year for the Center. The aggregate of office supplies and telephone costs cannot exceed $6,000 per year for the Center.

Amount of support per award: Up to $1,000,000 annually.

APPLICATION INFO:
Guidelines are available on the web site.

Duration: Five years.

Deadline: Letter of Intent: November 1. Notification sent to those selected for full application submission by December 31. Application: March 15.

ADDRESS INQUIRIES TO:
See e-mail address above.

LYMPHOMA RESEARCH FOUNDATION [2291]

115 Broadway, Suite 1301
New York, NY 10006
(212) 349-2910
Fax: (212) 349-2886
E-mail: researchgrants@lymphoma.org
Web Site: www.lymphoma.org

FOUNDED: 2001

AREAS OF INTEREST:
Lymphoma research.

CONSULTING OR VOLUNTEER SERVICES:
The LRF Ambassador program is comprised of individuals from around the country, each with a personal lymphoma story. The ambassadors represent several subtypes and treatment options for the disease. The group includes current patients, caregivers of patients and survivors. Ambassadors are able to share their individual stories and experiences navigating this diagnosis.

The LRF Advocacy Program offers volunteers a variety of opportunities, including attending in-person meetings with members of Congress and submitting letters to the editor and op-eds which cover issues important to the lymphoma community.

NAME(S) OF PROGRAMS:

- **Clinical Investigator Career Development Awards (CDA)**
- **Disease Focus Area Grants for Senior Investigators**
- **LRF Clinical Research Mentoring Program (LCRMP)**
- **Postdoctoral Fellowship Grants**

TYPE:
Fellowships; Research grants; Training grants.

YEAR PROGRAM STARTED: 1992

PURPOSE:
To support innovative lymphoma research in keeping with the Foundation's mission to eradicate lymphoma and serve those touched by this disease.

LEGAL BASIS:
Nonprofit organization.

ELIGIBILITY:
CDA: Advanced fellows or junior faculty with at least two years fellow/postdoctoral experience and no more than five years beyond completion of fellowship/postdoctoral; 35 to 50% protected time for research; must be licensed physicians at a nonprofit clinical research institution.

Disease Focus Area Grants: Open to licensed senior researchers (usually Assistant, Associate or Full Professor or their equivalent) at accredited, nonprofit research institutions; other restrictions vary by individual RFP.

LCRMP: At least second year of select ACGME fellowships (see RFP) and no more than three years in first faculty position. Applicants must be licensed physicians at a clinical research institution.

Postdoctoral Fellowship Grants: Advanced clinical fellows or those with postdoctoral experience (with no more than five years fellow/postdoctoral experience). M.D. applicants must have completed at least two years of clinical fellowship work. Faculty are not eligible for this grant.

CDA, Fellowship and LCRMP limited to applicants based at institutions in the U.S. or Canada for the duration of the grant. Citizenship not required. Other programs refer to RFP.

FINANCIAL DATA:
Amount of support per award: CDA: $225,000 total over three years, salary support and professional development expenses; Disease Focus Area Grants: Research expenses (personnel and nonpersonnel) vary by RFP; LCRMP: $10,000 total professional development expenses over two years plus travel to LCRMP workshops; Postdoctoral Fellowship Grants: $105,000 total over two years, salary support and professional development expenses.

Total amount of support: Varies.

NO. MOST RECENT APPLICANTS: 57.

NO. AWARDS: 13 grants in the fiscal year 2016.

REPRESENTATIVE AWARDS:
$225,000 CDA to Anita Kumar, M.D., Memorial Sloan Kettering Cancer Center for "A Multicenter Phase I Study of Ibrutinib in Relapsed and Refractory T-cell Lymphoma;" $105,000 Fellowship to Andrea Rabellino, Ph.D., University of Texas - Southwestern Medical Center for "Role of PIAS1 in c-MYC-driven lymphomagenesis;" $100,000 Disease Focus Area Grant (in Adolescent/Young Adult Lymphoma Correlative Studies) to David Scott, M.D., MBChB of British Columbia Cancer Agency for "Biomarkers predicting early treatment response in advanced stage classical Hodgkin lymphoma."

APPLICATION INFO:
Application information is available online.

Duration: CDA: Three years. Disease Focus Area Grants: Varies by RFP (usually two to three years). LCRMP and Postdoctoral Fellowship Grants: Two years.

Deadline: CDA, Postdoctoral Fellowship Grants and LCRMP generally open in early June and close in early September. Disease Focus Area Grants: Varies by RFP.

IRS I.D.: 95-4335088

BOARD OF DIRECTORS:
Steven J. Prince, Chairman
Michael Werner, Executive Vice President
John A. Nelson, Treasurer
Tom Condon, Secretary
Leo I. Gordon, M.D., Chairman, Scientific Advisory Board
Morton Coleman, M.D., Chairman, Medical Affiliates Board
Joseph R. Bertino, M.D.
Eric Cohen
Errol M. Cook
Kevin Fennessey
Joseph M. Ferraro
Robert E. Fischer
Barbara Freundlich
Jerry Freundlich
Tom Goldstone
Keith Hoogland
Bob McAuley
Lance Meyerowich
Leigh Olson
Miriam Phalen
Donna Reinbolt
Steven E. Rosen
Sheri Rosenfeld

ADDRESS INQUIRIES TO:
Whitney Steen
(See e-mail address above.)

NATIONAL HEADACHE FOUNDATION [2292]

820 North Orleans, Suite 411
Chicago, IL 60610-3132
(312) 274-2650
(888) 643-5552
Fax: (312) 640-9049
E-mail: info@headaches.org
Web Site: www.headaches.org

FOUNDED: 1970

AREAS OF INTEREST:
Headache and pain.

TYPE:
Research grants. Support for research in the field of headache and pain.

YEAR PROGRAM STARTED: 1970

PURPOSE:
To enhance the health care of individuals with headache; to provide a source of help to families, physicians and allied health care professionals who treat them, and to the public; to provide educational and informational resources, supporting headache research, and advocating for the understanding of headache as a legitimate neurobiological disease.

LEGAL BASIS:
Nonprofit organization.

ELIGIBILITY:
Investigators from departments of neurology and pharmacology are invited to apply. Submissions from other departments and individual investigators are also welcome. No funding for overhead, salaries, rent or indirect expenses. Grants may be used for data analysis, interpretation, reading of results, etc.

GEOG. RESTRICTIONS: United States.

FINANCIAL DATA:
Full or partial funding may be granted.

Amount of support per award: Varies depending on project.

NO. MOST RECENT APPLICANTS: 9.

NO. AWARDS: 2 for the year 2014-15.

REPRESENTATIVE AWARDS:
$49,544 to Harvard Medical School/Mayo Clinic for Functional and Morphometric Measures in Chronic Daily Headache; $49,544 to Children's Hospital of Denver for Adolescents with Migraine-What's Stress Got To Do With It?.

APPLICATION INFO:
Applicants must submit abstract of research proposal on Foundation form as well as protocol and proposed budget. Proposed projects will be evaluated at the winter board meeting of the NHF.

Duration: One year.

Deadline: October 1. Announcement December 1.

PUBLICATIONS:
Program announcement.

ADDRESS INQUIRIES TO:
Mary A. Franklin, Director of Operations
(See address above.)

NATIONAL HEART, LUNG AND BLOOD INSTITUTE (NHLBI) [2293]

Division of Blood Diseases and Resources
National Institutes of Health
6701 Rockledge Drive, Suite 9030
Bethesda, MD 20892
(301) 435-0080
Fax: (301) 480-0867
E-mail: hootsw@nhlbi.nih.gov
Web Site: www.nhlbi.nih.gov

FOUNDED: 1948

AREAS OF INTEREST:
Research on the causes, prevention, and treatment of nonmalignant blood diseases, including anemias, sickle cell disease, and thalassemia; premalignant processes such as myelodysplasia and myeloproliferative disorders; hemophilia and other abnormalities of hemostasis and thrombosis; and immune dysfunction.

NAME(S) OF PROGRAMS:

- **Blood Diseases and Resources Research**

TYPE:
Conferences/seminars; Demonstration grants; Fellowships; Grants-in-aid; Project/program grants; Training grants; Research contracts. Funding encompasses a broad spectrum of research ranging from basic biology to medical management of blood diseases.

YEAR PROGRAM STARTED: 1972

PURPOSE:
To develop programs that will reduce the morbidity and mortality caused by blood diseases, lead to the primary prevention of these diseases and ensure the availability of adequate supplies of safe and efficacious blood products.

LEGAL BASIS:
Public Health Service Act, Section 301(e) and Section 412; Public Law 78-410, as amended; 42 U.S.C. 241; 42 U.S.C. 287a; Public Health Service Act, Section 472; Public Law 78-410, as amended; 42 U.S.C. 289 1-1.

ELIGIBILITY:
Any nonprofit organization engaged in biomedical research and institutions (or companies) organized for profit may apply for grants with the exception of National Research Service Awards. Only citizens and noncitizen nationals are eligible for support by research training and career development programs. Other mechanisms are not restricted.

FINANCIAL DATA:
Grants may support salaries, equipment, supplies, travel and patient hospitalization as required to perform the research effort.

Amount of support per award: Varies by the type of grant.

APPLICATION INFO:
Application information is available on the web site.

Duration: One to five years. Renewable through reapplication.

Deadline: Varies.

PUBLICATIONS:
Annual report.

DIRECTORS:
W. Keith Hoots, M.D., Director
Donna DiMichele, M.D., Deputy Director

RESEARCH STAFF:
Simone Glynn, M.D., M.Sc., M.P.H., Branch Chief, Blood Epidemiology and Clinical Therapeutics Branch
Traci Mondoro, Ph.D., Branch Chief, Translational Blood Science and Resources Branch
Yu-Chung Yang, Ph.D., Branch Chief, Molecular, Cellular and Systems Blood Science Branch

ADDRESS INQUIRIES TO:
Division of Blood Diseases and Resources
(See address above.)

NEURO-DEVELOPMENTAL TREATMENT ASSOCIATION [2294]

1540 South Coast Highway
Suite 204
Laguna Beach, CA 92651
(800) 869-9295
Fax: (949) 376-3456
E-mail: membership@ndta.org
Web Site: www.ndta.org

AREAS OF INTEREST:
Neuro-Developmental Treatment.

TYPE:
Research grants.

PURPOSE:
To support the investigation of the effectiveness of Neuro-Developmental Treatment with pediatric and adult populations.

ELIGIBILITY:
Qualified investigators affiliated with appropriate institutions are eligible to apply. Applicants must have the approval of the institution and recommendation of the department head where the research training will be conducted.

FINANCIAL DATA:
The grant does not pay indirect, overhead or salary reimbursement costs.

Amount of support per award: Up to $5,000.

NO. AWARDS: Typically 1 annually.

APPLICATION INFO:
Send requests for a grant application and guidelines to the e-mail address above or to the attention of Janet Powell, Ph.D., OT, University of Washington, Division of Occupational Therapy, 1959 Northeast Pacific Street, Box 356490, Seattle, WA 98195.

Duration: Varies.

Deadline: December 1.

ADDRESS INQUIRIES TO:
Brad Lund, Executive Director
(See address above.)

Cardiovascular and pulmonary

AMERICAN COLLEGE OF CARDIOLOGY [2295]

2400 N Street, N.W.
Washington, DC 20037
(202) 375-6000 ext. 6538
Fax: (202) 375-7000
E-mail: kwest@acc.org
Web Site: www.cardiosource.org/researchawards

AREAS OF INTEREST:
Cardiology.

NAME(S) OF PROGRAMS:
- **ACCF/Merck Research Fellowships in Cardiovascular Disease**

TYPE:
Awards/prizes; Development grants; Endowments; Fellowships; Internships; Project/program grants; Research grants; Scholarships; Seed money grants; Technical assistance; Training grants; Travel grants; Visiting scholars; Work-study programs; Research contracts.

PURPOSE:
To advance research in cardiovascular disease.

ELIGIBILITY:
Anyone currently in an adult cardiology fellowship training program recognized by the Accreditation Council for Graduate Medical Education or the American Osteopathic Association and who has the recommendation and agreement of their training program director and institution is eligible to apply. Preference is given to individuals who have had no more than two years of prior full-time experience either in clinical or basic research.

GEOG. RESTRICTIONS: United States and Canada.

FINANCIAL DATA:
Fellowships must be used only for salary support.

Amount of support per award: $70,000 for one year of salary support.

NO. MOST RECENT APPLICANTS: 30.

NO. AWARDS: 4.

APPLICATION INFO:
Guidelines and application form are available online.

Duration: One year.

Deadline: September.

ADDRESS INQUIRIES TO:
Kristin West, Member Strategy Associate
(See e-mail address above.)

AMERICAN COLLEGE OF CARDIOLOGY [2296]

2400 N Street, N.W.
Washington, DC 20037
(202) 375-6000 ext. 6390
Fax: (202) 375-6842
E-mail: kroberts@acc.org
Web Site: www.cardiosource.org/researchawards

AREAS OF INTEREST:
Cardiology.

NAME(S) OF PROGRAMS:
- **ACC Young Investigators Awards Competition**

TYPE:
Awards/prizes. Awarded in four categories:
(1) Clinical Investigations, Congenital Heart Disease and Cardiac Surgery;
(2) Physiology, Pharmacology, and Pathology;
(3) Molecular and Cellular Cardiology and;
(4) Cardiovascular Health Heart Outcome and Population Genetics.

PURPOSE:
To encourage and recognize young scientific investigators of promise.

ELIGIBILITY:
Any physician or scientist presently in a residency or fellowship training program or who has been in such a program within the past three years, medical students, and Ph.D. candidates are eligible to apply.

FINANCIAL DATA:
Each candidate receives up to $1,500 reimbursement for travel to attend the annual meeting.

Amount of support per award: First Place: $2,000; Second Place: $1,000; Honorable Mention: $500.

NO. MOST RECENT APPLICANTS: 150.

NO. AWARDS: 20 awards; 5 awards per category.

APPLICATION INFO:
Guidelines and application form are available online.

Deadline: October.

ADDRESS INQUIRIES TO:
Kristen Robertson, Associate Director
(See address above.)

AMERICAN COLLEGE OF CARDIOLOGY [2297]

2400 N Street, N.W.
Washington, DC 20037
(202) 375-6000 ext. 6538
(800) 253-4636 ext. 6538
Fax: (202) 375-6842
E-mail: kwest@acc.org
Web Site: www.cardiosource.org/researchawards

AREAS OF INTEREST:
Cardiology.

NAME(S) OF PROGRAMS:
- **ACCF/William F. Keating, Esq. Endowment Award for Hypertension and Peripheral Vascular Disease**

TYPE:
Awards/prizes; Research grants. This is a career development award.

PURPOSE:
To recognize and provide financial support for research efforts by outstanding young cardiovascular scholars; to encourage junior faculty in the early phases of their careers in the field of cardiology.

ELIGIBILITY:
The award recipient must meet the following qualifications:
(1) hold the rank of instructor or assistant professor at the time of the initiation of the award and have completed adult, pediatric, surgical cardiology fellowship training in a program approved by the Accreditation Council for Graduate Medical Education or the American Osteopathic Association;
(2) be a member or be eligible to become a member of the American College of Cardiology (ACC);
(3) be no more than five years out of training;
(4) have the recommendation and agreement of his or her division chief and his or her chief's assurance that the award's support will provide protected time for the applicant to pursue his or her research program and;
(5) have an agreement with his or her institution that the full amount of the award will be designated for the salary support.

GEOG. RESTRICTIONS: United States and Canada.

FINANCIAL DATA:
Award funds can only be used for salary support. They cannot be used for any institutional or indirect costs.

Amount of support per award: $70,000.

NO. MOST RECENT APPLICANTS: 20.

NO. AWARDS: 1 per year.

APPLICATION INFO:
Guidelines and application form are available online.

Duration: One year, beginning July 1 through June 30.

Deadline: September.

ADDRESS INQUIRIES TO:
Kristin West, Member Strategy Associate
(See e-mail address above.)

AMERICAN HEART ASSOCIATION [2298]

AHA National Center
7272 Greenville Avenue
Dallas, TX 75231-4596
(214) 360-6100
E-mail: apply@heart.org
Web Site: my.americanheart.org

FOUNDED: 1948

AREAS OF INTEREST:
Research broadly related to cardiovascular function and disease and stroke, or to related clinical, basic science, bioengineering or biotechnology, and public health problems, including multidisciplinary efforts.

NAME(S) OF PROGRAMS:
- **Postdoctoral Fellowship**

TYPE:
Fellowships. Supports individuals before they are ready for some stage of independent research.

PURPOSE:
To help trainees initiate careers in cardiovascular and stroke research while obtaining significant research results under the supervision of a sponsor or mentor.

LEGAL BASIS:
Research association.

ELIGIBILITY:
Proposals are encouraged from all basic disciplines, as well as epidemiological, behavioral, community and clinical investigations that bear on cardiovascular and stroke problems. Applicants must:
(1) be a U.S. citizen or permanent resident;
(2) be individuals before they are ready for some stage of independent research;
(3) have M.D., Ph.D., D.O., D.V.M. (or equivalent) at activation and;
(4) have five years or less postdoctoral research experience at time of activation.

GEOG. RESTRICTIONS: United States.

FINANCIAL DATA:
Amount of support per award: Varies per initiative for each geographical area.

APPLICATION INFO:
Guidelines and application form are available on the web site.

Duration: Founders Affiliate, Midwest Affiliate, SouthWest Affiliate and Western States Affiliate: Two years; Great Rivers Affiliate and Greater Southeast Affiliate: One or two years.

Deadline: July.

ADDRESS INQUIRIES TO:
See e-mail address above.

AMERICAN HEART ASSOCIATION [2299]

AHA National Center
7272 Greenville Avenue
Dallas, TX 75231-4596
(214) 360-6100
E-mail: apply@heart.org
Web Site: my.americanheart.org

FOUNDED: 1948

AREAS OF INTEREST:
Research broadly related to cardiovascular function and disease and stroke, or related to clinical, basic science, bioengineering or biotechnology, and public health problems, including multidisciplinary efforts.

NAME(S) OF PROGRAMS:
- **Predoctoral Fellowship**

TYPE:
Fellowships.

PURPOSE:
To help students initiate careers in cardiovascular and stroke research by providing research assistance and training.

LEGAL BASIS:
Research association.

ELIGIBILITY:
Proposals are encouraged from all basic, behavioral, epidemiological, and community and clinical investigations that bear on cardiovascular and stroke problems.
Applicants must meet the following criteria:
(1) be a U.S. citizen or permanent resident;
(2) be post-Baccalaureate, predoctoral M.D., Ph.D., D.O., D.V.M. (or equivalent) student seeking research training with a sponsor/mentor prior to embarking on a research career and;
(3) be a full-time student working toward their degree.

GEOG. RESTRICTIONS: United States.

FINANCIAL DATA:
Amount of support per award: Varies per initiative for each geographical area.

APPLICATION INFO:
Guidelines and application form are available on the web site.

Duration: One to two years.

Deadline: July.

ADDRESS INQUIRIES TO:
See e-mail address above.

AMERICAN HEART ASSOCIATION [2300]

AHA National Center
7272 Greenville Avenue
Dallas, TX 75231-4596
(214) 360-6100
E-mail: apply@heart.org
Web Site: my.americanheart.org

FOUNDED: 1948

AREAS OF INTEREST:
Research broadly related to cardiovascular function and disease and stroke, and clinical, basic science, bioengineering or biotechnology, and public health problems, including multidisciplinary efforts.

NAME(S) OF PROGRAMS:
- **Beginning Grant-in-Aid**

TYPE:
Grants-in-aid. Beginning grant-in-aid for all basic disciplines as well as epidemiological, community and clinical investigations that bear on cardiovascular and stroke problems.

PURPOSE:
To promote the independent status of promising beginning scientists.

LEGAL BASIS:
Research association.

ELIGIBILITY:
Applicant must:
(1) be a U.S. citizen or permanent resident;
(2) at time of application have M.D., Ph.D., D.O., D.V.M. or equivalent initiating independent research career;
(3) hold position of assistant professor (or equivalent) or higher at activation and;
(4) have faculty/staff appointment at activation and meet institutional requirements for grant submission at time of application.

GEOG. RESTRICTIONS: Alaska, Arizona, Arkansas, California, Colorado, Hawaii, Idaho, Montana, Nevada, New Mexico, Oklahoma, Oregon, Texas, Utah, Washington and Wyoming.

FINANCIAL DATA:
Amount of support per award: $70,000 maximum per year (including $35,000 for salary/fringe and 10% indirect cost).

APPLICATION INFO:
Guidelines and application form are available on the web site.

Duration: Two years.

Deadline: July.

ADDRESS INQUIRIES TO:
See e-mail address above.

AMERICAN HEART ASSOCIATION [2301]

AHA National Center
7272 Greenville Avenue
Dallas, TX 75231-4596
(214) 360-6100
E-mail: apply@heart.org
Web Site: my.americanheart.org/fundingopportunities

FOUNDED: 1948

AREAS OF INTEREST:
Research broadly related to cardiovascular disease and stroke, and research in clinical, basic science, bioengineering or biotechnology, and public health problems.

NAME(S) OF PROGRAMS:
- **Greater Southeast Affiliate Medical and Health Sciences Fellowship Program**

TYPE:
Fellowships. Provides opportunities for health science students to work for 10 consecutive weeks with a faculty/staff member on any project related to the mission of the AHA.

PURPOSE:
To encourage students to consider a future academic career in health science.

LEGAL BASIS:
Research association.

ELIGIBILITY:
Proposals are encouraged from all basic disciplines, including multidisciplinary efforts, as well as epidemiological and clinical disciplines that bear on cardiovascular and stroke problems.

Applicant must be predoctoral M.D., D.O., D.D.S., Pharm.D. (or equivalent) health science student. At the time of application, student must be a U.S. citizen, permanent resident, pending permanent resident or hold one of the following visas: E-3, F-1, H1-B, J-1, O-1 or TN.

Award must be completed at any accredited institution in Alabama, Florida, Georgia, Louisiana, Mississippi, Puerto Rico, Tennessee or U.S. Virgin Islands.

FINANCIAL DATA:
Amount of support per award: $4,500 per student.

Total amount of support: $13,500 per year, per institution.

NO. AWARDS: Up to 3 student fellows per institution per year.

APPLICATION INFO:
Guidelines and application form are available on the web site.

Duration: Two years.

Deadline: Mid-September.

ADDRESS INQUIRIES TO:
See e-mail address above.

AMERICAN HEART ASSOCIATION [2302]

AHA National Center
7272 Greenville Avenue
Dallas, TX 75231-4596
(214) 360-6100
E-mail: apply@heart.org
Web Site: my.americanheart.org/fundingopportunities

FOUNDED: 1948

AREAS OF INTEREST:
Research broadly related to cardiovascular disease and stroke, and research in clinical, basic science, bioengineering or biotechnology, and public health problems.

NAME(S) OF PROGRAMS:
- **Great Rivers Affiliate Student Undergraduate Research Fellowship**

TYPE:
Fellowships. Institutional award to qualified research institutions, within the Affiliate's geographic boundaries, that can offer a meaningful research experience to undergraduate students.

PURPOSE:
To encourage promising students, including women and members of minority groups underrepresented in the sciences, from all disciplines to consider research careers while supporting the highest quality scientific investigation broadly related to cardiovascular disease and stroke.

LEGAL BASIS:
Research association.

ELIGIBILITY:
Applicant must be a U.S. citizen or permanent resident, pending permanent resident, J-1, E-3, H1-B, TN, O-1, or F-1 visa. To be eligible, undergraduate students should be currently classified at the junior or senior academic status at the time of award activation. Students must be enrolled full-time in an undergraduate degree program, at the time of application, in either a four-year college or university, or a two-year institution with plans to transfer to a four-year college or university by the fall semester immediately following the summer program.

The award may be completed at any accredited institution in Delaware, Kentucky, Ohio, Pennsylvania or West Virginia.

FINANCIAL DATA:
Amount of support per award: $4,000 per student; $20,000 maximum per year for institution; $40,000 maximum for a two-year award.

NO. AWARDS: Up to 5 per institution.

APPLICATION INFO:
Guidelines and application form are available on the web site.

Duration: Two years to qualified institutions.

Deadline: Mid-September.

ADDRESS INQUIRIES TO:
See e-mail address above.

AMERICAN HEART ASSOCIATION [2303]

AHA National Center
7272 Greenville Avenue
Dallas, TX 75231-4596
(214) 360-6100
E-mail: apply@heart.org
Web Site: my.americanheart.org/fundingopportunities

FOUNDED: 1948

AREAS OF INTEREST:
Research broadly related to cardiovascular function and disease and stroke, or related to clinical, basic science, bioengineering or biotechnology, and public health problems, including multidisciplinary efforts.

NAME(S) OF PROGRAMS:
- **Grant-in-Aid Program**

TYPE:
Grants-in-aid. Offered through Founders, Great Rivers, SouthWest and Western States Affiliates.

PURPOSE:
To encourage and adequately fund the most innovative and meritorious research projects from independent investigators.

LEGAL BASIS:
Research association.

ELIGIBILITY:
Proposals are encouraged from all basic disciplines, as well as epidemiological, behavioral, community and clinical investigations that bear on cardiovascular and stroke problems. At the time of application, the applicant must:
(1) hold a faculty/staff appointment of any rank (or equivalent), and must be conducting independent research. Not intended for individuals in research training or fellowship positions;
(2) hold an M.D., Ph.D., D.O., D.V.M. or equivalent post-Baccalaureate doctoral degree;
(3) meet institutional requirements for grant submission and;
(4) be a U.S. citizen, permanent resident, pending permanent resident or hold these visas: E-3, H1-B, J-1, O-1 or TN.

For the Founders Affiliate program, the award may be completed at any accredited institution in Connecticut, Maine, Massachusetts, New Hampshire, New Jersey, New York, Rhode Island or Vermont.

For the Great Rivers Affiliate program, the award may be completed at any accredited institution in Delaware, Kentucky, Ohio, Pennsylvania or West Virginia.

For the SouthWest Affiliate program, the award may be completed at any accredited institution in Arkansas, Colorado, New Mexico, Oklahoma, Texas or Wyoming.

For the Western States Affiliate program, the award may be completed at any accredited institution in Alaska, Arizona, California, Hawaii, Idaho, Montana, Nevada, Oregon, Utah or Washington.

FINANCIAL DATA:
Amount of support per award: Founders Affiliate: $66,000 per year (including up to $30,000 for salary/fringe and 10% indirect cost); Great Rivers Affiliate: $77,000 maximum per year (including up to $30,000 for salary/fringe and 10% indirect cost); SouthWest Affiliate: $70,000 maximum per year (including up to $28,636 for salary/fringe and 10% indirect cost and up to $3,000 for travel cost); Western States Affiliate: $70,000 maximum per year (including up to $35,000 for salary/fringe and 10% indirect cost).

APPLICATION INFO:
Guidelines and application form are available on the web site.

Duration: Founders Affiliate: Three years; Great Rivers Affiliate, SouthWest Affiliate and Western States Affiliate: Two years.

Deadline: July.

ADDRESS INQUIRIES TO:
See e-mail address above.

AMERICAN HEART ASSOCIATION [2304]

AHA National Center
7272 Greenville Avenue
Dallas, TX 75231-4596
(214) 360-6100
E-mail: apply@heart.org
Web Site: my.americanheart.org/fundingopportunities

FOUNDED: 1948

AREAS OF INTEREST:
Research broadly related to cardiovascular function and disease and stroke, or to related clinical, basic science, bioengineering or biotechnology, and public health problems, including multidisciplinary efforts.

NAME(S) OF PROGRAMS:
- **National Innovative Research Grant**

TYPE:
Research grants. Program aims to provide pilot or seed funding that should lead to successful competition for additional funding beyond the pilot period.

PURPOSE:
To support highly innovative, high-risk, high-reward research that could ultimately lead to critical discoveries or major advancements that will accelerate the field of cardiovascular and stroke research.

LEGAL BASIS:
Research association.

ELIGIBILITY:
Proposals are encouraged from all basic, behavioral, epidemiological, and community and clinical investigations that bear on cardiovascular and stroke problems. At the time of application, the applicant must:
(1) hold an M.D., Ph.D., D.O. or equivalent doctoral degree;
(2) meet institutional requirements for grant submission;
(3) be a U.S. citizen, permanent resident, pending permanent resident, or have one of the following visas: E-3, H-1B, J-1, O-1 or TN and;
(4) at the time of award activation, have a faculty (or faculty equivalent) appointment. This award is not intended for postdoctoral fellows or others in research training positions.

Eligibility for the grant is not restricted based upon experience level or seniority. Seniority will not be used as a criterion in evaluating an application's merit.

FINANCIAL DATA:
Amount of support per award: $75,000 per year (including 10% indirect costs).

APPLICATION INFO:
Guidelines and application form are available on the web site.

Duration: Two years.

Deadline: Mid-July.

ADDRESS INQUIRIES TO:
See e-mail address above.

AMERICAN HEART ASSOCIATION [2305]

AHA National Center
7272 Greenville Avenue
Dallas, TX 75231-4596
(214) 360-6100
E-mail: apply@heart.org
Web Site: my.americanheart.org/fundingopportunities

FOUNDED: 1948

AREAS OF INTEREST:
Research broadly related to cardiovascular function and disease and stroke, or related to clinical, basic science, bioengineering or biotechnology, and public health problems, including multidisciplinary efforts.

NAME(S) OF PROGRAMS:
- **National Established Investigator Award**

TYPE:
Research grants. Candidates for this award have a demonstrated commitment to cardiovascular or cerebrovascular science as indicated by prior publication history and scientific accomplishments. A candidate's career is expected to be in a rapid growth phase.

PURPOSE:
To support midcareer investigators with unusual promise and an established record of accomplishments.

LEGAL BASIS:
Research association.

ELIGIBILITY:
Proposals are encouraged from all basic disciplines as well as epidemiological, behavioral, community and clinical investigations that bear on cardiovascular and stroke problems.

At the time of application, the applicant must:
(1) have an M.D., Ph.D., D.O. or equivalent doctoral degree;
(2) be a faculty/staff member;
(3) meet institutional requirements for grant submission;
(4) have current national-level funding as a principal investigator (or co-PI) on an R01 grant or its equivalent;
(5) be a U.S. citizen or permanent resident and;
(6) at the time of award activation be at least four years, but no more than nine years, since the first faculty/staff appointment at the assistant professor level or equivalent (including, but not limited to, research assistant professor, research scientist, staff scientist, etc.). Instructor positions (or equivalent positions) do not count toward the four or nine years of eligibility.

Research awards are limited to nonprofit institutions, including medical, osteopathic and dental schools, veterinary schools, schools of public health, pharmacy schools, nursing schools, universities and colleges, public and voluntary hospitals and other nonprofit institutions that can demonstrate the ability to conduct the proposed research. Applications will not be accepted for work with funding to be administered through any federal institution or work to be performed by a federal employee, except for Veterans Administration employees.

Funding is prohibited for awards at non-U.S. institutions.

FINANCIAL DATA:
Amount of support per award: $80,000 per year (including up to 10% indirect costs).

APPLICATION INFO:
Guidelines and application form are available on the web site.

Duration: Five years. No renewals.

Deadline: Mid-July.

ADDRESS INQUIRIES TO:
See e-mail address above.

AMERICAN HEART ASSOCIATION [2306]

AHA National Center
7272 Greenville Avenue
Dallas, TX 75231-4596
(214) 360-6100
E-mail: apply@heart.org
Web Site: my.americanheart.org

FOUNDED: 1948

AREAS OF INTEREST:
Reducing disability and death from cardiovascular diseases and stroke; clinical, basic science, bioengineering/biotechnology, and public health problems; epidemiological, community and clinical investigations that bear on cardiovascular and stroke problems.

NAME(S) OF PROGRAMS:
- **Mentored Clinical and Population Research Award**
- **National Scientist Development Grant**

TYPE:
Awards/prizes; Development grants; Research grants. Mentored Clinical and Population Research Program is intended to encourage early career investigators who have appropriate and supportive mentoring relationships to engage in high-quality introductory and pilot clinical studies that will guide future strategies for reducing cardiovascular disease and stroke while fostering new research in clinical and translational science, and encouraging community- and population-based activities.

National Scientist Development Grant is intended to support highly promising beginning scientists in their progress toward independence by encouraging and adequately funding research projects that can bridge the gap between completion of research training and readiness for successful competition as an independent investigator.

YEAR PROGRAM STARTED: 1997

PURPOSE:
To support research activities broadly related to cardiovascular function and disease, stroke, or to related basic science, clinical, bioengineering/biotechnology and public health problems.

LEGAL BASIS:
Research association.

ELIGIBILITY:
Applicant must be U.S. citizen or permanent resident.

Mentored Clinical and Population Research Program: Open to health care professionals with a Master's or post-Baccalaureate doctoral degree, including M.P.H., R.N., Pharm.D., M.D., D.O. or Ph.D. Interdisciplinary research teams are eligible. Applicant must meet institutional requirements for grant submission at time of application.

National Scientist Development Grant: At the time of application, applicant must hold an M.D., Ph.D., D.O., D.V.M. or equivalent post-Baccalaureate doctoral degree and meet institutional requirements for grant submission. At the time of award activation, applicant must hold a faculty-staff position up to and including the rank of assistant professor (or equivalent). Applications may be submitted for review in the final year of a postdoctoral research fellowship or in the initial years of the first faculty/staff appointment. No more than four years can have elapsed since an applicant's first faculty/staff appointment (after receipt of doctoral degree) at the assistant professor level or its equivalent (including, but not limited to, research assistant professor, research scientist, staff scientist, etc.).

GEOG. RESTRICTIONS: United States.

FINANCIAL DATA:
Amount of support per award: Up to $35,000 per year (50%) of direct costs may be used for salary/fringe benefits, including allowance of up to $5,000 for mentor, indirect cost of $7,000 (10%), project support of up to $3,000 for travel and $5,000 computer limit, up to a maximum of $77,000 per year.

APPLICATION INFO:
Guidelines and application form are available on the web site.

Duration: Mentored Clinical and Population Research Program: Two years. National Scientist Development Grant: Four years.

Deadline: July.

ADDRESS INQUIRIES TO:
See e-mail address above.

THE AMERICAN LEGION NATIONAL HEADQUARTERS

P.O. Box 1055
Indianapolis, IN 46206
(317) 630-1209
Fax: (317) 630-1369
E-mail: scholarships@legion.org
Web Site: www.legion.org

TYPE:
Scholarships. Grants for registered nurses.

See entry 2407 for full listing.

AMERICAN LUNG ASSOCIATION [2307]

55 West Wacker Drive
Suite 1150
Chicago, IL 60601
E-mail: research@lung.org
Web Site: www.lung.org

FOUNDED: 1904

AREAS OF INTEREST:
Research and education for the prevention and control of lung disease.

NAME(S) OF PROGRAMS:
- **Dalsemer Research Grant**

TYPE:
Research grants.

PURPOSE:
To support research in interstitial lung disease.

LEGAL BASIS:
Nonprofit.

ELIGIBILITY:
At the time of application, applicant must:
(1) hold a doctoral degree and be assured of a faculty appointment or equivalent with demonstrated institutional commitment (salary support, research space) by the start of the award;
(2) have completed two years of postdoctoral research training;
(3) be U.S. citizens or foreign nationals holding one of the following visa immigration statuses: permanent resident (Green Card), exchange visitor (J-1), temporary worker in a specialty occupation (H-1, H-1B), Canadian or Mexican citizen engaging in professional activities (TC or TN), or temporary worker with extraordinary abilities in the sciences (O-1). Non-citizens must submit a notarized copy of proof of visa immigration status and;
(4) be employed by a U.S. institution.

Grantee organizations must be recognized academic or other nonprofit research entities.

Medical residents, those presently enrolled in a degree program (e.g., graduate students), and established investigators are not eligible to apply.

FINANCIAL DATA:
Amount of support per award: $40,000 per year.

NO. AWARDS: 1 to 2.

APPLICATION INFO:
Application information is available on the web site.

Duration: Up to two years.

Deadline: Varies.

PUBLICATIONS:
Program announcement.

ADDRESS INQUIRIES TO:
See e-mail address above.

AMERICAN LUNG ASSOCIATION [2308]

55 West Wacker Drive
Suite 1150
Chicago, IL 60601
E-mail: research@lung.org
Web Site: www.lung.org

FOUNDED: 1904

AREAS OF INTEREST:
Adult pulmonary medicine, lung biology, pediatric pulmonary medicine, and research and education for the prevention and control of lung disease.

NAME(S) OF PROGRAMS:
- **Senior Research Training Fellowships**

TYPE:
Fellowships.

YEAR PROGRAM STARTED: 1948

PURPOSE:
To prevent lung disease and promote lung health through research, education and advocacy.

LEGAL BASIS:
Nonprofit foundation.

ELIGIBILITY:
At the time of application, an applicant must hold a doctoral degree and must work in an academic or not-for-profit institution. M.D. or D.O. applicants must be in their third or fourth year of fellowship training. Ph.D. applicants must be in their first or second year of postdoctoral training.

GEOG. RESTRICTIONS: United States.

FINANCIAL DATA:
Amount of support per award: $32,500 per year.

APPLICATION INFO:
Application information is available on the web site.

Duration: Up to two years.

Deadline: November. Contact Association for exact date.

PUBLICATIONS:
Program announcement.

ADDRESS INQUIRIES TO:
See e-mail address above.

AMERICAN LUNG ASSOCIATION [2309]

55 West Wacker Drive
Suite 1150
Chicago, IL 60601
E-mail: research@lung.org
Web Site: www.lung.org

FOUNDED: 1904

AREAS OF INTEREST:
Research and education for the prevention and control of lung disease.

NAME(S) OF PROGRAMS:
- **Biomedical Research Grants**

TYPE:
Research grants.

YEAR PROGRAM STARTED: 1921

PURPOSE:
To prevent lung disease and promote lung health through research, education and advocacy.

LEGAL BASIS:
Nonprofit foundation.

ELIGIBILITY:
Intended for junior investigators researching the mechanisms of lung disease and general lung biology.

FINANCIAL DATA:
Amount of support per award: $40,000 per year.

APPLICATION INFO:
Application information is available on the web site.

Duration: Up to two years.

Deadline: November. Contact Association for exact date.

PUBLICATIONS:
Program announcement.

ADDRESS INQUIRIES TO:
See e-mail address above.

AMERICAN LUNG ASSOCIATION [2310]

55 West Wacker Drive
Suite 1150
Chicago, IL 60601
E-mail: research@lung.org
Web Site: www.lung.org/research

FOUNDED: 1904

AREAS OF INTEREST:
Research and education for the prevention and control of lung disease.

NAME(S) OF PROGRAMS:
- **Lung Health Dissertation Grant**

TYPE:
Research grants.

LEGAL BASIS:
Nonprofit organization.

ELIGIBILITY:
Grant is intended for predoctoral support for students with an academic career focus and/or nurses pursuing a doctoral degree. Research areas of particular interest to the Association include psychosocial, behavioral, health services, health policy, epidemiological, biostatistical and educational matters related to lung disease. Applicants must be matriculating in a full-time doctoral program. Individuals with an M.D. seeking a Ph.D. are not eligible.

Applicant must be a U.S. citizen or permanent resident or have a valid working visa. Research must be conducted in the U.S.

GEOG. RESTRICTIONS: United States.

FINANCIAL DATA:
Amount of support per award: Up to $21,000 ($16,000 stipend and $5,000 for research support).

NO. AWARDS: 1.

APPLICATION INFO:
Application information is available on the web site.

Duration: Up to two years.

Deadline: November. Contact Association for exact date.

ADDRESS INQUIRIES TO:
See e-mail address above.

THE CANADIAN LUNG ASSOCIATION (CLA) [2311]

1750 Courtwood Crescent
Suite 300
Ottawa ON K2C 2B5 Canada
(613) 569-6411
(888) 566-5864 (within Canada)
Fax: (613) 569-8860
E-mail: research@lung.ca
Web Site: www.lung.ca

FOUNDED: 1958

AREAS OF INTEREST:
Prevention and control of lung disease including asthma, emphysema, chronic bronchitis, tuberculosis and lung cancer; air pollution and smoking.

NAME(S) OF PROGRAMS:
- **Canadian Thoracic Society Fellowship**
- **Canadian Thoracic Society Studentship**

TYPE:
Fellowships. The Society offers a number of fellowships and studentships to support research training in pulmonary disease.

YEAR PROGRAM STARTED: 1959

PURPOSE:
To permit physicians and those holding Doctorate degrees in the health sciences to be funded for a period of research training so they may contribute to Canadian work in the area of respiratory disease.

LEGAL BASIS:
Not-for-profit, incorporated.

ELIGIBILITY:
A candidate/applicant must hold, or be completing, a Ph.D. or a health professional degree (or equivalent). The health professional degree must be in a field such as medicine, dentistry, pharmacy, optometry, veterinary medicine, chiropractic, nursing or rehabilitative science. For individuals that do not hold a health professional degree, awards will take effect only after the recipient has completed all requirements of the Ph.D. program, including the oral examination.

These awards are normally held at Canadian institutions. Canadian citizens and permanent residents may apply for awards to be held outside Canada. Candidates who are neither Canadian citizens nor permanent residents may apply only for awards to be held in Canada.

FINANCIAL DATA:
Amount of support per award: Fellowships: $45,000 to $55,000 (CAN) per year; Studentships: $21,000 (CAN) per year.

Total amount of support: Varies.

CO-OP FUNDING PROGRAMS: Partnerships include CIHR and the pharmaceutical industry (peer review only).

NO. MOST RECENT APPLICANTS: 60 for the year 2013.

NO. AWARDS: Approximately 6 each year.

APPLICATION INFO:
Application information is available on the web site.

Duration: One to two years. Competitive renewal.

Deadline: January 31.

PUBLICATIONS:
Canadian Respiratory Journal.

ADDRESS INQUIRIES TO:
The Canadian Thoracic Society
c/o Michelle McEvoy, Manager of Research
(See address above.)

THE CANADIAN LUNG ASSOCIATION (CLA)

1750 Courtwood Crescent
Suite 300
Ottawa ON K2C 2B5 Canada
(613) 569-6411
(888) 566-5864 (within Canada)
Fax: (613) 569-8860
E-mail: research@lung.ca
Web Site: www.lung.ca

TYPE:
Fellowships; Research grants. Fellowships are offered to registered nurses pursuing postgraduate education with a major component of the program involving respiratory nursing practice, physiotherapists pursuing postgraduate training with respiratory research as the major component, and respiratory therapists pursuing postgraduate education with a major component of the program involving respiratory therapy practice.

Grants for research and feasibility studies are offered to registered nurses undertaking research investigations related to nursing management of patients with respiratory disease and symptoms. Grants are also offered to physiotherapists undertaking investigations related to management of patients with respiratory disease. Respiratory therapists undertaking research investigations related to the management of patients with respiratory disease and symptoms may also qualify.

See entry 2410 for full listing.

THE CHEST FOUNDATION [2312]

2595 Patriot Boulevard
Glenview, IL 60026
(224) 521-9800
Fax: (224) 521-9801
E-mail: sreimbold@chestnet.org
Web Site: www.chestnet.org/foundation

FOUNDED: 1935

AREAS OF INTEREST:
All aspects of chest medicine and surgery.

NAME(S) OF PROGRAMS:

- **CHEST Foundation and the Alpha-1 Foundation Research Grant in Alpha-1 Antitrypsin Deficiency**
- **CHEST Foundation Research Grant in Chronic Obstructive Pulmonary Disease**
- **CHEST Foundation Research Grant in Lung Cancer**
- **CHEST Foundation Research Grant in Nontuberculous Mycobacteria**
- **CHEST Foundation Research Grant in Pulmonary Arterial Hypertension**
- **CHEST Foundation Research Grant in Pulmonary Fibrosis**
- **CHEST Foundation Research Grant in Venous Thromboembolism**
- **Chest Foundation Research Grant in Women's Lung Health**
- **Community Service Grant Honoring D. Robert McCaffree, M.D., Master FCCP**
- **GlaxoSmithKline Distinguished Scholar in Respiratory Health**

TYPE:
Research grants.

YEAR PROGRAM STARTED: 1996

PURPOSE:
To provide resources to advance the prevention and treatment of diseases of the chest: asthma, tuberculosis, end-of-life issues, smoking prevention and chronic obstructive pulmonary disease.

LEGAL BASIS:
Supporting organization.

ELIGIBILITY:
Applicant must be a CHEST member to apply for CHEST Foundation grants. For a community service grant, applicant or sponsor must be a current member of CHEST.

Special consideration will be given to applicants who are within five years of completing an advanced training program, or equivalent experience.

FINANCIAL DATA:
Amount of support per award: Varies by program.

Total amount of support: $475,000.

CO-OP FUNDING PROGRAMS: Actelion Pharmaceuticals, US, Inc.; Alpha-1 Foundation; The American Society of Transplantation; Astra Zeneca; Daiichi Sankyo; Genentech Inc.; Insmed.

APPLICATION INFO:
Application guidelines can be found on the Foundation web site.

Duration: One to three years.

Deadline: May 2.

PUBLICATIONS:
Call for Abstracts, brochure; also in *Ads in CHEST*, monthly publication of The American College of Chest Physicians (ACCP).

IRS I.D.: 36-3286520

ADDRESS INQUIRIES TO:
Sue Reimbold, Executive Director
(See address above.)

GREENBURG-MAY FOUNDATION

146 Central Park West
New York, NY 10023
(212) 451-3200
E-mail: pmay@trianpartners.com

TYPE:
Development grants; Research grants. Social services.

See entry 2364 for full listing.

HEART AND STROKE FOUNDATION OF CANADA [2313]

222 Queen Street
Suite 1402
Ottawa ON K1P 5V9 Canada
(613) 569-4361
Fax: (613) 569-3278
E-mail: research@hsf.ca
Web Site: www.hsf.ca/research

FOUNDED: 1956

AREAS OF INTEREST:
Cardiovascular/cerebrovascular research.

NAME(S) OF PROGRAMS:

- **Grant-in-Aid**

TYPE:
Grants-in-aid. Grants to support projects in areas of cardiovascular/cerebrovascular research.

YEAR PROGRAM STARTED: 1958

PURPOSE:
To reduce the morbidity and mortality from cardiovascular/cerebrovascular disease in Canada.

LEGAL BASIS:
Nonprofit.

ELIGIBILITY:
Qualified investigators affiliated with appropriate institutions are eligible.

GEOG. RESTRICTIONS: Canada.

FINANCIAL DATA:
Amount of support per award: Varies, depending upon the needs and nature of the request.

APPLICATION INFO:
Current guidelines and official application materials may be obtained online.

Duration: One to three years.

Deadline: Applications must be submitted online by the submission deadline (listed online) for funding to become effective on July 1 of the following year.

ADDRESS INQUIRIES TO:
Research Department
(See e-mail address above.)

HEART AND STROKE FOUNDATION OF CANADA [2314]

222 Queen Street
Suite 1402
Ottawa ON K1P 5V9 Canada
(613) 569-4361
Fax: (613) 569-3278
E-mail: research@hsf.ca
Web Site: www.hsf.ca/research

FOUNDED: 1956

AREAS OF INTEREST:
Cardiovascular and cerebrovascular research.

NAME(S) OF PROGRAMS:

- **New Investigator**

TYPE:
Awards/prizes; Scholarships. The New Investigator is the senior award offered by the Foundation.

YEAR PROGRAM STARTED: 1958

PURPOSE:
To reduce the morbidity and mortality from cardiovascular disease in Canada.

LEGAL BASIS:
Nonprofit.

ELIGIBILITY:
Individuals who have clearly demonstrated excellence during their predoctoral and postdoctoral training in cardiovascular or cerebrovascular research are eligible.

GEOG. RESTRICTIONS: Canada.

FINANCIAL DATA:
Amount of support per award: $60,000 (CAN) including employer's portion of fringe benefits.

APPLICATION INFO:
Official application materials may be obtained from the web site.

Duration: Five years.

Deadline: September 1, to become tenable July 1 of the following year.

ADDRESS INQUIRIES TO:
Research Department
(See e-mail address above.)

HEART AND STROKE FOUNDATION OF CANADA [2315]

222 Queen Street
Suite 1402
Ottawa ON K1P 5V9 Canada
(613) 569-4361
Fax: (613) 569-3278
E-mail: research@hsf.ca
Web Site: www.hsf.ca/research

FOUNDED: 1956

AREAS OF INTEREST:
Cardiovascular and cerebrovascular research.

NAME(S) OF PROGRAMS:
- **Research Fellowship**

TYPE:
Fellowships.

YEAR PROGRAM STARTED: 1958

PURPOSE:
To attract and foster the young investigator to initiate and/or continue training and competence in scientific method in a chosen area of the cardiovascular and cerebrovascular fields.

LEGAL BASIS:
Nonprofit organization.

ELIGIBILITY:
Intended for applicants with a Ph.D., M.D., or equivalent degree in cardiovascular or cerebrovascular field. Refer to guidelines for specific eligibility criteria.

GEOG. RESTRICTIONS: Canada.

FINANCIAL DATA:
Amount of support per award: Up to $50,000 (CAN) per year.

APPLICATION INFO:
Official application materials may be obtained from the web site.

Duration: Two to three years.

Deadline: November 1 for fellowships normally becoming tenable on July 1 of the following year.

ADDRESS INQUIRIES TO:
Research Department
(See e-mail address above.)

NATIONAL BLOOD FOUNDATION, A PROGRAM OF AABB [2316]

8101 Glenbrook Road
Bethesda, MD 20814-2749
(301) 215-6552
Fax: (301) 215-5751
E-mail: nbf@aabb.org
Web Site: www.aabb.org/nbf

FOUNDED: 1983

AREAS OF INTEREST:
Blood banking, blood safety, transfusion medicine, tissue transplantation, cellular therapy, and patient blood management.

NAME(S) OF PROGRAMS:
- **Scientific Research Grants Program**

TYPE:
Awards/prizes; Development grants; Research grants; Seed money grants. Basic medical research grants.

The focus of the NBF's Scientific Research Grants Program is to support early career researchers in the field of transfusion medicine, to include aspects of immunology, hematology, tissue and transplantation medicine, cellular therapies, emerging infectious disease, immunohematology, donor health and recruitment and retention, implementation of technological advances, and patient blood management. Priority is given to young investigators and innovative new projects with the potential to have a practical impact on patients and donors in transfusion medicine and cellular therapies.

YEAR PROGRAM STARTED: 1985

PURPOSE:
To actively support the leadership role of the AABB in establishing and promoting the highest standards of care for patients and donors by funding basic and applied scientific research, administrative research/projects, professional education in all aspects of blood banking, transfusion medicine, cellular therapies and patient blood management.

LEGAL BASIS:
Nonprofit association.

ELIGIBILITY:
Each applicant/researcher must be a doctor (M.D. or Ph.D.) or transfusion medicine, cellular therapies or patient blood management professional. Priority will be given to innovative, new projects. Funding will not be given to any one investigator more than two times. Awards will not be made to increase the funding available for currently funded research projects.

FINANCIAL DATA:
Grant awards may not cover indirect costs. Equipment expenditures cannot exceed $8,000 per grant.

Amount of support per award: Up to $75,000.

NO. MOST RECENT APPLICANTS: 40.

NO. AWARDS: 5.

APPLICATION INFO:
Required application forms are available from the Foundation. Electronic submission required as pdf (size restrictions). Application fee of $150 if applicant is not an AABB Individual Healthcare Professional or Physician in Residency member.

Duration: One to two years.

Deadline: December 31. Announcement in June for funds to be distributed in July.

PUBLICATIONS:
Application; program announcement.

IRS I.D.: 36-2384118

ADDRESS INQUIRIES TO:
Amy Quiggins, Manager
(See address above.)

NATIONAL HEART, LUNG AND BLOOD INSTITUTE (NHLBI) [2317]

National Institutes of Health
Grants Operations Branch, Room 7160
6701 Rockledge Drive, MSC 7926
Bethesda, MD 20892-7926
(301) 435-0166
Fax: (301) 451-5462
E-mail: lombardr@nhlbi.nih.gov
Web Site: www.nhlbi.nih.gov/research/funding

FOUNDED: 1948

AREAS OF INTEREST:
Diseases of the heart, blood vessels, lung and blood, sleep disorders, clinical use of blood and blood resources, and transfusion medicine.

TYPE:
Conferences/seminars; Fellowships; Project/program grants; Research grants; Training grants; Loan forgiveness programs. Career awards and other grant mechanisms to foster research on heart, vascular and lung diseases, and to develop scientists in these areas. Also, small business grants. Loan forgiveness programs are for research.

YEAR PROGRAM STARTED: 1948

PURPOSE:
To support research into the causes, improved diagnosis, treatment and prevention of cardiovascular diseases in arteriosclerosis, hypertension, cardiovascular disease, coronary heart disease, peripheral vascular disease, arrhythmias, heart failure and shock, congenital and rheumatic heart disease, cardiomyopathies and infections of the heart, circulatory assistance and AIDS.

LEGAL BASIS:
Public Health Service Act, Sections 301(c), 412 and 472.

ELIGIBILITY:
Any nonprofit or for-profit organization engaged in biomedical research may apply. An individual may apply for a fellowship award. Some restrictions may apply to foreign grantee institutions.

FINANCIAL DATA:
Amount of support per award: Varies by type of award.

APPLICATION INFO:
Application information is available on the web site.

Duration: Varies.

Deadline: Varies.

PUBLICATIONS:
NHLBI Fact Book; Annual Report of Director, NHLBI.

OFFICER:
Ryan Lombardi, Chief Grants Management Officer

ADDRESS INQUIRIES TO:
Ryan Lombardi
Chief Grants Management Officer
(See address above.)

NATIONAL HEART, LUNG AND BLOOD INSTITUTE (NHLBI) [2318]

Two Rockledge Center, Suite 10042
6701 Rockledge Drive, MSC 7952
Bethesda, MD 20892-7952
(301) 435-0202
Fax: (301) 480-3547
E-mail: nhlbi@nhlbi.nih.gov
Web Site: www.nhlbi.nih.gov

FOUNDED: 1948

AREAS OF INTEREST:
Pulmonary research, prevention, education and training programs in pulmonary diseases.

NAME(S) OF PROGRAMS:
- **Lung Diseases Research**

TYPE:
Project/program grants. Cooperative agreements.

YEAR PROGRAM STARTED: 1970

PURPOSE:
To use available knowledge and technology to solve specific disease problems of the lungs; to promote further studies on the structure and function of the lung; to achieve improvement in the prevention and treatment of lung diseases.

LEGAL BASIS:
Public Health Service Act, Section 301, 422 and 487, as amended, Public Laws 78-410 and 99-158, 42 U.S.C. 241, 42 U.S.C. 285, and 42 U.S.C. 288, as amended.

ELIGIBILITY:
Any nonprofit or for-profit organization engaged in biomedical research may apply for grants with the exception of NRSAs. An individual may apply for an NRSA or, in some cases, may qualify for a research grant if adequate facilities in which to perform the research are available.

Some grants are available to U.S. citizens or institutions only.

FINANCIAL DATA:
Grants may support salaries, equipment, supplies, travel, and patient hospitalization as required to perform the research effort.

APPLICATION INFO:
Research grant applications are submitted on designated forms to the Center for Scientific Review, National Institutes of Health, Bethesda, MD 20892. Forms for individual NRSA applications may be obtained from and submitted to the Office of Research Manpower, Center for Scientific Review, National Institutes of Health, Bethesda, MD 20892. For some special grant programs, applicants may be advised to submit directly to the Review Branch, Division of Extramural Affairs, National Heart, Lung, and Blood Institute, Bethesda, MD 20892. The standard application forms, as furnished by PHS and required by 45 CFR, Part 92, must be used for this program.

Duration: One to five years. Renewable.

PUBLICATIONS:
Annual Program Report.

STAFF:
James P. Kiley, Ph.D., Director, Division of Lung Diseases
Gail Weinmann, M.D., Deputy Director

ADDRESS INQUIRIES TO:
James P. Kiley, Ph.D., Director
Division of Lung Diseases
(See address above.)

THE POTTS MEMORIAL FOUNDATION [2319]

P.O. Box 1015
Hudson, NY 12534
(518) 851-2292
E-mail: pottsfoundation@outlook.com

FOUNDED: 1922

AREAS OF INTEREST:
Tuberculosis.

TYPE:
Fellowships; Grants-in-aid; Research grants; Seed money grants. At present, the program allows the Foundation to provide for the care, treatment and rehabilitation of persons afflicted with tuberculosis by methods selected by the trustees. This may include maintenance, operation of hospitals, research, vocational counseling and guidance, scholarships, subsidies for education and training, job placement, grants to hospitals and charitable institutions and the operation of sheltered workshops.

YEAR PROGRAM STARTED: 1922

PURPOSE:
To help people who are battling tuberculosis.

LEGAL BASIS:
Nonprofit corporation.

FINANCIAL DATA:
Amount of support per award: $1,000 to $30,000.

NO. MOST RECENT APPLICANTS: Under 50.

NO. AWARDS: 10 to 15.

APPLICATION INFO:
A letter of request and proposal should be furnished in as much detail as possible, including a detailed budget, to the Foundation. Eight (8) copies would be appreciated.

Duration: One year.

Deadline: 30 days prior to May 15 and October 15.

OFFICERS:
Brian Daggett, M.D., President
Kathleen A. McDonough, Ph.D., Vice President
Sidney D. Richter, Treasurer
Donna D. Klose, Secretary

TRUSTEES:
John Chan, M.D.
Richard Gullot, M.D.
Anthony Malanga, M.D.
Donna O'Hare, M.D.

ADDRESS INQUIRIES TO:
Donna D. Klose, Secretary
(See address above.)

THE SARNOFF CARDIOVASCULAR RESEARCH FOUNDATION [2320]

731 Walker Road
Suite G2
Great Falls, VA 22066
(703) 759-7600
Fax: (703) 759-7838
E-mail: dboyd@sarnofffoundation.org
Web Site: www.sarnofffoundation.org

FOUNDED: 1981

AREAS OF INTEREST:
Cardiovascular research.

NAME(S) OF PROGRAMS:
- **Sarnoff Fellowship Program**
- **Sarnoff Scholar Fellow-to-Faculty Transition Award**

TYPE:
Awards/prizes; Fellowships. Research Fellowship and Award.

PURPOSE:
To give medical students the opportunity to spend a year conducting intensive work in a biomedical research laboratory; to provide financial support to former Sarnoff Fellows committed to pursuing a career in cardiovascular research.

ELIGIBILITY:
Sarnoff Fellowship Program is for medical students enrolled in any accredited medical school in the U.S. Applications are encouraged from second- and third-year medical students. Fourth-year medical students are required to submit an official letter from their medical schools granting graduation deferment. There are no citizenship requirements for application, but those who are not U.S. citizens must have and maintain an appropriate visa. Applicants enrolled in an M.D./Ph.D. program are ineligible. The Foundation strongly encourages applicants from members of underrepresented or historically disadvantaged backgrounds.

Sarnoff Scholar Fellow-to-Faculty Transition Award applicant must be a former Sarnoff Fellow pursuing a career in cardiovascular research. Applicants may apply during the second half of their post-residency training/fellowship program and/or overlapping with the first two junior faculty years.

FINANCIAL DATA:
Amount of support per award: Fellowship: $30,000 stipend; $3,500 allowance for travel and moving expenses, and health insurance; financial support to attend the Sarnoff Annual Scientific Meeting and American Heart Association Scientific Sessions; and up to $1,350 for travel to present a paper, based on Fellowship research, at two national conferences.

Scholar: $50,000 in direct costs per year for salary support; $10,000 per year research supply budget; up to $1,500 annually to defray the cost of health insurance; travel funds up to $1,000 to enable the Scholar to present a paper at a national conference; and maximum of 10% indirect costs paid to the institution for handling the award.

Total amount of support: Varies.

NO. AWARDS: Fellowship: Up to 18 annually; Scholar: 1 to 2 annually.

APPLICATION INFO:
Applicants to the Fellowship Program must submit the following:
(1) one-page personal statement describing scholarly interests and career plans;
(2) three-page essay on the applicant's cardiovascular topic of interest;
(3) completed application form and signed statement of confidentiality;
(4) official medical school transcript;
(5) curriculum vitae;
(6) recommendation from the applicant's sponsor;
(7) two additional recommendations and;
(8) any other material that the applicant determines is appropriate to support the application.

Duration: Fellowship: One year; Scholar: Two years.

Deadline: Contact Foundation for exact dates.

ADDRESS INQUIRIES TO:
Dana Quinn Boyd, Executive Director
(See address above.)

SOCIETY OF CARDIOVASCULAR ANESTHESIOLOGISTS [2321]
8735 West Higgins Road
Suite 300
Chicago, IL 60631
(855) 658-2828
Fax: (847) 375-6323
E-mail: info@scahq.org
Web Site: www.scahq.org

AREAS OF INTEREST:
Cardiothoracic and vascular anesthesia.

NAME(S) OF PROGRAMS:
- **Roizen and Anesthesia Research Foundation New Investigator Grant**
- **SCA Starter Grants**
- **SCA-IARS Mid-Career Grant**

TYPE:
Research grants.

PURPOSE:
To promote excellence in patient care through education and research in perioperative care for patients undergoing cardiothoracic and vascular procedures.

ELIGIBILITY:
Grant applicants must be a member of Society of Cardiovascular Anesthesiologists and hold an M.D. or Ph.D. degree.

No part of the grant may be used for salary support of the principal investigator (or fellows or residents), travel or tuition expenses of the principal investigator, patient costs (except to pay for pertinent laboratory studies), consultant costs, alterations or renovations.

FINANCIAL DATA:
Amount of support per award: $25,000 to $50,000 per year.

Total amount of support: Up to $100,000 per recipient, depending on which grant is applied for.

NO. MOST RECENT APPLICANTS: 21.

NO. AWARDS: Maximum of 5 each year.

APPLICATION INFO:
Application information is available on the web site.

Duration: Up to two years.

Deadline: Varies.

IRS I.D.: 72-0863580

ADDRESS INQUIRIES TO:
Linda Caradine-Poinsett, MBA, Ph.D.
Executive Director
(See address above.)

Metabolism, gastroenterology, nephrology

A.S.P.E.N. RHOADS RESEARCH FOUNDATION [2322]
8630 Fenton Street
Suite 412
Silver Spring, MD 20910
(301) 587-6315
Fax: (301) 587-2365
E-mail: aspen@nutritioncare.org
Web Site: www.nutritioncare.org

FOUNDED: 1975

AREAS OF INTEREST:
Metabolic issues and nutrition support therapy.

TYPE:
Research grants. Annual support for nutritional research.

YEAR PROGRAM STARTED: 1992

PURPOSE:
To support the personal and professional development of nutrition researchers throughout their careers.

LEGAL BASIS:
Nonprofit foundation.

ELIGIBILITY:
Applicants are encouraged from the fields of medicine, dietetics, nursing and pharmacy. Grants are only given to individuals. There are no citizenship requirements. Preference is given to individuals who are active in developing a career in nutritional research. A.S.P.E.N. membership is required.

FINANCIAL DATA:
Amount of support per award: Up to $25,000.

Total amount of support: Up to $130,000 annually.

NO. AWARDS: Up to 4 at $25,000; 1 at $16,600; 2 at $5,000.

APPLICATION INFO:
Application form required. Contact the Foundation for additional information.

Duration: One year. Renewal possible up to two years.

Deadline: August; see program announcement for exact date.

PUBLICATIONS:
Application guidelines.

ADDRESS INQUIRIES TO:
Michelle Spangenburg
Director of Education and Research
(See address above.)

AMERICAN DIABETES ASSOCIATION [2323]
1701 North Beauregard Street
Alexandria, VA 22311
(703) 549-1500 ext. 5532
Fax: (703) 621-3759
E-mail: grantquestions@diabetes.org
Web Site: www.professional.diabetes.org/grants

FOUNDED: 1940

AREAS OF INTEREST:
Programs serving the needs of people with diabetes, their families, researchers, clinicians and the diabetic health care team.

CONSULTING OR VOLUNTEER SERVICES:
Various support and education programs carried out at affiliate level. Research program on national level.

NAME(S) OF PROGRAMS:
- **Innovative Basic Science Award (IBS)**
- **Innovative Clinical or Translational Science Award (ICTS)**
- **Junior Faculty Development Award (JFD)**
- **Minority Undergraduate Internship (MUI)**
- **Postdoctoral Fellowship (PDF)**
- **Postdoctoral Minority Fellowship (PMF)**

TYPE:
Fellowships; Research grants; Training grants.

YEAR PROGRAM STARTED: 1955

PURPOSE:
To aid in the search for a cure and prevention of diabetes; to help those with diabetes complications.

LEGAL BASIS:
Nonprofit voluntary health organization.

ELIGIBILITY:
Applicants must have a Ph.D., M.D., Pharm.D., D.O. or D.P.M. degree or appropriate health or science-related degrees and must hold full-time or clinical faculty positions or the equivalent at university-affiliated institutions within the U.S. or its possessions. Postdoctoral Fellowship applicants must hold a full-time postdoctoral fellowship or the equivalent.

All investigators must be legally authorized to work in the U.S. Institutional certification of work permission will be required for all funded awards.

For the Junior Faculty Development Award, applicants can have any level of faculty appointment up to and including Associate Professor and have no more than 10 years of research experience following receipt of their terminal degree.

For the Postdoctoral Minority Fellowship, underrepresented minorities are defined as the minority groups that are underrepresented in the area of biomedical and behavioral research: African American or Black, Hispanic/Spanish/Latino, American Indian/Alaskan Native, and Native Hawaiian or other Pacific Islander descent.

GEOG. RESTRICTIONS: United States.

FINANCIAL DATA:
Amount of support per award: Innovative Basic Science Award: Up to $115,000 per year; Innovative Clinical or Translational Science Award: Up to $200,000 per year; Junior Faculty Development Award: $138,000 per year, plus optional student loan repayment of $10,000 per year; Minority Undergraduate Internship: $3,000 stipend; Postdoctoral Fellowship and Postdoctoral Minority Fellowship: $42,000 to $55,272 per year salary stipend, plus $5,000 per year research and $5,000 per year fringe allowances.

NO. MOST RECENT APPLICANTS: 1,000.

APPLICATION INFO:
Applicants for all grants must submit application forms, a nontechnical description of the research project of less than 200 words and a scientific abstract of the proposal of no more than 200 words.

Duration: Innovative Basic Science Award, Innovative Clinical or Translational Science Award, Postdoctoral Fellowship and Postdoctoral Minority Fellowship: Up to three years; Junior Faculty Development Award: Two to four years; Minority Undergraduate Internship: Up to one year.

Deadline: April 15.

PUBLICATIONS:
Annual reports.

OFFICERS:
Janel Wright, J.D., Chairman of the Board
David Marrero, Ph.D., President, Health Care and Education
Samuel Dagogo-Jack, M.D., President, Medicine and Science

ADDRESS INQUIRIES TO:
Magda Galindo
Director Research Programs
(See address above.)

AMERICAN GASTROENTEROLOGICAL ASSOCIATION (AGA) [2324]

4930 Del Ray Avenue
Bethesda, MD 20814
(301) 222-4012
Fax: (301) 652-3890
E-mail: awards@gastro.org
Web Site: www.gastro.org/research-funding

FOUNDED: 1990

AREAS OF INTEREST:
Gastroenterology and related fields.

NAME(S) OF PROGRAMS:
- **AGA-R. Robert and Sally D. Funderburg Research Award in Gastric Cancer**

TYPE:
Research grants. Recognition award for an established investigator working on novel approaches in gastric cancer, including the fields of gastric mucosal cell biology, regeneration and regulation of cell growth (not as they relate to peptic ulcer disease or repair), inflammation as precancerous lesions, genetics of gastric carcinoma, oncogenes in gastric epithelial malignancies, epidemiology of gastric cancer, etiology of gastric epithelial malignancies or clinical research in diagnosis or treatment of gastric carcinoma.

YEAR PROGRAM STARTED: 1990

PURPOSE:
To support an established investigator in the field of gastric biology which enhances our fundamental understanding of gastric cancer pathobiology in order to develop a cure for the disease.

LEGAL BASIS:
Nonprofit foundation.

ELIGIBILITY:
Candidates must hold faculty positions at accredited North American institutions. Candidates may not hold other exclusively salary support awards on a similar topic from other agencies. In recognition of their underrepresentation in gastroenterology-related fields, women and minorities are strongly encouraged to apply. Applicant must also be a member of the AGA.

Awardees will be selected based on the novelty, feasibility and significance of the proposal, attributes of the candidate and the likelihood that support will lead the applicant toward a research career in the field of gastric cancer biology. Preference will be given to novel approaches.

GEOG. RESTRICTIONS: North America.

FINANCIAL DATA:
Funds are to be used for the salary, support, equipment and supplies of the investigator, to promote his or her involvement in the field. No indirect costs will be allowed.

Amount of support per award: $50,000 per year.

NO. MOST RECENT APPLICANTS: 12 for the year 2013.

NO. AWARDS: 1.

APPLICATION INFO:
Application forms can be obtained online.

Duration: Two years.

Deadline: Late August.

PUBLICATIONS:
Announcements.

ADDRESS INQUIRIES TO:
Wykenna S.C. Vailor
Senior Manager, Research Affairs and Awards
(See address above.)

AMERICAN GASTROENTEROLOGICAL ASSOCIATION (AGA) [2325]

4930 Del Ray Avenue
Bethesda, MD 20814
(301) 222-4012
Fax: (301) 652-3890
E-mail: awards@gastro.org
Web Site: www.gastro.org/research-funding

FOUNDED: 1990

AREAS OF INTEREST:
Gastroenterology and related fields.

NAME(S) OF PROGRAMS:
- **AGA-Athena Troxel Blackburn Research Award in Neuroenteric Disease**
- **AGA-Gilead Sciences Research Scholar Award in Liver Disease**
- **AGA-Takeda Pharmaceuticals International Research Scholar Award in Gut Microbiome Research**
- **AGA-Takeda Pharmaceuticals International Research Scholar Award in Neurogastroenterology**
- **Research Scholar Award**

TYPE:
Research grants. Awards for young investigators working in any area of gastroenterology, hepatology or in related areas.

YEAR PROGRAM STARTED: 1990

PURPOSE:
To provide salary support or, in special circumstances, research support to ensure that a major proportion of time is protected for research scholarship. The overall objective is to enable young investigators to develop independent productive research careers in gastroenterology-related fields.

LEGAL BASIS:
Nonprofit foundation.

ELIGIBILITY:
The applicant must hold an M.D., Ph.D. or equivalent degree, and a full-time faculty position at a North American university or professional institute at the time of application. Applicant must also be a member of the AGA. The award is not intended for fellows, but for young faculty who have demonstrated exceptional promise and have some record of accomplishment in research. Candidates should be early in their careers; therefore, established investigators are not appropriate candidates. Women, minorities and physician/scientist investigators are strongly encouraged to apply. Applicants working in a nonprofit institution in North America are eligible for this award (U.S. citizenship is not required). For M.D. applicants, no more than seven years shall have elapsed following the completion of clinical training (GI fellowship or its equivalent) at the start date of the award. For Ph.D. applicants, no more than seven years shall have elapsed following the awarding of the applicant's Ph.D. and the start date of the award. An appropriately documented parental leave of absence will not be counted toward the seven-year eligibility criteria. Exceptional circumstances may also be considered.

Applicants cannot hold or have held, prior to receiving the first payment of this award, an R01, R29, K-series award, VA career development award, or any award with similar objectives from non-federal sources. However, awards or grants obtained after receipt of the Research Scholar Award support by the RSA would be required to forfeit the remaining balance of award.

GEOG. RESTRICTIONS: North America.

FINANCIAL DATA:
Amount of support per award: $270,000 ($90,000 per year).

CO-OP FUNDING PROGRAMS: Jointly sponsored by the American Gastroenterological Association and participating pharmaceutical corporations.

APPLICATION INFO:
Completed application, letters of support or commitment, and other documents, as applicable, must be combined into and submitted as one PDF document to the e-mail address above. The document must be titled by the applicant's last name and first initial only. In the submission e-mail, applicant must include full name and project title. Hard copies are not accepted.

Duration: Three years.

Deadline: AGA-Athena Troxel Blackburn Award and AGA-Gilead Sciences Research Scholar Award: June for awards to begin the following October. AGA-Takeda Pharmaceuticals International Research Scholar Awards: August for awards to begin the following November. Research Scholar Award: September for awards to begin the following December.

ADDRESS INQUIRIES TO:
Wykenna S.C. Vailor
Senior Manager, Research Affairs and Awards
(See address above.)

AMERICAN GASTROENTEROLOGICAL ASSOCIATION (AGA) [2326]

4930 Del Ray Avenue
Bethesda, MD 20814
(301) 222-4012
Fax: (301) 652-3890
E-mail: awards@gastro.org
Web Site: www.gastro.org/research-funding

FOUNDED: 1990

AREAS OF INTEREST:
Gastroenterology and related fields.

NAME(S) OF PROGRAMS:
- **AGA Student Research Fellowship Award**

TYPE:
Research grants. Financial support for individuals to obtain research experience by spending some time in an active research environment. The proposed subjects of investigation should be related to a problem in digestive disease or nutrition. This award is not intended to provide salary for lab technicians.

YEAR PROGRAM STARTED: 1990

PURPOSE:
To stimulate interest in research careers in digestive diseases by providing salary support for research projects.

LEGAL BASIS:
Nonprofit foundation.

ELIGIBILITY:
Candidates may be high school students or undergraduate students at accredited North American (U.S. or Canada) institutions and must be in full-time research with a preceptor for a minimum of 10 weeks. Candidates holding advanced degrees must be enrolled as undergraduate students. In recognition of their underrepresentation in gastroenterology-related fields, women and minorities are strongly encouraged to apply. Candidates may not hold similar salary support awards from other agencies, e.g., American Liver Foundation and/or Crohn's and Colitis Foundation.

The preceptor must be a full-time faculty member who directs a research project in a gastroenterology-related area at an accredited North American institution. In addition, he/she must be an individual member of the AGA.

Awardees will be selected based on novelty, feasibility and significance of the proposal, attributes of the candidate, the record of the preceptor, evidence of institutional commitment and the laboratory environment.

GEOG. RESTRICTIONS: North America.

FINANCIAL DATA:
Amount of support per award: $2,500.

NO. AWARDS: 10 for the year 2015.

APPLICATION INFO:
Application forms can be obtained online.

Duration: One year.

Deadline: February 12.

PUBLICATIONS:
Announcement.

ADDRESS INQUIRIES TO:
Wykenna S.C. Vailor
Senior Manager, Research Affairs and Awards
(See address above.)

*SPECIAL STIPULATIONS:
Applicants must be sponsored by an AGA member.

AMERICAN GASTROENTEROLOGICAL ASSOCIATION (AGA) [2327]

4930 Del Ray Avenue
Bethesda, MD 20814
(301) 222-4012
Fax: (301) 652-3890
E-mail: awards@gastro.org
Web Site: www.gastro.org/research-funding

FOUNDED: 1990

AREAS OF INTEREST:
Gastroenterology and related fields.

NAME(S) OF PROGRAMS:
- **Elsevier Gut Microbiome Pilot Research Award**
- **Elsevier Pilot Research Award**

TYPE:
Research grants. Research initiative grants for investigators to work in gastroenterology- or hepatology-related areas.

YEAR PROGRAM STARTED: 1990

PURPOSE:
To provide non-salary funds to new investigators starting their research careers to help them establish their independence; to support pilot projects that represent new research directions for established investigators, with the intent of stimulating research in gastroenterology- or hepatology-related areas by permitting investigators to obtain new data which can ultimately provide the basis for subsequent grant applications of more substantial funding and duration.

LEGAL BASIS:
Nonprofit foundation.

ELIGIBILITY:
Open to investigators with M.Ds. or Ph.Ds. (or equivalent), who must hold full-time faculty positions at accredited North American institutions. They may not hold awards on a similar topic from other agencies. Applicant must also be a member of the AGA. In recognition of their underrepresentation in gastroenterology-related fields, women and minorities are strongly encouraged to apply.

Proposals will be selected on the basis of novelty, importance, feasibility, environment, commitment of the institution and overall likelihood that the projects will lead to more substantial, subsequent grant applications. Applicants may not submit the same research project for both of these awards.

GEOG. RESTRICTIONS: North America.

FINANCIAL DATA:
Funds may be used for salary (for lab personnel and technicians only), supplies or equipment. Indirect costs are not allowed.

Amount of support per award: $25,000 per year.

NO. MOST RECENT APPLICANTS: Varies.

NO. AWARDS: Elsevier Gut Microbiome Pilot Research Award: 1; Elsevier Pilot Research Award: 2.

APPLICATION INFO:
Application information is available on the web site.

Duration: One year.

Deadline: January 15.

ADDRESS INQUIRIES TO:
Wykenna S.C. Vailor
Senior Manager, Research Affairs and Awards
(See address above.)

AMERICAN GASTROENTEROLOGICAL ASSOCIATION (AGA) [2328]

4930 Del Ray Avenue
Bethesda, MD 20814
(301) 222-4012
Fax: (301) 652-3890
E-mail: awards@gastro.org
Web Site: www.gastro.org/research-funding

AREAS OF INTEREST:
Gastroenterology and related fields.

NAME(S) OF PROGRAMS:
- **AGA-Rome Foundation Functional GI and Motility Disorders Pilot Research Award**

TYPE:
Research grants. Award for early stage and established investigators to support pilot research projects pertaining to functional GI and motility disorders.

PURPOSE:
To provide investigators funds to help establish their research careers or support pilot projects that represent new research directions; to stimulate research in the areas of functional GI and motility disorders by providing time for investigators to obtain new data that can ultimately lead to subsequent grant applications for more substantial funding and duration.

ELIGIBILITY:
Applicants must hold an M.D., Ph.D. or equivalent degree and a full-time faculty position at an accredited institution. The applicant must also be a member of the AGA. International candidates may apply. Women and minorities are strongly encouraged to apply. Awardees will be selected based on novelty, importance, feasibility, environment and the overall likelihood that the project will lead to subsequent, more substantial grants in the areas of functional GI and motility disorders research.

Candidates may not hold awards directly related to the proposed research from other agencies. Rome Foundation board members are ineligible.

GEOG. RESTRICTIONS: North America.

FINANCIAL DATA:
Funds are to be used for salary support of the primary investigator, research assistants, biostatistics support, laboratory technicians, supplies and equipment. No indirect costs will be allowed.

Amount of support per award: $50,000.

CO-OP FUNDING PROGRAMS: Jointly sponsored by the Rome Foundation and the American Gastroenterological Association.

NO. AWARDS: 2.

APPLICATION INFO:
Completed application, letters of support or commitment, and other documents, as applicable, must be combined into and submitted as one PDF document to the e-mail address above. The document must be titled by the applicant's last name and first initial only. In the submission e-mail, applicant must include full name and project title. Hard copies are not accepted.

Duration: One year.

Deadline: January 15.

ADDRESS INQUIRIES TO:
Wykenna S.C. Vailor
Senior Manager, Research Affairs and Awards
(See address above.)

AMERICAN GASTROENTEROLOGICAL ASSOCIATION (AGA) [2329]

4930 Del Ray Avenue
Bethesda, MD 20814
(301) 222-4012
Fax: (301) 652-3890
E-mail: awards@gastro.org
Web Site: www.gastro.org/research-funding

AREAS OF INTEREST:
Gastroenterology and related fields.

NAME(S) OF PROGRAMS:

- **AGA Student Abstract Prizes**

TYPE:
Awards/prizes; Travel grants. Awards for high school, undergraduate, graduate and medical students who have submitted abstracts chosen by AGA to be presented during Digestive Disease Week (DDW).

PURPOSE:
To stimulate interest in gastroenterology/hepatology research careers through competition and recognition.

ELIGIBILITY:
Applicant must be high school, undergraduate, graduate or medical student or medical resident (up to and including postgraduate year three) who has performed original research related to diseases, structure or functioning of the digestive system. The applicant's sponsor must be a member of AGA. Applicants may only submit one abstract for consideration and must be the designated presenter or first author of the abstract. Women and minority students are strongly encouraged to apply. Awardees will be selected based on novelty, significance of the proposal, clarity of the abstract and contribution of the student.

Postdoctoral fellows, technicians, visiting scientists and M.D. research fellows are not eligible.

GEOG. RESTRICTIONS: North America.

FINANCIAL DATA:
Amount of support per award: Travel Award: $500; Best Student Abstract: $1,000.

NO. AWARDS: Travel Award: 8; Best Student Abstract: 3.

APPLICATION INFO:
Typed application, copy of accepted DDW abstract, copy of AGA acceptance notification and letter of support must be combined into and submitted as one PDF document to the e-mail address above. The document must be titled by the applicant's last name and first initial only. In the submission e-mail, applicant must include full name and project title. Hard copies are not accepted.

Deadline: March 4.

ADDRESS INQUIRIES TO:
Wykenna S.C. Vailor
Senior Manager, Research Affairs and Awards
(See address above.)

AMERICAN GASTROENTEROLOGICAL ASSOCIATION (AGA) [2330]

4930 Del Ray Avenue
Bethesda, MD 20814
(301) 222-4012
Fax: (301) 652-3890
E-mail: awards@gastro.org
Web Site: www.gastro.org/research-funding

AREAS OF INTEREST:
Gastroenterology and related fields.

NAME(S) OF PROGRAMS:

- **AGA-Moti L. and Kamla Rustgi International Travel Awards**

TYPE:
Awards/prizes; Travel grants. Awards for young basic, translational and clinical investigators residing outside North America to provide travel expenses to attend Digestive Disease Week (DDW).

PURPOSE:
To enable young investigators outside of North American institutions to attend DDW and encourage them to maintain a commitment to digestive disease research.

ELIGIBILITY:
The applicant must hold an M.D. or Ph.D. degree or a non-U.S. equivalent degree, be 35 years of age or younger at the time of DDW and be fluent in English. The applicant must be an AGA member, who is sponsored by an international AGA member. The applicant must be the first author of an abstract accepted by the AGA for presentation at DDW and provide evidence of abstract acceptance. Applicants must only submit one abstract for consideration.

Awardees will be selected based on the applicant's credentials and achievements as documented in their application.

GEOG. RESTRICTIONS: North America.

FINANCIAL DATA:
Amount of support per award: $750.

NO. AWARDS: 2.

APPLICATION INFO:
Typed application, curriculum vitae, copy of accepted DDW abstract, copy of AGA acceptance notification and letter of support must be combined into and submitted as one PDF document to the e-mail address above. The document must be titled by the applicant's last name and first initial only. In the submission e-mail, applicant must include full name and project title. Hard copies are not accepted.

Deadline: February 26.

ADDRESS INQUIRIES TO:
Wykenna S.C. Vailor
Senior Manager, Research Affairs and Awards
(See address above.)

AMERICAN GASTROENTEROLOGICAL ASSOCIATION (AGA) [2331]

4930 Del Ray Avenue
Bethesda, MD 20814
(301) 222-4012
Fax: (301) 652-3890
E-mail: awards@gastro.org
Web Site: www.gastro.org/research-funding

AREAS OF INTEREST:
Gastroenterology and related fields.

NAME(S) OF PROGRAMS:

- **AGA/AGA-GRG Fellow Travel and Abstract of the Year Awards**

TYPE:
Awards/prizes; Travel grants.

PURPOSE:
To encourage trainees to become more involved in digestive disease research.

ELIGIBILITY:
Applicants must be M.D. and/or Ph.D. postdoctoral fellows who are active or trainee members of AGA, and must be sponsored by a member of AGA. Applicants must be first author of an abstract accepted by AGA for oral or poster presentation, and must provide confirmation of AGA abstract acceptance.

Applicants may not apply for both the AGA Fellow Travel Awards and the AGA-GRG Fellow Travel Award. Individuals with faculty appointments are not eligible.

GEOG. RESTRICTIONS: North America.

FINANCIAL DATA:
Amount of support per award: Up to $1,000.

NO. AWARDS: 12.

APPLICATION INFO:
Copy of the submitted abstract, AGA acceptance confirmation and a letter of recommendation from the applicant's sponsor (one page or less) are required. The letter of recommendation must describe his or her role in the research being presented and detail how the award will benefit their career. Completed application and required documentation must be combined into and submitted as one PDF document to the e-mail address above. The document must be titled by the applicant's last name and first initial only. In the submission e-mail, applicant must include full name and project title. Hard copies are not accepted.

Deadline: February 26.

ADDRESS INQUIRIES TO:
Wykenna S.C. Vailor
Senior Manager, Research Affairs and Awards
(See address above.)

AMERICAN GASTROENTEROLOGICAL ASSOCIATION (AGA) [2332]

4930 Del Ray Avenue
Bethesda, MD 20814
(301) 222-4012
Fax: (301) 652-3890
E-mail: awards@gastro.org
Web Site: www.gastro.org/research-funding

AREAS OF INTEREST:
Gastroenterology and related fields.

NAME(S) OF PROGRAMS:

- **AGA-Caroline Craig Augustyn and Damian Augustyn Award in Digestive Cancer**

TYPE:
Research grants. Award for a young investigator, instructor, research associate or equivalent who currently holds a federal or non-federal career development award devoted to conducting research related to digestive cancer.

PURPOSE:
To support young investigators, research associates or equivalents conducting research relevant to the pathogenesis, prevention,

diagnosis, or treatment of digestive cancer; to supplement existing career development funding.

ELIGIBILITY:

Candidates must hold an M.D., Ph.D. or equivalent degree and a full-time position at a North American institution. Research must be conducted at a North American institution. Candidates must also be members of AGA. Candidates must hold an NIH K series or other federal or non-federal career development award of at least four years duration. There must be at least one remaining year on the award by the start date of this award. Women and underrepresented minority applicants are strongly encouraged to apply. Physician/scientist investigators and candidates interested in translational research are especially encouraged to apply. Awardees will be selected based on qualifications of the candidate, the novelty, feasibility and significance of their research and the potential for a future independent research career.

M.D. applicants: no more than seven years shall have elapsed following the completion of clinical training (GI fellowship or its equivalent) and the start date of this award. Ph.D. applicants: no more than seven years shall have elapsed following the awarding of the Ph.D. and the start date of this award. An appropriately documented parental leave of absence will not be counted toward the seven-year eligibility criteria. Exceptional circumstances may also be considered.

Candidates may not hold an R01 or equivalent, such as a VA Merit award; therefore, established investigators will not be considered for this award.

FINANCIAL DATA:

Funds are to be used to support direct research-related activities and may be used to support a new endeavor or an ongoing basic or clinical project. Funds may also be used for equipment, supplies, animal costs and other materials. No indirect costs will be allowed.

Amount of support per award: $40,000.

NO. AWARDS: 1.

APPLICATION INFO:

Completed application, letters of recommendation and other documents, as applicable, must be combined into and submitted as one PDF document to the e-mail address above. The document must be titled by the applicant's last name and first initial only. In the submission e-mail, applicant must include full name and project title. Hard copies are not accepted.

Deadline: January 29.

ADDRESS INQUIRIES TO:

Wykenna S.C. Vailor
Senior Manager, Research Affairs and Awards
(See address above.)

AMERICAN GASTROENTEROLOGICAL ASSOCIATION (AGA) [2333]

4930 Del Ray Avenue
Bethesda, MD 20814
(301) 222-4012
Fax: (301) 652-3890
E-mail: awards@gastro.org
Web Site: www.gastro.org/research-funding

AREAS OF INTEREST:

Gastroenterology and related fields.

NAME(S) OF PROGRAMS:

- **AGA-Boston Scientific Career Development Technology and Innovation Award**

TYPE:

Research grants. Award for young investigators working toward independent careers in gastroenterology, hepatology, or related areas focused on technology and innovation.

PURPOSE:

To enable young investigators to develop independent and productive research careers in the field of biomedical technology by ensuring that a major proportion of their time is protected for research.

ELIGIBILITY:

Candidates must hold an M.D., Ph.D. or equivalent and a full-time position at a North American institution. Candidates research must be conducted at a North American institution. Candidates must also be members of AGA. Women and underrepresented minority applicants are strongly encouraged to apply. Candidates with an active K12 may apply. Awardees will be selected based on significance, investigator, innovation, approach, environment, relevance to AGA's mission, and evidence of institutional commitment.

M.D. applicants: no more than seven years shall have elapsed following the completion of clinical training (GI fellowship or its equivalent) and the start date of this award. Ph.D. applicants: no more than seven years shall have elapsed following the awarding of the Ph.D. and start date of this award. An appropriately documented parental leave of absence will not be counted toward the seven-year eligibility criteria. Exceptional circumstances may also be considered.

Established investigators (fellows) are not eligible. Candidates may not hold or have held an NIH R01, R29, R21, K08, K23, Veterans Affairs Career Development Award or any award with similar objectives from non-federal sources.

GEOG. RESTRICTIONS: North America.

FINANCIAL DATA:

Amount of support per award: $150,000. ($75,000 per year).

NO. AWARDS: 1.

APPLICATION INFO:

Completed application, letters of support or commitment, and other documents, as applicable, must be combined into and submitted as one PDF document to the e-mail address above. The document must be titled by the applicant's last name and first initial only. In the submission e-mail, applicant must include full name and project title. Hard copies are not accepted.

Duration: Two years.

Deadline: June.

ADDRESS INQUIRIES TO:

Wykenna S.C. Vailor
Senior Manager, Research Affairs and Awards
(See address above.)

AMERICAN GASTROENTEROLOGICAL ASSOCIATION (AGA) [2334]

4930 Del Ray Avenue
Bethesda, MD 20814
(301) 222-4012
Fax: (301) 652-3890
E-mail: awards@gastro.org
Web Site: www.gastro.org/research-funding

NAME(S) OF PROGRAMS:

- **AGA Microbiome Junior Investigator Research Award**

TYPE:

Research grants. Award for junior investigators engaged in research related to the gut microbiome.

PURPOSE:

To enable investigators, especially those in the early stages of their careers, to develop and maintain independent and productive research programs in digestive diseases; to encourage and facilitate innovative research into relationships between the gut microbiome and functioning of the digestive system in health and disease.

ELIGIBILITY:

Applicants must hold an M.D., Ph.D. or equivalent degree and a full-time faculty position at a North American educational institute. Research must be conducted at a North American institution. Recipients of the award must also be members of AGA. Applicants must be in the early phase of their careers: clinicians who completed clinical training and investigators who received their final research degree no more than seven years before the application due date. The length of appropriately documented parental leave(s) of absence will not count toward the seven-year eligibility criteria. Exceptional circumstances may also be considered. Women and underrepresented minorities are strongly encouraged to apply.
Awardees are selected based on significance of the proposed research and implication for preventing or treating disease, innovation, scientific approach, institutional environment and support, and applicant potential commitment.

GEOG. RESTRICTIONS: North America.

FINANCIAL DATA:

Amount of support per award: $60,000 ($30,000 per year).

NO. AWARDS: 1.

APPLICATION INFO:

Completed application, letters of support or commitment, and other documents, as applicable, must be combined into and submitted as one PDF document to the e-mail address above. The document must be titled by the applicant's last name and first initial only. In the submission e-mail, applicant must include full name and project title. Hard copies are not accepted.

Duration: Two years.

Deadline: June.

ADDRESS INQUIRIES TO:

Wykenna S.C. Vailor
Senior Manager, Research Affairs and Awards
(See address above.)

AMERICAN GASTROENTEROLOGICAL ASSOCIATION (AGA) [2335]

4930 Del Ray Avenue
Bethesda, MD 20814
(301) 222-4012
Fax: (301) 652-3890
E-mail: awards@gastro.org
Web Site: www.gastro.org/research-funding

AREAS OF INTEREST:
Gastroenterology and related fields.

NAME(S) OF PROGRAMS:

- **AGA-Covidien Research and Development Pilot Award in Technology**

TYPE:
Research grants. Award for investigators to support the research and development of novel devices or technologies that will potentially impact the diagnosis or treatment of digestive disease.

PURPOSE:
To provide non-salary funds for new and established investigators to research and develop new devices, design and test a significant improvement to an existing technology, develop a new diagnostic, develop a novel research method technology, and/or investigate the application of nanotechnology or methodologies such as computational biology to the field of gastroenterology.

ELIGIBILITY:
Applicants must hold an M.D., Ph.D. or equivalent degree and a full-time faculty position at an accredited North American institution. Research must be conducted at a North American institution. Applicants must also be members of AGA. Women and minorities are strongly encouraged to apply. Awardee will be selected based on the potential impact of the study on diagnosing or treating digestive disease.
Candidates may not hold awards directly related to the proposed research from other agencies. Candidates may not submit the same research project for both the AGA-Elsevier Pilot Research Award and the AGA-Covidien Research and Development Pilot Award in Technology.

GEOG. RESTRICTIONS: North America.

FINANCIAL DATA:
Funds are to be used for salary support of research assistants, biostatistics support, laboratory technicians, supplies and/or equipment. No indirect costs will be allowed.

Amount of support per award: $30,000, plus $1,000 travel stipend.

NO. AWARDS: 1.

APPLICATION INFO:
Completed application, letters of support or commitment, and other documents, as applicable, must be combined into and submitted as one PDF document to the e-mail address above. The document must be titled by the applicant's last name and first initial only. In the submission e-mail, applicant must include full name and project title. Hard copies are not accepted.

Duration: One year.

Deadline: January 29.

ADDRESS INQUIRIES TO:
Wykenna S.C. Vailor
Senior Manager, Research Affairs and Awards
(See address above.)

AMERICAN GASTROENTEROLOGICAL ASSOCIATION (AGA) [2336]

4930 Del Ray Avenue
Bethesda, MD 20814
(301) 222-4012
Fax: (301) 652-3890
E-mail: awards@gastro.org
Web Site: www.gastro.org/research-funding

AREAS OF INTEREST:
Gastroenterology and related fields.

NAME(S) OF PROGRAMS:

- **AGA Investing in the Future Student Research Fellowship**

TYPE:
Fellowships. Fellowship is for underrepresented minority undergraduate and medical school students to perform eight to 10 weeks of research related to digestive diseases or nutrition.

PURPOSE:
To stimulate interest among underrepresented minority students in digestive disease and nutrition research.

ELIGIBILITY:
Underrepresented minority students from accredited U.S. institutions may apply. Eligible candidates include African Americans, Hispanic/Latino Americans, American Indians, Alaska Natives and natives of the U.S. Pacific Islands. Past recipients of the AGA Student Research Fellowship Award may reapply for continuous funding provided a scientific progress report was submitted for the previous project and other eligibility requirements are met.

Candidates may not hold similar salary support awards from other agencies. This award is not intended to provide salary support for laboratory technicians.

GEOG. RESTRICTIONS: North America.

FINANCIAL DATA:
Amount of support per award: $5,000.

NO. AWARDS: 12.

APPLICATION INFO:
Completed application, transcript and reference letters must be combined into and submitted as one PDF document to the e-mail address above. The document must be titled by the applicant's last name and first initial only. In the submission e-mail, applicant must include full name and project title. Hard copies are not accepted.

Duration: One year.

Deadline: February 5.

ADDRESS INQUIRIES TO:
Wykenna S.C. Vailor
Senior Manager, Research Affairs and Awards
(See address above.)

THE BROAD MEDICAL RESEARCH PROGRAM AT CCFA [2337]

733 Third Avenue, Suite 510
New York, NY 10017
(646) 484-1695
Fax: (310) 775-4067
E-mail: infoBMRP@ccfa.org
Web Site: www.broadmedical.org

FOUNDED: 2001

AREAS OF INTEREST:
Understanding and treating inflammatory bowel disease.

TYPE:
Research grants; Seed money grants. Designed to stimulate innovative research that will lead to both the prevention and successful therapy of inflammatory bowel disease.

YEAR PROGRAM STARTED: 2001

PURPOSE:
To understand and treat inflammatory bowel disease.

ELIGIBILITY:
Grants will only be awarded to nonprofit organizations, such as universities, hospitals and research institutes.

FINANCIAL DATA:
Amount of support per award: Average $114,082 per year.

Total amount of support: $2,000,000 for the year 2014.

NO. MOST RECENT APPLICANTS: 98.

NO. AWARDS: 20 new awards.

APPLICATION INFO:
Applicants should submit a brief Letter of Interest (up to three pages, not including attachments) as the initial request for funding. Investigators whose Letters of Interest fit the Program's criteria and areas of interest will be invited to submit a full grant application.

The following information is part of the three-page limit:
(1) title of the project;
(2) specific hypothesis or question to be investigated;
(3) methodology;
(4) data analysis and;
(5) anticipated outcomes.

Additionally, applicants are required to:
(1) state why the project fits the Program's criteria, including its relevance and likely benefits to patients with inflammatory bowel disease in the next several years;
(2) attach the investigator's curriculum vitae(s) or biographical sketch(es);
(3) briefly describe the laboratory or clinical environment;
(4) indicate the estimated total budget and the period for which funding is requested and;
(5) provide the principal investigator's e-mail and postal addresses.

Supportive information, such as references, preliminary data or recent publications, may be included. These will not be counted as part of the three-page limit.

Duration: Up to two years.

IRS I.D.: 13-6193105

ADDRESS INQUIRIES TO:
See e-mail address above.

CANADIAN DIABETES ASSOCIATION [2338]

National Life Building
522 University Avenue, Suite 1400
Toronto ON M5G 2R5 Canada
(416) 408-7090
Fax: (416) 363-7465
E-mail: research@diabetes.ca
Web Site: www.diabetes.ca

FOUNDED: 1953

AREAS OF INTEREST:
Medical research into the causes and cure of diabetes.

NAME(S) OF PROGRAMS:
- **Charles H. Best Research Fund**

TYPE:
Fellowships; General operating grants; Research grants; Training grants. Scholar awards. Support for new and ongoing research into better ways to prevent, treat, and manage diabetes and to ultimately find a cure.

YEAR PROGRAM STARTED: 1975

PURPOSE:
To promote the health of Canadians through diabetes research, education, service, and advocacy.

LEGAL BASIS:
Nonprofit.

ELIGIBILITY:
Individuals and groups may apply for research programs in Canada only.

GEOG. RESTRICTIONS: Canada.

FINANCIAL DATA:
Total amount of support: Varies.

NO. MOST RECENT APPLICANTS: 259.

APPLICATION INFO:
Guidelines and application form are available on the web site.

Duration: One to five years, depending on the type of grant/award.

ADDRESS INQUIRIES TO:
Tracy Barnes
Director, Research
Tel: (416) 408-7207
E-mail: tracy.barnes@diabetes.ca

Myrtella Hodge
Coordinator, Grants and Awards
Tel: (416) 408-7085
E-mail: myrtella.hodge@diabetes.ca

CANADIAN LIVER FOUNDATION [2339]

3100 Steeles Avenue East
Suite 801
Markham ON L3R 8T3 Canada
(416) 491-3353
(800) 563-5483 (within Canada and U.S.)
Fax: (905) 752-1540
E-mail: clf@liver.ca
Web Site: www.liver.ca

FOUNDED: 1969

AREAS OF INTEREST:
Research and education into the causes, diagnosis, prevention and treatment of diseases of the liver.

NAME(S) OF PROGRAMS:
- **Canadian Liver Foundation Operating Grant**

TYPE:
Research grants.

YEAR PROGRAM STARTED: 1970

PURPOSE:
To support research projects directed towards a defined objective, conducted by an investigator working alone or in collaboration with others.

LEGAL BASIS:
Registered Canadian charity.

ELIGIBILITY:
Hepatobiliary research investigators who hold an academic appointment in a Canadian university or affiliated institution are eligible to apply. Clinical investigators and basic scientists will be considered.

The applicant must designate the institution in which he or she holds an academic appointment. The institution is considered by the Foundation to be responsible for the provision of space, facilities, furniture and general services for the conduct of the research project described.

GEOG. RESTRICTIONS: Canada.

FINANCIAL DATA:
Amount of support per award: $60,000 (CAN) per year.

Total amount of support: Varies depending on the number of suitable candidates and the funds available.

NO. MOST RECENT APPLICANTS: 39 for the year 2015.

NO. AWARDS: 5 for the year 2015.

REPRESENTATIVE AWARDS:
Dr. Laura Arbour, University of British Columbia, "Genetic studies of primary biliary cirrhosis in First Nations peoples of the Pacific Northwest Coast;" Dr. Norman Kneteman, University of Alberta, "Transcriptional regulation of hepatic genes in response to hepatitis C infection and treatment with interferon alpha 2b;" Dr. Diana Mager, University of Alberta, "Altered fat metabolism as a mechanism for hepatic steatosis in children with non-alcoholic fatty liver disease."

APPLICATION INFO:
Grant application criteria and forms are available on the web site.

Duration: Two years.

Deadline: March 31, for awards to become tenable the following September 1.

PUBLICATIONS:
Program description and guidelines.

STAFF:
Billie Potkonjak, Research Grants Administrator

ADDRESS INQUIRIES TO:
Billie Potkonjak
Research Grants Administrator
(See address above.)

CANADIAN LIVER FOUNDATION

3100 Steeles Avenue East
Suite 801
Markham ON L3R 8T3 Canada
(416) 491-3353
(800) 563-5483 (within Canada and U.S.)
Fax: (905) 752-1540
E-mail: clf@liver.ca
Web Site: www.liver.ca

TYPE:
Scholarships.

See entry 2179 for full listing.

CANADIAN LIVER FOUNDATION

3100 Steeles Avenue East
Suite 801
Markham ON L3R 8T3 Canada
(416) 491-3353
(800) 563-5483 (within Canada and U.S.)
Fax: (905) 752-1540
E-mail: clf@liver.ca
Web Site: www.liver.ca

TYPE:
Scholarships.

See entry 2180 for full listing.

COOLEY'S ANEMIA FOUNDATION, INC. [2340]

330 7th Avenue
Suite 200
New York, NY 10001-5264
(212) 279-8090 ext. 201
Fax: (212) 279-5999
E-mail: info@thalassemia.org
Web Site: www.thalassemia.org

FOUNDED: 1954

AREAS OF INTEREST:
Cooley's anemia and all thalassemias.

TYPE:
Fellowships; Research grants. Clinical grants. Research, public and professional education, patient care and public information. Basic and clinical research and fellowships.

YEAR PROGRAM STARTED: 1954

PURPOSE:
To provide impetus to benefit the advancement of knowledge and the quality of care in Cooley's anemia and other thalassemias.

LEGAL BASIS:
Federal tax-exempt, nonprofit, voluntary health agency.

ELIGIBILITY:
Medical researchers who are interested in initiating a thalassemia related project or who have an existing project that requires additional funding may apply.

FINANCIAL DATA:
Amount of support per award: Fellowships: $32,500; Clinical grants: Up to $40,000.

NO. MOST RECENT APPLICANTS: 30.

APPLICATION INFO:
Applications are available on the web site.

Duration: One year. Possibility for renewal for second year.

Deadline: First Monday in February.

PUBLICATIONS:
Lifeline Newsletter; screening material; educational pamphlets.

IRS I.D.: 11-1971539

OFFICERS:
Tony Viola, President

ADDRESS INQUIRIES TO:
Craig Butler, National Executive Director
(See address above.)

CROHN'S AND COLITIS FOUNDATION OF AMERICA, INC. [2341]

733 Third Avenue, Suite 510
New York, NY 10017
(646) 943-7505
(800) 932-2423
Fax: (212) 779-4098
E-mail: grants@ccfa.org
Web Site: www.ccfa.org

FOUNDED: 1967

AREAS OF INTEREST:
Research and education in inflammatory bowel disease (Crohn's disease and ulcerative colitis).

CONSULTING OR VOLUNTEER SERVICES:
Medical committees (consisting of physician volunteers) provide services in the areas of patient and professional education, research development, grants review, etc.

NAME(S) OF PROGRAMS:
- **CCFA Career Development Award**
- **CCFA Research Fellowship Award**
- **CCFA Research Initiatives**
- **CCFA Senior Research Award**
- **CCFA Student Research Fellowship Awards**

TYPE:
Awards/prizes; Conferences/seminars; Fellowships; Project/program grants; Research grants; Scholarships; Training grants; Visiting scholars. Senior Research Award provides funds to enable established investigators to generate sufficient data to become competitive for funds from other sources, such as the National Institutes of Health.

Research Fellowship Awards and Career Development Awards encourage the early developmental stages of individuals with potential for a career of independent basic and/or clinical investigation in IBD.

Student Research Fellowship Awards are available for undergraduate, medical or graduate students (not yet engaged in thesis research) in accredited North American institutions to conduct full-time research with a mentor investigating a subject relevant to IBD.

YEAR PROGRAM STARTED: 1967

PURPOSE:
To fund research leading to understanding of and ultimate cure for Crohn's disease and ulcerative colitis.

LEGAL BASIS:
Nonprofit, special-interest foundation.

ELIGIBILITY:
For Career Development Awards, candidates must have at least five years of relevant postdoctoral experience prior to the beginning date of the awards and not in excess of 10 years beyond the attainment of their Doctorate degrees.

For Research Fellowship Awards, candidates must have two years of relevant postdoctoral experience prior to the beginning date of the award.

For Research Training Awards, candidates must be sponsored by a public or private nonprofit institution or a government institution engaged in health care and health-related research within the U.S. and its possessions. Individuals who already are well established in the field are not considered eligible for these awards. Applicants must hold M.D. or Ph.D. degrees and be employed within the U.S. at the time of submission. Eligibility is not restricted by citizenship.

For Senior Research Award, applicants must be established researchers in the field of inflammatory bowel disease.

FINANCIAL DATA:
Amount of support per award: Career Development Award: $90,000 per year; Research Fellowship Award: $58,250 per year; Senior Research Award: $115,830 per year; Student Research Fellowship Award: $2,500.

Total amount of support: Approximately $28,000,000 annually.

CO-OP FUNDING PROGRAMS:
NASPGHAN/CDHNF.

NO. MOST RECENT APPLICANTS: 500 to 600.

NO. AWARDS: 248.

APPLICATION INFO:
Before submitting a Letter of Intent or Full Proposal, applicants are urged to view the online policies and instructions. After the Letter of Intent is submitted and approved, CCFA Research Grants Administration will send an e-mail to the applicant with a link to complete and submit a Full Proposal.

Duration: Senior Research Awards: One to three years.

Deadline: Student Research Fellowship Awards: March 15. Awards begin on or about June 15. Career Development Award, Research Fellowship Award and Senior Research Award: January 14 for July 1 start date and July 1 for January 1 start date.

PUBLICATIONS:
Annual report; *Inflammatory Bowel Diseases*; *Foundation Focus*; brochures.

IRS I.D.: 13-6193105

STAFF:
Michael Osso, President

FOUNDERS:
Henry D. Janowitz, M.D.
William D. Modell
Irwin M. Rosenthal

ADDRESS INQUIRIES TO:
Moustafa Ibrahim, Senior Manager
(See address above.)

CYSTIC FIBROSIS FOUNDATION [2342]

6931 Arlington Road
Suite 200
Bethesda, MD 20814
(301) 951-4422
(800) 344-4823
Fax: (301) 951-6378; (301) 841-2605
E-mail: grants@cff.org
Web Site: www.cff.org

FOUNDED: 1955

AREAS OF INTEREST:
Research, care and education programs to benefit patients with cystic fibrosis.

NAME(S) OF PROGRAMS:
- **CFF/NIH Unfunded Grants**
- **Clinical Research Grants**
- **Leroy Matthews Physician/Scientist Award**
- **Pilot and Feasibility Awards**
- **Research Grants**
- **Harry Shwachman Clinical Investigator Award**

TYPE:
Fellowships; Research grants; Training grants. The CFF/NIH Unfunded Grants support excellent CF-related research projects that have been submitted to and approved by the National Institutes of Health (NIH) but cannot be supported by available NIH funds.

Clinical Research Grants offer support to clinical research projects directly related to cystic fibrosis treatment and care.

Leroy Matthews Physician/Scientist Award provides support for outstanding, newly trained pediatricians and internists (M.D. and M.D./Ph.D.) to complete subspecialty training, develop into independent investigators, and initiate a research program.

Pilot and Feasibility Awards are for developing and testing new hypotheses and/or new methods and to support promising new investigators as they establish themselves in research areas relevant to CF.

Research Grants are intended to encourage the development of new information that contributes to the understanding of the basic etiology and pathogenesis of cystic fibrosis.

The Harry Shwachman Award provides the opportunity for clinically-trained physicians to develop into independent biomedical research investigators who are actively involved in CF-related areas. It is also intended to facilitate the transition from postdoctoral training to a career in academic medicine.

YEAR PROGRAM STARTED: 1955

PURPOSE:
To encourage clinical research into the cause, care and treatment of cystic fibrosis; to train specialists for careers in academic medicine.

LEGAL BASIS:
501(c)(3) organization, incorporated as a nonprofit, tax-exempt organization.

ELIGIBILITY:
Contact the Foundation for specific eligibility details for the various grant programs.

FINANCIAL DATA:
Amount of support per award: CFF/NIH Unfunded Grants: $75,000 to $125,000 per year; Clinical Research Grants: Up to $150,000 per year (single-center) and up to $350,000 per year (multicenter); Leroy Matthews Physician/Scientist Award: $60,000 (stipend) plus $10,000 (research and development) for year one to $100,000 (stipend) plus $30,000 (research and development) for year six; Pilot and Feasibility Awards: Up to $50,000 per year; Research Grants: $100,000 per year; Harry Shwachman Clinical Investigator Award: Up to $100,000 per year plus $30,000 for supplies.

APPLICATION INFO:
Detailed information can be obtained from the CFF Grants and Contracts Office.

Duration: CFF/NIH Unfunded Grants: Up to two years (from CFF); Clinical Research Grants: Up to three years; Matthews Physician/Scientist Award: Up to six years; Pilot and Feasibility Awards: Up to two years; Research Grants: Two years with possible renewal for one additional year; Shwachman Clinical Investigator Award: Three years.

Deadline: CFF/NIH Unfunded Grants: Applications accepted January 1 through October 31; Clinical Research Grants: April 1; Matthews Physician/Scientist Award and

Shwachman Clinical Investigator Award: Second Wednesday in September for application; Pilot and Feasibility Award: April 6 for spring and September 4 for fall; Research Grants: April 6 for spring and September 7 for fall.

PUBLICATIONS:
Annual report; application form; guidelines.

IRS I.D.: 13-1930701

STAFF:
Preston W. Campbell, III, M.D., President and Chief Executive Officer
Marc S. Ginsky, Executive Vice President and Chief Operating Officer
Vera H. Twigg, Executive Vice President and Chief Financial Officer
Amy DeMaria, Senior Vice President of Communications
William Skach, M.D., Senior Vice President of Research Affairs
Marybeth McMahon, Ph.D., Chief of Staff

ADDRESS INQUIRIES TO:
Grants and Contracts Manager
(See address above.)

JDRF (JUVENILE DIABETES RESEARCH FOUNDATION INTERNATIONAL) [2343]

26 Broadway
14th Floor
New York, NY 10004
(212) 785-9500
(800) 533-2873
Fax: (212) 785-9595
E-mail: info@jdrf.org
Web Site: www.jdrf.org

FOUNDED: 1970

AREAS OF INTEREST:
To support research into the causes, treatment, prevention and cure of diabetes and its complications.

NAME(S) OF PROGRAMS:
- **Postdoctoral Fellowships**

TYPE:
Fellowships. Postdoctoral fellowships to attract qualified and promising scientists entering their professional career into fields of research in diabetes. The applicant is required to work with a sponsor who can provide a training environment most conducive to beginning a career in diabetes-relevant research. Fellowship research may be conducted at foreign and domestic, for-profit and nonprofit, public and private organizations such as universities, colleges, hospitals, laboratories, units of state and local governments, and eligible agencies of the federal government.

YEAR PROGRAM STARTED: 1973

PURPOSE:
To support advanced training in fields of research directly related to diabetes.

LEGAL BASIS:
Incorporated not-for-profit voluntary health agency.

ELIGIBILITY:
By the beginning of the period of support sought, the applicant must have a doctoral degree (M.D., D.M.D., D.V.M., Ph.D. or the equivalent) for no more than five years before the fellowship and may not have a faculty appointment. Each applicant must be sponsored by a scientist who is affiliated full-time with an accredited institution and who agrees to supervise that individual's training. JDRF welcomes applications from persons with disabilities, women and members of minority groups underrepresented in the sciences.

The applicant is responsible for selecting a research mentor and for making arrangements to work in this person's laboratory. The designated mentor must be the senior scientist who will directly supervise the proposed research.

FINANCIAL DATA:
The stipend is dependent on the number of years of relevant experience.

Amount of support per award: $43,692 to $57,504 per year, with a research allowance of $5,500 per year.

APPLICATION INFO:
Application forms are available from the address above. Applicants must submit a signed original with 15 copies. The applicant must include three letters of reference assessing the scientific abilities and potential of the applicant and a statement of career goals with the relevance to diabetes-related research. The sponsor must outline a specific training program, confirm the space and facilities for the research project, provide information on all sources of grant support (current or pending, federal or nonfederal) and must include the title, amounts, funding periods and abstract pages of all current and pending support.

Duration: Three years.

Deadline: Contact JDRF for up-to-date details.

PUBLICATIONS:
Annual report; policy statement; research appropriations sheet; *Countdown Magazine.*

ADDRESS INQUIRIES TO:
E-mail: preawardsupport@jdrf.org

*SPECIAL STIPULATIONS:
Awardees will be required to produce a progress report at the end of each funding year. Awardees must spend 100% of time and effort on the research project during the period of the award.

JDRF (JUVENILE DIABETES RESEARCH FOUNDATION INTERNATIONAL) [2344]

26 Broadway
14th Floor
New York, NY 10004
(212) 785-9500
(800) 533-2873
Fax: (212) 785-9595
E-mail: info@jdrf.org
Web Site: www.jdrf.org

FOUNDED: 1970

AREAS OF INTEREST:
Prevention and treatment of type I diabetes and its complications.

NAME(S) OF PROGRAMS:
- **Career Development Awards**

TYPE:
Development grants; Research grants; Training grants. Grants are awarded to promising scientists entering their professional career in the diabetes research field. In the five-year term, awardees will focus their research efforts in a subject directly related to JDRF's research mission goals and position themselves to work at the leading edge of diabetes research.

YEAR PROGRAM STARTED: 1979

PURPOSE:
To attract qualified and promising scientists early in their faculty careers and to give them the opportunity to establish themselves in areas that reflect the JDRF research mission goals.

LEGAL BASIS:
Charitable foundation.

ELIGIBILITY:
The individuals must be in a relatively early stage of their career who have demonstrated superior scholarship and show the greatest promise for future achievement in research, including either clinically relevant research or basic research. Ordinarily, their first degree (M.D., Ph.D., D.M.D., D.V.M. or equivalent) will have been received at least three, but not more than seven, years before the award. The applicant must hold an academic faculty-level position (including assistant professor or equivalent) at the time of the proposal, at a university, health science center or comparable institution with strong, well-established research and training programs for the chosen area of interest.

FINANCIAL DATA:
Indirect costs cannot exceed 10% of subtotal direct costs.

Amount of support per award: Up to $150,000 per year, including indirect costs; these funds may be used for a research allowance, which can include a technician, supplies, equipment and travel up to $2,000 per year. Salary for additional research personnel is permitted. Requests for equipment, in years other than the first year, must be strongly justified. Salary requests must be consistent with the established salary structure of the applicant's institution.

APPLICATION INFO:
Application forms are available from the address above. Applicants must submit a signed original with 15 copies and include three letters of reference assessing the candidate's scientific abilities, assurance from the university of an academic commitment to the applicant and the research project, all other sources of funding (current, federal and nonfederal), with the title, abstract, annual and total amount of support and inclusive funding periods of all current and pending grants.

Duration: One year. Renewable up to a maximum of four years pending satisfactory progress.

Deadline: Contact JDRF for up-to-date details.

PUBLICATIONS:
Annual report; policy statement; research appropriations sheet; *Countdown Magazine.*

ADDRESS INQUIRIES TO:
E-mail: preawardsupport@jdrf.org

JUVENILE DIABETES RESEARCH FOUNDATION INTERNATIONAL [2345]

26 Broadway
14th Floor
New York, NY 10004
(212) 785-9500
(800) 533-2873
Fax: (212) 785-9595
E-mail: info@jdrf.org
Web Site: www.jdrf.org

FOUNDED: 1970

AREAS OF INTEREST:
To support research into the causes, treatment, prevention and cure of diabetes and its complications.

NAME(S) OF PROGRAMS:
- **Regular Research Grant**

TYPE:
Project/program grants; Research grants. Support for a variety of needs, such as salaries for technical assistance, special equipment, animals and supplies for scientific investigations related to diabetes.

YEAR PROGRAM STARTED: 1973

PURPOSE:
To support scientific investigations of diabetes.

LEGAL BASIS:
Incorporated not-for-profit voluntary health agency.

ELIGIBILITY:
Grants are awarded to new or established researchers. Proposal must be for a scientific research project involving the cause, treatment, prevention, and/or cure of diabetes and its complications. Applicants must hold an M.D., D.M.D., D.V.M., Ph.D. or equivalent and have a full-time faculty position or equivalent at a college, university, medical school, company, or other research facility.

FINANCIAL DATA:
Salary support plus fringe benefits for the principal investigator may not exceed his or her percentage effort on the project multiplied by institutional base salary. Indirect costs (excluding equipment) may not exceed 10%. Funds may be used for salaries for technical assistant, special equipment, animals and supplies.

Amount of support per award: $110,000 per year for three years, including indirect cost.

APPLICATION INFO:
Application forms are available from the address above. The current JDF or NIH application may be used; however, for the NIH the research plan must include two abstracts (one written in scientific language and one in lay language) and cannot exceed 10 pages. Applicants must submit a signed original with 15 copies and include information regarding all other sources of support (current or pending) including title, abstract, annual total amount of grant, inclusive funding period and percentage effort of the applicant. In addition, applicants must include a detailed letter of intent outlining the rationale for the request, budgetary requirements, and curriculum vitae of the principal investigator. Applications from industry must also include the rationale of how the proposed device/technology will address an important issue in diabetes management or research and the potential to improve diabetes management or progress toward prevention or cure of diabetes and its complications.

Duration: One year with renewal by application for up to two additional years.

Deadline: Applications open May 1. Online applications due July 31, with review in November. Notification in January for start date of March 1.

PUBLICATIONS:
Annual report; policy statement; research appropriations sheet; *Countdown Magazine*.

ADDRESS INQUIRIES TO:
Director, Operations and Administration
(See address above.)

THE KIDNEY FOUNDATION OF CANADA [2346]

5160 Decarie Boulevard
Suite 310
Montreal QC H3X 2H9 Canada
(514) 369-4806
(800) 361-7494
Fax: (514) 369-2472
E-mail: research@kidney.ca
Web Site: www.kidney.ca

FOUNDED: 1964

AREAS OF INTEREST:
Research that may further the current knowledge pertaining to the kidney and urinary tract.

NAME(S) OF PROGRAMS:
- **Biomedical Research Grant**

TYPE:
Research grants. Provides funds to defray the cost of research, including the purchase and maintenance of experimental animals, the purchase of materials, supplies and equipment and the payment of laboratory assistants.

YEAR PROGRAM STARTED: 1972

PURPOSE:
To acquire a greater understanding of kidney diseases and the importance of the role of the kidneys in the human body.

LEGAL BASIS:
Corporation.

ELIGIBILITY:
Applicants must be Canadian citizens or landed immigrants. Research must be conducted within Canada and funding is limited to individuals holding staff appointments at Canadian universities or other recognized Canadian academic institutions.

Grant applications for equipment only will not be considered.

GEOG. RESTRICTIONS: Canada.

FINANCIAL DATA:
Amount of support per award: Maximum $50,000 (CAN) per year.

Total amount of support: $100,000.

NO. MOST RECENT APPLICANTS: 72.

NO. AWARDS: 20.

APPLICATION INFO:
Application information is available on the web site.

Duration: Up to three years. Grants run from July 1 to June 30.

Deadline: Registration: September 1; Full application: October 1.

ADDRESS INQUIRIES TO:
National Director of Research
(See address above.)

THE KIDNEY FOUNDATION OF CANADA [2347]

5160 Decarie Boulevard
Suite 310
Montreal QC H3X 2H9 Canada
(514) 369-4806
(800) 361-7494
Fax: (514) 369-2472
E-mail: research@kidney.ca
Web Site: www.kidney.ca

FOUNDED: 1964

AREAS OF INTEREST:
Research that may further the current knowledge pertaining to the kidney and urinary tract.

NAME(S) OF PROGRAMS:
- **Allied Health Research Grant**

TYPE:
Research grants. Funds allocated to assist in defraying the cost of research, including the purchase and maintenance of experimental animals, the purchase of materials, supplies and equipment and the payment of laboratory assistants. Travel assistance is also available.

YEAR PROGRAM STARTED: 1972

PURPOSE:
To foster and encourage research relevant to clinical practice in the area of nephrology and urology by allied health professionals.

LEGAL BASIS:
Corporation.

ELIGIBILITY:
Open to Canadian citizens. The Foundation will consider only those applications which prove scientific excellence where there is clear, demonstrated relevance of the project and its outcomes to the mission of The Kidney Foundation and the primary investigator is an allied health professional (e.g., nurses, technicians, dieticians, social workers).

Funds are available for research conducted within Canada.

The majority of applicants/co-applicants must be allied health professionals.

Priority will be given to applications submitted where the primary investigation has a demonstrated commitment to nephrology, urology or organ donation.

Under no circumstance should the grant application exceed the amount of $50,000. An investigator may not hold more than $50,000 per year from The Kidney Foundation as an award from a single grant or from multiple grants where the applicant is listed as an investigator or as a co-investigator.

GEOG. RESTRICTIONS: Canada.

FINANCIAL DATA:
Amount of support per award: Up to $50,000 (CAN) per year.

Total amount of support: Varies.

APPLICATION INFO:
Initial or renewal application must be made on the prescribed form and sent in 12 copies to The Kidney Foundation at the address above. Grant application must also include letters of intent to participate from collaborators who have a role in the research project. Additional documentation, in the future, may be requested from the applicant.

Duration: Up to two years. Grants run from July 1 to June 30.

Deadline: October 15.

ADDRESS INQUIRIES TO:
National Director of Research
(See address above.)

THE KIDNEY FOUNDATION OF CANADA [2348]

5160 Decarie Boulevard
Suite 310
Montreal QC H3X 2H9 Canada
(514) 369-4806
(800) 361-7494
Fax: (514) 369-2472
E-mail: research@kidney.ca
Web Site: www.kidney.ca

FOUNDED: 1964

AREAS OF INTEREST:
Research that may further the current knowledge pertaining to the kidney and urinary tract.

NAME(S) OF PROGRAMS:
- **Allied Health Doctoral Fellowship**

TYPE:
Fellowships. Designed to provide for full-time academic and research preparation at the doctoral level in Canada or abroad. The award is designed to encourage new students to enter doctoral programs, as well as support students currently enrolled in a program.

YEAR PROGRAM STARTED: 1991

PURPOSE:
To promote and enhance the development of nephrology/urology allied health investigators in Canada.

LEGAL BASIS:
Corporation.

ELIGIBILITY:
Open to nephrology/urology nurses and technicians, social workers, dietitians, transplant coordinators and other allied health professionals. Applicant must demonstrate commitment to the area of nephrology/urology with a minimum of two years direct clinic practice.

Applicant must intend to return to Canada, if studies are outside the country.

FINANCIAL DATA:
Amount of support per award: Up to $31,000 per year for fellowship, depending upon the applicant's qualifications.

APPLICATION INFO:
Applications must be made on the prescribed forms which are available from the National Office. The completed application must include a certified transcript of the applicant's postsecondary school academic records, a letter from the supervisor, dean or department chairperson outlining academic plan and possible research plans, a letter from the sponsoring institution confirming the acceptance of candidate by June 30 and two Assessment of Candidate forms from persons who can give an assessment of the applicant's ability.

Duration: One year. A second, third or fourth year may be obtained upon successful reapplication.

Deadline: March 15. Renewal possible.

PUBLICATIONS:
Guidelines; application form; annual report.

ADDRESS INQUIRIES TO:
National Director of Research
(See address above.)

THE KIDNEY FOUNDATION OF CANADA [2349]

5160 Decarie Boulevard
Suite 310
Montreal QC H3X 2H9 Canada
(514) 369-4806
(800) 361-7494
Fax: (514) 369-2472
E-mail: research@kidney.ca
Web Site: www.kidney.ca

AREAS OF INTEREST:
Research into the incidence and cure of kidney and urinary tract disease, patient services and public education.

NAME(S) OF PROGRAMS:
- **Allied Health Scholarship**

TYPE:
Scholarships. To promote and enhance the development of nephrology/urology allied health investigators in Canada.

YEAR PROGRAM STARTED: 1991

PURPOSE:
To assist the student with a demonstrated interest in nephrology/urology in pursuing education at the Master's or doctoral level.

LEGAL BASIS:
Corporation.

ELIGIBILITY:
Open to nurses and technicians, social workers, dietitians, transplant coordinators, and other allied health professionals who demonstrate commitment to the area of nephrology, urology or organ donation. Applicants who demonstrate a minimum of two years direct clinical practice are eligible. Must have Canadian citizenship or landed immigrant status.

FINANCIAL DATA:
Amount of support per award: Up to $5,000 per year for full-time studies and $2,500 per year for part-time studies up to a maximum of $10,000 (CAN).

NO. AWARDS: Varies depending on funding.

APPLICATION INFO:
Application information is available on the web site.

Duration: One year. Must reapply for second year of funding.

Deadline: March 15.

PUBLICATIONS:
Guidelines; application forms; annual report.

ADDRESS INQUIRIES TO:
National Director of Research
(See address above.)

NATIONAL KIDNEY FOUNDATION [2350]

30 East 33rd Street
New York, NY 10016
(212) 889-2210
(800) 622-9010
Fax: (212) 889-2038
E-mail: research@kidney.org
Web Site: www.kidney.org

AREAS OF INTEREST:
Improvement in the treatment and prevention of kidney disease.

NAME(S) OF PROGRAMS:
- **Young Investigator Grant Program**

TYPE:
Development grants; Project/program grants; Research grants; Seed money grants.

YEAR PROGRAM STARTED: 1987

PURPOSE:
To support research in the fields of nephrology, urology and related disciplines by individuals who have completed fellowship training and who hold junior faculty positions at university-affiliated medical centers in the U.S.

LEGAL BASIS:
Voluntary health agency.

ELIGIBILITY:
Applications will be considered from individuals who will have completed research training in nephrology or closely related fields prior to the start of the grant award and who intend to pursue research directly related to these areas. At the time funding begins (July 1), the applicant must hold a full-time appointment to a faculty position at a university or an equivalent position as a scientist on the staff of a research-oriented institution, e.g., National Institutes of Health (NIH) or other research organization, in the U.S. Customarily, the appropriate faculty rank is that of Assistant Professor. (In some institutions a title other than Assistant Professor, e.g., Instructor, is used to designate junior faculty status; individuals at that rank in such institutions are eligible to apply for a Young Investigator Grant). Qualifications should be documented in the bio-sketch (maximum four pages).

Young Investigator Grants will be awarded to individuals no later than four years after initial appointment to a faculty (or equivalent) position or after appointment to a staff scientist (or equivalent) position in a research organization. Because of this policy, candidates who received a faculty appointment before July 1, 2013 would not be eligible for this award in this funding cycle. It is the responsibility of the applicant to demonstrate that he or she satisfies the eligibility requirements for a Young Investigator Grant. Eligibility rules will be strictly enforced. Anyone who may not be certain as to his or her eligibility should request an advisory opinion from NKF staff before submitting an application.

Young Investigator Grants are primarily intended to support research by individuals holding M.D. or Ph.D. degrees who are commencing careers on the faculty of medical schools or research institutions. In all cases, the applicant's research and career goals must be directed to the study of normal or abnormal kidney function or of diseases of the kidney and urinary tract. Only one investigator in an institution will be supported in any funding cycle by a Young Investigator Grant. Since the NKF research support program is an integral part of the Foundation's overall scientific mission, it is expected that candidates for support pursuant to this funding mechanism participate as dues-paying professional members of the National Kidney Foundation, Inc.

GEOG. RESTRICTIONS: United States.

FINANCIAL DATA:
Amount of support per award: $40,000.

NO. AWARDS: 4.

APPLICATION INFO:
Application form, letter of commitment from the applicant's department and three letters of recommendation are required.

Duration: One year, with the opportunity to apply for a second year of funding.

Deadline: February 1.

PUBLICATIONS:
Program announcement.

STAFF:
Kerry Willis, Chief Scientific Officer
Jessica Joseph, Vice President, Scientific Activities

ADDRESS INQUIRIES TO:
Jessica Joseph, Vice President
Scientific Activities
(See address above.)

NATIONAL KIDNEY FOUNDATION [2351]

30 East 33rd Street
New York, NY 10016
(212) 889-2210
(800) 622-9010
Fax: (212) 889-2038
E-mail: research@kidney.org
Web Site: www.kidney.org

FOUNDED: 1993

AREAS OF INTEREST:
Function and diseases of the kidney.

NAME(S) OF PROGRAMS:

- **Satellite Dialysis Clinical Investigator Grant**

TYPE:
Research grants.

YEAR PROGRAM STARTED: 1993

PURPOSE:
To support investigators who have demonstrated outstanding clinical research potential to promote their continued success as independent investigators.

LEGAL BASIS:
Voluntary health agency.

ELIGIBILITY:
Applications will be considered from individuals who will have completed research training in nephrology, or closely related fields, prior to the start of the grant award and who intend to pursue research directly related to these areas. At the time funding begins, the applicant must hold a full-time appointment to a faculty position at a university or an equivalent position as a scientist on the staff of a research-oriented institution, e.g., National Institutes of Health (NIH) or other research organization, in the U.S. Customarily, the appropriate faculty rank is that of Assistant Professor. (In some institutions a title other than Assistant Professor, e.g. Instructor, is used to designate junior faculty status; individuals at that rank in such institutions are eligible to apply for a Satellite Dialysis Clinical Investigator Grant.) Qualifications should be documented in the biosketch (maximum four pages).

GEOG. RESTRICTIONS: United States.

FINANCIAL DATA:
Amount of support per award: $40,000.
Total amount of support: $40,000.

NO. AWARDS: 1.

APPLICATION INFO:
Applications will be reviewed by a committee designated by the National Kidney Foundation. During the peer review process, the responsiveness of the individual application to the research agendas of the NKF will be one of the elements used to judge merit and assign ranking. Applicants will be asked on the face sheet of the application to provide a description of the applicability of the application to the research agenda of the NKF, with specific reference to any KDOQI Guideline upon which the research project impacts.

Duration: One year, with the opportunity for a second year of funding.

Deadline: February 1.

STAFF:
Jessica Joseph, Vice President, Scientific Activities
Kerry Willis, Chief Scientific Officer

ADDRESS INQUIRIES TO:
Jessica Joseph, Vice President
Scientific Activities
(See address above.)

Oncology

AMERICAN ASSOCIATION FOR CANCER RESEARCH [2352]

615 Chestnut Street, 17th Floor
Philadelphia, PA 19106
(215) 440-9300
Fax: (267) 825-9550
E-mail: grants@aacr.org
Web Site: www.aacr.org

FOUNDED: 1907

AREAS OF INTEREST:
Cancer.

NAME(S) OF PROGRAMS:

- **Career Development Awards**
- **Innovator Awards in Cancer Research**
- **Research Grants and Fellowships**
- **Scholar-in-Training Awards**

TYPE:
Awards/prizes; Fellowships; Research grants; Travel grants. AACR Career Development Awards in Cancer Research support research by junior investigators. These awards, which include an annual stipend, provide important transitional support for direct research expenses as researchers move from the ranks of early career scientists to faculty status.

AACR Research Fellowships in Basic, Clinical and Translational Research foster cancer research throughout the world by scientists currently at the postdoctoral or clinical research fellow level.

AACR Scholar-in-Training Awards enhance the education and training of graduate students, medical students and residents, clinical fellows or equivalent, and postdoctoral fellows by facilitating their attendance at the Annual Meeting and Special Conferences of the American Association for Cancer Research. These awards are presented to scientists in training who are presenters of abstracts that have been highly rated by AACR.

Innovator Awards in Cancer Research are designed to foster innovation and collaboration in cancer research and support independent investigators early in their careers. The awards provide the recipients with the recognition they need to further their careers and possibly leverage additional funding.

PURPOSE:
To facilitate communication and dissemination of knowledge among scientists and others dedicated to the cancer problem; to foster research in cancer and related biomedical sciences; to encourage presentation and discussion of new and important observations in the field; to foster public education, science education and training; to advance the understanding of cancer etiology, prevention, diagnosis and treatment throughout the world.

LEGAL BASIS:
Not-for-profit society.

ELIGIBILITY:
Grants are given to individuals. For some programs, applicants must be working at an academic institution in the U.S. No grants to religious organizations. AACR Associate Members and persons who are not yet members of AACR are eligible for awards.

Fellowship candidates must have completed a Ph.D., M.D., or other doctoral degree. Candidates must be working as a postdoctoral or clinical research fellow at an academic facility, teaching hospital, or research institution, and must be in their second, third, or fourth year of a cancer research fellowship at the beginning of the award year. Academic faculty holding the rank of adjunct professor, associate professor, assistant professor, or higher, graduate or medical students, medical residents, permanent national government employees, and employees of private industry are not eligible. Candidates must be nominated by a member of AACR and must be an AACR member or apply for membership by the time the fellowship application is submitted. AACR Associate Members may not serve as nominators.

Career Development Award candidates must be full-time, junior faculty at the time the grant term begins. Candidates must also have completed productive postdoctoral research and demonstrated independent, investigator-initiated research. Employees of a national government and employees of private industry are not eligible. Candidates must be nominated by a member of AACR and must be an AACR member or apply for membership by the time the application is submitted. AACR Associate Members may not serve as nominators.

FINANCIAL DATA:
Amount of support per award: Fellowships: $45,000 to $50,000 salary support per year; Career Development Awards: $50,000 to $75,000 per year for first five years for salary or direct research expenses.

Total amount of support: Varies.

NO. MOST RECENT APPLICANTS: Over 250.

NO. AWARDS: Scholar-in-Training: Approximately 250 per year; Awards and Fellowships: Approximately 30 per year.

APPLICATION INFO:
Application form is available online.

Duration: Fellowships: One to three years; Scholar-in-Training Awards: One year.

Deadline: Scholar-in-Training: November of each year for Annual Meeting Awards, with notification the following February; Fellowships and Awards: Fall of each year, with notification the following February.

PUBLICATIONS:
Cancer Research, scientific journal; *Clinical Cancer Research*, journal; *Cell Growth and Differentiation*, journal; *Cancer Epidemiology, Biomarkers and Prevention*, journal.

ADDRESS INQUIRIES TO:
Deborah L. Crabtree
(See address above.)

AMERICAN BRAIN TUMOR ASSOCIATION

8550 West Bryn Mawr Avenue
Suite 550
Chicago, IL 60631
(773) 577-8750
Fax: (773) 577-8738
E-mail: info@abta.org
Web Site: www.abta.org

TYPE:
Fellowships; Seed money grants; Training grants. Medical Student Summer Fellowships support a 10- to 12-week summer laboratory experience.

See entry 2378 for full listing.

AMERICAN CANCER SOCIETY, INC. [2353]

250 Williams Street, N.W.
6th Floor
Atlanta, GA 30303-1002
(404) 329-7558
Fax: (404) 321-4669
E-mail: grants@cancer.org
Web Site: www.cancer.org/research

FOUNDED: 1946

AREAS OF INTEREST:
All forms of cancer and their cures.

NAME(S) OF PROGRAMS:
- **Postdoctoral Fellowship**

TYPE:
Fellowships.

YEAR PROGRAM STARTED: 1946

PURPOSE:
To speed the conquest of cancer by training and supporting personnel for cancer research.

LEGAL BASIS:
Nonprofit corporation.

ELIGIBILITY:
Applicants must be U.S. citizens or legal permanent residents. The latter must provide notarized evidence of their legal resident alien status. Applicants who hold doctoral degrees in appropriate disciplines are eligible to apply. Applicant shall have been awarded a doctoral degree prior to the activation of the grant.

GEOG. RESTRICTIONS: United States.

FINANCIAL DATA:
Amount of support per award: Award includes an annual stipend of $48,000 in the first year, $50,000 in the second and $52,000 in the third. Relocation travel expenses for fellow only and a fellowship allowance of up to $4,000 per year.

APPLICATION INFO:
Official application materials are available on the Society's web site.

Duration: Up to three years.

Deadline: For receipt of completed materials: April 1, for approved grants to be activated on or after January 1; and October 15, for approved grants to be activated on July 1.

ADDRESS INQUIRIES TO:
Shannon Pair
Operations Systems Specialist
(See address above.)

AMERICAN CANCER SOCIETY, INC. [2354]

250 Williams Street, N.W.
6th Floor
Atlanta, GA 30303-1002
(404) 329-7558
Fax: (404) 321-4669
E-mail: grants@cancer.org
Web Site: www.cancer.org/research

FOUNDED: 1946

AREAS OF INTEREST:
Cancer and its cures.

NAME(S) OF PROGRAMS:
- **Institutional Research Grants**

TYPE:
Block grants. Grants for institutional cancer research projects. Support is available for integration of varied efforts in cancer research within the institution and preliminary testing of new and venturesome ideas for research on cancer by junior investigators without other national research support.

YEAR PROGRAM STARTED: 1957

PURPOSE:
To eliminate cancer as a major health problem by preventing cancer, saving lives and diminishing suffering from cancer through research, education, advocacy and service.

LEGAL BASIS:
Nonprofit corporation.

ELIGIBILITY:
Institutions of higher learning in the U.S. and its territories are eligible to apply for support of appropriate research to be conducted by qualified investigators.

GEOG. RESTRICTIONS: United States.

FINANCIAL DATA:
Amount of support per award: Average $120,000 per year.

APPLICATION INFO:
Grant application materials become available January 1 and are accessible on the Society's web site.

Duration: One to three years. Renewable upon reapplication.

Deadline: April 1.

ADDRESS INQUIRIES TO:
Shannon Pair
Operations Systems Specialist
(See address above.)

AMERICAN GASTROENTEROLOGICAL ASSOCIATION (AGA)

4930 Del Ray Avenue
Bethesda, MD 20814
(301) 222-4012
Fax: (301) 652-3890
E-mail: awards@gastro.org
Web Site: www.gastro.org/research-funding

TYPE:
Research grants. Recognition award for an established investigator working on novel approaches in gastric cancer, including the fields of gastric mucosal cell biology, regeneration and regulation of cell growth (not as they relate to peptic ulcer disease or repair), inflammation as precancerous lesions, genetics of gastric carcinoma, oncogenes in gastric epithelial malignancies, epidemiology of gastric cancer, etiology of gastric epithelial malignancies or clinical research in diagnosis or treatment of gastric carcinoma.

See entry 2324 for full listing.

AMERICAN INSTITUTE FOR CANCER RESEARCH [2355]

1759 R Street, N.W.
Washington, DC 20009
(202) 328-7744
Fax: (202) 328-7226
E-mail: research@aicr.org
Web Site: www.aicr.org

FOUNDED: 1982

AREAS OF INTEREST:
Food, nutrition, physical activity and the prevention and treatment of cancer; food, nutrition, physical activity and cancer survivorship.

NAME(S) OF PROGRAMS:
- **Investigator Initiated Grants (IIG)**

TYPE:
Research grants. The Investigator Initiated Research Grant program is open to researchers at not-for-profit universities, hospitals or research centers. The Institute encourages new research on dietary means of preventing and treating cancer, or improving the life of the cancer patient or survivor.

YEAR PROGRAM STARTED: 1983

PURPOSE:
To foster research on diet, nutrition, physical activity and cancer and educate the public about the results.

ELIGIBILITY:
Institutions: Research grants are awarded to nonprofit institutions in the Americas. Grant applications will not be accepted from agencies of the federal government or agencies supported entirely by the federal government of any country. Proof of nonprofit status of the institution must be submitted with the grant application.

Investigators: The Principal Investigator must have a Ph.D. or equivalent degree or M.D. degree and be a research staff or faculty member at a nonprofit academic or research institution at the minimum level of an assistant professor (or its equivalent) or higher. The Principal Investigator at an institution in the U.S. must be a citizen of the U.S. or foreign national with a permanent residence visa that is valid for the duration of the grant award. In other countries, the Principal Investigator must meet the requirements of that country for permanent residency and employment.

GEOG. RESTRICTIONS: North, Central and South America and the Caribbean.

FINANCIAL DATA:
Amount of support per award: Up to $75,000 per year, plus 10% indirect costs.

Total amount of support: $165,000 to $247,500.

APPLICATION INFO:
Online application is required. There are two stages to the application process. Letter of Intent is required before full application invitation.

Duration: One to three years.

PUBLICATIONS:
Grant application package; recipients list.

STAFF:
Susan Higginbotham, Ph.D., R.D., Vice President of Research

ADDRESS INQUIRIES TO:
Research Department
(See address above.)

ASSOCIATION FOR RESEARCH OF CHILDHOOD CANCER, INC. (AROCC) [2356]

P.O. Box 251
Buffalo, NY 14225-0251
(716) 681-4433
E-mail: president@arocc.org
Web Site: www.arocc.org

FOUNDED: 1971

AREAS OF INTEREST:
Pediatric cancer research and parent support.

TYPE:
Seed money grants. Pilot projects.

YEAR PROGRAM STARTED: 1971

PURPOSE:
To fund pediatric cancer research institutions in New York state to find better treatment, and eventually a cure, for the types of cancer that afflict children.

LEGAL BASIS:
Tax-exempt, not-for-profit corporation in New York state.

ELIGIBILITY:
Awarded to qualified investigators in pediatric cancer research.

FINANCIAL DATA:
Amount of support per award: Varies.

Total amount of support: Varies.

NO. MOST RECENT APPLICANTS: 30.

NO. AWARDS: 3 to 5 per year.

APPLICATION INFO:
Application must be submitted on AROCC forms. All grants are evaluated by AROCC Medical Advisors.

Duration: One year average. Consideration for three years. Renewal is possible based on past progress supported by abstracts and publications.

Deadline: November 1. Announcement by June 30.

ADDRESS INQUIRIES TO:
Anne O'Donnell, President
(See address above.)

CANADIAN CANCER SOCIETY RESEARCH INSTITUTE [2357]

55 St. Clair Avenue West
Suite 300
Toronto ON M4V 2Y7 Canada
(416) 961-7223
Fax: (416) 961-4189
E-mail: research@cancer.ca
Web Site: www.cancer.ca/research

FOUNDED: 1947

AREAS OF INTEREST:
Cancer research.

TYPE:
General operating grants; Research grants; Travel grants. Innovation grants. Grants for support of clinical cancer research and basic research projects related to the problem of cancer.

PURPOSE:
To stimulate Canadian investigators in a very broad spectrum of cancer research, not limited to but including biological, chemical, physical, clinical and population health sciences.

LEGAL BASIS:
Registered charity.

ELIGIBILITY:
Applicants must be persons holding eligible appointments at Canadian universities or other recognized Canadian institutions. Basic equipment and research facilities and necessary administrative services must be available at the institution concerned.

GEOG. RESTRICTIONS: Canada.

FINANCIAL DATA:
Grants may be used for the purchase and maintenance of animals, for expendable supplies and minor items of equipment and for payment of graduate students, postdoctoral fellows and technical and professional assistants, but do not include personal support for the grantee.

Amount of support per award: Varies.

Total amount of support: Approximately $37,000,000 (CAN) for fiscal year ended January 2015.

NO. MOST RECENT APPLICANTS: Over 750.

NO. AWARDS: 357 new and continuing grants/awards for the fiscal year ended January 2015.

APPLICATION INFO:
Applications must be made via online application system available on Institute web site.

Duration: Up to five years.

Deadline: Varies.

PUBLICATIONS:
Research report/impact report.

BOARD OF DIRECTORS:
Marc Genereux, Chairperson

ADDRESS INQUIRIES TO:
Carol Bishop
Assistant Director, Research Operations
(See address above.)

CANCER RESEARCH INSTITUTE [2358]

One Exchange Plaza
55 Broadway, Suite 1802
New York, NY 10006
(212) 688-7515
(800) 992-2623
Fax: (212) 832-9376
E-mail: grants@cancerresearch.org
Web Site: www.cancerresearch.org

FOUNDED: 1953

AREAS OF INTEREST:
Tumor immunology.

NAME(S) OF PROGRAMS:

- **Cancer Research Institute Irvington Postdoctoral Fellowship**

TYPE:
Fellowships; Research grants; Training grants.

YEAR PROGRAM STARTED: 1971

PURPOSE:
To offer postdoctoral fellowships to qualified individuals in the formative stages of their career who wish to receive training in cancer immunology.

LEGAL BASIS:
Private, nonprofit organization.

ELIGIBILITY:
Applicants must have a doctoral degree and must conduct research under a sponsor who holds a formal appointment at the sponsoring institution. There are no nationality restrictions. Work may be carried out in the U.S. or abroad at nonprofit institutions and medical centers. Fellows with five or more years of postdoctoral experience are ineligible.

FINANCIAL DATA:
Amount of support per award: $55,000 stipend for the first year, $57,000 for the second year, and $59,000 for the third year. An institutional allowance of $1,500 is provided for the host institution to cover laboratory supplies, scientific travel and health insurance on behalf of the fellow.

Total amount of support: $4,361,500 for the year 2015.

NO. MOST RECENT APPLICANTS: 300 for the year 2015.

NO. AWARDS: 26 for the year 2015.

APPLICATION INFO:
Paper applications will not be accepted. Applicants must complete an electronic application form to be submitted with the following attachments:
(1) scanned copy of paper application form with signatures of certifying officers;
(2) brief description of the applicant's background;
(3) list of other funding sources to which applications have been submitted;
(4) applicant's curriculum vitae and bibliography;
(5) brief summary of project with description of how the proposed research is relevant to cancer immunology;
(6) abstract of research in nontechnical English;
(7) concise research proposal, not to exceed six pages;
(8) letter of introduction from sponsor;
(9) sponsor's curriculum vitae, bibliography and current support and;
(10) letters of reference from two individuals acquainted with applicant's work.

Duration: Up to three years.

Deadline: April 1 and October 1. Notification eight to 10 weeks after the deadline.

PUBLICATIONS:
Annual report; application guidelines.

IRS I.D.: 13-1837442

STAFF:
Jill O'Donnell-Tormey, Chief Executive Officer and Director, Scientific Affairs
Lynne Harmer, Director of Grants Administration

ADDRESS INQUIRIES TO:
Denise Upton, Grants Administrator
(See address above.)

CANCER RESEARCH INSTITUTE [2359]

One Exchange Plaza
55 Broadway, Suite 1802
New York, NY 10006
(212) 688-7515
Fax: (212) 832-9376
E-mail: grants@cancerresearch.org
Web Site: www.cancerresearch.org

FOUNDED: 1953

AREAS OF INTEREST:
Tumor immunology.

NAME(S) OF PROGRAMS:
- **Clinic and Laboratory Integration Program (CLIP)**

TYPE:
Awards/prizes; Research grants. This Program awards investigators at tenure-track assistant professor level or higher seeking to answer clinically relevant questions aimed at improving the effectiveness of cancer immunotherapies.

YEAR PROGRAM STARTED: 2011

PURPOSE:
To support qualified scientists who are working to explore clinically relevant questions aimed at improving the effectiveness of cancer immunotherapies; to support basic, preclinical and translational research, which will provide information that can be directly applied to optimizing cancer immunotherapy in the clinic.

ELIGIBILITY:
Investigators must be tenure-track assistant professors or higher when award activates. Eligible organizations must have IRS 501(c)(3) not-for-profit status. Grants are not made to religious organizations.

FINANCIAL DATA:
The award can be used at the recipient's discretion for salary, technical assistance, supplies and/or equipment.

Amount of support per award: Up to $100,000 per year for two years.

NO. MOST RECENT APPLICANTS: 200.

NO. AWARDS: 10.

APPLICATION INFO:
Letters of Intent are accepted November 1 annually. Candidates will be notified by December 15 whether or not they have been invited to submit a full grant proposal. An application form needs to be completed.

Duration: Up to two years. Grant is not renewable.

Deadline: Letters of Intent: November 1 annually. Full application: February 1.

ADDRESS INQUIRIES TO:
Denise Upton, Grants Administrator
Cancer Research Institute
(See address above.)

CANCER RESEARCH SOCIETY [2360]

625 President Kennedy Avenue
Suite 402
Montreal QC H3A 3S5 Canada
(514) 861-9227
Fax: (514) 861-9220
E-mail: grants@src-crs.ca
Web Site: www.cancerresearchsociety.ca

FOUNDED: 1945

AREAS OF INTEREST:
Cancer research.

NAME(S) OF PROGRAMS:
- **Scholarship for the Next Generation of Scientists**

TYPE:
Fellowships; Research grants. One year of salary award as a postdoctoral fellow and two years of operating grants as a researcher associated with an accredited institution.

YEAR PROGRAM STARTED: 2013

PURPOSE:
To support the future generation of Canadian researchers in the field of cancer research.

LEGAL BASIS:
Nonprofit registered fund-raising corporation.

ELIGIBILITY:
Holders of a Ph.D. or a professional diploma (M.D., D.M.V. or other) obtained in September 2010 or later and undergoing an additional postdoctoral training since a minimum of two years, each one of these two years having been completed uninterrupted, with at least 75% of the time devoted to research.

The candidate must obtain an academic appointment in a Canadian university or accredited institution and must begin his or her functions between January 1, 2017 and March 1, 2018.

FINANCIAL DATA:
Amount of support per award: $40,000 for the first year and $60,000 for the second and third year.

NO. MOST RECENT APPLICANTS: Varies.

NO. AWARDS: Varies.

APPLICATION INFO:
Application information is available on the web site.

Duration: Three years. No renewal possible.

Deadline: April 30.

ADDRESS INQUIRIES TO:
Lucille Beaudet, Ph.D., MBA
Scientific Advisor
(See address above.)

CANCER RESEARCH SOCIETY [2361]

625 President Kennedy Avenue
Suite 402
Montreal QC H3A 3S5 Canada
(514) 861-9227
Fax: (514) 861-9220
E-mail: grants@src-crs.ca
Web Site: www.cancerresearchsociety.ca

FOUNDED: 1945

AREAS OF INTEREST:
Cancer research.

NAME(S) OF PROGRAMS:
- **Grants for Cancer Research**

TYPE:
General operating grants.

YEAR PROGRAM STARTED: 1946

PURPOSE:
To find the cause, cure and prevention of cancer.

LEGAL BASIS:
Nonprofit registered fund-raising corporation.

ELIGIBILITY:
Any qualified researcher who is associated with an accredited institution may apply, provided the research is done in Canada.

GEOG. RESTRICTIONS: Canada.

FINANCIAL DATA:
Amount of support per award: $60,000 per year.

CO-OP FUNDING PROGRAMS: CURE Foundation, Government of Quebec, Myeloma Canada, Ovarian Cancer Canada, Pancreatic Cancer Canada and Quebec Breast Cancer Foundation.

NO. MOST RECENT APPLICANTS: Varies.

NO. AWARDS: Varies.

APPLICATION INFO:
Application information is available on the web site.

Duration: Two years. Renewal possible.

Deadline: February 15 for research grants.

BOARD OF DIRECTORS:
Domenic Pilla, President
Mike G. Bouchard, L.L.B., MBA, Vice President
Nathalie Labelle, C.A., B.A.A., Treasurer
Heidi Lange, C.R.H.A., Secretary
Francois Castonguay
Benoit Durocher
Philippe P. Huneault
Martin Langlais
Katia Marquier
Monique Mercier
Ivan Robert Nabi
Martin Thibodeau
Joanna Wilson
George Zogopoulos

ADDRESS INQUIRIES TO:
Lucille Beaudet, Ph.D., MBA
Scientific Advisor
(See address above.)

CANCER RESEARCH UK [2362]

Research Funding
Angel Building
407 St. John Street
London EC1V 4AD England
(44) 020 7242 0200
(44) 020 3469 5452 (grants helpline)
Fax: (44) 020 3469 6400
E-mail: grants.helpline@cancer.org.uk
Web Site: science.cancerresearchuk.org

FOUNDED: 2002

AREAS OF INTEREST:
Research into the causes, diagnosis, treatment and prevention of cancer.

TYPE:
Fellowships; Project/program grants; Research grants; Training grants; Travel grants. There are various grant programs for cancer research including clinical trials. Funding includes research groups, fellowships, programs and project grants.

YEAR PROGRAM STARTED: 2002

PURPOSE:
To carry out world-class research to improve understanding of cancer and find out how to prevent, diagnose and treat different kinds of cancer; to ensure that the findings are used to improve the lives of all cancer patients; to help people to understand cancer, the progress being made and the choices each person can make; to work in partnership with others to achieve the greatest impact in the fight against cancer.

LEGAL BASIS:
Charity (public-funded).

ELIGIBILITY:
Research should be conducted in the U.K. Awards are made to researchers in universities, medical schools and independent research organizations.

GEOG. RESTRICTIONS: United Kingdom.

FINANCIAL DATA:
Amount of support per award: Varies.

Matching fund requirements: Varies.

NO. MOST RECENT APPLICANTS: Over 800.

NO. AWARDS: Over 1,100 projects supported.

APPLICATION INFO:
Contact a member of Research Funding for a discussion prior to sending an application. Applications for funding must be made using the electronic Grants Management System (eGMS).

Duration: Two to six years (longer for clinical trials).

Deadline: Varies.

PUBLICATIONS:
Scientific Yearbook; *Annual Review.*

THE JANE COFFIN CHILDS MEMORIAL FUND FOR MEDICAL RESEARCH [2363]

333 Cedar Street
New Haven, CT 06510
(203) 785-4612
Fax: (203) 785-3301
E-mail: jccfund@yale.edu
Web Site: www.jccfund.org

FOUNDED: 1937

AREAS OF INTEREST:
Biomedical science, basic research and cancer research.

TYPE:
Fellowships. Postdoctoral fellowships for studies in the medical and related sciences bearing on cancer.

YEAR PROGRAM STARTED: 1944

PURPOSE:
To further research into the causes, origins and treatment of cancer.

LEGAL BASIS:
Private foundation.

ELIGIBILITY:
Applicants must be U.S. or foreign citizens holding the M.D. or Ph.D. degree in the proposed field of study (or the equivalent in training and experience) and have no more than one year postdoctoral experience. The prior sponsorship of the laboratory at which they promise to work must be obtained.

Awards to foreign nationals will be made only for work in the U.S., whereas fellowships to American citizens are tenable in the U.S. or any foreign country.

FINANCIAL DATA:
Amount of support per award: $51,500 annually. A grant of $2,000 per year to be applied toward the cost of research is usually made available to the sponsoring laboratory each year.

Total amount of support: $4,000,000.

NO. AWARDS: 25 to 30.

APPLICATION INFO:
Official application materials are available online.

Duration: Three years.

Deadline: February 1 to be considered at late spring meetings.

IRS I.D.: 06-6034840

OFFICERS:
James E. Childs, Chairman
Bronwen Childs, Treasurer

STAFF:
Stephen Elledge, Science Director
Kim Roberts, Administrative Director

ADDRESS INQUIRIES TO:
Kim Roberts, Administrative Director
(See address above.)

GREENBURG-MAY FOUNDATION [2364]

146 Central Park West
New York, NY 10023
(212) 451-3200
E-mail: pmay@trianpartners.com

FOUNDED: 1947

AREAS OF INTEREST:
Medical research, Parkinson's disease, with primary focus on research in cancer and heart disease, the aged, and Jewish institutions.

TYPE:
Development grants; Research grants. Social services.

PURPOSE:
To improve health conditions and expedite cures in many diseases through research.

ELIGIBILITY:
Eligible organizations must be IRS 501(c)(3) tax-exempt and be located in Florida or New York. No funding to individuals.

GEOG. RESTRICTIONS: Florida and New York.

FINANCIAL DATA:
Amount of support per award: Varies depending on project.

Total amount of support: Varies.

APPLICATION INFO:
Applicants must submit a copy of their tax-exempt determination letter. Contact the Foundation for further guidelines.

ADDRESS INQUIRIES TO:
Isabel May, President
(See address above.)

SUSAN G. KOMEN [2365]

5005 LBJ Freeway
Suite 250
Dallas, TX 75244
(972) 855-4390
(877) 465-6636
Fax: (972) 855-4302
E-mail: helpdesk@komengrantsaccess.org
Web Site: www.komen.org
www.komen.org/researchhelpdesk

FOUNDED: 1982

AREAS OF INTEREST:
Breast cancer research.

CONSULTING OR VOLUNTEER SERVICES:
Through a Komen Affiliate; find a Komen Affiliate on the Organization's web site.

NAME(S) OF PROGRAMS:
- **Career Catalyst Research Grants (CCR)**
- **Graduate Training in Disparities Research (GTDR)**
- **Postdoctoral Fellowship (PDF)**

TYPE:
Fellowships; Research grants; Training grants.

YEAR PROGRAM STARTED: 1982

PURPOSE:
To support breast cancer research and awareness.

LEGAL BASIS:
Texas nonprofit corporation.

ELIGIBILITY:
Varies with each award or grant.

FINANCIAL DATA:
Amount of support per award: $60,000 to $150,000 per year.

Total amount of support: Varies per program.

APPLICATION INFO:
Application information is available on the web site.

Duration: Two to three years.

PUBLICATIONS:
Annual report.

IRS I.D.: 75-1835298

LEUKEMIA RESEARCH FOUNDATION [2366]

191 Waukegan Road
Suite 105
Northfield, IL 60093
(847) 424-0600
Fax: (847) 424-0606
E-mail: info@lrfmail.org
Web Site: www.allbloodcancers.org

FOUNDED: 1946

AREAS OF INTEREST:
Curing all blood cancers.

NAME(S) OF PROGRAMS:
- **New Investigator Awards**

TYPE:
Research grants. The goal of the grant program is to support new investigators. It funds scientists and physicians around the world.

YEAR PROGRAM STARTED: 1946

PURPOSE:
To conquer all blood cancers by funding research into their causes and cures; to enrich the quality of life of those touched by these diseases.

ELIGIBILITY:
Preference will be given to applicants proposing new lines of investigation.

FINANCIAL DATA:
Amount of support per award: Up to $100,000.

Total amount of support: More than $1,000,000 annually.

NO. AWARDS: Varies.

APPLICATION INFO:
Applications will only be accepted electronically and should be e-mailed to grants@lrfmail.org. All applicants will receive a receipt via e-mail when their application is received. Hard copies of grant applications will not be accepted.

Duration: One year. Funding cycle begins July 1.

Deadline: Usually mid-February; varies each year.

IRS I.D.: 36-6102182

ADDRESS INQUIRIES TO:
Linda Kabot
Research Grants Administrator
(See address above.)

ONCOLOGY NURSING FOUNDATION [2367]

125 Enterprise Drive
Pittsburgh, PA 15275-1214
(412) 859-6298
Fax: (412) 859-6160
E-mail: jbrown@ons.org
Web Site: www.onsfoundation.org

FOUNDED: 1981

AREAS OF INTEREST:
Oncology nursing.

NAME(S) OF PROGRAMS:

- **Dissertation Research Grant**
- **ONF Foundation Research Grant Award**
- **Research Career Development Award**

TYPE:
Awards/prizes; Research grants. Dissertation Research Grant assists doctoral students with their dissertation.

YEAR PROGRAM STARTED: 1984

PURPOSE:
To support the professional development of oncology nurses around the world.

LEGAL BASIS:
National public, nonprofit, tax-exempt organization.

ELIGIBILITY:
An applicant must be a health professional actively involved in some aspect of cancer patient care, education or research. Membership in the Oncology Nursing Society is preferred but not required. Doctoral students are eligible. The Foundation does not fund completed projects or those nearing completion, tuition or conference registration fees, travel, the purchase of office equipment or institutional indirect costs.

FINANCIAL DATA:
Amount of support per award: Dissertation Research Grant: $5,000; ONF Foundation Research Grant Award: $25,000; Research Career Development Award: $20,000.

Total amount of support: $178,298 for the year 2013.

NO. MOST RECENT APPLICANTS: 25.

NO. AWARDS: Varies.

APPLICATION INFO:
Letters of Intent and applications must be submitted online, including:
(1) an e-mail address;
(2) $25 application fee (make checks payable to the Oncology Nursing Foundation);
(3) if a resubmission, attach a cover letter explaining the revisions to the application;
(4) title page with all signatures;
(5) an IRB or animal welfare committee approval letter;
(6) 500-word abstract;
(7) an eight-page project narrative describing purpose and specific aims, significance, background and review of literature, research design, experimental variables, instruments, facilities and resources;
(8) reference list;
(9) timetable;
(10) statement of scientific integrity;
(11) letters of support;
(12) form documenting the signature of the thesis or dissertation chairperson;
(13) biographical sketches (two-page limit) and;
(14) itemized budgets and budget narratives.

Duration: Dissertation Research Grant and Research Grant Award: Two years; Research Career Development Award: One year.

Deadline: Dissertation Research Grant and Research Grant Award: August 15 for Letter of Intent and September 15 for Application. Notification by January 1; Research Career Development Award: June 1 for Letter of Intent and July 1 for Application.

PUBLICATIONS:
Program announcement; applications; guidelines; *Recognition of Achievement: Awards, Grants, Honors, Scholarships.*

ADDRESS INQUIRIES TO:
Jenny Brown, Grants Specialist
Oncology Nursing Society Research Team
(See address above.)

THE ELSA U. PARDEE FOUNDATION [2368]

P.O. Box 2767
Midland, MI 48641-2767
(989) 832-3691
Fax: (989) 832-8842
Web Site: www.pardeefoundation.org

FOUNDED: 1944

AREAS OF INTEREST:
Research for control and cure of cancer.

TYPE:
Research grants. Grants for research projects relating to the cure and control of cancer and for the treatment needs of cancer victims.

The Foundation supports activities in two major areas:
(1) innovative and new approaches to cancer research and;
(2) Pardee Cancer Treatment Funds in six counties in central Michigan and one Texas county. The Treatment Funds assist cancer patients, who are residents of those counties, with their treatment expenses.

PURPOSE:
To promote the control and cure of cancer.

LEGAL BASIS:
Private foundation.

ELIGIBILITY:
Grants are limited under the terms of the charter to the cure and control of cancer, and in general do not provide for building funds, equipment (except that used in a specific project), fellowships or fund-raising campaign contributions.

Priority is given to researchers at nonprofit institutions in the U.S. who are new to the field of cancer research, or to established research investigators examining new approaches to cancer cure.

FINANCIAL DATA:
The Foundation has provided more than $132,000,000 since 1944 to support its purpose. Generally, two-thirds of the Foundation's annual gift giving is directed toward research.

Amount of support per award: Grants vary in amount, depending upon the needs and nature of the request.

REPRESENTATIVE AWARDS:
$125,000 to University of Chicago for the study of non-invasive delivery of stem cells as therapeutic vehicles to the brain tumors; $93,750 to Florida State University for the study of phosphoprotein signatures of human triple-negative breast cancer; $138,431 to Michigan State University for the study of using bioinformatic methods to dissect tumor development and develop therapy.

APPLICATION INFO:
Grant applications are required to be submitted online at the Foundation web site.

Duration: Typically one year.

Deadline: Grant applications are reviewed by the Medical Committee in April, August and November, with final approval occurring at the Board of Trustees meetings in May, September and December, respectively.

PUBLICATIONS:
Annual report; application guidelines.

OFFICERS AND TRUSTEES:

PREVENT CANCER FOUNDATION [2369]

1600 Duke Street, Suite 500
Alexandria, VA 22314
(703) 836-4412
Fax: (703) 836-4413
E-mail: caitlin.patterson@preventcancer.org
Web Site: www.preventcancer.org

FOUNDED: 1985

AREAS OF INTEREST:
Cancer prevention and cancer early detection.

TYPE:
Fellowships; Research grants. Grants/Fellowships are given for prevention and early detection of cancer through scientific research and education.

PURPOSE:
To support innovative projects in prevention and early detection of cancer through scientific research.

ELIGIBILITY:
Fellowships: Citizenship is unrestricted, but research must be conducted primarily in the U.S. Postdoctoral Fellows (graduate students who will have their doctoral degrees before the project start date) are eligible to apply. Individuals with academic or professional degrees (e.g., M.D., Phar.D., Ph.D.) who are conducting cancer prevention research under the guidance of a mentor are also eligible.

Grants: Citizenship is unrestricted, but research must be conducted primarily in the U.S. Researchers at the instructor or assistant professor level with relevant academic or professional degrees (e.g., M.D., Phar.D., Ph.D.) who are conducting cancer prevention research and researchers who are farther along in their careers and who are shifting their focus to cancer prevention are eligible to apply.

GEOG. RESTRICTIONS: United States.

FINANCIAL DATA:
Indirect costs will not be covered.

Amount of support per award: $40,000 per year.

Total amount of support: Varies.

APPLICATION INFO:
Electronic submissions are required, along with the original sent by mail.

Duration: Two years.

Deadline: February 28 and September 14.

STAFF:
Caitlin Patterson, Coordinator

ADDRESS INQUIRIES TO:
Caitlin Patterson, Coordinator
Research and Programs Administration
(See address above.)

PROSTATE CANCER RESEARCH AND EDUCATION FOUNDATION (PC-REF) [2370]

6823 Deer Hollow Place
San Diego, CA 92120-1605
(619) 906-4700
Fax: (619) 794-2100
E-mail: info@pcref.org
Web Site: www.pcref.org

FOUNDED: 1997

AREAS OF INTEREST:
Prostate cancer.

TYPE:
Seed money grants. The Foundation provides seed money to deserving researchers to help them generate preliminary results that are needed to obtain major grants in the field of prostate cancer.

PURPOSE:
To promote medical research and treatment regarding prostate cancer.

ELIGIBILITY:
The Foundation concentrates on projects that will help prostate cancer patients sooner rather than later. Grants are not made to individuals.

FINANCIAL DATA:
The Foundation funds direct expenses only, not overhead expenses.

Amount of support per award: Varies.

APPLICATION INFO:
Contact the Foundation.

Duration: Varies. Renewal possible.

IRS I.D.: 91-1863748

ADDRESS INQUIRIES TO:
Dr. Israel Barken
Founder and Medical Director
(See address above.)

DAMON RUNYON CANCER RESEARCH FOUNDATION [2371]

One Exchange Plaza
55 Broadway, Suite 302
New York, NY 10006-3720
(212) 455-0520
Fax: (212) 455-0529
E-mail: awards@damonrunyon.org
Web Site: www.damonrunyon.org

FOUNDED: 1946

AREAS OF INTEREST:
All theoretical and experimental research that is relevant to the study of cancer and the search for cancer causes, mechanisms, therapies and prevention.

NAME(S) OF PROGRAMS:

- **Damon Runyon Clinical Investigator Award**
- **Damon Runyon Dale F. Frey Award for Breakthrough Scientists**
- **Damon Runyon Fellowship Award**
- **Damon Runyon Physician-Scientist Training Award**
- **Damon Runyon-Rachleff Innovation Award**
- **Damon Runyon-Sohn Pediatric Cancer Fellowship Award**

TYPE:
Fellowships; Project/program grants; Research grants; Training grants. The Damon Runyon Clinical Investigator Award supports early career physician-scientists conducting patient-oriented research. The goal of this innovative program is to increase the number of physicians capable of moving seamlessly between the laboratory and the patient's bedside in search of breakthrough treatments.

Damon Runyon Dale F. Frey Award for Breakthrough Scientists provides additional funding to scientists completing a Damon Runyon Fellowship who are most likely to make paradigm-shifting breakthroughs. This funding is to accelerate their path to independence and their impact on cancer.

The Damon Runyon Fellowship Award supports the training of the brightest postdoctoral scientists as they embark upon their research careers. This funding enables them to be trained by established investigators in leading research laboratories across the country.

The Damon Runyon Physician-Scientist Training Award is designed to encourage outstanding physicians to pursue cancer research careers by providing them with the opportunity for a protected research training experience under the mentorship of a highly qualified and gifted mentor.

The Damon Runyon-Rachleff Innovation Award supports the next generation of exceptionally creative thinkers with high-risk/high-reward ideas that have the potential to significantly impact our understanding of and/or approaches to the prevention, diagnosis or treatment of cancer, but lack sufficient preliminary data to obtain traditional funding.

The Damon Runyon-Sohn Pediatric Cancer Fellowship Award provides funding to basic scientists and clinicians who conduct research with the potential to significantly impact the prevention, diagnosis, or treatment of one or more pediatric cancers.

YEAR PROGRAM STARTED: 1947

PURPOSE:
To advance cancer research through supporting the development of the most promising young talent in cancer research.

LEGAL BASIS:
501(c)(3) organization, classified as a publicly supported organization and not as a private foundation under Section 509(a)(1) of the IRS, incorporated in New York.

ELIGIBILITY:
Clinical Investigator Award: Each applicant must be nominated by his or her institution. Applicants must be conducting independent research at a U.S. research institution and be within the first four years of his or her initial full faculty appointment.

For the Fellowship Award, applicants must have completed one or more of the following degrees or its equivalent: M.D., M.D./Ph.D., Ph.D., D.D.S., D.V.M.

Level I Funding is for basic and physician scientist applicants who must have received their degrees within the year prior to the FAC meeting at which their applications are to be considered.

Level II Funding is for physician scientists (M.D.) and clinical scientists (M.D., M.D./Ph.D., D.D.S., D.V.M. or the equivalent) who have completed their residencies and clinical fellowship training, are board-eligible, and have not yet been appointed Assistant Professor (or equivalent).

The proposed investigation must be conducted at a university, hospital, or research institution. Foreign candidates may only apply to do research in the U.S.

Only candidates who are beginning their first full-time postdoctoral research fellowship are eligible.

Frey Award: Damon Runyon Fellows are eligible to apply in the fourth year of their Fellowship.

Innovation Award: Institutional nominations are not required and there is no limit to the number of applications that can be received from a particular institution. Applicants (including non-U.S. citizens) must be conducting independent research at a U.S. research institution.

Physician-Scientist Training Award: Applicant must have an M.D. degree. Applicants must have completed their residencies and clinical training and be U.S. Specialty Board eligible at the time of application.

FINANCIAL DATA:
Awards are made to institutions for the support of the Damon Runyon scientist, pursuant to the requirements of the specific award.

Amount of support per award: Clinical Investigator Awards: $150,000 per year. In addition, awardees may be eligible to retire up to $100,000 of their medical school debt.

Dale F. Frey Award: $100,000.

Fellowship Award: Level I stipend: $50,000 per year; Level II stipend: $60,000 per year.

Innovation Award: $150,000 per year.

Physician-Scientist Training Award: $460,000 over four years.

A sum of $2,000 is awarded each year to the laboratory in which the Fellow is working, and can be used by the Fellow for his or her educational and scientific expenses. With a written request to the Foundation from the Fellow, the expense allowance may be used to defray the cost of health benefits. The Fellow determines how he or she would like to spend the money with approval from his or her mentor. It is not an allowance for institutional overhead, postdoctoral scholar registration fees or postdoctoral fellowship taxes. Institutions may not automatically deduct any fees from this allowance without the Fellow's approval.

Additionally, the Foundation also provides a Dependent Child Allowance of $1,000 per child per year. (There is no allowance for a spouse.) Eligible Fellows must provide a copy of the birth or adoption certificate for each child.

Total amount of support: Approximately $4,050,000 in Clinical Investigator Awards; approximately $5,634,000 in Fellowship Awards, and approximately $2,700,000 in Innovation Awards for fiscal year 2014.

NO. MOST RECENT APPLICANTS: Clinical Investigator Awards: 52; Fellowship Awards: 314; Frey Awards: 13; Innovation Awards: 100; Physician-Scientist Awards: 30; Sohn-Pedriatic Fellowship Awards: 16.

NO. AWARDS: Clinical Investigator Awards: 4 new, 19 renewals; Fellowship Awards: 33 new, 87 renewals; Frey Awards: 6 new, 4 renewals; Innovation Awards: 6 new, 11 renewals; Physician-Scientist Awards: 3 new, no renewals; Sohn-Pedriatic Fellowship Awards: 4 new, 8 renewals.

REPRESENTATIVE AWARDS:
Damon Runyon Clinical Investigator Award: Carey K. Anders, M.D., "mTOR inhibition in the treatment of HER2-positive breast cancer brain metastases," with Lisa A. Carey, M.D., and Charles M. Peron, Ph.D., University of North Carolina, Chapel Hill, NC; Damon Runyon Postdoctoral Fellowship: Douglas H. Phanstiel, Ph.D., "Exploring the regulatory role of long-range chromatin interactions," with Michael P. Snyder, Ph.D., Stanford University School of Medicine, Stanford, CA.

APPLICATION INFO:
The following requirements apply:
(1) Online At-a-Glance form; the information submitted here must match one's application; therefore, bookmark the "Edit your response" link in case one needs to make changes;
(2) application cover sheet; applicants must submit a hard copy of the cover sheet with all required signatures; signatures can be ink or electronic, or a mix of the two; electronic signatures are acceptable but not required for the USB copy; (if applying under the mentorship of two Sponsors, one's second Sponsor must fill out the co-Sponsor cover sheet;)
(3) Sponsor's biographical sketch in NIH format and a list of current funding; do not include Sponsor's full bibliography; (if applying under the mentorship of two Sponsors, co-Sponsor must also submit a biosketch;)
(4) Sponsor's letter including: description of training plan for the candidate; and numerical percentage (_%) of proposal written by the candidate (if applying under the mentorship of two Sponsors, the training plan for the candidate must be written jointly and each co-Sponsor must submit his or her individual track record of mentorship with list of graduate and postdoctoral fellows trained;)
(5) Sponsor's mentorship track record with names and current positions of graduate and postdoctoral trainees from the past 10 years;
(6) applicant's curriculum vitae, including a bibliography of all published works;
(7) applicant's letter of approximately two pages including: description of previous research and teaching experience; statement on the transformative impact he or she had on his or her field of research as a graduate student; if applicant is training at the same institution in which he or she received his or her degree, an explanation of the reasons(s) for remaining at the same institution (can be copied for page 2 of cover sheet);
(8) statement of applicant's long-term commitment to a career in cancer research; this statement should be no longer than one paragraph and indicate what applicant plans to do after completing his or her postdoctoral experience;
(9) research proposal, not to exceed five pages of single-spaced, 12-point type with at least 1/2-inch margins; in the proposal, the applicant should: provide a summary of the research proposed (this is in addition to the required summary form); provide a brief background to the proposed research; state specific research objectives/aims; describe concisely the method of approach for the proposed research; explain the significance of the proposed research to the Foundation's goals: understanding the causes and mechanisms of cancer and developing more effective cancer therapies and prevention; demonstrate the relevance of his or her own background and the background and previous work of the Sponsor and any other investigators to the proposed research; list references including the full title of each work cited - references are not included in the five-page limit; figures or tables may be appended or incorporated into the text (not to exceed two extra pages); if the figures are incorporated into the text, the proposal may be up to seven pages;
(10) copy of the applicant's degree certificate; applicants who have not yet received their Ph.D. diploma but have successfully completed all Ph.D. requirements, including Ph.D. defense, may submit a letter from their graduate school explicitly stating such, with the dates of the Ph.D. defense and degree conferral;
(11) summary of Research Form, not to exceed one page - no attachments;
(12) if available, PDFs of up to three of applicant's published papers (no submitted manuscripts, no hard copies) and;
(13) if applicable, up to two letters from collaborators indicating their willingness to contribute equipment, materials or expertise (not reference letters).

Duration: Clinical Investigator Award: Three years. Awardees can apply for a two-year continuation grant. Damon Runyon-Sohn Fellowship, Fellowship Award and Physician-Scientist Training Award: Four years. Frey Award: Up to two years. Innovation Award: Two years with the possibility of two years additional funding.

Deadline: Clinical Investigator Award: February 2; Damon Runyon-Sohn Fellowship Award: March 15; Fellowship Award: March 15 and August 15; Frey Award: July 15; Innovation Award: July 1; Physician-Scientist Training Award: December 1.

PUBLICATIONS:
Annual report; award brochures.

BOARD OF DIRECTORS:
Alan M. Leventhal, Chairman
Sanford W. Morhouse, Esq., Vice Chairperson, Audit Committee and Secretary
Michael L. Gordon, Vice Chairperson, Board Development
David M. Beirne, Vice Chairperson, Development and Communications
Leon G. Cooperman, Vice Chairperson, Investments, and Treasurer
David M. Livingston, M.D., Vice Chairperson, Scientific Programs
Steven J. Burakoff, M.D.
Deborah J. Coleman
Gary E. Erlbaum
Thomas J. Fahey, Jr., M.D.
Buck French
Elaine V. Fuchs, Ph.D.
Richard B. Gaynor, M.D.
Todd R. Golub, M.D.
Scott Greenstein
Steve Hayden
Jay W. Ireland
William G. Kaelin, Jr., M.D.
Steven A. Kandarian
Noah Knauf
Gabrielle Layton
Ronald Levy, M.D.
David G. Marshall
John H. Myers
Richard J. O'Reilly, M.D.
Andrew S. Rachleff
William Raveis, Jr.
Michael V. Seiden, M.D., Ph.D.
Karen D. Seitz
Nancy Simonian, M.D.
Cynthia Sulzberger
Peter Van Camp
James Wells, Ph.D.

ADDRESS INQUIRIES TO:
Clare M. Cahill, Chief Administrative Officer
(See address above.)

THE SKIN CANCER FOUNDATION [2372]

149 Madison Avenue
Suite 901
New York, NY 10016
(212) 725-5176
Fax: (212) 725-5751
E-mail: acea@skincancer.org
Web Site: www.skincancer.org

FOUNDED: 1979

AREAS OF INTEREST:
To promote skin cancer research and public education.

NAME(S) OF PROGRAMS:
- **Heads-Up**
- **Hispanic-American Outreach**
- **Research Grant Award**
- **Road to Healthy Skin Tour**
- **Sun Smart U**

TYPE:
Awards/prizes; Challenge/matching grants; Conferences/seminars; Development grants; Exchange programs; General operating grants; Research grants; Seed money grants.

YEAR PROGRAM STARTED: 1981

PURPOSE:
To reduce the incidence, morbidity, and mortality of skin cancer.

LEGAL BASIS:
Nonprofit foundation.

ELIGIBILITY:
Applications must be for research projects relevant to skin cancer which address, at the basic science and clinical level, improved methods of prevention and detection of skin cancers.

GEOG. RESTRICTIONS: United States.

FINANCIAL DATA:
Amount of support per award: $10,000 to $25,000.
Total amount of support: $100,000 annually.

NO. MOST RECENT APPLICANTS: 39.

NO. AWARDS: 3 for the year 2015.

APPLICATION INFO:
Application information is available on the web site.
Duration: One year.

OFFICERS:
Perry Robins, M.D., President
Rex A. Amonette, M.D., Senior Vice President
C. William Hanke, M.D., Senior Vice President
Deborah S. Sarnoff, M.D., Senior Vice President
Leonard H. Goldberg, M.D., Vice President
Elizabeth K. Hale, M.D., Vice President

Allan C. Halpern, M.D., Vice President
Maritza Perez, M.D., Vice President
Susan H. Weinkle, M.D., Vice President
Michael J. Cosgrove, Treasurer
Elizabeth Robins, Esq., Secretary
Bennet Weiner, Esq., General Counsel

EXECUTIVE DIRECTOR:
Dan Latore

ADDRESS INQUIRIES TO:
Dan Latore, Executive Director
(See address above.)

*SPECIAL STIPULATIONS:
E-mail applications are not accepted. Because the amounts of the grants are small, the Foundation does not fund overhead or indirect costs.

LADY TATA MEMORIAL TRUST [2373]

c/o Mr. F.H. Parekh
Tata Limited
18 Grosvenor Place
London SW1X 7HS England
(020) 7235 8281
Fax: (020) 7259 5996
E-mail: sonia@tata.co.uk
pam@tata.co.uk
Web Site: www.ladytatatrust.org

FOUNDED: 1933

AREAS OF INTEREST:
Leukemia research.

TYPE:
Fellowships. Studentships (Ph.D.). Annual awards for postgraduate scientists of any nationality to support programs of research likely to throw light on the nature of leukemia. One or more grants of a studentship for a student entering an M.Phil./Ph.D. program is available. The Trustees especially wish to encourage studies on the leukaemogenic agents and on the epidemiology, pathogenesis, immunology and genetic basis of leukemia. The work may be done in any country or in an institution where the candidate has been accepted.

YEAR PROGRAM STARTED: 1933

PURPOSE:
To support research in leukemia.

LEGAL BASIS:
Registered charity.

ELIGIBILITY:
Suitably qualified medical or science graduates of any nationality, who are accepted in the institution where the work is to be undertaken, may apply.

FINANCIAL DATA:
Stipends are paid in quarterly installments. Since amounts vary according to age, qualifications, experience and the scales appropriate to the institution where the applicant has been accepted, intending applicants should try to find out the range of salary that would be appropriate before they apply.

Amount of support per award: GBP 25,000 to 35,000 per annum.

Total amount of support: GBP 350,000 per year.

NO. MOST RECENT APPLICANTS: 40 to 50.

NO. AWARDS: Approximately 10 per year.

APPLICATION INFO:
Applications are only accepted online during the current year schedule.

Duration: All awards are tenable for one academic year, October to September. Awards for two years may be given if considered by the Trust to be in best interests of a particular project.

Deadline: March 15. Announcements June 18.

OFFICERS:
Prof. Daniel Catovsky, Chairperson, Scientific Advisory Board
Prof. Barbara J. Bain, Secretary

ADDRESS INQUIRIES TO:
Professor D. Catovsky, Chairperson
c/o Mr. F.H. Parekh
(See address above.)

*SPECIAL STIPULATIONS:
Holders of awards are expected to submit yearly reports on their progress to the Scientific Advisory Committee and to acknowledge the support of the Trust in their publication.

UNION FOR INTERNATIONAL CANCER CONTROL (UICC) [2374]

62 route de Frontenex
1207 Geneva Switzerland
(41) 22 809 1842
(41) 22 809 1811
Fax: (41) 22 809 1810
E-mail: fellows@uicc.org
Web Site: www.uicc.org

FOUNDED: 1933

AREAS OF INTEREST:
Cancer research, clinical oncology, oncology nursing and voluntary cancer societies.

NAME(S) OF PROGRAMS:
- **American Cancer Society International Fellowships for Beginning Investigators (ACSBI)**
- **Asia-Pacific Cancer Society Training Grants (APCASOT)**
- **International Cancer Technology Transfer Fellowships (ICRETT)**
- **UICC Workshops**
- **Yamagiwa-Yoshida Memorial International Study Grants (YY)**

TYPE:
Fellowships. The UICC Fellowships Programme provides long-, medium- and short-term fellowships abroad to qualified investigators, clinicians, and nurses, who are actively engaged in cancer research, clinical oncology, or oncology nursing. Short-term scheme offers nonmedical training opportunities in the Asia-Pacific region.

YEAR PROGRAM STARTED: 1933

PURPOSE:
To enable qualified cancer investigators, doctors, nurses, cancer society staff or accredited volunteers to carry out specific research and clinical projects, or to obtain training in cancer society work in appropriate organizations abroad.

ELIGIBILITY:
Candidates must:
(1) possess appropriate professional qualifications and experience according to the specific fellowship applied for;
(2) be currently engaged in cancer research, clinical oncology practice, oncology nursing, or cancer society work;
(3) be on the staff payroll of a university, research laboratory or institute, hospital, oncology unit, or voluntary cancer society (or be accredited volunteers of such societies) to where they will return at the end of a fellowship and;
(4) have adequate fluency in a language that will permit effective communication at the host institute.
Candidates may submit application for only one fellowship scheme at a time. Applicants who have already obtained a UICC fellowship in the past may apply for further UICC awards only if they are members of the Association of UICC Fellows.

No distinction will be made among candidates on the basis of gender, ethnic origin, religious or political beliefs. Awards are made on the basis of scientific and expert evaluation of the application and the proposed work as set out by the candidate in the project description by reviewers of the highest international standing in their respective fields. Decisions are final and cannot be appealed.

Fellowships are conditional on Fellows returning to the home institutes at the end of the fellowship period. Awards are not granted for basic training courses, lectures, meetings, conferences, congresses or for visiting institutes. They cannot prolong or run concurrently with other awards and cannot be granted to candidates who are already physically present at the proposed host institute while their applications are under consideration. ICRETT Workshops and APCASOT may not be financially supplemented. Those programs terminated early must notify UICC immediately and appropriate funds be reimbursed. All awards require an end-of-the-project report in English, within one month at the end of the project.

FINANCIAL DATA:
Amount of support per award: ACSBI: $50,000 average; APCASOT: Up to $2,000 AUD; ICRETT: $3,400 average; UICC Workshops: $30,000 average; YY: $10,000 average.

NO. AWARDS: ACSBI: 6 to 8; APCASOT: 5 to 10; ICRETT: 120 to 150; UICC Workshops: 3 to 5 grants per round; YY: 14 to 16.

APPLICATION INFO:
Applications and all supporting documentation for ACSBI, YY, ICRETT and APCASOT must be submitted in English. Applications may be submitted using our online grant system (or by e-mail for APCASOT applications) and will be acknowledged promptly. Candidates will be advised if items are missing. Those proposals that have undergone a review and selection process and were not approved for funding cannot be resubmitted. However, candidates are encouraged to submit new applications for new work programs.

Duration: Fellowships and grants: Up to 12 months. ICRETT: One month; UICC Workshops: There is no limiting criteria related to the duration of the training.

Deadline: ACSBI: November 1. APCASOT: Late October. ICRETT: Applications accepted year-round. UICC Workshops: March 1, July 15 and November 1. YY: January 15 and July 15.

ADDRESS INQUIRIES TO:
UICC Fellowships Department
(See address above.)

*SPECIAL STIPULATIONS:
UICC requires an end-of-the-project report in English within one month of the end of the project.

Rheumatology

THE ARTHRITIS SOCIETY [2375]

393 University Avenue, Suite 1700
Toronto ON M5G 1E6 Canada
(416) 979-7228
Fax: (416) 979-1149
E-mail: research@arthritis.ca
Web Site: www.arthritis.ca

FOUNDED: 1948

AREAS OF INTEREST:
Arthritis medical and scientific research.

NAME(S) OF PROGRAMS:

- **The Arthritis Society Clinician Teacher Educator Grant**
- **The Arthritis Society Consumer Activity Grants**
- **The Arthritis Society Networking/Knowledge Translation Grants**
- **The Arthritis Society Strategic Operating Grants**
- **The Arthritis Society Young Investigator Operating Grant**
- **The Arthritis Society Young Investigator Salary Award**
- **CRA (CIORA) TAS New Clinical Investigator Grant**
- **Graduate Ph.D. Award**
- **Postdoctoral Fellowship Award**

TYPE:
Fellowships; General operating grants; Research grants; Scholarships.

PURPOSE:
To search for the underlying causes and subsequent cures for arthritis; to promote the best possible care and treatment for people with arthritis.

LEGAL BASIS:
Registered charity.

ELIGIBILITY:
Applicants are restricted to Canadian citizens and permanent residents of Canada. Applicants for research grants must hold faculty appointments at Canadian medical schools. Specific requirements vary by program.

GEOG. RESTRICTIONS: Canada.

FINANCIAL DATA:
Amount of support per award: Varies.
Total amount of support: Varies.

APPLICATION INFO:
Application information is available on the web site.
Duration: Varies by program.
Deadline: Varies by program.

PUBLICATIONS:
Annual report; regulations.

BOARD MEMBERS:
Drew McArthur, Chairperson
Janet Yale, President and Chief Executive Officer
Dr. Brian Feldman, Chairman of the Medical Advisory Committee
Jason J. McDougall, Ph.D., Chairman of Scientific Advisory Committee
Michael Whitcombe, Honourary Solicitor
Mary E. Hofstetter, C.M., Director at Large
Duncan Mathieson, Director at Large
Cathy McIntyre, Director at Large
Jeffrey Morton, Director at Large
Carmelita Thompson O'Neill, Director at Large
Ken Ready, Director at Large
Kenneth Smith, Director at Large
Ronald Smith, Director at Large

ADDRESS INQUIRIES TO:
The Research Department
(See e-mail address above.)

LUPUS FOUNDATION OF AMERICA, INC.

2000 L Street, N.W., Suite 410
Washington, DC 20036
(202) 349-1155
(202) 212-6771
(800) 875-2562 (customer support)
E-mail: pcsupport@altum.com
Web Site: www.lupus.org/finzifellowships

TYPE:
Summer Fellowship. The Gina M. Finzi Memorial Student Summer Fellowship Program proposes to foster an interest among students in the areas of basic, clinical, translational, epidemiological or behavioral research relevant to lupus under the sponsorship and supervision of an established, tenure-track Principal Investigator who directs a laboratory dedicated at least in part to the investigation of lupus at a U.S. or Canadian academic, medical or research institution.

See entry 2204 for full listing.

Neurology

ALZHEIMER'S ASSOCIATION [2376]

225 North Michigan Avenue, Suite 17
Chicago, IL 60601-7633
(312) 335-5747
E-mail: mepps@alz.org
grantsapp@alz.org
Web Site: www.alz.org

FOUNDED: 1980

AREAS OF INTEREST:
Basic biology; clinical, adoptive technology, social/behavioral and cognitive/functional.

NAME(S) OF PROGRAMS:

- **Everyday Technology for Alzheimer's Care (ETAC)**
- **Investigator-Initiated Research Grant (IIRG)**
- **Mentored New Investigator Research Grant to Promote Diversity (MNIRGD)**
- **New Investigator Research Grant (NIRG)**
- **New Investigator Research Grant to Promote Diversity (NIRGD)**
- **Zenith Fellows Award (ZNTH)**

TYPE:
Fellowships; Research grants; Seed money grants. International Research Grant Program funds investigations that advance our understanding of Alzheimer's disease, help identify new treatment strategies, provide information to improve care for people with dementia, and further our knowledge of brain health and disease prevention. Awards support investigators at every professional stage and always include categories specifically designed to help talented young scientists establish careers in Alzheimer's research. The Association's entire grant portfolio is structured to meet the needs of the field and to nurture fresh ideas.

YEAR PROGRAM STARTED: 1982

PURPOSE:
To accelerate the global effort to eliminate Alzheimer's disease; to connect with scientific, academic, government and industry thought-leaders and key stakeholders worldwide; to become a catalyst toward the time when there will be disease-modifying treatments, preventive strategies and gold-standard care for all people affected by Alzheimer's disease.

LEGAL BASIS:
Voluntary health association, not-for-profit 501(c)(3).

ELIGIBILITY:
Each program has specific requirements. Therefore, contact the Association for additional information.

FINANCIAL DATA:
Amount of support per award: ETAC, MNIRGD, NIRG and NIRGD: $100,000 per award; IIRG: $250,000; ZNTH: $450,000.

NO. MOST RECENT APPLICANTS: 731.

NO. AWARDS: Everyday Technology for Alzheimers Care (ETAC): Up to 3; Investigator-Initiated Research Grant (IIRG): Up to 3; New Investigator Research Grant (NIRG): Up to 20; Zenith Fellows Award: Up to 4.

APPLICATION INFO:
The first step in applying for any research grant is to submit a Letter of Intent (LOI) through the proposalCENTRAL online application system at proposalcentral.altum.com. Applications will not be accepted without an approved LOI. The Association requires all applicants be registered as a reviewer with the Association to submit an LOI. Additionally, it is required that the applicant review at least one grant proposal within their area of expertise, outside the grant competition to which they are applying.

LOI and completed application must be submitted by a single Principal Investigator. A PI cannot submit an LOI that had been approved or rejected during a previous grant cycle. All LOIs must be approved or rejected in the current grant cycle.

Applicants are responsible for adhering to the space limitations, as outlined in the Program Announcement.

Hard copies of the LOI will not be accepted. LOIs will not be accepted after the deadline date.

Duration: ETAC, IIRG, MNIRGD and NIRG: Two years; NIRGD: Up to three years; ZNTH: Three years.

Deadline: Varies per grant cycle.

PUBLICATIONS:
Annual report; application guidelines.

ADDRESS INQUIRIES TO:
E-mail: grantsapp@alz.org

ALZHEIMER'S ASSOCIATION [2377]

225 North Michigan Avenue, Suite 17
Chicago, IL 60601-7633
(312) 335-5747
E-mail: mepps@alz.org
grantsapp@alz.org
Web Site: www.alz.org

FOUNDED: 1980

AREAS OF INTEREST:
Basic biology; clinical, adaptive technology, social/behavioral and cognitive/functional.

NAME(S) OF PROGRAMS:
- **U.S.-U.K. Young Investigator Exchange Fellowship**

TYPE:
Fellowships. This fellowship funds research into the causes, diagnosis and treatment of Alzheimer's disease, while encouraging promising scientists as they establish their careers within Alzheimer's research internationally.

PURPOSE:
To accelerate the global effort to eliminate Alzheimer's disease; to connect with scientific, academic, government and industry thought-leaders and key stakeholders worldwide; to become a catalyst toward the time when there will be disease-modifying treatments, preventive strategies and gold-standard care for all people affected by Alzheimer's disease.

LEGAL BASIS:
Voluntary health association, not-for-profit 501(c)(3).

ELIGIBILITY:
Applicants must have less than 10 years of research experience after receipt of their terminal degree. Postdoctoral fellows are eligible to apply.

GEOG. RESTRICTIONS: Unites States and United Kingdom.

FINANCIAL DATA:
Amount of support per award: U.S.: Up to $300,000; U.K.: Up to GBP 160,000.

CO-OP FUNDING PROGRAMS: Alzheimer's Research UK.

APPLICATION INFO:
Applicants based in the U.S. must apply to the Alzheimer's Association. Those based in the U.K. must apply to Alzheimer's Research UK. Application and review procedures are broadly similar, but kept separate for ease of administration. Instructions can be found on the applicable web site.

Duration: Up to three years.

Deadline: April.

ADDRESS INQUIRIES TO:
U.S. Applicants:
E-mail: grantsapp@alz.org

U.K. Applicants:
E-mail: research@alzheimersresearchuk.org

AMERICAN BRAIN TUMOR ASSOCIATION [2378]

8550 West Bryn Mawr Avenue
Suite 550
Chicago, IL 60631
(773) 577-8750
Fax: (773) 577-8738
E-mail: info@abta.org
Web Site: www.abta.org

AREAS OF INTEREST:
Brain tumor research.

NAME(S) OF PROGRAMS:
- **Basic Research Fellowship Awards**
- **Discovery Grants**
- **Medical Student Summer Fellowships**

TYPE:
Fellowships; Seed money grants; Training grants. Medical Student Summer Fellowships support a 10- to 12-week summer laboratory experience.

PURPOSE:
To encourage talented scientists early in their careers to enter, or remain in, the field of brain tumor research; to facilitate the development of potentially important research studies; to support innovative brain tumor research.

ELIGIBILITY:
Varies by grant mechanism.

GEOG. RESTRICTIONS: United States and Canada.

FINANCIAL DATA:
Amount of support per award: Discovery Grants: $50,000; Research Fellowships: $100,000; Medical Student Summer Fellowships: $3,000.

NO. AWARDS: Varies.

APPLICATION INFO:
Contact the Organization for application procedures. Applications accepted by invitation only for Discovery Grants.

Duration: Discovery Grants: One year; Medical Student Summer Fellowships: 10 to 12 weeks over the summer; Research Fellowships: Two years.

Deadline: Discovery Grants: Letters of Intent due early fall. Research Fellowships: Applications should be submitted online in early January.

STAFF:
Alexandra Sierra, Research Grants Manager

ADDRESS INQUIRIES TO:
Alexandra Sierra, Research Grants Manager
Email: grants@abta.org

AMERICAN EPILEPSY SOCIETY (AES) [2379]

342 North Main Street
West Hartford, CT 06117-2507
(860) 586-7505 ext. 572
Fax: (860) 586-7550
E-mail: info@aesnet.org
Web Site: www.aesnet.org
epilepsyresearchresource.org

FOUNDED: 1936

AREAS OF INTEREST:
Study and acquisition, dissemination and application of knowledge concerning epilepsy in all its phases including biological, clinical and social.

NAME(S) OF PROGRAMS:
- **The Grass Foundation - AES Young Investigator Travel Award**
- **Lennox and Lombroso Postdoctoral Research Fellowship**
- **Postdoctoral Research Fellowship**
- **Predoctoral Research Fellowship**
- **Research and Training Workshops**
- **Seed Grants**
- **Susan S. Spencer Clinical Research Training Fellowship in Epilepsy**

TYPE:
Awards/prizes; Fellowships; Seed money grants. The American Epilepsy Society is one of the oldest neurological professional organizations in the U.S. The Society, in partnership with other organizations, funds Grants and Fellowships that are awarded to individuals with a professional degree whose research impacts an aspect of the study of, and work toward the cure for, epilepsy. Some funding programs are for Society members only.

The Grass Foundation - AES Young Investigator Travel Award: This award recognizes and honors outstanding young investigators conducting research in basic or clinical neuroscience related to epilepsy; the Grass Foundation and the Society have combined resources to present this annual meeting poster travel award.

Lennox and Lombroso Postdoctoral Research Fellowship: This one-year fellowship, administered by AES, is available to physicians or Ph.D. neuroscientists who desire postdoctoral research experience.

Postdoctoral Research Fellowship: This one-year fellowship, administered by AES, is available to physicians or Ph.D. neuroscientists who desire postdoctoral research experience.

Predoctoral Research Fellowship: This one-year fellowship, administered by AES, is offered to graduate students matriculating in a full-time doctoral (Ph.D.) program with an academic career focus, with dissertation research related to epilepsy.

Research and Training Workshops: The Society, through the Research and Training Committee, provides funding for targeted workshops, intended for clinical or scientific audiences and on specific collaborative topics in neuroscience.

Seed Grants: This grant is to foster collaborative interactions between two or more established investigators to make future grants related to epilepsy more competitive for larger awards and to fuel multi-investigator projects.

Susan S. Spencer Clinical Research Training Fellowship in Epilepsy: A two-year fellowship, administered by the American Academy of Neurology, to support clinical research training in the field of epilepsy.

YEAR PROGRAM STARTED: 1970

PURPOSE:
To promote interdisciplinary communications, scientific investigation and exchange of clinical information about epilepsy; to improve the quality of life for people with epilepsy; to provide those engaged in research with information and assistance of potential benefit in advancing their work.

LEGAL BASIS:
501(c)(3) organization.

ELIGIBILITY:
Details for the different programs can be found online.

FINANCIAL DATA:
Amount of support per award: Varies by mechanism.

Total amount of support: Varies.

CO-OP FUNDING PROGRAMS: The Society has formed alliances with other organizations that provide research funding, including the Grass Foundation, Epilepsy Foundation and other funding sources.

Susan S. Spencer Clinical Research Training Fellowship in Epilepsy is supported by the AAN Foundation, the American Epilepsy Society and the Epilepsy Foundation.

NO. MOST RECENT APPLICANTS: Varies.

NO. AWARDS: Varies.

APPLICATION INFO:
Application information is available on the web site.

Duration: One to two years.

Deadline: Varies.

IRS I.D.: 04-6112600

EXECUTIVE DIRECTOR:
Eileen M. Murray, MM, CAE

ADDRESS INQUIRIES TO:
Eileen M. Murray, MM, CAE
Executive Director
(See address above.)

AMERICAN PARKINSON DISEASE ASSOCIATION, INC. [2380]

135 Parkinson Avenue
Staten Island, NY 10305
(718) 981-8001
(800) 223-2732
Fax: (718) 981-4399
E-mail: hgray@apdaparkinson.org
Web Site: www.apdaparkinson.org

FOUNDED: 1961

AREAS OF INTEREST:
Parkinson's disease, medical neurology and neuropathology.

NAME(S) OF PROGRAMS:

- **Medical Student Summer Fellowships**

TYPE:
Fellowships. To assist investigators in establishing careers in the research of Parkinson's disease.

YEAR PROGRAM STARTED: 1965

PURPOSE:
To enable medical students to perform supervised laboratory or clinical research designed to clarify our understanding of Parkinson's disease, its nature, manifestations, etiology or treatment.

LEGAL BASIS:
Not-for-profit organization.

ELIGIBILITY:
Applicant should be a full-time medical student in good academic standing in an approved U.S. medical school. The proposed research project must be performed in an academic medical center or recognized research institute in the U.S. and be sponsored by a full-time faculty member or established institute scientist. The project must be part of the sponsor's ongoing research and be performed under the sponsor's direct supervision. Either laboratory or clinical research or a combination of both may be acceptable; however, merely reviewing literature or preparing reports will not be deemed acceptable.

GEOG. RESTRICTIONS: United States.

FINANCIAL DATA:
Amount of support per award: $4,000.

NO. AWARDS: Varies.

APPLICATION INFO:
The medical student should provide a brief description of the proposed work, not to exceed three pages, containing the following elements:
(1) title of the research study;
(2) location of where the study will be performed (i.e., department or laboratory);
(3) identify sponsor (include mailing address, phone number and e-mail address);
(4) background rationale including preliminary results of work completed by the sponsor;
(5) goals and objectives;
(6) investigative methods;
(7) data analysis method;
(8) significance of anticipated findings;
(9) institutional resources available and;
(10) description of study subjects (human or animal).

Application must be accompanied by a supporting letter from the sponsor, a letter of reference from another faculty member familiar with the student's previous academic performance, and a letter from the Dean's office assuring the student is in good academic standing.

Duration: Three months.

Deadline: January 31.

PUBLICATIONS:
Program announcement; guidelines.

ADDRESS INQUIRIES TO:
Heather Gray, Assistant Director of Scientific and Medical Affairs
(See address above.)

THE AMYOTROPHIC LATERAL SCLEROSIS ASSOCIATION [2381]

National Headquarters
1275 K Street, N.W., Suite 250
Washington, DC 20005
(202) 407-8580
Fax: (202) 289-6801
E-mail: researchgrants@alsa-national.org
Web Site: www.alsa.org

FOUNDED: 1985

AREAS OF INTEREST:
Amyotrophic lateral sclerosis (ALS) programs include research grants, patient services, public education and awareness, local chapter development, and advocacy.

NAME(S) OF PROGRAMS:

- **Research Grant Program**

TYPE:
Awards/prizes; Conferences/seminars; Fellowships; Project/program grants; Research grants; Technical assistance; Research contracts. Grants, for a specified number of years, to neuroscientific researchers to pursue a project of relevance to Amyotrophic Lateral Sclerosis. Both basic and clinical research supported (including postdoctoral fellowships). The ALS Association forms partnerships on clinical trials.

YEAR PROGRAM STARTED: 1985

PURPOSE:
To find the cause and cure of amyotrophic lateral sclerosis; to support research vital to this goal.

LEGAL BASIS:
Nonprofit voluntary health agency under IRS 501(c)(3).

ELIGIBILITY:
Applicant should be a faculty member at a reputable scientific facility.

FINANCIAL DATA:
Amount of support per award: Multiyear grants: Maximum $80,000 per year; Starter grants: Maximum $40,000 for 12-month period; Postdoctoral fellows: Maximum $40,000 per year for two years.

Total amount of support: Varies.

NO. MOST RECENT APPLICANTS: 650.

NO. AWARDS: 45.

REPRESENTATIVE AWARDS:
$120,000 to Joseph Beckman, Ph.D., University of Alabama at Birmingham; $80,000 to Laura Dugan, M.D., Massachusetts General Hospital; $35,000 to Charles Epstein, M.D., University of California at San Francisco.

APPLICATION INFO:
Request an abstract form from the e-mail address above. Submit a one-page abstract, via e-mail, describing the proposed project. An application form will be sent with the invitation to submit, after review and interest in abstract.

Duration: Two to three years; longer if justifiable. Renewable on occasion. Some starter grants for 12 months.

Deadline: Information available upon request to the e-mail address above.

PUBLICATIONS:
Research ALS Today, newspaper; miscellaneous ALS information and patient care brochures; *ALS Journal News*, monthly.

IRS I.D.: 13-3271855

STAFF:
Lucie Bruijn, Ph.D., Chief Scientist

ADDRESS INQUIRIES TO:
Lucie Bruijn, Ph.D., Chief Scientist
(See address above.)

BENIGN ESSENTIAL BLEPHAROSPASM RESEARCH FOUNDATION INC.

637 North 7th Street
Suite 102
Beaumont, TX 77702
(409) 832-0788
Fax: (409) 832-0890
E-mail: bebrf@blepharospasm.org
Web Site: www.blepharospasm.org

TYPE:
Fellowships; Project/program grants; Research grants; Seed money grants. The Foundation offers research fellowships to support the training of exceptionally qualified physicians or scientists who wish to focus on blepharospasm with and without oromandibular dystonia.

See entry 2429 for full listing.

BRIGHT FOCUS FOUNDATION [2382]

22512 Gateway Center Drive
Clarksburg, MD 20871
(301) 948-3244
Fax: (301) 948-4403
E-mail: researchgrants@brightfocus.org
Web Site: www.brightfocus.org

FOUNDED: 1973

AREAS OF INTEREST:
Alzheimer's disease research.

NAME(S) OF PROGRAMS:

- **Alzheimer's Disease Research**

TYPE:
Research grants. Awards for basic research into the causes and treatment of Alzheimer's.

YEAR PROGRAM STARTED: 1985

PURPOSE:
To develop treatments, preventions and cures for Alzheimer's disease.

LEGAL BASIS:
Nonprofit foundation.

ELIGIBILITY:
Grants are awarded on the basis of the proposal's scientific merit and its relevance to understanding the disease studied. No funds for large equipment, institutional overhead costs, construction or building expenses.

FINANCIAL DATA:
Amount of support per award: Fellows: Up to $100,000; Standard award: Up to $250,000.

Total amount of support: Varies.

NO. AWARDS: 29 for fiscal year 2015.

APPLICATION INFO:
Application information is available on the web site.

Duration: Three-year projects and two-year research fellowships.

Deadline: Contact the Foundation for exact dates.

PUBLICATIONS:
Annual report; clinical brochures; newsletters.

ADDRESS INQUIRIES TO:
Kara Summers, Program Officer
(See e-mail address above.)

CUREPSP FOUNDATION FOR PSP/CBD AND RELATED BRAIN DISEASES [2383]

404 Fifth Avenue, Third Floor
New York, NY 10018
(347) 294-2871
Fax: (410) 785-7009
E-mail: caruana@curepsp.org
Web Site: www.curepsp.org

FOUNDED: 1990

AREAS OF INTEREST:
Progressive supranuclear palsy and corticobasal degeneration.

TYPE:
Research grants.

YEAR PROGRAM STARTED: 1997

PURPOSE:
To provide support for basic and clinical research in progressive supranuclear palsy and corticobasal degeneration.

ELIGIBILITY:
Qualified investigators affiliated with appropriate institutions are eligible to apply. Applicants must have the approval of the institution where the research training will be conducted. Ph.D. or M.D. status is required.

FINANCIAL DATA:
Amount of support per award: Varies.

Total amount of support: Varies.

NO. MOST RECENT APPLICANTS: 10.

NO. AWARDS: 4 to 5 per year.

APPLICATION INFO:
Application information is available on the web site.

Duration: Varies.

Deadline: March 15, July 15 and November 15.

ADDRESS INQUIRIES TO:
Lawrence I. Golbe, M.D.
Director of Research and Clinical Affairs
CurePSP
E-mail: golbe@rutgers.edu
Alex Klein
Vice President of Scientific Affairs
E-mail: klein@curepsp.org

DYSAUTONOMIA FOUNDATION, INC. [2384]

315 West 39th Street
Suite 701
New York, NY 10018
(212) 279-1066
Fax: (212) 279-2066
E-mail: info@famdys.org
Web Site: www.familialdysautonomia.org

FOUNDED: 1951

AREAS OF INTEREST:
Familial dysautonomia.

CONSULTING OR VOLUNTEER SERVICES:
Dysautonomia Treatment and Evaluation Center at New York University Medical Center, 530 First Avenue, Suite 9Q, New York, NY 10016, under the direction of Felicia B. Axelrod, M.D.

NAME(S) OF PROGRAMS:
- **Dysautonomia Research Program**

TYPE:
Project/program grants; Research grants; Seed money grants. In addition to support for research and clinical study, the Foundation also provides financial support to the Dysautonomia Treatment and Evaluation Center at NYU and the Israeli FD Center in Tel Aviv.

YEAR PROGRAM STARTED: 1955

PURPOSE:
To fund research for treatment and/or cure for familial dysautonomia; to stimulate and promote medical research into familial dysautonomia (an inherited disease of the autonomic nervous system); to provide information to lay and medical public.

LEGAL BASIS:
Nonprofit, tax-exempt corporation.

ELIGIBILITY:
Researcher connected with a recognized medical and/or teaching institution may apply.

FINANCIAL DATA:
Amount of support per award: Varies, depending upon the needs and nature of the request.

Total amount of support: Varies.

NO. MOST RECENT APPLICANTS: 15.

NO. AWARDS: 6.

APPLICATION INFO:
Application forms are supplied upon request. Researchers must check online to see if the Foundation is soliciting research application before submitting.

Duration: One year with option to apply for ongoing research and/or renewal. Renewal application (with progress report) is required each year.

Deadline: Contact the Foundation.

IRS I.D.: 13-6145280

STAFF:
David Brenner, Executive Director

DYSTONIA MEDICAL RESEARCH FOUNDATION [2385]

One East Wacker Drive
Suite 2810
Chicago, IL 60601-1905
(312) 755-0198
Fax: (312) 803-0138
E-mail: dystonia@dystonia-foundation.org
Web Site: www.dystonia-foundation.org

FOUNDED: 1976

AREAS OF INTEREST:
Dystonia.

NAME(S) OF PROGRAMS:
- **Research Grants**

TYPE:
Project/program grants; Research grants. Research Grants to be used for hypothesis-driven dystonia relevant research.

YEAR PROGRAM STARTED: 1976

PURPOSE:
To fund research into the cause of, treatments and a cure for, dystonia.

LEGAL BASIS:
Private foundation.

ELIGIBILITY:
For all programs, all nonprofit institutions or organizations within the U.S., Canada and those foreign countries where supervision of grant administration is possible are eligible. For all investigations involving humans, approval by the institution's human subject protection committee is necessary. If research proposals involve human brain tissue, the Foundation will make every effort to obtain appropriate tissue from affected individuals and from controls. No support for medical care of dystonia patients, construction or alterations. Investigators must have M.D. or Ph.D. degrees.

FINANCIAL DATA:
Support cannot be used for indirect costs, new construction or renovation of existing facilities, consultant fees or travel costs unless specified in the original grant application.

Amount of support per award: Average $65,000.

Total amount of support: Varies.

APPLICATION INFO:
Application form required for all programs.

Duration: Up to two years.

PUBLICATIONS:
Guidelines.

IRS I.D.: 95-3378526

ADDRESS INQUIRIES TO:
Jody Roosevelt, Grants Manager
(See address above.)

EPILEPSY FOUNDATION OF AMERICA [2386]

8301 Professional Place, Suite 200
Landover, MD 20785-2353
(800) 332-1000
Fax: (301) 577-4941
E-mail: grants@efa.org
info@efa.org
Web Site: www.epilepsyfoundation.org

FOUNDED: 1968

AREAS OF INTEREST:
Epilepsy research and training.

TYPE:
Research grants; Seed money grants. Seed grants are awarded to clinical investigators or basic scientists for support of biological or behavioral research which will advance the understanding, treatment and prevention of epilepsy.

PURPOSE:
To provide funding for investigators in the early stages of their careers.

LEGAL BASIS:
Private foundation.

ELIGIBILITY:
This program supports newly independent faculty members entering the field of epilepsy research. Established investigators (associate professor level or above) are ineligible.

GEOG. RESTRICTIONS: United States.

FINANCIAL DATA:
Amount of support per award: Varies.

APPLICATION INFO:
Application forms and guidelines can be obtained from the address above.

Duration: One to two years.

Deadline: Spring cycle: April 4 for Letter of Intent. May to June for Application. Fall cycle: November 6 for Letter of Intent. February 15 for Application.

THE GRASS FOUNDATION [2387]

P.O. Box 241458
Los Angeles, CA 90024
(310) 266-0300
E-mail: info@grassfoundation.org
Web Site: www.grassfoundation.org

FOUNDED: 1955

AREAS OF INTEREST:
Research and education in neuroscience.

NAME(S) OF PROGRAMS:
- **Grass Fellowships in Neuroscience**

TYPE:
Fellowships; Research grants. Summer research support for independent research projects in neuroscience at the Marine Biological Laboratories, Woods Hole, MA.

YEAR PROGRAM STARTED: 1955

PURPOSE:
To encourage young investigators in the field of neuroscience.

LEGAL BASIS:
Private foundation.

ELIGIBILITY:
Applicants must be late predoctoral, postdoctoral, or early independent investigators. Fellow must be a U.S. citizen, permanent resident, or have proper visa.

FINANCIAL DATA:
The Grass Foundation pays traveling expenses, reasonable living expenses while at MBL and certain laboratory costs. There is a modest drawing account for personal expenses. Expenses of the spouse or domestic partner and dependent children are likewise paid.

Amount of support per award: Varies.

Total amount of support: Varies.

NO. AWARDS: 10 to 12.

APPLICATION INFO:
Application materials may be obtained from the Foundation's web site.

Duration: 14 weeks.

Deadline: December 5. Announcement in January.

SELECTION COMMITTEE:
Catherine E. Carr, Ph.D.
Graeme W. Davis, Ph.D.
Bernice Grafstein, Ph.D.
Henry J. Grass, M.D.
Gregory L. Holmes, M.D.
Ronald R. Hoy, Ph.D.
Kamran Khodakhah, Ph.D.
George M. Langford, Ph.D.
Richard Larkin, C.P.A.
Jeff Lichtman, Ph.D.
Edwin McCleskey, Ph.D.
Felix E. Schweizer, Ph.D.
Amy R. Segal, Esq.
Janis C. Weeks, Ph.D.
Steven J. Zottoli, Ph.D.

ADDRESS INQUIRIES TO:
Executive Assistant
(See address above.)

HUNTINGTON'S DISEASE SOCIETY OF AMERICA, INC. [2388]

505 Eighth Avenue, Suite 902
New York, NY 10018
(212) 242-1968
Fax: (212) 239-3430
E-mail: hdsainfo@hdsa.org
Web Site: www.hdsa.org

FOUNDED: 1967

AREAS OF INTEREST:
Research into Huntington's disease.

NAME(S) OF PROGRAMS:
- **HD Human Biology Project**
- **HDSA Berman-Topper Family Huntington's Disease Career Development Fellowship**
- **Donald King Summer Research Fellowship**

TYPE:
Fellowships; Research grants.

YEAR PROGRAM STARTED: 1986

PURPOSE:
To support and stimulate research into the cause, prevention and treatment of Huntington's disease.

LEGAL BASIS:
Nonprofit, tax-exempt voluntary health agency.

FINANCIAL DATA:
Amount of support per award: Human Biology Project: $75,000 per year. Summer Research Fellowship: $4,000.

Total amount of support: Varies.

APPLICATION INFO:
Application information is available on the web site.

Duration: Human Biology Project: One or two years. Nonrenewable. Summer Research Fellowship: 10 weeks.

Deadline: Human Biology Project: Letter of Intent must be received by May 23; full application deadline is July 31. Summer Research Fellowship: March 4.

PUBLICATIONS:
Annual report; application guidelines; *Toward a Cure*; *The Marker*.

IRS I.D.: 13-3349872

TRUSTEES:
Jang-Ho Cha, M.D., Ph.D., Chairman
Daniel S. Vandivort, Treasurer
Jennifer Leyton, Secretary
Claudia Adkison, J.D., Ph.D.
Hugh DeLoayza
Lawrence Fisher
Gerald Francese, Esq.
Samuel Frank, M.D.
Michelle Gray, Ph.D.
Donald Higgins, M.D.
Barbara Jacobs
Arik Johnson, Psy.D.
Bill Kline
Robert Millum
Steven V. Seekins
Arvind Sreedharan
David Waltermire

ADDRESS INQUIRIES TO:
George Yohrling, Ph.D.
Senior Director, Mission and Scientific Affairs
(See address above.)

THE MCKNIGHT ENDOWMENT FUND FOR NEUROSCIENCE [2389]

The McKnight Foundation
710 South Second Street, Suite 400
Minneapolis, MN 55401
(612) 333-4220
Fax: (612) 332-3833
E-mail: info@mcknight.org
Web Site: www.neuroscience.mcknight.org

FOUNDED: 1986

AREAS OF INTEREST:
Neuroscience.

NAME(S) OF PROGRAMS:
- **McKnight Neuroscience Scholar Award**

TYPE:
Awards/prizes; Research grants.

PURPOSE:
To encourage neuroscientists in the early stages of their careers to focus on disorders of learning and memory.

LEGAL BASIS:
Nonprofit.

ELIGIBILITY:
Applicants must hold an M.D. and/or Ph.D. degree, have completed formal postdoctoral training and be in the early stages of an independent research career. Applicants should show evidence of a commitment to a continuing career in neuroscience and be in a tenured or tenure-track position.

GEOG. RESTRICTIONS: United States.

FINANCIAL DATA:
Awards are made to the sponsoring institution.

Amount of support per award: $75,000 per year.

NO. MOST RECENT APPLICANTS: 45.

NO. AWARDS: Up to 6 annually.

APPLICATION INFO:
Application forms and guidelines are available in September.

Duration: Three years.

Deadline: Early January. Announcement by mid-May.

ADDRESS INQUIRIES TO:
Eileen Maler, Program Manager
(See address above.)

MONTREAL NEUROLOGICAL INSTITUTE [2390]

3801 University Street
Room 636
Montreal QC H3A 2B4 Canada
(514) 398-1903
(514) 398-5205
Fax: (514) 398-8248
E-mail: viviane.poupon@mcgill.ca
Web Site: www.mni.mcgill.ca

FOUNDED: 1934

AREAS OF INTEREST:
Neurology, neurosurgery and neuroscience.

NAME(S) OF PROGRAMS:
- **Jeanne Timmins Costello Fellowships**
- **Preston Robb Fellowship**

TYPE:
Exchange programs; Fellowships. Awards for research and study in the fields of clinical and basic neurosciences.

PURPOSE:
To provide the recipient with the experience of going from laboratory bench to the patient's bedside by exploiting the strengths of the Institute in basic and clinical science.

LEGAL BASIS:
University, research institute.

ELIGIBILITY:
For the Costello Fellowship, candidates must have an M.D. or Ph.D. degree. Those candidates with M.D. degrees will ordinarily have completed clinical studies in neurology or neurosurgery. Research themes at the MNI include neuroanatomy, neurochemistry, neurogenetics, molecular genetics, neuroimaging, neuroimmunology, epilepsy, neuromuscular disease, neuro-oncology, molecular and cellular biology and neuropsychology.

For the Robb Fellowship, candidates must have an M.D. degree with clinical studies in neurology or neurosurgery.

FINANCIAL DATA:
Amount of support per award: $40,000 per year.

NO. AWARDS: Jeanne Timmins Costello Fellowships: 4; Preston Robb Fellowship: 1.

APPLICATION INFO:
Application form and guidelines are available online from August 1 to October 31.

Duration: One year. Renewal possible for one additional year.

Deadline: October 31.

PUBLICATIONS:
Annual report.

ADDRESS INQUIRIES TO:
Viviane Poupon
Associate Director, Scientific Affairs
(See address above.)

MULTIPLE SCLEROSIS SOCIETY OF CANADA [2391]

250 Dundas Street West
Suite 500
Toronto ON M5T 2Z5 Canada
(416) 922-6065
(866) 922-6065
Fax: (416) 922-7538
E-mail: msresearchgrants@mssociety.ca
Web Site: www.mssociety.ca

FOUNDED: 1948

AREAS OF INTEREST:
Neurology, immunology, virology, pathology and biochemistry, fields of biomedical research, and clinical and population health research.

NAME(S) OF PROGRAMS:
- **endMS Doctoral Studentship Award**
- **endMS Master's Studentship Award**

TYPE:
Research grants. Studentships offered at the Master's and Ph.D. levels.

PURPOSE:
To find the cause and cure of multiple sclerosis.

LEGAL BASIS:
Charitable organization.

ELIGIBILITY:
Applicant must be a Canadian citizen, landed immigrant, or person holding a Canadian student visa who is going to school at a recognized Canadian research institute, or a Canadian citizen or landed immigrant who is going to school at a recognized foreign research institute.

FINANCIAL DATA:
Amount of support per award: Master's: $20,000 (CAN) per year; Ph.D.: $22,000 (CAN) per year; Ph.D. (who hold an M.D.): $50,500 (CAN) per year.

Total amount of support: Varies.

NO. MOST RECENT APPLICANTS: 90 for the year 2013-14.

NO. AWARDS: 30 for the year 2013-14.

APPLICATION INFO:
Applications are only accepted online.

Duration: endMS Master's Studentships: Up to two years. No renewals; endMS Doctoral Studentships: Up to four years. No renewals.

Deadline: October 1. Announcement the following March 1 to begin July 1.

ADDRESS INQUIRIES TO:
Research and Programs Department
(See e-mail address above.)

MULTIPLE SCLEROSIS SOCIETY OF CANADA [2392]

250 Dundas Street West
Suite 500
Toronto ON M5T 2Z5 Canada
(416) 922-6065
(866) 922-6065
Fax: (416) 922-7538
E-mail: msresearchgrants@mssociety.ca
Web Site: www.mssociety.ca

FOUNDED: 1948

AREAS OF INTEREST:
Neurology, immunology, virology, pathology and biochemistry.

NAME(S) OF PROGRAMS:
- **Biomedical Research Grants**
- **Clinical and Population Health Research Grants**

TYPE:
Research grants.

PURPOSE:
To find the cause and cure of multiple sclerosis.

LEGAL BASIS:
Charitable organization.

ELIGIBILITY:
Applicants must carry out research at a recognized Canadian research institute (e.g., university or hospital).

FINANCIAL DATA:
Amount of support per award: $10,000 to $100,000 (CAN) average per year.

Total amount of support: Varies.

NO. MOST RECENT APPLICANTS: 72 for the year 2013-14.

NO. AWARDS: 20 for the year 2013-14.

APPLICATION INFO:
Applications are only accepted online.

Duration: Biomedical Research Grants: Up to three years, beginning July 1. Clinical and Population Health Research Grants: Up to three years, beginning October 1 for Spring Competition; beginning July 1 for Fall Competition.

Deadline: Biomedical Research Grants: October 1, with announcement the following March 1. Clinical and Population Health Research Grants: Mid-May, with announcement in September for the Spring Competition; October 1, with announcement the following March 1 for the Fall Competition.

ADDRESS INQUIRIES TO:
Research and Programs Department
(See e-mail address above.)

MULTIPLE SCLEROSIS SOCIETY OF CANADA [2393]

250 Dundas Street West
Suite 500
Toronto ON M5T 2Z5 Canada
(416) 922-6065
(866) 922-6065
Fax: (416) 922-7538
E-mail: msresearchgrants@mssociety.ca
Web Site: www.mssociety.ca

FOUNDED: 1948

AREAS OF INTEREST:
Neurology, immunology, virology, pathology and biochemistry, fields of biomedical research, and clinical and population health research.

NAME(S) OF PROGRAMS:
- **endMS Postdoctoral Fellowship**

TYPE:
Fellowships. The program is intended to support research for training of postdoctoral fellows in studies related to MS.

PURPOSE:
To find the cause and cure of multiple sclerosis.

LEGAL BASIS:
Charitable organization.

ELIGIBILITY:
Applicant must be a Canadian citizen, landed immigrant or person holding a Canadian student visa who is working at a recognized Canadian research institute, or a Canadian citizen or landed immigrant who is working at a recognized foreign research institute. Applicant must have completed their doctoral degree within the last three years by the time of the competition deadline.

FINANCIAL DATA:
Amount of support per award: Postdoctoral Fellows: $41,000 (CAN) per year; Postdoctoral Fellows (for those who hold an M.D.): $50,500 (CAN) per year.

Total amount of support: Varies.

NO. MOST RECENT APPLICANTS: 21 for the year 2013-14.

NO. AWARDS: 12 for the year 2013-14.

APPLICATION INFO:
Applications are only accepted online.

Duration: Up to three years. No renewals.

Deadline: October 1. Announcement the following March 1 to begin July 1.

ADDRESS INQUIRIES TO:
Research and Programs Department
(See e-mail address above.)

MUSCULAR DYSTROPHY ASSOCIATION [2394]

222 South Riverside Plaza, Suite 1500A
Chicago, IL 60606
(312) 254-0632
E-mail: grants@mdausa.org
Web Site: www.mda.org

FOUNDED: 1950

AREAS OF INTEREST:
Research into diseases of the neuromuscular system.

NAME(S) OF PROGRAMS:
- **Neuromuscular Disease Research**

TYPE:
Research grants; Training grants. Translational Research Grants. Basic scientific and clinical research grants are offered.

MDA supports research into diseases of the neuromuscular system to develop effective treatments for the muscular dystrophies and related diseases which include spinal muscular atrophy and other motor neuron diseases, inflammatory myopathies, metabolic myopathies, diseases of the neuromuscular junction, certain peripheral neuropathies and basic research increasing general knowledge in the neuromuscular field.

YEAR PROGRAM STARTED: 1950

PURPOSE:
To find the causes of, and treatments for, neuromuscular diseases.

LEGAL BASIS:
Nonprofit, voluntary health agency.

ELIGIBILITY:
An applicant must be a professional or faculty member at an appropriate educational, medical or research institution and be qualified to conduct and supervise a program of original research, have access to institutional resources necessary to conduct the proposed research project and hold a Doctor of Medicine, Doctor of Philosophy, Doctor of Science or equivalent degree.

Proposals from applicants outside the U.S. will be considered only for projects of highest priority to MDA and when, in addition to the applicant's having met the eligibility requirements noted above, one or more of the following conditions exist: the applicant's country of residence has inadequate sources of financial support for biomedical research, collaboration with an MDA-supported U.S. investigator is required to conduct the project, or an invitation to submit an application has been extended by MDA.

FINANCIAL DATA:
Funding levels for Primary Research Grants are $100,000 including indirect costs per year for a maximum of three years. Overhead limited to a maximum of 10% of the total direct costs of the grant requested.

Amount of support per award: Development Grants: Up to $60,000 per year.

NO. MOST RECENT APPLICANTS: 612.

NO. AWARDS: Approximately 90.

APPLICATION INFO:
Guidelines are available on the web site.

Duration: One, two or three years.

Deadline: For Neuromuscular Disease Research, applications must be requested by December 15 and submitted by January 30 for funding to commence the following August 1. Applications must be requested by June 15 and submitted by July 15 for funding to commence the following February 1.

STAFF:
Steven Derks, President and Chief Executive Officer
Valerie A. Cwik, M.D., Executive Vice President and Chief Medical and Scientific Officer
Julie Faber, Chief Financial Officer

ADDRESS INQUIRIES TO:
See e-mail address above.

MYASTHENIA GRAVIS FOUNDATION OF AMERICA, INC. [2395]

355 Lexington Avenue
15th Floor
New York, NY 10017
(800) 541-5454
Fax: (212) 297-2159
E-mail: mgfa@myasthenia.org
Web Site: www.myasthenia.org

FOUNDED: 1952

AREAS OF INTEREST:
Myasthenia gravis and related neuromuscular conditions.

CONSULTING OR VOLUNTEER SERVICES:
Nationwide Support Group Network.

NAME(S) OF PROGRAMS:
- **Nurses Research Fellowship**

TYPE:
Fellowships; Research grants. Awards for research pertaining to problems faced by myasthenia gravis patients.

YEAR PROGRAM STARTED: 1988

PURPOSE:
To create an effective communications, service and human relations network for myasthenics, their families and friends; to educate both the lay and professional community about myasthenia gravis; to stimulate and support scientific inquiry, interchange and research in the quest for improved treatment techniques and a cure.

LEGAL BASIS:
Nonprofit corporate foundation.

ELIGIBILITY:
Candidates must be currently licensed as registered professional nurses. Fellowships are limited to U.S. or Canadian citizens or holders of bona fide permanent visas for training in U.S. institutions.

FINANCIAL DATA:
Amount of support per award: Up to $5,000.

NO. MOST RECENT APPLICANTS: 1.

NO. AWARDS: 1.

APPLICATION INFO:
Candidates should submit four copies of cover letter stating that he or she is applying for the Nurses Research Fellowship, proposed budget, curriculum vitae, research proposal and letters of approval to conduct research by appropriate parties (i.e., institution, physicians and educational facilities).

Duration: One year.

Deadline: July 1.

PUBLICATIONS:
Guidelines.

IRS I.D.: 13-5672224

ADDRESS INQUIRIES TO:
Anne Williams, R.N.
E-mail: annewilliams515@yahoo.com

NATIONAL ATAXIA FOUNDATION [2396]

2600 Fernbrook Lane, Suite 119
Minneapolis, MN 55447
(763) 553-0020
Fax: (763) 553-0167
E-mail: susan@ataxia.org
Web Site: www.ataxia.org

FOUNDED: 1957

AREAS OF INTEREST:
Cause and treatment of ataxia.

NAME(S) OF PROGRAMS:
- **National Ataxia Foundation Fellowship Award**
- **National Ataxia Foundation Pioneer SCA Translational Research Award**
- **National Ataxia Foundation Research Grant Program**
- **National Ataxia Foundation Young Investigator Award and Young Investigator Award for SCAs**

TYPE:
Fellowships; Research grants; Seed money grants. Young investigator award.

YEAR PROGRAM STARTED: 1978

PURPOSE:
To support research into hereditary and sporadic ataxia, as well as treatment, services, and education of the disorder.

LEGAL BASIS:
Nonprofit 501(c)(3) organization.

ELIGIBILITY:
Individuals and organizations, including religious, can apply.

FINANCIAL DATA:
Amount of support per award: Fellowship Award: Up to $35,000; Pioneer SCA Translational Research Award: $100,000; Research Grant Program: Up to $30,000; Young Investigator Award: $35,000; Young Investigator Award for SCAs: $50,000.

Total amount of support: $1,000,000 for the fiscal year 2014.

NO. MOST RECENT APPLICANTS: 55.

NO. AWARDS: 24 for the year 2014.

APPLICATION INFO:
Letter of Intent must be submitted one month prior to application deadlines.

Duration: Pioneer SCA Translational Award and Young Investigator Award: One year. Research Grant and Research Fellowship: One year. Renewals by reapplication each year for continuing support.

Deadline: Pioneer SCA Translational Award and Research Fellowship: September 15; Research Grant: August 15; Young Investigator: September 1.

PUBLICATIONS:
Annual report; application guidelines.

IRS I.D.: 41-0832903

ADDRESS INQUIRIES TO:
Susan Hagen, Patient Services Director
(See address and e-mail above.)

NATIONAL HEADACHE FOUNDATION

820 North Orleans, Suite 411
Chicago, IL 60610-3132
(312) 274-2650
(888) 643-5552
Fax: (312) 640-9049
E-mail: info@headaches.org
Web Site: www.headaches.org

TYPE:
Research grants. Support for research in the field of headache and pain.

See entry 2292 for full listing.

NATIONAL INSTITUTE OF NEUROLOGICAL DISORDERS AND STROKE [2397]

Building 31, Room 8A34
31 Center Drive, MSC 2540
Bethesda, MD 20892
(301) 435-7726
E-mail: frushouk@ninds.nih.gov
Web Site: www.ninds.nih.gov

FOUNDED: 1950

AREAS OF INTEREST:
Neurological disorders, including multiple sclerosis and amyotrophic lateral sclerosis, movement disorders, such as the dystonias and Tourette's syndrome and degenerative and dementing disorders such as Parkinson's, Huntington's and Alzheimer's diseases, stroke, spinal cord injury, neural regeneration and plasticity, coma, chronic pain, head injury, traumatic brain injury, peripheral nerve injury, tumors of the nervous system, brain edema and manipulative therapy, and convulsive, developmental and neuromuscular disorders.

TYPE:
Assistantships; Conferences/seminars; Fellowships; Project/program grants; Research grants; Training grants; Research contracts. Support for research, including neurological science basic research, which explores the fundamental structure and function of the brain and the nervous system, research to understand the causes and origins of pathological conditions of the nervous system with the goal of prevention of these disorders, research on the natural course of neurological disorders, research training in the basic neurological sciences and mechanisms associated with stroke and other cerebrovascular disorders, effects of trauma to the nervous system, neuroplasticity and regeneration and tumors of neural and sensory tissues.
Research may include:
(1) improved methods of disease prevention;
(2) new methods of diagnosis and treatment;
(3) clinical trials;
(4) drug development;
(5) development of neural prostheses for stroke and paraplegia;
(6) epidemiological research and;
(7) research training in the clinical sciences.

PURPOSE:
To support research on neurological diseases and stroke.

LEGAL BASIS:
PHS Act, Section 301, Section 431 and Section 433; Public Law 78-410, as amended; (42 U.S.C. 241), (42 U.S.C. 289C). PHS Act, Section 472; Public Law 78-410, as amended; (42 U.S.C. 289L-1).

ELIGIBILITY:
Research grants are available to any public or private nonprofit university, college, hospital, laboratory, or other institution, including state and local units of government, or to any individual. National Research Service Awards for the above areas may be made to individuals or to nonfederal public and private nonprofit institutions for the training of individuals at the pre- and postdoctoral levels.

FINANCIAL DATA:
Grants may be used for any usual research expenses including salaries, equipment supplies, travel to scientific meetings, patient care, publications, etc.

Amount of support per award: Approximately $380,000.

Total amount of support: $1.7 billion appropriated for fiscal year 2016.

APPLICATION INFO:
Application forms may be requested from the Division of Research Grants, National Institutes of Health, Bethesda, MD 20892.

Duration: One to five years. Renewal applications may be submitted.

Deadline: November 1, March 1, and July 1. Awards are announced throughout the year.

ADDRESS INQUIRIES TO:
Director, Division of Extramural Activities
NINDS, NIH MSC 9531
6001 Executive Boulevard
Rockville, MD 20892

NATIONAL MULTIPLE SCLEROSIS SOCIETY [2398]

733 Third Avenue, 3rd Floor
New York, NY 10017-3288
(212) 476-0536
Fax: (212) 986-7981
E-mail: douglas.landsman@nmss.org
Web Site: www.nationalmssociety.org

FOUNDED: 1946

AREAS OF INTEREST:
Multiple sclerosis.

NAME(S) OF PROGRAMS:
- **Postdoctoral Fellowships Program in Multiple Sclerosis Research**

TYPE:
Fellowships. Postdoctoral fellowships for training leading to an academic career involving clinical or basic research in multiple sclerosis.

YEAR PROGRAM STARTED: 1955

PURPOSE:
To support investigators for whom further assistance may be critical in obtaining the training required for a research or academic career, or for whom the additional training will increase research or teaching potential in areas related to multiple sclerosis.

LEGAL BASIS:
Voluntary health agency, tax status 501(c)(3).

ELIGIBILITY:
Qualified investigators holding a doctoral-level degree in medicine or appropriate biological fields are eligible to apply. Candidates must select their own training institutions and make all necessary arrangements for the conduct of proposed training or study program. Awards are based upon the applicant's professional status, training and experience.

FINANCIAL DATA:
Candidates must request all funds required.

Amount of support per award: Varies.

NO. MOST RECENT APPLICANTS: 44 for the year 2014.

NO. AWARDS: 15 for the year 2014.

APPLICATION INFO:
Instructions for completing the pre-application and full application are available on the Society's web site.

Duration: Up to three years.

Deadline: Mid-August. Pre-application one week prior to full application deadline.

OFFICERS OF THE BOARD:
Peter A. Galligan, Chairman
Cynthia Zagieboylo, President and Chief Executive Officer
Richard Knutson, Treasurer
Linda J. McAleer, Secretary

ADDRESS INQUIRIES TO:
Dr. Douglas Landsman
Director of Research Training Programs
(See telephone and e-mail address above.)

NATIONAL MULTIPLE SCLEROSIS SOCIETY [2399]

Research Programs
733 Third Avenue
New York, NY 10017-3288
(212) 986-3240
Fax: (212) 986-7981
E-mail: msresearch@nmss.org
Web Site: www.nationalmssociety.org

FOUNDED: 1946

AREAS OF INTEREST:
Multiple sclerosis.

NAME(S) OF PROGRAMS:
- **National Multiple Sclerosis Society Research Grants Program**

TYPE:
Awards/prizes; Fellowships; Research grants; Training grants; Research contracts. Grants for fundamental or applied research in scientific areas pertinent to multiple sclerosis. Grants are available for clinical or nonclinical studies, providing they show a reasonable relevance to the Society's interests.

YEAR PROGRAM STARTED: 1947

PURPOSE:
To support research into the cause, prevention, alleviation and cure of multiple sclerosis.

LEGAL BASIS:
Voluntary health agency, tax status 501(c)(3).

ELIGIBILITY:
Qualified investigators affiliated with appropriate institutions are eligible to apply. Institutions are the official recipients of grants. Some commercial partnerships supported.

FINANCIAL DATA:
The principal investigator and the grantee institution will be advised of the exact amount and duration of the grant award. Grant funds may be requested for professional and nonprofessional personnel, permanent equipment, consumable supplies, travel and other expenditures and indirect costs.

Amount of support per award: Varies.

Total amount of support: Varies.

NO. MOST RECENT APPLICANTS: 500 for the year 2014.

NO. AWARDS: 171 for the year 2014.

APPLICATION INFO:
Before submitting a proposal for research support, investigators must submit preapplication online to determine whether the research plan is appropriate and relevant to the Society's goals.

Duration: Maximum of five years.

Deadline: August and February for research grants. Quarterly for pilot research grants. Specific dates are posted online.

OFFICERS OF THE BOARD:
Peter A. Galligan, Chairman
Cynthia Zagieboylo, President and Chief Executive Officer
Richard Knutson, Treasurer
Linda J. McAleer, Secretary

ADDRESS INQUIRIES TO:
See e-mail address above.

NEUROSURGERY RESEARCH AND EDUCATION FOUNDATION [2400]

5550 Meadowbrook Drive
Rolling Meadows, IL 60008
(847) 378-0500
(888) 566-AANS
Fax: (847) 378-0600
E-mail: nref@aans.org
Web Site: www.nref.org

FOUNDED: 1982

AREAS OF INTEREST:
Neurosurgery.

NAME(S) OF PROGRAMS:
- **Research Fellowships**
- **Young Clinician Investigator Award**

TYPE:
Awards/prizes; Fellowships; Research grants.

YEAR PROGRAM STARTED: 1983

PURPOSE:
To advance the neurosciences.

LEGAL BASIS:
Private foundation.

ELIGIBILITY:
Applicants for the Research Fellowship must be M.Ds. who have been accepted into or who are in an approved residency training program in neurological surgery in North America.

Applicants for the Young Clinician Investigator Award must be neurosurgeons who are full-time faculty in North American teaching institutions in the early years of their careers. Those who accept grants from other sources for the same project are ineligible.

GEOG. RESTRICTIONS: North America.

FINANCIAL DATA:
Amount of support per award: $40,000.

NO. MOST RECENT APPLICANTS: 90.

NO. AWARDS: Typically 10 awards annually.

APPLICATION INFO:
Applicants must provide a proposal, budget, a current curriculum vitae and three letters of reference. Electronic applications are accepted.

Duration: One year beginning July 1.

Deadline: Approximately November 1. Call for exact deadline. Announcement by February 1.

ADDRESS INQUIRIES TO:
See e-mail address above.

PARKINSON'S DISEASE FOUNDATION, INC. [2401]

1359 Broadway, Suite 1509
New York, NY 10018
(212) 923-4700
Fax: (212) 923-4778
E-mail: bvernaleo@pdf.org
grants@pdf.org
Web Site: www.pdf.org

FOUNDED: 1957

AREAS OF INTEREST:
Basic and clinical research toward finding the cause and cure for Parkinson's disease.

CONSULTING OR VOLUNTEER SERVICES:
Information and referral service to Parkinson's disease patients and caregivers.

NAME(S) OF PROGRAMS:
- **Postdoctoral Fellowship**

TYPE:
Fellowships. The Postdoctoral Fellowship program has two distinct components: (1) Postdoctoral Fellowship for Basic Scientists and (2) Postdoctoral Fellowship for Neurologists.

YEAR PROGRAM STARTED: 1990

PURPOSE:
To provide support and training for Parkinson's disease researchers at early stages in their careers.

LEGAL BASIS:
Nonprofit organization.

ELIGIBILITY:
Postdoctoral Fellowship for Basic Scientists: The applicant must be within five years of receiving his or her Ph.D., and must identify an individual who will serve as his or her mentor and supervisor of the research.

Postdoctoral Fellowship for Neurologists: Applicants seeking a Postdoctoral Fellowship for Neurologists must possess an M.D. or equivalent and be within three years of having completed a residency in neurology. Applicants may not have their own lab and must identify an individual who will serve as his or her mentor and supervisor of their research.

FINANCIAL DATA:
The Postdoctoral Fellowship does not pay indirect or overhead costs and requires the grant recipient to account for all expenditures. The second year's funding is dependent upon submission of a satisfactory report covering the first year's work.

Amount of support per award: Postdoctoral Fellowship for Basic Scientists: Up to $45,000, plus $5,000 research allowance. Postdoctoral Fellowship for Neurologists: Up to $55,000, plus $5,000 research allowance.

Total amount of support: Approximately $500,000.

NO. MOST RECENT APPLICANTS: 86.

NO. AWARDS: 5 for the year 2016.

APPLICATION INFO:
Applications must be submitted online. Applicants for the Postdoctoral Fellowship must also submit the investigator's curriculum vitae, an outline of work to be undertaken and a detailed budget.

Duration: Two years.

Deadline: Letter of Intent: Early November, with notification in mid- to late December. Full Application: Mid-February, with award notification in mid-April.

PUBLICATIONS:
Annual reports; research reports; application guidelines.

ADDRESS INQUIRIES TO:
Research
(See address above.)

PARKINSON'S DISEASE FOUNDATION, INC. [2402]

1359 Broadway, Suite 1509
New York, NY 10018
(212) 923-4700
(800) 457-6676
Fax: (212) 923-4778
E-mail: bvernaleo@pdf.org
grants@pdf.org
Web Site: www.pdf.org

FOUNDED: 1957

AREAS OF INTEREST:
Basic and clinical research toward finding the cause and cure for Parkinson's disease.

CONSULTING OR VOLUNTEER SERVICES:
Information and referral service to Parkinson's disease patients and caregivers; counseling.

NAME(S) OF PROGRAMS:
- **Conference Awards**
- **PDF-PSG Mentored Clinical Research Award**

TYPE:
Conferences/seminars; Research grants.

ELIGIBILITY:
Conference Awards: Open to independent investigators, both nationally and internationally, possessing postdoctoral training or a medical degree (or the equivalent). The Award supports gatherings of experts in the field in order to address emerging clinical or basic science questions about Parkinson's. Award is not open to postdoctoral researchers or fellows.

PDF-PSG Mentored Clinical Research Award: Clinicians and scientists who are within five years of having completed formal training. Fellows may apply. Applicants must identify an appropriate mentor or mentors with extensive research experience. Either the applicant or the mentor must be a member of the PSG. An applicant may have co-mentors.

FINANCIAL DATA:
Amount of support per award: Conference Awards: Average award $10,000, with a maximum of $15,000. PDF-PSG Mentored Clinical Research Award: $50,000 per year.

CO-OP FUNDING PROGRAMS: PDF-PSG Mentored Clinical Research Award is funded by a grant from the PDF to the Parkinson Study Group (PSG).

APPLICATION INFO:
Conference Awards: Review program requirements and apply.

PDF-PSG Mentored Clinical Research Award: Review program overview and instructions, and apply directly to the PSG via e-mail to Roseanna.Battista@ctcc.rochester.edu.

Duration: Conference Awards: Up to one year. PDF-PSG Mentored Clinical Research Award: One year.

Deadline: Conference Awards: Applications will be accepted anytime, as long as they are submitted at least 90 days prior to proposed conference start date; award notification four to six weeks after application submission. PDF-PSG Mentored Clinical Research Award: Applications due January, with award notification in March.

ADDRESS INQUIRIES TO:
Beth A. Vernaleo, Ph.D.
Associate Director of Research Programs or
James Beck, Ph.D., Research Director
(See address above.)

PARKINSON'S DISEASE FOUNDATION, INC. [2403]

1359 Broadway, Suite 1509
New York, NY 10018
(212) 923-4700
(800) 457-6676
Fax: (212) 923-4778
E-mail: bvernaleo@pdf.org
grants@pdf.org
Web Site: www.pdf.org

FOUNDED: 1957

AREAS OF INTEREST:
Basic and clinical research toward finding the cause and cure for Parkinson's disease.

NAME(S) OF PROGRAMS:
- **Stanley Fahn Junior Faculty Award**

TYPE:
Research grants. Stanley Fahn Junior Faculty Award provides junior investigators - in conjunction with their institution's commitment - with the support necessary to develop their own independent funding source (such as an NIH R01 award) and stay in the field of Parkinson's disease research.

PURPOSE:
To act as a bridge to ensure that promising early career scientists stay in the field of Parkinson's research and help solve, treat and end the disease; to stem the loss of talent from Parkinson's research.

ELIGIBILITY:
Junior faculty members possessing a Ph.D., M.D. or equivalent are eligible to apply. Applicants must generally meet the NIH definition of a "new investigator." The Foundation anticipates the typical applicant will hold an assistant professor-level position with up to several years of experience. Earlier-stage faculty and those with more experience will be considered provided that the above eligibility criteria are met.

This Award is open to applicants, regardless of citizenship, who reside in the U.S. and are faculty members of U.S. institutions.

Applicants from Foundation Research Centers are eligible to apply. A letter of support from the applicant's department chair will be required to demonstrate level of institutional commitment to the applicant.

This program is restricted to full-time faculty members of U.S. institutions with a current post of instructor or assistant professor. As a career development initiative, the program is not open to current or prior holders of NIH R01 awards or their equivalent. In principle, only one award will be made per institution in a given year, but special exceptions may be considered.

FINANCIAL DATA:
Amount of support per award: $300,000 in total costs. Indirect costs, not exceeding 10% of direct costs, may be deducted from the total. Applicant salary support is permitted up to 40% of total salary.

NO. AWARDS: 3 in 2016.

APPLICATION INFO:
Application process is divided into two parts. Applicants first submit a letter of intent (LOI). Second, based on favorable peer review, applicants may then be invited to submit a full application, also for peer review. All materials must be submitted online at grants.pdf.org.

Duration: Three years, subject to review of annual progress. Submission of an NIH R01 or equivalent is a required milestone of this Award and upon which third year of funding is contingent.

Deadline: Letter of intent: November 11. Full application:Following February 15.

ADDRESS INQUIRIES TO:
Beth A. Vernaleo, Ph.D.
Senior Manager, Research Programs
(See address above.)

PARKINSON'S DISEASE FOUNDATION, INC. [2404]

1359 Broadway, Suite 1509
New York, NY 10018
(212) 923-4700
(800) 457-6676
Fax: (212) 923-4778
E-mail: bvernaleo@pdf.org
grants@pdf.org
Web Site: www.pdf.org

FOUNDED: 1957

AREAS OF INTEREST:
Basic and clinical research toward finding the cause and cure for Parkinson's disease.

CONSULTING OR VOLUNTEER SERVICES:
Information and referral service to Parkinson's disease patients and caregivers; counseling.

NAME(S) OF PROGRAMS:
- **PDF Summer Student Fellowship**

TYPE:
Fellowships. Supports medical students and undergraduates for study under the supervision of an established investigator.

YEAR PROGRAM STARTED: 2002

PURPOSE:
To seek the cause and cure of Parkinson's disease.

LEGAL BASIS:
Nonprofit organization.

ELIGIBILITY:
Undergraduate, graduate and medical students are eligible.

FINANCIAL DATA:
Amount of support per award: $4,000.
Total amount of support: $48,000.

NO. MOST RECENT APPLICANTS: 39.

NO. AWARDS: 12 for the year 2016.

APPLICATION INFO:
Application information is available on the web site.

Duration: 10 weeks.

Deadline: Late January, with award notification in mid-March.

PUBLICATIONS:
Annual reports; research reports; application guidelines and forms.

BOARD OF DIRECTORS:
Howard D. Morgan, Chairman of the Board
Constance Woodruff Atwell, Ph.D., Vice Chairman
Robin Anthony Elliott, President
Stephen Ackerman, Treasurer
Isobel Robins Konecky, Secretary
Stanley Fahn, M.D., Scientific Director

DIRECTORS:
Karen Elizabeth Burke, M.D., Ph.D.
Peter Dorn
George Pennington Egbert, III
Richard D. Field
Stephanie Goldman-Pittel
Arlene Levine
Marshall Loeb
Linda Morgan, R.Ph., MBA
Timothy A. Pedley, M.D.
Gregory Romero
Lewis P. Rowland, M.D.
Marie Schwartz
Melvin S. Taub

ADDRESS INQUIRIES TO:
Beth A. Vernaleo, Ph.D.
Associate Director of Research Programs or
James Beck, Ph.D.
Vice President, Scientific Affairs
(See address above.)

TOURETTE ASSOCIATION OF AMERICA, INC. [2405]

42-40 Bell Boulevard
Suite 205
Bayside, NY 11361-2820
(718) 224-2999
Fax: (718) 279-9596
E-mail: support@tourette.org
Web Site: www.tourette.org

FOUNDED: 1972

AREAS OF INTEREST:
Education, research and services relating to Tourette Syndrome and relevant scientific fields, such as biochemistry, neuroanatomy, neurophysiology, genetics, molecular biology, epidemiology, psychiatry, psychology, neuropsychology, neurology, neuroimaging, neuropathology, pharmacology and/or animal models.

NAME(S) OF PROGRAMS:
- **Tourette Syndrome Research Fellowships**
- **Tourette Syndrome Research Grants**

TYPE:
Fellowships; General operating grants; Research grants; Seed money grants; Technical assistance. Research grants available for Ph.D. and M.D. researchers in the following categories:
(1) proposals in basic neuroscience specifically relevant to Tourette Syndrome and;
(2) clinical studies related to the etiology, pathophysiology and treatment of Tourette Syndrome.

Fellowships provide one-year postdoctoral training.

YEAR PROGRAM STARTED: 1984

PURPOSE:
To support significant basic and clinical research in Tourette Syndrome.

LEGAL BASIS:
Not-for-profit organization.

ELIGIBILITY:
Open to Ph.D. and M.D. investigators from all areas of science who can contribute to the understanding of the genetics, pathogenesis, pathophysiology and the treatment of Tourette Syndrome. Investigators already studying Tourette Syndrome and those currently working in areas of science that can be applied to the problems of Tourette Syndrome are invited to apply.

FINANCIAL DATA:
These designated award levels can include indirect costs no greater than 10%. However, the total grant award cannot exceed $75,000 for a one-year research grant or $150,000 for a two-year award.

Amount of support per award: Research grants: Up to $75,000 for one year or up to $150,000 for two years. Fellowships: Up to $40,000 for one year.

Total amount of support: Varies.

NO. MOST RECENT APPLICANTS: 36.

NO. AWARDS: 10.

REPRESENTATIVE AWARDS:
$40,000 to Deanna Greene, Ph.D., Washington University School of Medicine, St. Louis, MO, for "Pathophysiological Markers in the 'Pre-Tourette' Population;" $150,000 to Izhar Bar-Gad, Ilan University, Ramat-Gan, Israel, for "Interaction of the Dopaminergic and GABAergic Systems in the Formation of Tics."

APPLICATION INFO:
Application information is available on the web site.

For preliminary screening, a preproposal is required. The approximate project funding level should be included. Inquirers will be informed as to whether to proceed with a full application.

Duration: One or two years.

Deadline: Preproposals are due in early November each year. Final proposals are due in February each year. Awards are announced in July.

PUBLICATIONS:
Brochure.

OFFICERS:
Michael Wolff, Chairperson
Rovena Schirling, First Vice Chairperson
Bruce Ochsman, Second Vice Chairperson
Alice Kane, Third Vice Chairperson
Cindy Kurtz, Fourth Vice Chairperson
Frederick Cook, Finance Committee Chairperson
Marcie Kirkpatrick, Secretary

ADVISORY BOARD:
Tamara Hershey, Ph.D., Co-Chairperson
Jonathan W. Mink, M.D., Ph.D., Co-Chairperson
Erika Augustine, M.D.
Nicole Calakos, M.D., Ph.D.
Robert Chen, M.A., M.B.B. Chir
Joseph Garner, Ph.D.
Aryn Gittis, Ph.D.
Denise Head, Ph.D.
Ellen Hess, Ph.D.
Peggy Nopoulos, M.D.
Laurie Ozelius, Ph.D.
David A. Peterson, Ph.D.
Rosalinda Roberts, Ph.D.
Jeremiah Scharf, M.D., Ph.D.
Tristram H. Smith, Ph.D.

ADDRESS INQUIRIES TO:
Marc Scullin, Manager of Research and Medical Programs
(See address above.)

Nursing

AMERICAN ASSOCIATION FOR THE HISTORY OF NURSING, INC. [2406]

10200 West 44th Avenue
Suite 304
Wheat Ridge, CO 80033
(303) 422-2685
Fax: (708) 881-6101
E-mail: dstumph@kellencompany.com
Web Site: www.aahn.org

FOUNDED: 1978

AREAS OF INTEREST:
Nursing historical research.

NAME(S) OF PROGRAMS:

- **Competitive Student Research H-31 Predoctoral Grant**
- **H-15 Grant for Faculty Members or Independent Researchers**

TYPE:
Awards/prizes; Research grants. Research awards.

PURPOSE:
To encourage and support research in nursing history.

ELIGIBILITY:
Competitive Student Research H-31 Predoctoral Grant: Student must be an AAHN member enrolled in an accredited Master's or doctoral program. Proposals must focus on a significant question in the history of nursing and the research advisor will be doctorally prepared with scholarly activity in the field of nursing history and prior experience in guidance of research training.

H-15 Grant: Applicant must be an AAHN member with a doctoral degree. Proposals will be judged for scholarly merit and significance to the field of nursing history.

FINANCIAL DATA:
Amount of support per award: Competitive Student Research H-31 Predoctoral Grant: $2,000; H-15 Grant: $3,000.

Total amount of support: $5,000.

NO. MOST RECENT APPLICANTS: 8 to 12.

NO. AWARDS: 3.

APPLICATION INFO:
Contact the Association.

Deadline: Spring.

ADDRESS INQUIRIES TO:
David L. Stumph, IOM, CAE
(See address above.)

THE AMERICAN LEGION NATIONAL HEADQUARTERS [2407]

P.O. Box 1055
Indianapolis, IN 46206
(317) 630-1209
Fax: (317) 630-1369
E-mail: scholarships@legion.org
Web Site: www.legion.org

FOUNDED: 1919

NAME(S) OF PROGRAMS:

- **Eight and Forty Lung and Respiratory Disease Nursing Scholarship Fund**

TYPE:
Scholarships. Grants for registered nurses.

YEAR PROGRAM STARTED: 1957

PURPOSE:
To allow registered nurses to further their education at the graduate level in the area of pediatric lung and respiratory diseases.

ELIGIBILITY:
Applicant must be a registered nurse, in adequate health and a U.S. citizen. Applicant must also have freedom to pursue full-time employment, have qualities of leadership and be able to attend classes full- or part-time at an accredited school of nursing.

FINANCIAL DATA:
Amount of support per award: Up to $3,000.

NO. MOST RECENT APPLICANTS: 43.

APPLICATION INFO:
Application forms may be obtained from the address above.

Duration: One school year.

Deadline: May 15. Announcement July 1.

PUBLICATIONS:
Brochure.

ADDRESS INQUIRIES TO:
Eight and Forty Scholarships
(See address above.)

AMERICAN NURSES FOUNDATION [2408]

8515 Georgia Avenue
Suite 400
Silver Spring, MD 20910
(301) 628-5227
Fax: (301) 628-5354
E-mail: anf@ana.org
gisele.marshall@ana.org
Web Site: www.givetonursing.org

FOUNDED: 1955

AREAS OF INTEREST:
Nursing research.

NAME(S) OF PROGRAMS:

- **Nursing Research Grants**

TYPE:
Research grants.

YEAR PROGRAM STARTED: 1955

PURPOSE:
To support research conducted by nurse investigators.

LEGAL BASIS:
Not-for-profit corporation under Section 501(c)(3) of the Internal Revenue Code.

ELIGIBILITY:
Applicant must be an R.N. with a minimum of a Baccalaureate degree in nursing.

FINANCIAL DATA:
Total funding is dependent, in part, on the participation of external sponsors.

Amount of support per award: Varies.

Total amount of support: Varies.

NO. MOST RECENT APPLICANTS: Varies.

NO. AWARDS: Varies.

APPLICATION INFO:
The application packet is available online beginning February 1.

Duration: One year.

Deadline: May 1. Award announcement: August 31.

PUBLICATIONS:
Annual report; newsletter; research publications.

ADDRESS INQUIRIES TO:
Gisele Marshall, Executive Assistant
(See address above.)

*PLEASE NOTE:
Some of the grants are restricted to a particular field of study.

ASSOCIATION OF WOMEN'S HEALTH, OBSTETRIC AND NEONATAL NURSES (AWHONN) [2409]

2000 L Street, N.W.
Suite 740
Washington, DC 20036
(202) 261-2400
Fax: (202) 728-0575
E-mail: researchprograms@awhonn.org
Web Site: www.awhonn.org

FOUNDED: 1969

AREAS OF INTEREST:
Women's health, obstetrics, neonatal nursing, newborns, nursing profession, advocacy, research and clinical resources for nurses.

NAME(S) OF PROGRAMS:
- **AWHONN Research Grants Program**

TYPE:
Research grants.

YEAR PROGRAM STARTED: 1993

PURPOSE:
To promote the advancement of nursing research among members.

ELIGIBILITY:
Applicant must be current member at the time of application and at time of selection and funding. Researchers who are currently principal investigators on a federally funded grant, or who have received an AWHONN-funded research grant within the past five years are ineligible to apply.

GEOG. RESTRICTIONS: United States.

FINANCIAL DATA:
Amount of support per award: $5,000 to $10,000.

NO. MOST RECENT APPLICANTS: 8 for the year 2015.

NO. AWARDS: 4 for the year 2015.

APPLICATION INFO:
Application information is available on the web site.

Duration: One year.

Deadline: December 1.

PUBLICATIONS:
Journal of Obstetric, Gynecologic and Neonatal Nursing; *Nursing for Women's Health.*

ADDRESS INQUIRIES TO:
Research Programs
(See e-mail address above.)

THE CANADIAN LUNG ASSOCIATION (CLA) [2410]

1750 Courtwood Crescent
Suite 300
Ottawa ON K2C 2B5 Canada
(613) 569-6411
(888) 566-5864 (within Canada)
Fax: (613) 569-8860
E-mail: research@lung.ca
Web Site: www.lung.ca

FOUNDED: 1977

AREAS OF INTEREST:
Respiratory health.

NAME(S) OF PROGRAMS:
- **The Canadian Respiratory Health Professionals Fellowships and Grants**

TYPE:
Fellowships; Research grants. Fellowships are offered to registered nurses pursuing postgraduate education with a major component of the program involving respiratory nursing practice, physiotherapists pursuing postgraduate training with respiratory research as the major component, and respiratory therapists pursuing postgraduate education with a major component of the program involving respiratory therapy practice.

Grants for research and feasibility studies are offered to registered nurses undertaking research investigations related to nursing management of patients with respiratory disease and symptoms. Grants are also offered to physiotherapists undertaking investigations related to management of patients with respiratory disease. Respiratory therapists undertaking research investigations related to the management of patients with respiratory disease and symptoms may also qualify.

PURPOSE:
To build research capacity in respiratory health; to support research excellence; to assist future researchers in their professional development in congruence with the mission of the Association; to increase the number of nurses with expertise in the clinical practice of respiratory nursing and as leaders in advancing knowledge, which will result in improved quality of care in respiratory nursing.

LEGAL BASIS:
Not-for-profit, incorporated.

ELIGIBILITY:
For Fellowships, an applicant must be a Canadian citizen or a permanent Canadian resident, a Registered Nurse, Registered Physiotherapist or Registered Respiratory Therapist, be enrolled or accepted for full-time studies in a graduate program at the Master's or Doctorate level and be a member of CRHP.

For Research Grants, the principal investigator must be a Canadian citizen or a permanent Canadian resident, a Registered Nurse, a Registered Physiotherapist or Registered Respiratory Therapist, hold an appointment in, or have an affiliation with, a health care agency, education institution, or other organization in Canada that can administer the funds in an approved manner and be a member of CRHP.

FINANCIAL DATA:
Amount of support per award: Varies.

Total amount of support: Varies.

NO. MOST RECENT APPLICANTS: Approximately 12.

NO. AWARDS: Approximately 8 each year.

APPLICATION INFO:
Application information is available on the web site.

Duration: One year.

Deadline: Contact the Foundation for exact dates.

PUBLICATIONS:
Brochure; newsletters.

OFFICERS:
Dr. Dina Brooks, Chairperson, CRHP Leadership Council
Mika Nonoyama, CRHP Research Committee Co-chair

ADDRESS INQUIRIES TO:
The Canadian Respiratory Health Professionals
c/o Michelle McEvoy
The Canadian Lung Association
(See address above.)

FOUNDATION FOR NEONATAL RESEARCH AND EDUCATION (FNRE) [2411]

200 East Holly Avenue
Sewell, NJ 08080
(856) 256-2343
Fax: (856) 589-7463
E-mail: contact@fnre.com
Web Site: ajj.com/fnre

FOUNDED: 1992

AREAS OF INTEREST:
Neonatal nursing.

TYPE:
Research grants; Scholarships.

YEAR PROGRAM STARTED: 1992

PURPOSE:
To support research and education in neonatal nursing; to promote the development of expertise in the neonatal profession; to raise awareness of the general public as consumers of neonatal services.

LEGAL BASIS:
Nonprofit.

ELIGIBILITY:
Members of the FNRE Research Review Committee and the FNRE Board members are not eligible to apply.

All grant applicants must be professionally active neonatal nurses. Applicant must be principal investigator of the project. If the principal investigator has limited research experience, it is expected that the application will reflect appropriate nursing research consultation.

Scholarship applicants must:
(1) be officially admitted to a college or school of higher education for Bachelor of Science in Nursing, Master in Science in Nursing for Advance Practice in Neonatal Nursing, Doctoral degree in Nursing, or Master's or Post-Master degree in Nursing

Administration or Business Management;
(2) have a 3.0 grade point average or higher;
(3) be a professionally active neonatal nurse and;
(4) not have received a FNRE scholarship or grant in the past five years.

GEOG. RESTRICTIONS: United States.

FINANCIAL DATA:
Amount of support per award: Grants: Up to $5,000 per project.

Total amount of support: Varies.

NO. AWARDS: 1 to 2.

APPLICATION INFO:
Grant applicants must submit:
(1) a research plan addressing the problem or significance of the project, literature review (five-page maximum), methodology, data collection instruments, data analysis and completion schedule;
(2) Institutional Review Board approval;
(3) documentation verifying that research procedures meet federal guidelines for animal protection if animals are to be used;
(4) detailed budget;
(5) one-page curriculum vitae of each principal investigator, co-investigator and support person;
(6) a conflict of interest disclosure and;
(7) the signature of their major advisor or dissertation/thesis/project committee chairperson.

Duration: One year. Extensions requested in writing may be granted.

Deadline: May 1. Award notifications will be mailed by September.

FOUNDATION OF THE NATIONAL STUDENT NURSES' ASSOCIATION, INC. [2412]

45 Main Street
Suite 606
Brooklyn, NY 11201-1075
(718) 210-0705
Fax: (718) 797-1186
E-mail: lauren@nsna.org
nsna@nsna.org
Web Site: www.nsna.org

FOUNDED: 1969

AREAS OF INTEREST:
Nursing education.

TYPE:
Scholarships. Scholarships are based on academic achievement, financial need and involvement in nursing student organizations and community activities related to health care. Additional criteria may be required by some sponsors.

PURPOSE:
To provide aid to nursing students.

LEGAL BASIS:
501(c)(3) charitable foundation.

ELIGIBILITY:
Applicants must be U.S. citizens or students with an Alien Registration number. They must also be currently enrolled in state-approved schools of nursing or pre-nursing in Associate degree, Baccalaureate, diploma, generic Doctorate, generic Master's and 16- to 18-month accelerated programs. Funds are not available for graduate study unless it is for a first degree in nursing. Graduating high school seniors are not eligible. Monies are awarded in the spring to be used in the next academic year and summer school. Monies can only be used for nursing or pre-nursing in one of the above-mentioned programs. No monies can be used for graduate education unless leading to a first degree in nursing. If applicant is matriculating into a nursing program, letter of acceptance must accompany this application. Proof of enrollment will be required at time of award. Current Association Board of Directors and Association Nominating and Elections Committee members are not eligible.

FINANCIAL DATA:
Amount of support per award: Scholarships: $1,000 to $7,500.

Total amount of support: Over $300,000 annually in the general scholarship program.

NO. MOST RECENT APPLICANTS: 648.

NO. AWARDS: 115.

APPLICATION INFO:
Applications can be completed online at the NSNA web site from August until the following January. Each completed application, when filed, must be accompanied by a $10 processing fee.

Applicants must submit a copy of their recent nursing school and college transcripts, or grade report. NSNA members must submit proof of their membership. Registered nurses in Baccalaureate programs and licensed practical/vocational nurses in programs leading to registered nurse licensure must submit a copy of their license to be considered for the Career Mobility Scholarships.

Duration: One year. Scholarships are awarded in the spring for use in the upcoming academic year.

Deadline: January.

ADDRESS INQUIRIES TO:
Lauren Sperle
Scholarship Program Committee
(See address above.)

*PLEASE NOTE:
The scholarships are based on academic achievement, financial need, and involvement in nursing student organizations and community activities related to health care. Additional criteria may be required by some sponsors.

INDEPENDENCE FOUNDATION

Offices at the Bellevue
200 South Broad Street, Suite 1101
Philadelphia, PA 19102
(215) 985-4009
Fax: (215) 985-3989
E-mail: ssherman@independencefoundation.org
Web Site: www.independencefoundation.org

TYPE:
Challenge/matching grants; Fellowships; General operating grants; Project/program grants.

See entry 165 for full listing.

MYASTHENIA GRAVIS FOUNDATION OF AMERICA, INC.

355 Lexington Avenue
15th Floor
New York, NY 10017
(800) 541-5454
Fax: (212) 297-2159
E-mail: mgfa@myasthenia.org
Web Site: www.myasthenia.org

TYPE:
Fellowships; Research grants. Awards for research pertaining to problems faced by myasthenia gravis patients.

See entry 2395 for full listing.

NATIONAL BLACK NURSES ASSOCIATION, INC. [2413]

8630 Fenton Street
Suite 330
Silver Spring, MD 20910
(301) 589-3200
Fax: (301) 589-3223
E-mail: info@nbna.org
Web Site: www.nbna.org

AREAS OF INTEREST:
HIV/AIDS, cardiovascular disease, women and children's health, cancer, substance abuse, diabetes, obesity, and violence in African American communities.

NAME(S) OF PROGRAMS:
- **Esther Colliflower/VITAS Scholarship**
- **Dr. Martha A. Dawson Genesis Nurse Leader Scholarship**
- **Maria Dudley Scholarship**
- **Martha R. Dudley Scholarship**
- **Sheila Haley Scholarship**
- **Rita E. Miller Scholarship**
- **NBNA Board of Directors Scholarship**
- **Margaret Pemberton Scholarship**
- **Della H. Raney Nursing Scholarship**
- **Dr. Lauranne Sams Scholarship**
- **United Health Foundation Scholarship**

TYPE:
Scholarships.

PURPOSE:
To advance nursing practice, improve health care for all Americans, particularly the unserved and the underserved, and shape health policy for the access and delivery of health care services.

LEGAL BASIS:
Nonprofit professional association.

ELIGIBILITY:
Awards are given primarily to African Americans enrolled at any level in a nursing program (AD, BSN or LPN/LVN). Applicant must be in good standing at the time of application and be a member of NBNA.

GEOG. RESTRICTIONS: United States.

FINANCIAL DATA:
Amount of support per award: $1,000 to $6,000.

NO. MOST RECENT APPLICANTS: 60.

NO. AWARDS: 39.

APPLICATION INFO:
Applicant must submit completed scholarship application form. The following items (not to exceed 10 pages) must be included:
(1) two letters of recommendation; letters from the school of nursing and a nurse in the area will suffice for candidates who have no local chapter in the area;
(2) head shot photo; if not included, application will be deemed not ready;
(3) official transcript from school;
(4) one-page biographical sketch and;
(5) two-page statement on why applicant wants to become a nurse.

Duration: One year. Nonrenewable.

Deadline: April 15. Awards are presented at the July/August conference.

BOARD OF DIRECTORS:
Dr. Eric Williams, President

ADDRESS INQUIRIES TO:
E-mail: millicent@nbna.org or
Scholarships Committee
(See address above.)

NATIONAL INSTITUTE OF NURSING RESEARCH [2414]

31 Center Drive, Room 5B-03
Bethesda, MD 20892-2178
(301) 496-0207
Fax: (301) 480-4969
E-mail: info@ninr.nih.gov
Web Site: www.ninr.nih.gov

FOUNDED: 1986

AREAS OF INTEREST:
Health of individuals, families, communities and populations.

CONSULTING OR VOLUNTEER SERVICES:
For potential principal investigators.

NAME(S) OF PROGRAMS:
- **Career Development Grants**
- **Research Grants**
- **Research Training Grants**
- **Small Business Innovation Research Grants**

TYPE:
Fellowships; Project/program grants; Research grants; Training grants. Funds may be used for salaries, consultation, equipment, travel and other usual costs, subject to federal regulations applicable to the grant. Fellowships are for postdoctoral research training; predoctoral support is also available.

YEAR PROGRAM STARTED: 1986

PURPOSE:
To support nursing research, research training at pre- and postdoctoral levels, and research related to patient care, the promotion of health, the prevention of disease and the mitigation of the effects of acute and chronic illnesses and disabilities.

LEGAL BASIS:
Public Health Service Act, Sections 301, 483, 484, and 487, as amended by Public Law 99-158.

ELIGIBILITY:
Applicant may be a for-profit organization, a nonprofit organization, a public or private institution such as a university, college, hospital and laboratory, a unit of state government, a unit of local government, an eligible agency of the federal government, a foreign institution, a domestic institution, a faith-based or community-based organization, an Indian/Native American tribal government (federally recognized), an Indian/Native American tribal government (other than federally recognized), or an Indian/Native American tribally designated organization.

FINANCIAL DATA:
Amount of support per award: Varies based on type of grant and duration.

Total amount of support: Varies.

CO-OP FUNDING PROGRAMS: Co-funding of research project grants with other NIH Institutes and Centers.

APPLICATION INFO:
With few exceptions, all types of grant applications are electronic. When determining which form to submit, applicants are encouraged to read the funding opportunity announcement.

Duration: Varies.

Deadline: Applications are accepted at any time for inclusion in one of the three annual review cycles (depending on the activity code).

PUBLICATIONS:
Investigators' publications.

STAFF:
Brian Albertini, Grants Manager

ADDRESS INQUIRIES TO:
Melissa Barrett, Chief, Office of Communications and Public Liaison
(See address above.)

NATIONAL SOCIETY DAUGHTERS OF THE AMERICAN REVOLUTION [2415]

1776 D Street, N.W.
Washington, DC 20006-5303
(202) 879-3263
Fax: (202) 879-3348
E-mail: scholarships@dar.org
Web Site: www.dar.org

FOUNDED: 1895

AREAS OF INTEREST:
Nursing.

NAME(S) OF PROGRAMS:
- **Madeline Pickett Cogswell Nursing Scholarship**
- **DAR American Revolution Nursing Scholarship**
- **Caroline E. Holt Nursing Scholarship**

TYPE:
Scholarships. Awarded to students who are enrolled or currently attending an accredited school of nursing.

PURPOSE:
To provide ways and means to help students to attain higher education; to perpetuate the memory and spirit of men and women who achieved American Independence by acquisition and protection of historical spots and erection of monuments; to carry out injunction of Washington in his farewell address to the American people; to maintain institutions of American Freedom; to aid liberty.

LEGAL BASIS:
Incorporated historical society.

ELIGIBILITY:
Scholarships are awarded without regard to race, religion, sex or national origin. Candidates must be U.S. citizens and must attend an accredited college or university in the U.S. Awards are judged on the basis of academic excellence, commitment to field of study, as required, and financial need.

Applicants for the Cogswell Nursing Scholarship must be members, descendants of members or eligible for membership in NSDAR. DAR member number must be on the application.

The DAR Nursing Scholarship is intended for minority students in need who are enrolled in or attending the University of the District of Columbia.

No affiliation or relationship to DAR is required for qualification for the Holt Nursing Scholarship, but candidate must be sponsored by a local DAR Chapter.

GEOG. RESTRICTIONS: United States.

FINANCIAL DATA:
Amount of support per award: $1,000.

Total amount of support: Cogswell and Holt Nursing Scholarships: Varies; DAR Nursing Scholarship: $2,500.

NO. AWARDS: Varies.

APPLICATION INFO:
Application information is available online. The application package must be completed. All transcripts, letters of recommendation and other required documents must be in a single package.

Included with the application packet is the list of DAR State Scholarship Chairmen. All scholarship applicants are required to have a letter of sponsorship from a chapter. Individuals interested in obtaining a letter of sponsorship from a local chapter are encouraged to contact the DAR State Chairman.

Duration: One academic year. Nonrenewable.

Deadline: February 15.

PUBLICATIONS:
American Spirit, magazine.

ADDRESS INQUIRIES TO:
Office of the Reporter General
DAR Scholarship Committee
(See address above.)

*PLEASE NOTE:
Awards are placed on deposit with the college or university. Any unused portion shall be returned to the National Society.

NATIONAL SOCIETY DAUGHTERS OF THE AMERICAN REVOLUTION

1776 D Street, N.W.
Washington, DC 20006-5303
(202) 879-3263
Fax: (202) 879-3348
E-mail: scholarships@dar.org
Web Site: www.dar.org

TYPE:
Scholarships.

See entry 2223 for full listing.

NURSES' EDUCATIONAL FUNDS, INC. [2416]

137 Montague Street, Suite 144
Brooklyn, NY 11201
(917) 524-8051
E-mail: info@n-e-f.org
Web Site: www.n-e-f.org

FOUNDED: 1912

AREAS OF INTEREST:
Graduate nursing studies.

TYPE:
Scholarships. Scholarships for registered nurses seeking Master's and Doctorate degrees in nursing.

YEAR PROGRAM STARTED: 1912

PURPOSE:
To increase the supply of nurses qualified for administrative, supervisory, teaching or research positions and clinical specialization in nursing.

LEGAL BASIS:
Private foundation.

ELIGIBILITY:
Registered nurses who are U.S. citizens, or who have officially declared intention of becoming citizens, are eligible to apply if they have been accepted into a Master's

program, or applying to a Master's program of nursing education accredited by NLNAC or CCNE, or enrolled full-time or part-time in a doctoral program in a field related to nursing. Applicants must be able to present proof of membership in a professional nursing association.

GEOG. RESTRICTIONS: United States.

FINANCIAL DATA:

Amount of support per award: Scholarships vary in amount, according to the funds available.

Total amount of support: Varies.

NO. MOST RECENT APPLICANTS: 250.

NO. AWARDS: 22 to 25 annually.

APPLICATION INFO:

Official application materials can be downloaded from the web site.

Duration: One academic year. Can reapply for one additional year provided two semesters remain before graduation.

Deadline: February 1.

BOARD OF DIRECTORS:

Susan Bowar-Ferres, Ph.D., R.N., President
Cynthia Sculco, R.N., Ed.D, Vice President
Joan Arnold, Ph.D., R.N., Treasurer
Rosanne Raso, M.S., R.N., Secretary
Allison Adams, B.A., B.S.
Karen Ballard, M.A., R.N.
Vincent Batyr, C.P.A.
Kathleen Dirschel, Ph.D., R.N.
Aida Egues, D.N.P., R.N.
M. Louise Fitzpatrick, Ed.D., R.N.
Joan Marren, M.Ed., R.N.
Margaret McClure, Ed.D., R.N.
Thelma Schorr, B.S.N., R.N.
Roy L. Simpson
Henry Spencer
Gerhard Stubi
Madeleine S. Sugimoto, M.Ed., R.N.
Judith Ann Vessey, Ph.D., R.N.

ADDRESS INQUIRIES TO:

Jerelyn Weiss, Executive Director
(See e-mail address above.)

REHABILITATION NURSING FOUNDATION (RNF) [2417]

8735 West Higgins Road
Suite 300
Chicago, IL 60631
(800) 229-7530
Fax: (847) 375-6435
E-mail: info@rehabnurse.org
Web Site: www.rehabnurse.org

FOUNDED: 1976

AREAS OF INTEREST:

Rehabilitation nursing.

NAME(S) OF PROGRAMS:

- **RNF Grant**

TYPE:

Project/program grants; Research grants.

YEAR PROGRAM STARTED: 1988

PURPOSE:

To promote and advance professional rehabilitation nursing practice through education, advocacy, collaboration, and research to enhance the quality of life for those affected by disability and chronic illness.

ELIGIBILITY:

The principal investigator for the research project must be a registered nurse who is active in rehabilitation or who demonstrates interest in and significant contributions to rehabilitation nursing. Graduate student researchers may be eligible for funding.

FINANCIAL DATA:

Amount of support per award: Up to $30,000.

NO. MOST RECENT APPLICANTS: 8.

NO. AWARDS: 1.

APPLICATION INFO:

Proposals must be typed and electronically submitted to the e-mail address above. All applicants must:
(1) complete a Summary Data Form;
(2) submit a typed, 250- to 350-word abstract;
(3) have the institution or agency named in the proposal complete the Administrative Approval Form to indicate acknowledgment and approval and;
(4) complete the Grant Contact Form regarding the contact person for the grant funding agreement and disbursement of funds should application be selected.

All forms and instructions can be downloaded from the web site.

Deadline: March 1.

ADDRESS INQUIRIES TO:

Mary Beth Benner, Director of Operations
(See e-mail address above.)

SIGMA THETA TAU INTERNATIONAL [2418]

Honor Society of Nursing
550 West North Street
Indianapolis, IN 46202
(317) 634-8171 (Local)
(888) 634-7575 (U.S./Canada)
Fax: (317) 634-8188
E-mail: research@stti.org
Web Site: www.nursingsociety.org

FOUNDED: 1922

AREAS OF INTEREST:

Nursing.

NAME(S) OF PROGRAMS:

- **Rosemary Berkel Crisp Research Award**
- **Doris Bloch Research Award**
- **Virginia Henderson Clinical Research Grant**
- **Small Grants**
- **Joan K. Stout, R.N., Research Grant**

TYPE:

Research grants.

YEAR PROGRAM STARTED: 1936

PURPOSE:

To encourage qualified nurses to contribute to the advancement of nursing through research.

LEGAL BASIS:

Incorporated.

ELIGIBILITY:

Applicants must meet the following requirements:
(1) be a registered nurse with a current license;
(2) hold a Master's or doctoral degree or be enrolled in a doctoral program;
(3) be ready to implement research project when funding is received and;
(4) complete the project within one year of funding.

For the Rosemary Berkel Crisp Research Award, applicant must be a member of Sigma Theta Tau International. Some preference will be given to applicants residing in Arkansas, Illinois, Kentucky, Missouri and Tennessee.

For the Virginia Henderson Clinical Research Grant, applicant must be a member of Sigma Theta Tau International and be actively involved in some aspect of health care delivery, education or research in a clinical setting.

FINANCIAL DATA:

Amount of support per award: $5,000 maximum.

Total amount of support: Varies.

NO. AWARDS: 10 to 15 Small Grants; 1 each for the others.

APPLICATION INFO:

Application information is available on the web site.

Duration: For approved research time.

Deadline: Joan K. Stout, R.N., Research Grant: July 1. All others: December 1.

PUBLICATIONS:

Guidelines; applications.

ADDRESS INQUIRIES TO:

Grants Coordinator
(See address above.)

U.S. DEPARTMENT OF HEALTH AND HUMAN SERVICES [2419]

HRSA/BHW, Division of Nursing and Public Health
Parklawn Building, Room 9-89
5600 Fishers Lane
Rockville, MD 20857
(301) 443-5688
Fax: (301) 443-0791
E-mail: jbrown@hrsa.gov
Web Site: www.bhpr.hrsa.gov/nursing

AREAS OF INTEREST:

Nursing education and practice.

TYPE:

Project/program grants; Training grants.

YEAR PROGRAM STARTED: 1965

PURPOSE:

To improve nursing practice and education through projects that increase the knowledge and skills of nursing personnel, enhance their effectiveness in primary care delivery, increase the number of qualified professional nurses and increase nursing workforce diversity.

LEGAL BASIS:

Amendment to Public Health Service Act, Title VIII, Section 820 by "The Health Professions Education Partnership Act of 1998" Public Law 105-392, Subtitle B.

ELIGIBILITY:

Eligible entities are schools of nursing, nursing centers, academic health centers, state or local governments, and other public or private nonprofit entities appropriate by the Secretary that submit an application in accordance with Section 802.

GEOG. RESTRICTIONS: United States.

FINANCIAL DATA:

Amount of support per award: Grants vary in amount, depending on the needs and nature of the project.

Total amount of support: Varies.

APPLICATION INFO:

Contact the U.S. Department of Health and Human Services.

Duration: Varies according to project.

ADDRESS INQUIRIES TO:
Division of Nursing and Public Health, BHW/HRSA
Nursing Education Practice Quality and Retention Branch
(See address above.)

VIRGINIA DEPARTMENT OF HEALTH [2420]

Office of Minority Health and Health Equity
109 Governor Street, Seventh Floor
Suite 714 West
Richmond, VA 23219
(804) 864-7422
Fax: (804) 864-7440
E-mail: incentiveprograms@vdh.virginia.gov
Web Site: www.vdh.virginia.gov/healthpolicy

NAME(S) OF PROGRAMS:
- **Commonwealth of Virginia Nurse Educator Scholarship Program**
- **Mary Marshall Nursing Scholarship/Practical Nurse Program**
- **Mary Marshall Nursing Scholarship/Registered Nurse Program**
- **Nurse Practitioner/Nurse Midwife Scholarship Program**

TYPE:
Awards/prizes; Challenge/matching grants; Scholarships; Technical assistance; Loan forgiveness programs. Awarded to eligible students enrolled in undergraduate or graduate nursing programs at schools of nursing approved by the Virginia State Board of Nursing to assist with their professional education.

Undergraduate nursing programs are defined as those leading to a licensed practical nurse, an Associate degree, diploma, or Baccalaureate degree in nursing.

YEAR PROGRAM STARTED: 1950

PURPOSE:
To provide the citizens of the state with more skilled and greater nursing care coverage.

LEGAL BASIS:
Funding is appropriated by the General Assembly of Virginia under code 23-35.9-23-35.13; code 32.1-122.6-01; and Title 32.1, Chapter 6, 32.1-122.6-02.

ELIGIBILITY:
Criteria vary for the different scholarships. Because of the strict nature of these criteria, it is vital that the applicant contact the Department for full particulars.

GEOG. RESTRICTIONS: Virginia.

FINANCIAL DATA:
Amount of scholarships varies, depending upon amount appropriated by the General Assembly, amount collected by the Board of Nursing and the number of qualified applicants. There are strict conditions attached to these scholarships. (They are not outright gifts; require service in the Commonwealth of Virginia.)

Amount of support per award: Varies each year.

Total amount of support: Varies each year.

NO. AWARDS: Varies each year.

APPLICATION INFO:
Applications are available online. Required data for application include most current transcript of grades (or last school attended if not currently enrolled), verification of need from the Financial Aid Officer and recommendation of the Director of the School of Nursing.

Duration: Each scholarship is awarded for a single year. Upon reapplication, scholarships may be awarded for succeeding years to a maximum of four years.

PUBLICATIONS:
Guidelines.

OFFICER:
Olivette Burroughs, Health Workforce Specialist

ADDRESS INQUIRIES TO:
Nursing Scholarships
(See address above.)

Obstetrics and gynecology

CENTRAL ASSOCIATION OF OBSTETRICIANS AND GYNECOLOGISTS [2421]

15 North Main
Minot, ND 58703
(701) 838-8323
Fax: (701) 852-8733
E-mail: rhickel@caog.org
Web Site: www.caog.org

FOUNDED: 1929

AREAS OF INTEREST:
Obstetrics and gynecology, including investigative and/or clinical work.

NAME(S) OF PROGRAMS:
- **Annual Central Prize Award**
- **Central Poster Award**
- **Community Hospital Award**
- **FAR Research Network Award**
- **President's Certificate of Merit Award**
- **Young Investigator's Award**

TYPE:
Awards/prizes. The Annual Central Prize Award, President's Certificate of Merit Award and Central Poster Awards are presented annually for manuscripts demonstrating outstanding investigative or clinical work in the field of obstetrics and gynecology.

The Community Hospital Award is presented annually for clinical study or research in the field of obstetrics and gynecology to members located in community hospitals who are not full-time faculty in medical schools. Preference for this award will be given to papers concerning gynecologic endoscopy or any other diagnostic or therapeutic procedures which enhance the quality of care of gynecologic or obstetric patients.

The Young Investigator's Award is presented annually for clinical study or research in the field of obstetrics and gynecology to residents, fellows, and clinicians residing in the geographic confines of the Central Association.

YEAR PROGRAM STARTED: 1929

PURPOSE:
To encourage original work in obstetrics and gynecology.

LEGAL BASIS:
Nonprofit medical organization.

ELIGIBILITY:
Those eligible to compete are accredited physicians, teachers, research workers and medical students whose work was done within the geographic area of the Association.

For the Community Hospital Award, at least one author must be a member of the Central Association. Manuscripts must be written expressly for this competition and they must be original, not having been previously presented or published. Manuscripts will be considered for both the general program and the award unless the author specifically requests otherwise in writing.

GEOG. RESTRICTIONS: Alabama, Arizona, Arkansas, Colorado, Idaho, Illinois, Indiana, Iowa, Kansas, Kentucky, Louisiana, Michigan, Minnesota, Mississippi, Missouri, Montana, Nebraska, Nevada, New Mexico, North Dakota, Ohio, Oklahoma, South Dakota, Tennessee, Texas, Utah, West Virginia, Wisconsin and Wyoming.

FINANCIAL DATA:
Amount of support per award: Annual Central Prize Award: $2,000; Central Poster Award: $500 each; Community Hospital Award and FAR Research Network Award: $1,000; President's Certificate of Merit Award: $1,500; Young Investigator's Award: $750.

NO. MOST RECENT APPLICANTS: 50.

NO. AWARDS: Annual Central Prize Award, Community Hospital Award, FAR Research Network Award, President's Certificate of Merit, and Young Investigator's Award: 1 of each annually. Central Poster Award: 2 annually.

APPLICATION INFO:
For consideration for these awards, an online abstract must be submitted. The abstract maximum length is 800 words.

Duration: One year. Nonrenewable.

Deadline: Mid-March each year. Award winners notified early May.

OFFICERS AND TRUSTEES:

ADDRESS INQUIRIES TO:
Rochelle Hickel
(See address above.)

THE LALOR FOUNDATION, INC. [2422]

c/o GMA Foundations
77 Summer Street, Eighth Floor
Boston, MA 02110
(617) 426-7080
Fax: (617) 426-7087
E-mail: fellowshipmanager@gmafoundations.com
Web Site: www.lalorfound.org

FOUNDED: 1935

AREAS OF INTEREST:
Sexual and reproductive health, contraception and pregnancy termination.

NAME(S) OF PROGRAMS:
- **The Anna Lalor Burdick Program**

TYPE:
Project/program grants.

PURPOSE:
To empower young women through education about healthy reproduction in order to broaden and enhance their options in life.

LEGAL BASIS:
Tax-exempt philanthropic foundation.

ELIGIBILITY:
Applicants must be tax-exempt under Section 501(c)(3) of the Internal Revenue Code and defined as "not a private foundation" under Section 509(a). Projects may take place outside of the U.S., but organization must be based in the U.S.

Grants are not normally made to individuals, research projects and scholarships, requests for endowment or major capital support, or general operating support for ongoing programs.

FINANCIAL DATA:
Amount of support per award: $10,000 to $35,000.

Total amount of support: $218,113 for fiscal year 2015.

NO. MOST RECENT APPLICANTS: 78 Spring and 65 Fall for fiscal year 2015.

NO. AWARDS: 3 Spring and 7 Fall for fiscal year 2015.

APPLICATION INFO:
Applicant must submit Letter of Intent online. Full application information is available on the web site.

Duration: One year.

Deadline: Letter of Intent: May 1 and November 1. Invitation for full proposals six to eight weeks later.

IRS I.D.: 51-6000153

OFFICERS:
Cynthia B. Patterson, President
Christopher Burdick, Vice President
Lalor Burdick, Secretary and Treasurer

BOARD OF TRUSTEES:
Christopher Burdick
Lalor Burdick
Carol Chandler, Esq.
Marnie Cochran
Cynthia B. Patterson
Sally H. Zeckhauser

ADDRESS INQUIRIES TO:
Fellowship Manager
(See address above.)

REPRODUCTIVE SCIENTIST DEVELOPMENT PROGRAM (RSDP) [2423]

Department of Obstetrics and Gynecology
Washington University, School of Medicine
BJC-IH, 10th Floor, Room 10631
425 South Euclid Avenue, Campus Box 8064
St. Louis, MO 63110
(314) 747-3598
Fax: (314) 747-0264
E-mail: heflina@wudosis.wustl.edu
Web Site: www.rsdp.wustl.edu/

FOUNDED: 1986

AREAS OF INTEREST:
Obstetric-gynecologic academic investigative careers in fundamental biomedical science.

NAME(S) OF PROGRAMS:

- **Reproductive Scientist Development Program**

TYPE:
Research grants. National career development program grant for full-time basic research under the mentorship of internationally recognized senior scientists.

YEAR PROGRAM STARTED: 1988

PURPOSE:
To train obstetrician-gynecologists committed to academic investigative careers in fundamental biomedical science.

ELIGIBILITY:
Candidates must be seeking a career in academic obstetrics and gynecology research and meet the following criteria:
(1) possess M.D. or D.O. degree;
(2) be a U.S. citizen, noncitizen national, verification as a permanent citizen at time of award;
(3) have completed a four-year internship and residency in obstetrics-gynecology approved by the Accreditation Council for Graduate Medical Education or the Royal College of Physicians and Surgeons of Canada and;
(4) submit a research proposal as part of application.

GEOG. RESTRICTIONS: United States.

FINANCIAL DATA:
Amount of support per award: Up to $125,000 for salary plus fringes and up to $25,000 for research support may be provided from NICHD funds for Phase I scholars.

Up to $100,000 for salary plus fringes and up to $25,000 for research support may be provided from NICHD funds for Phase II scholars. Phase II Scholars are also eligible to receive support from program sponsors of the RSDP Program. Award amounts vary.

NO. AWARDS: Up to 3 new positions are available each year.

APPLICATION INFO:
Applicant must submit a Letter of Intent to the RSDP office indicating the name of the Department of Ob/Gyn sponsor, name and address of proposal scientific mentor, and a brief description of the research project. This will be reviewed by the Executive Committee for appropriateness, and feedback will be provided to potential applicants.

Duration: Two to five years of support is available.

Deadline: Letter of Intent: August 15. Application: October 1.

ADDRESS INQUIRIES TO:
Amanda Heflin, MBA
Project Administrator
(See address above.)

U.S. DEPARTMENT OF HEALTH AND HUMAN SERVICES [2424]

Maternal and Child Health Bureau
Parklawn Building, Room 5C 26
5600 Fishers Lane
Rockville, MD 20857
(301) 443-2204
Fax: (301) 443-9354
E-mail: CallCenter@hrsa.gov (grants information)
Web Site: www.mchb.hrsa.gov
www.hrsa.gov

FOUNDED: 1936

AREAS OF INTEREST:
Health of mothers and children.

NAME(S) OF PROGRAMS:

- **Maternal and Child Health Services Block Grant**

TYPE:
Block grants. The Title V Block Grant Program has as a general purpose the improvement of the health of all mothers and children in the nation. The Block Grant Program has three components: Formula Block Grants to 59 states and other political jurisdictions, Special Projects of Regional and National Significance (SPRANS), and Community Integrated Service Systems (CISS) Grants.

PURPOSE:
To improve the health of all mothers and children; to create federal-state partnerships to develop service systems in U.S. communities that can meet the critical challenges facing maternal and child health.

LEGAL BASIS:
Title V, Section 501, of the Social Security Act, as amended by Public Law 101-239.

ELIGIBILITY:
State health agencies.

GEOG. RESTRICTIONS: United States and its territories.

FINANCIAL DATA:
Amount of support per award: Grants vary in amount, depending upon the number of children at the poverty level in the state.

Total amount of support: Varies.

Matching fund requirements: The Title V Block Grant Program requires that every four dollars of federal Title V money must be matched by at least three dollars of state and local money.

CO-OP FUNDING PROGRAMS: NICHD, CDC, Department of Education, ADAMHA and other inter-agency agreements.

NO. AWARDS: 59.

APPLICATION INFO:
Instructions available at grants.gov.

Duration: One to two years. Must reapply annually.

Deadline: July 15.

ADDRESS INQUIRIES TO:
Maternal and Child Health Bureau
(See address above.)

Ophthalmology and otolaryngology

THE ALCON FOUNDATION, INC. [2425]

6201 South Freeway
Fort Worth, TX 76134-2099
(817) 293-0450
E-mail: alcon.foundation@alcon.com
Web Site: www.alcon.com

AREAS OF INTEREST:
Ophthalmology and vision care.

TYPE:
Project/program grants.

YEAR PROGRAM STARTED: 1962

PURPOSE:
To support programs designed to improve the quality of eye care and patient access to eye care, advance eye health education, research

and awareness, and enhance and create sound communities where Alcon has a facility presence.

LEGAL BASIS:
Corporate foundation.

ELIGIBILITY:
Eligible organizations must be 501(c)(3) nonprofit entities. Grants are awarded for community activities of interest to Alcon employees in communities where Alcon has a facility. Generally, grants awarded outside of Alcon communities are for organizations with a national/international focus on eye care.

APPLICATION INFO:
Only online application will be accepted.

Duration: One year.

Deadline: July 31 for requests larger than $10,000.

ADDRESS INQUIRIES TO:
Bettina Maunz, Vice President
Global Head Communications
(See address above.)

AMERICAN ACADEMY OF OPTOMETRY [2426]

2909 Fairgreen Street
Orlando, FL 32803
(321) 710-3937
Fax: (407) 893-9890
E-mail: helenv@aaoptom.org
Web Site: www.aaopt.org

FOUNDED: 1922

AREAS OF INTEREST:
Vision science and vision care.

NAME(S) OF PROGRAMS:

- **Julius F. Neumueller Award in Optics**

TYPE:
Awards/prizes.

YEAR PROGRAM STARTED: 1969

PURPOSE:
To advance optometric education in optics.

LEGAL BASIS:
Tax-exempt corporation.

ELIGIBILITY:
Applicant must be a student pursuing an O.D. degree in a school of optometry recognized by the AOA Council on Optometric Education.

GEOG. RESTRICTIONS: Primarily United States and Canada.

FINANCIAL DATA:
Amount of support per award: Approximately $750.

Total amount of support: Approximately $750 annually.

NO. MOST RECENT APPLICANTS: 10.

NO. AWARDS: 1.

APPLICATION INFO:
Applicant must submit a paper, not to exceed 3,000 words, on Geometrical Optics, Physical Optics, Ophthalmic Optics or Optics of the Eye. Each school may submit two papers each year to the Chairman of the Awards Committee, which are judged by selected members of the American Academy of Optometry.

Duration: One-time award.

Deadline: April 2. Award announcement July 1.

ADDRESS INQUIRIES TO:
Helen Viksnins
Senior Director of Programs
(See address above.)

AMERICAN DIABETES ASSOCIATION

1701 North Beauregard Street
Alexandria, VA 22311
(703) 549-1500 ext. 5532
Fax: (703) 621-3759
E-mail: grantquestions@diabetes.org
Web Site: www.professional.diabetes.org/grants

TYPE:
Fellowships; Research grants; Training grants.

See entry 2323 for full listing.

AMERICAN OPTOMETRIC FOUNDATION [2427]

2909 Fairgreen Street
Orlando, FL 32803
(321) 710-3936
Fax: (407) 893-9890
E-mail: aof@aaoptom.org
Web Site: www.aaopt.org/aof/programs

FOUNDED: 1947

AREAS OF INTEREST:
Optometric research and education.

NAME(S) OF PROGRAMS:

- **Award of Excellence**
- **J. Pat Cummings Scholarships**
- **William C. Ezell Fellowship**
- **Residency Awards**
- **VSP/AOF Practice Excellence Scholarships**

TYPE:
Awards/prizes; Fellowships; Project/program grants; Research grants; Scholarships. Scholarships for individuals pursuing an O.D. degree and fellowships for graduate students.

YEAR PROGRAM STARTED: 1952

PURPOSE:
To encourage teaching careers in optometry and to further vision research, both basic and clinical.

LEGAL BASIS:
IRS tax status 501(c)(3).

ELIGIBILITY:
Applicants must be postgraduate students (i.e., those who have received the Doctor of Optometry degree) and must be entering or continuing a full-time academic program toward the Master's or Ph.D. degree. They must also be planning on a career in teaching and/or research at an optometric school or college.

GEOG. RESTRICTIONS: Canada, Puerto Rico and United States.

FINANCIAL DATA:
Full fellowships are available in amounts of up to $8,000, plus travel grants to the American Academy of Optometry and ARVO annual meetings.

Amount of support per award: Varies.

Total amount of support: Varies.

NO. MOST RECENT APPLICANTS: Ezell Fellowships: 36; Other awards: Varies.

NO. AWARDS: 125.

APPLICATION INFO:
Prospective applicants may obtain detailed information regarding application procedures from the optometric schools/colleges or the administrative offices of the AOF.

Duration: Fellowships are awarded for a period of one year.

Deadline: Varies.

PUBLICATIONS:
Application guidelines/criteria.

STAFF:
Lois Schoenbrun, C.A.E., FAAO, Executive Director, AAO
Maureen Dimont, Development Director
Jennifer Rubin, Foundation Coordinator

BOARD OF DIRECTORS AND OFFICERS:
David Kirschen, President
Judy Clay, President-Elect
Wendy Harrison, Secretary-Treasurer
Melissa Bailey
Dori Carlson
Kathy Dumbleton
Susan Eger
Pete Kollbaum
Richard Madonna
Jason Nichols
Jeffrey Walline

AMERICAN SPEECH-LANGUAGE-HEARING FOUNDATION [2428]

2200 Research Boulevard
Rockville, MD 20850-3289
(301) 296-8703
Fax: (301) 296-8567
E-mail: foundationprograms@asha.org
Web Site: www.ashfoundation.org

FOUNDED: 1946

AREAS OF INTEREST:
Communication sciences and disorders.

NAME(S) OF PROGRAMS:

- **Clinical Research Grant**
- **Louis M. DiCarlo Award for Recent Clinical Achievement**
- **Graduate Student Scholarship for International/Minority Students**
- **Graduate Student Scholarship for Minority Students**
- **Graduate Student Scholarship for NSSLHA Members**
- **Graduate Student Scholarship for Students with a Disability**
- **Graduate Student Scholarships**
- **Frank R. Kleffner Clinical Career Award**
- **New Century Scholars Doctoral Scholarship**
- **New Century Scholars Research Grant**
- **New Investigators Research Grant**
- **Speech Science Research Grant**
- **Student Research Grant in Audiology**
- **Student Research Grant in Early Childhood Language Development**
- **Rolland J. Van Hattum Award for Contribution in the Schools**

TYPE:
Research grants; Scholarships. Clinical achievement awards. Clinical Research Grants are awarded to researchers to advance knowledge of the efficacy of treatment and assessment practices in communication sciences and disorders.

Louis M. DiCarlo Award for Clinical Achievement recognizes individuals demonstrating outstanding achievement in the advancement of knowledge in clinical practice within the past three years.

Graduate Student Scholarships are available to students demonstrating outstanding academic achievement in communication sciences and disorders. These include general scholarships, scholarships for students with disabilities, scholarships for international and minority students, and scholarships for NSSLHA members.

Frank R. Kleffner Clinical Career Award recognizes outstanding lifetime achievement in clinical science and practice.

New Century Scholars Doctoral Scholarships are available to students enrolled in a research doctoral program (Ph.D. or equivalent) in communication sciences and disorders.

New Century Scholars Research Grants are awarded to individuals committed to teacher-investigator careers in the university or college environment or in external research institutes or laboratories.

New Investigators Research Grants are awarded to new scientists to pursue research in audiology or speech-language pathology.

Speech Science Research Grants are awarded to new investigators to encourage research activities in the area of speech science.

Student Research Grant in Audiology supports a proposed one-year study to conduct research in audiology.

Student Research Grant in Early Childhood Language supports a proposed one-year study to conduct research in early childhood language development.

Rolland J. Van Hattum Award for Contribution in the Schools recognizes professionals demonstrating significant contribution to the delivery of audiology and/or speech pathology services in the schools.

YEAR PROGRAM STARTED: 1979

PURPOSE:
To further education in speech, language and hearing through the provision of financial assistance; to recognize and support research and similar endeavors which contribute to the advancement of knowledge and improvement of practice in serving children and adults with speech, language, or hearing disorders; to identify and facilitate new directions in the field of communication sciences and disorders through support of such vehicles as conferences, publications and other activities.

LEGAL BASIS:
501(c)(3) association.

FINANCIAL DATA:
Amount of support per award: Research Grants: $2,000 to $75,000, depending on grant type; Scholarships: $5,000 to $10,000.

Total amount of support: Varies.

NO. MOST RECENT APPLICANTS: Approximately 300 for all programs.

NO. AWARDS: 70.

APPLICATION INFO:
Guidelines are available from the ASH Foundation web site. Required documentation for scholarships includes application form, academic documentation, faculty recommendation committee report, and student essay. Research grant submissions require a research proposal.

Duration: One year. Nonrenewable.

Deadline: Usually April or May. Awards presented in November.

PUBLICATIONS:
Annual report; program and application guidelines; fact sheet.

IRS I.D.: 52-6055761

ADDRESS INQUIRIES TO:
Program Administrator
(See address above.)

BENIGN ESSENTIAL BLEPHAROSPASM RESEARCH FOUNDATION INC. [2429]

637 North 7th Street
Suite 102
Beaumont, TX 77702
(409) 832-0788
Fax: (409) 832-0890
E-mail: bebrf@blepharospasm.org
Web Site: www.blepharospasm.org

FOUNDED: 1981

AREAS OF INTEREST:
Benign essential blepharospasm, Meige syndrome, hemifacial spasm and related disorders and infirmities of the facial musculature.

TYPE:
Fellowships; Project/program grants; Research grants; Seed money grants. The Foundation offers research fellowships to support the training of exceptionally qualified physicians or scientists who wish to focus on blepharospasm with and without oromandibular dystonia.

YEAR PROGRAM STARTED: 1985

PURPOSE:
To undertake, promote, develop and carry on the search for the cause and cure for benign essential blepharospasm and other related disorders and infirmities of the facial musculature.

LEGAL BASIS:
Foundation.

ELIGIBILITY:
For the Fellowship Program, physician applicants must be board certified or board eligible in neurology or ophthalmology, have completed a residency, and hold or be able to hold an unrestricted license to practice medicine in the U.S. Ph.Ds. should have completed their degree.

Research proposals must relate specifically to benign essential blepharospasm and Meige to include new treatments, pathophysiology and genetics, photophobia and dry eye.

FINANCIAL DATA:
Amount of support per award: Fellowships: Up to $75,000 per year; Grants: $10,000 to $150,000.

Total amount of support: $150,000.

NO. MOST RECENT APPLICANTS: 4 for the year 2013.

NO. AWARDS: 3 for the year 2014.

APPLICATION INFO:
Application information is available on the web site or by sending an e-mail to the address above.

Duration: Fellowships: Two years. Grants: One to two years. Extensions have been granted.

Deadline: August 31.

PUBLICATIONS:
Program announcement; application guidelines; brochure.

IRS I.D.: 74-2193322

BRIGHT FOCUS FOUNDATION

22512 Gateway Center Drive
Clarksburg, MD 20871
(301) 948-3244
Fax: (301) 948-4403
E-mail: researchgrants@brightfocus.org
Web Site: www.brightfocus.org

TYPE:
Research grants.

See entry 1386 for full listing.

BRIGHT FOCUS FOUNDATION [2430]

22512 Gateway Center Drive
Clarksburg, MD 20871
(301) 948-3244
Fax: (301) 948-4403
E-mail: researchgrants@brightfocus.org
Web Site: www.brightfocus.org

FOUNDED: 1978

AREAS OF INTEREST:
Glaucoma research.

NAME(S) OF PROGRAMS:

- **National Glaucoma Research Program**

TYPE:
Research grants. Support for basic research into the causes and potential treatments of glaucoma.

YEAR PROGRAM STARTED: 1978

PURPOSE:
To develop treatments, preventions and cures for glaucoma.

LEGAL BASIS:
Nonprofit foundation.

ELIGIBILITY:
Grants are awarded on the basis of the proposal's scientific merit and its relevance to understanding the disease studied. No funds for large equipment, institutional overhead costs, construction or building expenses.

FINANCIAL DATA:
Amount of support per award: Up to $75,000 per year.

Total amount of support: Varies.

NO. AWARDS: 13 for the year 2015.

APPLICATION INFO:
Application information is available on the web site.

Duration: Up to two years.

PUBLICATIONS:
Annual report; newsletters; clinical brochures.

ADDRESS INQUIRIES TO:
Kara Summers, Program Officer
(See e-mail address above.)

CANADIAN NATIONAL INSTITUTE FOR THE BLIND [2431]

1929 Bayview Avenue
Toronto ON M4G 3E8 Canada
(416) 486-2500 ext. 7622
Fax: (416) 480-7700
E-mail: shampa.bose@cnib.ca
Web Site: www.cnib.ca

FOUNDED: 1918

AREAS OF INTEREST:
Ophthalmic subspecialties, vision research and macular degeneration.

NAME(S) OF PROGRAMS:
- **CNIB Barbara Tuck MacPhee Award in Macular Degeneration**

TYPE:
Research grants. Award supports researchers in the field of macular degeneration.

YEAR PROGRAM STARTED: 1961

PURPOSE:
To conduct research focused on better serving and improving the quality of life for people with vision loss; to fund cutting-edge medical research aimed at improving our understanding of how to prevent, diagnose and treat eye disease.

LEGAL BASIS:
Registered charity.

ELIGIBILITY:
Applicants must be residents of Canada and research must be conducted primarily in Canada.

FINANCIAL DATA:
Amount of support per award: Fellowships: $25,000.

Total amount of support: Varies.

NO. AWARDS: 1 per year.

APPLICATION INFO:
Applications must be submitted online.

Duration: One year.

Deadline: January 15. Grant payments will begin July 1 of the same year.

PUBLICATIONS:
Guidelines.

ADDRESS INQUIRIES TO:
Ms. Shampa Bose, Grants Administrator
(See address above.)

EYE BANK ASSOCIATION OF AMERICA [2432]

1015 18th Street, N.W.
Suite 1010
Washington, DC 20036
(202) 775-4999
Fax: (202) 429-6036
E-mail: info@restoresight.org
Web Site: www.restoresight.org

FOUNDED: 1961

AREAS OF INTEREST:
Restoration of sight through eye banks.

NAME(S) OF PROGRAMS:
- **Richard Lindstrom Research Grant**
- **Networking Grants**

TYPE:
Research grants; Travel grants.

PURPOSE:
To promote scientific research in the fields of eye banking and corneal transplantation; to promote collaboration between eye banks.

ELIGIBILITY:
Lindstrom Grant applicant must be a physician, including corneal surgeon and other eye care specialist, basic scientist, including biomedical and social scientists, or eye-bank technician, nurse, fellow, ophthalmology fellow or medical student that is supervised by a physician.

FINANCIAL DATA:
Amount of support per award: Lindstrom Grant: Generally $3,000 to $5,000; Networking Grants: $1,500.

Total amount of support: Varies.

NO. AWARDS: Lindstrom Grant: 8 for the year 2015; Networking Grants: 2 annually.

APPLICATION INFO:
Application information is available on the EBAA web site.

Duration: Lindstrom Grant: One year.

Deadline: Lindstrom Grant: Early March.

ADDRESS INQUIRIES TO:
Stacey Gardner, Director of Education
(See address above.)

FIGHT FOR SIGHT, INC. [2433]

381 Park Avenue South
Suite 809
New York, NY 10016
(212) 679-6060
Fax: (212) 679-4466
E-mail: janice@fightforsight.org
Web Site: www.fightforsight.org

FOUNDED: 1946

AREAS OF INTEREST:
Ophthalmology and visual sciences.

NAME(S) OF PROGRAMS:
- **Research Awards Program**

TYPE:
Fellowships; Grants-in-aid; Research grants. Fight for Sight primarily supports new investigators, promoting the development of scientific findings and pilot studies necessary to successfully apply for more substantial federal and private funding such as that provided by the National Eye Institute and other divisions of the NIH.

YEAR PROGRAM STARTED: 1946

PURPOSE:
To support and inspire eye and vision research by funding promising young scientists early in their careers.

LEGAL BASIS:
501(c)(3) corporation.

ELIGIBILITY:
Summer Fellowships are open to undergraduate, graduate and medical students.

Postdoctoral Awards are offered to recent Ph.D., M.D., Dr.P.H., D.V.M., and O.D. graduates.

Grants-in-Aid are available for academic researchers within the first three years of their academic appointments.

GEOG. RESTRICTIONS: United States and Canada.

FINANCIAL DATA:
Funds are to be used to defray costs of equipment, consumable supplies and personnel (excluding applicant) for Postdoctoral Awards recipients.

Amount of support per award: Up to $22,500.

Total amount of support: Varies.

NO. MOST RECENT APPLICANTS: 90.

NO. AWARDS: 19.

APPLICATION INFO:
Application guidelines are available on the web site.

Duration: One year; Summer Fellowships: Eight to 12 weeks.

Deadline: November 15. Start date between July 1 and September 1.

PUBLICATIONS:
Brochure.

ADDRESS INQUIRIES TO:
Janice Benson, Associate Director
(See address above.)

FIGHT FOR SIGHT, INC. [2434]

381 Park Avenue South
Suite 809
New York, NY 10016
(212) 679-6060
Fax: (212) 679-4466
E-mail: janice@fightforsight.org
Web Site: www.fightforsight.org

FOUNDED: 1946

AREAS OF INTEREST:
Ophthalmology and visual sciences.

NAME(S) OF PROGRAMS:
- **Fight for Sight Postdoctoral Fellowship**

TYPE:
Fellowships; Grants-in-aid; Research grants; Seed money grants. Stipend to support individuals with a Doctorate who are interested in academic careers involving basic or clinical research in ophthalmology or visual sciences.

YEAR PROGRAM STARTED: 1953

PURPOSE:
To assist research and treatment aimed at eliminating blinding eye diseases and sight impairment.

LEGAL BASIS:
501(c)(3) corporation.

ELIGIBILITY:
Physicians or scientists holding a Doctorate and who are interested in academic careers involving fundamental or clinical research in ophthalmology or its related sciences are eligible to apply. If at the time of filing the applicant does not as yet have a Doctorate, it is required that a cover letter be submitted together with the application advising that the Doctorate will be conferred by the designated commencement date.

GEOG. RESTRICTIONS: United States and Canada.

FINANCIAL DATA:
Amount of support per award: Stipend up to $22,500.

NO. MOST RECENT APPLICANTS: 130.

NO. AWARDS: Approximately 15 to 20.

APPLICATION INFO:
Applications are available online. Completed applications should include:
(1) application face pages and related information completed online and including information about the applicant, his or her education and training, institution and sponsor;
(2) a research proposal of no more than six single-spaced pages, not including references;
(3) letters of support from a sponsor,

departmental chair, and a third reference. These letters should include an evaluation of the student, the role of the mentor in advising the applicant during the project, the training plan, any extracurricular training the student will receive and other information helpful to the committee in evaluating the mentor, the laboratory and the institutional resources in support of a FFS Postdoctoral Award. They should specifically address the suitability of the applicant's training, his or her academic achievements and, most importantly, his or her potential to develop into an independent eye and vision researcher and/or leader in academic ophthalmology;
(4) an NIH-style biosketch of the applicant and sponsor and;
(5) supplemental information, including relevant awards, previous research experience and academic or career goals.

Duration: One year.

Deadline: November 15. Start date is between July 1 and September 1.

PUBLICATIONS:
Brochure.

IRS I.D.: 23-7085732

ADDRESS INQUIRIES TO:
Janice Benson, Associate Director
(See address above.)

*SPECIAL STIPULATIONS:
Research work to be performed in the U.S. or Canada.

THE GLAUCOMA FOUNDATION [2435]

80 Maiden Lane, Suite 700
New York, NY 10038-4778
(212) 285-0080
Fax: (212) 651-1888
E-mail: info@glaucomafoundation.org
Web Site: www.glaucomafoundation.org

FOUNDED: 1984

AREAS OF INTEREST:
Glaucoma.

TYPE:
Research grants.

PURPOSE:
To fund research to determine the causes of glaucoma; to improve methods of treatment, and ultimately to develop cures for the various kinds of glaucoma.

ELIGIBILITY:
Applicants must have a full-time faculty position or the equivalent. Applicant must also demonstrate the Principal Investigator's understanding of glaucoma or his or her collaboration with an investigator who has experience in glaucoma research. If collaboration is warranted, a letter of support from the glaucoma researcher must be included in the application.

FINANCIAL DATA:
Amount of support per award: $40,000.

Total amount of support: Varies.

NO. MOST RECENT APPLICANTS: 20.

APPLICATION INFO:
Grant application and instructions are posted on the Foundation web site.

Duration: One year. Renewable.

Deadline: Varies.

GLAUCOMA RESEARCH FOUNDATION [2436]

251 Post Street, Suite 600
San Francisco, CA 94108
(415) 986-3162
Fax: (415) 986-3763
E-mail: research@glaucoma.org
Web Site: www.glaucoma.org

FOUNDED: 1978

AREAS OF INTEREST:
Research and education pertaining to glaucoma.

NAME(S) OF PROGRAMS:
- **Shaffer Fund for Innovative Glaucoma Research**

TYPE:
Research grants.

PURPOSE:
To protect the sight and independence of people with glaucoma through research and education; to provide funding for such research.

ELIGIBILITY:
Applicants must hold a graduate degree.

FINANCIAL DATA:
Amount of support per award: $40,000.

NO. MOST RECENT APPLICANTS: 90.

NO. AWARDS: 8.

APPLICATION INFO:
Preliminary proposals are accepted annually between June 1 and July 15, when a link to the online application will be available on the GRF web site. A link to the full online grant application will be e-mailed to those whose preliminary proposals meet the required criteria.

Applications received by mail will not be reviewed or returned.

Duration: One year.

Deadline: Preliminary proposals: June 1 to July 15. Full grant application: September 1 to September 30.

IRS I.D.: 94-2495035

ADDRESS INQUIRIES TO:
Catalina San Agustin, Director of Operations
(See e-mail address above.)

HEARING HEALTH FOUNDATION [2437]

363 Seventh Avenue, 10th Floor
New York, NY 10001-3904
(212) 257-6140
(866) 454-3924
Fax: (212) 257-6139
E-mail: info@hhf.org
Web Site: www.hhf.org

FOUNDED: 1958

AREAS OF INTEREST:
Research concerning the causes, treatment and prevention of hearing loss and related ear and balance disorders.

NAME(S) OF PROGRAMS:
- **Emerging Research Grants (ERG)**
- **Hearing Restoration Project (HRP)**

TYPE:
Research grants. Limited in amount and term, grants are awarded as seed funding in support of projects directed by new investigators or for promising new studies in areas of demonstrable basic science or clinical importance. It does include grant support for new research by established investigators.

Specifically, applications will be considered for research directed to any aspect of the ear; that is, investigation of the function, physiology, biochemistry, genetics, anatomy or pathology. Basic and applied research is welcome.

Through the Hearing Restoration Project (HRP), the Foundation is striving toward a cure for hearing loss and tinnitus, a promise that is very real. Underlying that promise is the discovery that chickens have the ability to spontaneously restore their hearing and the HRP is aiming to enable just that in humans.

YEAR PROGRAM STARTED: 1958

PURPOSE:
To prevent and cure hearing loss through groundbreaking research.

LEGAL BASIS:
Nonprofit public voluntary organization.

ELIGIBILITY:
ERG Program: Applications are accepted from all U.S. institutions, including universities, hospitals and nonprofit tax-exempt institutions, public or private.

The HHF's Scientific Review Committee will consider the subject of the research, the quality of its design, its potential for significant advance in basic knowledge or clinical application, the available facilities and personnel at the institution in which the research will be carried out and the qualifications of the investigators.

In accepting a research grant, the institution and the principal investigator are responsible for using grant funds only for those purposes set forth in the application and approved in the HHF award letter.

GEOG. RESTRICTIONS: United States.

FINANCIAL DATA:
Grant funds may be budgeted and used for direct costs of carrying out approved projects, including equipment purchases and supplies. Grant funds may not be used for the salary of principal investigator, travel, living expenses, printing costs, overhead costs exceeding 10% of project costs or public information/education programs.

Amount of support per award: Regardless of the indirect amount, the HHF award will not exceed $30,000.

Total amount of support: Varies.

NO. MOST RECENT APPLICANTS: ERG: 31 for the year 2015.

NO. AWARDS: ERG: 10 for the year 2015.

APPLICATION INFO:
New Project applications and Second-Year applications must be submitted using the current forms available on the web site.

Duration: One calendar year, July 1 to June 30.

Deadline: ERG: Late December. Principal investigators are notified in June.

PUBLICATIONS:
Hearing Health Magazine.

IRS I.D.: 13-1882107

STAFF:
Nadine Dehgan, Chief Executive Officer
Laura Friedman, Communcations and Programs Manager

ADDRESS INQUIRIES TO:
Laura Friedman, Communications and Programs Manager
(See address above.)

HEED OPHTHALMIC FOUNDATION [2438]

655 Beach Street
San Francisco, CA 94109
(415) 447-0249
Fax: (415) 561-8531
E-mail: admin1@heed.org
Web Site: www.heed.org

AREAS OF INTEREST:
Diseases and surgery of the eye or research in opthalmology.

NAME(S) OF PROGRAMS:
- **Heed Fellowship**

TYPE:
Fellowships.

PURPOSE:
To provide assistance to men and women who desire to further their education or to conduct research in opthalmology.

ELIGIBILITY:
Open to U.S. citizens who are graduates of an institution approved by the AMA.

FINANCIAL DATA:
Amount of support per award: $10,000 for the year 2016.

Total amount of support: $200,000 for the year 2016.

NO. MOST RECENT APPLICANTS: 100.

NO. AWARDS: 20 for the year 2016.

APPLICATION INFO:
Applicants are required to submit:
(1) a one-page statement setting forth the applicant's major ophthalmic interest, professional aims and objectives, and noting qualifications deserving of particular consideration;
(2) a letter of recommendation from the Chair of Ophthalmology who supervised residency training;
(3) a letter from the preceptor of the applicant's fellowship program describing the program, including a statement that a minimum of 20% of the fellowship will be spent in research;
(4) two additional letters of recommendation from physicians who have supervised the applicant;
(5) a letter of acceptance of the applicant at the institution where the fellowship is to be taken (this may be a copy of the applicant's match letter) and;
(6) a letter of recommendation from the Chairman of the department who has offered an academic appointment (optional).

Do not send curriculum vitae.

Facsimiles of application materials or letters of recommendation will not be accepted.

Duration: One year. Nonrenewable.

Deadline: February 1.

ADDRESS INQUIRIES TO:
Lisa Brown
Heed Administrator
(See e-mail address above.)

THE MARFAN FOUNDATION [2439]

22 Manhasset Avenue
Port Washington, NY 11050
(516) 883-8712 ext. 117
Fax: (516) 883-8040
E-mail: research@marfan.org
Web Site: www.marfan.org

FOUNDED: 1981

AREAS OF INTEREST:
Education, support and research relating to Marfan syndrome and related disorders.

NAME(S) OF PROGRAMS:
- **Early Investigator Grant Program**
- **Fellowship Grant Program**
- **The Marfan Foundation Faculty Grant Program**

TYPE:
Fellowships; Grants-in-aid; Project/program grants; Research grants. Basic and clinical research related to the Marfan syndrome and related connective tissue disorders. Areas include basic translational and clinical research in genetics, cardiology, ophthalmology and orthopaedic issues of the Marfan syndrome.

YEAR PROGRAM STARTED: 1986

PURPOSE:
To provide financial support for investigators, scientists and physicians studying any or all disciplines involved in Marfan syndrome research.

ELIGIBILITY:
The principal investigator must hold an M.D., D.O., Ph.D., Sc.D., D.D.S., D.V.M. or equivalent degree. The investigator must have proven ability to pursue independent research publications in peer-reviewed journals. Fellowships must be conducted in the U.S.

FINANCIAL DATA:
Amount of support per award: Early Investigator: $37,500; Faculty: $50,000; Fellowship: $50,000 to $75,000.

Total amount of support: Varies.

NO. MOST RECENT APPLICANTS: 40 for the year 2014.

NO. AWARDS: 4 Faculty, 4 Early Investigator and 1 Fellowship Awards for the year 2015.

APPLICATION INFO:
Application information is available on the web site.

Duration: Up to two years.

Deadline: Early Investigator and Fellowship: February; Faculty: April.

ADDRESS INQUIRIES TO:
Josephine Grima, Ph.D.
Chief Scientific Officer
(See address above.)

NATIONAL EYE INSTITUTE [2440]

National Institutes of Health
5635 Fishers Lane, Suite 1300
Bethesda, MD 20892
(301) 451-2020
Fax: (301) 496-2267
E-mail: wujekjer@mail.nih.gov
Web Site: www.nei.nih.gov

FOUNDED: 1968

AREAS OF INTEREST:
Vision research, cooperative clinical trials for evaluation, diagnosis and therapy of ocular diseases, and epidemiologic and risk factor studies of ocular diseases.

NAME(S) OF PROGRAMS:
- **Cooperative Clinical Research Grants**
- **Small Business Innovation Research Awards**

TYPE:
Conferences/seminars; Fellowships; Research grants; Training grants. Research Project Grants support individual investigators whose work is aimed at discovering means of improving the prevention, diagnosis and treatment of blinding and disabling eye and vision disorders.

Small Business Innovation Research Awards aim to stimulate technological innovations, to use small business to meet federal research-development needs that may ultimately lead to commercial products or services and to foster and encourage participation by minority and disadvantaged persons in technological innovations.

Areas of study include vision research, retinal diseases, corneal diseases, cataract, glaucoma, low vision and blindness rehabilitation, visual impairment and its rehabilitation, strabismus, amblyopia and visual processing.

YEAR PROGRAM STARTED: 1968

PURPOSE:
To gain new knowledge about normal and abnormal functioning of the eye and visual system; to support research aimed at improving the prevention, diagnosis and treatment of eye disease and disorders of vision. These are essential for progress against the major causes of blindness and visual disability.

ELIGIBILITY:
Research grants are available to any public or private university, college, hospital, laboratory, or other institution, including state and local units of government and federal institutions; eligibility is no longer restricted to nonprofit organizations.

GEOG. RESTRICTIONS: Cooperative Clinical Research Grants: Primarily United States; Small Business Innovation Research Awards: United States.

FINANCIAL DATA:
Amount of support per award: Grants vary in amount, depending upon the needs and nature of the request and the limitations of the program.

APPLICATION INFO:
Those interested in applying are encouraged to contact the NEI staff prior to submitting applications.

Duration: Cooperative Clinical Research Grants: Up to five years; Small Business Innovation Research Award: Six months to two years.

Deadline: Varies according to award.

IRS I.D.: 52-0858115

STAFF:
Paul Sieving, M.D., Director

ADDRESS INQUIRIES TO:
Jerome Wujek, Ph.D.
Research Resources Officer
(See address above.)

NATIONAL EYE INSTITUTE [2441]

National Institutes of Health
5635 Fishers Lane, Suite 1300
Bethesda, MD 20892
(301) 451-2020
Fax: (301) 402-0528
E-mail: esl@nei.nih.gov
Web Site: www.nei.nih.gov

AREAS OF INTEREST:
Vision research, cooperative clinical trials for evaluation, diagnosis and therapy of ocular diseases, and epidemiologic and risk factor studies of ocular diseases.

NAME(S) OF PROGRAMS:
- **Center Core Grants**

TYPE:
Research grants.

PURPOSE:
To support centralized resources and facilities shared by investigators with existing NINDS-funded research projects; to enrich the effectiveness of ongoing research; to promote new research directions.

FINANCIAL DATA:
Amount of support per award: Applicants may request up to $400,000 for less than 20 R01s or up to $500,000 for more than 20 R01s per year in direct costs.

Matching fund requirements: Cost sharing is not required to be eligible for this program. However, it is strongly encouraged for applicant organizations to make appropriate and needed commitments to the Center in order to maximize the effectiveness and utility of the shared resources.

APPLICATION INFO:
Contact NEI for details.

Duration: Maximum project period of five years.

ADDRESS INQUIRIES TO:
Ellen S. Liberman, Ph.D.
(See address above.)

RESEARCH FUND OF THE AMERICAN OTOLOGICAL SOCIETY, INC. [2442]

Administrative Office
4960 Dover Street, N.E.
St. Petersburg, FL 33703
(217) 638-0801
Fax: (727) 800-9428
E-mail: administrator@americanotologicalsociety.org
Web Site: www.americanotologicalsociety.org

FOUNDED: 1868

AREAS OF INTEREST:
Research related to any aspects of the ear, hearing and balance disorders.

NAME(S) OF PROGRAMS:
- **AOS Clinician-Scientist Award**
- **Clinical Investigations Research Grants**
- **Fellowship and Medical Student Training Grants**
- **Research Grants**

TYPE:
Fellowships; Research grants. AOS Clinician-Scientist Award: For salary and research support of a new academic clinician-scientist, at the Assistant Professor level, in order to facilitate development into an independent otologic investigator. Department chair guarantees at least 50% time commitment in research.

Clinical Investigations Research Grants: Intended to encourage and support academic research in sciences related to the ear.

Fellowship and Medical Student Training Grants: For physicians only (residents, medical students or fellows), to support one to two years of full-time research conducted outside of residency training.

Research Grants: Related to research on any aspects of the ear, hearing and balance disorders.

YEAR PROGRAM STARTED: 1926

PURPOSE:
To encourage research in otosclerosis, Meniere's disease and related ear disorders.

LEGAL BASIS:
Private foundation.

ELIGIBILITY:
AOS Clinician-Scientist Award: Applicant must
(1) hold or be approved for a full-time university faculty appointment at the rank of Assistant Professor in a department or division of Otolaryngology - Head and Neck Surgery;
(2) be citizens of the U.S., or have been lawfully admitted for permanent U.S. residency at the time of application;
(3) hold a Doctor of Medicine (M.D.) or equivalent degree from an accredited institution awarded within the last 10 years;
(4) have completed an ACGME-approved otolaryngology residency program and;
(5) have demonstrated the capacity or potential for a highly productive, independent research career with an emphasis in otology/neurotology.
Preference will be given to candidates who are currently enrolled in or have completed (within the preceding three years) a two-year otology/neurotology fellowship program.

Clinical Investigations Research Grants: Grant awards may involve research on any topic related to ear disorders. The research need not be directly on an otological disease but may explore normal functions of the cochlea, labyrinth or central auditory or vestibular systems. However, the applicant must describe how the proposed research will benefit the understanding, diagnosis or treatment of otological disorders. The Research Fund Advisory Board will review applications that propose, as a central focus, a clinical trial or other "hands-on" patient clinical investigative study. Applicants should follow general guidelines for research proposals and also include information about the clinical study design and ethical requirements regarding human research subject participation. Grants are available to physician or doctoral-level investigators in the U.S. and Canada only.

Fellowship and Medical Student Training Grants: Research must be conducted in U.S. or Canadian institutions. Applicants must be medical students, residents or fellows (not nonmedical postgraduate researchers). Recipients must be relieved of all clinical duties during the fellowship period.

Research Grants are available to physician or doctoral-level investigators in the U.S. and Canada only.

FINANCIAL DATA:
Amount of support per award: AOS Clinician-Scientist Award: Up to $80,000 for salary and research support; Clinical Investigations Research Grants: Up to $66,000 per year, including indirect costs (overhead); indirect costs not to exceed 10% of direct costs; Research Grants: $55,000 maximum per year, including indirect costs; Fellowship and Medical Student Training Grants: $35,000 stipend and $5,000 for supplies (plus up to 10% indirect costs).

APPLICATION INFO:
The American Otological Society can only accept grant applications and reference letters electronically. Applicant must prepare application electronically with his or her preferred word processor, and after that convert the final document to a PDF file using Adobe Acrobat or the free Abode Acrobat Reader. (Society discourages scanning paper documents, as lower quality resolution usually is the result.)

Applicant must submit final application by e-mail in the PDF format. Reference letters may be electronically prepared and signed as PDF documents, or may be scanned as PDF documents, in order that they may be submitted as part of the grant application. If one's application is accepted for funding, he or she is required to submit the original signature documents and reference letters to the American Otological Society Administrative Office at the address above.

The grants and reference letters are to be submitted via e-mail to Dr. John Carey, Executive Secretary of the American Otological Society Research Fund (jcarey@jhmi.edu) and to Kristen Bordignon, Administrator for the American Otological Society Research Fund (administrator@americanotologicalsociety.org).

Duration: AOS Clinician-Scientist Award: Up to three years; renewable annually. Clinical Investigations Research Grants: Renewable annually. Fellowship and Medical Student Training Grants: One to two years. Research Grants: Up to two years.

Deadline: Letter of Intent: December 31. Completed applications: January 31.

STAFF:
John P. Carey, M.D., Executive Secretary

ADDRESS INQUIRIES TO:
Kristen Bordignon, Administrator
American Otological Society
Research Fund
E-mail:
administrator@americanotologicalsociety.org

Osteopathy

AMERICAN OSTEOPATHIC FOUNDATION [2443]

142 East Ontario Street, Suite 1450
Chicago, IL 60611-2864
(312) 202-8235
Fax: (312) 202-8216
E-mail: info@aof.org
Web Site: www.aof.org

FOUNDED: 1949

AREAS OF INTEREST:
Osteopathic medical education and research.

TYPE:
Awards/prizes; Scholarships. Grants.

PURPOSE:
To assist and encourage osteopathic medical students, researchers and physicians; to

ensure the ideals of osteopathic medicine by initiating and supporting programs that enhance the profession, advance the quality of people's health, and recognize excellence in the areas of education and research.

LEGAL BASIS:
Private foundation.

ELIGIBILITY:
Specific requirements can be found on the Foundation web site.

FINANCIAL DATA:
Amount of support per award: Varies.
Total amount of support: Varies.

APPLICATION INFO:
Applications or nomination forms are available January 1 on the Foundation web site.
Duration: Varies.
Deadline: Varies.

PUBLICATIONS:
Application; brochure.

ADDRESS INQUIRIES TO:
Elizabeth Ortolano
Director of Internal and External Affairs
(See address above.)

FOUNDATION FOR OSTEOPATHIC EMERGENCY MEDICINE [2444]

142 East Ontario Street
Suite 1500
Chicago, IL 60611
Fax: (312) 587-9951
E-mail: swhitmer@foem.org
Web Site: www.foem.org

FOUNDED: 1998

AREAS OF INTEREST:
Osteopathic emergency medicine.

NAME(S) OF PROGRAMS:
- **Investigator Research Grant**
- **David A. Kuchinski Memorial Research Grant**
- **Resident Research Grant**
- **Young Investigator Research Grant**

TYPE:
Awards/prizes; Research grants.

YEAR PROGRAM STARTED: 1998

PURPOSE:
To improve patient care through quality research and education in osteopathic emergency medicine.

LEGAL BASIS:
501(c)(3).

ELIGIBILITY:
Grants are made to individuals or organizations that have tax-exempt status under Section 501(c)(3) of the Internal Revenue Code.

GEOG. RESTRICTIONS: United States.

FINANCIAL DATA:
Amount of support per award: Investigator Grant and Young Investigator Grant: $1,000 to $3,000; Kuchinski Memorial Research Grant: Varies; Resident Research Grant: $500 to $2,000.
Total amount of support: Varies.

NO. MOST RECENT APPLICANTS: 3.

NO. AWARDS: 1.

APPLICATION INFO:
Contact the Foundation for application procedures.
Duration: One-time grants.
Deadline: July 31. Reviewed in April, July and October.

PUBLICATIONS:
Research Beacon.

ADDRESS INQUIRIES TO:
Stephanie Whitmer
Assistant Executive Director
(See address above.)

MAINE OSTEOPATHIC ASSOCIATION [2445]

128 State Street
Augusta, ME 04330
(207) 623-1101
Fax: (207) 623-4228
E-mail: info@mainedo.org
Web Site: www.mainedo.org

FOUNDED: 1912

AREAS OF INTEREST:
Osteopathic medicine.

NAME(S) OF PROGRAMS:
- **Maine Osteopathic Association Scholarship**

TYPE:
Scholarships. The program is a tuition subsidy for eligible students who enroll in a qualifying medical school program.

LEGAL BASIS:
Nonprofit physician membership organization.

ELIGIBILITY:
Any Maine resident who will enroll in a participating accredited college of osteopathic medicine. School does not have to be located in Maine.

FINANCIAL DATA:
Amount of support per award: $1,000.
Total amount of support: Varies.

NO. AWARDS: Varies.

APPLICATION INFO:
Application is available online or by contacting the Association directly.
Duration: One year.
Deadline: June 1.

STAFF:
Angela Westhoff, Executive Director

ADDRESS INQUIRIES TO:
Angela Westhoff, Executive Director
(See address above.)

NEW JERSEY OSTEOPATHIC EDUCATION FOUNDATION [2446]

One Distribution Way
Suite 201
Monmouth Junction, NJ 08852-3001
(732) 940-9000 ext. 303
Fax: (732) 940-8899
E-mail: info@njosteo.com
Web Site: www.njosteo.com

FOUNDED: 1901

AREAS OF INTEREST:
Osteopathic education.

TYPE:
Scholarships. For students pursuing osteopathic medical education. A first-year scholarship will be awarded to New Jersey residents accepted to the fall class of any approved college of osteopathic medicine.

YEAR PROGRAM STARTED: 1965

PURPOSE:
To provide the means to promote education in the field of osteopathic medicine.

LEGAL BASIS:
Not-for-profit corporation.

ELIGIBILITY:
Applicants must be residents of New Jersey having completed four years of pre-medical education and entering their first year in an osteopathic college. Applicants must have a 3.0 grade point average on a 4.0 scale or be in the upper 25% of his or her class. Selections are based on class standing, financial need, high motivation and professional promise. Students accepting scholarships must agree to become members of the New Jersey Association of Osteopathic Physicians and Surgeons and the American Osteopathic Association.

GEOG. RESTRICTIONS: New Jersey.

FINANCIAL DATA:
The scholarship sum will be paid directly to the college to cover part of the first year's tuition.
Amount of support per award: $4,000 to $7,000.
Total amount of support: $29,000.

NO. MOST RECENT APPLICANTS: 20.

NO. AWARDS: Approximately 7 each year.

APPLICATION INFO:
To apply for a scholarship, qualified students must:
(1) submit a completed NJOEF scholarship application;
(2) provide four named references, at least one of whom is an osteopathic physician;
(3) provide four completed reference evaluation forms;
(4) supply MCAT scores with confirmation code;
(5) supply pre-med college transcripts directly from the college;
(6) compose an essay sharing his or her desire to become an osteopathic physician (why osteopathic medicine?) and;
(7) supply the prior year's tax return or that of the parent/guardian, if the student is claimed as a dependent.
Duration: One year.
Deadline: May 31.

IRS I.D.: 22-6088562

ADDRESS INQUIRIES TO:
Scholarship Program
(See address above.)

Pediatrics

ACADEMIC PEDIATRIC ASSOCIATION [2447]

6728 Old McLean Village Drive
McLean, VA 22101
(703) 556-9222
Fax: (703) 556-8729
E-mail: info@academicpeds.org
Web Site: academicpeds.org

FOUNDED: 1960

AREAS OF INTEREST:
General pediatrics.

NAME(S) OF PROGRAMS:

- **Young Investigator Grant Program**

TYPE:
Project/program grants; Research grants.

YEAR PROGRAM STARTED: 1994

PURPOSE:
To provide financial support to teaching, research and health care delivery projects in general pediatrics.

ELIGIBILITY:
The principal investigator of any proposal submitted must be a member of the APA or have submitted an application for membership. Preference will be given to new investigators, including those in training. Preference will be given to proposals that have the potential of leading to projects of a larger or longer-term nature.

FINANCIAL DATA:
Amount of support per award: Up to $10,000.

NO. AWARDS: Varies.

APPLICATION INFO:
Applicants must submit a two-page proposal. Only electronic submissions as an e-mail attachment are accepted. The proposals should contain a brief overview of the project including purpose, methods, evaluation and estimated budget. A curriculum vitae for the principal investigator must also be included with the proposal. Budget requests should not include overhead or salary for the principal investigator if they are full-time faculty. The review panel will identify those that warrant further elaboration. Re-submitted proposals can be no more than 10 pages in length including tables and appendices. They must contain background, hypothesis, description of key personnel, detailed budget with justification and methods.

Duration: One year. Renewal possible.

ADDRESS INQUIRIES TO:
Connie Mackay
Young Investigator Grant
(See address above.)

AMERICAN ACADEMY OF PEDIATRICS [2448]

141 Northwest Point Boulevard
Elk Grove Village, IL 60007
(847) 434-4000
(800) 433-9016 ext. 7134
Fax: (847) 434-8000
E-mail: kvandenbrook@aap.org
Web Site: www.aap.org/ypn

FOUNDED: 1930

AREAS OF INTEREST:
Pediatric training.

NAME(S) OF PROGRAMS:

- **American Academy of Pediatrics Residency Scholarships**

TYPE:
Residencies; Scholarships. Stipend for the support of pediatric residents.

YEAR PROGRAM STARTED: 1982

PURPOSE:
To enable young physicians to complete their pediatric training.

LEGAL BASIS:
Nonprofit organization.

ELIGIBILITY:
Applicant must have completed, or will have completed by July 1, a qualifying approved internship (PL-0) and have a definite commitment for a first-year pediatric residency (PL-1) accredited by the Residency Review Committee for Pediatrics. In addition, applicant must be a pediatric resident or chief resident (categorical pediatrics or combined-training program) in a training program and have made a definite commitment for another year of residency (not fellowship) in a U.S. or Canadian program accredited by the Residency Review Committee for Pediatrics, as well as have a substantial need for financial assistance.

GEOG. RESTRICTIONS: United States and Canada.

FINANCIAL DATA:
Amount of support per award: $1,000 to $5,000.

Total amount of support: Varies.

APPLICATION INFO:
Official application materials are available upon request in December. Applications must be supported by a form from the Department Head or the Chief of Service or the Residency Program Director addressing the financial need, commitment to pediatrics and performance in the program.

Duration: One year. Possible renewals.

Deadline: Last day in February.

ADDRESS INQUIRIES TO:
Kimberley VandenBrook
Program Coordinator, Resident Initiatives
(See address above.)

DYSAUTONOMIA FOUNDATION, INC.

315 West 39th Street
Suite 701
New York, NY 10018
(212) 279-1066
Fax: (212) 279-2066
E-mail: info@famdys.org
Web Site: www.familialdysautonomia.org

TYPE:
Project/program grants; Research grants; Seed money grants. In addition to support for research and clinical study, the Foundation also provides financial support to the Dysautonomia Treatment and Evaluation Center at NYU and the Israeli FD Center in Tel Aviv.

See entry 2384 for full listing.

FIRST CANDLE/SIDS ALLIANCE [2449]

9 Newport Drive, Suite 200
Forest Hill, MD 21050
(443) 640-1049
Fax: (443) 640-1031
E-mail: info@firstcandle.org
Web Site: www.firstcandle.org

FOUNDED: 1962

AREAS OF INTEREST:
Medical research into the cause and prevention of Sudden Infant Death Syndrome, counseling and information projects which aid parents and educate the public about SIDS and SIDS-related issues and education of relevant professionals on SIDS and about care for infants at-risk.

CONSULTING OR VOLUNTEER SERVICES:
Local chapters provide voluntary peer support to parents and National Office provides consulting services in the management of specialized services, seminars to health professionals, review of SIDS medical research proposals and clearinghouse for literature and films on SIDS and related issues.

NAME(S) OF PROGRAMS:

- **Professional Research**

TYPE:
Conferences/seminars; Research grants. Professional medical research for SIDS, stillbirths and related issues.

YEAR PROGRAM STARTED: 1963

PURPOSE:
To promote infant health and survival during the prenatal period through two years of age by means of advocacy, education and research; to provide SIDS and other infant death bereavement services.

LEGAL BASIS:
Not-for-profit corporation.

ELIGIBILITY:
Applicant reviews are made on an individual basis by the First Candle/SIDS Alliance and the Alliance Medical and Scientific Advisory Council.

FINANCIAL DATA:
Amount of support per award: Grants vary in amount depending upon proposals.

Total amount of support: Varies.

NO. AWARDS: 6 per year average.

APPLICATION INFO:
Letters soliciting Foundation interest prior to submission of proposals are welcome.

IRS I.D.: 52-1591162

ADDRESS INQUIRIES TO:
Alison Jacobson, Chief Executive Officer
(See address above.)

CHARLES H. HOOD FOUNDATION, INC. [2450]

95 Berkeley Street, 2nd Floor
Boston, MA 02116
(617) 695-9439
E-mail: glockwood@hria.org
Web Site: www.tmfgrants.org/hood

FOUNDED: 1942

AREAS OF INTEREST:
Child health research.

NAME(S) OF PROGRAMS:

- **Child Health Research Awards Program**

TYPE:
Research grants. Medical research grants that are relevant to child health. Projects must be hypothesis-driven clinical, basic science, public health, health services research or epidemiology.

YEAR PROGRAM STARTED: 1942

PURPOSE:
To improve the health and quality of life for children through grant support of New England-based pediatric researchers.

LEGAL BASIS:
Private family foundation.

ELIGIBILITY:
Investigators working in tax-exempt academic, medical and research institutions in New England are eligible. Grants must have relevance to child health. Investigators must be within five years of their first faculty appointment. In addition to basic science

research, grants are also given to researchers in public health, epidemiology, clinical research and health services research.

GEOG. RESTRICTIONS: New England.

FINANCIAL DATA:

Amount of support per award: $75,000 per year for two years (inclusive of 10% overhead).

Total amount of support: $1,500,000 over two years.

NO. MOST RECENT APPLICANTS: 45.

NO. AWARDS: 10 new grants for the year 2015.

REPRESENTATIVE AWARDS:

"Kisspeptin as a Novel Tool for the Evaluation of Delayed Puberty;" "The Effectiveness of Community Financing Approach in Improving Child Nutrition Status in Rwanda;" "Detecting and Correcting Errors During Cell Division;" "Prospective Study of Genomic Aberrations during Prenatal Gestation;" "The Impact of Genes and Experience on the Development of Brain Circuits."

APPLICATION INFO:

Application guidelines, instructions and forms are available on the web site.

Duration: Two years.

Deadline: Spring and Fall for Child Health Research Grants. Funding begins on July 1 and January 1. Deadlines and guidelines change each cycle.

PUBLICATIONS:

Application guidelines; alumni directory; summaries of current and previous funded projects.

IRS I.D.: 04-3507847

OFFICERS:

Neil Smiley, President and Treasurer
John Parker, Jr., Vice President and Clerk
Robert Sege, M.D., Ph.D., Secretary and Executive Director

TRUSTEES:

ADDRESS INQUIRIES TO:

See e-mail address above.

HUMAN GROWTH FOUNDATION [2451]

997 Glen Cove Avenue, Suite 5
Glen Head, NY 11545
(516) 671-4041
(800) 451-6434
Fax: (516) 671-4055
E-mail: hgf1@hgfound.org
Web Site: www.hgfound.org

FOUNDED: 1965

AREAS OF INTEREST:

Growth disorders and pediatrics.

NAME(S) OF PROGRAMS:

- **Small Grants for Research in Field of Short Stature**

TYPE:

Research grants.

YEAR PROGRAM STARTED: 1965

PURPOSE:

To help medical science better understand the process of growth and to help individuals with growth-related disorders, their families and health care professionals through education, research and advocacy.

ELIGIBILITY:

Applicants must be involved in research of the human growth process. Special consideration will be given to young investigators and to projects dealing with psychological, social, and educational aspects of dwarfism and its treatment and to new approaches to diagnosis and management, as well as clinical and basic research in the mechanisms of statural growth disorders of children including chondrodystrophies, genetic, or psychological causes.

FINANCIAL DATA:

Amount of support per award: $10,000 to $15,000.

NO. MOST RECENT APPLICANTS: Over 40.

NO. AWARDS: Up to 3.

APPLICATION INFO:

Application and guidelines are available from the Foundation. Applicants must first provide a Letter of Intent. Grant applications must be in NIH format.

Duration: One-time funding.

Deadline: Letter of Intent: May 15. Final application: September 1.

ADDRESS INQUIRIES TO:

Patricia D. Costa, Executive Director
(See address above.)

NATIONAL LEUKEMIA RESEARCH ASSOCIATION [2452]

585 Stewart Avenue
Suite LL-18
Garden City, NY 11530
(516) 222-1944
Fax: (516) 222-0457
E-mail: info@childrensleukemia.org
Web Site: www.childrensleukemia.org

FOUNDED: 1965

AREAS OF INTEREST:

Leukemia.

NAME(S) OF PROGRAMS:

- **Children's Leukemia Research Grants**

TYPE:

Research grants. Support for research efforts into the causes and cure of leukemia. Patient aid to families in need while meeting the expenses incurred in leukemia treatment.

YEAR PROGRAM STARTED: 1965

PURPOSE:

To work towards a cure for leukemia; to provide patient aid.

ELIGIBILITY:

Any doctor at the Ph.D. or M.D. level who is involved in research towards finding the causes and cure for leukemia may apply.

FINANCIAL DATA:

Amount of support per award: Up to $30,000 per year.

APPLICATION INFO:

Application form required. Contact Association for other requirements.

Duration: One year. Renewal for a second year is considered if other funding for promising projects has not been obtained.

Deadline: June 30.

ADDRESS INQUIRIES TO:

Anthony R. Pasqua, President
(See address above.)

SICKKIDS FOUNDATION

525 University Avenue, 14th Floor
Toronto ON M5G 2L3 Canada
(416) 813-6166 ext. 2354
(800) 661-1083
Fax: (416) 813-4912
E-mail: national.grants@sickkidsfoundation.com
Web Site: www.sickkidsfoundation.com/about-us/grants

TYPE:

Awards/prizes; Conferences/seminars; Project/program grants; Research grants. Community Conference Grants program brings together families with researchers and clinicians for medical presentations and family-oriented discussions. It helps ensure knowledge exchange with families so that they are able to access the most up-to-date information about their children's health.

New Investigator Research Grants program focus is to ensure that there continues to be well-trained researchers across the country working to address the most pressing childhood diseases and conditions.

See entry 1426 for full listing.

SOCIETY FOR PEDIATRIC DERMATOLOGY [2453]

8365 Keystone Crossing, Suite 107
Indianapolis, IN 46240
(317) 202-0224
Fax: (317) 205-9481
E-mail: info@pedsderm.net
Web Site: www.pedsderm.net/grants-awards/

FOUNDED: 1975

AREAS OF INTEREST:

Pediatric dermatology.

NAME(S) OF PROGRAMS:

- **Pilot Project Grants**
- **Team Grants**
- **Weston Pediatric Dermatology Career Development Award (CDA)**

TYPE:

Research grants; Seed money grants. Research grants for investigators on the faculty and postdoctoral levels.

PURPOSE:

To foster research in pediatric dermatology.

LEGAL BASIS:

Medical society.

ELIGIBILITY:

Applicants must have completed training in pediatrics or dermatology and be active in the investigation of pediatric dermatology. Importance of the project and feasibility within the timeframe available are selection criteria.

FINANCIAL DATA:

Amount of support per award: Pilot Project Grants: Up to $7,500; Team Grants: up to $25,000. Weston Pediatric Dermatology Career Development Award : $40,000.

Total amount of support: Varies.

NO. AWARDS: Pilot Project Award: Varies. Weston Pediatric Dermatology Career Development Award : 1 given every other (odd-numbered) year.

APPLICATION INFO:

Application form required. Notices also placed in various medical, dermatology and pediatrics publications.

Duration: Weston Pediatric Dermatology Career Development Award : One year.

Deadline: First cycle: May 1; notification in June. Second cycle: December 7; notification in the following February.

ADDRESS INQUIRIES TO:
Awards and Goals Committee
(See address above.)

THRASHER RESEARCH FUND [2454]

68 South Main Street, Suite 400
Salt Lake City, UT 84101
(801) 240-4753
Fax: (801) 240-1625
E-mail: martinezaf@thrasherresearch.org
Web Site: www.thrasherresearch.org

FOUNDED: 1977

AREAS OF INTEREST:
Pediatric medical research, with emphasis on clinical/translational research with potential findings that would be clinically applicable in a short period of time in the prevention, diagnosis and/or treatment of pediatric medical problems.

TYPE:
Research grants. Grants for support of research that addresses problems in children's health in areas of critical illnesses that have been insufficiently researched or investigated. The Fund assumes that significant solutions to children's health problems remain undiscovered and invites a broad array of applications designed to remedy these deficiencies.

YEAR PROGRAM STARTED: 1977

PURPOSE:
To provide grants for pediatric medical research that addresses problems in children's health that are significant in terms of either magnitude or severity.

LEGAL BASIS:
Private organization.

ELIGIBILITY:
The Fund supports medical research that seeks to prevent or cure children's critical illnesses, injuries and disabilities. Projects should:
(1) be scientifically sound and culturally appropriate;
(2) document methods and practices that have sustainable benefits;
(3) have specific aims and a well-designed methodology and;
(4) evaluate the significance of impact on children's health.

Funding is limited to research. The Fund does not award grants for general operations, construction or renovation of buildings or facilities, nor does the Fund award grants for general donations, loans, student aid, scholarships, educational programs or support of other funds or institutions.

The Fund excludes research using human fetal tissue, stem cell research, or behavioral science research.

FINANCIAL DATA:
Support may be provided for supplies, minor equipment and technical personnel assistance related to a specific Fund-sponsored project. Principal investigators in need of salary support for a specific project may apply for 20% support, based on federal guidelines.

Amount of support per award: $25,000 to $500,000. Typically $100,000 to $300,000.

Total amount of support: Varies.

NO. MOST RECENT APPLICANTS: 100.

NO. AWARDS: 18.

APPLICATION INFO:
Application guidelines are available on the Fund's web site. Potential applicants are encouraged to contact Fund staff prior to a formal submission to determine the potential fit of a project with current Fund interests.

Duration: Up to three years.

PUBLICATIONS:
Brochure; application information.

STAFF:
R. Justin Brown, M.P.H., President and Research Manager
Megan Duncan, M.P.H., Research Manager
Aaron V. Pontsler, M.S., MBA, Research Manager

U.S. DEPARTMENT OF HEALTH AND HUMAN SERVICES

Maternal and Child Health Bureau
Parklawn Building, Room 5C 26
5600 Fishers Lane
Rockville, MD 20857
(301) 443-2204
Fax: (301) 443-9354
E-mail: CallCenter@hrsa.gov (grants information)
Web Site: www.mchb.hrsa.gov
www.hrsa.gov

TYPE:
Block grants. The Title V Block Grant Program has as a general purpose the improvement of the health of all mothers and children in the nation. The Block Grant Program has three components: Formula Block Grants to 59 states and other political jurisdictions, Special Projects of Regional and National Significance (SPRANS), and Community Integrated Service Systems (CISS) Grants.

See entry 2424 for full listing.

Pharmacology

AMERICAN ASSOCIATION OF COLLEGES OF PHARMACY [2455]

1727 King Street, Floor 2
Alexandria, VA 22314
(703) 739-2330
Fax: (703) 836-8982
E-mail: nia@aacp.org
Web Site: www.aacp.org

FOUNDED: 1900

AREAS OF INTEREST:
Pharmaceutical education.

NAME(S) OF PROGRAMS:

- **New Investigator Award**

TYPE:
Research grants.

YEAR PROGRAM STARTED: 1985

PURPOSE:
To provide start-up funds for new faculty members to assist in establishing a research program; to assist new faculty in establishing themselves as independent investigators.

LEGAL BASIS:
Nonprofit foundation, tax-exempt under the IRS Code.

ELIGIBILITY:
Applicants must have earned terminal degrees in their disciplines (Pharm.D., Ph.D.), hold a regular full-time academic faculty appointment in a college or school of pharmacy, hold the rank of assistant professor, and be in the first to fifth year of their academic appointment. The applicant must be a current individual member of AACP. Only one application per investigator will be accepted for review.

A faculty member who has been a principle investigator on an AACP, NIA, NPFRAP or equivalent starter grant, on a professional (e.g., ACCP, ASHP, AAPS, PhRMA, etc.), organizational (e.g., American Heart or American Cancer) or federal grant (e.g., NIH, NSF, AHRQ, DOD, CDC, etc.) is not eligible to apply.

Intramural university or college/school start-up support may be used for supplementing the proposed research.

GEOG. RESTRICTIONS: United States.

FINANCIAL DATA:
No overhead allowed. In addition to grant monies, each award winner will receive $1,000 for required travel to the AACP Annual Meeting.

Amount of support per award: $10,000 maximum.

NO. MOST RECENT APPLICANTS: 100.

NO. AWARDS: Up to 18.

APPLICATION INFO:
Application specifics are available on the AACP web site.

Duration: One year.

Deadline: Letter of Intent: Early August. Full Proposal: Early September.

PUBLICATIONS:
Program announcement.

OFFICERS:
Lucinda Maine, Executive Vice President and Chief Executive Officer

ADDRESS INQUIRIES TO:
Kirsten Block, Associate Director of Research and Graduate Programs
(See address above.)

AMERICAN FOUNDATION FOR PHARMACEUTICAL EDUCATION (AFPE) [2456]

6076 Franconia Road, Suite C
Alexandria, VA 22310-1758
(703) 875-3095
Fax: (703) 875-3098
E-mail: info@afpenet.org
Web Site: www.afpenet.org

FOUNDED: 1942

AREAS OF INTEREST:
Pharmaceutical education.

NAME(S) OF PROGRAMS:

- **Phi Lambda Sigma-AFPE First Year Graduate Fellowship**
- **Rho Chi-AFPE First Year Graduate Fellowship**

TYPE:
Fellowships. Phi Lambda Sigma-AFPE First Year Graduate Fellowship encourages outstanding Phi Lambda Sigma members to pursue the Ph.D. in a college of pharmacy graduate program.

Rho Chi-AFPE First Year Graduate Fellowship encourages outstanding Rho Chi Honor Society members to pursue the Ph.D. in a college of pharmacy graduate program.

YEAR PROGRAM STARTED: 1985

PURPOSE:
To encourage outstanding Rho Chi and Phi Lambda Sigma members to continue their education in a graduate program for the Ph.D. in a college of pharmacy.

LEGAL BASIS:
Nonprofit foundation, tax-exempt under the IRS Code.

ELIGIBILITY:
Phi Lambda Sigma-AFPE Fellowship: Applicant must be a member of Phi Lambda Sigma and a pharmacy Pharm.D. degree student in the final year of professional studies who is planning to enroll full-time for the Ph.D. degree in the pharmaceutical sciences after graduation in a Ph.D. degree program at or affiliated with an accredited U.S. school/college of pharmacy or be a pharmacy Pharm.D. degree student in the final year of professional studies who is currently enrolled in a joint Pharm.D./Ph.D. degree program at or affiliated with an accredited U.S. school or college of pharmacy who will pursue full-time graduate study in the year the award is made. U.S. citizenship or permanent resident status is required.

Rho Chi-AFPE Fellowship: Applicants must be members of the Rho Chi Honor Society. Applicants must be a pharmacy student in the final year of professional studies or a professional pharmacy degree program graduate entering a pharmaceutical sciences (including social/administrative sciences) Ph.D. program in an accredited U.S. school or college of pharmacy as a full-time student. Pharmacy students who have initiated graduate work through a dual Pharm.D./Ph.D. degree pathway are eligible if they have completed their professional degree and will be pursuing full-time graduate study in the year the award is made. Applicants must be a U.S. citizen or permanent resident.

GEOG. RESTRICTIONS: United States.

FINANCIAL DATA:
Phi Lambda Sigma-AFPE: The scholarship may be used for any purpose decided by the awardee and faculty sponsor that will enable the student to have a successful program, i.e., student stipend, laboratory supplies, books, materials, travel, etc., related to the program of graduate study. None of the funds shall be used for indirect costs by the institution.

Amount of support per award: $7,500.

Total amount of support: $15,000.

NO. MOST RECENT APPLICANTS: 12.

NO. AWARDS: 1 of each.

APPLICATION INFO:
For the Phi Lambda Sigma-AFPE Fellowship, the following information should be sent to exec_director@philambdasigma.org:
(1) letters of recommendation from two college faculty members who are acquainted with the student and his or her potential for graduate study;
(2) name of the graduate school the student plans to attend (if known);
(3) a one- to two-page statement by applicant elaborating reasons for wishing to attend graduate school;
(4) a list of special honors, awards and accomplishments in high school and college reflecting achievement and ability to succeed in graduate school and;
(5) an official transcript of all collegiate grades and copies of GRE, SAT and other national achievement test scores.

For the Rho Chi Fellowship, application forms are available from Rho Chi Faculty Advisors or the Secretary of Rho Chi. Required information should be sent to: The Rho Chi Society National Office, UNC Eshelman School of Pharmacy, 3210 Kerr Hall, CB No. 7569, Chapel Hill, NC 27599-7569; Tel: (919) 843-9001; E-mail: rhochi@unc.edu. The packet should include the following:
(1) a completed application form;
(2) a one-page description of present academic status including all previous scholarships and fellowships and memberships in professional, scientific, scholastic and honor societies;
(3) a one-page account of involvement in professional and extracurricular activities, list of proposed expenses for the year; if married, include spouse and family expenses; list all sources and amounts of income;
(4) name of university to be attended and planned field of study;
(5) graduate record examination scores;
(6) a one- to two-page statement describing career goals;
(7) official transcripts from all colleges or universities attended and;
(8) letters of reference from three individuals who are directly familiar with the applicant and can speak specifically to educational achievements and capacity for graduate study.

Duration: One academic year.

Deadline: Phi Lambda Sigma-AFPE Fellowship: February 15. Rho Chi-AFPE Fellowship: February 1. Notification by April 15.

PUBLICATIONS:
Program announcement.

OFFICERS:
Ellen L. Woods, President and Secretary

AMERICAN FOUNDATION FOR PHARMACEUTICAL EDUCATION (AFPE) [2457]

6076 Franconia Road, Suite C
Alexandria, VA 22310-1758
(703) 875-3095
Fax: (703) 875-3098
E-mail: info@afpenet.org
Web Site: www.afpenet.org

FOUNDED: 1942

AREAS OF INTEREST:
Pharmaceutical education.

NAME(S) OF PROGRAMS:

- **Kappa Epsilon-AFPE-Nellie Wakeman First Year Graduate Fellowship**

TYPE:
Fellowships.

PURPOSE:
To encourage an outstanding pharmacy school graduate to pursue an advanced degree in the pharmaceutical sciences.

ELIGIBILITY:
An applicant must be in the final year of the Pharm.D. program or have completed a pharmacy degree. Consideration is given to those who need financial assistance to further their education in pharmacy. At the time of application, the Kappa Epsilon member must be in good financial standing with the KE Fraternity and planning to pursue a Doctor of Philosophy (Ph.D.) degree, a Master's degree, or a combined Residency/Master's degree program at a U.S. college or school of pharmacy.

FINANCIAL DATA:
The funds may be used for any purpose decided by the awardee and faculty sponsor that will enable the student to have a successful program, e.g., student stipend, laboratory supplies, books, materials, travel related to the program of study. None of the funds shall be used for indirect costs by the institution.

Amount of support per award: $7,500.

Total amount of support: $7,500.

NO. AWARDS: 1.

APPLICATION INFO:
Applications can be downloaded from the web site. Applications must include:
(1) a completed application form (application and reference forms available from a Kappa Epsilon faculty advisor or the Kappa Epsilon Executive Office, Tel: (913) 262-2749);
(2) a letter of recommendation from the faculty advisor and one other faculty member familiar with the applicant (both faculty members are to complete a letter of reference form) and;
(3) official transcripts of all collegiate grades, undergraduate and graduate.
Applications should be sent to the Kappa Epsilon Executive Office: 7700 Shawnee Mission Parkway, Suite 201, Overland Park, KS 66202.

Duration: One year.

Deadline: All application materials must be received by February 1. Notification end of April.

AMERICAN INSTITUTE OF THE HISTORY OF PHARMACY [2458]

University of Wisconsin School of Pharmacy
Rennebohm Hall
777 Highland Avenue
Madison, WI 53705-2222
(608) 262-5378
E-mail: gia@aihp.org
Web Site: www.aihp.org

FOUNDED: 1941

AREAS OF INTEREST:
History of pharmacy.

NAME(S) OF PROGRAMS:

- **Fischelis Grants for Research in the History of American Pharmacy**
- **History of Pharmacy Thesis Research Grants-in-Aid**

TYPE:
Grants-in-aid; Research grants.

PURPOSE:
To contribute to the understanding of the development of civilization by fostering the creation, preservation and dissemination of knowledge concerning the history and related humanistic aspects of the pharmaceutical field.

ELIGIBILITY:
For grants-in-aid, applicants must be Ph.D. students in good standing at an institution of the U.S. Students need not be American citizens, nor does the research topic have to be related to American history. Thesis research must be clearly related to some

aspect of pharmaceutical history or some other humanistic investigation that utilizes a pharmaco-historical approach.

For Fischelis Grants, applicants do not have to be U.S. citizens, but must attend American institutions.

FINANCIAL DATA:

Grants-in-Aid only cover direct costs of research attributable to supplies and other expenses that cannot be reimbursed by the degree-granting institution itself. These can include computer time and programming, obtaining a photocopy or microform of essential sources, travel and maintenance at a site away from the home university. Ineligible expenses include routine typing of the manuscript, living expenses at the home university, publication of research results or routine illustrations for the manuscript.

Amount of support per award: Fischelis Grants: Varies; Grants-in-Aid: Up to $2,500.

APPLICATION INFO:

Application forms required for both programs. For Grants-in-Aid, application must be no longer than four pages and must include identifying information of the graduate student, educational background, faculty reference information, thesis topic and description, estimate of expenses, statement of other financial support applied for and other information considered important to the proper consideration of the application.

Deadline: February 1.

ADDRESS INQUIRIES TO:

Beth D. Fisher
Director of Curatorial Affairs
(See address above.)

AMERICAN SOCIETY OF REGIONAL ANESTHESIA AND PAIN MEDICINE [2459]

4 Penn Center West
Suite 401
Pittsburgh, PA 15276
(412) 471-2718
Fax: (412) 471-7503
E-mail: asraassistant@asra.com
Web Site: www.asra.com

AREAS OF INTEREST:

Regional anesthesia and pain medicine.

NAME(S) OF PROGRAMS:

- **ASRA Carl Koller Memorial Research Grant**
- **ASRA Chronic Pain Research Grant**

TYPE:

Research grants.

PURPOSE:

To support research related to any aspect of regional anesthesia, acute and chronic pain medicine and their application to surgery, obstetrics and pain control; to encourage anesthesiologists and other researchers who are interested in the field.

ELIGIBILITY:

Applicant must be a member of the ASRA.

FINANCIAL DATA:

Amount of support per award: $500 to $200,000.

Total amount of support: Up to $200,000 biennially.

NO. MOST RECENT APPLICANTS: 17 for the year 2014.

NO. AWARDS: 1 for the year 2016.

APPLICATION INFO:

The application, which must be written by the applicant, should be accompanied by a complete narrative research protocol. The research proposal must be concerned with an original idea or concept. The research must be carried out primarily by the applicant.

Deadline: September 1.

ADDRESS INQUIRIES TO:

Angie Stengel, Executive Director
(See address above.)

PHARMACEUTICAL RESEARCH AND MANUFACTURERS OF AMERICA FOUNDATION, INC. [2460]

950 F Street, N.W.
Suite 300
Washington, DC 20004
(202) 572-7756
E-mail: foundation@phrma.org
Web Site: www.phrmafoundation.org

AREAS OF INTEREST:

Pharmacology and clinical pharmacology.

NAME(S) OF PROGRAMS:

- **The Paul Calabresi Medical Student Fellowship**

TYPE:

Fellowships.

PURPOSE:

To generate interest in research careers in pharmacology, including clinical pharmacology, among medical and dental students; to enable medical or dental students who have substantial interests in research and teaching careers in pharmacology/clinical pharmacology to pursue a specific research effort within a pharmacology or clinical pharmacology unit.

ELIGIBILITY:

Candidates must be enrolled in a U.S. medical/dental school and have finished at least one year of the school curriculum. Must be U.S. citizen or permanent resident and have firm commitment from an accredited U.S. school.

GEOG. RESTRICTIONS: United States.

FINANCIAL DATA:

Amount of support per award: Maximum stipend $18,000.

NO. AWARDS: 2 budgeted.

APPLICATION INFO:

Consult the Foundation web site.

Duration: Six months to two years.

Deadline: February 1.

ADDRESS INQUIRIES TO:

The Paul Calabresi Medical
Student Research Fellowship
(See address above.)

*SPECIAL STIPULATIONS:

Commitment must be full-time.

PHARMACEUTICAL RESEARCH AND MANUFACTURERS OF AMERICA FOUNDATION, INC. [2461]

950 F Street, N.W.
Suite 300
Washington, DC 20004
(202) 572-7756
E-mail: foundation@phrma.org
Web Site: www.phrmafoundation.org

FOUNDED: 1965

AREAS OF INTEREST:

Pharmaceutics.

NAME(S) OF PROGRAMS:

- **Post Doctoral Fellowships in Pharmaceutics**

TYPE:

Fellowships.

YEAR PROGRAM STARTED: 1992

PURPOSE:

To encourage more qualified graduates from Ph.D. programs in pharmaceutics to obtain postdoctoral research training in the area of pharmaceutics.

LEGAL BASIS:

501(c)(3) organization.

ELIGIBILITY:

Applicants must either hold a Ph.D. degree in a field of study logically or functionally related to the proposed postdoctoral activities or expect to receive such a degree before activating the fellowship. Suitable facilities for the necessary training and research must be available to the applicant. U.S. citizenship or permanent residency in the U.S. is required. Applicant must have firm commitment from a sponsor/mentor at an accredited U.S. university.

GEOG. RESTRICTIONS: United States.

FINANCIAL DATA:

The award is made to the institution on behalf of the Fellow. The program provides no other subsidies (travel, tuition, fringe benefit costs, etc.) and indirect costs are not paid to the institution.

Amount of support per award: Maximum $80,000 ($40,000 per year).

NO. AWARDS: 2 budgeted.

APPLICATION INFO:

Applications are to be submitted online by an accredited U.S. school.

Duration: Two years.

Deadline: September 1. Announcement December 15.

PUBLICATIONS:

Brochure.

IRS I.D.: 52-6063009

BOARD OF DIRECTORS:

Michael Rosenblatt, M.D., Chairman
Thomas O. Daniel, M.D.
Mikael Dolsten, M.D., Ph.D.
Betsy Garofalo, M.D.
Jan M. Lundberg, Ph.D.
Andrew Plump, M.D., Ph.D.
Alfred W. Sandrock, M.D., Ph.D.
Moncef Slaoui, Ph.D.
Joanne Waldstreicher, M.D.
Elias Zerhouni, M.D.

ADDRESS INQUIRIES TO:

Postdoctoral Fellowships in Pharmaceutics
(See address above.)

*SPECIAL STIPULATIONS:

The second year of this award is contingent upon a progress report approved by the Foundation and submission of a financial report.

PHARMACEUTICAL RESEARCH AND MANUFACTURERS OF AMERICA FOUNDATION, INC. [2462]

950 F Street, N.W.
Suite 300
Washington, DC 20004
(202) 572-7756
E-mail: foundation@phrma.org
Web Site: www.phrmafoundation.org

FOUNDED: 1965

AREAS OF INTEREST:
Pharmaceutics.

NAME(S) OF PROGRAMS:
- **Predoctoral Fellowships in Pharmaceutics**

TYPE:
Fellowships. Support for full-time research for promising students in the field of pharmaceutics during their thesis research.

YEAR PROGRAM STARTED: 1987

PURPOSE:
To support promising students in the area of pharmaceutics during their thesis research.

LEGAL BASIS:
501(c)(3) organization.

ELIGIBILITY:
Applicants must be full-time, in-residence Ph.D. candidates in the field of pharmaceutics who are enrolled in schools of pharmacy and who expect to complete the requirements for the Ph.D. in two years or less from the time the fellowship begins. The program seeks to support advanced students who will have completed the bulk of their pre-thesis requirements (generally two years of study) and are starting their thesis research by the time the award is activated. Students just starting in graduate school should not apply. Applicants must be U.S. citizens or permanent residents and have a firm commitment from an accredited U.S. university.

GEOG. RESTRICTIONS: United States.

FINANCIAL DATA:
The award is made to the university on behalf of the Fellow and provides a stipend, payable monthly, which includes $1,000 per year for incidentals directly associated with the thesis research preparation.

Amount of support per award: Maximum $40,000 ($20,000 per year), which includes up to $1,000 per year for expenses associated with thesis research.

APPLICATION INFO:
Applications are to be submitted on the Foundation web site.

Duration: Up to two years.

Deadline: September 1. Announcement by December 15.

PUBLICATIONS:
Brochure.

IRS I.D.: 52-6063009

BOARD OF DIRECTORS:
Michael Rosenblatt, M.D., Chairman
Thomas O. Daniel, M.D.
Mikael Dolsten, M.D., Ph.D.
Betsy Garofalo, M.D.
Jan M. Lundberg, Ph.D.
Andrew Plump, M.D., Ph.D.
Alfred W. Sandrock, M.D., Ph.D.
Moncef Slaoui, Ph.D.
Joanne Waldstreicher, M.D.
Elias Zerhouni, M.D.

ADVISORY COMMITTEE:
Darrell R. Abernethy, M.D., Ph.D.
Terry L. Bowlin, Ph.D.
Bill Chin, M.D.
Jean Paul Gagnon, Ph.D.
Michael J. Hageman, Ph.D.
Michael N. Liebman, Ph.D.

ADDRESS INQUIRIES TO:
See e-mail address above.

PHARMACEUTICAL RESEARCH AND MANUFACTURERS OF AMERICA FOUNDATION, INC. [2463]

950 F Street, N.W.
Suite 300
Washington, DC 20004
(202) 572-7756
E-mail: foundation@phrma.org
Web Site: www.phrmafoundation.org

FOUNDED: 1965

AREAS OF INTEREST:
Pharmacology, clinical pharmacology, drug toxicology, pharmaceutics, informatics and health outcomes.

NAME(S) OF PROGRAMS:
- **Research Starter Grants in Adherence Improvement**
- **Research Starter Grants in Health Outcomes**
- **Research Starter Grants in Informatics**
- **Research Starter Grants in Pharmaceutics**
- **Research Starter Grants in Pharmacology/Toxicology**
- **Research Starter Grants in Translational Medicine and Therapeutics**

TYPE:
Project/program grants; Research grants; Seed money grants. Starter grants to support research in the fields of pharmacology, clinical pharmacology, drug toxicology, pharmaceutics, informatics and health outcomes. The grants offer financial support to individuals beginning independent research careers at the faculty level.

YEAR PROGRAM STARTED: 1972

PURPOSE:
To offer financial support to individuals beginning their independent research careers at the faculty level.

LEGAL BASIS:
501(c)(3) organization.

ELIGIBILITY:
Applicant must be a U.S. citizen or permanent resident for all but the Research Starter Grants in Adherence Improvement, which has no citizenship requirement. Those holding the academic rank of instructor or assistant professor and investigators at the doctoral level with equivalent positions are eligible to apply, providing their proposed research is neither directly nor indirectly subsidized to any significant degree by an extramural support mechanism.

GEOG. RESTRICTIONS: United States.

FINANCIAL DATA:
Funds are generally unrestricted, to provide resources directly related to the proposed research. Funds may not be used as salary support of the grantee nor for indirect costs to the institution. No more than $1,500 per year may be used by the grantee for travel to professional meetings.

Funds may be used to support technical assistance, which may include hourly wages of a technician; however, funds may not be used to provide fringe benefits or cover indirect costs.

Amount of support per award: Research Starter Grants in Adherence Improvement: $50,000; all others: $100,000.

Total amount of support: Varies.

APPLICATION INFO:
Applications should be submitted on the Foundation web site.

Duration: One year.

Deadline: Adherence Improvement, Pharmaceutics, Pharmacology/Toxicology and Informatics: : September 1; Health Outcomes and Translational Medicine and Therapeutics: February 1.

PUBLICATIONS:
Brochure.

IRS I.D.: 52-6063009

BOARD OF DIRECTORS:
Michael Rosenblatt, M.D., Chairman
Thomas O. Daniel, M.D.
Mikael Dolsten, M.D., Ph.D.
Betsy Garofalo, M.D.
Jan M. Lundberg, Ph.D.
Andrew Plump, M.D., Ph.D.
Alfred W. Sandrock, M.D., Ph.D.
Moncef Slaoui, Ph.D.
Joanne Waldstreicher, M.D.
Elias Zerhouni, M.D.

ADVISORY COMMITTEE:
Darrell R. Abernethy, M.D., Ph.D.
Terry L. Bowlin, Ph.D.
Bill Chin, M.D.
Jean Paul Gagnon, Ph.D.
Michael J. Hageman, Ph.D.
Michael N. Liebman, Ph.D.

ADDRESS INQUIRIES TO:
See e-mail address above.

PHARMACEUTICAL RESEARCH AND MANUFACTURERS OF AMERICA FOUNDATION, INC. [2464]

950 F Street, N.W.
Suite 300
Washington, DC 20004
(202) 572-7756
E-mail: foundation@phrma.org
Web Site: www.phrmafoundation.org

FOUNDED: 1965

AREAS OF INTEREST:
Pharmacology or toxicology.

NAME(S) OF PROGRAMS:
- **Pre Doctoral Fellowships in Pharmacology/Toxicology**

TYPE:
Fellowships. Support for full-time research for promising students in the fields of pharmacology or toxicology during their thesis research.

YEAR PROGRAM STARTED: 1978

PURPOSE:
To support promising students during their thesis research.

LEGAL BASIS:
501(c)(3) organization.

ELIGIBILITY:
Applicants must be full-time, in-residence Ph.D. candidates in the fields of pharmacology or toxicology who are enrolled in schools of medicine, pharmacy, dentistry, or veterinary medicine. The program seeks to support advanced students who will have completed the bulk of their pre-thesis requirements (at least two years of study) and are starting their thesis research by the time the award is activated. Students just starting in graduate school should not apply.
Applicant must be a U.S. citizen or a permanent resident and must have a firm commitment from an accredited U.S. university. One application per institution accepted.

GEOG. RESTRICTIONS: United States.

FINANCIAL DATA:
The award is made to the university on behalf of the Fellow and provides a stipend which includes up to $1,000 a year for incidentals directly associated with the thesis research.

Amount of support per award: Maximum $40,000 ($20,000 per year).

NO. AWARDS: 9 budgeted.

APPLICATION INFO:
Applications should be submitted on the Foundation web site.

Duration: Up to two years.

Deadline: September 1. Announcement December 15.

PUBLICATIONS:
Brochure.

IRS I.D.: 52-6063009

BOARD OF DIRECTORS:
Michael Rosenblatt, M.D., Chairman
Thomas O. Daniel, M.D.
Mikael Dolsten, M.D., Ph.D.
Betsy Garofalo, M.D.
Jan M. Lundberg, Ph.D.
Andrew Plump, M.D., Ph.D.
Alfred W. Sandrock, M.D., Ph.D.
Moncef Slaoui, Ph.D.
Joanne Waldstreicher, M.D.
Elias Zerhouni, M.D.

ADVISORY COMMITTEE:
Darrell R. Abernethy, M.D., Ph.D.
Bill Chin, M.D.
Terry L. Bowlin, Ph.D.
Jean Paul Gagnon, Ph.D.
Michael J. Hageman, Ph.D.
Michael N. Liebman, Ph.D.

ADDRESS INQUIRIES TO:
See e-mail address above.

THE UNIVERSITY OF SYDNEY [2465]

Scholarships Office
Level 5, Jane Foss Russell Building G02
The University of Sydney N.S.W. 2006
Australia
(02) 8627 8112
Fax: (02) 8627 8485
E-mail: scholarships.officer@sydney.edu.au
Web Site: www.sydney.edu.au/scholarships/research

FOUNDED: 1850

AREAS OF INTEREST:
Pharmacy.

NAME(S) OF PROGRAMS:
- **Elizabeth Wunsch Postgraduate Research Scholarship in Pharmacy**

TYPE:
Scholarships.

YEAR PROGRAM STARTED: 1982

PURPOSE:
To promote and encourage research work within the Faculty of Pharmacy at the University of Sydney.

LEGAL BASIS:
University.

ELIGIBILITY:
Open to graduates of the University of Sydney or any other university who are eligible to enroll in a higher degree in the Faculty of Pharmacy on a topic approved by the Head of the Department.

FINANCIAL DATA:
The scholarship does not cover tuition fees payable by international students.

Amount of support per award: $25,849 AUD per annum for the year 2015.

NO. AWARDS: 1 offered as vacancy occurs and funds are available.

APPLICATION INFO:
Contact the University for guidelines.

Duration: Master's research degree: Two years; Ph.D. degree: Three years.

ADDRESS INQUIRIES TO:
Faculty of Pharmacy
The University of Sydney
N.S.W. 2006 Australia
Tel: (02) 9036 7243
Fax: (02) 9351 4391
E-mail: pharmacy.research@sydney.edu.au

*PLEASE NOTE:
Very few awards are available and competition for them is extremely keen. They are awarded strictly on academic merit and only graduates with First Class Honours or equivalent qualifications (e.g., graduation magna cum laude) will be considered.

*SPECIAL STIPULATIONS:
Scholarships are tenable at the University of Sydney. Holder is required to enroll for a higher degree.

Physical medicine and rehabilitation

AMERICAN BURN ASSOCIATION [2466]

311 South Wacker Drive
Suite 4150
Chicago, IL 60606
(312) 642-9260
Fax: (312) 642-9130
E-mail: info@ameriburn.org
Web Site: www.ameriburn.org

AREAS OF INTEREST:
Thermal injury.

NAME(S) OF PROGRAMS:
- **International Education Exchange Program**
- **Cheryl Jordan Scholarship Fund**
- **Visiting Professor Program**

TYPE:
Exchange programs; Professorships; Travel grants.

PURPOSE:
To support efforts that address the problems of burn injuries and burn victims; to provide care and rehabilitation to burn patients, conduct burn-related research, educate burn team members, develop and implement burn injury prevention programs, fight fires and address the psychosocial needs of burn victims.

ELIGIBILITY:
Institutions of higher learning in the U.S. and its territories are eligible to apply for support of appropriate research to be conducted by qualified investigators.

GEOG. RESTRICTIONS: United States and Canada.

FINANCIAL DATA:
Amount of support per award: $1,500 to $2,000, depending on the award.

NO. AWARDS: 1 each annually.

APPLICATION INFO:
Applicants must submit a brief letter outlining the purpose of the grant.

ADDRESS INQUIRIES TO:
John Krichbaum, Executive Director
(See address above.)

AMERICAN GERIATRICS SOCIETY [2467]

40 Fulton Street, 18th Floor
New York, NY 10038
(212) 308-1414
Fax: (212) 832-8646
E-mail: info.amger@americangeriatrics.org
Web Site: www.americangeriatrics.org

AREAS OF INTEREST:
Problems of the aged.

NAME(S) OF PROGRAMS:
- **AGS New Investigator Awards**
- **Clinical Student Research Award**
- **Clinician of the Year**
- **The Arnold P. Gold Foundation Humanism in Medicine Awards for Practicing Doctors**
- **Edward Henderson Student Award**
- **Dennis W. Jahnigen Memorial Award**
- **Nascher/Manning Award**
- **Outstanding Junior Clinical Education Manuscript**
- **Outstanding Junior Clinical Educator of the Year**
- **Outstanding Junior Investigator of the Year**
- **Outstanding Junior Research Manuscript**
- **Outstanding Mid-Career Clinical Teacher of the Year**
- **Outstanding Scientific Achievement for Clinical Investigation Award**
- **Scientist-in-Training Research Award**

TYPE:
Awards/prizes. AGS New Investigator Awards are presented to individuals whose original research, as presented in a submitted abstract, reflects new and relevant research in geriatrics.

The AGS Student Research Award is presented to the student who submitted the most outstanding student abstract for the AGS Annual Meeting.

Clinician of the Year was established to recognize the great contributions of practitioners to the delivery of quality health care to older people, and the importance of the geriatrics clinician in our health care delivery system.

Arnold P. Gold Foundation Award identifies and honors a practicing physician who best demonstrates the ideals of compassionate and respectful care for a patient's physical and emotional well-being.

Edward Henderson Student Award is presented to a medical student interested in pursuing a career in geriatrics who has demonstrated excellence in the field.

Dennis W. Jahnigen Memorial Award is given annually to an AGS member who has provided leadership to train students in geriatrics and has contributed significantly to the progress of geriatrics education in health professions schools.

Nascher/Manning Award recognizes distinguished, lifelong achievement in clinical geriatrics, including medicine, psychiatry, and all other related disciplines.

Outstanding Scientific Achievement for Clinical Investigation Award recognizes outstanding achievement in clinical research addressing health care problems of older adults by an investigator who is actively involved in direct patient care.

PURPOSE:
To encourage and promote the field of geriatrics and to stress the importance of medical research in the field of aging; to recognize individuals whose outstanding work in geriatrics education, research and clinical practice contribute to the delivery of high-quality care for older people.

FINANCIAL DATA:
Amount of support per award: AGS New Investigator Awards: $1,500; Clinical Student Research Award, Edward Henderson Student Award and Scientist-in-Training Research Award: $500; Clinician of the Year: $2,000; Arnold P. Gold Foundation Award: $1,000 stipend, plus up to $2,000 for travel expenses to attend AGS meeting; Dennis W. Jahnigen Memorial Award, Nascher/Manning Award and Outstanding Scientific Achievement for Clinical Investigation Award: travel expenses to attend the AGS meeting.

APPLICATION INFO:
Application is posted on the Society web site by mid-August.

Deadline: December 4.

ADDRESS INQUIRIES TO:
Dennise McAlpin, Senior Manager of Professional Education and Special Projects
(See address above.)

AMERICAN KINESIOTHERAPY ASSOCIATION, INC. [2468]

118 College Drive, Box No. 5142
Hattiesburg, MS 39406
(800) 296-2582
Fax: (601) 266-4445
E-mail: info@akta.org
Web Site: www.akta.org

FOUNDED: 1946

AREAS OF INTEREST:
Kinesiotherapy, including adaptive physical education.

NAME(S) OF PROGRAMS:

- **AKTA Lou Montalvano Memorial Scholarship**

TYPE:
Scholarships. Award for students in AKTA-accredited kinesiotherapy programs.

PURPOSE:
To recognize academic excellence and career planning through funding for educational needs.

LEGAL BASIS:
Incorporated, nonprofit organization.

ELIGIBILITY:
Candidate must be currently enrolled in an AKTA-accredited kinesiotherapy program in a university and have definite intentions to pursue certification and a career in kinesiotherapy. Candidate must be a current member of the AKTA. Past AKTA scholarship winners are ineligible to apply for further AKTA scholarships.

FINANCIAL DATA:
Amount of support per award: $500.

Total amount of support: $500.

NO. AWARDS: 1 annually.

APPLICATION INFO:
Application process includes college transcripts and three letters of recommendation. Further information is available from the Association.

Duration: One year.

Deadline: October 1.

ADDRESS INQUIRIES TO:
Melissa Ziegler, M.A., R.K.T.
Executive Director
(See e-mail address above.)

THE AMERICAN ORTHOPAEDIC SOCIETY FOR SPORTS MEDICINE (AOSSM) [2469]

9400 West Higgins Road
Suite 300
Rosemont, IL 60018
(877) 321-3500 (IL only)
(847) 292-4900
Fax: (847) 292-4905
E-mail: irv@aossm.org
Web Site: www.sportsmed.org

FOUNDED: 1972

AREAS OF INTEREST:
Sports medicine.

NAME(S) OF PROGRAMS:

- **AOSSM Young Investigator Grant**

TYPE:
Awards/prizes; Research grants. Grant is intended to encourage junior researchers.

PURPOSE:
To increase the knowledge of and improve the care of sports-related injuries and disease.

ELIGIBILITY:
Grants will be awarded to the principal investigators who fulfill the following criteria:
(1) has not received any peer-reviewed external funding nor any external funding greater than $15,000;
(2) must be an orthopaedic surgeon who has graduated from an approved residency program or is a resident currently in an approved program;
(3) must document and play the primary role in the proposed investigation and;
(4) must stay at the parent institution while completing the project.

FINANCIAL DATA:
Amount of support per award: Up to $50,000 over a 24-month period.

NO. AWARDS: 1 or 2.

APPLICATION INFO:
Online submission only.

Duration: Two years.

Deadline: Pre-review deadline: August 15. Final deadline: December 1.

ADDRESS INQUIRIES TO:
Irv Bomberger, Executive Director
(See address above.)

FOUNDATION FOR PHYSICAL THERAPY, INC. [2470]

1111 North Fairfax Street
Alexandria, VA 22314-1488
(703) 706-8505
(800) 875-1378
Fax: (703) 706-8587
E-mail: info@foundation4pt.org
Web Site: www.foundation4pt.org

FOUNDED: 1979

AREAS OF INTEREST:
Physical therapy research, investigative studies that add to or refine the body of clinical knowledge on which physical therapy practice is based, and intervention projects involving therapeutic procedures and modalities.

TYPE:
Research grants.

YEAR PROGRAM STARTED: 1998

PURPOSE:
To add to or refine the body of clinical knowledge on which physical therapy practice is based and to evaluate patient interventions.

LEGAL BASIS:
Foundation.

ELIGIBILITY:
Awards are made to qualified physical therapists and physical therapist assistants or groups of investigators. Must be a U.S. citizen or permanent resident. Projects must be sponsored by a U.S. institution or organization. No funds will be approved to finance cost overruns or deficits on existing projects or to finance projects already in progress.

GEOG. RESTRICTIONS: United States.

FINANCIAL DATA:
Amount of support per award: Maximum $40,000 to $80,000 per year.

NO. AWARDS: 2 for the year 2015.

APPLICATION INFO:
Application guidelines and access to the online application system are available on the Foundation's web site.

Duration: One to two years.

Deadline: Proposals are due first week in August for most types of grants. Contact Foundation for details.

PUBLICATIONS:
Application guidelines.

IRS I.D.: 13-6161225

ADDRESS INQUIRIES TO:
Dario Dieguez Ph.D.
Scientific Programs and Communications Manager
(See address above.)

*PLEASE NOTE:
Applicants can only apply to one grant mechanism per cycle.

FOUNDATION FOR PHYSICAL THERAPY, INC. [2471]

1111 North Fairfax Street
Alexandria, VA 22314-1488
(800) 875-1378
Fax: (703) 706-8587
E-mail: info@foundation4pt.org
Web Site: www.foundation4pt.org

FOUNDED: 1979

AREAS OF INTEREST:
Physical therapy.

NAME(S) OF PROGRAMS:

- **Florence P. Kendall Post-Professional Doctoral Scholarship**
- **New Investigator Fellowship Training Initiative (NIFTI)**
- **Promotion of Doctoral Studies Scholarships (PODS)**

TYPE:
Fellowships; Scholarships. Fellowships for postdoctoral physical therapy research. Scholarships for physical therapists who intend to pursue physical therapy research as a career.

YEAR PROGRAM STARTED: 1979

PURPOSE:
To provide scholarships that support physical therapists who wish to continue their doctoral coursework and enter the dissertation phase; to provide fellowships that support developing researchers and improve their competitiveness in securing external funding for future research.

LEGAL BASIS:
Foundation.

ELIGIBILITY:
Must be U.S. citizen or permanent resident. Scholarship applicants must be physical therapists or physical therapist assistants pursuing a doctoral degree in physical therapy or a related field with a research focus related to the clinical practice of physical therapy. Applicants must demonstrate a commitment to research.

Fellowship applicants must be physical therapists or physical therapist assistants who have completed Doctorate, or the professional education degree in physical therapy for those already holding a post-professional doctoral degree in the last five years.

One year of teaching is expected for each year of support.

FINANCIAL DATA:
Amount of support per award: Maximum of $15,000 for scholarships; $78,000 for fellowships.

Total amount of support: PODS I Scholarships: $7,500 annually for a maximum of three years (must reapply each year); PODS II Scholarships: Up to $15,000 annually for a maximum of two years (must reapply each year); Florence P. Kendall Doctoral Scholarships: $5,000; Fellowships: A two-year award totaling $78,000.

NO. AWARDS: 17 scholarships and 1 fellowship for the year 2015.

APPLICATION INFO:
Applicants must check the online eligibility guidelines, review the application instructions, then submit the online application.

Duration: Scholarships: One year; Fellowships: Two years.

Deadline: Mid-January for Promotion of Doctoral Studies (PODS) Scholarships and New Investigator Fellowship Training Initiative (NIFTI) Fellowships; Mid-August for Florence P. Kendall Doctoral Scholarships.

IRS I.D.: 13-6161225

ADDRESS INQUIRIES TO:
Dario Dieguez, Ph.D.
Scientific Programs and Communications Manager
(See address above.)

INTERNATIONAL ORDER OF ALHAMBRA [2472]

4200 Leeds Avenue
Baltimore, MD 21229-5496
(800) 478-2946
(410) 242-0660
Fax: (410) 536-5729
E-mail: salaam@orderofalhambra.org
Web Site: www.orderalhambra.org

FOUNDED: 1904

AREAS OF INTEREST:
Scholarships for those interested in teaching special education.

NAME(S) OF PROGRAMS:

- **Scholarship and Charity Fund**

TYPE:
Grants-in-aid; Scholarships.

YEAR PROGRAM STARTED: 1970

PURPOSE:
To further education in the field of the intellectually and developmentally disabled.

LEGAL BASIS:
A nonprofit 501(c)(3) fraternal organization of Catholic men and women dedicated to assisting intellectually disabled persons.

ELIGIBILITY:
Applicant should be attending college or postgraduate study. Applicants must be majoring in special education, which involves the mentally, physically or emotionally handicapped person, and must be eligible to teach special education upon graduation.

GEOG. RESTRICTIONS: United States and Canada.

FINANCIAL DATA:
Amount of support per award: Varies depending on the level of education.

NO. AWARDS: Varies.

APPLICATION INFO:
Students may only apply for one semester per application. Call (800) 478-2946 for further information.

Duration: One semester. Renewable by reapplication.

Deadline: March 1.

ADDRESS INQUIRIES TO:
Roger Reid, Executive Director
(See address above.)

NATIONAL AMBUCS, INC. [2473]

4285 Regency Drive
Greensboro, NC 27410
(336) 852-0052
Fax: (336) 852-6830
E-mail: scholars@ambucs.org
Web Site: www.ambucs.org

FOUNDED: 1948

AREAS OF INTEREST:
Physical therapy, occupational therapy, speech-language pathology and hearing audiology.

NAME(S) OF PROGRAMS:

- **AMBUCS Scholars-Scholarships for Therapists**

TYPE:
Scholarships. AMBUCS Scholars is the largest private single source of educational grants for therapists in America. The goal of this program is to provide financial assistance to needy students studying therapy, which in return places trained individuals in the therapy community to help people with disabilities.

YEAR PROGRAM STARTED: 1955

PURPOSE:
To financially assist students studying for qualification in one of the therapy professions.

LEGAL BASIS:
Private nonprofit association.

ELIGIBILITY:
Applicant must be a citizen of the U.S., document financial need, document good scholastic standing and be accepted at the junior or senior undergraduate or graduate level in an accredited program by the appropriate health therapy profession authority in occupational therapy, physical therapy, speech-language pathology or hearing audiology.

GEOG. RESTRICTIONS: United States.

FINANCIAL DATA:
Amount of support per award: $500 to $1,500, plus one two-year scholarship (awarded annually) of $6,000.

Total amount of support: $167,500 for the year 2015.

CO-OP FUNDING PROGRAMS: Funding for this scholarship program is provided entirely by individual AMBUCS chapters and private donations.

NO. MOST RECENT APPLICANTS: 1,267 for the year 2013.

NO. AWARDS: Approximately 200 scholarships each year.

APPLICATION INFO:
Applications must be submitted electronically. If the student is being sponsored by a local chapter, the student should give the local chapter a copy of the completed application, along with the most current IRS Form 1040, a narrative statement, and enrollment certification.

Duration: One academic year.

Deadline: Applications accepted from mid-January to April 15 only.

ADDRESS INQUIRIES TO:
Janice Blankenship
AMBUCS Scholarship Coordinator
AMBUCS Resource Center
P.O. Box 5127
High Point, NC 27262
E-mail: ambucs@ambucs.org

NATIONAL ASSOCIATION OF HEALTH SERVICES EXECUTIVES (NAHSE) [2474]

NAHSE National Office
1050 Connecticut Avenue, N.W.
5th Floor
Washington, DC 20036
(202) 772-1030
Fax: (202) 772-1072
E-mail: nahsehq@nahse.org
Web Site: www.nahse.org

AREAS OF INTEREST:
Health care.

TYPE:
Scholarships.

PURPOSE:
To promote the advancement and development of Black health care leaders and elevate the quality of health care services rendered to minority and underserved communities.

ELIGIBILITY:
Applicant must:
(1) be either enrolled or accepted in an accredited college or university program, pursuing a B.S., M.S. or Doctorate degree, majoring in computer science, management of information technology or information management, or provide proof of intent to pursue a major in one of the above areas of study;
(2) be able to demonstrate financial need;
(3) be an active NAHSE member;
(4) have a minimum academic grade point average of 3.0 or above on a scale of 4.0 and;
(5) submit a position paper examining new information and technology trends and their effects on health care.

To retain the scholarship for the second year, the recipient must maintain a 3.0 grade point average and produce a position paper on new technologies and present the position paper to an FCG or NAHSE panel.

FINANCIAL DATA:
Amount of support per award: $2,500.

Total amount of support: $7,500.

NO. MOST RECENT APPLICANTS: 12.

NO. AWARDS: 3.

APPLICATION INFO:
Contact the Association for guidelines.

Duration: One year.

Deadline: May 1.

ADDRESS INQUIRIES TO:
Beverly Glover, Manager
(See address above.)

NATIONAL MULTIPLE SCLEROSIS SOCIETY

Research Programs
733 Third Avenue
New York, NY 10017-3288
(212) 986-3240
Fax: (212) 986-7981
E-mail: msresearch@nmss.org
Web Site: www.nationalmssociety.org

TYPE:
Awards/prizes; Fellowships; Research grants; Training grants; Research contracts. Grants for fundamental or applied research in scientific areas pertinent to multiple sclerosis. Grants are available for clinical or nonclinical studies, providing they show a reasonable relevance to the Society's interests.

See entry 2399 for full listing.

NATIONAL SOCIETY DAUGHTERS OF THE AMERICAN REVOLUTION [2475]

1776 D Street, N.W.
Washington, DC 20006-5303
(202) 879-3263
Fax: (202) 879-3348
E-mail: scholarships@dar.org
Web Site: www.dar.org

FOUNDED: 1895

AREAS OF INTEREST:
Occupational and physical therapy.

NAME(S) OF PROGRAMS:
- **Occupational/Physical Therapy Scholarship**

TYPE:
Scholarships. Awarded to students who are in financial need and have been accepted or are attending an accredited school of occupational or physical therapy (including art, music, or physical therapy).

PURPOSE:
To provide ways and means to aid students in attaining higher education.

LEGAL BASIS:
Incorporated historical society.

ELIGIBILITY:
Scholarships are awarded without regard to race, religion, sex or national origin. Candidates must be U.S. citizens and must be enrolled in an accredited school of occupational or physical therapy in the U.S. No affiliation or relationship to DAR is required for qualification, but candidate must be sponsored by a local DAR Chapter.

Candidate must be majoring in occupational therapy or physical therapy and must be in financial need.

Awards are judged on the basis of academic excellence, commitment to field of study, as required, and need.

GEOG. RESTRICTIONS: United States.

FINANCIAL DATA:
Amount of support per award: Varies.

Total amount of support: Varies.

NO. AWARDS: Varies.

APPLICATION INFO:
Application information is available online. All scholarship applicants are required to have a letter of sponsorship from a chapter. Individuals interested in obtaining a letter of sponsorship from a local chapter are encouraged to contact the DAR State Chairman. A letter of acceptance into the occupational therapy program or the transcript stating the applicant is in the occupational therapy program must be included with the application.

Duration: One-time scholarship.

Deadline: February 15.

PUBLICATIONS:
American Spirit, magazine.

ADDRESS INQUIRIES TO:
Office of the Reporter General
DAR Scholarship Committee
(See address above.)

PHYSIOTHERAPY FOUNDATION OF CANADA [2476]

955 Green Valley Crescent
Suite 270
Ottawa ON K2C 3V4 Canada
(613) 564-5454 ext. 280
(800) 387-8679
Fax: (613) 564-1577
E-mail: foundation@physiotherapy.ca
Web Site: www.physiotherapyfoundation.ca

FOUNDED: 1982

AREAS OF INTEREST:
Canadian research and scholarship in physiotherapy.

NAME(S) OF PROGRAMS:
- **Constance Beattie Memorial Fund Bursary Program**
- **Alun Morgan Memorial Research Fund in Orthopaedic Physiotherapy**
- **NPAA Grant**
- **PFC Research Grants**
- **B.E. Schnurr Memorial Fund Research Grant**
- **Ann Collins Whitmore Memorial Fund Student Awards Competition**
- **Ann Collins Whitmore Memorial Scholarship**

TYPE:
Fellowships; Research grants; Scholarships. Beattie Memorial Fund Bursary Program is to provide support for continuing education courses that are relevant to applicants' career goals.

Alun Morgan Memorial Research Fund provides support for physiotherapy research projects that deal with the management of musculoskeletal problems in Canada.

NPAA Grant supports NPAA member(s) to pursue continuing professional development and translate learning in their local community and to recognize the contribution that NPAA members make to the profession and to CPA.

PFC Research Grants seek to encourage the development of new technology and treatment methods, develop methods for the prevention and early recognition of physical disabilities, evaluate the effectiveness and efficiency of both new and existing treatment methods, and encourage epidemiological studies on the incidence and prevalence of physical disabilities.

Schnurr Memorial Fund Research Grant provides for physiotherapy research projects, with special encouragement made for projects from Alberta.

Ann Collins Whitmore Memorial Fund Student Awards Competition is designed to encourage young researchers and is open to students pursuing a Baccalaureate degree in physiotherapy at one of the accredited university programs in Canada.

Ann Collins Whitmore Memorial Scholarship are for physiotherapists enrolled in a Ph.D. or Master's program. Special consideration will be made for blind physiotherapists.

YEAR PROGRAM STARTED: 1983

PURPOSE:
To develop the science of physiotherapy and expand knowledge and skills of individual physiotherapists.

LEGAL BASIS:
Public foundation.

GEOG. RESTRICTIONS: Canada.

FINANCIAL DATA:

Amount of support per award: Beattie Memorial Fund Bursary Program: Up to $1,500 for two recipients (up to $750 each); Morgan Memorial Research Fund: Up to $5,000; PFC Research Grants: $4,000; Schurr Memorial Fund Research Grant: Up to $3,500; Whitmore Memorial Fund: Up to $4,000.

Total amount of support: $1,300,000 since inception.

NO. MOST RECENT APPLICANTS: 15.

NO. AWARDS: 15.

APPLICATION INFO:

Applicant must use authorized application form.

Duration: One year. Renewal possible with reapplication.

Deadline: Contact the Foundation for exact dates.

GOVERNING BOARD:

Rob Werstine, President

ADDRESS INQUIRIES TO:

Rosalby Kelly, Grants Program Manager
(See address above.)

PVA RESEARCH FOUNDATION [2477]

801 Eighteenth Street, N.W.
Washington, DC 20006
(202) 416-7651
Fax: (202) 416-7641
E-mail: foundations@pva.org
Web Site: www.pva.org

FOUNDED: 1976

AREAS OF INTEREST:

Basic and applied research in spinal cord injury and diseases.

NAME(S) OF PROGRAMS:

- **Spinal Cord Injury Research Grants and Fellowships**

TYPE:

Awards/prizes; Conferences/seminars; Demonstration grants; Development grants; Fellowships; Project/program grants; Research grants; Seed money grants. The PVA Research Foundation funds research projects and fellowships relevant to spinal cord injury and diseases, in addition to sponsoring basic research that will increase scientific knowledge leading to a cure for spinal cord injury. The Foundation also funds research that deals with applied medical, psychological and technological areas of importance to persons with spinal cord injury or disease.

YEAR PROGRAM STARTED: 1976

PURPOSE:

To promote research to find better treatments and cures for paralysis; to support efforts to improve the quality of life of individuals with spinal cord dysfunction until cures are found.

LEGAL BASIS:

Tax-exempt corporation under Sections 170(c) and 501(c)(3) of the Internal Revenue Code. Incorporated in the District of Columbia as a nonprofit organization.

ELIGIBILITY:

All applications must be submitted by fiscally responsible organizational entities in the name of the Principal Investigator. Entities should be nonprofit academic institutions, health care providers, associations and/or organizations. Each application must include appropriate endorsement of an official who is responsible for the administration of awarded funds (hereafter called the "Grant Administrator").

Grantee institutions must be located in the U.S. or Canada. However, investigators and fellows are not required to be U.S. or Canadian citizens. The Foundation does not fund undergraduate or predoctoral students. Postdoctoral students who received their Ph.D. or M.D. within four years or less should apply for a fellowship grant, and may not be proposed as a Principal Investigator if they have not held such a position under previous funding (from any source). However, if a postdoctoral student has completed a postdoctoral fellowship under any source (please document), they may apply as a Principal Investigator. The Foundation is concerned about any Principal Investigator committing 5% effort or less in a project, with project activities falling primarily on less experienced investigators. Foreign nationals who will serve as a grant's Project Director (PD), Principal Investigator (PI), Research Fellow (RF) or a Significant Project Staff member(s) (20% of time) must provide verification that their U.S. or Canadian visa is current and that the visa will allow sufficient in-country (U.S. or Canada) time to complete the approved and funded grant project or fellowship award. Visa verification can be accomplished by submitting a letter from the PDs, PIs, RFs or significant staff on the sponsoring institution's letterhead that identifies the individual's visa expiration date. The letter must bear the individual's signature and the signature of the institution's grant administrator. The PD, PI, RF or significant staff person may also submit a copy of his or her current visa that identifies the visa's expiration date.

GEOG. RESTRICTIONS: United States and Canada.

FINANCIAL DATA:

Fringe benefits limited to 40%. Indirect cost limited to eight percent.

Amount of support per award: Fellowships: Maximum $50,000 per year; Basic science, clinical, design development: Maximum $75,000 per year.

NO. MOST RECENT APPLICANTS: 67.

NO. AWARDS: 8.

APPLICATION INFO:

All application submissions must be made online through the proposalCENTRAL/Altum web site, which can be accessed from the link on the Paralyzed Veterans' web site (click on "Research and Education"). Paper copy applications will be returned without review and will not satisfy the submission deadline. One may use either PC or Mac platforms and all standard operating systems.

The online application includes the following components:
(1) title page (title may not exceed 75 characters);
(2) applicant/Principal Investigator (PI);
(3) institution and contacts;
(4) letters of reference (required for fellowships; optional for others);
(5) abstract;
(6) organization assurances;
(7) proposal narrative (20-page maximum, including references) and supporting documents (including biosketches and budget) and;
(8) signature page(s).

All components of the application must be completed and submitted electronically. All submissions are considered confidential. Specific instructions for completing each component are included with the templates for each component. All applicants must use templates as appropriate for their application to ensure uniformity of presentation for reviewers. Some of the components have fixed-size templates one can complete online. Others are Microsoft Word templates that one may download to one's computer. One may complete these templates with any standard word processing software (e.g., MS Word or another), but one must convert completed documents to Adobe.pdf format to be uploaded to the web site. As the final step in submission, print, secure necessary signature(s) and send the original Signature Page(s) to the Foundation office. The signed Signature Page must be submitted by the deadline for submission of grant applications to make one's application complete. In order to meet the deadline, a fully signed copy of the form may be faxed to the fax number above, but the original signed form must immediately be mailed to the Foundation for inclusion in the Foundation's files.

Duration: One to two years.

Deadline: September 1.

PUBLICATIONS:

Annual report; application guidelines.

IRS I.D.: 52-1064398

DIRECTORS AND OFFICERS:

Al Kovach, Jr., Chairperson
Peter W. Axelson, M.S., M.E.
Rory A. Cooper, Ph.D.
Kenneth C. Curley, M.D.
Ken Ness
Eduardo M. Tinoco, M.L.I.S.
William Hodge Wood

ADDRESS INQUIRIES TO:

Frank Davis, Jr.
Grants Portfolio Manager
(See address above.)

CHRISTOPHER AND DANA REEVE FOUNDATION [2478]

636 Morris Turnpike, Suite 3A
Short Hills, NJ 07078
(973) 379-2690
(800) 225-0292
Fax: (973) 912-9433
E-mail: dvalente@christopherreeve.org
qol@christopherreeve.org
Web Site: www.paralysis.org
www.christopherreeve.org

FOUNDED: 1982

AREAS OF INTEREST:

Improving the quality of life for individuals living with paralysis, as well as their families.

NAME(S) OF PROGRAMS:

- **Quality of Life Grants**

TYPE:

Project/program grants. Provide funding to organizations nationwide that help improve opportunities, access and day-to-day quality of life for individuals with paralysis. The program recognizes the unique and numerous needs of these individuals and the importance of providing services that enable them to

participate in all areas of life. The awards fulfill a variety of needs for recipient organizations.

YEAR PROGRAM STARTED: 1999

PURPOSE:
To support exemplary organizations that provide valuable services to individuals with paralysis and their quality of life and health.

LEGAL BASIS:
Not-for-profit organization.

ELIGIBILITY:
Quality of Life Grants are awarded to 501(c)(3) organizations, as well as community parks, schools, veterans hospitals, tribal entities, etc.

GEOG. RESTRICTIONS: Support for programs outside of the United States is currently limited.

FINANCIAL DATA:
Amount of support per award: Up to $25,000. Partial grants may be awarded.

Matching fund requirements: Matching funds are not required. However, it is beneficial to seek funding from additional sources.

CO-OP FUNDING PROGRAMS: Quality of Life Grants are currently funded through a cooperative agreement with the Centers for Disease Control and Prevention.

NO. MOST RECENT APPLICANTS: Approximately 620.

NO. AWARDS: Approximately 200 per year.

REPRESENTATIVE AWARDS:
$5,000 to help support program of aquatic therapy sessions for community members with paralysis.

APPLICATION INFO:
All applications must be submitted online through the Reeve Foundation web site. Potential applicants may call to discuss proposed project if unsure of relevance to Foundation's funding goals.

Duration: One year.

Deadline: February 16 and August 15. Grants awarded in June and January.

PUBLICATIONS:
Guidelines; application form; final report form; People First; Language Guide; A Quick Guide to Establishing Evaluation Indicators.

IRS I.D.: 22-2939536

ADDRESS INQUIRIES TO:
Donna Valente, Director
E-mail: dvalente@christopherreeve.org

*SPECIAL STIPULATIONS:
Prior grant recipients must wait three grant cycles (two years) upon receiving grant to reapply for funding.

U.S. DEPARTMENT OF HEALTH AND HUMAN SERVICES [2479]

Administration for Community Living
400 Maryland Avenue, S.W., Room PCP-5020
Washington, DC 20202
(202) 245-7393
Fax: (202) 245-7590
E-mail: robert.groenendaal@acl.hhs.gov
Web Site: www.acl.gov

FOUNDED: 1978

AREAS OF INTEREST:
Priorities are established annually for certain programs.

NAME(S) OF PROGRAMS:
- **Assistive Technology Programs**

TYPE:
Project/program grants. Assistive Technology Program provides states with financial assistance that supports programs designed to maximize the ability of individuals with disabilities and their family members, guardians, advocates, and authorized representatives to obtain assistive technology devices and assistive technology services.

YEAR PROGRAM STARTED: 1978

PURPOSE:
To support state efforts to improve the provision of assistive technology devices and services to individuals with disabilities of all ages through comprehensive statewide programs of technology-related assistance.

LEGAL BASIS:
Assistive Technology Act of 1998, as amended by Public Law 108-364.

ELIGIBILITY:
Requirements vary according to program. Full information is available on the Administration for Community Living web site.

FINANCIAL DATA:
Amount of support per award: Grants vary in amount depending on type of program.

APPLICATION INFO:
Guidelines are available online.

Duration: Annual formula grant awards.

Deadline: Varies.

Psychiatry, psychology, mental health

AMERICAN ACADEMY OF CHILD AND ADOLESCENT PSYCHIATRY [2480]

3615 Wisconsin Avenue, N.W.
Washington, DC 20016-3007
(202) 966-7300 ext. 117
Fax: (202) 966-5894
E-mail: aarcher@aacap.org
Web Site: www.aacap.org

FOUNDED: 1953

AREAS OF INTEREST:
Child and adolescent psychiatry.

NAME(S) OF PROGRAMS:
- **Robinson-Cunningham Award**
- **Jeanne Spurlock Minority Medical Student Research Fellowship in Substance Abuse and Addiction**
- **Summer Medical Student Fellowship**

TYPE:
Awards/prizes; Conferences/seminars; Fellowships; Research grants; Travel grants. The Robinson-Cunningham Award recognizes a paper on some aspect of child and adolescent psychiatry started during residency and completed within three years of graduation.

Jeanne Spurlock Minority Medical Student Research Fellowship in Substance Abuse and Addiction provides support for research training in substance abuse and addiction under a mentor with experience in the type of research that is being proposed, and whose work includes children and adolescents participants.

Summer Medical Student Fellowship provides clinical or research training under a child and adolescent psychiatrist mentor.

YEAR PROGRAM STARTED: 1994

PURPOSE:
To increase the number of minority child and adolescent psychiatrists trained in research.

LEGAL BASIS:
Nonprofit organization.

ELIGIBILITY:
Robinson-Cunningham Award: Preference will be given to independent work. If the research is done as part of a collaborative team, the resident or recently trained child and adolescent psychiatrist should be the first author or principal investigator. The recipient is not required to attend the AACAP Annual Meeting. However, he or she must be an AACAP member by the time of the Annual Meeting in order to receive the award.

Spurlock Minority Medical Student Research Fellowship: Applications are considered from African American, Native American, Alaskan Native, Mexican American, Hispanic, Asian and Pacific Islander students in accredited U.S. medical schools or students whose research will focus on minorities.

GEOG. RESTRICTIONS: United States.

FINANCIAL DATA:
Amount of support per award:
Robinson-Cunningham Award: $1,000 honorarium, plus plaque presented at Annual Meeting. Spurlock Minority Medical Student Research Fellowship: Up to $4,000 per award, plus four days of paid travel and lodging to AACAP's Annual Meeting. Summer Medical Student Fellowship: Up to $3,500, plus four days of paid travel and lodging to AACAP's Annual Meeting.

Total amount of support: All awards contingent upon available funding.

NO. AWARDS: Robinson-Cunningham Award: 14; Spurlock Minority Medical Student Research Fellowship: 5. Summer Medical Student Fellowship: 21.

APPLICATION INFO:
E-mail training@aacap.org to receive application materials.

Duration: Spurlock Minority Medical Student Research Fellowship and Summer Medical Student Fellowship: Eight to 12 weeks.

Deadline: Spurlock Minority Medical Student Research Fellowship: February 2017; contact AACAP for exact date. Summer Medical Student Fellowship: February and May 2017; contact AACAP for exact date.

PUBLICATIONS:
Program announcement; *Research Notes*, newsletter.

ADDRESS INQUIRIES TO:
Anneke Archer
Training and Education Manager
(See address above.)

AMERICAN ACADEMY OF CHILD AND ADOLESCENT PSYCHIATRY [2481]

3615 Wisconsin Avenue, N.W.
Washington, DC 20016-3007
(202) 966-7300 ext. 117
Fax: (202) 966-5894
E-mail: aarcher@aacap.org
Web Site: www.aacap.org

FOUNDED: 1953

AREAS OF INTEREST:
Child and adolescent psychiatry.

NAME(S) OF PROGRAMS:
- **Educational Outreach Program**
- **Paramjit T. Joshi, M.D., International Scholars Award**
- **Junior Investigator Award**
- **Life Members Mentorship Grant for Medical Students**
- **Pilot Awards**
- **Ülkü Ülgür, M.D., International Scholar Award**

TYPE:
Conferences/seminars; Fellowships; Research grants; Travel grants. Educational Outreach Program is for both child and adolescent psychiatry residents and general psychiatry residents. It provides funding support to attend AACAP's Annual Meeting. Partnered with the Mentorship Program, these grants provide participants with networking opportunities, exposure to various specialties and interaction with a vibrant network of AACAP. This Program is instrumental in integrating residents into the field; 90% of general psychiatry residents who participate in the Program become child and adolescent psychiatrists.

Joshi International Scholars Award provides funding support for eligible international scholars to attend the Annual Meeting.

Junior Investigator Award is offered for one child and adolescent psychiatry junior faculty recipient (assistant professor level or equivalent).

Life Members Mentorship Grant for Medical Students provides funding support to attend AACAP's Annual Meeting. Partnered with the Mentorship Program, these grants provide participants with networking opportunities, exposure to various specialties and interaction with Life Members, along with a vibrant network of AACAP members.

Pilot Awards are offered for qualified residents and junior faculty who have an interest in beginning a career in child and adolescent mental health research.

Ülgür International Scholar Award recognizes a child psychiatrist or physician in the international community who has made significant contributions to the enhancement of mental health services for children and adolescents.

PURPOSE:
To increase the number of minority child and adolescent psychiatrists trained in research.

LEGAL BASIS:
Nonprofit organization.

ELIGIBILITY:
Joshi International Scholars Award: Qualified international physicians may include pediatricians, family medicine doctors, adult psychiatrists, child and adolescent psychiatrists and other physicians who primarily work with children and adolescents providing mental health services.

FINANCIAL DATA:
Joshi International Scholars Award: Funds will cover Annual Meeting registration, lodging and travel for AACAP's Annual Meeting.

Amount of support per award: Educational Outreach Program: Up to $1,000. Joshi International Scholars Award: Up to $2,500, plus a special award plaque at the Young Leaders Awards Ceremony held during AACAP's Annual Meeting. Junior Investigator Award: $30,000 per year, along with five days of paid travel and lodging to AACAP's Annual Meeting. The recipient has the opportunity to submit a poster presentation on his or her research for AACAP's Annual Meeting. Life Members Mentorship Grant for Medical Students: Up to $1,000. Pilot Awards: $15,000, plus five days of paid travel and lodging to AACAP's Annual Meeting during the second year; recipients have the opportunity to submit a poster presentation on their research at the Annual Meeting. Ülgür International Scholar Award: Up to $2,500 for reimbursement for registration and travel support to attend the AACAP Annual Meeting for five days including airfare, hotel, and up to $75 per day for meals; awardee will be recognized during AACAP Annual Meeting and presented with an engraved glass award.

NO. AWARDS: Educational Outreach Program: 54. Joshi International Scholars Award: 2. Life Members Mentorship Grant for Medical Students: 13. Pilot Awards: 14. Ülgür International Scholar Award: 1.

APPLICATION INFO:
E-mail training@aacap.org to receive application materials.

Duration: Educational Outreach Program, Joshi International Scholars, Life Members Mentorship Grant for Medical Students and Ülgür International Scholar Awards: Varies. Junior Investigator Award: Two years. Pilot Awards: One year.

Deadline: July 2017. Contact AACAP for exact deadline dates.

PUBLICATIONS:
Program announcement; *Research Notes*, newsletter.

ADDRESS INQUIRIES TO:
Anneke Archer
Training and Education Manager
(See address above.)

AMERICAN GROUP PSYCHOTHERAPY ASSOCIATION, INC. [2482]

25 East 21st Street, 6th Floor
New York, NY 10010
(212) 477-2677
Fax: (212) 979-6627
E-mail: dfeirman@agpa.org
Web Site: www.agpa.org

FOUNDED: 1942

AREAS OF INTEREST:
Group psychotherapy.

CONSULTING OR VOLUNTEER SERVICES:
Volunteer Program provided at Annual Conferences for local students. Specific duties are required in lieu of payment for events at Annual Conferences.

NAME(S) OF PROGRAMS:
- **The Anne Alonso Scholarship**
- **Donald T. Brown Memorial Scholarship**
- **The Barry Bukatman, M.D. Memorial AGPA Scholarship**
- **Josephine M. Cunningham-Tervalon Scholarship**
- **Durkin/Glatzer Scholarship**
- **The Howard and Barbara Goldstein Scholarship**
- **Ruth Hochberg Scholarship**
- **International Scholarship**
- **Susanne Jensen Scholarship**
- **Saul Scheidlinger Scholarship**
- **Mary M. Tanenbaum Scholarship**
- **The Robert E. White, M.D. and Sara Jane White, Ph.D. Scholarship**
- **The Wilkenfeld Psychiatric Resident Scholarship**

TYPE:
Scholarships; Travel grants; Visiting scholars. Special rates for students in addition to the volunteer program.

PURPOSE:
To enable professionals and other interested people to attend these professional meetings who would not otherwise be able to do so due to lack of funds.

LEGAL BASIS:
Incorporated, nonprofit, professional association.

ELIGIBILITY:
Financial need and proximity to location of annual meetings are considered.

For the Durkin-Glatzer Scholarship, applicants must be women entering or re-entering the field of group psychotherapy.

Josephine M. Cunningham Scholarship is for minority women.

Susanne Jensen Scholarship is for a foreign-born woman working or training in the U.S. as a group psychotherapist.

FINANCIAL DATA:
Amount of support per award: Tuition for Annual Meeting and travel stipend for Alonso Scholarship, Cunningham Scholarship, Durkin-Glatzer Scholarship, Hochberg Scholarship, and Wilkenfeld Scholarship.

Total amount of support: $8,000 to $25,000.

NO. AWARDS: 1 of each award or program.

APPLICATION INFO:
Current application guidelines are available on the Association's web site.

Duration: Two days for the Institute; three days for Conference.

Deadline: November 1.

PUBLICATIONS:
International Journal of Group Psychotherapy; *The Group Circle*, newsletter.

ADDRESS INQUIRIES TO:
Diane Feirman, CAE
Public Affairs Senior Director
(See address or e-mail above.)

AMERICAN PSYCHIATRIC FOUNDATION [2483]

1000 Wilson Boulevard, Suite 1825
Arlington, VA 22209-3901
(703) 907-8653
Fax: (703) 907-1089
E-mail: mking@psych.org
Web Site: www.psychfoundation.org
www.psych.org

AREAS OF INTEREST:
Psychiatric research.

NAME(S) OF PROGRAMS:
- **Kempf Fund Award for Research Development in Psychobiological Psychiatry**

TYPE:
Awards/prizes; Research grants. The Award supports the research-career development of a young research psychiatrist working in a

mentor-trainee relationship with the award winner on further research in the field of schizophrenia.

PURPOSE:
To recognize a senior researcher who has made a significant contribution to research on the causes and treatment of schizophrenia as both a researcher and a mentor.

ELIGIBILITY:
Applicants must be American Psychiatric Association members and citizens of the U.S. or Canada. Detailed guidelines are available from the Association. Contact the Association's Research Training Programs Office to obtain a copy of the printed announcement.

FINANCIAL DATA:
Amount of support per award: $1,500 award to the senior researcher, and $20,000 for support of the research-career development of a young research psychiatrist working in a mentor-trainee relationship with the award winner on further research in this field.

APPLICATION INFO:
Application information is available on the web site. Completed application materials required may be submitted online via a PDF format or by regular mail to: APA/Kempf Fund Award, American Psychiatric Association, at the address above.

Duration: One year. Nonrenewable.

Deadline: Postmarked by October 15.

ADDRESS INQUIRIES TO:
Director of Research Training
(See e-mail address above.)

AMERICAN PSYCHIATRIC FOUNDATION [2484]

1000 Wilson Boulevard, Suite 1825
Arlington, VA 22209
(703) 907-8622
(800) 852-1390
E-mail: apa@psych.org
Web Site: www.psychiatry.org/residents

AREAS OF INTEREST:
Psychiatric research.

NAME(S) OF PROGRAMS:

- **American Psychiatric Leadership Fellowship**
- **APA Child & Adolescent Psychiatry Fellowship**
- **APA Minority Fellowships**
- **APA Public Psychiatry Fellowship**

TYPE:
Fellowships. American Psychiatric Leadership Fellowship: This two-year fellowship offers psychiatric residents, with exceptional leadership potential, many different experiences that prepare them for leadership roles. Only the Chair of the Department or the Director of the Training Program can nominate.

APA Child & Adolescent Psychiatry Fellowship: This fellowship is designed to promote interest among general psychiatry residents in pursuing careers in child and adolescent psychiatry. Fellows will learn about new clinical research, successful treatments for children and adolescents with mental disorders and many other issues associated with child and adolescent mental health.

APA Minority Fellowships: These fellowships endeavor to eliminate racial and ethnic disparities in mental health and substance abuse care by providing specialized training to psychiatry residents and medical students interested in serving minority communities.

APA Public Psychiatry Fellowship: This two-year fellowship provides experiences that will contribute to the professional development of residents who will play future leadership roles within the public sector psychiatry and heighten awareness of the public psychiatry activities and career opportunities.

PURPOSE:
To promote psychiatric research.

APPLICATION INFO:
Duration: American Psychiatric Leadership and APA Public Psychiatry Fellowships: Two years.

Deadline: American Psychiatric Leadership and APA Public Psychiatry Fellowships: December 12, 2015. APA Child & Adolescent Psychiatry Fellowship: December 15, 2015. APA Minority Fellowships: January 30, 2016.

ADDRESS INQUIRIES TO:
APA Fellowship Programs
(See address above.)

AMERICAN PSYCHIATRIC FOUNDATION [2485]

1000 Wilson Boulevard, Suite 1825
Arlington, VA 22209
(703) 907-8622
(800) 852-1390
E-mail: apa@psych.org
Web Site: www.psychiatry.org/residents

AREAS OF INTEREST:
Psychiatric research.

NAME(S) OF PROGRAMS:

- **Psychiatric Research Fellowship**
- **Resident Psychiatric Research Scholars**
- **Jeanne Spurlock, M.D. Congressional Fellowship**

TYPE:
Fellowships; Travel grants. Psychiatric Research Fellowship sponsors two postgraduate psychiatry trainees specifically to focus on research and personal scholarship.

Resident Psychiatric Research Scholars is a one-year fellowship that provides mentoring and career enrichment opportunities and travel support to the APA Annual Meeting.

Jeanne Spurlock, M.D. Congressional Fellowship provides all psychiatry residents, fellows and early career psychiatrists an opportunity to work in a congressional office on federal health policy, particularly policy related to child and/or minority issues.

NO. AWARDS: Psychiatric Research Fellowship: 2.

APPLICATION INFO:
Duration: Resident Psychiatric Research Scholars: One year.

Deadline: Psychiatric Research Fellowship: November 17, 2015. Resident Psychiatric Research Scholars: January 16, 2016. Jeanne Spurlock, M.D. Congressional Fellowship: December 19, 2015.

ADDRESS INQUIRIES TO:
APA Fellowship Programs
(See address above.)

AMERICAN PSYCHOLOGICAL ASSOCIATION [2486]

Minority Fellowship Program/APA
750 First Street, N.E.
Washington, DC 20002-4242
(202) 336-6127
Fax: (202) 336-6012
E-mail: mfp@apa.org
Web Site: www.apa.org/pi/mfp

FOUNDED: 1892

AREAS OF INTEREST:
Psychology.

NAME(S) OF PROGRAMS:

- **MFP Services for Transition Age Youth**

TYPE:
Fellowships.

YEAR PROGRAM STARTED: 2014

PURPOSE:
To provide financial support, professional development activities, and guidance to promising doctoral students and postdoctoral trainees with the goal of moving them toward high achievement in areas related to ethnic minority behavioral health services.

LEGAL BASIS:
Nonprofit.

ELIGIBILITY:
Applicant must:
(1) be citizens, noncitizen nationals, or permanent residents of the U.S.;
(2) be enrolled in a terminal Master's Program in psychology that is on the APA eligible programs list (see web site for complete list) and;
(3) have a strong commitment to a career immediately after graduation in ethnic minority behavioral health services.

African-Americans, Alaskan Natives, Asian Americans, Latino-Hispanic, Native Americans and Pacific Islanders are especially encouraged to apply.

Person receiving Fellowship from MFP cannot be the recipient of federal funds.

FINANCIAL DATA:
Amount of support per award: $5,000.

CO-OP FUNDING PROGRAMS: Funding for services training is made available through Substance Abuse and Mental Health Services Administration allocations.

NO. MOST RECENT APPLICANTS: 68.

NO. AWARDS: 48.

APPLICATION INFO:
Applications are available October 1 to January 15. Guidelines are available online.

Duration: One academic year, in last year of Master's Program.

Deadline: January 15. Announcement by April.

ADDRESS INQUIRIES TO:
Minority Fellowship Program
(See telephone and e-mail address above.)

AMERICAN PSYCHOLOGICAL ASSOCIATION [2487]

Government Relations Office
Public Interest Directorate
750 First Street, N.E.
Washington, DC 20002-4242
(202) 336-5935
Fax: (202) 336-6063
E-mail: mhaskell-hoehl@apa.org
Web Site: www.apa.org/about/gr/fellows

FOUNDED: 1892

AREAS OF INTEREST:
Professional organization to advance psychology as a science and profession and as a means of promoting health, education and human welfare.

NAME(S) OF PROGRAMS:
- **APA Congressional Fellowship Program**

TYPE:
Fellowships. Program provides trained scientists and practitioners an opportunity for enhanced understanding of and involvement in the federal policymaking process by serving as congressional staff in Washington, DC.

YEAR PROGRAM STARTED: 1974

PURPOSE:
To provide an opportunity for psychologists to participate in the policymaking process.

LEGAL BASIS:
Nonprofit professional organization.

ELIGIBILITY:
Doctoral degree in psychology and APA membership required. Two years of postdoctoral experience is preferred. Individuals with sabbatical funds are eligible. Must be U.S. citizen and willing to relocate to Washington, DC.

GEOG. RESTRICTIONS: United States.

FINANCIAL DATA:
Amount of support per award: For the year 2015-16: $75,000 to $90,000, depending on years of postdoctoral experience. Up to $3,750 is allocated per Fellow for relocation to the Washington, DC area and for travel expenses during the year. Additional funds may be available for health insurance.

Total amount of support: Varies.

CO-OP FUNDING PROGRAMS: Fellowship is sponsored by the APA in cooperation with the American Association for the Advancement of Science and with funds from the ASA Goldman Fellowship.

NO. AWARDS: Up to 2.

APPLICATION INFO:
Completed online application form, curriculum vitae, three letters of reference and a statement of interest are required.

Duration: September through August. Nonrenewable.

Deadline: Early January. Announcement in March.

STAFF:
Micah Haskell-Hoehl, Program Administrator

ADDRESS INQUIRIES TO:
Micah Haskell-Hoehl, Program Administrator
APA Congressional Fellowship Program
(See telephone and e-mail address above.)

AMERICAN PSYCHOLOGICAL ASSOCIATION [2488]

Minority Fellowship Program/APA
750 First Street, N.E.
Washington, DC 20002-4242
(202) 336-6127
Fax: (202) 336-6012
E-mail: mfp@apa.org
Web Site: www.apa.org/pi/mfp

FOUNDED: 1892

AREAS OF INTEREST:
Psychology.

NAME(S) OF PROGRAMS:
- **MFP Mental Health and Substance Abuse Services Fellowship**

TYPE:
Fellowships. Fellowship is geared to those pursuing careers as practitioners specializing in the delivery of behavioral health services to ethnic minority populations. Students specializing in clinical, school and counseling psychology are encouraged to apply.

YEAR PROGRAM STARTED: 1974

PURPOSE:
To provide financial support, professional development activities, and guidance to promising doctoral students and postdoctoral trainees with the goal of moving them toward high achievement in areas related to ethnic minority behavioral health services.

LEGAL BASIS:
Nonprofit.

ELIGIBILITY:
Applicants must:
(1) be citizens, noncitizen nationals, or permanent residents of the U.S.;
(2) be enrolled full-time in a doctoral degree program in psychology (Ph.D. or Psy.D.); Mental Health Services applicants must be enrolled in an APA-accredited program and;
(3) have a strong commitment to a career in ethnic minority behavioral health services or policy.

African-Americans, Alaskan Natives, Asian Americans, Latino/Hispanic, Native Americans and Pacific Islanders are especially encouraged to apply.

Person receiving Fellowship from MFP cannot be the recipient of federal funds.

FINANCIAL DATA:
Amount of support per award: Follows NRSA guidelines.

CO-OP FUNDING PROGRAMS: Funding for services training is made available through the Substance Abuse and Mental Health Services Administration allocations.

NO. MOST RECENT APPLICANTS: 176.

NO. AWARDS: 9.

APPLICATION INFO:
Applications are available October 1 to January 15. Guidelines are available online.

Duration: One academic year. Renewable for up to two additional years.

Deadline: January 15. Announcement by April.

ADDRESS INQUIRIES TO:
Minority Fellowship Program
(See telephone and e-mail address above.)

AMERICAN PSYCHOSOMATIC SOCIETY [2489]

6728 Old McLean Village Drive
McLean, VA 22101
(703) 556-9222
Fax: (703) 556-8729
E-mail: info@psychosomatic.org
Web Site: www.psychosomatic.org

FOUNDED: 1942

AREAS OF INTEREST:
Psychosomatic medicine.

NAME(S) OF PROGRAMS:
- **Herbert Weiner Early Career Award for Contributions to Psychosomatic Society**

TYPE:
Awards/prizes.

PURPOSE:
To support individuals who show substantial promise in continuing study in psychosomatic medicine.

LEGAL BASIS:
Not-for-profit organization.

ELIGIBILITY:
Nominees must be fewer than 10 years past their final academic degree and must be members of the American Psychosomatic Society.

FINANCIAL DATA:
Amount of support per award: $1,000, plaque and an opportunity to present the research for which the award was given during the annual meeting of the Society.

NO. MOST RECENT APPLICANTS: 5.

NO. AWARDS: 1.

APPLICATION INFO:
Nominations must include a 500- to 1,000-word justification for the nomination, an updated curriculum vitae and reprints of the two to six publications of the work for which the nomination is being made. Two- to three-page proposal of the project and a copy of the curriculum vitae are due June 1 of each year.

Duration: One-time award.

Deadline: August 31.

PUBLICATIONS:
Award announcement.

IRS I.D.: 11-1866747

ADDRESS INQUIRIES TO:
Award Committee
(See address above.)

ANNA-MONIKA FOUNDATION [2490]

Kieshecker Weg 240
D-40468 Duesseldorf Germany
(49) 211 437187 13
Fax: (49) 211 437187 23
E-mail: m.bommers@gospax.com
Web Site: www.anna-monika-stiftung.com

FOUNDED: 1965

AREAS OF INTEREST:
Biochemistry, neurophysiology, neuropathology, psychopharmacology, psychiatry, depression and psychosomatic illnesses.

NAME(S) OF PROGRAMS:
- **The Anna-Monika Foundation Prize**

TYPE:
Awards/prizes. Prizes for research papers investigating the biological substrate and functional disturbances of depression. Prize-winning lectures will be published in *Pharmacopsychiatry*.

YEAR PROGRAM STARTED: 1966

PURPOSE:
To support international pioneering research in the area of depression research.

LEGAL BASIS:
Private foundation, authorized by the state of Nordrhein-Westfalen, Germany.

ELIGIBILITY:
As far as possible, the papers describing the studies should feature information about the recent advances and the knowledge that

should be helpful in promoting treatment and open new paths of scientific progress in depression. Papers published in the last two years in an international scientific peer-reviewed journal may be submitted. Papers may be written in German, French or English.

FINANCIAL DATA:
Total amount of support: EUR 25,000.

NO. AWARDS: Maximum of 3 biennially in odd-numbered years.

APPLICATION INFO:
A maximum of three publications (in sets of four copies) plus a short summary (approximately 600 words) emphasizing the relevance and importance of the research are required. A curriculum vitae and summary of achievements in the field should be added; hitherto unpublished studies or papers published in an international professional journal within the past two years may also be submitted. Papers may be written in English and should be submitted to the Executive Board only by e-mail to Rainer.Rupprecht@medbo.de.

Deadline: October 31.

ADDRESS INQUIRIES TO:
Michael Bommers, Managing Director
(See address above.)

ASSOCIATION FOR APPLIED PSYCHOPHYSIOLOGY AND BIOFEEDBACK [2491]

10200 West 44th Avenue
Suite 304
Wheat Ridge, CO 80033-2840
(303) 422-8436
Fax: (303) 422-8894
E-mail: info@aapb.org
Web Site: www.aapb.org

FOUNDED: 1969

AREAS OF INTEREST:
Biofeedback and psychophysiology.

NAME(S) OF PROGRAMS:
- **Student Travel Scholarship Program**

TYPE:
Travel grants.

PURPOSE:
To advance the development, dissemination and utilization of knowledge about applied psychophysiology and biofeedback to improve health and the quality of life through research, education and practice.

ELIGIBILITY:
Must be a full-time student pursuing a professional or doctoral degree in a health-related field.

FINANCIAL DATA:
Total amount of support: Varies.

NO. AWARDS: Varies.

APPLICATION INFO:
Contact the Organization for application procedures.

Deadline: October 1 for presentation. December 15 for scholarship application.

ASSOCIATION FOR BEHAVIORAL AND COGNITIVE THERAPIES [2492]

305 Seventh Avenue
16th Floor
New York, NY 10001
(212) 647-1890
Fax: (212) 647-1865
E-mail: mjeimer@abct.org
Web Site: www.abct.org

AREAS OF INTEREST:
Behavior therapy and cognitive behavior therapy.

NAME(S) OF PROGRAMS:
- **Virginia Roswell Dissertation Award**

TYPE:
Awards/prizes.

PURPOSE:
To explore the application of behavioral and cognitive sciences to understanding human behavior, developing interventions to enhance the human condition, and promoting the appropriate utilization of these interventions.

ELIGIBILITY:
Applicant must be an AABT student member who has already had their dissertation proposal approved and be investigating an area of direct relevance to behavior therapy or cognitive behavior therapy.

FINANCIAL DATA:
Amount of support per award: $1,000.

NO. AWARDS: 1.

APPLICATION INFO:
All candidates must be nominated. Contact the Organization for nomination procedures.

Deadline: March.

ADDRESS INQUIRIES TO:
M.J. Eimer, Executive Director
(See address above.)

ASSOCIATION FOR BEHAVIORAL AND COGNITIVE THERAPIES [2493]

305 Seventh Avenue
16th Floor
New York, NY 10001
(212) 647-1890
Fax: (212) 647-1865
E-mail: mjeimer@abct.org
Web Site: www.abct.org

AREAS OF INTEREST:
Behavior therapy and cognitive sciences.

NAME(S) OF PROGRAMS:
- **President's New Researcher Award**

TYPE:
Awards/prizes.

PURPOSE:
To explore the application of behavioral and cognitive sciences to understanding human behavior, developing interventions to enhance the human condition, and promoting the appropriate utilization of these interventions.

ELIGIBILITY:
Must be authored by an individual with five years or less posttraining experience and have been published in the last two years or currently in press.

FINANCIAL DATA:
Amount of support per award: $500.

APPLICATION INFO:
Contact the Organization for application procedures.

Deadline: August.

ADDRESS INQUIRIES TO:
M.J. Eimer, Executive Director
(See address above.)

AUTISM SPEAKS

1060 State Road, 2nd Floor
Princeton, NJ 08540
(609) 228-7313
E-mail: jnew@autismspeaks.org
Web Site: www.autismspeaks.org

TYPE:
Fellowships; Project/program grants; Research grants. Research grants that are in line with Autism Speaks research priorities.

Fellowship Training Grants provide predoctoral and postdoctoral research grants in response to periodical requests for applications.

See entry 2172 for full listing.

BRAIN & BEHAVIOR RESEARCH FOUNDATION [2494]

90 Park Avenue, 16th Floor
New York, NY 10016
(800) 829-8289
Fax: (646) 681-4891
E-mail: grants@bbrfoundation.org
Web Site: www.bbrfoundation.org

FOUNDED: 1987

AREAS OF INTEREST:
Mental health, brain and behavior disorders.

NAME(S) OF PROGRAMS:
- **Distinguished Investigator Grant**
- **Independent Investigator Grant**
- **Young Investigator Grant**

TYPE:
Research grants. Distinguished Investigator Grant supports senior investigators (professor or equivalent level) who maintain a laboratory and who propose an innovative and new direction in their research with a one-year grant to encourage pursuit of innovative projects in schizophrenia, affective disorders, or other serious mental illnesses.

Independent Investigator Grant is intended for the scientist at the academic level of associate professor or equivalent, who has won national competitive support as a principal investigator. Assistant professors who have NIH R01s and equivalent are also eligible. The program is intended to facilitate innovative research opportunities.

Young Investigator Grant enables promising investigators to either extend their research fellowship training or to begin careers as independent research faculty.

PURPOSE:
To raise and distribute funds for scientific research into the causes, cures, treatments and prevention of severe psychiatric brain disorders.

LEGAL BASIS:
Private, not-for-profit organization.

ELIGIBILITY:
Applicant must hold a doctoral-level degree and be affiliated with a university or research institution. For the Distinguished Investigator Grant, applicant must be a full professor (or professional equivalent) who maintains a laboratory. For the Independent Investigator Grant, applicant must be at associate professor level with national competitive

support as a principal investigator. Assistant professors who have NIH R01s and equivalent are also eligible. For the Young Investigator Grant, applicant must be advanced postdoctoral fellow through assistant professor (or equivalent) to either extend research fellowship training or to begin career as independent research faculty. Basic and/or clinical investigators are supported, but research must be relevant to schizophrenia, major affective disorders or other serious mental illnesses.

FINANCIAL DATA:
Amount of support per award: Distinguished Investigator: Up to $100,000 for one year; Independent Investigator: $50,000 per year for two years; Young Investigator: Up to $35,000 per year for up to two years.

NO. MOST RECENT APPLICANTS: Distinguished Investigator: 190 for the year 2013; Independent Investigator: 487 for the year 2012; Young Investigator: 1,030 for the year 2013.

NO. AWARDS: Independent Investigator: 42; Young Investigator: 202 for the year 2012.

APPLICATION INFO:
Guidelines are available on the Foundation web site.

Duration: Distinguished Investigator Grant: One-year, one-time award; Independent Investigator Grant: Two-year, one-time award; Young Investigator Grant: One or two years. May not apply more than twice for initial grant and more than once for second grant.

Deadline: Varies.

IRS I.D.: 31-1020010

STAFF:
Jeff Borenstein, President and Chief Executive Officer
Lou Innamorato, Vice President, Finance and Chief Financial Officer
Lauren Duran, Vice President, Communications, Marketing and Public Relations
Faith Rothblatt, Vice President of Development
Abbey Chakalis, Director of Special Events
Josh Okun, Associate Director of Web Services and Online Marketing
Sho Tin Chen, Associate Director, Research Grants
Nieves Ortiz, Manager of Donor-based Management
Laura Terio, C.S.W., Outreach Manager
John Bayat, Senior Accountant
Mike Kirsic, Senior Accountant
Grace Nagaur, Senior Associate, Research Grants

ADDRESS INQUIRIES TO:
Grants Management
(See address above.)

JAMES MCKEEN CATTELL FUND [2495]

Duke University
Genome Sciences Research Building II, 3rd floor
572 Research Drive, Box 91050
Durham, NC 27708
(919) 660-5713
(919) 660-5638
Fax: (919) 660-5726
E-mail: williams@psych.duke.edu
Web Site: www.cattell.duke.edu

FOUNDED: 1941

NAME(S) OF PROGRAMS:
- **James McKeen Cattell Fund Sabbatical Fellowships for Psychologists**

TYPE:
Fellowships. The fellowship provides funds to supplement the regular sabbatical allowance provided by the recipients' home institutions.

YEAR PROGRAM STARTED: 1942

PURPOSE:
To promote scientific research and the dissemination of knowledge with the object of obtaining results beneficial to the development of the science of psychology.

LEGAL BASIS:
Tax-exempt foundation.

ELIGIBILITY:
The awards are available to psychologists who are faculty members at colleges and universities in the U.S. and Canada and are eligible, according to the regulations of their own institutions, for a sabbatical leave or its equivalent.

GEOG. RESTRICTIONS: United States and Canada.

FINANCIAL DATA:
Amount of support per award: Up to $40,000.

Total amount of support: Varies.

NO. MOST RECENT APPLICANTS: Approximately 35.

NO. AWARDS: 1 to 4 per year.

APPLICATION INFO:
Fellowship application is available at the Fund web site.

Duration: One academic year.

Deadline: December 15.

TRUSTEES AND OFFICERS:
Peter A. Ornstein, Managing Trustee
Christina L. Williams, Secretary-Treasurer
Marcia K. Johnson
Robert W. Levenson
Scott E. Maxwell

ADDRESS INQUIRIES TO:
Dr. Christina L. Williams
Secretary-Treasurer
(See address above.)

COUNCIL ON SOCIAL WORK EDUCATION

1701 Duke Street, Suite 200
Alexandria, VA 22314-3457
(703) 683-8080
Fax: (703) 683-8099
E-mail: gmeeks@cswe.org
Web Site: www.cswe.org/mfp

TYPE:
Fellowships. Awards for minority doctoral-level studies in social work, specializing in mental health and substance abuse-related education, research, policy and practice.

See entry 963 for full listing.

DEPARTMENT OF VETERANS AFFAIRS [2496]

Associated Health Education (10A2D)
Office of Academic Affiliations
810 Vermont Avenue, N.W.
Washington, DC 20420
(202) 461-9493
Fax: (202) 461-9855
E-mail: kenneth.jones6@va.gov
Web Site: www.psychologytraining.va.gov

FOUNDED: 1946

AREAS OF INTEREST:
Veterans' mental health.

NAME(S) OF PROGRAMS:
- **VA Psychology Training Program**

TYPE:
Fellowships; Internships. Stipends for internship and postdoctoral training in clinical or counseling psychology. Provides one year of supervised training in the skills and techniques of these specialty areas. Participants have no obligation to remain with the VA after completion of training.

YEAR PROGRAM STARTED: 1946

PURPOSE:
To provide a source of highly qualified psychologists who are interested in the direct delivery of professional services in federal, state, and community facilities; to provide internship training to students enrolled in doctoral programs in clinical or counseling psychology from those schools accredited by the American Psychological Association; to provide postdoctoral fellowships to graduates of clinical or counseling psychology doctoral programs and internships that are accredited by the American Psychological Association.

LEGAL BASIS:
Federal agency.

ELIGIBILITY:
Applicant must be a U.S. citizen. Prospective intern must be enrolled in an academic graduate program leading to the doctoral degree in clinical or counseling psychology from an APA-accredited program. Prospective postdoctoral fellow must have completed a doctoral program and internship in clinical or counseling psychology accredited by the APA.

FINANCIAL DATA:
Amount of support per award: Stipend of $23,974 to $28,382 for full-time interns and $42,239 to $52,709 for full-time postdoctoral fellows.

Total amount of support: Varies.

NO. AWARDS: 598 intern positions at 115 sites and 349 postdoctoral fellow positions at 71 sites for academic year 2014-15.

APPLICATION INFO:
Interested persons should contact the Director of Psychology Training at the VA Medical Center they are interested in.

Duration: One year. Occasionally two years for postdoctoral fellowships.

Deadline: November.

ADDRESS INQUIRIES TO:
Chief of Psychology Service or
Director of Psychology Training
at a local VA Medical Center

ALBERT ELLIS INSTITUTE [2497]

145 East 32nd Street, 9th Floor
New York, NY 10016
(212) 535-0822
Fax: (212) 249-3582
E-mail: krisdoyle@albertellis.org
Web Site: www.albertellis.org

FOUNDED: 1968

AREAS OF INTEREST:
Psychotherapy.

CONSULTING OR VOLUNTEER SERVICES:
Work-study positions offered.

NAME(S) OF PROGRAMS:

- **Postgraduate Clinical Fellowship Training Program at the Albert Ellis Institute**

TYPE:
Conferences/seminars; Fellowships; Internships; Work-study programs. Postdoctoral fellowships and internships in cognitive behavior therapy for a comprehensive program, featuring intensive supervision of individual and group clients seen at the Institute's clinic, seminars and workshops.

YEAR PROGRAM STARTED: 1969

PURPOSE:
To train professionals in cognitive behavioral and Rational Emotive Behavior Therapy.

LEGAL BASIS:
501(c)(3) nonprofit organization.

ELIGIBILITY:
Applicant must have a Ph.D. in psychology, M.D., M.S.W. or R.N.

NO. MOST RECENT APPLICANTS: 30.

NO. AWARDS: 6.

APPLICATION INFO:
Application form and information are available online.

Duration: One to two years.

Deadline: February 15.

ADDRESS INQUIRIES TO:
Dr. Kristene Doyle, Director
(See address above.)

*PLEASE NOTE:
Training takes place in New York City.

FONDATION DES ETATS-UNIS

15, boulevard Jourdan
75014 Paris France
(33) 1 53 80 68 82
Fax: (33) 1 53 80 68 99
E-mail: culture@feusa.org
Web Site: www.feusa.org/harriet-hale-woolley-scholarship/

TYPE:
Awards/prizes; Development grants; Scholarships. Bequeathed to the Fondation des Etats-Unis, Cite Internationale Universitaire de Paris in the early 1930s, the Harriet Hale Woolley Scholarship is awarded annually to a select number of exceptional American artists and musicians who plan to pursue their studies in Paris.

A scholarship is also available to French, Swiss and American medical postgraduates specializing in psychiatry with an internship in a Parisian hospital.

The scholarship is not intended for research in art history or musicology, nor for dance or theater.

See entry 436 for full listing.

HEALTHY MINDS CANADA [2498]

1920 Yonge Street
3rd Floor
Toronto ON M4S 3E2 Canada
(416) 351-7757
E-mail: admin@healthymindscanada.ca
Web Site: www.healthymindscanada.ca/awards/

FOUNDED: 1980

AREAS OF INTEREST:
Biomedical research targeted in psychiatric disorders and addiction in Canada. Education and awareness activities in the mental illness and addictions space. Youth mental health; adult mental health; men's mental health; women's mental health; caregiver support; workplace mental health; mental health in the classroom; mental health-related online tools and apps.

NAME(S) OF PROGRAMS:

- **ACT! (Youth Program)**
- **Bell Let's Talk Awareness Campaign (Online Awareness Raising Campaign)**
- **Bright Futures Conference (Recovery)**
- **Healthy Minds Canada/Pfizer Canada Workplace Depression Research Awards (Grants)**
- **Lunch & Learns (Free Community Events)**
- **Movies for Mental Health (Universities and Colleges)**
- **Scotiabank Toronto Marathon (Volunteer and Awareness)**
- **Taking Charge (Adult Program)**
- **Teen ParticipACTION Program (Youth Wellness - Yoga)**

TYPE:
Awards/prizes; Conferences/seminars; Project/program grants; Research grants.

YEAR PROGRAM STARTED: 2016

PURPOSE:
To promote meritorious research into the neurobiology of psychiatric disorders and addictions, schizophrenia mood disorders, anxiety disorders (e.g., posttraumatic stress disorder) and addiction and co-morbidity.

ELIGIBILITY:
The focus of the research proposal must be in line with any of the following areas of research:
(1) research assessing the impact of rapid and early optimization of treatment on depression and level of functional improvement in workplace productivity, presenteeism and absenteeism;
(2) research assessing the impact of rapid and early optimization of treatment to minimize depression relapse in the workplace and;
(3) research exploring the impact of rapid and early optimization of treatment to minimize the incidence of/mitigate the risks for depression in the workplace (e.g., quality improvement research).

GEOG. RESTRICTIONS: Canada.

FINANCIAL DATA:
The two awards (grants) are up to $25,000 each. Award funds are intended to be operating grants and must contribute towards the direct costs of the research program or project for which the funds are granted. The budget must be inclusive of institutional overhead where applicable; this amount shall not exceed 20% of the grant application budget. Applicants may not receive a salary, a stipend or an honorarium from the award (grant).

Amount of support per award: Up to $25,000 per annum per research grant or event.

NO. AWARDS: 2.

APPLICATION INFO:
Refer to the web site address above.

Duration: One year.

Deadline: September 1.

ADDRESS INQUIRIES TO:
E-mail: Psychiatryawards@pfizer.com

INTERNATIONAL OCD FOUNDATION [2499]

18 Tremont Street, Suite 903
Boston, MA 02108
(617) 973-5801
Fax: (617) 973-5803
E-mail: info@iocdf.org
Web Site: www.iocdf.org

FOUNDED: 1986

AREAS OF INTEREST:
Obsessive-compulsive disorders and obsessive compulsive spectrum disorder.

NAME(S) OF PROGRAMS:

- **Annual Conference**
- **Behavior Therapy Training Institute (BTTI)**
- **Research Awards**

TYPE:
Awards/prizes; Conferences/seminars; Research grants.

YEAR PROGRAM STARTED: 1986

PURPOSE:
To disseminate information and to fund research for the ultimate causes and cures for obsessive-compulsive disorders.

ELIGIBILITY:
Research Awards: Investigators whose research focuses on the nature, causes and treatment of OCD and related disorders are eligible to apply. Senior investigators may also ask for grant funding for projects that would provide pilot data for future larger-scale federal grant applications.

FINANCIAL DATA:
Awards do not cover indirect or travel costs.

Amount of support per award: Varies.

Total amount of support: Varies.

NO. MOST RECENT APPLICANTS: 50.

NO. AWARDS: 5.

APPLICATION INFO:
Application information is available on the web site. Applicants can request application guidelines from the Foundation.

Duration: One to two years.

Deadline: January.

PUBLICATIONS:
OCD Newsletter.

IRS I.D.: 22-2894564

STAFF:
Jeff Szymanski, Ph.D., Executive Director
Melissa Smith, Event Manager

ADDRESS INQUIRIES TO:
See e-mail address or phone number above.

THE KLINGENSTEIN THIRD GENERATION FOUNDATION [2500]

125 Park Avenue
Suite 1700
New York, NY 10017-5529
(212) 492-6179
Fax: (212) 492-7007
E-mail: info@ktgf.org
Web Site: www.ktgf.org

FOUNDED: 1993

AREAS OF INTEREST:
Child and adolescent depression and ADHD.

TYPE:
Fellowships; Research grants. The Foundation funds research and other programs related to childhood and adolescent ADHD and depression. All funding is directed towards three research fellowship programs (funding postdoctoral research in ADHD, depression and access to care) and the medical student training program. The Foundation does not accept general applications for project or research funding.

YEAR PROGRAM STARTED: 1993

PURPOSE:
To address the need for further research in pediatric ADHD and pediatric depression, and the need to cultivate more child and adolescent psychiatrists and psychologists.

LEGAL BASIS:
Family foundation.

ELIGIBILITY:
The Foundation makes fellowship grants to medical institutions that have nominated research projects led by outstanding postdoctoral candidates.

The Foundation is prohibited from making grants to political action groups and from lobbying the government, and makes no grants to individuals.

FINANCIAL DATA:
Amount of support per award: Fellowships: $30,000 per year.

NO. AWARDS: Fellowships: Up to 5.

APPLICATION INFO:
Applications must be submitted online.

Duration: Fellowships: Two years.

Deadline: Fellowship nominations: November 15.

BOARD OF TRUSTEES:
Andrew D. Klingenstein, President
Susan Klingenstein, Vice-President
Thomas D. Klingenstein, Treasurer
Nancy K. Simpkins, Secretary
Sally Klingenstein Martell, Executive Director
Kathy Klingenstein

ADVISORY COMMITTEE:
Thomas F. Anders, M.D.
William R. Beardslee, M.D.
David A. Brent, M.D.
Kiki Chang, M.D.
Anne Glowinski, M.D.
Laurence L. Greenhill, M.D.
Jeffrey H. Newcorn, M.D.

*PLEASE NOTE:
The Foundation does not accept unsolicited applications.

DELLA MARTIN FOUNDATION [2501]

333 South Hope Street
43rd Floor
Los Angeles, CA 90071
(213) 617-4143
Fax: (213) 620-1398
E-mail: lgould@sheppardmullin.com

FOUNDED: 1975

AREAS OF INTEREST:
Mental health research.

TYPE:
Endowments; Fellowships; Professorships. Foundation has endowed four university chairs for mental health research and seven postdoctoral mental health research fellowships.

YEAR PROGRAM STARTED: 1975

PURPOSE:
To promote research into causes of and cures for mental illness.

LEGAL BASIS:
Nonprofit foundation.

ELIGIBILITY:
For southern California tax-exempt organizations only. No grants are made to individuals.

GEOG. RESTRICTIONS: Southern California.

FINANCIAL DATA:
Amount of support per award: Varies.

Total amount of support: $300,000 annually.

Matching fund requirements: Generally 1:1.

NO. MOST RECENT APPLICANTS: 20.

NO. AWARDS: 1 annually.

REPRESENTATIVE AWARDS:
$250,000 to University of California, Irvine to establish postgraduate research fellowship.

APPLICATION INFO:
Send brief letter to the Foundation describing grant request.

IRS I.D.: 23-7444954

TRUSTEES:
Laurence K. Gould, Jr.
Kelly Kinnon
James A. Lonergan
Allen W. Mathies, Jr., M.D.
Nancy B. Reimann
Eileen D. Sheppard
Philip A. Swan

ADDRESS INQUIRIES TO:
Laurence K. Gould, Jr., Trustee
(See address above.)

NATIONAL INSTITUTE OF MENTAL HEALTH [2502]

6001 Executive Boulevard, Room 6160
Bethesda, MD 20892
(301) 443-5047
Fax: (301) 443-9474
E-mail: jnoronha@mail.nih.gov
Web Site: www.nimh.nih.gov

FOUNDED: 1948

AREAS OF INTEREST:
Basic neuroscience, genetics, basic behavioral science aimed at understanding mental disorders, research training, resource and technology development and drug discovery; translational research on the mechanisms of adult psychopathology and the development of novel treatment approaches for adult mental disorders; integrated research and research training that translates knowledge from basic/behavioral science into a better understanding of pediatric psychopathology and the development of novel treatment and prevention strategies; research on mechanisms and interventions on the interrelationship of physical and mental health; mental health research on AIDS that includes studies that range from the molecular and cellular basis of HIV/AIDS CNS infection to the domestic and international dissemination of effective preventative interventions; research that evaluates the effectiveness of treatment and preventive mental health interventions and mental health services research.

TYPE:
Development grants; Fellowships; Project/program grants; Research grants; Training grants; Research contracts.

YEAR PROGRAM STARTED: 1948

PURPOSE:
To support innovative science that will profoundly transform the diagnosis, treatment and prevention of mental disorders, paving the way for a cure; to reduce the burden of mental illness and behavioral disorders through research on mind, brain and behavior.

LEGAL BASIS:
Government agency.

ELIGIBILITY:
Public, private, profit or nonprofit agencies, including state and local government agencies, eligible Federal agencies, universities, colleges, hospitals, and academic or research institutions may apply for research grants. SBIR grants can be awarded only to domestic small businesses, and STTR grants can be awarded only to domestic small businesses which partner with a research institution in cooperative research and development.

An applicant for individual predoctoral fellowship support must be enrolled in a research doctoral degree program by the proposed activation date of the fellowship. A postdoctoral applicant must have received a Ph.D., Psy.D., M.D., D.D.S., Sc.D., D.N.S., D.O., D.S.W., or equivalent degree from an accredited institution to be eligible for an individual postdoctoral fellowship.

All research training awards are made to appropriate domestic research centers, medical schools, departments of psychiatry, nonmedical academic departments, psychiatric hospitals or hospitals with psychiatric services, community mental health centers, and biomedical research institutes on behalf of individuals who need the opportunity to realize research potential. Except for the NIH Pathway to Independence Award, the individuals must be citizens or nationals of the U.S. or have been lawfully admitted for permanent residence. NIH Pathway to Independence Award is open to both U.S. citizens and non-U.S. citizens. Individuals must qualify by scholastic degree and previous training and/or experience.

FINANCIAL DATA:
Amount of support per award: Grants and awards vary in amount, depending upon the program and type of funding mechanism.

Total amount of support: Varies.

NO. AWARDS: Approximately 3,063 for the year 2013.

APPLICATION INFO:
Application materials are available on NIMH web site. Prospective applicants should contact NIMH staff prior to submission to ensure the area of research that they investigate is within NIMH priorities.

Duration: Varies, with project periods ranging one to five years. Funding commitments are made annually.

ADDRESS INQUIRIES TO:
Dr. Jean Noronha
Division of Extramural Activities
(See address above.)

NATIONAL INSTITUTE OF MENTAL HEALTH

Division of Translational Research (DTR)
6001 Executive Boulevard, Room 7111, MSC 9632
Bethesda, MD 20892-9632
(301) 443-9232
E-mail: ftuma@nih.gov
Web Site: www.nimh.nih.gov/about/organization/dtr/index.shtml

TYPE:
Fellowships; Project/program grants; Research grants; Technical assistance; Training grants; Visiting scholars; Research contracts.

See entry 1809 for full listing.

NATIONAL SCIENCE FOUNDATION [2503]

Directorate for Social Behavorial and Economic Sciences
4201 Wilson Boulevard, Room 995 N
Arlington, VA 22230
(703) 292-4636
Fax: (703) 292-9083
Web Site: www.nsf.gov

FOUNDED: 1950

AREAS OF INTEREST:
Social behavior and social development.

NAME(S) OF PROGRAMS:
- **Social Psychology Program**

TYPE:
Project/program grants; Research grants; Training grants; Travel grants; Visiting scholars. Support for laboratory and field research in all areas of human social behavior including social cognition, attitude formation and change, and social influence. The Program includes research on social, personality and emotional development in children and adults. Research to improve the conceptual and methodological base of social and developmental psychology is encouraged.

YEAR PROGRAM STARTED: 1972

PURPOSE:
To initiate and support scientific research and programs to strengthen research potential.

LEGAL BASIS:
National Science Foundation Act of 1950.

ELIGIBILITY:
Applicants may be colleges and universities on behalf of their staff members, nonprofit, nonacademic research institutions, such as independent museums, observatories, research laboratories, stock centers and similar organizations, private profit organizations, in exceptional circumstances, rarely, foreign institutions utilizing U.S. currency and, under special circumstances, unaffiliated U.S. scientists.

GEOG. RESTRICTIONS: United States.

FINANCIAL DATA:
Support may cover salaries, research assistantships, staff benefits if a direct cost, permanent equipment, travel, publication costs, computer costs and certain other direct and indirect costs.

Amount of support per award: Average $95,000 to $150,000 per year.

NO. MOST RECENT APPLICANTS: Approximately 2,000.

NO. AWARDS: 50.

APPLICATION INFO:
A proposal should include title and description of proposed research, information about the institution, principal investigator and business administrator, desired effective date of grant, duration of support, endorsement, facilities, personnel, current support and pending applications and budget.

Duration: Research grants may be awarded for periods of up to five years. Most grants are for two or three years.

Deadline: Target dates are January 15 and July 15.

ADDRESS INQUIRIES TO:
Program Director
(See address above.)

NATIONAL SCIENCE FOUNDATION [2504]

Division of Behavioral and Cognitive Sciences
4201 Wilson Boulevard, Room 995N
Arlington, VA 22230
(703) 292-7238
Fax: (703) 292-9068
Web Site: www.nsf.gov

FOUNDED: 1950

NAME(S) OF PROGRAMS:
- **Perception, Action & Cognition Program**

TYPE:
Research grants. Supports research on perception, action and cognition. Emphasis is on research strongly grounded in theory. Research topics include vision, audition, haptics, attention, memory, reasoning, written and spoken discourse, motor control, and developmental issues in all topic areas. The program encompasses a wide range of theoretical perspectives such as symbolic computation, connectionism, ecological, nonlinear dynamics, complex systems, and a variety of methodologies including both experimental studies and modeling. Research involving acquired or developmental deficits is appropriate if the results speak to basic issues of cognition, perception or action.

YEAR PROGRAM STARTED: 1976

PURPOSE:
To initiate and support scientific research and programs to strengthen research potential.

LEGAL BASIS:
National Science Foundation Act of 1950.

ELIGIBILITY:
Requirements vary according to program. Applicants should consult web site for current programs.

GEOG. RESTRICTIONS: United States.

FINANCIAL DATA:
Amount of support per award: Approximately $120,000 per year.

Total amount of support: Varies.

APPLICATION INFO:
Application should be submitted by FastLane or through Foundation's web site. Standard grant proposal guidelines apply.

Duration: 12 to 60 months, depending on the scientific merit and requirements of the project, and the type of program.

STAFF:
Betty Tuller, Program Director

ADDRESS INQUIRIES TO:
Betty Tuller, Program Director
(See address above.)

PSI CHI, THE INTERNATIONAL HONOR SOCIETY IN PSYCHOLOGY [2505]

825 Vine Street
Chattanooga, TN 37403
(423) 756-2044
Fax: (877) 774-2443
E-mail: awards@psichi.org
Web Site: www.psichi.org

FOUNDED: 1929

AREAS OF INTEREST:
Psychology.

NAME(S) OF PROGRAMS:
- **Psi Chi/APA Edwin B. Newman Graduate Research Award**

TYPE:
Awards/prizes. Provides recognition to the best published graduate research. Award includes benefits from Psi Chi and APA.

PURPOSE:
To give recognition to a graduate student for research in the field of psychology.

LEGAL BASIS:
Honor society.

ELIGIBILITY:
Psi Chi membership not required. The submitter of a research paper must:
(1) be a graduate student at the time the research was carried out and submitted for publication and/or presentation;
(2) be the primary and first author and;
(3) have presented the results of the research at a state, regional or national psychology convention, or have been published in a psychology journal.

FINANCIAL DATA:
Amount of support per award: $1,200 and two engraved plaques - one for the winner and one for the psychology department as a permanent honor - are awarded from Psi Chi. Up to $1,500 in travel reimbursement to attend the APA (American Psychological Association) National Convention, registration for the Convention, recognition during the APF Awards Ceremony, including the opportunity to give a short awards address, a framed APA Presidential Citation, and acceptance of the winning project in the APAGS poster session (as long as the work was not presented at a previous APA convention) are awarded by the APA.

NO. MOST RECENT APPLICANTS: 24 for the year 2016.

NO. AWARDS: 1.

APPLICATION INFO:
Submit online at the web site, under the Awards/Grants section. The link to submissions is available at least one month prior to the submission deadline.

Duration: One-time award.

Deadline: February 1.

PUBLICATIONS:
Eye on Psi Chi, magazine; *Journal of Undergraduate Research.*

ADDRESS INQUIRIES TO:
Jennifer Baldwin, Director of Awards/Grants
(See e-mail address above.)

*SPECIAL STIPULATIONS:
APA convention attendance for the winner is strongly encouraged. If the winner is unable to attend, the travel reimbursement and registration fees portion of the award will be forfeited.

SCOTTISH RITE CHARITABLE FOUNDATION OF CANADA [2506]

4 Queen Street South
Hamilton ON L8P 3R3 Canada
(905) 522-0033
Fax: (905) 522-3716
E-mail: grantsandawards@srcf.ca
info@srcf.ca
Web Site: www.srcf.ca

FOUNDED: 1970

AREAS OF INTEREST:
Biomedical research into intellectual impairment.

NAME(S) OF PROGRAMS:

- **Scottish Rite Charitable Foundation Major Research Grants**

TYPE:
Research grants. SRCFC grants support biomedical research into intellectual impairment focused on:
(1) the causes and eventual cure of intellectual impairment, such as autism and Down syndrome, especially as it affects children;
(2) the causes and eventual cure of Alzheimer's Disease and;
(3) research into other forms of intellectual impairment.

The focus should be on the causes and cure of the disease as opposed to the active treatment or palliative care.

YEAR PROGRAM STARTED: 1970

PURPOSE:
To provide financial support to researchers studying developmental disabilities.

LEGAL BASIS:
Nonprofit.

ELIGIBILITY:
The following criteria apply:
(1) applications are invited from researchers who hold, or have a firm offer of, at least a three-year academic appointment at a Canadian university or similar appointment at a Canadian research hospital;
(2) applicant must be a Canadian citizen or a permanent resident of Canada;
(3) special consideration will be given to applicants who have received their doctoral degree within the past five years;
(4) research projects must be endorsed by the research services department or equivalent of the university, hospital or research institute and;
(5) research must be carried out within Canada.

GEOG. RESTRICTIONS: Canada.

FINANCIAL DATA:
Amount of support per award: Up to $35,000 per year.

NO. AWARDS: Approximately 10 new and renewals per year.

APPLICATION INFO:
The research proposals submitted should be accompanied by an explanation of the relationship of the research to the areas of priority, a proposed budget, published papers of the applicant relevant to the proposed research and the time lines of the research. Applications should be submitted to the Chair of the Awards Committee at the address above.

Duration: One, two or three years. Renewal contingent on a progress report of the work and research results.

Deadline: April 30 each year.

OFFICERS:
Allard Loopstra, President

ADDRESS INQUIRIES TO:
The Awards Committee
(See address above.)

SOCIETY OF BIOLOGICAL PSYCHIATRY [2507]

Mayo Clinic - Jacksonville
Research-Birdsall 310
4500 San Pablo Road
Jacksonville, FL 32224
(904) 953-2842
Fax: (904) 953-7117
E-mail: maggie@sobp.org
Web Site: www.sobp.org

FOUNDED: 1945

AREAS OF INTEREST:
Biological psychiatry, neuropsychopharmacology and clinical neuroscience.

NAME(S) OF PROGRAMS:

- **A.E. Bennett Research Awards**

TYPE:
Awards/prizes. Awards for recent, unpublished research papers in the field of biological psychiatry.

YEAR PROGRAM STARTED: 1958

PURPOSE:
To promote research in biological psychiatry.

LEGAL BASIS:
Nonprofit foundation.

ELIGIBILITY:
Applicants must be qualified investigators with appropriate interests. Candidates shall either:
(1) have not passed their 45th birthday by January 1 for the year of the award or;
(2) have not been engaged in research for greater than 10 years following award of their terminal degree or the end of formal clinical/fellowship training, whichever is later.

Membership in the Society is not required. The prize will be awarded based on a body of work rather than a single paper.

FINANCIAL DATA:
Amount of support per award: $5,000 each for the best clinical paper and the best basic science paper submitted.

NO. AWARDS: 1 or 2 each year.

APPLICATION INFO:
Applications are submitted electronically.

Duration: One year.

Deadline: Nominations must be submitted online on or before September 30.

OFFICERS:
Kerry Ressler, M.D., Ph.D., President
Elliott Richelson, M.D., Treasurer
Trey Sunderland, Executive Secretary

STAFF:
Maggie Peterson, MBA, Executive Director

ADDRESS INQUIRIES TO:
Maggie Peterson, MBA, Executive Director
E-mail: sobp@sobp.org
(See telephone number above.)

SOCIETY OF BIOLOGICAL PSYCHIATRY [2508]

Mayo Clinic - Jacksonville
Research-Birdsall 310
4500 San Pablo Road
Jacksonville, FL 32224
(904) 953-2842
Fax: (904) 953-7117
E-mail: maggie@sobp.org
Web Site: www.sobp.org

FOUNDED: 1945

AREAS OF INTEREST:
Biological psychiatry, neuropsychopharmacology and clinical neuroscience.

NAME(S) OF PROGRAMS:

- **Ziskind-Somerfeld Research Award**

TYPE:
Awards/prizes. Award for recent, unsubmitted, unpublished research paper in the field of biological psychiatry.

YEAR PROGRAM STARTED: 1991

PURPOSE:
To stimulate investigations in biological psychiatry by senior investigators.

LEGAL BASIS:
Nonprofit.

ELIGIBILITY:
The award winner is the first author of the award paper. Special consideration is given to the originality of the approach and independence of thought in the archival report. The studies and the data must not have been published elsewhere.

FINANCIAL DATA:
Amount of support per award: $5,000.

Total amount of support: $5,000 annually.

NO. MOST RECENT APPLICANTS: 5.

NO. AWARDS: 1 each year.

APPLICATION INFO:
No application submission is required for the award. The Society provides a list of the top 15 articles to the Ziskind-Somerfeld Award Committee to review and make a final award selection.

Duration: One-time award.

Deadline: Announcement in May.

ADDRESS INQUIRIES TO:
Maggie Peterson, MBA, Executive Director
E-mail: sobp@sobp.org
(See telephone number above.)

SUBSTANCE ABUSE AND MENTAL HEALTH SERVICES ADMINISTRATION, DISASTER TECHNICAL ASSISTANCE CENTER [2509]

5600 Fishers Lane
Rockville, MD 20857
(800) 308-3515
Fax: (240) 276-1890
E-mail: dtac@samhsa.hhs.gov
Web Site: www.samhsa.gov/dtac

AREAS OF INTEREST:
Emergency mental health and crisis counseling.

NAME(S) OF PROGRAMS:
- **Crisis Counseling Assistance and Training Program**

TYPE:
Project/program grants. Grants to address the various dimensions of mental health crises affecting victims of presidentially declared major disasters. Support is available for development of training models and other psychological material for the delivery of crisis intervention services/outreach.

YEAR PROGRAM STARTED: 1974

PURPOSE:
To provide supplemental support to victims of major disasters and their families in emergency mental health and crisis intervention.

LEGAL BASIS:
Section 416 of The Robert T. Stafford Disaster Relief and Emergency Assistance Act (Public Law 100-707).

ELIGIBILITY:
Must be presidentially declared major disaster. U.S. territories and federally recognized tribes are also eligible.

FINANCIAL DATA:
Amount of support per award: Grants given according to justifiable need. Amounts vary in accordance with existing resources in stricken community.

Total amount of support: Varies.

CO-OP FUNDING PROGRAMS: Program funding is supplemental when existing programs are inadequate to meet the needs of the community.

APPLICATION INFO:
Contact the organization for guidelines.

Duration: Nine months; renewal possible upon approval of CMHS and SAMHSA. Extension of grant possible in limited circumstances.

Deadline: 60 days following the disaster.

ADDRESS INQUIRIES TO:
Nikki Bellamy, Project Officer
SAMHSA/CMHS
(See address above.)

VAN AMERINGEN FOUNDATION, INC. [2510]

509 Madison Avenue
Room 2010
New York, NY 10022
(212) 758-6221
Fax: (212) 688-2105
E-mail: info@vanamfound.org
Web Site: www.vanamfound.org

FOUNDED: 1950

AREAS OF INTEREST:
Mental illness and mental health.

TYPE:
Demonstration grants; Development grants; General operating grants; Project/program grants; Research grants; Seed money grants. Grants for projects and activities in areas of social welfare, with particular emphasis on mental health.

YEAR PROGRAM STARTED: 1950

PURPOSE:
To promote mental health through preventive medicine, research, treatment and rehabilitation.

LEGAL BASIS:
Private foundation.

ELIGIBILITY:
Tax-exempt organizations with appropriate interests are eligible. No grants are made to individuals.

GEOG. RESTRICTIONS: Metropolitan New York area and Philadelphia.

FINANCIAL DATA:
Amount of support per award: Up to $50,000, according to the needs and nature of the project.

Total amount of support: Approximately $4,500,000 for the year 2015.

NO. MOST RECENT APPLICANTS: 520.

NO. AWARDS: 89.

APPLICATION INFO:
No formal application forms are required. Proposals may be submitted in the form of a short descriptive letter, enclosing such pertinent background as tax status documentation and the organization's annual reports and financial statements. Proposals may be submitted to the president at the address above.

Deadline: Notification by December 1 for March Board meeting, April 1 for June meeting and July 1 for November meeting.

PUBLICATIONS:
Annual report; guidelines.

DIRECTORS:
Kenneth A. Kind, President and Treasurer
Steadman Westergaard, Vice President and Secretary
Judith Beck
Alexandra Herzan
Christina K. Kind
Patricia Kind
Valerie Kind-Rubin
Andrew Kindfuller
Laura K. McKenna
Clarence Sundram
Henry van Ameringen

ADDRESS INQUIRIES TO:
Kenneth A. Kind, President
(See address above.)

TECHNOLOGY AND INDUSTRY

Technology and industry

AGC EDUCATION AND RESEARCH FOUNDATION

2300 Wilson Boulevard, Suite 300
Arlington, VA 22201
(703) 837-5342
Fax: (703) 837-5451
E-mail: patricianm@agc.org
Web Site: www.agcfoundation.org

TYPE:

Awards/prizes; Internships; Project/program grants; Scholarships. Allhands Essay Competition: Awarded to a student essay on a specific topic that is deemed to be beneficial to the advancement of technological, educational or vocational expertise in the construction industry.

Faculty Internships: Grants for faculty through internships with AGC contractor-members.

Graduate Scholarship Program: Scholarships for students enrolled in ABET- or ACCE-accredited construction management or construction-related engineering programs.

Industry Case Studies: Commissioning case studies on industry scenarios.

Outstanding Educator Award: Awards to top competitors in essay competition for seniors and faculty nominated as Outstanding Educator.

Undergraduate Scholarship Program: Scholarships for students enrolled in ABET- or ACCE-accredited construction management or construction-related engineering programs.

Workforce Development Scholarship: Awarded for students entering craft training or technical programs.

See entry 2547 for full listing.

AIR & WASTE MANAGEMENT ASSOCIATION (A&WMA) [2511]

One Gateway Center, 3rd Floor
420 Fort Duquesne Boulevard
Pittsburgh, PA 15222
(412) 904-6006
Fax: (412) 232-3450
E-mail: sglyptis@awma.org
Web Site: www.awma.org

FOUNDED: 1907

AREAS OF INTEREST:

Air quality, waste management and/or environmental management/policy/law.

NAME(S) OF PROGRAMS:

- **Scholarship Endowment Trust Fund**

TYPE:

Scholarships.

PURPOSE:

To provide monies for students with interest in the area of air quality, waste management and/or environmental management/policy/law.

ELIGIBILITY:

Must be a full-time graduate student pursuing studies in the area of air quality, waste management and/or environmental management/policy/law.

FINANCIAL DATA:

Amount of support per award: $2,000 to $7,500.

Total amount of support: Approximately $26,000 annually.

NO. MOST RECENT APPLICANTS: 50.

NO. AWARDS: Approximately 10.

APPLICATION INFO:

Applications must be completed online.

Duration: One year. Renewal possible by reapplying.

Deadline: December 1.

ADDRESS INQUIRIES TO:

Stephanie Glyptis, Executive Director
(See address above.)

AIR TRAFFIC CONTROL ASSOCIATION (ATCA) [2512]

1101 King Street, Suite 300
Alexandria, VA 22314
(703) 299-2430 ext. 314
Fax: (703) 299-2437
E-mail: tim.wagner@atca.org
Web Site: www.atca.org

FOUNDED: 1956

AREAS OF INTEREST:

Air traffic control and aviation.

TYPE:

Scholarships. Scholarships to promising young men and women enrolled in programs leading to careers in aviation or air traffic control and scholarships for dependents of air traffic controllers pursuing a degree.

PURPOSE:

To promote careers in air traffic control or aviation disciplines.

LEGAL BASIS:

Private, 501(c)(3) charity.

FINANCIAL DATA:

Amount of support per award: $2,000 to $8,000.

Total amount of support: Varies.

NO. MOST RECENT APPLICANTS: 300.

NO. AWARDS: 8 to 12.

APPLICATION INFO:

Contact the Association.

Duration: One year.

Deadline: May 1.

ADDRESS INQUIRIES TO:

Tim Wagner, Membership Manager
(See address above.)

AMERICAN GROUND WATER TRUST [2513]

50 Pleasant Street, Suite 2
Concord, NH 03301-4073
(603) 228-5444
Fax: (603) 228-6557
E-mail: trustinfo@agwt.org
Web Site: www.agwt.org

FOUNDED: 1986

AREAS OF INTEREST:

Groundwater education, sustainable management and protection.

NAME(S) OF PROGRAMS:

- **AMTROL Scholarship**
- **Baroid Scholarship**
- **Thomas M. Stetson Scholarship**

TYPE:

Awards/prizes; Scholarships.

YEAR PROGRAM STARTED: 1986

PURPOSE:

To provide education outreach to inform the public about the optimal utilization and protection of groundwater for the benefit of mankind.

LEGAL BASIS:

501(c)(3) nonprofit organization.

ELIGIBILITY:

Applicants must be U.S. citizens, apply during their senior year in high school, and be enrolled the following year in an undergraduate program relevant to the groundwater industry.

GEOG. RESTRICTIONS: United States.

FINANCIAL DATA:

Amount of support per award: $1,000 to $2,000.

NO. MOST RECENT APPLICANTS: 40.

NO. AWARDS: 3.

APPLICATION INFO:

Applicant must submit only one application to be considered for all scholarships. Completed application form must be countersigned by a teacher at the applicant's high school and accompanied by two letters of recommendation. A 500-word essay and a 300-word description of the applicant's high school groundwater project and/or practical environmental work experience must accompany the application. Documentary evidence of scholastic achievements and references will be requested from finalists.

Duration: One academic year.

Deadline: June 1. The Trust will write to all applicants (successful and unsuccessful) at the end of August.

IRS I.D.: 23-7244958

STAFF:

Andrew W. Stone, Executive Director
Garret W. Graaskamp, Director of Programs

ADDRESS INQUIRIES TO:

Andrew W. Stone, Executive Director
(See address above.)

AMERICAN SOCIETY FOR ENOLOGY AND VITICULTURE

1784 Picasso Avenue, Suite D
Davis, CA 95618-0551
(530) 753-3142
Fax: (530) 753-3318
E-mail: society@asev.org
Web Site: www.asev.org

TYPE:

Scholarships. Awards for undergraduate or graduate students enrolled in enology or viticulture or in a curriculum which emphasizes a science basic to the wine and grape industry and who intend to pursue a career in research for the wine or grape industry after graduation from college or university.

See entry 2051 for full listing.

THE AMERICAN SOCIETY FOR NONDESTRUCTIVE TESTING, INC. [2514]

1711 Arlingate Lane
Columbus, OH 43228-0518
(614) 274-6003
(800) 222-2768
Fax: (614) 274-6899
E-mail: jvandervort@asnt.org
Web Site: www.asnt.org

FOUNDED: 1941

AREAS OF INTEREST:
Nondestructive testing.

NAME(S) OF PROGRAMS:
- **ASNT Fellowship Award**

TYPE:
Fellowships. Nondestructive evaluation and testing (NDE/NDT) is the science of examining components and systems in a manner that does not impair their further usefulness. NDE/NDT is a complex, multidisciplinary field offering exciting career opportunities. Current areas for applying new and advanced nondestructive testing technology include power plant life extension, aging aircraft and deteriorating civil engineering structures.

YEAR PROGRAM STARTED: 1981

PURPOSE:
To advance the examination of objects with technology that does not affect the object's future usefulness; to identify up to five ABET-accredited educational institutions that may receive one of the awards for NDT postgraduate research.

LEGAL BASIS:
Nonprofit organization.

ELIGIBILITY:
ABET-accredited academic institutions with graduate educational research programs are invited to submit proposals. Proposals are evaluated based on their soundness of approach, value of potential contribution, potential for successful completion, qualifications of potential student recipient, qualifications of advisor, adequacy of program of study, adequacy of facilities, and qualifications of faculty members.

FINANCIAL DATA:
Amount of support per award: $20,000.

Total amount of support: Up to $100,000.

NO. AWARDS: Up to 5 per year.

APPLICATION INFO:
The proposal, with all support materials, should not exceed 20 one-sided sheets. It must include a title page, table of contents, research proposal, program of study, research facilities, budget, research advisor, and recipient. The educational facility must submit a written report on the completed study within 24 months of the program's initiation. This report must be in a format suitable for publication in the Society's technical journal, *Materials Evaluation*. In addition, the postgraduate student must present his findings at an ASNT national conference. No more than one proposal per faculty member.

Duration: One year.

Deadline: October 15.

ADDRESS INQUIRIES TO:
Michelle Thomas
ASNT Administrative Assistant
ASNT Headquarters
(See address above.)

APICS SUPPLY CHAIN COUNCIL [2515]

8430 West Bryn Mawr Avenue
Suite 1000
Chicago, IL 60631-3439
(773) 867-1758
Fax: (773) 659-3058
E-mail: saspacher@apics.org
Web Site: www.apics.org/education/erfoundation

FOUNDED: 1965

AREAS OF INTEREST:
Applied resource management, manufacturing, service industries, production and inventory management.

NAME(S) OF PROGRAMS:
- **George and Marion Plossl Doctoral Dissertation Fellowship**

TYPE:
Awards/prizes; Conferences/seminars; Fellowships; Project/program grants; Research grants. Plossl Doctoral Dissertation Fellowship is in the area of operations management.

YEAR PROGRAM STARTED: 1965

PURPOSE:
To further develop the APICS body of knowledge; to develop professional efficiency in production and inventory management.

LEGAL BASIS:
Tax-exempt 501(c)(3) organization.

ELIGIBILITY:
To be eligible for consideration, a submission must meet the following criteria:
(1) an applicant must be a Ph.D. candidate in Operations Management (or a closely-related discipline) from a fully-accredited academic institution;
(2) doctoral dissertation proposal of the applicant must have been approved by the thesis committee and;
(3) doctoral dissertation research must not have been completed at the time of submission.

FINANCIAL DATA:
Amount of support per award: $2,500.

Total amount of support: $2,500 annually.

NO. MOST RECENT APPLICANTS: 8.

NO. AWARDS: 1.

APPLICATION INFO:
The following submission requirements must be strictly met:
(1) submission must include a nominating letter on university letterhead from the dissertation advisor of the doctoral student whose doctoral dissertation proposal is being entered for competition consideration;
(2) an executive summary which describes and justifies the importance of the pragmatic problem that the doctoral dissertation addresses, delineates the research questions that stem from this pragmatic problem, discusses critical insights from the literature that have a bearing on the research questions and/or pragmatic problem motivating the research questions, identifies and justifies the hypotheses to be examined, explains the methods to be used in data collection and data analyses to provide answers to the research questions, and discusses the managerial implications of potential findings. (Executive Summary must not exceed a maximum of 10 double-spaced, 8.5 x 11, pages with 1-inch margins, must include a footer showing the page number, and use Arial font, size 11 only.)

Letter of Introduction and the Executive Summary should be submitted to the e-mail address above as a single PDF attachment. Please name the submission using the following convention: LAST NAME_FIRST NAME-2015 Plossl Dissertation Fellowship. Once received, an e-mail confirmation will be sent to the applicant.

Submissions that do not comply with these requirements run the risk of being disqualified.

Deadline: August 30.

PUBLICATIONS:
Guidelines.

ADDRESS INQUIRIES TO:
Steve Aspacher, Senior Manager
Student Membership and Academic Services
(See address above.)

AWS FOUNDATION, INC. [2516]

8669 N.W. 36th Street
No. 130
Miami, FL 33166
(305) 443-9353
Fax: (305) 443-7559
E-mail: vpinsky@aws.org
Web Site: www.aws.org

FOUNDED: 1989

AREAS OF INTEREST:
Welding and materials joining.

NAME(S) OF PROGRAMS:
- **Howard E. and Wilma J. Adkins Memorial Scholarship**
- **Airgas-Jerry Baker Scholarship**
- **Airgas-Terry Jarvis Memorial Scholarship**
- **Arsham Amirikian Engineering Scholarship**
- **D. Fred and Marian L. Bovie Scholarship**
- **John C. Lincoln Memorial Scholarship**
- **Matsuo Bridge Company, Ltd. of Japan Scholarship**

TYPE:
Scholarships. Howard E. and Wilma J. Adkins Memorial Scholarship is awarded to a full-time college junior or senior pursuing a minimum four-year degree in welding engineering or welding engineering technology.

Airgas-Jerry Baker Scholarship is awarded to a full-time college undergraduate pursuing a minimum four-year degree in welding engineering or welding engineering technology; however, priority will be given to welding engineering students.

Airgas-Terry Jarvis Memorial Scholarship is awarded to a full-time college undergraduate pursuing a minimum four-year degree in welding engineering or welding engineering technology; however, priority will be given to welding engineering students.

Arsham Amirikian Engineering Scholarship is awarded to a college undergraduate pursuing a minimum four-year degree in civil engineering or welding engineering.

D. Fred and Marian L. Bovie Scholarship is awarded to a full-time college undergraduate pursuing a minimum four-year degree in welding engineering at The Ohio State University.

John C. Lincoln Memorial Scholarship is awarded to a college undergraduate pursuing a minimum four-year degree in welding engineering or welding engineering technology. Priority will be given to welding engineering students.

Matsuo Bridge Company Ltd. of Japan Scholarship is for a college junior, senior, or graduate student pursuing a minimum four-year degree in civil engineering, welding engineering, welding engineering technology or a related discipline.

PURPOSE:
To promote education in welding engineering.

ELIGIBILITY:
Howard E. and Wilma J. Adkins Memorial Scholarship: U.S. citizens with a 3.2 grade point average in engineering, scientific and technical subjects, with a 2.8 overall grade point average.

Airgas-Jerry Baker Scholarship and Airgas-Terry Jarvis Memorial Scholarship: U.S. or Canadian citizens/residents who maintain a minimum overall grade point average of 2.8 with a 3.0 in engineering courses. Essay required: "Why I want to pursue a career with an industrial gas or welding equipment distributor?"

Arsham Amirikian Engineering Scholarship: Applicant must be a U.S. citizen or resident and have a minimum 3.0 overall grade point average.

D. Fred and Marian L. Bovie Scholarship: U.S. citizen or resident welding engineering student at The Ohio State University with a 3.0 overall grade point average. Electrical engineering students at The Ohio State University may be considered if there is no qualified welding engineering applicant at The Ohio State University.

John C. Lincoln Memorial Scholarship: U.S. citizen or resident with a 2.5 overall grade point average.

Matsuo Bridge Company Ltd. of Japan Scholarship: Applicant must be a U.S. citizen with a 3.0 overall grade point average; preference given to students from California, Oregon, Texas and Washington.

GEOG. RESTRICTIONS: United States and Canada.

FINANCIAL DATA:
Amount of support per award: Howard E. and Wilma J. Adkins Memorial Scholarship, Airgas-Jerry Baker Scholarship, Airgas-Terry Jarvis Memorial Scholarship, Arsham Amirikian Engineering Scholarship and Matsuo Scholarship: $2,500; D. Fred and Marian L. Bovie Scholarship: $3,000; John C. Lincoln Memorial Scholarship: $3,500.

NO. MOST RECENT APPLICANTS: Adkins Scholarship: 12; Airgas-Jerry Baker Scholarship and Airgas-Terry Jarvis Memorial Scholarship: 5; Amirikian Scholarship: 20; Bovie Scholarship: 3; Lincoln Memorial Scholarship: 23; Matsuo Scholarship: 19.

NO. AWARDS: 1 award per scholarship program.

APPLICATION INFO:
Application must be made online: scholarship.aws.org.

Duration: Howard E. and Wilma J. Adkins Memorial Scholarship: One year; may reapply for second year. All others, one year and renewable up to three years.

Deadline: February 15.

ADDRESS INQUIRIES TO:
Vicki L. Pinsky
Associate Director, Scholarships
(See address above.)

AWS FOUNDATION, INC. [2517]

8669 N.W. 36th Street
No. 130
Miami, FL 33166
(305) 443-9353
Fax: (305) 443-7559
E-mail: vpinsky@aws.org
Web Site: www.aws.org

FOUNDED: 1989

AREAS OF INTEREST:
Welding and materials joining.

NAME(S) OF PROGRAMS:
- **Jack R. Barckhoff Welding Management Scholarship**
- **Edward J. Brady Memorial Scholarship**
- **William A. and Ann M. Brothers Scholarship**
- **Don and Shirley Hastings Scholarship**
- **Donald F. Hastings Scholarship**
- **William B. Howell Memorial Scholarship**
- **Miller Electric Mfg. Co. Scholarship**

TYPE:
Scholarships. Jack R. Barckhoff Welding Management Scholarship is awarded to a college junior pursuing a minimum four-year degree in welding engineering at The Ohio State University. Applicants will be expected to enroll and complete the two-hour course in Total Welding Management at The Ohio State University. Applicants must also complete an essay on how they see their role once they have graduated in improving the world of welding and the welding industry in the U.S., and how they will use their education to improve the U.S. competitive position in welding and manufacturing.

Edward J. Brady Memorial Scholarship is awarded to a college undergraduate pursuing a minimum four-year degree in welding engineering or welding engineering technology. Priority will be given to welding engineering students.

William A. and Ann M. Brothers Scholarship is awarded to a full-time college undergraduate pursuing a minimum four-year degree in welding or a related program.

Don and Shirley Hastings Scholarship is awarded to a college undergraduate pursuing a minimum four-year degree in welding engineering or welding engineering technology. Priority will be given to welding engineering students.

Donald F. Hastings Scholarship is awarded to a college undergraduate pursuing a minimum four-year degree in welding engineering or welding engineering technology. Priority will be given to welding engineering students.

William B. Howell Memorial Scholarship is awarded to a full-time college undergraduate pursuing a minimum four-year degree in a welding program at an accredited university.

Miller Electric Mfg. Co. Scholarship is awarded to a senior in a four-year Bachelor's program in welding engineering or welding engineering technology. Priority is given to Ferris State University.

PURPOSE:
To promote education in welding engineering.

ELIGIBILITY:
For all scholarships, applicants must be U.S. citizens/residents and have a minimum 2.5 grade point average.

Jack R. Barckhoff Welding Management Scholarship: Applicant must attend The Ohio State University.

William A. and Ann M. Brothers Scholarship: Priority will be given to those individuals residing or attending school in the state of Ohio.

Don and Shirley Hastings Scholarship: Priority will be given to those individuals who reside or attend school in the states of California, Iowa or Ohio.

Donald F. Hastings Scholarship: Priority will be given to those individuals who reside or attend school in California or Ohio.

William B. Howell Memorial Scholarship: Priority will be given to those individuals who reside or attend school in Florida, Michigan or Ohio.

Miller Electric Mfg. Co. Scholarship: Priority will be given to individuals attending Ferris State University.

GEOG. RESTRICTIONS: United States.

FINANCIAL DATA:
Amount of support per award: Jack R. Barckhoff Welding Management Scholarship, Edward J. Brady Memorial Scholarship, Don and Shirley Hastings Scholarship, Donald F. Hastings Scholarship and William B. Howell Memorial Scholarship: $2,500; William A. and Ann M. Brothers Scholarship: $6,000; Miller Electric Mfg. Co. Scholarship: $3,000.

NO. MOST RECENT APPLICANTS: Jack R. Barckhoff Welding Management Scholarship: 1; Edward J. Brady Memorial Scholarship: 14; William A. and Ann M. Brothers Scholarship: 23; Don and Shirley Hastings Scholarship: 20; Donald F. Hastings Scholarship and William B. Howell Memorial Scholarship: 24; Miller Electric Mfg. Co. Scholarship: 11.

NO. AWARDS: Jack R. Barckhoff Welding Management Scholarship and Miller Electric Mfg. Co. Scholarship: 2 per scholarship; All others: 1 per scholarship.

APPLICATION INFO:
Detailed information is available on the web site: scholarship.aws.org.

Duration: Jack R. Barckhoff Welding Management Scholarship: One year, with up to two years of scholarship support by reapplication; Edward J. Brady Memorial Scholarship, William A. and Ann M. Brothers Scholarship, Don and Shirley Hastings Scholarship, Donald F. Hastings Scholarship and William B. Howell Memorial Scholarship: One year, with up to four years of scholarship support by reapplication.

Deadline: February 15.

ADDRESS INQUIRIES TO:
Vicki L. Pinsky
Associate Director, Scholarships
(See address above.)

AWS FOUNDATION, INC. [2518]

8669 N.W. 36th Street
No. 130
Miami, FL 33166
(305) 443-9353
Fax: (305) 443-7559
E-mail: vpinsky@aws.org
Web Site: www.aws.org

FOUNDED: 1989

AREAS OF INTEREST:
Welding and materials joining.

NAME(S) OF PROGRAMS:
- **Past Presidents Scholarship**
- **Robert L. Peaslee Brazing Scholarship**
- **Praxair International Scholarship**
- **James A. Turner, Jr. Memorial Scholarship**

TYPE:
Scholarships. Past Presidents Scholarship is for a student in a four-year program in welding engineering, welding engineering technology, or an engineering program with an emphasis on welding, or a graduate student pursuing a Master's or Doctorate in engineering and/or management.

Robert L. Peaslee Brazing Scholarship is for a college junior or senior pursuing a minimum four-year degree, or a graduate student, in welding engineering, welding engineering technology, or materials joining science with an emphasis on brazing or soldering applications.

Praxair International Scholarship is for a full-time college student pursuing a minimum four-year degree in welding engineering or welding engineering technology; however, priority will be given to welding engineering students. Applicant must demonstrate leadership abilities through clubs, organizations, extracurricular academic activities, community involvement, etc.

James A. Turner, Jr. Memorial Scholarship is for a student pursuing a Bachelor's degree in business that will lead to a management career in welding store operations or welding distributorship.

PURPOSE:
To promote education in welding engineering.

ELIGIBILITY:
Past Presidents Scholarship: Applicant must be a U.S. citizen and write a 300- to 500-word essay on their career aspirations. Applicant must have demonstrated leadership qualities, i.e., community involvement, AWS Section or other professional society participation, industry leadership, and be an AWS member.

Robert L. Peaslee Brazing Scholarship: Applicant may be a citizen of any country and plan to attend a university in the U.S. or Canada; U.S. citizens will receive priority. Minimum grade point average of 3.0 in engineering courses.

Praxair International Scholarship: Applicant must be a U.S. or Canadian citizen with a minimum overall grade point average of 2.5.

James A. Turner, Jr. Memorial Scholarship: Applicant must be employed at least 10 hours per week at a welding store operation or welding distributorship.

GEOG. RESTRICTIONS: United States.

FINANCIAL DATA:
Amount of support per award: Robert L. Peaslee Brazing Scholarship and Praxair International Scholarship: $2,500. James A. Turner, Jr. Memorial Scholarship: $3,500.

NO. MOST RECENT APPLICANTS: Robert L. Peaslee Brazing Scholarship and James A. Turner, Jr. Memorial Scholarship: 1; Praxair International Scholarship: 22.

NO. AWARDS: 1 award per scholarship.

APPLICATION INFO:
Detailed information is available on the web site: scholarship.aws.org.

Past Presidents Scholarship: One or more recommendation letters must come from community members, local AWS Section Officers, and/or AWS District Director, attesting to leadership capability; one or more recommendation letters must come from faculty (if a student), or from employer (if employed).

Robert L. Peaslee Brazing Scholarship: Personal statement must include at least one paragraph on applicant's interest in brazing or soldering, any courses taken in related subjects, and any other information that would help the Selection Committee in selecting a recipient. Also, include a description of applicant's impressions of any experience he or she has had involving soldering or brazing.

Duration: Robert L. Peaslee Brazing Scholarship: Maximum of two years per award; Praxair International Scholarship and James A. Turner, Jr. Memorial Scholarship: Award recipients may reapply with a maximum of four years per award.

Deadline: February 15.

ADDRESS INQUIRIES TO:
Vicki L. Pinsky
Associate Director, Scholarships
(See address above.)

AWS FOUNDATION, INC. [2519]

8669 Doral Boulevard, Suite 130
Doral, FL 33166
(305) 443-9353 ext. 212
(800) 443-9353 ext. 212
Fax: (305) 443-7559
E-mail: vpinsky@aws.org
Web Site: www.aws.org/rwma

FOUNDED: 1935

AREAS OF INTEREST:
Resistance welding processes.

NAME(S) OF PROGRAMS:
- **Resistance Welding Manufacturing Alliance Scholarship**

TYPE:
Scholarships.

YEAR PROGRAM STARTED: 2005

PURPOSE:
To encourage the highest standards of ethics in the resistance welding industry; to encourage education pertaining to the resistance welding processes.

ELIGIBILITY:
Applicant must:
(1) be a junior-level student in a four-year program and working towards a degree in welding engineering or welding engineering technology;
(2) have a minimum 3.0 overall grade point average and;
(3) be a U.S. or Canadian citizen and plan to attend an academic institution in the U.S. or Canada.

FINANCIAL DATA:
Awards are for tuition and fees only and will be paid directly to the academic institution.

Amount of support per award: $2,500.

Total amount of support: $2,500.

NO. MOST RECENT APPLICANTS: 2.

NO. AWARDS: 1.

APPLICATION INFO:
Candidates must submit the following:
(1) a completed application form;
(2) an essay of 500 words or less about why the student wishes to become involved in the resistance welding industry;
(3) a letter of recommendation from an academic advisor or faculty member using the RWMA Scholarship Recommendation form;
(4) a second letter of recommendation from another party, such as an employer, using the RWMA Scholarship Recommendation form and;
(5) a personal statement.

Duration: One year. Renewal possible; must reapply.

Deadline: February 15.

ADDRESS INQUIRIES TO:
Vicki L. Pinsky, Manager
(See address above.)

CHARLES BABBAGE INSTITUTE [2520]

University of Minnesota
211 Elmer L. Anderson Library
222 21st Avenue South
Minneapolis, MN 55455
(612) 624-5050
E-mail: cbi@umn.edu
Web Site: www.cbi.umn.edu

FOUNDED: 1978

AREAS OF INTEREST:
History of computers and information technology.

NAME(S) OF PROGRAMS:
- **The Adelle and Erwin Tomash Fellowship in the History of Information Technology**

TYPE:
Fellowships.

YEAR PROGRAM STARTED: 1978

PURPOSE:
To advance the professional development of historians of information technology.

LEGAL BASIS:
University and research association.

ELIGIBILITY:
Open to graduate students whose dissertation addresses some aspect of the history of computers and information technology. Topics may be chosen from the technical history of hardware or software, economic or business aspects of the information technology industry or other topics in the social, institutional or legal history of computing. Theses that consider technical issues in their socio-economic context are especially encouraged.

Priority will be given to students who have completed all requirements for the doctoral degree except the research and writing of the dissertation.

The fellowship may be held at the home academic institution, the Babbage Institute or any other location where there are appropriate research facilities.

FINANCIAL DATA:
Amount of support per award: $14,000 stipend.

Total amount of support: $14,000.

NO. MOST RECENT APPLICANTS: 5.

NO. AWARDS: 1.

APPLICATION INFO:
Applicants should send biographical data and a research plan. The plan should contain a statement and justification of the research problem, a discussion of procedure for research and writing, information on availability of research materials and evidence of faculty support for the project. Applicants should arrange for three letters of reference and certified transcripts of college credits to be sent directly to the Institute. There is no special application form. A one-page flyer describing the fellowship is available.

Duration: One academic year.

Deadline: January 15.

PUBLICATIONS:
Newsletter.

ADDRESS INQUIRIES TO:
Jeffrey Yost, Associate Director
Charles Babbage Institute
(See address above.)

COIN-OP CARES CHARITABLE AND EDUCATION FOUNDATION [2521]

c/o Amusement & Music Operators Association
600 Spring Hill Ring Road, Suite 111
West Dundee, IL 60118
(847) 428-7699
(800) 937-2662
Fax: (847) 428-7719
E-mail: amoa@amoa.com
Web Site: www.amoa.com

FOUNDED: 1948

AREAS OF INTEREST:
Higher education.

NAME(S) OF PROGRAMS:
- **Wayne E. Hesch Memorial Scholarships**

TYPE:
Scholarships. Designed to provide financial support to students who are, or plan or hope to be, engaged in the profession.

PURPOSE:
To provide leadership for the amusement, music, entertainment and vending industry; to protect and promote the industry interests.

ELIGIBILITY:
Open to individuals in need of financial assistance who are attending or plan to attend an institution of higher education and have a 3.0 grade point average on a 4.0 scale.

FINANCIAL DATA:
Amount of support per award: $1,000 each.

Total amount of support: $50,000 annually.

APPLICATION INFO:
Application information is available online.

Duration: One year.

Deadline: February 12. Selection in late March. Announcement in April.

ADDRESS INQUIRIES TO:
Claudia Kaczmarek, Program Coordinator
(See address above.)

EARLY AMERICAN INDUSTRIES ASSOCIATION, INC. [2522]

P.O. Box 524
Hebron, MD 21830-0524
(703) 967-9399
E-mail: eaia1933@verizon.net
Web Site: www.eaiainfo.org

FOUNDED: 1933

AREAS OF INTEREST:
To encourage study and better understanding of early American industries in the home, shop, on the farm and the sea; to discover, identify, classify, preserve and exhibit obsolete tools, implements and mechanical devices used in early America, craft practices, and industrial technology.

NAME(S) OF PROGRAMS:
- **Research Grants Program**

TYPE:
Research grants. These are not scholarship or internship grants.

YEAR PROGRAM STARTED: 1977

PURPOSE:
To preserve and present historic trades, crafts and tools, and to interpret their impact on the present generation.

LEGAL BASIS:
Nonprofit corporation.

ELIGIBILITY:
Applicants may be sponsored by an institution or engaged in self-directed projects. Projects must relate to the purposes of the Association. Grants can supplement existing aid. These are not scholarship, fellowship or internship funds. A grant may not be used to pay for salaries, historical artifacts, software or equipment in whole or in part.

GEOG. RESTRICTIONS: United States.

FINANCIAL DATA:
Amount of support per award: Up to $3,000.

NO. MOST RECENT APPLICANTS: 8.

NO. AWARDS: 2.

APPLICATION INFO:
Application is available online, and must be completed and mailed to the above address.

Duration: One year. Nonrenewable.

Deadline: March 15 annually. Announcements in April annually.

PUBLICATIONS:
The Chronicle, quarterly journal; *Shavings*, newsletter for members; application guidelines; E.A.I.A. brochure.

OFFICERS:
John H. Verrill, Executive Director

ADDRESS INQUIRIES TO:
John H. Verrill, Executive Director
(See address above.)

*PLEASE NOTE:
A project report, including a statement of expenditures, must be filed by recipients.

FEDERAL HIGHWAY ADMINISTRATION [2523]

Technology Partnerships Programs
1310 North Court House Road, Suite 300
Arlington, VA 22201
(703) 235-0538
Fax: (703) 235-0593
E-mail: transportationedu@dot.gov
Web Site: www.fhwa.dot.gov/tpp/ddetfp.htm

AREAS OF INTEREST:
Transportation-related disciplines.

NAME(S) OF PROGRAMS:
- **Dwight David Eisenhower Transportation Fellowship Program**

TYPE:
Fellowships; Internships; Research grants. Dwight David Eisenhower Transportation Fellowship Program's objectives are to attract the nation's brightest minds to the field of transportation, to enhance the careers of transportation professionals by encouraging them to seek advanced degrees, and to retain top talent in the transportation industry of the U.S. This Program encompasses all areas of transportation. The Program has eight award categories:
(1) Eisenhower Graduate (GRAD) Fellowships enable students to pursue Master's degrees or Doctorates in transportation-related fields at the university of their choice;
(2) Eisenhower Grants for Research (GRF) Fellowships acquaint undergraduate and graduate students with transportation research, development and technology-transfer activities at the U.S. Department of Transportation facilities;
(3) Eisenhower Historically Black Colleges and Universities (HBCU) Fellowships provide HBCU students with additional opportunities to enter careers in transportation. The Fellowships also serve as a feeder for other Eisenhower fellowships;
(4) Eisenhower Hispanic Serving Institutions (HSI) Fellowships provide HSI students with additional opportunities to enter careers in transportation. The Fellowships also serve as a feeder for other Eisenhower fellowships;
(5) Eisenhower Tribal College and Universities Fellowships (TCU) provides students with additional opportunities to enter careers in transportation. The Fellowships also serve as a feeder for other Eisenhower fellowships;
(6) Eisenhower Intern Fellowships (EIF) provides students with opportunities to perform a wide range of transportation-related activities at public and private-sector transportation organizations;
(7) Eisenhower People with Disabilities (PWD) Fellowships provide additional opportunities for people with disabilities to enter careers in transportation. The Fellowships also serve as a feeder for other Eisenhower fellowships and;
(8) Eisenhower Community College Fellowships provide students at community colleges with opportunities to enter careers in transportation. The Fellowships also serve as a feeder for other Eisenhower fellowships.

YEAR PROGRAM STARTED: 1983

PURPOSE:
To attract the nation's brightest minds to the field of transportation; to enhance the careers of transportation professionals by encouraging them to seek advanced degrees; to retain top talent in the transportation industry of the U.S.

LEGAL BASIS:
Government agency.

ELIGIBILITY:
Applicants must be enrolled in transportation-related disciplines (e.g., engineering, computer science, physics, transportation planning) at accredited universities.

GEOG. RESTRICTIONS: United States.

FINANCIAL DATA:
Award may include an allowance for tuition, stipend and travel expenses for the student to attend the annual Transportation Research Board (TRB) conference held in Washington, DC every January.

Amount of support per award: $1,500 to $40,000.

Total amount of support: $2,200,000 per year.

NO. AWARDS: 171 for the fiscal year 2015.

APPLICATION INFO:
Undergraduate applicants must submit applications through their faculty advisors and be nominated for awards by their respective universities. Graduate applicants must apply to the Arlington, VA office. Further information is available from the Administration.

Duration: Minimum three months during the summer. Maximum three years of funding, with five years to complete the course.

Deadline: Varies.

PUBLICATIONS:
Application guidelines; brochures.

ADDRESS INQUIRIES TO:
Fawn Thompson, Program Manager
(See address above.)

FOUNDATION FOR TECHNOLOGY AND ENGINEERING EDUCATION

1914 Association Drive
Suite 201
Reston, VA 20191-1539
(703) 860-2100
Fax: (703) 860-0353
E-mail: iteea@iteea.org
Web Site: www.iteea.org

TYPE:
Scholarships. The scholarship is for an undergraduate student majoring in technology and engineering education teacher preparation.

See entry 1629 for full listing.

FOUNDATION FOR TECHNOLOGY AND ENGINEERING EDUCATION

1914 Association Drive
Suite 201
Reston, VA 20191-1539
(703) 860-2100
Fax: (703) 860-0353
E-mail: iteea@iteea.org
Web Site: www.iteea.org

TYPE:
Scholarships.

See entry 1499 for full listing.

FOUNDATION FOR TECHNOLOGY AND ENGINEERING EDUCATION

1914 Association Drive
Suite 201
Reston, VA 20191-1539
(703) 860-2100
Fax: (703) 860-0353
E-mail: iteea@iteea.org
Web Site: www.iteea.org

TYPE:
Scholarships.

See entry 1630 for full listing.

THE FOUNDATION OF FLEXOGRAPHIC TECHNICAL ASSOCIATION [2524]

3920 Veterans Memorial Highway, Suite 9
Bohemia, NY 11716
(631) 737-6020 ext. 36
Fax: (631) 737-6813
E-mail: srubin@flexography.org
Web Site: www.flexography.org

FOUNDED: 1958

AREAS OF INTEREST:
Flexographic printing.

NAME(S) OF PROGRAMS:
- **Flexographic Technical Association Scholarship**

TYPE:
Scholarships.

PURPOSE:
To support education in the study of flexography.

ELIGIBILITY:
Must be enrolled in a qualified school offering a study of flexography. Must have grade point average of 3.0 or better.

FINANCIAL DATA:
Amount of support per award: $3,000 per year.

Total amount of support: Varies.

NO. AWARDS: Varies.

APPLICATION INFO:
Contact the Organization for application procedures.

Duration: One year. Renewable upon reapplication.

Deadline: Usually March of each year.

ADDRESS INQUIRIES TO:
Shelley Rubin
Manager, Educational Services
(See address above.)

GREAT MINDS IN STEM [2525]

602 Monterey Pass Road
Monterey Park, CA 91754
(323) 262-0997
Fax: (323) 262-0946
E-mail: info@greatmindsinstem.org
Web Site: www.greatmindsinstem.org

FOUNDED: 1989

AREAS OF INTEREST:
Science, technology, computer science, engineering and math.

NAME(S) OF PROGRAMS:
- **HENAAC Scholars Program**

TYPE:
Scholarships.

YEAR PROGRAM STARTED: 2000

PURPOSE:
To provide undergraduate and graduate scholarships to students majoring in science, technology, computer science, engineering and math.

ELIGIBILITY:
Applicants must be of Hispanic origin and/or must significantly participate in and promote organizations and activities in the Hispanic community. Applicants must be enrolled in an undergraduate or graduate engineering or science program at a college or university and must be planning to pursue a career in either area. Selection is based on academic standing, financial need, career potential and character.

GEOG. RESTRICTIONS: United States.

FINANCIAL DATA:
Amount of support per award: $500 to $10,000.

Total amount of support: Varies.

NO. MOST RECENT APPLICANTS: 815.

NO. AWARDS: 108 for the year 2014.

APPLICATION INFO:
Application form required. If requesting an application in writing, send a self-addressed, stamped envelope. Absolutely no faxes will be accepted.

Duration: One academic year. Renewal possible.

Deadline: April 30.

STAFF:
Dr. Gary Cruz, Senior Manager

ADDRESS INQUIRIES TO:
HENAAC Scholars Program
(See address above.)

HIMSS FOUNDATION

33 West Monroe Street, Suite 1700
Chicago, IL 60603-5616
(312) 915-9515
(312) 664-4467
Fax: (312) 664-6143
E-mail: scholarships@himss.org
Web Site: www.himss.org

TYPE:
Awards/prizes; Conferences/seminars; Fellowships; Internships; Research grants; Scholarships.

See entry 2195 for full listing.

IEEE HISTORY CENTER

Stevens Institute of Technology
Samuel C. Williams Library, Third Floor
One Castle Point on Hudson
Hoboken, NJ 07030
(732) 562-5468
Fax: (732) 562-6020
E-mail: ieee-history@ieee.org
Web Site: www.ieee.org/history_center

TYPE:
Fellowships; Internships. Fellowship in the History of Electrical and Computing Technology: Award for one year of full-time doctoral or postdoctoral work in the history of electrical engineering and technology at a college or university of recognized standing.

Internship in Electrical History: Two-month internship for graduate research.

See entry 587 for full listing.

INSTITUTE OF FOOD TECHNOLOGISTS FOUNDATION [2526]

525 West Van Buren Street
Suite 1000
Chicago, IL 60607
(312) 782-8424
Fax: (312) 416-7919
E-mail: feedingtomorrow@ift.org
Web Site: www.ift.org/scholarships

FOUNDED: 1939

AREAS OF INTEREST:
Food science and technology.

NAME(S) OF PROGRAMS:
- **Freshman Scholarships**
- **Graduate Scholarships**
- **Undergraduate Scholarships**

TYPE:
Scholarships. Freshman Scholarships and Undergraduate Scholarships encourage undergraduate enrollment in food science and technology. Graduate Scholarships support advanced study in the field of food science and technology.

YEAR PROGRAM STARTED: 1950

PURPOSE:
To encourage and support outstanding research in food science/technology including such areas as food packaging, flavor chemistry, new food ingredients and products; to recognize scholastic achievement.

LEGAL BASIS:
Nonprofit 501(c)(3) foundation.

ELIGIBILITY:
Freshman scholarships are awarded to high school seniors entering college for the first time. Applicant must be a current high school senior and accepted into an IFT-approved undergraduate food science program, have at least a 3.0 cumulative grade point average, and become an IFT student member.

Graduate scholarships are awarded to outstanding M.S. and Ph.D. students pursuing research and education in the field of food science and technology. Student applicants must be pursuing a graduate with an emphasis in food science and related disciplines. They must be able to understand and appreciate the impact of their research on the global food supply. Research in such disciplines as genetics, horticulture, nutrition, microbiology, biochemistry, engineering, chemistry, etc. are not eligible unless it is directly related to the student's research program in food science, except as otherwise noted. The school of enrollment can be any educational institution conducting fundamental investigations for the advancement of food science and food technology, unless there are stated exceptions of scholarship criteria for sponsored scholarships. Applicant must be enrolled as a full-time M.S. or Ph.D. student, have at least a 3.0 cumulative grade point average, and be a student member of IFT at the time of application.

Undergraduate scholarships are awarded to sophomore, junior, and senior students enrolled as a full-time student pursuing an undergraduate degree in an IFT-approved undergraduate food science program, have at least a 3.0 cumulative grade point average, and be a student member of IFT at the time of application.

FINANCIAL DATA:
Amount of support per award: $1,000 to $5,000.

Total amount of support: Varies.

CO-OP FUNDING PROGRAMS: The scholarships are sponsored by Feeding Tomorrow donors.

NO. MOST RECENT APPLICANTS: Approximately 300.

NO. AWARDS: 75.

APPLICATION INFO:
Applications are available on the Institute's web site.

Duration: One year.

Deadline: Varies.

ADDRESS INQUIRIES TO:
Shannon Rodnick, Project Coordinator
(See address and e-mail above.)

THE INTERNATIONAL EXECUTIVE HOUSEKEEPERS ASSOCIATION [2527]

1001 Eastwind Drive
Suite 301
Westerville, OH 43081-3361
(614) 895-7166
Fax: (614) 895-1248
E-mail: excel@ieha.org
Web Site: www.ieha.org

FOUNDED: 1930

AREAS OF INTEREST:
Directors of housekeeping, environmental service and facilities management, and training.

NAME(S) OF PROGRAMS:
- **330-Hour Self Study Program**

TYPE:
Scholarships.

YEAR PROGRAM STARTED: 1960

PURPOSE:
To provide a professional organization for executive housekeepers, directors of environmental services, managers within the housekeeping or custodial activities, and suppliers of custodial goods and services.

ELIGIBILITY:
Must be a member of IEHA and be working towards any degree program at a university or college, in a certification program or engaged in self-study.

FINANCIAL DATA:
Amount of support per award: $800 to $1,500 per year.

Total amount of support: Varies.

NO. MOST RECENT APPLICANTS: 5.

NO. AWARDS: Approximately 3.

APPLICATION INFO:
Application may be requested from the e-mail address above.

Duration: One year.

Deadline: Must be postmarked by January 10.

INTERNATIONAL FOOD SERVICE EXECUTIVES ASSOCIATION, INC. (IFSEA) [2528]

4955 Miller Street, Suite 107
Wheat Ridge, CO 80033
(800) 893-5499
Fax: (303) 420-9579
E-mail: ifseahqoffice@gmail.com
Web Site: www.ifsea.com

FOUNDED: 1901

AREAS OF INTEREST:
Food service field.

NAME(S) OF PROGRAMS:
- **Worthy Goal Scholarship**

TYPE:
Scholarships. Tuition scholarships.

YEAR PROGRAM STARTED: 1939

PURPOSE:
To give needed assistance to qualified young people in furthering their careers in the food service field.

LEGAL BASIS:
Nonprofit.

ELIGIBILITY:
Students must be enrolled as or accepted as a full-time student in a food service-related major at a two- or four-year college/university.

GEOG. RESTRICTIONS: United States.

FINANCIAL DATA:
Amount of support per award: $250 to $1,500.

APPLICATION INFO:
Scholarship application is available at the Association web site.

Duration: One year. Renewable.

Deadline: March 1. The scholarship is awarded every spring for the following fall semester.

ADDRESS INQUIRIES TO:
Dr. Joan Johnson
Worthy Goal Scholarship Chairperson
E-mail: johnsojm@morrisville.edu

PRINT AND GRAPHICS SCHOLARSHIP FOUNDATION [2529]

301 Brush Creek Road
Warrendale, PA 15086
(412) 259-1740
(800) 910-4283
Fax: (412) 741-2311
E-mail: pgsf@printing.org
Web Site: www.printing.org/pgsf

FOUNDED: 1956

AREAS OF INTEREST:
Graphic communications, printing technology, printing management and publishing.

TYPE:
Fellowships. For advanced study relating to the printing, publishing and packaging industries. Support is provided for research and study in engineering, chemistry, physics, mathematics, industrial education or such business technology areas as systems analysis, operations research and marketing research, provided the area of study has potential application in the printing, publishing and packaging industries.

YEAR PROGRAM STARTED: 1956

PURPOSE:
To strengthen the print and graphics industry through scholarship assistance.

LEGAL BASIS:
Nonprofit organization.

ELIGIBILITY:
Applicants must be students who plan to major and have a career in graphic communications, printing technology, printing management or publishing. Must have and maintain a 3.0 grade point average or higher, submit two recommendations, and be a full-time student.

FINANCIAL DATA:
Amount of support per award: $1,000 to $5,000.

NO. AWARDS: Varies.

APPLICATION INFO:
Contact the Foundation.

Duration: One academic year. Renewable.

Deadline: February 15.

ADDRESS INQUIRIES TO:
Bernadine Eckert, Administrator
(See address above.)

PRINT AND GRAPHICS SCHOLARSHIP FOUNDATION [2530]

301 Brush Creek Road
Warrendale, PA 15086
(412) 259-1740
(800) 910-4283
Fax: (412) 741-2311
E-mail: pgsf@printing.org
Web Site: www.printing.org/pgsf

FOUNDED: 1956

AREAS OF INTEREST:
Graphic communications and graphic arts; printing technology and management.

NAME(S) OF PROGRAMS:
- **PGSF Undergraduate Awards**

TYPE:
Scholarships. Awarded to students who plan to major and have a career in graphic communications, printing technology, printing management or publishing.

YEAR PROGRAM STARTED: 1956

PURPOSE:
To encourage eligible students to enter the field of graphic communications in the printing and publishing industries.

LEGAL BASIS:
Nonprofit foundation.

ELIGIBILITY:
Applicants must be high school seniors who will graduate in January or June of current year or high school graduates. Grants are usually restricted to colleges and universities offering two-year and four-year degree programs recognized by the graphic communications industry. A limited number of awards also are available for students already enrolled in two-year or four-year college programs and for sons and daughters of employees of scholarship sponsors. Financial need is not a criterion for selection.

Applicant must be a full-time student and must have and maintain a 3.0 grade point average or higher.

GEOG. RESTRICTIONS: United States.

FINANCIAL DATA:
Awards are paid directly to colleges for payment of tuition, fees and other charges.

Amount of support per award: $500 to $5,000.

NO. MOST RECENT APPLICANTS: 600.

NO. AWARDS: Approximately 180 four-year scholarships annually.

APPLICATION INFO:
Applications and letters of recommendation must be submitted online.

Duration: Renewable for up to four years (unless otherwise specified).

Deadline: April 1. Decisions are announced in July or August.

PUBLICATIONS:
Annual reports; newsletter; career brochures.

IRS I.D.: 25-1668339

ADDRESS INQUIRIES TO:
Bernadine Eckert
Scholarship Administrator
(See address above.)

*SPECIAL STIPULATIONS:
Candidates must be pursuing a career in graphic communications or printing and must maintain a 3.0 grade point average.

SME-EF (SOCIETY OF MANUFACTURING ENGINEERS EDUCATION FOUNDATION) [2531]

One SME Drive
P.O. Box 930
Dearborn, MI 48121-0930
(313) 425-3300
Fax: (313) 425-3411
E-mail: foundation@sme.org
Web Site: www.smeef.org

FOUNDED: 1932

AREAS OF INTEREST:
Manufacturing and industrial engineering technology, machining technology, robotics, automated systems and technology.

NAME(S) OF PROGRAMS:
- **Connie and Robert T. Gunter Scholarship**
- **Clinton J. Helton Manufacturing Scholarship**
- **Kalamazoo Chapter No. 116-Roscoe Douglas Scholarship**
- **Lucille B. Kaufman Women's Scholarship**
- **E. Wayne Kay Scholarships**
- **St. Louis Chapter No. 17 Scholarship**
- **Myrtle and Earl Walker Scholarship**
- **William E. Weisel Scholarship**

TYPE:
Scholarships. Support for full- or part-time students seeking careers in manufacturing or industrial engineering technology or closely related fields.

YEAR PROGRAM STARTED: 1982

LEGAL BASIS:
Professional society.

ELIGIBILITY:
Applicants must reside in the U.S. or Canada, be a full- or part-time student pursuing a degree in manufacturing engineering, manufacturing engineering technology, or a closely related engineering field of study, and must attend an accredited institution in the U.S. or Canada. Applicants must have a minimum 2.5 grade point average.

GEOG. RESTRICTIONS: United States and Canada.

FINANCIAL DATA:
Amount of support per award: Varies according to scholarship.

Total amount of support: Over $60,000.

APPLICATION INFO:
Application must be completed online.

Duration: One year. Students may reapply for undergraduate scholarships.

Deadline: February 1. Announcements in May and June.

PUBLICATIONS:
Program announcement.

BOARD OF DIRECTORS:
Brian A. Ruestow, President
Kathy Burnham, Vice President and Secretary
Peter F. Mackie, Treasurer and Chair of Finance
Edward M. Swallow, Assistant Treasurer and Vice Chair of Finance
Ashok Agrawal
David P. Bozeman
Elizabeth Kautzmann
Lazaro J. Lopez, Ed.D.
Gwendolyn Malone
Mike Marlowe, CNM
Jennifer McNelly
Irving Pressley McPhail, Ed.D.
Karla E. Middlebrooks
John Miller
Ted Peachee
Pamela J. Ruschau, Esq.
Mike Schmidt
Susan E. Shimoyama
Roy Sweatman
Peter T. Zierhut

ADDRESS INQUIRIES TO:
Kathy Carter, Program Officer
(See address above.)

TRANSPORTATION ASSOCIATION OF CANADA FOUNDATION [2532]

2323 St. Laurent Boulevard
Ottawa ON K1G 4J8 Canada
(613) 736-1350
Fax: (613) 736-1395
E-mail: foundation@tac-atc.ca
Web Site: www.tac-foundation.ca

FOUNDED: 2003

AREAS OF INTEREST:
Transportation.

NAME(S) OF PROGRAMS:
- **TAC Foundation Scholarships and Bursaries**

TYPE:
Scholarships. Awards are provided for the study of road and transportation sciences, such as highway engineering, transport economics and administration.

YEAR PROGRAM STARTED: 2004

PURPOSE:
To encourage studies by Canadians in the field of transportation.

LEGAL BASIS:
Foundation.

ELIGIBILITY:
Applicants must be Canadian citizens or permanent residents in Canada who are enrolled in a university or college and pursuing studies full-time in some aspect of transportation.

GEOG. RESTRICTIONS: Canada.

FINANCIAL DATA:
Amount of support per award: $1,000 to $10,000.

Total amount of support: Over $140,000 annually.

NO. MOST RECENT APPLICANTS: Approximately 125.

NO. AWARDS: More than 40 annually.

APPLICATION INFO:
Full information is available on the Foundation web site.

Duration: One year. Applicants may apply at each level: college student, undergraduate and graduate.

Deadline: Second week of February.

ADDRESS INQUIRIES TO:
See e-mail address above.

THE UNIVERSITY OF CALGARY
Faculty of Graduate Studies
MacKimmie Library Tower, Room 213
2500 University Drive, N.W.
Calgary AB T2N 1N4 Canada
(403) 220-4938
Fax: (403) 289-7635
E-mail: gsaward@ucalgary.ca
Web Site: www.grad.ucalgary.ca/awards

TYPE:
Awards/prizes; Scholarships. Graduate scholarship for study in all areas relevant to the petroleum industry. Tenable at The University of Calgary. Award endowed through a bequest of the late Corinne Patteson.

See entry 1728 for full listing.

Aeronautics and astronautics

AIRCRAFT ELECTRONICS ASSOCIATION (AEA) [2533]
3570 N.E. Ralph Powell Road
Lee's Summit, MO 64064
(816) 347-8400
Fax: (816) 347-8405
E-mail: info@aea.net
Web Site: www.aea.net/scholarship

AREAS OF INTEREST:
Avionics and aircraft electronics.

NAME(S) OF PROGRAMS:
- **David Arver Memorial Scholarship**
- **Dutch and Ginger Arver Scholarship**
- **Johnny Davis Memorial Scholarship**
- **Duncan Aviation Scholarship**
- **Field Aviation Company Scholarship**
- **Garmin - Jerry Smith Memorial Scholarship**
- **Garmin Scholarship**
- **Lowell Gaylor Memorial Scholarship**
- **Gogo Business Aviation Scholarship**
- **Leon Harris/Les Nichols Memorial Scholarship**
- **L-3 Avionics Systems Scholarship**
- **Mid-Continent Instrument Scholarship**
- **Lee Tarbox Memorial Scholarship**
- **Universal Avionics Systems Corporation Scholarship**

TYPE:
Scholarships.

PURPOSE:
To provide funding for students seeking higher education in the fields of avionics and aircraft electronics.

LEGAL BASIS:
Nonprofit.

ELIGIBILITY:
Applicants for the Mid-Continent Instruments Scholarship and the Lowell Gaylor Memorial Scholarship can be anyone who plans to or is enrolled in an avionics program in an accredited U.S. or Canadian school.

Applicants for the Field Aviation Company Scholarship must attend an accredited vocational school located in Canada.

Applicants for Lee Tarbox Memorial, Garmin Scholarship, Johnny Davis Memorial and the Garmin-Jerry Smith Memorial Scholarships must be high school or vocational/technical school/college students who plan to or are attending an accredited vocational or technical school in an avionics or aviation-related program.

The Scholarships are not available to obtain pilot licenses.

GEOG. RESTRICTIONS: North America.

FINANCIAL DATA:
Amount of support per award: $1,000 to $30,000, depending on award.
Total amount of support: Varies.

NO. MOST RECENT APPLICANTS: 400.

NO. AWARDS: 15.

APPLICATION INFO:
Contact the Association.
Duration: One year.
Deadline: Approximately April 1.

ADDRESS INQUIRIES TO:
Educational Foundation
(See address above.)

THE AMERICAN HISTORICAL ASSOCIATION
400 A Street, S.E.
Washington, DC 20003
(202) 544-2422
Fax: (202) 544-8307
E-mail: awards@historians.org
Web Site: www.historians.org

TYPE:
Fellowships. The Association annually funds at least one fellow for a period of six to nine months, to undertake a proposed research project related to aerospace history. The Fellowship is supported by the National Aeronautics and Space Administration (NASA).

See entry 566 for full listing.

AMERICAN INSTITUTE OF AERONAUTICS AND ASTRONAUTICS [2534]
1801 Alexander Bell Drive
Suite 500
Reston, VA 20191
(703) 264-7577
Fax: (703) 264-7551
E-mail: rachela@aiaa.org
Web Site: www.aiaa.org

FOUNDED: 1977

AREAS OF INTEREST:
Arts, sciences, and technology of aeronautics and astronautics.

NAME(S) OF PROGRAMS:
- **American Institute of Aeronautics and Astronautics Undergraduate Scholarship Program**

TYPE:
Scholarships. Program presents yearly scholarship awards to college sophomores, college juniors and college seniors. Graduate awards are also offered.

YEAR PROGRAM STARTED: 1977

PURPOSE:
To encourage original research; to further dissemination of new knowledge; to foster the professional development of those engaged in scientific and engineering activities; to improve public understanding of the profession and its contributions; to foster education in engineering and science; to promote communication among engineers and scientists and with other professional groups; to stimulate outstanding professional accomplishments.

ELIGIBILITY:
The AIAA requirements are as follows:
(1) applicant must be an AIAA student member to apply;
(2) applicant's scholastic plan shall be such as to provide entry into some field of science or engineering encompassed by the technical activities of AIAA;
(3) applicant shall be enrolled in an accredited college or university in the U.S.;
(4) applicant shall not have or subsequently receive any other scholarship award which combined with the AIAA award would provide a stipend greater than the tuition plus direct educational expenses (such as books, lab fees, room, board, etc.) estimated by the educational institute he or she plans to attend;
(5) sophomore and junior students who receive one of these awards are eligible to reapply for these awards (until completion of their senior year) provided they maintain a 3.3 (B+) grade point average on a scale of 4.0. Continuation, however, is not automatic. Students must reapply each year;
(6) financial background will not be a factor for eligibility;
(7) student must have a college grade point average of at least a 3.3 on a 4.0 scale and;
(8) student must have completed one semester or quarter of full-time academic college work.

FINANCIAL DATA:
Amount of support per award: Up to $5,000.
Total amount of support: Varies.

NO. MOST RECENT APPLICANTS: 350.

NO. AWARDS: 9.

APPLICATION INFO:
Form and guidelines are available on the web site.
Duration: One year.
Deadline: Applications must be received by January 31.

ADDRESS INQUIRIES TO:
Rachel Andino, Student Programs Coordinator
(See address above.)

AMERICAN METEOROLOGICAL SOCIETY [2535]
45 Beacon Street
Boston, MA 02108-3693
(617) 226-3907
Fax: (617) 742-8718
E-mail: dfernandez@ametsoc.org
Web Site: www.ametsoc.org

FOUNDED: 1919

AREAS OF INTEREST:
Meteorology, atmospheric, hydrologic and oceanic sciences.

NAME(S) OF PROGRAMS:
- **AMS Freshman Undergraduate Scholarship Program**
- **AMS Graduate Fellowship in the History of Science**
- **AMS Graduate Fellowships**
- **AMS Minority Scholarship**
- **AMS Named Scholarships**
- **The Father James B. Macelwane Annual Awards in Meteorology**

TYPE:
Fellowships; Scholarships. AMS Freshman Undergraduate Scholarship Program awards

funding to high school seniors entering their freshman year of undergraduate study in the fall.

AMS Graduate Fellowship in the History of Science is awarded to a student wishing to complete a dissertation on the history of the atmospheric and related oceanic or hydrologic sciences.

AMS Graduate Fellowships are designed to attract students entering their first year of graduate study in the fall who wish to pursue advanced degrees in the atmospheric and related oceanic and hydrologic sciences.

AMS Minority Scholarship awards funding to high school minority students who have been traditionally underrepresented in the sciences, especially Hispanic, Native American and Black/African American students.

AMS Named Scholarships are directed to students entering their final year of undergraduate study in the fall.

The Father James B. Macelwane Annual Awards in Meteorology are intended to stimulate interest in meteorology among college students through the submission of original student papers concerned with some phase of the atmospheric sciences. The student must be enrolled as an undergraduate at the time the paper was written.

YEAR PROGRAM STARTED: 1965

PURPOSE:
To stimulate interest in meteorology among college students and to recognize academic excellence and achievement; to stimulate careers in atmospheric and related oceanic and hydrologic sciences.

LEGAL BASIS:
Nonprofit organization.

ELIGIBILITY:
Candidates must be U.S. citizens or hold permanent resident status.

AMS encourages applications from women, minorities and disabled students who are traditionally underrepresented in the atmospheric and related oceanic and hydrologic sciences.

AMS Freshman Undergraduate Scholarship Program makes awards on the basis of academic excellence.

AMS Graduate Fellowship in the History of Science: Candidate must be a graduate student in good standing who proposes to complete a dissertation on the history of the atmospheric, or related oceanic or hydrologic sciences.

AMS Graduate Fellowships: Applicants must be entering their first year of graduate study in the fall pursuing an advanced degree in the atmospheric and related oceanic and hydrologic sciences. Prospective candidates from the fields of chemistry, computer sciences, engineering, environmental sciences, mathematics or physics who intend to pursue careers in the atmospheric or related oceanic or hydrologic sciences are also encouraged to apply.

AMS Minority Scholarship: Funding to high school minority students who have been traditionally underrepresented in the sciences, especially Hispanic, Native American and Black/African American students. Minority students must be entering their freshman year of undergraduate study in the fall at a four-year U.S. accredited institution, and must plan to pursue a career in the atmospheric or related oceanic or hydrologic sciences.

AMS Named Scholarships: Candidates must be entering their final undergraduate year in the fall and majoring in the atmospheric or related oceanic or hydrologic sciences and/or must show clear intent to make atmospheric or related sciences their career.

Father James B. Macelwane Annual Awards in Meteorology: Student must be enrolled as an undergraduate at the time the paper is written. No more than two students from any one institution may enter papers in any one contest.

GEOG. RESTRICTIONS: United States.

FINANCIAL DATA:
Amount of support per award: AMS Freshman Undergraduate Scholarship Program: $2,500 per year (freshman and sophomore years); AMS Graduate Fellowship in the History of Science: $15,000 stipend; AMS Graduate Fellowships: $25,000 stipend; AMS Minority Scholarship: $3,000 per year (freshman and sophomore years); AMS Named Scholarships: Up to $7,500; Father James B. Macelwane Annual Awards in Meteorology: $1,000 stipend and partial travel support to the AMS Annual Meeting.

Total amount of support: Varies.

NO. MOST RECENT APPLICANTS: 340.

NO. AWARDS: 55.

APPLICATION INFO:
Those interested should apply online at the Society's web site. When writing for an application package, specify which application is being requested, and what year of academic study applicant will be entering in the fall. Submit a complete application form, written letters of reference and official transcripts.

Duration: AMS Freshman Undergraduate Scholarship Program: Up to two years; AMS Graduate History of Science Fellowship: One year; AMS Minority Scholarship: Two years; AMS/Industry/Government Graduate Fellowships: Nine months.

Deadline: Graduate Fellowship: January. Father James B. Macelwane: Mid-June. All other programs: February.

PUBLICATIONS:
Program announcement.

OFFICERS:
Dr. Keith L. Seitter, Executive Director

ADDRESS INQUIRIES TO:
Donna Fernandez, Development and Student Programs Manager
(See address/phone/e-mail above) or

Stephanie Armstrong
Director of Development
Tel: (617) 226-3906 or 3907
E-mail: armstrong@ametsoc.org

*SPECIAL STIPULATIONS:
Applicants must review program requirements before applying.

AVIATION DISTRIBUTORS AND MANUFACTURERS ASSOCIATION (ADMA) [2536]

100 North 20th Street, Suite 400
Philadelphia, PA 19103
(215) 564-3484
Fax: (215) 564-2175
E-mail: adma@fernley.com
Web Site: www.adma.org

FOUNDED: 1943

AREAS OF INTEREST:
Aviation and pilot education, mechanics and maintenance.

NAME(S) OF PROGRAMS:
- **ADMA Scholarship Programs**

TYPE:
Scholarships.

ELIGIBILITY:
Applicant must be one of following:
(1) third- or fourth-year B.S. candidate with Aviation Management major, emphasis in General Aviation, Airway Science Management, Aviation Maintenance or Airway Science Maintenance Management;
(2) third- or fourth-year B.S. candidate with major in Professional Pilot with any of the following emphases: General Aviation, Flight Engineer, Airway Science A/C Systems Management or;
(3) second-year student in A/P education program (two-year accredited aviation technical school).

Applicant must also have 3.0 grade point average or higher.

GEOG. RESTRICTIONS: United States.

FINANCIAL DATA:
Amount of support per award: $3,000.

Total amount of support: $12,000.

NO. AWARDS: 4.

APPLICATION INFO:
Detailed information is available from the Association.

Duration: One year.

ADDRESS INQUIRIES TO:
Tia Diggs, Executive Director
(See address above.)

AVIATION INSURANCE ASSOCIATION (AIA) [2537]

7200 West 75th Street
Overland Park, KS 66204
(913) 627-9632
Fax: (913) 381-2515
E-mail: mandie@aiaweb.org
Web Site: www.aiaweb.org

AREAS OF INTEREST:
Aviation insurance.

NAME(S) OF PROGRAMS:
- **AIA Scholarship**

TYPE:
Scholarships.

PURPOSE:
To help students with an interest in aviation insurance to continue on to higher education.

LEGAL BASIS:
Nonprofit association.

ELIGIBILITY:
Applicants must:
(1) be currently enrolled in an accredited undergraduate or graduate degree program;
(2) currently be an intern or recently completed an internship program within a facet of the aviation insurance industry;
(3) have completed at least 45 college credits and;
(4) have a minimum 2.5 grade point average on a 4.0 scale.

FINANCIAL DATA:
Amount of support per award: $2,500.

NO. AWARDS: 4.

APPLICATION INFO:
Applicants must submit five sets of the following documents to be considered a scholarship candidate:
(1) completed AIA Scholarship application;
(2) letter describing activities, indicating leadership qualities, goals, rolls and reason for applying;
(3) at least one letter of recommendation from a supervisor during the internship program and;
(4) latest transcript(s) from all universities and colleges attended.

Duration: One-time award.

Deadline: February 28.

ADDRESS INQUIRIES TO:
Mandie Bannwarth, Executive Director
(See address above.)

MCDONNELL CENTER FOR THE SPACE SCIENCES [2538]

Washington University, Campus Box 1105
One Brookings Drive
St. Louis, MO 63130-4899
(314) 935-5332
E-mail: trecia@physics.wustl.edu
Web Site: mcss.wustl.edu

FOUNDED: 1974

AREAS OF INTEREST:
Space sciences.

NAME(S) OF PROGRAMS:
- **McDonnell Astronaut Fellowships**
- **McDonnell Graduate Fellowships**

TYPE:
Fellowships. These fellowships are funded by a gift from the McDonnell Douglas Foundation to Washington University and provide tuition remission plus stipend for graduate students interested in pursuing research in the space sciences who are enrolled in the Washington University Departments of Physics or Earth and Planetary Sciences.

PURPOSE:
To support graduate students in the space sciences.

LEGAL BASIS:
University.

ELIGIBILITY:
All applicants for admission to graduate school in physics or earth and planetary sciences are considered for the McDonnell Graduate Fellowships if they are interested in pursuing research in the space sciences and note it on their application forms; only U.S. citizens are considered for the McDonnell Astronaut Fellowships.

GEOG. RESTRICTIONS: United States.

FINANCIAL DATA:
Amount of support per award: Varies.

Total amount of support: Varies.

APPLICATION INFO:
Application materials for the individual graduate school programs may be obtained at the web site.

Duration: Three years.

Deadline: January 15. Announcement by April 1.

ADDRESS INQUIRIES TO:
Ramanath Cowsik, Director
(See address above.)

NATIONAL BUSINESS AVIATION ASSOCIATION [2539]

1200 G Street, N.W.
Suite 1100
Washington, DC 20005
(202) 783-9000
(202) 783-9267
Fax: (202) 331-8364
E-mail: info@nbaa.org
scholarships@nbaa.org
Web Site: www.nbaa.org/scholarships

AREAS OF INTEREST:
Aviation.

NAME(S) OF PROGRAMS:
- **William M. Fanning Maintenance Scholarship**
- **Flight Attendants/Flight Technicians Scholarship**
- **International Operators Scholarship**

TYPE:
Scholarships. The William M. Fanning Maintenance Scholarship is for those who are pursuing careers as maintenance technicians.

The Flight Attendants/Flight Technicians Scholarship is dedicated to promoting education and training as a means to increase professionalism for business aviation flight attendants and flight technicians.

The International Operators Scholarship is dedicated to promoting education and training to increase safety and professionalism for business aviation professionals engaged in international operations.

PURPOSE:
To help students continue their education in aviation and advance in that field.

LEGAL BASIS:
Nonprofit association.

ELIGIBILITY:
Contact the Association for details.

GEOG. RESTRICTIONS: United States.

FINANCIAL DATA:
Amount of support per award: Fanning Maintenance Scholarship: $2,500; Flight Attendants/Flight Technicians Scholarship and International Operators Scholarship: Up to $9,000.

Total amount of support: Varies.

NO. AWARDS: Fanning Maintenance Scholarship: 2.

APPLICATION INFO:
Applications are available at the Association web site.

Duration: One-time award.

Deadline: Fanning Maintenance Scholarship: August 1; Flight Attendants/Flight Technicians Scholarship: March 16; International Operators Scholarship: November 30.

STAFF:
Tyler Austin, Professional Development Coordinator

ADDRESS INQUIRIES TO:
E-mail: info@nbaa.org

*PLEASE NOTE:
Awards will be made to U.S. citizens without regard to sex, race, religion or national origin.

NATIONAL BUSINESS AVIATION ASSOCIATION [2540]

1200 G Street, N.W.
Suite 1100
Washington, DC 20005
(202) 783-9000
(202) 783-9267
Fax: (202) 331-8364
E-mail: scholarships@nbaa.org
Web Site: www.nbaa.org/scholarships

AREAS OF INTEREST:
Aviation and business aviation.

NAME(S) OF PROGRAMS:
- **Lawrence Ginocchio Scholarship**
- **Schedulers & Dispatchers Scholarship**
- **UAA Janice K. Barden Scholarship**

TYPE:
Scholarships. Janice K. Barden Scholarship is presented to undergraduates who are studying aviation-related curricula.

Lawrence Ginocchio Scholarship honors individuals whose strength of character inspired a high standard. Applicants must be students at NBAA/UAA Member programs.

PURPOSE:
To help students continue their education in aviation and advance in that field.

LEGAL BASIS:
Nonprofit association.

ELIGIBILITY:
Contact the Association for details.

FINANCIAL DATA:
Amount of support per award: Janice K. Barden Scholarship: $1,000; Lawrence Ginocchio Scholarship: $4,500.

Total amount of support: Janice K. Barden Scholarship: $5,000; Lawrence Ginocchio Scholarship: $22,500.

NO. AWARDS: Janice K. Barden and Lawrence Ginocchio Scholarships: 5 each.

APPLICATION INFO:
Contact the Association for guidelines.

Deadline: Varies.

STAFF:
Tyler Austin, Professional Development Coordinator

ADDRESS INQUIRIES TO:
Tyler Austin
Professional Development Coordinator
(See address above.)

NATIONAL BUSINESS AVIATION ASSOCIATION [2541]

1200 G Street, N.W.
Suite 1100
Washington, DC 20005
(202) 783-9000
(202) 783-9267
Fax: (202) 331-8364
E-mail: scholarships@nbaa.org
Web Site: www.nbaa.org/scholarships

AREAS OF INTEREST:
Aviation.

NAME(S) OF PROGRAMS:
- **Donald A. Baldwin Sr. Business Aviation Management Scholarship**

TYPE:
Scholarships. Promotes professional development in business aviation.

YEAR PROGRAM STARTED: 2007

PURPOSE:
To benefit individuals seeking to become NBAA-Certified Aviation Managers (CAMs).

ELIGIBILITY:
Applicants must be U.S. citizens or permanent residents and must be eligible within two years of award date to take the CAM exam.

FINANCIAL DATA:
Amount of support per award: $1,225 per recipient.

NO. AWARDS: Varies.

APPLICATION INFO:
Applicants must submit their resume, a 250-word essay explaining their plans for a career in business aviation, two letters of recommendation in support, and meet minimum qualifications to take the CAM exam.

Duration: One year.

Deadline: Mid-November.

ADDRESS INQUIRIES TO:
Tyler Austin
Professional Development Coordinator
(See address above.)

RTCA [2542]

1150 18th Street, N.W.
Suite 910
Washington, DC 20036
(202) 330-0680
Fax: (202) 833-9434
E-mail: khofmann@rtca.org
Web Site: www.rtca.org

FOUNDED: 1935

AREAS OF INTEREST:
Aviation electronics, telecommunications, and other closely allied fields such as determination of common operational requirements, state-of-the-art developments and applications, other problems associated with air traffic control, navigation, communications, and efficient utilization of airports and airspace.

CONSULTING OR VOLUNTEER SERVICES:
Federal Advisory Committee under Federal Advisory Committee Act (FACA).

NAME(S) OF PROGRAMS:
- **The William E. Jackson Award**

TYPE:
Awards/prizes. Award for a paper by an outstanding graduate student in aviation electronics or telecommunications, in memory of William E. Jackson, an outstanding pioneer in the development and implementation of the present airways, air traffic control, and aviation communication systems.

YEAR PROGRAM STARTED: 1975

PURPOSE:
To honor an outstanding graduate student in aviation electronics or telecommunications.

LEGAL BASIS:
Nonprofit, 501(c)(3) organization.

ELIGIBILITY:
Open to any graduate student earning a degree in the field of aviation electronics or telecommunication systems. There are no restrictions as to race, creed, color, religious affiliation, national origin or citizenship. The sole basis for selection will be the written report, which must be in English.

FINANCIAL DATA:
The recipient will travel at the expense of RTCA to the location of the award presentation. Complimentary registration for any RTCA business meeting taking place concurrently is also awarded.

Amount of support per award: $4,000.

NO. MOST RECENT APPLICANTS: 10.

NO. AWARDS: 1.

APPLICATION INFO:
Submissions must be in the form of a thesis, project report, or paper in a technical journal. The work must have been completed no earlier than three years before the submission deadline and only those in English and without publication restrictions will be considered. Joint authors may submit if both or all qualify as students and candidates for undergraduate or graduate degrees in this field. Joint authors would share the award. Additionally, candidates must submit two copies (one paper and one electronic) of a one- to two-page summary of the written material, a biographical sketch of the candidate, and a letter of endorsement from the candidate's instructor, professor, or departmental head. Submit material to the address above.

Deadline: September 30.

OFFICERS:
Karan Hofmann, Program Director

ADDRESS INQUIRIES TO:
William E. Jackson Award Committee
(See address above.)

SMITHSONIAN NATIONAL AIR AND SPACE MUSEUM [2543]

P.O. Box 37012, MRC 312
Washington, DC 20013-7012
(202) 633-2648
Fax: (202) 786-2447
E-mail: nasm-fellowships@si.edu
Web Site: www.nasm.si.edu

FOUNDED: 1946

AREAS OF INTEREST:
Aeronautics.

NAME(S) OF PROGRAMS:
- **Aviation Space Writers Foundation Award**
- **Guggenheim Fellowship**
- **Charles A. Lindbergh Chair in Aerospace History**
- **Postdoctoral Earth and Planetary Sciences Fellowship**
- **A. Verville Fellowship**

TYPE:
Fellowships; Research grants. Aviation Space Writers Foundation Award, offered in even-numbered years, is intended to support research on aerospace topics.

The Guggenheim Fellowship is a competitive three- to 12-month in-residence fellowship for pre- or postdoctoral research in aviation and space history.

The Charles A. Lindbergh Chair in Aerospace History is a competitive 12-month fellowship.

Postdoctoral Earth and Planetary Sciences Fellowship supports scientific research in the area of earth and planetary sciences. Scientists in the Center for Earth and Planetary Studies concentrate on geologic and geophysical research of the earth and other terrestrial planets, using remote sensing data obtained from earth-orbiting and interplanetary spacecraft. Research also focuses on global environmental change.

The A. Verville Fellowship is a competitive nine- to 12-month in-residence fellowship intended for analysis of major trends, developments, and accomplishments in the history of aviation or space studies.

All candidates are encouraged to pursue programs of research and writing that support publication of works that are scholarly in tone and substance, and/or addressed to an audience with broad interests. Each fellow will work closely with staff members who share similar interests.

PURPOSE:
To promote research into, and writing about, the history of aviation and space flight.

ELIGIBILITY:
All applicants must be able to write and converse fluently in English. Additional information is available online.

Aviation Space Writers Foundation Award: The product created as a result of the grant must be in any form suitable for potential public dissemination in print, electronic, broadcast or other visual medium, including, but not limited to, a book manuscript, a video, or film script or monograph.

Guggenheim Fellowship: Predoctoral applicants should have completed preliminary course work and examinations and be engaged in dissertation research. Postdoctoral applicants should have received their Ph.D. within the past seven years.

Lindbergh Chair in Aerospace History: Open to senior scholars with distinguished records of publication who are at work on, or anticipate being at work on, books in aerospace history.

Verville Fellowship: Open to interested candidates with demonstrated skills in research and writing. Publishing experience should demonstrate either a mid-level academic record of accomplishment or proven ability to engage in a reliable manner broader audiences. An advanced degree in history or a related field is preferred but not a requirement.

FINANCIAL DATA:
Amount of support per award: Aviation Space Writers Foundation Award: Grant of $5,000. Guggenheim Fellowship: Annual stipend of $30,000 for predoctoral candidates and $45,000 for postdoctoral candidates. Lindbergh Chair in Aerospace History: Support is available for living expenses in the Washington, DC area up to a maximum of $100,000 a year. Postdoctoral Earth and Planetary Sciences Fellowship: Stipends are compatible with National Research Council postdoctoral fellowships in the applicant's field. Verville Fellowship: Annual stipend of $55,000 (for a 12-month fellowship tenure), with limited additional funds for travel and miscellaneous expenses.

NO. AWARDS: 1 each.

APPLICATION INFO:
Instructions and forms for each program are available on the web site.

Duration: Guggenheim Fellowship: three to 12 months; Lindbergh Chair in Aerospace History: typically for an academic year (September through August); Postdoctoral Earth and Planetary Sciences Fellowship: appointments can be made for one or more years; Verville Fellowship: nine to 12 months.

Deadline: Guggenheim and Verville Fellowships and Lindbergh Chair: January 15. Lindbergh deadline is January 15 of the year preceding the award of this fellowship.

PUBLICATIONS:
Brochure; application package.

ADDRESS INQUIRIES TO:
Aviation Space Writers Foundation Award:
Dr. Dominick A. Pisano
Aeronautics Department
National Air and Space Museum
E-mail: pisanod@si.edu

Guggenheim, Lindbergh and Verville Fellowships:
Collette Williams, Fellowship Program Coordinator
(See e-mail address above.)

Postdoctoral Earth and Planetary Sciences Fellowship: Rosemary Aiello
Center for Earth and Planetary Studies
National Air and Space Museum
Washington, DC 20560
E-mail: aiellor@si.edu

*PLEASE NOTE:
Applicants are restricted to applying for a single National Air and Space Museum fellowship grant at a time. Proposals must reflect that the research to be undertaken is intended for publication in peer-reviewed books and journals.

SMITHSONIAN NATIONAL AIR AND SPACE MUSEUM [2544]

601 Independence Avenue, S.W.
Room P700, MRC 305
Washington, DC 20560
(202) 633-2542
Fax: (202) 633-8928
E-mail: banksscottm@si.edu
Web Site: airandspace.si.edu/research/internships/

FOUNDED: 1946

AREAS OF INTEREST:
Aeronautics.

NAME(S) OF PROGRAMS:
- **Summer Internship Program**

TYPE:
Internships. Full-time interns work 40 hours per week from approximately the first week in June until the second week in August.

PURPOSE:
To give interns a firsthand opportunity to learn about the historic artifacts and archival materials housed in the Museum and to study the scientific and technological advances they represent.

ELIGIBILITY:
Applicant must be a high school graduate and be enrolled in, or recently graduated from, a degree-granting undergraduate or graduate program at an accredited college or university. Applicant is expected to have a strong academic record.

Applicants from outside the U.S. are welcome. International applicants must have the appropriate J-1 visa and are responsible for any other necessary official documents.

FINANCIAL DATA:
Interns are responsible for locating and securing lodging.

Amount of support per award: $5,500.

NO. MOST RECENT APPLICANTS: 288 in 2015.

NO. AWARDS: Varies; 41 paid internships in 2015.

APPLICATION INFO:
Application information is available on the web site. Visit the Smithsonian Online Academic Appointment System (SOLAA) web site, which opens January 15, to apply.

Duration: 10 weeks during the summer; schedule is flexible.

Deadline: Applications are accepted from January 15 to February 15 during the calendar year of the internship. Interns are notified of the status of their application by April 1.

ADDRESS INQUIRIES TO:
Myra Banks-Scott, Intern Manager or
Amy Stamm, Communications
E-mail: NASMInternships@si.edu

*SPECIAL STIPULATIONS:
A commitment of 10 weeks during the summer is required.

VERTICAL FLIGHT FOUNDATION [2545]

2701 Prosperity Avenue, Suite 210
Fairfax, VA 22031
(703) 684-6777
Fax: (703) 739-9279
E-mail: bchen@vtol.org
Web Site: www.vtol.org/vff

FOUNDED: 1967

AREAS OF INTEREST:
Support of scientific and educational activities related to VTOL (Vertical Take-Off and Landing) flight.

NAME(S) OF PROGRAMS:
- **Vertical Flight Foundation Engineering Scholarships**

TYPE:
Awards/prizes; Scholarships. Annual scholarships to undergraduate senior, Master's or Ph.D. students interested in pursuing careers in some technical aspect of helicopter or vertical flight engineering.

YEAR PROGRAM STARTED: 1967

PURPOSE:
To acquire the best technical experts for the vertical flight industry.

LEGAL BASIS:
Independent, charitable trust.

ELIGIBILITY:
Scholarships will be awarded to undergraduate, Master's and Ph.D. engineering students studying for a career in the rotorcraft or vertical takeoff and landing aircraft industry.

The scholarships are merit-based, and applicants need not be members of the American Helicopter Society International. Individuals will be eligible once for each academic level. Undergraduate students must be in at least the second semester of their program. Applicants must be a full-time student at an accredited school of engineering (U.S. or international), and they must be in school through the full academic year following receipt of the scholarship. Further information is available at the web site address above.

FINANCIAL DATA:
Amount of support per award: $1,000 to $5,000.

Total amount of support: $68,000 for the year 2015.

NO. AWARDS: 22 for the year 2015.

APPLICATION INFO:
Detailed instructions are available at the web site. Applicants can also download a copy of the application form.

Duration: One academic year.

Deadline: February 1 annually. Postmark governs timeliness. Notification by April 15.

PUBLICATIONS:
Applications.

IRS I.D.: 23-6428319

ADDRESS INQUIRIES TO:
Betty Chen, Scholarship Coordinator
(See address above.)

Engineering

ADSC: THE INTERNATIONAL ASSOCIATION OF FOUNDATION DRILLING [2546]

8445 Freeport Parkway
Suite 325
Irving, TX 75063
(469) 359-6000
Fax: (469) 359-6007
E-mail: adsc@adsc-iafd.com
Web Site: www.adsc-iafd.com

FOUNDED: 1972

AREAS OF INTEREST:
Civil, geotechnical and structural engineering.

TYPE:
Scholarships.

PURPOSE:
To promote the foundation drilling and anchored earth retention industry.

ELIGIBILITY:
Must be a graduate student studying civil engineering.

GEOG. RESTRICTIONS: United States or Canada.

FINANCIAL DATA:
Amount of support per award: Maximum $3,000; $1,500 per semester. Part-time scholarship program: Maximum $1,500; $750 per semester.

Total amount of support: Approximately $42,000 annually.

NO. AWARDS: Minimum of 14 per year.

APPLICATION INFO:
Applicants must submit a brief letter outlining personal goals, two letters of recommendation and a copy of their transcript with application. Further information and application may be obtained from the Association.

Duration: One year.

Deadline: Contact the Association for deadline.

ADDRESS INQUIRIES TO:
Emily Matthews, Marketing Administrator
(See address above.)

AGC EDUCATION AND RESEARCH FOUNDATION [2547]

2300 Wilson Boulevard, Suite 300
Arlington, VA 22201
(703) 837-5342
Fax: (703) 837-5451
E-mail: patricianm@agc.org
Web Site: www.agcfoundation.org

FOUNDED: 1968

AREAS OF INTEREST:
Construction and civic interest in improving the quality of educational programs for students specifically in the area of commercial construction and construction research.

NAME(S) OF PROGRAMS:

- **James L. Allhands Essay Competition**
- **Faculty Internships**
- **Graduate Scholarship Program**
- **Industry Case Studies**
- **Outstanding Educator Award**
- **Undergraduate Scholarship Program**
- **Workforce Development Scholarship**

TYPE:
Awards/prizes; Internships; Project/program grants; Scholarships. Allhands Essay Competition: Awarded to a student essay on a specific topic that is deemed to be beneficial to the advancement of technological, educational or vocational expertise in the construction industry.

Faculty Internships: Grants for faculty through internships with AGC contractor-members.

Graduate Scholarship Program: Scholarships for students enrolled in ABET- or ACCE-accredited construction management or construction-related engineering programs.

Industry Case Studies: Commissioning case studies on industry scenarios.

Outstanding Educator Award: Awards to top competitors in essay competition for seniors and faculty nominated as Outstanding Educator.

Undergraduate Scholarship Program: Scholarships for students enrolled in ABET- or ACCE-accredited construction management or construction-related engineering programs.

Workforce Development Scholarship: Awarded for students entering craft training or technical programs.

YEAR PROGRAM STARTED: 1968

PURPOSE:
To improve the science of construction through the funding of scholarships and construction research projects.

LEGAL BASIS:
501(c)(3).

ELIGIBILITY:
James L. Allhands Essay Competition is for seniors only in a four- or five-year ABET- or ACCE-accredited university construction management or construction-related engineering program.

Undergraduate scholarships are available to college sophomores and juniors enrolled or planning to enroll in a full-time, four- or five-year ABET- or ACCE-accredited construction or civil engineering program. High school seniors and college freshman are not eligible.

Graduate awards are available to college seniors enrolled in an undergraduate construction or civil engineering degree program, or others possessing an undergraduate degree in construction or civil engineering. The applicant must be enrolled, or planning to enroll, in a graduate-level construction or civil engineering degree program as a full-time student. All candidates must be U.S. citizens or permanent U.S. residents.

Workforce Development Scholarship is available to students already enrolled or planning to enroll in craft training or technical programs up to two years in length.

Contact the Foundation for details.

GEOG. RESTRICTIONS: United States.

FINANCIAL DATA:
Amount of support per award: Allhands Essay Competition: First Prize $1,000 and an expense-paid trip to the AGC Convention; Faculty Internships: Budget submitted by applicant (shared by academic institution, contractor and Foundation); Graduate Scholarships: Up to $7,500; Industry Case Studies: $9,000 grant; Outstanding Educator Award: $5,000 award and an expense-paid trip to the AGC Convention, plus two $2,500 scholarships for students of the educator; Undergraduate Scholarships: $2,500 per year renewable to a maximum of $7,500; Workforce Development Scholarship: $1,000 per year, renewable up to $2,000.

Total amount of support: $400,000 to $500,000 for all programs.

CO-OP FUNDING PROGRAMS: Faculty Internships budget shared with academic institution and participating contractor.

NO. MOST RECENT APPLICANTS: 400 (for graduate and undergraduate scholarships).

NO. AWARDS: First, second and third prizes awarded in Allhands Essay. Outstanding Educator: 1. Over 100 scholarships are awarded each year.

APPLICATION INFO:
Undergraduate and graduate applications are posted online after July 1. Online link: scholarship.agc.org. All other application links can be found at www.agcfoundation.org.

Duration: Varies.

Deadline: Allhands Essay Competition and Outstanding Educator Award: November 15; Graduate and Undergraduate Scholarships: Applications are accepted July 1 to November 1; Workforce Development Scholarship: Applications are accepted April 1 to June 1. Contact the Foundation for other deadlines.

IRS I.D.: 52-6083465

ADDRESS INQUIRIES TO:
Melinda Patrician, Director
(See address above.)

AMERICAN CHEMICAL SOCIETY

1155 16th Street, N.W.
Washington, DC 20036-4800
(202) 872-6283
Fax: (202) 776-8008
E-mail: awards@acs.org
Web Site: www.acs.org/awards

TYPE:
Awards/prizes.

See entry 1996 for full listing.

AMERICAN INSTITUTE OF CHEMICAL ENGINEERS (AICHE) [2548]

120 Wall Street, Floor 23
New York, NY 10005-4020
(646) 495-1384
Fax: (646) 495-1503
E-mail: awards@aiche.org
Web Site: www.aiche.org

FOUNDED: 1908

AREAS OF INTEREST:
Chemical engineering.

NAME(S) OF PROGRAMS:

- **Minority Scholarship Awards for College Students**

TYPE:
Scholarships.

YEAR PROGRAM STARTED: 1994

PURPOSE:
To encourage minority undergraduate study of chemical engineering.

LEGAL BASIS:
Nonprofit.

ELIGIBILITY:
Nominations are accepted from AIChE student chapters or chemical engineering clubs. Nominees must be AIChE national student members at the time of nomination, undergraduates in chemical engineering during the academic year, and members of a disadvantaged minority group that is underrepresented in chemical engineering. Chapters may nominate a student who will complete the chemical engineering Baccalaureate degree requirements in mid-year, but such nominees, if successful, will receive prorated awards. The selection of winners will be based on the nominee's academic record, participation in AIChE student and professional activities, career objectives, and financial need.

GEOG. RESTRICTIONS: United States.

FINANCIAL DATA:
Amount of support per award: $1,000.

NO. AWARDS: 13 for the year 2014.

APPLICATION INFO:
Contact the Institute.

Duration: One scholastic year. Renewable following year if student continues to meet eligibility requirements.

Deadline: July 1.

PUBLICATIONS:
AIChExtra; awards nomination form.

AMERICAN NUCLEAR SOCIETY (ANS) [2549]

555 North Kensington Avenue
LaGrange Park, IL 60526
(708) 352-6611
Fax: (708) 352-0499
E-mail: scholarships@ans.org
Web Site: www.ans.org

FOUNDED: 1954

AREAS OF INTEREST:
Nuclear science, nuclear engineering or nuclear-related field.

NAME(S) OF PROGRAMS:
- **Delayed Education for Women Scholarship**
- **John and Muriel Landis Scholarships**

TYPE:
Scholarships. Delayed Education for Women Scholarship is designed for women in a nuclear-related field whose formal studies have been delayed or interrupted for at least one year.

Landis Scholarships are administered by the ANS NEED Committee, and are awarded to undergraduate and graduate students who have greater-than-average financial need.

PURPOSE:
To encourage mature women whose formal studies in the field of nuclear science, nuclear engineering, or a nuclear-related field have been delayed or interrupted for at least one year; to provide financial aid to students with greater-than-average need.

ELIGIBILITY:
Applicants must be ANS student members. Delayed Education for Women Scholarship: Applicants must have experienced a minimum of a one-year delay or interruption of their undergraduate studies and must be entering a four-year curriculum. Those at graduate level of education can also apply. Applicants must also have proven academic ability as well as demonstrated financial need. An applicant must be a U.S. citizen or possess a permanent resident visa, be enrolled in a U.S. college or university, and must be sponsored by an ANS local section, division, student branch, committee or organization member. More than one applicant can be sponsored by any of these organizations. Those applying must be enrolled in a course of study relating to a degree in nuclear science or nuclear engineering in a U.S. institution. Applicants must be mature women whose undergraduate studies in nuclear science, nuclear engineering, or a nuclear-related field have been delayed.

Landis Scholarships: Applicants must be undergraduate or graduate students who have greater-than-average financial need. Consideration is given to conditions or experiences that render the student disadvantaged (poor high school/undergraduate preparation, etc.). Applicants should be planning a career in nuclear science, nuclear engineering, or a nuclear-related field and be enrolled or planning to enroll in a college or university located in the U.S. Applicants need not be U.S. citizens.

GEOG. RESTRICTIONS: United States.

FINANCIAL DATA:
Scholarship funds may be used by the student to defray any bona fide education costs including tuition, books, room and board.

Amount of support per award: $5,000.

CO-OP FUNDING PROGRAMS: Delayed Education for Women Scholarship: Sponsored jointly by the NEED and Professional Women in the ANS Committees.

NO. AWARDS: Delayed Education for Women Scholarship: 1; Landis Scholarships: Up to 9.

APPLICATION INFO:
Applications must be submitted online.

Duration: One year. Nonrenewable.

Deadline: February 1.

ADDRESS INQUIRIES TO:
Scholarship Coordinator
(See address above.)

*SPECIAL STIPULATIONS:
Student may receive no more than three NEED scholarships over the course of their undergraduate and graduate studies.

AMERICAN NUCLEAR SOCIETY (ANS) [2550]

555 North Kensington Avenue
LaGrange Park, IL 60526
(708) 352-6611
Fax: (708) 352-0499
E-mail: scholarships@ans.org
Web Site: www.ans.org

FOUNDED: 1954

AREAS OF INTEREST:
Nuclear science, nuclear engineering or nuclear-related fields.

NAME(S) OF PROGRAMS:
- **Decommissioning and Environmental Sciences (DESD) Undergraduate Scholarship**

TYPE:
Scholarships. For an undergraduate student pursuing a degree in engineering or science major with emphasis on decommissioning/decontamination, management/characterization of radioactive waste, restoration of the environment, or nuclear engineering.

ELIGIBILITY:
Applicant must be at junior or senior undergraduate level and must be a U.S. citizen or permanent resident. He or she must be enrolled in a course of study relating to a degree in nuclear science or nuclear engineering in a U.S. institution. Additional criteria to be met include:
(1) the student must be enrolled in a curriculum of engineering or science that is associated either with decommissioning/decontamination of nuclear facilities, management/characterization of nuclear waste, restoration of the environment, or nuclear engineering;
(2) the scholarship is limited to U.S. citizens who are enrolled in U.S. schools;
(3) the student will join the American Nuclear Society (ANS);
(4) the student will designate the ANS DDR Division as one of his or her professional divisions and;
(5) he or she will commit to provide student support to the ANS DDR Division at the next ANS meeting after receipt of the scholarship award. (DDR will provide funding for the student's travel to the ANS meeting, including student registration, reasonable transportation, food and lodging.)

FINANCIAL DATA:
Scholarship funds may be used by the student to defray any bona fide education costs including tuition, books, room and board.

Amount of support per award: $2,000.

NO. AWARDS: 1 annually.

APPLICATION INFO:
Applications must be submitted online.

Duration: One year. Nonrenewable.

Deadline: February 1.

ADDRESS INQUIRIES TO:
Scholarship Coordinator
(See address above.)

AMERICAN NUCLEAR SOCIETY (ANS) [2551]

555 North Kensington Avenue
LaGrange Park, IL 60526
(708) 352-6611
Fax: (708) 352-0499
E-mail: scholarships@ans.org
Web Site: www.ans.org

FOUNDED: 1954

AREAS OF INTEREST:
Nuclear science, nuclear engineering or nuclear-related field.

NAME(S) OF PROGRAMS:
- **Raymond DiSalvo Scholarship**
- **Robert T. Liner Scholarship**
- **Operations and Power Division Scholarship**
- **Charles (Tommy) Thomas Memorial Scholarship**

TYPE:
Scholarships. Award for a full-time undergraduate student in a program leading to a degree in nuclear science or nuclear engineering at an accredited institution in the U.S.

ELIGIBILITY:
U.S. and non-U.S. applicants must be ANS student members enrolled in an accredited institution in the U.S. Applicant must be a U.S. citizen or possess a permanent resident visa.

Academic accomplishments must be substantiated by transcript. Applicants must be sponsored by an ANS local section, division, student branch, committee or organization member.

Operations and Power Division Scholarship: Applicants must have completed a minimum of two complete academic years in a four-year nuclear science or engineering program.

Charles (Tommy) Thomas Memorial Scholarship: Undergraduate of at least junior-year status pursuing a degree in a discipline preparing them for a career dealing with the environmental aspects of nuclear science or nuclear engineering.

GEOG. RESTRICTIONS: United States.

FINANCIAL DATA:
Scholarship funds may be used by the student to defray any bona fide education costs including tuition, fees, books, room and board.

Amount of support per award: Raymond DiSalvo and Robert T. Liner Scholarships: $2,000; Operations and Power Division Scholarship: $2,500; Charles (Tommy) Thomas Memorial Scholarship: $3,000.

NO. AWARDS: 1 each.

APPLICATION INFO:
Applications must be submitted online.

Duration: One year. Nonrenewable.

Deadline: February 1.

ADDRESS INQUIRIES TO:
Scholarship Coordinator
(See address above.)

AMERICAN NUCLEAR SOCIETY (ANS)

555 North Kensington Avenue
LaGrange Park, IL 60526
(708) 352-6611
Fax: (708) 352-0499
E-mail: scholarships@ans.org
Web Site: www.ans.org

TYPE:
Scholarships. Scholarship award to recognize one outstanding undergraduate student or one graduate student pursuing a career in radioanalytical chemistry or analytical applications of nuclear science.

See entry 1997 for full listing.

AMERICAN NUCLEAR SOCIETY (ANS) [2552]

555 North Kensington Avenue
LaGrange Park, IL 60526
(708) 352-6611
Fax: (708) 352-0499
E-mail: scholarships@ans.org
Web Site: www.ans.org

FOUNDED: 1954

AREAS OF INTEREST:
Nuclear science, nuclear engineering or nuclear-related fields.

NAME(S) OF PROGRAMS:
- **ANS Undergraduate Scholarships**
- **Joseph R. Dietrich Memorial Scholarship**
- **Allan F. Henry/Paul A. Greebler Memorial Graduate Scholarship**
- **John R. Lamarsh Memorial Scholarship**

TYPE:
Scholarships.

ELIGIBILITY:
U.S. and non-U.S. applicants must be ANS student members enrolled in and attending an accredited institution in the U.S. Applicants must have completed a minimum of two complete academic years in a four-year nuclear engineering program and must be U.S. citizens or possess a permanent resident visa. Academic accomplishments must be substantiated by transcript. Applicant must be sponsored by an ANS local section, division, student branch, committee or organization member.

ANS Undergraduate Scholarships and Lamarsh Memorial Scholarship are open to full-time undergraduate students in a program leading to a degree in nuclear science or nuclear engineering at an accredited institution in the U.S.

Joseph R. Dietrich Scholarship is open to a full-time graduate student in a program leading to a degree in nuclear science or nuclear engineering at an accredited institution in the U.S.

Henry/Greebler Scholarship is open to a full-time graduate student of a North American university engaged in Master's or Ph.D. research in the area of nuclear reactor physics or radiation transport. Students of all nationalities are eligible.

FINANCIAL DATA:
Scholarship funds may be used by the student to defray any bona fide education costs including tuition, fees, room and board.

Amount of support per award: ANS Undergraduate, Joseph R. Dietrich Memorial and John R. Lamarsh Memorial Scholarships: $2,000; Alan F. Henry/Paul A. Greebler Memorial Graduate Scholarship: $3,500.

NO. AWARDS: ANS Undergraduate Scholarships: Up to 21; Dietrich, Greebler and Lamarsh Memorial Scholarships: 1 each.

APPLICATION INFO:
Applications must be submitted online.

Duration: One year. Nonrenewable.

Deadline: February 1.

ADDRESS INQUIRIES TO:
Scholarship Coordinator
(See address above.)

AMERICAN NUCLEAR SOCIETY (ANS) [2553]

555 North Kensington Avenue
LaGrange Park, IL 60526
(708) 352-6611
Fax: (708) 352-0499
E-mail: scholarships@ans.org
Web Site: www.ans.org

FOUNDED: 1954

AREAS OF INTEREST:
Nuclear science, nuclear engineering or nuclear-related field.

NAME(S) OF PROGRAMS:
- **Angelo F. Bisesti Memorial Scholarship**
- **Robert G. Lacy Memorial Scholarship**

TYPE:
Scholarships. Scholarship awards for undergraduate students who have completed two or more years in a course of study leading to a degree in nuclear science, nuclear engineering or a nuclear-related field.

PURPOSE:
To support higher education in the nuclear science field.

ELIGIBILITY:
U.S. and non-U.S. applicants must be ANS student members. Applicant must be a U.S. citizen or possess a permanent resident visa, be enrolled in an accredited institution in the U.S., and must be sponsored by an ANS local section, division, student branch, committee or organization member. More than one applicant can be sponsored by any of these organizations.

FINANCIAL DATA:
Amount of support per award: $2,000.

NO. AWARDS: 1 each.

APPLICATION INFO:
Applications must be submitted online.

Duration: One year. Nonrenewable.

Deadline: February 1.

ADDRESS INQUIRIES TO:
Scholarship Coordinator
(See address above.)

AMERICAN NUCLEAR SOCIETY (ANS) [2554]

555 North Kensington Avenue
LaGrange Park, IL 60526
(708) 352-6611
Fax: (708) 352-0499
E-mail: scholarships@ans.org
Web Site: www.ans.org

FOUNDED: 1954

AREAS OF INTEREST:
Nuclear science, nuclear engineering or nuclear-related field.

NAME(S) OF PROGRAMS:
- **ANS Graduate Scholarships**
- **Everitt P. Blizard Scholarship**
- **Robert A. Dannels Memorial Graduate Scholarship**
- **Verne R. Dapp Memorial Scholarship**
- **Walter Meyer Scholarship**
- **James F. Schumar Scholarship**

TYPE:
Scholarships. Blizard Scholarship is for students pursuing graduate studies in the field of radiation protection and shielding.

The Dapp is awarded in odd-numbered years. The Meyer is awarded in even-numbered years.

Schumar Scholarship is for a student pursuing graduate studies in material science and technology for nuclear applications.

PURPOSE:
To support higher education in the field of nuclear science.

ELIGIBILITY:
U.S. and non-U.S. applicants must be ANS student members. Applicant must be a U.S. citizen or possess a permanent resident visa, be enrolled in a U.S. university and must be sponsored by an ANS local section, division, student branch, committee or organization member. More than one applicant can be sponsored by any of these organizations.

The Dannels Scholarship is for a graduate-level course of study leading toward a degree in mathematics and computation. Only U.S. citizens or persons possessing a permanent resident visa are eligible. Nomination of handicapped persons is encouraged.

The Dapp Scholarship is awarded on the graduate level toward a degree in nuclear engineering at an accredited institution in the U.S. Only U.S. citizens or persons possessing a permanent resident visa are eligible.

GEOG. RESTRICTIONS: United States.

FINANCIAL DATA:
Scholarship funds may be used to defray any bona fide education costs including tuition, books, room and board.

Amount of support per award: Blizard, Dapp, Meyer, Schumar and ANS Graduate Scholarships: $3,000 each; Dannels Scholarship: $3,500.

NO. AWARDS: Blizard, Dannels, Dapp, Meyer and Schumar: 1 each; ANS Graduate Scholarships: Up to 29.

APPLICATION INFO:
Applications must be submitted online.

Duration: One year. Nonrenewable.

Deadline: February 1.

ADDRESS INQUIRIES TO:
Scholarship Coordinator
(See address above.)

AMERICAN NUCLEAR SOCIETY (ANS) [2555]

555 North Kensington Avenue
LaGrange Park, IL 60526
(708) 352-6611
Fax: (708) 352-0499
E-mail: scholarships@ans.org
Web Site: www.ans.org

FOUNDED: 1954

AREAS OF INTEREST:
Nuclear science, nuclear engineering and nuclear-related field.

NAME(S) OF PROGRAMS:
- **Pittsburgh Local Section Scholarship**

TYPE:
Scholarships. Two Pittsburgh Local Section Scholarships: one for a graduate student (studying nuclear science and technology) and one for an undergraduate student (studying nuclear science and technology) who either have some affiliation with western Pennsylvania or who attend school at a nearby university within the region.

PURPOSE:
To support higher education in nuclear science.

ELIGIBILITY:
Applicant must be a U.S. citizen or possess a permanent resident visa, be enrolled in a U.S. college or university, and must be sponsored by an ANS local section, division, student branch, committee or organization member. More than one applicant can be sponsored by any of these organizations.

GEOG. RESTRICTIONS: Western Pennsylvania.

FINANCIAL DATA:
Scholarship funds may be used to defray any bona fide education costs including tuition, books, room and board.

Amount of support per award: Undergraduate: $2,000; Graduate: $3,500.

NO. AWARDS: Undergraduate and Graduate: 1 each.

APPLICATION INFO:
Applications must be submitted online.

Duration: One year. Nonrenewable.

Deadline: February 1.

ADDRESS INQUIRIES TO:
Scholarship Coordinator
(See address above.)

AMERICAN PUBLIC POWER ASSOCIATION (APPA) [2556]

2451 Crystal Drive
Suite 1000
Arlington, VA 22202
(202) 467-2900
Fax: (202) 467-2910
E-mail: deed@publicpower.org
Web Site: www.publicpower.org/deed

FOUNDED: 1980

AREAS OF INTEREST:
Engineering, mathematics and computer science.

NAME(S) OF PROGRAMS:
- **DEED Scholarship**

TYPE:
Demonstration grants; Development grants; Internships; Project/program grants; Research grants; Scholarships.

YEAR PROGRAM STARTED: 1980

PURPOSE:
To promote the involvement of students studying in energy-related disciplines in the public power industry; to provide host utilities with technical assistance.

ELIGIBILITY:
Open to students conducting research on a project approved by the sponsoring utility who will then submit a final report on the project, describing the activities, cost, bibliography, achievements, problems, results and recommendations. Applicants will not be discriminated against on the basis of sex, race, religion, national origin or citizenship.

GEOG. RESTRICTIONS: Students must be accepted or enrolled in a full-time vocational or accredited college, university or high school in the United States.

FINANCIAL DATA:
Amount of support per award: $4,000.

Total amount of support: Up to $40,000 per year.

NO. MOST RECENT APPLICANTS: 20.

NO. AWARDS: 10.

APPLICATION INFO:
Applications must be sent from a DEED member utility and must be dated on the last page by an authorized individual at the utility.

Deadline: February 15 and October 15.

ADDRESS INQUIRIES TO:
Richelle Dodds, DEED Assistant
(See address above.)

AMERICAN SOCIETY FOR ENGINEERING EDUCATION [2557]

1818 N Street, N.W., Suite 600
Washington, DC 20036-2479
(202) 649-3831
Fax: (202) 265-8504
E-mail: ndseg@asee.org
Web Site: ndseg.asee.org

FOUNDED: 1893

AREAS OF INTEREST:
STEM disciplines.

NAME(S) OF PROGRAMS:
- **Department of Defense National Defense Science and Engineering Graduate Fellowship Program (NDSEG)**

TYPE:
Fellowships.

YEAR PROGRAM STARTED: 1964

ELIGIBILITY:
For students at or near the beginning of their doctoral study in science or engineering. Field of study must fit under one of 15 supported STEM disciplines. Applicants must be citizens or nationals of the U.S.

FINANCIAL DATA:
Provides competitive stipend and full tuition.

Amount of support per award: Varies.

Total amount of support: Varies.

NO. AWARDS: NDSEG: Approximately 200 annually.

APPLICATION INFO:
Application guidelines are available on the ASEE web site.

Deadline: Typically December. Applications open late summer/early fall.

ADDRESS INQUIRIES TO:
See e-mail address above.

AMERICAN SOCIETY FOR ENGINEERING EDUCATION [2558]

1818 N Street, N.W., Suite 600
Washington, DC 20036
(202) 350-5763
Fax: (202) 265-8504
E-mail: postdocs@asee.org
Web Site: www.asee.org/nrl

FOUNDED: 1893

AREAS OF INTEREST:
Engineering education programs, scientific research in government, industry and the military.

NAME(S) OF PROGRAMS:
- **Naval Research Laboratory (NRL) Postdoctoral Fellowship Program**

TYPE:
Fellowships. Offered at Naval research and development centers and laboratories. NRL is charged with developing technologies that will support Naval Forces in meeting future operational needs. Scientists and fellows working at NRL pursue research on subjects including, but not limited to, processing, biomedicine, logistics, command control and intelligence, training and oceanography.

YEAR PROGRAM STARTED: 2002

PURPOSE:
To significantly increase the involvement of creative and highly trained scientists and engineers from academia and industry in scientific and technical areas of interest and relevance to the Navy.

LEGAL BASIS:
Special interest society.

ELIGIBILITY:
Applicants must be U.S. citizens and permanent residents and must be eligible for a Department of Defense security clearance of "Secret." In most cases, participants will be permitted to do research pending completion of the security clearance. All appointments are contingent upon fellows obtaining the appropriate level of security clearance. Prior to appointment, participants must present evidence of having received the Ph.D., Sc.D. or other earned research doctoral degree recognized in U.S. as equivalent to the Ph.D. within seven years of the date of application or must present acceptable evidence of having completed all formal academic requirements for one of these degrees. No support to applicants who received prior postdoctoral appointment under any program at the same Navy laboratory. No appointments or denials based on grounds of race, creed, color, national origin, age or sex.

GEOG. RESTRICTIONS: United States.

FINANCIAL DATA:
Awards include stipend, insurance, relocation expenses and travel.

Amount of support per award: $75,621.

Total amount of support: Varies.

NO. AWARDS: Approximately 40 new appointments each year.

APPLICATION INFO:
Applicants should contact the research facility of interest to develop a suitable research proposal. Proposals developed closely with the proposed host facility stand the greatest chance of success in the selection process. A proposal should be no more than 10 pages, be concise, and address a problem of mutual interest to the applicant and Navy research facility.

Duration: One year. Renewable for a second and third year with satisfactory performance and availability of funds.

PUBLICATIONS:
Program announcement.

STAFF:
Shannon Koonce, Program Manager

ADDRESS INQUIRIES TO:
NRL Postdoctoral Program
Contracts/Grants Office
(See address above.)

THE AMERICAN SOCIETY FOR NONDESTRUCTIVE TESTING, INC.

1711 Arlingate Lane
Columbus, OH 43228
(614) 274-6003
(800) 222-2768
Fax: (614) 274-6899
E-mail: jvandervort@asnt.org
Web Site: www.asnt.org

TYPE:
Scholarships.

See entry 1604 for full listing.

AMERICAN SOCIETY OF CIVIL ENGINEERS [2559]

1801 Alexander Bell Drive
Reston, VA 20191-4400
(703) 295-6300 ext. 6382
(800) 548-2723
Fax: (703) 295-6144
E-mail: awards@asce.org
Web Site: www.asce.org

FOUNDED: 1852

AREAS OF INTEREST:
Civil engineering.

NAME(S) OF PROGRAMS:
- **O.H. Ammann Research Fellowship in Structural Engineering**
- **CI Construction Engineering Scholarship and Student Prizes**
- **Lawrence W. and Francis W. Cox Scholarship**
- **Trent R. Dames and William W. Moore Fellowship**
- **Eugene C. Figg, Jr. Civil Engineering Scholarship**
- **Freeman Fellowship**
- **Jack E. Leisch Memorial National Graduate Fellowship**
- **John Lenard Civil Engineering Scholarship**
- **Robert B.B. and Josephine N. Moorman Scholarship**
- **J. Waldo Smith Hydraulic Fellowship**
- **Samuel Fletcher Tapman ASCE Student Chapter Scholarship**
- **Arthur S. Tuttle Memorial Scholarship**
- **Y.C. Yang Civil Engineering Scholarship**

TYPE:
Fellowships; Grants-in-aid; Research grants; Scholarships. Scholarships, fellowships and grants for research; undergraduate and graduate studies in civil engineering fields from ASCE endowments, operation or other funds.

Fellowships and scholarships are awarded annually.

YEAR PROGRAM STARTED: 1924

PURPOSE:
To aid and encourage education, research and studies in civil engineering.

LEGAL BASIS:
Nonprofit professional organization.

ELIGIBILITY:
Qualified engineers or engineering undergraduate or graduate students with appropriate interests are eligible to apply. Undergraduate students must be enrolled at an ABET-accredited university, be a member of an ASCE student chapter and also be a national student member. (A list of schools that have student chapters is available from the address above.)

FINANCIAL DATA:
Amount of support per award: $2,000 to $10,000.

APPLICATION INFO:
Application forms are available at www.asce.org/student_resources/.

Deadline: Varies; majority due close of business February 10.

PUBLICATIONS:
Scholarships/Fellowships brochure.

OFFICERS:
Thomas Smith, Executive Director

ADDRESS INQUIRIES TO:
See e-mail address above.

*SPECIAL STIPULATIONS:
Requires ASCE membership of some kind.

THE AMERICAN SOCIETY OF MECHANICAL ENGINEERS AUXILIARY, INC. [2560]

2 Park Avenue, MS-RB
New York, NY 10016-5990
(212) 591-7650
Fax: (212) 591-7739
E-mail: bigleyr@asme.org
Web Site: go.asme.org/scholarships

FOUNDED: 1923

AREAS OF INTEREST:
Mechanical engineering students.

NAME(S) OF PROGRAMS:
- **Allen J. Baldwin Scholarship**
- **Berna Lou Cartwright Scholarship**
- **Lucy and Charles W.E. Clarke Scholarship**
- **Sylvia W. Farny Scholarship**
- **Agnes Malakate Kezios Scholarship**
- **Elisabeth M. and Winchell M. Parsons Scholarship**
- **Rice-Cullimore Scholarship**
- **Marjorie Roy Rothermel Scholarship**
- **Charles B. Scharp Scholarship**
- **Student Loan Fund**

TYPE:
Scholarships. Lucy and Charles W.E. Clarke Scholarship is for high school seniors participating on a FIRST team.

Baldwin, Cartwright, Farny, Kezios and Scharp Scholarships are for undergraduate students in mechanical engineering.

Parsons and Rothermel Scholarships are for graduate students with a degree in mechanical engineering, to be used to pursue a Master's degree in mechanical engineering.

Rice-Cullimore Scholarship is for foreign students at the graduate level.

Student Loan Fund is for juniors, seniors or graduate students enrolled as degree candidates in good standing.

YEAR PROGRAM STARTED: 1924

PURPOSE:
To give financial assistance to mechanical engineering students.

LEGAL BASIS:
Incorporated organization.

ELIGIBILITY:
Applicants must be U.S. citizens, enrolled in a degree program in a school with accredited mechanical engineering curriculum and members of the ASME for scholarships and student loans. Applicants must be foreign students, selected in their home country, who meet the requirements of the sponsor in their home country who holds a contract with the International Institute of Education for the Rice-Cullimore Scholarship.

FINANCIAL DATA:
Amount of support per award: Lucy and Charles W.E. Clarke Scholarship: $5,000. All other Scholarships: $3,000; Student Loans: $5,000 maximum.

Total amount of support: Varies.

NO. MOST RECENT APPLICANTS: Undergraduate Scholarships: 15; Rothermel: 1.

NO. AWARDS: Undergraduate Scholarships: 9; Rothermel: 1.

APPLICATION INFO:
Contact the Society.

Duration: One year. Nonrenewable.

Deadline: Contact the Auxiliary for individual scholarship deadlines and notification dates.

PUBLICATIONS:
Application guidelines; scholarship forms; applications.

OFFICERS:
Benetta Cook, President
Linda Sims, Executive Vice President
Jennifer Jewers Bowlin, Vice President, Members-at-Large
Stella Seiders, Treasurer
Ed Seiders, Student Loan Fund Treasurer
Ella Baldwin-Viereck, Recording Secretary
Vatsala Menon, Corresponding Secretary

ADDRESS INQUIRIES TO:
RuthAnn Bigley, Coordinator, Governance
(See address above.)

AMERICAN SOCIETY OF NAVAL ENGINEERS (ASNE) [2561]

1452 Duke Street
Alexandria, VA 22314-3458
(703) 836-6727
Fax: (703) 836-7491
E-mail: nlackey@navalengineers.org
Web Site: www.navalengineers.org

FOUNDED: 1888

AREAS OF INTEREST:
Naval Engineering includes all arts and sciences as applied in the research,

development, design, construction, operation, maintenance and logistic support of surface and sub-surface ships and marine craft, naval maritime auxiliaries, aviation and space systems, combat systems, command control, electronics and ordnance systems, ocean structures and associated shore facilities, which are used by naval and other military forces and civilian maritime organizations for the defense and well-being of the Nation.

CONSULTING OR VOLUNTEER SERVICES:
Volunteer Services.

NAME(S) OF PROGRAMS:
- **ASNE Scholarship Program**

TYPE:
Scholarships. Stipend for tuition, fees and expenses to follow a full-time or co-op program of study that applies to naval engineering, such as naval architecture, marine engineering, ocean engineering, mechanical engineering, structural engineering, electrical engineering, electronic engineering and the physical sciences, as well as other programs leading to careers with civilian and military maritime organizations supporting and developing work and life at sea.

YEAR PROGRAM STARTED: 1979

PURPOSE:
To encourage college students to enter the field of naval engineering; to support naval engineers seeking advanced education in the field.

LEGAL BASIS:
Nonprofit professional society.

ELIGIBILITY:
Support will be limited to the last year of undergraduate education or one year of graduate education in an accredited college or university. Candidates must be U.S. citizens and must have demonstrated or expressed a genuine interest in a career in naval engineering. Graduate students must be members of ASNE or SNAME and may apply at time of application.

Selection criteria will be based on academic record, work history, professional promise and interest in naval engineering, extracurricular activities, recommendations of college faculty, employers and other character references. Demonstrated financial need is not a requirement, but it may be taken into consideration by the Scholarship Committee.

A scholarship will not be awarded to a doctoral candidate or to a person already having an advanced degree.

GEOG. RESTRICTIONS: United States.

FINANCIAL DATA:
The award will be in the form of a check for the first academic period payable jointly to the awardee and the college or university that the student will attend. Transcripts showing satisfactory performance constitute the basis for further awards for subsequent academic periods.

Amount of support per award: Undergraduate: $3,000; Graduate: $4,000.

NO. AWARDS: Varies.

APPLICATION INFO:
Application information is available on the Society's web site.

Duration: One year.

Deadline: February 28. Notification by early May.

PUBLICATIONS:
Naval Engineers Journal.

IRS I.D.: 53-0229465

OFFICERS:
Capt. Dennis K. Kruse, USN (Ret.), Executive Director

ADDRESS INQUIRIES TO:
ASNE Scholarship Committee
(See address above.)

AMERICAN SOCIETY OF SAFETY ENGINEERS [2562]

520 North Northwest Highway
Park Ridge, IL 60068
(847) 699-2929
Fax: (847) 296-9221
E-mail: customerservice@asse.org
Web Site: www.asse.org

FOUNDED: 1911

AREAS OF INTEREST:
Occupational safety and health.

NAME(S) OF PROGRAMS:
- **Edgar Monsanto Queeny Safety Professional of the Year Award**

TYPE:
Awards/prizes. Cash honorarium to Society-selected award winners from Monsanto Co.

YEAR PROGRAM STARTED: 1980

PURPOSE:
To recognize exemplary achievements in Safety, Health and Environmental (SHE) Education.

LEGAL BASIS:
Not-for-profit professional society.

ELIGIBILITY:
Nominees must be active dues-paying professional members or members of the Society, domestic or international, and cannot have received this award within the past five years. The Society President is not eligible for the award until five years after he or she has left the Board of Directors. ASSE Fellows and members currently serving on the Society Technical and Professional Recognition Committee and/or the Board of Directors are ineligible.

FINANCIAL DATA:
Amount of support per award: $2,000 honorarium and an engraved statuette.

NO. MOST RECENT APPLICANTS: 9.

NO. AWARDS: 1 each year.

APPLICATION INFO:
Nominations must be submitted in writing to the ASSE Technical and Professional Recognition Committee Chairman, postmarked no later than November 1, to be considered that same year. Individual members, chapters, regions, practice specialty, councils or the Society Board of Directors may submit them. Must be accompanied by a letter of endorsement from the nominating colleague (Chapter, Regional Operating Committees, Practice Specialty, Councils or the Society Board of Directors), as well as the immediate employment supervisor, a single-page resume, plus a petition listing the nominee's achievements. Submit eight copies by mail or one single PDF electronically.

Deadline: November 1 by mail (postmarked) or November 7 electronically. Award announcement in early March.

ADDRESS INQUIRIES TO:
Dennis Hudson
Director, Professional Affairs
(See address above.)

ASHRAE [2563]

1791 Tullie Circle, N.E.
Atlanta, GA 30329
(404) 636-8400
E-mail: mvaughn@ashrae.org
Web Site: www.ashrae.org

FOUNDED: 1894

AREAS OF INTEREST:
Engineering, environmental technology, technical assistance, public health and conservation.

CONSULTING OR VOLUNTEER SERVICES:
Cooperative research with government agencies and other organizations by supplying ASHRAE expertise, usually in the form of an advisory committee.

NAME(S) OF PROGRAMS:
- **ASHRAE Research Grants**

TYPE:
Research contracts. Institutional grants for basic research and technical studies concerned with the arts and sciences of heating, refrigeration, air conditioning and ventilation.

YEAR PROGRAM STARTED: 1912

PURPOSE:
To increase the amount and accuracy of fundamental information in the fields of heating, refrigeration, air conditioning/ventilation and related areas and to make this information available.

LEGAL BASIS:
Organization exempt under 501(c)(3) of the Internal Revenue Code.

ELIGIBILITY:
Accredited institutions of higher learning may apply with appropriate proposals.

FINANCIAL DATA:
Amount of support per award: $5,000 to $250,000 per project.

Total amount of support: $2,500,000 to $3,000,000 annually.

NO. MOST RECENT APPLICANTS: 60.

NO. AWARDS: Approximately 20 grants annually.

APPLICATION INFO:
Applications take the form of a proposal. Detailed information concerning its preparation is available upon request to the Manager of Research at the address above.

Duration: Up to three years, with the possibility of extension.

Deadline: Applications may be submitted throughout the year. Proposals are generally acted upon only in January and June.

ADDRESS INQUIRIES TO:
Michael R. Vaughn, Manager of Research and Technical Services
(See address above.)

ASHRAE [2564]

1791 Tullie Circle, N.E.
Atlanta, GA 30329
(404) 636-8400
E-mail: mvaughn@ashrae.org
Web Site: www.ashrae.org

FOUNDED: 1894

AREAS OF INTEREST:
Engineering, environmental technology, technical assistance, public health and conservation.

NAME(S) OF PROGRAMS:
- **ASHRAE Graduate Student Grant-in-Aid Program**

TYPE:
Grants-in-aid. Support for projects of original research concerned with the arts and sciences of heating, refrigeration, air-conditioning/ventilation and related areas.

YEAR PROGRAM STARTED: 1968

PURPOSE:
To stimulate interest in the areas of heating, refrigeration, air-conditioning and ventilation through the encouragement of original research in these fields.

LEGAL BASIS:
Organization exempt under 501(c)(3) of the Internal Revenue Code.

ELIGIBILITY:
Qualified graduate engineering students capable of carrying out appropriate and scholarly research are eligible to apply.

FINANCIAL DATA:
Amount of support per award: $10,000 with the opportunity to earn an additional $1,500 honorarium for presentation of an authored research paper at an ASHRAE meeting.

Total amount of support: Approximately $200,000 annually.

NO. MOST RECENT APPLICANTS: 60.

NO. AWARDS: Approximately 20 per year.

APPLICATION INFO:
Prospective applicants should complete the official Grant-in-Aid application containing the following:
(1) significance of proposed research;
(2) outline or plan of procedure;
(3) approximate budget and extent to which the applicant's institution will support the work;
(4) plans for seeking other funds for this or related work;
(5) anticipated plans for publication of research results;
(6) student's name and qualifications;
(7) faculty advisor's and institution's qualifications to do the work and;
(8) copy of official transcripts.

Duration: Grants are usually awarded for a maximum period of one year. Students who have previously received grants may not reapply; one grant per student.

Deadline: Applications should be submitted by or before December 15, for consideration at review meeting held in January.

OFFICERS:
Tom Phoenix, President
David Underwood, President-Elect
Jeff Littleton, Executive Vice President and Secretary

ADDRESS INQUIRIES TO:
Michael R. Vaughn, Manager of Research and Technical Services
(See address above.)

ASM MATERIALS EDUCATION FOUNDATION

9639 Kinsman Road
Materials Park, OH 44073-0002
(440) 338-5151 ext. 5533
(800) 336-5152 ext. 5533
Fax: (440) 338-4634
E-mail: jeane.deatherage@asminternational.org
Web Site: www.asmfoundation.org

TYPE:
Scholarships.

See entry 2593 for full listing.

CANADIAN SOCIETY FOR CHEMICAL ENGINEERING [2565]

222 Queen Street
Suite 400
Ottawa ON K1P 5V9 Canada
(613) 232-6252 ext. 223
Fax: (613) 232-5862
E-mail: awards@cheminst.ca
Web Site: www.cheminst.ca/awards

FOUNDED: 1945

AREAS OF INTEREST:
Chemical engineering.

NAME(S) OF PROGRAMS:
- **The CSChE Chemical Engineering Local Section Scholarships**
- **SNC-LAVALIN Plant Design Competition**

TYPE:
Scholarships. The CSChE Chemical Engineering Local Section Scholarships are offered to undergraduate students in chemical engineering about to enter the final year of studies at a Canadian university and will be made for leadership qualities and demonstrated contributions to the Canadian Society for Chemical Engineering, such as participation in student chapters. Two scholarships will be given annually.

The SNC-LAVALIN Plant Design Competition is offered to students enrolled in undergraduate chemical engineering programs at Canadian universities.

PURPOSE:
To promote undergraduate study in chemical engineering and provide financial support for that study.

LEGAL BASIS:
Special interest society.

ELIGIBILITY:
Applicants for the CSChE Chemical Engineering Local Section Scholarships must be members of the Canadian Society for Chemical Engineering.

Applicants for the SNC-LAVALIN Plant Design Competition must be individuals and groups of undergraduate students registered in chemical engineering programs in Canadian universities during the current academic year. To minimize the number of projects to be judged, each chemical engineering department may submit no more than two entries.

GEOG. RESTRICTIONS: Canada.

FINANCIAL DATA:
Amount of support per award: Chemical Engineering Local Section: $2,000; SNC-LAVALIN Plant Design Competition: $1,000 to the team with the best design.

NO. AWARDS: Local Section Scholarships: 2; SNC-LAVALIN Plant Design Competition: 1.

APPLICATION INFO:
For the scholarships, applications should contain evidence of academic standing, description of work to be undertaken, letters of reference, and evidence of contributions to the Society.

Entries for the SNC-LAVALIN Plant Design Competition should contain copies of the following:
(1) a short summary, including a simplified flowsheet of the process;
(2) a copy of the final report submitted to the university at the end of the project;
(3) a list of students who performed the work, with their permanent addresses and phone numbers;
(4) the name of the collaborating organization and the engineers who assisted the students and;
(5) a brief description of the assistance provided by that organization.

The entry should be accompanied by a letter from the head of the department of chemical engineering indicating that the information is not confidential and that the summary may be published in *Canadian Chemical News.*

Deadline: Local Section Scholarships: April 30; SNC-LAVALIN Competition: May 30.

PUBLICATIONS:
Announcement.

ADDRESS INQUIRIES TO:
Gale Thirlwall, Awards Manager
(See address above.)

GEORGE WASHINGTON UNIVERSITY [2566]

Department of Electrical and Computer Engineering
Science and Engineering Hall
800 22nd Street N.W., Suite 5000
Washington, DC 20052
(202) 994-6083
Fax: (202) 994-0227
E-mail: ece@gwu.edu
Web Site: www.ece.seas.gwu.edu

FOUNDED: 1821

AREAS OF INTEREST:
Electrical engineering, computer engineering, and telecommunications.

NAME(S) OF PROGRAMS:
- **Graduate Teaching Assistantships**

TYPE:
Assistantships. Merit-based awards for graduate studies at George Washington University.

PURPOSE:
To attract high-quality graduate students.

LEGAL BASIS:
University.

ELIGIBILITY:
Usually for currently enrolled students. Some fellowships are limited to U.S. citizens. Must have a grade point average of 3.5 on a possible scale of 4.0 and have taken the Graduate Record Examination.

GEOG. RESTRICTIONS: United States.

FINANCIAL DATA:
Amount of support per award: Varies.

Total amount of support: Varies.

APPLICATION INFO:
Graduate students should submit an application for admission to the School of Engineering and Applied Science.

Duration: One academic year. Must reapply for additional funding.

ADDRESS INQUIRIES TO:
Dr. Ahmed Louri, Chairperson
(See address above.)

GREAT MINDS IN STEM

602 Monterey Pass Road
Monterey Park, CA 91754
(323) 262-0997
Fax: (323) 262-0946
E-mail: info@greatmindsinstem.org
Web Site: www.greatmindsinstem.org

TYPE:
Scholarships.

See entry 2525 for full listing.

INSTITUTE OF INDUSTRIAL AND SYSTEMS ENGINEERS (IISE) [2567]

3577 Parkway Lane
Building 5, Suite 200
Norcross, GA 30092
(770) 449-0461
Fax: (770) 441-3295
E-mail: bcameron@iienet.org
Web Site: www.iienet.org

FOUNDED: 1948

AREAS OF INTEREST:
The design, improvement and installation of integrated systems of people, material, information, equipment and energy, incorporating specialized knowledge and skills from the mathematical, physical and social sciences, together with the principles and methods of engineering analysis and design to specify, predict and evaluate the results to be obtained from such systems.

NAME(S) OF PROGRAMS:
- **CISE Undergraduate Scholarship**
- **John S.W. Fargher Scholarship**
- **C.B. Gambrell Undergraduate Scholarship**
- **Dwight D. Garden Scholarship**
- **Gilbreth Memorial Fellowship**
- **IIE Council of Fellows Undergraduate Scholarship**
- **John L. Imhoff Scholarship**
- **Henry and Elisabeth Kroeze Memorial Scholarship**
- **Harold and Inge Marcus Scholarship**
- **Marvin Mundel Memorial Scholarship**
- **Presidents Scholarship**
- **A.O. Putnam Memorial Scholarship**
- **E.J. Sierleja Memorial Fellowship**
- **Society for Health Systems Scholarship**
- **United Parcel Service Scholarship for Female Students**
- **United Parcel Service Scholarship for Minority Students**
- **Lisa Zaken Award of Excellence**

TYPE:
Fellowships; Scholarships. The Institute supports the advancement of engineering education and research through scholarships and fellowships to recognize and support these types of endeavors.

PURPOSE:
To recognize academic excellence and campus leadership.

LEGAL BASIS:
Nonprofit, international professional membership society.

ELIGIBILITY:
Candidates must be active Institute members enrolled full-time in graduate or undergraduate industrial engineering programs. The nominee's scholastic ability, character, leadership, service, and financial need are all considered.

Membership is not required for the Imhoff Scholarship.

FINANCIAL DATA:
Amount of support per award: Varies per award.

APPLICATION INFO:
Students may not apply directly for scholarships. They must be nominated by their department head or faculty advisor. Nominations must be mailed to the Institute. Call for nominations are sent out at the beginning of each school year in the fall.

Deadline: December 1 (postmark).

STAFF:
Don Greene, Chief Executive Officer

ADDRESS INQUIRIES TO:
Bonnie Cameron
Headquarters Operations Administrator
(See address above.)

THE JAMES F. LINCOLN ARC WELDING FOUNDATION [2568]

22801 St. Clair Avenue
Cleveland, OH 44117
(216) 481-8100
Fax: (216) 486-6476
E-mail: lori_hurley@lincolnelectric.com
Web Site: www.lincolnelectric.com
www.jflf.org

FOUNDED: 1936

AREAS OF INTEREST:
Engineering, welded design and fabrication.

NAME(S) OF PROGRAMS:
- **Awards for Achievement in Arc Welded Design, Engineering and Fabrication: College Division**

TYPE:
Awards/prizes. Awards to recognize and reward achievement by engineering and technology students (graduate and undergraduate) in solving design, engineering or fabricating problems involving the knowledge or application of arc welding.

YEAR PROGRAM STARTED: 1956

PURPOSE:
To recognize outstanding work in the welding design and fabrication field.

LEGAL BASIS:
Private corporate foundation.

ELIGIBILITY:
Graduate or undergraduate students enrolled in college or university programs leading to a Bachelor's, Master's or doctoral degree may submit papers completed within a one-year period, ending June 30 of the year of the contest. Papers should represent students' work on design, engineering or fabrication problems relating to any type of building, bridge or other generally stationary structure, any type of machine, product or mechanical apparatus or arc welding research, testing, procedure or process development.

Students to participate in the Undergraduate Division must be enrolled in a four-year or longer curriculum leading to a Bachelor's degree. Students to participate in the Graduate Division must be enrolled in a graduate program leading to a Master's or Doctorate degree. Qualified students may apply individually or jointly in groups of not more than five. Undergraduate students compete for 17 awards, and graduate students compete for 12 awards.

GEOG. RESTRICTIONS: United States.

FINANCIAL DATA:
Amount of support per award: $50 to $1,000.

Total amount of support: Varies.

NO. AWARDS: Varies.

APPLICATION INFO:
Official application materials are available upon request to the Secretary. Any number of entries may be submitted from one school, but no student may participate in more than one entry.

Deadline: June 30.

TRUSTEES:
Duane Miller

EXECUTIVE STAFF:
Leslie Brown, President
Carl Peters, Executive Director
Lori Hurley, Secretary

ADDRESS INQUIRIES TO:
Lori Hurley, Secretary
(See address above.)

LOS ALAMOS NATIONAL LABORATORY

P.O. Box 1663
MS-P125
Los Alamos, NM 87545
(505) 664-6947 ext. 05004
Fax: (505) 606-5901
E-mail: hrstaffing-postdocs@lanl.gov
Web Site: www.lanl.gov/science/postdocs

TYPE:
Fellowships. The Distinguished Postdoctoral Fellowships provide the opportunity for the recipients to collaborate with LANL scientists and engineers on staff-initiated research. Candidates for these awards must display extraordinary ability in scientific research and show clear and definite promise of becoming outstanding leaders in the research they pursue.

See entry 1774 for full listing.

NATIONAL ACTION COUNCIL FOR MINORITIES IN ENGINEERING, INC. (NACME)

One North Broadway
Suite 601
White Plains, NY 10601
(914) 539-4010 ext. 222
Fax: (914) 539-4032
E-mail: scholars@nacme.org
Web Site: www.nacme.org

TYPE:
Block grants; Endowments; Fellowships; Scholarships. NACME encourages students to consider engineering as a career and to pursue the requisite preparation in mathematics and science. It motivates high school students and channels them to engineering schools and provides scholarship support and leadership development seminars

to its university scholars. The retention of minority students in engineering is a priority issue for NACME.

See entry 979 for full listing.

THE NATIONAL GEM CONSORTIUM

1430 Duke Street
Alexandria, VA 22314
(703) 562-3646
Fax: (202) 207-2518
E-mail: info@gemfellowship.org
Web Site: www.gemfellowship.org

TYPE:
Fellowships; Internships. All-expense fellowship for graduate study (tuition and stipend) and paid summer work experience in a scientific or engineering environment.

See entry 982 for full listing.

NATIONAL RESEARCH COUNCIL OF CANADA

1200 Montreal Road, Building M-55
Room 369A
Ottawa ON K1A 0R6 Canada
(613) 949-4655
Fax: (613) 990-1286
E-mail: info@nrc-cnrc.gc.ca
racoordinator.hrb@nrc-cnrc.gc.ca
Web Site: www.nrc-cnrc.gc.ca

TYPE:
Associateships. Research Associate Program provides promising scientists and engineers with the opportunity to work in a challenging research environment during the early stages of their career. Applicants will be selected competitively and must demonstrate the ability to perform original, high-quality research in their chosen field.

Research Associates will be offered appointments to the staff of the National Research Council on a term basis and will be offered salaries and benefits currently available to Research Officers.

See entry 1779 for full listing.

NATIONAL SCIENCE FOUNDATION [2569]

Directorate for Engineering
Office of Assistant Director
4201 Wilson Boulevard, Room 505
Arlington, VA 22230
(703) 292-8300
(703) 292-8301
Fax: (703) 292-9013
Web Site: www.nsf.gov

FOUNDED: 1950

AREAS OF INTEREST:
Chemical, biochemical and thermal engineering, mechanics, structures and materials engineering, electrical, communications and systems engineering, design, manufacturing and computer engineering, emerging engineering systems, cross-disciplinary research, engineering research centers, civil and environment engineering, earthquake engineering and small business innovation research.

NAME(S) OF PROGRAMS:
- **Directorate for Engineering Grants Program**

TYPE:
Assistantships; Conferences/seminars; Fellowships; Internships; Project/program grants; Research grants; Travel grants; Visiting scholars.

YEAR PROGRAM STARTED: 1984

PURPOSE:
To strengthen U.S. engineering education and research; to focus on areas relevant to national problems by supporting research across the entire range of engineering disciplines and by identifying areas where results are expected to have timely applications.

LEGAL BASIS:
Government agency.

ELIGIBILITY:
Proposals may be submitted by colleges, universities, profit and nonprofit organizations and by state, local or regional governments. Industry, state and local governments and other organizations are eligible to participate. Joint proposals are encouraged.

NSF does not make loans or grants to develop or promote any business venture, technical assistance, pilot plant efforts, research requiring security classification, the development of products for commercial marketing or market research for a particular product or invention.

GEOG. RESTRICTIONS: United States and its territories.

FINANCIAL DATA:
Amount of support per award: $2,000 to $5,000,000. Average $63,000.
Total amount of support: Varies.

APPLICATION INFO:
Informal inquiry to the Directorate for Engineering may be made to determine whether or not a potential project would qualify for support.
Duration: One to five years. Average is approximately 30 months.
Deadline: Varies. Approximately six to eight months are required for consideration of formal proposals.

PUBLICATIONS:
Grants for Research and Education in Science and Engineering; Guide to Programs.

STAFF:
Pramod Khargonekar, Assistant Director, Engineering
Grace Wang, Deputy Assistant Director

ADDRESS INQUIRIES TO:
Directorate for Engineering
(See address above.)

NATIONAL SOCIETY OF PROFESSIONAL SURVEYORS (NSPS) [2570]

5119 Pegasus Court
Suite Q
Frederick, MD 21704
(240) 439-4615 ext. 105
Fax: (240) 439-4952
E-mail: trisha.milburn@nsps.us.com
Web Site: www.nsps.us.com

AREAS OF INTEREST:
Surveying.

NAME(S) OF PROGRAMS:
- **The Schonstedt Scholarship in Surveying**

TYPE:
Scholarships. For students enrolled in four-year degree programs in surveying or in closely related degree programs such as geomatics or surveying engineering.

PURPOSE:
To encourage and recognize students committed to a career in surveying.

LEGAL BASIS:
Nonprofit educational organization.

ELIGIBILITY:
The Schonstedt Scholarship is for students enrolled in four-year degree programs in surveying or in closely related degree programs such as geomatics or surveying engineering. Preference will be given to applicants with junior or senior standing.

GEOG. RESTRICTIONS: United States, Canada and South America.

FINANCIAL DATA:
Amount of support per award: $3,000.
Total amount of support: $3,000 annually.

CO-OP FUNDING PROGRAMS: Scholarship is made possible by a donation from the Schonstedt Instrument Company of Kearneysville, WV.

NO. MOST RECENT APPLICANTS: 21.

NO. AWARDS: 1 annually.

APPLICATION INFO:
Required documentation includes:
(1) a completed application form;
(2) proof of student membership in NSPS (this will be checked);
(3) a brief yet complete statement indicating educational objectives, future plans of study or research, professional activities and financial need;
(4) three letters of recommendation (at least two from faculty members familiar with the student's work) and;
(5) a complete original official transcript through the end of the school year prior to when the award will be presented; in addition, send unofficial transcripts for the fall semester when available.

Do not send applications by fax or e-mail. Mail all documents in one envelope. Incomplete or improperly completed applications will be discarded.
Duration: One academic year.
Deadline: April 29, 2017.

ADDRESS INQUIRIES TO:
Patricia Milburn, Office Manager
(See e-mail address and phone number above.)

NATIONAL SOCIETY OF PROFESSIONAL SURVEYORS (NSPS) [2571]

5119 Pegasus Court
Suite Q
Frederick, MD 21704
(240) 439-4615 ext. 105
Fax: (240) 439-4952
E-mail: trisha.milburn@nsps.us.com
Web Site: www.nsps.us.com

FOUNDED: 1941

AREAS OF INTEREST:
Surveying and surveying technology.

NAME(S) OF PROGRAMS:
- **The Berntsen International Scholarship in Surveying**
- **The Berntsen International Scholarship in Surveying Technology**

TYPE:
Scholarships. Berntsen International Scholarship in Surveying: Annual scholarship award for undergraduate study in four-year degree programs in surveying or in closely related degree programs such as geomatics or surveying engineering.

Berntsen International Scholarship in Surveying Technology: For students enrolled in two-year degree programs in surveying technology. Scholarship awarded in even years only.

PURPOSE:
To provide financial assistance to students pursuing two- or four-year degree programs in surveying, surveying technology or closely related fields.

LEGAL BASIS:
Nonprofit, educational organization.

ELIGIBILITY:
The Berntsen International Scholarship in Surveying: Student applicants must be enrolled in four-year degree programs in surveying or in closely related degree programs such as geomatics or surveying engineering.

The Berntsen International Scholarship in Surveying Technology: Student applicants must be enrolled in two-year degree programs in surveying technology.

GEOG. RESTRICTIONS: United States.

FINANCIAL DATA:
Amount of support per award: Berntsen International Scholarship in Surveying: $2,000; Berntsen International Scholarship in Surveying Technology: $2,000.

CO-OP FUNDING PROGRAMS: Scholarships are made possible by Berntsen International, Inc., of Madison, WI.

NO. MOST RECENT APPLICANTS: 21.

NO. AWARDS: The Berntsen International Scholarship in Surveying: 1 annually. The Berntsen International Scholarship in Surveying Technology: 1 in even-numbered years.

APPLICATION INFO:
Required documentation includes:
(1) a completed application form;
(2) proof of student membership in NSPS (this will be checked);
(3) a brief yet complete statement indicating educational objectives, future plans of study or research, professional activities and financial need;
(4) three letters of recommendation (at least two from faculty members familiar with the student's work) and;
(5) a complete original official transcript through the end of the school year prior to when the award will be presented; in addition, send unofficial transcripts for the fall semester when available.

Do not send applications by fax or e-mail. Mail all documents in one envelope. Incomplete or improperly completed applications will be discarded.

Duration: One academic year.

Deadline: April 29, 2017.

ADDRESS INQUIRIES TO:
Patricia Milburn, Office Manager
(See e-mail address and phone number above.)

NATIONAL SOCIETY OF PROFESSIONAL SURVEYORS (NSPS) [2572]

5119 Pegasus Court
Suite Q
Frederick, MD 21704
(240) 439-4615 ext. 105
Fax: (240) 439-4952
E-mail: trisha.milburn@nsps.us.com
Web Site: www.nsps.us.com

FOUNDED: 1941

AREAS OF INTEREST:
Surveying.

NAME(S) OF PROGRAMS:
- **NSPS Board of Directors Scholarship**
- **The NSPS Scholarship**

TYPE:
Scholarships.

PURPOSE:
To recognize outstanding surveying students; to encourage qualified candidates to pursue an undergraduate degree in surveying.

LEGAL BASIS:
Nonprofit foundation.

ELIGIBILITY:
NSPS Board of Directors Scholarship applicants must be enrolled in studies in surveying or in closely related degree programs and entering their junior year of study in a four-year degree program of their choice (either full- or part-time) and must have maintained a minimum 3.0 grade point average.

The NSPS Scholarship is awarded to students enrolled in four-year degree programs in surveying or in closely related degree programs such as geomatics or surveying engineering. The Scholarship is intended to recognize an outstanding student enrolled full-time in undergraduate surveying programs.

GEOG. RESTRICTIONS: United States.

FINANCIAL DATA:
Amount of support per award: $2,000 per scholarship.

NO. MOST RECENT APPLICANTS: 21.

NO. AWARDS: NSPS Board of Directors Scholarship: 1 (awarded in even-numbered years only); The NSPS Scholarship: 1.

APPLICATION INFO:
Applicants must submit (in the following order):
(1) a completed application form;
(2) proof of student membership in NSPS (this will be checked);
(3) a brief yet complete statement indicating educational objectives, future plans of study or research, professional activities and financial need;
(4) three letters of recommendation (at least two from faculty members familiar with the student's work) and;
(5) a complete original official transcript through the end of the school year prior to when the award will be presented; in addition, send unofficial transcripts for the fall semester when available.

Do not send applications by fax or e-mail. Mail all documents in one envelope. Incomplete or improperly completed applications will be discarded.

Duration: One academic year.

Deadline: April 29, 2017.

ADDRESS INQUIRIES TO:
Patricia Milburn, Office Manager
(See e-mail address and phone number above.)

NATIONAL SOCIETY OF PROFESSIONAL SURVEYORS (NSPS) AMERICAN ASSOCIATION FOR GEODETIC SURVEYING (AAGS) [2573]

5119 Pegasus Court
Suite Q
Frederick, MD 21704
(240) 439-4615 ext. 105
Fax: (240) 439-4952
E-mail: trisha.milburn@nsps.us.com
Web Site: www.aagsmo.org
www.nsps.us.com

FOUNDED: 1941

AREAS OF INTEREST:
Geodetic surveying.

NAME(S) OF PROGRAMS:
- **American Association for Geodetic Surveying (AAGS) Graduate Fellowship Award**

TYPE:
Fellowships. Annual fellowship award to support graduate study in a program with a significant focus on geodetic surveying or geodesy at a school of the recipient's choice.

PURPOSE:
To recognize outstanding graduate students committed to the pursuit of knowledge in geodetic surveying, thus enhancing the ability of the profession to better serve the needs of society.

LEGAL BASIS:
Nonprofit educational organization.

ELIGIBILITY:
Nominees must be members of the American Association for Geodetic Surveying (AAGS) and should be enrolled in or accepted by a graduate program in geodetic surveying or geodesy. Preference will be given to applicants having at least two years of employment experience in the surveying profession.

GEOG. RESTRICTIONS: United States, Canada and South America.

FINANCIAL DATA:
Amount of support per award: $2,000 and an appropriate citation to be presented at the annual meeting.

Total amount of support: $2,000 annually.

CO-OP FUNDING PROGRAMS: Provided by the American Association for Geodetic Surveying and administered by NSPS Foundation.

NO. MOST RECENT APPLICANTS: 21.

NO. AWARDS: 1 annually.

APPLICATION INFO:
Required documentation includes:
(1) a completed application form;
(2) proof of student membership in AAGS (this will be checked);
(3) a brief yet complete statement indicating educational objectives, future plans of study or research, professional activities and financial need;
(4) three letters of recommendation (at least two from faculty members familiar with the student's work) and;
(5) a complete original official transcript through the end of the school year prior to

when the award will be presented; in addition, send unofficial transcripts for the fall semester when available.

Do not send applications by fax or e-mail. Mail all documents in one envelope. Incomplete or improperly completed applications will be discarded.

Duration: One academic year.

Deadline: April 29, 2017.

PUBLICATIONS:
Surveying and Land Information Science Journal.

ADDRESS INQUIRIES TO:
Patricia Milburn, Office Manager
(See e-mail address and phone number above.)

NATIONAL SOCIETY OF PROFESSIONAL SURVEYORS (NSPS) AMERICAN ASSOCIATION FOR GEODETIC SURVEYING (AAGS) [2574]

5119 Pegasus Court
Suite Q
Frederick, MD 21704
(240) 439-4615 ext. 105
Fax: (240) 439-4952
E-mail: trisha.milburn@nsps.us.com
Web Site: www.aagsmo.org
www.nsps.us.com

AREAS OF INTEREST:
Geodetic surveying.

NAME(S) OF PROGRAMS:
- **AAGS Joseph F. Dracup Scholarship Award**

TYPE:
Scholarships. The award is intended for students enrolled in four-year degree programs in surveying or in closely related degree programs.

PURPOSE:
To promote study in the surveying and mapping professions.

LEGAL BASIS:
Nonprofit educational organization.

ELIGIBILITY:
Nominees must be members of the National Society of Professional Surveyors. Student applicants must be enrolled in four-year degree programs in surveying or in closely related degree programs such as geomatics or surveying engineering. Preference will be given to applicants from programs with a significant focus on geodetic surveying.

GEOG. RESTRICTIONS: United States, Canada and South America.

FINANCIAL DATA:
Amount of support per award: $2,000 and an appropriate citation to be presented at the annual meeting.

Total amount of support: $2,000 annually.

CO-OP FUNDING PROGRAMS: Provided by the American Association for Geodetic Surveying and administered by NSPS.

NO. MOST RECENT APPLICANTS: 21.

NO. AWARDS: 1 annually.

APPLICATION INFO:
Required documentation includes:
(1) a completed application form;
(2) proof of student membership in AAGS (this will be checked);
(3) a brief yet complete statement indicating educational objectives, future plans of study or research, professional activities and financial need;
(4) three letters of recommendation (at least two from faculty members familiar with the student's work) and;
(5) a complete original official transcript through the end of the school year prior to when the award will be presented; in addition, send unofficial transcripts for the fall semester when available.

Do not send applications by fax or e-mail. Mail all documents in one envelope. In addition, send unofficial transcripts for the fall semester when available. Incomplete or improperly completed applications will be discarded.

Duration: One academic year.

Deadline: April 29, 2017.

PUBLICATIONS:
Surveying and Land Information Science Journal.

ADDRESS INQUIRIES TO:
Patricia Milburn, Office Manager
(See e-mail address and phone number above.)

OAK RIDGE INSTITUTE FOR SCIENCE AND EDUCATION (ORISE) [2575]

MC-100-36
P.O. Box 117
Oak Ridge, TN 37831-0117
(865) 574-7798
(865) 576-3424
Fax: (865) 576-1609
E-mail: science.education@orau.org
Web Site: orise.orau.gov/science-education

FOUNDED: 1946

AREAS OF INTEREST:
Energy-related disciplines and technologies.

TYPE:
Fellowships; Internships; Scholarships. ORISE administers a broad range of internships, scholarships, fellowships and research experiences. ORISE programs include research experiences at Department of Energy national laboratories as well as other federal agencies with research facilities located across the country as well as some positions outside the U.S.

YEAR PROGRAM STARTED: 1950

PURPOSE:
To provide hands-on research training for students seeking Associate, Baccalaureate, or graduate degrees in appropriate disciplines relating to science and engineering education, training and management systems, energy and environment systems.

LEGAL BASIS:
Government agency.

ELIGIBILITY:
ORISE programs are available to science and engineering students and educators at every academic level from K-12th grade, to college students and postdoctoral researchers, to university faculty members.

APPLICATION INFO:
Contact ORISE for general information and application guidelines.

PUBLICATIONS:
Program announcement; ORISE Resource Guide.

ADDRESS INQUIRIES TO:
David Duncan, Director, Scientific Assessment
and Workforce Development
(See address above.)

PRECAST/PRESTRESSED CONCRETE INSTITUTE [2576]

200 West Adams Street
Suite 2100
Chicago, IL 60606
(312) 786-0300
Fax: (312) 621-1114
E-mail: rbecker@pci.org
Web Site: www.pci.org

AREAS OF INTEREST:
Research, design and construction of buildings, bridges and other structures using precast/prestressed concrete.

NAME(S) OF PROGRAMS:
- **Daniel P. Jenny Research Fellowships**

TYPE:
Fellowships.

YEAR PROGRAM STARTED: 1972

PURPOSE:
To support graduate students in civil engineering interested in research related to precast and prestressed concrete.

LEGAL BASIS:
Nonprofit trade association.

ELIGIBILITY:
Student applicants must be graduate students in civil engineering interested in research related to precast/prestressed concrete and enrolled in a U.S., Canadian or Mexican university. Religious organizations are ineligible.

GEOG. RESTRICTIONS: United States, Canada and Mexico.

FINANCIAL DATA:
Amount of support per award: $35,000.

NO. AWARDS: Up to 4.

APPLICATION INFO:
Application information is available online.

Duration: One to two years.

Deadline: Proposals are solicited in December. Deadline generally mid-February. Decision by end of April, with announcement in May for following academic year.

ADDRESS INQUIRIES TO:
Roger Becker, Managing Director
Research and Development
(See address above.)

THE SOCIETY OF NAVAL ARCHITECTS AND MARINE ENGINEERS [2577]

99 Canal Center Plaza, Suite 310
Alexandria, VA 22314
(703) 997-6709
Fax: (703) 997-6702
E-mail: bgreer@sname.org
Web Site: www.sname.org

FOUNDED: 1893

AREAS OF INTEREST:
Naval architecture, marine engineering, ocean engineering or marine industry-related fields.

NAME(S) OF PROGRAMS:
- **Graduate Scholarships**
- **Undergraduate Scholarships**

TYPE:
Scholarships. The Society annually awards both graduate and undergraduate scholarships to encourage study in naval architecture, marine engineering, ocean engineering or marine industry-related fields.

Graduate Scholarships are made for one year of study leading to a Master's in naval architecture, marine engineering, ocean engineering or in fields directly related to the marine industry.

Undergraduate Scholarships are administered by schools offering undergraduate programs on grants given to the schools.

YEAR PROGRAM STARTED: 1933

PURPOSE:
To encourage young men and women to enter the fields of naval architecture, marine engineering, ocean engineering or marine industry-related fields as a career by aiding them to pursue courses of study in these specialties and to provide the incentive and attractions for such a career.

LEGAL BASIS:
Technical Society.

ELIGIBILITY:
Society scholarships are based soley on merit, not financial need.

Graduate Scholarships: Open to U.S., Canadian, or international applicants. Awards are made for one year of study leading to a Master's degree in naval architecture, marine engineering, ocean engineering or in fields directly related to the marine industry. Society membership is required one year prior to application submission deadline. Applicants must not receive their Master's prior to October 1 of the year in which they are applying for their scholarship. Graduate scholarships are awarded to an individual only once. Non-U.S. or Canadian citizens must plan to study in U.S. or Canadian schools. Generally, applicants are not expected to receive their Master's Degree prior to April 15 of the academic year in which graduate study is undertaken.

Undergraduate Scholarships: Open to citizens of the U.S. and Canada, or study must be toward a degree in naval architecture, marine engineering or ocean engineering. The applicant must be entering his or her junior or senior year and must be a member in the Society for at least four months prior to the application submittal deadline. Scholarship awardees may repeat as an undergraduate recipient and subsequently apply for a graduate scholarship.

FINANCIAL DATA:
Amount of support per award: Graduate Scholarships: Up to $20,000 per year; Undergraduate Scholarships: Varies.

Total amount of support: Varies.

NO. AWARDS: Graduate Scholarships: At least 8 annually.

APPLICATION INFO:
Graduate Scholarships: Application may be downloaded from the Society web site or may be obtained by written request to the attention of the Chairperson, Scholarships Committee, at the address above. Applicants are required to provide GRE scores regardless of graduate school admission requirements. Application and supporting data are sent to the Scholarships Committee.

Undergraduate Scholarships: Requests are made directly to schools. The schools present their nominations in biographical form for each applicant and include a statement from the student indicating his or her career goals and why he or she is interested in the marine field. Selection of the recipients is made by the colleges in accordance with their established procedures.

Duration: Graduate Scholarships: One year. No renewals. Undergraduate Scholarships: One year. Awardee may repeat as an undergraduate recipient and subsequently apply for a Graduate Scholarship.

Deadline: Graduate Scholarships: Application prior to February 1; supporting data by February 15. Graduate Scholarships selected in April.

Undergraduate Scholarships: Application prior to June 1; supporting data by June 15. Nominations are presented to the Society's Scholarships Committee annually for approval in July.

SCHOLARSHIP COMMITTEE:
Dr. Walter Maclean, Chairman

ADDRESS INQUIRIES TO:
Estelle Lee, Scholarships Coordinator
(See address above.)

SOCIETY OF WOMEN ENGINEERS

203 North La Salle Street
Suite 1675
Chicago, IL 60601
(312) 596-5223
(877) 793-4636
Fax: (312) 596-5252
E-mail: scholarships@swe.org
Web Site: www.swe.org/scholarships

TYPE:
Awards/prizes; Conferences/seminars; Scholarships. Support for undergraduate and graduate engineering studies including women who have been out of the engineering job market and out of school for a minimum of two years and who will return to school for an engineering program.

See entry 1074 for full listing.

SYSTEMS PLUS, INC. [2578]

One Research Court
Rockville, MD 20850
(301) 948-4232
E-mail: afsffp@sysplus.com
Web Site: afsffp.sysplus.com

AREAS OF INTEREST:
Science, engineering and mathematics.

NAME(S) OF PROGRAMS:
- **USAF Summer Faculty Fellowship Program**

TYPE:
Fellowships. Research fellowship.

PURPOSE:
To complement research efforts and build critical links between Air Force scientists and counterparts in the academic community.

ELIGIBILITY:
Must be a full-time faculty member of an accredited Baccalaureate-granting U.S. college, university or technical institution, and have earned a Ph.D. in science or engineering. No other employment or remuneration is permitted during the period of the award, eight to 12 weeks from May through August.

GEOG. RESTRICTIONS: United States.

FINANCIAL DATA:
Amount of support per award: Assistant Professor: $1,500 per week; Associate Professor: $1,700 per week; Full Professor: $1,900 per week.

Total amount of support: Varies.

NO. MOST RECENT APPLICANTS: 203.

NO. AWARDS: Up to 150.

APPLICATION INFO:
Each applicant must get approval to apply to a program from the Advisor before uploading his or her proposal. Application opens September 1. Applications, curriculum vitae and references must be submitted electronically.

Duration: One summer.

Deadline: Late November.

ADDRESS INQUIRIES TO:
Imar Nkeba, Program Management Office
(See address above.)

THE TAU BETA PI ASSOCIATION, INC. [2579]

508 Dougherty Engineering Building
1512 Middle Drive - UTK
Knoxville, TN 37996-2215
(865) 546-4578
Fax: (865) 546-4579
E-mail: tbp@tbp.org
fellowships@tbp.org
Web Site: www.tbp.org

FOUNDED: 1885

AREAS OF INTEREST:
Engineering.

NAME(S) OF PROGRAMS:
- **Raymond A. and Ina C. Best Fellowship for MBA at Rensselaer Polytechnic Institute**
- **Graduate Fellowship in Engineering**
- **Tau Beta Pi Undergraduate Scholarship**

TYPE:
Fellowships; Scholarships. Fellowship awards are for one academic year of study in engineering for qualified graduate students.

Scholarships are awarded for senior year of full-time undergraduate study.

YEAR PROGRAM STARTED: 1928

PURPOSE:
To support the advancement of engineering education and the profession.

LEGAL BASIS:
Corporation.

ELIGIBILITY:
Candidate must be a member of Tau Beta Pi.

Scholarship applicants must be planning to return to school for at least one semester, one trimester, or two quarters of full-time undergraduate study in engineering on campus in the upcoming academic year.

FINANCIAL DATA:
Fellows having other graduate study financial aid that is in excess of tuition may be awarded Tau Beta Pi Fellowships without stipend. Persons supported by a salary from industry, government or other sources may not be entitled to the stipend.

Amount of support per award: Fellowships: $10,000. Scholarships: $2,000 for full year, $1,000 for one semester, one trimester or two quarters.

Total amount of support: $700,000 to $820,000 per year.

NO. MOST RECENT APPLICANTS: 1,175.

NO. AWARDS: 31 fellowships and 261 scholarships for the academic year 2015-16.

APPLICATION INFO:
Application forms are available November 1 for fellowships and January 15 for scholarships for the following academic year.

Duration: One academic year. Fellowships and scholarships are not renewable.

Deadline: Fellowships: February 1. Scholarships: April 1.

PUBLICATIONS:
The Bent of Tau Beta Pi, quarterly magazine.

IRS I.D.: 62-0479545

OFFICERS:
Curtis D. Gomulinski, Executive Director
Sally J. Steadman, Ph.D., Director of Fellowships

EXECUTIVE COUNCIL:
J.P. Blackford, President
Norman Pih, Vice President
Susan L.R. Holl, Ph.D., Councillor
George J. Morales, Ph.D., Councillor
Alan J. Passman, Councillor

ADDRESS INQUIRIES TO:
Director of Fellowships
The Tau Beta Pi Association, Inc.
P.O. Box 2697
Knoxville, TN 37901-2697
E-mail: fellowships@tbp.org

U.S. DEPARTMENT OF ENERGY [2580]

3610 Collins Ferry Road
P.O. Box 880
Morgantown, WV 26507-0880
(304) 285-4784
Web Site: www.netl.doe.gov

FOUNDED: 1979

AREAS OF INTEREST:
Materials development to support direct power extraction and low-cost distributed sensing of fossil energy power systems.

NAME(S) OF PROGRAMS:
- **University Coal Research Program**

TYPE:
Assistantships; Project/program grants; Research grants.

YEAR PROGRAM STARTED: 1980

PURPOSE:
To foster the highest quality fundamental research on coal at the university level; to ensure the continued training of researchers in the areas of fossil energy.

LEGAL BASIS:
Government agency.

ELIGIBILITY:
Open to U.S. colleges and universities only.

GEOG. RESTRICTIONS: United States.

FINANCIAL DATA:
Amount of support per award: Maximum DOE funding for grant applications submitted by one or two universities is up to $400,000 for a 36-month performance period.

Total amount of support: Approximately $2,100,000 for the year 2014.

Matching fund requirements: No matching fund requirements; however, cost-sharing and/or industrial collaboration is encouraged.

APPLICATION INFO:
Funding opportunities are posted on the web site above.

Duration: Up to 36 months. No renewals.

Deadline: Early February.

U.S. SOCIETY ON DAMS [2581]

1616 17th Street, Suite 483
Denver, CO 80202
(303) 628-5430
Fax: (303) 628-5431
E-mail: stephens@ussdams.org
Web Site: www.ussdams.org

AREAS OF INTEREST:
Dams and water resources.

NAME(S) OF PROGRAMS:
- **USSD Scholarship**

TYPE:
Scholarships.

PURPOSE:
To advance the technology of dam engineering, construction, operation, maintenance and dam safety; to foster socially and environmentally responsible water resources projects; to promote awareness of the role of dams in the beneficial and sustainable development of the nation's water resources.

ELIGIBILITY:
Open to U.S. college or university graduate students whose research studies have a potential for developing practical solutions to design and construction problems and other dam-related issues. Applicants must be U.S. citizens or permanent residents enrolled full-time in U.S. academic institutions which have programs related to dams.

GEOG. RESTRICTIONS: United States.

FINANCIAL DATA:
Amount of support per award: $10,000; three finalists receive $1,000.

Total amount of support: $13,000 for the year 2015.

NO. AWARDS: 4 for the year 2015.

APPLICATION INFO:
Applicants must submit a proposal describing a specific research topic. The proposed research work should be original and innovative. The proposed research can be part of an ongoing research project. Applicants are encouraged to submit proposals in topics that are related to their graduate research work. The application package must include the application form, a description of the proposed research work, an official set of academic transcripts and two letters of recommendation, one of which must be from the applicant's academic advisor.

ADDRESS INQUIRIES TO:
Kathleen Clarkson
Awards Committee
Tel: (503) 552-2723
E-mail: kathleen.clarkson@ferc.gov

THE UNIVERSITY OF SYDNEY [2582]

Scholarships Office
Level 5, Jane Foss Russell Building G02
The University of Sydney N.S.W. 2006
Australia
(02) 8627 8112
Fax: (02) 8627 8485
E-mail: scholarships.officer@sydney.edu.au
Web Site: www.sydney.edu.au/scholarships/research

FOUNDED: 1850

AREAS OF INTEREST:
Aerospace, electrical and information engineering, mechanical and mechatronic engineering.

NAME(S) OF PROGRAMS:
- **Norman I. Price Supplementary Scholarship**
- **Peter Nicol Russell Postgraduate Scholarship in Mechanical and Mechatronic Engineering**

TYPE:
Scholarships. Awarded for research leading to a higher degree. Tenable at the University of Sydney.

PURPOSE:
To promote and encourage research and study in various fields of engineering.

LEGAL BASIS:
University.

ELIGIBILITY:
Open to graduates of the University of Sydney or to any other person eligible for admission to full-time candidature for a higher degree by research in the Faculty of Engineering and Information Technologies at the University of Sydney.

FINANCIAL DATA:
This scholarship does not cover tuition fees payable by international students.

Amount of support per award: Varies.

NO. AWARDS: 1 offered as vacancy occurs.

APPLICATION INFO:
Contact the University.

Duration: One year. May be renewed for a second year in the case of a Master's degree, and for a third year for a Ph.D.

ADDRESS INQUIRIES TO:
Faculty of Engineering and Information Technologies
The University of Sydney
N.S.W. 2006 Australia
Tel: (02) 9351 8155
Fax: (02) 9351 7082
E-mail:
engineering.scholarships@sydney.edu.au

THE UNIVERSITY OF SYDNEY

Scholarships Office
Level 5, Jane Foss Russell Building G02
The University of Sydney N.S.W. 2006
Australia
(02) 8627 8112
Fax: (02) 8627 8485
E-mail: scholarships.officer@sydney.edu.au
Web Site: www.sydney.edu.au/scholarships/research

TYPE:
Scholarships. Awarded for research leading to a higher degree. Tenable at the University of Sydney.

See entry 2066 for full listing.

Home economics and nutrition

THE ACADEMY OF NUTRITION AND DIETETIC FOUNDATION [2583]

120 South Riverside Plaza, 20th Floor
Chicago, IL 60606
(312) 899-4773
Fax: (312) 899-4796
Web Site: www.eatright.org/foundation

FOUNDED: 1966

AREAS OF INTEREST:
Food, nutrition, dietetics and food service management.

TYPE:
Awards/prizes; Fellowships; Grants-in-aid; Research grants; Scholarships.

YEAR PROGRAM STARTED: 1966

PURPOSE:
To further progress in the educational and scientific advancement of dietetics.

LEGAL BASIS:
Public, not-for-profit foundation.

ELIGIBILITY:
Applicant must be a member of the Academy to qualify for its scholarships and (in general) for its awards as well.

GEOG. RESTRICTIONS: Primarily United States.

FINANCIAL DATA:
Amount of support per award: Scholarships: $500 to $10,000.

Total amount of support: Over $942,000.

CO-OP FUNDING PROGRAMS: Collaborative Consumer Research Program.

NO. MOST RECENT APPLICANTS: 1,000.

NO. AWARDS: 200.

APPLICATION INFO:
One common application form is used for all scholarships. Scholarship applications are available online to Academy members.

Awards applications are available online.

Deadline: Scholarships: February 15. Announcement in June; Awards and Fellowships: February 1; Grants: April 1.

PUBLICATIONS:
Annual report.

IRS I.D.: 36-6150906

ADDRESS INQUIRIES TO:
Martha Ontizeros
(See telephone number above.)

AMERICAN ASSOCIATION OF FAMILY AND CONSUMER SCIENCES (AAFCS)

400 North Columbus Street
Suite 202
Alexandria, VA 22314-2752
(703) 706-4600
(800) 424-8080
Fax: (703) 706-4663
E-mail: awards@aafcs.org
Web Site: www.aafcs.org/awards/index.asp

TYPE:
Fellowships. AAFCS awards fellowships to individuals who have exhibited the potential to make contributions to the family and consumer sciences profession.

See entry 935 for full listing.

AMERICAN ASSOCIATION OF FAMILY AND CONSUMER SCIENCES (AAFCS) [2584]

400 North Columbus Street
Suite 202
Alexandria, VA 22314-2752
(703) 706-4600
(800) 424-8080
Fax: (703) 706-4663
E-mail: awards@aafcs.org
Web Site: www.aafcs.org/awards/index.asp

FOUNDED: 1909

AREAS OF INTEREST:
Family and consumer sciences.

NAME(S) OF PROGRAMS:
- **National Teacher of the Year Award**

TYPE:
Awards/prizes. Recognizes exemplary teachers who utilize cutting-edge methods, techniques and activities to provide the stimulus for and give visibility to family and consumer sciences elementary and secondary education.

YEAR PROGRAM STARTED: 1972

PURPOSE:
To provide leadership and support for professionals whose work assists individuals, families and communities in making informed decisions about their well-being, relationships and resources to achieve optimal quality of life.

LEGAL BASIS:
501(c)(3) nonprofit charity.

ELIGIBILITY:
National-level competitors for this award must have been chosen as an Affiliate Teacher of the Year (through competitions run at the affiliate level); each affiliate may enter no more than one Affiliate Teacher of the Year into the national competition per year and the nomination must be submitted by the Affiliate Leader. An Affiliate Teacher of the Year who is eligible for the National Teacher of the Year Award:
(1) is employed as a full-time family and consumer sciences teacher of grades kindergarten through 12 at the time the nomination is submitted;
(2) is an AAFCS member at the time of nomination and for at least three consecutive years prior to nomination and;
(3) created and runs a family and consumer sciences program that focuses on one of the following five program areas: (a) career awareness/job skill training; (b) consumer education/family finance; (c) creative dimensions/alternative program designs; (d) family life/personal and social development and; (e) nutrition education/diet and health.

Members of the AAFCS Board of Directors, Awards and Recognition Committee, and Development Committee are not eligible for nomination during their terms of office. AAFCS staff members are not eligible for nomination during their periods of employment with the Association.

Award recipient must attend the AAFCS Annual Conference & Expo for presentation and recognition.

FINANCIAL DATA:
Amount of support per award: A commemorative plaque and a $2,500 award, plus up to $1,000 of support for one year of AAFCS membership and participation in the AAFCS Annual Conference & Expo.

NO. MOST RECENT APPLICANTS: 10.

NO. AWARDS: Up to 3 merit finalists, from whom 1 National Teacher of the Year is selected.

APPLICATION INFO:
Detailed guidelines and instructions are available from the Association.

ADDRESS INQUIRIES TO:
See e-mail address above.

CANADIAN FOUNDATION FOR DIETETIC RESEARCH (CFDR) [2585]

480 University Avenue
Suite 604
Toronto ON M5G 1V2 Canada
(416) 357-3022
Fax: (416) 596-0603
E-mail: info@cfdr.ca
Web Site: www.cfdr.ca

FOUNDED: 1991

AREAS OF INTEREST:
Applied research in food and nutrition/dietetic research.

NAME(S) OF PROGRAMS:
- **Research Grants in Dietetics**

TYPE:
Awards/prizes; Research grants.

YEAR PROGRAM STARTED: 1991

PURPOSE:
To promote and support dietetic research.

ELIGIBILITY:
For research awards, applicants must be practicing dietitians who are delivering direct/indirect client/patient public care or service. One of the investigators must be a member of the dietetic profession, as identified by membership in a professional association of dietitians and/or registration as a member of a Canadian dietetics regulatory body.

GEOG. RESTRICTIONS: Canada.

FINANCIAL DATA:
Amount of support per award: Research grants: $5,000 maximum small grants; $5,000 to $20,000 large grants.

APPLICATION INFO:
Completed letter of intent; completed full proposal.

Duration: Small grants: One year. Large grants: One to two years.

Deadline: Research grant letters of intent: Mid-September. Full proposal: March 1. Announcement in June.

PUBLICATIONS:
Canadian Journal of Dietetic Practice and Research (Revue Canadienne de la Pratique et de la Recherché en Dietetique).

STAFF:
Greg Sarney, Executive Director

ADDRESS INQUIRIES TO:
See e-mail address above.

CENTER FOR SCIENCE IN THE PUBLIC INTEREST [2586]

1220 L Street, N.W.
Suite 300
Washington, DC 20005
(202) 332-9110
Fax: (202) 265-4954
E-mail: coday@cspinet.org
Web Site: www.cspinet.org

FOUNDED: 1971

AREAS OF INTEREST:
Consumer advocacy on nutrition, diet and health, and food safety.

NAME(S) OF PROGRAMS:
- **Public Interest Internships**

TYPE:
Internships. These unpaid internships allow interns to work on specific projects under the direction of a Project Director or the Executive Director.

YEAR PROGRAM STARTED: 1978

PURPOSE:
To provide interns with direct, practical experience; to provide the Center with extra assistance.

LEGAL BASIS:
501(c)(3).

ELIGIBILITY:
Students in undergraduate, graduate, law and medical schools are eligible to apply. Requirements vary depending on specific internship applied for.

Must work out of the Washington, DC office.

NO. MOST RECENT APPLICANTS: 250.

NO. AWARDS: Varies.

APPLICATION INFO:
Cover letter should indicate preferred dates. Application materials should include the following:
(1) cover letter indicating issues of interest, future plans, and the dates that applicant is available;
(2) resume (experience with advocacy groups is not required, but would be advantageous) and;
(3) writing sample (a popularly written piece is preferred over a technical report).

Duration: 10 weeks. Renewal possible.

Deadline: Applicants are advised to follow the application guidelines and apply as soon as possible. Applications are taken on a rolling basis until all positions have been filled.

PUBLICATIONS:
Status report; general brochure; publications list; *Nutrition Action Healthletter.*

OFFICERS:
Michael F. Jacobson, Ph.D., Chief Executive Officer

ADDRESS INQUIRIES TO:
Colleen O'Day, Human Resources Director
(See address above.)

DIETITIANS OF CANADA (DC) [2587]

480 University Avenue
Suite 604
Toronto ON M5G 1V2 Canada
(416) 596-0857
Fax: (416) 596-0603
E-mail: contactus@dietitians.ca
Web Site: www.dietitians.ca

FOUNDED: 1935

AREAS OF INTEREST:
Dietetics and nutrition.

NAME(S) OF PROGRAMS:
- **Student Awards in Food and Nutrition**

TYPE:
Awards/prizes.

YEAR PROGRAM STARTED: 1966

PURPOSE:
To provide financial support to students in undergraduate and graduate levels of study.

LEGAL BASIS:
Incorporated under Canada Corporations Act.

ELIGIBILITY:
Applicants must be members of Dietitians of Canada and registered in a food and nutrition or related program.

GEOG. RESTRICTIONS: Canada.

FINANCIAL DATA:
Amount of support per award: $2,500 cash prize, plus $1,000 for travel support to attend the DC national conference.

NO. MOST RECENT APPLICANTS: 26.

NO. AWARDS: 5.

APPLICATION INFO:
Completed application form, academic transcript, and two recommendations are required.

ADDRESS INQUIRIES TO:
E-mail:centralinfo@dietitians.ca

FOOD AND DRUG LAW INSTITUTE (FDLI)

1155 15th Street, N.W., Suite 910
Washington, DC 20005-2706
(202) 371-1420
Fax: (202) 371-0649
E-mail: comments@fdli.org
Web Site: www.fdli.org/resources/academics/h-thomas-austern-memorial-writing-competition

TYPE:
Awards/prizes. The subject matter of the competition is an in-depth analysis of a current issue relevant to the food and drug field, including a relevant case law, legislative history and other authorities, particularly where the U.S. Food and Drug Administration is involved.

See entry 1913 for full listing.

HANNAFORD CHARITABLE FOUNDATION

145 Pleasant Hill Road
Scarborough, ME 04074
(207) 885-3834
Fax: (207) 885-3051
Web Site: www.hannaford.com

TYPE:
Capital grants. Employee scholarships. Long-term project/program grants.

See entry 1503 for full listing.

ILLINOIS RESTAURANT ASSOCIATION EDUCATIONAL FOUNDATION

33 West Monroe, Suite 250
Chicago, IL 60603
(312) 787-4000
Fax: (312) 845-1956
E-mail: ksummers@illinoisrestaurants.org
Web Site: www.illinoisrestaurants.org

TYPE:
Scholarships.

See entry 1637 for full listing.

INTERNATIONAL ASSOCIATION FOR FOOD PROTECTION [2588]

6200 Aurora Avenue
Suite 200W
Des Moines, IA 50322-2864
(515) 276-3344
(800) 369-6337
Fax: (515) 276-8655
E-mail: info@foodprotection.org
Web Site: www.foodprotection.org

FOUNDED: 1911

AREAS OF INTEREST:
Food science and research.

NAME(S) OF PROGRAMS:
- **Harold Barnum Industry Award**
- **Food Safety Innovation Award**
- **Harry Haverland Citation Award**
- **International Leadership Award**
- **Elmer Marth Educator Award**
- **Sanitarian Award**
- **Student Travel Scholarship Award**
- **Travel Award for State or Provincial Health or Agricultural Department Employees**
- **Maurice Weber Laboratorian Award**

TYPE:
Awards/prizes; Travel grants. Cash awards and plaques to outstanding members.

YEAR PROGRAM STARTED: 1973

PURPOSE:
To provide food safety professionals worldwide with a forum to exchange information on protecting the food supply; to recognize and reward outstanding member contributions in the specified award area.

LEGAL BASIS:
Nonprofit, incorporated professional association.

ELIGIBILITY:
Nominees must be members of the International Association for Food Protection.

FINANCIAL DATA:
Amount of support per award: $1,500 to $2,500 and plaque or travel expense paid.

NO. AWARDS: Generally, 1 of each award annually. Travel awards: Multiple.

APPLICATION INFO:
Deadline: February 23.

IRS I.D.: 35-0894354

OFFICERS:
Alejandro S. Mazzotta, President
Linda J. Harris, President-Elect
Mickey Parish, Vice President
Tim Jackson, Secretary

EXECUTIVE DIRECTOR:
David W. Tharp

ADDRESS INQUIRIES TO:
David W. Tharp, Executive Director
(See address above.)

KAPPA OMICRON NU HONOR SOCIETY [2589]

1749 Hamilton Road
Suite 106
Okemos, MI 48864
(517) 351-8335
Fax: (517) 351-8336
E-mail: info@kon.org
Web Site: www.kon.org

FOUNDED: 1912

AREAS OF INTEREST:
Home economics, family and consumer sciences, and human sciences.

NAME(S) OF PROGRAMS:
- **Marjorie M. Brown Dissertation Fellowship**
- **Ruth E. Hawthorne Research Grant**
- **Kappa Omicron Phi/Hettie M. Anthony Fellowship**
- **The KON/GEICO LeaderShape Undergraduate Scholarship**
- **Eileen C. Maddex Fellowship**
- **Dorothy I. Mitstifer Scholarship**
- **National Alumni Chapter Fellowship**
- **National Alumni Chapter Grant**
- **National Scholar Program**
- **New Initiatives Grant**
- **Omicron Nu Master's Fellowship**
- **Omicron Nu Research Fellowship**
- **Betty Jeanne Root Fellowship**
- **Undergraduate Research Award**

TYPE:
Fellowships; Project/program grants; Research grants; Scholarships. Awarded to members for graduate or postgraduate study and research in human sciences or one of its specializations at colleges or universities with strong research programs and supporting disciplines for the chosen major or topic.

YEAR PROGRAM STARTED: 1969

PURPOSE:
To promote research and graduate study in human sciences by recognizing and encouraging scholastic excellence.

LEGAL BASIS:
Nonprofit corporation, 501(c)(3) status.

ELIGIBILITY:
Fellowships/Grants: Applicant must be a member of Kappa Omicron Nu who has demonstrated scholarship, research and leadership potential.

FINANCIAL DATA:
Amount of support per award: $150 to $10,000 per year.

Total amount of support: $40,000 for the year 2016.

NO. MOST RECENT APPLICANTS: 6.

NO. AWARDS: Doctoral Fellowships: 4; Master's Fellowships: 3; Scholar Grants: 50; Marjorie M. Brown Dissertation Fellowship, Ruth E. Hawthorne Research Grant, Kappa Omicron Phi/Hettie M. Anthony Fellowship, Leadership Award, Dorothy I. Mitstifer Scholarship, National Alumni Chapter Grant, New Initiatives Grant and Betty Jeanne Root Fellowship: 1 per award or fellowship.

APPLICATION INFO:
Contact the Society.

Duration: One academic year. Nonrenewable.

Deadline: Research and Project Grants: February 15. Announcement April 15. Doctoral Fellowships: January 15. Announcement April 1. Master's Fellowships: April 1. Announcement May 15.

PUBLICATIONS:
Brochure.

IRS I.D.: 38-1245233

STAFF:
Lisa Wootton Booth, Interim Executive Director, Chief Operating Officer

BOARD OF DIRECTORS:
Bridget Clinton-Scott, Chairperson
Kendra Brandes, First Vice Chairperson
Katherine Shaw, Second Vice Chairperson
Bonita Manson, Secretary

ADDRESS INQUIRIES TO:
Lisa Wootton Booth
Interim Executive Director
and Chief Operating Officer
(See address above.)

NATIONAL CATTLEMAN'S BEEF ASSOCIATION [2590]

9110 East Nichols Avenue
Centennial, CO 80112-3450
(830) 569-0046
Fax: (303) 770-6921
E-mail: smcneill@beef.org
Web Site: www.beefresearch.org

FOUNDED: 1922

AREAS OF INTEREST:
Human nutrition, the relationship between nutrients in beef and health (including amino acids, vitamins and minerals), diet and health.

NAME(S) OF PROGRAMS:
- **Nutrition Research**

TYPE:
Grants-in-aid; Research grants; Research contracts. Research contracts and grants-in-aid for experimental projects in the areas of:
(1) beef as part of a balanced diet;
(2) parity studies;
(3) health benefits of beef lipids and;
(4) contribution of beef nutrients to total diet.

Proposals solicited via specific RFPs (request for proposals).

YEAR PROGRAM STARTED: 1923

PURPOSE:
To gain further knowledge of the value of beef in our diets; to develop research technology that can be applied to the areas noted above.

LEGAL BASIS:
Professional, nonprofit association.

ELIGIBILITY:
Open to qualified institutions (including universities, medical centers, nonprofit organizations and/or contract research laboratories) with appropriate interests.

GEOG. RESTRICTIONS: Primarily United States.

FINANCIAL DATA:
Amount of support per award: $20,000 to $50,000 for one year to $200,000 to $400,000 for multiyear awards. Most are $100,000 to $150,000.

Total amount of support: Varies.

CO-OP FUNDING PROGRAMS: Occasionally federally funded programs are under way that can be facilitated with other funds to expand the scope of the work.

APPLICATION INFO:
Official application materials are available upon request to NCBA at the address above, after it has been established that the proposal would be of mutual interest.

Duration: Support is provided for one to three years depending upon the project.

Deadline: Varies for RFPs.

PUBLICATIONS:
Annual research report.

OFFICERS AND STAFF:
Mandy Carr, Ph.D., Executive Director, Beef Safety Research
Shalene McNeill, Ph.D., Executive Director, Nutrition Research

ADDRESS INQUIRIES TO:
Shalene McNeill, Ph.D.
Executive Director, Nutrition Research
(See address above.)

NATIONAL DAIRY COUNCIL [2591]

10255 West Higgins Road
Suite 900
Rosemont, IL 60018-5616
(847) 627-3232
Fax: (847) 803-2077
E-mail: elieke.demmer@dairy.org
Web Site: researchsubmission.nationaldairycouncil.org

FOUNDED: 1915

AREAS OF INTEREST:
Independent research to aid in the ongoing discovery of information about dairy foods' important role in a healthy lifestyle. This research provides insights to industry for new dairy product innovation.

NAME(S) OF PROGRAMS:
- **Nutrition Research Program**

TYPE:
Research contracts. The National Dairy Council is the nutrition research, education and communications arm of Dairy Management Inc. On behalf of U.S. dairy farmers, the National Dairy Council provides science-based nutrition information to, and in collaboration with, a variety of stakeholders committed to fostering a healthier society, including health professionals, educators, school nutrition directors, academia, industry, consumers and media. The National Dairy Council comprises a staff of nutrition science researchers, registered dietitians and communications experts dedicated to educating the public on the health benefits of consuming milk and milk products throughout a person's lifespan.

YEAR PROGRAM STARTED: 1915

PURPOSE:
To research and discover health benefits for dairy foods and ingredients and advance scientific understanding of these benefits; to increase demand for dairy.

LEGAL BASIS:
Nonprofit educational-scientific institution under IRS 501(c)(3).

ELIGIBILITY:
Qualified investigators associated with accredited institutions of higher learning are eligible for support. Applicants must hold a Ph.D., M.D., D.D.S., D.V.M. or other degree, with experience demonstrating ability to conduct the proposed research.

Funds are not available for alteration of facilities or purchase of permanent equipment.

FINANCIAL DATA:
Amount of support per award: Administered research contracts vary in amount, depending upon the needs and nature of the request.

Total amount of support: Varies.

CO-OP FUNDING PROGRAMS: If research interests of additional organizations coincide, cooperative projects are preferred to enhance efficiency of funds utilized and to benefit the researcher through a broader base of support.

NO. MOST RECENT APPLICANTS: 85 preproposals; approximately 19 selected for full proposal submission.

NO. AWARDS: Varies.

APPLICATION INFO:
The National Dairy Council invites submission of two-page preproposals in the beginning of each calendar year, typically early July. Applications which meet the needs of the research program, which are stated in the guidelines for preproposal submission, will be reviewed. Approximately two to three weeks following the submission deadline, all applicants will receive notice of the outcome of this screening process. Applicants whose preproposals generated interest will receive further information and materials for submission of a detailed full research application to the program. Full proposals will be due approximately six to eight weeks later. All full proposals will be peer-reviewed for scientific merit by the Nutrition Research Scientific Advisory Committee, which is comprised of expert scientists from academia, government and industry. For information on the research program and research topics of interest in the next solicitation, please send a letter requesting the information and a self-addressed label to the address above or contact the NDC research office.

Duration: Projects supported on a yearly basis for up to three years.

Deadline: Preproposal: Typically middle of the year. Full proposal: Three months after preproposal deadline.

PUBLICATIONS:
Guidelines for application and administration.

ADMINISTRATION:
Elieke Demmer, Ph.D., R.D., Manager, Nutrition Research

ADDRESS INQUIRIES TO:
Elieke Demmer, Ph.D., R.D.
Manager, Nutrition Research
(See address above.)

THE NATIONAL RESTAURANT ASSOCIATION EDUCATIONAL FOUNDATION [2592]

2055 L Street, N.W.
Washington, DC 20036
(800) 424-5156
E-mail: scholars@nraef.org
Web Site: www.nraef.org/scholarships

FOUNDED: 1987

AREAS OF INTEREST:
Foodservice education and training.

NAME(S) OF PROGRAMS:

- **National Restaurant Association Educational Foundation (NRAE) Scholarship Program**

TYPE:
Scholarships. Provides scholarships for students who are pursuing an education and career in the foodservice industry.

YEAR PROGRAM STARTED: 1987

PURPOSE:
To encourage and support students pursuing an education and career in the foodservice industry.

LEGAL BASIS:
Not-for-profit organization.

ELIGIBILITY:
Applicant must be a U.S. citizen or permanent resident alien who is accepted and/or enrolled in a foodservice-related postsecondary program.

GEOG. RESTRICTIONS: United States and its territories.

FINANCIAL DATA:
Amount of support per award: Undergraduate Scholarships: $2,500.

NO. AWARDS: Approximately 400.

APPLICATION INFO:
All applicants need:
(1) a valid e-mail address;
(2) at least two letters of recommendation (please note, applicant can either attach the letters of recommendation or contact their references via the application to request that they send letter(s) of recommendation);
(3) current resume;
(4) proof of enrollment;
(5) student transcripts that include a cumulative grade point average (official or unofficial) and;
(6) Student Aid Report (generated by FAFSA).

Duration: Varies depending upon the award.

Deadline: Varies.

PUBLICATIONS:
Awards brochure.

ADDRESS INQUIRIES TO:
Scholarships
(See address above.)

USDA FOOD AND NUTRITION SERVICE

Child Nutrition Service
3101 Park Center Drive, Room 628
Alexandria, VA 22302
(703) 305-2054
Fax: (703) 305-2879
Web Site: www.fns.usda.gov/cnd

TYPE:
Formula grants; Grants-in-aid; Project/program grants. Reimbursement for the support of food service in schools, child and adult care institutions to improve nutrition.

The Child and Adult Care Food Program helps child care facilities and institutions serve nutritious meals and snacks to preschool and school-age children. To participate, facilities and institutions must be licensed or approved to provide child care services. They must also meet certain other eligibility requirements. The program operates in nonresidential day care centers, settlement houses, outside-school-hours care centers, family day care homes, institutions providing day care for handicapped children and others. Participating facilities and institutions get cash assistance, USDA-donated foods and technical guidance. In child care centers, the amount of cash assistance varies according to the family size and income of children served. In day care homes, the amount of cash assistance is based on a food service payment rate. Similar benefits are also now available to adult day care centers which serve functionally impaired adults or persons 60 years of age or older.

The Fresh Fruit and Vegetable Program introduces school children to a variety of produce that they otherwise might not have the opportunity to sample. The goal is to improve children's overall diet and create healthier eating habits to impact their present and future health.

The National School Lunch Program makes well-planned nutritious meals available to school children. Any public or nonprofit private schools of high school grade or under and licensed public or nonprofit private residential child care institutions are eligible to participate in the National School Lunch and School Breakfast Programs. Schools that participate are required to provide free and reduced-price meals to children unable to pay the full price. Eligibility is based on application information submitted by a parent or guardian. The household income limit for free lunches is set at or below 130% of the federal poverty level and for reduced price lunches household income must be above 130% or at or below 185% of the federal poverty level. Children from households not eligible for free or reduced-price meals must pay the school's full price charge for lunch. Cash and donated commodities are provided to participating schools and institutions according to the number of meals served.

The School Breakfast Program makes nutritious breakfasts available to school children under the same eligibility guidelines and general requirements as the National School Lunch Program.

The Special Milk Program for Children makes it possible for all children attending a participating school or institution to purchase milk at a reduced price or receive it free, if they are eligible. Reimbursement is provided for each half-pint of milk served under the program. Schools and institutions that participate in other federal child nutrition programs authorized under the National School Lunch Act or the Child Nutrition Act of 1966 may not participate in the Special Milk Program for Children, except for split-session kindergarten programs conducted in schools in which the children do not have access to the other meal program.

The Summer Food Service Program for Children helps communities serve meals to needy children when school is not in session. The program is sponsored by public or private nonprofit school food authorities or local, municipal, county or state governments. Public or private nonprofit residential camps, other private nonprofit organizations, colleges and universities which participate in the National Youth Sports Program also may be sponsors. The program operates in areas in which at least 50% of the children meet the income criteria for free and reduced-price school meals. USDA reimburses sponsors for operating costs of food services up to a specified maximum rate for each meal served. In addition, sponsors receive some reimbursement for planning, operating and supervising expenses.

See entry 1131 for full listing.

Mining and metallurgy

ASM MATERIALS EDUCATION FOUNDATION [2593]

9639 Kinsman Road
Materials Park, OH 44073-0002
(440) 338-5151 ext. 5533
(800) 336-5152 ext. 5533
Fax: (440) 338-4634
E-mail: jeane.deatherage@asminternational.org
Web Site: www.asmfoundation.org

FOUNDED: 1913

AREAS OF INTEREST:
Materials science and engineering in related fields such as metallurgy, metallurgical engineering, polymeric engineering, ceramic engineering, advanced composites engineering and engineering of electronic materials.

NAME(S) OF PROGRAMS:
- **ASM Outstanding Scholars**
- **David J. Chellman Scholarship**
- **Edward J. Dulis Scholarship**
- **William & Mary Dyrkacz Scholarships**
- **John M. Haniak Scholarship**
- **Ladish Co. Foundation Scholarships**
- **George A. Roberts Scholarship**
- **Lucille & Charles A. Wert Scholarship**
- **William Park Woodside Founder's Scholarship**

TYPE:
Scholarships.

YEAR PROGRAM STARTED: 1953

PURPOSE:
To encourage and support capable students with interest and potential in the field of metallurgy and materials science.

LEGAL BASIS:
501(c)(3) educational charity.

ELIGIBILITY:
Applicant must be a Material Advantage student member and have an intended or declared major in metallurgy/materials science engineering. Applicants majoring in related science or engineering disciplines will be considered if they demonstrate a strong academic emphasis and interest in materials science. Applicant must also be at the sophomore level or above. Open to U.S. and international students.

G.A. Roberts and W.P. Woodside Scholarship candidates must have a junior or senior standing in the fall at a North American university, have proof of financial need, and must be a citizen of the U.S., Canada or Mexico and attending school in one of these countries. University must have an accredited science and engineering program leading to a Bachelor's degree.

Applicants are eligible for ASM Scholar or ASM Outstanding Scholar award a total of two times.

Criteria for selection include the student's academic achievement, interest in the field, and personal qualities. Financial need is not a factor, except for the G.A. Roberts and W.P. Woodside Scholarships.

GEOG. RESTRICTIONS: United States.

FINANCIAL DATA:
Amount of support per award: Up to $10,000.

NO. AWARDS: Varies.

APPLICATION INFO:
Completed scholarship application (Part One), two letters of recommendation, transcript of college academic records, a photograph, and an individual statement that is no longer than two typewritten pages are required. For G.A. Roberts and W.P. Woodside Scholarships only, applicants should complete Part Two of the application form, including a personal statement and a financial aid officer contact, along with previous requirements.

Duration: Ladish Co. Foundation Scholarship: Up to two years; All others: One academic year.

Deadline: Application and materials must be sent by May 1. Award winners will be notified by mail by July 15.

IRS I.D.: 34-6541397

OFFICERS:
Charles R. Hayes, Executive Director and Secretary

ADDRESS INQUIRIES TO:
ASM Foundation Undergraduate Scholarship Program
(See e-mail address above.)

*SPECIAL STIPULATIONS:
Must have completed one year of undergraduate work.

INSTITUTE OF MATERIALS, MINERALS AND MINING [2594]

The Boilerhouse
Springfield Business Park
Caunt Road
Grantham Lincs NG31 7FZ England
(44) 0 1476 513886
Fax: (44) 0 1476 513899
E-mail: graham.woodrow@iom3.org
Web Site: www.iom3.org

FOUNDED: 1892

AREAS OF INTEREST:
Mining and metallurgy.

NAME(S) OF PROGRAMS:
- **Centenary Scholarship**
- **Stanley Elmore Fellowship Fund**
- **G. Vernon Hobson Bequest**
- **Mining Club Award**
- **Edgar Pam Fellowship**
- **The Tom Seaman Travelling Scholarship**
- **Bosworth Smith Trust Fund**

TYPE:
Awards/prizes; Fellowships; Research grants; Scholarships; Training grants; Travel grants. The Centenary Scholarship is restricted to first- or second-year undergraduates in student membership of the Institute and will be awarded for projects, visits, etc., in furtherance of applicants' career development.

Stanley Elmore Fellowship Fund offers fellowships (normally two for one year) applicable at a U.K. university for research into all branches of extractive metallurgy and mineral processing and, in special cases, for expenditure related to such research.

The G. Vernon Hobson Bequest awards are given for the advancement of teaching and practice of geology as applied to mining. One or more awards may be made for travel, research or other objects in accordance with the terms of the Bequest.

The Mining Club Award will be offered to British subjects 21 to 35 years of age who are actively engaged (in full- or part-time postgraduate study or in employment) in the minerals industry, as defined by the Institute, for travel purposes (for example, to study mineral industry operations in the U.K. or overseas, to present a paper at an international minerals industry conference or to assist the applicant in attending a full-time course of study related to the minerals industry outside the U.K.), or for any other similar purpose that may be regarded as being within the spirit of the award.

The Edgar Pam Fellowship is awarded for postgraduate study in subjects within the Institute's fields of interest, which range from exploration geology to extractive metallurgy. Those eligible for the award are young graduates, domiciled in Australia, Canada, New Zealand, South Africa and the U.K., who wish to undertake advanced study or research in the U.K.

The Tom Seaman Travelling Scholarship is awarded annually to a member, not older than 35 years of age, who is training or has been trained for a career in mining and/or related technologies. The scholarship shall be to assist the study for an aspect of engineering in the minerals industry, with the intention of advancing the associated standards or techniques.

The Bosworth Smith Trust Fund is given for the assistance of postgraduate research in metal mining, non-ferrous extraction metallurgy or mineral dressing. Applications will be considered for grants towards working expenses, the cost of visits to mines and plants in connection with such research, and purchase of apparatus.

ELIGIBILITY:
Applicants should note that, in general, preference will be given to members of the Institution (student membership is required for the Centenary Scholarship). Recipients of the awards will be required to submit summary reports of the ways in which such awards have been used for publication.

In judging the applications received for each award, the Institute will take into account academic excellence and scholarship. The application must, therefore, specify academic ability. Candidates merely seeking assistance for financial hardship will not be considered.

Applicants for awards must ensure that the particular fund from which support is being sought is relevant to their field(s) of interest. Applications not in accordance with the specified terms and conditions of the various funds, those which are received after the deadline, and those for which the appropriate letters of support have not been received by that date will not be submitted to the awards committee.

FINANCIAL DATA:
Amount of support per award: Centenary Scholarship: GBP 500; Stanley Elmore Fellowship Fund: Up to GBP 14,000 distributed between one or two awardees; G. Vernon Hobson Bequest: Up to GBP 1,300; Mining Club Award: Up to GBP 1,500; Edgar Pam Fellowship: Maximum GBP 2,000; Tom Seaman Travelling Scholarship: Up to GBP 5,500; Bosworth Smith Trust Fund: Approximately GBP 5,000 in grants.

APPLICATION INFO:
Application form required. Applications not in accordance with the specified terms and

conditions of the various funds, those which are received after the closing date each year, and those for which the appropriate levels of support have not been received by that date, will not be accepted for consideration.

Deadline: April 6.

PUBLICATIONS:
Guidelines.

ADDRESS INQUIRIES TO:
Dr. G.J.M. Woodrow
Deputy Chief Executive
(See address above.)

INTERNATIONAL CENTRE FOR DIFFRACTION DATA [2595]

12 Campus Boulevard
Newtown Square, PA 19073-3273
(610) 325-9814
Fax: (610) 325-9823
E-mail: info@icdd.com
Web Site: www.icdd.com

FOUNDED: 1991

AREAS OF INTEREST:
The science of crystallography.

NAME(S) OF PROGRAMS:

- **The Ludo Frevel Crystallography Scholarship Award**

TYPE:
Scholarships.

YEAR PROGRAM STARTED: 1991

PURPOSE:
To encourage promising graduate students to pursue crystallographically oriented research.

ELIGIBILITY:
Applicant should be a graduate student seeking a degree with major interest in crystallography, crystal structure analysis, crystal morphology, modulated structures, correlation of atomic structures with physical properties, systematic classification of crystal structures, phase identification and materials characterization. There are no restrictions on country, race, age or sex. Students with a graduation date prior to July 1 of the award year are not eligible.

Funds can be used for travel to conferences or for research-related purposes.

FINANCIAL DATA:
The scholarship stipend is to be used by the graduate student to help defray tuition and laboratory fees. A portion of the stipend may be applied to registration fees to accredited scientific meetings related to crystallography.

Amount of support per award: $2,500.

NO. MOST RECENT APPLICANTS: 59 for fiscal year 2016.

NO. AWARDS: 10 for fiscal year 2016.

APPLICATION INFO:
The following information must be prepared in advance of applying online:
(1) a description of the candidate's proposed research (limit two pages), including purpose and rationale for the research, proposed methodology to be used in the study, and references and/or descriptions of the scientific background for the proposed research and;
(2) a curriculum vitae, including educational preparation (institutions, dates, degrees obtained and in progress, and particularly pertinent coursework), awards/honors received, any research publications and/or presentations given, any work experience (dates, employers, positions), and professional activities and memberships.

Duration: One year. Renewals possible. Renewal applications will be considered on a competitive basis in conjunction with all applications that have been submitted up to the closing date.

Deadline: Late October. Contact Centre for exact date.

ADDRESS INQUIRIES TO:
Stephanie Jennings, Conference Assistant
(See address above.)

MINERALOGICAL ASSOCIATION OF CANADA [2596]

490, rue de la Couronne
Quebec QC G1K 9A9 Canada
(418) 653-0333
Fax: (418) 653-0777
E-mail: office@mineralogicalassociation.ca
Web Site: www.mineralogicalassociation.ca

FOUNDED: 1955

AREAS OF INTEREST:
Mineralogy.

NAME(S) OF PROGRAMS:

- **Leonard G. Berry Medal**
- **Hawley Medal**
- **MAC Foundation Scholarship**
- **MAC Student Travel/Research Grants**
- **Peacock Medal**
- **Pinch Medal**
- **Undergraduate Awards**
- **Young Scientist Award**

TYPE:
Awards/prizes; Grants-in-aid; Research grants; Scholarships; Travel grants.

PURPOSE:
To promote and advance the knowledge of mineralogy and the allied disciplines of crystallography, petrology, geochemistry and mineral deposits.

LEGAL BASIS:
Nonprofit scientific and charitable organization.

ELIGIBILITY:
The Leonard G. Berry Medal is awarded for distinguished service to the Mineralogical Association of Canada.

The Hawley Medal is presented to the author(s) of what is judged to be the best paper published in the preceding year's volume of *The Canadian Mineralogist.*

The MAC Foundation Scholarship is awarded to a graduate student involved in an M.Sc. or Ph.D. thesis program in the fields of mineralogy, crystallography, petrology, geochemistry or mineral deposits.

The MAC Student Travel/Research Grants are given to assist honours undergraduate and graduate students in the mineral sciences.

The Peacock Medal is awarded annually for excellence in research to a scientist who has made outstanding contributions to the mineralogical sciences in Canada.

The Pinch Medal is awarded every other year to recognize major and sustained contributions to the advancement of mineralogy by members of the collector-dealer community.

Undergraduate Awards are given to university students in mineralogy. The Association presents a MAC publication to the top student in the introductory mineralogy course at each Canadian university.

The Young Scientist Award is given to a young scientist who has made a significant international research contribution in a promising start to a scientific career.

FINANCIAL DATA:
Amount of support per award: Varies depending on award.

Total amount of support: $25,000.

NO. MOST RECENT APPLICANTS: MAC Travel/Research Grants: 20.

NO. AWARDS: Varies.

APPLICATION INFO:
Contact the Association.

Duration: Varies.

Deadline: Varies.

PUBLICATIONS:
The Canadian Mineralogist.

STAFF:
Lee A. Groat, Editor

ADDRESS INQUIRIES TO:
Johanne Caron, Business Manager
(See address above.)

Indexes

Entry Listing by Chapter

Subject Index

A

B

C

D

E

F

G

H

I

J

K

L

M

N

O

P

R

S

T

U

V

W

Y

Z

Organization and Program Index

The Organization and Program Index alphabetically lists grant programs in upper-lower case and funding organizations in upper case. In addition, programs also are listed following the organizations which sponsor them.

A

B

C

D

F

G

H

I

J

K

L

M

N

P

Q

R

S

T

U

V

X

Y

Z

Geographical Index

UNITED STATES

Alabama

Alaska

Arizona

Arkansas

California

Colorado

Connecticut

Delaware

District of Columbia

Florida

Georgia

Hawaii

Idaho

Illinois

Indiana

Iowa

Kansas

Kentucky

Louisiana

Maine

Maryland

Massachusetts

Michigan

Minnesota

Mississippi

Missouri

Montana

Nebraska

Nevada

New Hampshire

New Jersey

New Mexico

New York

North Carolina

North Dakota

Ohio

Oklahoma

Oregon

Pennsylvania

Rhode Island

South Carolina

South Dakota

Tennessee

Texas

Utah

Vermont

Virgin Islands

Virginia

Washington

West Virginia

Wisconsin

Wyoming

FOREIGN COUNTRIES

Australia

Austria

Belgium

Canada

England

France

Germany

Israel

Italy

Japan

The Netherlands

Scotland

Sweden

Switzerland

Personnel Index

A

B

C

D

E

F

G

H

I

J

K

L

M

N

O

P

Q

R

S

T

U

V

W

Y

Z